Bailey, Harris & Jones

Civil Liberties
Cases and Materials

Fifth edition

S H Bailey MA, LL B (Cantab)
Professor of Public Law and Pro-Vice-Chancellor,
University of Nottingham

D J Harris LL M, PhD (Lond), CMG
Professor of Public International Law,
University of Nottingham

D C Ormerod LL B (Essex)
Professor of Criminal Law,
University of Hull

Butterworths
LexisNexis™

Members of the LexisNexis Group worldwide

United Kingdom	Butterworths Tolley, a Division of Reed Elsevier (UK) Ltd, Halsbury House, 35 Chancery Lane, LONDON, WC2A 1EL, and 4 Hill Street, EDINBURGH EH2 3JZ
Argentina	Abeledo Perrot, Jurisprudencia Argentina and Depalma, BUENOS AIRES
Australia	Butterworths, a Division of Reed International Books Australia Pty Ltd, CHATSWOOD, New South Wales
Austria	ARD Betriebsdienst and Verlag Orac, VIENNA
Canada	Butterworths Canada Ltd, MARKHAM, Ontario
Chile	Publitecsa and Conosur Ltda, SANTIAGO DE CHILE
Czech Republic	Orac sro, PRAGUE
France	Editions du Juris-Classeur SA, PARIS
Hong Kong	Butterworths Asia (Hong Kong), HONG KONG
Hungary	Hvg Orac, BUDAPEST
India	Butterworths India, NEW DELHI
Ireland	Butterworths (Ireland) Ltd, DUBLIN
Italy	Giuffré, MILAN
Malaysia	Malayan Law Journal Sdn Bhd, KUALA LUMPUR
New Zealand	Butterworths of New Zealand, WELLINGTON
Poland	Wydawnictwa Prawnicze PWN, WARSAW
Singapore	Butterworths Asia, SINGAPORE
South Africa	Butterworths Publishers (Pty) Ltd, DURBAN
Switzerland	Stämpfli Verlag AG, BERNE
USA	LexisNexis, DAYTON, Ohio

© Reed Elsevier (UK) Ltd 2001

A CIP Catalogue record for this book is available from the British Library.

ISBN 0 406 90326 3

Typeset by Doyle & Co, Colchester
Printed and bound in Great Britain by The Bath Press, Bath

Visit Butterworths LexisNexis *direct* at www.butterworths.com

Preface

There has been a quiet revolution since the last edition of this casebook, with the entry into force of the Human Rights Act 1998. Although these are early days, practice has already demonstrated the considerably greater responsibilities that the courts have under the 1998 Act for the protection of human rights. The very first cases in which the courts have been called upon to exercise their larger role have been included in Chapter 1 of this new edition. In these, the judiciary have quickly spelt out the fundamentals of the approach they intend to apply, although the results in terms of declarations of incompatibility have so far been modest.

Quite apart from the Human Rights Act 1998, Parliament has enacted much legislation bearing upon civil liberties since the last edition of this casebook, with the result that almost all of its chapters have been substantially revised. Statutes from which extracts have been inserted include the Broadcasting Act 1996, the Police Act 1997, the Protection from Harassment Act 1997, the Crime and Disorder Act 1998, the Data Protection Act 1998, the Freedom of Information Act 2000, the Regulation of Investigative Powers Act 2000, the Terrorism Act 2000, the Criminal Justice and Police Act 2001 and the Race Relations (Amendment) Act 2001. Account has also been taken of the many judicial cases and reports, including, in the latter category, the report resulting from the Stephen Lawrence inquiry.

This new edition differs in several other respects, mainly because of pressure of space. For this reason, the chapter on immigration and nationality has been omitted, as has the separate chapter on the European Convention on Human Rights. As to the latter, the jurisprudence of the European Court of Human Rights is now so large that justice cannot properly be done to it in a single chapter in a book such as the present one. However, some European Court cases have been included in other chapters where they have particular relevance to the subject matter of the chapter. Even so, the book is now much longer than previously. This is partly because the size of print and the footnoting arrangements have been changed to make the book easier for the reader to use. But it also follows from the growth of legislation and other sources of English civil liberties law.

One sad fact that must be recorded is that Brian Jones was unable to contribute to the present, fifth edition of the book that bears his name. Brian made a large contribution to the development of the original conception of the book and played an invaluable part in the preparation of the first four editions. Fortunately, David Ormerod has agreed to step in and has contributed hugely to the present edition. Although, as in previous editions, each author has been primarily responsible for particular chapters, all three authors share general responsibility for the book as a whole.

It may be that this is the last edition of the book in its present form. It may be that in future editions, consideration will have to be given to organising the chapters on a basis of particular rights, following the pattern of the European Convention on

Human Rights, rather than along the traditional lines found in British constitutional law books. It might also be that the title should be re-thought, so as to refer to human rights. However, rather than anticipate developments over the next few years and irritate readers who are familiar with traditional ways and concepts, we have decided that the current edition, published while the Human Rights Act is still finding its feet, should follow its established pattern.

We would like to record our thanks for the assistance given in the preparation of the book in its final stages by Thomas Poole, lecturer in law, University of Nottingham; and Andrew Roberts and Julie Self, research students, School of Law, University of Nottingham. We would also like to thank our colleagues at Butterworths for their assistance and encouragement during the preparation of the manuscript for publication.

We are grateful to the following publishers for allowing publication of extracts in this book: the Incorporated Council of Law Reporting for England and Wales; Sweet & Maxwell Ltd (for extracts from the Criminal Appeal Reports); Times Newspapers Ltd; Justice of the Peace Ltd; Cambridge University Press (for an extract from Wardlaw, *Political Terrorism*); Mansell Publishers Ltd (for an extract from Hepple and Szyszczak, *Discrimination : The Limits of Law*); Penguin Books Ltd; Frank Cass; Macmillan Publishers Ltd; The Press Council; Pearson Education Ltd; and the Institute for Jewish Policy Research. Crown copyright material is reproduced with the permission of the Controller of HMSO.

We would also like to acknowledge the assistance given to us by a number of government departments and other bodies. These include the Home Office, the Cabinet Office, the Attorney General's Office, the Secretary of the Defence, Press and Broadcasting Committee, the Independent Commissioner for the Holding Centres, the British Board for Film Classification, the Press Complaints Commission, the Commission for Racial Equality and the Council of Europe.

The manuscript was delivered to the publishers in September 2001. It has been possible to note a few later developments at the proof stage.

S. H. Bailey
D. J. Harris   December 2001
D. C. Ormerod

Contents

Table of statutes

References in **bold** type indicate where the Act is set out in part or in full.

List of cases

Page references printed in **bold** type indicate where the case extracts are set out.

K

L

N

l *List of cases*

liv   *List of cases*

PAGE

CHAPTER 1

The method of protecting civil liberties in English law

1 The former method

Report of an Interdepartmental Working Group Concerning Legislation on Human Rights, with Particular Reference to the European Convention (1976-77) HL 81

Our arrangements for the protection of human rights are different from those of most other countries. The differences are related to differences in our constitutional traditions. Although our present constitution may be regarded as deriving in part from the revolution settlement of 1688-89, consolidated by the Union of 1707, we, unlike our European neighbours and many Commonwealth countries, do not owe our present system of government either to a revolution or to a struggle for independence. The United Kingdom—

(a) has an omnicompetent Parliament, with absolute power to enact any law and change any previous law; the courts in England and Wales have not, since the seventeenth century, recognised even in theory any higher legal order by reference to which Acts of Parliament could be held void;[1] in Scotland the courts, while reserving the right to treat an Act as void for breaching a fundamental term of the Treaty of Union [see *McCormick v Lord Advocate* 1953 SC 396], have made it clear that they foresee no likely circumstances in which they would do so;

(b) unlike other modern democracies, has no written constitution;

(c) unlike countries in civil law tradition, makes no fundamental distinction, as regards rights or remedies, between 'public law' governing the actions of the State and its agents, and 'private law' regulating the relationships of private citizens with one another; nor have we a coherent system of administrative law applied by specialised tribunals or courts and with its own appropriate remedies;[2]

(d) has not generally codified its law, and our courts adopt a relatively narrow and literal approach to the interpretation of statutes;

(e) unlike the majority of EEC countries and the United States, does not, by ratifying a treaty or convention, make it automatically part of the domestic law (nor do we normally give effect to such an international agreement by incorporating the agreement itself into our law).

In other countries the rights of the citizen are usually (thought not universally) to be found enunciated in general terms in a Bill of Rights or other constitutional document. The effectiveness of such instruments varies greatly. A Bill of Rights is not an automatic guarantee of liberty; its efficacy depends on the integrity of the institutions which apply it, and ultimately on the determination of the people that it should be maintained. The United Kingdom as such has no Bill of Rights of this kind. The Bill of Rights of 1688, though more concerned with the relationship between the English Parliament and the Crown, did contain some important safeguards for personal liberty—as did the Claim of Right of 1689, its Scottish equivalent. Among the provisions common to both the Bill of Rights and the Claim of Right are declarations that excessive bail is illegal and that it is the right of subjects to petition the Crown without

---

1   *Ed.* Following the European Communities Act 1972, the UK courts have recognised limitations upon parliamentary sovereignty that result from European Union law.

2   *Ed.* This ceased to be wholly true with the introduction of the present Order 53 remedy for judicial review and the distinction between public and private law used in its application: see *O'Reilly v Mackman* [1983] 2 AC 237, HL.

1

incurring penalties. But the protection given by these instruments to the rights and liberties of the citizen is much narrower than the constitutional guarantees now afforded in many other democratic countries.[3]

The effect of the United Kingdom system of law is to provide, through the development of the common law and by express statutory enactment, a diversity of specific rights with their accompanying remedies. Thus, to secure the individual's right to freedom from unlawful or arbitrary detention, our law provides specific and detailed remedies such as habeas corpus[4] and the action for false imprisonment. The rights which have been afforded in this way are for the most part negative rights to be protected from interference from others, rather than positive rights to behave in a particular way. Those rights which have emerged in the common law can always be modified by Parliament. Parliament's role is all-pervasive—potentially, at least. It continually adapts existing rights and remedies and provides new ones, and no doubt this process would continue even if a comprehensive Bill of Rights were enacted.

The legal remedies provided for interference with the citizen's rights have in recent times been overlaid by procedures which are designed to afford not so much remedies in the strict sense of the term as facilities for obtaining independent and impartial scrutiny of action by public bodies about which an individual believes he has cause for complaint, even though the action may have been within the body's legal powers. For example, the actions of central government departments are open to scrutiny by the Parliamentary Commissioner for Administration; and complaints about the administration of the National Health Service are investigated by the Health Service Commissioners.

NOTES

1. As the penultimate paragraph of the above extract from the Report[5] indicates, before the Human Rights Act 1998 civil liberties were protected in the UK law by a mixture of legislation and common law. Dicey pointed out over a century ago[6] that when providing such protection Parliament and the courts did not usually make general positive statements of a right. There is, for example, no statute providing for a 'right to freedom of assembly'. Instead the technique was to legislate in detailed terms, making particular legislative provision, as in the Public Order Act 1986, from which the general right might be inferred. The courts were similarly restrained when developing the common law.[7] While sometimes making general statements,[8] they preferred to formulate particular rules, shaped by the facts of the cases before them. Moreover, the focus of judgments was often, as it was in legislation, upon matters, such as the need to ensure public order, other than the protection of the civil liberty concerned. Another characteristic of the common law approach was that the individual's civil liberties were treated truly as liberties, not as rights. It was a negative approach by which a court, when faced with a civil liberties issue, sought to discover whether there is a limitation in law upon the challenged action and, if there is not, to

3   *Ed.* The Bill of Rights was relied upon (unsuccessfully) in *Williams v Home Office (No 2)* [1981] 1 All ER 1211, QBD.

4   *Ed.* Although habeas corpus is of value in some civil liberties contexts (e.g. obtaining the release of suspects being questioned by the police, and preventing deportation (*R v Secretary of State for the Home Department, ex p Muboyayi* [1992] QB 244, CA)), it has limitations in others (e.g. achieving the release of the mentally disordered: see *X v United Kingdom* (1981) EHRR 188). On habeas corpus, see R. J. Sharpe, *The Law of Habeas Corpus* (2nd edn, 1989) and A. Le Sueur, [1992] PL 13.

5   The Report was prepared in connection with the consideration of the question of a Bill of Rights by the House of Lords Select Committee on a Bill of Rights.

6   *An Introduction to the Study of the Law of the Constitution* (10th edn by E. C. S. Wade, 1959), p. 197. First edition, 1885.

7   See D. J. Harris, in F. Matscher (ed.), *The Implementation of Economic and Social Rights* (1991) p. 201.

8   See e.g. Lord Kilbrandon's reference in *Cassell v Broome* [1972] AC 1027, 1133, HL, to a 'constitutional right to free speech'.

conclude that the action was lawful. A weakness of this approach was that it permitted interferences with civil liberties as well as protection of them.[9] It was in direct contrast with the approach in the European Convention on Human Rights (ECHR), which lists in general terms the rights that it protects. The contrast was pointed out by Lord Goff in *A-G v Guardian Newspapers (No 2)*:[10]

'. . . I can see no inconsistency between English law on this subject and Article 10 of the [ECHR] . . . The only difference is that, whereas Article 10 . . . proceeds to state a fundamental right and then to qualify it, we in this country (where everybody is free to do anything, subject only to the provisions of the law) proceed rather upon an assumption of freedom of speech, and turn to our law to discover the established exceptions to it.'

The pre-Human Rights Act 1998 approach of Parliament and the courts that has been outlined in the preceding paragraph has been stated in the past tense. Obviously, some changes will occur under the new Act, with the courts, in particular, being likely to move to a more positive human rights based approach. It is predictable, however, that legislation on civil liberties matters that supplements the guarantee in the Human Rights Act will continue, at least at the outset, to take the same detailed and indirect approach as before.

2. As the Report also states, nearly all countries protect civil liberties by means of a Bill of Rights.[11] Lord Lloyd[12] defines a Bill of Rights as a 'constitutional code of human rights' that is binding in law, is (inevitably) generally worded and has the following other key characteristics:

'(a) The code should be given some sort of overriding authority over other laws.
(b) Power should be vested in the judiciary (whether generally or by way of a Constitutional or Supreme Court) to interpret the rights set forth in the Bill of Rights and to determine judicially their proper scope, extent and limits, and their relationship inter se.
(c) The judiciary will possess the power to declare legislation invalided which it holds to be repugnant to the rights guaranteed in the Bill of Rights.'

3. The United Kingdom had, and still has,[13] no bill of rights in the above sense. A power of judicial review over legislation was claimed by Coke CJ in *Dr Bonham's Case*:[14] 'When an Act of Parliament is against common right and reason, or repugnant, or impossible to be performed, the common law will control it, and adjudge such Act to be void.' Had this claim been pressed and accepted, the resulting power could

---

9 See E. C. S. Wade and A. W. Bradley, *Constitutional and Administrative Law* (11th edn. by A. W. Bradley and K. D. Ewing, 1993), p. 411, who refer to the *Malone* case as an example. See also *R v Kirkless Metropolitan Borough Council, ex p C* [1993] 2 FLR 187, CA, in which counsel for a detained, mentally disordered person argued that there was no legal basis for the detention, and Stuart-Smith LJ stated that counsel had asked the wrong question: 'The real question is, on what basis can it be said that the council acted unlawfully', and there was none.
10 [1990] 1 AC 109 at 283, HL.
11 Australia and Israel are among the few exceptions. Canada and New Zealand adopted bills of rights in 1982 and 1990 respectively. The Canadian and New Zealand models were taken into account when the Human Rights Act 1998 was enacted. Although the 1998 Act differs significantly from both, it contains some echoes of the New Zealand Bill of Rights and the experience of the courts in implementing both systems was instructive.
12 (1976) 39 MLR 121 at 122-123.
13 For the more limited powers of the courts under the Human Rights Act 1998, see below, p. 12. The definition is one that fits the bills of rights in states such as the United States and Germany. The courts in Canada can overturn federal or provincial legislation unless the legislature concerned expressly provides that it may not do so: Canadian Charter of Rights and Freedoms s. 33, which is enacted in Sch. B of the Canada Act 1982: see P. W. Hogg, *Constitutional Law of Canada* (4th edn, 1997), Chap. 36. The courts in New Zealand have no power to overturn statutes; they apply a rule of interpretation similar to that in s. 3 of the Human Rights Act: see M. Taggart, [1998] PL 266.
14 (1610) 8 Co Rep 114a, 118.

have been used to protect civil liberties in much the same way as a Bill of Rights does without any formal enactment. But it proved only to be rhetoric; no statute has ever been overturned on the basis of it. The position before the Human Rights Act 1998 was stated by Lord Reid in *British Railways Board v Pickin*:[15]

> 'The idea that a court is entitled to disregard a provision in an Act of Parliament on any ground must seem strange and startling to anyone with any knowledge of the history and law of our constitution . . . In earlier times many learned lawyers seem to have believed that an Act of Parliament could be disregarded in so far as it was contrary to the law of God or the law of nature or natural justice, but since the supremacy of Parliament was finally demonstrated by the Revolution of 1688 any such idea has become obsolete.'

In *Oppenheimer v Cattermole*[16] the question was whether English courts should recognise a Nazi law that deprived German Jews resident abroad of their nationality and confiscated their property. A majority of the House of Lords took the view that the law was 'so grave an infringement of human rights that the courts of this country ought to refuse to recognise it as a law at all'.[17]   Mann[18] refers to the case and notes that 'for more than 300 years England has been spared the necessity of facing' the question of the legality of such laws *within its own legal system*. He suggests that were it to arise 'English judges could no doubt find a legally convincing reason for reverting to the tradition of the fundamental law' and that the 'real question would be whether, in the condition which has been assumed, they would have the strength of character to search for it'.

4. Although subject to Parliament, the courts have always played an important role in the protection of civil liberties by the interpretation of statutes, the review of administrative action and the development of the common law. As far as the interpretation of statutes is concerned, the courts have developed certain presumptions that help. The presumption against the taking of property without compensation[19] is an example. So are the presumptions against the retrospective effect of legislation,[20] against denial of access to the courts,[1] against interference with the freedom from self-incrimination;[2] and against interference with the liberty of the subject.[3]   More generally, *Maxwell on Statutes*[4] reads: 'Statutes which encroach on the rights of the subject, whether as regards person or property, are subject to a strict construction in the same way as penal Acts.' The presumption that legislation complies with UK treaty obligations is important in that the UK is bound by a number of international human rights treaties, including the ECHR.[5]   There is also a

---

15 [1974] AC 765 at 765, 782, HL.
16 [1976] AC 249, HL.
17 Lord Cross at 278.
18 (1978) 94 LQR 512, 513–4.
19 *Central Control Board (Liquor Traffic) v Cannon Brewery Co Ltd* [1919] AC 744 at 752, HL, per Lord Atkinson. See also *R v Secretary of State for Transport, ex p de Rothschild* [1989] 1 All ER 933, CA.
20 *Waddington v Miah* [1974] 1 WLR 683, HL.
 1 *Raymond v Honey* [1983] 1 AC 1, HL.
 2 *Re O* [1991] 2 QB 520, CA.
 3 *R v Hallstrom, ex p W* [1986] QB 1090, QBD. This presumption does not apply in wartime: *R v Halliday* [1917] AC 270, HL.
 4 (12th edn, 1969), p. 251.
 5 Other human rights treaties in force protecting civil and political rights to which the UK is a party include the Genocide Convention 1948, UKTS 58 (1970), Cmnd 4421; the ILO Freedom of Association Convention (ILO 87), Cmnd 7638; the ILO Right to Organise Convention (ILO 98), Cmnd 7852; the International Covenant on Civil and Political Rights 1966, UKTS 6 (1977), Cmnd 6702; the Convention on the Elimination of All Forms of Racial Discrimination 1966, UKTS 77 (1969), Cmnd 4108; the Convention on the Elimination of All Forms of Discrimination against Women 1979, UKTS 2 (1989), Cm 643; the UN Convention Against

presumption that UK legislation complies with customary international law,[6] which contains a number of human rights guarantees (e.g. against torture).[7] Quite apart from such presumptions, a determined court may do a lot by way of interpretation of a statute that it considers infringes civil liberties (see the direction to the jury in *R v Bourne*,[8] interpreting the Offences against the Person Act 1861, s. 58 – an abortion, or women's rights, case). A court's attitude to the interpretation of ambiguous provisions in legislation aimed positively at protecting civil liberties can also be crucial. Consider, for example, the interpretation given to doubtful provisions in the Race Relations Acts 1965–76.[9] Although these presumptions and some other aspects of the courts' former approach to the interpretation of statutes are now overtaken by the stronger rule of interpretation in s. 3 of the Human Rights Act 1998 in the context of Convention rights, they well may still play a part in the interpretation of statutes in the area of non-Convention human rights, although it is possible that the courts will take it upon themselves to apply the approach in s. 3 of the Human Rights Act 1998 to non-Convention rights also.

5. The courts have a well established power of judicial review of administrative action taken by national or local or other government authorities, including action bearing upon civil liberties. This has long been so where the action is based upon *statutory* powers. More recently, it has been established that the exercise of *prerogative* powers may be subject to judicial review also, depending upon the subject matter of the power: *Council of Civil Service Unions v Minister of the Civil Service*.[10] The courts may quash or prevent executive decisions that are not authorised by law; that are not taken in accordance with the prescribed procedures; that are erroneous in law; that infringe the rules of natural justice; or that involve an exercise of discretion that is not in accordance with, in human rights cases, the 'heightened scrutiny' test that the courts had developed before the Human Rights Act 1998.[11] Although the 'heightened scrutiny' test has been replaced under the Act by a stricter proportionality test in respect of Convention rights, it may continue to apply for non-Convention rights unless the courts decide to apply the Human Rights Act proportionality test more generally.

Torture 1984, UKTS 107 (1991), Cm 1775; the European Convention for the Prevention of Torture 1987, UKTS 5 (1991), Cm 1634; and the Convention on the Rights of the Child 1989, UKTS 44 (1992), Cm 1976. The Universal Declaration of Human Rights 1948, GAOR, 3rd Sess, Part I, Resolutions, p. 71, is not a treaty and not in itself legally binding. However, it has come, at least in part, to be recognised as stating customary international law and British courts have made reference to it: see, e.g. Lord Reid in *Waddington v Miah* [1974] 1 WLR 683 at 964, HL.

6   *Mortensen v Peters* (1906) 8 F 93, Ct of Justiciary.

7   See T. Meron, *Human Rights and Humanitarian Norms of Customary Law* (1989), Chap. 2.

8   [1939] 1 KB 687, CCA.

9   Below, Chap. 10.

10 [1985] AC 374, HL. In the *Council of Civil Service Unions* case, the prerogative power to determine conditions of employment in the civil service was considered 'justiciable' and hence subject to judicial review, but the powers to make treaties and to defend the realm were given (per Lord Roskill) as examples of powers that involved 'high policy' so that their exercise would not be subject to judicial review. In *R v Secretary of State for Foreign and Commonwealth Affairs, ex p Everett* [1989] QB 811, CA, the prerogative power to issue a British passport was held to be subject to judicial review. So is the prerogative of mercy: *R v Secretary of State for the Home Department, ex p Bentley* [1994] QB 349, CA. There have been many orders made under the prerogative in recent years, including orders in civil liberties areas such as telephone tapping and defence matters: see (1993) 143 NLJ 656. For a debate on the scope of the prerogative, see 223 HC Debs, 21 April 1993, col. 487.

11 See below, p. 62.

6. The judges have a long and proud tradition of protecting civil liberties at common law against encroachment by the executive. *Entick v Carrington*[12] is a classic example. But although cases of this sort still occur,[13] some judges, before the Human Rights Act 1998, were less open to persuasion than others. It was a common complaint that the courts generally were not inclined to develop the law on a grand scale, at least in the field of civil liberties. Commenting upon the failure of the courts to develop a law of privacy in the way that the American courts have, Street[14] stated:

> 'But there is no spirit of adventure or progress, either in judges or counsel, in England today. Today's English judges are not the innovators that some of their distinguished predecessors were; in the hands of modern judges the common law has lost its capacity to expand. They have not been helped by counsel. Cases are argued and tried by a narrow circle of men who seldom look beyond the decided cases for guidance. The entire development of the American law of privacy can be traced to an article in a law periodical published by Harvard Law School.[15] It is inconceivable that the views of an academic journal would exercise similar influence in Britain. This inward- and backward-looking attitude of the English Bar serves only to increase the likelihood that the courts will fail to make the law fit the needs of the time.'

Later in the same book he wrote:[16]

> 'Our judges may be relied on to defend strenuously some kinds of freedom. Their emotions will be aroused where personal freedom is menaced by some politically unimportant area of the executive: a case of unlawful arrest by a policeman, for example.[17] Their integrity is, of course, beyond criticism. Yet there are obvious limitations to what they can be expected to do in moulding the law of civil liberties. Two factors stand in their way: their reluctance to have clashes with senior members of Government, their desire not to have a repetition of the nineteenth-century strife between Parliament and the courts; and secondly, their unwillingness to immerse themselves in problems of policy, which of course loom large in many of the issues examined here.'

It will be interesting to see whether Street's strictures will be justified as the courts apply the Human Rights Act 1998. No doubt Street would have approved of the good start made by the Court of Appeal in developing the law of privacy in *Douglas v Hello!*[18]

---

12   Below, p. 84.
13   See the remarkable case of *Re M* [1994] 1 AC 377, HL, in which the Home Secretary was held in civil contempt of court for disobeying a court injunction not to deport a Zairean whose application for judicial review of the Home Office decision not to grant him asylum was under consideration by the courts. See also *R v Secretary of State for the Home Department, ex p Fire Brigades Union* [1995] 1 All ER 888, CA (Home Secretary could not introduce under the prerogative a criminal injuries scheme that was radically different from the statutory scheme).
14   *Freedom, The Individual and the Law*, (5th edn, 1982), p. 263.
15   *Ed.* See below, p. 914.
16   pp. 318–319.
17   E.g. £40,000 exemplary damages were awarded against the police for oppressive conduct amounting to torture (suffocating with plastic bags to obtain confession): *Treadaway v Chief Constable of West Midlands* (1994) Independent, 23 September, QBD.
18   Below, p. 922.

2 The present method: the Human Rights Act 1998

Rights Brought Home: The Human Rights Bill, Cm 3782, pp. 4–7

The European Convention on Human Rights
1.1 The European Convention for the Protection of Human Rights and Fundamental Freedoms is a treaty of the Council of Europe. This institution was established at the end of the Second World War, as part of the Allies' programme to reconstruct durable civilisation on the mainland of Europe. The Council was established before the European Union and, although many nations are members of both, the two bodies are quite separate.

1.2 The United Kingdom played a major part in drafting the Convention, and there was a broad agreement between the major political parties about the need for it (one of its draftsmen later became, as Lord Kilmuir, Lord Chancellor in the Conservative Administration from 1954 to 1962). The United Kingdom was among the first group of countries to sign the Convention. It was the very first country to ratify it, in March 1951. In 1966 the United Kingdom accepted that an individual person, and not merely another State, could bring a case against the United Kingdom in Strasbourg (the home of the European Commission of Human Rights and Court of Human Rights, which were established by the Convention). Successive administrations in the United Kingdom have maintained these arrangements.

1.3 The European Convention is not the only international human rights agreement to which the United Kingdom and other like-minded countries are party, but over the years it has become one of the premier agreements defining standards of behaviour across Europe. It was also for many years unique because of the system which it put in place for people from signatory countries to take complaints to Strasbourg and for those complaints to be judicially determined. These arrangements are by now well tried and tested. The rights and freedoms which are guaranteed under the Convention are ones with which the people of this country are plainly comfortable. They therefore afford an excellent basis for the Human Rights Bill which we are now introducing.

1.4 The constitutional arrangements in most continental European countries have meant that their acceptance of the Convention went hand in hand with its incorporation into their domestic law. In this country it was long believed that the rights and freedoms guaranteed by the Convention could be delivered under our common law. In the last two decades, however, there has been a growing awareness that it is not sufficient to rely on the common law and that incorporation is necessary.

1.5 The Liberal Democrat Peer, Lord Lester of Herne Hill QC, recently introduced two Bills on incorporation into the House of Lords (in 1994 and 1996). Before that, the then Conservative MP Sir Edward Gardner QC introduced a Private Member's Bill on incorporation into the House of Commons in 1987. At the time of introducing his Bill he commented on the language of the Articles in the Convention, saying: 'It is language which echoes right down the corridors of history. It goes deep into our history and as far back as Magna Carta.' (Hansard, 6 February 1987, col. 1224). In preparing this White Paper the Government has paid close attention to earlier debates and proposals for incorporation.

The Convention rights
1.6 The Convention contains Articles which guarantee a number of basic human rights. They deal with the right to life (Article 2): torture or inhumane or degrading treatment or punishment (Article 3); slavery and forced labour (Article 4); liberty and security of person (Article 5); fair trial (Article 6); retrospective criminal laws (Article 7); respect for private and family life, home and correspondence (Article 8); freedom of thought, conscience and religion (Article 9); freedom of expression (Article 10); freedom of peaceful assembly and freedom of association, including the right to join a trade union (Article 11); the right to marry and to found a family (Article 12); and discrimination in the enjoyment of these rights and freedoms (Article 14).

1.7 The United Kingdom is also a party to the First Protocol to the Convention, which guarantees the right to the peaceful enjoyment of possessions (Article 1), the right to education (Article 2) and the right to free elections (Article 3).

1.8   The rights in the Convention are set out in general terms, and they are subject in the Convention to a number of qualifications which are also of a general character. Some of these qualifications are set out in the substantive Articles themselves (see, for example, Article 10, concerning freedom of expression); others are set out in Articles 16 to 18 of the Convention. Sometimes too the rights guaranteed under the Convention need to be balanced against each other (for example, those guaranteed by Article 8 and Article 10).

Applications under the Convention

1.9   Anyone within the United Kingdom jurisdiction who is aggrieved by an action of the executive or by the effect of the existing law and who believes it is contrary to the European Convention can submit a petition to the European Commission of Human Rights. The Commission will first consider whether the petition is admissible. One of the conditions of admissibility is that the applicant must have gone through all the steps available to him or her at home for challenging the decision which he or she is complaining about. If the Commission decides that a complaint is admissible, and if a friendly settlement cannot be secured, it will send a confidential report to the Committee of Ministers of the Council of Europe, stating its opinion on whether there has been a violation. The matter may end there, with a decision by the Committee (which in practice always adopts the opinion of the Commission), or the case may be referred on to the European Court of Human Rights[19] for consideration. If the Court finds that there has been a violation it may itself 'afford just satisfaction' to the injured party by an award of damages or an award of costs and expenses. The Court may also find that a formal finding of a violation is sufficient. There is no appeal from the Court.

Effect of a Court judgment

1.10   A finding by the European Court of Human Rights of a violation of a Convention right does not have the effect of automatically changing United Kingdom law and practice: that is a matter for the United Kingdom Government and Parliament. But the United Kingdom, like all other States who are parties to the Convention, has agreed to abide by the decisions of the Court . . . It follows that, in cases where a violation has been found, the State concerned must ensure that any deficiency in its internal laws is rectified so as to bring them into line with the Convention. The State is responsible for deciding what changes are needed, but it must satisfy the Committee of Ministers that the steps taken are sufficient. Successive United Kingdom administrations have accepted these obligations in full.

Relationship to current law in the United Kingdom

1.11   When the United Kingdom ratified the Convention the view was taken that the rights and freedoms which the Convention guarantees were already, in substance, fully protected in British law. It was not considered necessary to write the Convention itself into British law, or to introduce any new laws in the United Kingdom in order to be sure of being able to comply with the Convention.

1.12   From the point of view of the *international* obligation which the United Kingdom was undertaking when it signed and ratified the Convention, this was understandable. Moreover, the European Court of Human Rights explicitly confirmed that it was not a necessary part of proper observance of the Convention that it should be incorporated into the laws of the States concerned.

1.13   However, since its drafting nearly 50 years ago, almost all the States which are party to the European Convention on Human Rights have gradually incorporated it into their domestic law in one way or another. Ireland and Norway have not done so, but Ireland has a Bill of Rights which guarantees rights similar to those guaranteed by the Convention and Norway is also in the process of incorporating the Convention. Several other countries with which we have close links and which share the common law tradition, such as Canada and New Zealand, have provided similar protection for human rights in their own legal systems.

---

19   *Ed.* Protocol 11 to the Convention, which came into force on 1 November 1998, replaced the existing part-time European Commission and Court of Human Rights with a single full-time Court.

The case for incorporation

1.14 The effect of non-incorporation on the British people is a very practical one. The rights, originally developed with major help from the United Kingdom Government, are no longer actually seen as British rights. And enforcing them takes too long and costs too much. It takes on average five years to get an action into the European Court of Human Rights once all domestic remedies have been exhausted; and it costs an average of £30,000. Bringing these rights home will mean that the British people will be able to argue for their rights in the British courts – without this inordinate delay and cost. It will also mean that the rights will be brought much more fully into the jurisprudence of the courts throughout the United Kingdom, and their interpretation will thus be far more subtly and powerfully woven into our law. And there will be another distinct benefit. British judges will be enabled to make a distinctively British contribution to the development of the jurisprudence of human rights in Europe.

1.15 Moreover, in the Government's view, the approach which the United Kingdom has so far adopted towards the Convention does not sufficiently reflect its importance and has not stood the test of time.

1.16 The most obvious proof of this lies in the number of cases in which the European Commission and Court have found that there have been violations of the Convention rights in the United Kingdom. The causes vary. The Government recognises that interpretations of the rights guaranteed under the Convention have developed over the years, reflecting changes in society and attitudes. Sometimes United Kingdom laws have proved to be inherently at odds with the Convention rights. On other occasions, although the law has been satisfactory, something has been done which our courts have held to be lawful by United Kingdom standards but which breaches the Convention. In other cases against, there has simply been no framework within which the compatibility with the Convention rights of an executive act or decision can be tested in the British courts: these courts can of course review the exercise of executive discretion, but they can do so only on the basis of what is lawful or unlawful according to the law in the United Kingdom as it stands. It is plainly unsatisfactory that someone should be the victim of a breach of the Convention standards by the State yet cannot bring any case at all in the British courts, simply because British law does not recognise the right in the same terms as one contained in the Convention.

1.17 For individuals, and for those advising them, the road to Strasbourg is long and hard. Even when they get there, the Convention enforcement machinery is subject to long delays. This might be convenient for a government which was half-hearted about the Convention and the right of individuals to apply under it, since it postpones the moment at which changes in domestic law or practice must be made. But it is not in keeping with the importance which this Government attaches to the observance of basic human rights.

Bringing Rights Home

1.18 We therefore believe than the time has come to enable people to enforce their Convention rights against the State in the British courts, rather than having to incur the delays and expense which are involved in taking a case to the European Human Rights Commission and Court in Strasbourg and which may altogether deter some people from pursing their rights. Enabling courts in the United Kingdom to rule on the application of the Convention will also help to influence the development of case law on the Convention by the European Court of Human Rights on the basis of familiarity with our laws and customs and of sensitivity to practices and procedures in the United Kingdom. Our courts' decisions will provide the European Court with a useful source of information and reasoning for its own decisions. United Kingdom judges have a very high reputation internationally, but the fact that they do not deal in the same concepts as the European Court of Human Rights limits the extent to which their judgments can be drawn upon and followed. Enabling the Convention rights to be judged by British courts will also lead to closer scrutiny of the human rights implications of new legislation and new policies. If legislation is enacted which is incompatible with the Convention, a ruling by the domestic courts to that effect will be much more direct and immediate than a ruling from the European Court of Human Rights. The Government of the day, and Parliament, will want to minimise the risk of that happening.

1.19 Our aim is a straightforward one. It is to make more directly accessible the rights which the British people already enjoy under the Convention. In other words, to bring those rights home.

NOTES

1. The Human Rights Act 1998 had been preceded by a series of private members' bills during a period of 25 years or so proposing the introduction of a bill of rights.[20] Draft bills of rights had also been prepared by non-governmental organisations.[1] Parliamentary progress could not be made in the absence of support by the government of the day. The tide turned when the Labour Party decided to introduce a bill of rights[2] as party policy and later included it in its 1997 election manifesto. On coming to power in that year, the new Labour government acted to honour its election pledge to incorporate the ECHR into United Kingdom law. It prepared a White Paper, from which the above extract is taken. The extract indicates the general Convention background and the reasons for incorporating it.

2. Prior to the enactment of the Human Rights Act (HRA), there had been an extensive debate on the arguments for and against a bill of rights. Although the debate was conducted primarily with a bill of rights involving a judicial power to strike down, rather than interpret, legislation in mind, some of the issues raised are relevant to the model of the latter kind that was adopted in the HRA. Whereas most of the cases that will arise under the HRA may prove to be cases raising particular points of criminal procedure, others in time may concern larger issues and the rule of interpretation rule in HRA, s. 3, coupled with the continuing dynamic interpretation of the ECHR at Strasbourg on a broad range of social issues, may place the courts much more centre stage than they are now. Accordingly, and because the above extract from the White Paper includes only arguments for incorporation of the ECHR that do not address these issues, the following notes rehearse some of the points about the role of the judiciary under a bill of rights that have concerned commentators.

3. One objection to a bill of rights is that it involves the courts in politics. Although the British courts have always had to rule on matters of political and social controversy,[2a] a power of interpretation such as that in HRA, s. 3, based upon the standards of the ECHR, will inevitably increase their participation in such matters. The question raised is whether unelected judges, who are necessarily difficult to dismiss, should be given a political and social role on this scale. The contrary argument is that persons taking decisions on human rights matters (which often concern minority groups and the unpopular) should be free from the 'tyranny of the majority'.

4. Another concern has been that the judiciary is not a cross-section of society, as it should be to be properly qualified to take decisions that have great social impact. J. A. G. Griffiths states: [2b]

---

20 For details of the private bills introduced by Lord Wade, Sir Edward Gardner, Mr Graham Allen and Lord Lester, see M. Zander, *A Bill of Rights* (4th edn, 1996), Chap. 1.

1 See Institute for Public Policy Research, *A Written Constitution for the United Kingdom* (2nd revd edn, 1993), p. 34ff and National Council for Civil Liberties, *A Peoples' Charter* (1991). Charter 88 also advocated a bill of rights: see *New Statesman*, 2 December 1988, p. 4 and N. Stranger, 8 *Index on Censorship* 14.

2 See *A New Agenda for Democracy*, a party policy document adopted by the Party Conference in 1993.

2a See, e.g. the *Tameside* case [1977] AC 1014, HL (comprehensive schooling) and *R v Secretary of State for the Environment, ex p Hammersmith and Fulham Borough Council* [1990] 3 All ER 589, HL (charge-capping).

2b *The Politics of the Judiciary* (5th edn, 1996), p. 21. On steps taken more recently to encourage applications from women and ethnic minority groups, see below, Chap. 11.

'In January 1994 the average age, the number of women, and those from the ethnic minorities were:

	Average age	Women	Ethnic minorities	Total number
Law Lords	66.5	0	0	10
Heads of Division	63.0	0	0	4
Lords Justices	63.0	1	0	29
High Court Judges	57.6	6	0	95
				138

Of 514 Circuit judges in post on 1 December 1994, 29 were women, and 4 were of ethnic minority origin. In 1996 there were 7 female judges on the High Court bench.

In summary, 80 per cent of the senior judiciary are products of public schools and of Oxford or Cambridge, with an average age of about sixty; 5.1 per cent are women; 100 per cent are white. Some explanation of the gross disproportions in gender and colour can no doubt be found in the structure of the legal profession, in the financial and other difficulties facing those wishing to qualify as barristers, and then needing to support themselves in the early years of practice. Another part of the explanation is sexual and racial discrimination within the profession.'

5. Later in the same book, the same author, while recognising the independence of the judiciary, also expressed concern, as a commentator on the left, at entrusting judges with greater powers at the expense of Parliament because of their generally conservative (with a small 'c') philosophy:[2c]

'Judges in the United Kingdom are not beholden politically to the government of the day. And they have longer professional lives than most ministers. They, like civil servants, see governments come like water and go with the wind. They owe no loyalty to ministers, not even that temporary loyalty which civil servants owe. Coke said that Bracton said that the King ought to be under no man but under God and the law.[2d] Judges are also lions under the throne but that seat is occupied in their eyes not by the Prime Minister but by the law and by their conception of the public interest. It is to that law and to that conception that they owe allegiance. In that lies their strength and their weakness, their value and their threat.

By allegiance to "the law" judges mean the whole body of law, much of which has its origins in the judge-made common law. "The law" also means the rule of law and here the allegiance is to the philosophical ideal that we should be ruled by laws and not by men. If that means that power should not be exercised arbitrarily or on the whim of rulers and their officials but should be dependent on and flow from properly constituted authority and from rules written down and approved by some form of representative assembly, it is an admirable and necessary, if partial, safeguard against tyranny. The proposition can hardly be taken further because, in modern industrial society, it is impossible to avoid vesting considerable discretionary power in public officials if only because laws cannot be adequately framed to cover every eventuality.
. . .

When on 14 June 1995, it was put to the Lord Chief Justice that "the very top judges" had in recent years been more 'robust' in standing up to the executive, Lord Taylor said, "It is not that they have been more robust. We have developed judicial review. It did not exist as such before 1977."

The reply was significant but evasive, suggesting that the judicial attitude to the executive had not changed, only that the means of review at the disposal of the judiciary had improved. Later, in his evidence to the Select Committee, Lord Taylor emphasized that the courts "were

2c Ibid., pp. 296, 326–327, 340–341. See also J. A. G. Griffiths, (2000) 63 MLR 159.
2d *Prohibitions del Roy* (1607) 12 Co Rep 63.

very careful not to go too far" in overturning ministerial decisions and he cited challenges to Maastricht by Rees-Mogg, to the Anglo-Irish Agreement, and to the use of a statute brought in existence in 1939 for the national emergency. But these were surely examples of deliberate use of the courts for political propaganda. It was not surprising that the applications were dismissed.

However the question is answered, what is undeniable is that the courts have, during this decade, become more severe in their criticism and more strict in their scrutiny of the exercise of executive powers in some areas. . . .

To some, the judicial view of the public interest appears merely as reactionary conservativism. It is not the politics of the extreme right. Its insensitivity is clearly rooted more in the unconscious assumptions than in a wish to oppress. But it is demonstrable that on ever major social issue which has come before the courts during the last thirty years – concerning industrial relations, political protest, race relations, governmental secrecy, police powers, moral behaviour – the judges have supported the conventional, established and settled interest. And they have reacted strongly against challenges to those interests. This conservatism does not necessarily follow the day-to-day political policies currently associated with the party of that name. But it is a political philosophy none the less.'

K. Ewing and C. Gearty[2e] reach a similar conclusion: 'The harsh reality is that we need to be protected by Parliament from the courts, as much as we need to be protected from the abuse of executive power.'

Lord Denning has expressed opposition to a US-style bill of rights on the different ground of the effect upon judicial independence and public confidence in the courts:[2f]

'. . . if judges were given power to overthrow sections or Acts of Parliament, they would become political, their appointments would be based on political grounds and the reputation of our Judiciary would suffer accordingly. One has only to see, in the great Constitutions of the United States of America and of India, the conflicts which arise from time to time between the judges and the Legislature. I hope we shall not have such conflicts in this country. The independence of our judges and their reputation for impartiality depend on their obeying the will of Parliament and on their being independent. The independence of the judges is the other pillar of our Constitution.'

Human Rights Act 1998

Introduction

1. The Convention rights

(1) In this Act 'the Convention rights' means the rights and fundamental freedoms set out in—

    (*a*) Articles 2 to 12 and 14 of the Convention,

    (*b*) Articles 1 to 3 of the First Protocol, and

    (*c*) Articles 1 and 2 of the Sixth Protocol,

as read with Articles 16 to 18 of the Convention.

(2) Those Articles are to have effect for the purposes of this Act subject to any designated derogation or reservation (as to which see sections 14 and 15).

(3) The Articles are set out in Schedule 1.

(4) The Secretary of State may by order make such amendments to this Act as he considers appropriate to reflect the effect, in relation to the United Kingdom, of a protocol.

(5) In subsection (4) 'protocol' means a protocol to the Convention—

    (*a*) which the United Kingdom has ratified; or

    (*b*) which the United Kingdom has signed with a view to ratification.

2e *Freedom Under Thatcher* (1990), pp. 270–271.
2f 369 HL Deb, 25 March 1976, cols. 797–798.

(6) No amendment may be made by an order under subsection (4) so as to come into force before the protocol concerned in force in relation to the United Kingdom.

2. Interpretation of Convention rights

(1) A court or tribunal determining a question which has arisen in connection with a Convention right must take into account any—

  (*a*) judgment, decision, declaration or advisory opinion of the European Court of Human Rights,

  (*b*) opinion of the Commission given in a report adopted under Article 31 of the Convention,

  (*c*) decision of the Commission in connection with Article 26 or 27(2) of the Convention, or

  (*d*) decision of the Committee of Ministers taken under Article 46 of the Convention,

whenever made or given, so far as, in the opinion of the court or tribunal, it is relevant to the proceedings in which that question has arisen.

(2) Evidence of any judgment, decision, declaration or opinion of which account may have to be taken under this section is to be given in proceedings before any court or tribunal in such manner as may be provided by rules.

(3) In this section 'rules' means rules of court or, in the case of proceedings before a tribunal, rules made for the purposes of this section—

  (*a*) by the Lord Chancellor or the Secretary of State, in relation to any proceedings outside Scotland;

  (*b*) by the Secretary of State, in relation to proceedings in Scotland; or

  (*c*) by a Northern Ireland department, in relation to proceedings before a tribunal in Northern Ireland—

    (i) which deals with transferred matters; and

    (ii) for which no rules made under paragraph (a) are in force.

Legislation

3. Interpretation of legislation

(1) So far as it is possible to do so, primary legislation and subordinate legislation must be read and given effect in a way which is compatible with the Convention rights.

(2) This section—

  (*a*) applies to primary legislation and subordinate legislation whenever enacted;

  (*b*) does not affect the validity, continuing operation or enforcement of any incompatible primary legislation; and

  (*c*) does not affect the validity, continuing operation or enforcement of any incompatible subordinate legislation if (disregarding any possibility of revocation) primary legislation prevents removal of the incompatibility.

4. Declaration of incompatibility

(1) Subsection (2) applies in any proceedings in which a court determines whether a provision of primary legislation is compatible with a Convention right.

(2) If the court is satisfied that the provision is incompatible with a Convention right, it may make a declaration of that incompatibility.

(3) Subsection (4) applies in any proceedings in which a court determines whether a provision of subordinate legislation, made in the exercise of a power conferred by primary legislation, is compatible with a Convention right.

(4) If the court is satisfied—

  (*a*) that the provision is incompatible with a Convention right, and

  (*b*) that (disregarding any possibility of revocation) the primary legislation concerned prevents removal of the incompatibility,

it may make a declaration of that incompatibility.

(5) In this section 'court' means—

  (*a*) the House of Lords;

  (*b*) the Judicial Committee of the Privy Council;

  (*c*) the Courts-Martial Appeal Court;

  (*d*) in Scotland, the High Court of Justiciary sitting otherwise than as a trial court or the Court of Session;

  (*e*) in England and Wales or Northern Ireland, the High Court or the Court of Appeal.

(6) A declaration under this section ('a declaration of incompatibility')—
    (*a*) does not affect the validity, continuing operation or enforcement of the provision in respect of which it is given; and
    (*b*) is not binding on the parties to the proceedings in which it is made.

5. Right of Crown to intervene
(1) Where a court is considering whether to make a declaration of incompatibility, the Crown is entitled to notice in accordance with rules of court.
(2) In any case to which subsection (1) applies—
    (*a*) a Minister of the Crown (or a person nominated by him),
    (*b*) a member of the Scottish Executive,
    (*c*) a Northern Ireland Minister,
    (*d*) a Northern Ireland department,
is entitled, on giving notice in accordance with rules of court, to be joined as a party to the proceedings.
(3) Notice under subsection (2) may be given at any time during the proceedings.
(4) A person who has been made a party to criminal proceedings (other then in Scotland) as the result of a notice under subsection (2) may, with leave, appeal to the House of Lords against any declaration of incompatibility made in the proceedings.
(5) In subsection (4)—
    'criminal proceedings' includes all proceedings before the Courts-Martial Appeal Court; and
    'leave' means leave granted by the court making the declaration of incompatibility or by the House of Lords.

Public authorities

6. Acts of public authorities
(1) It is unlawful for a public authority to act in a way which is incompatible with a Convention right.
(2) Subsection (1) does not apply to an act if—
    (*a*) as the result of one or more provisions of primary legislation, the authority could not have acted differently; or
    (*b*) in the case of one or more provisions of, or made under, primary legislation which cannot be read or given effect in a way which is compatible with the Convention rights, the authority was acting so as to give effect to or enforce those provisions.
(3) In this section 'public authority' includes—
    (*a*) a court or tribunal, and
    (*b*) any person certain of whose functions are functions of a public nature,
but does not include either House of Parliament or a person exercising functions in connection with proceedings in Parliament.
(4) In subsection (3) 'Parliament' does not include the House of Lords in its judicial capacity.
(5) In relation to a particular act, a person is not a public authority by virtue only of subsection (3)(b) if the nature of the act is private.
(6) 'An act' includes a failure to act but does not include a failure to—
    (*a*) introduce in, or lay before, Parliament a proposal for legislation; or
    (*b*) make any primary legislation or remedial order.

7. Proceedings
(1) A person who claims that a public authority has acted (or proposes to act) in a way which is made unlawful by section 6(1) may—
    (*a*) bring proceedings against the authority under this Act in the appropriate court or tribunal, or
    (*b*) rely on the Convention right or rights concerned in any legal proceedings,
but only if he is (or would be) a victim of the unlawful act.
(2) In subsection (1)(a) 'appropriate court or tribunal' means such court or tribunal as may be determined in accordance with rules; and proceedings against an authority include a counterclaim or similar proceeding.
(3) If the proceedings are brought on an application for judicial review, the applicant is to be taken to have a sufficient interest in relation to the unlawful act only if he is, or would be, a victim of that act.

(4) If the proceedings are made by way of a petition for judicial review in Scotland, the applicant shall be taken to have title and interest to sue in relation to the unlawful act only if he is, or would be, a victim of that act.

(5) Proceedings under subsection (1)(a) must be brought before the end of—

    (*a*) the period of one year beginning with the date on which the act complained of took place; or

    (*b*) such longer period as the court or tribunal considers equitable having regard to all the circumstances,

but that is subject to any rule imposing a stricter time limit in relation to the procedure in question.

(6) In subsection (1)(b) 'legal proceedings' includes—

    (*a*) proceedings brought by or at the instigation of a public authority; and

    (*b*) an appeal against the decision of a court or tribunal.

(7) For the purposes of this section, a person is a victim of an unlawful act only if he would be a victim for the purposes of Article 34 of the Convention if proceedings were brought in the European Court of Human Rights in respect of that act.

(8) Nothing in this Act creates a criminal offence.

(9) In this section 'rules' means—

    (*a*) in relation to proceedings before a court or tribunal outside Scotland, rules made by the Lord Chancellor or the Secretary of State for the purposes of this section or rules of court,

    (*b*) in relation to proceedings before a court or tribunal in Scotland, rules made by the Secretary of State for those purposes,

    (*c*) in relation to proceedings before a tribunal in Northern Ireland—

        (i) which deals with transferred matters; and

        (ii) for which no rules made under paragraph (a) are in force,

    rules made by a Northern Ireland department for those purposes,

and includes provision made by order under section 1 of the Courts and Legal Services Act 1990.

(10) In making rules, regard must be had to section 9.

(11) The Minister who has power to make rules in relation to a particular tribunal may, to the extent he considers it necessary to ensure that the tribunal can provide an appropriate remedy in relation to an act (or proposed act) of a public authority which is (or would be) unlawful as a result of section 6(1), by order add to—

    (*a*) the relief or remedies which the tribunal may grant; or

    (*b*) the grounds on which it may grant any of them.

(12) An order made under subsection (11) may contain such incidental, supplemental, consequential or transitional provision as the Minister making it considers appropriate.

(13) 'The Minister' includes the Northern Ireland department concerned.

8. Judicial remedies

(1) In relation to ay act (or proposed act) of a public authority which the court finds is (or would be) unlawful, it may grant such relief or remedy, or make such order, within its powers as it considers just and appropriate.

(2) But damages may be awarded only by a court which has power to award damages, or to order the payment of compensation, in civil proceedings.

(3) No award of damages is to be made unless, taking account of all the circumstances of the case, including—

    (*a*) any other relief or remedy granted, or order made, in relation to the act in question (by that or any other court), and

    (*b*) the consequences of any decision (of that or any other court) in respect of that act,

the court is satisfied that the award is necessary to afford just satisfaction to the person in whose favour it is made.

(4) In determining—

    (*a*) whether to award damages, or

    (*b*) the amount of an award,

the court must take into account the principles applied by the European Court of Human Rights in relation to the award of compensation under Article 41 of the Convention.

(5) A public authority against which damages are awarded is to be treated—
   (*a*) in Scotland, for the purposes of section 3 of the Law Reform (Miscellaneous Provisions) (Scotland) Act 1940 as if the award were made in an action of damages in which the authority has been found liable in respect of loss or damage to the person to whom the award is made;
   (*b*) for the purposes of the Civil Liability (Contribution) Act 1978 as liable in respect of damage suffered by the person to whom the award is made.
(6) In this section—
   'court' includes a tribunal;
   'damages' means damages for an unlawful act of a public authority; and
   'unlawful' means unlawful under section 6(1).

9. Judicial acts
(1) Proceedings under section 7(1)(a) in respect of a judicial act may be brought only—
   (*a*) by exercising a right of appeal;
   (*b*) on an application (in Scotland a petition) for judicial review; or
   (*c*) in such other forum as may be prescribed by rules.
(2) That does not affect any rule of law which prevents a court from being the subject of judicial review.
(3) In proceedings under this Act in respect of a judicial act done in good faith, damages may not be awarded otherwise than to compensate a person to the extent required by Article 5(5) of the Convention.
(4) An award of damages permitted by subsection (3) is to be made against the Crown; but no award may be made unless the appropriate person, if not a party to the proceedings, is joined.
(5) In this section—
   'appropriate person' means the Minister responsible for the court concerned, or a person or government department nominated by him;
   'court' includes a tribunal;
   'judge' includes a member of a tribunal, a justice of the peace and a clerk or other officer entitled to exercise the jurisdiction of a court;
   'judicial act' means a judicial act of a court and includes an act done on the instructions, or on behalf, of a judge; and
   'rules' has the same meaning as in section 7(9).

Remedial action
10. Power to take remedial action
(1) This section applies if—
   (*a*) a provision of legislation has been declared under section 4 to be incompatible with a Convention right and, if an appeal lies—
       (i) all persons who may appeal have stated in writing that they do not intend to do so;
       (ii) the time for bringing an appeal has expired and no appeal has been brought within that time; or
       (iii) an appeal brought within that time has been determined or abandoned; or
   (*b*) it appears to a Minister of the Crown or Her Majesty in Council that, having regard to a finding of the European Court of Human Rights made after the coming into force of this section in proceedings against the United Kingdom, a provision of legislation is incompatible with an obligation of the United Kingdom arising from the Convention.
(2) If a Minister of the Crown considers that there are compelling reasons for proceeding under this section, he may by order make such amendments to the legislation as he considers necessary to remove the incompatibility.
(3) If, in the case of subordinate legislation, a Minister of the Crown considers—
   (*a*) that it is necessary to amend the primary legislation under which the subordinate legislation in question was made, in order to enable the incompatibility to be removed, and
   (*b*) that there are compelling reasons for proceeding under this section,
he may by order make such amendments to the primary legislation as he considers necessary.

(4) This section also applies where the provision in question is in subordinate legislation and has been quashed, or declared invalid, by reason of incompatibility with a Convention right and the Minister proposes to proceed under paragraph 2(b) of Schedule 2.

(5) If the legislation is an Order in Council, the power conferred by subsection (2) or (3) is exercisable by Her Majesty in Council.

(6) In this section 'legislation' does not include a Measure of the Church Assembly or of the General Synod of the Church of England.

(7) Schedule 2 makes further provision about remedial orders.

Other rights and proceedings

11. Safeguard for existing human rights

A person's reliance on a Convention right does not restrict—

    (*a*) any other right or freedom conferred on him by or under any law having effect in any part of the United Kingdom; or

    (*b*) his right to make any claim or bring any proceedings which he could make or bring apart from sections 7 to 9.

12. Freedom of expression

(1) This section applies if a court is considering whether to grant any relief which, if granted, might affect the exercise of the Convention right to freedom of expression.

(2) If the person against whom the application for relief is made ('the respondent') is neither present nor represented, no such relief is to be granted unless the court is satisfied—

    (*a*) that the applicant has taken all practicable steps to notify the respondent; or

    (*b*) that there are compelling reasons why the respondent should not be notified.

(3) No such relief is to be granted so as to restrain publication before trial unless the court is satisfied that the applicant is likely to establish that publication should not be allowed.

(4) The court must have particular regard to the importance of the Convention right to freedom of expression and, where the proceedings relate to material which the respondent claims, or which appears to the court, to be journalistic, literary or artistic material (or to conduct connected with such material), to—

    (*a*) the extent to which—

        (i) the material has, or is about to, become available to the public; or

        (ii) it is, or would be, in the public interest for the material to be published;

    (*b*) any relevant privacy code.

(5) In this section—

'court' includes a tribunal; and

'relief' includes any remedy or order (other than in criminal proceedings).

13. Freedom of thought, conscience and religion

(1) If a court's determination of any question arising under this Act might affect the exercise by a religious organisation (itself or its members collectively) of the Convention right to freedom of thought, conscience and religion, it must have particular regard to the importance of that right.

(2) In this section 'court' includes a tribunal.

Derogations and reservations

14. Derogations

(1) In this Act 'designated derogation' means—

    any derogation by the United Kingdom from an Article of the Convention, or of any protocol to the Convention, which is designated for the purposes of this Act in an order made by the Secretary of State.

(2) . . .

(3) If a designated derogation is amended or replaced it ceases to be a designated derogation.

(4) But subsection (3) does not prevent the Secretary of State from exercising his power under subsection [(1)] . . . to make a fresh designation order in respect of the Article concerned.

(5) The Secretary of State must by order make such amendments to Schedule 3 as he considers appropriate to reflect—

    (*a*) any designation order; or

    (*b*) the effect of subsection (3).

(6) A designation order may be made in anticipation of the making by the United Kingdom of a proposed derogation.[3]

15. Reservations

(1) In this Act 'designated reservation' means—

    (*a*)   the United Kingdom's reservation to Article 2 of the First Protocol to the Convention; and

    (*b*)   any other reservation by the United Kingdom to an Article of the Convention, or of any protocol to the Convention, which is designated for the purposes of this Act in an order made by the Secretary of State.

(2) The text of the reservation referred to in subsection (1)(a) is set out in Part II of Schedule 3.

(3) If a designated reservation is withdrawn wholly or in part it ceases to be a designated reservation.

(4) But subsection (3) does not prevent the Secretary of State from exercising his power under subsection (1)(b) to make a fresh designation order in respect of the Article concerned.

(5) The Secretary of state must by order make such amendments to this Act as he considers appropriate to reflect—

    (*a*)   any designation order; or

    (*b*)   the effect of subsection (3).

16. Period for which designated derogations have effect

(1) If it has not already been withdrawn by the United Kingdom, a designated derogation ceases to have effect for the purposes of this Act . . . at the end of the period of five years beginning with the date on which the order designating it was made.

(2) At any time before the period—

    (*a*)   fixed by subsection (1) . . ., or

    (*b*)   extended by an order under this subsection,

comes to an end, the Secretary of State may by order extend it by a further period of five years.

(3) An order under section 14(1) . . . ceases to have effect at the end of the period for consideration, unless a resolution has been passed by each House approving the order.

(4) Subsection (3) does not affect—

    (*a*)   anything done in reliance on the order; or

    (*b*)   the power to make a fresh order under section 14(1) . . .

(5) In subsection (3) 'period for consideration' means the period of forty days beginning with the day on which the order was made.

(6) In calculating the period for consideration, no account is to be taken of any time during which—

    (*a*)   Parliament is dissolved or prorogued; or

    (*b*)   both Houses are adjourned for more than four days.

(7) If a designated derogation is withdrawn by the United Kingdom, the Secretary of State must by order make such amendments to this Act as he considers are required to reflect that withdrawal.[4]

17. Periodic review of designated reservations

(1) The appropriate Minister must review the designated reservation referred to in section 15(1)(a)—

    (*a*)   before the end of the period of five years beginning with the date on which section 1(2)came into force; and

    (*b*)   if that designation is still in force, before the end of the period of five years beginning with the date on which the last report relating to it was laid under subsection (3).

(2) The appropriate Minister must review each of the other designated reservations (if any)—

    (*a*)   before the end of the period of five years beginning with the date on which the order designating the reservation first came into force; and

    (*b*)   if the designation is still in force, before the end of the period of five years beginning with the date on which the last report relating to it was laid under subsection (3).

3   The words omitted were repealed by the Human Rights (Amendment) Order 2001, S.I. 2001 No. 1216 (in force 1 April 2001). They provided for the UK derogation from its obligations under Art. 5(3) that was in issue in *Murray v United Kingdom* (1996) 22 EHRR 29. The derogation was withdrawn in 2001.

4   The words omitted were repealed by the Human Rights (Amendment) Order 2001, S.I. 2001 No. 1216 (in force 1 April 2001). They provided for the UK derogation from its obligations under Art. 5(3) that was in issue in *Murray v United Kingdom* (1996) 22 EHRR 29. The derogation was withdrawn in 2001.

(3) The Minister conducting a review under this section must prepare a report on the result of the review and lay a copy of it before each House of Parliament.

. . .

Parliamentary procedure

19. Statements of compatability

(1) A Minister of the Crown in charge of a Bill in either House of Parliament must, before Second Reading of the Bill—

    (*a*) make a statement to the effect that in his view the provisions of the Bill are compatible with the Convention rights ('a statement of compatibility'); or

    (*b*) make a statement to the effect that although he is unable to make a statement of compatibility the government nevertheless wishes the House to proceed with the Bill.

(2) The statement must be in writing and be published in such manner as the Minister making it considers appropriate.

. . .

21. Interpretation, etc

(1) In this Act—

. . .

    'primary legislation' means any—

        (*a*) public general Act;

        (*b*) local and personal Act;

        (*c*) private Act;

        (*d*) Measure of the Church Assembly;

        (*e*) Measure of the General Synod of the Church of England;

        (*f*) Order in Council—

            (i) made in exercise of Her Majesty's Royal Prerogative;

            (ii) made under section 38(1)(*a*) of the Northern Ireland Constitution Act 1973 or the corresponding provision of the Northern Ireland Act 1998; or

            (iii) amending an Act of a kind mentioned in paragraph (*a*), (*b*) or (*c*);

and includes an order or other instrument made under primary legislation (otherwise than by the National Assembly for Wales, a member of the Scottish Executive, a Northern Ireland Minister or a Northern Ireland department) to the extent to which it operates to bring one or more provisions of that legislation into force or amends any primary legislation;

. . .

    'subordinate legislation' means any—

    (*a*) Order in Council other than one—

        (i) made in exercise of Her Majesty's Royal Prerogative;

        (ii) made under section 38(1)(*a*) of the Northern Ireland Constitution Act 1973 or the corresponding provision of the Northern Ireland Act 1998; or

        (iii) amending an Act of a kind mentioned in the definition of primary legislation;

    (*b*) Act of the Scottish Parliament;

    (*c*) Act of the Parliament of Northern Ireland;

    (*d*) Measure of the Assembly established under section 1 of the Northern Ireland Assembly Act 1973;

    (*e*) Act of the Northern Ireland Assembly;

    (*f*) order, rules, regulations, scheme, warrant, byelaw or other instrument made under primary legislation (except to the extent to which it operates to bring one or more provisions of that legislation into force or amends any primary legislation);

    (*g*) order, rules, regulations, scheme, warrant, byelaw or other instrument made under legislation mentioned in paragraph (*b*), (*c*), (*d*) or (*e*) or made under an Order in Council applying only to Northern Ireland;

    (*h*) order, rules, regulations, scheme, warrant, byelaw or other instrument made by a member of the Scottish Executive, a Northern Ireland Minister or a Northern Ireland department in exercise of prerogative or other executive functions of Her Majesty which are exercisable by such a person on behalf of Her Majesty;

    'transferred matters' has the same meaning as in the Northern Ireland Act 1998; and

    'tribunal' means any tribunal in which legal proceedings may be brought.

(2) The references in paragraph (*b*) and (*c*) of section 2(1) to Articles are to Articles of the convention as they had effect immediately before the coming into force of the Eleventh Protocol.
(3) The reference in paragraph (d) of section 2(1) to Article 46 includes a reference to Articles 32 and 54 of the Convention as they had effect immediately before the coming into force of the Eleventh Protocol.
(4) The references in section 2(1) to a report or decision of the Commission or a decision of the Committee of Ministers include references to a report or decision made as provided by paragraphs 3, 4 and 6 of Article 5 of the Eleventh Protocol (transitional provisions).
(5) Any liability under the Army Act 1995, the Air Force Act 1955 or the Naval Discipline Act 1957 to suffer death for an offence is replaced by a liability to imprisonment for life or any less punishment authorised by those Acts; and those Acts shall accordingly have effect with the necessary modifications.

22. Short title, commencement, application and extent
(1) This Act may be cited as the Human Rights Act 1998.
(2) Sections 18, 20 and 21(5) and this section come into force on the passing of this Act.
(3) The other provisions of this Act come into force on such day as the Secretary of State may by order appoint; and different days may be appointed for different purposes.
(4) Paragraph (b) of subsection (1) of section 7 applies to proceedings brought by or at the instigation of a public authority whenever the act in question took place; but otherwise that subsection does not apply to an act taking place before the coming into force of that section.
(5) This Act binds the Crown.
(6) This Act extends to Northern Ireland.
(7) Section 21(5), so far as it relates to any provision contained in the Army Act 1955, the Air Force Act 1955 or the Naval Discipline Act 1957, extends to any place to which that provision extends.

SCHEDULES
SCHEDULE 1
THE ARTICLES
PART I
THE CONVENTION
RIGHTS AND FREEDOMS
ARTICLE 2
RIGHT TO LIFE
1. Everyone's right to life shall be protected by law. No one shall be deprived of his life intentionally save in the execution of a sentence of a court following his conviction of a crime for which this penalty is provided by law.
2. Deprivation of life shall not be regarded as inflicted in contravention of this Article when it results from the use of force which is no more than absolutely necessary:
    (a) in defence of any person from unlawful violence;
    (b) in order to effect a lawful arrest or to prevent the escape of a person lawfully detained;
    (c) in action lawfully taken for the purpose of quelling a riot or insurrection.

ARTICLE 3
PROHIBITION OF TORTURE
No one shall be subjected to torture or to inhuman or degrading treatment or punishment.

ARTICLE 4
PROHIBITON OF SLAVERY AND FORCED LABOUR
1. No one shall be held in slavery or servitude.
2. No one shall be required to perform forced or compulsory labour.
3. For the purpose of this Article the term 'forced or compulsory labour' shall not include:
    (a) any work required to be done in the ordinary course of detention imposed according to the provisions of Article 5 of this Convention or during conditional release from such detention;
    (b) any service of a military character or, in case of conscientious objectors in countries where they are recognised, service exacted instead of compulsory military service;
    (c) any service exacted in case of an emergency or calamity threatening the life or well-being of the community;
    (d) any work or service which forms part of normal civic obligations.

ARTICLE 5
RIGHT TO LIBERTY AND SECURITY

1. Everyone has the right to liberty and security of person. No one shall be deprived of his liberty save in the following cases and in accordance with a procedure prescribed by law:
   (a) the lawful detention of a person after conviction by a competent court;
   (b) the lawful arrest or detention of a person for non-compliance with the lawful order of a court or in order to secure the fulfilment of any obligation prescribed by law;
   (c) the lawful arrest or detention of a person effected for the purpose of bringing him before the competent legal authority on reasonable suspicion of having committed an offence or when it is reasonably considered necessary to prevent his committing an offence or fleeing after having done so;
   (d) the detention of a minor by lawful order for the purpose of educational supervision or his lawful detention for the purpose of bringing him before the competent legal authority;
   (e) the lawful detention of persons for the prevention of the spreading of infectious diseases, of persons of unsound mind, alcoholics or drug addicts or vagrants;
   (f) the lawful arrest or detention of a person to prevent his effecting an unauthorised entry into the country or of a person against whom action is being taken with a view to deportation or extradition.

2. Everyone who is arrested shall be informed promptly, in a language which he understands, of the reasons for his arrest and of any charge against him.

3. Everyone arrested or detained in accordance with the provisions of paragraph 1(c) of this Article shall be brought promptly before a judge or other officer authorised by law to exercise judicial power and shall be entitled to trial within a reasonable time or to release pending trial. Release may be conditioned by guarantees to appear for trial.

4. Everyone who is deprived of his liberty by arrest or detention shall be entitled to take proceedings by which the lawfulness of his detention shall be decided speedily by a court and his release ordered if the detention is not lawful.

5. Everyone who has been the victim of arrest or detention in contravention of the provisions of this Article shall have an enforceable right to compensation.

ARTICLE 6
RIGHT TO A FAIR TRIAL

1. In the determination of his civil rights and obligations or of any criminal charge against him, everyone is entitled to a fair and public hearing within a reasonable time by an independent and impartial tribunal established by law. Judgment shall be pronounced publicly but the press and public may be excluded from all or part of the trial in the interest of morals, public order or national security in a democratic society, where the interests of juveniles or the protection of the private life of the parties so require, or to the extent strictly necessary in the opinion of the court in special circumstances where publicity would prejudice the interests of justice.

2. Everyone charged with a criminal offence shall be presumed innocent until proved guilty according to law.

3. Everyone charged with a criminal offence has the following minimum rights:
   (a) to be informed promptly, in a language which he understands and in detail, of the nature and cause of the accusation against him;
   (b) to have adequate time and facilities for the preparation of his defence;
   (c) to defend himself in person or through legal assistance of his own choosing or, if he has not sufficient means to pay for legal assistance, to be given it free when the interests of justice so require;
   (d) to examine or have examined witnesses against him and to obtain the attendance and examination of witnesses on his behalf under the same conditions as witnesses against him;
   (e) to have the free assistance of an interpreter if he cannot understand or speak the language used in court.

ARTICLE 7
NO PUNISHMENT WITHOUT LAW

1. No one shall be held guilty of any criminal offence on account of any act or omission which did not constitute a criminal offence under national or international law at the time when it was committed. Nor shall a heavier penalty be imposed than the one that was applicable at the time the criminal offence was committed.

2. This Article shall not prejudice the trial and punishment of any person for any act or omission which, at the time when it was committed, was criminal according to the general principles of law recognised by civilised nations.

ARTICLE 8
RIGHT TO RESPECT FOR PRIVATE AND FAMILY LIFE

1. Everyone has the right to respect for his private and family life, his home and his correspondence.
2. There shall be no interference by a public authority with the exercise of this right except such as is in accordance with the law and is necessary in a democratic society in the interests of national security, public safety or the economic well-being of the country, for the prevention of disorder or crime, for the protection of health or morals, or for the protection of the rights and freedoms of others.

ARTICLE 9
FREEDOM OF THOUGHT, CONSCIENCE AND RELIGION

1. Everyone has the right to freedom of thought, conscience and religion; this right includes freedom to change his religion or belief and freedom, either alone or in community with others and in public or private, to manifest his religion or belief, in worship, teaching, practice and observance.
2. Freedom to manifest one's religion or beliefs shall be subject only to such limitations as are prescribed by law and are necessary in a democratic society in the interests of public safety, for the protection of public order, health or morals, or for the protection of the rights and freedoms of others.

ARTICLE 10
FREEDOM OF EXPRESSION

1. Everyone has the right to freedom of expression. This right shall include freedom to hold opinions and to receive and impart information and ideas without interference by public authority and regardless of frontiers. This Article shall not prevent States from requiring the licensing of broadcasting, television or cinema enterprises.
2. The exercise of these freedoms, since it carries with it duties and responsibilities, may be subject to such formalities, conditions, restrictions or penalties as are prescribed by law and are necessary in a democratic society, in the interests of national security, territorial integrity or public safety, for the prevention of disorder or crime, for the protection of health or morals, for the protection of the reputation or rights of others, for preventing the disclosure of information received in confidence, or for maintaining the authority and impartiality of the judiciary.

ARTICLE 11
FREEDOM OF ASSEMBLY AND ASSOCIATION

1. Everyone has the right to freedom of peaceful assembly and to freedom of association with others, including the right to form and to join trade unions for the protection of his interests.
2. No restrictions shall be placed on the exercise of these rights other than such as are prescribed by law and are necessary in a democratic society in the interests of national security or public safety, for the prevention of disorder or crime, for the protection of health or morals or for the protection of the rights and freedoms of others. This Article shall not prevent the imposition of lawful restrictions on the exercise of these rights by members of the armed forces, of the police or of the administration of the State.

ARTICLE 12
RIGHT TO MARRY

Men and women of marriageable age have the right to marry and to found a family, according to the national laws governing the exercise of this right.

ARTICLE 14
PROHIBITON OF DISCRIMINATION

The enjoyment of the rights and freedoms set forth in this Convention shall be secured without discrimination on any ground such as sex, race, colour, language, religion, political or other opinion, national or social origin, association with a national minority, property, birth or other status.

ARTICLE 16
RESTRICTIONS ON POLITICAL ACTIVITY OF ALIENS

Nothing in Articles 10, 11 and 14 shall be regarded as preventing the High Contracting Parties from imposing restrictions on the political activity of aliens.

ARTICLE 17
PROHIBITION OF ABUSE OF RIGHTS

Nothing in this Convention may be interpreted as implying for any State, group or person any right to engage in any activity or perform any act aimed at the destruction of any of the rights and freedoms set forth herein or at their limitation to a greater extent than is provided for in the Convention.

ARTICLE 18
LIMITATION ON USE OF RESTRICTIONS ON RIGHTS

The restrictions permitted under this Convention to the said rights and freedoms shall not be applied for any purpose other than those for which they have been prescribed.

PART II
THE FIRST PROTOCOL
ARTICLE 1
PROTECTION OF PROPERTY

Every natural or legal person is entitled to the peaceful enjoyment of his possessions. No one shall be deprived of his possessions except in the public interest and subject to the conditions provided for by law and by the general principles of international law.

The preceding provisions shall not, however, in any way impair the right of a State to enforce such laws as it deems necessary to control the use of property in accordance with the general interest or to secure the payment of taxes or other contributions or penalties.

ARTICLE 2
RIGHT TO EDUCATION

No person shall be denied the right to education. In the exercise of any functions which it assumes in relation to education and to teaching, the State shall respect the right of parents to ensure such education and teaching in conformity with their own religious and philosophical convictions.

ARTICLE 3
RIGHT TO FREE ELECTIONS

The High Contracting Parties undertake to hold free elections at reasonable intervals by secret ballot, under conditions which will ensure the free expression of the opinion of the people in the choice of the legislature.

PART III
THE SIXTH PROTOCOL
ARTICLE 1
ABOLITION OF THE DEATH PENALTY

The death penalty shall be abolished. No one shall be condemned to such penalty or executed.

ARTICLE 2
DEATH PENALTY IN TIME OF WAR

A State may make provision in its law for the death penalty in respect of acts committed in time of war or of imminent threat of war; such penalty shall be applied only in the instances laid down in the law and in accordance with its provisions. The State shall communicate to the Secretary General of the Council of Europe the relevant provisions of that law.

SCHEDULE 2
REMEDIAL ORDERS
Orders

1. (1) A remedial order may—
  (a) contain such incidental, supplemental, consequential or transitional provisions as the person making it considers appropriate;
  (b) be made so as to have effect from a date earlier than that on which it is made;
  (c) make provision for the delegation of specific functions;
  (d) make different provision for different cases.

(2) The power conferred by sub-paragraph (1)(a) includes—

    (a) power to amend primary legislation (including primary legislation other than that which contains the incompatible provision); and

    (b) power to amend or revoke subordinate legislation (including subordinate legislation other than that which contains the incompatible provision).

(3) A remedial order may be made so as to have the same extent as the legislation which it affects.

(4) No person is to be guilty of an offence solely as a result of the retrospective effect of a remedial order.

Procedure

2. No remedial order may be made unless—

    (a) a draft of the order has been approved by a resolution of each House of Parliament made after the end of the period of 60 days beginning with the day on which the draft was laid; or

    (b) it is declared in the order that it appears to the person making it that, because of the urgency of the matter, it is necessary to make the order without a draft being so approved.

Orders laid in draft

3. (1) No draft may be laid under paragraph 2(a) unless—

    (a) the person proposing to make the order has laid before Parliament a document which contains a draft of the proposed order and the required information; and

    (b) the period of 60 days, beginning with the day on which the document required by this sub-paragraph was laid, has ended.

(2) If representations have been made during that period, the draft laid under paragraph 2(a) must be accompanied by a statement containing—

    (a) a summary of the representations; and

    (b) if, as a result of the representations, the proposed order has been changed, details of the changes.

Urgent cases

4. (1) If a remedial order ('the original order') is made without being approved in draft, the person making it must lay it before Parliament, accompanied by the required information, after it is made.

(2) If representations have been made during the period of 60 days beginning with the day on which the original order was made, the person making it must (after the end of that period) lay before Parliament a statement containing—

    (a) a summary of the representations; and

    (b) if, as a result of the representations, he considers it appropriate to make changes to the original order, details of the changes.

(3) If sub-paragraph (2)(b) applies, the person making the statement must—

    (a) make a further remedial order replacing the original order; and

    (b) lay the replacement order before Parliament.

(4) If, at the end of the period of 120 days beginning with the day on which the original order was made, a resolution has not been passed by each House approving the original or replacement order, the order ceases to have effect (but without that affecting anything previously done under either order or the power to make a fresh remedial order).

Definitions

5. In this Schedule—

    'representations' means representations about a remedial order (or proposed remedial order) made to the person making (or proposing to make) it and includes any relevant Parliamentary report or resolution; and

    'required information' means—

    (a) an explanation of the incompatibility which the order (or proposed order) seeks to remove, including particulars of the relevant declaration, finding or order; and

    (b) a statement of the reasons for proceeding under section 10 and for making an order in those terms.

Calculating periods

6. In calculating any period for the purposes of this Schedule, no account is to be taken of any time during which—

    (a) Parliament is dissolved or prorogued; or

    (b) both Houses are adjourned for more than four days.

SCHEDULE 3

DEROGATION AND RESERVATION
PART I[5]
DEROGATION

· · ·

PART II
RESERVATION

At the time of signing the present (First) Protocol, I declare that, in view of certain provisions of the Education Acts in the United Kingdom, the principle affirmed in the second sentence of Article 2 is accepted by the United Kingdom only so far as is compatible with the provision of efficient instruction and training, and the avoidance of unreasonable public expenditure.
Dated 20 March 1952
Made by the United Kingdom Permanent Representative to the Council of Europe.

NOTES

1. The Human Rights Act (HRA) entered fully into force on 2 October 2000.[6] The Act applies to England and Wales, Scotland and Northern Ireland.[7] It does not apply to the Channel Islands or the Isle of Man.[8]

2. *The Scheme of the Human Rights Act.*[9] This is both complicated and unique. The HRA provides for the indirect incorporation of the rights in the European Convention on Human Rights into United Kingdom law as 'the Convention rights' (s. 1). This has two main consequences. First, in all cases coming before them, the United Kingdom courts must interpret primary legislation compatibly with Convention rights so far as is possible (s. 3), taking into account the interpretation that has been given to them at Strasbourg (s. 2). If, despite all efforts, primary legislation cannot be

5   Sch. 3, Part I, was repealed by the Human Rights (Amendment) Order 2001, S.I. 2001 No. 1216 (in force 1 April 2001). It contained the text of the UK derogation from its obligations under Art. 5(3) that was in issue in *Murray v United Kingdom* (1996) 22 EHRR 29. The derogation was withdrawn in 2001.

6   The main provisions entered into force on this date: Human Rights Act 1998 (Commencement No. 2) Order 2000, S.I. 2000 No. 1851. Some provisions entered into force on 9 November 1998, with the royal assent: see s. 22(2) HRA. Section 19 entered into force on 24 November 1998: Human Rights Act 1998 (Commencement) Order 2000, S.I. 2000 No. 2882.

7   On its application to Scottish, Northern Irish and Welsh devolution issues, see below, p. 55.

8   It is expected that these jurisdictions will enact their own similar legislation.

9   On the HRA, see C. Baker (ed.), *The Human Rights Act 1998: A Practitioner's Guide* (1998); L. Betten (ed.), *The Human Rights Act 1998: What it Means* (1999); F. Butler (ed.), *Human Rights for the New Millennium* (2000); C. Chandran (ed.), *A Guide to the Human Rights Act 1998* (1999); R. Clayton and H. Tomlinson, *The Law of Human Rights*, 2 vols (2000); J. Cooper and A. Marshall-Williams (eds.), *Legislating for Human Rights; the Parliamentary Debates on the Human Rights Bill* (2000); J. Coppel, *The Human Rights Act 1998: Enforcing the European Convention in Domestic Courts* (1999); R. English and P. Havers (eds.), *An Introduction to Human Rights and the Common Law* (2000); S. Greer, (1999) 24 ELR 3; S. Grosz, J. Beatson, and P. Duffy, *Human Rights: The 1998 Act and the European Convention* (2000); Sir John Laws, [1998] PL 258; Lord Lester and D. Pannick, *Human Rights Law and Practice* (1999); B. Markesenis (ed.), *The Impact of the Human Rights Bill on English Law* (1998); R. Singh, *The Future of Human Rights in the United Kingdom* (1998); A. T. H. Smith, (1999) Crim LR 251; K. Starmer, *European Human Rights Law* (1999) Chaps 1 and 2; J. Wadham and H. Mountfield, *The Human Rights Act 1998* (1999); Lord Woolf, [1997] Denning LJ. More generally, see F. Klug, *Values for a Godless Age: the Story of the United Kingdom's New Bill of Rights* (2000).

interpreted compatibly with Convention rights, the courts may make a 'declaration of incompatibility' (s. 4). This does not affect the validity, continuing operation or enforcement of the legislation concerned. Instead, the legislation continues to apply, but a Minister may decide to legislate to remove the incompatibility, with the possibility of using a 'fast track' legislative procedure to do so (s. 10). Subordinate legislation that is incompatible with Convention rights is, in most cases, invalid (s. 3).

Second, 'public authorities' must act in accordance with Convention rights, unless incompatible primary or subordinate legislation leaves them no choice (s. 6). If they do not do so, a 'victim' of the resulting breach of the HRA has a new public law right of action against the public authority concerned, or may rely on the Convention right in other legal proceedings (s. 7).[10] A court may award damages or grant other relief to the victim (s. 8).

There are also consequences for the common law, which must be applied and developed by the courts, as 'public authorities', in accordance with Convention rights.
3. *Section 1: The Convention rights.* The HRA applies to the Convention rights listed in s. 1. These are the rights in Arts. 2–12 and 14 of the ECHR, Arts. 1–3 of the First Protocol to the ECHR[11] and Arts. 1 and 2 of the 6th Protocol to the ECHR.[12] The HRA thus extends to almost all of the rights in the ECHR and its Protocols. The missing rights are the right to an effective remedy in national law guaranteed by Art. 13 of the ECHR,[13] and the rights in the 4th, 7th and 12th Protocols, which the United Kingdom has not ratified.[14] The Convention rights have to be read with Arts. 16–18, which permit restrictions on the political activities of aliens (Art. 16); prohibit the use of Convention rights so as to subvert other rights (Art. 17)[15]; and prohibit the use of a permitted restriction for an improper purpose (Art. 18).

The HRA does not apply to a Convention right to the extent of any derogation from it that the United Kingdom has made under Art. 15 of the ECHR and that has been 'designated' for this purpose under the HRA.[16] There is no such 'designated derogation' at present.[17]

---

10   E.g. criminal proceedings against the victim.
11   The inclusion of the right to education in Art. 2, First Protocol is subject to the reservation to that article made by the UK upon ratification of the ECHR: see s. 15(1)(a) HRA. For the text of the reservation, see Sch. 3, Pt. II HRA.
12   For the text see HRA, Sch. 1.
13   Lord Irvine LC explained the omission of Art. 13 as follows: 'The courts would be bound to ask what was intended beyond the existing scheme of remedies set out in the Act. It might lead them to fashion remedies other than clause [now section] 8 remedies, which we regard as sufficient and clear. We believe that clause 8 provides effective remedies before our courts … I cannot conceive of any state of affairs in which an English court, having held an act to be unlawful because of its infringement of a Convention right, would under clause 8(1) be disabled from giving an effective remedy': 583 HL Deb, 18 November 1997, cols. 475, 479. Cf. Lord Hope in *Montgomery v HM Advocate* [2001] 2 WLR 779 at 794, PC. However, Lord Irvine LC noted that although Art. 13 was not included as a Convention right, the courts may none the less 'have regard to Article 13' when applying the HRA: ibid., col. 477. See the reliance upon it by Lord Hope in *R v Lambert* [2001] 3 All ER 577 at 609, HL.
14   Ratification of the 4th and 7th Protocols is under consideration. Art. 1 of the ECHR is also omitted. This contains the basic obligation of ECHR parties to 'secure to everyone within their jurisdiction' all ECHR rights; it does not protect a particular right. Art. 1 can be used to interpret Convention rights: see Brooke LJ in *Douglas v Hello!*, below, p. 922.
15   E.g. by relying upon freedom of expression or association to replace a democratic society by one that does not protect Convention rights generally.
16   s. 14 HRA.
17   Originally, s. 14(1)(a) expressly designated the derogation from ECHR, Art. 5(3) that was in issue in *Murray v United Kingdom* (1999) 22 EHRR 29. However, in 2001 the UK withdrew this derogation and the HRA was amended accordingly, with s. 14(1)(a) being repealed: see S.I. 2001 No. 1216.

4. The HRA does not extend to all human rights. A small number of civil and political rights are omitted. In addition to the ECHR rights that are not incorporated (see preceding note), a few other civil and political rights that are not included in the ECHR are absent. For example, there is no guarantee of freedom of information, the right to recognition as a person in law, or the right of a detained person to be treated with humanity and dignity.[18]

Human rights include economic, social and cultural rights as well as civil and political rights.[19] The former are not protected by the ECHR[20] and hence the HRA. Instead, within the Council of Europe, economic, social and cultural rights are guaranteed by the European Social Charter 1961,[1] which is enforceable through the assessment of national reports by the European Committee of Social Rights in Strasbourg and a right of collective (but not individual) complaint.[2] The Charter has not been incorporated into United Kingdom law.[3]

5. Of course, United Kingdom law may protect these missing human rights, or may protect Convention rights more extensively than the ECHR requires, outside of the regime of the HRA.[4] In such situations, the advantages of the HRA are not available, including its rules of interpretation and remedies. Instead, the rules of interpretation that were developed by the United Kingdom courts in human rights cases before the HRA continue to apply,[5] as do the familiar, non-HRA judicial remedies in national law.

6. *Section 2: Reliance upon Strasbourg jurisprudence in the interpretation of Convention rights.* This section required a court (or tribunal) to 'take into account' the interpretation given to the ECHR by the European Court of Human Rights and

---

18 As so far interpreted, Art. 3 of the ECHR (prohibition of inhuman or degrading treatment or punishment) does not cover prison conditions as fully as the last of these rights, although the Strasbourg Court would appear to be moving in that direction. Contrast the International Covenant on Civil and Political Rights 1966, which does protect this right (Art. 10), as well as freedom from cruel, inhuman or degrading treatment or punishment (Art. 7). The UN Covenant has not been incorporated into United Kingdom law and the United Kingdom has not accepted its international right of individual petition. J. Wadham in R. Gordon and R. Wilmot-Smith (eds.), *Human Rights in the United Kingdom* (1996), p. 25 points to other gaps in the ECHR list of rights, including the lack of due process guarantees in extradition and immigration procedures and the right to jury trial. See also the criticism of the underlying ECHR ideology (individualistic, not socialist) in K. Ewing and C. Gearty, [1997] EHRLR 146.

19 See the Universal Declaration of Human Rights 1948, which extends to all five categories of rights.

20 But see the guarantees of the right to respect for family life (Art. 8 ECHR), the right to freedom of association (Art. 11 ECHR), the right to property (Art. 1, First Protocol) and the right to education (Art. 2, First Protocol), which, to some extent concern economic, social or cultural rights. On inadequacies of social rights protection in the United Kingdom, see K. Ewing, [1999] PL 104.

1 UKTS 38 (1965), Cmnd. 2643; 529 UNTS 89; ETS 35. In force 1965. 24 parties, including the UK. The Charter is being replaced for the parties thereto by the Revised European Social Charter 1996, ETS 163. In force 1999. Eight parties, but not the UK. See D. Harris, *The European Social Charter* (2nd edn., 2001, by D. Harris and J. Darcy).

2 See the 1995 Collective Complaints Protocol to the 1961 Charter, ETS 158. In force 1998. Ten states bound by it, as parties or having made declarations under the Revised Charter, but not the UK.

3 Nor has its UN counterpart, the International Covenant of Economic, Social and Cultural Rights 1996 (n. 5 above). The UK is a party to the Covenant.

4 This is recognised by s. 11 HRA. See also Art. 53 ECHR. See, e.g., the Sex Discrimination Act 1975, the Race Relations Act 1976, and the Freedom of Information Act 2000. Nearly all of the prohibitions of discrimination in the first two of these fall outside Art. 14 ECHR. Some of them (concerning *private* discrimination in employment, etc.) are not directly covered by the 12th ECHR Protocol either, although that Protocol is likely to be interpreted as imposing positive obligations on states to control private conduct.

5 See above, pp. 4–5.

other specified Strasbourg bodies. Strasbourg jurisprudence is thus persuasive but not legally binding.[6] In *R (on the application of Alconbury Developments Ltd) v Secretary of State for the Environment, Transport and the Regions*,[7] Lord Slynn stated:

> 'Although the Human Rights Act 1998 does not provide that a national court is bound by these decisions (of the European Court of Human Rights) it is obliged to take account of them so far as they are relevant. In the absence of some special circumstances it seems to me that the court should follow any clear and constant jurisprudence of the European Court of Human Rights. If it does not do so there is at least the possibility that the case will go to that court which is likely in the ordinary case to follow its own constant jurisprudence.'

In the same case, Lord Hoffmann stated:[8]

> 'The House is not bound by the decisions of the European Court and, if I thought that the Divisional Court was right (it was not) to hold that they compelled a conclusion fundamentally at odds with the distribution of powers under the British constitution, I would have considerable doubt as to whether they should be followed.'

Would the situation suggested by Lord Hoffmann be an example of the kind of 'special circumstances' imagined by Lord Slynn? British judges[9] were very critical of the Strasbourg judgment in *Osman v United Kingdom*[10] in which the common law rule of police immunity from liability in tort for negligence in the investigation of a crime[11] was held to be a breach of the right of access to a court in Art. 6 ECHR. Might that be another kind of case in which the United Kingdom courts might be tempted to disagree with Strasbourg? Note also that some Strasbourg decisions turn upon the application of the 'margin of appreciation' doctrine to the facts of the particular case in the state concerned, so that they might not be appropriate in the national United Kingdom context.[12]

As Lord Slynn indicates (above), if the United Kingdom courts adopt an interpretation that is less favourable to a litigant relying upon the ECHR than that adopted previously at Strasbourg, there is always the possibility of a successful challenge at Strasbourg. Generally, the reverse is not true: the United Kingdom courts are free to adopt an interpretation of the ECHR for the purposes of United Kingdom law that is more favourable to a litigant relying upon it without this being open to reconsideration at Strasbourg.[13] An exception is where the interpretation goes to the balance between two Convention rights. If, for example, a United Kingdom court were to interpret the right to respect for privacy (Art. 8 ECHR) more extensively than the European Court of Human Rights and at the expense of the right to freedom of expression (Art. 10), a newspaper might be able to bring a successful Strasbourg claim under Art. 10.[14]

The jurisprudence of the United Kingdom courts so far indicates a clear intent to follow the interpretation of the ECHR at Strasbourg. Where, as sometimes happens,

---

6 For the view that Strasbourg jurisprudence should have been made binding, see K. Ewing, (1999) 62 MLR 79, 86. The jurisprudence of the European Court of Justice is legally binding: see European Communities Act 1972, s. 3.
7 [2001] 2 WLR 1389 at 1399, HL.
8 Ibid., at 1413.
9 See, e.g., Lord Browne-Wilkinson in *Barrett v Enfield LBC* [1999] 3 All ER 193 at 198. Cf. Lord Hoffmann (1999) 62 MLR 159 at 162.
10 (1999) 29 EHRR 245. The European Court of Human Rights reversed *Osman* on this point in *Z v United Kingdom* [2001] ECHR 29392/95, acknowledging that it had misunderstood English law.
11 *Hill v Chief Constable of West Yorkshire* [1989] AC 53, HL.
12 On the absence of a 'margin of appreciation' doctrine under the HRA, see below, p. 57.
13 The UK government has no right of recourse to Strasbourg.
14 See, e.g., the facts of *Douglas v Hello!*, below, p. 922. Other examples would be cases concerning the balance between freedom of expression and the right to a fair trial (Art. 6 ECHR) or the right to freedom of religion (Art. 9 ECHR).

there is no Strasbourg precedent in point,[15] the United Kingdom courts adopt their own interpretation, applying any existing Strasbourg case law by analogy.[16] A lower United Kingdom court is bound by the interpretation and application of Strasbourg case law by a higher United Kingdom court in accordance with the ordinary rules of precedent.[17]

7. *Section 3: Interpretation of legislation compatibly with Convention rights.*[18] On the approach to be followed by a court (or tribunal) when applying the 'so far as it is possible' rule in s. 3 HRA to decide whether legislation is compatible with the Convention rights, see *R v A*[19] and the notes thereto. Although they do not apply a 'margin of appreciation' doctrine when deciding whether legislation is compatible with Convention rights, the courts have accepted that they should in appropriate cases defer to Parliament's legislative judgment as to whether a particular limitation upon a Convention right in a Westminster statute is compatible with it: see *Brown v Stott*[20] and the notes thereto.

The rule of interpretation in s. 3 HRA extends only to the compatibility of legislation[1] with Convention rights. As far as its compatibility with the United Kingdom's other human rights treaty obligations is concerned,[2] the position was explained by Lord Ackner in *R v Secretary of State for the Home Department, ex p Brind*[3] as follows:

'The Convention which is contained in an international treaty to which the United Kingdom is a party has not yet been incorporated into English domestic law. The appellants accept that it is a constitutional principle that if Parliament has legislated and the words of the statute are clear, the statute must be applied even if its application is in breach of international law. In *Salomon v Comrs of Customs and Excise* [1967] 2 QB 116 Diplock LJ at 143 stated:

"If the terms of the legislation are clear and unambiguous they must be given effect to, whether or not they carry out Her Majesty's treaty obligations."

Much reliance was placed upon the observations of Lord Diplock in *Garland v British Rail* [1983] 2 AC 751 when he said (at 771):

"… it is a principle of construction of United Kingdom statutes … that the words of a statute passed after the Treaty has been signed and dealing with the subject matter of the international obligation of the United Kingdom, are to be construed, if they are reasonably capable of bearing such a meaning, as intended to carry out the obligation, and not to be inconsistent with it."

I did not take the view that Lord Diplock was intending to detract from or modify what he had said in *Salomon*'s case.

It is well settled that the Convention may be deployed for the purpose of the resolution of an ambiguity in English primary or subordinate legislation. The case of *R v Chief Immigration Officer, Heathrow Airport, ex p Salamat Bibi* [1976] 1 WLR 979 concerned a lady who arrived at London Airport from Pakistan with two small children saying that she was married to a

---

15 See e.g. *R (on the application of DPP) v Havering Magistrates* [2001] 1 WLR 805, DC.
16 A problem is that the Strasbourg jurisprudence may be open to different interpretations: in *R (Alconbury Developments Ltd) v Secretary of State for the Environment, Transport and the Regions* [2001] 2 WLR 1389 and *Brown v Stott*, below, p. 51, the House of Lords and the Privy Council respectively differed from the lower courts in their interpretation of Strasbourg decisions.
17 *R v Central Criminal Court, ex p Bright* [2001] 2 All ER 244 (a pre-HRA case in which the House of Lords interpretation of Strasbourg case law was binding).
18 See F. Bennion, [2000] PL 77; G. Marshall, [1998] PL 167 and [1999] PL 377; Lord Lester, [1998] EHRLR 665; [1999] Stat LR 218; Sir W. Wade [1998] EHRLR 520.
19 Below, p. 40.
20 Below, p. 51.
1 This includes the HRA itself: *R v Lambert* [2001] 3 All ER 577 at 612, per Lord Hope.
2 For a list of relevant treaties, see above, p. 4.
3 [1991] 1 AC 696 at 760, HL.

man who was there and who met her. She was refused leave to enter and an application was made for an order of certiorari and also for mandamus on the ground that she ought to have been treated as the wife of the man who met her at the airport. During the course of the argument a question arose about the impact of the Convention and in particular Article 8 concerning the right to private and family life and the absence of interference by a public authority with that right.

In his judgment at p. 984 Lord Denning MR said:

> "The position as I understand it is that if there is any ambiguity in our statutes, or uncertainty in our law, then these courts can look to the Convention as an aid to clear up the ambiguity and uncertainty ... but I would dispute altogether that the Convention is part of our law. Treaties and declarations do not become part of our law until they are made law by Parliament."

In his judgment at p. 988 Geoffrey Lane LJ said:

> "It is perfectly true that the Convention was ratified by this country ... nevertheless, the Convention, not having been enacted by Parliament as a statute, does not have the effect of law in this country; whatever persuasive force it may have in resolving ambiguities it certainly cannot have the effect of overriding the plain provision of the Act of 1971 and the rules made thereunder. ...'"

The statements in the above extract concerning the (then) unincorporated ECHR must apply to other human rights treaties also. Note Lord Ackner's suggestion that Lord Diplock's dictum in the *Garland* case, which was made in the particular context of EC law, was not intended to depart from the established position that a treaty may only be looked at where legislation is ambiguous and, in particular, did not mean, as might well have been thought,[4] that a judge should strain to find an ambiguity. Whatever Lord Diplock's intention, the established rule, requiring ambiguity, continued to be applied post-*Garland*.[5]

Also relevant to the interpretation of legislation affecting non-Convention human rights is the fact that, prior to the HRA, the courts had adopted a principle of 'generous interpretation' of constitutional guarantees of human rights, originating in a Privy Council case interpreting an overseas constitution. In *Minister of Home Affairs v Fisher*[6] Lord Wilberforce stated:

> 'These antecedents,[7] and the form of Chapter I (the bill of rights) itself, call for a generous interpretation avoiding what has been called "the austerity of tabulated legalism", suitable to give to individuals the full measure of the fundamental rights and freedoms referred to.'

The 'generous interpretation' approach is overtaken by that in s. 3 HRA on a matter of the compatibility of legislation with Convention rights. Presumably, the courts are free, as a matter of common law, to extend the 'generous interpretation' approach in the interpretation of Westminster statutes such as the Sex Discrimination Act 1975 or the Race Relations Act 1976 in respect of their human rights provisions that do not fall with the HRA's Convention rights, even though these statutes might not be considered as constitutional guarantees. Certainly, the presumptions favouring civil liberties in the interpretation of statutes that the courts had developed at common law prior to the HRA continue to apply in respect of non-Convention human rights.[8]

4   See M Hunt, *Using Human Rights Law in English Courts* (1997), p. 18.
5   See, e.g., *Re M and H (Minors)* [1990] 1 AC 686 at 721, HL, per Lord Brandon: 'While English courts will strive when they can to interpret statutes as conforming with the obligations of the United Kingdom under the (European) Convention they are nevertheless bound to give effect to statutes which are free from ambiguity in accordance with their terms.' This statement can be taken to apply to human rights treaties generally.
6   [1980] AC 319 at 328, PC. Cf Lord Woolf in *A-G of Hong Kong v Lee Kwong-Kut* [1993] AC 951 at 966, PC.
7   I.e. the ECHR and the Universal Declaration of Human Rights that had inspired the Bermuda constitution that was being interpreted.
8   See above, p. 4. The 'heightened scrutiny' test for reviewing executive acts also applies: see below, p. 62.

8. *The HRA and the common law.* By virtue of s. 6 HRA, the courts, as public authorities,[9] must not act incompatibly with Convention rights. As far as their application of the common law is concerned, this means that the courts must not act inconsistently with Convention rights procedurally[10] or in the provision of remedies.[11] It also means that any existing substantive rule of common law that is incompatible with Convention rights must give way to them, with a court being obliged to ignore otherwise binding precedent to the contrary. Moreover, the substantive common law cannot be developed incompatibly with Convention rights.[12] More positively, Convention rights may be used by the courts as a basis for their taking the initiative to develop common law rules or causes of action that further those rights, as in *Douglas v Hello!*[13] However, s. 6 does not mean that the courts, as 'public authorities', must allow one private person to sue another for a breach of a Convention right.[14]

9. *Section 4: Declarations of incompatibility.* Primary legislation[15] that, despite the application of the rule of interpretation in s. 3, is incompatible with Convention rights is not thereby rendered invalid, inoperative or unenforceable.[16] Instead, a court may make a 'declaration of incompatibility', as to which see *Wilson v First County Trust Ltd*[17] and the notes thereto. The purpose of a declaration of incompatibility is to give notice of the incompatibility to the government, so that it may initiate remedial action, not to provide a remedy for any victim. In contrast, incompatible subordinate legislation is invalid, inoperative and unenforceable unless the incompatibility flows unavoidably from the enabling primary legislation,[18] in which latter case a declaration of incompatibility may be made.

10. *Section 6: Acts of public authorities.* Section 6(1) HRA makes it unlawful for a 'public authority' to act incompatibly with a Convention right. However, an act, which includes a failure to act, is not unlawful if the authority has no choice but to act in this way because of incompatible primary legislation.[19] In such a case, no claim may be brought by the victim of the act against the authority under s. 7 HRA; the only remedy is a declaration of incompatibility. For example, a court will not commit an unlawful act if it is required to take a decision or give judgment in a certain way by incompatible primary legislation.

---

9 See s 6(3) HRA.

10 E.g. in criminal proceedings in the application of common law rules of evidence.

11 E.g. the level of damages must comply with Convention rights: see *Tolstoy Miloslavsky v UK* (1995) 20 EHRR 442 and *Rantzen v Mirror Group Newspapers (1986) Ltd* [1994] QB 670, CA.

12 See Lord Irvine LC, 583 HL Debs, col 783, 24 November 1997: 'We also believe that it is right as a matter of principle for the courts to have the duty of acting compatibly with the Convention not only in cases involving other public authorities but also in developing the common law in deciding cases between individuals.'

13 For *Douglas v Hello!*, see below, p. 922.

14 See further, below. Contrast the position under s. 7 HRA, by which a private individual has a *statutory* cause of action against a *public authority* (but not a private individual) for conduct incompatible with a Convention right: see below, p. 33.

15 For the meaning of primary legislation, see s. 21(1) HRA. It includes Westminster statutes and prerogative orders in council. On the significance of placing prerogative orders on a par with a Westminster statute, see P. Billings and B. Pontin [2001] PL 21.

16 s. 3(2)(b) HRA.

17 Below, p. 63.

18 s. 3(2)(c) HRA. Incompatible subordinate legislation does not in itself render its enabling legislation incompatible: per Dame Elizabeth Butler-Sloss, in *Re K (a child) (secure accommodation: right to liberty)* [2001] 2 WLR 1144 at 1155, CA. For the meaning of subordinate legislation, see s. 21(1) HRA.

19 s. 6(2) HRA. However, in the case of executive acts, there will usually be some discretion which can be exercised consistently with Convention rights. As to the courts, they must apply the common law and, so far as possible, interpret legislation in accordance with Convention rights.

On the meaning of 'public authority', see *Donoghue v Poplar Housing Regeneration Community Association Ltd*,[20] and the notes thereto.
11. *Acts of private persons.* A consequence of limiting liability under s. 6 HRA to the acts of public authorities is that a claim may not be brought by one private person against another for a breach of a Convention right. The HRA has, that is, vertical, but not horizontal effect in this regard.[1] There was a possibility of the HRA being interpreted differently, so as to require its application by the Court to claims to be brought against private persons, on the basis that the courts are public authorities under s. 6 and must act compatibly with Convention rights.[2] The most obvious case in which this possibility was relevant was the invasion of privacy by the press, in the absence of a right to privacy in English law. However, the Court of Appeal in *Douglas v Hello!*[3] rejected such an approach, and in *Venables v News Group Newspapers Ltd*[4] Dame Elizabeth Butler-Sloss clearly stated that the courts' obligation to apply Convention rights does not 'encompass the creation of a free-standing cause of action based directly upon the articles of the Convention' that could be used by one private person to bring a claim against another. In the *Douglas* case, the Court of Appeal indicated that instead the courts would use the HRA to contribute to the development of existing or emerging causes of action at common law.[5]

As Hunt points out, the courts had already been moving in the direction of this kind of indirect horizontal effect of the ECHR before the HRA was enacted:[6]

'Arguably, even before the Human Rights Act, the position had already been reached in the development of a domestic human rights jurisdiction where courts considered it legitimate both to develop the common law and to exercise their own powers so as to be consistent with the Convention, including in cases involving wholly private parties. Indeed, it is one of the great ironies of it having taken so long for this country to make the Convention part of its domestic law that imaginative development of the common law by judges was for a long time the only way of giving some domestic effect to Convention rights. As a result, when the Act comes into effect, there will be nothing particularly novel about the courts taking an active role in developing the common law so as to achieve consistency with the Convention.'

Would this indirect effect extend to the following case, as Hunt suggests?[7]

---

20 Below, p. 76.
 1 Contrast the position under the Irish constitution: '... if a person has suffered damage by virtue of a breach of a constitutional right or the infringement of a constitutional right, that person is entitled to seek redress against the person or persons who infringed that right', per Walsh J in *Meskell v Coras Iompair Eireann* [1973] IR 121 at 133. See M. Hunt, [1998] PL 423 for a comparative survey of widely varying approaches to horizontal effect in different constitutions.
 2 See H. W. R. Wade, in J. Beatson, C. Forsyth and I. Hare (eds.), *Constitutional Reform in the United Kingdom: Practice and Principles* (1998), p. 61 and ibid., (2000) 116 LQR 217 (in favour of this interpretation); and R. Buxton, (2000) 116 LQR 48 (against). See also N. Bamforth, (1999) 58 CLJ 159; M. Hunt, [1998] PL 423; I. Leigh (1999) 48 ICLQ 57; S. Grosz, J. Beatson and P. Duffy, *Human Rights: the 1998 Act and the European Convention* (2000) para. 4–45; S. Kentridge, in J. Beatson, Forsyth and Hare, above; G. Phillipson, (1999) 62 MLR 824.
 3 Below, p. 922.
 4 Below, p. 973.
 5 Thus in the *Douglas* case the Convention right to respect for privacy in Art. 8 ECHR was seen as assisting in the crystalisation of a common law right to privacy that was emerging anyway (see Sedley LJ) or as extending the law of breach of confidence to protect privacy more fully than it had done previously (see Keene LJ). See also Sedley LJ's judgment, below, p. 926, on the significance of s. 12(4) HRA in confirming the application of the HRA to private litigation.
 6 [1998] PL 423, 435–436.
 7 Ibid. at 442 (footnote omitted).

'The example of the all-male golf club which does not allow women guests into its bar might help to illustrate the distinction. The new Human Rights Act will not confer any new cause of action on women who want to complain that such arrangements constitute a violation of their rights under Articles 11 and 14, to freedom of association without discrimination. But a woman who is physically ejected from the premises and sues for assault may argue that the common law of trespass cannot be interpreted and applied in such a way as to provide the club with a defence of lawful ejection to the assault claim, because the court to accede to the availability of such a defence would itself be in breach of the Convention. Once the club puts forward its defence, it is seeking to enlist the assistance of the state (in the form of the courts) in preserving its present freedom to discriminate, and that is something which section 6 of the Act arguably does not permit the courts to do.'

What if it is the defendant, not the plaintiff who wishes to rely upon a Convention right in a civil action against him? In the celebrated case of *Shelley v Kraemer*,[8] the US Supreme Court held that it would be unconstitutional state action contrary to the equal protection clause in the US Bill of Rights for a court to issue an injunction to a private person to enforce a restrictive covenant prohibiting the sale of land by another private person because of the race or colour of the purchaser. How would this case be dealt with under the HRA?[9] Note in this connection the following statement by Lightman J in *RSPCA v Attorney-General*:[10]

'The court is a public authority, but that status does not impinge on the question whether one party to the proceedings before it has a convention right to which another party is bound to give effect. The court is bound to give effect to such a convention right if established: in this context that is the full extent to which the status of the court as a public authority is engaged.'

Might the liability of a 'public authority' in s. 6 be availed of in some horizontal cases by focusing on a positive obligation of the state under the ECHR? For example, there is a positive obligation on the state to prevent, investigate and punish private domestic violence.[11] Might a claim be brought under s. 6 against the 'public authority' that has failed to carry out its obligation?

12. *Section 7. Claims by victims.* Section 7(1) allows a victim to claim in court that a public authority has acted unlawfully contrary to s. 6(1). A claim may be brought or made in one of two ways. First under s. 7(1)(a) a claim may be brought against a public authority before the appropriate court or tribunal.[12] The HRA thus introduces a new public law right of action for the breach of a Convention right by a public authority.[13]

---

8   334 US 1 (1948). Although it has not been reversed, *Shelley v Kraemer* has not been applied by the Supreme Court in recent years.

9   Suppose that the case might raise issues under Art. 1, First Protocol (right to property) and Art. 14 ECHR (non-discrimination).

10   [2001] All ER (D) 188, Ch D. In that case, the RSPCA, a charity, sought guidance as to whether a membership rule which excluded persons who might want to seek to change its policy against hunting with dogs would be incompatible with the Convention right to freedom of association (Art. 11 ECHR), as some members claimed.

11   See *A v United Kingdom* (1998) 27 EHRR 611 and *Z v United Kingdom* [2001] ECHR 29392/95. Cf. the positive obligation under Art. 2 ECHR to prevent and investigate killings: see *Osman v United Kingdom* (1998) 29 EHRR 245 and *McCann v United Kingdom*, below, p. 633.

12   Such claims are heard in the ordinary courts; no new constitutional court has been established. Legal aid is available to claimants. No rules have been made giving any tribunal jurisdiction to hear cases: see s. 7(2) and (11). Claims alleging that decisions under the Immigration Acts are incompatible with Convention rights may be brought before an immigration adjudicator or the Immigration Appeal Tribunal: Immigration and Asylum Act 1999, s. 65.

13   Lord Lester and D. Pannick, (2000) 116 LQR 380 at 382, refer to a 'new cause of action against public authorities (widely defined) for a new public law tort of acting in breach of the victim's Convention rights'. The tort is distinct from the tort of breach of statutory duty.

This new cause of action applies only to acts by public authorities; as noted above, it does not extend to acts by private persons. Moreover, a public authority is not liable where it cannot act otherwise because of the constraints of incompatible primary legislation.[14] Nor does s. 7(1) apply to judicial acts by courts or tribunals: instead a claim of incompatibility must be made on appeal to a higher court or tribunal or in judicial review proceedings.[15]

Second, a victim may raise an issue of incompatibility in legal proceedings that have been commenced on some other basis,[16] e.g. criminal proceedings in which the victim is a defendant, a civil claim in contract or tort to which the victim is a party, or judicial review proceedings brought on other established judicial review grounds.[17]

Claims under s. 7 may only be made by a 'victim' of the act. 'Victim' has the same meaning as it has in Art. 34 ECHR, which contains the locus standi requirement for bringing a Strasbourg application.[18] This requirement means essentially that the applicant must be directly affected by the act of the public authority. This is a more restrictive rule than that in judicial review proceedings under United Kingdom law, which allows non-governmental organisations to bring proceedings about a matter of general concern in respect of which they have a 'sufficient interest'.[19] The reason for limiting claims under s. 7 in this way was explained in Parliament as follows:[20]

'As a government, our aim is to grant access to victims. It is not to create opportunities to allow interest groups from SPUC to Liberty ... to venture into frolics of their own in the courts. The aim is to confer access to rights, not to license interest groups to clog up the courts with test cases.'

13. *Section 8. Damages or other relief.*[1] Where a claim succeeds under s. 7, the court or tribunal may award damages or grant such other remedy or relief as it considers 'just and appropriate'. Damages,[2] like other remedies or relief, are discretionary and may only be awarded by a court or tribunal with the power to award damages or compensation in civil proceedings.[3] Damages may not be awarded unless the court is satisfied that this is necessary to afford 'just satisfaction',[4] which is the criterion for the award of damages by the European Court of Human Rights.[5] When deciding whether to award damages, and the amount of any award, a court must 'take into account' the principles applied at Strasbourg.[6] These principles, which give rise to lower damages than would

---

14   s. 6(2) HRA. Where s. 6(2) applies, the remedy is a declaration of incompatibility under s. 4, not a claim under s. 7.

15   s. 9(1) HRA.

16   s. 7(1)(b) HRA.

17   The effect of the HRA is to add a new ground of illegality in judicial review proceedings, which a victim can raise by itself or in conjunction with other judicial review arguments. Where it is raised by itself, s. 7(1)(a) applies.

18   s. 7(7) HRA. On Art. 34 (formerly Art. 25), see D. Harris, M. O'Boyle and C. Warbrick, *The Law of the European Convention on Human Rights* (1995), pp. 630–638.

19   See, e.g. *R v Inspectorate of Pollution, ex p Greenpeace (No 2)* [1994] 4 All ER 329, QBD.

20   Mr O'Brien, Under Secretary of State, Home Office, 314 HC Deb, 24 June 1998, col. 1086.

1   On s. 8 see [2001] PL 210. On damages under s. 8, see M. Amos, [1999] EHRLR 178. On HRA remedies generally, see D. Feldman, [1998] EHRLR 691.

2   In accordance with the usual rule of judicial immunity, damages may not be awarded in respect of a judicial act done in good faith, except as compensation for detention contrary to Art. 5 ECHR: s. 9(3) HRA.

3   s. 8(2) HRA. Criminal courts are excluded.

4   s. 8(3) HRA.

5   Art. 41 ECHR.

6   s. 8(4) HRA. For the Strasbourg practice, see A. Mowbray, [1997] PL 647. See also Sir Robert Carnwath, (2000) 49 ICLQ 517.

normally be awarded in the English law of tort, are thus persuasive, but not legally binding; it would be open to a court to award higher damages.[7]
14. Section 10. Remedial action: legislation to remove an incompatibility. A declaration of incompatibility that is made by a court under s. 4 HRA does not render the legislation invalid, inoperative or ineffective.[8] Instead, the provision for 'remedial action' in s. 10 applies. By s. 10(2), after any appeal proceedings in the case have been completed, a Minister 'may'[9] proceed by 'remedial order' to amend the offending legislation to eliminate the incompatibility. The order may be given retrospective effect.[10] Section. 10(3) gives a similar power to correct primary legislation that prevents the alteration of incompatible subordinate legislation. A remedial order may be adopted by the use of a 'fast track' procedure, involving an affirmative resolution of each of the two Houses of Parliament.[11] However, a Minister may act by way of remedial order only if he considers that there are 'compelling reasons' for doing so; otherwise, a statute will be needed.[12] Lord Hoffmann has stated: 'If the courts make a declaration of incompatibility, the political pressure upon the government to bring the law into line will be hard to resist.'[13] Would this be true in all cases? What about a case involving a legal point that would not attract much public interest, such as that in the *Wilson* case?[14] The first remedial order under the HRA was made in 2001 in response to the declaration of incompatibility in *R (on the application of H v North and East Region Mental Health Review Tribunal.*[15]

The power to make a 'remedial order' is also available to a Minister where the European Court of Human Rights has given a judgment, whether against the United Kingdom or another state, which suggests that United Kingdom legislation is contrary to the ECHR.[16]
15. Section 12: Freedom of expression. Section 12 of the HRA was introduced because of concerns that the HRA might serve as a vehicle for the introduction of a right to privacy at the expense of the right to freedom of expression on the part of the media. However, the direction to 'have particular regard to the importance of the Convention right to freedom of expression' in the introductory wording of s. 12(4) has not had the desired effect. Instead, it was used to further the common law protection of privacy at the expense of the press in *Douglas v Hello!*,[17] the Court of

7 *Re Crawley Green Rd Cemetery, Luton* [2001] 2 WLR 1175, Ch D.
8 s. 4(6)(a) HRA. Nor is the declaration binding on the parties to the case: s. 4(6)(b) HRA.
9 The Minister thus has a power, not a duty, to initiate legislative change. Failure to make a remedial order is not a breach of s. 6(1): s. 6(5) HRA.
10 Sch. 2, para. 1(1)(b) HRA. A person cannot be convicted of a criminal offence by the retrospective application of a remedial order: para 1(3).
11 For the details of the procedure, see Sch. 2, HRA. The remedial order must be laid before both Houses of Parliament for 60 days: para 2(a). The 60-day period may be dispensed with in urgent cases: para 2(b).
12 The 'compelling reasons' limitation was inserted because Parliament was concerned about giving Ministers too wide a power to bypass ordinary legislative procedures. Lord Simon expressed concern about the use of Henry VIII clauses: 583 HL Deb, 27 November 1997, col. 1141. A decision on the existence of 'compelling reasons' may be subject to judicial review: see K. Ewing, (1999) 62 MLR 70 at 93.
13 (1999) 62 MLR 159 at 160.
14 Below, p. 63.
15 See below, p. 70.
16 s. 10(1)(b) HRA.
17 Below, p. 922. S. 12(4) does not 'require the court to treat freedom of speech as paramount' or 'direct the court to place even greater weight on the importance of freedom of expression than it does already'; instead, 'the requirement "to pay particular regard" contemplates specific and separate consideration being given to this factor': per Sir Andrew Morritt V-C, in *Imutran Ltd v Uncaged Campaigns Ltd* [2001] 2 All ER 385 at 391, Ch D. See also *Ashdown v Telegraph Group Ltd* [2001] EWCA Civ 1142, [2001] 2 All ER 370, Ch D, in which s. 12(4) did not prevent a successful breach of copyright claim for the unauthorised publication of a minute of a private meeting.

Appeal taking account of (i) the fact that the reference in s. 12(4) is to the 'Convention right' to freedom of expression, which includes the permissibility in Art. 10(2) of restrictions to protect the 'rights of others' (including the right to privacy), and (ii) the reference to 'any relevant privacy code' in s. 12(4), which includes the Press Complaints Commission Code.[18]

16. *Section 13: Freedom of religion.* Section 13 requires courts to have 'particular regard to the importance of' the right to freedom of religion in Art. 9 ECHR. It was introduced by the government in place of amendments that had been successfully promoted by the churches in the House of Lords who feared that their activities might be affected by the HRA by the guarantee of freedom of 'thought, conscience and religion' in Art. 9 and the prohibition on discrimination in Art. 14 ECHR.[19] For example, they were concerned that the HRA might limit their freedom to exclude persons as church members or employees,[20] or to decide who might be married in church.[1] The final text of s. 13 is unlikely to change the outcome of the application of the HRA to any case. The equivalent 'particular regard' wording in s. 12 HRA has not been understood to mean that freedom of expression is overriding or to be given special weight.[2] Moreover, churches are 'public authorities' in only a few contexts. In Parliament, Mr Straw stated:

> 'The two most obvious examples relate to marriages and to the provision of education in church schools ... We think it right in principle ... that people should be able to raise Convention points in respect of the actions of the churches in those areas on the same basis as they will be able to in respect of, the actions of other public authorities, however rarely such occasions may arise.'[3]

Religious 'organisations' were understood in Parliament during the drafting of s. 13 to include charities whose objects were the advancement of religion.[4] Whether an organisation is 'religious' goes to the definition of a 'religion' in English law.[5]

17. *Section 19: Parliamentary statements of compatibility.* Section 19 requires that when a Bill is introduced into Parliament, a Minister make a statement before the second reading on its compatibility with Convention rights. The Bill may proceed even though the statement is not able to confirm compatibility.[6] No such obligation exists in respect of any amendments introduced during the passage of the Bill. Section 19 statements are not binding on the courts and do not have persuasive authority.[7]

18. *Section 21(5): Abolition of the death penalty for military offences.* Following the abolition of the death penalty for treason and piracy with violence by the Crime and Disorder Act 1998, s. 36, the death penalty only remained in United Kingdom

---

18 As to which, see below, p. 992. However, the reference in s. 12(2) HRA to information being in the public domain was taken into account in *A-G v Times Newspapers* [2001] EWCA Civ 97, [2001] 1 WLR 885, CA, in favour of freedom of expression (spy revelations already published in a book in Russia).

19 For these concerns and generally on s. 13, see P. Cumper, [2000] PL 154.

20 E.g. an atheist as a church school headmaster, or women or homosexuals as priests.

 1 E.g. divorcees or a homosexual couple.

 2 See the *Imutran* case, above, p. 35, n. 17. See also *Ishak v Thowfeek* [1968] 1 WLR 1718, PC and other cases cited by Cumper, n. 19, above, pp. 262–263.

 3 312 HC Deb, 20 May 98, col. 1015. See also Mr Straw, 306 HC Deb, 16 February 98, col. 777. Arts. 9 and 14 ECHR have not yet been interpreted as guaranteeing a right to marriage for a homosexual couple, although this may happen as more European states accept the right in their law. The special privileges of established churches have not been questioned under Arts. 9 and 14 ECHR. What if a church were to accept state funding for its schools or its shelters for the homeless? Would this make it a 'public authority' under s. 6 HRA?

 4 See Cumper n. 19 above, pp. 260–261 above.

 5 As to which, see below, p. 1028.

 6 s. 19(2) HRA.

 7 Per Lord Hope in *R v A*, below, p. 40.

law for military offences such as mutiny. Section 21(5) repeals the death penalty in military law, thus completing the process of abolition.

19. *Section 22: Retrospective effect.* Section 22(4) means that a victim cannot bring proceedings under s 7(1)(a) in respect of acts by public authorities that occurred before the HRA entered into force on 2 October 2000. The HRA does apply to the conduct of criminal and other proceedings brought by a public authority after its entry into force, even though the facts of the case occurred before that date. However, the HRA does not apply to an appeal against a conviction by a court before 2 October 2000.[8]

20. *Repeal of the HRA.* The question arises whether the HRA can be repealed[9] by a Parliament that becomes dissatisfied with its interpretation and application by the courts, or that legislates inconsistently with a convention right. The possibility of entrenching a Westminster statute containing a Bill of Rights was addressed in the pre-HRA Report of the House of Lords Select Committee on a Bill of Rights[10] Rejecting such a possibility, the Committee stated:

'14. ... there is no way in which a Bill of Rights could be made immune altogether from amendment or repeal by a subsequent Act. That follows from the principle of the sovereignty of Parliament which is the central feature of our constitution. ... The usual way of entrenching provisions in countries with written constitutions is to require a special majority in the legislature, or in some cases a favourable vote in a referendum, for any Act amending or repealing, or otherwise overriding, the entrenched provision. The Committee think it is clear, however, that no such provision (e.g. a requirement for a two-thirds majority in the House of Commons for any Bill seeking to override a Bill of Rights) would be legally effective in the United Kingdom ...

15. The only other possibility is a provision such as is contained in clause 3 of Lord Wade's Bill.

16. If such a clause were effective, it would, in the Committee's view, in practice provide an important degree of entrenchment. In this regard, the Committee do not accept the view that has been expressed that, if such a clause were included in a Bill of Rights, Governments would have no hesitation in including in future Acts the necessary express formula to ensure that the Act would override the Bill of Rights. . . .

17. The Committee have, however, felt unable to accept the assumption ... that a Bill of Rights could protect itself from being overriden by implication. It is contrary to the principle of Parliamentary sovereignty as it has hitherto been understood in the United Kingdom. Under that principle, Parliament cannot bind itself as to the future and a later Act must always prevail over an earlier one if it is inconsistent with it, whether the inconsistency is express or implied. The Committee are aware that some legal writers have advanced the view that the principle of Parliamentary sovereignty does not preclude Parliament from laying down a binding requirement as to the manner or form of subsequent Acts of a particular kind. ... If this view prevailed in the courts, a provision like clause 3 of Lord Wade's Bill[11] would be efficacious in that it does no more than lay down the form in which a subsequent Act has to be framed if it is to override a Bill of Rights. The Committee are not, however, persuaded that the view is sound. [. . .]

23. It follows from the foregoing that the Committee conclude that the main scope for a Bill of Rights would be to operate on our existing law. The most that such a Bill could do

---

8 *R v Lambert* [2001] 3 All ER 577, HL. The comments on s. 22(4) made by Sir Andrew Morritt V-C in *Wilson v First County Trust Ltd (No 2)* below, n. 63, were approved in the *Lambert* case.

9 The term 'repeal' is used to include repeal of the whole statute or the amendment of any of its sections.

10 Report of the Select Committee on a Bill of Rights (1977–89) HL 176, pp. 22–26.

11 When considered by the Committee in 1977, cl. 3 of Lord Wade's Human Rights Bill had read: 'In case of conflict between any enactment subsequent to the passing of this Act and the provisions of the said Convention and Protocols, the said Convention and Protocols shall prevail unless subsequent enactment shall explicitly state otherwise.'

would be to include an interpretation provision which ensured that the Bill of Rights was always taken into account in the construction of later Acts ...'

As the House of Lords Select Committee Report indicates, there are differing views as to the nature of parliamentary sovereignty that bear upon the question whether a statute embodying a guarantee of human rights such as the HRA can be entrenched within the UK constitution. It is generally agreed that, under the rule of parliamentary sovereignty as it has been recognised by the courts to date, Parliament can always change its mind as to the *content* of legislation. It could, therefore, having passed the HRA, later enact a statute that expressly or by necessary implication contradicted it, and the later statute in time would prevail. Even an express provision in the HRA to the effect that the statute could not be repealed would not prevent this. The controversy concerns the question whether Parliament can bind itself as to the '*manner and form*' of subsequent legislation. Could it for example, require that a provision in a statute introducing a statute such as the HRA be repealed only by express (not implied) repeal (see Lord Wade's Bill), thus dictating the 'form' of legislation?[12] There are Commonwealth cases in which a special voting or referendum requirement has been held to be binding upon a legislature,[13] but the Select Committee (para. 14) clearly prefers H. W. R. Wade's view that these can be distinguished. An English case which supports Wade's view is *Ellen Street Estates Ltd v Minister of Health*.[14]

Although H. W. R. Wade rejects the view that Parliament can limit itself as to the 'manner and form' of subsequent legislation, he does so on the basis that this is the current rule of common law, which the judges can change. It is, he suggests, a special common law rule which results from an 'ultimate political fact'. It is a rule that reflects the political consensus in the country and one that should be changed by the judges if, and only if, a 'revolution' occurs by which parliamentary sovereignty in its present form (which was itself recognised by the courts only at the end of the seventeenth century as power shifted from the Crown to Parliament) no longer commands general support. So, if Parliament, speaking for the people, were to legislate, even by means of an ordinary statute, so as to introduce a Bill of Rights which was intended to limit Parliament's legislative sovereignty in the area of civil liberties, the courts should recognise it as indicating a change in the 'ultimate political fact' and modify the common law rule of parliamentary sovereignty accordingly.

With regard to the HRA, there is no clause comparable to clause 3 of Lord Wade's Bill, seeking to prevent implied repeal by later legislation, in the HRA. To the contrary, s. 3 HRA confirms that later primary legislation that is incompatible with the HRA is not thereby rendered invalid; instead a declaration of incompatibility must be made for the later legislation to be at risk.[15] Moreover, earlier incompatible primary legislation is neither expressly or impliedly repealed by the HRA; it too remains valid until replaced by remedial action in Parliament following any declaration of incompatibility. Parliamentary sovereignty is thus greatly respected.

But what if, as imagined above, Parliament decided to legislate to repeal the whole of the HRA or to amend it in such a way as significantly to weaken the scheme

---

12 Contrast, for example, the views of H. W. R. Wade (Lord Wade's cousin) [1955] CLJ 172 (Parliament cannot bind itself as to the manner and form of subsequent legislation) and R. F. V. Heuston, *Essays in Constitutional Law* (2nd edn., 1964) (Parliament can do so). See also Bradley, in J. Jowell and D. Oliver (eds.), *The Changing Constitution*, (2nd edn., 1989), Chap. 2, and Elkind, (1987) 50 MLR 158.

13 E.g. *A-G for New South Wales v Trethowan* [1932] AC 526, PC (referendum).

14 [1934] 1 KB 590, CA.

15 On the HRA, incompatible later legislation and parliamentary sovereignty, see A. W. Bradley, (2001) 151 NLJ 311 and M. Shrimpton, (2000) 151 NLJ 450.

of the Act, e.g. by abolishing the special rule of interpretation in s. 3 or deleting certain ECHR Articles as ones giving rise to Convention rights? What if it legislated to re-introduce capital punishment contrary to the Convention right in s. 2(1)(c) HRA?[16] Would the established rule of parliamentary sovereignty permit a change in the content of what is, after all, technically an ordinary statute? And would it permit such a change by a simple majority vote in each of the two House of Parliament, plus the royal assent? As to the latter question, the answer is 'Yes', not least because there are no special voting or other procedural rules in the HRA concerning its repeal. As to a change in its *content*, might it be relevant that the HRA has been judicially characterised as a 'constitutional instrument',[17] which might suggest that it has a special status, so that the established rule of express or implied repeal (see above) would not apply? Note also that the courts have recognised that the European Communities Act 1972 has modified the established doctrine of parliamentary sovereignty in relation to EU legislation, thereby recognising a change in the 'ultimate political fact'.[18] The Canadian judiciary have responded in this way in respect of the Canadian Charter of Rights and Freedoms, although it is true, as Hogg[19] notes, that the 'prolonged and highly public process by which the Charter was adopted' had 'fed the public expectation that a significant change in the Canadian Constitution occurred with the adoption of the Charter'. Note also, with regard to the EU, that British judges may have been influenced by the fact that UK entry into the EU was preceded by a referendum in which the public voted in its favour.

21. *Number of Strasbourg applications.* One objective of the HRA was to reduce the number of cases taken to Strasbourg, against the United Kingdom. Although many cases will now be resolved domestically,[20] might it be that the interest in human rights generally and the ECHR in particular that is generated by the HRA may act as a counterweight, causing the numbers not to decline?

22. *The Parliamentary Joint Committee on Human Rights.* The Joint Committee on Human Rights is a Select Committee of the two Houses of Parliament. It has a general competence to consider and report on matters relating to human rights in the United Kingdom, except that it cannot consider individual cases. It also considers and reports on remedial orders proposed and made under s. 10 HRA. It reports on the compatibility of selected bill with Convention rights[1] and has reported on the implementation of the HRA.[2]

23. *A Human Rights Commission.* The idea of a Human Rights Commission was considered, but not for the time being accepted, in the Government White Paper leading to the HRA,[3] and no provision for a Commission is made in it. The Parliamentary Joint Committee on Human Rights plans to report on the question of establishing a Commission. The Commission's role would be a promotional one.[4]

---

16 See D. Judge, [1999] PL 6.
17 Per Lord Woolf CJ in *R v Offen* [2001] 1 WLR 253 at 275, CA. See also D. Pannick [1998] PL 546.
18 See *Garland v British Rail Engineering Ltd* [1983] 2 AC 751, HL and *Factortame Ltd v Secretary of State for Transport* [1990] 2 AC 85, HL.
19 (1984) 32 AJCL 183, 204.
20 Note that the s. 7 right of action against public authorities will reduce considerably the previously large number of successful claims against the UK under Art. 13 ECHR (right to an effective remedy), in respect of which the UK has been the main customer.
1 The Committee's First Report was on the Criminal Justice and Police Bill 2001.
2 Report, HL 66–I, HC 332–1.
3 *Rights Brought Home*, Cm. 3782, p. 14.
4 See S. Spencer and I. Bynoe, *A Human Rights Commission: the Options for Britain and Northern Ireland* (1998).

R v A [2001] 2 WLR 1546, House of Lords

The defendant (respondent) was charged with raping the complainant (appellant). His defence was that sexual intercourse had occurred with the appellant's consent. He was alternatively going to rely on the defence that he believed that she consented. The defendant and his friend, X, first met the complainant on about 26 May 2000. X and the complainant began a sexual relationship. On 13 June, at about 9 pm, they had sexual intercourse in the flat shared by X and the defendant, when the defendant was not there. Later that evening, the three of them had a picnic on the riverbank at which X and the defendant drank a lot of alcohol. When the three of them returned to the flat, X collapsed and was taken to hospital by ambulance. In the early hours of the morning of 14 June, the defendant and the complainant decided to visit X in the hospital and, at the defendant's suggestion, walked along the river towpath en route. As they were doing so, the defendant fell down. The complainant alleged that when she tried to help him to his feet, the defendant pulled her down and had intercourse with her against her will. The defendant claimed that this was not correct; that the complainant had initiated sexual intercourse on this occasion. The defendant also claimed that he and the complainant had had consensual sexual relations at his flat over a period of about three weeks prior to 14 June including sexual intercourse on several occasions. The last instance of this had been about one week before 14 June.

In an appeal arising out of a preparatory hearing prior to the trial, the Court of Appeal upheld the ruling by the trial judge that the effect of s. 41 of the Youth Justice and Criminal Evidence Act 1999[5] was that the alleged sexual relationship between

---

5   s. 41 reads: '(1) If at a trial a person is charged with a sexual offence, then, except with the leave of the court—

  (a) no evidence may be adduced, and

  (b) no question may be asked in cross-examination,

by or on behalf of any accused at the trial, about any sexual behaviour of the complainant.

(2) The court may give leave in relation to any evidence or question only on an application made by or on behalf of an accused, and may not give such leave unless it is satisfied—

  (a) that subsection (3) or (5) applies, and

  (b) that a refusal of leave might have the result of rendering unsafe a conclusion of the jury or (as the case may be) the court on any relevant issue in the case.

(3) This subsection applies if the evidence or question relates to a relevant issue in the case and either—

  (a) that issue is not an issue of consent; or

  (b) it is an issue of consent and the sexual behaviour of the complainant to which the evidence or question relates is alleged to have taken place at or about the same time as the event which is the subject matter of the charge against the accused; or

  (c) it is an issue of consent and the sexual behaviour of the complainant to which the evidence or question relates is alleged to have been, in any respect, so similar—

    (i) to any sexual behaviour of the complainant which (according to evidence adduced or to be adduced by or on behalf of the accused) took place as part of the event which is the subject matter of the charge against the accused, or

    (ii) to any other sexual behaviour of the complainant which (according to such evidence) took place at or about the same time as that event,

that the similarity cannot reasonably be explained as a coincidence.

(4) For the purposes of subsection (3) no evidence or question shall be regarded as relating to a relevant issue in the case if it appears to the court to be reasonable to assume that the purpose (or main purpose) for which it would be adduced or asked is to establish or elicit material for impugning the credibility of the complainant as a witness.

(5) This subsection applies if the evidence or question—

  (a) relates to any evidence adduced by the prosecution about any sexual behaviour of the complainant; and

  (b) in the opinion of the court, would go no further than is necessary to enable the evidence adduced by the prosecution to be rebutted or explained by or on behalf of the accused. ...'

the defendant and the complainant was inadmissible on the issue of consent (but not the issue of belief in consent). However, in view of the Court of Appeal's view that this might result in a breach of the guarantee of the right to a fair trial in Art. 6 ECHR and the Human Rights Act 2000, the Crown appealed against the Court of Appeal's decision and the Court of Appeal certified the following question for the House of Lords:

'May a sexual relationship between a defendant and complainant be relevant to the issue of consent so as to render its exclusion under section 41 of the Youth Justice and Criminal Evidence Act 1999 a contravention of the defendant's right to a fair trial?'

Lord Steyn:
30. Although not an issue before the House, my view is that the 1999 Act deals sensibly and fairly with questioning and evidence about the complainant's sexual experience with other men. Such matters are almost always irrelevant to the issue whether the complainant consented to sexual intercourse on the occasion alleged in the indictment or to her credibility. To that extent the scope of the reform of the law by the 1999 Act was justified. On the other hand, the blanket exclusion of prior sexual history between the complainant and an accused in section 41(1), subject to narrow categories of exception in the remainder of section 41, poses an acute problem of proportionality.

31. As a matter of common sense, a prior sexual relationship between the complainant and the accused may, depending on the circumstances, be relevant to the issue of consent. It is a species of prospectant evidence which may throw light on the complainant's state of mind. It cannot, of course, prove that she consented on the occasion in question. Relevance and sufficiency of proof are different things. The fact that the accused a week before an alleged murder threatened to kill the deceased does not prove an intent to kill on the day in question. But it is logically relevant to that issue. After all, to be relevant the evidence need merely have some tendency in logic and common sense to advance the proposition in issue. It is true that each decision to engage in sexual activity is always made afresh. On the other hand, the mind does not usually blot out all memories. What one has been engaged on in the past may influence what choice one makes on a future occasion. Accordingly, a prior relationship between a complainant and an accused may sometimes be relevant to what decision was made on a particular occasion.

32. . . . Not surprisingly the legislative technique adopted in section 41 has been criticised. Professor Diane Birch ('A Better Deal for Vulnerable Witnesses?' [2000] Crim LR 223, 248), trenchantly commented:

'Under section 41, the complainant's sexual behaviour (including behaviour with the accused) has relevance to consent only where it took place at or about the same time as the event of the subject-matter of the charge, or where it is strikingly similar to behaviour of the subject-matter of the charge or to any other sexual behaviour alleged to have taken place at or about that time. All that can be revealed, it would seem, is evidence such as that the complainant was seen in a passionate embrace with the accused just before (or just after) the alleged offence; bizarre and unusual conduct like the much-discussed propensity to re-enact the balcony scene from *Romeo and Juliet*, and (perhaps) evidence that the complainant was picking up clients as a prostitute (if it is D's defence that he was so picked up). Along with all the complainant's other sexual doings, the remainder of the history of any sexual relationship the complainant has had with the accused will, it seems, have to be concealed from the jury or magistrates. It is not clear how this is to be done in a case where, for example the parties are living together: is the jury simply to be told what happened in the bedroom without any idea of whether D was a trespasser or an invitee? Presumably there will have to be some concept of background evidence that it is necessary for the jury to know in order to make sense of the evidence in the case.

Section 41 is well-intentioned, but the constraints laid on relevance go too far. . . .'

It is difficult to dispute this assessment. After all, good sense suggests that it may be relevant to an issue of consent whether the complainant and the accused were ongoing lovers or strangers. To exclude such material creates the risk of disembodying the case before the jury. It also increases the danger of miscarriages of justice. These considerations raise the spectre of the possible need for a declaration of incompatibility in respect of section 41 under section 4 of the Human Rights Act 1998. ...

34. In order to assess whether section 41 is incompatible with the Convention right to a fair trial, it is necessary to consider what evidence it excludes. The mere fact that it excludes some relevant evidence would not by itself amount to a breach of the fair trial guarantee. On the other hand, if the impact of section 41 is to deny the right to accused in a significant range of cases from putting forward full and complete defences it may amount to a breach.

35. Counsel for the Secretary of State has argued that unfairness to an accused will rarely arise because evidence of sexual experience between a complainant and an accused will almost always be admissible on the basis of the defence that the accused thought that the complainant consented. His argument has assumed that in practice an accused will almost invariably be able to put forward both defences. Counsel for the defendant has persuaded me that the defence of belief in consent would often have no air of reality and would in practice not be available, eg in cases where there are diametrically opposite accounts of the circumstances of the alleged rape, with the complainant insisting that it was perpetrated with great violence and the accused saying that the complainant took the initiative in an act of consensual intercourse. In any event, it does not meet the difficulty that the judge's direction to the jury would always have to be to the effect that the past experience between the complainant and the accused is irrelevant to the issue of consent. I would reject the submissions of counsel for the Secretary of State on this point. In these circumstances counsel for the Secretary of State accepts that, despite the interlocutory nature of the proceedings, the House must now grapple with the problem whether, measured against the guarantee of a fair trial, the breadth of the exclusionary provisions of section 41 in respect of sexual experience between a complainant and the defendant are justified and proportionate. The position of counsel for the Secretary of State on this point is realistic. To postpone the decision until after the conclusion of a number of pending trials, which raise the issue, would be unfair to individuals and contrary to the public interest.

36. Counsel for the Secretary of State further relied on the principle that, in certain contexts, the legislature and the executive retain a discretionary area of judgment within which policy choices may legitimately be made: see *Brown v Stott* [2001] 2 WLR 817. Clearly the House must give weight to the decision of Parliament that the mischief encapsulated in the twin myths[6] must be corrected. On the other hand, when the question arises whether in the criminal statute in question Parliament adopted a legislative scheme which makes an excessive inroad into the right to a fair trial the court is qualified to make its own judgment and must do so.

37. The methodology to be adopted is important. In a helpful paper under the title 'The Act of the Possible: Interpreting Statutes under the Human Rights Act' [1998] EHRLR 665 Lord Lester of Herne Hill QC has summarised the correct approach, at p 674:

'The first question the courts must ask is: does the legislation interfere with a Convention right? At that stage, the purpose or intent of the legislation will play a secondary role, for it will be seldom, if ever, that Parliament will have intended to legislate in breach of the Convention. It is at the second stage, when the Government seeks to justify the interference with a Convention right, under one of the exception clauses, that legislative purpose or intent becomes relevant. It is at that stage the principle of proportionality will be applied.'

See also Bertha Wilson J, 'The Making of a Constitution: Approaches to Judicial Interpretation' (1988) PL 370, 371–372; and David Feldman, 'Proportionality and The Human Rights Act 1998' in *The Principle of Proportionality in the Laws of Europe* (1999), pp. 117, 122–123.

38. It is well established that the guarantee of a fair trial under article 6 is absolute: a conviction obtained in breach of it cannot stand. *R v Forbes*, [2001] 2 WLR 1, 13, para 24. The only balancing permitted is in respect of what the concept of a fair trial entails: here account may be taken of the familiar triangulation of interests of the accused, the victim and society. In this context proportionality has a role to play. The criteria for determining the test of proportionality have been analysed in similar terms in the case law of the European Court of Justice and the European Court of Human Rights. It is not necessary for us to re-invent the wheel. In *de Freitas v Permanent Secretary of Ministry of Agriculture, Fisheries, Lands and Housing*

---

6   *Ed.* The 'twin myths' were that 'unchaste women were more likely to consent to intercourse and, in any event, were less worthy of belief': *R v Seaboyer* (1991) 83 DLR (4th) 193, 258 at 278, per McLachlin J, quoted by Lord Steyn (judgment, para 28).

[1999] 1 AC 69 Lord Clyde adopted a precise and concrete analysis of the criteria. In determining whether a limitation is arbitrary or excessive a court should ask itself:

'whether: (i) the legislative objective is sufficiently important to justify limiting a fundamental right; (ii) the measures designed to meet the legislative objective are rationally connected to it; and (iii) the means used to impair the right or freedom are no more than is necessary to accomplish the objective.'

The critical matter is the third criterion. Given the centrality of the right of a fair trial in the scheme of the Convention, and giving due weight to the important legislative goal of countering the twin myths, the question is whether section 41 makes an excessive inroad into the guarantee of a fair trial.

39. Subject to narrow exceptions section 41 is a blanket exclusion of potentially relevant evidence. Section 41 must however be construed in order to determine its precise exclusionary impact on alleged previous sexual experience between the complainant and the accused. Two processes of interpretation must be distinguished. First, ordinary methods of purposive and contextual interpretation may yield ways of minimising the prima facie exorbitant breadth of the section. Secondly, the interpretative obligation in section 3(1) of the 1998 Act may come into play. It provides that 'so far as it is *possible* to do so, primary legislation ... *must* be read and given effect in a way which is compatible with the Convention rights'. It is a key feature of the 1998 Act.

40. Three possible ways of minimising the excessive breadth of section 41 must be considered. The first possible gateway is to be found in section 41(3)(b), viz:

'it is an issue of consent and the sexual behaviour of the complainant to which the evidence or question relates is alleged to have taken place at or about the same time as the event which is the subject matter of the charge against the accused;'

An example covered by this provision would be where it is alleged that the complainant invited the accused to have sexual intercourse with her earlier in the evening. In my opinion, however, neither ordinary methods of interpretation nor the interpretative obligation under section 3 of the 1998 Act enables one to extend the temporal restriction to days, weeks or months. Section 41(3)(b) acknowledges by its own terms that previous sexual experience between a complainant and an accused may be relevant but then restricts the admission of such evidence by an extraordinary narrow temporal restriction.

41. The second gateway suggested by counsel for the Director of Public Prosecutions is the provision in section 41(5)(b) enabling evidence adduced by the prosecution to be rebutted or explained by or on behalf of the defence. The suggestion is that the Crown could adduce evidence which will enable the defence to lead evidence of previous sexual experience in rebuttal. This is not a coherent and satisfactory solution. It depends on the goodwill and co-operation of the prosecutor. A defendant has the *right* in a criminal trial to offer a full and complete defence. I would reject this suggested solution.

42. The third gateway is section 41(3)(c). It permits evidence where

'(c) it is an issue of consent and the sexual behaviour of the complainant to which the evidence or question relates is alleged to have been, in any respect, so similar –

(i) to any sexual behaviour of the complainant which (according to evidence adduced or to be adduced by or on behalf of the accused) took place as part of the event which is the subject matter of the charge against the accused ...

that the similarity cannot reasonably be explained as a coincidence.'

This gateway is only available where the issue is whether the complainant consented and the evidence or questioning relates to behaviour that is so similar to the defence's version of the complainant's behaviour at the time of the alleged offence that it cannot reasonably be explained as a coincidence. An example would be the case where the complainant says that the accused raped her; the accused says that the complainant consented and then after the act of intercourse tried to blackmail him by alleging rape; and the defence now wishes to ask the complainant whether on a previous occasion she similarly tried to blackmail the accused.

43. Rightly none of the counsel appearing before the House were prepared to argue that on ordinary methods of interpretation section 41(3)(c) can be interpreted to cover, for example, cases similar to the one before the House where it is alleged that there was a previous sexual

experience between the complainant and the accused on several occasions during a three week period before the occasion in question. ... In my view ordinary methods of purposive construction of section 41(3)(c) cannot cure the problem of the excessive breadth of the section 41, read as a whole, so far as it relates to previous sexual experience between a complainant and the accused. Whilst the statute pursued desirable goals, the methods adopted amounted to legislative overkill.

44. On the other hand, the interpretative obligation under section 3 of the 1998 Act is a strong one. It applies even if there is no ambiguity in the language in the sense of the language being capable of two different meanings. It is an emphatic adjuration by the legislature: *R v Director of Public Prosecutions, ex p Kebilene* [2000] 2 AC 326, per Lord Cooke of Thorndon, at p 373F; and my judgment, at p 366B. The White Paper made clear that the obligation goes far beyond the rule which enabled the courts to take the Convention into account in resolving any ambiguity in a legislative provision: see 'Rights Brought Home: The Human Rights Bill' (1997) (Cm 3782), para 2.7. The draftsman of the Act had before him the slightly weaker model in section 6 of the New Zealand Bill of Rights Act 1990 but preferred stronger language. Parliament specifically rejected the legislative model of requiring a reasonable interpretation. Section 3 places a duty on the court to strive to find a possible interpretation compatible with Convention rights. Under ordinary methods of interpretation a court may depart from the language of the statute to avoid absurd consequences: section 3 goes much further. Undoubtedly, a court must always look for a contextual and purposive interpretation: section 3 is more radical in its effect. It is a general principle of the interpretation of legal instruments that the text is the primary source of interpretation: other sources are subordinate to it: compare, for example, articles 31 to 33 of the Vienna Convention on the Law of Treaties (1980) (Cmnd 7964). Section 3 qualifies this general principle because it requires a court to find an interpretation compatible with Convention rights if it is possible to do so. In the progress of the Bill through Parliament the Lord Chancellor observed that 'in 99% of the cases that will arise, there will be no need for judicial declarations of incompatibility' and the Home Secretary said 'We expect that, in almost all cases, the courts will be able to interpret the legislation compatibility with the Convention': Hansard (HL Debates), 5 February 1998, col 840 (3rd Reading) and Hansard (HC Debates), 16 February 1998, col 778 (2nd Reading). For reasons which I explained in a recent paper, this is at least relevant as an aid to the interpretation of section 3 *against* the executive: 'Pepper v Hart: A re-examination' (2001) 21 Oxford Journal of Legal Studies 59. In accordance with the will of Parliament as reflected in section 3 it will sometimes be necessary to adopt an interpretation which linguistically may appear strained. The techniques to be used will not only involve the reading down of express language in a statute but also the implication of provisions. A declaration of incompatibility is a measure of last resort. It must be avoided unless it is plainly impossible to do so. If a *clear* limitation on Convention rights is stated *in terms*, such an impossibility will arise: *R v Secretary of State for the Home Department, ex p Simms* [2000] 2 AC 115, 132A–B per Lord Hoffmann. There is, however, no limitation of such a nature in the present case.

45. In my view section 3 requires the court to subordinate the niceties of the language of section 41(3)(c), and in particular the touchstone of coincidence, to broader considerations of relevance judged by logical and common sense criteria of time and circumstances. After all, it is realistic to proceed on the basis that the legislature would not, if alerted to the problem, have wished to deny the right to an accused to put forward a full and complete defence by advancing truly probative material. It is therefore possible under section 3 to read section 41, and in particular section 41(3)(c), as subject to the implied provision that evidence or questioning which is required to ensure a fair trial under article 6 of the Convention should not be treated as inadmissible. The result of such a reading would be that sometimes logically relevant sexual experiences between a complainant and an accused may be admitted under section 41(3)(c). On the other hand, there will be cases where previous sexual experience between a complainant and an accused will be irrelevant, eg an isolated episode distant in time and circumstances. Where the line is to be drawn must be left to the judgment of trial judges. On this basis a declaration of incompatibility can be avoided. If this approach is adopted, section 41 will have achieved a major part of its objective but its excessive reach will have been attenuated in accordance with the will of Parliament as reflected in section 3 of the 1998 Act. That is the approach which I would adopt. ...

46. It is of supreme importance that the effect of the speeches today should be clear to trial judges who have to deal with problems of the admissibility of questioning and evidence on alleged prior sexual experience between an accused and a complainant. The effect of the decision today is that under section 41(3)(c) of the 1999 Act, construed where necessary by applying the interpretative obligation under section 3 of the Human Rights Act 1998, and due regard always being paid to the importance of seeking to protect the complainant from indignity and from humiliating questions, the test of admissibility is whether the evidence (and questioning in relation to it) it nevertheless so relevant to the issue of consent that to exclude it would endanger the fairness of the trial under article 6 of the Convention. If this test is satisfied the evidence should not be excluded. ...

47. The appeal before the House concerns a concrete case. It involves the permissibility of questioning a complainant about an alleged recent sexual relationship between her and the defendant, and the admissibility of evidence on that point. These are matters for the trial judge to rule on at the resumed trial. But in my view he must do so on the broader interpretation of section 41(3)(c) required by section 3 of the 1998 Act. ...

48. ... Given the terms of this speech it is unnecessary to answer the certified question. I would dismiss the appeal.

Lord Hope:

69. It may be noted in passing that a statement of compatibility was attached to the Bill before second reading that its provisions were compatible with the Human Rights Act 1998. Statements to that effect are now required by section 19 of the Act, which was brought into force on 24 November 1998: (SI 1998/2882). But Mr Pannick QC for the Secretary of State did not seek to rely on this statement in the course of his argument. I consider that he was right not to do so. These statements may serve a useful purpose in Parliament. They may also be seen as part of the parliamentary history, indicating that it was not Parliament's intention to cut across a Convention right: Lord Irvine of Lairg LC 'The Development of Human Rights in Britain under an Unincorporated Convention on Human Rights' (1998) PL 221, 228. No doubt they are based on the best advice that is available. But they are no more than expressions of opinion by the minister. They are not binding on the court, nor do they have any persuasive authority. ...

99. It is plain that the question is in the end one of balance. Has the balance between the protection of the complainant and the accused's right to a fair trial been struck in the right place? ... if any doubt remains on this matter, it raises the further question whether Parliament acted within its discretionary area of judgment when it was choosing the point of balance indicated by section 41. The area is one where Parliament was better equipped than the judges are to decide where the balance lay. The judges are well able to assess the extent to which the restrictions will inhibit questioning or the leading of evidence. But it seems to me that in this highly sensitive and carefully researched field an assessment of the prejudice to the wider interests of the community if the restrictions were not to take that form was more appropriate for Parliament. An important factor for Parliament to consider was the extent to which restrictions were needed in order to restore and maintain public confidence.

104. But two important factors seem to me to indicate that prima facie the solution that was chosen was a proportionate one. The first is the need to restore and maintain public confidence in the system for the protection of vulnerable witnesses. Systems which relied on the exercise of a discretion by the trial judge have been called into question. Doubts have been raised as to whether they have achieved their object. I think that it was within the discretionary area of judgment for Parliament to decide not to follow these systems. The second is to be found in a detailed reading of the section as a whole. As I have tried to show in my analysis of the various subsections, it contains important provisions which preserve the defendant's right to ask questions about and adduce evidence of other sexual behaviour by the complainant where this is clearly relevant. While section 41(3) imposes very considerable restrictions, it needs to be seen in its context. I would hold that the required level of unfairness to show that in *every case* where previous sexual behaviour between the complainant and the accused is alleged the solution adopted is not proportionate has not been demonstrated.

105. I emphasise the words 'every case', because I believe that it would only be if there was a material risk of incompatibility with the article 6 Convention right in *all* such cases that it would be appropriate to lay down a rule of *general* application as to how, applying section 3

of the Human Rights Act 1998, section 41(3) ought to be read in a way that is compatible with the Convention right or, if that were not possible, to make a declaration of general incompatibility. I do not accept that there is such a risk. This is because I do not regard the *mere* fact that the complainant had consensual sexual intercourse with the accused on previous occasions as relevant to the issue whether she consented to intercourse on the occasion of the alleged rape.

106. For these reasons I consider that it has not been shown that, if the ordinary principles of statutory construction are applied to them, the provisions of section 41 which are relevant to the respondent's case are incompatible with his Convention right to a fair trial. I would hold that the question whether they are incompatible cannot be finally determined at this stage, as no attempt has been made to investigate the facts to the required level of detail to show that section 41 has made excessive inroads into the Convention right. It seems to me that it is neither necessary nor appropriate at this stage to resort to the interpretative obligation which is described in section 3 of the Human Rights Act in order to modify, alter or supplement the words used by Parliament. I think that it would only be appropriate to resort to surgery of that kind in this case if the words used by Parliament were unable, when they were given their ordinary meaning, to stand up to the test of compatibility. But that cannot, in my view be said of the allegations which the respondent makes as to the complainant'' sexual behaviour with him prior to the incident of the alleged rape. All he appears to be relying upon at present is the mere fact that on various occasions during the previous three weeks she had had consensual sexual intercourse with him in his flat. As I have said, I consider that this fact alone – and nothing else is alleged about it – is irrelevant to his defence of consent. So I would hold that the exclusion of evidence and questions which relate to it in regard to that defence (but not that of honest belief) is not incompatible with his right to a fair trial.

107. This does not mean that the question whether or not the respondent will have a fair trial is at an end. I agree with Mr Perry for the Crown that it will only be in rare and isolated cases, that the question of fairness will be capable of being determined before the trial. It was clearly right that this case should have been brought before your Lordships on appeal in view of the important issues of principle that were raised and the risk of exposing vulnerable witnesses to the risk of having to give evidence at a new trial. But now that these issues have been resolved the case must go back to the Crown Court for trial. The question whether the respondent did in the event have a fair trial will be open for consideration after the trial is over if he is convicted.

108. I should like to add however that I would find it very difficult to accept that it was permissible under section 3 of the Human Rights Act 1998 to read in to section 41(3)(c) a provision to the effect that evidence or questioning which was required to ensure a fair trial under article 6 of the Convention should not be treated as inadmissible. The rule of construction which section 3 lays down is quite unlike any previous rule of statutory interpretation. There is no need to identify an ambiguity or absurdity. Compatibility with Convention rights is the sole guiding principle. That is the paramount object which the rule seeks to achieve. But the rule is only a rule of interpretation. It does not entitle the judges to act as legislators. As Lord Woolf CJ said in *Poplar Housing and Regeneration Community Association Ltd v Donogue* [2001] EWCA Civ 595, section 3 does not entitle the court to legislate; its task is still one of interpretation. The compatibility is to be achieved only so far as this is possible. Plainly this will not be possible if the legislation contains provisions which expressly contradict the meaning which the enactment would have to be given to make it compatible. It seems to me that the same result must follow if they do so by necessary implication, as this too is a means of identifying the plain intention of Parliament: see Lord Hoffmann's observations in *R v Secretary of State for the Home Department, ex p Simms* [2000] 2 AC 115, 131F–G.

109. In the present case it seems to me that the entire structure of section 41 contradicts the idea that it is possible to read into it a new provision which would entitle the court to give leave whenever it was of the opinion that this was required to ensure a fair trial. The whole point of the section, as was made clear during the debates in Parliament, was to address the mischief which was thought to have arisen due to the width of the discretion which had previously been given to the trial judge. A deliberate decision was taken not to follow the examples which were to be found elsewhere, such as in section 275 of the Criminal Procedure (Scotland) Act 1995, of provisions which give an overriding discretion to the trial judge to allow the evidence or questioning where it would be contrary to the interests of justice to

exclude it. Section 41(2) *forbids* the exercise of such a discretion *unless* the court is satisfied as to the matters which that subsection identifies. It seems to me that it would not be possible, without contradicting the plain intention of Parliament, to read in a provision which would enable the court to exercise a wider discretion than that permitted by section 41(2).

110. I would not have the same difficulty with a solution which read down the provisions of subsections (3) or (5), as the case may be, in order to render them compatible with the Convention right. But if that were to be done it would be necessary to identify precisely (a) the words used by the legislature which would otherwise be incompatible with the Convention right and (b) how these words were to be construed, according to the rule which section 3 lays down, to make them compatible. That, it seems to me, is what the rule of construction requires. The court's task is to read and give effect to the legislation which it is asked to construe. The allegations about the complainant's previous sexual behaviour with the respondent are so exiguous that I do not think that it would be possible for your Lordships in this case with any degree of confidence to embark upon that exercise. I would leave that exercise to be undertaken by the trial judge in the light of such further information about the nature and circumstances of his relationship with the complainant that the respondent can make available if and when he renews his application. If he finds it necessary to apply the interpretative obligation under section 3 of the Human Rights Act 1998 to the words used in section 41(3)(c) of the 1999 Act, he should do so by construing those words, so far as it is possible to do so, by applying the test indicated in paragraph 46 of the speech of my noble and learned friend Lord Steyn. ...

122. ... I would dismiss the appeal. But I would hold that the respondent should be given an opportunity, in the light of the decision of this House, to renew his application to the trial judge for leave to be given under section 41(3)(c).

Lord Hutton:

155. ... on the basis that further evidence which the defendant may wish to give may be relevant I turn to consider whether such evidence is admissible under section 41. This gives rise to the following questions. The first is whether the evidence would be admissible under section 41 on ordinary principles of construction. If the answer to this question is in the negative the second question is whether the exclusion of the evidence infringes the defendant's right to a fair trial under article 6 of the Convention for the Protection of Human Rights and Fundamental Freedoms ('the Convention'). If the answer to this question is in the affirmative the third question is whether section 41 can be construed pursuant to section 3 of the Human Rights Act 1998 in such a way that it is compatible with article 6. If the answer to this question is in the negative it would be the duty of the House under section 4(2) of the 1998 Act to consider making a declaration that section 41 is incompatible with the Convention right given by article 6.

156. I consider it to be clear that if, as in this case, the defendant says that the most recent act of previous intercourse took place approximately one week before the date of the alleged offence, that sexual behaviour of the complainant cannot come within the scope of the word 'at or about the same time as the event which is the subject matter of the charge against the accused' in section 41(3)(b). This is so whether ordinary rules of construction are applied or the more expansive approach to construction is taken under section 3 of the 1998 Act.

157. A more difficult question arises under section 41(3)(c) because that paragraph is, in itself, a difficult one to construe in the context of the section. ...

158. It is to be noted that paragraph (c) does not contain the term 'strikingly similar' – it contains the less stringent words 'so similar ... that the similarity cannot reasonably be explained as a coincidence.' It also provides that it is sufficient if the sexual behaviour of the complainant is alleged to have been so similar 'in any respect'. Moreover section 42(1)(c) defines 'sexual behaviour' as being 'any sexual behaviour'.

159. I turn to consider the following hypothetical case. A defendant wishes to give evidence that for a number of months prior to the date of the alleged offence he had had a close and affectionate relationship with the complainant and that he had had frequent consensual intercourse with her during that period. Before intercourse he would kiss her and she would return his kisses. At the time of the alleged offence, before having intercourse, affectionate behaviour took place between them as it had done on the early occasions. Is this evidence admissible under section 41(3)(c)? It can be argued that the similarity between the sexual

behaviour of the woman on the earlier occasions and on the occasion in question cannot reasonably be explained as a coincidence: there is a causal connection which is that the woman was fond of the defendant and attracted to him and that is why intercourse has taken place on all occasions. But can it be said that the behaviour is 'so similar that the similarity cannot reasonably be explained as a coincidence'? Such behaviour is normal between a man and a woman and so it cannot be said to be 'strikingly similar', but that is not what the paragraph requires. Therefore I think there is an argument that such evidence would be admissible under section 41(3)(c). However I consider that some weight must be given to the word 'so', which I think was intended to emphasis that mere similarity was not sufficient. Moreover having regard to the way in which the mischief at which the section was directed was described by the Minister of State in the debate in the House of Lords, I do not think that Parliament intended that evidence such as that which I have described in the hypothetical case can be admitted under section 41(3)(c). Therefore I would hold that such evidence is not admissible under the paragraph. ...

160. In *Brown v Stott* [2001] 2 WLR 817 the Judicial Committee of the Privy Council considered the circumstances in which a particular right given by article 6 may be qualified by considerations of the public interest which Parliament has taken into account in enacting the statutory provision under consideration; in that case the public interest being the need to address in an effective way the high incidence of death and injury on the roads caused by the misuse of motor vehicles. But it is clear that in relation to a fair trial certain rights are absolute and cannot be qualified. Lord Bingham of Cornhill stated, at p 825A:

'There is nothing to suggest that the fairness of the trial itself may be qualified, compromised or restricted in any way, whatever the circumstances and whatever the public interest in convicting the offender. If the trial as a whole is judged to be unfair, a conviction cannot stand.

What a fair trial requires cannot, however, be the subject of a single, unvarying rule or collection of rules. It is proper to take account of the facts and circumstances of particular cases, as the European Court has consistently done.'

And, at p 836B:

'The jurisprudence of the European Court very clearly establishes that while the overall fairness of a criminal trial cannot be compromised, the constituent rights comprised, whether expressly or implicitly, within article 6 are not themselves absolute. Limited qualification of these rights is acceptable if reasonably directed by national authorities towards a clear and proper public objective and if representing no greater qualification than the situation calls for.'

Lord Hope of Craighead stated, at p 851A:

'A similar approach to the function of the rule of law can be seen in the fact that the court has consistently recognised that, while the right to a fair trial is absolute in its terms and the public interest can never be invoked to deny that right to anybody under any circumstances, the rights which it has read into article 6 are neither absolute nor inflexible.'

161. In the type of case which I have instanced where a man, who may be innocent, wishes to give evidence of previous acts of sexual intercourse with the complainant in the course of a recent close and affectionate relationship, such evidence would be a central and essential part of his defence, and I consider that to deny him the opportunity to cross-examine the complainant and to give such evidence would compromise the overall fairness of the hearing and would deny him the essence of a fair trial. In my opinion the right of a defendant to call relevant evidence, where the absence of such evidence may give rise to an unjust conviction, is an absolute right which cannot be qualified by considerations of public interest, no matter how well founded that public interest may be. ...

Therefore I would hold on ordinary principles of construction that section 41 is incompatible with the right to a fair trial given by article 6. ...

162. Section 3(1) provides:

'So far as it is possible to do so, primary legislation and subordinate legislation must be read and given effect in a way which is compatible with the Convention rights.'

As my noble and learned friend Lord Steyn stated in *R v Director of Public Prosecutions, ex p Kebilene* [2000] 2 AC 326, 366B, this subsection enacts a strong interpretative obligation, and Lord Cooke of Thorndon, at p 373F, described the subsection as an adjuration. It is clearly desirable that a court should seek to avoid having to make a declaration of incompatibility under section 4 of the 1998 Act unless the clear and express wording of the provision makes this impossible.

163. In paragraph 159 I have observed that on ordinary principles of construction and having regard to the change in emphasis in *Director of Public Prosecutions v P* [1991] 2 AC 447 away from 'striking similarity' to 'probative force' there is a possible argument that relevant evidence of a previous close and affectionate relationship in which sexual intercourse took place is admissible under section 41(3). Therefore pursuant to the obligation imposed by section 3(1) that section 41 must be read and given effect in a way which is compatible with article 6, I consider that section 41(3)(c) should be read as including evidence of such previous behaviour by the complainant because the defendant claims that her sexual behaviour on previous occasions was similar, and the similarity was not a coincidence because there was a causal connection which was her affection for, and feelings of attraction towards, the defendant. It follows that I am in full agreement with the test of admissibility stated by my noble and learned friend Lord Steyn in paragraph 46 of his speech.

164. Therefore I consider that the matter should be remitted to the trial judge in the Crown Court to consider if the evidence which the defendant wishes to give (as amplified by him if he wishes to do so) is admissible under that test. Having regard to the terms of this speech I think it is unnecessary to answer the certified question.

Lord Clyde delivered a concurring judgment.

Appeal dismissed.

NOTES

1. In this case, the House of Lords considered the approach to the interpretation of legislation to be taken by the courts when applying the requirement in s. 3(1) HRA that '[s]o far as it is possible to do so, primary legislation and subordinate legislation must be read and given effect in a way which is compatible with the Convention rights'.
2. The approach set out in Lord Steyn's judgment was accepted by the other four judges in the case. Applying this approach, Lords Slynn, Steyn, Clyde and Hutton considered that, whereas s. 41 of the Youth Justice and Criminal Evidence Act 1999 could not be interpreted as being compatible with the Convention right to a fair trial in Art. 6 ECHR on ordinary principles of statutory construction, it could be so interpreted on the basis of s. 3 HRA. This was because s. 41(3)(c) could be read as 'subject to the implied provision that evidence or questioning which is required to ensure a fair trial under article 6 of the Convention should not be treated as inadmissible' (Lord Steyn's judgment, para 45). Lord Hope (judgment para 106) considered that s. 41 could be interpreted as being consistent with Art. 6 using ordinary principles of interpretation, so that there was no need to resort to s. 3.
3. As *R v A* shows, a lot may be done in the application of s. 3 to temper legislation to achieve Convention compliance and so avoid the need for a declaration of incompatibility and new legislation. Section 3 takes matters much further than the longstanding rule of statutory interpretation by which any ambiguity in a statute must be resolved consistently with United Kingdom treaty obligations.[7] The rule in s. 3 also differs fundamentally from those which generally apply in the interpretation of statutes. These all give way where necessary to the overriding need to find a meaning, if at all possible and however strained, that is compatible with Convention

---

7   See above, p. 4.

rights. The difference was indicated by Dame Elizabeth Butler-Sloss in *Re K (a child)*[8] as follows:

> '41 ... The duty of the English court under the 1998 Act is to attempt to find a compatible interpretation. If a compatible interpretation can be found, there is no justification for a declaration of incompatibility. Mr Garnham referred us to an extra-judicial observation of Lord Cooke of Thorndon who said: "section 3(1) will require a very different approach to interpretation from that to which the United Kingdom courts are accustomed. Traditionally, the search has been for the true meaning; now it will be for a possible meaning that would prevent the making of a declaration of incompatibility": see Lester and Pannick *Human Rights Law and Practice* (1999), pp. 23–24, para 2.3, fn.2.
> 42. I respectfully agree with Lord Cooke.'

Note in connection the application of s. 3 the use by judges of the terms 'reading in' and 'reading down'.[9] 'Reading in' means reading words into a statute that will cause it not to be incompatible with Convention rights. 'Reading down' means reading wording that might lead to incompatibility in a limited way so as to prevent this.

4. In *R v A*, while approving Lord Steyn's approach, Lord Hope stated that, were he to have decided the case under s. 3, he would, in contrast with the other four judges, have found it impossible interpret s. 41(1)(c) in such as way as to have made s. 41 compatible with Art. 6 ECHR. In this connection, he commented (para. 108), approving Lord Woolf in the *Poplar Housing* case,[10] that 'section 3 does not entitle the court to legislate; its task is still one of interpretation'. Cf. the following comment by Lord Hoffmann in *R (Alconbury Developments Ltd) v Secretary of State for the Environment, Transport and the Regions*:[11] 'The Human Rights Act 1998 was no doubt intended to strengthen the rule of law but not to inaugurate the rule of lawyers.'

How close to the line between interpretation and legislation does the House of Lords decision in *R v A* come? Does it overstep that line? Is the role of the courts under s.3 to read into a statutory provision, if necessary, wording that makes it compatible with Convention rights so long as the statute does not contain express and clear wording to the contrary?[12] What wording in s. 41(3)(c) might have prevented the House of Lords from reading Lord Steyn's 'implied provision'[13] into it? For cases in which the wording of a statute was incompatible with Convention rights despite the rule in s. 3, see *Wilson v First County Trust Ltd (No 2)*[14] and *R (on the application of H v North and East Region Mental Health Review Tribunal*.[15] In Parliament, Lord Irvine suggested that, in view of s. 3, 'in 99 per cent. of the cases that will arise, there will be no need for judicial declarations of incompatibility.'[16]

5. The fact that a court is not able to interpret primary legislation[17] as being compatible with Convention rights does not affect its 'validity, continuing operation

8 [2001] 2 All ER 719 at 732, CA.
9 See, e.g., Lord Hope in *R v Lambert* [2001] 3 All ER 577 at 604, HL; and Lord Cooke in *R v DDP, ex p Kebilene* [2000] 2 AC 326 at 373, HL. As to whether s. 3 requires both reading down and reading in, see R. A. Edwards, [2000] 20 LS 353. See also Lord Clyde in *R (on the application of Wardle) v Crown Court at Leeds* [2001] 2 WLR 865 at 898, HL.
10 Below, p. 76.
11 [2001] 2 WLR 1389 at 1427, HL.
12 In *Ahmad v ILEA*, below, p. 1058, Lord Denning read into s. 30 of the Education Act 1944, the words 'if the timetable so permits.' If that were done to achieve compatibility with a Convention right (the reverse was true in that case), would that be in accord with the *R v A* approach to s. 3?
13 See above, p. 49.
14 Below, p. 63.
15 Below, p. 70.
16 585 HL Debs, 5 February 1998, col. 840.
17 These are mainly Westminster statutes and prerogative orders in council. See further, above, p. 31, n. 15.

or enforcement'.[18] Instead, the court must apply it in the case before the court and in subsequent cases, unless and until the competent Minister has taken remedial action under s. 10 HRA.[19] However, subordinate legislation[20] that is incompatible with a Convention right is invalid, etc., unless the 'primary legislation prevents the removal of the incompatibility'.[1] Subject to this exception, incompatible subordinate legislation is invalid whenever it is made and even though the statute authorising it post-dates the HRA.

6. The rule of interpretation in s. 3 applies to legislation whether it was enacted before or after the HRA[2] and to events occurring before as well as after the HRA entered into force.[3] A pre-HRA precedent establishing an interpretation of a statute may have to give way to a different interpretation if this is necessary for the statute to be compatible with Convention rights, with a lower court being free to deviate from even a House of Lords precedent.

Brown v Stott [2001] 2 All ER 97, [2001] 2 WLR 817, Privy Council

The defendant was suspected of stealing a bottle of gin from a superstore in the early hours. When asked by the police, who suspected she had been drinking alcohol, how she had reached the superstore, the defendant pointed to a car, which she said was hers. She was charged with theft and taken to the police station. There, under s. 172(2)(a) of the Road Traffic Act 1988, the defendant was required to indicate who had been driving the car when she travelled to the superstore, and admitted that it was her. After a positive breath test, the defendant was charged with driving while her breath alcohol level was above the legal limit. In the Scottish High Court of Judiciary, it was held that the evidence compulsorily obtained from her under s. 172(2)(a) could not be led by the procurator fiscal because s. 172(2)(a) infringed the defendant's Convention right to a fair trial in Art. 6 ECHR, particularly the implied right to freedom from self-incrimination that had been read into Art. 6(1) by the European Court of Human Rights. The procurator fiscal and the Advocate General appealed. The Privy Council first held that the case raised a devolution issue so that the question of the compatibility of s. 172(2)(a) with Convention rights could be raised. It then unanimously upheld an appeal from the decision of the High Court of Justiciary on the ground that, as read in accordance with s. 3 HRA, s. 172(2)(a) was not incompatible with Art. 6 ECHR.

Lord Steyn:
In the first real test of the Human Rights Act 1998 it is opportune to stand back and consider what the basic aims of the Convention are. One finds the explanation in the very words of the preambles of the Convention. There were two principal objectives. The first was to maintain and further realise human rights and fundamental freedoms. The framers of the Convention recognised that it was not only morally right to promote the observance of human rights but that it was also the best way of achieving pluralistic and just societies in which all can peaceably go about their lives. The second aim was to foster effective political democracy. This aim necessarily

---

18 s. 3(2)(b) HRA. The normal rule of implied repeal of statutes by later inconsistent statutes does not apply to a pre-HRA statute that is contrary to the HRA.

19 Per Lord Steyn, in *R v DPP, ex p Kebilene* [2000] 2 AC 326 at 367, HL. See further on this matter and on the position concerning unsafe convictions, below, p. 68–69.

20 Mainly regulations, statutory orders in council, devolved legislation in Scotland, Northern Ireland and Wales. See s. 21(1) HRA.

1 s. 3(2)(c) HRA.

2 s. 3(2)(a) HRA.

3 *JA Pye v Graham* [2001] EWCA Civ 117, [2001] 2 WLR 1293, CA. As Keene LJ stated, ibid. at 1310, a statute should not have different meanings depending on whether it is applied to events before or after the HRA entered into force.

involves the creation of conditions of stability and order under the rule of law, not for its own sake, but as the best way to ensuring the well being of the inhabitants of the European countries. After all, democratic government has only one raison d'être, namely to serve the interests of all the people. The inspirers of the European Convention, among whom Winston Churchill played an important role, and the framers of the European Convention, ably assisted by English draftsmen, realised that from time to time the fundamental right of one individual may conflict with the human right of another. Thus the principles of free speech and privacy may collide. They also realised only too well that a single-minded concentration on the pursuit of fundamental rights of individuals to the exclusion of the interests of the wider public might be subversive of the ideal of tolerant European liberal democracies. The fundamental rights of individuals are of supreme importance but those rights are not unlimited: we live in communities of individuals who also have rights. The direct lineage of this ancient idea is clear: the European Convention (1950) is the descendant of the Universal Declaration of Human Rights (1948) which in article 29 expressly recognised the duties of everyone to the community and the limitation on rights in order to secure and protect respect for the rights of others. It is also noteworthy that article 17 of the European Convention prohibits, among others, individuals from abusing their rights to the detriment of others. Thus, notwithstanding the danger of intolerance towards ideas, the Convention system draws a line which does not accord the protection of free speech to those who propagate racial hatred against minorities: article 10; *Jersild v Denmark* (1994) 19 EHRR 1, 26, para 31. This is to be contrasted with the categorical language of the First Amendment to the United States Constitution which provides that 'Congress shall make no law ... abridging the freedom of speech.' The European Convention requires that where difficult questions arise a balance must be struck. Subject to a limited number of absolute guarantees, the scheme and structure of the Convention reflects this balanced approach. It differs in material respects from other constitutional systems but as a European nation it represents our Bill of Rights. We must be guided by it. And it is a basic premise of the Convention system that only an entirely neutral, impartial, and independent judiciary can carry out the primary task of securing and enforcing Convention rights. This contextual scene is not only directly relevant to the issues arising on the present appeal but may be a matrix in which many challenges under the Human Rights Act 1998 should be considered. ...

The present case is concerned with article 6 of the Convention which guarantees to every individual a fair trial in civil and criminal cases. ...

It is well settled, although not expressed in the Convention, that there is an implied privilege against self-incrimination under article 6. Moreover, section 172(2) undoubtedly makes an inroad on this privilege. On the other hand, it is also clear that the privilege against self-incrimination is not an absolute right. While there is no decision of the European Court of Human Rights directly in point, it is noteworthy that closely related rights have been held not to be absolute. It is significant that the basic right of access to the courts has been held to be not absolute: *Golder v United Kingdom* 1 EHRR 524. The principle that everyone charged with a criminal offence shall be presumed innocent until proved guilty according to law is connected with the privilege against self-incrimination. Yet the former has been held not to be absolute: *Salabiaku v France* 13 EHRR 379. The European Court has also had occasion to emphasise the close link between the right of silence and the privilege against self-incrimination: *Murray v United Kingdom* 22 EHRR 29. In *Murray* the European Court held that the right of silence is not absolute.

In these circumstances it would be strange if a right not expressed in the Convention or any of its Protocols, but implied into article 6 of the Convention, had an absolute character. In my view the right in question is plainly not absolute. From this premise it follows that an interference with the right may be justified if the particular legislative provision was enacted in pursuance of a legitimate aim and if the scope of the legislative provision is necessary and proportionate to the achievement of the aim. ...

In considering whether an inroad on the privilege against self-discrimination can be justified, it is necessary to concentrate on the particular context. An intense focus on section 172(2) is required. It reads:

> 'Where the driver of a vehicle is alleged to be guilty of an offence to which this section applies—(a) the person keeping the vehicle shall give such information as to the identity of the driver as he may be required to give by or on behalf of a chief officer of police, and (b)

any other person shall if required as stated above give any information which it is in his power to give and may lead to identification of the driver.'

The penalty for failing to comply with section 172(2) is a fine of not more than £1,000. In addition an individual may be disqualified from driving and endorsement of the driver's licence is mandatory. It is well established that an oral admission made by a driver under section 172(2) is admissible in evidence: *Foster v Farrell* 1963 JC 46.

The subject of section 172(2) is the driving of vehicles. It is a notorious fact that vehicles are potentially instruments of death and injury. The statistics placed before the Board show a high rate of fatal and other serious accidents involving vehicles in Great Britain. The relevant statistics are as follows:

	1996	1997	1998
Fatal and serious accidents	40,601	39,628	37,770

The effective prosecution of drivers causing serious offences is a matter of public interest. But such prosecutions are often hampered by the difficulty of identifying the drivers of the vehicles at the time of, say, an accident causing loss of life or serious injury or potential danger to others. The tackling of this social problem seems in principle a legitimate aim for a legislature to pursue.

The real question is whether the legislative remedy in fact adopted is necessary and proportionate to the aim sought to be achieved. There were legislative choices to be made. The legislature could have decided to do no more than to exhort the police and prosecuting authorities to redouble their efforts. It may, however, be that such a policy would have been regarded as inadequate. Secondly, the legislature could have introduced a reverse burden of proof clause which placed the burden on the registered owner to prove that he was not the driver of the vehicle at a given time when it is alleged that an offence was committed. Thirdly, and this was the course actually adopted, there was the possibility of requiring information about the identity of the driver to be revealed by the registered owner and others. As between the second and third techniques it may be said that the latter involves the securing of an admission of a constituent element of the offence. On the other hand, such an admission, if wrongly made, is not conclusive. And it must be measured against the alternative of a reverse burden clause which could without further investigation of the identity of the driver lead to a prosecution. In their impact on the citizen the two techniques are not widely different. And it is rightly conceded that a properly drafted reverse burden of proof provision would have been lawful.

It is also important to keep in mind the narrowness of the interference. Section 172(2) is directed at obtaining information in one category, namely the identity of the driver at the time when an offence was allegedly committed. The most important part of section 172(2) is paragraph (a) since the relevant information is usually peculiarly within the knowledge of the owner. But there may be scope for using (b) in a limited category of cases, e g when only the identity of a passenger in the car is known. Section 172(2) does not authorise general questioning by the police to secure a confession of an offence. On the other hand, section 172(2) does, depending on the circumstances, in effect authorise the police officer to invite the owner to make an admission of one element in a driving offence. It would, however, be an abuse of the power under section 172(2) for the police officer to employ improper or overbearing methods of obtaining the information. He may go no further than to ask who the driver was at the given time. If the police officer strays beyond his power under section 172(2) a judge will have ample power at trial to exclude the evidence. It is therefore a relatively narrow interference with the privilege in one area which poses widespread and serious law enforcement problems.
...

Under the Convention system the primary duty is placed on domestic courts to secure and protect Convention rights. The function of the European Court of Human Rights is essential but supervisory. In that capacity it accords to domestic courts a margin of appreciation, which recognises that national institutions are in principle better placed than an international court to evaluate local needs and conditions. That principle is logically not applicable to domestic courts. On the other hand, national courts may accord to the decisions of national legislatures some deference *where the context justifies* it: see *R v Director of Public Prosecutions, Ex p Kebilene*

[2000] 2 AC 326, 380–381 per Lord Hope of Craighead; see also: Singh, Hunt and Demetriou, 'Is there a Role for the "Margin of Appreciation" in National Law after the Human Rights Act?' [1999] EHRLR 15. This point is well explained in *Lester & Pannick, Human Rights Law and Practice* (1999), p 74:

> 'Just as there are circumstances in which an international court will recognise that national institutions are better placed to assess the needs of society, and to make difficult choices between competing considerations, so national courts will accept that there are some circumstances in which the legislature and the executive are better placed to perform those functions.'

In my view this factor is of some relevance in the present case. Here section 172(2) addresses a pressing social problem, namely the difficulty of law enforcement in the face of statistics revealing a high accident rate resulting in death and serious injuries. The legislature was entitled to regard the figures of serious accidents as unacceptably high. It would also have been entitled to take into account that it was necessary to protect other Convention rights, viz the right to life of members of the public exposed to the danger of accidents: see article 2(1). On this aspect the legislature was in as good a position as a court to assess the gravity of the problem and the public interest in addressing it. It really then boils down to the question whether in adopting the procedure enshrined in section 172(2), rather than a reverse burden technique, it took more drastic action than was justified. While this is ultimately a question for the court, it is not unreasonable to regard both techniques as permissible in the field of the driving of vehicles. After all, the subject invites special regulation; objectively the interference is narrowly circumscribed; and it is qualitatively not very different from requiring, for example, a breath specimen from a driver. Moreover, it is less invasive than an essential modern tool of crime detection such as the taking of samples from a suspect for DNA profiling. If the matter was not covered by authority, I would have concluded that section 172(2) is compatible with article 6. ...

The decision of the European Court in *Saunders v United Kingdom* 23 EHRR 313 gave some support to the view of the High Court of Justiciary. With due respect I have to say that the reasoning in *Saunders* is unsatisfactory and less than clear: see the critique in Andrews, 'Hiding Behind the Veil: Financial Delinquency and the Law' (1997) 22 ELR 369; Eriksen and Thorkildsen, 'Self-Incrimination, The Ban on Self-Incrimination after the Saunders Judgment' (1997) 5 JFC 182; Davies, 'Do polluters have the right not to incriminate themselves?' (1999) 143 SJ 924. The European Court did not rule that the privilege against self-incrimination is absolute. Surprisingly in view of its decision in *Murray* 22 EHRR 29 that the linked right of silence is not absolute it left the point open in respect of the privilege against self-incrimination: 23 EHRR 313, 339–340, para 74. On the other hand, the substance of its reasoning treats both privileges are not absolute. The court observed, at p 337, para 68:

> 'The court recalls that, although not specifically mentioned in article 6 of the Convention, the right to silence and the right not to incriminate oneself, are generally recognised international standards which lie at the heart of the notion of a fair procedure under article 6. Their rationale lies, inter alia, in the protection of the accused against improper compulsion by the authorities thereby contributing to the avoidance of miscarriages of justice and to the fulfilment of the aims of article 6.'

The court emphasised the rationale of improper compulsion. It does not hold that *anything* said under compulsion of law is inadmissible. Admittedly, the court also observed, at para 68:

> 'The right not to incriminate oneself, in particular, presupposes that the prosecution in a criminal case seek to prove their case against the accused without resort to evidence obtained through methods of coercion or oppression in defiance of the will of the accused. In this sense the right is closely linked to the presumption of innocence contained in article 6(2) of the Convention.'

Again one finds the link with the non-absolute right of silence. In any event 'methods of coercion or oppression in defiance of the will of the accused' is probably another way of referring to improper compulsion. This is consistent with the following passage, at p 338, para 69:

'In the present case the court is only called upon to decide whether the use made by the prosecution of the statements obtained from the applicant by the inspectors amounted to an unjustifiable infringement of the right. This question must be examined by the court in the light of all the circumstances of the case. In particular, it must be determined whether the applicant has been subject to compulsion to give evidence and whether the use made of the resulting testimony at his trial offended the basic principles of a fair procedure inherent in article 6(1) of which the right not to incriminate oneself is a constituent element.'

The expression 'unjustifiable infringement of the right' implies that some infringements may be justified. In my view the observations in *Saunders* do not support an absolutist view of the privilege against self-incrimination. It may be that the observations in *Saunders* will have to be clarified in a further case by the European Court. As things stand, however, I consider that the High Court of Justiciary put too great weight on these observations. In my view they were never intended to apply to a case such as the present. ...

That brings me back to the decision of the High Court of Justiciary. It treated the privilege against self-incrimination as virtually absolute. That conclusion fits uneasily into the balanced. Convention system, and cannot be reconciled with article 6 in all its constituent parts and the spectrum of jurisprudence of the European Court on the various facets of article 6.

I would hold that the decision of the High Court of Justiciary on the merits was wrong. The procurator fiscal is entitled to lead the evidence of Miss Brown's admission under section 172(2). ...

I am in complete agreement with Lord Hope of Craighead that a devolution issue has been raised and I would respectfully endorse his reasons.

For these reasons, as well as the reasons given by Lord Bingham of Cornhill, I would allow the appeal and quash the declaration made by the High Court.

Appeal allowed.

Lord Bingham, **Lord Hope**, **Lord Clyde** and **the Right Honourable Ian Kirkwood** also delivered judgments allowing the appeal.

NOTES

1. Under the Scotland Act 1998, primary legislation of the Scottish Parliament (s. 29(2)(d)) and subordinate legislation and acts of members of the Scottish executive (s. 57(2)) on devolution issues are invalid if they are incompatible with Convention rights.[4] The Scotland Act 1998 entered into force in 1999 with the result that a number of cases, including *Brown v Stott*,[5] concerning compliance with Convention rights arose in Scottish cases before the HRA entered into force for the United Kingdom generally. Although *Brown v Stott* concerned Westminster legislation, the case raised a question of compliance with Convention rights in the exercise of a devolved power within the Scotland Act, viz. whether the procurator fiscal, acting for the Lord Advocate, a member of the Scottish executive, could lead evidence in a criminal

---

4   Similarly, the Welsh Assembly may not adopt legislation or act incompatibly with Convention rights: Government of Wales Act 1998, s. 107. Acts of the Northern Ireland Parliament, Measures of the Assembly established under the Northern Ireland Assembly Act 1973 and Acts of the Northern Ireland Assembly are subordinate legislation under the HRA: s. 21(1) HRA. On the position in Scotland, see A. Stewart, (2000) SLT 239 and Lord Hope, [1998] EHRLR 467. Curiously, human rights cases arising in respect of devolved powers under the Scotland Act go on appeal to the Privy Council; non-devolution HRA cases stop with the High Court of Justiciary in Scotland: see A. Stewart, ibid.
5   Another case was *Starrs v Ruxton* 2000 SLT 42, H Ct of Justiciary, in which a temporary sheriff was held not to constitute an 'independent and impartial tribunal' for the purposes of Art. 6 ECHR.

prosecution in Scotland. Declarations of incompatibility are not applicable to devolved acts, which are instead invalid.

2. *Deference to Parliament.* Lord Steyn's judgment in *Brown v Stott* articulates the 'deference to Parliament' principle that the courts apply when deciding whether Westminster legislation is incompatible with Convention rights. Lord Bingham spoke in *Brown v Stott*[6] in similar terms:

> 'While a national court does not accord the margin of appreciation recognised by the European Court as a supra-national court, it will give weight to the decisions of a representative legislature and a democratic government within the discretionary area of judgment accorded to these bodies: see Lester and Pannick, *Human Rights Law and Practice* (1999), pp. 73–76.'[7]

Earlier, Lord Hope had taken the same position in *R v DPP, ex p Kebilene*:[8]

> 'The doctrine of the "margin of appreciation" is a familiar part of the jurisprudence of the European Court of Human Rights. The European Court has acknowledged that, by reason of their direct and continuous contact with the vital forces of their countries, the national authorities are in principle better placed to evaluate local needs and conditions than an international court: *Buckley v United Kingdom* (1996) 23 EHRR 101, 129, paras. 74–75. Although this means that, as the European Court explained in *Handyside v United Kingdom* (1976) 1 EHRR 737, 753, para. 48, 'the machinery of protection established by the Convention is subsidiary to the national systems safeguarding human rights,' it goes hand in hand with a European supervision. The extent of this supervision will vary according to such factors as the nature of the Convention right in issue, the importance of that right for the individual and the nature of the activities involved in the case.
>
> This doctrine is an integral part of the supervisory jurisdiction which is exercised over state conduct by the international court. By conceding a margin of appreciation to each national system, the court has recognised that the Convention, as a living system, does not need to be applied uniformly by all states but may vary in its application according to local needs and conditions. This technique is not available to the national courts when they are considering Convention issues arising within their own countries. But in the hands of the national courts also the Convention should be seen as an expression of fundamental principles rather than as a set of mere rules. The questions which the courts will have to decide in the application of these principles will involve questions of balance between competing interests and issues of proportionality.
>
> In this area difficult choices may have to be made by the executive or the legislature between the rights of the individual and the needs of society. In some circumstances it will be appropriate for the courts to recognise that there is an area of judgment within which the judiciary will defer, on democratic grounds, to the considered opinion of the elected body or person whose act or decision is said to be incompatible with the Convention. This point is well made at p. 74, para. 3.21 of *Human Rights Law and Practice* (1999), of which Lord Lester of Herne Hill and Mr. Pannick are the general editors, where the area in which these choices may arise is conveniently and appropriately described as the "discretionary area of judgment". It will be easier for such an area of judgment to be recognised where the Convention itself requires a balance to be struck, much less so where the right is stated in terms which are unqualified. It will be easier for it to be recognised where the issues involve questions of social or economic policy, much less so where the rights are of high constitutional importance or are of a kind where the courts are especially well placed to assess the need for protection. But even where the right is stated in terms which are unqualified the courts will need to bear in mind the jurisprudence of the European Court which recognises that due account should be taken of

---

6   [2001] 2 WLR 817, 835, HL.

7   For other literature to the same effect, see Sir John Laws, in C. Forsyth and I. Hare (eds.), *The Golden Metwand and the Crooked Cord: Essays on Public Law in Honour of Sir William Wade QC* (1998), p. 201; D. Pannick, [1998] PL 545.

8   [2000] 2 AC 326 at 380, HL. Note, however, Lord Hope's reference to a margin of appreciation in *Montgomery v HM Advocate* [2001] 2 WLR 779 at 798, which was questioned by Lord Hoffmann, at 786.

the special nature of terrorist crime and the threat which it poses to a democratic society: *Murray v United Kingdom* (1994) 19 EHRR 193, 222, para. 47.'

See also Lord Hoffmann in *Montgomery v HM Advocate*:[9]

'The doctrine of a "margin of appreciation" exists to enable the concepts in the Convention to be given somewhat different content in the various contracting states, according to their respective histories and cultures. But the present issue is not one which raises the question of the content which should be given to a Convention concept. It would not come before the Strasbourg court at all. It is a purely United Kingdom question, brought into existence by the specific provisions for incorporating provisions of the Convention into the domestic laws of those parts of the United Kingdom having legislatures with devolved powers. As such, it involves simply the construction of United Kingdom legislation. I would be very reluctant, without further argument, to accept that the concept of a margin of appreciation should be employed to enable the same provision of the Convention to be given different meanings according to whether it has been incorporated into the law of one part of the United Kingdom rather than another.'

3. The 'margin of appreciation' doctrine to which their Lordships refer is well established in the jurisprudence of the European Court of Human Rights. It was formulated most famously in *Handyside v UK* in the context of limitations on freedom of expression (Art. 10 ECHR):[10]

'By reason of their direct and continuous contact with the vital forces of their countries, state authorities are in principle in a better position than the international judge to give an opinion on the exact content of those requirements [of morals] as well as on the "necessity" of a "restriction" or "penalty" intended to meet them ...

Nevertheless, Article 10(2) does not give the contracting states an unlimited power of appreciation. The Court, which, with the Commission, is responsible for ensuring the observance of those states' engagements, is empowered to give the final ruling on whether a "restriction" or "penalty" is reconcilable with freedom of expression as protected by Article 10. The domestic margin of appreciation thus goes hand in hand with a European supervision.'

By means of the doctrine, the European Court of Human Rights allows states, whether acting through their legislature, executive or judiciary, a certain degree of latitude in borderline cases in deciding whether a limitation upon a Convention right is justifiable by the public interest. It does so because of the local knowledge of state institutions. There is, as it were, a presumption in favour of their assessment of the facts and of what is called for in the light of them.[11] It is also used as a basis for not pressing a state on a matter of social policy where European values are in flux.[12] As Lord Steyn states, the margin of appreciation doctrine, or principle, is not 'logically applicable' in the different context of national courts assessing the compatibility of national legislation with Convention rights. However, the 'deference to Parliament' principle, while having a different justification, ie recognition of the special position of a democratically elected legislature 'where the context justifies it',[13] may lead to the same result on the facts of a particular case.

4. The deference principle was applied in *Pearson v Secretary of State for the Home Department*.[14] There the Divisional Court dismissed applications for judicial review in which the applicant convicted prisoners challenged decisions by the electoral registrar refusing to register them as voters because of s. 3(1) of the Representation

9   [2001] 2 WLR 779 at 786–787, PC.
10   [1976] 1 EHRR 737.
11   See D. Harris, M. O'Boyle and C. Warbrick, *The Law of the European Convention on Human Rights* (1995), pp. 12–15.
12   E.g. the legal status of transsexuals: see *Sheffield and Horsham v United Kingdom* (1998) 27 EHRR 163.
13   Per Lord Steyn, extract above.
14   [2001] EWHC Admin 239, [2001] 1 All ER (D) 22 (Apr), QBD.

of the People Act 1983, which denied such persons the right to vote. Deferring to Parliament, the court refused to make a declaration that s. 3 was incompatible with Art. 3 ECHR, First Protocol.

Kennedy LJ stated:

'As Parliament has the responsibility for deciding what shall be the consequences of conviction by laying down the powers and duties of a sentencing tribunal or other body it necessarily follows that lines have to be drawn, and that on subsequent examination a case can be made in favour of the line being drawn somewhere else, but in deference to the legislature courts should not easily be persuaded to condemn what has been done, especially where it has been done in primary legislation after careful evaluation and against a background of increasing public concern about crime.

... Of course as far as an individual prisoner is concerned disenfranchisement does impair the very essence of his right to vote, but that is too simplistic an approach, because what Article 3 of the First Protocol is really concerned with is the wider question of universal franchise, and 'the free expression of the opinion of the people in the choice of the legislature'. If an individual is to be disenfranchised that must be in pursuit of a legitimate aim. In the case of a convicted prisoner serving his sentence the aim may not be easy to articulate. Clearly there is an element of punishment, and also an element of electoral law. As the Home Secretary said, Parliament has taken the view that for the period during which they are in custody convicted prisoners have forfeited their right to have a say in the way the country is governed. The Working Group said that such prisoners had lost the moral authority to vote. Perhaps the best course is that suggested by Linden JA, namely to leave to philosophers the true nature of this disenfranchisement whilst recognising that the legislation does different things.

The European Court also requires that the means employed to restrict the implied Convention rights to vote are not disproportionate, and that is the point at which, as it seems to me, it is appropriate for this court to defer to the legislature. It is easy to be critical of a law which operates across a wide spectrum (e.g. in relation to its effect on post-tariff discretionary life sentence prisoners, and those detained under some provision of the Mental Health Act 1983), but, as is clear from the authorities those states which disenfranchise following conviction do not all limit the period of disenfranchisement to the period in custody. Parliament in this country could have provided differently in order to meet the objectives which it discerned, and ... I would accept that the tailoring process seldom admits of perfection, so the courts must afford some leeway to the legislator. As Mr Rabinder Singh submits, there is a broad spectrum of approaches among democratic societies, and the United Kingdom falls into the middle of the spectrum.'

5. *Executive action.* No deference principle applies in the assessment of the compatibility of *executive* action with Convention rights: see *R (on the application of Daly) v Secretary of State for the Home Department* and the notes thereto.[15]

R (on the application of Daly) v Secretary of State for the Home Department [2001] UKHL 26, [2001] 2 WLR 1622, House of Lords

Home Office policy on the searching of prisoners' cells in closed prisons was set out in a 1995 Security Manual. This provided that prisoners were not to be present when searches took place. This restriction was justified on the grounds that prison officers might be intimidated by prisoners who were present and that it was necessary to keep searching methods secret. Under the policy, officers could, *inter alia*, examine prisoners' correspondence with their legal advisers to check that it was bona fide legal correspondence and that it did not conceal anything else. However, they could not read it unless there was reasonable cause to suspect that its contents endangered prison security, or the safety of others, or was otherwise of a criminal nature.

In this case, the applicant applied for judicial review of the policy in so far as it concerned legal correspondence that he kept in his cell. The House of Lords upheld

---

15 Immediately below.

his appeal against a Court of Appeal decision dismissing his application for judicial review. It did so on the basis that the policy infringed the common law right of a prisoner to legal professional privilege in his communications with his legal adviser. This was because the possibility that a prison officer might, improperly, read the correspondence would have a chilling effect on freedom of communication. Although the general wording of the Prison Rules might justify some limitation on the common law right to professional legal privilege, they could not justify a policy that extended to all prisoners, whether or not there was reason to believe that they might be abusing their freedom of correspondence.

The House of Lords also held that the executive decision underlying the policy was an interference with a Convention right, viz. the right to respect for correspondence in Art. 8 ECHR. The following extract from Lord Steyn's judgment addresses the ECHR issue only. In particular, it indicates the judicial review criterion to be followed by the courts when considering whether an executive decision complies with the ECHR. The other members of the House of Lords concurred in his judgment on this point. The extracts from Lord Bingham's and Lord Cooke's judgment consider the overlap between the position at common law and under the HRA.

Lord Bingham:
23. I have reached the conclusions so far expressed on an orthodox application of common law principles derived from the authorities and an orthodox domestic approach to judicial review. But the same result is achieved by reliance on the European Convention. Article 8(1) gives Mr Daly a right to respect for his correspondence. While interference with that right by a public authority may be permitted if in accordance with the law and necessary in a democratic society in the interests of national security, public safety, the prevention of disorder or crime or for protection of the rights and freedoms of others, the policy interferes with Mr Daly's exercise of his right under article 8(1) to an extent much greater than necessity requires. In this instance, therefore, the common law and the Convention yield the same result. But this need not always be so. In *Smith and Grady v United Kingdom* (1999) 29 EHRR 493, the European Court held that the orthodox domestic approach of the English courts had not given the applicants an effective remedy for the breach of their rights under article 8 of the Convention because the threshold of review had been set too high. Now, following the incorporation of the Convention by the Human Rights Act 1998 and the bringing of that Act fully into force, domestic courts must themselves form a judgment whether a Convention right has been breached (conducting such inquiry as is necessary to form that judgment) and, so far as permissible under the Act, grant an effective remedy. On this aspect of the case, I agree with and adopt the observations of my noble and learned friend Lord Steyn which I have had the opportunity of reading in draft.

Lord Steyn:
24. My Lords, I am in complete agreement with the reasons given by Lord Bingham of Cornhill in his speech. For the reasons he gives I would also allow the appeal. Except on one narrow but important point I have nothing to add.
25. There was written and oral argument on the question whether certain observations of Lord Phillips of Worth Matravers MR in *R (Mahmood) v Secretary of State for the Home Department* [2001] 1 WLR 840 were correct. The context was an immigration case involving a decision of the Secretary of State made before the Human Rights Act 1998 came into effect. The Master of the Rolls nevertheless approached the case as if the Act had been in force when the Secretary of State reached his decision. He explained the new approach to be adopted. The Master of the Rolls concluded, at p 857, para 40:

'When anxiously scrutinising an executive decision that interferes with human rights, the court will ask the question, applying an objective test, whether the decision-maker could reasonably have concluded that the interference was necessary to achieve one or more of the legitimate aims recognised by the Convention. When considering the test of necessity in the relevant context, the court must take into account the European jurisprudence in accordance with section 2 of the 1998 Act.'

These observations have been followed by the Court of Appeal in *R (Isiko) v Secretary of State for the Home Department* The Times, 20 February 2001; Court of Appeal (Civil Division) Transcript No 2272 of 2000 and by Thomas J in *R (Samaroo) v Secretary of State for the Home Department* (unreported) 20 December 2000.

26. The explanation of the Master of the Rolls in the first sentence of the cited passage requires clarification. It is couched in language reminiscent of the traditional *Wednesbury* ground of review (*Associated Provincial Picture Houses Ltd v Wednesbury Corpn* [1948] 1 KB 223), and in particular the adaptation of that test in terms of heightened scrutiny in cases involving fundamental rights as formulated in *R v Ministry of Defence, Ex p Smith* [1996] QB 517, 554E–G per Sir Thomas Bingham MR. There is a material difference between the *Wednesbury* and *Smith* grounds of review and the approach of proportionality applicable in respect of review where Convention rights are at stake.

27. The contours of the principle of proportionality are familiar. In *de Freitas v Permanent Secretary of Ministry of Agriculture, Fisheries, Lands and Housing* [1999] 1 AC 69 the Privy Council adopted a three-stage test. Lord Clyde observed, at p 80, that in determining whether a limitation (by an act, rule or decision) is arbitrary or excessive the court should ask itself:

> 'whether: (i) the legislative objective is sufficiently important to justify limiting a fundamental right; (ii) the measures designed to meet the legislative objective are rationally connected to it; and (iii) the means used to impair the right or freedom are no more than is necessary to accomplish the objective.'

Clearly, these criteria are more precise and more sophisticated than the traditional grounds of review. What is the difference for the disposal of concrete cases? Academic public lawyers have in remarkably similar terms elucidated the difference between the traditional grounds of review and the proportionality approach: see Professor Jeffrey Jowell QC, 'Beyond the Rule of Law: Towards Constitutional Judicial Review' [2000] PL 671; *Craig, Administrative Law*, 4th ed (1999), pp 561–563; Professor David Feldman, 'Proportionality and the Human Rights Act 1998', essay in *The Principle of Proportionality in the Laws of Europe* edited by Evelyn Ellis (1999), pp 117, 127 et seq. The starting point is that there is an overlap between the traditional grounds of review and the approach of proportionality. Most cases would be decided in the same way whichever approach is adopted. But the intensity of review is somewhat greater under the proportionality approach. Making due allowance for important structural differences between various convention rights, which I do not propose to discuss, a few generalisations are perhaps permissible. I would mention three concrete differences without suggesting that my statement is exhaustive. First, the doctrine of proportionality may require the reviewing court to assess the balance which the decision maker has struck, not merely whether it is within the range of rational or reasonable decisions. Secondly, the proportionality test may go further than the traditional grounds of review inasmuch as it may require attention to be directed to the relative weight accorded to interests and considerations. Thirdly, even the heightened scrutiny test developed in *R v Ministry of Defence, ex p Smith* [1996] QB 517, 554 is not necessarily appropriate to the protection of human rights. It will be recalled that in Smith the Court of Appeal reluctantly felt compelled to reject a limitation on homosexuals in the army. The challenge based on article 8 of the Convention for the Protection of Human Rights and Fundamental Freedoms (the right to respect for private and family life) foundered on the threshold required even by the anxious scrutiny test. The European Court of Human Rights came to the opposite conclusion: *Smith and Grady v United Kingdom* (1999) 29 EHRR 493. The court concluded, at p 543, para 138:

> 'the threshold at which the High Court and the Court of Appeal could find the Ministry of Defence policy irrational was placed so high that it effectively excluded any consideration by the domestic courts of the question of whether the interference with the applicants' rights answered a pressing social need or was proportionate to the national security and public order aims pursued, principles which lie at the heart of the court's analysis of complaints under article 8 of the Convention.'

In other words, the intensity of the review, in similar cases, is guaranteed by the twin requirements that the limitation of the right was necessary in a democratic society, in the sense of meeting a pressing social need, and the question whether the interference was really proportionate to the legitimate aim being pursued.

28. The differences in approach between the traditional grounds of review and the proportionality approach may therefore sometimes yield different results. It is therefore important that cases involving Convention rights must be analysed in the correct way. This does not mean that there has been a shift to merits review. On the contrary, as Professor Jowell [2000] PL 671, 681 has pointed out the respective roles of judges and administrators are fundamentally distinct and will remain so. To this extent the general tenor of the observations in *Mahmood* [2001] 1 WLR 840 are correct. And Laws LJ rightly emphasised in *Mahmood*, at p 847, para 18, 'that the intensity of review in a public law case will depend on the subject matter in hand'. That is so even in cases involving Convention rights. In law context is everything.

Lord Cooke of Thorndon:

29. My Lords, having had the advantage of reading in draft the speeches of my noble and learned friends, Lord Bingham of Cornhill and Lord Steyn, I am in full agreement with them. I add some brief observations on two matters, less to supplement what they have said than to underline its importance.

30. First, while this case has arisen in a jurisdiction where the European Convention for the Protection of Human Rights and Fundamental Freedoms applies, and while the case is one in which the Convention and the common law produce the same result, it is of great importance, in my opinion, that the common law by itself is being recognised as a sufficient source of the fundamental right to confidential communication with a legal adviser for the purpose of obtaining legal advice. Thus the decision may prove to be in point in common law jurisdictions not affected by the Convention. Rights similar to those in the Convention are of course to be found in constitutional documents and other formal affirmations of rights elsewhere. The truth is, I think, that some rights are inherent and fundamental to democratic civilised society. Conventions, constitutions, bills of rights and the like respond by recognising rather than creating them.

31. To essay any list of these fundamental, perhaps ultimately universal, rights is far beyond anything required for the purpose of deciding the present case. It is enough to take the three identified by Lord Bingham: in his words, access to a court; access to legal advice; and the right to communicate confidentially with a legal adviser under the seal of legal professional privilege. As he says authoritatively from the woolsack, such rights may be curtailed only by clear and express words, and then only to the extent reasonably necessary to meet the ends which justify the curtailment. The point that I am emphasising is that the common law goes so deep.

32. The other matter concerns degrees of judicial review. Lord Steyn illuminates the distinctions between 'traditional' (that is to say in terms of English case law, *Wednesbury*) standards of judicial review and higher standards under the European Convention or the common law of human rights. As he indicates, often the results are the same. But the view that the standards are substantially the same appears to have received its quietus in *Smith and Grady v United Kingdom* (1999) 29 EHRR 493 and *Lustig-Prean and Beckett v United Kingdom* (1999) 29 EHRR 548. And I think that the day will come when it will be more widely recognised that *Associated Provincial Picture Houses Ltd v Wednesbury Corpn* [1948] 1 KB 223 was an unfortunately retrogressive decision in English administrative law, in so far as it suggested that there are degrees of unreasonableness and that only a very extreme degree can bring an administrative decision within the legitimate scope of judicial invalidation. The depth of judicial review and the deference due to administrative discretion vary with the subject matter. It may well be, however, that the law can never be satisfied in any administrative field merely by a finding that the decision under review is not capricious or absurd.

33. I, too, would therefore allow the present appeal.

Appeal allowed.

Lord Hutton and **Lord Scott** concurred.

NOTES

1. As Lord Steyn indicates in his judgment in the *Daly* case, in a passage that was accepted by the other four judges, the test to be used when deciding for the purposes of the HRA whether executive decisions are compatible with Convention rights is whether they are a proportionate response to a pressing social need (para 27). This test, which is stricter than the *Smith* test (see next note), is one that has been developed by the European Court of Human Rights when deciding whether a limitation on a Convention right is acceptable under Art 8(2), 9(2) and 10(2) ECHR, and one that it has required national courts to use when deciding whether a limitation on a Convention right is a breach of the ECHR. If they do not, they are not providing an effective remedy for the purposes of Art. 13 ECHR. As Lord Steyn states, the Strasbourg Court has made it clear in a number of British cases that the much more relaxed *Wednesbury* criterion for judicial review (see next note) is not rigorous enough for this purpose. Moreover, the stricter version of it in the *Smith* case was not good enough when that case went to Strasbourg as *Smith and Grady v United Kingdom*.[16] It was in this context that the proportionality test was introduced in the *Daly* case. Note that no 'margin of appreciation' language is used by Lord Steyn, and it is clear that no such margin applies. Nor does any doctrine of parliamentary deference, which obviously applies only to acts by an elected parliament. At the same time, as Lord Steyn indicates, the proportionality test does not mean substituting a judge's decision on the merits for one by a member of the executive. The court's power is still one of review, not of decision, and involves only deciding whether what has been done is one of possibly a number of proportionate responses.

2. The *Wednesbury* test to which Lords Steyn and Cooke refer is one of 'unreasonableness', or, in Lord Diplock's term, 'irrationality'. It was expounded by Lord Diplock in the following classic passage:[17]

'By "irrationality" I mean what can by now be succinctly referred to as "*Wednesbury* unreasonableness" (*Associated Provincial Picture Houses Ltd. v. Wednesbury Corporation* [1948] 1 KB 223). It applies to a decision which is so outrageous in its defiance of logic or of accepted moral standards that no sensible person who had applied his mind to the question to be decided could have arrived at it.'

The 'heightened scrutiny' version of the *Wednesbury* test that was adopted for a human rights case in *R v Ministry of Defence, ex p Smith*[18] was explained by Sir Thomas Bingham MR in that case as follows:

'Mr David Pannick QC (who represented three of the appellants, and whose arguments were adopted by the fourth) submitted that the court should adopt the following approach to the issue of irrationality:

"The court may not interfere with the exercise of an administrative discretion on substantive grounds save where the court is satisfied that the decision is unreasonable in the sense that it is beyond the range of responses open to a reasonable decision-maker. But in judging whether the decision-maker has exceeded this margin of appreciation the human rights context is important. The more substantial the interference with human rights, the more the court will require by way of justification before it is satisfied that the decision is reasonable in the sense outlined above.'

16 (1999) 29 EHRR 493. In *Smith*, the Court of Appeal had reluctantly held that it could not overturn the executive prohibition on homosexuals in the armed forces. At Strasbourg, the Court found a breach of Art. 8 ECHR: on the facts, even allowing for a margin of appreciation, the action, taken against the particular applicants had been disproportionate. Note that the 'heightened scrutiny' test did provide a remedy in *R v Lord Saville of Newdigate, ex p A* [1999] 4 All ER 860, CA (decision of the Bloody Sunday Tribunal of Inquiry not to allow soldiers to give evidence anonymously quashed as unreasonable).
17 *Council of Civil Service Unions v Minister for the Civil Service* [1985] AC 374 at 408, HL.
18 [1996] QB 517 at 554, CA.

This submission is in my judgment an accurate distillation of the principles laid down by the House of Lords in *Bugdaycay v Secretary of State for the Home Dept* [1987] 1 All ER 940, [1987] AC 514 and *Brind v Secretary of State for the Home Dept* [1991] 1 All ER 720, [1991] 1 AC 696. ...

It was argued for the ministry, in reliance on *Nottinghamshire CC v Secretary of State for the Environment* [1986] 1 All ER 199, [1986] AC 240 and *Hammersmith and Fulham London BC v Secretary of State for the Environment* [1990] 3 All ER 589, [1991] 1 AC 521, that a test more exacting than *Wednesbury* was appropriate in this case (see *Associated Provincial Picture Houses Ltd v Wednesbury Corp* [1947] 2 All ER 680, [1948] 1 KB 223). The Divisional Court rejected this argument and so do I. The greater the policy content of a decision, and the more remote the subject matter of a decision from ordinary judicial experience, the more hesitant the court must necessarily be in holding a decision to be irrational. That is good law and, like most good law, common sense. Where decisions of a policy-laden, esoteric or security-based nature are in issue, even greater caution than normal must be shown in applying the test, but the test itself is sufficiently flexible to cover all situations.

The present cases do not affect the lives or liberty of those involved. But they do concern innate qualities of a very personal kind and the decisions of which the appellants complain have had a profound effect on their careers and prospects. The appellants' rights as human beings are very much in issue. It is now accepted that this issue is justiciable. This does not of course mean that the court is thrust into the position of the primary decision-maker. It is not the constitutional role of the court to regulate the conditions of service in the armed forces of the Crown, nor has it the expertise to do so. But it has the constitutional role and duty of ensuring that the rights of citizens are not abused by the unlawful exercise of executive power. While the court must properly defer to the expertise of responsible decision-makers, it must not shrink from its fundamental duty to "do right to all manner of people".'

The 'heightened scrutiny' test in the *Smith* case continues to apply to the review of executive acts bearing upon human rights other than Convention rights. It is to be hoped, however, that the courts will go further and apply the proportionality test in the *Daly* case more generally, to all human rights cases. It is submitted that this should be so for all of the human rights in the Universal Declaration of Human Rights, including economic, social and cultural rights, and whether or not the United Kingdom has a treaty obligation in respect of them.

3. The *Daly* case is an example of the role of the courts in ensuring that acts of the executive are not incompatible with Convention rights. In that case, it would not have been difficult for Home Office policy on cell searching to have conformed with Convention rights within the limits of the enabling primary legislation, i.e. the Prison Act 1952. Generally, it will be very unusual for the powers given to the executive by primary legislation to be so tightly drawn that a Minister or other executive member will have no choice but to act incompatibly with Convention rights, particularly in view of the rule of interpretation in s. 3 HRA.[19] As a result, executive action incompatible with Convention rights will almost always be invalid, rather than lead to a declaration of incompatibility.[20]

Wilson v First County Trust Ltd [2001] EWCA Civ 633, [2001] 3 All ER 229, [2001] 3 WLR 42, Court of Appeal

A credit agreement between the claimant and the defendant pawnbrokers was improperly executed in breach of 1983 regulations made under s. 61 of the Consumer Credit Act 1974 because the amount of credit was incorrectly stated. In 1999 a district judge refused the claimant's application for a declaration that the rate of interest in the agreement was extortionate and that the agreement was unenforceable by court

---

19 Cf. K. Ewing (1999) 62 MLR 79, 87,
20 For this distinction in the HRA, see above, p. 31.

order by virtue of ss. 65(1) and 127(3) of the 1974 Act, which prohibited the making an order to enforce a credit agreement if s. 61 of the 1974 Act was not complied with. On appeal by the claimant, in an interim judgment in November 2000, the Court of Appeal was of the opinion that s. 127(3) might be incompatible with the ECHR and adjourned the appeal so as to allow a later hearing on the question of compatibility and whether it should make a declaration of incompatibility.

Sir Andrew Morritt V-C for the court:

9. We pointed out, in the judgments which we handed down on 23 November 2000, that the effect of sections 65(1) and 127(3) of the 1974 Act—in a case to which the latter section applied—is to deprive the court of any power to enforce a regulated agreement from which a prescribed term has been omitted, notwithstanding that no prejudice has been caused to anyone by that omission. We queried whether that was a proportionate response, having regard to the creditor's Convention rights. ...

10. Section 6(1) of the Human Rights Act 1998 makes it unlawful for a public authority to act in a way which is incompatible with a Convention right. In that context 'public authority' includes a court or tribunal: see section 6(3)(a) of the Act. but section 6(2)(b) excludes the application of section 6(1) where, in the case of one or more provisions of, or made under, primary legislation which cannot be read or given effect in a way which is compatible with the Convention rights, the court is acting so as to give effect to or enforce those provisions. That provision must be read in conjunction with section 3(1) of the Act, which requires that, so far as it is possible to do so, primary legislation must be read and given effect in a way which is compatible with the Convention rights. The position, therefore, is that, where a court is faced with a provision in primary legislation which appears to require it to make an order which would be incompatible with a Convention right, the court must consider whether it is possible to read and give effect to that provision in a way which does not lead to that result. If it is possible to do so, then the court must take that course. The court will make an order which is not incompatible with the Convention right. But if it is not possible to read and give effect to the primary legislation in a way which is compatible with the Convention right, then the court must make the order which the primary legislation requires. It will not, then, be acting unlawfully: see section 6(2)(b) of the 1998 Act.

11. It follows that, in any case where the court makes an order which is incompatible with a Convention right, it must, necessarily, first address the question whether it is required to do so by some provision in primary legislation. If satisfied that it is required to do so— that is to say, if satisfied that (notwithstanding the obligation imposed on the court by section 3(1) of the Act) the provision in primary legislation cannot be read and given effect in a way which is compatible with the Convention right—the court (if a court within section 4(5) of the Act) may make a declaration of that incompatibility: see section 4(2) of the Act. It does so, in part at least, in order to explain why it is not, itself, acting unlawfully: see sections 6(1) and 6(2)(b) of the Act. But, in so doing, it also enables remedial action to be taken by government, under section 10 of the Act. A declaration of incompatibility does not affect the validity, continuing operation or enforcement of the provision in respect of which it is given, nor is it binding on the parties to the proceedings in which it is made: see section 4(6) of the Act.

12. Section 5(1) of the 1998 Act requires that where a court is considering whether to make a declaration of incompatibility, the Crown is entitled to be given notice; and, in such a case, a Minister of the Crown (or a person nominated by him) is entitled to be joined as a party to the proceedings. In the present case, in response to the notice which we directed to be given under section 5 of the Act, the Secretary of State for Trade and Industry has been joined as a party to the appeal. Counsel instructed on his behalf has appeared at the further hearing to resist the making of a declaration of incompatibility. ...

13. The original respondent to the appeal, First County Trust, had not been represented by solicitors or counsel at the earlier hearing of the appeal and (in any event) would seem to have no interest in the question whether or not a declaration of incompatibility should be made. In those circumstances we thought it appropriate to invite the Attorney General to appoint an amicus curiae to assist the court. We have had that assistance, for which we are grateful. We have been assisted, also, by counsel now instructed on behalf of First County Trust and by

counsel who have accepted instructions pro bono publico on behalf of the appellant, Mrs Wilson. ...

23. We turn, therefore, to consider the ... issue ... whether the provisions in section 127(3) of the 1974 Act—read with those in Schedule 6 to the 1983 Regulations—would (but for the application of section 3(1) of the 1998 Act) be incompatible with the rights guaranteed to the pawnbroker by article 6(1) of the Convention and article 1 of the First Protocol [the right to property]. ...

28. It is the restrictions on enforcement which engage article 6(1) of the Convention. The guarantee, in relation to the determination of a party's civil rights, of a fair and public hearing by an independent and impartial tribunal is of no substance if the outcome is determined by a statutory inhibition which not only prevents the court from doing what is just in the circumstances, but does so (a) in the context of a legislative scheme which gives the court a discretion to do what is just in other, very similar, circumstances and (b) for reasons which (if they exist at all) are wholly opaque. If there is some legitimate aim in pursuit of which the guarantee enshrined in article 6(1) needs to be wholly or partially curtailed, then it is necessary to ask whether the statutory inhibition is proportionate to that aim. Is there a proper balance between ends and means? ...

31. The question, therefore, is whether the exclusion of any judicial remedy—indeed, the exclusion of any meaningful consideration by the court of the creditor's rights under the agreement—in a case where the document signed by the debtor does not include all the prescribed terms of the agreement is legitimate, having regard to the fundamental nature of the right guaranteed by article 6(1) of the Convention. The principle was expressed in the majority judgment in the European Court of Human Rights in *Osman v United Kingdom* (1998) 29 EHRR 245, 315, para 147:

> 'However, [the right of access to a court under article 6(1) of the Convention] is not absolute, but may be subject to limitations; these are permitted by implication since the right of access by its very nature calls for regulation by the state. In this respect, the contracting states enjoy a certain margin of appreciation, although the final decision as to the observance of the Convention's requirements rests with the court. It must be satisfied that the limitations applied do not restrict or reduce the access left to the individual in such a way or to such an extent that the very essence of the right is impaired. *Furthermore, a limitation will not be compatible with article 6(1) if it does not pursue a legitimate aim and if there is not a reasonable relationship of proportionality between the means employed and the aim sought to be achieved.*' (Emphasis added.)

As Lord [Hope] pointed out in *R v Director of Public Prosecutions, Ex p Kebilene* [2000] 2 AC 326, 380e–h, the doctrine of 'the margin of appreciation', while a familiar part of the jurisprudence of the Strasbourg Court, has no place, as such, in a consideration by a national court of a Convention issue arising within its own domestic jurisdiction. But he went on to say, at pp 380–381: ...

[This passage from Lord Hope's judgment is quoted above, p. 56]

33. Counsel for the Secretary of State urged, rightly, that the Consumer Credit Act 1974 is concerned with issues of social policy rather than matters of high constitutional importance. The issues fall within an area in which the courts should be ready to defer, on democratic grounds, to 'the considered opinion of the elected body or person'. We recognise the force of those arguments. But, unless deference is to be equated with unquestioning acceptance, the argument that an issue of social policy falls within a discretionary area of judgment which the courts must respect recognises, as it seems to us, the need for the court to identify the particular issue of social policy which the legislature or the executive thought it necessary to address, and the thinking which led to that issue being dealt with in the way that it was. It is one thing to accept the need to defer to an opinion which can be seen to be the product of reasoned consideration based on policy; it is quite another thing to be required to accept, without question, an opinion for which no reason of policy is advanced.

34. It was submitted on behalf of the Secretary of State that an attempt to investigate, through examination of preparatory materials and the content of debates in Parliament, what reason of policy led enacted legislation to take the precise form that it does is, itself, illegitimate. It is enough, he submits, that the legislation has been enacted. Because it has been enacted, it must be taken to represent the considered opinion of the elected body. It is not for the courts to

question the basis upon which that opinion was reached; nor even, it seems, to seek to understand the basis upon which that opinion was reached. For the reasons which we have already expressed, we reject that submission. We note that the European Court of Human Rights has thought it helpful to look at preparatory material in order to identify the policy aims and justification of social legislation: see *James v United Kingdom* 8 EHRR 123, 143, 146, paras 47–48, 52 and *Mellacher v Austria* (1989) 12 EHRR 391, 409, para 47. ...

[Sir Andrew Morritt V-C reviewed the legislative history of the 1974 Act, but found that it was of no assistance. He continued:]

37. In the present case, therefore, we are left without the assistance which examination of reports, preparatory material and debates in Parliament might have been expected to provide on the question: 'why was it thought necessary to deny to the courts the power to do what was just in those cases in which there was no document signed by the debtor which contained terms which would or might, at some future date, be prescribed by the Secretary of State?' Nor has the Secretary of State been able to explain to us, now, why it is thought necessary to deny to the courts the power to do what is just in those cases. We have been shown no material which helps us to understand why the executive thought it necessary to propose, or why Parliament thought it necessary to enact, section 127(3) of the 1974 Act in the form which it takes. Nor is there anything which indicates why the Secretary of State thought it appropriate to prescribe the terms which he did in the 1983 Regulations.

38. In the absence of extraneous assistance as to the policy aims of the legislation, or as to the justification for the exclusion of any judicial remedy in cases where there is no signed document which contains all the prescribed terms, we must decide the issue on the basis of the legislation as enacted. The policy aims for which sections 60, 61 and 65 of the 1974 Act were enacted are clear enough. Regulated agreements ought to be made with an appropriate degree of formality; that requires that the terms of the agreement should be set out in a document which is signed by the debtor; the document should contain information relevant to the transaction; and, where those requirements are not met, the agreement is not to be enforced against the debtor except through the court. It cannot be suggested that those are not legitimate objectives of social policy. Nor can it be suggested that judicial control, under section 127 and the other sections in Part IX of the Act, is not a legitimate means of pursuing those objectives. Indeed, it might be said that judicial control—under which, in the event that the requirements imposed by section 61 are not met, the court has power to do what is just—is an obviously legitimate and sensible way of implementing the policy aims.

39. But section 127(3) of the Act goes beyond that. The policy aim, reflected in that section, is to ensure that particular attention is paid to the inclusion in the document to be signed by the debtor of certain terms which will, or may, be prescribed by the Secretary of State in the future. Again, it cannot be suggested that that is not a legitimate policy objective. But it does not follow that the means by which that policy aim is to be achieved, under the provisions of section 127(3) of the Act are also legitimate. The means will not be legitimate if guaranteed Convention rights are infringed to an extent which is disproportionate to the policy aim. That, in our view, is the effect of the inflexible prohibition—imposed by the section 127(3) of the Act—against the making of an enforcement order in a case where the document signed by the debtor does not include the prescribed terms. There is no reason that we can identify—and, as we have said, no reason has been advanced—why an inflexible prohibition is necessary in order to achieve the legitimate policy aim. There is no reason why that aim should not be achieved through judicial control; by empowering the court to do what is just in the circumstances of the particular case.

40. For those reasons we are satisfied that (subject to the application of section 3(1) of the 1998 Act) the provisions in section 127(3) of the 1974 Act are incompatible with the rights guaranteed by article 6(1) of the Convention and article 1 of the First Protocol. ...

41. We can deal with [the section 3] issue shortly. Section 3(1) of the 1998 Act requires that, 'So far as it is possible to do so', primary legislation and subordinate legislation must be read and given effect in a way which is compatible with Convention rights. It follows, as we understand that requirement, that, where the court finds that what we may describe as a 'non-Convention' interpretation of the words used in legislation would lead to the conclusion that the legislative provision was incompatible with a Convention right, it must consider whether there is some other legitimate interpretation of those words which avoids

that conclusion. If there is, then the interpretation which avoids that conclusion must be adopted.

42. In that context, by 'some other legitimate interpretation' we mean some interpretation of the words used which is legally possible. The court is required to go as far as, but not beyond, what is legally possible. The court is not required, or entitled, to give to words a meaning which they cannot bear; although it is required to give to words a meaning which they can bear, if that will avoid incompatibility, notwithstanding that that is not the meaning which they would be given in a 'non-Convention' interpretation.

43. Section 127(3) of the 1074 Act falls into three parts: (i) 'The court shall not make an enforcement order under section 65(1)'; (ii) 'if section 61(1)(a) (signing of agreements) was not complied with'; (iii) 'unless a document ... itself containing all the prescribed terms of the agreement was signed by the debtor ...'. Section 61(1)(a) requires 'a document in the prescribed form itself containing all the prescribed terms and conforming to regulations under section 60(1) ... signed in the prescribed manner both by the debtor ... and by or on behalf of the creditor ...'. It is clear that, notwithstanding what we have identified as the second part of section 127(3), the prohibition in the first part of the section does not prevent the making of an enforcement order in all cases where section 61(1)(a) has not been complied with. But the irreducible minimum requirement is that spelt out in the third part of the section. No enforcement order can be made unless there is a document signed by the debtor which contains all the prescribed terms of the agreement. We can see no way in which it is possible to read and give effect to section 127(3) of the 1974 Act which avoids that irreducible minimum requirement; and none has been suggested to us in argument. Nor can we see any way in which it is possible to read and give effect to the 1983 Regulations which avoids the conclusion that the terms set out in Schedule 6 to those Regulations are 'prescribed terms' for the purposes of sections 61(1)(a) and 127(3) of the Act. ...

45. We conclude that it is not possible to read and give effect to the relevant provisions of the 1974 Act in a way which is compatible with the pawnbroker's Convention rights.

46. The court has power, if satisfied that a provision of primary legislation is incompatible with a Convention right, to make a declaration of that incompatibility: see section 4(2) of the 1998 Act. In the case of subordinate legislation—of which the 1983 Regulations are an example—the power is circumscribed. The court should not make a declaration of incompatibility in respect of a provision of subordinate legislation unless satisfied both that the provision is incompatible with a Convention right and that (disregarding any possibility of revocation) the primary legislation under which the subordinate legislation has been made prevents the removal of the incompatibility: see section 4(4) of the 1998 Act. In the present case, the incompatibility lies in the primary legislation. It is not the fact that there are prescribed terms which infringes Convention rights. Nor is it the content of the prescribed terms which leads to infringement. Rather, it is the fact that, where terms have been prescribed for the purposes of section 127(3) of the 1974 Act, the provisions of section 127(3) of that Act have the effect of excluding the creditor from any judicial remedy in aid of his rights.

47. The question, therefore, is whether, as a matter of discretion, a declaration of incompatibility should be made in the present case. In our view it is right to do so for three reasons. First, the point has been identified and fully argued at a further hearing appointed for that purpose. Second, in the circumstances that we have held that the order which a non-Convention interpretation of section 127(3) of the 1974 Act requires the court to make on this appeal would be incompatible with Convention rights, we could not lawfully make that order unless satisfied that the section cannot be read or given effect in a way which is compatible with Convention rights; and it is appropriate that that should be formally recorded by a declaration which gives legitimacy to the order. Third, a declaration serves a legislative purpose under the 1998 Act; in that it provides a basis, under section 10(1)(a) of that Act, for a Minister of the Crown to consider whether there are compelling reasons to make amendments to the legislation by remedial order (under Schedule 2 to the Act) for the purpose of removing the incompatibility which the court has identified. ...

50. We invite further submissions from the Secretary of State on the form of the declaration of incompatibility to be made. It may be of assistance, however, if we indicate our present view. We think that it would be appropriate to declare that, having regard to the terms prescribed by regulation 6(1) of the Schedule 6 to the 1983 Regulations, the provisions of section 127(3) of the 1974 Act, in so far as they prevent the court from making an enforcement order under section 65(1) of that Act unless a document containing all the prescribed terms of the agreement

has been signed by the debtor or hirer, are incompatible with the rights guaranteed to the creditor or hirer by article 6(1) of the Convention and article 1 of the First Protocol.

51. We allow the appeal against the order made on 24 September 1999 for the reasons given in our interim judgments [2001] QB 407 of 23 November 2000.

The other members of the court were **Chadwick** and **Rix LJJ**.

NOTES

1. The *Wilson* case was the second English case in which a declaration of incompatibility was made under the HRA. Earlier, in *R (on the application of Alconbury Developments Ltd) v Secretary of State for the Environment, Transport and the Regions*[1] the Divisional Court made a declaration to the effect that a statutory planning law procedure contravened the right to a fair trial in Art. 6 ECHR. However, the House of Lords reversed the Divisional Court ruling on the basis that the procedure complied with Art. 6.

2. The decision to make a declaration of incompatibility under s. 4(1) is discretionary ('may'), in line with the power of the courts to grant a declaration in other contexts.[2] The judgment in the *Wilson* case gives the reasons why the court exercised its discretion to make one.

3. A declaration of incompatibility may be only be made at the level of court indicated in s. 4(5), viz. in England and Wales, the High Court and above. A magistrates' court, Crown Court, county court or tribunal may not make such a declaration; instead, the point must be taken on appeal. In the *Wilson* case, the district judge could not have made one. As in that case, if the Crown is not a party, a court must give the Crown notice that it is considering making a declaration of incompatibility, and the Crown is entitled to be joined.[3]

4. As a declaration of incompatibility, like the initial judicial determination of incompatibility, does not affect the legal validity, operation or enforcement of the legislative provision concerned,[4] the curious result is that a litigant who successfully raises an issue of incompatibility may well not benefit.[5] For example, a person who successfully claimed that he was detained under legislation that was incompatible with the Convention right to freedom of the person in Art. 5 ECHR would none the less have no right to release; an order for his detention could be renewed under the incompatible law despite a declaration of incompatibility concerning it.[6] In such a case, it is much better for an alleged victim of a violation of a Convention right if the court, applying s. 3 HRA, manages to stretch the meaning of a statute in the victim's favour, rather than find an incompatibility. However, there is an important exception to the rule that a finding of incompatibility cannot work to the advantage of the

1   [2001] 2 WLR 1389, HL.
2   In Parliament, Lord Irvine LC stated: 'I certainly would expect courts generally to make declarations of incompatibility', but accepted that they should retain 'a discretion not to do so because of the particular circumstances of any case' (583 HL Deb, 18 Nov 1997, col 546). These circumstances might include cases where there was 'an alternative statutory appeal route which the court might think it preferable to follow, or there might be any other [sic] procedure which the court in its discretion thought the applicant should exhaust before seeking a declaration which would then put Parliament under pressure to follow a remedial route': ibid.
3   s. 5 HRA.
4   s. 4(6) HRA.
5   Damages or other relief would not be available under s. 3 because the act of the public authority would, if a case where a declaration of incompatibility is available, not be unlawful for the purposes of s. 6(1): s. 6(2) HRA.
6   Per Dame Elizabeth Butler-Sloss in *Re K (a child)* [2001] 2 WLR 1141 at 1148, CA (legislation authorising the detention of children in secure units; in fact held not contrary to Art. 5 ECHR). Moreover, the detainee would not have the Art. 5(5) ECHR right to compensation: ibid.

individual victim in the instant case. This concerns criminal convictions where the defendant has been denied a fair trial contrary to the Convention right in Art. 6 ECHR. In such cases, the conviction would be almost certainly be set aside as 'unsafe', as provided in s. 2 of the Criminal Appeal Act 1968.[7] In other, non-criminal cases, the only possibility is that any remedial action taken by the government following the declaration of incompatibility is given retroactive application, which the HRA allows.[8] Otherwise, in non-criminal cases the remedy for the litigant, as it was before the HRA was enacted, will be to take the case on the long road to Strasbourg, armed with a declaration of incompatibility, which will be a powerful weapon before the European Court. Although these considerations suggest that in some cases there may be insufficient incentive under the HRA for an individual[9] to raise a question of incompatibility, note that a 'compatibility' argument may be added to other arguments in criminal, civil or judicial review proceedings brought on some other legal basis without much trouble. A litigant who presents such an argument may be rewarded with a s. 3 reading of a statute that makes it compatible with Convention rights from which he or she can profit in the instant case.[10]

The device of the 'declaration of incompatibility' is ingenious and not found in any other legal system. It was prompted by a wish to respect the principle of parliamentary sovereignty.[11] As noted by Lord Steyn in *R v DPP, ex p Kebilene*:[12]

'It is crystal clear that the carefully and subtly drafted Human Rights Act 1998 preserves the principle of Parliamentary Sovereignty. In a case of incompatibility, which cannot be avoided by interpretation under section 3(1), the courts may not disapply the legislation. The court may merely issue a declaration of incompatibility which then gives rise a power to take remedial action: see section 10.'

Similarly, Lord Irvine LC stated in Parliament:[13]

---

7 *R v Togher* [2001] 3 All ER 463, CA. For example, in *R v A*, above, p. 40, had s. 41 been declared incompatible with Art. 6 ECHR and the trial of the defendant had still occurred on the basis of it, the conviction could have been set aside as 'unsafe'. What if the breach of Art. 6 (e.g. no trial within a reasonable time) does not in fact affect the safety of the conviction? Should the conviction be set aside as 'unsafe'? For differing views, see *Darmalinghum v The State* [2000] 1 WLR 2303, PC (conviction quashed seemingly automatically, applying a 'reasonable time' guarantee in Mauritian constitution) and *Flowers v R* [2000] 1 WLR 2396, PC (conviction not quashed in a case where the evidence was strong and the offence serious, applying a 'reasonable time' guarantee in the Jamaican constitution). Where a breach of Art. 6 would result from the application of a common law rule, rather than a statute, the rule (e.g. of evidence) should be reshaped to comply with the Convention right in the instant case by the trial or the appellate court; no question of a declaration of incompatibility arises.
8 See s. 10 and Sch. 2, para. 1(1)(b) HRA. The remedial order may also make 'different provision for different cases': para 1(1)(d). On the face of it, the wording of para. 1 would seem to allow (not require) the change in the incompatible law legislation to be applied to the case in which the question was raised where the circumstances make this appropriate. But see the statement by Lord Irvine in Parliament, below, p. 70.
9 A court, which must apply Convention rights, may raise a compatibility issue on its own initiative, as happened in the *Wilson* case. Note that at the outset the parties to that case did not appear greatly interested in being represented when the Court of Appeal was considering whether to make a declaration of incompatibility.
10 See *R v A*, above, p. 40, where evidence that might contribute to an acquittal was admissible.
11 Whether the motivation for doing so was a genuine respect for that principle or the need to ease the passage of the HRA through a Parliament that might not be sympathetic to a surrender of its powers, or a mixture of the two, is not clear. On parliamentary sovereignty and the HRA, see N. Bamforth, [1998] PL 572; M. Elliott, (1999) 115 LQR 119; K. Ewing, (1999) 62 MLR 79 at 91; S. Freeman, (1998) 114 LQR 538.
12 [2000] 2 AC 326 at 367, HL.
13 582 HL Debs, 3 November 1997, cols. 1228–1229.

'The design of the Bill is to give the courts as much space as possible to protect human rights, short of a power to set aside or ignore Acts of Parliament. In the very rare cases where the higher courts will find it impossible to read and give effect to any statute in a way which is compatible with convention rights, they will be able to make a declaration of incompatibility. Then it is for Parliament to decide whether there should be remedial legislation. Parliament may, not must, and generally will, legislate. If a Minister's prior assessment of compatibility (under Clause 19) is subsequently found by declaration of incompatibility by the courts to have been mistaken, it is hard to see how a Minister could withhold remedial action. There is a fast-track route for Ministers to take remedial action by order. But the remedial action will not retrospectively make unlawful an act which was a lawful act—lawful since sanctioned by statute. This is the logic of the design of the Bill. It maximises the protection of human rights without trespassing on parliamentary sovereignty.'

It is thus clear that the power given to the United Kingdom courts by ss. 3 and 4 HRA falls far short of the power of judicial review of legislation of certain other national courts such as the United States Supreme Court.[14] For example, in the famous case of *Roe v Wade*,[15] state criminal abortion statutes that interfered with a woman's constitutional right to privacy were struck down by the US Supreme Court, so that they did not apply to the petitioners' cases and had no further legal effect. Does the absence of such a power on the part of United Kingdom courts mean that the HRA is not a 'bill of rights'?[16]

Nonetheless, although the courts are not be empowered to strike down primary legislation, might not the combined effect of ss. 3, 4 and 10 HRA result over time in a considerable erosion in practice of the sovereignty of Parliament and an important constitutional shift in the balance of power between Parliament and the courts?[17]

R (on the application of H) v North and East Region Mental Health Review Tribunal [2001] EWCA Civ 415, [2001] 3 WLR 512, Court of Appeal

The appellant, H, was convicted of manslaughter in 1988 and ordered to be detained as a restricted patient in Broadmoor Hospital. In 2000, his application under s. 73 of the Mental Health Act 1983 to be discharged was rejected by the Mental Health Review Tribunal. His application for judicial review of the Tribunal decision was dismissed by Crane J, who also refused to grant declaratory relief as to the compatibility of s. 73 of the Mental Health Act with Art. 5(1) and (4) ECHR. H obtained permission to appeal to the Court of Appeal from Laws LJ, who stated that 'the appellant should be allowed to argue his Human Rights Act 1998 points'. Before the Court of Appeal, the only issue that was raised was whether s. 73 could be given an interpretation that was compatible with Convention rights. Having been given the required s. 5 notice, the Secretary of State participated in the hearing, through his counsel, Mr Rabinder Singh. The facts of the case are indicated in Lord Phillips' judgment.

Lord Phillips for the court:
2. There were reports from two psychiatrists before the tribunal. Dr Basson was H's responsible medical officer ('RMO'). In his report dated 25 January 2000, Dr Basson referred to the diagnosis of schizophrenia, and said that since the commencement of antipschycotic medication in 1990, there had been an improvement in his mental state, and a marked decrease

14 Remarkably, the Supreme Court's power is an implied one, read into the US constitution by the Supreme Court itself: *Marbury v Madison* 5 US 1 (1 Cranch) 137 (1803).
15 410 US 113 (1973).
16 On the definition of a bill of rights, see above, p. 3.
17 Cf. the consequences of the European Communities Act 1972, which also, technically, can be explained consistently with classical parliamentary sovereignty.

in the negative symptoms of his illness. He said that since the appellant was moved to the Windsor Ward, Broadmoor Hospital, in December 1996, there had been no positive symptoms of mental illness. He did, however, continue to show 'negative' symptoms of illness, and he still found it difficult to be motivated in relation to the future move to a regional secure unit. The negative symptoms were his lack of insight into (a) his illness, (b) his need for treatment and (c) the nature of his index offence. He concluded:

'Given [H's] recent improvement I think he may be able to be managed in a specialised hostel or hostel ward. I do not see him as being a danger to the general public. Those living in close proximity, if we take the index offence, are at risk if the living circumstances are inappropriate and/or the medication is inadequate.'

3. In an addendum dated 29 February 2000, Dr Basson reported that his earlier report had been seen by staff from the North London Forensic Service who unanimously recommended long term medium security. He said that this was also the option favoured by the majority of the clinical team on Windsor Ward. In the addendum report, Dr Basson expressed his conclusion as follows:

'Given the above, the North London Forensic Service and Rehabilitation team at Broadmoor, advise that hostel accommodation providing the care this patient needs on initially leaving Broadmoor is not a realistic option and we should pursue the line of long term medium security. We have contacted the local authority to confirm the above view and they will do the appropriate assessment.'

4. The second psychiatrist was Dr Somekh. In his report of 3 March 2000, he said that he was satisfied that H continued to suffer from a chronic paranoid schizophrenia which was currently well stabilised by his medication. It was noted that H was 'compliant with his medication even though he himself expresses doubts as to his need for it'. Dr Somekh raised the issue as to whether he needed continuing treatment in the hospital. He believed that the forensic psychiatry team were taking an unreasonably cautious approach in proposing a placement in long term medium security.

5. Both doctors gave evidence at the tribunal hearing. Both of them said that in their opinion H did not satisfy the conditions necessary for detention under the Act. Dr Basson said that he thought that if H went to a suitable hostel and continued to take his medication he would remain as well as he was at the present time.

6. Despite this evidence the tribunal concluded that H should not be discharged from hospital. In their written reasons the tribunal explained:

'The tribunal is of the opinion that this patient is (a) still exhibiting symptoms of his illness, namely the hearing of voices, (b) would not continue to take his medication ... The tribunal are clear that this patient needs to be detained in hospital for treatment for his own health and safety.'

7. The tribunal completed the standard Decision Form S73 by giving a negative answer to each of the following questions:

'A. Is the Tribunal satisfied that the patient is not now suffering from mental illness, psychopathic disorder, severe mental impairment, or mental impairment or from any of those forms of disorder of a nature or degree which makes it appropriate for the patient to be liable to be detained in a hospital for medical treatment?

B   Is the Tribunal satisfied that it is not necessary for the health or safety of the patient or for the protection of other persons that the patient should receive such treatment.'

8. Those questions reflect the provisions of section 73 of the Act. Before Crane J., junior counsel Mr Bowen, on behalf of H, argued that the jurisprudence of the Strasbourg Court demonstrated that those questions were not appropriate and that section 73 was not compatible with the Convention. Before us Mr Gordon, Q.C., who did not appear below, suggested that it might be possible to interpret section 73 in a way that was compatible with the Convention and that was satisfactory to his client, but that should we not feel able to achieve this, we should make a declaration of incompatibility. ...

11. H was admitted to hospital as a restricted patient pursuant to the provisions of sections 37 and 41 of the Act. For present purposes, however, it suffices to set out the following very

similar provisions of the Act dealing with compulsory admission of an unrestricted patient for treatment in hospital under section 3(2). Section 3(2) reads:

'An application for admission for treatment may be made in respect of a patient on the grounds that—

(a) he is suffering from mental illness, severe mental impairment, psychopathic disorder or mental impairment, and his mental disorder is of a nature or degree which makes it appropriate for him to receive medical treatment in a hospital; and

(b) in the case of psychopathic disorder or mental impairment, such treatment is likely to alleviate or prevent a deterioration of his condition; and

(c) it is necessary for the health or safety of the patient or for the protection of other persons that he should receive such treatment and it cannot be provided unless he is detained under this section.'

12. The relevant provisions for discharge of an unrestricted patient are set out in section 72(1)(b):

'The tribunal shall direct the discharge of a patient liable to be detained otherwise than under section 2 above if they are satisfied—

(i) that he is not then suffering from mental illness, psychopathic disorder, severe mental impairment or mental impairment or from any of those forms of disorder of a nature or degree which makes it appropriate for him to be liable to be detained in a hospital for medical treatment; or

(ii) that it is not necessary for the health or safety of the patient or for the protection of other persons that he should receive such treatment. …'

13. These apply to a restricted patient by virtue of section 73(1), which provides:

'Where an application to a Mental Health Review Tribunal is made by a restricted patient who is subject to a restriction order, or where the case of such a patient is referred to such a tribunal, the tribunal should direct the absolute discharge of the patient if satisfied—

(a) as to the matters mentioned in paragraph (b)(i) or (ii) of section 72(1) above; and

(b) that it is not appropriate for the patient to remain liable to be recalled to hospital for further treatment. …'

15. Mr Gordon's submission on behalf of H can be summarised as follows:

i)   The function of a Mental Health Review Tribunal in a case such as the present is to enable a patient who has been compulsorily admitted to a hospital to challenge the legality of his detention.

ii) In performing that function, the tribunal acts as 'a court' in enabling the patient to exercise the right conferred on him by Article 5(4) of the Convention.

iii) The criteria that the tribunal has to consider on an application under section 73 are the same criteria that have to be satisfied before a patient can be admitted under section 3.

iv) On a natural reading of section 73 a tribunal is not required to discharge a patient unless *satisfied* that at least one of these criteria *does not* exist. This has the effect of placing the burden of proof on the patient. The patient has to prove that the criteria for admission are not satisfied, whereas he should be entitled to be discharged if it cannot be demonstrated that the criteria are satisfied.

v)   This reversal of the burden of proof is incompatible with his rights under Article 5(1) and (4).

16. The position of the Secretary of State, as set out in the skeleton arguments submitted by Mr Singh, can be summarised as follows:

i)   To place the burden on a patient of proving that the conditions for detention are no longer met would be incompatible with Article 5(1) of the Convention, but

ii) It is possible to read the words of section 72 of the Act in such a way that it does not impose the burden of proof on the patient, albeit that to do so involves straining the natural meaning of the section.

17. It was this submission that led Mr Gordon to suggest that it might be possible to interpret section 73, which incorporates section 72, in a manner compatible with the Convention. He confessed in argument, however, that he was not able to see how this could be done. …

19. Under the Mental Health Act 1959 a patient under a restriction order had no right to apply to a tribunal for his discharge. He could require that his case be referred to a tribunal in order that it should *advise* the Secretary of State whether he should be discharged, but the Secretary of State was not required to follow the advice of the tribunal. In *X v United Kingdom* (1981) 4 EHRR the European Court of Human Rights held that this was not in conformity with Article 5(4) of the Convention. Article 5(4) required the court reviewing the lawfulness of the detention of a patient to have the power to order the discharge of the patient where that detention was unlawful. Sections 72 and 73 of the 1983 Act were enacted in response to the decision in *X*. Thus the first two heads of Mr Gordon's argument are made out ...

20. The third head of Mr Gordon's argument was founded on the decision of the House of Lords in *Reid v Secretary of State for Scotland* [1999] 2 AC 513. That case concerned provisions of the Mental Health (Scotland) Act 1984 which mirror those of sections 3 and 73 of the 1983 Act. Under the Scottish Act the application for discharge is made to the sheriff. The House of Lords held that, when considering whether a patient was entitled to discharge, the sheriff had to consider all three of the criteria which had to be established on an application for admission under the section equivalent to section 3. If the sheriff found that any one of those criteria was not satisfied, the patient was entitled to be discharged. It follows that the third head of Mr Gordon's argument is made out. ...

21. In *Reid* Lord Clyde observed at p. 533:

'... the decision is not one which is left to the discretion of the sheriff once he is satisfied on the particular criteria. If he is satisfied, he is obliged to grant a discharge. Secondly, the burden of establishing the particular propositions to the satisfaction of the sheriff will lie on the patient, although in practice it may well be that questions of the burden of proof will not often arise.'

22. In *Perkins v Bath District Health Authority* [1989] 4 BMLR 145 Counsel for the Tribunal conceded that they had wrongly ordered the discharge of a patient on the ground that they were not satisfied that the patient was suffering from a mental disorder which warranted his detention. In approving that concession, Lord Donaldson MR said:

'If a tribunal is to make an order under s72(1)(a)(i), clearly they have to be satisfied, and should state that they are satisfied, that he is not then suffering from mental disorder. That is not the same thing as saying the tribunal is not satisfied that he is so suffering.'

23. Reference to the 'reversed burden of proof' has been made in other cases, including a recent decision of Latham J. in a case that raised very similar issues to the present one: *R v London and South Western Mental Health Review Tribunal ex p M* [2000] Lloyd's LR Med 143 at p. 150.

24. In the course of argument it was suggested that, in the context of review of a patient's detention, the phrase 'burden of proof' was not appropriate. The phrase suggests an adversarial process, whereas proceedings of a Mental Health Review Tribunal are inquisitorial in nature. Furthermore, a reference under section 71 may not be made by the patient. There is some force in this. The essential question is the nature of the test to be applied when determining the entitlement of a patient to release. Does the tribunal have to order discharge of the patient if it is not satisfied that each of the criteria is made out, or is a patient only entitled to release if the tribunal is satisfied that at least one of the criteria is not made out. If the latter is the position, however, it is not inappropriate, where a patient makes an application under section 73, to say that the burden of proof is on the patient. To speak of reversing the burden of proof is a useful shorthand to describe the effect of the section.

25. Mr Gordon submitted that, having regard to the authorities to which we have referred, and to the natural meaning of the language, it was hard to accord to section 72 a meaning which did other than require the tribunal to be satisfied that one of the criteria was not made out before a patient was entitled to release—in other words the section placed the burden of proof on the patient.

26. The submission of the Secretary of State appears in the following passage of Mr Singh's skeleton argument:

'In the Secretary of State's submission, were it necessary to do so in order to secure compatibility with Convention rights, it would be possible to read and give effect to section 72 of the MHA as imposing the burden of proof on the hospital authorities and not on the patient. This is for the following reasons:

(1) The section does not in terms address the question of the burden of proof. It is silent on the point. It certainly does not in terms impose the burden of proof on the patient.
(2) The negative formulation used in section 72(1)(b) ("not then suffering ...") can be read as simply reflecting the fact that the criteria for admission (in section 3 of the MHA) are no longer present. The negative formulation does not compel the conclusion that the burden of proof lies on the patient.'

27. We are not persuaded by this submission. It is of course the duty of the court to strive to interpret statutes in a manner compatible with the convention and we are aware of instances where this has involved straining the meaning of statutory language. We do not consider however that such an approach enables us to interpret a requirement that a tribunal must act if satisfied that a state of affairs does not exist as meaning that it must act if not satisfied that a state of affairs does exist. The two are patently not the same. If the requirements of the Convention can only be satisfied if the tribunal is required to order the discharge of a patient unless satisfied that the three criteria justifying admission are made out, sections 72 and 73 are incompatible with the Convention. ...

28. The written submission of the Secretary of State on this issue was as follows:

'Although the point about the burden of proof has not been directly decided by the European Court of Human Rights the Secretary of State accepts that to place the burden on a patient to prove that the conditions for detention are no longer met would be incompatible with Article 5(1) of the Convention. This is ultimately a matter for the Court but it appears to follow from cases such as *Winterwerp v The Netherlands* [1979] 2 EHRR 387, para. 39–40, and *Johnson v United Kingdom* (1999) 27 EHRR 296, para. 60. In those cases the European Court has held that both the initial deprivation of a mental patient's liberty and the continued detention of a patient can only be lawful under Article 5(1)(e) of the Convention if it can "reliably be shown" that he or she suffers from a mental disorder sufficiently serious to warrant detention.'

29. In oral argument Mr Singh suggested that this concession went no further than accepting that it was inappropriate to speak of the plaintiff having to discharge a 'burden of proof'. As indicated above, we do not find it possible to divorce the concept of 'burden of proof' from the question of the test that the tribunal has to apply when considering whether a patient is entitled to be discharged. We understand the Secretary of State to concede that the same approach has to be applied when considering whether to admit a patient as that which has to be applied when considering whether the continued detention of the patient is lawful. In either case the test is whether it can be 'reliably shown' that the patient suffers from a mental disorder sufficiently serious to warrant detention.

30. Mr Gordon's submission mirrored the written submission of the Secretary of State. He submitted that the continued detention of a patient who had been compulsorily admitted was not lawful under Article 5(1) unless it could reliably be shown that the mental condition of the patient was such as to warrant detention. A test which allowed the continued detention of a patient simply because it could not be shown that his mental condition did not warrant detention violated Article 5(1). Mr Gordon also submitted that such a test violated Article 5(4), but invited us simply to record that he had taken this point rather than decide it.

31. We do not think it sensible to address the issue of compatibility without considering both the relevant paragraphs of Article 5. So far as 5(4) is concerned, it seems to us axiomatic that if the function of the tribunal is to consider whether the detention of the patient is lawful, it must apply the same test that the law required to be applied as a precondition to admission, unless it be the case that a patient once admitted can be lawfully detained provided that some other test is satisfied. We endorse the common submission of Mr Singh and Mr Gordon that it is contrary to the Convention compulsorily to detain a patient unless it can be shown that the patient is suffering from a mental disorder that warrants detention. Inasmuch as Sections 72 and 73 do not require the tribunal to discharge a patient if this cannot be shown we have concluded that they are incompatible with both Article 5(1) and Article 5(4). We think that this follows from the following statement of principle in the seminal case of *Winterwerp v Netherlands* [1979] 2 EHRR 387 at paragraph 39:

'In the Court's opinion, except in emergency cases, the individual concerned should not be deprived of his liberty unless he has been reliably shown to be of 'unsound mind'. The very nature of what has to be established before the competent national authority – that is, a true mental disorder – calls for objective medical expertise. Further, the mental disorder must be of a kind or degree warranting compulsory confinement. What is more, the validity of continued confinement depends upon the persistence of such a disorder. ...'

32. There are some further observations that we wish to make although we should record that they relate to matters to which Counsel for the Appellant did not address detailed argument. It does not follow from our conclusion that Article 5 requires that a patient be discharged whenever any one of the three criteria in section 3 cannot be demonstrated on balance of probability. Detention cannot be justified under Article 5(1)(e) unless the patient is 'of unsound mind', but once that is established we do not consider that the Convention restricts the right to detain a patient in hospital, as does section 3, to circumstances where medical treatment is likely to alleviate or prevent a deterioration of the condition. Nor is it necessary under the Convention to demonstrate that such treatment cannot be provided unless the patient is detained in hospital (see section 3(2)(c)).

33. The circumstances of the present case, which are similar to those considered by Latham J. in *M*, are not uncommon. A patient is detained who is unquestionably suffering from schizophrenia. While in the controlled environment of the hospital he is taking medication, and as a result of the medication is in remission. So long as he continues to take the medication he will pose no danger to himself or to others. The nature of the illness is such, however, that if he ceases to take the medication he will relapse and pose a danger to himself or to others. The professionals may be uncertain whether, if he is discharged into the community, he will continue to take the medication. We do not believe that Article 5 requires that the patient must always be discharged in such circumstances. The appropriate response should depend upon the result of weighing the interests of the patient against those of the public having regard to the particular facts. Continued detention can be justified if, but only if, it is a proportionate response having regard to the risks that would be involved in discharge.

34. Having regard to these considerations, we believe that it is only rarely that the provisions of sections 72 and 73 constrain a Mental Health Review Tribunal to refuse an order of discharge where the continued detention of the patient infringes Article 5. Indeed, in our experience where a tribunal refuses an application for a discharge it usually gives reasons for doing so that involve a positive finding that the patient is suffering from a mental disorder that warrants his or her continued detention. These may well be matters that the Secretary of State will wish to bear in mind when considering whether to take remedial action under section 10 of the Human Rights Act 1998. We have in mind the White Paper recently published on reforming the Mental Health Act and note that it does not appear to be proposed that the new Mental Health Tribunal will, when reviewing detention of a patient, apply a reversed burden of proof (see Part 1, 3.42).

35. For the reasons that we have given we consider that H has made out his case for a declaration of incompatibility. We shall hear Counsel on the precise form of the declaration.

NOTE

The above judgment was given in March 2001. Following a hearing the next month, the Court of Appeal made a declaration of incompatibility as follows:

'A declaration under section 4 of the Human Rights Act 1998 that sections 72(1) and 73(1) of the Mental Health Act 1983 are incompatible with Articles 5(1) and 5(4) of the European Convention of Human Rights in that, for the Mental Health Review Tribunal to be obliged to order a patient's discharge, the burden is placed upon the patient to prove that the criteria justifying his detention in hospital for treatment no longer exist; and that Articles 5(1) and 5(4) require the Tribunal to be positively satisfied that all the criteria justifying the patient's detention in hospital for treatment continue to exist before refusing a patient's discharge.'

Following the declaration of incompatibility, acting under s. 10 HRA, the Secretary of State for Health made a remedial order amending s. 73 of the Mental Health Act 1983. This was the first remedial order under the HRA.

Poplar Housing and Regeneration Community Association Ltd v Donoghue [2001] EWCA Civ 595, [2001] 4 All ER 604, Court of Appeal

The plaintiff housing association brought a claim before a district judge for possession of the dwelling house of which the defendant was the tenant. The weekly tenancy had been granted to the defendant by Tower Hamlets London Borough Council as the housing authority. The house was later transferred to the plaintiff association, which had been created by Tower Hamlets London Borough Council with a view to transferring to it most of the council's housing stock. The plaintiff's claim was brought under s. 21(4) of the Housing Act 1988 which provided that, on its termination or expiry, a 'court shall make an order for possession of a dwelling house let on an assured shorthold tenancy which is a periodic tenancy (as in this case)'. As stated by Lord Woolf CJ, under s. 21(4), 'the court's discretion not to make an order for possession is strictly limited'. The defendant, who was expecting her fourth child at the time of the claim for possession, applied for a declaration that s. 21(4) was incompatible with Art. 6 and 8 ECHR. The application was rejected by the district judge, who made an order for possession.

The defendant appealed to the Court of Appeal on the HRA point. As well as claiming that s. 21(4) was incompatible with Arts. 6 and 8 ECHR, she presented argument on the question whether the claim for possession was the act of a 'public authority' for the purposes of s. 6 HRA. The Court of Appeal held that s. 21(4) was not incompatible with the ECHR. The following extracts concern the court's consideration of (i) the question whether the plaintiff was a public authority and (ii) other aspects of the courts' role under the HRA.

Lord Woolf CJ:

32. In order to determine the remaining issues, it is critical to have in mind the manner in which the legislative framework, which sets out the duties which are owed to tenants in the position of the defendant, and under which a registered social landlord ('RSL') such as Poplar operates, has evolved. ...

49. ... Housing associations were very much 'the legal embodiment of the voluntary housing movement' as Mr Brockway, another witness on behalf of the Department, stated. Originally, many were small local charities, though others were large entities endowed by wealthy employers or philanthropists. The legal definition of a housing association is contained in section 1(1) of the Housing Association Act 1985. This section makes it clear that a housing association may be a charity, an industrial and provident society, or a company which does not trade for profit and which has among its objects the provision of housing accommodation. Some are fully mutual co-operative organisations. Throughout the 20th century many housing associations were funded by grants or loans usually through local authorities. In 1964, the Housing Corporation (the 'Corporation') was created and thereafter most of the public funding was channelled through the Corporation. The Corporation was granted supervisory powers by the Housing Act 1974. There are now 4000 housing associations, of which approximately 2200 are registered with the Corporation as RSLs. Since 1988, RSLs have been required to borrow funds in the private markets to supplement public funding. To date, some £20 billion has been raised outside the public sector borrowing requirement. The other major development has been the growth in the transfer of housing stock from local authorities to RSLs. Both under the previous and the present government, some 500,000 dwellings have been transferred in this way. Today, there are 1.5 million dwellings in the ownership of RSLs.

Under Part 1 of the 1996 Act, the Corporation is given two basic roles. These are to provide funding to RSLs and to regulate them. The funding is payable by way of grant under section 18 of the 1996 Act. Regulation covers the area of governance, finance and housing management.

If performance fails, the Corporation can exercise a number of powers: it can withdraw funding; make appointments to the governing body of the TSL and remove employees or governing body members (Schedule 1 to the 1996 Act). ...

Many local authorities have transferred some or all of their housing stock to one or more RSLs. This has happened so far as Poplar is concerned. Poplar was created for the purpose of taking over part of the housing stock of the borough of Tower Hamlets. It was a condition of Tower Hamlets receiving funding that this should happen. The funding came from the government under a scheme (the Estates Renewal Challenge Fund) designed to bring about the repair and improvement of the housing stock, the improvement of security for occupants of estates, to tackle anti-social behaviour and crime and to develop community initiatives. ...

55. The importance of whether Poplar was at the material times a public body or performing public functions is this: the HRA will only apply to Poplar if it is deemed to be a public body or performing public functions. HRA section 6(1) makes it unlawful for a public authority to act in a way which is incompatible with a Convention right. Section 6(3) states that a 'public authority'; includes '(6) any person certain of whose functions are functions of a public nature'. Section 6(5) provides that 'in relation to a particular act, a person is not a public authority by virtue only of subsection (3)(b) if the nature of the act is private.'

56. The defendant relies on the witness statements of Mr David Cowan, a lecturer of law at the University of Bristol (specialising in housing law and policy) and of Professor Alder of the University of Newcastle in support of her contention that Poplar is a public authority within section 6. Both Mr Cowan and Professor Alder acknowledge that the questions raised are ones of importance and of some debate in academic circles. However, Mr Cowan says it is 'tolerably clear that RSLs do fall within the definition of public authority under section 6(1)' as they are performing public functions.

57. Mr Cowan says:

'The obligation to provide interim accommodation under Part 7 (homelessness) of the Housing Act 1996 pending enquiries is owed by the local authority to the homeless applicant. That is clearly a public function. The accommodation can be provided by an RSL – see section 206(1)(b). An RSL which provides that accommodation is thus fulfilling a public function. Where, as here, the accommodation provided to the homeless household in satisfaction of the duty was originally owed by the local authority, but subsequently transferred to the RSL *whilst the duty was ongoing*, then the public nature of a function is made all the clearer. The decision to seek possession of the property once the relevant enquiries and a decision on the homelessness application have been made are all part and parcel of that function. It is therefore clear that this case does not fall within the exemption of activities covered by section 6(5).'

58. We agree with Mr Luba's submissions that the definition of who is a public authority, and what is a public function, for the purposes of section 6, should be given a generous interpretation. However, we would suggest that the position is not as simple as Mr Cowan suggests. The fact that a body performs an activity which otherwise a public body would be under a duty to perform, cannot mean that such performance is necessarily a public function. A public body in order to perform its public duties can use the services of a private body. Section 6 should not be applied so that if a private body provides such services, the nature of the functions are inevitably public. If this were to be the position, then when a small hotel provides bed and breakfast accommodation as a temporary measure, at the request of a housing authority that is under a duty to provide that accommodation, the small hotel would be performing public functions and required to comply with the HRA. This is not what the HRA intended. The consequence would be the same where a hospital uses a private company to carry out specialist services, such as analysing blood samples. The position under the HRA is necessarily more complex. Section 6(3) means that hybrid bodies, who have functions of a public and private nature are public authorities, but *not* in relation to acts which are of a private nature. The renting out of accommodation can certainly be of a private nature. The fact that through the act of renting by a private body a public authority may be fulfilling its public duty, does not automatically change into a public act what would otherwise be a private act. See, by analogy, *R v Muntham House School, ex parte R* [2000] LGR 255.

59. The purpose of section 6(3)(b) is to deal with hybrid bodies which have both public and private functions. It is not to make a body, which does not have responsibilities to the

public, a public body merely because it performs acts on behalf of a public body which would constitute public functions were such acts to be performed by the public body itself. An act can remain of a private nature even though it is performed because another body is under a public duty to ensure that that act is performed.

60. A useful illustration is provided by the decision of the European Court of Human Rights in *Costello-Roberts v United Kingdom* [1993] 19 EHRR 112. The case concerned a seven year old boy receiving corporal punishment from the headmaster of an independent school. The European Court made it clear that the State cannot absolve itself of its Convention obligations by delegating the fulfilment of such obligations to private bodies or individuals, including the headmaster of an independent school. However, if a local authority, in order to fulfil its duties, sent a child to a private school, the fact that it did this would not mean that the private school was performing public functions. The school would not be a hybrid body. It would remain a private body. The local authority would, however, not escape its duties by delegating the performance to the private school. If there were a breach of the Convention, then the responsibility would be that of the local authority and not that of the school.

61. The approach of Professor Alder differs from that of Mr Cowan. He states that there is no single factor that determined whether a function is a public function. He adds:

'The meaning of "public function" is not necessarily the same in the different contexts where the matter arises. ... Analogies, particularly in respect to the test for determining which bodies are susceptible to judicial review in the Administrative Court may be helpful, given that one purpose of judicial review, is to ensure that public bodies are subject to high standards of conduct the same being true of the ECHR. There is also an analogy with the test that is being developed in EC law for determining whether a body is a public body, namely "a body, whatever its legal form, which has been made responsible pursuant to a measure adopted by the state, for providing a public service under the control of the state, and has for that purpose special powers beyond those which result from the normal rules applicable in relation to individuals", (*Foster v British Gas plc*, case C-188/89 [1990] ECRI-3313, ECJ).'

62. In coming to his conclusion that in this case the activities of Poplar are within section 6, the Professor relies upon:
- the charitable status of Poplar
- the fact that Poplar is subject to the control of the Corporation
- the sanctions which the Corporation can apply
- the provision of public funding to Poplar
- the standards which Poplar is required to adopt in the exercise of its powers
- the control which the Corporation can exert over the exercise of Poplar's powers
- local authority involvement

Both the Department [for the Environment, Transport and the Regions] and Poplar dispute that Poplar is a public authority. Mr Philip Sales helpfully adopts the distinction correctly identified by *Clayton & Tomlinson, The Law of Human Rights* (at para 5.08) between *standard public* authorities, *functional* public authorities and courts and tribunals. Mr Sales submits, and we, like Professor Alder and Mr Holmes, would agree that housing associations as a class are not standard public authorities. If they are to be a public authority this must be because a particular function performed by an individual RSL is a public as opposed to a private act. The RSL would then be a functional, or hybrid, public authority.

64. In support of his contention, Mr Sales draws attention to the following features of housing associations;
  a)   They vary vastly in size.
  b)   Their structure is that of an ordinary private law entity.
  c)   As to regulation by the Corporation he points to the fact that many financial institutions are regulated by the Bank of England but this does not make them public bodies. Furthermore, the Corporation gives each RSL freedom to decide how it achieves what is expected of it.
  d)   Members of the RSL are not appointed by, or answerable to, the government but are private individuals who volunteer their services. Even in the rare cases were the Corporation makes appointments, the appointee owes his duty to the RSL.

e)   In *R (Louisa Goldsmith and Others) v Servite Houses and Wandsworth LBC* (Unreported, 12 May 2000) Moses J decided a housing association was not subject to judicial review.

f)   Although a RSL is funded in part out of public funds, the major source of its income is its rental income. In any event, this is not by any means conclusive: see *Peabody Housing Association Ltd v Green* (1978) 33 P & CR 644 at p 660 & 662.

65. In coming to our conclusion as to whether Poplar is a public authority within the HRA meaning of that term, we regard it of particular importance in this case that:

i)   While HRA section 6 requires a generous interpretation of who is a public authority, it is clearly inspired by the approach developed by the courts in identifying the bodies and activities subject to judicial review. The emphasis on public functions reflects the approach adopted in judicial review by the courts and text books since the decision of the Court of Appeal (the judgment of Lloyd LJ) in *R v Panel of Takeovers and Mergers, ex p Datafin* [1987] QB 815.

ii)   Tower Hamlets, in transferring its housing stock to Poplar, does not transfer its primary public duties to Poplar. Poplar is no more than the means by which it seeks to perform those duties.

iii)   The act of providing accommodation to rent is not, without more, a public function for the purpose of HRA section 6. Furthermore, that is true irrespective of the section of society for whom the accommodation is provided.

iv)   The fact that a body is a charity or is conducted not for profit means that it is likely to be motivated in performing its activities by what it perceives to be the public interest. However, this does not point to the body being a public authority. In addition, even if such a body performs functions, that would be considered to be of a public nature if performed by a public body, nevertheless such acts may remain of a private nature for the purpose of sections 6(3)(b) and 6(5).

v)   What can make an act, which would otherwise be private, public, is a feature or a combination of features which impose a public character or stamp on the act. Statutory authority for what is done can at least help to mark the act as being public; so can the extent of control over the function exercised by another body which is a public authority. The more closely the acts that could be of a private nature are enmeshed in the activities of a public body, the more likely they are to be public. However, the fact that the acts are supervised by a public regulatory body does not necessarily indicate that they are of a public nature. This is analogous to the position in judicial review, where a regulatory body may be deemed public but the activities of the body which is regulated may be categorised private.

vi)   The closeness of the relationship which exists between Tower Hamlets and Poplar. Poplar was created by Tower Hamlets to take a transfer of local authority housing stock; five of its board members are also members of Tower Hamlets; Poplar is subject to the guidance of Tower Hamlets as to the manner in which it act towards the defendant.

vii)   The defendant, at the time of transfer, was a sitting tenant of Poplar and it was intended that she would be treated no better and no worse than if she remained a tenant of Tower Hamlets. While she remained a tenant, Poplar therefore stood in relation to her in very much the position previously occupied by Tower Hamlets.

66. While these are the most important factors in coming to our conclusion, it is desirable to step back and look at the situation as a whole. As is the position on applications for judicial review, there is no clear demarcation line which can be drawn between public and private bodies and functions. In a borderline case, such as this, the decision is very much one of fact and degree. Taking into account all the circumstances, we have come to the conclusion that while activities of housing associations need not involve the performance of public functions in this case, in providing accommodation for the defendant and then seeking possession, the role of Poplar is so closely assimilated to that of Tower Hamlets that it was performing public and not private functions. Poplar therefore is a functional public authority, at least to that extent. We emphasise that this does not mean that all Poplar's functions are public. We do not even decide that the position would be the same if the defendant was a secure tenant. The activities of housing associations can be ambiguous. For example, their activities in raising

private or public finance could be very different from those that are under consideration here. The raising of finance by Poplar could well be a private function. ...

73. As we have decided that there is no contravention of Articles 6 and 8, strictly, there is no need for us to speculate as to whether, if there had been a contravention, this would have created a situation of incompatibility. We note that if we decided that there was a contravention of Article 8, the Department would prefer us not to interpret section 21(4) 'constructively' but instead to grant a declaration of incompatibility. However, so far, the sections of the HRA dealing with interpretation and incompatibility have been subject to limited guidance and for that reason we hope it will be helpful if we set out our views even though they are strictly obiter.

74. The relevant sections of the HRA are sections 3 and 4. ...

75. It is difficult to overestimate the importance of section 3. It applies to legislation passed both before and after the HRA came into force. Subject to the section not requiring the court to go beyond that which is possible, it is mandatory in its terms. In the case of legislation predating the HRA where the legislation would otherwise conflict with the Convention, section 3 requires the court to now interpret legislation in a manner which it would not have done before the HRA came into force. When the court interprets legislation usually its primary task is to identify the intention of Parliament. Now, when section 3 applies, the courts have to adjust their traditional role in relation to interpretation so as to give effect to the direction contained in section 3. It is as though legislation which predates the HRA and conflicts with the Convention has to be treated as being subsequently amended to incorporate the language of section 3. However, the following points, which are probably self evident, should be noted:

a) unless the legislation would otherwise be in breach of the Convention section 3 can be ignored; (so courts should always first ascertain whether, absent section 3, there would be any breach of the convention),

b) if the court has to rely on section 3 it should limit the extent of the modified meaning to that which is necessary to achieve compatibility;

c) section 3 does not entitle the court to *legislate*; (its task is still one of *interpretation*, but interpretation in accordance with the direction contained in section 3),

d) the views of the parties and of the Crown as to whether a 'constructive' interpretation should be adopted cannot modify the task of the court; (if section 3 applies the court is required to adopt the section 3 approach to interpretation),

e) where despite the strong language of section 3, it is not possible to achieve a result which is compatible with the convention, the court is not *required* to grant a declaration and presumably in exercising its discretion as to whether to grant a declaration or not it will be influenced by the usual considerations which apply to the grant of declarations.

76. The most difficult task which courts face is distinguishing between legislation and interpretation. Here practical experience of seeking to apply section 3 will provide the best guide. However, if it is necessary in order to obtain compliance to radically alter the effect of the legislation this will be an indication that more than interpretation is involved.

77. In this case Mr Luba contends that all that is required is to insert the words 'if it is reasonable to do so' into the opening words of section 21(4). The amendment may appear modest but its effect would be very wide indeed. It would significantly reduce the ability of landlords to recover possession and would defeat Parliament's original objective of providing certainty. It would involve legislating.

78. Finally, we are prepared to grant the parties declarations if this will assist them to seek permission to appeal. Despite this, the parties should not assume permission to appeal will be granted. The decision whether to grant permission or to leave the decision to grant permission to the Lords, should not be affected by the fact that the appeal involves the HRA. The House of Lords should normally be allowed to select for itself the appeals which it wishes to hear.

The Appeal is dismissed.

NOTE

As the *Donoghue* case demonstrates, the definition of 'public authority' in s. 6 HRA is such that, with certain exceptions, its meaning will need to be established on a case by case basis. A court[18] or tribunal[19] is a 'public authority', but 'either House of Parliament or a person exercising functions in connection with proceedings in Parliament' is not.[20] Otherwise, 'public authority' is defined in s. 6(3)(b) in functional terms, so as to refer to 'any person certain of whose functions are functions of a public nature'.[1] However, s. 6 will not apply to such a 'public authority' if the nature of the particular act is private.[2] The definition in s. 6(3)(b) was intended to include 'central government (including executive agencies); local government; the police; immigration officers; prisons; courts and tribunals themselves; and, to the extent that they are exercising public functions, companies responsible for areas of activity which were previously within the public sector, such as privatised utilities.'[3] In Parliament, Lord Irvine gave the following examples of this last category of hybrid 'public authorities':

'Railtrack would fall within that category because it exercises public functions in its role as a safety regulator, but it is acting privately in its role as a property developer. A private security company would be exercising public functions in relation to the management of a contract-out prison but would be acting privately when, for example, guarding commercial premises. Doctors in general practice would be public authorities in relation to their National Health Service functions, but not in relation to their private patients.'[4]

In addition, it was understood in Parliament that the Press Complaints Commission was a public authority,[5] as were the British Board of Film Classification,[6] the Jockey Club,[7] water companies,[8] the Royal National Lifeboat Institution,[9] and the churches,[10] in respect of certain of their functions. As to broadcasting, the Home Secretary said that this 'is ultimately a matter for the courts, but our judgment is that the BBC will be regarded as a public authority under clause 6; independent television companies will not, but the Independent Television Commission will be.'[11] But the courts will take their own decisions. So far, they have stated or supposed that the DDP (when consenting to a prosecution)[12] and a National Health Service Trust[13] are public authorities, but that the RSPCA[14] and a newspaper are not.[15]

---

18 An ecclesiastical court is included: *Re Crawley Green Rd Cemetery, Luton* [2001] 2 WLR 1175, QB (Art. 9 ECHR required that a faculty be granted to re-inter the body of a husband in non-church premises at the widow's request, contrary to normal practice).
19 These are likely to be those in Sch. 1 to the Tribunals and Inquiries Act 1992, but not domestic tribunals.
20 s. 6(3) HRA.
 1 The intention was to provide that 'liability in domestic proceedings should lie with bodies in respect of whose actions the United Kingdom Government were answerable in Strasbourg': Mr Straw, 314 HC Deb, 17 June 98, col. 406.
 2 s. 6(5) HRA.
 3 *Rights Brought Home*, Cm. 3782, p. 8.
 4 583 HL Deb, 24 November 97, col. 758. What different remedies would be available for NHS and private patients if a doctor revealed to a third party information given by the patient in breach of confidence?. On the law of breach of confidence, see below, p. 959.
 5 Mr Straw, Home Secretary, 315 HC Deb, 2 July 98, col. 545.
 6 Mr Straw, Home Secretary, 314 HC Deb, 17 June 1998, col. 413.
 7 Mr Straw, Home Secretary, 312 HC Deb, 20 May 1998, col. 1020.
 8 Mr Straw, Home Secretary, ibid., col. 409.
 9 Mr Straw, Home Secretary, 314 HC Deb, 17 June 1998, col. 407.
10 See above, p. 36.
11 Mr Straw, Home Secretary, 306 HC Deb, 16 February 98, col. 776. Cf. Lord Williams of Mostyn, Home Office Minister, 583 HL Deb, 3 November 97, col. 1309, who suggested that Channel 4 might be a public authority.
12 *R v DPP, ex p Kebilene* [2000] 2 AC 326, HL.
13 *Re A (children) (conjoined twins)* [2000] 4 All ER 961 at 1017, CA.
14 [2001] All ER (D) 188, ChD.
15 *Venables v News Group Newspapers Ltd*, below, p. 973.

As Lord Woolf CJ indicated in the *Donoghue* case, the distinction between public and private law that has been developed for the purposes of judicial review proceedings is likely to offer a guide to the meaning of public function.[16]

16 See H. W. R. Wade and C. F. Forsyth, *Administrative Law* (8th edn, 2000), p. 651.

CHAPTER 2

Policing

1 Introduction

Many organisations and state bodies serve to protect civil liberties and also have the potential to infringe them. The most conspicuous group is the police.[1] This chapter seeks to provide an understanding of the structure and organisation of the police so as to appreciate the impact they have on some of the citizen's most basic rights: liberty, protest and expression, privacy etc.

An immediate problem in exploring the role of the police is that it is almost impossible to provide a comprehensive definition or explanation of their function in modern society.

'In a democratic society, the police are first and foremost the guardians of law and order and of human rights and freedoms. In addition to keeping the peace and protecting public safety in the interest of society at large, they are also to guarantee individual and collective freedoms to protect people and their property and to defend the institutions on which their legitimacy is founded.'[2]

And, as R. Morgan and T. Newburn observe:

'Most realistic discussion of police work suggests that at the very least the police role includes: order maintenance; crime control; environmental and traffic functions; assistance in times of emergency; crime prevention; and conciliation in conflict resolution.'[3]

How can an organisation playing such a diverse role in society be effectively monitored and assessed to ensure that it remains subject to the rule of law?

The enactment of the Human Rights Act 1998 added to police responsibilities:

'[T]he police not only must refrain from breaching the convention, but are under a positive obligation to ensure that individuals are protected from having their rights infringed by the actions of others. Such positive obligation encompasses five duties:

(a) to put in place a legal framework to provide effective protection of Convention rights;
(b) to prevent breaches of convention rights;
(c) to provide information and advice relevant to the breach of convention rights;
(d) to respond to breaches of convention rights;
(e) to provide resources to individuals to prevent breaches of their convention rights.

In relation to the police, this translates into safeguarding the life and physical integrity of individuals known to be at risk, investigating crime effectively, and ensuring that individuals may enjoy their convention rights without interference.'[4]

---

1 For general information see www.police.uk/.
2 C. Diaz, *Police Ethics* (1999) p. 31.
3 R. Morgan and T. Newburn, *The Future of Policing* (1997), p. 74. See further the articles collected in R. Reiner, *Policing I* (1996) Part II, 'The Role of the Police in Practice'; R. Reiner, *The Future of Policing* (2000). For a recent illustration of the diversity see Home Office, *Diary of a Police Officer* (2001).
4 S. Khan and M. Ryder, (2000) Legal Action, September, p. 31.

The central theme running throughout this chapter will be to consider the ways in which the police are accountable for their actions, and a consideration of the efficacy of the accountability mechanisms.[5] The task of balancing efficiency and effectiveness whilst protecting rights is increasingly complex and it is vital that the police remain answerable for their actions. Accountability arises through central government's imposition of organisational structure, through its requirement of consultation and local policing policies, and through financial control. The police must also remain accountable in law through the 'ordinary law of the land' i.e. paying damages when torts are committed, being prosecuted when crimes are committed. Finally, the police must provide a degree of self-regulation – as with other major organisations and professions. The chapter concludes with a consideration of the problems associated with complaints and discipline within the police.

2   Accountable to law

The following case was a landmark in requiring clear legal authority to be shown to justify invasions of the rights of others:

Entick v Carrington (1765) 19 State Tr 1029, 2 Wils 275, 95 ER 807, Court of Common Pleas, Lord Camden CJ

On 6 November 1762, the Earl of Halifax, one of the principal Secretaries of State, issued a warrant to four King's messengers (Nathan Carrington, James Watson, Thomas Ardran and Robert Blackmore) 'to make strict and diligent search for John Entick, the author of, or one concerned in writing, several weekly very seditious papers, intitled the Monitor, or British Freeholder ...; and him, having found you are to seize and apprehend, and to bring, together with his books and papers, in safe custody before me to be examined ...' The messengers entered E's house, the outer door being open, apprehended him, and searched for his books and papers in rooms and in one bureau, one writing desk and several drawers. Where necessary these were broken open. They seized some books and papers and read others, remaining for about four hours. They then took E and the items seized to Lovel Stanhope, law-clerk to the Secretaries of State. E was released on 17 November. He subsequently brought an action in trespass against the messengers. The jury gave a special verdict and assessed the damages at £300. The defendants argued that their acts were done in obedience to a lawful warrant.

> **Lord Camden CJ:** ... [I]f this point should be determined in favour of the jurisdiction, the secret cabinets and bureaus of every subject in this kingdom will be thrown open to the search and inspection of a messenger, whenever the secretary of state shall think fit to charge, or even to suspect, a person to be the author or, printer, or publisher of a seditious libel.
>
> This power so assumed by the secretary of state is an execution upon all the party's papers, in the first instance. His house is rifled; his most valuable secrets are taken out of his possession, before the paper for which he is charged is found to be criminal by any competent jurisdiction, and before he is convicted either of writing, publishing, or being concerned in the paper. This power, so claimed by the secretary of state, is not supported by one single citation from any law book extant. ...
>
> The arguments, which the defendants' counsel have thought fit to urge in support of this practice, are of this kind.

---

5   See also Council of Europe 12th Proceedings, *Police Powers and Accountability in a Democratic Society* (1999).

That such warrants have issued frequently since the Revolution, which practice has been found by the special verdict; ....

That the case of the warrants bears a resemblance to the-case of search for stolen goods.

They say too, that they have been executed without resistance upon many printers, booksellers, and authors who have quietly submitted to the authority; that no action hath hitherto been brought to try the right; and that although they have been often read upon the returns of Habeas Corpus, yet no court of justice has ever declared them illegal.

And it is further insisted, that this power is essential to government, and the only means of quieting clamours and sedition. ...

If it is law, it will be found in our books. If it is not to be found there, it is not law.

The great end, for which men entered into society, was to secure their property. That right is preserved sacred and incommunicable in all instances, where it has not been taken away or abridged by some public law for the good of the whole. The cases where this right of property is set aside by positive law, are various. Distresses, executions, forfeitures, taxes, &c. are all of this description; wherein every man by every common consent gives up that right, for the sake of justice and the general good. By the laws of England, every invasion of private property, be it ever so minute, is a trespass. No man can set his foot upon my ground without my licence, but he is liable to an action, though the damage be nothing; which is proved by every declaration in trespass, where the defendant is called upon to answer for bruising the grass and even treading upon the soil. If he admits the fact, he is bound to show by way of justification, that some positive law has empowered or excused him. The justification is submitted to the judges, who are to look into the books; and see if such a justification can be maintained by the text of the statute law, or by the principles of common law. If no such excuse can be found or produced, the silence of the books is an authority against the defendant, and the plaintiff must have judgment.

Where is the written law that gives any magistrate such a power? I can safely answer, there is none, and therefore it is too much for us without such authority to pronounce a practice legal, which would be subversive of all the comforts of society.

But though it cannot be maintained by any direct law, yet it bears a resemblance, as was urged, to the known case of search and seizure for stolen goods.

I answer, that the difference is apparent. In the one, I am permitted to seize my own goods, which are placed in the hands of a public officer, till the felon's conviction shall intitle me to restitution. In the other, the party's own property is seized before and without conviction, and he has no power to reclaim his goods, even after his innocence is cleared by acquittal.

The case of searching for stolen goods crept into the law by imperceptible practice. It is the only case of the kind that is to be met with. No less a person than my lord Coke (4 Inst. 176,) denied its legality; and therefore if the two cases resembled each other more than they do, we have no right, without an act of parliament, to adopt a new practice in the criminal law, which was never yet allowed from all antiquity.

Observe too the caution with which die law proceeds in this singular case. ...

I come now to the practice since the Revolution, which has been strongly urged, with this emphatical addition, that an usage tolerated from the era of liberty and continued downwards to this time through the ages of constitution, must necessarily have a legal commencement. ...

With respect to the practice itself; if it goes no higher, every lawyer will tell you, it is much too modern to be evidence of the common law; and if it should be added, that these warrants ought to acquire some strength by the silence of those Courts, which have heard them read so often upon return without censure or animadversion. I am able to borrow my answer to that pretence from the Court of King's-bench, which lately declared with great unanimity in the Case of General Warrants, that as no objection was taken to them upon the returns, and the matter passed *sub silentio,* the precedents were of no weight. I most heartily concur in that opinion; ...

But still it is insisted, that there has been a general submission, and no action brought to try the right.

I answer, there has been a submission of guilt and poverty to power and the terror of punishment. But it would be strange doctrine to assert that all the people of this land are bound to acknowledge that to be universal law, which a few criminal booksellers have been afraid to dispute. ...

It is then said, that it is necessary for the ends of government to lodge such a power with a state officer; and that it is better to prevent the publication before than to punish the offender afterwards. I answer, if the legislature be of that opinion, they will revive the Licensing Act. But if they have not done that I conceive they are not of that opinion. And with respect to the argument of state necessity, or a distinction that has been aimed at between state offences and others, the common law does not understand that kind of reasoning, nor do our books take notice of any such distinction.

Serjeant Ashley was committed to the Tower in the 3d of Charles 1st, by the House of Lords only for asserting in argument, that there was a 'law of state' different from the common law; and the ShipMoney judges were impeached for holding, first that state-necessity would justify the raising money without consent of parliament; and secondly, that the king was judge of that necessity.

If the king himself has no power to declare when the law ought to be violated for reason of state, I am sure we his judges have no such prerogative...

[U]pon the whole we are all of opinion, that the warrant to seize and carry away the party's papers in the case of a seditious libel, is illegal and void. ...

NOTES

1. *Entick v Carrington* was one of four leading cases which followed the publication of No. 45 of the *North Briton*[6] – a weekly paper, of which John Wilkes was joint editor and a leading contributor. Its main purpose was to abuse and ridicule the recently appointed administration of the Earl of Bute. After No. 45 was published, the two Secretaries of State, Lords Egremont and Halifax, issued a general warrant for the arrest of its 'authors, printers and publishers'. Over 45 people were arrested under this warrant, including Wilkes. The warrant was held to be illegal, and damages were awarded for trespass.[7]

2. This case is a classic illustration of the principle that any public officer must be able to point to lawful authority for actions of his which infringe the rights of others, and not merely some general conception of state necessity. This is an important aspect of the rule of law. It also reflects an unwillingness to 'invent' or 'discover' lawful authority, which has not been shared by some judges in more recent cases. For example, in *Chic Fashions (West Wales) Ltd v Jones*[8] the Court of Appeal held, contrary to previous authority,[9] that:

'when a constable enters a house by virtue of a search warrant for stolen goods, he may seize not only the goods which he reasonably believes to be covered by the warrant, but also any other goods which he believes on reasonable grounds to have been stolen and to be material evidence on a charge of stealing or receiving against the person in possession of them or anyone associated with him.'[10]

Lord Denning MR noted, *inter alia*, there was 'ever-increasing wickedness ... about' and that if a constable who came across stolen goods not mentioned in the warrant was forced to leave in order to obtain such a warrant 'in nine cases out of ten, by the

6 See Sir William Holdsworth, *A History of English Law* (1938), Vol X, pp. 659–672; G. Rudé, *Wilkes and Liberty* (1962) Chap. II; A. Williamson, *Wilkes, A Friend to Liberty* (1974) Chap. IV.
7 See *Wilkes v Wood* (1763) 19 State Tr 1153; *Leach v Money* (1765) 19 State Tr 1002; and *Wilkes v Lord Halifax* (1769) 19 State Tr 1406.
8 [1968] 2 QB 299.
9 See L. H. Leigh, *Police Powers in England and Wales* (1975) pp. 189–190.
10 Per Lord Denning MR at 313.

time he came back . . . these other goods would have disappeared'.[11] These appear to be the kinds of arguments disapproved of in *Entick v Carrington*. In *Ghani v Jones*[12] Lord Denning MR, for the Court of Appeal, enunciated: (1) a broad principle extending the ambit of the power of a constable, executing a search or arrest warrant or effecting an arrest without warrant, to seize goods or evidence;[13] and (2) a series of five principles creating a new power to seize goods or evidence where there is no warrant or arrest, and even from a person not himself criminally implicated.[14] The first mentioned dictum was applied in *Garfinkel v Metropolitan Police Comr*[15] and *Frank Truman Export Ltd v Metropolitan Police Comr*[16] without consideration of its status as a precedent. Finally, the House of Lords in *Wills v Bowley*[17] held by three to two that the power of a constable under s. 28 of the Town Police Clauses Act 1847 to arrest any person who 'within his view commits' one of a series of offences (here, using profane or obscene language to the annoyance of passers-by) extended to cases where the constable honestly believed on reasonable grounds derived wholly from his own observation that an offence had been committed and even though the person arrested was subsequently acquitted of the offence.[18] The minority argued in vain that:

'Where the liberty of the subject is concerned, the Court should not go beyond the natural construction of the statute and the strict terms of the grant of the power to arrest without warrant.'[19]

The majority view, expressed by Lord Bridge, was that it would be 'nonsensical to construe such provisions 'in the sense that the legality of the arrest can only be established by an *ex post facto* verdict of guilty against the person arrested' and 'ridiculous' to do so in such a way as to force on the constable a choice between the risk of making an unlawful arrest and the risk of committing a criminal neglect of duty'.[20]

3. By contrast, the spirit of *Entick v Carrington* can be seen in the decisions of the House of Lords in *Morris v Beardmore*[1] and of the Divisional Court in *McLorie v Oxford*[2] (where *Ghani v Jones* was held not to have created a new right to *enter* premises as distinct from a right to *seize* goods). Moreover, a series of cases show that any unlawful act (subject to the *de minimis* principle) by a police officer will take him outside the execution of his duty.[3] In yet more recent cases, the courts have recognised the need for officers to explain more fully their reasons for entry to search to effect an arrest (PACE, s. 17), and to search after an arrest (s. 18).[4]

One of the issues to be addressed in this chapter is the extent to which the principle of *Entick* lives on, despite central government's increased powers to direct actions of the police and Police Authorities, and of the power to specify policing objectives.

11 Ibid.
12 [1970] 1 QB 693.
13 *Obiter*, at 706.
14 At 708–709.
15 [1972] Crim LR 44, Ackner J.
16 [1977] QB 952, Swanwick J.
17 [1983] 1 AC 57.
18 See commentary by D. J. Birch, [1982] Crim LR 580; A. Samuels, (1982) 98 LQR 537; J. L. Lambert, [1983] PL 234.
19 Per Lord Elwyn-Jones [1983] 1 AC 57 at 72.
20 At 680, 681.
1 Below, p. 362.
2 [1982] QB 1290, DC.
3 See below, p. 159.
4 See *O'Loughlin v Chief Constable of Essex* [1998] 3 WLR 374; *Lineham v DPP* [2000] Crim LR 861 and commentary, both discussed in Chap. 3 below, p. 251.

The relationships that exist between central and local government and the police and the influences exerted are crucial to this examination. In considering these relationships, it will also be necessary to explore the relationship of the police with the general public, with one of the perennial questions being to what extent there is policing 'by consent' of the citizens in England and Wales. Materials throughout this chapter, culminating in the Macpherson Report[5] into the murder of Stephen Lawrence, suggest that, to date, the police consultative process has failed to enable true policing by consent.[6]

3   Police structure and organisation

The effectiveness of the control of the police can only be properly examined with an understanding of the structure and organisation of the police. Similarly, the changes in the law relating to police powers discussed in the next chapter must be seen against the background of substantial and significant developments in policing in the last 20 years.[7] As the diversity and potential intrusiveness of police activity increases, the organisational structure of the police has come under close scrutiny and been the subject of much debate. The current basic structure was established by the Police Act 1964, but this was subject to modification by the Police and Magistrates' Courts Act 1994.[8] The relevant provisions of these Acts have been consolidated in the Police Act 1996.

The organisational debate has centred on the question whether elected (or mainly elected) Police Authorities should be given power to determine general policing policies.[9] In 1979, Jack Straw, then a backbench Labour MP, introduced a Bill designed to achieve this.[10] Others argued that this would not be a 'happy solution' and it would be more appropriate to seek 'better explanatory accountability and a

---

5 *The Stephen Lawrence Inquiry* (1999) Cm. 4262.

6 There is considerable confusion as to what that much-used expression means – see R. Morgan, 'Policing by Consent: Legitimating the Doctrine' in D. J. Smith (ed.), *Coming to Terms with Policing* (1989): 'establishing the degree to which there is policing by consent and whether it has changed over time is as difficult an enterprise as one can imagine' (p. 218).

7 On the historical context see: C. Emsley, *The English Police: A Political and Social History* (2nd edn, 1996); R. Morgan and T. Newburn, *The Future of Policing* (1997) Chap. 1.

8 See T. Jones and T. Newburn, *Policing After the Act* (1997).

9 For other contributions to the debate on police accountability, see T. Newburn and T. Jones, 'Police Accountability' in W. Saulsbury, J. Mott and T. Newburn (eds.), *Themes in Contemporary Policing* (1996); I. Oliver, 'Police Accountability in 1996' [1996] Crim LR 611; R. Morgan and T. Newburn, *The Future of Policing* (1997); J. Kleinig, *The Ethics of Policing* (1996) Chap.11; R. Baldwin and R. Kinsey, *Police, Powers and Politics* (1982); B. Loveday, (1983) 9 Local Government Studies 39; P. A. J. Waddington (1983) 10 Local Government Studies 27; B. Loveday, (1983) 10 Local Government Studies 43; T. Jefferson and R. Grimshaw, *Controlling the Constable* (1984); S. Spencer, *Called To Account* (1985); L. Lustgarten, *The Governance of Police* (1986); D. Downes and T. Ward, *Democratic Policing* (Labour Campaign for Criminal Justice) (1986); I. Oliver, *Police, Government and Accountability* (1987); S. Uglow, *Policing Liberal Society* (1988), Chaps. 7 and 8; R. Reiner, *Chief Constables* (1991), Chap. 11; R. Reiner *The Politics of the Police* (3rd edn, 2000), Chap. 6; R. Reiner and S. Spencer (eds.), *Accountable Policing* (1993); N. Walker, *Policing in a changing constitutional order* (2000); T. Jones, T. Newburn and D. J. Smith, *Democracy and Policing* (1994); I. Loader, 'Democracy, Justice and the Limits of Policing: Rethinking Police Accountability' (1994) 3 Social & Legal Studies 521; A. Brown, *Police Governance* (1998); W. Saulsbury, J. Mott and T. Newburn (eds.), *Themes in Contemporary Policing* (1996).

10 The approach has been favoured by the political left. See the discussions by M. Dean, (1982) 53 PQ 153; P. Hewitt, *The Abuse of Power* (1982), Chap. 3; S. Savage, (1984) 55 PQ 48, 51–56.

satisfactory solution to the problem of the complaints machinery procedure'.[11] The emphasis was on consultation. Reforms initially took this direction. The Police Act 1996, s. 96(1), replacing the Police and Criminal Evidence Act 1984, s. 106(1), provides that:

'Arrangements shall be made in each police area for obtaining the views of people in that area about matters concerning the policing of the area and for obtaining their co-operation with the police in preventing crime in the area.'

In all areas, the Police Authority facilitates this co-operation after consultation with the Chief Constable.[12] Prior to the legislative requirement for consultation with the community, arrangements were less formal. Lord Scarman in his report on The Brixton Disorders[13] stated that:

'If a rift is not to develop between the police and the public as a whole (not just the members of the ethnic minority communities) it is in my view essential that a means be derived of enabling the community to be heard not only in the development of policing policy but in the planning of many, though not all, operations against crime.'[14]

As the machinery for consultation became formalised, the Home Office issued guidelines on local consultation committees and their involvement in policing.[15] Through such guidelines central government was able to affect local accountability.

Subsequent research suggests that the members of these consultative committees tended to have had little experience as consumers of police service (i.e. as victims or offenders); they accordingly depended on the knowledge and expertise of the police officers present, who were then able to maintain control of the discussion. The social background of members tended not to be representative of the local community.[16] Similarly, a Policy Studies Institute study found that local representative bodies such as consultative committees, crime prevention panels and

11 G. Marshall, *Constitutional Conventions* (1984), p. 145.
12 In London, the Metropolitan Police Commissioner had, until July 2000, made arrangements in light of guidance from the Home Secretary, and following consultation with local councils. Part VI of the Greater London Authority Act 1999, and specifically s. 311, establishes a Metropolitan Police Authority to act in the same way as other area police authorities. For further information on the Metropolitan Police, see www.met.police.uk/.
13 Cmnd. 8427 (1981).
14 Para 5.56.
15 Home Office Circular 54/1982, *Local Consultation Arrangements Between the Community and the Police*. See also Home Office Circular 2/1985. Home Office Circulars are available at www.homeoffice.gov.uk/.
16 See E. Stratta, 'A Lack of Consultation?' (1990) 6 Policing 523. See further, R. Morgan and C. Maw, *Setting the PACE* (Bath Social Policy Papers 4); and (1985) 1 Policing 87; R. Morgan, (1986) 57 PQ 83; R. Morgan, 'The Local Determinants of Policing Policy' in P. Wilmott (ed.), *Policing and the Community* (1987); R. Morgan, (1987) BJ Crim L 87; R. Morgan, 'Policing by Consent' in R. Morgan and D. Smith (eds.), *Coming to Terms with Policing* (1989), Chap. 12; R. Morgan, 'Talking about Policing' in D. Downes (ed.), *Unravelling Criminal Justice* (1992), Chap. 7; G. Hughes, 'Talking Cop Shop? A Case-Study of Police Community Consultative Groups in Transition' (1994) 4 Policing and Society 253. See also N. Fielding, *Community Policing* (1995); R. Bradley, *Public Expectations and Perceptions of Policing* (1998) (Police Research Series Paper No 96); R. Elliott and J. Nicholls, *It's Good to Talk: Lessons in Public Consultation and Feedback* (1997) (Police Research Series Paper No 22); N. Bland, *Measuring Public Expectations of Policing: an evaluation of gap analysis* (1997) (Police Research Series No 24); R. Morgan and T. Newburn, *The Future of Policing* (1997). For studies of policing from sociological perspectives, see: S. Holdaway, *Inside the British Police* (1983); D. Hobbs, *Doing the Business* (1989); M. Young, *An Inside Job* (1991); R. Reiner, *Chief Constables* (1991); S Choongh, *Policing as Social Discipline* (1997); W. Lyons, *The Politics of Community Policing: rearranging the power to punish* (1999).

Neighbourhood Watch schemes 'made no discernible input into local policing policy'.[17]

The effectiveness of these liaison schemes in reducing crime and catching criminals is still hotly disputed. For example, T. Bennett has claimed that there is 'no strong evidence that Neighbourhood Watch has prevented a single crime in Britain since its inception in the early 80s'.[18] Arguably, the existence of schemes involving the local community serves a useful function in itself by giving members of the community a perception that they are playing a part in reducing crime.

(A) POLICE AUTHORITIES[19]

The major reforms effected by the Conservative government in the Police and Magistrates' Courts Act 1994 took matters in a different direction, with a change from elected (or partly elected) police authorities to smaller, appointed police authorities. [20] The reforms were based on the White Paper, *Police Reform*,[1] but the government's original Bill was amended significantly in a number of respects during its passage through the House of Lords following adverse criticism by influential Conservative peers, e.g. Lord Whitelaw. The result is regarded by many as a compromise 'between a government keen on "quangoisation" and a range of different bodies defending (for differing reasons) local electoral representation'.[2]

The provisions relating to police authorities have now been consolidated in the Police Act 1996. The key points are now as follows. England and Wales is divided into 43 police areas.[3] Apart from the Metropolitan Police District and the City of London police area, police areas are based on one or more counties.[4] There is a police force and police authority established for each area.[5] The police authority normally comprises 17 members.[6] Nine of these are to be members of a relevant council.[7] Five are 'independent members' appointed by the other members of the police authority

---

17 T. Johnson et al., *Democracy and Policing* (1994), p. 298 and Chap. 5. For further information on the Policy Studies Institute, see www.psi.org.uk.

18 T. Bennett, 'Community Policing on the Ground: Developments In Britain' in D. Rosenbaum (ed.), *The Challenge of Community Policing: Testing the Promises* (1994), p. 241.

19 For further information see www.apa.police.uk/.

20 R. Morgan and T. Newburn, *The Future of Policing* (1997) Chap. 4; R. Sullivan, 'The Politics of British Policing in the Thatcher/Major State' (1998) 37 Howard Journal 300.

1 Cm. 2281 (1993).

2 T. Jones and T. Newburn, *Policing After the Act* (1997), p. 15. See on the role of the police authority and the issue of police governance generally the articles collected in R. Reiner, *Policing II* (1996) Part V.

3 Police Act 1996, s. 1 and Sch. 1. Information on individual forces is available from www.police.co.uk/.

4 Police forces other than those governed by authorities under the Police Act include the Atomic Energy Authority Constabulary, British Transport Police, Ministry of Defence Police, Royal Parks Constabulary, as well as the many dock or port police and other geographically specific groups: e.g. Royal Borough of Kensington and Chelsea Parks Police.

5 Police Act 1996, ss. 2, 3.

6 The age limit of 70 for members was removed by s. 106 of the Criminal Justice and Police Act 2001. In the case of the Metropolitan Police Authority, there are 23 members (Greater London Authority Act 1999, s. 310, inserting s. 5A into the Police Act 1996). Twelve members are elected members of the Assembly and are appointed by the mayor; four magistrates members from the Greater London Magistrates Courts' Association and seven independent, with one being selected by the Home Secretary. This was welcomed by the MPS Commissioner, Sir John Stevens: 'for the first time in the Met's long history, there will be a statutory democratic accountability to Londoners for our policing policies.'

7 Section 4(4) and Sch. 2, para. 2. See the amendments made by the Criminal Justice and Police Act 2001, s. 105, providing for a more accurate reflection of the political balance of the relevant local council.

from a short-list prepared by the Secretary of State, taken in turn from a list of nominations made by specially constituted local selection panels.[8] Three are local magistrates appointed by selection panels established by regulations under s. 29(2) of the Justices of the Peace Act 1997.[9] Vice-chairmen may be appointed.[9a] The chairman is appointed by the authority from among its members.[10] The government's original proposal in the 1994 Act was that the Secretary of State should appoint the independent members and chairman. This approach was dropped following strong criticism in the House of Lords; instead, there is a somewhat complex and convoluted procedure to select independent members.[11] The selection panels must have regard to the desirability of ensuring that the persons nominated 'represent the interests of a wide range of people within the community in the police area'[12] and 'include persons with skills, knowledge or experience' in such fields as may be specified in regulations made by the Secretary of State[13] (a power not as yet exercised).

Soon after the Act T. Jones and T. Newburn observed that:

'One of the most controversial aspects of the reforms concerned the appointment of new independent members to police authorities . . . even with the watered down reform, that eventually became law. There was concern in some quarters that the arrival of the new, independent members would dilute the powers of the local police authority. There appears to be little evidence that this has occurred in practice.'[14]

They concluded that there was little evidence of a range of experience and expertise in independent authority members. Most are businessmen.[15] Despite the attempts to provide true representation of the community, recent statistics show that only 6.6% of all police authority members and 15.7% of independent members are from minority ethnic groups.[16] More recent research by T. Jones and T. Newburn examined the claims that the independent members are party political, but concluded that the 'introduction of independent members had led to . . . a dilution of party politics.'[16a]

The police authorities as managers

It is now to be the duty of every police authority 'to secure the maintenance of an efficient and effective [rather than "adequate and efficient"] police force for its area'.[17] In discharging its functions, the authority must have regard to any:

 8 Police Act 1996, s. 4(4), Sch. 2, para. 5, Sch. 3; Police Authority (Selection Panels) Regulations 1994 (S.I. 1994 No. 2023).
 9 Police Act 1996, Sch. 2, para. 8(2).
9a See Criminal Justice and Police Act 2001, s. 104.
10 Police Act 1996, s. 4(4), Sch. 2, para. 9(1), (2).
11 See Police Act 1996, Sch. 3, and the Police Authorities (Selection Panel) Regulations 1994, S.I. 1994 No. 2023, given effect by the Police Act 1996, s. 103(2), Sch. 8, Pt. I, para. 1(2). See T. Newburn and T. Jones, 'The Police and the New Magistracy: Independent Members and the New Police Authorities' (1999) Liverpool LR 241.
12 The Macpherson Report (Stephen Lawrence Inquiry Report (1999), Cmnd. 4262) recommended that 'the Home Secretary and Police Authorities should seek to ensure that the membership of police authorities reflects so far as possible the cultural and ethnic mix of the communities which those authorities serve'. (Recommendation No. 7).
13 Police Act 1996, Sch 3, para. 10.
14 *Policing After the Act* (1997), p. 204.
15 Ibid., Chap.4.
16 See Home Secretary's *First Annual Response to the Macpherson Report* (2000).
16a Op. cit., p 258, n. 50. On a challenge to the party politics of police authorities by an independent councillor, see *R (on the application of East Riding) v Joint Committee for the purposes of making appointments to the Humberside Police Authority* [2001] BLGR 292.
17 Police Act 1996, s. 6(1).

(a) *objectives for the policing of the areas of all police authorities* determined by the Secretary of State under Police Act 1996, s. 37.[18] These are currently:

'(1) to deal speedily and effectively with young offenders and to work with other agencies to reduce offending and re-offending by young people;
(2) to identify and reduce local problems of crime and disorder in partnership with local authorities, other local agencies and the public;
(3) to target and reduce drug-related crime in partnership with other local agencies, in particular local drug action teams or local drug and alcohol action teams and having regard to government strategy; and
(4) to increase trust and confidence in policing amongst minority ethnic communities.'[19]

(b) *local policing objectives* determined annually by the authority itself after consulting the Chief Constable and considering any views obtained in accordance with arrangements under the Police Act 1996, s. 96. (If these relate to the Secretary of State's objectives they must be consistent.[20]);

(c) *performance targets* determined by the authority; and

(d) *local policing plans* issued annually by the authority, setting out the proposed arrangements for the policing of the area during the year.[1]

NOTES

1. The local policing plan must include a statement of the authority's priorities for the year, of the financial resources expected to be available and the proposed allocation of those resources. It must also give details of the four matters listed above. A draft is prepared initially by the Chief Constable and submitted to the authority. All the accounts of the police authority are subject to audit in accordance with the Audit Commission Act 1998, s. 2.[2]

2. Where the Secretary of State has determined an objective under s. 37, he may direct police authorities to establish performance targets to be aimed at seeking to achieve the objective.[3] He may also issue codes of practice and give directions to police authorities after an adverse report by an Inspector of Constabulary under s. 39 of the 1996 Act. Police authorities must publish annual reports;[4] and must send a copy of the report to the Secretary of State.[5] In view of this, to what extent is the police authority independent of central government? Is there any point in local authorities if national objectives are prescribed?

3. Under s. 111(1), a police authority is authorised to use its finances to support its general function under s. 6. The courts have acknowledged that the police authority has considerable discretion to incur expenditure on items – e.g. by funding a police officer's defence in a private prosecution: *R v DPP, ex p Duckenfield*[6] (although this may be limited to defending senior officers only – see *R v South Yorkshire Police Authority, ex p Booth*[7]).

18 See the Police (Secretary of State's Objectives) (No 2) Order 1999, S.I. 1999 No. 1415.
19 S.I. 1999 No. 1415, Art 3. See also the Home Office, *Ministerial Priorities, Key Performance Indicators and Efficiency Planning for 1999-2000* (1999).
20 Police Act 1996, s. 7.
 1 Police Act 1996, s. 8.
 2 The Audit Commission encouraged implementation of performance targets in its papers: *Helping with Enquiries* (1993) and *Streetwise* (1996). Further Audit Commission material is available at www.audit-commission.gov.uk/.
 3 Police Act 1996, s. 38.
 4 Police Act 1996, s. 9(1).
 5 Police Act 1996, s. 9(3).
 6 [2000] 1 WLR 5, DC. The private prosecution followed the negligence of the South Yorkshire Police leading to the 96 deaths at the Hillsborough football stadium disaster.
 7 (2000) Times, 10 October, DC. See now H. O. Circular 43/2001.

(B) THE CHIEF CONSTABLE[8]

Section 10(1) of the Police Act 1996 provides that:

> 'a police force maintained under section 2 ... shall be under the direction and control of the Chief Constable. ...'

In discharging his functions, every Chief Constable shall have regard to the local policing plan.[9] The Chief Constable must submit an annual report on policing in that area to the police authority for which his force is maintained.[10] The Chief Constable is appointed by the police authority, but subject to the approval of the Secretary of State and such regulations as may be made under Police Act 1996, s. 50. The authority, also with the approval of the Secretary of State, may call upon the Chief Constable to retire 'in the interests of efficiency or effectiveness'.[11] Civilian employees of the authority are normally under the direction and control of the Chief Constable.[12]

The Criminal Justice and Police Act 2001 now requires every police force to appoint a Deputy Chief Constable, and provides for the appropriate powers for the deputy to exercise functions of the Chief Constable.[13]

T. Jones and T. Newburn suggest that the operational independence of the Chief Constable, which was threatened by the local authorities in the 1980s, has now come to be threatened by central government.[14] Given the policing objectives specified above, is it realistic to expect Chief Constables to have significantly different approaches to policing? To what extent can an individual Chief Constable's approach to policing still make a difference to the way his force operates? (Consider, for example, the policy of zero-tolerance[15] policing in Cleveland,[16] or the policing of Greater Manchester[17] under James Anderton.) Does diversity diminish accountability?

(C) THE SECRETARY OF STATE

In addition to the numerous powers already mentioned, the Secretary of State has power to: alter police areas;[18] determine the annual aggregate of grants and the amount of the grant to be made to each authority;[19] make regulations for police forces;[20] appoint inspectors of constabulary;[1] provide and maintain or contribute to the provision or maintenance of common organisations, facilities or services

---

8 See D. Wall, *The Chief Constables in England and Wales* (1998); R. Reiner, *The Chief Constable* (1991).
9 Police Act 1996, s. 10(2).
10 Police Act 1996, s. 22(1).
11 Police Act 1996, s. 11(2). See the resignation in 1998 of Ian Oliver, the Chief Constable of Grampian, after criticism of the force for its conduct of a murder investigation. See recently the resignation of P. Whitehouse from Sussex Police, June 2001.
12 Police Act 1996, s. 15(2).
13 Police Act 1996, ss. 123 and 124.
14 *Policing After the Act* (above), p. 6.
15 On zero-tolerance schemes, see A. Grady, (1998) 148 NLJ 1528; M. Innes, (1999) 38(4) Howard Journal 397; W. J. Bratton et al., *Zero-Tolerance: Policing a Free Society* (1998). See generally, G. Kelling and C. Coles, *Fixing Broken Windows* (1997). See also the comments against zero-tolerance made by Sir Paul Condon (1998) 148 NLJ 526.
16 See www.cleveland.police.uk/.
17 See www.gmp.police.uk/.
18 Police Act 1996, s. 31(1).
19 Police Act 1996, ss. 46, 47, 48. Annual funding figures for police forces are available from the Home Office. See www.homeoffice.gov.uk/ppd/pru/pgranta.htm/.
20 Police Act 1996, s. 50. See also Police Regulations 1995, S.I. 1995 No. 215, amended by S.I. 1995 No. 545 and S.I. 1995 No. 2020, S.I. 1996 No. 699, S.I. 1998 No. 493.
1 Police Act 1996, s. 54.

(e.g. training and hardware).[2] In addition, the Secretary of State may require a local inquiry to be held by any person appointed by him into any matter connected with policing in that area.[3]

The Secretary of State's position in the tripartite arrangements has, over the years, become increasingly significant, and, notwithstanding the efforts of the House of Lords, was further strengthened by the 1994 Act. Apart from formal legal powers, significant influence is maintained through Home Office circulars and arrangements for inspection by HM Inspectors of Constabulary,[4] and indirectly by its influence with the Association of Chief Police Officers (ACPO).[5] The Local Government Act 1999 gives the Secretary of State additional powers to order inspection of a police authority regarding its 'Best Value' – i.e. its efficient supply of services. This further control is another example of managerialism in policing control which has become a common theme. Is the *financial* accountability of the police a primary concern?

Despite the Home Secretary's very wide and diverse powers, it is nevertheless important to note that the Secretary of State (like police authorities) has only limited powers to give directions, and these do not extend to *operational* matters.[6]

(D) CONSTABULARY INDEPENDENCE

Despite the increasing statutory obligations of consultation and greater direction in broader areas from central government, much is still made of the so-called doctrine of 'constabulary independence' articulated most forcefully by Lord Denning MR in *R v Metropolitan Police Comr, ex p Blackburn*:[7]

'I have no hesitation in holding that, like every constable in the land, he should be, and is, independent of the executive. He is not subject to the orders of the Secretary of State, save that under the Police Act 1964, the Secretary of State can call upon him to give a report, or to retire in the interests of efficiency. I hold it to be the duty of the Commissioner of Police of the Metropolis, as it is of every Chief Constable, to enforce the law of the land. He must take steps so to post his men that crimes may be detected; and that honest citizens may go about their affairs in peace. He must decide whether or not suspected persons are to be prosecuted: and if need be, bring the prosecution or see that it is brought. But in all these things he is not the servant of anyone, save of the law itself. No Minister of the Crown can tell him that he must, or must not, keep observation on this place or that; or that he must, or must not, prosecute this man or that one. Nor can any police authority tell him so. The responsibility for law enforcement lies on him. He is answerable to the law and to the law alone. That appears sufficiently from *Fisher v Oldham Corporation* [1930] 2 KB 364, and *Attorney-General for New South Wales v Perpetual Trustee* Co Ltd [1955] AC 457, PC.'

Lustgarten[8] commented that 'seldom have so many errors of law and logic been compressed into one paragraph'. Among these are the points that the Commissioner of Police of the Metropolis was not a constable, was not subject to the Police Act 1964 powers and has been given orders by the Secretary of State.[9] Moreover, the

2 Police Act 1996, s. 57.
3 Police Act 1996, s. 49. See e.g. the *Stephen Lawrence Inquiry Report* (1999) (Cmnd 4262). Such inquiries are subject to the Tribunals and Inquiries Act 1992, ss. 1 and 9.
4 See www.homeoffice.gov.uk/hmic/hmic.htm/.
5 See www.acpo.police.uk/.
6 See below, p 95.
7 [1968] 2 QB 118 at 135–136.
8 *The Governance of Police* (1986), pp. 64–67.
9 See now Police Act 1996, s. 50 and the Greater London Authority Act 1999, ss. 315, 317–320. All Commissioners are now police officers.

cases cited merely stood for the proposition (in effect bypassed by s. 48 of the Police Act 1964) that there is no master and servant relationship between a police officer and the police authority.[10] Nevertheless:

> 'the reality is that *Blackburn No.1* has over nearly two decades embedded itself in the lore and learning of both judges and police, and it is inconceivable that, without parliamentary intervention, the courts would resile from the position they have reached.'[11]

To what extent do the amendments effected by the 1994 Act, as consolidated in the 1996 Act, impinge on constabulary independence? Note that it is a perfectly respectable principle of administrative law that, where a discretion is conferred on a particular official or body, he or it may not act under the dictation of a third party and may not fetter the exercise of that discretion by self-created rules of policy.[12] This applies as much to insulate police constables in the exercise of their powers 'from dictation by superiors as it does to insulate Chief Constables from dictation by the executive'. Is this the true essence of constabulary independence?[13] In *ex p Blackburn*, Lord Denning MR indicated that, in extreme cases, such as a directive from a Chief Constable 'that no person should be prosecuted for stealing any goods less than £100 in value', the courts might interfere.[14] In the case itself, the Commissioner's decision not to enforce certain gaming laws had already been rescinded, and no order of mandamus (an order compelling action from the Commissioner) was granted. In subsequent cases, the courts have declined to intervene.[15] Decisions to prosecute may be subject to judicial review under the *Wednesbury* doctrine, but the courts are similarly reluctant to interfere.[16]

(E) A NATIONAL POLICE FORCE?

The 1996 Act maintains the structure of individual locally based police forces, although there is provision for co-operation between forces.[17] Dr. A. L. Goodhart argued the case for a national force in a memorandum of dissent to the Royal Commission on the Police.[18] The majority of that Commission, while rejecting the argument that a national force would be a step towards a police state,[19] recommended a more limited programme of amalgamations and greater central control, preserving the partnership between local and central government. Reiner[20] identifies a whole series of factors in a 'trajectory of centralisation', including the *Northumbria* case concerning the equipping of the force;[1] stringent central controls over police manpower; the enhanced role of HM Inspectors 'as the linchpin of a more centralised co-ordination of standards and procedures'; the higher profile of the Association of

---

10 In *White v Chief Constable of South Yorkshire* [1999] 1 All ER 1, HL it was accepted that police officers are not servants of the Chief Constable (see Lord Steyn at 36). The tortious liability is discussed below; note that the Chief Constable is liable for the torts of his officers: Police Act 1996, s. 88.

11 Lustgarten, op. cit., p. 67.

12 See generally, Sir William Wade and C. Forsyth, *Administrative Law* (8th edn, 1999).

13 Cf. Lustgarten, op. cit., pp. 13–15.

14 Ibid. p.136.

15 *R v Metropolitan Police Comr, ex p Blackburn (No 3)* [1973] QB 241; *R v Chief Constable of Devon and Cornwall, ex p CEGB* [1982] QB 458.

16 See below, p. 119.

17 See Police Act 1996, s. 23.

18 Cmnd. 1728 (1962), and see B. Greenway, 'National Force' (1996) *Police Review*, 30 August, p. 16.

19 Ibid. pp. 45–46.

20 *The Politics of the Police* (2nd edn, 1992), pp. 236–249.

1 *R v Secretary of State for the Home Department, ex p Northumbria Police Authority* [1989] QB 26: Secretary of State entitled to supply CS gas and plastic baton rounds without Police Authority approval even if no emergency.

Chief Police Officers; the proliferation of specialist national policing units; and the informal development of a cadre of potential chief officers, given the Home Office's power to approve the shortlist of candidates interviewed by police authorities and to veto the authority's selection (a power exercised in 1990 in the case of Derbyshire).[2] Overall, while the 1962 Royal Commission rejected a *de jure* national police force it concluded:

'we have ended up with the substance of one, but without the structure of accountability for it which the explicit proposals embodied. ... The myth of a tripartite structure of governance for essentially local policing, with constabulary independence for operational decisions, is useful for legitimating a system of de facto national control.'[3]

This claim is even more valid in light of the establishment of a National Criminal Intelligence Service (NCIS), a National Crime Squad (NCS), a Central Police Training and Development Authority, and the deployment of MI5 in mainstream policing in England.

(i) National Criminal Intelligence Service and National Crime Squad

The Police Act 1997 established the National Crime Squad, and puts the National Criminal Intelligence Service (NCIS) (which had been a Home Office body since 1991) on a statutory footing,[4] created the relevant service authorities, similar to police authorities, to maintain them. The 1997 Act followed government proposals put forward in *Protecting the Public*.[5] The precise structure of the service authorities has been amended by the Criminal Justice and Police Act 2001 to reduce the number of members drawn from regional police authorities but to broaden the range of those eligible for membership.[6]

The functions of NCIS are specified in s. 2(2) of the 1997 Act:

'(1) to gather, store and analyse information in order to provide criminal intelligence; (2) to provide criminal intelligence to police forces; and (3) to act in support of those bodies in carrying out their criminal intelligence activities.'

In carrying out these functions NCIS must have regard to:

'(a) any objectives determined by the Secretary of State; (b) any objectives it determines; (c) any performance targets it establishes; and (d) any service plans it issues.'[7]

It plays an important role as the interface between UK police forces and Interpol[8] and Europol.[9]

The Secretary of State determines the objectives of NCIS after consultation with relevant bodies.[10] These are currently:

2 See R. Reiner, *The Chief Constables* (1991), p. 35.
3 R. Reiner, *The Politics of the Police* (2000), p. 249. See also B. Loveday, 'Reforming the police: from local service to state police?' (1995) PQ 141.
4 For detailed accounts of the 1997 Act, see S. Uglow with V. Telford, *The Police Act 1997* (1997); B. Emmerson, *Guide to the Police Act 1997* (1997). For further information on the working of NCIS, see the website www.ncis.co.uk and for the NCS see www.nationalcrimesquad.police.uk.
5 Cmnd. 3190, (1996) Chap. 3.
6 See ss. 108, 109.
7 Police Act 1997, s. 2(4).
8 The significance of international policing is well recognised: see M. Fooner, *Interpol: Issues in World Crime and International Criminal Justice* (1989); M. Anderson, *Policing the World: Interpol and the politics of international police co-operation* (1989); W. McDonald, *Crime and Law Enforcement in the Global Village*(1997); M. Anderson, *Policing the EU: Theory, Law and Practice* (1995).
9 See A. Brown, (1998) 148 NLJ 1404.
10 Police Act 1997, s. 26(2).

'(1) to provide high quality and relevant criminal intelligence leading to (a) the dismantling or disruption of criminal enterprises engaged in serious and organised crime; and (b) the arrest and prosecution of criminals whose activities take place in or impact on the UK; (2) to provide high quality and relevant criminal intelligence and information to law enforcement agencies, having regard to government strategy and in order to suppress the availability of controlled drugs in the UK.'[11]

The functions of the National Crime Squad (NCS) are 'to prevent and detect serious crime which is of relevance to more than one police area'.[12] The Secretary of State determines the objectives of the NCS after consultation with appropriate bodies.[13] These are currently:

'(1) to improve, in partnership, where appropriate, with other law enforcement agencies, the quality of operations leading to the arrest and prosecution of individuals, or the dismantling of or disruption of criminal enterprises engaged in serious and organised crime within or which impacts on the UK; (2) having regard to government strategy and in partnership, where appropriate, with other law enforcement agencies, to suppress the availability of controlled drugs in the UK (a) by reducing the unlawful manufacture and distribution of controlled drugs within the UK; (b) by reducing the quantity of such drugs entering the UK unlawfully; and (c) by the arrest and prosecution of individuals, leading to the dismantling or disruption of criminal enterprises engaged in serious and organised crime control with drug trafficking.'[14]

NOTES

1. Since these objectives all derive from central government, are there sufficient safeguards against their being used to further political objectives? In addition to fulfilling these objectives, NCS may respond to a request for assistance from a Chief Constable or the Director General of NCIS.[15] The National Crime Squad may also institute criminal proceedings.[16]

2. The Police Act 1997 establishes service authorities for both NCIS and NCS. These service authorities perform the functions of a police authority for the respective bodies.[17] The constitution of the bodies, and complex procedures for appointment, are provided in the Act. These differ between NCS and NCIS, but both are accountable to central government.[18]

3. The service authorities have similar obligations to produce plans and reports as a police authority[19] and have a duty to obtain the views of the police authorities.[20] Initially, they had the power to issue levies to each police authority, subject to the Secretary of State calculating and administering such levies and their apportionment.[1] Controversy followed the levels of funding provided to NCIS and NCS. In 1998, £125m was earmarked for them (NCIS £30m; NCS £95m). These sums were levied from police authorities, with police forces contributing on average 1.75% of their

11 See NCIS (Secretary of State's Objectives) Order 1999, S.I. 1999 No. 822. See, on the government's particular emphasis on drugs, *Tackling Drugs to Build a Better Britain – the Government's ten-year strategy for tackling drugs misuse* (Cmnd. 3945) (1998).
12 Police Act 1997, s. 48(2).
13 Police Act 1997, s. 71(1).
14 National Crime Squad (Secretary of State's Objectives) Order 1999, S.I. 1999 No. 821.
15 Police Act 1997, s. 48(3)(a), (b).
16 Police Act 1997, s. 48(3)(c).
17 However, they are not police authorities, and thus, for example, unable to claim VAT refunds: *R v HM Treasury, ex p Service Authority for NCS* (2000) 18 July.
18 Police Act 1997, s.1 (NCIS), s. 47 (NCS), as amended by the Criminal Justice and Police Act 2001, ss. 108 (not yet in force), 109 (in force).
19 Police Act 1997, ss. 3, 4, 5 (NCIS), ss. 49, 50, 51 (NCS).
20 Police Act 1997, s. 4 (NCIS), s. 85(1) (NCS). There are also powers for NCIS or NCS resources to be deployed by the relevant Director General to assist any police force or NCIS or NCS as appropriate: ss. 23, 69.
1 Police Act 1997, s. 17 (NCIS), s. 62 (NCS).

total budget.[2] Following the amendments introduced by the Criminal Justice and Police Act 2001, funding is by direct grant from the Secretary of State.[3]

4. The Secretary of State has other direct powers over NCIS and NCS. The powers include: the ability to require the relevant Director General to retire in the 'interests of efficiency and effectiveness';[4] to require the service authority or the Director General to submit reports on its functions;[5] to require HMIC to inspect and in the event of an adverse report to specify measures to be taken;[6] to direct the submission to him by NCIS of statistical information regarding offences, offenders, criminal proceedings and the state of crime;[7] to order an inquiry into any matter connected with NCIS or NCS;[8] to regulate equipment and services;[9] and to make regulation relating to the conduct of NCIS and NCS members.[10] The Directors General fulfil the role of Chief Constables, hold that rank, and are now appointed by the Secretary of State.[11] The Criminal Justice and Police Act 2001 gives the Home Secretary more control over NCS and NCIS. As noted, the system of funding by levies is replaced by a provision for grants made by the Secretary of State. Financial control will be with a permanent secretary of the Home Office (a Departmental Accounting Officer).[11a] The membership of the service authorities is altered to reflect this with a reduction in numbers appointed by virtue of their local police authority membership. This has given rise to concerns that all regional accountability will be lost. To what extent will NCIS and NCS become a central government police force – an English FBI?

5. Despite being launched as an 'elite squad', NCS soon ran into controversy when 52 detectives were removed from its ranks following allegations of corruption.[12] NCIS has maintained a high profile, with its focus on crimes such as Internet fraud[13] and pornography, drugs, counterfeiting etc. It also provoked controversy by investigating six city law firms believed to be involved in international money laundering.[14]

6. Part IV of the Criminal Justice and Police Act 2001 creates a new Central Police Training and Development Authority as a non-departmental public body. The Authority is to 'design, deliver and accredit' training programmes (s. 85). The Authority comprises at least 11 members, six are independent members, two represent chief police officers, two police authorities and one civilian. The Secretary of State has powers to establish a mandatory core curriculum (s. 99) to set performance targets (s. 91); to set objectives (s. 89); to require inspections by HMIC and to make relevant directions as a result of such inspections (s. 93); to appoint members of the Authority (Sch. 3); to require reports from the Authority (s. 94).

---

2 Home Office Press Release, 9 January 1998.
3 Criminal Justice and Police Act 2001, ss. 111 (NCIS); 114 (NCS). See also NCIS Service Authority (Budget Statement) Order 2001, S.I. 2001 No. 2428.
4 Police Act 1997, s. 29(1) (NCIS), s. 74(1) (NCS), as amended by the Criminal Justice and Police Act 2001, ss. 118, 121.
5 Police Act 1997, s. 32 (NCIS), s. 76 (NCS).
6 Police Act 1997, s. 30 (NCIS), s. 75 (NCS).
7 Police Act 1997, s. 33 (NCIS), s. 78 (NCS).
8 Police Act 1997, s. 34 (NCIS), s. 79 (NCS).
9 Police Act 1997, s. 35 (NCIS), s. 80 (NCS).
10 Police Act 1997, s. 37 (NCIS), s. 73 (NCS).
11 Police Act 1997, s. 6 (NCIS), s. 52 (NCS), as amended by the Criminal Justice and Police Act 2001, ss. 116, 119.
11a See Criminal Justice and Police Act 2001, ss. 111, 114.
12 *Observer*, 14 May 2000.
13 See e.g. the criticism of the three year study – Project Trawler study – in which NCIS reviewed the threat to computer networks, *Guardian*, 24 June 1999.
14 *Financial Times*, 8 December 1998.

The Authority must set annual objectives (s. 90) prepare an annual training and development plan (s. 92) and to report annually to the Secretary of State.

(ii) A de facto national force?

The trend towards establishing a national force that can be deployed by the government in response to specific crime and disorder concerns is also supported by the involvement of the security services (MI5[15]) to tackle serious crime in the UK. Although MI5 had been involved in counter-terrorist measures, the Security Services Act 1996 extends its responsibility to organised and serious crime generally.[16] Unlike the police, NCIS and NCS, the security services have no service authority, are not subject to inspections by HMIC, nor do they fall under the remit of the Police Complaints Authority. How can accountability of the security service be achieved in a policing context?

A further aspect of the centralisation of the police came in Pt III of the Police Act 1997, putting the Police Information Technology Organisation (PITO) on a statutory footing.[17] The primary function of the organisation is to deal with 'developing, procuring and managing the delivery of national information technology in support of the police'.[18] Unlike NCIS and NCS, the body has no service authority, and is run by an executive board.[19] Membership comprises three police members, three police authority members and others selected by the Home Office and the Secretaries of State for Scotland and Northern Ireland. The board has responsibilities of planning and reporting (to the Home Office). The Home Office again directs the activities of the organisation, regulates the finance – by levy from police authorities – and has power of appointment and removal of members.

There are numerous other examples of national policing initiatives, as with the establishment of an Animal Rights National Index, collating information on extreme activists. See also, for example, the National Automated Fingerprints Identification System. These systems give rise to broader concerns of privacy and potential abuse, in addition to the problems of inaccurate records being held.[20]

The government has announced its intention to review the workings of NCIS, NCS, MI5, Customs and Excise, and GCHQ.[1]

To what extent can it now be said that there is a national police force under the direct supervision of the Secretary of State? S. Uglow claims that '[t]he current

---

15 See www.mi5.gov.uk/. See also Chap. 8 below on security services.
16 s. 1 of the Security Services Act 1996 inserts into the Security Services Act 1989 a new s. 1(4), which provides that it 'shall also be the function of the service to act in support of the activities of police forces and other law enforcement agencies in the prevention and detection of serious crime'. See P. Leach, (1996) 146 NLJ 224. On the use of the Security Services in policing, see P. Duffy and M. Hunt, 'Goodbye Entick v Carrington: The Security Service Act 1996' [1997] EHRLR 11. See the revelations by Stella Rimmington regarding MI5 spying on miners during the national strike: *The Times*, 8 September 2001.
17 Police Act 1997, ss. 109, 110, Sch. 8 and PITO (Additional Bodies) Order 1998, S.I. 1998 No. 411.
18 s. Uglow, with V. Telford, *The Police Act 1997,* (1997) p.111.
19 There is a separate Home Office Science and Technology Unit that sponsors PITO. See www.pito.org.uk.
20 On crime recording and police responsibilities, see HMIC, *On the Record* (2000), a thematic inspection report on police crime recording. Error rates in crime records were found to be between 15% and 65% across the forces, with recording rates varying between 55% and 82%. See recently T. Thomas, 'Records playing out of tune – police records in disarray (2001) 151 NLJ 856. Similar concerns have been expressed regarding the European police database. See M. Colvin, 'The Schengen Information System: A Human Rights Audit' [2001] EHRLR 271.
1 *The Times*, 26 February 2000.

situation suits senior police management and the Home Office, leaving the former with operational autonomy and the latter with indirect control'.[2] How indirect is that control? Is it certain that a national force would bring clearer responsibility and accountability? It has been suggested that the debate about a national force should be conducted more thoroughly and with greater transparency. R. Morgan and T. Newburn suggest that a dual system with a national policing structure, debated and accountable to Parliament, implemented by local forces as at present, is a viable proposition and would 'better safeguard the local policing tradition' favoured in Britain.[3] Do you agree?

Ironically, as the Human Rights Act 1998 provides another level of legal control over police activity, it is likely to lead to more centralisation, with more standardisation of guidelines from the Home Office.

(F) EURO-POLICING[4]

In addition to the greater co-operation between regional forces in England and the centralisation of many policing tasks, there is the specific development of European policing initiatives:

> 'the creation of an internal market and freedom of movement, culminating in the creation of a common citizenship, has equally engendered vulnerabilities to criminality and an impetus towards policing co-operation in response to the threats. The outcome has already been institutionalised in structures such as TREVI, the Schengen agreement and EUROPOL.'[5]

The Europol objectives are:

> 'to improve the effectiveness and co-operation of the competent authorities in combating certain forms of crime – namely terrorism, drug trafficking and other serious forms of international crime – where an organised criminal structure is involved and 2 or more Member States are affected by the form of crime in question in such a way as to require a common approach owing to the scale, significance and consequences of the offences concerned. To achieve these aims the tasks of Europol are to:

- Facilitate the exchange of information between Member States
- Obtain, collate and analyse information and intelligence
- Notify the competent authorities of the member States of the information concerning them and of any connections identified between criminal offences
- Aid investigation in the Member States by forwarding all relevant information to the national units
- Maintain a computerised system of collected information.'[6]

---

2   S. Uglow, 'The Police Act 1997' [1997] 10 Arch News 6; S. Uglow with V. Telford, *The Police Act 1997* (1997).
3   *The Future of Policing,* op. cit., p. 200.
4   For further information, see www.europol.eu.int/.
5   C. Walker, [1997] CLJ 114. See further, N. Walker, 'European Integration and European Policing' in M. Anderson and M. den Boer, *Policing across National Boundaries* (1994); M. den Boer, 'Europe and the Art of International Police Cooperation' in D. O'Keefe and P. M. Twomey (eds.), *Legal Issues of the Maastricht Treaty* (1994); M. den Boer (ed.), *Schengen, Judicial cooperation and policy coordination* (1997). See further, J. Benyon et al., *Police Cooperation in Europe: An Investigation* (1993); R. Monaco, 'Europol: the culmination of the EU's International Police Cooperation Efforts' (1995) 19 Fordham Int LJ 247. See also C. S. Kurse, [2000] European Public Law 81, considering the Select Committee's review of Europol.
6   D. Chalmers and E. Szyszack, *EU Law Vol II: Towards a Euro Polity* (1998), p. 141. For comments on its objectives and organisation, see A. Brown, [1998] NLJ 1404.

NOTES

1. The Amsterdam Treaty provides for increased Europol powers moving towards a more operational body rather than an information-gathering unit.[7] The Third Pillar, 'Provisions on Police and Judicial Co-operation in Criminal Matters', has been extended by the Amsterdam Treaty to include other law enforcement agencies including the intelligence services:

'Article 29 TEU. Without prejudice to the powers of the European Community, the Union's objective shall be to provide citizens with a high level of safety within an area of freedom, security and justice by developing, common action among the member states in the fields of police and judicial cooperation in criminal matters and by preventing and combating racism and xenophobia.

That objective shall be achieved by preventing and combating crime, organised or otherwise, in particular terrorism, trafficking in persons and offences against children, illicit drug trafficking and illicit arms trafficking, corruption and fraud:

- through closer co-operation between police forces, customs authorities and other competent authorities in the member states, both directly and through the European police office (EUROPOL), in accordance with the provisions of articles 30 and 32;
- closer co-operation between judicial and other competent authorities of the member states in accordance with the provisions of article 31(a) to (d) and 32;
- approximation, where necessary, of rules on criminal matters in the member states, in accordance with the provisions of article 31(e).'

2. There is an even greater danger of less accountability from the police forces as this European influence increases.[8] The degree of supervision and scrutiny of some European policing initiatives has been questioned. For example, JUSTICE concluded that the Schengen information system database was in need of serious reform to guarantee accountability.

3. Given the widely reported British Euro-scepticism, to what extent will the British public be willing to devolve matters of policing to the EU? S. Peers argues that:

'while there is no record of any of Europol's supporters claiming, "Cross-border crime is a disease ... and Europol is the cure!" enthusiasm for Europol and other types of "European crime-fighting" is sometimes so fervent and uncritical that at least a few of them might as well have. Certainly the idea of preventing and combating cross-border crime is welcome in principle, but in every democratic society it is considered necessary to ensure proper accountability of the police and other law enforcement agencies to the legislature and judiciary. This should be no less true of European-level policing that aims to further the free movement of investigations.'[9]

'National police forces have historically represented the inner core of state sovereignty, but they can no longer be deployed purely in pursuit of national goals, with purely national decisions about operations and without any accountability to "foreign" citizens, governments or courts.'[10]

However, Peers also accepts that:

'a "Euro-FBI" prospect still looks unrealistic at present because of huge differences in national laws and a strong belief that the exercise of force by law enforcement agencies is an inherent expression of national sovereignty. However, there have been limited moves in this direction. ... Joint operations of national customs authorities are called "surveillance" operations but go

---

7 See generally, M. den Boer, 'An Area of Freedom, Security and Justice: Bogged Down by Compromise' in D. O'Keefe and P. Twomey (eds.), *The Legal Issues of the Amsterdam Treaty* (1999). EU Justice and Home Affairs ministers are set to approve a European prosecution unit – 'Eurojust'. See (2000) 10(3/4) Statewatch 28.
8 See M. den Boer, in D. O'Keefe and D. Twomey, op. cit., p. 315. On the protocol on privileges and immunities of Europol, see Cm 4733, Treaty Series (2000) No. 65.
9 S. Peers, *EU Justice and Home Affairs Law* (2000), p. 188.
10 Peers, op. cit., p. 192.

well beyond merely observing suspects as provided for in the surveillance provisions of the Schengen and Naples II Conventions. Rather, they are intended to lead directly to operational action by some authorities. For example, there were three joint operations in 1996: "Require" observed over 4,000 vessels, resulting in five seizures of cannabis and cigarettes; "Operation 96a" checked transit passengers from the Caribbean and South America in thirty-three airports in fourteen Member States over two days, resulting in large seizures in two airports and two controlled deliveries; and "Mercury 96" checked "correspondence and parcels sent by mail from problem areas" with the goal of prosecuting the eventual recipients.'[11]

4. Further amendments to the Europol powers are currently under consideration.[12] Note that under para. 5 of Art. 35, the European Court of Justice shall not:

'review the validity or proportionality of operations carried out by the police or other law enforcement services of a member state or the exercise of the responsibilities incumbent upon member states with regard to the maintenance of law and order and the safeguarding of internal security.'[13]

The ECJ's inability to deal with individuals affected by the actions of Europol has been called an 'insult to democracy'.[14]

4   Police accountability through auditing and local partnerships?

(A) TOWARDS 'MANAGERIAL' AND 'CONSUMERIST' POLICING

As part of its policy to 'get tough on crime and tough on the causes of crime', the Labour Government sought to enhance local authority involvement in policing strategies:[15]

'At the heart of the strategy are the new steps we will be taking to ensure that every local Crime & Disorder reduction partnership (of which there are 375 in England and Wales) and police force is performing to their maximum potential. This will involve both establishing clear arrangements for performance monitoring and providing effective support. One of the key aspects are the targets that the police and local authorities (through the Crime & Disorder reduction partnerships) will set themselves to reduce vehicle crime, domestic burglary and robberies. This together with the publication of crime statistics at the level of individual police divisions and by reference to partnership areas, will enable constructive debate about the performance of the key local services in reducing crime and disorder and help drive up their performance.

The drive for better performance goes hand in hand with support for the work of the partnerships and new resources, tools and technology for the police, and to this end we are providing: an extensive programme of research, training and seminars for the partnerships; establishing regional Crime Reduction Directors to provide a source of practical support for the partnerships at local level; a new national Crime Reduction Task Force to provide a focus for the work of the partnerships at national level; a new Crime Fighting Fund, part of which will be used to recruit, train and pay 5,000 police officers over and above the number that forces would otherwise have recruited, a huge injection of money to expand the DNA database, and an investment in a new national communications system.'[16]

The Crime and Disorder Act 1998 places each local authority under a specific duty to: 'exercise its various functions with due regard to the likely effect of the exercise

---

11 Ibid., p. 203.
12 See European Commission (555/01) 21 February 2001, Official Publication, and (5134/01) 6 February 2001, Official Publication.
13 M. den Boer, op. cit., p. 318.
14 D. Curtin and I. Dekker, 'The EU as a layered international organisation' in P. Craig and G. de Burca (eds), *The Evolution of EU Law* (1999), p. 129, referring to C. A. Groendijk and E. Guild, *A New Immigration Law for Europe* (1993), p. 193.
15 See most recently, *Criminal Justice: The Way Ahead* (Cm 5074) (2001).
16 *The Government's Crime Reduction Strategy: Raising the performance of the police and the Crime & Disorder reduction partnerships* (2000).

of those functions on, and the need to do all that it can to prevent, crime and disorder in its area.'[17]

NOTES

1. Furthermore, ss. 5 and 6 require local authorities and Chief Constables to co-operate in formulating and implementing a strategy for the reduction of crime and disorder in the area.[18] This complements the established duty of the police authorities to consult with the local community on policing issues[19] and to consult with the local communities on local crime and disorder strategies in co-operation with the Chief Constables and the local authorities.[20] This represents a further clear step towards imposing managerialism in policing with requirements for inter-agency co-operation, performance indicators, planning and monitoring.

2. Local authorities might be only too willing to support police initiatives, for example in providing more CCTV in town centres, and the partnerships encouraged by the Crime and Disorder Act provide an opportunity to further such ventures, but can the local agencies be trusted to have regard to the wider civil liberties implications of their actions?[21] Should the police be guided by populist pressures?

Some commentators have seen the moves as a de-politicisation of the police:

'The most striking factor in British police governance during the last decade has been the extent to which the formal apparatuses of local police accountability have been denuded of political content. For "political accountability" now read "balanced budgets", "financial propriety", "quality of service", "customer satisfaction" and "consumer sovereignty".'[1]

Others see this as a new form of accountability:

'Until now, the police were politically accountable to the [state] but operationally accountable to individuals. Community policing challenges again the customary distribution of authority over the coercive power of the state. If communities can define police work, a new centre of political power has been established. Community policing represents a regeneration of the social contract between the police and society.'[2]

3. To what extent will government (whether local or central) be better able to control police actions, even at an operational level, by the pressures of economics? One danger is that there is far less transparency in this method of controlling the police than by explicit direction or police objectives. Furthermore, the accountability of the police lies in terms of economic efficiency, rather than for its success in protecting rights and preventing crime. This is a difference of principle.

The service provider/consumer attitude to policing reflects the charterist move in other areas of the criminal justice system – see, for example, the *Victim's Charter*

---

17 See s. 17. On this, see further HORDS Briefing Note 11/00, K. Bullock, K. Moss and J Smith, 'Anticipating the Impact of Section 17 of the CDA' (2000); HORDS Briefing Note 9/00, A. Deehan, and E. Saville, 'Crime and Disorder Partnerships' (2000). See, more generally, A. Crawford, *The Local Governance of Crime: Appeals to Community and Partnerships* (1997).
18 These provisions are based on the recommendations in the Home Office Standing Committee Conference on Crime Prevention, *Safer Communities: The Local Delivery of Crime Prevention through the Partnership Approach* (1991) and the Home Office Consultation Paper, *Getting to grips with Crime: A New Framework for Local Intervention* (1997). See also HORDS Briefing Note 10/00, R. Hester, 'Crime and Disorder Partnerships' (2000).
19 Police Act 1996, ss. 7, 96.
20 Crime and Disorder Act 1998, ss. 5, 6.
21 See the willingness of local authorities to seek injunctions to prevent drug dealers within their locality: *Nottingham City Council v Z* [2001] EWCA 1248.
1 L. Johnson, *Policing Britain: Risk Security and Governance* (2000), p. 32.
2 D. Bayely, *Police for the Future* (1994), p. 120.

(1996), providing minimum standards of service to be expected by victims of crime.[3]
Such schemes are not without their critics: B. Williams argues that:

'citizens – and victims of crime – are more than merely consumers. To discuss citizenship
only in terms of consumer rights is to neglect important dimensions of the issue. . . . A narrow,
consumerist definition of citizenship creates a situation in which citizens are provided only
with limited information about the choices available to them , while government-promoted
charters employ a misleading rhetoric of choice and empowerment.'[4]

4. The 1998 Act aims to increase the involvement of ordinary people in policing
crime by making authorities 'take due account of the knowledge and experience of
persons on the area, and obtain their views on the report produced'.[5] The emphasis is
on policing to the demands of the residents. If this is to mean *all* residents, then, as
N. Hough and N. Tilley observe:

'Special arrangements may be needed in relation to hard to reach groups, such as the homeless
and members of the gay and lesbian community, where it may be useful to conduct or
commission focus groups. Focus groups may also be useful for tapping victims' views.'[6]

The Macpherson Report recommended that:

'in creating strategies under the provisions of the Crime and Disorder Act or otherwise Police
Services, local Government and relevant agencies should specifically consider implementing
community and local initiatives aimed at promoting cultural diversity and addressing racism
and the need for focused, consistent support for such initiatives. (Recommendation No 70).[7]

Is there a general awareness in England and Wales of the obligation to be consulted
regarding policing matters?
5. Although the Crime and Disorder Act results in greater involvement of local
authorities in policing, their role is largely as consultees. The explicit tripartite power
structure of the Home Office, the police authorities and the Chief Constables remains.
The Secretary of State may order that any relevant bodies be invited to participate in
formulating or implementing strategies,[8] and the statutory provisions are
supplemented by the Home Office guidelines: *Guidance on Statutory Crime and
Disorder Partnerships* (1998).
    The 1998 Act continues the process of formalising the police-community
consultative process. This is one aspect of a broader managerial shift to include a
rolling programme of consultation, auditing, setting and tackling of targets and
monitoring. R. Bradley[9] suggests that:

'police are more likely to influence the public's view of, and demand for, policing if the police
have a strong working relationship with the public. The research found, however, that while
the police already had good working relationships with some social groups, others, particularly
young people and ethnic minorities, believed that the police failed to address the concerns and
threats its members perceive. If the police service is to be in a position to influence the views
and expectations of these disaffected groups, it needs specifically to focus on their interests
and so build a working relationship with them.'

3   See B. Williams (1999) Howard JCJ 384.
4   Ibid., p. 395.
5   s. 6(2)(d).
6   N. Hough and N. Tilley, *Auditing Crime and Disorder: Guidance for Local Partnerships*
     (1998), p. 30.
7   See recently T. Jones and T. Newburn, *Widening Access: Improving Police Relations with
     Hard to Reach Groups* (2001) PRS No. 138.
8   Although the primary emphasis is on the local authority and the Chief Constables being more
     accountable to the local residents, the Home Secretary has the power to require reports from
     the responsible authorities (s. 7).
9   R. Bradley, *Public Expectations and Perceptions of Policing* (1998) PRS No. 96.

He concludes that the solution lies in 'segmented' policing with different styles for different groups. This represents a shift from 'product focus' to 'consumer focus'. In his view, it is essential that 'the police see the public as consumers with a particular mix of needs and concerns that require in-depth consideration and understanding to resolve successfully'.[10] Is this how the police see the public? Should it be?

6. Note that one important aim is to be able to influence the community's view as to what types of policing should be conducted. In March 2000[11] the Home Office reported that 61% of people thought the police were doing a good/excellent job. In earlier Home Office Research,[12] 81% of people thought that the police do a 'fairly good' (59%) or 'very good' (22%) job. The figures are heavily influenced by the public perception of crime rates. The Home Office claims that these are poor, with 80% of people overestimating the proportion of violent crime.[13] See also the study by R. Elliott and J. Nicholls,[14] in which the public perceptions of the police are broken down by age, gender and ethnic origin. On the public perception of crime, see generally *Digest 4*,[15] and the reports of the Home Office into the findings of the British Crime Survey 2000:[16] 78% of people in that survey said that local police do a very or fairly good job; but 20% of people could 'remember being really annoyed by a police officer's behaviour during the previous 5 years', and of these 20% made a formal complaint.[17] In 58% of recorded incidents, victims were very satisfied with the way police dealt with the matter. Levels of satisfaction were higher for women aged 60+, rural dwellers and the more affluent. Is accountability about more than satisfying the customer?

7. Recent reports have fuelled the controversy of the (in)efficiency of policing, with reports of the cost of crime at £60bn per annum.[18] A HMIC Thematic Report, *On the Record*, highlighted significant inconsistencies in the sample of reports examined. The inspection found between 55% and 82% of allegations of crime were ultimately recorded as such and that between 15% and 65% were wrongly classified. The report suggests that the recorded crime figures would increase significantly if all reported crimes were recorded and the official figure would move closer to that in the British Crime Survey.

8. A fundamental question underpinning this consumerist and community policing drive is whether the government's aim is to provide local communities with the policing policies they desire, or merely to alter the public's perception of policing policy. R. Reiner argues that:

---

10 p. 13. See also N. Bland, *Measuring Public Expectations of Policing: an evaluation of gap analysis* (1997) PRS No. 24; Morgan and Newburn, *Future of Policing*, op. cit., pp. 91–101.
11 30 March 2000, 078/2000. See the Home Office Research Study No. 200, *Attitudes to Crime and Criminal Justice: Findings from the 1998 British Crime Survey* (2000).
12 C. Mirrless-Black and T. Budd, *Policing of the Public: Findings from the 1996 British Crime Survey* Research Statistics Paper No. 6 (1997). See also T. Bucke, *Policing and the Public: Findings from the 1994 British Crime Survey* (1995). See further R. Reiner, *Policing I* (1996), Part III.
13 30 March 2000, 078/2000. Op. cit., n. 11.
14 R. Elliott and J. Nicholls, *Its Good to Talk: Lessons in Public Consultation Feedback* (1996) PRS No. 22, especially Chap. 8.
15 (1999). See also Home Office Research Findings, No. 83, *Concern about Crime: findings from the 1998 British Crime Survey* (1998); Home Office Statistical Bulletin 21/98, *1998 British Crime Survey*.
16 See also C. Mirrlees-Black, 'Confidence in the Criminal Justice System: Findings from the 2000 BCS' (2001) HORSD No. 137; L. Sims and A. Myhill, 'Policing and the Public: Findings from the 2000 BCS' (2001) HORSD No. 136. See also G. Barclay, C. Tavares and A. Siddique, *International comparisons of criminal justice statistics 1999* (2001).
17 L. Sims and A. Myhill, 'Policing and the Public: Findings from the 2000 BCS' (2001) HORSD No. 136.
18 See S. Brand and R. Price, *The Economic and Social Costs of Crime* (2000) HORS No. 217. Each homicide costs around £1.1m, with a burglary at £2,300 and a car theft at £4,700.

'In the past thirty years the process of growing acceptance of the police in Britain has been reversed. A number of changes have plunged them into acute controversy and conflict: corruption and miscarriage of justice scandals; accusations of race and sex discrimination; increasing public disorder and the militarization of police tactics; rising crime and an apparently declining police ability to deal with it; decreasing public accountability as forces have grown larger, more centralised and more reliant on technology. In recent years the leadership of police forces has recognised this problem and tried to introduce reforms to deal with it. They have sought to professionalise management standards, improve training, streamline working procedures, and become more open to the public through consultation of various kinds. They have tried to re-orient the culture of policing around an explicit mission of service and an ethos of consumerism.'[19]

R. Morgan and T. Newburn have confirmed earlier research findings that people continue to press for more visible police foot patrols:[20] 'presented with a choice, [the public] would choose problem-solving over crime fighting as the approach the police should adopt'.[1] Is the customer always right or do the police know best?

9. All customers want value of money, and, in addition to these formal procedures for receiving the views of the residents, the government has introduced mechanisms to ensure that the residents receive 'Best Value' policing. The local policing plan produced by the police authority must give details of the proposals for compliance with the 'best value' requirements of the Local Government Act 1999, Pt I.[2] The Act places a responsibility on all police authorities to ensure best value in all local policing services, i.e. that all local services are continually under review for improvement having regard to economy, efficiency and effectiveness.[3] In addition, all the accounts of the police authority are subject to audit in accordance with the Audit Commission Act 1998, s. 2, Sch. 2, para. 1(K).[4] Best Value adds to the other statutory obligations of consultation by requiring police authorities to consult with service users (local businesses, other criminal justice agencies, etc.). The courts have also acknowledged that the *efficient use* of resources is a proper matter for the police to consider when deploying its officers: *R v Chief Constable of Sussex, ex p Independent Traders Ferry Ltd.*[5] This empowers chief constables considerably.

To what extent can the assessments of efficiency provide a valid indicator of the success of the police from the perspective of civil liberties? This forms part of a much broader question about the production of policing plans. Fielding observes that:

'Because the resolution of conflict is central to the community police mission, and conflict is unpredictable, police initiated activity is hard to plan. It is therefore difficult to define a set of concrete tasks for community police.'[6]

---

19 R. Reiner, 'Policing and the Police' in M. Maguire, R. Morgan and R. Reiner (eds.), *Oxford Handbook of Criminology* (2nd edn, 1997), p. 1036 (references omitted).

20 p. 102.

1 Ibid., p. 102. See also the discussion of 'auxiliary police force patrols', pp 161–172. See also K. Lumb, 'Community Attitudes Regarding Police Responsibility for Crime Control' (1996) Pol J 319. See also J. Morton, (2000) 151 NLJ 289.

2 ss. 21–29.

3 On 'Best Value', see Home Office, *Best Value – The Police Authority Role* (1999): 'A key principle of best value is that local people should be the judge of the services they receive.' (p. 3). Section 6 of the Local Government Act requires the authority to publish an annual 'Best Value Performance Plan' covering a five-year period. The Act also empowers HMIC to inspect a police authority regarding its Best Value plan.

4 See *Best Value – The Police Authority Role* (1999); A. Leigh, G. Mundy and R. Tuffin, *Best Value Policing: Making Preparations* (1999).

5 [1998] 3 WLR 1260, HL.

6 *Community Policing* (1995), p. 45.

It is questionable whether it is possible, useful, or even appropriate to provide performance indicators for policing. 'If policing consists of a large number of diverse tasks then clearly there can be no single or overall measure of police performance'.[7] In addition, there remains the underlying question: to what extent is an economically efficient police force a 'better' police force?[8]

5 Judicial scrutiny of policing

Issues as to the *legality* (as distinct from the propriety) of police action may arise in a number of contexts. We give here some examples of the situations that are most likely to occur – actions in tort, criminal prosecutions and through judicial review. Note that breach of PACE Codes of Practice (discussed in Chapter 3) will not of itself give rise to liability in crime or tort: s. 67(10).

Bringing the police 'to book' through the courts is a very clear demonstration that they are subject to the rule of law, but are the obstacles inherent in the process of litigation too onerous for it to be an effective mechanism for securing accountability? It is important to note that few tort claims ever go to court. In 1998–99 there were 1,302 claims for assault, false imprisonment and malicious prosecution which were settled out of court.[8a]

(A) ACTIONS IN TORT[9]

A citizen may sue a police officer for trespass to the person (assault; false imprisonment[10]), trespass to goods or trespass to land, and the officer may seek to establish the defence that he had lawful authority for this action. Conversely, a police officer may wish to sue a citizen for assaulting him.[10a]

---

7   C. Horton and D. Smith, *Evaluating Police Work* (1988), p. 21. See also K. Thompson, 'Examining the proposition that police efficiency and legal and community accountability are inextricably interdependent' (1996) 69(2) Pol J 131.
8   On other aspects of economics and efficiency in policing, see J. Stockdale, C. Whitehead and P. Gresham, *Applying Economic Evaluation to Policing Activity* (1999) PRS No 103 – looking at the economic efficiency of pro-active policing, and introducing the concept of 'economic evaluation of policing'. More generally, see N. Lacey, 'Government as Manager, Citizen as Consumer' (1994) 57 MLR 534. See also the Audit Commission, *Helping with Enquiries* (1993) and C. Dunningham and C. Norris, 'The Nark's Game' (1996) 146 NLJ 402, 456. On costs of policing, see HMIC, *What Price Policing* (1998), in that year, 1997–98, £6,600m was spent on policing.
8a See *HMIC Annual Report 1998-99*.
9   See generally, W. V. H. Rogers, *Winfield and Jolowicz on Tort* (15th edn, 1998).
10 On which see N. Ley, *False Imprisonment* (2001).
10a Police officers can, obviously, bring actions against the force. See the award of £175,792 for a flying squad officer who developed tinnitus after prolonged use of an earpiece: *Dyer v Metropolitan Police Comr* (1998) Times, 27 October. One officer can sue the force for the failings of another officer that cause injury – see *Costello v Chief Constable of Northumbria Police* [1999] 1 All ER 550, CA, where an inspector failed to come to the assistance of a colleague being attacked. See also *Mullaney v Chief Constable of West Midlands* [2001] EWCA Civ 700, CA (Civ D). In *Schofield v Chief Constable of West Yorkshire* [1998] ICR 193, CA, S suffered post-traumatic stress disorder when a fellow officer fired three shots close to S without warning and for no apparent reason. In *Waters v Metropolitan Police Comr* [2000] 4 All ER 934 the House of Lords recognised the validity of a claim in negligence against the Police Commissioner where the police had failed to protect the claimant officer from victimisation and harassment of fellow officers. Police officers can also rely on the Police (Health and Safety) Act 1997, on which see R. Knowles, (1998) 162 JP 209. For comparison with payments made to those under the criminal injuries compensation scheme, see J. Morton, (2001) 151 NLJ 405. See recently *Cockram v MPC* (2001) 5 October, CA; *Rowntree v MPC* (2001) 26 October; *Robinson v Chief Constable of Northumbria* (2001) 12 October.

In its recent proposals for reform of police complaints, the Home Office commented:

'52. When civil cases against the police are lost or settled, the criminal and disciplinary issues need to be reviewed: on receipt of a notification of civil action, the appropriate authority will consider immediately the disciplinary and criminal issues and, if necessary, instigate an investigation; the appropriate authority will notify the IPCC [Independent Police Complaints Authority] of all civil cases at the outset and of the proposed action; and the IPCC will have the power to call in the case for supervision or independent investigation, according to the criteria used in complaints cases.

53. There was overwhelming support from both police and non-police bodies for the review of criminal and disciplinary issues when civil cases against the police were lost or settled. Many police forces do review such cases and sometimes investigations follow. They believe that this practice should be adopted across all forces and, if it became a statutory requirement, it would lead to greater public confidence.'[11]

(i) Recovering property

A citizen may sue to recover property in the possession of the police or may apply to a magistrates' court for its return under the Police (Property) Act 1897, as amended by the Police (Property) Act 1997. An application under the Act may be made by the claimant and the court may 'make an order for the delivery of the property to the person appearing ... to be the owner thereof, or, if the owner cannot be ascertained, make such order'.[12] Proceedings may be brought by complaint and the court may award costs: *R v Uxbridge Justices, ex p Metropolitan Police Comr.*[13] See also *Chief Constable of West Yorkshire v Singh*,[14] where it was held that the police may, if appropriate, be ordered to pay a sum of money equivalent to the value of the items (perishable consumables sold by the assumed owner). It was emphasised that magistrates ought not to accept jurisdiction where complex legal issues, such as a claim of right, are involved. Where the true owner of goods seized by the police remains unidentifiable, and the police right to retain comes to an end, the right to possession by the person from whom the police seized them is revived: *Verrechia v Metropolitan Police Comr.*[15]

In *Webb v Chief Constable of Merseyside Police*[16] the Court of Appeal held that the police were not entitled to retain moneys that they had seized from W when they were arresting him on drugs charges (of which he was later acquitted). The police power to seize the moneys was beyond question, but once the police power to hold for the purposes of the trial had terminated, W had a better claim than the police:

In the absence of any evidence that anybody else is the true owner, once the police right of retention comes to an end, the person from whom they were compulsory taken is entitled to possession.'[16a]

---

11 See *Complaints Against the Police: Framework for a New System* (2001).
12 See Police (Property) Regulations 1997, S.I. 1997 No. 1908. See also *General Accident v Chief Constable of Gloucester* (1997) CC at Gloucester, holding that there is no duty on the police to take property (a stolen caravan) into safe-keeping once it was discovered; cf. *Sutcliffe v Chief Constable of West Yorkshire* [1996] RTR 86, where a vehicle in a police yard was vandalised, but no breach of duty was found on the facts.
13 [1981] QB 829, CA.
14 (1997) 3 November, unreported.
15 (2001) 15 March, unreported.
16 [2000] 1 QB 427, CA.
16a See also *Clarke v Chief Constable of West Midlands* [2001] EWCA Civ 1169 and s. 99 of the Road Traffic Regulation Act 1984, reg. 4.

This was so even though the police had been able to establish, on the balance of probabilities, that the money was from drug dealing. There was no public policy exception of illegality allowing retention except where the material was itself illegal (e.g. drugs themselves or obscene books), in which case the police did not have to return them. The contention that the Chief Constable was entitled to retain the money until the true owner was found was said to be 'fanciful'.[17]

(ii) Malice?

There are a number of tortious actions that may be brought provided the claimant establishes malice, with the most obvious being a claim for malicious prosecution against a police officer.[18] The claimant must show that the criminal process was set in motion against him without reasonable and probable cause, that it was done maliciously (i.e. with spite or ill will against the claimant, or a motive other than bringing someone to justice), and that he suffered damage as a result.[19] Obviously, the criminal proceedings must have terminated in favour of the claimant.[20] Note that in *Abraham v Metropolitan Police Comr,*[1] A's acceptance of a formal caution did not prevent her from bringing a civil claim that denied the admissions made in that caution.[2] Similarly, being bound over to keep the peace does not prevent such a claim in malicious prosecution: *Hourihane and Hourihane v Metropolitan Police Comr.*[3] The question of whether the prosecution was without reasonable and probable cause is a matter of law to be decided by the judge considering the evidence available to the prosecutor at the time of charge: *Martin v Metropolitan Police Comr.*[3a]

The Privy Council has also recently affirmed the existence of a tort of maliciously procuring the issue of a search warrant.[4] In addition, there is the possibility of a claim of misfeasance in public office.[5] This requires proof that the claimant suffered loss as a result of unlawful administrative action. In *Gizzanio v Chief Constable of Derbyshire*[6] the court refused to recognise a tort of maliciously denying bail. Where the claimant had been held on remand but charges were subsequently dropped, the Court of Appeal held that the 'family of torts' included maliciously procuring an arrest, but that the bail decision was integral to the investigation procedure and immunity attached[7] unless there was no reasonable and probable cause for the prosecution.

---

17 See also *Malone v Metropolitan Police Comr* [1980] QB 49.
18 The scope of the tort was recently reviewed by the House of Lords, in a non-police context, and was held to be limited to criminal prosecutions not extending to civil or disciplinary proceedings: *Gregory v Portsmouth City Council* [2000] 2 WLR 306, HL.
19 On non-police witnesses who lie being sued for malicious prosecution, see *Martin v Watson* [1996] AC 74, HL.
20 As a recent example, where police were held to have had no honest suspicion for arrest during which they assaulted C, see *Smith v Chief Constable of Sussex* [1999] CLY 4852. See also the damages of £2,000 for malicious prosecution of D, not affected by his conduct on arrest: *Clark v Chief Constable of Cleveland* (1999) 7 May, CA (CivD).
 1 [2001] 1 WLR 1257, CA. The court distinguished *Saif Ali v Sydney Mitchell & Co* [1980] AC 198.
 2 See N. Parpworth, (2001) 165 JPN 138.
 3 (1994) Times, 27 December, CA.
3a (2001) 18 June.
 4 *Gibbs v Rea* [1998] AC 786, PC. See also *Reynolds v Metropolitan Police Comr* [1985] QB 881. Obviously, there can be no requirement for the search warrant proceedings to have concluded in the claimant's favour. On remedies for police searches, see R. Stone, *Entry Search and Seizure* (3rd edn, 1997) Chap.2.
 5 The police, unlike the CPS, have no general immunity from a suit of misfeasance in public office: *Bennett v Metropolitan Police Comr* (1998) 162 JPN 402. See also *Thomas v Chief Constable of Cleveland* (2001) 31 October, CA.
 6 (1998) Times, 29 April, CA (Civ D).
 7 Ibid.

An officer might also be liable for the tort of misfeasance in public office as in *Elliott v Chief Constable of Wiltshire*,[8] where an officer disclosed a person's convictions for an improper purpose and with intent to injure. See also the (discontinued) prosecution of a senior police officer for misfeasance where he used police vehicles to taxi his family to school, shops, etc.[9]

In *Kuddus v Chief Constable of Leicestershire Constabulary*[10] a police officer forged the claimant's signature on a form suggesting that the complaint of theft should be withdrawn. The House of Lords, overruling the Court of Appeal, held that exemplary damages are not necessarily unavailable in such circumstances.

There is immunity from misfeasance for acts in the preparation of evidence for a criminal trial,[11] but the House of Lords has recently restricted the scope of this immunity. In *Darker v Chief Constable of West Midlands Police*,[12] witness immunity was held not to extend to steps prior to the making of the statement of evidence where the steps were not for the purpose of making an accurate and truthful statement but for the purposes of fabricating false evidence. The police had fabricated informer evidence in an unsuccessful attempt to prosecute the claimant for drugs offences. Restricting the ambit of the earlier case of *Silcott v Metropolitan Police Comr*,[13] Lord Hutton (with whom the other Lords agreed), stated that:

'immunity should not extend to cover the wrongful fabrication of evidence or of a note which will purport to be used to refresh the memory of the witness in the witness box and which will give the impression to the jury that there is support for the witness's false statement that the suspect made an admission. This view is not in conflict with the principle that immunity (where it exists) is given to a malicious and dishonest witness as well as to an honest witness, and I think that the honest (though negligent) examination of articles to enable a statement of evidence to be made comes within the concept of the preparation of a statement of evidence, whereas the deliberate fabrication of evidence to be referred to in a statement of evidence does not come within that concept.' [14]

Such cases have an important symbolic function because of their explicit judicial recognition and condemnation of police malpractice.

(iii) Negligence

The police have always been subject to proceedings in negligence for activities they undertake other than the investigation of crime per se, as for example in failing to take reasonable care of prisoners or for negligence in driving. As in any negligence claim, the claimant would have to establish a duty of care, breach of that duty and a resultant loss to a recognised interest. The House of Lords in *Hill v Chief Constable of West Yorkshire*[15] established a 'blanket immunity' for negligence in police action regarding the job of fighting crime. In *Hill*, the plaintiff was the mother of a victim of the serial-killer Peter Sutcliffe, the 'Yorkshire Ripper'. She claimed that the police had been negligent in failing to apprehend him after his earlier killings, as a result of which her daughter, one of his later victims, was murdered. The House of Lords, heavily influenced by considerations of policy, held that police forces owe no general

8 (1996) Times, 5 December.
9 (2001) JPN 500.
10 [2001] UKHL 29.
11 *Taylor v SFO* [1998] 3 WLR 1040.
12 [2000] 3 WLR 747, HL.
13 [1996] 8 Admin LR 633, HL.
14 At 775.
15 [1989] 1 AC 53, HL.

duty of care to the general public to identify or apprehend an unknown criminal. This was applied in cases such as *Alexandrou v Oxford*[16] (no claim where police fail to attend and deal with burglar alarm).

The *Hill* immunity came under attack from the European Court of Human Rights.[17] In the bizarre case of *Osman v Ferguson*,[18] the offender had formed an obsessive attachment to a former pupil (the claimant) and had become violent towards the claimant and his family and their property. The police were alerted to this but did not detain the offender until he had shot and killed the father of the claimant. A civil claim against the police was struck out by the Court of Appeal, holding that although there was a 'very close degree of proximity amounting to a special relationship',[19] nevertheless, 'the House of Lords decision on public policy in *Hill's* case dooms this action to failure'.[20] The English Court of Appeal had treated *Hill v Chief Constable of Yorkshire* as granting blanket immunity to the police. The case was taken to the European Court of Human Rights,[1] where it was held, unanimously, that there was a denial of the right to a fair trial under Art. 6.[2] The blanket immunity was an 'unjustified restriction on an applicant's right to have a determination on the merits of his or her claim against the police in deserving cases'.

T. Weir comments that:

> 'nations should decide for themselves whether public funds should be directed to victims of past malfunction in public service or used to reduce the number of such malfunctions in the future ... In any case, to answer this question in terms of "human rights" is frankly absurd.'[3]

The decision was also heavily criticised by the then senior Law Lord, Lord Browne-Wilkinson, in his speech in *Barrett v Enfield London Borough Council*:[4]

> 'I confess that I find the decision of the Strasbourg court [in *Osman v UK*] extremely difficult to understand. Article 6(1) of the convention provides: "In the determination of his civil rights and obligations ... everyone is entitled to a fair and public hearing ..." At first sight this would seem to require that the applicant has, under the local *law*, a right (right A) enforceable in the local court. Under art 6 he is given as a separate right (right B) a right of access to the local courts to assert right A being a separate, free standing right. Thus one would assume that right A would consist of, for example, a contractual right or a tortious right not to be negligently injured. If a person is prevented from enforcing those rights that is not an infringement of right A but an infringement of right B, i.e. the right of access to the court. However, that is apparently not how the European Court of Human Rights construes art 6.'[5]

The courts have, since *Osman*, applied a test of balancing the policy grounds in individual cases, as for example in *Kinsella v Chief Constable of Nottinghamshire*,[6] where it was held that K's claim for damages for damage to property incurred in the course of a police search for terrorist offences should be struck out. This seems to represent a stricter approach then even *Hill* imposed,[7] where there was no suggestion

---

16 [1993] 4 All ER 328.
17 *Osman v United Kingdom* (1998) 29 EHRR 245.
18 [1993] 4 All ER 344, CA.
19 Per McCowan LJ at 350.
20 At 354.
1 See comments on the case: R. Bernstein 'Police Immunity Undermined' (1999) 143 SJ 10; E. Morgan, 'Police Immunity, Public Policy and Proportionality' (1999) 149 NLJ 13.
2 The court also considered, but rejected, a claim under Art. 2 – protecting the right to life.
3 [1999] 58 CLJ 4, 7.
4 [1999] 3 All ER 193. See also L. Hoyano, (1999) MLR 912.
5 Ibid., p. 198. Cf. the liability of the ambulance service (*Kent v Griffiths* [2000] WLR 1158, CA) and the fire service (*Capital and Counties plc v Hampshire County Council* [1997] QB 1004).
6 (1999) Times, 24 August.
7 On the interpretation of *Osman*, see P. Giliker, (2000) 20 LS 372, arguing for a proximity based assessment rather than one based on policy. See also C. Gearty, [2001] 64 MLR 159.

that damage to property by police negligence would ever be covered by an immunity. The most recent ruling from the European Court of Human Rights is a marked retreat from the broad statement in *Osman*: see *Z v United Kingdom*.[7a]

There are also suggestions that liability might be imposed in other diverse circumstances.[7b] Thus, the police have been held to have assumed responsibility for the psychiatric injury caused to the suspect and alleged victim of intrafamilial sex abuse that they caused to be prosecuted on unfounded allegations.[8] Furthermore, it has recently been suggested that a claim in negligence may be possible if police make an error in entering details onto the Police National Computer.[9] However, a failure of the police to keep the Police National Computer up to date, so that O was wrongly treated as a disqualified driver, did not give rise to an action for damages for distress and alarm by O: *Ogle v Chief Constable of Thames Valley Police*.[10]

The clearest examples of the imposition of a duty have arisen in the context of a duty to retain confidentiality to informants and in cases of very close proximity where a duty has been acknowledged by the police. In *Swinney v Chief Constable of Northumbria (No 2)*[11] the court found such duty satisfied where the information relating to the informant had been stolen from a locked police car. It should be noted that police also owe a duty not to disclose potentially damaging information about individuals except where this is necessary for the performance of police duties or for the duties of another public body. Thus, police should not disclose the paedophile tendencies of a person to the community: *R v Chief Constable of North Wales Police, ex p AB*.[12] In *A v Chief Constable of C*[13] the court upheld the legality of the transfer of information from one Chief Constable to another that was then divulged to a local education authority resulting in the claimant losing the prospect of employment. The failure to comply with HO Circular (9/93) was not actionable. There have been a series of interesting cases in which the police duty of confidentiality has been considered. In *Woolgar v Chief Constable of Sussex Police*[14] the court held that it was legitimate for the police to disclose confidential information which it reasonably believed to be in the public interest to disclose to a professional or regulatory body. In a later case, the court struck out an informer's claim for damages for breach of contract when the police failed to pay him full remuneration for his work. The public interest in withholding the evidence relating to specialist and confidential police operations outweighed the public interest in having the claim litigated: *Carnduff v Chief Constable of West Midlands Police*.[15]

A further example of the imposition of a duty is to safeguard against those in custody from coming to harm. In *Reeves v Metropolitan Police Comr*[16] the House of Lords held that the police owe a duty to prevent a suspect from committing suicide when they have recognised that he is a suicide risk. The police cannot claim that R's actions broke the chain of causation and absolved them of liability. This does not mean that the

---

7a [2001] 2 FLR 246; see p. 28 above.
7b And see *Cowan v Chief Constable of Avon and Somerset* (2001) Independent, 21 November, CA (Civ D).
 8 See *L v Reading Borough Council* [2001] 1 WLR 1575, CA.
 9 See Simon Brown LJ in *Hough v Chief Constable of Staffordshire* (2001) 15 February, CA (Civ D).
10 [2001] EWCA Civ 598, CA (Civ D).
11 (1999) Times, 25 May,
12 (1997) 147 NLJR 1061. Cf. *Preston v McGrath* (2000) 19 May, unreported, CA (CivD), recognising that the police were entitled, in the interests of justice, to disclose evidence of corruption to the council.
13 [2001] 1 WLR 461.
14 [1999] 3 All ER 604, CA (Civ D).
15 [2001] 1 WLR 1786. See C. Taylor, (2001) J Crim L 435.
16 [1999] 3 All ER 897, HL. See also *Kirkham v Chief Constable of Greater Manchester Police* [1990] 2 QB 283, CA.

police have to treat all prisoners as potential suicide risks: *Orange v Chief Constable of West Yorkshire Police.*[17] Similarly, the police do not owe a duty to an arrested person to take care that that person was not injured in a foreseeable attempt to escape from police custody: *Vellino v Chief Constable of Greater Manchester.*[18] See also *Leach v Chief Constable of Gloucestershire Constabulary*[19] on the duty of the police towards an appropriate adult present at interviews with a serial killer (Fred West) where that adult went on to develop psychiatric injury as a result of the failure to provide adequate counselling and support for her. See also the claim for negligence in *L v Reading London Borough Council,*[20] in which the claimant had been the victim of alleged sexual abuse but the police had concluded unsubstantiated.

Section 4 of the Race Relations Amendment Act 2000 inserts new ss. 76A and 76B into the Race Relations Act 1976 to make police authorities liable for acts done by constables, and for compensation to be paid out of police fund.

(iii) Damages

In 1998–99 claimants received nearly £4.5m in damages (excluding costs) in actions brought against the police.[21]

In recent years, many cases against the police have been reported as examples of appropriate damages awards. In *Thomas v Metropolitan Police Comr,*[22] an award of £36,401 was not perverse nor too low for a 'leading' limbo dancer who suffered injury and property damage on arrest; in *Gallagher v Merseyside Police*[23] damages of £1,000 were awarded to a 5-year-old who had been falsely imprisoned when taken to the station with his father who was arrested for smoking on a train and for non-payment of fines, the child was held for four hours before being taken to relatives; in *Burke v Metropolitan Police Comr,*[1] £20,000 general damages for the assault, £15,000 general damages for false imprisonment, and £15,000 for malicious prosecution against a 73-year-old grandmother when she was pulled to the ground and held down by three police officers when she had attempted to give her disabled husband (79) his diabetes tablets after having been arrested over a minor traffic accident; in *Barnett v Chief Constable of West Yorkshire*[2] awards to the two claimants were increased to £400 and £600 for their being held for 11¼ hours on unfounded suspicion of drug dealing (damages were low owing to the extent of the claimants' previous criminal records); a legal executive was awarded £45,000 by Essex police when she was falsely imprisoned for four hours;[3] a solicitor was awarded £30,000 by Thames Valley Police for a 14-hour false imprisonment;[4] £7,000 was paid to a 25-year-old woman injured when a door was broken down by police executing a search warrant.[5] R. Clayton and H. Tomlinson[6] list many cases of damages awards against the police; see also news

17 [2001] EWCA Civ 611, [2001] 3 WLR 736, CA.
18 [2001] EWCA Civ 1249, CA.
19 [1999] 1 WLR 1421, CA.
20 [2001] EWCA Civ 346, [2001] 1 WLR 1575, CA.
21 See *HMIC Annual Report 1998-99.* The Annual Report for 2000 is available from the Home Office website.
22 [1997] QB 813, CA.
23 (1994) Guardian, 9 November.
 1 (1992) Times, 20 March.
 2 (1998) 24 April, unreported.
 3 *The Times,* 1 March 1997.
 4 *Daily Telegraph,* 30 September 1999.
 5 *Walchester v Chief Constable of Staffordshire* (1998) 4 December, unreported.
 6 *Civil Actions against the Police* (3rd edn, 1999). See also R. Clayton and H. Tomlinson, *Police Actions* (1997).

reports[7] law reports and, for earlier examples, see the 4th edition of this work. These cases all turn on their own facts, and what is more significant is that the Court of Appeal has laid down guidelines governing directions to juries on the appropriate levels of damages to be awarded.

Thompson v Metropolitan Police Comr [1998] QB 498, Court of Appeal[8]

The case involved two co-joined appeals relating to damages awards against the Metropolitan Police Commissioner. In the case involving Mr Hsu, three officers assaulted Mr Hsu when he attempted to prevent them entering his house. His arms were twisted behind his back, he was placed in a headlock, he was punched in the face, struck across the face with a set of keys and kicked in the back (he later passed blood in his urine). He was also racially abused. His neighbours, a former lodger, and her father observed part of this conduct. He had a most uncomfortable journey to the police station, where he was placed in a cell for about one and a quarter hours. He was refused police transport home, although he had nothing on his feet. A friend took him home only to find that, in his absence, his house had been entered and, in addition to the belongings of the lodger being removed, some of his own property was missing. Mr Hsu sustained cuts, bruises, and a stiff neck. He had a predisposition to depression and was socially and culturally isolated and, three years after the incident, he was still suffering some symptoms of a post-traumatic stress disorder which would be alleviated by the disposal of this litigation. His award was reduced from £220,000 to £35,000.

Miss Thompson was lawfully arrested for a drink and driving offence to which she later pleaded guilty. 'Considerable and unnecessary' force was used to place Miss T in a cell with four or five officers involved. In the course of this, hair was pulled out and, in Miss Thompson's own words, 'it was like I was being abused physically and sexually by all of them'. As a result of this assault, in addition to the loss of hair, Miss Thompson was bruised and had pain in the back and hands. Her award of £45,000 was upheld.

Lord Woolf MR: This is the judgment of the court.

[After reviewing the circumstances in which the Court of Appeal can interfere with the jury's assessment of damages, and drawing comparisons with the Court of Appeal's preparedness to intervene in defamation awards.]

While there is no formula which is appropriate for all cases and the precise form of a summing-up is very much a matter within the discretion of the Trial Judge, it is suggested that in many cases it will be convenient to include in a summing-up on the issue of damages additional directions on the following lines. As we mention later in this judgment we think it may often be wise to take the jury's verdict on liability before they receive directions as to quantum.

...

In a straightforward case of wrongful arrest and imprisonment the starting point is likely to be about £500 for the first hour during which the plaintiff has been deprived of his or her liberty. After the first hour an additional sum is to be awarded, but that sum should be

---

7   Other recent examples of which include: a settlement of £200,000 from the West Midlands Police where the suspect had been induced to sign blank confession forms resulting in his being convicted of armed robbery and jailed for five years ((1998) 14 P& MILL 28); £55,000 settlement paid to 11 Kurdish refugees arrested when they were dressed in combat gear at a play rehearsal (*Independent*, 3 February 2000); £250,000 legal fees were paid by the police when Ian Anderson was awarded £100 for two tea bags and washing up after providing officers with tea when they unlawfully searched his home: *The Times*, 29 July 1999.

8   See G. Smith, (1997) 147 NLJ 287, 319.

on a reducing scale so as to keep the damages proportionate with those payable in personal injury cases and because the plaintiff is entitled to have a higher rate of compensation for the initial shock of being arrested. As a guideline we consider, for example, that a plaintiff who has been wrongly kept in custody for twenty-four hours should for this alone normally be regarded as entitled to an award of about £3,000. For subsequent days the daily rate will be on a progressively reducing scale. [These figures are lower than those mentioned by the Court of Appeal of Northern Ireland in *Oscar v Chief Constable of The Royal Ulster Constabulary* (1993) unreported, where a figure of about £600 per hour was thought to be appropriate for the first 12 hours. *That case, however only involved unlawful detention for two periods of 30 minutes in respect of which the Court of Appeal of Northern Ireland awarded £300 for the first period and £200 for the second period.* On the other hand, the approach is substantially more generous than that adopted by this court in the unusual case of *Cumber v Hoddinott* [(1995) 23 January (unreported) in which this court awarded £350 global damages where the jury had awarded no compensatory damages and £50 exemplary damages.]

...

Where exemplary damages are appropriate they are unlikely to be less than £5,000. Otherwise the case is probably not one which justifies an award of exemplary damages at all. In this class of action the conduct must be particularly deserving of condemnation for an award of as much as £25,000 to be justified and the figure of £50,000 should be regarded as the absolute maximum, involving directly officers of at least the rank of superintendent.

...

The figures given will of course require adjusting in the future for inflation. We appreciate that the guideline figures depart from the figures frequently awarded by juries at the present time. However they are designed to establish some relationship between the figures awarded in this area and those awarded for personal injuries. In giving guidance for aggravated damages we have attached importance to the fact that they are intended to be compensatory and not punitive although the same circumstances may justify punishment.

NOTES

1. Are the sums awarded to the claimants in this case adequate? Would higher awards deter the police from unlawful activity? In *Gerald v Metropolitan Police Comr*[9] the Court of Appeal held that the *Thompson* guidelines as to amount are not a rigid code and are not to be applied in a mechanistic manner, they do no more than provide for jury directions as to normal brackets for basic damages and maxima for aggravated and exemplary damages. See also the £50,000 out of court settlement in *Rutherford v Chief Constable of Kent*,[10] where the officers had falsified records and assaulted R. The 'Guildford Four' each received around £500,000 ex gratia payments after being wrongfully convicted of terrorist murders and serving 15 years' imprisonment.[11] Is it better to spend such sums on rectifying the wrongdoings of forces or to invest it in improving future policing?

2. A. Sanders and R. Young claim that the decision in *Thompson* is:

'a lost opportunity. The court is denying the organisation a role in preventing malpractice as a justification for limiting positive damages. In fact it should be doing the reverse, that is, ascribing to the organisation a role in preventing malpractice and backing this up by inflating punitive damages.'[12]

---

9 (1998) Times, 26 June, CA.
10 (2001) 15 May.
11 See news reports celebrating the tenth anniversary of their release, 19 September 1999, and the Prime Minister's apology: *Guardian*, 6 June 2000.
12 p. 679.

3. The Law Commission recently reviewed the law relating to awards of aggravated and exemplary damages and noted that:

'the availability of exemplary damages ... has played a significant role in buttressing civil liberties in claims for false imprisonment, assault and battery, and malicious prosecution, arising from police misconduct.'[13]

Note the decision of the House of Lords in *Kuddus* (above, p. 110).

4. Where claimants had been assaulted in the course of their attempted escape from prison, they were entitled to aggravated but not exemplary damages: *Russell v Home Office*.[14] In *Isaac v Chief Constable for West Midlands Police*[14a] the court held that there was nothing in *Thompson* that suggested that where an award of exemplary damages was made, it followed that an award of aggravated damages was also to be made.

5. In civil actions for damages, once the claimant has proved the wrong it is for the defendant to establish any justification in law.[15] However, if the defendant establishes the statutory conditions for the exercise of power which would justify the trespass, and the essence of the claimant's complaint is that there has been an *ultra vires* abuse of discretion, the onus lies on the claimant to establish the relevant facts.[16] Most of the cases in this area have issues as to whether the relevant statutory conditions have been fulfilled – commonly, whether an officer is able to satisfy the court that he has had 'reasonable cause' for his actions. A recent example is the successful appeal by the Chief Constable of West Yorkshire against the award of damages to P, who was bitten by a police dog during arrest. The Court of Appeal held that the use of a properly trained dog was not unreasonable force to effect an arrest of youths who had been smashing streetlights.[17] However, the decision of the House of Lords in *Holgate-Mohammed v Duke*[18] confirms that exercises of statutory powers by police officers are in addition subject to the principles expounded by Lord Greene MR in *Associated Provincial Picture Houses Ltd v Wednesbury Corporation*:[19]

'public authorities or officers must not exercise statutory discretions for improper purposes; they must not take legally irrelevant matters into account or fail to have regard to legally relevant matters; and an exercise of discretion must not be so unreasonable that no reasonable authority or officer could so decide.'

In the *Holgate-Mohammed* case itself, the House held that it was not an improper use of the power to detain after arrest where the officer did so because he believed that Mrs Holgate-Mohammed would be more likely to respond truthfully if she were questioned under arrest at the police station than if she were questioned at her home.[20]

6. The Police Authority is also liable to pay compensation where damage or loss occurs as a result of 'civil commotion': see the Riot (Damages) Act 1886, s. 2(1).

13 Law Commission Report No. 247, *Report on Exemplary, Aggravated and Restitutionary Damages*, (1997), para. 1.92.
14 [2001] All ER (D) 38 (Mar), CA (Civ D).
14a [2001] All ER (D) 331 (Jul), CA (Civ D).
15 *R v IRC, ex p Rossminster Ltd* [1980] 1002 at 1011, HL, per Lord Diplock.
16 *Greene v Secretary of State for Home Affairs* [1942] AC 284, HL, as explained in *R v Governor of Brixton Prison* [1969] 2 QB 222, DC. See generally Sir William Wade and C. Forsyth, *Administrative Law* (8th edn, 1999), Chap 12.
17 *Pollard v Chief Constable of West Yorkshire* [1999] PIQR 219.
18 [1984] AC 437.
19 [1948] 1 KB 223, CA.
20 See Commentary by D. J. Birch, [1984] Crim LR 419; G. Zellick, [1984] Crim LR 94 (on the Court of Appeal decision in the case).

7. Three final points need to be made in relation to tort actions against the police. First, s. 88 of the Police Act 1996 provides that a Chief Constable is vicariously liable in respect of torts committed by constables under his direction and control in the performance or purported performance of their functions.[1] This is the equivalent of an employer's liability for employees' torts, but no relationship of employer/employee, or principal and agent is created by the Act.[2] The ability to sue the Chief Constable is also important where the individual officer is not identifiable. See, for example, the claim for personal injuries sustained by a football supporter hit by a police truncheon without cause. The officer was recorded on CCTV hitting W: *Wilson v Metropolitan Police Comr.*[2a] Secondly, under s. 6 of the Constables Protection Act 1750, a police officer has a good defence to an action brought against him in respect of 'any thing done in obedience to any action brought under the hand or seal of any justice of the peace … notwithstanding any defect of jurisdiction in such justice'. The protection extends to 'any person or persons acting by his order and in his aid'. The defence is, however, only available if the limits of the warrant have been strictly observed. If this defence is available, the possible cause of action will be for malicious prosecution.[3] Thirdly, under the Human Rights Act 1998 all public authorities are required to act in compliance with the ECHR (see Chapter 1). Sections 7 and 8 of the Human Rights Act 1998 provide a right to claim damages against a public authority.[4]

(B) STATISTICS ON CIVIL ACTIONS

HMIC Annual Report 1999–2000

In 1999/2000, 12,133 civil claims were received by forces in England and Wales, of which 44% (5,375) were for malfeasance. The remaining were made up of 2,040 claims in relation to employer liability, 4,490 road traffic accidents and 228 employment tribunals. In 1999/2000 there were 540 fewer recorded civil claims than in 1998/1999. This includes a reduction in the number of complaints for malfeasance of 868. In April 1999 the Woolf Reforms introduced new Civil Justice Rules governing civil litigation. These are designed to reduce costs and delays by courts actively managing cases. Failure to comply with stringent time limits could result in cost penalties or loss of cases. We hope that the introduction of these procedures will lead to civil cases being dealt with far more effectively.

Figure 5 Civil Claims

	Claims Received (£) 1999/2000	Claims Received (£) 1998/99	Payments to Claimants (£) 1999/2000	Legal Costs to Forces (£) 1999/2000
Public Liability (Malfeasance)	5,375	6,243	6,897,876	6,601,630
Public Liability – Employer Liability	2,040	2,368	5,810,365	10,812,446
Road Traffic Accidents	4,490	3,868	3,221,605	172,448
Employment Tribunals	228	194	567,008	76,186

1 The Police Act 1997 creates similar relationships for the Directors General of NCIS and NCS regarding officers under their control. Police authorities are vicariously liable for police cadets' torts: Police Act 1996, s. 17(3).
2 *Farah v Metropolitan Police Comr* [1997] 2 WLR 824; *White v Chief Constable of South Yorkshire* [1991] 1 All ER 1.
2a (2001) 6 July.
3 See *Reynolds v Metropolitan Police Comr* [1984] 3 All ER 649.
4 See above, Chap. 1, p. 19 and Law Commission Report No. 266, *Damages under the Human Rights Act 1998* (1998).

To what extent are tort claims, which are primarily concerned with securing compensation for claimants, an effective mechanism for ensuring police accountability?

(C) CRIMINAL PROSECUTIONS

A citizen who resists police action may find himself prosecuted for assault on or obstruction of the police in the execution of their duty[5] or the common law offence of escaping from lawful custody: *R v Timmis*.[6] He may wish to establish that the police action was unlawful and that the resistance or escape was, as a consequence, lawful. Conversely, a prosecution may be brought against the police officer for assault or false imprisonment or other offences committed. In 1998–99 there were 38 successful prosecutions of police officers.[7] There is always the possibility of a private prosecution, as in *R v Duckenfield*.[8] That case resulted in an acquittal for one of the officers involved in the policing at Hillsborough Stadium in 1989 when 96 football fans died.

In many cases the police officer has been subject to internal discipline, but it has been claimed that there are too few prosecutions of those officers against whom disciplinary procedures have been brought.[9] The Butler Report, *Inquiry into Crown Prosecution Service Decision Making in Relation to Deaths in Custody and Related Matters* (1999) considered several high-profile cases in which no prosecution was brought following a death in custody. The application of the standard CPS procedure for determining whether to prosecute (asking whether there was a reasonable prospect of conviction and whether it was in the public interest to prosecute) came under close scrutiny:

'... It is almost inconceivable that the public interest test will not be satisfied in the case of a death in custody. The system employed by Central Casework to arrive at a decision as to whether or not to prosecute is "inefficient and fundamentally unsound". The vice of the system is clearly demonstrated by the cases of Mr. Lapite and Mr. O'Brien [two high profile deaths in custody] ... A decision not to prosecute, if erroneously made, can have even more undesirable consequences for the public interest than an erroneous decision to prosecute ... The advice of Counsel must be sought more often than it has in the past. ... The judicial review proceedings in the cases of Mr. Lapite and Mr. O'Brien were dealt with in an unsatisfactory manner by the CPS. But there was no dishonest or deceitful conduct. There are no guidelines in existence setting out the procedure to be followed when the CPS are made respondents to judicial reviews that raise matters of sensitivity, importance or complexity. In none of the cases ... considered, including those of Mr. Lapite and Mr. O'Brien, [was there] unfair bias. The overall standard of the review notes was adequate. This was found not to be so, however, in the case of *R v DPP, ex parte Treadaway*.'[10]

Judge Butler's recommendations included that all cases of death in custody, whether of the police or prison service, should be dealt with at CPS Central Casework, and that *every* case of a death in custody should be sent for decision as to whether or not to prosecute to the Assistant Chief Crown Prosecutor, who must consider *the whole*

---

5 Below, p. 156.
6 [1976] Crim LR 129. See further, *Archbold* (2001), para. 28-191.
7 Home Office Statistical Bulletin, *Police Complaints and Discipline 1998–99* (1999).
8 See news reports for 24 July 2000 and see *R v DPP, ex p Duckenfield* [2000] 1 WLR 55. See also P. Scratton, 'Policing with Contempt: the degrading truth and denial of justice in the aftermath of the Hillsborough disaster' (1999) 26(7) J Law and Soc 273.
9 See B. Hilliard, 'No Action is Being Taken' (1996) 146 NLJ 1092. See the discussion of the Stephen Lawrence inquiry below, in which the Metropolitan Police gave only a verbal warning for neglect of duty to the one officer who was actually disciplined: see *Independent*, 23 July 1999.
10 References omitted. See recently *R v HM Coroner for Coventry, ex p Marshall* [2001] EWHC Admin 804.

of the relevant documentation and prepare a report. If it decided not to prosecute, Senior Treasury Counsel should review that decision. If counsel advises that there should be a prosecution, the matter has to be reconsidered by the ACCP. In addition to guidelines for these procedures, there were recommendations for a compulsory training programme for CPS Central Caseworkers.[11]

It is not just in cases of deaths in custody that prosecutions are controversial; in the 20 cases of police shooting dead civilians in the last decade, only two have faced criminal prosecution. In one of the most infamous cases, in 1983, two police officers who shot Stephen Waldorf in the mistaken belief that he was a dangerous escaped prisoner, David Martin, were tried for attempted murder and wounding with intent to cause grievous bodily harm; one of the officers who pistol-whipped him after he had been shot was charged in addition with causing grievous bodily harm with intent: the officers were acquitted.[12] There have been many other cases in which calls for prosecution for outrageous police conduct were ignored. More recent examples include the Divisional Court's recommendation that the DPP reconsider prosecution in the case of *Treadaway*, who was tortured by the West Midlands Police Serious Crime Squad.[13]

There are also procedural problems with less serious charges against the police, particularly where the offence is summary only and no information is laid within the six-month time limit all of which reduces the number of prosecutions.[13a]

The most recent Home Office proposals for the reform of police complaints make the following comments on criminal proceedings:

'55. In cases investigated by the IPCC: the IPCC will be responsible for determining whether a case is submitted to the CPS for consideration and will have the power to submit it direct to the CPS.

56. It will remain a CPS responsibility to provide the proper scrutiny and challenge and to decide if criminal proceedings are brought in complaints cases investigated by either the IPCC or police forces. Location of IPCC offices.'[14]

How else could prosecutions against the police be initiated?

(D) APPLICATIONS FOR JUDICIAL REVIEW

A citizen may challenge executive action on the ground that it is *ultra vires* (and on certain other grounds) by making an 'application for judicial review' to the Administrative Court under CPR 54. A variety of remedies may be sought including an order, for example, to quash a warrant (see *R v IRC, ex p Rossminster Ltd*),[15] or a declaration (i.e. that a seizure of property is unlawful).[16] Note, however, that the House of Lords held that if there is a substantial conflict of evidence the matter is not suitable for resolution on an application for judicial review, where evidence is normally only received in affidavit form: the matter should instead be determined by a civil action for trespass. Proceedings for habeas corpus may be brought under CPR 54 to challenge the legality of personal detention.

11 See G. Smith, (1999) 149 NLJ 20; M. Burton, [2001] Crim LR 371. See also *Jordan v United Kingdom* (2001) ECtHR on the need for a proper investigation where a suspected terrorist had been shot in Northern Ireland.
12 *The Times*, 13–20 October 1983. It was reported that he subsequently received £120,000 damages plus legal expenses from the police in an out of court settlement (*The Times*, 8 March 1984).
13 *R v DPP, ex p Treadaway* (1997) Times, 31 October. See *Treadaway v Chief Constable of West Midlands Police* (1994) Independent, 23 September. See Chap. 1, p. 6.
13a See (1998) 162 JP 259.
14 (2001) op. cit., n. 188.
15 [1980] AC 952, HL.
16 Ibid.

6 Self-policing: accountability through internal monitoring of police conduct

In the last two decades police (mis)conduct has come under increasing scrutiny from the media and researchers. The RCCP and the RCCJ each commissioned research projects and the Home Office Research Unit has also issued a number of Research Studies in the area.[17] The Metropolitan Police commissioned a large-scale research project from the Policy Studies Institute, which was published in four volumes in 1983: *Police and People in London.* The report made many detailed findings and recommendations as to selection of recruits, training, management and policing methods. The Commissioner noted that:

'In places, the Report is sharply critical of the attitudes and behaviour of a worrying number of my officers, as well as of some organisational and management aspects of the force. Although there are occasional misconceptions, the notes of criticism have, for the most part, a ring of truth.'[1]

The Metropolitan Police Service suffered further damning criticism in the Macpherson Report on the investigation of the murder of Stephen Lawrence.[2] In response to some of the recommendations in that report, the Home Office has recently published a Code of Conduct for Police Officers.[3]

Police Code of Conduct

'(a) The primary duties of those who hold the office of constable are the protection of life and property, the preservation of the Queen's peace, and the prevention and detection of criminal offences. To fulfil these duties police officers are granted extraordinary powers; the public and the police service therefore have the right to expect the highest standards of conduct from them.

(b) This Code sets out the principles which guide police officers' conduct. It does not seek to restrict officers' discretion: rather, it aims to define the parameters of conduct within which that discretion should be exercised. However, it is important to note that any breach of the principles in this Code may result in action being taken by the organisation, which, in serious cases, could involve dismissal.

(c) This Code applies to the conduct of police officers in all ranks whilst on duty, or whilst off duty if the conduct is serious enough to indicate that an officer is not fit to be a police officer. It will be applied in a reasonable and objective manner. Due regard will be paid to the degree of negligence or deliberate fault and to the nature and circumstances of an officer's conduct. Where off duty conduct is in question, this will be measured against the generally accepted standards of the day.

Honesty and integrity
1. It is of paramount importance that the public has faith in the honesty and integrity of police officers. Officers should therefore be open and truthful in their dealings; avoid being improperly beholden to any person or institution; and discharge their duties with integrity.

Fairness and impartiality
2. Police officers have a particular responsibility to act with fairness and impartiality in all their dealings with the public and their colleagues.

17 See www.homeoffice.gov.uk/prgpubs.htm.
1 Report for 1983 (Cmnd. 9268), p. 44.
2 *The Stephen Lawrence Inquiry* (Cm. 4262) (1999). Available from www.official documents.co.uk/document/cm42/4262.
3 Home Office, *Guidance On Police Unsatisfactory Performance, Complaints and Misconduct Procedures* (2000).

Politeness and tolerance

3. Officers should treat members of the public and colleagues with courtesy and respect, avoiding abusive or deriding attitudes or behaviour. In particular, officers must avoid: favouritism of an individual or group; all forms of harassment, victimisation or unreasonable discrimination; and overbearing conduct to a colleague, particularly to one junior in rank or service.

Use of force and abuse of authority

4. Officers must never knowingly use more force than is reasonable, nor should they abuse their authority.

Performance of duties

5. Officers should be conscientious and diligent in the performance of their duties. Officers should attend work promptly when rostered for duty. If absent through sickness or injury, they should avoid activities likely to retard their return to duty.

Lawful orders

6. The police service is a disciplined body. Unless there is good and sufficient cause to do otherwise, officers must obey all lawful orders and abide by the provisions of Police Regulations. Officers should support their colleagues in the execution of their lawful duties, and oppose any improper behaviour, reporting it where appropriate.

Confidentiality

7. Information which comes into the possession of the police should be treated as confidential. It should not be used for personal benefit and nor should it be divulged to other parties except in the proper course of police duty. Similarly, officers should respect, as confidential, information about force policy and operations unless authorised to disclose it in the course of their duties.

Criminal offences

8. Officers must report any proceedings for a criminal offence taken against them. Conviction of a criminal offence may of itself result in further action being taken.

Property

9. Officers must exercise reasonable care to prevent loss or damage to property (excluding their own personal property but including police property).

Sobriety

10. Whilst on duty officers must be sober. Officers should not consume alcohol when on duty unless specifically authorised to do so or it becomes necessary for the proper discharge of police duty.

Appearance

11. Unless on duties which dictate otherwise, officers should always be well turned out, clean and tidy whilst on duty in uniform or in plain clothes.

General conduct

12. Whether on or off duty, police officers should not behave in a way which is likely to bring discredit upon the police service.

NOTES

1. There is no requirement to disclose membership of private/secret organisations such as the Freemasons. Should there be? The Home Office produced a Consultation Document on *Freemasonry in the Police Service.*[4] The policy objective certified in that document was to increase transparency in the police service so as to strengthen public confidence. There is a proposed registration scheme, which is extremely

4   (2000).

complex.[5] In 1999 a voluntary registration scheme achieved a very low national response rate. Should all officers be obliged to disclose any interest or membership of an organisation that might reasonably be perceived to affect their ability to perform their tasks? The APA favours a compulsory registration scheme.[6] Do police officers' rights of 'privacy' justify their withholding such information or do the public have a 'right' to know?

2. There is an expectation in the Code that officers report improper behaviour of colleagues. J. Kleinig[7] observes that 'the primary loyalty of police officers often seems to be the horizontal loyalty of peers'.[8] Will the publication of a Code of Conduct affect that? Is it ever likely to be possible to overcome the closing of ranks?

3. The shortfall in police recruitment persists. Despite the Labour government's commitment to an increase in numbers, the force has dropped in size from 127,158 to 124,418 between 1997 and 2000.[9] Is the image of the police irreparably tarnished? Consider also the significance of this in light of the public perception of crime rates.[9a]

(A) POLICE COMPLAINTS[10]

Arrangements for police discipline and the handling of complaints against the police overlap but are not coterminous. The police are subject to a code of discipline. Disciplinary proceedings may be instituted as the result of a complaint from a member of the public; more commonly, the force itself instigates them internally. Complaints may be resolved informally without recourse to disciplinary proceedings. Major reforms since 1964 first saw the establishment, by the Police Act 1976, of a Police Complaints Board with power to recommend, and in the last resort to direct, the institution of disciplinary proceedings in a particular case. The Board was replaced by the Police Complaints Authority (PCA), established by Pt IX of the Police and Criminal Evidence Act 1984. Its powers were further amended by the Police and Magistrates' Courts Act 1994. That Act also provided for changes to the police disciplinary arrangements.[11] The present system of complaints is governed by the Police Act 1996, Pt IV.[12]

A major survey of the complaints system over 1986-88 was conducted by M. Maguire and C. Corbett.[13] They reported that they were generally impressed with the commitment and abilities of both police investigators and PCA members.[14] However, apart from informally resolved cases, an overwhelming majority of complainants were dissatisfied. High proportions of both complainants and officers

---

5 See paras. 19–23.
6 See www.apa.uk/news/_views_papers/freemasonry.htm.
7 *The Ethics of Policing* (1996).
8 Ibid., p. 70.
9 See *Guardian*, 30 August 2000. See, however, B. Block, 'Do We Really Need More Police?' (2001) 165 JP 179.
9a Above, p. 105.
10 See R. Reiner, *Policing II* (1996), Part IV. On complaints in NI, see p. 569.
11 For further discussion of the system, see the fourth Report of the Home Affairs Committee, 1991–92 HC 179, *Police Complaints Procedures* and Government Reply (Cm. 1996) (1992); for comparative perspectives, see A. Goldsmith (ed.), *Complaints Against the Police: The Trend to External Review* (1991).
12 See Police Act 1996 (Commencement and Transition Provisions) Order 1999, S.I. 1999 No. 533. J. English, [2000] 101 Crim Law 6; S. Cragg, (1999) LA Dec 8–9; G. Smith, [2000] 99 Crim Law 4–6; G. Smith, (1999) 149 NLJ 1223; Home Office, *Guidance on Police Unsatisfactory Performance, Complaints and Misconduct Procedures* (2000).
13 *A Study of the Police Complaints System* (1991).
14 Ibid., pp. 193–201.

complained against felt excluded from the system, thought it too secretive and bureaucratic, thought that investigations took too long, that they were not kept informed of progress and that they received inadequate explanation of decisions. Only a minority of the population felt confident that, if they made a complaint, it would be investigated fairly. Maguire and Corbett concluded overall that the system had little effect in deterring police misconduct (given the extremely low proportion of substantiated complaints); did not satisfy complainants or inspire public confidence; and was only beginning to be used as a source of information by police managers in improving police performance. The greatest hope for convincing a wider public of the PCA's effectiveness appeared to lie in a greater use of 'intensive' or 'participant' supervision of investigations by PCA members, then adopted in a very small minority of cases given the PCA's resources. However, while the complaints system remained so closely interlinked with the disciplinary system (with the requirement at that time of proof beyond reasonable doubt), there was limited scope for making responses more akin to those provided by other 'consumer-oriented' organisations where satisfaction of the consumer was accorded high priority.

Since the Maguire and Corbett study, public attitude surveys conducted for the PCA have shown an increasing awareness of the PCA (62%) and of its role (30%). In 1993 47% of people surveyed believed the PCA to be impartial in the handling of complaints, but 30% felt that it favoured the police; 44% would trust police officers to investigate complaints while 41% would not.[15] By 1996, 40% did not trust the police to investigate themselves (37% did), and 37% thought the PCA was impartial and 39% thought it independent.[16]

To maintain public confidence in the police, it is vital that there is a mechanism for internal discipline and accountability which is respected.

(i) Functions

The PCA was set up under the Police and Criminal Evidence Act 1984 with three basic functions:

- to supervise investigations into the most serious complaints against police officers;
- to supervise investigations into serious matters voluntarily referred by the police (roughly 150 cases a year) such as: deaths in police custody; discharges of firearms against the public;[17] serious road traffic incidents involving police vehicles;
- to review all completed investigations and decide whether there is sufficient evidence to prefer misconduct proceedings or not.

(ii) Organisation

The Authority comprises a chairman (appointed by the Queen) and not fewer than eight other members appointed by the Home Secretary.[18] No member of the PCA can have served or be serving as a police officer.[19] The Home Secretary holds the power to dismiss a member from office for, *inter alia*, acting improperly in relation to his duties,[20]

---

15 *Annual Report of the PCA* (1993) 1993–94 HC 305, p. 47.
16 See PCA, *Annual Report 1995–96* (1996).
17 The police have shot dead 22 people in the last decade, some in very controversial circumstances: e.g. the shooting of Harry Stanley, who was carrying a table leg in a carrier bag, and was shot when it was mistaken for a shotgun.
18 Police Act 1996, s. 66(2) and Sch. 5, para. 1; Sch. 5 para. 3.
19 Police Act 1996, Sch. 5, para. 1(4).
20 Police Act 1996, Sch. 5, para. 3(4)(e).

or being convicted of a criminal offence.[1] The organisation is financed by central government through the Home Secretary.[2]

(iii) Recording of complaints

The 1996 Act defines a complaint as a 'complaint about the conduct of a member of a police force which is submitted—(a) by a member of the public, or (b) on behalf of a member of the public and with his written consent'.[3] Where a complaint is submitted to a police force, the appropriate authority – the Chief Constable if the complaint relates to an officer, and the police authority if it relates to the Chief Constable or assistant Chief Constables – must: first, take any steps that appear to him to be desirable for the purpose of obtaining or preserving evidence relating to the conduct complained of;[4] second, determine whether he is the appropriate authority in relation to the subject of the complaint.[5] If he concludes that he is not the appropriate authority, the complaint must be passed to the appropriate one, and the complainant (if there is one) notified.

(iv) Procedure for senior officers

Where the complaint relates to an officer of the rank of superintendent or above, the appropriate authority must, on receiving it, decide on one of three courses of action.

- '[I]f satisfied that the conduct complained of, even if proved, would not justify criminal or disciplinary proceedings, the appropriate authority may deal with the complaint according to the appropriate authority's discretion'.[6] The aim is to resolve the dispute quickly rather than seek evidence for disciplinary action. This gives enormous discretion to the Chief Constable to deal with matters within the force.
- In any other case, a member of the appropriate authority's force or of some other force (of at least the same rank) is appointed to investigate the complaint.[7]
- In some circumstances complaints *must* be referred to the PCA, or *may* be referred at the discretion of the appropriate authority.[8]

(v) Procedure for other officers – 'The Standard Procedure'

The appropriate authority must record the complaint and decide whether the complaint is suitable for 'informal resolution'.[9] Between 30–40% of cases are dealt with in this way.

- A complaint is not suitable for informal resolution unless: '(a) the member of the public concerned gives his consent, and (b) the chief officer of police is satisfied that the conduct complained of, even if proved, would not justify criminal or disciplinary proceedings.'

1   Police Act 1996, Sch. 5, para. 3(4), (77b).
2   Police Act 1996, s. 66(2), Sch. 5, paras. 12 and 13.
3   Police Act 1996, s. 65.
4   Police Act 1996, s. 67(1).
5   Police Act 1996, s. 67(2).
6   Police Act 1996, s. 68(2).
7   Police Act 1996, s. 69.
8   See below, p. 126.
9   The Police Act 1996, provides wide powers to the Secretary of State to make regulations governing the procedure for informal resolution.

- If the Chief Constable decides that informal resolution is unsuitable, he appoints a member of his own or some other force to investigate it formally. This procedure is also available where attempts have been made to resolve a complaint informally, but the Chief Constable decides that '(a) that informal resolution of the complaint is impossible, or (b) that the complaint is for any other reason not suitable for informal resolution'.[10] If an investigation occurs without PCA supervision, a report is sent to the Chief Constable and a memorandum explaining what if any disciplinary action will be taken is sent by the Chief Constable to the PCA. The PCA may recommend that disciplinary action occurs, and ultimately, may direct a Chief Constable to take such action.[11]

- As above, the appropriate authority may, in some circumstances be required to refer a complaint to the PCA, or may do so in its discretion.[12]

Should there be a different system of investigation for senior officers? If so, why?

Note that the police disciplinary procedure cannot be used against an officer once his contract with the force has expired: *Surrey Police Authority v Beckett*.[13]

Informal resolution can be seen as the police closing ranks and keeping investigations 'in house', but could also be regarded as a further indication of management ethics and practice at work, with a move towards restorative justice and conciliation:

'The restorative justice process normally involves a coming together of all those affected by an incident. A complainant and relevant family or friends might meet with the officer subject of the complaint together with relevant colleagues. All concerned would have a chance to air their views, understand how their actions have affected others and repair and move on from the damage that has been caused. We have been working on a joint project with Thames Valley Police to introduce the principles of restorative justice into the police complaints process. With its roots in local community solutions to crime and normally associated with bringing victims and offenders together, restorative justice offers a constructive and educational way of resolving complaints and an alternative to the current formal, legalistic, lengthy and punishment-based complaints process. Used appropriately, we believe that the restorative process offers a fair, open and immediate way of resolving many complaints. It can be a painful process, but the hope is that officers will, where necessary, change their attitudes and behaviour as a result of a meeting.'[14]

C. Corbett[15] claims that:

'locally-based informal resolution procedure not only better achieves the objective of satisfying the customer than withdrawal or formal investigation, but also fares relatively well in serving the other functions of complaints systems.'

Is informal resolution merely an opportunity for the police to keep things in-house and avoid public scrutiny? A complementary scheme of restorative justice has been proposed by the IPPA.[16] This has been piloted in Thames Valley and has been used by the New South Wales police.

---

10 s. 69(6). No duty of care is owed by the investigating officer to the officer under investigation: *Calvely v Chief Constable of Merseyside* [1989] AC 1228. Neither is a duty owed to the complainant: *W v Metropolitan Police Comr* (1997) Times, 21 July.
11 Police Act 1996, s. 76.
12 Police Act 1996, s. 70.
13 [2001] EWCA Civ 1253.
14 *PCA Annual Review 1999–2000* (2001), p. 19.
15 'Complaints Against the Police: The New Procedure of Informal Resolution' (1991) Policing and Society 47.
16 J. Dobry, *Restorative Justice and Police Complaints* (2001).

Should the complaints system focus on the needs of the particular complainant, or on the need to satisfy the public that police misconduct is punished? To what extent are these differing objectives?

(vi) Referrals to the PCA

By s. 70 of the Police Act 1996, a referral to the PCA must occur where the complaint alleges that conduct resulted in death,[17] or serious injury (defined as 'fracture, damage to internal organ, impairment of bodily function, a deep cut or deep laceration'[18]), and where any complaint concerns conduct 'of a description specified... by the Secretary of State' (these are currently: conduct amounting to an assault occasioning actual bodily harm;[19] offences under the Prevention of Corruption Act 1906, s. 1; or a serious arrestable offence[20]).

In addition, the appropriate authority has a discretion to refer *any* other complaint to the PCA.[1] An example, taken from the *PCA Annual Report for 1996-97*, was of the referral by a force of allegations that some of its officers had, when assisting at a road traffic incident, taken £420-worth of chocolates that had, literally, fallen off the back of a lorry and which were being transferred to another vehicle. The investigation led to eight officers being disciplined and four admonished.[2] There was a marked increase in the number of referrals of this type: 60 in 1992, and 194 in 1999, but recently figures have dropped: 144 in 1999–2000 and 125 in 2000–01.

There is also a very broad power in s. 71 to refer to the PCA cases which are not the subject of a complaint where it appears that a member of a police force 'may have committed a criminal offence or behaved in a manner which would justify disciplinary proceedings', and 'it appears to the appropriate authority that the matter ought to be referred by reason – (a) of its gravity, or (b) of exceptional circumstances'. The PCA must agree that it is desirable in the public interest that it should investigate the case.

Finally, the PCA has the power to require any case to be referred to it if it believes that to be in the public interest.[3]

Where an investigation is to be supervised by the authority, it has the power to veto appointments of investigating officers made by the appropriate authority.[4] The Secretary of State may make regulations to impose requirements on a particular investigation.[5] At the conclusion of the investigation, a report is sent to the PCA, the appropriate authority, to the subject of the investigation if practicable, and if prompted by a complaint, to the complainant.[6] On receipt of the report, the appropriate authority decides on the course of action:

---

17 See the ACPO guidelines on the use of firearms, discussed in Chap. 3 below, p. 198. Annex 6A to the ACPO *Manual of Guidance on Police Use of Firearms* (2001) explains the investigative procedures.

18 Police Act 1996, s. 65.

19 There are fewer allegations of actual bodily harm by officers because they are now equipped with CS sprays and can arrest without struggles. The introduction of CS spray in day-to-day policing has been very controversial. See *PCA Annual Report 1996–97* (1997), p. 36. The first officer to be charged with unlawful use of CS spray – against a pensioner parked on a double yellow line who became abusive – was acquitted: *The Times*, 19 June 1998.

20 See Police (Complaints) (Mandatory Referrals etc) Regulations 1985, S.I. 1985 No. 673, reg. 4(1). These have effect by virtue of Police Act 1996, s. 103(2), Sch. 8, Pt. I, para. 1(2). On the meaning of serious arrestable offence, see below, p. 201.

1 Police Act 1996, s. 70(1)(b).

2 *1995-96 Annual Report* (1996), p. 27.

3 Police Act 1996, s. 70(2).

4 Under Police Act 1996, s. 68(3) or s. 69(5), s. 72(3).

5 Police Act 1996, s. 72(4).

6 Police Act 1996, s. 73.

- If the case involves a senior officer, the case must be referred to the DPP unless satisfied that no criminal offence has been committed.[7]
- If the case involves non-senior officers, the Chief Constable refers to the DPP any cases in which a crime may have been committed.[8] If no crime has been committed, a memorandum explaining what, if any, disciplinary action will be taken is sent to the PCA.[9]
- The PCA may recommend (and ultimately direct) that disciplinary action be taken in cases involving non-senior officers.[10]

The complaints procedure may overlap with a civil action. The House of Lords has ruled, in *R v Chief Constable of the West Midlands Police, ex p Wiley*,[11] overruling a number of Court of Appeal authorities, that a class claim to public interest immunity does not attach generally to all documents coming into existence in consequence of an investigation under Pt IX of PACE (i.e. police complaints). The possibility of a class claim covering the report of the investigating officer, and of claims on a contents basis, was left open, and the first of these was subsequently recognised by the Court of Appeal in *Taylor v Anderton*.[12] The possible use by Chief Constables of such material in defending civil actions, although inhibited by the earlier Court of Appeal authorities, had deterred litigants or potential litigants from instituting complaints or co-operating with complaints investigations. The Macpherson Report recommended that investigating officers' reports should not attract public interest immunity as a class. They should be disclosed to complainants, subject only to the 'substantial harm' test for withholding disclosure.[13]

The PCA reports to the Home Secretary on any matter on which it is requested to do so, and in any event annually.

The PCA Annual Report 2000–2001

...

Workload

This year we supervised 38 investigations into road traffic incidents (RTIs) in which 31 members of the public died and 19 were seriously injured. These formed the single largest element of total referrals accepted. ...

There was a considerable and welcome reduction in the number of referrals of investigations into deaths in police care or custody, which fell by a third from 47 cases last year to 32 this year...

This year there were 946 referrals of cases requiring or inviting Authority supervised investigations, 246 (21 per cent) fewer than last year. Of these, we agreed to supervise 586 cases. ...

Openness

We have only a limited legal right to disclose information obtained during the course of an investigation. Nevertheless we believe that greater openness is essential to achieving public confidence in the complaints system. This year the Crown Prosecution Service (CPS), the Association of Chief Police Officers (ACPO) and the Coroners' Society approved our internal guidance to supervision members on disclosure during investigations of the most serious incidents. We continue to need the agreement of the police service, coroner (where a death has occurred) and CPS to give details confidentially to a complainant or bereaved family during

---

7 Police Act 1996, s. 74.
8 Police Act 1996, s. 75(3).
9 Police Act 1996, s. 75(5).
10 Police Act 1996, s. 76.
11 [1995] 1 AC 274, HL.
12 [1995] 2 All ER 420, CA.
13 Recommendation No. 10.

the course of an investigation, rather than at its conclusion. However we now have recognition of the importance of openness, and we trust that this will enable us to improve the assistance we provide to those needing information.

Supervision Project Group
A supervision project group has been formed during the year to review our arrangements for meeting statutory obligations to supervise investigations into certain categories of complaints and incidents and voluntary referrals by police forces. The group will evaluate how investigations are currently being supervised and make recommendations to improve the process by examining our internal working procedures and resources and our working relationship with the police forces, complainants and others. Work will continue this year.

Misconduct Review in Practice
Five Authority members and 20 caseworkers review formal investigations of complaints and serious incidents to ensure that all complaints are thoroughly investigated and that the conclusions and actions from the investigation are appropriate. We seek further information or work if we are not satisfied with the quality or adequacy of the investigation. Our members also raise concerns with senior police managers if the general standard of investigations is unsatisfactory or if investigating officers appear biased or prejudiced in their approach. We report annually to HM Inspectorate of Constabulary (HMIC) on the performance of complaints investigation departments.

Workload: fully investigated cases
During the year, we received 8,305 complaint cases and finalised 8,880 complaint cases, 363 fewer than last year (see Figure 3). These included misconduct reviews in 117 non-complaint cases voluntarily referred to us by police forces. This was 22 fewer than last year.

One case may contain several complaints and each must be considered separately. This year's 8,880 cases included 18,058 separate matters of complaint, an increase of 126 (one per cent) on last year's total. Approximately two thirds of our caseworker resources and half of our member resources are devoted to misconduct review. Each caseworker (civil servants at executive officer grade) considered, on average, 444 cases during the year.

Each member reviewed an average of 1,776 cases in the same period. Last year the respective totals were 462 for caseworkers and 1,849 for members.

Outcomes
We complete our misconduct review only after the CPS has considered whether to bring criminal proceedings. We reviewed and decided on the outcomes of 4,066 fully investigated cases, 279 (7 per cent) more than last year. This total, including 3,949 complaint cases and 117 voluntary referrals, does not include the large number of dispensation cases that we considered.

The 4,066 formal investigations resulted in disciplinary or other outcomes for 1,168 individual complaint allegations (see Table 2). These included 232 allegations referred to a misconduct hearing; 49 allegations attracting a formal written warning; 110 allegations resulting in an admonishment; 723 allegations leading to a verbal warning (called 'advice' in the police service); and 54 other outcomes which include guidance to staff, changes to force policy and additional training for officers. For minor misconduct due to ignorance or inexperience the most appropriate outcome may be advice or guidance to improve future performance rather than punishment. Some form of action was the result in more than one in four (28.7 per cent) cases we reviewed, on average.

Formal Proceedings Guidance
Recent analysis of 100 cases finalised since 1999, where misconduct was referred to a formal hearing, showed that we recommended or directed 19 per cent of the 211 charges and allegations preferred, rather than the police force. We introduced this year internal guidelines for staff and members on whether to recommend or direct a misconduct hearing. Modelled on the Code for Crown Prosecutors, the guidelines set out the necessary evidential and public interest tests before we can engage our statutory powers either to recommend a hearing or to direct a hearing where a recommendation is not accepted. The guidelines outline the factors for a hearing and balance them with other factors suggesting where a formal written warning would be more appropriate.

…

Learning the Lessons
In a study of 100 randomly chosen cases completed this year, 11 led to changes in force procedures. These changes included reviewing the aftercare provided to people sprayed with CS spray; identifying better training for criminal justice section staff in disclosure to the CPS; improving sensitivity in questioning members of ethnic minorities; and setting up a police service and mental health NHS Trust service level agreement concerning the treatment of mentally ill persons.

Complainants' profile
We have recorded statistics on the age and gender of complainants for seven years. We monitor how the complaints system is used to help us identify where a section of the community may not be benefiting from it. Our average complainant is still a white male, aged 25–44. Indeed, there is very little difference from last year in the gender and age of complainants.

Ethnicity
Last year, complaints from minority ethnic communities accounted for 23 per cent of the total, while 6 per cent were of unknown origin. This year, the figures are 19 per cent and 12 per cent, respectively. The biggest change has been the 3 per cent fall in the number of black complainants.

Other factors
For five years we have recorded the incidence of unemployment among complainants. In 1998–1999 nearly half of all complainants were unemployed. In 1999–2000 this fell to one third. This year, this figure is just below one third. However, this proportion is still significantly above the unemployment level for the population as a whole.

Alcohol is often associated with the circumstances giving rise to complaint. This year it featured in 1,738 cases that we considered, one in five of all cases.

Time taken
In 1992, we made a voluntary agreement with the police service, the CPS and the Home Office, laying down the target timescales for each stage of the complaints process. These are: to complete the investigation stage of supervised cases within 120 days of referral; and to undertake the misconduct review stage of all cases within 28 days of our receiving the case. Our capacity to meet the first target is limited since we do not have control over all external factors influencing the speed of investigation. The police conduct the investigations, not us. The second timescale is more achievable from within the Authority although our performance is affected by having sometimes to seek further information from the police force that conducts the investigation, or by the delays resulting from disagreement over conclusions and outcome.

Many investigations into serious allegations or incidents, particularly where a member of the public has died, must take longer than 120 days if we and the investigators are to be, and are seen to be, rigorous in our inquiries.

The number of people dying in police care or custody fell sharply again from 47 in 1999–2000 to 32 this year – the lowest number of such deaths since 1993. Of particular significance is the further fall in the number of people who died either in a cell, police station or following detention. We made 16 recommendations in our report published in 1999 to reduce the risks of cell deaths. Improved custody officer training, particularly in first aid and dealing with suicide risks, CCTV in cells, and improved procedures can significantly reduce the risks.

Cell deaths due to alcohol and drugs also fell significantly – down from 19 two years ago to seven this year. Eleven of the 32 deaths in police care or custody occurred when police were called to an incident in a public place and removed the member of the public directly to hospital. We argue that such deaths should usually be described as deaths 'following police attendance', to distinguish them from deaths in custody where the deceased person has been arrested. We understand that from April 2002, the Home Office may adopt a more meaningful definition of a death occurring in police custody, following our suggestions.

Ethnicity
In past years, the number of black and Asian people who died in custody has been disproportionate when compared with their representation in the total number of people arrested. This year's figures do not suggest any such disproportionality.

Restraint-related deaths
Special concerns arise when someone becomes seriously ill while physically restrained by the police and then, usually after a struggle, dies at the scene or some time later. Naturally, there will be suspicions that police used excessive force during the restraint or that, at least, police officers failed in their duty of care towards that person, particularly if they held him or her in an unsafe posture. Where neither post-mortem examination nor toxicological and other tests reveal any clear reason for death, it may be argued that the physical restraint either contributed to the sudden death or caused it. This year we supervised only one investigation where restraint was a relevant factor. Deaths associated with restraint have in the past included a disproportionate number of people from minority ethnic communities. This year the one death involving restraint was of a young white male. A major problem for investigators of restraint-related deaths is the lack of any consensus among pathologists about the cause of such deaths. In recent high profile cases, investigators had to seek up to five separate medical opinions to assist decision makers to determine the precise cause of death. Opinions have, however, often diverged. Some experts may suggest that 'excited delirium' caused or contributed to death while others point to 'positional' or 'postural asphyxia' as an important or single causative factor. The absence of any clear agreement among medical experts leads to suspicions that Authority-supervised investigations lack competence or integrity.

Mental illness and deaths in custody
Some recent deaths in custody exposed weaknesses in the collaboration between NHS Mental Health Trusts and police forces. We have highlighted to the Home Office and to the Metropolitan Police Commissioner the following areas of concern and we are contributing to a Home Office and Department of Health initiative to address them: the appropriate place of safety for section 136 Mental Health Act patients should be a designated hospital and not a police cell except where the individual is suspected of a serious criminal offence, such as murder, rape or a serious assault. To fulfill the requirement, NHS Trusts need the resources to staff section 136 rooms attached to accident and emergency departments; assessment for any underlying medical condition should precede a psychiatric examination of section 136 patients; NHS Trusts and police services need to agree a written protocol for the handover from police to medical staff of section 136 patients on arrival at the hospital; and NHS Trusts with responsibility for detained psychiatric patients and police services need to agree a written protocol to clarify the responsibilities of the hospital staff and police for returning to hospital detained patients who are absent without leave.

Road Traffic incidents
In last year's Annual Report we reported encouraging progress in implementing the recommendations of the ACPO (Lind) report, 1998, on pursuit driver training. In December 2000 ACPO launched its new police driver training course, introducing a universal standard for driving in England and Wales. It is an essential element of the course that officers recognise the need to give priority to public safety above all other considerations such as attending an incident or apprehending a suspect. Given this recognition that public safety is paramount, it is all the more disappointing to report that this year the number of incidents from pursuits has increased. We supervised investigations into 28 incidents and there were fatalities in 19 of them. Altogether, 25 people died and 16 were seriously injured. In 1999–2000, 22 people died. In 1998–1999 there were 17 fatalities and nine the year before. Therefore, over the past four years there has been an increase of 178 per cent in the number of deaths from road traffic incidents associated with police following a vehicle. It is important to emphasise that in most cases a police vehicle was not directly involved in a collision causing death or injury. Of the 27 people who died after being hit by, or crashing in, a non-police vehicle:
-   nine were driving the vehicle followed by the police;
-   nine were passengers in that vehicle;
-   six were pedestrians; and
-   three were in another vehicle.

Firearms Incidents Supervised investigations
During the year we began nine supervised investigations into firearms incidents. Police officers shot and killed two members of the public and seriously injured four others. Three incidents caused minor or no injury.

We were represented on the working group that revised ACPO's manual on firearms operations for forces. The revisions took effect from January 2001.

We had a particular interest in post-incident procedures and informed the debate from our wide knowledge of police firearms incidents. Practically all incidents involving the operational discharge of police firearms in England and Wales are referred to us for a supervised investigation.

Corruption

Historically, many corruption investigations have not been referred to the Authority for supervision, since there is only an obligation to do so if a complaint comes from a member of the public. The Home Office framework document for reform of the complaints system, however, includes allegations of serious corruption involving police officers as one of the categories proposed for mandatory referral to the proposed Independent Police Complaints Commission (IPCC), intended to replace the PCA when the complaints system is reformed. We suggest that this principle be adopted by police services ahead of the planned legislation. The limits on our resources will ensure that we only accept priority cases for supervision.

Race

This year the number of complaints of racially discriminatory behaviour rose from 579 in 1999–2000 to 647 this year. Such complaints remain three times higher than in 1998–1999. To prove an allegation of a *racist motive* for a neglect of duty or abuse of authority remains problematic. It may be possible to uphold an allegation of neglect, for example, or the use of unnecessary violence and yet be unable to prove that this conduct was racially discriminatory. The number of investigated complaints leading to misconduct action rose from 3.9 per cent in 1998–1999 to 5.9 per cent this year.

We give priority to supervising investigations of serious allegations involving racism. In some cases, a supervising member will involve an advisor or a consultant in the investigation. We aim to raise the investigators' awareness and understanding of the nature of discrimination and appropriate methods for investigating it effectively.

...

During the 1990s, we highlighted the disproportionate number of black people involved in stop and search complaints. This year the Home Office published extensive research into this issue. These studies examined the populations on the street and in vehicles as distinct from the residential population in different areas, and drew conclusions about the proportionality of stops and searches in relation to the available population. This year we researched 90 complaints cases involving such police action to examine the experiences of complainants, the justification for stop and search and to explore why stop and search complaints can or cannot be substantiated. We will publish the report from this study soon.

...

The proportion of those dying in police care or custody who were from an ethnic minority community fell from 19 per cent in 1999–2000 to 9 per cent this year (two black people and one Asian). (See 'Deaths in police care and custody')

...

Section 71 of the Race Relations (Amendment) Act 2000 imposes the following duties on authorities such as police authorities and chief police officers. To have due regard to the need: to eliminate unlawful racial discrimination; and to promote equality of opportunity and good relations between people of different racial groups.

The Secretary of State may impose other duties as appropriate. The Commission for Racial Equality (CRE) may issue codes of practice containing practical guidance on the performance of the above duties. We are represented on the CRE Working Group, which is drawing up the Code of Practice. The intention is to draft the Code by July 2001 ready for public consultation.

Other incidents

Allegations of sexual assaults by police officers by both members of the public and other police officers are invariably a matter of public concern. Many of the investigations into these matters are referred voluntarily to us for supervision

In our 1997–1998 Annual Report, we wrote that although the number of cases of sexual harassment formed only a tiny proportion of our workload they did cause concern. We said then: "They do suggest that some male police officers will display an outdated and unacceptable attitude towards women and that a few are prepared to betray their position of trust for personal sexual gratification."

We regret to report that some male officers' behaviour continues to damage the reputation of the police service. We see it not only in the cases that we supervise and review but also in the reports of tribunals hearing claims brought by women working in the service. Allegations of harassment and sexual assault go to the core of confidence in policing. If women cannot trust the police officers on whom they call for protection, who can they rely upon?

Restraint and self defence

Many of the complaints we considered concern how police officers have used force to effect an arrest or in self-defence. There are allegations that CS spray has been used excessively, that its use was unjustified, or that handcuffs or police batons have caused unnecessary injury. Many complaints arise from the use of unarmed self-defence or distraction techniques, which to the untrained eye can appear objectionable. The equipment provided to police officers and training they receive in its use plays a significant role in deciding the merits of such complaints. Innovations in equipment and its use affect how members of the public experience the use of force. Developments can influence the prevalence of complaints, particularly those alleging injury.

Handcuffs

We received 1,048 complaints this year about the use of handcuffs. The most common complaints alleged improper use of handcuffs, causing bruising or redness to the wrists. Rigid handcuffs can inflict such damage when they are not properly fitted, not double locked, or when the detainee struggles after being handcuffed. Officers must be able to justify the use of handcuffs on each occasion.

CS spray

We received 409 complaints this year about the use of CS spray by police officers. Controversy still surrounds the spray and the Home Office has now given approval to Sussex Police and Hertfordshire Constabulary to test PAVA, a synthetic pepper spray. Sussex have invited us to monitor its testing. When we researched the use of CS spray from complaints made about it, we found that many forces did not know how often they used it. All forces should monitor exceptional use by individual officers. During the past year, the first police officer was convicted and imprisoned for causing injury by an excessive and unjustified use of the spray.

Batons

The number of complaints of assault involving batons has fallen from 459 in 1997–1998 to 291 this year. It is reasonable to suppose that the changing complaints profile may reflect a parallel shift in the use of CS and batons. We note that MLA (a Yorkshire-based company) has brought out an extendable, relatively lightweight baton designed with our 1998 report on new batons in mind. We highlighted the small number of complaints generated by the relatively light, smooth Arnold baton. The extending section of the MLA model has no edges or sharp points so as to minimize injuries. It is, of course, for the police service to decide whether it is suitable for operational use but we will monitor any concerns that arise from its use.

Emergency Restraint Belt

In March 2001, Northamptonshire Constabulary began force-wide training with the alternative to VIPERS, the American-designed Emergency Restraint Belt (ERB). The belt had come through a three-month trial successfully, without public complaint, and 500 police services in North America use it.

The ERB is carried by each officer whereas VIPERS is held in a vehicle. The advantage of ERB for officers is that there is no possibility of getting free from it. The disadvantage is that detainees with their legs strapped find it very difficult to walk. We will monitor the introduction of both methods of restraint and any complaints from the public. The forces introducing the equipment believe it will reduce the number of injuries to the public and to police officers. We expect police officers to exercise caution whenever they use this new equipment, until it has been extensively tested in practice.

Improving the police complaints system

The Home Office approved an increase of £950,000 in our budget for 2001–2002. Our improved financial position meant we could appoint an additional five members and five casework staff. After several years of budget cuts we now have a real opportunity to improve our service to complainants, bereaved families and the police service. We will make our supervision of investigations more robust, increase personal contact with complainants, and improve completion times for investigations and misconduct review. This will benefit complainants and police officers subject to complaints. We are doing much of this work internally before consulting with ACPO and others. The Learning Lab, described below, will also make an important contribution.

The Learning Lab

The Modernising Government White Paper set up Learning Labs to raise the quality and responsiveness of public services. The Labs have evolved from experience of public service reforms in the USA. The concept is based on the premise that front-line staff are usually aware of the problems facing users. They can identify the barriers to better service delivery and have ideas to tackle them. Front-line staff in the PCA, the CPS and the Metropolitan Police Service, with the support of the Cabinet Office and Home Office, formed a Learning Lab to: review the processes arising from public complaints against police; identify and make recommendations on how to provide a better service to complainants and police officers subject to complaints; consult with stakeholders on those recommendations; and implement the recommendations and evaluate the results. The Lab first met in October 2000 and meets regularly. It addresses problems such as delays in the process, the format of reports and cumbersome bureaucratic procedures. The three agencies are aiming for investigation reports which are relevant, proportionate, streamlined and standardised, while taking into account the defined statutory responsibilities of the PCA and the CPS. It is anticipated that the outcomes of the Lab's work will be relevant to complaints investigation practice throughout the police service.

Table 1: Analysis of cases referred to the Authority and accepted for supervision 2000/2001

Type of referral	Number referred	per cent	Number accepted	per cent
Death or serious injury	366*	38.7	340	58.0
Actual bodily harm	330	34.9	54	9.2
Corruption	25	2.6	8	1.4
Serious arrestable offence	22	2.3	8	1.4
Complaint referred voluntarily	74	7.8	56	9.6
Referral required by the Authority	4	0.4	3	0.5
Voluntary referral of non-complaint matter	125	13.2	117	20.0
Total	946 (due to rounding)	99.9	586 (due to rounding)	100.1

* Includes some referred in this category but then reclassified

NOTES

1. Statistics on police complaints are revealing.[14] In 1999–2000 there were 21,000 complaints; 36% informally resolved; 38% withdrawn/dispensed with; 8,048

14 Statistics on police complaints and discipline are published annually in a Home Office Statistical Bulletin; statistics on the work of the Police Complaints Authority are set out in that body's annual report, available from www.pca.gov.uk/.

required investigation; 714 complaints were substantiated (i.e. 9% of those investigated), and 27% of those concerned oppressive behaviour, and around 50% involved failure in duty; disciplinary charges were proved against 353 officers, and 115 officers were dismissed/required to resign.[15] What would be an acceptable number of complaints found to be justified in an ideal police force?

2. The European Court of Human Rights has held that a PCA investigation does not provide an adequate remedy for Art. 13 of the Convention: *Sultan Khan v United Kingdom*.[16]

(B) AN INDEPENDENT INVESTIGATIVE BODY?

An issue perennially debated is whether the investigation of complaints by the police 'themselves' can ever command public confidence. It should be noted that, at present, the PCA supervises investigations – the police are still investigating their own alleged wrongdoing. It is often suggested that only the establishment of a fully independent system of investigation would secure public confidence. The difficulties have been summarised by the PCA.[17] A truly independent system would require substantial resources (both capital outlay and continuing commitment) in establishing its own accommodation and support services in regional centres;[18] retired or seconded police officers would not be seen to be independent, and investigators from other bodies such as Customs and Excise or the DSS would need in-depth training and might find it more difficult to secure police co-operation. In 1994, the PCA did not think such an allocation of resources was justified: 'we see no evidence to support the view that complaints against police officers are not thoroughly and impartially investigated'.

The Home Affairs Committee First Report *Police Disciplinary and Complaints Procedure* HC 258 (1998), recommended changes to the discipline process.[19]

Pressure for an independent system increased following the Macpherson Report, particularly Recommendation 58:

> 'That the Home Secretary, taking into account the strong expression of public perception in this regard, considers what steps can and should be taken to ensure that serious complaints against police officers are independently investigated. Investigation of police officers by their own or another Police Service is widely regarded as unjust, and does not inspire public confidence.'[20]

(i) A new independent complaints body?[21]

The Home Office published a consultation document in 2000, which was based on a KPMG study commissioned by the Home Office on 'Feasibility of an Independent System for Investigating Complaints Against the Police'[22] and a study by Liberty on 'An Independent Police Complaints Commission'.[1] As a result, the Home Office has published its final proposals for the Independent Police Complaints Commission.

---

15 J. Cotton and D. Povey Home Office Statistical Bulletin, Issue 14/00.
16 [2000] 8 BHRC 310. See recently *Jorden v United Kingdom* (2001) ECtHR, 4 May; see also J. Simor and J. Sawyer, (2001) NLJ 992.
17 *Triennial Review, 1991–94, 1993–94*, HC 396, pp. 15–16.
18 Currently, the PCA costs around £3m a year, excluding the costs of investigations of complaints by police forces, which far exceed that figure.
19 See below p. 135.
20 Op. cit.
21 *Complaints against the Police Framework for a New System* (2001).
22 HO PRS Paper No. 124 (2000).
 1 J. Harrison and M. Cunneen, *Liberty* (2000).

Objectives of a New Complaints Procedure

4. The proposed framework favoured by Ministers, if operated as we envisage, should lead to: increased public confidence and trust in the police and in the complaints system as a whole; increased accessibility, openness and independence; quicker resolution of complaints; improved communications with complainants; improved collection, collation and reporting of data.

5. Our starting point is the current legislation and this framework builds on that - but the result will be a fundamentally new system. These changes and additions will, inevitably, lead to an increase in the number of complaints and a proportion of them will be vexatious; this is the price of having a more accessible and more open procedure but the payback should be greater public confidence and trust in the police. All this will create additional pressure on resources, which we will have to manage. This will be a great incentive for forces to help themselves by providing leadership and training in order to combat misconduct by its officers.

A New Independent Body

6. There will be a new independent body which will replace the Police Complaints Authority. It will be known as the Independent Police Complaints Commission (IPCC). It will have a much more independent and proactive role to build a system in which all sections of the community, and the police service, can have confidence.

Definition of a Complaint

7. The present definition of a complaint will be extended as follows: a bystander who witnessed police misconduct will be allowed to make a complaint; the scope of the new complaints system will cover in all respects regular police officers, irrespective of rank, special constables and civilian employees; the IPCC will be expected to widen access to the complaints system by creating other gateways into it, and the IPCC will provide guidelines on how complaints can be made; and complainants will have a right to appeal to the IPCC against the refusal by the appropriate authority to record a complaint.

The complaints system will be made more accessible as the public will be able to make a complaint through other agencies, e.g. the Citizen's Advice Bureaux:

16. In order to have a speedy and understandable process as an alternative to formal investigations for resolving complaints, the informal resolution process: will be retained and renamed 'local resolution'; will continue to be used for allegations which, if proved, would not lead to criminal or disciplinary proceedings. However, where there are no prospects of obtaining the necessary evidence to substantiate complaints, the appropriate authority will be able to apply to the IPCC for authority to use local resolution instead of formal investigation; and will be strengthened to provide a range of different approaches: management resolution, restorative conference and mediation.

...

18. Local resolution provides a fast, efficient and effective method of resolving complaints and we should aim to use it as much as possible. At present, about a third of all complaints are resolved locally without the need for a formal investigation but there is scope to increase the numbers.

...

22. The IPCC will be the guardian of the use of local resolution by monitoring and audit. The IPCC will be expected to review how it functions and to ensure that processes are used in accordance with regulations and guidance. Therefore, the IPCC will have powers both to gather information from police forces and to present it for public consumption.

The IPCC investigation teams will comprise independent civilian investigation managers, seconded senior police officers and others drawn from police and non-police sources as appropriate. Non-police personnel will not have powers of constables, but the Secretary of State will have the power to bestow certain powers on them. Some matters will be referred to the IPCC automatically, and some at its discretion:

27. The proposed categories in which complaint and non-complaint cases will have to be referred to the IPCC are: deaths in police care or custody; fatal road traffic incidents in which a police vehicle is involved; shooting incidents in which a police officer discharges a firearm in the course of a police operation; allegations of serious corruption involving police officers; miscarriages of justice resulting allegedly from misconduct by a police officer; allegations of racist conduct; serious arrestable offences allegedly committed by a police officer; and allegations that serious injury to a member of the public has been caused by a police officer.
28. The IPCC will also have powers at its discretion to call in for independent investigation or supervision other complaints not falling within those specified categories. Views are invited on whether this discretionary call in power should extend to other matters not the subject of complaints.

Powers will be created to allow IPCC investigations to occur independently of the police:

33. The IPCC would be able to operate effectively and independently if the home force had a more proactive role in dealing with complainants on completion of an investigation and if the IPCC has appellate powers. In this respect, the home force will: make the provisional decision about any action in relation to the conduct of the officers in the case; if necessary, meet the complainant or family and explain the results of the investigation; send a full written account of the investigation to the complainant setting out the way the investigation had been conducted, a summary of the evidence, the conclusions – including the proposed action to be taken against the officer concerned, reasons for those conclusions and any action taken to prevent a recurrence; and advise the complainant of their right of appeal to the IPCC against the provisional decision.

There will be attempts to ensure greater openness and an appearance of such:

47. In cases where the complaint is investigated by a police force, the complainant will have a right of appeal to the IPCC if it is felt that the written account does not provide a satisfactory explanation of what has been done and why. The IPCC will be able to consider the details of the case and, if appropriate, provide additional information to the complainant.
48. We recognise that there will be some material or information which should not be disclosed; for example, details which might identify a potentially vulnerable witness or reveal the identity of a confidential police informant. The body which has investigated the complaint, whether it is the IPCC or a police force, should be entitled to keep such information confidential where necessary. There may also be internal personnel management matters which should be conveyed to the management of the force concerned, but will not be of direct interest to the complainant. Such matters could be included in a separate 'management memorandum' from the investigating officer to the responsible authority.
49. We do not propose, therefore, to compel the disclosure of all relevant evidence in every case. There must be discretion for those who have investigated the complaint to decide whether it is necessary in the public interest to keep some information confidential. When the new legislation is in place, we will issue guidance to the IPCC and to Chief Officers about what should be contained in the investigation report which is sent to the complainant, and what should be omitted or excluded.

NOTES

1. Truly independent complaints and investigation bureaux have been created in other jurisdictions, e.g. Canada.[2]
2. To what extent do the proposed changes make any substantial difference to the complaints procedure? Can all of the defects in the present procedure be remedied?

2   See A. Goldsmith and F. Farson, [1987] Crim LR 615.

3. Will the public perception of the procedure be improved? Will the public ever be satisfied that there is a fair system of policing the police? In practical terms, who is capable of policing the police?

4. In the absence of an effective complaints system, the victims of police misconduct have little option but to rely on formal legal processes for redress. Is this advantageous to either complainants or police?

(C) THE POLICE DISCIPLINARY PROCEDURE [3]

Significant changes have been made to the procedure for police disciplinary proceedings, these have been targeted to facilitate a more managerial approach.[4] There are three sets of regulations – one governing non-senior officers, one senior officer and one relating to the efficiency of non-senior officers.[5] The Police (Efficiency) Regulations 1999[6] establish procedures for resignation/reduction in rank for non-senior officers who have been proved to be 'inefficient'. After two interviews an 'inefficiency hearing is conducted with sanctions being to require resignation, reduce in rank or give a written warning'.

The most important recent changes to disciplinary hearings are that:

- The civil standard of proof on the balance of probabilities applies rather than the criminal standard of proof beyond reasonable doubt, as is the norm in employment cases.
- This resulted in the removal of the bar on 'double jeopardy' (that if convicted or acquitted of a criminal offence, no disciplinary charges could be brought in respect of an offence that was in substance the same).
- No officer of the rank of superintendent or below can be dismissed, required to resign or reduced in rank, unless he has been given an opportunity of legal representation.
- Hearings will be able to go ahead in the absence of the accused officer if necessary. This is designed to prevent false claims of ill-health to delay matters.
- Fast track procedures will be available for the most serious criminal allegations where the evidence is overwhelming and does not rely on witness testimony.

'The general effect of the new regulations has been to reduce the quasi-military police discipline process with employment–style labour relations practices, as urged by ACPO.'[6a]

The Chief Constable must follow the disciplinary procedure and cannot dismiss without any hearing at all – see the case of *R v Chief Constable of the British Transport Police, ex p Farmer,*[7] in which F, a probationer, was dismissed without hearing for allegedly cheating in an examination.

Note that neglect of duty is also a common law criminal offence: *R v Dytham.*[8] Prosecutions are rare.

---

3 See the Home Office Consultation Paper, *Review of Police Discipline Procedures,* February 1993; J. Harrison and S. Cragg, (1993) 143 NLJ 591.

4 The need for change was highlighted by the strong Report of the Home Affairs Committee into *Police Disciplinary and Complaints Procedures* (23 March 1999); see Police (Conduct) Regulations 1999, S.I. 1999 No. 730; Police (Conduct) (Senior Officers) Regulations 1999, S.I. 1999 No. 731.

5 Corresponding provisions exist for the officers in NCIS and NCS. See Sections 37–40 and 81–84 of the 1997 Act.

6 S.I. 1999 No. 732.

6a G. Smith, (2001) 64 MLR 385.

7 [1998] 36 LS Gaz R 31.

8 [1979] QB 722. An off-duty detective was recently convicted of this offence when he stood by as his friend attacked a curry-house owner: *Independent,* 11 April 2001.

In its Annual Report, the PCA describes its role regarding discipline:

'In many cases, although a complaint is upheld, the circumstances do not justify the officer responsible appearing at a hearing. Other misconduct action is available. For misconduct before 1 April 1999, the officer may be admonished by a senior officer, often an assistant chief constable. For substantiated misconduct after that date, there is a new, formal written warning procedure. In less serious cases, there is an oral warning or "advice", usually given by the divisional commander but sometimes by an assistant or deputy chief constable. For misconduct due to ignorance or inexperience the likely outcome is guidance or a "constructive discussion" to improve future performance. We recommend further training for officers whose conduct shows they need this and we will propose changes in procedures or management systems where appropriate.'

NOTES

1. The Macpherson Report recommended further change:

'Recommendation 56. That in order to eliminate the present provision, which prevents disciplinary action after retirement, disciplinary action should be available for at least five years after an officer's retirement.
Recommendation 57. That the Police Services should through the implementation of a Code of Conduct or otherwise ensure that racist words or acts proved to have been spoken or done by police officers should lead to disciplinary proceedings, and that it should be understood that such conduct should usually merit dismissal.'

2. In response, the latest Home Office proposals on Police Complaints propose further reform of the disciplinary procedure:

'Discipline
35. In order to build public confidence in the end process of the new complaints system, additional powers will be required by the IPCC and the presiding officer of a disciplinary panel in regards to complaints cases: the IPCC will have discretionary powers to present or to observe cases it investigated, and cases investigated by police, whether or not those cases were supervised; in disciplinary cases arising from a complaint, one of the three members of the panel to be independent of the police; as a consequence, Police Authorities to compile and maintain lists of independent people (excluding members of the police authority itself) eligible to sit on discipline panels; in attending a disciplinary hearing up to the point that a finding is reached, a complainant can be accompanied by up to three people of their choice; the presiding officer of a disciplinary hearing arising from a complaint to have the discretion to allow the complainant to be accompanied by more than three people if, in his/her opinion, the circumstances of the case justify it and there are no reasonable objections from the accused officer; and the presiding officer of a disciplinary hearing to have the discretion to exclude any persons.

Presenting Disciplinary Cases
36. As with the handling of complaints, the handling of discipline proceedings can make or break public confidence and trust in the police. Therefore, changes to the proceedings which will make them more open, but without detriment to the charged officer would be a step in the right direction. The complainant and the general public need to be assured that evidence in a disciplinary hearing will be presented fully and robustly. Therefore, giving the IPCC the option to present or observe disciplinary cases would provide the police with a strong incentive to do just that.

Constitution of a Disciplinary Panel
37. The Home Affairs Select Committee suggested that in a case arising from a complaint, there should be at least one independent member of the disciplinary panel, the Government saw merit in it and it received widespread support. The Police Authority is well placed to maintain a list of independent people who can sit on disciplinary panels in its area. Panel members will be trained to clear national standards. Comments on maintaining a list of trained, independent people would be welcomed.

Attendance at a Disciplinary Hearing

38. There was widespread support for extending the present arrangement where the complainant may attend disciplinary hearings up to the point that a finding is reached by allowing a representative and supporters (up to three people) to attend as well. The presiding officer will be expected to be even-handed when allowing the accused officer and the complainant to be accompanied by others.

Disciplinary Hearings in Public

39. In its response to the Home Affairs Select Committee report, the Government argued that the advantages in making disciplinary hearings open to the public at large were outweighed by the disadvantages with regard to the confidential nature of some aspects of most of the proceedings. It added that this would be allowing the public admittance to what is essentially a management exercise.

40. There are strong arguments on both sides; on the one hand, there are issues of greater openness and public confidence and, on the other, there are issues of police confidence and fairness to the accused officer. In general, the police oppose making disciplinary hearings open to the public but it is not opposed to exploring whether cases at the serious end of the scale should be open to the general public. Two questions remain: how to define which cases should be public? How will direction be given to make a hearing public? Further views are sought on this issue.'

(D) HER MAJESTY'S INSPECTORATE OF CONSTABULARY

Another mechanism for internal review and accountability of the police exists in the shape of Her Majesty's Inspectorate of Constabulary. HMIC was established 150 years ago, and it now derives its powers from the Police Act 1996, s. 54. It is responsible for examining the efficiency and effectiveness of the police service. It is independent of the tripartite structure of the police authority, Chief Constables and Home Office. The role of the Inspectorate is defined in the Police Acts (1994 and 1996) and the Local Government Act 1999, relating to 'Best Value'.

The Inspectorate is regionally based, with five inspectors and a Chief Inspector of Constabulary. Inspectors (HMIs) are appointed by the Crown on the recommendation of the Secretary of State and, until 1993, all were senior officers. Since 1993, several HMIs have been appointed from non-police backgrounds. HMIC plays an important role in ensuring police accountability. In April 2000, the inspectorate introduced a new 'diagnostic model of inspection', which measures each force's performance against approximately 60 established protocols. These are linked to 'ministerial priorities and objectives for policing':

'The model is a structured methodology to analyse, assess and score forces' performance against a number of protocols (statements of good practice in operational and organisational activities). The model will give a comprehensive analysis of performance which will allow us to judge the level of inspection needed. Poorer performing forces will receive a more rigorous inspection than high performers and some forces may not receive a visit at all. The model will highlight particular aspects of good and poor performance and HMIC will visit some forces to look specifically at these areas. Inspections under the new methodology will take place between September 2000 and April 2001.'

Poorer performing forces will be subjected to more rigorous inspections than successful forces. Note that between 1992 and 1995, HMIC refused a certificate of efficiency for Derbyshire Constabulary.

'Thematic inspections' are carried out on important issues, e.g. *Police Integrity*:[9]

---

9   (1999) These follow recommendations of the Masefield Scrutiny – a committee established in 1994 and reporting to the Prime Minister in 1995 on the administrative burdens on the police.

'. . . The approach was to examine 'integrity' in its broadest sense, encompassing subjects such as fairness, behaviour, probity, equal treatment and a range of operational and management issues. It is not about corruption in a narrow sense, rather how public confidence is secured and maintained.

. . . The public has a right to expect a high standard of behaviour from its Police Service, and generally speaking the Inspection confirmed the vast majority of men and women – police officers, civilian support staff and special constables – working within the 44 police forces in England, Wales and Northern Ireland, are honest, industrious and dedicated. Policing by consent relies on the overwhelming majority of the public, particularly minority groups and the disadvantaged, trusting and respecting individual officers and staff; the reality is this reputation can be seriously harmed if only a few fail. Regrettably, the Inspection found failings in the Service, some minor and others quite serious, all of which need to be addressed so public confidence can be re-established and the good reputation of the Service restored....

2.1 In a system of policing by consent, it is vital to have regular confirmation from all sections of the community that the traditional trust in the police is sustained. Trust depends on the strength of mutual understanding and respect between the police and the community they serve, and every time an individual officer behaves badly, public trust and confidence in the whole Service is affected. During this comprehensive Inspection, it quickly became clear to Her Majesty's Inspector and his team that in the day-to-day policing of their communities, the behaviour exhibited by police officers was of fundamental importance in maintaining public confidence. Poor behaviour was considered tantamount to any other breach of integrity.

2.2. It is self evident that every police officer and member of support staff should behave professionally, courteously and impartially to members of the public and colleagues alike. It is a sad fact, however, that during 1997 well over 6,000 complaints of alleged rudeness and incivility were recorded. How police officers behave is very much a matter of personal integrity, and in an environment where bullying, arrogance, rudeness, racist or sexist behaviour is tolerated, corruption and other wrongdoing will flourish, and is more likely to remain unreported.'

See also *Winning The Race: Policing Plural Communities*, HMIC Thematic Inspection Report On Police Community And Race Relations 1996/97:

'It must be recognised that racial discrimination, both direct and indirect, and harassment are endemic within our society and the police service is no exception. There was continuing evidence during the Inspection of inappropriate language and behaviour by police officers, but even more worrying was the lack of intervention by sergeants and inspectors. This was re-enforced during the observation of assessment panels for promotion to sergeant and inspector where potential supervisors demonstrated a reluctance to challenge colleagues who indulged in racist 'banter' and racist behaviour. Many ethnic minority officers felt unsupported by management and were left to rely on support from colleagues of a similar background. Some supervisors displayed little awareness or understanding of harassment and discrimination issues, and there was a lack of faith in the grievance procedure by many individuals.'

Some of its reports have been very critical, e.g. *Police Integrity: securing and maintaining public confidence*:[10]

'The behaviour and attitude of some police officers gives the public greatest concern.[11] "All forces are trying hard to consult their communities and to understand their needs and concerns, but each is failing to a greater or lesser extent in providing a better service to the disadvantaged groups in society, as well as ethnic minority groups".'[12]

10 (1999).
11 Ibid., p. 1.
12 Ibid., p. 3.

(E) CUSTODY VISITORS[13]

Yet another method of monitoring police action at the ground level is the custody visitors scheme, formerly known as the lay visitors scheme. These visitors are selected by the police authority from those who apply from the general community. A recent report has found that there was under-representation of the young and ethnic groups, and that more was needed to be done to encourage people to apply to be custody visitors.[14]

Visits to stations by custody visitors may be by prior arrangement or unannounced.[15] Weatheritt and Vieira found that 'a significant number of stations were visited rarely or not at all,[16] and that a 'frequent and consistently observed visiting programme' was needed across the board, with a recommendation of one visit per station per month.[17]

The new custody visitor scheme is described as follows:[18]

'6. Volunteers from the community are recruited and accredited by the police authority and organised into groups responsible for visiting a particular police station or stations. Unannounced visits are made at varying times of the day and night, with volunteers having immediate access to the custody area. The conditions of detention and the treatment of individual detainees are checked. As part of that process there will usually be discussion with custody staff and detainees who are required to give their consent before being spoken to. Visitors may raise issues needing immediate attention by the police. After every visit they will produce a written report of their findings. Arrangements will be in place for output from visits to be discussed by groups of visitors and communicated to the police at local, area and force level. There will also be regular feedback to the police authority and a commitment to publicising the work and, where appropriate, the findings of custody visitors.'

Its purposes are identified as:

'7. Custody visiting has a number of connected purposes. First, and most obviously, it offers an extra level of protection to detainees by providing independent scrutiny of their treatment and the conditions in which they are held. By giving members of the community an opportunity to observe, comment and report on these matters, it can improve citizens' understanding of procedures at police stations and strengthen their confidence that these are properly applied. From a police perspective, it is a clear demonstration of their commitment to transparency and openness in relation to this critical aspect of their duties. Furthermore, it can improve police management of their own performance by pointing out areas where problems have occurred and which may have implications for policy, training, communications or the daily work of officers responsible for custody at police stations.

8. For police authorities, custody visiting is an extremely important aid in fulfilling their responsibility to ensure that policing in their areas is carried out fairly, in accordance with statutory and other rules and with respect for the human rights of all those coming into contact with the police.

30. The key priority is for custody visitors to be recruited from and representative of the local community. Local groups should aim for a balance in terms of age range, gender and ethnic background. The scheme is likely to lack effectiveness and credibility if those participating are drawn from too narrow a section of the local community. This inclusive approach should extend to those with handicaps and those who do not have English as their first language. All reasonable efforts should be made to accommodate applicants in these categories as custody

---

13 S. James, [1988] PL 432; C. Kemp and R. Morgan, *Behind the Front Counter* (1989).
14 M. Weatheritt and C. Vieira, *Lay Visitors to Police Stations* (1998), Home Office Research Study No. 188.
15 See 97 HC Deb. 26 February 1986, Written Answer; revised guidelines have been issued by the Home Office: see Home Office Circular 992.
16 Op. cit., p. 15.
17 Ibid., p. 44. See also their calls for a general expansion of police authority support for visiting, clearer organisation, and better provision of information.
18 See H.O. Circular 15/2001, 4 May.

visitors where they are considered suitable candidates. However, it is important that custody visits are always conducted in English, with translation support where necessary. Visitors should be independent persons of good character who are able to make informed judgements in which the community can have confidence and which the police will accept as fair criticism when it is justified...'

It is expected that visits occur regularly (not less than one per month and in busier stations around once per week). On arrival, visitors are to be admitted to the custody area immediately unless there is a threat to their safety:

'66. Visitors should have access to all parts of the custody area including cells, detention rooms, charging areas, washing facilities and medical room (but not the drugs cabinet). Visitors will wish to satisfy themselves that these areas are clean, tidy and in a reasonable state of repair and decoration, and that bedding in cells is clean and adequate. Relevant storage areas may also be seen and visitors should check that there are adequate stocks of blankets, pillowcases and other necessary items. They should also verify that arrangements are established for the cleaning of blankets etc and for any necessary replacement of furnishings and equipment. They should check that any CCTV systems installed to observe the custody area or individual cells are operating properly. They may inspect empty cells and detention rooms to check heating/ventilation systems and that cell bells and toilet flushing mechanisms are working properly. They may visit interview rooms in the custody area if unoccupied, but it is not part of their role to attend police interviews with detainees. Visitors may not visit CID rooms or other operational parts of the station . . .

78. Conversations between detainees and custody visitors should normally take place in sight but out of hearing of the escorting officer. If for some reason the police decide that the escorting officer should remain within hearing, this decision must be taken by the duty officer or some other senior officer at the station. Visitors should bear in mind, however, that some detained persons may be violent or under the influence of drink or drugs and that the presence of a police officer may deter or frustrate assaults on the visitor . . .

80. Conversations should focus on checking whether or not detainees have been offered their rights and entitlements under PACE (including receipt of the necessary paperwork) and on confirming whether the conditions of detention are adequate. Custody visitors should do all they can to encourage an open exchange with the detainee and may wish to use a checklist to ensure that they cover all the relevant issues.

81. Visitors must remain impartial and should not seek to involve themselves in any way in the process of investigation. If detainees press them for advice about co-operating with the police, making a statement or anything in relation to their defence, they should explain that it is not part of their role. If the detainee's concerns are linked to not yet having received legal advice, that is something the visitors may wish to take up with the escorting or custody officer.'

7 Two specific issues highlighting the difficulties of control and accountability

Some high-profile issues are likely to have a significant impact in bringing about reform of the complaints system and police accountability. Two deserve further special mention: deaths in custody and police racism.

(A) DEATHS IN CUSTODY

In recent years the number of deaths in police custody rose sharply (1996/97 – 48; 1997/98 – 53; 1998/99 – 65). This represents a 41% increase in four years.[19] The Home

---

19 See PCA Report, *Deaths in Police Custody: Reducing the Risks* (1999); PCA, *One Year On, Deaths in Police Custody: the risks reduced* (2000).

Office *Deaths in Police Custody Statistics for England & Wales*, April 1998 to March 1999, confirm that in 1998/99, 67 people died in police custody or otherwise in the hands of the police. The number of people from ethnic minorities who died in police custody or otherwise in the hands of the police was 12, which forms 18% of the total. The number of persons who died in police stations was 16 (24%). Of the 67 deaths: 25 resulted from deliberate self harm; six followed car or motorcycle crashes; and 18 involved people arrested for being drunk and disorderly or found drunk in the street.[20] Despite the fact that in 1999/2000 the number of deaths in custody dropped slightly for the first time in years, this remains a significant problem for modern day policing.[21] A number of deaths in these circumstances is inevitable, given the volume of arrests each year. What is important is: (a) that the number of deaths is kept to an absolute minimum; and (b) that the deaths are thoroughly and openly investigated, and that if a death has been caused unlawfully, that there is an appropriate legal response.[22]

The latest recommendations to reduce deaths in custody are contained in a PCA publication *One Year On, Deaths in Police Custody: the risks reduced*.[1] The report notes that Art. 2 of the ECHR provides a right to life protected by law. Under the Human Rights Act 1998, 'any force failing to provide adequate training for officers, systems and medical care for the preservation of life of incapacitated prisoners may be exposed to legal action'.[2]

Specific proposals to safeguard against deaths in custody included: in-cell CCTV; life signs monitors; keeping cell hatches closed but ensuring adequate ventilation in cells; evaluation using nurses and community psychiatric nurses in cell suites; introducing the Association of Police Surgeons' medical forms; and recommending that forces consider establishing 'custody users groups'.[3] The Police Complaints Authority has recently produced further guidance on dealing with people with behavioural difficulties.[3a]

The second issue of concern with deaths in custody is that so few cases are prosecuted, even where the inquest records an unlawful killing. In *R v HM Coroner for Coventry, ex p Chief Constable of Staffordshire Police*[4] it was held that where there was evidence that the police had had an opportunity of doing something effective to prevent a death in custody, a verdict of accidental death aggravated by neglect could be left to a jury at an inquest. In that case, the deceased was an alcoholic

20 See Home Office Circular 20/1999, *Deaths In Police Custody: Guidance To The Police On Pre-Inquest Disclosure* (1999).
21 See Home Office, *Deaths in Custody 1999 (April) to 2000 (March)* (2000). The PCA Annual Report 2000–2001 records 32 deaths.
22 See recently the decision that it was appropriate to order an independent official investigation into the death of someone in custody where their death might have been contrary to Art. 2 and/or 3 of the ECHR: *R v Home Office, ex p Wright* (2001) 20 June.
1 (1999). On deaths in custody, see A. Leigh, G. Johnson and A. Ingram, *Deaths in Police Custody: Learning the Lessons* (1998) PRS No. 26, especially Chap. 6 on police restraint techniques and death and Chap. 7 on ethnicity and death. See also the press coverage of the death of Christopher Alder: *Independent*, 25 August 2000.
2 On Art. 2, see Chap. 1 above.
3 'The ethnic origin of those who die in police custody has attracted considerable public attention. This year a disproportionate number of people from black or other minority ethnic communities died in custody, although white people accounted for the vast majority of such deaths. The significant point is that several deaths of black people in custody in recent years have generated intense controversy, giving rise to inquest verdicts of unlawful killing and a sense of distrust if no criminal or disciplinary charges follow. These high profile cases tend to be those where a death follows a struggle between the detained person and police officers, whether or not the struggle resulted in serious or life-threatening injuries. This year, of the nine people who died following a struggle three were black.' *PCA Annual Report 1998–9*. For a medical review of the problem, see Sir Montague Levine, (1998) Medico-Legal Journal 97.
3a *Policing Acute Behavioural Disturbance* (2001).
4 (2000) 5 July, unreported.

with a history of recurrent epileptic fits who died in custody unsupervised in the police yard when a fit caused his fall and fractured his skull. The Divisional Court has also held that where an inquest culminates in a verdict of unlawful killing implicating an officer, the Director of Public Prosecutions was expected to give reasons for failing to prosecute: *R v DPP, ex p Manning*.[5] See also the discussion of the Butler Report.[6] Why should the DPP not give reasons in all cases in which a prosecution is not pursued? Do you agree that, in such cases, 'silence simply feeds suspicion of some political or ulterior motive'?[7]

(B) RACISM IN POLICING[7A]

Stephen Lawrence was murdered in a racist attack in London in 1993. No convictions were ever secured in relation to his death, despite substantial evidence against a number of individuals who were investigated. In February 1997, the Lawrence family made a formal complaint against the Metropolitan Police. The investigation was conducted by Kent County Constabulary, under the supervision of the PCA, and was completed in December 1997. The PCA provided a report, which concluded that the Metropolitan Police investigations had been seriously flawed by:

> 'errors of judgement; failure to acquire available evidence; weaknesses in organisation, management and supervision; failures in family liaison; and the failure of the internal review to reveal the serious weaknesses, omissions and lost opportunities of the earlier murder investigation.'[8]

The PCA recommended that one officer face seven charges of neglect of duty arising from the investigation. Four other senior officers would have faced charges had they not retired. The Detective involved was disciplined – he received a verbal warning for neglect of duty.[9] The PCA Report concluded that the 'investigation has not produced any evidence to support the allegations of racist conduct by police officers'.

A full public inquiry was ordered – chaired by Sir William Macpherson of Cluny[10] – which produced 70 recommendations.

The Macpherson Report[11]

> 'Para. 46.1. The conclusions to be drawn from all the evidence in connection with the investigation of Stephen Lawrence's racist murder are clear. There is no doubt but that there were fundamental errors. The investigation was marred by a combination of professional incompetence, institutional racism and a failure of leadership by senior officers. A flawed MPS review failed to expose these inadequacies. The second investigation could not salvage the faults of the first investigation
>
> Para. 46.26. At its most stark the case against the police was that racism infected the MPS and that the catalogue of errors could only be accounted for by something more than incompetence. If corruption and collusion did not play its part then, say the critics, the case must have been

---

5 (2000) 17 May, DC.
6 Above, p. 118.
7 L. Blom-Cooper, [2000] PL 560, 561.
7a See generally, on race and the criminal justice system, D. Smith, 'Ethnic Origins, Crime and Criminal Justice' in M. Maguire, R. Morgan and R. Reiner (eds.), *The Oxford Handbook of Criminology* (1997), pp. 703–759.
8 *Report by the PCA on the investigation of a complaint against the MPS by Mr N and Mrs D Lawrence* (1997) (Cm 3822).
9 *Independent*, 23 July 1999.
10 See *Stephen Lawrence Inquiry* references above.
11 On which see J. Robins, (2000) 97(8) LSG 22; R. Oakley, (1999) 72(4) Pol J 285; L. Bridges, 'The Lawrence Inquiry: incompetence, corruption and institutional racism' (1999) 26(3) J Law and Soc 298; A. Rutherford, (1999) NLJ 345.

thrown or at least slowed down because officers approached the murder of a black man less energetically than if the victim had been white and the murderers black.'

NOTES

1. J. Lea argues that:

'Racial prejudice among police officers, the association of black with underclass and disorder, is then reproduced in an occupational culture which legitimises stop and search as the policing of dangerous populations. Racism is thus genuinely institutional in that it arises out of the normal functioning of the institution rather than being seen as the disruption of that functioning or something parasitic upon it. It is Macpherson's failure to grasp this dynamic which undermines his whole project. By maintaining that stop and search is important for the control of crime despite its minimal yield of arrests and information, he misses the fact that stop and search as a form of generalised policing of whole communities and groups, however much it is formally regulated by rules, is a major factor in generating police racism.'[12]

2. Some of the most significant recommendations of the Macpherson Report will have far-reaching consequences:[13]

'Para. 6.4 "Racism" in general terms consists of conduct or words or practices which advantage or disadvantage people because of their colour, culture or ethnic origin. In its more subtle form it is as damaging as in its overt form.
Para. 6.34 "Institutional Racism" consists of the collective failure of an organisation to provide an appropriate and professional service to people because of their colour, culture or ethnic origin. It can be seen or detected in processes, attitudes and behaviour which amount to discrimination through unwitting prejudice, ignorance, thoughtlessness, and racist stereotyping which disadvantage minority ethnic people.'

The definition of a racist incident (recommendations 12-14); reporting and recording racist incidents and crimes (recommendations 15-17[13a]) are particularly important:

'12. That the definition should be: "A racist incident is any incident which is perceived to be racist by the victim or any other person".
13. That the term "racist incident" must be understood to include crimes and non-crimes in policing terms. Both must be reported, recorded and investigated with equal commitment.
14. That this definition should be universally adopted by the Police, local Government and other relevant agencies.'

3. Recommendations also related to training and recruitment,[14] especially as regards racism awareness and valuing cultural diversity (recommendation 48). Specific recommendations were made regarding police practice and the investigation of racist crime (recommendations 18-19) and that ACPO produce manuals and Codes of Practice governing the procedures. The Police Complaints Authority's *Annual Report* (2000) states that it dealt with 579 allegations of racist behaviour by officers,

12 [2000] Howard Journal 219, 231.
13 For examples of racist behaviour by police officers towards colleagues, see reports of the dismissal of one officer for calling an Asian colleague a 'wog' (*Guardian*, 16 June 2000), and another who was fined £50 when prosecuted for racial insults to a colleague when off duty (*Guardian*, 26 June 2000). See also *Chief Constable of Kent v Kufeji* (2001) 4 May, where a racist postcard amounted to unlawful discrimination.
13a See the new Code of Practice on reporting and recording racist incidents in response to recommendation 15 (2000).
14 There are currently 2,483 black or Asian officers in England, which represents 2% of the force, when the groups make up 5.6% of the population. See further N. Bland, J. Russell, and R. Tu, *Career Progression of Ethnic Minority Police Officers* (1999), PRS Paper No. 107. The proportion of minority groups represented in British police forces was addressed by the UK government in its 13th Periodic Report to the UN Committee for the Elimination of Racial Discrimination (1996). See further L. Parratt and C. Foley, [1996] 4 EHRLR 384.

compared to 331 the year before. This is an increase of approximately 75%. In its *Annual Report* (2001) the PCA recorded complaints from ethnic minorities making up 19% of the total.

4. Some of the Macpherson Report's more general conclusions impact on much broader issues of accountability in policing. For example, it was noted that:

> 'there is a striking and inescapable need to demonstrate fairness, not just by Police Services, but across the criminal justice system as a whole, in order to generate trust and confidence within minority ethnic communities, who undoubtedly perceive themselves to be discriminated against by *"the system"*. Just as justice needs to be *"seen to be done"*, so fairness must be *"seen to be demonstrated"* in order to generate trust. An essential first step in creating that trust is to ensure that it is a priority for all Police Services. The existing system of Ministerial Priority is the obvious route by which this may be achieved.'[15]

5. The Police Federation, in its response to the Macpherson Report, stated that:

> 'The Macpherson Report is the most searing indictment of policing ever published. It is a catalogue of professional incompetence which shows, with the benefit of hindsight, how mistake was piled on mistake, resulting in a miscarriage of justice that has seen Stephen Lawrence's murderers go free. Acceptance of the Report is the first step down a long road towards a society which can feel at ease with itself and confident that its police service is fair but firm for all.'

6. The report has prompted a number of responses. A Metropolitan Police Racial and Violent Crimes Task Force has been created, led by a Deputy Assistant Commissioner. The force, (CO24), aims:

> 'to provide a major new resource for tackling racial and violent crime based on extensive uses of intelligence gathering methods and the use of specialist officers available to carry out investigations and provide guidance to other officers. It aims to improve standards of victim care, in part by developing new training methods for officers in consultation with interested parties and lay representatives. The creation of the Task Force has already led to a dramatic increase in the reporting of race crime and charges for such crimes throughout London.'

The most significant response has been the Home Secretary's Action Plan. See the *First Annual Report on Progress* (2000). These plans include: a new ministerial priority to 'increase trust and confidence in policing amongst minority ethnic communities'; a Code of Practice on the reporting and recording of racist incidents and crimes; a statutory programme of 'citizenship education' for all 11-16 year olds, which involves 'teaching on diversity and the multi-cultural nature of Britain'; further research into the exercise of stop and search powers; and, most importantly, a new Race Relations (Amendment) Act 2000.

7. It is unlawful for an officer to discriminate in the provision of goods, facilities or services to the public or section of the public contrary to s. 20 of the Race Relations Act 1976: *Farah v Metropolitan Police Comr.*[16] The Race Relations (Amendment) Act 2000 extends the Race Relations Act 1976 in relation to public authorities, making Chief Constables vicariously liable for acts of racial discrimination by police officers. Section 19B makes it unlawful for a public authority directly to discriminate against a person or to victimise a person on racial grounds in carrying out any of its functions. By s. 19D, s. 19B does not apply to a decision not to institute criminal proceedings, or, where a decision not to institute criminal proceedings has been taken,

15 *Macpherson Report*, para. 46.30.
16 [1998] QB 65, CA.

to any act done for the purpose of making a decision about instituting criminal proceedings.[17]

8. Stephen Lawrence's murder was not a unique example of the failings of the police caused by racism.[18] See also the death of Ricky Reel in 1997[19] and the 'Telford hangings', in which two relatives were assumed to have committed suicide.[20] Delroy Lindo, a black activist, had been subjected to persistent harassment after his friend Winston Silcott had been wrongly convicted of a murder of police officer during the Broadwater Farm riots. He received an apology from the Metropolitan Police Commissioner after eight years of harassment (unfortunately, the apology was published on the Internet with Mr Lindo's address, and soon had to be removed).[1]

8 The future of policing[2]

R. Morgan and T. Newburn have claimed that there is 'little evidence that anything the police do has much more than a very marginal impact on crime levels'.[3] If this is the case, it raises fundamental questions about the role of the police and the public perceptions of policing. It is clear that policing will continue to change at a rapid pace. The material discussed in this chapter demonstrates that policing develops as a result of (sometimes unpredictable) political, economic and social factors. Some possible future developments have given rise to concern.[4] Some of these can be outlined briefly.

NOTES

1. The development of European policing seems inevitable, as the UK is a member of the Schengen policing and judicial co-operation arrangements.[5] One commentator has claimed that 'wide ranging proposals concerning the modernisation of the British police can ultimately only be understood by reference to the advent of a United Europe'.[6] It is not easy to see how a truly European police force will develop until there exists a greater level of European citizenship.[7] Concerns about increased

17 See *Chief Constable of Bedfordshire v Liversidge* (2001) 21 September (holding that no vicarious liability arose prior to the 2000 Act). The government has gone further than the Macpherson recommendation by bringing all public services within the scope of the Race Relations Act 1976. The government described its initial concerns that by including indirect discrimination in the Bill public bodies might be exposed to 'spurious challenges to regulatory, economic and social policies where these were entirely proper, in particular those that helped ethnic minorities the most'. However, the government concluded that the risk was outweighed by the value of including indirect discrimination in the Act.
18 The Lawrence family were paid £320,000 by the Metropolitan Police Service for its failings: *Guardian*, 20 December 2000.
19 HC Deb. 20 October 1999 (Mr J. McDonald).
20 See newspaper reports, particularly in the *Independent*, in July 1999.
1 *Guardian*, 31 January 2001.
2 See also on the future of policing L. Johnson, *Policing Britain: Risk Security and Governance* (2000), Part IV, and R. Reiner, *The Politics of the Police* (3rd edn, 2000), Chap. 7.
3 *The Future of Policing*, op. cit., p. 9.
4 See R. Reiner, *Policing I* (1996) Part V.
5 See Home Office Press Releases 29 May 2000 and 12 March 1999. See also recently the establishment of Eurodac, a system for comparison of fingerprints throughout Europe.
6 See E. McLaughlin, 'The Democratic Deficit: The EU and the Accountability of the British Police' (1992) 32 BJ Crim 473.
7 See N. Walker, 'European Integration and European Policing: A complex relationship' in M. Anderson and M. den Boer (eds.), *Policing Across National Boundaries* (1994), p. 39.

European policing are that different standards will be applicable, that informal arrangements will be condoned, and that there will be less obvious accountability and transparency in policing. 'Police cooperation in Europe has developed at a number of levels; and throughout these there appears to have been a widespread neglect of the mechanisms to ensure political and public accountability'.[8]

The significance of existing links is made clear in the NCIS *Annual Report 2000*:

'The UK Europol Liaison Officers work alongside forty other liaison officers from the fourteen other Member States. Between them thousands of cross-border cases are handled each year. Last year the UK was responsible for initiating 325 new cases through Europol, whilst receiving 336 others involving the UK from the other Member States. The work involved varied in significance from requests for routine information to the management of the controlled deliveries of drugs. In this reporting period 46 controlled deliveries were initiated by the UK and accepted by other Member States. These led to operations which culminated, in total, to the arrest of 27 suspected criminals and the seizure of nearly 50 kilos of drugs (of which almost 30 kilos were Class A drugs). These successes underline the virtues of the Europol Liaison Officer network. Through the co-location of officers drawn from all 15 Member States and through the experience and spirit of co-operation that they share, this network offers the most effective and efficient means by which to manage international operational co-operation within the EU.'[9]

2. Increased centralisation also seems inevitable. In its report in 1993, the Royal Commission on Criminal Justice was 'less satisfied' with arrangements for the supervision of routine police inquiries than with those for the most serious investigations. Indeed, research conducted for the RCCJ found little evidence of supervision as such.[10] Accordingly, a new approach to supervision was required throughout the police service, with improved training in the supervision of inquiries at all levels, and an overhaul of detective training and of training in investigations.[11] The HMIC Thematic Report *Managing Learning*[12] has provided a comprehensive appraisal of police training.[13] Two recent reports into police training[14] have spurred the government into implementing a National Training Scheme. Following a consultation document outlining a range of proposals to raise standards in police training, in May 2000 the government published *Police Training: The Way Forward*,[15] outlining the cost and efficiency savings that could be made through more effective collaboration between forces.

Part IV of the Criminal Justice and Police Act 2001 creates a new Central Police Training and Development Authority as a Non-Departmental Public Body.

8 J. Benyon, L. Turnbull, A. Willis and R. Woodward, *Understanding Police Cooperation in Europe: Setting A Framework for Analysis* (1993), p. 64.
9 p. 38.
10 J. Baldwin and T. Moloney, *The Supervision of Police Investigations in Serious Criminal Cases* (RCCJ Research Study No. 4) (1992); M. Maguire and C. Norris, *The Conduct and Submission of Criminal Investigations* (RCCJ Research Study No. 5) (1992); B. Irving and C. Dunnighan, *Human Factors in the Quality Control of CID Investigations* (RCCJ Research Study No. 21) (1993).
11 Cm. 2263, pp. 18–22.
12 (1999).
13 See also Home Affairs Committee in their inquiry into police training (June 1999) and Sir William Stubbs' report to the Home Secretary on *The Organisation and Funding of Police Training in England and Wales* (1999).
14 The Police Federation 'Project Forward' (May 1998) and 'Police Training – What Next?' (July 1999), the recommendations of the report of the inquiry into the death of Stephen Lawrence (February 1999), the first ever thematic inspection of training by HMIC (April 1999), a report by the Home Affairs Committee (June 1999), and a report from Sir William Stubbs (July 1999) on the organisation and funding of police training.
15 Home Office Communication Directorate; also available on the Home Office website at www.home.office.gov.uk.

'The Authority will build on the services currently provided by National Police Training, which was established by the Home Office in 1993 with a remit to design, deliver and accredit training programmes for core policing operations. As an NDPB, the new Authority will have greater independence from the Home Office. The Bill allows the Secretary of State, in consultation with stakeholders, to establish a mandatory core curriculum and a qualifications framework for police. It also strengthens the powers of the Secretary of State to require improvements in the quality of police training following and inspection undertaken by Her Majesty's Inspectorate of Constabulary (HMIC). Other plans include: A re-organised Police Training Council to provide the Home Secretary with strategic advice on training; An employer led Police National Training Organisation to promote skills and competencies within the sector; A national review team, managed by the APA and the ACPO, to identify opportunities to promote collaboration at a national, regional and local level; Improved use of information and communication technology and distance learning; Greater community involvement and co-operation in police training; The implementation of annual human resource plans for forces by Statutory Guidance to be issued under Best Value legislation.'[16]

It is intended that the Authority will serve as a centre of excellence for police training and development, promoting the value of police training and working to enhance the efficiency and effectiveness of forces in England and Wales. It will have regard to objectives set by the Secretary of State, the objectives set within the Authority's annual plan, any performance targets set, including any set in compliance with a direction given by the Secretary of State, and Authority's training and development plan, and to comply with Secretary of State's directions requiring the Authority to establish performance targets; responses to HMIC reports, and any other general or specific directions given.[17] The Police Training Inspectorate has announced that its first inspection will be of probation training in all forces.[17a]

3. The militarisation of the police is also predicted to increase. This is a concern that has been expressed especially since the miners' strike and in the wake of numerous public order incidents in which heavily armed police have adopted military tactics.[18] The Human Rights Act 1998 may well force reconsideration of the present approach to the use of firearms and other lethal weapons by the police. At present, the application of the 'citizen in uniform' doctrine, whereby the police are treated as any other citizen, creates difficulties.[19] There were 10,915 police operations in which firearms were issued to police officers between April 1999–March 2000. There were seven incidents where firearms were discharged with only three fatalities. There was an increase of 6.2% of operations in which Armed Response Vehicles were deployed (total 8,276).[20]

4. The increased use of surveillance techniques seems set to continue. Some argue that policing will shift to providing security by predicting and managing risks rather than providing crime control.[21] In a risk society:

'the traditional police focus on deviance, control, and order is displaced in favour of a focus on risk, surveillance and security. The concern is less with the labelling of deviants as outsiders and more on developing a risk-profile knowledge of individuals to ascertain and manage their place in institutions. The concern is not so much control of deviants in a repressive sense as

16 *Explanatory Notes on the Criminal Justice and Police Bill 2001*, Home Office (2001).
17 See *Police Training: The Way Forward* (2000).
17a See HMIC website press release 18 May 2001.
18 See R. Reiner, *Policing I* (1996), Part IV, and see T. Jefferson, *The Case Against Paramilitary Policing* (1990). On military intervention proper, rather than the militarisation of policing, see Chap. 4 below on public order, and HMSO, *The Manual of Military Law* (12th edn, 1993), Part II, Chap. 5.
19 See S. Skinner, [2000] PL 266; see Chap. 3 below.
20 See Home Office *Statistics on the Police Use of Firearms in England and Wales 1999–2000*, Table 1.
21 See R. V. Ericson and D. Haggerty *Policing the Risk Society* (1997).

surveillance that constitutes populations of individuals, organisations and institutions in their respective risk categories.'[1]

Another dimension to the development of police and risk management is the increasing use of civilian experts in policing. One example of this can be seen in the reliance on psychological advice in investigations[2] into serious crime, and the development of databases[3] that will help predict the likely characteristics of the offender. Unless properly monitored, these are open to abuse, and there is a real danger that the police 'round up the usual suspects', rather than investigate the crime thoroughly.

On intelligence-led policing, see the HMIC Thematic Report *Policing with Intelligence*, which encouraged the development of intelligence gathering systems and the proactive use of informants and the Internet for collecting information. ACPO recently proposed a National Public Order Intelligence System and Unit. The system would:

> 'draw intelligence from a number of sources, analyse assess and disseminate it ensuring forces, operational commanders and operational officers have access to a full and current intelligence picture to inform their decision making. The system will have checks and balances built in to it to ensure the integrity of the system and to protect intelligence gathered from sensitive sources or by sensitive means.'[4]

The shift towards intelligence-led policing leads to a greater risk of police abusing their powers than in circumstances where they exercise less discretion.

5. The rise in the private security industry has clear implications for public policing.[5] It affects the role the police perform and the public perception of the police more generally. Recognising the need to regulate the private security industry, the government has enacted a Private Security Industry Act 2001, which establishes a Security Industry Authority to licence, monitor and regulate the individuals ranging from door supervisors to wheel clampers and private investigators:

> 'Individuals will have to have a licence before becoming an employee or manager providing security services in the private security industry or setting up a private security firm. Licences will be based on consideration of whether the applicant is a "fit person" to be an employee or employer or manager in the industry. The Authority will issue licences after consideration of an applicant's full criminal record (exempt from the provisions of the Rehabilitation of Offenders Act 1974) obtained from the new Criminal Records Bureau to be set up under Part V of the Police Act 1997. For managers and directors, consideration will also be given to any records on Companies House registers of undischarged bankruptcy and/or disqualified director status. Successful applicants will be issued with a physical licence. A fee will be payable and licences will be valid for three years. An applicant will be able to appeal against the refusal or revocation of a licence.'

---

1   Ibid., p. 18.
2   See on psychological uses in police D. Oldfield, 'What Help do the Police Need with their Enquiries' in J. L. Jackson and D. A. Beckerian, *Offender Profiling, Theory Research and Practice* (1997).
3   On databases of this nature, see J. A. Stevens, 'Standard Investigatory Tools and Offender Profiling' and A. Davies, 'Specific profile Analysis: A Data based Approach to Offender Profiling' in J. L. Jackson and D. A. Beckerian, *Offender Profiling, Theory Research and Practice* (1997).
4   HMIC, *Keeping the Peace, Policing Disorder* (1999), p. 18.
5   See T. Jones and T. Newburn, *Private Security and Public Policing* (1998). See also the British Security Industry Association website: www.bsia.co.uk.

Enforcement

'Employing someone as a security operative who is unlicensed, offering security services or operating as a security operative without being licensed, providing false information to obtain a licence and breach of terms or conditions of a licence will be an offence. The Authority will publicise arrangements for licensing individuals in the private security industry and publicise the appearance of the licence issued by it. Businesses and members of the public will be encouraged to ask to see an individual's licence and be encouraged to contact the Authority if they have any suspicions about an individual or a company.'[6]

On the dangers of vigilantism generally, and its impact on local policing, see D. Sharp and D. Wilson,[7] considering a scheme in Doncaster which triggered considerable media interest.

A recent twist to this private security policing has appeared with the recent suggestion for an auxiliary police force of civilians or traffic wardens. The proposals are being reviewed by David Blunkett.[8]

(A) A ROYAL COMMISSION ON POLICING?

There are so many aspects of policing that are in controversy, including very fundamental issues such as the role, localisation and accountability of police forces, that it is not surprising to find repeated calls for a Royal Commission. The Police Federation has recently added its voice to these calls to examine the role of policing in the twenty-first century:

'The Police Federation of England and Wales has called on the Government to establish a Royal Commission on policing....

The renewed demand comes at a time when the country finds the service at its lowest ebb in recent memory and forty years after the recommendations of the last Royal Commission, undertaken between1960-62, have become redundant. "The country and the police service has changed out of all recognition since 1960. The recommendations and conclusions of the last Royal Commission relate to a police service that has long since disappeared. There was then no drugs problem, virtually no gun crime, almost no motorways, immigration was an issue in a few city areas but race relations were not considered. Eighty thousand police officers dealt with about half a million crimes a year. Last year five million crimes were reported to almost 125,000 officers. We now have 46,000 more officers to deal with four and a half million additional crimes. In simple terms, that means today's officers are dealing with ten times as many crimes. In 1960, the patrolling beat bobby was the foundation of policing, there were no personal radios, policewomen were employed only on duties relating to women and children, they had their own department and career structure, but not equal pay. The police use of firearms was virtually nil. There were no specialist squads. There was no public order training and no kind of riot gear." Mr Broughton said that society's transformation over the last 40 years has been accompanied by tinkering with policing, usually dictated by politicians, which has often satisfied neither police officers nor the public. "The police and the public it serves is crying out for redefined direction and the impetus to go forward with confidence in the difficult years ahead. A Royal Commission would set a reasoned, logical, balanced, and non-partisan agenda for the police service of this new century."

The Chairman believes the public's esteem for the police has gone into decline in recent years with the police service becoming the "fall guys" for many of the ills of society, social tensions and sustained under investment. If we look at some of the areas which attract criticism from the public, we find that we are seen as losing the fight against drugs. We are seen as remote and no longer omnicompetent. People say we have got our priorities wrong. The trouble is that different groups have different ideas of what police priorities should be. Years ago,

6   *The Government's Proposals on Regulating the Private Security Industry* (2000).
7   (2000) Howard JCJ 113.
8   See *The Sunday Times* 19 August 2001.

there was no ambivalence about the role of the police service. We were there to achieve the primary objectives - protecting life and property, preventing and detecting crime, prosecuting wrongdoers. The job description was simple, and the job was done. Today the terms of reference of policing have become muddied, and often contradictory. The service has become the handy dustbin for the insoluble problems for a wholly more complex society that the one that existed 40 years ago. Policing has diversified. Now we carry out a range of tasks that, admirable and essential as each might be, begs the question of whether the police should be doing them. Should, for example, police time and personnel be tied up in case conferences about young offenders? Why should the police be seen as part of the treatment of offenders? Mr Broughton said the time had now come for a wholesale review of policing which could include an examination of the structure of today's 43 forces, of police training which is currently failing the service, the status of the police constable - a rank which the vast majority of officers hold, a debate about the role, if any, of the private sector in future policing development, and the merits of patrolling and the extent to which technology plays an everyday part in policing. He said: We hear much talk about more changes in the offing. But why should we leave our futures, and the futures of those who come after us, to the politicians? It is forty years since the representatives of the police service had the chance to sit down with a body of independent and eminent Royal Commissioners, and set out our vision for the future of policing. A very large part of what we proposed was embodied in the Royal Commission's report. I am convinced the time is right for us to do an equally valuable job with another such Commission. The previous Royal Commission got it right when it said 'the maintenance of law and order ranks with national defence as a primary task of government. It is an essential condition of a nation's survival and happiness.'[9]

What are the most important changes that should be made to police structure and accountability: from the point of view of (a) the police (b) the citizen? To what extent are they irreconcilable aims?

The government has recently outlined plans for reform of policing and of the criminal justice system generally. The Home Office has established a dedicated website[10] to provide information on the proposals to modernise police working practices.

9 Police Federation Press Release 16 May 2000 (www.polfed.org/pressrel/releases/), quoting Chairman Fred Broughton.
10 www.homeoffice.gov.uk/policereform/.

CHAPTER 3

Police powers

1 Introduction and historical background

The materials in this chapter illustrate the powers and duties of the police in the enforcement of the criminal law.[1] The powers have undergone radical change in the last 20 years, and there is continuous expansion in this area. The position was transformed by the Police and Criminal Evidence Act 1984. In the first edition of this book, we described the previous law as follows:[2]

'The present law satisfies nobody. It is far too complex, contained in a miscellany of, often archaic, statutes and cases. Problems which are difficult enough as examination questions are trickier still for the "policeman on the beat" who will often have to act without prolonged deliberation. If the rules are known their precise meaning may be uncertain. And when their meaning is clear their content is often unsatisfactory. Many powers of the police are of unduly wide scope and yet, at the same time, the police do not possess certain powers which many would regard as necessary to the performance of their tasks. And when the law is reasonably clear and its content reasonably satisfactory there may be difficulties in ensuring compliance with those rules. Police officers perform their duties subject to the possibilities of prosecution, civil claim and internal disciplinary action if they exceed their powers. Yet for most of those with whom they deal the opportunity to prosecute or sue (notwithstanding possible punitive damages – see *Cassell & Co Ltd v Broome* [1972] AC 1027, HL) may be of little practical value, and, despite new arrangements, there still exists a division of opinion as to the way in which complaints against the police are handled. Moreover, with the exception of the rules about confessions, the judges have declined to use the rules about admissibility of evidence as a method of "policing" the police.

In the past a large amount of police work has relied on the co-operation and consent of citizens together with a certain amount of "bluff" as to the extent of police powers. With co-operation and consent apparently diminishing and a greater awareness of people as to their 'rights', the need grows for a thorough review and reform of the law of police powers.'

These matters were considered by the Royal Commission on Criminal Procedure (RCCP) that reported in 1981.[3] In a summary of the report, the RCCP outlined its task:

Royal Commission on Criminal Procedure; The Balance of Criminal Justice: Summary of the Report (HMSO, 1981)

The Royal Commission on Criminal Procedure began work in February 1978. Its terms of reference were:

---

1 See generally on police powers: the articles collected in R. Reiner, *Policing Vols I and II* (1996); N. Whitty, T. Murphy and S. Livingstone, *Civil Liberties Law: The Human Rights Act Era (2001)*; R. Clayton and H. Tomlinson, *Civil Actions Against the Police* (3rd edn, 1997); K. Lidstone and C. Palmer, *Bevan and Lidstone's Investigation of Crime: A Guide to Police Powers* (2nd edn., 1996); D. Feldman, *Civil Liberties and Human Rights in England and Wales* (1993), Chaps. 5, 9; M. Zander, *The Police and Criminal Evidence Act 1984* (4th edn, 2001); Symposia, [1985] PL 388ff; [1985] Crim LR 535ff; [1990] Crim LR 452ff.
2 p. 33.
3 *RCCP Report* (Cmnd. 8092, 1981); *Law and Procedure* volume (Cmnd. 8092–1, 1981).

'To examine, having regard both to the interests of the community in bringing offenders to justice and to the rights and liberties of persons suspected or accused of crime, and taking into account also the need for the efficient and economical use of resources, whether changes are needed in England and Wales in

i.   the powers and duties of the police in respect of the investigation of criminal offences and the rights and duties of suspect and accused persons, including the means by which these are secured;

ii.   the process of and responsibility for the prosecution of criminal offences; and

iii. such other features of criminal procedure and evidence as relate to the above; and to make recommendations.'

Matter of fact though these subjects may appear, they form one of the central threads in the history of liberty in Britain. Criminal justice has provided for centuries a natural arena in which the struggle to establish the rights of the individual citizen in relation to the security of society and the power of the state has been waged.

The Commission's task has been to try to achieve a balance between a host of competing rights and objectives, a task made the more difficult by the lack of consensus about the content or even the existence of some of the rights. On the one hand there are those who see the fight to bring criminals to justice as being of paramount necessity in today's society. They tend to see the police as struggling against increasing crime, shackled by laws and procedures which, during their investigations, their questioning of suspects, and finally at the trial, favour the criminal. On the other side are those who believe that the cards are in practice stacked against suspects and defendants, that the individual has insufficient legal protection against police power, and that the safeguards against abuse and oppression are inadequate. The majority of public and professional opinion is inevitably between the two. But where can a balance be found which will secure the confidence of the public?

In its review of investigation and prosecution, the Commission applies throughout three standards for judging both the existing system and its own recommendations. Are the arrangements, actual or proposed, fair and clear? Are they open, that is, not secret, and is there accountability? Are they workable and efficient?

The Commission recommended that police powers should be extended in a number of significant respects, but that this should be balanced by the improvement of safeguards against abuse and the extension of safeguards across the whole field of police powers. The government accepted many (although not all) of the recommendations concerning police powers and implemented them in the Police and Criminal Evidence Act 1984 (PACE), which received Royal Assent on 31 October 1984 and generally took effect on 1 January 1986. [4]

A common theme running through many of the commentaries on the RCCP Report was that police powers were to be extended but that the proposed safeguards requirements that a subject of the exercise of a power be informed of the reasons for it; the requirement that the reasons be recorded contemporaneously; periodic review by senior police officers or magistrates of exercises of power; improvement in complaints procedures; reliance on codes of conduct, breach of which by a police officer would constitute a disciplinary offence, were not as strong as at first sight might appear. McConville and Baldwin[5] argued (*inter alia*) that while the RCCP

4   On the Report of the Royal Commission see the symposium in the Criminal Law Review: [1981] Crim LR 445ff; L. H. Leigh, (1981) 44 MLR 296; B. Smythe, [1981] PL 184, 481; M. McConville and J. Baldwin, 10 Int J Sociology of Law 287. On the Police and Criminal Evidence Bill, see the *Police and Criminal Bill Briefing Guide* (Home Office, 1984); L. Bridges and T. Bunyan, (1983) 10 JLS 85; L. Christian, *Policing By Coercion* (GLC Police Committee Support Unit, 1983).

5   Op. cit., n. 4.

commissioned an extensive body of research, the results of that research were used selectively: for example, 'No evidence is adduced to demonstrate a need for the increased powers of stop and search, to arrest, to fingerprint, or to search property and seize goods and articles which are proposed'.[6]

Moreover,

'No research was conducted into the efficacy of police disciplinary procedures or of civil actions, either as means of inducing police compliance with the rules or as remedies to citizens in the event of breach. No research was conducted to test whether the Commission's confidence that requiring police officers to record in writing their reasons, say, for arrest, for prolonged interrogation of suspects, or for refusing access to a solicitor, would provide adequate opportunity for subsequent review was well-founded or not.'[7]

As was only to be expected, some took a more favourable view than others. Leigh[8] noted that the RCCP Report 'engendered strong reactions, some almost Pavlovian in character': in his view, the report, with some exceptions 'on balance would improve the present system and ought to be implemented'.

The arrangements under PACE have now been in operation for 15 years and it is easier to monitor their effect. The Home Office regularly publishes statistics on the use of certain powers under PACE. More significantly, the findings of a series of research projects on particular areas have been published and research is continuing.[9] The research on particular areas is noted at the appropriate points in the chapter. The structure of PACE has been extended to Northern Ireland, with some modifications.[10]

The role and powers of the police again came under a measure of scrutiny by the Royal Commission on Criminal Justice (RCCJ), chaired by Lord Runciman, which reported in 1993.[11] Its terms of reference were:

'to examine the effectiveness of the criminal justice system in England and Wales in securing the conviction of those guilty of criminal offences and the acquittal of those who are innocent, having regard to the efficient use of resources.'[12]

Furthermore, it was 'in particular to consider what changes are needed in eight specific areas of the criminal justice process'. The first of these was:

'the conduct of police investigations and their supervision by senior police officers, and in particular the degree of control that is exercised by those officers over the conduct of the investigation and the gathering and preparation of evidence.'

The background to the appointment of the RCCJ was the spate of high profile cases, many involving convictions for terrorist offences, in which the Court of Appeal had found there to have been a miscarriage of justice.[13] Police malpractice, in the form of

6 Ibid. p. 299.
7 M. McConville and J. Baldwin, 'The Research Programme' (1981) 131 NLJ 1117, 1118.
8 (1981) 44 MLR 296, 307–308.
9 See in particular the research produced by the Home Office Policing and Reducing Crime Unit. Their Police Research Series Reports are available at www.homeoffice.gov.uk/prghome.htm.
10 See the Police and Criminal Evidence (Northern Ireland) Order 1989, S.I. 1989 No. 1341 (N.I. 12) and subsequent amendments; Symposium, (1989) 40 NILQ 319ff.
11 Cm. 2263.
12 Ibid., p. i.
13 On these cases see J. Rozenberg, 'Miscarriages of Justice' in E. Stockdale and S. Casale (eds.), *Criminal Justice Under Stress* (1992); C. Walker 'Introduction' in C. Walker and K. Starmer, (eds.), *Justice in Error* (1993). See also the writings of the victims of these miscarriages: P. Hill and R. Burnett, *Stolen Years* (1990); G. Conlon, *Proved Innocent* (1990). Such cases continue to come to light: see e.g. the release of the Bridgewater Three (*Independent*, 5 March 1997). On 14 July 2000, ten-year jail sentences against three men convicted of armed robbery were quashed in the light of the discovery that flying squad officers had conspired in concocting evidence (*Guardian*, 15 July 2000).

the suppression or falsification of evidence, was a significant factor in several of these cases. By 1993, the emphasis of the government's concerns had shifted from the problem of miscarriages of justice to a perceived lack of effectiveness of the criminal justice system in controlling crime. The RCCJ made 352 recommendations. Commentators (other than the police) have been largely hostile, noting that the recommendations seemed directed more to promoting the efficiency of the system in obtaining convictions than to the prevention or remedying of miscarriages of justice.[14] This persistent drive for efficiency in the criminal justice system echoes the changes in policing considered in Chapter 2.

In the area of policing, Reiner[15] noted that the RCCJ appeared to have taken the view that the Report of the Philips Royal Commission, largely incorporated in PACE and the Prosecution of Offences Act 1985:

> 'laid down a framework which is broadly on the right lines. In this sense, the policing proposals of the Runciman Commission can largely be seen as a set of footnotes to Philips rather than a new departure.'

Many of the RCCJ recommendations have been accepted and incorporated in the Criminal Justice and Public Order Act 1994 or changes to regulations or practice. Even now, some eight years after the Report, the government is still seeking to implement some of the recommendations as, for example, with the Criminal Justice (Mode of Trial) (No. 2) Bill 2001.

In addition to reforms flowing from Royal Commissions, police powers in England and Wales have been influenced by relevant international standards. These include the protection of the right to life (Art. 2 ECHR; Art. 6 ICCPR); the prohibition of torture or inhuman or degrading treatment or punishment (Art. 3 ECHR; Art. 7 ICCPR (which also outlaws 'cruel' treatment or punishment); the right to liberty and security of person (Art. 5 ECHR; Art. 9 ICCPR); and the enjoyment of the protected rights and freedoms without discrimination (Art. 14 ECHR, cf. Art. 26 ICCPR (general entitlement without any discrimination to the equal protection of the law).[16] The implementation of the Human Rights Act 1998 has inevitably resulted in a much more direct influence of the ECHR jurisprudence on police powers, and its impact is considered throughout the chapter. Nevertheless, the trend of diluting safeguards for the suspect originally introduced in the 1984 Act continues; at the same time there is an expansion of the police powers with broader powers of search, more arrestable offences, wider powers to take samples and retain them, and to invite juries to draw inferences from the suspect's behaviour during the investigation.

2   Assaults on and obstruction of the police

Before examining the powers available to the police in terms of search, arrest, detention etc., it is worth considering the offences most often used to prosecute those who do not comply with police actions. Many of the cases in which the courts are

---

14 See generally, M. McConville and L. Bridges, *Criminal Justice in Crisis* (1994); S. Field and P. Thomas (eds.), 'Justice and Efficiency? The Royal Commission on Criminal Justice' (1994) 12 JLS 1–164 (special issue); Symposium [1993] Crim LR 808ff, 926 ff;L. Bridges and M. McConville, (1994) 57 MLR 75; M. Zander, ibid., p 264, reply by Bridges and McConville, ibid. p. 267.

15 [1993] Crim LR 808, 810.

16 See above, Chap. 1. The application of international standards to police powers is considered by R. Reiner and L. Leigh, 'Police Powers' in G. Chambers and C. McCrudden (eds.), *Individual Rights and the Law* in *Britain* (1993) and S. H. Bailey, 'Rights in the Administration of Justice' in D. J. Harris and S. Joseph (eds.), *The ICCPR and United Kingdom Law* (1995).

called upon to determine the lawfulness of police action involve prosecutions under s. 89 of the Police Act 1996, which replaced the offences in Police Act 1964, s. 51.[17]

(A) THE OFFENCES[18]

Police Act 1996, s. 89

(1) Any person who assaults a constable in the execution of his duty, or a person assisting a constable in the execution of his duty, shall be guilty of an offence and liable on summary conviction to imprisonment for a term not exceeding six months or to a fine not exceeding level 5 on the standard scale, or to both.

(2) Any person who resists or wilfully obstructs a constable in the execution of his duty, or a person assisting a constable in the execution of his duty, shall be guilty of an offence and liable on summary conviction to imprisonment for a term not exceeding one month or to a fine not exceeding level 3 on the standard scale, or to both.

(3) This section also applies to a constable who is a member of a police force maintained in Scotland or Northern Ireland when he is executing a warrant, or otherwise acting in England or Wales, by virtue of any enactment conferring powers on him in England and Wales.

'Assault'

This includes both a technical assault and a battery (the two are often misleadingly used interchangeably). Thus, an assault is committed where the defendant, D, intentionally or recklessly causes another person to apprehend immediate[19] and unlawful personal violence. As where D waves a weapon at V, or makes oral threats in such a way that V apprehends immediate violence.[20] A battery is committed when D intentionally or recklessly inflicts unlawful force on V, this is satisfied by the slightest touch, and there is no need to prove any injury. The offence under s. 89 requires proof of either an assault or a battery in the sense described here.

In the execution of his duty

Coffin v Smith (1980) 71 Cr App Rep 221, Queen's Bench Divisional Court

Police officers were summoned to a boys' club by the youth leader there to ensure that various people left before a disco started. S and H assaulted the officers. The magistrates dismissed charges under the Police Act 1964, s. 51(1) on the ground that the officers were not acting in the execution of their duty as they were doing something that they were not compelled by law to do.[1] The Divisional Court allowed the prosecutors' appeal.

Donaldson LJ: The modern law on the subject is, I think, to be found in two different cases. The first is a decision of the Court of Criminal Appeal, *Waterfield and Lynn* (1963) 48 Cr App Rep 42, [1964] 1 QB 164, where Ashworth J delivering the judgment of the Court, at p. 47 and 170 respectively, said: 'In the judgment of this court it would be difficult, and in

17 See also the offence of assault with intent to resist or prevent arrest contrary to s. 38 of the Offences Against the Person Act 1861.

18 See generally, G. Williams, *Textbook on Criminal Law* (2nd edn, 1983), pp. 199–205; J.C. Smith, *Smith and Hogan, Criminal Law* (9th edn, 1999), pp. 415–424; M. Supperstone, *Brownlie's Law Relating to Public Order* (2nd edn, 1981), pp. 105–119. On the older cases see: K. Lidstone, 'A Policeman's Duty Not to Take Liberties' [1975] Crim LR 617. On reform, see: 14th Report of the Criminal Law Revision Committee on Offences against the Person (Cmnd. 7844, 1980); Home Office *Consultation Paper on Violence* (1998) p. 9.

19 *R v Constanza* [1997] 2 Cr App R 492.

20 See *R v Ireland* [1998] AC 147, per Lord Steyn especially at p. 161. See also *Collins v Wilcock* [1984] 3 All ER 374.

1 As earlier cases had required: *R v Prebble* (1858) 1 F and F 325; *R v Roxburgh* (1871) 12 Cox CC 8.

the present case it is unnecessary, to reduce within specific limits the general terms in which the duties of police constables have been expressed. In most cases it is probably more convenient to consider what the police constable was actually doing and in particular whether such conduct was prima facie an unlawful interference with a person's liberty or property . If so, it is then relevant to consider whether (a) such conduct falls within the general scope of any duty imposed by statute or recognised at common law and (b) whether such conduct, albeit within the general scope of such a duty, involved an unjustifiable use of powers associated with the duty.'

Applying that basis, it is quite clear that these constables were on duty, they were in uniform, and they were not doing anything that was prima facie any unlawful interference with a person's liberty or property.

Further guidance on the scope of the police officer's duty in this context is I think to be derived from the judgment of Lord Parker CJ in *Rice v Connolly* [1966] 2 QB 414, and the passage to which I would like to refer is at p. 419 'It is also in my judgment clear that it is part of the obligations and duties of a police constable to take all steps which appear to him necessary for keeping the peace, for preventing crime or for protecting property from criminal injury. There is no exhaustive definition of the powers and obligations of the police, but they are at least those, and they would further include the duty to detect crime and to bring an offender to justice.'

In a word, a police officer's duty is to be a keeper of the peace and to take all necessary steps with that in view. These officers, just like the ordinary officer on the beat, were attending a place where they thought that their presence would assist in the keeping of the peace. I know that Mr Staddon says 'Oh no, this is all part and parcel of the assistance which they gave to the youth leader in ejecting these people'. Even if that was so, they would have been doing no more than a police officer's duty in all the circumstances. In fact it is clear that there was a break. Both the respondents went away and came back. The officers were in effect simply standing there on their beat in the execution of their duty when they were assaulted. This is a very clear case indeed.

Bristow J agreed.

Appeal allowed.

NOTES

1. The term 'duty' is ambiguous. It could mean:
(1) a function which in a general sense can be termed part of a police officer's job but without necessarily any element of obligation;
(2) the same as (1) but with the qualification that the officer be in the exercise of some specific legal power or performance of some specific legal duty;
(3) a function which an officer is specifically required by his superiors or police regulations to perform;
(4) a function which a police officer is obliged by law to perform in the sense that failure to do so constitutes a crime or tort.
Coffin v Smith appears to reject meanings (3) and (4).
2. The statement quoted from *R v Waterfield and Lynn*[2] and other cases makes the point that if a constable is acting in the purported exercise of specific legal powers or duties he must remain within the limits set by law to those powers or duties. For example, a constable has been held to have exceeded his powers and thus acted outside the execution of his duty where he has trespassed on private land: *Davis v Lisle*;[3] *McArdle v Wallace (No 2)*;[4] or assaulted someone: *Kenlin v Gardner*;[5] *Ludlow v*

Burgess;[6] *Ricketts v Cox;*[7] *McBean v Parker.*[8] Thus, a police officer is not acting in the execution of his duty if he restrains someone in the mistaken belief that another officer has already arrested that person.[9] If a police officer makes an unlawful arrest, he is not in the execution of his duty,[10] but where the arrest is lawful but it is impracticable for the officer to inform the suspect of the grounds for arrest he is still in the execution of his duty.[11] An officer is not in the execution of his duty where he searches a suspect without supplying his name and station,[12] nor where he searches premises under s. 17 or 18 of PACE without informing the occupier of the reasons for entry.[13] The prosecution must prove that the officer was acting in the execution of his duty.[14] The failure of the court in *Coffin v Smith* to provide precise guidance has led to further judicial disagreement, as seen in *Porter v Metropolitan Police Commissioner.*

(i) Police duty as 'keeping the peace'?

Porter v Metropolitan Police Commissioner (1999) 20 November, Court of Appeal, Civil Division, unreported

P was annoyed when the electricity board had failed to keep an appointment at her flat. She went to the electricity board shop to complain. She became very angry at her treatment and refused to leave until the board arranged for a visit to her flat. Police officers were called and forcibly removed her from the premises at the request of the staff. P bit one of the officers, but charges of assaulting an officer in the execution of his duty were dropped and she brought a civil action against the MPC claiming false imprisonment. The court discussed the question of whether the police officers were acting in the execution of their duty.

Judge LJ: Mr Blaxland [counsel for the claimant] suggested that although the police officers who attended the LEB showroom were on duty and in uniform, they were not present nor acting as police officers in the execution of their duty. They arrived to deal with the civil wrong of trespass. In that capacity they enjoyed no powers greater than those which could be exercised in ordinary circumstances by members of the LEB staff themselves, or if the LEB had arranged to use them, guards or attendants employed by 'civilian security' organisations. As a matter of public policy, so Mr Blaxland argued, it is undesirable for police officers to act at the behest of private individuals engaged in a private dispute, unless there is something to suggest an actual or pending breach of the peace. If they do, they are likely to be perceived by one side or the other to be taking sides. As the only report received by the police was that the plaintiff was refusing to leave the showroom and she was not causing any trouble beyond that, there was nothing requiring their attendance.

In my judgment the obvious organisation to be contacted for assistance in a troublesome situation like the ejection of a trespasser is the police. Indeed if the police response were to the effect that 'this is not police business', some might sensibly ask, 'Why ever not?' A good example of the consequences of police inertia is provided by the tendency in earlier days to regard threatened or actual violence between spouses, or partners, as 'only domestic'. With a more positive police response a number of unpleasant incidents of violence might have been discouraged, if not altogether avoided. Mr Blaxland's proposal, said to be based on public

---

6 Below, p.163.
7 Below, p. 171.
8 Below, p. 468. See also *Riley v DPP* (1989) 91 Cr App R 14.
9 *Kerr v DPP* [1995] Crim LR 394.
10 *DPP v Chapman* (1989) 89 Cr App R 190.
11 *DPP v Hawkins* [1988] 3 All ER 673.
12 *Osman v DPP* (1999) 163 JP 725.
13 *Lineham v DPP* [2000] Crim LR 861; *O'Loughlin v Chief Constable of Essex* [1998] 3 WLR 374.
14 *DPP v Chapman* (1988) 89 Cr App R 190.

policy, would create an environment in which the police would avoid, and be expected to keep clear of any involvement 'only civil', in an area of modern life affecting the community peace.

On analysis it is not strictly necessary to decide whether the police officers were acting in the execution of their duty when they first laid hands on the plaintiff, nor whether *Coffin v Smith* (1980) 72 Cr App R 221 correctly overruled *R v Prebble & Others* [1858] 1 F & F 325 and *R v Roxburgh* [1871] 12 Cox CC 8. In my judgment the critical question in this case is not whether they were acting in the execution of their duty, but rather whether they were acting lawfully when they seized the plaintiff physically in order to remove her from the premises.

On the question of the lawfulness of the police behaviour, whether or not *R v Roxburgh* was rightly or wrongly decided in relation to the execution of a police officer's duty, Cockburn CJ observed that

> 'Although, no doubt, the prosecutor might not have been acting strictly speaking in the execution of his duty as a police officer, since he was not actually obliged to assist in ejecting the prisoner, yet he was acting quite lawfully in doing so; for the landlord had a right to eject the prisoner under the circumstances, and the prosecutor might lawfully assist him in so doing.'

(For more recent examples of the practical application of this reasoning, see *Glasbrook v Glamorgan County Council* [1925] AC 270: *R v Chief Constable of Devon and Cornwall, ex p CEGB* [1982] 1QB 458, particularly per Templeman LJ at 479-480). The present case provides another example of the same principle in operation.

The officers were not only acting lawfully when they arrived at and eventually began to remove the plaintiff from the showroom, but while so acting, even if not strictly in the execution of their duty, they were also entitled to arrest any individual responsible for or threatening or likely to cause a breach of the peace.

> 'Every citizen in whose presence a breach of the peace is being, or reasonably appears to be about to be, committed has the right to take reasonable steps to make the person who is breaking or threatening to break the peace refrain from doing so; and those reasonable steps in appropriate cases will include detaining him against his will. At common law this is not only the right of every citizen, it is also his duty, although, except in the case of the citizen who is a constable, it is a duty of imperfect obligation.' (Per Lord Diplock in *Albert v Lavin* [1982] AC 546 at 565.)

In my judgment this is a straightforward case. The first police officers to attend the showroom did so in direct response to a request for assistance made to their police station by a member of the public. They were at work as police officers, on duty, in uniform, when the call was received, and when they arrived. The woman police officers responded to a request for assistance from their male colleagues. They too were at work, on duty, and in uniform. These police officers were present to sort out a problem between members of the public in which there was an inherent risk of trouble, and by their presence, as well as by their efforts at persuasion, were seeking to ensure so far as they could, that the peace was maintained. If the plaintiff persisted in her refusal to leave voluntarily they were ultimately entitled to lay hands on her and physically remove her from the showroom against her wishes, again, a situation fraught with potential difficulty. This, in the end, is what they did. For the reasons already given their actions were lawful.

As I understood it, Mr Blaxland's argument seemed to predicate that until grounds for arrest existed, the execution of the police officers' duty was somehow postponed or deferred. I do not accept that a police officer on duty, offering practical assistance to a member of the public enforcing his civil rights, is not acting in the execution of his duty as a police officer until grounds for arrest have arisen. Police officers on duty are required to maintain and preserve the peace, if possible, before it is broken, as well as to restore it after things have gone wrong.

As to authority, this view is supported by the decision in *Coffin v Smith* (above) where the argument that a police officer cannot be held to be acting in the execution of his duty unless he is doing something that he is 'compelled by law to do', was emphatically rejected.

May LJ: In principle, I think that there is every reason why the law should encourage those who are lawfully entitled to eject trespassers to ask the police to help them to do so. The dangers of individual self-help are obvious and it is far preferable for people to receive help from trained police officers than to look to friends, neighbours or passers by. In addition, since forcible ejection is inherently likely to lead to violent resistance, the police would be at hand to prevent or restrain violence in accordance with the law.

It is not, in my view, necessary in this appeal to decide whether a police officer who helps a proprietor to eject a peaceful but intransigent trespasser initially acts as an individual or as a police officer. The power to help would in practical terms be the same, whatever the answer to that question. The only likely relevance of the question would be if the trespasser assaulted the police officer or, possibly, if the trespasser obstructed what the police officer was doing. If there was an assault, there could be a question whether this was common assault or an assault on a police officer in the execution of his duty. In the present case, the appellant did not at the relevant time assault any of the police officers: so the question does not arise. Academically, *R v Prebble* (1858) 1 F& F 325 and *R v Roxburgh* (1871) 12 Cox CC8 support the proposition that the police officer is not acting in the execution of his duty. *Coffin v Smith* (1980) 72 Cr App R 221 decides otherwise and I am inclined to think that the conclusion was a necessary part of the court's decision. It was at least in response to what Donaldson LJ said at page 225 was 'the whole basis of Mr Staddon's argument' in opposition to the successful appeal by police prosecutors.

Intrinsically, I think that there would be strong common sense grounds for holding, if it were necessary, that the police officers in the present case were acting as police officers from the moment they entered the LEB showroom. They were in uniform and no one could have supposed that they were not police officers. They were responding to a sensible request for assistance when self-help by individuals would have been difficult and provocative. If there was violence or threatened violence, they would immediately be entitled and obliged to act as police officers to deal with the resulting breach of the peace. There is no practical sense in distinguishing their role at one moment from their role at the next. I am not persuaded that the practical and common sense answer in the present case would have any constitutional significance, nor would it adversely affect any one's civil rights and liberties. The position would probably be different, depending on the facts, if a police officer, accepting an invitation to help eject a trespasser, was off duty and in civilian clothes. He would then act as the individual which he appeared to be. If the time came when there was violence and the police officer disclosed that he was a police officer and made an arrest, he would then be acting as a police officer in the execution of his duty.

Sedley LJ: I agree with Lord Justice Judge that London Electricity were entitled to call the police and that the police were right to respond to the call. But it is important to be clear why this was so.

There is long-established authority that a constable may lawfully assist others in self-help, but acting as an individual and not as a constable: *R v Prebble* (1858) 1 F & F 325, *R v Roxburgh* (1871) 12 Cox CC 8. Equally, it is clear that everyone, whether a constable or not, has both a power and a duty to detain persons committing or provoking a breach of the peace, in order to abate or prevent it: *Albert v Lavin* [1982] AC 546. But neither of these powers is a power of arrest. The power of arrest, the purpose of which is to bring a person before a court, will arise if a person creates or threatens to create a fracas in the course of being lawfully removed, whether the police are assisting in the removal or (as they may be wiser sometimes to do) are standing by to keep the peace while the occupier removes the trespasser.

But it is argued by Mr McLeod for the Commissioner that a constable who assists in an eviction, provided he is present in performance of his general peacekeeping function, is acting in the execution of his duty even if no crime or breach of the peace has been committed and no power of arrest has arisen. If then, he argues, the trespasser fails to co-operate and compels the officers to use force, she has caused a breach of the peace. It is on this basis that he defends the judge's ruling, relying on the decision of a divisional court (Donaldson and Bristow JJ) in *Coffin v Smith* (1980) 72 Cr App R 221.

If it were necessary to analyse the reasoning in *Coffin v Smith*, I would have difficulty in accepting it as wholly correct, even though I have no doubt about the correctness of the conclusion. But as Lord Justice Judge has pointed out, the present case does not turn on whether the constables who removed Mrs Porter were acting in the execution of their duty: it turns on whether they were acting lawfully. In my judgment they were. By assisting London Electricity's staff to evict Mrs Porter they were acting as lawfully as the staff themselves would have been had they evicted her. This is established by the decisions in *Prebble* and *Roxburgh*, which I consider still to be good law. It was not necessary for the Divisional Court to overrule them in *Coffin v Smith* because there the constables were acting in the execution of their duty in standing by to keep the peace, not in taking any active part in the eviction of the youths.

In the present case, by contrast, a trespasser was being removed by police constables acting as voluntary agents for the occupiers of the premises. This they were free to do. If in the course of the eviction whoever was carrying it out a breach of the peace occurred or became imminent, their continuing duty as constables required them to intervene by detention or arrest. Such a breach of the peace 'is committed only when an individual causes harm, or appears likely to cause harm, to persons or property, or acts in a manner the natural consequence of which would be to provoke violence in others'

For these reasons I agree that the appeal must fail.

NOTES

1. See the discussion of the breach of the peace power, below, Chap. 4, p. 460.

2. When the police are called to a civil dispute of this nature, it is likely that they will choose to exercise a power of arrest for breach of the peace. Is that not very likely to provoke anger from one of the parties and lead to an obstruction charge out of what was a mere civil dispute? The arrest power for breach of the peace should be used exceptionally only.

(ii) Physical contact in the course of 'exercising' duty

The question whether an officer has exceeded his powers when making 'trivial' contact with another has come under close scrutiny in a series of cases beginning with *Donnelly v Jackman*[15] which was later interpreted as having created only a very limited exception: *Bentley v Brudzinski*.

Bentley v Brudzinski (1982) 75 Cr App Rep 217, Queen's Bench Divisional Court

At about 3.30 a.m. PC Phillips was looking for a vehicle reported to have been taken without consent. He saw the defendant and his brother running barefoot along certain streets. They broadly fitted the description of the two men said to have taken the vehicle. The constable questioned them. They denied, truthfully, any involvement with the vehicle and after various interchanges moved off. PC Butler, who had just arrived on the scene, said 'Just a minute' then, not in any hostile way, but merely to attract attention he placed his right hand on [the defendant's] left shoulder. The defendant punched PC Butler in the face. The magistrates held there was no case to answer on a charge under s. 51(1) on the ground that PC Butler was not acting in the execution of his duty. The prosecutor's appeal to the Divisional Court was dismissed.

> **McCullough J:** *Donnelly v Jackman* (1970) 54 Cr App Rep 229, [1970] 1 WLR 562 was in some ways similar case to the present on its facts. Mr Donnelly was charged with the same offence as here, assaulting a police constable in the execution of his duty. A Police Constable Grimmett had wanted to ask him certain questions. He had asked him to stop and tapped him on the shoulder. Mr Donnelly then tapped the officer's shoulder and said 'Now we are even, copper.' The police constable tapped Mr Donnelly on the shoulder a second time. It was found by the justices that his intention in so doing was to stop him and ask him further questions. Mr Donnelly's reaction was to strike the officer with some force. He was convicted, and appealed unsuccessfully by way of case stated to this Court.
>
> In giving the first judgment, with which Ashworth J and Lord Parker CJ both agreed, Talbot J said at p. 232 and p. 565 of the respective reports:
>
> 'Turning to the facts of this matter, it is not very clear what precisely the justices meant or found when they said the officer touched the defendant on the shoulder, but whatever it was they really did mean, it seems clear to me that they must have felt it was a minimal matter by

the way they treated this matter and the result of the case. When one considers the problem: was this officer acting in the course of his duty, one ought to bear in mind that it is not every trivial interference with a citizen's liberty that amounts to a course of conduct sufficient to take the officer out of the course of his duties. The facts that the magistrates found in this case do not justify the view that the police officer was not acting in the execution of his duty when he went up to the defendant and wanted to speak to him. Therefore the assault was rightly found to be an assault upon this officer whilst acting in the execution of his duty and I would dismiss this appeal.'

I observe that in that paragraph Talbot J simply referred 'to the officer going up to the defendant, wanting to speak to him and tapping him on the shoulder. He does not specifically advert in that paragraph, or anywhere in his judgment, to the justices' finding that the defendant was being stopped by the police officer.

I, for my part, think that in cases of this kind a great deal will inevitably turn on the impression that the witnesses have given to the justices. In *Donnelly*'s case (supra) this Court was plainly of the view that what had happened was trivial and was not enough to take the officer out of the ordinary scope of his duties. The fact that that was the decision in *Donnelly v Jackman* (supra) does not of course necessarily mean that the decision will be the same in every case in which an officer goes up to a person in the street to ask him questions.

In the next case, *Ludlow v Burgess* (1971) 25 Cr App Rep 227, which also is in many ways rather similar to the present case, the decision went the other way. It is only reported shortly in [1971] Crim LR 238. Again it is a decision of this Court with Lord Parker CJ presiding. What had happened was this. While a constable was getting on a bus he was kicked by a youth. The constable thought it was a deliberate kick but the defendant said it was accidental. The constable, who did not have his warrant card with him, told him not to use foul language and said that he was a police officer, whereupon the defendant began to walk away. The constable put a hand on his shoulder, not with the intention of arresting him, but to detain him for further conversation and inquiries. Then the defendant struggled and kicked the constable. Others joined in. In due course the defendant was charged with the same offence as here. He was convicted. His appeal was allowed by this Court, which said that 'the detention of a man against his will without arresting him was an unlawful act and a serious interference with the citizen's liberty. Since it was an unlawful act, it was not an act done in the execution of the constable's duty.'

Although the precise circumstances of the touching are not apparent from the very short report, *Ludlow v Burgess* (supra) when compared with *Donnelly v Jackman* (supra) demonstrates that the decision in any individual case will turn on the particular circumstances in which the police officer and the citizen come into, if I may use a neutral word, engagement with one another. I have no doubt, looking at the circumstances as a whole, that both constables were trying to stop the defendant and his brother from going home in order to detain them and to question them further.

We have to ask ourselves whether the justices arrived at a decision which no bench could reasonably have reached. I can well understand why they reached the decision they did. I would have reached the same decision myself.

Donaldson LJ: ... I entirely agree with McCullough J's conclusion and the reasons which led him to that conclusion.

NOTES

1. On *Donnelly v Jackman* see J. M. Evans,[16] and D. Lanham.[17] For a New Zealand decision approving, obiter, the approach taken in *Donnelly,* see *Pounder v Police.*[18] S. H. Bailey and D. J. Birch commented:[19]

16 (1970) 33 MLR 438.
17 [1974] Crim LR 288.
18 [1971] NZLR 1080.
19 [1982] Crim LR at 481–482.

'The facts of *Donnelly v Jackman* and *Bentley v Brudzinski* are, however difficult to reconcile. It is possible that the tap on the shoulder *(Donnelly)* was genuinely more 'trivial' than the hand *(Bentley)*. This would be a very fine distinction, and one arguably untenable as the intentions of the officers in the two cases seem the same, i.e. to stop for questioning. Perhaps the real explanation is that the facts of the two cases are essentially the same, that the two benches of magistrates took divergent views, and the Divisional Court was not in a position to say that either was so unreasonable or perverse as to enable it to impose a different view.'

2. In *Kerr v DPP*,[20] K struck an officer who took hold of her arm in order to detain her, and began to caution her, in the mistaken belief that she had already been placed under arrest by another officer. The Divisional Court set aside her conviction for assaulting the officer in the execution of his duty. The officer's conduct was not so trivial as to fall within *Donnelly v Jackman,* he was clearly exceeding his powers and his mistaken (albeit honest and reasonable) belief was insufficient to cause him to be acting in the execution of his duty.

3. Is it possible to lay down cast-iron rules on the degree of interference that will be necessary to take an officer outside the execution of his duty? Note the court's desire to maintain consistency between this offence and the mainstream offences of assault. A recent example of the problem was provided in *Mepstead v DPP*[1] in which police officers gave M a parking ticket having warned him about his parking. When M became abusive, one officer, L, took hold of M's arm and said 'Don't be silly, calm down, it's only a ticket'. The magistrates found that L was not seeking to arrest or detain M but held him solely in order to draw his attention to the content of what was being said to him and in attempt to calm the situation down. M assaulted L.

Balcombe LJ: The leading authority is *Collins v Wilcock* [1984] 3 All ER 374, [1984] 1 WLR 1172, a decision of the Divisional Court of the Queen's Bench Division consisting of Lord Justice Robert Goff and Lord Justice Mann. The judgment of the Court was given by Lord Justice Robert Goff in a reserved judgment, and it is sufficient, I think, if I quote from two passages.

At page 1177, just below letter B, Lord Justice Robert Goff says this: 'We are here concerned primarily with battery. The fundamental principle, plain and incontestable, is that every person's body is inviolate.' [A little later] 'But so widely drawn a principle must inevitably be subject to exceptions.'

Then he said, after referring to certain other exceptions: 'a broader exception has been created to allow for the exigencies of everyday life. Generally speaking, consent is a defence to battery; and most of the physical contacts of ordinary life are not actionable because they are impliedly consented to by all who move in society and so expose themselves to the risk of bodily contact.' Then after giving various examples of that type of bodily contact, just near the foot of the page, Lord Goff says this: 'Among such forms of conduct long held to be acceptable, is touching a person for the purpose of engaging his attention, though of course using no greater degree of physical contact than is reasonably necessary in the circumstances for that purpose.' Then he gives various examples of that. A little later: 'Furthermore, persistent touching to gain attention in the face of obvious disregard may transcend the norms of acceptable behaviour, and so be outside the exception. We do not say that more that one touch is never permitted; for example, the lost or distressed may surely be permitted a second touch, or possibly even more, on a reluctant or impervious sleeve or shoulder, as may a person who is acting reasonably in the exercise of a duty. In each case, the test must be whether the physical contact so persisted in has in the circumstances gone beyond generally acceptable standards of conduct; and the answer to that question will depend upon the facts of the particular case.' A little later on, at page 1178, just above letter E:

'police officers have for present purposes no greater rights than ordinary citizens. It follows that, subject to such cases, physical contact by a police officer with another person may be unlawful as a battery, just as it might be if he was an ordinary member of the public. But a police officer has his rights as a citizen, as well as his duties as a policeman. A police officer may wish to engage a man's attention, for example if he wishes to question him. If he lays his hand on the man's sleeve or taps his shoulder for that purpose, he commits no wrong. He may even do so more than once; for he is under a duty to prevent and investigate crime, and so seeking further, in the exercise of that duty, to engage a man's attention in order to speak to him may in the circumstances be regarded as acceptable: see *Donnelly v Jackman* [1970] 1 All ER 987, [1970] 1 WLR 562. But if taking into account the nature of his duty, his use of physical contact in the face of non-co-operation persists beyond generally acceptable standards of conduct, his action will become unlawful; and if a police officer restrains a man, for example by gripping his arm or his shoulder, then his action will also be unlawful, unless he is lawfully exercising his power of arrest. A police officer has no power to require a man to answer him, though he has the advantage of authority, enhanced as it is by the uniform which the state provides and requires him to wear, in seeking a response to his inquiry. What is not permitted, however, is the unlawful use of force or the unlawful threat, actual or implicit, to use force; and, excepting the lawful exercise of his power of arrest, the lawfulness of a police officer's conduct is judged by the same criteria as are applied to the conduct of any ordinary citizen of this country.'

I read that citation in full because it seems to me to lay down, quite clearly, what is the law relevant in this particular case. Having already read the facts in detail it seems to me that the answer to the question can only be one, that is, yes, the police officer who takes a man's arm, not intending to detain or arrest him, but in order to draw his attention to the content of what was being said to him can be seen as acting within the execution of his duty. It is, of course, for the tribunal of fact to decide whether the physical contact goes beyond what is acceptable by the ordinary standards of everyday life and, as I said a little earlier in this judgment, if the period of contact had gone on for any length of time it might well be said to be a finding of fact, to which no reasonable court would come, to say that there was not an intention to detain.

Buxton J agreed.

Appeal dismissed.

Commenting on the case D. J. Birch[2] observed that '*Collins v Wilcock* opens the door to the explicit argument that society should be more tolerant of direct and perhaps even slightly rough contact between a police officer and a citizen who is drunk or angry or otherwise behaving unreasonably'. Is that tolerance desirable?

(iii) There is no common law power to detain for questioning

Kenlin v Gardiner [1967] 2 QB 510, [1987] 2 WLR 129, [1966] 3 All ER 931, 131 JP 191, 110 Sol Jo 848, Queen's Bench Divisional Court

Two boys were visiting homes of members of their school rugby team to remind them of a forthcoming match. Two plain-clothed police officers became suspicious of the boys' behaviour. One approached the boys and asked them what they were doing. He stated that he was a policeman and showed his warrant card but this information did not register in the minds of the boys. One boy tried to run away but was restrained by the officer. The boy, not realising the restrainer was a police officer, struck the officer and escaped. Further struggle ensued. The boys were charged under s. 51(1) of the Police Act 1964. They appealed against conviction.

Winn LJ: [W]as this officer entitled in law to take hold of the first boy by the arm? I feel myself compelled to say that the answer to that question must be in the negative. This officer might or might not in the particular circumstances have possessed a power to arrest these boys. I leave that question open, saying no more than that I feel some doubt whether he would have had a power of arrest: but on the assumption that he had a power of arrest, it is to my

2 [1996] Crim LR 612.

mind perfectly plain that neither of these officers purported to arrest either of these boys. What was done was not done as an integral step in the process of arresting, but was done in order to secure an opportunity, by detaining the boys from escape, to put to them or to either of them the question which was regarded as the test question to satisfy the officers whether or not it would be right in the circumstances, and having regard to the answer obtained from that question, if any, to arrest them.

I regret to say that I think there was a technical assault by the police officer.

Widgery J and **Lord Parker CJ** agreed.

Appeal allowed.

NOTES

1. For further judicial denials of the existence of any power at common law to detain for questioning see *R v Lemsatef* [3] and *R v Francoisy.* [4]

2. In *DPP v L,* [5] because L had not been informed that she was under arrest, despite it being practicable for an officer to do so, her arrest was unlawful. However, that did not prevent her being convicted of assaulting a police officer in the execution of his duty, when the officer she assaulted was not the arrester but the custody officer at the station: the custody officer was in the execution of *his* duty. The Divisional Court held that a custody officer was entitled to assume that there had been a lawful arrest (see below). Cf. *Kerr v DPP* (above).

3. PACE Code of Practice A governing stop and search (discussed in full below) confirms that the Code does not 'affect the ability of an officer to speak to or question a person in the ordinary course of his duties (and in the absence of reasonable suspicion) without detaining him or exercising any element of compulsion'. [6]

4. Under Art. 5 of the European Convention on Human Rights, any detention by the police must conform with the lawful arrest procedures. Whether action involving touching a suspect and/or restricting his movement involves a detention is a question of degree. [7] See further the discussion in relation to stop and search and arrest below, pp. 204 and 175.

5. For powers in relation to terrorism, see the discussion of the Terrorism Act 2000, below, Chap. 5.

(B) ASSAULT ON A POLICE OFFICER

There will usually be little doubt that the defendant has assaulted the officer, but questions as to whether the officer was in the execution of his duty and of the defendant's mistaken beliefs frequently arise. A number of different mistakes might be made by the defendant: (1) that the act of assaulting the person is not an unlawful act – e.g. if it is done in self defence; (2) that the person is not a constable; (3) that the constable is not in the exercise of his duty when D assaults him.

As to (1), there will normally be a good defence if D assaults a constable in the honest belief that the constable is using unlawful force against him. His mistake does not prevent him setting up the defence of self-defence. [8] In *Albert v Lavin* [9] the

---

3 [1977] 1 WLR 812, per Lawton LJ at p. 816.
4 (1978) 68 Cr App Rep 197, per Lawton LJ at pp. 205–206.
5 [1999] Crim LR 752.
6 Para. 1 Note 1B.
7 See *Guzzardi v Italy* (1981) 3 EHRR 333, para. 63.
8 See A. Zuckerman, (1972) 88 LQR 246.
9 [1982] AC 546.

Divisional Court held that such a belief would only constitute a defence where it was based on reasonable grounds (the House of Lords affirmed the decision on different grounds: see below, p. 465). However, the limitation was disapproved by the Court of Appeal (Criminal Division) in *R v Kimber*[10] and *R v Gladstone Williams*,[11] where it was held that the reasonableness of a belief was material only to the question whether on the facts the belief was held at all. These cases concerned, respectively, the issue of consent in relation to a charge of indecent assault and a defence of using reasonable force in the prevention of crime in relation to a charge of assault occasioning actual bodily harm. In the recent case of *B v DPP* the House of Lords recognised that 'There has been a general shift from objectivism to subjectivism in this branch of the law. It is now settled as a matter of general principle that mistake, whether reasonable or not, is a defence where it prevents the defendant from having the mens rea which the law requires for the crime with which he is charged.'[12] Applying that principle, the honest but unreasonable mistake of the accused should result in acquittal in these circumstances. Note that the 'question whether in the circumstances which the defendant believed to exist it was justifiable to use the degree of force, still depends on whether it was reasonable to do so'.[13] *Williams* was approved by the Privy Council in *Beckford v R*[14] and applied by the Court of Appeal (Civil Division) to the charge of assaulting a court officer in the execution of his duty contrary to the County Courts Act 1984, s. 14(1)(b) in *Blackburn v Bowering*.[15]

It has been suggested that such a subjective test of mistake in relation to self-defence could be in contravention of Art. 2 of the ECHR if it concerns the use of lethal force. Professor Andrew Ashworth suggests that *Williams* might conflict with Art. 2,[16] but Sir John Smith regards this, if correct, as a 'grave setback' for English law. No doubt challenges will be made under the Human Rights Act 1998.

As for mistakes about the status of the officer, a person may be guilty under s. 89 even if he is unaware (whether reasonably or unreasonably) that the person he is assaulting is a constable.[17] This strict liability element of the offence has been strongly criticised[18] but remains the law.[19] It is arguable that this is merely a mistake of fact and, as such, should be governed by the more subjective approach adopted in *DPP v B* (above). In practice it will be much easier to establish a defence of self-defence founded on a mistake of fact where the defendant is unaware that the person assaulting or restraining him is a police officer, or honestly disbelieves the claim of, for example, a scruffy-looking individual to be a constable.

A mistake of *law* as to the extent of a police officer's duty cannot be a defence.[20] The defence of self-defence may, however, be established where there is a mistake of fact as to whether a constable is acting in the execution of his duty.[1] In reality there

---

10 [1983] 1 WLR 1118.
11 (1983) 87 Cr App Rep 276.
12 [2000] 2 WLR 452; [2000] 2 Cr App R 65.
13 See the commentary on *Williams* by J. C. Smith, [1984] Crim LR at pp. 163–164. This position has been confirmed in *R v Owino* [1996] 2 Cr App R 128.
14 [1988] AC 130.
15 [1994] 3 All ER 380. See also *R v Jackson (Kenneth)* [1984] Crim LR 674.
16 See his commentary on *Andronicou v Cyprus* [1998] Crim LR 823, p. 825. Cf. J. C. Smith, *Smith and Hogan Criminal Law* (9th edn, 1999), p. 254.
17 *R v Forbes and Webb* (1865) 10 Cox CC 362; *R v Maxwell and Clanchy* (1909) 2 Cr App R 26, CCA.
18 See e.g. J.C. Smith, *Smith and Hogan Criminal Law* (9th edn, 1999) pp. 419–414; G. Williams, op. cit., p. 157, n. 18, p. 200.
19 *Blackburn v Bowering* [1994] 3 All ER 380, CA (CD).
20 See G. Williams, op. cit., p. 157, n. 18, p. 513, see also p. 201, where it is noted that this rule operates with great rigour because the legal powers of the police are in doubt on many particulars; cf. R. Austin, [1982] CLP 187.
1   See Roch LJ in *Blackburn v Bowering* [1994] 3 All ER 380 at 389.

168 Police powers

are two situations: (a) where the defendant makes a mistake of fact which causes him to believe that the constable has no power to act as he does. In such cases the defendant's mistake should be treated as other mistakes of fact – adopting the subjective approach from *DPP v B* (above); (b) where the defendant makes a mistake of law because he believes that the police officer lacks power to act as he does (on the agreed facts), this should not afford the defendant a defence to the charge of assault. On policy grounds, the law should require him to submit to the arrest and challenge the legality of the police action through the normal legal processes. This distinction should it is submitted have been adopted by the Court of Appeal in *R v Lee*[2] in which D made a mistake about whether a breath test was positive, and concluded from that factual mistake that police had no power to arrest him. The court treated this as a mistake of law.[3]

'it was the prisoner's duty, whatever might be his consciousness of innocence, to go to the station house and hear the precise accusation against him. He is not to erect a tribunal in his own mind to decide whether he was legally arrested or not.'

There is a related rule based on policy that if a person 'is in police custody and not in imminent danger of injury there is no urgency of the kind which requires an immediate decision': another person who forcibly releases him 'does so at his peril', and that is so even if he genuinely believes on reasonable grounds that the restraint is unlawful: *R v Fennell.*[4]

The Court of Appeal has recently questioned the legitimacy of using the charge under s. 18 of the Offences Against the Person Act 1861 (wounding with intent to resist arrest), which carries a maximum of life imprisonment for cases of resisting arrest with violence. The defendant had caused her dog to bite the officer, but as she was only being arrested for breach of the peace (which is *not* an offence[4a]), the charge of resisting arrest for an offence under s. 38 of the Offences Against the Person Act 1861 was not available. The s. 18 conviction was upheld, but the court regarded it as an 'accidental and erratic provision'.[5]

Research by the Home Office has shown that, as one would expect, assaults on officers occur in a diverse range of circumstances. It was found that 'almost one third of all assaults occurred before officers had the opportunity to speak with assailants', and 'one fifth of assaults occurred when officers tried to calm or pacify individuals'.[6] In its report *Striking the Balance* (1998), the Police Complaints Authority (PCA) found that the total number of assaults on officers had fallen from 18,108 in 1992/3, to 14,840 in 1995/6.

(C) OBSTRUCTION OF A POLICE OFFICER[7]

The offence under s. 89(2) is broader in its scope than that under s. 89(1). In Scotland it has been confined to physical obstruction.[8] In England and Wales, however, a broader view has been taken. There is no need for proof of any physical contact, nor

---

2   [2001] 1 Cr App R 213, [2000] Crim LR 991, a case on s. 38 of the Offences Against the Person Act 1861.
3   See commentary by D. J. Birch at p. 992.
4   [1971] 1 QB 428. See the analysis by G. Williams, op. cit, pp. 513–515.
4a See below, p. 460.
5   *R v Ramsell* (1999) 25 May, CA (Cr D), unreported, per Buxton LJ, see below, p. 465.
6   B. Brown, *Assaults on Police Officers: An Examination of the Circumstances In Which Such Incidents Occur* (1993) (PRS 10).
7   On the obstruction offence see U. Ross, [1977] Crim LR 187; P. Murphy, [1978] Crim LR 474; R. C. Austin, [1982] CLP 187; T. Gibbons, [1983] Crim LR 21; K. Lidstone, [1983] Crim LR 29. For surveys of other offences of interfering with justice see G. Williams, [1975] Crim LR 430, 479, 608.
8   *Curlett v M'Kechnie* 1938 JC 176.

even an assault. The main cause for concern is whether it has been extended too far towards a position where simple disobedience to police instructions or even a lack of co-operation may constitute the offence. There would be little need for other specific legal powers if this were the case.

(i) Refusing to answer questions does not constitute obstruction

Rice v Connolly [1966] 2 QB 414, [1966] 2 All ER 649, [1966] 3 WLR 17, 130 JP 322, Queen's Bench Divisional Court

Police officers, patrolling late at night in an area where a number of break-in offences had just been committed, observed Rice loitering about the streets. The officers asked him where he was going to, where he had come from and for his name and address. Rice gave only his surname and the name of the street on which he said he lived. The officers asked Rice to accompany them to a nearby police-box so that this information could be checked. Rice refused to move unless arrested. The officers obliged. Rice appealed against conviction under s. 51(3) of the Police Act 1964.

Lord Parker CJ: What the prosecution have to prove is that there was an obstructing of a constable; that the constable was at the time acting in the execution of his duty and that the person obstructing did so wilfully. To carry the matter a little further, it is in my view clear that 'obstruct' under section 51(3) of the Police Act 1964, is the doing of any act which makes it more difficult for the police to carry out their duty. That description of obstructing I take from *Hinchliffe v Sheldon* [1955] 1 WLR 1207. It is also in my judgment clear that it is part of the obligations and duties of a police constable to take all steps which appear to him necessary for keeping the peace, for preventing crime or for protecting property from criminal injury. There is no exhaustive definition of the powers and obligations of the police, but they are at least those, and they would further include the duty to detect crime and to bring an offender to justice.

Pausing there, it seems to me quite clear that the defendant was making it more difficult for the police to carry out their duties, and that the police at the time and throughout were acting in accordance with their duties. The only remaining ingredient, and the one upon which in my judgment this case revolves, is whether the obstructing of which the defendant was guilty was a wilful obstruction. 'Wilful' in this context not only in my judgment means 'intentional' but something which is done without lawful excuse, and that indeed is conceded by Mr Skinner, who appears for the prosecution in this case. Accordingly, the sole question here is whether the defendant had a lawful excuse for refusing to answer the questions put to him. In my judgment he had. It seems to me quite clear that though every citizen has a moral duty or, if you like, a social duty to assist the police, there is no legal duty to that effect, and indeed the whole basis of common law is the right of the individual to refuse to answer questions put to him by persons in authority, and to refuse to accompany those in authority to any particular place; short, of course, of arrest.

In my judgment there is all the difference in the world between deliberately telling a false story – something which in no view a citizen has a right to do and preserving silence or refusing to answer something which he has every right to do.

Marshall J: I agree. In order to uphold this conviction it appears to me that one has to assent to the proposition that where a citizen is acting merely within his legal rights, he is thereby committing a criminal offence. Nor can I see that the manner in which he does it can make any difference whatsoever, and for me reasons given by my Lord I agree that this appeal should be allowed.

James J: Also for the reasons given by my Lord Chief Justice, I agree that this appeal should be allowed. For my own part, I would only add this, that I would not go so far as to say that there may not be circumstances in which the manner of a person together with his silence could amount to an obstruction within the section; whether it does remains to be decided in any case that happens hereafter, not in this case, in which it has not been argued.

Appeal allowed.

NOTES

1. The decision has been criticised on the ground that a sensible result was achieved by the doubtful mechanism of holding that the word 'wilfully' incorporated the concept of 'without lawful excuse'.

2. *Rice v Connolly* requires the courts to draw a distinction between certain acts of obstruction which s. 89(2) prohibits and other acts of obstruction which remain lawful notwithstanding the apparent terms of the subsection.

In accomplishing this task the courts have sometimes distinguished between active and passive obstruction. In *Dibble v Ingleton*,[9] in order to frustrate the administration of a breathalyser test, the defendant drank from a bottle of whisky. He was convicted under s. 51(3) of the Police Act 1964 and appealed. Giving the judgment of the Divisional Court, Bridge J said (at p. 488):

> 'I would draw a clear distinction between a refusal to act, on the one hand, and the doing of some positive act on the other. In a case, as in *Rice v Connolly* [1966] 2 QB 414 where the obstruction alleged consists of a refusal by the defendant to do the act which the police constable had asked him to do to give information, it might be, or to give assistance to the police constable can see readily the soundness of the principle that such a refusal to act cannot amount to a wilful obstruction under section 51 unless the law imposes upon the person concerned some obligation in the circumstances to act in the manner requested by the police officer.
>
> On the other hand, I can see no basis in principle or in any authority which has been cited for saying that where the obstruction consists of a positive act, it must be unlawful independently of its operation as an obstruction of a police constable under section 51. If the act relied upon as an obstruction had to be shown to be an offence independently of its effect as an obstruction it is difficult to see what use there would be in the provision of section 51 of the Police Act 1964.
>
> In my judgment the act of the defendant in drinking whisky when he did with the object and effect of frustrating the procedure under sections 2 and 3 of the Road Safety Act 1967 was a wilful obstruction of Police Constable Tully.'

However, although obstructive inaction is more likely to be excused by the courts than obstructive action, this is not always so. For example, in *Johnson v Phillips*,[10] in order to allow the passage of an ambulance, a police officer ordered the defendant to reverse the 'wrong way' down a one-way street. The defendant's refusal to do so was held to constitute an obstruction of the officer. The court asserted that a constable in purported exercise of his power to control traffic on a public road has the right to disobey a traffic regulation provided that he was acting to protect life and property and such a course of action was reasonably necessary: 'if he himself has that right then it follows that he can oblige others to comply with his instructions to disobey such a regulation.'[11] Similarly, in *Lunt v DPP*,[12] the Divisional Court held that a refusal to allow the police to exercise a right to enter his home could constitute obstruction.[13] However, in *Green v DPP*,[14] the Divisional Court confirmed that it was not obstruction to advise a third party of his right not to answer questions. The fact that G did so in abusive terms and also told the police to 'fuck off' did not make any difference; the justices' finding that G's behaviour made it impossible for the officers to confirm or allay their suspicions of the third party meant no more than that they were unable to obtain answers.

 9 [1972] 1 QB 480, DC.
10 [1975] 3 All ER 682.
11 At 685. Note the criticisms of this case by U. Ross, [1977] Crim LR 187.
12 [1993] Crim LR 534.
13 See further below, p. 252.
14 [1991] Crim LR 782.

3. In *Burton v DPP*[15] the defendant's brother, X, was arrested for a public order offence, and B tried to prevent the arrest. B's conduct was held to be an obstruction even though the officer was unaware of the obstruction by B at the time as he was restraining X, the Divisional Court dismissed his appeal.

Thomas J: In my view, the finding made by the Magistrates was sufficient for the Magistrates to be able to find the element of obstruction. There was no need for them to be sure that the officer being obstructed was aware of that fact. Proof of obstruction depends on an objective assessment of the action, said to amount to obstruction, and does not necessarily depend on the victim's awareness of the acts. Two simple examples will suffice. Assume that shortly after the obstruction, PC Henniker had sustained an injury that caused him amnesia and he was unable to recall what happened. It would be impossible to contend that because he had no recollection of what happened, even though others could give clear evidence of the obstruction, the offence could not be proved.

A second and more common example would be in circumstances were a police officer was struggling with a person who was violent and was pushed in the back or kicked, he had not appreciated the other blow because his attention was on the person with whom he was struck. In those circumstances again, it would be clear that there had been obstruction even though the police officer was unaware of this.

Appeal dismissed.

4. The decision in *Ricketts v Cox*[16] has been widely criticised. Here the justices found that two police officers approached Ricketts and another man, named Blake, explained that a serious assault had taken place and that it was believed that 'coloured' youths were responsible, and asked 'would you care to tell me where you have been?' R and B 'were abusive, uncooperative and positively hostile to the officers from the outset. They used obscene language calculated to provoke and antagonise the officers and ultimately made to walk away from the officers before the completion of their inquiries'. The justices held that the totality of this behaviour amounted to obstruction. R was convicted of this offence. (B was charged only with assault on the police officer in the execution of his duty, but was acquitted as the blow was in response to the unlawful act of one of the constables taking hold of his arm.) The Divisional Court merely asserted that the justices were entitled to reach this conclusion and that the case was of the kind envisaged by James J in *Rice v Connolly* (above, p. 169). On this basis the decision is highly doubtful. [17] If a refusal to answer questions is lawful it is difficult to see that accompanying it by abuse makes any difference. Ormrod LJ stated that the defendant had used threats,[18] although no weight was attached by either the justices or the court to the threats in isolation. In fact the stated case reveals that only B had appeared to use threats: 'You only think you're fucking big because you've got that uniform on man. I'll take you white blokes on any time'. [19] This could not be relevant to R's liability. Would it have justified the conviction of B for obstruction? G. Williams argues not: whatever was threatened, 'the police could not reasonably have believed that they were in danger of being assaulted, because they knew that all they had to do in order to close the incident was to cease pestering him with unwelcome questions.' [20]

However, the police are just as entitled to ask questions (provided they do not attempt to detain for questioning) as citizens are entitled to refuse to answer them (and, it appears, to tell the police to 'fuck off' or 'get stuffed' or whatever). Is it realistic

15 (1998) unreported, Lexis Transcript.
16 (1981) 74 Cr App Rep 298, DC.
17 See G. Williams, *Textbook of Criminal Law* (2nd edn, 1983), p. 204; J. C. Smith, *Smith and Hogan Criminal Law* (9th edn, 1999), pp. 419–420; K. Lidstone, [1983] Crim LR 29, 33–35.
18 See at 300.
19 At 299.
20 Op. cit., p. 204.

172   *Police powers*

to say that a threat to thump a police officer if he does not stop asking questions should not constitute an obstruction under s. 89(2)? Note that it is the threats in isolation that would constitute the obstruction, not the threats in conjunction with other lawful acts. K. Lidstone,[1] states that Ricketts should have been acquitted, as the police were not acting in the execution of their duty in 'requiring answers'. However, (1) it does not appear on the facts that the officers were 'requiring answers' up to the moment that one of the constables seized B's arm (which was held to be unlawful, see cases above, p. 162); and (2) even if they did, their conduct (assuming no physical force was used) would not constitute a crime or tort and therefore an *unlawful* act taking the constables outside the execution of their duty. Accordingly, while the decision appears to be wrong, it is not for this reason.

Threats may constitute an offence of assault, or an offence under the Public Order Act (see below, p. 490). For a recent example of an arrest for obstruction where the suspect had refused to reply to the officer's questions about his actions (walking down a street in the middle of the morning 50 yards from home) see *Samuels v Metropolitan Police Commissioner* (below).

5. The requirement of 'wilfulness' (which does not appear in s. 89(1)) is taken as requiring that the defendant know or at least be reckless as to whether the person he is obstructing is a police officer: *Ostler v Elliott.*[2] Here, the defendant had taken a prostitute by car to a secluded place. Three 'informally dressed' young officers opened the passenger door. One said that they were police officers and asked the prostitute to get out (their intention was to arrest her for soliciting); but no identification was shown. The defendant drove off and let her out of the car. The court held that he was rightly acquitted under a charge under s. 51(3). He had reasonably supposed that the officers were accomplices of the prostitute who intended to rob him.[3] Note that in *Osman v DPP*[4] the Divisional Court held that the officer's failure to provide his name and station meant that he was not in the execution of his duty when searching the suspect.[5]

(ii) The significance of the purpose of interference with police authority

Lewis v Cox [1985] QB 509, [1984] 3 WLR 875, 148 JP 601, Queen's Bench Divisional Court

A drunk was arrested and placed in the back of a police van. C opened the rear door to ask him where he was being taken. PC Lewis, the driver, closed the door, warned C that if he opened it again he would be arrested for obstruction. C did it again, and L arrested him. The justices acquitted C on a charge under s. 51 (3) of the Police Act 1964, holding that his conduct was not aimed at the police and that he did not intend to obstruct the police. The Divisional Court allowed the prosecutor's appeal.

Webster J: [T]here is a line of authority that the word 'wilfully' in the context of section 51(3) of the Police Act, 1964 connotes an element of mens rea. I find it necessary to consider this line of authority, although not every case in it, in some detail because it cannot, in my view, confidently be asserted that the test, whether the actions of the defendant are aimed at the Police', is the definitive and authoritative test.

It can, however, in my view be confidently stated, as I have already mentioned, that the word 'wilfully' imports an element of mens rea. In *Betts v Stevens* [1910] 1 KB I, a case arising out of the warnings given at the time by AA patrol men to those who were exceeding

1   Op. cit., p. 34.
2   [1980] Crim LR 584, DC.
3   Note that 'reasonableness' would not be necessary: cf. above, p. 167.
4   (1999) 163 JP 725.
5   See below p. 216.

the speed limit of the existence of a nearby police trap, Darling J, dealing with the question of intention, said at page 8: 'The gist of the offence to my mind lies in the intention with which the thing is done'.

In *Willmott v Atack* [1977] QB 498, [1976] 3 All ER 794, the defendant had intervened and obstructed a Police Officer while the Officer was attempting to restrain a man under arrest and take him to a police car. The Justices convicted him of an offence under section 51(3) of the Police Act, 1964. Although they found that the defendant had intervened in the belief that he could resolve the situation better than the Police, they concluded that his deliberate conduct had obstructed the Police, and that he was therefore guilty of wilful obstruction. This Court allowed him appeal against that conviction. Before this Court, Counsel for the defendant contended (see page 500), that: 'The proper interpretation of "wilfully obstructs" within section 51(3) of the Police Act 1964 is that there should not merely be an intention on the part of the defendant to do something which happens to result in an obstruction of a Police Officer in the execution of his duty, but that there should also be an element of hostility and criminal intent towards the Police Officer.'

Croom-Johnson J, who gave the first judgment, said at pages 504-5: 'When one looks at the whole context of section 51, dealing as it does with assaults upon Constables in sub-section (1) and concluding in sub-section (3) with resistance and wilful obstruction in the execution of the duty, I am of the view that the interpretation of this sub-section for which the defendant contends is the right one. It fits the words 'wilfully obstructs' in the context of the sub-section, and in my view there must be something in the nature of a criminal intent of the kind which means that it is done with the idea of some form of hostility to the Police with the intention of seeing that what is done is to obstruct, and that it is not enough merely to show that he intended to do what he did and that it did in fact have the result of the Police being obstructed'.

May J (as he then was) agreed. He observed that the word 'wilfully' had been inconsistently interpreted in various statutes which defined criminal offences, and continued: I agree with Croom-Johnson J that when one looks at the judgment of Darling J in *Betts v Stevens* [1910] 1 KB I (supra) it is clear that 'wilfully' in this particular statute does import a requirement of mens rea'.

Lord Widgery, in a very short judgment at page 505, agreed that the question posed should be answered in the negative, that question being (see page 502): 'whether upon a charge of wilfully obstructing a Police Officer in the execution of his duty it is sufficient for the prosecution to prove that the defendant wilfully did an act which obstructed the Police Officer in the execution of his duty , or must the prosecution further prove that the defendant intended to obstruct the Police Officer'.

In *Moore v Green* [1983] 1 All ER 663, DC, the facts of which are immaterial for present purposes, McCullough J, at page 665, having cited the passage from the judgment of Croom-Johnson J in *Willmott v Alatk* [1977] QB 498, DC (which I have just cited) said: 'I do not understand the reference to 'hostility' to indicate a separate element of the offence. I understand the word to bear the same meaning as the phrase which Croom-Johnson J used immediately afterwards, namely 'the intention of seeing that what is done is to obstruct'...

Griffiths LJ agreed with the judgment of McCullough J. Finally, on this aspect of the matter, I return to *Hills v Ellis* [1983] QB 680, [1983] 1 All ER 667. In that case the appellant, while leaving a football match, saw two men fighting and formed the view that one of them was the innocent party in the fight. He then saw a Police Officer arresting the man he thought was innocent. He approached them with the intention of intervening on the part of the arrested man and, being unable to make his voice heard above the noise of the crowd, he grabbed the Police Officer's elbow to draw the Officer's attention to the fact that he was arresting the wrong man.

Another Police Officer warned the appellant that if he did not desist, he might himself be arrested for obstructing the Police. The appellant persisted in trying to stop the arrest, and was charged with wilful obstruction of a Police Officer in the execution of his duty. The Magistrates convicted him.

On his appeal he contended, inter alia, that, since his motive was to correct the Police Officer's error in arresting the wrong person, he had not acted with hostility towards the Police Officer. It was conceded that the Officer was lawfully arresting that man.

Griffiths LJ at page 670 cited the same passage from the judgment of Croom-Johnson J in *Willmott v Atack*. ...and continued: 'The appellant's Counsel argues from that passage that, as the motive here was merely to correct the policeman's error, it cannot be said that he, the appellant, was acting with hostility towards the Police. But in my view the phrase hostility towards the Police in that passage means no more than that the actions of the defendant are aimed at the Police. There can be no doubt here that his action in grabbing a policeman's arm was aimed at that policeman. It was an attempt to get that policeman to desist from the arrest that he was making. In my view, this is as clear a case as we can have of obstructing a Police Officer in the course of his duty, and the Justices came to the right decision.'

McCullough J agreed with the judgment of Griffiths LJ, and added, at page 671: 'I am uncertain what Croom-Johnson J had in mind when he used the word 'hostility'. Hostility suggests emotion and motive, but motive and emotion are alike irrelevant in criminal law. What matters is intention that is what state of affairs the defendant intended to bring about. What motive he had while so intending is irrelevant. What is meant by 'an intention to obstruct'? I would construe 'wilfully obstructs' as doing deliberate acts with the intention of bringing about a state of affairs which, objectively regarded, amount to an obstruction as that phrase was explained by Lord Parker in *Rice v Connolly* [1966] 2 QB 414, [1966] 2 All ER 649 at 651, i.e. making it more difficult for the Police to carry out their duty. The fact that the defendant might not himself have called that state of affairs an obstruction is, to my mind, immaterial. That is not to say that it is enough to do deliberate actions which, in fact, obstruct; there must be an intention that those actions should result in the further state of affairs to which I have been referring'.

Lord Parker CJ, on the same page of his judgment in *Rice v Connolly* [1966] 2 QB 414 at page 419 said that 'wilful' in the context of this section 'not only in my judgment means "intentional" but something which is done without lawful excuse'; and Lord Parker's explanation of 'wilfully obstructs' as being something which makes it more difficult for the Police to carry out their duties was taken by him from the judgment of Lord Goddard CJ in *Hinchliffe v Sheldon* [1955] 3 All ER 406, [1955] 1 WLR 1207, where Lord Goddard said: 'Obstructing, for the present purpose, means making it more difficult for the Police to carry out their duties'.

For my part I conclude that, although it may not be unhelpful in certain cases to consider whether the actions of a defendant were aimed at the Police, the simple facts which the Court has to find are whether the defendant's conduct in fact prevented the Police from carrying out their duty, or made it more difficult for them to do so, and whether the defendant intended that conduct to prevent the Police from carrying out their duty or to make it more difficult to do so.

In the present case the test which the Justices applied was whether the defendant had deliberately done some act which was aimed at the Police, they found that his actions were not aimed at the Police and they accordingly dismissed the charge. In my view, for the reasons which I have given, the justices did not ask themselves the right question for the purposes of the present case, or the whole of the right question.

[His Lordship examined the facts. He noted, inter alia, that C must have known that the police van could not be driven away with the door open, and, before he opened the door the second time, that L was about to drive the van away. It was not suggested that C had a lawful excuse for his conduct.]

In my view, therefore, if the Justices had also asked themselves whether the respondent had, by opening the door, intended to make it more difficult for the Police to perform their duties in order to carry out his intention of asking where Marsh was to be taken they must, on the evidence, have been satisfied so as to feel sure that he had such an intention.

Although the question whether a defendant's conduct is aimed at the Police may not be an unhelpful question in certain circumstances, where, as here: a defendant intended to do one thing in order to carry out his intention of doing another, that test, which might be appropriate if the Court had to find what was the defendant's predominant intention, can, in my view, mislead the Court if it is not necessary to do that. For my part I conclude, therefore, that if the Justices had directed themselves properly in the way in which I have set out they must, on the evidence, have decided that the respondent, when he opened the door on the second occasion, intended to make it more difficult for the Police to carry out their duties, even though that was not his predominant intention, and they ought, therefore, to have convicted him of the charge against him.

Kerr LJ: I agree with Webster J's analysis of the authorities. The actus reus is the doing of an act which has the effect of making it impossible or more difficult for members of the Police to carry out their duty. The word 'wilfully' clearly imports an additional requirement of mens rea. The act must not only have been done deliberately, but with the knowledge and intention that it will have this obstructive effect. But in the absence of a lawful excuse, the defendant's purpose or reason for doing the act is irrelevant, whether this be directly hostile to, or 'aimed at', the Police, or whether he has some other purpose or reason. Indeed, in the majority of cases the intention to obstruct the Police will not be simply 'anti-Police', but will stem from some underlying reason or objective of the defendant which he can only achieve by an act of intentional obstruction. This may be to assist an offender, which could be termed 'hostile' to the Police. Equally, the motivation could be public-spirited, for instance, by intervening on behalf of someone whom the defendant believes to be innocent, as in *Hills v Ellis* [1983] QB 680, [1983] 1 All ER 667, DC. Or it may be for some neutral reason for instance because the defendant consider that something else should have a higher priority than the duty on which the Police Officer is immediately engaged. In all such cases, if the defendant intentionally does an act which he realises will, in fact, have the effect of obstructing the Police in we sense defined above, he will in my view be guilty of having done so 'wilfully', with the necessary mens rea. In the absence of a lawful excuse, the defendant's underlying intention, reason or purpose for intentionally obstructing the Police is irrelevant, because the intention to obstruct is present at the same time. *Willmott v Atack* [1977] QB 498, [1976] 3 All ER 794 only went the other way because the defendant's intention was in fact to assist the police.

Appeal allowed. Case remitted with a direction to convict.

NOTES

1. Some of the cases discussed raise the problem of defendants with mixed purposes. A person may: (1) (a) intend to obstruct a policeman in the performance of one task, (b) with the further intention of aiding him in the performance of another task;[6] or (2) (a) intend to obstruct a policeman in the performance of a task, (b) with the further intention of pursuing some private purpose of his own (e.g. *Lewis v Cox*). The law could say either (1) that the presence of an intention to obstruct is sufficient for liability, irrespective of any other purpose, or (2) that the presence of an intention to help is sufficient for an acquittal or (3) that the answer should depend upon which motive was dominant. *Hills v Ellis* seems to adopt the first of these approaches; *Willmott v Atack* the second. It is difficult to see that the conduct in *Willmott v Atack* is distinguishable from that in *Hills v Ellis* and one of the cases is accordingly wrongly decided. Which do you prefer? *Lewis v Cox* is rightly decided on either approach as the defendant clearly is not entitled to set his own private purposes above those of the officer.

2. Some of the cases also illustrate the point that no physical obstruction is necessary. For example, the offence under s. 89(2) may be committed where a warning is given in order that the commission of a crime may be suspended whilst there is a danger of detection, e.g. a warning to motorists who are speeding that a police speed trap is ahead: *Betts v Stevens*[7] a warning to a licensee suspected of serving drinks after hours that the police are outside (so that it could not then be proved that an offence had been committed). Similarly, warning a licensee during opening hours that the police intended to raid the premises after hours was held to be obstruction in *Moore v Green*.[8] The case had previously been before the Divisional Court: *Green v Moore*.[9] On the earlier occasion it had been held that there was no relevant distinction between a warning

6 E.g. *Hills v Ellis* [1983] QB 680, [1983] 1 All ER 667.
7 [1910] 1 KB 1.
8 [1983] 1 All ER 663, DC.
9 [1982] QB 1044, DC.

given in order to *suspend* the commission of an offence whilst there was a danger of detection and a warning given in order to *postpone* the commission of an offence until after the danger of detection had passed: moreover, the offence was not limited to an obstruction where a crime was being committed or had been committed.

> 'Police constables maintain the Queen's peace in many different ways besides by criminal investigation. They patrol beats. They direct traffic. Is it really to be said that a police constable on point duty is not acting in the execution of his duty and that someone who wilfully obstructs his field of vision is not obstructing him in the execution of that duty? Of course not.'[10]

Refusal to comply with police instructions given in order to prevent a breach of the peace may constitute an obstruction under s. 89(2).[11]

The police have no right to stop a defendant's solicitor from attempting to contact alibi witnesses, and such behaviour by the solicitor does not amount to an obstruction in the exercise of an officer's duty: *Connolly v Dale.*[12]

(iii) Arrests for obstruction

There is no specific power of arrest without warrant in respect of offences under s. 89 of the Police Act 1996. In respect of s. 89(1) the 'assault' will constitute a breach of the peace and so a power of contemporaneous arrest will exist (see below, pp. 460–470). In respect of offences under s. 89(2), if the obstruction does not involve an actual or apprehended breach of the peace no power of arrest exists. Unless an arrestable offence is reasonably suspected or a common law power of arrest arises, there is no power to arrest. The police do not seem to have been much aware of this. See the arrests made in, for example, *Tynan v Balmer*;[13] *Stunt v Bolton*;[14] *Johnson v Phillips*;[15] *Wershof v Metropolitan Police Comr*;[16] *Ledger v DPP*;[17] and *Green v DPP*.[18] Note also that in Moriarty, *Police Law*[19] there was an unqualified statement that a constable may arrest without warrant a person who obstructs him in the execution of his duty.

In *Wershof v Metropolitan Police Comr*, May J stated[20] that a police constable may only arrest without a warrant anyone who wilfully obstructs him in the execution of his duty if the nature of that obstruction is such that he actually causes, or is likely to cause, a breach of the peace or is calculated to prevent the lawful arrest or detention of another'. This proposition forms part of the *ratio* of May J's judgment. The authorities cited for the proposition about arrest for conduct calculated to prevent the lawful arrest or detention of another were *Levy v Edwards*[1] and *Mite v Edmunds*.[2]

The Divisional Court in *Edwards v DPP* held that if an officer purports to be arresting for 'obstruction', it is not possible for the court to infer another (legitimate) reason for the arrest.[3] In *Mullady v DPP*[4] the appellant was arrested for obstructing an officer in the execution of her duty after proffering the invitation: 'go on and

---

10 Donaldson LJ at p. 1052.
11 See *Duncan v Jones* (below, p. 531); *Piddington v Bates* (below, p. 535).
12 [1996] 1 QB 120.
13 [1967] 1 QB 91, DC.
14 [1972] RTR 435, DC.
15 [1975] 3 All ER 682, DC.
16 [1978] 3 All ER 540, DC.
17 [1991] Crim LR 439, DC.
18 [1991] Crim LR 782, DC.
19 23rd edn, 1976, p. 18.
20 At 550.
1 (1823) 1 C & P 40.
2 (1791) Peake 123.
3 See (1993) 97 Cr App R 301.
4 (1997) 3 July, DC, unreported.

fucking nick me then.' The appellant's conviction was quashed, because, following *Edwards*, the court was not prepared to infer a legitimate reason – breach of the peace – for arrest.

(iv) Arrest for anticipated breach of the peace

In *Riley v DPP*[5] police officers arrested R's brother, and then arrested R for obstruction when he attempted to push past other officers, including PC McDade, to go to his brother. R subsequently bit the thumb of PC Martin, who came to PC McDade's assistance in putting R into a police van, and was subsequently convicted of assaulting PC Martin in the execution of his duty. Watkins LJ (for the Divisional Court) stated: [6]

'In order for there to be a lawful arrest for wilful obstruction of a constable in the execution of his duty, the Crown has to prove, in addition to the fact that he was so acting, the physical and mental element of the obstruction and further that the constable reasonably believed that if he did not make an arrest there would, or might be, a breach of the peace or an attempt to impede a lawful arrest.'

The Divisional Court quashed R's conviction on the ground (inter alia) that there was no finding of fact by the justices that any officer had a reasonable apprehension that a breach of the peace might follow. (Is 'might' sufficient in this formulation? See below, p. 460 on breach of the peace.) Moreover, as no evidence was put before the justices as to the reasons for the arrest of R's brother, the arrest for obstruction could not be justified on the basis that R intended to impede a lawful arrest. Accordingly, it was not established that the officers who arrested R's brother, and PC McDade, were acting in the execution of their duty. PC Martin, in going to PC McDade's assistance was 'unwittingly acting in furtherance of an unlawful arrest of the defendant and could not consequently have been acting in the execution of his duty when he was bitten'.[7] The decision on this last part was criticised by Professor J. C. Smith:[8]

'when M saw his colleagues struggling with a man whom they had arrested, did he not have reasonable grounds for suspecting that an arrestable offence had been committed by that man? If he did, he would have had power to make an arrest under section 24(6) of PACE, had the man not already been under arrest. If it would have been lawful for him to make an arrest, it was surely also lawful for him to assist the (as he thought) lawful arrest which was taking place.'

It is submitted that this goes too far: it would mean that violence used to resist an unlawful arrest by constable A would become unlawful violence as against constables B and C who came to A's assistance. The requirement that there be evidence before the court establishing that constable A in such cases was acting in the execution of his duty is appropriate and reasonable. *Riley v DPP* was distinguished in *Plowden v DPP*.[9] During a large demonstration against the poll tax, P was observed by PC Corby holding on to the back of another (unidentified) uniformed police officer's jacket, shouting and using abusive language, apparently attempting to prevent an arrest. The Divisional Court held that the justices were entitled to infer that the unidentified officer was acting in the execution of his duty. The line between cases where the court can draw such inferences and cases where direct evidence must be presented is,

5 (1989) 91 Cr App Rep 14. Note the stricter attitude to the use of the power discussed below, pp. 460–470.
6 At 22.
7 At 23.
8 [1990] Crim LR 424–425.
9 [1991] Crim LR 850, DC.

however, fine, cf. *Griffiths v DPP*.[10] Note also that an officer can be obstructed without being aware that he is! *Burton v DPP*.[10a]

3　General aspects of police powers

(A)　THE CONCEPT OF 'REASONABLE SUSPICION'

Most of the coercive powers of the police are conditioned on the presence of reasonable 'suspicion', 'cause' or 'belief' in the existence of a state of affairs-commonly that the object of the power is involved, actually or potentially, in a particular criminal offence. The significance of this trigger should not be underestimated, especially since it forms the basis of one of the grounds upon which detention can occur within Art. 5 of the European Convention. See *Brogan v UK*[11] concerning arrests under the Prevention of Terrorism (Temporary Provisions) Act 1984 noting that reasonable suspicion in Art. 5 does not presuppose that the police should have obtained sufficient evidence to bring charges, either at the point of arrest or while applicants were in custody. See also *Fox, Campbell and Hartley v UK*:[12] 'reasonable suspicion presupposes the existence of facts or information which would satisfy an objective observer that the person concerned may have committed a criminal offence. What may be regarded as 'reasonable' will however depend on all the circumstances.'

In England, surprisingly little judicial guidance had been provided until recently.

Castorina v Chief Constable of Surrey (1988) NLJR 180, Lexis, Court of Appeal (Civil Division)

Detectives reasonably concluded that the burglary of a company's premises was an 'inside job'. The managing director told them that she had recently dismissed someone (the plaintiff) although she did not think it would have been her, and that the documents taken would be useful to someone with a grudge. The detectives interviewed the plaintiff having found out that she had no criminal record, and arrested her under the Criminal Law Act 1967, s. 2(4). She was detained for three and three-quarter hours at the police station and interrogated, and then released without charge. She claimed damages for wrongful arrest and detention. Judge Lermon QC held that the officers had a prima facie case for suspicion but the arrest was premature; he applied as a definition of reasonable cause 'honest belief founded on reasonable suspicion leading an ordinary cautious man to the conclusion that the person arrested was guilty of the offence', and stated that an ordinary man would have sought more information from the suspect, including an explanation for any grudge on her part. A jury awarded £4,500. The Court of Appeal (Purchas and Woolf LJJ, and Sir Frederick Lawton) allowed an appeal by the Chief Constable.

> **Purchas LJ:** The powers under which the police officers acted are contained in section 2(4) of the Criminal Law Act 1967. This section provides:
>
> '2(4) Where a constable, with reasonable cause, suspects that an arrestable offence has been committed, he may arrest without warrant anyone whom he, with reasonable cause, suspects to be guilty of the offence.'
>
> No question arises on the first part of this section, namely the commission of an arrestable offence. The debate centres solely around the words 'whom he, with reasonable cause, suspects

---

10　(1992) 8 December, DC, unreported.
10a Above, p. 171.
11　(1988) 11 EHRR 117.
12　(1990) 13 EHRR 157.

to be guilty of the offence'. These powers have now been replaced by section 24(6) of the Police and Criminal Evidence Act 1984 which, however, repeats in substance the same phrase 'he may arrest without a warrant anyone whom he has reasonable grounds for suspecting to be guilty of the offence'. The exercise, therefore, is to consider the information available to the arresting officer at the time when he makes his decision to arrest in order to see whether that information is sufficient to form 'reasonable' cause for the officer's suspicion.

Mr Wilson, who appeared for the appellant, submitted that the judge directed himself incorrectly on this aspect of the law. He submitted that the judge's definition extended the strictness of the requirements imposed upon the arresting officer beyond those imposed in the section in the respect that the honest belief must lead an ordinary cautious man to the conclusion that the person was guilty of the offence. Mr Wilson illustrated the distinction by reference to a police officer investigating a crime which could only have been committed by one individual but where there were two or more candidates in respect of whom it was perfectly possible to hold a reasonable suspicion that one or other was guilty, whilst it would be impossible to have reason to believe in the conclusion that more than one was guilty. A similar analogy, Mr Wilson submitted, was to be found in the case of a person charged who was found in the possession of stolen goods but who might, as a result of the doctrine of recent possession, be guilty of the theft rather than handling the goods.

I turn first to the judgment of Peter Pain J [in *Holtham v Metropolitan Police Comr* (1987) Times, 8 January] which, subsequently to the judgment of Judge Lermon QC, was reversed in the Court of Appeal on 25 November 1987 [(1987) Times, 28 November]. Mr Wilson referred to an extract from the judgment of Peter Pain J which was cited by the Master of the Rolls in the *Holtham* case. This passage was part of the transcript which was before the trial judge:

'the police do not have to have good evidence which would establish a prima facie case before they arrest. All they have to have is reasonable grounds for suspicion, which may be a good deal less. It may even involve matters which would not be admissible in evidence in court. But the statute requires them to have reasonable grounds for suspicion, and that, in my view, is something a good deal more than suspicion.'

The Master of the Rolls criticised this passage in the following terms:

'With all respect to the learned judge, I do not think that this is a correct statement of the law. As it was put by Lord Devlin in *Hussien v Chong Fook Kam* [1970] AC 942 at 948, "Suspicion in its ordinary meaning is a state of conjecture or surmise where proof is lacking: I suspect but I cannot prove". Suspicion may or may not be based upon reasonable grounds, but it still remains suspicion and nothing more. By applying a test of something which was not suspicion but was "something a good deal more than suspicion", I think that the learned judge erred and that this error was fundamental to his conclusion.'

Mr Wilson submitted that, following the approach of Peter Pain J, the judge in this case had relied upon a definition which required a state of mind higher than suspicion, namely a state of mind which concluded that the person arrested was in fact guilty of the offence.

It is clear from the notes made by the judge at the end of the evidence that the passage from the judgment of Lord Devlin in *Hussien v Chong Fook Kam* [1970] AC 942 was to the mind of the judge. It is helpful to read a little more of the context in which the passage cited by the Master of the Rolls is to be found. *Hussien's* case concerned sections of the criminal code in Malaysia but the equivalent sections dealing with malicious prosecution, on the one hand, and false imprisonment, on the other, carried similar distinctions to those present in the law of this country. Citing from the judgment of Lord Devlin at [1970] AC page 947H:

'Mr Gratiaen has criticised the test adopted in the Federal Court. Suffian FJ, who delivered the judgment of the court, said that the information available to the police "was insufficient to prove prima facie a case against the plaintiffs under section 304A of the Penal Code or under section 34A of the Road Traffic Ordinance". Mr Gratiaen submits that this is the test appropriate in actions for malicious prosecution and not in actions for false imprisonment.

Whether or not this is so-and their Lordships do not wish to add any further formulae to those already devised for the action for false imprisonment it would appear to be a much stiffer test than the reasonable suspicion, which is the foundation of the power given in section 23(i)(a) of the Criminal Procedure Code. Suspicion in its ordinary meaning is a state of conjecture or surmise where proof is lacking: "I suspect but I cannot prove". Suspicion arises at or near the starting-point of an investigation of which the obtaining of prima facie proof is the end. When such proof has been obtained, the police case is complete; it is ready for trial and passes on to its next stage. It is indeed desirable as a general rule that an arrest should not be made until the case is complete. But if arrest before that were forbidden, it could seriously hamper the police. To give power to arrest on reasonable suspicion does not mean that it is always or even ordinarily to be exercised. It means that there is an executive discretion on the exercise of it many factors have to be considered besides the strength of the case. The possibility of escape, the prevention of further crime and the obstruction of police inquiries are examples of those factors which all judges who have had to grant or refuse bail are familiar. There is no serious danger in a large measure of executive discretion in the first instance because in countries where common law principles prevail the discretion is subject indirectly to judicial control.'

There are two quite distinct considerations apparent in this passage, namely what is sufficient in order to establish the right in the arresting officer to make the arrest, namely suspicion on reasonable grounds, and the second stage, namely whether in all the circumstances the officer has in making his executive decision acted within his discretion or whether he is subject to criticism under the *Wednesbury* principle (See *Associated Provincial Picture Houses v Wednesbury Corpn* [1948] 1 KB 223, [1947] 2 All ER 680) for wrongful exercise of an executive discretion. In this appeal we are concerned solely with the first of these two aspects.

I now turn to *Dumbell v Roberts* [1944] 1 All ER 326 which was the third authority listed by the judge. It is to be remembered that this case concerned special powers of arrest contained in section 513, in association with section 507 of the Liverpool Corporation Act 1921. The effect of these sections is to give a power of arrest where a person was found in possession of, in that case, an excessive quantity of soap flakes for the possession of which he was unable to give a reasonable explanation. The passages upon which the judge appears to have relied in the judgment of Scott LJ are:

'The police are not called on before acting to have anything like a prima facie case for conviction; but the duty of making such inquiry as the circumstances of the case ought to indicate to a sensible man is, without difficulty, presently practicable, does rest on them; for to shut your eyes to the obvious is not to act reasonably.

They may have to act on the spur of the moment and have no time to reflect and be bound, therefore, to arrest, to prevent escape; but where there is no danger of the person who has ex hypothesi aroused their suspicion, that he is probably an "offender" attempting to escape, they should take all the presently practicable enquiries from persons present or immediately accessible who are likely to be able to answer their enquiries forthwith. I am not suggesting a duty on the police to try to prove innocence; that is not their function; but they should act on the assumption that their prima facie suspicion may be ill founded. That duty attaches particularly where slight delay does not matter because there is no probability, in the circumstances of the arrest or intended arrest, of the suspected person running away.'

Basing himself upon this passage from the judgment of Scott LJ, the learned judge formed his conclusion that the arrest was premature...

In the judgment of Goddard LJ, with whom Luxmoore LJ agreed, in *Dumbells* case it is made clear that the majority of the court dealt with the case as one arising particularly under the provisions of the Liverpool Corporation Act in which section 513 gave a power to arrest 'when the common law grounds are absent'. The remarks of Scott LJ did not, therefore, form part of the *ratio decidendi* of the majority of the court.

Mr Wilson also attacked the reference to 'honest belief in the legal definition of reasonable cause. The provided by the section requires that the suspicion must arise from reasonable cause. Reasonable cause, it is not disputed, is to be determined as an objective matter from the information available to the arresting officer and cannot have anything to do with the subjective state of the officer's mind. This may well be relevant in the offence of malicious prosecution. With all respect to the learned judge it appears that he has confused belief; which plays no part in the power of arrest under the section, and suspicion, based upon reasonable grounds which does. Honest belief; therefore, cannot be relevant. To the extent that the judge has specifically found honest belief and stated it in his judgment this is an indication that he has misdirected himself.

With respect to the judge I agree with Mr Wilson's submissions that, in concentration on what the officers might or might not have done by way of further inquiry before arrest, the judge's attention was deflected from the critical question, namely when they arrested her did they have reasonable cause for suspecting that the respondent was guilty of the offence? (See *Holgate-Mohammed v Duke* [1984] AC 437, [1984] 1 All ER 1054). In that case the trial judge had found that the detective constable had had reasonable cause to suspect the plaintiff of having committed an arrestable offence but, because the constable had decided not to interview her under caution but to subject her to the greater pressure of arrest and detention so as to induce a confession, there had been a wrongful exercise of the power of arrest. From the speech of Lord Diplock, who delivered the leading speech, it is clear that the failure to interrogate before arrest did not impair the lawfulness of the arrest in the first instance under the powers of section 2(4) but that the exercise of those powers before interrogation in order to enhance the chances of obtaining a confession had to be tested against the principles laid down in *Associated Provincial Picture Houses Ltd v Wednesbury Corpn* [1948] 1 KB 223, [1947] 2 All ER 680. Their Lordships decided that in the circumstances of that case there had been no such breach of the *Wednesbury* principle.

There is ample authority for the proposition that courses of inquiry which may or may not be taken by an investigating police officer before arrest are not relevant to the consideration whether, on the information available to him at the time of the arrest, he had reasonable cause for suspicion. Of course, failure to follow an obvious course in exceptional circumstances may well be grounds for attacking the executive exercise of that power under the *Wednesbury* principle. The position is very starkly pointed out in a passage from the judgment of Sir John Arnold P in *Mohammed-Holgate*'s case in the Court of Appeal [1984] 1 QB 209, [1983] 3 All ER 526 at page 216C of the former report:

'As to the proposition that there were other things which he might have done, no doubt there were other things which he might have done first. He might have obtained a statement from her otherwise than under arrest to see how far he could get. He might have obtained a specimen of her handwriting and sent that off for forensic examination against a specimen of the writing of the person who had obtained the money by selling the stolen jewellery, which happened to exist in the case. All those things he might have done. He might have carried out fingerprint investigations if he had first obtained a print from the plaintiff: but the fact that there were other things which he might have done does not, in my judgment, make that which he did do into an unreasonable exercise of the power of arrest if what he did do, namely to arrest, was within the range of reasonable choices available to him.'

At an earlier stage of the hearing in dealing with an argument as to a preliminary point, Sir John Arnold referred to the judgment of Scott LJ in *Dumbell*'s case confirming that the passage upon which the judge had relied went not to the question of suspicion on reasonable grounds but to the executive exercise of a discretionary power – see [1983] 3 All ER 526 at page 530F:

'The real reason why this line of argument fails is simply that the whole of what Scott LJ says is plainly directed in the context in which it was said not to the question of whether the police arrested with reasonable cause a person whom they suspected of having committed the crime, but whether it was reasonable to carry out the arrest even if the power were available, in other words the very point which was decided by the judge against the police and on which the main appeal is founded.'

This court has recently commented upon this part of the judgment of Scott LJ in the case of *Ward v Chief Constable of Avon and Somerset Constabulary* (unreported) Court of Appeal transcript for 25th June 1986. After pointing out that the arrest in *Dumbell*'s case was under the special powers of the Liverpool Corporation Act Croom-Johnson LJ said this:

'After saying the plaintiff's appeal would be allowed, and a new trial ordered, Lord Justice Scott made some general observations which were obiter, about what might amount to reasonable suspicion of guilt justifying an arrest. The passage relied on (p. 329G) stressed the need for the police to 'make all presently practicable enquiries from persons present or immediately accessible who are likely to be able to answer their enquiries forthwith.'

Thus is it said here that Det Sgt Edwards' enquiries were not detailed enough. But it is necessary for the police to probe every explanation. Section 2(4) of the Criminal Law Act 1967 requires the constable to have 'reasonable cause' for suspicion before he arrests.

With respect, I adopt the approach of Croom-Johnson LJ in this case. The strictures made by Judge Lermon about the failure of the arresting police officers to inquire of the respondent whether she did or did not actually have a grudge against her erstwhile employers fall within the criticism made more than once in this court of the approach based on the judgment of Scott LJ. It can be tested by asking whether the investigation would have been advanced if the police officers had pursued the point and were met with a flat denial. In my judgment, the judge was wrong to rely on the judgment of Scott LJ and this led him erroneously to conclude that the arrest was premature and, therefore, unlawful. I have, therefore, come to the conclusion that Mr Wilson's submissions on this aspect of the case are made out and that the learned judge misdirected himself in applying the provisions of section 2(4) of the Act.

[Purchas LJ then rejected the plaintiff's argument that the court should order a retrial before a jury; the primary facts were not in dispute, and it was 'open to the court to draw the necessary inferences of secondary fact in order to determine whether the arresting officers had reasonable cause to suspect'. On this question, he continued:]

Mr Scrivener urged upon us that there was a duty upon the police officers to have made these inquiries, in other words that the judge was right in holding that the arrest was premature. He also submitted that there had been no lie or inconsistency in the responses given by the respondent prior to arrest, or indeed subsequent thereto. His submissions were based on an assertion that at the time of arrest, without an inquiry as to whether or not the respondent held a grudge, there was insufficient information upon which the officers could have had reasonable cause to suspect that she had committed the offence. But, with respect to Mr Scrivener, this approach discloses the fallacy of looking at what the officers might have done by way of inquiry rather than looking at the information they had gained in order to apply the test required by section 2(4). Of course, if it was relevant to consider what inquiries the officers might have made, then it would be equally relevant to consider what the result of those inquiries might have been. The evidence led before the learned judge of the inquiries made by the police officers after receiving the respondent's emphatic denial that she had a grudge, disclosed further grounds for suspicion. The note of the evidence of DC Thorne reads:

'Further enquiries. 'Phoned Mrs Wilson [*sic. Ed.*] to learn more about ill feeling by the Plaintiff. Mrs Wilson told me that the Plaintiff had made false statements to other people about the Company. Specifically had told others within the Company that the Company was heading for financial ruin. That is the Plaintiff was running the Company down in a malicious way.'

The names of other people were obtained from Mrs Wilson but inquiries of these people did not prove fruitful. Mrs Wilson's evidence as noted by the judge was:

'Two days after the Plaintiff left I had telephone calls, one from our Manchester supervisor, Mrs Templeton. She said that the Plaintiff had told her that she had left the Company which was in financial difficulties and that it was unlikely that her interviewers would get paid for the work. Also two other telephone *calls,* one of a similar nature from another supervisor and one from the field director of NOP who had also been told that we were in financial difficulties. I understood then that rumours were going about the Company which concerned me. Prior to the burglary I had contacted my solicitor as a result of the 'phone calls. She suggested writing a letter threatening litigation. She drafted a letter which was sent to the Plaintiff together with her salary cheque "unless she stopped slandering the Company we would take further proceedings".'

Had the police officers pressed their inquiries further she may well have told them all of this. This evidence demonstrates the difficult and unsatisfactory waters into which the inquiry drifts if the approach advocated by the judge had been adopted. For the reasons already given in this judgment, however, I consider that the failure to carry out this line of inquiry is not relevant to considering the objective question of reasonable cause within the meaning of section 2(4). I, therefore, find myself unable to accede to Mr Scrivener's submissions in support of the judgment based on premature arrest.

This leaves the final inquiry to be made by this court as to whether or not as an objective criterion there was sufficient information available to the arresting officers to give them 'reasonable cause to suspect that the respondent was guilty of the burglary'. I have already outlined the unusual features of the burglary which became apparent to the arresting officers on their visit to the Company's premises on the morning of 23rd June. These features need not be repeated here. They do indicate a very specific and particular character which could safely be attributed to the burglar in a number of different respects, i.e. experience, motive and inside knowledge of affairs within the Company's premises. In addition to this the information also given to the arresting officers by Mrs Wilson at the first stage of their inquiries identified the respondent as the only person who possessed these particular qualities. In the circumstances of this case, and I emphasise that every case has to be determined upon its particular facts, I am satisfied that the arresting officers had reasonable cause to suspect that the respondent was guilty of this unusual burglary.

For these reasons, therefore, I would allow this appeal and set aside the award of damages made by the jury enshrined in the judge's order.

Woolf LJ and **Sir Frederick Lawton** delivered concurring judgments.

Appeal allowed.

NOTES

1. In his judgment, Woolf LJ stated that, in a case where it is alleged that there has been an unlawful arrest, there are three questions to be answered:

'1. Did the arresting officer suspect that the person who was arrested was guilty of the offence? The answer to this question depends entirely on the findings of fact as to the officer's state of mind.
2. Assuming the officer had the necessary suspicion, was there reasonable cause for that suspicion? This is a purely objective requirement to be determined by the judge, if necessary on facts found by a jury.
3. If the answer to the two previous questions is in the affirmative, then the officer has a discretion which entitles him to make an arrest and in relation to that discretion the question arises as to whether the discretion has been exercised in accordance with the principles laid down by Lord Greene MR in *Associated Provincial Picture Houses Ltd v Wednesbury Corpn* [1948] 1 KB 223, [1947] 2 All ER 680.'

A. R. Clayton and H. Tomlinson[13] argue that *Castorina* was incorrect in holding that the possibility of 'further inquiries' cannot be relevant to the question whether there are reasonable grounds for an arrest:

'It is clear law that reasonable cause will only be present if a reasonable man, in the position of the officer at the time of arrest, would have thought that the plaintiff was probably guilty of the offence: see *Dallison v Caffery* [1965] 1 QB 348, 371 and *Wiltshire v Barrett* [1966] 1 QB 312, 322.
   Thus, whether or not there is 'reasonable cause to suspect' depends on an overall assessment of the reliability of the evidence incriminating the suspect. [I]t is submitted that a reasonable man would, before thinking that a person was probably guilty of an offence, probe the evidence available to him by making any obvious and simply available inquiries.'[14]

They further submitted that *Castorina* was inconsistent with one of the justifications for the requirement that an officer give reasons for an arrest,[15] namely that the person arrested 'may be able to give more than a bare and unconvincing denial if he is in fact innocent' (per Sir John Donaldson in *Murphy v Oxford*[16]):

'If an arresting officer is obliged to give reasons on arrest he must be under a correlative obligation to consider any answers given by the suspect and, if appropriate, to investigate them. Otherwise, the giving of reasons would simply be an empty formality.'[17]

13 'Arrest and reasonable grounds for suspicion' (1988) 85 LS Gaz, 7 September, p. 22.
14 p. 25.
15 Op. cit., pp. 109–111.
16 (1988) 15 February 1988, DC, unreported.
17 p. 26.

Finally, the authors regard the conclusion that there was 'reasonable cause' on the facts as 'remarkable':

'If the police are justified in arresting a middle aged women of good character on such flimsy grounds, without even questioning her as to her alibi or possible motives, then the law provides very scant protection for those suspected of crime.'[18]

(i) Applying *Castorina*

Inevitably the application of the reasonable suspicion test will involve difficult borderline cases. In *Lyons v Chief Constable of West Yorkshire*[19] the Court of Appeal (Civil Division) held that the judge was right to accept that reasonable suspicion can be formed despite information from a third party claiming that the suspect had an alibi, but wrong to conclude that those comments were relevant to the decision to exercise the power of arrest. A relative of the suspect had told the police, before they had spoken to the suspect, that he had an alibi for the whole day in question. Hutchison LJ (with whom Hobhouse and Evans LJJ agreed) said:

'The officers had a number of grounds for regarding an arrest as desirable in the interests of furthering their inquiries and this new factor, insufficient as it was to undermine their belief, was in my view not material (save in the most general sense of being part of the overall picture) to the exercise of discretion. It is easy to envisage circumstances which may militate against exercising a power to arrest a person suspected on reasonable grounds to have committed on offence. Ordinarily those circumstances will be extraneous to the question of reasonable suspicion; for example that the suspect has the sole care of young children. I would not go so far as to say that the strength or weakness of the evidence justifying the reasonable suspicion can never be a material factor at this stage; but in most cases it will not be so, and will be material only to the question whether the conditions precedent to the exercise of the discretion existed.'

The danger of abuse of the discretion within the reasonable suspicion test and of the difficulty for the courts to monitor the use of the discretion are obvious. The objective element – that the grounds be reasonable – plays a vital role. There are numerous cases considering this element. In *King v Gardner*[20] officers received a radio message describing suspects loitering about, and Gardner, who fitted the description (blue jeans and long hair) was arrested after refusing to show them what was in a large canvas bag he was carrying when challenged. He was prosecuted for assaulting one of the officers. The sender of the message was not called to give evidence as to the identity of the defendant or as to acts which could be said to have given rise to reasonable suspicion. No evidence was called relating to the personal description given in the radio message, apart from PC Parker's bare assertion that Gardner fitted the description of the man in the area. The Divisional Court held that the Metropolitan Stipendiary Magistrate had been entitled to conclude that there was no satisfactory evidence that would constitute reasonable suspicion under s. 66 of the Metropolitan Police Act 1839 (below, pp. 209, 213). His decision was essentially one of fact that could only be upset if it was perverse.[1]

In *Monaghan v Corbett*[2] M's conviction for drink-driving was quashed. The Divisional Court held that the officer's reliance on a neighbour's information that M frequently drank and drove at Sunday lunch did not amount to reasonable suspicion

18 p. 26.
19 (1997) 24 April, unreported.
20 (1979) 71 Cr App Rep 13, DC.
 1 See also *R v Prince* [1981] Crim LR 638; *Ware v Matthews* (unreported); and *Pedro v Diss* [1981]
    2 All ER 59, DC, discussed by S. H. Bailey and D. J. Birch, [1982] Crim LR at pp. 476–477.
 2 (1983) 147 JP 545, DC.

that M had consumed alcohol on this occasion as it did not arise out of the driving of the motor vehicle at the relevant time. This appears to be an artificial limit, not imposed by the statute, on the information that may be relied upon by officer: it would be contrary to common sense to hold that on all the facts there was no reasonable suspicion.[3] Conversely, in *Ward v Chief Constable of Avon and Somerset Constabulary*,[4] the Court of Appeal held that there was sufficient evidence to show reasonable cause where the officer investigating a riot in which, inter alia, many Easter eggs had been stolen, found 13 eggs at D's premises and was unconvinced by the claim that they were bought for 37p each. In *Black v DPP*[5] the Divisional Court held that B's being at the house of his brother, who was a known drug dealer, could not give rise to a reasonable ground for suspicion that B was in possession of drugs. Nor could his aggressive behaviour on arrest retrospectively provide reasonable grounds to suspect. In *Parker v Chief Constable of Hampshire*[6] the court held that the armed arrest of P in Portsmouth on suspicion of firearms offences committed ten days earlier in Liverpool was reasonable because, although he did not fit the description, the car he was driving had been involved and the officer had reasonable grounds to think it 'possible' that one of the two people in the car was a suspect. Do you agree?

In *Samuels v Commissioner of Police for the Metropolis*[7] S was stopped when walking home along a London street in the middle of the morning, carrying no bags or other articles and in everyday casual clothes. The officer said that S looked suspicious because S was not 'walking purposefully', because he turned to look at the officer and when asked 'Why are you walking?' had replied, 'Am I not allowed to walk? I thought it was a free country'. The officer said he wanted to search S's pockets on suspicion of burglary. S told him he was not a burglar and that he lived in this area. He then took his keys out of his pocket and stepped into his front garden. The policeman grabbed hold of his arm and twisted it round his back. PC Senior later explained that he thought the claimant could possibly have had a screwdriver on him. The judge concluded that there were reasonable grounds to justify the officer in reaching the conclusion that he should stop and search S.

Brooke LJ: The only matter on which the judge appears to have relied in his ruling is the fact that when the officer asked the plaintiff if he minded telling him if he was going anywhere in particular the plaintiff said, 'It's a free country. I can go where I want' and moved away. The judge was rightly not willing to attach much significance to the fact that the plaintiff looked back, or that he was walking at a fairly leisurely pace, although these were matters to which the officer had referred when he was justifying the action he took. Indeed, the officer told the plaintiff that he wanted to search the plaintiff before ever he came up to talk to him.

Mr Buckett seeks to support the judge's ruling by relying also on other matters that were in evidence. First, that the area was known as a high risk burglary area by the police, and statistics were read to the jury which illustrated this fact. Next, that PC Senior told the plaintiff that it was a high risk burglary area, and made clear his wish to know what the plaintiff was doing. Thirdly, that the officer told the jury that he wanted to search the plaintiff in case he was carrying something with him to use in connection with burglary.

As I have made clear, in my judgment the judge was right to attach little significance to the evidence that the plaintiff looked round in the manner described, or that he was ambling along in a leisurely manner on this very hot day, as amounting to a reasonable ground for suspecting that he was going equipped for burglary. The fact that the police officer knew that this was a high risk area for burglary and told the plaintiff this fact cannot in my judgment in itself add anything. Everything turns on the behaviour of the plaintiff when he was stopped, since, in

3   Cf. *DPP v Wilson* [1991] Crim LR 441, DC.
4   (1986) Times, 26 June.
5   [1995] COD 381.
6   (1999) 25 June, CA (CD), unreported.
7   (1999) 3 March, Transcript from Lexis.

my judgement, the fact that the plaintiff, like many young men, had his hands in his pockets (if he did) cannot add anything.

[Brooke LJ referred to *Rice v Connolly* and the well established principle that a citizen is not obliged to answer police questions.]

It is unfortunate that the plaintiff gave the police officer unhelpful answers. In this, as Mr Buckett accepted, he would have been reacting in a manner no different to that of many young black men and indeed many young white men in London today when they feel that the police are picking on them. In my judgment, however, if the officer did not have reasonable grounds for suspecting that the plaintiff had a prohibited article on him before he came up to him, the fact that the plaintiff walked away after giving him a truthful answer that this was a free country could not turn what was an unreasonable suspicion into a reasonable suspicion that he was going equipped for burglary and does not add anything in the context of the present case.

Appeal allowed with costs.

What were the matters relied on by the officer as forming his reasonable suspicion? S had his hands in his pockets, was not walking purposefully, and was in an area of high crime? Would that *ever* be sufficient to amount to reasonable suspicion? Samuels was black. See the discussion below on the proportion of stop and searches carried out against minority ethnic communities. C. Phillips and D. Brown, found that the standard of reasonable suspicion to arrest a black or Asian person was lower than that required to arrest a white, and 'this was not explained by differences in the kinds of offence for which ethnic minority and white suspects were arrested'.[8]

(ii) Reasonable suspicion as an operational question

O'Hara v Chief Constable of the Royal Ulster Constabulary [1997] AC 286, [1997] 1 All ER 129, [1997] 2 WLR 1, Court of Appeal

O's house was searched early one morning by the RUC, and he was detained for questioning on suspicion of terrorist offences. He was released without charge. He sued the RUC for, inter alia, false imprisonment. At trial the judge found that the officers' arrest had been lawful, being based on a reasonable suspicion. The Court of Appeal upheld that decision.

Lord Steyn: So far as it is material section 12(1) [of the Prevention of Terrorism (Temporary Provisions) Act 1984] reads as follows:

'. . . a constable may arrest without warrant a person whom he has reasonable grounds for suspecting to be . . .
(b)   a person who is or has been concerned in the commission, preparation or instigation of acts of terrorism to which this Part of this Act applies; . . .'

The constable made the arrest in connection with a murder which was undoubtedly an act of terrorism within the meaning of section 12(1) of the 1984 Act. It was common ground that subjectively the constable had the necessary suspicion. The question was whether the constable objectively had reasonable grounds for suspecting that the appellant was concerned in the murder. The constable said in evidence that his reasonable grounds for suspecting the appellant were based on a briefing by a superior officer. He was told that the appellant had been involved in the murder. The constable said that the superior officer ordered him to arrest the appellant. He did so. Counsel for the appellant took the tactical decision not to cross-examine the constable about the details of the briefing. The trial judge described the evidence as scanty. But he inferred that the briefing afforded reasonable grounds for the necessary suspicion. In other words the judge inferred that some further details must have been given in the briefing. The legal burden was on the respondent to prove the existence of reasonable grounds for suspicion. Nevertheless I am persuaded that the judge was entitled on the sparse materials before him to infer the existence of reasonable grounds for suspicion. On this basis the Court of Appeal was entitled

8   p. 45.

to dismiss the appeal. That means that the appeal before your Lordships House must also fail on narrow and purely factual grounds.

[T]he decision of the House of Lords in *Mohammed-Holgate v Duke* [1984] AC 437 is of assistance. The House had to consider the issue whether an arrest was lawful in the context of a statutory provision which authorised arrest when a constable suspected on reasonable grounds that an arrestable offence had been committed. Lord Diplock made the following general observations, at p. 445B-E:

'My Lords, there is inevitably the potentiality of conflict between the public interest in preserving the liberty of the individual and the public interest in the detection of crime and the bringing to justice of those who commit it. The members of the organised police forces of the country have, since the mid-19th century, been charged with the duty of taking the first steps to promote the latter public interest by inquiring into suspected offences with a view to identifying the perpetrators of them and of obtaining sufficient evidence admissible in a court of law against the persons they suspect of being the perpetrators as would justify charging them with the relevant offence before a magistrates' court with a view to their committal for trial for it.

The compromise which English common and statutory law has evolved for the accommodation of the two rival public interests while these first steps are being taken by the police is two-fold:

(1) no person may be arrested without warrant (i.e. without the intervention of a judicial process) unless the constable arresting him has reasonable cause to suspect him to be guilty of an arrestable offence . . .

(2) a suspect so arrested and detained in custody must be brought before a magistrates' court as soon as practicable. . . .'

Lord Diplock made those observations in the context of statutes containing provisions such as section 12(1). He said that the arrest can only be justified if the constable arresting the alleged suspect has reasonable grounds to suspect him to be guilty of an arrestable offence. The arresting officer is held accountable. That is the compromise between the values of individual liberty and public order.

Section 12(1) authorises an arrest without warrant only where the constable 'has reasonable grounds for' suspicion. An arrest is therefore not lawful if the arresting officer honestly but erroneously believes that he has reasonable grounds for arrest but there are unknown to him in fact in existence reasonable grounds for the necessary suspicion, e.g. because another officer has information pointing to the guilt of the suspect. It would be difficult without doing violence to the wording of the statute to read it in any other way.

A strong argument can be made that in arresting a suspect without warrant a constable ought to be able to rely on information in the possession of another officer and not communicated to him: Feldman, *The Law Relating to Entry, Search & Seizure* (1986), pp. 204-205. Arguably that ought as a matter of policy to provide him with a defence to a claim for wrongful arrest. Such considerations may possibly explain why Art. 5(1) of the European Convention for the Protection of Human Rights and Freedoms 1950 contains a more flexible provision. It reads as follows:

'Everyone has the right to liberty and security of person. No one shall be deprived of his liberty save in the following cases and in accordance with a procedure prescribed by law: . . .

c. the lawful arrest or detention of a person effected for the purpose of bringing him before the competent legal authority on reasonable suspicion of having committed an offence or when it is reasonably considered necessary to prevent his committing an offence or fleeing after having done so; . . .'

It is clear from the drafting technique employed in Art. 5(1)*c*, and in particular the use of the passive tense, that it contemplates a broader test of whether a reasonable suspicion exists and does not confine it to matters present in the mind of the arresting officer. That is also the effect of the judgment of the European Court of Human Rights in *Fox v United Kingdom* (1990) 13 EHRR 157, 167-169, paras. 33-35. But section 12(1), and similar provisions, cannot be approached in this way: they categorise as reasonable grounds for suspicion only matters present in the mind of the constable. In *Civil Liberties & Human Rights in England and Wales*

(1993), Professor Feldman lucidly explained the difference between two classes of statutes, at p. 199:

> 'Where reasonable grounds for suspicion are required in order to justify the arrest of someone who turns out to be innocent, the [Police and Criminal Evidence Act 1984] requires that the constable personally has reasonable grounds for the suspicion, and it would seem to follow that he is not protected if, knowing nothing of the case, he acts on orders from another officer who, perhaps, does have such grounds. On the other hand, under statutes which require only the objective existence of reasonable grounds for suspicion, it is possible that the officer need neither have the reasonable grounds nor himself suspect anything; he can simply follow orders.'

Section 12(1) is undeniably a statutory provision in the first category. The rationale for the principle in such cases is that in framing such statutory provisions Parliament has proceeded on the longstanding constitutional theory of the independence and accountability of the individual constable: Marshall and Loveday, *The Police Independence and Accountability in The Changing Constitution*, (3rd edn, ed. by Jowell and Oliver, 295 et seq); Christopher L. Ryan and Katherine S. Williams, 'Police Discretion', [1986] Public Law 285, at 305. This case must therefore be approached on the basis that under section 12(1) the only relevant matters are those present in the mind of the arresting officer.

Certain general propositions about the powers of constables under a section such as section 12(1) can now be summarised. (1) In order to have a reasonable suspicion the constable need not have evidence amounting to a prima facie case. Ex hypothesi one is considering a preliminary stage of the investigation and information from an informer or a tip-off from a member of the public may be enough: *Hussien v Chong Fook Kam* [1970] AC 942, 949. (2) Hearsay information may therefore afford a constable a reasonable grounds to arrest. Such information may come from other officers: *Hussien's* case, ibid. (3) The information which causes the constable to be suspicious of the individual must be in existence to the knowledge of the police officer at the time he makes the arrest. (4) The executive 'discretion' to arrest or not as Lord Diplock described it in *Mohammed-Holgate v Duke* [1984] AC 437, 446, vests in the constable, who is engaged on the decision to arrest or not, and not in his superior officers.

Given the independent responsibility and accountability of a constable under a provision such as section 12(1) of the Act of 1984 it seems to follow that the mere fact that an arresting officer has been instructed by a superior officer to effect the arrest is not capable of amounting to reasonable grounds for the necessary suspicion within the meaning of section 12(1). It is accepted, and rightly accepted, that a mere request to arrest without any further information by an equal ranking officer, or a junior officer, is incapable of amounting to reasonable grounds for the necessary suspicion. How can the badge of the superior officer, and the fact that he gave an order, make a difference? In respect of a statute vesting an independent discretion in the particular constable, and requiring him personally to have reasonable grounds for suspicion, it would be surprising if seniority made a difference. It would be contrary to the principle underlying section 12(1) which makes a constable individually responsible for the arrest and accountable in law. In *R v Chief Constable of Devon and Cornwall, ex p Central Electricity Generating Board* [1982] QB 458, 474 Lawton LJ touched on this point. He observed:

> '[chief constables] cannot give an officer under command an order to do acts which can only lawfully be done if the officer himself with reasonable cause suspects that a breach of the peace has occurred or is imminently likely to occur or an arrestable offence has been committed.'

Such an order to arrest cannot without some further information being given to the constable be sufficient to afford the constable reasonable grounds for the necessary suspicion. That seems to me to be the legal position in respect of a provision such as section 12(1). For these reasons I regard the submission of counsel for the respondent as unsound in law. In practice it follows that a constable must be given some basis for a request to arrest somebody under a provision such as section 12(1), e.g. a report from an informer.

Subject to these observations, I agree that the appeal ought to be dismissed.

Lord Hope of Craighead: My Lords, the test which section 12(1) of the Act of 1984 has laid down is a simple but practical one. It relates entirely to what is in the mind of the arresting officer when the power is exercised. In part it is a subjective test, because he must have formed a genuine suspicion in his own mind that the person has been concerned in acts of terrorism. In part also it is an objective one, because there must also be reasonable grounds for the suspicion which he has formed. But the application of the objective test does not require the court to look beyond what was in the mind of the arresting officer. It is the grounds which were in his mind at the time which must be found to be reasonable grounds for the suspicion which he has formed. All that the objective test requires is that these grounds be examined objectively and that they be judged at the time when the power was exercised.

This means that the point does not depend on whether the arresting officer himself thought at that time that they were reasonable. The question is whether a reasonable man would be of that opinion, having regard to the information which was in the mind of the arresting officer. It is the arresting officer's own account of the information which he had which matters, not what was observed by or known to anyone else. The information acted on by the arresting officer need not be based on his own observations, as he is entitled to form a suspicion based on what he has been told. His reasonable suspicion may be based on information which has been given to him anonymously or it may be based on information, perhaps in the course of an emergency, which turns out later to be wrong. As it is the information which is in his mind alone which is relevant however, it is not necessary to go on to prove what was known to his informant or that any facts on which he based his suspicion were in fact true. The question whether it provided reasonable grounds for the suspicion depends on the source of his information and its context, seen in the light of the whole surrounding circumstances.

This approach to the wording of section 12(1) of the Act of 1984 is consistent with authority. In *Dallison v Caffery* [1965] 1 QB 348, which preceded the enactment of section 2(4) of the Criminal Law Act 1967, the arrest had been effected in the exercise of the common law power. Diplock LJ's description, at p. 354, of the test to be applied does however provide a useful starting point for the examination of the power which has been given by the statute. What he said was:

'The test whether there was reasonable and probable cause for the arrest or prosecution is an objective one, namely, whether a reasonable man, assumed to know the law and possessed of the information which in fact was possessed by the defendant, would believe that there was reasonable and probable cause.'

Many other examples may be cited of cases where the action of the constable who exercises a statutory power of arrest or of search is a member of a team of police officers, or where his action is the culmination of various steps taken by other police officers, perhaps over a long period and perhaps also involving officers from other police forces. For obvious practical reasons police officers must be able to rely upon each other in taking decisions as to whom to arrest or where to search and in what circumstances. The statutory power does not require that the constable who exercises the power must be in possession of all the information which has led to a decision, perhaps taken by others, that the time has come for it to be exercised. What it does require is that the constable who exercises the power must first have equipped himself with sufficient information so that he has reasonable cause to suspect before the power is exercised.

My Lords, in this case the evidence about the matters which were disclosed at the briefing session to the arresting officer was indeed scanty. But, as Mr. Coghlin pointed out, the trial judge was entitled to weigh up that evidence in the light of the surrounding circumstances and, having regard to the source of that information, to draw inferences as to what a reasonable man, in the position of the independent observer, would make of it. I do not think that either the trial judge or the Court of Appeal misdirected themselves as to the test to be applied. I would dismiss this appeal.

Lords Hoffmann, Mustill and **Goff** concurred.[8a]

NOTES

1. Hunt suggests that the case is a 'valiant attempt to reconcile the demands of operational context with traditional constitutional principle'.[9] Do you agree?
2. Research into stop and search distinguishes 'high' and 'low' exercises of discretion. A high discretion stop would be where an officer stops an unknown person late at

8a See now the ECtHR ruling (2001) Times, 13 November, upholding the finding of reasonable suspicion.
9   A. Hunt, (1997) 113 LQR 548, 550.

night in a high-crime area. A low discretion stop would be where the officer targeted a named individual on the basis of an instruction from fellow officers or the public. C. Phillips and D. Brown,[10] found that 28% of all arrests based on reasonable suspicion came from an instruction from the control room.[11] Fewer than 25% of all arrests were from pro-active policing.

3. How realistic is Lord Steyn's opinion that 'a mere request to arrest without any further information by an equal ranking officer, or a junior officer, is incapable of amounting to reasonable grounds for the necessary suspicion?' How likely is a junior officer to ignore such an instruction and go off in search of his own grounds for suspicion? Does the constitutional principle of constabulary independence discussed in Chap. 2 really reflect the way that modern policing is conducted?

4. In *French v DPP*[12] the Divisional Court held that a stop and search for drugs could lawfully be based on a reasonable suspicion if that was based on the 'unparticularised assertion' of other officers. Is the decision still good law?

5. Research by Phillips and Brown[13] found that of the 4,250 arrests they examined, in 71% of cases the arresting officer claimed that the basis of his reasonable suspicion was from only one source of evidence. In 21% of cases there were two sources and in 8% of cases three of more. In 40% of all cases the main ground for the suspicion derived from 'a police observation of the offence.'[14] Even such observation can lack objective bases: in *Slade v DPP*[15] the court upheld the trial judge's finding that reasonable grounds for suspicion to search under s. 23 of the Misuse of Drugs Act 1971 existed where an officer saw S in the vicinity of a house known for drug dealing, with his hand in his pocket and a 'smug' smile on his face. Can this ever be more than at best a hunch and at worst prejudice?

In deciding whether a reasonable suspicion exists, it is not legitimate for the court to consider evidence of subsequent conduct alleged to constitute a course of harassment by the officers: *Tomlinson v Chief Constable of Hertfordshire*.[16]

6. In *Clarke v Chief Constable of North Wales*[17] it was held that it was not really necessary for each officer to 'satisfy himself that the information conveyed by other officers comes from a reliable source'. Sedley LJ observed that:

> 'Of course if the briefing makes it apparent that the sources are unreliable or non-existent, the arresting constable's suspicion will not be reasonable in the absence of other grounds for it. And if the briefing officer has told the arresting officer that there is reliable information when there is not, the chief constable may become vicariously liable for a wrongful arrest but on behalf of the briefing officer not of the arresting officer. These, it seems to me are the protections the law affords against arrest on unjustified suspicion. They do not extend, and do not need to extend, to requiring each constable involved in an arrest and search operation to make an independent evaluation of the grounds for suspicion. Nothing in *O'Hara* suggests otherwise.'

Is this what you understand *O'Hara* to require?

7. That 'reasonable cause to suspect' may be based on hearsay evidence was confirmed by *Erksine v Hollin*[18] and in *O'Hara*. See also *Doorson v Netherlands*.[19] Reasonable

10 HORS No. 49, *Entry into the Criminal Justice System: a survey of arrests and their outcomes* (1998).
11 p. 34.
12 [1997] COD 174, DC.
13 Op. cit. n. 10.
14 Ibid., p. 41.
15 (1996) 22 October, DC, unreported.
16 [2001] All ER (D) 109 (Mar), CA (Cr D).
17 (2000) 5 April, CA (Cr D), unreported.
18 [1971] RTR 199, DC; *R v Evans* [1974] RTR 232, CA (Cr D): information supplied by a fellow police officer.
19 (1996) 22 EHRR 330.

suspicion can also be founded on 'fleeting glimpse eyewitness evidence' (*Brian Jones v Chief Constable of Bedfordshire*,[20] but see Sedley J's dissent). In *Hough v Chief Constable of Staffordshire*[21] the court held that the reasonable suspicion could arise from reliance on a Police National Computer (PNC) check for a vehicle – in that case it was an erroneous entry and H, who was completely innocent, was arrested by an armed police unit. Simon Brown LJ emphasised that, except in emergencies, the police ought to make checks beyond the PNC to found a reasonable suspicion.

8. In *Lamothe v Metropolitan Police Comr*[1] the Court of Appeal (Civil Division) struck down an *ex parte* order of a judge that the reason for an officer forming his reasonable suspicion was not to be the subject of cross-examination at the trial for false imprisonment brought by the claimant arrestee. How are officers supposed to demonstrate reasonable suspicion when the basis for that suspicion comes from an informer? Efforts must also be made to protect an informer, but this creates problems. In *R v Smith*[2] the Court of Appeal held that the judge could, in deciding whether the police had reasonable suspicion to arrest, rely on information received by the judge in the course of the public interest immunity hearing. There was no breach of Art. 6 in so doing.

9. Article 5 of the European Convention on Human Rights provides protection against unlawful detention. In *O'Hara* the House of Lords addressed the compatibility of the concept of 'reasonable suspicion' in English law with that under the Convention. Lord Hope of Craighead stated:

> 'I should add that I see no conflict in principle between the approach which has been taken in these cases and the judgment of the European Court of Human Rights in *Fox v United Kingdom* (1990) 13 EHRR 157 to which we were referred by Mr. Kennedy. The applicants had been detained without warrant under section 11 of the Northern Ireland (Emergency Provisions) Act 1978. As has already been noted, this section provided for the arrest without warrant of any person whom a constable suspected of being a terrorist. It was held that as the constable's suspicion had not been shown to be "reasonable", the United Kingdom were in breach of Article 5(1) of the Convention, which provides:

> "Everyone has the right to liberty and security of person. No one shall be deprived of his liberty save in the following cases and in accordance with the procedure prescribed by law:
> . . .
> *c.* The lawful arrest or detention of a person effected for the purpose of bringing him before the competent legal authority on reasonable suspicion of having committed an offence . . ."

> In that case, as was stated, at p. 169, para. 35 of the judgment, the arrest and detention of the applicants was based on a suspicion which was bona fide or genuine. But the court held that the Government had not provided sufficient material to support the conclusion that the suspicion was 'reasonable', and that its explanations did not meet the minimum standard set by Art. 5(1)*c.* for judging the reasonableness of a suspicion for the arrest of an individual. As to what these requirements are, they are to be found in the following passage in the judgment, at p. 167, para. 32:

> "The 'reasonableness' of the suspicion on which an arrest must be based forms an essential part of the safeguard against arbitrary arrest and detention which is laid down in Art. 5(1)*c.* The court agrees with the Commission and the Government that having a 'reasonable suspicion' presupposes the existence of facts or information which would satisfy an objective observer that the person concerned may have committed the offence. What may be regarded as 'reasonable' will however depend upon all the circumstances."

---

20 (1999) 30 July CA (Cr D).
21 [2001] EWCA Civ 39.
1 (1999) 25 October, unreported.
2 (2000) 15 December, unreported, CA (Cr D). See on this problem *O'Hara* in the European Court (2001) Times, 13 November.

What Parliament has enacted in section 12(1)(*b*) of the Act of 1984, as in the other statutes to which I have referred, is that the reasonable suspicion has to be in the mind of the arresting officer. So it is the facts known by or the information given to the officer who effects the arrest or detention to which the mind of the independent observer must be applied. It is this objective test, applying the criterion of what may be regarded as reasonable, which provides the safeguard against arbitrary arrest and detention. The arrest and detention will be unlawful unless this criterion is satisfied.'[3]

The European Court of Human Rights has held that the existence of a reasonable suspicion depends on all the circumstances of the case at the time of the action *Stogmuller v Austria*[4] and that the level of suspicion need not be as high as that required to prefer charges.[5] In *K-F v Germany*[6] the court held that reasonable suspicion presupposes the existence of facts or information that would satisfy an objective observer that the person concerned might have committed the offence. The degree of deprivation of the suspect's liberty is an important factor in assessing the existence of the reasonable suspicion. This was confirmed by the ECtHR in *O'Hara*.

(iii) Reasonable suspicion: an undefinable concept?

A question that has been debated since before the enactment of PACE is whether a definition of reasonable suspicion can ever be satisfactorily provided. It must be sufficiently flexible to allow the police to operate effectively, but it is important to ensure the protection of civil liberties that there are sufficient safeguards against its abuse. The Advisory Committee on Drug Dependence, *Powers of Arrest and Search in Relation to Drug Offences*[7] concluded (by a majority) that it would be impracticable to formulate standards for grounds of reasonable suspicion in a statute or code of practice. The Royal Commission on Criminal Procedure (RCCP) concluded that the requirements of notifying reasons, making records and the monitoring of such records by superior officers would be the most effective way of reducing the risk of random action.

Home Office research into stop and search has confirmed that officers' suspicions are aroused as a result of appearance, including: youth; type of vehicle; incongruence; 'in some cases' ethnicity; being known to the police; and fitting the suspect description.[8] Can officers be expected not to base suspicion on hunches?

In *Baker v Oxford*[9] the Divisional Court accepted that there was a distinction between requirements of reasonable cause to *suspect* and reasonable cause to *believe*.[10] No opinion was expressed on what the distinction might be although it had been suggested in argument that '"suspect" implied an imagination to exist without proof, whereas "belief" implied an acceptance of what was true'. In *Johnson v Whitehouse*[11] the Divisional Court confirmed that 'the greater force of the word "believe" [than "suspect"] is an essential part of the law'.[12] However, an arrest was not invalid merely because the constable used the wrong word provided that the

---

3 See also *K-F v Germany* (1998) 26 EHRR 390.
4 (1979–80) 1 EHRR 155.
5 *Murray v United Kingdom* (1995) 19 EHRR 193, para. 55.
6 (1998) 26 EHRR 390.
7 Home Office, 1970, paras. 111, 123–127 and the RCCP *Report*, Cmnd. 8092, p. 29.
8 See P. Quinton, N. Bland and J. Miller, *Police Stops, Decision-making in Practice* (2000) (HORS Paper No. 130).
9 [1980] RTR 315.
10 See S. H. Bailey and D. J. Birch, [1982] Crim LR at pp. 549–551.
11 [1984] RTR 38.
12 p. 47.

relevant grounds were present. In *Siddiqui v Swain*[13] the Divisional Court held that where an arrest required 'reasonable cause to suspect', it must be shown both that (1) there was 'reasonable cause' and (2) that the constable in fact 'suspected'.[14]

(iv) Reasonable suspicion and stereotypes

One of the most controversial areas in which the reasonable suspicion question arises is in relation to stop and search. Annex B to the original version of the Code of Practice for the Exercise by Police Officers of Statutory Powers of Stop and Search (Code A) sets out guidance on the question of reasonable suspicion. In the second and third editions of Code A, Annex B was omitted and the guidance reworded. The most recent version of Code A came into force on 1 March 1999. It takes account of the Knives Act 1997, s. 8, and the Crime and Disorder Act, s. 25 (see below). The changes (Parts 1.6A and 1.7AA) represent a significant qualification to the earlier version:

'1.6 Whether reasonable grounds for suspicion exist will depend on the circumstances in each case, but there must be some objective basis for it. An officer will need to consider the nature of the article. suspected of being carried in the context of other factors such as the time and the place, and the behaviour of the person concerned or those with him. Reasonable suspicion may exist, for example, where information has been received such as a description of an article being carried or of a suspected offender; a person is seen acting covertly or warily or attempting to hide something; or a person is carrying a certain type of article at an unusual time or in a place where a number of burglaries or thefts are known to have taken place recently. But the decision to stop and search must be based on all the facts which bear on the likelihood that an article of a certain kind will be found.

1.6A For example, reasonable suspicion may be based upon reliable information or intelligence which indicates that members of a particular group or gang, or their associates, habitually carry knives or weapons or controlled drugs.

1.7 Reasonable suspicion can never be supported on the basis of personal factors alone. For example, a person's colour, age, hairstyle or manner of dress, or the fact that he is known to have a previous conviction for possession of an unlawful article, cannot be used alone or in combination with each other as the sole basis on which to search that person. Nor may it be founded on the basis of stereotyped images of certain persons or groups as more likely to be committing offences.

1.7AA However, where there is reliable information or intelligence that members of a group or gang who habitually carry knives unlawfully or weapons or controlled drugs, and wear a distinctive item of clothing or other means of identification to indicate membership of it, the members may be identified by means of that distinctive item of clothing or other means of identification.'

In the notes for guidance, 1H, it is stated that 'other means of identification might include jewellery, insignias, tattoos, or other features which are known to identify members of the particular gang or group'.

NOTES

1. Do these amendments provide officers with an opportunity to harass certain groups within society because of the way they dress? Do they provide equal protection for Rastafarians, hell's angels and merchant bankers?

13 [1979] RTR 454.
14 See S. H. Bailey and D. J. Birch, op. cit, pp. 550–551. Cf. *Chapman v DPP* (1988) 89 Cr App Rep 190.

2. For difficulties that arose from the wording of the old Annex B, see D. Dixon, et al., 'Reality and Rules in the Construction and Regulation of Police Suspicion'.[15] They confirm that in practice, contrary to a provision of Annex B (para. 4) omitted from the revised version, the standard of suspicion applied by the police to justify a stop and search is lower (less individualised) than that applied to justify an arrest. Can this be justified on the argument that a stop and search is less intrusive than an arrest?[16] They argue that some of the problems in this area might appropriately be tackled by such steps as 'clearer statements of required standards, more testing judicial scrutiny, public education and new police training'[17] See further the discussion of stop and search below, p. 204.

3. Reasonable suspicion triggers the *possibility* for officers to use many powers under PACE. It does not *oblige* officers to use the powers. In addition to the very considerable scope of discretion in deciding whether there is a reasonable suspicion, there remains a large element of discretion in the way the officer then elects whether to use the power. As M. Wasik, T. Gibbons and M. Redmayne note:

> 'For serious matters it will be unreasonable and irregular not to take a suspect into custody for further investigation. That will also be the case with specialised offending which is enforced through dedicated policing, such as drugs, vice, or robbery squads. For the less serious kinds of suspected offending however the emphasis in policing decisions shifts to the moral worth of the individual rather than his or her behaviour. The outcome of an encounter may depend on the officer's assessment of the extent to which the individual deserves to be processed.'[18]

4. P. Waddington comments that 'if the police can use their extensive discretion to define crime, they can use that same discretion to concentrate attention on vulnerable sections of the population and cast them in the role of criminals'.[19] To what extent do powers triggered by a flexible standard like 'reasonable suspicion' allow the police to determine *what* is criminal? Does a requirement of accurate record keeping and monitoring of the use of the police powers provide adequate protection against abuse?

(B) THE CONCEPT OF 'SERIOUS ARRESTABLE OFFENCE'

The RCCP recommended that certain of the powers of the police should be available only in respect of 'grave offences'. This was where powers were to be used against persons not themselves reasonably suspected of complicity in an offence or where the powers were particularly intrusive. The RCCP did not list 'grave offences' but suggested which broad categories would be included.[20] The 1984 Act used instead the concept of 'serious arrestable offence' in relation to the powers given by ss. 4 (road checks), 8 (search warrants), 42 and 43 (continued detention), 56(2) (delay in informing a friend or relative that a person has been arrested), 58(6) (delayed access to legal advice). The term 'arrestable offence' is defined by s. 24.[1] The concept of 'serious arrestable offence' is defined as follows:

15 (1989) 17 International Journal of the Sociology of Law 185.
16 See pp. 194–195.
17 p. 204.
18 *Criminal Justice Text and Materials* (1999), p. 137.
19 *Policing Citizens* (1999), Chap. 2, p. 35. See also comments in J. Kleinig, *The Ethics of Policing* (1996), p. 86; Fielding, *Community Policing* (1995).
20 Report, paras. 3.7–3.9.
 1 Below, pp. 275.

Police and Criminal Evidence Act 1984

116. Meaning of 'serious arrestable offence'

(1) This section has effect for determining whether an offence is a serious arrestable offence for the purposes of this Act.

(2) The following arrestable offences are always serious

    (*a*) an offence (whether at common law or under any enactment) specified in Part I of Schedule 5 to this Act; and

    (*b*) an offence under an enactment specified in Part II of that Schedule; [and

    (*c*) any of the offences mentioned in paragraphs (*a*) to (*f*) of section 1(3) of the Drug Trafficking Act 1994.] [2]

(3) subject to subsections (4) [...] below, any other arrestable offence is serious only if its commission

    (*a*) has led to any of the consequences specified in subsection (6) below; or

    (*b*) is intended or is likely to lead to any of those consequences.

(4) An arrestable offence which consists of making a threat is serious if carrying out the threat would be to lead to any of the consequences specified in subsection (6) below.

(5) [repealed by the Terrorism Act 2000, s. 125, Sch. 15, para. 5(11)].

(6) The consequences mentioned in subsections (3) and (4) above are

    (*a*) serious harm to the security of the State or to public order;

    (*b*) serious interference with the administration of justice or with the investigation of offences or of a particular offence;

    (*c*) the death of any person;

    (*d*) serious injury to any person;

    (*e*) substantial financial gain to any person; and

    (*f*) serious financial loss to any person.

(7) Loss is serious for the purposes of this section if, having regard to all the circumstances, it is serious for person who suffers it.

(8) In this section 'injury' includes any disease or any impairment of a person's physical or mental condition.

NOTES

1. Schedule 5, Part I, mentioned in s. 116(2)(a), lists: (1) treason; (2) murder; (3) manslaughter; (4) rape; (5) kidnapping; (6) incest with a girl under the age of 13; (7) buggery with a person under 16; (8) indecent assault which constitutes an act of gross indecency. Those in Sch. 5, Part II, s. 116(2)(b) are: (1) causing an explosion likely to endanger life or property;[3] (2) intercourse with a girl under 13;[4] (3) possession of firearms with intent to injure, use of firearms and imitation firearms to resist arrest and carrying firearms with criminal intent;[5] (4) hostage taking;[6] (5) hi-jacking;[7] (6) torture;[8] (7) causing death by driving, causing death by careless driving when under the influence of drink or drugs;[9] (8) endangering safety at aerodromes, hijacking of ships and seizing or exercising control of fixed platforms;[10] (9) hijacking of Channel Tunnel trains, seizing or exercising control of the tunnel system;[11] (10) taking and

2 Inserted by the Drug Trafficking Act 1994, Sch. 1, para. 9.
3 Explosive Substances Act 1883, s. 2.
4 Sexual Offences Act 1956, s. 5.
5 Firearms Act 1968, ss. 16, 17(1), 18.
6 Taking of Hostages Act 1982, s. 1.
7 Aviation Security Act 1982, s. 1.
8 Criminal Justice Act 1988, s. 134.
9 Road Traffic Act 1988, ss. 1, 3A.
10 Aviation and Maritime Security Act 1990, ss. 1, 9, 10.
11 Channel Tunnel (Security) Order 1994, S.I. 1994 No. 570.

distribution of indecent photographs or pseudo-photographs of children;[12] (11) publication of obscene matter;[13] (12) (from a day to be appointed, as inserted by CJPA 2001, s. 72) offences of importing indecent or obscene goods contrary to s. 170 of the Customs and Excise Management Act 1979.

2. In *R v Central Criminal Court, ex p Bright*[14] Maurice Kay LJ, considering the expression 'likely to lead to serious harm to the security of the state', held that 'likely' should be taken to mean 'such as well might happen' rather than the higher standard of 'more probable than not'.

3. There have been few cases offering guidance on the conditions listed in sub-s. (6). In *R v Mclvor*[15] Lawton LJ, sitting at first instance, held that the theft of 28 beagles worth £880 from a hunt was not a serious arrestable offence: the theft of the dogs, owned collectively by the hunt did not cause 'serious financial loss'. In *R v Smith (Eric)*[16] a robbery from Woolworths involving two video recorders, valued at about £800, plus cash of £116, was regarded by the trial judge as probably not a serious arrestable offence: the gain to the robbers was not necessarily substantial and the loss would probably not be serious for a large store. In *R v Central Criminal Court, ex p Carr*,[17] a case concerning the validity of a search warrant regarding investigations of alleged fraud by the Broadwater Farm Youth Association, Glidewell LJ stated that:

> 'if it be proved that there has been a fraudulent misappropriation of part of the funds of an association designed to serve the members of a community, funds which are to a major extent provided by local authorities and thus indirectly by ratepayers and taxpayers, and if moreover it be proved that the accounts of the association have been deliberately drawn up in such a way as to conceal misappropriation, I have no doubt that a serious arrestable offence has been committed.'

4. In the House of Lords in *R v Manchester Stipendiary Magistrate, ex p Granada Ltd* it was accepted that the expression serious arrestable offence 'was designed for use in connection with offences alleged to have been committed in England and Wales only, not offences alleged to have been committed in Scotland'.[18] See the changes contained in the Criminal Justice and Police Act 2001 (below).

5. The consequences of an offence being categorised as a serious arrestable offence are significant. An incorrect classification would lead to the action of the police being unlawful, and could lead to the exclusion of evidence.[19]

(C) THE USE OF FORCE

Criminal Law Act 1967

3. Use of force in making arrest, etc

(1) A person may use such force as is reasonable in the circumstances in the prevention of crime, or in effecting or assisting in the lawful arrest of offenders or suspected offenders or of persons unlawfully at large.

(2) Subsection (1) above shall replace the rules of the common law on the question when force used for a purpose mentioned in the subsection is justified by that purpose.

---

12 Protection of Children Act 1978, s. 1.
13 Obscene Publications Act 1959, s. 2.
14 [2000] 1 WLR 662.
15 [1987] Crim LR 409.
16 [1987] Crim LR 579.
17 (1987) Independent, 5 March, DC.
18 [2000] 2 WLR 1 at 12, per Lord Hope of Craighead.
19 See below, p. 350.

NOTES

1. This section authorises the use of reasonable force in the making of an arrest.[20] It also authorises the use of reasonable force to resist an unlawful arrest, such force constituting force used in 'the prevention of crime'.[1] In a civil case the question of reasonable force is entirely objective. In a criminal case the reasonableness of the force the defendant used will be judged – by the jury (objectively) on the facts as the accused (subjectively) believed them to exist (however unreasonable the belief).

2. 'Reasonable force' presumably will not exceed the minimum necessary to make or resist an arrest. However, it may well be that the minimum force necessary to make or resist arrest will exceed what is reasonable. For example, a person unlawfully arrested (e.g. because no power of arrest exists in connection with the offence for which the arrest was made) might be regarded by a court as using unreasonable force in using even a small amount of force in trying to escape if in the circumstances it was likely that the mistake could be pointed out to superior officers and the arrested person be released within a brief period.

3. In *O'Connor v Chief Constable of Norfolk*,[2] the court held that a male officer, accompanied by another, had gone beyond what was reasonable when applying the 'Koti Hinari' grip to arrest a suspected woman drink driver whom he thought might try to escape even though she was out of her car and in the presence of two officers. The grip fractured her wrist. See also the decision in *Chief Constable of Lincolnshire v Glowacki*,[3] where an off-duty officer had used an unapproved method to restrain G, causing two fractures.

4. In the PCA Report *Striking the Balance: The police use of new batons*[4] concern is expressed about inadequate training of officers in relation to some types of the side-handled baton. In addition it is noted that batons should only be used at the final stages of the 'use of force continuum'. These being: level 1 – officer's presence; level 2 – tactical communications; level 3 – primary controls (armlocks, wristlocks, escort positions, handcuffs etc.); level 4 – secondary control (incapacitants); level 5 – defensive tatics (racking extendable batons, blocks/strikes and takedowns with or without batons); level 6 – deadly force.

5. The use of force under s. 3 is justified not only on what the person believed was being done to him, but what he feared was about to be done to him: *R v Hughes*[5] – a raised truncheon caused H to struggle with an officer and resist what H thought was going to be a battering.

6. J. Kleinig[6] asserts that 'To grant that police should have the authority to use force is only the first step in any justification of their use of that force'.[7] Does English law require sufficient justification of the use of force by police officers?

---

20 See J. C. Smith, 'Using Force in Self-Defence and the Prevention of Crime' (1994) 47 CLP 101.
1   See above, p. 167. See further J. C. Smith, *Smith and Hogan, Criminal Law* (9th edn, 1999), pp. 252–263; G. Williams, *Textbook of Criminal Law* (2nd edn, 1983), pp. 493–499; *R v Fennell* [1971] 1 QB 428, CA; *A-G for Northern Ireland's Reference (No 1 of 1975)* [1977] AC 105, *R v Jones* [1978] 3 All ER 1098, CA; *Allen v Metropolitan Police Comr* (1980) Times, 25 March, [1980] Crim LR 441.
2   (1997) 10 February, CA (Cr D).
3   (1998) 18 June, CA (Cr D).
4   (1998).
5   [1995] Crim LR 957.
6   *The Ethics of Policing* (1996).
7   p. 98.

7. On the use of police dogs to effect arrest compare *Coles v Chief Constable of South Yorkshire*[8] and *Pollard v Chief Constable of West Yorkshire*.[9] The question is one of fact as Swinton Thomas LJ stated in *Coles*:

> 'once the concept of reasonableness is introduced [in section 3] then whether it is reasonable to instruct the dog to bite a human being must depend on the circumstances. Police officers are accustomed to exercising their judgement, and for my own part, I doubt very much whether many cases will arise in which it is possible for a plaintiff to establish that that judgement has been exercised wrongly.'

In *Murgatroyd v Chief Constable of West Yorkshire Police*[10] the court held that the use of a police dog to disable a suicidal occupant of a house that the police had forcibly entered was unreasonable. The dog was used to protect the police from harm rather than to prevent the occupier self-harming, but the police were already adequately protected against a 'puny' man.

8. *Using lethal force.* Following the Waldorf shooting,[11] revised instructions in respect of the issue of firearms were brought into effect. The most recent version has been produced by the Association of Chief Police Officers (ACPO) in its *Manual of Guidance on Police Use of Firearms* (2001),[12] which seeks to ensure compliance with the ECHR. Firearms are issuable to authorised firearms officers (AFOs of which there are 6,262) where an authorising officer has reason to suppose that, in the course of his duty, the AFO may have to protect themselves or others from a person who is in possession of a firearm or has immediate access to a firearm or is otherwise so dangerous that the officer's use of a firearm may be necessary (or for the humane destruction of an animal in certain specified cases).[13] Between April 1999 and March 2000 there were 10,915 operations in which firearms were issued.[13a]

The command structure of those officers involved in firearms issue and use is spelt out in detail in the ACPO guidelines (Chap. 4) as are the requirements for documentation for issue and use.[14] There are some situations in which standing authority for issue/carriage of weapons is met (e.g. airports, nuclear plants, and in armed response vehicles (ARVs)[15]). In 1999–2000, 8,276 operations involved ARVs being deployed.[15a]

Guidance as to discharge of the firearms is provided in Chap. 5 of the guidelines. Firearms are to be fired by AFOs in the course of duty, only when 'absolutely necessary' after conventional methods have been tried and failed or must, from the nature of the circumstances, be unlikely to succeed if tried. Warning shots are strongly discouraged since they might escalate the situation, and cause the suspect to begin firing.[16] Oral warnings should be given that armed police are present unless it would endanger an officer or would be pointless. Officers are advised to target the central body mass rather than shooting to injure. The ACPO guidelines make it clear that the ultimate responsibility rests with the individual officer for his conduct. Chapter 6

8 (1998) CA (Cr D).
9 (1998) 28 April, CA (Cr D). No evidence that handler had intended or foresaw that dog might react otherwise than in accordance with training.
10 (2000) 8 November, CA (CD).
11 See above, p. 119.
12 See www.acpo.police.uk.
13 Para. 2.2–2.4.
13a See *Statistics on the Police use of Firearms in England and Wales 1999-2000* Table 1.
14 Para. 14.
15 On developments in the use of armed response vehicles (vehicles on patrol with a small armoury from which the officers can draw weapons if authorised to do so) see P. Southgate, *The Management and Deployment of Police Armed Response Vehicles* (HORPU Paper 67, 1992).
15a Op. cit., Table 3.
16 Op. cit., Annex 3B.

of the guidelines deals with the investigations into misuse and remedies available for such.[17]

9. The application of the ordinary criminal law in relation to the police and armed services when using weapons has provoked controversy. S. Skinner[18] argues that the 'citizens in uniform' doctrine, whereby police are not afforded special status, is potentially incompatible with the Human Rights Act 1998 and has a dubious pedigree in terms of precedent. He concludes:

> 'maintaining the citizens in uniform principle enables the judiciary to employ the rhetoric of the rule of law, without grasping the nettle of recognising the real disparity between ordinary citizens and state agents who use force.'[19]

See further J. Rogers,[20] discussing the Home Office Review Inter-Departmental review of the *Law on the Use of Lethal Force in Self Defence or the Prevention of Crime* (1996).

Rogers concludes that:

> 'when one combines the various features of the present law – a soldier may shoot in order to prevent a future, unspecified crime, the jury need only consider whether a reasonable man might have thought that the shooting was lawful (and should take into account all such factors as the short time available for reflection, and the defendant's belief that he had acted lawfully) and that a breach of the internal [i.e. police] instructions need carry no adverse consequences – the case for reform of some nature becomes unanswerable.'[1]

His suggestion is to refine the existing system to provide two new defences based on the reasonableness of the public servant's actions. Skinner approaches things from a human rights angle, and identifies advantages to that approach rather than one based on reasonableness:

> 'proportionality (and necessity) as the benchmark for legitimate interference with a positive right differ from reasonableness in three distinct ways. First, the starting point is the recognition of an individual right that it is to be protected (in addition to recognising competing, legitimate social aims) as opposed to the looser concept of harm as a by-product of state agents' action in the context of reasonableness. Second, proportionality involves recognition of an intrinsic hierarchy of rights. Thus depending on the right in question, it requires the importance of the right to be protected to be taken into account – rather than the importance of why interference with it occurred – thus necessitating a harder test for justifying interference with the right to life, namely "strict proportionality" or "absolute necessity". Third and above all in the context of this argument, because positive rights, especially Article 2, are primarily enforced vertically, a test of proportionality or necessity involves ab initio recognition of the different status of actors involved, one of whom (the state) is being judged in the context of a legal regime of rights that exists entirely to protect the other (the citizen). Reasonableness in the citizens in uniform doctrine ignores the status of the actors, in order to apply a universal legal standard.'[1a]

10. Concern over the use of armed police continues.[2] In a recent House of Commons debate, Mr Brian Sedgemore MP spoke of the:

> '22 people shot dead by police officers since 1990, some of them found to be unarmed and some armed with a toy replica gun. Prosecutions have been virtually non-existent. Indeed, in

---

17 On police and firearms generally see P.A.J. Waddington, '"Overkill" or "Minimum force"?' [1990] Crim LR 695 and, generally, *The Strong Arm of the Law* (1991). On the former ACPO guidelines for the use of firearms and plastic bullets, see *Statewatch* (1999) 9(5) 13.
18 [2000] PL 266.
19 p. 278.
20 (1998) 18 LS 486.
1 pp. 491–492.
1a Op. cit., n. 18.
2 HC Debates, 17 April 2000, col. 802.

only two of the cases has anyone been charged. In one case, the jury acquitted; in another, a trial is pending. Although each case must be considered on its merits, when the cases are examined collectively, the signal that goes out to the public is that the police have a licence to kill.'

The Minister of State, Home Office (Mr. Charles Clarke) replied:

'The use of firearms by police has been and remains a rare last resort. Neither in this case nor in any other have the police had a licence to kill; nor has the Home Secretary, any police authority or anyone else given them a licence to kill in any circumstances, general or particular. I feel I must rebut the suggestion that any police have a licence to kill, because it is simply wrong. The policy is that the police should not generally be armed, but that specialist firearms officers should be deployed when an operational need arises. The protection of officers and members of the public is clearly the highest priority whenever there is a firearms risk. It is against that background that chief officers must decide whether, in any given circumstances, the deployment of armed officers is justified. I think there is a consensus that that is far preferable to the routine arming of patrol officers, which happens in some countries.

It may be of interest to the House to know how it is all moving: what the statistics are. Last Wednesday, we released figures to show that the number of firearms operations had fallen from 11,842 in 1997-98 to 10,942 in 1998-99, a decrease of more than 7 per cent. There has been a 4 per cent. decrease in the number of authorised firearms officers in police forces and a 3 per cent. increase in the number of operations involving armed response vehicles. The number of authorised firearms officers continues to fall because of a trend towards concentrating police firearms capability in a smaller number of highly trained officers, and the replacement of many divisional firearms officers with a smaller number of armed response vehicle officers. The small rise in the number of operations involving armed response vehicles may have been due to more of those units being available to police. Many forces are increasing their numbers of armed response vehicles. The number of operations in which firearms are discharged by police remains very low. The number of operations in which firearms are issued has decreased again. Chief officers are continuing to concentrate their firearms capacity in a small number of highly trained officers.'

Note that an officer (or other) who uses excessive force will not be able to rely on a claim of self-defence. If he causes death, there is no special rule that he is to be convicted of manslaughter rather than murder: *R v Clegg*.[3] There have long been calls for a fall-back position where such cases would constitute only manslaughter.[4]

On Art. 2 of the European Convention on Human Rights and the use of force by the state see below, p. 628. The recent decisions of the European Court of Human Rights in *Jordan*, *Shanghan* and *Kelly* on the ineffectiveness of the Northern Ireland procedures for inquiry into deaths caused by the agencies of the state are discussed by P. Ferguson.[4a] The UK government was ordered to pay damages in these cases. In *Kelly v United Kingdom*, K had been shot by soldiers in Northern Ireland who believed he was a terrorist escaping (he was in fact a joyrider). It was claimed that the only way to stop the vehicle was to shoot. Should it be legitimate to shoot in such circumstances on the basis that the officers believed the occupants to be terrorists and thought they might be escaping to continue their illegal activity? Should the shooting be accepted as lawful if it is to kill: (a) to possible prevent future crimes as the officers believed; (b) to protect themselves from imminent danger; (c) to protect against imminent crime or a threat to others? For a critique of the much-publicised decision in the earlier case of *Kelly v United Kingdom*[4b] see Sir John Smith.[4c]

---

3 [1995] 1 All ER 334, HL; see also A. Ashworth, [1995] Crim LR 185.
4 See S. Doran, (1987) 7 LS 291, 302.
4a (2001) NLJ 808.
4b (1993).
4c (1994) NLJ 354.

Police and Criminal Evidence Act 1984

117. Power of constable to use reasonable force

Where any provision of this Act—

(a) confers a power on a constable; and

(b) does not provide that the power may only be exercised with the consent of some person, other than a police officer,

the officer may use reasonable force, if necessary, in the exercise of the power.

NOTE

Some specific police powers expressly authorise the use of force if the need arises.[5] There was probably a power at common law to use force to execute any search or arrest warrant provided that admittance had been demanded and refused: see *Launock v Brown*;[6] *Burdett v Abbot*.[7] In *Swales v Cox*,[8] the court held that the power to enter premises, 'if need be by force', to effect an arrest, conferred by the Criminal Law Act 1967, s. 2(6), was intended to be a 'comprehensive code' on the right to enter for this purpose. The right to use force was qualified only by the requirement that it be necessary. The court defined 'force' as the application of any energy to an obstacle, such as turning a door handle or the opening of a door or a window. There was no longer any *legal* requirement that there be a prior request before force might be used, but any person who sought to enter by force without a prior request would have a 'very severe burden to displace' in establishing 'necessity'.[9] An example of a case where this might be justified would be where it was essential for an officer's protection that he give no warning of his approach to a house where a very dangerous man was to be found.[10] What if the protection is for the occupant? In *Smith v DPP*[11] S was charged with an offence under s. 89 of the Police Act 1996 after police had been called to the house following an abandoned 999 call (i.e. one where the caller hung up). As Brooke LJ explained:

> 'The officers arrive wishing to enter the premises for the purposes of their duty to save life and limb. Secondly, PC Atkins was aware that Mr Smith lived at the premises. Thirdly, Mr Smith was shouting and banging at the door. Fourthly, Mr Smith was not impeding the officers from gaining access to the house, but he refused to move away from it, stating incorrectly that it was nothing to do with them. Fifthly, the stipendiary magistrate made a finding of fact as to PC Atkins state of mind when he found that he took Mr Smith by the arm because he wished to lead him away so that the police officers could deal with the abandoned 999 call without interference. Sixthly, that he was entitled to use reasonable force as a matter of law in the execution of his duty to enter the house and save life and limb. Seventhly, the stipendiary magistrate made a finding of fact that it was perfectly reasonable for the officer to require Mr Smith to move away to allow the police to execute their duty and investigate the call without his interference.'

In *O'Loughlin v Chief Constable of Essex*[12] it was held that 'unless circumstances made it impossible impracticable or undesirable, a police officer exercising powers

---

5 E.g. Public Order Act 1936, s. 2(5), below, p. 414.
6 (1819) 2 B & Ald 592; *Poster's Crown Cases* 136, 320.
7 (1811) 14 East 1.
8 [1981] QB 849, DC.
9 See Donaldson LJ at 1119.
10 See S. H. Bailey and D. J. Birch, [1982] Crim LR 475, 478–480.
11 (2001) 2 February, QBD, Admin Court.
12 [1998] 1 WLR 374.

of entry by force pursuant to section 17 of PACE should first give the occupier the true reason for seeking to enter'. (See below for discussion in context of search.)

There is no power under s. 117 to use force to compel a suspect to take part in an identification parade or other identification procedure: *R v Jones and Nelson*.[13]

'[S]ection 117 is not to be interpreted as giving a right to exercise force whenever the consent of a suspect to a course of action taken under the Act by a constable is not required.'[14]

(D) CODES OF PRACTICE

Police and Criminal Evidence Act 1984

CODES OF PRACTICE – GENERAL
66. Codes of Practice
[This section requires the Secretary of State to issue Codes of Practice in connection with the matters covered by Codes A to D: see n. 1, below.]

67. Codes of practice – supplementary
(1)–(7) [This prescribes the procedure for the issue of codes practice, with the approval of each House of Parliament.]
(9) Persons other than police officers who are charged with the duty of investigation offences or charging offenders shall in the discharge of that duty have regard to any relevant provision of such a code.
(10) A failure on the part
    (*a*) of a police officer to comply with any provision of such a code; or
    (*b*) of any person other than a police officer who is charged with the duty of investigating offences or charging offenders to have regard to any relevant position of such a code in the discharge of that duty.
shall not of itself render him liable to any criminal or civil proceedings.
(11) In all criminal and civil proceedings any such code shall be admissible in evidence; and if any provision of such a code appears to the court or tribunal conducting the proceedings to be relevant to any questions arising in the proceedings it shall be taken into account in determining that question.

NOTES

1. Four Codes of Practice were issued with effect from 1 January 1986; revised versions were issued with effect from 1 April 1991. These were (1) Code A: *Code of Practice for the Exercise by Police Officers of Statutory Powers of Stop and Search*; (2) Code B: *Code of Practice for the Searching of Premises by Police Officers and the Seizure of Property found by Police Officers on Persons or Premises*; (3) Code C: *Code of Practice for the Detention, Treatment and Questioning of Persons by Police Officers*; (4) Code D: *Code of Practice for the Identification of Persons by Police Officers*. Code E, on *Tape Recording*, was issued with effect from 29 July 1988. A further revision of the five Codes was issued with effect from 10 April 1995, further amendments are noted at relevant points in the text. It is vital to rely on the correct Code of Practice (see *R v Miller*[15] in which the trial judge had relied on the out of date version of Code C and failed to recognise breaches of the new Code). Similarly, the court should be sure to use the Queen's Printers copy rather than rely on those

---

reproduced in the textbooks: *R v Keriwala*.[16] A court should refer to a current code when considering events prior to the implementation of that code if it is necessary to do justice: *R v Ward*.[16a]

2. Codes A to D have been issued, with modifications, for Northern Ireland under the Police and Criminal Evidence (Northern Ireland) Order 1989 (S.I. 1989/134).

3. By virtue of the Police and Magistrates' Courts Act 1994, s. 37(a), repealing PACE, s. 67(8), breach of one of the Codes is not automatically a disciplinary office.

4. All Codes of Practice issued under the 1994 Act 'must be readily available at all police stations for consultation by police officers, detained persons and members of the public' (Codes A.1.1., B.1.1., C.1.2., D.1.1., E.1.1.).

5. It is a mixed question of fact and law whether a person is 'charged with the duty of investigation offices for the purpose of s. 67(9). It requires consideration of the statute or instrument under which the person purports to act, and the facts of the case, per Gage J in *DPP v G*.[17] Section 67(9) has been held to apply to Ladbrokes investigators,[18] the Federation against Copyright Theft Ltd,[19] and a store detective,[20] but not a supervising manager of the Bank of England in the course of acting to ensure that minimum criteria for authorisation by the Bank were met and maintained, under Sch. 3 to the Banking Act 1987.[1] An RSPCA inspector may be bound by the Codes in some circumstances: *RSPCA v Eager*.[2] A head teacher is not a person charged with the duty of investigating offences unless his contract expressly provides so: *DPP v G (Duty to Investigate)*.[3] This is true of an investigation into a teacher's alleged assault of a pupil (*DPP v G*) and of an investigation of an alleged theft by a pupil: *R v Headteacher of Dunraven School, ex p M*.[4] A police officer acting on a judge's direction to effect an arrest for contempt is not bound by the Codes as he is acting as a jailer: *R v Jones*.[5] Prison officers are not bound by the Codes of practice: *R v Taylor*.[6]

6. By s. 114, PACE applies to Customs and Excise investigations with appropriate amendments.

7. If a breach of the Codes is admissible as evidence in the proceedings, the judge should leave to the jury the question of the breach and its significance: *R v Kenny*.[7]

8. The Codes of Practice apply even where an investigative search is conducted in the belief that the occupier is a victim of the offence, so that when material is discovered implicating him as an offender, the evidence may be excluded if the Codes are breached: *R v Sanghera*.[8]

9. The Criminal Justice and Police Act 2001 will allow, amendments to the Codes of Practice for trial purposes, by negative resolution procedure.[9]

10. The question whether officers may be liable in negligence for a failure to comply with the Codes remains open: *Ahmed v Chief Constable of West Midlands*.[10]

16 (1991) Times, 4 January, CA.
16a(1994) 98 Cr App R 337, CA.
17 (1997) Times, 24 November.
18 *R v Twaites and Brown* (1990) 92 Cr App Rep 106.
19 *Joy v FACT* [1993] Crim LR 588, DC.
20 *R v Bayliss* (1993) 98 Cr App Rep 235.
1 *R v Smith (Wallace)* [1994] 1 WLR 1396, CA (Cr D).
2 [1995] Crim LR 59.
3 (1997) Times, 24 November.
4 (1999) 24 September, unreported. On PACE in schools, see J. Marston and K. Thompson, (1999) 163 JP 307.
5 [1996] Crim LR 806, CA (Cr D).
6 (2000) 16 March, CA (Cr D), unreported.
7 [1992] Crim LR 800, CA (Cr D).
8 [2001] Crim LR 480.
9 Criminal Justice and Police Act 2001, s. 77.
10 (1998) 28 July, CA (Cr D).

(E) CRIMINAL INVESTIGATIONS

Part II of the Criminal Procedure and Investigation Act 1996 provides statutory definitions of the duties of police investigators in relation to the collection, storage and disclosure of information and other material in an investigation. The statute is supplemented by a Code of Practice issued by the Home Secretary under powers in s. 23. Unlike PACE Codes examined in detail below, the CPIA Codes merely provide sets of examples of the duties and responsibilities of the police. The primary aim is to ensure that the material gathered in the course of the investigation is accurately recorded and stored so that adequate disclosure to the defence will be possible. Many of the miscarriages of justice that prompted the Royal Commission of Criminal Justice (RCCJ) resulted from failure to provide adequate disclosure and the 1996 Act provides a new scheme for disclosure. The scheme has not proved successful, and is currently under review.

An important feature of the 1996 Act is that in the course of defining the duties and responsibilities of the police in respect of disclosure, it provides a definition of criminal investigation, and makes it clear that the police are under a duty to investigate the crime not the individual suspect, so that all lines of inquiry must be pursued. Obligations under the ECHR to carry out effective investigation into crime have been considered in a number of cases see especially: *Osman v UK*;[11] *Labita v Italy*.[12] However, the cases are primarily concerned with the investigations into the wrongdoing of State agencies.

4 Powers to stop and search

Police and Criminal Evidence Act 1984

PART 1

POWERS TO STOP AND SEARCH

1. Power of constable to stop and search persons, vehicles etc
(1) A constable may exercise any power conferred by this section—
> (*a*)   in any place to which at the time when he proposes to exercise the power the public or any section of the public has access, on payment or otherwise, as of right or by virtue of express or implied permission; or
> (*b*)   in any other place to which people have ready access at the time when he proposes to exercise the power but which is not a dwelling.
(2) Subject to subsections (3) to (5) below, a constable—
> (*a*)   may search—
>> (i)   any person or vehicle;
>> (ii)   anything which is in or on a vehicle,
>> for stolen or prohibited articles [or any article to which subsection (8A) below applies]: and
> (*b*)   may detain a person or vehicle for the purpose of such a search.
(3) This section does not give a constable power to search a person or vehicle or anything in or on a vehicle unless he has reasonable grounds for suspecting that he will find stolen or prohibited articles [or any article to which subsection (8A) below applies].[13]
(4) If a person is in a garden or yard occupied with and used for the purposes of a dwelling or on other land so occupied and used, a constable may not search him in the exercise of the power conferred by this section unless the constable has reasonable grounds for believing–
> (*a*)   that he does not reside in the dwelling; and

---

11 (1998) 29 EHRR 245.
12 (2000) 6 April.
13 Inserted by the Criminal Justice Act 1988, s. 140.

(*b*) that he is not in the place in question with the express or implied permission of a person who resides in the dwelling.

(5) If a vehicle is in a garden or yard occupied and used for the purpose of a dwelling or on other land so occupied and used, a constable may not search the vehicle or anything in or on it in the exercise of the power conferred by this section unless he has reasonable grounds for believing–

    (*a*) that the person in charge of the vehicle does not reside in the dwelling; and

    (*b*) that the vehicle is not in the place in question with the express or implied permission of a person who resides in the dwelling.

(6) If in the course of such a search a constable discovers an article which he has reasonable grounds for suspecting to be a stolen or prohibited article [or any article to which subsection 8(A) below applies], he may seize it.

(7) An article is prohibited for the purposes of this Part of this Act if it is—

    (*a*) an offensive weapon; or

    (*b*) an article—

        (i) made or adapted for use in the course of or in connection with an offence to which this sub-paragraph applies; or

        (ii) intended by the person having it with him for such use by him or by some other person.

(8) The offences to which subsection (7)(*b*)(i) above applies are—

    (*a*) burglary;

    (*b*) theft;

    (*c*) offences under section 12 of the Act (taking motor vehicle or other conveyance without authority); and

    (*d*) offences under section 15 of that Act (obtaining property by deception).

[(8A) This subsection applies to any article in relation to which a person has committed, or is committing, or is going to commit an offence under section 139 of the Criminal Justice Act 1988.]

(9) In this Part of this Act 'offensive weapon' means any article—

    (*a*) made or adapted for use for causing injury to persons; or

    (*b*) intended by the person having it with him for such use by him or by some other person.

2. Provisions relating to search under section 1 and other powers

(1) A constable who detains a person or vehicle in the exercise—

    (*a*) of the power conferred by section 1 above; or

    (*b*) of any other power—

        (i) to search a person without first arresting him; or

        (ii) to search a vehicle without making an arrest,

need not conduct a search if it appears to him subsequently—

    (i) that no search is required; or

    (ii) that a search is impracticable

(2) If a constable contemplates a search, other than a search of an unattended vehicle, in the exercise–

    (*a*) of the power conferred by section 1 above; or

    (*b*) of any other power, except the power conferred by section 6 below and the power conferred by section 27(2) of the Aviation Security Act 1982—

        (i) to search a person without first arresting him; or

        (ii) to search a vehicle without making an arrest,

it shall be his duty, subject to subsection (4) below, to take reasonable steps before he commences the search to bring to the attention of the appropriate person—

    (i) if the constable is not in uniform, documentary evidence that he is a constable; and

    (ii) whether he is in uniform or not, the matters specified in subsection (3) below;

and the constable shall not commence the search until he has performed that duty.

(3) The matters referred to in subsection (2)(ii) above are—

    (*a*) the constable's name and the name of the police station to which he is attached;

    (*b*) the object of the proposed search;

    (*c*) the constable's grounds for proposing to make it; and

    (*d*) the effect of section 3(7) or (8) below, as may be appropriate.

(4) A constable need not bring the effect of section 3(7) or (8) below to the attention of the appropriate person if it appears to the constable that it will not be practicable to make the record in section 3(1) below.

(5) In this section 'the appropriate person' means—

    (a) if the constable proposes to search a person, that person; and

    (b) giving the name of the police station to which he is attached;

    (c) stating that an application for compensation for any damage caused by the search may be made to that police station; and

    (d) stating the effect of section 3(8) below.

(7) The constable shall leave the notice inside the vehicle unless it is not reasonably practicable to do so without damaging the vehicle.

(8) The time for which a person or vehicle may be detained for the purposes of such a search ins such time at is reasonably required to permit a search to be carried out either at the place where the person or vehicle was first detained or nearby.

(9) Neither the power conferred by section 1 above nor any other power to detain and search a person without first arresting him or to detain and search a vehicle without making an arrest is to be construed–

    (a) as authorising a constable to require a person to remove any of his clothing in public other than an outer coat, jacket or gloves; or

    (b) as authorising a constable not in uniform to stop a vehicle.

(10) This section and section 1 above apply to vessels, aircraft and hovercraft as they apply to vehicles.

3. Duty to make records concerning searches

(1) Where a constable has carried out a search in the exercise of any such power as is mentioned is section 2(1) above, other than a search—

    (a) under section 6 below; or

    (b) under section 27(2) of the Aviation Security Act 1982,

he shall make a record of it in writing unless it is not practicable to do so.

(2) If—

    (a) a constable is required by subsection (1) above to make a record of a search; but

    (b) it is not practicable to make the record on the spot,

he shall make it as soon as practicable after the completion of the search.

(3) the record of a search of a person shall include a note of his name, if the constable knows it, but a constable may not detain a person to find out his name.

(4) If a constable does not know the name of a person whom he has searched, the record of the search shall include a note otherwise describing that person.

(5) The record of a search of a vehicle shall include a note describing the vehicle.

(6) The record of a search of a person or a vehicle—

    (a) shall state—

        (i) the object of the search;

        (ii) the grounds for making it;

        (iii) the date and time when it was made;

        (iv) the place where it was made;

        (v) whether anything, and if so what, was found;

        (vi) whether any, and if so what, injury to a person or damage to property appears to the constable to have resulted from the search; and

    (b) shall identify the constable making it

(7) If a constable who conducted a search of a person made a record of it, the person who was searched shall be entitled to a copy of the record if he asks for one before the end of the period specified in subsection (9) below.

(8) If—

    (a) the owner of a vehicle which has been searched or the person who was in charge of the vehicle at the time when it was searched asks for a copy of the record of the search before the end of the period specified in subsection (9) below; and

    (b) that constable who conducted the search made a record of it,

the person who made the request shall be entitled to a copy.

(9) The period mentioned in subsections (7) and (8) above is the period of 12 months beginning with the date on which the search was made.

(10) The requirements imposed by this section with regard to records of searches of vehicles shall apply also to records of searches of vessels, aircraft and hovercraft.

4. Road checks[14]

(1) This section shall have effect in relation to the conduct of road checks by police officers for the purpose of ascertaining whether a vehicle is carrying–

    (*a*) a person who has committed an offence other than a road traffic offence or a vehicle excise offence;

    (*b*) a person who is a witness to such an offence;

    (*c*) a person intending to commit such an offence; or

    (*d*) a person who is unlawfully at large.

(2) For the purposes of this section a road check consists of the exercise in a locality of the power conferred by section [163] of the Road Traffic Act [1998] in such a way as to stop during the period for which its exercise in that way in that locality continues all vehicles selected by any criterion.

(3) Subject to subsection (5) below, there may only be such a road check if a police officer of the rank of superintendent or above authorises it in writing.

(4) An officer may only authorise a road check under subsection (3) above—

    (*a*) for the purpose specified in subsection (1)(*a*) above if he has reasonable grounds—

        (i) for believing that the offence is a serious arrestable offence; and

        (ii) for suspecting that the person is, or is about to be, in the locality in which vehicles would be stopped if the road check were authorised;

    (*b*) for the purpose specified in subsection (1)(*b*) above, if he has reasonable grounds for believing that the offence is a serious arrestable offence;

    (*c*) for the purpose specified in subsection (1)(*c*) above, if he has reasonable grounds—

        (i)   for believing that the offence would be a serious arrestable offence; and

        (ii) for suspecting that the person is, or is about to be in the locality in which vehicles would be stopped if the road check were authorised;

    (*d*) for the purpose specified in subsection (1)(*d*) above, if he has reasonable grounds for suspicion that the person is, or is about to be, in that locality.

(5) An officer below the rank of superintendent may authorise such a road check if it appears to him that it is required as a matter of urgency for one of the purposes specified in subsection (1) above.

(6) If an authorisation is given under subsection (5) above, it shall be the duty of the officer who gives it—

    (*a*) to make a written record of the time at which he gives it; and

    (*b*) to cause an officer of the rank of superintendent or above to be informed that it has been given.

(7) The duties imposed by subsection (6) above shall be performed as soon as it is practicable to do so.

(8) An officer to whom a report is made under subsection (6) above may, in writing, authorise the road to check to continue.

(9) If such an officer considers that the road check should not continue, he shall record in writing—

    (*a*) the fact it took place; and

    (*b*) the purpose for which it took place.

(10) An officer giving an authorisation under this section shall specify the locality in which vehicles are to be stopped.

(11) An officer giving an authorisation under this section, other than an authorisation under subsection (5) above–

    (*a*) shall specify a period, not exceeding seven days, during which the road check may continue; and

---

14 As amended by the Road Traffic (Consequential Provisions) Act 1998, Sch. 3, para. 27(1) and the Vehicle Excise and Registration Act 1994, s. 63, Sch. 3, para. 9.

    (*b*) may direct that the road check—
        (i) shall be continuous; or
        (ii) shall be conducted at specified times, during that period.

(12) If it appears to an officer of the rank of superintendent or above that a road check ought to continue beyond the period for which it has been authorised he may, from time to time, in writing specify a further period, not exceeding seven days, during which it may continue.

(13) Every written authorisation shall specify—
    (*a*) the name of the officer giving it;
    (*b*) the purpose of the road check; and
    (*c*) the locality in which vehicles are to be stopped.

(14) The duties to specify the purposes of a road check imposed by subsections (9) and (13) above include duties to specify any relevant serious arrestable offence.

(15) Where a vehicle is stopped in a road check, the person in charge of the vehicle at the time when it is stopped shall be entitled to obtain a written statement of the purpose of the road check if he applies for such a statement not later than the end of the period of twelve months from the day on which the vehicle was stopped.

(16) Nothing in this sections affects the exercise by police officers of any power to stop vehicles for purposes other than those specified in subsection (1) above.

Criminal Justice and Public Order Act 1994

Powers of police to stop and search

60. Powers to stop and search in anticipation of violence

[(1) If a police officer of or above the rank of inspector reasonably believes—
    (*a*) that incidents including serious violence may take place in any locality in his police area, and that it is expedient to give an authorisation under this section to prevent their occurrence or,
    (*b*) that persons are carrying dangerous instruments or offensive weapons in any locality in his police area without good reason

he may give an authorisation that the powers conferred by this section are to be exercisable at any place within that locality for a specified period not exceeding 24 hours.][15]

(3) If it appears to [an officer of or above the rank of] superintendent that it is expedient to do so, having regard to offences which have, or are reasonably suspected to have, been committed in connection with any activity falling within the authorisation, he may direct that the authorisation shall continue in being for a further 24 hours.[16]

(3A) If an inspector gives an authorisation under subsection (1) he must, as soon as practicable to do so, cause an officer of or above the rank of superintendent to be informed.[17]

(4) This section confers on any constable in uniform power—
    (*a*) to stop any pedestrian and search him or anything carried by him for offensive weapons or dangerous instruments;
    (*b*) to stop any vehicle and search the vehicle, its driver and any passenger for offensive weapons or dangerous instruments.

[(4A) This section also confers on any constable in uniform power—
    (*a*) to require any person to remove any items which the constable reasonably believes that person is wearing wholly or mainly for the purpose of concealing his identity;
    (*b*) to seize any items which the constable reasonably believes any person intends to wear wholly or mainly of that purpose.[18]]

(5) A constable may, in the excise of the powers conferred by subsection above,[19] stop any person or vehicle and make any search he thinks fit whether or not he has any grounds for suspecting that the person or vehicle is carrying weapons or articles of that kind.

15 As substituted by Knives Act 1997, s. 8(2).
16 As amended by Knives Act 1997, s. 8(4).
17 As inserted by Knives Act 1997, s. 8(5).
18 As inserted by Crime and Disorder Act 1998, s. 25(1).
19 As amended by the Crime and Disorder Act 1998, s. 25(2).

(6) If in the course of a search under this section a constable discovers a dangerous instrument or an article which he has reasonable grounds for suspecting to be an offensive weapon, he may seize it.

(7) This section applies (with the necessary modifications) to ships, aircraft and hovercraft as it applies to vehicles.

(8) A person who fails

    [(*a*) to stop, or to stop a vehicle; or

    (*b*) to remove any item worn by him[20]]

when required to do so by a constable in the exercise of his powers under this section shall be liable on summary conviction to imprisonment for a term not exceeding one month or to a fine not exceeding level 3 on the standard scale or both.

(9) Any authorisation under this section shall be in writing signed by the officer giving it and shall specify [the grounds on which it is given and][21] the locality in which and the period during which the powers conferred by this section are exercisable and a direction under subsection (3) above shall also be given in writing or, whether that is not practicable, recorded in writing as soon as it is practicable to do so.

(10) Where a vehicle is stopped by a constable under this section, the driver shall be entitled to obtain a written statement that the vehicle was stopped under the powers conferred by this section if he applies for such a statement not later than the end of the period of twelve months from the day on which the vehicle was stopped.[22]

[(10A) A person who is searched by a constable under this section shall be entitled to obtain a written statement that he was searched under the powers conferred by this section if he applies for such a statement not later than the end of the period of 12 months from the day on which he was searched.[23]]

(11) In this section—

    "dangerous instruments" means instruments which have a blade or are sharply pointed;

    "offensive weapon" has the meaning given by section 1 (9) of the Police and Criminal Evidence Act 1984;…and

    "vehicle" includes a caravan as defined I section 29 (1) of the Caravan Sites and Control of Development Act 1960.

[(11A) for the purpose of this section, a person carries a dangerous instrument or an offensive weapon if he has it in his possession.[1]]

(12)The powers conferred by this section are in addition to and not in derogation of, any power otherwise conferred.

[60(B) provides or power of arrest for failure to comply with s. 60(8)(*b*) ie. failing to remove a mask etc.[2]]

NOTES

1. Section 1(8A) of PACE, and the references to it, were added by the Criminal Justice Act 1988, s. 140. Section 139 of the 1988 Act makes it an offence for any person to have with him in a public place any article which has a blade or is sharply pointed (except a folding pocket knife whose blade does not exceed three inches). It is a defence for D to show that he had a good reason or lawful authority, or that he had the article with him for use at work, for religious reason, or as part of a national costume.

2. Section 5 requires the annual reports of chief officers of police to include information about the number of searches and road checks carried out under ss. 3 and 4. This should facilitate independent scrutiny by police authorities and Inspectors

---

20 As amended by the Crime and Disorder Act 1998, s. 25 (3).
21 As inserted by Knives Act 1997, s. 8 (6).
22 As amended by the Knives Act 1997, s. 8 (7).
23 As inserted by the Knives Act 1997, s. 8 (8).
 1 As inserted by the Knives Act 1997, s. 8 (10).
 2 Inserted by Crime and Disorder Act 1998, s. 27.

of Constabulary to ensure that the powers are not used randomly. Section 6 enables a 'constable employed by statutory undertakers' (such as railway police) to 'stop, detain and search any vehicle before it leaves a goods area included in the premises of the statutory undertaker'.

For the definitions of 'arrestable offence' and 'serious arrestable offence' see below.[3] At the last minute the House of Commons deleted a House of Lords amendment to the effect that the s. 1 powers could only be exercised by a constable *in uniform*. This issue remains relevant to s. 2(2) and 2(9)(*b*). Under the Road Traffic Act 1988 s. 6, only a constable 'in uniform' may require a person to provide a specimen of breath for a breath test. Whether a constable is in uniform is a question of fact. In *Wallwork v Giles*[4] it was held that a constable wearing his uniform except for his helmet was 'in uniform' as he was easily identifiable as a constable.[5] A court is entitled to assume that a constable is in uniform unless the point is challenged: *Cooper v Rowlands*;[6] *Richards v West*.[7] This limitation also applies to powers under the Criminal Justice and Public Order Act 1994, s. 60.

3. *Stop and search.* Section 1 of PACE extended the powers of the police to stop and search without warrant in a number of important respects. First, it gave power to search for any offensive weapon: previously, there was only a power to search for firearms.[8] Secondly, the power to search for stolen goods, previously available in the metropolitan area,[9] and in a number of other locations in the country (enshrined in local legislation) was extended throughout England and Wales, the earlier legislation being repealed.[10] Thirdly, there was a new power to stop and search for equipment used in offences such as burglary (e.g. jemmies or picklocks).

4. The new power conferred by s. 60 of the Criminal Justice and Public Order Act 1994 does not depend on any 'reasonable suspicion' held by the officer conducting the stop-search. The Minister of State at the Home Office, David Maclean MP, stated[11] that the government was:

'persuaded that the need to meet the tests of reasonable suspicion seriously inhibits effective preventive action by the police when they believe that violence is likely to break out.'

The power would, for example, enable the police to search a group of people where there are grounds to believe that some although not all are carrying a weapon. Given that the exercise of such a power involves detention while a search is conducted, does this comply with Art. 5 of the ECHR and Art. 9 of the ICCPR?

5. See also the new power to stop and search to prevent acts of terrorism: below, p. 583. Article 5 of the ECHR does not expressly authorise stops and searches. The ECHR powers are drafted in terms of 'deprivation of liberty' and 'detention'. Although most of the powers in England and Wales are exercisable only on proof of an officer's reasonable suspicion, some do not contain this requirement.[12] The Convention provides that a deprivation of liberty on reasonable suspicion is legitimate provided, under Art. 5(1)(c), that the detention relates to the commission of an offence *and* is

---

3   s. 4(4) see respectively below, p. 289 and above, pp. 195–196.
4   [1970] RTR 117, DC.
5   Cf *Taylor v Baldwin* [1976] RTR 265, DC.
6   [1971] RTR 291, DC.
7   [1980] RTR 215, DC.
8   Firearms Act 1968, ss. 47(3), 49(1) and (2): these powers continued to be available after the 1984 Act.
9   Metropolitan Police Act 1839, s. 66.
10 PACE, s. 7.
11 241 HC Deb, 12 April 1994, col. 69.
12 See Criminal Justice and Public Order Act 1994, s. 60.

with the purpose of bringing the suspect to court. Are stop and search powers usually exercised with a view to detaining a suspect with that purpose?

Does the stop and search amount to a sufficient deprivation of liberty as to fall within Art. 5? D. J. Harris, M. O'Boyle and C. Warbrick[13] stated that:

'a person who is made to believe that he is obliged to remain when stopped on the street . . . by the police for the purpose of being questioned, searched, or subjected to a test in the administration of the criminal law should be protected by Article 5.'[14]

In a recent Written Answer provided in the House of Commons, a Home Office Minister, Mr Charles Clarke, confirmed that the government believes that 'the police power of stop and search is compatible with the Convention, provided of course that it is exercised lawfully'.[15]

The purpose of an arrest is to bring the suspect before a competent judicial authority: *Lawless v Ireland.*[16] In *Brogan v United Kingdom*[17] it was recognised that the fact that arrest did not lead to a charge did not render it contrary to Art. 5 – by analogy stop and search would seem to be acceptable.

'there is no reason to believe that the police investigation in this case was not in good faith or that the detention of the applicants was not entitled to further that investigation by way of confirming, or dispelling, the concrete suspicions which, as the court has found, grounded the arrest.'[18]

Limited powers of pursuit and stop are contained in the EU Schengen Agreement.[19] It is unlikely that there will be many hot pursuits across the channel or indeed through the channel tunnel,[20] except perhaps of asylum seekers pursued by the French?

6. *Pre-emptive stops and searches.* The Knives Act 1997 and Crime and Disorder Act 1998 have extended stop and search powers quite significantly.

Authorisation now depends on a reasonable belief by an inspector. The authorisation had previously to come from a superintendent, and was limited to a six-hour period. The power is triggered by a belief that people are carrying offensive weapons, but there is no need to believe serious violence has occurred or will/might occur. The only safeguards with this new power are for the inspector to inform a senior officer and for a statement of having been searched to be provided.

The further extension made by the Crime and Disorder Act 1998 take the power to stop and search to a new level. The power is intended to allow the police to stop and search '*before* they have a reasonable suspicion against a person'.[1]

Whereas the Knives Act extended the situations in which authorisation could be given and by whom it can be given, the Crime and Disorder Act extends the powers of the officer conducting the stop and search. The new s. 60(4A) relating to the removal of face masks gives two powers – one to remove and one to seize items. These were

13 *Law of the European Convention on Human Rights* (1995).
14 p. 100. See further on stop and search and the European Court of Human Rights, D. Mead, [2000] 5 (1) J Civ Lib 5.
15 HC Written Answer, 13 March 2000, col. 76W.
16 (1961) 1 EHRR 1.
17 (1989) 11 EHRR 117.
18 (1989) 11 EHRR 117. Para. 53. See the discussion by B. Emmerson and A. Ashworth, *Human Rights and Criminal Justice* (2001), Chap. 5.
19 S. Peers, *European Union, Justice and Home Affairs Law* (2000), pp. 194–196.
20 The difficulties encountered by officers pursuing suspects across UK jurisdiction are considered by C. Walker, [1997] CLJ 114.
 1 M. O'Brien, Under Secretary of State for the Home Office, Commons Standing Committee B, 9 June 1998, col. 788.

explained as being targeted at 'youths with balaclavas covering their faces who hijack cars and drive them at high speed around housing estates.'[2] Could such people not have been arrested and searched under the general PACE powers or those in the Road Traffic Acts? Note the use of this power to arrest an individual who refused to remove his General Custer mask when on his way to a fancy dress party. He had been stopped by police on suspicion of being involved in the May Day protests.[3]

In *DPP v Avery*,[3a] the Court held that the officer exercising these powers was not required to give his name, station or reasons for his action.

Because of fears of insensitivity in relation to religious dress, a new Note for Guidance was included in the revised and latest version of Code A:

'Note 1AA: where there may be religious sensitivities about asking someone to remove a face covering using the power in section 25 of the Crime and Disorder Act 1998, for example in the case of a Muslim woman wearing a face covering for religious purposes, the officer should permit the item to be removed out of public view. Where practicable, the item should be removed in the presence of an officer of the same sex as the person and out of the sight of anyone of the opposite sex. In all cases the officer must reasonably believe that the person is wearing the item in question *wholly* or *mainly* to conceal his or her identity.'[4]

See also the Code, para. A1.8 on the authorisation to exercise these powers.

7. Recent Home Office research into the stop and search powers found that the power in s. 60 (and others that were not triggered by specific need for reasonable suspicion) was much less effective, and it was recommended that they be reviewed in light of their inefficiency and the negative impact they have on public confidence.[5]

8. PACE empowers officers to stop to search, rather than to stop per se. In the Police Research Group study into stop and search following the Macpherson Report, the pilot study recording monitoring adopted a working definition of a stop:

'when a police officer requests a person to account for their actions, behaviour, or possession of anything the encounter will be regarded as a stop. For the purposes of this pilot study this applies if the person is on foot, driving or riding any vehicle, or is a passenger in or on such a vehicle.'[6]

Should such a definition be contained in PACE? Should an officer only ever be entitled to stop on the basis of a reasonable suspicion? Should all stops be subject to the same recording and monitoring safeguards as searches? Note the generally acknowledged attitude of the public that searches were more intrusive than mere stops.[7]

9. Another important general stop and search power is contained in the Misuse of Drugs Act 1971:

'23(2). – If a constable has reasonable grounds to suspect that any person is in possession of a controlled drug in contravention of this Act of any regulations made there under, the constable may—
(a) search that person, and detain him for the purpose of searching him;
(b) search any vehicle or vessel in which the constable suspects that the drug may be found, and for that purpose require the person in control of the vehicle or vessel to stop it;

2   Ibid., col. 804.
3   See *The Times*, 2 May 2001.
3a [2001] EWCA Admin 748.
4   Emphasis in original.
5   J. Miller, N. Bland and P. Quinton, *The Impact of Stops And Searches on Crime and the Community* (2000), p. 59.
6   N. Bland, J. Miller and P. Quinton, *Upping the PACE? An Evaluation of the Recommendations of the Stephen Lawrence Inquiry on Stops and Searches* (2000) PRS No 128, p. 14.
7   See below.

(c) seize and detain, for the purposes of proceedings under this Act, anything found in the course of the search which appears to the constable to be evidence of an offence under this Act.

In this subsection 'vessel' includes a hovercraft within the meaning of the Hovercraft Act 1968; and nothing in this subsection shall prejudice any power of search or any power to seize or detain property which is exercisable by a constable apart from this subsection.'

This power, and certain other stop and search powers[8] survived the 1984 Act, but are subject to the safeguards set out in s. 2. Note that the requirements of s. 2 operate in respect of *searches* and therefore not where a *stop* does not lead to a search. In *French v DPP*[9] F successfully appealed against his conviction for obstructing an officer in the execution of his duty the officer had strip searched F at the police station after a different officer had detained F following his being stopped and searched under s. 23 by two further officers. Since the officer exercising the stop and search under s. 23 had not given evidence, it was not possible to conclude that the strip search was lawful.

10. Section 66 of the Metropolitan Police Act 1839 gave power to 'stop, search and detain' any person or vehicle on which there was a reason to suspect that there was stolen property: this was held to include impliedly a power to detain for questioning.[10] Section 1, by contrast, gives a power to detain for the express purpose of searching: is there room for an implied power to detain for questioning?

11. Compare ss. 44–47 of the Terrorism Act 2000, below, pp. 583–588 (replacing s. 13B of the Prevention of Terrorism (Temporary Provisions) Act 1989).

12. The *Code of Practice for Exercise by Police Officers of Statutory Powers of Stop and Search* (Code A) applies to all stop and search powers except the Aviation Security Act 1982, s. 27(2) and the Police and Criminal Evidence Act 1984, s. 6(1).[12]

The Code emphasises that there is no power to stop or detain a person against his will in order to find grounds for a search (Code A.2.1); in some circumstances preparatory questioning may be unnecessary, but in general a brief conversation or exchange will be desirable, not only as a means of avoiding unsuccessful searches, but to explain the grounds for stop and search, to gain co-operation and reduce any tension there might be surrounding the stop and search (Code A.2.A); reasonable grounds cannot be retrospectively provided by questioning during detention (Code A.2.3); every reasonable effort must be made to reduce to the minimum the embarrassment that a person being searched may experience (Code A.3.1); the co-operation of the person to be searched should be sought in every case, even if he initially objects; reasonable force may be used if necessary and only in the last resort (Code A.3.2); the person or vehicle may be detained for a time that is reasonable in all the circumstances, and not beyond the time taken for the search (Code A.3.3); in the case of stop-searches based on reasonable suspicion, the thoroughness and extent of a search must depend on what is suspected of being carried and by whom; where on reasonable grounds it is considered necessary to conduct a search more thorough than removal of an outer coat, jacket or gloves, such as removal of a T-shirt or headgear,[13] this should be done out of public view (e.g. in a police van or a nearby police station); searches in the street are in public even if the street is empty when the search begins (Code A.3AA); any search involving the removal of more than the items specified in s. 2(9)(a) or headgear or footwear may only be made by an officer

8 E.g. the Wildlife and Countryside Act 1981, s. 19; the Firearms Act 1968, ss. 47(3), 49(1), (2).
9 [1997] COD 174, DC.
10 *Daniel v Morrison* (1979) 70 Cr App Rep 142, DC.
11 Power to search airport employees etc. for stolen goods.
12 Powers of constables employed by statutory undertakers.
13 See s. 2(9)(a); Code A. 3.5.

of the same sex, and may not be made in the presence of anyone of the opposite sex unless requested by the person searched; the record should include, in addition to the matters in s. 3(3)–(6), a note of the person's ethnic origin (Code A.4.5); the record of grounds must 'briefly but informatively' explain the reason for suspecting the person concerned, whether by reference to his behaviour or other circumstances or, in the case of searches under the Criminal Justice and Public Order Act 1994, s. 60 state the authority provided to carry out such a search (Code A.4.7). In the case of enquiries linked to the investigation of terrorism, the officer is to give his warrant number and police station rather than his name (Code A.2.4 (i), 4(5)(x). Supervising officers monitoring stop and search powers should consider 'whether there is any evidence that officers are exercising their discretion on the basis of stereotyped images of certain persons or groups' contrary to the Code.[14]

(A) REASONABLE SUSPICION AND DISCRETION IN STOP AND SEARCH

'Stop and search epitomises the exercise of police discretion and the issues associated with it.'[15] It is important to consider to what extent the discretion is necessary for the power to be workable. With the maximum discretion given to the officer on the beat (at the lowest point in the organisational structure) is he or she capable of being monitored and supervised effectively?

P. Quinton, N. Bland, and J. Miller[16] concluded that their research demonstrated that:

'in practice, generalisations of various kinds play an important role in how officers form suspicion and decide to carry out stops and searches. However, we have observed that this involves a clear tension between:
-   the need to draw on generalisations for effective targeting of police activity; and
-   the alienation that generalisations, potentially, and negative stereotypes, in particular, cause.

For example, generalisations which link crime with age, appearance, time and place, and behaviour can sometimes provide a useful basis for the effective targeting of stops and searches. However, these generalisations (which in some sense might seem reasonable) will mean that people will be identified by the police as suspicious when they do not warrant police attention. This can be a cause of public resentment.

Secondly, we noted how the poor handling of stop or search encounters can impact negatively on public confidence. Research has shown that public satisfaction with encounters is dependent on the politeness of the officer, whether the person was given an acceptable reason for the stop and whether they were searched. As such, improving public confidence can be achieved in part by better handling of stops and searches. Some officers themselves provide a good indication of how public confidence and satisfaction can be strengthened based on their understanding on how a good search should be handled (e.g. building a good rapport and using appropriate language). . . .

Legality. We have seen that the notion of PACE reasonable suspicion in relation to searches, in practice, operates more along a continuum than as a simple dichotomy. The working practices of officers reveal that suspicion is based on a range of different factors in which a person might appear more or less suspicious to police officers. Furthermore, the research clearly showed differences in the level of suspicion required by different officers to do stops and searches. This is likely to be reflected across the police service. As such, the discretion that officers exercise in this respect can potentially be a risk to legality. Specifically, the report points out the following concerns.

First, the variation between officers in their decisions to carry out stops and searches raises questions about the rule of law and the extent to which police interventions are evenly

---

14 For the Code's provisions as to reasonable grounds, see above, p. 193.
15 P. A. J. Waddington, *Policing Citizens* (1999), p. 50.
16 *Police Stops, Decision-making and Practice* (2000) Police Research Series Paper No. 130.

applied. Secondly, it is clear that reasonable suspicion for searches is not, in some cases, being achieved. The levels of evidence recorded in grounds are also low: in both the lack of specific detail and a failure to refer to all the available direct and indirect evidence. This points to guidance both in the operational use of reasonable suspicion and in its written articulation for search records.

Effectiveness. Effectiveness is likely to be strongest when suspicion is well-informed, and decisions are based on direct and accurate information – maximising encounters with active offenders and minimising them with the general public.

Direct evidence, that is evidence pointing to specific individuals, is less ambiguous – there is a greater certainty about the person the police intend to stop. As such, the risks to effectiveness are lower when suspicion relies on direct evidence. Regardless of whether evidence is direct or indirect, the reliability of suspicion will be affected by the accuracy of the information and intelligence available to officers. The generalisations about current high-crime areas, for example, will be more reliable when based on up-to-date intelligence.

To reduce the risks to effectiveness and, in turn, public confidence, it is important that suspicions are, as far as possible, well-informed, reliable and based good quality information.

[The authors provided a series of Recommendations for the Home Office, National Police Training (NPT) and the Association of Chief Police Officers (ACPO):]

The legal concept of reasonable suspicion and its application needs to be further clarified to specify whether current officer practices are acceptable. Although the PACE Code clearly states that stereotyped images should not be used as a basis for suspicion, we have shown that generalisations are used by officers, in practice, as a basis for suspicions. As a result, the PACE Code needs to spell out whether, and to what extent, generalisations can be used to inform decisions to stop or search. This is not to say that the law should be relaxed, but that further clarification is required. If, however, generalisations are recognised as an acceptable practice, adequate safeguards need to be in place to ensure that they are reliable and not used unfairly.

The differences in the way reasonable suspicion is understood and applied by officers highlights the need for clearer guidance, training and supervision on what reasonable suspicion means in operational terms. Whilst the current PACE Code attempts to describe reasonable suspicion from a practical perspective, it might be useful to define the level of evidence required for a search (perhaps in terms of direct and indirect factors) and to mark out the differences in the level of suspicion needed for a stop and for a search.'[17]

The Notes for Guidance in Code A state that nothing in the Code affects the routine searching of persons entering sports grounds or other premises with their consent, or as a condition of entry, or the search of a person in the street on a voluntary basis (the officer should always make it clear that he is seeking the co-operation of the person concerned) (Code A.1D). If an officer acts in an improper manner this will invalidate a voluntary search (Code, Note 1E).

A failure to give grounds as required by s. 2(3)(c) will render the search unlawful: *R v Fennelley*.[18] However, a failure to make a written record does not: *Basher v DPP*,[19] where Waller J also indicated, without deciding the point, that he doubted whether a failure to give the grounds would render the search illegal.

(B) ADEQUATE RECORDING AND MONITORING?

In *Osman v DPP*[20] it was held that a stop and search was rendered unlawful where the officers had failed to identify themselves in accordance with s. 2(3)(a). The search was conducted under s. 60 of the 1994 Act.

17 pp. 64–67.
18 [1989] Crim LR 142 (Crown Ct). But note *DPP v Avery* [2001] EWCA Admin 748.
19 [1993] COD 372, DC.
20 (1999) 163 JP 725, DC.

Osman v DPP (1999) 163 JP 725, Divisional Court

Sedley LJ: [W]hat the officers are required by law to do is to take 'reasonable steps' before beginning the search to bring the prescribed data to the attention of the members of the public whom they are proposing to search. On the evidence set out in the Crown Court's findings, no step whatever was taken in this direction. It is impossible, therefore, to begin to attach the epithet 'reasonable' to what was done.

It seems to me, having heard Mr Boothby's submission, that while there is an element of formality and, perhaps, of excessive use of time in having to recite the constable's name and station to every person searched, it is nevertheless Parliament's view that such formality is of great importance in relation to civil liberties. There would be nothing, I would have thought, to prevent uniformed officers, who are sent out to make searches of this kind from carrying in their pocket slips of paper giving their name and station, so that the person searched not only is told what these are but can carry the information away with him or her, and the officer is saved the trouble of going through an oral rigmarole. That, however, is beside the present point. This search was unlawful for the reasons given.

This being so, the appellant's conduct in presenting himself as if he were consenting to the search – assuming that that was a legitimate finding – was nothing to the point. That he may have consented to being searched would not make the search that was being inaugurated and attempted by the officers a lawful one. What is more, I have the gravest doubts about whether the officers were entitled to infer from the conduct described that there was consent to the search, much less to infer from the appellant's resistance to being searched anywhere but at a police station that he might well be carrying a weapon. Nothing in the Crown Court's conclusions or in Mr Boothby's submissions is predicated upon any suggestion that some independent ground for search, based on reasonable suspicion, had arisen in the course of the confrontation – rightly so, in my judgment, because the questions posed to do not touch on the point.

It follows that I would answer the second question in the affirmative; that is to say, I would hold that the failure of the officers to supply details of their names and station rendered the search unlawful. The availability of information on the officer's lapels is in law neither here nor there; and in any case nothing that we know of suggests that these officers, uniquely, were carrying details of their names and station on their lapels. In the ordinary way, one would expect their numbers but no more to be visible there, and there is no different finding in this case.

This being so, I would, if necessary, answer the first pair of questions in the negative. I do not think that the appellant's conduct amounted to consent; nor, if it did amount to consent, would it have entitled the officers, without more, to commit what technically, on any view, would have been an assault on the appellant. The question, however, for the reasons I have given, is not a necessary question. The case is concluded in the appellant's favour by the answer to the second of the questions posed.

Accordingly, I would allow this appeal and quash both convictions.

Collins J: This is, no doubt, because Parliament has recognised that a search of a person is a serious interference with his liberty, and all proper safeguards must be followed. The facts found show that there was no reason why the officers could not have given the necessary information. It is not for the court to disapply the duties set out in the Act, but only to decide whether, in a given set of circumstances, the officers have taken all reasonable steps to do what Parliament has required them to do. I emphasise that we are not concerned with the admissibility of evidence found as a result of a search, but whether the search itself was lawful, so that the officers were acting in the execution of their duty when carrying it out.

The first question asked by the Crown Court concerns consent. Consent is not relevant. If the officer fails to comply with section 2, there can be no proper consent. The ordinary law-abiding citizen no doubt usually accepts the constable's word that he has the powers he asserts and, if he has nothing to hide, will accept that he can be searched. But that apparent consent cannot mean that the officer is acting in the execution of his duty in carrying out the search. In any event, I cannot see how the Crown Court could reasonably have found that the officers could have assumed consent. The respondent's reaction, when the officer took hold of him in order to search him, made it as clear as it could be that he was not consenting. He said, 'You cannot fucking search me here, take me to a fucking police station.'

NOTES

1. Is there a realistic likelihood that officers will comply with this approach? Will there be more 'consensual searches' as a result?

2. To what extent have the rights to be free from police interference in everyday life been substituted for a right to have a written record of its occurrence? Following the Macpherson Report recommendation, all stops and searches were recorded by some forces in a pilot scheme.[1] (See below p. 218).

3. In *R v McCarthy*,[2] the Court of Appeal refused to quash a conviction when evidence obtained during a search was admitted at trial. The search had been conducted by officers who were in fact conducting surveillance of the suspects regarding their drug dealing. The fact that the officers did not disclose their involvement and told the suspects that it was 'routine' did not affect the admissibility of the evidence discovered. Does the reason given by an officer affect the type of responses given by the suspect and affect his behaviour? Can the reason given affect the reliability of the evidence discovered?

4. From the outset, stop and search powers have been particularly controversial. A study of stops carried out over a few months in 1983 in four police stations, two in the provinces and two in the Metropolitan Police District[3] found that blacks, and particularly young black males, were much more likely to be stopped and searched by the police than whites. The notes for Guidance in Code A remind officers that:

'It is important to ensure that powers of stop and search are used responsibly by those who exercise them and those who authorise their use...Misuse of the powers is likely to be harmful to the police effort in the long term and can lead to mistrust of the police by the community.'[4]

(C) PUBLIC PERCEPTIONS OF STOP AND SEARCH

Although complaints about stop and search have declined over the years,[5] this may be a reflection of the 'acceptance among young people that being stopped is a fact of life'.[6] Is being stopped and searched in the street a fact of life? Should it be?

V. Stone and N. Pettigrew[7] explored public experiences of stop and search, particularly in light of the Stephen Lawrence Inquiry and perceptions of discrimination in police practice. The three main conclusions were:

'There is general support for stops and searches amongst all ethnic groups but only if there are fundamental changes in the way they are used by the police. Whilst the Inquiry's recommendations were perceived by the public as potentially enhancing accountability, it was important for the police to ensure that records are made by officers and effective monitoring occurs. Public confidence in police use of stops and searches is primarily based on being treated fairly and with respect, and being given a satisfactory reason for the stop or search.

1 See P. Quinton and N. Bland, *Modernising the Tactic: Improving the Use of Stop and Search* (1999).
2 [1996] Crim LR 818.
3 C. F. Willis, *The Use, Effectiveness and Impact of Police Stop and Search Powers, Research and Planning Unit Paper 15* (Home Office, 1983).
4 Code A.1AA.
5 See M. Fitzgerald, MPS Report, *Searches in London* (1999).
6 Peter Moorhouse, Chairman of the Police Complaints Authority, commenting on the release of M. Fitzgerald's report, press release of the PCA, 15 December 1999.
7 *The Views of the Public on Stops and Searches* (2000) Police Research Series Paper No. 129.

Public views on the use of stops and searches

There was a very strong perception that the way in which stops and searches are currently handled causes more distrust, antagonism, and resentment than any of the positive effects they can have. Despite this, respondents from all ethnic groups felt that if there were fundamental changes in the ways they are used, who they are targeted at, attitudes of the police, and reasons given, then there was a role for stops and searches. The following were felt to be the two most important factors that should change:

1. There were very strong views that there needed to be considerable changes in attitudes of the police during stops and searches.
2. Respondents believed that stops and searches should be carried out for legitimate reasons and that a person should be given a valid genuine and credible reason at all times whenever he/she is stopped or searched.'[8]

(D) INTELLIGENCE GATHERING AND STOP AND SEARCH

The Philips Commission recognised the need to balance the rights of suspects and the powers and duties of the police. This balance has been recognised subsequently in the context of stop and search by the Macpherson Report, which concluded that there is a 'need' for a stop and search power, and that the power has a 'genuine usefulness in the prevention and detection of crime.' Paul Boateng, a Home Office Minister, recently described the stop and search power as one of the most important available to the police.[9] In what sense is it 'important' when arrests rates from stops and searches are as low as 11%?[10] To what extent is it legitimate for stop and search powers to be used primarily as an intelligence-gathering tool? P. Quinton and N. Bland[11] found that some forces used the power to stop the same individuals repeatedly as a means of monitoring the whereabouts of 'known criminals'. This was recognised as an effective use of the power.

'**Operational effectiveness** One of the key concerns of forces is to maximise the impact searches have on people actively involved in crime and to minimise their use on law-abiding members of the public... We suggested that improved targeting of searches can help increase the arrest rate from searches. One useful way in which this might be achieved is by ensuring that individual searches are linked to intelligence-led patrols, as well as reliable and accurate information ... These might be based on effective structures for the sharing and dissemination of up-to-date and accurate intelligence, and specific intelligence-led patrol tasks. There might also be a role for linking searches with strategic and planned police operations, whereby individual searches are based on strong intelligence and observation with the consent of local communities. It is clear that efforts which emphasise the need to increase effectiveness need also to act against the potential development of perverse incentives and competition by, again, having an effective system for recording-keeping and supervision. The working practices of officers themselves can also be a useful avenue for identifying good practice. This might provide a good source of information for developing specific training packages which respond to local needs. However, as with all these interventions, forces need to ensure that interventions are implemented fully and their progress monitored.' [12]

Can civil liberties concerns be met by managerial monitoring? In further research on information gathering, P. Quinton, N. Bland, and J. Miller *Police Stops, Decision-making and Practice*[13] concluded:

8   pp. 52–54.
9   HC Standing Committee on Delegated Legislation (1999) 27 January 1999.
10 The use of stop and search has increased, but the hit rate has gradually declined: see D. Brown, *PACE Ten Years On: A Review of Research* (1997) HORSD No. 49.
11 *Modernising the Tactic* (1999).
12 p. 73.
13 (2000) Police Research Series Paper No. 130.

'The research has emphasised the need for stops and searches to be based on good quality information and intelligence that is up-to-date, detailed, accurate and reflects the needs of operational officers. For example, as officers will, in practice, make common sense generalisations about high-crime areas as a basis for suspicions, it is important that the information on which generalisations are based is current and specific. Rather than just knowing the broad high-crime areas, officers will need to know – where the current problems are in a high-crime area;

- the exact nature of the problem;
- when it occurs; and
- who the current active offenders are.

It is clear that though this does occur, it does not do so routinely and consistently across the police service. Forces should ensure that the systems they have in place provide officers with such information. A review of information and intelligence systems will need to examine the collection and storage process, and whether the information is disseminated and acted upon quickly and effectively.

The reliability of suspect descriptions is a key factor in suspicion. In order to improve, forces will need to clarify in more detail the central, necessary elements of a description to be usable by officers. This will also have training implications for call-handling staff, and more widely, for improving the way in which interactions with victims and witnesses are handled to maximise the quality and quantity of information about suspects.

Forces need to ensure that reasonable suspicion for searches has been fulfilled for each search and that the recorded grounds accurately reflect all the available direct and indirect factors in detail (e.g. recording the nature of a person's behaviour not just "suspicious behaviour"). Bland, et al. (above) examine in greater detail how this might be achieved through management interventions, looking in part at the role of the supervisor. Shift supervisors might provide, for example, a safeguard against unfair use of negative stereotypes by challenging broad generalisations made by officers and the information which they are based on. Forces could usefully produce guidance on the standards expected from officers and supervisors in this respect.'

(E) STATISTICS ON STOP AND SEARCH

Statistics on stop and search have been produced by a number of bodies. The Home Office Statistics Directorate publishes annual reports on the operation of 'certain police powers under PACE'.[14]

'In 1996 there were 814,500 stops of people/vehicles, which represented an 18% increase on the previous year. 11% of searches led to arrest. 36% of stops were on suspicion of stolen property; 31% for drugs; and 18% for going equipped.

In 1997–98 there were 1,050,700 stops of people/vehicles, which represented a 20% increase on the previous year. 10% of searches led to arrest. 38% of stops were on suspicion of stolen property; 33% for drugs; and 16% for going equipped.[15]

In 1998–99 there were 1,080,700 stops of people/vehicles, which represented a 3% increase on the previous year. 11% of searches led to arrest. 40% of stops were on suspicion of stolen property; 34% for drugs; and 14% for going equipped.[16]

In 1999–2000 there were 857,000 stops of people/vehicles, which represented a 21% decrease on the previous year. 13% of searches led to arrest. 43% of stops were on suspicion of stolen property; 32% for drugs; and 13% for going equipped.[17]

In 2000–01 there were 714,100 stops of people/vehicles, which represented a 17% decrease. 13% of searches led to arrest.[17a]

---

14 G. Wilkins and C. Addicott, *Operation of Certain Police Powers Under PACE: England and Wales.* See those for 2000–01 by M. Ayres, HORSD 19/01.

15 See HORSD paper 2/99 G. Wilkins and C. Addicott, *Operation of Certain Police Powers Under PACE: England and Wales.*

16 See HORSD paper 9/00 G. Wilkins and C. Addicott, *Operation of Certain Police Powers Under PACE: England and Wales.*

17 See HORSD Paper 03/01, G. Wilkins and P. Hayward *Operation of Certain Police Powers Under PACE: England and Wales.*

17a See M. Ayres et al., *Arrests for Notifiable Offences* (2001) HORSD 19/01,

Other search statistics: [18]

> 'Section 60 CJPOA stops: 1995 – 2,373; 1996 – 7,019; 1996/7 – 7,974; 1997/8 – 7,970; 1998/9 – 6,800; 1999/00 – 6,800.
>
> Section 13A and B of the Prevention of Terrorism Act 1989: 1995 – 6 (part year only); 1996 – 40,475 (power now includes pedestrian stops); 1996/7 – 43,674; 1997/8 15,400; 1998/9 – 3,300; 1999/00 – 1,900.
>
> Road checks under section 4, number of vehicles stopped: 1987 – 63,900; 1988 – 61,700; 1989 – 41,500; 1990 – 38,700; 1991 – 31,800; 1992 – 31,500; 1993 – 48,800; 1994 – 25,100; 1995 – 17,100; 1996 – 21,400; 1997/8 – 24,500; 1998/99 – 26,800; 1999/00 – 23,400.'

(F) WHO GETS STOPPED?

L. Sims and A. Myhill reported that:[1]

> 'the proportion of adults stopped by the police while on foot (3%) has remained constant throughout the 1990s, although the proportion stopped while in a vehicle (12%) has decreased. Young men aged 16–29 are particularly likely to be stopped by the police. In the 2000 BCS [British Crime Survey] a quarter (25%) said they had been stopped while in a vehicle and 15% while on foot. Young black males were much more likely to be stopped while in a vehicle (39%) than either Asian (29%) or young white males (25%). Even among those aged over 30, black males were more likely to be stopped.'

Other groups likely to be stopped were the unemployed, single adults and those living in private rented accommodation.

In her research, M. Fitzgerald[2] found that:

- Most searches occur between 2 p.m. and 6 p.m. and 10 p.m. and 2 a.m.
- Most searches were of men with an average age of 21/22.
- The proportion of those searched more than once was higher for white people.
- There had been a significant rise in the use of stops and searches as a tool to gain information by targeting those with criminal records.[3]
- There had been a significant improvement in supervising officers' use of the powers.[4]

In the months immediately following publication of the Macpherson Report, the number of stops and searches in some parts of London reduced by as much as 50%.[5] This decrease was explained on the basis of reluctance of officers to risk being perceived as racist if they stopped a black person. The drop was also influenced by the removal of stops and searches from the performance indicators used by the MPS to measure police performance.[6]

(G) ETHNICITY AND STOPS AND SEARCHES

Much has been written on the disproportionate number of stops and searches of ethnic minority groups.[7] Statistics on this issue should be treated with caution, since there

---

18 Op. cit., n. 17.
1 See L. Sims and A. Mayhill, *Policing and the Future: Findings From the 2000 BCS* (2001) HORDSD No 136.
2 *Searches in London* (1999).
3 p. 18, pp. 66–68.
4 Ibid.
5 HMIC, *Policing London, Winning Consent: A review of murder investigation and community and race relations issues in the Metropolitan Police Service*, (2000), p. 54.
6 See Fitzgerald, op. cit., pp. 32–34.
7 See Fitzgerald, Chap. 3; A. Marlow and J. Maddock (1998) 71 Pol J 317; Home Office, *Race and the Criminal Justice System* (1999), Chaps. 1 and 2.

is a greater likelihood that a stop of a black person will lead to a search and therefore a greater likelihood that it will be recorded. J. Miller[8] looked at the ethnicity of those stopped and searched and exposed the complexity behind the statistics:

'the resident population is not a reliable measure of the available population. However, the question remains as to whether police officers are more likely to stop or search those from minority ethnic backgrounds among those they actually encounter in the available population. This issue was investigated in depth in this study. Overall, across the five sites, the findings of this research did not suggest any general pattern of bias against those from minority ethnic backgrounds. This was true for minority ethnic groups as whole, as well as any particular minority ethnic group. Asian people tended to be under-represented in those stopped or searched, compared to their numbers in the available population, with some notable exceptions. The general picture for black people was mixed. Perhaps surprisingly, the most consistent finding across sites was that white people tended to be stopped and searched at a higher rate than their numbers in the available population would predict.[9]

The conclusions were that a disproportionate number of searches could be due to: ethnic bias in officers; a larger proportion of ethnic groups in the population available to be stopped and searched; and a higher concentration of minority groups in the areas targeted. But this raises the question why those areas are targeted:

'While the overall picture does not, on the face of it, suggest a general pattern of discrimination against those from minority ethnic groups, it is important to flag-up certain caveats. First, the findings do indicate there are some situations where ethnic bias does occur. While it should not be assumed that discrimination underlies such biases, it does remind us that we should not be complacent in assuming there is no problem.

In many respects, the findings of this research are a problem for the police. Most significantly, they suggest that disproportionality is, to some extent, a product of structural factors beyond the control of the police. Therefore, they may lack the power to eliminate disproportionality, based upon residential population measures, by changing their practices. So, despite the best efforts of police forces, those from minority ethnic backgrounds may continue to be stopped and searched more often than white people.'[10]

The Macpherson Report[11] recommended that:

'60. The powers of the police under current legislation are required for the prevention and detection of crime and should remain unchanged.

61. That the Home Secretary, in consultation with police services, should ensure that a record is made by police officers of all "stops" and "stops and searches" made under any legislative provision (not just PACE). Non-statutory or so-called "voluntary" stops must also be recorded. The record to include the reasons for the stop, the outcome, and the self-defined ethnic identity of the person stopped. A copy of the record shall be given to the person stopped.

62. that these records should be monitored and analysed by police services and police authorities, and reviewed by HMIC inspectors. The information and analysis should be published.

63. That police authorities be given a duty to undertake publicity campaigns to ensure that the public is aware of "stop and search" provisions and the right to receive a record in all the circumstances.'

---

8 *Profiling Populations Available for Stops and Searches* (2000) Police Research Series Paper No. 131. See also HO: *Crime Policing and Justice, the experience of ethnic minorities.*
9 p. 84.
10 p. 87.
11 Op. cit.

Following the pilot study to assess these recommendations, Home Office research has demonstrated that recording of stops and searches was unclear, and the level of recording recommended by Macpherson was complied with in only 27% of encounters in the pilot study.[12] Recording for searches was better than for stops. Reasons for such low rates included definitional and practical problems and the exercise of the officer's discretion not to record. There were particular problems with recording a person's ethnicity based on their own definition.[13] Officers were sometimes reluctant to ask the question for fear of aggravating a potentially hostile encounter, or provided insufficient explanation of why the material was being requested.[14]

Important results of the pilot study included evidence that because of the requirement officers were more likely to exercise caution in stopping and searching and were more likely to provide more information and explanation to the suspect.[15] One significant recommendation from the research was that a contemporaneous record should be made of every search.[16]

V. Stone and N. Pettigrew's research echoed these findings of difficulty in recording and monitoring effectively the race of the suspects: [17]

'Public views on the [Stephen Lawrence] Inquiry's recommendations

It was clear that people's initial reactions to the [ethnicity] form were related to the way officers introduced and explained the form at the time of the stop. This emphasises that the form needs to be explained fully for the public to see value in having a record of a stop or search. The purpose of the form was welcomed by respondents when explained during the research. They could see the various benefits to having a record, and identified additional benefits from a police perspective. The form, for example, was viewed as providing the police with a means of communicating that they were simply doing their job and might encourage a better atmosphere during stop and search encounters.

For the public, the key benefits were seen as having: information in writing about the stop encounter, and in particular the reason for it – helping people to better understand what had happened; details of people's rights during stops and searches; and a record of the police officer's name involved in the encounter, which might help should a complaint be made subsequently.

The perception amongst respondents was that the Inquiry's recommendations might enhance accountability in two broad ways:

Complaints

It was felt that that if a person was stopped repeatedly and was being harassed, they would be able to make a complaint if they had been given a record for each stop or search. However, respondents were concerned that this step forward could be undermined if the police were not giving the form to people at every stop or search encounter.

Monitoring

The study also highlighted the view that accountability might be increased through the monitoring of information collected on the forms. However, without regular monitoring of stops and searches, respondents felt that there could be little accountability. There were some doubts as to whether this apparent advantage of the Inquiry's recommendations would be of any benefit if the forms were not being completed and given out by the police. Even those who were regularly stopped by the police during the pilot period could only remember seeing, or being offered, the form once. Apart from ensuring that records are completed when they

12 In N. Bland, J. Miller and P. Quinton, *Upping the PACE? An Evaluation of the Recommendations of the Stephen Lawrence Inquiry on Stops and Searches* (2000) PRS No. 128.
13 See Appendix C of the research.
14 See p. 93.
15 p. 78.
16 p. 95.
17 *The Views of the Public on Stops and Searches* (2000) PRS No. 129, p. 68.

should be, respondents also mentioned the idea of having more publicity about the whole initiative (e.g. on television).

Public confidence in stops and searches

Overall, despite the potential value of the Inquiry's recommendations in terms of improving information and enhancing accountability of stops and searches, respondents felt that their confidence in the police relied on more than just receiving a form. The study shows that how an individual is treated by the police has an important role, affecting their confidence and trust in the police generally. Consequently, whilst the form was seen to be important, there was thought to be a strong need for use of the form to go hand-in-hand with a respectful attitude from officers and the provision of a valid reason for the stop or search.'

In earlier research, P. Quinton and N. Bland[18] noted that it is difficult to monitor stops when the forces fail to record stops and searches in a uniform manner.

It seems that the stop and search powers need to be further refined so as to ensure:
- that there is better information available to the public of their rights;
- that the right to 'stop' is adequately defined;
- that the bases on which the stop and search can be carried out are more clearly and expressed in Codes;
- that there is some effective method of recording and monitoring the exercise of discretion;
- that the officers executing the stop provide adequate explanation of the power and the reasons for their exercise of it to the suspect;
- that voluntary searches are subjected to some form of monitoring to prevent circumvention of the statutory scheme and prevent abuse;
- that records of stops/searches are provided to the suspect;
- that records are held of the stops/ searches and that these are monitored.

M. Fitzgerald in her research in 1999 recommended:[19]

'– Informal warnings should be given where people with no previous cautions or convictions are found in possession of cannabis. The substance should be disposed of on the spot under the supervision of a sergeant.
 – The collection and co-ordination of community intelligence generally should be improved; and available sources of intelligence should be used more systematically for the purposes of briefing officers in order to improve their efficiency in searching.
 – Arrest rates fail to measure the impact of searches; and the number of arrests alone is insufficient for this purpose. Systems should be developed to capture the yield from searches more fully.
 – Sergeants should be held directly and formally accountable for monitoring and directly supervising the search activity of the officers they are responsible for.'

(H) EFFECTIVENESS

The arrest rate from stops and searches is consistently found to be below 15%. There have been calls for a stricter application of the reasonable suspicion test so that 'hit rates' could be raised to around 50%.[20] It has been shown that stops and searches do have some effect on the crime rate in an area. M. Fitzgerald, found that there was a statistically significant rise in crime in 1999 corresponding to the decrease in stops and searches that year.

J. Miller, N. Bland and P. Quinton,[1] found there to be a 'substantial variation between forces in the extent to which searches are used'.[2] Most strikingly it was

18 See P. Quinton and N. Bland, *Modernising the Tactic: Improving the Use of Stop and Search* (1999).
19 *Searches in London* (1999) MPS Report.
20 HMIC, op. cit., p. 55.
 1 *The Impact of Stops and Searches on Crime and the Community* (2000) HOR No 127.
 2 p. 12.

found that 'searches appear to have a minor role in detecting offenders for the range of all crimes that they address, and a relatively small role in detecting offenders for such crimes that come to the attention of the police'.[3] Despite this some officers interviewed claimed that they would be powerless without the stop and search and that 'crime would go through the roof'.[4] Searches were found to have 'only a limited direct disruptive impact on crime by intercepting those going out to commit offences'[5] and it was estimated that only 0.2% of disruptable crimes were affected in 1997. Contrary to popular belief, and that of some officers interviewed, 'it is unlikely that searches make a substantial contribution to undermining drug-markets or drug related crime'.[6] In sum, 'there is little evidence' that searches have any 'marginal deterrent effect on offending'.[7]

(I)   ROAD CHECKS

Section 163 (1) of the Road Traffic Act 1988 provides that:

> 'A person driving a mechanically propelled vehicle on a road must stop the vehicle on being required to do so by a constable in uniform.'

Section 163(2) makes similar provision for a person riding a cycle and s. 163(3) makes failure to comply an offence. It has been held that it is not necessary for a constable acting under this section to be 'acting in the execution of his duty under some common law powers. It would seem on the face of it that the constable derives his duty as well as his power from the terms of s. 159 [now s. 163] itself'.[9] Accordingly, a constable may stop a vehicle to check whether the driver has valid documents, even though he has no reasonable grounds to suspect that he does not.[10] However, a constable may not act 'in bad faith' or 'capriciously':[11] the section does not give a constable ' a power willy-nilly to stop a motor vehicle'.[12] The result is that a motorist may be stopped more or less at random, provided that it is done for some purpose related to police duties. If the constable reasonably suspects the driver has been drinking the breathalyser legislation will become applicable. Although random *tests* are not permitted, (more or less) random stops are.[13] This position was confirmed in *Chief Constable of Gwent v Dash*,[14] where the Divisional Court confirmed that random stops made in order to detect whether drivers could be reasonably suspected of having alcohol in their bodies did not as such constitute 'malpractice'.[15] The reasonable suspicion may be based on such factors as the manner of driving, the smell of alcohol on the driver's breath or the admission by the driver that he has been drinking.[16] In the absence of reasonable cause, evidence subsequently obtained may be excluded under s. 78 of PACE.[17]

---

3 p. 27.
4 p. 16.
5 p. 45.
6 p. 45.
7 p. 33.
9 *Beard v Wood* [1980] RR 454 at 457–458, DC, per Wien J.
10 Ibid.
11 [1980] RTR 454 at 457–459.
12 *Winter v Barlow* [1980] RTR 209 at 213, DC, per Eveleigh LT. See also *Steel v Goacher* [1983] RTR 98, DC; Commentary by D. J. Birch, [1982] Crim LR 689 and D. P. J. Walsh, [1994] Crim LR 187.
13 D. J. Birch, [1982] Crim LR 689.
14 [1986] RTR 41.
15 [1991] RTR 284, DC (below, p. 355). See also *DPP v Wilson*.
16 *DPP v McGladrigan* [1991] RTR 297, DC.
17 *DPP v Godwin* [1991] RTR 303, DC; below, p. 355.

Section 163 is regarded as impliedly imposing a duty on the driver (or cyclist) to remain at rest for a reasonable period after having stopped, to enable the officer to complete any lawful inquiries; however, it does not confer on the officer a power to detain the vehicle for that purpose.[18]

When the s. 163 power is used to carry out general road checks the position is governed by s. 4 of the 1984 Act. The number of road checks rose dramatically in 1993 (from 445 in 1992 to 3,650), over 3,200 being conducted in the City of London following increased terrorist activity.[19] These 'rolling random road blocks' involved 'stretching PACE powers to their limit'.[20] The Commissioner subsequently used his powers under s. 12 of the Road Traffic Regulation Act [1984] to restrict vehicle access to the City to eight streets covered by CCTV cameras. This had the incidental effect of helping reduce crime by 17%.[1] Section 4 of the Prevention of Terrorism (Additional Powers) Act 1996 created a power to impose a police cordon on an area. The powers included those to require people to leave the area, remove vehicles, and to search premises in the area where there were reasonable grounds to believe that searches of premises/people will uncover material likely to be of substantial value to a terrorist investigation.[2]

On Road Traffic Measures, see generally HMIC Thematic Inspection, *Road Policing and Traffic.*[3] In *Sadiku v DPP*[4] it was held that the power in s. 67 of the Road Traffic Act 1988 for an officer to require an inspection of a vehicle was exercisable even when an ice-cream van was stationary in Trafalgar Square.

5 Entry, search and seizure

Police and Criminal Evidence Act 1984

PART II

POWERS OF ENTRY, SEARCH AND SEIZURE

Search warrants

8. Power of justice of the peace to authorise entry and search of premises
(1) If on an application made by a constable a justice of the peace is satisfied that there are reasonable grounds for believing—
    (*a*) that a serious arrestable offence has been committed; and
    (*b*) that there is material on premises specified in the application which is likely to be of substantial value (whether by itself or together with other material) to the investigation of the offence; and
    (*c*) that the material is likely to be relevant evidence; and
    (*d*) that it does not consist of or include items subject to legal privilege, excluded material or special procedure material; and
    (*e*) that any of the conditions specified in subsection (3) below applies,
he may issue a warrant authorising a constable to enter and search the premises.
(2) A constable may seize and retain anything for which a search has been authorised under subsection (1) above.

18 *Lodwick v Sanders* [1985] 1 All ER 577; *Saunders v DPP* [1988] Crim LR 605.
19 HOSB 15/94, Table B.
20 J. Owen (then Commissioner of the City of London Police), 'The IRA Threat to the City of London' (1994) 10 Policing 88, 93.
1 pp. 95–98.
2 See now the Terrorism Act 2000, ss. 33–36 discussed below, pp. 580–582.
3 (1998).
4 [2000] RTR 155, DC.

(3) The conditions mentioned in subsection (1) (*e*) above are—
- (*a*) that it is not practicable to communicate with any person entitled to grant entry to the premises;
- (*b*) that it is practicable to communicate with a person entitled to grant entry to the premises but it is not practicable to communicate with any person entitled to grant access to the evidence;
- (*c*) that entry to the premises will not be granted unless a warrant is produced;
- (*d*) that the purpose of a search may be frustrated or seriously prejudiced unless a constable arriving at the premises can secure immediate entry to them.

(4) In this Act 'relevant evidence' in relation to an offence, means anything that would be admissible in evidence at a trial for the offence.

(5) The power to issue a warrant conferred by this section is in addition to any such power otherwise conferred.

(6) This section applies in relation to a relevant offence [as defined in [s. 28 D(4) of the Immigration Act 1971] as it applies in relation to a serious arrestable offence.][5]

9. Special provisions as to access
(1) A constable may obtain access to excluded material or special procedure material for the purposes of a criminal investigation by making an application under Schedule 1 below and in accordance with the Schedule.

(2) Any Act (including a local Act) passed before this Act under which a search of premises for the purposes of a criminal investigation could be authorised by the issue of a warrant to a constable shall cease to have effect so far as it relates to authorisation of searches—
- (*a*) for items subject to legal privilege; or
- (*b*) for excluded material; or
- (*c*) for special procedure material consisting of documents or records other than documents.

10. Meaning of 'items subject to legal privilege'
(1) Subject to subsection (2) below, in this Act 'items subject to legal privilege' means—
- (*a*) communications between a professional legal advisor and his client or any person representing his client made in connection with the giving of legal advice to the client;
- (*b*) communications between a professional legal advisor and his client or any person representing his client or between such an advisor or his client or any such representative and any other person made in connection with or in contemplation of legal proceedings and for the purposes of such proceedings; and
- (*c*) items enclosed with or referred to in such communications and made—
  - (i) in connection with the giving of legal advice; or
  - (ii) in connection with or in contemplation of legal proceedings and for the purposes of such proceedings,

when they are in the possession of a person who is entitled to possession of them.

(2) Items held with the intention of furthering a criminal purpose are not items subject to legal privilege.

11. Meaning of 'excluded material'
(1) Subject to the following provisions of this section, in this Act 'excluded material' means—
- (*a*) personal records which a person has acquired or created in the course of any trade, business, profession or other occupation or for the purposes of any paid or unpaid office and which he holds in confidence;
- (*b*) human tissue or tissue fluid which has been taken for the purposes of diagnosis or medical treatment and which a person holds in confidence;
- (*c*) journalistic material which a person holds in confidence and which consists—
  - (i) of documents; or
  - (ii) of records other than documents

(2) A person holds material other than journalistic material in confidence for the purposes of this section if he holds it subject—
- (*a*) to an express or implied undertaking to hold it in confidence or

---

5　As inserted by Immigration and Asylum Act 1999, s. 169, Sch. 14, para. 80(2).

(*b*) to a restriction on disclosure or an obligation of secrecy contained in any enactment, including an enactment contained in an Act passed after this Act.

12. Meaning of 'personal records'

In this Part of this Act 'personal records' means documentary and other records concerning an individual (whether living or dead) who can be identified from them and relating—
(*a*) to his physical or mental health
(*b*) to spiritual counselling or assistance given or to be given to him; or
(*c*) to counselling or assistance given or to be given to him, for the purposes of his personal welfare, by any voluntary organisation or by any individual who—
  (i) by reason of his office or occupation has responsibilities for his personal welfare; or
  (ii) by reason of an order of a court has responsibilities for his supervision.

13. Meaning of 'journalistic material'

(1) Subject to subsection (2) below, in the Act 'journalistic material', means material acquired or created for the purpose of journalism.
(2) Material is only journalistic material for the purposes of this Act if it is in the possession of a person who acquired or created it for the purposes of journalism.
(3) A person who receives material from someone who intends that the recipient shall use it for the purposes of journalism is to be taken to have acquired it for those purposes.

14. Meaning of 'special procedure material'

(1) in this Act 'special procedure material' means—
(*a*) material to which subsection (2) below applies; and
(*b*) journalistic material, other than excluded material.
(2) Subject to the following provisions of this section, this subsection applies to material, other than items subject to legal privilege and excluded material, in the possession of a person who—
(*a*) acquired or created it in the course of any trade, business, profession or other occupation or for the purpose of any paid or unpaid office; and
(*b*) holds it subject—
  (i) to an express or implied undertaking to hold it in confidence; or
  (ii) to a restriction or obligation such as is mentioned in s. 11(2)(*b*) above.
(3) Where material is acquired—
(*a*) by an employee from his employer and in the course of his employment; or
(*b*) by a company from an associated company.
It is only special procedure material if it was special procedure material immediately before the acquisition.
(4) Where material is created by an employee in the course of his employment, it is only special procedure material if it would have been special procedure material had his employer created it.
(5) Where material created by a company on behalf of an associated company, it is only special procedure material if it would be been special procedure material had the associated company created it.
(6) A company is to be treated as another's associated company for the purposes of this section if it would be so treated under [s. 416 of the Income and Corporation Taxes Act 1988].[6]

15. Search warrants – safeguards

(1) This section and section 16 below have effect in relation to the issue to constables under any enactment, including an enactment contained in an Act passed after this Act, of warrants to enter and search premises; and an entry on or search of premises under a warrant is unlawful unless it complies with this section and s. 16 below.
(2) Where a constable applies for any such warrant, it shall be his duty—
(*a*) to state—
  (i) the ground on which he makes the application; and
  (ii) the enactment under which the warrant would be issued;

6 As substituted by Income and Corporation Taxes Act 1988, s. 844, Sch. 31.

(*b*) to specify the premises which it is desired to enter and search; and

(*c*) to identify, so far as is practicable, the articles or persons to be sought.

(3) An application for such warrant shall be made ex parte and supported by an information in writing.

(4) The constable shall answer on oath any question that the justice of the peace or judge hearing the application asks him.

(5) A warrant shall authorise an entry on one occasion only.

(6) A warrant—

(*a*) shall specify—

(i)   the name of the person who applies for it;

(ii) the date on which it is issued;

(iii) the enactment under which it is issued, and

(iv) the premises to be searched; and

(*b*) shall identify, so far as is practicable, the articles or persons to be sought.

(7) Two copies shall be made of a warrant.

(8) The copies shall be clearly certified as copies.

16. Execution of warrants

(1) A warrant to enter and search premises may be executed by any constable.

(2) Such a warrant may authorise persons to accompany any constable who is executing it.

(3) Entry and search under a warrant must be within one month from the date of issue.

(4) Entry and search under a warrant must be at a reasonable hour unless it appears to the constable executing it that the purpose of a search may be frustrated on an entry at a reasonable hour.

(5) Where the occupier of premises which are to be entered and searched is present at the time when a constable seeks to execute a warrant to enter and search them, the constable—

(*a*) shall identify himself to the occupier and, if not in uniform, shall produce to him documentary evidence that he is a constable;

(*b*) shall produce the warrant to him; and

(*c*) shall supply him with a copy of it.

(6) Where—

(*a*) the occupier of such premises is not present at the time when a constable seeks to execute such a warrant; but

(*b*) some other person who appears to the constable to be in charge of the premises is present,

subsection (5) above shall have effect as if any reference to the occupier were a reference to that other person.

(7) If there is no person present who appears to the constable to be in charge of the premises, he shall leave a copy of the warrant in a prominent place on the premises.

(8) A search under a warrant may only be a search to the extent required for the purpose of which the warrant was issued.

(9) A constable executing a warrant shall make an endorsement on it stating—

(*a*) whether the articles or persons sought were found; and

(*b*) whether any articles were seized, other than articles which were sought.

(10) A warrant which—

(*a*) has been executed; or

(*b*) has not been executed within the time authorised for its execution,

shall be returned—

(i)   if it was issued by a justice of the peace, to the chief executive to the justices[7] for the petty sessions area for which he acts; and

(ii) if it was issued by a judge, to the appropriate officer of the court from which he issued it.

(11) A warrant which is returned under subsection (10) above shall be retained for 12 months from its return—

(*a*) by the chief executive to the justices, if it was returned under paragraph (i) of that subsection; and

(*b*) by the appropriate officer, if it was returned under paragraph (ii).

---

7   Amended by the Access to Justice Act 1999, s. 90, Sch. 13, paras. 125, 6.

(12) If during the period for which a warrant is to be retained the occupier of the premises to which it relates asks to inspect it, he shall be allowed to do so.

Entry and search without search warrant

17. Entry for purpose of arrest etc

(1) Subject to the following provisions of this section, and without prejudice to any other enactment, a constable may enter and search premises for the purpose—

    (*a*) of executing—

        (i) a warrant of arrest issued in connection with or arising out of criminal proceedings; or

        (ii) a warrant of commitment issued under section 76 of the Magistrates' Courts Act 1980;

    (*b*) of arresting a person for an arrestable offence;

    (*c*) of arresting a person for an offence under—

        (i) Section 1 (prohibition of uniforms in connection with political object) [...] of the Public Order Act 1936.

        (ii) any enactment contained in sections 6 to 8 or 10 of the Criminal Law Act 1977 (offences relating to entering and remaining on property);

        [(iii) Section 4 of the Public Order Act 1986 (fear or provocation of violence)]:[8]

        [(iv) Section 76 of the Criminal Justice and Public Order Act 1994 (failure to comply with interim possession order)];[9]

    [(Ca) of arresting in pursuance of s. 32 (1A) of the CYPA 1969, any child or young person who has been remanded or committed to local authority accommodation under s. 23 (1) of that Act;

    (Cb) of recapturing any person who is, or is deemed for any purpose to be, unlawfully at large while liable to be detained;

        (i) in a prison, remand centre, young offenders institution or secure training unit, or

        (ii) in pursuance of [s. 92 of the Powers of Criminal Courts (Sentencing) Act 2000][10] (dealing with children and young persons guilty of grave crimes), in any other place;[11]]

    (*d*) of recapturing [any person whatever][12] who is unlawfully at large and whom he is pursing; or

    (*e*) of saving life or limb or preventing serious damage to property.

(2) Except for the purpose specified in paragraph (*e*) of subsection (1) above, the powers of entry and search conferred by this section—

    (*a*) are only exercisable if the constable has reasonable grounds for believing that the person whom he is seeking is on the premises; and

    (*b*) are limited, in relation to premises consisting of two or more separate dwellings, to powers to enter and search—

        (i) any parts of the premises which the occupiers of any dwelling comprised in the premises use in common with the occupiers of any other such dwelling; and

        (ii) any such dwelling in which the constable has reasonable grounds for believing that the person whom he is seeking may be.

(3) The powers of entry and search conferred by this section are only exercisable for the purposes specified in subsection (1)(*c*)(ii) [or (iv)][12a] above by a constable in uniform.

(4) The power of search conferred by this section is only a power to search to the extent that is reasonably required for the purpose for which the power of entry is exercised.

(5) Subject to subsection (6) below, all the rules of common law under which a constable has power to enter premises without a warrant are hereby abolished.

(6) Nothing in subsection (5) above affects any power of entry to deal with or prevent a breach of the peace.

---

8 Inserted by the 1986 Act, s. 40, Sch. 2, para. 7.
9 Inserted by the Criminal Justice and Public Order Act 1994, Sch. 10, para. 53.
10 As submitted by the Powers of Criminal Courts (Sentencing) Act 2000, s. 165(1).
11 As inserted by the Prisoners (Return to Custody) Act 1995, s. 2(1).
12 As inserted by the Prisoners (Return to Custody) Act 1995, s. 2(1).
12a Inserted by the Criminal Justice and Public Order Act 1994, Sch. 10, para. 53.

18. Entry and search after arrest

(1) Subject to the following provisions of this section, a constable may enter and search any premises occupied or controlled by a person who is under arrest for an arrestable offence, if he has reasonable grounds for suspecting that there is on the premises evidence, other than items subject to legal privilege, that relates—

(a) to that offence, or

(b) to some other arrestable offence which is connected with or similar to that offence

(2) A constable may seize and retain anything for which he may search under subsection (1) above.

(3) The power to search conferred by subsection (1) above is only a power to search to the extent that is reasonably required for the purpose of discovering such evidence.

(4) Subject to subsection (5) below, the powers conferred by this section may not be exercised unless an officer of the rank of inspector or above has authorised them in writing.

(5) A constable may conduct a search under subsection (1) above—

(a) before taking the person to a police station; and

(b) without obtaining an authorisation under subsection (4) above,

in the presence of that person at a place other than a police station is necessary for the effective investigation of the offence.

(6) If a constable conducts a search by virtue of subsection (5) above, he shall inform an officer of the rank of inspector or above that he has made the search as soon as practicable after he has made it.

(7) An officer who—

(a) authorises a search; or

(b) is informed of a search under subsection (6) above,

shall make a record in writing—

(i) of the grounds for the search; and

(ii) of the nature of the evidence that was sought,

(8) If the person who was in occupation or control of the premises at the time of the search is in police detention at the time of the record is to be made, the officer shall make the record as part of his custody record.

Seizure etc

19. General power of seizure etc.

(1) The powers conferred by subsections (2), (3) and (4) below are exercisable by a constable who is lawfully on any premises.

(2) The constable may seize anything which is on the premises if he has reasonable grounds for believing—

(a) that it has been obtained in consequence of the commission of an offence; and

(b) that it is necessary to seize it in order to prevent it being concealed, lost, damaged, altered or destroyed.

(3) The constable may seize anything which is on the premises if he has reasonable grounds for believing—

(a) that it is evidence in relation to an offence which he is investigating or any other offence; and

(b) that it is necessary to seize the evidence in order to prevent it being concealed, lost altered or destroyed.

(4) The constable may require any information which is contained in a computer and is accessible from the premises to be produced in a form in which it can be taken away and in which it is visible and legible if he has reasonable grounds for believing—

(a) that—

(i) it is evidence in relation to an offence which he is investigation or any other offence; or

(ii) it has been obtained in consequence of the commission of an offence; and

(b) that it is necessary to do so in order to prevent it being concealed, lost, tampered with or destroyed.

(5) The powers conferred by this section are in addition to any power otherwise conferred.

(6) No power of seizure conferred on a constable under any enactment (including an enactment contained in an Act passed after this Act) is to be taken to authorise the seizure of an item

which the constable exercising the power has reasonable grounds for suspecting to be subject to legal privilege.

20. Extension of powers of seizure to computerised information
(1) Every power of seizure which is conferred by an enactment to which this section applies on a constable who has entered premises in the exercise of a power conferred by an enactment shall be construed as including a power to require any information contained in a computer and accessible from the premises to be produced in a form in which it can be taken away and in which it is visible and legible.
(2) This section applies—
    (*a*) to any enactment contained in an Act passed before this Act;
    (*b*) to sections 8 and 18 above;
    (*c*) to paragraph 13 of Schedule 1 to this Act; and
    (*d*) to any enactment contained in an Act passed after this Act.

21. Access and copying
(1) A constable who seizes anything in the exercise of a power conferred by any enactment, including an enactment contained in an Act passed after this Act, shall if so requested by a person showing himself—
    (*a*) to be the occupier of premises on which it was seized; or
    (*b*) to have had custody or control of it immediately before the seizure,
provide that person with a record of what he seized.
(2) The officer shall provide the record within a reasonable time from the making of the request for it.
(3) Subject to subsection (8) below, if a request for permission to be granted access to anything which—
    (*a*) has been seized by a constable; and
    (*b*) is retained by the police for the purpose of investigating an offence,
is made to the officer in charge of the investigation by a person who had custody or control of the thing immediately before it was so seized or by someone acting on behalf of such a person, the officer shall allow the person who made the request access to it under the supervision of a constable.
(4) Subject to subsection (8) below, if a request for a photograph or copy of any such thing is made to the officer in charge of the investigation by a person who had custody or control of the thing immediately before it was so seized, or by someone acting on behalf of such a person, the officer shall—
    (*a*) allow the person who made the request access to it under the supervision of a constable for the purpose of photographing or copying it; or
    (*b*) photograph or copy it, or cause it to be photographed or copied.
(5) A constable may also photograph or copy, or have photographed or copied, anything which he has power to seize, without a request being made under subsection (4) above.
(6) Where anything is photographed or copied under subsection (4)(*b*) above, the photograph or copy shall be supplied to the person who made the request.
(7) The photograph or copy shall be so supplied within a reasonable time for the making of the request.
(8) There is no duty under this section to grant access to, or to supply a photograph or copy of, anything if the officer in charge of the investigation for the purposes of which it was seized has reasonable grounds for believing that to do so would prejudice—
    (*a*) that investigation;
    (*b*) the investigation of an offence other than the offence for the purposes of investigating which the thing was seized; or
    (*c*) any criminal proceedings which may be brought as a result of—
        (i) the investigation of which he is in charge; or
        (ii) any such investigation as is mentioned in paragraph (*b*) above.

22. Retention
(1) Subject to subsection (4) below, anything which has been seized by a constable or taken away by a constable following a requirement made by virtue of section 19 or 20 above may be retained so long as it is necessary in all the circumstance.
(2) Without prejudice to the generality of subsection (1) above—

(*a*) anything seized for the purposes of criminal investigation may be retained, except as provided by subsection (4) below,—
    (i) for use as evidence at a trial for an offence; or
    (ii) for forensic examination or for investigation in connection with an offence; and
(*b*) anything may be retained in order to establish its lawful owner, where there are reasonable grounds for believing that it has been obtained in consequence of the commission of an offence.
(3) Nothing seized on the ground that it may be used—
    (*a*) to cause physical injury to any person;
    (*b*) to damage property
    (*c*) to interfere with evidence; or
    (*d*) to assist in escape from police detention or lawful custody may be retained when the person from whom it was seized is no longer in police detention or the custody of a court or is in the custody of a court but has been released on bail.
(4) Nothing may be retained for either of the purposes mentioned in subsection (2)(*a*) above if a photograph or copy would be sufficient for that purpose.
(5) Nothing in this section affects any power of a court to make an order under section 1 of the Police (Property) Act 1897.
[(6) This section also applies to anything retained by the police under s. 28H(5) of the Immigration Act 1971.[13]]

Part II – Supplementary

23. Interpretation
In this Act—
'premises' includes any place and, in particular, includes—
    (*a*) any vehicle, vessel, aircraft or hovercraft
    (*b*) any offshore installation; and
    (*c*) any tent or movable structure; and
'offshore installation' has the meaning given to it by section 1 of the Mineral Working (Offshore Installations) Act 1971 [as repealed by Offshore Installations & Pipeline Works (Management & Administration) Regulations 1995, S.I. No. 1995/738, reg. 22 (1), Sch. 1, Part 1.]

SCHEDULE 1

SPECIAL PROCEDURE

Making of orders by circuit judge
1. If on an application made by a constable a circuit judge is satisfied that one or other of the sets of access conditions is fulfilled, he may make an order under paragraph 4 below.
2. The first set of access conditions is fulfilled if—
    (*a*) there are reasonable grounds for believing—
        (i) that a serious arrestable offence has been committed;
        (ii) that there is material which consists of special procedure material or includes special procedure material and does not also include excluded material on premises specified in the application;
        (iii) that the material is likely to be of substantial value (whether by itself or together with other material) to the investigation in connection with which the application is made; and
        (iv) that the material is likely to be relevant evidence;
    (*b*) other methods of obtaining the material—
        (i) have been tried without success; or
        (ii) have not been tried because it appeared that they were bound to fail; and
    (*c*) it is in the public interest, have regard—
        (i) to the benefit likely to accrue to the investigation if the material is obtained; and
        (ii) to the circumstances under which the person in possession of the material holds it, that the material should be produced or that access to it should be given.

13 Inserted by the Immigration and Asylum Act 1999, s. 169(1), Sch. 14, para. 80(3).

3. The second set of access conditions is fulfilled if—
  (*a*) there are reasonable grounds for believing that there is material which consists of or includes excluded material or special procedure material on premises specified in the application;
  (*b*) but for section 9(2) above a search of the premises for that material could have been authorised by the issue of a warrant to a constable under an enactment other than this Schedule; and
  (*c*) the issue of such a warrant would have been appropriate.
4. An order under this paragraph is an order that the person who appears to the circuit judge to be in possession of the material to which the application relates shall—
  (*a*) produce it to a constable for him to take away; or
  (*b*) give a constable access to it,
not later than the end of the period of seven days from the date of the order or the end of such longer period as the order may specify.
5. Where the material consists of information contained in a computer,
  (*a*) an order under paragraph 4(a) above shall have effect as an order to produce the material in a form in which it can be taken away and in which it is visible and legible; and
  (*b*) an order under paragraph 4(b) above shall have effect as an order to give a constable access to the material in a form in which it is visible and legible.
6. For the purposes of sections 21 and 22 above material produced in pursuance of an order under paragraph 4(a) above shall be treated as if it were material seized by a constable.

Notices of applications for orders
7. An application for an order under paragraph 4 above shall be made inter partes...
11. Where notice of an application for an order under paragraph 4 above has been served on a person, he shall not conceal, destroy, alter or dispose of the material to which the application relates except—
  (*a*) with the leave of a judge; or
  (*b*) with the written permission of a constable,
until—
  (i) the application is dismissed or abandoned; or
  (ii) he has complied with an order under paragraph 4 above made on the application.

Issue of warrants by circuit judge
12. If on an application made by a constable a circuit judge—
  (*a*) is satisfied—
    (i) that either set of access conditions is fulfilled; and
    (ii) that any of the further conditions set out in paragraph 14 below is also fulfilled; or
  (*b*) is satisfied—
    (i) that the second set of access conditions is fulfilled; and
    (ii) that an order under paragraph 4 above relating to the material has not been complied with,
he may issue a warrant authorising a constable to enter and search the premises.
13. A constable may seize and retain anything for which a search has been authorised under paragraph 12 above.
14. The further conditions mentioned in paragraph 12(a)(ii) above are—
  (*a*) that it is not practicable to communicate with any person entitled to grant entry to the premises to which the application relates;
  (*b*) that it is practicable to communicate with a person entitled to grant entry to the premises but it is not practicable to communicate with any person entitled to grant access to the material.
  (*c*) that the material contains information which—
    (i) is subject to a restriction or obligation such as is mentioned in section11(2)(*b*) above; and
    (ii) is likely to be disclosed in breach of it if a warrant is not issued;
  (*d*) that service of notice of an application for an order under paragraph 4 above may seriously prejudice the investigation.

15. (1) If a person fails to comply with an order under paragraph 4 above, a circuit judge may deal with him as if he had committed a contempt of the Crown Court...

Note also the new provisions in the Criminal Justice and Police Act 2001 discussed below.

NOTES

1. *The common law background.* Part II of PACE extended police powers in a number of significant respects. At common law there was no general power to enter premises to search for evidence, and there was no general power to obtain warrants to authorise such searches, although there were some specific powers. Lord Denning MR noted in *Ghani v Jones*,[14] that there was no power to search premises for evidence of murder. There was a power to search the premises of a person arrested there (perhaps only in his immediate vicinity) but it had to be exercised contemporaneously with the arrest.[15] If the police were lawfully on premises, whether by consent or in the execution of a warrant or a power to enter premises without a warrant, the decision in *Ghani v* Jones,[16] authorised the seizure of a wide range of material,[17] the ambit of the power to seize being wider than the powers of entry and search. The RCCP supported the extension of powers along the lines of Part II although they would have applied the special procedure involving a circuit judge to all warrants to search for evidence, and confined the power to 'grave offences'.[18]

2. The main features of Part II of PACE were (1) new general powers to search for evidence (ss. 8–14 and Sch. 1); (2) provisions applying generally to search warrants (ss. 15, 16); (3) general powers of entry (s. 17); a power to enter and search after arrest (s. 18); and (5) general powers of seizure (s. 19).

3. On the ECHR and search and seizure, see *Miailhe v France*,[19] where the indiscriminate seizure of 15,000 documents without a warrant was in breach of Art. 8. The court stressed that the derogations in Art. 8(2) are to be narrowly construed; (see also *Cremieux v France*.[20]) Article 8 protects against infringement of privacy unless prescribed by law and the infringement is necessary and proportionate to the legitimate aim. It is vital that there are adequate safeguards against abuse, notwithstanding the margin of appreciation; see *Niemitz v Germany*.[1] For cases involving over broad searches of premises see: *Ozgur Gundem v Turkey*;[2] *Camenzind v Switzerland*.[3] Warrants must be sufficiently clearly prescribed *Funke v France*;[4] and see also *Camenzind* on other procedural safeguards regarding search warrants.

4. *General Powers to obtain evidence.* Generally speaking, the police no longer can have direct access to items subject to legal privilege (s. 9(2)(*a*)). Access to excluded or special procedure material can only be authorised under s. 9(1) and Sch. 1. Of these two classes, excluded material is regarded as more sensitive, and may only be the subject of an order or warrant under Sch. 1 if, but for s. 9(2), a warrant could have

---

14 [1970] 1 QB 693, CA.
15 *McLorie v Oxford* [1982] QB 1290, DC.
16 [1970] 1 QB 693, CA.
17 See first edition of this book at pp. 94–103.
18 Cf. above, p. 195.
19 (1993) 16 EHRR 332.
20 (1993) 16 EHRR 357.
 1 (1992) 16 EHRR 97.
 2 (2000) 16 March.
 3 (1997) 28 EHRR 458.
 4 (1993) 16 EHRR 297, para. 56.

been used under a pre-existing power.[5] This restriction does not apply to special procedure material, and orders or warrants for the production of such material are much more common: see K. Lidstone[6] reporting on a survey, to which 39 of the 43 police forces of England and Wales responded, which showed that over 2,000 orders or warrants had been granted under the first set of access conditions, but only nine under the second set. Lidstone also notes that 'mortgage frauds were almost impossible to investigate before 1984, there being no legal machinery for obtaining access to material relating to such frauds held by solicitors, building societies, estate agents and the like'.[7] In a survey of two forces, s. 8 had been rarely used.[8]

Excluded or special procedure material can be seized during the course of a search under post-arrest powers (ss. 18, 32), or under any other warranted search and whenever a constable is lawfully on premises and comes across such material (s. 19): see Lidstone.[9] In a survey of two city forces involving over 860 searches of premises, 12% were conducted under a judicial warrant and 87% under post-arrest powers (75% under s. 18, 2% under s. 32, and 6% following and entry to arrest under s. 17).[10] There appears to be a steady decline in the use of warrants.[11] Excluded material can also be disclosed voluntarily by the maker or holder independently of s. 9(1) and Sch. 1: *R v Singleton*.[12]

5. The new powers to grant warrants to search for evidence under ss. 8 and 9 of PACE (and associated provisions) have given rise to a series of cases raising both procedural and substantive issues. Thus, it has been held that the material in question must be specified, either in the notice of application or otherwise: *R v Central Criminal Court, ex p Adegbesan*,[13] *R v Crown Court at Manchester, ex p Taylor*;[14] but the evidence on which the application is based need not: *R v Crown Court at Inner London Sessions, ex p Baines & Baines*,[15] (warrant quashed where its terms went beyond those of the sworn information on which it was based and where it would have been 'practicable' to identify the articles sought with much greater precision) and *R v Southampton Crown Court, ex p J and P*,[16] (warrants to search solicitors' premises quashed as they were wider than justified by the investigation, the judge had failed to consider the issue of legal privilege and the use of the ex parte procedure was not justified). The suspect need not be notified by the applicant if he is not the holder of the material: *R v Crown Court at Leicester, ex p DPP*,[17] and a bank is not impliedly under a contractual duty to notify its client or to contest the application: *Barclays Bank plc v Taylor*.[18] This position is strongly criticised by A. A. S. Zuckerman,[19] on the ground that the person most affected by the order is not given the opportunity to challenge it, and that if there is a risk that that person would impede or frustrate the

---

5 See *R v Central Criminal Court, ex p Brown* (1992) Times, 7 September, DC, where it was held that no production order could be made in respect of a medical report from a hospital administration for a murder investigation as no warrant could have been issued for its seizure prior to PACE.
6 (1989) 40 NILQ 333, 344, n. 35.
7 Ibid., p. 342, n. 29.
8 Ibid., p. 334.
9 Op. cit., p. 28.
10 Lidstone, op. cit., p. 355, n. 67.
11 Ibid., p. 362, n. 87.
12 [1995] 1 Cr App Rep 431, CA (Cr D) (dental records).
13 [1986] 1 WLR 1292.
14 [1988] 1 WLR 705.
15 [1988] QB 579; cf. *R v Central Criminal Court, ex p AJD Holdings Ltd* [1992] Crim LR 669.
16 [1993] Crim LR 962.
17 [1987] 1 WLR 1371.
18 [1989] 3 All ER 563.
19 [1990] Crim LR 472.

order if he were given notice, the warrant procedure is available under Sch. 1, paras. 12–14. In *R v Singleton*[20] it was held that excluded material could be voluntarily disclosed although an application under s. 9 would have been unsuccessful. No reference to *Barclays Bank v Taylor* was made. In *R v Crown Court at Lewes, ex p Weller*[21] it was emphasised that judges need to provide properly recorded reasons for decisions under s. 9.

As to substantive matters arising under Sch. 1, in *R v Crown Court at Bristol, ex p Bristol Press and Picture Agency Ltd*,[22] the Divisional Court upheld the decision of Stuart-Smith J to order the applicant to produce press photographs taken during the 1986 riots in the St. Pauls area of Bristol. This was special procedure material and the first set of access conditions in Sch. 1 were applied. The court held that the judge had been entitled to conclude that there were reasonable grounds to believe that the material was 'likely to be of substantial value...to the investigation in connection with which the application was made' and 'likely to be relevant evidence',[23] notwithstanding that it could not identify any particular photograph as relating to any particular incident of violence or other criminal offence; it was likely that the press would attempt to photograph 'newsworthy' incidents, some at least relating to the actions of those engaged in violence. As to the public interest under para. 2(c), the judge was entitled to conclude that the public interest in the conviction of those guilty of serious crimes here required an access order to be made. He had taken into account the applicant's arguments that allowing access would compromise the impartially of the press and increase the risk of injury to photographers, but had concluded: (1) that the former was not undermined, given that the press would not be handing over the material voluntarily but only in response to a court order; and (2) that any risk of injury to a photographer would arise from the attackers' wish not to appear on the transmitted part of the news rather than the untransmitted part.[1] R. Stone comments:

> 'Once the police have established that there are reasonable grounds for believing that serious arrestable offences have occurred, and that the material they are seeking is likely to be relevant evidence, it is difficult to imagine circumstances where the court is going to be prepared to refuse access.'

This balance must be struck by consideration of all the issues, not just legal privilege. A circuit judge hearing a s. 9 application should consider whether there should be an inter partes application for a production order: *R v Lewes Crown Court, ex p Weller*.[2] On the special problems of cases with legal privilege, see also *Kopp v Switzerland*.[2a]

Less protection is afforded to special procedure material and journalist's material than legally privileged material, but the courts claim that they will still require strong evidence before issuing an order. In *R v Central Criminal Court, ex p Bright*[3] the Divisional Court quashed a series of orders made against the Guardian and Observer newspapers requiring them to produce material relating to David Shayler, who was alleged to have committed offences under the Official Secrets Act 1989. The material included his email address and other letters and correspondence with the papers. The court stressed that the judge had to be satisfied that the statutory requirements had been established. The judge was not simply asking himself whether the decisions of

20 [1995] 1 Cr App Rep 431, CA.
21 (1999) 12 May, unreported, DC.
22 (1986) 85 Cr App Rep 190.
23 Para 2(a)(iii), (iv).
 1 See R. T. H. Stone, [1988] Crim LR 498, 500–501.
 2 (1999) 12 May, unreported, DC.
2a (1997) 24 EHRR 523.
 3 [2001] 2 All ER 244, DC.

the constable making the applications were reasonable. If the judge was satisfied that the access conditions existed, he was not bound to make the order, he had a discretion to refuse. The judge could take account of factors such as the impact on third parties, the antiquity of matters, the potentially nominal sentence that might be passed, the potential stifling of public debate and the risk of requiring a person to incriminate himself. However, the result is still that s. 9 allows for the production order even though it might involve an infringement of the privilege against self-incrimination.

See also *R v Central Criminal Court, ex p Carr*[4] and *R v Crown Court at Maidstone, ex p Waitt*,[5] and also discussed by Stone,[6] *R v Crown Court at Lewes, ex p Hill*;[7] *R v Crown Court at Leeds, ex p Switalski*;[8] *R v Central Criminal Court, ex p Hutchinson*;[9] *R v Crown Court at Northampton, ex p DPP*;[10] *R v Liverpool Crown Court, ex p George Wimpey plc*;[11] *R v Acton Crown Court, ex p Layton*.[12] In *ex p Waitt*, Macpherson J stated that Sch. 1 constitutes;

> 'a serious inroad upon the liberty of the subject. The responsibility for ensuring that the procedure is not abused lies with circuit judges. It is of cardinal importance that circuit judges should be scrupulous in discharging that responsibility.'

R. Costigan,[12a] argues that the judiciary have failed to provide adequate protection for journalist material, particularly film footage. The 'pragmatic judiciary has exploited the vague formulation of the special procedure in PACE ... to drive a coach and horses through the intended safeguards for journalists material in pursuit of crime control.'[12b]

In *R v Southwark Crown Court, ex p Sorksy-Defries*,[13] a warrant to search offices of a firm of accountants for material relating to money laundering was set aside because the Divisional Court was not satisfied that the judge issuing the warrant had satisfied himself (in a hearing lasting 15 minutes) that the material was of substantial value.

The House of Lords has held that s. 9(2) does not preclude the endorsement in England and Wales of a warrant issued in Scotland, where a TV company had guaranteed anonymity to a prisoner filmed about HIV, but the Scottish police suspected that he might be guilty of offences in that jurisdiction.[14] The Criminal Justice and Police Act 2001 amends PACE so that search warrants and production orders in respect of special procedure material can be endorsed for execution in Scotland. Part X of the Criminal Justice and Police Act 1994 deals with the enforcement of arrest warrants across UK jurisdictions. Section 86 of the 2001 Act amends PACE so that s. 4 of the Summary Jurisdiction (Process) Act 1881 applies to orders and warrants for special procedure and excluded material.[14a]

---

4 (1987) Independent, 5 March.
5 [1988] Crim LR 384, (1988) Times, 4 January.
6 Op. cit.
7 (1990) 93 Cr App Rep 60.
8 [1991] Crim LR 559.
9 [1996] COD 14.
10 (1991) 93 Cr App Rep 376.
11 [1991] Crim LR 635.
12 [1993] Crim LR 458.
12a [1996] Crim LR 231.
12b p. 232.
13 [1996] Crim LR 195. See on this E. Franey (1999) 149 NLJ 855.
14 *R v Manchester Stipendiary Magistrate, ex p Granada TV* [2000] 2 WLR 1, HL. For a full discussion of the many issues arising from the increasingly common phenomenon of UK forces encroaching into each other's jurisdiction, and the difficulties that causes, see C. Walker [1997] CLJ 114.
14a See also HO Circular 31/2001.

On s. 8, see *R v Billericay Justices and Dobbyn, ex p Frank Harris (Coaches) Ltd*,[15] where the Divisional Court held that, unlike the position under s. 9, it was not a condition precedent to the granting of a warrant that other methods had been tried without success or would be bound to fail.

6. Hospital records of patients' admission to and discharge from a mental hospital are 'personal records' within PACE, s. 12, as they are records 'relating to' their mental health: *R v Crown Court at Cardiff, ex p Kellam.*[16]

7. By s. 10(2), 'items held with the intention of furthering a criminal purpose are not items subject to legal privilege'. In *R v Central Criminal Court, ex p Francis & Francis*,[17] the House of Lords held by three to two (Lords Brandon, Griffiths and Goff, Lords Bridge and Oliver dissenting) that this exception (applied by the Drug Trafficking Offences Act 1986, s. 129(2)) takes effect even where the intention is that of a third party, and is not shared by either the solicitor holding the items in question or his client. Thus, production was ordered of documents held by solicitors relating to property transactions suspected to have been used by a relative of the client as a means of laundering the proceeds of drug trafficking. The majority argued that a construction that limited s. 10(2) to cases where the holder was party to the intention would lead to absurd consequences; as cases of solicitors having such an intention were 'happily rare' this 'would do little to assist' in achieving the purpose of Part II of PACE.[18] The minority argued, with some force, that the majority's interpretation could not be the grammatical meaning of the words actually used by Parliament. Does the privilege arise in such cases or is there an exception to the privilege? See the comprehensive discussion by J. Auburn,[19] concluding that the 'scope of the crime-fraud rule under section 10(2) of the Act is apparently not contiguous with the scope of the professional relationship'.[20]

An item is covered by legal professional privilege if it is a communication made in connection with the giving of advice; records of conveyancing transactions are themselves, accordingly, not privileged, although correspondence containing advice relating to such transactions would be: *R v Crown Court at Inner London Sessions, ex p Baines & Baines.*[1] See also *R v Guildhall Magistrates' Court, ex p Primlaks Holdings Co (Panama) Inc;*[2] but cf. the Court of Appeal recognising a solicitor's right to reveal fraudulent information to the possible victim of the fraud in *Finers v Miro.*[3] In *R v R*,[4] it was held that a blood sample provided by the defendant to his doctor at the request of his solicitors for the purposes of his defence was an item subject to legal privilege. In *R v Manchester Crown Court, ex p R*,[5] the police were granted an order to recover appointment records from a solicitor's office when investing a claim that a murder suspect, R, had visited the offices after the stabbing had taken place. The Divisional Court held that legal professional privilege only applies to communications made for the purpose of seeking and receiving legal advice. This purpose was to be determined by consideration of the function and nature of the documents in question. A record of the time of an appointment or fee record was not a communication concerned with obtaining legal advice.

15 [1991] Crim LR 472.
16 (1993) 16 BMLR 76, DC.
17 [1989] AC 346.
18 Per Lord Brandon at p. 381.
19 *Legal Professional Privilege: Law and Theory* (2000), Chap. 8.
20 p. 166.
 1 [1988] QB 579.
 2 [1990] 1 QB 261.
 3 (1990) 150 NLJ 1387.
 4 [1994] 1 WLR 758, CA (Cr D).
 5 [1999] 1 WLR 832, CA (Cr D).

In *R v Cottrill*,[6] it was held that no legal privilege attached to a defendant's written statement to his solicitor, voluntarily handed over to the prosecution.

An item not protected by legal professional privilege as a result of s. 10(2) (and so not immune from seizure) its nevertheless likely to be special procedure material, and so only obtainable via s. 9 and Sch. 1: *ex p Primlaks*.[7] However, forged material can neither be covered by legal privilege nor acquired or created in the course of the profession of a solicitor so as to be special procedure material: *R v Leeds Magistrates' Court, ex p Dumbleton*.[8] One issue that has created difficulty for the courts is the relationship between s. 8 and the power to seize items that might be legally privileged. Section 8 provides that the magistrates, before issuing a warrant, must be satisfied that the material to be searched for 'does not consist of or include items subject to legal privilege, excluded material or special procedure material.' (s. 8(1)(d)). Search warrants for such material are to be sought under s. 9. Research in the ten years since PACE has shown that searches on a magistrate's warrant have declined although entry, search and seizure powers are frequently used.[8a]

The question arose whether, when exercising a warrant under s. 8, an officer who discovers material that might be privileged has power to search or seize it. In *R v Chief Constable of Warwickshire, ex p Fitzpatrick*,[9] police acting under a warrant issued under s. 8 found that the amount of material at the premises was so great that they sealed it and removed it elsewhere to be searched. The warrant was challenged for being too wide. The Divisional Court held that, when executing a warrant under s. 8, the material seized must be something for which the search had been authorised. The officer conducting the search *must himself be satisfied* of the criteria in s. 8. Why should the officers' beliefs as to the search at the time of execution affect the legitimacy of the warrant lawfully issued by a magistrate? The relationship between the authority to search under s. 8 and the breadth of the power to seize under s. 19 also remained unclear. The matter came under closer scrutiny in the Divisional Court in *R v Chesterfield Justices, ex p Bramley*,[10] where the Divisional Court cast doubt on *Fitzpatrick*. It was accepted by all members of the court that the officer is entitled under s. 19 to seize material that he believes not to be legally privileged provided the other (broad) criteria of that section are satisfied. The Courts disagreed on the scope of seizure under s. 8(2). Should the officer executing the warrant have to be satisfied at the time of execution of the conditions in s. 8(1) before he may seize material under s. 8(2)?[11] Jowitt J preferred his own reasoning in *R v Chief Constable of Warwickshire, ex p Fitzpatrick* that the officer must, at the time of the execution of the warrant, be satisfied of the conditions necessary to cause a warrant to issue. Since any officer lawfully on the premises will be able to seize (under s. 19) material that he reasonably believes not to be legally privileged and should have a defence to an action for trespass, does it matter? Jowitt J poses the hypothetical scenario where, prior to a warrant being executed, it became obvious that the material listed for search was no longer relevant. Is it not the case that such a search would be unlawful because the officer would no longer be complying with the requirement in s. 16(8) that the search is for the purpose for which the warrant was issued? Is there a need to consider s. 8 at all?

6 [1997] Crim LR 56, CA.
7 [1990] 1 QB 261.
8 [1993] Crim LR 866.
8a D. Brown, *PACE Ten Years On: A Review of Research* (1997) HORS No. 49.
9 [1998] Crim LR 290, DC.
10 [2000] 1 All ER 411, DC.
11 See further commentary at [2000] Crim LR 385.

Under s. 19 the requirement is that the officer has no reasonable belief as to the privileged status of the items, and this renders the debate as to the belief under s. 8 unnecessary. In another recent case the Divisional Court held that if in the course of a legitimate search of a solicitor's office, particularly where the solicitor himself was alleged to be complicit in the offence being investigated, the officers inadvertently seized material which included items subject to legal privilege, the seizure of those items could not render the execution of the warrant unlawful: *R v H M Customs and Excise, ex p Popely.* [12] See also the decision in *R v Inland Revenue Commissioners, ex p Tamosius & Partners (a firm),* [13] dealing with a search and seizure under the Taxes Management Act 1970, s. 20C. There are important differences between the Taxes Management Act 1970 and comparable provisions in PACE, with the Taxes Management Act providing an absolute prohibition on the seizure of legally privileged material. Thus, even if the officer (perhaps on the advice of independently appointed counsel) has reasonable grounds to believe that the items are not legally privileged, there will be no defence to an action for trespass to goods if, once seized, they turn out to be so privileged. This is much stricter than the comparable provision of PACE (s. 19(6)). [14]

8. *Sifting legally privileged material.* There is a great practical difficulty that was obviously not foreseen by Parliament regarding the need for disputed material to be taken and scrutinised later. Section 15(5) provides that a warrant authorises only one entry, so that in a case with a large amount of material to search, unless the search is to be regarded as continuous over a number of days, the inability to remove material presents a real problem. Is it possible to remove such material under s. 19? The practical solution to this problem was to require that the disputed material is sealed prior to its being sifted, that sifting occurs in the presence of the suspect's legal advisor as soon as is practicable and that material is returned to the suspect as soon as possible. Additional safeguards could require the initial on-site sifting to be by a legal advisor and the later sifting to be by an independently appointed legal advisor. In *ex p Popely* the court acknowledged that the system devised by Customs and Excise of applying to the Attorney-General to nominate a member of the Bar to sift through the documents seized before a decision was made as to which should be retained, was a scheme which protected the solicitor concerned and Customs and Excise and substantially reduced the area of dispute.

The court in *ex p Popely* also held that the erroneous removal of legally privileged material will not render the whole search unlawful, thereby limiting the effect of s. 16(8) to the purpose of the search and not to matters of seizure (cf. *R v Chief Constable of Warwickshire, ex p Fitzpatrick*). [15]

Further problems of legally privileged material being seized have arisen where prisoners' cells have been searched and material relating to their pending appeals has been seized. In *R v Secretary of State for the Home Department, ex p Allan,* [16] the court considered that the use of independent counsel to sift through material to determine whether it was privileged provided a good solution to the problem. The House of

---

12 [2000] Crim LR 388, DC.
13 [2000] Crim LR 390, DC.
14 On the IRC powers of search and seizure, see J. Walters, [1998] BTR 213; S Matheson, [1998] BTR 278; B. Brown, [1999] BTR 16.
15 [1998] Crim LR 290, DC.
16 [1998] 2 All ER 491, CA.

Lords in *R (on the application of Daly) v Secretary of State for the Home Department*[17] recognised that it would be necessary on some occasions for prison officers to do more than examine a prisoner's legal documents. The House also recognised that this was bound to inhibit a prisoner's willingness to communicate freely with his legal adviser. Holding that there was no doubt that the policy infringed a prisoner's common law right to legal professional privilege, the House identified the key issue as whether there was justification for the infringement. One of the justifications for private searches was that the prison service alleged that there was intimidation and disruption from prisoners during a cell search. The House of Lords held that that was not sufficient for the implementation of a blanket policy. Section 47(1) of the Prison Rules Act 1952 did not provide authorisation for such excessive intrusion. Where a prisoner attempted to disrupt a cell search or their past conduct showed that they were likely to do so then that prisoner could properly be excluded whilst his cell was searched. That included the searching of his privileged correspondence. However, there was no justification for routinely excluding all prisoners whilst their privileged correspondence was searched. The infringement of prisoner's rights to maintain the confidentiality of their privileged legal correspondence was of greater significance than the legitimate objectives of excluding them from the cell.

9. *New Powers.* The Criminal Justice and Police Act 2001 contains provisions designed to resolve many of these difficulties, by providing the power to remove material to be examined elsewhere, and by allowing for the removal of intrinsically linked material (e.g. on a computer hard disk) some of which may be legally privileged.[18] Under s. 52, there is a requirement to give the occupier and/or some other person or persons from whom material has been seized under the new powers in s. 50 (property) or s. 51 (personal search) a notice specifying what has been seized and the grounds on which it has been seized. The information must include the notification of a right to apply to a judge for the return of seized material and an explanation of how to apply to be present at any examination of the material seized. Section 53 prescribes how the examination of the property seized under ss. 50 and 51 should take place and what material can be retained. Subsection (4) gives the occupier or some other person with an interest in the property an opportunity to be present at the examination. Under s. 54 specific protection is provided to legally privileged material which, under ss. 50 and 51 can be seized. Officers are obliged to return such material if seized, but sub-ss. (2) and (3) provide that legally privileged material can be retained if it is inextricably linked to other seizable material. This remedies the practical difficulty from cases like *ex p Bramley*, but does it provide sufficient protection for the legally privileged material?

Section 55 relates to special procedure and excluded material as defined in PACE. It aims to provide protections similar to those in PACE but does not apply where the underlying power of seizure is found in legislation where such protection is not afforded, e.g. the Financial Services and Markets Act 2000 or the Criminal Justice Act 1987. Section 56 sets out circumstances in which seized property may be retained. It parallels s. 19 of PACE and ensures that where a constable has been involved in the seizure of material under s. 50 or s. 51 it is possible to retain evidence of any offence or property obtained in consequence of the commission of an offence if it is necessary to do so to stop it being destroyed etc, even if it is not material originally being searched for.

Section 59 deals with applications to 'appropriate judicial authority' by those with a relevant interest in the seized property. The right to apply to the appropriate

17 [2001] 2 WLR 1622, HL, see above, p. 58.
18 See ss. 50–70.

judicial authority (as defined in s. 64) will provide the mechanism for challenging the use of the ss. 50 and 51 powers. The court, on a successful application can order the return of material or, *inter alia*, order that it be examined by an independent third party. Section 60 imposes a duty to secure the material seized pending the hearing of that application. There will be a New Code of Practice and Crown Court Rules providing guidance on the powers procedures linked to their application.

10. *Other statutory seizure powers.* Many such powers exist, for example, ss. 143 and 144 of the Powers of Criminal Courts (Sentencing) Act 2000 formerly, under s. 43 of the Powers of Criminal Courts Act 1973, to confiscate property lawfully seized or in the offender's possession when he was apprehended which was used for the purpose of committing, or facilitating the commission of, any offence or was intended to be used for that purpose; or the offence, or an offence which the court has taken into consideration in determining his sentence, consists of unlawful possession of property which has been lawfully seized from him or was in his possession when he was apprehended. Sections 2–10 of the Drug Trafficking Act 1994 provide complex powers to seize property, the essence is for confiscation orders in conjunction with the sentencing process of those who have been convicted of drug trafficking offences. Section 71 of the Criminal Justice Act 1988 contains similar confiscation provisions for offenders convicted of relevant offences other than specifically drug trafficking offences. There are various statutory provisions for the forfeiture and disposal of objects used in the perpetration of offences, such as firearms, offensive weapons, knives, drugs etc.[19]

11. *Specific powers to obtain search warrants.* There are many specific powers whereby a court, judge or magistrate may issue a search warrant in respect of an offence. They have different limitations as to the geographical area for which a warrant may be granted, the persons who may execute the warrant, and the items which may be seized. The safeguards and other provisions relating to execution contained in ss. 15 and 16 are applicable to all these powers, thus removing some of these variations.[20] Examples include the following:

Theft Act 1968

26. (1) If it is made to appear by information on oath before a justice of the peace that there is reasonable cause to believe that any person has in his custody or possession or on his premises any stolen goods, the justice may grant a warrant to search for and seize the same; but no warrant to search for stolen goods shall be addressed to a person other than a constable except under the authority of an enactment expressly so providing…

(3) Where under this section a person is authorised to search premises for stolen goods, he may enter and search the premises accordingly, and may seize any goods he believes to be stolen goods.

Subsection (3) goes beyond the *ratio* of *Chic Fashions (West Wales) Ltd v Jones*.[1] It is not clear whether it is an exhaustive statement of the items that may be seized under a warrant in addition to those specified in it. At common law a constable executing a warrant to search for stolen goods[2] could seize items 'likely to furnish evidence of the identity of the specified stolen goods as well as goods ' reasonably believed' to be those specified in the warrant.[3]

19　Section 52 of the Firearms Act 1968; s. 1(2) of the Prevention of Crime Act 1953; s. 6 of the Knives Act 1997; and s. 27 of the Misuse of Drugs Act 1971. Section 6 of the Criminal Justice Act 1972 provides for the making of restitution orders for the purpose of s. 28 of the Theft Act 1968 out of money taken from the offender on his apprehension.
20　See generally, D. Feldman, *The Law Relating to Entry, Search and Seizure* (1986); R. T. H. Stone, *Entry, Search and Seizure: A Guide to Civil and Criminal Powers of Entry.*
1　Above p. 86–87.
2　*Crozier v Cundey* (1827) 6 B & C 232.
3　*Chic Fashions*, above, pp. 86–87.

Section 26 is not limited to a power to search for a...
their rightful owner; it includes a general power to search ...
identified in the warrant or not: *R v Chief Constable of Ke...*

Misuse of Drugs Act 1971

23. Powers to search and obtain evidence

(1) A constable or other person authorised in that behalf by a general or ...
Secretary of State…shall, for the purposes of the execution of this Act, ha   ...er
the premises of a person carrying on business as a producer or supplier of c...   ... drugs
and to demand the production of, and to inspect, any books or documents relati.. ... to dealings
in any such drugs and to inspect any stocks of any such drugs.

(2) [Given above at p. 212]

(3) If a justice of the peace… is satisfied by information on oath that there is reasonable ground
for suspecting–

> (*a*) that any controlled drugs are, in contravention of this Act or of any regulations made
> there under, in the possession of a person on any premises; or
>
> (*b*) that a document directly or indirectly relating to, or connected with, a transaction or
> dealing which was, or an intended transaction or dealing which would if carried out
> be, an offence under this Act, or in the case of a transaction or dealing carried out or
> intended to be carried out in a place outside the United Kingdom, an offence against
> the provision of a corresponding law in force in that place, is in the possession of a
> person on any premises.

he may grant a warrant authorising any constable acting for the police area in which the premises
are situated at anytime or times within one month from the date of the warrant, to enter, if need
be by force, the premises named in the warrant, and to search the premises and any persons
found therein and, if there is reasonable ground for suspecting that an offence under this Act has
been committed in relation to any controlled drugs found on the premises or in the possession
of any such person, or that a document so found is such a document as is mentioned in paragraph
(b) above, to seize and detain those drugs on that document, as the case may be…[4a]

Note that sub-s. (3) expressly empowers a justice to issue a warrant authorising
the search of *persons* found on the premises specified. In *King v R*[5] the Privy Council
held that the search of persons by virtue of a warrant granted under similar Jamaican
legislation was not lawful unless the *warrant* expressly authorised such a search.
Not all search warrant provisions refer expressly to authority to search persons. Is it
proper to assume that these different formulations have been adopted deliberately
by Parliament, so as to deny the police power to search persons under a warrant unless
both the relevant statutory provisions and the warrant expressly authorise such search?
If a search warrant is secured for one purpose, when in reality it is for a different
purpose, (warrant purportedly for a drugs search under Misuse of Drugs Act 1971,
s. 23 but really for pirated software), the search will be unlawful and the court may
exclude the evidence under s. 78 if to admit it would render the proceedings unfair:
R v Rotherham Magistrates, ex p Todd.[6]

12. *The role of magistrates*. The assumption behind the requirement that warrants
must in many cases be obtained from a magistrate is that this operates as a safeguard.
In February 1968 four police officers went to the home of Lady Diana Copper and
executed a warrant to search for drugs. The police had acted on an anonymous
telephone call. The matter was raised in Parliament.[7] The Under Secretary of State

---

4   (2001) 19 February, CA (Civ D), unreported.
4a J. Corkery, HO Statistical Bulletin, 5/01, *Drug Seizure and Offender Statistics* (2001),
5   [1969] 1 AC 304.
6   (2000) 16 February, DC, unreported.
7   760 HC Deb, 7 March 1968, cols. 826–836.

...ne Department, Mr Dick Taverne, acknowledged that a serious mistake ...een made in relying on the anonymous call. There should have been an attempt o find corroborative evidence.

Following this case guidance was issued as set out in para. 40 of the *Home Office Evidence to the Royal Commission on Criminal Procedure, Memorandum, No. III*:

'40. The decision whether or not to issue a search warrant is a matter for the magistrate concerned. The Lord Chancellor has advised those responsible for the training of Justices of the Peace that:

a. it is the duty of a magistrate before issuing a warrant to satisfy himself that it is in all the circumstances right to issue the warrant;

b. a magistrate may question the person swearing the information to this end; and

c. although a police officer who applies for a warrant should not be expected to identify his informant, the magistrate may wish to know whether the informant is known to the officer, and whether it has been possible to make further enquiries to verify the information and, if so, with what result.

Chief officers of police have been informed that this advice has been given..'

A survey conducted by the Centre for Criminological and Socio-Legal Studies at the University of Sheffield indicated that 'magistrates are not at present the safeguard which constitutional theory supposes them to be'.[8] Only rarely was any solid information supplied by the police, and it did not seem that questioning by magistrates was at all intensive. Most seemed unwilling to go behind assertions on oath by police officers that they had reasonable grounds for suspicion 'as a result of information from a source which is reliable.' Lidstone[9] suggested that this could 'be changed by better training and the provisions of the Police and Criminal Evidence Bill could ensure that fuller information is provided.' Evidence from a later study by the same author 'suggests that this formula continues to be used, though less frequently, and that magistrates are no more questioning now than they were before the Act.'[10] Technical failings in the issue of a warrant are unlikely to render it invalid: *A-G of Jamaica v Williams*[11] (magistrate failing to specify precise section under which warrant issued). Magistrates are not obliged to engage in a specific inquiry into the issue of legal privilege in every case; only where there is some suggestion that such material might be involved: *R v Plymouth Magistrates, ex p Reuter*.[12]

13. The execution of warrants: PACE Code requirements. The *Code of Practice for the Searching of Premises by Police Officers and the Seizure of Property found by Police Officers on Persons or Premises*[13] applies to (a) searches of premises for the purposes of a criminal investigation, with the occupier's consent, other than routine scenes of crime searches and searches following the activation of fire or burglar alarms or calls to a fire or a burglary made on behalf of an occupier or bomb threat calls or searches under B. 44 (below); (b) searches under ss. 17, 18 and 32 of PACE; searches of premises by virtue of a warrant issued under s. 15 or Sch. 1 of PACE or under the Terrorism Act 2000 (see below pp. 614–618). Code B applies in relation to searches

---

8 K. Lidstone, 'Magistrates, Police and Search Warrants' [1984] Crim LR 449.
9 p. 457.
10 Lidstone, (1989) 40 NILQ 333, 351, n. 55.
11 [1998] AC 351.
12 (1997) 4 July, DC, unreported.
13 PACE Code B; Revised Edition, 1995.

falling within the scope of para. 1.3; it does not apply to searches conducted under other statutory powers, e.g. the Food and Safety Act 1990.[14]

Code B supplements the requirements of PACE in a number of respects. Thus, before applying for a warrant or production order, the officer must take reasonable steps to check his information is accurate, recent and has not been provided maliciously or irresponsibly; and an application may not be made on the basis of information from an anonymous source where corroboration has not been sought;[15] he must ascertain as specifically as is possible in the circumstances the nature and location of the articles concerned;[16] he must make reasonable inquiries about the likely occupier of the premises, and their nature, and whether they have been previously searched;[17] no application for a search warrant may be made without the authority of an officer of at least the rank of inspector (or, in cases of urgency where no inspector is readily available, the senior officer on duty), or, in the case of a production order or warrant under Sch. 1 to PACE, an officer of at least the rank of superintendent;[18] and, except in cases of urgency, the local police/community liaison officer must be consulted before a search if there is reason to believe that it might have an adverse effect on police/community relations.[19] If an application is refused, no further application may be made unless supported by additional grounds.[1]

If it is proposed to search premises with consent, that consent must be given in writing (on the Notice of Powers and Rights see below) before the search takes place; then the officer must make inquiries to satisfy himself that the person is in a position to give that consent;[2] and before seeking that consent, the officer in charge of the search must state its purpose, and inform the person concerned that he is not obliged to consent, that anything seized may be produced in evidence and, if it is so, that he is not suspected of an offence.[3] In *R v Barker*,[4] the court held that acquiescence by an occupier to a search which was in breach of Code B.4.2 should be sufficient to render the evidence discovered admissible. The court was persuaded that there was nothing to show that the occupier would have refused if B.4.2 had been complied with. An officer cannot enter and search, or continue to search premises by consent if the consent is given under duress or is withdrawn before the search is completed.[5] Consent need not be sought if this would cause disproportionate inconvenience to the person concerned (e.g. a brief check of gardens along the route of a pursuit).[6]

Where an entry is made without consent, the officer must first attempt to communicate with the occupier, or any other person entitled to grant access, unless (i) the premises are known to be unoccupied, (ii) the occupier etc. is known to be absent, or (iii) there are reasonable grounds for believing that to alert him would frustrate the object of the search or endanger the officers concerned or other people.[7] Where the premises are occupied, before the search begins the officer must identify himself, if not in uniform show his warrant card, and state the purpose of the search

---

14 See *Walkers Snack Foods Ltd v Coventry City Council* [1998] 3 All ER 163 DC; cf. *Dudley Metropolitan Borough Council v Debenhams plc* (1994) Times, 16 August.
15 Code B.2.1.
16 Code B.2.2.
17 Code B.2.3.
18 Code B.2.4.
19 Code B.2.5.
 1 Code B.2.8.
 2 Code B.4.1.
 3 Code B.4.2.
 4 (1996) 13 June, CA (Cr D), unreported.
 5 Code B.4.3.
 6 Code B.4.4. and 4C.
 7 Code B.5.4.

and the grounds for undertaking it (unless (iii) above applies).[8] See *O' Loughlin v Chief Constable of Essex*[9] discussed below.

The officer must, unless it is impracticable, provide the occupier with a Notice of Powers and Rights, (i) specifying whether the search is made under a warrant, or with consent or under ss. 17, 18 or 32 of PACE; (ii) summarising the extent of the powers of search and seizure under the Act; (iii) explaining the rights of the occupier and the owner of property seized; (iv) explaining that compensation maybe payable for damage; (v) stating that a copy of the Code is available at any police station.[10] If the occupier is present, copies of the Notice and the warrant (if any) should if practicable be given to him before the search starts, unless the officer in charge reasonably believes that this would frustrate the object of the search or endanger the officers concerned or other people. If he is not present, copies of the Notice and warrant (where appropriate) should be left in a prominent place on the premises and endorsed with the name of the officer in charge, his police station and the date and time of the search.[11] An inadvertent failure to leave a copy of the search warrant at the premises as required by s. 16(7) would be unlikely to render the search invalid *ab initio*: *Fisher v Chief Constable of Cumbria.*[12]

As to the conduct of searches, premises may be searched only to the extent necessary to achieve the object of the search, having regard to the size and nature of whatever is sought; a search under warrant may not continue under the authority of the warrant once all the things specified in it have been found, or the officer in charge is satisfied they are not there.[12a] Searches must be conducted with due consideration for the occupier's property and privacy, and with no more disturbance than necessary.[13] If the occupier wishes to ask a friend, neighbour or other person to witness the search he must be allowed to do, unless the officer in charge has reasonable grounds for believing that this would seriously hinder the investigation; a search need not be unreasonably delayed for this purpose.[14] Premises entered by force must be left secure.[15]

A full record must be kept of searches[16] and a search register must be maintained at each sub-divisional police station with copies of all records required by Code B.[17] In *Linehan v DPP,*[18] the Divisional Court held that the same requirements were applicable when entry was being effected under s. 18(4). Officers refused to slide a warrant under the door and the occupier refused to view the warrant pressed to the window. The officers failed to explain the reason for the search. However, record keeping under s. 18(7) is to be regarded as a directory rather than a mandatory requirement. Non-compliance will not invalidate a search: *Krohn v DPP.*[19] Is this decision now out of line with recent pronouncements in which the procedural and record keeping elements of PACE are emphasised: (*Linehan,*[20] *O'Loughlin,*[1] and *Osman*)?[2]

Under s. 18(1) the premises must be controlled by a person under arrest. There is no clear judicial guidance as to what degree of control is necessary.

---

8 Code B.5.5.
9 [1998] 1 WLR 374.
10 Code B.5.7.
11 Code B.5.8.
12 (1997) 29 July, CA (Civ D), unreported, *obiter dictum* of Roch LJ.
12a Code B.5.9.
13 Code B.5.10.
14 Code B.5.11.
15 Code B.5.12.
16 Code B.7.
17 Code B.5.8.
18 [2000] Crim LR 685.
19 [1997] COD 345, DC. Cf. the requirement in s. 18(4), which is mandatory.
20 [2000] Crim LR 685.
1 [1998] 1 WLR 374.
2 Above, p. 216.

14. In *R v Longman*[3] the Court of Appeal held that s. 16(5) was not to be interpreted as requiring the preliminaries set out in paras. (a) to (c) to be observed before *entry* to the premises; it was sufficient that this be done before the *search* begins, as set out in Code B. 5. 5.[4] The case concerned the execution of a warrant to enter and search L's premises for drugs. It was not the first time that the premises had been the subject of such a search and the police knew that there would almost certainly be great difficulty in effecting an entry. On this occasion, warnings were shouted as soon as the police entered. The court noted that a requirement that the preliminaries be observed before entry would stultify 'the whole object of the more important type of search operation',[5] particularly in drugs cases 'because unless the officers move very quickly indeed, by the time they have reached the back of the premises the offending drugs will be flushed down the lavatory pan...'[6] Other points made by the court were (1) that the police were entitled to subterfuge as an alternative to force (here, a police woman in plain clothes pretending to be delivering flowers from Interflora); and (2) that for a warrant to be 'produced' in accordance with s. 16(5)(b), it must be made available for inspection by and not merely shown to the occupier.

In *Heagren v Chief Constable of Norfolk*,[7] Kennedy LJ held that it was not necessary under s. 16(9) for an officer to give a copy of the warrant at the start of the search only to seek its return at the end. His Lordship commented that 'when Code B is next revised consideration should perhaps be given to the wording of paragraph 5.8.'

In *R v Chief Constable of Lancashire, ex p Parker*,[8] the Divisional Court held that entry, search and seizure purportedly authorised by warrants issued under s. 9 of and Sch. 1 to PACE were unlawful. The occupier was shown the original warrant, but only uncertified copies of schedules that had to be read in conjunction with the warrants to comply with s. 15(6)[9] and copies of the warrants only were left with the occupier.[10] The phrase in s. 15(1):

'an entry on or search of premises under a warrant is unlawful unless it complies with this section and s. 16 below.'

is ambiguous (to what is 'it' meant to refer?). However, this case makes it clear that breaches of s. 16 will render the execution of a warrant unlawful by virtue of s. 15(1).

Evidence of an armoury of weapons and drug paraphernalia was not to be excluded at his trial for drugs offences when D's property was searched when he was under arrest for a non-payment of a council tax bill. The Court of Appeal acknowledged that the officers had not acted within the 'spirit' of s. 16 and Code B.5.4 when they took the opportunity to search in D's absence when he was arrested under the warrant for the totally different offence: *R v Dennis*.[11]

The execution of search warrants cannot lawfully be delegated to other persons: see *R v Reading Justices, Chief Constable of Avon and Somerset and Intervention Board for Agricultural Produce, ex p South West Meat Ltd*,[12] where the Divisional

3 [1988] 1 WLR 619.
4 Under the revised Code B.5.5 even this is subject to the provision in Code B.5.4.(iii) (above, n. 8).
5 p. 153.
6 p. 153.
7 (1997) 8 July, CA (Civ D), unreported.
8 [1993] QB 577.
9 A breach of s. 16(5)(b).
10 A breach of s. 16(5)(c).
11 (2000) 13 April, CA (Civ D), unreported.
12 [1992] Crim LR 672.

Court granted declarations and awarded £25,000 damages in respect of a search under a warrant issued under PACE, s. 8, that was, *inter alia*, too general in its terms, where the search was conducted by Board Officials rather than the police; and the material was then retained unlawfully by the Board, the statutory power of retention being with the police. The presence of a film crew when a search warrant was being exercised was deplored but did not invalidate the warrant in *R v Marylebone Magistrates' Court & MPC, ex p Amdrell Ltd trading as Get Stuffed*.[13] In *ex p Get Stuffed*, the magistrate had not been informed of the involvement of the film crew when issuing the warrant. The Divisional Court emphasised that the operation of the execution of the search warrant was a matter for the police, not the magistrates, but a briefing to the magistrates of the media involvement would have been highly desirable.[14]

15. In *R v Atkinson*,[15] the Court of Appeal held that a warrant obtained under s. 23(3) for the search of 'Flat 45' in certain premises could not justify the search of Flat 30, even though the police bona fide believed that A's flat was Flat 45. However, misspellings or trivial errors in the description of premises would not necessarily invalidate a warrant. There has long been concern over searches of multiple occupancy premises. The Divisional Court in *R v South Western Magistrates' Court, ex p Coife*,[16] confirmed that where the officer wishes to search a part of the building which is divided into separate dwellings, or to search the communal areas (as in that case) this must be clearly specified in the warrant application.[17]

16. *Seizure.* The RCCP recommended that the ambit of the power of seizure under a warrant should extend to items which could be the subject of a warrant: i.e. on their recommendation, goods whose possession is an offence and material relating to 'grave offences'. The Act is wider in this respect (see ss. 19, 20). Sections 8(2) and 18(2), however, authorise the seizure of goods 'reasonably believed' to be the goods specified in the warrant. Should the courts permit a similar extension here, or should any seizure not justified by ss. 8(2) or 18(2) have to be justified under s. 19? Material unlawfully seized may not be retained under s. 22: *R v Chief Constable of Lancashire, ex p Parker.*[18]

Police owe a duty to the owner of seized property to take reasonable care to prevent damage during its retention: *Sutcliffe v Chief Constable of West Yorkshire*.[19]

It has been held that the police have powers under ss. 18 and 19 to seize the premises themselves where they are mobile. In *Cowan v Metropolitan Police Comr*,[20] a search of the suspect's premises was undertaken in respect of allegations of serious sexual abuse of children. It was believed that the suspect's car might yield vital forensic evidence. The police seized the vehicle. Under s. 23 of PACE, a vehicle is defined as being premises. The court held that the power to seize 'anything' which is on the premises included a power to seize the premises where movable. See also the statements of Lord Denning MR in *Ghani v Jones*,[21] recognising such a right at common law. Consider the implications for caravan dwellers and New Age travellers. On the potential challenges under protocol 1 of the ECHR compare *Hopping v Customs and Excise Comrs*.[1]

13 (1998) 162 JP 719, DC.
14 See the discussion by A. Lee, (1999) 10(1) Entertainment Law Rev 8.
15 [1976] Crim LR 307.
16 [1997] 1 WLR 885.
17 See also the difficulties under s. 8 of the Misuse of Drugs Act 1971, where questions might turn on the degree of control over the premises exercised by the occupant.
18 [1993] QB 577.
19 (1995) 159 JP 770, CA.
20 [2000] 1 WLR 254, CA (Civ D).
21 [1970] 1 QB 693.
 1 (2001) 9 October.

The Divisional Court has held that Leicester Square is not 'premises' for the purposes of the Act (attempt to seize busker's equipment with warrant drafted in terms of premises of Leicester Square).[2]

In *R v Chief Constable of Warwickshire, ex p Fitzpatrick*,[3] it was confirmed that the warrant under s. 8 and 15 must be drafted in terms of the premises not the material belonging to a named person.

17. *Retention.* In *Marcel v Metropolitan Police Comr*,[4] discussing the constraints placed on prosecuting authorities as to their use of material seized. Dillon LJ[5] stated that:

'Parliament should not be taken to have authorised use of seized documents for any purpose the police think fit.... Police are authorised to seize , retain and use documents only for public purposes related to the investigation and prosecution of crime and the return of stolen property to the true owner.'

In *Webb v Chief Constable of Merseyside*[6] the Court of Appeal held that the police were not entitled to retain monies that they had seized from W when they were arresting him on drugs charges (of which he was later acquitted). The police power to seize the moneys was beyond question, but once the police power to hold them for the purposes of the trial had come to an end, W had a better claim than the police. 'In the absence of any evidence that anybody else is the true owner, once the police right of retention comes to an end, the person from whom they were compulsory taken is entitled to possession.' This was so even though the police had been able to establish, on the balance of probabilities, that the money was from drug dealing. There was no public policy exception of illegality except where the material was itself illegal (e.g. drugs themselves or obscene books), in which case the police did not have to return them. The contention that the Chief Constable was entitled to retain the money until the true owner was found was 'fanciful'.[7]

Webb was followed in *Costello v Chief Constable of Derbyshire Constabulary*,[8] where it was held that the police must return to the claimant a car that was quite clearly stolen. The claimant had better title to the car than the police, and the owner (who had better title still) was unknown (the car had been 'ringed'). Why was *Webb* not distinguishable on the basis that the person who paid the money in that case intended to pass full possessory rights to the claimant? In *Costello* the car owner had no intention to pass any rights to the thief. See also *Verrechia v Metropolitan Police Comr*[8a] and *Customs and Excise Commissioners v Ghiselli*,[9] in which it was emphasised that in such cases it was still necessary for the claimant to prove title to the goods.

Challenges to the legality of seizure should be made in course of private law when seeking appropriate remedy rather than in judicial review: *R v Chief Constable of Warwickshire, ex p Fitzpatrick*.[10]

18. *Entry.* For entry to premises to be justified by reference to s. 17(1)(b), the police officer entering must have reasonable grounds to suspect the person sought to be guilty of the offence in question; the provision cannot justify entry to effect an

---

2 *R v Bow Street Magistrates' Court, ex p MacDonald* (1997) unreported, DC.
3 [1999] 1 All ER 65.
4 [1992] Ch 225.
5 At p. 234.
6 [2000] 1 QB 427; above p. 108.
7 See also *Malone v MPC* [1980] QB 49.
8 [2001] EWCA Civ 381, CA (Civ D).
8a (2001) 15 March, CA.
9 (2000) Mr B. Livesy QC.
10 [1999] 1 All ER 65.

unlawful arrest: *Kynaston v DPP*.[11] Here, the justices were held to be entitled to infer that the officers had the necessary reasonable suspicion . The officers knew a robbery had taken place; they desired to arrest one Doyle for it; they had reasonable grounds for believing he was in the premises; they stated when they entered that they wished to arrest him for robbery. 'If that does not raise an inference that they had reasonable grounds for suspecting him of the robbery, I am bound to say I do not know what else it would amount to...That is an inference which could have been rebutted but was not.'[12] Cf. *Chapman v DPP*,[13] where the Divisional Court held that an officer's entry to arrest a person for assault on another police officer could not be justified under s. 17(1)(b). There was no evidence that the arresting officer suspected that his colleague had been injured; assault occasioning actual bodily harm is an arrestable offence but common assault is not. Furthermore, there was no evidence that the arresting officer suspected that there had been an offence of violent disorder contrary to the Public Order Act 1986, s. 2. Whether there was a lawful arrest triggering the s. 18 power will often be critical to the case: see e.g. *Odewale v DPP*[13a] comparing *Kynaston* and *Riley* (inference of lawful arrest not permissible).

For entry to be justified by reference to s. 17(1)(d) ('recapturing a person who is unlawfully at large and whom [the police officer] is pursuing'), there must be 'pursuit': per Lord Lowry in *D'Souza v DPP*.[14]

> 'The verb in the clause 'whom he is pursing' is in the present continuous tense and therefore, give or take a few seconds or minutes – this is a question of degree – the pursuit must be almost contemporaneous with the entry into the premises. There must, I consider, be an act of pursuit, that is a chase, however short in time and distance. It is not enough for the police to form an intention to arrest, which they put into practice by resorting to the premises where they believe that the person whom they seek may be found.'

Accordingly, the House of Lords held that where a person admitted to hospital for psychiatric assessment under the Mental Health Act 1983, s. 2(4) returned home without leave granted under s. 17 of that Act, she was 'unlawfully at large': however, the police who subsequently on the same day went to her home could not justify forcible entry under s. 17(1)(d) as there was no element of 'pursuit'.[15] Note that there are many powers to enter premises granted by statute to public officials such as (to name a few) Customs and Excise officers, Inland Revenue officials, employees of gas and electric companies and trading standards officers.[16] There is no statutory power of entry for search without a warrant in an extradition context: *R v Metropolitan Police Comr, ex p Rottman*.[16a]

Should police officers seeking to exercise a right of entry be required to give reasons, by analogy with *Christie v Leachinsky?*[17] *Swales v Cox*[18] suggested not in respect of the power under the Criminal Law Act 1967, s. 2(6) to enter (if need be by force) to arrest for an arrestable offence. Section 2(6) provided a 'comprehensive code' which provided that the officer 'might enter without qualification but not that he might use force without qualification'.[19] Thus reasons might have to be given to

---

11 (1987) 87 Cr App Rep 200, DC.
12 Per Parker LJ at 206.
13 (1988) 89 Cr App Rep 190.
13a (2000) 28 November, DC.
14 [1992] 4 All ER 545 at 556.
15 For powers to enter premises to deal with or prevent breaches of the peace see below, pp. 548–556.
16 For a list, see RCCP, *Law and Procedure Volume*, Appendix 4.
16a (2001) 24 July, DC.
17 Below, p. 283.
18 [1981] 1 QB 849, DC.
19 Per Donaldson LJ at 854.

justify the use of force, but this would depend on the circumstances: it might be essential for the protection of an officer following a 'very dangerous man' that he should 'give no warning of his approach by asking the leave of the criminal to enter'. This approach was adopted in respect of the similarly worded power of entry under the Road Traffic Act 1988, s. 4(7), in *Lunt v DPP*.[1]

The question has been addressed by the Court of Appeal.

O'Loughlin v Chief Constable of Essex [1998] 1 WLR 374, Court of Appeal

Police attended O's house following a complaint from neighbours that Mrs O had smashed a car windscreen with a cricket bat. The police found O and Mrs O barricading themselves in behind the front door. The officers used force to gain entry and arrest O. The judge ruled that 'unless circumstances made it impossible, impracticable or undesirable, a police officer exercising powers of entry by force, pursuant to section 17 of PACE should first give the occupier the true reason for seeking to enter'. As police had not done so, O's claim for trespass succeeded.

The Court of Appeal (Thorpe LJ dissenting) agreed.

Buxton LJ: [His lordship referred to *Swales v Cox*]. Donaldson LJ did not refer to any authority in formulating the approach that the Divisional Court adopted in *Swales v Cox*, but in my view that approach is fully in line with the general law of police powers. As was made clear in *Christie v Leachinsky* the obligation to inform a citizen why his liberty is being interfered with is not absolute: circumstances may make communication impossible or unnecessary. Subject to that, however, it is a strong obligation, and one that Parliament must be taken to have had in mind when conferring the power on the police that it created in section 2 of the 1967 Act and continued in PACE. The very strong distinction between powers of arrest and powers of questioning recognised in *Rice v Connolly* must also have been in Parliament's mind when creating these powers of entry to effect *arrest*. It is wholly unlikely that Parliament would have thought that those powers could be exercised because of, or be adequately explained to the subject in terms of, a wish to investigate.

The position is no different under PACE. We were shown various sections of the Act where there is an express obligation to communicate, but those tend either to address limited situations, such as the use of search warrants, or to deal with *ex post facto* giving or recording of information, such as recording of reasons for delay in taking a person to the police station, or informing a detained person of the reasons for his detention. It is wholly unlikely that the presence of these sections in PACE indicates any intention on the part of Parliament to alter the implications for forcible entry to arrest contained in section 2 of the 1967 Act when that provision was replaced in substantially the same terms by sections 17 and 117 of PACE.

That is the effect of sections 17 and 117 of PACE is further reinforced by the terms of paragraph 5.4 of the *Code of Practice for Searching of Premises by Police Officers* formulated under PACE, paragraph 5.4 of which states, subject to certain exceptions not at present relevant, that the officer in charge shall first attempt to communicate with the occupier or any other person entitled to grant access to the premises by explaining the authority under which he seeks entry to the premises and ask the occupier to allow him in.

This paragraph strictly speaking did not apply in the present case, because no search was contemplated. It is, however, a strong indication of the importance and relevance of the officer who seeks entry explaining his authority, and certainly explaining the reason why he seeks entry.

I therefore respectfully agree with the burden of Donaldson LJ's judgment that a very important factor in deciding whether the police have proved that use of force to enter was necessary, as section 117 requires, is whether before using force the police have explained the (proper) reason why they require entry, and nonetheless had been refused.

---

1   [1993] COD 430, DC.

[The Chief Constable sought to resist that construction of PACE by relying on the unreported Divisional Court case of *Lunt v DPP* (1993). His lordship referred to that case].

If *Lunt v DPP* addressed the issue now before this court I do not need to say that I would be strongly disposed to follow it, even though it is not, strictly speaking, binding on us. But since the Divisional Court in that case was deprived of considering these issues because of the way in which the argument was presented to them, I cannot find the case of any assistance.

Lunt v DPP was the subject of an abbreviated report at [1993] Crim LR 534, where it attracted the considerable benefit of a note by Professor Sir John Smith. We were not shown that note, but it is of interest to see that in it Professor Smith, without suggesting that the point arose in *Lunt's case* itself, asks should it not be necessary, by analogy with the common law rule regarding arrest laid down in *Christie v Leachinsky* [1947] A.C. 573, for the officer to give reasons? Freedom of the home from invasion is an interest of comparable importance to freedom from arrest and is deserving of a comparable degree of protection.

I respectfully agree. But I go further, by saying that I consider that that important rule of the common law, applying not only to arrest but, as in *Brazil*, to other interferences with liberty, does indeed apply to the exercise of powers under sections 17 and 117 of PACE.

Roch LJ: [agreed with Buxton LJ]

Thorpe LJ: In my judgment, the trial in the court below was most unsatisfactory and resulted in a quite unjust conclusion. The facts of the case were exceptional and neither authority nor evidence compelled the defendant's case on liability to be determined by the judge without the involvement of the jury.

Section 17(1)(b) of the Police and Criminal Evidence Act 1984 allows entry and search. Section 117 permits the officer to use reasonable force, if necessary, in the exercise of the power conferred by section 117. The judgment of Donaldson LJ in the Divisional Court in 1980 suggests that where the issue in any case is 'was the force necessary' the burden of proof is on the officer who resorted to force and that is a very heavy burden: *Swales v Cox* [1981] Q.B. 849 at 855 B–D. Whilst that judgment is upon similar sections of the Criminal Law Act 1967, it obviously commands great respect. Nevertheless, I would not wish to see the severity of the burden exaggerated. It is essentially a burden to prove on the balance of probabilities that the use of force was indeed necessary. Applying the objective test, would the reasonable police constable standing in the defendant's shoes have concluded that the use of force was reasonably necessary? That the test is an objective test is clearly stated in the judgment of Diplock LJ in this court in the case of *Dallison v Caffery* [1965] 1 Q.B. 348 at 371 E–F. Although that statement is upon the exercise of the common law power of arrest, it seems to me equally applicable to the exercise of the statutory power under section 17.

On the question that diverted the judge's attention, namely as to whether the use of force must be preceded by a statement of the reason for requiring entry, I conclude that none of the authorities is directly in point.

Thus I am of the firm opinion that in determining any question as to whether or not the use of force was necessary the court should throughout restrict itself to that issue having established through the medium of the jury the relevant facts and circumstances to enable the issue to be approached and decided. Of course in many cases, the communication between the officer and the householder prior to the use of force will be a highly relevant factor. But in my judgment, it should never be elevated to the extent that it predetermines the essential issue. Even if an explanation was plainly required, in the absence of concession it is always for the jury to determine whether it was given. If the jury determines that it was not then the way is clear for the judge to decide that without it the use of force had not been proved to be necessary.

The relevance of Code 'B' made under the Police and Criminal Evidence Act 1984 was considerably debated in the court below. Section 67(11) of the Police and Criminal Evidence Act 1984 is generously drawn: [his Lordship referred to that section]

NOTES

1. Buxton LJ was unimpressed by the argument that although the police had not announced that they wished to enter to arrest her, the wish to talk to a suspect could 'be elided into a wish to arrest her'.

2. The requirement that entry under s, 18 be authorised in writing is not satisfied by a note in an officer's notebook recording an oral authorisation: an independent document is required: *R v Badham*.[2] A failure to make a record in the custody record will not necessarily lead to the exclusion of evidence from the search: *R v Wright*.[3]
3. *Consensual Searches.* Apart from any right to enter premises conferred by law, a police officer may enter premises with the express or implied permission (or licence') of the owner. This point was raised in the following case.
4. If an occupier is bringing a claim for damages for a wrongful search, it is not legitimate for the police to make an ex parte application for an order that the officer had reasonable grounds to search the premises for a murderer, and to request that that issue be free from challenge by the claimants at trial: *Lamothe v Metropolitan Police Comr.*[4]

Davis v Lisle [1936] 2 KB 434, [1936] 2 All ER 213, 105 LLKB 593, 155 LT 23, 52 TLR 475, 34 LGR 253, Cox CC, King's Bench Divisional Court

Sidney Davis was a member of a firm which occupied a railway arch as a garage. Two police officers entered the garage to make inquiries as to the person responsible for obstructing the highway with a lorry, which had subsequently been moved into the garage. D, using abusive and obscene language, told them to get out. L was in the act of producing his warrant card when D struck him in the chest and stomach with his fist, damaging his tunic. D was convicted by the justices of (1) assaulting a police officer in the execution of his duty contrary to the Metropolitan Police Act 1839, s. 18; n(2) obstructing an officer in the execution of his duty contrary to the Prevention of Crimes Amendment Act 1885, s. 2; and (3) maliciously damaging a serge tunic (by tearing it), to the amount of 7s 6d. D appealed unsuccessfully to quarter sessions, and then appealed to the Divisional Court by way of case stated.

Lord Hewart CJ: The point which is raised here with regard to the appellant's first two convictions is whether the officers were at the material time acting in the execution of their duty. In my opinion they were not, and there are no grounds on which they can be held to have been so acting. The only ground which is put forward in support of the contention that they were so acting seems to me to be quite beside the point. I feel a difficulty in envisaging the legal proposition that because the police officers had witnessed an offence being committed on the highway they were acting in the execution of their duty I entering and remaining on private premises because the offenders then were on those premises. Admittedly, the officers were at liberty to enter his garage to make an inquiry, but quite a different thing to say that they were entitled to remain when, not without emphasis, the appellant had said: 'Get outside. You cannot come here without a search warrant.' From that moment on, while the officers remained where they were, it seems to me that they were trespassers and it is quite clear that the act which the respondent was doing immediately before the assault complained of was tantamount to putting forward a claim as of right to remain where he was. The respondent was in the act of producing his warrant card. That was after the emphatic order to 'get out' had been made. Mr Raphael, with his usual candour, has admitted that, if the finding in the case that the respondent was in the act of producing his warrant card is fairly to be construed as meaning that he was asserting his right to remain on the premises, it is not possible to contend that at that moment the respondent was acting in the execution of his duty. I think it is quite clear that the act of producing his warrant card constituted the making of such a claim, I cannot think that there is any ambiguity about it...

In my opinion, it is not possible to maintain the conclusion that at the material time the respondent was acting in the execution of his duty as a constable. But that conclusion by no means disposes of everything contained in this case. It does not dispose of the question whether the assault which was in fact committed was justified. We have not the materials

2 [1997] Crim LR 202 (Wood Green Crown Court).
3 [1994] Crim LR 55, CA (Cr D).
4 (1999) 25 October, CA (Civ D).

before us which would enable us to determine that question. Nor was the appellant prosecuted for assault. He was prosecuted for assaulting and obstructing a police officer in the execution of his duty. Furthermore, the conclusion to which I have come does not affect the third conviction – that of damaging a tunic by 'wilfully and maliciously tearing' it. On that part of the case no question arises whether at that moment the officer was acting in the execution of his duty and I see no reason why we should interfere with that conviction...
Du Parq and Goddard JJ delivered concurring judgments.

Appeal allowed as to first two convictions.

NOTES

1. The officers in this case were not entering in order to prevent crime, but to investigate.[5]
2. In this case, the officers asserted a right to remain. Otherwise, persons requested to leave must be given reasonable time to depart. In *Robson v Hallett*,[6] a police sergeant was told to leave a private house where he was making inquiries. He at once turned and walked towards the front door but was then jumped on. Two constables went to his aid from the front path. The Divisional Court held that the sergeant had not become a trespasser the instant he was told to depart. Lord Parker CH stated:[7]

'When a licence is revoked as a result of which something has to be done by the licensee, a reasonable time must be implied in which he can do so, in this case to get off the premises; no doubt it will be a very short time, but he was doing here his best to leave the premises.'

The constables were lawfully in the front garden, as they, like any other members of the public, had implied leave and licence to walk up to the front door, and that implied licence had never been revoked.[8] They were acting in the execution of their duty in assisting the sergeant and avoiding any further breach of the peace. Lord Parker stated[9] that 'even if they had been outside the gate, it seems to me that they would have abundant right to come onto private property in those circumstances'. Diplock LJ said of the constables[10] that:

'once a breach of the peace was taking place under their eyes, they had not only an independent right but a duty to go and stop it, and it matters not from that moment onwards whether they started off on their journey to stop it from outside the premises...or...inside...'

Another example of a premature attack is *Kay v Hibbert*.[11]
   Robson v Hallett was distinguished by Eichelbaum J in the New Zealand High Court in *Edwards v A-G*,[12] where a traffic officer pursued a speeding motor cyclist, E, who returned to his friend's house, where he was staying, and drove into the garage. The officer followed E into the driveway, pushed the door up again and entered the garage. There he noticed that E had been drinking and subsequently arrested him under the drink/drive legislation. In proceedings by E for wrongful arrest, the judge held that the common law licence normally implied to permit a person to enter an unlocked gate and proceed to the door in order to make an inquiry did not extend to pursuit by a traffic officer of a suspected offender into a house or garage, or authorise

5 Cf. *Thomas v Sawkins*, below, pp. 548–550.
6 [1967] 2 QB 939 and see below, p. 938.
7 At 952–953.
8 See below, p. 256.
9 Obiter at 953.
10 At 954.
11 [1977] Crim LR 226, DC.
12 [1986] 2 NZLR 232.

forcible entry; the situation went beyond that of 'a driver, who seeking to elude a traffic officer, dodges onto the nearest private land' where an implied licence might arise. Then in *Howden v Ministry of Transport*[13] the New Zealand Court of Appeal held that it would not be reasonable to hold that an occupier gives any implied licence to police or traffic officers to enter:

'for random checking of a driver whose driving or other prior behaviour has given no cause for suspicion.'[14]

Bisson J also noted[15] that the implied licence recognised in *Robson v Hallet*: 'may only be exercised at a time of the day or night when it is reasonable for the lawful business to be conducted. In this case it was 1.30 in the morning which would not have been a reasonable hour to knock on the door for some lawful purpose not of an urgent nature...'

3. In *McArdle v Wallace*[16] a police constable entered a yard to inquire about some property in an adjourning passageway. The occupier's son told him to leave, and struck him when he did not. The magistrates found as a fact that the son had the implied authority of the father to ask the constable to leave. The Divisional Court held that the son was rightly acquitted of the charge of assaulting a police officer in the execution of his duty[17] albeit the constable did not know of the implied authority.

4. In *Jones and Jones v Lloyd*,[18] one Leach was seen by police officers attempting to open a car. He admitted that he was not the owner, and said that the owner was at a party in one of the houses in the street. Inspector Lloyd asked to be taken to see her. Leach invited the officer into the house. One of the guests told them to leave, but the officers, having satisfied themselves that she was not the owner of the house, ignored her. The officers satisfied themselves about Leach's possession of the car keys, and were leaving when they were assaulted by two guests at the party. The Divisional Court held that where a guest leaves a party and then gets into difficulty, any host would be 'presumed to have authorised the guests to bring the police back into the house in order to clear his name. The officers were, accordingly, not trespassers. S. H. Bailey and D. J. Birch commented:[19]

'This seems to be a broad view of the scope of the implied licence doctrine, but in any event it is arguable that the fact of trespass vis-à-vis the owner of the house should not affect the position vis-à-vis guests, [Cf. below, p. 153] unless, presumably, they are acting on behalf of the owner in ejecting officers who are in fact trespassers. It should be noted here that it did not appear that the owner of the house either knew of or objected to the officers' presence.'

5. In *R v Thornley*,[20] the Court of Appeal held that a licence to enter premises given by a wife in the course of a domestic dispute could not be revoked by the husband who had been the subject of a complaint to the police. It was accepted that the judge had been right to direct the jury that when the officers entered the house they were not trespassers because they had been invited to enter by the wife 'who was co-occupier'.

6. In *Riley v DPP*,[1] the Divisional Court held that police officers were lawfully on premises, when permitted to enter by the owner's son, and subsequently met by the

---

13 [1987] 2 NZLR 747.
14 Per Cooke P at 751.
15 At 754.
16 (1964) 108 Sol Jo 483, DC.
17 See above, p. 156.
18 [1981] Crim LR 340, DC.
19 [1982] Crim LR at 478.
20 (1980) 72 Cr App Rep 302, [1981] Crim LR 637.
 1 (1989) 91 Cr App Rep 14.

owner, who raised no objection to their presence. Moreover, s. 17 of PACE did not set out a complete code for entry by police officers, it only applied where entry was without the occupier's consent.[2]

7. A trespassing officer may not validly require a person to take a breath test: *Morris v Beardmore*.[3] Accordingly a number of cases have turned on whether the officer was a trespasser. It has been held that whether the words 'fuck off' used by the owner of the house constitute revocation of the implied licence to be in the driveway or mere vulgar abuse is a question of fact for the justices: *Snook v Mannion*,[4] *Gilham v Breidenbach*,[5] (both cases decided adversely to the defendant). (Quaere 'fuck off out of it'?). Moreover, in *Snook v Mannion*, it was not sufficient simply that the officer was aware that his presence on the driveway or his request for the owner to take a breath test was contrary to the owner's wishes; such a position would be 'unworkable'. Cf. *Pamplin v Faser*[6] (no revocation of implied licence where D merely wound up the window of his car and locked the doors while remaining inside). In *Faulkner v Willetts*,[7] D's wife opened the front door to a constable. He explained that he wished to interview D in connection with a road accident. She walked back into the house giving him the impression that it was an implied invitation to enter. No indication was subsequently given refusing him entry or requiring him to leave; indeed he was offered a cup of coffee. The court held the justices were entitled to conclude that this constituted implied permission to enter.

6 Surveillance

In addition to the more obvious forms of surveillance which are relied on by the police with increasing regularity (e.g. CCTV footage[8]) the police rely on more sophisticated devices and techniques. Until recently the only detailed regulation of intrusive surveillance was under the Interception of Communications Act 1985, and the Home Office guidelines which regulated other surveillance techniques.[9] The Regulation of Investigatory Powers Act 2000 provides a comprehensive new code dealing with surveillance. Its provisions are extremely complex, and are considered below.

(A) CCTV CAMERAS

The use of CCTV surveillance equipment in public places was recognised by *Liberty*, to give:

'rise to a complex balance between the rights of data subjects who are engaged in private activities (e.g. shopping) albeit in public spaces and the rights of data controllers whose surveillance is directed at one or more aspects of the public interest which may well include the preservation of certain rights (e.g. safety) of the data subjects themselves.

Liberty does not accept that [the police] should remain outside the scope of any relevant Code of Practice. Indeed there may well be a pressing need for such agencies to develop codes of practice governing specialised investigations and/or surveillance in particular.'[10]

---

2 *See O'Loughlin v Chief Constable of Essex* [1998] 1 WLR 374.
3 Below, p. 362.
4 [1982] RTR 321.
5 [1982] RTR 328n.
6 [1981] RTR 494, DC.
7 [1982] RTR 159, [1982] Crim LR 543, DC.
8 On which see D. Rogers, (1996) Police Review, 5 July p. 26; P. Edwards (1997) The Magistrate, April p. 64; J. Wadham, (2000) 150 NLJ 1173, 1236.
9 See below, Chap. 9 on privacy, p. 1020.
10 See the *Submission by Liberty to the Data Protection Registrar's consultation on the draft Code of Practice for CCTV* (2000).

The use of CCTV is regulated by the Data Protection Act 1998 and the Code of Practice for users of Close Circuit Television published by the Data Protection Commissioner. The Act covers all forms of CCTV except those for purely private use in personal, family or household affairs.

A new Code of Practice (Code of Practice for Users of CCTV) governing the use of CCTV cameras is extremely limited in effect, since it does not apply to the police and other security services.[10a] Liberty observed that:

'It is no substitute for such regulations and we are concerned that it will have little effect on the kind of abuse detailed so clearly in "The Maximum Surveillance Society: The Rise of CCTV", Clive Norris and Gary Armstrong, 1999. In addition, the absence of proper regulation and the interference with privacy created by CCTV may well violate the right to privacy which will be part of domestic law once the Human Rights Act comes into force in October 2000.'

Since the evidence generated by CCTV is likely to be very cogent and reliable, there is a strong incentive to admit it at trial, with the dangers of privacy infringements, although obvious, being unlikely to lead to exclusion. For example, the courts have accepted evidence of covertly filmed footage of the suspect used for identification purposes, in breach of Code D: *R v Perry*.[11] There is no rule of public policy that surveillance by video cannot be used at trial: *R v Wright*.[12]

(B) COVERT SURVEILLANCE

In the last few years a number of legislative reforms have been introduced. These have been prompted by the incorporation of the Human Rights Act 1998, and the increasing use of covert policing techniques. Under Art. 8, secret surveillance must be prescribed by law, necessary, and proportionate: *Kopp v Switzerland*;[13] *Klass v Germany*.[14] The ECHR and covert surveillance are reviewed by S. Uglow in *The Human Rights Act 1998: Part 4: Covert Surveillance And The European Convention On Human Rights*:[15]

'From the creation of the CID in the Metropolitan force in 1877, undercover work has been a normal part of policing. Over the past decades, however, the means available to the police for covert operations have become more specialised and technical with computer databases, electronic location monitoring, video and audio monitoring. New technologies have enhanced the ability not only to track people through their computerised record trail, which has become part of daily life, but also to see through walls, overhear conversations, and track movement. We are too familiar with advanced microphones and Circuit Television Cameras (CCTV) but there are other, more esoteric, examples of surveillance technology:
- BT have a system which can switch on the phone in your house in order to listen to any conversations in the vicinity.
- massive millimetre wave detectors use a form of radar to scan beneath clothing. By monitoring the millimetre wave portion of the electromagnetic spectrum emitted by the human body, the system can detect items such as guns and drugs from a range of 12 feet or more. It can also look through building walls and detect activity.
- Van Eck Monitoring works on the basis that every computer emits low levels of electromagnetic radiation from the monitor, processor, and attached devices. Although experts disagree whether the actual range is only a few yards or up to a mile, these signals can be remotely recreated on another computer. Aided by a transmitting device

10a Op. cit., n. 10.
11 (2000) 28 April, CA (Cr D), unreported.
12 (2001) 14 June, CA (Cr D), unreported.
13 (1998) 27 EHRR 91.
14 (1978) 2 EHRR 24.
15 [1999] Crim LR 287, pp. 287–294. See also the recent decision in *Amann v Switzerland* (2000) 30 EHRR 843, which seems to adopt a strict approach.

to enhance the signals, in the United States the FBI reportedly used Van Eck Monitoring to extract information from spy Aldrich Ames' computer and relay it for analysis.
- tracking devices of all kinds including cellular phones which transmit location information to the home system to determine call routing. These can also be used for automated tracking of the caller's movements. In 1993, fugitive Colombian drug kingpin Pablo Escobar was pinpointed through his cellular phone. Currently there is an effort to develop a system that would give location information for every cellular phone.

Such examples reveal that governments have at their disposal the capacity to make social control more penetrative and intrusive. The lesson of history is that governments are likely to use this armoury. As the means by which an individual's privacy can be invaded develop, it becomes of greater importance to define positively what our legitimate expectations of privacy may be. Yet these cannot be unfettered rights. Organised terrorism, trafficking in drugs and money laundering are real and present dangers for any society. Nor should the violent husband be allowed to rely on the privacy of the home to assault his wife or children. There is thus a public policy dilemma as we seek a balance between the public interest in the prevention of crime and the need for constraints on state power to intrude into individual life. Increasingly the courts will be required to balance the concerns about crime alongside the need to reinforce the values that are expressed in international documents such as the European Convention on Human Rights.

This dilemma is of particular importance in criminal investigation, which inevitably involves violation of fundamental rights, especially of the liberty of the person, of privacy and to a fair trial. But such rights are not absolute and the European Court has consistently stated that they must be weighed against the restrictions imposed on those rights to protect other members of society, especially where the police are investigating serious offences posing a danger for society…

But the European Court adopts the approach that procedural standards should be complied with and, in a recent report, JUSTICE summarises those as comprising:
- legality—that the possibility of such interference is clearly laid out in law, readily accessible and precise so that citizens are aware of the circumstances under which surveillance may be undertaken or communications intercepted. It should go without saying that legality requires that the grounds for surveillance should be subject to prior judicial scrutiny
- necessity—the interference should be necessary because less intrusive means have been tried and failed or are inappropriate and the operation is likely to produce valuable material which would aid the investigation
- proportionality—the intrusive measures should be proportional to the seriousness of the offence, bearing in mind the rights not only of the individual but also those of others likely to be affected
- accountability—there must be proper controls and adequate and effective remedies against abuse

Surveillance—the European Court
When considering covert police operations, Convention caselaw also reveals greater willingness to impose constraints upon the state either on the basis that the use of evidence gathered surreptitiously is in breach of the applicant's right to a fair trial under Article 6(1) or alternatively in violation of the applicant's right to privacy under Article 8. Examining Article 8, it is clear that the right to privacy is not absolute. The Convention lays down the conditions under which the state can depart from it—under Article 8(2) the state has the right to derogate from "respect for the right to a private life" in the interests of public safety, to prevent disorder or crime, or to protect health or morals. In Klass v. Germany the Court acknowledged the significance of the technical advances made in surveillance as well as the development of terrorism, and recognised that the state must be entitled to counter terrorism with secret surveillance of mail, post and telecommunications. But such measures must be taken in exceptional circumstances and the state does not have the right to adopt whatever measures it thinks appropriate in the name of counteracting espionage, terrorism or serious crime.'

In The House of Lords in *Khan v UK*,[16] Lord Nicholls expressed 'astonishment' that there was then no statutory regulation of the use of devices such as that used in the

16 [1997] AC 558, discussed below.

case to listen to conversations of K via a bugging device covertly fitted to an associate's house (the police committing a trespass, criminal damage and breaching Art. 8 of the ECHR in the process),[17] rendering English law incompatible with Art. 8.

R v Khan (Sultan) [1997] AC 558, [1996] 3 All ER 289, [1996] 3 WLR 162, House of Lords

Lord Nolan: The focal point of the appellant's case was the fact that there is no legal framework regulating the installation and use by the police of covert listening devices. This is in contrast to the use of such devices by the Security Service, which has been regulated by statute since 1989 under the Security Service Act of that year.

That is a matter to which I shall return. It should not be assumed, however, that the use by the police of such devices is wholly arbitrary and undisciplined. They are the subject of guidelines which were issued to police authorities by the Home Office in 1984, entitled 'Guidelines on the use of Equipment in Police Surveillance Operations.' They are also dealt with in standing orders issued by the South Yorkshire Police, but it is unnecessary to refer to these since they do not differ materially from the Home Office guidelines.

The guidelines amount to a detailed and comprehensive code restricting the authorised use of the devices in question. For present purposes it is, I think, sufficient to quote paragraphs 4, 5 and 6 which read as follows:

'4. In each case in which the covert use of a listening device is requested the authorising officer should satisfy himself that the following criteria are met: (*a*) the investigation concerns serious crime; (*b*) normal methods of investigation must have been tried and failed, or must, from the nature of things, be unlikely to succeed if tried; (*c*) their equipment would be likely to lead to an arrest and a conviction, or where appropriate, to the prevention of acts of terrorism; (*d*) use of equipment must be operationally feasible.

5. In judging how far the seriousness of the crime under investigation justifies the use of particular surveillance techniques, authorising officers should satisfy themselves that the degree of intrusion into the privacy of those affected by the surveillance is commensurate with the seriousness of the offence. Where the targets of surveillance might reasonably assume a high degree of privacy, for instance in their homes, listening devices should be used only for the investigation of major organised conspiracies and of other particularly serious offences, especially crimes of violence.

6. The covert use in operations of listening, recording and transmitting equipment (for example microphones, tape recorders and tracking equipment) requires the personal authority of the chief officer.'

In certain circumstances, which do not exist in the present case, this authority may be delegated to an assistant chief constable. As appears from the facts found by the judge, after the hearing on the voire dire, the installation of the listening device in Mr. Bashforth's premises was authorised by the Chief Constable of South Yorkshire on the grounds that there was good reason to suppose that Mr. Bashforth was dealing in heroin, but that conventional methods of surveillance were unlikely to provide proof that he was doing so. No suggestion was made in your Lordships' House that the South Yorkshire Police had operated otherwise than in accordance with the Home Office guidelines.

Even so, it was argued for the appellant, the evidence was unacceptable in principle and should not be admitted. Private conversations on private property of a kind which could not be overheard save by means of listening devices should be inviolate save where intrusion upon them was authorised by law. The procedure adopted in the present case should not be accepted as a means of obtaining evidence, the more so in a case, such as the present, where it involved trespass and, at least arguably, criminal damage to property.

Mr. Muller, representing the appellant, likened the case of a private conversation conducted in a private house to that of a private telephone conversation by means of the public telecommunications system. The interception of the latter was strictly regulated by the provisions of the Interception of Communications Act 1985. This Act had been passed as a result of the decision of the European Court of Human Rights in *Malone v. United Kingdom* (1984)

17 See *Khan v UK* [2000] Crim LR 684.

7 E.H.R.R. 14. In that case, the applicant's telephone calls and correspondence had been intercepted by the police. The interception had been carried out pursuant to a warrant issued by the Home Secretary, but there was no authority in statute or common law for such a warrant. The applicant had brought civil proceedings against the police in the High Court, but without success. Megarry J. concluded, after an extensive review of the authorities, that the applicant had no right of action against the police under English law: *Malone v. Metropolitan Police Commissioner* [1979] Ch. 344. In the course of his judgment, Megarry J. commented, at p. 380E–H, that telephone tapping was a subject which cried out for legislation, and that the requirements of the European Convention for the Protection of Human Rights and Fundamental Freedoms should provide a spur to action.

These comments were resoundingly echoed by the European Court of Human Rights. The court held that the tapping of the applicant's telephone amounted to a breach of his rights under article 8 of the Convention. That article provides as follows:

'1. Everyone has the right to respect for his private and family life, his home and his correspondence.

2. There shall be no interference by a public authority with the exercise of this right except such as is in accordance with the law and is necessary in a democratic society in the interests of national security, public safety or the economic well being of the country, for the prevention of disorder or crime, for the protection of health or morals, or for the protection of the rights and freedoms of others.'

The court held, at pp. 39–40, para. 66, that article 8.2 imposed requirements over and above compliance with the domestic law. These included the requirement that the law must be adequately accessible. The court added, at pp. 40–41, para. 67:

'the law must be sufficiently clear in its terms to give citizens an adequate indication as to the circumstances in which and the conditions on which public authorities are empowered to resort to the secret and potentially dangerous interference with the right to respect for private life and correspondence.'

Mr. Muller contended that in the present case there had been interception which was not in accordance with the law and further that there had been a breach of the requirement of accessibility to information about the conditions in which it took place. The Home Office circular was placed in the library of the House of Commons, but knowledge of its terms was not available to the general public.

Reverting to the Interception of Communications Act 1985, Mr. Muller pointed out that the use in evidence of material obtained by the interception of communications was expressly forbidden by section 9. He added that there had evidently been a similar restriction on material obtained by the use of surveillance devices in the years prior to 1984. He referred us in this connection to a Home Office letter dated 1 July 1977, addressed to chief constables, which appears to have been the precursor to the 1984 guidelines, and which stated that 'the primary purpose of using equipment for aural or visual surveillance should be to help confirm or dispel a suspicion of serious crime, and not to collect evidence (except where, as in blackmail, the spoken word is the kernel of the offence).' This is to be contrasted with the opening sentence of paragraph 10 of the 1984 guidelines which reads:

'It is accepted that there may be circumstances in which material obtained through the use of equipment by the police for surveillance as a necessary part of a criminal investigation could appropriately be used in evidence at subsequent court proceedings.'

In *Reg. v. Preston* [1994] 2 A.C. 130, 148 Lord Mustill, referring to paragraph 10, had said that this departure from previous practice was itself contradicted a few weeks later by the Home Office White Paper, The Interception of Communications in the United Kingdom (1985) (Cmnd. 9438) designed to lay the ground for the Bill which became the Interception of Communications Act 1985. Paragraph 12(*f*) of the White Paper had stated:

'The Bill will provide for controls over the use of intercepted material. By making such material generally inadmissible in legal proceedings it will ensure that interception can be used only as an aspect of investigation, not of prosecution.'

It is true that the Home Office guidelines were concerned with aural and visual surveillance devices whereas the Act of 1985 is concerned with telephone tapping and the interception of postal communications, but it is difficult to see why different rules should apply to the admissibility of evidence gained from these sources. The difficulty is compounded by the provisions of the Intelligence Services Act 1994 which govern the activities of the Secret Intelligence Service, the Government Communications Headquarters and the Security Service. One of the effects of section 2(2)(*a*) and section 5(4) of the Act is that information obtained by the Secret Intelligence Service or the Security Service through the use of listening devices may be disclosed not only for the purpose of preventing or detecting serious crime but also for the purpose of any criminal proceedings.

Finally, Mr. Muller turned to the decision of your Lordships' House in *Reg. v. Sang* [1980] A.C. 402. That decision is, of course, authority for the proposition that a judge has no discretion to refuse to admit relevant evidence on the ground that it was obtained by improper or unfair means. Lord Diplock said, at p. 437:

'(1) A trial judge in a criminal trial has always a discretion to refuse to admit evidence if in his opinion its prejudicial effect outweighs its probative value. (2) Save with regard to admissions and confessions and generally with regard to evidence obtained from the accused after commission of the offence, he has no discretion to refuse to admit relevant admissible evidence on the ground that it was obtained by improper or unfair means. The court is not concerned with how it was obtained.'

As to this, Mr. Muller submitted first that the general rule in *Sang* did not apply to the evidence with which the present case was concerned because that evidence fell within the category of admissions, confessions, and other evidence obtained from the accused after commission of the offence. In my judgment, this submission has no force. It is clear from an earlier passage in the speech of Lord Diplock, at p. 436, that the exceptional category which he had in mind consisted of:

'evidence tantamount to a self-incriminatory admission which was obtained from the defendant, after the offence had been committed, by means which would justify a judge in excluding an actual confession which had the like self-incriminating effect.'

He continued:

'My Lords, I propose to exclude, as the certified question does, detailed consideration of the role of the trial judge in relation to confessions and evidence obtained from the defendant after commission of the offence that is tantamount to a confession. It has a long history dating back to the days before the existence of a disciplined police force, when a prisoner on a charge of felony could not be represented by counsel and was not entitled to give evidence in his own defence either to deny that he had made the confession, which was generally oral, or to deny that its contents were true. The underlying rationale of this branch of the criminal law, though it may originally have been based upon ensuring the reliability of confessions is, in my view, now to be found in the maxim nemo debet prodere se ipsum, no one can be required to be his own betrayer or in its popular English mistranslation "the right to silence." That is why there is no discretion to exclude evidence discovered as the result of an illegal search but there is discretion to exclude evidence which the accused has been induced to produce voluntarily if the method of inducement was unfair.'

In the present case, I would regard it as a misuse of language to describe the appellant as having been 'induced' to make the admissions which were recorded on the tape. He was under no inducement to do so. But if this be too narrow a view, the only result would be to bring into play the judge's discretion as to whether or not the evidence should in fairness be admitted. It would not make the evidence intrinsically inadmissible. *Breach of Art. 8 of the Convention found.*

NOTES

1. Part III of the Police Act 1997 was a direct response to this judgment.[18] The scope of that Part of the Act is very limited. It does not attempt to provide a comprehensive

18 In addition, there are developments governing surveillance in the Security Services Act 1989 and the Intelligence Services Act 1994. See P. Carter, (1997) 113 LQR 468 on *Khan* and the 1997 Act.

Code, but merely to regulate surveillance involving entry on/interference with property, and to establish a Commission to regulate such matters. As the Bill passed through Parliament, there were many calls for an independent judicial body to authorise all covert surveillance. The resulting provisions represent a compromise whereby all authorisations are reviewed by an independent commission, but some of those reviews are conducted *after* the authorisation has been given by senior police officers. Is this a sufficient safeguard? See further Emerson and Ashworth.[19]

2. By s. 92: 'No entry on or interference with property or with wireless telegraphy shall be unlawful if it is authorised by an authorisation having effect under this Part.' The Act therefore provides immunity from civil and criminal liability for those acting under its terms. The Act does not affect the interception of post or public telecommunications which were then regulated by the Interception of Communication Act 1985, and are now regulated by the Regulation of Investigatory Powers Act 2000. The relationship between the Interception of Communications Act 1985 and the Police Act 1997 were spelt out in the Notes for Guidance in the Code of Practice issued under the Police Act, s. 101(3):

> '1A The question will frequently arise whether a surveillance device may legitimately be used in circumstances where the incidental effect will be to enable the overhearing of what is said by a party to a telephone conversation who is speaking from a location where a device is installed. The use of a surveillance device should *not* be ruled out simply because it may incidentally pick up one end of a telephone conversation. However, its use would not be appropriate where its purpose is to overhear speech which is being transmitted by a public telecommunications system. In such cases an application must be made for a warrant under the [Interception of Communications Act 1985] …'[20]

3. In the case of a non-sensitive surveillance (i.e. not relating to a dwelling, office, hotel bedroom or likely to involve confidential material), the 'authorising officer' (i.e. chief constable, Metropolitan Police Commissioner or Assistant Metropolitan Police Commissioner, Director Generals of NCIS and NCS etc.), or if that is not reasonably practicable a 'designated deputy' (assistant chief constable etc.) may issue an authorisation. The authorising officer must believe: that the investigation concerns serious crime as defined in the Act; that the action proposed is necessary because it is likely to be of substantial value in the prevention or detection of serious crime; and that the action seeks to achieve cannot reasonably be achieved by other means. 'Serious crime' is defined as conduct which constitutes one or more offences if, and only if: it involves the use of violence, results in substantial financial gain or is conduct by a large number of persons in pursuit of a common purpose, or the offence or one of the offences is an offence for which a person who has attained the age of 21 and has no previous convictions could reasonably be expected to be sentenced to imprisonment for a term of three years or more. In deciding whether to grant authorisation, the degree of intrusion into the privacy of those affected must be balanced against the gravity of the offence. Special care should be taken where religious ministers, medical or professional counsellors or therapists are involved. Similarly regard should be had to collateral intrusion into persons not suspected. Once the authorisation has been given, it must be reported to the Commissioners for scrutiny.

4. Cases of sensitivity must receive *prior* approval of the commissioner. This must occur in cases where:

> 'any of the property specified in the authorisation: is used wholly or mainly as a dwelling or as a bedroom in a hotel; or constitutes office premises; or the action authorised is likely to

19 Op. cit., paras. 7–22.
20 See now RIPA 2000.

result in any person acquiring knowledge of: matters subject to legal privilege; confidential personal information; or confidential journalistic material.'

Legal privilege is broadly defined as in PACE, s. 10. Confidential personal information:

'is information held in confidence concerning an individual (whether living or dead) who can be identified from it, and relating: (a) to his/her physical or mental health; or (b) to spiritual counselling or other assistance given or to be given; and which a person has acquired or created in the course of any trade, business, profession or other occupation, or for the purposes of any paid or unpaid office. It includes both oral and written information and also communications as a result of which personal information is acquired or created.'

Under the 1997 Act, information is held in confidence if: it is held subject to an express or implied undertaking to hold it in confidence; or it is subject to a restriction on disclosure or an obligation of secrecy contained in existing or future legislation.[1] Confidential journalistic material includes 'material acquired or created for the purposes of journalism and held subject to an undertaking to hold it in confidence, as well as communications resulting in information being acquired for the purposes of journalism and held subject to such an undertaking'.[2] In exceptional cases of urgency, an authorisation which should require prior approval can be given by the authorisating officer, but the Commissioner's approval must then be sought.

Applications should specify:

'the identity or identities of those to be targeted (where known); the property which the intrusive surveillance will affect; the identity of individuals and/or categories of people, where known, who are likely to be affected by collateral surveillance; details of the offence planned or committed; and of the intrusive surveillance involved; how the authorisation criteria have been met; any action which may be necessary to retrieve any equipment used in the surveillance. in case of a renewal, the results obtained so far, or a full explanation of the failure to obtain any results; and subsequently record whether authority was given or refused, by whom and the time and date.'[3]

The Commissioner must scrutinise the applications and authorisations given by officers 'as soon as is reasonably practicable'. The Commissioner notifies the authorising officer if valid or notifies the applicant whether the authorisation is given accordingly. Compare this with the procedure for searches involving protected material, as discussed above.

5. There are provisions governing the recording and reporting of authorisations, and regulating the renewal and cancellation of authorisations. They are normally of three months duration. The authorisation record should always record 'every occasion when interference with property or wireless telegraphy has occurred; the result of periodic reviews of the authorisation; and the date of every renewal'.[4] To meet the requirements of independent regulation for the process, the Act creates a complaints and appeals procedure. These are dealt with by the Chief Commissioner, who is also responsible for reviewing the performance and functions of commissioners and making an annual report to the Prime Minister on the discharge of functions of the commission. Is it appropriate to report to the PM?

6. In many ways, Pt III of the Police Act 1997 was a very short-sighted piece of legislation since it failed to deal with many types of surveillance that are claimed to be vital in the fight against crime; most notably those relating to access of electronic communication. This raises broader questions regarding the appropriate policing of

1 Code of Practice (2000), paras. 1.10, 2.10.
2 Code of Practice (2000), para. 2.11.
3 Para. 2.15.
4 Para. 2.32.

the Internet. The growth of 'cybercrime', coupled with the fact that ordinary forms of criminal activity can be facilitated by Internet use (especially fraud, counterfeiting etc.), means that this is area is in need of comprehensive review. See D. S. Wall,[5] for a discussion of cybercrimes (cybertrespass, cybertheft, cyberobscenity and cyberviolence) and the current methods of regulation and policing of the Internet, although his conclusion is that we need to adapt existing forms of policing rather than invent new ones. The police face an overwhelming task in seeking to regulate e-crime, which is sophisticated, technical and cross-jurisdictional.

(C) REGULATION OF INVESTIGATORY POWERS ACT 2000[6]

The latest step towards a comprehensive code of policing and surveillance, including surveillance of Internet data, is the Regulation of Investigatory Powers Act 2000, which is a more controversial piece of legislation. In a letter defending the Regulation of Investigatory Powers Bill against widespread criticism, the then Home Secretary, Jack Straw, wrote to the *Daily Telegraph*:[7]

'This is not *1984*. It is 2000 and we need to update vital law enforcement powers for the digital age. But we also need to ensure that we protect individuals' legitimate rights and not over-burden industry. The Regulation of Investigatory Powers Bill strikes this balance.'

The Bill was described as a snooper's charter, and was criticised for the costs it would impose on industry for them to be able to comply. The Home Office published a series of information sheets explaining and justifying the Bill,[8] and set aside £20m for compensation where necessary for the [Internet Service Providers] ISPs. Reference was made to the many countries (selected perhaps because they are perceived to be 'liberal') in which similar legislation already exists – Sweden, Holland, Canada, Australia, USA, France and Germany.

The 2000 Act seeks to regulate surveillance of the types of communication not dealt with in the Police Act 1997: pagers, emails, mobile phones etc. It extends the powers in relation to post and telecommunications surveillance by replacing the Interception of Communications Act 1985 which is repealed. The Act also aims to ensure compliance with the Human Rights Act 1998.

Part I of the 2000 Act deals with the extension of the powers of surveillance over post and telecommunications. The 1985 Act is replaced by a similar scheme that covers non-public telecommunications systems – including switchboards etc. The Secretary of State remains responsible for authorising all intercepts and his power is reviewed by the independent Interception Commissioner. There will be an office of Surveillance commissioners. The changes were proposed in the Consultation Paper *Interception of Communication in the UK*.[1] This part came into force in October 2000.

Part II deals with the regulation of covert human policing (undercover officers, informers entrapment etc.). All such policing was previously governed by Home Office guidelines.[2]

Part III governs the controversial powers to maintain effective policing by allowing enforcement agencies to require the disclosure of encryption keys for material or for a plain text copy. The government stated its considerable concern that the electronic

---

5   [1998] Crim LR (Special Edn) 79, and O. Ward, (2001) 151 NLJ 337.
6   See also Q. Whitaker, 'Surveillance: General Principles and the Police Act 1997' in K. Starmer et al., *Criminal Justice, Police Powers and Human Rights* (2001). On Part I see below, p. 998.
7   15 June 2000.
8   See www.homeoffice.gov.uk/oicd/snoopers.htm; www.homeoffice.gov.uk/oicd/pnrip.htm.
1   Cmd. 4368, 1999. See further below, Chap. 9 on privacy.
2   See below, under 'Admissibility of evidence', p. 349.

commerce that is now so vital to the country's economy was inadequately protected from fraud.[3] This part is yet to be brought into force.

Part IV provides powers for the Prime Minister to appoint Interception of Communications Commissioners. Provision is also made for the appointment of intelligence service commissioners and chief surveillance commissioners and a tribunal to consider complaints. There will be four separate commissioners, including those under the Police Act 1997. Would there be greater consistency and more effective monitoring with only one commissioner?

Part II of the 2000 Act provides a statutory framework governing the authorisation and use of covert surveillance, agents, informants and undercover officers. It is designed to provide appropriate regulation of the use of covert policing techniques and meet the demands of the Human Rights Act 1998 by providing adequate protection against invasions of privacy.

Regulation of Investigating Powers Act 2000

26. Conduct to which Part II applies

(1) This Part applies to the following conduct—
  (*a*) directed surveillance;
  (*b*) intrusive surveillance; and
  (*c*) the conduct and use of covert human intelligence sources.

(2) Subject to subsection (6), surveillance is directed for the purposes of this Part if it is covert but not intrusive and is undertaken—
  (*a*) for the purposes of a specific investigation or a specific operation;
  (*b*) in such a manner as is likely to result in the obtaining of private information about a person (whether or not one specifically identified for the purposes of the investigation or operation); and
  (*c*) otherwise than by way of an immediate response to events or circumstances the nature of which is such that it would not be reasonably practicable for an authorisation under this Part to be sought for the carrying out of the surveillance.

(3) Subject to subsections (4) to (6), surveillance is intrusive for the purposes of this Part if, and only if, it is covert surveillance that—
  (*a*) is carried out in relation to anything taking place on any residential premises or in any private vehicle; and
  (*b*) involves the presence of an individual on the premises or in the vehicle or is carried out by means of a surveillance device.

(4) For the purposes of this Part surveillance is not intrusive to the extent that—
  (*a*) it is carried out by means only of a surveillance device designed or adapted principally for the purpose of providing information about the location of a vehicle; or
  (*b*) it is surveillance consisting in any such interception of a communication as falls within section 48(4).

(5) For the purposes of this Part surveillance which—
  (*a*) is carried out by means of a surveillance device in relation to anything taking place on any residential premises or in any private vehicle, but
  (*b*) is carried out without that device being present on the premises or in the vehicle,
is not intrusive unless the device is such that it consistently provides information of the same quality and detail as might be expected to be obtained from a device actually present on the premises or in the vehicle.

(6) For the purposes of this Part surveillance which—
  (*a*) is carried out by means of apparatus designed or adapted for the purpose of detecting the installation or use in any residential or other premises of a television receiver (within the meaning of section 1 of the Wireless Telegraphy Act 1949), and
  (*b*) is carried out from outside those premises exclusively for that purpose,
is neither directed nor intrusive.

---

3   See the Home Office, *Building Confidence in Electronic Commerce: A Consultation Document* (1999).

(7) In this Part—

    (*a*) references to the conduct of a covert human intelligence source are references to any conduct of such a source which falls within any of paragraphs (*a*) to (*c*) of subsection (8), or is incidental to anything falling within any of those paragraphs; and

    (*b*) references to the use of a covert human intelligence source are references to inducing, asking or assisting a person to engage in the conduct of such a source, or to obtain information by means of the conduct of such a source.

(8) For the purposes of this Part a person is a covert human intelligence source if—

    (*a*) he establishes or maintains a personal or other relationship with a person for the covert purpose of facilitating the doing of anything falling within paragraph (*b*) or (*c*);

    (*b*) he covertly uses such a relationship to obtain information or to provide access to any information to another person; or

    (*c*) he covertly discloses information obtained by the use of such a relationship, or as a consequence of the existence of such a relationship.

(9) For the purposes of this section—

    (*a*) surveillance is covert if, and only if, it is carried out in a manner that is calculated to ensure that persons who are subject to the surveillance are unaware that it is or may be taking place;

    (*b*) a purpose is covert, in relation to the establishment or maintenance of a personal or other relationship, if and only if the relationship is conducted in a manner that is calculated to ensure that one of the parties to the relationship is unaware of the purpose; and

    (*c*) a relationship is used covertly, and information obtained as mentioned in subsection (8)(*c*) is disclosed covertly, if and only if it is used or, as the case may be, disclosed in a manner that is calculated to ensure that one of the parties to the relationship is unaware of the use or disclosure in question.

(10) In this section 'private information', in relation to a person, includes any information relating to his private or family life.

(11) References in this section, in relation to a vehicle, to the presence of a surveillance device in the vehicle include references to its being located on or under the vehicle and also include references to its being attached to it.

Authorisation of surveillance and human intelligence sources

27. Lawful surveillance etc

(1) Conduct to which this Part applies shall be lawful for all purposes if—

    (*a*) an authorisation under this Part confers an entitlement to engage in that conduct on the person whose conduct it is; and

    (*b*) his conduct is in accordance with the authorisation.

(2) A person shall not be subject to any civil liability in respect of any conduct of his which—

    (*a*) is incidental to any conduct that is lawful by virtue of subsection (1); and

    (*b*) is not itself conduct an authorisation or warrant for which is capable of being granted under a relevant enactment and might reasonably have been expected to have been sought in the case in question.

(3) The conduct that may be authorised under this Part includes conduct outside the United Kingdom.

(4) In this section 'relevant enactment' means—

    (*a*) an enactment contained in this Act;

    (*b*) section 5 of the Intelligence Services Act 1994 (warrants for the intelligence services); or

    (*c*) an enactment contained in Part III of the Police Act 1997 (powers of the police and of customs officers).

28. Authorisation of directed surveillance

(1) Subject to the following provisions of this Part, the persons designated for the purposes of this section shall each have power to grant authorisations for the carrying out of directed surveillance.

(2) A person shall not grant an authorisation for the carrying out of directed surveillance unless he believes—

    (*a*) that the authorisation is necessary on grounds falling within subsection (3); and

    (*b*) that the authorised surveillance is proportionate to what is sought to be achieved by carrying it out.

(3) An authorisation is necessary on grounds falling within this subsection if it is necessary

- (*a*) in the interests of national security;
- (*b*) for the purpose of preventing or detecting crime or of preventing disorder;
- (*c*) in the interests of the economic well-being of the United Kingdom;
- (*d*) in the interests of public safety;
- (*e*) for the purpose of protecting public health;
- (*f*) for the purpose of assessing or collecting any tax, duty, levy or other imposition, contribution or charge payable to a government department; or
- (*g*) for any purpose (not falling within paragraphs (*a*) to (*f*)) which is specified for the purposes of this subsection by an order made by the Secretary of State.

(4) The conduct that is authorised by an authorisation for the carrying out of directed surveillance is any conduct that—

- (*a*) consists in the carrying out of directed surveillance of any such description as is specified in the authorisation; and
- (*b*) is carried out in the circumstances described in the authorisation and for the purposes of the investigation or operation specified or described in the authorisation.

(5) The Secretary of State shall not make an order under subsection (3)(*g*) unless a draft of the order has been laid before Parliament and approved by a resolution of each House.

29. Authorisation of covert human intelligence sources

(1) Subject to the following provisions of this Part, the persons designated for the purposes of this section shall each have power to grant authorisations for the conduct or the use of a covert human intelligence source.

(2) A person shall not grant an authorisation for the conduct or the use of a covert human intelligence source unless he believes—

- (*a*) that the authorisation is necessary on grounds falling within subsection (3);
- (*b*) that the authorised conduct or use is proportionate to what is sought to be achieved by that conduct or use; and
- (*c*) that arrangements exist for the source's case that satisfy the requirements of subsection (5) and such other requirements as may be imposed by order made by the Secretary of State.

(3) An authorisation is necessary on grounds falling within this subsection if it is necessary–

- (*a*) in the interests of national security;
- (*b*) for the purpose of preventing or detecting crime or of preventing disorder;
- (*c*) in the interests of the economic well-being of the United Kingdom;
- (*d*) in the interests of public safety;
- (*e*) for the purpose of protecting public health;
- (*f*) for the purpose of assessing or collecting any tax, duty, levy or other imposition, contribution or charge payable to a government department; or
- (*g*) for any purpose (not falling within paragraphs (*a*) to (*f*)) which is specified for the purposes of this subsection by an order made by the Secretary of State.

(4) The conduct that is authorised by an authorisation for the conduct or the use of a covert human intelligence source is any conduct that—

- (*a*) is comprised in any such activities involving conduct of a covert human intelligence source, or the use of a covert human intelligence source, as are specified or described in the authorisation;
- (*b*) consists in conduct by or in relation to the person who is so specified or described as the person to whose actions as a covert human intelligence source the authorisation relates; and
- (*c*) is carried out for the purposes of, or in connection with, the investigation or operation so specified or described.

(5) For the purposes of this Part there are arrangements for the source's case that satisfy the requirements of this subsection if such arrangements are in force as are necessary for ensuring–

- (*a*) that there will at all times be a person holding an office, rank or position with the relevant investigating authority who will have day-to-day responsibility for dealing with the source on behalf of that authority, and for the source's security and welfare;
- (*b*) that there will at all times be another person holding an office, rank or position with the relevant investigating authority who will have general oversight of the use made of the source;

(c) that there will at all times be a person holding an office, rank or position with the relevant investigating authority who will have responsibility for maintaining a record of the use made of the source;

(d) that the records relating to the source that are maintained by the relevant investigating authority will always contain particulars of all such matters (if any) as may be specified for the purposes of this paragraph in regulations made by the Secretary of State; and

(e) that records maintained by the relevant investigating authority that disclose the identity of the source will not be available to persons except to the extent that there is a need for access to them to be made available to those persons.

(6) The Secretary of State shall not make an order under subsection (3)(*g*) unless a draft of the order has been laid before Parliament and approved by a resolution of each House.

(7) The Secretary of State may by order—

(a) prohibit the authorisation under this section of any such conduct or uses of covert human intelligence sources as may be described in the order; and

(b) impose requirements, in addition to those provided for by subsection (2), that must be satisfied before an authorisation is granted under this section for any such conduct or uses of covert human intelligence sources as may be so described.

(8) In this section 'relevant investigating authority', in relation to an authorisation for the conduct or the use of an individual as a covert human intelligence source, means (subject to subsection (9)) the public authority for whose benefit the activities of that individual as such a source are to take place.

(9) In the case of any authorisation for the conduct or the use of a covert human intelligence source whose activities are to be for the benefit of more than one public authority, the references in subsection (5) to the relevant investigating authority are references to one of them (whether or not the same one in the case of each reference).

32. Authorisation of intrusive surveillance

(1) Subject to the following provisions of this Part, the Secretary of State and each of the senior authorising officers shall have power to grant authorisations for the carrying out of intrusive surveillance.

(2) Neither the Secretary of State nor any senior authorising officer shall grant an authorisation for the carrying out of intrusive surveillance unless he believes—

(a) that the authorisation is necessary on grounds falling within subsection (3); and

(b) that the authorised surveillance is proportionate to what is sought to be achieved by carrying it out.

(3) Subject to the following provisions of this section, an authorisation is necessary on grounds falling within this subsection if it is necessary—

(a) in the interests of national security;

(b) for the purpose of preventing or detecting serious crime; or

(c) in the interests of the economic well-being of the United Kingdom.

(4) The matters to be taken into account in considering whether the requirements of subsection (2) are satisfied in the case of any authorisation shall include whether the information which it is thought necessary to obtain by the authorised conduct could reasonably be obtained by other means.

(5) The conduct that is authorised by an authorisation for the carrying out of intrusive surveillance is any conduct that —

(a) consists in the carrying out of intrusive surveillance of any such description as is specified in the authorisation;

(b) is carried out in relation to the residential premises specified or described in the authorisation or in relation to the private vehicle so specified or described; and

(c) is carried out for the purposes of, or in connection with, the investigation or operation so specified or described.

(6) For the purposes of this section the senior authorising officers are– [other specified senior officers]

33. Rules for grant of authorisations

(1) A person who is a designated person for the purposes of section 28 or 29 by reference to his office, rank or position with a police force, the National Criminal Intelligence Service or the National Crime Squad shall not grant an authorisation under that section except on an application made by a member of the same force, Service or Squad.

48. Interpretation of Part II

(1) In this Part–

'covert human intelligence source' shall be construed in accordance with section 26(8); 'directed' and 'intrusive', in relation to surveillance, shall be construed in accordance with section 26(2) to (6); 'private vehicle' means (subject to subsection (7)(*a*)) any vehicle which is used primarily for the private purposes of the person who owns it or of a person otherwise having the right to use it;

'residential premises' means (subject to subsection (7)(*b*)) so much of any premises as is for the time being occupied or used by any person, however temporarily, for residential purposes or otherwise as living accommodation (including hotel or prison accommodation that is so occupied or used);

'senior authorising officer' means a person who by virtue of subsection (6) of section 32 is a senior authorising officer for the purposes of that section;

'surveillance' shall be construed in accordance with subsections (2) to (4);

'surveillance device' means any apparatus designed or adapted for use in surveillance.

(2) Subject to subsection (3), in this Part 'surveillance' includes—

(*a*)   monitoring, observing or listening to persons, their movements, their conversations or their other activities or communications;

(*b*)   recording anything monitored, observed or listened to in the course of surveillance; and

(*c*)   surveillance by or with the assistance of a surveillance device.

(3) References in this Part to surveillance do not include references to—

(*a*)   any conduct of a covert human intelligence source for obtaining or recording (whether or not using a surveillance device) any information which is disclosed in the presence of the source;

(*b*)   the use of a covert human intelligence source for so obtaining or recording information; or

(*c*)   any such entry on or interference with property or with wireless telegraphy as would be unlawful unless authorised under—

(i)   section 5 of the Intelligence Services Act 1994 (warrants for the intelligence services); or

(ii)   Part III of the Police Act 1997 (powers of the police and of customs officers).

(4) References in this Part to surveillance include references to the interception of a communication in the course of its transmission by means of a postal service or telecommunication system if, and only if—

(*a*)   the communication is one sent by or intended for a person who has consented to the interception of communications sent by or to him; and

(*b*)   there is no interception warrant authorising the interception.

(5) References in this Part to an individual holding an office or position with a public authority include references to any member, official or employee of that authority.

(6) For the purposes of this Part the activities of a covert human intelligence source which are to be taken as activities for the benefit of a particular public authority include any conduct of his as such a source which is in response to inducements or requests made by or on behalf of that authority.

(7) In subsection (1)—

(*a*)   the reference to a person having the right to use a vehicle does not, in relation to a motor vehicle, include a reference to a person whose right to use the vehicle derives only from his having paid, or undertaken to pay, for the use of the vehicle and its driver for a particular journey; and

(*b*)   the reference to premises occupied or used by any person for residential purposes or otherwise as living accommodation does not include a reference to so much of any premises as constitutes any common area to which he has or is allowed access in connection with his use or occupation of any accommodation.

(8) In this section—

'premises' includes any vehicle or moveable structure and any other place whatever, whether or not occupied as land;

'vehicle' includes any vessel, aircraft or hovercraft.

NOTES

1. See further the discussion in Chap. 9 on Privacy. The bodies regulated by the Act include NCS, NCIS, Customs and Excise, MI5 and MI6. The Home Office is an authority whose actions are governed by the Act, and as such prison services are included in the scope of the protection.[4] See further the Draft Code of Practice issued pursuant to s. 71 of the Regulation of Investigating Powers Act 2000, published for public consultation 25 September 2000.[5]

2. Part II, which came into force on 25 October 2000, is intended to deal with all those aspects of surveillance not previously dealt with under the Police Act 1997 or the Intelligence Services Act 1994. What is immediately noticeable is that there is no criminal offence of unlawful intrusive surveillance – should there have been? What would be an appropriate remedy for unlawful police surveillance? Who would police such an offence? See also P. Mirfield,[6] who considers the evidential difficulties created by the Act and the many methods by which the admissibility of evidence discovered under the Act could be challenged.

3. The Commissioner has a duty to review the Secretary of State's role in the operation of warrants. Note the exception for urgent cases (s. 36). Can there be an effective safeguard against abuse of such an exception?

(D) THE DRAFT CODE OF PRACTICE

The Draft Code of Practice on covert surveillance provides that:

'Surveillance plays a necessary part in modern life. It is used not just in the targeting of criminals but as a means of protecting the public from harm and preventing crime.

The covert surveillance regulated by the 2000 Act and covered by this code is in two categories: intrusive surveillance and directed surveillance. The code explains the two categories and the authorisation procedures for each. Authorisation under the 2000 Act gives lawful authority to carry out surveillance. However, surveillance operations will often also involve interference with property. This may require separate authorisation and Part 5 of this code details the procedures which give lawful authority for the interference with property and wireless telegraphy.

General observation forms part of the duties of many law enforcement officers and other public bodies. Police officers will be on patrol at football grounds and other venues monitoring the crowd to maintain public safety and prevent disorder. Officers may also target a crime 'hot spot' in order to identify and arrest offenders committing crime at that location. Trading standards or HM Customs & Excise officers might covertly observe and then visit a shop as part of their enforcement function to verify the supply or level of supply of goods or services that may be liable to a restriction or tax. Such observation may involve the use of equipment to merely reinforce normal sensory perception, such as binoculars, or the use of cameras, where this does not involve systematic surveillance of an individual. It forms a part of the everyday functions of law enforcement or other public bodies. This low-level activity will not usually be regulated under the provisions of the 2000 Act.

Neither do the provisions of the 2000 Act or of this code of practice cover the use of overt CCTV surveillance systems. Members of the public are aware that such systems are in use, for their own protection, and to prevent crime.'

---

4   See Regulation of Investigatory Powers Act 2000 (Designation of Public Authorities for the Purposes of Intrusive Surveillance) Order 2001, S.I. 2001 No. 1126.
5   www.homeoffice.gov.uk/ripa/covhis.htm.
6   [2001] Crim LR 91.

The Code is admissible in evidence in criminal and civil proceedings. If any provision of the Code appears relevant to any court or tribunal considering any such proceedings, it must be taken into account.[7] However, the Act does not provide for the automatic exclusion of intercept material at trial.[8]

Very important guidance on authorisations is also provided in Chap. 2:

Draft Code of Practice on Covert Surveillance, Chapter 2

2.1 An authorisation will provide lawful authority for a public authority to carry out covert surveillance. Responsibility for authorising surveillance operations will vary, depending on whether the authorisation is for 'intrusive surveillance' or 'directed surveillance', and which organisation is involved. There is no requirement on the part of a public authority to obtain an authorisation for a covert surveillance operation and the decision not to obtain an authorisation would not, of itself, make an action unlawful. However, public authorities are strongly recommended to seek an authorisation where the purpose of the covert surveillance, wherever that takes place, is to obtain private information about a person, whether or not that person is the target of the investigation or operation. Obtaining an authorisation will ensure that the action is carried out in accordance with law and subject to stringent safeguards against abuse. It will also make the action less vulnerable to challenge under the Human Rights Act 1998.

2.2 Any person giving an authorisation should first satisfy him/herself that the authorisation is necessary on particular grounds and that the surveillance is proportionate to what it seeks to achieve.

2.3 Particular consideration should be given to collateral intrusion on or interference with the privacy of persons other than the subject(s) of surveillance. Such collateral intrusion or interference would be a matter of greater concern in cases where there are special sensitivities, for example in cases of premises used by lawyers or for any form of medical or professional counselling or therapy.

2.4 An application for an authorisation should include an assessment of the risk of any collateral intrusion or interference. This will be taken into account by the authorising officer, particularly when considering the proportionality of the surveillance.

2.5 Those carrying out the covert surveillance should inform the authorising officer if the operation/investigation unexpectedly interferes with the privacy of individuals who are not the original subjects of the investigation or covered by the authorisation in some other way. In some cases the original authorisation may not be sufficient and consideration should be given to whether a separate authorisation is required.

2.6 Any person giving an authorisation will also need to be aware of particular sensitivities in the local community where the surveillance is taking place or of similar activities being undertaken by other public authorities which could impact on the deployment of surveillance. In this regard, it is recommended that the authorising officers in NCIS, the National Crime Squad and HM Customs & Excise consult the local chief constable where the authorising officer considers that conflicts might arise.

Special Rules

2.7 The fullest consideration should be given in cases where the subject of the surveillance might reasonably expect a high degree of privacy, for instance in his/her home, or where there are special sensitivities.

The Code provides that operations will respect the seal of confession with ministers of religion.

---

7   Para. 1.3.
8   Para. 1.5.

NOTES

1. To what extent is the division of surveillance into 'directed' and 'intrusive' appropriate and/or successfully achieved by the Act? Y. Akdeniz, N. Taylor and C. Walker[9] in a comprehensive review of the Act consider the adequacy of the protections afforded in the Act. They describe the distinction between 'directed' and 'intrusive' surveillance as ambiguous, and point out that the protection is for places rather than people. Can the Act provide anything other than protection for places? Will that satisfy Art. 8? Directed surveillance is further explained in the Code:

> '3.2 Directed surveillance is conducted where it involves the observation of a person or persons with the intention of gathering private information to produce a detailed picture of a person's life, activities and associations. However, it does not include covert surveillance carried out by way of an immediate response to events or circumstances which, by their very nature, could not have been foreseen. For example, a plain clothes police officer would not require an authorisation to conceal himself and observe a suspicious person who he comes across in the course of a patrol.'

Y. Akdeniz, N. Taylor and C. Walker[10] also note a number of difficulties arising under s. 26(5) and the ambiguity of the protection turning on the quality of the device rather than the degree of intrusion. Should a citizen's freedom from intrusion depend on how strong the officer anticipates the signal from the bug will be?

2. In what circumstances should the Home Secretary have the power to authorise intrusive surveillance to 'protect the economic well being of the country' if that is not also a serious crime? Would this allow for the surveillance of fuel protestors?

3. Private information does not include business information – unless that relates to a person's private life. Whose private life is in issue? Is the discussion of a third parties' private life by the suspect protected?

4. The courts will be reluctant to exclude reliable evidence of the type generated by surveillance. In *R v Hallsworth*[11] H's incriminating comments made in the course of the investigation when his telephone was tapped were held admissible, the calls were not an interview under Code C of PACE, and there was no unfairness in the proceedings.

5. TV detector vans are not subject to the regime of the Act.[12]

(E) SURVEILLANCE – THE EU DIMENSION

S. Peers:[12a]

> 'The Naples II provisions allow surveillance where "there are serious grounds for believing [a person is] involved in one of the infringements" referred to in the special co-operation rules. Otherwise, the Naples II rules are the same as the Schengen rules, except that a Member State can opt out of the provisions entirely and host Member States can impose a general ban on home state officers carrying firearms.
>
> Undercover operations
> The Schengen Convention did not provide for "covert operations" outside the scope of simple observation, but the Naples II Convention does, although Member States may opt out of the relevant provision entirely. If a Member State wishes to "make contacts with subjects and other persons associated with them" in another Member State, it may ask another Member

9 [2001] Crim LR 73.
10 Ibid.
11 (1998) 3 April, CA (Cr D).
12 Regulation of Investigatory Powers Act (BBC) Order 2001, S.I. 2001 No. 1057.
12a *EU Justice and Home Affairs Law*, p. 196

State to allow its customs officers "or officers acting on behalf" of its administration to enter "under cover of a false identity".

There is no rule restricting covert investigations to certain types of offences and no list of general conditions attaching to the authorisation of the investigations. Instead, the host state's rules on such investigations apply and the host state is given great latitude to restrict or lay conditions upon the scope of the home state agents' undercover work. The host state must protect the home state officers and provide personnel and technical support, and the general liability and damage rules apply. Cross-border covert operations by the police would be authorised if the draft Convention on mutual criminal assistance is agreed. The draft rules are even vaguer than those in the Naples II Convention, leaving the duration, "the detailed conditions, the legal status of the officers concerned and liability for any offence committed or damage caused" to be agreed between the Member States concerned. It is not clear whether private detectives might be involved. In general, the investigation would again take place under the host state's rules with much latitude to the host state to set conditions. The accountability problems attached to undercover investigations by the police would be magnified if there is extensive use of cross-border requests for surveillance or enquiries. The Naples II Convention allows one Member State's customs investigators to request another's to carry out surveillance or enquiries on its territory. This is another type of limited transfer of investigation; it is, of course, distinct from allowing the investigating state's officers access to the requested state's territory to carry out operations themselves.'

The Schengen Information System is a database accessible to police forces throughout Europe. SIRENE is a similar Euro database of photographs and fingerprints. There are currently 9.8m files accessible from 50,000 terminals.[13] A recent Justice report revealed the absence of effective monitoring and the absence of judicial control of these systems.[14]

(F) COVERT HUMAN INTELLIGENCE SOURCES

The courts may face considerable difficulty in interpreting and applying the CHIS provisions and the number of operations of this nature will be high, particularly in the fight against drug crime.

The Code of Practice begins with the foreword:

'Up until now, the use of sources has never been the subject of statutory control in this country. Their continued use is, however, essential to the maintenance of law and order and for the protection of the public.

Nothing in the provisions of the Regulation of Investigatory Powers Act 2000, nor in this code of practice, affects statutory duties (such as under the Drug Trafficking Act 1994) to disclose information about, for example, suspicious financial transactions.

The provisions of the Regulation of Investigatory Powers Act 2000 are not intended to apply in circumstances where members of the public volunteer information to the police or other authorities, as part of their normal civic duties, or contact numbers specifically set up to receive anonymous information (such as Crimestoppers, the Anti Terrorist Hotline, the Security Service Public Telephone Number or the Customs Drugs Freephone). Members of the public acting in this way would not generally come within the definition of a covert source. However, someone might become a source as a result of a relationship with a public authority begun in this way.'

The Draft Code of Practice contains useful further guidance:

'1.5 There is no geographical limitation on the use or conduct of a source. Authorisations can be granted for the use or conduct of a source both inside and outside the United Kingdom.

1.7 There is also nothing in the 2000 Act which prevents any material obtained from the use or conduct of a source from being adduced as evidence in court proceedings.

---

13 See M. Colvin, [2001] EHRLR 270.
14 www.justice.org.uk.

1.8 The code should be readily available, for reference purposes, at public offices of public authorities designated in the 2000 Act to authorise the use or conduct of covert sources. Where this is not possible, copies should be made available by post or e-mail.'

NOTES

1. Paragraph 1.10 provides further guidance on interpreting key expressions – 'authorising officer', 'confidential material', etc.

2. Chapter 2 of the Code of Practice deals with authorisation for covert sources emphasising that the responsibility for authorising the use or conduct of a source rests with the authorising officer.[15] Before authorising the use or conduct of a source, the authorising officer should believe that the conduct/use including the likely degree of intrusion into the privacy of those potentially affected is proportionate to what the use or conduct of the source seeks to achieve. He should also take into account the risk of intrusion into the privacy of persons other than those who are directly the subjects of the operation or investigation (collateral intrusion). Measures should be taken, wherever practicable, to avoid unnecessary intrusion into the lives of those not directly connected with the operation.[16] Particular care should be taken in circumstances where people would expect a high degree of privacy or where, as a consequence of the authorisation, 'confidential material' is likely to be obtained,[17] and consideration should also be given to any adverse impact on community confidence that may result from the use or conduct of a source or information obtained from that source.[18]

3. It is important to note that the Code recognises the danger of sources becoming perpetrators of offences:

> 'A source may, in the context of an authorised operation, infiltrate existing criminal activity, or be a party to the commission of criminal offences, within the limits recognised by law. A source who acts beyond these limits will be at risk of prosecution. The need to protect the source cannot alter this principle.'[19]

The Code spells out the ways in which legitimate cultivation of a source can occur, noting that 'It may be necessary to infringe the personal privacy of the potential source in the process of cultivation. In such cases, authorisation is needed for the cultivation process itself, as constituting the conduct (by the person undertaking the cultivation) of a source'[20] and that it may be necessary to deploy directed surveillance against a potential source as part of the process of assessing their suitability for recruitment, or in planning how best to make the approach to them.

4. Authorisation for the use and conduct of a source is required prior to any 'tasking', i.e. an assignment given to the source, asking him or her to obtain information, to provide access to information or to otherwise act, incidentally, for the benefit of the relevant public authority.[1] It may involve the source infiltrating existing criminal activity in order to obtain that information.[2] Authorisations must be given in writing by the authorising officer. However, in urgent cases, they may be given orally by the authorising officer save where he is only entitled to act in urgent cases.[3] More disturbingly, an authorising officer may in certain circumstances act as the controller or handler of a source.[4]

15 Para. 2.1.
16 Para. 2.5.
17 Para. 2.6.
18 Para. 2.7.
19 Para. 2.4.
20 Para. 2.10.
 1 Para. 2.10.
 2 Para. 2.11.
 3 Para. 2.14.
 4 Para. 2.15.

Sources can include members of foreign law enforcement or other agencies or sources of those agencies.[5]

5. The Code also emphasises the need for special care 'where the target of the investigation is likely to be involved in handling confidential material', and when dealing with vulnerable individuals, such as the mentally impaired, and juvenile sources. It is clear that on 'no occasion should the use or conduct of a source under 16 years of age be authorised to give information against his or her parents'. Not quite 1984! The Code also provides detailed guidance on the management of sources and their welfare, the application for authorisation and its processes, and the retention of material.

6. The Code also appears to undermine what might be regarded as important protections, by allowing for sources to engage in directed surveillance:

> '3.15 The question will frequently arise whether a surveillance device may legitimately be used in circumstances where the incidental effect will be to enable the overhearing of what is said by a party to a telephone conversation who is speaking from a location where a device is installed. The use of a surveillance device should not be ruled out simply because it may incidentally pick up one end of a telephone conversation, and such product can be treated as having been lawfully obtained.'

7. Who is the covert human intelligence source? This character must have the covert purpose in setting up the relationship and use it covertly to obtain information. Does not the informer do this? Under s. 26(9)(b) the covert relationship must be calculated to ensure that one of the parties to the relationship is unaware of the purpose.

8. The authorisations for directed and covert human surveillance requires only that the authorising officer is satisfied that, *inter alia*, the surveillance is necessary to detect crime, not *serious* crime. The authorisation of the Home Secretary regarding intrusive surveillance is more limited – it must be necessary and proportionate to detect serious crime. Hopefully, the final versions of the Codes will be more tightly drawn than the Draft. Note that under the Draft Code, if a CHIS has surveillance cameras or equipment on his person, the use of the device is not treated as intrusive surveillance unless it is left on the premises after the CHIS departs.[6]

7 Arrest

Police and Criminal Evidence Act 1984

PART III

ARREST

24. Arrest without warrant for arrestable offences
(1) The powers of summary arrest conferred by the following subsections shall apply—
    (*a*) to offences for which the sentence is fixed by law;
    (*b*) to offences for which a person of 21[7] years of age or over (not previously convicted) may be sentenced to imprisonment for a term of five years (or might be so sentenced but for the restrictions imposed by section 33 of the Magistrates' Court Act 1980); and
    (*c*) to the offences to which subsection (2) below applies,
and in this Act 'arrestable offence' means any such offence.
(2) The offences to which this subsection applies are—

5 Para. 2.19.
6 See para. 2.34. See further Q. Whitaker, op. cit., p. 71.
7 As from a day to be appointed, s. 24(1)(b) is amended to '18' years: see Criminal Justice and Courts Services Act 2000, s. 74 and Sch. 7.

(*a*) offences for which a person may be arrested under the Customs and Excise Acts, as defined in section 1(1) of the Customs and Excise Management Act 1979;

(*b*) offences under the Official Secrets Act [...] 1920 that are not arrestable offences by virtue of the term of imprisonment for which a person may be sentenced in respect of them;

[(*bb*)offences under any provision of the Official Secrets Act 1989 except section 8 (1), (4) or (5);][8]

(*c*) offences under section [...][9] 22 (causing prostitution of women) or 23 (procuration of girl under 21) of the Sexual Offences Act 1956;

[(*ca*) an offence under section 46 of the Criminal Justice and Police Act 2001][10]

(*d*) offences under section 12(1) (taking motor vehicle or other conveyance without authority etc.) or 25 (1) (going equipped for stealing, etc.) of the Theft Act 1968; and

[(*e*) any offence under the Football Offences Act 1991;][11]

[(*f*) an offence under section 2 of the Obscene Publications Act 1959 (publication of obscene matter);

(*g*) an offence under section 1 of the Protection of Children Act 1978 (indecent photographs and pseudo-photographs of children);][12]

[(*ga*) an offence under section 1 of the Sexual Offences Act 1985 (kerb crawling)

(*gb*) an offence under subsection (4) of s. 170 of the Road Traffic Act 1988 (failure to stop and report an accident to which that section applies...)][13]

[(*h*) an offence under section 166 of the Criminal Justice and Public Order Act 1994 (sale of tickets by unauthorised persons);][14]

[(*i*) an offence under section 19 of the Public Order Act 1986 (publishing, etc. material intended or likely to stir up and racial hatred);][15]

[(*j*) an offence under section 167 of the Criminal Justice and Public Order Act 1994 (touting for hire car service).][16]

[(*k*) an offence under section 1(1) of the Prevention of Crime Act 1953 (prohibition of the carrying of offensive weapons without lawful authority or reasonable excuse);

(*l*) an offence under section 139(1) of the Criminal Justice Act 1988 (offence of having an article with a blade or point in a public place);

(*m*) an offence under section 139A (1) or (2) of the Criminal Justice Act 1988 (offence of having article with blade or point (or offensive weapon) on school premises).][17]

[(*n*) an offence under section 2 of the Protection from Harassment Act 1997;][18]

[(*o*) an offence under section 60(8)(*b*) of the Criminal Justice and Public Order Act 1994 (failing to comply with requirement to remove mask etc.);

(*p*) an offence falling within section 32(1)(*a*) of the Crime and Disorder Act 1998 (racially aggravated harassment);

(*q*) an offence under section 16(4) of the Football Spectators Act 1989 (failure to comply with reporting duty imposed by [international banning order][19]).][20]

[(*r*) [(*qa*) an offence under section 12(4) of the Criminal Justice and Police Act 2001][1]

[(*r*) [repealed by the Football (Disorder) Act 200 section 1(2)].]

---

 8 Inserted by the 1989 Act, s. 11(1).
 9 Repealed by the Sexual Offences Act 1985, s. 5(3).
10 As inserted by s. 46 of the Criminal Justice and Police Act 2001.
11 Inserted by the Football Offences Act 1991, s. 5.
12 Inserted by the Criminal Justice and Public Order Act 1994, s. 85(2).
13 As inserted by the Criminal Justice and Police Act 2001, s. 71.
14 Inserted by ibid., s. 166(4).
15 Inserted by ibid., s. 155.
16 Inserted by ibid., s. 167(7).
17 Inserted by the Offensive Weapons Act 1996, s. 1(1).
18 Inserted by the Protection from Harassment Act 1997, s. 2(3).
19 As amended by the Football (Offences and Disorder) Act 1999, s. 1(2)(f).
20 As inserted by the Crime and Disorder Act 1998, ss. 27(1), 84(2), 120(1).
 1 As inserted by the Criminal Justice and Police Act 2001.

[(*s*) an offence under sections 1(1) or (2) or 6 of the Wildlife and Countryside Act 1981 (taking, possessing, selling etc. wild birds) in respect of a bird included in Schedule 1 to the Act or any part of the, or anything derived from such a bird).

(*t*) an offence under any of the following provisions of the Wildlife and Countryside Act 1981—

(i) section 1(5) (disturbance of wild birds),

(ii) section 9 or 13(1)(*a*) or (2) (taking, possessing, selling etc. of wild animals or plants),

(iii) section 14 (introduction of new species etc.)."][2]

(3) Without prejudice to section 2 of the Criminal Attempts Act 1981, the powers of summary · arrest conferred by the following subsections shall also apply to the offences of—

(*a*) conspiring to commit any of the offences mentioned in subsection (2) above;

(*b*) attempting to commit any such offence [other than an offence under section 12(1) of the Theft Act 1968],[3]

(*c*) inciting, aiding, abetting, counselling or procuring the commission of any such offence;

and such offences are also arrestable offences for the purposes of this Act.

(4) Any person may arrest without a warrant—

(*a*) anyone who is in the act of committing an arrestable offence;

(*b*) anyone whom he has reasonable grounds for suspecting to be committing such an offence.

(5) Where are an arrestable offence has been committed, any person may arrest without a warrant—

(*a*) anyone who is guilty of the offence;

(*b*) anyone whom he has reasonable grounds for supecting to be guilty of it.

(6) Where a constable has reasonable grounds for suspecting that an arrestable offence has been committed, he may arrest without a warrant anyone whom he has reasonable grounds for suspecting to be guilty of the offence.

(7) A constable may arrest without a warrant—

(*a*) anyone who is about to commit an arrestable offence;

(*b*) anyone whom he has reasonable grounds for suspecting to be about to commit an arrestable offence.

25. General arrest conditions

(1) Where a constable has reasonable grounds for suspecting that any offence which is not an arrestable offence has been committed or attempted, or is being committed or attempted, he may arrest the relevant person if it appears to him that service of a summons is impracticable or inappropriate because any of the general arrest conditions are satisfied.

(2) In this section 'the relevant person' means any person whom the constable has reasonable grounds to aspect of having committed or having attempted to commit the offence or of being in the course of committing or attempting to commit it.

(3) The general arrest conditions are—

(*a*) that the name of the relevant person is unknown to, and cannot be readily ascertained by, the constable;

(*b*) that the constable has reasonable grounds for doubting whether a name furnished by the relevant person as his name is his real name;

(*c*) that—

(i) the relevant person has failed to furnish a satisfactorily address for service, or

(ii) the constable has reasonable grounds for doubting whether an address furnished by the relevant person is a satisfactory address for service;

(*d*) that the constable has reasonable grounds for believing that arrest is necessary to prevent the relevant person—

(i) causing physical injury to himself or any other person;

(ii) suffering physical injury;

(iii) causing loss of or damage to property;

(iv) committing an offence against public decency; or

(v) causing an unlawful obstruction of the highway;

2   As inserted by the Countryside and Rights of Way Act 2000, s. 81 and Sch. 12.

3   Inserted by the Criminal Justice 1998 Act, Sch. 15, para. 98.

    (*e*) that the constable has reasonable grounds for believing that arrest is necessary to protect a child or other vulnerable person from the relevant person.

(4) For the purposes of subsection (3) above an address is a satisfactorily address for service if it appears to a constable—

    (*a*) that the relevant person will be at it for a sufficiently long period for it to be possible to serve him with a summons; or

    (*b*) that some other person specified by the relevant person will accept service of a summons for the relevant person at it.

(5) Nothing in subsection (3)(*d*) above authorises the arrest of a person under sub-paragraph (iv) of that paragraph except where members of the public going about their normal business cannot reasonably be expected to avoid the person to be arrested.

(6) This section shall not prejudice any power of arrest conferred apart from this section.

26. Repeal of statutory powers of arrest without warrant or order

(1) Subject to subsection (2) below, so much of any Act (including a local Act) passed before this Act as enables a constable—

    (*a*) to arrest a person for an offence without a warrant; or

    (*b*) to arrest a person otherwise than for an offence without a warrant or an order of a court, shall cease to have effect.

(2) Nothing in subsection (1) above affects the enactments specified in Schedule 2 to this Act.

27. Fingerprinting of certain offenders

(1) If a person—

    (*a*) has been convicted of a recordable offence;

    (*b*) has not at any time been in police detention for the offence; and

    (*c*) has not had his fingerprints taken—

        (i) i n the course of the investigation of the offence by the police; or

        (ii) since the conviction,

any constable may at any time not later than one month after the date of the conviction require him to attend a police station in order that his fingerprints may be taken.

(2) A requirement under subsection (1) above—

    (*a*) shall give the person a period of at least 7 days within which he must so attend; and

    (*b*) may direct him to so attend at a specified time of day or between specified times of day.

(3) Any constable may arrest without warrant a person who has failed to comply with a requirement under subsection (1) above.

(4) The Secretary of State may by regulations make provision for recording in national police records convictions for such offences as are specified in the regulations.

[(4A) In subsection (4) above, 'conviction' includes—

    (*a*) a caution within the meaning of Part V of the Police Act 1997; and

    (*b*) a reprimand or warning given under section 65 of the Crime and Disorder Act 1998.][4]

(5) Regulations under this section shall be made by statutory instrument and shall be subject to annulment in pursuance of a resolution of either House of Parliament.[5]

28. Information to be given on arrest.

(1) Subject to subsection (5) below, where a person is arrested, otherwise than by being informed that he is under arrest, the arrest is not lawful unless the person arrested is informed that he is under arrest as soon as is practicable after his arrest.

(2) Where a person is arrested by a constable, subsection (1) above applies regardless of whether the fact of the arrest is obvious.

(3) Subject to subsection (5) below, no arrest is lawful unless the person arrested is informed of the ground for the arrest at the time of or as soon as is practicable after, the arrest.

(4) Where a person is arrested by a constable, subsection (3) above applies regardless of whether the ground for the arrest is obvious.

---

4   Inserted by the Crime and Disorder Act 1998, s. 119, Sch. 8, para. 61.
5   See further National Police Records (Recordable Offences) (Amendment) Regulations 1997, S.I. 1997 No. 556.

(5) Nothing in this section is to be taken to require a person to be informed—

    (*a*) that he is under arrest; or

    (*b*) of the ground for the arrest,

if it was not reasonably practicable for him to be so informed by reason of his having escaped from arrest before the information could be given.

29. Voluntary attendance at police station etc.

Where for the purpose of assisting with an investigation a person attends voluntarily at a police station or at any other place where a constable is present or accompanies a constable to a police station or any such other place without having been arrested—

    (*a*) he shall be entitled to leave at will unless he is placed under arrest;

    (*b*) he shall be informed at once that he is under arrest if a decision is taken by a constable to prevent him from leaving at will.

30. Arrest elsewhere than at police station

(1) Subject to the following provisions of this section, where a person—

    (*a*) is arrested by a constable for an offence; or

    (*b*) is taken into custody by a constable after being arrested for an offence by a person other than a constable.

at any place other than a police station, he shall be taken to a police station by a constable as soon as practicable after the arrest.

(2) Subject to subsections (3) and (4) below, the police station to which an arrested person is taken under subsection (1) above shall be a designated police station.

(3) A constable to whom this subsection applies may take an arrested person to any police station unless it appears to the constable that it may be necessary to keep the arrested person in police detention for more than six hours.

(4) Subsection (3) above applies—

    (*a*) to a constable who is working in a locality covered by a police station which is not a designated police station; and

    (*b*) to a constable belonging to a body of constables maintained by an authority other than a police authority.

(5) Any constable may take an arrested person to any police station if—

    (*a*) either of the following conditions is satisfied—

        (i) the constable has arrested him without the assistance of any other constable and no other constable is available to assist him;

        (ii) the constable has taken him into custody from a person other than a constable without the assistance of any other constable and no other constable is available to assist him; and

    (*b*) it appears to the constable that he will be unable to take the arrested person to a designated police station without the arrested person injuring himself, the constable or some other person.

(6) If the first police station to which an arrested person is taken after his arrest is not a designated police station not more than six hours after his arrival at the first police station unless he is released previously.

(7) A person arrested by a constable at a place other than a police station shall be released if a constable is satisfied, before the person arrested reaches a police station, that there are no grounds for keeping him under arrest.

(8) A constable who releases a person under subsection (7) above shall record the fact that he has done so.

(9) The constable shall make the record as soon as is practicable after his release.

(10) Nothing in subsection (1) above shall prevent a constable delaying taking a person who has been arrested to a police station if the presence of that person elsewhere is necessary in order to carry out such investigations as it is reasonable to carry out immediately.

(11) Where there is delay in taking a person who has been arrested to a police station after his arrest, the reasons for the delay shall be recorded when he first arrives at a police station.

(12) Nothing in subsection (1) above shall be taken to affect—

    (*a*) paragraphs 16(3) or 18(1) of Schedule 2 to the Immigration Act 1971;

    (*b*) section 34(1) of the Criminal Justice Act 1972; or

(*c*) [any provision of the Terrorism Act 2000.][6]
(13) Nothing in subsection (10) above shall be taken to affect paragraph 18(3) of Schedule 2 to the Immigration Act 1971.

31. Arrest for further offence
Where—
(*a*) a person—
(i)   has been arrested for an offence; and
(ii) is at a police station in consequence of that arrest; and
(*b*) it appears to a constable that, if he were released from that arrest, he would be liable to arrest for some other offence,
he shall be arrested for that other offence.

32. Search upon arrest
(1) A constable may search an arrested person, in any case where the person to be searched has been arrested at a place other than a police station, if the constable has reasonable grounds for believing that the arrested person may present a danger to himself or others.
(2) Subject to subsections (3) to (5) below, a constable shall also have power in any such case—
(*a*) to search the arrested person for anything–
(i)   which he might use to assist him to escape from lawful custody; or
(ii) which might be evidence relating to an offence; and
(*b*) to enter and search any premises in which he was when arrested or immediately before he was arrested for evidence relating to the offence for which he has been arrested.
(3) The power to search conferred by subsection (2) above is only a power to search to the extent that is reasonably required for the purpose of discovering any such thing or any such evidence.
(4) The powers conferred by this section to search a person are not to be construed as authorising a constable to require a person to remove any of his clothing in public other than an outer coat, jacket or gloves [but they do authorise the search of a person's mouth].[7]
(5) A constable may not search a person in the exercise of the power conferred by subsection (2)(*a*) above unless he has reasonable grounds for believing that the person to be searched may have concealed on him anything for which a search is permitted under that paragraph.
(6) A constable may not search premises in the exercise of the power conferred by subsection (2)(*b*) above unless he has reasonable grounds for believing that there is evidence for which a search is permitted under that paragraph on the premises.
(7) In so far as the power of search conferred by subsection (2)(*b*) above relates to premises consisting of two or more separate dwellings, it is limited to a power to search—
(*a*) any dwelling in which the arrest took place or in which the person arrested was immediately before his arrest; and
(*b*) any parts of the premises which the occupier of any such dwelling uses in common with the occupiers of any other dwellings comprised in the premises.
(8) A constable searching a person in the exercise of the power conferred by subsection (1) above may seize and retain anything he finds, if he has reasonable grounds for believing that the person searched might use it to cause physical injury to himself or to any other person.
(9) A constable searching a person in the exercise of the power conferred by subsection (2)(*e*) above may seize and retain anything he finds, other than an item subject to legal privilege, if he has reasonable grounds for believing—
(*a*) that he might use it to assist him to escape from lawful custody; or
(*b*) that it is evidence of an offence or has been obtained in consequence of the commission of an offence.
(10) Nothing in this section shall be taken to affect the power conferred by [section 43 of the Terrorism Act 2000].[8]

---

6   Substituted by the Terrorism Act 2000, s. 135, Sch. 15, para. 5(2).
7   Inserted by the Criminal Justice and Public Order Act 1994, s. 59(2).
8   Substituted by the Terrorism Act 2000, s. 125, Sch. 15, para. 5(3).

NOTES

1. Schedule 2 lists 42 provisions which provide for a power of arrest without warrant and which were preserved by virtue of s. 26. They include the Public Order Act 1936, s. 7(3); the Street Offences Act 1959, s. 1(3); the Immigration Act 1971, s. 24(2), Sch. 2, paras. 17, 24 and 33 and Sch. 3, para 7; the Criminal Law Act 1977, ss. 6(6), 7(11), 8(4), 9(7) and 10(5); and the Mental Health Act 1983, ss. 18, 35(10), 36(8), 38(7), 136(1) and 138. Powers of arrest without warrant included in Acts passed since PACE include the Sporting Events (Control of Alcohol etc.) Act 1985, s. 7(2); Public Order Act 1986, s. 3(6) (affray), s. 4(4) (fear of provocation of violence), s. 5(4) (harassment, alarm or distress) (these powers have proved especially useful to the police.[9] Phillips and Brown[9a] found that 13% of all arrests in their survey were under ss. 4 or 5 of the Act), ss. 12(7), 13(10) and 14(7) (processions and assemblies),[10] carrying offensive weapons (Offensive Weapons Act 1996, s. 1); carrying knives in public (Offensive Weapons Act 1996); harassment (Protection from Harassment Act 1997).[11]

Controversially, it has been held that s. 26 of PACE does not remove the power of arrest under the Vagrancy Act 1824, s. 6. In *Gapper v Chief Constable of Avon and Somerset*[12] it was held that s. 26 removed specific statutory powers of arrest for constables in statutes, but had no application to statutes which provide a power of arrest exercisable by the general public. Section 6 refers to 'any person whatsoever' being empowered to arrest. In *DPP v Kitching*,[13] the powers of arrest for being drunk and disorderly in public were held not to have been repealed by s. 26 of PACE. The new offences added to the list of arrestable offences by the Criminal Justice and Police Act 2001 demonstrate a willingness to empower the police to deal with offences of populist concern such as prostitutes' cards in telephone boxes and kerb crawling.

2. *Requisites of a valid arrest.* There are a number of elements which must be present for an arrest to be valid:

(1) There must be either an arrest warrant or a legal power to arrest without warrant (see ss. 24–26).

(2) The factual requirements of the relevant powers must be fulfilled: commonly the requirement of 'reasonable suspicion'.[14] If the arresting officer has made a reasonable but erroneous interpretation of the law, he will not have a reasonable suspicion and the arrest will be unlawful: *Todd v DPP*.[15] The reasonableness of the officer's decision is to be based on the information available to him at that time: *Redmond-Bate v DPP*.[16] The Divisional Court in *Clarke v DPP*,[17] described it as a 'golden rule' that the prosecution should ask the arresting officer when he is giving evidence at trial what he had in mind when arresting the suspect. Where there are no reasons to question what appears on the face of the warrant for arrest, a constable enforcing that warrant has no obligation to question it and is not to be regarded as acting unlawfully if it contains a wrong name: *McGrath v RUC*.[18]

---

9 See below, Chap. 4.
9a HORS No. 185 *Entry into the Criminal Justice System: a survey of police arrests and their outcomes* (1998).
10 Below, pp. 437–470.
11 Below.
12 [1999] 2 WLR 928.
13 (1990) 154 JP 293, DC.
14 See above, p. 178–194.
15 [1996] Crim. LR 344.
16 Below, pp. 526–530.
17 (1997) 14 November, unreported.
18 [2001] UKHL 39 (NI).

(3) At common law it was necessary for the arrestor to make it clear that the arrestee was under compulsion either (i) by physical means (such as taking him by the arm) or (ii) by notifying him of the fact of compulsion by word of mouth. There was a danger where the arrestor relied on words alone that the words might not sufficiently indicate compulsion. For example, in *Alderson v Booth*[19] following a positive breathalyser test a constable said to the defendant 'I shall have to ask you to come to the police station for further tests'. D accompanied the constable to the police station. At his trial the defendant defended charges of driving with an excess of alcohol in his blood by claiming that he had not been arrested by the constable (a lawful arrest having being made being a condition precedent to conviction under the drink and drive legislation). He was acquitted and the prosecution's appeal was dismissed. Lord Parker CJ (with whom Blain and Donaldson JJ agreed) said:

'...the narrow point here was whether the justices were right in holding, as they did, that there never had been an arrest.

In their opinion, which is clearly partly opinion and partly finding of fact, they say:

"We were of the opinion that when the respondent accompanied the constable to the police station it was not made clear to him either physically or by word of mouth that he was under compulsion. We consider that compulsion is a necessary element of arrest, and we therefore did not regard the respondent as a person who had been arrested."

...I for my part have little doubt that, just looking at the words used here, "I shall have to ask you to come to the police station for further tests," that they were in their context words of command which one would think would bring home to a defendant that he was under compulsion. But the justices here had the evidence not only of the police constable but of the defendant, and they were not satisfied, having heard him, that it had been brought home unequivocally to him that he was under compulsion. I confess it surprised me that he was believed but believed he was when he said or conveyed that he was not going to the police station because he thought he was under compulsion, but was going purely voluntarily. It seems to me that this is so much a question of fact for the justices that, surprising as this decision is, I feel that this court cannot interfere.

I would only say this, if what I have said is correct in law, it is advisable that police officers should use some very clear words to bring home to a person that he is under compulsion. It certainly must not be left in the state that a defendant can go into the witness-box and merely say "I did not think I was under compulsion." If difficulties for the future are to be avoided, it seems to me that by far and away the simplest thing is for a police officer to say "I arrest you." If the defendant goes to the police station after hearing those words, it seems to me that he simply could not be believed if he thereafter said "I did not think there was any compulsion, I was only going voluntarily."'

Furthermore, where words alone were used the arrestee had to accede to the detention: if the arrestor simply said 'I arrest you' and the arrestee ran off before he was physically touched, the arrest was not complete.[20]

These principles remain good law: see *Nichols v Bulman*[21] (words 'I arrest you' not sufficient to constitute a lawful arrest in the absence of any prior to subsequent submission to compulsion). See *Mepstead v DPP*[1] holding that for an officer to touch the arm of another is not an arrest nor actionable in trespass per se.

(4) There is a requirement now clearly distinct from element (3) that in *all* cases the arrestee must be informed of the *fact* of arrest, except where the arrest is made by a private citizen and the fact of arrest is obvious: s. 28(1), (2) and (5).

19 [1969] 2 QB 216, DC.
20 *Russen v Lucas* (1824) 1 C & P 153; *Sandon v Jervis* (1859) EB & E 942; Glanville Williams, [1954] Crim LR 6 at 12–14.
21 [1985] RTR 236.
1 Above, p. 164.

(5) The arrestee must be informed of the *ground* for arrest as soon as is practicable except where the arrest is by a private citizen and the ground of arrest is obvious. This was an important common law requirement (although the exception where the ground was 'obvious' applied to police arrests as well as citizen arrests): *Christie v Leachinsky*.[2] The reasons for the rule were stated as follows by Viscount Simon:[2a]

'[T]his is for the obvious purpose of securing that a citizen who is prima facie entitled to personal freedom should know why for the time being his personal freedom is interfered with. Scott LJ argued that if the law circumscribed the issue of warrants for arrest in this way it would hardly be that a policeman acting without a warrant was entitled to make an arrest without stating the charge on which the arrest was made... No one, I think, would approve a situation in which when the person arrested asked for the reason, the policeman replied "that has nothing to do with you: come along with me."...
...And there are practical considerations, as well as theory, to support the view I take. If the charge on suspicion of which the man is arrested is then and there made known to him, he has the opportunity of giving an explanation of any misunderstanding or of calling attention to other persons for whom he may have been mistaken, with the result that further inquiries may save him from the consequences of false accusation...'

His Lordship also stated that this 'does not mean that technical or precise language need be used'. Lord Simonds put the point like this (p. 593):

'[I]t is not an essential condition of lawful arrest that the constable should at the time of arrest formulate any charge at all, much less the charge which may ultimately be found in the indictment. But this, and this only, is the qualification which I would impose upon the general proposition. It leaves untouched the principle, which lies at the heart of the matter, that the arrested man is entitled to be told what is the act for which he is arrested. The "charge" ultimately made will depend upon the view taken by the law of his act. In ninety-nine cases out of a hundred the same words may be used to define the charge or describe the act, nor is any technical precision necessary: for instance, if the act constituting the crime is the killing of another man, it will be immaterial that the arrest is for murder and at a later hour the charge of manslaughter is substituted. The arrested man is left in no doubt that the arrest is for that killing. This is I think, the fundamental principle, viz.., that a man is entitled to know what... are "the facts which are said to constitute a crime on his part"...'

Explaining true grounds for arrest. In *R v Chalkey and Jeffries*,[3] the Court of Appeal considered that it was sufficient for a suspect to be told of the ground for his arrest even if there was an ulterior motive (to investigate his involvement in other serious crimes) that was not disclosed to him. Is it legitimate to inform a suspect of the valid reason for arrest even if it is not the true reason for the arrest? Note that under Art. 5(2) a suspect must be informed properly in a language he understands of the reason for his arrest: see also *Murray v UK*.[4]

In *R v Kirk*[5] a conviction for manslaughter was quashed where K had been arrested and cautioned in relation to a burglary and not cautioned in respect of the manslaughter even though the police had adequate information to arrest on that charge. The tactic was to keep K in custody on what he thought was a non-serious charge (so that he rejected legal advice). Kennedy LJ stated that:

'where the police, having made an arrest, propose to question a suspect or to question him further in relation to an offence which is more serious than the offence in respect of which the offence was made, they must, before questioning him or further questioning him, either charge

---

2   [1947] AC 573, HL.
2a pp. 585, 588.
3   [1998] QB 848, CA.
4   (1994) 19 EHRR 193.
5   [1999] 4 All ER 698, CA (Cr D).

the suspect with the more serious offence or… at least ensure that he is aware of the true nature of the investigation.'

Will a suspect's awareness of the true nature of the investigation render more reliable his answers in interview? Will the investigation be more fair? If an arresting officer is satisfied that the arrest conditions are met, his private views as to the likelihood of a charge resulting from that arrest are not relevant provided he is not acting mala fides or in the knowledge that no charge would result: *Martin v Metropolitan Police Comr.*[6]

It was not necessary for the arrestor to indicate the grounds upon which his 'reasonable suspicion' was based.[7] Is that required now? The difficulty faced by the officer in making the decision whether there is a reasonable suspicion is often lost when the case is considered in the calm of the courtroom. For example, the Court of Appeal allowed an appeal against dismissal of a claim for false imprisonment when the police had arrested B for theft of a cheque book despite his clear evidence that it was his girlfriend's and having shown them slips from his cheque book recording payments to her account: *Banjo v Chief Constable of Greater Manchester.*[8]

In *Gelberg v Miller*,[9] the appellant parked his car outside a restaurant in London while he had a meal. Police officers asked him to move the car. He refused, preferring to finish his meal first. On being told that the police would remove the car themselves he removed the rotor arm from the distributor mechanism. He also refused to give his name and address or show his driving licence and certificate of insurance. He was arrested by one of the officers. The officer said he was arresting the appellant for 'obstructing him in the execution of his duty by refusing to move his car and refusing his name and address'. The appellant was charged under a forerunner of s. 89 of the Police Act 1996.[10] The Attorney-General conceded that there was no power to arrest for obstruction of the police as no actual or apprehended breach of the peace was involved. However, the court held that this was a valid arrest for 'obstructing the thoroughfare' (an offence under s. 54(6) of the Metropolitan Police Act 1839). Lord Parker CJ stated:[1]

'To my mind it is clear that, by saying that he was arresting him for refusing to move his motor-car, he was informing the appellant of a fact which, in all circumstances, amounted to a wilful obstruction of the thoroughfare by leaving his car in that position. It seems to me to matter not that the respondent also coupled with that the refusal to give his name and address or the allegation of obstructing him in the execution of his duty. May I test it in this way: supposing the respondent had said nothing but had just arrested him, could it really be said that the appellant did not know all the facts constituting an alleged wilful obstruction of the thoroughfare without having that particular charge made against him at the time? In my judgment, what the appellant knew and what he was told was ample to fulfil the obligation as to what should be done at the time of an arrest without warrant.'

How would this case be decided now?[2]

In *R v Telfer*,[3] a police officer knew that the police wanted to interview the defendant in connection with a burglary. The officer encountered the defendant and when the defendant refused voluntarily to accompany the officer to the police station the officer arrested him 'on suspicion of burglary'. At the time of the arrest the officer did not know which particular burglary the defendant was suspected of having

---

6 (2001) 18 June, CA (Civ Div), unreported.
7 See Glanville Williams, [1954] Crim LR 161.
8 (1997) 24 June, CA (Civ D), unreported.
9 [1961] 1 WLR 153, DC.
10 See above.
1 At 161.
2 See *Ghafar v Chief Constable of West Midlands Police* (2000) 21 May, CA (Civ Div), unreported.
3 [1976] Crim LR 562 (Bristol Cr Ct).

committed. The officer could have ascertained these details fairly speedily had he asked his headquarters. Instead he had merely sought confirmation that the defendant was wanted. The arrest was held unlawful. A person arrested was entitled to be told the particular burglary of which he was suspected and on the facts such information could quite easily have been given to him. Would the obligation of the officer have been less if the information had been less readily available?

In *Abbassy v Metropolitan Police Comr*,[4] the Court of Appeal held that the trial judge in a civil action against the police, inter alia for unlawful arrest, had been wrong to hold that an arrest stated to be for 'unlawful possession' was *necessarily* insufficient as a reason for an arrest for theft of, receiving or unlawfully taking and driving away a motor vehicle. Immediately before A's arrest, he had been told by the officer that if he did not satisfy her with regard to the ownership of the vehicle he had been driving she would arrest him. (The matter was remitted for a new trial for a jury to determine as a matter of fact whether a sufficient reason had been given.) Cf. *Murphy v Oxford*.[5]

In *Wilson v Chief Constable of Lancashire*,[6] W was arrested on suspicion of theft of cheques from a supervisor at his training centre. There was video footage of W visiting the bank at which the withdrawals from the account had been made at the relevant time. When confronted by a police officer, W was not told any of this, he was simply told that he was under suspicion for theft of a cheque, and asked of his whereabouts on the day of the withdrawals. He was arrested when he made no mention of a visit to the bank. He was later able to provide a reason for the visit. Mance LJ concluded that W had not been adequately informed of the reason for arrest:

> 'the most that an innocent party would have gathered from what was actually said would have been that he was being charged with stealing cheques (or perhaps a cheque book) from or at a bank in Cleveleys on November 1st 1996. This is in marked contrast with the actual information which the officer had and which gave him his cause for reasonable suspicion.'

Thorpe LJ dissented on the application of the law to the facts, believing that the officer had done 'just enough'.

How specific should the officer be in explaining the grounds for his reasonable suspicion and the grounds for the arrest?

When arresting a suspect for drug dealing, it is not necessary to specify the class of drugs involved. To do so would be to require undue technicality: *Clarke v Chief Constable of North Wales*.[7] However, Sedley LJ took the view, *obiter*, that the –

> 'very fact that not every possession of controlled drugs is an arrestable offence... arguably made some greater specificity, however shortly expressed, essential. Without it, the argument goes, no court could determine whether the arrest was lawful without considering extrinsic evidence of what the ground of arrest actually was ... when the whole purpose of the principle now set out in section 28(3) of PACE is to make such inquiry inappropriate. The determination of what was conveyed to the person detained, as opposed to what was in the constable's mind, is a different question: hence the decision in *Abbassy*. I am also impressed by the consideration that to sanction the words used in the present case in the context in which they were used (which unlike the situation in Abbassy, conveyed no fuller information) as a sufficient compliance with the law may be to invite, in fact to initiate, the erosion of one of our most important historic safeguards of personal liberty. *Christie v Leachinsky* expressly brought the law of arrest into line with the longstanding principle that – in the words of Burrow's famous headnote to *Entick v Carrington* (1765) 19 St Tr. 1029 – general warrants are illegal. It seems to me at least arguable that to uphold this arrest will mean creating a distinction of law

---

4 [1990] 1 All ER 193.
5 (1985) 15 December.
6 (2000) 23 November, CA.
7 (2000) Independent, 22 May, CA (Civ D), per Brooke LJ, with whom Sir Christopher Staughton agreed.

between the unlawful use of general words in *Christie v Leachnisky* (where unlawful possession was quite large enough, in non-technical terms to embrace the arrestable as well as the non-arrestable offence. Put another way, I do not at present think that an intelligible line can be drawn between a case where the suspect is told the wrong ground for his arrest and a case where he is not told the right ground for his arrest – and that may be the difference between *Christie v Leachnisky* and this case.'

Do you agree with Sedley LJ? Could there have been any real doubt in the minds of the suspects why they were being deprived of their liberty? What else is the purpose of s. 28(3)? Does it matter if the police are consciously withholding details from the suspect rather than doing so without premeditation?[8]

In *R v Green*,[9] the Court of Appeal held that the trial judge should direct the jury whether the words of the officer are capable in law of amounting to a sufficient basis to inform the defendant of the arrest, but leave to the jury the decision as to whether they were spoken.

As to the requirement that suspects are informed of their arrest under Art. 5(2) of the ECHR, in *Fox, Campbell and Hartley v UK*[10] the ECHR held that an arrestee must be told in simple, non-technical language that he can understand, the essential legal and factual grounds for his arrest, so as to be able, if he sees fit, to challenge its lawfulness. Technical errors are unlikely to invalidate an arrest under the Convention: see *Douiyeb v Netherlands*.[11]

An arrest is unlawful if the person arrested is not told the ground of arrest in compliance with s. 28(3); however, the arrest becomes lawful once the ground is given: *Lewis v Chief Constable of the South Wales Constabulary*,[12] applying the pre-PACE decision in *R v Kulynycz*.[13] Moreover, if it is not practicable for the ground of arrest to be given at the time of arrest the arrest is not rendered unlawful retrospectively when the ground is not supplied when this does become practicable thereafter: *DPP v Hawkins*[14] (conviction for assault on a police officer under s. 51(1) of the Police Act 1964 upheld). Cf. *Edwards v DPP*.[14a] Failure to inform of the ground of arrest at the time does not taint all further police action. Where L was arrested and there was a failure to comply with s. 28, that did not prevent her later attack on the custody officer from being an assault on an officer in the execution of his duty: *DPP v L*.[15] Should subsequent findings of unlawfulness in the arrest procedure render the arrest void *ab initio*? If a suspect is arrested by one officer and informed of the ground of arrest by another, s. 28 is satisfied.[16]

In *Dawes v DPP*,[17] D took a car without authority; the vehicle had been prepared by the police so that when the door was opened, they were automatically informed, and after the car had been driven a few yards, the engine cut out and D was trapped inside. The police arrived on the scene within minutes and informed D that he was arrested and of the reason. The court held that D had been arrested when the doors locked on him, and that he had been given the reason as soon as practicable. Kennedy LJ did, however, say that if the police were slow to respond, a court might find that he was not informed as soon as practicable:

---

8 On the application of the *Christie v Leachinsky* principles to arrests under s. 25, see *Nicholas v Parsonage*, n. 6 below, and on arrests under the Road Traffic Act 1972 see S. H. Bailey and D. J. Birch, [1982] Crim LR at 551–554.
9 (1996) 15 October, CA (Cr D).
10 (1990) 13 EHRR 157, para. 19.
11 (1999) 30 EHRR 790.
12 [1991] 1 All ER 206.
13 [1971] 1 QB 367.
14 [1988] 1 WLR 1166.
14a Below, p. 293.
15 (1998) 14 December, DC.
16 *Dhesi v Chief Constable of West Midlands Police* (2000) Times 19 April, CA (Civ D).
17 [1994] RTR 209, DC.

'It may, therefore, be prudent for police forces who wish to use this type of device to consider whether it would be practicable to put in the car something which would advise the person detained that they are under arrest and the reason why they are under arrest, but that is a matter for them.'[18]

(A sealed envelope marked 'For the attention of any car thief'?)

(6) The arrestor must regard his action as an arrest in the sense of a possible first step in the criminal process. For example, if he simply detains someone to question him without any thought of arrest the action will be unlawful (see *Kenlin v Gardiner*[19] and *R v Brown*[20]).

(7) The exercise of discretion must not be an ultra vires abuse of power:[21] *Plange v Chief Constable of South Humberside Police*[1] (arrest where officer knew that there was no possibility of a charge would be unlawful as the officer had acted on some irrelevant consideration or for an improper purpose). See the *dicta* in *R v Chalkey and Jeffries*[2] regarding the legitimacy of a properly executed arrest for one offence with the real purpose being to investigate others:

'we acknowledge the importance of the liberty of the subject. It is a fundamental right of which he may only be deprived by the due process of law, which process includes an entitlement to be told why he is being deprived of it. However, a collateral motive for an arrest on otherwise good and stated grounds does not necessarily make it unlawful. It depends on the motive. That is clear from the materially different facts of *Christie v Leachnisky* and the qualified manner in which the Members of the Judicial Committee expressed the important principle for which the case is famous. [His lordship referred to the judgments in *Christie*]. The reasoning for that well-known and respectable aid to justice "a holding charge", seems to us equally appropriate to circumstances where, as here, the police have, and have so informed the subjects when arresting them, reasonable grounds for doing so, but were motivated by a desire to investigate and put a stop to further, far more serious, crime.'[3]

In Phillips and Brown's Home Office Study (above), 11% of people were arrested for two offences and 2% for three or more.[4]

The use of undue force does not itself render an arrest unlawful: *Simpson v Chief Constable of South Yorkshire Police*.[5]

4. Under s. 1 of the Magistrates' Courts Act 1980:

'Upon an information being laid before a justice of the peace…that any person has, or is suspected of having, committed an offence.'

the justice may either (1) issue a summons requiring that person to appear before a magistrates' court or (2) issue a warrant to arrest that person and bring him before a magistrates' court. There are geographical limitations to the justice's power (s. 1(2)) and the information must be in writing and substantiated on oath (s. 1(3).) Where the offence charged is an indictable offence, a warrant may be issued at any time notwithstanding that a summons has previously been issued (s. 1(6)). A decision to issue a warrant or summons is a 'judicial act' and cannot be delegated by a justice without express authority.[6] The Justices' Clerks Rules 1970[7] expressly authorise

---

18 p. 125.
19 Above, p. 165.
20 (1976) 64 Cr App Rep 231.
21 See above, p. 283.
 1 (1992) Times, 23 March, CA.
 2 [1998] QB 848, CA.
 3 Per Auld LJ.
 4 At p. 27.
 5 (1991) 135 Sol Jo 383, CA.
 6 Per Lord Roskill, *obiter*, in *Hill v Anderton* [1982] 2 All ER 963 at 971–972, HL.
 7 S.I. 1970 No. 231.

justices' clerks (but not their subordinates) to issue summonses (but not arrest warrants).

Section 125 of the Magistrates' Courts Act 1980, as amended by the 1984 Act, provides:

'(1) A warrant of arrest issued by a justice of the peace shall remain in force until it is executed or withdrawn or it ceases to have effect in accordance with the rules.

(2) A warrant of arrest, warrant of commitment, warrant of detention, warrant of distress or search warrant issued by a justice of peace may be executed anywhere in England and Wales by any person to whom it is directed or by any constable acting within his police area...

This subsection does not apply to a warrant of commitment, [warrant of detention][8] or a warrant of distress issued under Part VI of the General Rate Act 1967.

[(3) A warrant to [which this subsection applies] may be executed by a constable notwithstanding that it is not in his possession at the time; but the warrant shall, on the demand of the person arrested, be shown to him as soon as practicable...]'[9]

Subsection (4) lists the warrants to which sub-s. (3) applies, and includes arrest warrants and various other warrants under the 1980 Act and other Acts.

There are considerable variations among police forces as to the proportions of cases initiated by (i) an arrest without warrant and charge and (ii) the issue of a summons; the arrangements whereby the police decide to prosecute also vary according to which method is adopted: see S. H. Bailey and M. J. Gunn.[10]

5. *Powers of arrest without warrant.* The general powers to arrest without warrant for 'arrestable offences' are based on those contained in s. 2 of the Criminal Law Act 1967. Section 2 had replaced common law powers of arrest in respect of felonies following the abolition of the distinction between felonies and misdemeanours.[11] Sections 24(5) and 24(6) preserve a distinction that existed at common law in respect of the powers of constables and private individuals to arrest for felony. In *Walters v W H Smith & Son Ltd*[12] the defendants reasonably suspected that Walters had stolen books from a station bookstall. At Walters' trial the jury acquitted him, believing his statements that he had intended to pay for the books. Accordingly no crime had been committed in respect of the books. Walters sued the defendants, *inter alia*, for false imprisonment in having arrested him for an offence that had not been committed. Sir Rufus Isaacs CJ giving judgment for the Court of Appeal held that to justify the arrest a private individual had to show not only reasonable suspicion but also that the offence for which the arrested person was given into custody had in fact been committed, albeit by somebody else. In its Seventh Report, the Criminal Law Revision Committee commented:

'14. We gave serious consideration to recommending the abolition of the rule that, in order to justify an arrest, on reasonable suspicion that an offence had been committed, a private person unlike a constable, must prove that the offence was in fact committed by somebody. We recognise that there is a substantial case for abolishing the distinction. First, it seems anomalous that a private person should be liable for wrongful arrest by a constable. Secondly, it is argued that in *Walton's* case... the Court of Appeal, in affirming the existence of the distinction, accepted too uncritically statements to the same effect in Hale and Hawkins, without considering the question fully as one of principle; in that case however Sir Rufus Isaacs CJ said (p. 606) that he was "convinced on consideration that it [the rule] is based on sound

---

8 Inserted by the Access to Justice Act 1999, ss. 95(1); 97(4), 106, Sch. 15, Part V(8).
9 Prospectively repealed by the Access to Justice Act 1999, Sch. 15.
10 *Smith and Bailey on The Modern English Legal System* (3rd edn, 1995), Chap. 13.
11 See the Seventh Report of the Criminal Law Revision Committee (Cmnd. 2695, 1965) on Felonies and Misdemeanours.
12 [1914] 1 KB 595.

principle" and that, in the interests of the liberty of the subject, a person who arrested another without getting a warrant would have to take the risk of its turning out, contrary to appearance, that no felony had been committed. Thirdly, it is pointed out that the existence of the distinction maybe a trap to a private person who is careful instead of precipitate about deciding whether to arrest a person. If, for example, a store detective saw a person apparently shoplifting, he could arrest him under clause 2(2) on the ground that he had reasonable cause to suspect him of being in the act of committing an arrestable offence, and he would not be liable for unlawful arrest even if it turned out that he was wrong: but if he preferred out of caution to invite the other to the office to give him an opportunity of clearing himself, and then arrested him on being satisfied that he was guilty, the detective would be liable if this turned out to be wrong.

15. But the majority of the committee... are not in favour of recommending that the distinction should be abolished. They doubt whether it would be desirable, or acceptable to public opinion, to increase the powers of arrest enjoyed by private persons; and they think that there is a strong argument in policy that a private person should, if it is at all doubtful whether the offence was committed, put the matter in the hands of the police or, as Sir Rufus Isaacs CJ said, take the risk of liability if he acts on his own responsibility.'

The distinction between sub-s. (4) and (5) was crucial in *R v Self*.[13] S was seen by a store detective (Mrs Stanton) to put a bar of chocolate in his pocket and leave the store without paying for it. He was followed outside and along the street by the store detective and a shop assistant (Mr Frost). They saw him throw the chocolate away and approached him, F saying 'You have been seen shoplifting'. S punched and kicked F and ran off. This was observed by a passer-by, Mr Mole, who gave chase, caught S and told him he was making a citizen's arrest. S kicked M and struggled but was subsequently restrained. At trial S gave evidence that he had forgotten about the chocolate and had no intention to steal it. He was acquitted of theft, but convicted of assault with intent to resist or prevent his lawful apprehension contrary to s. 38 of the Offences against the Person Act 1861. The Court of Appeal quashed these convictions holding that the acquittal on the theft charge was fatal to the lawfulness of the arrest under s. 24(5) of PACE. The court dealt dismissively with an argument that the arrest might be justified by reference to s. 24(4).[14]

'...it is said on behalf of the Crown that the court should not be assiduous to restrict the citizen's powers of arrest and that, by going back to sub-s. (4) and looking at the words there, "anyone who is in the act of committing an arrestable offence", perhaps those words can be used to cover the sort of situation that arose in this case where somebody apparently making good his escape. Having committed the offence of theft, can it be said, asks Mr Sleeman, that the thief is not in substance still committing the offence while running away?

He asks, rhetorically, should the court have to inquire into the exact moment when the ingredients of the theft come together – dishonesty, appropriation, intention permanently to deprive – when to analyse the offence carefully may produce absurd results so that in one set of circumstances the offence may be complete and the situation fall within sub-s (5) and in another be still being committed and fall within sub-s (4).

The view of this court is that little profit can be had from taking examples and trying to reduce them to absurdity. The words of the statute are clear and applying those words to this case there was no arrestable offence committed.'

Is this convincing? Note that S was under the observation of the store detective throughout and so no issue of identity could arise as there might in respect of an offence that is clearly complete and in the past. Could it plausibly make a difference that the chocolate was no longer in S's possession when he was arrested? If the court's

---

13 [1992] 3 All ER 476, CA (Cr D).
14 Per Garland J at 480.

analysis is correct does it not illustrate the absurdity of the distinction between sub-ss. (4) and (5)?[15]

Later cases have interpreted *Self* more restrictively. Garland J's final sentence, quoted above, was explained as meaning 'no more than that it was necessary for it to mean for the purposes of the case the court was dealing with, namely, that the verdict convicting Mr Self of assault was, in view of the condition precedent in sub-s. (5), inconsistent with the verdict acquitting him of theft.'[16]

In *Stanley v Benning*[17] S was arrested by B, a shopkeeper, after S had been seen to take two pairs of trousers into a fitting cubicle and come out with only one pair. S was detained immediately outside B's shop and was found to be wearing the other pair underneath his own trousers. He was acquitted of theft by the magistrates. The question arose in civil proceedings brought by S was to whether the determination of not guilty was conclusive proof for s. 24(5). Sir Nicholas Scott V-C stated that as 'a matter of principle' no one in civil law can be debarred from alleging that an acquittal was incorrect. It is therefore always open to the defendant to challenge a claimant's acquittal in cases involving s. 24(5). The court distinguished *Self* on the ground that in the present case it was impossible to divide up the actions of S into a series of separate acts. As his actions were one continuous act, s. 24(4) applied:

'the intent of subsection (4) was to provide a power which citizens can exercise when they have reasonable grounds for suspecting that an arrestable offence is being committed before their eyes. If an individual sees somebody taking goods from a shop self, putting them in his or her pocket or his or her bag and leaving the shop without paying, it seems to me that the individual is able to rely on subsection (4) if he or she then and there endeavours to arrest the miscreant. It is not to the point that some analysis of the offence of theft might require the conclusion that the offence was complete when the article was taken from the shelf with the requisite dishonest intention. For the purposes of subsection (4), in my judgement, the question whether the act of committing the arrestable offence has continued up to the point at which the arrest was made raises a question of fact and degree fit to be put before a jury for decision.'

With the increasing trend towards private security (in shopping centres and other public places), the courts will be under a greater pressure to clarify the extent of the 'citizens' arrest' powers.[18] Does Art. 5 permit an arrest in the absence of reasonable suspicion? Are all citizen's arrests based on reasonable suspicion?[19]

6. The concept 'arrestable offence' includes most serious offences. For example, it includes murder, manslaughter, wounding with intend to do grievous bodily harm, unlawful wounding, criminal damage, robbery, burglary, blackmail, theft, handling stolen goods and obtaining a pecuniary advantage by deception. The reference to offences for which the penalty is fixed by law relates to murder,[1] and treason.

Under the 1967 Act the five-year imprisonment had to be available by virtue of an enactment. This requirement has been removed: accordingly, certain common law offences, including kidnapping, attempting to pervert the course of justice, conspiracy to defraud and false imprisonment, now fall within the concept of 'arrestable offence'. The RCCP thought that the concept should be widened to include all *imprisonable* offences: s. 24 retains the 'five-year' principle.

---

15 See Commentary by J. C. Smith, [1992] Crim LR 573–574 and J. E. Stannard, (1994) 58 JCL 393.
16 Per Sir Nicholas Scott V-C in *Stanley v Benning* (1998) 14 July, CA (Civ D).
17 (1998) 14 July, CA (Civ D).
18 See material in Chap. 2 above, and see proposals to require private companies to bring shoplifting prosecutions: Home Office, *Diary of a Police Officer* (2001).
19 See s. 24(4)(a).
1 Murder (Abolition of Death Penalty) Act 1965, s. 1(1).

7. *Section 25 (3) arrests.* Section 25 creates a power of arrest in respect of minor offences in circumstances where such a power is necessary if the suspect is to be brought to justice.[2] In *Nicholas v Parsonage*[3] N refused to give his name when stopped for riding his bicycle in a dangerous manner. P informed him of his powers of arrest under PACE, and request N's name and address. N again refused. P arrested him and told him he was being arrested for failing to give his name and address. The Divisional Court dismissed an appeal against conviction, holding that the arrest, under s. 25 of PACE, had been lawful. Among the points made by the Divisional Court were (1) a constable exercising the power under s. 25(3)(a) and (c) is not required to say why he wants the name and address; (2) N had been adequately informed of the ground of arrest under s. 28(3), (4). 'Failure to give name and address' is not itself the ground:

> 'at the time of the arrest the arresting constable must indicate in some words – and there is plenty of authority for the proposition that he does not need to specify it in detail – the offence for which the defendant is being arrested. If he goes on and says: "I am arresting you because you have not given your name and address", so much the better. He has then given all the detail that could possibly be required.'[4]

The requirement was satisfied here by the reference to N's riding in a dangerous manner only a very short time before the moment of arrest. The expression 'at the time of arrest'.

> 'comprehends a short but reasonable period of time around the moment of arrest, both before and, as the statute itself specifically says, after.'[5]

In *Ghafar v Chief Constable of West Midlands Police*[6] G was stopped while driving a car without wearing a seatbelt. He was asked for his name and address and refused to provide them. The officer arrested G on that basis. In G's claim for damages, the Recorder found that the police had not informed G of the ground for arrest. The Court of Appeal held that the officer should have explained both: (1) the offence which G was suspected of committing – the seatbelt offence, and (2) the power to request a name and address. It was not enough to simply say that the failure to provide a name and address was the cause of the arrest.

Ghafar v Chief Constable of West Midland Police (2000) 21 May, Court of Appeal (Civil Division)

Roch LJ: Mr. Perks makes two submissions: first, that section 28(3) requires an officer to tell the person he is arresting the ground for the arrest. The ground for the arrest in this case was the commission of the seat belt offence. That was all that PC Wilkes was required to tell the respondent. The second submission that Mr Perks makes is that if he is wrong about that submission, and the officer in addition to telling the respondent of the officer's suspicion that the respondent had committed a seat belt offence, had also to indicate the general arrest condition on which the officer was relying, then, submits Mr. Perks, both those matters were adequately conveyed to the respondent by the police officer at the time of the respondent's arrest. Mr. de Mello's submission is that the Recorder's ruling, that section 28(3) had not been fulfilled by the officer, should be upheld for the reasons that the Recorder gave. I would not accept the first submission made by Mr. Perks. The phrase, the ground of arrest, in section 28(3), must include the grounds of arrest, if more than one ground is required before the power to arrest arises. This was a case where two matters had to exist before the officer could exercise a power of arrest: first, that a seat belt offence had been committed or the officer reasonably suspected that such an offence had been committed and, secondly, that one of the general arrest conditions existed or appeared to the officer to have existed. Both those matters, in my judgment, had to be communicated to the respondent.

---

2 As advocated, e.g., by D. A. Thomas, [1966] Crim LR 639.
3 [1987] RTR 199.
4 Per Glidewell LJ at 204.
5 Ibid.
6 (2000) 21 May, CA (Civ D), unreported.

I would allow the appeal. The Recorder, in my view, misdirected himself in two ways. First, he adopted a too legalistic approach as to the words which the officer actually used. He required the officer to use words which approximated to the wording of section 25(1) and section 25(3)(a), whereas I would adopt the view of Glidewell L.J. in the case of *Nicholas v Parsonage*, that there is no obligation on the arresting officer to refer to the power of arrest as opposed to the matters which have to exist for the officer to lawfully exercise that power. Second, the Recorder thought that the officer had to bring to the respondent's attention a causal link between the offence the respondent was thought by the officer to have committed and the failure to provide a name and the reason for the arrest. There is no causal link between the offence and the failure to provide a name. They both have to exist if the arrest is to be lawful and they both have to be communicated to the person being arrested at the time of the arrest if the arrest is to be lawful. Here, the ground for the arrest had two aspects; first, that the respondent had driven the car without wearing a seat belt and, second, that he had refused to give the officer his name and he had been unable to produce any means of identification. Both those matters had to be communicated to the respondent at the time of his arrest, which includes a short period of time either side of the physical act of arrest. Neither matter had to be communicated in detail, nor is there any set formula for doing so.

Mr. de Mello referred us to the case of *Abbassy v Commissioner of Police of the Metropolis* [1991] WLR 385, a judgment of the Court of Appeal, consisting of Purchas, Mustill and Woolf LJJ. In the judgment of Woolf LJ at page 392B this passage appears:

'It should, however, be noted that although information has to be given for the reasons for the arrest, no reference need to be made as to the power of arrest, whether that power be under common law or statute. Whether or not the information which is given is adequate has to be assessed objectively having regard to the information which is reasonably available to the officer. Thus, for example, in dealing with a deaf person it will be sufficient if the arresting constable has done what a reasonable person would have done in the circumstances: see *Wheatley v Lodge* [1971] 1 WLR 29. Furthermore, it is not as Leonard J said a 'technical matter' but involves informing the person who is arrested in non-technical and not necessarily precise language of the nature of the offence said to constitute the crime for which he is being arrested.'

Although that case referred to events prior to the passing of the Police and Criminal Evidence Act 1984, I would adopt that passage as still representing the law as to the way in which the necessary information has to be conveyed by an arresting officer to a person being arrested. Police constables are not lawyers. When they are arresting a person they are acting, not in the calm atmosphere of a court of law, but often in a public place. Police constables can anticipate that, in effecting arrest, they may have to deal with physical resistance or an attempt to escape by the person being arrested, or physical interference by bystanders who may be sympathetic to the person being arrested. Again, I would refer to another passage in the judgment of Woolf L.J. in *Abbassy's* case at page 394F:

'While it is extremely important to recognize that the right to arrest without a warrant is an infringement of the liberty of the individual, it has also to be borne in mind that police officers have frequently to perform their duties in difficult circumstances when it is unreal to expect them to use precise legal language.'

In such circumstances all the law requires of the officer is that the gist or essentials of the ground or grounds of arrest are conveyed to the person being arrested. Here, these essentials were, first, that the respondent had committed an offence of driving without a seat belt, and, second, that the respondent's name had not been given to the officer.

The question whether an arrest was lawful is one of law for the judge to decide, but where there is a jury, the judge can only make such a determination on agreed facts. If there are disputed facts these must be resolved by the jury: *Balchin v Chief Constable of Hampshire Constabulary.*[7]

---

7   (2001) 5 April, CA (Civ D), unreported.

In *G v DPP*,[8] Gibson (G), Gill and others went to a police station to make a complaint. They refused to leave, and became abusive. Sergeant Jackson arrested Gill for violent behaviour in a police station.[9] G attempted to prevent this. His conviction for obstructing a police officer was subsequently quashed by the Divisional Court on the ground that Gill's arrest was unlawful. The s. 29 offence was non-arrestable. J gave evidence that, when he made the arrest, he believed the details of name and address that had been supplied by Gill when he first came to the station were false. The sole ground was that 'in the vast majority of cases...people who commit offences do not give their correct details'. The court found that J's suspicion was not 'reasonable' as here the details had been provided before Gill was suspected of any offence.

Aspects of both cases are criticised by A. Lawson.[10] She argues that for a valid arrest under s. 25, satisfaction of a *general arrest* condition is just as necessary as satisfaction of the *offence* condition.[11] Is this undermined by Glidewell LJ's suggestion in *Nicholas v Parsonage* that it is not essential to give as a 'ground' of arrest the relevant general arrest condition as well as the offence; and by the failure of the court in *G v DPP* to state that the sergeant's belief was in any event wholly unreasonable as in effect rendering the general arrest conditions superfluous?

More reassuringly, in *Edwards v DPP*,[12] the Divisional Court confirmed that, where it is sought to justify an arrest by reference to s. 25, there must be evidence that this was in the officer's mind at the time. Here, police officers sought to search three men suspected of possessing cannabis. One of them put the contents of his right hand in his mouth when asked by PC R to hand them over, and was arrested by R, who said 'You are nicked for obstruction'. The court held this arrest to be unlawful. There was no evidence of R's state of mind and it was not appropriate to infer what it was. Moreover, it was practicable for R to give a reason for the arrest, but he gave a reason that was not a valid one. E's conviction for obstruction of a police officer by intervening after the arrest was quashed. *Edwards* was applied in *Mullady v DPP*:[13] where an officer gives a specific, but invalid reason for arrest, a later (valid) reason cannot be substituted later. See also *Maudling v DPP*,[14] failure to request breath test meant the refusal to provide one was not an arrestable offence, so arrest unlawful even though officer could have relied on other powers.

8. It has been argued that a constable would have power to stop a vehicle in circumstances where he would have power to stop a person, e.g. to effect an arrest.[15] Similarly, once a vehicle has been stopped (e.g. under the Road Traffic Act 1988, s. 163[16]) and the constable reasonably suspects that it has or might have been stolen, the constable has power at common law to detain it for such reasonable time as will enable him to effect an arrest.[17]

9. As Lord Hope observed recently, any detention that is unlawful in domestic law will automatically be contrary to Art. 5 of the ECHR: see *R v HMP Brockhill, ex p Evans (No 2)*.[18]

---

8 [1989] Crim LR 150.
9 Contrary to s. 29 of the Town Police Clauses Act 1847.
10 'Whither the "General Arrest Conditions"?' [1993] Crim LR 567.
11 p. 571.
12 (1993) 94 Cr App Rep 301.
13 [1997] COD 422.
14 (1996) 4 December, DC, unreported.
15 R. Clayton and H. Tomlinson, *Civil Actions Against the Police* (2nd edn, 1992), p. 279.
16 Above, p. 224.
17 *Lodwick v Sanders* [1985] 1 All ER 577; *Sanders v DPP* [1988] Crim LR 605.
18 [2000] 3 WLR 843.

10. *Disposition after arrest.* A person arrested by or handed over to a constable must be taken to a police station as soon as 'practicable', unless his presence elsewhere 'is necessary in order to carry out such investigations as it is reasonable to carry out immediately'.[19] This appears to put into statutory form the dicta of Lord Denning MR in *Dallison v Caffery*[1] here, a suspect had been taken to check out an alibi instead of direct to the police station: however, as it had been done with his consent, he could not complain of it anyway. It does not appear that the suspect can require a constable to make a detour to check out an explanation of his conduct that would clear him: *McCarrick v Oxford*.[2]

In *R v Keane*,[3] the Court of Appeal inclined to the view that there had been breaches of s. 30 (1), (10) and (11) in that it had not been necessary to interview K at the flat he was occupying, following his arrest for possessing a gun and cannabis; moreover no reasons for the delay were ever recorded. Nevertheless, the court upheld the judge's refusal to exclude the confession made during the interview under s. 78 of PACE.[4] Cf. *R v Raphaie*,[4a] in which police delayed taking a suspect to the station for one and three-quarter hours during which time they asked 43 questions (and see *R v Hanchard*.[4b])

If a private person makes an arrest he 'must, as soon as he reasonably can, hand the man over to a constable or take him to the police station or take him before a magistrate'.[5] However, there is no requirement that this be done immediately: *John Lewis & Co v Tims*.[6] Here, Mrs Tims and her daughter were arrested for shoplifting by store detectives employed by the appellant firm. After being arrested they were taken to the office of the chief store detective. They were detained there until the chief detective and a manager arrived to give instructions whether to bring proceedings. They were handed into police custody within an hour of arrest. Mrs Tims claimed damages for false imprisonment. She alleged that the detectives were obliged to give her into the custody of the police immediately upon arrest. The House of Lords held that the delay was reasonable in the circumstances: 'there are advantages in refusing to give private detectives a free hand and leaving the determination of whether to prosecute or not to a superior official.'[7]

Under s. 31, a second arrest may be delayed until shortly before release from the first arrest is about to occur: *R v Samuel*.[8] Phillips and Brown,[9] found that 8% of suspects were re-arrested while in custody for offences additional to those for which they had been originally detained.[10]

In *Henderson v Chief Constable of Cleveland*[11] police arrested H on a default warrant only after they had completed other interviews with him. By that time it was too late to take him before a court that day, and he was held overnight until he was

19 s. 30(1), (10).
1   [1965] 1 QB 348 at 366–367, CA.
2   [1983] RTR 117, Commentary by D. J. Birch, [1982] Crim LR 751. See also the discussion of Art. 5 of the ECHR in Chap. 1 above.
3   [1992] Crim LR 306.
4   See, however, the Commentary by D. J. Birch, [1992] Crim LR 307, noting that the revised Code C.11.1. was even more specific in limiting interviews other than at a police station or other authorised place of detention. See also *R v Khan* [1993] Crim LR 54, and Commentary by D. J. Birch.
4a [1996] Crim LR 812, CA.
4b (1999) 6 December, CA (Cr D), unreported.
5   Per Lord Denning MR in *Dallison v Caffery* at pp. 366–367.
6   [1952] AC 676, HL.
7   Per Lord Porter at p. 691.
8   [1988] QB 615.
9   Above, p. 281.
10 p. 52.
11 (2001) 27 February, CA (Civ D).

bailed the next day. The Court of Appeal held that the police had a discretion when to execute such a warrant, and that the detainee need not be taken 'immediately' in the sense of 'at that precise second' before a court.

11. *Search on arrest.* The provisions of s. 32 are similar to the powers at common law,[12] but with some significant modifications.[13] Note there is no *automatic* right to search in every case. The search may extend to premises where the suspect had been 'immediately' before arrest; at common law it was apparently only possible to search premises where the arrestee was at the time of arrest (and possibly only in the 'immediate vicinity' of arrestee): see *McLorie v Oxford*;[14] cf. *Dillon v O'Brien and Davis*,[15] *Elias v Pasmore*.[16] If this is not done 'immediately' entry and search must be based instead on s. 18:[17] *R v Badham*[18] (is s. 32 *clearly* so limited?).

In *R v Beckford*,[19] police officers were observing premises where they believed the ground floor flat (which had been searched under a warrant on previous occasions) was being used for drug dealing. They arrested a man, Lamptey, who emerged from the premises and who, when intercepted, dropped a package of what appeared to be (and turned out to be) heroin. On arrest, L denied that he had dropped anything. They then searched the flat in reliance on their s. 32 powers and found B and others and quantities of heroin. The Court of Appeal held that the police were entitled to assume that L had come from the ground floor flat rather than either of the other two flats in the premises in view of their previous knowledge of the use of the ground floor flat.[20] Moreover, the police were entitled to rely on s. 32 if that 'genuinely [was] the reason why police officers made their entry and search'.[1] However, B's conviction was quashed as this issue was not left to the jury to consider. In argument, counsel for the Crown argued that the police officers entered the flat to look for evidence that would rebut L's denial that he had dropped a package of drugs, thus falling within s. 32. Counsel for B argued that the police were using L's arrest 'as a pretext for what they had really wanted to do all along, namely enter the premises without a warrant', avoiding the requirements of PACE Code B. It was difficult to imagine what further evidence was required against L; 'where a police officer knows he already has all the evidence he reasonable requires upon the arrestable offence he cannot possibly be said to believe that he needs to search for evidence relating to that offence'.[2]

Counsel suggested that the true state of affairs was that the police were really seeking evidence of *other* offences against *other* people, which was not within s. 32. These arguments were not considered by the court. In fact, they raise familiar public law issues as to overlapping statutory powers and exercise of powers for a plurality of purposes. If the police have two avenues lawfully open to them, one involving obtaining a warrant and the other not, why should they not chose what is to them the less burdensome.[3]

---

12 See *Dillon v O'Brien and Davis* (1887) 16 Cox CC 245; *Bessell v Wilson* (1853) 20 LTOS 233n; *Leigh v Cole* (1853) 6 Cox CC 329 at 332.
13 For searches *at* police stations see below, ss. 54, 55.
14 [1982] QB 1290.
15 (1887) 16 COX CC 245.
16 [1934] 2 KB 164, Horridge J.
17 Above, p. 249.
18 [1987] Crim LR 202 Wood Green Crown Court.
19 (1991) 94 Cr App Rep 43, CA (Cr D).
20 Note, however, that the true issue was where in fact he was immediately before the arrest not what was suspected by the police: see Commentary by D. J. Birch, [1991] Crim LR 919.
1 Per Watkins LJ at p. 49.
2 At p. 48.
3 Cf. In a different context *Westminster Bank Ltd v Beverley Borough Council* [1971] AC 509, HL.

If the police can properly undertake a s. 32 search, is it necessarily wrong for them to have in mind the point that, once lawfully on the premises, s. 19 of PACE confers very broad powers of seizure? If it is wrong, are the police nevertheless protected provided they 'genuinely' intend to act under s. 32; or is the exercise of power unlawful because a legally irrelevant consideration he has been taken into account?
12. Section 29 makes it clear that a person at a police station 'helping police with their inquiries' is not under arrest unless he is told to the contrary. This reflects the present position although many may not realise it. Note that the Act does not require the police to inform such a person of the position.[4] The Code on Detention etc., requires this is to be done if he is cautioned (C.10.2). The question of 'voluntary attendance' is considered by I. McKenzie, R Morgan and R.Reiner.[5] They argue that any encounter between the police and a suspect (as distinct from a witness) is inherently coercive and that all 'voluntary attendees' who are suspects should be told that they are free to leave at any time, are under obligation to answer questions, and are entitled to have someone told of their whereabouts and to consult a solicitor in private. They also commend a formal recording procedure adopted by one force for voluntary attendees.
13. Part X of the Criminal Justice and Public Order Act 1994 provides for the availability of the execution of search warrants in UK jurisdictions other than those in which they were issued. There are powers of arrest for officers of another UK jurisdiction.
14. *Statistics on arrest.* Recent Home Office Research conducted by C. Phillips and D. Brown[6] reviewed the procedures following arrest. Given that there are around 1.75m arrests each year, there had been surprisingly little earlier research. Phillips and Brown's paper contains comprehensive socio-demographic information on arrests and the circumstances leading to arrest. Some of the statistics are disturbing.[7]

Who is arrested?
– 85% of arrestees were male;
– 15% were juveniles (under 17);
– 54% were unemployed, 27% employed, and 14% pupils or students;[8]
– 78% were white, 13% black and 7% Asian (96% of whom were male);[9]
– Over 60% of those arrested had previous convictions;[10]
– 10% were known to be subject to a court order at the time of arrest.

4 Cf. M. Zander, *The Police and Criminal Evidence Act 1984* (2nd edn, 1990), pp. 65–67.
5 [1990] Crim LR 22 at 27–33.
6 Home Office Research and Statistics Paper 185, *Entry into the Criminal Justice System: a survey of police arrests and their outcomes* (1998).
7 Further statistics on arrest are available annually from the Home Office in its Statistical Bulletins on 'The Operation of Certain Police Powers in England and Wales'. See those referred to above in respect of stop and search. See most recently M. Ayres (above) p. 219.
8 'The present study was not designed to explore the links between unemployment and crime, but it does provide striking evidence of the high level of unemployment among criminal suspects.' p. 18.
9 The reason for disproportionate numbers is described as 'complex' p. 13. See also HO, *Findings from the 2000 BCS* (2001).
10 Whether suspects had a criminal history varied considerably according to the offence for which they had been arrested. Figures were higher for those arrested for prostitution, burglary, vehicle related crime and public order, but lower for shoplifting, criminal damage, other theft and offences of sex and violence (p. 20).

Why arrested?
- 87% of arrests were on suspicion of committing an offence;
- 13% under a warrant or other order (e.g. place of safety etc.);
- 16% appeared to be under the influence of drink/drugs at the time of arrest;
- 2% were treated as mentally disordered on arrest.

In a number of research studies, it has been suggested that PACE has led to a higher standard of evidence required for arrests.[11] Phillips and Brown still found that 87% of people had been arrested on the basis of suspicion of committing an offence.[12] See also D. Brown.[13]

8 Detention

Police and Criminal Evidence Act 1984

PART IV

DETENTION

Detention – Conditions and duration

34. Limitations on police detention
(1) A person arrested for an offence shall not be kept in police detention except in accordance with the provisions of this Part of this Act.
(2) Subject to subsection (3) below, if at any time a custody officer—
    (*a*) becomes aware, in relation to any person in police detention, that the grounds for the detention of that person have ceased to apply; and
    (*b*) is not aware of any other grounds on which the continued detention of that person could be justified under the provisions of this Part of this Act,
it shall be the duty of the custody officer, subject to subsection (4) below, to order his immediate release from custody.
(3) No person in police detention shall be released except on the authority of a custody officer at the police station where his detention was authorised or, if it was authorised at more than one station, a custody officer at the station where it was last authorised.
(4) A person who appears to the custody officer to have been unlawfully at large when he was arrested is not to be released under subsection (2) above.
(5) A person whose release is ordered under subsection (2) above shall be released without bail unless it appears to the custody officer—
    (*a*) that there is need for further investigation of any matter in connection with which he was detained at any time during the period of his detention; or
    (*b*) that proceedings may be taken against him in respect of any such matter,
    and, if it so appears, he shall be released on bail.
(6) For the purposes of this Part of this Act a person arrested under [section 6(5) for the Road Traffic Act 1998] is arrested for an offence.
[(7) For the purposes of this Part of this Act a person who returns to a police station to answer to bail or is arrested under section 46A below shall be treated as arrested for an offence and the offence in connection with which he was granted bail shall be deemed to be that offence.][14]

35. Designated police stations
(1) The chief officer of police for each police area shall designate the police stations in his area which, subject to section 30(3) and (5) above, are to be the stations in that area to be used for the purpose of detaining arrested persons.

---

11 B. L. Irving and I. K. McKenzie (1989); Bottomley (1989).
12 p. 27.
13 *Pace Ten Years On: A review of the Research* (1997), p. 2.
14 Inserted by the Criminal Justice and Public Order Act 1994, s. 29(3).

(2) A chief officer's duty under subsection (1) above is to designate police stations appearing to him to provide enough accommodation for that purpose.

(3) Without prejudice to section 12 of the Interpretation Act 1978 (continuity of duties) a chief officer—

   (a) may designate a station which was not previously designated; and

   (b) may direct that a designation of a station previously made shall cease to operate.

(4) In this Act 'designated police station' means a police station designated under this section.

35. Custody officers at police stations

(1) One or more custody officers shall be appointed for each designated police station.

(2) A custody officer for a designated police station shall be appointed—

   (a) by the chief officer of police for the area in which the designated police station is situated; or

   (b) by such other police officer as the chief officer of the police for that area may direct.

(3) No officer may be appointed a custody officer unless he is of at least the rank of sergeant.

(4) An officer of any rank may perform the functions of a custody officer at a designated police station if a custody officer is not readily available to perform them.

(5) Subject to the following provisions of this section and to section 39(2) below, none of the functions of a custody officer in relation to a person shall be performed by an officer who at the time when the function falls to be performed is involved in the investigation of an offence for which that person is in police detention at that time…

(7) Where an arrested person is taken to a police station which is not a designated police station, the functions in relation to him which at a designated police station would be the functions of a custody officer shall be performed—

   (a) by an officer who is not involved in the investigation of an offence for which he is in police detention, if such an officer is readily available; and

   (b) if no such officer is readily available, by the officer who took him to the station or any other officer.

(8) References to a custody officer in the following provisions of this Act include references to an officer other than a custody officer who is performing the functions of a custody officer by virtue of subsection (4) or (7) above.

(9) Where by virtue of subsection (7) above an officer of a force maintained by a police authority who took an arrested person to a police station is to perform the functions of a custody officer in relation to him, the officer shall inform an officer who—

   (a) is attached to a designated police station; and

   (b) is of at least the rank of inspector,

that he is to do so.

(10) The duty imposed by subsection (9) above shall be performed as soon as it is practicable to perform it.

37. Duties of custody officer before charge

(1) Where—

   (a) a person is arrested for an offence – (i) without a warrant, or (ii) under a warrant not endorsed for bail; [...]

the custody officer at each police station where he is detained after his arrest shall determine whether he has before him sufficient evidence to charge that person with the offence for which he was arrested and may detain him at the police station for such period as is necessary to enable him to do so.

(2) If the custody officer determines that he does not have such evidence before him, the person arrested shall be released either on bail or without bail, unless the custody officer has reasonable grounds for believing that his detention without being charged is necessary to secure or preserve evidence relating to an offence for which he is under arrest or to obtain such evidence by questioning him.

(3) If the custody officer has reasonable grounds for so believing, he may authorise the person arrested to be kept in police detention.

(4) Where a custody officer authorises a person who has not been charged to be kept in police detention, he shall, as soon as it is practicable, make a written record of the grounds for the decision.

(5) Subject to subsection (6) below, the written record shall be made in the presence of the person arrested who shall at that time be informed by the custody officer of the grounds for his detention.

(6) Subsection (5) above shall not apply where the person arrested is, at the time when the written record is made—

    (*a*) incapable of understanding what is said to him.

    (*b*) violent or likely to become violent; or

    (*c*) in urgent need of medical attention.

(7) Subject to section 41(7) below, if the custody officer determines that he has before him sufficient evidence to charge the person arrested with the offence for which he was arrested, the person arrested—

    (*a*) shall be charged; or

    (*b*) at the time of his release a decision whether he should be prosecuted for the offence for which he was arrested has not been taken,

it shall be the duty of the custody officer so to inform him.

(9) If the person arrested is not in a fit state to be dealt with under subsection (7) above, he may be kept in police detention until he is.

(10) The duty imposed on the custody officer under subsection (1) above shall be carried out by him as soon as it is practicable after the person arrested arrives at the police station or, in the case of a person arrested at the police station, as soon as it is practicable after arrest...

(15) In this Part of this Act—

    'arrested juvenile' means a person arrested with or without a warrant who appears to be under the age of 17[...];

    'endorsed for bail' means endorsed with a direction for bail in accordance with section 117(2) of the Magistrates' Courts Act 1980.

38. Duties of custody officer after charge

(1) Where a person arrested for an offence otherwise than under a warrant endorsed for bail is charged with an offence, the custody officer shall [, subject to section 25 of the Criminal Justice and Public Order Act 1994,][15] order his release from police detention, either on bail or without bail, unless—

    (*a*) if the person arrested is not an arrested juvenile—

        (i) his name or address cannot be ascertained or the custody officer has reasonable grounds for doubting whether a name or address furnished by him as his name or address is his real name or address;

        [(ii) the custody officer has reasonable grounds for believing that the person arrested will fail to appear in court to answer bail;

        (iii) in the case of a person arrested for an imprisonable offence, the custody officer has reasonable grounds for believing that the detention of the person arrested is necessary to prevent him from committing an offence;

        (iv) in the case of a person arrested for an offence which is not an imprisonable offence, the custody officer has reasonable grounds for believing that the detention of the person arrested is necessary to prevent him from causing physical injury to any other person or from causing loss of or damage to property;

        (v) the custody officer has reasonable grounds for believing that the detention of the person arrested is necessary to prevent him from interfering with the administration of justice or with the investigation of offences or of a particular offence; or

        (vi) the custody officer has reasonable grounds for believing that the detention of the person arrested is necessary for his own protection;][16]

    (*b*) if he is an arrested juvenile—

        (i) any of the requirements of paragraph (*a*) above is satisfied; or

        (ii) the custody officer has reasonable grounds for believing that he ought to be detained in his own interests.

15 Inserted by the Criminal Justice and Public Order Act 1994, Sch. 10, para. 54.
16 Substituted by the Criminal Justice and Public Order Act 1994, s. 28(2).

(2) If the release of a person arrested is not required by subsection (1) above, the custody officer may authorise him to be kept in police detention.

[(2A) The custody officer, in taking the decisions required by subsection (1)(*a*) and (*b*) above (except (*a*)(i) and (vi) and (*b*)(ii), shall have regard to the same considerations as those which a court is required to have regard to in taking the corresponding decisions under paragraph 2 of Part 1 of Schedule 1 to the Bail Act 1976.][17]

(3) Where a custody officer authorises a person who has been charged to be kept in police detention, he shall, as soon as it is practicable, make a written record of the grounds for the detention.

(4) Subject to subsection (5) below the written records shall be made in the presence of the person charged who shall at that time be informed by the custody officer of the grounds for his detention.

(5) Subsection (4) above shall not apply where the person charged is, at the time when the written record is made—

    (*a*) incapable of understanding what is said to him;

    (*b*) violent or likely to become violent; or

    (*c*) in urgent need of medical attention.

[(6) Where a custody officer authorises an arrested juvenile to be kept in police detention under subsection (1) above, the custody officer shall, unless he certifies—

    (*a*) that, by reason of such circumstances as are specified in the certificate, it is impracticable for him to do so; or

    (*b*) in the case of an arrested juvenile who has attained the [age of 12 years], that no secure accommodation is available and that keeping him in other local authority accommodation would not be adequate to protect the public from serious harm from him,

secure that the arrested juvenile is moved to local authority accommodation.]

[(6A) In this section—

    'local authority accommodation' means accommodation provided by or on behalf of a local authority (within the meaning of the Children Act 1989);

    'secure accommodation' means accommodation provided for the purpose of restricting liberty;

    'sexual offence' and 'violent offence' have the same meanings as in [the Powers of Criminal Courts (Sentencing) Act 2000.][18]

    and any reference, in relation to an arrested juvenile charged with a violent or sexual offence, to protecting the public from serious harm from him shall be construed as a reference to protecting members of the public from death or serious personal injury, whether physical or psychological, occasioned by further such offences committed by him.][19]

[(6B) Where an arrested juvenile is moved to local authority accommodation under subsection (6) above, it shall be lawful for any person acting on behalf of their authority to detain him.][20]

(7) A certificate made under subsection (6) above in respect of an arrested juvenile shall be produced to the court before which he is first brought thereafter.

[(7A) In this section 'imprisonable offence' has the same meaning as in Schedule 1 to the Bail Act 1976.][1]

(8) In this Part of this Act 'local authority' has the same meaning as in the [Children Act 1989].[2]

17 Inserted by ibid., s. 28(3).

18 Substituted by the Powers of Criminal Courts (Sentencing) Act 200, s. 165(1), Sch. 9, para. 96.

19 Inserted by the Criminal Justice Act 1991, s. 59, and amended by the Criminal Justice and Public Order Act 1994, s. 24.

20 Substituted by the Children Act 1989, Sch. 13, para. 53(3).

 1 Inserted by the 1994 Act, s. 28(4).

 2 Substituted by the Children Act 1989, Sch. 13, para. 53(3).

39. Responsibilities in relation to persons detained

(1) Subject to subsections (2) and (4) below, it shall be the duty of the custody officer at the police station to ensure—

    (*a*) that all person in police detention at that station are treated in accordance with this Act and any code of practice issued under it and relating to the treatment of persons in police detention; and

    (*b*) that all matters relating to such persons which are required by this Act or by such codes of practice to be recorded are recorded in the custody records relating to such persons.

(2) If the custody officer, in accordance with any code of practice issued under this Act, transfers or permits the transfer of a person in police detention—

    (*a*) to the custody of a police officer investigating an offence for which that person is in police detention; or

    (*b*) to the custody of an officer who has charge of that person outside the police station–

the custody officer shall cease in relation to that person to be subject to the duty imposed on him by subsection (1)(*a*) above; and

it shall be the duty of the officer to whom the transfer is made to ensure that he is treated in accordance with the provisions of this Act and of any such codes of practice as are mentioned in subsection (1) above.

(3) If the person detained is subsequently returned to the custody of the custody officer, it shall be the duty of the officer investigating the offence to report to the custody officer as to the manner in which this section and the codes of practice have been complied with while that person was in custody.

(4) If an arrested juvenile is [moved to local authority accommodation][3] under section 38(6) above, the custody officer shall cease in relation to that person to be subject to the duty imposed on him by subsection (1) above...

(6) Where—

    (*a*) an officer of higher rank than the custody officer gives directions relating to a person in police detention; and

    (*b*) the directions are at variance—

        (i) with any decision made or action taken by the custody officer in the performance of a duty imposed on him under this Part of this Act; or

        (ii) with any decision or action which would but for the directions have been made or taken by him in the performance of such a duty,

the custody officer shall refer the matter at once to an officer of the rank of superintendent or above who is responsible for the police station for which the custody officer is acting as custody officer.

40. Review of police detention

(1) Reviews of the detention of each person in police detention in connection with the investigation of an offence shall be carried out periodically. In accordance with the following provisions of this section—

    (*a*) in the case of a person who has been arrested and charged, by the custody officer; and

    (*b*) in the case of a person who has been arrested but not charged, by an officer of at least the rank of inspector who has not been directly involved in the investigation.

(2) The officer to whom it falls to carry out a review is referred to in this section as a 'review officer'.

(3) Subject to subsection (4) below—

    (*a*) the first review shall be not later than six hours after the detention was first authorised;

    (*b*) the second review shall be not later than nine hours after the first;

    (*c*) subsequent reviews shall be at intervals of not more than nine hours.

(4) A review may be postponed—

    (*a*) if, having regard to all the circumstances prevailing at the latest time for it specified in subsection (3) above, it is not practicable to carry out the review at the time;

    (*b*) without prejudice to the generality of paragraph (*a*) above–

---

3 Substituted by the Children Act 1989, s. 108(5), (7), Sch. 13, para. 54, Sch. 16.

     (i)   if at that time the person in detention is being questioned by a police officer and the review officer is satisfied that an interruption of the questioning for the purpose of carrying out the review would prejudice the investigation in connection with which he is being questioned; or

     (ii) if at that time no review officer is readily available.

(5) If a review is postponed under subsection (4) above it shall be carried out as soon as it is practicable after the latest time specified for it in subsection (3) above.

(6) If a review is carried out after postponement under subsection (4) above, the fact that it was so carried out shall not affect any requirement of this section as to the time at which any subsequent review is to be carried out.

(7) The review officer shall record the reasons for any postponement of a review in the custody record.

(8) Subject to subsection (9) below, where the person whose detention is under review has not been charged before the time of the review, section 37(1) to (6) above shall effect in relation to him, but with the substitution—

    (*a*) of references to the person whose detention is under review for references to the person arrested; and

    (*b*) of references to the review officer for references to the custody officer.

(9) Where a person has been kept in police detention by virtue of section 37(9) above, section 37(1) to (6) shall not have effect in relation to him but it shall be the duty of the review officer to determine whether he is yet in a fit state.

(10) Where the person whose detention is under review has been charged before the time of the review, section 38(1) to (6) above shall have effect in relation to him, but with the substitution of reference to the person whose detention is under review for references to the person arrested.

(11) Where—

    (*a*) an officer of higher rank than the review officer gives directions relating to a person in police detention; and

    (*b*) the directions are at variance—

     (i)   with any decision made or action taken by the review officer in the performance of a duty imposed on him under this Part of this Act; or

     (ii) with any decision or action which would but for the directions have been made or taken by him in the performance of such a duty,

the review officer shall refer the matter at once to an officer of the rank of superintendent or above who is responsible for the police station for which the review officer is acting as review officer in connection with the detention.

(12) Before determining whether to authorise a person's continued detention the review officer shall give—

    (*a*) that person (unless he is asleep); or

    (*b*) any solicitor representing him who is available at the time of the review,

an opportunity to make representations to him about the detention.

(13) Subject to subsection (14) below, the person whose detention is under review or his solicitor may make representations under subsection (12) above either orally or in writing.

(14) The review officer may refuse to hear oral representations from the person whose detention is under review if he considers that he is unfit to make such presentations by reason of his condition or behaviour.

41. Limits on period of detention without charge

(1) subject to the following provisions of this section and to sections 42 and 43 below, a person shall not be kept in police detention for more than 24 hours without being charged.

(2) The time from which the period of detention of a person is to be calculated (in this Act referred to as 'the relevant time')—

    (*a*) in the case of a person to whom this paragraph applies, shall be—

     (i)   the time at which that person arrives at the relevant police station; or

     (ii) the time 24 hours after the time of that person's arrest, whichever is the earlier;

    (*b*) in the case of a person arrested outside England and Wales, shall be—

     (i)   the time at which that person arrives at the first police station to which he is taken in the police area in England or Wales in which the offence for which he was arrested is being investigated; or

(ii)   the time 24 hours after the time of that person's entry into England and Wales, whichever is the earlier;

(*c*)   in the case of a person who—
(i)   attends voluntarily at a police station; or
(ii)   accompanies a constable to a police station without having been arrested,
and is arrested at the police station at the time of his arrest;

(*d*)   in any other case, except where subsection (5) below applies, shall be the time at which the person arrested arrives at the first police station to which he is taken after his arrest.

(3) Subsection (2)(*a*) above applies to a person if—
(*a*)   his arrest is sought in one police area in England and Wales.
(*b*)   he is arrested in another police area; and
(*c*)   he is not questioned in this area in which he is arrested in order to obtain evidence in relation to an offence for which he is arrested;

and in sub-paragraph (i) of that paragraph 'the relevant police station' means the first police station to which he is taken in the police area in which his arrest was sought.

(4) Subsection (2) above shall have effect in relation to a person arrested under section 31 above as if every reference in it to his arrest or his being arrested were a reference to his arrest or his being arrested for the offence for which he was originally arrested.

(5) If—
(*a*)   a person is in police detention in a police area in England and Wales ('the first area'); and
(*b*)   his arrest for an offence is sought in some other police area in England and Wales ('the second area'); and
(*c*)   he is taken to the second area for the purposes of investigating that offence, without being questioned in the first area in order to obtain evidence in relation to it...,

the relevant time shall be—
(i)   the time 24 hours after he leaves the place where he is detained in the first area; or
(ii)   the time at which he arrives at the first police station to which he is taken in the second area,

whichever is the earlier.

(6) When a person who is in police detention is removed to hospital because he is in need of medical treatment, any time during which he is being questioned in hospital or on the way there or back by a police officer for the purpose of obtaining evidence relating to an offence shall be included in any period which falls to be calculated for the purposes of this Part of this Act, but any other time while he is in hospital or on his way there or back shall not be so included.

(7) Subject to subsection (8) below, a person who at the expiry of 24 hours after the relevant time is in police detention and has not been charged shall be released at that time either on bail or without bail.

(8) Subsection (7) above does not apply to a person whose detention for more than 24 hours after the relevant time has been authorised or is otherwise permitted in accordance with section 42 or 43 below.

(9) A person released under subsection (7) above shall not be re-arrested without a warrant for the offence for which he was previously arrested unless new evidence justifying a further arrest has come to light since his release [; but this subsection does not prevent an arrest under section 46A below.][4]

42. Authorisation of continued detention

(1) Where a police officer of the rank of superintendent or above who is responsible for the police station at which a person is detained has reasonable grounds for believing that—
(*a*)   the detention of that person without charge is necessary to secure or preserve evidence relating to an offence for which he is under arrest or to obtain such evidence by questioning him;
(*b*)   an offence for which he is under arrest is a serious arrestable offence; and

4   Inserted by the Criminal Justice and Public Order Act 1994, s. 29(4).

    (*c*) the investigation is being conducted diligently and expeditiously,
he may authorise the keeping of that person in police detention for a period expiring at or
before 36 hours after the relevant time.

(2) Where an officer such as is mentioned in subsection (1) above has authorised the keeping
of a person in police detention for a period expiring less than 36 hours after the relevant time,
such an officer may authorise the keeping of that person in police detention for a further
period expiring not more than 36 hours after that time if the conditions specified in
subsection (1) above are still satisfied when he gives the authorisation.

(3) If it is proposed to transfer a person in police detention to another police area, the officer
determining whether or not to authorise keeping him in detention under subsection (1) above
shall have regard to the distance and the time the journey would take.

(4) No authorisation under subsection (1) above shall be given in respect of any person—
    (*a*) more than 24 hours after the relevant time; or
    (*b*) to record the grounds in that person's custody record.

(6) Before determining whether to authorise the keeping of a person in detention under
subsection (1) or (2) above, an officer shall give—
    (*a*) that person; or
    (*b*) any solicitor representing him who is available at the time when it falls to the officer
        to determine whether to give the authorisation,
an opportunity to make representations to him about the detention.

(7) Subject to subsection (8) below, the person in detention or his solicitor may make
representations under subsection (6) above either orally or in writing.

(8) The officer to whom it falls to determine whether to give the authorisation may refuse to
hear oral representations from the person in detention if he considers that he is unfit to make
such representations by reason of his condition or behaviour.

(9) Where—
    (*a*) an officer authorises the keeping of a person in detention under subsection (1) above;
        and
    (*b*) at the time of the authorisation he has not yet exercised a right conferred on him by
        section 56 or 58 below,
the officer—
    (i)   shall inform him of that right;
    (ii) shall decide whether he should be permitted to exercise it;
    (iii) shall record the decision in his custody record; and
    (iv) if the detention is to refuse to permit the exercise of the right, shall also record the
        grounds for the decision in that record.

(10) Where an officer has authorised the keeping of a person who has not been charged in
detention under subsection (1) or (2) above, he shall be released from detention, either on bail
or without bail, not later than 36 hours after the relevant time; or
    (*a*) has been charged with an offence; or
    (*b*) his continued detention is authorised or otherwise permitted in accordance with
        section 43 below.

(11) A person released under subsection (1) above shall not be re-arrested without a warrant
for the offence for which he was previously arrested unless new evidence justifying a further
arrest has come to light since his release [; but his subsection does not prevent an arrest under
section 46A below.][5]

43. Warrants of further detention

(1) Where, on an application on oath made by a constable and supported by an information,
a magistrates' court is satisfied that there are reasonable grounds for believing that the further
detention of the person to whom the application relates is justified, it may issue a warrant of
further detention authorising the keeping of that person in police detention.

(2) A court may not hear an application for a warrant of further detention unless the person
to whom the application relates—
    (*a*) has been furnished with a copy of the information; and
    (*b*) has been brought before the court for the hearing.

---

5   Inserted by the Criminal Justice and Public Order Act 1994, s. 29(4).

(3) The person to whom the application relates shall be entitled to be legally represented at the hearing and, if he is not so represented but wishes to be so represented—

    (*a*)   the court shall adjourn the hearing to enable him to obtain representations; and

    (*b*)   he may be kept in police detention during the adjournment.

(4) A person's further detention is only justified for the purposes of this section or section 44 below if—

    (*a*)   his detention without charge is necessary to secure or preserve evidence relating to an offence for which he is under arrest or to obtain such evidence by questioning him;

    (*b*)   an offence for which he is under arrest is a serious arrestable offence; and

    (*c*)   the investigation is being conducted diligently and expeditiously.

(5) Subject to subsection (7) below, an application for a warrant of further detention may be made—

    (*a*)   at any time before the expiry of 36 hours after the relevant time; or

    (*b*)   in a case where—

        (i)   it is not practicable for the magistrates' court to which the application will be made to sit at the expiry of 36 hours after the relevant time; but

        (ii)   the court will sit during the 6 hours following the end of that period, at any time before the expiry of the said 6 hours

(6) In a case to which subsection (5)(*b*) above applies—

    (*a*)   the person to whom the application relates may be kept in police detention until the application is heard; and

    (*b*)   the custody officer shall make a note in that person's custody record—

        (i)   of the fact that he was kept in police detention for more than 36 hours after relevant time; and

        (ii)   of the reason why he was so kept.

(7) If—

    (*a*)   an application for a warrant of further detention is made after the expiry of 36 hours after the relevant time; and

    (*b*)   it appears to the magistrates' court that it would have been reasonable for the police to make it before the expiry of that period,

the court shall dismiss the application.

(8) Where on an application such as is mentioned in subsection (1) above a magistrates' court is not satisfied that there are reasonable grounds for believing that the further detention of the person to whom the application relates is justified, it shall be its duty—

    (*a*)   state the time at which it is issued;

    (*b*)   authorise the keeping in police detention of the person to whom it relates for the period stated in it.

(11) Subject to subsection (12) below, the period stated in a warrant of further detention shall be such period as the magistrates' court thinks fit, having regard to the evidence before it.

(12) The period shall not be longer than 36 hours.

(13) If it is proposed to transfer a person in police detention to a police area other than that in which he is detained when the application for a warrant of further detention is made, the court hearing the application shall have regard to the distance and the time the journey would take.

(14) Any information submitted in support of an application under this section shall state—

    (*a*)   the nature of the offence for which the person to whom the application relates has been arrested;

    (*b*)   the general nature of the evidence on which that person was arrested;

    (*c*)   what inquiries relating to the offence have been made by the police and what further inquiries are proposed by them;

    (*d*)   the reasons for believing the continued detention of that person to be necessary for the purposes of such further inquiries.

(15) Where an application under this section is refused, the person to whom the application relates shall forthwith be charged or, subject to subsection (16) below, released, either on bail or without bail.

(16) A person need not be released under subsection (15) above—

    (*a*)   before the expiry of 24 hours after the relevant time; or

    (*b*)   before the expiry of any longer period for which his continued detention is or has been authorised under section 42 above.

(17) Where an application under this section is refused, no further application shall be made under this section in respect of the person to whom the refusal relates, unless supported by evidence which has come to light since the refusal.

(18) Where a warrant of further detention is issued, the person to whom it relates shall be released from police detention, either on bail or without bail, upon or before the expiry of the warrant unless he is charged.

(19) A person released under subsection (18) above shall not be re-arrested without a warrant of the offence for which he was previously arrested unless new evidence justifying a further arrest has come to light since his release [: but this subsection does not prevent an arrest under section 46A below.][6]

44. Extension of warrants of further detention

(1) On an application on oath made by a constable and supported by an information a magistrates' court may extend a warrant of further detention issued under section 43 above if it is satisfied that there are reasonable grounds for believing that the further detention of the person to whom the application relates is justified.

(2) Subject to subsection (3) below, the period for which a warrant of further detention may be extended shall be such period as the court thinks fit, having regard to the evidence before it.

(3) The period shall not—

    (*a*) be longer than 36 hours; or

    (*b*) end later than 96 hours after the relevant time.

(4) Where a warrant of further detention has been extended under subsection (1) above, or further extended under this subsection, for a period ending before 96 hours after the relevant time, on an application such as is mentioned in that subsection a magistrates' court may further extend the warrant if it is satisfied as there mentioned; and subsections (2) and (3) above apply to such further extensions as they apply to extensions under subsection (1) above.

(5) A warrant of further detention shall, if extended or further extended under this section, be endorsed with a note of the period of the extension.

(6) Subsection (2), (3) and (14) of section 43 above shall apply to an application made under this section as they apply to an application made under that section.

(7) Where an application under this section is refused, the person to whom the application relates shall forthwith be charged or, subject to subsection (8) below, released, either on bail or without bail.

(8) A person need not be released under subsection (7) above before the expiry of any period for which a warrant of further detention issued in relation to him has been extended or further extended on an earlier application made under this section.

45. Detention before charge – supplementary

(1) In sections 43 and 44 of this Act, 'magistrates' courts means a court consisting of two or more justices of the peace sitting otherwise than in open court.

(2) Any reference in this Part of this Act to a period of time of day is to be treated as approximate only.

Detention – miscellaneous

46. Detention after charge

(1) Where a person—

    (*a*) is charged with an offence; and

    (*b*) after being charged—

        (i) is kept in police detention; or

        (ii) is detained by a local authority in pursuance of arrangements made under section 38(6) above,

he shall be brought before a magistrates' court in accordance with the provisions of this section.

(2) If he is to be brought before a magistrates' court for the petty session area in which the police station at which he was charged is situated, he shall be brought before such a court as

---

6   Inserted by the Criminal Justice and Public Order Act 1994, s. 29(4).

soon as it is practicable and in any event not later than the first sitting after he is charged with the offence.

(3) If no magistrates' court for that area is due to sit either on the day on which he is charged or on the next day, the custody officer for the police station at which he was charged shall inform the clerk to the justices for that area that there is a person in the area to whom subsection (2) above applies.

(4) If the person charged is to be brought before a magistrates' court for a petty sessions area other than that in which the police station at which he was charged is situated, he shall be removed to that area as soon as it is practicable and brought before such a court as soon as it is practicable after his arrival in the area and in any event not later than the first sitting of a magistrates' court for that area after his arrival in the area.

(5) If no magistrates' court for that area is due to sit either on the day on which he arrives in the area or on the next day—

(*a*) he shall be taken to a police station in the area; and

(*b*) the custody officer at that station shall inform the clerk to the justices for the area that there is a person to the area to whom subsection (4) applies.

(6) Subject to subsection (8) below, where a clerk to the justices for a petty sessions area has been informed—

(*a*) under subsection (3) above that there is a person in the area to whom subsection (2) above applies;

(*b*) under subsection (5) above that there is a person in the area to whom subsection (4) above applies,

the clerk shall arrange for a magistrates' court to sit not later than the day next following 'the relevant day'—

(*a*) in relation to a person who is to be brought before a magistrates' court for the petty sessions area in which the police station at which he was charged is situated, means the day on which he was charged; and

(*b*) in relation to a person who is to be brought before a magistrates' court for any other petty sessions area, means the day on which he arrives in the area.

(8) Where the day next following the relevant day is Christmas Day, Good Friday or a Sunday, the duty of the clerk under subsection (6) above is a duty to arrange for a magistrates' court to sit not later than the first day after the relevant day which is not one of those days.

(9) Nothing in this section requires a person who is in hospital to be brought before a court if he is not well enough.

46A. [Power of arrest for failure to answer to police bail.

(1) A constable may arrest with a warrant any person who, having been released on bail under this Part of this Act subject to a duty to attend a police station, fails to attend at that police station at the time appointed for him to do so.

(2) A person who is arrested under this section shall be taken to the police station appointed as the place at which he is to surrender to custody as soon as it is practicable after the arrest.

(3) For the purposes of—

(*a*) section 30 above (subject to the obligation in subsection (2) above), and

(*b*) section 31 above,

an arrest under this section shall be treated as an arrest for an offence.][7]

NOTES

1. Part IV established a new system for police detention. It created a division of functions (wherever possible) between the officers conducting an investigation and a 'custody officer' responsible for supervision each suspect's detention, provided for written records to be kept and provided for periodic reviews of the need for the continued detention of the suspect. It does not affect 'any right of a person in

7   Inserted by the Criminal Justice and Public Order Act 1994, s. 29(2).

detention to apply for habeas corpus or other prerogative remedy' (s. 51(d)). Statistics of detention must be kept and published in the annual reports of chief officers of police (s. 50). Periods in police detention count towards custodial sentences (s. 49).

The grounds for continued detention after charge were extended by the Criminal Justice and Public Order Act 1994, s. 28(2).

2. The basic period of permitted detention without charge is limited to 24 hours from the 'relevant time': s. 41, usually the first time at which the arrestee arrives at the first police station to which he is taken after the arrest. In the case of 'serious arrestable offences'[8] an officer of the rank of superintendent or above may authorise detention up to 36 hours from the 'relevant time' (s. 42); a magistrates' court may issue a warrant of further detention for a period up to a further 36 hours (s. 43); and a magistrates' court may extend the warrant for a still further period up to 36 hours, provided that the total time does not exceed 96 hours from the 'relevant time' (s. 44). Times are to be treated as 'approximate only' (s. 45). A person must normally be brought before a magistrates' court as soon as it is practicable and in any event not later than the first sitting after he is charged with the offence (s. 46).[9]

3. The provisions of the Act are supplemented by the *Code of Practice for the Detention, Treatment and Questioning of Persons by Police Officers*,[10] which applies to persons who are in custody at police stations whether or not they have been arrested for an offence; and to those who have been removed to a police station as a place of safety under ss. 135 and 136 of the Mental Health Act 1983.[11] C. Phillips and D. Brown found that around 1% of suspects were believed to be suffering from a mental disorder on arrival at the station.[12] In total, 2% of arrestees were treated as mentally disordered.[13] The notes for Guidance state that those at a police station voluntarily to assist with an investigation should be treated with no less consideration than those in custody, and enjoy an absolute right to obtain legal advice or to communicate with anyone outside the station.[14]

4. A custody record must be opened as soon as it is practicable for each person who is brought to a police station under arrest or is arrested at the police station having attended there voluntarily.[15] The custody officer is responsible for the accuracy and completeness of the custody record and for ensuring that it accompanies the detained person on any transfer to another station.[16] C. Phillips and D. Brown found that 4% of arrestees were too drunk to be dealt with on arrival, 1% were violent and 1% were totally unco-operative with the custody officer.[17] There have been suggestions to 'divert' the people who are drunk from the police custody suite into a 'detoxification facility'.[18] Where the person leaves police detention, or is taken before a court, he, his legal representative or his appropriate adult[19] is entitled, on request, to be given

---

8 See above, pp. 194–196.
9 See below, p. 409.
10 PACE Code C, Revised Edition, 1995.
11 Code C.1. 10.
12 Op. cit., p. 281, p. 51.
13 Code C.1A.
14 Op. cit., p. 24.
15 Code C.2.1.
16 Code C.2.3.
17 Op. cit., p. 51. see also HORS Paper No 183, *Drugs and Crime: The Results of Research on Drug Testing and Interviewing Arrestees*. See also A. Sondhi et al., *Statistics from the arrest referral monitoring programme* (2001) (Home Office).
18 See further *Deaths in Custody Statistics for England and Wales Apr 1999–Mar 2000* (2000).
19 See below, p. 368.

a copy of the record and, on giving reasonable notice, to inspect the original.[20] The custody record will prove crucial if a challenge is made to the detention of the suspect in an attempt to have evidence excluded.[21] In *R v Heslop*,[22] the Court of Appeal dismissed H's appeal where his admission to murder was recorded in the officer's notebook and signed by H. H had claimed that it should also have been recorded in the custody record. The court denied any such statutory requirement. Cf. the Code of Practice C.11.13, which requires a record to be made – where is it to be made?

5. Section 15 of Code C covers reviews and extensions of detentions. Points additional to the provisions of PACE include the following. On a review of detention, persons other than a solicitor or appropriate adult who have an interest in the person's welfare may make representations;[1] before conducting a review, the review officer must ensure that the detained person is reminded of his entitlement to free legal advice.[2] The Notes for Guidance state that if the detained person is likely to be asleep at the latest time when a review of detention or an authorisation of continued detention may take place, then it should be brought forward so that the detained person can make representations without being woken up.[3] An application for a warrant of further detention or an extension should be made between 10 a.m. and 9 p.m. and if possible during normal court hours.[4]

6. In *R v Chief Constable of Kent, ex p Kent Police Federation*[5] it was held that the review under s. 40 could not occur by video-link. The review provisions are drafted in mandatory terms. The Divisional Court cast doubt on the legality of the telephone review as prescribed in Code C. As noted in the commentary on the case, although the primary purpose of the review is to assess the validity of the continued detention, the review officer also has a responsibility to monitor the welfare of the suspect. The Criminal Justice and Police Act 2001 (s. 73 inserting ss. 40A and 45A) reverses the decision, allowing for reviews to be conducted by telephone or by video-link where necessary. In addition, there is the opportunity to make custody decisions regarding charging, detention and bail by video-link where the custody officer is at a different station. Will a video-link provide an adequate guarantee of the welfare of the detainee? Will it render the system more efficient?

In *Roberts v Chief Constable of Cheshire Constabulary*,[6] R was arrested on suspicion of burglary at 10.50 p.m. and taken to a police station where detention was authorised at 11.25 p.m. At 1 a.m. he was transferred to another station and continued detention was authorised at 1.45 a.m. The first review was conducted at 7.45 a.m., and thereafter at 4.20 p.m. before R was released without charge at 6.55 p.m. R claimed that the first review should have occurred earlier. The Court of Appeal held that the police failure to comply with mandatory provisions in s. 34 rendered the detention unlawful and that it was irrelevant that the detention would have been lawfully continued had the review in fact taken place when it should have. The review should have occurred at 5.25 a.m. and the continued detention after that time was a false imprisonment (even though R was unaware of that at the time).

7. A further authorisation by a superintendent under s. 42(2) may be given even if the original 24-hour time limit has by then expired: *R v Taylor*.[7]

20 Code C.2.4, C.2.5.
21 See below, p. 367.
22 [1996] Crim LR 730.
1 Code C.15.1.
2 See below, Code C.15.3.
3 Code C.15A.
4 Code C.15B.
5 [2000] Crim LR 854.
6 [1999] 2 All ER 326, CA (Civ D).
7 [1991] Crim LR 541, CA (Cr D).

8. In *R v Slough Magistrates' Court, ex p Stirling*,[8] S was detained following his arrest for armed robbery for a total period for 36 hours expiring at approximately 12.53 p.m. on 30 May 1986. At 12.45 p.m. on that day an information was prepared by the police as the basis of an application to the court for a warrant of further detention. The justices were advised by their clerk that it was not practicable to hear the application at that time because the pressure of business, and the hearing was delayed until 2.45 p.m. The justices granted a warrant. This decision was quashed by the Divisional Court, which (1) rejected S's argument that s. 43(5)(b)(i) only applies where the justices are not sitting at all at the expiry of the 36-hour period, holding that the justices had a discretion to postpone a hearing to a later time (within the six hours permitted) where it was not practicable for them to hear the application immediately; but held that (2) s. 43(7) *required* the justices to dismiss an application if it appeared to them that it would have been reasonable for the police to apply within the 36-hour period; and (3) no reasonable bench of magistrates could have concluded that the police had acted reasonably here. G. Wilkins and P. Hayward report that the number of warrants for detention in recent years has been as follows: 1996 – 271 applications (8 refused); 1997/98 – 343 (5 refused); 1998/99 – 295 (4 refused); 1999/2000 – 224 (0 refused).[9]

9. The role of the custody officer was designed as a key element in the protection of the rights of the detainee. In *Clarke v Chief Constable of North Wales*,[10] the court held that the custody officer is entitled to assume, in the absence of any evidence to the contrary, that the arrest is lawful. Should the custody officer not make sure for himself in order to better protect the suspect?

The custody officer determines, in every case, whether there is sufficient evidence to charge the person (s. 37). Courts have provided little guidance as to what is sufficient evidence to charge. In *R v McGuiness*,[11] the court held that the words 'sufficient evidence to prosecute' and 'sufficient evidence for a prosecution to succeed' in Code C 16.1[12] had to involve some consideration of any explanation or lack of one from the suspect. Each case must turn on its own facts. The arrestee may benefit from a decision that there is already sufficient evidence to charge on arrival at the station, since this will prevent any further questioning of him. E. Cape has questioned whether the section is in conflict with the Code of Practice owing to the vagueness of the expression 'sufficient evidence to charge'.[13] In *Martin v Chief Constable of Avon and Somerset*,[14] M was arrested following the discovery of a small quantity of cannabis at his home. M immediately admitted possession for personal use, and signed the officer's pocketbook to that effect. He was nevertheless taken to the station and detained for four hours. The Court of Appeal were not prepared to find that the trial judge could not conclude that s. 37 was exercised properly on the evidence available. Why could M not have been charged immediately?

In *Vince v Chief Constable of the Dorset Police*,[15] the Court of Appeal held that s. 36(1) merely imposed a duty on the Chief Constable to appoint one custody officer for each designated police station and a discretion (to be reasonably exercised) to appoint more. The provision could not be read as imposing a duty to appoint a sufficient number of custody officers to ensure that the functions of such officers

---

8 (1987) 151 JP 603.
9 *Operation of Certain Police Powers Under PACE 1999–2000* Home Office 3/01 (2001). Note that the figures for 1999–2000 exclude Staffordshire and Cleveland constabularies.
10 (2000) 22 May, CA (Civ D), unreported.
11 [1999] Crim LR 318, CA.
12 Below.
13 [1999] Crim LR 874.
14 (1997) 29 October, CA (Civ D), unreported.
15 [1993] 2 All ER 321.

were ordinarily performed by duly appointed officers, and (for example) by untrained constables. Steyn LJ noted[16] that this conclusion showed:

'that a central provision of the Act is a less effective safeguard than many may have thought.'

The custody officer is not 'statutorily debarred' from participating with other officers in a ploy involving placing suspects in a bugged cell: *R v Bailey and Smith*.[17]

The RCCJ noted that the research evidence,[18] and their own observations on and discussions with custody officers:

'indicate that the police are not entirely comfortable with the role and that performance of it, though improving, still leaves something to be desired.'[19]

Moreover,

'it may also be unrealistic to expect a police officer to take an independent view of a case investigated by colleagues. As far as the evidence needed to substantiate a charge is concerned, the custody officer is hardly in a position to take a different view from the investigating officer because in the nature of things he or she will not have the same direct and detailed knowledge of the case.[1]

Nevertheless, they recommended that the custody officer role should remain with the police rather than be handed to the CPS or an independent body; the latter would also not have the same detailed knowledge of the case as investigating officers and it was not certain that they would be able to maintain the desired independence. The police should continue to take full responsibility for the integrity of evidence gathered, both through interviews and in other ways. Accordingly, steps should be taken to develop and strengthen the performance by the police of the custody officer role. This should include keeping the use of acting sergeants to a minimum; exploration of the possibility of delegating clerical and administrative tasks to civilians under the custody officer's control; refresher-training; the centralisation of custody functions within forces wherever practicable and their supervision as a separate specialist service, the introduction of computerisation of the custody record process to a national standard; continuous video recording (including sound-track) of all the activities in the custody office, the passages and stairways leading to the cells and, if feasible, the cell passage and doors of individual cells; the testing of a simplified version of the notice to detained persons.'[2]

10. In view of the importance of the role of the custody officer, ought the function to be performed by officers of an independent body? Would it be advantageous to have CPS legal advisers assisting custody officers with the decisions about charging? J. Baldwin and A. Hunt,[3] considered this as part of a pilot scheme and concluded that it is of 'limited' and 'inconsequential' impact.[4] Would there be anything more than a temporary removal of the perception of bias?

Custody officers were described by M. McConville, A. Sanders and R. Leng, as 'complicitous in the creation of an off-the-record interview by permitting the case officer to visit the suspect in the cells or by authorising his release to the interview room without recording it.'[5] How can the problem of bias or perceived bias towards the investigating officers be avoided unless the custody officer is a non-police role? Some problems can be addressed through the use of Custody Users Groups (officers,

16 At 335.
17 Below, p. 379.
18 Including the 1993 report by D. Brown et al. referred to at p. 320, n. 6.
19 Cm 2263, p. 31.
 1 Ibid.
 2 Devised by I. Clare and G. Gudjosson, RCCJ Study No. 7 (HMSO, 1993).
 3 [1998] Crim LR 521.
 4 p. 535.
 5 *The Case for the Prosecution* (1991), p. 58.

practitioners etc.) to resolve difficulties at a local level. Should there be more civilians employed to perform some of the tasks of the custody officer?

11. Statistics on detention times have been controversial since the original studies conducted for the RCCP. The RCCP found that about 75% of suspects were dealt with within six hours and about 95% within 24 hours. A survey conducted by the Metropolitan Police for three months in 1979 showed that only 0.4% of 48,343 persons had been held for over 72 hours without charge or release.[6]   A study by D. Brown[7] of ten forces found considerable variations from station to station in the length of detention without charge, this being strongly linked with the seriousness of the crime in question, but also perhaps with differences in the custody officer's approach to PACE. The RCCJ did not think any changes in detention limits was necessary although further national statistics should be maintained.[8]

12. *Further statistics on detention.*[9] The number of people detained for more than 24 hours before being released without charge was: 550 in 1996; 674 in 1997/8; 710 in 1998/99; 570 in 1999–2000.[10]

C. Phillips and D. Brown (above) found that the average time spent without charge was six hours 40 minutes. The average time for those who sought legal advice was just over nine hours while for those who did not it was five and a half hours. Other commentators have noted dramatic falls in the levels of complaints about treatment by the police in the charge room or cells[11] and improvements in arrangements for the welfare of suspects.[12] On the other hand the initial authorisation of detention by the custody officer is in practice a formality.[13] Phillips and Brown found it to be exceptional for the custody officer to refuse detention. Of the 4,250 cases examined, only one case was refused.[14] Brown[15] stated that 'custody officers show considerable independence in the way they carry out their job although practical constraints limit their examination of the evidence against a suspect when considering whether to authorise detention.'[16]

C. Philips and D. Brown examined the outcomes of arrests and report that 52% of those arrested in their survey were charged, 17% cautioned, and in 20% of cases there was no further action. Around 17% of suspects were initially bailed for further inquiries, but 44% of these led to no further action. Black and Asian suspects were more likely to be bailed than white suspects.[17]

On the role played by the custody officer in deciding whether a caution is a suitable outcome, see C. Phillips and D. Brown, reporting that the custody officer made the decision in around 80% of cases.[18]

---

6 RCCP Report, para. 3.96.
7 *Detention at the Police Station under the Police and Criminal Evidence Act 1984*, H.O. Research Study 104, 1989.
8 Cm. 2263, 1993, p. 30.
9 Taken from G. Wilkins and P. Hayward, Home Office Research Bulletin 03/01 (2001).
10 Excluding Staffordshire and Cleveland.
11 M. Maguire, (1988) 28 Br J Crim 19, 41.
12 Ibid; B. L. Irving and I. K. McKenzie, *Police Interrogation: the effects of the Police and Criminal Evidence Act 1984* (1989), pp. 196–198 (replicating the RCCP Research Study No. 2, 1980).
13 I. McKenzie, R. Morgan and R. Reiner, [1990] Crim LR 22, 22–27.
14 p. 49.
15 *Pace Ten Years On,* above p. 297, n. 13.
16 p. 2.
17 p. 82.
18 pp. 102–106. On bail decisions, see T. Bucke and D. Brown, *In police custody: police powers and suspects' rights under the revised PACE codes of practice* (1997), Chap. 7.

13. Release on police bail is governed by provisions of the Bail Act 1976, as amended by Part II of the Criminal Justice and Public Order Act 1994.[19]

14. A magistrates' court having power to remand a person in custody may, if the remand is for a period not exceeding three clear days, commit him to police detention for the purposes of inquiries into other offences.[20] In the case of children and young persons, 24 hours.[21] There is no power in s. 128(7) to remand to any other magistrates' court: *R v Penrith Justices, ex p Morley*.[1]

9 Questioning and treatment of persons in custody

Police and Criminal Evidence Act 1984

PART V

QUESTIONING AND TREATMENT OF PERSONS BY POLICE

53. Abolition of certain powers of constables to search persons

(1) Subject to subsection (2) below, there shall cease to have effect any Act (including a local Act) passed before this Act is so far as it authorises—

  (*a*) any search by a constable of a person in police detention at a police station; or

  (*b*) an intimate search of a person by a constable;

and any rule of common law which authorises a search such as is mentioned in paragraph (*a*) or (*b*) above is abolished . . .

54. Searches of detained persons

(1) The custody officer at a police station shall ascertain and record or cause to be recorded everything which a person has with him when he is—

  (*a*) brought to the station after being arrested elsewhere or after being committed to custody by an order or sentence of a court; or

  [(*b*) arrested at the station or detained there [, as a person falling within section 34(7), under section 37 above.][2]][3]

(2) In the case of an arrested person the record shall be made as part of his custody record.

(3) Subject to subsection (4) below, a custody officer may seize and retain any such thing or cause any such ting to be seized and retained.

(4) Clothes and personal effects may only be seized if the custody officer—

  (*a*) believes that the person from whom they are seized may use them—

    (i)   to cause physical injury to himself or any other person;

    (ii) to damage property; or

    (iii) to interfere with evidence; or

    (iv) to assist him to escape; or

  (*b*) has reasonable grounds for believing that they may be evidence relating to an offence.

(5) Where anything is seized, the person from whom it is seized shall be told the reason for the seizure unless he is—

  (*a*) violent or likely to become violent; or

  (*b*) incapable of understanding what is said to him.

---

19 ss. 25–30 and Sch. 3. (See PACE, s. 47, as amended by the 1994 Act, s. 27 and the Access to Justice Act 1999, s. 90, Sch. 13, paras. 125, 127.) Section 47A (added by the Crime and Disorder Act 1998, s. 119(1), Sch. 8, para. 62) provides that: 'Where a person has been charged with an offence at a police station, any requirement imposed under this Part, for the person to appear to be brought before a magistrates' court shall be taken to be satisfied if the person appears or is brought before the clerk to the justices for a petty sessions area in order for the clerk to conduct a hearing under section 50 of the Crime and Disorder Act 1998 (early administrative hearings).' Conditions may now be attached to police bail.

20 Magistrates' Court Act 1980, s. 128(7), (8), as inserted by the 1984 Act, s. 48.

21 Children and Young Persons Act 1969, s. 23(14).

1 (1991) 155 JPN 92, 155 JP 137.

2 Substituted by the Criminal Justice and Public Order Act 1994, Sch. 10, para. 55.

3 Inserted by the Criminal Justice Act 1988, s. 147(a).

(6) Subject to subsection (7) below, a person may be searched if the custody officer considers it necessary to enable him to carry out his duty under subsection (1) above and to the extent that the custody officer considers necessary for that purpose.

[(6A) A person who is in custody at a police station or is in police detention otherwise than at a police station may at any time be searched in order to ascertain whether he has with him anything which he could use for any of the purposes specified in subsection (4)(*a*) above.

(6B) Subject to subsection (6C) below, a constable may seize and retain, or cause to be seized and retained, anything found on such a search.

(6C) A constable may only seize clothes and personal effects in the circumstances specified in subsection (4) above.][4]

(7) An intimate search may not be conducted under this section.

(8) A search under this section shall be carried out by a constable.

(9) The constable carrying out a search shall be of the same sex as the person searched.

55. Intimate searches

(1) Subject to the following provisions of this section, if an officer of at least the rank of superintendent[4a] has reasonable grounds for believing—

   (*a*)   that a person who has been arrested and is in police detention may have concealed on him anything which—

      (i)   he could use to cause physical injury to himself or others; and

      (ii)   he might so use while he is in police detention or in the custody of a court; or

   (*b*)   that such a person—

      (i)   may have a Class A drug concealed on him; and

      (ii)   was in possession of it with the appropriate criminal intent before his arrest,

he may authorise [an intimate][5] search of that person.

(2) An officer may not authorise an intimate search of a person for anything unless he has reasonable grounds for believing that it cannot be found without his being intimately searched.

(3) An officer may give an authorisation under subsection (1) above orally or in writing but, if he gives it orally, he shall confirm it in writing as soon as it is practicable.

(4) An intimate search which is only a drug offence search shall be by way of examination by a suitable qualified person.

(5) Except as provided by subsection (4) above, an intimate search shall be by way of examinations by a suitably qualified person unless an officer of at least the rank of superintendent considers that this is not practicable.

(6) An intimate search which is not carried out as mentioned in subsection (5) above shall be carried out by a constable.

(7) A constable may not carry out an intimate search of a person of the opposite sex.

(8) No intimate search may be carried out except—

   (*a*)   at a police station;

   (*b*)   at a hospital;

   (*c*)   at a registered medical practitioner's surgery; or

   (*d*)   at some other place used for medical purposes.

(9) An intimate search which is only a drug offence search may not be carried out at a police station.

(10) If an intimate search of a person is carried out, the custody record relating to him shall state—

   (*a*)   which parts of his body were searched; and

   (*b*)   why they were searched.

(11) The information required to be recorded by subsection(10) above shall be recorded as soon as it is practicable after the completion of the search.

(12) The custody officer at a police station may seize and retain anything which is found on an intimate search of a person, or cause any such thing to be seized and retained—

   (*a*)   if he believes that the person from whom it is seized may use it—

      (i)   to cause physical injury to himself or any other person;

      (ii)   to damage property;

4   Inserted by the Criminal Justice Act 1988, s. 147(b).

4a   From a day to be appointed, this will be replaced by 'inspector': see the Criminal Justice and Police Act 2001, s. 79.

5   Inserted by the Criminal Justice Act 1988, Sch. 15, para. 99.

         (iii) to interfere with evidence; or

         (iv) to assist him to escape; or

   (*b*) if he has reasonable grounds for believing that it may be evidence relating to an offence.
(13) Where anything is seized under this section, the person from whom it is seized shall be told the reason for the seizure unless he is—

   (*a*) violent or likely to become violent; or

   (*b*) incapable of understanding what is said to him...

(17) In this section—
'the appropriate criminal intent' means an intent to commit an offence under—

   (*a*) section 5(3) of the Misuse of Drugs Act 1971 (possession of controlled drug with intent to supply to another); or

   (*b*) section 68(2) of the Customs and Excise Management Act 1979 (exportation etc. with intent to evade a prohibition or restriction);

'Class A drug' has the meaning assigned to it by section 2(1)(*b*) of the Misuse of Drugs Act 1971; 'drug offence search' means an intimate search for a Class A drug which an officer has authorised by virtue of subsection (1)(*b*) above; and
'suitably qualified person' means—

   (*a*) registered medical practitioner; or

   (*b*) a registered nurse.

56. Right to have someone informed when arrested

(1) Where a person has been arrested and is being held in custody in a police station or other premises, he shall be entitled, if he so requests, to have one friend or relative or other person who is known to him or who is likely to take an interest in his welfare told, as soon as it is practicable except to the extent that delay is permitted by this section, that he has been arrested and is being detained there.

(2) Delay is only permitted—

   (*a*) in the case of a person who is in police detention for a serious arrestable offence; and

   (*b*) if an officer of at least the rank of superintendent[5a] authorises it.

(3) In any case the person in custody must be permitted to exercise the right conferred by subsection (1) above within 36 hours from the relevant time, as defined in section 41(2) above.

(4) [Subject to subsection (5A) below][6] An officer may give an authorisation under subsection (2) above orally or in writing but, if he gives it orally, he shall confirm it in writing as soon as it is practicable.

(5) [Subject to subsection (5A) below an][6a] officer may only authorise delay where he has reasonable grounds for believing that telling the named person of the arrest –

   (*a*) will lead to interference with or harm to evidence connected with a serious arrestable offence or interfere with or physical injury to other persons; or

   (*b*) will lead to the alerting of other persons suspected of having committed such an offence but not yet arrested for it; or

   (*c*) will hinder the recovery of any property obtained as a result of such an offence.

[(5A) An officer may also authorise delay where the serious arrestable offence is a drug trafficking offence [or an offence to which Part VI of the Criminal Justice Act 1988 applies (offences in respect of which confiscation order under that Part may be made)] and the officer has reasonable grounds for believing—

   [(*a*) where the offence is a drug trafficking offence, that the detained person has benefited from drug trafficking and that the recovery of the value of that person's proceeds of drug trafficking will be hindered by telling the named person of the arrest; and

   (*b*) where the offence is one to which Part VI of the Criminal Justice Act 1988 applies that the detained person has benefited from the offence and that the recovery of the value of the property obtained by that person from or in connection with the offence

---

5a From a day to be appointed, this will be replaced by 'inspector': see the Criminal Justice and Police Act 2001, s. 74.

6   Inserted by the Drug Trafficking Offences Act 1986, s. 32, including substitutional words from Criminal Justice Act 1988, s. 99(1), (2).

6a Inserted by the Drug Trafficking Offences Act 1986, s. 32, including substitutional words from Criminal Justice Act 1988, s. 99(1), (2).

or of the pecuniary advantage derived by him from or in connection with it will be hindered by telling the named person of the arrest].]⁶ᵇ

(6) If a delay is authorised—

  (*a*) the detained person shall be told the reason for it; and

  (*b*) the reason shall be noted on his custody record.

(7) The duties imposed by subsection (6) above shall be performed as soon as it is practicable.

(8) The rights conferred by this section on a person detained at a police station or other premises are exercisable whenever he is transferred from one place to another; and this section applies to each subsequent occasion on which they are exercisable as it applies to the first such occasion.

(9) There may be no further delay in permitting the exercise of the right conferred by subsection (1) above once the reason for authorising delay ceases to subsist.

(10) [Nothing in this section applies to a person arrested or detained under the terrorisms provisions.⁷]

58. Access to legal advice

(1) A person arrested and held in custody in a police station or other premises shall be entitled, if he so requests, to consult a solicitor privately at any time.

(2) Subject to subsection (3) below, a request under subsection (1) above and the time at which it was made shall be recorded in the custody record.

(3) Such a request need not be recorded in the custody record of a person who makes it at a time while he is at a court after being charged with an offence.

(4) If a person makes such a request, he must be permitted to consult a solicitor as soon as it is practicable except to the extent that delay is permitted by this section.

(5) In any case he must be permitted to consult a solicitor within 36 hours from the relevant time, as defined in section 41(2) above.

[subsections (6), (7), (8), (8A), (9), (10) and (11) correspond, respectively, to s. 56(2), (4), (5), (5A), (6), (7) and (9)].

(12) [Nothing in this section applies to a person arrested or detained under the terrorism provisions.⁸]

60. Tape-recording of interviews

(1) It shall be the duty of the Secretary of State—

  (*a*) to issue a code of practice in connection with the tape-recording of interviews of persons suspected of the commission of criminal offences which are held by police officers at police stations; and

  (*b*) to make an order requiring the tape-recording of interviews of persons suspected of the commission of criminal offences, or of such descriptions of criminal offences as may be specified in the order, which are so held, in accordance with the code as it has effect for the time being.

(2) An order under subsection (1) above shall be made by statutory instrument and shall be subject to annulment in pursuance of a resolution of either House of Parliament.

65. Part V – supplementary

In this Part of this Act—

'appropriate consent' means—

  (*a*) in relation to a person who has attained the age of 17 years, the consent of that person;

  (*b*) in relation to a person who has not attained that age but has attained the age of 14 years, the consent of that person and his parent or guardian; and

  (*c*) in relation to a person who has not attained the age of 14 years, the consent of his parent or guardian;

['drug trafficking' and 'drug trafficking offence' have the same meaning as in the [Drug Trafficking Act 1994];]⁹...

6b Inserted by the Drug Trafficking Offences Act 1986, s. 32, including substitutional words from Criminal Justice Act 1988, s. 99(1), (2).

7 Substituted by the Terrorism Act 2000, s. 125, Sch. 15, para. 5(5).

8 Substituted by the Terrorism Act 2000, s. 125, Sch. 15, para. 5(6).

9 Inserted by the Drug Trafficking Offences Act 1986, s. 32, and amended by the 1994 Act, Sch. 1, para. 8.

['intimate sample' means—
  (*a*) a sample of blood, semen or any other tissue fluid, urine or pubic hair;
  (*b*) a dental impression;
  (*c*) a swab taken from a person's body orifice other than the mouth;][10]
['non-intimate sample' means—
  (*a*) a sample of hair other than pubic hair;
  (*b*) a sample taken from a nail or from under a nail;
  (*c*) a swab taken from any part of a person's body including the mouth but not any other body orifice;
  (*d*) saliva;
  (*e*) a footprint or a similar impression of a part of a person's body other than a part of his hand.]
['intimate search', in relation to a person's fingerprints or samples, means such a check against other footprints or samples or against information derived from other samples as is referred to in section 63A(1) above; 'sufficient' and 'insufficient', in relation to a sample, means sufficient or insufficient (in point of quantity or quality) for the purpose of enabling information to be produced by the means of analysis used or to be used in relation to the sample.][11]
['the terrorism provisions' means section 41 of the Terrorism Act 2000, and any provisions of Schedule 7] [given in section 1 of that Act.][12]
[…references in this Part to any person's proceeds of drug trafficking are to be construed in accordance with the [Drug Trafficking Act 1994].][13]

Code of Practice for the Detention, Treatment and Questioning of Persons by Police Officers [C] Revised edition, 1995

11. Interviews: general

(a) Action

11.1A An interview is the questioning of a person regarding his involvement or suspected involvement in a criminal offence or offences which, by virtue of paragraph 10.1 of Code C, is required to be carried out under caution. Procedures undertaken under section 7 of the Road Traffic Act 1998 do not constitute interviewing for the purpose of this code.

11.1 Following a decision to arrest a suspect he must not be interviewed about the relevant offence except at a police station or other authorised place of detention unless the consequent delay would be likely:
  (*a*) to lead to interference with or harm to evidence connected with an offence or interference with or physical harm to other people; or
  (*b*) to lead to the alerting of other people suspected of having committed an offence but not yet arrested for it; or
  (*c*) to hinder the recovery of property obtained in consequence of the commission of an offence.
Interviewing in any of these circumstances shall cease once the relevant risk has been averted or the necessary questions have been put in order to attempt to avert that risk.

11.2 Immediately prior to the commencement or re-commencement of any interview at a police station or other authorised place of detention, the interviewing officer shall remind the suspect of his entitlement to free legal advice and that the interview can be delayed for him to obtain legal advice (unless the exceptions in paragraph 6.6 or Annex C apply). It is the responsibility of the interviewing officer to ensure that all such reminders are noted in the record of interview.

10 Substituted by the Criminal Justice and Public Order Act 1994, s. 58.
11 Substituted by the Criminal Justice and Public Order Act 1994, ss. 58, 59(1).
12 Substituted by the Terrorism Act 2000, s. 115, Sch. 14, para. 5(10).
13 Inserted by the Drug Trafficking Offences Act 1986, s. 32, and amended by the 1994 Act, Sch. 1, para. 8.

11.2A At the beginning of an interview carried out in a police station, the interviewing officer, after cautioning the suspect, shall put to him any significant statement or silence which occurred before his arrival at the police station, and shall ask him whether he confirms or denies that earlier statement or silence and whether he wishes to add anything. A 'significant' statement or silence is one which appears to be capable of being used in evidence against the suspect, in particular a direct admission of guilt, or failure or refusal to answer a question or to answer it satisfactorily, which might give rise to an inference under Part III of the Criminal Justice and Public Order Act 1994.

11.3 No police officer may try to obtain answers to questions or to elicit a statement by the use of oppression. Except as provided for in paragraph 10.5C, no police officer shall indicate, except in answer to a direct question, what action will be taken on the part of the police if the person being interviewed answers questions, makes a statement or refuses to do either. If the person asks the officer directly what action will be taken in the event of his answering questions, making a statement or refusing to do either, then the officer may inform the person what action the police propose to take in that event provided that action is itself proper and warranted.

11.4 As soon as a police officer who is making enquiries of any person about an offence believes that a prosecution should be brought against him and that there is sufficient evidence for it to succeed, he shall ask the person if he has anything further to say. If the person indicates that he has nothing more to say the officer shall without delay cease to question him about that offence. This should not, however, be taken to prevent officers in revenue cases or acting under the confiscation provisions of the Criminal Justice Act 1988 or the Drug Trafficking Offences Act 1986 from inviting suspects to complete a formal question and answer record after the interview is concluded.

(b) *Interview records*

11.5(a) An accurate record must be made of each interview with a person suspected of an offence, whether or not the interview takes place at a police station.

  (b) The record must state the place of the interview, the time it begins and ends, the time the record is made (if different), any breaks in the interview and the names of all those present; and must be made o the forms provided for this purpose or in the officer's pocket-book or in accordance with the code of practice for the tape-recording of police interviews with suspects (Code E).

  (c) The record must be made during the course of the interview, unless in the investigating officer's view this would not be practicable or would interfere with the conduct of the interview, and must constitute either a verbatim record of what has been said or, failing this, an account of the interview which adequately and accurately summarises it.

11.6 The requirements to record the names of all those present at an interview does not apply to police officers interviewing persons detained under the Prevention of Terrorism (Temporary Provisions) Act 1999. Instead the record shall state the warrant or other identification number and duty station of such officers.

11.7 If an interview record is not made during the course of the interview it must be made as soon as it is practicable after its completion.

11.8 Written interview records must be timed and signed by the maker.

11.9 If an interview record is not completed in the course of the interview the reason must be recorded in the officer's pocket book.

11.10 Unless it is impracticable the person interviewed shall be given the opportunity to read the interview record and to sign it as correct or to indicate the respects in which he considers it inaccurate. If the interview is tape-recorded the arrangements set out in Code E apply. If the person concerned cannot read or refuses to read the record or to sign it, the senior police officer present shall read it over to him and ask him whether he would like to sign it as correct (or make his mark) or to indicate the respects in which he considers it inaccurate. The police officer shall then certify on the interview record itself what has occurred. [See *Note 11D*.]

11.11 If the appropriate adult or the person's solicitor is present during the interview, he should also be given an opportunity to read and sign the interview record (or any written statement taken down by a police officer).

11.12 Any refusal by a person to sign an interview record when asked to do so in accordance with the provisions of the code must itself be recorded.

11.13 A written record should also be made of any comments made by a suspected person, including unsolicited comments, which are outside the context of an interview but which might be relevant to the offence. Any such record must be timed and signed by the maker. Where practicable the person shall be given the opportunity to read that record and to sign it as correct or to indicate the respects in which he considers it inaccurate. Any refusal to sign should be recorded. [See *Note 11D.*]

(c) *Juveniles, the mentally disordered and the mentally handicapped*
11.14 A juvenile or a person who is mentally disordered or mentally handicapped, whether suspected or not, must not be interviewed or asked to provide or sign a written statement in the absence of the appropriate adult unless paragraph 11.1 or Annex C applies...[14]

11.16 Where the appropriate adult is present at an interview, he shall be informed that he is not expected to act simply as an observer; and also that the purposes of his presence are, first, to advise the person being questioned and to observe whether or not the interview is being conducted properly and fairly, and secondly, to facilitate communication with the person being interviewed.

Notes for Guidance
11A [Not used.]
11B It is important to bear in mind that, although juveniles or persons who are mentally disordered or mentally handicapped are often capable of providing reliable evidence, they may, without knowing or wishing to do so, be particularly prone in certain circumstances to provide information which is unreliable, misleading or self-incriminating. Special care should therefore always be exercised in questioning such a person, and the appropriate adult should be involved, if there is any doubt about a person's age, mental state or capacity. Because of the risk of unreliable evidence it is also important to obtain corroboration of any facts admitted whenever possible.

11C It is preferable that a juvenile is not arrested at his place of education unless this unavoidable. Where a juvenile is arrested at his place of education, the principle or his nominee must be informed.

11D When a suspect agrees to read records of interviews and of other comments and to sign them as correct, he should be asked to endorse the record with words as such as 'I agree that this is a correct record of what was said' and add his signature. Where the suspect does not agree with the record, the officer should record the details of any disagreement and then ask the suspect to read these details and then sign them to the effect that they accurately reflect his disagreement. Any refusal to sign when asked to do so shall be recorded.

NOTES

1. Under Code C,[15] where a person arrives at a police station under arrest, or is arrested there, the custody officer must tell him clearly of (1) his right to have someone informed of the arrest, (2) his right to consult privately with a solicitor, and the fact

14 *Ed.* Annex C applies where an officer of the rank of superintendent or above considers that delay will lead to the consequences set out in para. 11.1 or (a) to (c). Questioning may not continue once sufficient information to avert the immediate risk has been obtained.
15 See above, p. 317.

that independent legal advice is available free of charge, and (3) his right to consult the Codes of Practice.[16] He must be given (1) a written notice setting out these rights, his right to a copy of the custody record, the terms of the caution (see below), and the arrangements for obtaining legal advice; and (2) an additional notice setting out his entitlements while in custody.[17] Special arrangements apply where the person appears to be deaf, or there is doubt about his hearing, or is juvenile, or is mentally handicapped or suffering from a mental disorder, or is blind or seriously visually handicapped or unable to read.[18] These normally require the involvement of an independent third party such as an interpreter, an approved social worker or an 'approved adult' as the case may be.

A person who attends a police station voluntarily may leave at will unless arrested; if it is decided that he should not be allowed to leave, then he must at once be arrested and brought before the custody officer, if a person is not arrested, but is cautioned, the officer who cautions him must also inform him that he is not under arrest, that he is not obliged to remain at the police station, but that if he remains he may obtain free and independent legal advice.[19] C.3.15 was held not to apply to an interview carried out at a Social Security Benefits' Agency office: *R v Secretary of State for Social Security, ex p South Central Division Magistrates' Court.*[20] If a person at the station voluntarily asks about his entitlement to legal advice, he must be given a copy of the written notice explaining the arrangements for obtaining legal advice.[1]

The Notes for Guidance state that the right to consult the Codes of Practice does not entitle the person concerned to delay unreasonably any necessary investigate or administrative action while he does so; procedures requiring the provision of breath, blood or urine specimens under the Road Traffic Act 1998 need not be delayed.[2] Detailed rules govern the conditions of detention: for example, cells must be adequately heated, cleaned, ventilated and lit; bedding must be of a reasonable standard and in a clean and sanitary condition access to toilet and washing facilities must be provided; at least two light meals and one main meal must be offered in any period of 24 hours; brief outdoor exercise must be offered daily if practicable; detainees should be visited every hour (every half hour if drunk).[3] Any complaints must be reported to an officer of the rank of inspector or above not connected with the investigation.[4] There are detailed provisions governing the medical treatment of person in custody.[5] D. Brown et al.[6] found that there had been improvements in the range of information provided to suspects following the introduction of a revised PACE Code C in 1991; however, the required information was not always given and, in a quarter of cases, rights were not explained clearly.

---

16 Code C.3.1.
17 Code C.3.2.
18 Code C.3.6–C.3.14.
19 Code C.3.15.
20 (2000) 23 October, unreported, DC.
 1 Code C.3.16.
 2 Code C.3E, confirming *DPP v Billington* [1988] 1 All ER 435, criticised by D. Tucker, [1990] Crim LR 177. See also *DPP v Ward* [1999] RTR 11, DC 9: failure to supply a specimen under s. 8 of the Road Traffic Act cannot be justified on the basis of a suspect request to take time reading Codes of Practice.
 3 Code C.8.
 4 Code C.9.1.
 5 Code C.9.2–9.6.
 6 *Changing the Code: Police Detention under the Revised PACE Codes of Practice* (HORS No 129, HMSO, 1993.

2. *Searches of detained persons.* Sections 54 and 55 replace any statutory or common law powers of search of arrested persons at police stations. A *search* may be carried out in any case where the custody officer considers it necessary to enable him to perform his duty of recording everything the arrestee has with him: s. 51(1), (6). This reflects standard police practice, which was previously of doubtful legality. At common law a search could only take place if there was reasonable cause to suspect that the arrestee had on his person evidence, a weapon or some other object he could use to effect an escape.[7] The power to *seize* was similarly limited. Now, anything may be seized except that limiting conditions attach to clothes and personal effects: s. 54(3), (4). Under the common law, *R v Naylor*[8] it was held to be unlawful for the police to seize jewellery from a woman prisoner where there was no suggestion that the rings were in any way unusual or capable of causing injury or that the earrings or necklace could cause harm to the defendant or anyone else. Similarly, in *Lindley v Rutter*[9] it was doubted whether it could be justifiable to remove a woman's brassiere unless there was 'some evidence that female drunks in general were liable to injure themselves with their brassieres or that the defendant had shown a peculiar disposition to do so'.[10] *Lindley v Rutter* also made it clear that suspects could not be searched simply because that was required by police standing orders:

'the officer having custody of the prisoner must always consider...whether the special circumstances of the particular case justify or demand a departure from the standard procedure either by omitting what would otherwise be done or by taking additional measures.'[11]

This principle remains applicable: the powers to search are (1) discretionary and (2) to be exercised by the officers on the spot, and must not be fettered in advance by themselves or their superiors.[12] Some doubt was, however, cast on this by the Court of Appeal in *Middleweek v Chief Constable of the Merseyside Police*.[13] Here, the court rejected an argument that *Lindley v Rutter* was authority for the proposition that a search is unlawful if a standing instruction is followed without first giving consideration to the particular circumstances of the case; it was regarded as holding merely that compliance with a standing instruction is itself no conclusive answer to a complaint that a search is unlawful. If in fact there is a good reason for the search, the search will be lawful. It is submitted that this takes insufficient (or indeed any) account of the principle that statutory discretions should not be fettered and that Donaldson LJ's statement should be taken at face value.

The custody officer is responsible for ascertaining and safeguarding a detained person's property.[14] Personal effects are defined as items which a person may lawfully need or use or refer to while in detention, but not cash and other items of value.[15] The Notes of Guidance state that s. 54(1) of PACE does not require *every* detained person to be searched, but requires a search 'where it is clear that the custody officer will have continuing duties in relation to that person or where that person's behaviour or offence made an inventory appropriate'.[16] Does it?

---

7 See above, p. 295; *Lindley v Rutter* [1981] QB 128; *Brazil v Chief Constable of Surrey* [1983] 3 All ER 537.

8 [1979] Crim LR 532.

9 [1981] QB 128.

10 Per Donaldson LJ at 135.

11 Per Donaldson LJ at 135; see also *Brazil v Chief Constable of Surrey* [1983] 3 All ER 537.

12 This is a standard feature of all statutory discretionary powers: see above, p. 95.

13 [1990] 3 All ER 662 decided in 1985 and concerning events in 1980.

14 Code C.4.

15 Code C.4.3.

16 Code C.4A.

Intimate and strip searches must be conducted in accordance with Annex A to Code C. A strip search is a search involving the removal of more than outer clothing, and may take place only if the custody officer considers it to be necessary to remove an article which the detained person would not be allowed to keep.[17] Statistics must be kept of intimate searches under s. 55 and published in the annual reports of chief officers of police (s. 55(15)).

3. *Statistics on intimate searches.*[18] In 1999/2000 there were 170 intimate searches, 135 of which were for drugs, with 25 leading to the discovery of class A drugs; 20 other searches were conducted with no articles discovered. In 1999/2000 of the 170 searches, four were carried out by a police officer, 12 in the presence of a suitably qualified person, and 138 by the suitably qualified person.[19] Strip searches are conducted in around 3% of cases.[20] (Over 40% of suspects have their photographs taken, with around 10% having it taken without consent.[1])

Holding a suspect's nose to cause him to spit out material placed in the mouth is not an intimate search (see now s. 65 anyway). The Court of Appeal held that an intimate search required physical intrusion into the orifice rather than visual inspection.[2] Do you agree?

4. *Right to have someone informed when arrested.* Such a right was first created by the Criminal Law Act 1977, s. 62. On the meaning of 'held in custody' in ss. 56 and 58, see *R v Kerawalla*,[3] where it was held that this meant where an appropriate authority has authorised detention in custody in a police station.[4] One-fifth of suspects exercise the right.[5]

Under Code C, if the friend etc., chosen cannot be contacted, the person who made the request may choose up to two alternatives; attempts beyond these may be allowed as a matter of discretion.[5a] The person in custody may receive visits at the custody officer's discretion.[6] If a friend etc. makes inquiries about his whereabouts, the information must be given if he agrees and unless the right not to be held incommunicado can properly be delayed.[7] The person in custody should be supplied with writing materials on request, and allowed to speak on the telephone for a reasonable time to one person; a letter or call can be denied or delayed by an officer of the rank of inspector or above if he considers that they may result in either of the conditions in s. 56(5)(a) or (b) (in the case of a person detained for an arrestable or serious arrestable offence). The person must be informed that the letter, call or message (other than to a solicitor) may be read or listened to as appropriate and may be given in evidence; a telephone call may be terminated if abused; the costs can be at public expense at the discretion of the custody officer.[8]

17 C, Annex A.10.
18 G. Wilkins and P. Hayward, (2001), op. cit., p. 12.
19 Some data on those conducting searches was not available for 1999/2000. For a discussion of the ethical issues for medical practitioners who perform intimate searches see J. Marston, (1999) 163 JP 646.
20 T. Bucke and D. Brown, *In police custody: police powers and suspects' rights under the revised PACE codes of practice* (1997), p. 48.
1 T. Bucke and D. Brown, ibid, p. 49.
2 *R v Hughes* [1995] Crim LR 407.
3 [1991] Crim LR 451, CA (CR D).
4 Criticised as too narrow an interpretation by D. J. Birch, Commentary at p. 453.
5 D. Brown, *PACE Ten Years On* (above), p. 3.
5a Code C.5.1.
6 Code C.5.4.
7 Code C.5.5
7 Code C.5.6.
8 Code C.5.7. See now *R(M) v MPC* (2001) 13 July, CA (Cr D) holding that failure to provide the accused with a room for private consultation did not breach Art. 6(3). Note also *PG and JH v UK* (2001) 19 October, ECtHR finding a breach of Art. 8 where police cells were bugged.

Citizens of independent Commonwealth countries and foreign nations have special rights of access to the appropriate High Commission, Embassy or Consulate.[9]
5. *Right of access to legal advice.* Code C provides that all people in police detention must be informed that they may at any time consult and communicate privately, whether in person, in writing or on the telephone, with a solicitor and that independent legal advice is available free of charge from the duty solicitor.[10] The term 'solicitor' includes any trainee solicitor, a duty solicitor representative or an accredited representative included on the register of representatives maintained by the Legal Aid Board.[11] This right can only be delayed in accordance with s. 58(8), and provided that the suspect 'has not yet been charged with an offence'[12] ('an' here means 'any': *R v Samuel*.[13]) On the very strict interpretation of s. 58, see *R v Samuel*[14] in which it was noted that instances in which an officer could 'genuinely' believe that a solicitor *will* if allowed to consult with a suspect, commit an offence will be rare. Inadvertent or unwitting conduct apart, the police officer must believe that a solicitor *would*, if allowed to consult the person in police detention, commit a criminal offence. The grounds put forward would have to be by reference to a specific solicitor.[14a] C. Phillips and D. Brown[15] found no instance of this in their survey of 4,250 cases. A poster advertising the right to legal advice must be prominently displayed in the charging area of every police station.[16] No police officer must at any time do or say anything with the intention of dissuading a person in detention from obtaining legal advice.[17] A person who wants legal advice may not be interviewed or continue to be interviewed until he has received it unless:
–   Annex B to Code C applies (i.e. the right to legal advice can be delayed); or
–   an officer of the rank of superintendent or above has reasonable grounds for believing that (i) delay will involve an immediate risk of harm to persons or serious loss of, or damage to, property; or (ii) where awaiting the arrival of a solicitor who has agreed to attend would cause unreasonable delay to the process of investigations; or
–   the chosen solicitor (i) cannot be contacted; or (ii) has previously indicated that he does not wish to be contacted; or (iii) has declined to attend; and the person has been advised of the Duty Solicitor Scheme (if there is one) but has declined to ask for the duty solicitor, or the duty solicitor is unavailable. (Here, the interview may be started or continued on the authority of an inspector or above.); or
–   the person who wanted legal advice changes his mind. (Here, the interview may be started or continued on the authority of an inspector or above; having inquired into the change of mind, if the person agrees on tape or in writing.)[18]
The delay in providing legal advice is a very rare occurrence. In one research study, there was no such finding in a sample of 12,500 cases, and previous research has found the percentage of cases to be less than 1%.[19] On ECHR guarantees of free legal

9 Code C.7.
10 Code C.6.1.
11 Code C.6.12.
12 Code C, Annex B.A. (a) 1.
13 Below, p. 371.
14 [1988] QB 615.
14a *R v Silcott, Braithwaite and Raghip* (1991) Times, 9 December, CA.
15 Above, p. 281.
16 Code C.6.3.
17 Code C.6.4.
18 Code C.6.6.
19 T. Bucke and D. Brown, p. 23.

representation, see Art. 6 and *Pakelli v FRG*.[20] Where a person is permitted to consult a solicitor, who is available when the interview begins or is in progress, the solicitor must be allowed to be present at the interview.[1] The solicitor may only be required to leave if his conduct is such that the investigating officer is unable properly to put questions, and on the authority of an officer not below the rank of superintendent (if readily available), and otherwise an officer not below the rank of inspector who is not connected with the investigation.[2] A non-accredited or probationary representative is to be admitted to the police station to provide advice on behalf of a solicitor unless an officer of the rank of inspector or above considers that such a visit will hinder the investigation of crime and directs otherwise; that officer should consider whether the non-accredited or probationary representative's identity and status have been satisfactorily established, whether he is of suitable character to provide legal advice, and any other matters in any letter of authorisation sent by the solicitor, the solicitor and the detained person must be informed if access is refused.[3]

Note that it is not appropriate or lawful for a Chief Constable to place a blanket ban on a particular solicitor's representative from entering police stations to advise detainees. The Chief Constable is entitled to publish guidelines for officers to follow on such matters: *R (on the application of Thompson) v Chief Constable of Northumbria*.[4] The representative in question was a former police officer who had been dismissed following allegations of sexual misconduct.

The Notes for Guidance state that the solicitor may seek to intervene in order to seek clarification or to challenge an improper question to his client or the manner in which it is put, or advise his client not to reply to particular questions, or if he wishes to give his client further legal advice. Paragraph C.6.9 only applies if the solicitor's approach or conduct prevents or unreasonably obstructs proper questions being put to the suspect or his response being recorded.[5]

The holder of acting rank is to be treated as if he were the holder of the substantive rank (e.g. of inspector), unless the appointment to acting rank is a colourable pretence: *R v Alladice*.[6]

6. *Use of Legal Advice*. The Preamble to the Judges' Rules[7] previously provided that:

'every person at any stage of an investigation should be able to communicate and to consult privately with a solicitor. This is so even if he is in custody provided that no unreasonable delay or hindrance is caused to the processes of investigation or the administration of justice by his doing so.'

This was not a legal requirement. In practice few suspects asked to see a solicitor and most such requests were refused.[8] On police eavesdropping, see *S v Switzerland*.[9]

Phillips and Brown confirmed earlier research finding that those who might benefit most from legal advice 'often did not request it because they were anxious not to delay their time in custody or because they were told that they probably would not be charged'.[10] Requests for legal advice varied depending on the offence, and the

---

20 (1983) 6 EHRR 1.
 1 Code C.6.8.
 2 Code C.6.9, C.6.10.
 3 Code C.6.12–6.14.
 4 [2001] EWCA Civ 321, CA (Civ D).
 5 Code C.6D.
 6 (1989) 98 Cr App Rep 380, CA (Cr D).
 7 See below, p. 353.
 8 See M. Zander, [1972] Crim LR 342; J. Baldwin, M. McConville, [1979] Crim LR 145; P. Softley, *An Observation Study in Four Police Stations*, RCCP Research Study No. 4, 1981, p. 68.
 9 (1992) 14 EHRR 670 and *PG and JH v UK* (2001) 19 October, ECtHR.
10 p. 59.

station at which the suspect was held. In addition, 'significant predictors of demand for legal advice [included] ethnic[ity], employment status; previous convictions; condition on arrival at the station; and whether answering police bail.'[11] The use of unqualified legal advisers continues to present concern. 35% of cases where the suspect had requested his own solicitor involved unqualified advisers (prior to the Law Society's accreditation scheme). How can suspects be guaranteed prompt access to effective legal advice?

On occasion the advice received from the legal adviser has been so poor that the court has excluded evidence obtained from the suspect despite the legal advice. The advice must be so poor as to be tantamount to a denial of access to a lawyer: see, for example, a murder case which collapsed because of the poor legal advice, discussed in *Matter of a Solicitor and in the Matter of the Solicitors' Act 1974.*[12] The ECtHR has emphasised the importance of prompt access to legal advice: *Imbroscia v Switzerland;*[13] *Murray v United Kingdom.*[14] Should a suspect have a right to choose his own lawyer? See also *Schonenberger and Durmaz v Switzerland.*[15]

The right of access to a solicitor is backed by a statutory 24-hour duty solicitor scheme. Research on the operation of the new arrangements indicated that there was a significant increase in the number of suspects seeking legal advice, although they still only constituted a minority; that a variety of ploys were used by the police to discourage exercise of the right; that only a small proportion of suspects had a lawyer with them during police interrogation; and that there might have been a rise in the number of suspects who refused to make admissions.[16] The report by A. Sanders et al. was critical of the quality of service provided by duty solicitors, with a high proportion relying on telephoned advice rather than attendance in person. C. Phillips and D. Brown confirm that telephone advice is still much more likely from a duty solicitor than a suspect's own.[17] In the last few years there has been a rise in the number of face-to-face consultations, with a decline in telephone advice.[18] Moreover, the length of the consultation lasted, on average, 15 minutes, which represents a considerable increase than revealed in earlier research.[19] The Legal Aid Board changed the rules to require other than in exceptional circumstances attendance in person where the suspect is to be questioned about an arrestable offence or an identity parade is to be held, or the suspect complains of serious maltreatment by the police.[20] The revised version of Code C expressly requires the custody officer to act without delay to secure the provision of legal advice when requested; prohibits any attempt to dissuade the suspect from obtaining advice; and requires the suspect to be reminded at various stages of the right to free legal advice. A report by D. Brown et al. following the introduction of the revised Code C in 1991[1] revealed an increase in the proportion

---

11 p. 62.
12 (1999) DC, unreported.
13 (1993) 17 EHRR 444.
14 (1996) 22 EHRR 29.
15 (1989) 11 EHRR 200.
16 See A. Sanders and R. Young, *Criminal Justice* (2nd edn, 2000), pp. 491–492 and for earlier accounts see S. H. Bailey and M. J. Gunn, *Smith and Bailey on the Modern English Legal System* (3rd edn, 1995), pp. 503–507, citing D. Brown, *Detention at the Police Station under the Police and Criminal Evidence Act 1984* (HORS 104, 1989), Chap. 3 and HORPU Bulletin 26:26; A. Sanders et al. *Advice and Assistance at Police Stations and the 24 Hour Duty Solicitor Scheme* (LCD, 1989) and A. Sanders and L. Bridges, [1990] Crim LR 494; B.L. Irving and I. K. McKenzie, *Police Interrogation* (1989), pp. 53–59, 113–115, 157–164, 199–200.
17 Op. cit., p. 66.
18 T. Bucke and D. Brown, p. 24.
19 T. Bucke and D. Brown, p. 28.
20 See E. Cape, Legal Action, March 1991, p. 21.
1 *Changing the Code*, HORS No. 129, HMSO, 1992.

of suspects that requested legal advice from 24% to 32%: 25% of suspects having a legal consultation compared with 18%, two-thirds being seen in person; but legal advisers less often remaining to attend police interviews with their clients. Other research remained critical of the quality of legal advice made available.[2] D. Brown's review, in *PACE Ten Years On*, found that around 38% of suspects request legal advice and that the figure is rising. By 1997, T. Bucke and D. Brown reported that the figure was 40%.[3]

The RCCJ noted that 'there remains a substantial proportion of cases in which legal advice is neither asked for nor received'. Some of the steps they recommended[4] to improve arrangements for offering and securing access to legal advice have been incorporated by amendments to Code C. Accordingly, the right to waive legal advice is to be achieved by ticking alternative boxes on the custody record; the suspect should be reminded that he can speak with a duty solicitor on the telephone.[5] On the other hand, a recommended amendment to Code C to encourage the police to inform the suspect's solicitor of at least the general nature of the case and the *prima facie* evidence against the suspect[6] has not been made.

Of those who request legal advice, around 80% receive it.[7] Custody officers were successful in contacting advisers in 88% of cases in C. Phillips and D. Brown's study. The RCCJ found the evidence on the quality of legal advice to be 'disturbing' but, rather weakly, thought the answer lay in improved training, supervision and monitoring.[8] The right of access to a solicitor vests in the detainee alone, so that a solicitor has no right of access to a client in the custody area: *Rixon v Chief Constable of Kent.*[9]

The improper denial of the right to legal advice is likely to lead to exclusion of a confession under s. 78: see *R v Samuel.*[10] The courts have not taken a particularly strict line on the exclusion of evidence for refusal or delay regarding legal advice. In *R v Walsh*[11] Saville J. said:

'The main object of section 58 of the Act and indeed the Codes of Practice is to achieve fairness to an accused or suspected person so as, among other things, to preserve and protect his legal rights; but also fairness for the Crown and its officers so that again, among other things, there might be reduced the incidence or effectiveness of unfounded allegations of malpractice.'[12]

The right is recognised as important under the Convention, but is not absolute. It is of 'paramount importance' when inferences from silence are in issue: *Murray v United Kingdom.*[13] See also *Condron v United Kingdom*;[14] *Magee v United Kingdom*;[15] *Averill v United Kingdom.*[16] The right of access to legal advice under s. 58(1) does not extend to a person on remand in custody at a magistrates' court, but there is a

2 See J. Baldwin, *The Role of Legal Representation at the Police station* (RCCJ Research Study No. 3, HMSO, 1992); M. McConville and J. Hodgson, *Custodial Legal Advice and the Right to Silence* (RCCJ Research Study No. 16, HMSO, 1993).
3 On the legal profession's attitude to duty solicitor schemes see A. Sanders and R. Young, op. cit., pp. 228–230, and see the discussion of the impact of the new Criminal Defence Service.
4 Cm. 2263, pp. 35–37.
5 See Code C.3.5, C.6.1.
6 RCCJ P. 36.
7 D. Brown *PACE Ten Years On* (1997), p. 2.
8 pp. 37–39.
9 (2000) Times, 11 April 2000, CA (Civ D).
10 Below, p. 371.
11 (1990) 91 Cr App R 161, CA.
12 At p. 163.
13 (1996) 22 EHRR 29 at 67.
14 (2001) 31 EHRR 1; [2000] Crim LR 679.
15 [2000] Crim LR 681.
16 [2000] Crim LR 682.

right of access as soon as reasonably practicable at common law, not abrogated by the 1984 Act; accordingly, a police policy of refusing access to a solicitor on the sole ground that the request was made after 10 a.m. was unlawful: *R v Chief Constable of South Wales, ex p Merrick*.[17] As to a right to legal advice where the statute is silent on the matter see *R v RUC, ex p Begley*.[18]

7. Fingerprints and body samples. PACE made separate provision for the taking of fingerprints (s. 61), intimate samples (s. 62) and non-intimate samples (s. 63). The *fingerprints* of a person detained at a police station may be taken without consent (a) on the authority of a superintendent;[19] or (b) if he has been charged with or informed that he may be reported for a recordable offence and he has not already been fingerprinted during the investigation; any person's fingerprints may be taken without consent on his conviction for a recordable offence. 'Detained' at a police station has been held to include temporary detention after having been remanded by a magistrates' court: *R v Seymour*.[20] Section 78(8) CJPA 2001 extends the definition of fingerprints to 'a record of the skin pattern and other physical characteristics or features of the fingers or palms', and s. 78(7) allows for electronic fingerprinting. Section 78 also authorises fingerprints to be retaken from a person convicted or charged with any recordable offence if the quality was poor or the originals are unusable etc. Section 78 of the CJPA 2001 allows for compulsory fingerprinting in cases where the suspect has been cautioned or reprimanded for a recordable offence. Section 81 extends the circumstances in which speculative searches of individuals fingerprints can be made. Non-intimate samples are taken in around 7% of cases. Sampling was undertaken in a wide range of offences, but most often in cases of rape and other sexual offences.[1] Approximately 50% of these samples are taken consensually. In most cases, non-intimate samples are taken after charge rather than as a part of the investigation itself.[2] Section 80 of the CJPA 2001 allows an inspector to authorise a non-intimate sample. The definition of non-intimate sample is amended so that 'skin impressions' may be taken (previously footprints were the only listed non-intimate sample of this nature).

Intimate samples may be taken if there is (a) the authority of a superintendent[2a] (or above) and (b) consent. Authorisation need not precede consent: *R v Butt*.[3] Under PACE, the authorising officer had to have reasonable grounds to suspect involvement in a serious arrestable offence; this was broadened significantly to *any* recordable offence by the Criminal Justice and Public Order Act 1994, s. 54 amending s. 62. The definition of an 'intimate sample' was changed by the 1994 Act, s. 58. By comparison with the old definition, the reference to a dental impression was added, but mouth swabs switched to the non-intimate category.[4] Suspects should be cautioned in accordance with Code D Note for Guidance A ... 'You do not have to provide this sample ... but I must warn you that if you refuse without good cause your refusal may harm your case at trial'. If consent is refused, a court or jury may draw such inferences as appear proper (s. 62(1)). An intimate sample other than a sample of urine may only be taken by a registered medical practitioner (or registered dentist in the case of dental impressions) (s. 62(9), as amended by the 1994 Act, s. 54(5)).

---

17 [1994] 1 WLR 663, DC.
18 [1997] 1 WLR 1475, HL, below, p. 591.
19 The Criminal Justice and Police Act 2001 replaces this with 'inspector' (s. 78(2)).
20 [1995] 1 Arch News 1.
1 T. Bucke and D. Brown, p. 43.
2 Ibid., p. 45. On the powers to take samples etc from terrorist suspects, see below, Chap. 5.
2a The Criminal Justice and Police Act 2001 replaces this with 'inspector' (s. 80(1)).
3 [1999] Crim LR 414, CA (Cr D).
4 The latter change was effected in Northern Ireland by the Criminal Justice Act 1988, Sch. 14; for criticism see M. Gelowitz, [1989] Crim LR 198 and C. Walker and I. Cram, [1990] Crim LR 479.

Home office researchers found that intimate samples are taken 'very rarely'[5] with blood being the most common form of sample. (See also D. Miers.[6]) Under the 2001 Act, the taking of an intimate sample can be authorised by an inspector (only ever with the suspect's consent), and the sample can be taken by a registered nurse, whereas previously the requirement had been for a registered doctor.

The power to take *non-intimate samples* without consent was broadened by the 1994 Act to operate on a broadly similar basis to fingerprinting, *inter alia*, extending to any recordable offence. The definition of 'non-intimate sample' in s. 65 was amended by the 1994 Act, s. 58, which added the references to the mouth and saliva.

The 1994 Act added supplementary provisions in respect of both fingerprints and samples:[7]

'(1) where a person has been arrested on suspicion of being involved in a recordable offence or has been charged with such an offence, or has been informed that he will be reported for such an offence, fingerprints or samples or the information derived from samples.'

Thus fingerprints or samples may be checked against records held by or on behalf of the police or in connection with or as a result of an investigation of an offence. (The 2001 Act extends the circumstances in which speculative searches can be made: s. 81.) Samples of hair other than pubic hair maybe taken either by cutting or plucking, so long as no more are plucked than the person taking the sample reasonably considers to be necessary for a sufficient sample. A person not in detention or custody may in certain circumstances be required to attend a police station in order to have a sample taken. Failure to comply can lead to arrest. Note that the National Automated Fingerprints Identification System gives all forces access to a full national database of convicted criminals' fingerprints. The changes in definition of search are designed to facilitate the use of dental and DNA evidence, including the establishment of DNA databases, and to enable officers to remove drugs and other suspected substances from a suspect's mouth. They follow recommendations of the RCCJ,[8] except that the latter merely recommended the extension of sampling powers to assault and burglary. The Northern Ireland provision for the reclassification of mouth swabs as non-intimate samples was said to have 'worked satisfactorily there',[9] although the evidence for this was not stated. Code D: 4.1, 4.2 deal with taking photographs of suspects, and D: 4.3 makes clear that force may not be used to obtain such.

Provision was made for the destruction of fingerprints or samples unless the person concerned is convicted (PACE, s. 64, as amended by the 1994 Act, s. 57, to enable samples that would otherwise have to be destroyed to be retained for statistical purposes only). This applied to DNA profiles: *R v Nathaniel*.[10] It was however held that use of DNA from destroyed samples to create a database for statistical use is not in breach of s. 64: *R v Willoughby*.[11] The Criminal Evidence (Amendment) Act 1997 allows for non-intimate samples to be taken from a person to whom the Act applies (*inter alia*: those imprisoned for sexual, violent and other specified offences). On the 1997 Act, see M. Redmayne, who asserts that 'it is not obvious that the powers given to the police to take samples from suspects are unacceptable, although it is

---

5 T. Bucke and D. Brown, p. 46.
6 (1995) 2 J Clinical Forensic Medicine 93.
7 New s. 63A of PACE.
8 Cm. 2263, pp. 14–16.
9 [1998] Crim LR 437.
10 [1995] 2 Cr App R 565, CA.
11 [1997] 1 Arch News 2.

arguable that, in applying to a number of trivial offences, they are rather too wide'.[12] Do you agree? News reports have alleged that the police are holding large numbers of DNA samples.[13] Home Office research reports that:

'the vast majority of samples were taken in order to build up the DNA database and, while the proportion of suspects sampled appears relatively small, it should be noted that approximately 1.5 million people enter police custody every year. Selective sampling therefore is likely to add a substantial number of people to the database over the forthcoming years.'[14]

Are there adequate safeguards for the use of such information? The DNA is held by the Forensic Science Service, not an independent body.

In *R v Weir*[15] the Court of Appeal quashed a murder conviction which had relied in part on the DNA sample taken from W in 1997 in relation to a burglary investigation that led to no charges being pursued. These samples should have been destroyed under s. 64. They should not have been admitted at trial and no link to the DNA samples taken from the murder investigation should have been permitted under s. 63. The Court of Appeal reached an identical conclusion in *Attorney-General's Reference No 3 of 1999*,[16] where it held that there was no discretion in the trial judge to admit evidence which ought to have been destroyed. Section 64 did not allow for such discretion. The DNA sample from an investigation into burglary that led to acquittal was correctly rejected at the defendant's later trial for rape. The House of Lords reversed these decisions.[17] The House of Lords held that although the DNA samples should have been destroyed under s. 64, this did not prevent admissibility of the new samples gained from the investigation (which was itself prohibited by s. 64).[18]

'The police can do nothing until a further crime is committed. Even a consequential confession by X or a discovery of a murder weapon in the house of X could not be used. But one does not have to resort to hypothetical examples: on the interpretation of the judge and the Court of Appeal a case involving evidence of a very serious rape could never reach the jury and in *Weir* a conviction for a brutal murder was quashed on the ground that the DNA evidence should not have been placed before the jury. It must be borne in mind that respect for the privacy of defendants is not the only value at stake. The purpose of the criminal law is to permit everyone to go about their daily lives without fear of harm to person or property. And it is in the interests of everyone that serious crime should be effectively investigated and prosecuted. Their must be fairness to all sides. In a criminal case this requires the court to consider a triangulation of interests. It involves taking into account the position of the accused, the victim and his or her family, and the public. In my view the austere interpretation which the Court of Appeal adopted is not only in conflict with the plain words of the statute but also produces results which are contrary to good sense.'[19]

Do you agree? The House of Lords considered that the availability of exclusion under s. 78 provided adequate protection. Do you agree? Is this what Parliament intended? The House of Lords did not express any endorsement of the trial judge's view that the evidence ought to have been excluded under s. 78. Section 82 of the CJPA 2001 removes the obligation to destroy samples and prints where the suspect was cleared of an earlier offence. This puts the decision of the House of Lords in *Attorney-General's Reference No 3 of 1999* on a statutory footing. A new s. 64(3AA) is substituted for the old s. 3(A) and (B) and allows for samples from volunteer mass screenings to be

12 [1998] Crim LR 444.
13 *Observer*, 11 June 2000.
14 T. Bucke and D. Brown, p. 72.
15 (2000) Times 16 June 2000.
16 [2000] Crim LR 995 and commentary.
17 [2001] 2 WLR 56; [2000] 2 Cr App R 416; [2001] 2 AC 91.
18 For an application of the House of Lords decision, see *R v Langley* [2001] EWCA Crim 732, CA (Cr D).
19 [2001] 2 AC 91. Per Lord Steyn at 118.

retained if the person is convicted or has given consent (which cannot be withdrawn). Retention of samples and private data is subject to Art. 8 protections: *X v Germany*.[21]

Do you agree with M. Redmayne, who rejects as having little merit an argument that:

'it would be fairer to enter the DNA profiles of all the inhabitants of the UK on the database, because this would not only ensure equality of risk of misidentification, but would also allow us to be much more certain about the discriminating power of DNA profiling because the database would reveal whether DNA profiles do occur more frequently than is currently thought?'[20]

Note that matches have been identified in approximately 50% of targeted mass intelligence screens (voluntary schemes).[1]

In a speech to police officers the Prime Minister announced plans to spend £109m funding DNA samples, enabling the police to take them from 'virtually the entire criminally active population' by 2004. This would add three million samples to the existing 940,000 held. 'I believe that the civil liberties argument is completely misplaced. This is using technology to catch criminals' he said.[2] Do you agree? Note that the FSS is an executive agency of the Home Office, which provides a nationwide service.

The method by which DNA profiling is conducted is described in an accessible manner by Lord Taylor CJ in *R v Gordon*.[3]

The courts have occasionally been alert to the dangers of over-reliance on DNA. In *R v Walters*,[4] evidence of DNA from cigarette ends found at the scene of a series of burglaries was felt, on appeal, to be too weak to sustain conviction, particularly since there was a possibility that the defendant's brother had committed the crime.

The Home Office produced controversial *Proposals for Revising Legislative Measures on Fingerprints, Footprints and DNA Samples*.[5] The proposals included the power for officers to take fingerprints electronically, for the power to take fingerprints at any location (including in public) with an inspector's authorisation, for wider powers of retention and retaking to ensure best quality matches. In addition, there were proposals for footprints to be taken in the circumstances in which fingerprints are currently taken, and for the retention of volunteers' DNA samples with their consent. *Liberty* raised a number of strong objections to the proposals particularly the need to take fingerprints at any location. Doubting its operational benefit, and fearing the use of 'fishing expeditions' by the police with possibly disproportionate impact on minority groups, *Liberty* commented that 'it strikes us as being extra-ordinary that the attempted justification for the introduction of such an intrusive power, which would have a significant impact on individual privacy, amounts to just one paragraph'.[6] The 2001 Act introduces many of these proposals. The amendments lower the protection for the suspect by reducing the authorising rank required. It should also be noted that s. 81 of the CJPA 2001 allows a wider range of state agencies to conduct speculative searches of the database of samples. If DNA evidence is so reliable are there good reasons to extend the powers to obtain samples? Does it depend on how well drafted are the protections on storage and use? Are the protections adequate? If you volunteered to provide a sample in a mass-

20 [1998] Crim LR 441.
21 (1976) 3 DR 1024.
 1 See *The Magistrate*, March 2001, p. 73.
 2 *Guardian*, 1 September 2000.
 3 [1995] 1 Cr App R 290.
 4 [2001] EWCA Crim 1261, CA (Cr D).
 5 (1999).
 6 Para. 3.1.

screening, would you give consent for the sample to be retained? There is currently no PACE guidance on taking other samples (e.g. voice samples).[7]

Samples taken for the purposes of one inquiry may be used as evidence in another: *R v Kelt*.[8] In *DPP v Noe*,[9] it was held that the defendant was not entitled to verify, by looking in a 'law book', the legality of police requests for breath samples.

Section 57 of the Criminal Justice and Courts Act 2000 provides new powers for police to take non-intimate samples, including urine, to test for specified class A drugs. This followed widespread concern at the number of arrestees who tested positive for class A drugs in a pilot study: some areas had rates as high as 78%.[10] The power is subject to a number of conditions: (1) that the detainee is charged with a 'trigger offence' (essentially those related to class A drugs and theft offences), or another offence and an inspector or above has reasonable grounds to suspect that class A drug misuse caused or contributed to the offence charged; (2) that the detainee is over 18; (3) that the officer has requested a sample; (4) that the officer informs the detainee of the grounds for authorisation (if appropriate) and warns that a failure to provide a sample without good cause may render the person liable to prosecution. Subsection (8) provides an offence with maximum imprisonment of three months for failing to provide a sample. Samples are taken by persons as prescribed in regulations made by the Secretary of State. By sub-s. (7) the results can be used in sentencing, and in making decisions relating to bail and detention. There is no prohibition on using this in evidence.

The Secretary of State may amend the conditions so that samples can be taken from those arrested but not charged with an offence: s. 63B(5).

The use of intimate samples will not constitute a breach of any privilege against self-incrimination. As the ECtHR noted in *Saunders v UK*,[11] the right not to incriminate oneself does not extend to the use in criminal proceedings of material 'which may be obtained from the accused through the use of compulsory powers but which has an existence independent of the will of the suspect such as, *inter alia*, documents acquired pursuant to a warrant, breath, blood and urine samples, and bodily tissues for the purpose of DNA testing'.[12]

8. *The interrogation process.* Code C lays down detailed rules governing the conduct of interviews.[13] There are special requirements where an interpreter is needed (Code C.13). C. Phillips and D. Brown[14] found that an interpreter was required in 2% of cases.[1] Particular difficulty has been caused by the issue of what constitutes an 'interview' for the purpose of determining whether the requirements of Code C apply.[2] The term was not defined in the first version of Code C (see *R v Maguire*);[3] and a Note for Guidance in the second version (para. 11A), was rightly criticised as self-contradictory by the Court of Appeal (Criminal Division) in *R v Cox*.[4] The RCCJ

---

7 See on voice identification D. Ormerod, [2001] Crim LR 595.
8 (1993) 99 Cr App Rep 372, CA (Cr D).
9 [2000] RTR 351.
10 See *Drug Testing of Arrestees Research Programme* (1999).
11 (1997) 23 EHRR 313.
12 Para. 69.
13 Code C.11, above, pp. 317–319, and C.12.
14 Above, p. 281.
1 Ibid., p. 56.
2 See H. Fenwick, [1993] Crim LR 174 and S. Field, (1993) 13 LS 254.
3 (1989) 90 Cr App Rep 115, CA (Cr D).
4 (1992) 96 Cr App Rep 464.

recommended that the point be clarified,[5] and a definition is now found in Code C.11.1A. The matter is of importance because the close regulation of the conduct of interviews in the police station, including tape-recording, provide an incentive to the police to seek to obtain admissions on the way to the station, perhaps by the use of inducements or threats, or to invent confessions. The RCCJ found it impossible to estimate the frequency of such practices'.[6] Research studies showed that questioning outside the police station still occurred in a significant proportion of cases (10% in one study, 8% in another). The RCCJ did not wish to rule out carefully researched and monitored progress towards the greater use of tape recorders outside the police station'. If this proved to be feasible, the PACE Codes should be extended. Furthermore, on the RCCJ's recommendation, PACE Code C has been amended to require at the beginning of an interview carried out at the police station 'significant statements or silence' which occurred before the interview to be put to the suspect.[7] D. Brown[8] concluded that 'little supervision or monitoring of interviews occurs...[and] some unregulated interviewing continues to occur outside the interview room.' On continuing problems of the definition of interview see D. Wolchover and A. Heaton Armstrong,[8a] who consider the issue of C.11.14 applying to non-suspects and the problems of vulnerable suspects.

What may begin as a general inquiry may become an 'interview' (to which Code C applies) where answers to questions give rise to a suspicion that an offence has been committed. In *R v Blackford,*[9] the court noted that what amounts to grounds to suspect:

'has troubled this Court on a number of previous occasions. It has been described as a singularly imprecise concept. (See *R v James* 8 March (1996) per Simon Brown LJ at transcript p. 18.) It may range from the country house murder as recorded in fiction where all twelve occupants have had opportunity and motive to the case where the suspect is caught knife in hand standing over the prostrate body of his victim. So it is not surprising that some attempt has been made to give it shape. In *R v Shah* (1994) CLR 125 Jowitt J giving the judgment of the court stated at p. 4E:

"First, it is to be seen that paragraph 10.1 sets out an objective test. There must be grounds of suspicion. Secondly it is not enough that the questioner is suspicious. He must have grounds for that suspicion. Grounds, obviously may fall well short of evidence which would support a prima facie case of guilt. Nonetheless, they must exist. A mere hunch or a sixth sense that something is not as it should be is not, in the view of this Court such as to provide the grounds for bringing the case within paragraph 10.1 of Code C. Moreover the grounds have to be such as to lead to suspicion, not simply that an offence has been committed, but committed by the person who is being questioned. It seems to this Court that, in any event, it was perfectly proper for Mr Campbell to ask the questions he did, and to which objection was taken, about the ownership of the briefcase. In our judgment, at that time when he asked those questions, Mr Campbell had no grounds for suspicion. Mr Campbell had no grounds to suspect that an offence had been committed by the appellant. Accordingly, there was no need for a caution and we agree with the learned judges ruling that the evidence should be admitted."

James is binding upon this court. And, though he might not have known of it, it was also binding upon the trial judge. So it was legitimate for him to put the rhetorical question to the jury which he presumably put to himself. We paraphrase; without more would the grounds of suspicion in this case have justified the police officers in arresting the appellant and if not how can it be said that they were such as to bring C.10.1 into play?

5   Cm. 2263, p. 27.
6   Ibid., pp. 27–28.
7   Code C.11.2A.
8   *PACE Ten Years On* (1997), p. 30.
8a [1995] Crim LR 356.
9   [2001] EWCA Civ 1479, CA (Cr D).

It cannot be said, therefore, that the trial judge misdirected himself as to the proper approach. He reminded himself of the provisions of C10.1 and in particular of the need for the grounds of suspicion to have related to the appellant. He heard evidence. He reached certain findings of fact. Should this Court interfere? Although in James the matter was treated as one of discretion under section 78 of the 1984 Act whereas we are considering a prior determination of fact, it seems to us that the same principles apply. This court should be slow to interfere with the findings of the tribunal of fact reached after hearing evidence and on consideration of the relevant principles of law. It should only do so if the conclusions reached are unreasonable. As much is implicit in the judgment of this court in *R v Nelson & Rose* (1998) 2 Cr App R 399, where the court felt able to make its own finding in a case where the trial judge had failed to reach one of his own.'

In this situation, the Court of Appeal has suggested that a record should be made of the earlier questions and answers as soon as practicable, the reason for the absence of a contemporaneous note should be recorded and the suspect given the opportunity to check the record: *R v Park*.[10] The volunteering of information other than in response to questions is not an 'interview': *R v Menard*.[11] See also cases where confessions outside the police station have been excluded for breach of PACE requirements.[12]

Code C.12 applies to Interviews in Police Stations. The custody officer is responsible for deciding whether to deliver a detained person into the custody of an interviewing officer.[13] In any period of 24 hours, a detained person must normally be allowed eight hours rest free from questioning, travel or interruption arising out of the investigation.[14] No person unfit through drink or drugs to the extent that he is unable to appreciate the significance of questions put to him and his answers may be questioned except in accordance with Annex C.[15] Note that C. Phillips and D. Brown[16] found that 10% of suspects were suffering some degree of intoxication from alcohol; 4% were too drunk to be dealt with on arrival at the station and 2% were under the influence of drugs. Interview rooms must as far as practicable be adequately heated, lit and ventilated.[17] Interviewing officers should identify themselves and other officers present.[18] Provision is made for meal and refreshment breaks,[19] complaints of breaches of the Code[20] and documentation.[1]

Where an officer considers that there is sufficient evidence to prosecute a detained person, and that there is sufficient evidence for a prosecution to succeed, and that the person has said all he wished to say about the offence, he must without delay bring him before the custody officer, who is then responsible for considering whether he should be charged.[2] If he is detained in respect of more than one offence, it is permissible to delay until the conditions are satisfied in respect of all the offences.[3] When a detained person is charged with or informed that he may be prosecuted for an offence, he must be cautioned,[4] and if charged, given a written notice with the

---

10 (1994) 99 Cr App Rep 270, CA (Cr D).
11 [1995] 1 Cr App Rep 306, CA (Cr D).
12 Below, pp. 367–368.
13 C.12.1.
14 C.12.2.
15 C.12.3.
16 Op. cit., p. 51.
17 C.12.4.
18 C.12.6.
19 C.12.7.
20 C.12.8.
 1 C.12.9–C.12.13.
 2 Code C.16.1.
 3 Subject to Code C.11.4, above, p. 318, ibid.
 4 See below, p. 338 (Code C.16.2).

particulars of the offence and other specified information.[5] Questions relating to an offence may not be put to a person after he has been charged with, or informed that he may be prosecuted for that offence,

- unless they are necessary for the purpose of preventing or minimising harm or loss to some other person or to the public or for clearing up an ambiguity in a previous answer; or
- where it is in the interests of justice that the person should have put to him and have an opportunity to comment on information concerning the offence which has come to light since that time.[6]

The RCCJ recommended that questioning be permitted after charge provided the suspect is cautioned and has access to a solicitor.[7]

Non-compliance with Code C may lead to exclusion of a confession.[8]

Around 90% of suspects are questioned only once.[1] And research studies since the introduction of PACE have consistently recorded that confession rates are around 55–60%.[2] Of those who confess, women are more likely (65%) than men (55%) and juveniles more likely (65%) than adults (55%) to do so.[3] Of those who receive legal advice, 47% make a confession compared to 66% of those who do not receive legal advice.[4]

Rejecting the idea that verballing is perpetrated by rogue officers only M. McConville, A. Sanders and R. Leng claim[5] that 'police work is systematically geared to the construction of evidence: the creation of evidence in one way or another is not a deviant police act but a standard form of production'.

9. All interviews by police officers at police stations with persons suspected of an indictable offence must be tape-recorded in accordance with the provisions of the *Code of Practice on Tape Recording* (PACE Code E).[6] As a result, disputes over the contents of interviews at police stations should be rare.[7] The RCCJ unreservedly welcome[d] this advance'.[8] The main practical difficulties have arisen in respect of the preparation by the police of summaries (a 'written record of the interview'), originally required by PACE (Code E.5.3). The exercise is very time-consuming for the police; at the same time, research by John Baldwin found that in less than a third of the cases examined could the summaries be said to provide an accurate and succinct record of the interview.[9] Further guidance by the Home Office[10] was, however, said by them to have led to improvements. That circular has now been withdrawn and HO Circular 26/1995 provides national guidelines. These are to: clarify preparation of records where adverse inferences might be drawn.[11] Officers are instructed to take a verbatim record of key points (admission etc.) and not to discuss bail or alternative

---

5 Code C.16.3.
6 Code C.16.5.
7 Cm. 2263, pp. 16–17.
8 See below, pp. 373–376.
1 T. Bucke and D. Brown, op. cit., p. 31.
2 Ibid., p. 33.
3 Ibid., p. 33.
4 Ibid., p. 34.
5 *The Case for the Prosecution* (1991), pp. 83–87.
6 Police and Criminal Evidence Act 1984 (Tape-recording of Interviews) (No. 1) Order 1991, S.I. 1991 No. 2687 and (No. 2) Order 1992, S.I. 1992 No. 2803.
7 On the use to be made of tapes at trial and by the jury on retirement see *R v Rampling* [1987] Crim LR 823 (CA) and *R v Hogan* [1997] 1 Cr App R 464. See also the *Practice Direction Crime: Tape Recordings of Police Interviews: Preparation for Proceedings in the Crown Court* (1989) 89 Cr App R 132.
8 Cm. 2263, p. 39.
9 *Preparing the Record of Taped Interview*, RCCJ Study No. 2 HMSO, 1992.
10 Circular 21/1992.
11 The guidelines are reproduced in (1995) 159 JPN 303.

pleas or charges. The RCCJ[12] suggested that the Home Office conduct further work to establish the best practicable method for the future. The latest version of Code E merely requires that a written record be made in accordance with national guidelines approved by the Secretary of State.[13]

Debate has now moved on to the possible introduction of video-taping of interviews.[14] The Criminal Justice and Police Act 2001 makes provision for this (s. 76, inserting s. 60A into PACE), and provides for a code to be drafted. The RCCJ noted Baldwin's finding that there were additional benefits to video over audio-taping in some 20% of the cases studied, although showing such recordings to jurors and magistrates might have some prejudicial effect, for example, symptoms of nervousness might be mistaken for symptoms of guilt; a powerful visual impact might distract from what was said. The RCCJ majority recommended further research.[15] The video can only record what occurs in the room and when it is switched on.

10. The interrogation of persons in custody was originally discouraged by the judges, but came to be 'the principal interrogation strategy employed by the police'.[16] Confessions and incriminating statements have been found in some 60% of cases where there is an interrogation and around 80% of guilty pleas.[17] At the same time, the importance of confessions was probably overstated.[18] More recently, there has been growing recognition of the risk of false confessions.[19] Unreliable confessions, as a result of police pressure, mental instability or a combination of both, have been at the heart of many of the high profile miscarriage of justice cases.[20] Access to taped records of interviews has demonstrated the very poor quality of much of the interviewing conducted by police officers.[21] In response:

> 'the police service, on an official level at least, has been stressing of late that questioning a suspect is only part of the process of investigation – and a decreasingly important part'.[1]

Home Office Circular 22/1992 laid down Principles for Investigative Interviewing, emphasising, *inter alia*, the points that the role of interviewing should be to obtain accurate and reliable information in order to discover the truth about matters under police investigation, that interviewing should be approached with an open mind, that when questioning anyone a police officer must act fairly and that vulnerable people must be treated with particular consideration at all times. Home Office Circular 7/1993 announced the availability of a new national training package for basic interviewing skills. These developments were welcomed by the RCCJ.[2]

Notwithstanding the many concerns, the RCCJ (by majority) did not recommend introduction of a requirement that confessions be corroborated, but unanimously

---

12 Cm. 2263, pp. 41–42.
13 Note for Guidance *5A*.
14 See RCCJ, Cm. 2263, pp. 39–40; J. Baldwin, *Video Taping Police Interviews with Suspects: A National Evaluation,* Police Research Series Paper No. 1, Home Office, 1992; HO Circular 6/93.
15 See further A. Leonard, (1991) 141 NLJ 1512; M. McConville, [1992] Crim LR 532 and (1992) 142 NLJ 960 and 1120; J. Baldwin, (1991) 141 NLJ 1512 and (1992) 142 NLJ 1095.
16 M. McConville, et al., *The Case for the Prosecution* (1991), p. 56.
17 A. Sanders and R. Young, *Criminal Justice* (2000), p. 247.
18 See M. McConville and J. Baldwin, *Courts, Prosecution and Conviction* (1981), Chaps. 7, 8.
19 See G. Gudjonsson, *The Psychology of Interrogations, Confessions and Testimony* (1992).
20 Walker, in C. Walker and K. Starmer (eds.), *Justice in Error* (1993), p. 14, citing the *Guildford Four, Birmingham Six, Judith Ward, Tottenham Three* and *Cardiff Three* cases; see also I. Dennis, [1993] PL 291.
21 See J. Baldwin, 'Police Interview Techniques' (1993) 33 Brit J Crim 325.
1   Baldwin, op. cit., pp. 325–326.
2   Cm. 2263, pp. 11–14, (see T. Williamson, 'Reflections on Current Police Practice' in D. Morgan and G. M. Stephenson (eds.), *Suspicion and Silence* (1994), Chap. 7, noting (at p. 111) that the principles of investigative interviewing were not yet widely understood.

recommended that the judge should give a strong warning that great care is needed before convicting on the basis of a confession alone.[3]

11. *The 'Right to Silence'.* Code C provides that a person whom there are grounds to suspect of an offence must be cautioned before questions about it are put to him regarding his involvement or suspected involvement in that offence if his answers or silence may be given in evidence to a court in a prosecution (and not, for example, to establish his identity or his ownership of a vehicle or to search him in the exercise of a power of stop and search).[4] A person must be cautioned upon arrest for an offence unless it is practicable by reason of his condition or behaviour or he has already been cautioned under para. C.10.1.[5]

The caution was originally in the terms:

> 'You do not have to say anything unless you wish to do so, but what you say might be given in evidence.'

The 1984 Act did not seek to attenuate the accused's 'right to silence'. Proposals to this effect were made by the Criminal Law Revision Committee in its Eleventh Report,[6] but received much adverse criticism and were not implemented.[7] The RCCP noted that the right was not a right which the generality of suspects chose to exercise and recommended, by a majority, that the present law on the right of silence should not be altered.[8] In 1988, the Home Secretary announced (after a period of public debate in which widely divergent views were expressed) that the case for change was strong; he commissioned a report by a Working Group on the precise form the change should take. The Working Group reported in 1989 that the recommendations in the 11th Report should be implemented, with modifications.[9] The change was, however, postponed.[10] The position was changed in Northern Ireland in 1989.[11] The RCCJ majority[12] expressed the view that adverse inferences should not be drawn from silence at the police station because of the risk that this might result in more convictions of the innocent: however, once the prosecution case was fully disclosed, defendants should be required to offer an answer to the charges made against them at the risk of adverse comment at trial on any new defence then disclosed or any departure from the defence which they previously disclosed. Apart from the latter change, the position as to silence at trial should continue.

The position was controversially rejected by the government, and the Criminal Justice and Public Order Act 1994, ss. 34–39, extends the rules applying in Northern Ireland (with some modifications) to England and Wales. 'Such inferences as appear proper' may be drawn at various stages of the trial process by a court or jury (and in some circumstances, a judge) or a magistrates' court inquiring into the offence as examining justices[13] in four situations. By s. 34(1), the first is:

---

3 Cm. 2263, pp. 63–68. See further R. Pattenden, (1991) 107 LQR 317.
4 Code C.10.1.
5 Code C.10.3.
6 *Evidence (General)* (Cmnd. 4991, 1972).
7 See e.g. M. Zander in P. Glazebrook (ed.), *Reshaping the Criminal Law* (1978) pp. 349–354.
8 Report, pp. 80–91.
9 *Report of the Working Group on the Right of Silence* (Home Office, 1989).
10 For powerful adverse criticism of the proposals, see A. A. S. Zuckerman, [1989] Crim LR 855; J. Wood and A. Crawford, *The Right of Silence: The Case for Retention* (1989); S Greer, (1990) 53 MLR 709; and B. Irving and I. McKenzie, (1990) 1 J Foresenic Psychiatry 167. for arguments in favour of change, see G. Williams, 'The Right of Silence and the Mental Element' [1988] Crim LR 97.
11 See below, pp. 604–609.
12 Cm. 2263, pp. 49–56.
13 Inserted as s. 2(*a*) by the Criminal Procedure and Investigation Act 1996, s. 44(1), (3), (4), (7), Sch. 5(1).

'where, in any proceedings against a person for an offence, evidence is given that the accused –

(*a*) at any time before he was charged with the offence, on being questioned under caution by a constable trying to discover whether or by whom the offence had been committed, failed to mention any fact relied on in his defence in those proceedings; or

(*b*) on being charged with the offence or officially informed that he might be prosecuted for it, failed to mention any such fact,

being a fact which in the circumstances existing at the time the accused could reasonably have been expected to mention when so questioned, charged or informed, as the case may be.'

The second is where a person arrested by a constable fails or refuses to account on request for objects, substances or marks on his person, in or on his clothing or footwear, or otherwise in his possession, or in any place in which he is at the time of his arrest; the arresting or investigating officer must reasonably believe that the object etc. may be attributable to the suspect's participation in the commission of an offence specified by the officer who must inform the suspect that he so believes (s. 36(1)). This applies to the condition of clothing or footwear as it applies to a substance or mark thereon (s. 36(3)). The constable must inform the suspect in ordinary language of the effect of the section should he fail or refuse to comply with the request (s. 35(4)). Similar provisions apply to an accused's failure or refusal to account for his presence at a place at or about the time the offence for which he was arrested is alleged to have been committed (s. 37). Finally, inferences may be drawn from the accused's failure to give evidence at trial on his refusal, without good cause, to answer any question (s. 35). These provisions have been amended in to ensure compliance with the ECHR.

'34[(2A) where the accused was at an authorised place of detention at the time of the failure, subsections (1) and (2) above do not apply if he had not been allowed an opportunity to consult a solicitor prior to being questioned, charged, or informed as mentioned in subsection (1) above.]¹⁴

36[(4A) where the accused was at an authorised place of detention at the time of the failure or refusal, subsections (1) and (2) above do not apply if he had not been allowed an opportunity to consult a solicitor prior to the request being made.]¹⁵

37 [(3A) where the accused was at an authorised place of detention at the time of the failure or refusal, subsections (1) and (2) above do not apply if he had not been allowed an opportunity to consult a solicitor prior to the request being made.] ¹⁶

38 [(2A) in each of the sections 34(2A), 36(4A) and 37(4A) 'authorised place of detention' means (a) a police station; or (b) any other place prescribed for the purposes by order made by the Secretary of State.]'¹⁷

In each of the sections, if the accused was at an authorised place of detention (i.e. police station or other designated place), the drawing of inferences is prohibited unless he has been allowed the opportunity to consult a legal adviser prior to the questioning/request for material.¹⁸

Note that a failure to disclose the general nature of the defence can result in adverse comment and inferences being drawn at trial under the Criminal Procedure and Investigation Act 1996, s. 11. The power in s. 11(4) of the Criminal Procedure and Investigation Act 1996 is not limited to the court or jury drawing inferences on an explicit difference between a defence statement and the defence at trial, it includes a change in the general terms of the nature of the defence: *R v Tibbs*.¹⁹ The Court of

14 As inserted by the Youth Justice and Criminal Evidence Act 1999, s. 58(1), (2).
15 As inserted by the Youth Justice and Criminal Evidence Act 1999, s. 58(1), (3).
16 As inserted by the Youth Justice and Criminal Evidence Act 1999, s. 58(1), (4).
17 Inserted by the Youth Justice and Criminal Evidence Act 1999, s. 58(5).
18 This is a response to the judgment in *Murray v UK* (below).
19 (2000) 28 January, CA.

Appeal held that the provisions should be strictly construed. The aim of the 1996 Act had been to introduce a procedure to investigate facts relied on by the opposite party so to reduce the risk of a miscarriage of justice by a wrongful conviction or a wrongful acquittal. A defence statement had to include the nature of the defence, matters on which issue was taken and the reasons for taking issue. Under s.11(4) the court had to have regard to the extent of differences in the defences and to any justification for those differences. The discretion with the judge under s. 11(4) was adequate to protect the accused. In *R v Wheeler*[20] the Court of Appeal recommended that the defence should get the defendant to sign the defence statement so that it is clear that it represents his views. Will defendants be advised to comply with this?

The new caution
Note that s. 34 only applies where a person is 'questioned under caution' or charged. Note also that 'interviews outside the police station are not normally permitted,[1] to that extent restricting the operation of s. 34(1)(a) to interviews at the police station. Such interviews should be properly recorded; moreover, by that time the suspect should have had the opportunity to take legal advice.

The standard caution is now: 'You do not have to say anything. But it may harm your defence if you do not mention when questioned something which you later rely on in court. Anything you do say may be given in evidence.' Research suggests that the police and legal advisers doubt whether the majority of suspects understand the new caution.[2] In fact, there is some suggestion that the new caution is used as an intimidatory tactic by investigating officers, who repeat the terms of the caution to put pressure on suspects to speak. [3]

Who stays silent
T. Bucke et al.,[4] found that since the Act, there was no significant rise in the proportion of suspects requesting legal advice. The figure remained stable at around 40%.[5] The percentage of suspects exercising their right to silence has not altered dramatically since the Act. Before the Act, 10% of suspects refused to answer all questions, 13% refused to answer some, and 77% answered all. Under the Act, 6% refused to answer all questions, 10% refused to answer some, and 84% answered all.[6] Those who obtained legal advice were 'far more likely to refuse' all questions than those who had not.[7] More serious allegations were more likely to lead to silence as was a suspect having a previous record (13% as opposed to 5%). Of those who received legal advice before the Act, 20% refused to answer all questions, 19% refused to answer some, and 61% answered all. After the Act those figures are 13%, 9% and 78%. For those who did not receive legal advice, the figures before the 1994 Act were: 3% refused to answer all: 9% refused to answer some; and 88% answered all questions. After the Act, the figures are 2%, 6%, and 92%.[8] The Act seems to have had the greatest impact on black suspects far fewer of whom now refuse to answer questions.

In view of the fact that the Act was aimed at preventing 'hardened' or professional criminals playing the system, there is some suggestion that it has been successful in

20 (2000) 3 July.
 1 See above, p. 317.
 2 T. Bucke, R. Street, and B. Brown, *The Right to Silence: The Impact of the Criminal Justice and Public Order Act 1994* (2000), Chap. 1. See also T. Bucke and D. Brown, *In police custody: police powers and suspects' rights under the revised PACE codes of practice* (1997), Chap. 4.
 3 Ibid., p. 29.
 4 Above, n. 2.
 5 Ibid., p. 21.
 6 T. Bucke et al., p. 31.
 7 Ibid., p. 78.
 8 Ibid., p. 33.

meeting that aim. It is impossible to monitor whether the provisions have had an impact on case outcomes, since these depend on an infinite number of variables of the suspects' motivations and the many possible reasons for decisions by the trier of fact are not disclosed. Assumptions based on only those cases which are reported are unlikely to be reliable since such cases represent only the appeals on difficult points.

Sections 34–37 generally[8a]
The provisions are to be read strictly as they restrict a right which is recognised to protect against injustice: see Lord Bingham CJ in *R v Bowden*,[9] and Maurice Kay J in *R v Nickolson*.[10]

The ECtHR has delivered a number of important judgments on the silence of the suspect. In *Funke v France*,[11] which involved the legitimacy of the French tax authorities' investigative powers, the Court, recognised:

'the right of anyone charged with a criminal offence, within the autonomous meaning of the expression in Article 6, to remain silent and not to contribute to incriminating himself.'

In construing the Northern Irish legislation on which the current English provisions are constructed, the ECHR held in *Murray v UK*[12] that drawing inferences:

'is a matter to be determined in the light of all the circumstances of the case, having particular regard to the situations where inferences may be drawn, the weight to be attached to them by the national courts and their assessment of the evidence and the degree of compulsion inherent.'[13]

In *Saunders v UK*,[14] the defendant had been convicted of offences in relation to the Guinness-Distillers take-over. His conviction rested in part on the answers he provided to questions under compulsion – i.e. where the failure to answer is itself an offence. The European Court held that this constituted an infringement of the privilege against self-incrimination. The majority stated:

'the right not to incriminate oneself, in particular, presupposes that the prosecution in a criminal case seek to prove their case against the accused without resort to evidence obtained through means of coercion or oppression in defiance of the will of the accused. In this sense the right is closely linked to the presumption of innocence contained in article 6(2).'

8a For reviews of the issues surrounding the right to silence, see S. Greer and R. Morgan (eds.), *The Right of Silence* Debate (1990); S. M. Easton, *The Right to Silence* (1991); S. C. Greer, (1990) 53 MLR 709; R. Leng, *The Right to Silence in Police Interrogation: A Study of Some of the Issues Underlying the Debate* (RCCJ Research Study No. 10, HMSO, 1993); D. Morgan and G. M. Stephenson, *Suspicion and Silence* (1994); I. Dennis, [1995] Crim LR 4, 9–18. On the implementations of the silence provisions and the history see J. Wood and A. Crawford, *The Right to Silence* (1989); A. Zuckerman, [1989] Crim LR 855; J. Coldrey, (1991) 20 Anglo-Am LR; D. Morgan and G. Stephenson (eds.), *Suspicion or Silence: the right to silence in criminal investigations* (1994). For academic comment on the implementation and operation of the sections, see P. Mirfield, *Silence Confessions and Improperly Obtained Evidence* (1998). See also: I. Dennis, (1995) 54 CLJ 342, [1995] Crim LR 4; S. Easton, [1998] 2 Int J E & P; J. Jackson, [1993] 44 NILQ 103; R. Pattenden, [1995] Crim LR 602; R. Pattenden, [1998] 2 Int J of E & P 141; D. Birch, [1999] Crim LR 769. For a summary of the debate preceding enactment, see the Home Office Research Study, T. Bucke, R. Street, and B. Brown, *The Right to Silence: The Impact of the Criminal Justice and Public Order Act 1994* (2000), Chap. 1.
9 [1999] 2 Cr App R 176.
10 [1999] Crim LR 61 (CA).
11 (1993) 16 EHRR 297.
12 [1996] 22 EHRR 29.
13 Para. 61. See above for the legislative changes resulting from the decision.
14 (1997) 23 EHRR 313.

Once again, English law has responded by introducing legislative amendments to the 1994 Act. See below, p. 348. However, in the more recent case of *IJL, GMR AKP v UK*,[15] the European Court refused to accept the argument that 'a legal requirement for an individual to give information demanded by an administrative body necessarily infringes Article 6 of the Convention'. The Court restricted the scope of the protection of the privilege against self-incrimination to cases where the inquiry is a criminal one by a prosecutorial body. This has already been influential in the House of Lords' consideration of cases arising under the Human Rights Act 1998. In *R v Hertfordshire County Council, ex p Green Environmental Industries Ltd*[16] it was held that a notice to supply information under the Environmental Protection Act 1990, s. 71(2), was not a breach of Art. 6. This was an 'extra-judicial' inquiry, and s. 78 of PACE gave a discretion to exclude evidence which would therefore have ensured a fair trial.

For recent reviews of the impact of the provisions in Northern Ireland see M. Zander,[17] reviewing J. Jackson, M. Wolfe and K. Quinn, *Legislating Against Silence: The NI Experience*.[18] The conclusion was that 'whereas terrorism suspects had not greatly changed their approach to interviews, they were more likely to testify after the 1988 Order'– 54% in 1991 compared with 6% in 1987. In ordinary cases too the proportion had increased: 85% in 1991 compared with 77% in 1987.[19]

Section 34
The section applies to any suspect who has been cautioned, irrespective of whether an arrest has been made. The Court of Appeal provided guidance on the use of s. 34 in the case of *R v Argent*:[20]

> **Lord Bingham CJ:** What then are the formal conditions to be met before the jury may draw such an inference? In our judgment there are six such conditions. The first is that there must be proceedings against a person for an offence; that condition must necessarily be satisfied before section 34(2)(d) can bite. The second condition is that the alleged failure must occur before a defendant is charged. The third condition is that the alleged failure must occur during questioning under caution by a constable. The requirement that the questioning should be by a constable is not strictly a condition, as is evident from section 34(4). The fourth condition is that the constable's questioning must be directed to trying to discover whether or by whom the alleged offence had been committed. The fifth condition is that the alleged failure by the defendant must be to mention any fact relied on in his defence in those proceedings. That raises two questions of fact: first, is there some fact which the defendant has relied on in his defence; and second, did the defendant fail to mention it to the constable when he was being questioned in accordance with the section? Being questions of fact these questions are for the jury as the tribunal of fact to resolve. The sixth condition is that the appellant failed to mention a fact which in the circumstances existing at the time the accused could reasonably have been expected to mention when so questioned. The time referred to is the time of questioning, and account must be taken of all the relevant circumstances existing at that time. The courts should not construe the expression 'in the circumstances' restrictively: matters such as time of day, the defendant's age, experience, mental capacity, state of health, sobriety, tiredness, knowledge, personality and legal advice are all part of the relevant circumstances; and those are only examples of things which may be relevant. When reference is made to 'the accused' attention is directed not to some hypothetical, reasonable accused of ordinary phlegm and fortitude but to the actual accused with such qualities, apprehensions, knowledge and advice as he is shown to have had at the time. It is for the jury to decide whether the fact (or facts) which the defendant

---

15 [2000] 9 BHRC 222, [2001] Crim LR 133.
16 [2000] 2 WLR 373.
17 (2001) NLJ 138.
18 (2000).
19 p. 129.
20 [1997] 2 Cr App R 27. A failure to give an adequate warning could result in a conviction being quashed: *R v Gill* [2001] 1 Cr App R 11.

has relied on in his defence in the criminal trial, but which he had not mentioned when questioned under caution before charge by the constable investigating the alleged offence for which the defendant is being tried, is (or are) a fact (or facts) which in the circumstances as they actually existed the actual defendant could reasonably have been expected to mention.

The crucial questions are whether there is a 'fact' that is being relied on by the defence, and whether there are reasonable grounds for the silence. Lord Taylor CJ, in the debates in the House of Lords on the Criminal Justice and Public Order Bill 1994 stated that:

> 'if a defendant maintains his silence from the first to last, and does not rely on any particular fact by way of defence but simply puts the prosecution to proof, then [s. 34] would not bite at all.'[21]

The defendant will not be relying on a 'fact' where he puts the prosecution to proof of their case (*R v Moshaid;*[22] *R v Bowers*[23]). Nor where he puts forward a speculation or theory that is not a fact (*R v Nickolson*[1] (proffered explanation of seminal staining of night-dress was defendant's habitual masturbation in bathroom visited by victim)). Cf. where D does rely on a fact or incident to support a theory or speculation he is seeking to set up: *R v B*[2] (explanation of sex abuse victim's motive for allegedly 'false allegations' was her jealousy of the defendant, but conviction quashed since D could not have known of this at time of interview and could not therefore reasonably have been expected to mention it).[3] Difficulties arise because the 'fact' might not be identified with sufficient precision at the time of interview: see, for example, *R v O.*[4] In determining whether something relied on is a 'fact' for these purposes, the court applies a dictionary definition and this is not limited to events and acts: *R v Milford.*[5]

Defendants are not obliged to disclose responses to allegations until they have had adequate knowledge of the allegations. If the police do not put the allegations to the suspect in specific enough terms, his silence cannot found an inference under s. 34: *R v Bowers;*[6] cf. *R v Hussain*[7] (police do not have to disclose case prior to the interview). Similarly, it may be reasonable to fail to comment at the time of the interview if the case is a very complex one or the events occurred a long time ago: *R v Roble.*[8] Other factors that might provide a reasonable basis for a suspect's silence where referred to by Lord Bingham CJ in *R v Argent.*[9] These include the defendant's age and experience, his state of health and sobriety or tiredness, his personality and the legal advice he had been given and the wide range of circumstances existing at the time. Bucke et al. report that there is no reported 'miscarriage of justice' resulting from a vulnerable suspect losing his right to silence.[10]

The Court of Appeal held that if a legal adviser recommends silence, this does not in itself prevent an adverse inference from being drawn. Otherwise, the section could be very easily circumvented: *R v Condron and Condron.*[11] In that case the suspect was convicted of heroin dealing, and claimed that her silence during questioning was on the advice of her solicitor who believed her to be unfit owing to the heroin

---

21 HL Debs, Vol. 55, col. 519.
22 [1998] Crim LR 420.
23 [1998] Crim LR 817.
 1 [2000] 1 Cr App Rep 182.
 2 [2000] Crim LR 181.
 3 For a further discussion of the possible interpretations of 'fact' in this context, see P. Mirfield, *Silence Confessions and Improperly Obtained Evidence* (1998), p. 252.
 4 [2000] Crim LR 616.
 5 [2000] JPL 943, CA (Cr D).
 6 (1997) 163 JP 33.
 7 [1997] Crim LR 754, CA.
 8 [1997] Crim LR 449, CA.
 9 Above, p. 340.
10 *The Right to Silence – The Impact of the CJPOA (1994)* (2000).
11 [1997] 1 Cr App R 185.

withdrawal symptoms. The Court of Appeal felt that the conviction was not unsafe given the amount of other evidence, and the fact that a medical examiner had declared her fit for interview. Stuart-Smith LJ suggested, *obiter*, that the jury could be directed to draw adverse inferences where they concluded that the failure was attributable to the suspect having later fabricated the evidence.[12] When the case was taken to Strasbourg, the ECtHR ruled that this was a breach of Art. 6 and that the applicant had been denied a fair trial:

'The Court recalls that in its *John Murray* judgment it proceeded on the basis that the question whether the right to silence is an absolute right must be answered in the negative (pp. 49–50, § 47). It noted in that case that whether the drawing of adverse inferences from an accused's silence infringes Article 6 is a matter to be determined in the light of all the circumstances of the case, having regard to the situations where inferences may be drawn, the weight attached to them by the national courts in their assessment of the evidence and the degree of compulsion inherent in the situation (ibid. § 47). The Court stressed in the same judgment that since the right to silence, like the privilege against self-incrimination, lay at the heart of the notion of a fair procedure under Article 6, particular caution was required before a domestic court could invoke an accused's silence against him. Thus it observed that it would be incompatible with the right to silence to base a conviction solely or mainly on the accused's silence or on a refusal to answer questions or to give evidence himself. Nevertheless, the Court found that it is obvious that the right cannot and should not prevent that the accused's silence, in situations which clearly call for an explanation from him, be taken into account in assessing the persuasiveness of the evidence adduced by the prosecution (ibid. § 47).

58. The Court notes that the domestic law and practice of the respondent State attempts to strike an appropriate balance between the exercise by an accused of his right to silence during police interview and the drawing of an adverse inference from that fact at a jury trial.

59. It observes, in line with the Government' submissions, that the applicants were under no legal compulsion to co-operate with the police and could not be exposed to any penal sanction for their failure to do so. The police were required under domestic law to administer a clear warning to the applicants about the possible implications of withholding information which they might later rely on at their trial. The Court does not accept the applicants' argument that the caution was ambiguous or unclear as to the consequences of their refusal to answer police questions. Furthermore, the question whether the applicants were sufficiently lucid at the material time to comprehend the consequences of their silence, as opposed to their fitness for interview, is a separate consideration which must be examined from the standpoint of the trial judge's direction on this matter.

60. It must also be observed that the applicants' solicitor was present throughout the whole of their interviews and was able to advise them not to volunteer any answers to the questions put to them. The fact that an accused person who is questioned under caution is assured access to legal advice, and in the applicants' case the physical presence of a solicitor during police interview, must be considered a particularly important safeguard for dispelling any compulsion to speak which may be inherent in the terms of the caution. For the Court, particular caution is required when a domestic court seeks to attach weight to the fact that a person who is arrested in connection with a criminal offence and who has not been given access to a lawyer does not provide detailed responses when confronted with questions the answers to which may be incriminating (see the above-mentioned *John Murray* judgment[13], p. 55, § 66). At the same time, the very fact that an accused is advised by his lawyer to maintain his silence must also be given appropriate weight by the domestic court. There may be good reason why such advice may be given. The applicants in the instant case state that they held their silence on the strength of their solicitor's advice that they were unfit to answer questions. Their solicitor testified before the domestic court that his advice was motivated by his concern about their capacity to follow questions put to them during interview (see paragraph 18 above).

---

12 This was applied in *R v Daniel* [1998] 2 Cr App R 373, CA, to drawing an adverse inference where silence was attributable to an unwillingness to be subjected to additional questioning while in a vulnerable position.

13 [2000] 31 EHRR 1; [2000] Crim LR 679.

As with the issue of the applicants' lucidity at the time of interview, the question whether the trial judge gave sufficient weight to the applicants' reliance on legal advice to explain their silence at interview must equally be examined from the standpoint of his directions on this matter. The Court would observe at this juncture that the fact that the applicants were subjected to cross-examination on the content of their solicitor's advice cannot be said to raise an issue of fairness under Article 6 of the Convention. They were under no compulsion to disclose the advice given, other than the indirect compulsion to avoid the reason for their silence remaining at the level of a bare explanation. The applicants chose to make the content of their solicitor's advice a live issue as part of their defence. For that reason they cannot complain that the scheme of section 34 of the 1994 Act is such as to override the confidentiality of their discussions with their solicitor.

61. It is to be noted that the trial judge directed the jury on the issue of the applicants' silence in accordance with the terms of the relevant specimen direction at the time (see paragraph 32 above). The Court notes, however, that the formula employed by the trial judge cannot be said to reflect the balance which the Court in its *John Murray* judgment sought to strike between the right to silence and the circumstances in which an adverse inference may be drawn from silence, including by a jury. It reiterates that the Court stressed in that judgment that, provided appropriate safeguards were in place, an accused's silence, in situations which clearly call for an explanation, could be taken into account in assessing the persuasiveness of the evidence adduced by the prosecution against him (see paragraph 56 above). The Court further noted, with reference to Articles 4 and 6 of the Criminal Evidence (Northern Ireland) Order 1988, that those provisions only permitted a judge to draw common-sense inferences which he considered proper in the light of the evidence against the accused (ibid., p. 50, § 51). However, in the instant case the applicants put forward an explanation for their failure to mention during the police interview why certain items were exchanged between them and their co-accused, Mr Curtis (see paragraph 19 above). They testified that they acted on the strength of the advice of their solicitor who had grave doubts about their fitness to cope with police questioning (see paragraph 21 above). Their solicitor confirmed this in his testimony in the voir dire proceedings (see paragraph 18 above). Admittedly the trial judge drew the jury's attention to this explanation. However he did so in terms which left the jury at liberty to draw an adverse inference notwithstanding that it may have been satisfied as to the plausibility of the explanation. It is to be observed that the Court of Appeal found the terms of the trial judge's direction deficient in this respect (see paragraph 27 above). In the Court's opinion, as a matter of fairness, the jury should have been directed that it could only draw an adverse inference if satisfied that the applicants' silence at the police interview could only sensibly be attributed to their having no answer or none that would stand up to cross-examination.

62. Unlike the Court of Appeal, the Court considers that a direction to that effect was more than merely "desirable" (see paragraph 27 above). It notes that the responsibility for deciding whether or not to draw such an inference rested with the jury. As the applicants have pointed out, it is impossible to ascertain what weight, if any, was given to the applicants' silence. In its *John Murray* judgment the Court noted that the trier of fact in that case was an experienced judge who was obliged to explain the reasons for his decision to draw inferences and the weight attached to them. Moreover, the exercise of the judge's discretion to do so was subject to review by the appellate courts (ibid., p. 51, § 51). However, these safeguards were absent in the instant case. It was thus even more compelling to ensure that the jury was properly advised on how to address the issue of the applicants' silence. It is true that the judge was under no obligation to leave the jury with the option of drawing an adverse inference from their silence and, left with that option, the jury had a discretion whether or not to do so. It is equally true that the burden of proof lay with the prosecution to prove the applicants' guilt beyond reasonable doubt and the jury was informed that the applicants' silence could not "on its own prove guilt" (see paragraph 22 above). However, notwithstanding the presence of these safeguards, the Court considers that the trial judge's omission to restrict even further the jury's discretion must be seen as incompatible with the exercise by the applicants of their right to silence at the police station.'[14]

14 *Condron v United Kingdom*, paras. 56–62.

Prior to the ruling of the ECHR in *Condron*, the recommended direction to a jury where a defendant relies on his legal adviser's recommendation for silence, was:

> 'You should consider whether or not he is able to decide for himself what he should do or having asked for a solicitor to advise him he would not challenge that advice.'[15]

The question is not as to the correctness of the legal advice given but whether it is reasonable for the suspect to heed it. The defendant may wish to give an explanation as to why his legal adviser advised silence (for example, the police have not disclosed the case yet etc.). In doing so, he is waiving privilege if he goes beyond a simple explanation that he refused to answer on legal advice, and seeks to provide details of the advice (*R v Bowden*[16]), and there is unlikely to be a problem of inadmissibility of that as evidence on the grounds of hearsay: *R v Desmond*;[17] *R v Roble*.[18] Is it desirable that solicitors should have to give evidence to explain why they made professional decisions?[19] Research has shown that one impact of the provisions has been to encourage legal advisers to ask for more information at the time of the interviews.[20] This leads to greater pressure on the investigator – the reverse of the intended impact of the provisions. However, this has also made the legal advisers task more difficult, since 'wrong' advice on silence could lead to serious consequences at trial. A number of legal advisers have raised concerns at the implications for lawyer/client privilege.[21] A. Jennings, A. Ashworth and B. Emmerson,[22] review the recent ECtHR and domestic law relating to silence:

> 'The legislative changes to a defendant's right to silence, brought about by sections 34-38 of the Criminal Justice and Public Order Act 1994, represented one of the most controversial reforms of English criminal law in the last century. The new century has seen the European Court of Human Rights in *Condron v. U.K.*, the first test of the legislation at Strasbourg, find the United Kingdom Government to be in breach of Article 6 of the European Convention. Condron and the more recent decisions in *Magee v. U.K.* and *Averill v. U.K.*, raise fundamental questions in respect of the law governing the right to silence. Even more profound questions are raised by Condron concerning the test applied by the Court of Appeal in reviewing convictions. This latter question has been partially but disappointingly answered by the Court of Appeal in *Davis, Rowe and Johnson*. The Human Rights Act 1998 will undoubtedly ensure that the jurisprudence in these areas will continue to develop and grow.
>
> ...
>
> *The European Court*
> The European Court [has] reiterated that the right to silence is not an absolute right but nonetheless one that lies at the heart of the notion of a fair trial and therefore "particular caution" was required before drawing an adverse inference. The Court in Averill arguably went further when it said that "the extent to which adverse inferences can be drawn from an accused's failure to respond to police questioning must be necessarily limited". Although silence could not be the sole or the main basis for any conviction, the Court in Condron added that it was only right that it could be taken into account in a situation which clearly called for an explanation. Such silence was relevant in "assessing the persuasiveness of the evidence adduced by the prosecution".
>   The current specimen direction does not include a direction that an adverse inference cannot be the main basis for a conviction and in that respect it fails to curtail the adverse inference

---

15 Per Lord Bingham in *Argent*, above, p. 340, at 34.
16 [1999] 2 Cr App R 176.
17 [1998] Crim LR 659, CA.
18 [1997] Crim LR 449.
19 See D. Wright, [1998] Crim LR 44.
20 Bucke et al., p. 23.
21 See Bucke et al., p. 51.
22 'Silence And Safety: The Impact Of Human Rights Law' [2000] Crim LR 879.

sufficiently and we believe that the direction should be amended accordingly. The Court also went on to distinguish *Condron* from *Murray*: the Condrons gave evidence, they were tried by a jury that had to be directed in relation to adverse inferences and in evidence they gave the reasons for their silence in interview. The Court further noted that domestic law and practice attempted to strike an "appropriate balance" between the right to silence and drawing adverse inferences.

Legal advice

The presence of a solicitor at interview was a "particularly important safeguard" for dispelling any compulsion to speak which may be inherent in the terms of the caution and the fact that a person has remained silent following legal advice must be given "appropriate weight" by the domestic court as there may be good reason why such advice was given. In *Averill* the Court observed that an accused's silence may be based on "bona fide advice received from his lawyer" and "due regard" must be given to such a position

The Court in *Condron* also observed that the judge's directions did not reflect the required balance between the right to silence and the drawing of adverse inferences because although the judge reminded the jury of the Condrons' explanation for their silence, "he did so in terms which left the jury at liberty to draw an adverse inference notwithstanding that it may have been satisfied as to the plausibility of the explanation". This failure to restrict even further the jury's discretion to draw an adverse inference was incompatible with the right to silence.

We believe this suggests a two-stage test:

(i) the jury must take into account the fact that the defendant has been advised by his legal representative to remain silent;

(ii) if the defendant's resulting silence was or may have been because of the reason relied upon at trial, then no adverse inference should be drawn. Such a test must permit a jury to decline to draw an adverse inference where it believes the only reason for the defendant's silence was because he had followed legal advice. If, however, the jury concluded that the defendant had only latched on to legal advice to remain silent because he had no explanation to offer, then it could properly draw such an inference. The exercise of the right to silence must therefore be for reasons of guilt. The current specimen direction draws the jury's attention to the reason advanced for silence and then states that if the jury think that explanation "amounts to a reason why you should not hold the defendant's failure against him, do not do so". We believe that this direction fails to give appropriate weight to the fact of legal advice as it leaves the matter entirely to the discretion of the jury and does nothing to remind the jury of the importance of such advice.'[1]

After the decision of the ECtHR in *Condron*, the jury will have to be instructed that no adverse inference can be drawn against defendant's pre-trial silence unless the failure to answer the question is because they have no answer that will stand up to scrutiny. In *R v Morgan*,[2] D relied at trial on a fact not previously mentioned and claimed that this was a result of legal advice. The Court of Appeal held that the courts could assume that those who had legal advice to remain silent would also have been advised of the adverse inferences rule under s. 34. A solicitor could rebut this by giving evidence of his advice. Is it legitimate to hold the suspect's silence against him when he has acted in accordance with the advice of his legal representative?[3] In *R v Browne*[4] a trial judge declared that he thought that the innocent never relied on the right to silence and that it could not be lawful for a solicitor to advise a complete 'no comment interview'. The judge refused to disqualify himself from the case, and the Court of Appeal upheld the conviction and his decision to try the case. To what extent was the judge merely verbalising the thoughts of many jurors?

1   p. 882.
2   [2001] EWCA Crim 1194, CA (Cr D).
3   E. Cape, [1997] 1 Int J Evidence and Proof 386.
4   (1998) 10 Admin LR 418.

The Criminal Justice and Public Order Act 1994 has placed more pressure on legal advisers and suspects in the already strained environment of the police station. It leads to more tactical games being played at the police station.

If interviews are conducted beyond the point at which it has been established that there is sufficient evidence to charge, no inference can be drawn from such interviews (in breach of Code C.11.14) see *R v McGuiness*;[6] *R v Pointer*;[7] *R v Gayle*;[8] *R v Ioannou*.[9] But officers have the opportunity to investigate the offence where they have the belief that the prosecution should continue: *R v Odeyemi*.[10]

What inferences can be drawn?

At trial the court is entitled to draw inferences from silence in deciding whether there is a case to answer (s. 34(2)(c)) but this may not be the sole basis for a finding of a case to answer (s. 38(3)): *R v D*.[11] In practice s. 34 will usually only bite once the defendant provides a defence at trial – i.e. after submissions of no case have been rejected. There is no rule that the inferences cannot be drawn where a defendant does not testify at trial, provided he has relied on a 'fact' etc.: *R v Bowers*.[12] The jury do not need to be told that there is a case to answer before they rely on the silence: *R v Doldur*.[13] The inferences can be drawn even where the facts relied on by the defence were raised before the trial proper: *R v Daniel*;[14] *R v Montague and Beckles*.[15] Research suggests that there is often reluctance in the legal profession when prosecuting to rely on the provisions at trial out of a sense of 'fairness to the accused', and a fear of creating sympathy with the jury.[16] The Court of Appeal has provided guidance on the use of the adverse inferences at trial and approved a Judicial Studies Board direction:[17]

'[When arrested, and at the beginning of each interview] this defendant was cautioned, he was told that he need not say anything, but that it may harm his defence if he did not mention something when questioned which he later relied on in court. Anything he did say may be given in evidence. The defendant, as part of his defence, has relied upon [....] (here specify precisely the fact(s) to which this direction applies). But [the prosecution case is] [he admits] that he did not mention this [when he was questioned before being charged with the offence] [when he was charged with the offence] [when he was officially informed that he might be prosecuted for the offence]. The prosecution case is that in the circumstances, and having regard to the warning which he had been given, if this fact had been true, he could reasonably have been expected to mention it at that stage, and as he did not do so you may therefore conclude that [it has since been invented/tailored to fit the prosecution case/he believed that it would not then stand up to scrutiny]. If you are sure that he did fail to mention when he was [charged] [questioned] [informed], it is for you to decide whether in the circumstances it was

4a (1996) 22 EHRR 29.
 5 (1996) 23 EHRR 313.
 6 [1999] Crim LR 318, CA.
 7 [1997] Crim LR 676.
 8 [1999] Crim LR 502.
 9 [1999] Crim LR 586.
10 [1999] Crim LR 828.
11 [2000] Crim LR 178.
12 (1999) 163 JP 33.
13 [2000] Crim LR 178, CA.
14 [1998] 2 Cr App Rep 73.
15 [1999] Crim LR 148.
16 T. Bucke et al., p. 48.
17 www.jsboard.co.uk.

something which he could reasonably have been expected to mention at that time. If it was, the law is that you may draw such inferences as appear proper from his failure to do so. Failure to mention cannot on its own prove guilt. But, if you are sure that quite regardless of this failure, there is a case for him to meet, it is something which you are entitled to take into account when deciding whether his evidence about this matter is true, i.e. you may take it into account as some additional support for the prosecution's case. You are not bound to do so. It is for you to decide whether it is fair to do so. [There is evidence before you on the basis of which the defendant's advocate invites you not to hold it against him that he failed to mention this fact when he had the opportunity to do so. That evidence is. If you think this amounts to a reason why you should not hold the defendant's failure against him, do not do so. On the other hand, if it does not in your judgement provide an adequate explanation, and you are sure that the real reason for his failure was that he then had no innocent explanation to offer in relation to this aspect of the case, you may hold it against him.]'

In *R v Everson*[18] the Court of Appeal upheld a conviction but noted the need for the Judicial Studies Board direction to be modified so that jurors are warned that they should not convict mainly on the basis of silence. See *Condron* (above).

A direction may be unnecessary where the fact relied on by the defendant is so crucial that, if it is rejected, there is no question but that he will be found guilty: *R v Mountford*[19] (defendant did not mention until trial that his companion was the drug dealer, not he). If no adverse inferences can be drawn the judge must direct the jury of that: *R v McGarry*,[20] otherwise they are left without guidance, and, as before the Act they were instructed against drawing such inferences, that should continue to be the case where the statute does not apply.[1] A misdirection in these circumstances does not necessarily lead to a conviction being unsafe: *R v Francom*.[2] It is unclear whether juries are restricted to drawing an inference (only) that the accused's silence means that his defence or fact relied on is a lie (*R v Roble*,[3] *R v Nickolson*,[4] *R v Condron*[5]), or whether adverse inferences may be held against the defendant in more general terms (*R v Randall*;[6] *R v Taylor*;[7] *R v Daniel*;[8] *R v Montague and Beckles*.[9] For an argument that inferences on more than credit of an accused are contrary to Art. 6, see R. Pattenden.[9a]

The effectiveness of the provisions

'There are strong grounds for arguing that the provisions have led to greater efficiency in the investigative and prosecution process.'[10] In particular, the legal adviser is better able to advise his client because the police will have been compelled to disclose more of their case at an earlier stage. This leads to a more efficient decision-making process regarding charging. A benefit to the suspect is also that in more cases than before, the police are compelled to investigate the story provided by the suspect.

18 [2001] EWCA Crim 2262, CA (Cr D).
19 [1999] Crim LR 575.
20 [1999] 1 Cr App R 377, CA.
 1 [1999] 1 Cr App R 377, CA.
 2 [2000] Crim LR 1018.
 3 [1997] Crim LR 449.
 4 [1999] Crim LR 61.
 5 [1997] 1 Cr App R 185.
 6 [1998] 6 Arch News 1.
 7 [1999] Crim LR 77.
 8 [1998] 2 Cr App R 73.
 9 [1999] Crim LR 148.
9a (1998) 2 E & P 141.
10 T. Bucke et al., p. 70.

This leads to the weeding out of weaker cases and encourages investigation of all lines of inquiry relating to the crime rather than the suspect per se. In addition, the provisions lead to greater certainty of conviction in cases where the evidence is already strong.[11] T. Bucke et al. conclude that: 'whatever philosophical standpoint is adopted, it seems clear that the change in the law has not led to undue practical disadvantages to the defendant.'[12] However, D. Birch has argued that the sections are too costly in terms of the number of appeals that they generate and the collateral issues they produce at trial.[13] If there are efficiency gains in the pre-trial procedure that affect thousands, is this worth the additional expense incurred in appellate court time for a few dozen cases? To what extent is the restriction of the right to silence about increasing efficiency in the criminal justice system?[14]

Compulsory questions

In *Saunders v UK*[15] the ECtHR ruled that incriminating answers obtained under compulsory questioning (i.e. where a failure to answer is itself an offence) should not be admissible. The Attorney-General subsequently published guidelines preventing the use of answers obtained in such circumstances being used at trial unless the defendant himself introduced the answers or the prosecution was for an offence of refusing to answer etc. These guidelines have now been put on a statutory footing in the Youth Justice and Criminal Evidence Act 1999. For a case in which the trial judge and counsel were unaware of the guidelines and the conviction was quashed, see *R v Faryab*.[16] Section 59 of the Youth Justice and Criminal Evidence Act 1999, and Sch. 3 apply these rules to those statutes in which compulsory questioning is provided for.[17] The supply of documents to the receiver (under compulsion) does not amount to self-incrimination contrary to Art. 6: *Attorney-General's Reference (No. 7 of 2000)*.[18] The courts will still have to deal with cases in which the compulsory questions give rise to other evidence of an incriminating nature. The use of evidence which is uncovered as a result of compulsory questioning is particularly difficult. If inferences from the failure to answer the compulsory questions are forbidden, and the answers made in the absence of adequate legal advice etc are to be excluded, can use be made of the material uncovered? Does it depend on whether the evidence existed prior to the interview? Is the reliability of the evidence the key issue?

Sections 36 and 37

These sections have attracted far less attention. The special warning that must be given under Code C: 10.5B, is given in 39% of cases in which a suspect has remained silent.[19] The warning must explain the offence that is being investigated, what the suspect is to account for, the officer's belief that the fact may be due to the suspect's involvement in the offence, that a court may draw an inference from a refusal to account for the fact and that a record of the interview will be available as evidence. Research suggests that the warning is often not understood by the suspects.[20]

11 See T. Bucke et al., pp. 70–73.
12 Ibid., p. 73.
13 [1999] Crim LR 769.
14 The number of appeals in the first few years of the statute's life is likely to be higher.
15 (1995) 23 EHRR 313.
16 [2000] Crim LR 180.
17 On *Saunders*, see S. Nash and M. Furse, [1995] Crim LR 854. On the ECHR, implications for the 1994 provisions, see R. Munday, [1996] Crim LR 370; and A. Ashworth, [1999] Crim LR 261.
18 [2001] Crim LR 736 and commentary.
19 T. Bucke et al., p. 39.
20 Ibid., pp. 39–40.

10 Admissibility of evidence

Police and Criminal Evidence Act 1984

76. Confessions

(1) In any proceedings a confession made by an accused person may be given in evidence against him in so far as it is relevant to any matter in issue in the proceedings and is not excluded by the court in pursuance of this section.

(2) If, any proceedings where the prosecution proposes to give in evidence a confession made by an accused person, it is presented to the court that the confession was or may have been obtained—

   (*a*) by oppression of the person who made it; or

   (*b*) in consequence of anything said or done which was likely, in the circumstances existing at the time, to render unreliable any confession which might be made by him in consequence thereof,

the court shall not allow the confessions to be given in evidence against him except in so far as the prosecution proves to the court beyond reasonable doubt that the confession (notwithstanding that it may be true) was not obtained as aforesaid.

(3) In any proceedings where the prosecution proposes to give in evidence a confession made by an accused person, the court may of its own motion require the prosecution, as a condition of allowing it to do so, to prove that the confession was not obtained as mentioned in subsection (2) above.

(4) The fact that a confession is wholly or partly excluded in pursuance of this section shall not affect the admissibility in evidence—

   (*a*) of any facts discovered as a result of the confession; or

   (*b*) where the confession is relevant as showing that the accused speaks, writes or expresses himself in a particular way, of so much of the confession as is necessary to show that he does so.

(5) Evidence that a fact to which this subsection applies was discovered as a result of a statement made by an accused person shall not be admissible unless evidence of how it was discovered is given by him or on his behalf.

(6) Subsection (5) above applies—

   (*a*) to any fact discovered as a result of a confession which is wholly excluded in pursuance of this section; and

   (*b*) to any fact discovered as a result of a confession which is partly so excluded, if the fact is discovered as a result of the excluded part of the confession...

(8) In this section 'oppression' includes torture, inhuman or degrading treatment, and the use or threat of violence (whether or not amounting to torture).

[(9) Where the proceedings mentioned in subsection (1) above the proceedings before a magistrates' court inquiring into an offence as examining justices this section shall have effect with the omission of—

   (*a*) in subsection (i) the words 'and is not excluded by the court in pursuance of this section'; and

   (*b*) subsection (2) to (6) and (8).][1]

77. Confessions by mentally handicapped persons

(1) Without prejudice to the general duty of the court at a trial on indictment to direct the jury on any matter on which it appears to the court appropriate to do so, where at such a trial–

   (*a*) the case against the accused depends wholly or substantially on a confession by him; and

   (*b*) the court is satisfied –

      (i) that he is mentally handicapped; and

      (ii) that the confession was not made in the presence of an independent person,

---

1   Inserted by the Criminal Procedure and Investigation Act 1996, s. 47, Sch. 1, Part II, para. 25.

the court shall warn the jury that there is special need for caution before convicting the accused in reliance on the confession, and shall explain that the need arises because of the circumstances mentioned in paragraphs (*a*) and (*b*) above.

(2) In any case where at the summary trial of a person for an offence it appears to the court that a warning under subsection (1) above would be required if the trial were on indictment, the court shall treat the case as one in which there is a special need for caution before convicting the accused on his confession.

(3) In this section—

'independent person' does not include a police officer or a person employed for, or engaged on, police purposes;

'mentally handicapped', in relation to a person, means that he is in a state of arrested or incomplete development of mind which includes significant impairment of intelligence and social functioning; and 'police purposes' has the meaning assigned to it by [s. 101(2) of the Police Act 1996.][2]

78. Exclusion of unfair evidence

(1) In any proceedings the court may refuse to allow evidence on which the prosecution proposes to rely to be given if it appears to the court that, having regard to all the circumstances, including the circumstances in which the evidence was obtained, the admission of the evidence would have such an adverse effect on the fairness of the proceedings that the court ought not to admit it.

(2) Nothing in this section shall prejudice any rule of law requiring a court to exclude evidence.

[(3) This section shall not apply in the case of proceedings before a magistrates' court inquiring into an offence as examining justices.][3]

82. Part VIII – Interpretation

(1) In this Part of this Act—

'confession' includes any statement wholly or partly adverse to the person who made it, whether to a person in authority or not and whether made in words or otherwise;

'proceedings' means criminal proceedings including – [court martial proceedings: *Ed.*]...

(3) Nothing in this Part of this Act shall prejudice any power of a court to exclude evidence (whether by preventing questions from being put or otherwise) at its discretion.

NOTES

1. *Principles underlying the exclusion of admissible evidence.* Commentators have identified a number of principles that might underlie the existence of a discretion, exercisable by the judge at a criminal trial, to exclude evidence that would otherwise, according to the law of evidence, be admissible. To an extent some of these principles overlap.

Such a discretion might exist:

(i)   to ensure that evidence that is unreliable, although technically admissible, is not placed before a jury: the 'reliability' principle;

(ii) to deter the police or other law enforcement agencies from obtaining evidence by illegal or improper means or to 'punish' them for so acting: the 'disciplinary' principle;

(iii) to protect the rights of citizens to be treated in accordance with the standards prescribed by law for the conduct of criminal investigations: the 'protective' principle.[4] This can be seen as a corollary of (ii).

(iv) to protect an accused person from being compelled to incriminate himself: the 'privilege against self-incrimination' principle (this can be regarded as an example of (iii)).

---

2   Substituted by the Police Act 1996, s. 103. Sch. 7, Part II, para. 38.
3   Inserted by the Criminal Procedure and Investigation Act 1996, s. 47, Sch. 1, Part II, para. 26.
4   See A. Ashworth, [1977] Crim LR 723.

(v) to uphold the right of a person to be treated fairly: the 'fairness' principle, which may simply be a general principle underlying (*inter alia*) principles (i), (iii) and (iv) or may operate more narrowly to ensure simply that the trial proceedings are conducted 'fairly'.

(vi) to preserve the moral authority of the verdict.[5]

English common law has tended to confine the discretion so as to reflect only the reliability principle and the need to protect the right against self-incrimination, although there have been some statements that support the 'fairness' principle. There are many judicial statements to the effect that the court should not exclude evidence under PACE as a mark of disapproval for the way in which it was obtained.[6] Courts have an inherent power to stay proceedings for an abuse of process. The decision to stay proceedings may involve considering the manner in which evidence was obtained, but also includes the much broader considerations of policy that distinguish it from an exercise of discretion under s. 78.[7]

2. Admissibility of physical evidence at common law.[8] At common law there has been no general rule to the effect that all physical evidence obtained unlawfully or illegally is thereby inadmissible. The manner in which such evidence is obtained tends not to affect its reliability, and the exclusion of reliable evidence by a court would be done simply as a mechanism for disciplinary function to be fulfilled by prosecution, actions for damages or complaints against the police. In *Kuruma v R*[9] the Privy Council held that relevant evidence was admissible however it was obtained except that in a criminal trial the judge had a discretion to disallow evidence if the strict rules of admissibility:

'would operate unfairly against an accused...If, for instance, some...piece of evidence, e.g. a document, had been obtained from a defendant by a trick, no doubt the judge might properly rule it out'[10]

This was regarded as giving rise to a limited discretion to disallow evidence obtained oppressively, by force or by false representations: see Lord Parker CJ in *Callis v Gunn*.[11] In *R v Payne*[12] after P was involved in a car collision, he was examined by a doctor at a police station. The Court of Criminal Appeal held that the doctor's evidence as to P's fitness to drive should be excluded as P had only agreed to be examined by him on the understanding that the purpose of the examination was to see if he was suffering from any illness or disability.

However, in *R v Sang*[13] the House of Lords took a restrictive view of this discretion. The House held unanimously that there was no discretion to exclude evidence merely

---

5 See I. Dennis, (1989) CLP 21 and see I. Dennis, *The Law of Evidence* (1999).
6 See recently *R v Chalkey and Jeffries* [1998] QB 848.
7 *R v Chalkey and Jeffries* [1998] QB 848, CA. See also *R v Horseferry Road Magistrates' Court, ex p Bennett* [1994] AC 42; and A. Choo, *Abuse of Process and Judicial Stays of Criminal Proceedings* (1993). In *R (on the application of Saifi) v Governor of Brixton Prison* [2001] 4 All ER 168, DC, a writ of habeas corpus was granted when S had been committed for extradition on inadmissible evidence because the evidence had been obtained by the London police in bad faith. See also *R v Loosely* [2001] UKHL 53.
8 See generally, R. Pattenden, *Judicial Discretion and Criminal Litigation* (2nd edn, 1990), pp. 264–288; J. D. Heydon, [1973] Crim LR 603 at 690; A. Ashworth, [1977] Crim LR 723; R. Pattendon, (1980) 19 ICLQ 664; D. K. Allen, (1980) 43 MLR 450; M Loewenthal, (1980) 9 Anglo-American LR 238; M. H. Yeo, (1981) 13 Melb ULR 31 and (1982) 6 Crim LJ 89; M. J. Allen, (1982) NILQ 105; M. Hirst, *Andrews and Hirst on Criminal Evidence* (4th edn, 2001), Chap. 14.
9 [1955] AC 197.
10 Per Lord Goddard CJ at 204.
11 [1964] 1 QB 495 at 501, 502; cf. Lord Widgery CJ in *Jeffrey v Black* [1978] QB 490 at 498.
12 [1963] 1 WLR 637.
13 [1980] AC 402.

on the basis that it was given by an *agent provacateur*. Indeed, Lord Diplock and Viscount Dilhorne indicated that apart from the well established discretion to exclude evidence on the ground that its prejudicial effect outweighs its probative value, a discretion existed only 'with regard to admissions and confessions and generally with regard to evidence obtained from the accused after commission of the offence'.[14]

The essential purpose underlying the discretion was to ensure that an accused was not induced to incriminate himself by deception.[15] *R v Payne* was approved on this basis.[16]

The other members of the House appeared not to assent to this narrow proposition.[17] Lord Salmon stated that the category of cases in which it is the duty of the trial judge to ensure that the accused receives a fair trial can not be closed,[18] Lord Fraser stated that the discretion could extend to evidence obtained from 'the accused himself or from premises occupied by him';[19] and Lord Scarman indicated that he would not necessarily dissent from the dicta in *Kuruma v R, Callis v Gunn* and *Jeffrey v Black* provided they were treated 'as relating exclusively to the obtaining of evidence from the accused'.[20]

R v Payne[1] was distinguished in *R v Apicella*.[2] A sample of body fluid was taken from A by a consultant while A was in prison; the prison doctor suspected that A was suffering from gonorrhoea and the sample was taken for therapeutic reasons. The consultant assumed that A was consenting, but in fact he only submitted because he had been told by a prison officer that he had no choice. The sample was subsequently used at A's trial for three rapes as it showed that A was suffering from the same unusual strain of gonorrhoea as had been passed to the three victims by their attackers. The Court of Appeal (Criminal Division) held: (1) that there was no rule of law that an intimate sample is only admissible if taken with the suspect's consent; (2) that evidence was not inadmissible 'solely because it has been obtained as result of a crime, such as assault, or a tort';[3] and (3) that the use of this sample at the trial was not unfair: A 'was not tricked into submitting to the examination in the way which led [the court in *Payne*]... to exclude evidence'.[4]

The common law discretion to exclude extends only to prosecution evidence: *Lobban v R.*[5]

3. *Admissibility of confessions at common law.* At common law a person's confession was *admissible* provided the prosecution showed to the satisfaction of the judge that it had 'not been obtained from him either by fear of prejudice or hope of advantage exercised or held out by a person in authority.[6] This led to a series of cases on the definition of 'person in authority' and what was capable of amounting to an 'inducement' for these purposes, and the rule tended to be applied strictly. The courts assumed that a confession obtained in such circumstances would be unreliable,

---

14 [1980] AC at 437 at 442.
15 See Lord Diplock at 436.
16 See Lord Diplock at 435; cf. Lord Fraser at 440, Lord Scarman at 455; and see also the remarks in *R v Trump* (1979) 70 Cr App Rep 300 at 302–304, CA (Cr D); and *R v Fox* [1986] AC 281.
17 See J. Heydon, [1980] Crim LR 129 at 132–135.
18 [1980] AC 402 at 445.
19 At 449, 450.
20 At 456.
1 [1963] 1WLR 637.
2 (1985) 82 Cr App Rep 295.
3 Per Lawton LJ at 299–300.
4 Per Lawton LJ at 300.
5 [1995] 1 WLR 877, PC (no discretion to exclude parts of confession as one co-accused which he relies on although they incriminate a co-accused).
6 Per Lord Sumner in *Ibrahim v R* [1914] AC 599 at 609.

without considering whether the particular confession was unreliable. However, the decision in *DPP v Ping Lin*[7] made it clear that there had to be a casual link between the 'fear' or 'hope' and the confession for the confession to be excluded, and that the whole issue of 'voluntariness' was essentially one of fact that was not to be treated 'legalistically'. Furthermore, in *R v Rennie*[8] Lord Lane CJ stated that even where a confession was made with a hope that an admission may lead to an earlier release or a lighter sentence', and the hopes were prompted by something said or done by a person in authority, the confession would not *automatically* be regarded as involuntary. The position was the same where, as in the present case, a confession was prompted by a fear that otherwise the police would interview and perhaps arrest and charge further members of the defendant's family. The judge should 'apply his common sense' and 'remind himself that "voluntary" in ordinary parlance means "of one's own free will"'.[9] The result was to narrow still further the range of confessions that were likely to be held to be involuntary.

In addition to cases applying or developing the *Ibrahim* principle, it was also held that a confession obtained as a result of 'oppression' would be treated as involuntary and thus inadmissible: *R v Prager.*[10]

For the guidance of the police, a set of rules governing the interrogation process was promulgated by the Queen's Bench judges, together with administrative directions from the Home Office. The first set was published in two stages in 1912 and 1918. A revised set of Judges' Rules was issued in 1964; and the Directions were amended further in 1978: *See Judge's Rules and Administrative Directors to the Police,* Home Office Circular No. 89/1978. The rules imposed requirements as to cautioning etc. and the Directions covered such matters as the keeping of records, provision for comfort and refreshment and the interrogation of children or a mentally handicapped person. The position appeared to be that if the rules were complied with, a confession would be regarded as voluntary. However, the converse did not hold good: a confession might be held to be voluntary, and accordingly admissible, even if there had been a breach of the Judges' Rules: *R v Prager;*[11] *Greaves v D and P.*[12]

At the same time, there were frequent assertions by judges of a residual *discretion* to exclude confessions. There was, however, much confusion over the permissible grounds for such exclusion, the cases referring to such matters as oppression (which in truth was not a matter of discretion at all), the use of a trick, unfairness or just breaches of the Judge's Rules.[13] Where the case is before the court although the events occurred before PACE was in force, as with appeals referred by the Criminal Case Review Commission, the court can have regard to the provisions of PACE: *R v Bentley.*[14]

4. *Current approach.* The interrogation process is now regulated by ss. 56–60 and 76–78 of the 1984 Act and PACE Code C.[14a] the admissibility of the *other* evidence obtained improperly is governed by s. 78. In the interpretation of these sections it must be remembered that PACE is a codifying Act and the proper course is to look to the words of the statute and not how the law previously stood: *R v Fulling;*[15]

---

7 [1976] AC 574, HL.
8 [1982] 1 All ER 384, CA (Cr D).
9 At 389.
10 [1972] 1 All ER 1114, CA (Cr D).
11 [1972] 1 All ER 1118, CA (Cr D).
12 (1980) 71 Cr App Rep 232 at 236, DC.
13 On the admissibility of confessions at common law see R. Pattenden, op. cit., pp. 274–281;
   C. R. Williams, 'Judicial discretion in relation to confessions' (1983) 3 OJLS 222.
14 [1999] Crim LR 330, CA.
14a See above, p. 317ff.
15 Below, p. 363.

R v Smurthwaite and Gill.[16] See also *Thompson v R*[17] on the relationship between the common law power to include confessions and that contained in PACE. A vast body of case law has considered the application of these provisions and the courts have been considerably more active than was anticipated. The circumstances of each case are almost always different and the judges may well take different views in the proper exercise of their discretion even when the circumstances are similar. This is not an apt field for hard case law and well-founded distinctions between cases, per Auld LJ in *Jelen v Katz.*[18] 'Oppression' and 'unreliability' under s. 76 were considered in *R v Fulling,*[19] the question of the exclusion of confessions under s. 78 in *R v Samuel,*[20] and the use of trickery by police in *R v Christou and Wright.*[21] Section 78 has been used to exclude identification evidence where there are breaches of Code D (*the Code of Practice for the Identification of Persons by Police Officers*): see, for example, *R v Gall*[1] (investigating officer took part in the conduct of a parade); *R v Conway*[2] (parade not held when requested, although no good reason); *R v Nagah*[3] (street identification inadmissible as identity parade was practicable).[4]

In *R v Bazil,*[5] B's conviction from 1990 was quashed where the defendant had only been identified after being handcuffed. Section 78 will have a significant role to play in excluding identification evidence following the House of Lords decision in *Forbes,*[6] holding that even where the suspect is brought to police by the witness, there must be a formal identification parade, save in exceptional circumstances. Other situations in which s. 78 has been used to exclude prosecution evidence include depositions[7] and voice identification evidence.[8]

Where the police video-taped the defendant at court and adduced the evidence of a facial mapping expert, comparing it to that of CCTV footage from the crime scene, the Court of Appeal upheld the conviction for robbery despite the breaches of the Codes of Practice and Art. 8: *R v Loveridge and Lee.*[9] The courts have rarely used s. 78 to exclude real evidence on the ground that it has been obtained illegally or otherwise improperly. One relevant factor is whether police officers have acted in bad faith. In *Matto v Crown Court at Wolverhampton,*[10] the Divisional Court held that in circumstances where police officers knew they were trespassing on M's property when they required him to take a breath test it was open to the Crown Court to conclude that this adversely affected the fairness of proceedings for driving with excess alcohol based

---

16 [1994] 1 All ER 898.
17 [1998] AC 811, PC.
18 (1989) 90 Cr App R 456 at 465, CA.
19 Below, p. 363.
20 Below, p. 371.
21 Below, p. 376. For general surveys, see D. J. Birch, 'The Pace Hots Up' [1989] Crim LR 95; D. Feldman, 'Regulating Treatment of Suspects in Police Stations' [1990] Crim LR 452.
1 (1989) 90 Cr App Rep 64, CA (Cr D); (1990) 91 Cr App Rep 143, CA (Cr D).
2 (1990) 91 Cr App Rep 143, CA (Cr D).
3 (1990) 92 Cr App Rep 344, CA (Cr D).
4 See also *Powell v DPP* [1992] RTR, DC; *R v Finley* [1993] Crim LR 50, CA (Cr D); *R v Hope, Limburn and Bleasdale* [1994] Crim LR 188, CA (Cr D); but cf. *R v Quinn* [1990] Crim LR 581, CA (Cr D) (evidence of identification of Q while on trial in a Dublin court admitted); *R v Grannell* (1989) 90 Cr App Rep, CA (Cr D) (breach of Code D but no unfairness); *R v Brown* [1991] Crim LR, CA (Cr D); *R v Garner* (1998) 1 December (two police officers sharing car journey to identification suite not a breach of Code D12.1, 12.3).
5 (1996) 6 April, CA (Cr Div).
6 [2001] UKHL 40.
7 *O'Louglin v Chief Constable of Essex* [1998] 3 All ER 431, CA.
8 *R v Deenik* [1992] Crim LR 578.
9 [2001] EWCA Crim 1034.
10 [1987] RTR 337.

on a breath specimen obtained subsequently at the police station. The point was stressed that the officers had acted 'mala fides'. Woolf LJ stated:[11]

'Whatever is the right interpretation of section 78, I am quite satisfied that it certainly does not reduce the discretion of the court to exclude unfair evidence which existed at common law. Indeed, in my view in any case where the evidence would properly be excluded in common law, it can certainly be excluded under section 78.'

This may be compared with the common law decision of the House of Lords in *R v Fox*.[12] Here, following an accident, police officers entered F's house through the front door, which was closed but not locked, and required F to take a breath test. F refused, and was arrested and taken to the police station, where he provided specimens of breath that proved to be over the limit. His conviction for driving with excess alcohol was upheld, the House holding that the magistrates had been entitled to refuse to exclude the evidence in the exercise of their discretion. Lord Fraser stated that the Divisional Court had been right to treat the fact that he was in the police station because he had been unlawfully arrested:

'merely as a historical fact, with which the court was not concerned. The duty of the court is to decide whether the appellant has committed the offence with which he is charged, and not to discipline the police for exceeding their powers...
...of course, if the appellant had been lured to the police station by some trick or deception, or if the police officers had behaved oppressively towards the appellant, the justice's jurisdiction to exclude otherwise admissible evidence recognised in *R v Sang* might have come into play. But there is nothing of that sort suggested here. The police officers did no more than make a bona fide mistake as to their powers...'[13]

It has, however, been suggested that the presence of bad faith does not automatically lead to exclusion under s. 78.[14] On the other hand, subsequent cases have confirmed that evidence may be excluded under s. 78 even where it is not established that the police have acted in bad faith. See *DPP v McGladrigan*.[15] In the latter case, the Divisional Court upheld the decision of justices to exclude under s. 78 evidence of specimens obtained from G at the police station following his earlier refusal to take a breath test at the roadside; however, it was not established that the police had reasonable cause to suspect that G had alcohol in his body, specified by s. 6(1) of the Road Traffic Act 1998 as a precondition to requiring a breath test.[16]

'The justices were entitled to conclude that the substantial breach by the constable of the protection affordable to members of the public by section 6 was denied to the defendant, that as a result the prosecutor obtained evidence which he would not otherwise have obtained, and that as a result the defendant was prejudiced in a significant manner in resisting the charge against him.'

This may be compared with *DPP v Wilson*,[17] where a constable, acting on an anonymous telephone call that a particular car would be on the move any minute and he would catch a drink-driver, waited for over an hour for the car to move. He then stopped the car, spoke to the driver, noticed alcohol on his breath and administered a breath test which proved positive. The Divisional Court held that this did not constitute 'malpractice'. 'There is, in my view, no duty on a constable

---

11 At 346.
12 [1986] AC 281.
13 At 292, 293.
14 Per Buckley J in *Sharpe v DPP* [1993] RTR 392 at 398–399, DC.
15 [1991] RTR 297, DC (per Hodgson J at 301–302, citing *R v Samuel* (below, p. 371));
    DPP v Godwin [1991] RTR 303 at 308.
16 Per Bingham LJ at 308.
17 [1991] RTR 284.

to warn a potential offender of a potential offence nor, in my view, is it oppressive if a constable does not do so'.[18]

In *Khan*[19] the House of Lords held that the police recording of conversations made by K incriminating him in drug dealing were admissible even though they had been obtained by the police fixing a secret listening device to the private property of K's associate. The House recognised that the action was probably in breach of Art. 8 of the ECHR, but, although that was a relevant matter, the evidence was still correctly admitted by the trial judge.

R v Khan (Sultan) [1997] AC 558, House of Lords

Lord Nolan:... Finally, Mr. Muller turned to the decision of your Lordships' House in *R v. Sang* [1980] A.C. 402. That decision is, of course, authority for the proposition that a judge has no discretion to refuse to admit relevant evidence on the ground that it was obtained by improper or unfair means. Lord Diplock said, at p. 437:

> '(1) A trial judge in a criminal trial has always a discretion to refuse to admit evidence if in his opinion its prejudicial effect outweighs its probative value. (2) Save with regard to admissions and confessions and generally with regard to evidence obtained from the accused after commission of the offence, he has no discretion to refuse to admit relevant admissible evidence on the ground that it was obtained by improper or unfair means. The court is not concerned with how it was obtained.'

As to this, Mr. Muller submitted first that the general rule in *Sang* did not apply to the evidence with which the present case was concerned because that evidence fell within the category of admissions, confessions, and other evidence obtained from the accused after commission of the offence. In my judgment, this submission has no force. It is clear from an earlier passage in the speech of Lord Diplock, at p. 436, that the exceptional category which he had in mind consisted of

> 'evidence tantamount to a self-incriminatory admission which was obtained from the defendant, after the offence had been committed, by means which would justify a judge in excluding an actual confession which had the like self-incriminating effect.'

He continued:

> 'My Lords, I propose to exclude, as the certified question does, detailed consideration of the role of the trial judge in relation to confessions and evidence obtained from the defendant after commission of the offence that is tantamount to a confession. It has a long history dating back to the days before the existence of a disciplined police force, when a prisoner on a charge of felony could not be represented by counsel and was not entitled to give evidence in his own defence either to deny that he had made the confession, which was generally oral, or to deny that its contents were true. The underlying rationale of this branch of the criminal law, though it may originally have been based upon ensuring the reliability of confessions is, in my view, now to be found in the maxim *nemo debet prodere se ipsum*, no one can be required to be his own betrayer or in its popular English mistranslation "the right to silence." That is why there is no discretion to exclude evidence discovered as the result of an illegal search but there is discretion to exclude evidence which the accused has been induced to produce voluntarily if the method of inducement was unfair.'

In the present case, I would regard it as a misuse of language to describe the appellant as having been 'induced' to make the admissions which were recorded on the tape. He was under no inducement to do so. But if this be too narrow a view, the only result would be to bring into play the judge's discretion as to whether or not the evidence should in fairness be admitted. It would not make the evidence intrinsically inadmissible.

Secondly Mr. Muller submitted that the rule in *R v. Sang* [1980] A.C. 402 must be taken to have been modified by the enactment of section 9 of the Interception of Communications

---

18 Per Tudor-Evans J at 291.
19 [1997] AC 558, HL. See B. Fitzpatrick and N. Taylor, (2000) E & P 349.

Act 1985, prohibiting the admission of what would otherwise be admissible evidence. This too appears to me to be, with respect, a wholly unsustainable submission. If we were to have regard to the provisions of the Act of 1985 which prohibit the admission of evidence obtained by comparable means to those used in the present case why should we not also have regard to the provisions of the Intelligence Services Act 1994 which authorise the admission of evidence obtained by identical means? I am satisfied, for my part, that neither of these statutes should be regarded as affecting the common law principles laid down by your Lordships' House in *R v Sang*.

In truth, in the light of *R v Sang*, the argument that the evidence of the taped conversation is inadmissible could only be sustained if two wholly new principles were formulated in our law. The first would be that the appellant enjoyed a right of privacy, in terms similar to those of Art. 8 of the Convention, in respect of the taped conversation. The second, which is different that even if there were such a right the decision of your Lordships' House in *R v Sang* and the many decisions which have followed it make it plain that as a matter of English law evidence which is obtained improperly or even unlawfully remains admissible, subject to the power of the trial judge to exclude it in the exercise of his common law discretion or under the provisions of s. 78 of the Police and Criminal Evidence Act 1984.

If evidence obtained by way of entrapment is admissible, then a fortiori there can hardly be a fundamental objection to the admission of evidence obtained in breach of privacy. In *R v Sang* itself, at pp. 429–430, Lord Diplock noted that if evidence obtained by entrapment were inadmissible this would have the effect of establishing entrapment as a defence to a criminal charge. By parity of reasoning, if evidence obtained by a breach of privacy were inadmissible then privacy too would become a defence to a criminal charge where the substance of the charge consisted of acts done or words spoken in private. Such a proposition does not bear serious examination.

I conclude, therefore, that the appellant fails upon the first issue. The evidence of the taped conversation was clearly admissible as a matter of law.

I turn, then, to the second issue, namely whether the judge should nevertheless have excluded it in the exercise of his common law discretion or under the powers conferred upon him by s. 78. The only element of the common law discretion which is relevant for present purposes is that part of it which authorises the judge 'to exclude evidence if it is necessary in order to secure a fair trial for the accused,' as Lord Griffiths put it in *Scott v R* [1989] A.C. 1242, 1256. It is therefore unnecessary to consider the common law position separately from that which arises under s. 78, I would respectfully agree with Lord Taylor of Gosforth C.J. that the power conferred by s. 78 to exclude evidence in the interests of a fair trial is at least as wide as that conferred by the common law. I hope that I do not unduly condense the case put forward by Mr. Muller if I say that, whereas his submissions upon the first issue placed indirect reliance upon Art. 8 of the Convention, his submissions upon the second issue were based directly and almost exclusively upon the terms of that article read with s. 78. In considering the second issue I have been much assisted by the written submission put forward with the consent of your Lordships' House and of the parties by the National Council for Civil Liberties ('Liberty'). As Liberty has observed, this case raises for the first time the question whether a criminal court, in considering its power under s. 78 of the Police and Criminal Evidence Act 1984, is required to have regard to the European Convention and the jurisprudence of the European Court of Human Rights, and if so whether a violation of the Convention is to be regarded per se as a ground for excluding otherwise admissible evidence.

I take first the submissions on this question which were put forward by Mr. Muller on behalf of the appellant. He referred to the full terms of s. 78(1), which reads as follows:

'In any proceedings the court may refuse to allow evidence on which the prosecution proposes to rely to be given if it appears to the court that, having regard to all the circumstances, including the circumstances in which it was obtained, the evidence would have such an adverse effect on the fairness of the proceedings that the court ought not to admit it.'

The appellant contends that these words plainly require the court, in considering whether or not to allow the relevant evidence, to have regard to 'all the circumstances, including the circumstances in which the evidence was obtained.' If the circumstances in which the evidence was obtained amounted to an apparent invasion of the appellant's rights of privacy under Art. 8, that is accordingly something to which the court must have regard. The only remaining question is whether the evidence which was obtained in such circumstances would have such an adverse effect on the fairness of the proceedings that the court ought not to admit it. As to that, the appellant submits that since the proceedings themselves are only possible because of the improper conduct of the executive, the court should conclude that the admission of evidence obtained in these circumstances would have such an adverse effect on the fairness of the proceedings that the court ought not to admit it.

The argument put forward by Liberty similarly started from the premise that the duty of the court under s. 78 to have regard to the circumstances in which the evidence was obtained necessarily included a duty to have regard to the fact that the evidence was apparently obtained in circumstances which amounted to a breach of the provisions of Art. 8. As a result, the appellant was entitled to invoke article 13 of the Convention, which provides: 'Everyone whose rights and freedoms as set forth in this Convention are violated shall have an effective remedy before a national authority. . . .'

In *R v Secretary of State for the Home Department, Ex parte Brind* [1991] 1 A.C. 696, 747 Lord Bridge of Harwich had accepted that 'The obligations of the United Kingdom . . . are to secure . . . the rights which the Convention defines including . . . the right under article 13 to 'an effective remedy' . . . for any violation . . .' But the remedy which article 13 required, according provides an effective means of reviewing the admissibility of the evidence a review, and therefore satisfies the requirements of article 13.

In the present case the trial judge had substantially followed the view of the law advocated by Liberty. He had accepted that there was at any rate an arguable breach of Art. 8, but had concluded that neither this nor any of the other circumstances of the case required the exclusion of the taped evidence. In the Court of Appeal, however, Lord Taylor of Gosforth C.J. [1995] Q.B. 27, 40 had expressed himself somewhat differently. He said:

'As to the argument based on Art. 8 of the ECHR, counsel for the Crown rightly pointed out that it is not (as yet) part of the law of the United Kingdom since it has not been enacted into our statutory law. He referred us to *Chundawadra v. Immigration Appeal Tribunal* [1988] Imm.A.R. 161 and *Pan-American World Airways Inc. v. Department of Trade* [1976] 1 Lloyd's Rep. 257. From these authorities it is clear that it is permissible to have regard to the Convention, which is of persuasive assistance, in cases of ambiguity or doubt. In the circumstances of the present case the position is neither ambiguous nor doubtful; nor is it incumbent on us to consider whether there was a breach of Art. 8, and we do not propose to do so.'

Both Liberty and the respondent have taken these words as amounting to an assertion that Art. 8 is irrelevant to a court's exercise of its powers under s. 78. On that basis, say Liberty, Lord Taylor of Gosforth C.J. has fallen into error. If Art. 8 were 'irrelevant' to the exercise of the s. 78 power, then that power could not amount to an effective remedy for the purposes of article 13. The respondent, on the other hand, argues that the Lord Chief Justice was quite right to regard the Convention as irrelevant. In my judgment, both of these arguments proceed on a fallacious assumption. The Lord Chief Justice did not describe Art. 8 as 'irrelevant.' On the contrary he referred to it twice in the paragraph of his judgment immediately following that which I have quoted, and in which he sets out the ratio of the decision of the Court of Appeal. In the passage which I have quoted the Lord Chief Justice as I understand him was saying simply that Art. 8 forms no part of our law, that this was not a case of ambiguity or doubt in which it could be invoked as an aid to construction, and that it was no part of the function of the Court of Appeal to consider whether there was a breach of the article. The question whether there was a breach, and if so what the consequences should be, is solely one for the European Court of Human Rights.

That is not to say that the principles reflected in the Convention on Human Rights are irrelevant to the exercise of the s. 78 power. They could hardly be irrelevant, because they embody so many of the familiar principles of our own law and of our concept of justice. In particular, of course, they assert the right of the individual to a fair trial, that is to say, in the words of article 6.1 'a fair and public hearing within a reasonable time by an independent and impartial tribunal established by law.'

My Lords, I think it is of interest in the present case that the appellant makes no complaint of an infringement of his rights under article 6.1. I also note with interest the decision of the

European Court of Human Rights in *Schenk v. Switzerland* (1988) 13 E.H.R.R. 242. In that case the applicant had complained that the making and use as evidence against him of an unlawfully obtained recording of a telephone conversation violated his right to a fair trial under article 6 and his right to confidentiality of telephone communications under Art. 8. Rejecting the complaint under article 6 the court said, at pp. 265–266, paras. 46 and 47:

'46. While article 6 of the Convention guarantees the right to a fair trial, it does not lay down any rules on the admissibility of evidence as such, which is therefore primarily a matter for regulation under national law. The court therefore cannot exclude as a matter of principle and in the abstract that unlawfully obtained evidence of the present kind may be admissible. It has only to ascertain whether Mr. Schenk's trial as a whole was fair.

'47. Like the Commission it notes first of all that the rights of the defence were not disregarded. The applicant was not unaware that the recording complained of was unlawful because it had not been ordered by the competent judge. He had the opportunity—which he took—of challenging its authenticity and opposing its use, having initially agreed that it should be heard. The fact that his attempts were unsuccessful makes no difference.'

The court went on to hold, at p. 268, para. 63, that it was not necessary to consider the complaint under Art. 8 'as the issue is subsumed under the question (already dealt with from the point of view of article 6) of the use made of the cassette during the judicial investigation and the trial.'

The submission put forward on behalf of Liberty suggests that the European Court of Human Rights would not necessarily have reached the same conclusion under article 6 in the circumstances of the present case, first because in the present case (unlike *Schenk's* case) there was no evidence, against the accused other than the tape-recorded conversation and secondly because whilst the interception in *Schenk* was conceded by the Swiss government to have been in breach of domestic law safeguards, in the present case there are no domestic law safeguards and for that reason the breach is arguably of a more fundamental character. I would, for my part, find it difficult to attach very great significance to either of these distinguishing features, but in any event we are not concerned with the view which the European Court of Human Rights might have taken of the facts of the present case. Its decision is no more a part of our law than the Convention itself. What is significant to my mind is the court's acceptance of the proposition that the admissibility of evidence is primarily a matter for regulation under national law, and its rejection of the proposition that unlawfully obtained evidence is necessarily inadmissible.

Further, it is to be noted in this connection that although the recording of the relevant conversation in the present case was achieved by means of a civil trespass and, on the face of it, criminal damage to property, Mr. Muller accepted at the outset that these matters were not fundamental to his argument. His submissions would have been essentially the same if the surveillance device had been lawfully positioned outside the premises, or, for that matter, if the conversation had been overheard by a police officer with exceptionally acute hearing listening from outside the window.

This brings one back to the fact that, under English law, there is in general nothing unlawful about a breach of privacy. The appellant's case rests wholly upon the lack of statutory authorisation for the particular breach of privacy which occurred in the present case, and the consequent infringement, as the appellant submits, of Art. 8.

My Lords, I am satisfied, for my part, that in these circumstances the appellant can no more succeed upon the second issue than upon the first. I am prepared to accept that if evidence has been obtained in circumstances which involve an apparent breach of Art. 8, or, for that matter an apparent breach of the law of a foreign country, that is a matter which may be relevant…mean that the trial judge is obliged to decide whether or not there has been a breach of the Convention or of the foreign law. That is not his function, and it would be inappropriate for him to do so. By the same token, it would have been inappropriate for the judge in the present case to have decided whether the admitted damage caused by the police to Mr. Bashforth's property amounted to a criminal offence under section 1 of the Criminal Damage Act 1971. But if the behaviour of the police in the particular case amounts to an apparent or probable breach of some relevant law or convention, common sense dictates that this is a consideration which may be taken into account for what it is worth. Its significance, however, will normally be determined not so much by its apparent unlawfulness or irregularity as upon its effect, taken as a whole, upon the fairness or unfairness of the proceedings. The fact that the behaviour in question constitutes a breach of the Convention or of a foreign law can plainly be of no greater significance per se than if it constituted a breach of English law. Upon the facts of the present case, in agreement with the Court of Appeal, I consider that the judge was fully entitled to hold that the circumstances in which the relevant evidence was obtained, even if they constituted a breach of Art. 8, were not such as to require the exclusion of the evidence.

I confess that I have reached this conclusion not only quite firmly as a matter of law, but also with relief. It would be a strange reflection on our law if a man who has admitted his participation in the illegal importation of a large quantity of heroin should have his conviction set aside on the grounds that his privacy has been invaded.

There is only one further word which I would add. The sole cause of this case coming to your Lordships' House is the lack of a statutory system regulating the use of surveillance devices by the police. The absence of such a system seems astonishing, the more so in view of the statutory framework which has governed the use of such devices by the Security Service since 1989, and the interception of communications by the police as well as by other agencies since 1985. I would refrain, however, from further comment because counsel for the respondent was able to inform us, on instructions, that the government proposes to introduce legislation covering the matter in the next session of Parliament.

My Lords, I would dismiss the appeal.

NOTES

1. The European Court of Human Rights ruled, unanimously, that there had been a breach of Art. 8 in that K's right to respect for his private and family life had been violated. There was no statutory regime governing the English police use of such equipment at the time, and therefore the court was not prepared to accept that the interference was 'in accordance with the law'. The court held that there was no breach of Art. 6, since the s. 78 discretion meant that the proceedings were not wholly unfair. Moreover, it was not the task of the European Court of Human Rights to rule on admissibility in domestic proceedings.

2. In *R v McDonald and McDonald*[20] the Court of Appeal held that the police could record an interview between an accused and a third party in order to obtain an admission by the accused to the third party where the third party was not recruited by the police, nor acted as their agent. The police had 'seized an opportunity of eavesdropping upon a conversation independent of their inquiry'.

There is one decision at the Crown Court level where evidence obtained as the result of stop and search in the street and a strip search at the police station was excluded on the ground that the suspect was not told why he was stopped, searched and arrested: *R v Fennelly*,[1] the case was disapproved by the Court of Appeal in *R v Khan*.[2] By contrast, in *R v Cooke (Stephen)*[3] the court agreed with the trial judge that even if the plucking of a sample of C's hair from his scalp for DNA testing had been unlawful, the evidence resulting from it should not have been excluded under s. 78; that there would have been an assault did not in any way cast doubt upon the accuracy of the evidence. The court in fact held that the hair and its sheath had lawfully been taken as a non-intimate sample.[4] Commenting on *R v Cooke*,[5] D. J. Birch observed

---

20 (1999) 29 June, CA (Cr D).
1 [1989] Crim LR 142 (Acton Crown Court), criticised by D. J. Birch, ibid., pp. 143–144.
2 [1997] Crim LR 508.
3 [1995] 1 Cr App Rep 318, CA (Cr D).
4 See above, p. 327.
5 [1995] Crim LR 497.

that the 'courts are as reluctant as they were at common law to exclude scientific evidence which clearly shows that an accused person has committed a serious offence such as rape'.[6] Nevertheless, the court would seem to contemplate the admissibility of an *intimate* sample taken without consent. Is that acceptable in view of the clear requirements of PACE? (but cf. the position at common law: *R v Apicella*[7]). Similarly, evidence was admitted where there were breaches of Code B (search) because these had no impact on the reliability of the material seized: *R v Stewart*.[8]

If the courts are concerned only with the reliability of the evidence the protections for the suspect will be of little value in the criminal trial. Should breaches of privacy etc. give rise to a remedy by way of an exclusion of evidence or a stay of proceedings? An interesting feature of the decision in *Khan* is the explicit balancing of factors for and against exclusion. For a case in which the court considered whether there was a breach of Art. 8, but concluded not, therefore admitting the evidence obtained from telephone tapping in Holland, see *R v Aujla*.[10]

'Fairness' in s. 78 comprises both fairness to the accused and fairness to the prosecution; *R v O'Loughlin and McLaughlin*;[11] *R v Hughes*.[12] See also K. Grevling[13] considering the history of the section and whether it is appropriate to treat the discretion as requiring fairness for the prosecution as well as the defence. One dimension of the question is whether the seriousness of the offence should feature in the judge's decision under s. 78.[14] Is it any fairer to admit illegally obtained evidence of a murder than of shoplifting? Should s. 78 be restructured so that courts were able to take account of broader issues of fairness?[15]

For a discussion of the relationship between abuse of process and s. 78, see A. Choo and S. Nash,[16] arguing that courts should adopt an approach more akin to that when considering abuse of process – with the focus on the pre-trial conduct of the police rather than the resulting evidence, and that s. 78 requires consideration of the fairness of the whole proceedings, not just the trial. The Human Rights Act 1998 has forced the Court of Appeal to address the relationship between fairness, safety and abuse of process doctrines.[17] Professor Colin Tapper, author of the leading treatise on evidence concludes that 'in England, illegally obtained evidence is admissible as a matter of law, provided that it involves neither a reference to an inadmissible confession, nor the commission of an act of contempt of court'.[18] Do you agree?

A trial within a trial must be held if an issue is raised under s. 76 and whether trial is at the Crown Court or before magistrates (*R v Liverpool Juvenile Court, ex p R*;[19] cf. *R v Oxford City Justices, ex p Berry*[20]). This is, however, discretionary where a

---

6 At 499.
7 Above, p. 352.
8 [1995] Crim LR 500, CA.
9 [1997] AC 558, HL.
10 [1998] 2 Cr App R 16.
11 (1987) 85 Cr App Rep 157 at 163.
12 [1988] Crim LR 519, CA (Cr D).
13 (1997) 113 LQR 667.
14 Ibid., p. 681.
15 Ibid., p. 685.
16 [1999] Crim LR 929.
17 See *R v Francom* [2000] Crim LR 1018; *R v Togher* [2001] Crim LR 140.
18 C. Tapper, *Cross and Tapper on Evidence* (9th edn, 1999), p. 501.
19 [1988] QB 1.
20 [1988] QB 507.

challenge is made under s. 78;[1] *Vel v Chief Constable of North Wales.*[2] The procedure in the magistrates' court is more complicated since the bench will have to hear the evidence which it might then decide to exclude. More detailed guidance is provided on the correct procedure in *Halaw v Federation Against Copyright Theft.*[3] Where magistrates were wrongly advised that they had no discretion under s. 78 regarding evidence of a breath test, it was not for the Divisional Court to open the issue anew: *Braham v DPP.*[4]

There is considerable confusion as to the correct test to be applied in deciding whether to interfere with the decision not to exclude evidence under s. 78. One line of authority suggests that the court should only interfere where there has been *Wednesbury* unreasonableness in the decision: (*R v Christou,*[5] *R v Khan*[6]). Other cases suggest that the correct question is whether the appellate court was 'satisfied that no reasonable judge, having heard the evidence that the judge heard, could not have reached the conclusion that he did' (per Taylor LCJ in *R v Quinn*[7] cited with approval by Rose LJ in *R v Dures.*)[8] Other cases have suggested that the question is simply one of whether the conviction is 'unsafe' within the meaning of the Criminal Appeal Act 1995. (See suggestions in *R v Callaghan*[9] that the question is whether the evidence was reliable, and see *R v Mullen.*[10]) Note also the comments of Auld LJ in *R v Chalkey and Jeffries,*[11] that there is no real discretion in the section since once a court has decided that the evidence would adversely affect the fairness of the proceedings such that it should be excluded, it must exclude it; there is no remaining discretion to speak of. Commenting on the case, Professor Sir John Smith wrote:

'The logic is compelling. The judge can hardly say, "I ought not to admit this evidence, but I am jolly well going to so there." Any discretion he has must lie in his decision that the effect would be, not merely unfair, but so unfair that he ought not to admit it. If the Wednesbury principle applies it must be at this stage.'[12]

3. In the context of the breathalyser laws, a distinction is drawn between prosecutions for refusal to provide a specimen of breath and prosecutions for driving with excess alcohol based on the evidence of a specimen that is provided. In the case of the former, a requirement to provide a specimen imposed by an officer while trespassing unlawfully in the suspect's home is itself unlawful and cannot form the basis of a conviction.[13] The issue 'related to the ingredients of the offence itself rather than evidence adduced in proof of the offence charged'.[14] In the case of the latter, exclusion of evidence of a specimen is regulated by the discretion to exclude evidence at common law[15] or under s. 78 of PACE.[16] Is this distinction tenable?

The practical effect of the decision in *Morris v Beardmore*[16a] was reduced by amendments to the breathalyser legislation introduced by the Transport Act 1981.

 1 *R v Beveridge* (1987) 85 Cr App Rep 255 (at the Crown Court).
 2 (1987) 151 JP 510 (before magistrates).
 3 [1993] 1 Cr App R 21, DC.
 4 [1996] RTR 30.
 5 (1992) 95 Cr App R 264.
 6 [1997] Crim LR 508.
 7 [1995] 1 Cr App R 480 at 489.
 8 [1997] 2 Cr App R 247, CA.
 9 (1999) 5 March.
10 [1999] 3 WLR 777.
11 [1998] QB 848.
12 [1998] Crim LR 216.
13 *Morris v Beardmore* [1981] AC 446, HL.
14 Per Lord Edmund-Davies at 459.
15 *R v Sang*, above, p. 351; *R v Fox* [1986] AC 281, HL.
16 Above.
16a [1981] AC 446, HL.

See now the Road Traffic Act 1998, ss. 4–11. In particular, s. 6 gives a right of entry (if need be by force) to require the provision of a breath specimen in cases of accidents involving injury to a person other than the driver or person in charge.[17] However, if there is no accident involving injury, the *Morris v Beardmore* principle remains applicable: *Fox v Chief Constable of Gwent.*[18]

Morris v Beardmore does not, of course, apply if the officers are not trespassers,[19] and has been stated to be concerned only with the 'sanctity of a man's home' and not applicable where a motorist who was affected by drink was still driving his car elsewhere.[20] It was also stated obiter in *Morris v Beardmore* that the principle only applied where the officer was a trespasser vis-à-vis the defendant.[1]

R v Fulling [1987] QB 426 [1987] 2 All ER 65, [1987] 2 WLR 923 (pet dis) [1987] 1 WLR 1196, HL, Court of Appeal (Criminal Division)

F claimed over £5,000 from an insurance company in respect of a burglary at her flat. An informant subsequently told the police that the burglary was bogus, and had been instigated by one Drewery, with whom F had been living and with whom she was infatuated. F was arrested and interviewed. She initially said nothing, but eventually confessed. At her trial for obtaining property by deception, she argued that the confession was or might have been obtained by oppression. She claimed that during a break in an interview, one of the police officers told her that Drewery, her lover, had for the last three years or so been having an affair with a Christine Judge, who had also been arrested in the light of the informant's disclosures and was occupying the next cell. This so distressed her that 'she just couldn't stand being in the cells any longer', and so she agreed to make a statement. The trial judge assumed, without deciding, that her claims were true, but ruled that the confession was admissible. The Court of Appeal dismissed her appeal.

> **Lord Lane CJ** delivered the judgment of the court (**Lord Lane CJ**, **Taylor** and **Henry JJ**): The material part of the [trial judge's] ruling runs:

>> 'Bearing in mind that whatever happens to a person who is arrested and questioned is by its very nature oppressive, I am quite satisfied that in section 76(2)(*a*) of the Police and Criminal Evidence Act, the word oppression means something above and beyond that which in inherently oppressive in police custody and must import some impropriety, some oppression actively applied in an improper manner by police. I do not find that what was done in this case can be so defined and, in those circumstances, I am satisfied that oppression cannot be made out on the evidence I have head in the context required by the statutory provision. I go on to add simply this, that I have not addressed my mind as to whether or not I believe the police or the defendant on this issue because my ruling is based exclusively upon the basis that, even if I wholly believed the defendant, I do not regard oppression as having been made out. In those circumstances, her confession – if that is the proper term for it – the interview in which she confessed, I rule to be admissible.'

> Mr. Davey has drawn our attention to a number of authorities on the meaning of 'oppression'. Sachs L.J. in *R v Priestly (Note)* (1965) 51 Cr App R 1 said, at pp. 1, 2–3:

>> 'to my mind [oppression] in the context of the principles under consideration imports something which tends to sap, and has sapped, that free will which must exist before a confession is voluntary... the courts are not concerned with ascertaining the precise motive

---

17 See sub-ss. (2) and (6).
18 [1985] 1 All ER 230, DC (this point did not arise before the House of Lords: *R v Fox* [1986] AC 281, HL).
19 See pp. 254–256.
20 Per Griffiths LJ in *Steel v Goacher* [1993] RTR 98 at 104–105.
 1 See Lord Roskill at 467–468.

of a particular statement. The question before them is whether the prosecution have shown the statement to be voluntary, whatever the motive may be, and that is always the point to which all arguments must return. To solve it, the court has to look to the questions which I have already mentioned. First, was there in fact something which could properly by styled or might well be oppression? Secondly, did whatever happened in the way of oppression or likely oppression induce the statement in question?'

R v Prager [1972] 1WLR 260, was another decision on note (*e*) to the Judges' Rules 1964, which required that a statement by the defendant before being admitted in evidence must be proved to be 'voluntary' in the sense that it has not been obtained by fear or prejudice or hope of advantage or being oppressed. Edmund Davies LJ, who delivered the judgment of the court, said, at p. 266:

'As we have already indicated, the criticism directed in the present case against the police is that their interrogation constituted 'oppression'. This word appeared for the first time in the Judge's Rules 1964, and it closely followed the observation of Lord Parker CJ in *Callis v Gunn* [1964] 1 QB 495, 501, condemning confessions "obtained in an oppressive manner".'

In an address to the Bentham Club in 1968, Lord MacDermott described 'oppressive questioning' as 'questioning which by its nature, duration, or other attendant circumstances (including the fact of custody) excites hopes (such as the hope of release) or fears, or so affects the mind of the subject that his will crumbles and he speaks when otherwise he would have stayed silent'. We adopt these definitions or descriptions...

DPP v Ping Lin [1976] AC 574, was again a case in which the question was whether a statement by the defendant was shown to be voluntary. It was held that a trial judge faced by the problem should approach the task in a common sense way and should ask himself whether the prosecution had proved that the contested statement was voluntary in the sense that it was not obtained by fear of prejudice or hope of advantage excited or held out by a person in authority. Lord Wilberforce, Lord Morris or Borth-y-Gest and Lord Hailsham of St. Marylebone expressed the opinion that

'it is not necessary, before a statement is held to be inadmissible because not shown to have been voluntary, that it should be thought or held that there was impropriety in the conduct of the person to whom the statement was made.'

What has to be considered is whether a statement is shown to have been voluntarily rather than one brought about in one of the ways referred to.

Finally Mr. Davey referred us to a judgment of this court in *R v Rennie* [1982] 1 WLR 64. Mr Davey submits to us that on the strength of those decisions the basis of the judge's ruling was wrong, in particular when he held that the word 'oppression' means something above and beyond that which is inherently oppressive in police custody and must import some impropriety, some oppression actively applied in an improper manner by the police. It is submitted that that files in the face of the opinions of their Lordships in *DPP v Ping Ling* [1976] AC 574.

The point is one of statutory construction. The wording of the Act of 1984 does not follow the wording of earlier rules or decisions, nor is it expressed to be a consolidating Act, nor yet to be declaratory of the common law...

It is a codifying Act, and there the principles set out in *Bank of England v Vagliano Bros* [1891] AC 107, 144 apply. Lord Herschell, having pointed out that the Bills of Exchange Act 1882 which was under consideration was intended to be a codifying Act, said, at pp. 144–145:

'I don't think the proper cause is in the first instance to examine the language of the statute and to ask what is its natural meaning, uninfluenced by any considerations derived from the previous state of the law, and not to start with inquiring how the law previously stood, and then, assuming that it was probably intended to leave it unaltered, to see if the words of the enactment will bear an interpretation in conformity with this view. If a statute, intended to embody in a code a particular branch of the law, is to be treated in this fashion, it appears to me that its utility will be almost entirely destroyed, and the very object with which it was enacted will be frustrated. The purpose of such a statute surely was that on any point specifically dealt with by it, the law should be ascertained by interpreting the language used instead of, as before, by roaming over a vast number of authorities in order to discover what the law was, extracting it by a minute critical examination of the prior decisions, dependant upon a knowledge of the exact effect even of an obsolete proceeding such as a demurrer to evidence'…

Section 76(2) of the Act of 1984 distinguishes between two different ways in which a confession may be rendered inadmissible: (a) where it has been obtained by oppression; (b) where it has been made in consequence of anything said or done which was likely in the circumstances to render unreliable any confession which might be made by the defendant in consequence thereof. Paragraph (b) is wider than the old formulation, namely that the confession must be shown to be voluntary in the sense that it was not obtained by fear of prejudice or hope of advantage, executed or held out by a person in authority. It is wide enough to cover some of the circumstances which under the earlier rule were embraced by what seems to us to be the artificially wide definition of oppression approved in *R v Prager* [1972] 1 WLR 360.

This in turn leads us to believe that 'oppression' in section 76(2)(*a*) should be given its ordinary dictionary meaning. The *Oxford English Dictionary* as its third definition of the word runs as follows; 'Exercise of authority of power in a burdensome, harsh, or wrongful manner; unjust or cruel treatment of subjects, inferiors, etc.; the imposition of unreasonable or unjust burdens.' One of the questions given under that paragraph runs as follows: 'there is not a word in our language which expresses more detestable wickedness than oppression.'

We find it hard to envisage any circumstances in which such oppression would not entail some impropriety on the part of the interrogator. We do not think that the judge was wrong in using that test. What, however, is abundantly clear is that a confession may be invalidated under section 76(2)(*b*) where there is no suspicion of impropriety. No reliance was placed on the words of section 76(2)(*b*) either before the judge at trial or before this court. Even if there had been such reliance, we do not consider that the policeman's remark was likely to make unreliable any confession of the appellant's own criminal activities, and she expressly exonerated – or tried to exonerate – her unfaithful lover.

In those circumstances, in the judgment of this court, the judge was correct to reject the submission made to him under section 76 of the Act of 1984. The appeal is accordingly denied.

Appeal dismissed.

NOTES

1. The partial definition in s. 76(8) was not mentioned. Might that have made a difference? To date, there are very few decisions in which a confession has been excluded on this ground. Breaches of the law or codes will not necessarily constitute oppression: *R v Parker*.[2] In *R v Hughes*,[3] through a misunderstanding, D did not see the duty solicitor; it was held that in the absence of police misconduct, there was no oppression. In *R v Emmerson*,[4] it was held that the use by a police officer of a raised voice and bad language, expressing impatience and irritation, for a short time during an otherwise low-key interview, did not amount to oppression.[5] Counsel for the defendant in *R v Samuel*[6] felt unable to argue that the conduct of the police there amounted to oppression. Do you agree? Note that it is for the prosecution to prove that the confession was not obtained by oppression or in circumstances of unreliability. The standard of proof is beyond reasonable doubt.

2   [1995] Crim LR 233, CA.
3   [1988] Crim LR 545, CA (Cr D).
4   (1990) 92 Cr App Rep 284, CA (Cr D).
5   See also *R v Heaton* [1993] Crim LR 593, CA (Cr D); and *R v L* [1994] Crim LR 839, CA (Cr D) (pressure applied in interview did not cross the threshold of what was acceptable); *R v Paris* (below) distinguished.
6   [1988] QB 615.

An example of exclusion on this ground is *R v Beales*[7] where an officer deliberately misstated evidence in order to pressurise a person suspected of assaulting a two-year-old boy.[8] The most notorious case where oppression has been found is *R v Paris, Abdullahi and Miller*,[9] where the Court of Appeal (Criminal Division) quashed the convictions of the three appellants for murder. M was interviewed for some 13 hours. Having denied involvement well over 300 times, he was finally persuaded to make admissions. Lord Taylor CJ stated[10] that each member of the court had been 'horrified' by what they had heard in the tape recording of one interview.

> 'Miller was bullied and hectored. The officers…were not questioning him so much as shouting at him what they wanted him to say. Short of physical violence, it is hard to conceive of a more hostile and intimidating approach by officers to a suspect.'

Moreover, M's solicitor:

> 'appears to have been gravely at fault for sitting passively through this travesty of an interview.'[11]

The Court concluded that the tenor and length of all the interviews would have been oppressive and the confessions obtained unreliable even with a suspect of normal mental capacity; in fact there was evidence that M was on the border of mental handicap. The convictions of P and A were quashed as the jury might have been prejudiced by the evidence of M's interviews.

It was stressed in *Paris*[12] that 'it is perfectly legitimate for officers to pursue their interrogation of a suspect with a view to eliciting his account or gaining admissions. They are not required to give up after the first denial or even after a number of denials'. The distinction between oppressive and non-oppressive conduct is a matter of degree.[13] Interviews that were constructed in a tendentious, persistent, aggressive and prurient manner would be excluded: *R v Ridley*.[14] Oppression in one interview may taint subsequent interviews and lead to their exclusion: *Burut v Public Prosecutor*[15] (manacled and hooded suspects being interrogated suffered oppression).[16] Note that torture is an offence contrary to s. 134 of the Criminal Justice Act 1988.

2. It is unclear whether 'confession' within s. 82 includes statements made by an accused which he intended to be explanatory but later prove to be evidence against him, for example, because they expose inconsistency or lies: *R v Sat Bhambra*.[17]

3. The 'unreliability' hurdle has been invoked more frequently than the 'oppression' hurdle. 'The word "unreliable" … means "cannot be relied upon as being the truth".'[18] Moreover, the question is whether *any* confession which the accused might make in consequence of anything said or done was likely to be rendered unreliable, not whether the confession made was unreliable.[19] The thing 'said or done' must be by someone other than the accused himself.[20]

---

7   [1991] Crim LR 118 (Norwich Crown Court).
8   See also *R v Ismail* [1990] Crim LR 109, (Cr D).
9   (1992) 97 Cr App Rep 99 (The 'Cardiff Three').
10   At 103.
11   At 104.
12   Per Lord Taylor CJ at 104.
13   Cf. *R v Emmerson* and *R v Heaton*, above.
14   (1999) 17 December unreported, CA (Cr D).
15   [1995] 2 AC 579, PC.
16   [1995] 2 AC 579, PC.
17   (1988) 88 Cr App R 55, CA. On *Sat Bhambra*, see A. Vahit Bicak, (2001) J Crim Law 85.
18   Per Stuart-Smith LJ in *R v Crampton* (1990) 92 Cr App Rep 369 at 372.
19   Ibid.
20   *R v Goldenberg* (1988) 88 Cr App Rep 285, CA (Cr D); *R v Crampton*, above (doubtful whether merely holding an interview with a suspect undergoing withdrawal symptoms is something 'done' within the meaning of s. 76(2)).

In *R v Walker*,[21] W claimed to have been under the influence of crack cocaine at the time of the interview, having smuggled it into the station to take. Psychiatric evidence demonstrated that she suffered from a personality disorder that could render her admissions unreliable, and that this was exacerbated by her drug taking. The judge rejected the evidence of the psychiatrist and of her having taken drugs. The Court of Appeal held that the conviction should be quashed: the judge had failed to recognise that the 'anything said or done' need not be done or said by the police. The drug taking was a relevant consideration. Cf. *R v Goldenberg*.[1]

In *R v Bow Street Magistrates, ex p Proulx*[2] the court confirmed that the question was as to the reliability of 'any' confession made in 'such' circumstances as those alleged. Examples of possible unreliability include cases:

(1) where a child has been interviewed in the absence of an 'appropriate adult';[3]
(2) where there have been doubts about the reliability of a confession by a person of low intelligence;[4]
(3) where proper records of the confession have not been kept;[5]
(4) where there has been an improper inducement;[6]
(5) where a drug addict was held in custody for 18 hours without being allowed the prescribed rest periods;[7] and
(6) where access to a lawyer has been wrongfully denied.[8] Under this head, a confession may be excluded where there has been no police impropriety: *R v Fulling*;[9]
(7) A confession was held to be unreliable where the defendant's solicitor had interjected in terms hostile to the defendant during the interview: *R v M*.[9a]

---

21 [1998] Crim LR 211.
1 (1988) 88 Cr App R 285.
2 [2000] Crim LR 997.
3 *DPP v Blake* [1989] 1 WLR 432, CA (Cr D); *R v Morse* [1991] Crim LR 195 (Wisbech Crown Court).
4 *R v Harvey* [1988] Crim LR 241, Central Criminal Court (psychopathic woman of low intelligence may have confessed after hearing her lover confess, in order to protect him); *R v Everett* [1988] Crim LR 826, CA (Cr D) (man of 42 with mental age of eight: judge had taken no account of his mental condition); *R v Delaney* (1988) 88 Cr App Rep 338, CA (Cr D) (D educationally subnormal and proper records not kept); *R v Cox* [1991] Crim LR 276, CA (Cr D); *R v Raghip* (1991) Times, 9 December, CA (Cr D) (psychological evidence of mental condition admissible and court not bound by whether D's IQ was above an arbitrary figure for the mentally defective: see P. Mirfield, (1992) 109 LQR 528); *R v Kenny* [1994] Crim LR 284, CA (Cr D) (absence of appropriate adult); *R v Walker* [1998] Crim LR 211, CA (W having taken cocaine before interview relevant to the circumstances); *R v Souteri* (1995) Crim LR 729 (confessions by soldier when in circumstances of extreme distress, statements made to officer sent to calm S: no caution, no legal advice); *Harold M v DPP* [1988] Crim LR 653, DC (failure to inform appropriate adult of role required of him).
5 *R v Doolan* [1988] CA (Cr D) (W was also wrongly questioned after charge); *R v Chung* (1990) 92 Cr App Rep 314, CA (Cr D); *R v Joseph* [1993] Crim LR 205, CA (Cr D).
6 *R v Phillips* (1987) 86 Cr App Rep 18, CA (Cr D) (statement that if D confessed, offences could be taken into consideration rather than prosecuted); cf. *R v Howden-Simpson* [1991] Crim LR 49, CA (Cr D)); *R v Barry* (1991) 95 Cr App Rep 384, CA (Cr D) (prosecution unable to prove beyond reasonable doubt that statement was not made in response to offer of assistance in obtaining bail). *R v Weeks* [1995] Crim LR 52, CA (police implying continued detention unless W confessed, but confession admissible since W continued to refuse to answer some questions); *R v Metropolitan Police Comr, ex p Thompson* [1997] 2 Cr App R 49, DC (offer of a formal caution rendered confession unreliable).
7 *R v Trussler* [1988] Crim LR 446, Reading Crown Court.
8 *R v McGovern* (1990) 92 Cr App Rep 228, CA (Cr D); there were also breaches of the recording provisions; these matters more commonly lead to exclusion under s. 78 below, pp. 373–375.
9 Above p. 363.
9a [2000] 8 Arch News 2.

4. Breaches of Code C may make it more likely that a confession may be excluded under s. 76(2)(*b*): see, e.g. *R v Doolan*.[10]

Section 76 is drafted in terms of its application only to prosecution evidence, and the House of Lords refused to decide whether it applies to defence evidence where co-accused's confessions relied on by an accused even though the confessions were obtained in breach of Codes: *R v Myers*.[11]

5. Where an interview is improperly conducted this may lead to the exclusion as 'tainted' of subsequent interviews even though they are conducted according to the rules: see, for example, *R v Ismail*;[12] *R v McGovern*;[13] *R v Glaves*;[14] *R v Neil*;[15] *R v Conway*;[15a] but cf. *R v Gillard and Barrett*;[16] *R v Hoyte*.[17] This is a question of fact and degree: *R v Neil*.[18] The extent to which the factors which led to the exclusion of the first interview impact on the others will be a crucial factor, as will the extent to which the suspect had an opportunity to exercise informed and independent choice regarding the subsequent interview: *R v Nelson and Rose*.[19] The opportunity to seek legal advice before the subsequent interview is also very important: see *Prouse v DPP*.[20]

6. *Protection for vulnerable suspects.* The interests of mentally handicapped defendants are also subject to the limited protection afforded by s. 77 of PACE,[1] which requires a warning to the jury of the need for caution in the circumstances set out in the section. A suspect's mental handicap is to be proved by medical expertise not by a police officer testifying: *R v Ham*.[2] In *R v Bailey*,[3] s. 77 was applied where a suspect had confessed to a member of the public, but without an appropriate adult present. Is this what s. 77 was intended to guard against?

In *R v Aspinall*[4] there had been a clear breach of the Code when a schizophrenic had been interviewed without an appropriate adult or solicitor. The trial judge had been wrong to deny the need for an appropriate adult, and should have asked whether the fairness of the trial was affected by the police interview, bearing in mind that the suspect might appear normal to a lay person. The court also held that there had been a breach of Art. 6 because the denial of access to a legal adviser was particularly important in a vulnerable suspect case. In deciding whether the confession is reliable in these circumstances, the judge should hear evidence of the interviews that have been conducted in the absence of an appropriate adult: *R v Cornish*.[5]

10 [1988] Crim LR 747, CA (Cr D).
11 [1998] AC 124.
12 [1990] Crim LR 109, CA (Cr D).
13 (1990) 92 Cr App Rep 228, CA (Cr D).
14 [1993] Crim LR 685, CA (Cr D).
15 [1994] Crim LR 441, CA (Cr D).
15a [1994] Crim LR 838, CA (Cr D).
16 (1990) 92 Cr App Rep 61, CA (Cr D).
17 [1994] Crim LR 215, CA (Cr D).
18 [1994] Crim LR 441, CA (Cr D).
19 [1998] 2 Cr App R 399, CA (Cr D).
20 (1999) All ER (D) 748. See further P. Mirfield, *Silence, Confessions and Improperly Obtained Evidence* (1998).
 1 Above, p. 349.
 2 (1995) 36 BMLR 169, CA.
 3 [1995] 2 Cr App R 262, CA.
 4 [1999] Crim LR 741.
 5 (1997) 27 January, DC.

Note that no adverse inferences can be drawn from a failure to testify at trial (i.e. under s. 35 of the Criminal Justice and Public Order Act 1994) if the defendant is mentally abnormal. See also *R v BJ Friend*.[6] Adverse inferences under s. 34 can only be drawn where the defendant does not have a reasonable explanation for failing to disclose the fact relied on earlier – mental illness could be a sufficient explanation.

Failure to give the required warning may lead to the quashing of a conviction: *R v Lamont*;[7] *R v Bailey*.[8] A warning is not needed unless the case for the Crown is substantially less strong without the confession: *R v Campbell*.[9]

Note that this section does not extend to the mentally ill. The RCCJ recommended that this point should be reconsidered, as it is inconsistent with other provisions in PACE and the PACE Codes.[10] Brown,[11] found that 2% of detainees are mentally handicapped/disordered, with 33% being detained as a safety measure rather than for commission of an offence. There have been numerous calls for review of the procedures by which vulnerable suspects are identified as such.

Under PACE, an appropriate adult must be provided for juveniles and mentally disordered and mentally handicapped suspects.[12] The person should be an adult, i.e. over 18: *R v Palmer*.[13] Recent research found that in the majority of cases, the appropriate adult for juveniles was a parent or guardian (59%). Social workers were used in 23% of cases.[14] In the case of mentally disordered detainees, 60% of appropriate adults were social workers. However, in only 66% of cases did appropriate adults attend the station in the case of mentally disordered suspects.[15] There is very strong evidence that adults (other than social workers) who were acting as appropriate adults were often unaware of the role they should fulfil, and in many cases they behave inappropriately – for example, being threatening towards or even assaulting the child for whom they are the appropriate adult.[16] Brown concluded that 'there is a particular risk of interviews with mentally handicapped suspects producing unreliable evidence and the passivity of appropriate adults during interviews suggests that they do not provide an adequate safeguard against this danger'.[17]

In *DPP v Blake*[18] the court noted that 'there is no point in police officers seeking to protect a juvenile by persisting with steps to facilitate the attendance of an adult … whom the juvenile has made plain he or she does not want present'. For criticism of the potential conflict with the welfare-based role of appropriate adults and the requirement under the Crime and Disorder Act 1998 that they be present at formal punitive cautioning, see J. Williams.[19]

There have been several suggestions for improved procedures. In particular, it has been proposed that social services departments could be responsible for the quality of the provision of the services and for training custody officers, and that greater

---

6 [1997] 1 WLR 1433.
7 [1989] Crim LR 813, CA (Cr D).
8 [1995] 2 Cr App Rep 262, CA.
9 [1995] 1 Cr App Rep 522, CA (Cr D).
10 Cm. 2263, p. 59.
11 *PACE Ten Years On* (above).
12 On vulnerable groups in detention see T. Bucke and D. Brown, *In police custody: police powers and suspects' rights under the revised PACE codes of practice* (1997), Chap. 2.
13 (1991) Legal Action, September, p. 21.
14 T. Bucke and D. Brown, Chap. 2.
15 Ibid., p. 8.
16 Ibid., Chap. 2.
17 Ibid., p. 3. See also the danger of authority figures as appropriate adults for those with disability: J. Williams, [2000] Crim LR 910.
18 [1989] WLR 432.
19 [2000] Crim LR 910.

input from psychiatric professionals is necessary.[20] C. Palmer,[1] critical of the way that appropriate adults are selected, states that:

> '[i]n the absence of any clearly defined role or formal training, the presence of an independent person during interviews will be simply a formality: safeguards as presently constructed appear to be more a matter of form than of substance.'[2]

The absence of an appropriate adult is not necessarily fatal if the suspect's solicitor is present[3] nor even where the confession was obtained from a mentally handicapped person in the absence of a solicitor and appropriate adult.[4] Although a solicitor is technically excluded from acting as an appropriate adult, a solicitor may act as the equivalent by safeguarding the suspect: see *R v Martin*.[5] In *R v Aspinall*[6] the Court of Appeal held that there was still the need for an appropriate adult where A, who was mentally disordered, showed no acute symptoms of disorder and was certified fit to be interviewed by a doctor. In *R v H and M*,[7] the court recognised that it might be necessary in some circumstances to have more than one appropriate adult present. The Court held that although the officer had failed to spell out the function of the appropriate adult precisely, and had failed to identify one of the three adults present as the appropriate one, the convictions were safe. W-Z, although not the father of either boy, had a better command of English, and his presence, along with the father's, did not render the procedure improper. The absence of an appropriate adult from an interview with a 17-year-old has been held not to be fatal where there was a 'reliable confession': *R (on the application of DPP) v Stratford Youth Court*.[7a] Is this what s. 77 was intended to allow?

The Court of Appeal has also stated that a judge should withdraw a case from the jury where the prosecution case depends wholly on vulnerable confessions. The defendant suffered from a significant degree of mental handicap, and the confessions were unconvincing to the point where a jury, properly directed, could not properly convict: *R v Mackenzie*.[8] This principle can apply independently of any question as to the admissibility of the confessions. Cf. *R v Moss;*[9] *R v Brine;*[10] *R v Wood*.[11] In these cases, convictions were quashed as unsafe and unsatisfactory. In *R v Ham*,[12] the police thought that H was not mentally handicapped. The trial judge admitted the evidence without considering whether H was mentally handicapped, and the Court of Appeal quashed the conviction holding that the judge should first have heard evidence on the matter.

Excluding material obtained from an inadmissible confession

Section 76(4)(a) allows for the admissibility of material discovered as a result of inadmissible confessions – e.g. where a confession has been excluded on grounds of

20 B. Littlechild, [1995] Crim LR 540; J. Laing, [1997] Crim LR 785; H. Pierrepoint, (2000) JSWFL 383; B. Littlechild, *The PACE 1984: Role of the Appropriate Adult* (1996).
 1 [1996] Crim LR 633.
 2 Ibid., p. 644; On vulnerable suspects, see also P. Mirfield, *Silence, Confessions and Improperly Obtained Evidence* (1997), Chap. 10. See also J. Lain, *Mentally Disordered Offenders in the Criminal Justice System* (1999).
 3 *R v Law Thompson* [1997] Crim LR 674, CA.
 4 *R v Ali* [1999] 2 Arch News 2, CA.
 5 [1996] Crim LR 260, CA.
 6 [1999] 2 Cr App Rep 115.
 7 [1998] Crim LR 653, CA.
7a [2001] EWCA Admin 615, DC.
 8 (1992) 96 Cr App Rep 98, CA (Cr D).
 9 (1990) 91 Cr App Rep 371, CA (Cr D).
10 [1992] Crim LR 122, CA (Cr D).
11 [1994] Crim LR 222, CA (Cr D).
12 [1997] 36 BMLR 169.

oppression, but the confession revealed the whereabouts of the weapon involved in the crime, the weapon can be admitted but no reference can be made by the prosecution as to the inadmissible confession. This follows the common law: *R v Warwickshall*.[13] Section 76(4)(b) also follows the common law by allowing the prosecution to adduce evidence of the manner in which a suspect expresses himself even if the confession in which that is revealed is inadmissible (e.g. suspect's unusual spelling ('Blady Belgiam') identical to that used by the offender: *R v Voisin*).[14]

If a confession is excluded under s. 78, there is no comparable statutory mechanism for admitting material discovered or expressions of the suspect. The common law should apply, in which case both should be admissible.

R v Samuel [1988] QB 615, [1988] 2WLR 920, [1988] 2 All ER 135, (1988) 87 Cr App Rep 232, Court of Appeal (Criminal Division)

S was arrested for armed robbery of a building society and after being questioned asked to see a solicitor. His request was refused under s. 58 by Superintendent Cresswell, who certified, *inter alia*, that there was a 'likelihood of other suspects to be arrested being inadvertently warned'. S had two further interviews, at the second of which he confessed to two burglaries, while denying the robbery. After he was charged with the burglaries his solicitor telephoned, but was refused access. Shortly afterwards S confessed to the robbery at a third interview, and was subsequently convicted of that offence.

The Court of Appeal quashed the conviction.

The judgment of the court (**Glidewell LJ, Hodgson** and **Rougier JJ**) was given by **Hodgson J** [who stated the facts and held (1) that the superintendent was entitled to conclude that the robbery had been a serious arrestable offence given the use of a shotgun and hand gun and the intention to cause serious financial loss to the society; (2) that the right to delay access to a lawyer could not be denied once S had been charged with the burglaries in view of para. 1 of Annex B(A)(*a*) of code C, which provided that the right could only be delayed, *inter alia*, if the suspect 'has not yet been charged with an offence'. His Lordship continued:]

Mr. Escott Cox's second point raises, in the judgment of this Court, more fundamental and important issues. He challenged on the voire dire and challenged before us the correctness of both Mr. Cresswell's first decision to delay access and, even more emphatically, the decision to refuse access to Mr. Warner at 4.45 p.m. on 7 August.

Perhaps the most important right given (or rather renewed) to a person detained by the police is his right to obtain legal advice. That right is given in section 58 of the Act, subsection (1) of which is precise and unambiguous.

[His Lordship read s. 58:]

The words of the section clearly imply that the officer does so believe. Therefore a court which has to decide whether denial of access to a solicitor was lawful has to ask itself two questions: 'did the officer believe?', a subjective test, 'were there reasonable grounds for that belief?,' an objective test.

What it is the officer must satisfy the court that he believed is this: (1) that delaying consultation with a solicitor (2) will (3) lead to or hinder one or more of the things set out in (8)(*a*) to (*c*). The use of the word 'will' is clearly of great importance. There were available to the draftsman many words or phrases by which he could have described differing nuances as to the officer's state of mind, for example 'might', 'could', 'there was a risk', 'there was a substantial risk', etc. The choice of 'will' must have been deliberately restrictive.

Of course, anyone who says that he believes that something will happen, unless he is speaking of one of the immutable laws of nature, accepts the possibility that it will not happen,

13 (1783) 1 Leach 263.
14 [1918] 1 KB 531.

but the use of the word 'will' in conjunction with belief implies in the believer a belief that it will very probably happen.

What is it that the officer has to satisfy the court he believed? The right denied is a right 'to consult a solicitor privately'. The person denied that right is in police detention. In practice, the only way that the person can make any of (*a*) to (*c*) happening he will, almost inevitably, commit a serious criminal offence. Therefore, inadvertent or unwitting conduct apart, the officer must believe that a solicitor will, if allowed to consult with a detained person, thereafter commit a criminal office. Solicitors are officers of the court. We think that the number of times that a police officer could genuinely be in that state of belief will be rare. Moreover it is our view that, to sustain such a basis for refusal, the ground put forward would have to have reference to a specific solicitor. We do not think they could ever be successfully advanced in relation to solicitors generally.

However, the experience of some members of this court and, so he tells us, of Mr. Escott Cox, is that the practice adopted in this case is becoming more and more usual. An officer's 'reasonable belief' is more and more being based upon the 'inadvertent' or 'unwitting' conduct of a solicitor.

At first sight the wording of the subsection does not seem apt to cover inadvertent or unwitting conduct by a solicitor. But what is said is that the detained person will be able to bring about one or more of the happenings (*a*) to (*c*) by causing the solicitor to pass on unwittingly some form of coded message. Whether there is any evidence that this has or may have happened in the past we have no way of knowing. Solicitors are intelligent professional people; persons detained by the police are frequently not very clever and the expectation that one of (*a*) to (*c*) will be brought about in this way seems to contemplate a degree of intelligence and sophistication in persons detained, and perhaps a naiveté and lack of common sense in solicitors, which we doubt often occurs. When and if it does, we think it would have to have reference to the specific person detained. The archetype would, we imagine, be the sophisticated criminal who is known or suspected of being a member of a gang of criminals.

The task of satisfying a court that reasonable grounds existed at the time the decision was made, either in respect of intentional or inadvertent conduct will, we think, prove even more formidable. Any officer attempting to justify his decision to delay the exercise of this fundamental right of a citizen will, in our judgment, be unable to do so save by reference to specific circumstances including evidence as to the person detained or the actual solicitor sought to be consulted.

In this connection it is relevant to note that at many police stations a duty solicitor scheme is in operation…

Duty solicitors will be well known to the police, and we think it will therefore be very difficult to justify consultation with the duty solicitor being delayed. If the duty solicitor has the reputation, deserved or not, for advising persons detained to refuse to answer questions that would, of course, be no reason for delaying consultation.

[On the facts, His Lordship concluded that whoever had decided to refuse access before the third interview could not have had reasonable grounds for the belief required by s. 58(8): by this time 'the police knew the identity of the solicitor, a highly respected and very experienced professional lawyer, unlikely to be hoodwinked by a 24-year old'. That person was 'very probably motivated by a desire to have one last chance of interviewing the appellant in the absence of a solicitor'.]

Having ruled against the defence submissions on both the construction point and the more fundamental submission on the exercise of the power under section 58(8), the trial judge briefly considered his discretion. He said:

'However, had I decided that "an offence" meant any offence I would, in the exercise of the discretion which I undoubtedly have, have exercised it on the basis of justice, fairness and common sense and would in any event have allowed the evidence to be given to the jury.'

It is to be noted that he there makes no reference to his decision on the second ground. Mr. Escott Cox submits that it is clear that the judge did not consider how he would have exercised his discretion if he had applied his mind to the situation at 4.45 p.m. and still held that the refusal at that time was proper. Secondly, he submits that, having found wrongly on both submissions, it was really impossible for him properly to consider how he would have exercised his discretion.

Mr. Warner gave evidence. He said it was not his policy always to advice a client not to answer questions put to him by the police. In his view, in many cases, it was of advantage to someone in detention to answer proper questions put to him. However on this occasion, knowing that his client had already been interviewed on four occasions and at each had strenuously denied complicity in the robbery and had already been charged with two serious offences, he would probably, after consultation, have advised his client, for the time being at any rate, to refuse to answer further questioning. The probable result of allowing the appellant to exercise his right would therefore, in all probability, have been that, had a further interview taken place (and we think it improbable that the police would, in those circumstances, have thought it worth their while to interview him further) no incriminating replies would have been given.

Mr. Esscot Cox further submits that he was handicapped in his conduct of the appellant's defence by the judge's ruling on the construction of the Annex. That was a ruling on a point of law and therefore prevented him cross-examining the police on the propriety of the refusal of access on that ground.

It is undesirable to attempt any general guidance as to the way in which a judge's decision under section 78 or his inherent powers should be exercised. Circumstances vary infinitely. Mr. Jones has made the extreme submission that, in the absence of impropriety, the discretion should never be exercised to exclude admissible evidence. We have no hesitation in rejecting that submission, although the propriety or otherwise of the way in which the evidence was obtained is something which a court is, in terms, enjoined by the section 58(8) point, the judge failed properly to address his mind to the point in time which was most material and did not in terms give consideration to what his decision would have been had he ruled in favour of the defence on this more fundamental issue before him.

In this case this appellant was denied improperly one of the most important and fundamental rights of a citizen. The trial judge fell into error in not so holding. If he had arrived at correct decisions on the two points argued before him he might well have concluded that the refusal of access and consequent unlawful interview compelled him to find that the admission of evidence as to the final interview would have 'such an adverse effect on the fairness of the proceedings' that he ought not to admit it. Such a decision would, of course, have very significantly weakened the prosecution case (the failure to charge earlier ineluctably shows this), in those circumstances this court feels that it has no alternative but to quash the appellant's conviction on count 1 in the indictment, the charge of robbery.

Appeal allowed.

Conviction quashed.

NOTES

1. The largest number of cases in which a confession has been excluded involve exclusion under s. 78. Examples include the following situations:

(1) Where the police have denied access to a solicitor in breach of s. 58: *R v Samuel,*[15] *R v Parris*[16] (superintendent's order that D to be kept incommunicado under s. 56 wrongly assumed to exclude access to a solicitor under s. 58); *R v Walsh;*[17] *R v Chung;*[18] *R v Braithwaite.*[19] Exclusion is not, however, automatic, and may not follow where D is aware of his rights: *R v Alladice*[20] (D admitted he was well able to cope with the interviews, that he understood the caution and was aware of his rights); *R v Dunford*[1] (D had a record and was aware of his right not to answer questions);

15 (1988) 87 Cr App Rep 232.
16 (1988) 89 Cr App Rep 68, CA (Cr D).
17 (1989) 91 Cr App Rep 161, CA (Cr D).
18 (1990) 92 Cr App Rep 314, CA (Cr D).
19 (1991) Times, 9 December, CA (Cr D).
20 (1988) 87 Cr App Rep 380, CA (Cr D).
 1 (1990) 91 Cr App Rep 150, CA (Cr D).

R v Oliphant[2] (presence of a solicitor would have added nothing to what O knew of his legal rights); *R v Anderson*[3] (even if a solicitor had been present and advised silence, A would not have acted on such advice). See H. Fenwick,[4] arguing for more use of the bad faith doctrine to exclude evidence in such cases.

   A confession may also be excluded where a suspect is not told that a solicitor has come to the police station at another person's request, contrary to Code C, Annex B, para. 3: *R v Franklin*.[5]

(2) Where D has not been advised of the right to legal advice: *R v Absolam*;[6] *R v Beycan*.[7]

(3) Where a proper record of the interview was not made: *R v Abolsam*[8] (no caution before questioning; no proper record); *R v Keenan*[9] (officers unaware of Code C); *R v Walsh*;[10] *R v Canale*[11] (where the breaches were described as 'flagrant', 'deliberate', and 'cynical'); *R v Bryce*[12] (interview after tape recorder switched off at B's request; no fresh caution and no contemporaneous record); *R v Cox*[13] (questioning before arrival at police station held to be 'interview' to which Code C.11 requirements applied); *R v Joseph*[14] (interview after arrest away from police station not shown to be necessary, accordingly, no justification for absence of contemporaneous note); *R v Goddard*[15] (questions to elicit admissions after arrest and caution held to be an interview; G given no opportunity to take legal advice and no contemporaneous note). In *R v Keenan*,[16] Hodgson J emphasised the importance of these provisions as safeguards against 'verballing' by the police (i.e. 'the police inaccurately recording or inventing the words used in questioning a detained person'). Cf. *R v Matthews, Dennison, Voss*,[17] where the Court of Appeal declined to interfere with the trial judge's exercise of discretion to admit a confession notwithstanding breach of the recording requirements (the confession included correct details as to where the victim's clothes were found); and *R v Dunn*,[18] where there were breaches of the recording requirements but a confession was held to be admissible as D's solicitor's clerk was present at the interview and so able to protect his interests.

(4) Where there was a breach of Code C.11.3:[19] *R v Howden-Simpson*[20] (the police indicated they would proceed on only two of a series of non-payments if D admitted theft.[1]

(5) Where there is a breach of a requirement to caution: *R v Absolam*;[2] *R v Hunt*[3] (H seen by a police officer to have a flick knife and asked what it was for; it was held

2 [1992] Crim LR 40, CA (Cr D).
3 [1993] Crim LR 447, CA (Cr D).
4 [1995] Crim LR 132.
5 (1994) Times, 16 June, CA (Cr D) (proviso applied).
6 (1988) 88 CR App Rep 332, CA (Cr D).
7 [1990] Crim LR 185, CA (Cr D).
8 Above.
9 [1990] 2 QB 54, CA (Cr D).
10 Above.
11 [1990] 2 All ER 187, CA (Cr D).
12 [1992] 4 All ER 567, CA (Cr D).
13 (1992) 96 CR App Rep 464, CA (Cr D).
14 [1993] Crim LR 206, CA (Cr D).
15 [1994] Crim LR 46, CA (Cr D).
16 [1990] 2 QB 54, 63.
17 (1989) 91 Cr App Rep 43.
18 (1990) 91 Cr App Rep 237, CA (Cr D).
19 Above, p. 317.
20 [1991] Crim LR 49, CA (Cr D).
1 Note the criticism by D. J. Birch, [1991] Crim LR 50–51.
2 (1988) 88 Cr App Rep 332, CA (Cr D).
3 [1992] Crim LR 582, CA (Cr D).

that there was ample evidence to suspect commission of an offence and he should have been cautioned): *R v Bryce*;[4] *R v Okafor*[5] (proviso applied); cf. *R v Shah*[6] (customs officer's suspicion that S might be a drugs courier not sufficient to require a caution. See also *R v James*[7] (questioning suspects' business partner regarding inconsistencies without caution); *R v Kirk*[8] (unfair to caution in relation to lesser offence when sufficient to caution on much more serious offence at that time). The correct time to caution is when there are grounds for suspicion (objectively assessed) but insufficient evidence to support a prima facie case of guilt: *R v Nelson and Rose*;[9] *R v Blackford*;[10] a second caution may be necessary on arrival at the station if conversations with the suspect then occur: *R v Miller*.[11] Breaches of the international convention relating to diplomatic immunity will not lead to exclusion: *R v Khan*;[12] a roadside confession will be admissible where it is made prior to the driver being given a breath test and then being cautioned: *R v Wheelan*.[13]

Much of the controversy over the scope of what constitutes an interview has been resolved by the definition in the 1995 revision of the Code. In *Batley v DPP*[14] it was stated that a conversation is an interview if a suspect is being asked to incriminate himself (police questioning landlord with 60 people drinking in his pub after hours). If the police only had a hunch that there was an illegal act, that would not trigger the suspicion necessary to activate the code.

(6) Where a juvenile is interviewed in the absence of an appropriate adult: *R v Weekes*.[15]

2. In some early cases, particularly at first instance, courts seem to have been too ready to assume that breaches of Code C render it unfair for a confession to be admitted.[16] The Court of Appeal has emphasised that 'not every breach or combination of breaches of the codes will justify the exclusion of interview evidence under section 76 or section 78... they must be significant and substantial' (per Hodgson J in *R v Keenan*).[17]

Furthermore, exclusion will not follow automatically even where there is a 'significant or substantial breach':

'The task of the court is not merely to consider whether there would be an adverse effect on the fairness of the proceedings, but such an adverse effect that justice requires the evidence to be excluded.'[18]

The nature rather than the number of breaches is what matters: *R v Stewart*.[19]

On the other hand, 'if the police have acted in bad faith, the court will have little difficulty in ruling any confession inadmissible under section 78, if not under section 76'.[20]

4 [1992] 4 All ER 567, CA (Cr D).
5 [1994] 3 All ER 741, CA (Cr D).
6 [1994] Crim LR 125, CA (Cr D).
7 [1996] Crim LR 650, CA (Cr D).
8 [1999] 4 All ER 698, CA (Cr D).
9 [1998] 2 Cr App Rep 399, CA (Cr D).
10 Above, p. 332.
11 [1998] Crim LR 209, CA (Cr D).
12 [1997] Crim LR 508.
13 [1995] RTR 177.
14 (1998) Times, 5 March, DC.
15 (1992) 97 Cr App Rep 222, CA (Cr D).
16 See D. J. Birch, [1989] Crim LR 95 at 105–106.
17 [1990] 2 QB 54 at 69.
18 Per Saville J, in *R v Walsh* (1989) 91 Cr App Rep 161 at 163, CA (Cr D).
19 [1995] Crim LR 500, CA.
20 Per Lord Lane CJ in *R v Alladice* (1988) 87 Cr App Rep 380 at 386, CA (Cr D).

3. The 'burden of proof' under s. 78 is unclear, in contrast to the position under s. 76.[1]

There is no academic consensus as to where the burden of proof lies in s. 78. Zander[2] and Andrews and Hirst[3] suggest that it lies on the accused, May[4] asserts that it is on the prosecution, and Tapper[5] is equivocal. It is submitted that the courts are likely to follow the normal practice 'he who asserts must prove'. In *R (on the application of Saifi) v Governor of Brixton Prison*[6] the Court of Appeal doubted whether there was truly a 'burden of proof issue'. Is there a burden of proving the facts on which the judge must exercise the discretion?

Section 78 has no application to proceedings before a magistrates' court sitting as examining justices (s. 78(3)). In *R v Governor of Brixton Prison, ex p Levin*,[7] Lord Hoffmann thought that the section was therefore also of no application in the case of extradition proceedings: cf. *R v Bow Street Magistrates' Court, ex p Proulx*.[8]

Admissibility of evidence derived from police deception

R v Christou and Wright [1992] QB 979, [1992] 3 WLR 228, [1992] 4 All ER 559, CA (Cr D)

In 1990, in order to combat a high rate of burglary and robbery in North London, police set up an undercover operation. A shop ('Stardust Jewellers') was established in Tottenham, run by two undercover officers ('Gary' and 'Aggi') who purported to be shady jewellers willing to buy in stolen property. Over three months, a series of transactions was recorded by cameras and sound recording equipment. The conversations included questions that would be asked by shady jewellers, such as the area of London in which it would be unwise to resell the goods. The officers also required the vendors to sign receipts recording the money paid and the specific goods. This was something which shady jewellers would be likely to do, but also had the effect of obtaining fingerprints. In the event the fingerprints were not used. C and W were vendors of stolen property charged in respect of a number of transactions. At their trial for handling stolen goods, the judge ruled that the evidence from the operation was admissible, and they accordingly pleaded guilty. Their appeal to the Court of Appeal was dismissed.

The judgment of the court (**Lord Taylor of Gosforth CJ, Boreham** and **Auld JJ**) was delivered by **Lord Taylor of Gosforth CJ**:

[His Lordship referred to dicta in *R v Sang* (above, pp. 351–352) and continued:]

In view of the terms of those dicta, the paucity of cases in which the discretion had been exercised so as to exclude legally admissible evidence is not surprising. In the present case the judge decided that, since the evidence from Stardust Jewellers had admittedly been obtained from the appellants by a trick and after the offences charged had been committed, he had a discretion to exclude the evidence if its admission would prejudice a fair trial. He also considered the alternative submission that, pursuant to section 78 of the Act of 1984, he ought to exclude the evidence…

---

1   See *R v Anderson* [1993] Crim LR 447.
2   M. Zander, *The Police and Criminal Evidence Act 1984* (3rd edn, 1994), p. 246.
3   M. Hirst, *Andrews and Hirst on Criminal Evidence* (4th edn, 2001), para. 14.29.
4   R. May, *Criminal Evidence* (4th edn, 1999), p. 307.
5   C. Tapper, *Cross and Tapper on Evidence* (9th edn, 1999), p. 188.
6   [2001] 4 All ER 168, CA (Cr D).
7   [1997] AC 741.
8   [2001] 1 All ER 57, DC.

The judge held that the discretion under section 78 may be wider than the common law discretion identified in *R v Sang* [1980] AC 402, the latter relating solely to evidence obtained from the defendant after the offence is complete, the statutory discretion not being so restricted. However, he held that the criteria of unfairness are the same whether the trial judge is exercising his discretion at common law or under the statute. We agree. What is unfair cannot sensibly be subject to different standards depending on the source of the discretion to exclude it.

In the result the judge concluded that to admit the challenged evidence would not have an adverse effect on the fairness of the trial. He said:

'Nobody was forcing the defendants to do what they did. They were not persuaded or encouraged to do what they did. They were doing in that shop exactly what they intended to do and in all probability, what they intended to do from the moment they got up that morning. They were dishonestly disposing of dishonest goods. If the police had never set up the jewellers shop, they would, in my judgment, have been doing the same thing, though of course they would not have been doing it in that shop, at that time. They were not tricked into doing what they would not otherwise have done, they were tricked into doing what they wanted to do in that place and before witnesses and devices who can now speak of what happened. I do not think that is unfair or leads to an unfairness in the trial.'

Putting it in different words, the trick was not applied to the appellants; they voluntarily applied themselves to the trick. It is not every trick producing evidence against an accused which results in unfairness. There are, in criminal investigations, a number of situations in which the police adopt ruses or tricks in the public interest to obtain evidence. For example, to trap a blackmailer, the victim may be used as an agent of the police to arrange an appointment and false or marked money may be laid as bait to catch the offender. A trick, certainly; in a sense too, a trick which results in a form of self-incriminations; but not one which could reasonably be thought to involve fairness. Cases such as *R v Payne* [1963] 1 WLR 637 and *R v Mason (Carl)* [1988] 1 WLR 139 are very different from the present case or the blackmail example. In *R v Mason* as in *R v Payne* [1963] 1 WLR 637, the defendant was in police custody at a police station. Officers lied to both the defendant and his solicitor. Having no evidence against the defendant, they falsely asserted that his fingerprints had been found in an incriminating place in order to elicit admissions from him. After advice from his solicitor, the defendant made admissions. This court quashed his conviction.

In the present case the argument was at one stage canvassed that requesting the receipt with the consequence obtaining of fingerprints, should be regarded separately from the main issue, that it amounted to a separate trick within a trick. However, Mr. Thornton made clear that in his submission requesting the receipt was merely an incident in the operation of the shop. The whole operation was a single trick, all the fruits of which should be excluded. We agree that the operation should be considered as a whole. In the end, the judge treated the receipts as 'part of the general deceit concerning the dishonest jewellers, the general pretence by them that it was a proper jeweller's shop'. It was not unfair. He gave, as a further reason, that had no request been made for a receipt, fingerprints could easily have been obtained in other ways, e.g. by dusting the counter. For this he relied upon *R v Apicella* (1985) 82 Cr App Rep R 295 and *Director of Public Prosecutions v Marshall* [1988] 3 All ER 683.

The judge's exercise of his discretion could only be impugned if it was unreasonably according to *Wednesbury* principles (*Associated Provincial Picture Houses Ltd v Wednesbury Corporation* [1948] 1 KB 223): see *R v O'Leary* (1988) 87 Cr App R 387, 391. In our judgment, not only can the judge's conclusion on this issue not be so stigmatised, we think he was right.

[The other ground of appeal turns on paragraph 10.1 of Code C of the PACE Codes [above, p. 332].]

It is submitted that the first sentence of that paragraph applied to the conversations in the shop. Accordingly, a caution should have been given. It is obvious that if this submission is correct, setting up Stardust Jewellers would have been pointless. Mr. Thornton and Mr. Taylor grasped that nettle. They say that the operation should not have been undertaken. If a caution was required, it cannot be dispensed with simply to facilitate the operation. It is accepted that Gary and Aggi had grounds to suspect each of the appellants of an offence. The issue is whether the Code applied to this situation at all. The judge concluded it did not…

In our view, although the Code extends beyond the treatment of those in detention, what is clear is that it was intended to protect suspects who are vulnerable to abuse or pressure from police officers or who may believe themselves to be so. Frequently, the suspect will be a detainee. But the Code will also apply where a suspect, not in detention, is being questioned about an offence by a police officer acting as a police officer for the purpose of obtaining evidence. In that situation, the officer and the suspect are not on equal terms. The officer is perceived to be in a position of authority; the suspect may be intimidated or undermined.

The situation at Stardust Jewellers was quite difficult. The appellants were being questioned by police officers acting as such. Conversation was on equal terms. There could be no question of pressure or intimidation by Gary or Aggi as persons actually in authority or believed to be so. We agree with the judge that the Code simply was not intended to apply in such a context.

In reaching that conclusion, we should ourselves administer a caution. It would be wrong for police officers to adopt or use an undercover pose or disguise to enable themselves to ask questions about an offence uninhibited by the requirements of the Code and with the effect of circumventing it.

Were they to do so, it would be open to the judge to exclude the questions and answers under section 78 of the Act of 1984. It is therefore necessary here to see whether the questioning by Gary and Aggi was such as to require the judge in his discretion to exclude the conversation. The judge carefully reviewed the evidence on this issue. He concluded that the questions and comments from Gary and Aggi were for the most part simply those necessary to conduct the bartering and maintain their cover. They were not 'about the offence'. The only exception was the questioning about which area should be avoided in reselling the goods. However, even that was partly to maintain cover since it was the sort of questioning to be expected from a shady jeweller.

We are of the view that the judge's approach to the aspect of the case concerned with the Code cannot be faulted...

Appeals dismissed.

NOTES

1. *Christou and Wright* deals with two distinct, but related issues: (1) the discretion to exclude evidence obtained by a trick; and (2) the question of 'entrapment'. The evidence obtained may in either event by confession or real evidence.[9] To what extent is it fair to say that the defendants in *Christou* applied the trick to themselves?

2. *Tricks.* In *R v Mason*,[10] mentioned by Lord Taylor CJ in *R v Christou and Wright*, Watkins LJ described the conduct of the police as 'most reprehensible'. The trial judge in exercising his discretion under s. 78 had failed to take any account of the deceit practised upon M's solicitor. If he had done so, he would clearly have ruled the confession inadmissible. The court stated that 'this was not the place to discipline the police' but they hoped 'never again to hear of deceit such as this being practised upon an accused person, and more particularly possibly on a solicitor, whose duty it is to advise him unfettered by false information from the police'.[11] The court also confirmed that s. 78 could be used to exclude evidence of confessions and admissions.

Lord Taylor in *Christou and Wright* emphasised that undercover operations must not be employed to enable police officers to ask questions about an offence uninhibited by the requirements of Code C. That line was crossed in *R v Bryce*,[12] where an undercover police officer posed as a potential buyer and agreed by telephone to buy a stolen car (actually worth £23,000) from B for £2,800. When they met, the officer asked B (*inter alia*) how long the car had been stolen, and was told two or

9 See p. 376.
10 [1988] 1 WLR 139.
11 At 144.
12 [1992] 4 All ER 567, CA (Cr D).

three days. Lord Taylor noted that: 'Those questions went to the heart of the vital issue of dishonesty. They were not even necessary to the undercover operation.'[13] They were also hotly disputed, and there was no contemporary record (unlike the position in *Christou and Wright* where the conversations were recorded). The court held that the answers should have been excluded.

Other cases where evidence obtained by tricks or deception has been held admissible include *DPP v Marshall*,[14] where the Divisional Court held that justices had been wrong to exclude evidence of test purchases made by police officers, without revealing their identity, as evidence for a prosecution for selling liquor without a licence; it had not been shown that admission of the evidence would adversely affect the fairness of proceedings.[15] (Note that under s. 31 of the Criminal Justice and Police Act 2001 there is a specific defence to a charge of using an under-18-year-old to buy alcohol in such cases.) Then, in *Williams and O'Hare v DPP*,[16] the Divisional Court upheld the admissibility of evidence of interfering with a vehicle with intent to commit theft, where the police left a van unattended, with what seemed to be a valuable load of cigarettes, and W and O'H succumbed to the temptation. Have the police incited theft? Does this render the situation different from *Christou* in which the police had no intention to encourage the crime?[17] See also *R v Maclean and Kosten*.[18] In a number of cases, covertly recorded conversations in situations set up by the police have been held to be admissible. See *R v Jelen, R v Katz*[19] (tape recorded telephone conversations with a witness who had been charged and released on bail); *R v Ali (Shaukat)*[20] (covertly recorded conversation between A and his family in the interview room at the police station after charge); *R v Bailey and Smith*[1] (covertly recorded conversations between the two appellants placed together in a police cell with the connivance of the custody officer, after being charged and remanded by the magistrates). Code C is held not to apply to such situations. The case that goes furthest is *R v Bailey and Smith* where the situation followed interviews in which B and S exercised their right to silence and involved a stratagem whereby the investigating officers, in order to avoid arousing their suspicions, pretended that they had been forced to place the appellants together by an unco-operative custody officer. However, their solicitors were not given any false information or deceived, nothing had been done oppressively or so as to render unreliable any admissions made. There was no reason to doubt the essential fairness of the evidence having been held admissible.[2] See also *R v Cadette*;[3] *R v Edwards*[4] (officers posing as drugs purchasers maintained cover by pursuing conversation with E).

In *R v Roberts*,[5] R and a fellow suspect, C, were charged with robbery. C then asked to be placed in a cell with R in the hope that R would admit the offence and exculpate C. R did make incriminating remarks, which were recorded as the cell had been bugged. The Court of Appeal upheld the trial judge's decision to admit the recordings since proper authorisation had been obtained to bug the cell and the trial judge had found

13 At 571–572.
14 [1988] 3 All ER 683.
15 Cf. *Ealing London Borough v Woolworths plc* [1995] Crim LR 58, DC.
16 (1993) 98 Cr App Rep 209.
17 See also D. Birch, [1994] 47 CLP 73.
18 [1993] Crim LR 775, CA (Cr D).
19 (1989) 90 Cr App Rep 456, CA (Cr D).
20 (1991) Times, 19 February, CA (Cr D).
 1 [1993] 3 All ER 513, CA (Cr D).
 2 Simon Brown LJ at 523.
 3 [1995] Crim LR 229, CA (Cr D).
 4 [1997] Crim LR 348.
 5 [1997] 1 Cr App R 217.

that there had been no deception by the police, because C was a suspect and not a police informer. Would R have said what he did had he known that C had requested to be put in a bugged cell? Did the breaches of the Code not affect the fairness of admitting this evidence?

3. *Entrapment and agents provocateurs.* In *R v Smurthwaite, R v Gill*[6] the Court of Appeal confirmed that s. 78 had not altered the common law rule laid down in *Sang*[7] that entrapment or the use of an agent provocateur does not per se afford a defence in law to a criminal charge. However, if the judge considered that in all the circumstances the obtaining of the evidence in that way had such an adverse affect on the fairness of the proceedings that the court ought not to admit it, it could be excluded under s. 78.[8]

His Lordship continued:[9]

'In exercising his discretion whether to admit the evidence of an undercover officer, some, but not an exhaustive list, of the factors that the judge may take into account are as follows. Was the officer acting as an agent provocateur in the sense that he was enticing the defendant to commit an offence he would not otherwise have committed? What was the nature of any entrapment? Does the evidence consist of admissions to a completed offence, or does it consist of the actual commission of an offence? How active or passive was the officer's role in obtaining the evidence? Is there an unassailable record of what occurred, or is it strongly corroborated? In *R v Christou* [1992] 4 All ER 559, [1992] QB 979 this court held that discussions between suspects and undercover officers, not overtly acting as police officers, were not within the ambit of the codes under the 1984 Act. However, officers should not use their undercover pose to question suspects so as to the circumvent the code. In *R v Bryce* [1992] 4 All ER 567 the court held that the undercover officer had done just that. Accordingly, a further consideration for the judge in deciding whether to admit an undercover officer's evidence is whether he has abused his role to ask questions which ought properly to have been asked as a police officer and in accordance with the codes.'

Here, police officers in two separate cases posed as contract killers, and were solicited by S and G to kill their respective spouses. On the facts in each case, tape-recorded conversations 'showed no sign of an unwilling defendant being persuaded or cajoled into an agreement to a murder she [or he] would not otherwise have entered'.[10] In S's case, all the conversations were recorded; in G's case an unrecorded conversation given in evidence by the officer was corroborated by later recorded conversations and held to be admissible. 'Agent provocateur' was defined in the *Royal Commission on Police Powers*[11] as ' a person who entices another to commit an express breach of the law which he would not otherwise have committed and then proceeds to inform against him in respect of such an offence'.

Although the matter was considered by the House of Lords in *Sang*, the House again addressed it in *R v Latif and Shazad*.[12] The defendants had been involved in a conspiracy to import heroin, and the British Customs and US Drug Enforcement Agency had participated. One of the officers had actually imported the drugs without a licence (the House of Lords was prepared to assume that he was guilty of an offence although that had not been argued at trial). The House held that the trial judge had exercised the discretion whether to stay the proceedings for abuse and had conducted the correct balancing of the interests involved, including the need for the law

---

6 [1994] 1 All ER 898.
7 Above, p. 351.
8 Lord Taylor CJ at 902.
9 At 903.
10 Lord Taylor CJ at 909.
11 (1928) (Cmnd. 3297).
12 [1996] 2 Cr App Rep 92.

enforcement agencies to fight serious crime. The same balance needed to be struck with s. 78 and the trial judge was right not to exclude the evidence.

S. Sharpe,[13] has argued that 'although in theory s. 78 allows for the exclusion of evidence obtained by entrapment, it is rare for a defence application to succeed'.[14] It is difficult to substantiate any claims. If a defence application succeeds, the case will probably collapse and there can be no appeal so no case will be reported. The number of cases where the defence applications do not succeed that are appealed is the only foundation for the claim. Commenting on *Latif*[15] Sir John Smith stated that 'the graver the offence to be prevented, the more the law enforcement authorities can get away with. It is a question of expediency'.[16] Is it? Should it be?

Police use of deceptive practices is not a new phenomenon. R. Plehwe,[17] noted that the Home Secretary in 1881, Sir William Harcourt, announced that police authorities had been instructed not to use entrapment without direct authorisation by the Home Office.

As the pressure to combat crime, and particularly those types of crime in which detection is very difficult – drug dealing being a prime example – the use of entrapment techniques has increased in recent years. There are an increasing number of cases being brought before the appellate courts because of this, and at present, because of an increased awareness of the ECHR. The impact of the ECHR has been considerable. The leading decision of the European Court of Human Rights is that in *Teixiera de Castro v Portugal*,[18] in which there was found to be a breach of Art. 6 where the undercover officers incited the offender to commit an offence which he would not otherwise have committed. The police had relied on T's predisposition to commit other offences:

> 'the use of undercover agents must be restricted and safeguards put in place even in cases concerning the fight against drug trafficking. While the rise in organised crime undoubtedly requires that appropriate measures be taken, the right to a fair administration of justice nevertheless holds such a paramount place that it cannot be sacrificed for the sake of expedience. The general requirements of fairness embodied in Article 6 apply to proceedings concerning all types of criminal offence, from the most straightforward to the most complex. The public interest cannot justify the use of evidence obtained as a result of police incitement.'

The European Court of Human Rights distinguished the earlier case of *Ludi v Switzerland*,[19] where the undercover police officer had actively been involved in buying drugs from someone who was already dealing drugs, and this case, in which the police had initiated the deal with someone who was not engaged in drug dealing. The European approach focuses on whether the suspect is 'predisposed' to commit the crime. Does this mean: (a) has a general disposition towards crime; (b) has a disposition towards this type of crime; (c) has a disposition to commit this specific crime on this occasion?[20] What are the implications for those with a criminal record? Can the police now round up the potential suspects – perhaps those known to have a criminal record and to be easily led into criminal acts[1] – encourage them to commit a crime and then arrest them?

---

13 [1997] Crim LR 848.
14 Ibid., p. 854.
15 [1996] Crim LR 446.
16 Ibid.
17 [1974] PL 316 at 329.
18 (1998) 28 EHRR 101.
19 (1993) 15 EHRR 173.
20 See A. Ashworth, [1999] 10 Arch News p. 5.
 1 Alternatively, drug addicts who can be encouraged to deal?

The concept of predisposition owes much to the US literature and case law. The difficulty in transposing that to English law is that there is a fundamental difference between the jurisdictions: the USA has a defence (in substantive criminal law) of entrapment; English law deals with the matter as one of procedure and evidence.[2] In *Jacobson v US*[3] the Supreme Court held that the defendant was not pre-disposed to commit the offence involving the transmission of pornographic material through the mail, on the basis of a single piece of conduct several years earlier at a time when the distribution of such material was not illegal.

A. Ashworth has examined the many arguments that can be advanced for and against deceptive police practices.[4] These include arguments that: criminals deserve reduced rights only, so no harm is done to them by police deception; the criminal relies on deception, so it is not unfair for him to be treated in similar fashion; entrapment and deception might be wrong in general, but in the specific context they will benefit the community. On the other hand, by deceiving suspects, the police infringe the integrity principle, they abuse the power of the state, and reduce confidence in the criminal justice system. There are arguments that deceptive practices ought to be used only exceptionally (Who decides? Is it fair to treat some crimes differently in terms of investigations? Which crimes and why?). He concludes that:

'there will doubtless be those who believe that this attempt to sift through the arguments…is pusillanimous and, ultimately, unrealistic. The main plank of this belief would probably be the maxim that the end justifies the means: in other words, if the police can discover the truth by indulging in a little deception, this constitutes a significant contribution to law enforcement which overshadows the method by which it was obtained. The whole thrust of this article is that the issues are more complex than this apparently tempting argument suggests. It fails to recognise the existence of rights, and its logic might lead to the approval of violence so long as the end was thought satisfactory.'

Having examined the types of trick, Ashworth concludes:

'(i) that lying in court is absolutely wrong because it compromises the integrity of the criminal justice system, and any attempt to justify it in terms of convicting the factually guilty is constitutionally and morally unsustainable;

(ii) that at any earlier stage in the criminal process 'tricks about rights' are wrong for similar reasons, insofar as the rights are recognised in the ECHR, in domestic legislation or in the Codes of Practice;

(iii) that for this purpose a trick should be defined so as to include any deception, including a failure to inform a suspect when there is a duty to do so; but

(iv) that there are distinctly fewer moral objections to the use of disguises, informers, or other agents at the investigative stage, so long as this does not involve prompting or questioning a suspect in relation to an incident in a way that undermines rights that should be protected; and

(v) that there are also fewer moral objections to a covert tape recording or electronic surveillance, although moral objections to 'bugging' private premises remain strong and should only be overcome in situations where the justifications for invading privacy are powerful and properly tested.'[6]

The English courts are faced with having to make some hard decisions on entrapment, and to apply this predisposition formula. In *Nottingham City Council v Amin*[7] the

---

2   See Donnelly, (1951) 60 Yale LJ 1091.
3   (1992) 503 US 118.
4   See (1998) 114 LQR 108.
5   Ibid., p.123.
6   Ibid., p.138.
7   [2000] 1 WLR 1071.

defendant was a taxi driver who was driving outside his licensed area when he was hailed by a plain clothes officer. The taxi took the fare and was charged with operating without a licence. The magistrate refused to accept the officer's evidence, since it amounted to an entrapment. The Divisional Court allowed the prosecutor's appeal.

One fundamental problem is that it remains unclear what the term 'entrapment' means, or what type of test is being applied to determine whether case should be stayed.

In *Amin*, Lord Bingham stated that:

'it has been recognised as deeply offensive to ordinary notions of fairness if a defendant were to be convicted and punished for committing a crime which he only committed because he had been incited, instigated, persuaded and pressured, or wheedled into committing it by a law enforcement officer [but it is] unobjectionable if a law enforcement officer gives a defendant an opportunity to break the law of which the defendant freely takes advantage, in circumstances where it appears that the defendant would have behaved in the same way if the opportunity had been offered by anyone else.'[8]

In *R v Lawrence and Nash*[9], Leggatt LJ observed that:

'Agent provocateur "entices another to commit an offence which he would not otherwise have committed". An example of an offence which would, in any event have been committed, is the offer by a person to sell drugs to an undercover officer in a public house, mistaking him for a user. Of that supply it could fairly be said that such an offence would have been committed in any event, but where a police officer prompts others to obtain drugs for him, believing them to be suppliers, it is not apparent without more that they would, in any event have supplied others.'

Are these satisfactory definitions?

The House of Lords has recently provided further clarification on the entrapment issues. In *R v Loosely*[10] the House held that English law, applying cases such as *Amin*, was not in conflict with the ECtHR approach in *Teixeira*. The Lords held that the officers in *Loosely* had not overstepped the mark since they had made one approach to a person who was suspected of drug dealing and had bought drugs on their first request. In *A-G's Reference (No. 3 of 2000)*,[11] the officers had overstepped the mark when they had pressurised the suspect over a period of time and offered inducements.

It was held that it would be unfair (and should lead to an abuse of process) for an undercover officer to incite or instigate an offence that the suspect would not otherwise have committed. If the officer merely provides an unexceptional opportunity for the suspect to take advantage there would be no unfairness in admitting the evidence at trial and no stay of proceedings.

The House of Lords also emphasised that the previous record of the accused is not determinative, but that a reasonable suspicion of offending or willingness to offend is important.

The House of Lords emphasised that in *Teixeira* the officers had been acting without judicial supervision and had no reasonable grounds to suspect T of drug dealing.

8 On *Amin* see J. Spencer, [2001] CLJ 30.
9 (1993) unreported, 14 December.
10 [2001] UKHL 53, HL.
11 [2001] UKHL 53.

The decision is a welcome one, but there are issues of entrapment that still need to be resolved. These might be best clarified in a Code of Practice or statute as suggested by D. Ormerod and A. Roberts.[12] They argue that:

'In addition to this unsatisfactory application of existing law, the decision is deficient in failing to explain how a defendant's "freedom" to take advantage of the offer is to be proved otherwise than by reference to a previous disposition and/or by post-rationalising from the fact of commission on this occasion. Similarly, there is no clarification of why the police conduct must be "unworthy" as well as being causative of an offence before a stay of proceedings should be granted.

...

The wealth of case law and academic writing point to three issues in need of resolution:
 –   In what circumstances is it permissible for the State to deploy entrapment techniques?
 –   What types of entrapment are legitimate in the course of an operation?
 –   What remedy is available where the State fails to comply with the legitimate entrapment procedures?
The European Court and Court of Appeal failed to unravel these questions. Although other jurisdictions, most notably the United States, have adopted a defence of entrapment based on a subjective enquiry there is no reason why such a one-dimensional approach should be adopted. The subjective and objective dimensions to the entrapment debate warrant more subtle exposition, since it seems that there are subjective and objective elements in all three issues requiring resolution. There can be no meaningful assessment of either the police conduct or the suspect's response in isolation of the other.

[One approach to a]... more principled base is the decision of the Supreme Court in *Mack*, which recognised these subtleties in proposing a test of entrapment where:
 a)   the authorities provide an opportunity to persons to commit an offence without reasonable suspicion or acting mala fides, ... or
 b)   having a reasonable suspicion or acting in the course of a bona fide inquiry, they go beyond providing an opportunity and induce the commission of an offence.[13]'

Referring back to the underlying principles concerned with the admissibility of evidence, entrapment evidence provides a clear example of the various approaches. Ian Dennis has written that:

'the evidence secured through the investigation of an offence may be wholly reliable in proving that the defendant in fact committed the offence, It is difficult to argue with say, film from a hidden camera, which shows the defendant handing over a quantity of heroin to undercover officers in exchange for money. However, the promotion of a crime that would not otherwise have taken place at all strikes at the core reason for the existence of criminal law. A guilty verdict in such a case cannot function as an expressive message that the values of the criminal law are to be respected if the sole reason for the occurrence of the offence is that it was procured by state officials whose duty is to uphold the law. In this way the state forfeits its moral authority to call for the imposition of blame and punishment of the defendant. Because the moral and expressive functions of the verdict would be undermined by the way the evidence was obtained, it would be right for the court to exclude it.'[14]

Should evidence from entrapment be received because it is reliable? Should it be excluded by way of disciplining the police for engaging in deceit? Does the deceit involved render a conviction morally flawed? A. Ashworth has recently written that:

---

12 (2002) E & P (Jan).
13 (1988) CCC 3d 513, para. 123.
14 I. Dennis, *The Law Of Evidence* (1999), p. 259.

'a disciplinary approach, designed to discourage unacceptable police behaviour has not generally been favoured in the UK. However, the disadvantage of such an approach is that the boundaries of acceptability become unclear. In the absence of any statutory framework or judicial supervision, the police are inclined to engage in ever more sophisticated forms of entrapment until the courts tell them to stop. As our unwritten constitution based on negative liberty enters its final historical moments, it is important that the courts begin to delineate the mechanisms in which the defendant's fundamental right to a fair trial can be positively protected.'[15]

In *R v Smith*,[16] the court was prepared to exclude evidence if it was obtained by the use of an agent provocateur inciting the offence prior to the involvement of the undercover officer who did not incite it. *R v Callaghan*[17] similarly led to the exclusion of evidence where the initial agent provocateur was not called as a witness. The danger in admitting evidence in such cases is that the initial police informer is never subjected to cross-examination at trial, and it is therefore impossible to discover what degree of entrapment was employed. The police prevent and detect crime, is it ever legitimate for them to cause it?[18]

The courts take a much stricter approach to officers targeting an individual not to incite him to commit an offence, but to question him about an offence that has already occurred. In such cases, the statutory procedures for questioning must be complied with. See *R v Stagg*,[19] and *R v Bow Street Magistrates Court, ex p Proulx*.[20]

J. Kleinig has written that:

'the proliferation of undercover operations, although intended to counter the increasing sophistication of criminal activity and to avoid the use of 'strong arm' or unconstitutional tactics by police, may have unpleasant side-effects on our social ethos – how we view and what we expect of each other, our leaders, and so on. Do we want to live in a society in which police engage in the kind of deceptive tactics that we sometimes read about? Maybe we think the cost is worth it: a bit of moral tattiness is not too heavy a price to pay for crime control, particularly if the deception in question is intended to control activities that cause injury, create fear, and erode social trust. But maybe we will find the moral shabbiness of some forms of police deception too threatening to a social self-image that we have, and we would be willing to put up with a higher level of the criminal activity in question, if that is what is at stake.'[21]

Is the law capable of drawing such a distinction with sufficient certainty to be of any practical use to the courts and police officers?

English law has rejected the possibility of a defence of entrapment in the criminal law. See *R v Sang*[22] and the statements of Lord Taylor in *R v Smurthwaite*: 's. 78 has not altered the substantive law, that entrapment or the use of an agent provocateur does not per se afford a defence to a criminal charge.'[23] Whether the issue will need to be reopened in the light of the Human Rights Act 1998 is unclear. Should there be a defence of entrapment in the substantive criminal law rather than a series of ill-defined discretions to exclude evidence?

15 [1999] 10 Arch News 8.
16 [1995] Crim LR 658.
17 [1999] 5 Arch News 2, CA.
18 See A. Ashworth, [2000] 63 MLR 633.
19 (1994) CCC, unreported, 14 September. See D. Ormerod, [1996] Crim LR 863.
20 [2001] 1 All ER 57, DC; [2000] Crim LR 997 and commentary.
21 J. Kleinig, *The Ethics of Policing* (1976), pp. 136–137.
22 Above pp. 351–352.
23 [1994] 1 All ER 898 confirmed by the House of Lords in *R v Loosely* [2001] UKHL 53.

To what extent is it legitimate to rely on mitigation in sentencing as an adequate compensation for the state entrapping someone into committing a crime? English cases have done this: see *R v Tonnessen*[1] where a drug addict was encouraged to deal by *News of the World* journalists; and see the suspension of the sentence of the Earl of Hardwicke where he had been entrapped by the *News of the World*. In that case and the similar one of *R v Shannon*,[2] the Court of Appeal upheld convictions where journalists had incited offences by celebrities with the sole aim of entrapping them.

There are at least now some published guidelines on the technique and its proper limits: The ACPO and Customs and Excise *Public Statement on Standards in Covert Law Enforcement Techniques*[3] states that:

'The principal United Kingdom law enforcement agencies are committed to the maintenance of working practices which observe their obligations under the ECHR. Those working practices seek to achieve a balance between the requirement to work within a defined framework for the safeguarding of civil liberties and the maintenance of a robust approach to the tackling of crime and criminality...

Serious crime and organised criminality are corrosive of civilised society. The growth in the threat from crime has been acknowledged both by Parliament and the courts in the provision of increased powers for law enforcement and in support for the principle of public interest immunity in the defence of both intelligence sources and those sensitive investigative techniques, the revelation of which to determined criminals would undermine the continuing operational effectiveness of the techniques. The law enforcement agencies seek to tackle the consequences of serious crime and organised criminality at several levels simultaneously:

"to mitigate the effects of criminal behaviour and violent disorder which degrade environments and diminish the quality of life whether through the reality or the fear of crime or through the destruction of the ambition and opportunities of the young by the marketing of narcotics; to mitigate the damage done to the administrative, financial and business infrastructure of society by the corruption of legitimate authority and business activity, and by the siphoning of profits; to mitigate the damage done to public confidence in the criminal justice system and to the rule of law by those who intimidate or suborn witnesses, who promote the corruption of law enforcement officers, who exploit weaknesses in national and international jurisdictions and who seek to discover and disable advances in investigative techniques."

The challenge offered to law enforcement agencies is to design and sustain, within the rule of law, preventive and investigative techniques that meet the requirements of each of the described levels. The key to effective law enforcement stratagems is the ability to describe and analyse the nature of the criminal problem....

The following specific commitments to standards give effect to the fundamental ethical precepts set out above:

- **justification** – the law enforcement agencies will establish "sufficient cause", based on a suspect's previous criminal history or on reasonable suspicion of criminal activity or association, before collecting and recording personal information on the suspect in intelligence systems;
- **proportionality** – the "covert techniques" referred to in this document will be applied only where criminal activity is sufficiently serious to justify the degree of intrusion into privacy which the technique entails;
- **necessity** – the "covert techniques" referred to in this document will be applied only where it appears that what the action seeks to achieve could not reasonably be achieved by other means;

1   [1998] 2 Cr App R (S) 217.
2   [2000] Crim LR 1001.
3   (1999) available at www.ncis.org.uk.

- **accuracy** – the provenance, accuracy and value of such information will be assessed and recorded, subject to the proviso that, where a requirement to protect a source's identity arises, access to source identity may be restricted;
- **review** – where authorisation is given to target an individual for the collection of intelligence or evidence, that investigation will be subject to appropriate reviews of the requirement to continue; the agencies do not favour the introduction of independent, external authorisation of covert activity beyond that currently required by law. The volume and speed of activity involving the use of informants, basic surveillance and the exchange of intelligence between agencies make such a proposal impractical. The agencies are, however, committed to scrutiny of adherence to the declared standards;
- **security** – personal information recorded in intelligence systems will be maintained in such a manner as to ensure security and prevent unauthorised disclosure;
- **integrity** – information recorded in digital format will be stored in such a manner as to prevent unauthorised manipulation of the data. . .'

See also *R v Latif and Shahzad*,[4] in which Lord Steyn observed that the judge must weigh in the balance the public interest is ensuring that those that are charge with grave crimes should be tried and competing public interest is not conveying the impression that the court will adopt the approach that the ends justify the means.[5] *R v Pattemore*;[6] *R v Dixon (Paul), R v Mann (Harbel)*;[7] and *R v Lawrence and Nash*.[8] In the last of these cases, convictions for conspiracy to supply cannabis to an undercover police officer were quashed where the officer 'persistently and vigorously pressed the appellant to supply it' and the relevant conversations had not been recorded. It is not always necessary to call the original inciter of the offence if there is an unassailable record of events. There may be good public policy reasons for not calling informers: however, this will leave a missing link in the investigation which cannot be examined orally at trial.

Similarly, the ACPO and Customs and Excise *Code Of Practice* (1999) Part 5, *Undercover Operations*, states that:

'1.4 The term "undercover operations" includes the activity of trained undercover officers, test purchasers and decoys as defined below. Such activity will only be authorised and conducted in accordance with this code of practice.

1.5 Authorisations for undercover operations will only be given in connection with national security, for the prevention or detection of crime, for the maintenance of public order, for the maintenance of community safety, in the case of a significant public interest, or in co-operation with foreign law enforcement agencies in these matters.

1.6 The primary purpose of undercover operations is to secure evidence to bring offenders before the Courts. Such operations may also be conducted in order to gather intelligence in support of the prevention or detection of crime.

1.7 Undercover operations will only be used by the law enforcement agencies where they judge such use to be proportionate to the seriousness of the crime being investigated, and the history and character of the individual(s) concerned.

1.8 Before authorising any undercover operations, authorising officers will take into account the risk of intrusion into privacy of persons other than the specified target of the undercover operation (collateral intrusion). Measures will be taken wherever practicable to avoid collateral intrusion.

1.9 All undercover operatives will be trained to approved standards.

---

4 [1996] 1 All ER 353.
5 At 361.
6 [1994] Crim LR 836, CA (Cr D).
7 [1995] Crim LR 647, CA.
8 (1993) unreported, cited by G. Robertson QC in 'Entrapment Evidence' [1994] Crim LR 805 at 811.

1.10 The objectives of an undercover operation may not be furthered by attempts to incite the commission of offences, which would not otherwise have been committed, nor by attempts to entrap offenders who were not otherwise disposed to the commission of such offences.

1.11 The undercover officer or test purchaser may be a party to the commission of criminal offences only within the limits recognised by case law and specified by the authorising officer.

Undercover officer means: a specially trained law enforcement officer working under direction in an authorised investigation in which the officer's identity is concealed from third parties by the use of an alias and false identity so as to enable:

- infiltration of an existing criminal conspiracy;
- the arrest of a suspected criminal or criminals;
- the countering of a threat to national security, or a significant threat to community safety or the public interest.'[9]

NOTES

1. Can the end justify the means?

2. As in other areas of police powers the regulation of police conduct is increasingly governed by Codes of Conduct rather than primary statutory material. Can the courts ensure the same accountability of the police?

9   www.ncis.co.uk/PDFS/COPsection5.pdf.

CHAPTER 4

Public order

1 Introduction[1]

The liberty of the people to assemble in public in order to express their views on political matters is generally regarded as an essential element in a free and open society. It is recognised in such international standards as Art. 11 of the ECHR [2] and Art. 21, ICCPR. K. Ewing and C. Gearty distinguish between primary civil liberties – those which deal with the right of the individual to participate directly in the process of government – and secondary liberties – those which deal with the right to influence the government, including such matters as freedom of expression and assembly. [3] Public order law often involves both types of liberty. The extent to which they may be exercised in this country depends partly on the existing state of the law, and partly on the way in which the law is enforced by police, prosecutors and courts. As this chapter shows, there are many ways in which public meetings or processions may fall foul of the law, both civil and criminal. Just as important is what is likely to happen in practice. On this latter point it is extremely difficult to generalise. Much (many would say too much) depends on 'the policeman on the spot'. [4] Moreover, the attitude of the authorities seems to vary according to current political circumstances. The more stable the political system, the greater is the toleration of political protest. As the effectiveness, or likely or even feared effectiveness, of protest increases, so

---

1 The main works cited in this chapter are: *Williams*: D.G.T. Williams, *Keeping the Peace* (1967); *Brownlie*: M. Supperstone, *Brownlie's Law of Public Order and National Security* (2nd edn, 1981); J. C. Smith, *Smith and Hogan: The Criminal Law* (9th edn, 1999). K. D. Ewing and C. A. Gearty, *The Struggle for Civil Liberties* (2000); Works published since the Public Order Act 1986 include R. Card, *Public Order Law* (2000); A. T. H. Smith, *Offences against Public Order* (1987) (hereafter cited as *Smith*); A. Sherr, *Freedom of Protest, Public Order and the Law* (1989); and P. Thornton, *Public Order Law* (1987). See also: R. Benewick and T. Smith (eds.), *Direct Action and Democratic Politics* (1972); V. T. Bevan, [1979] PL 163; D. Feldman, *Civil Liberties and Human Rights in England and Wales*; W. Finnie, 'Public Order Law in Scotland and England 1980–1990' in Finnie, *et al.*, *Edinburgh Essays in Public Law* (1991), pp. 251–277; A. D. Grunis, (1978) 56 Can Bar Rev 393; E. R. H. Ivamy, (1949) CLP 183; P. E. Kilbride and P. T. Burns, (1966) 2 NZULR 1; O. Hood Phillips, (1970) 86 LQR 1; A. T. H. Smith, [1984] Crim LR 643; C. Townshend, *Making the Peace* (1993); R. Vogler, *Reading the Riot Act* (1991); D. G. T. Williams, [1970] CLJ 96; [1974] Crim LR 635–8; (1975) 1 UNSW Law Journal 94. On the *White Paper*, see P. Scraton, (1985) 12 JLS 385. On the 1986 Act, see D. Bonner and R. Stone, [1987] PL 449; Symposium, [1987] Crim LR 153ff; J. Driscoll, [1987] JSWL 280. See also D. Gallighan, 'Preserving Public Protest: The Legal Approach' in L. Gostin, (ed.) *Civil Liberties in Conflict* (1988); P. A. J. Waddington, *Policing Citizens: Authority and Rights* (1999) Chap. 3; and D. Waddington, 'Key Issues and Controversies' in C. Critcher and D. Waddington (eds.) *Policing Public Order: Theoretical and Practical Issues* (1996); N. Whitty, T. Murphy and S. Livingstone, *Civil Liberties Law: The Human Rights Era* (2001). The constitutional status of public protest in Britain and the US is discussed by D. G. Barnum at [1977] PL 310 and (1981) 29 Am J Comparative Law 59.

2 Above, Chap. 1.

3 Op. cit., p.18.

4 See *Williams*, Chap. 5, and see the articles in R. Reiner, *Policing*, vol II (1996) Part I on police discretion.

toleration is reduced: the law is enforced more rigorously, and may be strengthened.[5] In addition to being concerned with the mechanics of protest (how many protestors? where are they? are they disorderly? are they violent?), the authorities may be more inclined to focus their attention on the content of the protest (is it seditious? does it incite to disaffection?).

Professors Ewing and Gearty have recently questioned the extent to which civil liberties have been accurately defined in English law, even in the course of academic scholarship. Much of their discussion is based on public order issues where they comment:

> 'the tendency to conflate civil liberties with human rights [is] deeply and profoundly mistaken: the two are different disciplines serving different and sometimes contradictory goals ... the main purpose of civil liberties is to promote political participation and that as such it is a discipline which encourages the development of an active political culture: it is about freedom *to* rather than freedom *from*.' [6]

Do you agree? Consider throughout the chapter the extent to which the courts and the proliferation of public order legislation seeks to support such liberties.[7] Can a clear division between rights and liberties be drawn, particularly in a public order context? Is there a freedom to stand and protest in public or a freedom from arrest in doing so?

At present, most of the law in the context of political protest relates to its 'public order' aspect. A major theme is the control of the advocacy or use of violence as a means of obtaining political change (in other words the prevention of breaches of the peace).[8] Another theme is the protection of other legitimate interests of citizens (e.g. the right to use the highway; the right not to have an unwanted crowd gathering in one's own front garden).

This concentration on the 'public order' aspect has three consequences. First, the control of political assemblies is seen as part of the general police function of keeping the peace. The problems posed by disorderly political demonstrators are regarded as analogous to those posed by vandals, quarrelling neighbours, 'mods' and 'rockers', 'football hooligans' and drunks. The laws applicable are the same for all. It is open to argument whether the law should operate in the same way in relation to all the categories mentioned, although this is a point on which a very firm view was expressed in *R v Caird*.[9]

> 'In considering laws relating to public disorder, we meet a problem of identification: how are we to identify "public order law"? The idea of "public disorder" can extend to almost any behaviour which violates criminal law and which can therefore be constructed as a "law and order" problem. Thus, it incorporates not only instances such as violent behaviour or vandalism, which affect public order in the "simple sense" of peace and tranquility in public places; but also obscenity, blasphemy, indecency, behaviour seen as affecting "public morals" or "public decency", and political acts of treason and sedition, all of which adversely affect public order in a broader sense.' [10]

Secondly, by checking violent protest, it is possible that the law checks the very kind of protest which is most likely to obtain fundamental change. The justifications

---

5 On the fragility of the Rule of Law in times of state emergency, see K. D. Ewing and C. A. Gearty, op. cit.
6 Ewing and Gearty, op. cit., p. 33.
7 For a discussion of the theoretical issues relating to civil disobedience, rights of free speech and constitutional principle, see T. R. S. Allan, [1996] CLJ 89. See also A. Sherr, *Freedom of Protest, Public Order and the Law* (1989).
8 See pp. 460–471 and 526–541.
9 (1970) 54 Cr App Rep 499 (below, p. 504).
10 N. Lacey and C. Wells, *Reconstructing Criminal Law: Text and Materials* (2nd edn, 1998), p. 115.

advanced are that any violence in society is unacceptable, and that violence in this context distorts the 'proper' democratic political process for obtaining reform.

'protesters who meekly assemble to hear speeches protesting at some grievance are not only acting lawfully, they are acting virtuously for they are actively engaged in the political process – the right peacefully to protest or mobilise political opinion is the quintessence of citizenship.
. . . [but it is that political dimension] that makes public disorder ambiguous: any crowd activity could be an assertion of political rectitude, an understandable albeit mistaken response to provocation, or an orgy of mindless violence, depending on which interpretation ultimately prevails.' [11]

A recent example of the control of protest is the reform of the public order laws to protect against the increasingly violent campaign conducted by some animal rights protestors. [12] How important is the right to dissent with force?

Thirdly, laws which seek to maintain public order are easier to justify than those which impinge directly on freedom of expression. Indeed, free expression is essential to the operation of those democratic processes which the maintenance of order is supposed to facilitate. However, laws preserving public order may have significant effects on freedom of expression (1) if they are enforced discriminatorily according to the nature of the political opinions held by particular individuals; [13] (2) if they interfere with the *effective* communication of views; [14] and (3) in so far as the use of words which incite or provoke violence is proscribed. [15]

The law relating to public order was modified and extended by the Public Order Act 1986 [16] and by the Criminal Justice and Public Order Act 1994, by the Crime and Disorder Act 1998 and again by the Criminal Justice and Police Act 2001. In addition, the particular menace of 'stalking' was tackled by the Protection from Harassment Act 1997, and continued efforts to combat football hooliganism can be seen in the Football (Offences and Disorder) Act 1999 and the Football (Disorder) Act 2000. Each of these has proved controversial in its own way. In these Acts, the government has proscribed a wide range of conduct, but, predictably, there has been no attempt to define liberties. The list of arrestable offences grows ever longer. The 1994 Act significantly extends the ambit of the criminal law in seeking to control, *inter alia*, acts of trespass and acts that disrupt lawful activities. The 1994 Act was particularly controversial, attracting opposition from such diverse quarters as members of the House of Lords, 'clergy, lawyers, police, MPs, civil rights groups, ecology groups and the disaffected young'. [17] Mike Bennett, then chairman of the Metropolitan Police Federation, described the public order provisions as unworkable, being 'legislation

---

11 P. A. J. Waddington, *Policing Citizens: Authority and Rights* (1999) pp. 66–67.
12 See the discussion in the Home Office Consultation Document *Animal Rights Extremism: Government Strategy* (2001). See *The Times,* 29 August 2000, and Home Office Press Release 26 April 2001: www.homeoffice.gov.uk.
13 As has frequently been alleged: see R Kidd, *British Liberty in Danger* (1940) Chap. 5; B. Cox, *Civil Liberties in Britain* (1975) Chap. 1 and see Ewing and Gearty, op. cit., n 5.
14 See, e.g. *Duncan v Jones* [1936] 1 KB 218, DC, below, p. 531, and *DPP v Redmond-Bate,* below, p. 526.
15 See e.g. *Wise v Dunning* [1902] 1 KB 167, DC, below, p. 526, Public Order Act 1986, ss. 4, 4A, 5, below, pp. 481–504; the law of sedition and incitement to disaffection.)
16 This was preceded by the *Review of the Public Order Act 1936 and related legislation* (Green Paper, Cmnd. 7891, 1980); the Fifth Report from the Home Affairs Committee, Session 1979–80, *The Law Relating to Public Order* (1979–80 HC 756: the Committee had a Conservative majority and divided on party lines on many issues); the Law Commission's Report, *Criminal Law: Offences Relating to Public Order* (Law Com No. 123, 1983) and the White Paper, *Review of Public Order Law* (Cmnd. 9510, 1985). Hereafter these are cited as *Green Paper, HAC Report, Law Com No. 123* and *White Paper.*
17 *Independent,* 4 November 1994.

directed against a certain section of the population ... people whose lifestyle, culture and attitude to life differs from other people'. On the day it was passed, 'other campaigners started a series of rolling protests across the country ... with "mass trespass" – a new offence created under the Act – at road construction sites'. [18] The following day, five people climbed on the roof of Westminster Hall in protest against the Act. [19] The most recent moves have been to tackle low-level antisocial behaviour, although these have often involved over-hasty reactions with little consideration for broader implications on civil liberties. The Crime and Disorder Act 1998 introduced novel powers for courts to make 'anti-social behaviour orders' in an effort to combat repeated acts of harassment and disorder on housing estates. The Act also includes a series of racially aggravated offences where assaults, public order offences or damage are caused with racial hostility. The Protection from Harassment Act 1997 is a very specific piece of legislation designed to tackle a particular problem. Unfortunately, the difficulty in defining 'stalking' behaviour means that the Act has broad provisions which impact on protestors. These Acts contain many examples of the recent emphasis on legislating to combat persistent low level disorder.

The Criminal Justice and Police Act 2001 contains several examples of the willingness to expand police powers, sometimes leaving incredible discretion to the officer. In particular, the new fixed penalty notice scheme which is contained in Part I empowers an officer to issue a fixed penalty notice (i.e. fixed fine) to any person he has reasonable grounds to believe to be committing a specified offence (including being drunk in a public place and causing harassment, alarm and distress contrary to s. 5 of the Public Order Act 1986 (see below)). This again has significant implications for protestors. The Fixed Penalty Notice is not a crime and no criminal record results from paying it – merely 'an opportunity to discharge liability' (what liability? is there a crime or tort proved against D?). The recipient may contest the notice and demand a trial, in which case the full penalty for the offence is available on conviction. Failure to pay the fine may lead to the imposition of a fine of 1.5 times the penalty. [20] Will such powers withstand challenge under the Human Rights Act 1998 and ECHR? [21] It is notable that a further element of discretion exists in that the Home Secretary can fix the level of the penalty up to the maximum of one quarter of the maximum fine for the offence. [1]

Other powers in the 2001 Act include measures to prevent consumption of alcohol in public places. Local authorities will be able to designate areas in which it will be an offence to consume alcohol after having been told not to do so by an officer (s. 13). The police officer will have a power to dispose of alcohol confiscated (s. 12). The Act also introduces broader offences of selling alcohol to minors and for imposing closure orders on licensed premises to prevent disturbance. These are good examples of the recent trend for creating criminal sanctions for non-compliance with police instructions. Other examples considered in the chapter come from the 1994 Act and the Crime and Disorder Act 1998.

This chapter also examines the development of police organisation, equipment and tactics in dealing with disorder.

---

18 Ibid.
19 *The Times*, 5 November 1994
20 For comment on the provisions see P. Tain, (2001) SJ 548.
21 See further the Home Office Consultation Paper *Reducing Public Disorder: The Role of Fixed Penalty Notices* (2000).
 1 And can amend by order subject to affirmative resolution the offences for which the penalty notice applies.

The Red Lion Square Disorders of 15 June 1974:Report of Inquiry by the Rt. Hon. Lord Scarman OBE (Cmnd. 5919, 1975)

First principles

5. Amongst our fundamental human rights there are, without doubt, the rights of peaceful assembly and public protest and the right to public order and tranquillity. Civilised living collapses – it is obvious – if public protest becomes violent protest or public order degenerates into the quietism imposed by successful oppression. But the problem is more complex than a choice between two extremes – one, a right to protest whenever and wherever you will and the other, a right to continuous calm upon our streets unruffled by the noise and obstructive pressure of the protesting procession. A balance has to be struck, a compromise found that will accommodate the exercise of the right to protest within a framework of public order which enables ordinary citizens, who are not protesting, to go about their business and pleasure without obstruction or inconvenience. The fact that those who at any one time are concerned to secure the tranquillity of the streets are likely to be the majority must not lead us to deny the protesters their opportunity to march: the fact that the protesters are desperately sincere and are exercising a fundamental human right must not lead us to overlook the rights of the majority.

6. This Inquiry has been concerned to discover where the balance should be struck, and the role of the police in maintaining it. Indiscipline amongst demonstrators, heavy-handed police reaction to disorder are equally mischievous: for each can upset the balance. Violent demonstrators by creating public disorder infringe a fundamental human right which belongs to the rest of us: excessively violent police reaction to public disorder infringes the rights of the protesters. The one and the other are an affront to civilised living.

The role of the police

7. The police are not to be required in any circumstances to exercise political judgment. Their role is the maintenance of public order—no more, and no less. When the National Front marches, the police have no concern with their political message; they will intervene only if the circumstances are such that a breach of the peace is reasonably apprehended. Even if the message be 'racist', it is not for the police to 'ban the march' or compel it to disperse unless public order is threatened. If, of course, the message appears to infringe the race relations legislation, the police have a duty to report the facts so that consideration may be given to subsequent prosecution: moreover in such circumstances a senior police officer, accompanying the march, might think it wise to warn the organisers of the march that, if it proceeds with its slogans, he will report the fact. But it is vital, if the police are to be kept out of political controversy, that in a public order situation their sole immediate concern is, and is seen to be, with public order.

The current law and its application can only be fully appreciated when set in the context of public disorder incidents of the 1980s. These have influenced the development of the legislation and the manner in which public order is policed in the UK. This is not to ignore the significance of the numerous earlier civil liberties struggles within the field of public order. [2]

2 See Ewing and Gearty, op. cit. For sociological studies of these incidents of public disorder, including case studies, see G. Gaskell and R. Benewick (eds.), *The Crowd in Contemporary Britain* (1987); D. Waddington, et al., *Flashpoints: Studies in Public Disorder* (1989); D. Waddington (ed.), *Contemporary Issues in Public Disorder* (1992); E.G. Dunning, et al., *The Social Roots of Football Hooliganism* (1987); P. Joyce, 'A decade of disorder' (1992) 8 Policing 232; M. Keith, *Race, Riots and Policing* (1993); P. A. J. Waddington, *Liberty and Order* (1994). The use of protest by the peace movement is described in J. Dewar, et al. (eds.), *Nuclear Weapons, the Peace Movement and the Law* (1986), Part III and J. Hinton, *Protests and Visions: Peace Politics in Twentieth-Century Britain* (1989). For comparative perspectives, see J. Roach and J. Thomaneck (eds.), *Police and Public Order in Europe* (1985) and J. Brewer, et al., *The Police, Public Order and the State* (1988); Sherr, op. cit., p. 51.

2 Demonstrations and riots

In general, contrary to the popular image, in the period 1900 to 1975 there was a marked and generally downward trend in the number of violent disorders, from a high point in the first two decades of the century.[3] The same point is made in respect of industrial disputes by Geary.[4]

In 1974, a serious public order incident at Red Lion Square led to an Inquiry chaired by Lord Scarman. Prior to the Red Lion Square disorder there had been only 54 incidents of protest giving rise to disorder (with a total of 623 arrests) in the previous three years. The MPC Report[5] attributed such low rates of disorder, arrest and injury to the 'unique relationship' between police and protestors who rely on mutual goodwill:

'13. Political demonstrations seem to give satisfaction in the main to those taking part. The public as a whole are usually not interested unless affected by inconvenience or aroused by disorder and violence. Nevertheless, the right to hold them is much valued and jealously preserved. In the event of violence there is usually much comment on the extent to which the police exercised or failed to exercise control. Speculation as to whether the police should have prohibited or regulated a political demonstration usually betrays a lack of knowledge of the law or of the difficulties of applying it. No useful purpose is achieved by prohibitions or regulations incapable of enforcement, or in respect of which judicial penalties are likely to be slight. Demonstrators who can rely on massive support, such as The Committee of 100 in the sixties, are unlikely to be deterred by such restrictions and political extremists are likely to welcome them. For both, disregard or defiance is sure to achieve maximum publicity at very little cost ....

16. When considering what action to take in respect of the declared intention to hold extremist demonstrations in support of any political persuasion, police observe scrupulously the principle declared to the House of Commons by a former Home Secretary:—

"If this is indeed a free country and we are free people, a man is just as much entitled to profess the Fascist philosophy as any other, and he is perfectly entitled to proclaim it and expound it so long as he does not exceed the reasonable bounds which are set by law."

18. The Metropolitan Police have always been disinclined to seek the approval of the Secretary of State for an Order prohibiting political processions for a specified period on the grounds that this encourages extremist minority groups to threaten violence with the object of achieving the suppression of opposition opinion. We believe that attempts by coercion or force to suppress free speech are not only wrong but unlawful and that behaviour of that kind must be resisted no matter what the inconvenience or cost. To give way to such threats is not just to defer to mob-rule but to encourage it ....'

Since the Red Lion Square disorder there have been numerous other serious incidents – some localised to riots on housing estates, some national trade union disputes (e.g. the miners' strike). In 1981 there was rioting in many parts of the country.

Report of Her Majesty's Chief Inspector of Constabulary for 1981 (1981–82 HC 463)

The civil disturbances
8.1 1981 saw the most serious outbreaks of public disorder in England and Wales since the end of the Second World War. The first disturbances took place at Brixton in April. No other outbreaks occurred at that time.

---

3   See E. Dunning et al., 'Violent disorders in twentieth-century Britain', in G. Gaskell and R. Benewick (eds.), *The Crowd in Contemporary Britain* (1987).
4   R. Geary, *Policing Industrial Disputes* (1985).
5   See Sir Robert Mark CPM, 'The Metropolitan Police and political demonstrations' (Appendix 8 to the Report of the Commissioner of Police of the Metropolis for the year 1974).

8.2 In July, however, disturbances occurred in many parts of the country. The first outbreak outside London began on 3 July in Toxteth, in Liverpool. A group of officers were attacked whilst attempting to arrest a youth believed to have stolen a motor cycle, and had to call for assistance. In the resulting struggle one officer sustained a broken nose. Following a warning of further trouble on the following day the police, including reinforcements from the Greater Manchester Police, were placed on standby. The disorders began in the evening, when the police were attacked with bricks and other missiles, including petrol bombs. A number of buildings were set alight. The area was then cordoned off and order restored. A reduced presence was maintained on 5 July, but was increased following warnings of further trouble. At about 5pm, some 100 youths created disorder, which spread and soon became a concerted attack on the police. Street lighting was extinguished, oil was poured onto the road and petrol used to ignite it. Buildings were set on fire and police attempting to cordon off the area and contain the disorders were ferociously attacked: stolen vehicles, including mechanical diggers and a bulldozer, were driven at their cordons. The fire service was unable to enter the area in order to fight the fires, and the occupants of an old peoples' home had to be evacuated because of neighbouring fires. To prevent further damage and violence, the Chief Constable authorised the use of CS which resulted in the dispersal of the crowds. This was the first use on the British mainland of CS to control public disorder. Further serious outbreaks of disorder occurred on a number of nights.

8.3 At Moss Side, in Manchester the violence spread over a number of areas for the three nights of 7–9 July. A typical series of incidents occurred on 8 July, when about 100 youths set fire to a shop and stoned the fire appliance which arrived to deal with the fire. After setting fire to neighbouring shops, the gang moved to a nearby shopping precinct, looted shops and set them on fire. Similar incidents occurred elsewhere in the area but police reinforcements arrived and the area was calm by 5am. The next day the police successfully adopted positive tactics. Sixty vans, each containing 11 officers equipped with protective equipment patrolled the area, dispersing groups before they could create serious disorder. Although some shops were damaged there were no major incidents; over 150 arrests were made and 2 police officers received minor injuries.

8.4 These disorders were the most serious which occurred outside London: their most worrying feature was the savagery of the attacks made upon the police. There were also, however, many other incidents of public disorder in other parts of the country between 3–15 July, among the most serious being those in the West Midlands, Bedfordshire, Hampshire, Kent, Leicestershire, West Yorkshire, Nottinghamshire and Derbyshire.

NOTES

1. These disturbances were foreshadowed by serious disorder in 1979 in Southall[6] and arising out of meetings held during the General Election by the National Front in Leicester, West Bromwich and Bradford.[7] On 2 April 1980, there was serious disorder in the St. Paul's district of Bristol.[8] C. Harlow[9] noted the inadequacy of inquests and the police complaints system as mechanisms for investigating events of this kind.

6 See *Southall 23 April 1979:The Report of the Unofficial Committee of Enquiry* (NCCL, 1980); *The Death of Blair Peach: The Supplementary Report of the Unofficial Committee of Inquiry* (NCCL, 1980); C. Harlow, [1980] PL 241.
7 See the *Report of H M Chief Inspector of Constabulary for 1979* (1979–80 HC 725), p. 50.
8 See 983 HC Deb, 28 April 1980 ,cols. 971–981; M. Kettle and L. Hodges, *Uprising!* (1982), Chap. 1.
9 [1980] PL 241.

2. The Brixton riots were the subject of an inquiry by Lord Scarman under the power in what was then the Police Act 1964, s. 32. [10] He concluded that the riots were not premeditated, not race riots, although having a strong racial element, and were largely caused by the hostility between black youths and the police as a result of a breakdown of communication with the community and a loss of confidence in the police. [11] An increase in crime, especially mugging, had been met by the deployment of officers of the Special Patrol Group, and this in turn provoked the hostility of young black people. Tension increased further as a result of 'Operation Swamp 81' in which over a hundred officers (not SPG) were deployed in Lambeth to detect and arrest burglars and robbers, relying on powers to stop and search for unlawfully obtained property under s. 66 of the Metropolitan Police Act 1839. [12] This was done without any warning to community leaders or local police officers. Overall Lord Scarman found that the Metropolitan Police were not racist although prejudice did manifest itself in the behaviour of some officers. [13] The conclusion was that the police had not over-reacted in handling the disorders. Broadly, 'the police response to the disorders, once they broke out, is to be commended, not criticised'. He recommended (*inter alia*) that there should be an urgent study of ways of improving ethnic minority recruitment into the regular police (but no quota of places reserved for ethnic minorities and no lowering of standards for recruitment); police training in community relations and in the handling of public disorder should be improved; it should be understood throughout the police that the normal penalty for racially prejudiced behaviour is dismissal; methods of policing, especially in inner city areas, should be re-examined; and arrangements for consultation between police and local community should be improved. [14] He also drew attention to failures in social policy concerning inner cities and ethnic minorities:

'there is a lack of a sufficiently well co-ordinated and directed programme for combating the problem of racial disadvantage. It is clear from the evidence of ethnic minority deprivation I have received that, if the balance of racial disadvantage is to be redressed, positive action is required.' [15]

---

10 *The Brixton Disorders 10–12 April 1981* (Cmnd. 8427, 1981).
   On the Scarman Report see (1981) 78 LS Gaz 1443–1445; G. J. Zellick, [1982] PL 1 (on Part VII, concerning the law reform proposals); S. Saeed, [1982] PL 198; (1981–82) IX(3) *New Community* 344–377 (various authors); (1982) 53 *Political Quarterly* 111–152 (various authors); M. Cain and S. Sadigh, (1982) 9 JLS 87; R. Baldwin and R. Kinsey, *Police Powers and Politics* (1982) Chap. 8; J. Benyon (ed.), *Scarman and After* (1984); 13 HC Deb cols. 891–900 and 425 HL Deb cols. 769–778 (25 November 1981); 13 HC Deb 26 November 1981 col. 1009 ff (debate on law and order); 14 HC Deb 10 December 1981 col. 1001; 426 HL Deb 4 February 1982 cols. 1396–1474.
   On the Toxteth riots see M. Jefferson, 'The Toxteth Riots: A Select Bibliography' [1983] V(2)Liverpool LR 203; P. J. Waller, (1981–82) IX(3) *New Community* 344; and M. Brogden *The Police: Autonomy and Consent* (1982): Postscript by A. and M. Brogden (pp. 239–250). For a survey of the views and experiences of male residents in relation to the disturbances of July 1981 in Handsworth, Birmingham, see P. Southgate in *Public Disorder* (Home Office Research Study No. 72, 1982, Part II). Part I (by S. Field) is a review of research concerning Urban Disorders in Britain and America.
   The 1981 riots generally are analysed by D. Cowell (et al) (eds.), *Policing the Riots* (1982); M. Kettle and L. Hodges, *Uprising!* (1982); M. Keith, *Race, Riots and Policing* (1993); J. Lea and J. Young, 'Urban Violence and Political Marginalisation: The Riots in Britain; Summer 1981' (1982) I (3) Critical Social Policy 59.
11 See para. 8.13; see also B. Bowling *Violent Racism* (1998).
12 Above, p. 213.
13 pp. 127–134.
14 See above. Compare the recommendation of the Lawrence Inquiry, Chap. 2 above, p. 144.
15 Para. 8.50.

Finally, he considered a number of proposals for law reform.

3. C. Unsworth [16] regards the riots as:

'not sudden explosions of violence within normally peaceful and harmonious communities, but a temporary cluster of upsurges punctuating a chronic reality of tension and aggression in the inner city.... The escalation ... may be attributed to the intersection of ... several developments ... provocative policing, insecurity and increasing resistance in the black communities, and traditions of resistance in white working class youth exacerbated by steeply and disproportionately rising unemployment.'[17]

See also J. Rex,[18] who brings out differences in the background to the riots in the different parts of England. Statistics of charges arising out of the riots were given in the Home Office Statistical Bulletin No. 20/82.[19]

4. Large scale public disorder leads to enormous pressure on the courts: especially the magistrates' courts. There are dangers that as a consequence cases will not be given the individual consideration that would normally be expected in relation to applications for bail and legal aid, determining guilt and in sentencing.[20] For example, the Nottinghamshire Law Society expressed concern at the procedure adopted by the police and Nottingham City Magistrates' Court in dealing with cases arising from street disturbances in Nottingham in July 1981.[1]

The next major influence on public order legislation and policing was the miners' strike, which was to alter radically policing practices and public perceptions of policing; particularly policing of public disorder.

Report of Her Majesty's Chief Inspector of Constabulary for 1984 (1984–85 HC 469)

PUBLIC ORDER

General

8.1 ... the NUM dispute dominated public order policing in 1984, and was the greatest challenge to the police capacity to deal with disorder since the civil disturbances in 1981. In some ways its presented a more gruelling test of determination and stamina as the months continued and the overall levels of disorder did not significantly decrease. The largest concentration of demonstrators was at Mansfield on 14 May when 12,000 attended an NUM rally. In the disorder that followed, several hundred of those who had attended threw bricks and bottles at the police and attacked others as well, including an ITV crew who were filming the incident. More than 1,000 officers, some mounted officers among them, were deployed to deal with the disorder: 87 arrests were made and 88 officers were injured. On 29 and 30 May and 1 June thousands of pickets gathered at the Orgreave coking plant to try to prevent convoys of coke-carrying lorries from leaving the works. The attempts were unsuccessful but, over the 3 days, there was considerable violence as bricks and petrol bombs were thrown at the police. In all there were more than 100 arrests and more than 50 police injuries. On 18 June 10,000

16 'The Riots of 1981: Popular Violence and the Politics of Law and Order' (1982) 9 JLS 63.
17 p. 71.
18 'The 1981 urban riots in Britain' (1982) 6 Int J Urban and Regional Research 99.
19 See (1982) 132 NLJ 977.
20 These difficulties have been reflected throughout modern times; see K. D. Ewing and C. A. Gearty, op. cit.
1 See (1982) 79 LS Gaz 102; Correspondence: [1982] Crim LR 255; (1982) 132 NLJ 1; (1982) 146 JPN 64. See, generally, *LAG Bulletin*, September 1981, p. 199; December 1981, p. 275; November 1982 pp. 5, 10–15. For criticism of the operation of magistrates' courts dealing with cases arising out of the miners' strike, see Legal Action, August 1984, p. 9 and September 1984 pp. 4–5; S. McCabe and P. Wallington, *The Police, Public Order and Civil Liberties* (1988), Chap. 7.

pickets demonstrated at Orgreave and again the ensuing violence was such that mounted officers with shields and helmets had to be deployed to disperse the crowds. The incident caused 28 police injuries and led to 93 arrests.

8.2 In addition to these instances of particularly serious disorders, there were many occasions on which large numbers of pickets congregated outside collieries and elsewhere, and the tactics adopted included not just missile-throwing but the building of barricades, the spilling of oil and nails on the roads and the placing of tripwires. In the first stages of the dispute such picketing was largely in Nottinghamshire as, for example, when on 9 April 2,000 pickets demonstrated at Babbington colliery, but as the return to work spread more widely, other police force areas also faced disorder. On 2 November, for example, 3 police force areas had sites which were the targets for more than 1,000 demonstrators – Arkwright in Derbyshire, Woolley in West Yorkshire and Steetley Quarry in Durham. On other occasions pickets tried to block major routes such as the A1/M by moving slowly in convoys of large numbers. The continuing scenes of public disorder, of which the above are just a few examples, took place against a background of individual acts of criminal damage, assault and intimidation in connection with the dispute, and were on such a scale that on some days more than 8,000 officers were deployed on mutual aid. Every police force in England and Wales either provided or received mutual aid, and by 21 December the dispute had led to 1,294 police injuries and 8,945 arrests.

8.3 By comparison, the anti-nuclear demonstrations were significantly smaller in scale....

8.4 Despite the different tactics and approaches adopted in the various forms of demonstration and picketing described above, the police forces continued to rely on the traditional methods of public order policing in this country, using the minimum of force to deal with violent disorder, and seeking to maintain order by co-operation and agreement whenever possible. For the most part demonstrations and pickets were policed using officers wearing ordinary uniform and in close contact with the demonstrators. Protective equipment such as overalls, shields and helmets were used where necessary, and the horses of the mounted branches again proved their worth in dispersing crowds of disorderly demonstrators. Ironically for an operation which involved such large-scale mutual aid, the policing of the NUM dispute also demonstrated chief officers' awareness of the importance of policing communities by local officers as far as possible.

Report of Her Majesty's Chief Inspector of Constabulary for 1985 (1985–86 HC 437)

NUM dispute

8.2 The decision in March by the National Union of Mineworkers to return to work ended one of the longest and most bitter industrial disputes ever seen in this country. The public order problems presented to the police were unprecedented in their scale and duration. The early and middle phases of the dispute, characterised by mass picketing and by attempts to stop supplies reaching steelworks, were covered in my report for 1984. In the final phase, as miners began to return to work at collieries which had been strike-bound, bitterness between working and striking miners intensified. There were more instances of attempted intimidation involving, in some cases, personal assaults and attacks on homes. The main centres of violence were in Yorkshire, Northumberland and Durham and, to a lesser extent, in South Wales. The role of the police throughout the dispute remained constant: to maintain public order, to enforce the criminal law and to ensure that those who wished to work or otherwise to go about their lawful business could do so. Despite physical discomfort and inevitable domestic upheaval, the police sought throughout to maintain the rule of law. I was heartened by the overall level of professionalism which was displayed.

8.3 The success of the police in meeting the formidable challenges of the dispute undoubtedly owes much to the effectiveness of the mutual aid arrangements which enabled over 7,000 officers to be deployed for sustained periods on such duties. Despite misunderstanding and misrepresentation of its roles, the National Reporting Centre efficiently fulfilled its function of co-ordinating requests from Chief Officers for mutual aid. The more professional arrangements for public order training and tactics, which had followed the inner-city riots of

1981, meant that the police were much better able to handle the disorder. Protective equipment again proved its worth. It was notable that, despite the severity of the disorders, the police were able to cope without resort to the use of CS smoke, water cannon and similar equipment. It is unlikely that other police forces in Europe would have been able to cope with such disorder without the use of much more aggressive measures. I have mentioned elsewhere, however, that if the scale of violence increases in these situations the use of this type of equipment may be inevitable.

8.4 In 1985 the dispute led to a further 96 police injuries and 863 arrests. The totals for the whole dispute were 1,390 and 9,808 respectively.

8.5 The dispute also took its toll on ordinary policing throughout the country but it is not possible to say what effect, if any, the dispute had on national crime figures. The financial and resource consequences were severe, despite the scale of central assistance, and there were increased stress and welfare implications for those officers left in forces due to additional workloads and extended hours of duty.

NOTES

1. Peter Wallington's 'overview' was as follows: [2]

'The policing of the dispute has attracted strong comments, many almost as partisan as the positions of the protagonists to the dispute itself. The police deserve much of the praise they received for undertaking a task of such daunting magnitude and complexity. Many of the criticisms of their behaviour, unfortunately, are also deserved, and the police are not well served by the crude loyalty of some of their supporters. But the real issue for those concerned with the lessons of the policing of the dispute was whether the police role was a proper one. Effectively they filled the vacuum created by the failure of the N.C.B. and others to use the civil law; effectively they became, wittingly or otherwise, the agency by which the strike was contained and eventually broken. How far this was an inexorable product of the circumstances, and in particular the strike leaders' own tactical choices, will continue to be a matter of controversy.

The police were given whatever resources they needed to preserve law and order and access to the pits. This enabled them to make the choice to preserve order by containment or prevention of picketing. With fewer resources it might in some cases have been necessary, and would certainly have been lawful, to preserve the peace by preventing individual returning miners from attempting to pass through picket lines. Resources enabled a choice to be made as to whose activities were to be curtailed, even (certainly in the case of the operation of a blanket turn-back policy) whose lawful activities were to be curtailed. Those critics of the police who argue that they took a partisan position can at least point to legal authority that would have justified a different approach. It is scarcely conceivable in the political climate of the time that the alternative would have been adopted as a matter of policy, but that it was avoided at the cost of serious reductions in the level of policing in much of the country suggests a conscious choice.'

2. For statistics of the miners' dispute see McCabe and Wallington.[3] In England and Wales, 9,808 people were arrested, of whom 7,917 (81%) were charged with over 10,000 offences, including conduct likely to cause a breach of the peace (4,107); obstructing a constable (1,682); criminal damage (1,019); obstructing the highway (640); unlawful

2   'Policing the Miners' Strike' (1985) 14 ILJ 145, 1591. For other appraisals, from varying standpoints, of the policing of the miners' strike, see B. Fine and R. Millar (eds.), *Policing the Miners' Strike* (1985); P. Scraton and P. Thomas (eds.), *The State v The People: Lessons from the Coal Dispute* (1985) 12 JLS, Winter issue; S. Spencer, *Police Authorities during the Miners' Strike* (Cobden Trust, 1985); P. A. J. Waddington, *The Effects of Police Manpower Depletion during the NUM Strike 1984–88* (Police Foundation, 1985); Welsh Council for Civil and Political Liberties, *Striking Back* (1985); S. McCabe and P. Wallington, *The Police, Public Order and Civil Liberties: Legacies of the Miners' Strike* (1988).
3   Op. cit., Appendix 1.

assembly (509); actual bodily harm (429); assaulting police (360); theft (352); watching and besetting/intimidation (275); breach of the peace (207) and riot (137). All the riot charges failed or were dropped. The overall acquittal rate was estimated at about 25%. Conspiracy charges were 'conspicuous by their absence'. [4]

3. Since the Red Lion Square disorders in 1974 [5] there have been three significant areas of development in policing disturbances.

Police equipment

First, there have been changes in equipment. Better protective headgear and flame resistant clothing have been supplied and widely used. Protective shields were first used in disturbances arising out of a National Front march in Lewisham in 1977, and were used again at the Notting Hill carnival in the same year. The Commissioner stated in his Report for 1977 that it 'was with extreme reluctance that the Force had to resort to the use of defensive equipment and I must stress that it does not mean that we have forsaken traditional methods of policing demonstrations and the like'. [6] The police now have at their disposal a wide range of equipment for use in policing public order incidents. In addition to the use of CS gas and batons, some forces are being equipped with rubber bullets – baton guns which fire solid polyurethane rubber cylinders; this in spite of the EU Parliament's view that such weapons involve excessive force. [7] There have been a number of deaths resulting from the use of these weapons in Northern Ireland. [8] The government refused to release the contents of the police scientific development branch report 'Plastic Baton Round Equipment for the Police' Part 2, No. 6/90. [9] The HMIC Report *Keeping the Peace* (1999) revealed that:

> 'with just two exceptions, none of the forces inspected had the ability to respond to serious disorder with police baton round launchers or CS gas dispersed by police firearms marksmen. Some of these forces possessed baton round launchers and ammunition, but they had not trained officers in their use . . . ' [10]

Water cannons have recently been deployed in Northern Ireland (having been borrowed from Belgian police). [11]

In *R v Secretary of State for the Home Department, ex p Northumbria Police Authority* [12] the Court of Appeal held that the Home Secretary had power by a circular to authorise the Home Office to supply CS gas and plastic baton rounds to a chief constable for operational use by the police, even though the local police authority declined to approve the supply of such equipment. The power was available either under s. 41 of the Police Act 1964 or under the royal prerogative to keep the peace. [13]

---

4 P. Wallington, (1985) 14 ILJ 145, 150.
5 Cf. above, pp. 393–394.
6 Cmnd. 7238, p. 6.
7 See *Guardian*, 2 August 1999.
8 See *Statewatch Bulletin*, Vol 8 No. 5, 1998.
9 See *Hansard*, HC, Written Answer, 11 Dec 1996, col. 264. On the use of plastic bullets see P. Waddington (1999), p. 88, and more generally, P. Waddington, *The Strong Arm of the Law* (1991). On the involvement of the military (army) in strikes and civil disorder, see S. Peak, *Troops in Strikes,* (1984); G. S. Morris, *Strikes in Essential Services* (1986); C. J. Whelan, (1979) 8 Ind LJ 222; C. J. Whelan, 'Armed Forces, Industrial Disputes and the law in Great Britain' in P. J. Rowe and C. J. Whelan (eds.), *Military Intervention in Democratic Societies* (1985); S. C. Greer, [1983] PL 573; Ministry of Defence, *Military Aid to the Civil Community in the UK* (3rd edn, 1989); Sherr, op. cit., Chap. 7.
10 p. 49.
11 See news reports 2 July 1999.
12 [1989] QB 26.
13 For criticism see H. J. Beynon, [1987] PL 146 (on the decision of the Divisional Court in this case) and A.W. Bradley, [1988] PL 298.

On the use of baton rounds, see B. Robertson. [14] On CS smoke, see L. Jason-Lloyd, [15] noting that it is significantly more indiscriminate in its effects to be suitable for use in public disorder situations (as distinct from sieges). Indeed it has not been used in such situations in Great Britain or Northern Ireland since the introduction of baton rounds. The current guidelines for their use are as follows: [16]

'CS or baton rounds are to be used only with the express authority of the chief officer of police (or, in his absence, his deputy), under the direction and control of a senior officer whom he has designated as officer in charge, and by police officers who have been trained in the use of the equipment and know its characteristics. CS or baton rounds are to be used only as a last resort where conventional methods of policing have been tried and failed, or must from the nature of the circumstances obtaining be unlikely to succeed if tried, and where the chief officer judges such action to be necessary because of the risk of loss of life or serious injury or widespread destruction of property. Wherever practicable, a public warning of their use is to be given.'

A distinction should be drawn between individual officers being equipped with CS sprays and the use of tear-gas type canisters being fired into crowds of protestors. The use of CS sprays is now commonplace: all but three of the police forces now issue them to officers.

CS sprays

The introduction of CS sprays has been extremely controversial. [17] In particular, there have been fears about the medical effects of the use of the spray. See especially the concern expressed after the death of Ibrahima Sey, an asylum seeker who was sprayed with the gas. [18] Although when introducing the equipment, the Home Office assured the public that the sprays had been found to be safe, [19] later scientific research has shown that there has been suffering even by those who were testing the spray for the Home Office. [20] The PCA has also been concerned by the use of CS gas. In its report, *CS Spray: Increasing Public Safety*[1] the authority draws attention to the lack of research into the interaction of CS and anti-psychotic medicines taken by mentally disturbed citizens.[2] In its Annual Report for 2000, the PCA noted that there were six out of 135 complaints regarding CS spray that involved mentally ill citizens, three of whom the spray did not incapacitate.[3]

The 1996 ACPO guidelines on the use of CS spray emphasised that it was to provide officers with a tactical advantage in a violent encounter and to restrain violent people who could not otherwise be safely detained. Its primary purpose was for self-defence. The new ACPO guidelines issued in 1999 omit any mention of the primary purpose being for self-defence. The PCA has been analysing every complaint related to CS since 1998, and records that some form of disciplinary action was taken in 10% of

14 (1991) 141 NLJ 340.
15 (1991) 141 NLJ 1043.
16 Cited by L. Jason-Lloyd, op. cit., pp. 1044–1045.
17 On the campaign against the use of cs gas see www.blink.org.uk/campaign/csspray.html.
18 *Statewatch*, February 1997. See the written answer from the Home Office reporting that there was nothing in the coroner's comments to attribute the death to CS. *Hansard* HC, written answer, 11 November 1997, col. 459.
19 See PCA Report, *CS Spray: Increasing Public Safety* (2000), p. 1.
20 *Statewatch*, February 1997, L. Jason-Lloyd, 'CS gas – an indiscriminate weapon?' (1991) 141 NLJ 1043. See the questions raised in Parliament: *Hansard*, HC Debates, 18th July 1995, col. 1026; HC, written answer, 11 January 1997, col. 442.
1 (2000).
2 p. 11.
3 p. 43.

cases in which the spray was used. Complaints are made about CS spray in about 5% of the cases in which it is used.[4] 39% of cases examined by the PCA involved the use of the spray otherwise than for self-defence. 49% of the cases in which it was used related to public disorder. Over half the complaints related to the use of the spray in confined spaces, with 6% complaining that it had been used in a vehicle. In addition, there are fears regarding cross-contamination, with innocent bystanders and other officers being affected by the spray.[5] 6% of cases resulted in serious injury – injury lasting longer than two to three hours and/or requiring hospitalisation.[6]

Since the introduction of CS sprays, the number of assaults on officers has gone down, whereas there has been a slight increase in such assaults in the three forces in which CS has not been introduced.[7] The PCA concluded 'that CS incapacitant spray does not appear to present a serious risk to the public . . . [and it] has made a real impact in making life safer for police officers.'[8] In one case in which the CS spray was used against a pensioner who had parked on a double yellow line to deliver his invalid wife to the hairdresser, the prosecution of the officer led to acquittal.[9] There are also reports of it being used on juveniles as young as 13.[10] The spray is used at least 5,000 times each year.[11] On the use of firearms in police operations see Chap. 2, above.

Mutual assistance

The second major development in the last 20 years concerns the mutual aid arrangements under which one chief officer of police provides assistance to another whose force is under pressure. The co-operation between forces is sanctioned by the Police Act 1996.[12] The development of NCIS and NCS have also played a significant part in the ability to police public order incidents, through the availability of national intelligence and specialist registers such as those for animal rights protestors.[13]

Training and militarisation

The third development has been in the training of police officers in public order policing. Police Support Units were established in all forces, each typically comprising an inspector, two sergeants and 20 constables, trained to work as a group. Some forces have established elite groups under various names (e.g. the Territorial Support Group in the Metropolitan Police). These have been associated with a more aggressive approach to disturbances –

'and represent a significant move away from the traditional approach to public order policing which was based on containment and the use of minimum force.'[14]

The use of militarised policing has been referred to in Chap. 2.[15] See also K. Reid and C. Walker,[16] identifying five constitutional precepts for the use of military

---

4 p. 3.
5 p. 10.
6 p. 3.
7 p. 25.
8 p. 27.
9 See *Hansard*, HL Debates, 27 July 1998, col. 1190.
10 See *Hansard*, HC Debates, 12 May 2000, col. 1186.
11 Ibid.
12 See above, Chap. 2, p. 95.
13 See above, Chap. 2, p. 96.
14 K. D. Ewing and C. D. Gearty, *Freedom under Thatcher* (1990), p. 105. See also T. Jefferson, *The Case Against Paramilitary Policing* (1990), Chap. 1. See also below, pp. 632–634.
15 On the use of military policing techniques that had been developed for civil defence strategies during the Cold War, see P. Waddington (1999), p. 82.
16 (1998) Anglo-American LR 133–168 at 136.

intervention in the UK. The legal framework must: (a) specify legitimate uses; (b) provide a clear basis in detailed law for intervention; (c) clarify the chain of command; (d) specify the available powers which arise; (e) ensure accountability to a democratic body. To what extent does English law satisfy these fundamental requirements?

The PCA has found that in some cases the use of riot gear has been excessive, as where it was used to break up a pub fight between rival football supporters in April 1998. The PCA found that none of the officers had later completed the use of force forms as required by regulation 5. The PCA 'regretted' that, because of the headgear they were wearing, it was impossible to identify any of the officers involved. [17]

The PCA in its report *The Police Use of New Batons* in 1998 considered the use of the different types of baton currently available and used in different forces, and recommended that forces reconsider the 'designation of target areas with a view to certain vulnerable parts of the body' (especially the shin). The report further acknowledged that there are more complaints generated by the use of some types of baton, and that forces using these ought to consult with forces using the others with a view to reducing complaints. [18]

New techniques, involving special formations of officers and the use of police horses, were incorporated in the revised *Public Order Manual of Tactical Options and Related Matters* prepared by the Association of Chief Police Officers. [19] The government has formally rejected the option of establishing a 'third force' to deal specifically with public disorder, modelled on forces in European countries, such as the French CSU. [20] The arguments against a 'third force' were summarised by the Chief Inspector of Constabulary in his Report for 1984: [1] mutual aid arrangements were effective in practice; we could not afford to have a large body of law enforcement officers kept in reserve for public order situations; and such a force would come under centralised control and consequently be more readily susceptible to political influence. The various developments outlined above seem to be steps towards at least the de facto establishment of the equivalent of a 'third force'. [2] For the argument that paramilitary policing is the most effective way of maintaining impartial and consensual public order policing, see P. A J. Waddington. [3]

The changing face of protest

It is not just the policing that has changed in recent years, the nature of protest has also evolved. Other major instances of public disorder in the last 20 years have included: (1) anti-nuclear demonstrations at Greenham Common and other RAF bases (1984); 'Stop the City' demonstrations (1984); serious riots at Handsworth, Brixton and Broadwater Farm, Tottenham, in which four people died (a press photographer in Brixton, two shopkeepers in a sub-post office in Handsworth and P.C. Keith Blakelock at Tottenham) (1985); the 'Peace Convoy' in the vicinity of Stonehenge (1986, 1988); [4] the News International dispute at Wapping (1986); the poll tax riot

---

17 *Guardian*, 7 March, 2000.
18 On the inadequacy of police training with the PR 24 side-handled baton, see HMIC Thematic Report, *Keeping the Peace* (1999), p. 56.
19 K. D. Ewing and C. D. Gearty, op. cit., pp. 105–106; G. Northam, *Shooting in the Dark: Riot Police in Britain* (1988).
20 T. Jefferson, op. cit., p. 2, referring to a Home Office Working Party between 1961 and 1971.
1 1984–85 HC 469, pp. 4–5.
2 For criticism, see T. Jefferson, *The Case Against Paramilitary Policing* (1990).
3 'Towards paramilitarism? Dilemmas in policing civil disorder' (1987) 27 B J Criminol 37. See also, P. Waddington, *The Strong Arm of the Law* (1991); K. Bryett, 'Who Polices Violence' (1991) 1 Policing & Society 285.
4 See p. 454.

in central London on 31 March 1990;[5] and an increasing number of 'free festivals' attracting 'New Age travellers' (e.g. Castlemorton in May 1992);[6] others include mass public protests at GM crops, road development, anti-globalisation and anti-capitalism protests, demonstrations against paedophile residents on housing estates, transportation of live animals, and petrol prices.

H. Fenwick has written that:

'public protest occurs in various forms, ranging from the peaceful expression of views to rioting; it can be categorised as: peaceful persuasion, offensive or insulting persuasion, intimidation, symbolic or persuasive physical obstruction or interference, actual physical obstruction or interference, forceful obstruction and violence.'[7]

If there are so many activities categorized as protest, can they be effectively policed by a non-specialised force, or is the diversity an argument against such a force?

More recently, there appears to have been a fundamental shift in the types of public disorder occurring. The dramatic increase in the number of environmental campaign groups in the 1990s and their liaison with other campaign groups has led to much larger and targeted protests. The use of email and the widespread ownership of mobile phones has revolutionised the way in which protests are organised, advertised, and executed. In addition, the targets of the protests have shifted. The focus now tends to be on individual companies or development sites rather than 'State' or 'establishment' institutions. The impact this has had on policing is considerable. There are less readily identifiable leaders and organisers, less information available to the police and greater unpredictability as to the size and location of the protests. Any symbol of capitalism (e.g. McDonalds) might be the target and the protest arranged exclusively by email contact of millions within a few minutes.

The HMIC Report, *Keeping the Peace*[8] acknowledges the changing face of disorder:

'the nature of potential disorder is broadening with the involvement of a wider and better informed representation of the public in single cause protests, especially environmental and animal rights issues.'[9]

In addition, the Report addresses the police response to protests that have a more international and 'quasi-terrorist' approach.[10] The emphasis has moved to an operation of greater intelligence gathering and disseminating information – facilitated by NCIS – and a greater need for inter-force co-operation.

The Report also acknowledged that more specialist training would be required for officers who command public order disputes in light of the change in the nature of such incidents. One factor of significance in leading to this recommendation was the increased likelihood of civil litigation following protests.[11]

In the Home Office Consultation Paper on Animals Rights protest (above), the police described typical conduct as follows:

'The targeting of protest activity is directed towards Primary and Secondary sites consisting of:
Day to day activities, the normal protesting by local group members at the primary and sometimes secondary sites.

---

5 See D. Burns, *Poll Tax Rebellion* (1992), Chaps. 4, 5.
6 See J. Baxter, 'Castlemorton and beyond' (1992) 8 Policing 222 and P. Cumper and K. Stevenson, (1992) 89 LS Gaz, 7 October, p. 23.
7 H. Fenwick, (1999) MLR 491, 494.
8 (1999).
9 p. 9.
10 p. 14.
11 p. 48.

Regional and National days of action, where substantially larger numbers of protesters gather together or in organised groups. They will target both primary and secondary sites. Often the majority of the protesters are not locals and there is more likelihood of more extremist activists' involvement.

1.1 Primary sites. This will consist of the main target premises where the activity of that business is the direct issue against which the protest is directed.

1.2 Secondary sites. These will consist of all other sites, which are linked in any whatsoever to the primary target site, for example: home addresses of directors, shareholders, employees of the primary target; home addresses of directors, shareholders, employees of any secondary sites; the neighbours of any above; suppliers of primary/secondary targets; customers of primary/secondary targets; local authorities; solicitors; banks; shops; public places; the police. The list of potential secondary targets is endless. It is generally any target which will have a direct impact or assist in the continuing and increasing pressure to bring about the closure of that primary target business.

2. Protester tactics. It is well recognised that the vast majority of the members of the protest groups are law-abiding citizens, actioning their right in this free democracy to voice their opinions and concerns about what they see is cruelty towards animals. However, amongst these protest groups are those who are willing to use more extreme methods to achieve their aims. Methods ranging from the harassment of others to outright terrorism. The severity of the protest will be affected by the significance of the target and whether the action is a day to day activity or a regional/national day of action.

2.1 Meet and greet. Groups of protestors will gather outside the primary and secondary sites and petition directors and employees of those businesses going to and from work, to encourage them to cease the activity towards which the protest is directed. This protest action will range in its extreme with reasonable verbal discussion to extreme abuse and threats. Protester numbers will vary from just a few people to several hundred, sometimes tactically splitting into several groups.

2.2 Home visits. Via their own significant intelligence gathering systems, the protest organisation will identify the names and addresses of people concerned with those primary and secondary target sites, i.e. activists will follow them home, use the electoral role; website informants within the business. An evolving tactic is for protestors to gather outside the home addresses of directors, employees and shareholders of target sites. The number of protesters will vary according to activity planned outside the address. The activity may involve the protesters standing in the street making no sound at all. More often it involves protestors shouting towards the address, knocking on doors and windows, knocking on neighbours' doors, displaying banners with pictures of animals or allegations of cruelty against the target resident. The passive protest outside houses poses challenges and questions as to use of legislation (or whether such legislation in fact presently exists).

2.3 Posters and leaflets. Activists prepare and display posters and banners with pictures relating to the target business. These will be pictures of animals including some from within the business and may range from animals at play to mutilated animals which could be considered upsetting by much of the general public. Activists will also distribute leaflets containing such pictures and allegations against the target business or person.

2.4 Public places. Protest activists will target town and city centres often near the primary or secondary target business. Their activities will include static protests in small groups sometimes outside banks; shops or other premises, which they believe, support their target. They may organise marches in large numbers holding Regional/National days of marching and protesting in town centres. Often these gatherings occur as secondary activities with the protesters splitting into small groups from the primary site, gathering at a local town centre.

2.5 Harassment of Police. Activists will target and harass police officers in the front line of the operation. The activists are well aware that offensive conduct towards officers may lead to instant arrest. And some may be willing to do this to reduce police numbers and vehicles. The activists will also target a few identified officers and constantly question them about their activity, motivation, use of powers etc. Over a time this can be very stressful to officers at the forefront of the police operation. One particular target for the activists will be the Police commander. Activist leaders will identify the Bronze commander and engage him/her in conversation about the protest, police powers etc with the sole intention to distract the officer from their real job to command the incident therefore affecting the police operation.

2.6 Phone calls. Phone calls will be made to the primary or secondary sites. These will range from polite discussion to persuade the target to desist, through to abuse and threats of impending harm or violence. The calls will occur at any time of day or night.

2.7 Fax. Protest activists will make use of fax facilities and their practices include sending offensive pictures to sending a black sheet of paper, which is taped so as to form a loop. This has the result in a constant print of black sheet at the target fax which puts the machine out of use for receiving other faxes and uses up all of the printer ink.

2.8 Web-sites. As with any organisation, protest groups make great use of the Internet and maintain their own web-sites. These sites contain information on the protest issue and advertise days of action. Some sites have developed and encourage use of more direct action against targets including the advertising of names, addresses and phone numbers. They also include details of tactics such as mentioned above.

2.9 Cause damage. More radical direct action protesters will claim that any law, which protects those who abuse animals, is not a law to be obeyed. They will claim a legitimate right to damage the very systems and structures which involve this abuse. Activists will damage site fencing, attempt site invasions to liberate the animals and damage equipment and security cameras, damage business vehicles, and break windows. Radical activists will damage vehicles outside or en-route to home addresses even whilst the driver is still in the vehicle.'

Despite the centralisation of the police information and resources, and greater emphasis on police intelligence, the Internet and mobile telephones have made truly spontaneous protest possible. Even where protest is anticipated, the unpredictability over numbers leads to huge numbers of police being deployed as a precautionary measure. In the 2000 May Day protests, 5,500 were available for the policing operation. [12]

On several occasions, attention has been drawn in Parliament to the difficulty in policing protests. In particular there is a growing concern that animal rights demonstrations are infiltrated by violent activists. [13] The HMIC Thematic report *Keeping the Peace* (1999) recognised the difficulty and the need to be:

'flexible enough to provide a positive response to the specific types of disorder that have emerged in recent years from the newer forms of mass non-violent protest surrounding for example, animal exports, to environmental concerns and other single cause issues. The mobility of protesters provides a fresh challenge for the Service in that supporters form an ideological community that only becomes geographically based for relatively short periods before moving on to the next protest site. Forces have had to deal with protest and potential disorder that relate to issues and incidents outside their force area and even outside the UK, particularly in relation to animal and environmental protest groups. These groups have adopted a strategic, long-term approach to their protests employing new and innovative tactics to frustrate authorities and achieve their objective. There is evidence that some elements operate in cell like structures in a quasi-terrorist mode to keep secret their movements and intentions. The police response has to be equally focused and determined with energy directed to intelligence gathering and dissemination at a local and national level.'

Particular emphasis is placed on intelligence-led policing:

'Her Majesty's Inspector was pleased to note that, in the main, the recommendations contained in "**Policing with Intelligence**" have been adopted in the forces visited. These recommendations together with the implications of the Crime and Disorder Act have led some forces to enhance and focus their intelligence systems with a view to gathering information and intelligence from a wide number of sources, to provide a clearly defined output standard. The proactive use of informants and community contacts is an area most officers are familiar with, but the use of the internet, activist magazines and news sheets provides a valuable insight to potential new and emerging causes that may present operational problems for forces and their local

12 See *Hansard*, HC Deb, 2 May 2000, col. 27.
13 See *Hansard*, HC Deb, 22 February 1995, col. 268. See also the discussion of the Terrorism Bill: 2000 *Hansard*, HC Deb, 14 December 1999, col. 155.

population. . . . At present "public order" intelligence is gathered, analysed and disseminated from a number of sources. These may include National Criminal Intelligence Service (NCIS), Special Branches, the Northern and Southern Intelligence Units, the Metropolitan Police Service (MPS) Public Order Intelligence System, and several different data systems within each force. Each unit has different terms of reference for collecting, analysing, and storing intelligence giving scope for duplication on some aspects and omission on others. The lack of a single point of reference for people, places and events related or linked to public order intelligence has hindered the policing of public order incidents for some years. Recent examples include the policing of animal exports, when protests occurred in several forces throughout the country. A national intelligence system could have given police early warning that trouble was imminent giving forces the opportunity to take action to prevent or reduce the disorder which followed. In July 1998 the ACPO Council agreed to requests from ACPO Public Order, and Terrorism and Allied Matters committees, to explore the possibility of a national public order intelligence system.

1.2.4. It is planned that this system will draw intelligence from a number of sources, analyse assess and disseminate it, ensuring forces, operational commanders and operational officers have access to a full and current intelligence picture to inform their decision making. The system will have checks and balances built into it to ensure the integrity of the system and to protect intelligence gathered from sensitive sources or by sensitive means. The proposed National Public Order Intelligence Unit will be established at New Scotland Yard and will incorporate the Animal Rights National Index (ARNI). It is planned that public order intelligence officers in each force area will have access to the unit via a secure network. Her Majesty's Inspector welcomes the proposal to bring some rationalisation to the present disparate system, but notes that the new unit will operate independently from NCIS, whilst football intelligence will remain a function of NCIS. In the longer term further consideration will need to be given to this system.

1.2.5 A common problem is the lack of a force level strategic overview to link emerging disorder issues at different locations within a force. The management of football intelligence best illustrated this; at present football intelligence is centrally collected and disseminated in NCIS. This intelligence is sometimes passed direct to divisions, by-passing the force intelligence bureau, thus depriving the force of the opportunity for a consolidated overview to properly assess the potential. Her Majesty's Inspector does not support such action whether in relation to football or any other activity. Forces that maintain a strategic overview of football related disorder are able to give a more effective and flexible response, through proactive policing, sometimes even at some distance from the stadium. Her Majesty's Inspector repeats the recommendation made in 'Policing with Intelligence' that each force should appoint an officer of ACPO rank to take overall responsibility for force intelligence and its co-ordination in order to achieve effective policing and value for money.' [14]

The Report recommends that greater communication with the community and use of the media can assist in minimising the risk of disorder. [15] Can the media be trusted to minimise the risk of disturbance? (Recall the *News of the World*'s publicity of those on the sex offenders' register in 2000.)

The investigation of offences arising out of major disorder is difficult in practice, despite the advances in policing with advanced equipment and mutual assistance between the forces.

'Frankly, the police record for successfully prosecuting those who engage in serious public disorder is dismal. Currently, where a senior investigating officer (SIO) is appointed after the event, suspects who plead "not guilty" stand only a one in five chance of being convicted.' [16]

However, modern practice includes the use of police officers and civilian photographers as 'evidence gatherers', the use of static video cameras, the power to

14 pp. 15-16.
15 p. 26.
16 Det. Supt. E. Williams, 'Investigating major disorder' (1994) 10 Policing 134. On police tactics see M. King and M. Brearley (eds.), *Public Order Policing* (1996).

seek a production order for press material under PACE [17] the organisation of hospital welfare teams to question casualties (police and public) and the establishment of charge centres. [18] Use of CCTV cameras has become more prevalent, and evidence from such cameras/recordings is routinely admitted as evidence in criminal trials, even in relation to disputed identification. On 17 January 2000, the government announced major funding for new CCTV projects around the country.[1] Over £59m of funding was made available in 1999–2000.[2]

The Crime and Disorder Act 1998 assists policing major disorder of this type by empowering officers to require a person to remove a face mask or covering (see below). In *Friedl v Austria*[3] the Court of Human Rights considered the practice of the Austrian police in video-recording and taking still photographs of the protestors at a homelessness demonstration. These images were used in the subsequent prosecution of the demonstrators for breaches of the relevant criminal offences relating to unauthorised demonstrations. The Commission found that there had been no breach of Art. 8.[4]

Football spectators and disorder

Football hooliganism has been a continuing concern. The increased use of closed-circuit television systems in football grounds; extensive covert operations to act against hooligan ringleaders (although a number of trials collapsed as a result of evidential difficulties); and the establishment of a National Football Intelligence Unit, operational as from March 1990, to collate police intelligence on persistent hooligans are all new measures to combat an old problem. Steps taken include improved liaison between the football and public authorities and the passing of the Sporting Events (Control of Alcohol etc.) Act 1985, controlling the sale and possession of alcohol inside grounds, on entry to grounds and on football special coaches and trains. Section 1 creates offences in relation to knowingly permitting alcohol to be carried on a public service vehicle/train or to carry alcohol thereon to be drunk on such a vehicle when it is being used to transport passengers to a sporting event. Section 1A, as inserted by the Public Order Act 1986, creates similar offences in relation to private vehicles (capable of carrying eight or more). Other offences include possession of alcohol in the ground, and possession of fireworks. For other regulation of behaviour at and admission to football stadiums see the Football Spectators Act 1989, and the Public Order Act 1986 [5] enabling exclusion orders to be made by the courts preventing persons convicted of football-related offences attending 'prescribed' football matches. The Football (Offences and Disorder) Act 1999 amended the Football Spectators Act 1989. That Act, as now amended by the Football (Disorder) Act 2000, provides courts with a power to make a 'banning order' against a person who is convicted of a 'relevant offence'. The court must be satisfied that there are reasonable grounds to believe that the order will prevent violence or disorder in connection with football matches: (s .1). The period of such an order and its form are subject to ss. 3 and 4. The 'relevant offences' for the purposes of this Act [6] include causing harassment alarm or distress and racial hatred committed within 24 hours of and in relation to a football match. The Act also empowers

---

17 Above, p. 235.
18 Ibid.
1 See Home Office Press Release, 13 January 2000.
2 See *Hansard*, HC Written Answers, 6 July 2000, col. 297W, and see www.homeoffice.gov.uk/crimeprev/crpinit13.htm. On the use of CCTV and even airship surveillance in combating public disorder, see *Keeping the Peace* (1999) p. 55.
3 (1995) 21 EHRR 83.
4 On the photographing of individuals in custody see Chap. 3 above and *Murray v UK* (1994) 19 EHRR 193.
5 ss. 30–37 as substituted by the Football (Offences and Disorder) Act 1999, ss. 6(1), 7(1).
6 Extended by s. 2 beyond those originally listed in Sch. 1 to the 1989 Act.

a court to make a banning order and provides a power of arrest for the breach of such an order (ss. 6–8).

The banning orders, as now available for international matches, represent a much greater potential restriction on liberty available in broader circumstances, and yet the legislation was rushed through Parliament as a knee-jerk response to the Euro-2000 hooliganism.[7]

Indecent or racial chanting is made an offence capable of commission by a sole individual.[8] This has become a problem not only for racial and indecent taunts of opposing fans, but also of the players – witness the complaints made by David Beckham when fans chanted indecent remarks about his wife.[9]

NCIS statistics for the 1998–99 season record 3,341 arrests for football-related incidents. In 1999/00 the number fell to 3,138, but that may be a reflection of the diminished police presence at games.[10]

G. Pearson,[11] concludes that

'even the most basic attempts of the Football (Offences) Act and the Sporting Events (Control of Alcohol) Act to prohibit specific actions within football stadiums have been thwarted by both over-ambitious drafting and the non-enforcement of their provisions by police and match-day stewards. In addition, the extent of the failure of these Acts is so manifest that their deterrent function is minimal. Of more concern than this is the way in which the phenomenon of football-related disorder more generally appears to have side-stepped the legislative measures imposed upon football crowds ... Serious violence within grounds does not occur as regularly as it did during the early 1970s or the early 1980s; but since the relatively "quiet" days of the early 1990s, violent disorder outside grounds appears to be as serious as ever, and is quite possibly on the increase. The failure of legislation to address this problem is a serious issue. The Football (Offences) Act 1991 has been completely unable to achieve its own specific crowd control objectives, and the Football Spectators Act 1989 has continually failed to prevent convicted hooligans from travelling abroad with England.'[12]

The Football (Disorder) Act 2000 was introduced in the light of the persistent episodes of disorder involving English football supporters during the European Championships in June 2000. The Act received Royal Assent on 28 July 2000, having been introduced only two weeks before. It is a temporary Act, amending the Football Spectators Act 1989 and expires in two years unless renewed by affirmative resolution.[13] A magistrates' court may make a banning order on the basis of a complaint rather than a conviction, provided that it believes that such an order would help to prevent violence or disorder at or in connection with football matches.[14] The Act also empowers authorities to require those subject to a banning order to surrender their passports. It provides power of arrest and a power to require a person to appear before a magistrates' court within 24 hours to answer a complaint for the making of a banning order.[15]

As with the ASBO (discussed below), proof is on the civil standard, and the order is available against a person who has not committed a criminal offence, or is even

---

7 For an interesting analysis of football hooliganism and criminal law theory see also N. Lacey and C. Wells, *Reconstructing Criminal Law* (2nd edn, 1998), Chap. 2.
8 s 9 amending the Football (Offences) Act 1991, s. 3.
9 See *Guardian*, 8 August 2000.
10 See NCIA Press Release, 12 August 2000. For a survey of the numerous legislative attempts to regulate spectating, see G. Osborn, 'Football's Legal Legacy: Recreation, Protest and Disorder' in S. Greenfield and G. Osborn (eds.), *Law and Sport in Contemporary Society* (2000), and S. Hall, 'The Treatment of "Football Hooligans" in the Press' in R. Ingram et al., *Football Hooliganism: The Wider Context* (1978).
11 'Legislating for the Football Hooligan: A Case for Reform' in S. Greenfield and G. Osborn (eds.), *Law and Sport in Contemporary Society* (2000).
12 p. 196
13 See Football (Disorder) (Duration of Powers) Order 2001, S.I. 2001 No. 2646.
14 s. 14.
15 The legislation is considered by S. Gardiner, (2000) 144 SJ 655.

suspected of one. Many civil liberties issues arise: Are such draconian measures necessary? Are there adequate safeguards against misuse? With some clubs, it might even be possible to argue that all supporters should be banned from an away-match because it is more probable than not (civil standard) that disorder and or violence will be prevented. Can these orders be imposed on players who are involved in violence? [16]Are these provisions compatible with Art. 5 of the ECHR? The Divisional Court has confirmed that the international banning order does not contravene EU law nor the ECHR: *Gough v Chief Constable of the Derbyshire Constabulary*. [17]

On the football riots which prompted the legislative response, see news reports for June 2000. The original provisions in the Bill sparked widespread controversy. In particular, cl. 14c, which provided that people could be banned from travel abroad if they displayed 'any writing, sign, or visible representation which is threatening, abusive or insulting'. Lord Bassam of Brighton was reported as saying that 'people making a "V" sign and acting aggressively would be enough evidence for police to stop them travelling'. The Home Secretary, Jack Straw, made several concessions in the Bill to gain opposition support so that the legislation would be in force in the summer of 2000. [18] He restricted the availability of issuing a banning order to magistrates' courts rather than individual police officers; and limited the police power to detain a person under this Act to four hours (six with an inspector's authorisation). Furthermore, the officer must now have reasonable grounds to believe that the person may have contributed to violence or disorder in the past before he can seek a banning order. A 21-year-old football fan was the first to receive an international banning order on 31 August 2000. [19]

How does the power to arrest simply to make inquiry about someone's past satisfy Art. 5 of the ECHR? Is the requirement that someone surrender his passport compatible with the ECHR or the International Covenant on Civil and Political Rights, Art. 12?

Lord Bassam's *Working Group on Football Disorder* [20] reviewed the disorder at Euro-2000 and recommended, *inter alia*, a multi agency approach to 'combat xenophobic, racist and threatening images of national identity'. [21]

'English football disorder cannot be removed from its wider social context. In many ways it is a manifestation of a wider social problem of alienated young males demonstrating their frustration in an anti-social and violent way. It occurs in high streets up and down the country every weekend. Mediterranean holiday resorts are equally at risk. Football is not immune and football cannot be expected to eliminate its disorder problems until the wider social causes have been tackled. But football can play an important role in that process, particularly in helping to reduce the alienation of fans who travel abroad in support of the national side. Communicating an anti-violence message and other positive images of English football is integral to this task.' [22]

3 Freedom of association

The ECHR guarantees a right of assembly. Article 11 provides:

'Everyone has the right to freedom of peaceful assembly and to freedom of association with others, including the right to form and to join trade unions for the protection of his interests.'

16 See the Liberty Briefing document (*Briefing on the Draft Football Disorder Bill* (2000) www.liberty-human-rights.org.uk/mlobby21.html) for examples of players' conduct that might lead to a ban.

17 [2001] EWHC Admin 554, [2001] 4 All ER 289. See I. Blackshaw, (2001) NLJ 1562.

18 See the Liberty *Briefing on the Draft Football Disorder Bill* (2000) www.liberty-human-rights.org.uk/mlobby21.html.

19 See *Guardian*, 1 September 2000.

20 (2001).

21 p. 9.

22 p. 15. See further the Football (Disorder) (Amendment) Bill 2001.

As far as English law is concerned, there are few express legal limits on the freedom of people to associate together for political purposes. The criminal law of conspiracy only applies to agreements to commit a crime, to defraud or to do an act which tends to corrupt public morals.[23] Accordingly, the fact that people associate to perform certain acts will not render them criminally liable unless those acts would be illegal if performed by an individual, subject to the two limited exceptions stated. The tort of conspiracy is committed where two or more people agree to do an unlawful act, or to do a lawful act by unlawful means, or to perform acts other than for their own legitimate benefit, with the object of inflicting damage on a third party.[24] The tort of conspiracy is thus now appreciably wider in scope than the crime, although it is necessary in tort for the claimant to prove that he has suffered damage.

The following section illustrates some statutory limitations on freedom of association in the public order context.

Public Order Act 1936

An Act to prohibit the wearing of uniforms in connection with political objects and the maintenance by private persons of associations of military or similar character; and to make further provision for the preservation of public order on the occasion of public processions and meetings and in public places.

1. Prohibition of uniforms in connection with political objects

(1) Subject as hereinafter provided, any person who in any public place or at any public meeting wears uniform signifying his association with any political organisation or with the promotion of any political object shall be guilty of an offence:

Provided that, if the chief officer of police is satisfied that the wearing of any such uniform as aforesaid on any ceremonial, anniversary, or other special occasion will not be likely to involve risk of public disorder, he may, with the consent of a Secretary of State, by order permit the wearing of such uniform on that occasion either absolutely or subject to such conditions as may be specified in the order....

9. Interpretation, etc

(1) In this Act the following expressions have the meanings hereby respectively assigned to them, that is to say—

'Meeting' means a meeting held for the purpose of the discussion of matters of public interest or for the purpose of the expression of views on such matters;

'Private premises' means premises to which the public have access (whether on payment or otherwise) only by permission of the owner, occupier, or lessee of the premises;

'Public meeting' includes any meeting in a public place and any meeting which the public or any section thereof are permitted to attend, whether on payment or otherwise;

['Public place' includes any highway and any other premises or place to which at the material time the public have or are permitted to have access, whether on payment or otherwise;]....

NOTES

1. The maximum penalty under s. 1 is currently three months' imprisonment, a fine not exceeding level 4 on the standard scale or both (1936 Act, s. 7 as amended by the Criminal Law Act 1977, s. 31, Sch. 6 and the Criminal Justice Act 1982, s. 46). The

23 Criminal Law Act 1977, Part I; *Smith and Hogan*, pp. 294–296.
24 M. Brazier (ed.) *Clerk and Lindsell on Torts*, 17th edn, paras 23.76–23.90; *Hubbard v Pitt* [1976] QB 142, CA, below, p. 182; *Lonrho Ltd v Shell Petroleum Co Ltd (No 2)* [1982] AC 173; *Lonrho plc v Fayed* [1992] 1 AC 448. The Court of Appeal recently clarified the elements of conspiracy in *Kuwait Oil Tanker Co Sak v Al Bader* [2000] 2 All ER (Comm) 271, CA (Civ D).

consent of the Attorney-General is required for a prosecution: s. 1(2). Section 7(3) gives a power of arrest.

2. The Public Order Acts 1936 and 1986 (for the most part: see s. 42) do not extend to Northern Ireland. The equivalent legislation there is the Public Order (Northern Ireland) Order 1987. [1] See also the Terrorism Act 2000. [2]

3. Section 1 was introduced in response to the increasing use of uniforms by political groups, notably the Fascists. [3] 'In the year following enactment of the POA 1936, there were no fewer than 12,011 meeting in the Metropolitan Police district alone, 3,094 of them fascist, 4,364 of them anti-facist with a further 4,553 connected with neither political position.' [4] The first prosecutions were of Blackshirts: *R v Wood* [5] (D sold Fascist newspapers while wearing a black peak cap with two emblems, black shirt, tie and leather motoring coat, dark trousers and dark footwear: fined £2); *R v Charnley* [6] (at public meetings D wore black trousers, dark navy blue pullover, and red brassard on his left arm: convicted and bound over). [7] Thus the wearing of a complete outfit is not necessary for a conviction. The section has also been used against members of the Ku Klux Klan [8] and supporters of the Irish republican movement. [9] See the detailed discussion of the background to the enactment in R. D. Ewing and C. A. Gearty. [10]

In *O'Moran*,[10a] members of a funeral party accompanying the body of Michael Gaughan, a self-confessed IRA member who died on a hunger strike while in Parkhurst prison, wore black or dark blue berets, dark glasses and dark clothing. They were not identically dressed. An oration beside the coffin referred to the Irish republican movement, and an Irish tricolour flag was placed on the coffin. In *Whelan*,[10b] the defendants assembled with others at Speakers' Corner in order to march as a protest on the first anniversary of internment in Northern Ireland. The march was organised by Provisional Sinn Fein and other groups. The leaders all wore black berets and some also wore dark clothing, dark glasses and carried Irish flags and banners. The Divisional Court upheld convictions under s. 1(1). Per Lord Widgery CJ: [11]

> '"Wearing" in my judgment implies some article of wearing apparel. I agree with the submission made in argument that one would not describe a badge pinned to the lapel as being a uniform worn for present purposes. In the present instance however the various items relied on, such as the beret, dark glasses, the pullovers and the other dark clothing, were clearly worn and therefore satisfy the first requirement of the section.
>
> The next requirement is that that which was worn was a uniform, ... the policeman or the soldier is accepted as wearing uniform without more ado, but the isolated man wearing a black beret is not to be regarded as wearing a uniform unless it is proved that the beret in its association has been recognised and is known as the uniform of some particular organisation, proof of which would have to be provided by evidence in the usual way.
>
> In this case [*O'Moran*] the eight men in question were together. They were not seen in isolation. Where an article such as a beret is used in order to indicate that a group of men are

---

1 S.I. 1987 No. 463: see B. Hadfield, (1987) 38 NILQ 86 and [1993] Crim LR 915. See also the Public Order (Amendment) (Northern Ireland) Order 1997, S.I. 1997 No. 1181.
2 Below, Chap. 5.
3 See *Williams*, pp. 216–220.
4 R. D. Ewing and C. A. Gearty, op. cit., p. 325.
5 (1937) 81 Sol Jo 108.
6 (1937) 81 Sol Jo 108.
7 See also *R v Wright* (1937) 81 Sol Jo 509; E. R. Ivamy, [1949] CLP 184–187; cf. *R v Taylor, Ward and Hawthorne* (1937) 81 Sol Jo 509: Social Credit Party members in green shirts, ties and armlets found not guilty.
8 *The Times*, 8 October 1965.
9 *O'Moran v DPP, Whelan v DPP* [1975] QB 864, DC.
10 Op. cit., pp. 300–320.
10a [1975] QB 864, DC.
10b [1995] RTR 177.
11 At pp. 873–874.

together and in association, it seems to me that that article can be regarded as uniform without any proof that it has been previously used as such. The simple fact that a number of men deliberately adopt an identical article of attire justifies in my judgment the view that that article is uniform if it is adopted in such a way as to show that its adoption is for the purposes of showing association between the men in question. Subject always to the de minimis rule, I see no reason why the article or articles should cover the whole of the body or a major part of the body, as was argued at one point, or indeed should go beyond the existence of the beret by itself. In this case the articles did go beyond the beret. They extended to the pullover, the dark glasses and the dark clothing, and I have no doubt at all in my own mind that those men wearing those clothes on that occasion were wearing uniform within the meaning of the Act.

Evidence has been called in this case from a police sergeant to the effect that the black beret was commonly used, or had been frequently used, by members of the IRA, and I recognise that it is possible to prove that an article constitutes uniform by that means as well.

The next point, and perhaps the most difficult problem of all, is the requirement of the section that the uniform so worn shall signify the wearer's association with any political organisation. This can be done in my judgment in two ways. The first I have already referred to. It is open to the prosecution, if they have the evidence and wish to call it, to show that the particular article relied upon as uniform has been used in the past as the uniform of a recognised association, and they can by that means, if the evidence is strong enough, and the court accepts it, prove that the black beret, or whatever it may be, is associated with a particular organisation. In my judgment it is not necessary for them to specify the particular organisation because in many instances the name of the organisation will be unknown or may have been recently changed. But if they can prove that the article in question has been associated with a political organisation capable of identification in some manner, then that would suffice for the purposes of the section.

Alternatively, in my judgment the significance of the uniform and its power to show the association of the wearer with a political organisation can be judged from the events to be seen on the occasion when the alleged uniform was worn. In other words, it can be judged and proved without necessarily referring to the past history at all, because if a group of persons assemble together and wear a piece of uniform such as a black beret to indicate their association one with the other, and furthermore by their conduct indicate that that beret associates them with other activity of a political character, that is enough for the purposes of the section.'

Could the wearing of any clothing or badge constitute an offence under ss. 4 or 5 of the Public Order Act 1986 (causing harassment, alarm or distress)? Could the offence under s. 1 of the Public Order Act 1936 be committed by wearing animal masks at an anti-vivisectionist protest?

Public Order Act 1936

2. Prohibition of quasi-military organisations
(1) If the members or adherents of any association of persons, whether incorporated or not, are—

    (*a*) organised or trained or equipped for the purpose of enabling them to be employed in usurping the functions of the police or of the armed forces of the Crown; or

    (*b*) organised and trained or organised and equipped either for the purpose of enabling them to be employed for the use or display of physical force in promoting any political object, or in such manner as to arouse reasonable apprehension that they are organised and either trained or equipped for that purpose;

then any person who takes part in the control or management of the association, or in so organising or training are aforesaid any members or adherents thereof, shall be guilty of an offence under this section:

Provided that in any proceedings against a person charged with the offence of taking part in the control or management of such an association as aforesaid it shall be a defence to that charge to prove that he neither consented to nor connived at the organisation, training, or equipment of members or adherents of the association in contravention of the provisions of this section.

(2) No prosecution shall be instituted under this section without the consent of the Attorney-General.

(3) [This authorises the forfeiture of the property of an association which is unlawful under this section] ...

(5) If a judge of the High Court is satisfied by information on oath that there is reasonable ground for suspecting that an offence under this section has been committed, and that evidence of the commission thereof is to be found at any premises or place specified in the information, he may, on an application made by an officer of police of a rank not lower than that of inspector, grant a search warrant authorising any such officer as aforesaid named in the warrant together with any other persons named in the warrant and any other officers of police to enter the premises or place at any time within one month from the date of the warrant, if necessary by force, and to search the premises or place and every person found therein, and to seize anything found on the premises or place or on any person which the officer has reasonable ground for suspecting to be evidence of the commission of such an offence as aforesaid:

Provided that no woman shall, in pursuance of a warrant issued under this subsection, be searched except by a woman.

(6) Nothing in this section shall be construed as prohibiting the employment of a reasonable number of persons as stewards to assist in the preservation of order at any public meeting held upon private premises, or the making of arrangements for that purpose or the instruction of the persons to be so employed in their lawful duties as such stewards, or their being furnished with badges or other distinguishing signs.

NOTES

1. The maximum penalties under this section are six months' imprisonment, a £5,000 fine or both on summary conviction, and two years, a fine of any amount or both on conviction on indictment. [12]

2. This section was passed to meet the growth of private armies, in particular Fascist groups, between 1933 and 1936. [13]

3. Note that there is no reference to the promotion of a political object in s. 2(1)(a). Vigilante groups might accordingly offend against this provision.

4. The first prosecution under s. 2(1)(b) was *R v Jordan and Tyndall*. [14] J and T took part in the organisation of 'Spearhead', part first of the British National Party and later of the National Socialist Movement. At various times in 1961 and 1962 uniformed members of Spearhead were seen practising foot drill, carrying out attack and defence exercises at a tower building and exchanging Nazi salutes. At a camp near Cheltenham, the Horst Wessel song was sung and cries of 'Sieg Heil' were heard. The police searched the Movement's headquarters under a warrant issued under s. 2, and found documents referring to the former German National Socialist Storm Troopers and containing phrases such as 'Task Force', 'Front Line Fighters' and 'Fighting Efficiency'. They also found tins of sodium chlorate (weed killer) which could be used in making bombs. On one tin, the words 'Jew Killer' had been written. J and T were convicted of organising Spearhead members in such a way as to arouse reasonable apprehension that they were organised to be employed for the use or display of physical force promoting a political object. The Court of Criminal Appeal approved the trial judge's direction that: 'reasonable apprehension means an apprehension or fear which is based not upon undue timidity or excessive suspicion or still less prejudice but one which is founded on grounds which to you appear to be

---

12 Public Order Act 1936, s. 7(1); Criminal Law Act 1977, ss. 28(2), 32(1); Magistrates' Courts Act 1980, s. 32; Criminal Justice Act 1991, s. 17(2)(c).

13 *Williams*, pp. 220–221; R. Benewick, 'The Threshold of Violence' in Benewick and Smith (eds.), *Direct Action and Democratic Politics* (1972). See K. D. Ewing and C. A. Gearty, op. cit.

14 [1963] Crim LR 124, CCA; *Williams* pp. 222–223.

reasonable. Moreover the apprehension or fear must be reasonably held by a person who is aware of all the facts.... You must try to put yourselves in the position of a sensible man who knew the whole of the facts.' J was sentenced to nine, and T to six months' imprisonment, the Court of Criminal Appeal regarding it as an appropriate occasion for the imposition of deterrent sentences. [15] The prosecution of members of the 'Free Wales Army' under s. 2 is described by D. G. T. Williams. [16] The section has also been employed in respect of the organisers of IRA units. [17]

5. Unauthorised meetings of persons for the purpose of being trained in the use of arms or of practising military exercises, are still prohibited by the Unlawful Drilling Act 1819, s. 1. Prosecutions under the Act were not brought against those responsible for drilling the Ulster Volunteer Force in resistance to Home Rule before the First World War, or in relation to the military activities of the British Fascists in the 1930s, despite, in the latter case, assurances from the Home Secretary that appropriate action would be taken. [18]

6. On the proscription of organisations in Northern Ireland, see below, p. 573. In the *Review of the Public Order Act 1936 and related legislation* [19] the government rejected an argument that since much recent disorder had resulted from confrontations between the supporters of the National Front and others, including members of the Socialist Workers Party, there were grounds for banning one or both of these organisations. Proscription had been confined to organisations openly and avowedly dedicated to violent terrorist acts and to the overthrow of the civil authorities. [20] See now Terrorism Act 2000 (Proscribed Organisations) (Amendment) Order 2001. [1]

4 Public meetings and processions

In this country there are no unfettered legal rights to hold public meetings or processions. The law regulates (1) the location and (2) the conduct of public assemblies.

To date, most challenges under Art. 11 of the ECHR to English law's approach to public meetings have arisen in the context of major trade union disputes. Challenges have, however, also arisen in relation to public disorder, including recently under Art. 10, *Steel v United Kingdom*, [2] where protestors had disrupted a grouse shoot and were arrested for breach of the peace. The court applied principles derived from cases dealing with freedom of expression in this case of physical demonstration by impeding the shoot. The Court accepted that 'a breach of the peace is committed only when an individual causes harm, or appears likely to cause harm, to persons or property or acts in a manner the natural consequence of which would be to provoke others to violence'. [3]

The potential for challenges under the Human Rights Act 1998 to a wide range of public meetings is also demonstrated by cases such as *Anderson v United Kingdom*. [4] It was held that Art. 11 did not give rise to a right to loiter in a shopping centre. See

---

15 See further M. Walker, *The National Front* (1977), pp. 39–42, 44–45.
16 At [1970] CLJ 103.
17 *R v Callinan* (1973) Times, 20 January, C Cr Ct; *R v Kneafsey* (1973) Times, 23 October; *R v Fell* [1974] Crim LR 673, CA (CrD).
18 28 HC Deb 31 January 1934 cols. 360–361.
19 Cmnd. 7891, 1980, p. 11.
20 Compare K. D. Ewing and C. A. Gearty, op. cit., Chaps. 3 and 6, discussing the difficulties in policing the Communist Party and Fascist supporters in the 1920s and 1930s.
1 S.I. 2001 No. 1261.
2 [1999] EHRLR 109, (1997) 5 BHRC 339.
3 Para. 55.
4 (1997) 25 EHRR CD 172.

the comprehensive discussion of this case and comparisons with approaches in other jurisdictions to 'quasi public space' by K. Gray and S. Gray (below).[5] What is the difference between loitering and window-shopping? Should the purpose of assembly affect its legality?

Article 11 applies in a diverse range of circumstances including where the assembly is alleged to be illegal,[6] and applies to both public and private assemblies.

Challenge to public meeting and protest arising in public order situations may include other 'rights' such as those involving freedom of religion. In *Pendragon v UK*[7] the application of Arthur U. Pendragon, a druid, challenging the banning order under s. 14A, POA 1986 (below) relating to Stonehenge, was declared inadmissible. P was arrested at a 'service' he was conducting for druids, and he claimed that his right to religion under Art. 9 was infringed, along with his rights under Arts. 10, 11, and 14. The Commission found that the order under s. 14A complied with a sufficiently clear procedure, was limited and could be challenged before the courts.

H. Fenwick has argued that the impact of the Human Rights Act 1998 on the right to protest in the UK will, ironically, depend on the 'readiness of the domestic judiciary to disregard much of the current Strasbourg public protest jurisprudence'.[8]

(A) THE LOCATION OF MEETINGS AND PROCESSIONS

All land is vested in some person or institution. People may be permitted to assemble at the landowner's discretion. Assembling without permission is a trespass, although proceedings may well not be taken.[9] Meetings and processions must also conform to the common law of nuisance and to any specific statutory restrictions as to location. The residual freedom or 'liberty' to assemble must be exercised without infringement of the rights of others, and with due regard for their liberties. It is an important question whether English law gives sufficient weight to freedom of assembly. It is also open to argument whether judges have attached sufficient importance to this interest where the law only proscribes conduct that is 'unreasonable', and the conflicting interests of different people have accordingly to be balanced. The materials considered here illustrate the courts' heavy reliance on property law rather than constitutional principles to resolve public order disputes and the limits of freedom to assemble.

(i) The highway

1. Tort

The use of the highway for meetings and processions is restricted by both the law of tort and the criminal law. Aspects of the law of tort which are theoretically relevant include trespass, public nuisance and private nuisance.

Trespass

The House of Lords confirmed in *DPP v Jones*[10] that a peaceful non-obstructive demonstration on a road is not a trespassory assembly for the purposes of s. 14A of

---

5 [1999] EHRLR 46–102.
6 *G v Germany* (1989) 60 DR 256.
7 [1999] EHRLR 223.
8 [1999] 62 MLR 513.
9 But see *Department of Transport v Williams* (1993) 138 Sol Jo LB5, where the Court of Appeal upheld the grant of interlocutory injunctions against persons demonstrating against the motorway constructions at Twyford Down to restrain trespasses and, in one case, interference with business.
10 [1999] 2 AC 240.

the Public Order Act 1986.[11] The majority held that there was no limitation that the use of the highway had to be restricted to passage and repassage or to uses incidental or ancillary thereto. It is a question of fact and degree for the magistrates in each case whether a particular use is reasonable. Lords Irvine and Hutton acknowledged a right of peaceful assembly, provided that it does not obstruct the public right of passage. Lord Clyde, the other member of the majority found that there was no trespass on the facts. Will a protestor be confident that he is not a trespasser?

Where a highway is maintainable at the public expense, as is usually the case with made up roads, it vests in the highway authority.[12] There is in fact no reported case of such an authority suing demonstrators or the participants in a meeting for trespass. In *Hubbard v Pitt*[13] the defendants picketed a firm of estate agents as part of a campaign against property developers. The estate agents brought an action alleging nuisance, libel and conspiracy, and were granted an interlocutory injunction by the Court of Appeal (affirming Forbes J, although not necessarily agreeing with all aspects of his judgment). Do you think that the highway authority *could* successfully have sued for trespass in this case? Why should orderly picketing not constitute 'a reasonable and usual mode of using a highway'?

Public nuisance

To constitute *public nuisance*, the misuse of a highway must amount to 'unreasonable user'.[14] In *Hubbard v Pitt* Forbes J assumed that 'unreasonableness' was established if it could be shown that passage was obstructed. That assumption has been criticised.[15] Wallington argues:

'The test is ... not whether a demonstration is something reasonably incidental to passage, but whether it is reasonable in the context of rights of highway users generally. If passers-by must make a detour, their inconvenience must be balanced against the interest in allowing the demonstration; it will be relevant to consider the degree of obstruction and whether the demonstration could conveniently have been held at a less obstructive venue or off the highway.'[16]

A civil action may be brought in respect of a public nuisance only by the Attorney-General, or by a person who suffers some particular or special loss over and above the inconvenience suffered by the public at large.[17] A local authority is entitled to seek an injunction to restrain an individual from committing a public nuisance (including criminal activity such as drug dealing): *Nottingham City Council v Z*.[18]

Private nuisance

Private nuisance is described in *Winfield and Jolowicz on Tort*[19] as 'unlawful interference with a person's use or enjoyment of land, or some right over, or in connection with it'. This includes infringement of a servitude.[20] Only those who have a right to exclusive possession of the land can sue in nuisance.[21] The person who creates the nuisance may be liable whether or not he is in occupation of the land on

11 See below, p. 446.
12 Highways Act 1980, ss. 1, 263, 265–267.
13 [1976] QB 142.
14 *Lowdens v Keaveney* [1903] 2 IR 82; *R v Clark (No 2)* [1964] 2 QB 315, CCA.
15 See P. Wallington, [1976] CLJ 82, 101–106.
16 Ibid., p. 104.
17 W. V. H. R. Rogers, *Winfield and Jolowicz on Tort* (15th edn, 1998), p. 490.
18 (2001) 31 July, CA (CivD).
19 15th edn, 1998, p. 490.
20 Ibid., pp. 495–496.
21 *Hunter v Canary Wharf Ltd* [1997] 2 All ER 426; see below, p. 939.

which it originates. [1] The blocking of access to private premises is an example of private nuisance. [2] Watching and besetting may constitute private nuisance [3] (but Lord Denning MR took a different view in *Hubbard v Pitt*).

A course of conduct amounting to harassment may also give rise to criminal or tortious liability under the Protection from Harassment Act 1997. [4]

Recent attempts to use the law of nuisance in respect of anti-social behaviour have met with limited success. In *Hussain v Lancaster City Council* [5] the landlord council was not liable in the tort of nuisance for activities of tenants not involving use of their land. In that case literally hundreds of council tenants from a housing estate had racially harassed the claimant, their acts included verbal abuse, criminal damage, arson, and threats of violence.

> 'In the present case the acts complained of unquestionably interfered persistently and . . . with the plaintiff's enjoyment of the plaintiff's land, but they did not involve the tenants' use of the tenants' land and therefore fell outside the scope of the tort.' [6]

However, in *Lippiatt v South Gloucestershire County Council* [7] a group of travellers on council land adversely affected the workability of adjoining land occupied by tenant farmers. The court held that there was no rule of law which prevents an owner/occupier of land being liable in nuisance by reason of the activities of his licensees taking place on the land. Distinguishing *Hussain v Lancaster City Council*, the court held that in this case the nuisance emanated from the travellers' use of the land. Are these cases so readily distinguishable on the basis of the use of the land from which the activities emanated?

Note the rights of access to open land under the Countryside and Rights of Way Act 2000, and the restrictions available to landowners (below, p. 428).

NOTES

1. *Harrassment.* In *Thomas v National Union of Mineworkers (South Wales Area)* [8] Scott J granted interlocutory injunctions against the branch union and its servants, agents and officers, from, *inter alia*, assisting, encouraging or organising members of the branch union to assemble at or near the colliery gates of each of five collieries in the area, in numbers greater than six or for any purpose outside s. 15 of the Trade Union and Labour Relations Act 1974. [9] The judge held that the unreasonable harassment of workers who wished to use the highway to go to work was tortious: 'the tort might be described as a species of private nuisance'. [10] The plaintiffs (working miners) were unable to establish a cause of action for obstructing the highway, as their entry into and egress from the colliery was not physically prevented; if the pickets were obstructing the highway, the plaintiffs had not suffered any special damage. [11] His Lordship also held that (1) regular picketing of the home of a working miner, regardless of the number of people involved and regardless of the peaceful

---

1 Ibid., 514–522.
2 Ibid., pp. 528–537.
3 Ibid., p. 531, based on *J. Lyons & Sons v Gullifer* [1914] 1 Ch 631.
4 See below, p. 506.
5 [1999] 77 P & CR 89.
6 Per Hirst LJ.
7 [2000] QB 51, CA (Civ D).
8 [1985] 2 All ER 1.
9 See now the Trade Union and Labour Relations (Consolidation) Act 1992, s. 220, below p. 419.
10 At 23.
11 At 21.

nature of their conduct, would constitute a common law nuisance;[12] and (2) mass picketing would constitute both common law nuisance and an offence under s. 7 of the Conspiracy, and Protection of Property Act 1875 (now s. 241 of the Trade Union and Labour Relations (Consolidation) Act 1992).[13] Section 241 is not restricted to use in the context of trade disputes, it can be applied to protestors who obstruct construction workers: *DPP v Todd.*[14] On the modern tactics of protest including intimidation of individuals' homes, etc see the discussion of the animals rights protests above.[15]

In *News Group Newspapers Ltd v Society of Graphical and Allied Trades '82 (No 2),*[16] Stuart-Smith J held that the daily mass picketing and demonstrations at the first plaintiff's Wapping plant constituted unreasonable use of the highway and public and private nuisance. The demonstrations arose out of the move of the printing of *The Times* and other newspapers published by the News International Group to Wapping, and the introduction of new technology. The judge held that the plaintiffs had, unlike the plaintiffs in *Thomas v NUM (South Wales Area)*, above, suffered special damage: *The Times* had lost journalists and expense had been incurred in busing in employees in vehicles with protective grilles over the windows. The judge granted interlocutory injunctions against the unions and certain individuals in a form that permitted their continuing to organise peaceful picketing and marches. It was not necessary for Stuart-Smith J to express a final view on the 'unreasonable harassment' basis of liability identified by Scott J in *Thomas v NUM (South Wales Area)*, above. However, he noted criticisms expressed by the defendants, who submitted that:

'Scott J should not have invented a new tort and that it is not sufficient to found liability that there has been an unreasonable interference with the rights of others, even though when a balance is struck between conflicting rights and interests the scale comes down in favour of the plaintiffs, unless those rights are recognised by the law and fall within some accepted head of tort.'

Stuart-Smith J commented:[17]

'I think there is force in these criticisms, especially where it does not appear that damage is a necessary ingredient of the tort.'[18]

2. *Crime.* The Protection from Harassment Act 1997[19] establishes a tort and criminal offences of pursuing a course of conduct that harasses another.[20] The Criminal Justice and Police Act 2001 extends the harassment legislation in a way that will be particularly significant for protestors. The 2001 Act provides a power for an officer to direct persons to leave the vicinity of premises used as a dwelling or to follow other directions given by the officer to prevent harassment, alarm or distress to persons in a dwelling. The power exists whenever there are people present 'in the vicinity' of

---

12 p. 23.
13 p. 30
14 [1996] Crim LR 344, DC.
15 See p. 405.
16 [1987] ICR 181.
17 At 206.
18 For a discussion of the issues arising out of these cases, see H. Carty, [1985] PL 542; S. Auerbach, (1987) 16 ILJ 227; K.D. Ewing and B. Napier, [1986] CLJ 285. For criticism of the policing of the dispute, in particular in relation to restrictions placed on the free movement of residents, see NCCL, *No Way in Wapping* (1986).
19 See P. Infield and G. Platford, *The Law of Harassment and Stalking* (2000); T. Lawson-Cruttenden and N. Addison, *Blackstone's Guide to the Protection from Harassment Act 1997* (1997); C. Wells, [1997] Crim LR 463.
20 See below, p. 506.

a dwelling[21] and the officer has reasonable grounds to believe that those present are there for the purpose:

> 'by his presence or otherwise of representing to the resident or another individual (whether or not one who uses the premises as his dwelling), or of persuading the resident or such another individual: (i) that he should not do something that he is entitled to or required to do; or (ii) that he should do something that he is not under any obligation to do'

and that the officer reasonably believes that the presence of the person (alone or with others) or their behaviour is likely to cause harassment, alarm or distress to people in the dwelling. Officers exercising the power may give such directions as they consider necessary to prevent harassment alarm or distress to the residents and may specify distances to which the protestors must withdraw. It is an arrestable offence to fail to comply with such an order. [22]

The provisions are, obviously, designed to deal with the animal rights protestors' tactics of standing outside the houses of employees and shareholders of relevant companies with placards of animals and vivisection activity. As is typical of much recent legislation designed to tackle public disorder concerns, the legislation is drafted very broadly and has the potential to stifle public protest. Are republican protests outside Buckingham Palace caught by this power? What of protestors outside No. 10 Downing Street? As in many public order contexts, the discretion of the officer on the spot is extremely broad.

In addition, s. 44 of the 2001 Act extends the harassment provisions to render it an offence to aid, abet, counsel or procure an harassing course of conduct. Conduct by one person shall be taken at the time it occurs to be conduct by another if it is aided, abetted, counselled or procured by that other. To make the offence even broader still, the knowledge and purpose of accessories is assessed by reference to what was contemplated or reasonably foreseeable at the time of the assistance. In terms of criminal law principle such extensions are very unsatisfactory.

In view of the power to arrest for breach of the peace (below), which includes situations in which there is a threat of a future breach of the peace was this extension of the harassment legislation necessary? It is arguable that the police would prefer to be granted powers to direct activities of protestors rather than have to resort to arrest. In practical terms it is often difficult for the police to execute arrests of large numbers.

Criminal nuisance

As we have seen, obstruction of the highway may constitute public nuisance. A public nuisance may be the subject of criminal proceedings. There are numerous statutory provisions which create offences of nuisance, usually where they relate to endangerment of health. [1] In addition, the common law offence of public nuisance continues to be used in a versatile fashion: in *R v Johnson*[2] it was used successfully where multiple indecent telephone calls had been made to women. See also *R v Eskdale*,[3] where a sentence of nine years was not manifestly excessive for 1,000 calls over a two-week period to numerous women, threatening to rape and stab them unless they continued to talk to E, who claimed to them to be outside their homes. See also

---

21 As defined in the Public Order Act 1986, s. 8 to include 'any structure or part of a structure occupied as a person's home or as other living accommodation (whether the occupation is separate or shared with others) but does not include any part not so occupied . . .'

22 ss. 42, 43, 44. See Home Office Circulars 29/2001; 24/2001.

1 See especially the Environmental Protection Act 1990, ss. 79–82.

2 [1997] 1 WLR 367, CA.

3 (2001) 8 May, CA (Cr D), unreported.

the charges of conspiracy to commit public nuisance in *R v Chee Kew Ong*,[4] where C agreed to switch off floodlights at a premiership football match.

Remedies for neighbourhood disturbances include the Night Noise Act 1996, which provides a power for local authorities to deal with domestic noise by, *inter alia,* seizing equipment if necessary.[5]

Highway obstruction

In *R v Clark (No 2)*,[6] C, the field secretary of the Campaign for Nuclear Disarmament, led a crowd through various streets in London in the course of a Committee of 100 demonstration during the visit of the King and Queen of Greece. Several streets were partially or completely blocked. C was convicted on a charge of inciting persons to commit a public nuisance by obstructing the highway and sentenced to 18 months' imprisonment. His conviction was quashed as the deputy chairman at the London Sessions had failed to direct the jury on the question whether, granted obstruction, there was an unreasonable user of the highway. He had merely directed that if there was a physical obstruction, that constituted nuisance, and that C, if he incited it, was guilty.

One of the difficulties with the application of offences dealing with the highway in the context of public protest is that the focus of the legal inquiry is on technical issues. For example, in *Clarke v Kato*[7] the House of Lords held that only exceptionally would a car park qualify as a road. Although primarily concerned with the definition of 'road', the House of Lords noted that 'the element of public access has to be tested by reference to *the facts* as well as rights. The question in this context is whether the public *actually* and legally have access . . .'[8]

Much more commonly, criminal proceedings for obstruction of the highway are brought under the following provision.

Highways Act 1980

137. Penalty for wilful obstruction

(1) If a person, without lawful authority or excuse, in any way wilfully obstructs the free passage along a highway he shall be guilty of an offence and shall be liable in respect thereof to a fine not exceeding level 3 on the standard scale.

NOTES

1. This section was formerly s. 121 of the Highways Act 1959. It is much used in respect of demonstrations – particularly where people sit down in the street. A power of arrest is available under the Police and Criminal Evidence Act 1984, s. 25(3)(d)(v),[9] replacing a power conferred by s. 137(2).

2. It is not open to the local authority to authorise an obstruction of the highway so as to afford a defence to criminal proceedings: *Redbridge London Borough v Jacques*;[10] *Cambridgeshire and Isle of Ely County Council v Rust*.[11]

4 [2001] 1 Cr App R (S) 117.
5 On public nuisance generally, see J. C. Smith, *Smith and Hogan* (9th edn, 1999), p. 756.
6 [1964] 2 QB 315.
7 [1998] 1 WLR 1647.
8 Per Lord Clyde at 1652.
9 Above, p. 278.
10 [1970] 1 WLR 1604, DC.
11 [1972] 2 QB426, DC. See A. J. Ashworth, [1974] Crim LR 652; A. T. H. Smith, (1985) 14 Anglo-Am LR 3.

3. Cases under s. 137 and analogous statutory provisions have consistently taken the line that the obstruction of any part of the highway constitutes obstruction for these purposes, notwithstanding that there is room for persons to pass by, or that delay is minimal. Consider the extent to which the House of Lords' decision in *DPP v Jones* (below) undermines these decisions.

In *Homer v Cadman* [12] H marched into the Bull Ring, Sedgley, an irregular triangle where six highways converge. He was accompanied by a band. He stood on a chair and addressed a crowd of between 150 and 200 people for an hour and a half. There was space between the crowd and the footpaths for vehicles or pedestrians to pass. H was convicted under the Highway Act 1835, s. 72. His appeal to the Divisional Court failed. Per Smith J: [13]

'The appellant was only entitled to use the highway in an authorised manner, that is, to pass over it to and fro. He certainly had used it in an unauthorised manner, and the magistrate has found that, as no person could have gone across that part of the highway where the appellant and his band were without considerable inconvenience and danger, there was an obstruction to the highway. The fact that only a part of the highway was so obstructed seems to me to make no difference.'

Cf. *Aldred v Miller*. [14]

4. Reasonable user of the highway will constitute 'lawful excuse' under s. 137. In *Nagy v Weston*, [15] Lajos Nagy parked his van in a lay-by where there was a bus stop, in order to sell hot-dogs from it. He was there for five minutes before he was arrested under s. 121 of the 1959 Act. The justices found that although the road was wide, it was nevertheless busy at that time of night (10.15 p.m.), carrying heavy traffic including buses which would be pulling out of the lay-by. There was therefore unreasonable user by parking a van even for five minutes. His conviction under s. 121 was affirmed by the Divisional Court. Per Lord Parker CJ: [16]

'There must be proof that the use in question was an unreasonable use. Whether or not the user amounting to an obstruction is or is not an unreasonable use of the highway is a question of fact. It depends upon all the circumstances, including the length of time the obstruction continues, the place where it occurs, the purpose for which it is done, and of course whether it does in fact cause an actual obstruction as opposed to a potential obstruction . . . [T]he justices . . . have clearly found that in the circumstances of this case there was an unreasonable use of the highway. Indeed, on the facts stated, it is difficult to see how they could conceivably arrive at any other conclusion.'

Examples of the magistrates exercising their judgement on this matter include determining whether a handgrip on an electric fence was sufficiently easy to operate that the fence did not present an obstruction. [17] See also *Kent County Council v Holland*, [18] holding that the menacing behaviour of K's rottweiler dogs jumping at the fence of his property adjoining the highway was not an obstruction. The protrusion of the dogs' heads over the fence was no more than minimal. On the *de minimis* rule in this context, see also *Torbay BC v Cross*, [19] on shop window displays on the footpath (5% of the footpath). What is the relationship between the degree of obstruction and the reasonableness of use of the highway?

12 (1886) 16 Cox CC 51, DC.
13 At 54.
14 1925 JC 117 (High Court of Justiciary).
15 [1965] 1 All ER 78, [1965] 1 WLR 280.
16 At 284.
17 *Kent County Council v Neeson* (1996) 10 May, DC, unreported.
18 [1996] COD 469.
19 (1995) 159 JP 682.

Wallington[20] argues that the term 'lawful excuse' could be interpreted more generously to cover all demonstrations reasonably conducted with due regard to the interests of others. The following decision acknowledges that some weight must be attached to the right of free speech.

Hirst and Agu v Chief Constable of West Yorkshire (1986) 85 Cr App Rep 143, (1986) 151 JP 304, Queen's Bench Divisional Court

H, A and four others were convicted by magistrates of obstructing the highway contrary to the Highways Act 1980, s. 137. They were members of a group of animal rights supporters who protested in Bradford City Centre outside and in the doorway of 'Lady at Lord John', a shop which sold furs. The defendants stood in varying parts of Darley Street, a spacious but busy pedestrian precinct, offering leaflets or holding a banner. A and others were arrested for conduct likely to cause a breach of the peace. H and others gathered in the shop's doorway to protest against this arrest and were in turn arrested for conduct likely to cause a breach of the peace and obstruction of the highway. In the event, only obstruction of the highway charges were brought. The defendants appealed unsuccessfully to the Crown Court, which found that their actions were not incidental to lawful user of the highway. H and A appealed to the Divisional Court by way of case stated.

Glidewell LJ: ... [stated the facts, referred to the authorities: *Lowdens v Keaveney* [1903] 2 IR 82; *Nagy v Weston* [1965] 1 All ER78; *Hubbard v Pitt* [1975] 3 All ER1; *Jones v Bescoby* (8 July 1983, unreported); *Waite v Taylor* (1985) 149 JP 551; *Cooper v Metropolitan Police Comr* (1985) 82 Cr App Rep 238, and continued:]
 Now it is clear in the present case that the Crown Court did not consider whether the defendants' user of the highway was reasonable or not, because that Court, considering itself bound by *Waite v Taylor* (supra), decided that handing out leaflets and holding banners was not incidental to the lawful use of the highway to pass and re-pass and, therefore, that the reasonableness of that activity was not relevant.
 As I have already said, in my judgment *Nagy v Weston* (supra) is the leading modern authority and it does not apply so rigid a test as that found in the judgment of May LJ in *Waite v Taylor*, with the greatest respect to him. In *Nagy v Weston* itself, the activity being carried on, that is to say the sale of hot dogs in the street, could not in my view be said to be incidental to the right to pass and re-pass along the street. Clearly, the Divisional Court took the view that it was open to the magistrates to consider, as a question of fact, whether the activity was or was not reasonable. On the facts the magistrates had concluded that it was unreasonable (an unreasonable obstruction) but if they had concluded that it was reasonable then it is equally clear that in the view of the Divisional Court the offence would not have been made out.
 That is the way Tudor Evans J approached the matter in the recent decision of *Cooper v MPC* (supra) and I respectfully agree with him.
 As counsel pointed out to us in argument, if that is not right, there are a variety of activities which quite commonly go on in the street which may well be the subject of prosecution under section 137. For instance, what is now relatively commonplace, at least in London and large cities, distributing advertising material or free periodicals outside stations, when people are arriving in the morning. Clearly, that is an obstruction; clearly, it is not incidental to passage up and down the street because the distributors are virtually stationary. The question must be: is it reasonable use of the highway or not? In my judgment that is a question that arises. It may be decided that if the activity grows to an extent that it is unreasonable by reason of the space occupied or the duration of time for which it goes on that an offence would be committed, but it is a matter on the facts for the magistrates, in my view.
 To take another even more mundane example, suppose two friends meet in the street, not having seen each other for some time, and stop to discuss their holidays and are more or less stationary for a quarter of an hour or 20 minutes. Obviously, they may well cause an obstruction

to others passing by. What they are discussing has nothing to do with passing or re-passing in the street. They could just as well have the conversation at the home of one or other of them or in a coffee shop nearby. Is it to be said that they are guilty of an offence and the reasonableness of what they are doing is not in issue? In my judgment it cannot be said.

Some activities which commonly go on in the street are covered by statute, for instance, the holding of markets or street trading, and thus they are lawful activities because they are lawfully permitted within the meaning of the section. That is lawful authority. But many are not and the question thus is (to follow Lord Parker's dictum): have the prosecution proved in such cases that the defendant was obstructing the highway without lawful excuse? That question is to be answered by deciding whether the activity in which the defendant was engaged was or was not a reasonable user of the highway.

I emphasise that for there to be a lawful excuse for what would otherwise be an obstruction of the highway, the activity in which the person causing the obstruction is engaged must itself be inherently lawful. If it is not, the question whether it is reasonable does not arise. So an obstruction of the highway caused by unlawful picketing in pursuance of a trade dispute cannot be said to be an activity for which there is a lawful excuse. But in this case it is not suggested that the activity itself – distributing pamphlets and displaying banners in opposition to the wearing of animal furs as garments – was itself unlawful.

I suggest that the correct approach for justices who are dealing with the issues which arose and arise in the present case is as follows. First, they should consider: is there an obstruction? Unless the obstruction is so small that one can consider it comes within the rubric *de minimis*, any stopping on the highway, whether it be on the carriageway or on the footway, is prima facie an obstruction. To quote Lord Parker: 'Any occupation of part of a road thus interfering with people having the use of the whole of the road is an obstruction.'

The second question then will arise: was it wilful, that is to say, deliberate? Clearly, in many cases a pedestrian or a motorist has to stop because the traffic lights are against the motorist or there are other people in the way, not because he wishes to do so. Such stopping is not wilful. But if the stopping is deliberate, then there is wilful obstruction.

Then there arises the third question: have the prosecution proved that the obstruction was without lawful authority or excuse? Lawful authority includes permits and licences granted under statutory provision, as I have already said, such as for market and street traders and, no doubt, for those collecting for charitable causes on Saturday mornings. Lawful excuse embraces activities otherwise lawful in themselves which may or may not be reasonable in all the circumstances mentioned by Lord Parker in *Nagy v Weston* (supra). In the present case the Crown Court never considered this question. In my judgment, carefully though they dealt with the matter, they were wrong not to do so, and I would, therefore, allow the appeal.

Otton J: I agree. The courts have long recognised the right to free speech to protest on matters of public concern and to demonstrate on the one hand and the need for peace and good order on the other.

In *Hubbard v Pitt* [1975] 3 All ER 1, to which Glidewell LJ has already referred, Lord Denning MR at another passage at pp. 10D and 11B said as follows:

'Finally, the real grievance of the plaintiffs is about the placards and leaflets. To restrain these by an interlocutory injunction would be contrary to the principle laid down by the court 85 years ago in *Bonnard v Perryman* [1891] 2 Ch 269 and repeatedly applied ever since. That case spoke of the right of free speech. Here we have to consider the right to demonstrate and the right to protest on matters of public concern. These are rights which it is in the public interest that individuals should possess; and indeed, that they should exercise without impediment so long as no wrongful act is done. It is often the only means by which grievances can be brought to the knowledge of those in authority – at any rate with such impact as to gain a remedy. Our history is full of warnings against suppression of these rights. Most notable was the demonstration at St. Peter's Fields, Manchester, in 1819 in support of universal suffrage. The magistrates sought to stop it. Hundreds were killed and injured. Afterwards the Court of Common Council of London affirmed "the undoubted right of Englishmen to assemble together for the purposes of deliberating upon public grievances." Such is the right of assembly. So also is the right to meet together, to go in procession, to demonstrate and to protest on matters of public concern. As long as all is done peaceably and in good order without threats or incitement to violence or obstruction to traffic, it is not prohibited: see *Beatty v Gillbanks* (1882) 9 QBD 308. I stress the need for peace and good order. Only too often violence may break out: and then it should be firmly handled and severely punished. But, so long as good order is maintained, the right to demonstrate must be preserved. In his recent inquiry [(1975) Cmnd. 5919] on the Red Lion Square disorders, Scarman L.J. was asked to recommend "that a positive right to demonstrate should be enacted." He said at p. 28 that it was unnecessary: "The right of course exists, subject only to limits required by the need for good order and the passage of traffic." In the recent report on Contempt of Court, the committee considered the campaign of the Sunday Times about thalidomide and said that the issues were "a legitimate matter for public comment." It recognised that it was important to maintain the "freedom of protest on issues of public concern." It is time for the courts to recognise this too. They should not interfere by interlocutory injunction with the right to demonstrate and to protest any more than they interfere with the right of free speech; provided that everything is done peaceably and in good order.'

Although Lord Denning was dealing with the use of an interlocutory injunction, I consider that the passage is of importance when considering whether persons behaving like these appellants have committed a criminal offence of wilful obstruction where there is under section 137(2) of the Act a statutory right of arrest without warrant.

On the analysis of the law, given by Glidewell LJ and his suggested approach with which I totally agree, I consider that this balance would be properly struck and that the 'freedom of protest on issues of public concern' would be given the recognition it deserves.

Appeal allowed.

Convictions quashed.

NOTES

1. See G. Holgate; [21] P. Copling; [1] I. Bing; [2] S. Bailey. [3]

2. In *Waite v Taylor* [4] a busker juggling with lighted fire sticks in a pedestrian precinct was held to be guilty of the offence as he had occupied part of the highway for a purpose that could not properly be said to be ancillary to the exercise of his right to pass and repass. In *Cooper v Metropolitan Police Comr* [5] the Divisional Court held that the Crown Court was entitled to find that the action of a club tout in engaging people in conversation on the highway to try and persuade them to enter the club constituted an unreasonable user. Note that the House of Lords has since held in *DPP v Jones* [6] that a peaceful non-obstructive demonstration on a road is not a trespassory assembly for the purposes of s. 14A of the Public Order Act 1986. [7] Is it practical for decisions under s. 137 to focus on the reasonableness of the activity?

In *Birch v DPP* [8] B had sat down in the road outside the premises being targeted as part of a demonstration and was arrested for obstruction. He sought to challenge the arrests under s. 137(1) by adducing evidence of the unlawful activities occurring within the premises. The magistrates declined to allow the evidence and the Divisional Court approved this decision. The case was distinguishable from *Hirst* (above) where the activity (handing out leaflets) was lawful in itself.

21 (1987) 151 JPN 568.
1 Ibid., p. 579.
2 Ibid., p. 628.
3 [1987] PL 495.
4 (1985) 149 JP 551, DC.
5 (1985) 82 Cr App Rep 238.
6 [1999] 2 AC 240.
7 See below, p. 446.
8 [2000] Crim LR 301.

The Divisional Court referred to the decision of the House of Lords in *Jones* and concluded that:

> 'Rose LJ: In my judgment it is apparent from the authorities to which we have been referred that no one may unreasonably obstruct the highway. There is no right to demonstrate in a way which obstructs the highway. There may be a lawful excuse for an obstruction which occurs in the highway and *Hirst and Agu* provides a good example of that. . . .
>
> Whether or not preventing crime affords a defence to a particular charge must depend on the circumstances.
>
> There may be circumstances in which preventing an actual, or imminently apprehended, breach of the peace or other serious offence, on or near the highway, will afford a lawful excuse for obstructing the passage along the highway of one or more vehicles.
>
> But that is not the present case. An honest and reasonable belief that the progress of a vehicle may contribute to criminal activity not amounting to an imminent breach of the peace or other serious offence is not, in my judgment, capable of affording lawful excuse for obstructing the passage along the highway of that vehicle, still less of other vehicles unconnected with it.
>
> A demonstration involving lying down in the road, as it seems to me, may possibly draw attention to crime but it cannot, in my judgment, give rise to the prevention of crime within either the [common law] principle . . . or section 3 of the [Criminal Law Act 1967] Act. As Mr Perry points out, there was, at the time of this lying down, no crime occurring in the road. There was an obstruction not only of a vehicle destined for SARP's premises but a considerable number of other vehicles which were entitled to pass and repass on the highway.
>
> [The magistrate] was, in my judgment, entitled to decline to hear the evidence which was proffered because it was not capable of giving rise to a defence in law to the offence with which the appellant was charged. For these reasons I would dismiss this appeal.
>
> **Smith J**: I agree and add only this: before there can be a conviction under section 137 of the Highways Act 1980 the prosecution must show that the defendant had no lawful excuse for obstructing the highway. Although the burden lies on the prosecution there will be an evidential burden on the defendant to show the circumstances relied upon.
>
> I agree with my Lord in accepting that the prevention of crime may in some circumstances amount to a lawful excuse for causing an obstruction of the highway; however, it will not be the prevention of any crime which would be capable of amounting to such a lawful excuse and I agree with what my Lord has said that it will only be where there is an imminent danger of a breach of the peace or some other serious crime being committed that the possibility will arise of those circumstances amounting to a lawful excuse to obstruct the highway.
>
> Where that defence is to be raised, it will be necessary for evidence to be called to establish the facts necessary to show that a breach of the peace or serious crime was about to be committed and that the defendant's actions were no more than was reasonably necessary to prevent that crime. The fact finding tribunal would then have to decide whether the actions in obstructing the highway did amount to lawful excuse. However, the facts on which this appellant wished to rely to raise a defence of lawful excuse did not approach anywhere near the type of circumstances which could amount to lawful excuse. The argument he would have wished to raise was obviously hopeless and in my view the magistrate was acting with good sense when he refused to hear the evidence which the appellant wished to call.'

NOTE

The offence under s. 137 seems to reverse the burden of proof – i.e. impose a burden on the defendant in a criminal trial to establish his innocence. It is debatable whether this is a true legal burden, or merely an evidential burden to raise the issue of the defence. If it is the former, this runs counter to the fundamental principle of English criminal law established in *Woolmington v DPP*.[9] Serious doubts as to the legitimacy

9   [1935] AC 462. See J. C. Smith, 'The Presumption of Innocence' (1987) 78 NILQ 223.

of the such a burden being placed on the defendant flow from the decision of the House of Lords in *R v DPP, ex p Kebilene* [10] and the requirements of a presumption of innocence in Art. 6(2) of the ECHR. The courts have been reluctant to regard English statutes as being incompatible with the ECHR on this basis: see e.g. the less than helpful advice of the House of Lords in *R v DPP, ex p Kebilene*: [11]

> 'as a matter of general principle . . . a fair balance must be stuck between the demands of the general interest of the community and the protection of the fundamental rights of the individual.'

In *R v Lambert*, decided in the House of Lords, [12] the majority held that the legal burden of proof should be on the prosecution, any burden on the defendant should, save in exceptional circumstances, be evidential. On the facts, they found that the section under the Misuse of Drugs Act 1971 (s. 28) provided no such special exception. [13]

Arrowsmith v Jenkins [1963] 2 QB 561, [1963] 2 All ER 210, [1963] 2 WLR 856, 127 JP 289, 61 LGR 312, Queen's Bench Divisional Court

On 13 April 1962, a meeting was held in Nelson Street, Bootle, at which the main speaker was Pat Arrowsmith. This street linked two main roads. Meetings had been held there from time to time and police officers had on occasions attended to ensure the free passage of traffic. There was no evidence that these meetings had led to prosecutions for obstruction. At this meeting the carriageway and pavements were completely blocked from 12.35 p.m. to 12.40 p.m. A passageway for vehicles was then cleared by the police and a fire engine and other vehicles were guided through the crowd. Police officers requested the defendant to ask her audience to draw closer to her to help clear the carriageway and the defendant did so by means of a loud-hailer through which she was addressing the crowd. But the carriageway remained partly obstructed until after 12.55 p.m. when the defendant finished speaking. If it had not been for the fact that the defendant was speaking, the crowd would have dispersed and the highway would have been cleared.

A was convicted under the Highways Act 1959, s. 121. She appealed unsuccessfully to quarter sessions and to the Divisional Court.

Lord Parker CJ: I think that the defendant feels that she is under a grievance because – and one may put it this way – she says: 'Why pick on me? There have been many meetings held in this street from time to time. The police, as on this occasion, have attended those meetings and assisted to make a free passage, and there is no evidence that anybody else has ever been prosecuted. Why pick on me?' That, of course, has nothing to do with this court. The sole question here is whether the defendant has contravened section 121(1) of the Highways Act, 1959....

I am quite satisfied that section 121(1) of the Act of 1959, on its true construction, is providing that if a person, without lawful authority or excuse, intentionally as opposed to accidentally, that is, by an exercise of his or her free will, does something or omits to do something which will cause an obstruction or the continuance of an obstruction, he or she is guilty of an offence. Mr. Wigoder, for the defendant, has sought to argue that if a person – and I think that this is how he puts it – acts in the genuine belief that he or she has lawful authority to do what he or she is doing then, if an obstruction results, he or she cannot be said to have wilfully obstructed the free passage along a highway.

Quite frankly, I do not fully understand that submission. It is difficult, certainly, to apply in the present case. I imagine that it can be put in this way: that there must be some mens rea

10 [1999] 4 All ER 801.
11 See commentary at [2000] Crim LR 486.
12 [2001] UKHL 37, 5 July; [2001] 3 WLR 206.
13 See A. Ashworth, [2001] 7 Arch News 5.

in the sense that a person will only be guilty if he knowingly does a wrongful act. I am quite satisfied that that consideration cannot possibly be imported into the words 'wilfully obstructs' in section 121(1) of the Act of 1959. If anybody, by an exercise of free will, does something which causes an obstruction, then an offence is committed. There is no doubt that the defendant did that in the present case....

Ashworth and **Winn JJ** agreed.

Appeal dismissed.

NOTES

1. A. T. H. Smith comments [14] that:

'Although it could undoubtedly be said that she intended to cause an obstruction in the sense that she intended that the crowd should gather around her, it may be doubted whether in the circumstances her conduct in causing the obstruction was properly described as "wilful" ... [W]here no contemporaneous objection is taken by those whose official function it is to preserve the way free from obstruction, it is unduly restrictive of freedom of speech for the courts to hold that the obstruction is wilful when the speaker acts in reliance on that official, and perfectly proper, connivance.'

2. The European Court has held that 'the right of a peaceful assembly stated in [Art. 11] is a fundamental right in a democratic society and, like the right to freedom of expression, is one of the foundations of such society . . . as such this right covers both private meetings and meetings in public thoroughfares.' [15]

(ii) Open spaces

Open spaces, parks, recreation grounds and the like are usually vested in the Crown, or in a local authority. They may be subject to regulations or byelaws made under a variety of statutory powers. [16] The Local Government Act 1972, s. 235 empowers district and London borough councils to make byelaws for the 'good rule and government' of the whole or any part of their area, 'and for the prevention and suppression of nuisances therein'. These commonly cover such topics as the use in public of musical instruments, amplifiers or indecent language.

The Countryside and Rights of Way Act 2000 introduces a statutory right of access to open land (as defined in Part I of the Act), and provides for landowners to exclude or restrict access for any reason for up to 28 days per year, and to impose other specific restrictions relating to dogs on specified land at certain times of the year. Landowners may gain permission from the Countryside Agency to exclude the public for other reasons. [17] The public's right of access to land is for the purposes of 'open air recreation' and on condition that they enter without damaging any wall, fence or gate and that they comply with the restrictions in Sch. 2 (not committing criminal offences including bylaws and restricting use of vehicles, horses, bikes, etc.). Breach of a restriction will lead to the loss of a right of access for 72 hours, and to the wrongdoer being treated as a trespasser (s. 2(4)).

14 *Smith*, pp. 204–205.
15 *Rassemblement Jurassien and Unite Jurassienne v Switzerland* (1979) 17 DR 93, p. 119.
16 See *Brownlie*, pp. 35–38; Public Health Act 1875, s. 164; Open Spaces Act 1906, s. 15.
17 See on the controversial background to the Bill *Access to the Open Countryside in England and Wales* (1998); *The Government's Framework for Action: Access to the Countryside in England and Wales* (1999); and www.wildlife-countryside.detr.gov.uk/c1/index.

The general public may not acquire a private law right to hold meetings on land. [18] 'No such right ... is known to the law'. [19] Moreover, challenges to byelaws which prohibit the holding of meetings at particular places or without prior consent have generally been unsuccessful. [20] Conversely, byelaws restricting access to RAF Greenham Common, made under the Military Lands Act 1892, s. 17(2), were held to be *ultra vires* in *DPP v Hutchinson*; *DPP v Smith*. [21] The byelaws on their face prejudicially affected rights of common, and this was specifically prohibited by the enabling Acts. The appellants, who did not assert any right of common, were nevertheless entitled to argue in their defence that the byelaws were *ultra vires*. [22] The House of Lords in *Boddington v British Transport Police* [1] recognised that 'any system of law under which the individual was convicted and made subject to a criminal penalty for breach of an unlawful byelaw would be inconsistent with the rule of law.' [2] It is therefore possible for a defendant in a criminal trial to challenge, on any ground, the validity of a byelaw, subject to the statute precluding such challenge. [3] The defence will always bear the burden of proving the invalidity of the subordinate legislation.

Bailey v Williamson [4] concerned the validity of regulations under the Parks Regulation Act 1872 which (*inter alia*) prohibited public addresses in Hyde Park except at certain places. Section 1 of the Act provided that nothing in the Act authorised 'any interference with any right whatever to which any person or persons may be by law entitled'. The Court of Queen's Bench held that there was no 'right' to hold public meetings in the Park. Cockburn CJ said: [5] '... whatever enjoyment the public have been allowed to have of these parks and royal possessions for any purpose has been an enjoyment which the public have had by the gracious concession of the Crown.' The use of Hyde Park is now regulated by the Royal and Other Parks and Gardens Regulations 1977. [6]

The Trafalgar Square Regulations 1952, S.I. 1952 No. 776

The Minister of Works in exercise of the powers conferred upon him by the Trafalgar Square Act 1844, and the Parks Regulation Acts 1872 and 1926, and of all other powers enabling him in that behalf, hereby makes the following Regulations: ...
2. Prohibited Acts.—Within the Square the following acts are prohibited:
    (1) wilfully interfering with the comfort or convenience of any person in the Square;
    (2) dropping or leaving litter or refuse except in a receptacle provided for the purpose;
    (3) polluting any water;
    (4) walking on any shrubbery or flower bed;
    (5) damaging, cutting or picking any tree or plant;
    (6) damaging, defacing or climbing on any structure, seat or other Government property;
    (7) bathing or paddling.
3. Acts for which Written Permission is required.—Within the Square the following acts are prohibited unless the written permission of the Minister has first been obtained:

---

18 *De Morgan v Metropolitan Board of Works* (1880) 5 QBD 155, DC, and *Brighton Corporation v Packham* (1908) 72 DP 318, Ch D.
19 Per Lush J in *De Morgan* at 157.
20 *De Morgan*, above; *Slee v Meadows* (1911) 75 JP 246, DC; *Aldred v Miller* 1925 JC 21; *Aldred v Langmuir* 1932 JC 22.
21 [1990] 2 AC 783, HL.
22 See A. W. Bradley, [1989] PL 1 and [1990] PL 193. Cf. *Bugg v DPP* [1993] 2 All ER 815, DC.
1 [1998] 2 WLR 639.
2 Per Lord Irving of Lairg, LC at 645.
3 *R v Wicks* [1998] AC 92.
4 (1873) LR 8 QB 118.
5 At 125.
6 S.I. 1977 No. 217.

(1) selling or distributing anything or offering anything for sale or hire;
(2) carrying on any trade or business;
(3) using artificial light or a tripod or stand for photography;
(4) organising, conducting or taking part in any assembly, parade or procession;
(5) making or giving a public speech or address;
(6) placing or exhibiting any display or representation;
(7) erecting or using any apparatus for the transmission, reception, reproduction or amplification of sound or speech by electrical or mechanical means unless the sound emitted is audible to the user only;
(8) causing any obstruction to free passage;
(9) singing or playing a musical instrument.

NOTES

1. The regulations were made on 8 April 1952, and came into operation on 8 June 1952. The Trafalgar Square Regulations 1952 were revoked by the Royal Parks and Open Spaces Regulations 1997.[7] The regulations were re-enacted (with minor amendments) by the same provision, which placed the control of the Square under the management of the Secretary of State. The management of the Square is now under the authority of the Mayor of London.[8]

2. In *Rai, Allmond and Negotiate Now v UK*[9] a challenge to the Trafalgar Square Statutory Instrument on grounds that it was not adequately clearly prescribed by law was rejected by the European Commission. The statutory instrument has sufficient precision to alert individuals to its effect. This is yet another example of the Strasbourg jurisprudence taking a very generous view of whether English law adequately defines its proscribed activities in public order contexts. Note that the Human Rights Act 1998 applies to all public authorities, therefore all local byelaws and local Acts must be compatible.

3. The history of Trafalgar Square as a place of public meeting is discussed in R. Mace, *Trafalgar Square*.[10] Appendix 5 gives a list of applicants for the use of the Square for political meetings. A small minority of applications have been refused since 1952.

4. Two cases in 1888 confirmed that there was no 'right' of public meeting in Trafalgar Square. In *R v Cunninghame Graham and Burns*[11] Charles J directed the jury that there was no right of public meeting 'either in Trafalgar-square' or any other public thoroughfare . . . . '[T]he use of public thoroughfares is for people to pass and repass along them'.[12] In *Ex p Lewis*[13] L sought summonses against Henry Matthews, the Home Secretary, and Sir Charles Warren, the Metropolitan Police Commissioner, alleging, *inter alia*, conspiracy to prevent Her Majesty's subjects from exercising their constitutional and lawful rights, to endanger the public peace,

---

7 S.I. 1997 No. 1639.
8 Greater London Authority Act 1999 (Commencement No. 4 and Adaptation) Order 2000, S.I. 2000 No. 801.
9 81-A Dand R 146 (1995).
10 (1976).
11 (1888) 16 Cox CC 420.
12 At 429.
13 (1888) 21 QBD 191, DC.

and to inflict grievous bodily harm, and nuisance. The allegations were based upon the conduct of the authorities in relation to the Trafalgar Square riots of 13 November 1887. [14] The Divisional Court declined to interfere with the magistrate's decision to refuse the summonses, and rejected the claim that there was a right of public meeting. Wills J pointed out [15] that Trafalgar Square was vested by statute in the Crown with the powers of control and management exercised by the Commissioners of Works.

'Trafalgar Square ... is completely regulated by Act of Parliament and whatever rights exist must be found in the statute if at all. The right of public meeting is not among them. The right of control appears to be unqualified except by what else is to be found in the Acts [53 Geo 3, c 121, 7 & 8 Vict c 60 and 14 & 15 Vict c 42] and must therefore cover the right of saying under what circumstances, and for what purposes, other than the public rights of passage given by the Acts, it shall be used ....'

(iii) Near Parliament

In addition to the legislative provisions mentioned below, both Houses of Parliament at the commencement of each session direct the Metropolitan Police Commissioner to keep the streets leading to Parliament open and order that the access to Parliament of Lords and members is not to be obstructed. The power to give such sessional orders derives from parliamentary privilege. [16] The Commissioner enforces these orders by giving directions under s. 52 of the Metropolitan Police Act 1839. [17]

Sessional Order of the House of Commons[17a]

METROPOLITAN POLICE

Motion made, and Question proposed
That the Commissioner of the Police of the Metropolis do take care that during the Session of Parliament the passages through the streets leading to this House be kept free and open, and that no obstruction be permitted to hinder the passage of Members to and from this House, and that no disorder be allowed in Westminster Hall, or in the passages leading to this House, during the Sitting of Parliament, and that there be no annoyance therein or thereabouts; and that the Serjeant at Arms attending this House do communicate this Order to the Commissioner aforesaid.

Metropolitan Police Act 1839

52. Commissioners may make regulations for the route of carriages, and persons, and for preventing obstruction of the streets during public processions, etc., or in the neighbourhood of public buildings, etc.
... It shall be lawful for the commissioners of police from time to time, and as occasion shall require, to make regulations for the route to be observed by all carts, carriages, horses, and persons, and for preventing obstruction of the streets and thoroughfares within the metropolitan police district, in all times of public processions, public rejoicings, or illuminations, and also to give directions to the constables for keeping order and for preventing any obstruction of the thoroughfares in the immediate neighbourhood of her Majesty's palaces and the public offices, the High Court of Parliament, the courts of law and equity, the [magistrates' courts] [18]

---

14 Below.
15 At 198.
16 See D. Limon and W. McKay (eds.), *Erskine May, Parliamentary Practice* (22nd edn, 1997), p. 180.
17 Below.
17a See *Erskine May*, op. cit., p. 180.
18 As substituted by the Access to Justice Act 1999, s. 78(2), Sch. 11, paras. 1, 2.

the theatres, and other places of public resort, and in any case when the streets or thoroughfares may be thronged or may be liable to be obstructed.

NOTES

1. By s. 54(9) of this Act, 'every person' commits an offence 'who, after being made acquainted with the regulations or directions' made under s. 52, 'shall wilfully disregard or not conform himself thereunto'. The maximum penalty is a fine not exceeding level 2 on the standard scale.

2. The following direction was made by the Commissioner on 21 April 1966:

> '*Processions prohibited during the sitting of Parliament.* By virtue of the powers conferred on me by section 52 of the Metropolitan Police Act 1839, I the undersigned Commissioner of Police of the metropolis do hereby give directions to all constables that during the session of Parliament the following sessional order shall be enforced: [the order was recited] And I further direct all constables in pursuance of the said order and by virtue of my powers under the said Act:(1) That all assemblies or processions of persons shall be dispersed and shall not be in or proceed along any street, square or open place within the area specified hereunder on any day on which Parliament is sitting: south side of the river Thames between Waterloo and Vauxhall Bridges, Vauxhall Bridge Road, Victoria Street (between Vauxhall Bridge Road and Buckingham Palace Road), Grosvenor Gardens, Grosvenor Place, Piccadilly, Coventry Street, New Coventry Street, Leicester Square (north side), Cranbourn Street, Long Acre, Bow Street, Wellington Street, crossing Strand and Victoria Embankment west of Waterloo Bridge. Provided that processions may be routed along the thoroughfares named except Victoria Embankment west of Waterloo Bridge. (2)That they shall prevent or remove any cause of obstruction within the area named in paragraph (1) hereof, so that every facility shall be afforded for the free passage of members to and from the Houses of Parliament on any day on which Parliament is sitting.'

This direction was at issue in *Papworth v Coventry*.[19] P and others took part in a 'vigil' in Whitehall on both sides of Downing Street to call attention to the situation in Vietnam. They were spaced (i.e. spread) out and stationary, and were not disorderly. They refused to move when requested and were prosecuted under s. 54(9) for failure to comply with the direction. The court held: (1) that the sessional order itself could have no effect outside the walls and precincts of the Houses of Parliament; and (2) that the direction was to be construed as if it referred only to such assemblies or processions of persons as are capable of causing consequential obstruction to the free passage of members to and from the Houses of Parliament or their departure therefrom, or disorder in the neighbourhood or annoyance thereabouts. Any wider sense would have been *ultra vires* the Commissioner. The case was remitted to the stipendiary magistrate to determine whether the conduct 'constituted an assembly which was capable of giving rise consequentially either to obstruction of streets and thoroughfares in the immediate neighbourhood of the Houses of Parliament, or to disorder, annoyance of the kind itself likely to lead to a breach of the peace.' Papworth was subsequently acquitted.[20]

See also *Needham v DPP*[21] where the Divisional Court held that it was sufficient to 'acquaint' someone of a direction to summarise it (and it would be insufficient merely to state its existence). However, N's conviction under s. 54(9) in respect of her participation in a sit-down protest in the roadway in Parliament Square was quashed as the Commissioner's direction in force on that day enabled the police to

19 [1967] 2 All ER 41, [1967] 1 WLR 663, DC.
20 *Brownlie*, p. 60.
21 11 March 1994, unreported.

stop or divert 'pedestrian traffic' but did not apply to persons sitting down on the thoroughfare.

3. The power to give directions was relied on as the basis of the use of roadblocks in the Wapping area during the News International dispute. These had a significant effect on the freedom of movement of residents. [22] The directions were not published and copies were not given to residents. The analogous power in the City of London Police Act 1839, s. 22, was used to combat 'Stop the City' demonstrations in the City. [23]

4. The enforcement of sessional orders has also been secured by the prosecution of persons for wilfully obstructing the police in the execution of their duty. See *Pankhurst v Jarvis*, [1] and *Despard v Wilcox*, [2] cases concerning suffragettes.

5. Processions are stopped at the boundary of the 'Sessional Area' and marchers are allowed to proceed independently to Parliament to lobby MPs. [3]

6. Disorder within the precincts of Parliament is dealt with by police under the direction of the Serjeant at Arms, as in 1966, where some members of the Committee of 100 attempted to make speeches in the House of Commons, and others sat down in Old Palace Yard. [4] The police on duty in the House are technically under the direction of the Serjeant at Arms. Both Houses have power to imprison any person offending the privileges of the House concerned or anyone in contempt of the House. The power has not been exercised since 1880. [5]

(iv) Publicly owned premises

As the holding of street meetings is likely to be unlawful, [6] and therefore dependent in practice upon the goodwill of the police, it becomes even more crucial to those that wish to organise meetings that premises be available. Political meetings today seem to arouse such little public enthusiasm that finding premises is less of a problem than filling them. Extremist groups which are likely to arouse opposition naturally have most difficulty. One of the contributory factors in the decline of Mosley's British Union of Fascists after 1936 was the difficulty in hiring halls for their rallies. [7] Prior to the Olympia meeting in June 1934, [8] the police prevented a BUF rally at White City by persuading the chairman of the White City Board to demand so high a bond upon the safety of the hall that Mosley had to decline the booking.

The traditional importance of meetings during elections is recognised by ss. 95 and 96 of the Representation of the People Act 1983 (as amended by the Representation of the People Act 1985 and the Greater London Authority Act 1999, s. 17), which entitle candidates during election campaigns (including European Parliamentary Elections) to the use of a suitable school room or meeting room (maintained at public expense) for the purpose of holding public meetings. Expenses are payable and damage must be paid for but the use is otherwise free of charge. In

---

22 See NCCL, *No Way in Wapping* (1986).
23 *New Statesman*, 11 May 1984, p. 5.
1 (1910) 22 Cox CC 228, DC.
2 (1910) 22 Cox CC 258, DC.
3 See P. A. J. Waddington, *Liberty and Order* (1994), pp.66–68.
4 *Report of the Commissioner of Police of the Metropolis for 1966*, Cmnd. 3315, p. 13.
5 On the Serjeant at Arms' power to take into custody any person misconducting himself in the public gallery, see HC Standing Orders (Public Business) 1997 No. 161, and the similar powers of the Gentleman of the Black Rod. See HL Standing Orders (Public Business) (1994) No. 104.
6 See above, pp. 416–418.
7 J. Stevenson and C. Cook, *Britain in the Depression* (1994), p. 233. See also K. D. Ewing and C. A. Gearty, op. cit., Chap. 6.
8 See below, p. 535.

434 Public order

addition the discretionary powers of management of public premises must be exercised within the constraints of the ultra vires doctrine. Accordingly, a fixed policy to refuse the use of premises to particular groups or for particular purposes may fall foul of the rule that requires individual exercises of discretion,[9] and decisions based on improper considerations may also be challenged.[10] Section 97 of the Representation of the People Act 1983 provides that acting or inciting others to act in a disorderly manner for the purposes of preventing such a meeting is an illegal practice.

In *R v Historic Buildings and Ancient Monuments Commission for England (English Heritage), ex p Firsoff*[11] the Court of Appeal dismissed a renewed application for leave to apply for judicial review of English Heritage's decision to close Stonehenge over the night of the summer solstice on 21–22 June 1991. EH's decision was taken on the advice of the police in view of disorder attending this occasion in previous years.[12] Under the Ancient Monuments and Archaeological Areas Act 1979, as amended by the National Heritage Act 1983, the public had access to Stonehenge, but EH had statutory power, if it considered it necessary or expedient to do so in the interest of safety or for the maintenance or preservation of the monument, to exclude the public from access for such period as it thought fit. The court held that there was no arguable case on any of the judicial review grounds.[13]

NOTES

1. Local councils with a general policy of refusing to allow their premises to be used for National Front meetings have been compelled to accede to requests to hold election meetings where the Front have had candidates in parliamentary elections.[14] In *Webster v Southwark London Borough Council*[15] Forbes J granted a declaration that a National Front candidate at a parliamentary by-election was entitled to use a room in accordance with the equivalent provision in the Representation of the People Act 1949.[16] In the light of continued refusal to make a room available leave was given for the issue of a writ of sequestration, although disobedience to a declaration, as a non-coercive order, did not amount to contempt of court. In *Ettridge v Morrell*,[17] the Court of Appeal held that the right of a local election candidate to have a suitable school room made available was a private right enforceable by an action in the Queen's Bench Division and not a public law right to be protected by an application for judicial review. The court permitted the meeting to take place.[18]

What is the position if the organisers of a National Front meeting, purportedly held under s. 95 of the Representation of the People Act 1983, only allow Front members or ticket holders into the meeting? What if the decision is taken by police outside in order to preserve the peace? Would the police be entitled to be present in the meeting in case of a breach of the peace.[19] In July 1978, Manchester City Council

9 J. M. Evans, *de Smith's Judicial Review of Administrative Action* (4th edn, 1980), pp. 311–317. See also, H. Woolf, J. Jowell and A. P. Le Sueur, *Principles of Judicial Review* (1999).
10 Ibid., pp. 322–343.
11 19 June 1991, unreported.
12 See *DPP v Jones*, p. 446.
13 See also *R v Commissioners of English Heritage, ex p Chappell*, 19 June 1986, unreported, CA, referred to in the 1991 case.
14 E.g. Manchester City Council: *The Times*, 20 April 1978.
15 [1983] QB 698, QBD.
16 s. 82.
17 (1986) 85 LGR 100.
18 P. Thornton, *Public Order Law* (1987), p. 162.
19 See *McLeod*, below, p. 552.

refused the National Front permission to hold an election meeting in a local school claiming that it would not be a public meeting, and that council employees had said they would refuse to take the steps necessary to make the room available such as opening the school. The local county court judge held that he had no jurisdiction to entertain the Front's claim for damages for breach of statutory duty. [20]

R. J. Clayton [21] argues that the expression 'public meeting', which is not defined, should be construed as 'a meeting to which the public have access' rather than 'a meeting which a section of the public is permitted to attend, whether on payment or otherwise':

> 'it would seem proper to construe the words narrowly so that section 95 is not construed as giving a candidate a right to use a room, on payment of bare expenses only, for the purpose of addressing the party faithful.'

See also P. Thornton. [1]

2. In October 1979, the Court of Appeal held that the Labour-controlled Great Yarmouth Council could not veto a booking for the annual conference of the National Front which had been accepted by the council when the Conservatives had been in power. The NF had paid over £6,000 for the booking fee and insurance to cover the risk of damage to council property. Lord Denning MR stated that the conference should go ahead in the interests of freedom of speech and assembly and of the importance of upholding a contract: *Verrall v Great Yarmouth Borough Council*; [2] cf. *Webster v Newham London Borough* Council. [3] Note again the reliance on private law (contract) to substantiate an important issue of constitutional principle.

3. See the *Green Paper*; [4] *HAC Report*; [5] *White Paper*. [6] The *HAC* proposed a procedure similar to s. 3(2) of the Public Order Act 1936 [7] to enable the Home Secretary to require a candidate to hold his meeting elsewhere in the constituency or electoral area. [8] This was rejected by the government on the ground that it would 'encroach upon the right of the candidate to convey his message to the electorate in the area of his choice; and it would involve the police and the public authorities in decisions bearing upon the political fortunes of particular candidates.'

4. Concerns regarding the freedom of expression in universities resulted in legislation.

Education (No. 2) Act 1986

43. Freedom of speech in universities, polytechnics and colleges
(1) Every individual and body of persons concerned in the government of any establishment to which this section applies shall take such steps as are reasonably practicable to ensure that freedom of speech within the law is secured for members, students and employees of the establishment and for visiting speakers.
(2) The duty imposed by subsection (1) above includes (in particular) the duty to ensure, so far as is reasonably practicable, that the use of any premises of the establishment is not denied to any individual or body of persons on any ground connected with—
    (a) the beliefs or views of that individual or of any member of that body; or

---

20 *The Times* 8 and 11 July 1978; J.F. Garner (1978) *Local Government Chronicle*, p. 778.
21 *Parker's Conduct of Parliamentary Elections* (1983), pp. 101–102.
1 Op. cit., pp. 162–163.
2 [1981] QB 202, CA.
3 (1980) Times, 22 November, CA.
4 pp. 24–26.
5 pp. xxv–xxvii.
6 pp. 36–37.
7 Below, p. 437.
8 p. xxvi.

(*b*)   the policy or objectives of that body.

(3) The governing body of every such establishment shall, with a view to facilitating the discharge of the duty imposed by subsection (1) above in relation to that establishment, issue and keep up to date a code of practice setting out—

   (*a*)   the procedures to be followed by members, students and employees of the establishment in connection with the organisation—

      (i)   of meetings which are to be held on premises of the establishment and which fall within any class of meeting specified in the code; and

      (ii)   of other activities which are to take place on those premises and which fall within any class of activity so specified; and

   (*b*)   the conduct required of such persons in connection with any such meeting or activity;

and dealing with such other matters as the governing body consider appropriate.

(4) Every individual and body of persons concerned in the government of any such establishment shall take such steps as are reasonably practicable (including where appropriate the initiation of disciplinary measures) to secure that the requirements of the code of practice for that establishment, issued under subsection (3) above, are complied with....

(6) In this section—

   'governing body', in relation to any university, means the executive governing body which has responsibility for the management and administration of its revenue and property and the conduct of its affairs (that is to say the body commonly called the council of the university);

   'university' includes a university college and any college, or institution in the nature of a college, in a university....

(8) Where a students' union occupies premises which are not premises of the establishment in connection with which the union is constituted, any reference in this section to the premises of the establishment shall be taken to include a reference to the premises occupied by the students' union.

NOTES

1. By sub-s. (5), as amended, the section applies to any university, any institution other than a university within the higher education sector; any establishment of higher or further education maintained by a local education authority; and any institution within the further education sector. An LEA maintaining or assisting an institution is taken to be concerned in its government.

2. For comments on this section, see E. Barendt,[9] who notes that this section –

'will principally benefit controversial politicians and students disposed to listen to them. There is therefore little case in principle for imposing these unusual duties to secure free speech on university premises, when the law otherwise almost always treats freedom of speech as a mere liberty and is unwilling to recognise rights of access.'[10]

3. In *R v University of Liverpool, ex p Caesar-Gordon*,[11] the university authorities granted permission to the student Conservative Association to hold a meeting subject to conditions that information about the meeting be treated as confidential until 9 a.m. on the day of the meeting; that the meeting be open only to those producing a valid staff or student card; and that the university reserved the right to charge the Association with the cost of security. Permission was subsequently withdrawn on the ground that it was likely that good order would not be maintained. The Divisional Court granted a declaration that the university was not entitled to take account of the risk of disorder other than on the university's premises, and there occasioned by

9 'Free Speech in the Universities' [1987] PL 344.
10 Ibid., pp. 349–350.
11 [1990] 3 All ER 821.

members of the public over whom the university had no control. (The university had taken account of the serious concern expressed by the police at the risk of disorder in nearby Toxteth.) However, the court held that the conditions were intra vires. The courts have held that a decision to expel a person from university as a result of his verbally abusive behaviour was not amenable to judicial review. The court denied that the 1986 Act gave a public law dimension to the actions of a students' union: *R v Thames Valley University Students Union, ex p Ogilvy.* [12]

4. Copies of relevant codes of practice should be available from the university or college authorities and may be set out in the institution's Calendar or Regulations.

(v) Powers to ban or control processions and assemblies

There are no general powers whereby public bodies or officials may prohibit in advance the holding of a *meeting*, although there are such powers in relation to land whose management or control is vested in the state. [13] General statutory powers to ban or control *processions* were provided in s. 3 of the Public Order Act 1936. The 1986 Act remodelled and extended those powers and introduced new powers to control (although not ban) meetings and static demonstrations. Moreover, any meeting or procession which constitutes an unlawful assembly may be dispersed, and it may be lawful to disperse a lawful assembly where necessary to prevent a breach of the peace. [14]

The European Court of Human Rights has recognised the compatibility with Art. 11 of prior notice requirements, and, in some circumstances, a ban for a procession:

'a general ban on demonstrations can only be justified if there is a real danger of their resulting in disorder which cannot be prevented by other less stringent measures. In this connection, the authority must also take into account the effect of a ban on procedures which do not themselves constitute a danger for public order. Only if the disadvantage of such processions being caught by the ban is clearly outweighed by the security consideration justifies the issue of the ban, and if there is no possibility of avoiding such undesirable side-effects of the ban by a narrow circumspection of its scope in terms of its territorial application and duration, can the ban be regarded as necessary [under Art. 11(2)].' [15]

Public Order Act 1986

PART II

PROCESSIONS AND ASSEMBLIES

11. Advance notice of public processions
(1) Written notice shall be given in accordance with this section of any proposal to hold a public procession intended—
    (*a*) to demonstrate support for or opposition to the views or actions of any person or body of persons,
    (*b*) to publicise a cause or campaign, or
    (*c*) to mark or commemorate an event,
unless it is not reasonably practicable to give any advance notice of the procession.
(2) Subsection (1) does not apply where the procession is one commonly or customarily held in the police area (or areas) in which it is proposed to be held or is a funeral procession organised by a funeral director acting in the normal course of his business.

---

12 [1997] CLY 2149.
13 See, for example, pp. 428–430.
14 See pp. 526–530.
15 *Christians against Racism and Fascism v United Kingdom* (1980) 21 DR 148, para. 5.

(3) The notice must specify the date when it is intended to hold the procession, the time when it is intended to start it, its proposed route, and the name and address of the person (or of one of the persons) proposing to organise it.

(4) Notice must be delivered to a police station—

(a) in the police area in which it is proposed the procession will start, or

(b) where it is proposed the procession will start in Scotland and cross into England, in the first police area in England on the proposed route.

(5) If delivered not less than 6 clear days before the date when the procession is intended to be held, the notice may be delivered by post by the recorded delivery service; but section 7 of the Interpretation Act 1978 (under which a document sent by post is deemed to have been served when posted and to have been delivered in the ordinary course of post) does not apply.

(6) If not delivered in accordance with subsection (5), the notice must be delivered by hand not less than 6 clear days before the date when the procession is intended to be held or, if that is not reasonably practicable, as soon as delivery is reasonably practicable.

(7) Where a public procession is held, each of the persons organising it is guilty of an offence if—

(a) the requirements of this section as to notice have not been satisfied, or

(b) the date when it is held, the time when it starts, or its route, differs from the date, time or route specified in the notice.

(8) It is a defence for the accused to prove that he did not know of, and neither suspected nor had reason to suspect, the failure to satisfy the requirements or (as the case may be) the difference of date, time or route.

(9) To the extent that an alleged offence turns on a difference of date, time or route, it is a defence for the accused to prove that the difference arose from circumstances beyond his control or from something done with the agreement of a police officer or by his direction....

12. Imposing conditions on public processions

(1) If the senior police officer, having regard to the time or place at which and the circumstances in which any public procession is being held or is intended to be held and to its route or proposed route, reasonably believes that—

(a) it may result in serious public disorder, serious damage to property or serious disruption to the life of the community, or

(b) the purpose of the persons organising it is the intimidation of others with a view to compelling them not to do an act they have a right to do, or to do an act they have a right not to do,

he may give directions imposing on the persons organising or taking part in the procession such conditions as appear to him necessary to prevent such disorder, damage, disruption or intimidation, including conditions as to the route of the procession or prohibiting it from entering any public place specified in the directions.

(2) In subsection (1) 'the senior police officer' means—

(a) in relation to a process being held, or to a procession intended to be held in a case where persons are assembling with a view to taking part in it, the most senior in rank of the police officers present at the scene, and

(b) in relation to a procession intended to be held in a case where paragraph (a) does not apply, the chief officer of police.

(3) A direction given by a chief officer of police by virtue of subsection (2)(b) shall be given in writing.

(4) A person who organises a public procession and knowingly fails to comply with a condition imposed under this section is guilty of an offence, but it is a defence for him to prove that the failure arose from circumstances beyond his control.

(5) A person who takes part in a public procession and knowingly fails to comply with a condition imposed under this section is guilty of an offence, but it is a defence for him to prove that the failure arose from circumstances beyond his control.

(6) A person who incites another to commit an offence under subsection (5) is guilty of an offence....

13. Prohibiting public processions

(1) If at any time the chief officer of police reasonably believes that, because of particular circumstances existing in any district or part of a district, the powers under section 12 will not be

sufficient to prevent the holding of public processions in that district or part from resulting in serious public disorder, he shall apply to the council of the district for an order prohibiting for such period not exceeding 3 months as may be specified in the application the holding of all public processions (or of any class of public procession so specified) in the district or part concerned.

(2) On receiving such an application, a council may with the consent of the Secretary of State make an order either in the terms of the application or with such modifications as may be approved by the Secretary of State.

(3) Subsection (1) does not apply in the City of London or the metropolitan police district.

(4) If at any time the Commissioner of Police for the City of London or the Commissioner of Police of the Metropolis reasonably believes that, because of particular circumstances existing in his police area or part of it, the powers under section 12 will not be sufficient to prevent the holding of public processions in that area or part from resulting in serious public disorder, he may with the consent of the Secretary of State make an order prohibiting for such period not exceeding 3 months as may be specified in the order the holding of all public processions (or of any class of public procession so specified) in the area or part concerned.

(5) An order made under this section may be revoked or varied by a subsequent order made in the same way, that is, in accordance with subsections (1) and (2) or subsection (4), as the case may be.

(6) Any order under this section shall, if not made in writing, be recorded in writing as soon as practicable after being made.

(7) A person who organises a public procession the holding of which he knows is prohibited by virtue of an order under this section is guilty of an offence.

(8) A person who takes part in a public procession the holding of which he knows is prohibited by virtue of an order under this section is guilty of an offence.

(9) A person who incites another to commit an offence under subsection (8) is guilty of an offence....

14. Imposing conditions on public assemblies

(1) If the senior police officer, having regard to the time or place at which and the circumstances in which any public assembly is being held or is intended to be held, reasonably believes that—

    (*a*) it may result in serious public disorder, serious damage to property or serious disruption to the life of the community, or

    (*b*) the purpose of the persons organising it is the intimidation of others with a view to compelling them not to do an act they have a right to do, or to do an act they have a right not to do,

he may give directions imposing on the persons organising or taking part in the assembly such conditions as to the place at which the assembly may be (or continue to be) held, its maximum duration, or the maximum number of persons who may constitute it, as appear to him necessary to prevent such disorder, damage, disruption or intimidation.

(2) In subsection (1) 'the senior police officer' means—

    (*a*) in relation to an assembly being held, the most senior in rank of the police officers present at the scene, and

    (*b*) in relation to an assembly intended to be held, the chief officer of police.

(3) A direction given by a chief officer of police by virtue of subsection (2)(*b*) shall be given in writing.

(4) A person who organises a public assembly and knowingly fails to comply with a condition imposed under this section is guilty of an offence, but it is a defence for him to prove that the failure arose from circumstances beyond his control.

(5) A person who takes part in a public assembly and knowingly fails to comply with a condition imposed under this section is guilty of an offence, but it is a defence for him to prove that the failure arose from circumstances beyond his control.

(6) A person who incites another to commit an offence under subsection (5) is guilty of an offence....

[14A. Prohibiting trespassory assemblies

(1) If at any time the chief officer of police reasonably believes that an assembly is intended to be held in any district at a place on land to which the public has no right of access or only a limited right of access and that the assembly—

    (*a*) is likely to be held without the permission of the occupier of the land or to conduct itself in such a way as to exceed the limits of any permission of his or the limits of the public's right of access, and

    (*b*) may result—

        (i) in serious disruption to the life of the community, or

        (ii) where the land, or a building or monument on it, is of historical, architectural, archaeological or scientific importance, in significant damage to the land, building or monument,

he may apply to the council of the district for an order prohibiting for a specified period the holding of all trespassory assemblies in the district or a part of it, as specified.

(2) On receiving such an application, a council may—

    (*a*) in England and Wales, with the consent of the Secretary of State make an order either in the terms of the application or with such modifications as may be approved by the Secretary of State; ...

(3) Subsection (1) does not apply in the City of London or the metropolitan police district.

(4) If at any time the Commissioner of Police for the City of London or the Commissioner of Police of the Metropolis reasonably believes that an assembly is intended to be held at a place on land to which the public has no right of access or only a limited right of access in his police area and that the assembly—

    (*a*) is likely to be held without the permission of the occupier of the land or to conduct itself in such a way as to exceed the limits of any permission of his or the limits of the public's right of access, and

    (*b*) may result—

        (i) in serious disruption to the life of the community, or

        (ii) where the land, or a building or monument on it, is of historical, architectural, archaeological or scientific importance, in significant damage to the land, building or monument,

he may with the consent of the Secretary of State make an order prohibiting for a specified period the holding of all trespassory assemblies in the area or a part of it, as specified.

    n order prohibiting the holding of trespassory assemblies operates to prohibit any bly which—

      / is held on land to which the public has no right of access or only a limited right of access, and

    (*b*) takes place in the prohibited circumstances, that is to say, without the permission of the occupier of the land or so as to exceed the limits of any permission of his or the limits of the public's right of access.

(6) No order under this section shall prohibit the holding of assemblies for a period exceeding 4 days or in an area exceeding an area represented by a circle with a radius of 5 miles from a specified centre.

(7) An order made under this section may be revoked or varied by a subsequent order made in the same way, that is, in accordance with subsection (1) and (2) or subsection (4), as the case may be.

(8) Any order under this section shall, if not made in writing, be recorded in writing as soon as practicable after being made.

(9) In this section and sections 14B and 14C—

    'assembly' means an assembly of 20 or more persons;

    'land' means land in the open air;

    'limited', in relation to a right of access by the public to land, means that their use of it is restricted to use for a particular purpose (as in the case of a highway or road) or is subject to other restrictions;

    'occupier' means—

    (*a*) in England and Wales, the person entitled to possession of the land by virtue of an estate or interest held by him; ...

and in subsections (1) and (4) includes the person reasonably believed by the authority applying for or making the order to be the occupier;

    'public' includes a section of the public; and

    'specified' means specified in an order under this section....

(11) In relation to Wales, the references in subsection (1) above to a district and to the council of the district shall be construed, as respects applications on and after 1 April 1996, as references to a county or county borough and to the council for that county or county borough.

14B. Offences in connection with trespassory assemblies and arrest therefor
(1) A person who organises an assembly the holding of which he knows is prohibited by an order under section 14A is guilty of an offence.
(2) A person who takes part in an assembly which he knows is prohibited by an order under section 14A is guilty of an offence.
(3) In England and Wales, a person who incites another to commit an offence under subsection (2) is guilty of an offence....][16]

[14C. Stopping persons from proceeding to trespassory assemblies
(1) If a constable in uniform reasonably believes that a person is on his way to an assembly within the area to which an order under section 14A applies which the constable reasonably believes is likely to be an assembly which is prohibited by that order, he may, subject to subsection (2) below—
　　(*a*)　stop that person, and
　　(*b*)　direct him not to proceed in the direction of the assembly.
(2) The power conferred by subsection (1) may only be exercised within the area to which the order applies.
(3) A person who fails to comply with a direction under subsection (1) which he knows has been given to him is guilty of an offence....][17]

15. Delegation
(1) The chief officer of police may delegate, to such extent and subject to such conditions as he may specify, any of his functions under sections 12 to [14A][18] to a deputy or assistant chief constable; and references in those sections to the person delegating shall be construed accordingly.
(2) Subsection (1) shall have effect in the City of London and the metropolitan police district as if 'a deputy or assistant chief constable' read 'an assistant commissioner of police'.

16. Interpretation
In this Part—
　　'the City of London' means the City as defined for the purposes of the Acts relating to the City of London police;
　　'the metropolitan police district' means that district as defined in section 76 of the London Government Act 1963;
　　'public assembly' means an assembly of 20 or more persons in a public place which is wholly or partly open to the air;
　　'public place' means—
　　　　(*a*)　any highway, or in Scotland any road within the meaning of the Roads (Scotland)Act 1984, and
　　　　(*b*)　any place to which at the material time the public or any section of the public has access, on payment or otherwise, as of right or by virtue of express or implied permission;
　　'public procession' means a procession in a public place....

NOTES

1. *Penalties and powers of arrest.* A person guilty of an offence under ss. 11(7), 12(5), 13(8), 14(5), 14B(2), 14C(3) is liable on summary conviction to a fine not exceeding

16　Inserted by the Criminal Justice and Public Order Act 1994, s. 70.
17　Inserted by 1994 Act, s. 71.
18　Substituted by 1994 Act, Sch. 10, para. 60.

level 3 on the standard scale; and under ss. 12(4), (6), 13(7), (9), 14(4), (6), 14B(1), (3) on summary conviction to a fine not exceeding level 4 on the standard scale, or three months' imprisonment, or both. [19] A constable in uniform may arrest without warrant anyone he reasonably suspects is committing an offence under ss. 12(4)–(6), 13(7)–(9), 14(4)–(6), 14B and 14C. [20] The Crime and Disorder Act 1998 creates new powers relating to stop and search. [21] These include the power for a constable to require a person to remove a face mask or other covering which he believes is worn to conceal the person's identity.

Banning orders

2. Section 3 of the Public Order Act 1936 gave powers to a chief officer of police to give directions to those organising or taking part in a procession if he had reasonable grounds to apprehend that it might occasion serious public disorder. If he was 'of opinion' that this would not be sufficient, he could apply for an order to ban all or any class of public processions in the area for a specified period. These powers were introduced in response, *inter alia*, to disturbances arising from the activities of the British Union of Fascists in the 1930s. [22]

The main changes effected by Part II of the 1986 Act were (1) the introduction of advance notice requirements for *processions*; [23] (2) the extension of the circumstances in which conditions may be imposed on *processions*; [24] and (3) a new power to impose conditions on (but not to ban) public *assemblies*. [25] A power to ban 'trespassory assemblies' was added by the Criminal Justice and Public Order Act 1994.

The provisions governing banning orders [26] are very similar to the old s. 3. The government considered but rejected adding further grounds for banning orders, [1] e.g. (1) 'that the views to be expressed would be seriously offensive: this would place an impossible task upon the police and be an unacceptable infringement of freedom of speech'; (2) a test of disruption: 'too restrictive'; (3) disproportionate cost: 'this would be haphazard in its effect and tend to concentrate major marches in the areas with larger forces'; (4) the procession 'would incite racial hatred': this 'would present insuperable problems of enforcement and could easily backfire by creating martyrs for free speech out of groups' whose policies had been decisively rejected by the electorate.

The power to impose conditions now extends to (1) 'serious damage to property'; (2) 'serious disruption to the life of the community' and (3) 'intimidation'. Ground (2) enables the police to impose conditions 'to re-route a procession in order to limit traffic congestion, or to prevent a bridge from being blocked, or to reduce the severe disruptions sometimes suffered by pedestrians, business and commerce'. [2]

Examples include the policy of the Metropolitan Police to discourage demonstrators from using Oxford Street during business hours. Ground (3) enables conditions to be imposed 'to prevent the coercion of individuals', e.g. where a march is organised to 'stop' or 'smash' opponents; where the National Front organise a march

19 1986 Act, ss. 11(10), 12(8)–(10), 13(11)–(13), 14(8)–(10), 14B(5)–(7), 14C(5).
20 1986 Act, ss. 12(7), 13(10), 14(7), 14B(4) and 14C(4).
21 See above.
22 See J. Stevenson and C. Cook, *Britain in the Depression: Society and Politics, 1929–1939* (2nd edn, 1994), Chaps 11, 12; R. Thurlow, *The Secret State* (1994), Chap. 5; and see the comprehensive discussion by K. D. Ewing and C. A. Gearty, op. cit., especially Chap. 6.
23 s. 11: see below, p. 445.
24 s. 12.
25 s. 14.
26 s. 13.
1   *White Paper*, Chap. 4.
2   *White Paper*, p. 27.

through Asian districts, and the response of the local community is to board up their shops and businesses and to stay at home; where animal rights protesters march on furriers' shops or food factories with the intention of preventing the employees from working; or where a very large crowd marches on the home of an individual councillor or inquiry inspector.[3] How these powers are used in practice is obviously of great importance. A. T. H. Smith commented on their introduction:[4]

'There is a danger that, if the powers are used too freely, the symbolic significance of a demonstration may be lost. For example, if the proposed route of the march takes the participants past an embassy or a particular factory against whose occupants the organisers wish to protest, the prescription of a different route or terminus may obviate the whole point of the demonstration, and amount to in effect a disguised ban.'

The new power to impose conditions on static demonstrations and meetings was justified in the *White Paper*[5] on the ground that they:

'may just as frequently be the occasion of public disorder as marches.... Since 1980 some of the most serious public order problems have been associated with static demonstrations – at Greenham Common, the picketing at Warrington, and of the course the mass pickets during the miners' dispute'.

The government did not then propose a power to ban, noting that:

'Meetings and assemblies are a more important means of exercising freedom of speech than are marches.'[6]

Nevertheless, the power to ban *trespassory assemblies* was added in 1994, prompted particularly by concern over the disruption caused by 'free festivals'.[7]

Waddington refers to the growth in police negotiation pre-protest, and how this gives the activity an air of respectability and renders it institutionalised. By compelling the protesters to take part in such democratic negotiations, the police control 'ordinary decent protestors' and will guarantee their protection – even where the protest is one challenging lawful activity and/or 'fundamental state interests'.[8]

See generally on Part II of the 1986 Act, D. G. T. Williams.[9]

3. May a specified procession be banned under s. 13(1)? If it is known that only one group is planning a march on a particular day, would it be lawful to ban 'all marches' on that day? The *White Paper*[10] proposed that the law be amended to allow a single march to be banned; this change did not appear in the Act on the ground that 'it would place the police in a situation where they would be subject to allegations of political motivation and partiality whenever they exercised the power to seek a ban on a particular march'.[11]

4. Directions and orders under these sections are potentially reviewable in the courts under the ultra vires doctrine. A challenge might be made directly, on an application for judicial review under CPR 54, or collaterally, as a defence to a prosecution. There is, however, no challenge on the merits.[12] It will, however, be difficult in practice to

---

3 *White Paper*, p. 28.
4 *Public Order Offences* (1987), p. 134.
5 p. 31.
6 *White Paper*, pp. 31–32.
7 See above, p. 176, and below, p. 454.
8 Op. cit., p.73. Note also the power to direct protestors away from a dwelling under s. 42 of the Criminal Justice and Police Act 2001.
9 [1987] Crim LR 167.
10 p. 25.
11 *Smith*, pp. 136–137, citing the Minister of State at the Home Office.
12 Cf. *The Times*, 21 April 1980, p. 2.

establish that a ban or other order is ultra vires. In *Kent v Metropolitan Police Comr,* [13] a ban was made under s. 3(3) of the Public Order Act 1936 in the aftermath of the Brixton (and other) disorders, prohibiting all processions within the Metropolitan Police District (786 square miles) 'except those traditionally held on May 1 to celebrate May Day and those of a religious character customarily held'. This had the incidental effect of preventing a planned CND procession. CND sought a declaration that the ban was ultra vires on the ground that in imposing such a wide ban the Commissioner had not directed himself properly as to the matters to be considered. The Court of Appeal rejected the claim: he had considered the relevant matters, the court could not substitute its judgment for his and CND could apply under s. 9(3) [14] for the order to be relaxed. The Commissioner was entitled to conclude that there was a risk that either the march or the police escorting the march would be attacked by hooligans. Moreover he was entitled to ban a 'class' of marches by exclusion.

It will similarly be difficult to establish on judicial review that a refusal to ban or impose conditions is *ultra vires*. See the discussion of two cases under analogous legislation in Northern Ireland, the Public Order (N.I.) Order 1987 [15] by B. Hadfield in 'Public Order Police Powers and Judicial Review'. [16]

5. In *Application No 8440/78 Christians against Racism and Fascism v United Kingdom* [17] the Commission held inadmissible a claim that a ban under s. 3(3) of the Public Order Act 1936 in February 1978 was contrary to ECHR Arts. 5(1), 10, 11 and 14, on the ground that the claim was manifestly ill-founded. On Art. 11 the Commission noted that the right of peaceable assembly guaranteed by Art. 11(1) could not as such be taken away simply by the prospect of violent counter-demonstrations. However, the ban was justified under Art. 11(2) as it complied with the principle that:

'a general ban on demonstrations can only be justified if there is real danger of their resulting in disorder that cannot be prevented by other less stringent measures'. [18]

6. In *Flockhart v Robinson* [1] F was prosecuted under s. 3 of the Public Order Act 1936. The Metropolitan Police Commissioner on 3 October 1949 banned all public processions of a political character within the Metropolitan Police District. On 15 October, F organised a procession of members of a political group, the Union Movement, which procession lawfully dispersed on reaching Temple Bar. Later that day he met about 150 members at Hyde Park Corner who followed him in loose formation when he moved along Piccadilly, and then closed ranks. He gave signals to guide them through the traffic and direction signals. Members other than F sang the Horst Wessel song and shouted political slogans. F led them round Piccadilly Circus and into Coventry Street, where they were broken up by the police. F's conviction for 'organising' a procession contrary to s. 3(4) was upheld by the Divisional Court. [2] Lord Goddard CJ stated: [3] 'A procession is not a mere body of persons: it is a body of persons moving along a route. Therefore the person who organises the route is the person who organises the procession'. In *Kent v MPC* [4] Lord Denning adopted a dictionary definition of procession:

13 *The Times*, 15 May, 1981.
14 See now s. 13(5), 1986 Act.
15 S.I. 1987 No. 463 (*Re Murphy* [1991] 5 NIJB 72, QBD (NI), and 88, CA(NI)); *Re Armstrong* (27 August 1992, unreported, QBD(NI)).
16 [1993] Crim LR 915.
17 (1981) 21 DR 148.
18 p. 198. See also *Pendragon v UK* (above, p. 416).
 1 [1950] 2 KB 498, DC.
 2 Lord Goddard CJ and Morris J, Finnemore J dissenting.
 3 At 502.
 4 Above.

'A public procession is the act of a body of persons marching along in orderly succession – see the *Oxford English Dictionary*. All kinds of processions take place every day up and down the country – carnivals, weddings, funerals, processions to the Houses of Parliament, marches to Trafalgar Square and so forth.'

7. Before 1981 bans under s. 3(2) and (3) of the 1936 Act were uncommon. However, in that year 39 banning orders were made in England and Wales, 7 inside and 32 outside the Metropolitan Police District and the City of London. 'Many of the orders were in response to tension following the civil disturbances'.[5] The figure fell to 13 (7 + 6) in 1982, 9 (2 + 7) in 1983 and 11 (3 + 8) in 1984. The commonest wording of a ban was 'all public processions except those of a religious, educational, festive or ceremonial character customarily held'. The Metropolitan police have on recent occasions resisted pressure to seek bans, claiming that the requirements were 'so onerous that it was a practical impossibility' and that enforcement was 'more trouble than it was worth': P. A. J. Waddington, *Liberty and Order*.[6]

Conditions on processions and assemblies

In practice, the power to impose conditions under the 1936 Act was rarely used, the police preferring to discuss the plans for a march with the organisers and to negotiate an informal agreement about the route and other matters.[7] Compare the power to impose conditions under ss. 12 and 14 with the common law powers of the police to preserve the peace.[8]

Section 11 of the 1986 Act introduced a general requirement of advance notice of public processions. This replaced notice requirements (in varying terms) in many local Acts. Lord Scarman, in his Report on the Red Lion Square disorders,[9] had rejected suggestions for notice requirements on the ground that the need for them had not been established.[10] In 1981, he took a different view.[11] Section 11 is incapable of dealing with spontaneous protests of the type which are becoming increasingly common. There is no opportunity for advance notice. The section leaves the scope of the exemption for processions 'commonly or customarily' held ambiguous.[12] Conditions under s. 12 can be imposed on the officers' 'reasonable belief'. The limiting factor is that there must be a belief in 'serious' disruption; every procession leads to some disruption. Furthermore, the conditions must be necessary (in the officer's opinion?). Will this broad power withstand challenge under the ECHR?

The House of Lords considered the interpretation of s. 14A and 14B in *DPP v Jones*.[13]

---

5 *Report of HM Chief Inspector of Constabulary for 1981* (1981–82 HC 463), para. 8.6.
6 (1994), pp. 58–61.
7 *White Paper*, pp. 26–27.
8 Below, pp. 524–541.
9 Cmnd. 5919, 1975.
10 Paras. 128, 129.
11 The Brixton Disorders (Cmnd. 8427, p.124) as did the Home Affairs Committee (*HAC*, pp. xii–xv) and the *White Paper*, pp. 21–22. See *Legal Action* June 1991, p.13, noting a case where a prosecution for breach of s. 11 in respect of a 'small and peaceful march' was dropped by the CPS; the police appeared to be aware of what was planned even though written notice had not been given. On the process of negotiation between the Metropolitan police and the organisers of demonstrations, see P. A. J. Waddington, *Liberty and Order*, Chap. 4.
12 See further R. Card, *Public Order Law*, Chap. 6. Presumably religious festivals are the principal category.
13 [1999] 2 AC 240.

DPP v Jones [1999] 2 AC 240, [1999] 2 WLR 625, House of Lords

On 1 June 1995, at about 6.40 p.m. Police Inspector Mackie counted 21 people on the roadside verge of the southern side of the A344, adjacent to the perimeter fence of the monument at Stonehenge. Some were bearing banners with the legends, 'Never Again', 'Stonehenge Campaign 10 years of Criminal Injustice' and 'Free Stonehenge'. He concluded that they constituted a 'trespassory assembly' and told them so. When asked to move off, many did, but some, including the Appellants, Mr Lloyd and Dr Jones, were determined to remain and put their rights to the test. They were arrested for taking part in a 'trespassory assembly' and convicted by the Salisbury Justices on 3 October, 1995. Their appeals to the Salisbury Crown Court, however, succeeded. The court held that neither of the appellants, nor any member of their group, was 'being destructive, violent, disorderly, threatening a breach of the peace or, on the evidence, doing anything other than reasonably using the highway'. About an hour before, a different group of people had scaled the fence of the monument and entered it. They had been successfully escorted away by police officers without any violence or arrests; but there were no grounds for apprehension that any of the group of which Mr Lloyd and Dr Jones were members proposed an incursion into the area of the monument.

Their convictions were overturned by the Crown Court, restored by the Divisional Court and finally, by a bare majority, quashed by the House of Lords.

Lord Irvine of Lairg LC: My Lords, this appeal raises an issue of fundamental constitutional importance: what are the limits of the public's rights of access to the public highway? Are these rights so restricted that they preclude in all circumstances any right of peaceful assembly on the public highway?

. . . [In the Divisional Court] it was assumed for the purposes of that appeal . . . that: (a) the grass verge constituted part of the public highway; and (b) the group was peaceful, did not create an obstruction and did not constitute or cause a public nuisance. . . .   The central issue in the case thus turns on two interrelated questions: (i) what are the 'limits' of the public's right of access to the public highway at common law? and (ii) what is the 'particular purpose' for which the public has a right to use the public highway? . . .   [I]n broad terms the basis of the Divisional Court's decision is the proposition that the public's right of access to the public highway is limited to the right to pass and repass, and to do anything incidental or ancillary to that right. Peaceful assembly is not incidental to the right to pass and repass. Thus peaceful assembly exceeds the limits of the public's right of access and so is conduct which fulfils the actus reus of the offence of 'trespassory assembly'.

The position at common law
The Divisional Court's decision is founded principally on three authorities. In *Ex parte Lewis* (1888) 21 Q.B.D. 191 the Divisional Court held obiter that there was no public right to occupy Trafalgar Square for the purpose of holding public meetings. However, Wills J, giving the judgment of the court, had in mind, at p. 197, an assembly ' . . . to the detriment of others having equal rights . . . in its nature irreconcilable with the right of free passage'. Such an assembly would probably also amount to a public nuisance, and, today, involve the commission of the offence of obstruction of the public highway contrary to section 137(1) of the Highways Act 1980 ('the 1980 Act'). Such an assembly would probably also amount to unreasonable user of the highway. It by no means follows that this same reasoning should apply to a peaceful assembly which causes no obstruction nor any public nuisance.

In *Harrison v. Duke of Rutland* [1893] 1 Q.B. 142 the plaintiff had used the public highway, which crossed the defendant's land, for the sole and deliberate purpose of disrupting grouse-shooting upon the defendant's land, and was forcibly restrained by the defendant's servants from doing so. The plaintiff sued the defendant for assault; and the defendant pleaded justification on the basis that the plaintiff had been trespassing upon the highway. Lord Esher M.R. held, at p. 146:

'. . . on the ground that the plaintiff was on the highway, the soil of which belonged to the Duke of Rutland, not for the purpose of using it in order to pass and repass, *or for any*

reasonable or usual mode of using the highway as a highway, I think he was a trespasser.'
(Emphasis added.)

Plainly Lord Esher M.R. contemplated that there may be 'reasonable or usual' uses of the highway beyond passing and repassing. He continued, at pp. 146-147:

'Highways are, no doubt, dedicated prima facie for the purpose of passage; but things are done upon them by everybody which are recognised as being rightly done, and as constituting a reasonable and usual mode of using a highway as such. If a person on a highway does not transgress such reasonable and usual mode of using it, I do not think that he will be a trespasser.'

Lopes LJ, by contrast, stated the law in more rigid terms, at p. 154:

'. . . if a person uses the soil of the highway for any purpose other than that in respect of which the dedication was made and the easement acquired, he is a trespasser. The easement acquired by the public is a right to pass and repass at their pleasure for the purpose of legitimate travel, and the use of the soil for any other purpose, whether lawful or unlawful, is an infringement of the rights of the owner of the soil . . .'

Similarly, Kay L.J. stated, at p. 158:

'. . . the right of the public upon a highway is that of passing and repassing over land the soil of which may be owned by a private person. Using that soil for any other purpose lawful or unlawful is a trespass.'

The rigid approach of Lopes L.J. and Kay L.J. would have some surprising consequences. It would entail that two friends who meet in the street and stop to talk are committing a trespass; so too a group of children playing on the pavement outside their homes; so too charity workers collecting donations; or political activists handing out leaflets; and so too a group of members of the Salvation Army singing hymns and addressing those who gather to listen.

The question to which this appeal gives rise is whether the law today should recognise that the public highway is a public place, on which all manner of reasonable activities may go on. For the reasons I set out below in my judgment it should. Provided these activities are reasonable, do not involve the commission of a public or private nuisance, and do not amount to an obstruction of the highway unreasonably impeding the primary right of the general public to pass and repass, they should not constitute a trespass. Subject to these qualifications, therefore, there would be a public right of peaceful assembly on the public highway.

The third authority relied upon by the Divisional Court is the decision of the Court of Appeal in *Hickman v Maisey* [1900] 1 Q.B. 752. In that case, the defendant, a racing tout, had used a public highway crossing the plaintiff's property for the purpose of observing racehorses being trained on the plaintiff's land. A. L. Smith L.J. expressly followed the approach of Lord Esher M.R. in *Harrison*. Applying that reasoning, he accepted, at p. 756, that a man resting at the side of the road, or taking a sketch from the highway, would not be a trespasser. The defendant's activities, however, fell outside 'an ordinary and reasonable user of the highway' and so amounted to a trespass. Collins L.J. similarly approved Lord Esher M.R.'s approach, noting, at pp. 757-758, that:

'. . . in modern times a reasonable extension has been given to the use of the highway as such . . . The right of the public to pass and repass on a highway is subject to all those reasonable extensions which may from time to time be recognised as necessary to its exercise in accordance with the enlarged notions of people in a country becoming more populous and highly civilised, but they must be such as are not inconsistent with the maintenance of the paramount idea that the right of the public is that of passage.'

Romer L.J. was to similar effect, at p. 759.

I do not, therefore, accept that, to be lawful, activities on the highway must fall within a rubric incidental or ancillary to the exercise of the right of passage. The meaning of Lord Esher's judgment in *Harrison*, at pp. 146-147 is clear: it is not that a person may use the highway only for passage and repassage and acts incidental or ancillary thereto; it is that any 'reasonable and usual' mode of using the highway is lawful, provided it is not inconsistent with the general public's right of passage. I understand Collins L. J.'s acceptance in *Hickman*, at pp. 757-758, of Lord Esher's judgment in *Harrison* in that sense.

To commence from a premise, that the right of passage is the only right which members of the public are entitled to exercise on a highway, is circular: the very question in this appeal is whether the public's right is confined to the right of passage. I conclude that the judgments of Lord Esher M.R. and Collins L.J. are authority for the proposition that the public have the right to use the public highway for such reasonable and usual activities as are consistent with the general public's primary right to use the highway for purposes of passage and repassage.

Nor can I attribute any hard core of meaning to a test which would limit lawful use of the highway to what is incidental or ancillary to the right of passage. In truth very little activity could accurately be described as 'ancillary' to passing along the highway; perhaps stopping to tie one's shoe lace, consulting a street-map, or pausing to catch one's breath. But I do not think that such ordinary and usual activities as making a sketch, taking a photograph, handing out leaflets, collecting money for charity, singing carols, playing in a Salvation Army band, children playing a game on the pavement, having a picnic, or reading a book, would qualify. These examples illustrate that to limit lawful use of the highway to that which is literally 'incidental or ancillary' to the right of passage would be to place an unrealistic and unwarranted restriction on commonplace day-to-day activities. The law should not make unlawful what is commonplace and well accepted.

Nor do I accept that the broader modern test which I favour materially realigns the interests of the general public and landowners. It is no more than an exposition of the test Lord Esher proposed in 1892. It would not permit unreasonable use of the highway, nor use which was obstructive. It would not, therefore, afford carte blanche to squatters or other uninvited visitors. Their activities would almost certainly be unreasonable or obstructive or both. Moreover the test of reasonableness would be strictly applied where narrow highways across private land are concerned, for example, narrow footpaths or bridle-paths, where even a small gathering would be likely to create an obstruction or a nuisance.

Nor do I accept that the 'reasonable user' test is tantamount to the assertion of a right to remain, which right can be acquired by express grant, but not by user or dedication. That recognition, however, is in no way inconsistent with the 'reasonable user' test. If the right to use the highway extends to reasonable user not inconsistent with the public's right of passage, then the law does recognise, (and has at least since Lord Esher's judgment in *Harrison* recognised), that the right to use the highway goes beyond the minimal right to pass and repass. That user may in fact extend, to a limited extent, to roaming about on the highway, or remaining on the highway. But that is not of the essence of the right. That is no more than the scope which the right might in certain circumstances have, but always depending on the facts of the particular case. On a narrow footpath, for example, the right to use the highway would be highly unlikely to extend to a right to remain, since that would almost inevitably be inconsistent with the public's primary right to pass and repass.

. . . I conclude therefore the law to be that the public highway is a public place which the public may enjoy for any reasonable purpose, provided the activity in question does not amount to a public or private nuisance and does not obstruct the highway by unreasonably impeding the primary right of the public to pass and repass: within these qualifications there is a public right of peaceful assembly on the highway.

Since the law confers this public right, I deprecate any attempt artificially to restrict its scope. It must be for the magistrates in every case to decide whether the user of the highway under consideration is both reasonable in the sense defined and not inconsistent with the primary right of the public to pass and repass. In particular, there can be no principled basis for limiting the scope of the right by reference to the subjective intentions of the persons assembling. Once the right to assemble within the limitations I have defined is accepted, it is self-evident that it cannot be excluded by an intention to exercise it. Provided an assembly is reasonable and non- obstructive, taking into account its size, duration and the nature of the highway on which it takes place, it is irrelevant whether it is premeditated or spontaneous: what matters is its objective nature. To draw a distinction on the basis of anterior intention is in substance to reintroduce an incidentality requirement. For the reasons I have given, that requirement, properly applied, would make unlawful commonplace activities which are well accepted. Equally, to stipulate in the abstract any maximum size or duration for a lawful assembly would be an unwarranted restriction on the right defined. These judgments are ever ones of fact and degree for the court of trial.

Further, there can be no basis for distinguishing highways on publicly owned land and privately owned land. The nature of the public's right of use of the highway cannot depend upon whether the owner of the sub-soil is a private landowner or a public authority. Any fear, however, that the rights of private landowners might be prejudiced by the right as defined are unfounded. The law of trespass will continue to protect private landowners against unreasonably large, unreasonably prolonged or unreasonably obstructive assemblies upon these highways.

Finally, I regard the conclusion at which I have arrived as desirable, because it promotes the harmonious development of two separate but related chapters in the common law. It is neither desirable in theory nor acceptable in practice for commonplace activities on the public highway not to count as breaches of the criminal law of wilful obstruction of the highway, yet to count as trespasses (even if intrinsically unlikely to be acted against in the civil law), and therefore form the basis for a finding of trespassory assembly for the purposes of the Public Order Act. A system of law sanctioning these discordant outcomes would not command respect.

Article 11 of the European Convention on Human Rights
    . . . Unless the common law recognises that assembly on the public highway *may* be lawful, the right contained in Article 11(1) of the Convention is denied. Of course the right may be subject to restrictions (for example, the requirements that user of the highway for purposes of assembly must be reasonable and non-obstructive, and must not contravene the criminal law of wilful obstruction of the highway). But in my judgment our law will not comply with the Convention unless its *starting-point* is that assembly on the highway will not necessarily be unlawful. I reject an approach which entails that such an assembly will always be tortious and therefore unlawful. The fact that the letter of the law may not in practice always be invoked is irrelevant: mere toleration does not secure a fundamental right. Thus, if necessary, I would invoke Article 11 to clarify or develop the common law in the terms which I have held it to be; but for the reasons I have given I do not find it necessary to do so. I would therefore allow the appeal.

Lord Clyde: [having referred to earlier cases] In the generality there is no doubt but that there is a public right of assembly. But there are restrictions on the exercise of that right in the public interest. There are limitations at common law and there are express limitations laid down in Article 11 of the Convention on Human Rights. I would not be prepared to affirm as a matter of generality that there is a right of assembly on any place on a highway at any time and in any event I am not persuaded that the present case has to be decided by reference to public rights of assembly. If a group of people stand in the street to sing hymns or Christmas carols they are in my view using the street within the legitimate scope of the public right of access to it, provided of course that they do so for a reasonable period and without any unreasonable obstruction to traffic. If there are shops in the street and people gather to stand and view a shop window, or form a queue to enter the shop, that is within the normal and reasonable use which is matter of public right. A road may properly be used for the purposes of a procession. It would still be a perfectly proper use of the road if the procession was intended to serve some particular purpose, such as commemorating some particular event or achievement. And if an individual may properly stop at a point on the road for any lawful purpose, so too should a group of people be entitled to do so. All such activities seem to me to be subsidiary to the use for passage. So I have no difficulty in holding that in principle a gathering of people at the side of a highway within the limits of the restraints which I have noted may be within the scope of the public's right of access to the highway.

In my view the argument for the appellants, and indeed the reasoning of the Crown Court, went further than it needed to go in suggesting that any reasonable use of the highway, provided that it was peaceful and not obstructive, was lawful, and so a matter of public right. Such an approach opens a door of uncertain dimensions into an ill-defined area of uses which might erode the basic predominance of the essential use of a highway as a highway. I do not consider that by using the language which it used Parliament intended to include some distinct right in addition to the right to use the road for the purpose of passage.

I am not persuaded that in any case where there is a peaceful non-obstructive assembly it will necessarily exceed the public's right of access to the highway. The question then is, as in this kind of case it may often turn out to be, whether on the facts here the limit was passed and the exceeding of it established. The test then is not one which can be defined in general terms but has to depend upon the circumstances as a matter of degree. It requires a careful assessment of the nature and extent of the activity in question. If the purpose of the activity becomes the predominant purpose of the occupation of the highway, or if the occupation becomes more than reasonably transitional in terms of either time or space, then it may come to exceed the right to use the highway.

The only point which has caused me some hesitation in the circumstances of the present case is the evident determination by the two appellants to remain where they were. That does seem to look as if they were intending to go beyond their right and to stay longer than would constitute a reasonable period. But I find it far from clear that there was an assembly of twenty or more persons who were so determined and in light of the fluidity in the composition of the grouping and in the consistency of its component individuals I consider that the Crown Court reached the correct conclusion.

I do not find it possible to return any general answer to the certified question. The matter is essentially one to be judged in light of the particular facts of the case. But I am prepared to hold that a peaceful assembly which does not obstruct the highway does not necessarily constitute a trespassory assembly so as to constitute the circumstances for an offence where an order under section 14A(2) is in force. I would allow the appeal.

Lord Hutton:
. . . My Lords, I consider that in the light of the well known authorities cited to the House the present state of the law is correctly stated in the following passage in *Halsbury's Laws of England* 4th ed. Vol. 21 para. 110:

'The right of the public is a right to pass along a highway for the purpose of legitimate travel, not to be on it, except so far as the public's presence is attributable to a reasonable and proper user of the highway as such. A person who is found using the highway for other purposes must be presumed to have gone there for those purposes and not with a legitimate object, and as against the owner of the soil he is to be treated as a trespasser.'

However I consider that there are indications in the authorities that the public's right to use the highway may be extended and I consider that the important issue before your Lordships' House is whether that right should be extended so that the public has a right in some circumstances to hold a peaceful assembly on the public highway provided that it does not obstruct the use of the highway.

[His Lordship referred to *Harrison v. Duke of Rutland* and other cases]   Therefore, as I have stated, the issue which arises in the present appeal is whether the right of the public to use the highway, as stated by Lopes L.J. in *Harrison v. Duke of Rutland,* should be extended and should include the right to hold a peaceful public assembly on a highway, such as the A344, which causes no obstruction to persons passing along the highway and which the Crown Court found to be a reasonable user of the highway.

In my opinion your Lordships' House should so hold for three main reason which are as follows. First, the common law recognises that there is a right for members of the public to assemble together to express views on matters of public concern and I consider that the common law should now recognise that this right, which is one of the fundamental rights of citizens in a democracy, is unduly restricted unless it can be exercised in some circumstances on the public highway. Secondly, the law as to trespass on the highway should be in conformity with the law relating to proceedings for wilful obstruction of the highway under section 137 of the Highways Act 1980 that a peaceful assembly on the highway may be a reasonable use of the highway. Thirdly, there is a recognition in the authorities that it may be appropriate that the public's right to use the highway should be extended, in the words of Collins L. J. in *Hickman v. Maisey* at p. 758:

'in accordance with the enlarged notions of people in a country becoming more populous and highly civilised, but they must be such as are not inconsistent with the maintenance of the paramount idea that the right of the public is that of passage.'

. . . I would not hold that a peaceful and non-obstructive public assembly on a highway is always a reasonable user and is therefore not a trespass.

It is for the tribunal of fact to decide whether the user was reasonable. In *Hirst and Agu* at p. 150 Glidewell L. J. makes it clear that a reasonable activity in the street may become unreasonable by reason of the space occupied or the duration of time for which it goes on, 'but it is a matter on the facts for the magistrates, in my view'.

If members of the public took part in an assembly on a highway but the highway was, for example, a small, quiet country road or was a bridleway or a footpath, and the assembly interfered with the landowner's enjoyment of the land across which the highway ran or which it bordered, I think it would be open to the Justices to hold that, notwithstanding the importance of the democratic right to hold a public assembly, nevertheless in the particular circumstances of the case the assembly was an unreasonable user of the highway and therefore constituted a trespass.

... I consider that there is an argument of some force that a reasonable user of the highway by an assembly may become an unreasonable user so that the non-trespassory assembly becomes a trespassory assembly if it appears that members of the assembly are about to commit unlawful acts. However, this point did not arise in the questions stated for the opinion of the Divisional Court and was not argued before the Divisional Court, and the point does not arise on the question stated for the opinion of your Lordships' House. Therefore it would not be right to decide the appeal on this point. Accordingly I express no concluded opinion on the point or on the circumstances in which a non-trespassory assembly may become a trespassory assembly.

NOTES

1. Lord Slynn, dissenting, held that:

'The fact that the purpose of the demonstration or assembly is one which most or many people would approve does not change what is otherwise a trespass into a legal right. Nor does the fact that an assembly is peaceful or unlikely to result in violence, or that is not causing an obstruction at the particular time when the police intervene, in itself change what is otherwise a trespass into a legal right of access.

It is objected that very often people on the highway singly or in groups take part in activities which go beyond passage and repassage and are not stopped. That is no doubt so, but reasonable tolerance does not create a new right to use the highway and indeed may make it unnecessary to create such a right which in its wider definition goes far beyond what is justified or needed.'

Lord Hope, dissenting, held that:

'The proposition that the public are entitled to do anything on the highway which amounts in itself to a reasonable user may seem at first sight to be an attractive one. But it seems to me to be tantamount to saying that members of the public are entitled to assemble, occupy and remain anywhere upon a highway in whatever numbers as long as they wish for any reasonable purpose so long as they do not obstruct it. I do not think that there is any basis in the authorities for such a fundamental rearrangement of the respective rights of the public and of those of public and private landowners.'

2. The case is not one in which there is a simple division with a bare majority; there is a spectrum of opinion from Lord Irvine's very broad approach to Lord Slynn's very narrow one. Even within the majority, it is difficult to discern a ratio. Whereas the majority required the use of the highway to be reasonable and usual, the minority focused on whether the use was associated with the passage. What sorts of activity are so connected with passage and re-passage on the highway? Is there a clear majority agreeing that there is a right to assemble in English law?
3. G. Clayton [14] describes the case as 'an endorsement of the right to peaceful assembly ... and an important vindication of a fundamental civil liberty'. Do you share this enthusiasm? Is the decision an invitation for hot-dog stand owners to set up shop anywhere they fancy? Is the case decided on principles of land law or principles of constitutional law? Is the average protestor any better informed of his rights?

14 [2000] MLR 252. See also I. Hare, [1999] CLJ 265; H. Fenwick and G. Phillipson, [2000] PL 627.

4. There is surprisingly little discussion of the ECHR from the Law Lords. Writing before the case, B. Fitzpatrick and N. Taylor questioned whether 'section 14A could indeed be the object of a successful challenge under the European Convention'.[15] To what extent has the decision in *Jones* assuaged those fears? The authors argue that

> 'The new powers conferred by the Act to restrict assemblies pose a considerable threat to the right to engage in even the most peaceful of gatherings, and contend that these powers represent an inappropriate balance between the rights of those seeking to participate in assemblies and the rights of the "community" within which the assembly takes place.
>
> Contemporary society is witnessing a decline in the amount of space that can meaningfully be called "public". However, needless to say, this decline is not accompanied by a reduction in the number of issues that are the legitimate subject of public concern or discussion. It follows that opportunities to assemble, protest, or demonstrate in public in respect of these issues are themselves becoming increasingly limited. Under such circumstances, one might consider it appropriate that some degree of legal protection was afforded to the right of assembly. The Supreme Court of the United States has recognised the utility of public space for the airing of public issues:
>
> "Wherever the title of streets and parks may rest, they have immemorially been held in trust for the use of the public, and time out of mind, they have been used for the purposes of assembly, communicating thought between citizens, and discussing public questions".
>
> However, in England and Wales this is neither the present case, nor has it ever been historically so. Such is the nature of rights in our jurisdiction, that the ability to assemble has always been the subject of considerable legal circumscription. History reveals both a failure, on the part of the domestic judiciary and legislature, to assert the fundamentality of this liberty, and, arguably, to appreciate its value. On the other hand, the right to assemble is granted an express measure of protection by Article 11 of the European Convention on Human Rights, though to date, its influence on domestic jurisprudence has been limited.'

5. Has *Jones* recognised the utility of the public space for the airing of public issues? Sir John Smith, commenting on the case, stated:

> 'It surely remains a fundamental constitutional principle that we can do anything we like unless the act is a crime or a tort or otherwise prohibited by law. It is to be hoped that this principle will survive the coming of the Human Rights Act 1998 and that we will not have to look, (as Collins J appeared to do in the Divisional Court) for a positively declared right to justify conduct which has not been declared to be unlawful. The premise of the present decision is that the conduct did not create an unreasonable obstruction of the highway or amount to a public nuisance. That may, on the facts, have been too generous a conclusion, but that is not the point.'[16]

6. In *Broadwith v Chief Constable of Thames Valley Police*[17] an order was imposed under s. 14 which specified a particular place of assembly and a designated route for the protesters to take to another specified site. B travelled to the area to take part in the demonstration, and, despite being told of the orders in place by the officers on duty, B nevertheless entered a road closed off by the police and was arrested. The fact that B had not first gone to the assembly point and that at that time no assembly had actually taken place, did not prevent the prohibition applying to him. The Divisional Court noted:

> 'groups, whether they be of 20 or more or less than that size, can only consist of individuals. It may be necessary according to the particular circumstances, in order to ensure that an assembly proceeds on permitted lines, to take steps in relation to controlling the movements of particular individuals.

---

15 [1998] EHRLR 292 at 297.
16 [1999] Crim LR 672.
17 [2000] Crim LR 924; cf. *Ezelin v France* (1992) 14 EHRR 362.

Furthermore, it is not, to my mind, an accurate description of the appellant as being not part of an assembly because he was walking away from the other larger group. The fact is that, although he was so walking, he had come with others intending to demonstrate and was deliberately seeking to enter the part of Burford Road which was closed by the police presence, in accordance with the notice which had been served, and was doing so prior to the time of 1.30, when an assembly in Burford Road was, in accordance with the notice, to be permitted.'

Under what circumstances will an individual protestor who has had a change of heart and who wishes to leave a march be allowed to do so? Does this lead to too much discretion in the hands of the officer on duty at the scene? One of the criteria for an order under s. 14 is that there will be serious disruption to the community. Does this prevent an order being sought when all of those in the immediate vicinity are part of the protest?

Earlier decisions on the exercise of s. 14 provide useful examples. An exercise of the power under s. 14 was considered in *Brickley and Kitson v Police*.[1] The defendants' convictions were quashed on appeal to the Crown Court, that court not being satisfied that there had been sufficient communication to B and K (via a megaphone) to make clear to them that there was a s. 14 condition in force which applied to them. The court was therefore not sure that they had *knowingly* been in breach of the condition when the police had sought to impose the condition by addressing the demonstrators through a megaphone.

In *Police v Reid*[2] R was acquitted by the magistrate of a charge under s. 14(5). This case arose out of a demonstration outside the South African Embassy. The chief inspector in charge imposed a condition when R, with about 20 others, demonstrated outside the embassy on the occasion of a reception, shouting slogans (e.g. 'Apartheid murderers, get out of Britain'), raising their arms and waving their fingers at arriving guests. The magistrates held that this conduct was intended to cause 'discomfort' and not 'intimidation': the chief inspector had equated the two, and that was the wrong test.

In *DPP v Baillie*[3] the court upheld the decision of the Crown Court to allow B's appeal against conviction for failing to comply with a s. 14 notice. B published his telephone number as a declared source of information and advice as to the time and location of free festivals. He directed callers (in fact police officers) on a Friday to Andover, and then to Crawley Down, with instructions to ring back, indicating that there was to be a festival that weekend. Police served a s. 14 notice imposing conditions requiring, *inter alia*, that any event be licensed under the Local Government (Miscellaneous Provisions) Act 1982, that there be advance agreement with the police as to maximum numbers in attendance and duration and that there be no damage or disruption to the life of the community resulting from inadequate sanitary arrangements. He continued to give these directions, and was arrested. The Divisional Court held that there was just sufficient evidence for a *prima facie* case that B was an organiser as his 'role as the purveyor of information as to the time and place of the festival was of crucial importance', but that there was insufficient evidence to show that the police were 'having regard to the time or place at which and the circumstances in which any public assembly is being held or intended to be held' in the terms of s. 14(1): 'to this day no one knows, save possibly the organisers, where or when any such public assembly was to be held.... [W]e do not even know that the intended assembly was going to be held in a public place as defined in s. 16 of the Act.'[4] The court left open the argument that, in any event at the time of B's arrest, there was still time for compliance with the conditions.

---

1   *Legal Action* July 1988, p. 21 (Knightsbridge Crown Court).
2   [1987] Crim LR 702.
3   [1995] Crim LR 446, DC.
4   Per McCowan LJ.

Trespass and assembly

It is increasingly common for legislation to provide police with specific powers to direct the conduct of meetings and processions. Section 39 of the Public Order Act 1986 enabled a senior police officer to direct trespassers to leave land. The officer had reasonably to believe that two or more persons had entered land as trespassers and were present there with the common purpose of residing there for any period; that reasonable steps had been taken by or on behalf of the occupier to ask them to leave; and that any of those persons had caused damage to property on the land or used threatening, abusive or insulting words or behaviour towards the occupier, a member of his family or an employee or agent of his, or that those persons had between them brought 12 or more vehicles on to the land. It was an offence to fail to leave the land as soon as reasonably practicable or, having left, to return as a trespasser within three months. This provision was designed as a response to large incidents of mass trespass involving such groups as Hell's Angels and hippies. In particular, in 1986, a 'Peace Convoy' of hippies attempting a pilgrimage to Stonehenge, trespassed on a farm owned by a Mr. Attwell with over 100 buses, trucks, caravans and other assorted vehicles. They stayed for seven days, and left peacefully when a High Court eviction order was granted.[5] It was doubted whether the creation of this offence was necessary,[6] given the existence of recently streamlined civil remedies, the very wide criminal damage offence and the powers of the police to deal with breaches of the peace.

Travellers

Section 39 was used by the police in subsequent years to discourage mass trespass and other disorderly activity by the Peace Convoy and others in the period leading up to the summer solstice.[7] In 1989, processions and marches within a 4-mile radius of Stonehenge were banned over a short period around the summer solstice under s. 13 of the Public Order Act 1986.[8] The 'reasonable steps' referred to in s. 39(1) should be taken by the occupier before the direction is given by the senior police officer.[9] An exercise of discretion to serve a notice is open to challenge on an application for judicial review, although it has been described as 'an entirely unfettered discretion to act on the information which is available': *R v Wiltshire Constabulary*.[10]

Disturbances in the early 1990s involving new age travellers (in particular, the encampment at Castelmorton, Worcestershire, with 20,000 people attending a free festival) provoked widespread concern.[11] Section 39 was replaced by much more draconian powers under the Criminal Justice and Public Order Act 1994. Section 61 is similar to the old s. 39, except that the officer must reasonably believe that two or more persons 'are trespassing'; the presence of six vehicles rather than 12 is sufficient to trigger the power; there is express power to direct the removal of vehicles or other property; there is express provision in respect of common land; the term 'vehicle' includes any vehicle whether or not in a fit state for use on roads and any chassis or

---

5 See P. Vincent-Jones, 'Private Property and Public Order: The Hippy Convoy and Criminal Trespass' (1986) 13 JLS 343; NCCL, *Stonehenge* (1986); K. D. Ewing and C. D. Gearty, *Freedom under Thatcher* (1990), pp. 125–128. For charges under s. 51(3) of the Police Act 1964, now s. 89 of the Police Act 1996, arising out of the Peace Convoy, see *Smith v Reynolds* [1986] Crim LR 559, DC.
6 *Smith*, 1st edition, pp. 259–260.
7 *Reports of the Chief Inspector of Constabulary for 1987* (1987–88 HC 521), pp. 57–58; *1988* (1988–89 HC 449), p. 66.
8 *Report of the Chief Inspector of Constabulary for 1989* (1989–90 HC524), p. 67.
9 *Krumpa and Anderson v DPP* [1989] Crim LR 295, DC.
10 (1992) 25 February, unreported, DC, per Kennedy J.
11 J. Baxter, (1992) Policing 222; *Hansard* HL, 25 April 1994, col. 584.

body, with or without wheels, appearing to have formed part of such a vehicle, and any load carried by, and anything attached to, such a vehicle; and there is a power for a constable to seize and remove any vehicle not removed in accordance with a direction, or taken with a person subject to a direction re-entering within three months. [12]

The 1994 Act provisions have been the subject of a detailed Home Office Research Study. [13] The provisions have been heavily criticised for criminalising 'lifestyles' (gypsies and new age travellers). [14] On the impact on gypsies see S. Campbell, arguing that:

'in respect of Gypsies, conform or be criminalised is the message. By their very unwillingness to model their lifestyles upon those of the sedentary majority, Gypsies and travellers are regarded as social outcasts whose values are inferior to those of the vocal majority.' [15]

Bucke and James found that the 1994 Act provisions were applied to both new age travellers and gypsies, although some forces felt that it was inappropriate to apply them to gypsies. The report also demonstrated that the provisions are now well known by many of the new age travellers against whom the police sought to enforce them. [16] The provisions were used in respect of a wide range of land types, with action usually prompted by damage to the property rather than threats to the occupier. [17] The police are much more likely to act under the provisions when the site belongs to an individual or small company than a major landowner, whom police felt were capable of protecting their own interests through the civil courts. [18]

ACPO guidelines on the use of s. 61 state that the police 'as officers of the law, are responsible for public order, and the prevention and detection of crime. It is therefore only in such circumstances that the use of s. 61 should be considered as a primary response'. [19] Bucke and James report that one force has adopted a policy of not using the s. 61 power, leaving responsibility with landowners and local authorities.[1] Some landowners have used innovative means of removal including for example, spraying trespassers with pig manure.[2]

The police have established a unit to monitor new age travellers – the northern intelligence unit – hosted by Cumbria police. In 1995, 15 forces in England and Wales issued a total of 67 directions under s. 61. The number of people involved in each case ranged from three to 46. In no case in which the powers were used was there a site that was not successfully cleared. Only four prosecutions occurred in 1995, with three convictions. Four prosecutions occurred in 1996 and 15 in 1997.[3] These figures represent a drop in prosecutions from those under the old s. 39 powers.[4] Numerous examples of new age travellers continuing to trespass are reported in the

---

12 s. 62.
13 T. Bucke and Z. James, *Trespass and Protest: policing under the Criminal Justice and Public Order Act 1994* (1998).
14 See Liberty, *Criminalising Diversity, Criminalising Dissent: a report on the use of the public order provisions of the Criminal Justice and Public Order Act 1994* (1995). See also R. Geary and C. O'Shea, (1995) 17 JSW and Fam Law 67.
15 [1995] Crim LR 28, 37. For further information on the impact of the Act on the lives of travellers see the Traveller Law Research Unit, Cardiff University: www.cf.ac.uk/claws/tlru/.
16 p. 10.
17 p. 8.
18 p. 9.
19 (1996).
 1 p. 10.
 2 *Daily Mail*, 8 August 2000.
 3 See *Hansard*, HC Written Answer, 22 Feb 1999 col. 125.
 4 Bucke and James, op. cit., p. 17.

press and referred to in Parliament. See in particular the discussion of the 'Exodus Collective', who trespassed in Bedfordshire for over two years.[5]

The Home Office has issued guidelines emphasising the importance of making adequate inquiry into the welfare of trespassers before the exercise of the power.[6] These issues involve the presence of the elderly, invalid, and in particular, pregnant women. Section 61 imports a *discretion* to direct the trespassers to leave – whether the police decide to order them to leave is an operational decision. The factors the police take into account should include considerations of 'common humanity' such as those listed in the circular. In *R v MAFF, ex p Callaghan, Shough, Tramoni*[7] concerning the local authority powers under the 1994 Act, the court noted that:

'The [Dept of Environment] Circular 18/94 offers guidance on the provisions in section 77 to 80 of the Criminal Justice and Public Order Act 1994 [powers relating to local authorities not the police]. Again it is to be noticed that that Circular is primarily directed towards local authorities, see for example the section under the heading "Policy of Toleration Towards Unauthorised Gypsy Encampment". Paragraphs 6 and 7 are directed towards local authorities. Paragraph 8, relied upon in this case because by its terms it is expressly directed towards government owned land, where it is provided that:

8. Where gypsies are unlawfully camped on Government-owned land, it is for the local authority, with the agreement of the land owning Department, to take any necessary steps to ensure that the encampment does not constitute a hazard to public health. It will continue to be the policy of the Secretaries of State that Government Departments should act in conformity with the advice that gypsies should not be moved unnecessarily from unauthorised encampments when they are causing no nuisance.

9. The Secretaries of State continue to consider that local authorities should not use their powers to evict gypsies needlessly. They should use the powers in a humane and compassionate fashion and primarily to reduce nuisance and to afford a higher level of protection to private owners of land.'[8]

It has been claimed that the decision 'as well as those in the ECHR, have largely emasculated the [Criminal Justice and Public Order Act] powers, because, now, unless a raft of social welfare conditions are taken into account, the local authority risks a challenge in the courts'.[9] There are no plans to amend the circular.[10]

The Metropolitan Police issued the following guidance to their officers in 1995:

'The powers under section 61 are discretionary. . . . It may be more appropriate to use the powers where trespassers "invade" a person's front garden than if they are camping on derelict land. . . . It will be much less appropriate to use the powers if the trespassers have been on the land for several weeks than if they have just arrived. Policing problems which arise from the presence of the trespassers on the land, namely public disorder, crime or obstruction of the highway (bearing in mind that the offence does not relate to the highway) there may be good policing reasons for moving the trespassers... It should be borne in mind that the use of the power under the Act may have the effect only of moving the problem to a different site. Indeed it could make matters worse. The police should not usurp the functions of the civil courts. The use of the powers under section 61 are not appropriate where there may be a genuine dispute as to the right to the possession of the land. In such a case, the matter should be left to the civil courts to determine in the normal way. The officers should certainly consider the effect of a direction to leave land. If the trespassers comply with the direction, the use of it may well be successful. However, if they do not comply the officer should consider what

---

5 See *Hansard*, HC Debates, 13 December 1999, col. 122. *Hansard*, HC Debates, 19 June 1995, col. 128, and the particularly disturbing account of the disruption of a small company as a result of an encampment on their premises discussed in debates: *Hansard*, HC Debates, 19 July 1999, col. 940.
6 H.O. Circular 45/1994.
7 8 December 1998, unreported.
8 Per Turner J.
9 See Mr Tim Loughton MP, *Hansard*, HC Debates, 10 May 1999 col. 85.
10 See *Hansard*, HC, written answer, 15 June 1998, col. 36.

steps it is proposed to take. It may not be practical to arrest all the trespassers, there may well be children or animals involved. Arresting adults may mean that provision will have to be made for the care of children or animals. Furthermore, arresting large numbers could lead to major disorder with the resulting problems that that would cause. If it is decided to arrest some or a large number of the trespassers, consideration should be given as to what will happen to vehicles and other property. It must be remembered that some of these vehicles will be used as homes by the trespassers. Even though section 62 provides a power to remove the vehicles, they have to be put somewhere. It would seem undesirable that police stations yards or car pounds should be turned into encampments for travellers or gipsies.' [11]

The power to issue the three-month ban under s. 61 is reported to be used very rarely, since it is almost impossible to prove an individual's identity in such cases because no record of identity is kept at the time of the initial expulsion. [12] In order to ensure that the direction to leave the site could be proved in court, police now routinely video-record their giving such directions. [13]

Police forces have expressed reservation regarding the use of the seizure power in s. 62, [14] claiming that they are administratively complicated and expensive. Only one case of seizure was reported by Bucke and James: gypsies with 30 vehicles had camped on a school playing field. Ultimately, this led to further public order problems when the gypsies seized back their vehicles from the police pound!

The HMIC Report *Keeping the Peace* [15] recommended 'that the Home Office consider . . . the need for new legislation designed to allow pre-emptive action to prevent the fortification process' that has become common with environmental protesters at sites of construction or development. [16] However, the government has stated that there are no 'plans to make damage to land by travelling people a specific criminal offence, nor to introduce compensation for private landowners and local authorities who have suffered damage to their land. Trespassers on land are bound by the general criminal law as is anyone else. If they behave in a threatening or violent way, or commit offences such as criminal damage, the police may take appropriate action to deal with them'. [17] Is there a clear case for further legislation increasing police powers?

Raves

Sections 63–66 confer powers in relation to 'raves'. These are defined as gatherings on land in the open air (which includes a place partly open to the air) of 100 or more persons (whether or not trespassers) at which amplified music is played during the night and as such is, by reason of its loudness and duration and the time at which it is played, likely to cause serious distress to the inhabitants of the locality; the term 'music' 'includes sounds wholly or predominantly characterised by the emission of a succession of repetitive beats'. If, as respects any land in the open air, a police officer of at least the rank of superintendent believes that two or more persons are making preparations for the holding of a 'rave' or ten or more persons are waiting for the rave to begin, or are attending a rave in progress, he may give a direction requiring any such persons to leave the land and remove any vehicle or property. The direction can be communicated by any constable at the scene. Persons are treated as having had a direction communicated to them if reasonable steps have been taken to bring it to their attention. Failure to comply with a direction, or re-entry within seven days,

11 *Hansard*, HC, written answer, 10 July 1998.
12 T. Bucke and Z. James, op. cit., p. 11.
13 p. 10.
14 p. 12.
15 (1999).
16 p. 50.
17 *Hansard*, HC, Written Answer, 3 March 1998, col. 548.

is an offence, subject to a defence of reasonable excuse. The section does not apply to a gathering with an entertainment licence granted by the local authority, and a direction cannot be given to an 'exempt person' (i.e. the occupier of the land, any member of his family and any employee or agent of his and any person whose home is situated on the land) (s. 63). A superintendent can authorise a constable to enter the land, and there is similar power to seize vehicles and sound equipment to that conferred by s. 62 (s. 64). Section 65 enables a constable to stop persons from proceeding to a rave in respect of which a direction is in force; this power may only be exercised within five miles of the boundary of the site of the gathering, and no direction may be given to an 'exempt person'. A person who, knowing that a constable has given him a direction, fails to comply, commits an offence. Section 66 enables the court to order forfeiture of sound equipment used at a rave following a conviction under s. 63. According to Earl Ferrers, speaking for the government in the House of Lords [18]

> 'unlicensed night time parties ... have caused appalling misery to local residents where the peaceful lives of rural societies have suddenly been ripped apart by the all-pervasive sound of what is sometimes delicately described as "music", the noise of which travels for miles, affecting everyone in its path – both man and beast – and from which it is impossible to escape. It can be a modern-day torture for the unwilling and the unwitting.'

On raves generally see M. Collin. [19] Bucke and James' research confirmed that the very specific drafting of the offence means that it has limited application, and that by the time the Act was in force 'illegal raves had become a rare phenomenon compared with the late 1980s'. [20] However newspaper reports of raves causing major disturbances to residents continue. Between 1994 and 1998 there were five occasions on which coroners commented that deaths had occurred at raves. [21] The cost of policing raves is substantial: two rave parties held at motorway service stations in Cheshire in 1997 cost approximately £3,600 to police. [1]

Research into the s. 62 power revealed that police forces adopted tactics of either stopping or containing raves by using ss. 63–65. In addition, forces often use a charge of conspiracy to create public nuisance at a time when the musical equipment is still in transit. The definition of 'open air' has created some difficulties for the police with partially enclosed buildings such as barns and marquees. [2] Police video-tape senior officers delivering instructions to leave so that proof of the direction is available in court. [3] The power to seize sound equipment [4] is rarely used because of practical and legal considerations. [5] Officers interviewed felt that the powers gave them much stronger legal grounds than they had previously had when struggling to police raves using common law and existing 1986 Act powers. [6]

In 1995, nine authorisations under s. 63 were made by eight different forces. There was only one seizure of sound equipment under s. 64. Thirty-two authorisations under s. 65 occurred and no prosecutions resulted from the directions not to proceed to a rave. In 1995 there were no prosecutions under s. 63. In 1996, seven prosecutions

---

18 554 HL Deb, 25 April 1994, col 384.
19 *Altered State, The Story of Ecstasy and Acid House* (1997).
20 p. 21.
21 See *Hansard*, HC written answer 28 Oct 1998, col. 177.
 1 See *Hansard*, HC, written answer 5 Nov 1997, col. 215.
 2 T. Bucke and Z. James, op. cit., p. 25.
 3 p. 26.
 4 s. 64.
 5 p. 26.
 6 p. 29.

resulted in four convictions and one caution.[7] Should the provisions be retained? Was their implementation more trouble than it was worth?

(B) THE CONDUCT OF PROCESSIONS AND ASSEMBLIES

(i) Introduction

There are many criminal offences which may be committed by those who take part in or disrupt meetings, processions and other activities. Some have already been mentioned, including the Police Act 1996, s. 89[8] and the Highways Act 1980, s. 137.[9] The Criminal Damage Act 1971 makes it an offence to destroy or damage property belonging to another without lawful excuse (s. 1(1); it is no defence that the defendant believes that he has the consent of God (to writing a Biblical quotation on a concrete pillar at the perimeter of the Houses of Parliament in protest at the Gulf War): *Blake v DPP*.[10] In *R v Hill & Hall*[11] CND protesters were caught in possession of wire cutters. They intended to cut through the perimeter fence of a USAF base, believing that if the base closed there would be less likelihood of a Soviet nuclear attack directed at the area and that therefore their houses would be safe. The defence in s. 5(2)(b) of the Criminal Damage Act 1971 that the houses were in need of protection from immediate danger failed:

'In our view that must mean evidence that the [accused] believed that immediate action had to be taken to do something which would otherwise be a crime in order to prevent the immediate risk of something worse happening.'[12]

See also the rejection of the argument that the criminal damage caused to the perimeter fence was lawful because the storing of atomic warheads at Aldermaston was contrary to international law: *Huthinson v Newbury Magistrates' Court,*[13] and see the similar arguments in *HM Advocate v Zelter et al.*[14]

Criminal damage is a very broad offence and has been used in numerous prosecutions of protestors,[15] as for example with charges brought against an animal rights protester who damaged an angler's rod at a fishing competition.[16]

It is also an offence for a person to have with him in any public place an offensive weapon without lawful authority or reasonable excuse (Prevention of Crime Act 1953, s. 1). If found in possession of an offensive weapon, it is no defence to claim a lack of knowledge that the item is a weapon: *R v Densu*[17] (telescopic expandable baton ordinarily used by D as a car jack) and *R v Deegan.*[18] The strictness of this rule is considered by Sir John Smith.[19]

The Criminal Law Act 1977 made it an offence for any person other than the displaced residential occupier or a protected intending occupier to use or threaten violence to secure entry to premises (s. 6, as amended by the Criminal Justice and

---

7 p. 30.
8 Above, p. 156.
9 Above, p. 421.
10 [1993] Crim LR 586.
11 [1989] Crim LR 136, CA.
12 Per Lane LCJ at 80.
13 (2000) Independent, 20 November, DC.
14 (2001) 30 March.
15 On the acquittal of GM crop destroyers charged under the Criminal Damage Act 1971, see news reports for 21 September 2000.
16 *The Times*, 27 June 2000.
17 [1998] 1 Cr App R 400, CA.
18 [1998] 2 Cr App R 121. Lack of knowledge of possession is a defence: *R v Daubney* (2001) 25 May, CA (Cr D).
19 [1998] Crim LR 346.

Public Order Act 1994, s. 72 (s. 6 is very wide since no actual entry is required and a threat of violence will suffice; the offence clearly covers the threat of a demonstration or 'sit in'; [20] s. 7 provides an immediate remedy to deal with squatters)); to occupy premises as a trespasser and fail to leave on being required to do so by a displaced residential occupier or a protected intending occupier (s. 7, as substituted by the 1994 Act, s. 73); to trespass with a weapon of offence (s. 8); to trespass upon consular or diplomatic premises (s. 9); and to obstruct court officers executing process for possession against unauthorised occupiers (s. 10). A local authority may direct unauthorised campers (i.e. persons residing in a vehicle or vehicles) to leave land, and seek an order from a magistrates' court for the removal of persons and their vehicles unlawfully on land in contravention of a direction (Criminal Justice and Public Order Act 1994, ss. 77–79). See *R v Wealden District Council, ex p Wales, R v Lincolnshire County Council, ex p Atkinson,* [21] in which the council used ss. 77 and 78 to remove new age travellers but the orders were quashed because they had failed to take account of the Department of Environment circular (18/94) [1] advising on the welfare considerations to be considered – several women in the group were pregnant. [2]

We deal in more detail with arrest for breach of the peace; the main offences under the Public Order Act 1986; and the disruption of lawful meetings and other activities.

(ii) Powers to deal with breaches of the peace

Halsbury's Laws of England [3] states that:

'the primary function of the constable remains, as in the 17th century, the preservation of the Queen's Peace. . . . the first duty of a constable is always to prevent the commission of crime. If a constable reasonably apprehends that the action of any person may result in a breach of the peace, it is his duty to prevent that action.'

It is interesting to note that the ACPO sub committee on Public Order has a working definition of disorder as 'a breach of the peace of which the police are aware, which may require police intervention or action in partnership with others'. [4]

The European Court in *Steel v UK* [5] acknowledged the development and clarification of the powers governing arrest for breach of the peace in the last decade, and held that they were sufficiently clear to comply with the requirements of the ECHR. The applicants in this case were involved in quite separate incidents. Steel, together with approximately 60 others, took part in a protest against a grouse shoot on Wheeldale Moor, Yorkshire. An officer began warning the protesters, through a public address system, to stop their behaviour. The protesters ignored this request and the police made a total of 13 arrests. Steel was arrested by a police officer for 'breach of the peace': according to the police, she was intentionally impeding the progress of a member of the shoot by walking in front of him as he lifted his shotgun to take aim, thus preventing him from firing. Lush took part in a protest against the building of an extension to the M11 motorway in Wanstead, London. During the course of that day a group of 20 to 25 protesters repeatedly broke into a construction site, where they climbed into trees which were to be felled and onto some of the

20 See further, E. Griew, *The Criminal Law Act 1977* (1977); A. Prichard, *Squatting* (1980). See also *Ropaigealach v Barclays Bank plc* [2000] 1 QB 263 on the protection of s. 6.
21 (1996) 8 Admin LR 529. See recently *Ward v Hillingdon London Borough Council* [2001] EWHC 91, for an unsuccessful ECtHR challenge.
1 Above, p. 456.
2 See further S. Cragg and R. Low-Beer, (1995) NLJ 1342, and Bucke and James op. cit., p. 14.
3 36(1) *Halsburys Laws* 4th edn, 1999, re-issue.
4 HMIC, *Keeping the Peace* (1999), p. 8.
5 (1998) 28 EHRR 603, [1998] Crim LR 893, ECtHR.

stationary machinery. On each occasion they were removed by security guards. The protesters did not offer any resistance and there were no incidents of violence or damage to machinery. Ms Lush was arrested while standing under the 'bucket' of a 'JCB' digger, for conduct 'likely to provoke a disturbance of the peace'. Needham, Polden and Cole attended the Queen Elizabeth Conference Centre in Westminster, London, where the 'Fighter Helicopter II' Conference was being held, in order to protest with three others against the sale of fighter helicopters. The protest took the form of handing out leaflets and holding up banners saying: 'Work for Peace and not War.' The three applicants were arrested by police officers. Ms Needham was holding a banner and Mr Polden and Mr Cole were distributing leaflets.

The European Court held:

'1. Breach of the peace is not classed as a criminal offence under English law . . . However, the Court observes that the duty to keep the peace is in the nature of a public duty; the police have powers to arrest any person who has breached the peace or who they reasonably fear will breach the peace; and the magistrates may commit to prison any person who refuses to be bound over not to breach the peace where there is evidence beyond reasonable doubt that his or her conduct caused or was likely to cause a breach of the peace and that he or she would otherwise cause a breach of the peace in the future . . .

2. Bearing in mind the nature of the proceedings in question and the penalty at stake, the Court considers that breach of the peace must be regarded as an "offence" within the meaning of Article 5 § 1 (c) (see, *mutatis mutandis*, the *Benham v. the United Kingdom* judgment of 10 June 1996, *Reports* 1996-III, p. 756, § 56).

3. The Court therefore finds that each applicant was arrested and detained with the purpose of bringing him or her before the competent legal authority on suspicion of having committed an "offence" or because it was considered necessary to prevent the commission of an "offence".

It will consider whether this suspicion was "reasonable" below, in connection with the issue of lawfulness . . .

2.   Lawfulness of the arrests and initial detention

4. The Government submitted that the applicants' arrests and initial detention complied with a well-established common-law power of arrest in respect of actual or reasonably apprehended breaches of the peace which had been preserved by the Police and Criminal Evidence Act 1984 . . . The conditions in which this power of arrest might be exercised had been clarified by the national courts in the cases of *Howell*, *Percy* and *Nicol* . . . with the result that the law was sufficiently certain and precise.

At the hearing before the Court, in respect of the detention of the third, fourth and fifth applicants, the Government pointed out that if the police officers' belief that these applicants' actions had been likely to cause a breach of the peace had lacked objective justification, it would have been open to the applicants to challenge the legality of their arrests in the domestic courts. Since they had failed to take such proceedings, it had to be presumed that their arrests had been objectively justified.

5. The applicants contended that their arrests and initial periods of detention had not been "lawful", since the concept of breach of the peace and the attendant powers of arrest were insufficiently certain under English law.

First, they submitted that if, as appeared from the national case-law . . . an individual committed a breach of the peace when he or she behaved in a manner the natural consequence of which was that others would react violently, it was difficult to judge the extent to which one could engage in protest activity, in the presence of those who might be annoyed, without causing a breach of the peace. Secondly, the power to arrest whenever there were reasonable grounds for apprehending that a breach of the peace was about to take place granted too wide a discretion to the police. Thirdly, there had been conflicting decisions at Court of Appeal level as to the definition of breach of the peace . . .

6. The Commission found that there had been no violation of Article 5 § 1 since the arrests and initial detention had not been arbitrary and there had been no suggestion of any lack of conformity with domestic law.

7. The Court recalls that the expressions "lawful" and "in accordance with a procedure prescribed by law" in Article 5 § 1 stipulate not only full compliance with the procedural and substantive rules of national law, but also that any deprivation of liberty be consistent with the purpose of Article 5 and not arbitrary (see the above-mentioned Benham judgment, pp. 752–53, § 40). In addition, given the importance of personal liberty, it is essential that the applicable national law meet the standard of "lawfulness" set by the Convention, which requires that all law, whether written or unwritten, be sufficiently precise to allow the citizen – if need be, with appropriate advice – to foresee, to a degree that is reasonable in the circumstances, the consequences which a given action may entail (see the *S.W. v. the United Kingdom* judgment of 22 November 1995, Series A no. 335-B, pp. 41–42, §§ 35–36, and, *mutatis mutandis*, the *Sunday Times v. the United Kingdom (no. 1)* judgment of 26 April 1979, Series A no. 30, p. 31, § 49, and the *Halford v. the United Kingdom* judgment of 25 June 1997, *Reports* 1997-III, p. 1017, § 49).

8. In this connection, the Court observes that the concept of breach of the peace has been clarified by the English courts over the last two decades, to the extent that it is now sufficiently established that a breach of the peace is committed only when an individual causes harm, or appears likely to cause harm, to persons or property or acts in a manner the natural consequence of which would be to provoke others to violence . . . It is also clear that a person may be arrested for causing a breach of the peace or where it is reasonably apprehended that he or she is likely to cause a breach of the peace . . .

Accordingly, the Court considers that the relevant legal rules provided sufficient guidance and were formulated with the degree of precision required by the Convention (see, for example, the *Larissis and Others v. Greece* judgment of 24 February 1998, *Reports* 1998-I, p. 377, § 34).

9. When considering whether the arrest and detention of each applicant was carried out in accordance with English law, the Court recalls that it is in the first place for the national authorities, notably the courts, to interpret and apply domestic law. However, since failure to comply with domestic law entails a breach of Article 5 § 1, the Court can and should exercise a certain power of review in this matter (see the above-mentioned Benham judgment, p. 753, § 41).'

The decision of the European Court might be regarded as surprising in view of the continuing confusion over the limits of the power as interpreted in English cases. Does the following case provide adequate definition?

R v Howell (Erroll) [1982] QB 416, [1981] 3 All ER 383, Court of Appeal (Criminal Division)

H and others had been making a disturbance at a street party. After complaints by neighbours the police arrived and told them to leave or be arrested for breach of the peace. They slowly moved off, stopping in their tracks to swear at the constables. PC Hammersley said to H 'if you swear once more you will be arrested for disturbing public order'. H said that his language was not disturbing public order, to which PC Hammersley replied 'At 4 am in the morning, and in the middle of the street, it is.' H continued to swear, whereupon the constable took hold of him in order to arrest him. In response H struck the constable in the face. H was convicted of assault occasioning actual bodily harm. He appealed to the Court of Appeal (Criminal Division) contending (*inter alia*) that the arrest was unlawful. Two issues were: (1) was there a power of arrest in relation to an anticipated breach of the peace?; and (2) what was the correct definition of 'breach of the peace'? On issue (1) a recorder had held in *R v Podger*[6] that the power to arrest for breach of the peace at common law was confined to cases in which a breach was committed in the presence of the arrestor or where one had been committed and its renewal was threatened.

6   [1979] Crim LR 524.

[The judgment of the court (**Watkins LJ**, **Cantley** and **Hollings JJ**) was given by **Watkins LJ**:] We entertain no doubt that a constable has a power of arrest where there is reasonable apprehension of imminent danger of a breach of the peace, so for that matter has the ordinary citizen. *R v Podger* [1979] Crim LR 524 was in our opinion wrongly decided. We hold that there is power of arrest for breach of the peace where:(1) a breach of the peace is committed in the presence of the person making the arrest or (2) the arrestor reasonably believes that such a breach will be committed in the immediate future by the person arrested although he has not yet committed any breach or (3) where a breach has been committed and it is reasonably believed that a renewal of it is threatened.

The public expects a police officer not only to apprehend the criminal but to do his best to prevent the commission of crime, to keep the peace, in other words. To deny him, therefore, the right to arrest a person who he reasonably believes is about to breach the peace would be to disable him from preventing that which might cause serious injury to someone or even to many people or to property. The common law, we believe, whilst recognising that a wrongful arrest is a serious invasion of a person's liberty, provides the police with this power in the public interest.

In those instances of the exercise of this power which depend upon a belief that a breach of the peace is imminent it must, we think we should emphasise, be established that it is not only an honest albeit mistaken belief but a belief which is founded on reasonable grounds.

A comprehensive definition of the term 'breach of the peace' has very rarely been formulated so far as, with considerable help from counsel, we have been able to discover from cases which go as far back as the 18th century. The older cases are of considerable interest but they are not a sure guide to what the term is understood to mean today, since keeping the peace in this country in the latter half of the 20th century presents formidable problems which bear upon the evolving process of the development of this branch of the common law. Nevertheless, even in these days when affrays, riotous behaviour and other disturbances happen all too frequently, we cannot accept that there can be a breach of the peace unless there has been an act done or threatened to be done which either actually harms a person, or in his presence his property, or is likely to cause such harm, or which puts someone in fear of such harm being done. There is nothing more likely to arouse resentment and anger in him, and a desire to take instant revenge, than attacks or threatened attacks upon a person's body or property.

In *Halsbury's Laws of England*, 4th edn, vol. 11 (1976), para. 108, it is stated:

'for the purpose of the common law powers of arrest without warrant, a breach of the peace arises where there is an actual assault, or where a public alarm and excitement are caused by a person's wrongful act. Mere annoyance and disturbance or insult to a person or abusive language, or great heat and fury without personal violence, are not generally sufficient.'

That is an amalgam of opinions expressed in various old cases which is principally criticised by Mr. Engels for its failure to attach the actual commission of violence to all acts which are said to be capable of causing a breach of the peace.

He makes a similar criticism of the crisp definition provided by the Attorney-General, Sir Reginald Manningham-Buller, referred to in *Gelberg v Miller* [1961] 1 WLR153 with reference to the word 'disturbance'. Lord Parker CJ said, at p. 158:

'The Attorney-General, to whom the court is grateful for his assistance, has appeared and has told the court that he feels unable to contend that a constable is entitled to arrest somebody for obstructing him in the course of his duty which, of course, is a misdemeanour under the Prevention of Crimes Amendment Act 1885, unless the circumstances show that a breach of the peace or an apprehended breach of the peace is involved, meaning by that some affray or violence or possibly disturbance.'

The statement in *Halsbury* is in parts, we think, inaccurate because of its failure to relate all the kinds of behaviour there mentioned to violence. Furthermore, we think, the word 'disturbance' when used in isolation cannot constitute a breach of the peace.

We are emboldened to say that there is a breach of the peace whenever harm is actually done or is likely to be done to a person or in his presence to his property or a person is in fear of being so harmed through an assault, an affray, a riot, unlawful assembly or other disturbance.

It is for this breach of the peace when done in his presence or the reasonable apprehension of it taking place that a constable, or anyone else, may arrest an offender without warrant....

The recorder directed the jury that in order for there to have been a lawful arrest it had to be proved that P.C. Hammersley was a witness to the shouting and swearing of the defendant and had, therefore, reasonable grounds for believing, and did believe, that the defendant's conduct, either alone or as part of a general shouting and swearing, was likely to lead to the use of violence by the defendant or somebody else in the officer's presence.... In our view it was a clear, correct and, in the circumstances of the case, wholly appropriate direction according to law.

Appeal dismissed.

NOTES

1. See Glanville Williams, 'Dealing with Breaches of the Peace'.[7] Williams notes (*inter alia*) that there may have been 'faulty draftsmanship' in the omission of the requirement of 'immediacy' from head (3) by comparison with head (2): the distinction (if intended) 'seems pointless' (but see *Foulkes v Chief Constable of Merseyside*).[8] He suggests moreover that it 'would have been better to define a breach as an actual breach, while asserting the power to arrest and to bind over for an apprehended breach'.[9] The latter approach was adopted by the Court of Appeal in *Lewis v Chief Constable of Greater Manchester*.[10] Farquharson LJ referred to passages in *Howell*:[11]

> 'which appear to say that an act constituting a threat of violence or which puts somebody in fear of violence is itself a breach of the peace with the definition of that offence. The act which puts someone in fear of violence taking place entitles a police officer or a member of the public to detain the actor but it is not itself a breach of the peace, for the violence has not yet occurred.'

This case confirms that loud noises and disturbance (here, loud music and screaming) do not of themselves constitute a breach of the peace, the court upholding an award of £2,500 for wrongful arrest and substituting an award of £5,000 (for £17,500) for false imprisonment, in respect of L's arrest in these circumstances. The jury rejected the police claim that they honestly believed on reasonable grounds that a breach of the peace (in the narrower *Howell* sense) was imminent.

2. A further point made in *R v Howell*[12] was that a person making an arrest when he reasonably believes a breach of the peace is about to be committed complies with the requirements of *Christie v Leachinsky*[13] if he says merely 'I am arresting you for a breach of the peace.' Moreover, the court[14] expressed the 'tentative view' that this would also suffice for an arrest under s. 5 of the Public Order Act 1936.[15]

3. *R v Howell* brought some clarification to an area of the law that previously was in doubt: see G. Williams.[16] Nevertheless, many 'question marks' remain.[17]

7 (1982) 146 JPN 199–200, 217–219.
8 Below, p. 466.
9 Ibid, p. 200.
10 (1991) Independent, 23 October.
11 p. 427.
12 [1982] QB 416 at 427–428, CA (Cr D).
13 [1947] AC 573, HL (see above, p. 283).
14 At 423–424.
15 See now s. 4 of the 1986 Act.
16 [1954] Crim LR 572; L.H. Leigh, *Police Powers in England and Wales* (2nd edn, 1985) pp. 185–190.
17 G. Williams, (1982) 146 JPN 199. For further criticism, see also D. Nicholson and K. Reid [1996] Crim LR 764. See R. Stone, [2001] 2 Web JCLI calling for abolition of the breach of the peace powers.

4. In *Albert v Lavin*, [18] A, in an attempt to board a bus, pushed past a number of people standing in a bus queue. Several objected, and L, a police constable in plain clothes, reasonably apprehended that there would be a breach of the peace. He prevented A from boarding the bus, and, after a struggle, pulled him away from the queue. He told A he was a police officer and that, if he did not stop struggling, he would arrest him. A (as the magistrates found) honestly, but unreasonably, disbelieved him and hit him five or six times. He was convicted of assaulting a police officer in the execution of his duty. The Divisional Court dealt with the case on the basis that the issue was whether an honest but unreasonable mistake was sufficient to ground a defence of self-defence: the court held that only a reasonable mistake would suffice. (The defence of self-defence is now available where a person has an honest belief in the need to use force: *R v Williams*.) [19]

The House of Lords held that this issue did not arise: [20]

'every citizen in whose presence a breach of the peace is being, or reasonably appears to be about to be, committed has the right to take reasonable steps to make the person who is breaking or threatening to break the peace refrain from doing so; and those reasonable steps in appropriate cases will include detaining him against his will. At common law this is not only the right of every citizen, it is also his duty, although, except in the case of a citizen who is a constable, it is a duty of imperfect obligation.'

Accordingly L's status as a constable was irrelevant, and A's mistake on the point was consequently also irrelevant. Note that the case also makes it clear that the steps that may be taken include detention 'without arrest'. [1] Glanville Williams [2] argues that Lord Diplock's statement is narrower than *R v Howell* in that it 'does not cover past breaches of the peace, but only those presently continuing or those feared for the future'. There is some authority to support a power of arrest *immediately* after a breach of the peace even if renewal is not apprehended. [3] On the other hand there are many statements to the effect that there is no such power where a breach of the peace has occurred but it is over and there is no ground for believing that it will be renewed. [4] The latter view was taken in the Commentary on *R v Podger* [5] and the Commentary was endorsed in *R v Howell*, [6] although it should be noted that this point did not arise for consideration and that the formulation 'is committed' in *Howell* [7] might be regarded as extending to cover an immediate arrest for a concluded breach committed in the arrestor's presence. Recent cases support a very narrow view.

Anticipatory arrest

5. The power to arrest in anticipation of a breach should be exercised with great restraint. In *R v Ramsell*, [8] which involved a domestic dispute the court noted that:

'It is not surprising to find that, where a person is not himself going to be violent but is simply being arrested in order to prevent violence on the part of others, such a power ought to be exercised only in very narrow circumstances. It may well be the case that in that category of

18 [1982] AC 546.
19 (1984) 87 Cr App R (see above, p. 167).
20 Per Lord Diplock at 565.
 1 See Lord Diplock at 564 D–F.
 2 (1982) 146 JPN 217.
 3 See G. Williams [1954] Crim LR 578 at 586–587.
 4 See G. Williams, op. cit.
 5 [1979] Crim LR 524.
 6 [1982] QB 416, 426, CA (Cr D).
 7 Above, p. 462.
 8 (1999) 25 May, CA.

breach of the peace there must be a sufficiently real and present threat to justify an extreme step. At the same time, however, it is important to note that, having sounded its words of warning, the Court of Appeal [in *Howell*] nonetheless still adopted and followed the test of Watkins LJ that the breach of the peace, be it committed by the person arrested or be it committed by others upon him, must be imminent; and did not impose any further limitations on that requirement.

What was the position here? The officers had good grounds to suspect that there had been an assault of some sort on Mr Vallender. Very shortly after that they interviewed Mrs Ramsell. She apparently was not prepared to discuss the matter with them but said that she was going to sort the matter out herself. They reasonably concluded that what she intended to do was there and then to go round to Mr Vallender's house. They had every reason, in our judgment, to fear that what might happen what she arrived at Mr Vallender's was something of the order that had happened on the previous occasion. They also had every reason to fear or every reason to think that that breach of the peace was 'imminent'. That word cannot mean 'there and then' and the requirement cannot be limited to acts in the presence of the person making the arrest, because in his judgment in *Howell* Watkins LJ made a clear distinction between a breach of the peace being committed in the presence of the person making the arrest and the second case stated by him, of imminent breach, where the arrester believes that such breach will be committed in the immediate future by the person arrested.

In our view, in the circumstances of this case, it was entirely open to the police and entirely open to a jury to think that the feared breach of the peace was indeed imminent or as the judge put it 'about to take place'. The judge correctly directed the jury on that point and it was a matter for them to decide.

Nothing that we have said is intended to undermine the warnings about the care that must be taken in dealing with this anomalous power of arrest. But within the limits laid down by this court, which we have sought to set out, we consider that this arrest was indeed lawful and was properly found to be so by the jury.

We mention one other point which in fact was not debated before us and which is a separate point from the decision we have already made. It will be recalled that paragraph 3 of Watkins LJ's analysis was directed to a case where a breach has been committed and it is reasonably believed that a renewal of it is threatened. Although this was not debated at the trial and we do not rely on it, it seems to us that the present may well have been a case where a breach had already been committed in the shape of the attack on Mr Vallender and a further breach might well have been about to occur.

The court went on to express concern that there was a possibility of conviction under the very serious offence of resisting an arrest contrary to s. 18 of the Offences Against the Person Act 1861 which carries a maximum of life imprisonment, but no conviction for the lesser crime of resisting arrest for an offence, because breach of the peace was not a crime.'[9]

6. In *Foulkes v Chief Constable of Merseyside*[10] the Court of Appeal confirmed that there must be a real and present threat to the peace to justify an arrest for an apprehended breach of the peace. The power should only be exercised exceptionally. In that case F had been arrested when he had tried to re-enter his own home, following a family dispute in which the police had already been called by him to remove his teenage children.

'a constable may exceptionally have power to arrest a person whose behaviour is lawful but provocative, it is a power which ought to be exercised by him only in the clearest of circumstances and when he is satisfied on reasonable grounds that a breach of the peace is imminent. ... there must be a sufficiently real threat to the peace to justify the extreme step of depriving of his liberty a citizen who is not at the time acting unlawfully.'[11]

---

9 Per Buxton LJ.
10 [1998] 3 All ER 705, CA (Civ D).
11 Per Beldam LJ, p. 711.

7. Another recent review of the law was conducted in *Bibby v Chief Constable of Essex.* [12] B, a bailiff, who was present at D's premises to levy distress against his property, was told to leave by D. The police were called and arrested B apprehending a breach of the peace. B claimed false imprisonment. The Court of Appeal held that the arrest was not justified. B had been acting lawfully, and the threat came from D.

The court approved six points submitted by counsel as summarising the law:

'1. There must be the clearest of circumstances and a sufficiently real and present threat to the peace to justify the extreme step of depriving of his liberty a citizen who is not at the time acting unlawfully. *Foulkes*

2. the threat must be coming from the person who is to be arrested. *Redmond-Bate*

3. the conduct must clearly interfere with the rights of others. *Redmond-Bate*

4. the natural consequence of the conduct must be violence from a third party. *Redmond-Bate*

5. the violence in 4 must not be wholly unreasonable. *Redmond-Bate*

6. the conduct of the person to be arrested must be unreasonable. *Redmond-Bate.*'

8. Should there be a requirement of 'unlawfulness' in any activity before it triggers a power of arrest? In earlier cases the court had upheld arrests as lawful where the behaviour was 'lawful but provocative and the exceptional circumstances where violence was imminent.' [13] In *Kelly v Chief Constable of Hampshire,* [14] the Court of Appeal upheld the dismissal of K's claim in damages in respect of his arrest to prevent a breach of the peace. PC Cutts came upon the scene of a heated altercation between K, a hunt saboteur, and a huntsman on horseback. K was holding the horse's reins. C arrested K 'within seconds' for conduct likely to cause a breach of the peace. Lloyd LJ stated that:

'If, on the information known to [the constable], he has reasonable cause to believe that a breach of the peace is about to occur, he is entitled to arrest one or more of the participants in order to prevent that occurrence.'

Here, C had the necessary 'reasonable cause'. The fact that, immediately prior to this incident and before C arrived, the huntsman had assaulted K with his whip (for which, indeed, K had been awarded £25 damages) was irrelevant; the answer to the question whether there was reasonable cause to believe that a breach of the peace was about to occur:

'does not depend on who started the altercation or who was responsible for the apprehended violence. Where violence is imminent, the police officer does not have time to hold an inquiry or conduct an investigation. As Lord Denning said in [the *CEGB* case [15]], the law does not require the constable to go into the right and wrongs of the matter at that stage. The officer has to act promptly as seems best to him in all the circumstances. The rights and wrongs as between the parties come later.'

(Lloyd LJ also stated, obiter, that if the constable *had* seen the whipping incident, that would not have been relevant. Do you agree?) [16]

The Court of Appeal also upheld the trial judge's view that K's subsequent detention was lawful. After 20 minutes, he was taken to a police station, where he was kept for a further two hours or so. The judge rejected K's argument that after

---

12 (2000) 164 JP 297.

13 *Maguire v Chief Constable of Cumbria Constabulary*(2001) 26 April, unreported, CA (Civ D).

14 (1993) Independent, 25 March.

15 *R v Chief Constable of Devon and Cornwall, ex p Central Electricity Generating Board* [1982] QB 458.

16 See also *Edwards v DPP* (1996) 24 April, DC.

20 minutes the situation was calmer and he should have been released then. He admitted in cross-examination that if he had not been arrested he would have stayed with the hunt for the rest of the day with the possibility of a further confrontation between himself and the huntsmen. Accordingly, PC Cutts: [17]

> 'was clearly justified in forming the view which he did, that the best way to secure the situation and to prevent a further breach of the peace was to continue the plaintiff's detention.'

9. In *McBean v Parker*, [18] the Divisional Court held that 'harm' for the purpose of the definition of 'breach of the peace' in *R v Howell* 'must be unlawful harm' [19] and not, as on the facts of that case, the use of reasonable force to resist an unlawful police search. What would the position be where the force used was excessive? [20]

10. In civil proceedings arising out of an arrest for breach of the peace, it is for the judge to decide whether there was the necessary reasonable cause and for the jury to decide any disputed issues of fact relevant to the judge's decision: *Kelly v Chief Constable of Hampshire* [1] applying *Dallison v Caffery* [2] (an authority on arrest for felony at common law). Diplock LJ's reasoning was of general application.

11. Note that the power to arrest for breaches of the peace was not removed by the Police and Criminal Evidence Act 1984: s. 26 [3] repealed only statutory powers. Although mere shouting and swearing will not alone constitute a breach of the peace, it is an offence under s. 28 of the Town Police Clauses Act 1847 and may lead to an arrest under s. 25 of PACE. [4] If it causes harassment, alarm or distress it may constitute an offence under s. 5 of the Public Order Act 1986. [5] Several other powers of arrest have been held to be unaffected by PACE. These include the power to arrest for being drunk and disorderly, and the powers to arrest under the Vagrancy Act 1824. (See *Gapper v Chief Constable of Avon and Somerset*. [6]) Similarly, in *Alveranga v Metropolitan Police Comr*, [7] the court again confirmed that:

> 'The Police and Criminal Evidence Act 1984 leaves intact a police constable's common law power to intervene to prevent or stop a breach of the peace. A constable may arrest a person who commits a breach of the peace in his presence provided he makes the arrest when or immediately after the offence is committed or while there is a danger of its renewal, though it may be that he is not entitled to make an arrest at all if there is no danger of a further breach. When a constable reasonably believes that a breach of the peace is about to take place, he may take any reasonable measures necessary to prevent such a breach.' [8]

Although the criminal law now recognises that assault can occur by words alone and threatening words will constitute an assault, that provides no power of arrest.

The ECHR recognised the legitimacy of the power to arrest for breach of the peace despite concerns that English law was too ambiguous, [9] in *Steel v UK*. [10] The European

---

17 Per Lloyd LJ.
18 (1983) 147 JP 205, DC.
19 At 208.
20 Cf. Commentary [1983] Crim LR at 401.
1 Above, p. 467.
2 [1965] 1 QB 348 at 371, per Diplock LJ.
3 Above, p. 281.
4 General arrest conditions: above, p. 281: see *Smith*, p. 182 n. 74.
5 Below, p. 490. Cf. the facts of *G v Chief Superintendent of Police, Stroud* (1986) 86 Cr App Rep 92, DC, decided before the 1986 Act came into force.
6 [1998] 4 All ER 248.
7 (2000) 10 March, CA (Cir Div).
8 Per Swinton Thomas LJ.
9 See D. Nicholson and K. Reid, [1996] Crim LR 764.
10 [1999] EHRLR 109, (1997) 5 BHRC 339.

Court of Human Rights accepted that 'a breach of the peace is committed only when an individual causes harm, or appears likely to cause harm, to persons or property or acts in a manner the natural consequence of which would be to provoke others to violence'.[11] Following that case and the decision in *DPP v Redmond-Bate*[12] is the English law of breach of the peace now safe from ECHR challenge? Note that the Court of Human Rights has accepted that under Art. 11 a peaceful assembly may be restricted if the conditions are lawful, necessary and proportionate.[13]

13. A person may be bound over by magistrates to keep the peace.[14] On powers of entry to preserve the peace see below.[15] Compare the power to arrest to prevent a breach of the peace with: (1) the use of reasonable force in the prevention of crime;[16] and (2) the power to take other (? necessary and proportionate) steps to preserve the peace.[17] See below in relation to ss. 68 and 69 of the Criminal Justice and Public Order Act 1994.

Breach of the peace in private

13. At common law, a breach of the peace can occur on private premises. This had been assumed in statements in *Wilson v Skeock*;[18] *Robson v Hallett*[19] and *R v Chief Constable of Devon and Cornwall, ex p Central Electricity Generating Board*,[20] but the point was only taken in *McConnell v Chief Constable of the Greater Manchester Police*.[1] The manager of a carpet store asked McC to leave, but he refused. PC Smith took McC outside, and, when he attempted to re-enter, arrested him on the ground that he was guilty of conduct whereby a breach of the peace might be occasioned, or, if he allowed him to re-enter, such a breach might take place. McC was taken before the magistrates to be bound over, but the magistrates declined to make a binding-over order. McC sued the police for false imprisonment claiming that the arrest was unlawful. His argument that a breach of the peace could not take place on private premises, such as a carpet store, was taken as a preliminary point, but ultimately rejected. The Court of Appeal also rejected the alternative contention that for there to be a breach of the peace on private premises, it is necessary for there to be some disturbance which would affect members of the public, or at least one other person, outside the premises themselves. Glidewell LJ pointed out[2] that this would lead to an unsatisfactory distinction between the case of an abusive altercation arising between two people in an isolated house and a similar altercation between the same two people in a terraced house with thin walls and neighbours who could hear everything that was going on. The possible effect on the public would therefore only be relevant to the factual question whether the constable reasonably apprehended that a breach of the peace might occur.[3]

---

11 Para. 55.
12 Below.
13 *Choherr v Austria* (1993) 17 EHRR 358.
14 See below, p. 541.
15 pp. 548–556.
16 Above, pp. 196–200.
17 Below, pp. 523–541.
18 (1949) 113 JP 294 at 296.
19 [1967] 2 QB 939 at 953, 954–955.
20 [1982] QB 458 at 471, 479.
1 [1990] 1 All ER 423, CA. The headnote in [1990] 1 WLR 364 is misleading.
2 At 429.
3 There is no requirement that there is any disturbance off the premises for there to be a breach of the peace on private premises: *McQuade v Chief Constable of Humberside Police* [2001] EWCA Civ 1330, (2001) Times, 3 September.

The question whether a breach of the peace can arise in private and quasi-private areas also fell to be reviewed in *Porter v Metropolitan Police Comr.* [4] The claimant brought an action for false imprisonment following her arrest for breach of the peace when she refused to leave the electricity board shop in which she was complaining. The staff called the police who arrested her when she refused to leave. Judge LJ held:

> 'refusal to leave the showroom did not itself constitute a breach of the peace nor justify her arrest, unless and until she resisted lawful efforts to remove her and a breach of the peace became imminent or actually occurred.'

The court was referred to the article by K. Gray and S. Gray, [5] in which it is argued, relying on European Court of Human Rights jurisprudence, that the owner of quasi-public premises has more limited powers to exclude and remove members of the public than private premises. Gray and Gray contrast:

> 'the position in the English law of trespass, which permits arbitrary exclusion, with the approach as taken in the USA, Canada and Australia where the courts have recognised a doctrine of reasonable access, under which owners of quasi-public property may exclude members of the public only on the grounds that are objectively reasonable.'

Can such rights be recognised in relation to the law governing police powers and public order if they are not also recognised in property law? Is the guarantee of a right of 'reasonable access' to 'quasi-public' space a sufficiently clear and workable concept for the courts to adopt? At a more principled level, the authors argue:

> 'During the last 20 years in Britain the increasing privatisation of urban space has vested new and enormous powers of social regulation in the hands of large, publicly unaccountable corporations. The essential thrust of the article is, at one level, that the law of civil wrongs—in the form of strict doctrines of trespass law—can no longer serve as an instrument for the curtailment of various kinds of civil right. Only a society deeply misguided or cynical would today consign the freedoms of its citizens to the uncontrolled discretion of a generation of property developers. The untenability of arbitrary trespass rules in relation to quasi-public land is merely one index of the constant need to monitor the distribution of social and economic power between corporate and non-corporate persons and, equally, to invigilate the allocation of police power between non- governmental entities and the state itself. It may be that only a clearer acknowledgement of the concept of the "corporate citizen"—until now virtually a contradiction in terms—can enable a range of civil freedoms to be moderated both fairly and consistently with fundamental principles of liberal democracy.
> At a different, but related, level, it is indeed striking that common law discourse on matters traditionally regarded as central to private law has been invaded by the once unfamiliar terminology of public law. Concerns with "reasonableness", legitimate expectation, "rights to interchange", due process and proportionality have noticeably begun to infiltrate the heartland of private law, transforming the property talk not merely of theorists but of common law courts as well. The emergence of recognisable species of "quasi- public" space underscores the fact that a starkly dichotomous view of the public/private distinction is nowadays impossible to sustain. Even within the hallowed territory of real property it is no longer heretical to suggest that the domains of the public and the private are separated, not by a clean cut, but rather by incremental gradations which only superficially conceal the interpenetrating nature of some of our most cherished legal categories. One inevitable effect of this evolutionary process has been the increasing politicisation of property; and the modern jurisprudence of quasi-public property is indeed the by-product of rejuvenated ideas of moral and social community. But this development need not, itself, strike terror into the hearts of the conservative; it highlights only the fact that, in the Britain of the last 20 years, a remarkably new order of things has come about.'

---

4   (1999) 20 Oct, CA (Civ D).
5   [1999] 1 EHRLR 46.

(iii) Part I of the Public Order Act 1986

Public Order Act 1986

PART I

NEW OFFENCES

1. Riot

(1) Where 12 or more persons who are present together use or threaten unlawful violence for a common purpose and the conduct of them (taken together) is such as would cause a person of reasonable firmness present at the scene to fear for his personal safety, each of the persons using unlawful violence for the common purpose is guilty of riot.

(2) It is immaterial whether or not the 12 or more use or threaten unlawful violence simultaneously.

(3) The common purpose may be inferred from conduct.

(4) No person of reasonable firmness need actually be, or be likely to be, present at the scene.

(5) Riot may be committed in private as well as in public places.

(6) A person guilty of riot is liable on conviction on indictment to imprisonment for a term not exceeding ten years or a fine or both.

2. Violent disorder

(1) Where 3 or more persons who are present together use or threaten unlawful violence and the conduct of them (taken together) is such as would cause a person of reasonable firmness present at the scene to fear for his personal safety, each of the persons using or threatening unlawful violence is guilty of violent disorder.

(2) It is immaterial whether or not the 3 or more use or threaten unlawful violence simultaneously.

(3) No person of reasonable firmness need actually be, or be likely to be, present at the scene.

(4) Violent disorder may be committed in private as well as in public places.

(5) A person guilty of violent disorder is liable on conviction on indictment to imprisonment for a term not exceeding 5 years or a fine or both, or on summary conviction to imprisonment for a term not exceeding 6 months or a fine not exceeding the statutory maximum or both.

3. Affray

(1) A person is guilty of affray if he uses or threatens unlawful violence towards another and his conduct is such as would cause a person of reasonable firmness present at the scene to fear for his personal safety.

(2) Where 2 or more persons use or threaten the unlawful violence, it is the conduct of them taken together that must be considered for the purposes of subsection (1).

(3) For the purposes of this section a threat cannot be made by the use of words alone.

(4) No person of reasonable firmness need actually be, or be likely to be, present at the scene.

(5) Affray may be committed in private as well as in public places.

(6) A constable may arrest without warrant anyone he reasonably suspects is committing affray.

(7) A person guilty of affray is liable on conviction on indictment to imprisonment for a term not exceeding 3 years or a fine or both, or on summary conviction to imprisonment for a term not exceeding 6 months or a fine not exceeding the statutory maximum or both.

4. Fear or provocation of violence

(1) A person is guilty of an offence if he—

(a) uses towards another person threatening, abusive or insulting words or behaviour, or

(b) distributes or displays to another person any writing, sign or other visible representation which is threatening, abusive or insulting,

with intent to cause that person to believe that immediate unlawful violence will be used against him or another by any person, or to provoke the immediate use of unlawful violence by that person or another, or whereby that person is likely to believe that such violence will be used or it is likely that such violence will be provoked.

(2) An offence under this section may be committed in a public or a private place, except that no offence is committed where the words or behaviour are used, or the writing, sign or other

visible representation is distributed or displayed, by a person inside a dwelling and the other person is also inside that or another dwelling.

(3) A constable may arrest without warrant anyone he reasonably suspects is committing an offence under this section.

(4) A person guilty of an offence under this section is liable on summary conviction to imprisonment for a term not exceeding 6 months or a fine not exceeding level 5 on the standard scale or both.

[4A. Intentional harassment, alarm or distress

(1) A person is guilty of an offence if, with intent to cause a person harassment, alarm or distress, he—

(*a*)   uses threatening, abusive or insulting words or behaviour, or disorderly behaviour, or

(*b*)   displays any writing, sign or other visible representation which is threatening, abusive or insulting,

thereby causing that or another person harassment, alarm or distress.

(2) An offence under this section may be committed in a public or a private place, except that no offence is committed where the words or behaviour are used, or the writing, sign or other visible representation is displayed, by a person inside a dwelling and the person who is harassed, alarmed or distressed is also inside that or another dwelling.

(3) It is a defence for the accused to prove—

(*a*)   that he was inside a dwelling and had no reason to believe that the words or behaviour used, or the writing, sign or other visible representation displayed, would be heard or seen by a person outside that or any other dwelling, or

(*b*)   that his conduct was reasonable.

(4) A constable may arrest without warrant anyone he reasonably suspects is committing an offence under this section.

(5) A person guilty of an offence under this section is liable on summary conviction to imprisonment for a term not exceeding 6 months or a fine not exceeding level 5 on the standard scale or both.][6]

5. Harassment, alarm or distress

(1) A person is guilty of an offence if he—

(*a*)   uses threatening, abusive or insulting words or behaviour, or disorderly behaviour, or

(*b*)   displays any writing, sign or other visible representation which is threatening, abusive or insulting,

within the hearing or sight of a person likely to be caused harassment, alarm or distress thereby.

(2) An offence under this section may be committed in a public or a private place, except that no offence is committed where the words or behaviour are used, or the writing, sign or other visible representation is displayed, by a person inside a dwelling and the other person is also inside that or another dwelling.

(3) It is a defence for the accused to prove—

(*a*)   that he had no reason to believe that there was any person within hearing or sight who was likely to be caused harassment, alarm or distress, or

(*b*)   that he was inside a dwelling and had no reason to believe that the words or behaviour used, or the writing, sign or other visible representation displayed, would be heard or seen by a person outside that or any other dwelling, or

(*c*)   that his conduct was reasonable.

(4) A constable may arrest a person without warrant if—

(*a*)   he engages in offensive conduct which [a][7] constable warns him to stop, and

(*b*)   he engages in further offensive conduct immediately or shortly after the warning.

(5) In subsection (4) 'offensive conduct' means conduct the constable reasonably suspects to constitute an offence under this section, and the conduct mentioned in paragraph (*a*) and the further conduct need not be of the same nature.

(6) A person guilty of an offence under this section is liable on summary conviction to a fine not exceeding level 3 on the standard scale.

6   Inserted by the Criminal Justice and Public Order Act 1994, s. 154.
7   Substituted by the Public Order (Amendment) Act 1996, s. 1.

6. Mental element: miscellaneous

(1) A person is guilty of riot only if he intends to use violence or is aware that his conduct may be violent.

(2) A person is guilty of violent disorder or affray only if he intends to use or threaten violence or is aware that his conduct may be violent or threaten violence.

(3) A person is guilty of an offence under section 4 only if he intends his words or behaviour, or the writing, sign or other visible representation, to be threatening, abusive or insulting, or is aware that it may be threatening, abusive or insulting.

(4) A person is guilty of an offence under section 5 only if he intends his words or behaviour, or the writing, sign or other visible representation, to be threatening, abusive or insulting, or is aware that it may be threatening, abusive or insulting or (as the case may be) he intends his behaviour to be or is aware that it may be disorderly.

(5) For the purposes of this section a person whose awareness if impaired by intoxication shall be taken to be aware of that of which he would be aware if not intoxicated, unless he shows either that his intoxication was not self-induced or that it was caused solely by the taking or administration of a substance in the course of medical treatment.

(6) In subsection (5) 'intoxication' means any intoxication, whether caused by drink, drugs or other means, or by a combination of means.

(7) Subsections (1) and (2) do not affect the determination for the purposes of riot or violent disorder of the number of persons who use or threaten violence.

7. Procedure: miscellaneous

(1) No prosecution for an offence of riot or incitement to riot may be instituted except by or with the consent of the Director of Public Prosecutions.

(2) For the purposes of the rule against charging more than one offence in the same count or information, each of sections 1 to 5 creates one offence.

(3) If on the trial on indictment of a person charged with violent disorder or affray the jury find him not guilty of the offence charged, they may (without prejudice to section 6(3) of the Criminal Law Act 1967) find him guilty of an offence under section 4.

(4) The Crown Court has the same powers and duties in relation to a person who is by virtue of subsection (3) convicted before it of an offence under section 4 as a magistrates' court would have on convicting him of the offence.

8. Interpretation

In this Part—

> 'dwelling' means any structure or part of a structure occupied as a person's home or as other living accommodation (whether the occupation is separate or shared with others) but does not include any part not so occupied, and for this purpose 'structure' includes a tent, caravan, vehicle, vessel or other temporary or movable structure;
>
> 'violence' means any violent conduct, so that—
>
> (*a*) except in the context of affray, it includes violent conduct towards property as well as violent conduct towards persons, and
>
> (*b*) it is not restricted to conduct causing or intended to cause injury or damage but includes any other violent conduct (for example, throwing at or towards a person a missile of a kind capable of causing injury which does not hit or falls short).

9. Offences abolished

(1) The common law offences of riot, rout, unlawful assembly and affray are abolished.

(2) The offences under the following enactments are abolished—

(*a*) section 1 of the Tumultuous Petitioning Act 1661 (presentation of petition to monarch or Parliament accompanied by excessive number of persons),

(*b*) section 1 of the Shipping Offences Act 1793 (interference with operation of vessel by persons riotously assembled),

(*c*) section 23 of the Seditious Meetings Act 1817 (prohibition of certain meetings within one mile of Westminster Hall when Parliament sitting), and

(*d*) section 5 of the Public Order Act 1936 (conduct conducive to breach of the peace).

10. Construction of other instruments
(1) In the Riot (Damages)Act 1886 . . .[8] (compensation for riot damage) 'riotous' and 'riotously' shall be construed in accordance with section 1 above.
(2) In Schedule 1 to the Marine Insurance Act 1906 (form and rules for the construction of certain insurance policies) 'rioters' in rule 8 and 'riot' in rule 10 shall, in the application of the rules to any policy taking effect on or after the coming into force of this section, be construed in accordance with section 1 above unless a different intention appears.
(3) 'Riot' and cognate expressions in any enactment in force before the coming into force of this section (other than the enactments mentioned in subsections (1) and (2) above) shall be construed in accordance with section 1 above if they would have been construed in accordance with the common law offence of riot apart from this Part.
(4) Subject to subsections (1) to (3) above and unless a different intention appears, nothing in this Part affects the meaning of 'riot' or any cognate expression in any enactment in force, or other instrument taking effect, before the coming into force of this section.

NOTES

1. Part I of the 1986 Act replaces the common law offences of riot, rout, unlawful assembly and affray and (*inter alia*) the statutory offence under s. 5 of the Public Order Act 1936 (the use of threatening, abusive or insulting words or behaviour with intent to provoke a breach of the peace or whereby a breach of the peace is likely to be occasioned). It is based on the recommendations of the Law Commission,[9] with some modifications. See generally on Part I;[10] E. Rees.[11]

Riot

2. At common law, there were five necessary elements:(1) three or more persons; (2) a common purpose; (3) execution or inception of the common purpose; (4) an intent to help one another by force if necessary against any person who might oppose them in the execution of their common purpose; and (5) force or violence displayed in such a manner as to alarm at least one person of reasonable firmness and courage.[12] The statutory offence is similar, but with a requirement of 12 or more persons rather than three. By contrast with the offence of violent disorder (below), the riot offence applies only to those who *use* violence. It is the most serious of the public order offences, being triable only on indictment. The consent of the DPP is required, but; that may be expressed by any Crown Prosecutor.[13]

The Law Commission regarded riot charges as appropriate where there is evidence of prolonged, active and direct participation in the organisation of a major public disturbance.[14] 'In many respects, riot is simply an aggravated form of violent disorder.'[15] The distinguishing features are (1) its scale, with the involvement of 12 or more; (2) the requirement of common purpose; and (3) the requirement that the defendant be shown to have *used* or threatened unlawful violence.[16] The common purpose relates to the violence, not the presence of the 12. A defendant who does not *use* unlawful violence may, nevertheless, be convicted of riot as an aider and abettor

8 Words omitted repealed by the Merchant Shipping Act 1995, s. 314(1), Sch. 12.
9 Law Com. No. 123.
10 A. T. H. Smith, [1987] Crim LR 156.
11 *Legal Action*, December 1989, p. 17.
12 *Field v Metropolitan Police Receiver* [1907] 2 KB 853.
13 Prosecution of Offences Act 1985, s. 7(1).
14 Law Com. No. 123, paras. 6.7–6.10.
15 *Smith*, p. 78.
16 *White Paper*, p. 17.

if he encourages the use of violence by others: *R v Jefferson*,[17] where the court confirmed that s. 8 of the Accessories and Abettors Act 1861 was potentially applicable to each of the offences in ss. 1–5 of the 1986 Act.

The principles set out in *Mahroof*[18] in respect of the number of persons involved in a disturbance in relation to charges of violent disorder presumably would apply, *mutatis mutandis*, to riot. The requirement of 'common purpose' may be very general, for example 'celebrating the victory of England over Egypt in their World Cup match',[19] and 'demonstrating against the poll tax':[20] The purpose may be of any character, it does not matter whether it is public or private, lawful or unlawful.[1] It does not matter that some of the 12 are acting without the intent to use violence or awareness that conduct is violent if they use violence for the common purpose. The hypothetical person of reasonable firmness who must fear for his personal safety need not be present at the scene. This is an important aspect of the offence, reflecting the fact that the offence is against the state rather than an individual victim. The section, read in conjunction with s. 6, renders voluntarily intoxicated offenders very easily prosecuted, even where their intoxication through drink or drugs is such that they were unaware of what they were doing.

3. In practice the authorities have found difficulty in securing convictions for riot following outbreaks of serious disorder. For example, in the riots in the St. Paul's district of Bristol in 1980, 134 arrests were made. The DPP decided that 16 should be charged with the common law offence of riotous assembly.[2] The trial lasted over seven weeks. The judge directed the acquittal of 3 defendants for lack of evidence, the jury acquitted 5 and failed to agree a verdict on the rest: the trial collapsed, having cost around £500,000 (the same as the cost of the riot damage). The result was seen as a 'resounding victory for black people and the rioters, and led the DPP ... to comment that it may have been a mistake to bring riot charges.' It appeared that a number of the jurors were not convinced that a common purpose of 'a show of strength against the police' was sufficient to constitute a riot, even though the judge had directed that it could be.[3] Similarly, all the charges of riotous assembly (and most of those of unlawful assembly) brought in consequence of violence during the 1984–85 miners' strike failed.[4] The Attorney-General commented that 'the law of riot creates some grave evidential problems'.[5] Several convictions followed the 'Tottenham Riots', but these are a rare example of prosecutors overcoming the problems. These problems appear to remain under the 1986 Act. The number found guilty or cautioned each year has remained small, although the number of public order offences generally has risen.[6]

Public order offences rose by 15% in 1996–97, with a total of 16,240 offences recorded.[7] In 1997-98, the police recorded six offences of riot, and in 1998–99, there were only three riot offences recorded.[8]

---

17 [1994] 1 All ER 270, CA (Cr D).
18 Below, p. 477.
19 *Jefferson*, above.
20 *R v Tyler* (1993) 96 Cr App Rep 332, CA (Cr D).
1 Law Comm No. 123, paras. 6.24, 6.25.
2 See M. Kettle and L. Hodges, *Uprising!* (1982), pp. 34–38.
3 Kettle and Hodges, op. cit., p. 38.
4 See S. McCabe and P. Wallington, *The Police, Public Order and Civil Liberties* (1988), pp. 99–100; S. Kavanagh and R. Malcolm, *Legal Action*, September 1985, p. 6.
5 63 HC Deb, 9 July 1984, col. 691.
6 E.g. 3 in 1990, 31 in 1992 and 18 in 1993: *Criminal Statistics: England and Wales 1993* (Cm. 2680, 1994), p. 119.
7 *Digest 4*, Chap. 1; *Criminal Statistics of England and Wales* (1997).
8 D. Povey and J. Prime, Home Office Research Statistics Issue 18/99, *Recorded Crime Statistics* (1999), p.18.

4. Most of the recent reported cases on riot have concerned claims under the Riot (Damages) Act 1886,[9] as amended by the Police Act 1996, ss. 103(1) and 63. That Act was passed to remedy defects in the previous legislation [10] under which compensation was paid by the hundred only in cases of the felonious destruction of certain specified kinds of property by persons riotously and tumultuously assembled. Pressure from people whose property was damaged in the Trafalgar Square riots of 8 February 1886, and who had no claim under the previous legislation, led to special provision being made for them by the Metropolitan Police (Compensation) Act 1886. The general legislation followed shortly afterwards. Claims are met by the police authority. See the discussion by P. Lewis on whether the anti-capitalism demonstration in London on 18 June 1999 (J-18) was a riot for the purposes of the Riot (Damages) Act 1886, s. 2. [11]

Other cases under this Act include *Gunter v Metropolitan Police District Receive*; [12] *Rance v Hastings Corpn* [13] (attack on a hotel where three ladies, wrongly thought by the mob to be militant suffragettes, had taken refuge: claim successful); *Ford v Metropolitan Police District Receiver* [14] (a 'good humoured' crowd, some armed with crowbars and pickaxes, took woodwork and floorboards from an empty house as fuel for a 'peace night' bonfire; a neighbour gave evidence that he was afraid: claim successful); *Munday v Metropolitan Police District Receiver* [15] (crowd unable to get into Chelsea F.C.'s ground to see a match against Moscow Dynamo broke into neighbouring premises in order to watch from there, the owner's daughter was held against a wall, and gave evidence that she was afraid: claim successful). In order to establish a claim, the conduct must be 'tumultuous' as well as 'riotous' (*JW Dwyer Ltd v Metropolitan Police District Receiver*).[16] This was endorsed by the Court of Appeal in *D H Edmonds Ltd v East Sussex Police Authority*, [17] when holding that the three or four robbers who had committed a smash and grab raid at the plaintiff's jewellery shop were assembled 'riotously' but not 'tumultuously'. To be 'tumultuous' an assembly should be of considerable size, excited and emotionally aroused and, generally although not necessarily, accompanied by noise. 'Riot' and 'riotously' in the 1886 Act are to be interpreted in accordance with s. 1: 1986 Act, s. 10(1).

Violent disorder

5. The violent disorder offence replaced the common law offence of unlawful assembly. This offence required (1) an assembly of three or more persons; (2) a common purpose (a) to commit a crime of violence or (b) to achieve some other object, whether lawful or not, in such a way as to cause reasonable men to apprehend a breach of the peace; and (3) an intention to use or abet the use of violence, or to do or abet acts which D knows to be likely to cause a breach of the peace. [18] There was, however, some uncertainty as to its exact scope. It was used as a charge following serious outbreaks of disorder such as Chartist disturbances in Newport; [19] the Trafalgar Square

---

9   See A. Samuels, [1970] Crim LR 336.
10   1827, 7 & 8 Geo IV c 31.
11   *The Times*, 13 July 1999.
12   (1888) 53 JP 249, Mathews J.
13   (1913) 136 LT Jo 117, Hastings Cty Ct.
14   [1921] 2 KB 344, Bailhache J.
15   [1949] 1 All ER 337, Pritchard J.
16   [1967] 2 QB 970, Lyell J.
17   (1988) Times, 15 July.
18   *Smith and Hogan* (6th edn, 1988), p. 745.
19   *R v Vincent* (1839) 9 C&P 91.

riots on 'Bloody Sunday', 13 November 1887; [20] the disturbance at the Garden House Hotel, Cambridge; [1] the Shrewsbury pickets case. [2] *Beatty v Gillbanks* [3] was also commonly regarded as an authority on unlawful assembly.
6. The *White Paper* stated: [4]

> '3.13. Violent disorder will be the main successor offence to unlawful assembly, and to some cases currently charged as riot. Like the Law Commission, the Government anticipates that it will be used in the future as the normal charge for serious outbreaks of public disorder. But it will be capable of being applied over a wide spectrum of situations ranging from major public disorder to minor group disturbances involving some violence.'

The offence is triable either way, but the *Practice Note* (*Offences Triable Either Way: Mode of Trial*) [5] states that cases of violent disorder 'should generally be committed for trial'. In practice, it has been used as a charge much more frequently than unlawful assembly. In 1997–98 there were 2,113 recorded offences of violent disorder, and in 1998–99, 2,500. [6]
7. The violent disorder offence requires three or more persons together using or threatening violence. In *R v Mahroof* [7] three defendants were charged jointly on one indictment with violent disorder, but M alone was convicted, with both his co-accused acquitted. The court held that there was a sufficient allegation made in the indictment to support M's conviction:

> 'subject to two very important qualifications: first of all, that there is evidence before the jury that there were three people involved in the criminal behaviour, though not necessarily those named in the indictment; secondly, that the defence are apprised of what it is they have to meet.' [8]

On the facts there had been evidence of the involvement of others, but the defence had not been sufficiently apprised. M's conviction under s. 2 of the 1986 Act was quashed, and a conviction under s. 4 substituted (by reference to s. 7(3)). The court indicated that the best way of 'apprising' the defence was by adding the words 'and others' to the indictment, enabling the defence then to seek particulars.

Section 7(3) permits the jury to return a conviction under s. 4 where the defendant has been acquitted of a charge under s. 2: this can apply where the acquittal has been directed by the judge [9] and without empanelling a jury. [10] Where the evidence which led to the conviction under s. 2 relates to violence to property, the court may decline to substitute verdicts under s. 3, since that offence is limited to violence to people. [11] The judge must direct the jury adequately on the relevant parts of s. 4. [12]

In *R v Fleming and Robinson* [13] four persons were involved in a fight: F and R were convicted of violent disorder; one other was acquitted and the jury was unable to agree a verdict on the fourth. Applying *Mahroof*, the convictions were quashed, and convictions for affray under s. 3 substituted. Where there are three defendants

20 See *R v Cunninghame Graham and Burns* (1888) 16 Cox CC 420; V. Bailey (ed.), *Policing and Punishment in Nineteenth Century Britain* (1981), Chap. 5.
1 See *R v Caird*, below, p. 504.
2 *R v Jones* [1974] ICR 310, CA (Cr D).
3 Below p. 526.
4 p. 15.
5 [1990] 3 All ER 979.
6 D. Povey and J. Prime, Home Office Research Statistics Issue 18/99, *Recorded Crime Statistics* (1999), p. 18.
7 (1988) 88 Cr App Rep 317, CA (Cr D).
8 At 321.
9 *R v Carson* (1990) 92 Cr App Rep 236, CA (Cr D).
10 *R v O'Brien* (1992) 156 JP 925, CA (Cr D).
11 *R v McGuigan and Cameron* [1991] Crim LR 719.
12 *R v Perrins* [1995] Crim LR 432.
13 (1989) 153 JP 517, CA (Cr D).

under s. 2, the judge should warn the jury specifically that if any one of them should be acquitted, they must necessarily acquit the others unless satisfied that some other person not charged was taking part in the violent disorder. [14] There need not be three *defendants* – one may have escaped detection. The defences of self defence, reasonable defence of another person and the 'taking of necessary steps to preserve the peace' may be raised: *R v Rothwell and Barton*. [15]

Section 2 has been used in cases of violent animal rights protests – e.g. *R v Crown Court at Oxford, ex p Monaghan* [16] throwing stones over the fence in an aimless manner at police and using fences as battering rams. Section 2 has also been charged where the defendant was part of a gang which had used violence by slashing people and attacking them with axes at the Notting Hill Carnival, even though the defendant did not assault anyone, but merely 'ran with the group'. The court referred to the judgment of Kerr LJ in *Allan v Ireland*: [17]

> 'a defendant's voluntary presence during an affray as part of crowd engaged in threatening behaviour is capable of raising a *prima facie* case of participation against the defendant . . . but that mere voluntary presence is not sufficient to convict a defendant unless the court is satisfied that he at least also gave some overt encouragement to the others who were directly involved in the affray or threatening behaviour. Thus, it would obviously be open to any individual defendant . . . to give evidence that he was not only innocent of any threatening behaviour himself, but that he had also not in any way encouraged any acts of threatening behaviour by others, and that he was merely swept up in the crowd without any opportunity of dissociating himself from what others were doing.'

Affray

8. This offence is typically used in respect of fights, although cases involving very serious violence are likely to lead to charges of violent disorder or riot rather than affray. Before the 1986 Act, affray was 'by far the most important of the common law public order offences, charged against some 1,000 people per year'. [18] It covered unlawful fighting or violence or an unlawful display of force, in such a manner that a bystander of reasonably firm character might reasonably be expected to be terrified. Statutory affray is triable either way and carries a maximum sentence (when tried on indictment) of three years (in comparison with life imprisonment at common law). Section 3(1) appears to contemplate both a person to whom the violence or threat is directed and a hypothetical third party of reasonable firmness as well as the defendant. It is this requirement that keeps all fights between just two participants from becoming an affray. It has been emphasised on a number of occasions that the hypothetical person is one who must fear for his safety not the victim. [19] In considering whether a person fears for his personal safety under s. 3, the bystander who must be imagined, 'though hypothetical, is not necessarily hypothetically a white bystander'. [20] Being armed with baseball bats and following a victim with menace late at night in a deserted area was capable of amounting to conduct which would put a hypothetical bystander in fear.[1] (How can the reasonable bystander be in fear for *his* safety if it is clear that

---

14 *R v Worton* (1989) 154 JP 201, CA (Cr D).
15 [1993] Crim LR 662, CA (Cr D).
16 (1998) 18 June, DC.
17 (1984) 79 Cr App R 206.
18 *White Paper*, p. 16.
19 *R v Sanchez* (1996) JP 321, [1996] Crim LR 572, CA (S attacked V, her former partner with whom she was arguing in a car park in the early hours – hypothetical reasonable bystander unlikely to be threatened; this was a very personal fight).
20 *Gray v DPP* (1999) 1 July unreported, DC.
 1 *R v Brodie* [2000] Crim LR 775.

only one person is being targeted, and the bystander has no knowledge of any weapon that D is carrying?) Accordingly, the offence will not cover every case of assault, as the circumstances may not be such as to cause a third party to fear for his own safety. Section 3 has been held to be committed in a prison cell, and in light of s. 3(4), the court felt it unnecessary to postulate what might have happened if someone else had been present.[2] Nevertheless, the offence may be committed in the course of domestic incidents and not just occasions of public disorder. See *R v Davison*,[3] and Commentary by Sir John Smith, and *DPP v Cotcher and Cotcher*.[4] In *R v Connor*[5] Buxton LJ reiterated the view in *R v Davison*,[6] that simple assaults ought not to be elevated to public order charges. The offence has also been used in relation to behaviour on an aircraft.[7]

Difficulties have arisen where a series of incidents give rise to a charge under s. 3. Is it necessary to the jury to agree on which of the incidents amounted to the affray, or can different jurors rely on different ones? The Lord Chief Justice recently described the problem with the offence in these terms:

> 'it is essential in considering this submission to bear in mind the nature of the offence of affray. It typically involves a group of people who may well be shouting, struggling, threatening, waving weapons, throwing objects, exchanging and threatening blows etc. Again, typically it involves a continuous course of conduct, the criminal character of which depends on the general nature and effect of the conduct as a whole and not on particular incidents and events which may take place in the course of it. Where reliance is placed on such a continuous course of conduct it is not necessary for the Crown to identify and prove particular incidents. To require such proof would deprive section 3(1) of the 1986 Act of its intended effect, and deprive law-abiding citizens of the protection which this provision intends that they should enjoy. It would be asking the impossible to require a jury of 12 men and women to be satisfied beyond reasonable doubt that each or any incident in an indiscriminate melee such as constitutes the typical affray was proved to the requisite standard.
>
> Different conclusions may, however, arise where the conduct which is alleged to constitute an affray is not continuous but falls into separate sequences. The character of the conduct relied on in each sequence may in such a case be quiet different and so may the effect on the persons who are (or may hypothetically be) present at the scene. The possibility then arises that half the jury may be persuaded that the first sequence of events amounted to an affray and the second did not, and the second half of the jury may be persuaded that the second sequence amounted to an affray and the first did not the result would then be that there was no unanimous jury verdict in support of conviction based on either sequence.'[8]

In *R v Hunter*[9] the court suggested that:

> 'in a continuous incident case we suggest that it would have been permissible to direct the jury (a) to be sure that acts of unlawful violence had been used or threatened and (b) that the defendants were parties to the incidents in which that unlawful violence was used or threatened even if they were not unanimous as to precisely which defendant had used to threatened to act with unlawful violence.'

On the limitation in s. 3(3) that for the purposes of affray a threat cannot be made by words alone, see *R v Dixon*[10] (encouragement of dog to attack police officers sufficient even in the absence of evidence that the dog's subsequent attack was in response to

2 *R v Beaumont and Correlli* (1999) 12 February unreported, CA (Cr D).
3 [1992] Crim LR 31.
4 [1993] COD 181.
5 (2000) 13 March, CA (Cr D).
6 [1992] Crim LR 33.
7 *R v Oliver* [1999] 1 Cr App R (S) 394.
8 *R v Smith (CFA)* [1996] Crim LR 893; *R v Chalcraft* (1996) 8 October, CA (Cr D).
9 (1999) 21 December, CA.
10 [1993] Crim LR 579, CA (Cr D).

the encouragement), and *R v Robinson*[11] (adoption of an aggressive tone of voice insufficient), and Commentaries by Sir John Smith.

The leading case on the scope of s. 3 must now be seen as *DPP v I, M and H.*[12] Police approached a gang of 40 to 50 Asian youths outside a residential block in east London, eight or nine of the youths, including the three applicants, were carrying what appeared to be petrol bombs, milk bottles with liquid inside and corked with paper; they were 'milling around'; none of them lit or brandished a petrol bomb in a threatening way or, at that stage, threw a petrol bomb. There was no fighting or shouting; One of several officers who saw the petrol bombs thought that there could be a disturbance. However, there was no other gang or anyone other than the police at the scene. On the arrival of the officers, the gang of youths dispersed. The police followed the three applicants and a number of others who remained in a group. As they ran off, the three applicants and others threw away their petrol bombs. In that part of the East End street gangs were territorial and there was bad blood between the various gangs.

> **Lord Hutton**: . . . My Lords, the issue which arises on the first certified question is whether, as a matter of law, the carrying of petrol bombs by a group of persons can constitute a threat of violence where those petrol bombs are not being waved or brandished. I consider that giving the words 'threatens unlawful violence' in section 3(1) their ordinary and natural meaning the carrying of dangerous weapons, such as petrol bombs by a group of persons can, in some circumstances, constitute the threat of violence, without those weapons being waved or brandished.
>
> . . . it is apparent that the Law Commission and Parliament intended that the offence set out in section 3 should penalise those who engage in a fight, whether they are landing blows, or attempting to land blows, or threatening to land blows, but it is also clear that in such circumstances the victim or victims are bound to be present with the offender or offenders. Accordingly I regard it as clear that the section does not make guilty of an affray a person whose conduct constitutes a threat of violence to persons who are not present. This conclusion also derives support from the requirement in subsection (1) that the conduct of the offender is such that it would cause a bystander 'present at the scene' to fear for his personal safety. The concept of presence at the scene suggests that the notional bystander would be in the presence of both the offender and the victim. It is also relevant to observe that there is no reported case of affray where the victim was not present at the scene where the accused threatened violence. . . .
>
> In order to constitute an offence under section 3 there must be a threat of violence towards another person. Whilst the carrying of petrol bombs can constitute a threat of violence, it does not necessarily follow that because a person is present at a location where a gang are carrying petrol bombs there is a threat of violence towards that person. Whether there is a threat of violence towards a person present at the scene constituted by the carrying of a weapon or weapons will depend on the facts of the actual case, but that issue does not arise in the present case because, apart from the police officers towards whom there was no threat, no one was present at the scene.

Research on the use of charges under ss. 2 and 3 of the 1986 Act[13] confirms that statutory affray has been 'downgraded' in comparison to common law affray. 14% of the sample studied were charged under s. 3; the vast majority of incidents were generally relatively minor in character, involving little violence at most and often only the threat of violence. Section 2 (used in 6% of the cases in the sample) was employed in more serious cases, usually involving a greater number of people. Most of the incidents involved fights between groups of youths which, on occasion, resulted in quite serious injuries. A further distinction, suggested by one custody officer, was

11   [1993] Crim LR 581, CA (Cr D).
12   [2001] 2 WLR 765, HL.
13   T. Newburn et al, (1990) 29 HORB 10 (see below, p. 492 n. 2).

that spontaneous violence would be likely, depending on its extent, to result in s. 3 charges; anything premeditated or planned, as long as sufficient numbers were involved, would be charged under s. 2. Sections 2 or 3 would also be used as an alternative to a charge of actual or grievous bodily harm if there was doubt about the sufficiency of the evidence of these offences. With regard to statistics on affray, the Home Office Report [14] does not list affray as a separate notifiable offence. Other than riot and violent disorder, there were 16,763 'offences against the state or public order' in 1997–98 and 18,638 in 1998–99. [15]

9. Section 4 of the 1986 Act was considered in *Atkin v DPP* [16] and *R v Horseferry Road Metropolitan Stipendiary Magistrate, ex p Siadatan.* [17] Section 5 was considered in *DPP v Orum.* [18]

Section 4A, an offence of intentionally causing harassment, alarm or distress, was added by the Criminal Justice and Public Order Act 1994, s. 154. The aim was to provide higher penalties where harassment etc was deliberately inflicted, and to:

> 'enable the courts to deal more effectively with serious racial harassment, particularly where it is persistent.' [19]

Atkin v DPP (1989) 89 Cr App Rep 199, 158 JP 383, Queen's Bench Divisional Court

Two Customs and Excise officers, accompanied by a bailiff, went to the defendant's farm to recover outstanding value added tax. The two officers conducted their business in the farmhouse while the bailiff waited outside in the car. The car was parked in the farmyard where the bailiff was unable to hear any of the conversation in the farmhouse. When the officers ascertained from the defendant that he was unable to pay the VAT due they informed him that the bailiff would have to enter the farmhouse to distrain on his goods. The defendant replied: 'If the bailiff gets out of the car he's a dead un.' No threats were made to the two officers. One of the officers noticed a gun in the corner of the room and that officer, on the instructions of her colleague, left the farmhouse and told the bailiff that the defendant had threatened him. The bailiff did not get out of the car as he felt threatened and all three then left the farm. The defendant was charged with contravening section 4 of the Public Order Act 1986. The justices were of opinion that threatening words were used in the farmhouse. The defendant did not want the bailiff to enter his house and therefore the defendant must have intended the officers to convey the threat to the bailiff in a bid to keep him out. The defendant, therefore, used threatening words towards the bailiff with intent to cause him to believe that immediate unlawful violence would be used against him. The bailiff was not in the farmhouse, so section 4(2) of the 1986 Act did not apply. The justices, therefore, convicted the defendant who appealed by way of case stated. The Divisional Court allowed the appeal.

> **Taylor LJ**: ... In this Court, Mr. Murray on behalf of the defendant, has highlighted the phrase in section 4(1)(*a*) 'used towards another person threatening words.' He submits that the plain and natural meaning of that phrase is that the threatening words have to be addressed directly to another person who is present and either in earshot or aimed at as being putatively in earshot.

---

14 D. Povey and J. Prime, Issue 18/99, *Recorded Crime Statistics* (1999).
15 Ibid., p. 19.
16 Below.
17 Below, p. 483.
18 Below, p. 488.
19 Earl Ferrers, 555 HL Deb, 16 June 1994, col. 1864.

The phrase does not equate with 'used in regard to another person' or 'used concerning another person'.

He submits that approached in that way the phrase here clearly related to the use of the words within the house to those who were in earshot. The only persons in earshot were the two Customs and Excise officers. If one therefore follows through the section, the alleged offence was using 'towards those officers threatening words with intent to cause those officers to believe that immediate unlawful violence would be used against them or another person', presumably the bailiff. However, subsection (2) of section 4 provides that no offence is committed where the words are used by a person inside the dwelling and the other person is also inside that or another dwelling.

The question then arises who is meant by the phrase 'the other person'? Mr. Murray submits that the other person there must refer to the opening words of the whole section in subsection (1)(*a*) 'uses towards another person', the two people identified in subsection (2) being the person using the words who has to be inside the dwelling and the other person, the person towards whom they are used.

Viewed in that way the correct decision of this case would be an acquittal because the other person in section (2) would be the Customs and Excise officers and they were inside the dwelling so no offence would be committed.

We were referred to decisions of different divisions of this Court in previous cases, *Parkin v Norman* [1983] QB 92 and *Masterson v Holden* [1986] 1 WLR 1017. We have not found those citations particularly helpful as they were both concerned with an earlier Act, the Public Order Act 1936. The 1986 Act in sections 4 and 5 supersedes section 5 of the 1936 Act. The wording in the new Act is quite different. The phrase 'uses towards another person' is entirely new and the construction of section 4 is therefore not assisted, in my judgment, by considering decisions of this Court in regard to the construction of an earlier statute. This statute has, we are told, not been construed by any court and the phrase 'uses towards another person' has not been found by counsel in any other statutory provision which would give any helpful indication as to its true meaning in this context. So the exercise is one of purely looking at the wording of the section and deciding what the plain and natural meaning of the words is, bearing in mind that if there were any doubt that doubt would have to be resolved, since this is a penal provision, in favour of the appellant.

In my judgment the submissions made by Mr. Murray are correct. The phrase 'uses towards another person' means, in the context of section 4(1)(*a*) 'uses in the presence of and in the direction of another person directly'. I do not think, looking at the section as a whole, the words can bear the meaning 'concerning another person' or 'in regard to another person'. That conclusion is assisted by comparing sub-paragraph (*a*) and sub-paragraph (*b*) of subsection (1). If one looks at sub-paragraph (*b*) which concerns distributing or displaying to 'another person' any writing, it is clear that the distribution or display must be directly made to the other person. That being so, one would be surprised to find that another person had a different meaning in paragraph (*a*) from the meaning it holds in paragraph (*b*). Accordingly, I consider that when one construes in the context of this case section 4(1)(*a*) and the phrase 'uses towards another person' it cannot be right to regard the bailiff as being that other person because he was not in earshot and the words were not directed towards him.

Once it has been decided that the words, in the context of this case, refer to the Customs and Excise officers in 4(1)(*a*) one then has to look at the meaning of section 4(2). Who is the other person? Again, looking solely at the words of the section it seems to me clear that the other person refers back to section 4(1)(*a*), 'the other person' being the person to whom the person charged addresses or uses the words, whether they be threatening, abusive or insulting. Accordingly the conclusion I reach on this case is that 'the other person' in subsection (2), being the Customs and Excise officer, and that other person being inside the dwelling, the offence is not proved because all concerned within the ambit of the section are inside a dwelling. That being so, no offence is committed.

The other question which was raised is an academic question and suggests that it might be possible for the phrase, 'the other person' to refer back not to the person referred to in section 4(1)(*a*) but to 'another' later on in subsection (1) where that word is used twice; in other words the suggestion is that the other person in sub-section (2) may be the bailiff notwithstanding that the court might decide, as it has, that 'towards another person' in section 4(1)(*a*) referred to the Customs and Excise officers. As already indicated that would not be my construction and accordingly, although it is not specifically raised as the question in the case, I would answer the second question which the justices raised in accordance with the reasoning I have just given.

To deal with the specific question they have asked ... in my judgment the justices were not correct in convicting the defendant on the facts outlined and accordingly I would quash this conviction.

Henry J: I agree with everything Taylor LJ has said....

When one looks at the words of the exception of s. 4(2) ... it is clear that the intention of Parliament was to exclude domestic quarrels conducted within the home even in circumstances where such words or behaviour would, if repeated outside the dwelling create an offence. It also seems to me to follow from the clear words of the statute that it was the intention to exclude such domestic quarrels from criminal liability attaching to such domestic quarrels, even where the threat uttered, though spoken to the person sharing the dwelling was related to violence against someone who was not in the dwelling at the time.

For those additional reasons I agree with the conclusion of Taylor LJ as reached.

Appeal allowed.

Conviction quashed.

R v Horseferry Road Metropolitan Stipendiary Magistrate, ex p Siadatan [1991] 1 All ER 324, [1991] 1 QB 260, [1990] 3 WLR 1006, Queen's Bench Divisional Court

The applicant, Sayid Mehdie Siadatan, laid an information against Penguin Books Ltd, the publishers of *Satanic Verses* by Salman Rushdie, and sought a summons accusing them of distributing a book written by the author which contained abusive and insulting writing whereby it was likely that unlawful violence would be provoked, contrary to s. 4(1) of the Public Order Act 1986. The book was offensive to many Muslims and a bookshop owned by the publishers was subjected to a fire bomb attack while the book was on sale. The magistrate hearing the information refused to issue the summons on the ground that the information disclosed no offence because it was not alleged that 'immediate' unlawful violence would be provoked. The applicant applied for judicial review to quash the magistrate's decision, but the Divisional Court dismissed the application.

The judgment of the court (**Watkins** and **Stuart-Smith LJJ** and **Roch J**) was delivered by **Watkins LJ**: ...

[His Lordship noted that it was not contended that distribution of the book would provoke 'immediate' unlawful violence, and continued:]

Mr Nice [counsel for the applicant] referred to the short history of the legislation as follows. Section 4(1) of the 1986 Act replaced s. 5 of the Public Order Act 1936, the offence created by which was abolished by s. 9(2)(*d*) of the 1986 Act. Section 5 provided:

'Any person who in any public place or at any public meeting—(*a*) uses threatening, abusive or insulting words or behaviour, or (*b*) distributes or displays any writing, sign or visible representation which is threatening, abusive or insulting, with intent to provoke a breach of the peace or whereby a breach of the peace is likely to be occasioned, shall be guilty of an offence ...'

Clearly s. 5 did not require that the breach of the peace which was either intended or likely to be occasioned should follow immediately upon the actions of the defendant....

[His Lordship read s. 6(3) of the 1986 Act]

In the light of those provisions Mr Nice submits that a person who intends written words to be threatening, abusive or insulting, or who is aware that written words may be threatening, abusive or insulting, should not escape criminal liability under s. 4(1) simply because the violence which the written words are likely to provoke will not be immediate. If, he said, the construction of the section for which he contended is rejected, there will be a gap in the law which did not exist under the 1936 Act, a gap which Parliament, when passing the 1986 Act, could not have intended to create.

A consequence of construing the words 'such violence' in s. 4(1) as meaning 'immediate unlawful violence' will be that leaders of an extremist movement who prepare pamphlets or banners to be distributed or carried in public places by adherents to that movement will not be committing any offence under s. 4(1) albeit that they intend the words in the pamphlets or on the banners to be threatening, abusive or insulting and it is likely that unlawful violence will be provoked by the words in the pamphlet or on the banners.

Thus, whilst recognising the right to freedom of expression which the law confers on all persons within the United Kingdom, Mr Nice argues that such rights do not include a freedom to insult or abuse other persons in such a way that it is likely that violence will be provoked. Section 4(1) provides, he said, only a partial and imperfect protection against conduct which is insulting and abusive and likely to lead to violence unless his construction of the section is correct.

He argued strongly that, whether the court seeks the 'natural and ordinary meaning' of the words of s. 4(1) or whether we construe the words of s. 4(1) 'according to the plain literal and grammatical meaning of the words', the proper construction is that 'such violence' means 'unlawful violence' unqualified in any other way.

He divided the second part of the subsection into these four parts:

'With intent:(i) to cause that person to believe that immediate unlawful violence will be used against him or another by any person, or (ii) to provoke the immediate use of unlawful violence by that person or another, or whereby:(iii) that person is likely to believe that such violence will be used, or (iv) it is likely that such violence will be provoked.'

That makes plain, he said, that the words in part (iv) 'such violence' refer back to a previous use of the word 'violence', that the normal rules of grammatical construction require a reader to look at the most recent use of the word 'violence' prior to the phrase 'such violence'. The most recent use of that word appears in part (ii), where the word 'violence' is qualified only by the word 'unlawful'.

Furthermore, he argued that the phrase 'immediate unlawful violence' could have been used expressly in each of the parts (i) to (iv). Alternatively, the phrase 'immediate unlawful violence' having been used in part (i) the words 'such violence' could have been used in parts (ii), (iii) and (iv). The change from 'immediate unlawful violence' in part (i) to 'immediate use of unlawful violence' in part (ii) can only be explained because Parliament intended the words 'such violence' where they occurred in the remainder of the subsection to refer to 'unlawful violence' and not to 'immediate unlawful violence'.

Persuasive though those somewhat intricate arguments appeared to be, as presented by Mr Nice, the contrary construction advanced for the respondents by Mr Fitzgerald and by the amicus curiae, Mr Paget, is, we think, to be preferred. In our judgment the phrase 'such violence' in s. 4(1) means 'immediately unlawful violence'. We now give our reasons for that conclusion.

We were referred to the Law Commission's report entitled *Criminal Law Offences Relating to Public Order* (Law Com no. 123 (1983)). The content and structure of s. 4(1) is foreshadowed in the very clearly expressed para 5.43 of that report thus:

'*Fear of violence and provoking violence:*

5.43 The offence requires that each defendant use threatening etc. words or behaviour which is intended or is likely—(a) to cause another person to fear immediate unlawful violence, or (b) to provoke the immediate use of unlawful violence by another person.'

That the parliamentary draftsman, when drafting the last part of s. 4(1), did not achieve the same clarity and precision found in that paragraph is, we think, most regrettable.

The context in which s. 4(1) appears in the 1986 Act is the first matter which leads us to our conclusion. The title to the Act recounts that it is 'An Act to abolish ... certain statutory offences relating to public order; to create new offences relating to public order ...' Section 4 appears in the first part of the Act together with the creation of new offences, namely riot by s. 1, violent disorder by s. 2, affray by s. 3, harassment, alarm or distress by s. 5. The provisions of those sections are such that the conduct of the defendants must produce in an actual or notional person of reasonable firmness fear in relation to ss. 1, 2 and 3 which is contemporaneous with the unlawful violence being used by the defendants or harassment, alarm or distress which is contemporaneous with the threatening, abusive or insulting conduct under s. 5. We consider it most unlikely that Parliament could have intended to include, among sections which undoubtedly deal with conduct having an immediate impact on bystanders, a section creating an offence for conduct which is likely to lead to violence at some unspecified time in the future.

The second reason is that, in our view, by itself a proper reading of s. 4(1) leads to this conclusion. We accept the submission of Mr Paget that the words 'immediate unlawful violence' and the words 'the immediate use of unlawful violence' have precisely the same meaning. The change in the phraseology used by Parliament is simply a matter of style. The only violence mentioned in s. 4(1) is 'immediate unlawful violence'. The words 'such violence' refer back to the earlier use or uses of the word 'violence' in the subsection as qualified by the other words which appear in the same phrases as the word 'violence'. On the first occasion that the word 'violence' is used it is qualified by the words 'immediate unlawful' and on the second it is qualified by the words 'the immediate use of unlawful'. In our opinion, praying in aid Mr Nice's useful partition of the subsection, it is not possible in construing the words 'such violence' in part (iv), which reads 'it is likely that such violence will be provoked', to return to part (ii) and ignore the words 'the immediate use'. Parts (iii) and (iv) must have been intended by Parliament to be mirror images of parts (i) and (ii) of the subsection.

A third and very compelling reason for our conclusion on the correct construction of this subsection is that here we are construing a penal statute, of which there are, or may be, two possible readings. It is an elementary rule of statutory construction that, in a penal statute where there are two possible readings, the meaning which limits the scope of the offence thus created is that which the court should adopt. It would surely be strange indeed, if, where it could be shown that a defendant has an intent to provoke unlawful violence by another person, Parliament required the prosecution to establish an intent to provoke the immediate use of unlawful violence, but in a situation where a defendant had no such intent, but nevertheless it was likely that violence would be provoked, there was no requirement that such violence be immediate.

For these reasons we hold that the magistrate was right to refuse to issue a summons.

Finally, we consider it advisable to indicate our provisional view on the meaning of the word 'immediate'. In the Law Commission's report to which reference has already been made, at para 5.46 the Law Commission indicated that in their opinion the new offence to replace that created by s. 5 of the 1936 Act should include the element of immediacy; in the case of behaviour provoking the use of violence, it must be the immediate use of such violence. Nevertheless, the Law Commission in para 5.44 gave an example of a gang in one part of a town uttering threats directed at persons, for example, of a particular ethnic or religious group resident in another part, and stated that that would be an offence, although the threat would not be capable of being performed until the gang arrived in the other part of the town. So the Law Commission recommended there that Parliament enact a law to create an offence of the making of threats which lead to the fear of violence to the person simpliciter as opposed to an offence of the making of threats, causing fear of violence to the person hearing the threats.

It seems to us that the word 'immediate' does not mean 'instantaneous', that a relatively short time interval may elapse between the act which is threatening, abusive or insulting and the unlawful violence. 'Immediate' connotes proximity in time and proximity in causation, that it is likely that violence will result within a relatively short period of time and without any other intervening occurrence....

Application dismissed.

NOTES

1. Section 4 was designed to be the direct replacement for s. 5 of the Public Order Act 1936, as amended. This had provided as follows:

'Any person who in any public place or at any public meeting—
　　(*a*)　uses threatening, abusive or insulting words or behaviour, or

(*b*) distributes or displays any writing, sign or visible representation which is threatening, abusive or insulting,

with intent to provoke a breach of the peace or whereby a breach of the peace is likely to be occasioned, shall be guilty of an offence.'

'Public place' was defined in s. 9.[20] Section 5 was modelled on the Metropolitan Police Act 1839, s. 15(13) and similar offences in local legislation.

The main changes appearing in the new s. 4 were: (1) that the offence can be committed in a public or *private* place (except inside a dwelling house); (2) that it is not confined to situations where a third party is likely to be *provoked* into violence, but extends also to cases where a third party *fears* violence; and (3) that the 'breach of the peace' concept is not employed. The first point was in response to the dismissal by magistrates of charges under the old s. 5 during the miners' dispute where the defendants showed that they were on National Coal Board or other private property, while the victims of the threats were on the public highway.[1] (In fact, there was clear authority that s. 5 applied where threats etc. were directed *to* a person in a public place: *Ward v Holman*;[2] *R v Edwards*; *R v Roberts*.[3] Threatening behaviour may be committed in a public or private place under s. 4. But, if the threatening words and behaviour are used by an accused inside a dwelling house, the offence cannot be committed if the other person is also inside that (or another) dwelling: *R v Barber*.[4] In this sense it is a truly 'public' order crime, unlike riot, violent disorder and affray. The second point responded to case law such as *Marsh v Arscott*[5] and *Parkin v Norman*[6] which suggested 'that in certain circumstances intimidatory conduct may not be caught by section 5 if the victim (for example, a policeman, or an elderly lady) is someone who is not likely to be provoked into violence by the defendant's behaviour. This is clearly a loophole which needs to be closed. . . .'[7] The requirement of immediacy was found in the Law Commission's proposals, rejected in the *White Paper*[8] but restored to the Bill.[9] This is a requirement of the offence of assault contrary to s. 39 of the Criminal Justice Act 1988.

2. The phrase 'threatening, abusive or insulting' is common to both the old s. 5 and the new s. 4. Authorities on this aspect of the old s. 5 accordingly appear still to be relevant. See *Brutus v Cozens*[10] and *Parkin v Norman*.[11] The phrase 'uses towards another person' did not appear in the old s. 5, and has the effect of narrowing s. 4 by comparison.[12]

3. The old s. 5 was the key public order offence, and was used in preference to the more serious charges of riot, unlawful assembly and affray.

4. The exception in s. 4(2) was also applied in *R v Va Kun Hau*,[13] where the defendant became excited and aggressive when visited at home by a bailiff, accompanied by a police officer, in connection with an unpaid parking fine. He wielded and then put down, in succession, a kitchen cleaver and a kitchen knife. His conviction by the jury under s. 4 (as an alternative to the offence charged, affray, under s. 3) had to be

20 Above, p. 473.
 1 *White Paper*, p. 14.
 2 [1964] 2 QB 580.
 3 (1978) 67 Cr App Rep 228.
 4 [2001] EWCA Crim 838.
 5 (1982) 75 Cr App Rep 211.
 6 [1983] QB 92.
 7 *White Paper*, p. 14.
 8 p. 15.
 9 See *R v Horseferry Road Metropolitan Stipendiary Magistrates, ex p Siadatan*, above.
10 Below, p. 494.
11 Below, p. 496.
12 See *Smith*, pp. 98–99 and *Atkin v DPP*, above.
13 [1990] Crim LR 518, CA (Cr D).

quashed as the events took place inside a dwelling house. [14] The communal landing outside the front door of a flat in a block of flats is not part of a 'dwelling' for the purposes of s. 4(2). [15]

5. The s. 4 offence may be committed in four different ways (see the wording of s. 4(1)). In *Winn v DPP*, [16] W was convicted by justices on evidence that he threatened and abused a process server attempting to serve a county court summons, causing him to feel that W was 'going to get him'. However, the charge alleged that it was likely that unlawful violence would be provoked. W's conviction was quashed as the variation between the facts found and the particulars alleged was so substantial that the information should have been amended.

On the question of what constitutes immediacy for the purposes of s. 4, in *DPP v Ramos*[1] the defendant had written letters containing threats of violence to an Asian support group shortly after the Brixton nail bomb attack in 1999. The question arose as to whether the letters gave rise to a fear of immediate violence. The Divisional Court held that the magistrates were entitled to infer that from the facts. The court referred to the width of the definition of assault following the House of Lords ruling in *R v Ireland*,[2] and that the 1986 Act deals with 'the state of mind of the victim which is crucial rather than the statistical risk of violence actually occurring within a very short space of time'. [3] A similarly broad interpretation was taken in *Valentine v DPP*,[4] where V had said to a neighbouring family 'next time you go [to work] we're going to burn your house. You are all going to fucking die'. The Court held that the magistrates were entitled to infer that these words gave rise to a fear of immediate violence.

The section is not limited to rowdy or abusive behaviour. In *R v Taft*[5] the defendant was prosecuted having driven erratically alongside lone women drivers on country roads while masturbating or pretending to. It has also been used in respect of air rage disturbances caused by passengers. [6] Disturbances on airlines have also been charged under the Public Order Act 1986, s. 5. [7]

In *Vigon v DPP*[8] surreptitious viewing of customers changing into swimwear in a market stall cubicle was capable of being insulting behaviour for the purposes of the Act. It is sufficient that the defendant is aware that his conduct may be insulting, so there is no need to prove that he intended to insult the customer – it is no defence that he concealed the camera. See also the conviction under the common law offence of outraging public decency, where the defendant secretly filmed women urinating in a supermarket toilet. Disgusting conduct was held to be that which fills an onlooker with loathing or extreme distaste or causes the onlooker extreme annoyance.[9] The Home Office, in its recent Consultation Document, *Setting the Boundaries: Reforming the Law on Sexual Offences*[10] recommends a new offence of voyeurism, where a person in the interior of a building or structure has a reasonable expectation of privacy and is observed without their knowledge or consent, whether by remote or mechanised

---

14 See also *R v Barber* [2001] EWCA Crim 838.
15 *Rukwira v DPP* (1993) 158 JP 65, DC.
16 (1992) 156 JP 881.
 1 [2000] Crim LR 768.
 2 [1997] AC 148.
 3 Per Kennedy LJ.
 4 [1997] COD 339, DC.
 5 [1997] 2 Crim App Rep (S) 182, CA (Cr D).
 6 See *R v Harlow Magistrates' Court, ex p O'Farrell* (2000) 28 March.
 7 *R v Fisher* (1999) 4 November, unreported, CA (Cr D).
 8 [1998] Crim LR 289, DC.
 9 *R v Choi* [1999] 8 Arch News 3.
10 (2000).

means or not. There will be an exception for authorised surveillance. [11] Note also the recommendations for new sex offences in public, including exposing the penis where D knew or ought to have known that he might cause fear, alarm or distress by so doing. [12]

DPP v Orum [1988] 3 All ER 449, [1989] 1 WLR 88, Queen's Bench Divisional Court

O was charged with (1) an offence under s. 5(1)(a) of the Public Order Act 1986; and (2) assaulting a police officer in the execution of his duty, contrary to s. 51(1) of the Police Act 1964. The magistrates dismissed the charges, and the DPP appealed by case stated to the Divisional Court.

Glidewell LJ: ... The magistrates heard the two charges together and found the following facts. At 1.15 am on 9 November 1987 the respondent was standing by a garden wall in a road in Victoria Park, Bristol in the company of his girlfriend. The road has terraced houses on both sides of it. The respondent and his girlfriend were eight to ten feet away from the nearest house. They were engaged in an argument and the respondent was using abusive language. He had consumed a quantity of alcohol during the course of the evening. PCs Hickman and Crossan arrived at the scene. PC Hickman approached the respondent and said: 'Quiet, you are disturbing the neighbours.' The respondent replied: 'You fuck off. This is a domestic and you can't do nothing.' PC Hickman said: 'Quiet, you are causing a breach of the peace. Quiet down, go home and sleep it off.' The respondent replied:' You can't fucking arrest me. I know my rights. If you don't go away I am going to hit you.' PC Hickman then arrested the respondent for causing a breach of the peace and cautioned him.

The only persons present in the street were the respondent, his girlfriend and the two police constables. The respondent was placed in the rear of a police vehicle. As PC Crossan entered the vehicle, the respondent kicked him in the stomach and hit him on the head and body. The respondent was finally subdued and handcuffed....

[The magistrates dismissed both charges.]

The main question which we have to answer is: can a police officer be a person who is likely to be caused harassment, alarm or distress by the threatening, abusive or insulting words or behaviour? It is apparent, as counsel who appears for the respondent sensibly concedes, that in the first part of the passage in which they set out their opinion, the magistrates firstly had taken the view that they can discount any question of harassment, alarm or distress to people living in and presumably mostly asleep in the nearby dwelling houses, because there is no evidence that any such person was likely to be caused harassment etc. Secondly, they appear to have totally discounted the effect of the respondent's conduct on his girlfriend. What they concerned themselves with, and what we are asked to concern ourselves with, is the impact of that conduct on either or both of the two police constables.

The magistrates seem to have been advised by their clerk that they could not properly, presumably as a matter of law, conclude that either of the constables was likely to be caused harassment, alarm or distress by the words or behaviour of the respondent. Counsel for the respondent argues that that is a proper conclusion provided that s. 5 of the 1986 Act is to be interpreted on the same lines as its predecessor, namely s. 5 of the Public Order Act 1936. I say 'on the same lines': what I mean is that it is conduct likely to involve a breach of the peace.

In the decision of this court in *Marsh v Arscott* (1982) 75 Cr App Rep 211 the defendant was charged under s. 5 of the Public Order Act 1936....

The defendant was slumped over the bonnet of a car late on a Saturday night in the car park of a shop. The police officers who found him asked the defendant questions and received only abusive replies. The question was whether the defendant's language and behaviour was such that a breach of the peace was likely to be occasioned notwithstanding that the only witnesses to the behaviour were the police officers. McCullough J, giving the first judgment, said (at 216):

'In the circumstances here, assuming the defendant to have been acting unlawfully in using threatening words and behaviour, no breach of the peace was likely to have been occasioned.

11 Recommendation No. 55.
12 Para. 8.2.9.

No other person was likely to have broken the peace, and all that the police were likely to do was arrest him, as they did. On that basis too an acquittal would, in my judgment, have been inevitable.'

If I may say so, respectfully, that is common sense as well as good law. However, with respect to counsel for the respondent, his argument is not. In my view, the very different wording of s. 5 of the 1986 Act, which makes no reference at all in sub-s (1) to a breach of the peace, does not allow the importation of the concept or that phrase in its interpretation.

I find nothing in the context of the 1986 Act to persuade me that a police officer may not be a person who is caused harassment, alarm or distress by the various kinds of words and conduct to which s. 5(1) applies. I would therefore answer the question in the affirmative, that a police officer can be a person who is likely to be caused harassment and so on. However, that is not to say that the opposite is necessarily the case, namely it is not to say that every police officer in this situation is to be assumed to be a person who is caused harassment. Very frequently, words and behaviour with which police officers will be wearily familiar will have little emotional impact on them save that of boredom. It may well be that, in appropriate circumstances, magistrates will decide (indeed, they might decide in the present case) as a question of fact that the words and behaviour were not likely to cause harassment, alarm or distress to either of the police officers. That is a question for the magistrates to decide having regard to all the circumstances: the time, the place, the nature of the words used, who the police officers are and so on.

It seems to me that the magistrates were advised by their clerk that they could not find that police officers could be caused harassment and so on by such words and behaviour as a matter of law. It may be that the clerk was thinking of *Marsh v Arscott* and he had in his mind the argument which counsel for the respondent advanced to us. If he did, I have already indicated that I think he was wrong so to do.

Counsel for the prosecution poses for our consideration a second question: if in fact a police officer is not likely to be caused harassment etc does he then have any power to arrest under s. 5(4)? Theoretically, the answer to that question may be Yes, but in practice, in my view, it must almost invariably be No. The reason is this. If an officer is not caused harassment alarm or distress, it is difficult to see how he can reasonably suspect, if he is the only person present, that an offence against s. 5(1) has been committed since such causation is a necessary element in the offence. If he does not reasonably suspect that such an offence has been committed, then he has no power of arrest under s. 5(4).

[His Lordship then held that the constable had lawfully arrested O for causing a breach of the peace as his conduct fell within the definition of a 'breach of the peace' set out in *R v Howell*.[13] The case was remitted to the magistrates with a direction to convict on the charge of assaulting a police officer; the acquittal on the s. 5 charge was set aside, but it was not thought necessary to send the matter back to the magistrates to determine on the facts whether the officers had been caused harassment etc.]

McCullough J: I agree both with the proposed orders and with the judgment of Glidewell LJ and would only add a few words since I was party to the decision in *Marsh v Arscott* (1982) 75 Cr App Rep 211. In enacting s. 5 of the Public Order Act 1986 in place of s. 5 of the Public Order Act 1936, Parliament advisedly deleted the requirement that a breach of the peace was either intended by the defendant or was likely to result from his conduct. In its place was put the requirement that someone within sight or sound of the defendant at the material time would be likely to be caused harassment, alarm or distress by his conduct. Thus, what matters now is not the likely physical reaction to the conduct complained of, but the likely mental reaction to it. It is improbable in the extreme that any police officer would ever be provoked by threatening, abusive or insulting words or behaviour to cause a breach of the peace, but it is by no means impossible that such an officer may not feel harassed, alarmed or distressed as a result of such words or behaviour. This distinguishes the present case from *Marsh v Arscott*.

Appeal allowed.

---

13 Above, p. 462.

NOTES

1. Section 5 of the Public Order Act 1986 was a controversial extension of the law, designed to deal with 'minor acts of hooliganism'. [14] Instances of such behaviour might include:

> 'hooligans on housing estates causing disturbances in the common parts of blocks of flat, blockading entrances, throwing things down the stairs, banging on doors, peering in at windows, and knocking over dustbins; groups of youths persistently shouting abuse and obscenities or pestering people waiting to catch public transport or to enter a hall or cinema; someone turning out the lights in a crowded dance hall, in a way likely to cause panic; rowdy behaviour in the streets, late at night which alarms local residents.' [15]

This control was:

> 'particularly needed when the behaviour is directed at the elderly and others who may feel especially vulnerable, including members of ethnic minority communities.' [16]

Thus, the new s. 5 extends to cover 'disorderly' behaviour as well as threatening, abusive or insulting words or behaviour, provided it is within the hearing or sight of a person likely to be caused harassment, alarm or distress thereby. The *White Paper* had suggested that the behaviour must *actually* cause someone to feel harassed etc., and described this as a safeguard lest the criminal law be extended widely to cover conduct not deserving of criminal sanctions; [17] the Act's provisions on this point are weaker, and avoid any need to call the victim as a witness. Victims may well be reluctant to testify in the kinds of case for which s. 5 was purportedly designed. Unlike s. 4, the words or behaviour need not be shown to be 'used towards' a particular person, but note that there is no strict requirement that the victim is called to testify in a prosecution under s. 4. [18]

'Disorderly' is presumably to be treated as an ordinary English word for the purpose of the approach in *Brutus v Cozens*. [19] Decisions on differently worded 'disorderly behaviour' offences in other jurisdictions are not likely to be appropriate authorities: see P. Sefton, [20] on what he regards as doubtful references to New Zealand authorities in connection with the disorderly behaviour offence found in the Public Order (Northern Ireland) Order 1987. [1] For example, the Northern Ireland disorderly behaviour offence can be committed by words alone: see *Chief Inspector Clinton v Watts*. [2] Can that be the case under s. 5 in view of its express wording? In *Chambers and Edwards v DPP* [3] 'disorderly' was held to be a question of fact for the trial court to determine (defendants standing peacefully to block surveyor's theodolite beam convicted despite absence of threat or fear of violence). It has been held that the ss. 5 and 4A offence can be committed where there is a general confrontation between the police and protesters and the fact that the victim perceives the behaviour through CCTV at the scene does not prevent a conviction. [4]

---

14 *White Paper*, p. 18.
15 Ibid.
16 Ibid.
17 p. 19.
18 *Swanston v DPP* (1996) 161 JP 203, DC.
19 Below, p. 494.
20 (1988) 39 NILQ 292.
 1 S.I. 1987 No. 463.
 2 [1992] NI 208.
 3 [1995] Crim LR 896.
 4 *Rogers v DPP* (1999) 22 July, DC.

2. In the House of Lords debate, Lord Denning welcomed the new offence, saying that it was 'high time that our law did something to put down disorderly behaviour'. He gave as examples of cases that would be covered: the conduct of the defendant in *Brutus v Cozens*;[5] disorderly pickets; hippies invading a person's land against the owner's will; and students who do all they can to stop freedom of speech in the universities. Lord Scarman opposed the introduction of the offence:

> 'A very good reason for that submission I find in the entertaining and fascinating account of cases that the noble and learned Lord, Lord Denning has just given to the Committee. The Committee will have noted the extraordinary range of activities which are covered by those cases and, which it is said that this clause would cover.'[6]

3. In practice, there were many examples of cases where magistrates had convicted defendants under the old s. 5 without sufficient regard to the requirements (1) that the defendant's conduct had been more than merely 'offensive' or 'annoying' and (2) that there had been some threat to the peace. See D. G. T. Williams[7] and A. Dickey.[8] In the more recent cases, the Divisional Court has taken steps to reassert these requirements, particularly the latter.[9]

There are indications that the fears expressed at the time of its enactment concerning the breadth of the new s. 5 have been borne out. According to Peter Thornton, a former NCCL chair:

> 'In fact it had been used quite indiscriminately, for example against juveniles for throwing fake snowballs, against a man who had a birthday party for his son in his back garden (he was charged even though he agreed to turn the music down), against two 19 year old males for kissing in the street, against a nudist on a beach and against another nudist in his own house, and, most sinisterly, in the so-called Madame M case (successfully taken up by NCCL) against four students who were in the process of putting up a satirical poster during the last general election. It depicted the Prime Minister as a sadistic dominatrix.'[10]

It is not clear how many of these cases ended in convictions. The *Madame M* case did not, the police officers who saw the poster testified to no more than an attack of mirth (rather than harassment, alarm or distress).[11]

Prosecutions have been launched under s. 5 against anti-abortion protesters picketing abortion clinics, and variously displaying plastic models of human foetuses, photographs of dead foetuses and placards, and shouting slogans such as 'you are evil God will punish you' and 'do you know they are going to kill your baby?', and approaching women attending the clinics. The outcomes have been mixed. In *DPP v Clarke*[12] the Divisional Court upheld the acquittal of protesters (in a peaceful and orderly group) in respect of the display to a police officer of pictures of aborted foetuses. The justices accepted the officer's evidence that he 'found the pictures insulting to him as a father and felt abused by them and found them distressing'. Applying an objective test, they found that the defendants' conduct was not 'reasonable' within s. 5(3)(c). However, they also held, applying a subjective test, that the defendants did not intend the displays to be threatening, abusive or insulting, nor were they aware that they might be so. The Divisional Court endorsed the approach of the justices on all three points. Nolan LJ confessed 'to a feeling of

---

5 Below, p. 494.
6 478 HL Deb, 16 July 1986, cols. 935–938.
7 [1967] Crim LR 385.
8 [1971] Crim LR 265.
9 See *Marsh v Arscott* (1982) 75 Cr App Rep 211 (above, p. 488).
10 *Decade of Decline: Civil Liberties in the Thatcher Years* (Liberty, 1990), p. 37.
11 (1988) 17(8) *Index on Censorship*, pp. 12, 13. See C. Douzinas, *et al.*, 'The shrinking scope of public protest'.
12 (1991) 94 Cr App Rep 359.

some surprise' that the police officer and the justices found the pictures abusive and insulting, but stated that the question was essentially one for the justices. [13] (Presumably the more 'surprising' the view that conduct is threatening, abusive or insulting, the less likely it is that D will have the requisite intention; however, future protesters would have to take note.)[14] See also *DPP v Fidler* [15] (membership of a group of anti-abortion protesters sufficient to establish a prima facie case under s. 5; offence under s. 7 of the Conspiracy and Protection of Property Act 1875 [16] not made out where evidence shows only 'persuasion' and not 'compulsion'); *Morrow, Geach and Thomas v DPP* [17] (anti-abortion protesters' conduct in shouting slogans, waving banners and preventing staff and patients from entering a clinic found to be disorderly and to have caused distress; no defence established under s. 5(3)(c) or s. 3 of the Criminal Law Act 1967); [18] *Morrow v DPP* [19] (convictions under s. 5 upheld in respect of the invasion of a clinic by protesters). In *Lewis v DPP* [20] the protestors outside an abortion clinic displayed placards including one of an aborted 21-week foetus in pools of blood. The Divisional Court held that this could constitute abusive and insulting behaviour:

> 'the point taken is that the photograph on the placard was an accurate representation of the result of an abortion, and that what is truthful cannot be abusive or insulting. . . . A Patient . . . (or . . . someone visiting . . . the clinic) may be abused or insulted in having the activities (lawful activities in this case) depicted in the way that they were on the placard.'[1]

What are the implications of this for anti-vivisectionist campaigners? If these individuals are expressing true fact rather than an opinion, should the law not allow them to do so in public? Would s. 5 withstand challenge on this basis under the ECHR Art. 10?

Could the offence under s. 5 be committed by wearing clothing or emblems that were, in context, likely to cause offence?

A survey of 470 public order cases from the 1988 records at five police stations in two force areas showed that 56% of the sample led to charges under s. 5 and 24% under s. 4. [2] The authors note that during the period 1986–88 the number of prosecutions for public order offences doubled. Generally, the officers they interviewed did not feel that there had been a rise in public disorder, and suggested that the rise in the number of prosecutions was due more to the nature of the new legislation. The research supported the view 'that low-level nuisances of widely varying kinds have increasingly been brought within the ambit of the law'. Certain offences that would not formerly have led to formal action were now subject to arrest and charge; s. 5 could be used where the evidence might not support more serious charges (e.g. where a person was sexually harassed in a public place but it had been difficult for the police to secure sufficient evidence to support a charge of indecent assault); under s. 5 police officers could now be regarded as people who might be harassed, alarmed or distressed (this was seen by the police as being 'crucially important'); [3] s. 5 was regarded as constituting a helpful advance in relation to 'domestic' cases given that it extended to private premises (subject to the domestic

---

13 *Brutus v Cozens*, below, p. 494.
14 See Nolan LJ at 366.
15 (1991) 94 Cr App Rep 286.
16 Now s. 241 of the Trade Union and Labour Relations (Consolidation) Act 1992, see below, p. 537.
17 [1994] Crim LR 58.
18 Above.
19 [1993] Crim LR 58.
20 (1995) unreported, DC.
 1 Per Pill LJ.
 2 T. Newburn et al., 'Policing the Streets' (1990) 29 HORB 10 and 'Increasing Public Order' (1991) 7 Policing 22.
 3 p. 14.

dwelling exception); it was suggested that s. 5 siphoned off cases that would formerly have been dealt with by arrest for common law breach of the peace. See also D. Brown and T. Ellis,[4] noting variations in the use of s. 5 in different police areas and some evidence that Afro-Caribbeans were over-represented among those arrested and proceeded against.

4. In *Lodge v DPP*[5] the Divisional Court held that the person caused 'alarm' for the purposes of s. 5 need not be concerned at physical danger to himself; it can be alarm about the safety of an unconnected third party. A policeman saw L walking into the middle of the road, shouting, kicking and gesticulating. A car approached and the police officer was seriously concerned that an accident might happen. L appeared to be at risk and a danger to traffic and he was arrested. The Divisional Court upheld L's conviction under s. 5, holding that there was ample evidence on which the justices could have concluded that alarm was likely to have been caused so far as both the policeman and the driver were concerned. Jaywalkers beware! On the power of arrest under s. 5(4), see *Groom v DPP*.[6] The amendment made by the Public Order (Amendment) Act 1996, s. 1 reverses the decision of the Court in *DPP v Hancock*.[7] Any officer can now exercise the power of arrest. K. Reid[8] discussing the Act, laments the ease with which such an extension to the law was added by Parliament, and doubts whether a power of arrest is warranted for such a trivial offence. It is not possible to prove whether *Hancock* was a major obstacle to the effective use of s. 5.

5. The exception enshrined in s. 5(2) was considered by the Divisional Court in *Chappell v DPP*,[9] in holding that the deposit of a letter containing threatening, abusive or insulting words through the letter box of a house, with its recipient reading it and being alarmed or distressed by it, could not constitute an offence under s. 5(1)(a) in view of the exception.[10] Other points made in *Chappell* were (1) that the justices had been right to hold that the deposit of the letter had been a 'display in writing' within the meaning of s. 5(1)(b); and (2) that a person writing and/or delivering a letter to another, who opens it in the absence of the sender, cannot be said to be a person who 'uses ... words or behaviour ... within the hearing or sight of a person ...' who receives it. The court noted that the conduct would now fall within the provisions of the Malicious Communications Act 1988.

6. On the defence that D's conduct was reasonable, see *DPP v Clarke* and *Morrow, Geach and Thomas v DPP*.[11] The reasonableness of the defendant's conduct under s. 5(3) must be judged objectively: *DPP v Clarke*.[12] See also *Poku v DPP*,[13] where the Divisional Court held that it was open to D to argue in defence to a s. 5 charge arising out of his resistance to the seizure of his ice cream van by police ('You're not taking my fucking van' etc.) that the seizure (for unlicensed street trading) was in fact unlawful and his response therefore reasonable.

---

4 *Policing low-level disorder* (HORS No. 135, 1994) and see D. Brown and T. Ellis, *Policing low-level disorder: Police use of the Public Order Act 1986* (1996) (HORS, 38 (1996)).
5 (1988) Times, 26 October.
6 (1991) 155 JPN 403, DC.
7 [1995] Crim LR 139, DC.
8 [1998] Crim LR 864.
9 (1988) 89 Cr App Rep 82.
10 Cf. *Atkin v DPP* (above, p. 481) under s. 4.
11 Above, n. **3**.
12 (1992) 94 Cr App R 359, DC.
13 [1993] Crim LR 705.

Brutus v Cozens [1973] AC 854, [1972] 2 All ER 1297, [1972] 2 WLR 521, 56 Cr App Rep 799, House of Lords

Members of the public were admitted to watch the annual open tennis tournament at Wimbledon from stands around the courts. They were not allowed access to the courts. During a tennis match involving Drysdale, a South African, B stepped on to No. 2 Court blowing a whistle. He threw around leaflets, attempted to give one to a player and sat down on the court. Upon the blowing of the whistle other persons, some bearing banners or placards on which slogans were written, came on to the court and more leaflets were distributed. Play was stopped. The appellant was charged with using insulting behaviour whereby a breach of the peace was likely to be occasioned contrary to s. 5 of the Public Order Act 1936. The justices held that his behaviour had not been insulting, and dismissed the information without calling on him to give evidence.

On appeal by the respondent prosecutor, the Divisional Court held that 'insulting ... behaviour' in section 5 of the 1936 Act was behaviour which affronted other people and evidenced a disrespect or contempt for their rights, and which reasonable persons would foresee as likely to cause resentment or protest; that on the findings of the justices, which were to be regarded as provisional, insulting behaviour by the appellant had been established and the case would be sent back to them to continue the hearing. B appealed to the House of Lords.

Lord Reid: ... It appears that the object of this demonstration was to protest against the apartheid policy of the Government of South Africa. But it is not said that that government was insulted. The insult is said to have been offered to or directed at the spectators.

The spectators at No. 2 Court were upset: they made loud shouts, gesticulated and shook their fists and while the appellant was being removed some showed hostility and attempted to strike him....

It is not clear to me what precisely is the point of law which we have to decide. The question in the case stated for the opinion of the court is, 'Whether, on the above statement of facts, we came to a correct determination and decision in point of law.' This seems to assume that the meaning of the word 'insulting' in section 5 is a matter of law. And the Divisional Court appear to have proceeded on that footing.

In my judgment that is not right. The meaning of an ordinary word of the English language is not a question of law. The proper construction of a statute is a question of law. If the context shows that a word is used in an unusual sense the court will determine in other words what that unusual sense is. But here there is in my opinion no question of the word 'insulting' being used in any unusual sense. It appears to me, for reasons which I shall give later, to be intended to have its ordinary meaning. It is for the tribunal which decides the case to consider, not as law but as fact, whether in the whole circumstances the words of the statute do or do not as a matter of ordinary usage of the English language cover or apply to the facts which have been proved. If it is alleged that the tribunal has reached a wrong decision then there can be a question of law but only of a limited character. The question would normally be whether their decision was unreasonable in the sense that no tribunal acquainted with the ordinary use of language could reasonably reach that decision.

Were it otherwise we should reach an impossible position. When considering the meaning of a word one often goes to a dictionary. There one finds other words set out. And if one wants to pursue the matter and find the meaning of those other words the dictionary will give the meaning of those other words in still further words which often include the word for whose meaning one is searching.

No doubt the court could act as a dictionary. It could direct the tribunal to take some word or phrase other than the word in the statute and consider whether that word or phrase applied to or covered the facts proved. But we have been warned time and again not to substitute other words for the words of a statute. And there is very good reason for that. Few words have exact synonyms. The overtones are almost always different.

Or the court could frame a definition. But then again the tribunal would be left with words to consider. No doubt a statute may contain a definition—which incidentally often creates more problems than it solves—but the purpose of a definition is to limit or modify the ordinary meaning of a word and the court is not entitled to do that.

So the question of law in this case must be whether it was unreasonable to hold that the appellant's behaviour was not insulting. To that question there could in my view be only one answer—No.

But as the Divisional Court [1972] 1 WLR 484, have expressed their view as to the meaning of 'insulting' I must, I think, consider it. It was said at 487:

'The language of section 5, as amended, of the Public Order Act 1936, omitting words which do not matter for our present purpose, is: "Any person who in any public place ... uses ... insulting ... behaviour, ... with intent to provoke a breach of the peace or whereby a breach of the peace is likely to be occasioned, shall be guilty of an offence." It therefore becomes necessary to consider the meaning of the word "insulting" in its context in that section. In my view it is not necessary, and is probably undesirable, to try to frame an exhaustive definition which will cover every possible set of facts that may arise for consideration under this section. It is, as I think, quite sufficient for the purpose of this case to say that behaviour which affronts other people, and evidences a disrespect or contempt for their rights, behaviour which reasonable persons would foresee is likely to cause resentment or protest such as was aroused in this case, and I rely particularly on the reaction of the crowd as set out in the case stated, is insulting for the purpose of this section.'

I cannot agree with that. Parliament had to solve the difficult question of how far freedom of speech or behaviour must be limited in the general public interest. It would have been going much too far to prohibit all speech or conduct likely to occasion a breach of the peace because determined opponents may not shrink from organising or at least threatening a breach of the peace in order to silence a speaker whose views they detest. Therefore vigorous and it may be distasteful or unmannerly speech or behaviour is permitted so long as it does not go beyond any one of three limits. It must not be threatening. It must not be abusive. It must not be insulting. I see no reason why any of these should be construed as having a specially wide or a specially narrow meaning. They are all limits easily recognisable by the ordinary man. Free speech is not impaired by ruling them out. But before a man can be convicted it must be clearly shown that one or more of them has been disregarded.

We were referred to a number of dictionary meanings of 'insult' such as treating with insolence or contempt or indignity or derision or dishonour or offensive disrespect. Many things otherwise unobjectionable may be said or done in an insulting way. There can be no definition. But an ordinary sensible man knows an insult when he sees or hears it.

Taking the passage which I have quoted, 'affront' is much too vague a word to be helpful; there can often be disrespect without insult, and I do not think that contempt for a person's rights as distinct from contempt of the person himself would generally be held to be insulting. Moreover, there are many grounds other than insult for feeling resentment or protesting. I do not agree that there can be conduct which is not insulting in the ordinary sense of the word but which is 'insulting for the purpose of this section'. If the view of the Divisional Court was that in this section the word 'insulting' has some special or unusually wide meaning, then I do not agree. Parliament has given no indication that the word is to be given any unusual meaning. Insulting means insulting and nothing else.

If I had to decide, which I do not, whether the appellant's conduct insulted the spectators in this case, I would agree with the magistrates. The spectators may have been very angry and justly so. The appellant's conduct was deplorable. Probably it ought to be punishable. But I cannot see how it insulted the spectators.

I would allow the appeal with costs.

Lords Morris of Borrth-y-Gest and **Kilbrandon** and **Viscount Dilhorne** delivered concurring speeches. **Lord Diplock** agreed.

Appeal allowed.

Parkin v Norman; Valentine v Lilley [1983] QB 92, [1982] 2 All ER 583, Divisional Court

In separate incidents, each of the defendants, P and V, was found masturbating in a public lavatory in a manner which clearly indicated that he wanted his behaviour to be seen only by the one other person present there at the time. Unknown to the defendants, the other person present in each case was a police officer in plain clothes. Both defendants were convicted of using threatening, abusive or insulting words or behaviour whereby a breach of the peace was likely to be occasioned contrary to s. 5 of the Public Order Act 1936. P's appeal to the Crown Court was dismissed. Both appealed by case stated to the Divisional Court. Counsel for P submitted (1) that there was no insulting behaviour: the officer was not insulted, P had desisted while a third person was present and there was no reason to suppose that he would not have desisted had anyone else entered; (2) that 'an insult requires an intention to insult'; and (3) that no breach of the peace was likely to be occasioned.

McCullough J read the judgment of the court (**Donaldson LJ** and **McCullough J**): ...
In our judgment, threats, abuse and insults are within the section whether or not they were intended to be threats, abuse or insults. 'Threatening, abusive or insulting words or behaviour' are simply words or behaviour that are threatening, abusive or insulting in character.... If the conduct in question is of this character it does not, in our judgment, matter whether anyone feels himself to have been threatened, abused or insulted. Insulting behaviour does not lose its insulting character simply because no one who witnessed it was insulted, any more than it would lose its liability to provoke a breach of the peace merely because no one who witnessed it broke the peace. In *Ballard v Blythe* (3 November 1980, unreported) the appellant insulted, abused, threatened and spat at a man who, unknown to him, was a headmaster, and who reacted with an unusual degree of self-restraint. In dismissing his appeal, Donaldson LJ said:

> 'the court has to find the circumstances in which the conduct takes place and to consider the question posed by the statute: is this conduct such as is inherently likely to occasion a breach of the peace? ... the general test is "What is the natural and probable result of the conduct?"'

Where the defendant is addressing an audience which he knows has special susceptibilities, a breach of the peace may be the natural and probable result of behaviour which would not provoke an audience not having this susceptibility in such a way....

The Act does not make it criminal to use offensive or disgusting behaviour whereby a breach of the peace is likely to be occasioned. It requires in the circumstances material to this case, 'insulting behaviour'. What then is an insult? We do not propose to attempt any sort of definition, particularly after the speeches in *Brutus v Cozens* [1973] AC854, but some consideration of its characteristics are necessary in the light of counsel's submissions that behaviour of the type here is not insulting.

One cannot insult nothing. The word presupposes a subject and an object and, in this day and age, a human object. An insult is perceived by someone who feels insulted. It is given by someone who is directing his words or his behaviour to another person or persons. When A is insulting B, and is clearly directing his words and behaviour to B alone, if C hears and sees is he insulted? He may be disgusted, offended, annoyed, angered and no doubt a number of other things as well; and he may be provoked by what he sees and hears into breaking the peace. But will he be insulted?

One must take care not to become too analytical or too refined about these things, and we are not beginning to attempt either to define or to lay down any sort of principle, but these considerations may help to clear the mind before one asks oneself whether homosexual behaviour of the type in question here is really properly described as 'insulting.'

At one stage, a third person did come in, but he, so far as we know, saw nothing. So he was not insulted, nor was he likely to have been. Had further people come in the position would no doubt have been the same. If, by chance, anyone had surprised the defendant and seen what was happening, we think it would be difficult to say that he would have been insulted.

The defendant's conduct was aimed at one person and only one person. He obviously hoped, and after a little while would presumably have believed, that the person to whom it was directed was another homosexual. Whatever he was trying to do, he was not trying to insult him. Whatever another homosexual would have felt, he would not, presumably, have felt insulted. In fact, the second person was a police officer. Was he insulted? He had gone there in plain clothes to catch anyone whom he saw doing this sort of thing, and he caught one. It seems to us quite unrealistic to say that he would have felt insulted. Suppose, as was possible, that the person to whom the behaviour was directed had been a heterosexual using the lavatory for its proper purpose. He would almost certainly have felt disgusted and perhaps angry, but would he have felt insulted? The argument that he would, is that the behaviour was tantamount to a statement: 'I believe you are another homosexual,' which the average heterosexual would surely regard as insulting. We regard this as the only basis upon which the behaviour could fairly be characterised as 'insulting'. However, that did not happen in this case. The only person importuned, for that is what it comes to, was the police officer, but the person importuned might very well have been an ordinary heterosexual using the lavatory for its proper purpose. On this basis we think that the behaviour can fairly be regarded as potentially insulting, and we would regard this as sufficient to give it the description 'insulting behaviour'.

For this reason, and this reason alone, we are not prepared to say that the court was in error in making a finding that there had been 'insulting behaviour'. And as has already been indicated, we do not think the court was prevented from making this finding by the fact that the defendant did not intend to insult, nor by the fact that no one was insulted, nor by his having taken steps to ensure that no third person saw what he was doing. This is not to hold that such a finding was inevitable. It was for the court to decide on the whole of the evidence. We could only interfere if it had been demonstrated that the finding must have been wrong.

But was a breach of the peace likely to result? Neither the defendant nor the police officer was likely to break the peace. No third party was likely to have seen. One came in and the defendant desisted. Had others come in, he would no doubt have done the same. It is true that someone might have caught him unawares and there must have been a possibility that such a person might have gone so far as to cause a breach of the peace, i.e., to use or threaten violence, but we think counsel for the defendant is right in saying that on the evidence, as we assume it to have been, no court could have been sure that this was likely. It our judgment the court can only have reached the conclusion that it did by treating 'likely' as if it had read 'liable', which it does not.

We therefore quash this conviction.

Appeal allowed.

NOTES

1. The appeal in *Valentine v Lilley* [14] was allowed on the ground that the justices had not applied the test for a 'breach of the peace' laid down in *R v Howell,* [15] in determining whether such a breach was 'likely' for the purpose of the old s. 5. Note that ss. 4 and 5 require D to intend his words etc. to be threatening, abusive or insulting etc. or to be aware that they may be. [16]

2. The decision of magistrates on a question of fact will only be reversed on appeal to the High Court if it is one which no reasonable bench of magistrates could reach or if it is totally unsupported by evidence (*Bracegirdle v Oxley*). [17] In most cases it is accepted that different magistrates may reasonably come to different conclusions, and the court will not interfere solely because the judges would personally have taken a different view.

---

14 [1983] QB 92, DC.
15 [1982] QB 416, CA (above, p. 462).
16 1986 Act, s. 6(3), (4).
17 [1947] KB 349, DC.

An example of a case where a conviction was upset is *Hudson v Chief Constable, Avon and Somerset Constabulary*. [18] H was on the terraces at a football match. He became excited, jumping up and down and clapping his hands above his head. He fell forward and knocked the persons in front, causing a surge in the crowd. He was convicted of using threatening behaviour whereby a breach of the peace was likely to be occasioned, but the Divisional Court held that the facts found contained nothing which constituted a threat. Conversely, in *Simcock v Rhodes* [19] the Divisional Court upheld a conviction under the old s. 5. A police sergeant instructed a disorderly group of about 15 young people who had emerged from a dance hall to be quiet and go home. The defendant shouted to him to 'fuck off'. The words were insulting and could have resulted in a breach of the peace. In *Maile v McDowell* [1] the Divisional Court held that an acquittal had been perverse. The defendant had been one of a crowd of 'away' supporters at a football match who had been jumping up and down, waving their fists and shouting aggressive slogans. The justices held that D's behaviour had 'not been threatening since the crowd habitually behaved in that manner, and in any event it had not been likely to occasion a breach of the peace because of a fence separating the rival groups of supporters'. The court allowed the prosecutor's appeal, holding that everybody had been guilty of threatening behaviour and that the 'presence of a Berlin-type wall to separate rival groups should not be necessary and the fact that such fencing stopped different groups from reaching each other could not of itself prevent a breach of the peace'. [2] More doubtful cases where the High Court has declined to interfere with the justices' decision are *DPP v Clarke*; [3] and *Herrington v DPP*. [4] In the latter case, H stood naked in his back garden, staring for some time in the direction of his neighbour's kitchen window, where he was observed by her while at her kitchen sink. This was found to be 'threatening' behaviour; although H could not have seen her at that distance as he was without his glasses, he must have been aware that his behaviour might be threatening. [5] In determining a defendant's awareness under s. 6(4), a subjective test should be applied: *DPP v Clarke*. [6]

3. In *Bryan v Robinson*, [7] a hostess at a non-alcoholic refreshment house in Dean Street London stood at the doorway, leaned out, smiled, beckoned and spoke to three men in the street. The men were annoyed and walked across the street. The Divisional Court allowed the hostess's appeal against conviction under the Metropolitan Police Act 1839, s. 54(13). [8] Per Lord Parker CJ: [9]

> 'I find it very difficult to see how a mere leaning out, smiling and beckoning without more could amount to such insulting behaviour of a character whereby a breach of the peace may be occasioned. It is true that three men were annoyed, but clearly somebody can be annoyed

---

18 [1976] Crim LR 451.
19 (1977) 66 Cr App Rep 192, [1977] Crim LR 751.
 1 [1980] Crim LR 586.
 2 Note the offences of chanting indecent or racist remarks in the Football (Offences and Disorder) Act 1999, s. 9 and the Football (Offences) Act 1991, s. 3.
 3 Above, p. 491: display of photograph of aborted foetus found to be 'insulting'.
 4 23 June 1992, unreported, DC.
 5 The CPS recently decided not to prosecute a doctor who had hidden a camera in a shampoo bottle in a nurses' shower cubicle. The CPS claimed to have no offence available. See news reports 29 January 2001.
 6 (1992) Cr App R 359.
 7 [1960] 1 WLR 508, DC.
 8   Above, p. 432.
 9 At 509.

by behaviour which is not insulting behaviour. The mere fact that they were annoyed really carries the matter no further. Even if it can be said that a reasonable person would be likely to treat the gestures as insulting, they were certainly not, in my judgment, of such a character whereby a breach of the peace may be occasioned.'

This approach is difficult to reconcile with a later decision under s. 54(13), *Masterson v Holden*. [10] The two defendants, both men, were standing by a bus stop in Oxford Street at about 2 a.m., kissing and cuddling and one fondling the other. They appeared to be unaware of others in the vicinity. They were seen by two young women, who stopped. One of them raised a hand to her mouth and both then ran to tell two young men whom they were with. The men then walked towards the defendants and one shouted 'You filthy sods. How dare you in front of our girls?' The defendants were then arrested by police officers. The justices convicted them of using 'insulting behaviour whereby a breach of the peace may be occasioned', ordered absolute discharges, and bound them over to keep the peace and be of good behaviour. The Divisional Court dismissed the defendants' appeal. Glidewell LJ rejected an argument that McCullough J's judgment in *Parkin v Norman* was:

'authority for the proposition that in the case of some sort of overt behaviour between two male persons that behaviour could only be said to be insulting if it amounts to a statement that they believe that the person who sees it is a homosexual.'

That was a correct appreciation of the situation where only two persons are present in a public lavatory and one displays some homosexual activity; it was not applicable to the conduct here: 'it was in the open street, one of the busiest streets in the United Kingdom, although it was 1.55 a.m.'. [11]

The other argument was that in order to be insulting, conduct must be directed at another person or persons; the defendants could not be said to be directing the insult at anybody given the findings that they appeared wholly unaware of other persons in the vicinity. The response of Glidewell LJ was as follows: [12]

'the magistrates were perfectly entitled to infer that the two appellants must have known that other people would be likely to be present and if they had glanced up for a moment they would have seen that four people were present. Their conduct, therefore, if in the ordinary sense it was capable of being insulting, would be likely to make some impact upon anybody who was nearby in the vicinity. In that sense, while not disagreeing with the way McCullough J. put it, in circumstances such as this it can properly be said that the conduct could be insulting, albeit it was not deliberately aimed at a particular person or persons if in fact it could be insulting to any member of the public who might be passing by. So one comes back to this. Was it conduct which within the ordinary meaning of the word could be said to be insulting? The magistrates have found as a question of fact that it was. In my judgment, they were entitled so to find. Overt homosexual conduct in a public street, indeed overt heterosexual conduct in a public street, may well be considered by many persons to be objectionable, to be conduct which ought to be confined to a private place. The fact it is objectionable does not constitute an offence. But the display of such objectionable conduct in a public street may well be regarded by another person, particularly by a young woman, as conduct which insults her by suggesting that she is somebody who would find such conduct in public acceptable herself. The magistrates do not say that that was the reason for their finding. We cannot say for certain that that was their reasoning. Certainly it may have been. I content myself with saying that in my view in the ordinary use of the word "insulting" on the material in this case they were perfectly entitled to conclude that the conduct was insulting.'

10 [1986] 3 All ER 39, DC.
11 p. 43.
12 p. 44.

Could this argument not be used to turn any objectionable conduct into 'insulting' conduct? Could it have been applied in *Bryan v Robinson*? Consider whether the defendants here would have been guilty under (1) s. 4 or (2) s. 5 of the 1986 Act. Could this interpretation withstand scrutiny under the Human Rights Act 1998? Is it realistic to claim that the overt displays of heterosexual behaviour would be prosecuted?

4. In *Jordan v Burgoyne* [13] J, a leader of the National Socialist movement, was addressing a rally in Trafalgar Square. A group of young people near the speakers' platform contained many Jews, supporters of CND and communists who intended to prevent the meeting. When J used the words:

> '... more and more people every day ... are opening their eyes and coming to say that Hitler was right. They are coming to say that our real enemies ... were not Hitler and the National Socialists of Germany but world Jewry and its associates in this country'

there was complete disorder, an outcry and a general surge forward by the crowd towards the speakers' platform. The police stopped the meeting. J was convicted of using insulting words whereby a breach of the peace was likely to be occasioned, contrary to s. 5 of the Public Order Act 1936. Quarter Sessions allowed his appeal holding that while his words were highly insulting they were not likely to lead ordinary reasonable persons to commit breaches of the peace. This decision was reversed by the Divisional Court.

Lord Parker LJ said: [14]

> 'I cannot myself, having read the speech, imagine any reasonable citizen, certainly one who was a Jew, not being provoked beyond endurance, and not only a Jew but a coloured man, and quite a number of people of this country who were told that they were merely tools of the Jews, and that they had fought in the war on the wrong side, and matters of that sort.
>
> But, be that as it may, in my judgment, there is no room here for any test as to whether any member of the audience is a reasonable man or an ordinary citizen....
>
> This is ... a Public Order Act, and if in fact it is apparent that a body of persons are present – and let me assume in the defendant's favour that they are a body of hooligans – yet if words are used which threaten, abuse or insult – all very strong words – then that person must take his audience as he finds them, and if those words to that audience or that part of the audience are likely to provoke a breach of the peace, then the speaker is guilty of an offence.'

Accordingly, on the assumption that the body of young persons near the platform was a body of hooligans ('I am not saying that they were') and assuming that they had come with the preconceived idea of preventing him from speaking, J committed the s. 5 offence when he addressed to them these words:

> 'As for the red rabble here present with us in Trafalgar Square it is not a very good afternoon at all. Some of them are looking far from wholesome, more than usual I mean. We shall of course excuse them if they have to resort to smelling salts or first aid. Meanwhile, let them howl these multi-racial warriors of the Left. It is a sound that comes natural to them, it saves them from the strain of thinking for themselves.'

These words were:

> 'intended to be and were deliberately insulting to that body of persons being restrained by the police ...'

His Lordship denied that there was any inroad into the doctrine of free speech:

> 'A man is entitled to express his own views as strongly as he likes, to criticise his opponents, to say disagreeable things about his opponents and about their policies, and to do anything of

13 [1963] 2 QB 744, DC.
14 At 748, 749.

that sort. But what he must not do is – and these are the words of the section – he must not threaten, he must not be abusive and he must not insult them, "insult" in the sense of "hit by words".' [15]

How would this case be decided under the new s. 4 (or s. 5)?

A. T. H. Smith argues [16] that, notwithstanding Lord Parker's statement, there is room for a 'reasonable man' test in determining whether words are 'insulting' in the first place. This question 'must be assessed objectively, by the standards of ordinary people'. He also suggests [17] that the change in language from 'occasioned' in the old s. 5 to 'provoked' in the new s. 4:

'might be an occasion for the rethinking of the doctrine enunciated by Lord Parker ... that the speaker must take his audience as he finds it.'

There was no doubt that Jordan intended to provoke part of his audience; however,

'a person may be the occasion of violence without necessarily provoking it.'

Lord Parker's dictum:

'has dire consequences for those who would seek to exercise freedom of speech in public. Effectively it confers on those who seek to disrupt a "heckler's veto".' [18]

5. On the facts of *Beatty v Gillbanks*, [19] would the Salvationists have committed any offence under Part I of the Public Order Act 1986?

Racially aggravated disorder

The Crime and Disorder Act 1998 creates new offences where a person commits a s. 4, 4A or 5 offence where the offence is 'racially aggravated'.[20] An offence is defined in s. 28 as being racially aggravated where:

'(1) (*a*) at the time of committing the offence, or immediately before or after doing so, the offender demonstrates towards the victim of the offence hostility based on the victim's membership (or presumed membership) of a racial group; or
(*b*) the offence is motivated (wholly or partly) by hostility towards members of a racial group.
(2) ... "membership", in relation to a racial group includes association with members of that group; 'presumed' means presumed by the offender.
(3) It is immaterial [for these purposes] whether or not the offender's hostility is also based to any extent on -
(*a*) the fact or presumption that any person or group of persons belonging to any religious group; or
(*b*) any other factors not mentioned in [subsection 1(*a*) or (*b*)]
(4) In this section "racial group" means a group of persons defined by reference to race, colour, nationality, including citizenship or ethnic or national origins.'

The racially aggravated offence carries a maximum sentence on summary conviction of six months' imprisonment or a fine not exceeding the statutory maximum or both, and on indictment to a maximum sentence of two years' imprisonment to both.[1] The *1996 British Crime Survey*[2] found that there were 143,000 crimes committed in which the victim felt that the offence was racially motivated.

---

15 See D. G. T. Williams, (1963) 26 MLR 425; A. Dickey, [1971] Crim LR 265, 272–275.
16 *Offences against Public Order* (1987), p. 14.
17 Ibid., pp. 110–111.
18 Ibid., p. 13.
19 Below, p. 526.
20 s. 31.
1 On difficulties in the magistrates' court see P. Tain, (1998) SJ 1063.
2 s. 31(4).

In *CPS v Weeks*[3] a charge under s. 4A failed on the facts where the defendant had said 'watch out the nights are getting dark' to his victim, and called him a 'black bastard'. Holland J noted that:

'No doubt there are many situations in which the use of the words "black bastard" do indicate an intention to cause harassment, alarm or distress. It is not in the least surprising if harassment, alarm and distress are caused to a black person if someone calls him a black bastard. But, whether or not it was the intention of the user of those words in the context and circumstances in which they were used, to cause harassment, alarm or distress, must, as it seems to me, be, in every case, a question for the fact finding tribunal to decide.'

The magistrates were entitled to find the defendant not guilty. Should the use of the expression 'black bastard' necessarily result in a conviction under the 1986 Act?

6. On race crimes generally, see J. Jacobs and K. Potter.[4] F. Brennan[5] argues that the provisions in the 1998 Act are well intentioned, but fraught with difficulty.[6] In particular, she identifies the deficiency in the lack of definition of racial motivation in the Act. The racial group membership that is used is based on the House of Lords decision in *Mandla v Dowell Lee*[7] excludes some groups – such as Muslims – and leaves them without protection under the Act:

'. . . limiting the provision in this way is an arbitrary and unjustified line to draw given the overwhelming evidence of "Muslimophobia". If one takes the term ethnicity as defined by the House of Lords to its logical conclusion there is no reason why a group of racists could not seek protection of the Act by claiming they were an ethnic group.[8]

On whether Muslims are covered by the 1986 Act see *R v DPP, ex p London Borough of Merton*.[9] How can race be defined for these purposes? How would the courts respond to a neo-Nazi group claiming that they were a race (Aryan?) that was being harassed by anti-Nazi protestors?[10] In *DPP v Pal*[11] P was alleged to have assaulted E, the caretaker at a community centre. P and E were both Asian. P called E a 'brown Englishman' and a 'white man's arse-licker'. The Divisional Court held that the element of racial aggravation was not proved: what P was demonstrating 'was not hostility towards Asians, but hostility towards Mr E's conduct that night'. In *R v White*[12] the defendant, a West Indian, had assaulted a woman and in the process called her a 'stupid African bitch'. The Court of Appeal upheld the conviction for racially aggravated assault, taking a broad interpretation of the offence. W's claims that the offence could not apply since both he and the victim were of the same racial group were rejected, as were his arguments that Africa did not constitute a culture or race, because it included a diverse collection of cultures. X says to a Malaysian: 'you stupid Chinese'; to a Columbian: 'you stupid South American'; and to a Pakistani: 'you stupid Asian'. Are these all aggravated offences? Should they be? Section 31 has been used in respect of racial taunts at police officers.[13] It was reported in *The*

---

3 (1997) Home Office. See also *Racially Motivated Crime: A British Survey* (1994) HORP No 28.
4 (2000) 14 June, DC.
5 *Hate Crimes, Criminal Law and Identity Politics* (1998).
6 [1999] Crim LR 17.
7 p. 27.
8 At 24. See also M. Idriss, (2001) 165 JP 618. See the recent proposals to introduce crimes related to religious hatred following the terrorist attacks on the USA on 11 September 2001, and news reports for 27 November 2001.
9 [1998] EWHC Admin 846.
10 See also the discussion by M. Malik, (1999) 62 MLR 409, and see the discussion of race in Chap. 11 below.
11 [2000] Crim LR 756.
12 [2001] 1 WLR 1352.
13 *R v Jesson* (2000) 17 January, CA (Cr D), unreported; *R v Jacobs* (2000) Times, 28 December.

Herald[14] that a Kilmarnock sheriff had questioned whether England was a nation for the purposes of the Act.

It is questionable why racial aggravation should attract special attention from the criminal law when other types of discrimination evident when crimes are committed do not: e.g. gender and homophobic prejudices. Sentencing practice seems to be an adequate method of dealing with the problem. Racially aggravated crimes are monitored by the Racist Incident Monitoring Scheme. The annual report for 1998–99 shows that police are identifying 58% of racially motivated offences. [15] The additional sentencing power for *any* racially aggravated offence in the Crime and Disorder Act 1998 prompted an increase in sentence in 21.6% of racially aggravated cases. [16] Guidelines on sentencing were issued by the Court of Appeal in *R v Saunders*: [17]

> 'One of the most important lessons of this century, as it nears its end, is that racism must not be allowed to flourish. The message must be received and understood, in every corner of our society, in our streets and prisons, in the services, in the workplace, on public transport, in our hospitals, public houses and clubs, that racism is evil. It cannot co-exist with fairness and justice. It is incompatible with a democratic civilisation. The courts must do all they can, in accordance with parliament's recently expressed intention, to convey that message clearly, by the sentences which they pass in relation to racially aggravated offences. Those who indulge in racially aggravated violence must expect to be punished severely, in order to discourage the repetition of that behaviour by them or others.'

Statistics on the use of racially aggravated offences in their first year of operation record: 5,385 offences of harassment; 2,279 cases of assault; 1,971 cases of criminal damage and 1,352 other racially aggravated offences. The total is 10,982 offences. The Sentencing Advisory Panel is reviewing the existing approach and will propose a structured approach for the courts to consider. [18] The CPS guidance manual reminds prosecutors not to accept a plea to lesser offences or to minimise or omit information for the sake of expediency in racially aggravated incidents. [19]

One of the more controversial recommendations of the Macpherson report was that consideration should be given to amending the law to allow for the prosecution of offences involving racist language or behaviour. [20] Some interpreted this as an attempt to outlaw racist language per se, even when spoken in a private dwelling and causing no offence to those present. Michael Mansfield QC, in a letter to the *Guardian*, wrote that the present private dwelling exceptions allow:

> 'racist organisations and individuals who do intend to stir up racial hatred (viz video surveillance material in the Lawrence case) to evade prosecution. Either we are serious about the eradication of deep-seated racism, or the battle that was fought to place this on the statute book in the first place will have been in vain.' [21]

Should use of racist language be an offence irrespective of whether it causes harassment etc.? Can criminal offences of such a nature be investigated and enforced without inappropriate intrusive policing?

---

14 14 June 2000.

15 See on the Racist Incident Monitoring Scheme, P. Jepson, (2001) 151 NLJ 562.

16 s. 82 of the Act requires the Court to treat racial aggravation (as defined in s. 28) as an aggravating factor when it is considering the seriousness of any other offence than the specific racially aggravated ones.

17 [2000] 1 Cr App R 458. See also *R v Bell* [2001] 1 Cr App R (S) 108; *R v Kelly* [2001] Crim LR 411.

18 See (2000) JP 156.

19 Para. 3.9

20 No. 39.

21 25 March 1999. See more generally on hate speech crimes, I. Hare, (1997) 17 OJLS 415.

Sentencing of public order offences

Some general considerations as regards sentencing for serious offences arising out of public protest were canvassed by Sachs LJ in *R v Caird*.[22]

R v Caird (1970) 54 Cr App Rep 499, Court of Appeal (Criminal Division)

The eight applicants were convicted of a variety of offences arising out of a disturbance at the Garden House Hotel, Cambridge. The hotel planned a dinner and dance to coincide with a 'Greek week' in Cambridge. A crowd of about 300 or 400 people assembled. The following facts were stated in the judgment. From the outset there was shouting. Soon it became clear that a large number of them had developed a common purpose of wrecking the dinner. They tried to stop people entering the hotel. One person was injured and others were frightened. A proportion of those present were determined to break through the police cordon and into the hotel. Some pounded on the windows, others climbed onto the roof. The dining room windows were broken and various missiles thrown in, including rocks, clods of earth and lighted mole fuses. Inside, tables were overturned, glass and crockery smashed, chairs brandished and thrown and curtains torn down. A constable and a proctor received serious injuries; many others received minor injuries. Many of the guests were terrified. The disturbance lasted over two and a half hours.

Fifteen defendants were tried at Hertford Assizes before Melford Stevenson J on a variety of charges. Seven were acquitted on all charges. Caird was convicted of riot, assaulting a police constable in the execution of his duty, and possessing an offensive weapon; John of riot and malicious damage; Household of unlawful assembly; Lagden of riot and malicious damage; Emley of riot and assaulting a police constable in the execution of his duty; Williams of possessing an offensive weapon; Bodea and Newton of unlawful assembly. Caird was sentenced to a total of two years' imprisonment; John and Emley to borstal training; Lagden to a total of fifteen months' imprisonment; and the others to nine months' imprisonment each. Williams and Bodea were recommended for deportation. They appealed to the Court of Appeal (Criminal Division).

Sachs LJ delivered the judgment of the court (**Sachs LJ**, **Lyell** and **Cusack JJ**): ... That on 13 February at Cambridge there was an unlawful and riotous assembly of most serious proportions at the Garden House Hotel is something which is obvious. It has not been and could not have been disputed in this Court....

Before now turning to individual sentences, it is appropriate first to mention certain general points which have been much canvassed. First, it should be observed that a plea in mitigation of 'provocation' made at one stage by Mr Myers was very properly withdrawn shortly after having been put forward. This Court could not entertain a political plea of that sort in the circumstances of this case as constituting mitigation, whatever other views it may have on it. Any suggestion that a section of the community strongly holding one set of views is justified in banding together to disrupt the lawful activities of a section that does not hold the same views so strongly or which holds different views cannot be tolerated and must unhesitatingly be rejected by the courts. When there is wanton and vicious violence of gross degree the Court is not concerned with whether it originates from gang rivalry or from political motives. It is the degree of mob violence that matters and the extent to which the public peace is being broken. It makes no difference whether the mob has attacked a first-class hotel in Cambridge or some dance hall frequented by the less well-circumstanced.

The next point to be mentioned is what might be called the 'Why pick on me?' argument. It has been suggested that there is something wrong in giving an appropriate sentence to one convicted on an offence because there are considerable numbers of others who were at the same time committing the same offence, some of whom indeed, if identified and arrested and established

22   (1970) 54 Cr App Rep 499, CA (Cr D) (below).

as having taken a more serious part, could have received heavier sentences. This is a plea which is almost invariably put forward where the offence is one of those classed as disturbances of the public peace—such as riots, unlawful assemblies and affrays. It indicates a failure to appreciate that on these confused and tumultuous occasions each individual who takes an active part by deed or encouragement is guilty of a really grave offence by being one of the number engaged in a crime against the peace. It is, moreover, impracticable for a small number of police when sought to be overwhelmed by a crowd to make a large number of arrests. It is indeed all the more difficult when, as in the present case, any attempt at arrest is followed by violent efforts of surrounding rioters to rescue the person being arrested. It is worse still when steps have been taken, as in the present case, to immerse the mob in darkness.

If this plea were acceded to, it would reinforce that feeling which may undoubtedly exist that if an offender is but one of a number he is unlikely to be picked on, and even if he is so picked upon, can escape proper punishment because others were not arrested at the same time. Those who choose to take part in such unlawful occasions must do so at their peril.

The present case was one of a long-lasting concerted attempt of grave proportions by aggressive force of numbers of overpower the police, to embark on wrecking, and to terrify citizens engaged in following peaceable and lawful pursuits. Any participation whatever, irrespective of its precise form, in an unlawful or riotous assembly of this type derives its gravity from becoming one of those who, by weight of numbers, pursued a common and unlawful purpose. The law of this country has always leant heavily against those who, to attain such a purpose, use the threat that lies in the power of numbers.

The general scale of the sentences adopted by the trial judge on this particular occasion was stern—but correctly so. The occasion was far more serious than that of most affrays and other disturbances of the public peace that have become all too common. In this connection it must also be emphasised that neither on the law applicable to ascertaining guilt, or on the matter of sentencing, is an adult student in any better position than any other citizen. He most certainly cannot by virtue of his education claim preferential treatment—as, for instance, to receive lighter punishment than one less well educated....

It is to be emphasised that in each and every case where the jury convicted one of the seven applicants either of riotous or unlawful assembly the person convicted had been in the very forefront of the mob and had been an active participator in attempts to get past and override the police in their protective tasks. It was indeed because he was thus in the forefront that he could be identified and in certain instances seized or arrested, often after a turbulent struggle in which those alongside attempted to rescue him. Moreover, each applicant was taking his part in the course of a protracted attack, and it was of no avail to plead sudden impulse. On that footing immediately custodial sentences were clearly required....

[The sentences were confirmed except that Lagden was put on probation and the recommendation for deportation of Bodea was quashed.]

NOTES

1. For a critical comment on *R v Caird*, see S. Sedley.[23]
2. The point that in sentencing a participant in public disorder the court must consider not only the defendant's precise individual acts, but also the fact that these were part of a wider disturbance, was confirmed by the Court of Appeal (Criminal Division) in *R v Hebron and Spencer*.[24] H and S were convicted of violent disorder following a disturbance in Hereford city centre on New Year's Eve in which up to 40 or so people among a large crowd were fighting. When the police intervened there were shouts and chants of 'Kill the Bill' and missiles were thrown at them. The police conducted three baton charges to restore order. S was shaking his fists and chanting 'Kill the Bill' with the others. Stuart-Smith LJ said.[1]

23 *The Listener* (1970) pp. 469–472, 783, 911; cf. A. W. Bradley, ibid., pp. 734–736; F. Bresler, ibid. pp. 736–737, 847.
24 (1989) 11 Cr App Rep (S) 226.
 1 At 228.

'... in cases of violent crowd disorder, it is not only the precise individual acts that matter. It is the fact that he is taking part in violent disorder, threatening violence against other people, and is part and parcel of the whole threatening and alarming activity.'

Accordingly, a custodial sentence was justified even though S was a young offender.

On sentencing for violent disorder, see also *R v Tyler*;[2] *R v Tomlinson, Mackie and Gladwell*.[3]

Other low level disorder offences

In recent years the government has sought to tackle low level disorder and harassment through a number of legislative measures. One of the most controversial was the response to the media fuelled panic about stalking.

Protection from Harassment Act 1997

1. Prohibition of harassment
(1) A person must not pursue a course of conduct—
  (*a*)   which amounts to harassment of another, and
  (*b*)   which he knows or ought to know amounts to harassment of the other.
(2) For the purposes of this section, the person whose course of conduct is in question ought to know that it amounts to harassment of another if a reasonable person in possession of the same information would think the course of conduct amounted to harassment of the other.
(3) Subsection (1) does not apply to a course of conduct if the person who pursued it shows—
  (*a*)   that it was pursued for the purpose of preventing or detecting crime.
  (*b*)   that it was pursued under any enactment or rule of law or to comply with any condition or requirement imposed by any person under any enactment, or
(c) that in the particular circumstances the pursuit of the course of conduct was reasonable.

2. Offence of harassment
(1) A person who pursues a course of conduct in breach of section 1 is guilty of an offence.
(2) A person guilty of an offence under this section is liable on summary conviction to imprisonment for a term not exceeding six months, or a fine not exceeding level 5 on the standard scale, or both.

3. Civil remedy
(1) An actual or apprehended breach of section 1 may be the subject of a claim in civil proceedings by the person who is or may be the victim of the course of conduct in question.
(2) On such a claim, damages may be awarded for (among other things) any anxiety caused by the harassment and any financial loss resulting from the harassment.
(3) Where—
  (*a*)   in such proceedings the High Court or a county court grants an injunction for the purpose of restraining the defendant from pursuing any conduct which amounts to harassment, and
  (*b*)   the plaintiff considers that the defendant has done anything which he is prohibited from doing by the injunction,
  the plaintiff may apply for the issue of a warrant for the arrest of the defendant.
(4) An application under subsection (3) may be made—
  (*a*)   where the injunction was granted by the High Court, to a judge of that court, and
  (*b*)   where the injunction was granted by a county court, to a judge or district judge of that or any other county court.
(5) The judge or district judge to whom an application under subsection (3) is made may only issue a warrant if—
  (*a*)   the application is substantiated on oath, and
  (b)   the judge or district judge has reasonable grounds for believing that the defendant has done anything which he is prohibited from doing by the injunction.

2   (1992) 96 Cr App Rep 332, CA (Cr D).
3   (1992) Times, 2 December, CA (Cr D).

4. Putting people in fear of violence

(1) A person whose course of conduct causes another to fear, on at least two occasions, that violence will be used him is guilty of an offence if he knows or ought to know that his course of conduct will cause the other so to fear on each of those occasions.

(2) For the purposes of this section, the person whose course of conduct is in question ought to know that it will cause another to fear that violence will be used against him on any occasion if a reasonable person in possession of the same information would think the course of conduct would cause the other so to fear on that occasion.

(3) It is a defence for a person charged with an offence under this section to show that—

(*a*) his course of conduct was pursued for the purpose of preventing or detecting crime.

(*b*) His course of conduct was pursued under any enactment or rule of law or to comply with any condition or requirement imposed by any person under any enactment, or

(*c*) the pursuit of his course of conduct was reasonable for the protection of himself or another or for the protection of his or another's property.

NOTES

1. The courts had developed a tort of harassment at common law.[4] In *Burris v Azadani*[5] the then Master of the Rolls, Sir Thomas Bingham, stated that 'in the light of ... authority' it can no longer be claimed 'that there is no tort of harassment'.[6] Further, his Lordship referred to the victim being 'adequately protected by an injunction which restrains the tort which is or is likely to be committed, whether trespass to the person or to land, interference with goods, harassment, intimidation or as the case may be'.[7] The use of the tort to tackle behaviour which amounted to stalking was severely curtailed by the decision of the House of Lords in *Hunter v Canary Wharf*[8] The House held that only those who had a right to exclusive possession of the land could sue in nuisance.

2. The Act is very badly drafted and displays many of the deficiencies typical of over-hasty legislative response to moral panics. Part of the problem lies in the intractable difficulty of trying to define the prohibited conduct:

'Stalkers do not stick to activities on a list. Stalkers and other weirdos who pursue women, [sic] cause racial harassment and annoy their neighbours have a wide range of activity which it is impossible to define.'[9]

The Act was preceded by the Home Office/Lord Chancellors' Department consultation paper, *Stalking – the solutions*.[10]

3. Celia Wells wrote that the Act 'follows a pattern witnessed in other areas (hunt saboteurs, joy riding and dangerous dogs come to mind) of addressing a narrowly conceived social harm with a widely drawn provision often supplementing and overlapping with existing offences'.[11] However, recent Home Office research has found that the CPS, police and magistrates are generally positive about the Act.[12]

---

4 N. Fricker, [1992] Fam Law 158; M. Brazier, [1992] Fam Law 346. See further J. Murphy, (1993) NLJ 926, 1685; M. Noble, (1993) NLJ 1685; A. Cooke, (1994) 57 MLR 289.

5 [1995] 1 WLR 1372.

6 At 1378.

7 At 1380. See further T. Lawson-Cruttenden, (1996) 146 NLJ 418 and 1776. On the civil law generally, see J. Bridgman and M. Jones 'Harassing Conduct and outrageous acts: a cause of action for intentionally inflicted mental distress' (1994) LS 180. See also R. Townshend-Smith 'Harassment as a tort in English and American Law: The Boundaries of *Wilkinson v Downton*' (1995) Anglo-American LR 299.

8 [1997] 2 All ER 426.

9 D. MacLean, Home Office Minister, HC 17 December 1996, col. 827.

10 (1996). For a comparative analysis of stalking legislation, see B. MacFarlane, (1997) UBC LR 37.

11 [1997] Crim LR 463, 464.

12 J. Harris, *An Evaluation of the Use and effectiveness of the Protection from Harassment Act 1997* (2000), p. 41.

4. Section 1 of the Act defines the conduct of harassment which is then applicable for both criminal and civil proceedings by ss. 2 and 3 respectively. Note that the offence and tort are objectively determined. The blurring of the crime/civil law divide is unsatisfactory, and Harris found that there was a lack of consensus among members of the police and CPS as to when a civil claim should be adequate: [13]

> 'It certainly appears that the crossover between criminal and civil law in the field of harassment sometimes poses problem. Some prosecutors called for improved police training about when it was appropriate to use the civil rather than the criminal law.' [14]

The effect of this was reported to have created a 'degree of inconsistency in decision-making between police, CPS magistrates and judges'. [15] There is no requirement that the harasser intended or directed his conduct; it is sufficient that 'a reasonable person in possession of the same information would think the course of conduct amounted to harassment of another'. [16]

The test in s. 1(2) is an objective one, with no requirement that the reasonable person be endowed with any of the defendant's characteristics: *R v Colohan* [17] (schizophrenic who could not help sending threatening letters to his MP).

5. Furthermore, there is no requirement that any violence is threatened (or feared) for the offence under s. 2. This criminalises conduct such as that in *Chambers and Edwards v DPP*, [18] where protestors persistently but non-violently blocked a surveyor's theodolite beam, since the Divisional Court held that such conduct would amount to harassment for the purposes of the Public Order Act 1986. Note also the statements of Eady J in *Huntingdon Life Sciences v Curtin* [19] that the offence was not intended by Parliament to be used to clamp down on the discussion of matters of public interest or upon public protest and public demonstration that formed a part of the democratic tradition. This interpretation of the Act is doubtful following the extension of the provisions by the Criminal Justice and Police Act 2001 specifically introduced to cover animal rights protest (discussed above).

The harassment offence can be committed by text messaging a mobile phone and by any other means of communication. [20] Note also that s. 43 of the Criminal Justice and Police Act 2001 extends the Malicious Communications Act 1988 to conduct involving electronic messages.

At the core of both the crime and the tort is a 'course of conduct', which is further explained in s. 7(1) such that it 'must involve conduct on at least two occasions'. The provision is very unclear. Are two incidents separated by one year a course of conduct? Is one protest outside a laboratory for several days a 'course of conduct' or one occasion? Recent research has found that in one third of cases brought under the Act, the suspect was arrested on the third occasion of their acting. [21]

6. The course of conduct must relate to 'another'. In *DPP v Williams* [22] W had put his hand through a bathroom window, startling the occupant, M, who was showering, who then informed H, her flatmate, who was scared by the event. Two days later he peered through the bedroom window, this time frightening H. The magistrate

---

13 p. 44.
14 p. 45.
15 p. 53.
16 s. 1(2).
17 [2001] Crim LR (Nov).
18 [1995] Crim LR 896.
19 (1997) Times, 11 December.
20 K. Parsons, (2001) 145 SJ 281.
21 J. Harris, *An Evaluation of the Use and Effectiveness of the Protection from Harassment Act 1997* (2000), p. 20.
22 (1998) unreported.

convicted, holding that 'another' could be read as 'others'. The Divisional Court decided the case on the basis that H had been distressed on both occasions and therefore the offence was made out. Is there any limit to the number of intermediaries through which an indirect stalking can occur? Is there a requirement that the indirect victim be informed contemporaneously? There could also be difficulties with mens rea: unless it can be established that D knew he was harassing M on the second occasion, it is by no means clear that a reasonable man would say that D ought to have realised that his conduct would have harassed M. The result in *Williams* may be laudable, but at the cost of certainty and, it may also be that D has a defence in relation to one of the occupants. If it is felt appropriate to criminalise such behaviour, resort should be had to other offences (e.g. assault). The magistrate's interpretation does extend the offence quite considerably. A charge under the 1997 Act might be bad for duplicity where it names two complainants unless they are members of a 'close knit identifiable group': *Mills v DPP*. [23]

'This is a vague qualification. Is there a numerical limit to a "close knit" group? Must the group perceive itself to be such? What degree of "nexus" must the group have? To take an example from the case of *DPP v Williams* (1997) (unreported, CO/2203/98, DC), is D's stalking of a nurses home with 50 occupants a course of conduct against a "close knit identifiable group"? A further difficulty may arise if D has a statutory defence under section 1(3) in respect of one of the members of the group. Does his defence in relation to that individual nullify the course of conduct in respect of the whole? . . . The term is not in the statutory formula and could be very difficult to prove. Would it not be better for the courts to keep the offence within strict limits by holding that the information must be specific as to which individual has been the victim on two occasions? If small are the complainants it will usually be the case that D harasses the group together (in which case numerous separate charges could be spelt out) or at worst the prosecutor would have to wait for a member of the group to be on the receiving end of D's attentions on two occasions. In the rather fanciful situations with a determined stalker of a nurses' home who diligently approaches a different window on each occasion so as to avoid harassing the same individual there is no reason why the courts should strive to extend the 1997 Act. There are other offences that could be used: for example, Public Order Act 1986 sections 4A or 5, or even public nuisance following the decision in *Johnson* [1996] 2 Cr App R 434.' [24]

7. How closely connected must the incidents forming the course of conduct be? In *Lau v DPP* [25] two incidents four months apart were held to be capable of amounting to a course of conduct: 'One can conceive of circumstances where incidents, as far apart as a year, could constitute a course of conduct'. The example given was of racial harassment outside a synagogue on the Day of Atonement. Is the only connecting factor that must be shown for harassment that the two events related to the same person? See also *R v Henley*. [1] Persistent following of former partner in *R v Wass* [2] led to conviction where W followed his victim on her bus journey and then immediately she alighted he remonstrated with her. The magistrates found this to constitute a course of conduct. In *King v DPP* [3] the alleged harassment was by offering the victim a plant; writing letters to her; rummaging in her rubbish and stealing her discarded underwear from those bags; and by filming her secretly. The Divisional Court held that:

---

23 (1998) 17 December, DC.
24 Commentary on *DPP v Dunn* [2001] Crim LR 130.
25 [2000] Crim LR 580–582.
 1 Below.
 2 (2000) 11 May, CA (Cr D) .
 3 (2000) 20 June, DC. See also recently *Pratt v DPP* [2001] EWHC Admin 438.

'repeated offers of unwelcome gifts or the repeated sending of letters could well amount to harassment, nevertheless, the single offer of a gift of modest value and the sending of one innocuous letter in the circumstances of this case cannot amount to harassment within the meaning of the 1997 Act. Nor could the letter and the gift be treated as the first stage or the first two stages of a course of conduct amounting to harassment . . . '

The magistrates were wrong to treat these incidents as forming a part of a course of conduct. The decision does not stand up to close scrutiny. There is no limitation as to the types of conduct amounting to harassment in the statute. Two bunches of flowers should trigger the offence provided the mens rea is present. In *DPP v Woolford*[4] D was convicted of harassing his former partner after sending her two cards with innocuous messages and leaving her one voice mail message:

'A further difficulty with the lack of definition in the Act is to identify whether conduct of the parties might break the chain of what would otherwise be regarded as a course of conduct. In this case the unsatisfactory nature of the evidence prevents the problem arising head on. Consider D who twice sends flowers to V and is rebuffed on each occasion (at least one act of the course of conduct, cf. *King* (2000)) and who then has a non-hostile encounter with V, say an innocuous chat over coffee. D then sends another bunch of flowers. Is that an harassing course of conduct? Without the intervening coffee it certainly looks to be. The problem will be especially acute where D behaves in a non-hostile way towards V throughout, and never grasps that the conduct is harassing despite V's complaints. V maintaining civility should not prevent her being able to rely on the protection of the Act. The position could also arise where V is unaware of who her stalker is, and maintains a civil relationship with him (e.g. in the workplace) and is at that time also being harassed by him.'[5]

8. In many cases the Act has been used successfully in respect of 'classic' stalking behaviour. *Hall v Tanner*[6] provides an example of a female harassing her male ex-partner with 41 telephone calls in two hours on one occasion; in *R v Miah*[7] M harassed a 15-year-old school girl, assaulting her and threatening her with a knife and verbally abusing and threatening her on many occasions, resulting in an 18-month sentence. There is no doubt that harassment may occur by a course of conduct comprising speech (only) or even silence (e.g. silent telephone calls). However, simply to withdraw the social grace of speaking to one's neighbour is not harassment: *Morris v Knight*.[8] Other cases leading to charges under the Protection from Harassment Act 1997 demonstrate how broad the offence is. For example, in one case it has been used in respect of a defendant delivering sexually explicit artwork to nursing homes, causing distress to residents.[9] A company may be the victim of harassment: *Huntingdon Life Sciences Ltd v British Union for the Abolition of Vivisection.*[10]

There have been attempts to use the Act in relation to newspapers publishing details of individuals causing the individual to be likely to receive hate mail: *Esther v News Group Newspapers.*[11]

9. The offence in s. 4 is much more serious, although recent research found that not all officers were aware of the difference between ss. 2 and 4.[12] The essential difference between this offence and the crime in s. 2 (and under tort in s. 3) is that the victim

---

4   (2000) 9 May, DC.
5   Commentary on *R v Hills* [2001] Crim LR 318.
6   (2000) 20 July, CA (Civ D).
7   [2001] EWCA Crim 228.
8   (1998) 22 October, CC Bournemouth.
9   *R v Swayzi* (1998) 4 December, unreported, CA (Cr D).
10 (1998) unreported.
11 (2001) 18 July.
12 J. Harris, *An Evaluation of the Use and Effectiveness of the Protection from Harassment Act 1997* (2000), p. 25.

must be caused to fear, on at least two occasions, that violence will be used against him. The other important difference is that the defences available to this charge that the harasser proves that his conduct was for the purpose of preventing or detecting crime, was lawfully authorised, or was reasonable for the protection of himself or another or of property. Section 4 has no requirement of immediacy as found in the offence of assault, and offences of 'violence' under the Public Order Act 1986. Whereas violence is defined in s. 8 of the Public Order Act 1986 for the purposes of that Act, no such definition appears in the Protection from Harassment Act 1997. In *R v Henley*[13] H's harassment of the complainant and her family included threats to kill. He was charged under s. 4. The trial judge failed to direct the jury on the section and confused the word 'violence' by telling the jury that an intention to 'seriously frighten her as to what might happen' was sufficient. The judge also confused the jury by failing to clarify that the person must fear violence against himself, not violence towards others.

In *R v DPP, ex p Moseley*[14] D was convicted of the offence under s. 4 when he threatened to cut V's throat and threatened to blow her dog's brains out. Was this a threat causing the victim to fear violence to her?

'A narrow interpretation of section 4 is that the prosecution must prove that the behaviour caused the victim to fear that violence would result directly from that incident forming part of the harassing course of conduct. Beyond direct threats to the victim, only certain threats to property/others would suffice – e.g. threats to torch the victim's home. A wider interpretation of section 4 suggests that is sufficient that the victim fears that personal violence *will* occur by some unspecified means at some unspecified time in the future. On this interpretation, conduct of any description, whether threats to property or another could suffice to trigger the offence. The limiting factor would lie in the requirement that the reasonable man would have to think that the fear would be caused. In this case the court seems to favour the wider interpretation without explicit acknowledgment, but because the ruling relates to the threat made to the dog *in the presence of* the victim, it could be seen as a generous application of the narrow view. On either interpretation the fear of personal violence is a matter of fact, and the court is right to accept it can be inferred from the evidence. The proximity of the victim to the property/person threatened and the manner in which the threat is to be carried out will be important factors.'[15]

10. The defences in s. 1(3) will prove very important in cases under the Act. Can an anti-vivisectionist claim that his demonstrations outside the houses of vivisectionist workers are reasonable? The burden is on the defendant to prove, on the balance of probabilities, that the section is satisfied. To what extent can the protester prove that his pursuit of a particular course of conduct is 'reasonable' if it causes harassment? Are magistrates to begin weighing the niceties of vivisectionism and animal rights? Will this reverse burden withstand challenge under the ECHR Art. 6(2)?

Pursuit of conduct in breach of an injunction will preclude a defence under s. 1(3)(c). In *R v DPP, ex p Moseley*[16] protests outside a mink farm led to prosecutions under the Act. The defence relied on ss. 1(3)(c) and (a), claiming that they sought to detect unlawful activity on the farm by their actions. The magistrate concluded that the protest was reasonable, even though an injunction had already been issued to prohibit the conduct. The Divisional Court accepted the DPP's argument that it cannot be reasonable to harass by conduct in breach of an injunction. Picketers, however, ought to be able to rely on the defence in s. 1(3)(b). Research has shown that in those cases where a defence was put forward, nearly half of the defendants claimed that

---

13 [2000] Crim LR 582–584.
14 [2001] Crim LR 397.
15 Commentary on *R v DPP* (ibid.).
16 (1999) 9 June, DC.

their behaviour was reasonable. [17] The defences of 'reasonableness' in s. 1(3) are not to be confused by courts drawing comparisons with provocation and duress defences in which attempts to introduce the subjective characteristics of the defendants into the objective tests of reasonableness have created considerable difficulty: *R v Colohan* [18]

One of the first cases in which the Act was considered involved anti-vivisection protesters being restrained under s. 3. The Court of Appeal held that the conduct of the protesters could amount to harassment of the claimant. [19] However, Eady J in the hearing relating to the injunction, commented that the Act was not intended to be used to stifle discussion of public interest on public demonstration. [20]

In *Baron v DPP* [21] two letters sent by B to a member of staff at the Benefit Agency, included violent threats and disclosing B's knowledge of the woman's private life. After conviction under the Malicious Communication Act 1988, B had intimidated the complainant during the trial by cross-examination that had to be stopped. Threats to bully again in cross-examination at the appeal were contained in one letter, but that did not, on the facts, fall within s. 1(3)(c). The court nevertheless emphasised that:

> 'a line must be drawn between legitimate expression of disgust at the way a public agency has behaved and conduct amounting to harassment. The right to free speech requires a broad degree of tolerance in relation to communications. It is a legitimate exercise of that right to say things which are unpleasant or possibly hurtful to the recipient. Persons in the public service, in my view, are used to rudeness, aggression and unpleasantness of every form and the courts are likely in my judgment to expect of them a high degree of robustness and fortitude beyond that which other members of the public may be expected to show.
>
> The legitimate right of free speech is given effect to by subsection 1(3)(*b*). But if the line is crossed an offence will have been committed because there is in my judgment, a limit to what is lawful to say in written communications. Equally, citizens have an unfettered right access to the courts to resolve disputes and to conduct those proceedings forcefully, causing legitimate aggravation to the other party within the procedural rules. Persons will or may feel harassed as a result of the lawful conduct of forcefully conducted litigation. On the other hand, if proceedings are used for an ulterior purpose, namely not to air legitimate grievances but to cause distress to those involved in the process, then the line may be crossed and the acts may become unlawful under the [1997] Act.' [22]

Note that there is the possibility of the local authority seeking to use the 1997 Act where tenants are harassing neighbouring tenants. [1]

11. Where the tort of harassment is proved, the court is empowered to award damages under s. 3 for 'any anxiety caused by the harassment and any financial loss resulting from the harassment'. In addition, the court can issue an injunction restraining the defendant from behaving in any particular way. These remedies are available where the court is satisfied that there has been 'an actual or apprehended' breach of s. 1. Nuisance had been used by claimants as a cause of action against stalkers before the protection from Harassment Act 1997. In *Perharic v Hennessey* [2] the Court of Appeal upheld the claimant's injunction and awarded £5,000 for abusive calls. In *B v MHA Ltd* [3] the

---

17 J. Harris, *An Evaluation of the Use and Effectiveness of the Protection from Harassment Act 1997* (2000), p. 36.
18 [2001] EWCA Crim 1251, CA.
19 [1998] Env LR D9.
20 *Huntingdon Life Sciences v Curtin* (1997) Times, 11 December.
21 (2000) 13 June, DC.
22 Per Morison J.
 1 On this, see D. Hughes, (1997) Anglo-Am LR 167, 196.
 2 [1997] CLY 4859.
 3 [1999] 2 CL 372.

claimant's action for nuisance and under s. 3 was dismissed where the conduct complained of was noisy neighbouring tenants, who did not maintain the property. The district judge restricted the Act to conduct 'aimed' at a person. Here the landlord/ tenants had not aimed their behaviour at anyone. This is, with respect, misleading: many stalkers do not intend to aim harassing behaviour.[4] The statute is to be confined to use against neighbour disputes and anti-social activities: *Tuppen v Microsoft*.[5]

In some cases courts have imposed psychiatric treatment as a condition of probation orders when conviction under the Act has occurred. Under the Protection from Harassment Act 1997, see for example *R v Melbourne*.[6] It may be necessary for the court to make a hospital order under s. 37 of the Mental Health Act 1983, or a restriction order under s. 41 of that Act. It has recently been suggested that a stalkers' register could be established to assist police in tracking persistent offenders.[7]

12. Section 2 of the Act is triable summarily only and carries a maximum six months or fine exceeding level 5 or both. Section 4 is triable either way, carrying a maximum sentence on indictment of five years or a fine or both. Further guidance on sentencing was provided in *R v Liddle, R v Hayes*.[8]

'We turn to a summary of considerations for sentencers to bear in mind for defendants who may be convicted of any of [the harassment] offences or plead guilty to them. We would identify these considerations: first, is the offence a s. 2 or a s.4 offence? Secondly, is there a history of disobedience to court orders in the past, whether they are orders under the Act or civil orders? Thirdly, the seriousness of the defendants' conduct, which can of course range from actual violence through to threats, down to letters, which of course may even express affection rather than any wish to harm the victim. Fourthly, is there persistent misconduct by the defendant or a solitary instance of misbehaviour? Fifthly, the effect upon the victim, whether physical or psychological?

Question: does the victim require protection? Further question: what is the level of risk posed by the defendant? Usually that risk is to the victim, but it may of course include the children or family of the victim. Sixthly, the mental health of the offender, and a sentencer should devote his attention to whether the defendant is willing to undergo treatment or have the necessary help from the probation service which is readily available under special schemes. Per Curtis. J. Seventhly, what is the offenders reaction to the court proceedings? First, is there a plea of guilty? Second, is there remorse? Thirdly, is there recognition of the need for help?

A court may also issue a restraining order protecting the victim by prohibiting the defendant from behaving in the prescribed way (e.g. visiting home or work of victim). (Section 5). Penalties for breaching restraining orders are criminal with maxima as with section 4.'

Of those convicted, restraining orders were issued in 56% of cases.[9] Where the defendant's harassment led to his being convicted and a restraining order prohibited from being within 50 yards of his victim's house, he was, by that order, physically unable to live in his council owned accommodation. The council's repossession of the property was regarded as entirely appropriate and not in breach of Art. 8 of the ECHR: *Lambeth London Borough Council v Howard*.[10]

---

4 On the use of s. 5 orders in the Act, see P. Tain, (1998) SJ 465, and on remedies generally, see P. Glover, (1998) SJ 988 comparing remedies under the Family Law Act 1996.
5 (2000) 15 November.
6 (2000) 25 January, CA (Cr D).
7 *Guardian*, 2 August 2000.
8 [1998] 3 All ER 816.
9 J. Harris, *An Evaluation of the Use and Effectiveness of the Protection from Harassment Act 1997* (2000), p. 37.
10 (2001) 6 March, unreported, CA (Civ D).

13. In 1998, 5,800 people were convicted of 'stalking' offences: 4,300 of the s. 2 charge and the remainder under s. 4. In the first six months of the Act being in force:

Section 2:   456 men and 51 women prosecuted

                225 men and 23 women convicted

Section 4:   231 men and 12 women prosecuted

                65 men and 9 women convicted

In 1998 there were 4,355 prosecutions under s. 2, with 2,221 convictions. Section 4 led to 1,505 summary proceedings with 420 convicted, and 167 Crown Court proceedings with 102 convictions. Between January and September 1999 there were 3,813 prosecutions under s. 2 with 1,867 convictions. Section 4 led to 1,176 proceeded against, with 281 convictions in this period.

E. von Heussen[11] provides an overview of the academic studies into stalking. The most recent research by the Home Office[12] examined 167 prosecutions during 1998. The study found that the Act is 'being used to deal with a variety of behaviour other than stalking, including domestic violence and inter-neighbour disputes, and rarely for stalking itself'.[13] A much higher proportion of cases charged were later dropped by the CPS than with other offences – this was often as a result of the complainant withdrawing the complaint.[14] The report concludes that the:

> 'use being made of the Act's criminal provisions is valid but that there is a need to clear up the confusion that exists among practitioners. This might be achieved by issuing some form of guidance or clarification from the centre about what the Act is intended to cover and through enhanced training for all practitioners, as and when opportunities arise.'[15]

On the relationship between the harassment legislation and the public and participants perception of stalking, see L. Sheridan and G. M. Davies.[16]

The Crime and Disorder Act 1998, s. 32 included a new offence of racially aggravated harassment (contrary to ss. 2 and 4).[17]

(iv) Anti-social behaviour orders

The Crime and Disorder Act 1998[18] introduced a novel form of quasi criminal order: the anti-social behaviour order, designed to deal with low level repeated disorder. Under s. 1 of the Act a local authority or police force can apply for an anti-social behaviour order (ASBO).[19] The application is made to the magistrates' court and, if successful, will prohibit the specified person from behaving in an anti social manner for two or more years. These are based on the model of the community safety order.

Section 1 provides:

---

11 [2000] Web JCLI.
12 J. Harris, *An Evaluation of the Use and Effectiveness of the Protection from Harassment Act 1997* (2000).
13 p. v.
14 p. viii.
15 p. x.
16 (2001) 6 Legal and Criminological Psychology 3.
17 See above, p. 501.
18 See R. Leng, R. Taylor and M. Wasik, *Blackstone's Guide to the Crime and Disorder Act 1998* (1998).
19 See generally on ASBOs, D. Hughes, V. Karn and R. Lickliss, [1994] JSWFL 201; S. Cracknell, [2000] JSWFL 108.

'(1) An application for an order under this section may be made by a relevant authority if it appears to the authority that the following conditions are fulfilled with respect to any person aged 10 or over, namely—

    (a) that the person has acted, since the commencement date, in a manner that caused or was likely to cause harassment, alarm or distress to one or more persons not of the same household as himself; and

    (b) that such an order is necessary to protect persons in the local government area in which the harassment, alarm or distress was caused or was likely to be caused or was likely to be caused from further anti-social acts by him.'

NOTES

1. In this section 'relevant authority' means the council for the local government area or any chief officer of police any part of whose area lies within that area. Failure to comply with such an order revokes the person liable to a term of imprisonment. The application is civil in nature in that it requires proof only on the balance of probabilities. No 'conviction' occurs with the granting of such an order. Suggestions that the criminal standard of proof should apply in these cases or they might fall foul of the ECHR have been scorned by Jack Straw, having described the challenge as 'hogwash', he continued:

'An order for eviction takes place in the civil courts, it uses a civil remedy and you use the civil rules of evidence just as an anti-social behaviour order does. I have not heard any of these so-called civil liberty lawyers say that an order for eviction is against the ECHR.'[20]

2. In *McCann v Manchester Crown Court*[1] the Court of Appeal held that ASBO proceedings are civil – approving the decision of the Divisional Court. In the Divisional Court, Lord Woolf CJ said:

'What are criminal as opposed to civil proceedings is a matter which can be difficult to determine. There is no one overriding test within our domestic law for determining whether proceedings are civil or criminal. To some extent it is like describing an elephant; it is recognised when seen but it is difficult effectively to describe.
    ASBO proceedings are civil:
    (i)   they involve a two-stage exercise: the obtaining of the order, and proceedings for breach of the order;
    (ii) the process is one which is generally used for civil proceedings;
    (iii) there is no punishment properly involved merely a restriction on activities;
    (iv) the objective of making an order is designed not to punish but to protect;
    (v) the proceedings are administrative in nature.'

3. The Court of Appeal relied heavily on the absence of punitive intent and the protective nature of the order. Cases have tried to challenge the admissibility of civil hearsay under the Human Rights Act 1998, but without success. In *R v Marylebone Magistrates' Court, ex p Clingham*[2] the court stated that:

'We do not think that there is anything in the Human Rights Act 1998 or the jurisprudence of the E.Ct.H.R which leads either to the automatic exclusion of hearsay evidence in civil proceedings or to any requirement to give the civil evidence legislation any meaning which it does not naturally bear. The fact that some of the evidence is hearsay without the possibility of cross-examination does not have the automatic result that the trial is not a fair trial as Article 6(1) requires. Nor was the complainant local authority acting in breach of the appellant's rights under Article 6 in seeking to adduce the hearsay evidence.'

20 *Hansard*, House of Commons Home Affairs Committee *Minutes of Evidence*, 26 Oct 1999, Qn 48.
  1 [2001] 1 WLR 1084.
  2 (2001) 11 January, DC.

4. It has also been argued that such orders might infringe Arts. 11 and 8 of the ECHR because they will restrict the freedom of family and private life of the individual. Since the orders are 'prescribed by law and are necessary in a democratic society . . . for the prevention of crime and disorder', it is unlikely that such challenges will succeed provided Orders are drafted sufficiently clearly.

5. The ASBO, which was something of a flagship for the Labour government's strategy against crime and disorder, has been little used.[3] This despite HMIC[4] concluded that ASBOs will 'assist considerably in tackling disorder and anti-social behaviour'. Home Office Minister, Mr Charles Clarke, reported that there have been at least 80 such orders, at least 27 of which have been issued against under 18-year-olds.[5] The Home Secretary took the step of writing to authorities to urge them to make more use of the order.[6] The Home Secretary is reported to have blamed the low numbers of such orders on the 'trendy civil rights lawyers who, having defended such people, jumped into their BMWs and went back to the leafy suburbs where they did not have to suffer from anti-social behaviour'.[7] North Somerset District Council were the first to be granted an ASBO, in that case against a man persistently harassing housing office officials.[8] In 1999 two Liverpool teenagers were made subject to an ASBO banning them from walking in two specified streets and from urinating and spitting in public.[9] Other examples include the case from Birmingham in which a 'prolific' car thief was banned from every car park in the city. He has since been convicted for breaching the order.[10] An ASBO was issued against a 14-year-old Nottingham boy who had been convicted of offences 55 times in the previous two years.[11] A woman who was suspected of drug dealing was banned from occupying council property and from having more than eight visitors per day.[12] It has been reported that the ASBOs have had little effect as regards 'nuisance neighbours'. The research into the use of the power suggests that those who have been evicted by councils have moved to privately rented homes in the same area.[13] There have been claims that the power is no real deterrent since the sentence for a breach of an order is too steep and is not taken seriously, particularly by youths.[14] On the ASBOs as a 'false dawn' being used only 177 times by December 2000, see D. Collins.[15]

6. The Crime and Disorder Act 1998 also introduced a power under s. 16 to remove truants and take them back to school. It is not a power of arrest, nor does it make truancy an offence.[16] In addition, the Act provides powers in relation to Local Child Curfews (ss. 14 and 15). These were stated to be designed to deal with the problem of unsupervised children under the age of 10 on the streets late at night who may be at risk of becoming involved in anti-social behaviour.[17] Schemes are drawn up by the

3 But see Home Office Press Release 19 November 2001 claiming use is on the increase.
4 *Keeping the Peace* (1999).
5 *Hansard*, HC, Written Answer, 6 July 2000, col. 296 W.
6 *The Times*, 15 September 1999.
7 See *Hansard*, HC Deb, 1 February 2000, col. 153 WH.
8 See news reports for 4 June 1999.
9 Hughes, op. cit., p. 21.
10 *Daily Telegraph*, 2 February 2001.
11 See *Hansard*, HC Deb, 1 February 2000, col. 139 WH.
12 *The Times*, 6 January 2001.
13 *Guardian*, 5 July 2000.
14 See *Hansard*, HC Deb, 1 February 2000, col. 145 WH. For calls for a wider power for ASBOs with less bureaucracy and complexity, see *Hansard*, HC Deb, 1 February 2000, col. 140 WH.
15 D. M. Collins, (2001) 151 NLJ 876; see also R. White, [1999] 1 EHRLR 55.
16 See further Home Office, Guidance Document, 'Power for the Police to Remove Truants', www.homeoffice.gov.uk/cdact/truancy.htm.
17 See further www.homeoffice.gov.uk/cdact/guidlcc.htm. See now Criminal Justice and Police Act 2001, s. 48.

authority in conjunction with the police and the local community.[18] By the end of 1999, there had been no child curfew orders issued.[19]

7. Other legislative provision for common annoyances include the Housing Act 1996, s. 152(1), which empowers a High Court or county court to grant an injunction prohibiting a person from:

> '(a) engaging in or threatening to engage in conduct causing or likely to cause a nuisance or annoyance to a person residing in, visiting or otherwise engaging in a lawful activity in residential premises to which this section applies or in the locality of such premises,
>
> (b) using or threatening to use residential premises to which this section applies for immoral or illegal purposes, or
>
> (c) entering residential premises to which this section applies or being found in the locality of any such premises.
>
> (3) The court shall not grant an injunction under this section when it is of the opinion that
>
> (a) the respondent has used or threatened to use violence against any person of a description mentioned in subsection 1 (a); and
>
> (b) there is a significant risk of harm to that person or a person of a similar description if the injunction is not granted.'

These powers may be exercised only on application by a local authority in respect of protecting their tenants or licensees.[20]

8. Low-level disorder continues to provide an easy target for politicians anxious to be seen to be 'dealing with crime'. The Prime Minister, Tony Blair, announced radical plans to introduce on the spot fines:[21] 'A thug might think twice about kicking in your gate, throwing traffic cones around your street or hurling abuse into the night sky if he thought he might get picked up by the police, taken to a cash point and asked to pay an on the spot fine.'[1]

What are the difficulties with introducing such a scheme? The plan was modified considerably, and the resulting fixed penalty notice scheme is now contained in the Criminal Justice and Police Act 2001 (see above, p. 392).

As a further measure against public disorder, particularly the perennial problem of youths' acts of vandalism and unruly behaviour, the Confiscation of Alcohol (Young Persons) Act 1997 was enacted. This provides officers with a power to confiscate 'intoxicating liquor' from any person under 18, in public, or from any person who intends it to be consumed by an under 18-year-old. The power is triggered by an officer's reasonable suspicion, and applies in any public place except licensed premises and to any place to which the person has unlawfully gained access. See also the Home Office Circular 38/97, which suggests that the power is not to be used when there is no perception of a problem arising from the underage drinking – e.g. at a family picnic.

(v) Disruption of lawful activities

The statutory provisions given below afford a measure of protection to lawful meetings. Those who disrupt lawful meetings may commit other criminal offences

---

18 See the Home Office Guidance Document, 'Local Child Curfews', www.homeoffice.gov.uk/cdact/curfews.htm.

19 *Hansard*, HC Deb, 6 December 1999, col. 551.

20 Note that the local authority is not obliged to act: *Hussain v Lancaster City Council* [1999] 4 All ER 125, CA.

21 On Tony Blair's proposed on-the-spot fines, see the questions posed by the Shadow Home Secretary (Miss Widdecombe), and the response of Mr Charles Clarke, *Hansard*, HC, Written Answer, 10 July 2000, 432W.

1 *Observer*, 2 July 2000.

not related in particular to meetings[2]. They may be ejected, and those who organise a meeting on private premises may employ stewards to preserve order.[3] It is arguable that the police should act first against persons who disrupt or threaten to disrupt a lawful meeting, and disperse the meeting itself only if necessary in the last resort.[4] As to police powers of entry to prevent disorder, see *Thomas v Sawkins*.[5] The Criminal Justice and Public Order Act 1994[6] introduced new provisions in respect of disruptive trespasses.

Public Meetings Act 1908

1. Penalty on endeavour to break up public meeting

(1) Any person who at a lawful public meeting acts in a disorderly manner for the purpose of preventing the transaction of the business for which the meeting was called together shall be guilty of an offence ....

(2) Any person who incites others to commit an offence under this section shall be guilty of a like offence.

(3) If any constable reasonably suspects any person of committing an offence under the foregoing provisions of this section, he may if requested so to do by the chairman of the meeting require that person to declare to him immediately his name and address and, if that person refuses or fails so to declare his name and address or gives a false name and address he shall be guilty of an offence under this subsection and liable on summary conviction thereof to a fine not exceeding [level 1 on the standard scale.]

(4)This section does not apply as respects meetings to which section 97 of the Representation of the People Act 1983 applies.

NOTES

1. Subsection (3) was added by the Public Order Act 1936, s. 6. The maximum penalty under s. 1(1) is now six months' imprisonment, a fine not exceeding level 5 on the standard scale. The Act does not apply to election meetings, but they are protected by analogous provisions in the Representation of the People Act 1983, s. 97, as amended by the Representation of the People Act 1985, Sch. 4, para. 39. Breach of s. 97 is an 'illegal practice' under election law (see the 1983 Act, ss. 169, 173, 174). A power to arrest a suspect for failure to give a satisfactory name and address was repealed by the Police and Criminal Evidence Act 1984, Sch. 7, and replaced, in effect, by the 1984 Act, s. 25.[7]

2. In *Burden v Rigler*[8] justices hearing a prosecution brought under the Act held that any meeting on the highway was *ipso facto* unlawful. The Divisional Court held that the justices had 'no right to assume that, simply because the meeting was held on a highway it could be interrupted notwithstanding the provisions of the Public Meeting Act 1908'.[9] The case was remitted for the justices to consider *inter alia* whether there was an obstruction.

3. The House of Lords has recently held that the police had not aided a council to perform an unlawful act under s. 33 of the Race Relations Act 1976 where the police had deliberately supplied the council with false information in a successful attempt

---

2   See above, pp. 411–415.
3   Public Order Act 1936, s. 2(6), above, p. 414.
4   See below, pp. 523–526.
5   Below, pp. 548–556.
6   Below.
7   Above, p. 277.
8   [1911] 1 KB 337, DC.
9   Lord Alverstone CJ at 340.

to persuade the council to impose conditions on the hiring of a facility to host a Romany wedding. [10]

Criminal Justice and Public Order Act 1994

Disruptive trespassers

68. Offence of aggravated trespass

(1) A person commits the offence of aggravated trespass if he trespasses on land in the open air and, in relation to any lawful activity which persons are engaging in or are about to engage in on that or adjoining land in the open air, does there anything which is intended by him to have the effect—

    (*a*) of intimidating those persons or any of them so as to deter them or any of them from engaging in that activity,

    (*b*) of obstructing that activity, or

    (*c*) of disrupting that activity.

(2) Activity on any occasion on the part of a person or persons on land is 'lawful' for the purposes of this section if he or they may engage in the activity on the land on that occasion without committing an offence or trespassing on the land....

(5) In this section 'land' does not include—

    (*a*) the highways and roads excluded from the application of section 61 by paragraph (*b*) of the definition of 'land' in subsection (9) of that section; [11] . . .

69. Powers to remove persons committing or participating in aggravated trespass

(1) If the senior police officer present at the scene reasonably believes—

    (*a*) that a person is committing, has committed or intends to commit the offence of aggravated trespass on land in the open air; or

    (*b*) that two or more persons are trespassing on land in the open air and are present there with the common purpose of intimidating persons so as to deter them from engaging in a lawful activity or of obstructing or disrupting a lawful activity,

he may direct that person or (as the case may be) those persons (or any of them) to leave the land.

(2) A direction under subsection (1) above, if not communicated to the persons referred to in subsection (1) by the police officer giving the direction, may be communicated to them by any constable at the scene.

(3) If a person knowing that a direction under subsection (1) above has been given which applies to him—

    (*a*) fails to leave the land as soon as practicable, or

    (*b*) having left again enters the land as a trespasser within the period of three months beginning with the day on which the direction was given,

he commits an offence....

(4) In proceedings for an offence under subsection (3) it is a defence for the accused to show—

    (*a*) that he was not trespassing on the land, or

    (*b*) that he had a reasonable excuse for failing to leave the land as soon as practicable or, as the case may be, for again entering the land as a trespasser....

(6) In this section 'lawful activity' and 'land' have the same meaning as in section 68.

NOTES

1. The penalties for offences under ss. 68 and 69 are three months' imprisonment or a fine not exceeding level 4 on the standard scale or both (ss. 68(3), 69(3)). A constable

---

10 See *Hallam v Avery* [2001] UKHL 15, [2001] 1 WLR 655, HL.

11 I.e. highways other than a footpath, bridleway, by-way open to all traffic, road used as a public place or cycle track.

in uniform who reasonably suspects that a person is committing an offence may arrest him without a warrant (ss. 68(4), 69(5)).

2. Where the activity being disrupted is lawful in principle, the fact that minor breaches of laws of a collateral nature will not be a defence for someone charged under s. 68. Thus, the courts rejected an argument from demonstrators that the constructors at the Newbury Bypass were acting unlawfully where one of the chainsaw operators was not wearing gloves contrary to Health and Safety Regulations. [12]

3. Note that s. 68 creates a single offence capable of being committed by either intimidation, obstruction or disruption: see *Nelder v DPP*. [13] Note that the Trade Union Labour Relations (Consolidation) Act 1992, s. 241 creates an offence of hindering another in that other's work with a view to compelling him to abstain from that work. In *Todd v DPP* [14] T was arrested for the offence when in protesting at a motorway construction site, he prevented a crane operator from working. The magistrates held that the offence only applied in trade disputes, but the Divisional Court reversed that decision, holding that the offence should not be artificially confined. The offence is triable only summarily and carries a six-month maximum sentence.

4. In the debates on the 1994 Act in the House of Commons, the Home Secretary, Michael Howard, noted: [15]

> 'In recent months we have seen many examples of disruptive and threatening behaviour – at the Grand National, during country sports and even fishing. Those who dislike such activities have a perfect right to campaign to change the law, but they do not have the right to trespass, threaten and intimidate.'

The main target, however, appears to have been hunt saboteurs, and the new powers were so employed immediately when they came into force on the passing of the Act on 3 November 1994. [16] Note that a *trespassing* hunt is not a lawful activity. In *Nelder v CPS* [17] a group of protestors had sought to disrupt a fox hunt. They had done so when a section of the hunt was crossing a railway which the hunt had no right to do. The hunt had the authority to use all the adjoining land. The magistrate concluded that, since the initial purpose of the demonstration was to disrupt the hunt in general, and that was achieved while the hunt was, as a whole, still in progress, the fact that the disruption occurred in relation to only one part of the hunt at a point when that part of the hunt was trespassing, was not fatal to the charge. The court also held that there was no need to charge obstructing or disrupting on two separate offences. Does this mean that obstructing one horse or one hound is sufficient?

5. How will an officer know, under s. 68, whether someone is a trespasser unless he has the express information from the landowner? By requiring that the activity being disrupted is lawful, the Act raises the familiar issue of whether the activity must be something that is not expressly forbidden, or whether it is necessary for the those taking part in the activity to point to a specific legal right to act in that way. Note the ambiguity of the protection – it is afforded where people are 'about to engage in' the activity in question. Does this allow pre-emptive arrests the day before a hunt? Other words in the offence are equally vague – i.e. doing 'anything' intended to 'obstruct or disrupt'. Was the new offence necessary given the full breadth of s. 5 and the extremely broad powers of arrest for breach of the peace? Do all 'streakers' at cricket

---

12 *Hibberd v DPP* (1996) 27 November.
13 (1998) Times, 8 June, DC.
14 [1996] Crim LR 344.
15 235 HC Deb, 11 January 1994, col. 29.
16 See *Civil Liberty Agenda* 13 March 1995, p.7.
17 (1998) Times, 8 June, DC.

or other sporting events commit offence?[18] If the senior police officer's 'reasonable belief' is in fact incorrect, could that be raised as a matter of 'reasonable excuse' under sub-s. (4)? A person cannot be convicted under s. 68 unless the person engaged in the relevant lawful activity was present on the land at the time of the alleged trespass.[19]

6. The s. 68 offence has been used extensively in relation to anti-hunt demonstrators. In *Winder v DPP*[20] it was held that running towards a hunt in order to prevent it happening amounted to disruption. In that case the Divisional Court gave two examples of the breadth of the offences:

'Suppose a trespasser on open land says to a third party "go over the brow of that hill and there throw some stink bombs" so as to disrupt the lawful activity – be it a hunt, be it a concert, be it a birthday celebration for the farmer's daughter which is going on there. Is the trespasser guilty of the s. 68 offence, whether or not the third party throws the stink bombs and whether or no the members of the hunt know of the trespassers existence? Clearly the act of giving the instruction does not in itself disrupt but it is intended in due course to result in acts which have that effect. We think that the trespasser is guilty". The same goes for a trespasser who, wishing to disrupt a lawful activity, but out of sight, picks up a stone with a view to throwing it in the midst of those carrying out the lawful activity. We do not consider that the drafting of the section would require a court to hold that since picking up a stone in itself harmed no-one no offence was committed.'

The protesters in that case were trespassing, had an intention to disrupt the hunt and were running to the hunt to fulfil that purpose. The running, although not itself intended to disrupt the hunt, was sufficiently closely connected. An overt act which is intended to have the effect either of intimidating persons doing a lawful activity so as to deter them from engaging in it, or of disrupting or obstructing the activity is required in addition to trespass on land: *DPP v Barnard*[21] (mere 'occupation' of an open cast mine without proof of intimidation was insufficient). Note that since the lawful activity being disrupted must be in the open air, trespassing to intimidate those in animal research laboratories or hunt kennels will not fall within the offence.

7. In *Capon v DPP*[1] it was held that the actual commission of an offence of aggravated trespass was not a pre-condition to an officer issuing a direction under s. 69. The direction would be lawful where the officer had a genuine belief that the lawful activity would be obstructed. Anti-hunt campaigners stood by with a video camera to record a huntsman digging out a fox and were arrested for refusing to leave the land. The huntsman claimed that the video recording and presence was intimidating. The fact that the officer did not give details of the reason for arrest over and above a reference to 'aggravated trespass' did not render it invalid. The Crown Court held that the protesters were not in fact committing an offence under s. 68, but that did not affect the validity of the officers direction or arrest for failure to comply. The Divisional Court held that there was evidence to support the officer's belief that the protestors were committing the offence under s. 68. Furthermore, the officer's instruction, 'you either leave the land or you are arrested', was sufficient for a s. 69 direction. The case is discussed by D. Mead,[2] who is critical of the opportunity provided to the police to use vague language of this type to direct under the statute. He also points to the opportunity for the police to have 'two bites at the cherry' where the fact that they have arrested under the wrong power does not affect the validity of

18 On the campaign to allow nakedness in public, see the news reports for 29 August 2000, where Vincent Bethell's continued protests led to his imprisonment. These convictions were subsequently quashed.
19 *DPP v Tilly* [2001] EWHC Admin 821.
20 (1996) 160 JP 713.
21 (1999) Times, 9 November, DC.
1 (1998) Independent, 23 March, DC.
2 [1998] Crim LR 870.

their action. This is inconsistent with other arrest powers where the courts have required the correct offence to be specified. [3] He concludes that the case 'indicates a dangerous erosion by the higher courts of the freedom to protest peacefully by widening broad statutory wording even further and increasing the ambit of police discretion'. Would the case withstand challenge under Arts. 10 and 11?

8. The application of the sections has focused on the activities of hunt saboteurs and environmental protesters. [4] The introduction of the provisions has been reported as leading hunters to have high expectations about policing saboteurs. [5] Violence between hunt saboteurs and field sports enthusiasts nevertheless continues to occur. [6]

Sections 68–69 have also been used in relation to many high-profile environmental protests, notably the Newbury Bypass protests in 1996. The protest led to 988 arrests, including 356 for aggravated trespass. [7] Two hundred and fifty-eight were prosecuted and 59 cautioned. Bail conditions were imposed so as to prevent those charged returning to the site. [8] The conviction rate was 83%. [9] The s. 69 powers were less commonly applied, partly because of trespassers 'resident' at the site. [10] In 1995, 122 people were arrested for aggravated trespass. In 1996, 359 were prosecuted. In 1995 58% and in 1996 59% were convicted. [11] Only four people of those convicted received a prison sentence. T. Bucke and Z. James concluded that the power to issue directions was vital. It was used frequently, and meant that few arrests and prosecutions had to take place. [12]

> 'Contrary to what is sometimes thought, the CJPOA does not appear to have brought a wider range of public disorder within the orbit of policing. Nor does the CJPOA appear to have led to a significant change in the police preparedness to take action in those public order situations.' [13]

To what extent are these powers necessary? Are they compatible with Art. 11?

9. A problem with aggravated trespass powers (as with those in relation to removing trespassers) is that the arrest power, although a useful threat, is in practice unusable because it requires too many officers to be removed from the incident to escort arrestees. [14] The effect is that officers 'sought to keep the peace rather than enforce the law' when policing trespass. [15] Successful policing of these events also relies on the use of inter-force and national intelligence data – from the Animal Rights National Index. Some forces have teams of officers deployed on hunting throughout the season. An alternative approach adopted in some forces was to negotiate and coerce the parties and encourage the use of stewards at hunts. [16] The Criminal Justice and Public Order Act 1994 provides a 'bargaining chip' for police in such negotiations. [17] Some officers

---

3 See above, p. 285.
4 For an outline of the background regarding hunting and hunt saboteurs, see T. Bucke and Z. James, op. cit., pp. 34–36.
5 T. Bucke and Z. James, op. cit., p. 37.
6 See also details published on the Hunt Saboteurs Association website, www.enviroweb.org/has/. See also the Hunt Saboteurs Association response to the Criminal Justice and Police Act 2001: www.enviroweb.org/has/legal/endterm.html, claiming that arrests have been made under the Act on public roads.
7 T. Bucke and Z. James, op. cit., p. 49.
8 p. 50. See also the orders for costs against 75 defendants in *Department of Trade v Williams* (1995) 31 July, unreported.
9 p. 51.
10 See also CLA 1977, s. 6 (on restrictions regarding violent removal from premises). T. Bucke and Z. James, op. cit., p. 50.
11 p. 53.
12 p. 57.
13 p. 6.
14 Bucke and James, op. cit., p. 38.
15 p. 39.
16 p. 40.
17 p. 41.

regarded the provisions as extremely successful, others as 'difficult to enforce' and 'poorly worded'. [18] The evidential difficulties have been overcome in part by video-recording saboteurs. [19] The provisions are capable of very wide interpretation; the forms of intimidation referred to in the research conducted by T. Bucke and Z. James included 'wearing balaclavas'. [1]

The s. 69 power to direct protesters to leave has also proved difficult for the police to use, with saboteurs video recording the direction to challenge discrepancies and this has led the police to use a pre-printed form of words.[2] There has been controversy over who was the senior officer present at the scene, with some cases collapsing because magistrates interpreted that as meaning the officer in charge of the operation. One magistrate also took into account length of service in deciding the issue.[3] The power to arrest for returning to land after a direction to leave is very difficult to enforce because no personal details are recorded at the time (only one arrest was recorded by T. Bucke and Z. James).[4]

10. In *Percy v Hall*[5] P claimed that he had been falsely imprisoned by Ministry of Defence officers when present at the Menwith Hill Station. The arrests made by the officers under the relevant byelaws were held to be void for uncertainty in the earlier case of *Bugg v DPP,*[6] and P claimed that this rendered the arrests unlawful. The Court of Appeal reversed the trial judge's decision to follow *Bugg* and held the byelaws invalid. The fact that the byelaws were declared void in later proceedings did not render the officers liable for the tort of false imprisonment if they reasonably believed that byelaws were being broken. The court also rejected the decision in *Bugg* that the failure to define adequately the boundary of the area protected by the byelaw rendered it void for uncertainty.

(C) PREVENTIVE POWERS

(i) Powers of dispersal

According to the cases in this section, police or magistrates may take direct action against persons not acting unlawfully where necessary to preserve the peace. This action may include committing what would otherwise be assaults. [7] *Duncan v Jones* [8] goes one step further: it supports the proposition that resistance to a police order to disperse may constitute the offence of obstruction of the police in the execution of their duty. These cases have been adversely criticised by commentators, and recently the courts have recognised the need to clarify and restrict the law.

Humphries v Connor (1864) 17 ICLR 1, Court of Queen's Bench in Ireland

Anne Humphries sued Daniel Connor for assault. C pleaded that he was a sub-inspector of Constabulary in Cavan; and at the time of the committing of the alleged assault, H was walking through Swanlinbar at about noon wearing a party emblem (an orange lily) the wearing of which 'was calculated and tended to provoke animosity between different classes of Her Majesty's subjects'. A number of people were provoked by

---

18 p. 42.
19 p. 46.
 1 p. 43.
 2 p. 44.
 3 p. 45.
 4 p. 45.
 5 [1997] QB 924.
 6 [1993] QB 473.
 7 *Humphries v Connor*, below; *O'Kelly v Harvey*, below, p. 526.
 8 Below, p. 531.

the emblem, followed her, caused great noise and disturbance and threatened her with personal violence. She refused C's request to remove the emblem. C's pleadings continued:

'Whereupon the defendant ... in order to preserve the public peace, which was likely to be broken by and in consequence of the said conduct of the plaintiff, and to protect the plaintiff from the said threatened violence, and which violence the said several persons who were provoked by the conduct of the plaintiff, as aforesaid, in consequence of her said conduct, were likely to inflict on the plaintiff, and in order to restore order and tranquillity in said town, then gently and quietly, and *necessarily and unavoidably*, removed said emblem from the plaintiff, doing her no injury whatever; and in so doing, and for the purpose of so doing, *necessarily* committed the said alleged trespass ... and thereby protected the plaintiff from said threatened personal violence, which would otherwise have been inflicted on her, and preserved the public peace, which was likely to be, and would otherwise have been broken.'

The plaintiff demurred to this defence on the grounds that the wearing of the lily was a perfectly legal act, and afforded no excuse for any turbulence on the part of others, and that it was the duty of the defendant to protect the plaintiff and not to assault or restrain her in the exercise of a legal right. The court held that, on the assumption that the facts alleged were true, the defence was good in law.

O'Brien J: ... With respect to the first ground ... that it was defendant's duty as a constable to preserve the public peace, and to prevent the breach of it by disturbance or otherwise; and it appears to me that some of the authorities cited in the argument show that, under the circumstances stated in the defence, he was justified in acting as therein mentioned. The observations of Baron Alderson in *Cook v Nethercote* (1835) 6 C&P 741), and in *R v Brown* ((1841) Car &M 314), and those of Baron Parke, in *Ingle v Bell* ((1836) 1 M&W 516), show the power which policemen have, even to arrest a party, in order to prevent a breach of the peace being committed or renewed. In another case—*R v Hagan* ((1837) 8 C&P 167)—where it appeared that a man playing the bagpipes at night had attracted a crowd of dissolute persons about him, Coltman J, held that a constable who had directed the man to move on did not exceed his duty by merely laying his hand on the man's shoulder, with that view only.

According to the statements in this defence now before us, the act complained of ... though an assault in point of law, was not a greater one than those complained of in some of the cases referred to; and it was done by defendant for the purpose of preventing a breach of the public peace, &c., and was necessary for that purpose. It has, however, been urged by plaintiff's Counsel that injurious consequences would result from our decision in defendant's favour—giving to constables a power so capable of being abused. I think it sufficient, in answer to this argument, to say that our decision would not be applicable to a state of facts where the power was abused; and that it would not protect a constable from any unnecessary, excessive, or improper exercise of such power in other cases.

Hayes J: ... A constable, by his very appointment, is by law charged with the solemn duty of seeing that the peace is preserved. The law has not ventured to lay down what precise measures shall be adopted by him in every state of facts which calls for his interference. But it has done far better; it has announced to him, and to the public over whom he is placed, that he is not only at liberty, but is bound, to see the peace be preserved, and that he is to do everything that is necessary for that purpose, neither more nor less. What he does, he does upon the peril of answering to a jury of his country, when his conduct shall be brought into question, and he shall be charged either with exceeding or falling short of his duty. In the present case it is said that it would be a lamentable thing if an individual were to be obstructed and assaulted when doing a perfectly legal act; and that there is no law against wearing an emblem or decoration of one kind or another. I agree with that in the abstract; but I think it is not straining much the legal maxim, *sic utere tuo ut alienum non lædas*—to hold that people shall not be permitted to use even legal rights for illegal purposes. When a constable is called upon to preserve the peace, I know no better mode of doing so than that of removing what he sees to be the provocation to the breach of the peace; and, when a person deliberately refuses to acquiesce in such removal, after warning so to do, I think the constable is authorised to do everything necessary and proper to enforce it. It would seem absurd to hold that a constable may arrest a person whom he finds committing a breach of the peace, but that he must not interfere with the individual who has wantonly provoked him to do. But whether the act which he did was or was not, under all the circumstances, *necessary* to preserve the peace, is for the jury to decide. The defendant in his defence asserts that it was; and, for the purposes of this demurrer, we must take that assertion to be true. In my opinion the plea is good.

Fitzgerald J: ... I entertain a doubt—and I may add a very serious doubt—as to the correctness of the judgment of the Court, though I defer to the greater experience and sounder opinions of my Brothers.... With respect to a constable, I agree that his primary duty is to preserve the peace; and he may for that purpose interfere, and, in the case of an affray, arrest the wrong-doers; or, if a breach of the peace is imminent, may, if necessary, arrest those who are about to commit it, if it cannot otherwise be prevented. But the doubt which I have is, whether a constable is entitled to interfere with one who is not about to commit a breach of the peace, or to do, or join in any illegal act, but who is likely to be made an object of insult or injury by other persons who are about to break the Queen's peace....

I do not see where we are to draw the line. If a constable is at liberty to take a lily from one person, because the wearing of it is displeasing the others, who may make it an excuse for a breach of the peace, where as we to stop? It seems to me that we are making, not the law of the land but the law of the mob supreme, and recognising in constables a power of interference with the rights of the Queen's subjects, which, if carried into effect to the full extent of the principle, might be accompanied by constitutional danger. If it had been alleged that the lady wore the emblem with an intent to provoke a breach of the peace, it would render her a wrongdoer; and she might be chargeable as a person creating a breach of the peace.

NOTES

1. According to the pleadings the plaintiff's conduct was 'calculated and tended' to provoke animosity. The term 'calculated' normally means 'likely' rather than 'intended'. See G. Williams, *Textbook on Criminal Law*.[9] Note the difference of view as to the relevance of the plaintiff's intentions. What would be the position where a person totally unwittingly provokes a breach of the peace, as where a person wears an emblem unaware of any political connotations? Should the availability of this defence depend upon the state of mind of the person against whom the action is taken? If so, what should the relevant state of mind be? Note that assault can be committed by words alone.[10]

2. In *Hughes v Casares*,[11] the defendant, a police officer, was struggling with a person under arrest in the course of transferring him to a police car. The plaintiff stood in front of the door and did not move when requested. The defendant pushed the plaintiff aside and the latter fell injuring his ankle. His claim for damages failed. Blain J held that there was no evidence of deliberate or unnecessary violence, and that the defendant's reaction was reasonable and 'no more than the occasion demanded'.

3. The courts have, on a number of occasions, been faced with the difficult question of whether the police should exercise a power of arrest against:

(a) those exercising lawful free speech/assembly/procession, but who in doing so provoke hostile reactions from others; and/or

(b) those who are provoked by the speech/assembly/processions of those going about their lawful activity.

In considering the cases, some of which are among the most famous 'civil liberty' cases of the century, it is important to bear in mind several factors:

9 2nd edn, 1983, p. 141.
10 *R v Ireland* [1997] AC 148.
11 (1967) 111 Sol Jo 637.

(i)   Was the act of the speech/assembly/procession lawful?
(ii) Was the act intended to provoke violence (was it targeted at a group etc.)?
(iii) Was the act likely to provoke such violence?
(iv) Was there a reasonable opportunity for those provoked to avoid the provocative behaviour?

The leading case is now that of *DPP v Redmond Bate*.[12] For a detailed analysis of the earlier cases *Beatty v Gillbanks*,[13] *Wise v Dunning*,[14] *Duncan v Jones*[15] and *O'Kelly v Harvey*[16] see the fourth edition of this work[17] and K. D. Ewing and C. A. Gearty.[18] The European Court of Human Rights has also recognised that the right to assembly applies if there is a peaceful activity even if it results in disorder: *Christians against Racism and Fascism v United Kingdom*.[19]

In *Beatty v Gillbanks*[20] the Divisional Court had quashed the order against members of the Salvation Army, binding them over to keep the peace, when they had conducted marches which had provoked (predictable) violent response from the Skeleton Army. The case was regarded as a classic demonstration of the English common law protecting civil liberties.[21] *Wise v Dunning* distinguished *Beatty*. In that case a 'protestant crusade' through Roman Catholic areas produced violence. The Divisional Court held that, unlike in *Beatty*, the breaches of the peace were a natural consequence of the actions. See also the decision of the court in *O'Kelly v Harvey*[1] concerning a meeting of the Land League (an Irish organisation concerned with tenants rights) which was met by a counter demonstration. A magistrate laid a hand on the plaintiff member of the Land League to instruct them to disperse, and an action was brought for assault. The action failed, with the court holding that the magistrate was under a duty to disperse the crowd to prevent a breach of the peace.[2]

Redmond-Bate v DPP [1999] Crim LR 998, Queen's Bench Divisional Court

Three women Christian fundamentalists belonging to a small organisation called Faith Ministries preached to passers-by in the street. They had agreed with the local police that they would do this on occasion from the steps of Wakefield Cathedral. On Thursday 2 October 1997, the three women were preaching from the steps. A couple complained about them to PC Tennant. He investigated and as no crowd had gathered, he merely warned the three women not to stop people. Since they were not doing so, he left. Twenty minutes later he returned to find that a crowd of more than a hundred had gathered. Another of the women was now preaching, and some of the crowd were showing hostility towards them. Fearing a breach of the peace, PC Tennant asked the women to stop preaching, and when they refused to do so arrested them all for breach of the peace, Ms. Redmond-Bate was subsequently charged with obstructing a police officer in the execution of his duty.

Sedley LJ: She was convicted, and her appeal to the Crown Court was dismissed. By case stated she now appeals to this Court on the following questions of law:

12 [1999] Crim LR 998.
13 (1882) 9 QBD 308, DC.
14 [1902] KB 167, DC.
15 [1936] 1 KB 218.
16 (1883) 15 Cox CC 435, CA(I).
17 See S. H. Bailey, D. J. Harris and B. L. Jones, *Civil Liberties Cases and Materials* (4th edn, 1995), pp. 244–247.
18 Op. cit.
19 (1980) 21 DR 138, para. 4.
20 (1882) 9 QBD 308, DC.
21 See K. D. Ewing and C. A. Gearty, op. cit., pp. 30–33.
1   (1883) 15 Cox CC 435.
2   See 4th edn, op. cit.

(1) In the circumstances of this case, was it reasonable for the police officer to arrest the appellant who had not conducted herself in a manner which would be said to constitute an offence under the Public Order Act 1986 when any apprehension by the police officer of violence or threat of violence which could be said to likely to breach criminal law emanated from others present?

(2) Whether it was proper for the Court to conclude that such actual or threatened violence was or would be the natural consequence of the appellant's actions?

These questions are not ideally formulated. It has emerged by common consent in the course of argument that the underlying question is whether it was reasonable for PC Tennant in the light of what he perceived to believe that the appellant was about to cause a breach of the peace. To explain why, it is necessary first to consider the present law and then to look in a little more detail at the facts.

The law

Section 89(2) of the Police Act 1996 makes it an offence wilfully to obstruct a police constable in the execution of his duty. Among the duties of a constable is the prevention of breaches of the peace. A member of the public who fails to comply with a reasonable request properly made by a constable to this end is therefore guilty of obstructing the constable in the execution of his or her duty.

Counsel are agreed, and I agree, that the test of the reasonableness of the constable's action is objective in the sense that it is for the Court to decide not whether the view taken by the constable fell within the broad band of rational decisions but whether in the light of what he knew and perceived at the time the Court is satisfied that it was reasonable to fear an imminent breach of the peace. Thus although reasonableness of belief, as elsewhere in the law of arrest, is a question for the court, it is to be evaluated without the qualifications of hindsight.

But a judgment as to the imminence of a breach of the peace does not conclude the constable's task. The next and critical question for the constable, and in turn for the Court, is where the threat is coming from, because it is there that the preventive action must be directed. Classic authority illustrates the point. In *Beatty v. Gilbanks* (1882) 9 QBD 308 this Court (Field J. and Cave J.) held that a lawful Salvation Army march which attracted disorderly opposition and was therefore the occasion of a breach of the peace could not found a case of unlawful assembly against the leaders of the Salvation Army. Field J., accepting that a person is liable for the natural consequences of what he does, held nevertheless that the natural consequences of the lawful activity of the Salvation Army did not include the unlawful activities of others, even if the accused knew that others would react unlawfully. By way of contrast, in *Wise v. Dunning* [1902] 1 KB 167 a Protestant preacher in Liverpool was held by this Court (Lord Alverstone CJ., Darling and Channell JJ.) to be liable to be bound over to keep the peace upon proof that he habitually accompanied his public speeches with behaviour calculated to insult Roman Catholics. The distinction between the two cases is clear enough: the reactions of opponents would in either case be unlawful, but while in the first case they were the voluntary acts of people who could not properly be regarded as objects of provocation, in the second the conduct was calculated to provoke violent and disorderly reaction.

The facts in *Duncan v. Jones* [1936] 1 KB 218 were a sharper example of the second category: the appellant was about to make a public address in a situation in which the year before a disturbance had been incited by her speaking. This Court (Lord Hewart CJ., Humphreys and Singleton JJ.) cast its reasoning somewhat wider than – as it seems to me – is consonant with modern authority. Lord Hewart CJ., without explanation, described the decision in *Beatty v. Gilbanks* as 'somewhat unsatisfactory' – I confess that I do not understand why: it may have had to do with the Irish cases to which Mr. F. E. Smith, the appellant's counsel, had drawn the court's attention in *Wise v. Dunning*, citing Dicey in order to distinguish and criticise them. That *Beatty v. Gilbanks* was distinguishable, as Lord Hewart CJ went on to hold, is clear. But Humphreys J. added that the case had 'nothing to do with the law of unlawful assembly'. For reasons to which I now turn, I respectfully disagree. Although public order is now largely governed by statute, the law of unlawful assembly, upon which *Beatty v. Gillbanks* was decided, depended upon the liberty of the Salvation Army to march peacefully, albeit in large numbers and with much noise (described with perhaps a touch of colour in paragraph (f) of the case stated by the Weston-super-Mare Justices) through public streets: unless their doing so either amounted to a breach of the peace or was in the nature of things going to cause one, they were guilty of no offence. Exactly the same was true of Mrs. Duncan, with this qualification: she, like the present appellant, was charged with police obstruction, raising the question not directly of the quality of her conduct but of the reasonableness of the constable's apprehension of it. What the constable had to evaluate however, in that case as in this, was the reality of the risk of a breach of the peace. Where this case differs from *Duncan v. Jones* and resembles *Beatty v. Gilbanks* is in the source of the threat to public order: in the former case, on the Justices' findings, it was the appellant herself; in the present case the critical issue, if there was a true threat of breach of the peace, was where the threat was coming from.

. . . The foregoing is sufficient to enable us to deal with this case, but I believe that it is important for us before doing so to look at the human rights dimension of it. Parliament has now enacted the Human Rights Act 1998, requiring every public authority, including the police and the courts, to give effect to the scheduled Convention rights unless statutory provision makes it impossible to do so. The bulk of the Act is not yet in force: Ministers have announced their intention to bring it into force on 2nd October 2000. But in this interregnum it is far from immaterial. Not only is it now accepted that the common law should seek compatibility with the values of the Convention insofar as it does not already share them; executive action which breaches the Convention already runs the risk, if uncorrected by law, of putting the United Kingdom in breach of the Convention and rendering it liable to proceedings before the European Court of Human Rights. There is therefore, and has been for a long time, good reason for policing and law in this field to respect the Convention.

[His Lordship referred to Articles 9 and 10 of the ECHR]

For the appellant, Mr. Rouse initially placed Article 9 in the forefront of his argument. When the Act comes into force, Article 9 may become prominent in a case such as the present because of the presence in the Act of Section 13, which reads:

'(1) If a court's determination of any question arising under this Act might affect the exercise by a religious organisation (itself or its members collectively) of the Convention right to freedom of thought, conscience and religion [i.e. Article 9] it must have particular regard to the importance of that right.'

Without anticipating the problem which may arise of a conflict between section 13 and Article 17, it is sufficient that for the present section 13 cannot be relied on to prioritise Article 9 rights, with the result that in a case like the present they do not usefully add to the rights recognised by Article 10.

To speak of rights at all in this context is to recognise the constitutional shift which is now in progress. The old order is crystallised in Lord Hewart CJ's opening remarks in his judgment in *Duncan v. Jones*:

'There have been moments during the argument in this case when it appeared to be suggested that the court had to do with a grave case involving what is called the right of public meeting. I say "called" because English law does not recognise any special right of public meeting for political or other purposes. The right of assembly, as Professor Dicey puts it [*Law of the Constitution*, 8th Edition, page 499] is nothing more than a view taken by the court of the individual liberty of the subject.'

A liberty, as A. P. Herbert repeatedly pointed out, is only as real as the laws and bylaws which negate or limit it. A right, by contrast, can be asserted in the face of such restrictions and must be respected, subject to lawful and proper reservations, by the courts.

It is therefore both relevant and reassuring that the European Court of Human Rights in the case of *Steel and others v. The United Kingdom* (Case No. 67/1997 185111058, judgment given on 23rd September 1998), following its decision in *Benham v. United Kingdom*, has accepted that the concept of breach of the peace in English law is sufficiently certain to pass muster under Article 5 because it is confined to persons who cause or appear to be likely to cause harm to others or who have acted in a manner 'the natural consequence of which was to provoke others to violence'. Of the five applicants before the court, two had obstructed the lawful activities of others (in one case grouse shooting, in the other civil engineering) but three had peacefully handed out leaflets and manifested their opposition to arms sales in a public place. The first two were held to have been victims neither of a violation of Article 5 nor of Article 10 of the Convention; the other three were held to have been victims of breaches of both. Additionally the court held that the arrest and detention of the latter three protesters (the prosecution had been dropped) had been disproportionate to the aim of preventing disorder or of protecting the rights of others. One may venture the comment that the proportionality decision was no more than another way of saying that in the absence of any ground to anticipate violent or provocative behaviour from the three applicants, there was nothing by which the appropriateness of intervention in the interests of public order could be gauged. This apart, the decision demonstrates that the common law . . . is in conformity with the Convention.

This proposition has in my judgment no basis in law. A police officer has no right to call upon a citizen to desist from lawful conduct. It is only if otherwise lawful conduct gives rise to a reasonable apprehension that it will, by interfering with the rights or liberties of others, provoke violence which, though unlawful, would not be entirely unreasonable that a constable is empowered to take steps to prevent it.

. . . Before I set out my conclusion on the present case, two general comments may be in place. Police officers in a situation like this have difficult on-the-spot judgments to make. Because they are judgments which impinge directly on important civil liberties and human rights, the courts must in their turn scrutinise them with care. There is, however, nothing particularly obscure in the law as it now stands and as the Human Rights Act will shortly reinforce it. The question for PC Tennant was whether there was a threat of violence and if so, from whom it was coming. If there was no real threat, no question of intervention for breach of the peace arose. If the appellant and her companions were (like the street preacher in *Wise v. Dunning*) being so provocative that someone in the crowd, without behaving wholly unreasonably, might be moved to violence he was entitled to ask them to stop and to arrest them if they would not. If the threat of disorder or violence was coming from passers-by who were taking the opportunity to react so as to cause trouble (like the Skeleton Army in *Beatty v. Gilbanks*), then it was they and not the preachers who should be asked to desist and arrested if they would not.

The second general reflection is that the Crown Court was right to be alert to the fact that ours is a society of many faiths and none, and of many opinions. If the public promotion of one faith or opinion is conducted in such a way as to insult or provoke others in breach of statute or common law, then the fact that it is done in the name of religious manifestation or freedom of speech will not necessarily save it. It may forfeit the protection of Articles 9 and 10 by reason of the limitations permitted in both Articles (provided they are necessary and proportionate) in the interests of public order and the protection of the rights of others.

But turning to the facts of this case, I am unable to see any lawful basis for the arrest or therefore the conviction. PC Tennant had done precisely the right thing with the three youths and sent them on their way. There was no suggestion of highway obstruction. Nobody had to stop and listen. If they did so, they were as free to express the view that the preachers should be locked up or silenced as the appellant and her companions were to preach. Mr. Kealy for the prosecutor submitted that if there are two alternative sources of trouble, a constable can properly take steps against either. This is right, but only if both are threatening violence or behaving in a manner that might provoke violence. Mr. Kealy was prepared to accept that blame could not attach for a breach of the peace to a speaker so long as what she said was inoffensive. This will not do. Free speech includes not only the inoffensive but the irritating, the contentious, the eccentric, the heretical, the unwelcome and the provocative provided it does not tend to provoke violence. Freedom only to speak inoffensively is not worth having. What Speakers' Corner (where the law applies as fully as anywhere else) demonstrates is the tolerance which is both extended by the law to opinion of every kind and expected by the law in the conduct of those who disagree, even strongly, with what they hear. From the condemnation of Socrates to the persecution of modern writers and journalists, our world has seen too many examples of state control of unofficial ideas. A central purpose of the European Convention on Human Rights has been to set close limits to any such assumed power. We in this country continue to owe a debt to the jury which in 1670 refused to convict the Quakers William Penn and William Mead for preaching ideas which offended against state orthodoxy.

To proceed, as the Crown Court did, from the fact that the three women were preaching about morality, God and the Bible (the topic not only of sermons preached on every Sunday of the year but of at least one regular daily slot on national radio) to a reasonable apprehension that violence is going to erupt is, with great respect, both illiberal and illogical. The situation perceived and recounted by PC Tennant did not justify him in apprehending a breach of the peace, much less a breach of the peace for which the three women would be responsible. No more were the Magistrates justified in convicting the appellant or the Crown Court in upholding the conviction. For the reasons I have given, the constable was not acting in the execution of his duty when he required the women to stop preaching, and the appellant was therefore not guilty of obstructing him in the execution of his duty when she refused to comply.

Although, therefore, the Crown Court's questions do not pose the key issue, I would answer both questions in the negative and allow this appeal.

NOTES

1. Who interprets which of the parties is behaving unreasonably? The decision is an important demonstration by the English courts of a willingness to protect dissent in the public protest. The difficulty lies in determining whether the dissent was reasonable.[3] Do you agree with Selley LJ's view of the reasonableness of the conduct in *Duncan v Jones* and *Wise v Dunning*?

2. Note that the European Court of Human Rights has recognised that the protection of free speech extends to ideas which offend shock or disturb.[4]

3. In *Nicol and Selvanayagam v DPP*[5] the court held that because of the protestors' throwing of sticks into the water from which anglers were fishing in an attempt to prevent the fishing, there was likely to be a breach of the peace provoked by the protest. Do angler's have a right to fish? is it a contractual right with the landowner only, or something more fundamental? Should they have to identify a right to act in this way? Cf. the comments on *DPP v Jones* (above).

4. In *R v Coventry City Council, ex p Phoenix Aviation*[6] it was held that port and airport authorities were not entitled to bar live animal exports in response to unlawful threats.[7] A threat to disrupt imports and exports by protest could amount to a breach of EU law. If the law enforcement agency do not take appropriate measures to enable free movement of goods, the community rights of the importer will be infringed. The European Court has recognised that 'it is not impossible that the threat of serious disruption to public order may, in appropriate cases, justify non-intervention by the police': *EC Commission v France*.[8]

P. A. J. Waddington[9] has commented that:

'the ambiguous status of those who engage in illegal protest places the police in an equally ambiguous position. Confronting an unambiguous criminal, like the hypothetical armed robber, is morally straightforward: the police wear the proverbial white hat and the robber is the "bad guy" in the black hat - police use coercive force, possibly lethal, so as to protect the rest of us. However, if police intervene against protesters who are acting illegally, then they might find themselves wearing the "black hat". A nice illustration of the difficulty arose in the mid-1990s when protests were held at several British seaports against the export of live animals to

3   Compare Fitzgerald J in *O'Kelly*, above, p. 525.
4   *Müller v Switzerland* [1991] 13 EHRR 212.
5   [1996] Crim LR 318, DC.
6   [1995] All ER 37, DC.
7   On the Divisional Court and Court of Appeal decisions, see C. Barnard and I. Hare, (1997) 60 MLR 394, and on the EU dimension to the case see E. Baker, [2000] Crim LR 95. In *R v Chief Constable of Sussex, ex p International Traders Limited* [1999] 1 All ER 129; see E. Baker [2000] Crim LR 95 the House of Lords recognised the discretion of the Chief Constable to deploy his forces in operational matters.
8   [1997] ECR I-6959, para. 54.
9   P. A. J. Waddington, (1999) p. 68. See also on these disputes: C. Critcher, 'On the Waterfront: Applying the Flashpoints Model to Protest Against Live Animal Exports' in C. Critcher and D. Waddington (eds.), *Policing Public Order: Theoretical and Practical Issues* (1996).

continental Europe. There was almost universal agreement that the conditions that these animals would suffer at their destination was morally indefensible; indeed had been illegal in Britain since 1990. By enabling exporters to continue their trade, despite the opposition of protesters, the police effectively ensured that morally indefensible treatment of animals could continue. It was implausible for the police to shield behind the justification that they were merely enforcing the law, since in this case the law that sanctioned the suffering of animals was widely regarded as itself unjust (an alien imposition of the EU). Thus, by enforcing the law against protestors who were clearly acting illegally, the police found themselves "defending injustice" by coercing those who were upholding moral virtue.' [10]

Restriction on movement

Duncan v Jones [1936] 1 KB 218, 105 LJKB 71, 154 LT 110, 99 JP 399, 52 TLR 26, 79 Sol Jo 903, 33 LGR 491, 30 Cox CC 279, King's Bench Divisional Court

Case stated by the County of London Quarter Sessions.

At 1 p.m. on 30 July 1934, about thirty people, including the appellant, Mrs Katherine Duncan, collected with a view to holding a meeting in Nynehead Street, New Cross, Deptford, a cul-de-sac, near to the entrance to an unemployed training centre. The meeting was to protest against the Incitement to Disaffection Bill. At the entrance to Nynehead Street a notice was written across the roadway as follows:—

'SEDITION'

Meeting at the Test Centre to-day (now) 1 p m

Speakers:

A. Bing (Barrister-at-Law),
E. Hanley (Amalgamated Engineers' Union),
K. Duncan (National Unemployed Workers' Movement),
Defend the right of free speech and public meeting.

A box was placed in the roadway opposite the entrance to the training centre, on which the appellant was about to mount, when the chief constable of the district, with whom was Inspector Jones, told her that a meeting could not be held in Nynehead Street, but that it could be held in Desmond Street, some 175 yards distant. The appellant then said: 'I'm going to hold it,' stepped on to the box, and started to address the people who were present, when the respondent immediately took her into custody, to which she submitted without resistance.

D was convicted by a magistrate of obstructing J in the execution of his duty contrary to the Prevention of Crimes Act 1871, s. 12, as amended by the Prevention of Crimes Amendment Act 1885, s. 2. She was fined 40*s*, and appealed to London Quarter Sessions.

At the hearing of the appeal it was not alleged . . . that there was any obstruction of the highway or of the access to the training centre, save in the sense of the obstruction necessarily caused by the box which was placed in the roadway and by the presence of the people surrounding it. Neither was it alleged that the appellant nor any of the persons present at the meeting had either committed, incited or provoked any breach of the peace.

It was proved or admitted that on 25 May 1933, a meeting had been held opposite the entrance to the training centre, and the appellant had addressed that meeting. Following the meeting and on the same day a disturbance took place inside the training centre. The superintendent of the training centre, who attributed the disturbance to the meeting, sent for the police to prevent a breach of the peace. Subsequently, and in spite of the disturbance and

---

10 Ibid., p. 68. See also on these disputes C. Critcher, 'On the Waterfront: Applying the Flashpoints Model to Protest Against Live Animal Exports' in C. Critcher and D. Waddington (eds.), *Policing Public Order: Theoretical and Practical Issues* (1996).

of warnings by the police, the appellant, for some reason unexplained by her, made one or more attempts to hold a meeting at the same spot, which were frustrated by the police. Before 30 July 1934, the superintendent of the training centre, who feared a repetition of the previous disturbance, communicated with the police, and by reason of such communication and of reports by the police in the course of their duty, the chief constable of the district and the respondent apprehended that a breach of the peace would result if the meeting now in question were held.

The deputy-chairman of quarter sessions was of opinion: (1.) that in fact (if it be material) the appellant must have known of the probable consequences of her holding the meeting—namely, a disturbance and possibly a breach of the peace—and was not unwilling that such consequences should ensue; (2.) that in fact the respondent reasonably apprehended a breach of the peace; (3.) that in law it thereupon became his duty to prevent the holding of the meeting; and (4.) that in fact, by attempting to hold the meeting, the appellant obstructed the respondent when in the execution of his duty. The appeal was, therefore, dismissed. A case was stated for the opinion of the Court whether there was evidence on which the deputy-chairman could so decide in point of law.

Lord Hewart CJ: There have been moments during the argument in this case when it appeared to be suggested that the Court had to do with a grave case involving what is called the right of public meeting. I say 'called,' because English law does not recognize any special right of public meeting for political or other purposes. The right of assembly, as Professor Dicey puts it (Dicey's Law of the Constitution, 8th edn., p. 499), is nothing more than a view taken by the Court of the individual liberty of the subject. If I thought that the present case raised a question which has been held in suspense by more than one writer on constitutional law—namely, whether an assembly can properly be held to be unlawful merely because the holding of it is expected to give rise to a breach of the peace on the part of persons opposed to those who are holding the meeting—I should wish to hear much more argument before I expressed an opinion. This case, however, does not even touch that important question.

Our attention has been directed to the somewhat unsatisfactory case of *Beatty v Gillbanks* ((1882) 9 QBD 308). The circumstances of that case and the charge must be remembered, as also must the important passage in the judgment of Field J, in which Cave J concurred. Field J said (Ibid. 314): 'I entirely concede that everyone must be taken to intend the natural consequences of his own acts, and it is clear to me that if this disturbance of the peace was the natural consequence of acts of the appellants they would be liable, and the justices would have been right in binding them over. But the evidence set forth in the case does not support this contention; on the contrary, it shows that the disturbances were caused by other people antagonistic to the appellants, and that no acts of violence were committed by them.' Our attention has also been directed to other authorities where the judgments in *Beatty v Gillbanks* have been referred to, but they do not carry the matter any further, although they more than once express a doubt about the exact meaning of the decision. In my view, *Beatty v Gillbanks* is apart from the present case. No such question as that which arose there is even mooted here.

The present case reminds one rather of the observations of Bramwell B in *R v Prebble* ((1858) 1 F&F 325 at 326), where, in holding that a constable, in clearing certain licensed premises of the persons thereon, was not acting in the execution of his duty, he said:' It would have been otherwise had there been a nuisance or disturbance of the public peace, or any danger of a breach of the peace.'

The case stated which we have before us indicates a causal connection between the meeting of May 1933, and the disturbance which occurred after it—that the disturbance was not only *post* the meeting but was also *propter* the meeting. In my view, the deputy-chairman was entitled to come to the conclusion to which he came on the facts which he found and to hold that the conviction of the appellant for wilfully obstructing the respondent when in the execution of his duty was right. This appeal should, therefore, be dismissed.

Humphrey J: I agree. I regard this as a plain case. It has nothing to do with the law of unlawful assembly. No charge of that sort was even suggested against the appellant. The sole question raised by the case is whether the respondent, who was admittedly obstructed, was so obstructed when in the execution of his duty.

It does not require authority to emphasize the statement that it is the duty of a police officer to prevent apprehended breaches of the peace. Here it is found as a fact that the respondent reasonably apprehended a breach of the peace. It then, as is rightly expressed in the case, became his duty to prevent anything which in his view would cause that breach of the peace. While he was taking steps so to do he was wilfully obstructed by the appellant. I can conceive no clearer case within the statutes than that.

Singleton J: On the facts stated in the case I am satisfied that the respondent at the material time was doing that which it was his duty to do, and that, therefore, the obstruction of him by the appellant constituted obstruction of him when in the execution of his duty. Authorities in other branches of the law do not carry the matter any further. I agree that the appeal should be dismissed.

Appeal dismissed.

NOTES

1. This case has received widespread condemnation from academic commentators. See E. C. S. Wade; [12] *Williams*; [13] *Brownlie*; [14] T. C. Daintith. [15]
2. An alternative version of events is given in A. Barrister. [16] See also *Williams*, [17] on the ban on meetings.
3. 'The police are set up by this judgment as the arbiters of what political parties or religious sects shall and shall not be accorded the rights of freedom of speech and freedom of assembly.' [18] Do you agree?
4. How convincing is the finding of fact that a breach of the peace was reasonably apprehended? Consider the width of the discretion which may be exercised by the police. Is there any suggestion that the police action was *necessary* in the *last resort*? Should this be a precondition to dispersal of a lawful meeting? Note that the meeting in *Duncan v Jones* was not alleged to be unlawful. On the facts given, however, what offences might have been committed? To what extent is the decision reconcilable with *Redmond-Bate?* Was Mrs Duncan's behaviour any more likely to cause a breach of the peace than the preachers on the steps of Wakefield Cathedral?
5. K. D. Ewing and C. A. Gearty[1] note that much of the writing on *Duncan v Jones* was devoted to attempts to reconcile the case with *Beatty v Gillbanks*. They comment that the case represents 'the common law at its least persuasive' in its attempts to distinguish *Beatty*. They refer to the fact that the case provides the police with tremendously wide powers to deal with gatherings, and that the limits to these are kept vague. Indeed the 'last thing the authorities wanted' was precise clarification of the police powers by a detailed judgment of the court.[2] They also reveal that Home Office files show some anxiety about the extent of the decision and whether the police power to intervene was exercisable only on evidence of a previous disturbance. An official memo concluded that this was not a prerequisite and ended 'with an assurance to colleagues that "we may sleep in our beds"'![3]
6. Is it possible to reconcile *Duncan v Jones* with *Beatty v Gillbanks*[4] or *Redmond-Bate v DPP* (1) in law; (2) in spirit?[5] Does it matter, given that both are merely

12 (1937) 6 CLJ 175.
13 pp. 119–123.
14 pp. 111–115.
15 [1966] PL 248.
16 *Justice in England* (1938) pp. 247–260.
17 pp. 127–128.
18 R. Kidd, *British Liberty in Danger* (1940), p. 24.
 1 Op. cit., pp. 260–270.
 2 p. 269.
 3 p. 270.
 4 Above, p. 241.
 5 See T. C. Daintith, [1966] PL 248; S. A. de Smith, *Constitutional and Administrative Law*, (5th edn, 1985), pp. 513–518 (a passage omitted from subsequent editions).

decisions of the Divisional Court? An important point made by Daintith is that obstructing the police in the execution of their duty was a summary offence under a variety of statutory provisions at the time of *Beatty v Gillbanks* and could have been used by the prosecutor in that case. [6] He suggests that the reason why it was not used was that 'not until 1936 was it revealed that facts insufficient to establish the offence of unlawful assembly might yet amount to obstruction of the police in the execution of their duty .... [U]nless an assembly was unlawful, the police had no duty to disperse it ...'. [7]

7. Compare the reasoning in *Duncan v Jones* with that of *Thomas v Sawkins*, [8] and that of *R v Waterfield*. [9] Note that other cases have taken a more restrictive view of what conduct, and in particular, disobedience to what commands, may amount to obstruction of the police in the execution of their duty. [10]

8. D. N. Pritt, who defended Mrs Duncan in the court, sponsored by the NCCL, told the House of Commons: 'You can always lend an air of plausibility to the enterprise of stopping the meeting by offering ... an alternative site 175 yards away .... [I]f you cannot get an audience 175 yards away you might as well be 175 miles away'. [11]

9. The basic issue could be regarded as one of policy. Where X 'innocently' provokes Y to commit breaches of the peace, and the police wish to take direct action against X, the alternatives are (1) the police pay compensation (damages) to X (who is after all 'innocent'), with the money coming out of public (police) funds; or (2) the police needn't pay damages; [12] or (3) the police needn't pay damages, and any resistance is an offence. [13]

10. The police in practice rely on *Duncan v Jones* to control the numbers of pickets outside places of work, and the judges do not show much inclination to challenge assertions by police officers that they had reasonable grounds to apprehend breaches of the peace. See *Piddington v Bates*. [14] It has been extended to persons stopped at some distance from the place they appear to be intending to picket. [15] These cases should be read with caution in light of *DPP v Redmond-Bate*.

11. In *Forbutt v Blake, Reid v Eggins, Vickers v Pearson* [16] Connor ACJ in the Supreme Court of the Australian Capital Territory declined to follow *Duncan v Jones*. The case provides an excellent example of the clash of interests that might arise in these breach of peace cases. The appellants had been part of a group of about 15 young women who wished to protest about women raped in war. They proposed to march in or alongside the Anzac Day parade (which is equivalent to a Remembrance Day parade). They were dressed in black and some carried placards with inscriptions such as 'Patriots kill' and 'Heroes rape'. On the day in question they disobeyed an instruction from a police officer not to march and they were subsequently convicted of obstructing a police officer in the execution of his duty. Connor ACJ allowed their appeal. He held that there was prima facie evidence:

6 Op. cit., p. 251.
7 Op. cit., pp. 251–252.
8 Below, p. 548.
9 [1964] 1 QB 164.
10 Above, pp. 168–177.
11 314 HC Deb, 10 July 1936, col. 1551.
12 *Humphries v Connor*, above, p. 523.
13 *Duncan v Jones*, above, p. 531.
14 Below, p. 251.
15 See *Moss v McLachlan*, below, p. 538.
16 (1980) 51 FLR 465.

(1) that the police officer had reasonable grounds to believe that some members of the public might be provoked into committing acts against the group which would constitute a breach or breaches of the peace;
(2) that this was 'imminent': 'Imminence must be a relative concept and in these circumstances I would not hesitate to describe a breach of the peace which might well have occurred during the ensuing five to ten minutes as "imminent"'; [17]
(3) that the arrests were 'necessary to preserve the peace': it could not be said: 'that the peace could have been preserved equally well by less drastic means such as perhaps removing the placards and the wreath and ordering the members of the group to disperse'; [18]
(4) that the women were not committing an offence at the time the order was given and were not suspected to be about to commit any offence.

However, disobedience to the police order could not in these circumstances constitute the offence charged: the most the police 'could legally have done was to arrest the appellants in order to bring them before a court to seek to have them bound over to keep the peace': [19]

'If this were not so it seems to me that quite extraordinary results would follow. A policeman might bona fide form the view that the attendance of a person, holding an exalted public office, at an official function might provoke some errant members of the public to commit breaches of the peace. He could presumably order that person to stay away from the function and, if he disobeyed, could charge him with obstructing the police in the execution of their duty. Members of Parliament could thus be forbidden to address hostile audiences during election campaigns. It is to be observed that the penalty for the offence of obstructing the police, if tried on indictment, is imprisonment for two years. I am quite unable to attribute an intention to the legislature to expose a person to such a penalty for disobeying a police order to cease a lawful activity in circumstances where the only relevant police duty is to prevent a breach of the peace by other citizens against him. What was said by O'Brien J in *R v Londonderry Justices* (1891) 28 LR Ir 440 seems much in point: "If danger arises from the exercise of lawful rights resulting in a breach of the peace, the remedy is the presence of sufficient force to prevent the result, not the legal condemnation of those who exercise those rights".' [20]

His Lordship regarded *Wise v Dunning* [1] as authority for the proposition that:

'a binding over order may be available against a person who has not committed any offence in circumstances where the consequences of his lawful conduct is likely to produce a breach of the peace by other persons.' [2]

12. Article 11 sometimes requires the state to take positive measures to protect those seeking to exercise their right to peaceful assembly in the face of dissent: *Plattform 'Ärzte für das Leben' v Austria*. [3]

Piddington v Bates [1960] 3 All ER 660, [1961] 1 WLR 162, Queen's Bench Divisional Court

Eighteen men arrived to picket a printer's works where about eight of the normal complement of 24 were working. Chief Inspector Bates told the appellant that two

17 p. 471.
18 Ibid.
19 p. 476.
20 Ibid, at p. 450.
 1 [1902] 1 KB 167, DC (above, p. 526).
 2 p. 476.
 3 (1988) 13 EHRR 204, para. 32.

pickets at each of the two entrances were sufficient. He replied 'I'm going there and you can't stop me', 'I know my rights', and 'I can stand by the gate if I want to' and finally, 'I'm going to join them. If you don't want me to, you'd better arrest me'. He then pushed gently past the prosecutor and was gently arrested. He was convicted of obstructing the prosecutor in the execution of this duty, and appealed.

Lord Parker CJ:... First, the mere statement by a constable that he did anticipate that there might be a breach of the peace is clearly not enough. There must exist proved facts from which a constable could reasonably anticipate such a breach. Secondly, it is not enough that his contemplation is that there is a remote possibility; there must be a real possibility of a breach of the peace. Accordingly, in every case, it becomes a question of whether, on the particular facts, it can be said that where there were reasonable grounds on which a constable charged with this duty reasonably anticipated that a breach of the peace might occur ... The magistrate found, so far as it is material: 'Having regard to the whole of the evidence the [prosecutor] was in my opinion justified in anticipating the possibility of a breach of the peace unless steps were taken to prevent it, and in my opinion it was his duty to decide what those steps should be.' That is challenged by the defendant on two grounds. The first and lesser ground is a criticism of the word 'possibility' of a breach of the peace. It is said that there must be something more than a mere possibility. I agree with that, but I do not read the finding of the magistrate as saying that it was just a mere remote possibility. I think he was referring to it as a real possibility.

The other point goes to an analysis of the evidence, from which it is said that no reasonable man could possibly anticipate a breach of the peace. It is pointed out that there was no obstruction in the street; that there was no actual intimidation; and that there were no threats or intimations of violence. It is said that there was really nothing save the fact that picketing was going on to suggest that a breach of the peace was a real possibility.

As I have said, every case must depend upon its exact facts, and the matter which influences me in this case is the matter of numbers. It is, I think, perfectly clear from the wording of the case, although it is not expressly so found, that the police knew that in these small works there were only eight people working. They found two vehicles arriving, with 18 people milling about the street, trying to form pickets at the doors. On that ground alone, coupled with the telephone call which, I should have thought, intimated some sense of urgency and apprehension, the police were fully entitled to think as reasonable men that there was a real danger of something more than mere picketing to collect or impart information or peaceably to persuade. I think that in those circumstances the prosecutor had reasonable grounds for anticipating that a breach of the peace was a real possibility. It may be, and I think this is the real criticism, that it can be said: Well, to say that only two pickets should be allowed is purely arbitrary; why two? Why not three? Where do you draw the line? I think that a police officer charged with the duty of preserving the Queen's peace must be left to take such steps as on the evidence before him he thinks are proper. I am far from saying that there should be any rule that only two pickets should be allowed at any particular door. There, one gets into an arbitrary area, but so far as this case is concerned I cannot see that there was anything wrong in the action of the prosecutor.

Finally, I would like to say that all these matters are so much matters of degree that I would hesitate, except on the clearest evidence, to interfere with the findings of magistrates who have had the advantage of hearing the whole case and observing the witnesses....

Ashworth and **Elwes JJ** agreed.

Appeal dismissed.

NOTES

1. See also *Tynan v Balmer*[4] and *Kavanagh v Hiscock*.[5] P. Wallington[6] observes that 'any form of mass picketing almost inevitably involves the commission of offences,

4   [1967] 1 QB 91, DC.
5   [1974] QB 600, DC.
6   [1972] 1 ILJ 219, 222.

unless the pickets remain quiet and orderly, do not obstruct the street or the footway, and do as they are told by the police.'

2. *Duncan v Jones* appears to have been relied upon by the police during operations in respect of the miners' strike. For example, on 18 March 1984 the police attempted to stop anyone who appeared to be a miner or who was travelling north to aid the strike from crossing the Thames via the Dartford Tunnel. [7] Miners claimed that they had been told they would be arrested if they crossed the county boundary; the police claimed that they were warned that they could later be arrested for causing a breach of the peace. On the assumption that the miners' version is correct, would that fall within the principle of *Duncan v Jones*? Would the police be entitled to prevent a 'working miner' entering a pit on the ground that this would provoke pickets to commit breaches of the peace? [8] Why do you think the police did not take such action? [9] On the use of bail conditions to restrict picketing, see *R v Mansfield Justices, ex p Sharkey.* [10]

3. The current statutory protection for peaceful picketing is s. 220 of the Trade Union and Labour Relations (Consolidation) Act 1992:

'(1) It shall be lawful for a person in contemplation or furtherance of a trade dispute to attend
    (a) at or near his own place of work; or
    (b) if he is an official of a trade union, at or near the place of work of a member of that union whom he is accompanying and whom he represents,
for the purpose only of peacefully obtaining or communicating information, or peacefully persuading any person to work or abstain from working.'

This protects pickets from civil actions in trespass or for inducing breaches of contract, but not in respect of unreasonable obstruction of access to premises, unreasonable obstruction of the highway or simply attendance in large numbers (whose purposes will not be regarded as 'peacefully obtaining or communicating information' etc.: *Thomas v National Union of Mineworkers (South Wales Area).* [11] It also absolves a picket from criminal liability 'where an act which is reasonably necessary for the communication of information involves a criminal act, such as technical obstruction'. [12] Again this will not extend to unreasonable obstructions of the highway [13] or offences such as breaches of the Public Order Act 1986, [14] and breaches of s. 241 of the Trade Union and Labour Relations (Consolidation) Act 1992; [15] *Galt v Philp.* [16] In 1980, the government (with Parliament's approval) issued a Code of Practice on picketing and a revised version was issued in 1992 [17] which, *inter alia*, states that 'pickets and their organisers should ensure that in general the number of pickets does not exceed six at any entrance to or exit from a workplace; frequently a smaller number will be appropriate'. [18] A person's failure to observe the code 'shall not of itself render him liable to any proceedings' but in proceedings before a court

7 See S. Miller and M. Walker, *A State of Siege* (A Report to the Yorkshire Area NUM) (1984) pp. 19–23.
8 Cf. (1984) 134 NLJ 325–326.
9 See also *Moss v McLachlan* below, pp. 538–541.
10 [1985] 1 All ER 193, DC.
11 [1985] 2 All ER 1 at 20. P. Wallington, *Butterworth's Employment Law Handbook* (1999).
12 R. Kidner, *Trade Union Law* (2nd edn, 1983) p. 187; G. Pitt, *Employment Law* (2000) pp. 436–446.
13 *Tynan v Balmer* [1967] 1 QB 91.
14 Above.
15 See Kidner, pp. 194–198.
16 [1984] IRLR 156; K. Miller, (1984) 13 ILJ 111.
17 P. Wallington, op. cit., para. 4066, Employment Code of Practice (Picketing) Order 1992, S.I. 1992 No. 476.
18 Para. 51.

or tribunal the code is admissible in evidence and, if relevant, is to be 'taken into account'.[19] The code has been used as the basis of the grant of injunctions limiting the number of pickets in attendance at a particular place to six.[20] No one can be obliged to stop and listen[21] and s. 220 does not confer a right to attend on land against the wishes of the owner of that land.[1] Note the possibility of prosecution under the Protection from Harassment Act 1997, or civil action under that statute.

Moss v McLachlan (1984) 149 JP 167, [1985] IRLR 76, Queen's Bench Divisional Court

During the miners' strike a number of police officers were stationed at Junction 27 on the M1, which was $1^1/_2$–2 miles from two collieries, which were $^1/_2$ mile away from each other, and 4–5 miles from two others, also $^1/_2$ mile apart. Their object was to stop cars carrying persons who appeared to be striking miners. Those who satisfied them that they were not were allowed to proceed; the rest would be turned back. Moss and three others were travelling in a convoy of 25 cars carrying 60–80 striking miners (clearly identifiable as such from their badges and stickers on their cars). The police told them of their fear that a breach of the peace would occur if they continued, and that if they did so they would be liable to arrest for obstructing the police in the execution of their duty. After 40 minutes or so, 40 miners who attempted to force their way through the police cordon were arrested on the ground that the police feared a breach of the peace at one of the four collieries. Moss and three others were among those subsequently convicted of obstruction offences and appealed to the Divisional Court by case stated. They conceded that they had wilfully obstructed the officers but argued that the latter had not been acting in the execution of their duty. The Divisional Court dismissed the appeal.

The judgment of the court (**Skinner** and **Otton JJ**) was delivered by **Skinner J**: ....

Subject to one submission by Mr. Mansfield, to which I shall return later, the law on this subject is clear. If a constable apprehends, on reasonable grounds, that a breach of the peace may be committed, he is not only entitled but is under a duty to take reasonable steps to prevent that breach occurring.

The magistrates concluded that 'The police honestly and on reasonable grounds feared that there would be a breach of the peace if there were a mass demonstration at whichever Nottinghamshire colliery the appellants and their colleagues chose to congregate.'

The appellants submit that there was no finding of fact by the magistrates to support that conclusion: there was no conduct from which any constable could reasonably have apprehended a breach of the peace. Mr. Mansfield submits that the conduct in question must be conduct by the appellants themselves in the presence of the arresting officer, though he concedes that the latter is entitled to take into account the conduct of a group of which the appellants were members. He also contends that the fears must be specific. It is not enough, he says, to fear a breach of the peace at one or more of the collieries involved by some or all of the miners involved. The officer must be able to say which pit, which miners and when.

Mr. Milmo replies that a police officer has to look at all the facts within his knowledge. He has the power to act if they raise in his mind a fear that the person or persons he is dealing with may cause a breach of the peace, even if he cannot precisely pinpoint when and where.

---

19 1992 Act, s. 207.
20 *Thomas v NUM (South Wales Area)*, above; *News Group Newspapers Ltd v Society of Graphical and Allied Trades 1982* [1986] ICR 716.
21 *Broome v DPP* [1974] AC 587, HL; *Kavanagh v Hiscock* [1974] QB 600, DC.
 1 *British Airports Authority v Ashton* [1983] 3 All ER 6, DC. See further on picketing: G. Pitt, op. cit.; N. Selwyn, *Law of Employment* (11th edn, 2000), pp. 500–507; P. Davies and M. Freedland, *Labour Law: Text and Materials*, (1984), pp. 842–861; R. Kidner, *Trade Union Law* (2nd edn, 1983), Chap. 11.

On this basis he relies on the magistrates' findings that: (a) there were four pits within five miles of the cordon; (b) over 25 cars carrying over 60 striking miners were involved in the attempt to break through the police cordon; (c) while waiting at the junction, angry shouts from the National Union of Mineworkers members at passing National Coal Board lorries and other comments by them made it plain that the police's suspicions that the men were intent on a mass demonstration or picket were justified; (d) the police suspicions that the gathering of a large picket would lead to a breach of the peace were based on their own experiences in the current and other trade disputes, on the knowledge gleaned from those experiences, from their colleagues and from the widespread public dissemination of the news that there had been severe disruptions of the peace, including many incidents of violence, at collieries within the Nottinghamshire coalfield area in the days and weeks of the dispute before April 20, 1984. The officers however had no way of knowing which colliery it was the intention of the miners to picket.

The appellants say this is not enough. The police were not entitled to take into account the experience of others or what they had heard or read on television or in the press. They could only prevent the men from proceeding if it was clear from the words and deeds of the men at the junction that a breach of the peace was intended.

In our judgment there was ample evidence before the magistrates to support their conclusion. That is enough to dispose of Mr. Mansfield's argument that the magistrates here were dealing with action by the police to prevent the appellants from exercising their undoubted right to demonstrate peacefully in order to show support for and solidarity with fellow trade unionists.

On the magistrates' findings of fact anyone with knowledge of the current strike would realize that there was a substantial risk of an outbreak of violence. The mere presence of such a body of men at the junction in question in the context of the current situation in the Nottinghamshire coalfields would have been enough to justify the police in taking preventive action. In reaching their conclusion the police themselves are bound to take into account all they have heard and read and to exercise their judgment and common sense on that material as well as on the events which are taking place before their eyes.

The situation has to be assessed by the senior police officers present. Provided they honestly and reasonably form the opinion that there is a real risk of a breach of the peace in the sense that it is in close proximity both in place and time, then the conditions exist for reasonable preventive action including, if necessary, the measures taken in this case.

The findings of fact by the magistrates therefore dispel any suggestion that (1) the belief of the officers present was other than honest or reasonable, or (2) that the steps taken were other than reasonable.

But, says Mr. Mansfield, the police can only take preventive action if a breach of the peace is imminent and there was no such imminence here. In support of this proposition he relied on a passage in the judgment of Watkins LJ in *R v Howell* (1982) 146 JP 13, [1981] 3 All ER 383 at p 388: '... there is a power of arrest for breach of the peace where ... (2) the arrestor reasonably believes that such a breach will be committed in the immediate future by the person arrested although he has not yet committed any breach ....'

This passage must be read in the light of the judgment of Parker LCJ in *Piddington v Bates* [1960] 3 All ER 660 at 663, in which he says the police must anticipate 'a real, not a remote, possibility' of a breach of the peace before they are justified in taking preventive action.

We do not think that there is any conflict between the two approaches. The possibility of a breach must be real to justify any preventive action. The imminence or immediacy of the threat to the peace determines what action is reasonable. If the police feared that a convoy of cars travelling towards a working coal field bearing banners and broadcasting, by sight or sound, hostility or threats towards working miners might cause a violent episode, they would be justified in halting the convoy to inquire into its destination and purpose. If, on stopping the vehicles, the police were satisfied that there was a real possibility of the occupants causing a breach of the peace one and a half miles away, a journey of less than five minutes by car, then in our judgment it would be their duty to prevent the convoy from proceeding further and they have the power to do so.

If and in so far as there may be any differences between the two approaches (and we do not believe there is), we respectfully prefer that of Lord Parker LCJ in *Piddington v Bates*.

We also repeat the words of Parker LCJ, at p. 663 of that case: 'For my part, I think that a police officer charged with the duty of preserving the Queen's peace must be left to take such steps as, on the evidence before him, he thinks proper.'

For the reasons we have given, on the facts found by the magistrates, a breach of the peace was not only a real possibility but also, because of the proximity of the pits and the availability of cars, imminent, immediate and not remote. In our judgment the magistrates were correct in their reasoning and conclusions and we would dismiss these appeals.

NOTES

1. See the generally critical comments of R. East and P. A. Thomas;[2] G. S. Morris;[3] F. P. Davidson;[4] A. L. Newbold.[5]

2. How can this decision stand alongside *Foulkes v Chief Constable of Merseyside* (above, p. 466) requiring an immediate threat to the peace?

3. Following *Redmond-Bate*, are *Piddington v Bates* and *Moss v McLachlan* good law?

4. *Duncan v Jones* and *Moss v McLachlan* were relied upon in *R v Secretary of State for Northern Ireland, ex p Atkinson.*[6] Hutton J as he then was, rejected A's application for judicial review seeking a declaration that the police had acted unlawfully in preventing the Magherafelt Ulster Democratic Unionist Party Flute Band joining a band parade at Keady, County Armagh. The great majority of the citizens of Keady were Nationalist, but the Keady No Surrender Branch Club of the Apprentice Boys of Derry decided to hold a very large parade at Keady on 8 August 1986, to which over 100 Apprentice Boys of Derry Clubs and over 100 bands and Orange Lodges were invited. Conditions were attached to the route of the parade under Art. 4(1) of the Public Order (Northern Ireland) Order 1981[7] on the ground that the parade might occasion a breach of the peace or serious public disorder (the test under Art. 4(1)). Concerned that there was still a risk of very serious public disorder, and unwilling to seek a ban on the parade, the police decided that in an attempt to prevent or minimise the risk, bands which had a reputation for, and record of, disorderly behaviour should be prevented from travelling to Keady to take part in the parade. (In the event, serious disorder did indeed occur.) The Magherafelt band was stopped by the police between Moneymore and Cookstown, but allowed to proceed to take part in the parade having left their instruments at Magherafelt.

Hutton J held: (1) that there were ample facts from which police officers could reasonably have anticipated a grave breach of the peace in Keady that evening; (2) that this risk was a strong probability and not merely a remote possibility; (3) that the police had reasonable grounds for believing their actions in stopping the band were necessary to preserve the peace (a test derived from *O'Kelly v Harvey*[8] to be applied in preference to that of Lord Parker in *Piddington v Bates*[9] ('such steps as, on the evidence before him, he thinks are proper') in so far as the tests were different); (4) that this was so notwithstanding that the distance at which the band was stopped was much further than that in *Moss v McLachlan*: 'the police had reasonable grounds for fearing that their task of seeking to preserve the peace in Keady and limiting the spread of disorder, if a breach of the peace occurred, would be much more difficult if they stopped the bus in close proximity to Keady ...';[10] (5) that the band had a record

2 (1985) 135 NLJ 63, (1985) 12 JLS 77.
3 (1985) 14 ILJ 109.
4 (1985) 19 LT 142.
5 [1985] PL 30.
6 [1987] 8 NIJB 6, Queen's Bench Division (Crown Side), High Court in Northern Ireland.
7 See now Art. 4 of the 1987 Order.
8 Above, p. 526.
9 Above, p. 535.
10 p. 23.

of disorderly behaviour and the police had reasonable grounds for fearing that it would have an inflammatory effect if it took part in the parade.

5. *Holmes v Bournemouth Crown Court*[11] is a particularly disturbing decision. H, a 'scruffy' anti-smoking campaigner, took up a position within five or six feet of delegates attending the Conservative Party conference rather than in a designated lobbying area further away. He held up a placard and shouted messages about the danger of smoking but at no time used, offered or threatened violence or did anything amounting to a breach of the peace. He refused to comply with the request of police officer, PC Caddy, that he move into the designated area, and was arrested, and subsequently convicted of obstructing PC Caddy in the execution of his duty. The judges of the Crown Court accepted PC Caddy's evidence that if H stayed in his original position he feared 'there might be a breach of the peace', and stated that they considered it reasonable for PC Caddy to entertain that fear, and found that he was acting in the execution of his duty. The Divisional Court (Kennedy LJ and Pill J) upheld the decision. Pill J stated:

'The police have a duty to take all reasonable steps which appear to be necessary to keep the peace. It needs no underlining in this Court that there are security risks at the annual conferences of the major political parties. The police must take reasonable steps to keep the peace and prevent crimes being committed against those lawfully attending conferences, whether they do so as delegates or in any other capacity. The proper discharge of that duty may involve placing restrictions upon the positions which may be taken up by those wishing to lobby delegates and others attending the conference centres. The police clearly must plan a security operation in advance if security at such a conference is to be effective. It does not necessarily take action outside the proper discharge of police duties that the effect of the measures they take may be to exclude law-abiding members of the public from certain areas.'

Here the attention of the court seems focused on the facilitation of the security operation rather than (as it should have been) on the question whether H's conduct gave rise to a risk of a breach of the peace. Is the conclusion of the judges of the Crown Court remotely plausible? What breach of the peace was to be anticipated – that smokers among the delegates might stub out their cigarettes on H in annoyance at his slogans? Was H's conduct ever anything other than reasonable?

(ii) Binding over [12]

The English Law Commission has recommended the abolition of the binding over power on following grounds: (1) the criminal sanctions now applicable to many of the forms of anti-social practice for which a binding-over was formerly used (e.g. the Public Order Act, ss. 4, 5, the Sexual Offences Act 1985 (kerb crawling), the Malicious Communications Act 1988 (poison pen letters), the Telecommunications Act 1984, s. 43 (covering, *inter alia*, persistent telephoning to cause annoyance, inconvenience or distress)); (2) modern developments in cautioning and diverting anti-social offenders from the criminal court system; (3) the many defects in practice in procedure which could not satisfactorily be cured without 'depriving the procedure of the informality which is regarded as one of its main attractions'. The conclusion in favour of abolition was buttressed by the belief that binding-over fell short of the requirements of the European Convention on Human Rights (in fact here reflecting fundamental principles

11 (1993) 6 October, unreported, DC.
12 On binding-over generally see G. Williams, 'Preventive Justice and the Rule of Law' (1953) 16 MLR 417; *Williams*, Chap. 4; *Brownlie*, pp. 312–315; (1961) 25 J Cr L 220; A. D. Grunis, [1976] PL 16; D. G. T. Williams, [1970] CLJ 96, 104–106; M. Dodds, (1985) 149 JPN 259, 278; Law Commission Report No. 222, *Binding Over* (Cm. 2439, 1994). On the historical origins, see D. Feldman, 'The King's Peace, the Royal Prerogative and Public Order: the Roots and Early Development of Binding Over Powers' [1988] CLJ 101.

of English law) as to the certainty and ascertainability of a citizen's obligations, the limitations on arrest and detention (Art. 5), the requirements of a fair trial (Art. 6) and the guarantees of free expression and assembly (Arts. 10 and 11). [13]

> 'These objections are, in summary, that the conduct which can be ground for a binding over order is too vaguely defined; that binding over orders when made are in terms which are too vague and are therefore potentially oppressive; that the power to imprison someone if he or she refuses to consent to be bound over is anomalous; that orders which restrain a subject's freedom can be made without the discharge of the criminal, or indeed any clearly defined, burden of proof; and that witnesses, complainants or even acquitted defendants can be bound over without any adequate prior information of any charge or complaint against them.' [14]

In light of this, is it not odd that the Court of Human Rights condoned the use of the power in *Steel*? [15]

The common law power of justices (and any court of record having a criminal jurisdiction: Justices of the Peace Act 1968, s. 1(7); Administration of Justice Act 1973, Sch. 5) to bind persons over to keep the peace, and their wider power under the Justices of the Peace Act 1361 (34 Edw III c 1) to bind persons over to be of good behaviour, have frequently been employed in the context of public order. The power to require a person to enter into a recognisance to keep the peace, either generally, or towards a particular person, may be exercised where there is reasonable apprehension of a future breach of the peace. [16] The recognisance may be forfeited by any unlawful action that 'either is or tends to a breach of the peace'. [17]

The statutory power 'to take of all of them that be [not] of good fame, where they shall be found, sufficient surety and mainprise of their good behaviour towards the King and his people ...', according to *Blackstone*, [18] may be exercised:

> 'for causes of scandal, *contra bonos mores*, as well as *contra pacem*: as, for haunting bawdy-houses with women of bad fame; or for keeping such women in his own house; or for words tending to scandalize the government, or in abuse of the officers of justice, especially in the execution of their office. Thus also a justice may bind over all night-walkers; eavesdroppers; such as keep suspicious company, or are reported to be pilferers or robbers; such as sleep in the day, and wake in the night; common drunkards; whore-masters; the putative fathers of bastards; cheats; idle vagabonds; and other persons whose misbehaviour may reasonably bring them within the general words of the statute, as persons not of good fame ...'

NOTES

1. An order may be made on a complaint to a magistrates' court under s. 115 of the Magistrates' Courts Act 1980; however, the binding-over powers may be exercised by justices of the peace at any stage of other proceedings. An appeal lies against a binding-over order made by a magistrates' court to the Crown Court (Magistrates' Courts (Appeals from Binding Over Orders) Act 1956; the appeal should be conducted by way of rehearing: *Shaw v Hamilton*), [19] or, by case stated on a point of law, to the Divisional Court (e.g. *Beatty v Gillbanks*; [20] *Wise v Dunning*). [21] An order may be

13 Op. cit., pp. 59–67.
14 Law Commission, Report No 222, *Binding Over* (1994), para. 6.27.
15 Above.
16 See above pp. 466–469.
17 *Blackstone*, Book IV, Chap. XVIII.
18 Ibid.
19 [1982] 2 All ER 718, DC.
20 Above, p. 526.
21 Above, p. 526.

challenged on an application for judicial review (see *R v Londonderry Justice*;[22] *R v Central Criminal Court, ex p Boulding*;[1] *R v Ilminster Justices, ex p Hamilton*[2] (binding-over orders quashed on the ground of breach of natural justice); *R v Morpeth Ward Justices, ex p Ward*[3] (the court noting, however, that the appeal by case stated was normally the appropriate method of challenge)). The common law powers date back to time immemorial.[4] Early statutes empowered Justices of the Peace to prevent, and punish, threats to the 'king's peace'. Justices could require a person to enter into a recognisance, with or without sureties to 'keep the peace' or 'be of good behaviour'.
2. The person bound over must be one who is or whose case is before the court, but no conviction is required.[5] The Justices of the Peace Act 1361 does not require any complaint to have been made before a magistrates' court has the power to bind someone over. However, under s. 115 of the Magistrates' Courts Act 1980, a binding-over order can only be made after a complaint has been made and adjudged to be true.[6] In *R v Coventry Magistrates' Court, ex p CPS*[7] the difficulty in defining whether the power was criminal or civil arose when issues of costs were disputed. Although breach of the peace is not an offence, the complaint under s. 115 of the Magistrates' Courts Act 1980 is a criminal matter.

In *R v South Molton Justices, ex p Ankerson*,[8] Taylor LJ stated[9] that when justices are minded to order a binding-over (sc. to keep the peace):

'(1) there should be material before them justifying the conclusion that there is a risk of a breach of the peace unless action is taken to prevent it. (2) They must indicate to the defendant their intention to bind him over and the reasons for it so that he or his lawyer can make representations. (3) They must obtain consent to the bind-over from the defendant himself. (4) Before fixing the amount of the recognisance they should inquire as to the defendant's means. (5)The binding-over should be for a finite period.'

Point (4) has been emphasised on a number of occasions: see *R v Central Criminal Court, ex p Boulding*;[10] *R v Atkinson*;[11] *R v Crown Court at Nottingham, ex p Brace*.[12] In *R v Clerkenwell Metropolitan Stipendiary Magistrate, ex p Hooper*[13] the Divisional Court held that legal representatives should be given an opportunity to make representations before making an order requiring a defendant to provide a surety with a term of imprisonment in default. See also the decision in *R v Lincoln Crown Court, ex p Jude*,[14] emphasising the importance of allowing representation and inquiry into means.
3. The binding over power has been subjected to scrutiny by the European Court of Human Rights on a number of occasions.[15] In *Steel v United Kingdom*[16] the Court reviewed the position of breach of the peace:

22 (1891) 28 LR Ir 440.
 1 [1984] 1 All ER 766, DC.
 2 (1983) Times, 23 June, DC.
 3 (1992) 95 Cr App Rep 215, DC.
 4 D. Feldman, op. cit.
 5 *R v Kingston upon Thames Crown Court, ex p Guarino* [1986] Crim LR 325.
 6 *CPS v Speede* (1997) 17 December, DC. See *R v Middlesex CC, ex p Khan* (1997) 161 JP 240, DC – holding that a mere belief that the defendant might pose a threat was insufficient.
 7 [1996] Crim LR 723.
 8 (1989) 90 Cr App Rep 158.
 9 At 162.
10 Above.
11 (1988) 10 Cr App Rep (S) 470, CA (Cr D).
12 (1989) 154 JP 161, CA.
13 [1998] 1 WLR 800.
14 [1998] 1 WLR 24.
15 See D. Mead, [1999] J Civ Lib Law 7.
16 Above, p. 460.

'10. The Government submitted that it was clear from national case-law that an order to be bound over to keep the peace and be of good behaviour required the person bound over to avoid conduct involving violence or the threat of violence or unreasonably giving rise to a situation where there was a real risk that violence might occur. The magistrates had acted within the law in committing Ms Steel and Ms Lush to prison for refusing to be bound over.

11. The applicants argued that it was unclear, first, what conduct could trigger an order to be bound over to keep the peace and be of good behaviour and, secondly, what conduct would amount to a breach of such an order; the expression *contra bonos mores* in particular was very vague . . . In addition, there was no limit to the possible duration of an order, the amount of the recognizance or, under the common law, the length of detention following refusal to enter into an order.

12. The Court will also examine whether the binding-over orders applied to the applicants were specific enough properly to be described as "lawful order[s] of a court".

In this respect it notes that the orders were expressed in rather vague and general terms; the expression "to be of good behaviour" was particularly imprecise and offered little guidance to the person bound over as to the type of conduct which would amount to a breach of the order. However, in each applicant's case the binding-over order was imposed after a finding that she had committed a breach of the peace. Having considered all the circumstances, the Court is satisfied that, given the context, it was sufficiently clear that the applicants were being requested to agree to refrain from causing further, similar, breaches of the peace during the ensuing twelve months.

13. Finally, the Court observes that there is no evidence to suggest that the magistrates acted outside their jurisdiction or that the binding-over orders or the applicants' subsequent detention failed to comply with English law for any other reason.

14. It follows that there has been no violation of Article 5 § 1 in respect of the detention of the first and second applicants following their refusal to be bound over.'

4. Most recently, the European Court of Human Rights ruled in *Hashman v United Kingdom*[17] that being bound over to 'be of good behaviour' was too imprecise to provide sufficient guidance on the limits of the defendant's future conduct.

Hashman v United Kingdom (2000) 30 EHRR 241, European Court of Human Rights

. . . On 3 March 1993 the applicants blew a hunting horn and engaged in hallooing with the intention of disrupting the activities of the Portman Hunt. A complaint was made to the Gillingham magistrates that the applicants should be required to enter into a recognizance with or without sureties to keep the peace and be of good behaviour pursuant to the Justices of the Peace Act 1361.

The applicants were bound over to keep the peace and be of good behaviour in the sum of 100 pounds sterling (GBP) for 12 months on 7 September 1993. They appealed to the Crown Court, which heard their appeals on 22 April 1994 at Dorchester.

15. The Crown Court, comprising a Crown Court judge and two magistrates, found that the applicants had not committed any breach of the peace, and that their conduct had not been likely to occasion a breach of the peace . . .

'(a) The [applicants'] behaviour had been a deliberate attempt to interfere with the Portman Hunt and to take hounds out of the control of the huntsman and the whippers-in.

(b) That in this respect the actions of the [applicants] were unlawful, and had exposed hounds to danger.

(c) That there had been no violence or threats of violence on this occasion, so that it could not be said that any breach of the peace had been committed or threatened.

(d) That the [applicants] would repeat their behaviour unless it were checked by the sanction of a bind over.

(e) That the [applicants'] conduct had been *contra bonos mores*.

17 (2000) 30 EHRR 241.

(f)   That *R. v. Howell* [see above] was distinguishable in that it related to the power of arrest for breach of the peace, which could only be exercised if there was violence or the immediate likelihood of violence.

(g)   That the power to bind over "to keep the peace and be of good behaviour" was wider than the power of arrest and could be exercised whenever it was proved either that there had been a breach of the peace or that there had been behaviour *contra bonos mores*, since a breach of the peace is *ex hypothesi contra bonos mores*, and the words "to keep the peace" added nothing to what was required of the defendant by the words "to be of good behaviour".'

17.   The court noted that neither the Law Commission's Report on Binding Over nor the European Convention was part of domestic law.

18.   The Crown Court judge agreed to state a case to the High Court, but legal aid for the case stated was refused on 5 August 1994. The applicants' appeals against the decisions were dismissed on 19 September 1994 . . .

19.   Behaviour *contra bonos mores* has been described as 'conduct which has the property of being wrong rather than right in the judgment of the majority of contemporary fellow citizens' (*per* Lord Justice Glidewell in *Hughes v. Holley* [1988] 86 Criminal Appeal Reports 130).

20.   In *R. v. Sandbach ex parte Williams* ([1935] 2 King's Bench Reports 192) the Divisional Court rejected the view that a person could not be bound over to be of good behaviour when there was no reason to apprehend a breach of the peace. As in the case of binding over to keep the peace, there must be some reason to believe that there might be a repetition of the conduct complained of before an order to be of good behaviour can be made.

B.   Binding over

21.   Magistrates have powers to 'bind over' under the Magistrates' Courts Act 1980 ('the 1980 Act'), under common law and under the Justices of the Peace Act 1361 ('the 1361 Act').

A binding-over order requires the person bound over to enter into a 'recognizance', or undertaking secured by a sum of money fixed by the court, to keep the peace or be of good behaviour for a specified period of time. If he or she refuses to consent to the order, the court may commit him or her to prison, for up to six months in the case of an order made under the 1980 Act or for an unlimited period in respect of orders made under the 1361 Act or common law. If an order is made but breached within the specified time period, the person bound over forfeits the sum of the recognizance. A binding-over order is not a criminal conviction (*R. v. County of London Quarter Sessions, ex parte Metropolitan Police Commissioner* [1948] 1 King's Bench Reports 670). [The court referred to the relevant statutes] . . .

4.   *The Law Commission's Report on Binding Over*

24.   In response to a request by the Lord Chancellor to examine binding-over powers, the Law Commission (the statutory law reform body for England and Wales) published in February 1994 its report entitled "Binding Over", in which it found that:

'4.34 We regard reliance on *contra bonos mores* as certainly, and breach of the peace as very arguably, contrary to elementary notions of what is required by the principles of natural justice when they are relied on as definitional grounds justifying the making of a binding-over order. Because an order binding someone to be of good behaviour is made in such wide terms, it fails to give sufficient indication to the person bound over of the conduct which he or she must avoid in order to be safe from coercive sanctions . . . ' (Law Commission Report no. 222)

The Law Commission recommended abolition of the power to bind over.

II.   ALLEGED VIOLATION OF ARTICLE 10 OF THE CONVENTION

25.   The applicants alleged a violation of Art. 10 of the Convention. In particular, they claimed that the finding that they had behaved in a manner *contra bonos mores* and the subsequent binding-over order constituted an interference with their rights under Article 10 which was not 'prescribed by law' within the meaning of that provision.

A.   As to the existence of an interference with the applicants' freedom of expression

26.   The Court recalls that proceedings were brought against the applicants in respect of their behaviour while protesting against fox hunting by disrupting the hunt. It is true that the protest took the form of impeding the activities of which they disapproved, but the Court considers nonetheless that it constituted an expression of opinion within the meaning of Article 10 (see,

for example, the *Steel and Others v. the United Kingdom* judgment of 23 September 1998, *Reports* 1998-VII, p. 2742, § 92). The measures taken against the applicants were, therefore, an interference with their right to freedom of expression.

B.   Whether the interference was 'prescribed by law'

27.   The Government submit that the concepts of breach of the peace and behaviour *contra bonos mores* are sufficiently precise and certain to comply with the requirement under Article 10 § 2 that any limitations on freedom of expression be 'prescribed by law'. With particular reference to the concept of behaviour *contra bonos mores*, the Government accept that the power is broadly defined, but claim that the breadth is necessary to meet the aims of the power, and sufficient to meet the requirements of the Convention. They state that the power to bind over to be of good behaviour gives magistrates a vital tool in controlling anti-social behaviour which has the potential to escalate into criminal conduct. They also note that the breadth of the definition facilitates the administration of justice as social standards alter and public perception of acceptable behaviour changes. The Government disagree with the Commission's conclusion that there is no objective element to help a citizen regulate his conduct: they point to the Chorherr case, where an administrative offence of causing 'a breach of the peace by conduct likely to cause annoyance' fell within the scope of the concept of 'prescribed by law' (*Chorherr v. Austria* judgment of 25 August 1993, Series A no. 266-B, pp. 35-36, § 25). They also point to the test under English law of whether a person has acted 'dishonestly' for the purpose of the Theft Acts 1968 and 1978 which is at least in part the standard of ordinary reasonable and honest people (*R. v. Ghosh* [1982] Queen's Bench Reports 1053), and to the test for whether a publication is defamatory, namely whether the statement concerned would lower a person in the opinion of right thinking members of society. Finally, the Government submit that on the facts of the case, the applicants should have known that what they had done was *contra bonos mores* and they should have known what they should do to avoid such behaviour in the future: they had acted in a way intended to disrupt the lawful activities of others, and should not have been in any doubt that their behaviour was unlawful and should not be repeated. The Government recall that the Court is concerned with the case before it, rather than abstract concerns about the compatibility of domestic law with the Convention *in abstracto*.

. . .

28.   The Court recalls that one of the requirements flowing from the expression 'prescribed by law' is foreseeability. A norm cannot be regarded as a 'law' unless it is formulated with sufficient precision to enable the citizen to regulate his conduct. At the same time, whilst certainty in the law is highly desirable, it may bring in its train excessive rigidity and the law must be able to keep pace with changing circumstances. The level of precision required of domestic legislation – which cannot in any case provide for every eventuality – depends to a considerable degree on the content of the instrument in question, the field it is designed to cover and the number and status of those to whom it is addressed (see generally in this connection, the *Rekvényi v. Hungary* judgment of 20 May 1999, to be published in the Court's official reports, § 34).

29.   The Court further recalls that prior restraint on freedom of expression must call for the most careful scrutiny on its part (see, in the context of the necessity for a prior restraint, the *Sunday Times v. the United Kingdom (No. 2)* judgment of 26 November 1991, Series A no. 217, pp. 29-30, § 51).

30.   The Court has already considered the issue of 'lawfulness' for the purposes of Article 5 of the Convention of orders to be bound over to keep the peace and be of good behaviour (in its above-mentioned Steel and Others judgment, pp. 2738-40, §§ 71-77). In that case, the Court found that the elements of breach of the peace were adequately defined by English law (ibid., p. 2739, § 75).

31.   The Court also considered whether the binding-over orders in that case were specific enough properly to be described as 'lawful order[s] of a court' within the meaning of Article 5 § 1(b) of the Convention. It noted at paragraph 76 of the judgment that:

'. . . the orders were expressed in rather vague and general terms; the expression "to be of good behaviour" was particularly imprecise and offered little guidance to the person bound over as to the type of conduct which would amount to a breach of the order. However, in each applicant's case the binding-over order was imposed after a finding that she had committed a breach of the peace. Having considered all the circumstances, the Court is satisfied that, given the context, it was sufficiently clear that the applicants were being requested to agree to refrain from casing further, similar, breaches of the peace during the ensuing twelve months.'

The Court also noted that the requirement under Article 10 § 2 that an interference with the exercise of freedom of expression be 'prescribed by law' is similar to that under Article 5 § 1 that any deprivation of liberty be 'lawful' (ibid., p. 2742, § 94).

32. It is a feature of the present case that it concerns an interference with freedom of expression which was not expressed to be a 'sanction', or punishment, for behaviour of a certain type, but rather an order, imposed on the applicants, not to breach the peace or behave *contra bonos mores* in the future. The binding-over order in the present case thus had purely prospective effect. It did not require a finding that there had been a breach of the peace. The case is thus different from the case of Steel and Others, in which the proceedings brought against the first and second applicants were in respect of breaches of the peace which were later found to have been committed.

33. The Court must consider the question of whether behaviour *contra bonos mores* is adequately defined for the purposes of Article 10 § 2 of the Convention.

34. The Court first recalls that in its Steel and Others judgment, it noted that the expression 'to be of good behaviour' 'was particularly imprecise and offered little guidance to the person bound over as to the type of conduct which would amount to a breach of the order' (ibid., p. 2739, § 76). Those considerations apply equally in the present case, where the applicants were not charged with any criminal offence, and were found not to have breached the peace.

35. The Court next notes that conduct *contra bonos mores* is defined as behaviour which is 'wrong rather than right in the judgment of the majority of contemporary fellow citizens' (see paragraph 13 above). It cannot agree with the Government that this definition has the same objective element as conduct 'likely to cause annoyance', which was at issue in the case of Chorherr (see paragraph 29 above). The Court considers that the question of whether conduct is 'likely to cause annoyance' is a question which goes to the very heart of the nature of the conduct proscribed: it is conduct whose likely consequence is the annoyance of others. Similarly, the definition of breach of the peace given in the case of *Percy v. Director of Public Prosecutions* (see above) – that it includes conduct the natural consequences of which would be to provoke others to violence – also describes behaviour by reference to its effects. Conduct which is 'wrong rather than right in the judgment of the majority of contemporary citizens', by contrast, is conduct which is not described at all, but merely expressed to be 'wrong' in the opinion of a majority of citizens.

36. Nor can the Court agree that the Government's other examples of behaviour which is defined by reference to the standards expected by the majority of contemporary opinion are similar to conduct *contra bonos mores* as in each case cited by the Government, the example given is but one element of a more comprehensive definition of the proscribed behaviour.

37. With specific reference to the facts of the present case, the Court does not accept that it must have been evident to the applicants what they were being ordered not do for the period of their binding over. Whilst in the case of Steel and Others the applicants had been found to have breached the peace, and the Court found that it was apparent that the bind over related to similar behaviour (ibid.), the present applicants did not breach the peace, and given the lack of precision referred to above, it cannot be said that what they were being bound over not to do must have been apparent to them.

38. The Court thus finds that the order by which the applicants were bound over to keep the peace and not to behave *contra bonos mores* did not comply with the requirement of Article 10 § 2 of the Convention that it be 'prescribed by law'.

39. In these circumstances, the Court is not required to consider the remainder of the issues under Article 10 of the Convention.

40. It follows that there has been a violation of Article 10 of the Convention.

NOTES

1. Buxton LJ has written (extra judicially) that 'should the facts of *Hashman* repeat themselves, the English Court should simply refuse to enforce or apply the law of binding over.'[18] See also the comments of A. Ashworth on the case.[19] It is reassuring to see the European Court of Human Rights restricting some vague English powers.

2. Binding-over orders have been made in many cases following conviction for a criminal offence against public order.[20] In addition, they have been made against persons who incite disorder. The most celebrated instance is *Lansbury v Riley*[1] where George Lansbury spoke in support of militant suffragettes at a time when there were many attacks on property. He said that women 'ought to break the law on every possible occasion, short of taking human life'.[2] He was bound over in the sum of £1,000 with two sureties of £500. In the 1930s, several officers of the National Unemployed Workers' Movement were imprisoned for refusing to be bound over.[3] See also *Wise v Dunning*,[4] and *Beatty v Gillbanks*.[5] A survey conducted for the Law Commission[6] showed that a large majority (79%) of orders were made both to keep the peace and be of good behaviour; 12% were to keep the peace and 9% to be of good behaviour.[7] For a list of examples of public order and other cases where orders have been used see ibid.[8]

(iii) Powers of entry to preserve the peace

Thomas v Sawkins [1935] 2 KB 249, 104 LJKB 572, 153 LT 419, 99 JP 295, 51 TLR 514, 33 LGR 330, 30 Cox CC, King's Bench Divisional Court

Case stated by Glamorgan (Newcastle and Ogmore) justices.

On 17 August 1934 a public meeting was held at the Large Hall of the Caerau Library to protest against the Incitement to Disaffection Bill then before Parliament and to demand the dismissal of the chief constable of the county of Glamorgan, at which meeting between 500 and 700 people were present. The principal speaker was to be Alun Thomas (the appellant). He had previously addressed meetings at Nantymoel (9 August), Caerau (14 August) and Maesteg (15 August). He had lodged a written complaint against the refusal of police officers to leave the Nantymoel meeting, had threatened physically to eject the police if they attended the meeting on 17 August, and had stated at the Maesteg meeting: 'If it were not for the presence of these people' – pointing to police officers – 'I could tell you a hell of a lot more.'

The Library Hall was hired by one Fred Thomas, and the public were invited to attend, free of charge. The meeting was convened by (among others) Fred Thomas and Alun Thomas. Sergeant Sawkins (the respondent), together with Inspector Parry and Sergeant Lawrence, was refused admission by Fred Thomas. Nevertheless, the three officers entered the hall and sat on the front row. They also refused to leave on two occasions when requested to do so by Alun Thomas. Alun Thomas then stated that the police officers would be ejected, and he laid his hand on Inspector Parry to eject him. Sergeant Sawkins thereupon pushed Alun Thomas's arm and hand from

---

18 [2000] Crim LR 331, 335.
19 [2000] Crim LR 185.
20 See *Williams*, pp. 94–95.
 1 [1914] 3 KB 229, DC.
 2 *Williams*, p. 97.
 3 Wal Hannington in 1922 and 1931; Sid Elias in 1931; Tom Mann and Emrhys Llewellyn in 1932: see *Williams*, pp. 99–100; J. Stevenson and C. Cook, *Society and Politics, 1929–1939, Britain in the Depression* (1994), p. 251.
 4 Above, p. 526.
 5 Above, p. 526.
 6 See below.
 7 Law Commission Working Paper No. 103, 1987, pp. 31–35 (Statistical Survey).
 8 pp. 39–43.

Parry, saying: 'I won't allow you to interfere with my superior officer.' About 30 other police officers entered with batons drawn, and no further attempt was made to eject the police. In attempting to remove Parry, Alun Thomas used no more force than was reasonably necessary for that purpose, and Sawkins used no more force than was reasonably necessary (assuming that he and Parry had a right to be there) to protect Parry and to prevent him from being ejected.

The respondent did not allege that any criminal offence was committed. There was no breach of the peace or disorder at any time.

Alun Thomas preferred an information against Sergeant Sawkins alleging that Sawkins had committed assault and battery contrary to s. 42 of the Offences against the Person Act 1861. He claimed that the police officers were trespassers. If that was correct, he would be entitled to use reasonable force to eject them, and forcible resistance by the police officers would be illegal. The justices concluded (33 LGR at 333):

'Upon the above facts and evidence given before us we were and are of the opinion that the respondent and other police officers had reasonable grounds for believing that if they were not present at the meeting seditious speeches would be made and/or incitements to violence and/or breaches of the peace would take place and that they were entitled to enter and remain in the said hall and meeting.'

They dismissed the information. Alun Thomas appealed. It was argued, *inter alia*, on behalf of Sawkins that:

'The respondent was entitled to be present at the meeting. A constable by his oath swears to cause the peace to be preserved and to prevent the commission of all offences. Where, therefore, the police have reasonable grounds for believing that an offence may be committed or a breach of the peace occur, they have a right to enter private premises to prevent the commission of the offence or the ocurrence of the breach of the peace. If that were not so, it would be extremely difficult for the police to exercise their powers of watch and ward and their duty of preventive justice' ([1935] 2 KB at 253).

Lord Hewart CJ: It is apparent that the conclusion of the justices in this case consisted of two parts. One part was a conclusion of fact that the respondent and the police officers who accompanied him believed that certain things might happen at the meeting which was then about to be held. There were ample materials on which the justices could come to that conclusion. The second part of the justices' finding is no less manifestly an expression of opinion. Finding the facts as they do, and drawing from those facts the inference which they draw, they go on to say that the officers were entitled to enter and to remain on the premises on which the meeting was being held.

Against that determination, it is said that it is an unheard-of proposition of law, and that in the books no case is to be found which goes the length of deciding, that, where an offence is expected to be committed, as distinct from the case of an offence being or having been committed, there is any right in the police to enter on private premises and to remain there against the will of those who, as hirers or otherwise, are for the time being in possession of the premises. When, however, I look at the passages which have been cited from Blackstone's Commentaries, vol. i., p. 356, and from the judgments in *Humphries v Connor* (1864) 17 ICLR 1 [above, p. 523] and *O'Kelly v Harvey* (1883) 14 LR Ir 105 [above, p. 526] and certain observations of Avory J in *Lansbury v Riley* [1914] 3 KB 229 at 236, 237, I think that there is quite sufficient ground for the proposition that it is part of the preventive power, and, therefore, part of the preventive duty, of the police, in cases where there are such reasonable grounds of apprehension as the justices have found here, to enter and remain on private premises. It goes without saying that the powers and duties of the police are directed, not to the interests of the police, but to the protection and welfare of the public.

It was urged in one part of the argument of Sir Stafford Cripps that what the police did here amounted to a trespass. It seems somewhat remarkable to speak of trespass when members of the public who happen to be police officers attend, after a public invitation, a public meeting which is to discuss as one part of its business the dismissal of the chief constable of the county.

It is elementary that a good defence to an action for trespass is to show that the act complained of was done by authority of law, or by leave and licence.

I am not at all prepared to accept the doctrine that it is only where an offence has been, or is being, committed, that the police are entitled to enter and remain on private premises. On the contrary, it seems to me that a police officer has ex virtute officii full right so to act when he has reasonable ground for believing that an offence is imminent or is likely to be committed.

I think, therefore, that the justices were right and that this appeal should be dismissed.

Avory J: I am of the same opinion. I think that it is very material in this particular case to observe that the meeting was described as a public meeting, that it was extensively advertised, and that the public were invited to attend. There can be no doubt that the police officers who attended the meeting were members of the public and were included in that sense in the invitation to attend. It is true that those who had hired the hall for the meeting might withdraw their invitation from any particular individual who was likely to commit a breach of the peace or some other offence, but it is quite a different proposition to say that they might withdraw the invitation from police officers who might be there for the express purpose of preventing a breach of the peace or the commission of an offence.

With regard to the general question regarding the right of the police to attend the meeting notwithstanding the opposition of the promoters, I cannot help thinking that that right follows from the description of the powers of a constable which Sir Stafford Cripps relies on in Stone's Justices' Manual, 1935, p. 208, where it is said that when a constable hears an affray in a house he may break in to suppress it and may, in pursuit of an affrayer, break in to arrest him. If he can do that, I cannot doubt that he has a right to break in to prevent an affray which he has reasonable cause to suspect may take place on private premises. In other words, it comes within his duty, as laid down by Blackstone (Commentaries, vol. i., p. 356), to keep the King's peace and to keep watch and ward. In my view, the right was correctly expressed in *R (Feehan) v Queen's County JJ* (1882) 10 LR Ir 294 at 301 where Fitzgerald J said: 'The foundation of the jurisdiction [to bind persons to be of good behaviour] is very remote, and probably existed prior to the statute of 1360–61; but whatever its foundation may be, or by whatever language conveyed, we are bound to regard and expound it by the light of immemorial practice and of decision, and especially of direct modern decisions. It may be described as a branch of preventive justice, in the exercise of which magistrates are invested with large judicial discretionary powers, for the maintenance of order and the preservation of the public peace.' That passage was expressly approved in *Lansbury v Riley* [1914] 3 KB 229 at 236 and the statement of the law which it contains was adopted by Lord Alverstone CJ in *Wise v Dunning* [1902] 1 KB 167 at 175; *R v Queen's County JJ* is there referred to sub nom *R v Cork JJ* (1882) 15 Cox CC 149. In principle I think that there is no distinction between the duty of a police constable to prevent a breach of the peace and the power of a magistrate to bind persons over to be of good behaviour to prevent a breach of the peace.

I am not impressed by the fact that many statutes have expressly given to police constables in certain circumstances the right to break open or to force an entrance into private premises. Those have all been cases in which a breach of the peace was not necessarily involved and it, therefore, required express statutory authority to empower the police to enter. In my opinion, no express statutory authority is necessary where the police have reasonable grounds to apprehend a breach of the peace, and in the present case I am satisfied that the justices had before them material on which they could properly hold that the police officers in question had reasonable grounds for believing that, if they were not present, seditious speeches would be made and/or that a breach of the peace would take place. To prevent any such offence or a breach of the peace the police were entitled to enter and to remain on the premises, and I agree that this appeal should be dismissed.

Lawrence J: As my Lord has pointed out, our judgment proceeds on the particular facts of this case, and on those facts I agree with the conclusion. I will only add that I am unable to follow the distinction which Sir Stafford Cripps has drawn between the present matter and the cases which have been cited. If a constable in the execution of his duty to preserve the peace is entitled to commit an assault, it appears to me that he is equally entitled to commit a trespass.

Appeal dismissed.

NOTES

1. Background information not available from the law reports is given in D. G. T. Williams, *Keeping the Peace*.[9] The case was adversely criticised by A. L. Goodhart.[10]
2. What is the *ratio decidendi* of the judgment of Lord Hewart CJ? Is it the *ratio decidendi* of the case? Is it a clear *ratio*? See *McLeod*.[10a]
3. Where Lord Hewart states that a police officer may enter and remain on private premises 'when he has reasonable ground for believing that an offence is imminent or is likely to be committed', do you think that the point he was considering was (a) the *point of time* at which the police may intervene, or (b) the nature of the *offence* which has to be anticipated, or (c) both? Does Lord Hewart's judgment amount to an endorsement of the argument of counsel for Sawkins that there is a power to enter premises to prevent *any* offence? Note that the Police and Criminal Evidence Act 1984, s. 17(5), (6) abolishes all common law powers of entry except to deal with or prevent a breach of the peace.[11] Does s. 17(6) constitute an endorsement of *Thomas v Sawkins*?
4. Could Alun Thomas have been convicted of the offences of assaulting or obstructing a police officer in the execution of his duty?[12]
5. In principle, the occupier of land may grant or refuse permission (a 'licence') to someone seeking to go on to the land according to his own wishes, unless that other has a right to enter conferred by law. A gratuitous licence may be revoked at any time provided that reasonable notice is given.[13] A licensee must be given reasonable time to depart before his continued presence on the land constitutes trespass.[14]

Apart from the situation where there is a right to remain conferred by law, a licence will only be irrevocable where (a) it is protected by estoppel or equity; (b) the licence is coupled with a proprietary interest in other property; or (c) (in some circumstances) where the licence is granted by contract.[15] In view of this, would it be correct to say that the persons who hired the hall could *only* 'withdraw their invitation from any particular individual who was likely to commit a breach of the peace or some other offence'?[16] How is the position of the organiser of a *public* meeting different from that of a *private* meeting? Is it not simply the difference between a meeting to which there is a general invitation to the public, and one to which specific invitations are given? Can the fact that a meeting is 'public' limit the power of the *occupier* to refuse entry or to eject, as distinct (possibly) from marking the limit of the right of the *police* to enter private premises in anticipation of the commission of offences?
6. The ambiguity regarding the power to enter private premises whether or not there was a public meeting occurring was resolved by the Court of Appeal in *McLeod v MPC*.[17] The court held that there was a power to enter and remain on premises to deal with an apprehended breach of the peace. The Court of Appeal's decision as to the application of that principle to the facts was rejected by the European Court.[18]

9 (1967), pp. 142–149, and (1985) Cambrian LR 116.
10 (1936–38) CLJ 22.
10a Below, p. 552.
11 See above, p. 229.
12 Cf. *Duncan v Jones* [1936] 1 KB 218, above, p. 531.
13 Megarry and Wade, *The Law of Real Property* (5th edn, 1984), p. 799; N. Gravells, *Land Law: Text and Materials* (2nd edn, 1999), p. 490.
14 *Robson v Hallett* [1967] 2 QB 939, above, p. 254; unless he makes it clear that he will not leave voluntarily (*Davis v Lisle* [1936] 2 KB 434, above, p. 158).
15 See Megarry and Wade, pp. 801–805; N. Gravells, op. cit., pp. 489–534.
16 Cf. Avory J.
17 [1994] 4 All ER 553.
18 See below, p. 552.

7. Consider the statement of Lawrence J that if a constable is 'entitled to commit an assault, ... he is equally entitled to commit a trespass' in the light of s. 3 of the Criminal Law Act 1967. [18]

8. What is the position where a police officer has no legal right of entry but obtains permission to enter premises:

(1) by concealing the fact that he is a police officer in circumstances where he knows that a policeman would not be admitted; or

(2) by a false representation of fact (e.g. 'I thought I saw a burglar'); or

(3) by a false representation of law (e.g. 'I have a legal power to enter'); or

(4) by acquiescing in the self deception of the occupier (e.g. 'You've a right to come in so I suppose I'd better let you'). [19]

9. In *Handcock v Baker*[20] the defendants were held entitled to break into a house where they had reasonable cause to believe that the occupier was about to kill his wife. Moreover, a constable may enter premises in fresh pursuit of a person who has committed a breach of the peace within his view. [1]

10. In *McGowan v Chief Constable of Kingston-upon-Hull*[2] the Divisional Court held that police officers were entitled to enter and remain in a private house where they feared there would be a breach of the peace arising out of a domestic quarrel. *Thomas v Sawkins* was not mentioned in the report, but was presumably the relevant authority.

McLeod v United Kingdom (1999) 27 EHRR 493, European Court of Human Rights

The applicant, Mrs McLeod, had been ordered by the court to return specified property to her former husband by a certain date as part of a divorce settlement. Mr McLeod believed that the applicant had consented to his taking the property. Owing to previous difficulties between the couple, Mr McLeod's solicitors had arranged for police officers to be present because of the potential for a breach of the peace. When Mr McLeod and the police arrived, Mrs McLeod was absent. The police entered and remained on the premises during the removal of the property by Mr McLeod. When Mrs McLeod arrived home, she objected to the removal of the property. The police ensured that Mr McLeod was allowed to remove the property and instructed Mrs McLeod that if she obstructed him, there was likely to be a breach of the peace for which she would be arrested. The applicant brought criminal proceedings against the police, but when they failed, she brought a civil action for trespass to her property – hat also failed. The Court of Appeal dismissed her appeal: *McLeod v Metropolitan Police Commissioner.*[3] She took the case to the European Court of Human Rights, alleging a breach of Art. 8. The European Court of Human Rights held that the entry onto the applicant's premises violated Art. 8 of the ECHR, what was of more significance was whether the interference was justifiable under Art. 8(2) as being 'in accordance with the law and is necessary in a democratic society in the interests of national security, public safety or the economic well-being of the

---

18 Above, p. 196.
19 See above, Chap. 3, p. 253.
20 (1800) 2 Bos & P 260.
 1 See *R v Walker* (1854) Dears CC 358; *R v Marsden* (1868) LR 1 CCR 131.
 2 [1967] Crim LR 34.
 3 [1994] 4 All ER 553, CA.

country, for the prevention of disorder or crime, for the protection of health or morals, or for the protection of the rights and freedoms of others':

'41. The applicant submitted that the common-law power of the police to enter private premises on the grounds of an anticipated breach of the peace was not "in accordance with the law" within the meaning of Article 8 § 2. In this regard she argued, first, that the meaning of the concept "breach of the peace" was insufficiently clear and precise and that, in particular, there was inconsistent jurisprudence as to the meaning of "breach of the peace". An element of apprehension by another was included in the definition of "breach of the peace", which made it difficult in many cases for an individual to foresee the consequences of his acts; the degree of imminence required was uncertain; and it was not clear who of one or more individuals involved in an incident would be held responsible for causing the breach of the peace. Secondly, she maintained that the scope of the discretionary power of the police to enter private premises was not sufficiently clearly defined to provide protection from arbitrary interference.

42. The Government contested this allegation, maintaining that the interference with the applicant's rights was in accordance with the law. The common-law power of the police to enter private premises without a warrant to prevent a breach of the peace had been preserved by section 17(6) of the 1984 Act (see paragraph 23 above). This provision, which was unequivocal in its terms, reflected the rule laid down in *Thomas v. Sawkins* . . . ; a rule that was formulated with sufficient precision to enable persons – including the police – to regulate their conduct.

Furthermore, they stressed that there was no ambiguity in the power of the police to enter private premises to prevent a breach of the peace. If there had been, Parliament would have clarified the power when the common-law powers of the police to enter private premises were reviewed in connection with the 1984 Act.

43. The Commission considered that the rule in *Thomas v. Sawkins*, as recognised in *McGowan v. Chief Police Constable of Kingston Upon Hull* . . . , had enabled the applicant reasonably to foresee that the police had had the right to enter and remain on her property to prevent a breach of the peace arising when her former husband collected his property from her home.

44. The Court recalls that the expression "in accordance with the law", within the meaning of Article 8 § 2, requires firstly that the impugned measures should have a basis in domestic law. It also refers to the quality of the law in question, requiring that it be accessible to the persons concerned and formulated with sufficient precision to enable them – if need be, with appropriate advice – to foresee, to a degree that is reasonable in the circumstances, the consequences which a given action may entail (see, amongst many others, the *Margareta and Roger Andersson v. Sweden* judgment of 25 February 1992, Series A no. 226-A, p. 25, § 75). However, those consequences need not be foreseeable with absolute certainty, since such certainty might give rise to excessive rigidity, and the law must be able to keep pace with changing circumstances (see, *mutatis mutandis*, the *Sunday Times v. the United Kingdom (No. 1)* judgment of 26 April 1979, Series A no. 30, p. 31, § 49).

45. In this connection, the Court observes that the concept of breach of the peace has been clarified by the English courts over the last two decades, to the extent that it is now sufficiently established that a breach of the peace is committed only when an individual causes harm, or appears likely to cause harm, to persons or property, or acts in a manner the natural consequence of which would be to provoke violence in others . . .

46. Furthermore, the English courts have recognised that the police have a duty to prevent a breach of the peace that they reasonably apprehend will occur and to stop a breach of the peace that is occurring. In the execution of this duty, the police have the power to enter into and remain on private property without the consent of the owner or occupier (see paragraphs 28 and 29 above). Despite the general abolition of common-law powers of entry without warrant, this power was preserved by section 17(6) of the 1984 Act (see paragraph 23 above).

47. When considering whether the national law was complied with, the Court recalls that it is primarily for the national authorities, notably the courts, to interpret and apply domestic law (see, as a recent authority, the *Kopp v. Switzerland* judgment of 25 March 1998, *Reports of Judgments and Decisions* 1998-II, p. 541, § 59). In this regard, the Court notes that in its decision the Court of Appeal took into account the criticisms of the common-law power of

the police to enter private premises to prevent a breach of the peace cited by the applicant in her memorial to the Court, and found that the common-law power was applicable in situations involving domestic disturbance (see paragraph 21 above).

48. In conclusion, the Court finds that the power of the police to enter private premises without a warrant to deal with or prevent a breach of the peace was defined with sufficient precision for the foreseeability criterion to be satisfied. The interference was, therefore, "in accordance with the law".

(b)   Legitimate aim

49. The applicant contended that, while the prevention of crime or disorder might be the objective behind the existence of the power, it was not the aim of the interference that took place in the present case. She submitted that the term "prevention" should be interpreted narrowly and should not encompass a situation where police officers by their own actions caused a risk of disorder and then assumed powers of entry to prevent it.

50. The Government maintained that the purpose of the police officers' entry into the applicant's property was to prevent disorder or crime. In this regard, they drew attention to the fact that domestic strife was often the cause of considerable disorder and occasionally led to serious violence against persons or property. The Commission accepted this submission.

51. The Court is of the view that the aim of the power enabling police officers to enter private premises to prevent a breach of the peace is clearly a legitimate one for the purposes of Article 8, namely the prevention of disorder or crime, and there is nothing to suggest that it was applied in the present case for any other purpose.

(c)   "Necessary in a democratic society"

52. The applicant contended that, since section 17(1)(e) of the 1984 Act enabled the police to enter private premises to save life or limb or prevent serious damage to property, the power of the police to enter private premises in circumstances other than when there was a risk of physical harm to persons or property was not "necessary in a democratic society".

Notwithstanding this contention she argued that, if the police chose to exercise their power of entry when there was no risk of physical injury or damage to property – which entailed a major infringement of the rights guaranteed under Article 8 of the Convention – the justification for the interference should be significant and indisputable. Furthermore, justification for the entry had to be made by reference to the degree of risk that existed at the time the police entered the property. In the present case, since there was no history of violence between the applicant and her ex-husband and the only person present at the house at the time of entry was her 74-year-old mother, the risk of harm was minimal or non-existent. Weighing this against the seriousness of the interference, the actions of the police could not be regarded as proportionate. In addition, they demonstrated such a lack of impartiality as to render the exercise of the powers disproportionate to the aim pursued.

53. The Government claimed that, because there was a clear pressing social need to prevent disorder or crime, the power of the police to enter private premises without permission to prevent a breach of the peace was "necessary in a democratic society". With regard to the present case, they submitted that the interference was proportionate to the legitimate aim pursued, as demonstrated by the fact that the visit to the applicant's home by her former husband to collect his possessions was made in the genuine, albeit mistaken, belief that she had agreed to the arrangement; the ex-husband's solicitors feared that a breach of the peace might occur because of the history of the court proceedings between their client and the applicant; the police officers attended the applicant's home not to assist in the removal of the property but to maintain the peace; they acted in a discreet and reasonable manner; and the applicant's conduct on her return did call for their intervention.

54. The Commission, placing emphasis on the risk of disturbance that might have arisen if the applicant's ex-husband and his party had gained access on their own, found that the measures taken by the police officers – who acted, in its opinion, with restraint throughout the incident – were not disproportionate to the legitimate aim pursued. Although the police officers had had limited possibilities of knowing the precise nature of private relations between the couple, they were under a duty to take seriously an indication from one party that trouble might arise.

55. The Court recalls that, according to its established case-law, the notion of necessity implies that the interference corresponds to a pressing social need and, in particular, that it is proportionate to the legitimate aim pursued (see, *inter alia*, the *Olsson v. Sweden (No. 1)* judgment of 24 March 1988, Series A no. 130, pp. 31–32, § 67).

1. The Court's task accordingly consists in ascertaining whether, in the circumstances of the present case, the entry of the police into the applicant's home struck a fair balance between the relevant interests, namely the applicant's right to respect for her private life and home, on the one hand, and the prevention of disorder and crime, on the other.

. . .

56. However, the Court observes that, notwithstanding the facts that the police were contacted in advance by Mr McLeod's solicitors and that the solicitor's clerk offered to return to his office and collect the court order . . . , the police did not take any steps to verify whether Mr McLeod was entitled to enter her home on 3 October 1989 and remove his property. Sight of the court order would have indicated that it was for the applicant to deliver the property, and not for her former husband to collect it, and moreover that she had three more days in which to do so (see paragraph 11 above). Admittedly, the court order would not have enabled the police officers to ascertain the correctness of Mr McLeod's genuinely held belief that an agreement had been made between himself and his ex-wife allowing him to remove his property from the former matrimonial home on 3 October 1989 – a belief that was communicated to the police officers upon their arrival (see paragraph 12 above). Nonetheless, given the circumstances of the interference, and the fact that the applicant was not present and that her mother lacked any knowledge of the agreement (see paragraph 13 above), the police should not have taken it for granted that an agreement had been reached superseding the relevant parts of the court order.

58. The Court considers further that, upon being informed that the applicant was not present, the police officers should not have entered her house, as it should have been clear to them that there was little or no risk of disorder or crime occurring. It notes in this regard that the police officers remained outside the property for some of the time, suggesting a belief on their part that a breach of the peace was not likely to occur in the absence of the applicant (see paragraph 14 above). The fact that an altercation did occur upon her return (see paragraph 15 above) is, in its opinion, immaterial in ascertaining whether the police officers were justified in entering the property initially.

59. For the above reasons, the Court finds that the means employed by the police officers were disproportionate to the legitimate aim pursued. Accordingly, there has been a violation of Article 8 of the Convention.'

NOTES

1. The two dissenting judges took the view that the police were 'fully entitled on the evidence to fear a breach of the peace'.[4] They expressed concern that the majority's ruling may significantly weaken the position of the police in dealing with cases of domestic violence. They stated[5] that there were clear dangers of escalation in this situation.

2. Professor Ashworth[6] notes that the court was much more interventionist in this case than it has been in other breach of the peace cases. He concludes that: 'All of this means that "breach of the peace" can no longer be treated by the police as a wide-ranging justification for all manner of actions.' Do you share this view?

3. Before *Thomas v Sawkins*, it was generally accepted that the police had no power to enter meetings on private premises unless they had reason to believe that a breach of the peace was *actually taking place*. This was stated to be the position by the *Departmental Committee on the Duties of the Police with respect to the Preservation*

4 Para. 2.
5 Para. 4.
6 [1999] Crim LR 156.

of Order at Public Meetings,[7] and by the Home Secretary, Sir John Gilmour, in a debate arising out of the Fascist meeting at Olympia on 7 June 1934 where there was considerable violence.[8] Cf. *Robson v Hallett.*[9]

4. Contrary to expectations which might be engendered by *Thomas v Sawkins,* D. G. T. Williams has noted 'the apparent determination of the police to avoid wherever possible any entanglement in the protests and demonstrations taking place on private property'.[10] This was particularly marked in relation to sit-ins at universities in the late 1960s. Cf. *R v Dytham,*[11] where a constable was convicted of the common law misdemeanour of misconduct of a public officer in that he failed to fulfil his duty to preserve the peace. He had witnessed a man being beaten and kicked to death outside a club, but had taken no steps to intervene.

5. The breach of the peace powers discussed in many of the cases dealt with in this chapter typify the problems of public order law. They provide incredibly broad discretion to the officer on the spot, they remain ill-defined – unless handled with a careful balance they can operate to stifle dissent as well as provocative comment.

There is a very strong case for further research to clarify the frequency with which these powers are exercised and in what circumstances. Only then can an effective evaluation of the power occur.

6. There is some indication from cases which such as *Redmond-Bate,*[12] *Bibby v Chief Constable of Essex*[13] and *Foulkes v Chief Constable of Merseyside*[14] that the domestic courts are seeking to restrict the scope of the breach of the peace power to cases of immediate threats of violence.

---

7 Cd. 4673, 1909, p. 6.
8 290 HC Deb, 14 June 1934, col. 1968.
9 Above, p. 254.
10 [1970] CLJ 96, 116.
11 [1979] QB 722, CA (CrD).
12 Above, p. 526.
13 Above, p. 467.
14 Above, p. 466.

CHAPTER 5

Emergency powers; the problem of political terrorism

1 Introduction

The most extreme form of emergency which the country may face is war. In earlier times, the Crown relied on prerogative powers to take steps necessary for the conduct of war.[1] Each of the two world wars saw the creation of a complex edifice of statutory powers, mostly contained in delegated legislation made under the Defence of the Realm Acts 1914–15 and the Emergency Powers (Defence) Acts 1939–40. Every aspect of national life was closely regulated. Commentators were able to poke fun at the inevitable fatuity of some of the controls.[2] The interest of civil liberties was equally inevitably and equally swiftly relegated to a lesser rank in the order of national priorities. These measures have attracted both support, inasmuch as Britain had 'created the means of preserving itself from disaster without sacrificing the essential processes of democracy'[3] and stringent criticism.[4] Economic difficulties caused certain aspects of wartime regulation to be prolonged after the cessation of hostilities.

In addition, the Emergency Powers Act 1920[5] enables the state to obtain wide ranging powers by regulation to meet peacetime emergencies. Section 1(1) of the Act[6] provides that

> 'If at any time it appears to His Majesty that [there have occurred, or are about to occur, events of such a nature] as to be calculated, by interfering with the supply and distribution of food, water, fuel, or light, or with the means of locomotion, to deprive the community, or any substantial portion of the community, of the essentials of life, His Majesty may, by proclamation (hereinafter referred to as a proclamation of emergency) declare that a state of emergency exists....'

A proclamation may not be in force longer than a month, without prejudice to the issue of further proclamations[7]. During the currency of a proclamation, regulations may be made by Order in Council 'for securing the essentials of life to the community'. The Act has been used solely in relation to major strikes. The most recent proclamation was in the winter of 1973/1974.[8]

That the royal prerogative is also a source of legal powers in relation to the maintenance 'of what is popularly called the Queen's peace within the realm' was

---

1   See Wade and Bradley, *Constitutional and Administrative Law* (12th edn, 1997), pp. 679–681.
2   See, e.g. C. K. Allen, *Law and Disorder* (1954).
3   C. P. Cotter, (1953) 5 Stanford LR 382, 416.
4   See C. K. Allen, *Law and Order* (1st edn, 1945); R. Kidd, *British Liberty in Danger* (1940), Part Two; N. Stammers, *Civil Liberties in Britain during the Second World War* (1983).
5   See generally, G. Morris, [1979] PL 317 and *Strikes in Essential Services* (1986), Chap. 3; K. Jeffery and P. Hennessy, *States of Emergency* (1983); S. Peak, *Troops in Strikes* (Cobden Trust, 1984); D. Bonner, *Emergency Powers in Peacetime* (1985), Chap. 5.
6   As amended by the Emergency Powers Act 1964.
7   Ibid.
8   The regulations were contained in S.I. 1974 No. 350.

affirmed by the Court of Appeal in *R v Secretary of State for the Home Department,
ex p Northumbria Police Authority.*[9] The court held that:

> 'the Crown does have a prerogative power to keep the peace, which is bound up with its
> undoubted right to see that crime is prevented and justice administered;'

that the power could be used by the Home Secretary to make plastic baton rounds
and CS gas available to chief constables, without the approval of the police authority,
the prerogative not having been curtailed by s. 4(4) of the Police Act 1964 (which
gave the police authority power to provide equipment); and that the power was not
confined to use *in* an emergency, but could be used:

> 'in times when there is reason to apprehend outbreaks of riot and serious civil disturbance.'[10]

The court could have dealt with the matter simply by reference to the Secretary of
State's statutory powers under the Police Act 1964 but chose to deal with the prerogative
issue as well. Note A. W. Bradley's criticism that in several respects the judges' approach
to the subject failed to conform with important constitutional traditions'.[11]

This chapter concentrates in particular on how the pressures for additional legal
powers to combat terrorism can be reconciled with legitimate demands for the
protection of civil liberties. The international standards applicable to the exercise
of police powers[12] apply here, subject to the point that some may be (and have been)
the subject of derogation by the UK.[13]

2 Political terrorism[14]

Political terrorism has been defined as:

> 'the use, or threat of use, of violence by an individual or a group, whether acting for or in
> opposition to established authority, when such action is designed to create extreme anxiety
> and/or fear-inducing effects in a target larger than the immediate victims with the purpose of
> coercing that group into acceding to the political demands of the perpetrators.'[15]

While the systematic employment of terrorist tactics can be traced back to the French
Revolution and various political movements in late nineteenth century Europe, there
has over the last 30 years been both a dramatic increase in the incidence of terrorism
in the world, and significant changes in its nature. These changes are related to various
factors, including technological developments in weaponry, the increasing
sophistication of the news media (media coverage often being a major objective of
terrorists), the dependence of heavily industrialised societies on a decreasing number
of critical locations or processes (e.g. commercial aircraft, gas pipelines, electric power
grids, government computers) and the development of links between terrorist groups

---

9 [1989] QB 26.
10 Per Croom-Johnson LJ at pp. 563–565.
11 A. W. Bradley, [1988] PL 298.
12 Above, p. 156.
13 See above, p. 26.
14 For general surveys, see R. Clutterbuck (ed.), *The Future of Political Violence* (1986) and
Terrorism and Guerilla Warfare (1990); C. Gearty, *Terror* (1991); J. Lodge (ed.), *The Threat
of Terrorism* (1988); G. Wardlaw, *Political Terrorism* (2nd edn, 1989); P. Wilkinson, *Political
Terrorism* (1974), *Terrorism and the Liberal State* (2nd edn, 1986), (ed.), *British Perspectives
on Terrorism* (1981) and *Lloyd Inquiry*, vol. 2 (Report on current and future threat to the UK
from international and domestic terrorism (other than that concerned with the affairs of Northern
Ireland)); P. Wilkinson and A. M. Stewart (eds.), *Contemporary Research on Terrorism* (1987).
15 G. Wardlaw, *Political Terrorism* (2nd edn, 1989), p. 16.

in different countries.[16] For liberal democracies, the choice of appropriate measures poses problems:

'The primary objective of counter-terrorist strategy must be the protection and maintenance of liberal democracy and the rule of law. It cannot be sufficiently stressed that this aim overrides in importance even the objective of eliminating terrorism and political violence as such. Any bloody tyrant can "solve" the problem of political violence if he is prepared to sacrifice all considerations of humanity, and to trample down all constitutional and judicial rights.'[17]

This point is developed in the following extract:[18]

'However serious the threat of terrorism, we must not be tempted to use repressive methods to combat it. To believe that we can 'protect' liberal democracy by suspending our normal rights and methods of government is to ignore the numerous examples in contemporary history of countries where 'temporary', 'emergency' rule has subsided quickly and irrevocably into permanent dictatorial forms of government. While we must avoid the easy move to repression as a counter to terrorism, it is equally vital that we do not allow ourselves to be so overcome by our democratic sensibilities that our response is weak and vacillating, and characterised by inaction. It is as much a betrayal of our beliefs and responsibilities to do not enough as to do too much. We must uphold constitutional authority and law and order, and we must do so with firmness and determination. To do so requires political will; but most importantly it requires citizen support. To gain such support the political will must be translated into effective action. First, the government must be open and honest about its policies and objectives. As will be stressed when we come to examine the role of the army in counter-terrorism, it is particularly important in a society such as ours to spell out clearly the circumstances under which military aid to the civil power would be invoked, the rights and responsibilities of military personnel operating in an internal security role, and the lines of control and command.

Second, the government must accord full and proper support to its civil and security force personnel who are involved in counter-terrorist operations. In particular, it is necessary to avoid sudden changes in security policy which could undermine both official and public confidence in the government's ability to handle difficult situations. Policy vacillations also expose weaknesses and differences within the government ranks which can be exploited by terrorists.

Third, any anti-terrorist measures must be, and be seen to be, directed only at terrorists. The response must be limited, well-defined, and controlled. It must also, wherever at all possible, be publicly explained....

It is most important that executive control of anti-terrorist and security policy rests with the civil authorities (the elected government) who are accountable to the people for their actions. Further, it should be both policy and practice for the government and its security forces to act within the law. Not only does failure to do so place the government in a morally difficult position (if it does not obey the law, why should anyone?) but also such action is likely to undermine their support and provide valuable ammunition for a terrorist cause. Propaganda capital can very easily be made out of violations of the law by government servants, and such propaganda can be used as additional justification for a terrorist campaign. While the law can be a refuge for the law-breaker and a hindrance to the law enforcement official, the law is the basis of our system of government and must be upheld. Otherwise are we any better than the terrorist who also argues on the grounds of expediency?'

In the United Kingdom the major problem of terrorism has been created by the Northern Ireland conflict, although there have, in addition, been a number of terrorist incidents reflecting struggles between groups of foreign nationals,[19] and, following the terrorist actions in the US on 11 September 2001, increased fears of campaigns directed at the UK government. Up to the enactment of the Terrorism Act 2000,

---

16 See G. Wardlaw, op. cit., Chap. 3.
17 P. Wilkinson, *Terrorism and the Liberal State* (1977) p. 121.
18 G. Wardlaw, op. cit., pp. 69–70.
19 E.g. the Iranian Embassy siege in 1980 (see G. Brock et al., *Siege* (1980)) and the Libyan Embassy siege in 1984.

distinctly different legal regimes designed to deal with terrorism applied respectively in Northern Ireland and in the rest of the United Kingdom. 'Emergency powers' or 'special powers' had existed in Ireland without a break from the nineteenth century. The latest was a series of Northern Ireland (Emergency Provisions) Acts; the first was passed in 1973 and the last in 1996 (amended in 1998). Elsewhere in the United Kingdom, legislation was enacted in response to perceived threats. In 1974, Parliament passed the Prevention of Terrorism (Temporary Provisions) Act following the Birmingham pub bombings. It was, in turn, replaced by Acts of 1984 and 1989. Some of its provisions extended to Northern Ireland; others did not. Both sets of provisions were subject to annual renewal.

The Terrorism Act 2000 puts a body of measures to combat terrorism drawn from both regimes on the statute book as permanent legislation; the dual arrangement whereby certain additional powers are available in Northern Ireland is reflected in their continuation in Part VII of the Act, which is subject to annual renewal.

Following the 11 September terrorist attacks in the US, an Anti-Terrorism, Crime and Security Bill was rushed through Parliament.

3   The Northern Ireland context[20]

Current provisions for Northern Ireland are contained in the Terrorism Act 2000.

The materials which follow concentrate upon Northern Ireland's security problems. This is not the whole picture. Between the inception of the state of Northern Ireland in 1921 and 1972 its government was in the hands of the Protestant Ulster Unionist party. The decision that Northern Ireland should comprise six of the nine counties in the Province of Ulster was indeed based on the desire to ensure a Unionist majority in the Parliament of Northern Ireland. The voting strength of Unionists and Nationalists in Ulster as a whole was roughly equal.[1] The Catholic minority during this period was the object of serious discrimination in a number of important areas. Official recognition of this came in 1969 with the report of the Cameron Commission on *Disturbances in Northern Ireland*, whose conclusions in this regard are summarised below. Both before and after the imposition of direct rule in 1972 a number of legislative measures sought to end the regime of discrimination. Fourteen reforms are listed in the Report of the Standing Advisory Commission on Human Rights on

---

20 For general surveys of the operation of the Northern Ireland system in relation to terrorism see K. Boyle, T. Hadden and P. Hillyard, op. cit.; K. Boyle, T. Hadden and P. Hillyard, *Ten Years On in Northern Ireland* (1980); K. Boyle 'Human Rights and the Northern Ireland Emergency' in J. A. Andrews (ed.), *Human Rights in Criminal Procedure* (1982), pp. 144–164; D. P. J. Walsh, *The Use and Abuse of Emergency Legislation in Northern Ireland* (1983); C. Palley in *International Commission of Jurists, States of Emergency: Their Impact on Human Rights* (1983) pp. 217–246; D. Bonner, *Emergency Powers in Peacetime* (1985), Chap. 3; G. Hogan and C. Walker, *Political Violence and the Law in Ireland* (1989) (hereafter, Hogan and Walker); A. Jennings (ed.), *Justice Under Fire: The Abuse of Civil Liberties in Northern Ireland* (rev. edn, 1990) (hereafter, Jennings); Amnesty International, *United Kingdom: Human Rights Concerns* (1991); *Human Rights in Northern Ireland: A Helsinki Watch Report* (1991); Liberty, *Broken Covenants: Violations of International Law in Northern Ireland* (1993); Lawyers Committee for Human Rights, *At the Crossroads* (1996). The constitutional background to 1972 is considered by C. Palley, (1972) 1 Anglo-Am LR 368–476. For contributions to the debate on ways out of the current political situation, see A. Pollak (ed.), *A Citizens' Inquiry: The Opsahl Report on Northern Ireland* (1993) (considered by B. Thompson, [1993] PL 588); B. O'Leary et al., *Northern Ireland: Sharing Authority* (IPPR, 1993); K. Boyle and T. Hadden, *Northern Ireland: The Choice* (1994); *Frameworks for the Future* (1995).

The problems of the control of emergency powers are considered by M. P. O'Boyle, (1977) 28 NILQ 160; C. Warbrick in F. E. Dowrick (ed.), *Human Rights* (1979), Chap. 7; and for a comparative survey see G. J. Alexander, 'The Illusory Protection of Human Rights by National Courts during Periods of Emergency' (1984) 5 HRLJ 1.

1 See N. Mansergh, *The Irish Question 1840–1921* (3rd edn, 1975) Chap. VI.

The protection of human rights by law in Northern Ireland[2] covering such matters as universal adult suffrage in local elections, and the establishment of a Parliamentary Commissioner for Administration (government departments), a Commissioner for Complaints (local councils and public bodies), a Police Complaints Board, a central housing authority, an independent police authority, a Director of Public Prosecutions and a Fair Employment Agency. All legislative and execution actions of central and local government and statutory bodies which are discriminatory on religious or political grounds have been unlawful under Part III of the Northern Ireland Constitution Act 1973 and now Part VII of the Northern Ireland Act 1998. Nevertheless, as the Advisory Commission pointed out:[3]

'What might have succeeded at another time or in different circumstances has not been sufficient to change a situation where violence has become a way of life for some and perpetual terror for others.... The continuing state of emergency has not only seriously impaired the effectiveness of the substantial legislative and administrative reforms which have been made since 1969 for the better protection of human rights but has also inevitably resulted in the restriction of certain basic rights and freedoms in Northern Ireland.'

One matter for concern for those who believe that legal processes may be of value in the protection of civil liberties has been why the minority did not seek legal redress for such of their grievances as lay against public authorities. The discriminatory abuse of statutory powers is potentially reviewable under the ultra vires doctrine. Judicial review of administrative action may in theory at least be used as a vehicle for civil rights litigation. The Government of Ireland Act 1920 contained specific guarantees against discriminatory legislation. However, commentators have pointed to the absence of 'the necessary confidence in the judicial system as a means of securing justice'.[4] The possibilities of judicial review have, however, been illustrated in a series of cases in which the courts have upheld and enforced the legal rights of Sinn Fein councillors (the government having decided not to ban the political activities of members of Sinn Fein), and in cases vindicating prisoners' rights.[5] However, C. Hill and S. Lee argue that the judges 'might be accused of being less successful in policing the criminal justice system itself, in policing (or judging) themselves'.[6]

In 1994 ceasefires were announced by both Republican and Loyalist paramilitary groups. *Framework Documents* were launched by the British and Irish governments in 1995 and the decommissioning of some weapons was set by the Secretary of State as a condition for Sinn Fein's entry into all-party talks. The PIRA ended its ceasefire on 9 February 1996 with the bombing at South Quay, but resumed it on 20 July 1997. The *Good Friday Agreement*[7] was announced on 10 April 1998 at the end of talks among 18 parties chaired by Senator George Mitchell. Referendums on 22 May in

---

2 Cmnd. 7009, 1977, pp. 11–14.
3 At p. 14.
4 K. Boyle, T. Hadden and P. Hillyard, *Law and State* (1975), p. 1. On the avenues of legal redress, see also Boyle, Hadden and Hillyard, Chap. 2; W. D. Carroll, (1973) 6 NY Univ Journal of International Law and Politics pp. 28, 47–53; T. Hadden and P. Hillyard, *Justice in Northern Ireland* (1973) Chap. II; *Purvis v Magherafelt District Council* [1978] NI 26.
5 See C. Hill QC and S. Lee, 'Without Fear or Favour? Judges and Human Rights in Northern Ireland' (Annex B to the SACHR 18th Report, 1992–93 HC 739, p. 81 at 83–90).
6 Ibid., at 90–92. See also B. Dickson, 'Northern Ireland's Troubles and the Judges' in B. Hadfield (ed.), *Northern Ireland, Politics and the Constitution* (1992), Chap. 9. For criticism of the general reluctance of the House of Lords to scrutinise closely the exercise of emergency powers, to ensure the individual rights are only derogated from the extent clearly mandated by Parliament, see S. Livingstone, 'The House of Lords and the Northern Ireland Conflict' (1994) 57 MLR 333.
7 See below, pp. 564–566.

both Northern Ireland and the Republic of Ireland endorsed the Agreement by large majorities.

This led to elections to the Northern Ireland Assembly in June 1998. On 15 August, 29 people were killed in Omagh by a bomb planted by the Real IRA. In July 1999 the Northern Ireland Executive collapsed following a boycott by the Ulster Unionist Party. However, following a review of implementation of the Good Friday Agreement by George Mitchell and agreement between UUP and Sinn Fein, ministers were elected to the Executive and powers were transferred to it on 2 December. On 11 February 2000, the Executive was suspended following PIRA's failure to start decommissioning weapons or to indicate a date by which a start would be made. Following a further PIRA statement on 6 May, devolved powers were restored on 30 May.[8]

Key elements of the *Good Friday Agreement* were: (1) a new British-Irish Agreement recognising the legitimacy of whatever choice is freely exercised by a majority of the people of Northern Ireland with regard to its status and that it is for the people of the island of Ireland alone, by agreement between the two parts, to bring about a united Ireland, if that is their wish; (2) a democratically elected Assembly in Northern Ireland and an Executive with ministers from all parties wishing to nominate; (3) legislative powers expressly made subject to the ECHR and any Bill of Rights for Northern Ireland; (4) a North/South Ministerial Council; (5) a British-Irish Council and Intergovernmental Conference; (6) new arrangements for the protection of human rights; (7) a commitment to the total disarmament of all para-military organisations; (8) progress towards the normalisation of security arrangements and practice; (9) the review of policing structures and the criminal justice system; (10) mechanisms for the accelerated release of prisoners convicted of scheduled offences or the equivalent; (11) referenda and review procedures.

The institutional framework of the Good Friday Agreement was established by the Northern Ireland Act 1998, which provided for devolved legislative powers; the Executive and Assembly; the NSMC, BIC and BIIC; and a new Northern Ireland Human Rights Commission (replacing the SACHR) and Equality Commission for Northern Ireland. Policing arrangements were reformed by the Police (Northern Ireland) Act 1998 (*inter alia* establishing a Police Ombudsman for Northern Ireland to deal with complaints) and the Police (Northern Ireland) Act 2000 (implementing certain of the recommendations of the Independent Commission on Policing for Northern Ireland chaired by Chris Patten).[9]

Disturbances in Northern Ireland: Report of a Commission appointed by the Governor of Northern Ireland, Chairman: Lord Cameron [Cmd. 532, 1969]

SUMMARY OF CONCLUSIONS ON CAUSES OF DISORDERS

(a) General
(1) A rising sense of continuing injustice and grievance among large sections of the Catholic population in Northern Ireland, in particular Londonderry and Dungannon, in respect of (i) inadequacy of housing provision by certain local authorities (ii) unfair methods of allocation of houses built and let by such authorities, in particular, refusals and omissions to adopt a 'points' system in determining priorities and making allocations (iii) misuse in certain cases of discretionary powers of allocation of houses in order to perpetuate Unionist control of the local authority.
(2) Complaints, now well documented in fact, of discrimination in the making of local government appointments, at all levels but especially in senior posts, to the prejudice of non-

---

8 This chronology is based on M. Cox, A. Guelke and F. Stephen (eds.), *A farewell to arms?* (2000), Appendix 1.
9 Report, September 1999.

Unionists and especially Catholic members of the community, in some Unionist controlled authorities.

(3) Complaints, again well documented, in some cases of deliberate manipulation of local government electoral boundaries and in others a refusal to apply for their necessary extension, in order to achieve and maintain Unionist control of local authorities and so to deny to Catholics influence in local government proportionate to their numbers.

(4) A growing and powerful sense of resentment and frustration among the Catholic population at failure to achieve either acceptance on the part of the Government of any need to investigate these complaints or to provide and enforce a remedy for them.

(5) Resentment, particularly among Catholics, as to the existence of the Ulster Special Constabulary (the 'B' Specials) as a partisan and para-military force recruited exclusively from Protestants.

(6) Widespread resentment among Catholics in particular at the continuance in force of regulations made under the Special Powers Act, and of the continued presence in the statute book of the Act itself.

(7) Fears and apprehensions among Protestants of a threat to Unionist domination and control of Government by increase of Catholic population and powers, inflamed in particular by the activities of the Ulster Constitution Defence Committee and the Ulster Protestant Volunteers, provoked strong hostile reaction to civil rights claims as asserted by the Civil Rights Association and later by the People's Democracy which was readily translated into physical violence against Civil Rights demonstrators....

Report of a Committee to consider, in the context of civil liberties and human rights, measures to deal with terrorism in Northern Ireland, Chairman: Lord Gardiner (Cmnd. 5847, 1975)

CIVIL LIBERTIES AND HUMAN RIGHTS

15. Our terms of reference require us to consider the problem of terrorism and subversion ... with due consideration for the preservation of civil liberties and human rights. We have been set the difficult task of maintaining a double perspective; for, while there are policies which contribute to the maintenance of order at the expense of individual freedom, the maintenance without restriction of that freedom may involve a heavy toll in death and destruction. Some of those who have given evidence to us have argued that such features of the present emergency provisions as the use of the Army in aid of civil power, detention without trial, arrest on suspicion and trial without jury are so inherently objectionable that they must be abolished on the grounds that they constitute a basic violation of human rights. We are unable to accept this argument. While the liberty of the subject is a human right to be preserved under all possible conditions, it is not, and cannot be, an absolute right, because one man may use his liberty to take away the liberty of another, and must be restricted from doing so. Where freedoms conflict, the state has a duty to protect those in need of protection....

17. The suspension of normal legal safeguards for the liberty of the subject may sometimes be essential, in a society faced by terrorism, to counter greater evils. But if continued for any period of time it exacts a social cost from the community; and the price may have to be paid over several generations. It is one of the aims of terrorists to evoke from the authorities an over-reaction to the violence, for which the terrorists are responsible, with the consequence that the authorities lose the support of those who would otherwise be on the side of government.

18. In the present situation there are neighbourhoods in Northern Ireland where natural social motivation is being deployed against lawful authority rather than in support of it. Any good society is compounded of a network of natural affection and loyalties; yet we have seen and heard of situations in which normal human responses such as family affection, love of home, neighbourliness, loyalty to friends and patriotism are daily invoked to strengthen terrorist activity.

19. The imposition of order may be successful in the short term; but in the long term, peace and stability can only come from that consensus which is the basis of law. The tragedy of Northern Ireland is that crime has become confused with politically motivated acts. The common criminal can flourish in a situation where there is a convenient political motive to cover anti-social acts; and the development of a 'prisoner-of-war' mentality among prisoners with social approval and the hope of an amnesty, lends tacit support to violence and dishonesty.

20. We acknowledge the need for firm and decisive action on the part of the security forces; but violence has in the past provoked a violent response. The adoption of methods of interrogation 'in depth', which involved forms of ill-treatment that are described in the Compton Report (Cmnd. 4823), did not last for long. Following the Report of the Parker Committee in 1972 (Cmnd. 4901) these methods were declared unlawful and were stopped by the British Government; but the resentment caused was intense, widespread and persistent.

21. **The continued existence of emergency powers should be limited both in scope and duration.** Though there are times when they are necessary for the preservation of human life, they can, if prolonged, damage the fabric of the community, and they do not provide lasting solutions. **A solution to the problems of Northern Ireland should be worked out in political terms, and must include further measures to promote social justice between classes and communities. Much has been done to improve social conditions in recent years, but much remains to be done.**[10]

The Good Friday Agreement: agreement reached in the multi-party negotiations

6. RIGHTS, SAFEGUARDS AND EQUALITY OF OPPORTUNITY

Human Rights

1. The parties affirm their commitment to the mutual respect, the civil rights and the religious liberties of everyone in the community. Against the background of the recent history of communal conflict, the parties affirm in particular:

- the right of free political thought;
- the right to freedom and expression of religion;
- the right to pursue democratically national and political aspirations;
- the right to seek constitutional change by peaceful and legitimate means;
- the right to freely choose one's place of residence;
- the right to equal opportunity in all social and economic activity, regardless of class, creed, disability, gender or ethnicity;
- the right to freedom from sectarian harassment; and
- the right of women to full and equal political participation.

United Kingdom Legislation

2. The British Government will complete incorporation into Northern Ireland law of the European Convention on Human Rights (ECHR), with direct access to the courts, and remedies for breach of the Convention, including power for the courts to overrule Assembly legislation on grounds of inconsistency.

3. Subject to the outcome of public consultation underway, the British Government intends, as a particular priority, to create a statutory obligation on public authorities in Northern Ireland to carry out all their functions with due regard to the need to promote equality of opportunity in relation to religion and political opinion; gender; race; disability; age; marital status; dependants; and sexual orientation. Public bodies would be required to draw up statutory schemes showing how they would implement this obligation. Such schemes would cover arrangements for policy appraisal, including an assessment of impact on relevant categories, public consultation, public access to information and services, monitoring and timetables.

4. The new Northern Ireland Human Rights Commission (see paragraph 5 below) will be invited to consult and to advise on the scope for defining, in Westminster legislation, rights supplementary to those in the European Convention on Human Rights, to reflect the particular circumstances of Northern Ireland, drawing as appropriate on international instruments and experience. These additional rights to reflect the principles of mutual respect for the identity and ethos of both communities and parity of esteem, and – taken together with the ECHR – to constitute a Bill of Rights for Northern Ireland. Among the issues for consideration by the Commission will be:

---

1 0 Para. 21 was endorsed as 'no less relevant today than at the time when they were made' by the Standing Advisory Commission on Human Rights (17th Report, 1991–92 HC 54, p. 12).

- the formulation of a general obligation on government and public bodies fully to respect, on the basis of equality of treatment, the identity and ethos of both communities in Northern Ireland; and
- a clear formulation of the rights not to be discriminated against and to equality of opportunity in both the public and private sectors.

New Institutions in Northern Ireland

5. A new Northern Ireland Human Rights Commission, with membership from Northern Ireland reflecting the community balance, will be established by Westminster legislation, independent of Government, with an extended and enhanced role beyond that currently exercised by the Standing Advisory Commission on Human Rights, to include keeping under review the adequacy and effectiveness of laws and practices, making recommendations to Government as necessary; providing information and promoting awareness of human rights; considering draft legislation referred to them by the new Assembly; and, in appropriate cases, bringing court proceedings or providing assistance to individuals doing so.

6. Subject to the outcome of public consultation currently underway, the British Government intends a new statutory Equality Commission to replace the Fair Employment Commission, the Equal Opportunities Commission (NI), the Commission for Racial Equality (NI) and the Disability Council. Such a unified Commission will advise on, validate and monitor the statutory obligation and will investigate complaints of default.

7. It would be open to a new Northern Ireland Assembly to consider bringing together its responsibilities for these matters into a dedicated Department of Equality.

8. These improvements will build on existing protections in Westminster legislation in respect of the judiciary, the system of justice and policing.

Comparable Steps by the Irish Government

9. The Irish Government will also take steps to further strengthen the protection of human rights in its jurisdiction. The Government will, taking account of the work of the All-Party Oireachtas Committee on the Constitution and the Report of the Constitution Review Group, bring forward measures to strengthen and underpin the constitutional protection of human rights. These proposals will draw on the European Convention on Human Rights and other international legal instruments in the field of human rights and the question of the incorporation of the ECHR will be further examined in this context. The measures brought forward would ensure at least an equivalent level of protection of human rights as will pertain in Northern Ireland. In addition, the Irish Government will:

- establish a Human Rights Commission with a mandate and remit equivalent to that within Northern Ireland;
- proceed with arrangements as quickly as possible to ratify the Council of Europe Framework Convention on National Minorities (already ratified by the UK);
- implement enhanced employment equality legislation;
- introduce equal status legislation; and
- continue to take further active steps to demonstrate its respect for the different traditions in the island of Ireland.

A Joint Committee

10. It is envisaged that there would be a joint committee of representatives of the two Human Rights Commissions, North and South, as a forum for consideration of human rights issues in the island of Ireland. The joint committee will consider, among other matters, the possibility of establishing a charter, open to signature by all democratic political parties, reflecting and endorsing agreed measures for the protection of the fundamental rights of everyone living in the island of Ireland.

Reconciliation and Victims of Violence

11. The participants believe that it is essential to acknowledge and address the suffering of the victims of violence as a necessary element of reconciliation. They look forward to the results of the work of the Northern Ireland Victims Commission.

12. It is recognised that victims have a right to remember as well as to contribute to a changed society. The achievement of a peaceful and just society would be the true memorial to the victims of violence. The participants particularly recognise that young people from areas affected

by the troubles face particular difficulties and will support the development of special community-based initiatives based on international best practice. The provision of services that are supportive and sensitive to the needs of victims will also be a critical element and that support will need to be channelled through both statutory and community-based voluntary organisations facilitating locally-based self-help and support networks. This will require the allocation of sufficient resources, including statutory funding as necessary, to meet the needs of victims and to provide for community-based support programmes.

13. The participants recognise and value the work being done by many organisations to develop reconciliation and mutual understanding and respect between and within communities and traditions, in Northern Ireland and between North and South, and they see such work as having a vital role in consolidating peace and political agreement. Accordingly, they pledge their continuing support to such organisations and will positively examine the case for enhanced financial assistance for the work of reconciliation. An essential aspect of the reconciliation process is the promotion of a culture of tolerance at every level of society, including initiatives to facilitate and encourage integrated education and mixed housing . . .

8. SECURITY

1. The participants note that the development of a peaceful environment on the basis of this agreement can and should mean a normalisation of security arrangements and practices.

2. The British Government will make progress towards the objective of as early a return as possible to normal security arrangements in Northern Ireland, consistent with the level of threat and with a published overall strategy, dealing with:

- (i)　the reduction of the numbers and role of the Armed Forces deployed in Northern Ireland to levels compatible with a normal peaceful society;
- (ii)　the removal of security installations;
- (iii)　the removal of emergency powers in Northern Ireland; and
- (iv)　other measures appropriate to and compatible with a normal peaceful society.

3. The Secretary of State will consult regularly on progress, and the response to any continuing paramilitary activity, with the Irish Government and the political parties, as appropriate.

4. The British Government will continue its consultation on firearms regulation and control on the basis of the document published on 2 April 1998.

5. The Irish Government will initiate a wide-ranging review of the Offences Against the State Acts 1939–85 with a view to both reform and dispensing with those elements no longer required as circumstances permit.

4　The Terrorism Act 2000[11]

Terrorism Act 2000

PART I
INTRODUCTORY
1. Terrorism: interpretation

(1) In this Act 'terrorism' means the use or threat of action where—
- (a)　the action falls within subsection (2),
- (b)　the use or threat is designed to influence the government or to intimidate the public or a section of the public, and
- (c)　the use or threat is made for the purpose of advancing a political, religious or ideological cause.

(2) Action falls within this subsection if it—
- (a)　involves serious violence against a person,
- (b)　involves serious damage to property,
- (c)　endangers a person's life, other than that of the person committing the action,
- (d)　creates a serious risk to the health or safety of the public or a section of the public, or
- (e)　is designed seriously to interfere with or seriously to disrupt an electronic system.

11　See J. J. Rowe, *Current Law Statutes Annotated 2000*; H.O. Circular 03/01. See generally N. Whitty, T. Murphy and S. Livingstone, *Civil Liberties Law: The Human Rights Act Era* (2001), Chap. 3.

(3) The use or threat of action falling within subsection (2) which involves the use of firearms or explosives is terrorism whether or not subsection (1)(b) is satisfied.

(4) In this section—

    (a) 'action' includes action outside the United Kingdom,

    (b) a reference to any person or to property is a reference to any person, or to property, wherever situated,

    (c) a reference to the public includes a reference to the public of a country other than the United Kingdom, and

    (d) 'the government' means the government of the United Kingdom, of a Part of the United Kingdom or of a country other than the United Kingdom.

(5) In this Act a reference to action taken for the purposes of terrorism includes a reference to action taken for the benefit of a proscribed organisation.

NOTES (PART I: INTRODUCTORY)

1. The Terrorism Act 2000[12] repealed the Prevention of Terrorism (Temporary Provisions) Act 1989 (with effect from its commencement by order) and the Northern Ireland (Emergency Provisions) Act 1996 (with effect from royal assent). However, most of the provisions of these Acts as they applied in Northern Ireland were continued in force between royal assent and commencement,[13] which took place on 19 February 2001.[14] Part VII ceases to have effect at the end of 12 months from its commencement, but it may be extended by order of the Secretary of State approved by an affirmative resolution of each House, subject to a maximum term of five years.[15] The 2000 Act was enacted following a review of terrorism legislation by Lord Lloyd[16] and the publication of a consultation paper.[17] The government agreed with Lord Lloyd that 'there will be a continuing need for counter-terrorist legislation for the foreseeable future,' regardless of the threat of terrorism related to Northern Ireland, and that the time had come for it to be put on a permanent footing.[18]

2. *Historical origins*

(i) *Prevention of terrorism legislation.* The Prevention of Terrorism (Temporary Provisions) Act 1989 had its origins in the Prevention of Violence (Temporary Provisions) Act 1939[19] which was also designed to deal with terrorism relating to Irish affairs, and was in force between 1939 and 1954. The Prevention of Terrorism (Temporary Provisions) Act 1974[20] was passed in the aftermath of the Birmingham public house bombings of 21 November 1974 when 21 people were killed and over 180 injured. The Bill was introduced on 27 November and received the Royal Assent on 29 November. It was re-enacted, with some amendments, as the Prevention of Terrorism (Temporary Provisions) Act 1976.[1] The 1976 Act was replaced by the

---

12 s. 2.

13 Sch. 1.

14 Terrorism Act 2000 (Commencement No. 3) Order 2001, S.I. 2001 No. 421.

15 s. 112.

16 *Inquiry into legislation against terrorism*, Cm. 3420, 1996 (hereafter, *Lloyd Inquiry*).

17 *Legislation Against Terrorism*, Cm. 4178, 1998.

18 Ibid., Introduction. Vol. 2 of the *Lloyd Inquiry* comprised an assessment by Professor Paul Wilkinson of the current and potential future terrorist threat to the UK from both international and domestic groups.

19 See O.G. Lomas, [1980] PL 16.

20 See H. Street, [1975] Crim LR 192.

1 The operation of the 1976 Act was monitored by the National Council for Civil Liberties (see C. Scorer, *The Prevention of Terrorism Acts 1974 and 1976* (NCCL, 1976) and was reviewed by Lord Shackleton in a report for the Home Office (*Review of the Operation of the Prevention of Terrorism (Temporary Provisions) Acts 1974 and 1976* (Cmnd. 7324, 1978). The provisions concerning exclusion orders were discussed by D. Bonner, [1982] PL 262.

Prevention of Terrorism (Temporary Provisions) Act 1984 following Lord Jellicoe's *Review of the Operation of the Prevention of Terrorism (Temporary Provisions) Act 1976*.[2] The 1984 Act was in turn replaced by the 1989 Act[3], following Lord Colville's *Review of the Operation of the Prevention of Terrorism (Temporary Provisions) Act 1984*.[4] The Labour Party was committed to the repeal of the 1989 Act[5] but the Labour government elected in 1997 did not take this step and, indeed, secured the passage of new permanent legislation.

(ii) *Northern Ireland Emergency Provisions legislation*. There have been many occasions in Irish history when the government of the day has secured the enactment of wider statutory powers to deal with the problem of security than those normally available in Great Britain.[6] In the nineteenth century, for example, the protection of Persons and Property Act (Ireland) 1881,[7] the Peace Preservation (Ireland) Act 1881,[8] the Prevention of Crime (Ireland) Act 1882,[9] and the Criminal Law and Procedure (Ireland) Act 1887,[10] included many provisions similar to those contained in the Northern Ireland (Emergency Provisions) Act 1996, including powers of detention, arrest and search, and trial without a jury for certain kinds of offence. In addition there were at various times powers to prohibit meetings, provisions as to special juries and the change of venue of trials, and provisions making intimidation an offence.

In the twentieth century, the main piece of 'emergency' legislation in Northern Ireland was the Civil Authorities (Special Powers) Act (NI) 1922 and the regulations made thereunder. This was originally intended as a temporary measure, but was renewed annually until 1928 and then for five years to 1933. It was then provided that the Act 'shall continue in force until Parliament otherwise determines' by the Civil Authorities (Special Powers) Act (NI) 1933.[11] The content of the regulations was altered from time to time, and certain features were strongly criticised.[12] One of the most objectionable provisions was s. 2(4) of the 1922 Act which provided that:

'If any person does any act of such a nature as to be calculated to be prejudicial to the preservation of the peace or maintenance of order in Northern Ireland and not specifically provided for in the regulations, he shall be deemed to be guilty of an offence against the regulations.'

This has had no counterpart in the successive Northern Ireland (Emergency Provisions) Acts.

2 Cmnd. 8803, 1983. See D. Bonner, 'Combating Terrorism: The Jellicoe Approach' [1983] PL 224; C. P. Walker, (1983) 46 MLR 484; J. Sim and P. Thomas, (1983) 10 JLS 71; *Current Law Statutes 1984* (annotations by D.S. Greer); C. Walker, (1984) 47 MLR 704; A. Samuels, [1984] PL 365; D. Bonner, *Emergency Powers in Peacetime* (1985), Chap. 4.

3 On the 1989 Act, see D. Bonner, [1989] PL 440; W. Finnie, 1990 JR 1; B. Dickson, (1989) 40 NILQ 250; C. Walker, *The Prevention of Terrorism in British Law* (2nd edn, 1992). The case for repeal without replacement was argued by C. Scorer and P. Hewitt, *The New Prevention of Terrorism Act: The Case for Repeal* (3rd edn, 1985). The impact on individuals' lives of the operation of the legislation was documented by P. Hillyard, *Suspect Community* (1993).

4 Cm. 264, 1987 (hereafter, *Colville Review (PTA)*).

5 See H. Arnott, 'Breaking the Silence', *Legal Action*, May 1990, p. 25.

6 See generally C. Townshend, *Political Violence in Ireland* (1983).

7 44 Vict c4.

8 45 Vict c5.

9 45 & 46 Vict c25.

10 50 & 51 Vict c20.

11 s. 2.

12 See the *Report of a Commission of Inquiry appointed to examine the purpose and effect of the Civil Authorities (Special Powers) Acts (NI) 1922 and 1933* (NCCL, 1936); *A Review of the 1936 NCCL Commission of Inquiry into the light of subsequent events* (NCCL, 1972); J. Ll. J. Edwards, [1956] Crim LR 7; H. Calvert, *Constitutional Law in Northern Ireland* (1968), pp. 380-386; *Emergency Powers: A Fresh Start*, Fabian Tract 416 (1972).

The legal procedures to deal with terrorist activities were reviewed by the Diplock Commission.[13] The Northern Ireland (Emergency Provisions) Act 1973 (which repealed the Special Powers Acts) was based upon their recommendations. The legislation was amended in 1975, consolidated in 1978, amended again in 1987, [14] consolidated with yet further amendments in 1991, consolidated again in 1996 and amended in 1998. It has been the subject of major reviews.[15] One of its features was a steady increase in size and scope.

The 1991 Act was analysed by B. Dickson,[16] who argued[17] that:

'Whatever the position in the early 1970s, the objective behind anti-terrorist legislation today, whether in Northern Ireland or in Great Britain, is no longer the prevention of atrocities or the detection and punishment of those who perpetrate them. Its real purpose is to placate the electorate, as well as some of the elected, who demand that some steps must be taken by the law to counteract terrorism, regardless of how effective these might prove in practice. Emergency law, in other words, is being exploited for its symbolic significance.'

3. *Statistics and monitoring.* Statistics as to the operation of the PTA 1989 were given regularly in Home Office Statistical Bulletins. Annual reviews of that Act were conducted, successively, by Sir Cyril Philips (1984–1985), Lord Colville (1986–1992) and John Rowe QC (1993–1999). Similar reviews of the EPA were conducted by Colville (1987–1992) and Rowe (1993–1999) and published by the Northern Ireland Office. These reports formed the background to the annual renewal debates. The 2000 Act requires that a report on its working be laid before Parliament at least once in every 12 months.[18] There were also, periodically, major reviews of each legislative regime.[19]

Issues arising out of special or emergency powers may arise in prosecutions or civil actions by or against the authorities. In addition, there are separate procedures for dealing with non-criminal complaints against the police and the army. The former may involve the Police Complaints Authority in England and Wales[20] and the Police Ombudsman for Northern Ireland.[1] Complaints against the army in Northern Ireland are monitored by the Independent Assessor of Military Complaints Procedure in Northern Ireland.[2] Unlike the case for police complaints, the Assessor has no power to oversee particular investigations and has no power of direction.[3]

4. *Definition of terrorism.* The definition of terrorism in s. 1 is both broader and narrower than previous definitions. Section 20 of the PTA 1989 and s. 58 of the EPA 1996 referred to 'the use of violence for political ends [including] any use of violence for the purpose of putting the public, or any section of the public in fear'. The PTA also conferred powers only in respect of terrorism connected with the affairs

---

13 Report, Cmnd. 5185, 1972; see W. L. Twining, [1972] Crim LR 407.
14 On the 1987 Act, see J. D. Jackson, (1988) 39 NILQ 235.
15 The Gardiner Committee (Cmnd. 5847, 1975; above, p. 563; the Bennett Committee Inquiry into *Police Interrogation Procedures in Northern Ireland* (Cmnd. 7497, 1989); Sir George Baker, *Review of the Operation of the Northern Ireland (Emergency Provisions) Act 1978* (Cmnd. 9222, 1984) Viscount Colville, *Review of the Northern Ireland (Emergency Provisions) Act 1978 and 1987* (Cm. 1115, 1990); J. J. Rowe QC, *Review of the Northern Ireland (Emergency Provisions) Act 1991* (Cm. 2706, 1995) (hereafter, *Rowe Review (EPA)*).
16 'Northern Ireland's Emergency Legislation' [1992] PL 592.
17 p. 597.
18 s. 126.
19 See above.
20 See pp. 126–134.
 1 Police (Northern Ireland) Act 1998.
 2 Originally appointed under s. 60 of the EPA 1991; now the Terrorism Act 2000, s. 98 and Sch. 11.
 3 See B. Dickson, [1992] PL 592.

of Northern Ireland or international terrorism. The 2000 Act applies to *serious* violence etc. but introduces a reference to religious and ideological purposes and the Act applies to both domestic and international terrorism. In which circumstances could an industrial dispute fall within the definition? Or the disruption of fuel supplies?

In justifying the extension, the government noted that the methods employed by terrorists and the effects of their actions were common whatever the cause espoused by them. Furthermore, there was a sufficient threat from domestic terrorists, including animal rights activists and to a lesser extent environmental rights activists to justify special powers. The threat of Scottish and Welsh nationalist extremists had considerably diminished, but there was a possibility that terrorist groups might develop in other contexts, such as in opposition to abortion (where there had been bombings and murders in the United States).[4]

Part II
Proscribed Organisations
Procedure
3. Proscription
(1) For the purposes of this Act an organisation is proscribed if—
  (*a*) it is listed in Schedule 2, or
  (*b*) it operates under the same name as an organisation listed in that Schedule.
(2) Subsection (1)(*b*) shall not apply in relation to an organisation listed in Schedule 2 if its entry is the subject of a note in that Schedule.
(3) The Secretary of State may by order—
  (*a*) add an organisation to Schedule 2;
  (*b*) remove an organisation from that Schedule;
  (*c*) amend that Schedule in some other way.
(4) The Secretary of State may exercise his power under subsection (3)(*a*) in respect of an organisation only if he believes that it is concerned in terrorism.
(5) For the purposes of subsection (4) an organisation is concerned in terrorism if it—
  (*a*) commits or participates in acts of terrorism,
  (*b*) prepares for terrorism,
  (*c*) promotes or encourages terrorism, or
  (*d*) is otherwise concerned in terrorism.

4. Deproscription application
(1) An application may be made to the Secretary of State for the exercise of his power under section 3(3)(*b*) to remove an organisation from Schedule 2.
(2) An application may be made by—
  (*a*) the organisation, or
  (*b*) any person affected by the organisation's proscription.
(3) The Secretary of State shall make regulations prescribing the procedure for applications under this section.
(4) The regulations shall, in particular—
  (*a*) require the Secretary of State to determine an application within a specified period of time, and
  (*b*) require an application to state the grounds on which it is made.

5. Deproscription appeal
(1) There shall be a commission, to be known as the Proscribed Organisations Appeal Commission.
(2) Where an application under section 4 has been refused, the applicant may appeal to the Commission.
(3) The Commission shall allow an appeal against a refusal to deproscribe an organisation if it considers that the decision to refuse was flawed when considered in the light of the principles applicable on an application for judicial review.
(4) Where the Commission allows an appeal under this section by or in respect of an organisation, it may make an order under this subsection.

---

4 *Legislation against Terrorism*, Chap. 3.

(5)Where an order is made under subsection (4) the Secretary of State shall as soon as is reasonably practicable—

    (*a*) lay before Parliament, in accordance with section 123(4), the draft of an order under section 3(3)(*b*) removing the organisation from the list in Schedule 2, or

    (*b*) make an order removing the organisation from the list in Schedule 2 in pursuance of section 123(5).

(6)Schedule 3 (constitution of the Commission and procedure) shall have effect.

6. Further appeal

(1)A party to an appeal under section 5 which the Proscribed Organisations Appeal Commission has determined may bring a further appeal on a question of law to—

    (*a*) the Court of Appeal, if the first appeal was heard in England and Wales,

    (*b*) the Court of Session, if the first appeal was heard in Scotland, or

    (*c*) the Court of Appeal in Northern Ireland, if the first appeal was heard in Northern Ireland.

(2)An appeal under subsection (1) may be brought only with the permission—

    (*a*) of the Commission, or

    (*b*) where the Commission refuses permission, of the court to which the appeal would be brought.

(3)An order under section 5(4) shall not require the Secretary of State to take any action until the final determination or disposal of an appeal under this section (including any appeal to the House of Lords).

7. Appeal: effect on conviciton, etc.

(1)This section applies where—

    (*a*) an appeal under section 5 has been allowed in respect of an organisation,

    (*b*) an order has been made under section 3(3)(*b*) in respect of the organisation in accordance with an order of the Commission under section 5(4) (and, if the order was made in reliance on section 123(5), a resolution has been passed by each House of Parliament under section 123(5)(*b*)),

    (*c*) a person has been convicted of an offence in respect of the organisation under any of sections 11 to 13, 15 to 19 and 56, and

    (*d*) the activity to which the charge referred took place on or after the date of the refusal to deproscribe against which the appeal under section 5 was brought.

[Subsections (2) to (5) and s. 8 provide for the person convicted to have the right to appeal against the conviction to the Court of Appeal or the Crown Court, (in England and Wales), the High Court of Justiciary (in Scotland) and the Court of Appeal of Northern Ireland and the County Court (in Northern Ireland), and for the court to be required to allow the appeal.]

9. Human Rights Act 1998

(1)This section applies where rules (within the meaning of section 7 of the Human Rights Act 1998 (jurisdiction)) provide for proceedings under section 7(1) of that Act to be brought before the Proscribed Organisations Appeal Commission.[5]

(2)The following provisions of this Act shall apply in relation to proceedings under section 7(1) of that Act as they apply to appeals under section 5 of this Act—

    (*a*) section 5(4) and (5),

    (*b*) section 6,

    (*c*) section 7, and

    (*d*) paragraphs 4 to [7] of Schedule 3.

(3)The Commission shall decide proceedings in accordance with the principles applicable on an application for judicial review.

(4)In the application of the provisions mentioned in subsection (2)—

    (*a*) a reference to the Commission allowing an appeal shall be taken as a reference to the Commission determining that an action of the Secretary of State is incompatible with a Convention right, and

5 See the Proscribed Organisations Appeal Commission (Human Rights Act Proceedings) Rules 2001, S.I. 2001 No. 127, which provide that the Commission is an appropriate tribunal for the purposes of s. 7 in relation to any proceedings under s. 7(1)(*a*) against the Secretary of State in respect of a refusal to deproscribe.

(b)   a reference to the refusal to deproscribe against which an appeal was brought shall be taken as a reference to the action of the Secretary of State which is found to be incompatible with a Convention right.

10. Immunity

(1) The following shall not be admissible as evidence in proceedings for an offence under any of sections 11 to 13, 15 to 19 and 56—

(a)   evidence of anything done in relation to an application to the Secretary of State under section 4,

(b)   evidence of anything done in relation to proceedings before the Proscribed Organisations Appeal Commission under section 5 above or section 7(1) of the Human Rights Act 1998,

(c)   evidence of anything done in relation to proceedings under section 6 (including that section as applied by section 9(2)), and

(d)   any document submitted for the purposes of proceedings mentioned in any of paragraphs (a) to (c).

(2) But subsection (1) does not prevent evidence from being adduced on behalf of the accused.

Offences
11. Membership

(1) A person commits an offence if he belongs or professes to belong to a proscribed organisation.

(2) It is a defence for a person charged with an offence under subsection (1) to prove—

(a)   that the organisation was not proscribed on the last (or only) occasion on which he became a member or began to profess to be a member, and

(b)   that he has not taken part in the activities of the organisation at any time while it was proscribed.

(3) A person guilty of an offence under this section shall be liable—

(a)   on conviction on indictment, to imprisonment for a term not exceeding ten years, to a fine or to both, or

(b)   on summary conviction, to imprisonment for a term not exceeding six months, to a fine not exceeding the statutory maximum or to both.

(4) In subsection (2) 'proscribed' means proscribed for the purposes of any of the following—

(a)   this Act;

(b)   the Northern Ireland (Emergency Provisions) Act 1996;

(c)   the Northern Ireland (Emergency Provisions) Act 1991;

(d)   the Prevention of Terrorism (Temporary Provisions) Act 1989;

(e)   the Prevention of Terrorism (Temporary Provisions) Act 1984;

(f)   the Northern Ireland (Emergency Provisions) Act 1978;

(g)   the Prevention of Terrorism (Temporary Provisions) Act 1976;

(h)   the Prevention of Terrorism (Temporary Provisions) Act 1974;

(i)   the Northern Ireland (Emergency Provisions) Act 1973.

12. Support

(1) A person commits an offence if—

(a)   he invites support for a proscribed organisation, and

(b)   the support is not, or is not restricted to, the provision of money or other property (within the meaning of section 15).

(2) A person commits an offence if he arranges, manages or assists in arranging or managing a meeting which he knows is—

(a)   to support a proscribed organisation,

(b)   to further the activities of a proscribed organisation, or

(c)   to be addressed by a person who belongs or professes to belong to a proscribed organisation.

(3) A person commits an offence if he addresses a meeting and the purpose of his address is to encourage support for a proscribed organisation or to further its activities.

(4) Where a person is charged with an offence under subsection (2)(c) in respect of a private meeting it is a defence for him to prove that he had no reasonable cause to believe that the address mentioned in subsection (2)(c) would support a proscribed organisation or further its activities.

(5) In subsections (2) to (4)—
    (*a*) 'meeting' means a meeting of three or more persons, whether or not the public are admitted, and
    (*b*) a meeting is private if the public are not admitted.
(6) A person guilty of an offence under this section shall be liable—
    (*a*) on conviction on indictment, to imprisonment for a term not exceeding ten years, to a fine or to both, or
    (*b*) on summary conviction, to imprisonment for a term not exceeding six months, to a fine not exceeding the statutory maximum or to both.

13. Uniform
(1) A person in a public place commits an offence if he—
    (*a*) wears an item of clothing, or
    (*b*) wears, carries or displays an article,
in such a way or in such circumstances as to arouse reasonable suspicion that he is a member or supporter of a proscribed organisation . . .
(3) A person guilty of an offence under this section shall be liable on summary conviction to—
    (*a*) imprisonment for a term not exceeding six months,
    (*b*) a fine not exceeding level 5 on the standard scale, or
    (*c*) both.

NOTES (PART II: PROSCRIBED ORGANISATIONS)

1. *Proscribed organisations.* Powers to proscribe organisations were conferred by both the EPA (in Northern Ireland) and PTA (elsewhere in the UK). They only applied in respect of terrorism related to Northern Irish affairs.

The 'Irish Republican Army' (which term covers both the 'Official' and 'Provisional' wings) was proscribed under the PTA 1974. The Irish National Liberation Army was proscribed in July 1979.[6] The group had claimed responsibility for the killing of Mr Airey Neave, Opposition spokesman on Northern Ireland. They remained proscribed throughout the operation of the PTA 1989 and are proscribed under the 2000 Act. These and a number of other organisations were proscribed by the EPA. Neither Lord Jellicoe[7] nor Lord Colville[8] saw any need for symmetry for proscription under the two regimes given that the difference reflected the activities of terrorist organisations in different parts of the UK. Such symmetry is now introduced by the 2000 Act, which establishes one regime for proscribed organisations and extends its scope to cover domestic and international terrorism in addition to Northern Ireland-related terrorism.

Schedule 2 of the 2000 Act proscribes the IRA, Cumann na mBan, Fianna na hEireann, the Red Hand Commando, Saor Eire, the Ulster Freedom Fighters, the Ulster Volunteer Force, the INLA, the Irish People's Liberation Organisation, the Ulster Defence Organisation, the Loyalist Volunteer Force, the Continuity Army Council, the Orange Volunteers, and the Red Hand Defenders. All were previously proscribed under the PTA or EPA. The criteria for proscription are not set out in the Act (beyond s. 3(4), (5)). From 29 March 2001, 21 international organisations were also proscribed.[9] It was stated in Parliament that the Secretary of State would take account of such factors as the nature and scale of the group's activities, the specific threat they pose to the UK and British nationals abroad, the extent of their presence in the UK and the need to support other members of the international community in the global fight

6 S.I. 1979 No. 745.
7 1983 Report, para. 2-11.
8 *Colville Review (EPA)*, p. 5.
9 Terrorism Act 2000 (Proscribed Organisations) (Amendment) Order 2001, S.I. 2001 No. 1261.

against terrorism.[10] A novel feature is that a refusal by the Secretary of State to deproscribe an organisation may be subject to an appeal to the Proscribed Organisation Appeals Commission. The Commission is to apply judicial review principles (including principles arising out of the Human Rights Act 1998). The Commission's members are appointed by the Lord Chancellor; it sits in panels of three, one of whom must be a person who holds or has held high judicial office.[11] Procedural rules are made by the Lord Chancellor, and may include limits on the reasons and evidence disclosed to the organisation or applicant concerned and provision for a lawyer to be appointed by the relevant Law Officer to represent the interests of but not be responsible to the organisation or applicant concerned.[12]

Under the PTA and EPA, convictions for membership or support of a proscribed organisation were relatively rare.[13] An offence of contributing to the resources of a proscribed organisation[14] led to more convictions.[15] The Criminal Justice (Terrorism and Conspiracy) Act 1998[16] inserted provisions into the EPA[17] and PTA[18] making the opinion of a senior police officer that a person belonged to a 'specified organisation' admissible as evidence of the matter stated. A 'specified organisation' was one which was (1) specified under s. 3(8) of the Northern Ireland (Sentences) Act 1998 or under (respectively) the PTA 1989, s. 2B(2) or EPA 1996, s. 30B(2); and (2) is or is part of a proscribed organisation. The criterion for specification was that the Secretary of State believed that the organisation was concerned in terrorism connected with the affairs of Northern Ireland, or in promoting or encouraging it, and had not established or was not maintaining a complete and unequivocal ceasefire.[19] The Act was passed in the immediate aftermath of the Omagh bombing. Parliament's wish to be seen to act is understandable. However, it is very doubtful whether any significant use of these provisions would comply with Art. 6 of the ECHR given the practical difficulty if not impossibility for the defendant to challenge the evidence on which the opinion is based.[20] They were not used in practice.[1]

A similar provision appears in the 2000 Act (s. 108), but only in respect of Northern Ireland. Serious doubts as to its compliance now with the Human Rights Act 1998 remain.

The justification advanced for proscription is as follows:[2]

---

10 Charles Clarke, 341 HC Deb, col. 227 (in respect of international terrorism); Adam Ingram, Standing Committee D, col. 79 (in respect of domestic terrorism). This approach was confirmed in HO News Release, 28 March 2001, on S.I. 2001 No. 1261.

11 Sch. 3, paras. 1, 4.

12 Ibid., paras. 5–8. See the Proscribed Organisations Appeal Commission (Procedure) Rules 2001, S.I. 2001 No. 443. See also the Proscribed Organisations (Applications for Deproscription) Regulations 2001, S.I. 2001 No. 107. Cf. arrangements for the handling of appeals in other security-sensitive contexts: below, p. 807.

13 In *R v Adams* [1978] 5 NIJB, Belfast City Commission, Lowry LCJ declined to infer IRA membership from the defendant's conduct in parading in a compound of the Maze prison run by the inmates on quasi-military lines.

14 PTA 1989, s. 10.

15 *Walker*, p. 125.

16 ss. 1, 2. See annotations by C. Walker in *Current Law Statutes Annotated 1998*; 24th Annual Report of the SACHR for 1998–99, Annex F (papers by C. Campbell and B. J. McDonald); C. Campbell, [1999] Crim LR 941 and C. Walker, (1999) 62 MLR 879.

17 ss. 2A, 2B.

18 ss. 30A, 30B.

19 See *Re Williamson* [2000] NI 281 where the Court of Appeal in Northern Ireland held that the Secretary of State had been entitled not to specify the PIRA notwithstanding that she was satisfied of their involvement in arms smuggling and a murder in breach of the ceasefire; this did not necessarily mean that the PIRA was not maintaining an unequivocal ceasefire.

20 See C. Walker, op cit, pp. 40-10–40-11; J. J. Rowe, *1998 EPA Report*, paras. 27–29.

1 J. J. Rowe, op cit, para. 61 and *1999 PTA Report*, para. 51.

2 *Legislation against Terrorism*, paras. 4.7, 4.8.

'Should the proscription powers be retained in respect of Irish terrorism?

4.7 In Northern Ireland, in particular, proscription has come to symbolise the community's abhorrence of the kind of violence that has blighted society there for over 30 years. The indications are that the proscription provisions have made life significantly more difficult for organisations to which they have been applied. Whilst the measures may not in themselves have closed down terrorist organisations, a knock on effect has been to deny the proscribed groups legitimate publicity and with it lawful ways of soliciting support and raising funds. Many activities by, or on behalf of, such groups are made more difficult by proscription, and that in itself aids the law enforcement effort in countering them. But perhaps more importantly the provisions have signalled forcefully the government's, and society's, rejection of these organisations' claims to legitimacy.

4.8 There have been no convictions for proscription-related offences in GB since 1990, though, in the same period, 195 convictions in Northern Ireland (usually as the second count on the charge sheet). But the indications are that the provisions have produced some less quantifiable but still significant outcomes. In particular it is suggested they have led proscribed organisations to tone down overt promotion and rallies. Although it is less easy to measure what has *not* happened because the proscription provisions have been in place, or to calculate the numbers deterred from supporting proscribed organisations because of the penalties if convicted (up to 10 years' imprisonment and an unlimited fine), the government still believes these factors to be very important.'

The government thought the arguments for and against extending proscription powers to other organisations were finely balanced[3] but ultimately decided in favour of extension. Advantages in extension was that condemnation of any terrorist organisation could be signalled whatever its origin and motivation, and that it could become easier to tackle fundraising. On the other hand, a large number of groups could be candidates and it would be difficult to keep the list up to date. Only Northern Ireland related groups are specified in the Act itself.

2. Compare the offences under ss. 12 and 13 with s. 1 of the Public Order Act 1936, banning political uniforms[4]. Are these offences necessary or desirable?[5]

PART III
TERRORIST PROPERTY
Interpretation
14. Terrorist property
(1) In this Act 'terrorist property' means—
    (*a*) money or other property which is likely to be used for the purposes of terrorism (including any resources of a proscribed organisation),
    (*b*) proceeds of the commission of acts of terrorism, and
    (*c*) proceeds of acts carried out for the purposes of terrorism.
(2) In subsection (1)—
    (*a*) a reference to proceeds of an act includes a reference to any property which wholly or partly, and directly or indirectly, represents the proceeds of the act (including payments or other rewards in connection with its commission), and
    (*b*) the reference to an organisation's resources includes a reference to any money or other property which is applied or made available, or is to be applied or made available, for use by the organisation.

Offences
15. Fund-raising
(1) A person commits an offence if he—
    (*a*) invites another to provide money or other property, and

---

3   Ibid., paras. 4.12–4.17. Lord Colville had previously argued against the extension of proscription to international terrorism: *Colville Review (PTA)*, p. 46.
4   Above, pp. 411–413.
5   See the debate in respect of the offences under PTA 1989, s. 3 by W. Finnie, [1990] JR 1, 6; B. Robertson, [1991] JR 250; C. Walker, [1993] JR 90; and W. Finnie, [1994] JR 118. Cf. the EPA 1996, s. 31; s. 3 was summary only, s. 31 triable either way.

     (*b*)   intends that it should be used, or has reasonable cause to suspect that it may be used, for the purposes of terrorism.

(2) A person commits an offence if he—

     (*a*)   receives money or other property, and

     (*b*)   intends that it should be used, or has reasonable cause to suspect that it may be used, for the purposes of terrorism.

(3) A person commits an offence if he—

     (*a*)   provides money or other property, and

     (*b*)   knows or has reasonable cause to suspect that it will or may be used for the purposes of terrorism.

(4) In this section a reference to the provision of money or other property is a reference to its being given, lent or otherwise made available, whether or not for consideration.

16. Use and possession

(1) A person commits an offence if he uses money or other property for the purposes of terrorism.

(2) A person commits an offence if he—

     (*a*)   possesses money or other property, and

     (*b*)   intends that it should be used, or has reasonable cause to suspect that it may be used, for the purposes of terrorism.

17. Funding arrangements

A person commits an offence if—

     (*a*)   he enters into or becomes concerned in an arrangement as a result of which money or other property is made available or is to be made available to another, and

     (*b*)   he knows or has reasonable cause to suspect that it will or may be used for the purposes of terrorism.

18. Money laundering

(1) A person commits an offence if he enters into or becomes concerned in an arrangement which facilitates the retention or control by or on behalf of another person of terrorist property—

     (*a*)   by concealment,

     (*b*)   by removal from the jurisdiction,

     (*c*)   by transfer to nominees, or

     (*d*)   in any other way.

(2) It is a defence for a person charged with an offence under subsection (1) to prove that he did not know and had no reasonable cause to suspect that the arrangement related to terrorist property.

19. Disclosure of information: duty

(1) This section applies where a person—

     (*a*)   believes or suspects that another person has committed an offence under any of sections 15 to 18, and

     (*b*)   bases his belief or suspicion on information which comes to his attention in the course of a trade, profession, business or employment.

(2) The person commits an offence if he does not disclose to a constable as soon as is reasonably practicable—

     (*a*)   his belief or suspicion, and

     (*b*)   the information on which it is based.

(3) It is a defence for a person charged with an offence under subsection (2) to prove that he had a reasonable excuse for not making the disclosure.

(4) Where—

     (*a*)   a person is in employment,

     (*b*)   his employer has established a procedure for the making of disclosures of the matters specified in subsection (2), and

     (*c*)   he is charged with an offence under that subsection,

it is a defence for him to prove that he disclosed the matters specified in that subsection in accordance with the procedure.

(5) Subsection (2) does not require disclosure by a professional legal adviser of—

     (*a*)   information which he obtains in privileged circumstances, or

     (*b*)   a belief or suspicion based on information which he obtains in privileged circumstances.

(6) For the purpose of subsection (5) information is obtained by an adviser in privileged circumstances if it comes to him, otherwise than with a view to furthering a criminal purpose—

    (*a*)   from a client or a client's representative, in connection with the provision of legal advice by the adviser to the client,

    (*b*)   from a person seeking legal advice from the adviser, or from the person's representative, or

    (*c*)   from any person, for the purpose of actual or contemplated legal proceedings.

(7) For the purposes of subsection (1)(*a*) a person shall be treated as having committed an offence under one of sections 15 to 18 if—

    (*a*)   he has taken an action or been in possession of a thing, and

    (*b*)   he would have committed an offence under one of those sections if he had been in the United Kingdom at the time when he took the action or was in possession of the thing.

(8) A person guilty of an offence under this section shall be liable—

    (*a*)   on conviction on indictment, to imprisonment for a term not exceeding five years, to a fine or to both, or

    (*b*)   on summary conviction, to imprisonment for a term not exceeding six months, or to a fine not exceeding the statutory maximum or to both.

20. Disclosure of information: permission

(1) A person may disclose to a constable—

    (*a*)   a suspicion or belief that any money or other property is terrorist property or is derived from terrorist property;

    (*b*)   any matter on which the suspicion or belief is based.

(2) A person may make a disclosure to a constable in the circumstances mentioned in section 19(1) and (2).

(3) Subsections (1) and (2) shall have effect notwithstanding any restriction on the disclosure of information imposed by statute or otherwise.

(4) Where—

    (*a*)   a person is in employment, and

    (*b*)   his employer has established a procedure for the making of disclosures of the kinds mentioned in subsection (1) and section 19(2),

subsections (1) and (2) shall have effect in relation to that person as if any reference to disclosure to a constable included a reference to disclosure in accordance with the procedure.

21. Cooperation with police

(1) A person does not commit an offence under any of sections 15 to 18 if he is acting with the express consent of a constable.

(2) Subject to subsections (3) and (4), a person does not commit an offence under any of sections 15 to 18 by involvement in a transaction or arrangement relating to money or other property if he discloses to a constable—

    (*a*)   his suspicion or belief that the money or other property is terrorist property, and

    (*b*)   the information on which his suspicion or belief is based.

(3) Subsection (2) applies only where a person makes a disclosure—

    (*a*)   after he becomes concerned in the transaction concerned,

    (*b*)   on his own initiative, and

    (*c*)   as soon as is reasonably practicable.

(4) Subsection (2) does not apply to a person if—

    (*a*)   a constable forbids him to continue his involvement in the transaction or arrangement to which the disclosure relates, and

    (*b*)   he continues his involvement.

(5) It is a defence for a person charged with an offence under any of sections 15(2) and (3) and 16 to 18 to prove that—

    (*a*)   he intended to make a disclosure of the kind mentioned in subsections (2) and (3), and

    (*b*)   there is reasonable excuse for his failure to do so.

(6) Where—

    (*a*)   a person is in employment, and

    (*b*)   his employer has established a procedure for the making of disclosures of the same kind as may be made to a constable under subsection (2),

this section shall have effect in relation to that person as if any reference to disclosure to a constable included a reference to disclosure in accordance with the procedure.

(7) A reference in this section to a transaction or arrangement relating to money or other property includes a reference to use or possession.

22. Penalties

A person guilty of an offence under any of sections 15 to 18 shall be liable—

    (*a*) on conviction on indictment, to imprisonment for a term not exceeding 14 years, to a fine or to both, or

    (*b*) on summary conviction, to imprisonment for a term not exceeding six months, to a fine not exceeding the statutory maximum or to both.

[Section 23 enables the court to make a forfeiture order following a conviction under any of sections 15 to 18. Sections 24 to 31 enable an 'authorised officer' (ie. a constable, customs officer or immigration officer) to siege and detain cash, for up to 48 hours, if he has reasonable grounds for suspecting that it is intended to be used for the purpose of terrorism, if it forms the whole or part of the resources of a proscribed organisation, or it is terrorist property within s. 14(1)(*b*) or (*c*).[6] An order for continued detention of the cash for up to three months may be made by a magistrates court;[7] further orders may be made in respect of particular cash, up to a total maximum period of two years. An application may be made to the magistrates' court for a forfeiture order, which may be granted if the court is satisfied that the cash falls within s. 25 (1)(*a*), (*b*) or (*c*). An appeal lies to the Crown Court (in England and Wales) or the county court (in Northern Ireland).]

Part IV

Terrorist Investigations

Interpretation

32. Terrorist investigation

In this Act 'terrorist investigation' means an investigation of—

    (*a*) the commission, preparation or instigation of acts of terrorism,

    (*b*) an act which appears to have been done for the purposes of terrorism,

    (*c*) the resources of a proscribed organisation,

    (*d*) the possibility of making an order under section 3(3), or

    (*e*) the commission, preparation or instigation of an offence under this Act.

Cordons

33. Cordoned area

(1) An area is a cordoned area for the purposes of this Act if it is designated under this section.

(2) A designation may be made only if the person making it considers it expedient for the purposes of a terrorist investigation.

(3) If a designation is made orally, the person making it shall confirm it in writing as soon as is reasonably practicable.

(4) The person making a designation shall arrange for the demarcation of the cordoned area, so far as is reasonably practicable—

    (*a*) by means of tape marked with the word 'police', or

    (*b*) in such other manner as a constable considers appropriate.

34. Power to designate

(1) Subject to subsection (2), a designation under section 33 may only be made—

    (*a*) where the area is outside Northern Ireland and is wholly or partly within a police area, by an officer for the police area who is of at least the rank of superintendent, and

    (*b*) where the area is in Northern Ireland, by a member of the Royal Ulster Constabulary who is of at least the rank of superintendent.

(2) A constable who is not of the rank required by subsection (1) may make a designation if he considers it necessary by reason of urgency.

---

6   s. 25(1)(*a*), (*b*), (*c*).

7   See the Magistrates' Courts (Detention and Forfeiture of Terrorist Cash) Rules 2001, S.I. 2001 No. 194.

(3) Where a constable makes a designation in reliance on subsection (2) he shall as soon as is reasonably practicable—

(*a*) make a written record of the time at which the designation was made, and

(*b*) ensure that a police officer of at least the rank of superintendent is informed.

(4) An officer who is informed of a designation in accordance with subsection (3)(b)—

(*a*) shall confirm the designation or cancel it with effect from such time as he may direct, and

(*b*) shall, if he cancels the designation, make a written record of the cancellation and the reason for it.

35. Duration

(1) A designation under section 33 has effect, subject to subsections (2) to (5), during the period—

(*a*) beginning at the time when it is made, and

(*b*) ending with a date or at a time specified in the designation.

(2) The date or time specified under subsection (1)(b) must not occur after the end of the period of 14 days beginning with the day on which the designation is made.

(3) The period during which a designation has effect may be extended in writing from time to time by—

(*a*) the person who made it, or

(*b*) a person who could have made it (otherwise than by virtue of section 34(2)).

(4) An extension shall specify the additional period during which the designation is to have effect.

(5) A designation shall not have effect after the end of the period of 28 days beginning with the day on which it is made.

36. Police powers

(1) A constable in uniform may—

(*a*) order a person in a cordoned area to leave it immediately;

(*b*) order a person immediately to leave premises which are wholly or partly in or adjacent to a cordoned area;

(*c*) order the driver or person in charge of a vehicle in a cordoned area to move it from the area immediately;

(*d*) arrange for the removal of a vehicle from a cordoned area;

(*e*) arrange for the movement of a vehicle within a cordoned area;

(*f*) prohibit or restrict access to a cordoned area by pedestrians or vehicles.

(2) A person commits an offence if he fails to comply with an order, prohibition or restriction imposed by virtue of subsection (1).

(3) It is a defence for a person charged with an offence under subsection (2) to prove that he had a reasonable excuse for his failure.

(4) A person guilty of an offence under subsection (2) shall be liable on summary conviction to—

(*a*) imprisonment for a term not exceeding three months,

(*b*) a fine not exceeding level 4 on the standard scale, or

(*c*) both.

Information and evidence . . .

39. Disclosure of information, etc.

(1) Subsection (2) applies where a person knows or has reasonable cause to suspect that a constable is conducting or proposes to conduct a terrorist investigation.

(2) The person commits an offence if he—

(*a*) discloses to another anything which is likely to prejudice the investigation, or

(*b*) interferes with material which is likely to be relevant to the investigation.

(3) Subsection (4) applies where a person knows or has reasonable cause to suspect that a disclosure has been or will be made under any of sections 19 to 21.

(4) The person commits an offence if he—

(*a*) discloses to another anything which is likely to prejudice an investigation resulting from the disclosure under that section, or (*b*)   interferes with material which is likely to be relevant to an investigation resulting from the disclosure under that section.

(5) It is a defence for a person charged with an offence under subsection (2) or (4) to prove—

    (*a*)   that he did not know and had no reasonable cause to suspect that the disclosure or interference was likely to affect a terrorist investigation, or

    (*b*)   that he had a reasonable excuse for the disclosure or interference.

(6) Subsections (2) and (4) do not apply to a disclosure which is made by a professional legal adviser—

    (*a*)   to his client or to his client's representative in connection with the provision of legal advice by the adviser to the client and not with a view to furthering a criminal purpose, or

    (*b*)   to any person for the purpose of actual or contemplated legal proceedings and not with a view to furthering a criminal purpose.

(7) A person guilty of an offence under this section shall be liable—

    (*a*)   on conviction on indictment, to imprisonment for a term not exceeding five years, to a fine or to both, or

    (*b*)   on summary conviction, to imprisonment for a term not exceeding six months, to a fine not exceeding the statutory maximum or to both.

(8) For the purposes of this section—

    (*a*)   a reference to conducting a terrorist investigation includes a reference to taking part in the conduct of, or assisting, a terrorist investigation, and

    (*b*)   a person interferes with material if he falsifies it, conceals it, destroys it or disposes of it, or if he causes or permits another to do any of those things.

NOTES (PARTS III AND IV: TERRORIST PROPERTY AND TERRORIST INVESTIGATIONS)

1. *Terrorist property.*[8] Part III of the Act develops and adds to powers previously contained in PTA 1989, Part III. It now extends to include domestic terrorism, and there are new powers to seize cash in transit,[9] modelled on those in the Drug Trafficking Offences Act 1994. By 1998, there had been four convictions in Great Britain for any of the fundraising offences in the previous 11 years, but 169 in Northern Ireland since 1989.[10] Sections 15–28 (and 39) may be applied to Crown servants by regulations made by the Secretary of State under s. 119.[11] Section 118, under which certain reversed burdens of proof are to be evidential only, does *not* apply to ss. 18(2), 19(3) and 21(5).

2. *Terrorist investigations.* 'Cordoning powers' were first introduced by the Prevention of Terrorism (Additional Powers) Act 1996,[12] following the IRA's ending of its ceasefire in that year with the South Quay bomb. The powers have been used but the extent of that use is not documented.

Schedule 5 is modelled on Sch. 7 to the PTA 1989 and enables a constable to obtain a warrant authorising, for the purposes of a terrorist investigation, entry to premises, the search of the premises and any person found there, and the seizure and retention of any 'relevant material' found. The material is 'relevant' if the constable

---

8 See *Lloyd Inquiry*, Chap. 13; *Legislation Against Terrorism*, Chap. 6.
9 See the Code of Practice for Authorised Officers under the Terrorism Act 2000, made under Sch. 14, para. 6(1), operative by virtue of S.I. 2001 No. 425.
10 *Legislation Against Terrorism*, para. 6.14.
11 See the Terrorism Act 2000 (Crown Servants and Regulators) Regulations 2001, S.I. 2001 No. 192.
12 See K. Reid, [1996] 4 Web JCLI.

has reasonable grounds for believing that it is likely to be of substantial value to a terrorist investigation and that it must be seized to prevent it from being concealed, lost, damaged, altered or destroyed. It must, not, however, be subject to legal privilege. A justice of the peace may grant a warrant if satisfied: (a) that it is sought for the purposes of a terrorist investigation; (b) that there are reasonable grounds for believing that there is relevant material (other than excluded material, items subject to legal privilege or special procedure material) on the premises; and (c) that the issue of the warrant is likely to be necessary in the circumstances of the case. Where the applicant is a senior officer (superintendent or above), and the application does not relate to residential premises, condition (c) need not be satisfied.[13] A senior officer (a constable in a case of urgency) may also authorise similar searches of premises within a condoned area.[14] Access to excluded or special procedure material may be ordered by a circuit judge (or county court judge in Northern Ireland), and a warrant may be issued if there is non-compliance with an access order or such an order would not be appropriate.[15] A circuit judge may by order require a person to provide an explanation of any material seized under a warrant or order.[16] A senior officer may by a written order confer the same authority as a search warrant where he has reasonable grounds for believing the case to be of 'great emergency' where 'immediate action is necessary.'[17] Note that the Sch. 5 powers are not confined to 'serious arrestable offences' and 'relevant material' need not be 'evidence'.[18] The powers in Sch. 5 are broader in many respects than those in PACE.[19] It was established in respect of the powers under PTA 1989, Sch. 7 that applications are made ex parte but there may be an inter partes hearing of an application to discharge or vary an order (see *R v Crown Court at Middlesex Guildhall, ex p Salinger,*[20] where the Divisional Court gave guidance as to the procedure to be adopted, stating that the nature of the information on which the application is based, but not the nature and identity of its source, should normally be disclosed). Disobedience to a production order is a contempt.[1]

In Northern Ireland only, a 'Secretary of State's production order' may be made in relation to an investigation of the commission, preparation or instigation of any offence under ss. 15–18 (terrorist finance) or s. 56 (directing a terrorist organisation). It must appear to the Secretary of State that the information which it would be necessary to provide to the court in support of a warrant application would, if disclosed, be likely to place any person in danger or prejudice the capability of the RUC to investigate the offence in question. In what kind of circumstances could recourse to the Secretary of State rather than a judge be justified in practice?

Production and explanation orders have been regularly used.[2]

Sch. 6 provides a new general power for a constable to obtain an order (a 'general bank circular') from a circuit judge (county court judge in Northern Ireland) requiring a financial institution to provide 'customer information' for the purpose of a terrorist investigation. An application may only be made by an officer of the rank of

---

13 Sch. 5, paras. 1, 2.
14 Sch. 5, para. 3.
15 Sch. 5, paras. 5–12.
16 Sch. 5, paras. 13, 14.
17 Sch. 5, paras. 15, 16.
18 Cf. PACE, above, pp. 225–242.
19 See the detailed analysis by J. J. Rowe, *Current Law Statutes Annotated 2000*, pp. 11-45–11-47.
20 [1993] 2 All ER 310.
1 See *DPP v Channel 4 Television Co Ltd*, below, p. 802.
2 237 in GB in 1996, over 150 in 1997 and well over 100 in 1998: J. J. Rowe, *Annual Reports on the PTA 1996–98*. 'A production order played a part in almost every terrorist investigation in Great Britain': *1997 PTA Report*, para. 39.

superintendent or above. An order overrides any restriction on disclosure imposed by statute or otherwise. 'Customer information' means information whether a business relationship exists with a particular person, his account number, full name, date of birth, address or former address, the date on which a business relationship begins or ends, evidence of identity obtained under money laundering legislation and the identity of any person sharing an account with that person. Customer information is not admissible in evidence in criminal proceedings against the institution or its officers or employees.

These powers are designed to be used at an earlier stage than Sch. 5 powers; the latter would have to be used, for example, to obtain details of transactions. The Sch. 6 powers are similar to but broader than powers of investigation in Northern Ireland in respect of proceeds of crime.[3]

PART V
COUNTER-TERRORIST POWERS
Suspected terrorists
40. Terrorist: interpretation
(1) In this Part 'terrorist' means a person who—
  (*a*) has committed an offence under any of sections 11, 12, 15 to 18, 54 and 56 to 63, or
  (*b*) is or has been concerned in the commission, preparation or instigation of acts of terrorism.
(2) The reference in subsection (1)(b) to a person who has been concerned in the commission, preparation or instigation of acts of terrorism includes a reference to a person who has been, whether before or after the passing of this Act, concerned in the commission, preparation or instigation of acts of terrorism within the meaning given by section 1.

41. Arrest without warrant
(1) A constable may arrest without a warrant a person whom he reasonably suspects to be a terrorist.
(2) Where a person is arrested under this section the provisions of Schedule 8 (detention: treatment, review and extension) shall apply.
(3) Subject to subsections (4) to (7), a person detained under this section shall (unless detained under any other power) be released not later than the end of the period of 48 hours beginning—
  (*a*) with the time of his arrest under this section, or
  (*b*) if he was being detained under Schedule 7 when he was arrested under this section, with the time when his examination under that Schedule began.
(4) If on a review of a person's detention under Part II of Schedule 8 the review officer does not authorise continued detention, the person shall (unless detained in accordance with subsection (5) or (6) or under any other power) be released.
(5) Where a police officer intends to make an application for a warrant under paragraph 29 of Schedule 8 extending a person's detention, the person may be detained pending the making of the application.
(6) Where an application has been made under paragraph 29 or 36 of Schedule 8 in respect of a person's detention, he may be detained pending the conclusion of proceedings on the application.
(7) Where an application under paragraph 29 or 36 of Schedule 8 is granted in respect of a person's detention, he may be detained, subject to paragraph 37 of that Schedule, during the period specified in the warrant.
(8) The refusal of an application in respect of a person's detention under paragraph 29 or 36 of Schedule 8 shall not prevent his continued detention in accordance with this section.
(9) A person who has the powers of a constable in one Part of the United Kingdom may exercise the power under subsection (1) in any Part of the United Kingdom.

---

3 Proceeds of Crime (Northern Ireland) Order 1996, S.I. 1996 No. 1299. See *Re Devine* [1999] NIJB 128 (issue of code of practice not a necessary precondition for exercise of power by investigator; investigator entitled to use a pseudonym).

42. Search of premises

(1) A justice of the peace may on the application of a constable issue a warrant in relation to specified premises if he is satisfied that there are reasonable grounds for suspecting that a person whom the constable reasonably suspects to be a person falling within section 40(1)(*b*) is to be found there.

(2) A warrant under this section shall authorise any constable to enter and search the specified premises for the purpose of arresting the person referred to in subsection (1) under section 41 . . .

43. Search of persons

(1) A constable may stop and search a person whom he reasonably suspects to be a terrorist to discover whether he has in his possession anything which may constitute evidence that he is a terrorist.

(2) A constable may search a person arrested under section 41 to discover whether he has in his possession anything which may constitute evidence that he is a terrorist.

(3) A search of a person under this section must be carried out by someone of the same sex.

(4) A constable may seize and retain anything which he discovers in the course of a search of a person under subsection (1) or (2) and which he reasonably suspects may constitute evidence that the person is a terrorist.

(5) A person who has the powers of a constable in one Part of the United Kingdom may exercise a power under this section in any Part of the United Kingdom.

44. Authorisations

(1) An authorisation under this subsection authorises any constable in uniform to stop a vehicle in an area or at a place specified in the authorisation and to search—

    (*a*)   the vehicle;

    (*b*)   the driver of the vehicle;

    (*c*)   a passenger in the vehicle;

    (*d*)   anything in or on the vehicle or carried by the driver or a passenger.

(2) An authorisation under this subsection authorises any constable in uniform to stop a pedestrian in an area or at a place specified in the authorisation and to search—

    (*a*)   the pedestrian;

    (*b*)   anything carried by him.

(3) An authorisation under subsection (1) or (2) may be given only if the person giving it considers it expedient for the prevention of acts of terrorism.

(4) An authorisation may be given—

    (*a*)   where the specified area or place is the whole or part of a police area outside Northern Ireland other than one mentioned in paragraph (*b*) or (*c*), by a police officer for the area who is of at least the rank of assistant chief constable;

    (*b*)   where the specified area or place is the whole or part of the metropolitan police district, by a police officer for the district who is of at least the rank of commander of the metropolitan police;

    (*c*)   where the specified area or place is the whole or part of the City of London, by a police officer for the City who is of at least the rank of commander in the City of London police force;

    (*d*)   where the specified area or place is the whole or part of Northern Ireland, by a member of the Royal Ulster Constabulary who is of at least the rank of assistant chief constable.

(5) If an authorisation is given orally, the person giving it shall confirm it in writing as soon as is reasonably practicable.

45. Exercise of power

(1) The power conferred by an authorisation under section 44(1) or (2)—

    (*a*)   may be exercised only for the purpose of searching for articles of a kind which could be used in connection with terrorism, and

    (*b*)   may be exercised whether or not the constable has grounds for suspecting the presence of articles of that kind.

(2) A constable may seize and retain an article which he discovers in the course of a search by virtue of section 44(1) or (2) and which he reasonably suspects is intended to be used in connection with terrorism.

(3) A constable exercising the power conferred by an authorisation may not require a person to remove any clothing in public except for headgear, footwear, an outer coat, a jacket or gloves.

(4) Where a constable proposes to search a person or vehicle by virtue of section 44(1) or (2) he may detain the person or vehicle for such time as is reasonably required to permit the search to be carried out at or near the place where the person or vehicle is stopped.

(5) Where—

(*a*) a vehicle or pedestrian is stopped by virtue of section 44(1) or (2), and

(*b*) the driver of the vehicle or the pedestrian applies for a written statement that the vehicle was stopped, or that he was stopped, by virtue of section 44(1) or (2),

the written statement shall be provided.

(6) An application under subsection (5) must be made within the period of 12 months beginning with the date on which the vehicle or pedestrian was stopped.

46. Duration of authorisation

(1) An authorisation under section 44 has effect, subject to subsections (2) to (7), during the period—

(*a*) beginning at the time when the authorisation is given, and

(*b*) ending with a date or at a time specified in the authorisation.

(2) The date or time specified under subsection (1)(*b*) must not occur after the end of the period of 28 days beginning with the day on which the authorisation is given.

(3) The person who gives an authorisation shall inform the Secretary of State as soon as is reasonably practicable.

(4) If an authorisation is not confirmed by the Secretary of State before the end of the period of 48 hours beginning with the time when it is given—

(*a*) it shall cease to have effect at the end of that period, but

(*b*) its ceasing to have effect shall not affect the lawfulness of anything done in reliance on it before the end of that period.

(5) Where the Secretary of State confirms an authorisation he may substitute an earlier date or time for the date or time specified under subsection (1)(*b*).

(6) The Secretary of State may cancel an authorisation with effect from a specified time.

(7) An authorisation may be renewed in writing by the person who gave it or by a person who could have given it; and subsections (1) to (6) shall apply as if a new authorisation were given on each occasion on which the authorisation is renewed.

47. Offences

(1) A person commits an offence if he—

(*a*) fails to stop a vehicle when required to do so by a constable in the exercise of the power conferred by an authorisation under section 44(1);

(*b*) fails to stop when required to do so by a constable in the exercise of the power conferred by an authorisation under section 44(2);

(*c*) wilfully obstructs a constable in the exercise of the power conferred by an authorisation under section 44(1) or (2).

(2) A person guilty of an offence under this section shall be liable on summary conviction to—

(*a*) imprisonment for a term not exceeding six months,

(*b*) a fine not exceeding level 5 on the standard scale, or

(*c*) both.

Parking

[ss. 48–52 enable a constable in uniform to be authorised by a commander or assistant chief constable if he considers it expedient for the prevention of acts of terrorism, to prohibit or restrict the parking of vehicles on a specified road.]

Port and border controls

[s. 53 and Sch. 7 provide for port and border controls.]

NOTES (PART V: COUNTER-TERRORIST POWERS)

1. *Arrest and detention.* Sections 40 and 41 and Sch. 8 confer powers of arrest and extended detention analogous to those previously available under PTA 1989, s. 14. The arrest power by virtue of s. 40 (1)(*b*) extends to persons not suspected of a specific crime; Sch. 8 provides for extended detention.

(i) *Use of and justification for the powers.* To the end of 1982, 5,555 people were detained in Great Britain under the PTA: exclusion orders were made against 261 (nearly 5%) and 394 (about 7%) were charged with a criminal offence; the equivalent figures for Northern Ireland (to 30 September) were 1,975 – 24 (all exclusions whether or not following arrest under PTA 1976, s. 12) and 847 (about 40%).[4] Lord Jellicoe came 'to the firm conclusion that if the power of extended detention were abolished, the police both in Northern Ireland and on the mainland would be seriously handicapped in dealing with terrorists'.[5] He continued:

'66. In evidence to this review, witnesses critical of the power of extended detention have deployed a number of arguments, amounting to a claim that the power is abused or is open to abuse. Some have suggested, on the basis of statistical or anecdotal evidence, that the power is used in many if not most cases with no prospect of a criminal charge resulting. Witnesses have given as evidence for this the alleged fact that questioning has focussed more on the arrested persons' political beliefs and activities than on possible terrorist involvement. There have been claims that many arrested people have simply been held in custody for seven days, without any attempt to question them at all, suggesting the use of the power as a form of preventive detention; and that it has been used for low-level intelligence gathering, with detention for up to seven days (rather than any physical maltreatment) employed as a means of putting pressure on arrested persons to provide information about their associates. Finally, critics of the power as applied on the mainland have claimed that is has been used largely as a means of harassing the Irish population in Great Britain.

67. It would be wrong to suggest that abuses of the power have never occurred. But I am satisfied on the basis of wide consultation, examination of individual cases, and the statistical evidence set out in the previous chapter than in the great majority of cases arrests are made and extensions of detention sought under section 12 because the police believe this to be necessary to prevent terrorist acts or to bring to justice those responsible for the commission. ... Clearly, extended detention should not be used for the purpose of gleaning minor information. But good intelligence can save lives, and if sensitive use of this power, under careful supervision, can aid the collection of such information from individuals who are themselves involved in terrorism, I see no objection to this.'

Nevertheless, the police should be reminded that the power of arrest under PTA 1976, s. 12 'should be exercised only where the use of no other power is appropriate to the end sought', 'wherever possible, applications for extended detention should specify the period required (which in many cases ought to be less than five days) and justify this by reference to the results anticipated', 'where circumstances permit, all applications should be seen and approved by the appropriate secretary of state personally, and not by a junior minister alone';[6] and a full five-day extension should only be granted 'when he is satisfied that this, rather than a lesser period, is necessary'.[7] It would not, however, be appropriate for extensions to be granted by a court rather than a Minister.[8]

Between 1989 and the end of 1999, 958 people were detained in Great Britain in connection with Northern Irish terrorism, leading to 43 exclusion orders (not used after 1995), 163 persons charged with an offence, and 752 (78%) persons not excluded or charged. Comparative figures for those detained in Great Britain in connection with international terrorism between 1984 and 1999 were 247 detained, seven deported, excluded or removed, 106 charged and 134 (54%) persons not deported etc. or charged. By contrast, in Northern Ireland, 369 persons were detained, with

---

4   Jellicoe Report, Annex D, Tables 1, 10 and 11.
5   Ibid., p. 22.
6   Extended detention could, however, lawfully be authorised by a junior minister: *R v Harper* [1980] 4 NIJB 75.
7   pp. 23, 24–25.
8   Cf. PACE, s. 43 above, pp. 304–306.

125 charged, in 1999 alone.[9]   In Northern Ireland, s. 14 became the major terrorist arrest power following the repeal of EPA 1978, s. 11.

Lord Colville reported that the arrest power under s. 12 of the 1984 Act (see now s. 41 of the 2000 Act) was justified as it enabled the police to arrest on reasonable suspicion 'at the preparatory stage of the commission of offences of violence'; reliance on ordinary powers to arrest for an attempt would be 'leaving things rather late' and proving conspiracy 'will often be more difficult than proving an attempt' and was surrounded by jurisdictional and other difficulties.[10] There were still good reasons for permitting a period of detention of up to seven days.[11]

In 1998, the government justified the existence of extended arrest powers as follows:[12]

'Whilst the ordinary powers of arrest are extensive, the government believes they may not be sufficient to deal effectively with all the problems posed by terrorism. Terrorist groups are frequently highly organised with well practised procedures for thwarting police actions against them. Many of those who have operated in the UK (including non-Irish terrorist groups) have been trained to evade surveillance and their operations have been meticulously planned both to minimise the risk of arousing suspicion before the terrorist act is undertaken and to minimise the chance of leaving forensic evidence. Communications may be in an encrypted form and, especially where international groups are involved, foreign languages may be deployed. Information about these sorts of techniques is increasingly available (for instance on the Internet and in exchanges between like-minded activists). The police are therefore, (and are likely to continue to be) up against groups skilled in, and dedicated to, evading detection. Although some of the factors may also apply in the disruption and investigation of serious non-terrorist crime it still remains the case that terrorist crime is often of a quite different order both in terms of the sophistication of the techniques deployed and the (potential) harm caused.'

(ii) *Reviews of detention.* The powers providing for extended detention without the authority of a judicial officer have been held by the European Court of Human Rights (in *Brogan v United Kingdom*[13]) to be contrary to the ECHR. The government's response was for the UK to derogate from the relevant provisions of the ECHR and the International Covenant on Civil and Political Rights.[14] This move was criticised by the SACHR, who argued that the initial period of detention should be limited to 48 hours, with extensions for further periods up to 120 hours in all permitted on application to a magistrates' court.[15] Alternatively, the establishment of a special tribunal could be considered.[16] Periodic reviews of detention were introduced by Sch. 3 to PTA 1989, modelled on the provisions of PACE.[17] Under the 2000 Act, a detention must be reviewed as soon as reasonably practicable after arrest and subsequently at interviews of not more than 12 hours.[18] In contrast with PACE provisions, all reviews under the PTA were conducted by police officers, albeit senior officers not directly involved with the case; there was no requirement for authorisation by magistrates or another judicial officer at the later stages of detention. Moreover, even if the review officer refused to authorise an extension of detention, an extension might still be granted by the Secretary of State.[19] However, under the 2000 Act,

9 Home Office Statistical Bulletin 5/00, *Statistics on the Operation of the Prevention of Terrorism Legislation – 1999*; J. J. Rowe, *1999 PTA Report*, Table 1.
10 *Colville Review (PTA)* (1987), Chap. 4.
11 Ibid., Chap. 5.
12 *Legislation Against Terrorism*, para. 7.8.
13 (1988) 11 EHRR 117. Also *O'Hara v United Kingdom*, Judgment of 16 October 2001.
14 See p. 26.
15 17th Report, 1991–92 HC 54, p. 217.
16 18th Report, 1992–93, HC 739.
17 ss. 40–44, above, pp. 301–306.
18 Sch. 8, para. 21.
19 PTA 1989, Sch. 3, para. 3(1)(b).

provision has now been made for warrant of further detention in respect of detention beyond 48 hours up to a maximum of seven days to be granted (in England and Wales) by the Senior District Judge (Chief Magistrate) or his deputy, or a District Judge (Magistrates' Court) who is designated for this purpose by the Lord Chancellor. In Northern Ireland a warrant may be granted by a county court judge or a designated resident magistrate. The judicial authority may order that the applicant and/or his representative be excluded from any part of the hearing and that specified information is not to be disclosed to them. This is one of three options proposed by the government to enable there to be compliance with the ECHR and ICCPR.[20]

Do these provisions now comply with Art. 5 ECHR? The government's position is that an arrest power without an explicit link to a specific offence is compatible with Art. 5(1)(c), citing the decision in *Brogan* where in the circumstances of the case (where the applicants were suspected of being members of a proscribed organisation), the European Court of Human Rights held that their arrest under PTA 1984, s. 12 was not in breach of Art. 5(1)(c).[1] However, it has been pointed out that the Court noted in *Brogan* that the definition of acts of terrorism was 'well in keeping with the idea of an offence' and that after arrest the applicants were asked about specific offences; the definition of 'terrorism' is now broader and a person arrested might not of course in another case be questioned so specifically. It is accordingly doubtful that there is compliance here.[2] The government intends by the introduction of the requirement of judicial authority for extended detention to be able to withdraw the ECHR and ICCPR derogations and this took place on 19 February 2001. However, the fact that detention may continue beyond 48 hours while a warrant is sought may itself come to be a breach of Art. 5(3).[3]

(iii) *Other points.* The PTA 1989, s.14 arrest power (then PTA 1976, s. 12) was considered by the Northern Ireland Court of Appeal in *Ex p Lynch*.[4] The court held that the arresting officer complied with the requirements of *Christie v Leachinsky*[5] by telling L that he was arresting him under s. 12 as he suspected him of being involved in terrorism:

> 'an arrest [under s. 12] is not necessarily ... the first step in a criminal proceeding against a suspected person on a charge which was intended to be judicially investigated. Rather it is usually the first step in the investigation of the suspected person's involvement in terrorism.'[6]

In *Fox, Campbell and Hartley v United Kingdom*,[7] the Court of Human Rights held that the use of this formula (in respect of an arrest under EPA 1978, s. 11, since repealed)[8] was not sufficient to comply with Art. 5(2) of the ECHR. However, it was not necessary for compliance that the required information be supplied on arrest; here, the information had been provided during interrogation, and in the present context 'intervals of a few hours [between arrest and interrogation] cannot be regarded as falling outside the constraints of time imposed by the notion of promptness in Article 5(2)'.[9] Then in *Oscar v Chief Constable of the Royal Ulster Constabulary* [10]

---

20 *Lloyd Inquiry*, Chap. 9; *Legislation Against Terrorism*, Chap. 8. Video links may be used: Criminal Justice and Police Act 2001, s. 75.
1 Lord Bassam of Brighton, 613 HL Deb, col 682; *Brogan v UK* (1988) 12 EHRR 371.
2 H. Fenwick, *Civil Rights* (2000), p. 247; *Lloyd Inquiry*, para. 8.13 (Lord Lloyd recommended as a result the creation of a new criminal offence of being concerned in the preparation of an act of terrorism; this was not accepted by the government).
3 Ibid., p 251.
4 [1980] NI 126 (see W. Finnie, (1982) 45 MLR 215).
5 Above, p. 283.
6 Per Lord Lowry LCJ at 131.
7 (1990) 13 EHRR 157.
8 See p. 610.
9 p. 171.
10 [1992] 9 NIJB 27.

the Northern Ireland Court of Appeal held it sufficient for an arrest under PTA for the arresting officer to say:

> 'I arrest you under section 12(1)(b) of the Prevention of Terrorism (Temporary Provisions) Act 1984 as I have reasonable grounds for suspecting you have been concerned in the commission, preparation or investigation of acts of terrorism.'

The arrest:

> 'was not unlawful because the constable failed to tell him of the nature of the terrorist acts which he was suspected to have committed.'[11]

The principle of *McKee v Chief Constable of the RUC* [12] that bona fide acceptance of instructions from a superior officer may amount to reasonable suspicion, has been applied in subsequent cases involving arrests under the Prevention of Terrorism legislation.[13] The outcome in *O'Hara* was that:

> 'the information given at the briefing to the arresting officer was admissible and although [in the words of the trial judge] "scanty", it was sufficient to constitute the required state of mind of an arresting officer under s. 12(1)(b) of the [1984] Act.'[14]

The arresting officer was simply briefed that O'Hara had been 'involved in' a particular murder. The decision in *O'Hara* was upheld by the House of Lords.[15] The House held that the mere fact that the arresting officer had been instructed to effect an arrest or had been told that the person in question had been concerned in the commission etc. of acts of terrorism was not itself sufficient. However, the trial judge had been entitled to find that the information provided at the briefing was on the facts of the particular case sufficient.

2. *Conditions in detention*

(i) *PTA detention in England and Wales.*[16] Detention under the PTA in England and Wales was regulated by the PACE regime, albeit with modifications.[17] A two-year experiment with audio-taping of interviews began on 1 December 1992.[18] Research on PTA detentions in England and Wales[19] showed that the exercise of rights to legal advice and to have someone notified of their detention were delayed in a far higher proportion of PTA than ordinary PACE detentions (26%, 44% of the sample), and a far higher percentage (40%) were held for more than 24 hours. The report also noted shortcomings in record-keeping. However, nearly 40% of detainees successfully obtained legal advice (a far higher proportion than for PACE prisoners) and:

> 'scrupulous attention to the detainee's physical well-being through regular medical examination and reviews by senior officers was also common, particularly where detention was lengthy.'[20]

11 Per Hutton LCJ at 54.
12 Below, p. 613.
13 See *Clinton v Chief Constable of the Royal Ulster Constabulary* [1991] 2 NIJB 53, QBD (NI); *Bradley v Chief Constable of the Royal Ulster Constabulary* [1991] 2 NIJB 22, QBD (NI) (see 'A barrister', (1992) 43 NILQ 66); *Oscar v Chief Constable of the RUC* [1992] NI 209, CA (NI); *O'Hara v Chief Constable of the RUC* (6 May 1994, unreported, CA (NI)).
14 Per Kelly LJ.
15 [1997] 1 All ER 129. Applied in *Porter v Chief Constable of the RUC* (unreported, 24 February 1999, QBD (NI)). The ECtHR subsequently found no breach of Art. 5(1): *O'Hara v United Kingdom*, Judgment of 16 October 2001.
16 For frequently critical views and experiences of conditions in PTA detention, see P. Hillyard, *Suspect Community* (1993), Chap. 7.
17 See PACE, Part V and Code C.
18 See Home Office Circular 108/1992.
19 D. Brown, *Detention under the Prevention of Terrorism (Temporary Provision) Act 1989: Access to Legal Advice and Outside Contact* (HORPU Paper 75, 1993).
20 p. 56.

(ii) *Treatment in detention in Northern Ireland.* In *Ireland v United Kingdom* [1] the European Court of Human Rights found that the adoption of the 'five techniques' in the operation of the policy of internment and detention in 1971 constituted inhuman treatment. The use of these techniques was officially abandoned following the Parker Report.[2] Allegations of ill-treatment in the period following that considered by the European Court were substantiated.[3] The Bennett Committee's examination of medical evidence revealed 'cases in which injuries, whatever their precise cause, were not self-inflicted and were sustained in police custody'.[4] The Committee made a number of suggestions for improving the supervision of interrogations and the police complaints procedures. For example, interviews should not last longer than the interval between normal meal times or extend over meal breaks or continue after midnight except for urgent operational reasons; not more than two officers at a time or six in all should interview a prisoner; prisoners should be seen by a medical officer at least every 24 hours; interrogation rooms should be covered by closed-circuit television and monitored by uniformed, supervisory officers; a training programme should be introduced for interrogators, and a code of conduct incorporated into the RUC Code. In addition, prisoners should be given an unconditional right of access to a solicitor after 48 hours and every 48 hours thereafter, although the solicitor should not be permitted to be present at interviews.

These recommendations were mostly accepted, and implemented by changes to the RUC Code.[5]

Following the implementation of the Bennett recommendations, the number of allegations of physical abuse declined significantly. Lord Jellicoe reported that the Bennett recommendations had 'on the whole ... been implemented fully and fairly ... Even witnesses in other respects strongly critical both of the continued existence of the emergency legislation and of its application assured me that well-founded allegations of mistreatment during interview were now rare and justified complaints of physical assault virtually non-existent'.[6] Nevertheless, there were persistent allegations of verbal abuse and the application of pressure on suspects to act as informers,[7] and indeed, continuing allegations of assaults against persons in detention at the 'holding centres' (Castlereagh and Gough Barracks, Londonderry) where most terrorist suspects were taken when arrested. In the period 1990–93 there were over 1,000 allegations of assault by persons detained in the holding centres, although none were substantiated, the proof required being 'beyond reasonable doubt'.[8] Moreover, in the 1989–92 period, the Police Authority settled 18 civil claims in which one factor in the calculation of damages was an allegation of assault in a holding centre.[9] In *R v Nash* [10] the trial judge, Hutton LCJ, excluded N's confession under EPA 1991, s. 11 on the ground that it was not proved beyond reasonable doubt that an assault had not been committed on him. Evidence was given that the officers

---

1 See A. Mowbray, *Cases and Materials on the European Convention on Human Rights* (2001), pp. 73–84.
2 Cmnd. 4901.
3 See the *Report of an Amnesty International Mission to Northern Ireland* (1978), the Bennett Report, (Cmnd. 7497, 1979) and P. Taylor, *Beating the Terrorists?* (1980).
4 Bennett Report, p. 136.
5 See Lord Jellicoe's *Review of the Operation of the Prevention of Terrorism (Temporary Provisions) Act 1976* (Cmnd. 8803) pp. 29–35, 39–44.
6 Report, pp. 30, 31.
7 See D. P. J. Walsh, *The Use and Abuse of Emergency Legislation in Northern Ireland* (1983), pp. 54–78; G. Hogan and C. Walker, p. 118.
8 B Dickson, (1994) 45 NILQ 210, 216.
9 Ibid.
10 Unreported, December 1992, Cr Ct.

with responsibility for watching CCTV monitors spent up to 20 minutes patrolling the corridors rather than watching the screens. In July 1993, the European Committee for the Prevention of Torture and Inhuman or Degrading Treatment or Punishment visited Northern Ireland and was told by both medical staff and senior paramilitaries 'that instances of physical ill-treatment had sharply decreased in recent times'. However, many allegations were made of various forms of psychological ill-treatment and this gave rise to 'legitimate concern'.[11] The government responded that there had been no specific complaints of psychological ill-treatment since 1993 and that all complaints were fully investigated.[12]

Steps taken to improve the regulation of detention at the holding centres include the introduction of a Code of Practice under EPA 1991, s. 61 and the appointment under the royal prerogative of an Independent Commissioner for the Holding Centres. His terms of reference state that his principal purpose is:

> 'to provide further assurance to the Secretary of State that persons detained in Holding Centres are fairly treated and that both statutory and administrative safeguards are being properly applied.'[13]

He (and his deputy) make irregular visits to the centres, normally without prior notice, inspect records and interview detainees (with their consent). The person appointed was Sir Louis Blom-Cooper QC. His deputy was a consultant psychiatrist. In his first annual report to the Secretary of State for Northern Ireland he reported:

> 'I have found absolutely nothing that might give anyone the slightest cause for concern about the care and treatment of detainees held in the custody of uniformed officers of the RUC.'[14]

The few complaints that were received related either to incidents on arrest, on the journey to the holding centre or during interviews by detectives. As regards the last of these:

> 'in 1994 public confidence can only be secured only if there is in place a form of surveillance over and a method of accountability for the conduct of non-uniformed police officers conducing interrogations in the interview rooms of the Holding Centres.'[15]

This has remained his position.[16] Proposals which were made by a number of persons and bodies over many years that interviews at the holding centres be recorded on audio and video tape were belatedly accepted. Silent video-recording was introduced in March 1998;[17] audio-taping in May 1999.[18] Sir Louis Blom-Cooper subsequently recommended that all activity in the interview room be recorded, not just interviews, to deal with claims of unauthorised interview 'off tape'.[19] Furthermore, the possibility of a pilot study by the Independent Commissioner of random samples of taped interviews to assist him informing a view of the extent of any improper treatment was held up following disagreement as to whether the relevant detainees' consent was necessary.[20]

(iii) *Access to legal advice in Northern Ireland.* A legal right of access was conferred by EPA 1991, s. 45 (EPA 1996, s. 47). Statements given some 24 hours beyond the

---

11 Report to the UK Government, CPT/Inf (94)17.
12 Response, CPT/Inf(94) 18, pp. 8–9.
13 2nd Annual (1994) Report, Annex.
14 1st Annual (1993) Report, p. 118.
15 p. 120.
16 7th Annual (1999) Report, p. 23.
17 EPA 1996, s. 53; S.I. 1998 Nos. 312 and 313. See now the 2000 Act, s. 100.
18 Ibid., s. 53A, inserted by the EPA 1998, s. 5; S.I. 1999 Nos. 1151 and 1172.
19 7th Annual (1999) Report, p. 26.
20 Ibid., pp. 27–31.

legal 48-hour deferral period permitted by s. 45(6) were excluded by Judge Russell in *R v Gilgunn* [1] and by Pringle J in *R v Lynch*. [2]

It was held that breach of the right of access to a solicitor did not give rise to an action for damages for breach of statutory duty or at common law, whether for false imprisonment or for an innominate tort.[3] However, the decision to delay access to a lawyer was subject to judicial review.[4] Such a decision had to be made in response to a request for access; there was no provision for an anticipatory deferral.[5]

Restrictions that did not apply in ordinary cases were that consulting with a lawyer normally took place in the hearing of an officer and that lawyers were not normally present during interrogations. The SACHR regarded the former limitation as contrary to international standards[6] and expressed concern on the latter,[7] noting that these restrictions did not apply to interrogations of terrorist suspects in Great Britain (the power to require consultation to be in the sight and hearing of an officer being very seldom used).[8]

In *R v Chief Constable of the RUC, ex p Begley, R v McWilliams* [9] the House of Lords confirmed that a person arrested under the PTA had no common law right to have a solicitor present during police interviews, and that this remained the case notwithstanding the introduction of the Criminal Evidence (Northern Ireland) Order 1988[10] enabling inferences to be drawn from silence. There was no previous decision or dictum in support of such a right and no academic support for it. Furthermore, recognition of such a right in Northern Ireland would be inconsistent with the will of Parliament, which had expressly provided for such a right in England and Wales[11] and in Northern Ireland as regards defendants other than those arrested or detained under the terrorism provisions.[12] A decision to refuse to allow a solicitor to be present was, however, subject to judicial review[13] and an unjustified decision to delay access could lead to the exclusion of statements made by the defendant.[14]

In *Magee v United Kingdom* [15] the European Court of Human Rights held that the denial of access by M to a lawyer for more than 48 hours following his arrest in 1988 under the PTA constituted in the circumstances a breach of Art. 6 ECHR. M confessed before access was allowed. The court stated:

1 19 October 1991, unreported, Cr Ct.
2 19 October 1993, unreported, Cr Ct, discussed in the SACHR 19th Report, 1993–94 HC 495, p. 11.
3 *Cullen v Chief Constable of the Royal Ulster Constabulary* [1999] NI 237, CA (NI).
4 See *Re McKenna's Application* [1992] NIJB, QBD (NI); *Re Duffy's Application* (20 September 1991, unreported, QBD (NI)) (authorisation quashed); *Re Application by Maher and others* (25 March 1992, unreported, QBD (NI)) (authorisation upheld; the *bona fides* of the solicitor were not challenged but the police were found to have had reasonable grounds for believing that INLA would force him to reveal information).
5 *R v McWilliams* [1996] NI 545, 556–557; *Cullen v Chief Constable of the RUC* [1999] NI 237.
6 17th Report, 1991–92 HC 54, pp. 218–219.
7 18th Report, 1992–93 HC 739, p. 24.
8 In 2% of 384 consultations in the study by D. Brown, *Detention under the Prevention of Terrorism (Temporary Provisions) Act 1989: Access to Legal Advice and Outside Contact*, HORPU Paper 75, 1992).
9 [1997] 4 All ER 833.
10 Below, p. 607.
11 PACE, s. 58.
12 PACE (Northern Ireland) Order 1989, S.I. 1989 No. 134, Art. 59(12).
13 *Re Floyd's Application* [1997] NI 414, QBD (NI) (application for judicial review rejected).
14 *R v McKeever & Taylor* (20 March 1995, Belfast Crown Court).
15 Judgment of 6 June 2000. See to similar effect *Averill v UK*, Judgment of 6 June 2000 (denial of access for 24 hours after PTA arrest found to violate Art. 6(3)(c) taken in conjunction with Art. 6(1)). The court did not deal with a separate complaint concerning refusal to allow a solicitor to be present at interview.

'43. The Court observes that prior to his confession the applicant had been interviewed on five occasions for extended periods punctuated by breaks. He was examined by a doctor on two occasions including immediately before the critical interview at which he began to confess. Apart from his contacts with the doctor, the applicant was kept incommunicado during the breaks between bouts of questioning conducted by experienced police officers operating in relays. It sees no reason to doubt the truth of the applicant's submission that he was kept in virtual solitary confinement throughout this period. The Court has examined the findings and recommendations of the European Committee for the Prevention of Torture and Inhuman or Degrading Treatment and Punishment ('CPT') in respect of the Castlereagh Holding Centre. It notes that the criticism which the CPT levelled against the Centre has been reflected in other public documents ... The austerity of the conditions of his detention and his exclusion from outside contact were intended to be psychologically coercive and conducive to breaking down any resolve he may have manifested at the beginning of his detention to remain silent. Having regard to the considerations, the Court is of the opinion that the applicant, as a matter of procedural fairness, should have been given access to a solicitor at the initial stages of the interrogation as a counterweight to the intimidating atmosphere specifically devised to sap his will and make him confide in his interrogators. Irrespective of the fact that the domestic court drew no adverse inferences under Article 3 of the 1988 Order, it cannot be denied that the Article 3 caution administered to the applicant was an element which heightened his vulnerability to the relentless rounds of interrogation on the first days of his detention.

44.In the Court's opinion, to deny access to a lawyer for such a long period and in a situation where the rights of the defence were irretrievably prejudiced is – whatever the justification for such denial – incompatible with the rights of the accused under Article 6 (see, *mutatis mutandis*, the above-mentioned John Murray judgment, p. 55 § 66).

45.It is true that the domestic court found on the facts that the applicant had not been ill-treated and that the confession which was obtained from the applicant had been voluntary. The Court does not dispute that finding. At the same time, it has to be noted that the applicant was deprived of legal assistance for over forty-eight hours and the incriminating statements which he made at the end of the first twenty-four hours of his detention became the central platform of the prosecution's case against him and the basis for his conviction.

46.Having regard to the above considerations, the Court concludes that there has been a violation of Article 6§ 1 of the Convention in conjunction with Article 6 § 3(c) thereof as regards the denial of access to a solicitor.'

Accordingly, denial of access is not automatically a breach of Art. 6, but a significant use at trial of evidence obtained during that period is likely to be held to be unfair. (iv) *Detention under the Terrorism Act 2000.* All detentions under the 2000 Act are regulated by the regime established by Sch. 8 to the Act, rather than by PACE (or its Northern Ireland equivalent). This confers rights to have one named person informed of the detention as soon as reasonably practicable and to consult a solicitor as soon as reasonably practicable, privately and at any time. A delay may be authorised by a senior officer, but in Northern Ireland it is now not possible to impose a delay or further delay once access is allowed, bringing the position into line with that in England and Wales. Note the restrictions on the use of evidence obtained during the period of the delay that will apply by virtue of *Magee v UK*.[16] Provision is also made in respect of fingerprinting and samples. The 2000 Act provides that the Secretary of State (1) must issue a code of practice about the audio recording of interviews in a police station by a constable of a person detained under Sch. 7 or s. 41 and must make an order requiring compliance with the Code;[17] (2) may make an order requiring video recording of such interviews (or such interviews in a particular part of the UK), specifying whether recording is to be silent or with sound, and if he does so he must

16 Above.
17 See the Terrorism Act 2000 (Code of Practice on Audio Recording of Interviews) Order 2001, S.I. 2001 No. 159; *Code of Practice for the Audio Recording of Interviews under the Terrorism Act 2000.*

issue a code of practice and require that it be followed.[18] The Secretary of State has required the video–taping with sound of such interviews at a police station in Northern Ireland.[19]

The Castlereagh Holding Centre was closed by the Chief Constable as from 31 December 1999. Physical conditions there had long been adversely criticised.[20] The Patten Independent Commission on Policing for Northern Ireland had recommended that the three holding centres should be closed forthwith.[1] The Secretary of State has stated that the two other centres will be closed as soon as practicable.[2]

The Patten Commission recommended that responsibility for inspecting all PACE custody suites, including those used for those detained under terrorism legislation, should be with the proposed Policing Board and Lay Visitors (a scheme for Lay Visitors to police stations having been established in 1991).[3] Sir Louis Blom-Cooper has, however, argued that there is a continued need for his office in some form given the special circumstances of the extended detention of terrorist suspects.[4]

3. *Travel controls.*[5] Section 53 and Sch. 7 set out a system of travel controls based on those previously found in PTA1989, s. 16 and Sch. 5. An 'examining officer'[6] may question a person for the purpose of determining whether he appears to be a person who is or has been concerned in the commission, preparation or instigation of acts of terrorism. The person must be at a point (including an airport or hoverport) or in the 'border area'[7] or on a ship or aircraft which has arrived in Great Britain or Northern Ireland. There need be no prior suspicion. An examining officer may also question a person in the border area for the purpose of determining whether his presence in the area is connected with his entering or leaving Northern Ireland. For the purpose of exercising these powers an officer may stop a person or vehicle or detain a person for up to nine hours.[8] The detention regime is that prescribed by Sch. 8, Part I.[9] There are extensive powers to search, to detain property and to require the production of information, and controls over journeys by ship or aircraft between Great Britain and the Republic of Ireland, Northern Ireland or the Islands and between Northern Ireland and any of those places. Such journeys must be to designated ports or otherwise as approved by an examining officer, or where the passengers are not carried for reward, on 12 hours' notice. Passengers may be required to complete embarkation or

---

18 Sch. 8, paras. 3, 4.

19 See the Terrorism Act 2000 (Code of Practice on Video Recording of Interviews) (Northern Ireland) Order 2001, S.I. 2001 No. 402; Code of Practice on Video Recording of Interviews.

20 See 7th Annual (1999) Report of the Independent Commissioner for the Holding Centres, Chap. 1.

1 Report, September 1999, para. 8.15.

2 7th Annual (1999) Report, p. 1.

3 Para. 8.16.

4 7th Annual (1999) Report, Chaps. II, IV; see also to a similar effect C. Walker and B. Fitzpatrick, [1998] PL 106.

5 See *Legislation Against Terrorism*, Chap. 11; *Code of Practice for Examining Officers under the Terrorism Act 2000*, made operative by S.I. 2001 No. 427.

6 I.e. a constable, immigration officer or designated customs officer. Their Sch. 7 functions may be conferred on members of HM Forces by an order made by the Secretary of State under s. 97.

7 I.e. in an area no more than one mile from the border between Northern Ireland and the Republic of Ireland or the first stopping place for a train going into Northern Ireland from the Republic.

8 Reduced from the PTA period of 12 hours, which could be extended where there were reasonable grounds to suspect terrorist involvement. In such a case now the person would have to be arrested under s. 41. Lord Lloyd had recommended a six-hour maximum period: *Lloyd Inquiry*, p.66.

9 Below, p. 619.

landing cards. However, under the 2000 Act, these arrangements now only apply where the Secretary of State has made an order subject to the affirmative resolution procedure bringing them into effect.[10]

Lord Lloyd reported that the port powers were among the less controversial of the PTA provisions and that 'there are sound strategic reasons for an island nation to carry out checks of this kind at ports. They provide a first line of defence against the entry of terrorists, and serve a useful function against crime as a by product.'[11]

PART VI
MISCELLANEOUS
Terrorist offences

54. Weapons training

(1) A person commits an offence if he provides instruction or training in the making or use of—

    (*a*) firearms,
    (*b*) explosives, or
    (*c*) chemical, biological or nuclear weapons.

(2) A person commits an offence if he receives instruction or training in the making or use of—

    (*a*) firearms,
    (*b*) explosives, or
    (*c*) chemical, biological or nuclear weapons.

(3) A person commits an offence if he invites another to receive instruction or training and the receipt—

    (*a*) would constitute an offence under subsection (2), or
    (*b*) would constitute an offence under subsection (2) but for the fact that it is to take place outside the United Kingdom.

(4) For the purpose of subsections (1) and (3)—

    (*a*) a reference to the provision of instruction includes a reference to making it available either generally or to one or more specific persons, and
    (*b*) an invitation to receive instruction or training may be either general or addressed to one or more specific persons.

(5) It is a defence for a person charged with an offence under this section in relation to instruction or training to prove that his action or involvement was wholly for a purpose other than assisting, preparing for or participating in terrorism.

(6) A person guilty of an offence under this section shall be liable—

    (*a*) on conviction on indictment, to imprisonment for a term not exceeding ten years, to a fine or to both, or
    (*b*) on summary conviction, to imprisonment for a term not exceeding six months, to a fine not exceeding the statutory maximum or to both.

(7) A court by or before which a person is convicted of an offence under this section may order the forfeiture of anything which the court considers to have been in the person's possession for purposes connected with the offence.

(8) Before making an order under subsection (7) a court must give an opportunity to be heard to any person, other than the convicted person, who claims to be the owner of or otherwise interested in anything which can be forfeited under that subsection.

(9) An order under subsection (7) shall not come into force until there is no further possibility of it being varied, or set aside, on appeal (disregarding any power of a court to grant leave to appeal out of time).

55. Weapons training: interpretation

[s. 55 defines 'biological', 'chemical' and 'nuclear' weapons by reference, respectively to the Biological Weapons Act 1974, s. 1(1)(*b*), the Chemical Weapons Act 1996, s. 1 and the Nuclear Material (Offences) Act 1983, Schedule.]

10 See the Terrorism Act 2000 (Carding) Order 2001, S.I. 2001 No. 426.
11 *Lloyd Inquiry*, pp. 59–66.

56. Directing terrorist organisation

(1) A person commits an offence if he directs, at any level, the activities of an organisation which is concerned in the commission of acts of terrorism.

(2) A person guilty of an offence under this section is liable on conviction on indictment to imprisonment for life.

57. Possession for terrorist purposes

(1) A person commits an offence if he possesses an article in circumstances which give rise to a reasonable suspicion that his possession is for a purpose connected with the commission, preparation or instigation of an act of terrorism.

(2) It is a defence for a person charged with an offence under this section to prove that his possession of the article was not for a purpose connected with the commission, preparation or instigation of an act of terrorism.

(3) In proceedings for an offence under this section, if it is proved that an article—

    (a) was on any premises at the same time as the accused, or

    (b) was on premises of which the accused was the occupier or which he habitually used otherwise than as a member of the public,

the court may assume that the accused possessed the article, unless he proves that he did not know of its presence on the premises or that he had no control over it.

(4) A person guilty of an offence under this section shall be liable—

    (a) on conviction on indictment, to imprisonment for a term not exceeding 10 years, to a fine or to both, or

    (b) on summary conviction, to imprisonment for a term not exceeding six months, to a fine not exceeding the statutory maximum or to both.

58. Collection of information

(1) A person commits an offence if—

    (a) he collects or makes a record of information of a kind likely to be useful to a person committing or preparing an act of terrorism, or

    (b) he possesses a document or record containing information of that kind.

(2) In this section 'record' includes a photographic or electronic record.

(3) It is a defence for a person charged with an offence under this section to prove that he had a reasonable excuse for his action or possession.

(4) A person guilty of an offence under this section shall be liable—

    (a) on conviction on indictment, to imprisonment for a term not exceeding 10 years, to a fine or to both, or

    (b) on summary conviction, to imprisonment for a term not exceeding six months, to a fine not exceeding the statutory maximum or to both.

(5) A court by or before which a person is convicted of an offence under this section may order the forfeiture of any document or record containing information of the kind mentioned in subsection (1)(a).

(6) Before making an order under subsection (5) a court must give an opportunity to be heard to any person, other than the convicted person, who claims to be the owner of or otherwise interested in anything which can be forfeited under that subsection.

(7) An order under subsection (5) shall not come into force until there is no further possibility of it being varied, or set aside, on appeal (disregarding any power of a court to grant leave to appeal out of time).

Inciting terrorism overseas
59. England and Wales

(1) A person commits an offence if—

    (a) he incites another person to commit an act of terrorism wholly or partly outside the United Kingdom, and

    (b) the act would, if committed in England and Wales, constitute one of the offences listed in subsection (2).

(2) Those offences are—

    (a) murder,

    (b) an offence under section 18 of the Offences against the Person Act 1861 (wounding with intent),

 (*c*) an offence under section 23 or 24 of that Act (poison),
 (*d*) an offence under section 28 or 29 of that Act (explosions), and
 (*e*) an offence under section 1(2) of the Criminal Damage Act 1971 (endangering life by damaging property).

(3) A person guilty of an offence under this section shall be liable to any penalty to which he would be liable on conviction of the offence listed in subsection (2) which corresponds to the act which he incites.

(4) For the purposes of subsection (1) it is immaterial whether or not the person incited is in the United Kingdom at the time of the incitement.

(5) Nothing in this section imposes criminal liability on any person acting on behalf of, or holding office under, the Crown.

[Sections 60 and 61 make similar provision to s. 59 in respect of Northern Ireland and Scotland.]

Terrorist bombing and finance offences
62. Terrorist bombing: jurisdiction
(1) If—
 (*a*) a person does anything outside the United Kingdom as an act of terrorism or for the purposes of terrorism, and
 (*b*) his action would have constituted the commission of one of the offences listed in subsection (2) if it had been done in the United Kingdom,
he shall be guilty of the offence.
(2) The offences referred to in subsection (1)(*b*) are—
 (*a*) an offence under section 2, 3 or 5 of the Explosive Substances Act 1883 (causing explosions, &c),
 (*b*) an offence under section 1 of the Biological Weapons Act 1974 (biological weapons), and
 (*c*) an offence under section 2 of the Chemical Weapons Act 1996 (chemical weapons).

63. Terrorist finance: jurisdiction
(1) If—
 (*a*) a person does anything outside the United Kingdom, and
 (*b*) his action would have constituted the commission of an offence under any of sections 15 to 18 if it had been done in the United Kingdom,
he shall be guilty of the offence.
(2) For the purposes of subsection (1)(*b*), section 18(1)(*b*) shall be read as if for 'the jurisdiction' there were substituted 'a jurisdiction'.

[Sections 65–80 contain various provisions as to proceedings for 'scheduled offences' i.e. those listed in Sch. 9. These are the crimes commonly committed by terrorists, including, for example, murder, manslaughter, riot, kidnapping, false imprisonment, various assaults, theft of nuclear material, robbery with weapons, intimidation, offences concerning explosives, petrol bombs, criminal damage and firearms, hijacking, computer misuse and various offences under the 2000 Act. In relation to some of these the Attorney-General may certify that a particular case is not to be treated as a scheduled offence. Trials on indictment of scheduled offences are normally held at the Belfast Crown Court (s. 74) and are conducted by a judge sitting without a jury (s. 75). Reasons for convictions must be given (s. 75(7)). A person convicted may appeal to the Court of Appeal on any ground without leave.]

NOTES (PART VI: MISCELLANEOUS)

1. *Weapons training.* This offence (ss. 54, 55) formerly applied only in Northern Ireland[12] and has been extended to include chemical, biological and nuclear weapons. It was noted in *Legislation Against Terrorism*[13] that the Kurdistan Workers Party poisoned the water supply of a Turkish military base in 1992 and the Aum Shinrikyo cult used Sarin gas in attacking the Tokyo underground in 1995. The offence has been difficult to prove.[14]

12 EPA, s. 34.
13 Para. 12.13.
14 *Lloyd Inquiry*, p. 95. In the absence of evidence that this offence would be of substantial value, Lord Lloyd did not recommend its inclusion in the permanent legislation.

2. *Directing terrorist organisation.* This offence (s. 56) formerly applied only in Northern Ireland.[15] It was first introduced in the EPA 1991[16] and was criticised by C. Walker and K. Reid[17] on the grounds that it was too wide in that it was not limited to proscribed organisations and all directions were penalised even if lawful. By 1998 there had been two convictions, with long sentences imposed in each case.[18] Its retention was supported by Lord Lloyd who thought it had 'real value.'[19]

3. *Possession for terrorist purposes; collection of information.* These offences (ss. 57, 58) are based on the PTA, ss. 16A, 16B,[20] and the EPA, ss. 32, 33. They are controversial to the extent that they involve a reversal of the burden of proof. The possession offence enables action to be taken, for example, in respect of commonplace articles that are well known to be used in bomb manufacture.

The collection of information offence would cover, for example, targeting lists. In *R v Lorenc*,[1] the Northern Ireland Court of Appeal held that the EPA offence (then s. 22 of the EPA 1978) was committed when L was found in possession of three Army Manuals pertaining to the use of rifles, booby traps and incendiaries. The court rejected an argument that the offence only applied to information likely or intended to be used in planning or carrying out an act of violence. Conversely, in *R v McLoughlin*[2] the court quashed McLoughlin's conviction under this provision in respect of his collection of a list of radio frequencies used by the RUC. The court was satisfied that he had established on the balance of probabilities the 'reasonable excuse' of being a 'radio buff' and not a terrorist.

By 1996 there had been no convictions for the PTA versions of these offences but 24 and 8 respectively for the EPA versions since 1991; Lord Lloyd recommended both should be retained.[3]

In *R v DPP, ex p Kebilene*[4] the House of Lords left open the question whether the PTA, s. 16A was compatible with ECHR, Art. 6(2). Lord Hope made it clear that imposition of an evidential burden only on the defendant would not breach the ECHR. Section 118, which applies (inter alia) to both provisions, now expressly provides that the burden place on the defendant is only an evidential burden.

4. *Inciting terrorism overseas.* Sections 59–61 extend the circumstances in which a UK court may exercise jurisdiction in respect of offences committed abroad.

PART VII

NORTHERN IRELAND

Scheduled offences . . .

76. Admission in trial on indictment

(1) This section applies to a trial on indictment for—

    (*a*) a scheduled offence, or

    (*b*) two or more offences at least one of which is a scheduled offence.

(2) A statement made by the accused may be given in evidence by the prosecution in so far as—

    (*a*) it is relevant to a matter in issue in the proceedings, and

    (*b*) it is not excluded or inadmissible (whether by virtue of subsections (3) to (5) or otherwise).

(3) Subsections (4) and (5) apply if in proceedings to which this section applies—

    (*a*) the prosecution gives or proposes to give a statement made by the accused in evidence,

---

15 EPA, s. 29.

16 s. 27.

17 [1993] Crim LR 669. B. Dickson [1992] PL at 617 regarded it as 'symbolic law-making'.

18 *Legislation Against Terrorism*, para. 12.8.

19 *Lloyd Inquiry*, para. 6.10.

20 Introduced by the Criminal Justice and Public Order Act 1994, s. 82.

1 [1988] NI 96.

2 8 October 1993, unreported, CA (Cr D) (NI).

3 *Lloyd Inquiry*, pp. 91–92.

4 [1999] 4 All ER 801.

   (*b*)   prima facie evidence is adduced that the accused was subjected to torture, inhuman or degrading treatment, violence or the threat of violence in order to induce him to make the statement, and

   (*c*)   the prosecution does not satisfy the court that the statement was not obtained in the manner mentioned in paragraph (b).

(4) If the statement has not yet been given in evidence, the court shall—

   (*a*)   exclude the statement, or

   (*b*)   direct that the trial be restarted before a differently constituted court (before which the statement shall be inadmissible).

(5) If the statement has been given in evidence, the court shall—

   (*a*)   disregard it, or

   (*b*)   direct that the trial be restarted before a differently constituted court (before which the statement shall be inadmissible).

(6) This section is without prejudice to any discretion of a court to—

   (*a*)   exclude or ignore a statement, or

   (*b*)   direct a trial to be restarted,

where the court considers it appropriate in order to avoid unfairness to the accused or otherwise in the interests of justice.

77. Possession: onus of proof

(1) This section applies to a trial on indictment for a scheduled offence where the accused is charged with possessing an article in such circumstances as to constitute an offence under any of the enactments listed in subsection (3).

(2) If it is proved that the article—

   (*a*)   was on any premises at the same time as the accused, or

   (*b*)   was on premises of which the accused was the occupier or which he habitually used otherwise than as a member of the public,

the court may assume that the accused possessed (and, if relevant, knowingly possessed) the article, unless he proves that he did not know of its presence on the premises or that he had no control over it.

(3) The following are the offences mentioned in subsection (1)—

The Explosive Substances Act 1883

Section 3, so far as relating to subsection (1)(b) thereof (possessing explosive with intent to endanger life or cause serious damage to property).

Section 4 (possessing explosive in suspicious circumstances).

The Protection of the Person and Property Act (Northern Ireland) 1969

Section 2 (possessing petrol bomb, &c in suspicious circumstances).

The Firearms (Northern Ireland) Order 1981

Article 6(1) (manufacturing, dealing in or possessing certain weapons, &c).

Article 17 (possessing firearm or ammunition with intent to endanger life or cause serious damage to property).

Article 18(2) (possessing firearm or imitation firearm at time of committing, or being arrested for, a specified offence).

Article 22(1), (2) or (4) (possession of a firearm or ammunition by a person who has been sentenced to imprisonment, &c).

Article 23 (possessing firearm or ammunition in suspicious circumstances) . . .

Powers of arrest, search, &c

81. Arrest of suspected terrorists: power of entry

A constable may enter and search any premises if he reasonably suspects that a terrorist, within the meaning of section 40(1)(b), is to be found there.

82. Arrest and seizure: constables

(1) A constable may arrest without warrant any person if he reasonably suspects that the person is committing, has committed or is about to commit—

   (*a*)   a scheduled offence, or

   (*b*)   a non-scheduled offence under this Act.

(2) For the purpose of arresting a person under this section a constable may enter and search any premises where the person is or where the constable reasonably suspects him to be.

(3) A constable may seize and retain anything if he reasonably suspects that it is, has been or is intended to be used in the commission of—

   (*a*) a scheduled offence, or

   (*b*) a non-scheduled offence under this Act.

83. Arrest and seizure: armed forces

(1) If a member of Her Majesty's forces on duty reasonably suspects that a person is committing, has committed or is about to commit any offence he may—

   (*a*) arrest the person without warrant, and

   (*b*) detain him for a period not exceeding four hours.

(2) A person making an arrest under this section complies with any rule of law requiring him to state the ground of arrest if he states that he is making the arrest as a member of Her Majesty's forces.

(3) For the purpose of arresting a person under this section a member of Her Majesty's forces may enter and search any premises where the person is.

(4) If a member of Her Majesty's forces reasonably suspects that a person—

   (*a*) is a terrorist (within the meaning of Part V), or

   (*b*) has committed an offence involving the use or possession of an explosive or firearm,

he may enter and search any premises where he reasonably suspects the person to be for the purpose of arresting him under this section.

(5) A member of Her Majesty's forces may seize, and detain for a period not exceeding four hours, anything which he reasonably suspects is being, has been or is intended to be used in the commission of an offence under section 93 or 94.

(6) The reference to a rule of law in subsection (2) does not include a rule of law which has effect only by virtue of the Human Rights Act 1998.

84. Munitions and transmitters

Schedule 10 (which confers power to search for munitions and transmitters) shall have effect.

85. Explosives inspectors

[This section gives powers of entry, search and seizure in respect of explosives to inspectors appointed under section 53 of the Explosives Act 1875.]

86. Unlawfully detained persons

(1) If an officer reasonably believes that a person is unlawfully detained in such circumstances that his life is in danger, the officer may enter any premises for the purpose of ascertaining whether the person is detained there.

(2) In this section 'officer' means—

   (*a*) a member of Her Majesty's forces on duty, or

   (*b*) a constable.

(3) A dwelling may be entered under subsection (1) only by—

   (*a*) a member of Her Majesty's forces authorised for the purpose by a commissioned officer of those forces, or

   (*b*) a constable authorised for the purpose by an officer of the Royal Ulster Constabulary of at least the rank of inspector.

87. Examination of documents

(1) A member of Her Majesty's forces or a constable who performs a search under a provision of this Part—

   (*a*) may examine any document or record found in order to ascertain whether it contains information of the kind mentioned in section 58(1)(*a*) or 103(1)(*a*), and

   (*b*) if necessary or expedient for the purpose of paragraph (a), may remove the document or record to another place and retain it there until the examination is completed.

(2) Subsection (1) shall not permit a person to examine a document or record if he has reasonable cause to believe that it is an item subject to legal privilege (within the meaning of the Police and Criminal Evidence (Northern Ireland) Order 1989).

(3) Subject to subsections (4) and (5), a document or record may not be retained by virtue of subsection (1)(*b*) for more than 48 hours.

(4) An officer of the Royal Ulster Constabulary who is of at least the rank of chief inspector may authorise a constable to retain a document or record for a further period or periods.

(5) Subsection (4) does not permit the retention of a document or record after the end of the period of 96 hours beginning with the time when it was removed for examination under subsection (1)(*b*).

(6) A person who wilfully obstructs a member of Her Majesty's forces or a constable in the exercise of a power conferred by this section commits an offence.
(7) A person guilty of an offence under subsection (6) shall be liable—
  (*a*) on conviction on indictment, to imprisonment for a term not exceeding two years, to a fine or to both, or
  (*b*) on summary conviction, to imprisonment for a term not exceeding six months, to a fine not exceeding the statutory maximum or to both.

88. Examination of documents: procedure
(1) Where a document or record is examined under section 87—
  (*a*) it shall not be photographed or copied, and
  (*b*) the person who examines it shall make a written record of the examination as soon as is reasonably practicable.
(2) The record shall—
  (*a*) describe the document or record,
  (*b*) specify the object of the examination,
  (*c*) state the address of the premises where the document or record was found,
  (*d*) where the document or record was found in the course of a search of a person, state the person's name,
  (*e*) where the document or record was found in the course of a search of any premises, state the name of a person appearing to the person making the record to be the occupier of the premises or to have had custody or control of the document or record when it was found,
  (*f*) where the document or record is removed for examination from the place where it was found, state the date and time when it was removed, and
  (*g*) where the document or record was examined at the place where it was found, state the date and time of examination.
(3) The record shall identify the person by whom the examination was carried out—
  (*a*) in the case of a constable, by reference to his police number, and
  (*b*) in the case of a member of Her Majesty's forces, by reference to his service number, rank and regiment.
(4) Where a person makes a record of a search in accordance with this section, he shall as soon as is reasonably practicable supply a copy—
  (*a*) in a case where the document or record was found in the course of a search of a person, to that person, and
  (*b*) in a case where the document or record was found in the course of a search of any premises, to a person appearing to the person making the record to be the occupier of the premises or to have had custody or control of the document or record when it was found.

89. Power to stop and question
(1) An officer may stop a person for so long as is necessary to question him to ascertain—
  (*a*) his identity and movements;
  (*b*) what he knows about a recent explosion or another recent incident endangering life;
  (*c*) what he knows about a person killed or injured in a recent explosion or incident.
(2) A person commits an offence if he—
  (*a*) fails to stop when required to do so under this section,
  (*b*) refuses to answer a question addressed to him under this section, or
  (*c*) fails to answer to the best of his knowledge and ability a question addressed to him under this section.
(3) A person guilty of an offence under this section shall be liable on summary conviction to a fine not exceeding level 5 on the standard scale.
(4) In this section 'officer' means—
  (*a*) a member of Her Majesty's forces on duty, or
  (*b*) a constable.

90. Power of entry
(1) An officer may enter any premises if he considers it necessary in the course of operations for the preservation of the peace or the maintenance of order.
(2) In this section 'officer' means—
  (*a*) a member of Her Majesty's forces on duty, or
  (*b*) a constable.

95. Sections 81 to 94: supplementary

(1) This section applies in relation to sections 81 to 94.

(2) A power to enter premises may be exercised by reasonable force if necessary.

(3) A power to search premises shall, in its application to vehicles (by virtue of section 121), be taken to include—

    (*a*) power to stop a vehicle (other than an aircraft which is airborne), and

    (*b*) power to take a vehicle or cause it to be taken, where necessary or expedient, to any place for the purpose of carrying out the search.

(4) A person commits an offence if he fails to stop a vehicle when required to do so by virtue of this section.

(5) A person guilty of an offence under subsection (4) shall be liable on summary conviction to—

    (*a*) imprisonment for a term not exceeding six months,

    (*b*) a fine not exceeding level 5 on the standard scale, or

    (*c*) both.

(6) In the application to a place or vehicle (by virtue of section 121) of a power to search premises—

    (*a*) a reference to the address of the premises shall be construed as a reference to the location of the place or vehicle together with its registration number (if any), and

    (*b*) a reference to the occupier of the premises shall be construed as a reference to the occupier of the place or the person in charge of the vehicle.

(7) Where a search is carried out under Schedule 10 in relation to a vehicle (by virtue of section 121), the person carrying out the search may, if he reasonably believes that it is necessary in order to carry out the search or to prevent it from being frustrated—

    (*a*) require a person in or on the vehicle to remain with it;

    (*b*) require a person in or on the vehicle to go to and remain at any place to which the vehicle is taken by virtue of subsection (3)(*b*);

    (*c*) use reasonable force to secure compliance with a requirement under paragraph (a) or (b) above.

(8) Paragraphs 4(2) and (3), 8 and 9 of Schedule 10 shall apply to a requirement imposed under subsection (7) as they apply to a requirement imposed under that Schedule.

(9) Paragraph 8 of Schedule 10 shall apply in relation to the search of a vehicle which is not habitually stationary only if it is moved for the purpose of the search by virtue of subsection (3)(b); and where that paragraph does apply, the reference to the address of the premises shall be construed as a reference to the location where the vehicle is searched together with its registration number (if any).

(10) A member of Her Majesty's forces exercising any power when he is not in uniform shall, if requested to do so by any person at or about the time of exercising the power, produce to that person documentary evidence that he is a member of Her Majesty's Forces.

Miscellaneous

96. Preservation of the peace: regulations

(1) The Secretary of State may by regulations make provision for promoting the preservation of the peace and the maintenance of order.

(2) The regulations may authorise the Secretary of State to make orders or give directions for specified purposes.

(3) A person commits an offence if he contravenes or fails to comply with—

    (*a*) regulations under this section, or

    (*b*) an order or direction made or given under regulations made under this section.

(4) A person guilty of an offence under this section shall be liable on summary conviction to—

    (*a*) imprisonment for a term not exceeding six months,

    (*b*) a fine not exceeding level 5 on the standard scale, or

    (*c*) both. . . .

103. Terrorist information

(1) A person commits an offence if—

    (*a*) he collects, makes a record of, publishes, communicates or attempts to elicit information about a person to whom this section applies which is of a kind likely to be useful to a person committing or preparing an act of terrorism, or

    (*b*) he possesses a document or record containing information of that kind.

(2) This section applies to a person who is or has been—
- (*a*)   a constable,
- (*b*)   a member of Her Majesty's Forces,
- (*c*)   the holder of a judicial office,
- (*d*)   an officer of any court, or
- (*e*)   a full-time employee of the prison service in Northern Ireland.

(3) In this section 'record' includes a photographic or electronic record.

(4) If it is proved in proceedings for an offence under subsection (1)(*b*) that a document or record—
- (*a*)   was on any premises at the same time as the accused, or
- (*b*)   was on premises of which the accused was the occupier or which he habitually used otherwise than as a member of the public,

the court may assume that the accused possessed the document or record, unless he proves that he did not know of its presence on the premises or that he had no control over it.

(5) It is a defence for a person charged with an offence under this section to prove that he had a reasonable excuse for his action or possession.

(6) A person guilty of an offence under this section shall be liable—
- (*a*)   on conviction on indictment, to imprisonment for a term not exceeding 10 years, to a fine or to both, or
- (*b*)   on summary conviction, to imprisonment for a term not exceeding six months, to a fine not exceeding the statutory maximum or to both.

(7) A court by or before which a person is convicted of an offence under this section may order the forfeiture of any document or record containing information of the kind mentioned in subsection (1)(a).

(8) Before making an order under subsection (7) a court must give an opportunity to be heard to any person, other than the convicted person, who claims to be the owner of or otherwise interested in anything which can be forfeited under that subsection.

(9) An order under subsection (8) shall not come into force until there is no further possibility of it being varied, or set aside, on appeal (disregarding any power of a court to grant leave to appeal out of time).

104. Police powers: records
The Chief Constable of the Royal Ulster Constabulary shall make arrangements for securing that a record is made of each exercise by a constable of a power under this Part in so far as—
- (*a*)   it is reasonably practicable to do so, and
- (*b*)   a record is not required to be made under another enactment.

105. Powers
A power conferred on a person by virtue of this Part—
- (*a*)   is additional to powers which he has at common law or by virtue of any other enactment, and
- (*b*)   shall not be taken to affect those powers or Her Majesty's prerogative. ...

Specified organisations

107. Specified organisations: interpretation
For the purposes of sections 108 to 111 an organisation is specified at a particular time if at that time—
- (*a*)   it is specified under section 3(8) of the Northern Ireland (Sentences) Act 1998, and
- (*b*)   it is, or forms part of, an organisation which is proscribed for the purposes of this Act.

108. Evidence
(1) This section applies where a person is charged with an offence under section 11.

(2) Subsection (3) applies where a police officer of at least the rank of superintendent states in oral evidence that in his opinion the accused—
- (*a*)   belongs to an organisation which is specified, or
- (*b*)   belonged to an organisation at a time when it was specified.

(3) Where this subsection applies—

(*a*)   the statement shall be admissible as evidence of the matter stated, but

(*b*)   the accused shall not be committed for trial, be found to have a case to answer or be convicted solely on the basis of the statement.

(4) In this section 'police officer' means a member of—

(*a*)   a police force within the meaning of the Police Act 1996 or the Police (Scotland) Act 1967, or

(*b*)   the Royal Ulster Constabulary.

109. Inferences

(1) This section applies where a person is charged with an offence under section 11.

(2) Subsection (4) applies where evidence is given that—

(*a*)   at any time before being charged with the offence the accused, on being questioned under caution by a constable, failed to mention a fact which is material to the offence and which he could reasonably be expected to mention, and

(*b*)   before being questioned the accused was permitted to consult a solicitor.

(3) Subsection (4) also applies where evidence is given that—

(*a*)   on being charged with the offence or informed by a constable that he might be prosecuted for it the accused failed to mention a fact which is material to the offence and which he could reasonably be expected to mention, and

(*b*)   before being charged or informed the accused was permitted to consult a solicitor.

(4) Where this subsection applies—

(*a*)   the court, in considering any question whether the accused belongs or belonged at a particular time to a specified organisation, may draw from the failure inferences relating to that question, but

(*b*)   the accused shall not be committed for trial, be found to have a case to answer or be convicted solely on the basis of the inferences.

(5) Subject to any directions by the court, evidence tending to establish the failure may be given before or after evidence tending to establish the fact which the accused is alleged to have failed to mention.

110. Sections 108 and 109: supplementary

(1) Nothing in section 108 or 109 shall—

(*a*)   prejudice the admissibility of evidence admissible apart from that section,

(*b*)   preclude the drawing of inferences which could be drawn apart from that section, or

(*c*)   prejudice an enactment providing (in whatever words) that an answer or evidence given by a person in specified circumstances is not admissible in evidence against him or some other person in any proceedings or class of proceedings (however described, and whether civil or criminal).

(2) In subsection (1)(c) the reference to giving evidence is a reference to giving it in any manner (whether by giving information, making discovery, producing documents or otherwise).

111. Forfeiture orders

(1) This section applies if—

(*a*)   a person is convicted of an offence under section 11 or 12, and

(*b*)   at the time of the offence he belonged to an organisation which was a specified organisation.

(2) The court by or before which the person is convicted may order the forfeiture of any money or other property if—

(*a*)   he had it in his possession or under his control at the time of the offence, and

(*b*)   it has been used in connection with the activities of the specified organisation or the court believes that it may be used in that connection unless it is forfeited.

(3) Before making an order under this section the court must give an opportunity to be heard to any person, other than the convicted person, who claims to be the owner of or otherwise interested in anything which can be forfeited under this section.

(4) A question arising as to whether subsection (1)(b) or (2)(a) or (b) is satisfied shall be determined on the balance of probabilities.

(5) Schedule 4 shall apply (with the necessary modifications) in relation to orders under this section as it applies in relation to orders made under section 23.

NOTES (PART VII: NORTHERN IRELAND)

1. Part VII continues a number of powers in Northern Ireland only. It has effect for one year from the day on which it is brought into force but may be extended.[5]
2. *Trial by judge alone.*[6] This was introduced following recommendations of the Diplock Commission.[7] The Commission took the view that there was a serious threat of intimidation to jurors, and a danger of perverse acquittals of 'loyalist extremists' by the predominantly Protestant juries. The Gardiner Committee concluded[8] that the new system 'has worked fairly and well', that 'the right to a fair trial has been respected and maintained and that the administration of justice has not suffered'. Accordingly they supported the continuation of these provisions. K. Boyle[9] gave figures which showed a pattern of declining acquittal rates for trials by judge alone over the period 1973–1977, and noted that 'concern has been voiced over the specture of judges becoming case-hardened ...'. Cf. D. Greer,[10] who argued that comparisons of acquittal rates were 'not entirely valid and the allegation of case-hardening cannot be regarded as having been established.' Sir George Baker[11] stated that each Northern Ireland judge ' is continually thinking of the possibility and warning himself against leaning or even appearing to lean to the prosecution or against the defence', that the fall in acquittal rates might be explained by greater care taken by the prosecuting authorities in the preparation or selection of cases, and that the rates had in fact risen in 1981 and 1982. He concluded that the time was not ripe for a return to jury trials: 'the over-whelming weight of opinion from those best qualified to judge is that members of juries in serious cases would be in more danger today than ever before.' He also rejected the alternative possibilities of courts comprising two or three judges or a judge with assessors or resident magistrates. The same position was taken in the *Colville Review (EPA)*,[12] There was insufficient judge-power to support two- or three-judge panels. A proposal for anonymous juries, hidden from the public was also rejected:

> 'It is far from certain ... that a person who suddenly deserts his normal way of life and disappears for five days a week ... is safe from the deduction that he is on jury service.'[13]

The acquittal rate in contested 'Diplock' cases has fluctuated, increasing in the early 1980s, most markedly in 1984 and 1985 (mainly as a result of the rejection of 'supergrass' evidence[14]), but then falling (in most years, although not to the low levels of the late 1970s);[15] There have been limited additions to the lists of offences that may be 'certified-out', but also additions to the list of scheduled offences. Many have argued in support of the restoration of trial by jury.[16] G. Hogan and H. Walker[17] argue that special trials are overused, and that the problem should be tackled by providing further protection for

---

5 See s. 112.
6 See J. Jackson and S. Doran, *Judge Without Jury; Diplock Trials in the Adversary System* (1995).
7 Cmnd. 5185, pp. 17–19.
8 Cmnd. 5847, p. 11.
9 Current Law Statutes Annotated 1978, note to 2.7.
10 (1980) 31 NILQ 205, 233.
11 Report, pp. 30–39.
12 Cm. 1115, 1990, Chap. 9.
13 Ibid., para. 9.1.
14 See p. 609.
15 See G. Hogan and H. Walker, op. cit., Table 4.2 (p. 104); A. Jennings, op cit., p. xxvii; J. Jackson and S. Doran, op. cit. p. 35.
16 See A. Jennings and D. Wolchover, (1984) 134 NLJ 659, 687 and S. Greer and A. White, *Abolishing the Diplock Courts* (Cobden Trust, 1986) and A. Jennings, op cit., Chap. 3.
17 pp. 100–109.

juries, the descheduling of certain offences, the extension of certification powers to any scheduled offence and, possibly, moving to a requirement of certifying-in.[18]

J. Jackson and S. Doran[19] undertook a detailed comparison of the Diplock and ordinary trial processes but found no conclusive evidence on the 'case-hardening' issue. Acquittal rates remain lower in Diplock trials.[20] However, there was evidence that judges '*did* adopt an approach towards the evidence which could be described as 'case-hardened', not in the commonly understood sense of being prosecution-minded, but in the sense of confining their consideration to the issue of legal guilt on the offences charged'.[1] This could work both ways: on the one hand, defendants could not benefit from a jury acquittal based on wider moral considerations; on the other, judges might be more effective than a jury in adopting a proper approach in handling certain kinds of evidence, such as identification evidence.[2] Overall, there were not dramatic differences between the professional conduct of Diplock and jury trials, but considerable variations in the degree of intervention by individual judges whatever the mode of trial.

The government is committed to move as quickly as circumstances allow to jury trial for all offences.[3] However, in July 2000 the government accepted the recommendation of a Review Group that the time was not yet right for such a move.[4] The number of Diplock trials has been declining as the security situation has improved.[5]

3. *Admissions*.[6] Section 76 of the 2000 Act is drawn from the EPA 1996, s. 12.[7] The reference to 'torture or inhuman or degrading treatment' is taken from Art. 3 ECHR. In *R v McCormick*,[8] McGonigal LJ stated that the EPA 1978, s. 6 left 'it open to an interviewer to use a moderate degree of physical maltreatment for the purpose of inducing a person to make a statement'. This observation was based on the view of the European Commission that assaults did not necessarily amount to 'inhuman treatment' under Art. 3 ECHR.[9] However, McGonigal LJ's view was doubted by Lord Lowry CJ in *R v O'Halloran*:[10]

'This court finds it difficult in practice to envisage any form of physical violence which is relevant to the interrogation of a suspect in custody and which, if it had occurred could at the same time leave a court satisfied beyond reasonable doubt in relation to the issue for decision under section 6.'

It was unclear how far s. 8 permitted psychological pressure to be applied to a suspect.[11]

In *R v McGrath*[12] the Northern Ireland Court of Appeal endorsed the view of the trial judge that:

18 Cf. *Colville Review (EPA)*, Chap. 8. For a critical analysis of the scheduling system in the light of research on the operation of juries in ordinary cases, see J. Jackson and S. Doran, 'Diplock and the Presumption Against Jury Trial' [1992] Crim LR 755.

19 *Judge without Jury* (1995).

20 pp. 33–36.

1 pp. 290–291.

2 pp. 224–240.

3 *Legislation Against Terrorism*, para. 13.5.

4 HC Deb, 18 July 2000, col. *124w*, Adam Ingram.

5 *Annual Statistics on the Operation of the Northern Ireland (Emergency Provisions) Act 1996* (1999), Table 4.

6 See generally D. S. Greer, (1973) 24 NILQ 199 and (1980) 31 NILQ 205; G. Hogan and H. Walker, pp. 109–119; J. Jackson and S. Doran, pp. 36–43.

7 Previously EPA 1973, s. 6, EPA 1978, s. 8 and EPA 1991, s. 11.

8 [1977] NI 105, 111, Belfast City Commission.

9 See e.g. Application No. 4220/69, *X v United Kingdom* 14 YBECHR, p. 250; L. Doswald-Beck, (1978) 25 Ned Int LRev 24.

10 [1979] NI 45, 47, (NI). See also the cases cited by D. S. Greer, (1980) 31 NILQ 205, 213, n. 37.

11 See D. S. Greer, op. cit., pp. 213–215.

12 [1980] NI 91.

'the ill-treatment which would fall within the section must be done with the intention of causing either physical or mental suffering and that physical or mental suffering must be of a very high degree and it must have been done also as the section indicates with the purpose of inducing a statement.'[13]

Accordingly suffering inflicted through negligence or lack of judgment or sensitivity did not come within s. 8; there had to be an intention to cause suffering. The object of Art. 3, and accordingly, s. 8(2), 'was to outlaw certain forms of conduct and not simply to obviate the admission of unreliable evidence'. Moreover, there had to be an intention, by causing that suffering, to induce the suspect to confess[14] and a causal link between the ill-treatment and the statement.[15] However, once a prima facie case had been raised that defendant had been subjected to improper treatment under the section, the onus shifted to the Crown to establish *beyond reasonable doubt* that admissions were not so obtained.[16]

There was an important qualification to these principles: it was held that while s. 8 had replaced the common law test of voluntariness, the judges retained their discretion to disallow relevant evidence 'on the ground that ... its prejudicial effect outweighs its probative value and that to admit the evidence would not be in the interests of justice'.[17] Indeed, the discretion seemed a little broader than this wording would suggest. In *R v Culbert* [18] Lord Lowry CJ referred without disapproval to the formulation of O'Donnell J in *R v McCracken* [19] where he stated that there was:

'an overall discretion to exclude statements which have been unfairly obtained which might prejudice the fair trial of the defendant even if not induced by torture, inhuman or degrading treatment.'

In *R v McCormick* [20] McGonigal LJ stated that this discretion should not be used so as to negative the effects of s. 6 of the 1973 Act 'and under the guise of the discretionary power have the effect of reinstating the old common law test in so far as it depended on the proof of physical or mental maltreatment'. It should only be exercised where maltreatment has rendered a statement 'in itself' suspect by reason of the method as a result of which it was obtained.[1] The existence of the discretion was affirmed by the Northern Ireland Court of Appeal in *R v Dillon* [2] and *R v McBrien and Harman*.[3]

The Bennett Committee concluded that reports of cases decide by the judges as to the discretion to exclude evidence 'necessarily leave areas of uncertainty from the point of view of police practice'.[4] This led the Committee 'to consider whether the control exercised by the court over the means by which statements are induced and obtained should be supplemented by more direct regulation operating immediately on the interviewing officers'.[5]

Sir George Baker[6] recommended that EPA 1978, s. 8 should be redrafted to prohibit violence and include the judges' discretion expressly. This change was effected by the EPA 1987. The discretion under this provision was held to be no wider than that

13 p. 92.
14 See also on this point *R v Milne* [1978] NI 110 at 117, Belfast City Commission.
15 D. S. Greer, (1980) 31 NILQ 205, 215–217.
16 *R v Hetherington* [1975] NI 164 at 166, Belfast City Commission; *R v Brophy* [1982] AC 476, Belfast City Commission.
17 *R v Corey* (1973) reported at [1979] NI 49 (Note), Belfast City Commission; *R v Hetherington* [1975] NI 164 at 169–180.
18 [1982] NI 90, 93, CA (NI).
19 Unreported, 1975.
20 [1977] NI 105 at 114.
1 See also *R v Milne* [1978] NI 110, Belfast City Commission, and *R v O'Halloran* [1979] NI 45, CA (NI) and D. S. Greer, (1980) 31 NILQ 205, 217–244.
2 [1984] NI 292.
3 [1984] NI 280.
4 Bennett Report (1979), p. 136.
5 Ibid., p. 31: see above, pp. 589–590.
6 Report (1984) pp. 54–58 and Appendix J.

arising in respect of the earlier statutes or at common law.[7] Note that the 2000 Act, s. 76(3)(b) is not confined to actual or threatened physical violence, but is limited to deliberate violence.[8] The question of the admissibility of confessions in cases where s. 76 does not apply is now determined by Arts. 74–76 of the PACE (Northern Ireland) Order 1989).[9] The Colville Review (EPA) recommended that 'an enabling power to transfer to the PACE standard, if it becomes appropriate to do so, should ... be made'.[10] Boyle[11] argues that there 'can be little doubt that the PACE standards are more demanding'. Is there any justification now for maintaining different standards?[12]

The Court of Appeal in Northern Ireland has held that the use of foul and obscene language by interrogating officers was on the facts of the case not 'degrading treatment' for the purposes of EPA 1978, s. 8 and not sufficient to justify exclusion in the exercise of discretion.[13] Moreover, searching and persistent questioning over a period which causes an accused to speak when otherwise he would have remained silent should not of itself be regarded as 'oppression' so as to justify discretionary exclusion[14] (although it might have constituted 'oppression' at common law: see *R v Priestley*[15]). Similarly, the offering of an inducement does not necessarily require exclusion.[16] Reliance 'on the threat of unlawful vengeance from a third party as a lever with which to apply pressure on a suspect' has, however, been held to be improper and to justify exclusion.[17]

Dermot P. J. Walsh[18] is critical of what became s. 11 and its interpretation by the judges:

'The cumulative effect of these judicial interpretations is that the RUC can subject a prisoner to lengthy, repetitive and debilitating interrogations, threats, bribes, trickery, verbal abuse and possibly even a moderate degree of physical ill-treatment to obtain a confession without that confession being ruled inadmissible.'[19]

Lord Lloyd found no evidence that the Northern Ireland courts were prepared to admit statements under the EPA standard that they would not have allowed under PACE. The EPA standard had been introduced at a time when voluntariness was the applicable test under the common law; with the arrival of the PACE Order the argument for maintaining a separate EPA standard had weakened and would be unsustainable in a lasting peace.[20]

Is there any justification for its retention in the 2000 Act? The SACHR was against its re-enactment.[1]

4. *The 'right to silence'.* Apart from the question of the admissibility of confessions, the Criminal Evidence (Northern Ireland) Order 1988[2] enables a court in any criminal trial to draw adverse inferences from an accused's failure to mention a relevant fact during police questioning or when charged;[3] his refusal to give evidence at trial;[4] his failure to

---

7 *R v Brennan* (unreported, 24 September 1996, CA (NI)).
8 Cf. G. Hogan and C. Walker, op. cit., p. 114.
9 S.I. 1989 No. 1341 (cf. above, pp. 349–388).
10 Cm. 1115, para. 10.5.7.6.
11 *Current Law Statutes Annotated 1987*, note to s. 5.
12 See the *Rowe Review (EPA)*, pp. 17–19.
13 *R v Mullan* (1988) 10 NIJB 36.
14 *R v McBrien and Harman* [1984] NI 280; *R v Dillon* [1984] NI 292.
15 (1967) 51 Cr App Rep 1n, above p. 363.
16 *R v Cowan* [1987] NI 338.
17 *R v Howell* [1987] 5 NIJB 10.
18 In *Jennings*, op cit., Chap. 2.
19 p. 38.
20 *Lloyd Inquiry*, paras. 16.20–16.22. Cf. J. J. Rowe, *EPA Review 1998*, para. 54, concluding that there was in fact a difference in practice.
1 E.g. Report for 1995–96 (1995–96 HC 467), p. 26.
2 S.I. 1988 No. 1987 (NI 20). See J. D. Jackson (1989) 40 NILQ 105, 105–118 and [1995] Crim LR 587; *Colville Review* (EPA), para. 10.6.
3 Art. 3.
4 Art. 4.

account for the presence of an object, substance or mark on his person, in or on his clothing or footwear, otherwise in his possession or in any place in which he is at the time of his arrest;[5] or his failure to account for his presence when found by a constable at a place at or about the time the offence for which he was arrested is alleged to have been committed.[6] After initial caution,[7] the judges have drawn inferences under Art. 4 in a series of cases.[8] In *Murray v DPP*[9] the House of Lords upheld M's convictions for the attempted murder of a soldier and possession of a firearm with intent to endanger life where the trial judge had drawn an inference under Art. 4. Lord Slynn (for a unanimous House of Lords) noted that the prosecutor must first establish a prima facie case (otherwise there could be a successful submission of no case to answer by the defence). The judge (as trier of fact) could then draw 'such inferences from the refusal [to testify] as appear proper'.[10] This would 'depend on the circumstances of the particular case and is a question to be decided by applying ordinary common sense'.[11] Here, there was forensic evidence linking M with the attempted murder (especially a thumb print on the mirror of the car used by the attackers, cartridge residue and mud on his jeans) and the trial judge was entitled 'to infer that there was no innocent explanation to the prima facie case and that the accused was guilty'. The judge had clearly not proceeded on the erroneous basis that 'simply because the accused did not give evidence he was therefore guilty'.[12] Moreover, it was not necessary for the judge to spell out what precise inference he drew from each aspect of the circumstantial evidence relied on; he was:

'entitled to have regard to the circumstantial evidence as a whole and to conclude that a refusal to deal with it or any of it justified an inference of guilt.'[13]

J. D. Jackson[14] argues that the House in *Murray* could have adopted a narrower approach, limiting the operation of Art. 4 to cases where the prosecution case is otherwise 'on the brink of proof beyond reasonable doubt'[15] or to inferences which undermine the defence case as distinct from inferences drawn directly to bolster the prosecution case.[16] He also criticises the lack of any guidelines on the application of 'common sense'.

Note that a prima facie case here means:

'a case consisting of direct evidence which, if believed and combined with legitimate inferences based upon it, could lead a properly directed jury to be satisfied beyond reasonable doubt ... that each of the essential elements of the offence is proved.'[17]

The Northern Ireland provisions were subsequently adopted for England and Wales (with modifications that were also made in Northern Ireland).[18]

The *Murray* case was taken to Strasbourg,[19] where the Court of Human Rights held: (1) by 14 to 5 that there had been no violation of Art. 6(1) and (2) arising out

5 Art. 5.
6 Art. 6.
7 J. D. Jackson, [1991] Crim LR 404.
8 J. D. Jackson, [1995] Crim LR 587, 595–599.
9 [1994] 1 WLR, 97 Cr App Rep 151.
10 Art. 4(4)(b).
11 Per Lord Slynn at 160, citing Lord Diplock in *Haw Tua Tau v Public Prosecutor* [1982] AC 136 at 153.
12 Lord Slynn at 161.
13 Ibid.
14 'Inferences from Silence: from Common Law to Common Sense' (1993) 44 NILQ 103.
15 pp. 107–108.
16 p. 108.
17 Per Lord Mustill at 154.
18 Above., pp. 336–348.
19 *John Murray v UK* (1996) 22 EHRR 29, Judgment of 8 February 1996. See C. Bell, 'Complying with European Court of Human Rights Decisions: An Assessment of *McCann v UK* and *Murray v UK*' 22nd Report of SACHR, 1996–97 (1997–98 HC 402), Annex B.; R. Munday [1996] Crim LR 370.

of the drawing of adverse inferences; (2) by 12 to 7 that there had been a violation of Art. 6(1) in conjunction with Art. 6(3)(c) as regards M's lack of access to a lawyer during the first 48 hours of his detention. The court stated that while a conviction solely or mainly based on the accused's silence would breach Art. 6, the right to silence was not an absolute. Whether there was a breach:

'was a matter to be determined in all the circumstances of the case, having particular regard to the situations where inferences may be drawn, the weight attached to them by the national court in their assessment of the evidence and the degree of compulsion inherent in the situation.'[20]

On the facts of *Murray*, the court noted that he had maintained his silence and that this was not itself an offence or a contempt of court; under national law, silence in itself could not be regarded as an indication of guilt; the drawing of inferences was subject to an 'important series of safeguards'; there was a strong case against M apart from the inferences from silence; the drawing of inferences was a matter of common sense.[1]

Following the decision in *Murray*, Arts. 3, 5 and 6 of the 1989 Order were amended[2] to provide that an adverse inference may not be drawn in any case where the accused was at an authorised place of detention at the time of the relevant failure or refusal and had not been allowed (lawfully or unlawfully) an opportunity to consult a solicitor prior to the questioning or charge or prior to the request to account for the relevant facts (as the case may be).

Research on the effects of the 1988 Order showed that following its introduction fewer scheduled defendants refused to give evidence at trial although there was little evidence that it increased the likelihood of terrorist suspects to answer police questions and no evidence of any impact on the conviction rate. There was also little evidence that the Order was used to fill a large evidential gap.[3]

5. *'Supergrasses'*.[4] From 1981 onwards, a number of trials, commonly involving large numbers of defendants, were conducted on the basis of the evidence of informers variously termed 'converted terrorists', 'accomplices' or 'supergrasses'. The Attorney-General[5] explained that the principles governing accomplice evidence were the same in England and Northern Ireland, in that the judge was required to warn the jury (or himself, if the trier of fact) that, although it (or he) may convict on such evidence, it is dangerous to do so unless it is corroborated. It was for the DPP:

'to consider each case on its own facts and in the light of the interest of the public that criminals, and particularly dangerous criminals, should be brought to justice. Where the evidence of an accomplice appears to be credible and cogent and relates to serious terrorist crime, there is an overriding public interest in having charges brought before the court.'

Any immunity from prosecution would only be given in respect of offences which the witness discloses and of which he has given a truthful account. The prospect of saving lives would weight heavily in making such a decision.

---

20 Para. 47.
1 See also *Fox v United Kingdom*, 9 November 1999, where the ECtHR declared F's application inadmissible; an adverse inference drawn by the trial judge was 'an additional element which went to the weight of the already substantial case'.
2 Criminal Evidence (Northern Ireland) Order 1999, S.I. 1999 No. 2789, Art. 36; the same change was effected for England and Wales by the Youth Justice and Criminal Evidence Act 1999, s. 58.
3 *Research and Statistical Series: No. 1 – Legislating Against Silence: the Northern Ireland Experience* (2000) (research conducted by J. D. Jackson, et al). See M. Zander, (2001) 151 NLJ 138.
4 See P. Hillyard and J. Percy-Smith, (1984) 11 JLS 335; S. C. Greer, *Supergrasses* (1994) and A. Jennings, Chap. 4; D. Bonner, (1988) 51 MLR 23; A. Boyd, *The Informers* (1984); G. Hogan and C. Walker, op cit., pp. 123–126.
5 47 HC Deb, 24 October 1983, cols. 3–5, written answer.

Critics stressed the dangers of relying on the evidence of accomplices.[6] It was suggested that the judges were not always sufficiently discriminating in accepting some parts of an accomplice's testimony while rejecting others, and in convicting on some counts without corroboration.[7] Indeed, the Northern Ireland Court of Appeal subsequently quashed convictions where they were based on the uncorroborated testimony of a 'supergrass' or other informer,[8] and the use of 'supergrasses' ceased. Whether this was simply to be explained by an absence of informers willing to testify, or a change in prosecution policy in the light of the critical response of the judiciary was unclear. The Attorney-General stated in 1986 that it was unlikely that there would be any further prosecutions in Northern Ireland based solely on accomplice evidence.[9]

6. *Possession: onus of proof.* Section 77 only imposes an evidential burden (s. 118).[10]

7. *Arrest.*

(i) *EPA arrests.* A wide power of arrest was conferred by the EPA 1978, s. 11: 'Any constable may arrest without a warrant any person whom he suspects of being a terrorist.'

It was designed to be used as the start of the procedure leading to internment, although it was also widely used to lead to questioning and, possibly, proceedings for a specific criminal offence. Over time, the RUC made increasing use of the power to arrest under PTA 1984, s. 12. It was indeed RUC policy to arrest every terrorist suspect, even if caught in the act of committing a specific offence, under one of these powers, as they gave more time in which to conduct investigations. Arrest powers under the EPA 1978, s. 13,[11] or s. 2 of the Criminal Law Act (Northern Ireland) 1967 were rarely used.[12] The EPA 1987 abolished the arrest power under s. 11, leaving arrests to be made either under PTA 1989, s. 14[13] or under specific arrest powers.[14]

In *Fox, Campbell and Hartley v United Kingdom*[15] the ECtHR held that the arrest of the complainants under the EPA 1978, s. 11 on suspicion of being terrorists was unlawful as contrary to Art. 5(1)(c) of the ECHR, which required 'reasonable suspicion' to justify detention, the matter being judged by reference to the facts of the case rather than any form of the legislation.[16]

(ii) *Army arrests and searches.* The 2000 Act, s. 83(2)[17] dispenses with the normal *Christie v Leachinsky* requirements.[18] This was justified by the Diplock

---

6 See D. P. J. Walsh, op. cit., pp. 90–92; T. Gifford, *Supergrasses: The Use of Accomplice Evidence in Northern Ireland* (1984).

7 See the comments by Gifford on the cases concerning the informers Bennett (*R v Graham* [1983] 7 NIJB, Belfast Cr Ct), Black, and McGrady (*R v Gibney* [1983] 13 NIJB, Belfast Cr Ct). (Cf. the Baker Report, pp. 47–50).

8 See *R v McCormack* [1984] NI 50; *R v Graham* [1984] 18 NIJB 23; *R v Donnelly* [1986] 4 NIJB 32; *R v Gibney* [1986] 4 NIJB 1; *R v Crumley* (1987) 3 BNIL n. 83.

9 94 HC Deb, 19 March 1986, col. 186, written answer.

10 Cf. p. 617.

11 Subsequently EPA 1991, s. 17, EPA 1996, s. 18.

12 See D. P. J. Walsh (1982) 9 JLS, 37, 41.

13 Which replaced PTA 1984, s. 12.

14 E.g. those conferred by the PACE (Northern Ireland) Order 1989, S.I. 1989 No. 1341 (NI 12) or EPA 1996, s. 18, now the 2000 Act, s. 82. For a detailed comparison of the EPA 1978, s. 11 and what became the PTA 1989, s. 14, see G. Hogan and C. Walker, op cit., pp 47–50.

15 (1990) 13 EHRR 157.

16 See W. Finnie, (1991) 54 MLR 288.

17 Formerly EPA, 1996, s. 19(2) and EPA 1991, s. 18(2). The army power under s. 19 and its predecessors has been exercised in a much reduced number of cases since the early 1980s: *Annual Statistics on the Operation of the Northern Ireland (Emergency Provision) Act 1996* (1999), Tables 7a, 7b.

18 See above, pp. 283–287. But note s. 83(6).

Commission[19] on the ground that it was not practicable for the initial arrest of a suspected terrorist in 'extremist strongholds' to be effected by a police officer:

'45. It is, we think, preposterous to expect a young soldier making an arrest under these conditions to be able to identify a person whom he has arrested as being a man whom he knows to be wanted for a particular offence so as to be able to inform him accurately of the grounds on which he is arresting him. It is impossible to question arrested persons on the spot to establish their identity. In practice this cannot usually be ascertained until they have been taken to the safety of battalion headquarters. Even here it may be a lengthy process, as suspects often give false names or addresses, or give their true names, which are often very common ones, assert that some relation or other person of the same name is the real person who is 'wanted' for a particular offence. It is only when his identity has been satisfactorily established that it is possible to be reasonably certain of the particular ground on which he was liable to arrest and inform him of it.'

The House of Lords has held, moreover, that the observance of even the limited requirements of EPA 1991, s. 18(2) can be delayed.[20] The House approved what appeared to be the army's standard practice when effecting an arrest at the home of a person suspected of an offence in connection with the IRA: the suspect was identified on entry to the house, but the house was searched, with its occupants detained in the living room, before the ground of arrest was given. This procedure was justified by the House of Lords on the ground that there would be a real risk that the alarm might be raised and an attempt made to resist arrest.[1]

A further deviation from normal standards was formerly found in ss. 13, 14 and 15(2) of the 1978 Act[2] in that the powers of arrest and search there were exercisable on the basis of 'suspicion'. This was changed to a requirement of 'reasonable suspicion' by the Northern Ireland (Emergency Provisions) Act 1978, Sch. 1.

(iii) *Arrest-search procedure.* The House of Lords in *Murray v Ministry of Defence*[3] held that the search procedure summarised above was lawful by reference to the power of search in s. 14(3) of the 1978 Act,[4] notwithstanding that the search was conducted after the person whom the army had come to arrest had been identified. The House accepted that there was no power to search for incriminating evidence, but held that:

'It is … a proper exercise of the power of search for the purpose of effecting the arrest to search every room for other occupants of the house in case there may be those there who are disposed to resist the arrest. The search cannot be limited solely to looking for the person to be arrested and must also embrace a search whose object is to secure that the arrest should be peaceable.'[5]

C. Walker[6] argues that this:

'improperly widens the notion of the 'purpose' to include the rounding up of possible malcontents removed from the arrest scene. … Furthermore, the search was unnecessary in *Murray v Ministry of Defence* since the arrest had already been executed without demur.'

The House also indicated, *obiter*, that the detention of the occupants of the house in one room while the rest of the house was searched was lawful. These dicta were

19 Cmnd. 5185.
20 *Murray v Ministry of Defence* [1988] 2 All ER 521.
1 For criticism of this 'new exception to *Christie v Leachinsky*', see C. Walker, (1989) 40 NILQ 1, 6–10, pointing out that the House 'applied a plausible reason for delay which did not in fact pertain' (p. 10), and G. Williams, (1991) 54 MLR 408.
2 Subsequently ss. 17, 18 and 19(2) of the 1991 Act.
3 [1988] 2 All ER 521.
4 Subsequently EPA 1991, s. 18(3) and EPA 1996, s. 19(3).
5 Per Lord Griffiths at 527.
6 (1989) 40 NILQ 1, 18.

applied by the High Court in Northern Ireland in the context of an alleged detention, ancillary to a munitions search in *Kirkpatrick v Chief Constable of the Royal Ulster Constabulary.* [7] Kelly LJ stated that:

> 'there must necessarily be some degree of control over the activities of the members of the household, especially at the outset of the search, when certain preliminaries and formalities are gone through. Such degree of control will be slight and minimal and must substantially depend on the consent, tacit or passive though it may be, of the household. The interference with the habits and convenience of the household will also be minimal and must at all times be justified on the grounds that it is reasonably necessary for the execution of a speedy and efficient search.' [8]

On the facts, however, the court found that the level of restraint imposed on the occupants did not amount to a detention or imprisonment; the occupants had consented in acceding to a request to assemble in one room at the start of the search. [9] Express authority was subsequently given for some of these matters in connection with munitions searches (but not searches on arrest). [10]

C. Walker [11] argues that 'the reasoning supporting both these judicially created powers is profoundly wrong' and that the issues would have been more appropriately dealt with 'as an aspect of the use of reasonable force in making an arrest, as governed by section 3(1) of the Criminal Law Act (Northern Ireland) 1967'. [12] In *Murray v UK* [13] the European Court of Human Rights rejected claims that the arrest and the arrest procedure violated Arts. 5 and 8 ECHR.

(iv) *Former army arrest powers.* Many regulations made under the Civil Authorities (Special Powers) Act (NI) 1922 purported to give powers to members of the armed forces on duty. It was held in *R (Hume) v Londonderry Justices* [14] that such regulations were ultra vires in view of the government of Ireland Act 1920, s. 4(1), which provided that the Northern Ireland Parliament was not to have power to make laws in respect of 'the navy, the army, the air force ... or the defence of the realm, or any other naval, military, or air force matter ...'.

Parliament immediately passed legislation to regularise the position retrospectively in the Northern Ireland Act 1972, s. 1. An application in which the Republic of Ireland argued that the 1972 Act conflicted with Art. 7 ECHR was withdrawn when the UK Attorney-General gave an undertaking in proceedings before the Commission that no one had or would be held guilty as a result of the 1972 Act for an act or omission which did not constitute a criminal offence at the time it was committed. [15]

In *Re McElduff* [16] McGonigal J held that the usual common law requirements as to arrests were applicable to arrests under the Civil Authorities (Special Powers) Act Regulations. Accordingly, a person could not be validly arrested unless: (1) the arrestor took reasonable steps to bring the fact of the arrest to the notice of the person arrested; (2) the person arrested was informed at the time of the arrest or at the earliest opportunity thereafter, (i) under what powers he had been arrested, and (ii) of the

---

7 [1988] NI 421.
8 pp. 429–430.
9 p. 428.
10 PTA 1989, s. 21; see subsequently EPA 1991, ss. 19(4), (5), 26(6); EPA 1996, ss. 20(4), (5), 28(6); 2000 Act, Sch. 10, para. 4.
11 (1989) 40 NILQ 1, 11–18.
12 p. 18.
13 (1994) 19 EHRR 193, Series A No. 300-A.
14 [1972] NI 91, QBD (NI).
15 A 5451/72 41 CDE Comm HR, pp. 82–83 (1972).
16 [1972] NI 1, QBD (NI).

general nature of the suspicion leading to the arrest. McElduff was arrested on 9 August 1971 under reg. 10 (power to arrest and detain for up to 48 hours for the purposes of interrogation) as part of 'Operation Demetrius'.[17] Later the same day, he was purportedly rearrested under reg. 11(1) (power to arrest persons suspected of acting in a manner prejudicial to peace or order). The arresting officer did not sufficiently distinguish this from the earlier arrest, merely stating that McElduff was 'being arrested' under the Special Powers Act. As a valid and subsisting arrest under reg. 11(1) was a necessary prerequisite for a valid detention order under Reg. 11(2), habeas corpus was granted. McGonigal J stated, *obiter*, that the power to arrest a person whom the arrestor suspects of acting in the prescribed manner did not import a standard of reasonableness:

> 'The test is therefore whether the arrestor suspected. That does not appear to me to be open to an objective test. It may be based on purely arbitrary grounds, on grounds on which the court, if this were an objective test of reasonableness, might consider unreasonable. ... What is required by the regulation is a suspicion existing in the mind of the constable. That is a subjective test. If that is correct, the courts enquiring into the exercise of the power, can only enquire as to the bona fides of the existence of the suspicion. Did the constable in his own mind suspect? And in my view the only other question for the court is, "Was this an honest suspicion".'[18]

(v) *Reasonable suspicion for EPA arrests.* In *McKee v Chief Constable*[19] the majority of the Northern Ireland Court of Appeal (Kelly J and O'Donnell LJ, Jones LJ dissenting) held that suspicion that a person was a member of a proscribed organisation was insufficient to constitute suspicion that he was a 'terrorist' (as defined in s. 31 of the 1978 Act[20]); for that, he had to be suspected of the commission or attempted commission of an act of terrorism or of the directing, organising or training of persons for the purpose of terrorism. A further point that the court unanimously accepted was that 'when a Constable receives instructions from a superior officer or an equal it is sufficient if he bona fide accepts the suspicion that those instructions contain or imply. The suspicion of the other becomes the arrestor's suspicion when accepted'.[1] An appeal to the House of Lords was allowed.[2] The decision on the second point was affirmed. However, the House held that the arresting officer at the time of arrest did in fact suspect that McKee was an active terrorist; the correctness of the Court of Appeal's interpretation of 'terrorism' was left open.[3] It is not clear whether it is applicable to an arrest under the 2000 Act, s. 41 as the power expressly applies in respect of the preparation or instigation of terrorism.[4]

Where the arresting officer relies on the suspicions of another officer in accordance with the decision in *McKee*, it is not necessary in defending an action for false imprisonment that the other officer be called as a witness to establish that he had reasonable grounds for suspicion: *Stanford v Chief Constable of the Royal Ulster Constabulary*.[5] If that officer were to supply false information to the arresting officer, an action might lie against the former for maliciously and without reasonable cause procuring his arrest.[6]

17 See *Ireland v United Kingdom*, below, p. 617.
18 p. 19. An earlier attempt by McElduff to obtain habeas corpus from the High Court in London failed on jurisdictional grounds: In *Re Keenan* [1972] 1 QB 533. See K. Boyle, (1972) 23 NILQ 334 and *Kelly v Faulkner* [1973] NI 31, QBD (NI).
19 [1983] 11 NIJB.
20 Subsequently s. 66 of the 1991 Act.
1 Per Kelly J at p. 3 of his judgment.
2 [1984] 1 WLR 1358.
3 For criticisms of this interpretation, see C. Walker, (1985) 36 NILQ 145.
4 G. Hogan and C. Walker, op cit., p. 48.
5 [1988] NI 361.
6 Ibid. at p. 364. See further above, p. 109.

(vi) *Purpose of arrest.* The Army have found it necessary to obtain information about the population in Republican areas. Indeed, a population census has been described as 'the fundamental tool for defeating terrorism and insurrection'.[7] One aspect of this has been the use of the EPA arrest powers to detain people in Republican areas for questioning.[8] The use of powers of arrest for purposes other than that of commencing criminal proceedings is of dubious legality. Moreover, according to Evelegh (who commanded an army battalion in Belfast in 1972 and 1973) 'the vast majority of those arrested by the Army in Northern Ireland were arrested without being suspected of anything except in the most general sense'.[9] Is the proper response to criticise the illegality, or to argue the case for the extension of powers to detain for questioning, or both?

The use of arrest powers solely for the purpose of general intelligence gathering would seem to be a use of power for an improper purpose, and thus ultra vires.[10] It will, however, be difficult in practice for the arrestee to establish that this was the sole purpose. In *Murray v Ministry of Defence*[11] the trial judge was satisfied that the soldier who arrested M under the EPA 1978, s. 14 did genuinely suspect M of having committed offences involving the collection of money for the IRA, and that the subsequent interrogation of M was at least in part directed to those offences, although much of it ranged over her private life. The House of Lords upheld the conclusion that the interrogation was lawful, declining to hold that the permitted scope of questioning was confined to matters directly related to the suspected offence.[12]

(vii) It was held in *Re Gillen's Application*[13] that where it is established that a prisoner is seriously assaulted during interrogation, the detention becomes unlawful and the detainee is entitled to the issue of a writ of habeas corpus. Here, G made out a strong prima facie case of a serious assault on him, based on medical reports, and an interlocutory injunction was restraining police from interrogating him, while his allegations were investigated by the Chief Constable, and pending a final ruling by the court on whether they were made out. In the event, the Chief Constable did not subsequently file affidavits contesting the allegations, and G was released. In 1990, G received an out of court settlement of £7,500.[14] However, *Re Gillen* was overruled by the Court of Appeal in Northern Ireland in *Cullen v Chief Constable of the RUC*[15] in the context of an action for damages.

8. *Search and the examination of documents.* Powers of entry and search in relation to arrests are conferred by the 2000 Act, ss. 81–83.[16] Schedule 10[17] gives powers to search for munitions, transmitters and scanning receivers. The power to enter and search any place other than a dwelling-house and the power to stop-search in any 'public place' do not require reasonable grounds to suspect that munitions etc. are to be found. 'Public place' is not defined, but includes a public house (*McShane v Chief Constable of the RUC*[18]). Entry for this purpose into a dwelling-house does

---

7 R. Evelegh, *Peace-Keeping in a Democratic Society* (1978), p. 119.
8 See K. Boyle, T. Hadden and P. Hillyard, *Law and State* (1975), pp. 41–48; R. Evelegh, op. cit., pp. 63–67, 119–122.
9 Op. cit., p. 120.
10 Cf. *Holgate-Mohammed v Duke*, above, p. 116.
11 [1988] 2 All ER 521.
12 p. 530. For further discussion of this question see C. Walker, (1989) 40 NILQ 1. 18–24; G. Hogan and C. Walker, op cit., pp. 53–54.
13 [1988] NI 40.
14 *Just News*, Vol. 5 No. 11/Vol. 6 No. 1, p. 4.
15 [1999] NI 237, following *R v Deputy Governor of Parkhurst Prison, ex p Hague* [1992] 1 AC 58.
16 Cf. EPA 1996, ss. 17, 18, 19.
17 Cf. EPA 1996, ss. 20, 21.
18 15 December 1993, unreported, QBD (NI).

require reasonable grounds and the authorisation of a commissioned officer (for a member of HM forces) or an officer not below the rank of inspector (for a constable).[19]

A power to examine documents (s. 87) was introduced by the EPA 1991.[20] The SACHR recommended that exercise be made conditional on reasonable suspicion.[1]

9. *Other powers.* If the Secretary of State considers it necessary for the preservation of the peace or the maintenance of order, he may authorise a person to take possession of land or other property, carry out works etc. (s. 91); an officer may, if he considers it immediately necessary for these purposes, close a road or prohibit or restrict the exercise of a right of way (s. 92); the Secretary of State may by order direct a road to be closed wholly or to a specified extent (s. 94(1)). Interference with such works is an offence (ss. 93, 94(2), (3)). The Secretary of State may make codes of practice in connection with the exercise of powers by the police and members of HM Forces (s. 99) and video recording (s. 100). There is a right to compensation where property is taken, occupied, destroyed or damaged or private right of property are otherwise infringed under Part VII (s. 102, Sch. 12). Private security services are regulated (s. 106, Sch. 13).

PART VIII
GENERAL
114. Police powers
(1) A power conferred by virtue of this Act on a constable—
- (*a*) is additional to powers which he has at common law or by virtue of any other enactment, and
- (*b*) shall not be taken to affect those powers.

(2) A constable may if necessary use reasonable force for the purpose of exercising a power conferred on him by virtue of this Act (apart from paragraphs 2 and 3 of Schedule 7).

(3) Where anything is seized by a constable under a power conferred by virtue of this Act, it may (unless the contrary intention appears) be retained for so long as is necessary in all the circumstances . . .

116. Powers to stop and search
(1) A power to search premises conferred by virtue of this Act shall be taken to include power to search a container.

(2) A power conferred by virtue of this Act to stop a person includes power to stop a vehicle (other than an aircraft which is airborne).

(3) A person commits an offence if he fails to stop a vehicle when required to do so by virtue of this section.

(4) A person guilty of an offence under subsection (3) shall be liable on summary conviction to—
- (*a*) imprisonment for a term not exceeding six months,
- (*b*) a fine not exceeding level 5 on the standard scale, or
- (*c*) both ...

118. Defences
(1) Subsection (2) applies where in accordance with a provision mentioned in subsection (5) it is a defence for a person charged with an offence to prove a particular matter.

(2) If the person adduces evidence which is sufficient to raise an issue with respect to the matter the court or jury shall assume that the defence is satisfied unless the prosecution proves beyond reasonable doubt that it is not.

(3) Subsection (4) applies where in accordance with a provision mentioned in subsection (5) a court—

---

19 On 'authorisation' see *Kirkpatrick v Chief Constable of the RUC* [1988] NI 421 (EPA 1978, s. 15(2); entry by officer not named in written authority held to be a trespass); cf. *Dooley v Darcy* (unreported, 19 May 1995, CA (NI)); superintendent entitled to give general authorisation with names of officers specified by an inspector under his command).
20 s. 22; subsequently EPA 1996, s. 24.
1 16th Report, 1990–91 HC 488, p. 91; see B. Dickson, [1992] PL 592 at 618–619.

(*a*) may make an assumption in relation to a person charged with an offence unless a particular matter is proved, or

(*b*) may accept a fact as sufficient evidence unless a particular matter is proved.

(4) If evidence is adduced which is sufficient to raise an issue with respect to the matter mentioned in subsection (3)(*a*) or (*b*) the court shall treat it as proved unless the prosecution disproves it beyond reasonable doubt.

(5) The provisions in respect of which subsections (2) and (4) apply are—

(*a*) sections 12(4), 39(5)(*a*), 54, 57, 58, 77 and 103 of this Act, and

(*b*) sections 13, 32 and 33 of the Northern Ireland (Emergency Provisions) Act 1996 (possession and information offences) as they have effect by virtue of Schedule 1 to this Act.

121. Interpretation

In this Act—

'act' and 'action' include omission,

'article' includes substance and any other thing,

'customs officer' means an officer commissioned by the Commissioners of Customs and Excise under section 6(3) of the Customs and Excise Management Act 1979,

'dwelling' means a building or part of a building used as a dwelling, and a vehicle which is habitually stationary and which is used as a dwelling,

'explosive' means—

(*a*) an article or substance manufactured for the purpose of producing a practical effect by explosion,

(*b*) materials for making an article or substance within paragraph (*a*),

(*c*) anything used or intended to be used for causing or assisting in causing an explosion, and

(*d*) a part of anything within paragraph (*a*) or (*c*),

'firearm' includes an air gun or air pistol,

'immigration officer' means a person appointed as an immigration officer under paragraph 1 of Schedule 2 to the Immigration Act 1971,

'the Islands' means the Channel Islands and the Isle of Man,

'organisation' includes any association or combination of persons,

'premises' includes any place and in particular includes—

(*a*) a vehicle,

(*b*) an offshore installation within the meaning given in section 44 of the Petroleum Act 1998, and

(*c*) a tent or moveable structure,

'property' includes property wherever situated and whether real or personal, heritable or moveable, and things in action and other intangible or incorporeal property,

'public place' means a place to which members of the public have or are permitted to have access, whether or not for payment,

'road' has the same meaning as in the Road Traffic Act 1988 (in relation to England and Wales), the Roads (Scotland) Act 1984 (in relation to Scotland) and the Road Traffic Regulation (Northern Ireland) Order 1997 (in relation to Northern Ireland), and includes part of a road, and

'vehicle', except in sections 48 to 52 and Schedule 7, includes an aircraft, hovercraft, train or vessel.

124. Directions

A direction given under this Act may be varied or revoked by a further direction …

NOTES (PART VIII: GENERAL)

1. Section 115 and Sch. 14 enable an authorised officer or an examining officer to enter a vehicle and use reasonable force (other than in respect of Sch. 7, paras. 2 and 3 (port and border controls)). The Secretary of State may issue codes of practice. The consent of the DPP or DPP for Northern Ireland is necessary in respect of most offences under the Act; where it appears to him that an offence is committed for a purpose connected with the affairs of a country other than the UK, the consent of the

Attorney-General or the Attorney-General for Northern Ireland is required (s. 117). Section 118 is an important provision restricting the number of provisions that impose anything more than an evidential burden on the defendant.[2]

2. The 2000 Act does not contain provisions for internment without trial, exclusion orders or a general offence of withholding information in connection with acts of terrorism.

(i) *Internment.* The detention of persons without trial has been employed by the authorities in both Northern Ireland and the Republic of Ireland.[3] The changes in legislation authorising the 'extrajudical deprivation of liberty' are traced in the Judgment of the European Court of Human Rights in *Ireland v United Kingdom*.[4] These were in turn: (1) reg. 12(1) of the Special Powers Regulations; (2) the Detention of Terrorists (Northern Ireland) Order 1972 (made under the Northern Ireland (Temporary Provisions) Act 1972 and in operation between 7 November 1972 and 8 August 1973); (3) the Northern Ireland (Emergency Provisions) Act 1973, s. 10(5) and Sch. 1 (7 August 1973–21 August 1975); and (4) the Northern Ireland (Emergency Provisions) (Amendment) Act 1975, s. 9 and Sch. 1a (21 August 1975–8 April 1998).[5]

The internment powers were invoked on 9 August 1971.[6]

In 1975, the Gardiner Committee concluded:

'148. After long and anxious consideration, we are of the opinion that detention cannot remain as a long-term policy. In the short term, it may be an effective means of containing violence, but the prolonged effects of the use of detention are ultimately inimical to community life, fan a widespread sense of grievance and injustice, and obstruct those elements in Northern Ireland society which could lead to reconciliation. Detention can only be tolerated in a democratic society in the most extreme circumstances; it must be used with the utmost restraint and retained only as long as it is strictly necessary. We would like to be able to recommend that the time has come to abolish detention; but the present level of violence, the risks of increased violence, and the difficulty of predicting events even a few months ahead make it impossible for us to put forward a precise recommendation on the timing.'

Should such measures still be regarded as necessary, the Committee recommended a return to the system where the sole and ultimate responsibility for detention should be that of the Secretary of State, advised by a Detention Advisory Board, but with no attempt to emulate, even approximately, quasi-judicial procedures of the kind operative between 1972 and 1975.[7] Revised arrangements were incorporated in the 1975 and 1978 statutes but were not used. The last detainees were released on 5 December 1975, and the policy of 'internment' abandoned.[8]

The relevant provisions remained on the statute book, were not brought into force and were repealed by EPA 1998. Their repeal was recommended by many commentators.[9]

(ii) *Exclusion orders.*[10] These were perhaps the most controversial provisions of the PTA regime.[11] The Secretary of State had power to make an exclusion order if he was

---

2 See above, p. 597.

3 See J. McGuffin, *Internment* (1973).

4 (1978) pp. 31–39.

5 Subsequently consolidated in EPA 1991 s. 34 and Sch. 3 and EPA 1996, s. 36 and Sch. 3.

6 See The Sunday Times Insight Team, *Ulster* (1972) Chap. 15; *Ireland v United Kingdom* (1978) pp. 16–18.

7 Cmnd. 5847, pp. 45–49.

8 See E. Rauch, (1973) 6 NY Univ J Int Law and Politics 1; R. J. Spjut, (1975) 10 Irish Jurist (ns) 272 and (1986) 49 MLR 712; K. Boyle, T. Hadden and P. Hillyard, *Law and State* (1975), Chap. 5.

9 Sir George Baker (Report, Chap. 6); *Colville Review (EPA)* (Cm 1115), Chap. 11; SACHR, 17th Report 1991–92 HC 54, pp. 222–223; *Rowe Review (EPA)*, pp. 32–33; cf. *Lloyd Inquiry*, paras. 16.5–16.8 (recommending they should not be included in permanent legislation but might be justified in an emergency).

10 See C. Walker, op cit., Chap. 6; Bonner, op cit., pp. 191–209; D. Bonner, [1989] PL 440 at 452–456; P. Hillyard *Suspect Community* (1993), Chaps. 9, 10.

11 PTA 1989, ss. 4–8.

satisfied that a person was or had been concerned in the commission, preparation or instigation of acts of terrorism connected with the affairs of Northern Ireland, or was attempting or might attempt to enter Great Britain or Northern Ireland for such a purpose. A person could be excluded from Great Britain or Northern Ireland or, in certain cases not involving a British citizen, the UK. The person concerned was entitled to make representations to an adviser nominated by the Secretary of State. A British citizen could not be excluded from part of the UK in which he had been ordinarily resident for the previous three years. The Secretary of State was not required to give reasons for his decisions.[12] The ECJ ruled that, save in cases of urgency, an order should not be made before the Secretary of State had considered the independent advice[13] and the legislation was amended accordingly.[14] The Court of Appeal[15] subsequently held that this non-compliance did not justify an award of compensation under the *Brasserie du Pecheur* principle, given that it had not affected the outcome so far as G was concerned; it was not a 'sufficiently serious' breach. No new orders were made after 1995 and all had lapsed by the end of 1997.[16]

The continuation of exclusion orders was supported by Lord Jellicoe[17] and J. J. Rowe[18] but opposed by Lord Colville[19] and the SACHR.[20] Lord Lloyd recommended they should not be included in permanent legislation.[1]

(iii) *Withholding information.* The PTA 1989, s. 18 [2] created a general offence for a person to withhold information which might be of assistance in preventing the commission by another of an act of terrorism connected with Northern Ireland affairs or in securing the apprehension, prosecution or convictions of any other person for an offence involving the commission, preparation or instigation of such an act. This was criticised because of the pressure it might place, for example, on a relative of a terrorist and was hardly used in practice. Its repeal was recommended by Lord Colville[3] and Lord Lloyd thought it should not be included in permanent legislation.[4]

---

12 *R v Secretary of State for the Home Department, ex p Stitt* (1987) Times, 3 February; *R v Secretary of State for the Home Department, ex p Gallagher* (1994) Times, 16 February.

13 *R v Secretary of State for the Home Department, ex p Gallagher* [1994] 3 CMLR 295, CA; preliminary ruling by the ECJ (1995) Times, 13 December. See also *R v Secretary of State for the Home Department, ex p Adams* (1995) Independent, 28 April (judicial review proceedings, dismissed and reference to ECJ withdrawn following revocation of exclusion order).

14 Prevention of Terrorism (Exclusion Orders) Regulations 1996, S.I. 1996 No. 892.

15 *R v Secretary of State for the Home Department, ex p Gallagher* (1996) Independent, 10 June.

16 *Statistics on the Operation of the Prevention of Terrorism Legislation* (1999), para. 8.

17 1983 Report, Chap. 9.

18 1997 PTA Report, Chap. 6.

19 *Colville Review (PTA)* (1987), p. 40.

20 19th Report, 1993–94, pp. 14–15.

1 *Lloyd Inquiry*, paras. 16.2–16.4.

2 Formerly PTA 1984, s. 11.

3 *Colville Review (PTA)* (1987), Chap. 15.

4 *Lloyd Inquiry*, paras. 14.16–14.23.

SCHEDULE 8

Detention

Part I

Treatment of Persons Detained under Section 41 or Schedule 7

Place of detention
1. (1)　The Secretary of State shall designate places at which persons may be detained under Schedule 7 or section 41.
(2) In this Schedule a reference to a police station includes a reference to any place which the Secretary of State has designated under sub-paragraph (1) as a place where a person may be detained under section 41.
(3) Where a person is detained under Schedule 7, he may be taken in the custody of an examining officer or of a person acting under an examining officer's authority to and from any place where his attendance is required for the purpose of—
　　(*a*)　his examination under that Schedule,
　　(*b*)　establishing his nationality or citizenship, or
　　(*c*)　making arrangements for his admission to a country or territory outside the United Kingdom.
(4) A constable who arrests a person under section 41 shall take him as soon as is reasonably practicable to the police station which the constable considers the most appropriate.
(5) In this paragraph 'examining officer' has the meaning given in Schedule 7.
(6) Where a person is arrested in one Part of the United Kingdom and all or part of his detention takes place in another Part, the provisions of this Schedule which apply to detention in a particular Part of the United Kingdom apply in relation to him while he is detained in that Part.

Identification
2. (1)　An authorised person may take any steps which are reasonably necessary for—
　　(*a*)　photographing the detained person,
　　(*b*)　measuring him, or
　　(*c*)　identifying him.
(2) In sub-paragraph (1) 'authorised person' means any of the following—
　　(*a*)　a constable,
　　(*b*)　a prison officer,
　　(*c*)　a person authorised by the Secretary of State, and
　　(*d*)　in the case of a person detained under Schedule 7, an examining officer (within the meaning of that Schedule).
(3) This paragraph does not confer the power to take—
　　(*a*)　fingerprints, non-intimate samples or intimate samples (within the meaning given by paragraph 15 below), or
　　(*b*)　[applies to Scotland.] ...

Status
5. A detained person shall be deemed to be in legal custody throughout the period of his detention.

Rights: England, Wales and Northern Ireland
6. (1)　Subject to paragraph 8, a person detained under Schedule 7 or section 41 at a police station in England, Wales or Northern Ireland shall be entitled, if he so requests, to have one named person informed as soon as is reasonably practicable that he is being detained there.
(2) The person named must be—
　　(*a*)　a friend of the detained person,
　　(*b*)　a relative, or
　　(*c*)　a person who is known to the detained person or who is likely to take an interest in his welfare.

(3) Where a detained person is transferred from one police station to another, he shall be entitled to exercise the right under this paragraph in respect of the police station to which he is transferred.

7. (1)   Subject to paragraphs 8 and 9, a person detained under Schedule 7 or section 41 at a police station in England, Wales or Northern Ireland shall be entitled, if he so requests, to consult a solicitor as soon as is reasonably practicable, privately and at any time.

(2) Where a request is made under sub-paragraph (1), the request and the time at which it was made shall be recorded.

8. (1)   Subject to sub-paragraph (2), an officer of at least the rank of superintendent may authorise a delay—

    (*a*)   in informing the person named by a detained person under paragraph 6;

    (*b*)   in permitting a detained person to consult a solicitor under paragraph 7.

(2) But where a person is detained under section 41 he must be permitted to exercise his rights under paragraphs 6 and 7 before the end of the period mentioned in subsection (3) of that section.

(3) Subject to sub-paragraph (5), an officer may give an authorisation under sub-paragraph (1) only if he has reasonable grounds for believing—

    (*a*)   in the case of an authorisation under sub-paragraph (1)(*a*), that informing the named person of the detained person's detention will have any of the consequences specified in sub-paragraph (4), or

    (*b*)   in the case of an authorisation under sub-paragraph (1)(*b*), that the exercise of the right under paragraph 7 at the time when the detained person desires to exercise it will have any of the consequences specified in sub-paragraph (4).

(4) Those consequences are—

    (*a*)   interference with or harm to evidence of a serious arrestable offence,

    (*b*)   interference with or physical injury to any person,

    (*c*)   the alerting of persons who are suspected of having committed a serious arrestable offence but who have not been arrested for it,

    (*d*)   the hindering of the recovery of property obtained as a result of a serious arrestable offence or in respect of which a forfeiture order could be made under section 23,

    (*e*)   interference with the gathering of information about the commission, preparation or instigation of acts of terrorism,

    (*f*)   the alerting of a person and thereby making it more difficult to prevent an act of terrorism, and

    (*g*)   the alerting of a person and thereby making it more difficult to secure a person's apprehension, prosecution or conviction in connection with the commission, preparation or instigation of an act of terrorism.

(5) An officer may also give an authorisation under sub-paragraph (1) if he has reasonable grounds for believing that—

    (*a*)   the detained person has committed an offence to which Part VI of the Criminal Justice Act 1988, Part I of the Proceeds of Crime (Scotland) Act 1995, or the Proceeds of Crime (Northern Ireland) Order 1996 (confiscation of the proceeds of an offence) applies,

    (*b*)   the detained person has benefited from the offence within the meaning of that Part or Order, and

    (*c*)   by informing the named person of the detained person's detention (in the case of an authorisation under sub-paragraph (1)(*a*)), or by the exercise of the right under paragraph 7 (in the case of an authorisation under sub-paragraph (1)(*b*)), the recovery of the value of that benefit will be hindered.

(6) If an authorisation under sub-paragraph (1) is given orally, the person giving it shall confirm it in writing as soon as is reasonably practicable.

(7) Where an authorisation under sub-paragraph (1) is given—

    (*a*)   the detained person shall be told the reason for the delay as soon as is reasonably practicable, and

    (*b*)   the reason shall be recorded as soon as is reasonably practicable.

(8) Where the reason for authorising delay ceases to subsist there may be no further delay in permitting the exercise of the right in the absence of a further authorisation under sub-paragraph (1).

(9) In this paragraph 'serious arrestable offence' has the meaning given by section 116 of the Police and Criminal Evidence Act 1984 (in relation to England and Wales) and by Article 87 of the Police and Criminal Evidence (Northern Ireland) Order 1989 (in relation to Northern Ireland); but it also includes—

(*a*) an offence under any of the provisions mentioned in section 40(1)(a) of this Act, and

(*b*) an attempt or conspiracy to commit an offence under any of the provisions mentioned in section 40(1)(*a*).

9. (1) A direction under this paragraph may provide that a detained person who wishes to exercise the right under paragraph 7 may consult a solicitor only in the sight and hearing of a qualified officer.

(2) A direction under this paragraph may be given—

(*a*) where the person is detained at a police station in England or Wales, by an officer of at least the rank of Commander or Assistant Chief Constable, or

(*b*) where the person is detained at a police station in Northern Ireland, by an officer of at least the rank of Assistant Chief Constable.

(3) A direction under this paragraph may be given only if the officer giving it has reasonable grounds for believing that, unless the direction is given, the exercise of the right by the detained person will have any of the consequences specified in paragraph 8(4) or the consequence specified in paragraph 8(5)(*c*).

(4) In this paragraph 'a qualified officer' means a police officer who—

(*a*) is of at least the rank of inspector,

(*b*) is of the uniformed branch of the force of which the officer giving the direction is a member, and

(*c*) in the opinion of the officer giving the direction, has no connection with the detained person's case.

(5) A direction under this paragraph shall cease to have effect once the reason for giving it ceases to subsist.

PART II

REVIEW OF DETENTION UNDER SECTION 41

Requirement

21. (1) A person's detention shall be periodically reviewed by a review officer.

(2) The first review shall be carried out as soon as is reasonably practicable after the time of the person's arrest.

(3) Subsequent reviews shall, subject to paragraph 22, be carried out at intervals of not more than 12 hours.

(4) No review of a person's detention shall be carried out after a warrant extending his detention has been issued under Part III.

Postponement

22. (1) A review may be postponed if at the latest time at which it may be carried out in accordance with paragraph 21—

(*a*) the detained person is being questioned by a police officer and an officer is satisfied that an interruption of the questioning to carry out the review would prejudice the investigation in connection with which the person is being detained,

(*b*) no review officer is readily available, or

(*c*) it is not practicable for any other reason to carry out the review.

(2) Where a review is postponed it shall be carried out as soon as is reasonably practicable.

(3) For the purposes of ascertaining the time within which the next review is to be carried out, a postponed review shall be deemed to have been carried out at the latest time at which it could have been carried out in accordance with paragraph 21.

Grounds for continued detention

23. (1) A review officer may authorise a person's continued detention only if satisfied that it is necessary—

(*a*) to obtain relevant evidence whether by questioning him or otherwise,

(*b*) to preserve relevant evidence,

(*c*)   pending a decision whether to apply to the Secretary of State for a deportation notice to be served on the detained person,

(*d*)   pending the making of an application to the Secretary of State for a deportation notice to be served on the detained person,

(*e*)   pending consideration by the Secretary of State whether to serve a deportation notice on the detained person, or

(*f*)   pending a decision whether the detained person should be charged with an offence.

(2) The review officer shall not authorise continued detention by virtue of sub-paragraph (1)(a) or (b) unless he is satisfied that the investigation in connection with which the person is detained is being conducted diligently and expeditiously.

(3) The review officer shall not authorise continued detention by virtue of sub-paragraph (1)(c) to (f) unless he is satisfied that the process pending the completion of which detention is necessary is being conducted diligently and expeditiously.

(4) In sub-paragraph (1)(*a*) and (*b*) 'relevant evidence' means evidence which—

(*a*)   relates to the commission by the detained person of an offence under any of the provisions mentioned in section 40(1)(*a*), or

(*b*)   indicates that the detained person falls within section 40(1)(*b*).

(5) In sub-paragraph (1) 'deportation notice' means notice of a decision to make a deportation order under the Immigration Act 1971.

Review officer

24. (1) The review officer shall be an officer who has not been directly involved in the investigation in connection with which the person is detained.

(2) In the case of a review carried out within the period of 24 hours beginning with the time of arrest, the review officer shall be an officer of at least the rank of inspector.

(3) In the case of any other review, the review officer shall be an officer of at least the rank of superintendent.

25. (1) This paragraph applies where—

(*a*)   the review officer is of a rank lower than superintendent,

(*b*)   an officer of higher rank than the review officer gives directions relating to the detained person, and

(*c*)   those directions are at variance with the performance by the review officer of a duty imposed on him under this Schedule.

(2) The review officer shall refer the matter at once to an officer of at least the rank of superintendent.

Representations

26. (1) Before determining whether to authorise a person's continued detention, a review officer shall give either of the following persons an opportunity to make representations about the detention—

(*a*)   the detained person, or

(*b*)   a solicitor representing him who is available at the time of the review.

(2) Representations may be oral or written.

(3) A review officer may refuse to hear oral representations from the detained person if he considers that he is unfit to make representations because of his condition or behaviour.

Rights

27. (1) Where a review officer authorises continued detention he shall inform the detained person—

(*a*)   of any of his rights under paragraphs 6 and 7 which he has not yet exercised, and

(*b*)   if the exercise of any of his rights under either of those paragraphs is being delayed in accordance with the provisions of paragraph 8, of the fact that it is being so delayed.

(2) Where a review of a person's detention is being carried out at a time when his exercise of a right under either of those paragraphs is being delayed—

(*a*)   the review officer shall consider whether the reason or reasons for which the delay was authorised continue to subsist, and

(*b*)   if in his opinion the reason or reasons have ceased to subsist, he shall inform the officer who authorised the delay of his opinion (unless he was that officer).

(3) In the application of this paragraph to Scotland, for the references to paragraphs 6, 7 and 8 substitute references to paragraph 16.

(4) The following provisions (requirement to bring an accused person before the court after his arrest) shall not apply to a person detained under section 41—

    (*a*)   section 135(3) of the Criminal Procedure (Scotland) Act 1995, and

    (*b*)   Article 8(1) of the Criminal Justice (Children) (Northern Ireland) Order 1998.

(5) Section 22(1) of the Criminal Procedure (Scotland) Act 1995 (interim liberation by officer in charge of police station) shall not apply to a person detained under section 41.

Record

28. (1) A review officer carrying out a review shall make a written record of the outcome of the review and of any of the following which apply—

    (*a*)   the grounds upon which continued detention is authorised,

    (*b*)   the reason for postponement of the review,

    (*c*)   the fact that the detained person has been informed as required under paragraph 27(1),

    (*d*)   the officer's conclusion on the matter considered under paragraph 27(2)(*a*),

    (*e*)   the fact that he has taken action under paragraph 27(2)(*b*), and

    (*f*)   the fact that the detained person is being detained by virtue of section 41(5) or (6).

(2) The review officer shall—

    (*a*)   make the record in the presence of the detained person, and

    (*b*)   inform him at that time whether the review officer is authorising continued detention, and if he is, of his grounds.

(3) Sub-paragraph (2) shall not apply where, at the time when the record is made, the detained person is—

    (*a*)   incapable of understanding what is said to him,

    (*b*)   violent or likely to become violent, or

    (*c*)   in urgent need of medical attention.

PART III

EXTENSION OF DETENTION UNDER SECTION 41

Warrants of further detention

29. (1) A police officer of at least the rank of superintendent may apply to a judicial authority for the issue of a warrant of further detention under this Part.

(2) A warrant of further detention—

    (*a*)   shall authorise the further detention under section 41 of a specified person for a specified period, and

    (*b*)   shall state the time at which it is issued.

(3) The specified period in relation to a person shall end not later than the end of the period of seven days beginning—

    (*a*)   with the time of his arrest under section 41, or

    (*b*)   if he was being detained under Schedule 7 when he was arrested under section 41, with the time when his examination under that Schedule began.

(4) In this Part 'judicial authority' means—

    (*a*)   in England and Wales, the Senior District Judge (Chief Magistrate) or his deputy, or a District Judge (Magistrates' Courts) who is designated for the purpose of this Part by the Lord Chancellor,

    (*b*)   in Scotland, the sheriff, and

    (*c*)   in Northern Ireland, a county court judge, or a resident magistrate who is designated for the purpose of this Part by the Lord Chancellor.

Time limit

30. (1) An application for a warrant shall be made—

    (*a*)   during the period mentioned in section 41(3), or

    (*b*)   within six hours of the end of that period.

(2) The judicial authority hearing an application made by virtue of sub-paragraph (1)(*b*) shall dismiss the application if he considers that it would have been reasonably practicable to make it during the period mentioned in section 41(3).

(3) For the purposes of this Schedule, an application for a warrant is made when written or oral notice of an intention to make the application is given to a judicial authority.

Notice
31. An application for a warrant may not be heard unless the person to whom it relates has been given a notice stating—
- (*a*) that the application has been made,
- (*b*) the time at which the application was made,
- (*c*) the time at which it is to be heard, and
- (*d*) the grounds upon which further detention is sought.

Grounds for extension
32. (1) A judicial authority may issue a warrant of further detention only if satisfied that—
- (*a*) there are reasonable grounds for believing that the further detention of the person to whom the application relates is necessary to obtain relevant evidence whether by questioning him or otherwise or to preserve relevant evidence, and
- (*b*) the investigation in connection with which the person is detained is being conducted diligently and expeditiously.

(2) In sub-paragraph (1) 'relevant evidence' means, in relation to the person to whom the application relates, evidence which—
- (*a*) relates to his commission of an offence under any of the provisions mentioned in section 40(1)(*a*), or
- (*b*) indicates that he is a person falling within section 40(1)(*b*).

Representation
33. (1) The person to whom an application relates shall—
- (*a*) be given an opportunity to make oral or written representations to the judicial authority about the application, and
- (*b*) subject to sub-paragraph (3), be entitled to be legally represented at the hearing.

(2) A judicial authority shall adjourn the hearing of an application to enable the person to whom the application relates to obtain legal representation where—
- (*a*) he is not legally represented,
- (*b*) he is entitled to be legally represented, and
- (*c*) he wishes to be so represented.

(3) A judicial authority may exclude any of the following persons from any part of the hearing—
- (*a*) the person to whom the application relates;
- (*b*) anyone representing him.

Information
34. (1) The officer who has made an application for a warrant may apply to the judicial authority for an order that specified information upon which he intends to rely be withheld from—
- (*a*) the person to whom the application relates, and
- (*b*) anyone representing him.

(2) Subject to sub-paragraph (3), a judicial authority may make an order under sub-paragraph (1) in relation to specified information only if satisfied that there are reasonable grounds for believing that if the information were disclosed—
- (*a*) evidence of an offence under any of the provisions mentioned in section 40(1)(*a*) would be interfered with or harmed,
- (*b*) the recovery of property obtained as a result of an offence under any of those provisions would be hindered,
- (*c*) the recovery of property in respect of which a forfeiture order could be made under section 23 would be hindered,
- (*d*) the apprehension, prosecution or conviction of a person who is suspected of falling within section 40(1)(*a*) or (*b*) would be made more difficult as a result of his being alerted,

(*e*) the prevention of an act of terrorism would be made more difficult as a result of a person being alerted,

(*f*) the gathering of information about the commission, preparation or instigation of an act of terrorism would be interfered with, or

(*g*) a person would be interfered with or physically injured.

(3) A judicial authority may also make an order under sub-paragraph (1) in relation to specified information if satisfied that there are reasonable grounds for believing that—

(*a*) the detained person has committed an offence to which Part VI of the Criminal Justice Act 1988, Part I of the Proceeds of Crime (Scotland) Act 1995, or the Proceeds of Crime (Northern Ireland) Order 1996 (confiscation of the proceeds of an offence) applies,

(*b*) the detained person has benefited from the offence within the meaning of that Part or Order, and

(*c*) the recovery of the value of that benefit would be hindered, if the information were disclosed.

(4) The judicial authority shall direct that the following be excluded from the hearing of the application under this paragraph—

(*a*) the person to whom the application for a warrant relates, and

(*b*) anyone representing him.

Adjournments

35. (1) A judicial authority may adjourn the hearing of an application for a warrant only if the hearing is adjourned to a date before the expiry of the period mentioned in section 41(3).

(2) This paragraph shall not apply to an adjournment under paragraph 33(2).

Extensions of warrants

36. (1) A police officer of at least the rank of superintendent may apply to a judicial authority for the extension or further extension of the period specified in a warrant of further detention.

(2) Where the period specified is extended, the warrant shall be endorsed with a note stating the new specified period.

(3) The specified period shall end not later than the end of the period of seven days beginning—

(*a*) with the time of the person's arrest under section 41, or

(*b*) if he was being detained under Schedule 7 when he was arrested under section 41, with the time when his examination under that Schedule began.

(4) Paragraphs 30(3) and 31 to 34 shall apply to an application under this paragraph as they apply to an application for a warrant of further detention.

(5) A judicial authority may adjourn the hearing of an application under sub-paragraph (1) only if the hearing is adjourned to a date before the expiry of the period specified in the warrant.

(6) Sub-paragraph (5) shall not apply to an adjournment under paragraph 33(2).

Detention—conditions

37. A person detained by virtue of a warrant issued under this Part shall (unless detained in accordance with section 41(5) or (6) or under any other power) be released immediately if the officer having custody of him becomes aware that any of the grounds under paragraph 32(1)(*a*) and (b) upon which the judicial authority authorised his further detention have ceased to apply.

5 The use of force[8]

Attorney-General for Northern Ireland's Reference (No 1 of 1975) [1977] AC 105, [1976] 2 All ER 937, [1976] 3 WLR 235, House of Lords (NI)

A British soldier on patrol in Northern Ireland in the exercise of his power to prevent crime under s. 3(1) of the Criminal Law Act (NI) 1967 (which is in the same terms as the Criminal Law Act 1967, s. 3(1))[9] shot and killed an unarmed man, who had run

---

8 See also pp. 196–202.
9 Above, p. 196.

away when challenged. The soldier had the honest and reasonable, though mistaken, belief that he was a terrorist. A judge sitting without a jury acquitted him of murder holding that he had no conscious intention to kill or seriously injure and that the killing was justifiable. The Attorney-General referred two matters to the Court of Criminal Appeal in Northern Ireland, and an appeal was taken to the House of Lords. The House held that the first matter raised no point of law, since it was in essence whether or not the soldier had used reasonable force, and that was a question of fact for the judge. The second matter accordingly did not arise. Lord Diplock made some observations as to the legal position.

Lord Diplock: ... There is little authority in English law concerning the rights and duties of a member of the armed forces of the Crown when acting in aid of the civil power; and what little authority there is relates almost entirely to the duties of soldiers when troops are called upon to assist in controlling a riotous assembly. Where used for such temporary purposes it may not be inaccurate to describe the legal rights and duties of a soldier as being no more than those of an ordinary citizen in uniform. But such a description is in my view misleading in the circumstances in which the army is currently employed in aid of the civil power in Northern Ireland.... In theory it may be the duty of every citizen when an arrestable offence is about to be committed in his presence to take whatever reasonable measures are available to him to prevent the commission of the crime; but the duty is one of imperfect obligation and does not place him under any obligation to do anything by which he would expose himself to risk of personal injury, nor is he under any duty to search for criminals or seek out crime. In contrast to this a soldier who is employed in aid of the civil power in Northern Ireland is under a duty, enforceable under military law, to search for criminals if so ordered by his superior officer and to risk his own life should this be necessary in preventing terrorist acts. For the performance of this duty he is armed with a firearm, a self-loading rifle, from which a bullet, if it hits the human body, is almost certain to cause serious injury if not death....

What amount of force is 'reasonable in the circumstances' for the purpose of preventing crime, is in my view, always a question for the jury in a jury trial, never a 'point of law' for the judge.

The form in which the jury would have to ask themselves the question in a trial for an offence against the person in which this defence was raised by the accused, would be: Are we satisfied that no reasonable man (a) with knowledge of such facts as were known to the accused or reasonably believed by him to exist (b) in the circumstances and time available to him for reflection (c) could be of opinion that the prevention of the risk of harm to which others might be exposed if the suspect were allowed to escape justified exposing the suspect to the risk of harm to him that might result from the kind of force that the accused contemplated using?

The jury would have also to consider how the circumstances in which the accused had to make his decision whether or not to use force and the shortness of the time available to him for reflection, might affect the judgment of a reasonable man. In the facts that are to be assumed for the purposes of the reference there is material upon which a jury might take the view that the accused had reasonable grounds for apprehension of imminent danger to himself and other members of the patrol if the deceased were allowed to get away and join armed fellow-members of the Provisional IRA who might be lurking in the neighbourhood, and that the time available to the accused to make up his mind what to do was so short that even a reasonable man could only act intuitively. This being so, the jury in approaching the final part of the question should remind themselves that the postulated balancing of risk against risk, harm against harm, by the reasonable man is not undertaken in the calm analytical atmosphere of the court-room after counsel with the benefit of hindsight have expounded at length the reasons for and against the kind and degree of force that was used by the accused; but in the brief second or two which the accused had to decide whether to shoot or not and under all the stresses to which he was exposed.

In many cases where force is used in the prevention of crime or in effecting an arrest there is a choice as to the degree of force to use. On the facts that are to be assumed for the purposes of the reference the only options open to the accused were either to let the deceased escape or to shoot at him with a service rifle. A reasonable man would know that a bullet from a self-loading rifle if it hit a human being, at any rate at the range at which the accused fired, would be likely to kill him or to injure him seriously. So in one scale of balance the harm to which the deceased would be exposed if the accused aimed to hit him was predictable and grave and the risk of its occurrence high. In the other scale of the balance it would be open to the jury to take the view that it would not be unreasonable to assess the kind of harm to be averted by preventing the accused's escape as even graver—the killing or wounding of members of the patrol by terrorists in ambush, and the effect of this success by members of the Provisional IRA in encouraging the continuance of the armed insurrection and all the misery and destruction of life and property that terrorist activity in Northern Ireland has entailed. The jury would have to consider too what was the highest degree at which a reasonable man could have assessed the likelihood that such consequences might follow the escape of the deceased if the facts had been as the accused knew or believed them reasonably to be.

Lords Simon of Glaisdale, Edmund-Davies and **Russell of Killowen** expressed their agreement with **Lord Diplock's** opinion.

NOTES

1. In *R v MacNaughton*[10], a sergeant was tried by Lowry LCJ (sitting without a jury) on charges of attempted murder and causing grievous bodily harm. He was in command of a foot patrol in South Armagh. They met a man, W, coming from the direction of an explosion and, suspecting him of being implicated in it, arrested him. The defendant claimed that W then tried to escape over a fence, and that he had shot at W after calling on him to stop. Lowry LCJ held that there had been a lawful arrest, that the defendant's evidence raised a triable issue that the force used was reasonable, and that the prosecution had been unable to prove beyond reasonable doubt that the degree of force was not reasonable on this occasion.

His Lordship took into account the factors that the patrol was working in active service conditions in a hostile area; that judging by the explosion, it was operating in the possible presence of an ambush; that there was a danger of booby-traps; that there was a possibility of masking a line of fire; the gravity of the suspected offence; and the likelihood that if W escaped he would undertake terrorist acts.

2. In *Farrell v Secretary of State for Defence*[11] the commanding officer of an army unit (X) received information that a bomb attack would be made by three men on a bank in Newry. He instructed an NCO, soldier A, and three other soldiers to take up a position on the roof of a building opposite the bank. During the night, soldier B saw two men attempt to open the bank's night safe; they were then attacked by three other men. B called soldier A, who saw only the second group. He called on them to halt. They stopped and looked up and down the street. One of them shouted 'run' and they made off. Soldier A shouted 'Halt, I am ready to fire'. They did not stop. A opened fire, as did his colleagues, and all three were killed. The widow of one of them sued the Secretary of State. The jury held that the soldiers had reasonable cause to suspect that the three men were attempting to place at the bank an explosive device that would endanger life, and that it was reasonable in the circumstances for the soldiers to shoot to kill, in the prevention of crime or in effecting a lawful arrest.[12] The Northern

1 0 [1975] NI 203. See also *R v Bohan* [1979] 5 NIJB, Belfast Crown Court; *McLaughlin v Ministry of Defence* [1978] 7 NIJB, (NI CA): on appeal, *Farrell v Secretary of State for Defence* [1980] 1 All ER 1667, HL; *McGuigan v Ministry of Defence* [1982] 19 NIJB, QBD (NI); *Lynch v Ministry of Defence* [1983] NI 216; *R v Hegarty* [1986] NI 343; *Magill v Ministry of Defence* [1987] NI 194; *Hegarty, Doyle and Kelly v Ministry of Defence* [1989] 9 NIJB 88.
1 1 [1980] 1 All ER 1667.
1 2 s. 3(1) of the Criminal Law Act (Northern Ireland) 1967: in the same terms as s. 3(1) of the Criminal Law Act 1967, above, p. 196.

Ireland Court of Appeal ordered a new trial on the ground that the jury should have been invited to consider whether there had been negligence in the planning of the operation: it had emerged that X had only given instructions to one soldier, A; that he had given no instructions about summoning help; that there was no agreed procedure for the four soldiers reporting back to base; only four soldiers out of 80 in X's command were selected for the operation; all four were ordered to go on the roof; they did not have a loud hailer; they were left in a situation where the only way to stop a suspected terrorist if he refused to stop was by firing at him. The House of Lords allowed an appeal, holding (1) that the term 'circumstances' in s. 3(1) did not extend to include the planning of the operation; and (2) that negligence had not been pleaded against any person other than the four soldiers at the scene. On the first point, Viscount Dilhorne stated:[13]

> 'I am unable to agree that the phrase "in the circumstances" in s. 3(1) should be given the wide interpretation given to it in the Court of Appeal. That section is contained in a statute dealing with the criminal law. It may provide a defence for a person sued. In each case when such a defence is put forward the question to be determined is whether the person who is accused or sued used such force as was reasonable in the circumstances in which he was placed in the prevention of crime or in bringing about a lawful arrest of an offender or suspected offender.
>
> Section 3(1) would provide no defence to soldier X in respect of a claim for negligence in the planning of the operation. It can only provide a defence for those who have used force and if the force the four soldiers used was reasonable in the circumstances in which they used it, the defects, if there were any, in the planning of the operation would not deprive them of that defence and render the force used unreasonable.'

This narrow approach has been criticised.[14] Many commentators, including D. S. Greer, C. P. Walker, G. Bennett and P. Rowe and the Standing Advisory Commission on Human Rights[15] have argued that s. 3(1) provides insufficient guidance on the general nature of the circumstances in which potentially lethal force may be used.[16] It has, furthermore, been argued that different standards should be applicable to the use of force by agents of the state as distinct from other citizens.[17] Can this be right? If Art. 2 ECHR[18] requires a certain standard in the case of the taking of life by state agents should the state not protect citizens by applying the same standards in its domestic law to the taking of life by a citizen?

3. The *Farrell* case was taken to Strasbourg and a claim under Art. 2 ECHR admitted for consideration on the merits.[19] The case was then the subject of a friendly settlement, the British government agreeing to pay substantial damages to Mrs Farrell. In *Stewart v United Kingdom*[20] the applicant's son died after being struck on the head by a plastic bullet fired by a British soldier in Northern Ireland. It was held that the use of plastic bullets was not per se contrary to Arts. 2 or 3 ECHR. Then, in *Kelly v United Kingdom*[1] the Commission found that the shooting dead of a joyrider attempting to

---

13 At p. 172.
14 D. S. Greer, (1980) 31 NILQ 151, 154–155. See also on the *Farrell* case C. P. Walker, (1980) 43 MLR 591 and G. Bennett and P. Rowe, (1981) 131 NLJ 991.
15 9th Annual Report for 1982–83 (1983–84 HC 262) pp. 21–23 and Appendix B.
16 See also G. Williams, *Textbook of Criminal Law* (2nd edn, 1983), pp. 493–500; J. C. Smith and B. Hogan, *Criminal Law* (9th edn, 1999) pp. 252–263; P. J. Rowe and C. J. Whelan (eds.), *Military Intervention in Democratic Societies* (1985), Chap. 9; *Hogan and Walker*, pp. 64–69; R. J. Spjut, [1986] PL 38; J. C. Smith, (1994) 47(2) CLP 101.
17 See J. Rogers, (1998) 18 LS 486 and S. Skinner [2000] PL, 266. Skinner argues that the 'citizen in uniform' concept applied to soldiers and police officers is 'based on an anachronistic fiction' and is 'an historically dubious precedent'. See further, p. 199.
18 See below, pp. 633–646.
19 *Farrell v United Kingdom* (1983) 5 EHRR 466.
20 Decn admiss of 10 July 1984.
1 App. No. 17579/90.

evade an army checkpoint did not contravene Art. 2 ECHR, as the soldiers had a genuine and reasonable belief that the youth was a terrorist and had fired 'in order to effect a lawful arrest' within Art. 2(2). This has been cogently criticised[2] on the ground that the national court had rejected a claim for damages on the basis of the force being reasonable force in the prevention of crime (a basis not found in Art. 2), and that the soldiers were neither seeking nor had power to arrest in the circumstances. The key decision of the Court of Human Rights is now that in *McCann v United Kingdom*.[3] It is argued that s. 3 is broader than the test prescribed by Art. 2 ECHR.[4] However, it must by virtue of the Human Rights Act 1998 now be interpreted and applied so as to conform with Art. 2 ECHR.

4. According to A. Jennings,[5] writing in 1988, over 270 individuals, at least 155 of them 'civilians', had been killed by the security forces in Northern Ireland since 1969. Between 1982 and 1985, 35 individuals were so killed, 23 in covert operations. Twenty-one members of the security forces had been prosecuted for killings using firearms on duty, of whom one was convicted of manslaughter[6] and one of murder.[7] There were suspicions of the existence of a 'shoot-to-kill' policy in the 1982–85 period, associated particularly with undercover surveillance units. John Stalker, then Deputy Chief Constable of Greater Manchester, conducted an inquiry into a series of killings, including those at two incidents where prosecutions of members of the security forces ended in acquittals.[8] The terms of reference did not, however, include an investigation of the existence of a shoot-to-kill policy. The inquiry was completed by Colin Sampson, Chief Constable of West Yorkshire, following Stalker's suspension for alleged disciplinary offences. The outcome of the inquiry was not made public. However, the Attorney-General announced in 1988 that eight RUC officers involved in a conspiracy to pervert the course of justice and responsible for obstructing the Stalker inquiry would not be prosecuted for reasons of national security. There was no evidence of a shoot-to-kill policy.[9]

John Stalker has subsequently suggested that there was:

'no written instruction, nothing pinned upon a noticeboard. But there was a clear understanding on the part of the men whose job it was to pull the trigger that that was what was expected of them.'[10]

Jennings concludes that:

'The sheer number of incidents and the circumstances in which they occurred during 1977–78 and 1982–85 points towards the deliberate planning of operations in which opportunities for the use of lethal force would arise.'[11]

Similar controversy was caused by the killing by the army of three members of the Provisional IRA in Gibraltar in 1988, and the programme about the shootings, 'Death

2 Sir John Smith, (1994) 144 NLJ 354; D. J. Harris, (1994) 1 Maastricht J European and Comparative Law 123 at 134–137.
3 Below, p. 633.
4 See e.g. SACHR, 18th Report, 1992–93 HC 739, p. 12, and n. 8, below.
5 'Shoot to Kill: The Final Courts of Justice' in Jennings (ed.) *Justice under Fire* (revd. edn, 1990), Chap. 5.
6 *R v Davidson* (1981, unreported).
7 *R v Thain* [1985] NI 457.
8 *R v Robinson* [1984] 4 NIJB; *R v Montgomery* (1984, unreported).
9 126 HC Deb, 25 January 1988, cols 21–35.
10 *The Times*, 9 February 1988, cited by A. Jennings, op. cit., p. 120.
11 Op. cit., p. 123. See also *Shoot to Kill? International Lawyers' Inquiry into the Lethal Use of Firearms by the Security Forces in Northern Ireland* (Chairman, Kader Asmal, 1985) and M. Urban, *Big Boys' Rules* (1992). On the Stalker affair, see J. Stalker, *Stalker* (1988); P. Taylor, *Stalker: The Search for the Truth* (1987); K. Taylor, *The Poisoned Tree* (1990); D. Murphy, *The Stalker Affair and the Press* (1991).

on the Rock', subsequently made by Thames Television. An inquest jury returned majority verdicts of lawful killing.[12] The Court of Human Rights subsequently found, on narrow grounds, there to have been a violation of Art. 2 ECHR.[13]

More recently, one member of the Parachute Regiment was convicted of murder and another of attempted murder.[14] In this case 'the crucial evidence ... came from a policeman, on patrol with the army unit on the night the incident occurred, who was unable to sustain the army's version of events'.[15] The victims were teenage joyriders in a stolen car. Campbell J held that the defendants were justified in firing shots at the car when speeding towards them, but not in shooting after the car had passed their patrol. On appeal, the Northern Ireland Court of Appeal dismissed C's appeal but substituted a conviction for malicious wounding for A's conviction for attempted murder.[16] The House of Lords dismissed an appeal.[17] Following a campaign on his behalf, C was released on licence in July 1995. The case was referred back to the Court of Appeal (Criminal Division) in Northern Ireland, which ordered a new trial in the light of fresh forensic evidence which cast doubt on whether C had indeed shot the deceased from behind.[18] At the retrial C was acquitted of murder but convicted of attempting to wound the driver of the car by firing from behind. This conviction was set aside by the Court of Appeal (Criminal Division) on the ground that it was unsafe.[19]

In 1995, two members of the Scots Guards (Fisher and Wright) were convicted of the murder of Peter McBride while on patrol. Kelly LJ found that they had lied about critical elements of their version of events, and that both had had sufficient time to decide whether or not to fire and had been aware when they discharged aimed shots at PM that he posed no threat to them. The Court of Appeal rejected an appeal and the House of Lords refused leave to appeal. An Army Board subsequently decided that they should not be discharged from the army but this was quashed on an application for judicial review brought by PM's mother on the ground that the Board had misinterpreted the findings of the trial judge.[20] The Board subsequently reached the same decision and this too was challenged on judicial review.[1]

By early 1994, the number of deaths caused by the security forces had risen to 351.[2]

5. Of enormous and lasting significance in the history of Northern Ireland has been the killing by members of the Parachute Regiment (and, it is alleged, another regiment) on 30 January 1972 of 13 persons attending a peaceful civil rights protest in Derry/Londonderry. The subsequent inquiry by Lord Widgery CJ largely

12 See A. Jennings (ed.), *Justice under Fire* (revd. edn, 1990), pp. xx–xxii; Amnesty International, *Investigating Lethal Shootings: the Gibraltar Inquest* (1989); *The Windelsham/ Rampton Report on 'Death on the Rock'* (1989); NCCL, *The Gibraltar Report*; R. Bolton, *Death on the Rock and other stories* (1990) and below, p. 633.
13 Below, p. 633.
14 *R v Clegg and Aindow* (4 June 1993, unreported, Cr Ct).
15 *Just News* (1993) Vol. 8 No. 6, p. 3.
16 Unreported, 30 March 1994.
17 [1995] 1 All ER 334.
18 Unreported, 27 February 1998.
19 *R v Clegg* [2000] NI 305.
20 *Re McBride's Application for Judicial Review* [1999] NI 299.
1 *Just News* Vol. 16 No. 2, pp. 4–5.
2 *Just News* (1994) Vol. 9 No. 2, p. 1. Compare the acquittals in *R v Elkington and Callaghan* (23 December 1993, unreported, Cr Ct; *Just News* (1994) Vol. 9 No. 1, p. 1) and *R v Hanley* (25 January 1994, unreported, Cr Ct; *Just News* (1994) Vol. 9 No. 2, p. 4). For a critical overview, see Amnesty International, *Political Killings in Northern Ireland* (1994), and F. Ní Aoláin, *The Politics of Force* (2000).

exonerated the army, although firing by some soldiers 'bordered on the reckless.'[3] No prosecutions followed. The government subsequently settled civil actions and formally acknowledged that all those killed 'should be regarded as having been found not guilty of the allegation of having been shot whilst handling a firearm or bomb'.[4]

The Widgery Report has been subjected to devastating criticism[5] and a new Tribunal of Inquiry has been appointed, chaired by Lord Saville of Newdigate. It began its work in 1998.[6] The families and the wounded have been accorded extended legal representation. The tribunal was required to reconsider a decision to withdraw anonymity from individual soldiers who admitted firing, or were alleged to have fired, live rounds.[7]

6. On the possible liability of members of the armed forces in negligence see the Court of Appeal in *McLaughlin v Ministry of Defence*.[8] In *McGuigan*, Hutton J noted that while in a criminal case, once the accused has raised by evidence the defence of reasonable force under s. 3(1) the onus rests on the *prosecution* to prove beyond a reasonable doubt that the force used was not reasonable in the circumstances, in a civil case the onus lies on the *defence* to establish a defence of reasonable force on the balance of probabilities. In *Copeland v Ministry of Defence* [9] Shiel J held the Ministry of Defence vicariously liable: (1) in trespass, in respect of the shooting of the plaintiff by Private Clarke from an army land rover without any justification; and (2) in negligence in respect of the failure of the Corporal in charge of the vehicle to disarm C following an earlier comment 'I'm going to get them when we go round next'. The judge based this on ordinary principles of vicarious liability but also stated that he considered that:

'as a matter of public policy ... when the State sends out a soldier or police officer armed with a lethal weapon which he is authorised to use in certain circumstances and that soldier or police officer, while on duty, intentionally or otherwise fires that weapon injuring a third party in circumstances which are not authorised and in which, as in the present case, there is no justification or defence for so doing, the State should be liable in damages at common law for any injury, loss or damage sustained by that third party.'

7. Where a plaintiff establishes a case in trespass against the police, the damages may be reduced on account of the plaintiff's contributory negligence. Thus in *Wasson v Chief Constable of the Royal Ulster Constabulary*[10] the plaintiff was taking part in a 'very serious' riot, when he was struck on the head by a baton round and badly injured. The police were held liable in trespass, having failed to show on a balance of probabilities that the baton round was not fired above leg level, and, as a result,

3 *Report of the Tribunal appointed to inquire into the events on Sunday, 30 January 1972, which led to the loss of life in connection with the procession in Londonderry on that day by the Rt Hon Lord Widgery* (1972) HC (22).
4 Dermot P. J. Walsh, *Bloody Sunday and the Rule of Law in Northern Ireland* (2000), p. 285.
5 S. Dash, *Justice Denied* (NCCL, 1972); E. McCann, *Bloody Sunday in Derry* (1992); D. Mullan, *Eyewitness Bloody Sunday: The Truth* (1997); P. Pringle and P. Jacobson, *Those are real bullets aren't they?* (2000); Walsh, op, cit.; B. M. E. McMahon, (1974) *The Human Context*, p. 681. See also *Ireland v United Kingdom* (Application No. 5310/7141) CDE Comm HR, p. 3 (1972) (application order Art. 2 ECHR in respect of the death of certain persons in Northern Ireland declared inadmissible).
6 See *Just News*, January 2001.
7 *R v Lord Saville of Newdigate, ex p B (No 2)* [1999] 4 All ER 860, CA.
8 (1978) 7 NIJB; Greer (1980) 31 NILQ 151, 156–159; *Doherty v Ministry of Defence* (1980, unreported, HL), noted by P. J. Rowe, (1981) 44 MLR 466; *McGuigan v Ministry of Defence*, [1982] 19 NIJB.
9 19 May 1999, unreported, QBD (NI).
10 [1987] NI 420.

being unable to establish a defence under s. 3(1) of the 1967 Act. However, the plaintiff's damages were halved in view of his participation in the riot.[11]

8. The absence of clear guidelines has been criticised by a number of commentators.[12] The SACHR has recommended that a specific code of conduct to govern the use of legal force should be introduced, and has prepared a draft code for consideration.[13] This code is based in part on the *Yellow Card* for 1972 and for 1980 (internal guidance for the armed forces) and on the terms of the *United Nations Instrument on Basic Principles on the Use of Force and Firearms by Law Enforcement Officials*.[14] Further recommendations by the Commission are that:

'(i)   The Government should review the law on the use of lethal force and publish the outcome of its deliberations.

(ii)   Section 3 of the Criminal Law Acts should be amended to meet the United Kingdom's obligations under the European Convention on Human Rights.

(iii) A specific detailed statutory code on the use of force by soldiers, police officers and other law enforcement officials should be enacted. The sanction for breach of this code in cases where a charge of murder or manslaughter is not appropriate should be limited to internal army or police disciplinary proceedings.

(iv)   Consideration should be given to the general law relating to murder and manslaughter in the whole of the United Kingdom.

(v)   Following on from (iv) above, charges of murder should be reserved for cases in which there is a preplanned intention to kill regardless of the legality of such action or at least of a deliberate disregard of the law in circumstances in which there was ample time for those responsible to decide whether to use lethal force.

(vi)   A charge of manslaughter should be made available in cases in which the soldier or police officer in using lethal force acted honestly though in excess of what the circumstances would have warranted. This would require the introduction of a specific statutory provision of general application.

(vii) The Government should issue a detailed response on the Commission's earlier recommendations on reform of the law on inquests.'[15]

On the other hand, the Commission is against the creation of a new offence of the reckless or dangerous use of firearms, or any offence which relates only to the actions of soldiers or police officers.[16]

In *R v Clegg and Aindow*[17] the Northern Ireland Court of Appeal endorsed the view that Parliament should consider a change in the existing law to permit a conviction for manslaughter where a soldier or police officer causes death with the intention to kill or cause grievous bodily harm, reacting wrongly but without malice or evil motive to a situation arising in the course of his duty. The House of Lords stated that any change should be made by Parliament and not by the House in its judicial capacity.[18]

---

11 Cf. *Tumelty v Ministry of Defence* [1988] 3 NIJB 51, where in a somewhat similar case, an 80% reduction in damages was made.

12 See n. **2**, above.

13 16th Report, 1990–91 HC 488, Annex C, Appendix 2.

14 Adopted in the 8th UN Congress on the Prevention of Crime and the Treatment of Offenders, Havana, 7 September 1990.

15 18th Report, 1992–93 HC 739, pp. 11–15.

16 See S. Doran, 'The doctrine of excessive defence: developments past, present and potential' (1985) 36 NILQ 314 and 'The use of force by the security forces in Northern Ireland: a legal perspective' (1987) 7 LS 291; Lord Colville's Annual Reports on the Northern Ireland (Emergency Provisions) Acts for 1987, pp. 28–30, 1988, pp. 34–38; paper by T. Hadden, SACHR 18th Report, Annex E.

17 Above, p. 630.

18 [1995] 1 All ER 334 at 345–347.

The government's subsequent response on inquests was that 'the present arrangements generally work well in practice',[19] a view disputed by the SACHR[20] and the NIHRC.[1]

9. The gap between theory and practice as regards military aid to the civil power is discussed by R. Evelegh.[2] 'By contrast with 19th century practice, the "civil power" that may call in the armed forces appears no longer to be the local magistracy, but the Home Secretary, acting on a request from a chief officer of police'.[3]

McCann v United Kingdom, ECtHRR A324, European Court of Human Rights, (1995) 21 EHRR 97

The facts of those cases as found by the Court were as follows. Prior to March 1988, the UK, Spanish and Gibraltar authorities became aware that the Provisional IRA were planning a terrorist attack in Gibraltar. It appeared that the target would be a changing of the guard ceremony carried out every Tuesday in an assembly area. The Gibraltar Commissioner of Police was advised by a group that included a senior military advisor (an SAS officer, soldier F), an SAS attack commander (Soldier E) and a bomb-disposal adviser (Soldier G). The Ministry of Defence issued Soldier F with Rules of Engagement under which military forces were to assist the Gibraltar police to arrest the IRA active service unit involved. The Rules provided '*inter alia*':

'Use of force
4. You and your men will not use force unless requested to do so by the senior police officer(s) designated by the Gibraltar Police Commissioner; or unless it is necessary to do so in order to protect life. You and your men are not then to use more force than is necessary in order to protect life ...

Opening fire
5. You and your men may only open fire against a person if you or they have reasonable grounds for believing that he/she is currently committing, or is about to commit, an action which is likely to endanger your or their lives, or the life of any other person, and if there is no other way to prevent this.

---

19 229 HC Deb, 27 July 1993, col 753, written answer.
20 19th Report, 1993–94 HC 495, p. 17.
1 Below, p. 645, n. 13.
2 Op. cit.
3 A. W. Bradley and K. Ewing, *Wade and Bradley: Constitutional and Administrative Law* (12th edn., 1997), pp. 668–669. See also the *Manual of Military Law*, Part II, Section V, (1968); Queen's Regulations for the Army, Reg. J. 11.002; Report of the Committee appointed to inquire into the Circumstances connected with the Disturbances at Featherstone on 7th of September, 1893 (C 7234); R. Neville, 'The Yorkshire Miners and the 1893 Lockout: The Featherstone "Massacre"' (1976) XXI International Review of Social History, 337; Report of the Departmental Committee on Riot (1895, C 7650); Report of the Commissioner of Police of the Metropolis for 1875, Cmnd. 6496, Appendix 9; Report of the Tribunal of Inquiry into Violence and Civil Disturbances in Northern Ireland (Chairman, Scarman J) (Cmd. 566, 1972) especially Part VI, and pp. 193–195, 201–206, 220–221; K. Jeffery in P. J. Rowe and C. J. Whelan, *Military Intervention in Democratic Societies* (1985), Chap. 2; A. Babington, *Military Intervention in Britain* (1990); C. J. Whelan, (1979) 8 ILJ 222; C. Townshend, (1982) 25 Historical Journal 167; S. Greer, 'Military Intervention in Civil Disturbances: the Legal Basis Reconsidered' [1983] PL 573, criticised by B. Robertson, (1990) xxix Military Law and Law of War Rev 309; C. Walker, 'The Role and Powers of the Army in Northern Ireland' in B. Hadfield (ed.), *Northern Ireland: Politics and the Constitution* (1992), Chap. 8, pp. 113–116; K. Reid and C. Walker, 'Military Aid in Civil Emergencies: Lessons from New Zealand' (1998) 27 Anglo-Am LR 133.

Firing without warning
6. You and your men may fire without warning if the giving of a warning or any delay in firing could lead to death or injury to you or them or any other person, or if the giving of a warning is clearly impracticable.

Warning before firing
7. If the circumstances in paragraph 6 do not apply, a warning is necessary before firing. The warning is to be as clear as possible and is to include a direction to surrender and a clear warning that fire will be opened if the direction is not obeyed.'

There was a reported sighting of the ASU on 4 March in Malaga in Spain. An operational briefing took place on 5/6 March. The Security Service assessment stated that the IRA intended to attack the parade on 8 March; that an ASU of three (Daniel McCann, Sean Savage (an 'expert bomb maker) and a third member, later identified as Mairead Farrell) would carry out the attack; that they were believed to be dangerous terrorists who would almost certainly be armed and who, if confronted by security forces, would be likely to use their weapons; that the attack would be by way of a car bomb; that it was possible, but unlikely, that a 'blocking car' would be parked earlier to save a space later to be used by a second car with the bomb. It was thought that the use of a remote-control device to detonate the bomb was more likely that a timer device or control wire. The military witnesses present were convinced it would be a remote-control device and that it was likely that if confronted the person with the device would seek to detonate it. Arrangements were made for surveillance at the border and a plan formulated for the arrest of the ASU members on foot in the assembly area after parking a car which the intended to leave. In the afternoon of 6 March, Savage was identified as a man who had earlier parked a car in the assembly area. At about the same time, there was a possible sighting of McCann and Farrell crossing the frontier on foot into Gibraltar. It was then reported that the three had met and were looking at a car in the assembly area. They then moved off. The identification was confirmed. Soldier G inspected the car, noted that it had a rusty aerial out of place with the car's age and reported that it was a 'suspect car bomb'. This information was passed on but understood by Soldiers A, B, C and D from Soldier E to be confirmation that there was a car bomb that could be detonated by one of the three suspects. It was subsequently established that Solder G was neither a radio-communicator nor explosives expert.

The Commissioner requested the military to arrest the suspects. Soldiers A and B and C and D, operating in pairs, were so instructed. Soldiers A and B approached McCann and Farrell. According to their evidence at the inquest, McCann and Farrell made movements which were interpreted as going for the button to detonate the bomb. Both were shot a number of times by each solder. The soldiers subsequently denied the allegations of some witnesses that McCann and Farrell had been shot while attempting to surrender and had then been shot while lying on the ground. Soldiers C and D followed Savage. They gave evidence that they heard gunfire, C shouted 'Stop', Savage spun round, his arm went down towards his right hand hip area and they shot him, believing he was going for a detonator. They denied the allegation of a witness that they shot him while on the ground.

When the bodies of McCann, Farrell and Savage were searched no weapons or detonating devices were found. Car keys were found in Farrell's handbag. The relevant car was subsequently found in La Linea; inside this car were the keys to another car in Marbella which was found to contain an explosive device with a timer set to explode at the time of the parade on 8 March. This second car had been rented by 'Katherine Smith', the name on the passport in Farrell's handbag.

An inquest was held in September. The jury returned verdicts of lawful killing by nine to two. Actions for damages were commenced in the High Court in Northern

Ireland on behalf of the estates of the deceased against the MoD; these were blocked by certificates of the Secretary of State for Foreign and Commonwealth Affairs issued under the s. 40(3) Crown Proceedings Act 1947 which stated conclusively that any alleged liability of the Crown arose neither in respect of HM Government in the UK or in Northern Ireland.

Evidence was subsequently made available that the UK police had briefed the Spanish police that McCann, Farrell and Savage were possible ASU members; the Spanish police had observed them arrive at Malaga Airport on 4 March. It was alleged that the car had been under surveillance by the Spanish authorities and that it would have been impossible for the three suspects to have detonated the bomb in the assembly area from the places where they were shot.

The applicants complained that the killings violated Art. 2 ECHR. The Commission found by 11 to 6 that there had been no violation.

Judgment of the Court

AS TO THE LAW

I. ALLEGED VIOLATION OF ARTICLE 2 (ART. 2) OF THE CONVENTION
145. The applicants alleged that the killing of Mr McCann, Ms Farrell and Mr Savage by members of the security forces constituted a violation of Article 2 (art. 2) of the Convention
…

A. *Interpretation of Article 2 (art. 2)*

1. *General approach*
146. The Court's approach to the interpretation of Article 2 (art. 2) must be guided by the fact that the object and purpose of the Convention as an instrument for the protection of individual human beings requires that its provisions be interpreted and applied so as to make its safeguards practical and effective (see, inter alia, the *Soering v. the United Kingdom* judgment of 7 July 1989, Series A no. 161, p. 34, para. 87, and the *Loizidou v. Turkey* (Preliminary Objections) judgment of 23 March 1995, Series A no. 310, p. 27, para. 72).
147. It must also be borne in mind that, as a provision (art. 2) which not only safeguards the right to life but sets out the circumstances when the deprivation of life may be justified, Article 2 (art. 2) ranks as one of the most fundamental provisions in the Convention – indeed one which, in peacetime, admits of no derogation under Article 15 (art. 15). Together with Article 3 (art. 15+3) of the Convention, it also enshrines one of the basic values of the democratic societies making up the Council of Europe (see the above-mentioned Soering judgment, p. 34, para. 88). As such, its provisions must be strictly construed.
148. The Court considers that the exceptions delineated in paragraph 2 (art. 2-2) indicate that this provision (art. 2-2) extends to, but is not concerned exclusively with, intentional killing. As the Commission has pointed out, the text of Article 2 (art. 2), read as a whole, demonstrates that paragraph 2 (art. 2-2) does not primarily define instances where it is permitted intentionally to kill an individual, but describes the situations where it is permitted to 'use force' which may result, as an unintended outcome, in the deprivation of life. The use of force, however, must be no more than 'absolutely necessary' for the achievement of one of the purposes set out in sub-paragraphs (a), (b) or (c) (art. 2-2-a, art. 2-2-b, art. 2-2-c) (see application no. 10044/82, *Stewart v. the United Kingdom*, 10 July 1984, Decisions and Reports 39, pp. 169-71).
149. In this respect the use of the term 'absolutely necessary' in Article 2 para. 2 (art. 2-2) indicates that a stricter and more compelling test of necessity must be employed from that normally applicable when determining whether State action is 'necessary in a democratic society' under paragraph 2 of Articles 8 to 11 (art. 8-2, art. 9-2, art. 10-2, art. 11-2) of the Convention. In particular, the force used must be strictly proportionate to the achievement of the aims set out in sub-paragraphs 2 (a), (b) and (c) of Article 2 (art. 2-2-a-b-c).
150. In keeping with the importance of this provision (art. 2) in a democratic society, the Court must, in making its assessment, subject deprivations of life to the most careful scrutiny, particularly where deliberate lethal force is used, taking into consideration not only the actions

of the agents of the State who actually administer the force but also all the surrounding circumstances including such matters as the planning and control of the actions under examination.

2. The obligation to protect life in Article 2 para. 1 (art. 2-1)
[The Court found that there was no breach of Art. 2(1). The difference between Art. 2, ECHR and Art. 2 of the Gibraltar Constitution (which provided for a 'reasonably justifiable' standard rather than 'absolutely necessary' was) was 'not sufficiently great that a violation of Art. 2(1) could be found on this ground alone' (para. 155). The alleged shortcomings in the inquest proceedings had not 'subsequently hampered the carrying out of a thorough, impartial and careful examination of the circumstances surrounding the killings'(para. 163).

B Application of Article 2 (art.2) to the facts of the case

1. General approach to the evaluation of the evidence
[The Court concluded that the Commission's establishment of the facts could be taken as 'an accurate and reliable account' (para. 169), but that it was for the Court to assess whether they disclosed a violation of Art. 2 ECHR (para. 171).]

2. Applicants' allegation that the killings were premeditated ...
178. The Commission concluded that there was no evidence to support the applicants' claim of a premeditated plot to kill the suspects.
179. The Court observes that it would need to have convincing evidence before it could conclude that there was a premeditated plan, in the sense developed by the applicants.
180. In the light of its own examination of the material before it, the Court does not find it established that there was an execution plot at the highest level of command in the Ministry of Defence or in the Government, or that Soldiers A, B, C and D had been so encouraged or instructed by the superior officers who had briefed them prior to the operation, or indeed that they had decided on their own initiative to kill the suspects irrespective of the existence of any justification for the use of lethal force and in disobedience to the arrest instructions they had received. Nor is there evidence that there was an implicit encouragement by the authorities or hints and innuendoes to execute the three suspects.
181. The factors relied on by the applicants amount to a series of conjectures that the authorities must have known that there was no bomb in the car. However, having regard to the intelligence information that they had received, to the known profiles of the three terrorists, all of whom had a background in explosives, and the fact that Mr Savage was seen to 'fiddle' with something before leaving the car (see paragraph 38 above), the belief that the car contained a bomb cannot be described as either implausible or wholly lacking in foundation.
182. In particular, the decision to admit them to Gibraltar, however open to criticism given the risks that it entailed, was in accordance with the arrest policy formulated by the Advisory Group that no effort should be made to apprehend them until all three were present in Gibraltar and there was sufficient evidence of a bombing mission to secure their convictions (see paragraph 203 above).
183. Nor can the Court accept the applicants' contention that the use of the SAS, in itself, amounted to evidence that the killing of the suspects was intended. In this respect it notes that the SAS is a special unit which has received specialist training in combating terrorism. It was only natural, therefore, that in light of the advance warning that the authorities received of an impending terrorist attack they would resort to the skill and experience of the SAS in order to deal with the threat in the safest and most informed manner possible.
184. The Court therefore rejects as unsubstantiated the applicants' allegations that the killing of the three suspects was premeditated or the product of a tacit agreement amongst those involved in the operation.

3. Conduct and planning of the operation ...

(b) The Court's assessment

(1) Preliminary considerations
192. In carrying out its examination under Article 2 (art. 2) of the Convention, the Court must bear in mind that the information that the United Kingdom authorities received that there

would be a terrorist attack in Gibraltar presented them with a fundamental dilemma. On the one hand, they were required to have regard to their duty to protect the lives of the people in Gibraltar including their own military personnel and, on the other, to have minimum resort to the use of lethal force against those suspected of posing this threat in the light of the obligations flowing from both domestic and international law.

193. Several other factors must also be taken into consideration. In the first place, the authorities were confronted by an active service unit of the IRA composed of persons who had been convicted of bombing offences and a known explosives expert. The IRA, judged by its actions in the past, had demonstrated a disregard for human life, including that of its own members. Secondly, the authorities had had prior warning of the impending terrorist action and thus had ample opportunity to plan their reaction and, in co-ordination with the local Gibraltar authorities, to take measures to foil the attack and arrest the suspects. Inevitably, however, the security authorities could not have been in possession of the full facts and were obliged to formulate their policies on the basis of incomplete hypotheses.

194. Against this background, in determining whether the force used was compatible with Article 2 (art. 2), the Court must carefully scrutinise, as noted above, not only whether the force used by the soldiers was strictly proportionate to the aim of protecting persons against unlawful violence but also whether the anti-terrorist operation was planned and controlled by the authorities so as to minimise, to the greatest extent possible, recourse to lethal force. The Court will consider each of these points in turn.

(2) Actions of the soldiers

195. It is recalled that the soldiers who carried out the shooting (A, B, C and D) were informed by their superiors, in essence, that there was a car bomb in place which could be detonated by any of the three suspects by means of a radio-control device which might have been concealed on their persons; that the device could be activated by pressing a button; that they would be likely to detonate the bomb if challenged, thereby causing heavy loss of life and serious injuries, and were also likely to be armed and to resist arrest (see paragraphs 23, 24-27, and 28-31 above).

196. As regards the shooting of Mr McCann and Ms Farrell, the Court recalls the Commission's finding that they were shot at close range after making what appeared to Soldiers A and B to be threatening movements with their hands as if they were going to detonate the bomb (see paragraph 132 above). The evidence indicated that they were shot as they fell to the ground but not as they lay on the ground (see paragraphs 59-67 above). Four witnesses recalled hearing a warning shout (see paragraph 75 above). Officer P corroborated the soldiers' evidence as to the hand movements (see paragraph 76 above). Officer Q and Police Constable Parody also confirmed that Ms Farrell had made a sudden, suspicious move towards her handbag (ibid.).

197. As regards the shooting of Mr Savage, the evidence revealed that there was only a matter of seconds between the shooting at the Shell garage (McCann and Farrell) and the shooting at Landport tunnel (Savage). The Commission found that it was unlikely that Soldiers C and D witnessed the first shooting before pursuing Mr Savage who had turned around after being alerted by either the police siren or the shooting (see paragraph 132 above).

Soldier C opened fire because Mr Savage moved his right arm to the area of his jacket pocket, thereby giving rise to the fear that he was about to detonate the bomb. In addition, Soldier C had seen something bulky in his pocket which he believed to be a detonating transmitter. Soldier D also opened fire believing that the suspect was trying to detonate the supposed bomb. The soldiers' version of events was corroborated in some respects by Witnesses H and J, who saw Mr Savage spin round to face the soldiers in apparent response to the police siren or the first shooting (see paragraphs 83 and 85 above).

The Commission found that Mr Savage was shot at close range until he hit the ground and probably in the instant as or after he had hit the ground (see paragraph 132 above). This conclusion was supported by the pathologists' evidence at the inquest (see paragraph 110 above).

198. It was subsequently discovered that the suspects were unarmed, that they did not have a detonator device on their persons and that there was no bomb in the car (see paragraphs 93 and 96 above).

199. All four soldiers admitted that they shot to kill. They considered that it was necessary to continue to fire at the suspects until they were rendered physically incapable of detonating a device (see paragraphs 61, 63, 80 and 120 above). According to the pathologists' evidence

Ms Farrell was hit by eight bullets, Mr McCann by five and Mr Savage by sixteen (see paragraphs 108-10 above).

200. The Court accepts that the soldiers honestly believed, in the light of the information that they had been given, as set out above, that it was necessary to shoot the suspects in order to prevent them from detonating a bomb and causing serious loss of life (see paragraph 195 above). The actions which they took, in obedience to superior orders, were thus perceived by them as absolutely necessary in order to safeguard innocent lives.

It considers that the use of force by agents of the State in pursuit of one of the aims delineated in paragraph 2 of Article 2 (art. 2-2) of the Convention may be justified under this provision (art. 2-2) where it is based on an honest belief which is perceived, for good reasons, to be valid at the time but which subsequently turns out to be mistaken. To hold otherwise would be to impose an unrealistic burden on the State and its law-enforcement personnel in the execution of their duty, perhaps to the detriment of their lives and those of others.

It follows that, having regard to the dilemma confronting the authorities in the circumstances of the case, the actions of the soldiers do not, in themselves, give rise to a violation of this provision (art. 2-2).

201. The question arises, however, whether the anti-terrorist operation as a whole was controlled and organised in a manner which respected the requirements of Article 2 (art. 2) and whether the information and instructions given to the soldiers which, in effect, rendered inevitable the use of lethal force, took adequately into consideration the right to life of the three suspects.

(3) Control and organisation of the operation

202. The Court first observes that, as appears from the operational order of the Commissioner, it had been the intention of the authorities to arrest the suspects at an appropriate stage. Indeed, evidence was given at the inquest that arrest procedures had been practised by the soldiers before 6 March and that efforts had been made to find a suitable place in Gibraltar to detain the suspects after their arrest (see paragraphs 18 and 55 above).

203. It may be questioned why the three suspects were not arrested at the border immediately on their arrival in Gibraltar and why, as emerged from the evidence given by Inspector Ullger, the decision was taken not to prevent them from entering Gibraltar if they were believed to be on a bombing mission. Having had advance warning of the terrorists' intentions it would certainly have been possible for the authorities to have mounted an arrest operation. Although surprised at the early arrival of the three suspects, they had a surveillance team at the border and an arrest group nearby (see paragraph 34 above). In addition, the Security Services and the Spanish authorities had photographs of the three suspects, knew their names as well as their aliases and would have known what passports to look for (see paragraph 33 above).

204. On this issue, the Government submitted that at that moment there might not have been sufficient evidence to warrant the detention and trial of the suspects. Moreover, to release them, having alerted them to the authorities' state of awareness but leaving them or others free to try again, would obviously increase the risks. Nor could the authorities be sure that those three were the only terrorists they had to deal with or of the manner in which it was proposed to carry out the bombing.

205. The Court confines itself to observing in this respect that the danger to the population of Gibraltar – which is at the heart of the Government's submissions in this case – in not preventing their entry must be considered to outweigh the possible consequences of having insufficient evidence to warrant their detention and trial. In its view, either the authorities knew that there was no bomb in the car – which the Court has already discounted (see paragraph 181 above) – or there was a serious miscalculation by those responsible for controlling the operation. As a result, the scene was set in which the fatal shooting, given the intelligence assessments which had been made, was a foreseeable possibility if not a likelihood.

The decision not to stop the three terrorists from entering Gibraltar is thus a relevant factor to take into account under this head.

206. The Court notes that at the briefing on 5 March attended by Soldiers A, B, C, and D it was considered likely that the attack would be by way of a large car bomb. A number of key assessments were made. In particular, it was thought that the terrorists would not use a blocking car; that the bomb would be detonated by a radio-control device; that the detonation could be effected by the pressing of a button; that it was likely that the suspects would detonate the

bomb if challenged; that they would be armed and would be likely to use their arms if confronted (see paragraphs 23-31 above).

207. In the event, all of these crucial assumptions, apart from the terrorists' intentions to carry out an attack, turned out to be erroneous. Nevertheless, as has been demonstrated by the Government, on the basis of their experience in dealing with the IRA, they were all possible hypotheses in a situation where the true facts were unknown and where the authorities operated on the basis of limited intelligence information.

208. In fact, insufficient allowances appear to have been made for other assumptions. For example, since the bombing was not expected until 8 March when the changing of the guard ceremony was to take place, there was equally the possibility that the three terrorists were on a reconnaissance mission. While this was a factor which was briefly considered, it does not appear to have been regarded as a serious possibility (see paragraph 45 above).

In addition, at the briefings or after the suspects had been spotted, it might have been thought unlikely that they would have been prepared to explode the bomb, thereby killing many civilians, as Mr McCann and Ms Farrell strolled towards the border area since this would have increased the risk of detection and capture (see paragraph 57 above). It might also have been thought improbable that at that point they would have set up the transmitter in anticipation to enable them to detonate the supposed bomb immediately if confronted (see paragraph 115 above).

Moreover, even if allowances are made for the technological skills of the IRA, the description of the detonation device as a 'button job' without the qualifications subsequently described by the experts at the inquest (see paragraphs 115 and 131 above), of which the competent authorities must have been aware, over-simplifies the true nature of these devices.

209. It is further disquieting in this context that the assessment made by Soldier G, after a cursory external examination of the car, that there was a 'suspect car bomb' was conveyed to the soldiers, according to their own testimony, as a definite identification that there was such a bomb (see paragraphs 48, and 51-52 above). It is recalled that while Soldier G had experience in car bombs, it transpired that he was not an expert in radio communications or explosives; and that his assessment that there was a suspect car bomb, based on his observation that the car aerial was out of place, was more in the nature of a report that a bomb could not be ruled out (see paragraph 53 above).

210. In the absence of sufficient allowances being made for alternative possibilities, and the definite reporting of the existence of a car bomb which, according to the assessments that had been made, could be detonated at the press of a button, a series of working hypotheses were conveyed to Soldiers A, B, C and D as certainties, thereby making the use of lethal force almost unavoidable.

211. However, the failure to make provision for a margin of error must also be considered in combination with the training of the soldiers to continue shooting once they opened fire until the suspect was dead. As noted by the Coroner in his summing-up to the jury at the inquest, all four soldiers shot to kill the suspects (see paragraphs 61, 63, 80 and 120 above). Soldier E testified that it had been discussed with the soldiers that there was an increased chance that they would have to shoot to kill since there would be less time where there was a 'button' device (see paragraph 26 above). Against this background, the authorities were bound by their obligation to respect the right to life of the suspects to exercise the greatest of care in evaluating the information at their disposal before transmitting it to soldiers whose use of firearms automatically involved shooting to kill.

212. Although detailed investigation at the inquest into the training received by the soldiers was prevented by the public interest certificates which had been issued (see paragraph 104, at point 1. (iii) above), it is not clear whether they had been trained or instructed to assess whether the use of firearms to wound their targets may have been warranted by the specific circumstances that confronted them at the moment of arrest.

Their reflex action in this vital respect lacks the degree of caution in the use of firearms to be expected from law enforcement personnel in a democratic society, even when dealing with dangerous terrorist suspects, and stands in marked contrast to the standard of care reflected in the instructions in the use of firearms by the police which had been drawn to their attention and which emphasised the legal responsibilities of the individual officer in the light of conditions prevailing at the moment of engagement (see paragraphs 136 and 137 above).

This failure by the authorities also suggests a lack of appropriate care in the control and organisation of the arrest operation.

213. In sum, having regard to the decision not to prevent the suspects from travelling into Gibraltar, to the failure of the authorities to make sufficient allowances for the possibility that their intelligence assessments might, in some respects at least, be erroneous and to the automatic recourse to lethal force when the soldiers opened fire, the Court is not persuaded that the killing of the three terrorists constituted the use of force which was no more than absolutely necessary in defence of persons from unlawful violence within the meaning of Article 2 para. 2 (a) (art. 2-2-a) of the Convention.

214. Accordingly, the Court finds that there has been a breach of Article 2 (art. 2) of the Convention.

FOR THESE REASONS, THE COURT

1. Holds by ten votes to nine that there has been a violation of Article 2 (art. 2) of the Convention;

2. Holds unanimously that the United Kingdom is to pay to the applicants, within three months, £38,700 (thirty-eight thousand seven hundred) for costs and expenses incurred in the Strasbourg proceedings, less 37,731 (thirty-seven thousand seven hundred and thirty-one) French francs to be converted into pounds sterling at the rate of exchange applicable on the date of delivery of the present judgment;

3. Dismisses unanimously the applicants' claim for damages;

4. Dismisses unanimously the applicants' claim for costs and expenses incurred in the Gibraltar inquest;

5. Dismisses unanimously the remainder of the claims for just satisfaction.

JOINT DISSENTING OPINION OF JUDGES RYSSDAL, BERNHARDT, THÓR VILHJÁLMSSON, GÖLCÜKLÜ, PALM, PEKKANEN, SIR JOHN FREELAND, BAKA AND JAMBREK

8. Before turning to the various aspects of the operation which are criticised in the judgment, we would underline three points of a general nature.

First, in undertaking any evaluation of the way in which the operation was organised and controlled, the Court should studiously resist the temptations offered by the benefit of hindsight. The authorities had at the time to plan and make decisions on the basis of incomplete information. Only the suspects knew at all precisely what they intended; and it was part of their purpose, as it had no doubt been part of their training, to ensure that as little as possible of their intentions was revealed. It would be wrong to conclude in retrospect that a particular course would, as things later transpired, have been better than one adopted at the time under the pressures of an ongoing anti-terrorist operation and that the latter course must therefore be regarded as culpably mistaken. It should not be so regarded unless it is established that in the circumstances as they were known at the time another course should have been preferred.

9. Secondly, the need for the authorities to act within the constraints of the law, while the suspects were operating in a state of mind in which members of the security forces were regarded as legitimate targets and incidental death or injury to civilians as of little consequence, would inevitably give the suspects a tactical advantage which should not be allowed to prevail. The consequences of the explosion of a large bomb in the centre of Gibraltar might well be so devastating that the authorities could not responsibly risk giving the suspects the opportunity to set in train the detonation of such a bomb. Of course the obligation of the United Kingdom under Article 2 para. 1 (art. 2-1) of the Convention extended to the lives of the suspects as well as to the lives of all the many others, civilian and military, who were present in Gibraltar at the time. But, quite unlike those others, the purpose of the presence of the suspects in Gibraltar was the furtherance of a criminal enterprise which could be expected to have resulted in the loss of many innocent lives if it had been successful. They had chosen to place themselves in a situation where there was a grave danger that an irreconcilable conflict between the two duties might arise.

10. Thirdly, the Court's evaluation of the conduct of the authorities should throughout take full account of (a) the information which had been received earlier about IRA intentions to mount a major terrorist attack in Gibraltar by an active service unit of three individuals; and

(b) the discovery which (according to evidence given to the inquest by Witness O) had been made in Brussels on 21 January 1988 of a car containing a large amount of Semtex explosive and four detonators, with a radio-controlled system – equipment which, taken together, constituted a device familiar in Northern Ireland.

In the light of (a), the decision that members of the SAS should be sent to take part in the operation in response to the request of the Gibraltar Commissioner of Police for military assistance was wholly justifiable. Troops trained in a counter-terrorist role and to operate successfully in small groups would clearly be a suitable choice to meet the threat of an IRA active service unit at large in a densely populated area such as Gibraltar, where there would be an imperative need to limit as far as possible the risk of accidental harm to passers-by.

The detailed operational briefing on 5 March 1988 (paragraphs 22-31) shows the reasonableness, in the circumstances as known at the time, of the assessments then made. The operational order of the Gibraltar Commissioner of Police, which was drawn up on the same day, expressly proscribed the use of more force than necessary and required any recourse to firearms to be had with care for the safety of persons in the vicinity. It described the intention of the operation as being to protect life; to foil the attempt; to arrest the offenders; and the securing and safe custody of the prisoners (paragraphs 17 and 18).

All of this is indicative of appropriate care on the part of the authorities. So, too, is the cautious approach to the eventual passing of control to the military on 6 March 1988 (paragraphs 54-58).

11. As regards the particular criticisms of the conduct of the operation which are made in the judgment, foremost among them is the questioning (in paragraphs 203-05) of the decision not to prevent the three suspects from entering Gibraltar. It is pointed out in paragraph 203 that, with the advance information which the authorities possessed and with the resources of personnel at their disposal, it would have been possible for them 'to have mounted an arrest operation' at the border.

The judgment does not, however, go on to say that it would have been practicable for the authorities to have arrested and detained the suspects at that stage. Rightly so, in our view, because at that stage there might not be sufficient evidence to warrant their detention and trial. To release them, after having alerted them to the state of readiness of the authorities, would be to increase the risk that they or other IRA members could successfully mount a renewed terrorist attack on Gibraltar. In the circumstances as then known, it was accordingly not 'a serious miscalculation' for the authorities to defer the arrest rather than merely stop the suspects at the border and turn them back into Spain.

12. Paragraph 206 of the judgment then lists certain 'key assessments' made by the authorities which, in paragraph 207, are said to have turned out, in the event, to be erroneous, although they are accepted as all being possible hypotheses in a situation where the true facts were unknown and where the authorities were operating on the basis of limited intelligence information. Paragraph 208 goes on to make the criticism that 'insufficient allowances appear to have been made for other assumptions'.

13. As a first example to substantiate this criticism, the paragraph then states that since the bombing was not expected until 8 March 'there was equally the possibility that the ... terrorists were on a reconnaissance mission'.

There was, however, nothing unreasonable in the assessment at the operational briefing on 5 March that the car which would be brought into Gibraltar was unlikely, on the grounds then stated, to be a 'blocking' car (see paragraph 23, point e). So, when the car had been parked in the assembly area by one of the suspects and all three had been found to be present in Gibraltar, the authorities could quite properly operate on the working assumption that it contained a bomb and that, as the suspects were unlikely to risk two visits, it was not 'equally' possible that they were on a reconnaissance mission.

In addition, Soldier F, the senior military adviser to the Gibraltar Commissioner of Police, gave evidence to the inquest that, according to intelligence information, reconnaissance missions had been undertaken many times before: reconnaissance was, he had been told, complete and the operation was ready to be run. In these circumstances, for the authorities to have proceeded otherwise than on the basis of a worst-case scenario that the car contained a bomb which was capable of being detonated by the suspects during their presence in the territory would have been to show a reckless failure of concern for public safety.

14. Secondly, it is suggested in the second sub-paragraph of paragraph 208 that, at the briefings or after the suspects had been spotted, 'it might have been thought unlikely that they would have been prepared to explode the bomb, thereby killing many civilians, as Mr McCann and Ms Farrell strolled towards the border area since this would have increased the risk of detection and capture'.

Surely, however, the question is rather whether the authorities could safely have operated on the assumption that the suspects would be unlikely to be prepared to explode the bomb when, even if for the time being moving in the direction of the border, they became aware that they had been detected and were faced with the prospect of arrest. In our view, the answer is clear: certainly, previous experience of IRA activities would have afforded no reliable basis for concluding that the killing of many civilians would itself be a sufficient deterrent or that the suspects, when confronted, would have preferred no explosion at all to an explosion causing civilian casualties. It is relevant that, according to Soldier F's evidence at the inquest, part of the intelligence background was that he had been told that the IRA were under pressure to produce a 'spectacular'. He also gave evidence of his belief that, when cornered, the suspects would have no qualms about pressing the button to achieve some degree of propaganda success: they would try to derive such a success out of having got a bomb into Gibraltar and that would outweigh in their minds the propaganda loss arising from civilian casualties.

15. The second sub-paragraph of paragraph 208 goes on to suggest that 'it might also have been thought improbable that at that point' – that is, apparently, as McCann and Farrell 'strolled towards the border' – '[the suspects] would have set up the transmitter in anticipation to enable them to detonate the supposed bomb immediately if confronted'.

Here, the question ought, we consider, to be whether the authorities could prudently have proceeded otherwise than on the footing that there was at the very least a possibility that, if not before the suspects became aware of detection then immediately afterwards, the transmitter would be in a state of readiness to detonate the bomb.

16. It is next suggested, in the third sub-paragraph of paragraph 208, that 'even if allowances are made for the technological skills of the IRA, the description of the detonation device as a "button job" without the qualifications subsequently described by the experts at the inquest ..., of which the competent authorities must have been aware, over-simplifies the true nature of these devices'. The exact purport of this criticism is perhaps open to some doubt. What is fully clear, however, is that, as the applicants' own expert witness accepted at the inquest, a transmitter of the kind which was thought likely to be used in the present case could be set up so as to enable detonation to be caused by pressing a single button; and in the light of past experience it would have been most unwise to discount the possibility of technological advance in this field by the IRA.

17. Paragraph 209 of the judgment expresses disquiet that the assessment made by Soldier G that there was a 'suspect car bomb' was conveyed to the soldiers on the ground in such a way as to give them the impression that the presence of a bomb had been definitely identified. But, given the assessments which had been made of the likelihood of a remote control being used, and given the various indicators that the car should indeed be suspected of containing a bomb, the actions which the soldiers must be expected to have taken would be the same whether their understanding of the message was as it apparently was or whether it was in the sense which Soldier G apparently intended. In either case, the existence of the risk to the people of Gibraltar would have been enough, given the nature of that risk, justifiably to prompt the response which followed.

18. Paragraph 209, in referring to the assessment made by Soldier G, also recalls that while he had experience with car bombs, he was not an expert in radio communications or explosives. In considering that assessment, it would, however, be fair to add that, although his inspection of the car was of brief duration, it was enough to enable him to conclude, particularly in view of the unusual appearance of its aerial in relation to the age of the car and the knowledge that the IRA had in the past used cars with aerials specially fitted, that it was to be regarded as a suspect car bomb.

The authorities were, in any event, not acting solely on the basis of Soldier G's assessment. There had also been the earlier assessment, to which we have referred in paragraph 13 above, that a 'blocking' car was unlikely to be used. In addition, the car had been seen to be parked by Savage, who was known to be an expert bomb-maker and who had taken some time (two to three minutes, according to one witness) to get out of the car, after fiddling with something between the seats.

19. Paragraph 210 of the judgment asserts, in effect, that the use of lethal force was made 'almost unavoidable' by the conveyance to Soldiers A, B, C and D of a series of working hypotheses which were vitiated by the absence of sufficient allowances for alternative possibilities and by 'the definite reporting ... of a car bomb which ... could be detonated at the press of a button'.

We have dealt in paragraphs 13-16 with the points advanced in support of the conclusion that insufficient allowance was made for alternative possibilities; and in paragraphs 17 and 18 with the question of reporting as to the presence of a car bomb.

We further question the conclusion that the use of lethal force was made 'almost unavoidable' by failings of the authorities in these respects. Quite apart from any other consideration, this conclusion takes insufficient account of the part played by chance in the eventual outcome. Had it not been for the movements which were made by McCann and Farrell as Soldiers A and B closed on them and which may have been prompted by the completely coincidental sounding of a police car siren, there is every possibility that they would have been seized and arrested without a shot being fired; and had it not been for Savage's actions as Soldiers C and D closed on him, which may have been prompted by the sound of gunfire from the McCann and Farrell incident, there is every possibility that he, too, would have been seized and arrested without resort to shooting.

20. The implication at the end of paragraph 211 that the authorities did not exercise sufficient care in evaluating the information at their disposal before transmitting it to soldiers 'whose use of firearms automatically involved shooting to kill' appears to be based on no more than 'the failure to make provision for a margin of error' to which the beginning of the paragraph refers. We have dealt already with the 'insufficient allowances for alternative possibilities' point (see, again, paragraphs 13-16 above), which we take to be the same as the alleged failure to provide for a margin of error which is referred to here. Any assessment of the evaluation by the authorities of the information at their disposal should, in any event, take due account of their need to reckon throughout with the incompleteness of that information (see paragraph 8 above); and there are no cogent grounds for any suggestion that there was information which they ought reasonably to have known but did not.

21. Paragraph 212, after making a glancing reference to the restrictive effect of the public interest certificates and saying that it is not clear 'whether the use of firearms to wound their targets may have been warranted by the specific circumstances that confronted them at the moment of arrest', goes on to say that 'their reflex action in this vital respect lacks the degree of caution ... to be expected from law-enforcement personnel in a democratic society, even when dealing with dangerous terrorist suspects, and stands in marked contrast to the standard of care reflected in the instructions in the use of firearms by the police'. It concludes with the assertion that this 'failure by the authorities also suggests a lack of appropriate care in the control and organisation of the arrest operation'.

22. As regards any suggestion that, if an assessment on the issue had been required by their training or instruction to be carried out by the soldiers, shooting to wound might have been considered by them to have been warranted by the circumstances at the time, it must be recalled that those circumstances included a genuine belief on their part that the suspects might be about to detonate a bomb by pressing a button. In that situation, to shoot merely to wound would have been a highly dangerous course: wounding alone might well not have immobilised a suspect and might have left him or her capable of pressing a button if determined to do so.

23. More generally as regards the training given, there was in fact ample evidence at the inquest to the effect that soldiers (and not only these soldiers) would be trained to respond to a threat such as that which was thought to be posed by the suspects in this case – all of them dangerous terrorists who were believed to be putting many lives at immediate risk – by opening fire once it was clear that the suspect was not desisting; that the intent of the firing would be to immobilise; and that the way to achieve that was to shoot to kill. There was also evidence at the inquest that soldiers would not be accepted for the SAS unless they displayed discretion and thoughtfulness; that they would not go ahead and shoot without thought, nor did they; but they did have to react very fast. In addition, evidence was given that SAS members had in fact been successful in the past in arresting terrorists in the great majority of cases.

24. We are far from persuaded that the Court has any sufficient basis for concluding, in the face of the evidence at the inquest and the extent of experience in dealing with terrorist activities which the relevant training reflects, that some different and preferable form of training should have been given and that the action of the soldiers in this case 'lacks the degree of caution in the use of firearms to be expected of law-enforcement personnel in a democratic society'. (We also question, in the light of the evidence, the fairness of the reference to 'reflex action in this vital respect' – underlining supplied. To be trained to react rapidly and to do so, when the needs of the situation require, is not to take reflex action.)

Nor do we accept that the differences between the guide to police officers in the use of firearms (paragraph 137 of the judgment) and the 'Firearms – rules of engagement' annexed to the Commissioner's operational order (paragraph 136), when the latter are taken together (as they should be) with the Rules of Engagement issued to Soldier F by the Ministry of Defence (paragraph 16), can validly be invoked to support a contention that the standard of care enjoined upon the soldiers was inadequate. Those differences are no doubt attributable to the differences in backgrounds and requirements of the recipients to whom they were addressed, account being taken of relevant training previously given to each group (it is to be noted that, according to the evidence of Soldier F at the inquest, many lectures are given to SAS soldiers on the concepts of the rule of law and the use of minimum force). We fail to see how the instructions for the soldiers could themselves be read as showing a lack of proper caution in the use of firearms.

Accordingly, we consider the concluding stricture, that there was some failure by the authorities in this regard suggesting a lack of appropriate care in the control and organisation of the arrest operation, to be unjustified. 25. The accusation of a breach by a State of its obligation under Article 2 (art. 2) of the Convention to protect the right to life is of the utmost seriousness. For the reasons given above, the evaluation in paragraphs 203 to 213 of the judgment seems to us to fall well short of substantiating the finding that there has been a breach of the Article (art. 2) in this case. We would ourselves follow the reasoning and conclusion of the Commission in its comprehensive, painstaking and notably realistic report. Like the Commission, we are satisfied that no failings have been shown in the organisation and control of the operation by the authorities which could justify a conclusion that force was used against the suspects disproportionately to the purpose of defending innocent persons from unlawful violence. We consider that the use of lethal force in this case, however regrettable the need to resort to such force may be, did not exceed what was, in the circumstances as known at the time, 'absolutely necessary' for that purpose and did not amount to a breach by the United Kingdom of its obligations under the Convention.

NOTES[4]

1. This was the first leading case on Art. 2 ECHR. The decision was described as the court's 'most politically controversial decision for a decade'. It was strongly criticised by the Conservative government and by Unionists, although not by the Labour opposition.[5] However, the judgment 'accepted almost all of the arguments put forward by the government and placed the finding of a violation on the narrowest possible ground.[6] Subsequent European Court of Human Rights cases have developed the points that states must 'take all feasible precautions in the choice of means and methods of a security operation mounted against an opposing group with a view to

4   See F. Ní Aoláin, *The Politics of Force* (2000), pp. 198–205; S. Joseph, 'Denouement of the Deaths on the Rock: the Right of Life of Terrorists' (1996) 14 NQHR 5; J. Merrills, (1996) 67 BYBIL 609; P. Cumper, (1995) Nott LJ 207; A. Mowbray, *Cases and Materials on the European Convention on Human Rights* (2001), Chap. 2.
5   P. Cumper, op cit., pp. 207–208.
6   J. Merrills, op cit., p. 612.

avoiding and, in any event, to minimising, incidental loss of civilian life'[.7] and must conduct effective investigations into unlawful killings, whether or not by state agents.[8]

The Court accepted the government's claim that the domestic standard of 'reasonable justification' was interpreted and applied in such a way as to negate any difference in protection from Art. 2 ECHR. It has been argued that such claims should be the subject of substantive examination.[9] Note Joseph's argument[10] that the finding of a violation by implication indicates that the *Kelly* case[11] was wrongly decided. The increase of risk to the ASU's lives that arose from the failure to arrest them at the border could not on the facts be justified by the argument that had they been arrested they would have had to be released for lack of evidence and that this would increase the risk that they or other IRA members could mount a renewed terrorist attack on Gibraltar.

The European Court of Human Rights has declared admissible a series of applications raising issues under Art. 2 arising out of deaths in Northern Ireland.[12] The cases raised issues as to the proportionality of the use of force and the thoroughness of the investigation following death (Art. 2), the discriminatory use of force (Art. 14) and the lack of an effective remedy, including criticisms of arrangements for inquests (Art. 13). The Northern Ireland Human Rights Commission submitted to the Court that the UK is 'failing to protect the rights to life by failing to ensure that its mechanisms of accountability are open, accountable, prompt and facilitating punitive sanctions when death has been caused by an agent of the state'.[13] The Court subsequently found the UK to have breached Art. 2, in respect of the inadequencies of the investigations.[14]

Compare, however, the decision on *Caraher v United Kingdom*[15] where the Court declared inadmissible a claim by the widow of Fergal Caraher, who had been shot by soldiers in 1990, as she had accepted £50,000 in settlement of a civil claim, and so could no longer claim to be a 'victim'. This would not have applied if it could have been shown that a breach of Art. 2 was authorised by domestic law or there was an administrative practice whereby such conduct was authorised or tolerated by the higher authorities of the state.[16] However, neither could be established. In acquitting the soldiers on charges of murder, Hutton LCJ had held that there was a reasonable

---

7 *Ergi v Turkey*, Judgment of 28 July 1998, para. 79.
8 *Kaya v Turkey* (1998) 28 EHRR1; *Kurt v Turkey* (1998) 27 EHRR 91; *Yasa v Turkey* (1998) 28 EHRR 408.
9 F. Ní Aoláin, op. cit., p. 200.
10 Op. cit., p. 17.
11 Above, p. 628.
12 *Jordan v United Kingdom*; (Application No. 24746/94) (arising out of the shooting of Pearse Jordan by RUC officers in 1992); *McKerr v United Kingdom* (Application No. 28883/95) (arising out of the shooting of Gervaise McKerr, Eugen Toman and Sean Burns by a RUC Home Support Unit in 1982; John Stalker regarded the investigation of the matter as slipshod and in some aspects woefully inadequate: *Stalker* (1988), pp. 40–43); *Kelly v United Kingdom* (Application No. 30054/96) (arising out of the deaths of nine men killed by the security forces in an operation at Loughgall in 1987); *Shanaghan v United Kingdom* (Application No. 37715/97) (arising out of the shooting of Patrick Shanaghan, for which responsibility was claimed by the UFF; RUC collusion was alleged); *McShane v United Kingdom* (Application No. 43290/98) (arising out of the death of Dermot McShane, who in 1996 at a major disturbance in Derry fell under a hoarding over which an armoured personnel carrier advanced).
13 *Submission to the European Court of Human Rights*, 23 March 2000 (published on the NICHR website).
14 Judgments of 4 May 2001. See p. 200.
15 Application No. 24520/94, 11 January 2000.
16 *Donnelly v United Kingdom*, Application Nos. 5577–5583/72, dec. 15.12.75, DR 4 p. 4, at pp. 78–79.

possibility that they had fired at the driver of a car because they honestly believed it necessary to do so to save another soldier from death or serious injury and that in the circumstances as they honestly believed them to be there was a reasonable possibility that this constituted reasonable force. The Court held that this approach was compatible with the principles established in *McCann*. Furthermore, there was insufficient evidence to establish a 'pattern or system' on the part of the authorities.

CHAPTER 6

Freedom of expression: censorship and obscenity

This chapter, and the ones which immediately follow, have as a unifying theme the issue of 'freedom of expression'. This freedom is commonly considered to be of fundamental importance in Western-style democracies.[1] The First Amendment to the US Constitution includes the slogan 'Congress shall make no law ... abridging the freedom of speech, or of the press'; Art. 19(2) of the International Convenant on Civil and Political Rights provides that 'everyone shall have the right to freedom of expression: this right shall include freedom to seek, receive and impart information and ideas of all kinds, regardless of frontiers, either orally, in writing or in print, in the form of art, or through any other media of his choice'; and Art. 10 of the European Convention on Human Rights proclaims: 'Everyone has the right to freedom of expression. This right shall include freedom to hold opinions and to receive and impart information and ideas without interference by public authority.'[2]

The philosophical underpinnings of this freedom have been much discussed.[3] Desire to protect freedom of speech is to an extent simply an aspect of the more general ideal that individual freedom of behaviour be protected: that incursions on an individual's liberty should be permitted only in situations where this is necessary to prevent harm to another, or where one person's liberty must be curtailed in order to preserve the liberty of others.

However, in addition to this general reason for seeking to protect liberty of expression, other more specific justifications may be offered. Some have pointed to the importance of freedom of expression in terms of the 'fulfilment' and 'development' of the individual in society, by means of the exposure of individuals to a free and wide-ranging flow of information, experience, ideas and opinions. Such exposure should at one and the same time both provide a stimulus to individual personality

---

1 In August 1994 the French Constitutional Council held that certain recently enacted laws, designed to purge English words and phrases from the French language, were invalid as contrary to the freedom of expression guarantees of the Declaration of the Rights of Man of 1789, protected under the French Constitution. The law had purported to outlaw the use of 'unapproved' foreign words on television, on radio, and in the press. The law was upheld, however, to the extent that it applied to the language which the state required to be used by its own officials in the performance of their duties.

2 Note also decisions of the High Court of Australia which recognise the notion of 'implied' rights to freedom of expression within the Australian Constitution: such rights being implicit in the Constitution's fundamental principles of governmental accountability and representative government. See *Australian Capital Television Pty Ltd v The Commonwealth* (1992) 177 CLR 506; *Theospharious v Herald and Weekly Times Ltd* (1994) CLR 104; *Lange v Australian Broadcasting Corpn* (1997) 189 CLR 520; *Levy v Victoria* (1997) 189 CLR 579. The *Lange* case affirmed that the freedom of political communication now recognised was to be interpreted only by reference to those aspects of representative and responsible government that could be identified in the 'text and structure' of the Constitution. For criticism, see A. Stone, (1999) 23 MULR 668.

3 See, for excellent surveys, E. Barendt, *Freedom of Speech* (Oxford, 1985), Chap. 1; G. Marshall, [1992] PL 40; D. Feldman, *Civil Liberties and Human Rights in England and Wales* (1993), Part IV.

development, and also act as a safeguard against an unduly restricted diet of 'information' and 'opinion' fed from official sources. It follows that there is a need, in a society which places a high value on the individual, for there to be freedom of artistic, literary and political expression. An adjunct to this is that the operation of democracy requires that there should be both open and informed discussion of issues of contemporary significance. Well known are the words of Mr Justice Brandeis of the US Supreme Court in *Whitney v California*,[4] speaking of those whose ideals had shaped the terms of the US Constitution. They:

> 'believed that freedom to think as you will and to speak as you think are means indispensable to the discovery and spread of political truth: that without free speech and assembly, discussion would be futile: that with them, discussion affords ordinarily adequate protection against the dissemination of noxious doctrine: that the greatest menace to freedom is an inert people: that public discussion is a political duty; and that this should be a fundamental principle of the American government....'

And in the still stronger words of Alexander Meiklejohn:

> 'when a question of policy is "before the house", free men choose it not with their eyes shut, but with their eyes open. To be afraid of ideas, any idea, is to be unfit for self-government.'[5]

This is not, of course, to suggest that there should be no limits to this liberty: only that in assessing the limits which should be drawn it is well to remember what may be the reasons underlying this ideal. In the sections which follow in this chapter we shall look at liberty of expression in the theatre, the cinema, on video and in the broadcasting media, in the published media and in the world of art. There then follows a chapter which looks at the extent to which free expression may be restricted in the interests of the due administration of justice; and this in turn is followed by a chapter which addresses these issues in the context of the 'openness' or otherwise of governmental information and activity.

In principle, the imposition of prior restrictions on freedom of expression requires particularly strong justification.[6] Given the value of expression, the harm or offence it causes may only justify the imposition of a penalty after the event; there may not in any event be a prosecution; prior restraint substitutes the view of an (often unaccountable) censor of the worth of the material for that of society; prior restraint often takes place at an interim stage. Nevertheless, subsequent restrictions may well of course inhibit expression, and prior restraints can be justified where there is a pressing need. Illustrations of these issues are considered below.[7] In the context of indecency and obscenity, prior restraint in the form of state censorship is now limited in England and Wales to videos, DVDs and certain computer games; the arrangements for the censorship of films are technically extra-statutory but do have a statutory underpinning in practice through the cinema licensing powers of local authorities.[8] In the US, most state visual prior censorship laws and procedures have been held unconstitutional.[9] By contrast, Australia has developed arrangements for censorship. Films, videos and computer games must be pre-rated by the government Office of Film and Literature Classification; it is also illegal to sell publications (including greeting cards, posters, magazines and books) which might be rated unsuitable for

---

4   274 US 357 (1927).
5   Free Speech and its Relation to Self-Government (New York, 1948, p. 19).
6   See E. Barendt, *Freedom of Speech* (1999), pp. 114–125; D. Feldman, *Civil Liberties and Human Rights in England and Wales* (1993), pp. 555–558.
7   pp. 721, 850.
8   See below, pp. 650–652.
9   *Kingsley International Pictures v Regents* 360 US 684 (1959) (film); *Southeastern Promotions Ltd v Conrad* 419 US 892 (1975) (theatre).

minors unless they have been pre-rated by the OFLC. It is an offence to distribute material other than in accordance with the rating; or to sell or exhibit material refused a rating. X-rated videos cannot be sold in the six states outside the two Territories. In one state, Queensland, it is illegal to sell to adults publications rated as unsuitable for minors.[10]

1 Theatre censorship

Theatres Act 1968

1. Abolition of censorship of the theatre
(1) The Theatres Act 1843 is hereby repealed; and none of the powers which were exercisable thereunder by the Lord Chamberlain of Her Majesty's Household shall be exercisable by or on behalf of Her Majesty by virtue of Her royal prerogative.
(2) In granting, renewing or transferring any licence under this Act for the use of any premises for the public performance of plays or in varying of the terms, conditions or restrictions on or subject to which any such licence is held, the licensing authority shall not have power to impose any term, condition or restriction as to the nature of the plays which may be performed under the licence or as to the manner of performing plays thereunder:
  Providing that nothing in this subsection shall prevent a licensing authority from imposing any term, condition or restriction which they consider necessary in the interests of physical safety or health or any condition regulating or prohibiting the giving of an exhibition, demonstration or performance of hypnotism within the meaning of the Hypnotism Act 1952.

NOTES

1. The Theatres Act 1968 ended official censorship of plays. Originating in legislation of 1737 (provoked by Sir Robert Walpole's sensitivity to his caricaturisation in plays), and extended in 1843 for the preservation of 'good manners' and 'decorum', the power of the Lord Chamberlain as regards the licensing of plays was, even in the years immediately preceding the 1968 Act, certainly no dead letter. Political characterisation, let alone satire, was closely controlled by the Lord Chamberlain, thus imposing significant restrictions on dramatic treatment of political issues of the day. Equally, the Lord Chamberlain firmly acted as guardian of the theatre-going public's 'decency'. A particularly strict line was taken as regards any allusions to homosexuality, with little or no regard taken to considerations of dramatic or other merit.
  Although unpopular with dramatists and directors, commercial theatre managers quite favoured the Lord Chamberlain's activities. It was unlikely that any prosecution (e.g. for obscenity) would be brought in respect of the performance of any play in respect of which he had granted his approval. Managers could therefore feel confident that they would only be involved in the presentation of 'safe' plays unlikely to cause much controversy amongst audiences or the public at large.[11] Writers and directors took a less sanguine view of the restrictions imposed by this licensing control, and, following a campaign mounted by the state-subsidised Royal Shakespeare Company,

10 See the website on Australia's Censorship System, libertus.net/censor/auscensor © Irene Graham; Classification (Publications, Films and Computer Games) Act 1995 (Cth), Classification of Publications Act 1991 (Qd). See *Michael Brown v Members of the Classification Review Board of the Office of Film and Literature* [1998] 319 FCA (24 March 1998), where the Federal Court upheld the refusal of classification to a student newspaper that contained a 'step by step guide to shoplifting'.
11 Compare the establishment, by the film industry itself, of the British Board of Film Censors.

the matter was considered by a Parliamentary Joint Committee which reported in 1967. The Committee's recommendation that theatre censorship be abolished was implemented by the 1968 Act. It remains, however, the case that a theatrical performance may involve the commission of a criminal offence, although the opportunity was taken in the Theatres Act 1968 to modify legislation on obscenity and incitement to racial hatred as it applies to the theatre.[12]

The absence of 'official' censorship of the theatre does not, of course, mean that writers and directors may not encounter difficulties staging plays with controversial content. Commercial theatre managers may prefer to present pieces with more assured audience attraction, and even the subsidised theatre has from time to time been said to act with one eye on the attitude of its funding bodies.[13]

2 Film censorship[14]

Cinemas Act 1985

Control of exhibitions

1. Licence required for exhibitions

(1) Subject to sections 5 to 8 below, no premises shall be used for a film exhibition unless they are licensed for the purpose under this section.

(2) A licensing authority may grant a licence under this section to such a person as they think fit to use any premises specified in the licence for the purpose of film exhibitions on such terms and conditions and subject to such restrictions as, subject to regulations under section 4 below, they may determine.

(3) Without prejudice to the generality of subsection (2) above, it shall be the duty of a licensing authority, in granting a licence under this section as respects any premises,—

    (*a*) to impose conditions or restrictions prohibiting the admission of children to film exhibitions involving the showing of works designated, by the authority or by such other body as may be specified in the licence, as works unsuitable for children; and

    (*b*) to consider what (if any) conditions or restrictions should be imposed as to the admission of children to other film exhibitions involving the showing of works designated, by the authority or by such other body as may be specified in the licence, as works of such other description as may be so specified.

2. Consent required for exhibitions for children

(1) Subject to sections 5 and 6 below, premises shall be used, except with the consent of the licensing authority, for a film exhibition organised wholly or mainly as an exhibition for children.

(2) Subject to regulations under section 4 below, a licensing authority may, without prejudice to any conditions or restrictions imposed by them on the granting of a licence, impose special conditions or restrictions on the granting of a consent under this section.

---

12 See below, pp. 704–707.

13 For accounts of the Lord Chamberlain's exercise of his powers of censorship, see R. Findlater, *Banned! A Review of Theatrical Censorship in Britain* (1967); N. De Jongh, *Politics, prudery and perversions : the censoring of the English Stage 1901–1968* (2000); P. O'Higgins, *Censorship* (1972), pp. 95–99; G. Robertson, *Freedom, the Individual and the Law* (7th edn, 1993), pp. 238–241.

14 See further on film censorship, N. March Hunnings, *Film Censors and the Law* (1967), pp. 29–148; Williams Committee on Obscenity and Film Censorship (1979) Cmnd. 7772 Appendix 2; J. Trevelyan, *What the Censor Saw* (1973) and 'Film Censorship and the Law' in R. Dhavan and C. Davies (eds.) *Censorship and Obscenity* (1978), pp. 98–108; G. Phelps, *Film Censorship* (1975); B. Brown, *Screen*, Vol. 23 No. 5 p. 2; E. Wistrich, *I Don't Mind the Sex it's the Violence* (1972); G. Robertson, *Freedom, the Individual and the Law* (7th edn, 1993), pp. 258–272; James C. Robertson, *The British Board of Film Censors: Film Censorship in Britain 1896–1950*, and *The Hidden Cinema: British Film Censorship in Action 1913–1975* (2nd edn, 1993); A. Aldgate, *Censorship and the Permissive Society: British Cinema and Theatre 1955–1965* (1995); S. Brody, *Screen Violence and Film Censorship* (HMSO).

NOTES

1. The Cinemas Act 1985 consolidates earlier legislation dating from 1909. By 'film exhibition' is meant any exhibition of moving pictures, but not the simultaneous reception and transmission of television programmes included in a programme service within the meaning of the Broadcasting Act 1990.[15] The licensing authorities are, now, the London boroughs and the common council of the City of London, the district councils elsewhere in England and county and county borough councils in Wales. A right of appeal against refusal, or against conditions imposed, lies to the Crown Court.[16] An appeal lies on behalf of 'any person aggrieved'.[17] Would (should) the following have standing to appeal against a restrictive licensing decision: film distributors; a local resident annoyed at being denied a local opportunity to view a film?[18] Central government responsibility for censorship and video classification now lies with DCMS.

2. In addition to the express obligation imposed on licensing authorities to exercise their functions so as to protect children (under 16), the Act authorises the Secretary of State to make regulations in respect of the 'safety', 'health' and 'welfare' of children attending film exhibitions.[19]

3. Sections 5 and 6 exclude from licensing control certain film exhibitions to which the public are not admitted and which are not presented for private gain. This applies, in particular, to domestic presentations and to members-only, non-commercial, cinema clubs (e.g. non-profit-making film societies). However, since 1982, 'commercial' cinema clubs have been subject to these local authority licensing controls.[20]

4. In *R v Greater London Council, ex p Blackburn*[21] Lord Denning MR said:[1]

'... [The Cinematograph Act 1909] was passed in the early days and was concerned with safety in cinemas, not with censorship.... Although the Act was concerned with safety, nevertheless the courts two years later held that a county council could impose conditions which related to other matters so long as they were not unreasonable. So, in 1911, the courts held that a condition saying that premises should not be opened on Sundays was valid: see *LCC v Bermondsey Bioscope Co Ltd* [1911] 1 KB 445. Soon afterwards the county councils began to insert a condition that no film shown should be of a licentious or indecent character. Such a condition was accepted as valid, but it did not permit any censorship beforehand. Next the county councils tried to insert a power of censorship by delegating it to three justices. This was held to be invalid: see *R v Burnley JJ, ex p Longmore* [1916–17] All ER Rep 346. Once again they tried. They sought to hand over all power of censorship to the British Board of Film Censors, but this was held invalid because the county councils were not allowed to delegate their powers: see *Ellis v Dubowski* [1921] 3 KB 621. But in 1924 there was a breakthrough. The courts gave a decision which allowed censorship by the British Board of Film Censors provided that that body did not have the final say, but was subject to review by the county council itself: see *Mills v LCC* [1925] 1 KB 213. That decision has held the field since that time and must, I think, be accepted as good law. It was recognised as such by Parliament itself[2] when it made it compulsory for conditions to be imposed for the protection

15 1985 Act, s. 21(1); 1990 Act, s. 201.
16 s. 16.
17 For modern judicial discussion of this phrase, see *Cook v Southend Borough Council* [1990] 2 WLR 61.
18 For the scope of appellate review in the Crown Court, see *Sagnata Investments Ltd v Norwich Corpn* [1971] 2 QB 614.
19 s. 4.
20 See s. 20 – restrictive definition of 'private gain'.
21 [1976] 1 WLR 550, CA.
1 At 553.
2 *Ed.* In the Cinematograph Act 1952.

of children. Under that section the county council are under a duty to impose conditions so as to ensure that, if a film is designated as unsuitable for children, then children are not to be admitted to see it. Such designation is to be done 'by the licensing authority or such other body as may be specified in the licence'. In speaking of such other body Parliament no doubt had in mind the British Board of Film Censors. To that extent, therefore, the Board has Parliamentary approval.... The British Board of Film Censors ... goes back for 60 years. There is a president, ... who is responsible for broad policy. There is a secretary, ... who makes executive decisions. There are ... film examiners.... They put films into ... categories, according to their suitability for various age groups.... They sometimes require cuts before giving a certificate. The examiners are recruited from outside the film industry....

I do not think the county councils can delegate the whole of their responsibilities to the board ... but they can treat the board as an advisory body whose views they can accept or reject, provided that the final decision – aye or nay – rests with the county council. If the exhibitor – or any member of the public – brings the film up before the county council, they ought themselves to review the decision of the British Board of Film Censors and exercise their own judgment on it. That is, I think, the right way to interpret *Mills v LCC*. When the Board issues a certificate permitting the exhibition of a film – and the county council take no objection – that is equivalent to a permission by the county council themselves. When the board refuses a certificate, the exhibitor can appeal to the county council....

The upshot of it all is this. The county council are in law the body which has the power to censor films for exhibitions in cinemas, but in practice it is the board which carries out the censorship, subject to review by the county council.'

Most local authorities have adopted the model licensing conditions suggested by the Home Office, which include the following:

(1) no film, other than a current newsreel, shall be exhibited unless it has received a certificate of the British Board of Film Classification or is the subject of the licensing authority's permission;

(2) no young people shall be admitted to any exhibition of a film classified by the Board as unsuitable for them (e.g. no person apparently under 18 to be admitted to an 18 certificate film), unless with the local authority's permission;

(3) no film shall be exhibited if the licensing authority gives notice in writing prohibiting its exhibition on the ground that it 'would offend against good taste or decency or would be likely to encourage or incite to crime or to lead to disorder or to be offensive to public feeling';

(4) the nature of the certificate given to any film shall be indicated in any advertising for the film, at the cinema entrance (together with an explanation of its effect), and on the screen immediately before the film is shown;

(5) displays outside the cinema shall not depict any scene or incident not in the film as approved;

(6) no advertisement shall be displayed at the premises if the licensing authority gives notice in writing objecting to it on the same grounds as apply to the prohibition of films.

Cinema licences in London carry the following additional conditions:

'No film shall be exhibited at the premises—
  (1) which is likely—
       (a) to encourage or to incite to crime; or
       (b) to lead to disorder; or
       (c) to stir up hatred against any section of the public in Great Britain on grounds of colour, race or ethnic or national origins, or sexual orientation or sex; or
       (d) to promote sexual humiliation or degradation of or violence towards women; or
  (2) the effect of which is, if taken as a whole, such as to tend to deprave and corrupt persons who are likely to see it; or
  (3) which contains a grossly indecent performance thereby outraging the standards of public decency.'

5. The film industry established the British Board of Film Censors in 1912 as a response to the assertion, under the 1909 Act, of censorship powers by local authorities. The aim was to establish a body which would be independent of both central and local government and which might help to secure achievement of reasonably informed, and reasonably uniform, decision-making on this matter by councils across the country. Being a non-statutory body its powers (in relation to film) are only those of advice, but in the main, its objectives seem to have been achieved. Councils have been willing to accept the classification decisions of the BBFC in most cases, and film makers have gained familiarity with the criteria adopted by the BBFC in deciding whether or not to grant a certificate, and if so, what viewing classification to impose. Inevitably, not all film makers (as compared with film distributors) have been happy with this system of 'control'. As the previous President of the BBFC, the Earl of Harewood, explained, 'one man's safeguards are another's shackles'. Controversy has arisen, over the years, in connection with numerous films. In some cases councils have chosen to ban a film from being shown in their areas even though it was passed by the BBFC – e.g. *Straw Dogs, Clockwork Orange, Life of Brian*. In other cases councils have chosen to allow films to be shown despite the fact that the BBFC felt unable to grant a certificate – e.g. *More about the Language of Love, Texas Chain Saw Massacre*[3] (both passed by the former Greater London Council). In truth, however, it appears that most councils have no wish to devote resources to the regular scrutiny of films and have been pleased to rely on the judgment of the BBFC.[4]

A virtue of the BBFC system is that decisions are taken by persons who have actually seen the film in question. Film examiners are drawn from outside the film industry, with a balance kept between men and women. They comprise persons with a broad range of ages and backgrounds (including from the ethnic minority communities: note that many films and videos are in foreign languages, designed for Hindi and Cantonese audiences). The examiners usually work in pairs but viewing by one examiner is used where the examination work is known not to be difficult. All proposals from examiners require the approval of a member of BBFC's senior staff (the director, the deputy director and senior examiners) to whom the President of the BBFC has delegated his authority. The BBFC views over 500 films annually; the numbers of videos examined has risen sharply from 3,000 in 1998 to 6,300 in 2000.[5]

By contrast to these arrangements, there have been occasions where a local council has banned the showing of a feature film, basing its decision upon press reports of the film's nature and content alone.[6] In 1988 concern was expressed in the press about the allegedly blasphemous content of a film, *The Last Temptation of Christ* (directed by Martin Scorsese). The Board received some 1,870 letters and petitions about the film even prior to its arrival in the UK. On viewing the film the BBFC came to the conclusion that it was a 'reinterpretation' of Christ's life and passion rather than a scurrilous attack on the Christian religion! An '18' certificate was granted. The BBFC took the view that the film did not contravene the offence of blasphemy. This was, however, not sufficient to prevent the film being banned by a number of local authorities.

3   *The Texas Chain Saw Massacre* was subsequently classified by the BBFC in 1999.
4   See D. Holbrook, (1973) 123 NLJ 701 and correspondence at pp. 754, 775, 794, 833, and 915; and Report of the Williams Committee on Obscenity and Film Censorship (1979) Cmnd. 7772 p. 27.
5   In 2000, 520 cinema features were classified (with only 12 (2.3%) cut and 1 rejected); 5,566 certificates were issued (4 refused) for video (with cuts to 173 (3.1%)); 28 digital works (games and interactive CD-Roms) were classified (with 1 cut): Annual Report for 2000.
6   See, e.g., G. Phelps, *Sight and Sound*, Vol. 42 No. 3 p. 138, discussing press reports about, and local authority decisions in respect of, *Last Tango in Paris*.

The functions of the BBFC (renamed the British Board of Film Classification) were significantly extended in 1985 by the Video Recordings Act 1984.[7] In this connection the BBFC takes decisions which themselves have legal effect under the Act. As regards films it continues to have no more than the power of recommendation to local authorities as to the exercise of their functions.

The Classification Guidelines were reviewed, after public consultation; and a revised paper published in September 2000.[8] This explains the background and role of the BBFC and the legal considerations to which it must have regard.[9] The Classification Principles and Guidelines are as follows:

Classification Principles
In classifying films, videos or digital media, the BBFC also gives consideration to the following basic principles
- – adults should be free to choose what they see, providing that it remains within the law and is not potentially harmful to society
- – works should be allowed to reach the widest audience that is appropriate for their theme and treatment
- – the context in which something (e.g. sex or violence) is presented is central to the question of its acceptability
- – the BBFC's Guidelines will be reviewed periodically in the light of changes in public taste, attitudes and concerns.

The Guidelines
   (i)   There are seven classification categories
   - •   U, Uc and PG which are advisory only
   - •   12, 15 and 18 which restrict viewing by age
   - •   R18 which is only available to adults in licenced outlets
   (ii) Occasionally, a work lies on the margin between the two categories. In making a final judgement, the BBFC takes into account the intentions of the film-maker, the expectations of the public in general and the work's audience in particular, and any special merits of the work.
   (iii) Classification decisions may be stricter on video than on film. This is because of the increased possibility of under-age viewing recognised in the Video Recordings Act, and of works being replayed or viewed out of context. Accordingly, a work may receive a higher age classification on video, or require heavier cuts.
   (iv) Classification decisions are most strict on trailers and advertisements. This is because difficult content, which may be mediated by the context of the original work, may have a much starker effect in the brief and unprepared context of the trailer/advertisement.
   (v)   Classification decisions may be less strict where they are justified by context.
   (vi) Anything not permitted in these Guidelines at a particular category (PG to 18) is unacceptable also at **all** preceding lower categories. Similarly, anything permitted at one level is acceptable at all higher levels.

Main Concerns
This section of the Guidelines sets out some concerns which apply, to a greater or a lesser degree, at all classification levels. The concerns are listed in the same order on the pages following, which provide **specific** guidance for 'U' through to '18'. The guidance there should be read in the light of this more general advice.

---

7   See further, below, p. 663.
8   See the BBFC website, www.bbfc.co.uk.
9   Under the Video Recordings Act 1984, the Cinematography Films (Animals) Act 1937 (which makes it illegal to show any scene 'organised or directed' to involve actual cruelty to animals; this was applied in requiring a cut to the film *Before Night Falls* in June 2001), the Protection of Children Act 1978, the Obscene Publications Act 1959 and 'other unlawful material' (i.e. 'material which is itself unlawful, or has arisen from the commission of an unlawful act').

Theme
The acceptability of a theme is determined by its treatment i.e. the context and sensitivity of its presentation. However, the most problematic themes (for example drug abuse or paedophilia) are unlikely to be appropriate at the most junior levels of classification. Correspondingly, there is no reason in principle why **any** theme, however difficult, could not be satisfactorily handled at '18' or even '15'.

Language
Many people are offended, some of them deeply, by bad language, including the use of expletives with a religious association. The extent of that offence varies according to age, background and beliefs. Different groups (for example, a minority ethnic community) have their own, separate standards of acceptability. Additionally, the severity of any particular word or expression will depend upon the **context** within which it is used.

For these reasons, it is impossible to set out comprehensive lists of acceptable words or expressions which will satisfy all sections of the public. The advice at different classification levels, therefore, provides general guidance with reference to specific terms only where there is a reasonable consensus of opinion.

Nudity
Natural nudity, providing there is no sexual context or sub-text, is acceptable at all classification levels.

Sex
The portrayal of human sexual activity is not permitted at 'U', 'Uc' or 'PG'. In '12' rated works it may be implied only. Progressively more graphic portrayal may be included at '15' and '18' depending on the emphasis given to responsible, loving and developing relationships. There is equality in terms of the standards set for legal heterosexual and homosexual behaviour.

The 'R18' category, required by the Video Recordings Act, is primarily for explicit videos of consenting sex between adults. 'R18' videos may be supplied only in licensed sex shops which no-one under 18 can enter.

Violence
Violence has been a feature of entertainment for children and adults since the first stories were told. It is an element in many serious representations of the human condition. We can, however, address the degree and nature of violence through our classification system.

In making decisions, our concerns include
- portrayal of violence as a normal solution to problems
- heroes who inflict pain and injury
- callousness towards victims
- encouraging aggressive attitudes
- taking pleasure in pain or humiliation

Works which glorify or glamorise violence will receive a more restrictive classification and may even be cut.

SEXUAL VIOLENCE
The BBFC has a strict policy on rape and sexual violence. Where the portrayal eroticises or endorses sexual assault, the Board is likely to require cuts at any classification level. This is more likely with video than film, because video scenes can be replayed repeatedly.

Any association of sex with **non-consensual** restraint, pain or humiliation may be cut.

Imitable Techniques
The BBFC is also concerned about detailed portrayal of criminal and violent techniques and the glamorisation of weapons. The use of weapons which are easily accessible to young people will be restricted. Imitable combat techniques may be cut.

Any action which would be likely to promote illegal or anti-social behaviour in real life is of particular concern. Imitable detail of criminal techniques may be unacceptable at any classification level. Potentially dangerous activity presented as safe and exciting is of particular concern in works aimed at children.

The BBFC is most concerned about videos, where a technique can be watched again and again until the lesson is learned.

Horror
Horror films are subject to the same Guideline constraints as all other films. The BBFC recognises that audiences pay to see horror films because they like being frightened. The Board does not cut films simply because they alarm or shock. Instead, it classifies them to ensure that the young and vulnerable are protected.

Drugs
No work taken as a whole, even at '18', may promote or encourage the use of illegal drugs. Clear instructive detail is unacceptable at all levels up to '15'. Even at '18', such detail may only be acceptable if there are exceptional considerations of context. Glamorising detail is a particular concern.

The dangers of showing instructive detail are particularly acute in videos where scenes can be replayed over and over again.

The Categories

Suitable for all

'U' Universal
It is impossible to predict what might upset any particular child. But a 'U' film should be suitable for audiences aged four years and over. Works aimed at children should be set within a positive moral framework and should offer reassuring counterbalances to any violence, threat or horror.

Theme
Treatment of problematic themes must be sensitive and appropriate to a younger audience.

Language
Infrequent use only of very mild bad language.

Nudity
Occasional natural nudity, with no sexual context.

Sex
Mild sexual behaviour (e.g. kissing) and references only (e.g. to 'making love').

Violence
Mild violence only.
Occasional mild threat or menace only.

Imitable techniques
No emphasis on realistic weapons.

Horror
Horror effects should be mild and brief and should take account of the presence of very young viewers. The outcome should be reassuring.

Drugs
No references to illegal drugs or drug use.

VIDEOS CLASSIFIED 'Uc' ARE PARTICULARLY SUITABLE FOR PRE-SCHOOL CHILDREN[10]

General viewing, but some scenes may be unsuitable for some children

'PG' Parental Guidance
Unaccompanied children of any age may watch. A 'PG' film should not disturb a child aged around eight or older. However, parents are advised to consider whether the content may upset younger or more sensitive children.

---

10 The Uc classification was introduced in 1985 at the request of the video industry.

Theme
More serious issues may be featured, e.g. crime, domestic violence, racism (providing nothing in their treatment condones them).

Language
Mild bad language only.

Nudity
Natural nudity, with no sexual context.

Sex
Sexual activity may be implied, but should be discreet and infrequent. Mild sexual references and innuendo only.

Violence
Moderate violence, without detail, may be allowed – if justified by its setting (e.g. historic, comedy or fantasy).

Imitable techniques
No glamorisation of realistic, contemporary weapons. No detail of fighting or other dangerous techniques.

Horror
Frightening sequences should not be prolonged or intense. Fantasy settings may be a mitigating factor.

Drugs
No references to illegal drugs or drug use unless entirely innocuous.
Suitable only for 12 years and over

'12'[11]
No-one younger than 12 may see a '12' film in a cinema or rent or buy a '12' rated video.

Theme
Mature themes are acceptable, but their treatment must be suitable for younger teenagers.

Language
The use of strong language (e.g. 'fuck') should be rare and must be justified by context.

Nudity
Nudity is allowed, but in a sexual context will be brief and discreet.

Sex
Sexual activity may be implied. Sexual references may reflect the familiarity of most adolescents today with sex education through school.

Violence
Violence must not dwell on detail. There should be no emphasis on injuries or blood. Sexual violence may only be implied or briefly indicated and without physical detail.

Imitable techniques
Dangerous techniques (examples include: combat, hanging, suicides) should contain no imitable detail. Realistic and contemporary weapons should not be glamorised.

Horror
Sustained threat and menace is permitted. Occasional gory moments only.

Drugs
Brief and occasional references to, and sight of, 'soft' drug-taking (e.g. cannabis) are allowed, but must be justified by context and should indicate the dangers. No instructional elements are permitted.

---

11 The '12' category was introduced for films in 1989 to deal with the film *Batman*. It was extended to videos in 1994. The Board is experimenting with a PG12 category.

Suitable only for 15 years and over

'15'
No-one younger than 15 may see a '15' film in a cinema or rent or buy a '15' rated video.

Theme
No theme is prohibited, provided the treatment is appropriate to 15 year olds.

Language
There may be frequent use of strong language; the strongest terms (e.g. 'cunt') are only rarely acceptable. Continued **aggressive** use of strong language and sexual abuse is unacceptable.

Nudity
There are no constraints on nudity in a non-sexual or educational context.

Sex
Sexual activity and nudity may be portrayed but without strong detail. The depiction of casual sex should be handled responsibly. There may be occasional strong verbal references to sexual behaviour.

Violence
Violence may be strong but may not dwell on the infliction of pain, and of injuries. Scenes of sexual violence must be discreet and brief.

Imitable techniques
Dangerous combat techniques such as ear claps, head-butts and blows to the neck are unlikely to be acceptable. There may be no emphasis on the use of easily accessible lethal weapons (in particular, knives).

Horror
Sustained or detailed infliction of pain or injury is unacceptable.

Drugs
Drug taking may be shown but clear instructive detail is unacceptable. The film as a whole must not promote or encourage drug use.

Suitable only for adults

'18'
No-one younger than 18 may see an '18' film in a cinema or rent or buy an '18' rated video.

The BBFC respects the rights of adults to choose their own entertainment, within the law. It will therefore expect to intervene **only rarely** in relation to '18' rated cinema films. In the case of videos, which are more accessible to younger viewers, intervention may be more frequent.
There are no constraints at this level on theme, language, nudity or horror.
The Board may, however, cut or reject the following content:
  - any detailed portrayal of violent or dangerous acts which is likely to promote the activity. This includes also instructive detail of illegal drug use
  - the more explicit images of sexual activity – unless they can be exceptionally justified by context

Sex Education at '18'
Where sex material genuinely seeks to inform and educate in matters such as human sexuality, safe sex and health, exceptions to the normal constraints on explicit images may be made in the public interest. Such explicit detail must be kept to the minimum necessary to illustrate the educational or instructional points being made.

Sex Works at '18'
Material which appears to be simulated is generally passed '18', while images of real sex are confined to the 'R18' category.

To be supplied only in licensed sex shops to adults of not less than 18 years

'R18'

The 'R18' category is a special and legally restricted classification primarily for explicit videos of consenting sex between adults. Such videos may be supplied to adults only in licensed sex shops, of which there are currently about 90 in the UK.[12] 'R18' videos may not be supplied by mail order.

(i)   The following content is not acceptable
- any material which is in breach of the criminal law
- material likely to encourage an interest in abusive sexual activity (e.g. paedophilia, incest) which may include depictions involving adults role-playing as non-adults
- the portrayal of any sexual activity, whether real or simulated, which involves lack of consent
- the infliction of pain or physical harm, real or (in a sexual context) simulated. Some allowance may be made for mild consensual activity
- any sexual threats or humiliation which do not form part of a clearly consenting role-playing game
- the use of any form of physical restraint which prevents participants from withdrawing consent, for example, ball gags
- penetration by any object likely to cause actual harm or associated with violence
- activity which is degrading or dehumanising (examples include the portrayal of bestiality, necrophilia, defecation, urolagnia)

(ii)   The following content, subject to the above, may be permitted
- aroused genitalia
- masturbation
- oral-genital contact including kissing, licking and sucking
- penetration by finger, penis, tongue, vibrator or dildo
- non-harmful fetish material
- group sexual activity
- ejaculation and semen

(iii)   These guidelines make no distinction between heterosexual and homosexual activity.

The Board gives 'consumer advice' about the content of classified works to the public. The policy on 'rejects' is as follows:

'Rejects
Films or videos which are unlawful or potentially harmful will, where possible, be cut. If this is not possible or not acceptable to the distributor, they may be refused classification altogether. 'Taboo' themes are acceptable, but not if their treatment is likely to encourage harm to viewers or, through their behaviour, to society. The following are of greatest concern: graphic rape or torture; sadistic violence or terrorisation; illegal or instructive drug use; material likely to incite racial violence; portrayals of children in a sexualised or violent content; sex accompanied by non-consensual pain, injury or humiliation; bestiality or necrophillia, or other material likely to be found obscene by the courts.'

An appeal lies to the Board or (in the case of videos) the Video Appeals Committee and in the case of films a submission can be made to the licensing authority.
6. If a film or video is considered to be obscene within the meaning of the Obscene Publications Acts,[13] or is considered to offend against some other aspect of the criminal law, a certificate will be refused altogether. In 1989 the BBFC refused a certificate to an 18-minute erotic video, *Visions of Ecstasy*, on grounds of blasphemy.

12 See n. **6** below.
13 See further, below, pp. 682–704.

Its nudity and sexual imagery were well within the normal bounds of an '18' classification. However, the sexual imagery focused on the crucified figure of Christ, and featured overt expressions of sexuality on the part of a nun. Having taken legal advice on the issue of blasphemy the BBFC[14] denied a certificate, and the decision was upheld by the Video Appeals Committee.

The BBFC has been willing in its Annual Reports, press releases and elsewhere, to explain its approach to certain issues which it has to tackle. One long-term theme is that there has been a dramatic decline in the number of films cut for cinema release, from 40% of the total in 1974 to under 4% in 1999.[15] James Ferman, who was Director of the BBFC between 1975 and 1999, regarded violence as the key issue during his tenure, particularly sexual violence,[16] and this concern has continued.[17] The public consultation and research that led to the adoption of the new BBFC Classification Guidelines showed that the large majority of the public wanted 12, 15 and 18 classification categories to remain mandatory; the public wanted more consumer information, did not want the BBFC to intervene unnecessarily at '18', continued to be concerned about children, but did not mind explicit portrayals of sexual activity in adult films.[18] The consultation involved the publication of draft guidelines followed by a series of public meetings or 'road shows', and was a model of its kind.

Examples of issues arising in recent years include the following. In 1997 there was much media and public concern about such films as *Lolita*, *Crash*,[19] *Gummo* and *Kissed*; all were classified '18' and 'public complaints evaporated once they had been released.' Following extensive test screenings to 478 children aged 6 to 11 and consultation with their teachers, *The Lost World – Jurassic Park* was classified 'PG'.[20] In 1998, the Board was 'at pains to moderate the levels of "violence as entertainment" in films like *Lethal Weapon 4*, where the distributors collaborated with the Board in toning down the blood-letting, cutting neck-breaks, head butts, garottings, eye-gougings, and the noisy breaking of bones' in order to achieve a '15' rather than an '18'. *Saving Private Ryan* was welcomed for exploring rather than exploiting violence and was deemed appropriate for a mid-teens audience. A cut to a 'vicious head-butt' was needed in *Mulan* in view of the risks of copycat violence. Five videos were refused certificates; two were serial killer-films in which sex was linked with the pleasure of killing and this juxtaposition was likely to have a dangerous impact on some vulnerable viewers; *Changing Room Exposed* was rejected on the ground that a video which invaded the privacy of a men's changing room without the knowledge or consent of those being photographed breached Art 8 ECHR; *Deadbeat at Dawn* was so incessantly violent that it breached the harm condition in the 1984 Act; *Makin' Whoopee* was an explicit sex video, where refusal of classification was overturned on appeal.[1] 1999 generated rather more controversy. Two videos were rejected, *Banned From Television*, a compilation of real scenes of extremely violent death, injury and mutilation and *Bare Fist – The Sport That Wouldn't Die*, a documentary on the illegal sport of bare-fist fighting. *A Clockwork Orange*, previously passed 'X' in 1971 and subsequently withdrawn by its director, Stanley Kubrick, was resubmitted for a modern classification and classified '18', being regarded as a serious exploration

---

14 See below.
15 Annual Reports for 1997–98 and 1999.
16 Annual Report for 1998.
17 Annual Report for 1999.
18 Ibid.
19 See BBFC Press Notice, 18 March 1997, summarising the legal and other expert advice taken by the Board. Most of the unsolicited advice received was from people 'troubled or outraged by rumours'.
20 Annual Report for 1997–98.
 1 Annual Report for 1998; see below, p. 666.

of both individual and state violence. *The Exorcist* was classified at '18' for video release. *The Texas Chain Saw Massacre* was classified at '18' uncut for both cinema and video release; it had been approved for showing by a number of local authorities in the 1970s but contained much less graphic violence than many subsequent works passed at '18'. Other notorious 'video nasties' from the 1980s were passed after cuts made by the distributor prior to submission to the BBFC. *A Cat in the Brain* was rejected because of the profusion of gross sexual violence. Overall, cuts were required in 22 videos on sexual violence grounds, although fewer problematic videos were submitted than in previous years. *Straw Dogs* was refused a '18' certificate following the distributor's refusal to make extensive cuts to a rape sequence filmed in a manner which could arouse some viewers and endorse the male myth that women enjoy being raped. Particular difficulties were encountered in respect of the sexual content of three foreign language 'art house' films, *The Idiots*, *Romance*, and *Seal Contre Tous*, but all were passed at '18' with minimal or no cuts.[2] Similarly, in 2001, the film *Baise Moi* was passed '18' with one cut to a scene of violent rape. This involved extreme sexual imagery that caused the scene to take on a more explicitly pornographic dimension. However, brief graphic sexual images elsewhere in the film were acceptable; none occurred in a context of rape or violence, the female protagonists remained in control of events and the film had a serious cultural purpose; the images did not have the primary purpose of providing sexual satisfaction to the viewer.[3] *The Lord of the Rings – The Fellowship of the Ring* was given a PG rating with consumer advice.

Illustrative of other concerns of the BBFC, the film *Amores Perros* was passed '18' uncut, the Board being satisfied that no animals were harmed during the making of the film.[4] Cuts to films for young people and children in respect of neck chops and double ear-claps, which may result in serious harm, were seen to be vindicated when several children were taken to hospital with punctured ear drums following the depiction of such action during an advertisement for Tango orange drink.[5]

6. The Local Government (Miscellaneous Provisions) Act 1982, s. 2 provides that district councils,[6] the London boroughs, and the Common Council of the City of London may by resolution, followed by public notice, adopt the provisions of Sch. 3 to the Act relating to the 'Control of Sex Establishments'. This Schedule provides, on pain of criminal penalty, that 'no person shall knowingly ... use any premises, vehicle, vessel or stall as a sex establishment except under and in accordance with the terms of a licence granted' by the local authority.[7] Paragraphs 8–11 lay down in some detail the procedure for applying for the grant, renewal or transfer of such a licence, and for the handling of such applications by the local authority (e.g. public notice of the application, account to be taken of objectors' views, rights of appearance for the applicant prior to an adverse decision). Paragraph 12 lists persons and bodies to whom licences 'shall not be granted' (e.g. persons under 18, bodies incorporated outside the UK), and states, in respect of eligible applicants, the grounds on which applications may be refused (e.g. the unsuitability of the applicant; the number of sex establishments in the locality already being such as the local authority thinks appropriate – which number may be nil; the character of the locality; the use to which premises in the vicinity are put). Paragraph 13 empowers local authorities to make

2 Annual Report for 1999.
3 BBFC Press Notice, 26 February 2001.
4 BBFC Press Notice, 26 February 2001.
5 Annual Report for 1992.
6 In Wales, the county and county borough councils.
7 Para. 6(1). For the requirement of mens rea see *Westminster City Council v Croyalgrange Ltd* [1986] 2 All ER 353, HL.

regulations prescribing standard conditions applicable to licences granted (e.g. relating to displays, or the visibility of the interior to passers-by). Paragraphs 17 and 18 provide for the variation and revocation of licences, and para. 19 authorises authorities to charge for licences 'a reasonable fee' – a power interpreted by some authorities as authorising annual fees of several thousand pounds. Paragraph 27 provides that unsuccessful applicants, applicants aggrieved by conditions, and holders whose licences have been revoked may appeal on the 'merits' to the magistrates' court, with a further right of appeal to the Crown Court.

Note that the possession of a licence under the Schedule provides no legal immunity in respect of charges of any offence at common law or under any enactment (except, of course, the offence under the Schedule itself). Nor does it protect against forfeiture proceedings under, e.g., the Obscene Publications Act 1959.[8]

The expression 'sex establishment' means a 'sex cinema' or a 'sex shop', and these terms are themselves further defined. 'Sex cinema' means premises etc. used to a 'significant degree' (a much criticised expression) for the exhibition of 'moving pictures, by whatever means produced' which:

(1) are concerned primarily with the portrayal of, or primarily deal with or relate to, or are intended to stimulate or encourage –

    (i)   sexual activity; or

    (ii)   acts of force or restraint which are associated with sexual activity; or

(2) are concerned primarily with the portrayal of, or primarily deal with or relate to, genital organs or urinary or excretory functions.

Likewise, 'sex shop' means premises etc. used for a 'business which consists to a significant degree of selling, hiring, exchanging, lending, displaying or demonstrating 'sex articles' (itself further defined) or 'other things intended for use in connection with, or for the purpose of stimulating or encouraging (i) sexual activity; or (ii) acts of force or restraint which are associated with sexual activity'. The local authority may only refuse a licence on one or more of the grounds set out in the Act. There is no discretion to refuse a licence simply on the basis of the disapproval of sex establishments on moral grounds.[9] In 2000 there were about 90 licensed sex shops in the country.

By virtue of the Greater London Council (General Powers) Act 1986, London borough councils may, by adopting the amendment to Sch. 3 to the 1982 Act embodied in s. 12(4) of the 1986 Act, exercise still further controls. The amended Sch. 3 extends, for the benefit of such adopting councils, the notion of 'sex establishment' to embrace also what are called 'sex encounter establishments'. Such premises comprise, *inter alia*, those at which:

'performances ... are given by one or more persons present and performing, which wholly or mainly comprise the sexual stimulation of persons admitted to the premises (whether by verbal or any other means); or, ... [where] any services ... which do not include sexual activity are provided by one or more persons who are without clothes or who expose their breasts or genital, urinary or excretory organs at any time while they are providing the service;

---

8   Below, p. 698.

9   *R v Newcastle upon Tyne City Council, ex p the Christian Institute* [2001] LQR 165; cf. *R v Birmingham District Council, ex p Sheptonhurst Ltd* (1989) 87 LGR 830 (council entitled to refuse renewal of licence notwithstanding lack of any change in the locality's character, provided it gave rational reasons and had regard for the fact that licence had previously been granted); *R v Bridgenorth City Council, ex p Prime Time Promotions Ltd* [1990] 1 All ER 1026 (refusal of a licence to supply R18 videos by mail order quashed as irrational); *R v Wandsworth London Borough Council, ex p Darker Enterprises Ltd* (1999) 1 LGLR 601 (council entitled to refuse renewal where character of locality had improved).

or ... [where] entertainments ... are provided by one or more persons who are without clothes...'[10]

Finally, it should be noted that a local authority may attach conditions to entertainment licences granted under Part I of the Local Government (Miscellaneous Provisions) Act 1982 regulating the sexual content of the entertainment.[11] For example, the City of Nottingham has a no-nudity policy, to which exceptions can be made in appropriate cases, such as a piece of performance art about lap dancers and strippers presented at Nottingham Trent University's Bonington Gallery.[12]

7. *Videos.* The Video Recordings Act 1984 established 'censorship' controls over the distribution of video recordings. The need felt for some such control stemmed from concern over 'video-nasties'; and, in particular, newspaper assertions as to the large numbers of children who were viewing such videos.[13] The provisions of the 1984 Act, superseding an earlier 'voluntary' BBFC classification system, extend beyond those necessary simply to deal with the 'video-nasties' problem, and have introduced for video a thorough-going statutory system of video classification and censorship modelled on that which has long applied to the cinema.

The basic offences under the Act are those of (i) supplying, or offering to supply, a video recording of an unclassified work, (ii) possessing such a recording for the purposes of supply, and (iii) supplying a video recording in breach of its classification.[14] The Act provides quite complex definitions of terms used. 'Video recording' refers to the disc, tape or any other device capable of storing data electronically containing the 'video work': any 'series of visual images' that is 'produced electronically by the use of information contained on any disc and shown as a moving picture,[15] magnetic tape or any other device capable of storing data electronically'. 'Supply' need not be for reward, and includes sales, lettings on hire, exchanges and loans.[16] 'Classified' means that a 'classification certificate' has been issued by the BBFC. Where such a certificate is issued it must state (i) that the work is suitable for general viewing and unrestricted supply, or (ii) that the work is suitable for viewing only by persons above an age specified in the certificate (not being more than 18) and that no recording containing the work is to be supplied to any person below that age, or (iii) that in addition to the statement in (ii) above, no recording containing the work is to be supplied other than in a licensed sex shop (the R18 category).[17] Some video works will be refused classification certificates altogether. In reaching its decisions the designated authority is required to have 'special regard to the likelihood of video works ... being viewed in the home'.[18] The letter of designation to the BBFC specifically enjoins it 'to seek to avoid classifying works which are obscene within the meaning of the Obscene Publications Acts 1959 and

10 For prosecution of the proprietor of an unlicensed Soho 'peep-show', see *McMonagle v Westminster City Council* [1990] 1 All ER 991, HL; see also *Smakowski v Westminster City Council* (1989) 154 JP 345 (no need to adduce evidence of actual stimulation of a member of the audience); *Willowcell v Westmister City Council* (1996) 94 LGR 83 (peep-shows with sexually explicit performances by naked or semi-naked women not covered by music and dancing licence but required licence as sex encounter establishment).
11 Cf. *North v Westminster City Council* (unreported, 30 March 1994), in respect of public entertainment licences in London.
12 *Nottingham Evening Post*, 14 March 2001.
13 See further, J. Petley, *Screen*, Vol. 25 No. 2 p. 68.
14 ss. 9–11.
15 The brevity of the display of the images is irrelevant provided the sequence is long enough to show continuity of movement: *Meechie v Multi-Media Market (Canterbury) Ltd* (1995) 94 LGR 474.
16 s. 1, as amended by the Criminal Justice and Public Order Act 1994, s. 89.
17 s. 7; see above, p. 659.
18 s. 4(1)(a).

1964 or which infringe other provisions of the criminal law'. This includes the law of blasphemy.[19]

The certification requirements do not, however, apply to 'exempted works' or to 'exempted supplies'. The former are works which, taken as a whole, are designed to 'inform, educate or instruct', are concerned with 'sport, religion or music' or are 'video games'. However, such works are not exempt if to any significant extent they depict 'human sexual activity[20] or acts of force or restraint associated with such activity; mutilation or torture of, or other acts of gross violence towards, humans or animals; human genital organs or human urinary or excretory functions; or techniques likely to be useful in the commission of offences. Exemption is also forfeit if a work is likely to any significant extent to stimulate or encourage sexual activity, is likely to any extent to encourage gross violence to humans or animals, or depicts criminal activity which is likely to stimulate or encourage commission of offences.[1] 'Exempted supplies' include supplies other than for reward and not in the course or furtherance of business, and supplies to participants of recordings of events or occasions so long as not significantly depicting anything referred to in s. 2,[2] i.e. the video-recording of a wedding ceremony but not the honeymoon. If dissatisfied with a decision of the BBFC in relation to a video recording an appeal may be taken to the Video Appeals Committee. Enforcement of the provisions of the 1984 Act became in 1988 a matter for local 'weights and measures' authorities.[3]

A general defence was added by the Video Recordings Act 1993: it is a defence to a charge of committing any offence under the 1984 Act 'to prove (a) that the commission of the offence was due to the act or default of a person other than the accused, and (b) that the accused took all reasonable precautions and exercised all due diligence to avoid the commission of the offence by any person under his control'.[4]

In the autumn of 1993 two young boys were convicted of the murder of two-year-old James Bulger. In passing sentence the trial judge, Morland J, commented that there might have been some connection between the behaviour of the two boys and the fact that the father of one of them had over the previous year rented several hundred 'adult' videos, including one of particular notoriety.[5]

Subsequently, there was much press coverage of a report authored by Professor Elizabeth Newson, a professor of developmental psychology, in which, purporting to speak also for others in her profession, she wrote:

'Many of us hold our liberal freedom of expression dear, but begin to feel we were naive in our failure to predict the extent of damaging material and its all too free availability to children. It now seems that professionals in child health and psychology underestimated the degree of brutality and sustained sadism that film makers were capable of inventing and willing to portray ... and we certainly underestimated how easy would be children's access to them.'[6]

---

19 This includes the law of blasphemous libel: see *Wingrove v United Kingdom* (1996) 24 EHRR 1, where the ECtHR found no violation of Art. 10 ECHR in the refusal to classify a video, the Visions of Ecstasy, which included erotic scenes involving St Teresa and Christ.
20 Activity short of masturbation may qualify for this description: *Meechie v Multi-Media Marketing (Canterbury) Ltd* (1995) 94 LGR 474.
1 s. 2.
2 Above.
3 s. 16A, as amended by the Criminal Justice Act 1988, s. 162 and the Criminal Justice and Public Order Act 1994, s. 91.
4 s. 14A.
5 *Child's Play 3.*
6 *Sunday Times*, 3 April 1994. See E. Newson, *Video Violence and the Protection of Children*, Report of the Home Affairs Committee, 29 June 1994.

This apparent change of stance amongst child development professionals at one and the same time spurred on those who sought tighter controls over video content and availability, and also produced a critical response on the part of those who had studied the evidence as regards the particular effect of film on children and others. For example, Dr Guy Cumberbatch (an academic applied psychologist) was quoted as commenting that although research showed that violent children liked violent films there was no firm evidence to show that such films cause violent or criminal behaviour. Studies suggesting the contrary, mostly American, have been difficult to replicate this side of the Atlantic.[7] Further concern was expressed by film-makers themselves. In a letter to *The Times*[8] nine leading film directors commented,

'This is the most heavily censored country in Europe and also the one with the largest prison population. We only have to point to the lower crime rates in countries such as Japan and Holland, where there is minimal censorship, to question the validity of any further restrictive measures. Although there is no conclusive research that the viewing of violent images results in violent activity, there is research that shows that deprivation within society and the family can lead to criminality.... The Victorian era is often referred to with nostalgia but juvenile crime and child prostitution were rife—and there were no videos, TV or films to blame then. Freedom of expression is essential for any democracy and trying to cover the wounds in our society by curtailing that freedom is dangerous and short-sighted.'

The response of Government was to incorporate the following provisions into the Criminal Justice and Public Order Bill, then before the House of Commons. Section 4A of the 1984 Act, inserted by s. 90 of the 1994 Act, now provides matters to which the BBFC is required to have 'special regard' in the exercise of its functions under the 1984 Act. Such special regard shall be had to:

'any harm that may be caused to potential viewers or, through their behaviour, to society by the manner in which the work deals with – (a) criminal behaviour, (b) illegal drugs, (c) violent behaviour or incidents, (d) horrific behaviour or incidents, or (e) human sexual activity.'

For the purposes of this section, 'potential viewer' means 'any person (including a child or young person) who is likely to view the video work in question' if a certificate (or one of a particular description) were issued.

The 1994 Act also stiffened the penalties which may be imposed following conviction for offences under the 1984 Act. Thus, for example, in relation to the principal offence under s. 9 (supplying video recording of an unclassified work) trial may now be on indictment (formerly summary only); and in either case a prison term may be imposed (maximum two years and six months respectively).

The Video Appeals Committee has overturned decisions of the BBFC in a number of cases.

In 1989 the BBFC refused a certificate to *International Guerrillas*, a video which appeared to depict the author, Salman Rushdie, as a drunken murderer of muslims. The BBFC feared that the video might be blasphemous. The Appeals Committee rejected this view.[9] A second refusal by the Board was based upon the view that the video involved a *criminal* libel of Rushdie. This decision was also overturned by the Appeals Committee, following a plea against such censorship from Rushdie himself.

---

7   For a critical response to the Newson Report, see M. Barker and J. Petley, *Ill Effects: The Media Violence Debate* (1997), discussed by L. Bibbings, (1998) 3 Communications Law 103. Bibbings also reviews a series of other reports on media violence, noting the difficulties of defining and coding 'violence' and the continuing absence of cogent evidence that video violence causes crime.

8   28 May 1994.

9   See further on blasphemy, below, pp. 1045–1053.

In 1997, the BBFC unilaterally relaxed its guidelines, and classified a number of videos containing more explicit material than previously classified, including scenes of actual penetration and oral sex. The Home Secretary was concerned that this was inconsistent with the approach taken by the customs and police in seizing material under, respectively, the Customs Consolidation Act 1876 and the Obscene Publications Act 1959. He instructed the BBFC to rescind the policy change. Accordingly, in 1998, the BBFC refused to classify *Makin' Whoopee!* that had been given an interim classification certificate under the revised guidelines. However the publishers successfully appealed to the Video Appeal Committee, which took the view that it was not obscene. The Board gave it a R18 classification, but refused to regard the decision as a precedent. Further explicit videos were refused classification. Seven were the subject of successful appeals to the VAC. The BBFC's application for judicial review of the VAC's decision was dismissed by Hooper J in *R v Video Appeals Committee of the British Board of Film Classification, ex p British Board of Film Classification*.[10] It was found that the VAC had applied the s. 4A criteria and was entitled to conclude that the risk of the videos being viewed by and causing harm to children and young persons was, on the present evidence, insignificant, and so a R18 classification should be granted. The approach adopted by the BBFC was that where the risk of harm to children was unquantifiable (as here) certification should be refused until the risk was quantified and shown to be acceptable in the light of the other factors. This approach was itself reasonable, but the VAC was entitled not to adopt it. Where harm is thought to be certain to even a small number of children, what justifications are there for the classification of highly explicit videos? The BBFC decided not to appeal and reconsidered the R18 Guidelines in the light of the judgment.[11] New guidelines were published that spelled out clearly what was *not* acceptable as well as what was allowed.[12]

The VAC's decision led to the issue of a consultation paper by the Home Office,[13] which noted that 'there remains substantial public concern that such material may fall into the hands of children' and 'that the mechanistic and impersonal way sexual activity can be portrayed in the videos could cause harm to children if they view it.'[14]

Options for reform involved: (1) amending s. 4A so that at 'potential viewer' would be 'any person (including a child or young person) who *may* view the video work in question'; (2) the creation of criminal offences of showing a R18 video to a child, allowing a child to watch an R18 video; and failing to take reasonable care to prevent a child from watching a R18 video; (3) re-establishing the VAC as a statutory body or modernising its existing recruitment and appointment procedures. As to (3), the Home Office had received a large number of letters to the effect that the VAC was unrepresentative and unaccountable, although it also noted it reported annually and held hearings in public. The BBFC's response was that option (1) would not have a useful effect, and suggested some different changes, but noted that there would still be the fundamental difficulty of providing firm evidence of harm. The law enforcement agencies would comment on whether offences likely to take place in the privacy of the home would be enforceable. It did not support the criticisms of the VAC. However, as the BBFC's decisions were based on Guidelines based on research and consultation, it recommended that the VAC's jurisdiction be limited to deciding

10 [2000] COD 239.
11 BBFC News Release, 22 May 2000.
12 BBFC News Release, 18 July 2000. Incorporated in the September 2000 reissue: above, p. 654.
13 *Home Office, Consultation Paper on the Regulation of R18 Videos*, July 200.
14 Para. 2.7.

whether the BBFC had been fair, consistent and legally correct in the application of the published policy and guidelines.[15]

Research published in 2000 based on interviews with 38 leading psychiatrists, psychologists and social workers showed that while a majority believed that pornography would be harmful to any child, case load evidence to that effect was rare; the majority of children being exposed to pornography were usually being harmed in other ways.[16]

The BBFC is assisted in this aspect of its work by a Video Consultative Council (established under the 1984 Act), with members from local authorities, the industry and other areas of expertise, and an Advisory Panel on Children's Viewing (set up in 1999).[17]

3 Broadcasting

In this section we shall be principally concerned with the following issues – (i) the independence of broadcasting authorities from governmental influence and control; (ii) the political impartiality of the broadcasting media – issues of political 'neutrality' and political 'balance'; and (iii) the regulation and enforcement of standards to be observed by broadcasters as regards matters of sex, violence, taste and decency.

The importance of these issues is easily demonstrated. In the modern world most people obtain the bulk of their information on matters of contemporary interest from the broadcasting media. A state which controls the broadcasters thereby possesses considerable power to manipulate opinion. There should, therefore, be a presumption in any Western-style democracy against governmental influence over broadcasters. Any influence or control should be restricted to wholly exceptional or emergency situations; and even then the fact of influence should, wherever possible, be declared to viewers and listeners.

As worrying as governmental influence over broadcasting is the possibility of limits being imposed, on what is broadcast, by those in control of the broadcasting stations. How independent, and how influential, are the, government appointed, Governors of the BBC? Who owns the 'independent' television and radio channels? Might the identity of the corporate owner make certain issues taboo? Might ownership of a broadcasting station be regarded as a way of wielding corporate political influence? These questions have commonly been raised in Britain in relation to ownership of the press. They are coming to be asked in relation to television and radio. During the 1980s, and also now in the 1990s, the BBC has, on several occasions, encountered the hostility of members of the Government and of the Conservative Party; and it was not clear to all observers that the Governors were as resistant to governmental influence and as supportive of broadcasters as might have been the case.

The 1990s have seen new arrangements for the franchising of independent television and radio. Provided a 'quality control' threshold is satisfied, the franchise under the terms of the Broadcasting Act 1990, goes to the highest bidder. Some safeguards are, however, provided. Provisions exist to prevent any individual or corporation achieving an excessive degree of media dominance. Also, the tradition in British broadcasting that no overt editorial stance shall be taken continues in force. Moreover, the new legislation preserves, and elaborates upon, the traditional obligation, as a part of the requirement of station neutrality, to achieve 'political balance' in programmes.

15 BBFC News Release, 26 October 2000.
16 BBFC News Release, 2000.
17 BBFC Annual Report for 1999.

As well as being of prime significance in the way in which it informs us, and moulds our ideas, the broadcasting medium is unique in the way in which it 'intrudes' into our homes. Individuals can quite easily choose to avoid reading books, or looking through magazines, or watching films or videos, if these will offend them. By contrast, there appears to be a public expectation that television and radio should, although 'invited' into the home, behave there as reasonable guests, not offending or outraging those who might be expected to be watching at the time in question. Controversy here, inevitably, concerns the point at which the mark is overstepped. What one person may regard as an appropriately forceful presentation, in dramatic form or as a news or current affairs item, of an important issue of the day, will likely shock or affront another. Difficulty in drawing this line should not mean that such issues be avoided, nor that they should be treated in a wholly anodyne way.[18]

Broadcasting Act 1990

[Section 1[19] established, as from 1 January 1991, the Independent Television Commission. This public body has replaced the former Independent Broadcasting Authority and the Cable Authority. It licenses and regulates non-BBC and S4C television services – these include Channels 3 and 4 and 5 and cable and satellite services (including multiplex and digital services). Section 2 and teletext services requires that the ITC discharge its licensing functions under Part I of the 1990 Act and Part I of the Broadcasting Act 1996 in the manner it considers best to ensure that a wide range of television programme services is available throughout the UK, and that the programmes (taken as a whole) are of high quality and calculated to appeal to a variety of tastes and interests. During 1991 the ITC was engaged in allocating 16 new Channel 3 licences, operative from 1 January 1993. The ITC was required to allocate these by competitive tender (i.e. to the highest bidder), subject to the tenderer satisfying certain threshold qualifying criteria. Thus, the ITC may not grant a licence to any person unless 'satisfied that he is a fit and proper person to hold it'; moreover, the ITC must do all it can to ensure that a franchise owner is not a person falling within Sch. 2 of the Act, imposing restrictions on the holding of licences (non-EEC nationals, political bodies, religious bodies, advertising agencies, prevention of accumulations of interests in licensed services, and restrictions on controlling interests in both the press and broadcasting services). Licences are not transferable except with the consent of the ITC.]

6. General requirements as to licensed services

(1) The Commission shall do all that they can to secure that every licensed service complies with the following requirements, namely—

    (*a*) that nothing is included in its programmes which offends against good taste or decency or is likely to encourage or incite to crime or to lead to disorder or to be offensive to public feeling;

    (*b*) that any news given (in whatever form) in its programmes is presented with due accuracy and impartiality;

    (*c*) that due impartiality is preserved on the part of the person providing the service as respects matters of political or industrial controversy or relating to current public policy;

    (*d*) that due responsibility is exercised with respect to the content of any of its programmes which are religious programmes, and that in particular any such programmes do not involve—

18 See generally T. Gibbons, *Regulating the Media* (2nd edn, 1998); M. Feintuck, *Media Regulation, Public Interest and the Law* (1999); N. Reville, *Broadcasting Law and Practice* (1997).

19 As amended by the Broadcasting Act 1996, Schs. 10, 11, S.I. 1997 No. 1682 and S.I. 1998 No. 3196.

      (i)   any improper exploitation of any susceptibilities of those watching the programmes, or

     (ii)   any abusive treatment of the religious views and beliefs of those belonging to a particular religion or religious denomination; and

  (*e*)   that its programmes do not include any technical device which, by using images of very brief duration or by any other means, exploits the possibility of conveying a message to, or otherwise influencing the minds of, persons watching the programmes without their being aware, or fully aware, of what has occurred.

(2) In applying subsection (1)(*c*) a series of programmes may be considered as a whole.

(3) The Commission shall—

  (*a*)   draw up, and from time to time review, a code giving guidance as to the rules to be observed in connection with the application of subsection (1)(c) in relation to licensed services; and

  (*b*)   do all that they can to secure that the provisions of the code are observed in the provision of licensed services;

and the Commission may make different provision in the code for different cases or circumstances.

(4) Without prejudice to the generality of subsection (1), the Commission shall do all that they can to secure that there are excluded from the programmes included in a licensed service all expressions of the views and opinions of the person providing the service on matters (other than the provision of programme services) which are of political or industrial controversy or relate to current public policy.

(5) The rules specified in the code referred to in subsection (3) shall, in particular, take account of the following matters—

  (*a*)   that due impartiality should be preserved on the part of the person providing a licensed service as respects major matters falling within subsection (1)(*c*) as well as matters falling within that provision taken as a whole; and

  (*b*)   the need to determine what constitutes a series of programmes for the purposes of subsection (2).

(6) The rules so specified shall, in addition, indicate to such extent as the Commission consider appropriate—

  (*a*)   what due impartiality does and does not require, either generally or in relation to particular circumstances;

  (*b*)   the ways in which due impartiality may be achieved in connection with programmes of particular descriptions;

  (*c*)   the period within which a programme should be included in a licensed service if its inclusion is intended to secure that due impartiality is achieved for the purposes of subsection (1)(*c*) in connection with that programme and any programme previously included in that service taken together; and

  (*d*)   in relation to any inclusion in a licensed service of a series of programmes which is of a description specified in the rules—

      (i)   that the dates and times of the other programmes comprised in the series should be announced at the time when the first programme so comprised is included in that service, or

     (ii)   if that is not practicable, that advance notice should be given by other means of subsequent programmes so comprised which include material intended to secure, or assist in securing, that due impartiality is achieved in connection with the series as a whole;

and those rules shall, in particular, indicate that due impartiality does not require absolute neutrality on every issue or detachment from fundamental democratic principles.

(7) The Commission shall publish the code drawn up under subsection (3)....

7. General code for programmes

(1) The Commission shall draw up, and from time to time review, a code giving guidance—

  (*a*)   as to the rules to be observed with respect to the showing of violence, or the inclusion of sounds suggestive of violence, in programmes included in licensed services, particularly when large numbers of children and young persons may be expected to be watching the programmes;

(b) as to the rules to be observed with respect to the inclusion in such programmes of appeals for donations; and

(c) as to such other matters concerning standards and practice for such programmes as the Commission may consider suitable for inclusion in the code;

and the Commission shall do all that they can to secure that the provisions of the code are observed in the provision of licensed services.

(2) In considering what other matters ought to be included in the code in pursuance of subsection (1)(c), the Commission shall have special regard to programmes included in licensed services in circumstances such that large numbers of children and young persons may be expected to be watching the programmes.

(3)...

(4)The Commission shall publish the code ...

8. General provisions as to advertisements

(1)The Commission shall do all that they can to secure that the rules specified in subsection (2) are complied with in relation to licensed services.

(2)Those rules are as follows—

(a) a licensed service must not include—

(i) any advertisement which is inserted by or on behalf of any body whose objects are wholly or mainly of a political nature,

(ii) any advertisement which is directed towards any political end, or

(iii) any advertisement which has any relation to any industrial dispute (other than an advertisement of a public service nature inserted by, or on behalf of, a government department);

(b) in the acceptance of advertisements for inclusion in a licensed service there must be no unreasonable discrimination either against or in favour of any particular advertiser; and

(c) a licensed service must not, without the previous approval of the Commission, include a programme which is sponsored by any person whose business consists, wholly or mainly, in the manufacture or supply of a product, or in the provision of a service, which the licence holder is prohibited from advertising by virtue of any provision of section 9.

(3) Nothing in subsection (2) shall be construed as prohibiting the inclusion in a licensed service of any party political broadcast which complies with the rules (so far as applicable) made by the Commission....

9. Control of advertisements

(1)It shall be the duty of the Commission—

(a) after the appropriate consultation, to draw up, and from time to time review, a code—

(i) governing standards and practice in advertising and in the sponsoring of programmes, and

(ii) prescribing the advertisements and methods of advertising or sponsorship to be prohibited, or to be prohibited in particular circumstances; and

(b) to do all that they can to secure that the provisions of the code are observed in the provision of licensed services ...

and the Commission may make different provision in the code for different kinds of licensed services.

(7) The Commission may give directions to persons holding any class of licences with respect to the times when advertisements are to be allowed.

(8) Directions under this section may be, to any degree, either general or specific and qualified or unqualified; and directions under subsection (7) may, in particular, relate to—

(a) the maximum amount of time to be given to advertisements in any hour or other period,

(b) the minimum interval which must elapse between any two periods given over to advertisements and the number of such periods to be allowed in any programme in any hour or day,

(c) the exclusion of advertisements from a specified part of a licensed service,

and may make different provision for different parts of the day, different days of the week, different types of programmes or for other differing circumstances ...

10. Government control over licensed services

(1) If it appears to him to be necessary or expedient to do so in connection with his functions as such, the Secretary of State or any other Minister of the Crown may at any time by notice require the Commission to direct the holders of any licences specified in the notice to publish in their licensed services, at such times as may be specified in the notice, such announcement as is so specified, with or without visual images of any picture, scene or object mentioned in the announcement; and it shall be the duty of the Commission to comply with the notice.

(2) Where the holder of a licence publishes any announcement in pursuance of a direction under subsection (1), he may announce that he is doing so in pursuance of such a direction.

(3) The Secretary of State may at any time by notice require the Commission to direct the holders of any licences specified in the notice to refrain from including in the programmes included in their licensed services any matter or classes of matter specified in the notice; and it shall be the duty of the Commission to comply with the notice.

(4) Where the Commission—

    (*a*) have given the holder of any licence a direction in accordance with a notice under subsection (3), or

    (*b*) in consequence of the revocation by the Secretary of State of such a notice, have revoked such a direction,

or where such a notice has expired, the holder of the licence in question may publish in the licensed service an announcement of the giving or revocation of the direction or of the expiration of the notice, as the case may be.

11. Monitoring by Commission of programmes included in licensed services

(1) For the purpose of maintaining supervision over the programmes included in licensed services the Commission may make and use recordings of those programmes or any part of them.

(2) A licence shall include conditions requiring the licence holder—

    (*a*) to retain, for a period not exceeding 90 days, a recording of every programme included in the licensed service;

    (*b*) at the request of the Commission, to produce to them any such recording for examination or reproduction;

    (*c*) at the request of the Commission, to produce to them any script or transcript of a programme included in the licensed service which he is able to produce to them.

(3) Nothing in this Part shall be construed as requiring the Commission, in the discharge of their duties under this Part as respects licensed services and the programmes included in them, to view such programmes in advance of their being included in such services.

NOTES

1. The provisions set out above are closely paralleled in Part III of the 1990 Act by provisions establishing the Radio Authority, and conferring upon it licensing and regulatory functions in respect of independent radio services.[1]

2. These provisions of the 1990 Act relate to non-BBC broadcasting. The BBC, by contrast, is a body established under Royal Charter, which operates under the terms of that Charter and also its Licence and Agreement from the Home Secretary.[2]

3. The formal power of 'veto', described above, has rarely been used by government. In the early days of broadcasting, in 1927, the BBC was directed not to broadcast matters of political, industrial or religious controversy. This directive only lasted

1   See ss. 83–97.
2   See, Cmnd. 8313 and 8233 respectively. These instruments impose on the BBC obligations similar to those outlined above (e.g. in relation to programme quality, variety of content, good taste and decency, encouragement to crime, offence to public feeling, due impartiality, avoidance of editorial opinion, scheduling of programmes to protect children, and obligations to broadcast Ministerial announcements and to comply with any 'veto' imposed by the Home Secretary on the broadcasting of any matter or class of matter).

until 1928. Later, in 1955, the BBC and the independent broadcasting authorities were ordered not to derogate from the primacy of Parliament as the proper forum for debating the affairs of the nation by broadcasts of their own programmes or discussions on the matter without 14 days of the Parliamentary debate. This embargo on discussion of issues of current concern also lasted for only a short period.

More recently this formal power has been used by government to seek to deprive terrorists of the 'oxygen of publicity'. In October, 1988, the Home Secretary ordered that the BBC and the independent companies refrain from broadcasting words spoken by representatives, or purported representatives, of certain specified organisations, or words spoken in support of, or which solicited or invited support for such an organisation. Words spoken by representatives were only proscribed when the representative was speaking in that capacity rather than in a personal capacity – a distinction requiring of broadcasters a careful exercise of judgment. When speaking as a representative of such an organisation the ban applied however innocent the actual content of the words. The organisations covered were those proscribed under the terms of the Northern Ireland (Emergency Provisions) legislation[3] as well as Sinn Fein, Republican Sinn Fein and the Ulster Defence Association. The directions did not extend to words spoken in the UK Parliament, nor words spoken by or in support of a candidate pending a Parliamentary, European Parliamentary or a local election. The directions applied only to direct statements, not to reported speech. In other words, it was permitted to show a film of a proscribed speaker, together with a 'voice-over' reading verbatim the speaker's words. The directions applied equally to current matters and to programmes about events of the past. In September 1990 Ulster Television discovered it could not broadcast directly the words of Eamonn de Valera or Sean McBride in its proposed six-part school history of Ulster.

For an early list of programmes which could not be broadcast in their original form, see *Index on Censorship*.[4] The ban was unsuccessfully challenged by the National Union of Journalists and others, but not the broadcasting organisations themselves, in judicial review proceedings in *R v Secretary of State for the Home Department, ex p Brind*.[5] Following the IRA declaration of a total cessation of violence, in September 1994, the ban was lifted.

4. The 1988 ban followed a considerable period of tension between broadcasters and government about the broadcasting of Irish affairs. As far back in the present troubles as 1972 controversy arose over a proposed BBC programme, *The Question of Ulster*: a programme in which both loyalist and republican proponents were to be given full opportunity to argue their cases. Following representations from the Home Secretary about the proposed programme, the Chairman and Director-General met the minister and told him that if the government felt that the programme should not be shown the proper course was for the minister to ban the programme and for the BBC to broadcast the fact of the ban. The Home Secretary apparently made further representations about the programme but declined to exercise his powers to prevent it from occurring.

In 1978 the BBC was criticised by government for having broadcast an interview with a member of the outlawed Irish National Liberation Army. In 1979, controversy surrounded the filming by a Panorama film crew (reporter, Jeremy Paxman) of an IRA road block at Carrickmore. It was alleged that the BBC had liaised with the IRA in staging the event. The Governors set up an inquiry and, in due course, denied the main charges. The filmed footage was not broadcast. However, the terms of the denial

3   See, above, pp. 570–575.
4   (1988) Vol. 17 No. 8.
5   [1991] 2 WLR 588.

were seen as a message to documentary film-makers to avoid issues likely to engender governmental criticism. In 1985, the Home Secretary, Leon Brittan, wrote an open letter to the Chairman of the BBC contending that a proposed programme[6] in a series called *Real Lives* should not be broadcast. The programme was to feature interviews with both Martin McGuinness (IRA) and Gregory Campbell, a hardline loyalist. The Governors immediately took the highly unusual step of previewing the programme themselves, rather than referring the matter for the judgment of the Director-General. In this case the Director-General was, in fact, temporarily unavailable and the preview took place in his absence. Following their viewing of the film the Governors withdrew the programme from the schedules. The Home Secretary denied having brought improper pressure on the BBC, claiming that it was appropriate for a minister to let the government's opinion on broadcasting by terrorists be known. He denied that the decision to ban the programme was anything other than the exercise of independent judgment by the Governors. Nevertheless, journalists at both the BBC and independent television staged a one-day strike a week after this action of the Governors, protesting at the failure of the Board to take a clear stance to protect news and current affairs journalism from government pressures. In due course the programme was shown, minor cuts having been made.[7] In 1988, Thames Television broadcast a *This Week* documentary, *Death on the Rock*, investigating the circumstances of the shooting of three, as it transpired unarmed, members of the IRA in Gibraltar earlier in the year. Government explanations were that the killings were of members of an active service unit of the IRA intent on planting a bomb on the island; and that they were shot by members of the SAS acting in self defence. The documentary, however, included evidence from a 'new' witness to the events who asserted that those killed had been shot without warning and with their hands in the air. The documentary rekindled debate about the existence of a 'shoot-to-kill' policy on the part of the security forces in dealing with terrorists. The documentary was strongly denounced by the Prime Minister, Mrs Thatcher; and similar material in a BBC programme shown in Northern Ireland met with expressions of disapproval from the Foreign Secretary, Sir Geoffrey Howe. The IBA (the forerunner of the ITC) supported the showing of the Thames documentary. Thames later set up an independent inquiry under Lord Windlesham. His report largely exonerated the documentary makers.[8]

In addition to these events in connection with Irish affairs a number of other recent examples of government seeking to interfere with broadcasting freedom (or of governmental annoyance at broadcasting bias!) may be noted. In 1986 a critical analysis of television news coverage was published by the Conservative Party. This followed strong criticism by Mr Tebbitt of the BBC's coverage of the US air raid, launched from UK bases, on Tripoli earlier in the year. In 1987, the BBC responded to government concerns and banned the showing of a documentary, on the secret *Zircon* spy-satellite project, made by Duncan Campbell in his *Secret Society* series.[9] The film was eventually shown, in slightly altered form, in 1988. Also not shown in this series was a documentary on the working of Cabinet government. The film was re-made by Channel 4 and eventually broadcast in 1991.[10] Note also the decision of the IBA not to permit the broadcast of a programme in the *20/20 Vision* series in

---

6 *At the Edge of the Union.*
7 See further, C. Horrie and S. Clarke, *Fuzzy Monsters: Fear and Loathing at the BBC* (1994) pp. 47–49.
8 Windlesham Report, *Death on the Rock* (1989). See also, R. Bolton, *Death on the Rock and Other Stories* (1990).
9 See further, below, pp. 821–822.
10 See further, P. Fiddich, 'Broadcasting: A Catalogue of Confrontation', in N. Buchan and T. Sumner (eds.) *Glasnost in Britain: Against Censorship and in Defence of the Word* (1989).

which a former employee of MI5, Cathy Massiter, had spoken of the very wide scope of that body's surveillance activities. The ban was eventually lifted following wide knowledge of the contents of the programme. Was this an example of undue deference to governmental desire for secrecy as regards the activities of the security services, or simply proper action on the part of a regulatory body in response to evidence of clear breach of the Official Secrets legislation? Over the years a number of Panorama programmes have been substantially revised following an elaborate 'referral up' process within the BBC.[11]

5. The ITC published its Programme Code in February 1991: the current version dates from April 2001, having been reviewed to take account of the Human Rights Act 1998. It has sections on: (1) family viewing policy, offence to good taste and decency, portrayal of violence and respect for human dignity; (2) privacy, fairness and the gathering of information; (3) impartiality; (4) party political and parliamentary broadcasting; (5) terrorism, crime, anti-social behaviour etc.; (6) charitable appeals and publicity for charity; (7) religion; and (8) commercial references in programmes.

The section which deals with impartiality on matters of political or industrial controversy and current public policy provides that: there are times when the principal opposing viewpoints are reflected in a single programme or item, either because it is not likely the licensee will soon return to the subject or because the issues are of current and active controversy. At other times a narrower range of views may be appropriate within individual programmes. A clearly linked series of programmes on the same channel may be considered as a whole. Any news, given in whatever form, must be presented with due accuracy and impartiality. Reporting must be dispassionate and judgements based on the need to give viewers an even-handed account of events. 'Personal view' programmes must be clearly identified as such, facts respected and a suitable opportunity for response provided.

6. The ITC Programme Code deals also with matters of good taste and decency, the portrayal of violence and respect for human dignity. It requires that early evening broadcasts conform to the requirements of the Family Viewing Policy. Material unsuitable for children must not be transmitted at times when large numbers of children (aged 15 and under) may be expected to be watching. The Policy assumes a progressive decline through the evening in the proportion of children viewing, matched by a progression towards material more suitable for adults. 9 p.m. is normally fixed as the time to which licensees are responsible for ensuring that nothing is shown that is unsuitable for children; the earlier in the evening a programme is shown, the greater the care required. After the watershed, and until 5.30 a.m., material more suitable for an adult audience may be shown, although there should be a gradual transition after it. Material which is particularly adult in tone should be schedule appropriately and clearly signposted. Particular care should be taken in respect of violence. Bad language should not be used in programmes made for children. Dangerous or harmful behaviour easily imitated by children should be avoided, especially before the watershed, and must be excluded entirely from children's programmes. Smoking and drinking should be avoided in children's programmes. Appropriate information, advice and warnings should be employed.

As regards films, BBFC's classifications (the video classification if there is one) should be used as a guide. Leaving aside 'pay per view' services, no '12' rated version should normally start before 8 p.m., no '15' rated version before 9 p.m. (8 p.m. on

---

11 E.g. in 1990 'Who Pays for the Party' – an investigation of Conservative Party finances; and an episode on the Iraqi Super-gun. Note also the controversy following the Panorama film, 'Maggie's Militant Tendency' (1984). See C. Horrie and S. Clarke, *Fuzzy Monsters: Fear and Loathing at the BBC* (1994), passim.

premium rate subscription services, content permitting); no '18' rated version before 10 p.m. (this can be relaxed if the classification was made over 10 years ago and the film is now clearly suitable for earlier transmission). No R18 film or film refused certification should ever be shown. These should be regarded as minimum requirements.

There is further specific guidance on bad language, sex and nudity and violence, and respect for human dignity and treatment of minorities. Bad language must be defensible in terms of context and scheduling; the most offensive language must not be used before the watershed. Some nudity before the watershed may be justifiable in a non-sexual and relevant context; representations of sexual intercourse should not occur then unless there is a serious educational purpose; more graphic and prolonged sex scenes must be limited to much later in the schedule.

Channel 4 has shown sex scenes excluded from the TV version of a film, *The Idiots*, on its website.[12]

7. Similar principles are found in the BBC's Producers' Guidelines.[13] Complaints concerning breaches of the guidelines can be raised with the BBC's own Programme Complaints Unit and then through the BBC Governors' Programme Complaints Committee. Regular Programme Complaints Bulletins are published on the web. Complaints can also be raised with the independent Broadcasting Standards Commission.[14]

8. Unlike its predecessor, the Independent Broadcasting Authority, the ITC, which is not itself the broadcaster will not act as censor in the sense of itself becoming involved in the previewing of scheduled programmes and determining whether or not to allow transmission. For cases challenging, unsuccessfully, the exercise by the IBA of these powers, see *A-G (ex rel McWhirter) v Independent Broadcasting Authority*,[15] and *R v Independent Broadcasting Authority, ex p Whitehouse*.[16] In both cases the court decided that the IBA had not broken, or failed to perform, its statutory duties in allowing transmission. The latter decision made clear that the IBA was not required by the legislation then in force to involve itself in 'day to day' editorial decisions on programmes. Such involvement by the IBA, both in relation to drama and current affairs programmes, had brought upon it much criticism from programme makers for meddling too closely in their freedom of communication. By contrast, the ITC has from 1993 no longer involved itself in the vetting of programmes. It has, however, sanctions which it is able to impose in relation to any programme which breaches the provisions of the legislation or the Code. These sanctions include the issue of a formal warning, a required on-screen apology, forbidding a repeat, the imposition of fines on the company in default, and the revocation, shortening or non-renewal of its broadcasting licence. Examples of sanctions include the revoking of MedTV's licence,[17] financial penalties of £2m imposed on Central Television for breaches of the Programme Code in a documentary, *The Connection*, [18] and of £½m on Granada Television for undue prominence and sponsorship code breaches in *This Morning*.[19]

1 2 Guardian Unlimited, Special report, 27 April 2000.
1 3 www.bbc.co.uk/info/editorial/prodgl/index.shtml.
1 4 Below, p 676.
1 5 [1973] QB 629, CA (proposed showing of documentary film about Andy Warhol).
1 6 (1985) Times, 4 April, CA (showing on Channel 4 of controversial, X-certificate, feature film *Scum* – film based on television play which the BBC had in 1978 decided not to transmit – depiction of violence within penal institution).
17 ITC news release 28/99.
18 ITC news release 118/98.
19 ITC news release 82/94. Other examples are summarised in *ITC Notes: ITC Regulation*.

9. Examples of drama programmes commissioned but not broadcast by the BBC or independent television include – *The War Game* (1965), a film depicting the horrific nature of nuclear war – made but not shown for some 20 years; *Brimstone and Treacle* (1976), a play by Dennis Potter which the BBC considered would outrage viewers in a way which was unjustifiable – play subsequently made into feature film – play eventually broadcast in 1987; *Scum* (1978), a play by Roy Minton and Alan Clarke;[20] *Solid Geometry* (1978), a play by Ian McEwan banned by BBC at rehearsal stage, objection being taken to certain lines about menstruation and the proposed appearance on screen of a preserved penis in a specimen jar; *Headcrash* (1987), a play by Michael Wall – cancelled after Wall refused to agree to cuts in violence in the script. In other instances programmes have been shown, albeit after cuts have been ordered against the wishes of the programme's writers and makers. Thus, for example, in 1978 a play, *The Legion Hall Bombing*, was broadcast in a shorter version than had been made by author Caryl Churchill and director Roland Joffe. The cuts removed criticisms of the fairness of the court system in Northern Ireland (non-jury 'Diplock' courts). Churchill and Joffe took proceedings to have their names removed from the play's credits and released the full script to the press. In 1983, the BBC cut some two-and-a-half minutes from a play, *The Falklands Factor*. Its author, Don Shaw, considered this to be 'political censorship': the BBC explained the decision as a desire not to cause distress to families of soldiers.

10. *Broadcasting Standards Commission.* The Broadcasting Standards Commission was established by Part V of the Broadcasting Act 1996 (ss. 106-130). It replaced two bodies, the Broadcasting Standards Council and the Broadcasting Complaints Commission. The Council was set up by government in 1988 as a consumer 'watchdog' over the activities of the broadcasters as regards matters of sex, violence, taste and decency. It was put on a statutory basis in the Broadcasting Act 1990 (Sch. 14). It published a Code of Practice. Part V of the 1990 Act provided for the continued existence of the BCC, first established under the Broadcasting Act 1981. Its function was to consider and adjudicate on complaints of unjust or unfair treatment in TV and radio programmes or of unwarranted infringement of privacy in (or in connection with the obtaining of material included in) such programmes.

The new BSC comprises a chairman and up to 14 other members appointed by the Secretary of State. It must, after consultation, draw up and publish a code of practice giving guidance as to principles to be observed, and practices to be followed, in connection with the avoidance of (a) unjust or unfair treatment[1] in programmes; or (b) unwarranted infringement of privacy in, or in connection with the obtaining of material included in, programmes.[2] The BSC must also draw up and publish a code giving guidance as to practices to be followed in connection with the portrayal of violence or sexual conduct[3] in programmes and standards of taste and decency for such programmes generally.[4] The BBC, the Welsh Authority, the ITC and the Radio Authority must where relevant reflect the general effect of these codes in drawing up their own codes. The BSC must monitor programmes covered by s. 108 with a view to enabling it to make reports on the portrayal of violence and sexual conduct in, and the standards of taste and decency obtained by, such programmes generally, and

---

20 See above, n. 8.

1 This includes treatment which is unjust or unfair because of the way in which material included in a programme has been selected or arranged: s. 130(1).

2 s. 107. This covers programmes broadcast by the BBC or the Welsh Authority or included in a licensed service.

3 This means 'any form of sexual activity or other sexual behaviour': s. 130(1).

4 s. 108. This covers the same programmes as s. 107 with the addition of certain local delivery services.

may publish reports. It also has a monitoring duty, so far as reasonably practicable, in respect of TV and sound programmes received from abroad.[5]

The BSC must consider and adjudicate on complaints ('fairness complaints') relating to unjust or unfair treatment or unwarranted infringement of privacy, and must consider and make findings on complaints ('standards complaints') relating to the portrayal of violence or sexual conduct or alleged failures on the part of programmes to attain standards of taste and decency. A fairness complaint may be made by a person or body of persons, but must be brought by the person affected[6] or a person authorised by him to make the complaint for him; where the person affected has died or is unable to act, a complaint may be made on his behalf. Where a complaint concerns the broadcasting of a programme or its inclusion in a licensed service, it must normally be brought within five years, and the BSC may refuse to entertain it if it appears to them not to have been made within a reasonable time after the broadcast. It may also refuse to entertain a complaint of unjust or unfair treatment if the person named as the affected was not himself the subject of the treatment and it appears to the BSC that he did not have a sufficiently direct interest in the subject-matter of that treatment to justify the making of a complaint by him as the person affected. The BSC must not entertain a standards complaint made more than two months after a TV programme or three weeks after a sound programme, unless it appears to them that in the particular circumstances it is appropriate to do so. Complaints must be in writing and must give particulars. The BSC must not consider a complaint if (a) the matter is the subject of UK court proceedings; (b) it could give rise to a remedy in a UK court and in the circumstances it is not appropriate for the BSC to consider a complaint about it; (c) it is frivolous; or (d) for any other reason it is inappropriate for them to deal with it.[7] A complaint may be dealt with at a private hearing or without a hearing; in the case of a standards complaint the BSC may decide to hold a public hearing. After the complaint has been considered, the BSC may direct the broadcaster to publish a summary of the complaint and the BSC's findings (without comment by the broadcaster). The BSC must also publish regular summaries of complaints and outcomes. Where a direction has been given, reports on action taken voluntarily in response to the findings by the relevant regulatory body, broadcaster or programme maker or provider must be given to the BSC.[8]

11. Section 177 of the Broadcasting Act 1990 enables the Secretary of State to make orders proscribing unacceptable foreign satellite services. Such a service may be drawn to the attention of the Secretary of State by the ITC, where it is satisfied:

> 'that there is repeatedly contained in programmes included in the service matter which offends against good taste or decency or is likely to encourage or incite to crime or to lead to disorder or to be offensive to public feeling.'

---

5   s. 109.
6   I.e. in relation to unjust and unfair treatment, a participant in the programme who was the subject of that treatment or who, whether a participant or not, had a direct interest in the subject matter of that treatment; or a person whose privacy was infringed: s. 130(1). See *R v Broadcasting Complaints Commission, ex p BBC* [1994] EMLR 497 (in a treatment case where the complainant is not a participant he must have a direct interest in the contents of the programme itself); *R v Broadcasting Complaints Commission, ex p BBC* [1995] EMLR 241 (National Council for One Parent Families had only an indirect interest in a programme about single parent families); cf. *R v Broadcasting Complaints Commission, ex p Channel Four Television Corporation* [1995] EMLR 163.
7   On the exercise of the discretion not to proceed, see *R v Broadcasting Complaints Commission, ex p Owen* [1985] QB 1153.
8   ss. 110–121.

The Secretary of State may, however, only make an order if he is satisfied that it is in the public interest and is compatible with any international obligation of the UK.[9] The Broadcasting Directive (*Television without frontiers*) 89/552, as amended by Directive 97/36, provides[10] that the responsibility for regulating television broadcasts within the jurisdiction of a member state lies with that state. Member states must ensure freedom of reception and must not restrict retransmissions on their territory of television broadcasts from other member states for reasons which fall within the fields co-ordinated by the directive. However, member states may 'provisionally' derogate from this last requirement where a broadcast coming from another member state 'manifestly, seriously and gravely' infringes Arts. 22 and/or 22a. Article 22 provides:

'1. Member States shall take appropriate measures to ensure that television broadcasts by broadcasters under their jurisdiction do not include any programmes which might seriously impair the physical, mental or moral development of minors, in particular programmes that involve pornography or gratuitous violence.

2. The measures provided for in paragraph 1 shall also extend to other programmes which are likely to impair the physical, mental or moral development of minors, except where it is ensured, by selecting the time of broadcast or by any technical measure, that minors in the area of transmission will not normally hear or see such broadcasts.'

In *R v Secretary of State for Culture, Media and Sport, ex p Danish Satellite Television*[11] the Court of Appeal held that the Secretary of State was entitled to proscribe the 'Eurotic Rendez-Vous' series containing explicit pornography, mostly beyond that which a R18 video certificate would be given. It was transmitted from Denmark and receivable, by those given a smart card, between midnight and 4 a.m. The court held that (1) the derogation whereby in certain circumstances member states could take action against foreign services extended (by way of both a literal and purposive construction) to direct transmission services as well as retransmission services; (2) the Secretary of State had based the order on the protection of minors and not some wider grounds as offence against good taste and decency; (3) the order was justified by reference to Arts. 8(2) and 10(2) of the ECHR; and (4) the order was 'provisional' in the sense that it would have been revoked if the Commission had not approved it. Other channels proscribed have been *Red Hot Dutch* (1993), *TV Erotica* (1995), the *Rendezvous Channel* (1996) and *Eros TV* (1998).[12]

12. *Licensed adult channels.* A number of specialist adult cable and satellite channels have been licensed by the ITC, including the Adult Channel, Babylon Blue, Television X and Playboy TV. Others have been licensed but have ceased to operate. These must comply with the ITC Code.

13. *The Internet.*[13] The development of the Internet has posed particular challenges with the rapid growth in the number of sites devoted to pornographic material, which are, in the nature of things, easily accessible. Various proprietary rating and filtering systems have been developed to manage access to the Internet. These may, for example,

---

9 s. 177(3).

10 Arts. 2 and 2a. The directive was amended in the light of issues as to the interpretation of the original directive raised in the *Red Hot Dutch* case: *R v Secretary of State for National Heritage, ex p Continental Television* [1993] 2 CMLR 333, DC; [1994] COD 121, CA (upholding the refusal of an interim injunction pending an A177 reference). On the background to this case see the previous edition of this book at p. 345.

11 9 July 1999, CA (CD).

12 S.I. 1993 No. 1024; S.I. 1995 No. 2917; S.I. 1996 No. 2557; S.I. 1998 No. 1865.

13 See Y. Akdeniz, 'Governance of Pornography and Child Pornography on the Global Internet: A Multi-Layered Approach' in L. Edwards and C. Waelde (eds.), *Law and the Internet* (1997), Chap. 13; Y. Akdeniz, C. Walker and D. Wall (eds.), *The Internet, Law and Society* (2000).

bar access to specified unsuitable sites, or by reference to particular words or phrases in the text, or to all unrated sites. The Internet Watch Foundation[14] was established in 1996 by Internet Service Providers. It was reconstituted with an independent chair in 1999. It has a hotline that enables members of the public to report child pornography or other illegal material on the web. IWF liaises with law enforcement agencies and notifies UK ISPs that they should take the material down from their servers. In IWF's Annual Report for 2000 it stated that, since its establishment in late 1996, 16,244 reports had been made; 28,675 items were judged potentially illegal; 25,790 items were found to be hosted in the UK and taken down; and 1,020 items originated in the UK.[15] The number of reports is increasing but the number of potentially illegal items hosted on originated in the UK is falling, and this is taken by IWF as a positive sign of the impact of its work.[16] The European Commission has funded work on how to make rating and filtering systems more effective. A new content labelling system was launched by the Internet Content Rating Association in December 2000 with a filtering system to follow in 2001.[17] These developments have been encouraged by the government.[18]

Robin Duval, the current Director of the BBRC has argued that concerns that the Internet is 'beyond regulation' are misplaced:

'Of course, eventually the Internet will begin to fulfil its promise. But by then, the major companies will have got their act together as they generally do, and the famous Internet freedoms may seem a quaint hippy memory.'

He cited the concerted actions in the US courts of the major music companies against Napster and www.MP3.com and proceedings by major film companies against Scour.com, responsible for new technologies which allowed website users to download film content on to ordinary CDs in their PCs, which proceedings led to Scour's collapse. If the Internet can be managed by corporations then it can also be regulated.[19] Further examples were provided by the closing of international paedophile rings such as the Wonderland Club and the Rhino Corporation.

Other jurisdictions have addressed the issues of pornography on the Internet in different ways. For example, in Australia, the Internet has been brought within its national censorship structure by the Broadcasting Services Amendment (Online Services) Act 1999 (Cth).[20] In the US, the Communications Decency Act 1996 created offences: (1) knowingly, by means of a telecommunications device, to make, create or solicit and initiate the transmission of any obscene or indecent communication, knowing that the recipient is under 18; (2) knowingly to use an interactive computer service to send or display to a person under 18 any communication that depicts or describes in terms patently offensive as measured by contemporary community standards, sexual or excretory activities or organs; or (3) knowing to permit any telecommunications facility under the defendant's control to be used, with intent, for either purpose. However, these provisions were struck down by the Supreme Court

---

14 www.iwf.org.uk.
15 Examples of successful international co-operation include the closing down of the Wonderland Club, an international online paedophile ring; seven British paedophiles were convicted at Kingston Crown Court.
16 The Report is available on the IWF's website.
17 www.icra.org. The IWF was instrumental in the formation of ICRA and also INHOPE (Internet Hotline Providers in Europe; www.inhope.org).
18 See the Communications White Paper, below. A new taskforce on improving child protection on the Internet has been set up: Home Office News Release, 29 March 2001.
19 RSA Lecture, 21 February 2001, available on the BBFC website.
20 For a critical appraisal see P. Chen, 6(1) UNSWLJ characterising the Act as an example of 'symbolic' legislation; K. Heitman, 6(1) UNSWLJ.

on the grounds that they were an unconstitutional interference with freedom of speech. They involved the unnecessarily broad suppression of speech addressed to adults and the government had failed to establish that there were not provisions that were less restrictive of such speech but also as effective in protecting children (such as 'tagging' indecent material).[1] Following this decision, Congress enacted the Child Online Protection Act 1998, which was narrowly drafted to protect minors from 'harmful material' measured by contemporary community standards knowingly posted on the web for commercial purposes. The US Court of Appeals for the Third Circuit granted an injunction to restrain its enforcement on the ground of its likely unconstitutionality; as web publishers could not restrict access by reference to a particular geographic locale they would have to abide by the most restrictive and conservative state's community standards.[2]

14. *Communications White Paper.* In December 2000, the DTI and DCMS published a White Paper, *A New Future for Communications.*[3] It proposed the establishment of a new body, the Office for Communications (OFCOM) to have concurrent powers with the OFT to exercise Competition Act powers for the communications sector and additional powers to promote effective competition in the communications services sector for the benefit of consumers. Policies would be monitored and developed to ensure universal access to public service broadcasting channels, telephone services and (by 2005) the Internet, and to maintain diversity and plurality (including a new system for ensuring plurality in TV services and reform of the cross-media ownership rules). The system of regulation of broadcasting would be rationalised so that it is more coherent across all broadcasters. It would have a new three-tier structure with the basic tier supporting standards across all services and further tiers applicable to public service broadcasters. OFCOM would be responsible for maintaining content standards in the electronic media, taking full account of the differences between services and people's expectations of them.[4] A set of objectives and principles would be established which would apply to all content delivered by electronic communications. These would be applied by OFCOM, which would develop codes, underpinned by statute, for the most pervasive services, and work with industry to ensure effective co- and self-regulatory approaches to protection for other services, such as the Internet. It would be able to commission research, would establish bodies to reflect public interest in the content of communications services and would consider and adjudicate on complaints on content, if unresolved by the service provider in a timely manner. It would also inherit the functions of the Broadcasting Standards Commission in considering complaints of unfair treatment or unwarranted infringement of privacy where no other legal remedy was being pursued. The principles of accuracy and impartiality would remain applicable as would the ban on political advertising and controls on religious advertising and programmes. OFCOM would assume principal responsibility for regulating advertising. It would ensure continuing and effective mechanisms for tackling illegal material on the Internet, such as those being pursued by the IWF, and promote rating and filtering systems.

---

1   *Reno v ACLU* 521 US 844 (1997). See E. Volokh, 'Freedom of Speech, Shielding Children and Transcending Balancing' [1997] The Supreme Court Rev 141 (arguing that the decision was right but the reasoning wrong, and that no substantial burden on speech should be constitutionally acceptable); T. O'Donnell, (1998) 27 Anglo-Am LR 397; D. W. Vick, (1998) 61 MLR 414.
2   *ACLU v Reno* 217 F3d 162 (2000).
3   Cm. 5010.
4   Para. 6.3.1 of the White Paper refers to research that showed that different standards were applied by audience groups to explicit sexual material according to the nature of the service, the means of access to it and whether it involved additional payment; similarly different expectations as regards swearing and offensive language and violence; and that viewers were generally more tolerant of challenging material on Channel 4 than BBC 1.

The government's proposals as to the objectives and principles were these:

'6.3.6 We propose that the high level objectives should be to:
- maintain freedom of expression and the right to impart and receive information and ideas;
- ensure the protection of children;
- prevent crime and disorder;
- provide protection from unwarranted invasions of privacy;
- ensure consumer protection;
- maintain generally accepted community standards;
and that these should be reflected within the regulator's central objectives.

6.3.7 We propose that the principles which OFCOM should consider in drawing up detailed rules should be:
- the likely degree of harm/offence;
- the extent of choice about access, including any likelihood of accidental access;
- known expectations about content on that medium, and the degree to which that content can be signalled in advance;
- the power of the medium – whether mass audience or not and the number of alternative channels/media to which consumers can migrate;
- the general desirability of upholding journalistic standards;
- the need to avoid unfairness and unwarranted intrusiveness;
- the desirability of maintaining accuracy and impartiality in communications services.'

The White Paper also proposed that the pre-classification system for videos, DVDs and computer games should be reviewed:

'6.11.1… There is nevertheless an argument that judgements about the suitability of material should be made on a more consistent and coherent basis across the media, according to our proposed set of statutory objectives and principles for content regulation (section 6.3).
6.11.2 There is a range of possibilities for the British Board of Film Classification in the proposed regulatory framework. One possible model is for the BBFC to remain as a separate body responsible, as now, for classifying films and videos, albeit within the framework of the statutory principles referred to above. It might, in effect, act as OFCOM's agent for these purposes. Another possible approach would be for OFCOM to take over the pre-classification work of the BBFC. In either case, we would expect the current enforcement arrangements to apply, with video classification certificates being backed up by a system of statutory controls on sale and distribution.'

Following publication of the White Paper, a new Memorandum of Understanding has been reached by the existing regulators (BSC, ITC, OFTEL, the Radio Authority and the Radiocommunications Agency) setting out arrangements for them to work closely together, including the development, wherever possible, of common positions.[5]

The BBFC has argued in favour of its retention of a 'one-stop shop' covering both cinema classification (outside the scope of the White Paper) and the video/DVD stage. The assumption by OFCOM of responsibility for the pre-classification of videos/DVDs would sit oddly with its other responsibilities which are centred on post hoc content regulation. However, the BBFC's guidelines should be allied to those of OFCOM. The BBFC would also welcome an independent appeals body which would arbitrate on public complaints in the cinema sector, alongside the Video Appeals Committee (available only to the video industry).[6]

---

5   ITC News Release, 18/01, 28 March 2001.
6   *The Government's White Paper 'A New Future for Communications': The BBFC's response* Lecture by Robin Duval, 21 February 2001 (www.bbfc.co.uk/website).

4 Obscenity and indecency

(A) INTRODUCTION

The extent to which it is appropriate for the law to impose criminal penalties in relation to the publication or display of material which is obscene or indecent has been, and remains, a matter of acute theoretical and practical debate. In terms of theory, a helpful discussion may be found in Joel Bakan.[7] Bakan identifies three principal factions in this 'law and morality' debate: 'liberals', 'legal moralists' and 'feminists'. He writes, perhaps a little over-simply,

> 'all appear to agree that, in certain circumstances, restrictions on pornography are justified, but they vehemently disagree as to why and in what circumstances such restrictions are justified. Liberals argue that restricting pornography means curtailing freedom of expression and the right to individual liberty, and that such restrictions are only justified where the exercise of these rights and freedoms can be shown to cause harm.... Legal moralists, on the other hand, argue that restrictions on pornography are necessary even where no harm to individuals can be shown. Pornography, they claim, is immoral, and the law must protect society from breaches of its moral standards. Feminists are not concerned with the moral or the immoral nature of pornography, but with the harm that pornography causes to ... women. In this sense the feminist position is consistent with liberal theory....'

Note that for 'liberals' any restraints imposed (whether pre-publication censorship or post-publication sanctions) may infringe both their cherished 'freedom of expression' and also the more general notion of 'liberty of the individual'. This will be the case at any rate in circumstances where the obscene material can be regarded as an 'expressive' act.[8]

As regards the liberal thesis much may depend on what is meant by 'harm to others': their accepted justification for constraints. Two particular arguments are commonly deployed in attempts to justify aspects of obscenity/indecency laws in terms of liberal principles. First, it is argued by some that pornographic material does indeed have an adverse and harmful effect on those who are its consumers. The truth or falsity of this assertion has long been controversial, and will probably remain so. At the time of the Williams Committee Report (1979) the prevailing view appeared to be that no causal link had been clearly demonstrated between pornography and such 'harm', either in terms of intrinsic 'corruption' of the mind of the individual consumer – arguably not harm in the liberal sense – or in terms of harm being caused by such persons to others. The difficult matter is the demonstration of causality. To some it is highly plausible that one who has exposed himself to, for example, violent and sadistic pornography may go on to commit sex offences (and, of course, from time to time it is discovered that such offenders have indeed collected such material). To others, in contrast, it may seem inconceivable that any person without a propensity to such criminal behaviour might be driven to commit such acts as a result of exposure to such material. A middle view, albeit in a context where middle views tend not to be voiced, might be to believe that for some people at least such exposure might just 'tip the scales'. A further complication, however, to note in this discussion of pornography and harm is the contrary view that for some persons who may have a propensity towards anti-social/criminal sexual behaviour the availability of pornography may constitute a 'safety-valve', offering catharsis to help them to refrain from such harmful behaviour.

---

7   (1984) 17 Ottawa Law Review 1.
8   See further, below.

Over the past decade those who assert a causal connection between pornography, violence and anti-social/criminal behaviour have become inclined to assert that studies are tending to support their contentions. Compare in this connection the approach to this issue of the (US) Federal Commission on Obscenity and Pornography (1970) and the (UK) Williams Committee (1979), with that of the (US) Meese Commission in 1986. However, many remain sceptical, arguing that research findings from US studies have been difficult to replicate, and may be flawed in terms of methodology.

It will be apparent that the range of possible connections between pornography and behaviour, and the difficulties of proof of causality, are considerable. This leads discussion on to the question: assuming that clear proof of a connection is not possible, what stance should the law take? Should it strive to offer protection to those who may be the victims of pornography on the basis that even in the absence of a proven connection a 'precautionary' approach is appropriate. Or should freedom of liberty/expression be regarded as inviolable in the absence of clear proof of harm?

Another 'harm' argument, and this time one commonly accepted by the liberal camp, involves the harm of causing offence by foisting obscene or indecent displays onto unwitting and undesiring individuals. It is one thing for images to be presented on the inside pages of a magazine which would only be opened by a person well aware of the likely contents; it is another, as one writer has put it, to utilise a 'billboard on Times Square to promulgate to the general populace the techniques and the pleasures of sodomy'. This notion of harm justifies controls on the basis of the nuisance caused by unsolicited experience of obscene and indecent material. As will be seen in the materials which follow it forms the basis of several pieces of legislation over the past two decades. It is not, however, a justification which is without some theoretical difficulty: at any rate in so far as we may be considering material which may be said to intend to communicate ideas or seek to promote some set of values. To proscribe involuntary exposure of others to such material is to accept that one person's liberty to express those ideals/values may be restrained because another person may thereby hear and see things which he or she does not wish to hear and see. The right to be an ostrich takes precedence over the liberty to bring before others one's ideas of right and wrong, of moral and immoral, or whatever. Perhaps most people would defend an individual's right of choice not to be unwittingly exposed to ideas which may be shocking and disturbing: and some have, in any event, argued that pornography does not express ideas and values, and so does not warrant protection on the grounds of freedom of expression – a protection to be afforded, in principle, to even the most offensive views and opinions. But this may be too easy an escape from the problem. Civil rights organisations have long wrestled with the tricky question of their attitude towards the pornographer. Some have taken up controversial stances, acknowledging that the issues are difficult ones which cannot be simply resolved. A spokesperson for the American Civil Liberties Union not so long ago made clear that whatever, ultimately, should be the law relating to pornography it was not right to seek to deny that pornography (and other lewd and indecent entertainment) presents and promotes to the world certain ideas, implicit within its explicitness, of the legitimacy of particular kinds of sexual behaviour.

A further notion of harm is that which has attracted the attention of feminist writers. This literature, which is itself quite diverse, has enhanced the debate by focusing on additional and rather different and subtle notions of harm which may be a consequence of pornography. In particular, feminists have argued that pornography has potential, by its demeaning and degrading images of women and in some instances in the hatred of women it seems to display, to provoke misogynist attitudes in men. In other words, over and above the fear of particular incidents of anti-social/criminal sexual conduct, exposure to pornography may also harm women by its influence on the way in which men perceive women. Additionally, feminists have argued strongly that it must be considered to be harmful to the female portion of the population that they have to live in a community which appears (because men make and enforce the laws) to tolerate a substantial and profitable industry sector which is involved in the production for men of material which, at best, does little to foster respect and mature relations between the sexes.

It is at this point that considerations of the gender equality under the law come into the picture. Feminists have argued that to debate the pornography issue in terms of protecting individual liberty and protecting freedom of expression is to debate in terms of constitutional libertarian principles devised essentially for men and by men. Once the debate is turned towards equal treatment under the law, and the promotion of fairness and equity within the state, different considerations may apply and different conclusions be drawn.

In *R v Butler*,[9] the Canadian Supreme Court considered the relationship between the Constitutional Guarantees of the Charter of Rights and the obscenity offences of the Canadian Criminal Code; it held that offences were prima facie in violation of freedom of expression guarantee, but 'saved' because the provisions constituted a reasonable limit prescribed by law. The Court reviewed carefully the scope and definition of the matter which might fall within the obscenity offences, and concluded that the offence was reasonably restricted to kinds of material in respect of which it was fair to presume that harm of various kinds might result, and therefore that criminal sanction was legitimate. Note that the court referred expressly to the idea that the kinds of material covered by the offences under the Code were such as to undermine the ideas of equality and dignity of all human beings, and referred to the 'equality' guarantees of the Charter: 'There is a substantial body of opinion that holds that the portrayal of persons being subjected to degrading and dehumanising sexual treatment results in harm, particularly to women, and therefore to society as a whole'.

Note also the New Zealand decision in *Comptroller of Customs v Gordon and Gotch (NZ) Ltd*[10] in which the High Court held that under New Zealand legislation defining indecency for purposes of customs control – in this case, importation of issues of *Knave* and *Fiesta* – in terms of injury to the public good, it was not necessary that any actual injury be proven by evidence: it was for the decision-making body to use its experience and judgment to determine whether such harm was likely. However, the Court considered that the approach of the minority of the Tribunal below had been misconceived. The minority had erred in adopting a feminist approach (and without alerting counsel to their thinking on this issue) of supposing that material 'depicting a representational view of women that degraded all women' (i.e. as the sexual playthings of men) could thereby be indecent under the Act. The minority had stated that some of the portfolios of photographs of women in the magazines were:

> 'injurious to the public good because of: the contrived positions the women are placed in ... the surrounding context of the photographs, and the symbolic representation of women depicted. Such portfolios promote social values which degrade, not just the single model posing, but all women as a social class. Women are portrayed as subordinates who are always sexually available and have limited choice ... The total effect of such representation suggests that women have an inferior social status and lack autonomy ... Publications which promote social values degrading a class or group would be considered harmful to the public good (and discriminatory) if that group were a racial or religious group. Similarly when the group is determined by sex.... We do not consider that, for the requirement of injury to be satisfied, the harm must be manifest by action. Injury may occur in the province of attitudes or perceptions,

9 (1992) 89 DLR 449.
10 [1987] 2 NZLR 80.

particularly if these are widely shared, and consistently suggest that one class is inferior to another.'

The extent to which the possession and publication of indecent or obscene material may be criminalised has caused much difficulty in the US in the light of the First Amendment's guarantee of freedom of speech.[11] The Supreme Court has held that obscene material, defined narrowly, is not speech for this purpose.[12] The test is (a) whether the average person, applying contemporary community standards (local or state) would find that the work, as a whole, appeals to the prurient interest; (b) whether the work depicts or describes, in a patently offensive way, sexual conduct specifically defined by the applicable state law; and (c) whether the work, taken as a whole, lacks serious literary, artistic, political or scientific value. However, private possession of obscene matter cannot be criminalised,[13] unless it is child pornography.[14] A state can make it a crime knowingly to sell material to minors under 17 that is obscene to them, whether or not it would be obscene to adults.[15] Material that is *indecent* but not obscene is constitutionally protected. However, it may be regulated by the state where there is a compelling government interest and there are no other, less restrictive, measures that would be as effective.[16] Lesser constitutional protection is afforded to broadcast radio and television than other media, including the Internet.[17]

The arguments of some feminists that the constitution should be interpreted as permitting laws that proscribe the distribution of pornography, 'the graphic sexually explicit subordination of women, whether in pictures or words' have not prevailed.[18]

11 See generally, H. Abraham and B. Perry, *Freedom and the Court* (7th edn, 1998), pp. 200–217; E. Volokh, [1997] Supreme Court Rev 141.
12 *Miller v California* 413 US 15 (1973) and *Paris Adult Theatre I v Slaton* 413 US 49 (1973). The common law *Hicklin* test based on a tendency to deprave and corrupt had previously been rejected in *Roth v United States; Alberts v California* 354 US 476 (1957).
13 *Stanley v Georgia* 394 US 557 (1969).
14 *Osborne v Ohio* 495 US 103 (1990). This does not apply to materials possessed by the child's parents or used for a bona fide artistic, educational or scientific purpose. See also *United States v Matthews* 209 F3d 338 (2000) (conviction of journalist for trading in child pornography upheld); *United States v Fox* 248 F3d 394 (prohibition on knowing receipt via computer of visual depictions that 'appear to be' or 'convey the impression of' minors engaging in sexually explicit conduct held constitutional).
15 *Ginsberg v New York* 390 US 629 (1968); cf. *Butler v Michigan* 352 US 380 (1957) (law cannot ban *all* distribution to any one of material unsuitable for children); *New York v Ferber* 458 US 747 (1982) (state can ban production, sale and distribution of child pornography whether or not legally obscene).
16 See e.g. *Pacifica Foundation v FCC* 348 US 726 (1978) (federal regulators may restrict the times for the broadcasting of words that depict sexual and excretory activities in a potentially offensive manner (and that are, accordingly, indecent and not obscene because of the lack of prurient appeal)). Cf. *Sable Communications v FCC* 492 US 115 (1989) (federal anti-dial-a-porn law that extended to indecency held unconstitutional); *Reno v ACLU*, above, p. 680; *United States v Playboy Entertainment Group Inc* 529 US 803 (2000) (requirement that channel that showed indecent material be transmitted either scrambled with no 'signal bleed' or at certain times of the day held unconstitutional by 5-4; the government failed to show that signal blocking by viewers on a household-by-household basis was an ineffective alternative).
17 Cf. *Pacifica Foundation v FCC*, above; *Reno v ACLU*, above.
18 An Indianapolis ordinance based on this approach was held unconstitutional in *American Booksellers Association v Hudnut* 771 F2d 323 (7th Cir 1985), aff'd 475 US 1001 (1986). For discussions of the issues see Catherine A. MacKinnon, *Only words* (1993); J. Weinstein, *Hate Speech, Pornography and the Radical Attack on Free Speech Doctrine* (1999); D.A.J. Richards, *Free Speech and the Politics of Identity* (1999).

(B) OBSCENE PUBLICATIONS ACTS 1959 AND 1964

(i) The Offences

Obscene Publications Act 1959

An Act to amend the law relating to the publication of obscene matter; to provide for the protection of literature; and to strengthen the law concerning pornography.

2. Prohibition of Publication of Obscene Matter
(1) Subject as hereinafter provided, any person who, whether for gain or not, publishes an obscene article [or who has an obscene article for publication for gain (whether gain to himself or gain to another)][19] shall be liable—

  (a) on summary conviction to a fine not exceeding [£5,000] or to imprisonment for a term not exceeding six months;
  (b) on conviction on indictment to a fine or to imprisonment for a term not exceeding three years or both. ...

(3) A prosecution ... for an offence against this section shall not be commenced more than two years after the commission of the offence.

[(3A)][20] Proceedings for an offence under this section shall not be instituted except by or with the consent of the Director of Public Prosecutions in any case where the article in question is a moving picture film of a width of not less than sixteen millimetres and the relevant publication or the only publication which followed or could reasonably have been expected to follow from the relevant publication took place or (as the case may be) was to take place in the course of a [film exhibition]; and in this subsection 'the relevant publication' means—

  (a) in the case of any proceedings under this section for publishing an obscene article, the publication in respect of which the defendant would be charged if the proceedings were brought; and
  (b) in the case of any proceedings under this section for having an obscene article for publication for gain, the publication which, if the proceedings were brought, the defendant would be alleged to have had in contemplation.]

(4) A person publishing an obscene article shall not be proceeded against for an offence at common law consisting of the publication of any matter contained or embodied in the article where it is of the essence of the offence that the matter is obscene.

[(4A)][1] Without prejudice to subsection (4) above, a person shall not be proceeded against for an offence at common law—

  (a) in respect of a [film exhibition] or anything said or done in the course of a [film exhibition], where it is of the essence of the common law offence that the exhibition or, as the case may be, what was said or done was obscene, indecent, offensive, disgusting or injurious to morality; or
  (b) in respect of an agreement to give a [film exhibition] or to cause anything to be said or done in the course of such an exhibition where the common law offence consists of conspiring to corrupt public morals or to do any act contrary to public morals or decency.]

(5) [See below, p. 704]
(6) [See below, p. 691]
(7) [In this section 'film exhibition' has the same meaning as in the Cinemas Act 1985].[2]

NOTES

1. The Obscene Publications Act 1964, s. 1(2) provides that for the purpose of any proceedings for an offence under s. 2 of the 1959 Act 'a person shall be deemed to

---

19 Words in square brackets added by the Obscene Publications Act 1964, s. 1(1).
20 Added by the Criminal Law Act 1977, s. 53.
 1 Ibid.
 2 See above, p. 650.

have an article for publication for gain if with a view to such publication he has the article in his ownership, possession or control'.

2. The Obscene Publications Act 1964, s. 1(5) provides that the term 'publication for gain' shall mean 'any publication with a view to gain, whether the gain is to accrue by way of consideration for the publication or in any other way'.

3. The Obscene Publications Acts 1959 and 1964 have superseded, though without actually abolishing, the common law offence of obscene libel. The 1959 Act followed recommendations of a committee set up by the Society of Authors[3] in response to a 'spate' of prosecutions of 'serious literature' during 1954, and the deliberations of a Parliamentary Select Committee[4]. The 1954 prosecutions revealed various unsatisfactory features of the common law offence.[5] Summing-up of Stable J in *R v Martin Secker Warburg*[6] was, however, much praised. The 1964 Act was passed to remedy certain flaws that had become apparent in the provisions of the 1959 Act.[7]

The 1959 Act was intended to provide greater safeguards for those who create or deal in works of 'art' or 'literature' whilst, at the same time, making better provision for the effective prosecution of those who create or deal in 'pornography' and for the seizure and forfeiture of such material. Neither aim appears to have been achieved. The protection afforded to literature depends more on levels of tolerance of jurors and magistrates than on the law itself, and pornography is such profitable business that the possibility of conviction, or forfeiture of material, provides no real deterrent. Moreover, the publicity which such proceedings bring may well provide a more than compensatory boost to future sales. The difficulties of enforcing the obscenity laws prompted Sir Robert Mark, then Metropolitan Police Commissioner, to describe the task as 'a self-defeating attempt to eradicate the ineradicable'.[8] See also *R v Metropolitan Police Comr, ex p Blackburn (No 3)*.[9] A further difficulty for the police was the vigilance necessary to ensure that their own officers did not succumb to offers of bribes held out by the pornographers.[10]

Inevitably there have been many proposals for reform of the law. Some have sought to provide a more workable legal formula for distinguishing what is permissible from what is not.[11] Others have favoured relaxation of the obscenity laws, though usually recognising the need to afford children some protection. A distinction has commonly been drawn between those who *foist* offensive displays on others and those who simply supply material to those who *actively seek* it.[12] A committee, chaired by Professor Bernard Williams, was appointed in 1977 to review, *inter alia*, 'the laws concerning

3 Chairman, Sir Alan Herbert.
4 1956–57 HC 245; 1957–58 HC 122 and 123.
5 See C. H. Rolph, *Books in the Dock* (1969), pp. 93–109; N. St. John-Stevas, [1954] Crim LR 817 and *Obscenity and the Law* (1956); series of unattributed articles in (1954) 118 JPN at 664, 680, 694, 709, 725, 812; G. Robertson, *Obscenity* (1979), Chap. 2.
6 [1954] 2 All ER 683, [1954] 1 WLR 1178.
7 See e.g. *R v Clayton and Halsey* [1963] 1 QB 163, CCA and *Mella v Monahan* [1961] Crim LR 175, DC.
8 Sir R. Mark, *Policing a Perplexed Society* (1977) p. 60.
9 [1973] QB 241, CA.
10 For accounts of such corruption and its 'rooting out' see B. Cox, J. Shirley and M. Short, *The Fall of Scotland Yard* (1977); Sir R. Mark, *In the Office of Constable* (1978), pp. 173–174, 263–269; Report of the Williams Committee on Obscenity and Film Censorship (Cmnd. 7772, 1979), pp. 39–41.
11 See e.g. *Pornography: The Longford Report* (1972); *The Pollution of the Mind: New Proposals to Control Public Indecency and Obscenity* – Society of Conservative Lawyers (1972); Obscene Publications Bill 1986.
12 See e.g. *The Obscenity Laws: Report of Arts Council Working Party* (1969); proposals of the Defence of Literature and the Arts Society (DLAS), reported at (1978) 128 NLJ 423. For appraisals of a variety of possible reforms see C. H. Rolph, *Books in the Dock* (1969), Chap. 6; G. Robertson, *Obscenity* (1979), Chap. 11.

obscenity, indecency and violence in publications, displays and entertainments in England and Wales, except in the field of broadcasting'. It reported in 1979.[13] It recommended that the existing variety of laws be scrapped and a fresh start made, avoiding the uncertainties resulting from couching criminal laws in terms like 'obscene', 'indecent', 'deprave' and 'corrupt'. In determining the scope of laws on these matters the committee considered that the following basic principles should govern. It was necessary to draw a clear distinction between material which should be 'prohibited', and thereby denied even to those who wish access to it; and material which should not be prohibited but merely 'restricted' – which should not be thrust, so as to cause offence, on to the ordinary public. Material should only be 'prohibited', and denied to those who wish to see it, where harm is likely to be caused by the material. The committee regarded the current state of scientific evidence as justifying only very limited prohibitions on adult access to material. The committee acknowledged, however, that the law should provide for broader categories of material to be kept from, more vulnerable, young persons. The committee also felt that a distinction should also be drawn between the printed word and other material. It recommended that the former should never be prohibited nor restricted. By its very nature it is not 'immediately offensive' in the way in which other material foisted on an unsuspecting public might be; and a specially protected status is justified for the written word because of its importance in conveying ideas. The many detailed recommendations of the Williams Committee, fleshing out these principles into more concrete proposals, have not, in terms, been implemented. Note, however, that certain of these ideas, but not the whole 'balanced package', have been implemented in the sex cinema/sex shop licensing legislation, in the R18 film and video classification system and the Video Recordings Act 1984, and in the Indecent Displays (Control) Act 1981.[14]

The Earl of Halsbury, on two occasions, proposed a private member's bill.[15] In 1999 it passed the House of Lords, albeit without much support. It sought to list material, such as 'display of human genital organs' and 'mutilation, torture or other acts of gross violence towards humans or animals, whether real or simulated,' that would be deemed obscene, 'including much that has been available in books, paintings and on film for many years'.[16]

4.   Research by Edwards[17] shows that it is not possible to assess the effectiveness of the obscenity laws by reliance on the official statistics. She argues that the ambiguity of the 'deprave and corrupt' test for obscenity results in practices which divert cases from jury trial. However, there were convictions in four of the five cases in the study that went to jury trial. Other defendants were acquitted by direction of the judge because of such matters are breaches of PACE.

5. The provisions in s. 2(4) of the 1959 Act were intended to prevent defendants being denied the various safeguards contained in the 1959 Act by being charged at common law with obscene libel. It has, however, been held that the subsection does not prevent charges of conspiracy to corrupt public morals or conspiracy to outrage public decency since in such cases the essence of the offence is not the *publication* of obscene matter

---

13 Cmnd. 7772.
14 See further, pp. 661, 663 and 715. For discussion of the Williams Report see C. Manchester, (1980) 31 NILQ 103 and (1980) 14 UWAL Rev 172; S. Coldham, (1980) 43 MLR 306; A.W.B. Simpson, *Pornography and Politics – the Williams Report in Retrospect* (1983) – discussion by member of the committee; R. Dworkin, (1981) 1 OJLS 177.
15 See HL Deb, 18 December 1996, cols. 1593ff (second reading debate); HC Deb, 9 March 1999, cols. 180–193 (second reading) and 27 May 1999, cols. 1132–1134 (third reading).
16 Lord Carter, HL Deb, 27 May 1999, col. 1134.
17 'On the Contemporary Application of the Obscene Publications Act 1959' [1998] Crim LR 843.

but the *agreement* to act in a corrupting or outrageous manner. See *Shaw v DPP*;[18] and *Knuller (Publishing, Printing and Promotions Ltd) v DPP*[19] per Lord Reid: 'Technically the distinction ... is correct but it appears to me to offend against the policy of the Act....'. Fears lest the bringing of such charges might circumvent the Obscene Publications Acts led to assurances to Parliament from the Law Officers that such charges would not be brought where to do so would deprive defendants of those Acts' safeguards.[20] Note, however, the prosecution brought, and the decision of the Court of Appeal in *R v Gibson*.[1] Two defendants were convicted of having outraged public decency contrary to common law. The charges followed the display at an art gallery run by one of the defendants of an item made by the other defendant. The offending item was a pair of earrings, each of which was made out of a freeze-dried foetus of three or four months gestation. The gallery was in a parade of shops and was open to the public to enter to browse. On appeal it was argued that the charges brought were precluded by the terms of s. 2(4) above. The Court of Appeal began by confirming that there was an offence at common law of outraging public decency, adopting the words of Lord Reid in *Shaw*'s case: 'it is an indictable offence to say or do or exhibit anything in public which outrages public decency, whether or not it also tends to corrupt and deprave those who see or hear it'. The next issue was whether, as was required for s. 2(4) to apply, the obscenity of the earrings was the essence of the offence charged. This depended, the Court held, on whether the word 'obscenity' was used in the subsection in its colloquial sense (which would cover an item's tendency to outrage public decency), or in its narrower sense, as defined in s. 1(1) of the Act, as depending solely on an item's tendency to deprave or corrupt. There being no suggestion that the display was likely to corrupt or deprave any member of the public, the court held that the essence of the offence was the likely outrage to decency caused by the display. Interpreting s. 2(4) the court held that there was no reason to depart from the Act's usual meaning of the term 'obscene'. Accordingly, the appellants' arguments failed. The court was unwilling to accept that this interpretation denied a defendant the 'artistic' merit safeguard intended by the enactment of the 1959 Act. It took the view that in the kind of case where a prosecution for outraging public decency might succeed it was 'unlikely that a defence of public good could possibly arise'.

Would the court have been able to have come to the same decision had the charge at common law been that of '*corruption*' of public morals? Note that the 'public good' defence proceeds on the basis that an admittedly obscene publication should not constitute the commission of a criminal offence because of its aesthetic value. In other words the defence does not negative obscenity – it justifies obscenity. Does this not suggest that the view of the court in *Gibson*, that this defence would be inapplicable in the case of an item which outrages decency, is misguided?[2]

The court also ruled that it was not necessary for the prosecution to prove that the defendant intended to outrage public decency (or was reckless).

In *S and G v United Kingdom*[3] the European Commission of Human Rights held that complaints by the art gallery curator and the artist that their convictions were contrary to Art. 10, ECHR were inadmissible. The convictions had involved an

---

18 [1962] AC 220, HL, at 268, 290, 291.
19 [1973] AC 435, HL, at 456.
20 See 695 HC Deb, 3 June 1964, col. 1212; 698 HC Deb, 7 July 1964, cols. 315–6.
1 [1990] 2 QB 619.
2 See also, on *Gibson*, M. Childs, [1991] PL 20 (and P. Kearns, [2000] Crim LR 652 (criticising the absence of the opportunity to give evidence of artistic merit)). For full discussion of these conspiracy offences see Smith and Hogan *Criminal Law* (7th edn, 1992), pp. 291–293, 748; Law Commission Report No. 76 *Conspiracy and Criminal Law Reform* (1976), pp. 74–80; G. Robertson, *Obscenity* (1979), pp. 210–236.
3 App. No. 17634/91.

690 Freedom of expression: censorship and obscenity

interference with freedom of expression, but that interference was prescribed by law, the offence having been clear or 'accessible' at least since *Knuller*. It would have been open to the defendants to have submitted to the trial court that the sculpture was not an outrage to public decency given that the atmosphere of tolerance was in itself part of public decency in a plural society, and so freedom of expression was not wholly irrelevant. Furthermore, the restriction was a proportionate act taken for the protection of morals, within the wide margin of appreciation in such cases.

Note the more comprehensive words in the 1959 Act, s. 2(4A),[4] and also in the Theatres Act 1968, s. 2(4)[5] in respect of obscene plays.

6. The time limit on prosecutions contained in the 1959 Act, s. 2(3) protects those who 'publish' or 'have for publication' rather than secondary parties who aid and abet such 'publication', e.g. authors, cameramen, actors. Time runs from the 'publication' or 'having for publication' rather than from the, perhaps much earlier, date of the secondary party's contribution to that eventual 'having' or 'publication'.[6] The Court of Appeal suggested that a person will not be regarded as having aided or abetted publication if he 'disassociated' himself from such publication, but did not give guidance as to what conduct would amount to such a 'disassociation'.

7. On the appropriate sentences to be imposed in respect of offences under the Obscene Publications Acts note the guidance of Lawton LJ in *R v Holloway*:[7]:

'Experience has shown, ... that fining these pornographers does not discourage them. Fines merely become an expense of the trade and are passed on to purchasers of the pornographic matter, so that prices go up and sales go on.

... the only way of stamping out this filthy trade is by imposing sentences of imprisonment on first offenders and all connected with the commercial exploitation of pornography: otherwise front men will be put up and the real villains will hide behind them. It follows ... that the salesmen, projectionists, owners and suppliers behind the owners should on conviction lose their liberty. For first offenders sentences need only be comparatively short, but persistent offenders should get the full rigour of the law. In addition courts should take the profit out of this illegal filthy trade by imposing very substantial fines.

... We wish to make it clear that the guidelines we have indicated apply to those who commercially exploit pornography. We do not suggest that sentences of imprisonment would be appropriate for a newsagent who is carrying on a legitimate trade in selling newspapers and magazines and who has the odd pornographic magazine in his possession ... [H]e can be discouraged ... by a substantial fine from repeating his carelessness. Nor do we suggest that a young man who comes into possession of a pornographic video tape and who takes it along to his rugby or cricket club to amuse his friends by showing it should be sentenced to imprisonment. On conviction he too can be dealt with by the imposition of a fine. The matter might be very different if owners or managers of clubs were to make a weekly practice of showing 'blue' films to attract custom.... When news of this judgment reaches Soho it is to be hoped, and we think it is likely, that there will be a considerable amount of stocktaking within the next 72 hours; because if there is not there is likely to be a depletion in the population of that area in the next few months.'

Consecutive sentences of six and twelve months' imprisonment were imposed in *R v Ibrahim*[8] on a 'front man' in respect of three separate occasions. Stephane Perrin,

---

4   The parallel provisions relating to prosecutions in respect of films added by Criminal Law Act 1977, s. 53.
5   Below, p. 704.
6   See G. Robertson, *Obscenity* (1979) at pp. 74–76 quoting from transcript of the Court of Appeal judgment in *R v Barton* [1976] Crim LR 514.
7   (1982) 4 Cr App Rep (S) 128, CA at 131.
8   [1998] 1 Cr App Rep (S) 157 ('Offences of this nature in the absence of exceptional circumstances, call for a custodial penalty'). Cf. *R v Pace* [1998] 1 Cr App Rep (S) 121; *R v Tunnicliffe and Greenwood* [1999] 2 Cr App Rep (S) 88.

an 'Internet pornographer', was sent to prison for 30 months in November 2000. His activities generated substantial profits. The site in question was hosted in the US and contained 'extreme and repulsive' material. The jury convicted under s. 1 of the 1959 Act in respect of material on a 'preview' page but acquitted in respect of 'pay-to-view' pages.[9]

8. Challenges to convictions under the Obscene Publications Acts have been rejected by the ECtHR. In *Handyside v United Kingdom*[10] the applicant was the publisher of the *Little Red Schoolbook*. The book, which was aimed at children, had chapters on education, learning, teachers, pupils and 'the system'. The chapters on pupils had subsections giving advice on sexual matters. H was convicted of having in his possession obscene articles for gain. The Court held by 13 to 1 that this could be justified as being for the protection of morals, the state in such cases having a wide margin of appreciation. There is no uniform European conception of morals. 'By reason of their direct and continuous contract with the vital force of their countries, State authorities are in principle in a better position than the international judge to give an opinion on the exact content of [the requirements of morals] as well as on the "necessity" of a "restriction" or "penalty" intended to meet them.'[11] Similarly, in *Hoare v United Kingdom*[12] the Commission declared inadmissible a complaint by a person convicted under s. 2 of the 1959 Act in respect of the distribution of hard-core videos to persons who responded to advertisements in *The Sport* newspaper. The conviction was proportionate given the risk that the videos might fall into the hands of minors and that there was no claim to artistic merit.

(ii) The Definition of 'obscene'

Obscene Publications Act 1959

1. Test of obscenity

(1)For the purposes of this Act an article shall be deemed to be obscene if its effect or (where the article comprises two or more distinct items) the effect of any one of its items is, if taken as a whole, such as to tend to deprave and corrupt persons who are likely, having regard to all relevant circumstances, to read, see or hear the matter contained or embodied in it.

(2) In this Act 'article' means any description of article containing or embodying matter to be read or looked at or both, any sound record, and any film or other record of a picture or pictures ...

2. Prohibition of publication of obscene matter ...

(6) In any proceedings against a person under this section the question whether an article is obscene shall be determined without regard to any publication by another person unless it could reasonably have been expected that the publication by the other person would follow from publication by the person charged.

---

9 *Guardian Unlimited*, 6 November 2000.
10 (1976) 1 EHRR 737. See also *Müller v Switzerland* (1988) 13 EHRR 212 (confirming that indecent or obscene art is not excluded from the definition of 'expression' but upholding convictions in respect of paintings of, *inter alia*, sexual relations between men and animals, found by the Swiss courts to be obscene); cf. *Scherer v Switzerland* (1994) 18 EHRR 276 (Commission found conviction of sex-shop owner for showing pornographic films in his unmarked shop not 'necessary in a democratic society'; case subsequently struck out on S's death).
11 Para. 48.
12 App. No. 31211/96 [1997] EHRLR 678.

Obscene Publications Act 1964

1. Obscene articles intended for publication for gain

(3) In proceedings brought against a person under the said section 2[13] for having an obscene article for publication for gain the following provisions shall apply in place of subsections (5) and (6) of that section, that is to say,—

(*a*)[14]

(*b*) the question whether the article is obscene shall be determined by reference to such publication for gain of the article as in the circumstances it may reasonably be inferred he had in contemplation and to any further publication that could reasonably be expected to follow from it, but not to any other publication.

NOTES

1. The Obscene Publications Act 1964, s. 2(1) extends the meaning of 'article' as defined in s. 1(2) of the 1959 Act. It provides:

'The Obscene Publications Act 1959 (as amended by this Act), shall apply in relation to anything which is intended to be used, either alone or as one of a set, for the reproduction or manufacture therefrom of articles containing or embodying matter to be read, looked at or listened to, as if it were an article containing or embodying that matter so far as that matter is to be derived from it or from the set.'

Whether or not such an article is obscene is to be determined in accordance with the Obscene Publications Act 1964, s. 2(2) which provides:

'For the purposes of the Obscene Publications Act 1959 (as so amended), an article shall be deemed to be had or kept for publication if it is had or kept for the reproduction or manufacture therefrom of articles for publication; and the question whether an article so had or kept is obscene shall—

(*a*) for the purposes of section 2 of the Act be determined in accordance with section 1(3)(*b*) above as if any reference to publication of them were a reference to publication of articles reproduced or manufactured from it; and

(*b*) for purposes of section 3 of the Act by determined on the assumption that articles reproduced or manufactured from it would be punished in any manner likely having regard to the circumstances in which it was found, but in no other manner.'[15]

2. In *A-G's Reference (No 5 of 1980)*[16] it was held that a video-cassette was an 'article' within s. 2(1) above in that it was a 'record of ... pictures'; and that a cinema showing video films was 'publishing' such article because the cassettes were being 'played or projected'.[17]

3. In *DPP v Whyte*,[18] Lord Wilberforce, commenting on the statutory test of obscenity, said:

'... the Act has adopted a relative conception of obscenity. An article cannot be considered obscene in itself: it can only be so in relation to its likely readers ... in every case, the magistrates, or the jury are called upon to ascertain who are likely readers and then to consider whether the article is likely to deprave and corrupt them.'

An example of the application of the test was given by Lord Pearson:[19]

13 I.e. Obscene Publications Act 1959, s. 2.
14 See below, p. 704.
15 For the Obscene Publications Act 1959, s. 3, see below, p. 699.
16 [1980] 3 All ER 816, CA(CD).
17 As required by section 1(3), below, p. 698.
18 [1972] AC 849, HL at 860.
19 At 864.

'The question whether an article is obscene depends not only on its inherent character but also on what is being or is to be done with it. Suppose that there is a serious book on *Psychopathia Sexualis* designed to be read only by medical men or scientists concerned with such matters, and that it is kept in the library of a hospital or university and so far as possible reserved for use by such medical men or scientists. Such a book should not be regarded as obscene for the purpose of the Act, because it is not likely to come (though possibly it might come) into the hands of anyone who might be corrupted by it.'

Lord Simon commented:[20]

'The intention of the Act was ... to enable serious literary, artistic, scientific or scholarly work to draw on the amplitude of human experience without fear of allegation that it could conceivably have a harmful effect on persons other than those to whom it was in truth directed ...'

The defence raised in *Whyte*, which the magistrates had accepted, was that by virtue of a policy of excluding young persons from the defendant's bookshop, the likely purchasers of the pornographic books were males of middle age and upwards described by the magistrates as 'inadequate, pathetic, dirty-minded men ... addicts to this type of material, whose morals were already in a state of depravity and corruption'. Since this likely audience was no longer open to immoral influence (being already corrupt and depraved) the articles could not be considered obscene within the meaning of the 1959 Act. The prosecutor appealed to the House of Lords. The majority held that the facts as found by the magistrates were sufficient to constitute the offence charged. The minority (Lords Simon and Salmon) held that the magistrates' conclusions on the facts could not be interfered with, as it had not been shown that they lacked any evidential basis. Their Lordships were generally agreed that the Act covered more than cases of once and for all corruption. Lord Wilberforce explained:[21]

'... the Act's purpose is to prevent the depraving and corrupting of men's minds by certain types of writing: it could never have been intended to except from the legislative protection a large body of citizens merely because, in different degrees, they had previously been exposed, or exposed themselves, to the "obscene" material. The Act is not merely concerned with the once and for all corruption of the wholly innocent; it equally protects the less innocent from further corruption, the addict from feeding or increasing his addiction.'

Lord Simon said:[22]

'... a defence is available not merely that the likely exposé is too aesthetic, too scientific or too scholarly to be likely of corruption by the particular matter in question, but also that he is too corrupt to be further corrupted by it. I would, however, express my concurrence with the view ... that the language of the statute is apt to extend to the maintenance of a state of corruption which might otherwise be escaped, and ... that a person can be recorrupted ...'

Lord Salmon commented:[1]

'... there was no finding that these dirty minded old men were other than depraved and corrupted long before they became customers of the respondents, nor that what they found there made them any worse than they already were or kept them in a state of depravity or corruption from which they might otherwise have escaped.'

4. The courts have deprecated judicial attempts to explain to juries the meaning of the terms 'corrupt and deprave'.[2] In general the matter should be left at large for the

20 At 867.
21 At 863.
22 At 867.
1 At 876.
2 See, for example, Salmon LJ in *R v Calder and Boyars Ltd* [1969] 1 QB 151 at 168 referring to 'attempts to improve upon or re-define' the statutory formula.

jury.[3] However judges have, from time to time, stressed the seriousness of the terms. For example, in *Knuller v DPP*[4] Lord Reid commented that one may 'lead persons morally astray without depraving and corrupting them.' On the other hand, in *DPP v Whyte*[5] the House of Lords stressed that the formula covered moral or spiritual corruption and depravity not manifesting itself in corrupt and depraved conduct. If an article produces in the minds of its audience thoughts which a magistrate or jury, as the case may be, regards as having corrupted and depraved the audience's minds, the article is obscene.

How far, and in what ways, might it be possible to define more precisely the content of an obscenity law? Consider the principle that justice requires that the criminal law should be clear in its terms. An American judge once despaired of the search for a judicial yardstick to delimit the extent to which obscenity laws might make inroads on freedom of expression: 'I know it when I see it.'[6]

5. A consequence of defining obscenity in terms of tendency to deprave and corrupt is that the concept is not confined to sexual matters. In *Calder (John) (Publications) Ltd v Powell* Lord Parker CJ said:[7]

'In my judgment it is perfectly plain that depravity, and, indeed, obscenity (because obscenity is treated as a tendency to deprave) is quite apt to cover what was suggested by the prosecution in this case. This book – the less said about it the better – concerned the life, or imaginary life, of a junkie in New York, and the suggestion of the prosecution was that the book high-lighted the favourable effects of drug-taking and, so far from condemning it, advocated it, and that there was a real danger that those into whose hands the book came might be tempted at any rate to experiment with drugs and get the favourable sensations high-lighted by the book.

In my judgment there is no reason whatever to confine obscenity and depravity to sex, and there was ample evidence upon which the justices could hold that this book was obscene.'

During 1984 a number of comics and pamphlets dealing with the taking of drugs were the subject of prosecutions at the Old Bailey. Note criticisms of the trials in the *New Statesman*.[8] What other matter might be regarded as having a tendency to deprave and corrupt? Violence? See *DPP v A and BC Chewing Gum Ltd*.[9]

6. Some guidance has been given by the courts as to what proportion of an article's audience a magistrate or jury need regard as being susceptible to an article's corrupting and depraving effect for the article to be obscene. In *R v Calder and Boyars Ltd*[10] Salmon LJ said at 168: 'the jury should have been directed to consider whether the effect of the book was to tend to deprave and corrupt a significant proportion of those persons likely to read it. What is a significant proportion is a matter entirely for the jury to decide.' Earlier he had said that the term 'persons' in s. 1 of the 1959 Act 'clearly ... cannot mean all persons, nor can it mean any person, for there are individuals who may be corrupted by almost anything. On the other hand, it is difficult to construe "persons" as meaning the majority of persons or the average reader...'. Salmon LJ's formulae were approved by the House of Lords in *DPP v Whyte*,[11] Lord Cross explaining that 'a significant proportion of a class means a part which is not numerically negligible but which may be much less than half' and Lord Pearson

---

3 See *R v O'Sullivan* (1994) Times, 3 May: judge's summing-up should inform juries of the words of 1959 Act, s. 1(1) and 1(3), and 1964 Act, s. 1(3)(b), adding only a comment about the proportion of the audience which need be shown to have been corrupted – see below, n. 6.
4 [1973] AC 435, HL at 456.
5 [1972] AC 849.
6 Per Stewart J, *Jacobellis v Ohio* (1964) 378 US 184.
7 [1965] 1 QB 509, DC at 515.
8 June 8 and August 3, 1984. See *R v Skirving* [1985] QB 819, CA, below, p. 697.
9 [1968] 1 QB 159, DC.
10 [1969] 1 QB 151, CA (Cr D).
11 [1972] AC 849.

stating that 'if a seller of pornographic books has a large number of customers who are not likely to be corrupted by such books, he does not thereby acquire a licence to expose for sale or sell such books to a small number of customers who are likely to be corrupted by them'. The concept of 'more than a negligible number' was approved in the Court of Appeal in *R v O'Sullivan*.[12]

7. A defence sometimes raised is that an article does not deprave and corrupt its audience if it so revolts them that it averts them from the sort of conduct it depicts. In *R v Calder and Boyars Ltd*, Salmon LJ said:[13]

'The defence ... was that the book ... gave a graphic description of the depths of depravity and degradation in which life was lived in Brooklyn. This description was compassionate and condemnatory. The only effect that it would produce in any but a minute lunatic fringe of readers would be horror, revulsion and pity; it was admittedly and intentionally disgusting, shocking and outrageous; it made the reader share in the horror it described and thereby so disgusted, shocked and outraged him that, being aware of the truth, he would do what he could to eradicate those evils and the conditions of modern society which so callously allowed them to exist. In short, according to the defence, instead of tending to encourage anyone to homosexuality, drug-taking or senseless, brutal violence, it would have precisely the reverse effect. Unfortunately, whilst the judge told the jury in general terms that it was not enough for the Crown to prove merely that the book tended to horrify, shock, disgust or nauseate, he never put a word of the specific defence to the jury when he summed up on the issue of obscenity.

This is a serious defect in the summing-up.... With a book such as this, in which words appear on almost every page and many incidents are described in graphic detail which, in the ordinary, colloquial sense of the word, anyone would rightly describe as obscene, it is perhaps of particular importance to explain to the jury what the defendant alleges to be the true effect of those words and descriptions within their context in the book.'

In *R v Anderson*,[14] Lord Widgery CJ said:

'... the defence ... said this material in the magazine [Oz No. 28 School Kids Issue] was not likely to deprave or corrupt; that it may shock is accepted, but it is not likely to cause people to act in a depraved or corrupted fashion. One of the arguments advanced in support of that line of defence was that many of the illustrations in the magazine were so grossly lewd and unpleasant that they would shock in the first instance and then would tend to repel. In other words, it was said that they had an aversive effect and that far from tempting those who had not experienced the acts to take part in them, they would put off those who might be tempted so to conduct themselves. The argument which Mr Mortimer [counsel for the defendant] put forward on this point is that the trial judge never really got over to the jury this argument of aversion, ... Strangely enough the same situation arose in [an] earlier decision in this court ... *R v Calder and Boyars Ltd* ... was in fact a then well-publicised criminal trial dealing with the book *Last Exit to Brooklyn* and Mr Mortimer appeared for the defence, and in this court Mr Mortimer argued, and this court held rightly argued, that the failure of the judge to put what one might call the aversion argument was fatal to the retention of the conviction.'

The appellants' convictions under s. 2 were accordingly quashed.[15]

8. Section 1(1) of the 1959 Act requires that an article be considered as a whole in estimating its effect on its likely audience. This contrasts with the position prior to 1959 in trials for obscene libel when prosecutors might read 'purple passages' in isolation from their context to juries. Note the effect, however, of s. 1(1) of the 1959 Act on articles comprising more than one item. In *R v Anderson*[16] Lord Widgery CJ said:

12 [1995] 1 Cr App Rep 455.
13 [1969] 1 QB 151, CA (Cr D), at 168.
14 [1972] 1 QB 304 at 314, CA (Cr D).
15 Cf. below, p. 696.
16 [1972] 1 QB 304 at 312 CA (Cr D).

'... At the trial the prosecution accepted the proposition that in deciding whether the offences under the Act of 1959 had been made out, it was right for the jury to consider the magazine as a whole and not to look at individual items in isolation. That was a proposition accepted by the prosecution ... largely in fairness to the defence, and, being accepted by both parties, it was a proposition which was accepted by the judge as well. It certainly did the defence no harm; it was much to their interests; but in the judgment of this court it was entirely wrong. It is in our view quite clear from section 1 that where you have an article such as this comprising a number of distinct items, the proper view of obscenity under section 1 is to apply the test to the individual items in question. It is equally clear that if, when so applied, the test shows one item to be obscene that is enough to make the whole article obscene.

Now that may seem unfair at first reading, but it is the law in our judgment without any question. A novelist who writes a complete novel and who cannot cut out particular passages without destroying the theme of the novel is entitled to have his work judged as a whole, but a magazine publisher who has a far wider discretion as to what he will, and will not, insert by way of items is to be judged under the Act on what we call the "item by item" basis. This was not done in this case. Our main concern in mentioning the point now is to ensure that it will be done in future....'

It is for the judge to rule whether as a matter of law a work is capable of comprising more than one item, and a question for fact for the jury whether that is indeed the case; where this arises, the Crown should make clear what it contends to be the separate items.[17]

9. The courts have usually refused to permit expert evidence as to the effect that an article may have on its likely audience. The matter is one for the jury to assess without expert guidance.[18] In *R v Anderson* Lord Widgery CJ said:[19]

'... a majority of the expert evidence called by the defence in this case ... was ... directed to showing that the article was not obscene. In other words, it was directed to showing that in the opinion of the witness it would not tend to deprave or corrupt. Now whether the article is obscene or not is a question exclusively in the hands of the jury, and it was decided in this court in *R v Calder and Boyars Ltd* [1969] 1 QB 151 that expert evidence should not be admitted on the issue of obscene or no. It is perfectly true that there was an earlier Divisional Court case in which a somewhat different view had been taken. It was *DPP v A and BC Chewing Gum Ltd* [1968] 1 QB 159. That case in our judgment should be regarded as highly exceptional and confined to its own circumstances, namely, a case where the alleged obscene matter was directed at very young children, and was of itself of a somewhat unusual kind. In the ordinary run of the mill cases in the future the issue "obscene or no" must be tried by the jury without the assistance of expert evidence on that issue, and we draw attention to the failure to observe that rule in this case in order that that failure may not occur again.

We are not oblivious of the fact that some people, perhaps many people, will think a jury, unassisted by experts, a very unsatisfactory tribunal to decide such a matter. Those who feel like that must campaign elsewhere for a change of the law. We can only deal with the law as it stands, and that is how it stands on this point.'

In *DPP v Jordan* Viscount Dilhorne expressed some doubt about the correctness of the *Chewing Gum* case and felt the exception certainly should not be extended. Lord Wilberforce stated the alleged exception to the general rule and commented:[20]

'we are not obliged to validate, or otherwise this exception or to define its scope, because the evidence was not directed to showing that the class of likely readers consisted of, or as to a significant number included, sexual abnormals or deviants. The case was one of normal readers,

---

17 *R v Goring (Jonathan)* [1999] Crim LR 670.
18 Cf. the use of expert testimony under s. 4 of the 1959 Act, see below, p. 702.
19 [1972] 1 QB 304, CA (Cr D), at 313.
20 [1977] AC 699, HL, at 718.

and was to be judged by the jury in relation to them, and, since normal readers were in question here, [expert] evidence ... was inadmissible at the stage when section 1 was being considered.'

Note, however, the decision in *R v Skirving*.[21] The appellants, partners in a book distribution business, had been convicted of having an obscene article for publication for gain, contrary to s. 1(1) of the 1959 Act. The article in question was a pamphlet entitled '*Attention Coke Lovers – Freebasing, the Greatest Thing Since Sex*', copies of which had been discovered by police following a search of their office premises. The pamphlet contained instructions ('recipes') as to how to take cocaine to maximum effect – in particular, how to smoke or 'freebase' the drug. The prosecution had, at the trial, obtained leave to adduce expert evidence from a professor of addiction behaviour as to the effects of taking cocaine. This had been permitted by the trial judge on the ground that the jury would need to consider the effects of 'freebasing', and that this was not within the knowledge or experience of the ordinary person. On appeal, the appellants argued that such evidence should not have been admitted. The Court of Appeal upheld the decision of the trial judge, holding that unlike the sexual obscenity cases (such as *Anderson* and *Jordan*) where the jury were in a reasonable position to assess from their own experience the likely effect of material, in this case the jury would have been 'in the dark' 'guessing and no more' at its likely effect. The Court of Appeal did emphasise, however, that the proper question for the jury was not whether the act of taking cocaine 'corrupted or depraved', but, rather, the linked but separate question whether the pamphlet itself could be said to have that effect. The court was content, however, that the trial judge had properly distinguished these questions in his summing-up.

10. For summaries of research into the effect of the portrayal of sex and violence in the various media see M. Yaffé, Appendix 5 to *Pornography: the Longford Report* (1972), and Appendix V to the *Williams Committee Report*; S. Brody, *Screen Violence and Film Censorship* – Home Office Research Study No. 40 (1977); E. Wistrich, *I Don't Mind the Sex it's the Violence – Film Censorship Explored* (1978), pp. 45–47, 83–89, 96–101; R. Dhavan and C. Davies (eds.), *Censorship and Obscenity* (1978), pp. 111–182; Belson, *Television Violence and the Adolescent Boy* (1978); G. Cumberpatch and D. Howitt, *A Measure of Uncertainty – The Effects of the Mass Media* (1989); Report of the Williams *Committee on Obscenity and Film Censorship* (1979) Cmnd. 7772, Chap. 6 and para. 10.8 (burden of proving harm caused by pornography fairly clearly not discharged). Contrast, however, Lawton LJ in *R v Holloway*:[1]

'In the course of our judicial experience we have dealt with cases of sexual offenders who have undoubtedly been incited to engage in criminal conduct by pornographic material ... Pornography, and particularly the type known as "hard porn," in our experience has a corrupting influence. Those of us who have had to deal with matrimonial cases in the Family Division ... know that sometimes matrimonial troubles are started by husbands who have been reading or seeing this kind of material and try to introduce in the matrimonial bed what they have read or seen. There is an evil in this kind of pornography. It is an evil which in our opinion has to be stopped.'

Note also feminist writing since the mid-1970s. Compare the opposing approaches (evident from their titles) of Andrea Dworkin, *Pornography: Men Possessing Women* (1981) and Carole Vance (ed.), *Pleasure and Danger: Exploring Female Sexuality* (1984).

---

21 [1985] QB819, CA (Cr D).
1 (1982) 4 Cr App Rep (S) 128.

(iii) The Definition of 'Publication'

Obscene Publications Act 1959

1. Test of obscenity

(3) For the purposes of this Act a person publishes an article who—

    (*a*) distributes, circulates, sells, lets on hire, gives, or lends it, or who offers it for sale or for letting on hire; or

    (*b*) in the case of an article containing or embodying matter to be looked at or a record, shows, plays or projects it, [or, where the matter is data stored electronically, transmits that data]:[2]

Provided that[3] ....

NOTE

1. In *R v Taylor (Alan)*[4] T had developed and printed photographic films depicting obscene acts. The Court of Appeal held that the sale of the prints to the owners of the developed film constituted a 'publication'. 'High Street' photographic developing-processing outlets have long exercised some caution in the material they are willing to return to customers. Periodically, press reports appear of difficulties experienced by would-be serious artists in securing the return, for self-portrait purposes, of 'snaps' they have taken of themselves. Camcorders have, no doubt, eased the difficulties of others with less legitimate purposes.

2. In *R v Fellows and Arnold*[5] the Court of Appeal (Criminal Division) held that the making available of a computer archive of obscene photographs constituted the 'publication' of the obscene articles by 'sharing or projecting' them. See further below[6] in respect of offences under the Protection of Children Act 1978. The transmission of data to a website in the US from which it is downloaded in the UK constitutes a publication in the UK.[7]

(iv) Forfeiture of Obscene Articles

Obscene Publications Act 1959[8]

3. Powers of search and seizure

(1) If a justice of the peace is satisfied by information on oath that there is reasonable ground for suspecting that, in any premises in the petty sessions area for which he acts, or on any stall or vehicle in that area, being premises or a stall or vehicle specified in the information, obscene articles are, or are from time to time, kept for publication for gain, the justice may issue a warrant under his hand empowering any constable to enter (if need be by force) and search the premises, or to search the stall or vehicle, ... and to seize and remove any articles found therein or thereon which the constable has reason to believe to be obscene articles and to be kept for publication for gain.

(2) A warrant issued under the foregoing subsection shall, if any obscene articles are seized under the warrant, also empower the seizure and removal of any documents found in the

---

2   Words added by Criminal Justice and Public Order Act 1994, Sch. 9, para. 3.
3   Proviso excluded television and radio from scope of Act: proviso ceased to have effect as from 1 January 1991: Broadcasting Act 1990, s. 162.
4   (1994) Times, 4 February 1994, CA.
5   [1997] 2 All ER 548.
6   p. 711.
7   *R v Waddon (Graham Lester Ian)* (unreported, 6 April 2000).
8   Words in square brackets and second proviso added by Criminal Law Act 1977.

premises or, as the case may be, on the stall or vehicle which relate to a trade or business carried on at the premises or from the stall or vehicle.

(3) [Subject to subsection (3A) of this section] any articles seized under subsection (1) of this section shall be brought before a justice of the peace acting for the same petty sessions area as the justice who issued the warrant, and the justice before whom the articles are brought may thereupon issue a summons to the occupier of the premises or, as the case may be, the user of the stall or vehicle to appear on a day specified in the summons before a magistrates' court for that petty sessions area to show cause why the articles or any of them should not be forfeited; and if the court is satisfied, as respects any of the articles, that at the time when they were seized they were obscene articles kept for publication for gain, the court shall order those articles to be forfeited:

[Provided that if the person summoned does not appear, the court shall not make an order unless service of the summons is proved.

Provided also that this subsection does not apply in relation to any article seized under subsection (1) of this section which is returned to the occupier of the premises or, as the case may be, the user of the stall or vehicle in or on which it was found.]

Obscene Publications Act 1964

1. Obscene articles intended for publication for gain
(4) Where articles are seized under section 3 of the Obscene Publications Act 1959 ... and a person is convicted under section 2 of that Act of having them for publication for gain, the court on his conviction shall order the forfeiture of those articles: ...

Obscene Publications Act 1959

3. Powers of search and seizure
[(3A)[9] Without prejudice to the duty of a court to make an order for the forfeiture of an article where section 1(4) of the Obscene Publications Act 1964 applies (orders made on conviction), in a case where by virtue of subsection (3A) of section 2 of this Act proceedings under the said section 2 for having an article for publication for gain could not be instituted except by or with the consent of the Director of Public Prosecutions, no order for the forfeiture of the article shall be made under this section unless the warrant under which the article was seized was issued on an information laid by or on behalf of the Director of Public Prosecutions.]

(4) In addition to the person summoned, any other person being the owner, author or maker of any of the articles brought before the court, or any other person through whose hands they had passed before being seized, shall be entitled to appear before the court on the day specified in the summons to show cause why they should not be forfeited.

(5) Where an order is made under this section for the forfeiture of any articles, any person who appeared, or was entitled to appear, to show cause against the making of the order may appeal to the Crown Court;....

(6) If as respects any articles brought before it the court does not order forfeiture, the court may if it thinks fit order the person on whose information the warrant for the seizure of the articles was issued to pay such costs as the court thinks reasonable to any person who has appeared before the court to show cause why those articles should not be forfeited; and costs ordered to be paid under this subsection shall be enforceable as a civil debt.

(7) For the purposes of this section the question whether an article is obscene shall be determined on the assumption that copies of it would be published in any manner likely having regard to the circumstances in which it was found, but in no other manner.

(8) The Obscene Publications Act 1857 is hereby repealed, ...

9 s. 3(3A) added by the Criminal Law Act 1977, s. 53.

NOTES

1. The Criminal Justice Act 1967, s. 25 provides that a warrant under s. 3 may not be issued except on an information laid by or on behalf of the DPP or by a constable. This restriction followed the successful private forfeiture proceedings, in 1966, against *Last Exit to Brooklyn*. These proceedings forced the hand of the DPP to reverse his original decision not to prosecute the publishers under s. 2.[10] The use made of the seizure and forfeiture procedure has increased considerably. In 1969 only 31 forfeiture orders were made throughout England and Wales compared with 550 in 1978. The number of items seized by the Metropolitan Police increased from 35,390 in 1969 to 1,229,111 in 1978,[11] and rose further to 2,071,190 in 1983. More recently, in 1989, the volume of figures fell to some 185,000 articles, as the police concentrated resources on investigating child pornography. In view of the volume of material seized, the Divisional Court has upheld the practice of magistrates and judges not examining each and every item, but reaching decisions having examined representative samples selected by the police and the defendant.[12]
2. Geoffrey Robertson has criticised the way in which magistrates operate the burden of proof under s. 3.[13]
3. The provision in s. 3(4) of the 1959 Act granting rights to appear to interested parties other than the occupier of the premises searched was regarded as an important new provision in the 1959 Act. The opportunity it provides to authors etc. to defend their work is somewhat diminished by the absence of any procedure for making such interested persons aware of the existence of the forfeiture proceedings. Much depends on press publicity of the seizure or the actions of the person from whom the articles were seized in contacting such other interested parties.
4. Prior to the 1959 Act a practice had developed whereby the police, having discovered articles which they and the DPP considered obscene, would persuade the occupier of the premises to sign a form disclaiming any interest in the articles. The police would then destroy the articles and no court proceedings would take place. This practice was disapproved by the 1957 *Parliamentary Select Committee on Obscene Publications*.[14] Section 3(3) of the 1959 Act (as amended) requires articles seized to be returned to the occupier or brought before the magistrates. See also the adverse comments of the Court of Appeal concerning the 'disclaimer' practice in *R v Metropolitan Police Comr, ex p Blackburn (No 3)*.[15]
5. It not uncommonly appears that there are differences between the attitudes of magistrates and juries in their application of the test of obscenity. For example, comment was aroused when magistrates at Watford ordered forfeiture of an edition of the magazine *Men Only* at about the time that an Old Bailey jury acquitted the editors of *Nasty Tales* of the offence under s. 2.[16] Note also the jury acquittal of the publishers of *Inside Linda Lovelace* in 1976 and comment[17] and in the Williams Committee Report:[18]

'... the view was expressed to us by representatives of the Metropolitan Police that the failure of that prosecution meant that the law was unlikely to be invoked again against the written word. Their view (which appeared from his summing up to have been shared by the trial

10 See further *R v Calder and Boyars Ltd* [1969] 1 QB 151, CA (Cr D).
11 Williams Report, Appendix 7.
12 See *R v Crown Court at Snaresbrook, ex p Metropolitan Police Comr* (1984) 148 JP 449.
13 *Obscenity* (1979), pp. 93–100.
14 1957–58 HC 123–1.
15 [1973] QB 241 at 252–254.
16 See (1973) 127 JPN 82.
17 (1976) 126 NLJ 126.
18 At p. 35.

judge) was that it was difficult to imagine what written material would be regarded as obscene if that was not.'

In the proceedings on the 1964 Obscene Publications Bill, the Solicitor General gave a undertaking that:

'If the prosecuting authority has evidence of a deliberate breach of the law, or of breach of the law and a determination to persist in that breach, it will ordinarily proceed by way of prosecution rather than by forfeiture. In the absence of special circumstances, and if satisfactory evidence of the offence is available, the ordinary policy of the Director of Public Prosecutions will be to proceed against the publisher by way of prosecution: First, where an article has been seized under a warrant from a retailer or printer and the publisher, before the case is brought before the justices under section 3 of the 1959 Act, indicates his intention to continue publishing whatever the result of forfeiture proceedings; and, secondly, where inquiries are being made about an article which the prosecution considers to be, prima facie, obscene and the publisher indicates his determination to publish, and continue to publish, in circumstances which would constitute a criminal offence.'[19]

However, in *Britton v DPP*[20] the Divisional Court held that B was not entitled to challenge the decision of the magistrate in forfeiture proceedings by claiming that the proceedings were in breach of this undertaking. B was both the seller and co-publisher of obscene magazines. Schiemann LJ said that the magistrates could not be bound by the Solicitor General's undertaking. The CPS had in fact decided against a prosecution and, in any event, did not have power to discontinue the forfeiture proceedings. Brian Smedley LJ stated that the 1964 undertaking should not be 'so interpreted or applied as to result in section 3 being thwarted at the option of the person from whose possession to obscene material has been seized so that he is entitled to have that material returned to him.' Is the undertaking, accordingly, valueless?

6. In *Darbo v DPP*[21] D was convicted under Police Act 1964, s. 51(3) for having obstructed a police officer in the execution of his duty. The officer had been seeking to execute a warrant which purported to authorise the search for 'any other material of a sexually explicit nature ...'. D's appeal succeeded. Under the 1959/1964 Acts it was not possible to equate the notions of 'obscene' and 'sexually explicit': and only searches for, and seizure of, material of the former kind could be authorised by a s. 3 warrant.[1]

7. Section 3 was relied upon controversially by the police in 1998 in seizing a book of homoerotic photographs by the late Robert Mapplethorpe from the Library of the University of Central England. The Vice Chancellor, Dr Peter Knight, indicated that any proceedings would be resisted and bought another copy from Waterstones to replace the one seized. Proceedings were subsequently dropped.

(v) Defence of 'Public Good'

Obscene Publications Act 1959

4. Defence of Public Good[2]

(1) [Subject to subsection (1A) of this section] a person shall not be convicted of an offence against section two of this Act, and an order for forfeiture shall not be made under the foregoing section, if it is proved that publication of the article in question is justified as being for the public good on the ground that it is in the interests of science, literature, art or learning, or of other objects of general concern.

---

19 HC Deb, 7 July 1964, col. 302.
20 Unreported, 26 July 1996.
21 (1994) Times, 11 July.
1 See further on what is now the Police Act 1996, s. 89, above, p. 157.
2 Words in square brackets, s. 4(1A) and s. 4(3) added by the Criminal Law Act 1977, s. 53.

[(1A) Subsection (1) of this section shall not apply where the article in question is moving picture film or soundtrack, but—

    (*a*) a person shall not be convicted of an offence against section 2 of this Act in relation to any such film or soundtrack, and

    (*b*) an order for forfeiture of any such film or soundtrack shall not be made under section 3 of this Act,

if it is proved that publication of the film or soundtrack is justified as being for the public good on the ground that it is in the interests of drama, opera, ballet or any other part, or of literature or learning.][3]

(2) It is hereby declared that the opinion of experts as to the literary, artistic, scientific or other merits of an article may be admitted in any proceedings under this Act either to establish or to negative the said ground.

[(3) In this section 'moving picture soundtrack' means any sound record designed for playing with a moving picture film, whether incorporated with the film or not.]

NOTES

1. Section 4 provides that the publication of an article which, taken as a whole, is regarded by a magistrate or a jury as having a tendency to corrupt and deprave its likely audience may nevertheless be found to be justified as being for the public good as furthering certain objects or ends. Expert evidence may be presented as to the merit (or lack of merit) of the articles, although the ultimate question whether such merit justifies the adverse effect of the articles is one for the court or jury and not a matter for expert opinion. In *R v Calder and Boyars Ltd* Salmon LJ explained:[4]

'... In the view of this court, the proper direction on a defence under section 4 in a case such as the present is that the jury must consider on the one hand the number of readers they believe would tend to be depraved and corrupted by the book, the strength of the tendency to deprave and corrupt, and the nature of the depravity or corruption; on the other hand, they should assess the strength of the literary, sociological or ethical merit which they consider the book to possess. They should then weigh up all these factors and decide whether on balance the publication is proved to be justified as being for the public good. A book may be worthless; a book may have slight but real merit; it may be a work of genius. Between those extremes the gradations are almost infinite. A book may tend to deprave and corrupt a significant but comparatively small number of its readers or a large number or indeed the majority of its readers. The tendency to deprave and corrupt may be strong or slight. The depravity and corruption may also take various forms. It may be to induce erotic desires of a heterosexual kind or to promote homosexuality or other sexual perversions or drug-taking or brutal violence. All these are matters for the jury to consider and weigh up; it is for them to decide in the light of the importance they attach to these factors whether or not the publication is for the public good. The jury must set the standards of what is acceptable, of what is for the public good in the age in which we live....'[5]

2. In *DPP v Jordan* the defence sought to argue that the publication of the articles in question, which they admitted to be 'hard pornography', was justified in that the articles had 'some psychotherapeutic value for various categories of persons of heterosexual taste unable to achieve satisfactory heterosexual relationships, for persons of deviant sexuality, and for homosexuals and other perverts ... providing ... appropriate material to relieve their sexual tensions by way of sexual fantasy and masturbation'. Also 'that such release was beneficial to such persons and would act

3   Added by the Criminal Law Act 1977, s. 53(6), (7).

4   [1969] 1 QB 151, CA(Cr D), at 171.

5   See generally on the role of the expert witness in obscenity cases, F. Bates, (1977–78) CLQ 250.

as a safety valve to save them from psychological disorders and ... divert them from anti-social and possibly criminal activities directed at others'. The House of Lords rejected this argument. Lord Wilberforce said:[6]

'... Whatever the exact meaning of the expressions used in section 4 may be, one thing is apparent. The section is dealing with a different range, or dimension, of considerations from that with which section 1 is concerned.... It assumes that, apart from what section 4 itself may do, that issue would be resolved in favour of "deprave and corrupt" and having assumed that, it allows a contention to be made and evidence to be given that publication of the material is, on specified grounds, for the public good.

Each of its subsections provides guidance as to the conception of public good which is in mind. Subsection (1) provides a list which one may suspect (from the long title) started with "literature" and was expanded to include science, art and learning and still further to include "other objects of general concern". The latter phrase is no doubt a mobile phrase; it may, and should, change in content as society changes. But ... even if this is not strictly a case for applying a rule of eiusdem generis (the genus being one of intellectual or aesthetic values), the structure of the section makes it clear that the other objects, or, which is the same argument, the nature of the general concern, fall within the same area, and cannot fall in the totally different area of effect on sexual behaviour and attitudes, which is covered in section 1. In other words it introduces a new type of equation—possibly between incommensurables—between immediate and direct effect on people's conduct or character (section 1) and inherent impersonal values of a less transient character assumed, optimistically perhaps, to be of general concern (section 4). ... The judgment to be reached under section 4(1), and the evidence to be given under section 4(2), must be in order to show that publication should be permitted in spite of obscenity—not to negative obscenity. Section 4 has been diverted from its proper purpose, and indeed abused, when it has been used to enable evidence to be given that pornographic material may be for the public good as being therapeutic to some of the public. I respectfully agree with the observations to this effect of Lord Denning MR and of Phillimore and Roskill LJJ in *R v Metropolitan Police Comr, ex p Blackburn (No 3)* [1973] QB 241 and I consider that such cases as *R v Gold* (unreported), 3 November, 1972, Central Criminal Court (see [1973] QB 241 and 250) took a wrong turning. Indeed, I have the impression that if those cases are right the more "obscene" an article, the more likely it would be that the appellant's defence would apply to it. To produce such a result would in my opinion involve a total alteration in the Act....'

3. In *A-G's Reference (No 3 of 1977)* the respondents had been allowed to produce at their trial expert witnesses as to the merit of the magazines, which they had sold, in providing information to their readers about sexual matters. They had contended, successfully before the trial judge, that this sex-education role of the magazines brought them within the term 'learning' in s. 4(1). On appeal, Lord Widgery CJ, giving the judgment of the court:[7]

'... it seems to us that the fundamental question is whether "learning" in this context is a noun, in which case ... it must mean the product of scholarship. The only possible meaning of "learning" as a noun ... would have been something whose inherent excellence is gained by the work of the scholar. I would reject at once the idea that "learning" in this context is a verb.'

Accordingly, since 'learning' could not be equated with 'teaching' or 'education' the trial judge had been wrong in allowing the expert testimony.

---

6   [1977] AC 699, at 718, HL.
7   [1978] 3 All ER 1166 at 1169, CA (Cr D).

(vi) Ignorance as to nature of article

Obscene Publications Act 1959

2. Prohibition of obscene matter
(5) A person shall not be convicted of an offence against this section if he proves that he had not examined the article in respect of which he is charged and had no reasonable cause to suspect that it was such that his publication of it would make him liable to be convicted of an offence against this section.

Obscene Publications Act 1964

1. Obscene articles intended for publication for gain
(3) In proceedings brought against a person under the said section 2[8] for having an obscene article for publication for gain the following provisions shall apply in place of subsections (5) and (6) of that section, that is to say—
  (*a*) he shall not be convicted of that offence if he proves that he had not examined the article and had no reasonable cause to suspect that it was such that his having it would make him liable to be convicted of an offence against that section; and
  (*b*) [above, p. 692]

(C) THEATRES ACT 1968

Theatres Act 1968

2. Prohibition of presentation of obscene performances of plays
(1) For the purpose of this section a performance of a play shall be deemed to be obscene if, taken as a whole, its effect was such as to tend to deprave and corrupt persons who were likely, having regard to all the circumstances, to attend it.
(2) Subject to sections 3 and 7 of this Act, if an obscene performance of a play is given, whether in public or private, any person who (whether for gain or not) presented or directed that performance shall be liable—
  (*a*) on summary conviction, to a fine not exceeding [£5,000] or to imprisonment for a term not exceeding six months;
  (*b*) on conviction on indictment, to a fine or to imprisonment for a term not exceeding three years, or both.
(3) A prosecution on indictment for an offence under this section shall not be commenced more than two years after the commission of the offence.
(4) No person shall be proceeded against in respect of a performance of a play or anything said or done in the course of such a performance—
  (*a*) for an offence at common law where it is of the essence of the offence that the performance or, as the case may be, what was said or done was obscene, indecent, offensive, disgusting or injurious to morality;
and no person shall be proceeded against for an offence at common law of conspiring to corrupt public morals, or to do any act contrary to public morals or decency, in respect of an agreement to present or give a performance of a play, or to cause anything to be said or done in the course of such a performance.

3. Defence of public good
(1) A person shall not be convicted of an offence under section 2 of this Act if it is proved that the giving of the performance in question was justified as being for the public good on the ground that it was in the interests of drama, opera, ballet or any other art, or of literature or learning.
(2) It is hereby declared that the opinion of experts as to the artistic, literary or other merits of a performance of a play may be admitted in any proceedings for an offence under section 2 of this Act either to establish or negative the said ground.

8 I.e. Obscene Publications Act 1959, s. 2.

6. Provocation of breach of peace by means of public performance of a play
(1) Subject to section 7 of this Act, if there is given a public performance of a play involving the use of threatening, abusive or insulting words or behaviour, any person who (whether for gain or not) presented or directed that performance shall be guilty of an offence under this section if—
    (*a*) he did so with intent to provoke a breach of the peace; or
    (*b*) the performance, taken as a whole, was likely to occasion a breach of the peace.
(2) A person guilty of an offence under this section shall be liable—
[on summary conviction to a fine not exceeding level 5 on the standard scale [currently £5,000] or to imprisonment for a term not exceeding 6 months or to both].

7. Exceptions for performances given in certain circumstances
(1) Nothing in sections 2 to 4 of this Act shall apply in relation to a performance of a play given on a domestic occasion in a private dwelling.
(2) Nothing in sections 2 to 6 of this Act shall apply in relation to a performance of a play given solely or primarily for one or more of the following purposes, that is to say—
    (*a*) rehearsal; or
    (*b*) to enable—
        (i) a record or cinematograph film to be made from or by means of the performance; or
        (ii) the performance to be broadcast; or
        (iii) the performance to be included in a programme service (within the meaning of the Broadcasting Act 1990) other than a sound or television broadcasting service,
but in any proceedings for an offence under section 2 or 6 of this Act alleged to have been committed in respect of a performance of a play or an offence at common law alleged to have been committed in England and Wales by the publication of defamatory matter in the course of a performance of a play, if it is proved that the performance was attended by persons other than persons directly connected with the giving of the performance or the doing in relation thereto of any of the things mentioned in paragraph (*b*) above, the performance shall be taken not to have been given solely or primarily for one or more of the said purposes unless the contrary is shown.
(3) In this section—
    'broadcast' means broadcast by wireless telegraphy (within the meaning of the Wireless Telegraphy Act 1949), whether by way of sound broadcasting or television;
    'cinematograph film' means any print, negative, tape or other article on which a performance of a play or any part of such a performance is recorded for the purposes of visual reproduction;
    'record' means any record or similar contrivance for reproducing sound, including the sound-track of a cinematograph film;

8. Restriction on institution of proceedings
Proceedings for an offence under section 2 or 6 of this Act or an offence at common law committed by the publication of defamatory matter in the course of a performance of a play shall not be instituted in England and Wales except by or with the consent of the Attorney-General.

18. Interpretation
(1) In this Act ...
    'play' means—
        (*a*) any dramatic piece, whether involving improvisation or not, which is given wholly or in part by one or more persons actually present and performing and in which the whole or a major proportion of what is done by the persons performing, whether by way of speech, singing or acting, involves the playing of a role; and
        (*b*) any ballet given wholly or in part by one or more persons actually present and performing, whether or not it falls within paragraph (*a*) of this definition;
    'premises' includes any place;
    'public performance' includes any performance in a public place within the meaning of the Public Order Act 1936 and any performance which the public or any section thereof are permitted to attend, whether on payment or otherwise;

(2) For the purposes of this Act—
    (*a*) a person shall not be treated as presenting a performance of a play by reason only of his taking part therein as a performer;
    (*b*) a person taking part as a performer in a performance of a play directed by another person shall be treated as a person who directed the performance if without reasonable excuse he performs otherwise than in accordance with that person's direction; and
    (*c*) a person shall be taken to have directed a performance of a play given under his direction notwithstanding that he was not present during the performance;
and a person shall be not treated as aiding or abetting the commission of an offence under section 2 ... or 6 of this Act in respect of a performance of a play by reason only of his taking part in that performance as a performer.

NOTES

1. For the prosecution of indecent performances not coming within the terms of the 1968 Act see R. T. H. Stone.[9]

2. In 1981 a play, *The Romans in Britain*, containing a scene depicting the homosexual rape of a young druid priest by three Roman soldiers, was presented at the National Theatre. Mrs Mary Whitehouse called upon the Attorney-General to bring, or consent to, a prosecution under the Theatres Act 1968.[10] Such consent was refused on the ground that a prosecution was not likely to succeed. Mrs Whitehouse thereupon commenced a private prosecution under s. 13 of the Sexual Offences Act 1956 – alleging the procurement by the (male) director, Michael Bogdanov, of the commission by one male actor of an act of gross indecency with another male actor. Since this was not a charge under the Theatres Act 1968 the consent of the Attorney-General was not necessary; and since it was not a charge of an offence of indecency at *common law* the provisions of s. 2(4) were not applicable. At the conclusion of the prosecution case Staughton J held that there was a case to answer: at which point the prosecution was dropped. Accordingly, no decision was reached as to whether or not the performance had involved commission of the offence charged. In particular, the defence was denied the opportunity to argue that there was no 'procurement' by the director because the scene had taken place with the actors' fullest agreement; and further, that the scene was not grossly indecent because of the serious manner of its performance, involving nothing by way of eroticism or titillation.[11] Note also that it was reported that the leader of the Greater London Council, Sir Horace Cutler, who had walked out of a performance in disgust, had subsequently threatened termination of the Council's substantial grant to the National Theatre.[12]

Public Order Act 1986

20. Public performance of play
(1) If a public performance of a play is given which involves the use of threatening, abusive or insulting words or behaviour, any person who presents or directs the performance is guilty of an offence if—
    (*a*) he intends thereby to stir up racial hatred, or
    (*b*) having regard to all the circumstances (and, in particular, taking the performance as a whole) racial hatred is likely to be stirred up thereby.

9 (1977) 127 NLJ 452.
10 E.g. for the offence under s. 2.
11 See further, G. Zellick, [1982] PL 165–167; G. Robertson and A. Nicol, *Media Law* (3rd edn, 1992), pp. 144–147.
12 See P.R MacMillan, *Censorship and Public Morality* (1983), p. 308.

(2) If a person presenting or directing the performance is not shown to have intended to stir up racial hatred, it is a defence for him to prove—

(*a*)   that he did not know and had no reason to suspect that the performance would involve the use of the offending words or behaviour, or

(*b*)   that he did not know and had no reason to suspect that the offending words or behaviour were threatening, abusive or insulting, or

(*c*)   that he did not know and had no reason to suspect that the circumstances in which the performance would be given would be such that racial hatred would be likely to be stirred up.

(3) This section does not apply to a performance given solely or primarily for one or more of the following purposes—

(*a*)   rehearsal,

(*b*)   making a recording of the performance, or

(*c*)   enabling the performance to be [included in a programme service];[13]

but if it is proved that the performance was attended by persons other than those directly connected with the giving of the performance or the doing in relation to it of the things mentioned in paragraph (*b*) or (*c*), the performance shall, unless the contrary is shown, be taken not to have been given solely or primarily for the purposes mentioned above.

(4) For the purposes of this section—

(*a*)   a person shall not be treated as presenting a performance of a play by reason only of his taking part in it as a performer,

(*b*)   a person taking part as a performer in a performance directed by another shall be treated as a person who directed the performance if without reasonable excuse he performs otherwise than in accordance with that person's direction, and

(*c*)   a person shall be taken to have directed a performance of a play given under his direction notwithstanding that he was not present during the performance;

and a person shall not be treated as aiding or abetting the commission of an offence under this section by reason only of his taking part in a performance as a performer.

(5) In this section 'play' and 'public performance' have the same meaning as in the Theatres Act 1968.

(D) OFFENCES INVOLVING INDECENCY

Post Office Act 1953[14]

11. Prohibition on sending by post of certain articles

(1) A person shall not send or attempt to send or procure to be sent a postal packet which—

(*a*)   ...; or

(*b*)   encloses any indecent or obscene print, painting, photograph, lithography, engraving, cinematograph film, book, card or written communication, or any indecent or obscene article whether similar to the above or not; or

(*c*)   has on the packet, or on the cover thereof, any words, marks or designs which are grossly offensive or of an indecent or obscene character.

(2) If any person acts in contravention of the foregoing subsection, he shall be liable on summary conviction to a fine not exceeding [£5,000] or on conviction on indictment to imprisonment for a term not exceeding twelve months.

NOTES

1. The meaning of the words 'indecent or obscene' was considered in *R v Stanley*. Lord Parker CJ explained:[15]

---

13 Substituted by the Broadcasting Act 1990, s. 164(1), (2)(b).
14 See C. Manchester, [1983] Crim LR 64.
15 [1965] 2 QB 327, CCA, at 335.

'... The words "indecent or obscene" convey one idea, namely, offending against the recognised standards of propriety, indecent being at the lower end of the scale and obscene at the upper end of the scale ... As it seems to this court, an indecent article is not necessarily obscene, whereas an obscene article almost certainly must be indecent....'

Lord Parker also quoted with approval the following passage from Lord Sands' judgment in *McGowan v Langmuir*:[16]

'I do not think that the two words "indecent" and "obscene" are synonymous. The one may shade into the other, but there is a difference of meaning. It is easier to illustrate than define, and I illustrate thus. For a male bather to enter the water nude in the presence of ladies would be indecent, but it would not necessarily be obscene. But if he directed the attention of a lady to a certain member of his body his conduct would certainly be obscene....'

In *R v Anderson*[17] it was held to have been no misdirection on the charge under the Post Office Act 1953 for the trial judge to have directed the jury to consider whether the material was 'repulsive', 'filthy' 'loathsome' or 'lewd'.

In assessing 'indecency' under this section the courts have refused to look beyond the intrinsic qualities of the material itself to consider the circumstances of its distribution – e.g. to consider its effect on its recipient. See *Kosmos Publications v DPP*.[18] Such effect would be crucial to a charge under the Obscene Publications Act 1959, s. 2.

In *Customs and Excise Comrs v Sun and Health Ltd*[19] a book comprising 122 photographs of naked boys, with their genitals as the focal point of interest, was held indecent under the customs legislation.[20] Bridge J accepted that the book could not be regarded as 'obscene'.

Note also the words of Lord Bridge in *McMonagle v Westminster City Council*:[21]

'Newspapers and magazines which in varying degrees overtly exploit nudity for the purposes of titillating the sexual appetite, and many of which, in the first half of this century, would certainly have led to prosecution of the publisher, are now on sale in any newsagent's shop. So also, in films, on television and on the stage varying degrees of nudity have come to be accepted as commonplace. In saying this I do not overlook, of course, that there are strongly held opinions in some sections of society which deplore this state of affairs and actively campaign for the restoration of what they regard as minimal standards of decency. It is nevertheless inevitable that in the current climate of opinion prosecutions for public indecency offences have become rare and since any such prosecution will, if the defendant so elects, be tried by jury the standard likely to be applied in determining what amounts to a public indecency offence is in a high degree unpredictable.'

Customs Consolidation Act 1876

42. Prohibitions and restrictions
The goods enumerated and described in the following table of prohibitions and restrictions inwards are hereby prohibited to be imported or brought into the United Kingdom, save as thereby excepted ...

Goods prohibited to be imported
Indecent or obscene prints, paintings, photographs, books, cards, lithographic and other engravings, or any other indecent or obscene articles.

16 1931 JC 10.
17 [1972] 1 QB 304, CA (Cr D).
18 [1975] Crim LR 345, DC.
19 (1973), cited in G. Robertson and A. Nicol, *Media Law* (3rd edn, 1992), p. 131.
20 See below.
21 [1990] 1 All ER 993.

Customs and Excise Management Act 1979

49. Forfeiture of goods improperly imported

(1) Where—

    (*a*) ...

    (*b*) any goods are imported, landed or unloaded contrary to any prohibition or restriction for the time being in force with respect thereto under or by virtue of any enactment; or

    (*c*) ...

those goods shall ... be liable to forfeiture.

NOTES

1. The forfeiture of indecent material under the customs legislation set out above has been challenged as being in breach of EC obligations. In Case 121/85, *Conegate Ltd v Customs and Excise Comrs*[1] the appellants had sought to import into the UK from West Germany a quantity of life-size rubber dolls of a sexual nature and other erotic articles. The items were forfeited by customs officers at Heathrow airport. The appellants contended that the prohibition imposed by s. 42 of the 1876 Act constituted a quantitative restriction on imports between EC states contrary to Art. 30 of the EC Treaty (now Art. 28EC). Although there is a provision in Art. 36 (now Art. 30EC) which permits restrictions where this is justified on grounds, *inter alia*, of public morality, the appellants argued that this could not protect the seizure because at least in so far as the materials were indecent rather than obscene such materials could be manufactured and sold perfectly legally within the UK (though certain restrictions might apply to the public display of the items, or to sending them through the post). In other words the restriction on importation was in reality an act of discrimination in favour of domestic producers of such items and against foreign competitors. The matter was referred to the Court of Justice of the European Communities. The ECJ upheld the contentions of the appellants, and when the case returned to the English courts the forfeiture order was quashed and the goods returned. Following this decision the customs authorities could have operated a differential policy depending on whether the import is from an EC or non-EC country. The Customs & Excise Guidance (para. C4-34) refers to s. 42 of the 1876 Act and states:

> 'In order to comply with EC legislation in free trade between Member States, the United Kingdom can only prohibit the import of the type of material which cannot lawfully be marketed or manufactured in the UK. To ensure consistency and as a matter of policy, we apply the same test to imports from outside the Community.'

It remains the case that where an item is obscene within the meaning of the 1959 legislation its forfeiture may be justified under Art. 30EC.[2] Customs forfeitures of 'obscene' material were upheld in *R v Bow St Metropolitan Stipendiary Magistrate, ex p Noncyp Ltd*[3] and in *R v Uxbridge Justices, ex p David Webb*.[4] Both these cases involved proceedings in respect of explicit homosexual material. In the former the court refused to admit evidence on the issue of 'public good', holding that there

---

1 [1987] QB 254.

2 See also *R v Henn and Darby* [1981] AC 850, [1980] 2 All ER 166, ECJ and HL: affirming that for the purpose of Art. 36 (now Art. 30EC) each Member State may determine the requirements of public morality in accordance with its own scale of values.

3 [1990] 1 QB 123.

4 [1994] CMLR 288 DC appeal dismissed, 26 January 1996, CA (CD).

could be no lawful trade in obscene articles within the UK even in circumstances
where a public good defence might succeed. It appears that it is necessary only to
find that an article is itself obscene within the meaning of s. 1(1) of the 1959 Act: i.e.
that its publication in the UK would be an offence. It is not necessary to show that a
person in whose possession it is found on importation into the UK was at that time
also committing an offence under the 1959 or 1964 Acts.[5]

2. Note that a directive issued by the Customs Department in 1978 instructs officers
to ignore the importation by individuals of small quantities of single copies of
prohibited material if imported purely for personal use.[6] Note also the marked fall in
the number of items seized in the decade prior to the *Williams Report*: 2,252,173 in
1969 compared with 125,394 in 1978. The Customs and Excise Commissioners have
noted that with paedophiles making increasing use of the Internet, the quantity of
obscene and indecent material detected at the physical frontier has fallen
significantly, and that they believe this trend will continue; emphasis at the frontier
has shifted further towards identifying active child molesters.[7]

3. For offences relating to breach of s. 42 see the Customs and Excise Management Act
1979, ss. 50 and 170.[8] Note also the provisions of the 1979 Act, s. 154(2), which places
a burden of proving that goods are not obscene on the importer. In *Wright
v Commissioners of Customs & Excise*[9] the Divisional Court held that the reverse burden
was 'of no consequence in terms of European (Community) Law.' Kennedy LJ said:

> 'In reality if the owner challenges the Customs Officer's conclusion in relation to any article
> then the court will examine it, and reach its own conclusion in relation to it, but there is an
> obvious advantage in not requiring the court to re-examine every article in every case.'

How should Art 6(1) ECHR apply in this situation? While it makes sense for the
courts to be involved only if a forfeiture decision is challenged, why should the
customs officer get the benefit of the doubt?

For severity of sentence in relation to commercial importation of pornography,
see *R v Nooy and Schyff*, per Lawton LJ:[10]

> 'The word should go round the Continent of Europe and the Americas that importing on a
> commercial basis indecent and obscene matter into the United Kingdom is nearly as hazardous
> an operation as importing dangerous drugs – ie sentences of imprisonment and heavy fines to
> be imposed in order to stamp out the "flood of filth".'

4. In *Little Sisters Book and Art Emporium v Canada (Minister of Justice)*[11] the
Supreme Court of Canada held that the reverse onus provision in s. 152(3) of the
Canadian Customs Act (placing the burden of proof in any question in relation to
the compliance with the legislation in respect of any goods on the importer) was
contrary to the guarantee of free expression in s. 2(b) of the Charter; the majority[12]

---

5 See *R v Uxbridge Justices, ex p Webb*, above; *Wright v Commissioners of Customs and Excise*
  [1999] 1 Cr App Rep 69 (importation of obscene horror films for applicant's private collection
  liable to forfeiture; not necessary to consider the purpose for which the particular goods would
  be used, but there was sufficient to invoke the 'public morality' exception in the potential for
  distribution and the purpose of protecting the less innocent from further corruption).
6 See G. Robertson, *Obscenity* (1979), p. 194. And see, generally, C. Manchester, [1981] Crim
  LR 531.
7 91st Report for 1999–2000, pp. 15–16.
8 See *R v Forbes* [2001] UKHL 40 (for s. 170 offence of being 'knowingly concerned in any
  fraudulent evasion' of a prohibition or restriction it is not necessary to prove knowledge of
  the precise nature of the article carried).
9 [1999] 1 Cr App Rep 69.
10 (1982) 4 Cr App Rep (S) 308, 311.
11 [2000] 2 SCR 1120, 2000 SCC 69.
12 McLachlin CJ and L'Hureaux-Dubé, Gonthier, Major, Bastarache and Binnie JJ.

held that, otherwise, the legislation constituted a reasonable limit prescribed by law justified under s. 1. However, the manner of its application, which had involved discrimination against the importers of homosexually explicit material, violated s. 15(1) of the Charter.

Protection of Children Act 1978[13]

1. Indecent photographs of children[14]

(1) It is an offence for a person—

    (a) to take, or permit to be taken [or to make], any indecent photograph [or pseudo photograph] of a child; or

    (b) to distribute or show such indecent photographs or [pseudo-photographs]; or

    (c) to have in his possession such indecent photographs or [pseudo-photographs], with a view to their being distributed or shown by himself or others; or

    (d) to publish or cause to be published any advertisement likely to be understood as conveying that the advertiser distributes or shows such indecent photographs or [pseudo-photographs], or intends to do so.

(2) For purposes of this Act, a person is to be regarded as distributing an indecent photograph or [pseudo-photograph] if he parts with possession of it to, or exposes or offers it for acquisition by, another person.

(3) Proceedings for an offence under this Act shall not be instituted except by or with the consent of the Director of Public Prosecutions.

(4) Where a person is charged with an offence under subsection (1)(b) or (c), it shall be a defence for him to prove—

    (a) that he had a legitimate reason for distributing or showing the photographs [or pseudo-photographs] or (as the case may be) having them in his possession; or

    (b) that he had not himself seen the photographs [or pseudo-photographs] and did not know, nor had any cause to suspect, them to be indecent ...

2. Evidence ...[15]

(3) In proceedings under this Act [relating to indecent photographs of children] a person is to be taken as having been a child at any material time if it appears from the evidence as a whole that he was then under the age of 16.

6. Punishments

(1) Offences under this Act shall be punishable either on conviction on indictment or on summary conviction.

(2) A person convicted on indictment of any offence under this Act shall be liable to imprisonment for a term of not more than three years, or to a fine or to both.

(3) A person convicted summarily of any offence under this Act shall be liable—

    (a) to imprisonment for a term not exceeding 6 months; or

    (b) to a fine not exceeding the prescribed sum [currently £5,000] ..., or to both.

7. Interpretation[16]

(1) The following subsections apply for the interpretation of this Act.

(2) References to an indecent photograph include an indecent film, a copy of an indecent photograph or film, and an indecent photograph comprised in a film.

---

13 See M. D. A. Freeman, *Current Law Statutes Annotated 1978* and, on the events leading to the passage of the Act, M. A. McCarthy and R. A. Moodie, (1981) 34 *Parliamentary Affairs* 47. See generally S. S. M. Edwards, 'Prosecuting child pornography' (2000) 22 JSWL 1.

14 Words in square brackets added by the Criminal Justice and Public Order Act 1994, s. 84, Sch. 11.

15 Words in square brackets added by the Criminal Justice and Public Order Act 1994, s. 84, Sch. 11.

16 Words in square brackets added by the Criminal Justice and Public Order Act 1994, s. 84, Sch. 11.

(3) Photographs (including those comprised in a film) shall, if they show children and are indecent, be treated for all purposes of this Act as indecent photographs of children [and so as respects pseudo-photographs].[17]

[(4) References to a photograph include—

(a) the negative as well as the positive version; and

(b) data stored on a computer disc or by other electronic means which is capable of conversion into a photograph.][18]

(5) 'Film' includes any form of video-recording.

[(6) 'Child', subject to subsection (8), means a person under the age of 16.

(7) 'Pseudo-photograph' means an image, whether made by computer graphics or otherwise howsoever, which appears to be a photograph.

(8) If the impression conveyed by a pseudo-photograph is that the person shown is a child, the pseudo-photograph shall be treated for all the purposes of this Act as showing a child and so shall a pseudo-photograph where the predominant impression conveyed is that the person shown is a child notwithstanding that some of the physical characteristics are those of an adult.

(9) References to an indecent pseudo-photograph include—

(a) a copy of an indecent pseudo-photograph; and

(b) data stored on a computer disc or by other electronic means which is capable of conveying information as a pseudo-photograph.][19]

Criminal Justice Act 1988

160. Summary offence of possession of indecent photograph of child

(1) It is an offence for a person to have any indecent photograph or pseudo-photograph of a child in his possession.

(2) Where a person is charged with an offence under subsection (1) above, it shall be a defence for him to prove—

(a) that he had a legitimate reason for having the photograph or pseudo-photograph in his possession; or

(b) that he had not himself seen the photograph or pseudo-photograph and did not know, nor had any cause to suspect, it to be indecent; or

(c) that the photograph or pseudo-photograph was sent to him without any prior request made by him or on his behalf and that he did not keep it for an unreasonable time.

(3) A person shall be liable on summary conviction of an offence under this section to imprisonment for a term not exceeding six months or a fine not exceeding level 5 on the standard scale or both [currently, £5,000].

(4) Sections 1(3), 2(3), 3 and 7 of the Protection of Children Act 1978 shall have effect as if any reference in them to that Act included a reference to this section.

NOTES

1. Sections 4 and 5 of the 1978 Act provide powers to entry, search, seizure and forfeiture in terms substantially similar to the provisions of the Obscene Publications Act 1959, s. 3.[20]

17 Words in square brackets added by the Criminal Justice and Public Order Act 1994, s. 84, Sch. 11.

18 Words in square brackets added by the Criminal Justice and Public Order Act 1994, s. 84, Sch. 11.

19 Words in square brackets added by the Criminal Justice and Public Order Act 1994, s. 84, Sch. 11.

20 Above, p. 698.

2. In *R v Graham-Kerr*[1] a naturist was convicted under s. 1(1) of the above Act of having taken photographs of a naked seven-year-old boy at a naturists-only session at a swimming pool. The prosecution at the trial adduced evidence of the purpose and motive for having taken the photos (i.e. sexual gratification) in order to seek to show that the pictures were indecent. The Court of Appeal, allowing the appeal against conviction, held that the photos should be considered objectively, as to whether they infringed recognised standards of propriety, without consideration being given to the motivation of the person who had taken them. That person's state of mind would only be relevant where an issue arose as to whether pictures were taken intentionally or by accident.

4. In *R v Fellows and Arnold*[2] the Court of Appeal (Criminal Division) held that, even prior to the amendments effected by the 1994 Act, the words of the statute covered the storage of a large archive of indecent photographs on a computer disk. The disk itself was not a 'photograph' as there was no 'picture or other image' on the or in the disk. However, it was a 'copy of an indecent photograph,' analogous to a piece of work with invisible ink, in that it contained data not visible to the eye which could be converted by appropriate technical means into a screen image and a print; the data itself 'represents the original photograph, in another form.'[3] The 1978 Act was to be interpreted as covering forms of photographs not in existence at the time the Act was passed. The court held, further, that the words 'with a view to them being distributed or shown by himself' extended to cover the situation where the defendant made available the archive to be downloaded by those to whom a password was given. If active conduct on the part of the defendant were required, the email correspondence with and the giving of a password to others was sufficient. Moreover, the fact that the downloading of material involved a fresh reproduction of data did not mean that the defendant had not possessed photographs with a view to those same (copy) photographs being shown to others: 'the same data is transmitted to the recipient so that he shall see the same visual reproductions as is available to the sender whenever he has access to the archive himself.'[4] The court also upheld a sentence of two years' concurrent on offences under the 1978 Act (with 12 months consecutive for offences under the Obscene Publications Act 1959) on the first defendant, who had stored an archive of some 11,650 pictures, including 1,875 pictures of children. They were made available to those willing to supply additional pictures in return, but not sold.

A photograph or pseudo-photograph can be 'made' by downloading it and creating a file on a computer disk.[5] However, 'making' under s. 1(1)(a) of the 1978 Act requires an intentional act of creation; unknowingly storing images in a cache is not sufficient.[6] Furthermore, the 'possession' offence under s. 160 of the 1988 Act is not committed unless the defendant knows he has photographs in his possession (or knows he once had them).[7]

The offence under s. 1(1)(c) of the 1978 Act does not arise where photographs (here, a cine film) are only to be 'shown' to the defendant himself.[8]

Whether there is a 'legitimate reason' under s. 1(4)(a) of the 1978 Act or s. 160(2)(a) of the 1988 Act is a question of fact. The central issue where the defence is legitimate

1   [1988] 1 WLR 1098.
2   [1997] 2 All ER 548. On the ruling at trial, see C. Manchester, [1996] Crim LR 645.
3   Per Evans LJ at 557.
4   At 558.
5   *R v Bowden* [2000] 2 All ER 418, CA (Cr D) and *Atkins v DPP* [2000] 2 All ER 425, DC (rejecting the argument that 'make' only applied to pseudo-photographs); *R v Mould (David Frederick)* (6 November 2000, unreported).
6   *Atkins v DPP*, above.
7   Ibid.
8   *R v T (Child Pornography)* (1999) 163 JP 349.

research is whether 'the defendant is essentially a person of unhealthy interests in possession of indecent photographs in the pretence of undertaking research, or by contrast a genuine researcher with no alternative but to have this sort of unpleasant material in his possession'.[9] For the defence under s. 1(4)(b) to be established, it is not enough that the defendant does not know there are indecent images of children in material where he does know there are indecent images.[10]

Section 2(3) makes it clear that it is a question of fact, based on inference, whether a person is a 'child' for these purposes; paediatric or expert evidence is not required.[11]

An item that is obviously comprised of parts of two different photographs cannot 'appear to be a photograph' for the purposes of s. 7(7) of the 1978 Act.[12]

5. The 1978 Act was invoked by the police in requiring the Saatchi Gallery in London to remove two photographs by the American photographer Tierney Gearon of his children (in various states of undress) from the *I Am A Camera* exhibition and the international fine art publisher Edward Booth-Clibborn to withdraw the book of the exhibition. The CPS subsequently ruled that there was no realistic prospect of any conviction and no charges were brought.[13] Would artistic expression amount to a 'legitimate reason' under s. 1(4)? Note that s. 1(4) does not apply to taking or making the photograph. It has been argued that this might render a conviction in some circumstances contrary to Art. 10 ECHR.[14] In *R v Smethhurst (John)*[15] the Court of Appeal held, however, that the offence did not contravene Arts. 8 and 10 ECHR. The concept of 'indecent' was sufficiently certain, as assessed objectively by the jury; there was no need to imply a requirement that the photograph should be intended for an indecent purpose; and the offence was justified under Art. 10(2) as being for the protection of children.

6. As to sentencing, 'sentences up to the statutory maximum should be imposed where there is a contested case, and there is evidence of commercial or large scale exploitation, and the amount of material is significant, especially if the offender has previous convictions'. Non custodial disposals should normally be reserved for isolated offences, concerning very small amounts of material for personal use, or use within a very restricted circle, with no commercial element and a plea of guilty.[16] A prison sentence may be imposed in respect of the making of a large collection of 'pornographic paedophiliac images' for the defendant's own use, given that such offences encourage the abuse of children.[17]

7. In *R v Sharpe*[18] the Supreme Court of Canada held that provision of the Criminal Code criminalising the possession of child pornography did not infringe the Canadian Charter of Rights and Freedoms, notwithstanding the infringement of the rights to free expression, as they fell within the exception prescribed by s. 1 of 'such reasonable limits prescribed by law as can be demonstrably justified in a free and democratic society'. It was not necessary for there to be scientific proof that this caused harm to children; it was sufficient that there was a 'reasoned risk of harm to children'. Such a risk arose from the facts that child pornography: (1) promotes cognitive distortions; (2) fuels fantasies that incite offenders to offend; (3) is used for grooming and seducing

9 Per Simon Brown LJ in *Atkins v DPP*, above at 432–433.
10 *R v Matrix (Billy)* [1997] Crim LR 901.
11 *R v Land (Michael)* [1998] QB 65.
12 *Goodland v DPP* [2000] 2 All ER 425 (heard with *Atkins v DPP*).
13 *Index on Censorship*, 20 March 2001.
14 A. Nicol, G. Millar and A. Sharland, *Media Law & Human Rights* (2001), pp. 119-120.
15 [2001] EWCA Crim 722.
16 *R v Toomer; R v Powell; R v Mould* [2001] 2 Cr App Rep (S) 30, CA (Cr D); cf. *R v Wild* [2000] EWCA Crim 1272.
17 *R v Thompson (David John)* [2001] EWCA Crim 1073.
18 2001 SCC 2.

victims; and that (4) children are abused in the production of child pornography involving real children. Criminalising possession might reduce the market for child pornography and the abuse of children often involved. However, a majority of the court[19] was of the view that it was necessary to read limitations to the legislation so that it did not apply to: (1) written materials or visual representations created and held by the accused alone, exclusively for personal use; and (2) visual recordings created by or depicting the accused that do not depict unlawful sexual activity and are held by the accused exclusively for private use. The minority[20] did not regard these exemptions as necessary.

Indecent Displays (Control) Act 1981[1]

1. Indecent Displays

(1) If any indecent matter is publicly displayed the person making the display and any person causing or permitting the display to be made shall be guilty of an offence.

(2) Any matter which is displayed in or so as to be visible from any public place shall, for the purposes of this section, be deemed to be publicly displayed.

(3) In subsection (2) above, 'public place', in relation to the display of any matter, means any place to which the public have or are permitted to have access (whether on payment or otherwise) while that matter is displayed except—

(*a*) a place to which the public are permitted to have access only on payment which is or includes payment for that display; or

(*b*) a shop or any part of a shop to which the public can only gain access by passing beyond an adequate warning notice;

but the exclusions contained in paragraphs (*a*) and (*b*) above shall only apply where persons under the age of 18 years are not permitted to enter while the display in question is continuing.

(4) Nothing in this section applies in relation to any matter—

[(*a*) included by any person in a television broadcasting service or other television programme service (within the meaning of Part I of the Broadcasting Act 1990);][2]

(*b*) included in the display of an art gallery or museum and visible only from within the gallery or museum; or

(*c*) displayed by or with the authority of, and visible only from within a building occupied by, the Crown or any local authority; or

(*d*) included in a performance of a play (within the meaning of the Theatres Act 1968); or

[(*e*) included in a film exhibition as defined in the Cinemas Act 1985—

(i) given in a place which as regards that exhibition is required to be licensed under section 1 of that Act or by virtue only of sections 5, 7, or 8 of that Act, is not required to be so licensed; or

(ii) which is an exempted exhibition to which section 6 of that Act applies given by an exempted organisation as defined in subsection (6) of that section.][3]

(5) In this section 'matter' includes anything capable of being displayed, except that it does not include an actual human body or any part thereof; and in determining for the purpose of this section whether any displayed matter is indecent—

(*a*) there shall be disregarded any part of that matter which is not exposed to view; and

(*b*) account may be taken of the effect of juxtaposing one thing with another.

(6) A warning notice shall not be adequate for the purposes of this section unless it complies with the following requirements—

(*a*) The warning notice must contain the following words, and no others—

---

19 McLachlin CJ and Iacobucci, Major, Binnie, Arbour and Le Bel JJ.
20 L'Heureux-Dubé, Gonthier and Bastarache JJ.
 1 See C. Manchester, [1982] Stat LR 31; R. Stone, (1981) 45 MLR 62, and annotations to the Act in *Current Law Statutes Annotated 1981*; C. Munro, (1981) 132 NLJ 629.
 2 As substituted by Broadcasting Act 1990, Sch. 20, para. 30.
 3 As substituted by Cinemas Act 1985, Sch. 2, para. 13.

'WARNING

Persons passing beyond this notice will find material on display which they may consider indecent. No admittance to persons under 18 years of age.'

(*b*)   The word 'WARNING' must appear as a heading.

(*c*)   No pictures or other matter shall appear on the notice.

(*d*)   The notice must be so situated that no one could reasonably gain access to the shop or part of the shop in question without being aware of the notice and it must be easily legible by any person gaining such access.

NOTES

1. Section 2(2) authorises constables to seize articles reasonably believed to be, or to contain, indecent matter and to have been used in the commission of an offence under the Act. Section 2(3) authorises justices of the peace to issue warrants authorising any constable to enter specified premises (if need be by force) and to seize any article reasonably believed to be, or to contain, indecent matter and to have been used in the commission of an offence under the Act. The justice of the peace must be satisfied that there are reasonable grounds for suspecting commission of an offence under the Act.

2. Section 3 provides for the criminal liability of directors, managers, secretaries and other officers of corporate bodies which commit offences under the Act. The consent, connivance or neglect of the individual in question must be proved.

4.   In *R v South Western Magistrates' Court, ex p Heslop* [4] the Divisional Court held that a stipendiary magistrate had been entitled to find, applying *R v Stanley*,[5] that a poster featuring a well known model dressed only in underwear, to which offensive graffiti had been added, was not 'indecent'.

5. The practical difficulties in applying a number of distinct legal regimes to control the display of prostitutes' cards in telephone boxes are addressed in a Home Office Consultation Paper,[6] proposing as options: (1) a new offence of unauthorised advertising in phone boxes (for adoption where needed); (2) a new offence prohibiting the advertising of sexual services in phone boxes; and (3) a new civil remedy through the statutory designation of prostitutes' cards as a nuisance. Section 46 of the Criminal Justice and Police Act 2001 creates a new arrestable offence of placing an advertisement relating to prostitution on or in the immediate vicinity of a public telephone. It may be extended, by order, to other public structures (s. 47).

4   18 May 1994, unreported.
5   [1965] 1 All ER 1035, above, p. 707.
6   *New Measures to Control Prostitutes' Cards in Phone Boxes*, May 1999.

CHAPTER 7

Freedom of expression: contempt of court

1 Introduction[1]

It is obvious that the administration of justice must be preserved free from improper interference and obstruction, and it is more or less inevitable that the courts will play a significant part in securing that end. There are a number of substantive criminal offences relating to the administration of justice, for example, perjury, subornation (i.e. inducing a witness to commit perjury), embracery (i.e. attempting to corrupt or improperly to influence a jury), perversion or obstruction of the course of public justice, and impeding the prosecution of a person who has committed an arrestable offence, contrary to s. 4(1) of the Criminal Law Act 1967. These offences have been considered by the Law Commission, who proposed the creation or retention of over 20 specific offences in order to bring more certainty into this area of the law.[2]

Superimposed upon these criminal offences is the power of the superior courts to punish contempts. The contempt power is of wide and uncertain scope, and in the United Kingdom is exercised according to a summary procedure unknown to any other branch of the law. Trial on indictment is a theoretical possibility, but proceedings are today almost invariably conducted summarily.[3] The summary procedure is of doubtful historical origin.[4] However, it is now too late to argue that the courts may

---

1 The main works cited in this chapter are: *Abraham*: H. J. Abraham and B. A. Perry, *Freedom and the Court* (7th edn, 1998); *Arlidge, Eady and Smith:* Sir David Eady and A. T. H. Smith, *Arlidge, Eady and Smith on Contempt* (2nd edn, 1999); *Borrie and Lowe and B. Sufrin*: N. Lowe, *Borrie and Lowe's Law of Contempt* (3rd edn, 1996); *Dobbs*: D. B. Dobbs, 'Contempt of Court: A Survey' (1971) 56 Cornell LR 183; *Goldfarb*: R. L. Goldfarb, *The Contempt Power* (1963); *Miller*: C. J. Miller, *Contempt of Court* (3rd edn, 2000); *Phillimore: Report of the Committee on Contempt of Court* (Cmnd. 5794, 1974); *Smith and Hogan*: J. C. Smith and B. Hogan, *Criminal Law* (6th edn, 1988): subsequent editions omit coverage of contempt of court. In addition, see: Zelman Cowen, *Individual Liberty and the Law* (1977), Chaps. 6 and 7; Zelman Cowen, *Sir John Latham and other papers* (1965) Chap. 2; *Contempt of Court: A Discussion Paper* (Cmnd. 7145, 1978); D. Feldman, *Civil Liberties and Human Rights in England and Wales* (1993), Chap. 16; A. L. Goodhart, (1935) 48 Harv LR 885; A. E. Hughes, (1900) 16 LQR 292; T. Ingman, 'Interference with the Proper Administration of Justice: Some Recent Developments' (1992) 11 CJQ 175; JUSTICE Report on Contempt of Court (1959); JUSTICE Report on Law and the Press (1965) pp. 5–17; H. J. Laski, (1928) 41 Harv LR 1031; J. Laws, (1990) 43 CLP 99; M. Lippman and T. Weber, [1978] 2 Crim LJ 198; Oswald, *Contempt of Court* (3rd edn, 1910); C. J. Miller, [1992] Crim LR 107; G. Robertson, *Freedom, the Individual and the Law* (7th edn, 1993), pp. 326–338; G. Robertson and A. G. L. Nicol, *Media Law* (3rd edn, 1992), Chaps. 6–8; S. Walker, 'Freedom of Speech and Contempt of Court: The English and Australian Approaches Compared' (1991) 40 ICLQ 583.
2 See *Law Commission Report No. 96 on Offences Relating to Interference with the Course of Justice* (1979); R. Leng, [1981] Crim LR 151.).
3 See below, pp. 803–804.
4 See *R v Almon* (1765) Wilm 243; Sir John Fox, *Contempt of Court* (1927); Frankfurter and Landis, 37 Harv LR 1010, 1046ff.

not punish contempts summarily, given that many judges of high authority have acted on the then unchallenged assumption that they could.[5]

Classification of contempt is not easy. A basic distinction is drawn in England (although not in Scotland) between 'civil' and 'criminal' contempts. The former are cases of disobedience to an order of a court made in civil proceedings such as an injunction, the object of such contempt proceedings being essentially coercive (although occasionally punitive[6]). Other illustrations of civil contempts include breaches of undertakings given by litigants or their lawyers, illustrated graphically by the decision of the House of Lords in *M v Home Office*[7] that Ministers of the Crown are amenable to this aspect of the contempt jurisdiction.[8] Criminal contempts are cases of interference with the administration of justice, and the aims of the proceedings are punitive and deterrent. There are some minor differences between the two forms. The most significant used to be that in civil contempt, committals could be *sine die*, until the contempt is purged: in criminal contempts, committals could only be for a fixed term.

Criminal contempts may be grouped under five headings:[9] (1) publications prejudicial to a fair criminal trial; (2) publications prejudicial to fair civil proceedings; (3) publications interfering with the course of justice as a continuing process; (4) contempt in the face of the court; and (5) acts which interfere with the course of justice. The materials given here concentrate on the first three aspects, as these tend to impinge most on freedom of expression, and the fourth, as this generates problems of natural justice and the right to a fair trial under Art. 6(1) ECHR. The general principles underlying the law of contempt are discussed in *A-G v Times Newspapers Ltd*[10] the first contempt case to reach the House of Lords.

The contempt power gives rise to concern on a number of points. Firstly, there is uncertainty as to its scope, which is undesirable given the heavy punishments that may be imposed. Secondly, it may inhibit unduly freedom of expression. Thirdly, the summary process may lack the qualities of procedural fairness that are essential for orthodox criminal proceedings. These considerations led the Phillimore Committee on Contempt of Court[11] to recommend that conduct *intended* to pervert the course of justice should be dealt with as a criminal offence unless there are compelling reasons requiring it to be dealt with as a matter of urgency by means of summary contempt procedures. Where there is no such intention, then the law of contempt should apply, but on a narrower basis than previously. Accordingly, strict liability should only attach to publications (and no other kinds of conduct) which create a risk of serious prejudice to the course of justice and which are addressed to the public at large during the currency of proceedings. The relevant time limits should be more narrowly drawn than the existing sub judice period. 'Scandalising the court' should no longer be punished as contempt, but as a criminal offence. Contempt in the face of the court should where appropriate be dealt with as a criminal offence, and where dealt with summarily there should be additional procedural safeguards

---

5   See *James v Robinson* (1963) 109 CLR 593; Frankfurter J in *Green v United States* 356 US 165 at 189 (1958).
6   See *Enfield London Borough Council v Mahoney* [1983] 2 All ER 901, CA.
7   [1994] 1 AC 377.
8   See also *Harman v Secretary of State for the Home Department* [1983] 1 AC 280, HL; CPR 31.22; *Miller*, pp. 338-342. A civil contempt is not a criminal offence but does give rise to the privilege against self incrimination: *Cobra Golf Ltd v Rata* [1997] 2 All ER 150.
9   See *Borrie and Lowe.*
10 [1974] AC 273. See below, p. 759.
11 Cmnd. 5794, 1974.

for the defendant. The distinctions between 'civil' and 'criminal' contempt should be abolished. Many of these proposals were implemented in the Contempt of Court Act 1981,[12] although the government took the view that on a number of points the Phillimore proposals for reducing the scope of contempt were too radical.[13] The 1981 Act has had some effect in narrowing and clarifying the law of contempt. However, recent decisions have shown that the common law of contempt, outside the 1981 Act, is by no means defunct. There have been important decisions dealing with publications *intended* to interfere with the administration of justice[14] and conduct which involves failure to respect the terms of an injunction directed to third parties.[15] The latter in particular has opened up what is in effect a new field of criminal contempt.

Ultimately, in this context the law must draw an appropriate balance between the protection of free expression and ensuring fairness in the administration of justice. Both interests are reflected in explicit guarantees in the European Convention on Human Rights (Arts. 10 and 6).[16] The first case before the European Court of Human Rights from the UK dealing with these issues, *Sunday Times v UK*[17] led to the Contempt of Court Act 1981[18] but whether English law has yet got the balance right remains controversial.

In the United States of America, the contempt power has been much more narrowly defined by comparison with the British position. The Supreme Court has applied the Constitution's First Amendment guarantees of freedom of speech and of the press strictly against exercises of the contempt power. In *Bridges v California; Times-Mirror v California*[19] the Court held by 5–4 that utterances can only be punished as contempt where there is a clear and present danger to the orderly and fair administration of justice in relation to pending litigation: 'The substantive evil must be extremely serious and the degree of imminence extremely high before utterances can be punished.'[20] A 'reasonable tendency' is not sufficient. Subsequent cases have shown that the law of contempt is virtually a dead letter in protecting the trial process from prejudicial comment.[1] In addition, the constitutional right to jury trial in serious criminal cases (Fifth, Sixth and Fourteenth Amendments) has been held applicable to contempt cases.[2] In federal courts, the summary contempt power is limited by statute[3] to: '(1) Misbehaviour of any person in its presence or so near thereto as to obstruct the administration of justice; (2) Misbehaviour of any of its officers in their official transactions; (3) Disobedience or resistance to its lawful writ, process, order, rule, decree, or command.' The words 'so near thereto' have been held by the Supreme Court to bear a geographical rather than a causative meaning.[4] Some states have similar legislation narrowing the scope of the contempt power.

The *Sunday Times* case did not raise directly issues under Art. 6(1) ECHR. The relationship between Arts. 6(1) and 10 was discussed by the Court of Human Rights

12 See below, pp. 724–730.
13 Cmnd. 7145.
14 pp. 755–758.
15 pp. 766–773.
16 See above, pp. 21, 22.
17 Below, p. 721.
18 Below, p. 724.
19 314 US 252 (1941).
20 Per Black J at 263.
 1 See below, p. 752.
 2 *Bloom v Illinois* 391 US 194 (1968); *Miller*, pp. 136–138.
 3 18 US Code, Section 401, as derived originally from an Act of 1831.
 4 *Nye v United States* 313 US 33 (1941).

in *Worm v Austria*.[5] During the trial of a former minister for tax evasion W wrote an article asserting his guilt. The court found that W's conviction for an offence of having exercised prohibited influence on criminal proceedings did not violate Art. 10. The court stated:

> '50. Restrictions on freedom of expression permitted by the second paragraph of Article 10 "for maintaining the authority and impartiality of the judiciary" do not entitle States to restrict all forms of public discussion on matters pending before the courts.
>
> There is general recognition of the fact that the courts cannot operate in a vacuum. Whilst the courts are the forum for the determination of a person's guilt or innocence on a criminal charge . . . this does not mean that there can be no prior or contemporaneous discussion of the subject matter of criminal trials elsewhere, be it in specialised journals, in the general press or amongst the public at large (see, *mutatis mutandis*, the *Sunday Times* (no. 1) p. 40 § 65 [see below]).
>
> Provided that it does not overstep the bounds imposed in the interests of the proper administration of justice, reporting, including comment, on court proceedings contributes to their publicity and is thus perfectly consonant with the requirement under Article 6 § 1 of the Convention that hearings be public. Not only do the media have the task of imparting such information and ideas: the public also has a right to receive them (ibid.). This is all the more so where a public figure is involved, such as, in the present case, a former member of the Government. Such persons inevitably and knowingly lay themselves open to close scrutiny by both journalists and the public at large (see, among other authorities, the *Lingens v Austria* judgment of 8 July 1986, Series A no. 103, p. 26, § 42). Accordingly, the limits of acceptable comment are wider as regards a politician as such than as regards a private individual (ibid.).
>
> However, public figures are entitled to the enjoyment of the guarantees of a fair trial set out in Article 6, which in criminal proceedings include the right to an impartial tribunal, on the same basis as every other person. This must be borne in mind by journalists when commenting on pending criminal proceedings since the limits of permissible comment may not extend to statements which are likely to prejudice, whether intentionally or not, the chances of a person receiving a fair trial or to undermine the confidence of the public in the role of the courts in the administration of criminal justice.'

Accordingly, there is no room for 'balancing'. This point was confirmed by the Privy Council in *Montgomery and Coulter v HM Advocate*.[6] Here the Privy Council upheld the decision of the High Court of Justiciary that to proceed to the trial of the applicants for murder notwithstanding considerable prejudicial publicity would not breach Art. 6(1). Lord Hope stated:

> 'Reference was also made to Application No. 17265/90 *Baragiola v Switzerland* (1993) 75 D.R. 76. In that case the Commission observed, at p. 120, that, while particular importance should be attached to the freedom of the press because of the public's right to information, a fair balance must nevertheless be struck between that freedom and the right to a fair trial guaranteed by article 6 of the Convention and that a restrictive interpretation of article 6(1) would not correspond to the aim and purpose of that provision. As I understand these observations, however, they were intended to emphasise the point that primacy must be given to the right to a fair trial. Article 6, unlike articles 8 to 11 of the Convention, is not subject to any words of limitation. It does not require, nor indeed does it permit, a balance to be struck between the rights which it sets out and other considerations such as the public interest. In so far as the *Baragiola* case may be taken as suggesting that in the application of article 6(1) a balance must be struck between the right of an individual to a fair trial and the freedom of the press or the public's right to information, I would be inclined not to follow it on the ground that this suggestion is inconsistent with the wording of the Convention. The suggestion is not, so far as I am aware, supported by any other authority.'

---

5   (1997) 25 EHRR 454. See A. Mowbray, *Cases and Materials on the European Convention on Human Rights* (2001), pp. 357–358.
6   DRA Nos. 1 and 2 of 2000, [2001] 2 WLR 779.

Even without balancing, however, the European Court of Human Rights has yet to find a breach of Art. 6(1) arising from prejudicial publicity.[7] The court will take account of the role of the judge in giving directions to the jury in ensuring a fair trial.[8]

2 The Sunday Times case

Sunday Times v United Kingdom, E Ct HRR A 30; (1979) 2 EHRR 245, European Court of Human Rights

Following *A-G v Times Newspapers Ltd*[9] the present application was brought by the publisher, editor, and a group of journalists of *The Sunday Times*. The Commission expressed the opnion, by 8 votes to 5, that the injunction granted by the House of Lords against *The Sunday Times* was a breach of Article 10. The case was referred to the Court by the Commission. The Court held that Article 10 had been infringed because the restriction, although 'prescribed by law' and imposed for a legitimate purpose, was not 'necessary in a democratic society' for the maintenance of the 'authority ... of the judiciary'. The full Court reached this conclusion by 11 votes to 9.

JUDGMENT OF THE COURT

49. In the Court's opinion, the following are two of the requirements that flow from the expression 'prescribed by law'. Firstly, the law must be adequately accessible: the citizen must be able to have an indication that is adequate in the circumstances of the legal rules applicable to a given case. Secondly, a norm cannot be regarded as a law unless it is formulated with sufficient precision to enable the citizen to regulate his conduct: he must be able—if need be with appropriate advice—to foresee, to a degree that is reasonable in the circumstances, the consequences which a given action may entail. Those consequences need not be foreseeable with absolute certainty: experience shows this to be unattainable. Again, whilst certainty is highly desirable, it may bring in its train excessive rigidity and the law must be able to keep pace with changing circumstances. Accordingly, many laws are inevitably couched in terms which, to a greater or lesser extent, are vague and whose interpretation and application are questions of practice.

[The Court, having confirmed that the term 'law' in the above phrase included unwritten law such as the common law, concluded that although the English law of contempt was not as clear as it might be, the applicants 'were able to foresee to a degree that was reasonable in the circumstances, a risk that publication of the draft article' might be contempt. The Court also held that the injunction could be justified as having an aim permitted by Article 10(2), viz. 'the maintenance of the authority ... of the judiciary'. More difficult was the question whether it was 'necessary,' etc., to achieve that aim:]

59. ... The Court has noted[10] that, whilst the adjective 'necessary,' within the meaning of Article 10 § 2, is not synonymous with 'indispensable' neither has it the flexibility of such expressions as 'admissible', 'ordinary', 'useful', 'reasonable', or 'desirable' and that it implies the existence of a 'pressing social need ...'

---

7 See D. J. Harris, M. O'Boyle and C. Warbrick, *The European Convention on Human Rights* (1995), p. 216, noting that the Commission seemed to require proof of a prejudicial effect on a jury in fact rather than just an indication that it is likely.

8 Cf. *Pullar v United Kingdom* (1996) 22 EHRR 391 (P's misgivings about the impartiality of a juror could not be objectively justified).

9 Below, p. 759.

10 *Ed.* In *Handyside v UK* (1976) 1 EHRR 737 (see A. Mowbray, *Cases and Materials on the European Convention on Human Rights* (2001), p. 443ff).

In the second place, the Court has underlined that the initial responsibility for securing the rights and freedoms enshrined in the Convention lies with the individual Contracting States. Accordingly, 'Article 10 § 2 leaves to the Contracting States a margin of appreciation. This margin is given both to the domestic legislator ... and to the bodies, judicial amongst others, that are called upon to interpret and apply the laws in force ...'

'Nevertheless, Article 10 § 2 does not give the Contracting States an unlimited power of appreciation:' 'The Court ... is empowered to give the final ruling on whether a "restriction" ... is reconcilable with freedom of expression as protected by Article 10 ...

The Court has deduced from a combination of these principles that 'it is in no way [its] task to take the place of the competent national courts but rather to review under Article 10 the decisions they delivered in the exercise of their power of appreciation ...'

This does not mean that the Court's supervision is limited to ascertaining whether a respondent State exercised its discretion reasonably, carefully and in good faith. Even a Contracting State so acting remains subject to the Court's control as regards the compatibility of its conduct with the engagements it has undertaken under the Convention ...

Again, the scope of the domestic power of appreciation is not identical as regards each of the aims listed in Article 10 § 2. The *Handyside* case concerned the 'protection of morals'. The view taken by the Contracting States of the 'requirements of morals', observed the Court, 'varies from time to time and from place to place, especially in our era'. Precisely the same cannot be said of the far more objective notion of the 'authority' of the judiciary. The domestic law and practice of the Contracting States reveal a fairly substantial measure of common ground in this area. This is reflected in a number of provisions of the Convention, including Article 6, which have no equivalent as far as 'morals' are concerned. Accordingly, here a more extensive European supervision corresponds to a less discretionary power of appreciation ...

60. Both the minority of the Commission and the Government attach importance to the fact that the institution of contempt of court is peculiar to common-law countries and suggest that the concluding words of Article 10 § 2 were designed to cover this institution which has no equivalent in many other member States of the Council of Europe.

However, even if this were so, the Court considers that the reason for the insertion of those words would have been to ensure that the general aims of the law of contempt of court should be considered legitimate aims under Article 10 § 2 but not to make that law the standard by which to assess whether a given measure was 'necessary.' ...

62. It must now be decided whether the 'interference' complained of correspond to a 'pressing social need', whether it was 'proportionate to the legitimate aim pursued ...'

63. ... The speeches in the House of Lords emphasised above all the concern that the processes of the law may be brought into disrespect and the functions of the courts usurped either if the public is led to form an opinion on the subject-matter of litigation before adjudication by the courts or if the parties to litigation have to undergo 'trial by newspaper'. Such concern is in itself 'relevant' to the maintenance of the 'authority of the judiciary.' ...

Nevertheless, the proposed *Sunday Times* article was couched in moderate terms and did not present just one side of the evidence or claim that there was only one possible result at which a court could arrive ... Accordingly, eve to the extent that the article might have led some readers to form an opinion on the negligence issue, this would not have had adverse consequences for the 'authority of the judiciary' especially since, as noted above, there had been a nationwide campaign in the meantime.

65. ... Whilst ... [the courts] are the forum for the settlement of disputes, this does not mean that there can be no prior discussion of disputes elsewhere, be it in specialised journals, in the general press or amongst the public at large. ... Not only do the media have the task of imparting such information and ideas: the public also has a right to receive them. ... The Court observes ... that, following a balancing of the conflicting interests involved, an absolute rule was formulated by certain of the Law Lords to the effect that it was not permissible to prejudge issues in pending cases. ... Whilst emphasising that it is not its function to pronounce itself on an interpretation of English law adopted in the House of Lords ... the Court points out that it has to take a different approach. The Court is faced not with a choice between two conflicting principles but with a principle of freedom of expression [in Article 10] that is subject to a number of exceptions which must be narrowly interpreted ... the Court has to be satisfied that the interference was necessary having regard to the facts and circumstances

prevailing in the specific case before it ... the families of numerous victims of the tragedy, who were unaware of the legal difficulties involved, had a vital interest in knowing all the underlying facts and the various possible solutions. They could be deprived of this information, which was crucially important for them, only if it appeared absolutely certain that its diffusion would have presented a threat to the 'authority of the judiciary'.

66. The thalidomide disaster was a matter of undisputed public concern ... fundamental issues concerning protection against and compensation for injuries resulting from scientific developments were raised and many facets of the existing law on these subjects were called in question.

... the facts of the case did not cease to be a matter of public interest merely because they formed a background to pending litigation. By bringing to light certain facts, the article might have served as a brake on speculative and unenlightened discussion.

67. Having regard to all the circumstances of the case ... the Court concludes that the interference complained of did not correspond to a social need sufficiently pressing to outweigh the public interest in freedom of expression within the meaning of the Convention. The Court therefore finds the reasons for the restraint imposed on the applicants not to be sufficient under Article 10 § 2. That restraint proves not to be proportionate to the legitimate aim pursued; it was not necessary in a democratic society for maintaining the authority of the judiciary.

NOTES[11]

1. In their joint dissenting opinion, the nine dissenting judges, who included Judge Sir Gerald Fitzmaurice, disagreed with the majority essentially on the question whether the injunction was 'necessary' and on the latitude to be given to the defendant state under the 'margin of appreciation' doctrine. They pointed out that the 'authority and impartiality of the judiciary' exception allowed by Art. 10(2) was inserted on the proposal of the United Kingdom when the Convention was drafted to take account of the common law of contempt which is 'peculiar to the legal traditions of the common-law countries ... and ... is unknown in the law of most of the member states'. In the opinion of the dissenting judges, the conclusion of the majority that the 'authority ... of the judiciary' was a far more objective notion than that of 'the protection of morals' (so that less discretion should be allowed to the defendant state) was erroneous. It was 'by no means divorced from national circumstances and cannot be determined in a uniform way'. Evidence for this was to be found in the different ways in which states went about protecting the authority. A state such as the United Kingdom that relied upon the law of contempt to protect it should be given sufficient latitude to apply it as national circumstances warranted or required.

2. The *Sunday Times* case was the first in which the Court was called upon to consider whether a judgment applying a rule of common law complied with the Convention. Crucial to the Court's decision was its understanding of the difference between the approach that it could adopt under Art. 10 and that open to the House of Lords at common law. Whereas it had to give priority to freedom of expression, the House of Lords could give equal weight to two competing freedoms. Even so, it is difficult to avoid the conclusion that had the House of Lords been applying Art. 10 (and it is interesting to note that the Convention was not referred to by any of their Lordships) it would have found the injunction to have been 'necessary' in the sense in which the Court interpreted that term. It would seem, moreover, that when applying the 'margin of appreciation' doctrine in this context, the Court reduced it almost to vanishing point. It appears to have made its own assessment of the situation *de novo* and simply to have disagreed with that of the House of Lords. This raises the question

11 For casenotes, see P. J. Duffy, (1980) 5 H Rts Rev 17; F. A. Mann, (1979) 95 LQR 348; W. W. M. Wong, (1984) 17 NY Univ JIL & Pol. 35. On Art. 10, see D. Korff, (1988) 9 J Media L & P 143.

of the relationship between the Strasbourg authorities and local courts. (Cf. the *Handyside* case,[12] in which a court judgment applying statutory law was in issue.) As the Court indicated in the *Sunday Times* case,[13] it is not a court of appeal from national courts. It seems likely that the Court found confidence to disagree with the House of Lords from the lack of unanimity among English judges on the proper scope of the law of criminal contempt and its application in this case. Certainly it was affected by the fact, to which it refers, that the Phillimore Committee had suggested that the 'prejudgment' principle should be considered[14] and that the British government White Paper[15] had not called in question this suggestion. The Contempt of Court Act 1981 was enacted partly to bring United Kingdom law into line with the Convention.

3   The Contempt of Court Act 1981[16]

In this section we set out the provisions of the Contempt of Court Act 1981. This Act does not codify the whole of the law of contempt of court. It simply modifies certain aspects of the previously existing law. One significant feature that should be noted is that the first seven sections deal with what the Act terms the 'strict liability rule', as defined in s. 1. Accordingly, conduct *intended* to interfere with the course of justice will be regulated by (1) the common law of contempt except insofar as it is modified by the remaining provisions of the 1981 Act or (2) the substantive offences relating to the administration of justice.[17]

In the remaining sections (3–8) of the chapter we consider in turn the main varieties of criminal contempt, and within each section the position at common law is set out first, followed by a summary of the position following the enactment of the Contempt of Court Act 1981.

Contempt of Court Act 1981

Strict liability

1. The strict liability rule
In this Act 'the strict liability rule' means the rule of law whereby conduct may be treated as a contempt of court as tending to interfere with the course of justice in particular legal proceedings regardless of intent to do so.

2. Limitation of scope of strict liability
(1) The strict liability rule applies only in relation to publications, and for this purpose 'publication' includes any speech, writing, [programme included in a programme service][18] or other communication in whatever form, which is addressed to the public at large or any section of the public.
(2) The strict liability rule applies only to a publication which creates a substantial risk that the course of justice in the proceedings in question will be seriously impeded or prejudiced.

---

12 (1976) 1 EHRR 737.
13 Para. 59.
14 Cmnd. 5794, para. 111.
15 Cmnd. 7145, para. 43.
16 The Act is considered in the following works: *Borrie and Lowe; Miller; Arlidge, Eady and Smith, Current Law Statutes Annotated 1981* (annotations by A. G. L. Nicol and (for Scotland) C. H. W. Gane); N. Lowe, [1982] PL 20; C. J. Miller, [1982] Crim LR 71; S. H. Bailey, (1982) 45 MLR 301; P. J. Cooke, [1983] V (1) Liverpool LR 35.
17 See above, p. 717.
18 Substituted by the Broadcasting Act 1990, Sch. 20, para. 31.

(3) The strict liability rule applies to a publication only if the proceedings in question are active within the meaning of this section at the time of the publication.

(4) Schedule 1 applies for determining the times at which proceedings are to be treated as active within the meaning of this section.

[(5) In this section 'programme service' has the same meaning as in the Broadcasting Act 1990.][19]

3. Defence of innocent publication or distribution

(1) A person is not guilty of contempt of court under the strict liability rule as the publisher of any matter to which that rule applies if at the time of publication (having taken all reasonable care) he does not know and has no reason to suspect that relevant proceedings are active.

(2) A person is not guilty of contempt of court under the strict liability rule as the distributor of a publication containing any such matter if at the time of distribution (having taken all reasonable care) he does not know that it contains such matter and has no reason to suspect that it is likely to do so.

(3) The burden of proof of any fact tending to establish a defence afforded by this section to any person lies upon that person. . . .

4. Contemporary reports of proceedings

(1) Subject to this section a person is not guilty of contempt of court under the strict liability rule in respect of a fair and accurate report of legal proceedings held in public, published contemporaneously and in good faith.

(2) In any such proceedings the court may, where it appears to be necessary for avoiding a substantial risk of prejudice to the administration of justice in those proceedings, or in any other proceedings pending or imminent, order that the publication of any report of the proceedings, or any part of the proceedings, be postponed for such period as the court thinks necessary for that purpose.

[(2A) Where in proceedings for any offence which is an administration of justice offence for the purposes of section 54 of the Criminal Procedure and Investigations Act 1996 (acquittal tainted by an administration of justice offence) it appears to the court that there is a possibility that (by virtue of that section) proceedings may be taken against a person for an offence of which he has been acquitted, subsection (2) of this section shall apply as if those proceedings were pending or imminent.][20]

(3) For the purposes of subsection (1) of this section [...][1] a report of proceedings shall be treated as published contemporaneously—

    (*a*) in the case of a report of which publication is postponed pursuant to an order under subsection (2) of this section, if published as soon as practicable after that order expires;

    (*b*) in the case of a report of [an application for dismissal under section 6 of the Magistrates' Courts Act 1980][2] of which publication is permitted by virtue only of [subsection (5) or (7) of section 8A of that Act],[3] if published as soon as practicable after publication is so permitted. . . .

5. Discussion of public affairs

A publication made as or as part of a discussion in good faith of public affairs or other matters of general public interest is not to be treated as a contempt of court under the strict liability rule if the risk of impediment or prejudice to particular legal proceedings is merely incidental to the discussion.

6. Savings

Nothing in the foregoing provisions of this Act—

    (*a*) prejudices any defence available at common law to a charge of contempt of court under the strict liability rule;

---

19 Added by the Broadcasting Act 1990, Sch. 20.
20 Added by the Criminal Procedure and Investigations Act 1996, s. 57(3).
1 Words repealed by the Defamation Act 1996, Sch. 2.
2 Substituted for 'commital proceedings' by the Criminal Justice and Public Order Act 1994, Sch. 4, para. 50, from a day to be appointed.
3 Substituted for a reference to s. 8(3) of the 1980 Act by the Criminal Justice and Public Order Act 1994, Sch. 4, para. 50, from a day to be appointed.

(b)   implies that any publication is punishable as contempt of court under that rule which would not be so punishable apart from those provisions;

(c)   restricts liability for contempt of court in respect of conduct intended to impede or prejudice the administration of justice.

7. Consent required for institution of proceedings

Proceedings for a contempt of court under the strict liability rule (other than Scottish proceedings) shall not be instituted except by or with the consent of the Attorney-General or on the motion of a court having jurisdiction to deal with it.

Other aspects of law and procedure

8. Confidentiality of jury's deliberations

(1) Subject to subsection (2) below, it is a contempt of court to obtain, disclose or solicit any particulars of statements made, opinions expressed, arguments advanced or votes cast by members of a jury in the course of their deliberations in any legal proceedings.

(2) This section does not apply to any disclosure of any particulars—

(a)   in the proceedings in question for the purpose of enabling the jury to arrive at their verdict, or in connection with the delivery of that verdict, or

(b)   in evidence in any subsequent proceedings for an offence alleged to have been committed in relation to the jury in the first mentioned proceedings,

or to the publication of any particulars so disclosed.

(3) Proceedings for a contempt of court under this section (other than Scottish proceedings) shall not be instituted except by or with the consent of the Attorney-General or on the motion of a court having jurisdiction to deal with it.

9. Use of tape recorders

(1) Subject to subsection (4) below, it is a contempt of court—

(a)   to use in court, or bring into court for use, any tape recorder or other instrument for recording sound, except with the leave of the court;

(b)   to publish a recording of legal proceedings made by means of any such instrument, or any recording derived directly or indirectly from it, by playing it in the hearing of the public or any section of the public, or to dispose of it or any recording so derived, with a view to such publication;

(c)   to use any such recording in contravention of any conditions of leave granted under paragraph (a).

(2) Leave under paragraph (a) of subsection (1) may be granted or refused at the discretion of the court, and if granted may be granted subject to such conditions as the court thinks proper with respect to the use of any recording made pursuant to the leave; and where leave has been granted the court may at the like discretion withdraw or amend it either generally or in relation to any particular part of the proceedings.

(3) Without prejudice to any other power to deal with an act of contempt under paragraph (a) of subsection (1), the court may order the instrument, or any recording made with it, or both, to be forfeited; and any object so forfeited shall (unless the court otherwise determines on application by a person appearing to be the owner) be sold or otherwise disposed of in such manner as the court may direct.

(4) This section does not apply to the making or use of sound recordings for purposes of official transcripts of proceedings.

10. Sources of information

No court may require a person to disclose, nor is any person guilty of contempt of court for refusing to disclose, the source of information contained in a publication for which he is responsible, unless it be established to the satisfaction of the court that disclosure is necessary in the interests of justice or national security or for the prevention of disorder or crime.

11. Publication of matters exempted from disclosure in court

In any case where a court (having power to do so) allows a name or other matter to be withheld from the public in proceedings before the court, the court may give such directions prohibiting the publication of that name or matter in connection with the proceedings as appear to the court to be necessary for the purpose for which it was so withheld.

12. Offences of contempt of magistrates' courts

(1) A magistrates' court has jurisdiction under this section to deal with any person who—

    (a) wilfully insults the justice or justices, any witness before or officer of the court[4] or any solicitor or counsel having business in the court, during his or their sitting or attendance in court or in going to or returning from the court; or

    (b) wilfully interrupts the proceedings of the court or otherwise misbehaves in court.

(2) In any such case the court may order any officer of the court, or any constable, to take the offender into custody and detain him until the rising of the court; and the court may, if it thinks fit, commit the offender to custody for a specified perod not exceeding one month or impose on him a fine not exceeding [£2,500] or both. . . .

[(2A) A fine imposed under subsection (2) above shall be deemed, for the purposes of any enactment, to be a sum adjudged to be paid by a conviction.][5]

(4) A magistrates' court may at any time revoke an order of committal made under subsection (2) and, if the offender is in custody, order his discharge.

(5) [Section 135 of the Powers of the Criminal Courts (Sentencing) Act 2000 (limit on fines in respect of young persons) and] the following provisions of the Magistrates' Courts Act 1980 apply in relation to an order under this section as they apply in relation to a sentence on conviction or finding of guilty of an offence [; and those provisions of the Magristrates' Courts Act 1980 are] sections 75 to 91 (enforcement); section 108 (appeal to Crown Court); section 136 (overnight detention in default of payment); and section 142(1) (power to rectify mistakes). . . .

Penalties for contempt and kindred offences

14. Proceedings in England and Wales

(1) In any case where a court has power to commit a person to prison for contempt of court and (apart from this provision) no limitation applies to the period of committal, the committal shall (without prejudice to the power of the court to order his earlier discharge) be for a fixed term, and that term shall not on any occasion exceed two years in the case of committal by a superior court, or one month in the case of committal by an inferior court.

(2) In any case where an inferior court has power to fine a person for contempt of court and (apart from this provision) no limit applies to the amount of the fine, the fine shall not on any occasion exceed [£2,500]. . . .

[(2A) A fine imposed under subsection (2) above shall be deemed, for the purposes of any enactment, to be a sum adjudged to be paid by a conviction.][6]

(4) and (4A) [*Persons suffering from mental illness or severe mental impairment*]

[(4A) For the purposes of the preceding provisions of this section a county court shall be treated as a superior court and not as an inferior court.] . . .

19. Interpretation

In this Act

    'court' includes any tribunal or body exercising the judicial power of the State, and 'legal proceedings' shall be construed accordingly;

    'publication' has the meaning assigned by subsection (1) of section 2, and 'publish' (except in section 9) shall be construed accordingly; . . .

    'the strict liability rule' has the meaning assigned by section 1;

    'superior court' means the Court of Appeal, the High Court, the Crown Court, the Courts-Martial Appeal Court, the Restrictive Practices Court, the Employment Appeal Tribunal and any other court exercising in relation to its proceedings powers equivalent to those of the High Court, and includes the House of Lords in the exercise of its appellate jurisdiction . . .

---

4   The reference to any officer of the court includes a reference to any court security officer assigned to the court-house in which the court is sitting: Criminal Justice Act 1991, Sch. 11, para. 29. On court security officers, see the 1991 Act, ss. 76–79.

5   Substituted by the Criminal Justice Act 1993, Sch. 3, para. 6(4).

6   Substituted by the Criminal Justice Act 1993, Sch. 3, para. 6(5).

SCHEDULES

SCHEDULE 1

Preliminary
1. In this Schedule 'criminal proceedings' means proceedings against a person in respect of an offence, not being appellate proceedings or proceedings commenced by motion for committal or attachment in England and Wales or Northern Ireland; and 'appellate proceedings' means proceedings on appeal from or for the review of the decision of a court in any proceedings.
2. Criminal, appellate and other proceedings are active within the meaning of section 2 at the times respectively prescribed by the following paragraphs of this Schedule; and in relation to proceedings in which more than one of the steps described in any of those paragraphs is taken, the reference in that paragraph is a reference to the first of those steps.

Criminal proceedings
3. Subject to the following provisions of this Schedule, criminal proceedings are active from the relevant initial step specified in paragraph 4 [or 4A][7] until concluded as described in paragraph 5.
4. The initial steps of criminal proceedings are:—
    (*a*) arrest without warrant;
    (*b*) the issue, or in Scotland the grant, of a warrant for arrest;
    (*c*) the issue of a summons to appear, or in Scotland the grant of a warrant to cite;
    (*d*) the service of an indictment or other document specifying the charge;
    (*e*) except in Scotland, oral charge.
[(4A) Where as a result of an order under section 54 of the Criminal Procedure and Investigations Act 1996 (acquittal tainted by an administration of justice offence) proceedings are brought against a person for an offence of which he has previously been acquitted the initial step of the proceedings is a certification under subsection (2) of that section; and paragraph 4 has effect subject to this.][8]
5. Criminal proceedings are concluded
    (*a*) by acquittal or, as the case may be, by sentence;
    (*b*) by any other verdict, finding, order or decision which puts an end to the proceedings;
    (*c*) by discontinuance or by operation of law.
6. The reference in paragraph 5(*a*) to sentence includes any order or decision consequent on conviction or finding of guilt which disposes of the case, either absolutely or subject to future events, and a deferment of sentence under [section 1 of the Powers of Criminal Courts (Sentencing) Act 2000], section 219 or 432 of the Criminal Procedure (Scotland) Act 1975 or Article 14 of the Treatment of Offenders (Northern Ireland) Order 1976.
7. Proceedings are discontinued within the meaning of paragraph 5(*c*)—
    (*a*) in England and Wales or Northern Ireland, if the charge or summons is withdrawn or a *nolle prosequi* entered;
    [(*aa*)in England and Wales, if they are discontinued by virtue of section 23 of the Prosecution of Offences Act 1985;][9]
    (*b*) in Scotland, if the proceedings are expressly abandoned by the prosecutor or are deserted *simpliciter*;
    (*c*) in the case of proceedings in England and Wales or Northern Ireland commenced by arrest without warrant, if the person arrested is released, otherwise than on bail, without having been charged.
8. Criminal proceedings before a court-martial or standing civilian court are not concluded until the completion of any review of finding or sentence.
9. Criminal proceedings in England and Wales or Northern Ireland cease to be active if an order is made for the charge to lie on the file, but become active again if leave is later given for the proceedings to continue.

7   Added by the Criminal Procedure and Investigations Act 1996, s. 57(4).
8   Ibid.
9   Added by the Prosecution of Offences Act 1985, Sch. 1, para. 4.

[9A. Where proceedings in England and Wales have been discontinued by virtue of section 23 of the Prosecution of Offences Act 1985, but notice is given by the accused under subsection (7) of that section to the effect that he wants the proceedings to continue, they become active again with the giving of that notice.][10]

10. Without prejudice to paragraph 5(*b*) above, criminal proceedings against a person cease to be active—

(*a*) if the accused is found to be under a disability such as to render him unfit to be tried or unfit to plead or, in Scotland, is found to be insane in bar of trial; or

(*b*) if a hospital order is made in his case under [section 51(5) of the Mental Health Act 1983] . . .

but become active again if they are later resumed.

11. Criminal proceedings against a person which become active on the issue or the grant of a warrant for his arrest cease to be active at the end of the period of twelve months beginning with the date of the warrant unless he has been arrested within that period, but become active again if he is subsequently arrested.

Other proceedings at first instance

12. Proceedings other than criminal proceedings and appellate proceedings are active from the time when arrangements for the hearing are made or, if no such arrangements are previously made, from the time the hearing begins, until the proceedings are disposed of or discontinued or withdrawn; and for the purposes of this paragraph any motion or application made in or for the purposes of any proceedings, and any pre-trial review in the county court, is to be treated as a distinct proceeding.

13. In England and Wales or Northern Ireland arrangements for the hearing of proceedings to which paragraph 12 applies are made within the meaning of that paragraph—

(*a*) in the case of proceedings in the High Court for which provision is made by rules of court for setting down for trial, when the case is set down;

(*b*) in the case of any proceedings, when a date for the trial or hearing is fixed.

14. In Scotland arrangements for the hearing or proceedings to which paragraph 12 applies are made within the meaning of that paragraph—

(*a*) in the case of an ordinary action in the Court of Session or in the sheriff court, when the Record is closed;

(*b*) in the case of a motion or application, when it is enrolled or made;

(*c*) in any other case, when the date for a hearing is fixed or a hearing is allowed.

Appellate proceedings

15. Appellate proceedings are active from the time when they are commenced—

(*a*) by application for leave to appeal or apply for review, or by notice of such an application;

(*b*) by notice of appeal or of application for review;

(*c*) by other originating process,

until disposed of or abandoned, discontinued or withdrawn.

16. Where, in appellate proceedings relating to criminal proceedings, the court—

(*a*) remits the case to the court below; or

(*b*) orders a new trial or a *venire de novo*, or in Scotland grants authority to bring a new prosecution,

any further or new proceedings which result shall be treated as active from the conclusion of the appellate proceedings.

NOTES

1. By mistake, two subsections (4A) have been inserted in s. 14. The second (the one printed here) was introduced by the County Court (Penalties for Contempt) Act 1983 and was enacted to deal with the restriction on the powers of county courts to deal with civil contempts highlighted by the decision of the House of Lords in *Peart*

10 Added by the Prosecution of Offences Act 1985, Sch. 1, para. 5.

v Stewart.[11] The fines in ss. 12(2) and 14(2) were increased by the Criminal Justice Act 1991, Sch. 4. The limits to the penalties for contempt apply to civil as well as criminal contempts.[12] A judge may not impose on one occasion consecutive sentences which cumulatively exceed two years.[13] A person found guilty of criminal contempt is not 'convicted of an offence' and so may not be put on probation.[14]

2. The real impetus to reform seems to have been the decision of the European Court of Human Rights in the *Sunday Times* case[15] that the restriction placed upon freedom of speech by the injunction against the newspaper, upheld by the House of Lords in *A-G v Times Newspapers Ltd*[16] was contrary to Art. 10 of the European Convention on Human Rights. The Bill was introduced in the House of Lords by Lord Hailsham of St Marylebone LC.[17] He said that his 'poor little ewe lamb' of a Bill was intended to be a liberalising measure. The three main purposes of the first group of sections, dealing with the so-called rule of strict liability in criminal contempt, were: (1) implementation of the main recommendations of the Phillimore report, with 'minor deviations'; (2) harmonisation of the law of England and Wales with the European Court's judgment in the *Sunday Times* case; and (3) harmonisation of the laws of England, Scotland and Northern Ireland into a coherent set of rules. The other sections either sought to implement other recommendations of the Phillimore Committee or to deal with problems that had arisen since the Committee reported. The Act came into force on 27 August, 1981. It has been a mAatter of debate whether the Act does enough to bring English law into conformity with the European Convention on Human Rights.[18]

4 Publications prejudicial to a fair criminal trial

The main area where uncertainties in the law of contempt cast a shadow over free expression is that of publications which tend to prejudice the fair trial of either criminal or civil proceedings, or otherwise interfere with the course of justice. The important criticisms made to the Phillimore Committee were (1) 'the lack of clear definition of the kind of statement, criticism or comment which will be held to amount to contempt'[19] and (2) 'the uncertainty as to the time when the law of contempt applies'.[20] Where it is sought to hold persons liable under the 'strict liability rule'[1] the law on these points has been modified by ss. 2 and 3 of and Sch. 1 to the 1981 Act.[2] Prior to the 1981 Act it was more or less settled that the common law imposed strict liability for this form of contempt, subject to certain statutory defences.[3] Strict liability can now only be imposed by virtue of ss. 1 to 7 of the 1981 Act. Recent cases have made it clear that publications (and indeed other conduct) *intended* to interfere with justice can still be dealt with under the common law of contempt. Here,

---

11 [1983] 2 AC 109, HL.
12 *Linnett v Coles* [1987] QB 555, CA.
13 *Re R (a minor) (contempt: sentence)* [1994] 2 All ER 144; *Villiers v Villiers* [1994] 2 All ER 149, CA.
14 *R v Palmer* [1992] 3 All ER 289, CA(CrD).
15 Above, p. 721.
16 Below, p. 759.
17 415 HL Deb, December 9 1980, cols. 657–665.
18 See the articles cited below, p. 765 n. 5.
19 Para. 83.
20 Para. 84.
 1 Contempt of Court Act 1981, s. 1; above p. 724.
 2 Above, pp. 724–725 and below pp. 730–742, and 754.
 3 See below, pp. 754–755.

the issues of what constitutes contempt, when the sub judice rule applies and the scope of liability are regulated by the common law and not the 1981 Act.[4]

The balance between freedom of expression and the right to a fair trial is different in the UK and the United States, and there are important sectors of opinion in each country which express dissatisfaction with their country's own position.

(A) WHAT CONSTITUTES CONTEMPT?

(i) At common law

R v Evening Standard Co Ltd [1954] 1 QB 578, [1954] 1 All ER 1026, [1954] 2 WLR 861, Queen's Bench Divisional Court

On 23 February 1954, a Mr Kemp was indicted at Chelmsford Assizes for the murder of his wife, who had been dead for a considerable time before his arrest and whose body was discovered in a trunk which the defendant had caused to be moved with his effects. Part of the case for the Crown was that the defendant had told many lies with regard to the disappearance of his wife. A Miss Briggs gave evidence that the defendant had told her that he was unmarried, and a Mrs Darmody said that he had told her that he had been married but that his wife had died. That evening, the *Evening Standard* carried a report of the trial under the headline 'Trunk Trial Story of Marriage Offer – Husband is Accused', which stated that Mrs Darmody 'said at the assizes that a man accused of murdering his wife asked her to marry him.'

In fact, Mrs Darmody had not given that evidence. Miss Briggs had given evidence before the examining justices that the prisoner had, after the death of his wife, asked her to marry him; but at the trial, when Miss Briggs had just begun to give evidence, the judge ruled, after a discussion in the absence of the jury, that that part of her evidence should not be given as it was highly prejudicial to the defendant; and no such evidence was given at the trial.

The reporter at the trial was responsible for the error – he had attended the committal proceedings, and had left the trial during the discussion as to the admissibility of part of Miss Briggs' evidence, returning just after she had completed her evidence. In fact the jury found the defendant not guilty.

The Attorney-General applied for leave to issue a writ of attachment against the Evening Standard Co Ltd, the editor of the *Evening Standard* and the reporter.

According to an affidavit filed by the editor the reporter had for 10 years been a trusted reporter on the staff of the newspaper and had previously reported many trials without any complaint as to the accuracy of his reports, and had proved himself a thoroughly competent and reliable reporter. He had thought the report perfectly accurate and genuine and he and the proprietors had published it in good faith.

Lord Goddard CJ delivered the judgment of the court (**Lord Goddard CJ**, **Hilbery** and **Hallett JJ**): . . .

This is surely a proper matter to bring before this court. It is just as well that the nature of the jurisdiction which this court exercises on these occasions with regard to reports of trials in newspapers should be understood. It is called contempt of court, and that is a convenient expression because it is akin to a contempt. But the essence of the jurisdiction is that reports, if they contain comments on cases before they are tried, or alleged histories of the prisoner who is on trial—such as in the case of the *Daily Mirror* (*R v Bolam, ex p Haigh* (1949) 93 Sol Jo 220), in which this court had to intervene about five years ago—and all misreports are matters which tend to interfere with the due course of justice. The foundation of the jurisdiction is that such reports are an interference with the due course of justice, and one of

4   See below, pp. 753–754, 735–758.

the earliest cases, if not the earliest, in which this jurisdiction was invoked was in 1742, in a case known as *The St. James Evening Post* ((1742) 2 Atk 469) before that great judge, Lord Hardwicke LC. In that case there was a motion to commit an editor for publishing a libel upon a litigant and it was objected that it was not a matter for the summary jurisdiction of the court because there was a remedy at law for libel. Lord Hardwicke pointed out that he was dealing with the matter of the publication of a libel upon a litigant in a case which had not then come to a conclusion or been heard. He started his judgment by saying (ibid.): 'Nothing is more incumbent upon courts of justice, than to preserve their proceedings from being misrepresented;—that is, of course, what has happened here—'nor is there any thing of more pernicious consequence, than to prejudice the minds of the public against persons concerned as parties in causes, before the cause is finally heard.' After rejecting the argument that he could not deal summarily with the case because there was a remedy at law, he considered the different sorts of contempt. The last one was (ibid. p. 471): 'There may be also a contempt of this court, in prejudicing mankind against persons before the cause is heard. There cannot be any thing of greater consequence, than to keep the streams of justice clear and pure, that parties may proceed with safety both to themselves and their characters.' . . .

We have said, perhaps more frequently in recent years, that the summary jurisdiction of this court should only be invoked and will only be exercised in cases of real and serious moment; and have deprecated in certain cases a motion to attach where there has not really been a serious interference with justice. This case might have been a disastrous interference with justice; but, as Lord Hewart CJ said in *R v Editor of the New Statesman, ex p DPP* (1928) 44 TLR 301 at 303 the gravity of the penalty or sanction which the court will impose must depend upon the circumstances of each particular case. If a comment is gratuitously published either in a newspaper or in any other form of public dissemination, this court would not hesitate to impose a severe penalty, and even, as in the recent case of the *Daily Mirror* (*R v Bolam, ex p Haigh* (1949) 93 Sol Jo 220) to inflict the penalty of imprisonment. In this case, however, I am glad to be able to come to the conclusion that there was here no intentional interference with the course of justice. I cannot believe that the reporter for a moment deliberately or intentionally sent out false information. He, as a responsible journalist, would know that doing so would land him in the gravest possible difficulty. Nor can one attach moral blame, if I may use that expression, to the editor, who had no reason to suppose that a reporter of the 'Standard' had sent him information in an inaccurate form. There are, therefore, mitigating circumstances, and one can only be thankful that the matter did not react unfavourably on the prisoner, though, as I have said whether it reacts favourably or unfavourably upon the prisoner is not the test.

Sir Hartley Shawcross said that, while his clients desired to abide by the well understood rule of journalism that the editor and proprietors of papers must in a case such as this take responsibility, he would suggest to the court that vicarious liability, as it is called, ought not in law to be visited upon them and that they ought not to be made vicariously liable for the mistake or misconduct of the reporter. I do not think that we can possibly agree with that submission, which seems contrary to what Lord Russell and Wright J said in *R v Payne* [1896] 1 QB 577 where they pointed out that the court would interfere where the publication was intended or calculated or likely to interfere with the course of justice. Wright J (ibid. p. 582) used the word 'likely,' Lord Russell (ibid. p. 580) used the word 'calculated'.

[The court held that all the defendants were guilty of contempt, but that no penalty should be imposed on the editor and reporter. The publishers were fined £1,000.]

NOTES

1. Note that the Divisional Court was not concerned with the actual effect upon proceedings, but the potential effect, particularly on a jury.[5]

The cases show that the test at common law was whether a publication was 'calculated' or 'likely' to interfere with the course of justice or, in other words, whether

---

5   Cf. *A-G for New South Wales v John Fairfax & Sons Ltd* [1980] 1 NSWLR 362, 368 (NSWCA).

it created a real risk that the fair and proper trial of pending proceedings might be prejudiced. This remains the test where contempt proceedings are taken in respect of conduct *intended* to interfere with the course of justice, with the possible qualification that the proceedings need not be pending or imminent.[6] The common law is also of relevance in as much as s. 6(b) of the Contempt of Court Act 1981 provides that nothing in ss. 1–5 implies that any publication is punishable as contempt of court under the strict liability rule which would not have been so punishable apart from those provisions: i.e. at common law.

2. The following are some examples of contempt in cases decided before the 1981 Act came into operation. Some involved prejudging the merits of cases at common law. In *R v Bolam, ex p Haigh*[7] B, the editor of the *Daily Mirror*, was imprisoned for three months, and the proprietors were fined £10,000 for describing Haigh as a 'vampire' and, after saying that he was charged with one murder, stating that he had committed others, giving the names of the victims.[8]

In the 1920s, various newspapers conducted systematic 'criminal investigations' whose results were then published. This led to fines of £1,000 imposed on the *Evening Standard*, and of £300 on two other newspapers, with a warning that repetition of the offence would lead to imprisonment.[9]

In the *Sunday Times* case,[10] the House of Lords held that prejudgment of the merits amounted to a contempt of court. The facts concerned civil proceedings, but a distinction between civil and criminal proceedings was not drawn for this purpose. However, in subsequent cases the Divisional Court held that prejudgment only amounted to contempt where it created a real risk that the fair and proper trial of pending proceedings might be prejudiced. So, in *Blackburn v BBC*[11] James Ferman, secretary designate of the British Board of Film Censors, referred in a television interview to pending criminal proceedings instituted by B in relation to the showing of the film 'The Language of Love', and said 'The context of the film was seriously educational and could do nothing but good in the board's opinion and my opinion'. The court held that there was no risk of prejudice given that the words were spoken in the middle of a general discussion about film censorship and were immediately followed by an expression of F's opinion that the courts should be the final arbiter. Moreover, the programme was only shown in the south-west, and it was unlikely that a prospective Old Bailey juror would see or recollect the words. The same test was applied in *R v Bulgin, ex p BBC*.[12]

Other examples include comments on a defendant's character,[13] the revelation of guilty plea during a trial that had been kept from the jury[14] and the publication of a photograph of a person on the day he was due to take part in an identification parade.[15]

3. As discussed below[16] common law liability for contempt may arise from conduct (including publications) which, with the requisite intent, 'frustrates, thwarts or subverts the purpose of the court's order and thereby interferes with the due

---

6 See below, pp. 755–759.
7 (1949) 93 Sol Jo 220.
8 Cf. *R v Odham's Press Ltd, ex p A-G* [1957] 1 QB 73.
9 *R v Evening Standard, ex p DPP* (1924) 40 TLR 833.
10 Below p. 759.
11 (1976) Times, 15 December.
12 (1977) Times, 14 July.
13 *R v Thomson Newspapers, ex p A-G* [1968] 1 All ER 268; the defendant's appeal against conviction was, however, rejected: *R v Malik* [1968] 1 All ER 582n.
14 *R v Border Television Ltd, ex p A-G*; *R v Newcastle Chronicle and Journal Ltd, ex p A-G* (1978) 68 Cr App Rep 375, DC.
15 *R v Evening Standard Co Ltd, ex p A-G* (1976) Times, 3 November, DC.
16 pp. 766–773.

administration of justice in the particular action'; 'purpose' here means the purpose the court was intending to fulfil: *A-G v Times Newspapers Ltd*.[17] This principle applies where the order in question is directed at persons other than the respondent to the contempt proceedings (see further *A-G v Newspaper Publishing plc*[18] and *A-G v Times Newspapers Ltd*[19] concerning orders made in civil proceedings). In *A-G v Newspaper Publishing plc*,[20] the Court of Appeal (Criminal Division) at the end of the hearing of the appeals of four persons connected with Ordtech Ltd against convictions for conspiracy to export armaments to Iraq in breach of control orders, ordered that various documents previously the subject of PII claims but now disclosed for the purpose of the appeal only should be returned. Lord Taylor CJ also expressed the hope 'that we will not see any more of the documents appearing on television or in the newspapers'. Subsequently the *Independent* published a facsimile of part of one of these documents and some sentences from another, including words that had not been quoted in the judgment. The Court of Appeal (Criminal Division) held that these publications did not constitute contempt. For contempt the order in question had to be clear and infringement would have to have 'some significant adverse effect on the administration of justice' (although not necessarily that it had been 'wholly frustrated or rendered utterly futile').[1] 'Recognising that the restraints upon freedom of expression should be no wider than are truly necessary in a democratic society, we do not accept that conduct by a third party which is inconsistent with a court order in only trivial or technical way should expose a party to conviction for contempt.'[2] The breaches here were very minor: the publication of a few additional sentences and the reproduction of the form of documents did not amount to a significant interference with the administration of justice. Furthermore, *mens rea* was not established given that the respondents were genuinely uncertain as to the effect of the order.[3]

(ii) Under the 'strict liability rule'

Section 2 of the Contempt of Court Act 1981[4] provides that there can only be liability for contempt under the strict liability rule where a 'publication' (see s. 2(1)) 'creates a substantial risk that the course of justice in the proceedings in question will be seriously impeded or prejudiced' (s. 2(2)). This is more stringent than the test at common law.

NOTES

1. This test was based on that recommended by the Phillimore Committee[5] but with the addition of the word 'substantial'. Note that strict liability is now confined to 'publications', as recommended by the Phillimore Committee[6] whose view was that strict liability should be confined to public conduct.

17 [1992] 1 AC 191, 222–223, per Lord Oliver, cited by Lord Bingham CJ in *A-G v Newspaper Publishing plc* [1997] 3 All ER 159 at 168.
18 [1988] Ch 333.
19 [1992] 1 AC 191, below, pp. 768.
20 Above.
 1 [1997] 3 All ER 159, 168.
 2 Ibid.
 3 See further on *mens rea*, below, pp. 755–758, 772–773.
 4 Above, p. 724.
 5 Cmnd. 5794, 1974, pp. 44–49.
 6 pp. 33–35.

2. To what extent does the new test constitute a real and not merely a 'semantic' or 'cosmetic' relaxation in the application of the law of contempt? See *Borrie and Lowe*.[7] Do you think that any of the cases where D was convicted at common law would have been decided differently had the new test been in operation? Section 2(2) has been applied in *A-G v English*[8] and *A-G v Times Newspapers*.[9] As to its application in respect of civil cases, see below.[10]

A-G v English [1983] 1 AC 116, [1982] 2 All ER 903, [1982] 3 WLR 278, House of Lords

In October 1981 the *Daily Mail* published an article under the heading 'The vision of life that wins my vote' written by the journalist and broadcaster Malcolm Muggeridge in support of a parliamentary candidate, Mrs Marilyn Carr, who was seeking election as a pro-life candidate. The article was concerned with preserving the sanctity of human life. It also noted that Mrs Carr had been born without arms and continued: 'Today the chances of such a baby surviving would be very small indeed. Someone would surely recommend letting her die of starvation, or otherwise disposing of her.' The article was published on the third day of the trial of a consultant paediatrician, Dr Leonard Arthur, for the murder of John Pearson, a baby suffering from Down's syndrome. The trial judge, Farquharson J, referred the article to the Attorney-General, who applied to the Divisional Court for an order of committal against the editor of the *Daily Mail*, David English, and the newspaper's owners. He relied on the 'strict liability rule' contained in s. 1 of the Contempt of Court Act 1981. The defendant relied on s. 5 of the 1981 Act.[11] The Divisional Court held that the publication amounted to contempt. No penalty was imposed on the editor; he had been absent from the office at the relevant times and was not personally responsible for the publication. A 'nominal' fine of £500 was imposed on the owners. The defendants appealed to the House of Lords.

Lord Diplock: ... There is, of course, no question that the article in the *Daily Mail* of which complaint is made by the Attorney-General was a 'publication' within the meaning of section 2(1). That being so, it appears to have been accepted in the Divisional Court by both parties that the onus of proving that the article satisfied the conditions stated in section 2(2) lay upon the Attorney-General and that, if he satisfied that onus, the onus lay upon the appellants to prove that it satisfied the conditions stated in section 5. For my part, I am unable to accept that this represents the effect of the relationship of section 5 to section 2(2). Section 5 does not take the form of a proviso or an exception to section 2(2). It stands on an equal footing with it. It does not set out exculpatory matter. Like section 2(2) it states what publications shall *not* amount to contempt of court despite their tendency to interfere with the course of justice in particular legal proceedings.

[L]ogically the first question always is: has the publication satisfied the criterion laid down by section 2(2) i.e. that it 'creates a substantial risk that the course of justice in the proceedings in question will be seriously impeded or prejudiced.'

My Lords, the first thing to be observed about this criterion is that the risk that has to be assessed is that which was created by the publication of the allegedly offending matter at the time when it was published. The public policy that underlies the strict liability rule in contempt of court is deterrence. Trial by newspaper or, as it should be more compendiously expressed today, trial by the media, is not to be permitted in this country. That the risk that was created by the publication when it was actually published does not ultimately affect the outcome of the proceedings is, as Lord Goddard CJ said in *R v Evening Standard Co Ltd* [1954] 1 QB 578, 582 'neither here nor there.' If there was a reasonable possibility that it might have done so if in the period subsequent to the publication the proceedings had not taken the course that in fact they did and Dr Arthur was acquitted, the offence was complete. The true course of justice must not at any stage be put at risk.

Next for consideration is the concatenation in the subsection of the adjective 'substantial' and the adverb 'seriously', the former to describe the degree of risk, the latter to describe the degree of impediment or prejudice to the course of justice. 'Substantial' is hardly the most apt word to apply to 'risk' which is a noumenon. In combination I take the two words to be intended to exclude a risk that is only remote. With regard to the adverb 'seriously' a perusal of the cases cited in *A-G v Times Newspapers Ltd* [1974] AC 273 discloses that the adjective 'serious' has from time to time been used as an alternative to 'real' to describe the degree of risk of interfering with the course of justice, but not the degree of interference itself. It is, however, an ordinary English word that is not intrinsically inapt when used to describe the extent of an impediment or prejudice to the cause of justice in particular legal proceedings, and I do not think that for the purposes of the instant appeal any attempt to paraphrase it is necessary or would be helpful. The subsection applies to all kinds of legal proceedings, not only criminal prosecutions before a jury. If, as in the instant case and probably in most other criminal trials upon indictment, it is the outcome of the trial or the need to discharge the jury without proceeding to a verdict that is put at risk, there can be no question that that which in the course of justice is put at risk is as serious as anything could be.

My Lords, that Mr Malcolm Muggeridge's article was capable of prejudicing the jury against Dr Arthur at the early stage of his trial when it was published, seems to me to be clear. It suggested that it was a common practice among paediatricians to do that which Dr Arthur was charged with having done, because they thought that it was justifiable in the interest of humanity even though it was against the law. At this stage of the trial the jury did not know what Dr Arthur's defence was going to be; and whether at that time the risk of the jury's being influenced by their recollection of the article when they came eventually to consider their verdict appeared to be more than a remote one, was a matter which the judge before whom the trial was being conducted was in the best position to evaluate, even though this evaluation, although it should carry weight, would not be binding on the Divisional Court or on your Lordships. The judge thought at that stage of the trial that the risk was substantial, not remote. So, too, looking at the matter in retrospect, did the Divisional Court despite the fact that the risk had not turned into an actuality since Dr Arthur had by then been acquitted. For my part I am not prepared to dissent from this evaluation. I consider that the publication of the article on the third day of what was to prove a lengthy trial satisfied the criterion for which section 2(2) of the Act provides.

The article, however, fell also within the category dealt with in section 5. It was made, in undisputed good faith, as a discussion in itself of public affairs, viz, Mrs Carr's candidature as an independent pro-life candidate in the North West Croydon by-election for which the polling day was in one week's time. It was also part of a wider discussion on a matter of general public interest that had been proceeding intermittently over the last three months, upon the moral justification of mercy killing and in particular of allowing newly born hopeless handicapped babies to die. So it was for the Attorney-General to show that the risk of prejudice to the fair trial of Dr Arthur, which I agree was created by the publication of the article at the stage the trial had reached when it was published, was not 'merely incidental' to the discussion of the matter with which the article dealt.

My Lords, any article published at the time when Dr Arthur was being tried which asserted that it was a common practice among paediatricians to let severely physically or mentally handicapped new born babies die of starvation or otherwise dispose of them would (as, in common with the trial judge and the Divisional Court, I have already accepted) involve a substantial risk of prejudicing his fair trial. But an article supporting Mrs Carr's candidature in the by-election as a pro-life candidate that contained no such assertion would depict her as tilting at imaginary windmills. One of the main planks of the policy for which she sought the suffrage of the electors was that these things did happen and ought to be stopped.

I have drawn attention to the passages principally relied upon by the Divisional Court as causing a risk of prejudice that was not 'merely incidental to the discussion'. The court described them as 'unnecessary' to the discussion and as 'accusations'. The test, however, is not whether an article could have been written as effectively without these passages or whether some other phraseology might have been substituted for them that could have reduced the risk of prejudicing

Dr Arthur's fair trial; it is whether the risk created by the words actually chosen by the author was 'merely incidental to the discussion', which I take to mean: no more than an incidental consequence of expounding its main theme. The Divisional Court also apparently regarded the passages complained of as disqualified from the immunity conferred by section 5 because they consisted of 'accusations' whereas the court considered, [1983] 1 AC p. 128e–f, that 'discussion' was confined to 'the airing of views and the propounding and debating of principles and arguments'. I cannot accept this limited meaning of 'discussion' in the section. As already pointed out, in the absence of any accusation, believed to be true by Mrs Carr and Mr Muggeridge, that it was a common practice among some doctors to do what they are accused of doing in the passages complained of, the article would lose all its point whether as support for Mrs Carr's parliamentary candidature or as a contribution to the wider controversy as to the justifiability of mercy killing. The article would be emasculated into a mere contribution to a purely hypothetical problem appropriate, it may be, for debate between academic successors of the mediaeval schoolmen, but remote from all public affairs and devoid of any general public interest to readers of the *Daily Mail*.

My Lords, the article that is the subject of the instant case appears to me to be in nearly all respects the antithesis of the article which this House (pace a majority of the judges of the European Court of Human Rights) held to be a contempt of court in *A-G v Times Newspapers Ltd* [1974] AC 273. There the whole subject of the article was the pending civil actions against Distillers Co. (Biochemicals) Ltd, arising out of their having placed upon the market the new drug thalidomide, and the whole purpose of it was to put pressure upon that company in the lawful conduct of their defence in those actions. In the instant case, in contrast, there is in the article no mention at all of Dr Arthur's trial. It may well be that many readers of the *Daily Mail* who saw the article and had read also the previous day's report of Dr Arthur's trial, and certainly if they were members of the jury at that trial, would think, 'that is the sort of thing that Dr Arthur is being tried for; it appears to be something that quite a lot of doctors do.' But the risk of their thinking that and allowing it to prejudice their minds in favour of finding him guilty on evidence that did not justify such a finding seems to me to be properly described in ordinary English language as 'merely incidental' to any meaningful discussion of Mrs Carr's election policy as a pro-life candidate in the by-election due to be held before Dr Arthur's trial was likely to be concluded, or to any meaningful discussion of the wider matters of general public interest involved in the current controversy as to the justification of mercy killing. To hold otherwise would have prevented Mrs Carr from putting forward and obtaining publicity for what was a main plank in her election programme and would have stifled all discussion in the press upon the wider controversy about mercy killing from the time that Dr Arthur was charged in the magistrates' court in February 1981 until the date of his acquittal at the beginning of November of that year; for those are the dates between which, under section 2(3) and Schedule 1, the legal proceedings against Dr Arthur would be 'active' and so attract the strict liability rule.

Such gagging of bona fide public discussion in the press of controversial matters of general public interest, merely because there are in existence contemporaneous legal proceedings in which some particular instance of those controversial matters may be in issue, is what section 5 of the Contempt of Court Act 1981 was in my view intended to prevent. I would allow this appeal.

Lords Elwyn-Jones, Keith, Scarman and **Brandon** agreed with **Lord Diplock**'s speech.

Appeal allowed.

NOTES

1. The word 'noumenon' means an 'object of intellectual intuition devoid of all phenomenal attributes' (OED).
2. Are the interpretation and application of s. 2(2) satisfactory?[12] In the Divisional Court, Watkins LJ noted[13] that while the article made no express reference to the

12 See G. J. Zellick, [1982] PL 343; A. Ward, (1983) 46 MLR 85; M. Redmond, [1983] CLJ 9.
13 [1983] 1 AC at 123–125.

Arthur trial, the circumstances of the trial were 'unusual' and 'had received very great publicity'. It seemed to their Lordships 'inevitable that all sensible people, including the jurors at the Crown Court at Leicester, would conclude' that assertions in the article such as 'someone would surely recommend letting her die of starvation' referred to the Arthur trial. The article 'contains undisguised assertions or insinuations that babies who are born with certain kinds of handicaps are caused or allowed by those in charge of them to die within days of birth of starvation among other means'. Such statements 'may wrongly prejudice jurors'. The 'poison of prejudice' must be kept away from the 'well of justice'. 'If it is not, then the possibility of a miscarriage of justice inevitably accompanies prejudice.' Accordingly, the Divisional Court was satisfied 'beyond reasonable doubt' that the publication 'created a substantial risk of serious prejudice in the trial of Dr Arthur'. Consider (1) whether the word 'substantial' in s. 2(2) should have been accorded such a narrow interpretation by the House of Lords and (2) whether, even on that narrow approach, you would be satisfied the publication created the necessary risk. (See Zellick,[14] who argues that the decision on this point 'seriously misinterpreted the subsection and confirms the traditional breadth of the contempt law which Parliament had been at pains to curb', and Redmond.[15])

4. *A-G v English* may be contrasted with the decisions of the Divisional Court in *A-G v Times Newspapers Ltd* (heard with four other cases).[16] The Attorney-General brought contempt proceedings under the strict liability rule against the publishers of five newspapers in respect of news stories and articles about Michael Fagan, an intruder into the Queen's bedroom. He had already been charged with offences arising out of three previous incidents: (1) a charge of burglary in respect of a previous entry into Buckingham Palace, during which he had drunk some wine; (2) a charge of taking a motor vehicle without the owner's consent; and (3) a charge of assaulting his stepson. Lord Lane CJ noted that under s. 2(2) a slight or trivial risk of serious prejudice was not enough nor was a substantial risk of slight prejudice. Five cases were heard together.

(1) The *Sun* was prosecuted in respect of assertions that Fagan had a long standing drug problem, was a glib liar and had stolen cigars from the Palace. Lord Lane 'accepted the view that jurors were to be credited with more independence of mind than was sometimes suggested'. The risk that the fair trial on the burglary charge would be prejudiced was 'too remote to qualify for the description of substantial'.

(2) The *Daily Star* had published allegations similar to the *Sun* and was accordingly acquitted in respect of those. In addition, it had asserted (i) that Fagan admitted to stealing the wine and (ii) that he intended to commit suicide, the inferential suggestion being that he was unbalanced. Assertion (i) amounted to contempt, but assertion (ii) did not: 'However independent minded a jury might be and however cynical about the accuracy of newspaper reporting nevertheless there would inevitably be a real risk, whether the judge gave a warning about disregarding extraneous facts or not, that the memory of [assertion (i)] would remain in the jurors' minds and would affect the outcome of their deliberations.' It was conceded that s. 5 provided no defence. Nevertheless, no penalty was imposed.

(3) Neither of the matters complained of against the *Sunday People* amounted to contempt: (i) allegations that Fagan had been addicted to drugs were similar to those made by the *Sun* and the *Daily Star*; (ii) reported comments, said to have emanated from a Palace spokesman, that some of Fagan's reported statements were 'quite absurd

14 Op. cit., p. 344.
15 Op. cit., pp. 12–13.
16 (1983) Times, 12 February, DC.

and fanciful suggestions' (thus implying that he was untruthful) were not likely to influence a juror.

(4) The *Mail on Sunday* had published an article by Lady Falkender which contained the clear suggestion of a possible homosexual liaison between Fagan and Commander Trestrail, who had recently resigned as Queen's Police Officer because of a homosexual relationship with a male prostitute. It also referred to Fagan as a 'rootless neurotic with no visible means of support'. The court held that this could not fail to have an effect on anyone considering Fagan's honesty. Although the burglary charge was not mentioned, everybody reading any newspaper would be well aware of it. 'Accordingly the article had the necessary ingredient under s. 2.' However, it fell within s. 5: 'the appalling state of the safeguards designed to protect Her Majesty together with the proclivities of her bodyguard were matters which were of the greatest public concern' and 'the article was part of the discussion about the Queen's safety'.

(5) *The Sunday Times* had alleged that Fagan was charged with stabbing his stepson in the neck with a screwdriver: it was now conceded that there was never any such allegation and that the only allegation was one of assault. This inaccuracy 'on its own did not cause the publication to amount to contempt. Where however the inaccuracy was of that extent and was given front-page prominence then the publisher put himself at risk'. A second article repeated the false suggestion that Fagan was charged with wounding and also stated that the whole affair arose out of a genuine misunderstanding that the boy had received his injuries not at Fagan's hands but in some earlier incident before Fagan arrived on the scene. These statements were held to be prejudicial to the trial of the assault charge. The second article also stated, falsely, that the charge of taking a motor vehicle had been dropped. This was held to be prejudicial to the prosecution in respect of this charge. Section 5 was not applicable. The alleged assault was no more than a domestic fracas that was irrelevant to the public discussion of the matter of the Queen's security. The articles nevertheless went into great detail about it and could not be described as 'merely incidental' to the expounding of the main theme. Ackner LJ agreed with Lord Lane CJ. Oliver LJ generally agreed, but doubted whether the *Mail on Sunday* article fell foul of s. 2, and held that the first *Sunday Times* article did so not because of any possible influence on jurors but because it caused Fagan, on legal advice, to elect for jury trial rather than summary trial: any extraneous factor which impeded or restricted the defendant's right of election was a serious prejudice. Cf. the placing of improper pressure on litigants in civil proceedings.[17] Oliver LJ's approach was followed in *A-G v Unger*[18] (no contempt on the facts).

Borrie and Lowe[19] note that: if s. 2(2) was thought to be restrictively interpreted in *A-G v English*, it must be considered to be generously interpreted in the *Fagan* cases. Do you agree?

The pattern of subsequent case law suggests that it has been increasingly difficult for the Attorney-General to secure convictions under the strict liability rule other than in very clear cut cases. Successful prosecutions include the following *A-G v BBC*; *A-G v Hat Trick Productions Ltd*:[20] (presenter of *Have I Got News for You* referred to sons of Robert Maxwell as 'heartless scheming bastards' six months before their trial for conspiracy to defraud; programme repeated notwithstanding protest from their solicitor; respondents each fined £10,000); *A-G v Associated Newspapers Ltd*[21]

17 Below, p. 765.
18 [1998] 1 Cr App Rep 308.
19 p. 150.
20 [1997] EMLR 76.
21 [1998] EMLR 711.

(acknowledged breach by the *Evening Standard* of s. 4 order prohibiting publication of terrorist background of prisoners to be tried for offences arising out of a break-out from Whitemoor Prison led to permanent stay of proceedings; £40,000 fine imposed); *A-G v Morgan; AG v News Group Newspapers Ltd*[1] (publication in the *News of the World* of the results of journalist's investigations into conspiracy to distribute counterfeit money the day after the alleged conspirators were arrested, treating the alleged conspiracy as a fact and referring to the defendants' criminal records, led to stay of proceedings and was held to be a contempt; £50,000 fine imposed); *A-G v Birmingham Post and Mail Ltd*[2] (publication during murder trial suggesting that the murder was carried out by members of a notorious criminal gang connected with drug dealing and gangland activities led to retrial; £20,000 fine); *A-G v Associated Newspapers Ltd*[3] (£35,000 fine for acknowledged breach of s. 4(2) order by the *Sun*).

A significant number of the reported cases have, however, been unsuccessful. The courts have examined in detail the nature and circumstances of the publication and its likely impact on jurors and parties and consequently on the course of proceedings. The grant before or at trial of a temporary or permanent stay of proceedings has not *automatically* been taken to prove the existence of a 'substantial risk of serious prejudice' under s. 2(2), although is a strong pointer in that direction.

In *A-G v Guardian Newspapers*,[4] the publication of the fact that one unidentified defendant out of six on trial in Manchester was awaiting trial in the Isle of Man on other charges was held not to give rise to any practical risk of engendering bias in a juror of ordinary good sense. In *A-G v Independent Television News Ltd*[5] TV news and newspapers (the *Daily Mail*, *Today*, *Daily Express* and *Northern Echo*) published the fact that Patrick Magee, who had been arrested for the murder of a special constable and the attempted murder of a police constable, was a convicted IRA terrorist who had escaped from jail in Belfast where he was serving a life sentence for the murder of an SAS officer. The court held that there was no contempt given the likely (and actual) lapse of time of over nine months before any trial, the ephemeral nature of a single news item on TV news, and the limited circulation of the first (and only offending) editions of the newspapers in question. In particular in the case of the *Northern Echo*, where only 146 copies were distributed in London, at King's Cross Station, there was no risk. In *A-G v MGN Ltd*,[6] coverage (accurate and inaccurate) in the *Daily Mirror*, the *Daily Star*, the *Sun*, *Today* and the *Daily Mail* in April and May 1995 of aspects of an alleged assault by Geoffrey Knights on Martin Davies led to an indefinite stay of proceedings being ordered by Judge Sanders in October of that year. However, the Divisional Court held that this coverage did not constitute contempt in view of the earlier saturation media coverage of Knights and his 'erstwhile girl friend' Gillian Taylforth who had had 'a major role in a popular television programme'. The publicity had included frequent references to Knights' prison record for violence. See also *A-G v Unger*[7] (no contempt where newspaper story setting out evidence, but not any inadmissible evidence, was published many months before an possible trial); *A-G v Sunday Business Newspapers Ltd*[8] (no contempt by 'obscure weekly publication').

1   [1998] EMLR 294.
2   [1998] 4 All ER 49.
3   Unreported, 16 April 1999.
4   [1992] 3 All ER 38.
5   [1995] 2 All ER 370, DC.
6   [1997] 1 All ER 456.
7   [1998] 1 Cr App Rep 308.
8   Unreported, 20 January 1998.

5. Varying views have been expressed on the relationship between the approaches that should be taken on: (1) proceedings for contempt; (2) applications for a stay of proceedings; and (3) appeals against conviction. Some have accepted that a publication may constitute a contempt without being sufficient to undermine the safety of a subsequent conviction. According to Simon Brown LJ in *A-G v Birmingham Post and Mail Ltd*,[9] this 'can only be because s. 2(2) postulates a lesser degree of prejudice than is required to make good an appeal against conviction' or a stay. Conversely, 'to create a seriously arguable ground of appeal is a sufficient basis for finding strict liability contempt'.

However, in *A-G v Guardian Newspapers Ltd*,[10] for Collins J and Sedley LJ the prejudice required by s. 2(2) is not in itself different; instead, the difference lies in the point that the risk ordinarily has to be gauged prospectively in a contempt case and retrospectively in a criminal appeal. Collins J agreed with Simon Brown LJ that creation of a seriously arguable ground of appeal was sufficient for contempt; for Sedley LJ, however, the issue turned on whether or not a ground of appeal was made out: 'any substantial risk ... that a conviction has been contributed to by a prejudicial publication will ordinarily make it unsafe.' Collins J. deferred to Sedley LJ's view that on the facts here no contempt was established. Collins J implicitly and Sedley LJ expressly adopted as a test (anticipating implementation of the Human Rights Act 1998) whether either prior restraint or subsequent punishment would be 'a proportionate response in a society which, as a democracy, values and protects freedom of the press'.

6. *The s. 5 defence.* In *A-G v TVS Television Ltd*,[11] TVS broadcast a programme, 'The New Rachman', on 29 January 1988, exposing certain landlords in Reading who were alleged to be obtaining money by deception from the DHSS, as part of a general discussion of the causes of a new wave of Rachmanism in Southern England. The trial of one of the landlords, which had commenced on 4 January, had to be aborted (at a cost of £215,000). TVS accepted that the broadcast was a publication which had created a substantial risk of serious prejudice, and the Attorney-General accepted that TVS had acted in good faith. The court held that the s. 5 defence was not available: the reference to the landlords was not 'merely incidental' to the matter of general public interest discussed in the programme: the thrust of the discussion was directed to the Reading landlords. TVS were fined £25,000.

To what extent is the defendant's intention relevant to the s. 5 limitation?[12] Is the test for 'good faith' objective or subjective?[13] Note that s. 5 was held to be applicable in the *Mail on Sunday* case[14] notwithstanding that the article mentioned the accused.[15] In *A-G v TVS Television Ltd*[16] Lloyd LJ stated that in determining whether a risk was merely incidental:

> '... a better and surer test is simply to look at the subject matter of the discussion and see how closely it relates to the particular legal proceedings. The more closely it relates the easier it will be for the Attorney-General to show that the risk of prejudice is not merely incidental to the discussion. The application of the test is largely a matter of first impression.'

9 [1998] 4 All ER 49, 57.
10 [1999] EMLR 904.
11 (1989) Times, 7 July, DC.
12 See M. Redmond, [1983] CLJ 9, 11–12.
13 See N. Lowe, (1981) 131 NLJ 1167, 1169.
14 Above, n. 4.
15 Cf. *A-G v English*, above, p. 735.
16 (1989) Times, 7 July.

In *A-G v Guardian Newspapers*, Mann LJ[17] agreed that the application of the test was largely one of impression. The Divisional Court held that the s. 5 defence was made out where in the course of an article criticising the alleged propensity of judges in major fraud trials to impose reporting restrictions, reference was made to a particular case where restrictions were imposed because a defendant was awaiting trial elsewhere. Brooke J stated[18] that the inclusion of examples was 'no more than an incidental consequence of expounding the main theme of the article'. On the burden of proof, Professor J. C. Smith,[19] points out that while s. 3(3)[20] states explicitly that the onus of proving the defence of innocent publication or distribution is on the defendant there is no such provision in ss. 4 or 5. Nevertheless, in *A-G v TVS Television Ltd*,[1] the Attorney-General accepted that the burden of proving liability rested on him for the purposes of both ss. 2(2) and 5 of the 1981 Act. Professor Smith also considers whether an article written with reference to the issue of principle raised by the trial itself would amount to contempt:

> 'Arguably, proceedings are not "impeded" or "prejudiced" by a discussion in good faith of issues of principle, even if it is intended to influence the court to reach a "correct" decision. Many commentaries on decisions of the Court of Appeal published in this *Review* have been written in the hope they might influence the House of Lords, either directly or through their adoption by counsel, to reach a particular decision and have not (so far) been treated as contemptuous. If, in the course of the published debate following the acquittal of Dr. Arthur, a similar charge had been brought against another doctor, would it have been necessary to suspend the debate? It is submitted that it would not.'

Does s. 5 apply only in respect of incidental risks created by the continuation of an *existing* public debate or does it extend in addition to articles which *initiate* such a debate?[2]

(iii) Other aspects of contempt

NOTES

1. *Protection of inferior courts and tribunals.* Inferior courts generally only have power to punish contempts in the face of the court.[3] However, the Divisional Court fulfils a protective role over the proceedings of inferior courts and tribunals. Accordingly, it has been held that that court can punish publications likely to prejudice proceedings before quarter sessions,[4] consistory courts,[5] coroners courts,[6] courts martial[7] and county courts.[8] However, in *A-G v BBC*[9] the House of Lords held that the contempt jurisdiction was not co-extensive with the High Court's general supervisory jurisdiction, but was only exercisable in relation to 'inferior courts'.[10]

---

17 [1992] 3 All ER 38 (see above, p. 740), at 45.
18 At 49.
19 [1982] Crim LR 744.
20 Above, p. 725.
 1 (1989) Times, 7 July, DC.
 2 See C. J. Miller, [1982] Crim LR 71, 78–79.
 3 See below, p. 787ff.
 4 See *R v Davies* [1906] 1 KB 32.
 5 *R v Daily Herald, ex p Bishop of Norwich* [1932] 2 KB 402.
 6 See *R v Clarke, ex p Crippen* (1910) 103 LT 636, 641, per Lord Coleridge CJ; *Peacock v London Weekend Television* (1985) 150 JP 71, CA.
 7 See *R v Daily Mail, ex p Farnsworth* [1921] 2 KB 733.
 8 See *R v Edwards, ex p Welsh Church Temporalities Comrs* (1933) 49 TLR 383 and *Manchester City Council v McCann* [1999] 2 WLR 590 (below, p. 791).
 9 [1981] AC 303.
10 See RSC Ord. 52, r. 1(2)(a)(iii).

The House was unanimous in holding that this contempt power did not apply to local valuation courts.

In *Pickering v Liverpool Daily Post and Echo Newspapers plc*,[11] the Court of Appeal held the definition in s. 19 of the Contempt of Court Act 1981[12] 'must be intended to reflect the common law concept of what is a "court" for the purposes of the common law jurisdiction of the courts in relation to contempt of court'.[13] Applying that definition, a Mental Health Review Tribunal was to be regarded as a 'court' for these purposes. Since the passing of the Mental Health (Amendment) Act 1982 (consolidated in the Mental Health Act 1983), these tribunals had been given power to determine whether a restricted patient should be released from detention; previously they had only had the power to make recommendations. Indeed this change had been necessitated by the ruling of the European Court of Human Rights in *X v United Kingdom*,[14] which had applied Art. 5(4) of the Convention to decisions of Mental Health Review Tribunals: this entitled persons deprived of their liberty by arrest or detention to have the lawfulness of the detention 'decided speedily by a court'. Lord Donaldson pointed out that if a Tribunal were not a 'court' for all purposes, the Convention would not be complied with. The decision of the Court of Appeal on this point was approved on appeal by the House of Lords.[15] An industrial tribunal is an 'inferior court' for these purposes,[16] but the Professional Conduct Committee of the General Medical Council is not.[17]

2. Powers to sit in camera. In general court proceedings must take place in public. However, courts have inherent power to sit in private where that is necessary to serve the ends of justice, and there are also statutory exceptions. The principles were stated as follows by Lord Diplock in *A-G v Leveller Magazine Ltd.*[18]

'The application of this principle of open justice has two aspects: as respects proceedings in the court itself it requires that they should be held in open court to which the press and public are admitted and that, in criminal cases at any rate, all evidence communicated to the court is communicated publicly. As respects the publication to a wider public of fair and accurate reports of proceedings that have taken place in court the principle requires that nothing should be done to discourage this.

However, since the purpose of the general rule is to serve the ends of justice it may be necessary to depart from it where the nature or circumstances of the particular proceedings are such that the application of the general rule in its entirety would frustrate or render impracticable the administration of justice or would damage some other public interest for whose protection Parliament has made some statutory derogation from the rule. Apart from statutory exceptions, however, where a court in the exercise of its inherent power to control the conduct of proceedings before it departs in any way from the general rule, the departure is justified to the extent and to no more than the extent that the court reasonably believes it to be necessary in order to serve the ends of justice.'

---

11 [1991] 2 AC 370, [1990] 1 All ER 335.
12 Above, p. 727.
13 Per Lord Donaldson MR at 341.
14 (1981) 4 EHRR 188.
15 [1991] 2 AC 370.
16 *Peach Grey & Co (a firm) v Sommers* [1995] 2 All ER 513.
17 *General Medical Council v BBC* [1998] 3 All ER 426.
18 [1979] AC 440 at 450. See also *Scott v Scott* [1913] AC 417, HL; *B (otherwise P) v A-G* [1965] 3 All ER 253; *R v Ealing Justices, ex p Weafer* (1982) 74 Cr App Rep 204, [1983] Crim LR 182, DC; *R v Reigate Justices, ex p Argus Newspapers and Larcombe* (1983) 147 JP 385, DC; *R v Chief Registrar of Friendly Societies, ex p New Cross Building Society* [1984] QB 227; *Polly Peck International plc v Nadir* (1991) Times, 11 November; Law Commission *Report on the Powers of Appeal Courts to Sit in Private and the Restrictions upon Publicity in Domestic Proceedings* (Cmnd. 3149, 1966); *Robertson and Nicol*, pp. 309–323.

This last stated point may in appropriate circumstances justify a decision to sit *in camera* or the imposition of restrictions on the reporting of certain matters.[19]

Where the prosecutor or defendant intends to apply for an order that all or part of a trial be held in camera for reasons of national security or the protection of the identity of a witness or any other person, notice must be served and a copy displayed within the court.[20]

A decision to sit *in camera* may be challenged (in the case of an inferior court or tribunal) on an application for judicial review or (in the case of a trial on indictment) an appeal to the Court of Appeal under the Criminal Justice Act 1988, s. 159. See, e.g. *Re Crook*,[1] where the Court of Appeal gave guidance as to the circumstances in which applications in connection with trials on indictment could properly be heard in chambers. If the public are excluded from a hearing, the Press should be excluded as well.[2] The policy of a particular bench to withhold the names of justices during the hearing of cases and from both public and press afterwards was held to be unlawful (as contrary to the principles of open justice) in *R v Felixstowe Justices, ex p Leigh*.[3]

3. *Powers to prohibit reporting; Contempt of Court Act 1981, s. 11*. It has been established that a judge has jurisdiction to order that the name of a witness should not be disclosed in the proceedings if there is a danger that a lack of anonymity would deter such witnesses from coming forward. Disclosure may then amount to contempt. In *R v Socialist Worker Printers and Publishers Ltd, ex p A-G*,[4] prosecution witnesses at the trial of Janie Jones on charges (*inter alia*) of blackmail were referred to in court as 'Y' and 'Z' by direction of the judge. Their names were published in the *Socialist Worker*. There was no specific direction to the press not to publish the names. Nevertheless, the publishers and editor (Paul Foot) were each fined £250 for contempt. This was both 'an affront to the authority of the court' and 'an act calculated to interfere with the due course of justice'.[5]

The New Zealand Court of Appeal has similarly held that it is contempt to disobey directions not to reveal the identities of members of the NZ Security Intelligence Service who were prosecution witnesses in a well publicised trial.[6]

In *A-G v Leveller Magazine Ltd*,[7] three newspapers (*Leveller, Peace News* and *Journalists*) published the name of a witness in the committal proceedings which led to the 'ABC trial'.[8] He had been allowed to give evidence as 'Colonel B' for security reasons. They were convicted of contempt and fined, on the ground that flouting (or deliberate disregard) outside the court will be a contempt if it frustrates the court's ruling'.[9] The House of Lords allowed the defendants' appeals on a variety of grounds.

(1) (Lord Diplock, Viscount Dilhorne and Lord Russell). In evidence at the committal proceedings 'Colonel B' gave the name and number of his unit and referred to the fact that his posting was recorded in a particular issue of 'Wire', the Royal Signals

---

19 See n. 3.
20 Crown Court Rules 1982, r. 28 (1), (2). This covers 'all or part of the trial process': *Ex p Guardian Newspapers Ltd* [1999] 1 All ER 65, CA (Cr D) (the court also gave guidance on the procedure to be followed).
1 (1989) 93 Cr App Rep 17.
2 Ibid.
3 [1987] QB 582. See also *R v Malvern Justices, ex p Evans*, below, p. 747.
4 [1975] QB 637, DC.
5 Per Lord Widgery CJ at 151.
6 *A-G v Taylor* [1975] 2 NZLR 675; *A-G v Hancox* [1976] 1 NZLR 171; W. C. Hodge, (1976) 7 NZ Universities LR 171.
7 [1979] 1 All ER 745, HL; R. T. H. Stone, (1980) 96 LQR 22.
8 Below, p. 825.
9 [1978] 3 All ER 731 at 736, per Lord Widgery CJ.

magazine, which was available to the general public. His identity could thus be deduced from evidence given in open court without objection from the prosecution. Accordingly, the disclosure could not interfere with the due administration of justice and could not amount to contempt. In the words of Lord Russell, 'the gaff was already blown'.[10] Viscount Dilhorne[11] and Lord Russell[12] gave this as the only reason for their decision.

(2) (Lord Edmund-Davies). The Attorney-General had sought the orders of committal on the basis that the defendants had ignored an explicit *direction* of the magistrates. It subsequently appeared from the affidavit of the court clerk that no such direction had been given. Lord Edmund-Davies held that:[13]

> 'it was not open to the Divisional Court (and particularly after refusing to allow him to amend his grounds of application) to entertain an entirely different case on which to commit the appellants for criminal contempt.... Persons charged with criminal misconduct are entitled to know with reasonable precision the basis of the charge.'

The speeches of their Lordships do not, however, give clear guidance as to when a publication of information will amount to contempt. Would it be sufficient for the court simply to rule that a witness's name should not be revealed in the court? Publication of the name, following such a ruling, might well amount *ipso facto* to contempt in the opinions of Viscount Dilhorne[14] and Lord Russell of Killowen.[15] The speeches of the other members of the House seemed to require further conditions to be fulfilled before a conviction for contempt. Lord Edmund-Davies' view was nearest to that of Viscount Dilhorne and Lord Russell, although he did express doubts as to the *ratio decidendi* of *R v Socialist Worker*. Viscount Dilhorne[16] (as did Lord Scarman) expressly approved the decision in that case and Lord Russell can be taken as having done so by implication.

Lord Diplock:

... [W]here (1) the reason for a ruling which involves departing in some measure from the general principle of open justice within the courtroom is that the departure is necessary in the interests of the due administration of justice and (2) it would be apparent to anyone who was aware of the ruling that the result which the ruling is designed to achieve would be frustrated by a particular kind of act done outside the courtroom, the doing of such an act with knowledge of the ruling and of its purpose may constitute a contempt of court, not because it is a breach of the ruling but because it interferes with the due administration of justice.

What was incumbent on [the magistrates] was to make it clear to anyone present at, or reading an accurate report of, the proceedings, what in the interests of the due administration of justice, was the result that was intended by them to be achieved by the limited derogation from the principle of open justice within the courtroom which they had authorised, and what kind of information derived from what happened in the courtroom would if it were published frustrate that result.

There may be many cases in which the result intended to be achieved by a ruling by the court as to what is to be done in court is so obvious as to speak for itself; it calls for no explicit statement. Sending the jury out of court during a trial within a trial is an example of this; so may be the common ruling in prosecutions for blackmail that a victim called as a witness be referred to in court by a pseudonym ...

10 At 764.
11 At 754.
12 At 764.
13 At 759.
14 At 755, 756.
15 At 764.
16 At 756.

Lord Edmund-Davies: . . .

For [contempt] to arise something more than disobedience of the court's direction needs to be established. That something more is that the publication must be of such a nature as to threaten the administration of justice either in the particular case in relation to which the prohibition was pronounced or in relation to cases which may be brought in the future. . . .

[N]othing I have said should be regarded as implying that there can be no committal for contempt unless there has been some sort of warning against publication. While, it would be wise to warn, the court is under no obligation to do so. And there will remain cases where a court could not reasonably have considered a warning even desirable, such as where the later conduct complained of should not have been contemplated as likely to occur. *R v Newcastle Chronicle and Journal Ltd*[17] is an example of such a case . . .

Lord Scarman: . . .

If a court is satisfied that for the protection of the administration of justice from interference it is necessary to order that evidence either be heard in private or be written down and not given in open court, it may so order. Such an order or ruling may be the foundation of contempt proceedings against any person who, with knowledge of the order, frustrates its purpose by publishing the evidence kept private or information leading to its exposure. The order or ruling must be clear and can be made only if it appears to the court reasonably necessary. There must be material (not necessarily evidence) made known to the court on which it could reasonably reach its conclusion, and those who are alleged to be in contempt must be shown to have known, or to have had a proper opportunity of knowing of the existence of the order. . . .

Note that there are three distinct statements by justices which are possible: (a) a 'ruling' that a witness should be allowed to remain anonymous in court; (b) a 'direction' that the witness's identity should not be published in or out of court; (c) a 'warning' that publication may amount to or be dealt with as contempt. Which of these statements do you think each of their Lordships has in mind as a precondition of liability in contempt? There seemed to be general agreement that disobedience to statements of any of these kinds would not *automatically* constitute contempt.[18] (Contrast the New Zealand decision in *A-G v Taylor*[19] where it was held that the court had power to make an order binding on outsiders disobedience to which would automatically constitute contempt.)

It would seem that in order for contempt proceedings to succeed (1) there must be a valid anonymity order (not a mere request) (see Lord Scarman); (2) D must know or (per Lord Scarman) must have had the opportunity of knowing of the order; (3) either there must be a warning from the court that the order is made to protect the administration of justice and that publication will constitute contempt or the object of the order must be apparent to anyone; and (4) (per Lord Edmund-Davies) the publication must constitute a real risk of interfering with the administration of justice.[20]

The difficulties of the *Leveller* case are not solved by s. 11 of the Contempt of Court Act 1981.[21] Note that s. 11 does not *confer* any power to withhold information in court, does not indicate what consequences are to flow from a breach of a direction made under the section, and does not make it clear whether the deliberate publication of matter withheld in court may constitute contempt where there has not also been an express direction to the press to refrain from publication. It has, however, been

---

17 Above, p. 733.
18 See Viscount Dilhorne at 734, Lord Edmund-Davies at 761 and Lord Scarman at 768. Lord Diplock at 751 left the point open.
19 [1975] 2 NZLR 675.
20 See *Borrie and Lowe*, pp. 276–278.
21 See above, p. 726.

held that an order cannot be made under s. 11 prohibiting the publication of a name in connection with proceedings unless the name has been withheld during the proceedings.[1] Anonymity orders have been made, for example, to protect witnesses in blackmail trials,[2] in connection with security matters,[3] in pornography trials[4] to prohibit the publication of the name and address of a person with a notifiable disease against whom an *ex parte* order was made under the Public Health (Control of Disease) Act 1984, s. 37, requiring his removal to hospital[5] and where there was a risk of psychological harm to an applicant for judicial review with advanced HIV disease should his identity be publicised.[6] Anonymity orders may also be justified where a witness is in fear for himself or his family.[7] The growing use of powers to sit *in camera*[8] and to make orders under s. 11 was viewed with concern by the National Union of Journalists, the Association of British Editors and the Press Council. However, the tide was to an extent stemmed by two decisions of the Divisional Court.

In *R v Malvern Justices, ex p Evans*,[9] the Divisional Court affirmed the jurisdiction of a magistrates' court to sit *in camera* if the administration of justice so required, but doubted that the court's discretion to do so had been properly exercised in the circumstances of the case. A woman pleaded guilty to driving with excess alcohol but sought to advance special reasons why she should not be disqualified which concerned embarrassing and intimate details of her personal life with her husband and her pending divorce proceedings. The justices acceded to her request that this be heard *in camera*. The case was only argued on the question of jurisdiction, but Watkins LJ also indicated that he regarded the justices' reason for sitting *in camera* as 'wholly unsustainable and out of accord with principle'.[10] Moreover, it was held in *R v Evesham Justices, ex p McDonagh*,[11] that a magistrates' court has no power to make a s. 11 order prohibiting publication of the defendant's address merely on the ground that he feared he would be subjected to severe harassment by his ex-wife if his address were made public; it could not be said that the application of the general rule requiring openness would in this case 'frustrate or render impracticable the administration of justice' (the test suggested by Lord Diplock in *A-G v Leveller Magazines Ltd*[12] for departing from the principle of open justice).[13]

An application for a hearing to be held *in camera*, or for suppression of (for example) a name or address, should itself be heard *in camera*: the court can then

1 *R v Arundel Justices, ex p Westminster Press Ltd* [1985] 2 All ER 390, DC, following dicta in *R v Central Criminal Court, ex p Crook* (1984) Times, 8 November, DC.
2 *R v Socialist Worker*, above.
3 *A-G v Leveller*, above.
4 *R v Hove Justices, ex p Gibbons* (1981) Times, 19 June.
5 *Birmingham Post and Mail Ltd v Birmingham City Council* (1993) Times, 25 November: the s. 11 order was, however, not to be continued once all reasonable opportunity to challenge the hospital order had passed.
6 *Re D* (1997) 45 BMLR 191.
7 *R v Watford Magistrates' Court, ex p Lenman* [1993] Crim LR 388 [1992] COD 474, DC; *R v Taylor (Gary)* (1994) Times, 17 August, CA(Cr D).
8 See nn. 2 above and 5 below.
9 [1988] QB 540.
10 At 550.
11 [1988] QB 553, DC.
12 Above, p. 745.
13 See also *R v Dover Justices, ex p Dover District Council* (1991) 156 JP 433 (justices could not prevent or restrict publicity of proceedings against a restaurant business alleging food hygiene offences on account of the very severe economic damage caused); *R v Westminster City Council, ex p Castelli* (1995) 30 BMLR 123 (no anonymity for HIV positive applicant; ordinarily, a litigant's name will be published); *R v Legal Aid Board, ex p Kaim Todner* [1998] 3 All ER 541 (no special treatment for legal profession).

determine whether there is any substance in the application without prejudicing the applicant: *R v Tower Bridge Magistrates' Court, ex p Osborne*.[14] Here a woman defendant sought to conceal her current address from her husband. The stipendiary magistrate refused to hear her application for a s. 11 order *in camera*, and her solicitor was obliged to reveal what were, in the words of Watkins LJ, 'very sensitive matters indeed, the publication of which could, in my view, have had serious consequences for the applicant'.[15] The magistrates in the event refused to make a s. 11 order. The court granted an injunction preventing (with certain exceptions) publication of any matter revealed in the making of the application before the magistrate. The decision to refuse the s. 11 order was not, apparently, challenged.

4. *Statutory reporting restrictions.* There are various statutory provisions which impose reporting restrictions disobedience to which constitutes a statutory offence.[16] See e.g. the Magistrates' Court Act 1980, s. 8A[17] (applications for dismissal); ibid., s. 71 (family proceedings); the Criminal Justice Act 1987, s. 11 (applications to the Crown Court for dismissal of charges and preparatory hearings in serious fraud cases); Children and Young Persons Act 1933, ss. 39[18] (children or young persons involved in court proceedings) and 49[19] (youth court and other proceedings[20]); Judicial Proceedings (Regulation of Reports) Act 1926 (indecent matter); Sexual Offences (Amendment) Act 1992;[1] victims of sexual offences; the Youth Justice and Criminal Evidence Act 1999, ss. 44–52 (restrictions on reporting alleged offences involving persons under 18; power to restrict reporting of criminal proceedings involving persons under 18; power to restrict reporting about vulnerable adult witnesses).[2] The position as to reporting proceedings properly held in private is governed by s. 12 of the Administration of Justice Act 1960.[3]

---

14 (1987) 88 Cr App Rep 28, DC.
15 At 30.
16 See generally M. Jones, *Justice and Journalism* (1974); B. Harris, *The Courts, the Press and the Public* (1976); *Borrie and Lowe*, pp. 281–333; G. Robertson and A. Nicol, *Media Law* (3rd edn, 1992), Chap. 7; D. Brogarth and C. Walker, (1988), 138 NLJ 909; *Reporting Restrictions in the Crown Court* (Guidelines endorsed by the Senior Presiding Judge, 30 August 2000); *Miller*, Chap. 10.
17 Substituted by the Criminal Justice and Public Order Act 1994, Sch. 4, Part I.
18 See *R v Tyne Tees Television* (1997) Times, 20 October, CA (Cr D) (fine of £10,000 for contempt of court for breach of s. 39 quashed; summary proceedings should have been taken under s. 39(2) where the maximum fine was £5,000); *R v Crown Court at Manchester, ex p H* [2000] 2 All ER 166 (decision to lift s. 39 order at the end of trial open to judicial review and held to be wrong as the judge had failed to take the possibility of a retrial properly into account); cf. *R v Central Criminal Court, ex p W, B and C* [2001] 1 Cr App Rep 7 (discretion to lift restrictions not confined to rare and exceptional circumstances, unlike the position in the youth court). Section 39 was amended by the Youth Justice and Criminal Evidence Act 1999, Sch. 2, para. 2, to apply only to civil proceedings.
19 Substituted by the Criminal Justice and Public Order Act 1994, s. 49 and amended by the Youth Justice and Criminal Evidence Act 1999, Sch. 2, para. 3.
20 See *McKerry v Teesdale and Wear Valley Justices* [2000] Crim LR 594 (partial lifting of reporting restrictions upheld although no place for a 'naming and shaming' approach; the power to lift restrictions as regards proceedings in the youth court should be exercised rarely).
1 As amended by the Youth Justice and Criminal Evidence Act 1999, Sch. 2, paras. 6–14.
2 See D. Birch and R. Leng, *Blackstone's Guide to the Youth Justice and Criminal Evidence Act 1999* (2000), Chap. 8.
3 See *Re F (a minor) (Publication of Information)* [1977] Fam 58; *Re L (a minor) (wardship: freedom of publication)* [1988] 1 All ER 418; *Pickering v Liverpool Daily Post and Echo Newspapers plc* [1991] 2 AC 370, HL; *Hodgson v Imperial Tobacco Ltd* [1998] 2 All ER 673 (holding there is no restriction on the publication of information from hearings in chambers apart from the limitation in s. 12(1) and comments that substantially prejudice the administration of justice) and below, p. 951.

5. *Powers to delay reporting; Contempt of Court Act 1981, s. 4.* Distinct from the powers set out in the previous note are the powers of a court to *postpone* publication of certain matters. The position at common law was uncertain.[4]

Apart from those authorities, it was accepted that a criminal court had power to hold a 'trial within a trial' in the absence of the jury (e.g. to determine whether evidence is legally admissible) and to withhold information from a jury (e.g. that the accused has pleaded guilty to some but not all the charges). The premature publication of these matters was regarded as an obvious contempt.[5]

The position is now regulated by s. 4 of the Contempt of Court Act 1981.[6] Section 4 was considered by the Court of Appeal in *R v Horsham Justices, ex p Farquharson*,[7] where a journalist and others sought judicial review to quash an order made by magistrates under s. 4(2). The court held that an order could validly be made under s. 4(2) restricting the reporting of 'old style' committal proceedings notwithstanding that the restrictions imposed by s. 3 of the Criminal Justice Act 1967 (now the Magistrates' Courts Act 1980, s. 8) had been lifted under s. 3(2). The two sections were regarded as applying in different situations and for different purposes. However, the magistrates' order was quashed on the ground that it was too wide. Another point concerned the relationship between s. 4(2) and s. 6(b). Counsel for the applicants argued that breach of a s. 4(2) order could only amount to contempt if it (a) constituted a breach of the 'strict liability rule' (s. 2(2)) and (b) that the conduct would have amounted to contempt at common law (s. 6(b)). Lord Denning MR[8] accepted this argument, but it was rejected by his brethren. Ackner LJ held that 'a new head of contempt of court has been created, separate and distinct from the strict liability rule. . . . If a journalist reports proceedings that are the subject matter of a postponement order under s. 4(2) then he is guilty of a contempt of court'.[9] Shaw LJ stated that 'a premature publication in contravention of an order of which the publisher is aware could not be said to be in good faith'[10] and would accordingly fall outside the protection of s. 4(1). Both the Divisional Court and the Court of Appeal were, however, agreed that the press are entitled under s. 4(1) to publish anything occurring in open court unless an order has been made under s. 4(2); accordingly an order is now necessary to prohibit reporting of a 'trial within a trial' or guilty pleas.[11] An order can only be made under s. 4(2) to postpone publication of reports of 'legal proceedings held in public'; this term means proceedings held in court at a hearing, and does not enable a court to ban the showing of a film of the defendant's arrest.[12]

In 1982 a Practice Direction was made by Lord Lane CJ in respect of orders under ss. 4(2) and 11:[13]

'It is necessary to keep a permanent record of such orders for later reference. For this purpose all orders made under section 4(2) must be formulated in precise terms, having regard to the decision of *R v Horsham Justices, ex p Farquharson* [1982] QB 762, and orders under both sections must be committed to writing either by the judge personally or by the clerk of the court under the judge's directions. An order must state (a) its precise scope, (b) the time at which it shall cease to have effect, if appropriate, and (c) the specific purpose of making the order.

4 See *R v Clement* (1821) 4 B & Ald 218; *R v Poulson* [1974] Crim LR 141; cf. *R v Kray* (1969) 53 Cr App Rep 412, CA(Cr D).
5 See above, p. 733.
6 Above, p. 725.
7 [1982] QB 762, CA.
8 At pp. 790–795.
9 At 805.
10 At 798.
11 Cf. above, p. 726: the *Border TV* case would now be decided differently.
12 *R v Rhuddlan Justices, ex p HTV Ltd* [1986] Crim LR 329.
13 *Practice Direction (Contempt: Reporting Restrictions)* [1982] 1 WLR 1475.

Courts will normally give notice to the press in some form that an order has been made under either section of the Act and court staff should be prepared to answer any inquiry about a specific case, but it is, and will remain, the responsibility of those reporting cases, and their editors, to ensure that no breach of any order occurs and the onus rests with them to make inquiry in any case of doubt.'

On a number of occasions newspapers and journalists have applied successfully to the trial judge for the order to be revoked.[14] It was subsequently stated that representations to a trial judge should only be made by counsel for the prosecution or counsel for a defendant; counsel acting on behalf of the media or a witness did not have standing.[15] A different view was, however, taken by the Divisional Court in *R v Clerkenwell Metropolitan Stipendiary Magistrate, ex p Telegraph plc*,[16] which held that the court had a discretion to hear representations from the media, which should ordinarily be exercised when the media asked to be heard either on the making of an order or in regard to its continuance. (For subsequent proceedings, see *R v Clerkenwell Justices, ex p Trachtenberg*,[17] where the Divisional Court upheld the magistrate's decision to revoke a s. 4(2) order.)

Orders under ss. 4 or 11 imposed by inferior courts or the Crown Court (other than in respect of a trial on indictment) may be challenged on an application for judicial review under the ultra vires doctrine. Orders in relation to a trial on indictment[18] can now be challenged by a 'person aggrieved' by way of an appeal to the Court of Appeal,[19] under which the role of the court is to form its own view and not merely review the decision of the trial judge.[20] Applications for leave to appeal and appeals under s. 159 are determined on written submissions without a hearing.[1]

In *Re Central Independent Television plc*,[2] the Court of Appeal allowed an appeal against an order under s. 4(2) which prohibited the reporting of a trial by radio or television on the evening that the jury had to spend at a hotel after having retired to consider their verdict. The judge had taken the view that they should be able to relax and watch television or listen to the radio; the Court of Appeal held there was no substantial risk of prejudice to the administration of justice to justify an order.

The Court of Appeal (Criminal Division) also took a robust approach in setting aside or restricting s. 4(2) orders in *R v Beck, ex p Daily Telegraph plc*[3] and *Ex p Telegraph plc*.[4] In *Beck*, the court set aside an order restricting reporting of the trial of three social workers on the first of three indictments alleging serious offences of sexual and physical abuse of children in the care of Leicestershire Social

---

14 *Robertson and Nicol*, 3rd edn, pp. 345–350.

15 *R v Central Criminal Court, ex p Crook* (1984) Times, 8 November.

16 [1993] QB 462.

17 [1993] COD 93.

18 But not a refusal to make an order or a decision to discharge one previously made: *R v S* [1995] 2 Cr App Rep 347; cf. *Re Saunders* (1990) Times, 8 February (decision to refuse s. 4(2) order at preparatory hearing under Part I of the Criminal Justice Act 1987 can be challenged on appeal under s. 9(11) of that Act, but only if erroneous in law).

19 Criminal Justice Act 1988, s. 159.

20 *Ex p Telegraph plc* [1993] 2 All ER 971, 977, CA (Cr D).

1 Criminal Appeal Rules 1968, S.I. 1968 No. 1262, r. 16B(6),(7): upheld as *intra vires* by the Divisional Court in *Ex p Guardian Newspapers* (1993) Times, 26 October.

2 [1991] 1 All ER 347.

3 [1993] 2 All ER 177. See also *MGN Pension Trustees Ltd v Bank of America National Trust and Savings Association* [1995] 2 All ER 355 (s. 4(2) order refused); *R v News Group Newspapers Ltd* (1999) Times, 21 May (s. 4(2) order set aside on appeal). On s. 4(2) orders and committal proceedings see *R v Beaconsfield Justices, ex p Westminster Press Ltd* (1994) 158 JP 1055, QBD.

4 [1993] 2 All ER 971.

Services, until end of the trial, when the matter would be reconsidered. The court had to consider separately (1) whether there was a substantial risk of prejudice and (2) whether, if so, it was necessary to make an order. The latter step involving balancing the considerations that supported a fair trial against the requirement of open justice and a legitimate public interest and concern in the matters in question. Here, there was a substantial risk of prejudice if the first trial were reported, but in view of the widespread public concern over the circumstances that gave rise to the trial, no order should be made. A similar approach was adopted in *Ex p Telegraph plc*, confirming that the question of the court's discretion was in practice merged with the requirement of necessity.[5] The court removed restrictions on the identification of the principal prosecution witness (an alleged accomplice) at the first of what was to be a series of major trials in respect of the importation, manufacture and supply of the drug 'Ecstasy'. There was no substantial risk of prejudice and, even if there had been, the case was important and one in which there was a considerable and legitimate public interest because of the nature and quantity of the drug involved; the restrictions in question would make the case almost impossible to report.

It has been proposed that there should be a unified statutory code governing the reporting of criminal cases.[6]

6. Media coverage *during* a trial that creates a real risk of prejudice against the defendant may cause the conviction to be quashed as unsafe. In *R v McCann*,[7] convictions of the 'Winchester three' for conspiracy to murder Tom King, the Secretary of State for Northern Ireland, were quashed following extensive media coverage during the trial of the government's proposals to change the law on the right to silence. This included interviews with Tom King and Lord Denning, expressing in strong terms the view that in terrorist cases a failure to answer questions or to give evidence was tantamount to guilt; two defendants had refused to answer questions and all had elected not to give evidence at trial. The Court of Appeal held that the jury should have been discharged. The risk of prejudice could not be eliminated by the judge's direction.

In *R v Taylor and Taylor*[8] coverage had been sensational and inaccurate, with headlines such as 'Love Crazy Mistress Butchered Rival Wife Court Told' (the court 'had been told no such thing'[9]). Apart from the effect on the fairness of the trial, the court also declined to order a retrial on the ground that a fair trial would not now be possible. The papers were sent to the Attorney-General, but he decided that no further action should be taken. An application for judicial review of that decision was dismissed, *inter alia* on the ground that the court had no jurisdiction to review the Attorney-General's decision because of his unique constitutional position.[10] In subsequent cases, however, the courts have been more sceptical of arguments that a fair retrial will not be possible.[11]

7. In an appropriate case the High Court may grant an injunction to restrain a publication that would be a contempt of court by prejudicing criminal proceedings: see *Coe v Central Television*,[12] where the Court of Appeal discharged an injunction

5 Lord Taylor CJ at 975.
6 C. Walker, I. Cram and D. Brogarth, 'The Reporting of Crown Court Proceedings and the Contempt of Court Act 1981' (1992) 55 MLR 647. See also M. J. Beloff, 'Fair Trial – Free Press? Reporting Restrictions in Law and Practice' [1992] PL 92.
7 (1990) 92 Cr App R 239, CA (Cr D).
8 (1993) 98 Cr App R 361, CA (Cr D). See B. Naylor, [1994] CLJ 492.
9 Per McCowan LJ at 369.
10 *R v Solicitor-General, ex p Taylor* (1995) Times, 14 August.
11 *R v Stone* [2001] Crim LR 465.
12 (1993) Independent, 11 August.

restraining the broadcasting of material in the 'Cook Report' relating to allegations against Coe of computer pornography. Proceedings had not yet been instigated, and the court was not satisfied on the evidence that the publication risked prejudice to the administration of justice and was motivated by an intention to create that risk of prejudice so as to amount to contempt at common law. On injunctions in the context of publications in respect of civil proceedings, see below.[13]

8. The strong line taken by the Supreme Court of the United States against inhibitions on freedom of expression and freedom of the press[14] has meant that broadcasting and press publication of prejudicial material have been a considerable problem. There has been an extensive debate on whether the balance between the right of free expression and the right to a fair trial is correctly drawn.[15] The Supreme Court has had to quash convictions in some extreme *causes célèbres: Irwin v Dowd*;[16] *Estes v Texas*[17] (where the courtroom, according to the *New York Times*, 'was turned into a snake-pit by the multiplicity of cameras, wires, microphones and technicians milling about the chamber');[18] and *Sheppard v Maxwell*.[19] In the last case, Sheppard's conviction was quashed after he had been in prison for ten years convicted of murder after a sensationalised 'circus-like' trial. He was acquitted following a re-trial. The disquiet engendered by such cases has led to the employment of a number of safety devices: use of the voir dire examination of jurors to determine whether they are capable of ignoring pre-trial publicity; sequestration of the jury during the trial; transferring a case to another county; and the exercise of control by judges and public authorities over police officers, lawyers and court officials to prevent the release of prejudicial information. In addition, there is the encouragement of self-regulation by the press – the voluntary observation of proper standards of press coverage. These devices are constitutional, but doubts are expressed as to their efficacy. Following *Sheppard v Maxwell*, with its emphasis on the defendant's right to a fair trial under the Sixth and Fourteenth Amendments, trial courts have imposed specific reporting restrictions ('gag orders') on the press in individual cases where prejudicial publicity is apprehended. In *Nebraska Press Association v Stuart*,[20] the Supreme Court held that a 'gag order' will normally be an unconstitutional restriction on press freedom.[1]

(B) WHEN DOES THE SUB JUDICE RULE APPLY?

(i) At common law

1. Commencement

There were uncertainties both as to the commencement and the conclusion of the period within which matters were sub judice so as to render comments or acts that were prejudicial, contempts. If proceedings were 'pending' they were clearly sub judice. Proceedings were held to be 'pending' where a defendant had been arrested by virtue of a warrant (*R v Clarke, ex p Crippen*[2]), and it was suggested obiter in the same case that they were 'pending' from the time the warrant was issued. The

13 pp. 774–775.
14 See above, p. 719.
15 See e.g. *Abraham*, pp. 174–183; Donnelly and Goldfarb, (1961) 24 MLR 239.
16 366 US 717 (1961).
17 381 US 532 (1965).
18 *Abraham*, p. 177.
19 384 US 333 (1966).
20 427 US 539 (1976).
1 See A. M. Schatz, (1975) 10 Harv Civ Rights–Civ Lib LR 608; Note (1977) 87 Yale LJ 342.
2 (1910) 103 LT 636, DC.

authorities conflicted on the question whether matters were sub judice when proceedings were merely 'imminent'. In *James v Robinson*,[3] the High Court of Australia held that, as a matter of law, contempt of court could not be committed before the proceedings in question began. The view that the law of contempt applied when proceedings were merely imminent was expressed in *R v Savundranayagan*,[4] but those were not contempt proceedings. In *R v Beaverbrook Newspapers Ltd*,[5] Sheil and McVeigh JJ held that the word 'imminent' in s. 11 of the Administration of Justice Act 1960[6] 'cannot be ignored if effect is to be given to the section as a whole. Whatever may be said to be the distinction between "proceedings pending" and "proceedings imminent", it is clear from the use of the words "as the case may be" that a distinction was intended'.[7] The *Daily Express* published photographs and other details (including the past criminal record) of a man who was arrested and charged with murder within two days of the publication. At the time of the publication, the reporter who supplied the material knew that the man was under close police surveillance, and indeed the *Daily Express* referred to him as the 'No. 1 Suspect'. Fines were imposed on the editors and proprietors of the *Daily Express*.

The Phillimore Committee concluded[8] that the application of the concept of 'imminence' presented too many problems, and that the right starting point in England and Wales was the moment when the suspected man was charged or a summons served.

2. Conclusion

Technically, the proceedings were not over until the trial had been completed and either the time for appealing had expired, or any appeals had finally been determined.[9] However, it was unlikely that any comment would be regarded as giving rise to any risk of prejudice to the fair conduct of proceedings. 'A judge is in a very different position to a juryman. Though in no sense superhuman, he has by his training no difficulty in putting out of his mind matters which are not evidence in the case.'[10] The Phillimore Committee recommended that the law of contempt should cease to apply at the conclusion of the trial or hearing at first instance unless: (1) sentence is postponed, in which case restrictions should continue until sentence is passed; or (2) no verdict is reached, in which case restrictions should continue unless and until it is clear that there will be no further trial; or (3) a new trial is ordered on appeal, in which case restrictions should again apply; or (4) there is an appeal from a magistrates' court to the Crown Court, in which case restrictions should apply from the moment the appeal is set down.[11]

(ii) Publications intended to interfere with justice

In *A-G v News Group Newspapers plc*,[12] the Divisional Court indicated[13] that where a publication was intended to interfere with justice and created a real risk of prejudice

---

3 (1963) 109 CLR 593.
4 [1968] 3 All ER 439n.
5 [1962] NI 15, QBD (NI).
6 See below, p. 755.
7 Shiel J at 21.
8 pp. 49–52.
9 See *Delbert-Evans v Davies and Watson* [1945] 2 All ER 167, DC; *R v Duffy, ex p Nash* [1960] 2 QB 188, DC.
10 Per Lord Parker CJ in *R v Duffy, ex p Nash* [1960] 2 QB 188 at 198.
11 Para. 132.
12 [1989] QB 110.
13 Below, p. 755.

to proceedings, contempt proceedings could be taken notwithstanding that proceedings were neither pending nor imminent. On the facts, however, the proceedings were properly to be regarded as 'imminent'. However, in *A-G v Sport Newspapers Ltd*,[14] the Divisional Court was divided on the point, Bingham LJ following the *News Group* case (with some reluctance), but Hodgson J holding that proceedings had to be pending. The court was agreed that the requisite intention had not been proved.[15]

(iii) Under the 'strict liability rule'

The time limits for the sub judice period in relation to the 'strict liability rule' are now to be found in s. 2(3), (4) of and Sch. 1 to the Contempt of Court Act 1981.[16]

NOTES

1. The government took the view that the Phillimore proposal in relation to commencement went 'too far in allowing prejudicial publication before a formal charge is made, so endangering the trial of accused persons'.[17] Accordingly the provisions in Sch. 1, para. 4 were enacted. It should be noted that proceedings are not technically 'active' while a person is voluntarily 'helping police with their inquiries'. It may be difficult for outsiders to discover whether an arrest warrant has been issued or an arrest without warrant effected. Note the defence in s. 3 of the 1981 Act.[18] This defence was found to be established by the Divisional Court in *R v Duffy; A-G v News Group Newspapers Ltd*,[19] where the *News of the World* in November 1994 published a story alleging that D had committed drugs offences for which he had, unknown to the journalist, already been arrested. The court found the s. 3 defence made out. The journalist had discussed D and the proposed publication with senior officers involved in his case and the officers had failed to mention the arrest, thus leading the journalist to believe that proceedings were not active. The journalist was found to have taken all reasonable care.
2. The rules for the conclusion of the sub judice period are found in Sch. 1, paras. 5–11. The provision in para. 11 was intended to cover the 'Lucan situation' i.e. where a suspect remains undiscovered or goes abroad and cannot be extradited.
3. Appellate proceedings will be 'active' according to the provisions of Sch. 1, para. 15.[20] These are wider than those recommended by the Phillimore Committee.[1] Do you think that the possible effect of comments on appellate judges is sufficient to justify this?[2]

(C) THE SCOPE OF LIABILITY

(i) At common law generally

A defendant was liable for contempt if he published matter in circumstances where such publication, objectively judged, created a real risk that the fair trial of proceedings might be prejudiced. An intention to prejudice proceedings was not apparently

---

14 [1992] 1 All ER 503.
15 See below, p. 758.
16 See above, pp. 724, 728–729.
17 Cmnd. 7145, 1978, para. 14.
18 Above, p. 725.
19 Unreported, 9 February 1996.
20 Above, p. 729.
 1 See above, p. 753.
 2 Cf. below, pp. 776–778.

enough if there was in fact no risk of prejudice.[3] However authorities to the contrary collected in *Borrie and Lowe*[4] were not mentioned by the members of the Divisional Court in *R v Ingrams*,[4a] and Eveleigh J was reported as saying that he did not think the article in question 'would – or had been intended to – prejudice the fair trial of the litigation' against *Private Eye*.

There appeared to be no requirement of *mens rea* beyond an intention to publish the matter in question and no defence of 'innocent dissemination' at common law.[5] However, s. 11 of the Administration of Justice Act 1960 provided defences in two situations where publication could be said to be 'innocent': (1) where the defendant 'did not know and had no reason to suspect that the proceedings were pending, or that such proceedings were imminent, as the case may be' (s. 11(1)); and (2) where the distributor of a publication 'did not know that it contained any [matter calculated to interfere with the course of justice in connection with any proceedings pending or imminent at the time of publication] and had no reason to suspect that it was likely to do so' (s. 11(2)).

It was also argued that the person who supplied information to a newspaper should not be held liable unless he had *mens rea*.[6]

The Phillimore Committee recommended that the unintentional creation of a risk of prejudice should continue to be regarded as contempt:

> 'The risk of damage resulting from potentially prejudicial publications is such that we are sure that, broadly speaking, no change of principle is required. A liability which rested only on proof of intent or actual foresight would favour the reckless at the expense of the careful. Most publishing is a commercial enterprise undertaken for profit, and the power of the printed or broadcast word is such that the administration of justice would not be adequately protected without a rule which requires great care to be taken to ensure that offending material is not published.'[7]

This recommendation was taken up: see section (iii)[8] on the strict liability rule.

(ii) Common law liability for intended contempt

This category is of significance where the circumstances fall outside the scope of the 'strict liability rule'. The leading cases are *A-G v Times Newspapers Ltd*[9] and *A-G v News Group Newspapers plc*.[10]

A-G v News Group Newspapers plc [1989] QB 110, [1988] 2 All ER 906, [1988] 3 WLR 163, 132 Sol Jo 934, 87 Cr App Rep 323, Queen's Bench Divisional Court

The respondents, proprietors of the *Sun*, published articles entitled 'Rape Case Doc: Sun Acts', 'He's a real swine' and 'Beast must be named says MP', accusing a Dr B of raping an eight-year-old girl. The second article, 'Rape Case Doc' and 'Doc groped me, says girl', named the girl and accused him of the indecencies. NGN wrote to the

---

3 *R v Ingrams, ex p Goldsmith* [1977] Crim LR 40, DC.
4 At 79–80.
4a [1977] Crim LR 40, DC.
5 *R v Odhams Press Ltd* [1957] 1 QB 73, DC; *R v Griffiths, ex p A-G* [1957] 2 QB 192, DC
6 See *Smith and Hogan* (6th edn, 1988) p. 776, criticising *R v Evening Standard Co Ltd* [1954] 1 QB 578; but cf. *Borrie and Lowe*, pp. 389–393.
7 Para. 74.
8 Below, p. 758.
9 [1992] 1 AC 191 (below p. 766) in the section on publications prejudicial to civil proceedings.
10 [1989] QB 110, DC (below).

girl's mother's solicitor offering to fund a private prosecution, as the police and the DPP had decided, in the absence of corroboration, not to prosecute Dr B. Nine months later, a private prosecution of the doctor resulted in his acquittal. The Attorney-General applied to the court for NGN to be fined for contempt of court at common law, proceedings not having been active for the purposes of the strict liability rule. NGN argued that at the time of publication proceedings were neither pending nor imminent.

Watkins LJ: . . . The Contempt of Court Act 1981 made fairly extensive provision for what might be called statutory contempts but by section 6 it made the following material saving, namely:

'Nothing in the foregoing provisions of this Act—. . . (c) restricts liability for contempt of court in respect of conduct intended to impede or prejudice the administration of justice.'

In order to tell whether it has been established that a contempt has been committed by reason of a newspaper publication, it is a first and necessary finding that the contents of the publication present a risk of prejudice to a fair trial assuming that at the time of publication, proceedings have commenced or there has been an arrest and the commencement of proceedings is thereafter inevitable. The risk predicated must be real as opposed to a remote possibility: see *R v Duffy, ex p Nash* [1960] 2 QB 188, 200.

No one could possibly resist the conclusion that in the circumstances I have assumed for the present purpose that the contents of the articles complained of here posed a real risk of prejudice to a fair trial of Dr B. Publication of them during pending proceedings could not, in my view, have failed to have had that effect, so grave are the allegations made against the doctor and so prominent, widespread and so savage, in headline at least, is the publicity given to them. . . .

. . . I feel bound to say that I should be surprised if the law were authoritatively declared to be that something less than a specific intent will do. After all, what is in contemplation here, as has been in some previous cases of criminal contempt, is serious criminal conduct accompanied by the possibility of the infliction of drastic penalty.

The ascertainment of the existence of intention is, of course, quite a different matter. . . .

Mr Alexander [counsel for NGN] submits that it would be wrong to infer the required intent from the contents of the articles, for which proposition he relies on *R v Moloney* [1985] AC 905.

If, in so submitting, he intended us to conclude that the contents are all we have to consider, I cannot agree with him, nor do I accept that the contents of these articles are not alone capable of giving rise to the inference that the respondent intended to prejudice the fair trial of Dr. B, if and when that proceeding took place. I agree with Mr. Pannick, who appeared with Mr. Laws [counsel for the A-G], that we are not bound to accept the editor's assertion that he did not intend to interfere with the course of administration of justice. But the articles do not stand alone. The respondent's affidavits and financial support to the mother stand with them in forming the whole of the circumstances to be considered for the purpose of ascertaining by inference whether the intent required was present.

Mr. Laws submits that we should draw the inference that the respondent intended to prejudice the fair trial because (1) the contents of the articles strikingly showed that it took the view that Dr B. was guilty; in paragraph 11 of his affidavit, Mr Mackenzie states: 'I believe that what we were publishing was true;' (2) although the risk of being in contempt was never mentioned, so they say, in discussions between him and Mr Crone [NGN's deputy legal manager], Mr Crone thought there would be an answer to an allegation of being in contempt in regard to which he states in paragraph 10 of his affidavit that he dismissed this as a likely danger since the proceedings were not in an active period under Schedule 1 to the Act of 1981 and that any proceedings likely to ensue were a long way off; (3) Mr Mackenzie and Mr Crone thought proceedings were likely to ensue otherwise why go to the lengths they did to put the mother in funds and, further, they could only have printed articles of such a kind if they were campaigning for a conviction, as they clearly were.

I regard that as a powerful and persuasive submission. I simply cannot accept that an experienced editor such as Mr. Mackenzie could have failed to have foreseen that the material which he published in the articles complained of and the steps he announced he was taking to assist the mother to prosecute would incur a real risk of prejudicing the fairness of a trial of Dr B. The inescapable inference is, in my judgment, that Mr Mackenzie became so convinced of Dr. B's guilt and incensed by that and the failure to prosecute him that he endeavoured to persuade readers of 'The Sun' to take a similar view. Some of those obviously could possibly have formed part of a jury to try the doctor. That is trial by newspaper, a form of activity which strikes directly at a jury's impartiality.

Furthermore, what conceivable reason could there be for publishing the article headed 'Doc groped me, says girl' unless it was intended to prejudice a fair trial by bringing to the notice of readers of 'The Sun,' including possibly potential jurors, extremely damaging matter affecting Dr. B. which would be inadmissible as evidence in his trial. . . .

[His Lordship then held that recklessness was insufficient for mens rea for this form of contempt, expressing agreement with Lloyd LJ in *A-G v Newspaper Publishing plc* [1988] Ch 333, 381–383. He then proceeded to consider whether this head of contempt only applies where proceedings are pending or imminent and if so whether the proceedings here satisfied that test.]

Mr Pannick, who, as I have said, appeared with Mr. Laws, most impressively submitted that 'imminent proceedings' is a vague and uncertain phrase which cannot be confined to any particular length of time as a matter of principle. Its application depends on all the circumstances of the case. The concept is necessarily imprecise because it is intended to be applied by reference to its purpose. There are cases, he said, where although proceedings are not yet active, they are likely to be commenced in the near future. Some proceedings are imminent when there is a likelihood or a real risk that they will be instituted in the near future and when there is a real risk that the kind of publication as here would interfere with the course of justice.

In the present case, he submitted, proceedings were imminent, the respondent intended they should be commenced at their expense as soon as possible and actively pursued that goal because they were determined to see Dr B. charged, tried and convicted. The possibility of counsel advising against proceedings did not remove the likelihood or real risk that proceedings would be instituted in the near future.

Alternatively, he argued, that if the proceedings here could not be said to be imminent, common law contempt applied nonetheless in the whole of the circumstances of this case. This is because the purpose of the contempt jurisdiction is to prevent interference with the course of justice. The more distant the commencement of proceedings, the less likely such interference. But here, he said, the contents of the articles created a real risk that a fair trial would be impeded.

There is, he contended, no authority which states that common law contempt cannot be committed where proceedings cannot be said to be imminent, but where there is a specific intent to interfere with the course of justice accompanied by a real risk that the published matter will impede a fair trial, the occurrence of which is in contemplation. The authorities are not concerned with the scope of common law contempt where such an intent exists in relation to proceedings in the contemplation of a respondent who deliberately assists a private prosecutor to prosecute as soon as possible.

I have found that a formidable contention. The circumstances in which a criminal contempt at common law can be committed are not necessarily, in my judgment, confined to those in which proceedings are either pending or imminent, 'an imprecise word by which to mark out a period of time,' *per* Windeyer J in *James v Robinson* (1963) 109 CLR 593, 618. The common law surely does not tolerate conduct which involves the giving of encouragement and practical assistance to a person to bring about a private prosecution accompanied by an intention to interfere with the course of justice by publishing material about the person to be prosecuted which could only serve to and was so intended to prejudice the fair trial of that person. This is especially so where the publisher of them makes it plain that he believes the person referred to in the articles is guilty of serious crime, is deserving of punishment for that and that he has committed some other similar crime.

The common law is not a worn out jurisprudence rendered incapable of further development by the ever increasing incursion of Parliamentary legislation. It is a lively body of law capable of adaptation and expansion to meet fresh needs calling for the exertion of the discipline of law. . . .

The need for a free press is axiomatic, but the press cannot be allowed to charge about like a wild unbridled horse. It has, to a necessary degree, in the public interest, to be curbed. The curb is in no circumstance more necessary than when the principle that every man accused of crime shall have a fair trial is at stake. It is a principle which, in my experience, newspaper proprietors and editors are usually as alert as anyone to avoid violating.

There may not have been in fact, as was suggested, another case quite like this, but the kind of threat which the articles complained of posed to the proper administration of justice is by no means novel, as reports of previous cases of criminal contempt committed by publishers of newspaper articles show.

The respondent here had very much in mind particular proceedings which it was determined, as far as it lay within its power and influence, to ensure took place. If it is necessary for the Attorney-General to establish that proceedings were imminent, he has, I think, done so. In my judgment, where a prosecution is virtually certain to be commenced and particularly where it is to be commenced in the near future, it is proper to describe such proceedings as imminent. Such was the case here.

Thus, for the reasons I have explained, I find that the Attorney-General justifiably complains of the conduct of the respondent whom I would hold is in contempt of court at common law and liable to be punished therefor.

Mann LJ agreed.

NOTES

1. The respondent was fined £75,000, with costs. The House of Lords refused leave to appeal.[11] In *A-G v Sport Newspapers*,[12] the Divisional Court dismissed the Attorney-General's application against the publishers and editors of the *Sport*, a tabloid newspaper that carried 'some general news stories, many of them with a sexual slant and generally written in a sensational style'.[13] The Attorney-General alleged that the deliberate publication of a wanted man's previous convictions, contrary to the wishes of the police expressed at a press conference, amounted to common law contempt. The court, however, held that it had not been proved beyond reasonable doubt that at the date of publication the editor had the specific intention to prejudice the fair conduct of proceedings, whose existence he regarded at that time as being speculative and remote. (An arrest warrant was issued two days after publication of the article; the wanted man, David Evans, was arrested three days later in France, extradited, and subsequently convicted of murder.)[14]

2. On the difficulties surrounding use of the term 'specific intent', see *Smith and Hogan*.[15] Smith and Hogan state that:[16]

> 'Where D has an "intent" to interfere with the course of justice, he may be liable whatever form his conduct takes, whether or not there is a substantial risk that the course of justice will be impeded, or the impediment serious. . . .'

(iii) The 'strict liability rule'

By virtue of s. 1 of the Contempt of Court Act 1981[17] conduct may be treated as a contempt of court as tending to interfere with the course of justice 'regardless of intent to do so'. However, it will still be necessary to prove that the defendant intended to

11 [1989] QB 135.
12 [1992] 1 All ER 503.
13 Bingham LJ at 506.
14 See A. T. H. Smith, [1992] CLJ 203.
15 pp. 70–71.
16 6th edn, 1988, p. 779. Cf. Below, pp. 772–773.
17 Above, p. 724.

publish the material in question.[18] Moreover, the 1981 Act enacts a number of defences and limitations to liability under the 'strict liability rule' (but not other aspects of the law of contempt, e.g. scandalising the court).[19] These provisions follow the recommendations of the Phillimore Committee.[20] Section 3[1] corresponds to s. 11 of the Administration of Justice Act 1960 (which is now repealed). Section 4(1)[2] enacts what was probably a defence at common law;[3] s. 5[4] enacts a limitation to the scope of liability which is recognised in the Commonwealth[5] and might have been recognised in this country.[6] The leading case on s. 5 is *A-G v English*.[7]

5 Publications prejudicial to civil proceedings

(A) AT COMMON LAW

As the jury is today rarely used in civil proceedings, so the risk of prejudice to the fairness of trials from the publication of information and comments concerning pending litigation is accordingly reduced. However, where there is trial by jury the law of contempt obviously applies in the same way as in criminal proceedings,[8] and the *Sunday Times* case (below) illustrated that the law protected litigants and witnesses from improper pressure, and indeed protected the administration of justice from being devalued by the development of 'trial by newspaper'.

A-G v Times Newspapers Ltd [1974] AC 273, [1973] 3 All ER 54, [1973] 3 WLR 298, House of Lords

In 1958, Distillers, a drug company, began to make and sell in the United Kingdom a sedative which contained the drug thalidomide. The product was prescribed for many pregnant women for whom it was said to be quite safe. Many of the mothers who had taken the drug gave birth to babies suffering from grave deformities. It was subsequently established that the deformities were caused by the action of thalidomide on the unborn child at certain stages of the pregnancy. As soon as that was realised Distillers withdrew the product in 1961. Between 1962 and 1968 some 70 actions for negligence were brought against Distillers on behalf of the deformed children. Early in 1968 a settlement was reached in those proceedings. Subsequently further writs were issued; by February 1969, 248 writs had been issued in proceedings which were not covered by the 1968 settlement. Negotiations took place with a view to a settlement and no further steps were taken in the proceedings in which writs had been issued to bring the actions to trial. Distillers made it a condition of any settlement that all claimants should accept it. The parties were, however, unable to come to agreement. In June 1972 Distillers made new proposals but they were not accepted; there were then some 389 claims outstanding. The editor of the *Sunday Times* took a keen interest in the matter. On 24 September 1972 the newspaper published a long and powerful article which criticised the law relating to the liability of drug companies and the methods of assessing damages. The sting of the article was however contained in a paragraph which stated that 'the thalidomide children shame Distillers' and urged Distillers to offer much more than they

---

18 See *Borrie and Lowe*, pp. 92–94.
19 Below pp. 779–786.
20 pp. 52–62.
1 Above, p. 725.
2 Above, p. 725.
3 See *Borrie and Lowe*, pp. 267–275.
4 Above, p. 725.
5 *Re Truth and Sportsman Ltd, ex p Bread Manufacturers Ltd* (1937) 37 SRNSW 242.
6 Cf. Lord Simon in *A-G v Times Newspapers Ltd* [1974] AC 273 at 321.
7 Above, p. 735.
8 See above, p. 731ff.

had done so far. The paragraph continued: '. . . the law is not always the same as justice. There are times when to insist on the letter of the law is as exposed to criticism as infringement of another's legal rights. The figure in the proposed settlement is £3.25 million, spread over 10 years. This does not shine as a beacon against pre-tax profits last year of £64.9 million and company assets worth £421 million. Without in any way surrendering on negligence, Distillers could and should think again.' Distillers brought the article to the attention of the Attorney-General maintaining that it was a contempt of court. The Attorney-General decided to take no action and Distillers let the matter drop. The editor of the *Sunday Times* was, however, minded to publish a further article of a different character. That article consisted in the main of detailed evidence and argument intended to show that Distillers had not exercised due care to see that thalidomide was safe for pregnant mothers before they put it on the market. The editor sent the article to the Attorney-General who commenced proceedings for an injunction against the respondents, the proprietors of the *Sunday Times*, restraining them from publishing that article. The Divisional Court ([1972] 3 All ER 1136) granted an injunction but the Court of Appeal ([1973] 1 All ER 815) allowed the respondents' appeal and discharged the injunction on the grounds, *inter alia*, that the article contained comments which the authors honestly believed to be true on matters of outstanding public interest and did not prejudice pending litigation since the litigation had been dormant for several years and no active steps had been taken or were likely to be taken to bring it before the courts. The Attorney-General appealed.

The House held unanimously (1) that the Attorney-General was a proper person to commence contempt proceedings, and (2) that an injunction should be granted to restrain publication of the second article. Lords Reid and Cross of Chelsea stated obiter that the first article did not amount to contempt. Lords Diplock and Simon of Glaisdale disagreed. They held that the first article improperly held Distillers up to public obloquy. Lord Simon would in addition have held that 'private pressure' to forgo legal rights was in general impermissible, and could only be justified within narrow limits as where there existed such a common interest that fair, reasonable and moderate personal representations could be appropriate. Lord Diplock took the view that 'private pressure' could not constitute contempt.

Lord Reid: . . . The law on this subject is and must be founded entirely on public policy. It is not there to protect the private rights of parties to a litigation or prosecution. It is there to prevent interference with the administration of justice and it should, in my judgment, be limited to what is reasonably necessary for that purpose. Public policy generally requires a balancing of interests which may conflict. Freedom of speech should not be limited to any greater extent than is necessary but it cannot be allowed where there would be real prejudice to the administration of justice. . . .

We are particularly concerned here with 'abusing parties' and 'prejudicing mankind' against them. Of course parties must be protected from scurrilous abuse: otherwise many litigants would fear to bring their cases to court. But the argument of the Attorney-General goes far beyond that. His argument was based on a passage in the judgment of Buckley J in *Vine Products Ltd v Green* [1966] Ch 484 at 495–496:

'It is a contempt of this court for any newspaper to comment on pending legal proceedings in any way which is likely to prejudice the fair trial of the action. That may arise in various ways. It may be that the comment is one which is likely in some way or other to bring pressure to bear upon one or other of the parties to the action, so as to prevent that party from prosecuting or from defending the action, or encourage that party to submit to terms of compromise which he otherwise might not have been prepared to entertain, or influence him in some other way in his conduct in the action, which he ought to be free to prosecute or to defend, as he is advised, without being subject to such pressure.'

I think that this is much too widely stated. It is true that there is some authority for it but . . . it does not seem to me to be in accord with sound public policy. Why would it be contrary to public policy to seek by fair comment to dissuade Shylock from proceeding with his action? Surely it could not be wrong for the officious bystander to draw his attention to the risk that, if he goes on, decent people will cease to trade with him. Or suppose that his best customer ceased to trade with him when he heard of his lawsuit. That could not be contempt of court. Would it become contempt if, when asked by Shylock why he was sending no more business his way, he told him the reason? Nothing would be more likely to influence Shylock to discontinue his action. It might become widely known that such pressure was being brought to bear. Would that make any difference? And though widely known must the local press keep silent about it? There must be some limitation of this general statement of the law.

And then suppose that there is in the press and elsewhere active discussion of some question of wide public interest, such as the propriety of local authorities or other landlords ejecting squatters from empty premises due for demolition. Then legal proceedings are begun against some squatters, it may be by some authority which had already been criticised in the press. The controversy could hardly be continued without likelihood that it might influence the authority in its conduct of the action. Must there then be silence until that case is decided? And there may be a series of actions by the same or different landlords. Surely public policy does not require that a system of stop and go shall apply to public discussion.

I think that there is a difference between direct interference with the fair trial of an action and words or conduct which may affect the mind of a litigant. Comment likely to affect the minds of witnesses and of the tribunal must be stopped for otherwise the trial may well be unfair. But the fact that a party refrains from seeking to enforce his full legal rights in no way prejudices a fair trial, whether the decision is or is not influenced by some third party. There are other weighty reasons for preventing improper influence being brought to bear on litigants, but they have little to do with interference with the fairness of a trial. There must be absolute prohibition of interference with a fair trial but beyond that there must be a balancing of relevant considerations. . . .

So I would hold that as a general rule where the only matter to be considered is pressure put on a litigant, fair and temperate criticism is legitimate, but anything which goes beyond that may well involve contempt of court. But in a case involving witnesses, jury or magistrates, other considerations are involved: there even fair and temperate criticism might be likely to affect the minds of some of them so as to involve contempt. But it can be assumed that it would not affect the mind of a professional judge. . . .

The crucial question on this point of the case is whether it can ever be permissible to urge a party to a litigation to forgo his legal rights in whole or in part. The Attorney-General argues that it cannot and I think that the Divisional Court has accepted that view. In my view it is permissible so long as it is done in a fair and temperate way and without any oblique motive. The *Sunday Times* article of 24 September 1972, affords a good illustration of the difference between the two views. It is plainly intended to bring pressure to bear on Distillers. It was likely to attract support from others and it did so. It was outspoken. It said: 'There are times when to insist on the letter of the law is as exposed to criticism as infringement of another's legal rights' and clearly implied that that was such a time. If the view maintained by the Attorney-General were right I could hardly imagine a clearer case of contempt of court. It could be no excuse that the passage which I quoted earlier was combined with a great deal of other totally unobjectionable material. And it could not be said that it created no serious risk of causing Distillers to do what they did not want to do. On the facts submitted to your Lordships in argument it seems to me to have played a large part in causing Distillers to offer far more money than they had in mind at that time. But I am quite unable to subscribe to the view that it ought never to have been published because it was in contempt of court. I see no offence against public policy and no pollution of the stream of justice by its publication.

Now I must turn to the material to which the injunction applied. . . . [I]t consists in the main of detailed evidence and argument intended to show that Distillers did not exercise due care to see that thalidomide was safe before they put it on the market.

If we regard this material solely from the point of view of its likely effect on Distillers I do not think that its publication in 1972 would have added much to the pressure on them created, or at least begun, by the earlier article of September 24. . . .

But, to my mind, there is another consideration even more important than the effect of publication on the mind of the litigant. The controversy about the tragedy of the thalidomide children has ranged widely but as yet there seems to have been little, if any, detailed discussion of the issues which the court may have to determine if the outstanding claims are not settled. The question whether Distillers were negligent has been frequently referred to but, so far as I am aware, there has been no attempt to assess the evidence. If this material were released now, it appears to me to be almost inevitable that detailed answers would be published and there would be expressed various public prejudgments of this issue. That I would regard as very much against the public interest.

There has long been and there still is in this country a strong and generally held feeling that trial by newspaper is wrong and should be prevented. I find, for example, in the report in 1969 of Lord Salmon's committee dealing with the Law of Contempt in relation to Tribunals of Inquiry (Cmnd. 4078) a reference to the 'horror' in such a thing (p. 12, para. 29). What I think is regarded as most objectionable is that a newspaper or television programme should seek to persuade the public by discussing the issues and evidence in a case before the court, whether civil or criminal, that one side is right and the other wrong. If we were to ask the ordinary man or even a lawyer in his leisure moments why he has that feeling, I suspect that the first reply would be—'well, look at what happens in some other countries where that is permitted.' As in so many other matters, strong feelings are based on one's general experience rather than on specific reasons, and it often requires an effort to marshal one's reasons. But the public policy is generally the result of strong feelings, commonly held, rather than of cold argument. . . .

There is ample authority for the proposition that issues must not be prejudged in a manner likely to affect the mind of those who may later be witnesses or jurors. But very little has been said about the wider proposition that trial by newspaper is intrinsically objectionable. That may be because if one can find more limited and familiar grounds adequate for the decision of a case it is rash to venture on uncharted seas.

I think that anything in the nature of prejudgment of a case or of specific issues in it is objectionable, not only because of its possible effect on that particular case but also because of its side effects which may be far reaching. Responsible 'mass media' will do their best to be fair, but there will also be ill-informed, slapdash or prejudiced attempts to influence the public. If people are led to think that it is easy to find the truth, disrespect for the processes of the law could follow, and, if mass media are allowed to judge, unpopular people and unpopular causes will fare very badly. Most cases of prejudging of issues fall within the existing authorities on contempt. I do not think that the freedom of the press would suffer, and I think that the law would be clearer and easier to apply in practice if it is made a general rule that it is not permissible to prejudge issues in pending cases. . . .

There is no magic in the issue of a writ or in a charge being made against an accused person. Comment on a case which is imminent may be as objectionable as comment after it has begun. And a 'gagging' writ ought to have no effect.

But I must add to prevent misunderstanding that comment where a case is under appeal is a very different matter. For one thing it is scarcely possible to imagine a case where comment could influence judges in the Court of Appeal or noble and learned Lords in this House. And it would be wrong and contrary to existing practice to limit proper criticism of judgments already given but under appeal.

Now I must deal with the reasons which induced the Court of Appeal to discharge the injunction. It was said that the actions had been dormant or asleep for several years. Nothing appears to have been done in court, but active negotiations for a settlement were going on all the time. No one denies that it would be contempt of court to use improper pressure to induce a litigant to settle a case on terms to which he did not wish to agree. So if there is no undue procrastination in the negotiations for a settlement I do not see how in this context an action can be said to be dormant.

Then it was said that there is here a public interest which counter-balances the private interests of the litigants. But contempt of court has nothing to do with the private interests of the litigants. I have already indicated the way in which I think that a balance must be struck between the public interest in freedom of speech and the public interest in protecting the administration of justice from interference. I do not see why there should be any difference in principle between a case which is thought to have news value and one which is not. Protection of the administration of justice is equally important whether or not the case involves important general issues. . . .

Lord Diplock: . . .

The due administration of justice requires *first* that all citizens should have unhindered access to the constitutionally established courts of criminal or civil jurisdiction for the determination of disputes as to their legal rights and liabilities; *secondly*, that they should be able to rely upon obtaining in the courts the arbitrament of a tribunal which is free from bias against any party and whose decision will be based upon those facts only that have been proved in evidence adduced before it in accordance with the procedure adopted in courts of law; and *thirdly* that, once the dispute has been submitted to a court of law, they should be able to rely upon there being no usurpation by any other person of the function of that court to decide it according to law. Conduct which is calculated to prejudice any of these three requirements or to undermine the public confidence that they will be observed is contempt of court. . . .

My Lords, to hold a party up to public obloquy for exercising his constitutional right to have recourse to a court of law for the ascertainment and enforcement of his legal rights and obligations is calculated to prejudice the *first* requirement for the due administration of justice: the unhindered access of all citizens to the established courts of law. Similarly, 'trial by newspaper,' i.e., public discussion or comment on the merits of a dispute which has been submitted to a court of law or on the alleged facts of the dispute before they have been found by the court upon the evidence adduced before it, is calculated to prejudice the *third* requirement: that parties to litigation should be able to rely upon there being no usurpation by any other person of the function of that court to decide their dispute according to law. If to have recourse to civil litigation were to expose a litigant to the risk of public obloquy or to public and prejudicial discussion of the facts or merits of the case before they have been determined by the court, potential suitors would be inhibited from availing themselves of courts of law for the purpose for which they are established.

It is only where a case is to be heard by a tribunal which may be regarded as incapable of being influenced by public criticism of the parties or discussion of the merits or the facts and any witnesses likely to be called are similarly immune, that conduct of this kind does not also offend against the *second* requirement for the due administration of justice; . . .

[His Lordship went on to hold that the second article was in contempt as it 'discussed prejudicially the facts and merits of Distillers' defence to the charge of negligence brought against them in the actions before these have been determined by the court or the actions disposed of by settlement'. The first article was also in contempt as a passage in it 'does hold Distillers up to public obloquy for . . . relying upon the defence, available to them under the law as it stands, that they were not guilty of any negligence. . . .' That did not mean that action should have been taken as it was a 'short passage in a long and trenchant article which was otherwise unobjectionable'.]

Lord Cross of Chelsea: . . . I agree with my noble and learned friend [Lord Reid] that we should maintain the rule that any 'prejudging' of issues, whether of fact or of law, in pending proceedings—whether civil or criminal—is in principle an interference with the administration of justice although in any particular case the offence may be so trifling that to bring it to the notice of the court would be unjustifiable . . . .

Appeal allowed.

NOTES

1. The injunction was discharged in 1976,[9] and the article subsequently appeared in the *Sunday Times*.[10]

2. The Phillimore Committee did not like the 'prejudgment' test propounded by the House of Lords, while recognising the force of the policy arguments against 'trial by newspaper' or 'trial by television':

'111. The test of prejudgment might well make for greater certainty in one direction – provided a satisfactory definition of prejudgment could be found – but it is by no means clear that it is

---

9 *The Times*, 24 June.
10 See casenotes by C. J. Miller, (1974) 37 MLR 96; M. O'Boyle, (1974) 25 NILQ 57; D. G. T. Williams, [1973] CLJ 177; and see C. J. Miller, [1975] Crim LR 132 and M. Rosen, *The Sunday Times Thalidomide Case* (1979).

satisfactory in others, for instance, in the case of the "gagging" writs. . . . It can be arbitrary in its application. For example, an opinion expressed on a legal issue in a learned journal would fall within the description of prejudgment given by Lord Cross of Chelsea. Again, there has been much discussion and expression of opinion in scientific journals as to the manner in which thalidomide operates to produce deformities. These, too, would fall within the test of prejudgment and would therefore be contempts. Furthermore, the scope and precise meaning of the words "prejudge" or "prejudgment" as used in the House of Lords are no easier to determine in practice than the phrase "risk of prejudice". At what point does legitimate discussion or expression of opinion cease to be legitimate and qualify as prejudgment? This may depend as much upon the quality and the authority of the party expressing the opinion as upon the nature of the opinion and the form of its expression. . . . Further, the expression of opinion and even its repetition can be so framed as to disclaim clearly any intention to offer a concluded judgment and yet be of highly persuasive and influential character. The simple test of prejudgment therefore seems to go too far in some respects and not far enough in others. We conclude that no satisfactory definition can be found which does not have direct reference to the mischief which the law of contempt is and always has been designed to suppress. That mischief is the risk of prejudice to the due administration of justice.'

The Committee's preferred test for contempt under the strict liability rule formed the basis of what is now s. 2(2) of the Contempt of Court Act 1981.[11]

3. It was formerly thought that once a writ for libel was issued, subsequent repetition of the libel would amount to contempt of court. So, persons with little or no intention of pursuing proceedings issued so-called 'gagging' writs in order to stifle further comment. The best view, prior to the 1981 Act, was that the issue of a writ did not *automatically* render repetition of the alleged libel contempt, but that repetition might be contempt if there was a risk of prejudice to the pending proceedings. If a court was not convinced that the plaintiff genuinely intended to proceed, or if the repetition was well before the trial, then there was likely to be no risk of prejudice and so no contempt. Salmon LJ seemed to go further when he offered the following encouragement to the press (obiter) in *Thomson v Times Newspapers Ltd*:[12]

'It is a widely held fallacy that the issue of a writ automatically stifles further comment. There is no authority that I know of to support the view that further comment would amount to contempt of court. Once a newspaper has justified, and there is some prima facie support for the justification, the plaintiff cannot obtain an interlocutory injunction to restrain the defendants from repeating the matters complained of [under the rule in *Bonnard v Perryman*].[13] In these circumstances it is obviously wrong to suppose that they could be committing a contempt by doing so. It seems to me to be equally obvious that no other newspaper that repeats the same sort of criticism is committing a contempt of court. They may be publishing a libel, and if they do so, and they have no defence to it, they will have to pay whatever may be the appropriate damages; but the writ does not, in my view, preclude the publication of any further criticism: it merely puts the person who makes the further criticism on risk of being sued for libel; and he takes the same risk whether or not there has been any previous publication. I appreciate that very often newspapers are chary about repeating criticism when a writ for libel has been issued because they feel they are running some risk of being proceeded against for contempt. Without expressing any final view, because the point is not before this court for decision, I think that in this they are mistaken. No doubt the law relating to contempt could and should be clarified in this respect.'

This was approved by Lord Denning MR in *Wallersteiner v Moir*.[14] Note also Lord Reid's remark in the *Sunday Times* case[15] that 'a gagging writ ought to have no effect.'

---

11 See p. 724.
12 [1969] 3 All ER 648 at 651, CA.
13 Below, p. 944.
14 [1974] 3 All ER 217 at 230, CA.
15 Above, p. 762.

There is now less scope for 'gagging writs' (or now, presumably, 'gagging claim forms') in view of the provisions of the Contempt of Court Act 1981 that: (1) delay commencement of the sub judice period in civil cases (Sch. 1); (2) strengthen the test for contempt (s. 2(2);[16] and (3) establish a public interest defence (s. 5).[17] However, it has been held that the rule in *Bonnard v Perryman* does not apply if there is an infringement of the strict liability rule.[18]

4. The *Sunday Times* case was distinguished in *Schering Chemicals Ltd v Falkman Ltd*.[19] Here, the Court of Appeal declined to grant an injunction to prevent the showing of a television film about a drug ('Primodos') that had been alleged to be harmful to unborn children, sought on the ground that it would be in contempt of court in relation to pending civil litigation. There was no risk of prejudice as the issues were not prejudged, there was no improper pressure and it would be arranged that the judge who tried the action would not have seen the broadcast. (An injunction was, however, granted (Lord Denning MR dissenting) on the ground of breach of confidence[20]).

5. The decision of the European Court of Human Rights in the *Sunday Times* case is considered above.[1] The Contempt of Court Act 1981 was intended to fulfil the requirements of that decision. It has been a matter of debate whether this has been achieved.[2]

6. *Borrie and Lowe*[3] argue that in *A-G v Times Newspapers*[4] Lords Reid, Cross and Morris took the view that fair and temperate criticism of a litigant, whether public or private, designed, for example, to encourage him to settle or not to insist on his strict legal rights, is not contempt.[5] For an example of illegitimate pressure, see *Dove Group plc and Jaguar Cars Ltd v Hynes*,[6] where H conducted a campaign of harassment against Dove Jaguars in respect of a Jaguar Sovereign car which was the subject of pending litigation between the parties in the county court. H's actions included driving the car around with a large cardboard box on the roof simulating a battery and making it clear that it was insufficiently powered, arranging for the car to be towed around the streets by shire horses having alerted the media beforehand, interfering with car salesmen and visiting Mr Dove's country home in his absence to Mrs Dove's alarm. H was fined. The Phillimore Committee[7] recommended that only conduct directed against a litigant which amounts to intimidation or unlawful threats should be capable of being treated as a contempt. The Green Paper[8] expressed the view that this would tip the balance too far against the interests of justice. The Law Commission[9] proposed an offence of making an unwarranted demand with menaces that a person should either not institute judicial proceedings, or should withdraw or should settle those proceedings. No action has been taken on these recommendations.

7. The following case considers liability for intentional contempt at common law.

16 See *A-G v News Group Newspapers Ltd* below, p. 774 n. 3.
17 Above, p. 724.
18 *A-G v News Group Newspapers Ltd*, below, p. 774 n. 3. See further on 'gagging writs': *Borrie and Lowe*, pp. 189–196; *Miller*, pp. 385–390.
19 [1982] QB 1, CA.
20 See (1982) 98 LQR 5–8.
1 At p. 721.
2 See N. V. Lowe in M. P. Furmston et al. (eds.), *The Effect on English Domestic Law of Membership of the European Communities and of Ratification of the European Convention on Human Rights* (1983), Chap. 10.
3 pp. 204–210.
4 Above.
5 Cf. Hunt J in *Commercial Bank of Australia Ltd v Preston* [1981] 2 NSWLR 554, Sup Ct NSW.
6 [1993] COD 174.
7 pp. 25–30.
8 Cmnd. 7145, pp. 15–17.
9 Law Com No. 96, pp. 59–62.

A-G v Times Newspapers Ltd [1991] 2 All ER 398, [1992] 1 AC 191, [1991] 2 WLR 994, House of Lords

In 1985, the Attorney-General obtained an interim injunction in Australia restraining Peter Wright from publishing *Spycatcher: The Candid Memoirs of an Intelligence Officer.* In June 1986, before the trial of the Australian proceedings, the *Guardian* and the *Observer* published articles outlining allegations contained in the Wright memoirs. The Attorney-General obtained interlocutory injunctions against the newspapers restraining them, with certain exceptions, from disclosing any information obtained by Wright in his capacity as a member of the security service (*A-G v Observer Newspapers Ltd and the Guardian* [1986] NLJ Rep 799, CA). He intended to seek final injunctions, based on Mr Wright's breach of confidence. In April 1987, the *Independent*, the *London Evening Standard* and the *London Daily News*, who were not parties to the 1986 injunctions, published further material derived from Wright's memoirs. The Attorney-General brought proceedings for contempt of court. A preliminary issue of law was tried, namely whether a publication made in knowledge of an outstanding injunction against another party and which if made by that party would be in breach of the injunction, could constitute a criminal contempt of court on the ground that it interfered with the process of justice in relation to that injunction. Sir Nicolas Browne-Wilkinson V-C held that the law of contempt did not apply where the only act complained of was not a breach of the express terms of the order and the alleged contemnor was neither party nor privy to any breach of the order by others. The Attorney-General appealed. He conceded that the strict liability rule did not apply as proceedings were not active, but argued that the defendants could be liable for contempt at common law as their conduct was intended to impede or prejudice the administration of justice. On 15 July 1987, the Court of Appeal[10] held that the respondents' publications could amount to contempt of court, and remitted the case for trial. Meanwhile, on 12 July, the *Sunday Times*, having been advised by leading counsel that it would not constitute contempt, published extracts from *Spycatcher*. On 13 July, the Attorney-General commenced contempt proceedings against the publishers of the *Sunday Times* (Times Newspapers Ltd) and its editor, Andrew Neil.

Both sets of proceedings were heard by Morritt J. At this stage the Attorney-General pressed for substantive relief only against the *Independent* and the *Sunday Times*. Morritt J held[11] that the publishers and editors of these papers had been guilty of contempt by publishing extracts from or summaries of *Spycatcher*. The respective publishers were each fined £50,000. On appeal, the Court of Appeal[12] upheld the finding of contempt, but discharged the fines. Times Newspapers appealed to the House of Lords. The only matter at issue was whether the appellants had committed the actus reus of contempt. The House of Lords unanimously dismissed the appeal.

Lord Oliver: . . . The appellants' primary submission is that it not only was not, but was not capable of being, a contempt of court because, although they were fully aware of the orders which had been made against 'The Guardian' and the 'Observer,' they were not themselves bound by those orders nor were they assisting in or procuring or inciting a breach of those orders by the two newspapers which were bound.

The submission involves some analysis of the particular type of contempt with which the appeal is concerned. A distinction (which has been variously described as 'unhelpful' or 'largely meaningless') is sometimes drawn by what is described as contempt,' that is to say, contempt by a party to proceedings in matters of procedure, and 'criminal contempt.' One particular form of contempt by a party to proceedings is that constituted by an intentional act which is

10 [1988] Ch 333.
11 [1989] 1 FSR 457.
12 *A-G v Newspaper Publishing plc* (1990) Times, 28 February.

in breach of the order of a competent court. Where this occurs as a result of the act of a party who is bound by the order or of others acting at his direction or on his instigation, it constitutes a civil contempt by him which is punishable by the court at the instance of the party for whose benefit the order was made and can be waived by him. The intention with which the act was done will, of course, be of the highest relevance in the determination of the penalty (if any) to be imposed by the court, but the liability here is a strict one in the sense that all that requires to be proved is service of the order and the subsequent doing by the party bound of that which is prohibited. When, however, the prohibited act is done not by the party bound himself but by a third party, a stranger to the litigation, that person may also be liable for contempt. There is, however, this essential distinction that his liability is for criminal contempt and arises not because the contemnor is himself affected by the prohibition contained in the order but because his act constitutes a wilful interference with the administration of justice by the court in the proceedings in which the order was made. Here the liability is not strict in the sense referred to, for there has to be shown not only knowledge of the order but an intention to interfere with or impede the administration of justice – an intention which can of course be inferred from the circumstances.

The distinction is very well brought out in the judgment of Eveleigh LJ in *Z Ltd v A-Z and AA-LL* [1982] QB 558, where the question arose whether a third party could be liable for contempt in doing, at a time before the party enjoined had himself received notice of the order, that which was prohibited by the order. Eveleigh LJ observed, at p. 578:

'It was argued that the liability of a third party arose because he was treated as aiding and abetting the defendants (i.e. he was an accessory) and as the defendant could himself not be in breach unless he had notice it followed that there was no offence to which the third party could be accessory. In my opinion this argument misunderstands the true nature of the liability of the third party. He is liable for contempt of court committed by himself. It is true that his conduct may very often be seen as possessing a dual character of contempt of court by himself and aiding and abetting the contempt by another, but the conduct will always amount to contempt of court by himself. It will be conduct which knowingly interferes with the administration of justice by causing the order of the court to be thwarted.'

Mr Lester, on behalf of the appellants, accepts this as an accurate statement of the principle but nevertheless contends that it is restricted to cases in which it can be demonstrated that the third party was privy in some way to a breach by the party enjoined and that therefore the decision of the Court of Appeal in the instant case constituted an unwarranted extension of the law of contempt in a way which is both contrary to principle and unwarranted by authority. That submission is encapsulated in paragraph 19 of the appellants' printed case where it is asserted:

'The authorities decide that a third party is not liable for contempt by performing an act prohibited by the court except where he has aided and abetted (or incited or otherwise assisted) the performance of the act by the party enjoined.'

I will consider in a moment the authorities upon which Mr Lester relies for this proposition, but a moment's reflection will, I think, demonstrate that it cannot possibly be valid as a general proposition. Of course, aiding and abetting or inciting a breach is an obvious example of the sort of situation in which a third party will subject himself to liability, but if the underlying basis of his liability is, as Mr Lester accepts that it is, that stated by Eveleigh LJ, there can be no logical reason for restricting the liability in the way that he suggests. Take a simple example. A has a right of way over a roadway on C's land which constitutes the only access to his premises. A, having built a wall on his premises which obstructs the light of his next-door neighbour B, B commences proceedings for an injunction. On motion in that action A proffers and the court accepts an undertaking by A to use his best endeavours to remove the wall by a given date. A accordingly instructs contractors to carry out the work of demolition. C, who knows of the undertaking but wishes to pursue a private spite against B, in order to prevent the demolition of the wall, obstructs the access to the premises by blocking the right of way and employs security guards to prevent A's contractors from removing the obstruction. C is not bound by the terms of the undertaking nor can he conceivably be under any obligation to assist A in fulfilling it. Nor, obviously, does he aid and abet a breach by A of his undertaking, which the latter has in fact fulfilled by instructing contractors. But equally obviously C has impeded the administration of justice by deliberately thwarting an undertaking given to the court and designed to secure the removal of the wall. In circumstances such as these, it would seem to me unarguable that C is not in contempt of court in exactly the same way as if he had obstructed an officer of the court and I cannot imagine any court accepting as a defence to a motion for committal the proposition that no contempt is committed because C was not a party to the action or the undertaking.

Nor, in my judgment, do the authorities cited by Mr. Lester support the broad proposition for which he contends. *Lord Wellesley v Earl of Mornington* (1848) 11 Beav 181 was a case in which the earl's agent had cut wood with notice of an injunction against the earl. It was certainly said that the agent was liable to be committed for contempt as a third party who had aided and abetted a breach by the earl, but there is in fact nothing in the report of the proceedings to suggest that the earl was even aware of the agent's acts much less that he had authorised them. *Seaward v Paterson* [1897] 1 Ch 545, was a case where the contemnors had actively aided and abetted the defendant in the action in a breach of the injunction and it is not surprising therefore that the judgments treat of contempt in that context. But the principle enunciated by the Court of Appeal, and which is expressed in the judgments of both Lindley LJ and Rigby LJ, was the quite general one that any member of the public is under a duty not to obstruct the course of justice. . . .

[His Lordship referred to *A-G v Leveller Magazine Ltd.*[13]]

My Lords, there can be no logical distinction between a case where the court seeks to protect or preserve the interests of justice by a procedural ruling in the course of a hearing and one where it seeks to achieve the same end by a formal prohibition directed to one of the parties. Once one gets away, as these authorities compel, from the notion that the binding effect of an order is an essential ingredient in the offence of contempt, Mr Lester's proposition that the actus reus of contempt is narrowly confined solely to those who aid, abet or incite breaches by the party bound is seen to be untenable. It could not have made the slightest difference to the liability of Murray and Shepherd in *Seaward v Paterson* [1897] 1 Ch 545, if they had arranged and conducted the offending boxing match without Paterson's knowledge or authority. Both had been served with copies of the order made for the protection of the plaintiffs from disturbance and restraining Paterson from using or suffering the premises to be used otherwise than as a private club and their use of the premises for the holding of a boxing match was an intentional act having the inevitable consequence of frustrating the very purpose for which the court had made its order.

Once the conclusion is reached that the fact that the alleged contemnor is not party to or personally bound by the court's order then, given the intention on his part to interfere with or obstruct the course of justice, the sole remaining question is whether what he has done has that effect in the particular circumstances of the case. In the Court of Appeal it was said that the administration of justice was interfered with because the publication, as it was variously put, 'rendered nugatory the trial of the action' [[1988] Ch 358, 373 per Sir John Donaldson MR], 'destroyed in whole or in part the subject matter of the action' [Lloyd LJ, at pp. 378–380] or 'rendered the trial . . . pointless' [Balcombe LJ, at p. 387]. I respectfully question, however, whether the mere fact that an act of a third party foreseeably has the result that the issue in the action becomes academic or that it is no longer worth pursuing, so that the court's order ceases to fulfil any useful purpose, necessarily involves the conclusion that it constitutes the actus reus of contempt. It is not difficult to imagine circumstances in which a stranger to litigation acting in the pursuit of his own interests can quite permissibly take steps which he knows perfectly well will render pending litigation pointless or destroy, for practical purposes, the subject matter of a pending action. For example, in the course of argument, I instanced the case of an action in which a company obtains an ex parte injunction until the next motion day to prevent a creditor whose debt is disputed from presenting and advertising a winding-up petition. A petition presented the next day with knowledge of the injunction by an unpaid creditor whose debt is not capable of being disputed would clearly have the effect of rendering any further proceeding in the action entirely pointless. But it would be absurd to suggest that a perfectly proper use of the court's own machinery, even if for the express purpose of affecting the course of other pending litigation, could constitute the actus reus of contempt. Other examples are not difficult to come by and they illustrate the difficulty and, sometimes, the danger of attempting to formulate a universal test of what constitutes interfering with or impeding the administration of justice.

For my part, I doubt the value of cataloguing a series of hypothetical circumstances which can do no more than serve as illustrations of conduct which can or may fall on one side of the line or the other. I think that a more dependable guide is to be found in the way in which the gravamen of the offence is expressed in the respondent's case and which, I think, must be based upon the speeches in this House in the *Leveller Magazine* case, [1979] AC 440: 'The publication . . . frustrates, thwarts, or *subverts the purpose* of the court's order and thereby interferes with the due administration of justice in the particular action.' 'Purpose,' in this context, refers, of course, not to the litigant's purpose in obtaining the order or in fighting the action but to the purpose which, in seeking to administer justice between the parties in the particular litigation of which it had become seized, the court was intending to fulfil.

The appellants raise two principal objections to addressing the purpose of the order in this context. In the first place, it is said that the purpose of an order is something which can be gathered only from its terms and thus becomes synonymous with the text of the order. By that test, of course, the act of a third party, not an aider or abettor, has no effect upon the order at all. If the order forbids the doing of an act by A, A has done nothing and remains bound by the order which thus cannot be said to be frustrated. It was, on its face, designed to inhibit A. It achieves that purpose. Any other approach, it is said, leads to uncertainty, but how otherwise is the court's purpose to be ascertained? And can it be right in the context of a criminal offence that members of the public should be obliged to enquire beyond the terms of the order itself?

I can see the force of this in a case where the court's purpose is not manifest from the mere making of the order and this was, indeed, one of the matters which troubled Lord Edmund-Davies in the *Leveller Magazine* case [1979] AC 440. But the difficulty is more imaginary than real. None of their lordships who decided the *Leveller Magazine* case experienced any difficulty where the purpose of the order or ruling is obvious and manifest. Where there is room for genuine doubt about what the court's purpose is, then the party charged with contempt is likely to escape liability, not because of failure to prove the actus reus but for want of the necessary mens rea, for an intention to frustrate the purpose of the court would be difficult to establish if the purpose itself was not either known or obvious. In the instant case, there could never have been any doubt in anybody's mind what the court's purpose was in making the order. It was to preserve, until the trial of the action, the plaintiff's right to keep confidential and unpublished the information obtained by Mr Wright in the course of his employment – a right which the plaintiff enjoyed against all the world but which had been specifically threatened by the defendants in the action. . . .

The appellants fairly take the point that the third party who learns of the order and is thus put in the position of considering whether he is at liberty to do that which the party to the order is forbidden to do, has not been heard by the court and has, thus, not had the opportunity of putting before the court any arguments which he may have for contending that he is free to do what he desires in his own interest to do. That is perfectly true, but the answer is surely that that is by his own choice. 'The Sunday Times' in the instant case was perfectly at liberty, before publishing, either to inform the respondent and so give him the opportunity to object or to approach the court and to argue that it should be free to publish where the defendants were not, just as a person affected by notice of, for example, a *Mareva* injunction is able to, and frequently does, apply to the court for directions as to the disposition of assets in his hands which may or may not be subject to the terms of the order. In the end, therefore, I find myself unpersuaded by this argument. . . .

[His Lordship then rejected the argument that the effect of the present decision was to criminalise an act retroactively: there was nothing retroactive about 'the application of perfectly well known principles to a novel set of circumstances – novel only in the sense that no precise analogue can be found in any previously reported proceedings.' The argument that maintenance of the injunctions was in conflict with Article 10 of the ECHR was precluded by the statement to the contrary by Lord Templeman in *A-G v Guardian Newspapers Ltd.*[14]]

Finally, it is said that, because of the impending publication of Mr Wright's book in the United States, 'The Sunday Times' publication did not in fact interfere with the administration of justice since such confidentiality as remained was about to be destroyed in any event. The short answer to this is that the act has to be looked at at the date when it was performed. It cannot be open to one who has frustrated the court's order to excuse himself by saying that someone else was about to do the same thing.

It seems, at first sight, a startling proposition that the doing by a person not a party to an action of an act which he is at liberty, in his own interests, to do and which he is not prohibited by order from doing, should subject him to proceedings for contempt merely because he is affected by knowledge that an order has been made against somebody else. But the circumstances are unusual and I cannot readily envisage circumstances likely in practice to occur, apart from claims for breach of confidence, where such an act would have the effect of impeding the administration of justice. As the Master of the Rolls observed in the instant case, breach of confidence is a uniquely fragile cause of action and the publication, once made, can have the effect of destroying for good and all the right which the law seeks to protect. Whilst newspapers have a legitimate interest and an important and necessary function in disseminating information, their rights are no higher than the right of a private individual to preserve the inviolability of that which he has imparted to another under an obligation of confidence and ought not to be permitted to override that right save where the public interest compulsively demands. A fortiori is that the case where a competent court has intervened to protect such right. The respondent to this appeal is the Attorney-General, but it has to be stressed as was emphasised in both the courts below, that in this case he was in no different position from any other private citizen entitled to preserve the sanctity of confidential information. In the end, I have found the logic of the respondent's arguments inescapable and I accordingly agree that the Court of Appeal reached the right conclusion and that the appeal must be dismissed. I confess, however, that I do so with a measure of disquiet, not because I doubt the validity of the conclusion, but because of the possibilities that open up. As I have said, I think that this sort of question is unlikely to arise except in cases of threatened publication of confidential material. But in those cases the important stage of the proceedings is almost always and inevitably the interlocutory one and it is, I think, important that a vigilant eye should be kept on the possibility that the law of contempt may be invoked in support of claims which are in truth insupportable. The guidelines laid down by this House in *American Cyanamid Co v Ethicon Ltd* [1975] AC 396, have come to be treated as carved on tablets of stone, so that a plaintiff seeking interlocutory relief has never to do more than show that he has a fairly arguable case. Thus the effect in a contest between a would-be publisher and one seeking to restrain the publication of allegedly confidential information is that the latter, by presenting an arguable case, can effectively through the invocation of the law of contempt, restrain until the trial of the action, which may be two or more years ahead, publication not only by the defendant but by anyone else within the jurisdiction and thus stifle what may, in the end, turn out to be perfectly legitimate comment until it no longer has any importance or commands any public interest. In cases where there is a contest as to whether the information is confidential at all or whether the public interest in any event requires its publication despite its confidentiality, this could be very important and experience shows that orders for speedy trial do not always achieve the hoped for result. I speak only for myself, but I cannot help feeling that in cases where it is clearly of importance that publication, if it takes place at all, should take place expeditiously, it may be necessary for courts to balance the rights of the parties and to decide the issue, as they sometimes did before the *Cyanamid* case, at the interlocutory stage on the prima facie merits and on the evidence then available.

Lords Brandon, Ackner and **Jauncey** delivered concurring speeches. **Lord Keith** concurred.

Appeal dismissed.

NOTES

1. The other members of the House of Lords did not express any misgiving of the kind mentioned by Lord Oliver, although Lord Jauncey did say[15] that it 'can only be in a limited type of case that independent action by a third party will have the effect

15 At 427.

of interfering with the operation of an order to which he is not a party. Cases involving confidential information are obvious examples.' Others might include destruction of a valuable object or demolition of a listed building, but it would 'only be in exceptional circumstances that a third party would be free to achieve this result without also incurring liabilities other than for contempt of court'.

The same principles apply in respect of orders made in criminal proceedings: *A-G v Newspaper Publishing plc.*[16]

2. The 1991 *Spycatcher* contempt case was analysed by the Court of Appeal in *Steen v A-G.*[17] The publishers of *Punch* and S, then the editor, were fined £20,000 and £5,000 respectively by Silber J for contempt in respect of the publication of an article by David Shayler that 'defeated the purposes of the court' in ordering injunctions against Shayler.[18] The Court of Appeal (Lord Phillips MR and Longmore LJ, Simon Brown LJ dissenting) allowed an appeal. Lord Phillips MR said:

'What is the ratio?

84. I asked Mr Crow whether the principle upon which he relied in this case was restricted to the publication of material which was subject to an interlocutory injunction, or whether it extended also to the situation where a court had granted a final injunction against publication. With a degree of hesitation he plumped for the latter. I am not surprised that he did. All too often in these cases, the claimant's object is achieved when an interlocutory injunction is granted and the stage of a substantive hearing is never reached. It seems to me that in ordering an interim injunction in a case such as this the primary object of the court is to prevent what will arguably constitute a legal wrong for which damages will not be an adequate remedy. The party against whom the injunction is granted will be in criminal contempt if he breaches the injunction. The effect and, so it seems to me, the primary purpose, of the third party contempt jurisdiction is to render it a criminal offence for any third party who is aware of the injunction to commit the potential wrong which the injunction is designed to prevent. That surely is the most serious aspect of the contempt, and the fact that it will at the same time render the litigation pointless is a subsidiary consideration.

85. Some of the reasoning of the House of Lords might appear to support the following principle:

Where the Court makes an order prohibiting a defendant from infringing a right, or potential right, of the plaintiff on the ground that damages will not be an adequate remedy, the Court thereby rules on the requirement of justice. Any third party who, with knowledge of the injunction, intentionally destroys the plaintiff's right, thereby interferes with the ends of justice and commits a contempt of court.

86. That principle, however, would run foul of the established principle of English law that an injunction does not bind a third party, a principle acknowledged by both the Court of Appeal and the House of Lords in Spycatcher. For this reason the House of Lords judgment cannot support a principle of that width.

87. I have some difficulty with the reliance placed by the House of Lords on cases where contempt was established in relation to final orders. Notwithstanding these problems, I have reached the following conclusions in relation to the basis of the House of Lords' finding that contempt of court was established in Spycatcher.

(a) Intentional interference with the manner in which a judge is conducting a trial can amount to a contempt of court.

(b) When in the course of a trial a judge makes an order with the purpose of furthering some aspect of the conduct of the trial, a third party who, with knowledge of that purpose, intentionally acts in such a way as to defeat that purpose can be in contempt of court.

(c) When a plaintiff brings an action to preserve an alleged right of confidentiality in information and the court makes an order that the information is not to be published pending trial, the purpose of the order is to protect the confidentiality of the information

16 [1997] 3 All ER 159, above, p. 734.
17 [2001] EWCA Civ 403.
18 Below, pp. 835–837.

pending trial. A third party who, with knowledge of the order, publishes the information and thereby destroys its confidentiality will commit a contempt of court. The contempt is committed not because the third party is in breach of the order the order does not bind the third party. The contempt is committed because the purpose of the judge in making the order is intentionally frustrated with the consequence that the conduct of the trial is disrupted.

88. The speeches of the House of Lords make it plain that the offence lies not simply in the commission of the act prohibited by the Order, but in the effect that the act has of interfering with the conduct of the trial.'

Hooper J's purpose in granting the injunctions 'was to prevent the disclosure of any matter that *arguably risked* harming the national interest'. It was not the broader purpose of prohibiting publication of any matter covered by the injunctions unless, in effect, cleared by the Attorney General under the terms of the proviso to the injunctions. Such an approach would subject 'the press to the censorship of the Attorney General' and would involve 'the imposition of a restriction on freedom of the press that is disproportionate to any public interest and thus in breach of Art. 10, ECHR' contrary to the duty imposed on the court by the Human Rights Act 1998, s.12(3). Accordingly, the republication by *Punch* of material already in the public domain could not (contrary to Silber J's view) form the actus reus of contempt. However, three matters not previously published, concerning: (1) the identity of two suspects in relation to the Bishopsgate bombing; (2) further information about one of the suspects; and (3) the way in which the Security Service surveillance operated, did defeat the purpose of the injunction as it arguably posed a risk of damaging national security. Here, the actus reus was established, but mens rea was not, as it was not established that S knew that the publication would interfere with the course of justice by defeating the purpose underlying the injunction. Lord Phillips noted that as the article had been written by Shayler, the appellants could have been prosecuted on the basis that they had aided and abetted S's breach of the injunctions. However, the Attorney had not chosen to proceed on this basis. Simon Brown LJ agreed with the analysis of *Spycatcher* and that republication of material (extensively as opposed to cursorily) in the public domain could not constitute contempt. However, S did have the necessary mens rea in respect of the 'three matters'. He knew there was a bar on publication unless the Attorney General consented; there was nothing intrinsically objectionable in such an arrangement; and it did not appear that the Attorney here could not properly have refused consent. S accordingly 'intended to take upon himself the responsibility for determining whether national security was risked and thereby he thwarted the court's intention'. The clarification of the narrow scope of this form of liability is welcome.

3. The question of mens rea was considered by the Court of Appeal.[19] It was common ground by this stage that recklessness was insufficient for mens rea and that what was necessary was a 'specific intent' to impede or prejudice the administration of justice.[20] What was in issue was how that intention was to be established. In the present case, the Court of Appeal held that the following passage from the judgment of Lord Lane CJ in *R v Nedrick*,[1] was applicable to criminal contempt of court.

'When determining whether the defendant had the necessary intent, it may therefore be helpful for a jury to ask themselves two questions. (1) How probable was the consequence which resulted from the defendant's voluntary act? (2) Did he foresee that consequence?

---

19 (1990) Times, 28 February.
20 In accordance with observations in *A-G v Newspaper Publishing plc* [1988] Ch 333 at 374 (Sir John Donaldson MR), 382 (Lloyd LJ), 387 (Balcombe LJ).
1   [1986] 3 All ER 1 at 3–4.

If he did not appreciate that death or serious harm was likely to result from his act, he cannot have intended to bring it about. If he did, but thought that the risk to which he was exposing the person killed was only slight, then it may be easy for the jury to conclude that he did not intend to bring about that result. On the other hand, if the jury are satisfied that at the material time the defendant recognised that death or serious harm would be virtually certain (barring some unforeseen intervention) to result from his voluntary act, then that is a fact from which they may find it easy to infer that he intended to kill or do serious bodily harm, even though he may not have had any desire to achieve that result.

As Lord Bridge said in *R v Moloney* [1985] 1 All ER 1025 at 1036, [1985] AC 905 at 925:

> "... the probability of the consequence taken to have been foreseen must be little short of overwhelming before it will suffice to establish the necessary intent."

Later he uses the expression 'moral certainty' (see [1985] 1 All ER 1025 at 1037, [1985] AC 905 at 926) and says, 'will lead to a certain consequence unless something unexpected supervenes to prevent it' (see [1985] 1 All ER 1025 at 1039, [1985] AC 905 at 929).

Where the charge is murder and in the rare cases where the simple direction is not enough, the jury should be directed that they are not entitled to infer the necessary intention unless they feel sure that death or serious bodily harm was a virtual certainty (barring some unforeseen intervention) as a result of the defendant's actions and that the defendant appreciated that such was the case.

Where a man realises that it is for all practical purposes inevitable that his actions will result in death or serious harm, the inference may be irresistible that he intended that result, however little he may have desired or wished it to happen. The decision is one for the jury to be reached on a consideration of all the evidence.'[2]

4. Is there any room in the law on intentional contempt for any public interest defence analogous to s. 5 of the Contempt of Court Act 1981.[3] J. Laws[4] argues that public interest considerations cannot affect the actus reus of intended contempt (if D intends to impede justice he can hardly argue that he was discussing *in good faith* matters of general public interest). They might, however, tend to negative the necessary intent. In *A-G v Times Newspapers Ltd*, Lord Jauncey did consider the public interest, and concluded 'that in these cases the public interest in having justice done unimpeded between parties must prevail over that interest in the freedom of the press'.

(B) UNDER THE STRICT LIABILITY RULE

The test for contempt under the 'strict liability rule' is to be found in s. 2(2) of the Contempt of Court Act 1981[5] and is the same as for criminal cases.[6] The time limits are enacted in Sch. 1, paras. 12–14 and (for appellate proceedings) paras. 15 and 16.[7] These largely follow the recommendations of the Phillimore Committee, which took the view that in the light of the length of civil as compared with criminal proceedings, the decrease in jury trials and the unlikelihood that judges will be improperly influenced, strict liability need not be imposed from the commencement of proceedings in civil cases. The defences under ss. 3, 4(1) and 5 of the 1981 Act are available.[8]

---

2   See further, J. Laws, (1990) 43 CLP 99, 105–110 and above, pp. 755–758.
3   Above, p. 725.
4   (1990) 43 CLP 99, 110–111.
5   Above, p. 724.
6   Above, pp. 734–742.
7   Above, pp. 728–730.
8   See above, p. 725.

NOTES

1. How would the *Sunday Times* case be decided under the 1981 Act? Consider (1) the test for contempt; (2) the time limits; (3) the defences. Note Lord Diplock's remarks in *A-G v English*[9] and *Re Lonrho plc*.[10]

2. Coroners' inquests are active once they have opened, and until they have been closed by a finding as to the cause of death; they remain active even though adjourned *sine die* while police investigations take place: *Peacock v London Weekend Television*.[11] In this case, an injunction was granted to prevent a televised reconstruction of events that led to the death of a black Hell's Angel in police custody; this was held to constitute a substantial risk that the coroner's proceedings would be seriously impeded or prejudiced. Watkins LJ regarded the proposed programme as 'very emotive': 'newspapers and broadcasters must beware of wittingly or unwittingly usurping the functions of courts. In our land we do not allow trial by television or newspaper'.[12] Croom-Johnson LJ did not regard the programme as 'balanced'. As to the suggestion that the passage of time would cause the memories of watchers to fade, 'nowadays one has to remember the existence of the video'.[13]

3. The relationship between the rule in *Bonnard v Perryman*[14] and the law of contempt of court was considered by the Court of Appeal in *A-G v News Group Newspapers Ltd*.[15] In 1984, Ian Botham, the England Test cricketer, began libel proceedings in respect of an article in the *Mail on Sunday* alleging, *inter alia*, the misuse of drugs while on tour in New Zealand. The defendants intended to plead justification and the case was set down for trial no earlier than March 1987. Under the rule in *Bonnard v Perryman*, applicable under the law of defamation, the plaintiff would not be able to seek an interlocutory injunction restraining the defendants from repeating the allegations subsequently. On 6 April 1986, the *News of the World* repeated the allegations, and a further story, with further details, was intended for publication on 13 April. The Attorney-General sought an injunction restraining the defendants from publishing allegations covering substantially the same ground as the *Mail on Sunday* allegations of 1984. The Court of Appeal held that the rule in *Bonnard v Perryman* was decisive only in so far as the strict liability rule was not invoked. However, on the facts here, the proposed publication by the *News of the World* at this time would not involve a breach of the strict liability rule. Per Sir John Donaldson:[16]

> 'There has to be a *substantial* risk that the course of justice in the proceedings in question will be *seriously* impeded or prejudiced. This is a double test. First, there has to be some risk that the proceedings in question will be affected at all. Second, there has to be a prospect that, if affected, the effect will be serious. The two limbs of the test can overlap, but they can be quite separate. I accept Mr Laws' submission that "substantial" as a qualification of "risk" does not have the meaning of "weighty," but rather means "not insubstantial" or "not minimal". The "risk" part of the test will usually be of importance in the context of the width of the publication. To declare in a speech at a public meeting in Cornwall that a man about to be tried in Durham is guilty of the offence charged and has many previous convictions for the same offence may well carry no substantial risk of affecting his trial, but, if it occurred, the prejudice would be most serious. By contrast, a nationwide television broadcast at peak viewing time of some far more innocuous statement would certainly involve a substantial risk of having some effect on

9 Above, p. 735.
10 Below, p. 776.
11 (1985) 150 JP 71, CA.
12 p. 80.
13 pp. 82–83.
14 Below, p. 944.
15 [1987] QB 1.
16 At 15, 16.

a trial anywhere in the country and the sole effective question would arise under the "seriousness" limb of the test. Proximity in time between the publication and the proceedings would probably have a greater bearing on the risk limb than on the seriousness limb, but could go to both. . . .

. . . Whatever else may be said about the "News of the World," it is a newspaper with a nationwide circulation and there is a reasonable chance that it will have been read by at least one member of the jury which eventually hears Mr Botham's claims against the "Mail on Sunday." Whilst it is true that these actions are not yet in the jury list, I wholly reject Mr Gray's suggestion that there is any significance in the time at which the case comes into that list or in a period of about three months before trial. To accept such a submission would be to substitute a new test for "activity" for the purposes of the Act of 1981.

However, proximity to the trial is clearly a factor of great importance and this trial will not take place for at least 10 months, by which time many wickets will have fallen, not to mention much water having flowed under many bridges, all of which would blunt any impact of the publication. Furthermore, whilst I have never been a great believer in the efficacy of a conscious effort to put something out of one's mind—an acceptance of the fact that it is likely to remain there, but a determination not to take it into account, is more effective—and whilst I fully accept that judges may have an exaggerated belief in the extent to which juries are prepared to be guided by them in such mental gymnastics, the fact is that for one reason or another a trial, by its very nature, seems to cause all concerned to become progressively more inward looking, studying the evidence given and submissions made to the exclusion of other sources of enlightenment. This is a well-known phenomenon. As Lawton J put it on the basis of vast experience of jury trials, both at the Bar and on the Bench: "the drama, if I may use that term, of a trial almost always has the effect of excluding from recollection that which went before": *R v Kray* (1969) 53 Cr App Rep 412, 415.

The time may well come when a national newspaper would be in breach of the strict liability rule if it referred to the disputed incidents which are the subject matter of the "Mail on Sunday" actions. But in my judgment that day has not yet arrived, because it is not at present possible to say that there is a substantial risk of the "Mail on Sunday" trials being seriously prejudiced.'

See also *Pickering v Liverpool Daily Post and Echo Newspapers plc*,[17] where the plaintiff, a restricted mental patient detained under the Mental Health Act 1983 following his brutal killing of a 14-year-old girl, sought an injunction restraining the defendants from publishing the fact that he had applied to a Mental Health Review Tribunal for his discharge, the date of the hearing or the tribunal's decision. Previous applications by him had given rise to considerable media controversy. The Court of Appeal held that such an injunction could not be granted here on the basis of a threatened breach of the strict liability rule: the publication of the information 'would not *necessarily* impede or prejudice the course of justice, although, according to when, and where and how it is published, considerable discretion and restraint may have to be exercised if it is not to do so'.[18] A modified injunction was, however, granted under the specific procedural rules applicable to Mental Health Appeal Tribunals, and the court indicated, obiter, that a deliberate breach of restrictions imposed by those rules might constitute contempt of court by virtue of s. 12 of the Administration of Justice Act 1960.[19] The injunction was in turn set aside by the House of Lords[20] on the grounds (1) that breach of the rules did not itself give rise to a cause of action; and (2) that in any event the rules would not be breached by the publication of the information in question. Cf. *A-G v Associated Newspapers Group plc*[21] where proceedings for criminal contempt arising out of publicity

---

17 [1990] 1 All ER 335.
18 Per Lord Donaldson MR at 342.
19 See above, p. 748.
20 [1991] 2 AC 370.
21 [1989] 1 All ER 604, DC.

surrounding a previous application by the plaintiff to a Mental Health Review Tribunal were dismissed, *inter alia*, on the ground that any risk of prejudice by any effect on the tribunal or expert witnesses was remote.

4. The application of the strict liability rule to appellate proceedings was considered by the Appellate Committee of the House of Lords in *Re Lonrho plc*.[22] This case arose out of the long campaign by Lonrho to acquire House of Fraser, the owners of a series of stores including Harrods. In 1985, House of Fraser was acquired by the Al Fayed brothers. In 1987 the Secretary of State appointed inspectors under the Companies Act 1985, s. 432(2), to investigate and report on this acquisition. In 1988, the Secretary of State received this report, and sent a copy to the Serious Fraud Office. He decided that it should not be published while this might hinder the S.F.O.'s investigation and the fair trial of anyone prosecuted in consequence. He also decided not to refer the acquisition to the Monopolies and Mergers Commission. Lonrho sought judicial review of these decisions. They succeeded in the Divisional Court but the Secretary of State's appeal to the Court of Appeal was allowed. Lonrho's appeal to the House of Lords was fixed for hearing on 10 April 1989. On 23 March, Lonrho's chief executive, 'Tiny' Rowland, came into possession of two unauthorised copies of the report. On 30 March, a special edition of the *Observer* (a Lonrho subsidiary) was published containing extracts from and comments on the report. An injunction was obtained against the *Observer* but too late to prevent widespread distribution. 3,000 copies were sent by Lonrho to various recipients including four of the five Law Lords who were due to hear the appeal. Further campaign literature against the Al Fayeds was subsequently sent to some of the Law Lords. The Appellate Committee that was due to hear the judicial review appeal commenced contempt proceedings against Lonrho, Rowland, three Lonrho directors, The Observer Ltd, the editor of the *Observer*, Donald Trelford, and two lawyers. An amicus curiae was instructed to present the case. The Committee subsequently held: (1) that the proceedings should be heard by the House, no other court having jurisdiction; and (2) that although there was nothing to prevent the Committee itself from determining impartially whether there had been a contempt, the alleged contemnors should not be left with a sense of grievance, and so proceedings should be heard before a differently constituted Committee.

A fresh Committee, comprising Lords Bridge, Goff and Jauncey, held that the respondents' conduct had not constituted contempt of court. Charges relating to the material sent to Law Lords were not proceeded with: the copies of the special edition had been sent to the Law Lords by mistake, steps having been taken to remove them from the mailing list; the subsequent sending of propaganda material did not fall within the original order of the House authorising contempt proceedings.

The Committee considered whether the publication of the special edition constituted contempt under the strict liability rule (1) by prejudging these issues; or (2) by pre-empting the outcome of the judicial review proceedings. On prejudgment, the Committee noted that the test for contempt under the strict liability rule (s. 2(2)) had to be applied without any preconception derived from *A-G v Times Newspapers Ltd*[1] as to what kind of publication is likely to impede or prejudice the course of justice:

> '7.3 . . . Whether the course of justice in particular proceedings will be impeded or prejudiced by a publication must depend primarily on whether the publication will bring influence to bear which is likely to divert the proceedings in some way from the course which they would

22   [1990] 2 AC 154.
1   Above, p. 759.

otherwise have followed. The influence may affect the conduct of witnesses, the parties or the court. Before proceedings have come to trial and before the facts have been found, it is easy to see how critical public discussion of the issues and criticism of the conduct of the parties, particularly if a party is held up to public obloquy, may impede or prejudice the course of the proceedings by influencing the conduct of witnesses or parties in relation to the proceedings. If the trial is to be by jury, the possibility of prejudice by advance publicity directed to an issue which the jury will have to decide is obvious. The possibility that a professional judge will be influenced by anything he has read about the issues in a case which he has to try is very much more remote. He will not consciously allow himself to take account of anything other than the evidence and argument presented to him in court.

7.4 After an action has been tried or an application for judicial review determined and when proceedings are pending on appeal from the decision of first instance or, as here, from the Court of Appeal to the House of Lords, the possibility that a publication which discusses the issues arising on the appeal or the merits of the decision appealed against or of the conduct of the parties in relation thereto will impede or prejudice the course of justice in those proceedings is very much narrower. In the ordinary case, as here, there will be no question of influencing witnesses. In general terms the possibility that the parties will be influenced is remote. When a case has proceeded so far it is unlikely, save in exceptional circumstances, that criticism would deter an appellant from pursuing his appeal or induce a respondent to forgo the judgment in his favour or to reach a compromise of the appeal. So far as the appellate tribunal is concerned, it is difficult to visualise circumstances in which any court in the United Kingdom exercising appellate jurisdiction would be in the least likely to be influenced by public discussion of the merits of a decision appealed against or of the parties' conduct in the proceedings. Discussion and criticism of decisions of first instance or of the Court of Appeal which are subject to pending appeals are a commonplace in legal journals, but on matters of more general public interest examples also readily spring to mind of criticism in the general press directed against, for example, criminal convictions, sentences imposed, damages awarded in libel actions and other court decisions which arouse public controversy. No case was drawn to our attention in which public discussion of the issues arising in, or criticism of the parties to, litigation already decided at first instance has been held to be a contempt on the ground that it was likely to impede or prejudice the course of justice in proceedings on appeal from that decision.

7.5 The publication in "The Observer" special edition of extracts from the inspectors' report falls for consideration as possible contempt under the heading of "pre-emption". The vice at which the strictures in the speeches in *A-G v Times Newspapers Ltd* against "trial by newspaper" and "prejudgment" were directed is exhibited, if at all, in the editorial comment, in particular the accusation that the Secretary of State acted in bad faith in deciding to defer publication of the inspectors' report. . . . Having heard full argument, we do not consider that the editorial comment in "The Observer" special edition, however intemperate the language in which it was expressed may have been, created any risk that the Secretary of State, having succeeded in the Court of Appeal in both appeals, would be deterred from seeking to uphold those decisions in opposition to the appeals or deflected from the course he would otherwise have followed in relation to the appellate proceedings. Nor was the publication in this regard capable of exerting any influence on the decision of the Appellate Committee on either appeal.'

As to the argument that the publication of the special edition 'pre-empted' the ruling of the House on the legality of the Secretary of State's decision to defer publication, the Committee commented:

'8.4 In the light of these apparent anomalies we must ask whether there is any support in principle or authority for the proposition that a litigant who seeks a judicial remedy compelling a certain course of action creates a risk that the course of justice in the proceedings in which the remedy is sought would be impeded or prejudiced if he takes direct action to secure for himself the substance of the remedy sought without the assistance of the court. The example was put in the course of argument of the plaintiff who complains that his neighbour has built a wall obstructing his right of way and seeks an injunction to have it removed. He succeeds at first instance, loses in the Court of Appeal and appeals to the House of Lords. While the appeal is still pending he loses patience and knocks the wall down. In this example, if the plaintiff succeeds in the appeal, he will no longer need a mandatory injunction. If he loses, he will have rendered himself liable in damages and possibly criminally. In either event, however deplorable his conduct, it is difficult to see how the course of justice, in determining the legal rights of the parties is likely to have been impeded or prejudiced in any way. It is easy to think of many other examples of litigants resorting to this kind of self-help. In all or nearly all of them their conduct may involve a breach of civil or criminal law or both. But so far as we are aware, no case has ever been before the court in which conduct of this character has been held to amount to contempt of court. We think that it would be a novel extension of the law of contempt to hold that direct action taken by a litigant to secure the substance of a remedy which he was seeking in judicial proceedings amounted to a contempt in relation to those proceedings and that the publication of extracts from the inspectors' report in "The Observer" special edition did not create any risk that the course of justice in the appellate proceedings challenging the lawfulness of the Secretary of State's decision to deter publication would be impeded or prejudiced.'

(In this case an injunction was obtained *after* publication; had one been obtained *before* publication, would the principle of *A-G v Times Newspapers Ltd*[2] have been applicable?)

In *R v Bow Street Magistrates' Court, ex p Mirror Group Newspapers Ltd*,[3] the Divisional Court quashed an order under s. 4(2) of the 1981 Act[4] in so far as it prevented the applicants from publishing the magistrates' reasons for ordering that committal proceedings of four police officers charged with conspiracy to pervert the course of justice be stayed as an abuse of process. The purpose of the s. 4 order was to prevent prejudice to the administration of justice in the Divisional Court, to which the DPP was expected to apply for judicial review of the stay. However, it was doubtful whether such publicity could properly be considered by the Divisional Court when reviewing the validity of the stay; in any event, it could not be said that the s. 4 order was 'necessary' or the risk of prejudice 'substantial'.

5. In *A-G v Hislop*,[5] Ian Hislop and Pressdram Ltd, respectively editor and publisher of *Private Eye*, were fined £10,000 each in respect of two articles relating to Sonia Sutcliffe, the wife of Peter Sutcliffe, the so-called 'Yorkshire Ripper'. They were published in 1989, when the trial of a libel action by Mrs Sutcliffe against *Private Eye*, arising out of allegations that she had sold her story to the *Daily Mail* for £250,000, was about three months away. The articles alleged that Mrs Sutcliffe had provided a false alibi for her husband, knew about his activities before his arrest and was defrauding the DSS. Mrs Sutcliffe was successful in the first action, although the damages were reduced by consent following an appeal to the Court of Appeal, and a second libel action arising out of 1989 articles was settled in her favour. In the present proceedings, the Court of Appeal, reversing Popplewell J, held that the articles constituted both common law contempt and contempt under the strict liability rule in that they constituted improper pressure on Mrs Sutcliffe to discontinue the first libel action; and contempt under the strict liability rule in that they created a substantial risk that a juror or jurors might be prejudiced against her. On the first point Parker LJ noted that the articles 'went far further than fair and temperate criticism. They were plain abuse'.[6] There was no defence under s. 5 of the 1981 Act: 'Mr Hislop's intention negatived the existence of good faith'.[7] On the second point, Parker LJ commented:[8]

2   Above, pp. 766–770.
3   [1992] COD 15.
4   See above, p. 725 and pp. 749–751.
5   [1991] 1 QB 514.
6   At 527.
7   Per Nicholls LJ at 532.
8   At 528.

'That anyone reading the articles might be prejudiced is, as it seems to me, beyond doubt. The impact of the charges was great. They were admittedly very damaging to Mrs. Sutcliffe and blackened her character. The trial was only three months away and Mr. Sutcliffe was notorious. I am fully satisfied that anyone who happened to read the articles and found himself on a jury three months later would be likely to remember them and in that case to mention the content of them to other jurors. I am also satisfied that there was a substantial risk of one or more jurors having read one or both of the articles. With the trial in London and the readership of the magazine as large as it was, I cannot accept that the risk was only a remote possibility.'

6 Publications interfering with the course of justice as a continuing process

(A) SCANDALISING THE COURT[9]

R v Gray [1900] 2 QB 36, 69 LJQB 502, 82 LT 534, 64 JP 484, Queen's Bench Divisional Court

On 15 March 1900, one Wells was tried before Darling J at Birmingham Assizes for publishing certain obscene and filthy words, and for publishing an obscene libel. Before the trial commenced Darling J made some observations in court, pointing out that, whatever might be the rights of the case, it was inexpedient that the press should give anything like a full or detailed account of what passed at the trial, and that, although a newspaper had the right to publish accounts of proceedings in a law court, and for many purposes was protected for doing so, there was absolutely no protection to a newspaper for the publication of objectionable, obscene, and indecent matter, and any newspaper which did so might as easily be prosecuted as anybody else. He further said that, although he hoped and believed that his advice would be taken, if it was disregarded he should make it his business to see that the law was in that respect enforced.

The following day, after the Wells trial was over, Gray wrote and published in the *Birmingham Daily Argus* an article which included the following passage (printed in 82 LT 534):

'No newspaper can exist except upon its merits, a condition from which the Bench, happily for Mr Justice Darling, is exempt. There is not a journalist in Birmingham who has anything to learn from the impudent little man in horsehair, a microcosm of conceit and empty-headedness, who admonished the Press yesterday. It is not the credit of journalism, but of the English Bench, that is imperilled in a speech like Mr Justice Darling's. One is almost sorry that the Lord Chancellor had not another relative to provide for on that day that he selected a new judge from among the larrikins of the law. One of Mr Justice Darling's biographers states that "an eccentric relative left him much money". That misguided testator spoiled a successful bus conductor. Mr Justice Darling would do well to master the duties of his own profession before undertaking the regulation of another.'

The Attorney-General brought the matter to the attention of the Queen's Bench Divisional Court on 27 March.

Lord Russell of Killowen CJ delivered the judgment of the court (**Lord Russell CJ, Grantham** and **Phillimore JJ**): . . .

Any act done or writing published calculated to bring a Court or a judge of the Court into contempt, or to lower his authority, is a contempt of Court. That is one class of contempt.

9 On the historical background to this head of contempt, see D. Hay, 'Contempt by Scandalizing the Court: A Political History of the First Hundred Years' (1987) 25(3) OHLJ 431 and, for Australia, H. Burmester, (1985) 15 Melb ULR 313. On the position more recently, see C. Walker, 'Scandalising in the Eighties' (1985) 101 LQR 359.

Further, any act done or writing published calculated to obstruct or interfere with the due course of justice or the lawful process of the Courts is a contempt of Court. The former class belongs to the category which Lord Hardwicke LJ characterised as 'scandalising a Court or a judge' (*Re Read and Huggonson* (1742) 2 Atk 291, 469). That description of that class of contempt is to be taken subject to one and an important qualification. Judges and Courts are alike open to criticism, and if reasonable argument or expostulation is offered against any judicial act as contrary to law or the public good, no Court could or would treat that as contempt of Court. The law ought not to be astute in such cases to criticise adversely what under such circumstances and with such an object is published; but it is to be remembered that in this matter the liberty of the press is no greater and no less than the liberty of every subject of the Queen. Now, as I have said, no one has suggested that this is not a contempt of Court, and nobody has suggested, or could suggest, that it falls within the right of public criticism in the sense I have described. It is not criticism: I repeat that it is personal scurrilous abuse of a judge as a judge. We have, therefore, to deal with it as a case of contempt, and we have to deal with it brevi manu. This is not a new-fangled jurisdiction; it is a jurisdiction as old as the common law itself, of which it forms part. . . . It is a jurisdiction, however, to be exercised with scrupulous care, to be exercised only when the case is clear and beyond reasonable doubt; because, if it is not a case beyond reasonable doubt, the Courts will and ought to leave the Attorney-General to proceed by criminal information.
[The court fined Gray £100, with £25 costs]

R v Metropolitan Police Commissioner, ex p Blackburn (No 2) [1968] 2 QB 150, [1968] 2 All ER 319, [1968] 2 WLR 1204, Court of Appeal

In January 1968 the Court of Appeal delivered judgment in an application by a private citizen, [Raymond Blackburn], for an order of mandamus against the Metropolitan Police Commissioner in connection with the non-enforcement of the Gaming Acts. In their judgments the court expressed opinions on the conduct of the police and on earlier decisions on the Acts in the Queen's Bench Divisional Court [see [1968] 2 QB 118]. After reports of the judgments had appeared in the Press, [Quintin Hogg], a Privy Councillor who was also a Member of Parliament and Queen's Counsel, wrote an article in the weekly newspaper *Punch* in a section entitled 'Political Parley' in which he vigorously criticised the Court of Appeal and its dicta, wrongly attributing to that court decisions of the Divisional Court.

The applicant applied to the same Court of Appeal for an order that the writer had been guilty of contempt of court in (a) that the article falsely stated that the Act was 'rendered virtually unworkable by the unrealistic, contradictory and, in the leading case, erroneous decisions of the courts, including the Court of Appeal' and ridiculed that court by suggesting that it should apologise for the expense and trouble to which it had put the police; (b) that without proper knowledge of the facts the writer sought to ridicule the court for its alleged 'blindness'; and (c) that the writer had stated that 'a prudent policeman may well turn a somewhat blind eye towards a law which does not make sense and which Parliament may be about to repeal,' thereby encouraging police officers to flout the court's decision and commit breaches of their duty to enforce the law. For the writer it was stated that no disrespect of the court was intended but that he was exercising his right to criticise on a matter which he believed to be of public importance.

Lord Denning MR: . . .
That article is certainly critical of this court. In so far as it referred to the Court of Appeal, it is admittedly erroneous. This court did not in the gaming cases give any decision which was erroneous, nor one which was overruled by the House of Lords. But is the article a contempt of court?

This is the first case, so far as I know, where this court has been called on to consider an allegation of contempt against itself. It is a jurisdiction which undoubtedly belongs to us but which we will most sparingly exercise: more particularly as we ourselves have an interest in the matter.

Let me say at once that we will never use this jurisdiction as a means to uphold our own dignity. That must rest on surer foundations. Nor will we use it to suppress those who speak against us. We do not fear criticism, nor do we resent it. For there is something far more important at stake. It is no less than freedom of speech itself.

It is the right of every man, in Parliament or out of it, in the Press or over the broadcast, to make fair comment, even outspoken comment, on matters of public interest. Those who comment can deal faithfully with all that is done in a court of justice. They can say that we are mistaken, and our decisions erroneous, whether they are subject to appeal or not. All we would ask is that those who criticise us will remember that, from the nature of our office, we cannot reply to their criticisms. We cannot enter into public controversy. Still less into political controversy. We must rely on our conduct itself to be its own vindication.

Exposed as we are to the winds of criticism, nothing which is said by this person or that, nothing which is written by this pen or that, will deter us from doing what we believe is right; nor, I would add, from saying what the occasion requires, provided that it is pertinent to the matter in hand. Silence is not an option when things are ill done.

So it comes to this: Mr Quintin Hogg has criticised the court, but in so doing he is exercising his undoubted right. The article contains an error, no doubt, but errors do not make it a contempt of court. We must uphold his right to the uttermost.

I hold this not to be a contempt of court, and would dismiss the application.

Salmon LJ: The authority and reputation of our courts are not so frail that their judgments need to be shielded from criticism, even from the criticism of Mr Quintin Hogg. Their judgments, which can, I think, safely be left to take care of themselves, are often of considerable public importance. It is the inalienable right of everyone to comment fairly upon any matter of public importance. This right is one of the pillars of individual liberty—freedom of speech, which our courts have always unfailingly upheld.

It follows that no criticism of a judgment, however vigorous, can amount to contempt of court, providing it keeps within the limits of reasonable courtesy and good faith. The criticism here complained of, however rumbustious, however wide of the mark, whether expressed in good taste or in bad taste, seeems to me to be well within those limits. . . .

No one could doubt Mr Hogg's good faith. I, of course, entirely accept that he had no intention of holding this court up to contempt; nor did he do so. Mr Blackburn complains that Mr Hogg has not apologised. There was no reason why he should apologise, for he owes no apology, save, perhaps, to the readers of *Punch* for some of the inaccuracies and inconsistencies which his article contains. I agree that this application should be dismissed.

Edmund Davies LJ delivered a concurring judgment.

Application dismissed.

NOTES

1. In *McLeod v St Aubyn*,[10] attacks upon the competence and partiality of St Aubyn, the Acting Chief Justice of St Vincent, appeared in the *Federalist* newspaper. McLeod gave a copy of the newspaper to a librarian. It was not alleged that he was the author of either the article or the letter in question, although he was the paper's agent and correspondent in St Vincent. Neither was he aware of the contents of the offending issue. The Privy Council held that McLeod was not guilty of contempt. 'A printer and publisher intends to publish, and so intending cannot plead as a justification that he did not know the contents. The appellant in this case never intended to publish'.[11] Lord Morris also stated:[12]

'The power summarily to commit for contempt of Court is considered necessary for the proper administration of justice. It is not to be used for the vindication of the judge as a person. He

10 [1899] AC 549, PC.
11 Per Lord Morris at 562.
12 At 561.

must resort to action for libel or criminal information. Committal for contempt of Court is a weapon to be used sparingly, and always with reference to the interests of the administration of justice. Hence, when a trial has taken place and the case is over, the judge or the jury are given over to criticism.

It is a summary process, and should be used only from a sense of duty and under the pressure of public necessity, for there can be no landmarks pointing out the boundaries in all cases. Committals for contempt of Court by scandalising the Court itself have become obsolete in this country. Courts are satisfied to leave to public opinion attacks or comments derogatory or scandalous to them. But it must be considered that in small colonies, consisting principally of coloured populations, the enforcement in proper cases of committal for contempt of Court for attacks on the Court may be absolutely necessary to preserve in such a community the dignity of and respect for the Court.'

The case of *R v Gray*,[12a] decided the following year, showed that this aspect of contempt was not obsolete. A. E. Hughes[13] argued strongly that Lord Morris's view was to be preferred. According to Abel-Smith and Stevens:[14] 'within a decade [of *R v Gray*] the criticism of judicial behaviour which had been so outspoken was replaced in the press by almost unbroken sycophantic praise for the judges'.
3. In *Ambard v A-G for Trinidad and Tobago*,[15] a reasoned criticism of the sentences passed in two cases in a Port of Spain court was held by the Privy Council not to constitute contempt. There was no evidence to support the finding of the Supreme Court of Trinidad that the article was written 'with the direct object of bringing the administration of the criminal law in this Colony by the judges into disrepute and disregard'. Lord Atkin stated:[16]

'But whether the authority and position of an individual judge, or the due administration of justice, is concerned, no wrong is committed by any member of the public who exercises the ordinary right of criticising, in good faith, in private or public, the public act done in the seat of justice. The path of criticism is a public way: the wrong headed are permitted to err therein: provided that members of the public abstain from imputing improper motives to those taking part in the administration of justice, and are genuinely exercising a right of criticism, and not acting in malice or attempting to impair the administration of justice, they are immune. Justice is not a cloistered virtue: she must be allowed to suffer the scrutiny and respectful, even though outspoken, comments of ordinary men.'

4. In *R v New Statesman Editor, ex p DPP*,[17] the defendant wrote that the verdict in a libel action against Marie Stopes was a miscarriage of justice – prejudice against her work 'ought not to be allowed to influence a court of justice in the manner in which they appeared to influence Mr Justice Avory in his summing-up. . . . [A]n individual owning to such views as those of Dr Stopes cannot apparently hope for a fair hearing in a Court presided over by Mr Justice Avory – and there are so many Avorys'. The Divisional Court held this to be a contempt, although they imposed no penalty in view of the editor's unqualified expressions of regret, and the absence of any intention to interfere with the performance of Avory J's judicial duties.
5. The last successful contempt proceedings of this nature in England were in the 1930s.[18] It is noteworthy that contempt proceedings were not instituted in respect of attacks on the National Industrial Relations Court which were at times virulent (see *Phillimore*[18a]). In 1997, the Attorney-General commenced proceedings for

12a [1900] 2 QB 36, above p. 779.
13 (1900) 16 LQR 292.
14 *Lawyers and the Courts* (1967) pp. 126–127.
15 [1936] AC 322, PC.
16 At 335.
17 (1928) 44 TLR 301, DC.
18 *R v Wilkinson* (1930) Times, 16 July; *R v Colsey* (1931) Times, 9 May.
18a Para. 160 and Chap. 11.

scandalising the court against Geoffrey Scriven, a frustrated litigant who had made repeated allegations of corruption against judges involved in various pieces of litigation. The contempt proceedings were dropped on the basis of S's undertaking not to allege corruption and the like against judges. He continued to litigate and broke that undertaking, and the Attorney-General moved to commit him for contempt of breach of it. The Divisional Court was 'troubled' by the motion to commit given that the Attorney-General was not prepared to assert that S's underlying conduct constituted contempt. The court had granted a separate application by the Attorney-General to have S declared a vexatious litigant, and the Attorney-General accepted that that order proceeded 'sufficient protection in the public interest in relation to Mr Scrivin's litigious activities'. The court discharged the undertaking. There have, however, been examples in the Commonwealth.[19] However, in *R v Kopyto*,[20] following the dismissal of a civil action against the police, the plaintiff's lawyer, K, criticised the decision in a newspaper interview as a 'mockery of justice. It stinks to high hell ... [the plaintiff and I are] wondering what is the point of appealing and continuing this charade of the Courts in this country which are warped in favour of protecting the police.' A majority of the Ontario Court of Appeal held that K's conviction for scandalising the court in respect of his expression of opinion was contrary to the guarantee of freedom of expression in s. 2(b) of the Canadian Charter of Rights and Freedoms. While the objective of protecting the administration of justice was of sufficient importance to warrant overriding a constitutionally protected right or freedom, the means chosen were not reasonable and demonstrably justified. In particular, the scandalising offence did not require the Crown to prove that the statements actually constituted a serious danger to the administration of justice, merely that they were 'calculated' to have that effect. Of the three judges in the majority on this point two (Cory and Goodman JJA) thought that the offence could be redefined so as to meet constitutional standards (e.g. where statements cause a clear, significant and imminent or present danger to the fair and effective administration of justice); the third (Houlden JA) thought that it could not, stating that the Canadian judiciary and courts were strong enough to withstand criticism after a case has been decided no matter how outrageous or scurrilous.

6. *Mens rea.* It is not clear whether mens rea is required for liability for this form of contempt.[1] *R v New Statesman Editor, ex p DPP*[2] seems to indicate that it does not. This was followed in New Zealand in *Solicitor General v Radio Avon Ltd.*[3] In *Ahnee v DPP*[4] the Privy Council asserted without examining the authorities that mens rea was not a requirement:

> 'The publication was intentional. If the article was calculated to undermine the authority of the court, and if the defence of fair criticism in good faith was inapplicable, the offence was established. There is no additional element of mens rea.'

Authorities to the contrary are *S v Van Niekerk*[5] (T) and *Re Ouellet.*[6]

---

19 See *R v Glanzer* (1963) 38 DLR (2d) 402; *Re Wiseman* [1969] NZLR 55; *Re Borowski* (1971) 19 DLR (3d) 537; *Re Ouellet* (1976) 67 DLR (3d) 73; and *Gallagher v Durack* (1983) 57 ALJR 191, HCA (see T. Caillard, (1983) 14 Melb ULR 311) and *Nationwide News Pty. Ltd v Wills* (1992) 177 CLR 1, HCA.

20 (1987) DLR 213.

1 See *Miller*, pp. 581–583; *Borrie and Lowe*, pp. 359–360; *Arlidge, Eady and Smith*, pp. 352–353.

2 (1928) 44 TLR 301, above p. 782.

3 [1978] 1 NZLR 225, NZCA.

4 [1999] 2 AC 294 at 307.

5 [1970] 3 SA 655.

6 (1976) 67 DLR (3d) 73, 91–92 (Qu Sup Ct).

In *S v Van Niekerk*[7] (T), the defendant, a senior lecturer in law, wrote in an article in the South African Law Journal[8] that a significant proportion of judges and advocates who responded to a questionnaire believed that justice as regards capital punishment was meted out to the different races on a deliberately differential basis. Claassen J held[9] that 'before a conviction can result the act complained of must not only be wilful and calculated to bring into contempt but must also be made with the intention of bringing the judges in their judicial capacity into contempt or of casting suspicion on the administration of justice'. As Van N did not have that intention he was not convicted.[10]

7. There is some Commonwealth authority in support of a defence of fair comment.[11] and of a defence that the statement was true and for the public benefit: *Nationwide News Pty Ltd v Wills*[12] per Brennan J. Arlidge, Eady and Smith[13] doubt that such a restrictive rule would accord with the requirements of Art. 10 ECHR.

8. This variety of the law of contempt is virtually a dead letter in the United States. In *Bridges v California; Times-Mirror Co v California*,[14] in applying the 'clear and present danger' test,[15] Black J discounted 'disrespect for the judiciary' as a 'substantive evil' which could properly be averted by restricting freedom of expression: 'The assumption that respect for the judiciary can be won by shielding judges from published criticism wrongly appraises the character of American public opinion. For it is a prized American privilege to speak one's mind, although not always with perfect good taste, on all public institutions. And an enforced silence, however limited solely in the name of preserving the dignity of the bench, would probably engender resentment, suspicion, and contempt much more than it would enhance respect.'[16]

Press allegations of judicial bias, directed to pending proceedings, have been held not to constitute a clear and present danger to the administration of justice.[17]

9. Does the law on scandalising the court comply with Art. 10 ECHR? Cf. *Barfod v Denmark*[18] where the court held that a conviction in the Greenland High Court for defaming two lay judges (imputing biased voting in a tax case in favour of their employer, the Greenland Local Government) did not violate Art. 10. The interference with freedom of expression was prescribed by law, and justifiable as necessary in a democratic society for the protection of the reputation of others and, indirectly, the maintenance of the authority of the judiciary. B was perfectly entitled to question the composition of the court, but not to allege actual bias without any supporting evidence. In *Ahnee v DPP*,[19] the Privy Council upheld A's conviction for scandalising the court in respect of a newspaper article alleging, incorrectly, that the Chief Justice of Mauritius had improperly fixed the date of the hearing of a defamation action

---

7 [1970] 3 SA 655.
8 (1969) 86 SALJ 457 and (1970) 87 SALJ 60.
9 At 657.
10 See H. R. Hahlo, (1971) 21 U of Toronto LJ 378 and J. R. L. Milton, (1970) 87 SALJ 424.
11 Per Griffith CJ in *R v Nicholls* (1911) 12 CLR 280 at 286; *A-G for New South Wales v Mundey* [1972] 2 NSWLR 887 at 910; *Solicitor-General v Radio Avon Ltd* [1978] 1 NZLR 225 at 231.
12 (1992) 177 CLR 1 at 39, per Brennan J.
13 Op. cit., p. 354.
14 314 US 252 (1941).
15 See above, p. 719.
16 pp. 270–271.
17 *Pennekamp v Florida* 328 US 331 (1946); *Re Turner* 174 NW (2d) 895 (1969).
18 (1989) 13 EHRR 493, ECtHR (Series A No. 149).
19 [1999] 2 AC 294. See also *Badry v DPP of Mauritius* [1983] 2 AC 297, PC (holding that this head of contempt applies only to 'courts of justice properly so called' and not a judge in his capacity as a Commissioner conducting a statutory inquiry).

brought by himself, and had chosen the judges and that the appointed judges would hear the case despite the fact they would be witnesses. The Supreme Court found the article imputed improper motives, and had been calculated to bring into contempt the administration of justice in Mauritius; that the journalist had failed to make reasonable enquiries; and that he had not acted in good faith but with the intention to mislead. The Privy Council found that the jurisdiction to punish for this form of contempt still existed in Mauritius and rejected the claim that the offence was inconsistent with the protection of freedom of expression guaranteed by s. 12 of the Constitution. This provided, *inter alia*, that nothing contained in or done under the authority of any law should be held to be inconsistent with that guarantee to the extent that the law in question made provision 'for the purpose ... of maintaining the authority and independence of the courts' unless this was 'shown not to be reasonably justifiable in a democratic society.' The Privy Council noted that 'the need for the offence of scandalising the court on a small island is greater' than in the UK.[20] The judgment continued:

> 'Moreover, it must be borne in mind that the offence is narrowly defined. It does not extend to comment on the conduct of a judge unrelated to his performance on the bench. It exists solely to protect the administration of justice rather than the feelings of judges. There must be a real risk of undermining public confidence in the administration of justice. The field of application of the offence is also narrowed by the need in a democratic society for public scrutiny of the conduct of judges, and for the right of citizens to comment on matters of public concern. There is available to a defendant a defence based on the 'right of criticising, in good faith, in private or public, the public act done in the seat of justice': see *R. v Gray* [1900] 2 Q.B. 36, 40; *Ambard v Attorney-General for Trinidad and Tobago* [1936] AC 322, 335 and *Badry v Director of Public Prosecutions* [1983] 2 AC 297. The classic illustration of such an offence is the imputation of improper motives to a judge. But, so far as *Ambard's* case [1936] AC 322 may suggest that such conduct must invariably be an offence their Lordships consider that such an absolute statement is not nowadays acceptable. For example, if a judge descends into the arena and embarks on extensive and plainly biased questioning of a defendant in a criminal trial, a criticism of bias may not be an offence. The exposure and criticism of such judicial misconduct would be in the public interest. On this point their Lordships prefer the way of the Australian courts that such conduct is not necessarily an offence: *R v Nicholls* (1911) 12 CLR 280. Given the narrow scope of the offence of scandalising the court, their Lordships are satisfied that the constitutional criterion that it must be necessary in a democratic society is in principle made out. The contrary argument is rejected.'

10. *Reform.* The Phillimore Committee recommended that attacks on courts or judges should not be dealt with under the law of contempt, unless there is a risk of serious prejudice to particular proceedings in progress. However, there should be a substantive criminal offence consisting of the publication of matter imputing improper or corrupt judicial conduct with the intention of impairing confidence in the administration of justice. It should be triable only on indictment, and only with the leave of the Attorney-General or the Lord Advocate. The Law Commission[1] took the view that there would be difficulties in interpreting the 'intent' provision, and that it would be too wide to include imputations of 'improper' conduct. Accordingly they recommended that it should be an offence to publish or distribute false matter, with intent that it be taken as true and knowing it to be false or being reckless whether it is false, when it imputes corrupt judicial conduct to any judge, tribunal or member of a tribunal. A prosecution could only be brought with the consent of the Attorney-General but the offence would be triable either way.

20 At 306.
1 Report (No. 96) on *Offences Relating to Interference with the Course of Justice*, pp. 67–68.

11. (i) Is the law of defamation sufficient to protect the judges from scurrilous abuse, or do you agree with either proposal for a criminal offence to replace contempt proceedings in this context?

(ii) Does the present law of contempt give sufficiently clear guidance to those who wish to criticise the judiciary?

(iii) Do you agree with Harold Laski's view that 'To argue that the expression, even the strong expression, of . . . doubts [as to judicial impartiality] is an "interference with the course of justice" because the result is to undermine public confidence in the judiciary is to forget that public confidence is undermined not so much by the comment, as by the habit which led to the comment. . . .'[2]

(iv) Should reports of research into the administration of justice ever be regarded as contempt (cf. *S v Van Niekerk*)?

(B) PUBLICATION OF JURY SECRETS[2a]

This is now regulated by s. 8 of the Contempt of Court Act 1981.[3] The section as originally drafted incorporated the limitation that it was not to apply to publications which did not identify the proceedings, or the names of particular jurors, and which did not enable such matters to be identified. Moreover, the disclosure or the solicitation of the disclosure of particulars was only to be an offence when done in the contemplation that they would be published. Neither the Criminal Law Revision Committee,[4] the Phillimore Committee nor the Law Commission had recommended legislation. Interesting accounts by jurors of their jury service had indeed been published.[5] However, the publication in the *New Statesman* of an interview with a juror after the trial of Jeremy Thorpe and others led to contempt proceedings against the newspaper.[6] The juror was interviewed after the trial was over and no money was paid. It was conceded that the publication could not in any respect interfere with the administration of justice in the *Thorpe* case and that the juror's comments showed that the jury had approached its task in a sensible and reasonable manner, but it was contended that any disclosure of jury-room secrets would tend to imperil the finality of jury verdicts and affect adversely the attitude of future jurymen. The Divisional Court held that if a publication had that tendency it was capable of being a contempt, but did not accept that the disclosure of jury-room secrets would necessarily have that effect, and did not accept that the article in question constituted contempt. The court did not explain why it thought the article in question was not objectionable; it indicated that no exception could be taken to disclosures which did not indentify the persons concerned, but the *New Statesman* article could not of course be exonerated on that ground.

It was argued by some that the exceptions built into the original clause were too narrow. However, Lord Hutchinson and Lord Wigoder persuaded the House of Lords at the last minute to remove the exceptions altogether on the ground that any approaches to jurors were undesirable, whether by 'respectable professors from Birmingham', 'Marxist professors from the English Faculty at Cambridge', by 'any

---

2   (1928) 41 Harv LR 1031 at 1036.
2a   See generally J. Baldwin and M. McConville, *Jury Trials* (1979) Chap. 1, pp. 130–134 and (1981) 145 JPN 575; E. Campbell, (1985) 11(4) Monash ULR 169; Mr. Justice McHugh in M. Findlay and P. Duff (eds.), *The Jury Under Attack* (1988), Chap. 4; P. Robertshaw, (1993) 14 J Media L & P 114.
3   Above, p. 726.
4   Tenth Report: Secrecy of the Jury Room, Cmnd. 3750, 1968.
5   See e.g. E. Devons, (1965) 28 MLR 561.
6   *A-G v New Statesman* [1981] QB 1; M. J. Richardson, [1980] II Liverpool LR 126.

scribbler or any journalist,' or by that 'most dangerous animal, the sociologist'.[7] Accordingly, it is now a contempt for any juror to disclose particulars of a case to anyone, even a spouse or a friend. The only safeguard is the requirement of the Attorney-General's consent to prosecution, and even this is not necessary where proceedings are instituted on the motion of a court. It is appropriate to rely upon that safeguard where the ambit of a law is uncertain and the considerations to be borne in mind when exercising the discretion to prosecute are particularly sensitive. It is clearly undesirable to have to rely upon that safeguard in relation to an offence that is drawn so widely that it catches many situations about which there is general agreement that they should not be regarded as criminal at all.

In *A-G v Associated Newspapers Ltd*,[8] the House of Lords held that the prohibition against 'disclosure' in s. 8 extended to the publication by a newspaper of the deliberations of jurors in the jury room, obtained from a source other than the jurors. The *Mail on Sunday* had published material from transcripts of interviews apparently conducted by independent 'researchers' with jurors at the 'Blue Arrow' fraud trial. The House rejected the argument that s. 8 should be construed narrowly to apply only to a revelation by a juror to another person; the section was not ambiguous and what the appellants had done amounted to 'disclosure' within the ordinary meaning of that word. The House upheld fines of £30,000 on the publishers, £20,000 on the editor, Stewart Steven, and £10,000 on the responsible journalist, Clive Wolman.

Inquiries of jurors concerning matters other than juror deliberations (here, the use of a mobile telephone by a juror in the jury room) do not infringe s. 8, but should only be undertaken with the leave of the trial court or (after verdict and sentence) the Court of Appeal.[9]

The Royal Commission on Criminal Justice[10] recommended[11] that s. 8 should be amended to enable research to be conducted into juries' reasons for their verdicts.

7 Contempt in the face of the court

It is obvious that the public interest in the due administration of justice requires that legal proceedings be free from disruption or direct interference. Some kinds of disruption are ordinary criminal offences, for example violent attacks on judges or jurors. All kinds of disruption will also amount to contempt in the face of the court, and may be dealt with summarily (e.g. *Balogh v Crown Court at St Albans*[12]). The law of contempt in this context does to an extent inhibit freedom of expression, such as the expression of the views of a disappointed litigant as to the defects of the English legal system in general, and the defects of the judge who has just tried his case in particular. Moreover, the disruption of legal proceedings in order to gain publicity for a particular cause has been roundly condemned in the Court of Appeal.[13] However, the law here cannot convincingly be criticised on the basis of interference with free speech. Most of the criticism has centred on the summary nature of the procedure. The two main criticisms made to the Phillimore Committee were, 'first,

---

7 416 HL Deb, 20 January 1981, col. 371, 422 HL Deb, July 1981, cols. 239–254.
8 [1994] 2 AC 238.
9 *R v McCluskey* (1993) 94 Cr App R 216, CA(Cr D). See also *R v Mickleburgh* [1995] 1 Cr App Rep 297, CA (Cr D); *R v Young (Stephen)* [1995] (use of ouija board by jurors in hotel overnight; conviction quashed); *R v Miah* [1997] 2 Cr App Rep 12 (held in *R v Qureshi (Sajid)* [2001] EWCA Crim 1807 still to be good law after implementation of the Human Rights Act 1998).
10 Cm. 2263, 1993.
11 p. 2.
12 [1975] QB 73, below, p. 788.
13 *Morris v Crown Office* [1970] 2 QB 114, below p. 791.

that the judge appears to assume the role of prosecutor and judge in his own cause, especially where the missile or insult is directed against him personally; and secondly, that the contemnor usually has little or no opportunity to defend himself or make a plea in mitigation'.[14] The refusal of a witness to answer a question or produce a document may also constitute contempt in the face. This can pose particular problems for journalists, who may be required to divulge their sources of information. This is now regulated by s. 10 of the Contempt of Court Act 1981,[15] which was considered by the House of Lords in *X Ltd v Morgan-Grampian (Publishers) Ltd*.[16]

(A) THE SCOPE OF CONTEMPT IN THE FACE OF THE COURT

Balogh v St Albans Crown Court [1975] QB 73, [1974] 3 All ER 283, [1974] 3 WLR 314, Court of Appeal

Balogh, a temporary clerk in a solicitor's office, while attending a criminal trial at a Crown Court, devised a plan to enliven the proceedings by releasing nitrous oxide ('laughing gas') down a ventilation duct on the roof into the trial court. He stole a cylinder of the gas from a hospital lorry and climbed up on to the roof at night to locate the particular inlet duct. The next morning he left the cylinder in his briefcase in the public gallery of the court next door (Court 1) from which there was access to the roof, intending to carry out his plan later in the day. Police, who had seen him on the roof, found his brief case, opened it, and later cautioned Balogh who at once admitted what he had done and planned to do. He was charged with theft of the cylinder. The police reported the matter to Melford Stevenson J, the senior judge, who was presiding in Court 1. Balogh was brought before the judge who said that his admitted conduct was a serious contempt of court and that he would consider the penalty overnight. Balogh was to be kept in custody.

The next morning Balogh told the judge that he did not feel competent to conduct his own case on contempt and that he understood that the only charge against him was theft. The judge said that he would not deal with that charge, but committed him to six months' imprisonment for contempt of court. Balogh then said: 'You are a humourless automaton. Why don't you self-destruct.' Subsequently, he wrote from prison to the Official Solicitor asking to be allowed to apologise in the hope that his contempt would be purged. Accordingly, he appealed to the Court of Appeal.

Lord Denning MR: . . .

The jurisdiction of the Crown Court
The Crown Court is a superior court of record: section 4(1) of the Courts Act 1971. In regard to any contempt of court, it has the like powers and authority as the High Court: section 4(8) [see now the Supreme Court Act 1981, s. 45(1)(4)]. . . .

[RSC Order 52, r. 5] . . . preserves the power of the High Court 'to make an order of committal of its own motion against a person guilty of contempt of court'. . . .

In what circumstances can the High Court make an order 'of its own motion?' In the ordinary way the High Court does not act of its own motion. An application to commit for contempt is usually made by motion either by the Attorney-General or by the party aggrieved: . . . and such a motion can, in an urgent case be made ex parte: see *Warwick Corpn v Russell* [1964] 2 All ER 337, [1964] 1 WLR 613. . . . All I find in the books is that the court can act upon its own motion when the contempt is committed 'in the face of the court'. Wilmot CJ in his celebrated opinion in *R v Almon* (1765) Wilm 243 at 254 said: 'It is a necessary incident to every court of justice to fine and imprison for a contempt to the court, acted in the face of it.'

---

14 *Phillimore*, para. 29.
15 Above, p. 726.
16 [1991] 1 AC 1, below, p. 796.

Blackstone in his *Commentaries*, 16th edn. (1825), Book IV, p. 286, said: 'If the contempt be committed in the face of the court, the offender may be instantly apprehended and imprisoned, at the discretion of the judges'. In *Oswald on Contempt*, 3rd edn. (1910), p. 23 it is said: 'Upon contempt in the face of the court an order for committal was made instanter' and not on motion. But I find nothing to tell us what is meant by 'committed in the face of the court'. It has never been defined. Its meaning is, I think, to be ascertained from the practice of the judges over the centuries. It was never confined to conduct which a judge saw with his own eyes. It covered all contempts for which a judge of his own motion could punish a man on the spot. So 'contempt in the face of the court' is the same thing as 'contempt which the court can punish of its own motion'. It really means 'contempt in the cognisance of the court'.

Gathering together the experience of the past, then, whatever expression is used, a judge of one of the superior courts or a judge of Assize could always punish summarily of his own motion for contempt of court whenever there was a gross interference with the course of justice in a case that was being tried, or about to be tried or just over—no matter whether the judge saw it with his own eyes or it was reported to him by the officers of the court, or by others—whenever it was urgent and imperative to act at once. This power has been inherited by the judges of the High Court and in turn by the judges of the Crown Court. To show the extent of it, I will give some instances:

(i) *In the sight of the court.* There are many cases where a man has been committed to prison at once for throwing a missile at the judge, be it a brickbat, an egg, or a tomato. Recently, too, when a group of students broke up the trial of a libel action Lawton J very properly sent them at once to prison: see *Morris v Crown Office* [1970] 2 QB 114. There is an older case, too, of great authority, where a witness refused to answer a proper question. The judge of Assize at York Castle at once sentenced him to prison for six months and imposed a fine of £500: see *Ex p Fernandez* (1861) 10 CBNS 3.

(ii) *Within the court room but not seen by the judge.* At the Old Bailey a man distributed leaflets in the public gallery inciting people to picket the place. A member of the public reported it to a police officer, who reported it to the judge. The offender denied it. Melford Stevenson J immediately heard the evidence on both sides. He convicted the offender and sentenced him to seven days' imprisonment. The man appealed to this court. His appeal was dismissed: *Lecointre v Court's Administrator of the Central Criminal Court* (1973) 8 February Bar Library Transcript No 57A (unreported).

(iii) *At some distance from the court.* At Bristol 22 men were being tried for an affray. The first witness for the prosecution was a school girl. After she had given her evidence, she went to a café for a meal. A man clenched his fist at her and threatened her. She told the police, who told the judge. Park J had the man arrested. He asked counsel to represent him. He broke off the trial. He heard evidence of the threat. He committed the man. He sentenced him to three months' imprisonment. The man appealed to this court. His appeal was dismissed: *Moore v Clerk of Assize, Bristol* [1972] 1 All ER 58. Another case was where a man was summoned to serve on a jury. His employer threatened to dismiss him if he obeyed the summons. Melford Stevenson J said it was a contempt of court which made him liable to immediate imprisonment: see 'The Rule of Law and Jury Service' (1966) 130 JP 622.

Those are modern instances. I have no doubt that there were many like instances in the past which were never reported, because there was until recently no right of appeal. They bear out the power which I have already stated—a power which has been inherited by the judges of the Crown Court.

This power of summary punishment is a great power, but it is a necessary power. It is given so as to maintain the dignity and authority of the court and to ensure a fair trial. It is to be exercised by the judge of his own motion only when it is urgent and imperative to act immediately—so as to maintain the authority of the court—to prevent disorder—to enable witnesses to be free from fear—and jurors from being improperly influenced—and the like. It is, of course, to be exercised with scrupulous care, and only when the case is clear and beyond reasonable doubt: see *R v Gray* [1900] 2 QB 36 at 41 by Lord Russell of Killowen CJ. But properly exercised it is a power of the utmost value and importance which should not be curtailed.

Over 100 years ago Erle CJ said that '. . . these powers, . . . as far as my experience goes, have always been exercised for the advancement of justice and the good of the public': see

Ex p Fernandez (1861) 10 CBNS 3 at 38. I would say the same today. From time to time anxieties have been expressed lest these powers might be abused. But these have been set at rest by section 13 of the Administration of Justice Act 1960, which gives a right to appeal to a higher court.

As I have said, a judge should act of his own motion only when it is urgent and imperative to act immediately. In all other cases he should not take it upon himself to move. He should leave it to the Attorney-General or to the party aggrieved to make a motion in accordance with the rules in RSC Ord 52. The reason is that he should not appear to be both prosecutor and judge: for that is a role which does not become him well.

Returning to the present case, it seems to me that up to a point the judge was absolutely right to act of his own motion. The intention of Mr Balogh was to disrupt the proceedings in a trial then taking place. His conduct was reported to the senior judge then in the court building. It was very proper for him to take immediate action, and to have Mr Balogh brought before him. But once he was there, it was not a case for summary punishment. There was not sufficient urgency to warrant it. Nor was it imperative. He was already in custody on a charge of stealing. The judge would have done well to have remanded him in custody and invited counsel to represent him. If he had done so counsel would, I expect, have taken the point to which I now turn.

The conduct of Mr Balogh
Contempt of court is a criminal offence which is governed by the principles applicable to criminal offences generally. In particular, by the difference between an attempt to commit an offence and an act preparatory to it.
[His Lordship held that B's conduct amounted at most to 'acts preparatory'] . . .

So here Mr Balogh had the criminal intent to disrupt the court, but that is not enough. He was guilty of stealing the cylinder, but no more.

On this short ground we think the judge was in error. We have already allowed the appeal on this ground. But, even if there had not been this ground, I should have thought that the sentence of six months was excessive. Balogh spent 14 days in prison: and he has now apologised. That is enough to purge his contempt, if contempt it was.

Conclusion
There is a lesson to be learned from the recent cases on this subject. It is particularly appropriate at the present time. The new Crown Courts are in being. The judges of them have not yet acquired the prestige of the Red Judge when he went on Assize. His robes and bearing made eveyone alike stand in awe of him. Rarely did he need to exercise his great power of summary punishment. Yet there is just as much need for the Crown Court to maintain its dignity and authority. The judges of it should not hesitate to exercise the authority they inherit from the past. Insults are best treated with disdain—save when they are gross and scandalous. Refusal to answer with admonishment—save where it is vital to know the answer. But disruption of the court or threats to witnesses or to jurors should be visited with immediate arrest. Then a remand in custody and, if it can be arranged, representation by counsel. If it comes to a sentence, let it be such as the offence deserves—with the comforting reflection that, if it is in error, there is an appeal to this court. We always hear these appeals within a day or two. The present case is a good instance. The judge acted with a firmness which became him. As it happened, he went too far. That is no reproach to him. It only shows the wisdom of having an appeal.

Stephenson and **Lawton LJJ** delivered concurring judgments.

Appeal allowed.

NOTES

1. Lord Denning MR equates 'contempt in the face of the court' and the power to the High Court to 'make an order of committal on its own motion'. *Borrie and Lowe*[17] argue that the concept of 'contempt in the face' should be construed more narrowly, particularly in the context of the inherent powers of *inferior* courts to punish

17 pp. 12–15.

contempts, to cover misconduct in the court room and (perhaps) other misbehaviour that actually interrupts proceedings or where there is an admission by the defendant or all the witnesses are before the court. In *McKeown v R*[18] Laskin J (in a dissenting judgment) held that the concept of contempt in the face was confined to cases where 'all the circumstances are in the personal knowledge of the court'.[19]

2. In *Morris v Crown Office*,[20] a group of young Welsh students interrupted the proceedings in a libel action (*Broome v Cassell & Co*) being heard by Lawton J. They shouted slogans, scattered pamphlets and sang songs. The judge adjourned the hearing. When order was restored, the judge returned to court and sentenced three students to three months' imprisonment each for contempt. At the rising of the court, he dealt with 19 others. Eight apologised, and were fined £50 each and bound over to keep the peace. Eleven did not apologise, saying that they acted as a matter of principle on behalf of the Welsh language. They each received three month sentences. The eleven students appealed to the Court of Appeal, arguing (*inter alia*) (1) that s. 39(1) and (3) of the Criminal Justice Act 1967 required the sentences to be suspended, and (2) that the sentences were too severe. The Court of Appeal held that the 1967 Act was not applicable as there was no machinery for following up a suspended sentence passed in such circumstances, and that the sentences when passed were appropriate. However, as the students had spent a week in prison, and shown respect to the court, the prison sentences were remitted and the defendants bound over to be of good behaviour, to keep the peace, and to come up to judgment if called on to do so.[1]

3. In *R v Powell*,[2] the Court of Appeal (Criminal Division) upheld P's conviction for contempt in the face of the court in respect of a loud wolf-whistle at a female juror as the jury came into court to deliver its verdict. The court stated that while the general principles applicable were to be found in the *Balogh* and *Morris* cases (above), 'when it comes to the detail [s. 12 of the Contempt of Court Act] gives a good indication of the sort of behaviour which should be considered contempt of that nature'.[3] Here, the wolf-whistle was:

> 'potentially an insult and potentially offensive, and a serious interference with the administration of justice and the process of the court.... [J]urors do not come to these courts, as they are under a duty to do when summoned, in order to have comments, even flattering comments, publicly made on their personal appearance. The administration of justice is not to be interrupted at the tense moment when the jury return with their verdict.'[4]

However, the judge's sentence of 14 days' imprisonment was quashed as excessive. As P had served one day in custody before his release on bail by Russell LJ of the Court of Appeal, no further penalty was imposed.

4. In England, inferior courts have statutory power to punish certain kinds of conduct amounting to contempt in the face. For county courts see the County Courts Act 1984, ss. 14(1) (assault on officer of the court), 55(1) (refusals to produce documents, to be sworn or to give evidence), 118(1) (insults towards judge, juror, witness or officer of the court whether in court or in going to or returning from the court,[5] and

---

18 (1971) 16 DLR (3d) 390, 408.

19 Contra, *Registrar, Court of Appeal v Collins* [1982] 1 NSWLR 682, NSWCA.

20 [1970] 2 QB 114, CA.

  1 On the problem of disruptive defendants see G. Zellick, (1980) 43 MLR 121 and 284; *R v Logan* [1974] Crim LR 609; *R v Aquarius* (1974) 59 Cr App Rep 165.

  2 (1993) 98 Cr App R 224.

  3 Per Staughton LJ at 227.

  4 Ibid., at 228.

  5 The statutory powers supersede any inherent power (*R v Lefroy* (1873) 8 QB 134, 138); however, s. 118 extends more broadly than contempt in the face at common law (*Manchester City Council v McCann* [1999] 2 WLR 590) and 'insults' includes 'threatens' (ibid.).

misbehaviour in court). For magistrates' courts see the Magistrates' Courts Act 1980, s. 97(4) (refusals to produce documents, to be sworn or to give evidence) and s. 12 of the Contempt of Court Act 1981.[6] Binding-over powers may be used, and offenders can be removed from the court. The Phillimore Committee recommended that magistrates courts be given statutory power to punish contempt in the face of the court with a maximum penalty the same as that prescribed by s. 77(4) of the 1952 Act,[7] namely seven days' imprisonment, with an alternative of a £20 fine. In the event, the penalties prescribed by s. 12 of the 1981 Act were much higher than those recommended, and this was a cause of criticism.[8] The penalty under s. 97(4) was increased in line with s. 12 by the Criminal Justice Act 1991, Sch. 4, Pt. I. In Parliament, the main point of controversy was whether the power to deal with insults was necessary or even desirable. Where the object of the insult is the magistrate he will be 'the victim, the witness, the prosecution, the judge and the jury'.[9] This is already accepted to be the main cause of concern with the law of contempt in the face of the court, but one may perhaps have greater confidence in the objectivity of High Court judges than of magistrates. In 1981 a man was reported to have been imprisoned for one month for refusing to stand while certain charges against him were read out in court.[10] In *Re Hooker (Patricia) and the Contempt of Court Act 1981*,[11] the Divisional Court set aside a conviction under s. 12(1)(b) of the 1981 Act and a £500 fine in respect of the use of a tape recorder by H, a court reporter, without leave, contrary to s. 9(1)(a).[12] In construing the words 'otherwise misbehaves' in s. 12(1)(b), regard had to be had to the fact that this was a criminal statute and that the other prohibitions in s. 12 were qualified by the word 'wilfully'. Accordingly, there had to be some other element of defiance, or at least conduct such that the court could not reasonably be expected to tolerate. Neither element was present here.

In *R v Tamworth Justices, ex p Walsh*,[13] the Divisional Court quashed the justices' order that a solicitor be detained in custody under s. 12(2) until the rising of the court following an insult to the clerk of the court (a reference to 'ridiculous listing' by the clerk). The court noted that the justices could have ordered the solicitor's removal from the court (should he have refused to withdraw the remark), reported him to the Law Society or adjourned the matter to another day. Instead, they 'had taken a sledgehammer to crack a nut'.

Threats to a witness outside the court have been held not to constitute 'insults' which can be dealt with under s. 12(1)(a): *R v Havant Justices, ex p Palmer*.[14] The statutory powers supersede any inherent power (*R v Lefroy*[14a]); however, s.118 extends more broadly than contempt in the face at common law (*Manchester City Council v McCann*[15]) and 'insults' includes 'threatens' (ibid.).[15a] Proceedings can be 'interrupted' under s. 12(1)(b) by acts done outside, as well as inside the court: *Bodden v Metropolitan Police Comr*[16] (use of loudhailer in the street outside court preventing witness being heard). The interruption is 'wilful' if the defendant commits

---

6   Above p. 727.
7   Now s. 97(4) of the 1980 Act.
8   G. J. Zellick, [1981] PL 148.
9   Lord Gifford, 416 HL Deb, 20 January 1981, col. 385.
10 (1981) Times, 19 December.
11 [1993] COD 190.
12 See above, p. 726.
13 (1994) Times, 3 March.
14 (1985) 149 JP 609.
14a (1873) 8 QB 134 at 138.
15 [1999] 2 WLR 590.
15a [1999] 2 WLR 590.
16 [1990] 2 QB 397, CA.

the acts causing the interruption deliberately with the intention that they should interrupt proceedings or if, knowing that there was a risk of interruption, he nevertheless goes on deliberately to do those acts.[17] The power under s. 12(1) includes all incidental powers necessary to enable the court to exercise its jurisdiction in a judicial manner, such as power to direct an officer of the court to bring a person reasonably believed to be responsible for a wilful interruption before the court.[18]

5. Section 41 of the Criminal Justice Act 1925 prohibits (in general) photography and sketching in court. Tape-recording in court is now regulated by s. 9 of the Contempt of Court Act 1981.[19]

6. The fact that many examples of contempt in the face of the court have their humorous side should not conceal the very real difficulties faced by judges in 'political' trials. These seem to be more endemic in the United States than in Britain.[20]

7. An excellent illustration of the dangers inherent in use of the summary procedures in this context is *McKeown v R*,[1] where the Supreme Court of Canada managed to uphold a contempt conviction based on slender evidence, over strong dissents by Spence and Laskin JJ. See also *Maharaj v A-G for Trinidad and Tobago (No 2)*,[2] where the Privy Council held that the failure of a judge to make plain the specific nature of the contempt with which M was being charged vitiated the judge's order committing M to the 'Royal Goal' [sic] for contempt in the face of the court. Subsequently the Privy Council held that M was entitled to claim damages for the imprisonment, under the Constitution of Trinidad and Tobago, on the ground that he had been deprived of his liberty otherwise than by due process of law (*Maharaj v A-G for Trinidad and Tobago (No 2)*).[3]

8. The Phillimore Committee recommended[4] that the practice whereby the judge deals with contempts in the face of the court himself should continue, and that:

'(a) the judge should always ensure that the contemnor is in no doubt about the nature of the conduct complained of, and give him an opportunity of explaining or denying his conduct, and of calling witnesses;

(b) before any substantial penalty is imposed there should be a short adjournment, with power to remand the contemnor in custody. The judge should have power to obtain a background report on the contemnor, and the contemnor should be entitled to speak in mitigation of sentence;

(c) for the purposes of defending himself and of making a plea in mitigation the contemnor should be entitled to legal representation, and the court should have power to grant legal aid immediately for this purpose where appropriate;

(d) if the contempt also amounts to a criminal offence, the judge should consider referring it to the prosecuting authorities to be dealt with under the ordinary criminal law, and should so refer it in serious cases unless reasons of urgency or convenience require that it be dealt with summarily'.[5]

17 Ibid.
18 Ibid.
19 Above, p. 726. See *Practice Direction* [1981] 3 All ER 848 (applicable to the Supreme Court and county courts), Home Office Circular No. 79/1981 (26 August 1981) (magistrates' courts) and *Re Hooker*, above.
20 See, for example, the *Transcript of the Contempt Citations, Sentences, and Responses of the Chicago Conspiracy 10* (1970). For entertainment, see R. E. Megarry, *A Second Miscellany-at-Law* (1973), pp. 70–83.
1 (1971) 16 DLR (3d) 390.
2 [1979] AC 385.
3 [1979] AC 385, PC. For a discussion of the problems arising out of alleged misconduct by lawyers in the face of the court, see P. Butt, [1978] Crim LR 463.
4 In Chap. 3.
5 p. 95.

Provisions for legal aid is made by s. 29 of the Legal Aid Act 1988.[6] Recent cases have emphasised the need for natural justice to be observed in summary contempt proceedings. The defendant must be given the chance to defend himself and in appropriate cases, should be given the opportunity of being legally represented. In *R v K*,[7] K refused to testify against a fellow inmate of Camp Hill prison at the latter's trial on a charge of wounding K: the judge did not offer him legal representation, brusquely prevented him from giving any explanation for his refusal and sentenced him to a further three months' imprisonment. The Court of Appeal (Criminal Division) quashed the conviction. In fact, K could have presented evidence of duress which might have constituted a valid defence. Per Watkins LJ:[8] 'calm reflection and consideration of how best to deal with such a situation is called for. The rules of natural justice obviously apply in these circumstances and have as much force as they do in any other proceedings in our courts and tribunals.'[9] In *R v Phillips*[10] the Court of Appeal (Criminal Division) stated that it was advisable in cases of refusals to testify to deal with the matter at the conclusion of the trial or, at the very soonest, the end of the prosecution case: to do so earlier, at the end of the second day of a five-day trial, was 'precipitous'. Moreover, the effect on the course of the trial was a relevant consideration when considering sentence: here, it transpired that P's evidence would have added little or nothing by way of weight, support or confirmation of other witnesses. Accordingly, the sentence of four months' imprisonment was replaced by one of 14 days' detention. See also *R v Moran*[11] (order of committal quashed where the judge had acted precipitately, failed to give an opportunity to apologise and did not ask anyone in court to offer advice to the defendant); *R v Hill*[12] (insults from public gallery, committal to prison for seven days upheld); *R v Griffin*[13] (committal for nine months for threatening witness outside court quashed: summary process not well suited in the circumstances, and should in any event have been postponed to the end of the trial); *R v Selby JJ, ex p Frame*[14] (no opportunity for F to deny or admit his disturbance of the court; no representation; committals under s. 12 of the 1981 Act quashed); *Re Hooker*[15] (legal representation not permitted); *R v Schot (Bonnie Belinda); R v Barclay (Carole Andrea)*[16] (jurors who refused to reach a verdict due to their 'conscious beliefs' should have been excused not sent to prison for 30 days for contempt; judge should not have dealt with the matter as there was a real danger of bias); *R v Moore (Peter Oliver Stace)*[17] (letter from juror's employer should not have been construed to be a contempt; no urgency to justify use of summary procedure); *R v Stafforce Personnel Ltd*[18] (finding of contempt in respect of dismissal of juror while on jury service quashed; no urgency

---

6 See *R (on the application of Daltry) v Selby Magistrates' Court* (2000) Times, 1 December (clerk to justices wrong to advise that because no contempt had been found there was no need to grant legal aid to cover the legal representation at a s.12 hearing that had actually been provided by D's own solicitor).
7 (1983) 78 Cr App Rep 82.
8 At 87.
9 See also *Re Dr A S Rayan* (1983) 148 JP 569, and *R v Chowdhury; R v Crone* (1984) Times, 29 March.
10 (1983) 78 Cr App Rep 88.
11 (1985) 81 Cr App Rep 51, CA (Cr D).
12 [1986] Crim LR 457, CA (Cr D).
13 (1988) 88 Cr App Rep 63, CA (Cr D).
14 [1992] QB 72.
15 [1993] COD 190 (see n. **4**).
16 (1997) 161 JP 473.
17 Unreported, 12 September 2000.
18 Unreported, 24 November 2000.

to justify use of summary procedure); cf. *R v MacLeod (Calum Iain)*[19] (judge entitled to deal with intimidation of witness in corridor outside the courtroom). In *R v Renshaw*,[20] a case widely publicised at the time, Judge Pickles found R to be in contempt, and sentenced her to seven days' imprisonment, when she refused to testify for the prosecution in respect of an assault on her by W, with whom she had cohabited. The Court of Appeal held that she had not had a fair trial: the judge had interrupted excessively; R had been threatened, apparently by W's friends; W had agreed to be bound over. In *R v Montgomery*,[1] the Court of Appeal (Criminal Division) set out sentencing guidelines in respect of witnesses refusing to testify, stating, *inter alia*, that an immediate custodial sentence was the only appropriate sentence unless the circumstances were wholly exceptional.

In cases of sudden outbursts in court that interrupt proceedings it has been said that it may be necessary for the court to take swift punitive action without affording an opportunity of legal representation.[2] In the *Newbury* case 11 women created a disturbance in court which seriously disrupted the court's business and were removed to the cells. Three subsequently apologised and were released; eight refused and were committed for 14 days for contempt. They were not afforded access to legal advice. The Divisional Court, however, held that in the circumstances this was not a requirement of natural justice. Given that order had been restored (as in the *Morris* case) is this decision justifiable?

In *R v MacLeod (Calum Iain)*[3] the Court of Appeal (Criminal Division) stated that in the context of contempt in the face of the court Art. 6 ECHR does not add to or alter the normal requirement of English law that proceedings should be conducted fairly before an independent and impartial tribunal. As the trial judge did not himself observe what had taken place in the corridor 'we see no reason why he should not be regarded as an independent and impartial tribunal for the purposes of the contempt proceedings'. Should it now be regarded as the norm that a judge should not act summarily in any case where he is a witness to events?

9. Is it contempt of court for a member of the public to raise two fingers in the direction of a limousine carrying two High Court judges on their way to court? Should it make any difference that the member of the public believes the car to be that of the local mayor, whom he regards as responsible for the latest increase in rates? Cf. the case of Mr Bangs,[4] who spent two hours in a cell before being admonished by Lawson J.

10. *Mens rea.* It is clear that it must be shown that the accused intended to do the act in question. At common law it was uncertain whether it was necessary to prove in addition an intention to interfere with the course of justice.[5] It does seem that such an intention must be shown where it is sought to hold an advocate or witness in contempt for failure to attend court:[6] or interference with jurors is alleged: *R v Giscombe*.[7] It has also been argued that the Contempt of Court Act 1981, by limiting the scope of strict liability in relation to conduct alleged to interfere with

---

19 (2000) Times, 20 December.
20 [1989] Crim LR 811.
1 [1995] 2 All ER 28.
2 Per Stephenson LJ (*obiter*) in *Balogh v St Albans Crown Court* [1975] QB 73 (citing *Morris v Crown Office* as an example); per Watkins LJ (*obiter*) in *R v K* (1983) 78 Cr App Rep 82, 87; *R v Newbury Justices, ex p Du Pont* (1983) 148 JP 248; *R v Moran* (1985) 81 Cr App Rep 51, 53.
3 (2000) Times, 20 December.
4 *Miller*, pp. 156–157, *The Times*, 24 May 1973, *Daily Telegraph*, 23 May 1973.
5 *A-G v Butterworth* [1963] 1 QB 696; *Borrie and Lowe*, pp. 64–65, 410–412.
6 *Weston v Central Criminal Court Courts' Administrator* [1976] QB 32, 43 (per Lord Denning MR); *Re Dr A S Rayan* (1983) 148 JP 569, DC.
7 (1985) 79 Cr App Rep 79, CA (Cr D).

the course of justice in particular proceedings,[8] now imports a full mens rea requirement for contempt in the face of the court.[9] In principle, however, there should be a full mens rea requirement, although this might properly extend to include recklessness.[10] Cf. Arlidge, Eady and Smith,[11] suggesting that the same approach is likely to be adopted as in common law publication cases, where recklessness is insufficient for mens rea.

(B) PROTECTION OF JOURNALISTS' SOURCES[12]

X Ltd v Morgan-Grampian (Publishers) Ltd [1991] 1 AC 1, [1990] 2 WLR 421, [1990] 1 All ER 616, House of Lords

A highly confidential draft business plan was stolen from the plaintiffs, two associated private companies. The following day, the third defendant, William Robin Goodwin, a trainee journalist employed by the first and second defendants, publishers of *The Engineer*, was telephoned by an unidentified source and given information which could be inferred to have been obtained from the stolen plan. He decided to write an article based on the information and contacted the plaintiffs to check certain facts. The plaintiffs immediately sought and obtained an ex parte injunction against the publishers restraining them from publishing information derived from the draft plan, on the ground that the information had been imparted to them in breach of confidence.

It being their intention to bring proceedings against the source for recovery of the plan, they applied for an order requiring the journalist and publishers to disclose the source, and sought discovery of Mr Goodwin's notes of the telephone conversation as a means of discovering the source's identity. The publishers did not know the source's identity and had no means of coercing Mr Goodwin. Accordingly, the plaintiffs directed their attention on Mr Goodwin. Hoffmann J granted the orders sought;[13] on appeal, the Court of Appeal varied the order by giving him the option of disclosing the notes, or delivering them to court in a sealed envelope which would remain sealed until final determination of his appeal against the order. Mr Goodwin declined to comply. The Court of Appeal dismissed the defendants' appeal against the orders.[14] The defendants appealed to the House of Lords. The House of Lords held unanimously that the court had jurisdiction to make an order against the defendants requiring disclosure of the source's identity: the defendants were parties to the injunction proceedings for breach of confidence, and were in any event 'mixed up in the tortious acts' of the source.[15] The House also considered the scope of s. 10 of the Contempt of Court Act 1981.

---

8 See ss. 1, 2: above p. 724.
9 *Borrie and Lowe*, ibid.; cf. *Miller*, p. 197, suggesting that the 1981 Act affords at best a weak inference to this effect.
10 See *Miller*, p. 199.
11 Op. cit., pp. 632–633.
12 See T. R. S. Allan, 'Disclosure of Journalists' Sources, Civil Disobedience and the Rule of Law' [1991] CLJ 131; S. Palmer, 'Protecting Journalists' Sources: Section 10, Contempt of Court Act 1981' [1992] PL 61; see also I. Cram, (1992) 55 MLR 400 (casenote on *X v Morgan-Grampian*) and S. Walker, (1991) 14(2) UNSWLJ 302. For cases at common law in this area, which have now been superseded by s. 10, see pp. 307–308 of the 2nd edition of this book.
13 [1990] 1 All ER 608.
14 [1991] 1 AC 1.
15 Cf. Lord Reid in *Norwich Pharmacal Co v Customs and Excise Comrs* [1974] AC 133, 175.

Lord Bridge: . . .

Privilege from disclosure

The courts have always recognised an important public interest in the free flow of information. How far and in what circumstances the maintenance of this public interest operated to confer on journalists any privilege from disclosure of their sources which the common law would recognise admitted of no short and simple answer on the authorities. But the matter is no longer governed by the common law and I do not think any assistance is to be gained from the authorities preceding the coming into force of section 10 of the Contempt of Court Act 1981 which is in these terms: [see above, p. 377].

It has been accepted in this case at all levels that the section applies to the circumstances of the instant case notwithstanding that the information obtained by Mr Goodwin from the source has not been 'contained in a publication'. The information having been communicated and received for the purposes of publication, it is clearly right to treat it as subject to the rule which the section lays down, since the purpose underlying the statutory protection of sources of information is as much applicable before as after publication. It is also now clearly established that the section is to be given a wide, rather than a narrow, construction in the sense that the restriction on disclosure applies not only to direct orders to disclose the identity of a source but also to any order for disclosure of material which will indirectly identify the source and applies notwithstanding that the enforcement of the restriction may operate to defeat rights of property vested in the party who seeks to obtain that material: *Secretary of State for Defence v Guardian Newspapers Ltd* [1984] Ch 156, 166–167, per Griffiths LJ; [1985] AC 339, 349–350, per Lord Diplock. As a statement of the rationale underlying this wide construction I cannot do better than quote from the passage in the judgment of Griffiths LJ to which I have referred, where he said:

'The press have always attached the greatest importance to their ability to protect their sources of information. If they are not able to do so, they believe that many of their sources would dry up and this would seriously interfere with their effectiveness. It is in the interests of us all that we should have a truly effective press, and it seems to me that Parliament by enacting section 10 has clearly recognised the importance that attaches to the ability of the press to protect their sources. . . . I can see no harm in giving a wide construction to the opening words of the section because by the latter part of the section the court is given ample powers to order the source to be revealed where in the circumstances of a particular case the wider public interest makes it necessary to do so.'

It follows then that, whenever disclosure is sought, as here, of a document which will disclose the identity of a source within the ambit of section 10, the statutory restriction operates unless the party seeking disclosure can satisfy the court that 'disclosure is necessary' in the interests of one of the four matters of public concern that are listed in the section. I think it is indisputable that where a judge asks himself the question: 'Can I be satisfied that disclosure of the source of *this* information is necessary to serve *this* interest?' he has to engage in a balancing exercise. He starts with the assumptions, first, that the protection of sources is itself a matter of high public importance, secondly, that nothing less than necessity will suffice to override it, thirdly, that the necessity can only arise out of concern for another matter of high public importance, being one of the four interests listed in the section.

What assistance is to be derived from the authorities as to the proper tests to be applied in carrying out this balancing exercise?

[His Lordship referred to Lord Diplock and himself in *Secretary of State for Defence v Guardian Newspapers Ltd* [1985] AC 339, 345, 372; Lord Griffiths and Lord Oliver in *Re an Inquiry under the Company Securities (Insider Dealing) Act 1985* [1988] AC 660, 704, 708–709, and continued:]

. . . I cannot help wondering whether these dicta do not concentrate attention too much on only one side of the picture. They suggest that in determining whether the criterion of necessity is established one need only look at, in the one case, the interests of national security and, in the other case, the prevention of crime. In the context of cases dealing with those two grounds of exception to the protection of sources, it is perfectly understandable that they should do so. For if non-disclosure of a source of information will imperil national security or enable a crime to be committed which might otherwise be prevented, it is difficult to imagine that any judge would hesitate to order disclosure. These two public interests are of such overriding importance that once it is shown that disclosure will serve one of those interests, the necessity of disclosure follows almost automatically; though even here if a judge were asked to order disclosure of a source of information in the interests of the prevention of crime, he 'might properly refuse to do so if, for instance, the crime was of a trivial nature': [1988] AC 660, 703, per Lord Griffiths.

But the question whether disclosure is necessary in the interests of justice gives rise to a more difficult problem of weighing one public interest against another. A question arising under this part of section 10 has not previously come before your Lordships' House for decision. In discussing the section generally Lord Diplock said in *Secretary of State for Defence v Guardian Newspapers Ltd* [1985] AC 339, 350:

> 'The exceptions include no reference to "the public interest" generally and I would add that in my view the expression "justice", the interests of which are entitled to protection, is not used in a general sense as the antonym of "injustice" but in the technical sense of the administration of justice in the course of legal proceedings in a court of law, or, by reason of the extended definition of "court" in section 19 of the Act of 1981 before a tribunal or body exercising the judicial power of the state.'

I agree entirely with the first half of this dictum. To construe 'justice' as the antonym of 'injustice' in section 10 would be far too wide. But to confine it to 'the technical sense of the administration of justice in the course of legal proceedings in a court of law' seems to me, with all respect due to any dictum of the late Lord Diplock, to be too narrow. It is, in my opinion, 'in the interests of justice', in the sense in which this phrase is used in section 10, that persons should be enabled to exercise important legal rights and to protect themselves from serious legal wrongs whether or not resort to legal proceedings in a court of law will be necessary to attain these objectives. Thus, to take a very obvious example, if an employer of a large staff is suffering grave damage from the activities of an unidentified disloyal servant, it is undoubtedly in the interests of justice that he should be able to identify him in order to terminate his contract of employment, notwithstanding that no legal proceedings may be necessary to achieve that end.

Construing the phrase 'in the interests of justice' in this sense immediately emphasises the importance of the balancing exercise. It will not be sufficient, per se, for a party seeking disclosure of a source protected by section 10 to show merely that he will be unable without disclosure to exercise the legal right or avert the threatened legal wrong on which he bases his claim in order to establish the necessity of disclosure. The judge's task will always be to weigh in the scales the importance of enabling the ends of justice to be attained in the circumstances of the particular case on the one hand against the importance of protecting the source on the other hand. In this balancing exercise it is only if the judge is satisfied that disclosure in the interests of justice is of such preponderating importance as to override the statutory privilege against disclosure that the threshold of necessity will be reached.

Whether the necessity of disclosure in this sense is established is certainly a question of fact rather than an issue calling for the exercise of the judge's discretion, but, like many other questions of fact, such as the question whether somebody has acted reasonably in given circumstances, it will call for the exercise of a discriminating and sometimes difficult value judgment. In estimating the weight to be attached to the importance of disclosure in the interests of justice on the one hand and that of protection from disclosure in pursuance of the policy which underlies section 10 on the other hand, many factors will be relevant on both sides of the scale.

It would be foolish to attempt to give comprehensive guidance as to how the balancing exercise should be carried out. But it may not be out of place to indicate the kind of factors which will require consideration. In estimating the importance to be given to the case in favour of disclosure there will be a wide spectrum within which the particular case must be located. If the party seeking disclosure shows, for example, that his very livelihood depends upon it, this will put the case near one end of the spectrum. If he shows no more than that what he seeks to protect is a minor interest in property, this will put the case at or near the other end. On the other side the importance of protecting a source from disclosure in pursuance of the policy underlying the statute will also vary within a wide spectrum. One important factor will be the nature of the information obtained from the source. The greater the legitimate public interest in the information which the source has given to the publisher or intended publisher, the greater will be the importance of protecting the source. But another and perhaps more significant factor which will very much affect the importance of protecting the source will be the manner in which the information was itself obtained by the source. If it appears to the court that the information was obtained legitimately this will enhance the importance of protecting the source. Conversely, if it appears that the information was obtained illegally, this will diminish the importance of protecting the source unless, of course, this factor is counterbalanced by a clear public interest in publication of the information, as in the classic case where the source has acted for the purpose of exposing iniquity. I draw attention to these considerations by way of illustration only and I emphasise once again that they are in no way intended to be read as a code.

In the circumstances of the instant case, I have no doubt that Hoffmann J and the Court of Appeal were right in finding that the necessity for disclosure of Mr Goodwin's notes in the interests of justice was established. The importance to the plaintiffs of obtaining disclosure lies in the threat of severe damage to their business, and consequentially to the livelihood of their employees, which would arise from disclosure of the information contained in their corporate plan while their refinancing negotiations are still continuing. This threat, accurately described by Lord Donaldson of Lymington MR, ante p. 28E, as 'ticking away beneath them like a time bomb' can only be defused if they can identify the source either as himself the thief of the stolen copy of the plan or as a means to lead to the identification of the thief and thus put themselves in a position to institute proceedings for the recovery of the missing document. The importance of protecting the source on the other hand is much diminished by the source's complicity, at the very least, in a gross breach of confidentiality which is not counterbalanced by any legitimate interest which publication of the information was calculated to serve. Disclosure in the interests of justice is, on this view of the balance, clearly of preponderating importance so as to override the policy underlying the statutory protection of sources and the test of necessity for disclosure is satisfied. . . .

The position of Mr. Goodwin . . .

The maintenance of the rule of law is in every way as important in a free society as the democratic franchise. In our society the rule of law rests upon twin foundations: the sovereignty of the Queen in Parliament in making the law and the sovereignty of the Queen's courts in interpreting and applying the law. While no one doubts the importance of protecting journalists' sources, no one, I think seriously advocates an absolute privilege against disclosure admitting of no exceptions. Since the enactment of section 10 of the Act of 1981 both the protection of journalists' sources and the limited grounds on which it may exceptionally be necessary to override that protection have been laid down by Parliament. I have not heard of any campaign in the media suggesting that the law itself is unjust or that the exceptions to the protection are too widely drawn. But if there were such a campaign, it should be fought in a democratic society by persuasion, not by disobedience to the law. Given the law as laid down by section 10, who, if not the courts, is to interpret it and to decide in the circumstances of any given case whether the protection is to prevail or whether the case is brought within one of the exceptions? The journalist cannot be left to be judge in his own cause and decide whether or not to make disclosure. This would be an abdication of the role of Parliament and the courts in the matter and in practice would be tantamount to conferring an absolute privilege. Of course the courts, like other human institutions, are fallible and a journalist ordered to disclose his source may, like other disappointed litigants, feel that the court's decision was wrong. But to contend that the individual litigant, be he a journalist or anyone else, has a right of 'conscientious objection' which entitles him to set himself above the law if he does not agree with the court's decision, is a doctrine which directly undermines the rule of law and is wholly unacceptable in a democratic society. Any rule of professional conduct enjoining a journalist to protect his confidential sources must, impliedly if not expressly, be subject to whatever exception is necessary to enable the journalist to obey the orders of a court of competent jurisdiction. Freedom of speech is itself a right which is dependent on the rule of law for its protection and it is paradoxical that a serious challenge to the rule of law should be mounted by responsible journalists.

Lords Templeman, Oliver and **Lowry** delivered concurring speeches. **Lord Griffiths** agreed.

Appeal dismissed.

NOTES

1. On 10 April 1990, the High Court fined Goodwin £5,000 for contempt of court. The European Court of Human Rights[16] subsequently found (by 11 to 7) that both the order requiring Goodwin to reveal his source and the fine imposed for having to do so violated Art. 10, ECHR. It was undisputed that the measures interfered with Goodwin's rights to freedom of expression. The Court decided that, notwithstanding, that s.10 conferred a discretion, the measures were 'prescribed by law': 'the interpretation of the relevant law made by the House of Lords in the applicant's case did not go beyond what could be reasonably foreseen in the circumstances.... Nor does [the Court] find any other indication that the law in question did not afford the applicant adequate protection against arbitrary interference.'[17] It was not disputed that the interference pursued a 'legitimate aim', the protection of the plaintiffs' rights. The Court did not reach a conclusion on the government's claim that the measures were also taken for the prevention of crime. However, the Court found that the interference was not 'necessary in a democratic society'. The plaintiffs' interests were largely protected by the ex parte injunction against Goodwin and the publishers of *The Engineer*. This had been notified to all the national newspapers and relevant journals:

> 'The Court cannot find that [the plantiffs'] interests in eliminating, by proceedings against the source, the residual threat of damage through dissemination of the confidential information otherwise than by the press, in obtaining compensation and in unmasking a disloyal employee or collaborator were, even if considered cumulatively, sufficient to outweigh the vital public interest in the protection of the applicant journalist's source.'

There was thus not 'a reasonable relationship of proportionality between the legitimate aim pursued by the disclosure order and the means deployed to achieve that aim.'[18] Seven judges dissented, noting that the majority had undertaken no detailed assessment of the plaintiffs' interests in securing the additional measures of protection sought and concluding that the conclusion of the House of Lords fell within the margin of appreciation allowed to national authorities. Which view do you prefer?

UK courts have failed to discern little if any difference in the principles stated by the House of Lords and by the Court of Human Rights. In *Camelot Group plc v Centaur Communications Ltd*[19] Schiemann LJ said: 'The difference of opinion between the House of Lords and the Court of Human Rights seems to me in large measure to be attributable to [a] different view taken of the facts' (i.e. of the significance to the plaintiffs of the additional protection that might be secured through a disclosure order).

In *Ashworth Hospital Authority v MGN Ltd*[20] Lord Phillips MR agreed with this point, but added that he was inclined to accept that ECtHR decisions 'demonstrate that the freedom of the press has in the past carried greater weight in Strasbourg than it has in the courts of this country'.[1]

2. As Lord Bridge points out, where disclosure is necessary in the interests of national security or the prevention of crime, the courts are unlikely to allow sources to be protected. Where one of the other interests specified in s. 10 is invoked, the picture

---

16 *Goodwin v UK* (1996) 22 EHRR 123.
17 Para 33.
18 Paras 45, 56.
19 [1998] 1 All ER 251 at 257–260. See T. R. S. Allan, [1998] CLJ 235.
20 [2001] 1 All ER 991.
 1 At 1012.

is more mixed. In most of the reported cases the courts have found disclosure not to be necessary. For example, in *X v Y*,[2] Rose J refused to order the disclosure of the source of stories in a national newspaper identifying two doctors who were carrying on general practice despite having contracted AIDS. The stories were based on information obtained from hospital records by one or more employees of the plaintiff health authority, and passed to the newspaper for payment. The health authority argued that disclosure was necessary 'for the prevention of crime'; there was prima facie evidence of offences of corruption under the Public Bodies Corrupt Practices Act 1889 and the Prevention of Corruption Act 1906, and they wished to ensure that such disclosures in breach of confidence did not happen again. Rose J held that the evidence adduced fell short of establishing necessity; prevention of crime was not one of the health authority's tasks and it was not clear that criminal investigation was the intended or likely consequence of disclosure. In *Saunders v Punch Ltd (t/a Liberty Publishing)*[3] Lindsay J held that disclosure was not necessary where injunction had already been granted restraining further publication of documents protected by legal professional privilege; while the protection of legal professional confidence was a 'towering public interest' it was still necessary for a balancing exercise to be undertaken and it was unlikely that S would suffer foreseeable damage if the order was refused.

In *John v Express Newspapers plc*[4] the Court of Appeal declined to order disclosure of the source of a copy of draft legal advice prepared for Sir Elton John by junior counsel that came into the possession of a journalist; other means of identifying the source through inquiries in chambers had not been pursued.

By contrast, in *Re an Inquiry under the Company Securities (Insider Dealing) Act 1985*,[5] Jeremy Warner, a financial journalist, was required by inspectors appointed under the 1985 Act to investigate suspected leaks from government departments of price-sensitive information about take-over bids, to reveal the sources of information on which he had based articles in *The Times* and the *Independent*. The inspectors certified his refusal to answer questions to the High Court under s. 178 of the Financial Services Act 1986, the High Court having power to punish a person who refuses to answer questions, without reasonable excuse, as if he had been guilty of contempt. The House of Lords held that the test set out in s. 10 should be applied to determine whether Mr Warner had a 'reasonable excuse', but that disclosure would here be 'necessary . . . for the prevention of . . . crime'. The House rejected a narrow construction of this test that would have limited it to a situation where disclosure would lead to the prevention of a particular identifiable future crime or crimes; it was sufficient that it would lead to the prevention of leaks of information and criminal insider dealing generally. Mr Warner persisted in his refusal, and was fined £20,000 (*Re an Inquiry under the Company Securities (Insider Dealing) Act 1985*).[6] See also *John Reid Enterprises Ltd v Pell*;[7]

---

2 [1998] 2 All ER 648. See also *Maxwell v Pressdram Ltd* [1987] 1 All ER 656 (disclosure of course of libellous *Private Eye* article not necessary as it related only to whether there was liability for aggravated and exemplary damages and the matter could be dealt with adequately by a strong direction to the jury); *Chief Constable of Leicestershire Constabulary v Garavelli* [1997] EMLR 543.
3 [1998] 1 All ER 234.
4 [2000] 3 All ER 257. See also *Special Hospital Services Authority v Hyde* (1994) 20 BMLR 75.
5 [1988] AC 660.
6 (1988) Times, 27 January.
7 [1999] EMLR 675.

Camelot Group plc v Centaur Communications Ltd;[8] *Michael O'Mara Books Ltd v Express Newspapers*[9] and *Ashworth Hospital Authority v MGN Ltd.*[10]

4. Disobedience to an order made by a circuit judge under the Prevention of Terrorism (Temporary Provisions) Act 1989, Sch. 7, para. 3,[11] requiring the production of information is punishable as a contempt. Such proceedings should invariably be heard in the Divisional Court; that court has no jurisdiction in contempt proceedings to review the exercise of the circuit judge's discretion – the order must be obeyed until set aside. These propositions were established in *DPP v Channel 4 Television Co Ltd,*[12] where the Divisional Court fined Channel 4 and Box Productions £75,000 for refusing to divulge material collected in the preparation of a programme in the 'Dispatches' series which made allegations of widespread and systematic collusion between members of the RUC and loyalist terrorists. The companies feared that the disclosure of their source would imperil both his life and that of their researcher, and had promised the source anonymity. Woolf LJ stated[13] that the companies should not have given unqualified assurances in view of the terms of the 1989 Act and the fact than an inquiry into the allegations was inevitable. Accordingly, they were responsible for their own dilemma of being compelled for genuinely held moral considerations to disobey what they knew to be their legal duty, and had to accept the consequences. However, the court refused the Attorney-General's application for sequestration orders against the companies, accepting the reality that they would not now change their stance. Section 10 of the 1981 Act was not relied on by the companies 'since, presumably, it was accepted it provided no protection'.[14] According to C. J. Miller,[15] s. 10 was not pleaded as it was regarded as disapplied by the Prevention of Terrorism (Temporary Provision) Act 1989, Sch. 7, para. 5(5)(b). This case has been described as dealing 'a severe blow to investigative journalism'.[16]

8 Interference with the course of justice

This head of contempt covers a variety of matters including interference with witnesses,[17] jurors[18] and judges and court officers,[19] whether the interference takes place before, during or after the relevant proceedings. In *R v Runting,*[20] the Court of Appeal quashed a conviction for contempt of court of a *Sun* photographer who

---

8 [1999] QB 124 (order granted for return of documents to plaintiff company to enable it to identify disloyal employee who had leaked draft accounts with information that was embarrassing to the company directors, but did not disclose iniquity).

9 [1999] FSR 49 (order granted for disclosure of course of copies of typescript of a book acquired in breach of copyright).

10 [2001] 1 All ER 991 (order granted for disclosure of identity of intermediary that would lead to identification of source of confidential medical records concerning Ian Brady leaked from Ashworth and published with *Daily Mirror*).

11 See now the Terrorism Act 2000, Sch. 5 above, pp. 580–582.

12 [1993] 2 All ER 517.

13 At 529.

14 Woolf LJ at 530.

15 All ER Review 1993 at p. 95.

16 R. Costigan, (1992) 142 NLJ 1417, 1418.

17 E.g. *A-G v Butterworth* [1962] 3 All ER 326; *Moore v Clerk of Assize, Bristol* [1972] 1 All ER 58 (above, p. 789); *R v Mulvaney* [1982] Crim LR 462, DC; *A-G v Jackson* [1994] COD 171, DC).

18 *R v Martin* (1848) 5 Cox CC 356; *R v Owen* [1976] 3 All ER 239; *R v Goult* (1982) 76 Cr App Rep 140; *A-G v Judd* (1994) Times, 15 August.

19 E.g. an assault on the Clerk of the Lists: *Re De Court* (1997) Times, 27 November.

20 (1988) 89 Cr App Rep 243.

pursued a defendant outside court in an attempt to take a close-up picture. The photographer had not struck or physically jostled his quarry; there were no intentional acts of sufficient gravity to amount to the actus reus of contempt of court by way of an interference with the course of justice.

Intentional interferences are clearly contempts: it is unclear, however, how far mens rea is a requirement, both at common law and after the enactment of the 1981 Act.[1] The issue of mens rea was left open in *R v Runting,* above.

Other illustrations include bringing improper pressure to bear on parties (cf. *A-G v Times Newspapers*[2]) and interfering with a prisoner's right of access to the courts;[3] and inspecting documents on a court file if it was known that leave was required or to gain access to a court file by deception or subterfuge.[4]

Intimidation of persons assisting in the investigation of offences, jurors and potential witnesses or jurors is now a substantive offence. Similarly, it is an offence to harm or threaten to harm a person because they have been so involved. This is in addition to any offence at common law. See the Criminal Justice and Public Order Act 1994, s. 51.

9 Jurisdiction

The position as to the jurisdiction to deal with criminal contempts is complex.[5] In brief, the superior courts of record (e.g. House of Lords, Court of Appeal, High Court) have inherent power, acting on their own motion, to punish contempts committed both in the face and outside the court. Formal applications for committal, as by the Attorney-General[6] must be made to the Queen's Bench Divisional Court: (1) if the alleged contempt is committed in connection with criminal proceedings (except where the contempt is committed in the face of the court or consists of disobedience to a court order or breach of an undertaking[7]); (2) if the alleged contempt concerns an inferior court;[8] or (3) if the contempt is committed otherwise than in connection with any proceedings.[9] However, the Court of Appeal may also exercise jurisdiction in relation to contempt of itself.[10] Criminal contempts committed in relation to civil proceedings may be dealt with by a High Court judge of the appropriate Division.[11] Inferior courts have inherent or statutory powers to deal with contempt in the face.[12] Applications for injunctions (e.g. by the Attorney-General: *A-G v Times Newspapers*[13]) should be made to the High Court.[14] Proceedings under the strict liability rule can

---

1 See *Borrie and Lowe*, pp. 410–412, 414–416; *A-G v Butterworth*, above.
2 [1974] AC 273, HL, above, p. 759.
3 *Raymond v Honey* [1983] 1 AC 1, HL.
4 *Dobson v Hastings* [1992] Ch 394 (on the facts there was no contempt as a journalist had obtained access to a court file without deception or trickery, and the editor responsible for the subsequent publication of information acquired from the file had no intention to interfere with the course of justice). For consideration of whether the victimisation of anti-discrimination complainants may amount to contempt, see E. Ellis and C. J. Miller, [1993] PL 80.
5 See *Borrie and Lowe*, Chap. 12.
6 Cf. s. 7 of the Contempt of Court Act 1981, above, p. 726.
7 Civil Procedure Rules, Sch. 1, RSC Ord. 52 r. 1(2)(a)(ii).
8 Ibid., r. 1(2)(a)(iii); above p. 742.
9 Ibid., r. 1(2)(b).
10 Ibid.
11 Ibid., r. 1(3).
12 See above, pp. 791–793.
13 Above, p. 759.
14 On the role of the Attorney-General in contempt proceedings, see J. Ll J. Edwards, *The Attorney-General, Politics and the Public Interest* (1984) pp. 161–176.

only be brought by or with the consent of the Attorney-General or on the motion of a court with jurisdiction to deal with such a contempt.[15] This restriction does not, however, apply to proceedings for an injunction to restrain the likely commission of an offence under the Act: *Peacock v London Weekend Television*.[16]

Appeals are governed by s. 13 of the Administration of Justice Act 1960. In most cases they lie to the Court of Appeal (Civil Division) but appeals against decisions of the Crown Court lie to the Court of Appeal (Criminal Division)[17] and against the decisions of some inferior courts to the Queen's Bench Divisional Court. Appeals lie from the Divisional Court or Court of Appeal to the House of Lords.

The possibility of trial on indictment for contempt was thought to be obsolete, the last such prosecution being *R v Tibbits and Windust*.[18] In *R v D*[19] a contempt of court count was included in an indictment charging a variety of offences arising out of D's conduct in taking his child, a ward of court, out of her mother's care and control and outside England and Wales without the consent of the court. The Court of Appeal (Criminal Division) quashed (*inter alia*) the conviction for contempt, holding that it was 'highly undesirable that that form of proceeding should be resorted to'.[20] (The House of Lords restored a conviction for kidnapping but the decision on the contempt point was not certified for consideration by the House.[1])

15 1981 Act, s. 7, above p. 726; *Taylor v Topping* (1990) Times, 15 February.
16 (1985) 150 JP 71, CA, above p. 774.
17 Supreme Court Act 1981, s. 53(2)(b); Criminal Justice Act 1988, s. 159.
18 [1902] 1 KB 77.
19 [1984] 1 All ER 574.
20 p. 583.
 1 [1984] 2 All ER 449.

CHAPTER 8

Government secrecy and national security

1 Introduction[1]

The materials in this chapter illustrate a variety of legal and extra-legal inhibitions on freedom of expression and access to information which protect the interest of the state in keeping certain matters secret. At the heart of the legal restrictions are the Official Secrets Acts[2] which cover matters ranging from serious breaches of national security to the unauthorised disclosure of certain classes of official information. These have reinforced the tendency towards excessive secrecy which has been one of the hallmarks of the public service. There have been moves towards more open government.[3] Government departments are prepared (and obliged) to release more information than formerly. The Official Secrets Act 1989, which repealed the 'catch all' provisions of s. 2 of the Official Secrets Act 1911, narrowed the scope of criminal sanctions. A Freedom of Information Act received royal assent in 2000 but is not yet in force. The courts have restricted the circumstances in which a public authority may decline to divulge information in the course of legal proceedings on the ground that it would be contrary to the public interest.[4] At the same time, the state has taken advantage of the developing law relating to the restraint by injunction of breaches of confidence.[5]

Extra-legal factors are equally significant in the maintenance of secrecy and security. The press have to an extent acceded to a system of self-censorship in defence and security matters ('D' (now 'DA') Notices[6]). There are extensive measures for maintaining the physical security of classified information. There are procedures for vetting applicants for positions in the Civil Service that have been aimed in particular at excluding persons with Communist associations or character defects from sensitive positions. Civil Servants responsible for unauthorised disclosures may be disciplined or dismissed.

Traditionally, the courts have adopted a deferential stance where the government seeks to justify a decision by reference to considerations of national security.

---

1 See generally, D. G. T. Williams, *Not in the Public Interest* (1965), (1968) 3 Federal LR 20 and 'Official Secrecy and the Courts' in P. Glazebrook (ed.), *Reshaping the Criminal Law* (1978) (hereafter cited as *D. G. T. Williams* (1978)); G. Robertson, *Freedom, the Individual and the Law* (7th edn, 1993), Chap. 4; D. Leigh, *The Frontiers of Secrecy* (1980); J. Michael, *The Politics of Secrecy* (1982); A. Nicol and G. Robertson, *Media Law* (3rd edn, 1992), Chap. 10; D. Hooper, *Official Secrets* (1987); P. Birkinshaw, *Freedom of Information: The Law, the Practice and the Ideal* (3rd edn, 2001), *Government and Information* (2nd edn, 2001) and *Reforming the Secret State* (1990); J. D. Baxter, *State Security, Privacy and Information* (1990); S. Shetreet (ed.), *Free Speech and National Security* (1991); P. Gill, *Policing Politics: Security Intelligence and the Liberal Democratic State* (1994); L. Lustgarten and I. Leigh, *In from the Cold: National Security and Parliamentary Democracy* (1994); H. Fenwick, *Civil Rights* (2000), Chap. 8; N. Whitty, T. Murphy and S. Livingstone, *Civil Liberties Law: The Human Rights Act Era* (2001), Chap. 7).
2 Below, pp. 808–837.
3 Below, pp. 893–908.
4 Below, p. 907.
5 Below, pp. 848–863.
6 Below pp. 843–848.

However, there are indications that the judges may adopt a more assertive role.[7] Accordingly, the House of Lords in *Council of Civil Service Unions v Minister for the Civil Service*[8] held that the government would need to adduce evidence that a decision was in fact based on national security grounds if the adoption of an unfair procedure was to be justified.[9] However, that case also established that once such evidence was adduced, the decision in question was not justiciable and so was not open to challenge on *Wednesbury* grounds. The courts have insisted on a certain level of evidence beyond the government's *ipse dixit* on this question.[10] The position of non-justiciability is, however, difficult to defend given the flexibility of the *Wednesbury* doctrine[11] and the vagueness of 'national security' as a concept. An alternative and more defensible approach (although expressly rejected by Jowitt J in *R v Secretary of State for the Home Department, ex p Manelfi*[11a]) would, even in a national security case, require the government to give reasons for a decision that interfered with fundamental rights subject to its duty in a proper case to make a claim of public interest immunity.

Under the ECHR, certain rights are non-derogable while others can be infringed by reference to a range of considerations that include national security (Arts. 6(1), 8, 9, 10, 11). National security has been advanced as a justification for such actions as barring access to the courts and the maintenance of arrangements for the secret surveillance of and the keeping of files on citizens. The European Court of Human Rights has taken a firmer line in the former than the latter. As to the former it held in *Chahal v United Kingdom*[12] that the exclusion of persons deported on grounds of national security from access to the courts violated Arts. 5(4) and 13 ECHR. In *Tinnelly and McElduff v United Kingdom*[13] the Court held that the issue of certificates under s. 42 of the Fair Employment (Northern Ireland) Act 1976 that decisions not to award certain building contracts to the applicants were acts 'done for the purpose of safeguarding national security or of protecting public safety or public order' was a disproportionate restriction on their right of access to a court or tribunal, contrary to Art. 6(1). Such a certificate was conclusive evidence that the act was done for the stated purpose. The 1976 Act conferred rights to complain of unlawful religious or political discrimination, but did not apply in respect of acts done for any of the stated purposes. There was no provision for any independent scrutiny of the facts which led to the Secretary of State issuing the certificates. As in *Chahal v United Kingdom*,[14] the Court stated[15] that:

---

7 B. Dickson, 'Judicial review and National Security', in B. Hadfield (ed.), *Judicial Review: A Thematic Approach* (1995).

8 [1985] AC 374.

9 Per Lord Fraser at 402. See also Taylor J in *R v Secretary of State for the Home Department, ex p Ruddock* [1987] 1 WLR 482, below, p. 877; *R v Secretary of State for the Home Department, ex p Chahal* [1995] 1 All ER 658; *R v Director of GCHQ, ex p Hodges*, below, p. 875; *R v Secretary of State for Foreign and Commonwealth Affairs, ex p Manelfi* (unreported, 25 October 1996).

10 *CCSU*: affidavit evidence that the Minister considered that prior consultation with GCHQ staff before decision to ban trade unions could have involved a risk of precipitating disruption; *Manelfi*: affidavit from Head of Security Division (R) at GCHQ that the nationality rule and waiver policy applied in recruitment were maintained to ensure loyalty, in the interest of national security. Cf. *R v Secretary of State for the Home Department, ex p McQuillan* [1995] 4 All ER 400, where Sedley J felt constrained by authority to hold that detailed reasons for an exclusion order could not be given as this 'might well lead to the discovery of sources of information available, and so possibly compromise police operations and/or put at risk the lives of informants, or their families.'

11 *R v Ministry of Defence, ex p Smith* [1996] QB 517.

11a 25 October 1996, unreported.

12 Judgment of 15 November 1996 (1997) 23 EHRR 418.

13 Judgment of 10 July 1998 (1998) 27 EHRR 249. See C. White, [1999] PL 406. Followed in the context of a refusal to appoint the applicant to a junior civil service post in *Devlin v United Kingdom*, Judgment of 30 October 2001.

14 Para. 131.

15 Para. 77.

'The right guaranteed to an applicant under Article 6§ 1 of the Convention to submit a dispute to a court or tribunal in order to have a determination of questions of both fact and law cannot be displaced by the *ipse dixit* of the executive.'

The need to protect the security of the process of intelligence gathering and vetting of potential contractors that lay behind the decisions was not sufficient to justify a complete exclusion of access to a court or tribunal. Alternative models could be adopted whereby sensitive cases are heard by a special tribunal in the absence (in whole or in part) of the applicant and his advisers, with limitations on the disclosure of evidence and with a special advocate appointed by the Attorney-General to represent the applicant's interests, albeit without responsibility to him. Such a model has indeed been adopted in each of these situations,[16] and extended to others.[17] These arrangements would seem to comply with Art. 6, but a supposedly adversarial arrangement from which one party is partially excluded is inevitably compromised although the gap may be reduced if the tribunal adopts an inquisitorial approach.[18]

By contrast the Court has tended to uphold arrangements for secret surveillance themselves.[19] Such arrangements do interfere with private life, home and correspondence (Art. 8) but the protection of national security is a legitimate aim and arrangements are justified if they are 'in accordance with the law' and 'necessary in a democratic society'. On the first of these points, the law must be accessible to the individual and its consequences for him must also be foreseeable. However, the requirement of foreseeability in the national security context cannot mean that an individual should be able to foresee precisely what checks will be made on him. It is enough in the case of a system applicable to citizens generally that the law is:

'sufficiently clear in its terms to give them an adequate indication as to the circumstances in which and the conditions on which the public authorities are empowered to resort to this kind of secret and potentially dangerous interference with private life.'

Where implementation of such a law consists of secret measures, the law must:

'indicate the scope of any discretion conferred on the competent authority with sufficient clarity, having regard to the legitimate aim of the measure in question, to give the individual adequate protection against arbitrary interference.'[20]

As to 'necessity', the Court accepts that arrangements for security vetting are indeed necessary for the protection of national security and that:

'the margin of appreciation available to the respondent State in assessing the pressing social need in the present case, and in particular in choosing the means for achieving the legitimate aim of protecting national security, was a wide one'.[1]

However, the Court must be satisfied that there exist adequate and effective guarantees against abuse.[2] In *Leander v Sweden*, the Court rejected challenges to security vetting arrangements in Sweden.[3]

1 6 Special Immigration Appeals Act 1997; Northern Ireland Act 1998, s. 90 and Fair Employment and Treatment (NI) Order 1998, S.I. 1998 No. 3162 (NI 21).
1 7 See below, pp. 840–841.
1 8 See C. White, [1999] PL 406, 413.
1 9 *Leander v Sweden*, Judgment of 25 Febuary 1997 (1987) 9 EHRR 433.
2 0 *Leander*, para. 51.
 1 Ibid., para. 59.
 2 Ibid., para. 60; *Klass v Germany*, Judgment of 6 September 1978, (1978) EHRR 214, paras. 49–50.
 3 (1987) 9 EHRR 433. Cf. *Amann v Switzerland*, Judgment of 16 February 2000 (violation of Art. 8 in respect of telephone tapping and creation and storage of a card with information about A as Swiss law did not indicate with sufficient clarity the scope of the authorities' discretion); *Rotaru v Romania*, Judgment of 4 May 2000 (violation of Arts. 8, 13 and 6(1) in respect of Romanian Intelligence Service's holding of information concerning his private life: insufficient clarity in authority's discretion; lack of safeguards against abuse).

2 The Official Secrets Acts

(A) THE OFFICIAL SECRETS ACTS 1911–1989

Official Secrets Act 1911[4]

1. Penalties for spying

(1) If any person for any purpose prejudicial to the safety or interests of the State—

    (*a*) approaches, [inspects, passes over] or is in the neighbourhood of, or enters any prohibited place within the meaning of this Act; or

    (*b*) makes any sketch, plan, model, or note which is calculated to be or might be or is intended to be directly or indirectly useful to an enemy; or

    (*c*) obtains, [collects, records, or publishes,] or communicates to any other person [any secret official code word, or pass word, or] any sketch, plan, model, article, or note, or other document or information which is calculated to be or might be or is intended to be directly or indirectly useful to an enemy;

he shall be guilty of felony . . . .

(2) On a prosecution under this section, it shall not be necessary to show that the accused person was guilty of any particular act tending to show a purpose prejudicial to the safety or interests of the State, and, notwithstanding that no such act is proved against him, he may be convicted if, from the circumstances of the case, or his conduct, or his known character as proved, it appears that his purpose was a purpose prejudicial to the safety or interests of the State; and if any sketch, plan, model, article, note, document, or information relating to or used in any prohibited place within the meaning of this Act, or anything in such a place [or any secret official code word or pass word], is made, obtained, [collected, recorded, published], or communicated by any person other than a person acting under lawful authority, it shall be deemed to have been made, obtained, [collected, recorded, published] or communicated for a purpose prejudicial to the safety or interests of the State unless the contrary is proved. . . .

3. Definition of prohibited place

For the purposes of this Act, the expression 'prohibited place' means—

    [(*a*) Any work of defence, arsenal, naval or air force establishment or station, factory, dockyard, mine, minefield, camp, ship, or aircraft belonging to or occupied by or on behalf of His Majesty, or any telegraph, telephone, wireless or signal station, or office so belonging or occupied, and any place belonging to or occupied by or on behalf of His Majesty and used for the purpose of building, repairing, making, or storing any munitions of war, or any sketches, plans, models, or documents relating thereto, or for the purpose of getting any metals, oil, or minerals of use in time of war]; and

    (*b*) any place not belonging to His Majesty where any [munitions of war], or any [sketches, models, plans] or documents relating thereto, are being made, repaired, [gotten] or stored under contract with, or with any person on behalf of, His Majesty, or otherwise on behalf of His Majesty; and

    (*c*) any place belonging to [or used for the purposes of] His Majesty which is for the time being declared [by order of a Secretary of State] to be a prohibited place for the purposes of this section on the ground that information with respect thereto, or damage thereto, would be useful to an enemy; and

    (*d*) any railway, road, way, or channel, or other means of communication by land or water (including any works or structures being part thereof or connected therewith), or any place used for gas, water, or electricity works or other works for purposes of a public character, or any place where any [munitions of war], or any [sketches, models, plans] or documents relating thereto, are being made, repaired, or stored otherwise than on behalf of His Majesty, which is for the time being declared [by order of a Secretary of State] to be a prohibited place for the purposes of this section, on the ground that information with respect thereto, or the destruction or obstruction thereof, or interference therewith, would be useful to an enemy. . . .

---

4   The words in square brackets were added by the Official Secrets Act 1920.

6. Power to arrest
Any person who is found committing an offence under this Act . . . or who is reasonably suspected of having committed, or having attempted to commit, or being about to commit, such an offence, may be apprehended and detained. . . .

7. Penalty for harbouring spies
If any person knowingly harbours any person whom he knows, or has reasonable grounds for supposing, to be a person who is about to commit or who has committed an offence under this Act, or knowingly permits to meet or assemble in any premises in his occupation or under his control any such persons, or if any person having harboured any such person, or permitted to meet or assemble in any premises in his occupation or under his control any such persons, [wilfully omits or refuses] to disclose to a superintendent of police any information which it is in his power to give in relation to any such person he shall be guilty of a misdemeanour. . . .

8. Restriction on prosecution
A prosecution for an offence under this Act shall not be instituted except by or with the consent of the Attorney-General.

9. Search warrants
(1) If a justice of the peace is satisfied by information on oath that there is reasonable ground for suspecting that an offence under this Act has been or is about to be committed, he may grant a search warrant authorising any constable . . . to enter at any time any premises or place named in the warrant, if necessary, by force, and to search the premises or place and every person found therein, and to seize any sketch, plan, model, article, note, or document, or anything of a like nature or anything which is evidence of an offence under this Act having been or being about to be committed, which he may find on the premises or place or on any such person, and with regard to or in connexion with which he has reasonable ground for suspecting that an offence under this Act has been or is about to be committed.

(2) Where it appears to a superintendent of police that the case is one of great emergency and that in the interests of the State immediate action is necessary, he may by a written order under his hand give to any constable the like authority as may be given by the warrant of a justice under this section. . . .

12. Interpretation
In this Act, unless the context otherwise requires,—

Any reference to a place belonging to His Majesty includes a place belonging to any department of the Government of the United Kingdom or of any British possessions, whether the place is or is not actually vested in His Majesty; . . .

Expressions referring to communicating . . . include any communicating . . . whether in whole or in part, and whether the sketch, plan, model, article, note, document, or information itself or the substance, effect, or description thereof only be communicated . . . expressions referring to obtaining or retaining any sketch, plan, model, article, note, or document, include the copying or causing to be copied the whole or any part of any sketch, plan, model, article, note, or document; and expressions referring to the communication of any sketch, plan, model, article, note or document include the transfer or transmission of the sketch, plan, model, article, note or document;

The expression 'document' includes part of a document;

The expression 'model' includes design, pattern, and specimen;

The expression 'sketch' includes any photograph or other mode of representing any place or thing;

[The expression 'munitions of war' includes the whole or any part of any ship, submarine, aircraft, tank or similar engine, arms and ammunition, torpedo, or mine, intended or adapted for use in war, and any other article, material or device, whether actual or proposed, intended for such use;]

The expression 'superintendent of police' includes any police officer of a like or superior rank [and any person upon whom the powers of a superintendent of police are for the purposes of this Act conferred by a Secretary of State];

The expression 'office under His Majesty' includes any office or employment in or under any department of the Government of the United Kingdom, or of any British possession;

The expression 'offence under this Act' includes any act, omission, or other thing which is punishable under this Act.

Official Secrets Act 1920

1. Unauthorised use of uniforms; falsification of reports, personation, and false documents

(2) If any person—

(*a*) retains for any purpose prejudicial to the safety or interests of the State any official document, whether or not completed or issued for use, when he has no right to retain it, or when it is contrary to his duty to retain it, or fails to comply with any directions issued by any Government Department or any person authorised by such department with regard to the return or disposal thereof; or

(*b*) allows any other person to have possession of any official document issued for his use alone, or communicates any secret official code word or pass word so issued, or, without lawful authority or excuse, has in his possession any official document or secret official code word or pass word issued for the use of some person other than himself, or on obtaining possession of any official document by finding or otherwise, neglects or fails to restore it to the person or authority by whom or for whose use it was issued, or to a police constable; or

(*c*) without lawful authority or excuse, manufactures or sells, or has in his possession for sale any such die, seal or stamp as aforesaid;

he shall be guilty of a misdemeanour.

(3) In the case of any prosecution under this section involving the proof of a purpose prejudicial to the safety or interests of the State, subsection (2) of section one of the principal Act shall apply in like manner as it applies to prosecutions under that section.

6. Duty of giving information as to commission of offence[5]

[(1) Where a chief officer of police is satisfied that there is reasonable ground for suspecting that an offence under section one of the principal Act has been committed and for believing that any person is able to furnish information as to the offence or suspected offence, he may apply to a Secretary of State for permission to exercise the powers conferred by this subsection and, if such permission is granted, he may authorise a superintendent of police, or any police officer not below the rank of inspector, to require the person believed to be able to furnish information to give any information in his power relating to the offence or suspected offence, and, if so required and on tender of his reasonable expenses, to attend at such reasonable time and place as may be specified by the superintendent or other officer; and if a person required in pursuance of such an authorisation to give information, or to attend as aforesaid, fails to comply with any such requirement or knowingly gives false information, he shall be guilty of a misdemeanour.

(2) Where a chief officer of police has reasonable grounds to believe that the case is one of great emergency and that in the interest of the State immediate action is necessary, he may exercise the powers conferred by the last foregoing subsection without applying for or being granted the permission of the Secretary of State, but if he does so shall forthwith report the circumstances to the Secretary of State.

(3) References in this section to a chief officer of police shall be construed as including references to any other officer of police expressly authorised by a chief officer of police to act on his behalf for the purposes of this section when by reason of illness, absence, or other cause he is unable to do so.]

7. Attempts, incitements, etc.

Any person who attempts to commit any offence under the principal Act or this Act, or solicits or incites or endeavours to persuade another person to commit an offence, or aids or abets and does any act preparatory to the commission of an offence under the principal Act or this Act, shall be guilty of a felony or a misdemeanour or a summary offence according as the offence in question is a felony, a misdemeanour or a summary offence, and on conviction shall be

5   Substituted by the Official Secrets Act 1939, s. 1.

liable to the same punishment, and to be proceeded against in the same manner, as if he had committed the offence.

Official Secrets Act 1989

1. Security and intelligence
(1) A person who is or has been—
    (*a*) a member of the security and intelligence services; or
    (*b*) a person notified that he is subject to the provisions of this subsection,
is guilty of an offence if without lawful authority he discloses any information, document or other article relating to security or intelligence which is or has been in his possession by virtue of his position as a member of any of those services or in the course of his work while the notification is or was in force.

(2) The reference in subsection (1) above to disclosing information relating to security or intelligence includes a reference to making any statement which purports to be a disclosure of such information or is intended to be taken by those to whom it is addressed as being such a disclosure.

(3) A person who is or has been a Crown servant or government contractor is guilty of an offence if without lawful authority he makes a damaging disclosure of any information, document or other article relating to security or intelligence which is or has been in his possession by virtue of his position as such but otherwise than as mentioned in subsection (1) above.

(4) For the purposes of subsection (3) above a disclosure is damaging if—
    (*a*) it causes damage to the work of, or of any part of, the security and intelligence services; or
    (*b*) it is of information or a document or other article which is such that its unauthorised disclosure would be likely to cause such damage or which falls within a class or description of information, documents or articles the unauthorised disclosure of which would be likely to have that effect.

(5) It is a defence for a person charged with an offence under this section to prove that at the time of the alleged offence he did not know, and had no reasonable cause to believe, that the information, document or article in question related to security or intelligence or, in the case of an offence under subsection (3), that the disclosure would be damaging within the meaning of that subsection.

(6) Notification that a person is subject to subsection (1) above shall be effected by a notice in writing served on him by a Minister of the Crown; and such a notice may be served if, in the Minister's opinion, the work undertaken by the person in question is or includes work connected with the security and intelligence services and its nature is such that the interests of national security require that he should be subject to the provisions of that subsection.

(7) Subject to subsection (8) below, a notification for the purposes of subsection (1) above shall be in force for the period of five years beginning with the day on which it is served but may be renewed by further notices under subsection (6) above for periods of five years at a time.

(8) A notification for the purposes of subsection (1) above may at any time be revoked by a further notice in writing served by the Minister on the person concerned; and the Minister shall serve such a further notice as soon as, in his opinion, the work undertaken by that person ceases to be such as is mentioned in subsection (6) above.

(9) In this section 'security or intelligence' means the work of, or in support of, the security and intelligence services or any part of them, and references to information relating to security or intelligence include references to information held or transmitted by those services or by persons in support of, or of any part of, them.

2. Defence
(1) A person who is or has been a Crown servant or government contractor is guilty of an offence if without lawful authority he makes a damaging disclosure of any information,

document or other article relating to defence which is or has been in his possession by virtue of his position as such.

(2) For the purposes of subsection (1) above a disclosure is damaging if—

    (*a*) it damages the capability of, or of any part of, the armed forces of the Crown to carry out their tasks or leads to loss of life or injury to members of those forces or serious damage to the equipment or installations of those forces; or

    (*b*) otherwise than as mentioned in paragraph (*a*) above, it endangers the interests of the United Kingdom abroad, seriously obstructs the promotion or protection by the United Kingdom of those interests or endangers the safety of British citizens abroad; or

    (*c*) it is of information or of a document or article which is such that its unauthorised disclosure would be likely to have any of those effects.

(3) It is a defence for a person charged with an offence under this section to prove that at the time of the alleged offence he did not know, and had no reasonable cause to believe, that the information, document or article in question related to defence or that its disclosure would be damaging within the meaning of subsection (1) above.

(4) In this section 'defence' means—

    (*a*) the size, shape, organisation, logistics, order of battle, deployment, operations, state of readiness and training of the armed forces of the Crown;

    (*b*) the weapons, stores or other equipment of those forces and the invention, development, production and operation of such equipment and research relating to it;

    (*c*) defence policy and strategy and military planning and intelligence;

    (*d*) plans and measures for the maintenance of essential supplies and services that are or would be needed in time of war.

3. International relations

(1) A person who is or has been a Crown servant or government contractor is guilty of an offence if without lawful authority he makes a damaging disclosure of—

    (*a*) any information, document or other article relating to international relations; or

    (*b*) any confidential information, document or other article which was obtained from a State other than the United Kingdom or an international organisation,

being information or a document or article which is or has been in his possession by virtue of his position as a Crown servant or government contractor.

(2) For the purposes of subsection (1) above a disclosure is damaging if—

    (*a*) it endangers the interests of the United Kingdom abroad, seriously obstructs the promotion or protection by the United Kingdom of those interests or endangers the safety of British citizens abroad; or

    (*b*) it is of information or of a document or article which is such that its unauthorised disclosure would be likely to have any of those effects.

(3) In the case of information or a document or article within subsection (1)(*b*) above—

    (*a*) the fact that it is confidential, or

    (*b*) its nature or contents,

may be sufficient to establish for the purposes of subsection (2)(*b*) above that the information, document or article is such that its unauthorised disclosure would be likely to have any of the effects there mentioned.

(4) It is a defence for a person charged with an offence under this section to prove that at the time of the alleged offence he did not know, and had no reasonable cause to believe, that the information, document or article in question was such as is mentioned in subsection (1) above or that its disclosure would be damaging within the meaning of that subsection.

(5) In this section 'international relations' means the relations between States, between international organisations or between one or more States and one or more such organisations and includes any matter relating to a State other than the United Kingdom or to an international organisation which is capable of affecting the relations of the United Kingdom with another State or with an international organisation.

(6) For the purposes of this section any information, document or article obtained from a State or organisation is confidential at any time while the terms on which it was obtained require it to be held in confidence or while the circumstances in which it was obtained make it reasonable for the State or organisation to expect that it would be so held.

4. Crime and special investigation powers

(1) A person who is or has been a Crown servant or government contractor is guilty of an offence if without lawful authority he discloses any information, document or other article to which this section applies and which is or has been in his possession by virtue of his position as such.

(2) This section applies to any information, document or other article—

    (*a*) the disclosure of which—

        (i) results in the commission of an offence; or

        (ii) facilitates an escape from legal custody or the doing of any other act prejudicial to the safekeeping of persons in legal custody; or

        (iii) impedes the prevention or detection of offences or the apprehension or prosecution of suspected offenders; or

    (*b*) which is such that its unauthorised disclosure would be likely to have any of those effects.

(3) This section also applies to—

    (*a*) any information obtained by reason of the interception of any communication in obedience to a warrant issued under section 2 of the Interception of Communications Act 1985 [or under the authority of an interception warrant under section 5 of the Regulation of Investigatory Powers Act 2000],[6] any information relating to the obtaining of information by reason of any such interception and any document or other article which is or has been used or held for use in, or has been obtained by reason of, any such interception; and

    (*b*) any information obtained by reason of action authorised by a warrant issued under section 3 of the Security Services Act 1989 [or under section 5 of the Intelligence Services Act 1994 or by an authorisation given under section 7 of that Act],[7] any information relating to the obtaining of information by reason of any such action and any document or other article which is or has been used or held for use in, or has been obtained by reason of, any such action.

(4) It is a defence for a person charged with an offence under this section in respect of a disclosure falling within subsection (2)(*a*) above to prove that at the time of the alleged offence he did not know, and had no reasonable cause to believe, that the disclosure would have any of the effects there mentioned.

(5) It is a defence for a person charged with an offence under this section in respect of any other disclosure to prove that at the time of the alleged offence he did not know, and had no reasonable cause to believe, that the information, document or article in question was information or a document or article to which this section applies.

(6) In this section 'legal custody' includes detention in pursuance of any enactment or any instrument made under an enactment.

5. Information resulting from unauthorised disclosures or entrusted in confidence

(1) Subsection (2) below applies where—

    (*a*) any information, document or other article protected against disclosure by the foregoing provisions of this Act has come into a person's possession as a result of having been—

        (i) disclosed (whether to him or another) by a Crown servant or government contractor without lawful authority; or

        (ii) entrusted to him by a Crown servant or government contractor on terms requiring it to be held in confidence or in circumstances in which the Crown servant or government contractor could reasonably expect that it would be so held; or

        (iii) disclosed (whether to him or another) without lawful authority by a person to whom it was entrusted as mentioned in sub-paragraph (ii) above; and

    (*b*) the disclosure without lawful authority of the information, document or article by the person into whose possession it has come is not an offence under any of those provisions.

(2) Subject to subsections (3) and (4) below, the person into whose possession the information, document or article has come is guilty of an offence if he discloses it without lawful authority knowing, or having reasonable cause to believe, that it is protected against disclosure by the

6   Inserted by the 2000 Act, Sch. 4, para. 5.
7   Inserted by the Intelligence Services Act 1994, Sch. 4, para. 4.

foregoing provisions of this Act and that it has come into his possession as mentioned in subsection (1) above.

(3) In the case of information or a document or article protected against disclosure by sections 1 to 3 above, a person does not commit an offence under subsection (2) above unless—

    (*a*) the disclosure by him is damaging; and

    (*b*) he makes it knowing, or having reasonable cause to believe, that it would be damaging;

and the question whether a disclosure is damaging shall be determined for the purposes of this subsection as it would be in relation to a disclosure of that information, document or article by a Crown servant in contravention of section 1(3), 2(1) or 3(1) above.

(4) A person does not commit an offence under subsection (2) above in respect of information or a document or other article which has come into his possession as a result of having been disclosed—

    (*a*) as mentioned in subsection (1)(*a*)(i) above by a government contractor; or

    (*b*) as mentioned in subsection (1)(*a*)(iii) above,

unless that disclosure was by a British citizen or took place in the United Kingdom, in any of the Channel Islands or in the Isle of Man or a colony.

(5) For the purposes of this section information or a document or article is protected against disclosure by the foregoing provisions of this Act if—

    (*a*) it relates to security or intelligence, defence or international relations within the meaning of section 1, 2 or 3 above or is such as is mentioned in section 3(1)(*b*) above; or

    (*b*) it is information or a document or article to which section 4 above applies;

and information or a document or article is protected against disclosure by sections 1 to 3 above if it falls within paragraph (*a*) above.

(6) A person is guilty of an offence if without lawful authority he discloses any information, document or other article which he knows, or has reasonable cause to believe, to have come into his possession as a result of a contravention of section 1 of the Official Secrets Act 1911.

6. Information entrusted in confidence to other States or international organisations

(1) This section applies where—

    (*a*) any information, document or other article which—

        (i) relates to security or intelligence, defence or international relations; and

        (ii) has been communicated in confidence by or on behalf of the United Kingdom to another State or to an international organisation,

          has come into a person's possession as a result of having been disclosed (whether to him or another) without the authority of that State or organisation or, in the case of an organisation, of a member of it; and

    (*b*) the disclosure without lawful authority of the information, document or article by the person into whose possession it has come is not an offence under any of the foregoing provisions of this Act.

(2) Subject to subsection (3) below, the person into whose possession the information, document or article has come is guilty of an offence if he makes a damaging disclosure of it knowing, or having reasonable cause to believe, that it is such as is mentioned in subsection (1) above, that it has come into his possession as there mentioned and that its disclosure would be damaging.

(3) A person does not commit an offence under subsection (2) above if the information, document or article is disclosed by him with lawful authority or has previously been made available to the public with the authority of the State or organisation concerned or, in the case of an organisation, of a member of it.

(4) For the purposes of this section 'security or intelligence', 'defence' and 'international relations' have the same meaning as in sections 1, 2 and 3 above and the question whether a disclosure is damaging shall be determined as it would be in relation to a disclosure of the information, document or article in question by a Crown servant in contravention of sections 1(3), 2(1) and 3(1) above.

(5) For the purposes of this section information or a document or article is communicated in confidence if it is communicated on terms requiring it to be held in confidence or in circumstances in which the person communicating it could reasonably expect that it would be so held.

7. Authorised disclosures
(1) For the purposes of this Act a disclosure by—
    (*a*) a Crown servant; or
    (*b*) a person, not being a Crown servant or government contractor, in whose case a notification for the purposes of section 1(1) above is in force,
is made with lawful authority if, and only if, it is made in accordance with his official duty.
(2) For the purposes of this Act a disclosure by a government contractor is made with lawful authority if, and only if, it is made—
    (*a*) in accordance with an official authorisation; or
    (*b*) for the purposes of the functions by virtue of which he is a government contractor and without contravening an official restriction.
(3) For the purposes of this Act a disclosure made by any other person is made with lawful authority if, and only if, it is made—
    (*a*) to a Crown servant for the purposes of his functions as such; or
    (*b*) in accordance with an official authorisation.
(4) It is a defence for a person charged with an offence under any of the foregoing provisions of this Act to prove that at the time of the alleged offence he believed that he had lawful authority to make the disclosure in question and had no reasonable cause to believe otherwise.
(5) In this section 'official authorisation' and 'official restriction' mean, subject to subsection (6) below, an authorisation or restriction duly given or imposed by a Crown servant or government contractor or by or on behalf of a prescribed body or a body of a prescribed class.
(6) In relation to section 6 above 'official authorisation' includes an authorisation duly given by or on behalf of the State or organisation concerned or, in the case of an organisation, a member of it.

8. Safeguarding of information
(1) Where a Crown servant or government contractor, by virtue of his position as such, has in his possession or under his control any document or other article which it would be an offence under any of the foregoing provisions of this Act for him to disclose without lawful authority he is guilty of an offence if—
    (*a*) being a Crown servant, he retains the document or article contrary to his official duty; or
    (*b*) being a government contractor, he fails to comply with an official direction for the return or disposal of the document or article,
or if he fails to take such care to prevent the unauthorised disclosure of the document or article as a person in his position may reasonably be expected to take.
(2) It is a defence for a Crown servant charged with an offence under subsection (1)(*a*) above to prove that at the time of the alleged offence he believed that he was acting in accordance with his official duty and had no reasonable cause to believe otherwise.
(3) In subsections (1) and (2) above references to a Crown servant include any person, not being a Crown servant or government contractor, in whose case a notification for the purposes of section 1(1) above is in force.
(4) Where a person has in his possession or under his control any document or other article which it would be an offence under section 5 above for him to disclose without lawful authority, he is guilty of an offence if—
    (*a*) he fails to comply with an official direction for its return or disposal; or
    (*b*) where he obtained it from a Crown servant or government contractor on terms requiring it to be held in confidence or in circumstances in which that servant or contractor could reasonably expect that it would be so held, he fails to take such care to prevent its unauthorised disclosure as a person in his position may reasonably be expected to take.
(5) Where a person has in his possession or under his control any document or other article which it would be an offence under section 6 above for him to disclose without lawful authority, he is guilty of an offence if he fails to comply with an official direction for its return or disposal.
(6) A person is guilty of an offence if he discloses any official information, document or other article which can be used for the purpose of obtaining access to any information, document or other article protected against disclosure by the foregoing provisions of this Act and the

circumstances in which it is disclosed are such that it would be reasonable to expect that it might be used for that purpose without authority.

(7) For the purposes of subsection (6) above a person discloses information or a document or article which is official if—

    (*a*) he has or has had it in his possession by virtue of his position as a Crown servant or government contractor; or

    (*b*) he knows or has reasonable cause to believe that a Crown servant or government contractor has or has had it in his possession by virtue of his position as such.

(8) Subsection (5) of section 5 above applies for the purposes of subsection (6) above as it applies for the purposes of that section.

(9) In this section 'official direction' means a direction duly given by a Crown servant or government contractor or by or on behalf of a prescribed body or a body of a prescribed class.

9. Prosecutions

(1) Subject to subsection (2) below, no prosecutions for an offence under this Act shall be instituted in England and Wales or in Northern Ireland except by or with the consent of the Attorney General or, as the case may be, the Attorney General for Northern Ireland.

(2) Subsection (1) above does not apply to an offence in respect of any such information, document or article as is mentioned in section 4(2) above but no prosecution for such an offence shall be instituted in England and Wales or in Northern Ireland except by or with the consent of the Director of Public Prosecutions or, as the case may be, the Director of Public Prosecutions for Northern Ireland.

10. Penalties

(1) A person guilty of an offence under any provision of this Act other than section 8(1), (4) or (5) shall be liable—

    (*a*) on conviction on indictment, to imprisonment for a term not exceeding two years or a fine or both;

    (*b*) on summary conviction, to imprisonment for a term not exceeding six months or a fine not exceeding the statutory maximum or both.

(2) A person guilty of an offence under section 8(1), (4) or (5) above shall be liable on summary conviction to imprisonment for a term not exceeding three months or a fine not exceeding level 5 on the standard scale or both.

11. Arrest, search and trial

(3) Section 9(1) of the Official Secrets Act 1911 (search warrants) shall have effect as if references to offences under that Act included references to offences under any provision of this Act other than section 8(1), (4) or (5); and the following provisions of the Police and Criminal Evidence Act 1984, that is to say—

    (*a*) section 9(2) (which excludes items subject to legal privilege and certain other material from powers of search conferred by previous enactments); and

    (*b*) paragraph 3(*b*) of Schedule 1 (which prescribes access conditions for the special procedure laid down in that Schedule),

shall apply to section 9(1) of the said Act of 1911 as extended by this subsection as they apply to that section as originally enacted....

(4) Section 8(4) of the Official Secrets Act 1920 (exclusion of public from hearing on the grounds of national safety) shall have effect as if references to offences under that Act included references to offences under any provision of this Act other than section 8(1), (4) or (5).

(5) Proceedings for an offence under this Act may be taken in any place in the United Kingdom.

12. 'Crown servant' and 'government contractor'

(1) In this Act 'Crown servant' means—

    (*a*) a Minister of the Crown;

    [(*aa*)a member of the Scottish Executive or a junior Scottish Minister;][8]

    (*b*) [...];[9]

8 Inserted by the Scotland Act 1998, Sch. 8, para. 26(2), (3).
9 Repealed by the Northern Ireland Act 1998, Sch. 13, para. 9(2).

(c) any person employed in the civil service of the Crown, including Her Majesty's Diplomatic Service, Her Majesty's Overseas Civil Service, the civil service of Northern Ireland and the Northern Ireland Court Service;

(d) any member of the naval, military or air forces of the Crown including any person employed by an association established for the purposes of [the Reserve Forces Act 1996];[10]

(e) any constable and any other person employed or appointed in or for the purposes of any police force (including a police force within the meaning of the Police Act (Northern Ireland) 1970) [or of the National Criminal Intelligence Service or the National Crime Squad];[11]

(f) any person who is a member or employee of a prescribed body or a body of a prescribed class and either is prescribed for the purposes of this paragraph or belongs to a prescribed class of members or employees of any such body;

(g) any person who is the holder of a prescribed office or who is an employee of such a holder and either is prescribed for the purposes of this paragraph or belongs to a prescribed class of such employees.[12]

(2) In this Act 'government contractor' means, subject to subsection (3) below, any person who is not a Crown servant but who provides, or is employed in the provision of, goods or services—

(a) for the purposes of any Minister or person mentioned in paragraph (a) or (b) of subsection (1) above, [of any office-holder in the Scottish Administration,][13] of any of the services, forces or bodies mentioned in that subsection or of the holder of any office prescribed under that subsection; or

[(aa) for the purpose of the National Assembly for Wales];[14]

(b) under an agreement or arrangement certified by the Secretary of State as being one to which the government of a State other than the United Kingdom or an international organisation is a party or which is subordinate to, or made for the purposes of implementing, any such agreement or arrangement.

(3) Where an employee or class of employees of any body, or of any holder of an office, is prescribed by an order made for the purposes of subsection (1) above—

(a) any employee of that body, or of the holder of that office, who is not prescribed or is not within the prescribed class; and

(b) any person who does not provide, or is not employed in the provision of, goods or services for the purposes of the performance of those functions of the body or the holder of the office in connection with which the employee or prescribed class of employees is engaged,

shall not be a government contractor for the purposes of this Act.

[(4) In this section 'office-holder in the Scottish Administration' has the same meaning as in section 126(7)(a) of the Scotland Act 1998.][15]

[(5) This Act shall apply to the following as it applies to persons falling within the definition of Crown servant—

(a) the First Minister and deputy First Minister in Northern Ireland; and

(b) Northern Ireland Ministers and junior Ministers.][16]

13. Other interpretation provisions

(1) In this Act—

---

10 Substituted by the Reserve Forces Act 1996, Sch. 10, para. 22.
11 Inserted by the Police Act 1997, Sch. 9, para. 62.
12 Other officials are taken to be 'Crown servants' by virtue of specific provisions: see e.g. Government of Wales Act 1998, ss. 53 (National Assembly for Wales First Secretary and Assembly Secretaries), 90 (Auditor General for Wales), 92 (Auditor General's staff), Sch. 9, Pt. I (Welsh Administration Ombudsman), Sch. 10 (Health Service Commissioner for Wales).
13 Inserted by the Scotland Act 1998, Sch. 8, para. 26(2), (3).
14 Inserted by the Government of Wales Act 1998, Sch. 12, para. 30.
15 Inserted by the Scotland Act 1998, s. 125, Sch. 8, para. 26(4).
16 Inserted by the Northern Ireland Act 1998, s. 99, Sch. 13, para. 9(1), (3).

'disclose' and 'disclosure', in relation to a document or other article, include parting with
    possession of it;
'international organisation' means, subject to subsections (2) and (3) below, an organisation
    of which only States are members and includes a reference to any organ of such an
    organisation;
'prescribed' means prescribed by an order made by the Secretary of State;
'State' includes the government of a State and any organ of its government and references
    to a State other than the United Kingdom include references to any territory outside
    the United Kingdom.
(2) In section 12(2)(*b*) above the reference to an international organisation includes a reference
to any such organisation whether or not one of which only States are members and includes
a commercial organisation.
(3) In determining for the purposes of subsection (1) above whether only States are members
of an organisation, any member which is itself an organisation of which only States are
members, or which is an organ of such an organisation, shall be treated as a State. . . .

15. Acts done abroad and extent
(1) Any act—
    (*a*)   done by a British citizen or Crown servant; or
    (*b*)   done by any person in any of the Channel Islands or the Isle of Man or any colony,
shall, if it would be an offence by that person under any provision of this Act other than
section 8(1), (4) or (5) when done by him in the United Kingdom, be an offence under that
provision.
(2) This Act extends to Northern Ireland. . . .

16. Short title, citation, consequential amendments, repeals, revocation and commencement
(1) This Act may be cited as the Official Secrets Act 1989.
(2) This Act and the Official Secrets Acts 1911 to 1939 may be cited together as the Official
Secrets Acts 1911 to 1989. . . .

NOTES

1. The maximum penalty under s. 1 of the 1911 Act is 14 years' imprisonment, and
for the other offences under the two Acts (other than ss. 4 and 5 of the 1920 Act) is
two years' imprisonment.
   There are special provisions concerning atomic energy.[17] Section 11 of the Atomic
Energy Act 1946 makes it an offence to communicate to an unauthorised person
information relating to atomic energy plant.[18] Section 13 makes it an offence for any
person to disclose, without authority, any information obtained in the exercise of
powers under the Act. Any place belonging to or used for the purposes of the
Authority may be declared to be a prohibited place under the Official Secrets Act
1911, s. 3(c).[19] Similar provisions apply to the Civil Aviation Authority (Civil
Aviation Act 1982, s. 18), the holders of a nuclear site licence[20] and public
telecommunications operators.[1] It is also an offence for a member of any Euratom
institution or committee, an officer or servant of Euratom or a person who has dealings

17 On the implications for civil liberties generally of nuclear power see J. C. Woodliffe, [1983]
    PL 440; JUSTICE Report on *Plutonium and Liberty* (1978); M. Flood and R. Grove-White,
    Nuclear Prospects (1976).
18 See S. R. & O. 1947 No. 100.
19 Atomic Energy Authority Act 1954, s. 6(3).
20 Nuclear Installations Act 1965, Sch. 1.
1 Telecommunications Act 1984, Sch. 4, para. 12(2).

with Euratom to disclose classified information acquired from that source (European Communities Act 1972, s. 11(2)). The current orders under s. 3(c) are The Official Secrets (Prohibited Places) Orders 1955 and 1994.[2] They cover the Capenhurst and Sellafield works of British Nuclear Fuels Ltd, and various establishments of the Atomic Energy Authority, including Dounreay, Windscale and Harwell.

2. It is an offence under section 1(1) of the 1920 Act to use specified false pretences for the purpose of gaining admission to a prohibited place or for any other purpose prejudicial to the safety or interests of the State. These include the use without lawful authority of official uniform (e.g. military or police) or any uniform so nearly resembling it as to be calculated to deceive; making false statements; tampering with a pass (or similar document); possessing a pass (or similar document) that has been forged, altered or is otherwise 'irregular'; personating a person holding office under the Crown or a person entitled to use an official pass (or similar document), code word, or pass word; unauthorised use or possession of any die, seal or stamp of a government department or any diplomatic, naval, military or air force authority under the Crown, or die, seal or stamp so closely resembling one as to be calculated to deceive.

It is also an offence to obstruct, knowingly mislead or otherwise interfere with or impede any police officer, or any member of the forces on guard, patrol or similar duty, 'in the vicinity of a prohibited place'.[3]

3. The fact that a person has been in communication with a foreign agent constitutes evidence in proceedings against him under s. 1 of the 1911 Act that he has for a purpose prejudicial to the safety or the interests of the State, obtained or attempted to obtain information which may be useful to an enemy.[4] There is also a power whereby a Secretary of State may require the production of telegrams.[5] Persons who carry on the business of receiving postal packets for delivery or forwarding must be registered with the police.[6]

4. If, in the course of any court proceedings under the Acts:

'... application is made by the prosecution, on the ground that the publication of any evidence to be given or of any statement to be made in the course of the proceedings would be prejudicial to the national safety, that all or any portion of the public shall be excluded during any part of the hearing, the court may make an order to that effect, but the passing of sentence shall in any case take place in public.' (1920 Act, s. 8(4)).

5. The 1911 Official Secrets Bill[7] was presented by the government as a measure which was aimed at spying and was essential on grounds of national security.[8] Section 2[9] was not mentioned. It passed all its Commons stages in less than an hour. The files show that the legislation had been desired for some time by governments, the Official Secrets Act 1889 having proved inadequate to prevent the leakage of official information by civil servants, and that it had been carefully prepared over a period of years.[10] The background to the 1989 Act is discussed below.[11]

---

2 S.I.s 1955 No. 1497 and 1994 No. 968.
3 1920 Act, s. 3.
4 1920 Act, s. 2.
5 1920 Act, s. 4.
6 1920 Act, s. 5.
7 The origins of the Officials Secrets Acts are discussed in D. G. T. Williams, *Not in the Public Interest* (1965), Chap. 1; Report of the Franks Committee on Section 2 of the Official Secrets Act 1911, Cmnd. 5104, Chap. 4 and Appendix III; D. French, 'Spy Fever in Britain, 1900–1915', *The Historical Journal*, 21, 2 (1978), p. 355; K. G. Robertson, *Public Secrets* (1982), Chaps. 4 and 5.
8 Franks Report, p. 24.
9 See below, p. 827.
10 Franks Report, p. 25.
11 pp. 827–834.

6. *Aspects of interpretation.* The term 'enemy' includes a potential enemy, and so all the provisions of s. 1 are applicable in peace time.[12] The leading case on s. 1, *Chandler v DPP,* is given below.[13] Section 3 of the 1920 Act was used in a prosecution of four members of the Committee of 100, including Pat Arrowsmith, in 1964. They were fined £25 for inciting people to obstruct police officers at the USAF base at Ruislip in connection with a demonstration there.[14] Williams points out[15] that it was not necessary for the Official Secrets Acts to be invoked against the nuclear disarmers in the 1960s, in preference to prosecutions for the general public order offences.

In *Adler v George,*[16] A obstructed a member of the armed forces engaged in security duty while within the boundaries of Marham RAF station. His conviction under s. 3 of the 1920 Act was upheld by the Divisional Court, which held that the words 'in the vicinity of' had to be read as meaning 'in or in the vicinity of'.

Another alteration in the statutory language to the detriment of a defendant was made by the Court of Criminal Appeal in *R v Oakes.*[17] The court treated section 7 of the 1911 Act as if it read 'aids or abets *or* does any act preparatory' so as to render liable a person who had done an 'act preparatory' without 'aiding or abetting'.

'It seems to the court that it is quite clear in the present case what the intention was, and that there has been merely a faultiness of expression.'[18]

O had also been convicted under s. 2 of the 1911 Act. In *R v Bingham*[19] the Court of Appeal (Criminal Division) held that an 'act preparatory' was 'an act done by the accused with the commission of an offence under the principal Act in mind', and that it was sufficient to show that the transmission of prejudicial information was 'possible' and not 'probable'.[20] Is it necessary for something to be an offence which is even more remote from the substantive offence than an attempt to commit it?

7. *Powers of search.* The powers of search granted by s. 9 of the 1911 Act were relied upon by the police in the 'Zircon affair'.[1] In 1986 the BBC commissioned Duncan Campbell to make a series of programmes entitled *Secret Society.* One of these revealed the existence of a secret Ministry of Defence project, Project Zircon, to put a spy satellite in space. The programme also revealed its cost (c. £500m) and the fact that the existence and cost of the project had been concealed from Parliament, but not its technical details. On 15 January 1987, the programme was banned on national security grounds by Alasdair Milne, the BBC's Director General (having previously been cleared by Assistant Director General Alan Protheroe). An injunction was obtained against Duncan Campbell on 21 January, but not served in time to prevent the Zircon story being told in the *New Statesman* of 23 January 1987 ('Spy in the Sky'), published on 22 January. On the same day, the Attorney-General failed to obtain an injunction to prevent the programme being shown in the Palace of

---

12 *R v Parrott* (1913) 8 Cr App Rep 186, CCA.
13 p. 821.
14 D. G. T. Williams, *Not in the Public Interest* (1965), p. 109.
15 At p. 111.
16 [1964] 2 QB 7.
17 [1959] 2 QB 350.
18 Per Lord Parker CJ at 357.
19 [1973] QB 870.
20 Per Lord Widgery CJ at 875.
 1 See generally the *New Statesman* for 23 and 30 January and 6 February 1987; P. Thornton, *The Civil Liberties of the Zircon Affair* (NCCL, 1987); P. Gill, (1987) 9 Liverpool LR 189; debates on the Special Branch Raids, 109 HC Deb 2 and 3 February 1987, cols. 691–700, 815–858; K. D. Ewing and C. A. Gearty, *Freedom Under Thatcher* (1990), pp. 147–152.

Westminster, Ian Kennedy J stating that it was for the House to regulate its own proceedings; but persuaded the Speaker, after a briefing 'on Privy Counsellor terms', to impose a ban on its being shown while the injunction against Campbell was in force (it was lifted on 25 February in the light of a detailed undertaking given by Campbell).

Over the weekend of 24–25 January, Special Branch police officers searched the offices of the *New Statesman*; on 25 January, officers searched Duncan Campbell's home, and on 31 January, the Glasgow offices of BBC Scotland. Substantial quantities of documents were removed, especially from the BBC. The London warrants were granted under the Police and Criminal Evidence Act 1984, s. 9 and Sch. 1 under the warrant procedure exceptionally available as an alternative to obtaining an order inter partes. The basis of the warrant in Glasgow was s. 9 of the 1911 Act, the PACE provisions not extending to Scotland.[2] It was claimed that the legal proceedings involved were instigated by the Attorney-General in England and the Lord Advocate in Scotland rather than Ministers.[3]

The government's actions were widely criticised as an attempt to intimidate the press, particularly in view of the broad terms in which the search warrants were granted. The question why the authorities, who had known about the proposed programme since the middle of 1986, waited until early 1987 to take any action was never satisfactorily answered.

A majority of the Committee of Privileges subsequently concluded that the Speaker had acted 'wholly correctly in this matter', and stated that the private showing of the programme could not constitute a 'proceeding in Parliament' protected by Parliamentary privilege.[4]

Section 9(2) and Sch. 1, para. 3(b) of PACE now apply to warrants under s. 9(1) of the 1911 Act.[6]

(B) SECTION 1 OF THE OFFICIAL SECRETS ACT 1911: ESPIONAGE, SABOTAGE AND WHAT ELSE?

Chandler v Director of Public Prosecutions [1964] AC 763, [1962] 3 All ER 142, [1962] 3 WLR 702, House of Lords

The appellants, five men and a woman, were members of the Committee of 100 who sought to further the aims of the Campaign for Nuclear Disarmament by non-violent demonstrations of civil disobedience. They took part in organising a demonstration held on 9 December 1961, at Wethersfield Airfield, which was a 'prohibited place' within section 3 of the Official Secrets Act 1911, and which was occupied at the material time by United States Air Force squadrons assigned to the Supreme Commander Allied Forces, Europe. The plan was that on 9 December 1961, some demonstrators would take up a position outside the entrances to the airfield and would remain there sitting for five hours, while others would enter the airfield and, by sitting in front of the aircraft, would prevent them from taking off. On that date, many demonstrators did travel to Wethersfield, but were prevented from entering the airfield. The admitted objects were to ground all aircraft, to immobilise the airfield and to

2 See G. J. Zellick, (1987) 137 NLJ 160.
3 See e.g. 110 HC Deb, 19 February 1977, cols. 796–798, written answer by Malcolm Rifkind MP, Secretary of State for Scotland.
4 See *First Report from the Committee of Privileges 1986–87, Speaker's Order of 22 January 1987 on a Matter of National Security* (1986–87 H.C. 365); A. W. Bradley, [1987] PL 1 and 488.
5 Official Secrets Act 1989, s. 11(3). See above, pp. 225, 232.

reclaim the base for civilian purposes. The appellants were charged with conspiring together to incite diverse persons to commit, and with conspiring together and with others to commit, 'a breach of section 1 of the Official Secrets Act 1911, namely, for a purpose prejudicial to the safety or interests of the State to enter a Royal Air Force Station . . . at Wethersfield'. A prosecution witness, Air Commodore Magill, gave evidence that interference with the ability of aircraft to take off was prejudicial to the safety or interests of the State. The judge refused to allow counsel for the defence to cross-examine or call evidence as to the appellants' beliefs that their acts would benefit the State or to show that the appellants' purpose was not in fact prejudicial to the safety or interests of the State. The appellants were convicted and sentenced to terms of imprisonment (18 months each for the men and 12 for the woman).

They appealed on the grounds that the facts did not disclose a conspiracy to commit a breach of section 1 of the Act of 1911, and that the judge was wrong in excluding cross-examination and evidence as to the facts on which the appellants' beliefs were based, and as to whether the appellants' purpose was in fact prejudicial to the State. Their appeals were dismissed by the Court of Criminal Appeal[6] and the House of Lords.

Lord Reid: . . . In cross-examination [of Air Commodore Magill] objection was taken to his being asked as to the armament of these squadrons. Counsel for the accused said that they sought to adduce evidence that their purpose was not prejudicial to the interests of the State, and that the basis of the defence was that these aircraft used nuclear bombs and that it was not in fact in the interests of the State to have aircraft so armed at that time there. So, he said, it would be beneficial to the State to immobilise these aircraft. Then counsel further submitted that he was entitled to adduce evidence to show that the accused believed, and reasonably believed, that it was not prejudicial but beneficial to the interests of the State to immobilise these aircraft: the jury were entitled to hold that no offence had been committed because the accused did not have a purpose prejudicial to the State, and it was for the jury to determine their purpose. . . . [C]ounsel said that his evidence would deal with the effect of exploding a nuclear bomb and . . . reference was made to the possibility of accident or mistake, and other reasons against having nuclear bombs. He said that he wished to cross-examine as to the basic wrongness of the conception of a deterrent force and the likelihood of it attracting hostile attack. In reply the Attorney-General submitted that an objective test must determine whether the purpose of grounding aircraft was a prejudicial purpose, that the accuseds' beliefs were irrelevant and so was the reasonableness of their beliefs. Havers J then ruled that the defence were not entitled to call evidence to establish that it would be beneficial for this country to give up nuclear armament or that the accused honestly believed that it would be. . . . [Section 1 of the Official Secrets Act 1911] has a side note 'Penalties for spying', and it was argued that this limits its scope. In my view side notes cannot be used as an aid to construction. They are mere catchwords and I have never heard of it being supposed in recent times that an amendment to alter a side note could be proposed in either House of Parliament. Side notes in the original Bill are inserted by the draftsman. During the passage of the Bill through its various stages amendments to it or other reasons may make it desirable to alter a side note. In that event I have reason to believe that alteration is made by the appropriate officer of the House—no doubt in consultation with the draftsman. So side notes cannot be said to be enacted in the same sense as the long title or any part of the body of the Act. Moreover, it is impossible to suppose that the section does not apply to sabotage and what was intended to be done in this case was a kind of temporary sabotage.

The first word in the section that requires consideration is 'purpose'. . . . The accused both intended and desired that the base should be immobilised for a time, and I cannot construe purpose in any sense that does not include that state of mind. A person can have two different purposes in doing a particular thing and even if their reason or motive for doing what they did is called the purpose of influencing public opinion that cannot alter the fact that they had a purpose to immobilise the base. And the statute says 'for any purpose'. There is no question here of the interference with the aircraft being an unintended or undesired consequence of carrying out a legitimate purpose.

Next comes the question of what is meant by the safety or interests of the State. 'State' is not an easy word. It does not mean the Government or the Executive. And I do not think that it means, as counsel argued, the individuals who inhabit these islands. The statute cannot be referring to the interests of all those individuals because they may differ and the interests of the majority are not necessarily the same as the interests of the State. . . . Perhaps the country or the realm are as good synonyms as one can find and I would be prepared to accept the organised community as coming as near to a definition as one can get.

Who, then, is to determine what is and what is not prejudicial to the safety and interests of the State? The question more frequently arises as to what is or is not in the public interest. I do not subscribe to the view that the Government or a Minister must always or even as a general rule have the last word about that.

But here we are dealing with a very special matter—interfering with a prohibited place which Wethersfield was. The definition in section 3 shows that it must either be closely connected with the armed forces or be a place such that information regarding it or damage to it or interference with it would be useful to an enemy. It is in my opinion clear that the disposition and armament of the armed forces are and for centuries have been within the exclusive discretion of the Crown and that no one can seek a legal remedy on the ground that such discretion has been wrongly exercised. I need only refer to the numerous authorities gathered together in *China Navigation Co Ltd v A-G* [1932] 2 KB 197. Anyone is entitled, in or out of Parliament, to urge that policy regarding the armed forces should be changed; but until it is changed, on a change of Government or otherwise, no one is entitled to challenge it in court.

Even in recent times there have been occasions when quite large numbers of people have been bitterly opposed to the use made of the armed forces in peace or in war. The 1911 Act was passed at a time of grave misgiving about the German menace, and it would be surprising and hardly credible that the Parliament of that date intended that a person who deliberately interfered with vital dispositions of the armed forces should be entitled to submit to a jury that Government policy was wrong and that what he did was really in the best interests of the country, and then perhaps to escape conviction because a unanimous verdict on that question could not be obtained. Of course we are bound by the words which Parliament has used in the Act. If those words necessarily lead to that conclusion then it is no answer that it is inconceivable that Parliament can have so intended. The remedy is to amend the Act. But we must be clear that the words of the Act are not reasonably capable of any other interpretation.

I am prepared to start from the position that, when an Act requires certain things to be established against an accused person to constitute an offence, all of those things must be proved by evidence which the jury accepts, unless Parliament has otherwise provided. But normally such things are facts and where questions of opinion arise they are on limited technical matters on which expert evidence can be called. Here the question whether it is beneficial to use the armed forces in a particular way or prejudicial to interfere with that use would be a political question—a question of opinion on which anyone actively interested in politics, including jurymen, might consider his own opinion as good as that of anyone else. Our criminal system is not devised to deal with issues of that kind. The question therefore is whether this Act can reasonably be read in such a way as to avoid the raising of such issues.

The Act must be read as a whole and paragraphs (*c*) and (*d*) of section 3 appear to me to require such a construction. Places to which they refer become prohibited places if a Secretary of State declares that damage, obstruction or interference there 'would be useful to an enemy'. Plainly it is not open to an accused who has interfered with or damaged such a place to a material extent to dispute the declaration of the Secretary of State and it would be absurd if he were entitled to say or lead evidence to show that, although he had deliberately done something which would be useful to an enemy, yet his purpose was not prejudicial to the safety or interests of the State. So here at least the trial judge must be entitled to prevent the leading of evidence and to direct the jury that if they find that his purpose was to interfere to a material extent they must hold that his purpose was prejudicial. If that be so, then, in view of the matters which I have already dealt with, it appears to me that the same must necessarily apply to the present case.

I am therefore of opinion that the ruling of Havers J excluding evidence was right and that his direction to the jury was substantially correct. . . . I think it was proper to give to the jury a direction to the effect that if they were satisfied that the intention and desire of the accused was to procure the immobilisation of these aircraft in a way which they knew would or might substantially impair their operational effectiveness then the offence was proved and they should convict.

Viscount Radcliffe: ... When a man has avowed that his purpose in approaching an airfield forming part of a country's defence system was to obstruct its operational activity, what, if any, evidence is admissible on the issue as to the prejudicial nature of his purpose? In my opinion the correct answer is, virtually none. This answer is not surprising if certain considerations that lie behind the protection of official secrets are borne in mind. The defence of the State from external enemies is a matter of real concern, in time of peace as in days of war. The disposition, armament and direction of the defence forces of the State are matters decided upon by the Crown and are within its jurisdiction as the executive power of the State. So are treaties and alliances with other States for mutual defence. An airfield maintained for the service of the Royal Air Force or of the air force of one of Her Majesty's allies is an instrument of defence, as are the airplanes operating from the airfield and their armament.

It follows, I think, that if a man is shown to the satisfaction of the jury to have approached an airfield with the direct purpose of obstructing its operational use, a verdict of guilty must result, provided that they are also satisfied that the airfield belongs to Her Majesty and was at the relevant date part of the defence system maintained by the Crown for the protection of the realm. . . .

[E]ven if all these matters [on which the accused wished to adduce evidence] were to be investigated in court, they would still constitute only various points of consideration on the ultimate general issue, is it prejudicial to the interests of the State to include nuclear armament in its apparatus of defence? I do not think that a court of law can try that issue or, accordingly, can admit evidence upon it. It is not debarred from doing so merely because the issue is what is ordinarily known as 'political'. Such issues may present themselves in courts of law if they take a triable form. Nor, certainly, is it because Ministers of State have any inherent general authority to prescribe to the courts what is or is not prejudicial to the interests of the State. But here we are dealing with a matter of defence of the realm and with an Act designed to protect State secrets and the instruments of the State's defence. If the methods of arming the defence forces and the disposition of those forces are at the decision of Her Majesty's Ministers for the time being, as we know that they are, it is not within the competence of a court of law to try the issue whether it would be better for the country that that armament or those dispositions should be different.

Lords Hodson, Devlin and **Pearce** delivered concurring speeches.

Appeal dismissed.

NOTES

1. Lord Devlin's reasoning differed in some respects from the other members of the House, although he concurred in the result. The question whether an act was for a prejudicial purpose was for the jury to consider, and they should take account of all the consequences of the act which were reasonably to be apprehended. There was no justification for restricting the relevant consequences, as the Crown had argued, to those which occurred in the prohibited place or which could otherwise be regarded as 'immediate'. Whether the general immobilisation of nuclear weapons would be a good thing for the country would have had to be considered by the jury had it not been for the words 'to the safety and interests of the State'. In this context, the term 'state' denoted 'the organs of government', which in relation to the armed forces meant the Crown:

'So long as the Crown maintains armed forces for the defence of the realm, it cannot be in its interests that any part of them should be immobilised.'[7]

7   At 807.

It was for the Crown to indicate, and not for the jury to determine, what its 'interests' were:

'Suppose that the statute made it an offence to be in a factory for a purpose prejudicial to the interests of the owner, I should not allow the accused to cross-examine the owner to suggest that the factory was unprofitable and that the sooner it closed down the better for the owner, nor to call expert evidence to show that his views were economically sound. A man is entitled to decide for himself how he should govern his life, his business and his other activities, and when the decision is taken, it dictates what his interests are. It is not to the point to say that if the decision had been a better one, his interests would have been different.'. . .[8]

'In a case like the present, it may be presumed that it is contrary to the interests of the Crown to have one of its airfields immobilised just as it may be presumed that it is contrary to the interests of an industrialist to have his factory immobilised . . . But the presumption is not irrebuttable. Men can exaggerate the extent of their interests and so can the Crown. It is the duty of the Courts to be as alert now as they have always been to prevent abuse of the prerogative. But in the present case there is nothing at all to suggest that the Crown's interest in the proper operation of its airfields is not what it may naturally be presumed to be or that it was exaggerating the perils of interference with their effectiveness.'[9]

2. The decision in this case has been severely criticised by D. Thompson.[10] He points out that Parliament had been assured by two Attorneys-General (Sir Gordon Hewart and Sir Hartley Shawcross) and Lord Maugham LC that s. 1 applied only to espionage, and that the expression 'for a purpose prejudicial to the safety or interests of the state' would be for the courts to construe and determine. Indeed the current form of s. 6 of the 1920 Act was adopted in order to limit its operation to cases of espionage, and linking it with s. 1 of the 1911 Act was thought to have that effect. While reference to proceedings in Parliament was not permissible as an aid to construction, 'it was indefensible on the part of the Attorney-General to press arguments upon the courts to give the section a wider meaning'.[11] Thompson also challenges the legal reasoning.[12]

3. Apart from *Chandler v DPP*, prosecutions under s. 1 have generally been confined to cases of espionage. It is certainly open to the Attorney-General to have regard to assurances given to Parliament in exercising the discretion whether to authorise a prosecution. However, the then Attorney-General, Sir Reginald Manningham-Buller said:

'In considering whether or not to prosecute, I must direct my mind to the language and spirit of the Acts and not to what my predecessors said about them many years ago in an entirely different context.'[13]

Persons convicted for contravening or conspiring to contravene s. 1 since the war include Dr Fuchs, the members of the Portland 'spy ring', George Blake,[14] and W. J. C. Vassall.[15] In 1978 proceedings were instituted under ss. 1 and 2 against John Berry, a former corporal in the Intelligence Corps, and two journalists, Duncan Campbell and Crispin Aubrey. B communicated information to the journalists concerning Britain's Signals Intelligence Organization. Mars-Jones J hinted that the

8 At 807.
9 At 809.
10 [1963] PL 201.
11 At 210–211.
12 Cf. J. C. Smith and B. Hogan, *Criminal Law* (6th edn, 1988), pp. 839–841; G. Marshall in R. F. Bunn and W. G. Andrews (eds.), *Politics and Civil Liberties in Europe* (1967), pp. 5–35.
13 657 HC Deb, 5 April 1962, col. 611.
14 Sentenced to 14 years' imprisonment on each of five separate counts the first three to run consecutively: (1961) 45 Cr App Rep 292.
15 See the Report of the Radcliffe Tribunal of Inquiry, Cmnd. 2009, 1963.

use of charges under s. 1 was oppressive in a non-spying case. None of the defendants intended to use the information to assist an enemy. Counsel for the prosecution offered to prove that the defendants' conduct was prejudicial, notwithstanding that the burden of proof as to this matter technically lay on the defendants under s. 1(2). Mars-Jones J was unable to accept this arrangement in view of the clear words of s. 1(2). The Attorney-General decided to drop the s. 1 charges.[16] See further, below. Other matters of significance were (1) the proceedings for contempt of court brought in relation to the disclosure of the identity of one of the witnesses;[17] and (2) the revelation that the potential jurors had been vetted for their potential loyalty or disloyalty.[18]

More recent prosecutions under s. 1 have related to espionage. In 1982, Geoffrey Arthur Prime pleaded guilty to seven counts on an indictment charging offences under s. 1. He had been engaged in signals intelligence work at Government Communications Headquarters (GCHQ) in Cheltenham and had passed a vast quantity of information concerning this work to the Russian Intelligence Service. He was sentenced to a total of 35 years' imprisonment (consecutive terms of 14, 14 and 7 years' imprisonment with other terms concurrent), with an additional three years for indecently assaulting three young girls. The Lord Chief Justice commented that he had done 'incalculable harm to the interests of security of this country . . . and of our friends and allies'. An application for leave to appeal against the sentence was dismissed.[19] Shortly afterwards, a Canadian economist, Professor Hugh Hambleton, admitted passing secret NATO documents to KGB agents and was sentenced to ten years' imprisonment.[1] Lance-Corporal Philip Aldridge pleaded guilty to doing an act preparatory to the commission of an offence under s. 1 in abstracting a highly classified document with the intention of communicating it to the Russian Intelligence Service; he was sentenced to four years' imprisonment.[2] Michael Bettaney, an MI5 counter-espionage officer, was convicted of six charges under s. 1(1) of the 1911 Act and four under s. 7 of the 1920 Act, and was sentenced to a total of 23 years' imprisonment. He had communicated some secret information to the Russians and had collected much more for the purposes of becoming an agent for them. Lord Lane CJ ruled that most of the trial should be held *in camera*, apart from a brief opening statement by the Attorney-General and the delivery of the verdict.[3] Sentences of ten years' imprisonment on two East Germans who settled in England with a view to espionage were upheld in *R v Schulze and Schulze*.[4]

In 1984 and 1985, prosecutions under s. 1 of eight young servicemen from the Cyprus Signals Intelligence base, for passing official secrets in return for 'favours', failed after lengthy trials estimated to have cost £5m, doubts having been cast on the reliability of confessions they had made. In one case the judge had ruled the defendant's statements inadmissible, the rest were acquitted by the jury. An inquiry by David Calcutt QC[5] found that they had all or most of the time been held in custody unlawfully, and interrogated oppressively (albeit without the use of sensory

16 *The Times*, 31 October 1978.
17 See above, pp. 744–746.
18 See H. Harman and J. Griffith, *Justice Deserted* (NCCL, 1979).
19 *The Times*, 11, 12 November 1982; *The Sunday Times*, 14 November 1982; *R v Prime* (1983) 5 Cr App Rep (S) 127; Report of the Security Commission, May 1983 (Cmnd. 8876); Statement by the Prime Minister, 42 HC Deb, 12 May 1983, cols. 431–434, written answer.
1 *The Times*, 30 November and 1, 2, 3, 7, 8 December 1982.
2 *The Times*, 19 January 1983; Report of the Security Commission, March 1984 (Cmnd. 9212, 1984).
3 *The Sunday Times*, 25 March 1984; *The Times*, 9, 11, 17 April 1984.
4 (1986) 8 Cr App Rep (S) 463.
5 Cmnd. 9781, 1986.

deprivation techniques or physical violence). Ex gratia payments were made.[6] The Security Commission criticised the lack of knowledge of officers and senior NCOs about the behaviour of the young servicemen under their command and recommended, *inter alia*, that so far as possible postings of very young servicemen and women to sensitive locations should be avoided.

In 1993, Michael John Smith, who worked for two top defence research companies, was sentenced to 25 years' imprisonment for spying for the Russians, reduced to 20 years on appeal.[7]

4. The failure of the authorities to prosecute individuals who have been identified as spies has attracted criticism. Material in the archive of Vasili Mitrokhin, a KGB officer who defected to the West in 1992, showed that Mrs Melita Norwood had revealed secrets between 1945 and 1949 while working for the British Non-Ferrous Metal Research Association; her security clearance was revoked in 1951 and suspicions about her were confirmed by the Mitrokhin archive. This did not, however, include original documents and was not itself of evidential value. The Intelligence and Security Committee[8] was critical of the 'serious failure' of the Security Service to consult the Law Officers in mid 1993 about a possible prosecution, the Service taking the view that police action was inappropriate given in particular Mrs Norwood's age and the passage of time since her espionage activities; by the time they were consulted, in March 1999, the Law Officers were of the view that it was now too late to institute proceedings. The ISC reaffirmed the point that prosecution decisions were for the Law Officers not the Security Service. The government agreed.[9] Political criticism of the failure to prosecute agents of the Stasi, the East German intelligence organisation has continued.[10]

(C) UNAUTHORISED DISCLOSURES: THE OFFICIAL SECRETS ACT 1989

The Official Secrets Act 1989 replaced, at long last, s. 2 of the Official Secrets Act 1911. Section 2, as amended by the Official Secrets Act 1920, was the product of a highly convoluted piece of draftsmanship. However, its essence was simple and breathtakingly wide in its scope. Section 2(1) penalised the disclosure of official information by D to anyone 'other than a person to whom he is authorised to communicate it, or a person to whom it is in the interest of the State his duty to communicate it'. The categories of protected information in question included any information which was obtained in contravention of the Act or owing to D's position or former position as an office holder under the Crown or as a government contractor. Section 2(2) penalised the receipt of any information by D, knowing or having reasonable ground to believe that the information was communicated to him in contravention of the Act, unless he proved that the communication was contrary to his desire.

The breadth of these provisions was widely regarded as unsatisfactory. The Franks Committee on s. 2 of the Official Secrets Act 1911[11] recommended the repeal of s. 2 and its replacement by narrower and more specific provisions. Various bills, both government and private member's, designed to secure reform, failed. Ultimately, the government, following the White Paper, *Reform of Section 2 of the Official Secrets*

---

6 See A. W. Bradley, [1986] PL 363 and the Report of the Security Commission, October 1986, Cmnd. 9923.

7 *The Times*, 19 November 1993; Report of the Security Commission, July 1995, (n. 2930).

8 *The Mitrokhin Inquiry Report*, Cm. 4764, 2000.

9 *Government Response*, Cm. 4765, 2000.

10 *The Times*, 18 September 2000, referring to decoded Stasi files.

11 Cmnd. 5104, 1972.

Act 1911,[12] secured the passage of the Official Secrets Act 1989. The extent to which this would prove in practice to be a liberalising measure was, however, hotly debated.

NOTES

1. The breadth of s. 2 of the 1911 Act was often emphasised.[13] Sir Lionel Heald, a former Attorney-General, commented that s. 2 'makes it a crime, without any possibility of defence, to report the number of cups of tea consumed per week in a government department, or the details of a new carpet in the Minister's room. . . . The Act contains no limitation as to materiality, substance or public interest'.[14] 'The Act has been variously described as a "blunderbuss", a "mangy old sheep", a "punt gun", and a "fishing net"; and that only includes the more recent and polite terms'.[15] The Franks Committee noted that over 2,000 differently worded charges could be brought under s. 2 and described it as a 'catch-all'[16] and a 'mess'.[17] The only significant safeguard was that a prosecution under the Acts might only be brought by or with the consent of the Attorney-General.[18]

About a third of the prosecutions between 1945 and 1983 concerned the improper disclosure of police information for the purposes of crime or to journalists or private detectives. Among the others, in 1981 a DHSS employee and a private detective were convicted summarily of communicating and retaining personal information about members of the public stored on the DHSS computer and a former detective sergeant, Edward Dodsworth, was fined £750 for disclosing information concerning the 'Yorkshire Ripper' inquiry to a journalist.[19] In 1982, Rhona Ritchie, formerly a second secretary at the British embassy in Tel Aviv, was convicted under s. 2 for wrongfully communicating confidential information to her lover, an official in the Egyptian embassy in Tel Aviv. She was given a nine month suspended prison sentence; he was promoted.[20] In 1983, Robin Gordon-Walker, a government information officer, was fined £500 for failing to take reasonable care of classified Foreign Office papers, which he lost on the way to Heathrow: a report on the papers and extracts from them were published in the magazine *City Limits* and on the same day the Crown obtained an injunction banning further publication. This was a rare example of a prosecution under s. 2(1)(c), which made it an offence to fail to take reasonable care of official documents or information.[1]

In *Loat v Andrews*,[2] the Divisional Court held that a civilian who operated police computers under the supervision of police officers was thereby employed 'under' a person who held office under Her Majesty. Accordingly, he was properly convicted

---

12 Cm. 408, 1988.

13 Summaries of prosecutions under the Acts (including all since 1945) are given in the Franks Report, Appendix II (1911–1971); 955 HC Deb, 1 August 1978, cols. 230–231, written answer (1972–78); and 36 HC Deb, 9 February 1983, cols. 367–368, written answer (1978–83). See also D. Hooper, *Official Secrets* (1987), Appendix I, which summarises many of the cases brought under s. 2 between 1915 and 1987.

14 *The Times*, 20 March 1970, cited in D. G. T. *Williams* (1978), pp. 160–161.

15 J. Michael, *The Politics of Secrecy* (1982), p. 36.

16 Cmnd. 5104, 1972, p. 14.

17 Ibid., p. 37.

18 1911 Act, s. 8.

19 *The Times*, 28 May 1981.

20 See *The Times*, 30 November 1982; Report of the Security Commission, 46 HC Deb, 28 July 1983, cols. 517–523, written answer.

 1 *The Times*, 7 January 1983; cf. *R v Treu* (1979) 49 CCC (2d) 222, Qu CA.

 2 [1986] ICR 679.

under s. 2 of the 1911 Act and s. 7 of the 1920 Act for passing information from the computer about the location of recent burglaries to the representative of a burglar alarm company.

2. In some cases prosecutions under s. 2 either failed spectacularly or attracted criticism even though successful. In *R v Aitken*[2a] a confidential assessment of the situation in Nigeria during the Biafran conflict, written by the Defence Adviser at the British High Commission in Lagos, was passed through various hands to Jonathan Aitken, a journalist (subsequently an MP and cabinet Minister). Aitken passed copies to the *Sunday Telegraph*, which gave the report wide coverage. The report contained information at variance with statements made by the government to Parliament and included various criticisms of the Nigerian government. Aitken, Brian Roberts (the editor of the *Sunday Telegraph*) and others were prosecuted for various offences under s. 2, but acquitted by the jury. The trial judge, Caulfield J, ruled that mens rea was a necessary requirement and left to the jury Aitken's defence that it was his duty in the interest of the State to communicate the report to the *Sunday Telegraph*. His Lordship's suggestion that the government consider whether s. 2 'should be pensioned off' and replaced by a provision of greater clarity was followed by the appointment of the Franks Committee.

The defendants in *R v Berry*[3] were John Berry, a former corporal in the Intelligence Corps, Duncan Campbell, a journalist with the *New Statesman*, and Crispin Aubrey, a journalist with *Time Out*. B communicated information to the journalists concerning Britain's signals intelligence (SIGINT) organisation. They were convicted under s. 2. The journalists were given conditional discharges, and B a six-month suspended prison sentence. The outcome, given that charges were originally brought under s. 1[4] was less than a triumph for the prosecution. As to mens rea, Mars-Jones J rejected B's argument that he was entitled to be acquitted if he honestly believed that in the interests of the State it was his duty to communicate the information to C. What was in the interests of the State was a wholly inappropriate question for a jury. He followed *R v Fell*[5] where the Court of Criminal Appeal stated that the offence under s. 2(1) 'is absolute and is committed whatever the document contains, whatever the nature of the disclosure and whether or not the disclosure is prejudicial to the state'. Contra, *R v Aitken*, above.

Also controversial was the prosecution of Sarah Tisdall, a clerk in the Foreign Secretary's private office, who leaked copies of two documents to the *Guardian*. One related to the delivery of cruise missiles to the RAF base at Greenham Common, naming the date when the first would arrive, and the other concerned the security arrangements at the base connected with the deliveries. Both were classified SECRET. The text of the first was printed in the *Guardian*; the other was destroyed. The Court of Appeal, on the application of the Secretary of State for Defence, ordered the *Guardian* to return the photocopy of the first document: *Secretary of State for Defence v Guardian Newspapers Ltd*.[6] From markings on the photocopy the police were able to narrow down the source to one small group of civil servants, including Miss Tisdall, and she confessed. She subsequently explained that she had learned from the memorandum that the Secretary of State proposed to delay the announcement of the arrival of the cruise missiles until after they had arrived, to make the announcement at the end of question time when there would be no time for him to answer questions, and to leave the House immediately. She regarded this as objectionable 'political subterfuge'. She pleaded guilty to a charge under s. 2 and was sentenced to six

---

2a (1971).
3   The *ABC* case: A. Nicol, [1979] Crim LR 284 and C. Aubrey, *Who's Watching You?* (1981).
4   See above, pp. 825–826.
5   [1963] Crim LR 207.
6   [1984] Ch 156 (see above, p. 797).

months' imprisonment. The judge stated that she had known that she was committing a criminal offence and a breach of trust. It was not possible to decide that such an action would do no harm. If secret documents were leaked for publication, that would weaken the confidence of this country's allies in the trustworthiness of the government. Unless other arrangements could be made in time, people fundamentally opposed to the missiles would have obstructed the arrival, and this had involved the danger of violent confrontation.

> '[U]nfortunately in these days it is necessary to make perfectly clear by example that any person in contact with material classified as secret, who presumes to give himself permission to decide to publish, will not escape from a custodial sentence, however honestly he thought it would do no harm.'[7]

When questioned in the House of Commons the Prime Minister said that no government could carry on its business unless it could trust civil servants to keep classified documents to themselves.[8] The Attorney-General defended his decision to prosecute and indicated that it was based on the same general guidelines on the criteria for prosecution which he had issued in March 1983 and which were applicable to all criminal cases.[9] He used s. 2 'sparingly and only when absolutely necessary'.[10]

Some critics argued that the prosecution should not have been brought, claiming that the disclosure had caused much political embarrassment rather than constituting a serious threat to national security; a larger number thought that the sentence was excessive. Some expressed surprise that the *Guardian* had not been prosecuted.

Among comments about the sentence, *The Times*[11] stated that 'a month's imprisonment, with strict warning that heavier sentences could be expected by anyone else who acted as she had done, . . . would almost certainly have been sufficient to meet . . . [the judge's] own purpose of setting an example'. Lord Hunt, a former member of the Parole Board, argued that, in his experience, exemplary sentences were 'unlikely to have any generally deterrent effect'.[12] Sir Douglas Wass, former Joint Head of the Home Civil Service, commented: 'I would have sacked her summarily. But sending her to jug for six months is absurd'.[13] The Court of Appeal (Criminal Division) refused Miss Tisdall's application for leave to appeal against the sentence.[14]

3. The last straw for the government was the acquittal of Clive Ponting: *R v Ponting*.[15] Ponting was an Assistant Secretary at the Ministry of Defence. In the belief that the government was deliberately misleading Parliament, the Select Committee on Foreign Affairs and the public on the circumstances of the sinking of the Argentinian warship, the *General Belgrano*, during the Falklands campaign, he sent two documents to Tam Dalyell MP, a known critic of the government on the *Belgrano* sinking. Ponting

---

7 *Guardian*, 24 March 1984; *The Times*, 26 and 27 March 1984.
8 57 HC Deb, 27 March 1984, col. 138.
9 See (1983) 127 Sol Jo 134.
10 58 HC Deb, 9 April 1984, cols. 13–15.
11 26 March 1984.
12 *The Times*, 29 March 1984.
13 *The Times*, 11 May 1984.
14 *The Times*, 10 April 1984. See *Hooper*, Chap. 11 and R. Pyper, (1985) 57 PQ 72.
15 [1985] Crim LR 318. See generally, C. Ponting, *The Right to Know* (1985) and (1987) 14 JLS 366; R. Norton-Taylor, *The Ponting Affair* (1985); *Hooper*, Chap. 12; R. Thomas, 'The British Official Secrets Act 1911–1939 and the Ponting Case' [1986] Crim LR 491 and pp. 95–122 of R. Chapman and M. Hunt (eds.), *Open Government* (1987); G. Drewry, [1985] PL 203; N. MacCormick in P. Wallington and R. Merkin (eds.), *Essays in Memory of F. H. Lawson* (1986); on parliamentary privilege in the context of 'leaks' to Parliament, A. I. L. Campbell, [1985] PL 212; and Y. Cripps, 'The Consequences of disclosure in the public interest' in C. Forsyth and I. Hare (eds.) *The Golden Metwand and the Crooked Cord* (2001).

was prosecuted under s. 2(1) of the 1911 Act. His defence was that Dalyell was a person to whom it was his duty in the interest of the state to pass the information. It was accepted that the leak itself had not damaged national security. McCowan J directed the jury that mens rea was not required under s. 2(1) and that the interests of the state were synonymous with the interests of the government of the day (following the approach of Lord Reid in *Chandler v DPP*,[16] on the interpretation of 'interests of the state' under s. 1). The jury acquitted, notwithstanding the fact that the judge's ruling on the law had favoured the prosecution. It has been suggested that the acquittal 'no doubt related to a jury refusing to be browbeaten by a judge, prosecution handling the case less adroitly than it should, a feeling that the Government was actively involved in manipulating an outcome, and the Attorney-General appearing to prejudge guilt in a radio broadcast. And Ponting's lawyers mounted a very successful campaign outside the courtroom'.[17]

Following Ponting's acquittal, it was noteworthy that no prosecution under the Official Secrets Acts was brought in respect of revelations by Cathy Massiter, formerly an officer in the Security Service, and an anonymous retired MI5 clerk, in a Channel 4 programme, *MI5's Official Secrets*, prepared by the 20/20 Vision production company. Massiter claimed that MI5 tapped telephones of trade unionists involved in strike action, and, in one case had burgled the house of Ken Gill, general secretary of TASS, in order to plant a bugging device; persistently disregarded the rules as to telephone tapping;[18] had placed leading CND members under surveillance; and had maintained files on NCCL officers such as Patricia Hewitt, its general secretary, and Harriet Harman, its legal officer. The terms of reference of MI5 provided that its task was the defence of the realm from espionage, sabotage and subversion; the peaceful activities of CND and the NCCL did not fall within this definition. The IBA initially banned the programme, pending a decision as to whether Massiter and the producers would be prosecuted. It was, however, screened in the House of Commons and elsewhere. On 5 March 1985, Sir Michael Havers announced his decision that there would be no prosecution, and the programme was shown on 8 March. Lord Bridge, following an inquiry begun on 28 February and concluded on 6 March, reported that all authorised taps had in fact been properly authorised. Given the large number of taps (6,129) that apparently had to have been checked, and the point that the allegations were that there had been *un*authorised taps, Lord Bridge's report was widely criticised. (In fact all that Lord Bridge had done was to look at the files of the individuals (about a dozen) named by Massiter[19]).

The prosecutions of Sarah Tisdall and Clive Ponting can also be contrasted with the lack of any prosecution of two cabinet Ministers, Cecil Parkinson and Leon Brittan. Parkinson was alleged to have revealed information to his lover, Sarah Keays, concerning the Falklands campaign (Parkinson being then a member of the War Cabinet).[20] Brittan, as Secretary of State for Trade and Industry, authorised the selective leaking of a confidential letter written by the Solicitor-General to Michael Heseltine, the Secretary of State for Defence, in connection with the proposed sale of Westland Helicopters, in order to discredit Heseltine. Heseltine was in favour of a bid by a European consortium, and Brittan a bid by Sikorski/Fiat. The Prime Minister maintained subsequently that she was not aware of the proposed leak (her Press Secretary, Bernard Ingham, was); Brittan was, however, under the impression that the leak had her approval. On one view, the disclosure was not in breach of s. 2 as it

16 Above, p. 821.
17 P. Birkinshaw, *Freedom of Information* (1988), p. 81.
18 See below, p. 1009.
19 See Lustgarten and Leigh, op. cit., p. 489.
20 See *Hooper*, Chap. 15.

was authorised by a cabinet Minister; the better view is, however, that such authorisation could only properly have been given by the Prime Minister. The Westland affair led to the resignation of both Ministers.[1]

4. The Official Secrets Act 1989[2] was based on the government's White Paper, *Reform of Section 2 of the Official Secrets Act 1911*.[3]

The Act narrows the scope of protection of official information by the criminal law to categories: (1) security and intelligence; (2) defence; (3) international relations; (4) information obtained in confidence from other states or international organisations; (5) information disclosure of which is likely to result in the commission of an offence or to impede the prevention or detection of offences; and (6) information obtained by special investigations authorised by warrant.[4] The categories reflect the post-Franks consensus that Cabinet documents and economic information should not automatically be protected. The unauthorised disclosure of information in these categories by a Crown servant or government contractor is an offence. In categories (2) to (5), the disclosure must be 'damaging' in the ways specified in the sections. The tests for 'damage' are more precise but less strict than those envisaged by Franks, and there is no system of ministerial certification.[5] In category (1), the unauthorised disclosure or purported disclosure by a member of the security and intelligence services, and others notified that they are subject to this provision, of information obtained by virtue of their work, is an offence without any proof of damage; damage must, however, be proved where a disclosure of information relating to security and intelligence is otherwise made by a Crown servant or government contractor. Similarly, there is no requirement to prove damage in respect of category (6). It is also an offence in certain circumstances for any person to make, without authority, (1) a damaging disclosure of protected information that has come into his possession following an unauthorised disclosure by a current (not former) Crown servant or government contractor, or the breach of a requirement of confidence imposed by a Crown servant or government contractor, or (2) a disclosure of information acquired as a result of a breach of s. 1 of the 1911 Act.[6] It is an offence for a person to make, without authority, a damaging disclosure of information in categories (1) to (3) communicated in confidence by the UK to another state or an international organisation and disclosed without the authority of that state or organisation.[7] There are also offences relating to the retaining or failure to take care of protected documents and articles and disclosing information which facilitates unauthorised access to protected material.[8] Mere receipt of information is no longer an offence.

It is generally a defence for the accused to prove that he did not know that the information fell into the protected category in question, or that disclosure would be damaging in the relevant sense.[9] Under s. 5, it is for the prosecution to prove that the accused knew or had reasonable cause to believe that the information was protected

1   See M. Linklater and D. Leigh, *Not with Honour: The Inside Story of the Westland Scandal* (1986); *Hooper*, Chap. 15; R. Austin, (1986) 39 CLP 269.
2   See generally on the 1989 Act, J. A. G. Griffith, (1989) 16 JLS 273; S. Palmer, [1990] PL 243; Annotations by J. Mayhew and P. O'Higgins in *Current Law Statutes Annotated 1989*; I. N. Stevens, (1989) Denning LJ 169; P. Birkinshaw, *Reforming the Secret State* (1990), pp. 15–29. On the White Paper, see S. Palmer, [1988] PL 523.
3   Cm. 408, 1988.
4   1989 Act, ss. 1–4.
5   Except, in effect, under s. 1(4)(b): see P. Birkinshaw, *Reforming the Secret State* (1990), pp. 11, 20.
6   1989 Act, s. 5.
7   1989 Act, s. 6.
8   1989 Act, s. 8.
9   1989 Act, ss. 1(5), 2(3), 3(4), 4(4), (5).

against disclosure and that disclosure would be damaging.[10] There is no defence that disclosure was in the public interest or (except in the limited situation covered in s. 6(3)) that the information had previously been published. As to the first, the government argued that such a defence would make the law less clear and was in any event inappropriate given that the criminal law would be confined to 'information which demonstrably requires its protection in the public interest'; as to the second, prior publication should at most be regarded as a factor in determining whether a disclosure would be damaging in a relevant way.[11]

The narrowing of the scope of the criminal law in the area can only be welcomed. There are, however, a number of criticisms that were forcefully articulated during the passage of the Bill but which left the government unmoved. These include:

(1) the blanket prohibition of disclosure of information by members of the security and intelligence services irrespective of damage;
(2) the blanket prohibition of disclosure of information derived from e.g. authorised telephone tapping, also irrespective of damage;
(3) the absence of any public interest defence and any general defence of prior publication;
(4) the imposition of the burden of proof to establish certain defences on the accused, contrary to normal principle.

As to (1), the absolute prohibition would extend to prevent, for example, the exposure of unlawful behaviour and thus is to be contrasted with the law of confidence.[12] Amendments proposed to prevent the Secretary of State from unreasonably withholding consent to the disclosure of information (e.g. in memoirs) by a former member of the security and intelligence services, or to establish a Publications Review Board with power to authorise disclosure, were rejected. A mechanism for considering complaints was, however, established by the Security Service Act 1989,[13] although this fell short of providing independent scrutiny. The absence of a public interest defence is designed to discourage 'whistleblowers'. Again, a mechanism has been created whereby members and former members of the security and intelligence services may approach a 'staff counsellor' with any grievance about their work. The counsellor has unrestricted access to the Prime Minister, and access to all documents, to all levels of management and the Cabinet Secretary.[14] Public disclosure is not, however, to be available in the last resort where other avenues have been exhausted.

5. Prosecutions under the 1989 Act have been relatively rare. In 1991, Arthur Henry Price and Joseph Terrence Wilson pleaded guilty to making a damaging disclosure to a foreign power. W, a security guard at the VSEL shipyard in Barrow-in-Furness, stole an acoustic tile used on submarines from the yard. W and F (a mini-cab driver) subsequently offered to sell it to a man (Nick) believed to be a Russian for £3m. The man turned out to be a British security agent. W's counsel said that the exercise had been conceived and executed as a joke. 'My indications are that Nick's Russian accent was wholly unconvincing. He kept saying "Ja" as in German, and he couldn't pronounce "Moscow".' The security services had got in touch with W and P via an advert in the local press. W had subsequently seen police officers enter the phone booths they had just left and start dusting for fingerprints. Nevertheless, the matter was not treated as a joke by Brooke J, who sentenced each of them to 15 months'

---

10 s. 5(2), (3); cf. similar provisions in s. 6(2).
11 White Paper, paras. 58–64.
12 Below, pp. 848–863.
13 Below, p. 885.
14 See 121 HC Deb, cols. 508 (2 November 1987) and 796 (3 November 1987).

imprisonment. Charges of conspiracy to contravene the 1911 Act were changed to charges under the 1989 Act, with the authority of the Attorney-General.[15]

In 1998, Chief Petty Officer Steven Hayden was sent to prison for 12 months for an offence against s. 1(3) of the 1989 Act for leaking to the *Sun* (for £10,000) a report about an alleged Iraqi anthrax threat. Also in 1998, MoD police searched the home of journalist Tony Geraghty in relation to the publication of *The Irish War*, which gave details of army computer surveillance in Northern Ireland. He was charged under s. 5 of the 1989 Act but proceedings were subsequently dropped.[16] Nigel Wylde, a retired colonel who was formerly a bomb disposal officer in Northern Ireland, was charged with disclosing classified documents to Geraghty and was due to stand trial in November 2000, after the implementation of the Human Rights Act 2000. This too was dropped after the prosecution read a report from Duncan Campbell, due to be an expert witness for the defence, explaining why there was nothing in the book that the PIRA did not know or had not worked out for itself 20 years earlier.

6. *Tomlinson.*[17] Further difficulties for the intelligence services have been caused by disaffected former officers. Richard Tomlinson was dismissed by SIS in 1995 having not satisfactorily completed a probationary period. Like all intelligence officers he had signed a confidentiality undertaking. He commenced proceedings for unfair dismissal. SIS complained that he then breached the Official Secrets Act by retaining material and preparing material for a book on SIS, and disclosing information to *The Sunday Times*. In September 1996 the High Court granted final injunctions restraining him from further disclosing information obtained by him in the course of his employment with SIS, apart from his lawyers for the purpose of legal proceedings. Further court orders led to recovery of a copy of the book and computer disks disclosing contacts with a New York literary agent. The unfair dismissal proceedings were settled. T obtained some financial benefits (subsequently said to be a loan and a job outside SIS) undertook to deliver to SIS any material relating to his work in and the activities of SIS, assigned copyright to the Crown, acknowledged his obligations under the Official Secrets Act and undertook to observe confidentiality and contractual undertakings. However, in 1997, while in Australia he disclosed confidential information to publishers. This led to a conviction under the 1989 Act on 18 December 1997 for which he was sentenced to 12 months' imprisonment. After his release in May 1998 he went to France. He had continued to discuss publication of a book with publishers. On 2 August 1998 *The Sunday Times* published an article attributing to T statements that he had plans to reveal details of a MI6 plot to murder Col. Gaddafi and details of MI6 operations. T flew to New Zealand, where the Attorney General obtained an interim injunction in similar terms to the High Court orders. T left New Zealand without then defending the proceedings. Further disclosures followed in magazines in New Zealand and England. He also revealed the names of MI6 officers on his website in Switzerland. The Attorney-General obtained an interim injunction in Geneva to close it down but the information subsequently appeared on a US website. The New Zealand Court of Appeal held that T's application to extend time to defend the injunction proceedings be stayed until such time as he returned to New Zealand and submitted to the jurisdiction of the

15 See the *North-Western Evening Mail*, 8–11 July 1991.
16 HC Deb, 23 May 2000, col. 462w.
17 *A-G for England and Wales v Tomlinson* [1999] 3 NZLR 722; *Guardian Unlimited*, 2 November 2000. See A. Reid and N. Ryder, (2000) I & CTL 61.

court and purged his contempt. In May 1999, John Wadham, his solicitor, stated that since being:

> 'banned from going to the industrial tribunal ... he feels he has been harassed by the authorities. He has had injunctions against him in every country he has visited, been ejected from Australia, the US and France, and has not been able to obtain a visa to settle anywhere to build a new life.'[18]

Legal remedies can thus be used across the world against the disaffected, but publication on the internet is obviously difficult to control. In January 2001, T's book *The Big Breach* was published in Russia. The Court of Appeal ruled that once the book was in the public domain, extracts could be published in the press.[19] Copies of the book were imported into the UK.[1] The FCO did not seek an injunction to restrain publication of the book but action was taken to freeze profits from the memoirs.[2]

7. *Shayler.* Even more publicity has attended the activities of David Shayler.[3] Shayler joined MI5 in 1991. At different times he worked in branches that dealt with subversion (since disbanded), Irish terrorism and international terrorism. He became disillusioned with the Service, taking the view that it was in many respects overly bureaucratic, incompetent and poorly managed. He resigned in 1997, having already decided to take steps to publish his criticisms but without endangering MI5 operations. He made contact with the *Mail on Sunday*, which on Sunday, 24 August 1997 published a story based on information provided by him. It included revelations that MI5 had placed a phone tap on Peter Mandelson, had maintained files on Mandelson and Jack Straw (now Home Secretary), had kept a *Guardian* journalist, Victoria Brittain, under surveillance for over a year and allegations of further MI5 'blunders'. He left for Amsterdam shortly before the story appeared. He was paid a total of £39,000. The legal moves that followed included the launch of a police investigation into breaches of the Official Secrets Act 1989, the obtaining of production orders under s. 93H of the Criminal Justice Act 1988 against the *Mail on Sunday*, the BBC and three banks requiring them to supply details of payments made to Shayler, and the grant by Keene J of a temporary injunction against the *Mail on Sunday*. The injunction restrained the *Mail on Sunday* from publishing further information Shayler had gained as a result of his employment with MI5 and Shayler himself from disclosing such information to anyone. On 4 September the injunction was continued, by consent, by Hooper J. Provision was made, however, for particular stories to be published if no objection was raised by the Home Secretary.[4] Shayler's flat was searched under a warrant granted under s. 9(1) of the Official Secrets Act 1911. Shayler had transferred the money received to friends. These were arrested on money-laundering charges, which were subsequently dropped.

In November 1997, a further story was published, following an indication by the Home Secretary that the government would not seek to restrain publication. This concerned allegations that MI5 had ignored warnings of a bomb at the Israeli Embassy in 1994. In 1998, steps were taken by the *Mail on Sunday* to hand over to the Treasury Solicitor 28 MI5 documents that had been passed to them by Shayler. These had

---

18 *Guardian Unlimited Archive*, 13 May 1999.
19 *A-G v Times Newspapers* [2001] EWCA Civ 97.
1 *Guardian Unlimited Special Report*, 30 January 2001.
2 *Guardian Unlimited Special Report*, 3 February 2001.
3 The following summary is based on M. Hollingsworth and N. Fielding, *Defending the Realm: MI5 and the Shayler Affair* (1999).
4 The writ against the *Mail on Sunday* claiming damages for breach of confidence and demanding the return of documents was dropped in December 2000: *Guardian Unlimited Special Report*, 2 December 2000 (R. Norton-Taylor).

been recognised as sensitive and stored securely in accordance with the terms of the 4 September injunction. A further development in 1998 was the publication by the BBC *Panorama* programme and the *Guardian* (following appearance of the story in the *New York Times*) of Shayler's allegations of MI6 involvement in a plot by dissidents to kill the Libyan leader, Colonel Gaddafi. (The Foreign Office denied that there was an official plot to kill Gaddafi.) Shayler subsequently sent a dossier concerning the allegations to the Home Secretary. In August, a warrant was issued for the arrest of Shayler for two offences under s. 1(1)(a) of the 1989 Act. He was now in France. The UK sought his extradition and he was arrested and held in custody, but the French court ultimately ruled that the case fell within the 'political offence' exception to extradition arrangements.

In August 2000, Shayler returned to the UK following negotiations between his lawyers and the government. On 21 August he was charged with two s. 1 offences of disclosing information in the *Mail on Sunday* and passing documents to newspapers, which were obtained by virtue of being a member of the Security Service. A third charge, of passing on material obtained through telephone tapping contrary to s. 4 of the 1989 Act, was added when, on 21 September, he was committed for trial. No charges have been laid in respect of the Gaddafi allegation. The Metropolitan Police Special Branch has conducted an investigation into the alleged MI6 involvement in the Gaddafi plot and sent a report to the CPS.[5]

Another related matter was the arrest during a lecture of Julie Ann Davies, a mature engineering student at Kingston University, who had been an active campaigner in support of Shayler. She was questioned about an MI6 report concerning the Gaddafi plot that appeared on the Internet. Charges were dropped on 21 August 2000, by which time she had dropped out of her course.

The book by Hollingsworth and Fielding, which repeats Shayler's revelations, was published with some of the deletions suggested by the Secretary to the Defence, Press and Broadcasting Committee and following an assurance by the Attorney-General that an injunction would not be sought. *Punch* magazine and its editor, James Steen, were found guilty of contempt of court in publishing an article by Shayler, but this was set aside on appeal.[6] Production orders under PACE, obtained by the police against the *Guardian*, following publication of a letter by Shayler confirming his account of the alleged Gaddafi plot, and against the *Observer*, following an article by Martin Bright which stated that Shayler had revealed to them the name of two serving intelligence officers involved in the plot, were quashed by the Divisional Court on the ground that the access conditions were not fulfilled.[7]

The prosecution of Shayler will be a test case on the compatibility of the 1989 Act with the Human Rights Act 1998. The government position is that Shayler's disclosures have been damaging to national security. In the application for a temporary injunction, the government alleged damage in four areas:

'(a) enabling targets of investigations to become aware of the particular surveillance used against them and therefore avoid them; (b) enabling targets to identify sources from which information has come into the possession of the Security Service, thereby jeopardising the usefulness of such sources; (c) jeopardising the confidence of the Service of those who assist it in operational matters; (d) a similar loss of confidence on the part of potential future informers.'[8]

---

5   *Guardian Unlimited Special Report*, 1 September 2000.
6   See above, p. 771.
7   *R v Central Criminal Court, ex p Rushbridger, Alton and Bright* [2001] 2 All ER 244. See above, pp. 236–237.
8   M. Hollingsworth and N. Fielding, op. cit., pp. 176–177.

Charges under s. 1(1)(a) do not require the prosecution to prove that a disclosure was damaging. This makes it vulnerable to attack under the ECHR and the Human Rights Act 1998. Following rulings by Moses J at a preparatory case management hearing, an appeal was taken to the Court of Appeal.[9] The Court ruled: (1) (reversing Moses J) that an extended defence of duress or necessity of circumstances was available under ss. 1(1) and 4(1), this providing a defence in respect of proportionate steps taken in response to imminent peril of death or serious injury to the defendant or those for whom he reasonably regards himself as being responsible; but (2) that this defence was not available on the facts; (3) that the restriction on freedom of expression under ss. 1(1) and 4 was proportionate and justified given the ability of individuals to obtain authorisation for disclosure and to make their voice heard 'by those of undoubted integrity and independence'. A refusal of authorisation would be challengeable on judicial review. The House of Lords gave permission to appeal.

There was speculation that the 1989 Act would be reformed should the Labour government be returned in the 2001 general election.[10] The Intelligence and Security Committee has volunteered to examine the Acts and make changes to ensure that the Acts protect secret information, having been concerned over a number of years that they are not capable of protecting the secrets they are designed to protect.[11]

8. A number of persons and bodies are prescribed under s. 12(1)(f) and (g) of the 1989 Act by the Official Secrets Act 1989 (Prescription) Order 1990.[12] These include (under s. 12(1)(f)) employees and Board members of British Nuclear Fuels plc and Urenco Ltd., and members, officers and employees of the UK Atomic Energy Authority and (under s. 12(1)(g)), the Comptroller and Auditor General and the staff of the National Audit Office, their Northern Ireland equivalents, officers of the Parliamentary Commissioner for Administration, the Health Service Commissioner and the Northern Ireland PCA not otherwise Crown servants, and a private Secretary to the sovereign.

9. *Civil servants and Ministers.* Following the Ponting affair,[13] the Head of the Home Civil Service, Sir Robert Armstrong, issued Notes for Guidance on *The Duties and Responsibilities of Civil Servants in Relation to Ministers.*[14] The Armstrong Memorandum stated, *inter alia*, that the duty of the individual civil servant was first and foremost to the Minister at the head of his department and that there was an obligation to keep confidences. However, a civil servant should not be required to do anything unlawful. Issues of conscience should be raised within the department with, from 1987, the possibility of an appeal to the head of the Civil Service.[15] These arrangements were replaced by the Civil Service Code[16] with effect from 1 January 1996. The Code was revised on 13 May 1999 to take account of devolution.

---

9 (2001) Times, 10 October.

10 *Guardian Unlimited Special Report*, 31 December 2000 (M. Bright).

11 *Interim Report 2000–01* (Cm. 5126, 2001), p. 10.

12 S.I. 1990 No. 200, as amended by S.I. 1993 No. 847 and the Intelligence Services Act 1994, Sch. 4, para. 5.

13 Above, p. 830.

14 Reproduced at 74 HC Deb, 26 February 1985, cols. 128–130, written answer.

15 123 HC Deb, 2 December 1987, cols. 572–575, written answer; Treasury and Civil Service Committee, 7th Report, *Civil Servants and Ministers: Duties and Responsibilities*, 1985–86 HC92 I, II; G. Drewry, [1986] PL 514.

16 Based on a proposal from the Treasury and Civil Service Committee, 5th Report, 1994–95 HC 27-I. For further discussion, see O. McDonald, *The Future of Whitehall* (1992), Chap. 5 (on 'Civil Service Ethics'); R. A. Chapman (ed.), *Ethics in Public Service* (1993); N. Lewis and D. Longley, 'Ethics and the Public Service' [1994] PL 596. For further discussion, see O. McDonald, *The Future of Whitehall* (1992), Chap. 5 (on 'Civil Service Ethics'); R. A. Chapman (ed.), *Ethics in Public Service* (1993); N. Lewis and D. Longley, 'Ethics and the Public Service' [1994] PL 596.

The Civil Service Code

The Civil Service Code sets out the constitutional framework within which all civil servants work and the values they are expected to uphold…

1. The constitutional and practical role of the Civil Service is, with integrity, honesty, impartiality and objectivity, to assist the duly constituted Government of the United Kingdom, the Scottish Executive or the National Assembly for Wales[17] constituted in accordance with the Scotland and Government of Wales Acts 1998, whatever their political complexion, in formulating their policies, carrying out decisions and in administering public services for which they are responsible.

2. Civil servants are servants of the Crown. Constitutionally, all the Administrations form part of the Crown and, subject to the provisions of this Code, civil servants owe their loyalty to the Administrations[18] in which they serve.

3. This Code should be seen in the context of the duties and responsibilities set out for UK Ministers in the Ministerial Code, or in equivalent documents drawn up for Ministers of the Scottish Executive or for the National Assembly for Wales, which include:

    – accountability to Parliament[19] or, for Assembly Secretaries, to the National Assembly;

    – the duty to give Parliament or the Assembly and the public as full information as possible about their policies, decisions and actions, and not to deceive or knowingly mislead them;

    – the duty not to use public resources for party political purposes, to uphold the political impartiality of the Civil Service, and not to ask civil servants to act in any way which would conflict with the Civil Service Code;

    – the duty to give fair consideration and due weight to informed and impartial advice from civil servants, as well as to other considerations and advice, in reaching decisions; and

    – the duty to comply with the law, including international law and treaty obligations, and to uphold the administration of justice;

    together with the duty to familiarise themselves with the contents of this Code.

4. Civil servants should serve their Administration in accordance with the principles set out in this Code and recognising:

    – the accountability of civil servants to the Minister[20] or, as the case may be, to the Assembly Secretaries and the National Assembly as a body or to the office holder in charge of their department;

    – the duty of all public officers to discharge public functions reasonably and according to the law;

    – the duty to comply with the law, including international law and treaty obligations, and to uphold the administration of justice; and

    – ethical standards governing particular professions.

5. Civil servants should conduct themselves with integrity, impartiality and honesty. They should give honest and impartial advice to the Minister or, as the case may be, to the Assembly Secretaries and the National Assembly as a body or to the office holder in charge of their department, without fear or favour, and make all information relevant to a decision available to them. They should not deceive or knowingly mislead Ministers, Parliament, the National Assembly or the public.

---

17 In the rest of this Code, we use the term 'Administration' to mean Her Majesty's Government of the United Kingdom, the Scottish Executive or the National Assembly for Wales as appropriate.

18 In the rest of this Code, we use the term 'Administration' to mean Her Majesty's Government of the United Kingdom, the Scottish Executive or the National Assembly for Wales as appropriate.

19 In the rest of this Code, the term Parliament should be read, as appropriate, to include the Parliament of the United Kingdom and the Scottish Parliament.

20 In the rest of this Code, Ministers encompasses members of Her Majesty's Government or of the Scottish Executive.

6. Civil servants should endeavour to deal with the affairs of the public sympathetically, efficiently, promptly and without bias or maladministration.
7. Civil servants should endeavour to ensure the proper, effective and efficient use of public money.
8. Civil servants should not misuse their official position or information acquired in the course of their official duties to further their private interests or those of others. They should not receive benefits of any kind from a third party which might reasonably be seen to compromise their personal judgement or integrity.
9. Civil servants should conduct themselves in such a way as to deserve and retain the confidence of Ministers or Assembly Secretaries and the National Assembly as a body, and to be able to establish the same relationship with those whom they may be required to serve in some future Administration. They should comply with restrictions on their political activities. The conduct of civil servants should be such that Ministers, Assembly Secretaries and the National Assembly as a body, and potential future holders of these positions can be sure that confidence can be freely given, and that the Civil Service will conscientiously fulfil its duties and obligations to, and impartially assist, advice and carry out the lawful policies of the duly constituted Administrations.
10. Civil servants should not without authority disclose official information which has been communicated in confidence within the Administration, or received in confidence from others. Nothing in the Code should be taken as overriding existing statutory or common law obligations to keep confidential, or to disclose, certain information. They should not seek to frustrate or influence the policies, decisions or actions of Ministers, Assembly Secretaries or the disclosure outside the Administration of any information to which they have had access as civil servants.
11. Where a civil servant believes he or she is being required to act in a way which:
    –   is illegal, improper, or unethical;
    –   is in breach of constitutional convention or a professional code;
    –   may involve possible maladministration; or
    –   is otherwise inconsistent with this Code;
    he or she should report the matter in accordance with procedures laid down in the appropriate guidance or rules of conduct for their department or Administration. A civil servant should also report to the appropriate authorities evidence of criminal or unlawful activity by others and may also report in accordance with the relevant procedures if he or she becomes aware of other breaches of this Code or is required to act in a way which, for him or her, raises a fundamental issue of conscience.
12. Where a civil servant has reported a matter covered in paragraph 11 in accordance with the relevant procedures and believes that the response does not represent a reasonable response to the grounds of his or her concern, he or she may report the matter in writing to the Civil Service Commissioners, Horse Guards Road, London SW1P 3AL. Telephone: 0171-270 5066.
13. Civil servants should not seek to frustrate the policies, decisions or actions of the Administrations by declining to take, or abstaining from, action which flows from decisions by Ministers, Assembly Secretaries or the National Assembly as a body. Where a matter cannot be resolved by the procedures set out in paragraphs 11 and 12 above, on a basis which the civil servant concerned is able to accept, he or she should either carry out his or her instructions, or resign from the Civil Service. Civil servants should continue to observe their duties of confidentiality after they have left Crown employment.

Civil Service Commissioners require internal procedures to be exhausted first. A civil servant can write directly to them or through the person within the department or agency who considered the matter internally; the latter may add comments but cannot amend the appeal itself. The Commissioners, directed by their staff, will examine the papers, may inspect other papers and files and may interview the civil servant in question and other officials. If the Commissioners support the appeal they make recommendations to the department or agency; otherwise the civil servant 'should abide by [their] department's or agency's instructions on the matter.'[21] The Commissioners reports annually to Parliament in general terms on the outcome of appeals.[1]

Civil servants, other than employees of the Security Service, SIS and GCHQ,[2] are also now protected by the Public Interest Disclosure Act 1998[3] which provides that dismissals as a result of 'protected disclosures' are unfair and confers a right not to suffer detriment on the ground of such a disclosure. Civil Servants are advised to use the procedure under the Civil Service Code to make protected disclosures.[4] An important limitation, however, is that 'a disclosure of information is not a qualifying disclosure if the person making the disclosure commits an offence by making it'.[5] This would include a breach of the Official Secrets Acts.

10. *Other means of maintaining security.* The Franks Committee proposals were shaped by their view that s. 2 was properly described as 'a long stop or a safety net. ... Section 2 is not the main protection: its function is to provide an extra margin of protection, in case other measures should fail'.[6] The 'other measures' are discussed in Chap. 5 of the Committee's report. They point out that a civil servant who is regarded as unreliable, or who tends to overstep the mark and talk too freely, may fail to obtain promotion or may be given less important and attractive jobs. Breach of the formal discipline code[7] may lead to penalties ranging from reprimand to dismissal. Employment legislation has, however, applied subject to limitations and restrictions where national security is concerned. Action taken for the purpose of safeguarding national security may not form the basis of a complaint for unfair dismissal[8] or detriment in respect of trade union membership[9] by virtue of s. 10(1) of the Employment Tribunals Act 1996.[10]

2 1 OCSC, *Appeal to the Civil Service Commissioners under the Civil Service Code* (www.open.gov.uk/ocsc/appeal.htm).

1 *Annual Reports of the Civil Service Commissioners to Her Majesty the Queen.* By 2000, three appeals had been investigated and all were upheld, in whole or in part. Two concerned the deliberate misrepresentation by civil servants of statistics relating to a performance measure; the third, difficulties arising from the interpretation of statutory regulations.

2 Employment Rights Act 1996, s. 191, as amended by the 1998 Act, s. 10, and s.193, as substituted by the Employment Relations Act 1999, Sch. 8, para. 1.

3 Inserting Part IVA and s. 47B in the 1996 Act. See J. Bowers, J. Mitchell and J. Lewis, *Whistleblowing: the new law* (1999) and Y. Cripps in J. Beatson and Y. Cripps (eds.), *Freedom of Expression and Freedom of Information* (2000), Chap. 17; R. A. Parker, 'Whistleblowing legislation in the United States: a preliminary appraisal' (1988) 41 *Parliamentary Affairs* 149; G. Zellick, [1987] PL 311; (1989) 63 ALJ 592; J. G. Starke, 'Public Service Whistleblowers' (1991) 65 ALJ 205, 252; R. Fox, 'Protecting the Whistleblower' (1993) 15(2) Adelaide LR 137; J. McMillan, 'The Whistleblower versus the Organisation – Who should be Protected?' in T. Campbell and W. Sadurski (eds.), *Freedom and Communication* (1994) and see 'Canadian law reform report on "Whistleblowing" by public servants' (1987) 61 ALJ 319. See R. A. Parker, 'Whistleblowing legislation in the United States: a preliminary appraisal' (1988) 41 *Parliamentary Affairs* 149; G. Zellick, [1987] PL 311; (1989) 63 ALJ 592; J. G. Starke, 'Public Service Whistleblowers' (1991) 65 ALJ 205, 252; R. Fox, 'Protecting the Whistleblower' (1993) 15(2) Adelaide LR 137; J. McMillan, 'The Whistleblower versus the Organisation – Who Should be Protected?' in T. Campbell and W. Sadurski (eds.), *Freedom and Communication* (1994) and see 'Canadian law reform report on "Whistleblowing" by public servants' (1987) 61 ALJ 319.

4 *Directory of Civil Service Guidance Vol. 2* 'Whistleblowing', www.cabinet-office.gov.uk/guidance/two/19.htm.

5 1996 Act, s. 43B(3), inserted by the 1998 Act, s. 1.

6 Franks Committee, p. 30.

7 See n. 9, above.

8 Employment Rights Act 1996, s. 111.

9 Trade Union and Labour Relations (Consolidation) Act 1992, s. 146.

1 0 As substituted by the Employment Relations Act 1999, Sch. 8, para. 3.

However, the Minister no longer has power to issue a conclusive certificate that specified action was taken for that purpose,[11] or, more generally, to issue a certificate excepting employment of a specified description from provisions of the Employment Rights Act 1996 on national security grounds.[12] Employment tribunal procedure regulations may provide for an employment tribunal to be specially composed where this is directed by a Minister or ordered by a President of Employment Tribunals or a Regional Chairman on the grounds that he considers it expedient in the interests of national security; a direction by a Minister must relate to 'particular Crown employment proceedings'. A Minister may also direct a tribunal to sit in private or exclude the applicant and/or his representatives from all or part of such proceedings, to conceal the identity of a particular witness and to keep secret all or part of its reasons. A tribunal can be enabled to do any of these of its own motion. Where a person has been excluded, regulations may provide for the appointment by the Attorney General of a person to represent his interests, about the publication and registration of reasons for its decision and permitting the person to make a statement to the tribunal. Proceedings are 'Crown employment proceedings' if the employment is Crown employment or is connected with the performance of functions on behalf of the Crown.[13] These arrangements replace one whereby a Minister could direct a case, on grounds of national security, to be heard by a President of the Employment Tribunals alone.

These provisions are an improvement on the pre-1999 Act arrangements. However, the Intelligence and Security Committee was strongly critical of the government's introduction of these changes at the Report Stage of the Bill in the House of Lords without consultation with the Committee on the drafting. The Committee did not see any need for power to exclude from *all* (as opposed to part) of proceedings and was of the view that use of the powers of exclusion should be subject to examination by the Commissioners for the Security Service Act 1989 and the Intelligence Services Act 1994.[14] Action taken for the purpose of safeguarding national security may not form the basis of a complaint for unfair dismissal under

The government's recruitment procedures are designed to ensure fitness for appointment. There are vetting procedures to check the suitability of those with access to particularly sensitive information.[15] Precautions are also taken to ensure the physical security of documents according to their classification. Following the report of the Security Commission on the Prime case[16] random searches have been made of staff leaving GCHQ premises, a practice also followed by the security service and SIS.[17]

In 1994, the government revised its approach to the classification of documents, as explained by John Major in a written answer:[18]

'**The Prime Minister:** In recent years, the nature of the threats of Government security has changed. While some of the traditional threats to national security may have somewhat reduced, others have not. The security of Government is also increasingly threatened by, for example, theft, copying and electronic surveillance, as well as by terrorism.

---

11 Employment Tribunals Act 1996, s. 10(5), repealed by the 1999 Act, Sch. 8, para. 3.

12 Employment Rights Act 1996, s. 193, replaced by differently worded provisions by the 1999 Act, Sch. 8, para. 1.

13 Employment Tribunals Act 1996, s. 16(2)–(9), substituted by the 1999 Act, Sch. 8, para. 3.

14 Annual Report 1998–99, Cm. 4532, paras. 31–34.

15 See below, pp. 868–877.

16 Cmnd. 8876, 1983: see above, p. 826.

17 Report of the Security Commission on Steven Hayden (2000), pp. 17–18. The Commission endorsed the agencies' view that more intrusive searching could not be justified.

18 240 HC Deb, 23 March 1994, cols. 259–260.

To ensure that one approach to security reflects current threats, the Government have recently completed a review of arrangements for the management of protective security in Departments and agencies. This has recommended a new protective marking system for documents which will help identify more precisely those which need protecting, enabling them to be protected more effectively according to their value. The new system will also be more closely related to the code of practice on Government information announced in the Government's White Paper on openness [below, p. 893].

In addition, the review has concluded that existing security measures should be examined closely to ensure they are necessary in relation to today's threats; that commercially available security equipment should be more widely used; and that personnel vetting enquiries should be streamlined particularly in routine cases. Overall, the aim is to give departments and agencies, and management units within them, greater responsibility for assessing the nature of the risks they face and for making decisions, within the framework of common standards of protection, about the security measures they need to put in place. Substantial cost savings will result.

The first stage of the implementation of the proposals of this review will be the introduction of a new protective marking system with effect from 4 April 1994 alongside the code of practice on access to Government information. The new definitions, which will allow fewer Government documents to be classified, particularly at the higher levels, are set out. The other elements of the new approach to protective security will be put in place in due course.

The four categories of protective marking: Definitions
The markings to be allocated to any asset, including information, will be determined primarily by reference to the practical consequences that are likely to result from the compromise of that asset or information. The levels in the new protective marking system are defined as follows:

TOP SECRET: the compromise of this information or material would be likely: to threaten directly the internal stability of the United Kingdom or friendly countries; to lead directly to widespread loss of life; to cause exceptionally grave damage to the effectiveness or security of United Kingdom or allied forces or to the continuing effectiveness of extremely valuable security or intelligence operations; to cause exceptionally grave damage to relations with friendly governments; to cause severe long-term damage to the United Kingdom economy.

SECRET: the compromise of this information or material would be likely: to raise international tension; to damage seriously relations with friendly governments; to threaten life directly, or seriously prejudice public order, or individual security or liberty; to cause serious damage to the operational effectiveness or security of United Kingdom or allied forces or the continuing effectiveness of highly valuable security or intelligence operations; to cause substantial material damage to national finances or economic or commercial interests.

CONFIDENTIAL: the compromise of this information or material would be likely: materially to damage diplomatic relations (ie cause formal protest or other sanction); to prejudice individual security or liberty; to cause damage to the operational effectiveness or security of United Kingdom or allied forces or the effectiveness of valuable security or intelligence operations; to work substantially against national finances or economic and commercial interests; substantially to undermine the financial viability of major organisations; to impede the investigation or facilitate the commission of serious crime; to impede seriously the development or operation of major government policies; to shut down or otherwise substantially disrupt significant national operations.

RESTRICTED: the compromise of this information or material would be likely: to affect diplomatic relations adversely; to cause substantial distress to individuals; to make it more difficult to maintain the operational effectiveness or security of United Kingdom or allied forces; to cause financial loss or loss of earning potential to or facilitate improper gain or advantage for individuals or companies; to prejudice the investigation or facilitate the commission of crime; to breach proper undertakings to maintain the confidence of information provided by third parties; to impede the effective development or operation of government policies; to breach statutory restrictions on disclosure of information; to disadvantage government in commercial or policy negotiations with others; to undermine the proper management of the public sector and its operations.'

3 DA Notices

Defence Press and Broadcasting Advisory Committee[19]

General introduction to DA-Notices
1. Public discussion of the United Kingdom's defence and counter-terrorist policy and overall strategy does not impose a threat to national security and is welcomed by Government. It is important however that such discussion should not disclose details which could damage national security. *The DA Notice System* is a means of providing advice and guidance to the media about defence and counter-terrorist information the publication of which would be damaging to national security. The system is voluntary, it has no legal authority and the final responsibility for deciding whether or not to publish rests solely with the editor or publisher concerned.
2. DA-Notices are issued by the Defence, Press and Broadcasting Advisory Committee (*DPBAC*), an advisory body composed of senior civil servants and editors from national and regional newspapers, periodicals, news agencies, television and radio. It operates on the shared belief that there is a continuing need for a system of guidance and advice such as the DA-Notice System, and that a voluntary, advisory basis is best for such a system.
3. When these notices were first published under their new title of Defence Advisory Notices in 1993, they reflected the changed circumstances following the break-up of the Soviet Union and the Warsaw Pact. The 2000 revision has allowed an overall reduction in the scope of the notices while retaining those parts that are appropriate for the current level of threat that involves grave danger to the State and/or individuals. Compliance with the DA-Notice system does not relieve the editor of responsibilities under the Official Secrets Act.
4. *The Secretary DPBAC (the DA-Notice Secretary)* is the servant of the Government and the Press and Broadcasting sides of the Committee. He is available at all times to Government departments and the media to give advice on the system and, after consultation with Government departments as appropriate, to help in assessing the relevance of a DA-Notice to particular circumstances. Within this system, all discussions with editors, publishers and programme makers are conducted in confidence…

Purpose
1. The Defence, Press and Broadcasting Advisory Committee oversees a voluntary code which operates between those Government departments which have responsibilities for national security and the media; using as its vehicle the DA-Notice system.

Composition
2. The Committee is chaired by the Permanent Under-Secretary of State for Defence.
3. Membership may be varied from time to time by agreement. At present there are three members representing Government departments, one each from the Home Office, the Ministry of Defence and the Foreign and Commonwealth Office.
4. At present there are thirteen members nominated by the media; three by the Newspaper Publishers Association, two by the Newspaper Society, two by the Periodical Publishers Association and one each by the Scottish Daily Newspaper Society, the Press Association, the BBC, ITN, ITV, and Sky TV. The Publishers Association was invited in 1993 and in 2000 to nominate a representative but declined.
5. The press and broadcasting members select one of their number as Chairman of their side and Vice Chairman of the Committee. He leads for their side at Committee meeting and provides a point of day-to-day contact for them and for the Secretary.
6. The Committee is served by a full-time *Secretary* and part-time Deputy Secretary who substitutes in the Secretary's absence on leave etc.…

Responsibility of Membership
7. The Press and Broadcasting members respond to proposals from the government departments concerned and advise the Committee on those areas of information in which it may be reasonable to invite guidance reflecting the interests of national security. Official

19 www.dnotice.org.uk.htm. Minutes of meetings of the Committee are published on this site.

proposals may not be issued in DA-Notice form without the consent of the Press and Broadcasting members.

Meetings
8. The Committee normally has a Spring and an Autumn meeting each year. It reviews the Secretary's report of guidance sought and advice offered over the previous six months. It also reviews the content of the DA-Notices as necessary to ensure that amendments are made to meet the changing needs of national security....

DA-Notices
9. The DA-Notices are intended to provide to national and provincial newspaper editors, to periodicals editors, to radio and television organisations and to relevant book publishers, general guidance on those areas of national security which the Government considers it has a duty to protect. *The Notices*, together with a General Introduction, *details of the Committee* and *how to contact the Secretary*, are widely distributed to editors, producers and publishers and also to officials in Government departments, military commanders, chief constables and some institutions. The Notices have no legal standing and advice offered within their framework may be accepted or rejected partly or wholly.
10. Although the system is normally applied through the standing DA-Notices, should it be found necessary to issue a DA-Notice on a specific matter, the Government department concerned will agree a draft of the proposed Notice with the Secretary who, from his experience, can advise upon the form and content which are likely to make it acceptable to the press and broadcasting members. The Secretary will then seek the agreement of both sides of the DPBAC to the draft and, if it is obtained, issue the text as a DA-Notice...

Secretary DPBAC
11. The Secretary is normally a retired two-star officer from the Armed Forces, employed as a Civil Servant on the budget of the Ministry of Defence. He is the servant of the Government and Press and Broadcasting sides of the Committee, a fact which is recognised by the Vice Chairman being involved in the process of his selection. Similar arrangements apply for the Deputy Secretary who is also normally a retired service officer.
12. *The Secretary* (or Deputy Secretary) is available at all times to Government departments and the media to give advice on the system, taking into account the general guidance given to him by the Committee. DA-Notices are necessarily drafted in somewhat general terms and it is the application of a DA-Notice to a particular set of circumstances on which the Secretary is expected to give guidance, consulting as necessary with appropriate department officials. He is not invested with the authority to give rulings nor to advise on considerations other than national security.
13. If the Secretary agrees that a Government Department may quote the DA-Notices in release of information to the media, he should ensure that the Department makes it clear that it is doing so on his authority and therefore that of the Committee. ...

NOTES

1. The pre-1965 position as to D Notices is discussed in D. G. T. Williams, *Not in the Public Interest* (1965).[20] The Report of the (Radcliffe) Committee of Privy Counsellors[1] concerned the revelation by Chapman Pincher in the *Daily Express* that private cables and telegrams were vetted by the security authorities. The government claimed, and persisted in claiming notwithstanding the contrary view expressed by the Radcliffe Committee, that this contravened two D Notices.[2]

20 pp. 80–87.
1 Cmnd. 3309, 1967.
2 See the White Paper, Cmnd. 3312 (1967); P. Hedley and C. Aynsley, *The D Notice Affair* (1967); Chapman Pincher, *Inside Story* (1978); M. Creevy, 'A Critical review of the Wilson Government's Handling of the D-Notice Affair 1967' (1999) 14 Intelligence and National Security 209.

Chapman Pincher suggested that the minority of government representatives on the Committee almost always got their way and that prior to 1967, journalists tended to rely heavily on the view of the Secretary as to whether a story was covered by a D Notice, confident that clearance by the Secretary would cover them in practice as regards possible prosecution under the Official Secrets Act (although it could not affect the legal position). According to Pincher, the affair, 'effectively destroyed the D-notice system', which he thereafter 'virtually ignored'.[3] This seems to stem from his loss of confidence in the changed role of the Secretary and the emphasis in the revised arrangements that clearance by the Secretary would not affect the position under the Official Secrets Act. In the Oral Evidence to the Franks Committee the Chairman of the Defence, Press and Broadcasting Committee, Sir James Dunnett, stated that it would be an 'extreme case' in which the DPP would want to prosecute an editor where clearance had been given, and that the Attorney-General in deciding to give his fiat under the Act would wish to know whether the editor had been in touch with the Secretary to the Committee.[4]

2. The system was reviewed by the House of Commons Defence Committee in its Third Report.[5] The Committee concluded that the system as at present constituted was failing to fulfil the role for which it was created, but concluded that it was necessary that advice should continue to be given to the press and broadcasting on what could be disseminated without damage to national security, and (by the Conservative majority) that the Committee should be retained at least until there was a fundamental review of the Official Secrets Acts. An internal review led to the publication of a Revised Introduction to the D Notices and a reduction in their number from 12 to 8, phrased in more general terms.[6]

3. The D Notice system was again put under strain in 1987 over a proposed BBC radio series, *My Country Right or Wrong*, which was to examine issues raised by the *Spycatcher* litigation. On the eve of the first programme, Henry J granted an interlocutory injunction sought by the Attorney-General to prevent the broadcasting of any interviews with or information derived from members or past members of the security and intelligence services relating to any aspect of the work of the services, including their identity as members. The terms of the injunction were subsequently modified by agreement to permit fair and accurate reports of proceedings in Parliament and the courts.[7] The injunction was subsequently continued by Owen J.[8] The injunction was lifted in respect of one of the programmes in March 1988, and the others in May 1988, after the scripts had been vetted.[9] The programme's producer had previously obtained an indication from the Secretary to the D Notice Committee that he did not advise that the broadcast would be potentially prejudicial to national security.[10] The apparent contradiction was subsequently explained by the Secretary on the basis that his advice concerned the lack of a threat to national security whereas the government's claim to an injunction was based on breach of confidence. It was, he said, 'a pity that the two issues have become entwined'.[11] Nevertheless, as Fairley comments,

---

3 Op. cit., p. 244.

4 p. 57.

5 1979–80 HC 773, 640 i–v, *The D Notice System*.

6 See J. Jaconelli, [1982] PL 37.

7 See D. Oliver in D. Kingsford-Smith and D. Oliver (eds.), *Economical with the Truth* (1990), p. 43.

8 *A-G v BBC* (1987) Times, 18 December, applying the *American Cyanamid* principles (below, p. 859) and *A-G v Guardian Newspapers* [1987] 1 WLR 1248 (below, pp. 860–862).

9 See P. Thornton, *Decade of Decline* (1989), pp. 9–11.

10 The nearest the Secretary gets to giving a 'clearance': see D. Fairley, (1990) 10 OJLS 430, 431, 435.

11 *Guardian*, 10 December 1987.

'Given that the policy argument upon which the existence and scope of the alleged duty of confidentiality depended in *Spycatcher* was that of potential damage to national security, it is hard to see how there can be two separate issues . . .'.[12]

He argues that the real difference lay in the approach to the assessment of the implications for national security; the Secretary was concerned solely with prejudice arising from the *contents* of the particular document or broadcast, whereas the government was asserting the broader basis for the duty of confidence also put forward in *A-G v Guardian Newspapers Ltd (No 2)*[13] and *Lord Advocate v Scotsman Publications Ltd*,[14] namely that there would be long term damage to the security service as a result of media pressure on MI5 members for similar disclosures, and loss of confidence in MI5 on the part of other countries and potential informants. This broader basis was ultimately rejected by the House of Lords in the *Scotsman* case (where, again, the editor had obtained a 'no advice' response from the D Notice Secretary before publication). This does not, however, remove the difficulty: Fairley argues that a claim to confidentiality based on the *contents* of a document would be likely to succeed before the courts even if the Secretary had offered 'no advice'.[15]

Fairley's survey of newspaper and periodical editors showed that formal participation in the system was fairly widespread, but actual use infrequent: most of the respondents:

'felt that, in the light of recent Government behaviour, they would be more influenced by the advice of their lawyers than by that of the Secretary of the D Notice Committee.'[16]

The effect of the government's increasing use of the civil courts has been to 'marginalize the significance of the D Notice system and to destroy the atmosphere of mutual trust' between press and government on which voluntary prior restraint can be based. Nevertheless, evidence of a 'no advice' response by the Secretary still may be of relevance to a civil action, or to a prosecution under the Official Secrets Act 1989 (e.g. in respect of an argument that there was no reasonable cause to believe that damage would result from disclosure of information), or in respect of sentence.[17]

4. The system was again reviewed by the Committee in 1992, leading to a number of changes.[18] The aim of the review 'was to make the system more transparent and relevant in the light of international changes and the increased emphasis on openness in Government'. The Notices were revised, reduced in number from 8 to 6 and renamed Defence Advisory Notices 'better to reflect the voluntary and advisory nature of the system'. They were revised again in 2000 and the number reduced to five. The introduction and procedure are set out above (p. 470). The content of the six DA Notices is now freely published. They cover: No. 1, Military Operations, Plans and Capabilities; No. 2, Nuclear and Non-Nuclear Weapons and Equipment; No. 3, Ciphers and Secure Communications; No. 4, Sensitive Installations and Home Addresses; and No. 5, United Kingdom Security and Intelligence Services and Special Forces. Each notice is accompanied by a stated 'rationale'. For example, DA Notice No. 5 states:

---

12 (1990) 10 OJLS 430, 435.
13 Below, p. 850.
14 Below, p. 862.
15 (1990) 10 OJLS 430, 437.
16 Ibid., p. 438.
17 Ibid., pp. 439, 440.
18 See *The Defence Advisory Notices: A Review of the D Notice System* (Ministry of Defence Open Government Document No. 93/06).
19 Letter to *The Times*, 25 April 1984.

DA-Notice No. 5: United Kingdom Security and Intelligence Services and Special Forces
1. Information falling within the following categories is normally regarded as being highly classified. It is requested that such information, unless it has been the subject of an official announcement or has been widely disclosed or discussed, should not be published without first seeking advice:

(a) specific covert operations, sources and methods of the Security Service, SIS and CGHQ, and those involved with them, including the Special Forces, the application of those methods, including the interception of communications, and their targets; the same applies to those engaged on counter-terrorist operations;

(b) the identities, whereabouts and tasks of people who are or have been employed by these services or engaged on such work, including details of their families and home addresses, and any other information, including photographs, which could assist terrorist or other hostile organisations to identify a target;

(c) addresses and telephone numbers used by these services, except those now made public.

2. *Rationale.* Identified staff from the intelligence and security services, others engaged sensitive counter-terrorist operations, including the Special Forces, and those who are likely targets for attack are at real risk from terrorists. Security and intelligence operational contacts and techniques are easily compromised, and therefore need to be pursued in conditions of secrecy. Publicity about an operation which is in train finishes it. Publicity given even to an operation which has been completed, whether successfully or not, may well deny the opportunity for further exploitation of a capability, which may be unique against other hostile and illegal activity. The disclosure of identities can prejudice past present and future operations. Even inaccurate speculation about the source of inforamtion on a given issue can put intelligence operations (and, in the worst case, lives) at risk and/or lead to the loss of information which is important in the interests of national security. Material, which has been the subject of an official announcement is not covered by this notice.

5. Some journalists and writers have expressly disassociated themselves from the D Notice system. J. Bloch and P. Fitzgerald, authors of *British Intelligence and Covert Action* (1983), which named British officials it claimed were, or had been, involved in British Intelligence, 'freely admit ignoring D Notice No. 6 (and several others besides). Neither ourselves nor our publishers are represented on the D Notice Committee, nor are we party to any other cosy agreement between Whitehall and the media'.[19] In response to this book preparatory work was apparently undertaken on a draft law to prohibit the naming in public of MI5 and MI6 officers and agents.[20] The Whitehall consensus on this book was that 'its publication was "indefensible" as unlike most other studies of British intelligence, it covered events and personalities "so near to the present day", as one insider put it'.[1] The DA Notice 'request' that nothing shall be published without reference to the DPBAC Secretary which identifies officers can be contrasted with the US Intelligence Identities Protection Act 1982, which makes it an offence for persons with access to classified information intentionally to reveal the identities of covert agents working outside the USA for agencies such as the CIA, and for other persons to do so 'in the course of a pattern of activities intended to identify and expose covert agents . . . with reason to believe that such activities would impair or impede the foreign intelligence activities of the United States'.[2] The maximum penalties are (1) $50,000/ten years' imprisonment/both for 'insiders' who have had access to classified information which identifies the agent(s); (2) $25,000/five years' imprisonment/both for 'insiders' who learn the identity as a result of their access to classified information in general; and (3) $15,000/three years' imprisonment/both for 'outsiders'. The legislation is directed at those

20 P. Hennessy, *The Times*, 9 April 1984.
1 Ibid.
2 50 USC § 421–426.

such as the former CIA agent, Philip Agee, who wished to expose and nullify covert political intervention in the affairs of other countries.[3]

6. Note that the revised DA Notice documentation states that systems provides advice as to whether a publication would *actually* involve 'grave damage to the State and/ or individuals'. This is recognised by the Committee to be narrower than the test applicable under the Official Secretary Act 1989, and it decided that this should be brought to the attention of officials.[4]

4 Breach of confidence

The use of the law of breach of confidence to protect official secrets was thrown into prominence in the *Spycatcher* litigation, in which the Attorney-General, in a number of jurisdictions throughout the world, sought to restrain the publication of the memoirs of Peter Wright, a former member of MI5. As the chronology set out below shows, the litigation was lengthy and complex, and saw the invocation of the law of contempt as well as the law of confidence against a variety of parties. So far as the UK and the law of breach of confidence was concerned, the matter culminated in the decision of the House of Lords in *A-G v Guardian Newspapers Ltd (No 2)*.[5]

Chronology of the Spycatcher litigation

1985	A-G commences proceedings in NSW against Peter Wright and Heinemann Publishers Australia Pty Ltd seeking an injunction restraining publication of *Spycatcher* or, alternatively, an account of profits. Pending trial, undertakings restraining publication of the book or disclosure of information obtained by W as a MI5 officer were given by W, H, and Malcolm Turnbull, the solicitor acting for them.
22, 23 June 1986	the *Observer* and the *Guardian* publish articles reporting on the forthcoming hearing.
27 June 1986	Ex parte injunctions against the newspapers granted by Macpherson J.
11 July 1986	Inter partes injunctions against the newspapers granted by Millett J, restraining them from disclosing any information obtained by W as an MI5 officer or from attributing any information about MI5 to him, with certain exceptions: [1989] 2 FSR 3.
25 July 1986	The Court of Appeal upholds the injunctions, with slight modifications: *A-G v Observer Newspapers Ltd* (1986) Times, 26 July, [1986] NLJ Rep 799, [1989] 2 FSR 15.
17 November 1986	NSW trial begins before Powell J.
13 March 1987	A-G's action dismissed: (1987) 8 NSWLR 341. Undertakings continued pending appeal.
27 April 1987	Articles published by the *Independent*, the *Evening Standard* and the *London Daily News* based on the contents of the book.
3 May 1987	The *Washington Post* publishes extracts from the manuscript of *Spycatcher*.
7 May 1987	Proceedings for contempt commence against the newspapers in respect of the articles of 27 April.

---

3   The Act's constitutionality is considered by S. D. Charkes, (1983) 83 Colum L Rev 727.
4   Record of meeting held 5 December 2000.
5   Below, p. 850.

14 May 1987	Viking Penguin Inc announces its intention to publish *Spycatcher* in the US.
2 June 1987	Sir Nicolas Browne-Wilkinson V-C holds on a preliminary point of law that contempt proceedings against the *Independent*, the *Evening Standard* and the *London Daily News* cannot succeed as they were not party to the Millett injunctions: *A-G v Newspaper Publishing plc* [1988] Ch 333.[6]
12 July 1987	*The Sunday Times*, having obtained a copy of the manuscript from Viking Penguin in the US, publishes extracts from *Spycatcher* in its second edition.
13 July 1987	A-G commences contempt proceedings against *The Sunday Times*.
15 July 1987	*Spycatcher* on sale in the US. (Reasons given 17 July.) Court of Appeal allows an appeal against the decision of the Vice-Chancellor, holding that the publication of the 27 April articles could constitute contempt: *A-G v Newspaper Publishing plc* [1988] Ch 333.
16 July 1987	A-G granted interlocutory injunction restraining *The Sunday Times* from publishing further extracts from *Spycatcher*.
22 July 1987	Sir Nicolas Browne-Wilkinson V-C discharges the Millett injunctions on the ground that the book was now 'freely available to all': *A-G v Guardian Newspapers Ltd* [1987] 3 All ER 316.
24 July 1987	Millett injunctions restored by the Court of Appeal: [1987] 3 All ER 316, in modified form, permitting the publication of a 'summary in very general terms' of W's allegations.
30 July 1987	(reasons given 13 August) Appeal to the House of Lords dismissed by 3–2. Millett injunctions endorsed, and without the exceptions, *inter alia*, permitting the reporting of what had taken place in open court in the Australian proceedings: [1987] 3 All ER 316.
2 August 1987	*News on Sunday* publishes an article with quotations from the *Sunday Times* article of 12 July.
24 September 1987	New South Wales Court of Appeal dismisses A-G's appeal: *A-G for the United Kingdom v Heinemann Publishers Australia Pty Ltd* (1987) 75 ALR 353.
29 September 1987	Deane J in the High Court of Australia declines to grant temporary injunctions pending the hearing of an application by the A-G for leave to appeal to the HCA.
12, 13 October 1987	*Spycatcher* goes on sale in Ireland and Australia.
27 October 1987	A-G commences proceedings against *The Sunday Times* for breach of confidence.
21 December 1987	Scott J discharges the interlocutory injunctions against the *Observer* and the *Guardian*, holds that *The Sunday Times* is accountable for profits resulting from the first extract of the serialisation on 12 July, and refuses the A-G an injunction restraining future publication of information derived from W: *A-G v Guardian Newspapers Ltd (No 2)* [1990] 1 AC 109, [1988] 3 All ER 545.
10 February 1988	Decision of Scott J upheld by Court of Appeal: *A-G v Guardian Newspapers Ltd (No 2)* [1990] 1 AC 109, [1988] 3 All ER 545 at 594.

2 June 1988	High Court of Australia dismisses A-G's appeal: *A-G for the United Kingdom v Heinemann Publishers Australia Pty Ltd (No 2)* (1988) 165 CLR 30, 78 ALR 449.
13 October 1988	Decision of Scott J and the Court of Appeal upheld by the House of Lords (4–1): [1990] 1 AC 109, [1988] 3 All ER 545 at 638 (below).
8 May 1989	the *Independent, The Sunday Times* and the *News on Sunday* each fined £50,000 for contempt by Morritt J; contempt proceedings against the *Evening Standard*, the *London Daily News* and the *Daily Telegraph* dismissed: *A-G v Newspaper Publishing plc*: [1989] FSR 457.
27 February 1990	Decision of Morritt J upheld by the Court of Appeal: *A-G*
11 April 1991	*v Newspaper Publishing plc* (1990) Times, 28 February; and the House of Lords: *A-G v Times Newspapers Ltd*.[7]
26 November 1991	European Court of Human Rights gives judgment in *Observer and Guardian v UK* (Series A No. 216) and *Sunday Times v UK (No 2)* (Series A No. 217).[8]

A-G v Guardian Newspapers Ltd (No 2) [1990] 1 AC 109, [1988] 3 All ER 545, House of Lords

The facts are set out in Lord Keith's speech. The House of Lords held:

(1) (Lord Griffiths dissenting) that the publications by *The Observer* and *The Guardian* on 22 and 23 June 1986 did not constitute an actionable breach of confidence, as they were not damaging to the public interest;

(2) that *The Sunday Times*' publications on 12 July 1987 did constitute a breach of confidence, for which the Crown was entitled to an account of profits;

(3) that no injunction should lie against (a) *The Observer* and *The Guardian* or (b) (Lord Griffiths dissenting) *The Sunday Times* to prevent any future serialisation of the book; neither would the newspaper be liable for any account of profits: the information was now in the public domain;

(4) that the A-G was not entitled to any general injunction restraining future publication of information derived from Mr Wright or other members or ex-members of the security service.

Lord Keith of Kinkel: My Lords, from 1955 to 1976 Peter Wright was employed in a senior capacity by the counter-espionage branch of the British Security Service known as MI5. In that capacity he acquired knowledge of a great many matters of prime importance to the security of the country. Following his retirement from the service he went to live in Australia and later formed the intention of writing and publishing a book of memoirs describing his experiences in the service. He wrote the book in association with a man named Paul Greengrass, and it was accepted for publication by Heinemann Publishers Pty. Ltd., the Australian subsidiary of a well known English publishing company. The Attorney-General in right of the Crown, learning of the intended publication of the book, instituted in 1985 proceedings in New South Wales against Mr. Wright and Heinemann Publishers claiming an injunction to restrain the publication in Australia or alternatively an account of profits. Pending trial, Mr. Wright, the publishers and their solicitors gave undertakings not to reveal the contents of the book. The Attorney-General's action failed before Powell J and again before the Court of Appeal of New South Wales. Special leave to appeal was granted by the High Court of Australia, but

6   Above, p. 766.
7   Ibid.
8   Below, p. 862.

the respondents were released from their undertakings. So the book was published in Australia on 13 October 1987, under the title of *Spycatcher*. On 2 June 1988 the High Court dismissed the Attorney-General's appeal upon the sole ground that an Australian court should not accept jurisdiction to enforce an obligation of confidence owed to a foreign government so as to protect that government intelligence secrets and confidential political information. In the meantime *Spycatcher* had on 14 July 1987 been published in the United States of America by Viking Penguin Inc., a subsidiary of an English publishing company. Her Majesty's Government had been advised that, in view of the terms of the First Amendment to the United States Constitution, any attempt to restrain publication there would be certain to fail. Publication also took place in Canada, the Republic of Ireland, and a number of other countries. Her Majesty's Government decided that it was impracticable and undesirable to take any steps to prevent the importation into the United Kingdom of copies of the book, and a very substantial number of copies have in fact been imported. So the contents of the book have been disseminated world-wide and anyone in this country who is interested can obtain a copy without undue difficulty.

... The issues raised in the litigation are thus summarised in the judgment of Sir John Donaldson M.R. in the Court of Appeal, ante, pp. 180H–181C:

'(1) Were the "Observer" and "The Guardian" in breach of their duty of confidentiality when, on 22 and 23 June 1986, they respectively published articles on the forthcoming hearing in Australia? If so, would they have been restrained from publishing if the Attorney-General had been able to seek the assistance of the court? ... (2) Was "The Sunday Times" in breach of its duty of confidentiality when, on 12 July 1987 it published the first extract of an intended serialisation of *Spycatcher*? ... (3) Is the Attorney-General now entitled to an injunction (a) in relation to the "Observer" and "The Guardian" and (b) in relation to "The Sunday Times" with special consideration to further serialisation? ... (4) Is the Attorney-General entitled to an account of the profits accruing to "The Sunday Times" as a result of the serialisation of *Spycatcher*? ... (5) Is the Attorney-General entitled to some general injunction restraining future publication of information derived from Mr. Wright or other members or ex-members of the Security Service?'

As regards issue (1) Scott J. and the majority of the Court of Appeal (Dillon and Bingham L.JJ.; Sir John Donaldson M.R. dissenting) held that the publication of the articles in question was not in breach of an obligation of confidence.

On issue (2) Scott J. and the majority of the Court of Appeal (Bingham L.J. dissenting) held that the publication of the first extract from *Spycatcher* was in breach of an obligation of confidence.

Upon issue (3) Scott J. and the Court of Appeal held that the Attorney-General was not entitled to an injunction against the 'Observer' and 'The Guardian' nor (Sir John Donaldson M.R. dissenting) against further serialisation of *Spycatcher* by 'The Sunday Times'.

As to issue (4) Scott J. and the majority of the Court of Appeal (Bingham L.J. dissenting) decided this in favour of the Attorney-General.

Issue (5) was decided against the Attorney-General both by Scott J. and by the Court of Appeal.

The Attorney-General now appeals to your Lordships' House upon all the issues on which he failed below. 'The Sunday Times' cross-appeals against the decision on account of profits.

The Crown's case upon all the issues which arise invokes the law about confidentiality. So it is convenient to start by considering the nature and scope of that law. The law has long recognised that an obligation of confidence can arise out of particular relationships. Examples are the relationships of doctor and patient, priest and penitent, solicitor and client, banker and customer. The obligation may be imposed by an express or implied term in a contract but it may also exist independently of any contract on the basis of an independent equitable principle of confidence: *Saltman Engineering Co Ltd v Campbell Engineering Co Ltd* (1963) 65 RPC 203. It is worthy of some examination whether or not detriment to the confider of confidential information is an essential ingredient of his cause of action in seeking to restrain by injunction a breach of confidence. Presumably that may be so as regards an action for damages in respect of a past breach of confidence. If the confider has suffered no detriment thereby he can hardly be in a position to recover compensatory damages. However, the true view may be that he would be entitled to nominal damages. Most of the cases have arisen in circumstances where there has been a threatened or actual breach of confidence by an employee or ex-employee of the plaintiff, or where information about the plaintiff's business affairs has been given in confidence to someone who has proceeded to exploit it for his own benefit: an example of the latter type of case is *Seager v Copydex Ltd* [1967] 1 WLR 923. In such cases the detriment to the confider is clear. In other cases there may be no financial detriment to the confider, since the breach of confidence involves no more than an invasion of personal privacy. Thus in *Duchess of Argyll v Duke of Argyll* [1967] Ch 302 an injunction was granted against the revelation of marital confidences. The right to personal privacy is clearly one which the law should in this field seek to protect. If a profit has been made through the revelation in breach of confidence of details of a person's private life it is appropriate that the profit should be accounted for to that person. Further, as a general rule, it is in the public interest that confidences should be respected, and the encouragement of such respect may in itself constitute a sufficient ground for recognising and enforcing the obligation of confidence even where the confider can point to no specific detriment to himself. Information about a person's private and personal affairs may be of a nature which shows him up in a favourable light and would by no means expose him to criticism. The anonymous donor of a very large sum to a very worthy cause has his own reasons for wishing to remain anonymous, which are unlikely to be discreditable. He should surely be in a position to restrain disclosure in breach of confidence of his identity in connection with the donation. So I would think it a sufficient detriment to the confider that information given in confidence is to be disclosed to persons whom he would prefer not to know of it, even though the disclosure would not be harmful to him in any positive way.

The position of the Crown, as representing the continuing government of the country may, however, be regarded as being special. In some instances disclosure of confidential information entrusted to a servant of the Crown may result in a financial loss to the public. In other instances such disclosure may tend to harm the public interest by impeding the efficient attainment of proper governmental ends, and the revelation of defence or intelligence secrets certainly falls into that category. The Crown, however, as representing the nation as a whole, has no private life or personal feelings capable of being hurt by the disclosure of confidential information. In so far as the Crown acts to prevent such disclosure or to seek redress for it on confidentiality grounds, it must necessarily, in my opinion, be in a position to show that the disclosure is likely to damage or has damaged the public interest. How far the Crown has to go in order to show this must depend on the circumstances of each case. In a question with a Crown servant himself, or others acting as his agents, the general public interest in the preservation of confidentiality, and in encouraging other Crown servants to preserve it, may suffice. But where the publication is proposed to be made by third parties unconnected with the particular confidant, the position may be different. The Crown's argument in the present case would go to the length that in all circumstances where the original disclosure has been made by a Crown servant in breach of his obligation of confidence any person to whose knowledge the information comes and who is aware of the breach comes under an equitable duty binding his conscience not to communicate the information to anyone else irrespective of the circumstances under which he acquired the knowledge. In my opinion that general proposition is untenable and impracticable, in addition to being unsupported by any authority. The general rule is that anyone is entitled to communicate anything he pleases to anyone else, by speech or in writing or in any other way. That rule is limited by the law of defamation and other restrictions similar to these mentioned in article 10 of the Convention for the Protection of Human Rights and Fundamental Freedoms (1953) (Cmd. 8969). All those restrictions are imposed in the light of considerations of public interest such as to countervail the public interest in freedom of expression. A communication about some aspect of government activity which does no harm to the interests of the nation cannot, even where the original disclosure has been made in breach of confidence, be restrained on the ground of a nebulous equitable duty of conscience serving no useful practical purpose.

There are two important cases in which the special position of a government in relation to the preservation of confidence has been considered. The first of them is *A-G v Jonathan Cape Ltd* [1976] QB 752. That was an action for injunctions to restrain publication of the political diaries of the late Richard Crossman, which contained details of Cabinet discussions held some ten years previously, and also of advice given to Ministers by civil servants. Lord Widgery C.J. said, at pp. 770–771:

'In these actions we are concerned with the publication of diaries at a time when 11 years have expired since the first recorded events. The Attorney-General must show (a) that such publication would be a breach of confidence; (b) that the public interest requires that the publication be restrained, and (c) that there are no other facets of the public interest contradictory of and more compelling than that relied upon. Moreover, the court, when asked to restrain such a publication, must closely examine the extent to which relief is necessary to ensure that restrictions are not imposed beyond the strict requirement of public need.'

Lord Widgery went on to say that while the expression of individual opinions by Cabinet Ministers in the course of Cabinet discussions were matters of confidence, the publication of which could be restrained by the court when clearly necessary in the public interest, there must be a limit in time after which the confidential character of the information would lapse. Having read the whole of volume one of the diaries he did not consider that publication of anything in them, ten years after the event, would inhibit full discussion in the Cabinet at the present time or thereafter, or damage the doctrine of joint Cabinet responsibility. He also dismissed the argument that publication of advice given by senior civil servants would be likely to inhibit the frankness of advice given by such civil servants in the future. So in the result Lord Widgery's decision turned on his view that it had not been shown that publication of the diaries would do any harm to the public interest.

The second case is *Commonwealth of Australia v John Fairfax & Sons Ltd* (1980) 147 CLR 39. That was a decision of Mason J. in the High Court of Australia, dealing with an application by the Commonwealth for an interlocutory injunction to restrain publication of a book containing the texts of government documents concerned with its relations with other countries, in particular the government of Indonesia in connection with the 'East Timor Crisis'. The documents appeared to have been leaked by a civil servant. Restraint of publication was claimed on the ground of breach of confidence and also on that of infringement of copyright. Mason J. granted an injunction on the latter ground but not on the former. Having mentioned, at p. 51, an argument for the Commonwealth that the government was entitled to protect information which was not public property, even if no public interest is served by maintaining confidentiality, he continued, at pp. 51–52:

'However, the plaintiff must show, not only that the information is confidential in quality and that it was imparted so as to import an obligation of confidence, but also that there will be "an unauthorised use of that information to the detriment of the party communicating it" (*Coco v A N Clark (Engineers) Ltd* [1969] RPC 41, 47). The question then, when the executive government seeks the protection given by equity, is: What detriment does it need to show?

'The equitable principle has been fashioned to protect the personal, private and proprietary interests of the citizen, not to protect the very different interests of the executive government. It acts, or is supposed to act, not according to standards of private interest, but in the public interest. This is not to say that equity will not protect information in the hands of the government, but it is to say that when equity protects government information it will look at the matter through different spectacles.

'It may be a sufficient detriment to the citizen that disclosure of information relating to his affairs will expose his actions to public discussion and criticism. But it can scarcely be a relevant detriment to the government that publication of material concerning its actions will merely expose it to public discussion and criticism. It is unacceptable in our democratic society that there should be a restraint on the publication of information relating to government when the only vice of that information is that it enables the public to discuss, review and criticise government action.

'Accordingly, the court will determine the government's claim to confidentiality by reference to the public interest. Unless disclosure is likely to injure the public interest, it will not be protected.

'The court will not prevent the publication of information which merely throws light on the past workings of government, even if it be not public property, so long as it does not prejudice the community in other respects. Then disclosure will itself serve the public interest in keeping the community informed and in promoting discussion of public affairs. If, however, it appears that disclosure will be inimical to the public interest because national security, relations with foreign countries or the ordinary business of government will be prejudiced, disclosure will be restrained. There will be cases in which the conflicting considerations will be finely balanced, where it is difficult to decide whether the public's interest in knowing and in expressing its opinion, outweighs the need to protect confidentiality.'

I find myself in broad agreement with this statement by Mason J. In particular I agree that a government is not in a position to win the assistance of the court in restraining the publication of information imparted in confidence by it or its predecessors unless it can show that publication would be harmful to the public interest.

In relation to Mr. Wright, there can be no doubt whatever that had he sought to bring about the first publication of his book in this country, the Crown would have been entitled to an injunction restraining him. The work of a member of MI5 and the information which he acquires in the course of that work must necessarily be secret and confidential and be kept secret and confidential by him. There is no room for discrimination between secrets of greater or lesser importance, nor any room for close examination of the precise manner in which revelation of any particular matter may prejudice the national interest. Any attempt to do so would lead to further damage. All this has been accepted from beginning to end by each of the judges in this country who has had occasion to consider the case and also by counsel for the respondents. It is common ground that neither the defence of prior publication nor the so called 'iniquity' defence would have availed Mr. Wright had he sought to publish his book in England. The sporadic and low key prior publication of certain specific allegations of wrongdoing could not conceivably weigh in favour of allowing publication of this whole book of detailed memoirs describing the operations of the Security Service over a lengthy period and naming and describing many members of it not previously known to be such. The damage to the public interest involved in a publication of that character, in which the allegations in question occupy a fairly small space, vastly outweighs all other considerations. The question whether Mr. Wright or those acting for him would be at liberty to publish *Spycatcher* in England under existing circumstances does not arise for immediate consideration. These circumstances include the world-wide dissemination of the contents of the book which has been brought about by Mr. Wright's wrongdoing. In my opinion general publication in this country would not bring about any significant damage to the public interest beyond what has already been done. All such secrets as the book may contain have been revealed to any intelligence services whose interests are opposed to those of the United Kingdom. Any damage to the confidence reposed in the British Security and Intelligence Services by those of friendly countries brought about by Mr. Wright's actions would not be materially increased by publication here. It is, however, urged on behalf of the Crown that such publication might prompt Mr. Wright into making further disclosures, would expose existing and past members of the British Security and Intelligence Services to harassment by the media and might result in their disclosing other secret material with a view, perhaps, to refuting Mr. Wright's account and would damage the morale of such members by the spectacle of Mr. Wright having got away with his treachery. While giving due weight to the evidence of Sir Robert Armstrong on these matters, I have not been persuaded that the effect of publication in England would be to bring about greater damage in the respects founded upon than has already been caused by the widespread publication elsewhere in the world. In the result, the case for an injunction now against publication by or on behalf of Mr. Wright would in my opinion rest upon the principle that he should not be permitted to take advantage of his own wrongdoing.

The newspapers which are the respondents in this appeal were not responsible for the world-wide dissemination of the contents of *Spycatcher* which has taken place. It is a general rule of law that a third party who comes into possession of confidential information which he knows to be such, may come under a duty not to pass it on to anyone else. Thus in *Duchess of Argyll v Duke of Argyll* [1967] Ch 302 the newspaper to which the Duke had communicated the information about the Duchess was restrained by injunction from publishing it. However, in that case there was no doubt but that the publication would cause detriment to the Duchess in the sense I have considered above. In the present case the third parties are 'The Guardian' and the 'Observer' on the one hand and 'The Sunday Times' on the other hand. The first two of these newspapers wish to report and comment upon the substance of the allegations made in *Spycatcher*. They say that they have no intention of serialising it. By virtue of section 6 of the Copyright Act 1956 they might, without infringing copyright, quote passages from the book for purposes of 'criticism or review'. 'The Sunday Times' for their part, wish to complete their serialisation of *Spycatcher*. The question is whether the Crown is entitled to an injunction restraining the three newspapers from doing what they wish to do. This is the third of the issues identified by Sir John Donaldson MR in the court below. For the reasons which I have indicated in dealing with the position of Mr. Wright, I am of the opinion that the reports and comments proposed by 'The Guardian' and the 'Observer' would not be harmful to the public interest, nor would the continued serialisation by 'The Sunday Times'. I would therefore refuse an injunction against any of the newspapers. I would stress that I do not base this upon any balancing of public interests nor upon any considerations of freedom of the press, nor upon any possible defences of prior publication or just cause or excuse, but simply upon the view that all possible damage to the interest of the Crown has already been done by the publication of *Spycatcher* abroad and the ready availability of copies in this country.

It is possible, I think, to envisage cases where, even in the light of widespread publication abroad of certain information, a person whom that information concerned might be entitled to restrain publication by a third party in this country. For example, if in the *Argyll* case the Duke had secured the revelation of the marital secrets in an American newspaper, the Duchess could reasonably claim that publication of the same material in England would bring it to the attention of people who would otherwise be unlikely to learn of it and who were more closely interested in her activities than American readers. The publication in England would be more harmful to her than publication in America. Similar considerations would apply to, say, a publication in America by the medical adviser to an English pop group about diseases for which he had treated them. But it cannot reasonably be held in the present case that publication in England now of the contents of *Spycatcher* would do any more harm to the public interest than has already been done.

In relation to future serialisation by 'The Sunday Times' the Master of the Rolls took the view that this newspaper stood in the shoes of Mr. Wright by virtue of the licence which it has been granted by the publishers. The cost of this licence was £150,000 of which £25,000 was to be paid at once and the balance after the serialisation. So Mr. Wright and his publishers will benefit from future instalments of it. The Master of the Rolls considered that there was a strong public interest in preventing Mr. Wright and his publishers from profiting from their wrongdoing. There can be no doubt that the prospect of Mr. Wright receiving further sums of money from 'The Sunday Times' as a reward for his treachery is a revolting one. But a natural desire to deprive Mr. Wright of profit does not appear to me to constitute a legally valid ground for enjoining the newspaper from a publication which would not in itself damage the interests of the Crown. Indeed, it appears that Mr. Wright would have no legally enforceable claim against 'The Sunday Times' for payment, upon the principle of ex turpi causa non oritur actio. Whether 'The Sunday Times' is bound to account for the profits of serialisation I shall consider later.

The next issue for examination is conveniently the one as to whether 'The Sunday Times' was in breach of an obligation of confidentiality when it published the first serialised extract from *Spycatcher* on 12 July 1987. I have no hesitation in holding that it was. Those responsible for the publication well knew that the material was confidential in character and had not as a whole been previously published anywhere. Justification for the publication is sought to be found in the circumstance that publication in the United States of America was known to be imminent. That will not hold water for a moment. It was Mr. Wright and those acting for him who were about to bring about the American publication in breach of confidence. The fact that a primary confidant, having communicated the confidential information to a third party in breach of obligation, is about to reveal it similarly to someone else, does not entitle that third party to do the same. The third party to whom the information has been wrongfully revealed himself comes under a duty of confidence to the original confider. The fact that his informant is about to commit further breaches of his obligation cannot conceivably relieve the third party of his own. If it were otherwise an agreement between two confidants each to publish the confidential information would relieve each of them of his obligation, which would be absurd and deprive the law about confidentiality of all content. The purpose of 'The Sunday Times' was of course to steal a march on the American publication so as to be the first to reveal, for its own profit, the confidential material. The evidence of Mr. Neil, editor of 'The

Sunday Times', makes it clear that his intention was to publish his instalment of *Spycatcher* at least a full week before the American publication and this was in the event reduced to two days only because circumstances caused that publication to be brought forward a week. There can be no question but that the Crown, had it learned of the intended publication in 'The Sunday Times', would have been entitled to an injunction to restrain it. Mr. Neil employed peculiarly sneaky methods to avoid this. Neither the defence of prior publication nor that of just cause or excuse would in my opinion have been available to 'The Sunday Times'. As regards the former, the circumstance that certain allegations had been previously made and published was not capable of justifying publication in the newspaper of lengthy extracts from *Spycatcher* which went into details about the working of the Security Service. As to just cause or excuse it is not sufficient to set up the defence merely to show that allegations of wrongdoing have been made. There must be at least a prima facie case that the allegations have substance. The mere fact that it was Mr. Wright, a former member of MI5 who, with the assistance of a collaborator, had made the allegations, was not in itself enough to establish such a prima facie case. In any event the publication went far beyond the mere reporting of allegations, in so far as it set out substantial parts of the text of *Spycatcher*. For example, the alleged plot to assassinate Colonel Nasser occupies but one page of a book, in paperback of 387 pages, and the alleged plot to destabilise Mr Wilson's government about five pages. In this connection it is to be noted that counsel for 'The Sunday Times' accepted that neither of the two defences would have availed Mr. Wright had he sought to publish the text of *Spycatcher* in England. There is no reason of logic or principle why 'The Sunday Times' should have been in any better position acting as it was under his licence.

This leads on to consideration of the question whether 'The Sunday Times' should be held liable to account to the Crown for profits made from past and future serialisation of *Spycatcher*. An account of profits made through breach of confidence is a recognised form of remedy available to a claimant: *Peter Pan Manufacturing Corpn v Corsets Silhouette Ltd* [1963] 3 All ER 402, [1964] 1 WLR 96; cf. *Reading v A-G* [1951] AC 507. In cases where the information disclosed is of a commercial character an account of profits may provide some compensation to the claimant for loss which he has suffered through the disclosure, but damages are the main remedy for such loss. The remedy is, in my opinion, more satisfactorily to be attributed to the principle that no one should be permitted to gain from his own wrongdoing. Its availability may also, in general, serve a useful purpose in lessening the temptation for recipients of confidential information to misuse it for financial gain. In the present case 'The Sunday Times' did misuse confidential information and it would be naive to suppose that the prospect of financial gain was not one of the reasons why it did so. I can perceive no good ground why the remedy should not be made available to the Crown in the circumstances of this case, and I would therefore hold the Crown entitled to an account of profits in respect of the publication on 12 July 1987. I would add that in my opinion 'The Sunday Times', in the taking of the account, is not entitled to deduct in computing any gain the sums paid to Mr. Wright's publishers as consideration for the licence granted by the latter, since neither Mr. Wright nor his publishers were or would in the future be in a position to maintain an action in England for recovery of such payments. Nor would the courts of this country enforce a claim by them to the copyright in a work the publication of which they had brought about contrary to the public interest: cf. *Glyn v Weston Feature Film Co* [1916] 1 Ch 261, 269. Mr. Wright is powerless to prevent anyone who chooses to do so from publishing *Spycatcher* in whole or in part in this country, or to obtain any other remedy against them. There remains of course, the question whether the Crown might successfully maintain a claim that it is in equity the owner of the copyright in the book. Such a claim has not yet been advanced, but might well succeed if it were to be.

In relation to future serialisation of further parts of the book, however, it must be kept in mind that the proposed subject matter of it has now become generally available and that 'The Sunday Times' is not responsible for this having happened. In the circumstances 'The Sunday Times' will not be committing any wrong against the Crown by publishing that subject matter and should not therefore be liable to account for any resultant profits. It is in no different position from anyone else who now might choose to publish the book by serialisation or otherwise.

The next matter for consideration, though the point is not now of any practical importance is whether the 'Observer' and 'The Guardian' were in breach of an obligation of confidence by the publication of their articles on 22 and 23 June 1986. The circumstances were that Mr. Wright and Heinemann and their solicitors had given to the New South Wales court, pending trial of the action there, undertakings not to disclose any information gained by Mr. Wright in the course of his service with MI5. Scott J. found, and it has never been disputed by counsel for the two newspapers, that information about the allegations described in the two articles must have been obtained from someone in the office of the publishers or in that of their solicitors. Scott J. also inferred that the newspapers must have known of the undertakings that had been given. There can be no question of the articles having been a fair and accurate report of proceedings in the New South Wales court. Such a report could only cover matters which had actually been divulged in open court. The newspapers knew that the information in question was of a confidential nature, deriving as it did from Mr. Wright and relating to his experiences in MI5. Some of the allegations, albeit of minor significance, had never previously been published at all. The allegations about Sir Roger Hollis had received quite widespread publicity in various books and newspapers and had been made by Mr. Wright himself on a Granada television programme in July 1984. Allegations about the Nasser plot and the Wilson plot and the bugging of embassies and other places had been made in a number of published books, but had been attributed to Mr. Wright only in an 'Observer' article of 15 March 1985 and another of 9 February 1986, and then only in a somewhat oblique fashion. I do not consider that an injunction would have been granted against publication of the fact that Mr. Wright was repeating in his memoirs the allegations about Sir Roger Hollis, because it was quite well known that he had been making that allegation for a considerable time. The specific attribution to Mr. Wright of the other allegations is perhaps a different matter. But I would regard it as highly doubtful that the publication of that attribution could reasonably be regarded as damaging to the public interest of the United Kingdom in the direct sense that the information might be of value to unfriendly foreign intelligence services, or as calculated to damage that interest indirectly in any of the ways spoken of in evidence by Sir Robert Armstrong. I consider that on balance the prospects are that the Crown would not have been held entitled to a permanent injunction. Scott J. and the majority of the Court of Appeal took that view, and I would not be disposed to differ from them.

The final issue is whether the Crown is entitled to a general injunction against all three newspapers restraining them from publishing any information concerned with the *Spycatcher* allegations obtained by any member or former member of the Security Service which they know or have reasonable grounds for believing to have come from any such member or former member, including Mr. Wright, and also from attributing any such information in any publication to any member or former member of the Security Service. The object of an injunction on these lines is to set up a second line of defence, so to speak, for the confidentiality of the operations of the Security Service. The first and most important line of defence is obviously to take steps to secure that members and ex-members of the service do not speak about their experiences to the press or anyone else to whom they are not authorised to speak. Obviously the Director-General of the Service is in a position to impose a degree of discipline upon the existing members of the service so as to prevent unauthorised disclosures, and it is reasonable to suppose that in any event the vast majority of these members are conscientious and would never consider making such disclosures. In so far as unconscientious ex-members are concerned, in particular Mr. Wright, the position under existing circumstances is more difficult, although measures may now be introduced which are apt to discourage breaches of confidence by such people. There are a number of problems involved in the general width of the injunction sought. Injunctions are normally aimed at the prevention of some specific wrong, not at the prevention of wrongdoing in general. It would hardly be appropriate to subject a person to an injunction on the ground that he is the sort of person who is likely to commit some kind of wrong, or that he has an interest in doing so. Then the injunction sought would not leave room for the possibility that a defence might be available in a particular case. If Mr. Wright were to publish a second book in America or Australia or both and it were to become readily available in this country, as has happened in regard to his first book, newspapers which published its contents would have as good a defence as the respondents in the present case. It would not be satisfactory to have the availability of any defence tested on contempt proceedings. In my opinion an injunction on the lines sought should not be granted.

A few concluding reflections may be appropriate. In the first place I regard this case as having established that members and former members of the Security Service do have a lifelong obligation of confidence owed to the Crown. Those who breach it, such as Mr. Wright, are guilty of treachery just as heinous as that of some of the spies he excoriates in his book. The case has also served a useful purpose in bringing to light the problems which arise when the obligation of confidence is breached by publication abroad. The judgment of the High Court of Australia reveals that even the most sensitive defence secrets of this country may not expect protection in the courts even of friendly foreign countries, although a less extreme view was taken by Sir Robin Cooke P. in the New Zealand Court of Appeal (*A-G v Wellington Newspapers Ltd (No 2)* [1988] 1 NZLR 180). The secrets revealed by Mr. Wright refer to matters of some antiquity, but there is no reason to expect that secrets concerned with matters of great current importance would receive any different treatment. Consideration should be given to the possibility of some international agreement aimed at reducing the risks to collective security involved in the present state of affairs. The First Amendment clearly poses problems in relation to publication in the United States of America, but even there there is the prospect of defence and intelligence secrets receiving some protection in the civil courts, as is shown by the decision of the Supreme Court in *Snepp v United States* (1980) 444 US 507. Some degree of comity and reciprocity in this respect would seem desirable in order to promote the common interests of allied nations. . . .

Lords Brightman, Goff and **Jauncey of Tullichettle** delivered generally concurring speeches. **Lord Griffiths** dissented in part.

Appeal and cross-appeal dismissed.

NOTES

1. The important question of the circumstances in which the duty of confidence owed by an officer of the security and intelligence services might be overridden was addressed more explicitly by Scott J at first instance, who stated that this:

'would not extend to information of which it could be said that, notwithstanding the needs of national security, the public interest required disclosure. Nor, in my opinion, would the duty extend to information which was trivial or useless or which had already been disclosed under the authority of the government.'

For example, the duty of confidence could not be used to prevent the press from informing the public of the allegation of a plot to assassinate President Nasser, and the press were entitled to report the fact that allegations of an MI5 plot to destabilise the Wilson government had been repeated by an insider:

'The press has a legitimate role in disclosing scandals by government. An open democratic society requires that that be so. If an allegation be made by an insider that, if true, would be a scandalous abuse by officers of the Crown of their powers and functions, and the allegation comes to the attention of the press, the duty of confidence cannot, in my opinion, be used to prevent the press from repeating the allegation. . . . Nor is it, in my opinion, necessarily an answer to say that the allegation should not have been made public but should have been reported to some proper investigating authority. In relation to some, perhaps many, allegations made by insiders, that may be the only proper course open to the press. But the importance to the public of this country of the allegation that members of MI5 endeavoured to undermine and destroy public confidence in a democratically elected government makes the public the proper recipient of the information'.[9]

In the House of Lords, Lord Griffiths denied the existence of an exception for trivia. He was, however, prepared to countenance a public interest defence, while finding it very difficult to envisage the circumstances where the facts would justify it:

9   [1988] 3 All ER 545 at 585, 588–589.

'But, theoretically, if a member of the service discovered that some iniquitous course of action was being pursued that was clearly detrimental to our national interest, and he was unable to persuade any senior member of his service or any member of the establishment, or the police, to do anything about it, then he should be relieved of his duty of confidence so that he could alert his fellow citizens to the impending danger.'[10]

However, no such considerations arose in *Spycatcher*. Lord Goff's position was similar.[11] Lord Keith was more concerned with the point that the public interest defence would not in any event have been open to Mr Wright on the facts.

2. Opinions were expressed on a number of other points that did not directly arise for consideration.

(1) Would Peter Wright or his publishers be restrained now from publishing *Spycatcher* in the UK? Lord Griffiths and Lord Jauncey of Tullichettle were clear that he would, on the ground that his duty of confidence persisted;[12] Lord Goff was very doubtful;[13] Lord Keith and Lord Brightman left the point open, but indicated that such an injunction would be based on the principle that he should not be permitted to take advantage of his own wrongdoing, and not on the basis of breach of confidence.[14]

(2) The position as to copyright. The House was clear that neither Wright nor his publishers had any copyright in *Spycatcher* that was enforceable in the UK[15] and, indeed, it was suggested that copyright might well be vested in the Crown.[16] See Y. Cripps,[17] noting that the government had based its claim for an account of profits on breach of confidence and not on a constructive trust imposed on any copyright which Wright or his publishers might hold. In a future case, the law of copyright might prove more fruitful, especially as there is no 'public domain' defence.[18]

3. The question for the House of Lords at the 'interlocutory stage' was whether the Millett interlocutory injunctions should be continued or discharged. The general approach to be adopted when considering whether an interlocutory injunction should be granted was laid down by the House of Lords in *American Cyanamid Co v Ethicon Ltd*,[19] and requires the judge to consider: (1) whether the plaintiff applicant for the injunction has an arguable case in law; (2) if so, whether damages would be an adequate or appropriate remedy should an interlocutory injunction be refused and the plaintiff ultimately succeed at trial; and (3) if not, where the balance of convenience lay. Sir Nicolas Browne-Wilkinson V-C held that since the Millett

---

10 [1988] 3 All ER 545, 650.
11 [1988] 3 All ER 545, 660–661.
12 [1990] 1 AC 109, 271, 293.
13 [1990] 1 AC 109, 284–289.
14 [1990] 1 AC 109, 259, 265–266.
15 See Lord Keith at 262–263, Lord Brightman at 267, Lord Griffiths at 275–276 and Lord Jauncey at 294.
16 See Lord Keith at 263, Lord Brightman at 266, Lord Griffiths at 276 and Lord Goff at 288.
17 [1989] PL 13.
18 Ibid., pp. 14–15, 19–20. The various stages of the *Spycatcher* litigation are considered by D. G. T. Williams, [1988] CLJ 2, 329, [1989] CLJ 1 and (1989) 12 Dalhousie LJ 209; Y. Cripps, [1989] PL 13 (on breaches of copyright and confidence) and E. Barendt, [1989] PL 204 (on freedom of speech); S. Lee, (1987) 103 LQR 506 (on the interlocutory stage); F. A. Mann, (1988) 104 LQR 497; M. Turnbull and M. Howard (1989) 19 UWALR 117, (1989) 105 LQR 382 (on the Australian decisions); P. Birks, (1989) 105 LQR 501; J. Michael, (1989) 52 MLR 389; B. J. Narain, (1988) 39 NILQ 73; D. Burnet and R. Thomas, (1989) 16 JLS 210; Lord Oliver of Aylmerton, (1989) 23 Israel LR 409; G. Jones (1989) 42 CLP 49; D. Kingsford-Smith and D. Oliver (eds.), *Economical with the Truth* (1990), chapters by D. Pannick and R. Austin; K. D. Ewing and C. D. Gearty, *Freedom under Thatcher* (1990), pp. 152–169. See also M. Turnbull, *The Spycatcher Trial* (1988).
19 [1975] AC 396.

injunctions had been granted in 1986 there had been a material change in the circumstances, given the publicity given to the Australian trial, the widespread publication of *Spycatcher* material in the foreign press and the publication of *Spycatcher* itself in the US. The government had taken the view that proceedings in the US to restrain publication would be doomed to failure, in the light of the 1st Amendment guarantees of freedom of speech. It also decided not to seek to prevent importation of *Spycatcher*, which could accordingly be obtained in the UK by mail order or simply brought back by travellers (it was apparently a best seller on the bookstall at JF Kennedy Airport). The Vice-Chancellor (*A-G v Guardian Newspapers Ltd*)[20] concluded, with reluctance, that the A-G had an arguable case for permanent injunctions; it was clear that damages would not be an appropriate remedy. However, the balance of convenience was against continuing the injunctions: the public interest in terms of deterring the publication of memoirs by members of the security service was small compared with the public interest in freedom of the press: 'One of the safeguards of our country and our system is to have a press that can search matters out, disclose them, and give rise to informed public discussion. . . . [O]ne should not restrain publication in the press unless it is unavoidable.'[1] Moreover, 'If the courts were to make orders manifestly incapable of achieving their avowed purpose, such as to prevent the dissemination of information which is already disseminated, the law would to my mind indeed be an ass'.[2]

The Court of Appeal allowed an appeal by the A-G, and a further appeal by the newspapers was dismissed by the House of Lords (*A-G v Guardian Newspapers Ltd*[3] by 3–2, Lords Brandon, Templeman and Ackner, Lords Bridge and Oliver dissenting. The decision was announced on 30 July with reasons given later. Their Lordships were agreed that the injunctions had originally properly been granted and that the compromise solution adopted by the Court of Appeal, permitting publication of 'a summary in very general terms' of the *Spycatcher* allegations, was unworkable. The majority were agreed that the A-G still had an arguable case for permanent injunctions. Lord Brandon argued that discharge of the injunctions now would cause permanent and irrevocable damage to the A-G's case for permanent injunctions; their continuance would merely postpone reporting by the newspapers, should *they* ultimately prevail at trial. The potential injustice to the A-G of the first course of action outweighed the potential injustice to the newspapers of the second. The approaches of Lord Templeman and Lord Ackner were more robust. Lord Templeman condemned Peter Wright's 'treachery' and held that there were good reasons for continuing the injunctions: the mass circulation of extracts from *Spycatcher* in the UK would expose members of the security service to the harassment of accusations to which they could not respond; discharge of the injunctions would create an 'immutable precedent' for 'any disgruntled public servant or holder of secret or confidential information relating to the security service' to 'achieve mass circulation in this country of damaging truths and falsehoods by the device of prior publication anywhere else abroad'; the newspaper reports were contrary to the object and purpose of the Millett injunctions, had originated with Wright and his publishers abroad, and were intended to bring pressure on the English courts to allow *Spycatcher* to be published here. Moreover, these reasons would make the interference with freedom

20 [1987] 3 All ER 316.
 1 [1987] 3 All ER 316 at 331.
 2 Ibid., at 332.
 3 [1987] 3 All ER 316.

of expression 'necessary in a democratic society in the interests of national security' and thus justified in terms of Art. 10 of the European Convention on Human Rights. Finally, the injunctions should be modified so as to prevent reporting of extracts from *Spycatcher* read in open court in Australia. Lord Ackner's speech was on similar lines, although he was even more critical of the conduct of the press, in particular in their response to the decision to continue the injunction that was announced on 30 July:

> 'It has required no imagination to anticipate the resentment which the newspaper, and, indeed, the entire media, would feel and vociferously express if we ultimately imposed a restraint on publication, albeit a temporary restraint. Moreover, it is a fact of life, however regrettable, that there are elements in the press as a whole which lack not only responsibility but integrity. . . It would have been absurd and naive of your Lordships not to have appreciated that every attempt would inevitably have been made to frustrate your Lordship's orders. The "antic disposition" of the press and the media following the announcement of the orders establishes this fully'.[4]

The modification to the injunctions was necessary to close a 'loophole' that might have been used by such elements to nullify the temporary damage limitation operation determined essential by the majority.

The speeches of the minority provided a stark contrast. Given the publication of *Spycatcher* in the US, an injunction would, in the view of Lord Bridge, now be 'futile'. Any remaining national security interest which the Millett injunctions were capable of protecting was of insufficient weight 'to justify the massive encroachment on freedom of speech' which their continuance would necessarily involve. He continued:[5]

> 'Having no written constitution, we have no equivalent in our law to the First Amendment to the Constitution of the United States of America. Some think that puts freedom of speech on too lofty a pedestal. Perhaps they are right. We have not adopted as part of our law the European Convention on Human Rights (Convention for the Protection of Human Rights and Fundamental Freedoms (Rome, 4 November 1950; TS 71 (1953); Cmd 8969)) to which this country is a signatory. Many think that we should. I have hitherto not been of that persuasion, in large part because I have had confidence in the capacity of the common law to safeguard the fundamental freedoms essential to a free society including the right to freedom of speech which is specifically safeguarded by art. 10 of the convention. My confidence is seriously undermined by your Lordships' decision. All the judges in the courts below in this case have been concerned not to impose any unnecessary fetter on freedom of speech. I suspect that what the Court of Appeal would have liked to achieve, and perhaps set out to achieve by its compromise solution, was to inhibit the Sunday Times from continuing the serialisation of *Spycatcher*, but to leave the press at large at liberty to discuss and comment on the *Spycatcher* allegations. If there were a method of achieving these results which could be sustained in law, I can see much to be said for it on the merits. But I can see nothing whatever, either in law or on the merits, to be said for the maintenance of a total ban on discussion in the press of this country of matters of undoubted public interest and concern which the rest of the world now knows all about and can discuss freely. Still less can I approve your Lordships' decision to throw in for good measure a restriction on reporting court proceedings in Australia which the Attorney General had never even asked for.
>
> Freedom of speech is always the first casualty under a totalitarian regime. Such a regime cannot afford to allow the free circulation of information and ideas among its citizens. Censorship is the indispensable tool to regulate what the public may and what they may not know. The present attempt to insulate the public in this country from information which is freely available elsewhere is a significant step down that very dangerous road. The maintenance

---

4   At 365.
5   At 346–347.

of the ban, as more and more copies of the book *Spycatcher* enter this country and circulate here, will seem more and more ridiculous. If the government are determined to fight to maintain the ban to the end, they will face inevitable condemnation and humiliation by the European Court of Human Rights in Strasbourg. Long before that they will have been condemned at the bar of public opinion in the free world.'

Lord Oliver endorsed the approach that had been taken by the Vice-Chancellor. Continuance of the injunctions 'on which I may call the Admiral Byng principle, "pour encourager les autres"' would involve misuse of the injunctive remedy, as would be its use to punish Mr Wright. (Lord Goff expressly agreed with this view in *A-G v Guardian Newspapers Ltd (No 2)*[6]). The newspapers were not responsible for the publication of *Spycatcher* in the US. He did not think the A-G would have an arguable case for a permanent injunction at trial. In the event, of course, permanent injunctions were refused.

4. In *Observer and Guardian v United Kingdom*,[7] and *Sunday Times v United Kingdom*,[8] the grant of the interlocutory injunctions was considered by the European Court of Human Rights. The court concluded by 14 to 10 that the injunctions up until the publication of *Spycatcher* in the United States in July 1987 did not violate Art 10 ECHR, but concluded unanimously that the continuation of the injunctions thereafter was such a violation.[9]

5. It was clear in the outcome of the *Spycatcher* litigation that the law of confidence, like the criminal law, will be ineffective in reaching persons outside the jurisdiction. Lord Oliver, for one, argued that 'in the end, the preservation of security secrets has to depend on the imposition on members of the security services of extremely tight *contractual* obligations which can be enforced interlocutorially without the assumption of any burden beyond the proof of the contract'[10] (cf. the position in the US).[11] Section 1 of the Official Secrets Act 1989[12] now imposes a 'lifelong duty of confidence' on members of the security services.

6. *A-G v Guardian Newspapers Ltd (No 2)* was applied by the House of Lords in *Lord Advocate v Scotsman Publications Ltd*.[13] Anthony Cavendish was an officer of MI6 from 1948 to 1953. In 1987 he sought authorisation for the publication of his memoirs, *Inside Intelligence*, which included some information about his time in MI6. Authorisation was refused. He distributed 279 of 500 copies he had printed at his own expense to private individuals. One of them gave a copy to the *Scotsman*, which published an article including some material from the book on 5 January 1988. The Lord Advocate sought an interim interdict restraining the *Scotsman* and any person having notice of the interdict from publishing (with certain exceptions) any information obtained by C in the course of his employment in MI6. The Lord Ordinary and the Second Division of the Court of Session refused the application.[14] The Lord Advocate appealed without success to the House of Lords. During argument before the Second Division, the Crown conceded that the book contained no information the disclosure of which was capable of damaging national security. In the light of this, the House held that the public interest did not require publication by the

---

6 [1990] 1 AC 109, 288.

7 Judgment of 26 November 1991, Series A No. 216.

8 Judgment of 26 November 1991, Series A No. 217.

9 See J. McDermott, (1992) J Media L & P 137 and S. Colyer, ibid., p. 142.

10 (1989) 23 Israel LR at 424.

11 Below, p. 867.

12 Above, p. 811.

13 [1990] 1 AC 812.

14 1988 SLT 490.

Scotsman to be restrained. Lord Keith[15] pointed out that the decision did not mean that any newspaper which received such an unsolicited book of memoirs by an intelligence officer would be free to publish: if there had been no previous publication, and no concession that the contents were innocuous, 'the newspaper would undoubtedly itself come under an obligation of confidence and be subject to restraint. If there had been a minor degree of prior publication, and no such concession, it would be a matter for investigation whether further publication would be prejudicial to the public interest, and interim interdict would normally be appropriate'.

Lords Griffiths and Goff agreed with Lord Keith. Lords Templeman and Jauncey noted that the decision mirrored the provision of ss. 1 and 5 of the Official Secrets Act 1989 (not then in force): under that provision, members and former members of the security services can be liable notwithstanding that no damage is proved; a third party could only be liable if a disclosure is damaging. See N. Walker, 'Spycatcher's Scottish Sequel',[16] noting the confusion between contents-based and non-contents-based arguments put forward by the Crown, and criticising the reliance on the terms of legislation in determining the scope of private law.

7. *Cabinet documents.* The foundation for the use of the law of confidence by the Crown was provided by the decision of Lord Widgery CJ in *A-G v Jonathan Cape Ltd*[17] (the Crossman Diaries case), discussed by Lord Keith.[18]

8. Cabinet documents may also be protected from disclosure in litigation by a claim that disclosure would be contrary to the public interest.[19] Note that in relation to both claims of public interest immunity and government applications to restrain threatened breaches of confidence the courts must balance competing interests. In the former, the public interest in the proper administration of justice is balanced against the public interest in keeping certain matters confidential. In the latter the public interest in confidentiality is balanced against other public interests, such as the freedom of speech.

9. The conventions as to the publication of ministerial memoirs were considered by the *Committee of Privy Counsellors on Ministerial Memoirs*.[20] The committee endorsed the view taken by the Cabinet in 1946 that it was necessary

'to keep secret information of two kinds, disclosure of which would be detrimental to the public interest:

(*a*) In the international sphere, information whose disclosure would be injurious to us in our relations with other nations, including information which would be of value to a potential enemy.

(*b*) In the domestic sphere, information the publication of which would be destructive of the confidential relationships on which our system of government is based and which may subsist between Minister and Minister, Ministers and their advisers, and between either and outside bodies or private persons.'[21]

The committee suggested further 'working rules' as to the reticence due from an ex-Minister:

15 pp. 858–859.
16 [1990] PL 354.
17 [1976] QB 752.
18 Above, p. 852. On this case see Hugo Young, *The Crossman Affair* (1976); R. K. Middlemass, (1976) 47 PQ 39; M. W. Bryan, (1976) 92 LQR 180; D. G. T. Williams, [1976] CLJ 1; D. L. Ellis, 'Collective Ministerial Responsibility and Collective Solidarity' [1980] PL 367.
19 See below, p. 907.
20 Chairman, Lord Radcliffe Cmnd. 6386, 1976.
21 p. 7.

'(*a*) In dealing with the experience that he has acquired by virtue of his official position, he should not reveal the opinions or attitudes of colleagues as to the Government business with which they have been concerned. That belongs to their stewardship, not to his. He may, on the other hand, describe and account for his own.

(*b*) He should not reveal the advice given to him by individuals whose duty it has been to tender him their advice or opinions in confidence. If he wishes to mention the burden or weight of such advice, it must be done without attributing individual attitudes to identifiable persons. Again, he will need to exercise a continuing discretion in any references that he makes to communications received by him in confidence from outside members of the public.

(*c*) He should not make public assessments or criticisms, favourable or unfavourable, of those who have served under him or those whose competence or suitability for particular posts he has had to measure as part of his official duties.'[1]

As to enforcement, the committee did not regard the legal principles expounded by Lord Widgery CJ in the Crossman Diaries case as providing 'a system which can protect and enforce those rules of reticence that we regard as called for when ex-Ministers compose their memoirs. . . .' According to his Lordship, each case would have to be decided on its own facts – there were 'no fixed principles of legal enforceability'.[2] The committee did not regard a judge as 'so equipped as to make him the best arbitrator of the issues involved. The relevant considerations are political and administrative. . . .' Moreover, the legal principles did not protect confidences of or about civil servants. Neither did legislation offer the right solution. The 'burden of compliance' should be 'left to rest on the free acceptance of an obligation of honour'.[3] Whenever a former Minister intends to publish information derived from his ministerial experience he should submit the full text in advance to the Secretary of the Cabinet. If clearance is refused in relation to information concerning national security or international affairs, the Minister may appeal to the Prime Minister, whose decision is final. If clearance is refused in relation to other information it is for the Minister to decide whether to publish; moreover, the information may be published after 15 years in any event, except that beyond that point he should not reveal the advice tendered by individuals who are still members of the public service nor make public assessment or criticisms of them. The government accepted these recommendations[4] and they remain operative.[5] The Labour government has no plans to change them.[6] However, not all ministers have observed them.[7] 'Everything which the Government failed to have decided in its favour in the *Crossman Diaries* case was duly enshrined in [these] constitutional conventions.'[8]

The current guidance as to publication by civil servants is set out in the *Directory of Civil Service Guidance 2000*:[9]

Memoirs and Books: Publication by Civil Servants

1. Section 4.2 of the Civil Service Management Code sets out the rules relating to civil servants' duties of confidentiality and their use of official information.

2. Serving civil servants who wish to publish books or other works which draw on official information or experience must apply for permission to do so by submitting their text for

1   pp. 20–21.
2   p. 24.
3   p. 26.
4   903 HC Deb, 22 January 1976, cols. 521–523.
5   Code of Conduct for Ministers, para. 103 c, www.cabinet-office.gov.uk/central/1997/mcode; *Directory of Civil Service Guidance*, vol. 2, 'Ministerial Memoirs.'
6   HC Deb, 10 November 1999, col. 581, written answer.
7   See B. Castle, *The Castle Diaries* (1980), H. Jenkins, *The Culture Gap* (1979).
8   G. Robertson, *Freedom, the Individual and the Law* (7th edn, 1993), p. 194. See further R. Brazier, *Constitutional Practice* (3rd edn, 1999), pp. 127–129.
9   Vol. 2, www.cabinet-office.gov.uk/guidance/two/12.htm.

scrutiny by the appropriate department. No civil servant may publish his or her memoirs while still in the Service, because public responsibility for the actions of their departments rests with Ministers.

3. Former members of the Home Civil Service must continue to observe their duties of confidentiality after they have left Crown employment. In particular, they must supply to the Head of their former Department, in good time before publication, a copy of the text or other recorded form of any material which they intend to make public and which draws, or appears to draw, on official information or experience. They are also urged to seek the advice of the Head of their former Department before entering any commitment to publish or broadcast personal accounts of their experience in Crown employment. In clearing material for publication, the Head of the Department and the Head of the Home Civil Service will have regard to the factors set out in section 4.2 of the Civil Service Management Code. Parallel rules apply to former members of the Diplomatic Service, for whom the final authority is the Head of the Diplomatic Service.

4. Former civil servants must abide by the decision of the Head of their Service in respect not only of State secrets, or information whose disclosure would be prejudicial to the UK's international relations, but also in respect of matters of trust and confidentiality (official advice, the views of Ministers or of colleagues, or judgements on the qualities or abilities of Ministers or of colleagues) which fall within the period of 15 years recommended by the Radcliffe Committee (see *Ministerial Memoirs: the "Radcliffe Rules" and their application*). As also recommended by the Radcliffe Committee, this period can be extended for disclosures relating to public servants who are still serving. A similar extension applies to disclosures by former public servnts relating to Ministers or former Ministers still actively engaged in politics.

5. Heads of Department should ensure that guidance on the lines of the preceding paragraphs is given to civil servants whose work brings them into close contact with Ministers e.g. senior civil servnts, private secretaries, press officers. It should also go to temporary civil servants in the same position, including special advisers. It should be repeated from time to time to ensure that it is not forgotten.'

For example, Professor A. V. Jones' book, *Most Secret War*, which concerned Britain's secret scientific intelligence operations during the Second World War, was cleared by the Cabinet Office, MI6 and the D Notice Committee.[10] The power has been used 'to delete or dilute criticisms of still-serving ministers'.[11] The criteria for authorising publications by former members of the security and intelligence services were set out by the Foreign Secretary, Douglas Hurd, in a written answer.[12] The statement noted the duty of confidence and obligations under s. 1(1) of the Official Secrets Act 1989 applicable to former employees of the security and intelligence agencies. It continued:

'The need to protect sensitive information is fully recognised in the Intelligence Services Bill, as it is in the Security Service Act 1989. The Bill defines strictly the circumstances under which information may properly be disclosed by the intelligence services including disclosure of records in accordance with the Public Records Act 1958 and 1967, which of course applies only to matters over 30 years old.

Authorisation for publication or other disclosure will accordingly be especially rare and exceptional with regard to events which happened less than 30 years ago. In any case where a former member of the security and intelligence agencies or a person notified under section 1(1)(b)[of the 1989 Act] ... wishes to publish or otherwise disclose material relating to his official duties, whether older than 30 years or not, he will need to apply to his former employer for authority to disclose. But there may, in the case of older material, be more likelihood that there will be no objection to disclosure. Any applications made in good faith would be looked at on their individual merits, and would still be judged on whether disclosure

10 *The Times*, 10 May 1977; *Brownlie*, pp. 266–267.
11 Robertson, op. cit., in relation to the autobiography of Bernard Ingham, Mrs Thatcher's press secretary.
12 241 HC Deb, 20 April 1994, cols. 539–540, written answer.

of any particular piece of information would jeopardise national security, whether directly or indirectly. If not, the service would be able so to inform the prospective author and give him authority to make the disclosure, so that it would not be contrary to section 1(1) of the Official Secrets Act 1989 nor in breach of his civil duty of confidence. Authorisation would imply only that there were no concerns about national security. It would not imply that the Crown had endorsed the publication or confirmed the accuracy of its contents. The Crown would reserve the right not to give authorisation in cases where an officer had committed breaches of the criminal law or his civil obligations.'

Particular consternation has been caused in some quarters by the determination of Stella Rimington, former head of MI5, to publish her memoirs, albeit after clearance. It was reported that the views in Whitehall were mixed, but that MI6 was strongly against publication and leaked the story to the press.[13] Injunctions have been obtained preventing former members of special forces from publishing memoirs.[14] There has been speculation that the rules will be relaxed following the return of the Labour government at the 2001 general election.[15]

10. An injunction will only rarely be granted by a civil court to restrain a threatened breach of the criminal law, such as a breach of the Official Secrets Acts.[16] In the *Gouriet* case[17] Lord Wilberforce stated that it is:

'an exceptional power confined, in practice, to cases where an offence is frequently repeated in disregard of a, usually, inadequate penalty – see *A-G v Harris* [1961] 1 QB 74; or to cases of emergency – see *A-G v Chaudry* [1971] 1 WLR 1614.'

Threatened breaches of the Official Secrets Acts might well count as an 'emergency' for these purposes, at least where 'grave and irreparable' harm[18] would be caused. Cf. *Commonwealth of Australia v John Fairfax & Sons Ltd*.[19] Here, the federal government discovered that long extracts from unpublished government documents were to be printed in two newspapers and a book. The documents related to various defence and foreign affairs issues, but did not contain technical information of military significance. Many of them were classified. The government sought an interim injunction on three grounds: (1) the threatened breach of s. 79 of the Crimes Act 1914 (Cth), which is similar in terms to the Official Secrets Act 1911, s. 2(1)(a) and (b); (2) breach of confidence; and (3) breach of copyright. Mason J acceded to the application on ground (3) alone. On ground (1) his Lordship stated:[20]

'It may be that in some circumstances a statutory provision which prohibits and penalizes the disclosure of confidential government information or official secrets will be enforceable by injunction. This is more likely to be the case when it appears that the statute, in addition to creating a criminal offence, is designed to provide a civil remedy to protect the government's right to confidential information. I do not think that s. 79 is such a provision. It appears in the *Crimes Act* and its provisions are appropriate to the creation of a criminal offence and to that alone. The penalties which it imposes are substantial. There is nothing to indicate that it was intended in any way to supplement the rights of the Commonwealth to relief by way of injunction to restrain disclosure of confidential information or infringement of copyright. There is no

1 3 *The Sunday Times*, 21 May 2000; *Guardian Unlimited Special Report*, 2 June 2000 (R. Norton-Taylor).
1 4 Ibid.
1 5 *Guardian Unlimited Special Report*, 31 December 2000 (M. Bright).
1 6 See *Gouriet v Union of Post Office Workers* [1978] AC 435; D. G. T. Williams, [1977] Crim LR 703; D. Feldman, (1979) 42 MLR 369; J. M. Evans, *de Smith's Judicial Review of Administrative Action* (4th edn, 1980), pp. 455–457. (The 5th edition, by Jowell and Woolf, deals with this area briefly at pp. 731–732.)
1 7 *Gouriet v Union of Post Office Workers* [1978] AC 435 at 481.
1 8 See *de Smith*, p. 456.
1 9 (1980) 55 ALJR 45, 147 CLR 39; HCA.
2 0 147 CLR at 50.

suggested inadequacy in these two remedies which would lead me to conclude that it is inappropriate to regard s. 79 as a foundation for injunctive relief.'

Do you think these observations would be applicable to a threatened breach of the Official Secrets Acts? Are they unduly restrictive? This case was referred to by Lord Keith on the breach of confidence point.[1] On the copyright point, note that actual Crown documents were involved, and not merely a work written by a former Crown servant.

An attempt by the Court of Appeal to extend this jurisdiction to freeze the proceeds of a spy's autobiography was rejected by the House of Lords.[2]

11. In the United States there is a heavy presumption against any prior restraint on the freedom of the press guaranteed by the First Amendment. In *New York Times v United States*[3] the Supreme Court rejected by 6–3 the government's application for an injunction to prevent publication of the 'Pentagon Papers', a series of secret government documents dealing with the origins of the United States' involvement in Vietnam. Black and Douglas JJ held that the First Amendment prevented any judicial restraint on speech and press. Brennan, Stewart and White JJ held, in varying degrees, that the government had failed to show that publication *would* (not could) cause direct, immediate and irreparable harm to the nation. Marshall J held that an injunction could not be issued in the absence of the specific statutory authority of Congressional legislation. Burger CJ and Harlan and Blackmun JJ held that the courts should not refuse to enforce the executive branch's claim, provided that a Cabinet-level officer personally so decided.[4] It was left unclear whether the strict tests propounded by Brennan, Stewart and White would be applicable where there was a specific statutory provision.

In 1979 a US district judge granted an injunction to restrain publication of materials on the hydrogen bomb: these had been specifically defined as 'restricted data' in the Atomic Energy Authority Act 1954, and the Act had also empowered the courts to issue injunctions against the publication of such material.[5]

Then in 1980 the Supreme Court held that an agreement requiring CIA employees not to publish any information about the agency without specific prior approval was a judicially enforceable contract applicable to both classified and non-classified information. Moreover, CIA employees were in a fiduciary position. An ex-employee of the CIA published without permission a highly critical account (*Decent Interval*) of the CIA's evacuation of South Vietnam after the fall of Saigon. The Supreme Court imposed a constructive trust on all profits from the sales in favour of the CIA and permanently enjoined the author from publishing future writings concerning the CIA or intelligence activities without submitting them to the CIA for prepublication review. This was notwithstanding the concession that the book contained no information that the CIA could have suppressed under the secrecy agreement.[6]

A similar outcome to that reached in *Snepp* was achieved by the House of Lords in *A-G v Blake (Jonathan Cape Ltd, third party).*[7] George Blake was a member of SIS

---

1 Above, p. 853.
2 *A-G v Blake* [2000] 4 All ER 385, below.
3 403 US 713 (1971).
4 See N. Sheehan et al., *The Pentagon Papers* (1971); L. Henkin, (1971) 120 U Pa L Rev 271; Nimmer, (1974) 26 Stan L Rev 311; M. Supperstone, *Brownlie's Law of Public Order and National Security* (2nd edn, 1981), pp. 271–274; C. R. Sunstein, 74 Calif LR 889.
5 42 USC §, 2014(y)–2162, 2274, 2280: *United States v Progressive Inc* 467 F Supp 990 (1979) (the litigation was dropped after similar materials were published elsewhere).
6 *Snepp v United States* 444 US 507 (1980) (see Comment, (1979) 14 Harv Civ Rights–Civ Lib L Rev 665; Comment, (1980) 32 Stan L Rev 409; D. F. Orentlicher, (1981) 81 Colum LR 662; C. R. Sunstein, 74 Calif LR 889, 912–921).
7 [2000] 4 All ER 385.

from 1944 to 1961. He had signed an Official Secrets Act declaration by which he agreed not to divulge any official information gained as a result of his employment either in the press or in book form. In 1951 he became an agent for the Soviet Union. In 1961 he was convicted under s. 1 of the Official Secrets Act 1911.[8] In 1966 he escaped to Moscow. In 1989 he wrote his autobiography (*No Other Choice*) and agreed to its publication by JC. No injunction to restrain publication was sought as the information was no longer confidential. However, his actions were in breach of contract. JC agreed to pay £150,000 as advance against the royalties. The House of Lords held by 4 to 1[9] that the Attorney-General was entitled, exceptionally, to restitutionary damages for the breach of contract.[10] The trial judge and the Court of Appeal[11] had rejected the Attorney's original case based on a breach of fiduciary duty (B was no longer an employee of the Crown) or breach of confidence (the information was no longer confidential). The Court of Appeal had upheld an alternative, public law, basis of claim flowing from the Attorney-General's capacity as guardian of the public interest, and granted an injunction freezing (but not confiscating) payments resulting from exploitation of *No Other Choice*. This basis was unanimously disapproved by the House of Lords on the ground that the court had no common law power to make what was in substance, albeit not in form, a confiscation order. 'There is no common law power to take or confiscate property without compensation.'[12]

It has been argued that there was no principled basis for the decision of the House, it being new law made to fit Blake's case.[13]

5 Security vetting

Processes by which individuals are 'vetted' by the state to ensure that they are not employed in situations that might compromise security have existed in one form or another for many years. From, at the latest, 1937, a relatively obscure branch (later C Division) of the Security Service conducted checks of the names of new civil servants against MI5 files. Analogous organisations in the US and Canada in addition, in a proportion of cases, took positive steps to investigate the backgrounds of individuals.[14] As matters turned out, the record of MI5 was mixed. On the one hand there was little if any evidence of penetration by enemy agents during the war; on the other hand a number of persons with known Communist backgrounds succeeded in joining the Security Service or the Secret Intelligence Service and subsequently operated successfully as agents for the USSR. After the war vetting procedures in the UK were applied more rigorously and arrangements for positive vetting were introduced.

---

8 Above, p. 825.

9 Lords Nicholls, Goff, Browne-Wilkinson and Steyn, Lord Hobhouse dissenting.

10 A declaration that the Attorney-General was entitled to be paid a sum equal to whatever amount was due and owing to B from JC Ltd under the 1989 publishing agreement.

11 [1997] Ch 84; [1998] Ch 439.

12 Per Lord Nicholls at 402, citing *A-G v De Keyser's Royal Hotel Ltd* [1920] AC 508 and *Burmah Oil Co v Lord Advocate* [1965] AC 75.

13 S. Hedley, (2000) 4 Web JCLI, noting that while Blake's treachery was very serious it was not so clear that the breach of his contractual undertaking was. See also D. Fox, [2001] CLJ 333, noting the deterrent effect of the award.

14 See L. Hannant, 'Inter-war security screening in Britain, the United States and Canada' (1991) 6(4) Intelligence and National Security 711.

(A) THE 'PURGE' PROCEDURE

In 1945, the defection of Igor Gouzenko stimulated a chain of events which led to the unravelling of major spy rings in Canada, the United States and Britain. This included the arrest and conviction in 1946 of Dr Alan Nunn May, a nuclear scientist who had spied for Russia while working in Canada. A number of civil servants, suspected of communist or fascist sympathies, were transferred to non-sensitive posts.[15] 'MI5 feared its covert purge might be "blown" as the number of transferees grew.' Accordingly, in 1948 the prime Minister, Mr Attlee, made a public statement to the effect that:

'the only prudent course to adopt is to ensure that no one who is known to be a member of the Communist Party, or to be associated with it in such a way as to raise legitimate doubts about his or her reliability, is employed in connection with work, the nature of which is vital to the security of the state.'[16]

The same rule was to govern persons known to be actively associated with Fascist organisations. These were included to give the appearance of impartiality: Communists were considered the real threat. 'The security authorities were overjoyed when they eventually found a fascist in one of the service departments.'[17] The procedure was revised in 1957, 1962 and 1985. Where the Minister ruled that there was a prima facie case, but the allegation was not accepted by the public servants, the matter would be referred to the 'Three Advisers' who would hear representations from the individual without disclosing the sources of evidence. The Three Advisers would report to the Minster but the final decision lay with him. If he upheld the ruling the public servant would be transferred to non-secret work or dismissed. The procedure applied also to certain cases of employment outside the public service, including employees of firms engaged in classified government contracts.[18] By November 1954, 124 civil servants had been removed from their posts for security reasons. Between 20 and 30 were dismissed; almost as many resigned; the remainder were transferred.[19] There were no cases under the purge procedure after 1969; this case was not, in the end, referred to the Three Advisers.[20] The procedure declined in importance with the introduction of positive vetting and can now be regarded as having lapsed.[1]

(B) POSITIVE VETTING

'By today's standards, the purge procedure was rudimentary, almost naive.'[2] The United States authorities regarded it as 'feeble'.[3] The arrest and conviction of Klaus Fuchs in 1950, a nuclear scientist who had leaked atomic secrets to the Russians, led

15 See P. Hennessy and G. Brownfeld, 'Britain's Cold War Security Purge: The Origins of Positive Vetting' (1982) 25(4) Historical Journal 965–973; R. J. Aldrich, *The Hidden Hand* (2001), pp. 117–121.
16 448 HC Deb, 15 March 1948, cols. 1703–1704.
17 P. Hennessy and G. Brownfeld, op. cit., p. 968.
18 Statement of the procedure to be followed when the reliability of a public servant is thought to be in doubt on security grounds (Cabinet Office). See D. G. T. Williams, *Not in the Public Interest* (1965), pp. 170–185; D. C. Jackson, (1957) 20 MLR 346; [1963] PL 51; I. Linn, *Application Refused* (1990); NCCL Trade Union Liaison Committee, *The Purging of the Civil Service* (1985).
19 D. G. T. Williams, op. cit., p. 171.
20 Information supplied by the Cabinet Office. The Three Advisers last sat in 1967.
1 Information supplied by the Security Vetting Appeals Panel.
2 P. Hennessy and G. Brownfeld, op. cit., p. 967.
3 Ibid., p. 969.

to the introduction of 'positive vetting'. Instead of simply ensuring that the security service had no adverse record of a candidate, a conscious effort should be made to confirm his reliability. The introduction of positive vetting was announced in a press statement released on 8 January 1952. The arrangements have been revised on a number of occasions, the latest being in 1994, as explained in the following extract from *Hansard*.

Vol. 251 HC Deb, cols. 764–766, written answer, 15 December 1994

The Prime Minister: [... To] ensure that security measures and procedures reflect current threats, the Government have recently completed a fundamental review of their arrangements for the management of protective security in Departments and agencies. In the area of personnel security, the review concluded that the vetting process served a worthwhile purpose, not only in disclosing circumstances which might lead to breaches of security but as a deterrent to those who might otherwise seek to undermine that security. The review recommended, however, that there should be a streamlining of the procedures that made up the vetting process. That work has now been completed.

The new framework should ensure that personnel security objectives are properly defined and that responsibility for achieving them is clearly established. There will be a greater emphasis on ensuring that personnel security resources are targeted on, and proportionate to, the threat and add necessarily and cost-effectively to the protection of government assets. Between 1 January and 31 March 1995, the existing arrangements will be replaced by a new personnel security regime which will consist of two levels of vetting, a security check and developed vetting. A security check will be similar to the current PV(S) – positive vetting (secret) – clearance, but will in addition include a check on the financial status of the individual. Developed vetting will replace the present PV(TS) – positive vetting (top secret) – and EPV – extended positive vetting – levels of vetting. The current system of counter terrorist checks will remain unchanged, but will be subject to review.

As at present, all candidates for security vetting will be asked to complete a security questionnaire which will explain the purpose of the procedure and invite them to provide the personal details required for the necessary checks to be carried out. Vetting will then be carried out on the basis of the statement of policy set out below.

Statement of HM Government's vetting policy
In the interests of national security, safeguarding the Parliamentary democracy and maintaining the proper security of the Government's essential activities, it is the policy of HMG that no one should be employed in connection with work the nature of which is vital to the interests of the state who:

is, or has been involved in, or associated with any of the following activities:
—   espionage,
—   terrorism,
—   sabotage,
—   actions intended to overthrow or undermine Parliamentary democracy by political, industrial or violent means; or
is, or has recently been:
—   a member of any organisation which has advocated such activities; or
—   associated with any organisation, or any of its members in such a way as to raise reasonable doubts about his or [sc. her] reliability; or
is susceptible to pressure or improper influence, for example because of current or past conduct; or
has shown dishonesty or lack of integrity which throws doubt upon their reliability; or
has demonstrated behaviour, or is subject to circumstances which may otherwise indicate unreliability.

In accordance with the above policy, Government departments and agencies will carry out a Security Check (SC) on all individuals who require long term, frequent and uncontrolled access to SECRET information or assets. A Security Check may also be applied to staff who are in a position directly or indirectly to bring about the same degree of damage as such individuals or who need access to protectively marked material originating from other countries or international organisations. In some circumstances, where it would not be possible for an individual to make reasonable progress in their career without clearance to SECRET level, it may be applied to candidates for employment whose duties do not, initially, involve such regular access.

An SC clearance will normally consist of:

a check against the National Collection of Criminal Records and relevant departmental and police records;
    in accordance with the Security Service Act 1989, where it is necessary to protect national security, or to safeguard the economic well-being of the United Kingdom from threats posed by persons outside the British Islands, a check against Security Service records; and
credit reference checks and where appropriate, a review of personal finances.

In some circumstances further enquiries, including an interview with the subject, may be carried out.

Individuals employed on government work who have long term, frequent and uncontrolled access to TOP SECRET information or assets, will be submitted to the level of vetting clearance known as Developed Vetting (DV). This level of clearance may also be applied to people who are in a position directly or indirectly to cause the same degree of damage as such individuals and in order to satisfy the requirements for access to protectively marked material originating from other countries and international organisations. In addition to a Security Check, a DV will involve:

an interview with the person being vetted; and
references from people who are familiar with the person's character in both the home and work environment. These may be followed up by interviews. Enquiries will not necessarily be confined to past and present employers and nominated character referees.

It is also the Government's policy that departments and agencies will carry out Counter Terrorist Checks (CTC) in the interest of national security before anyone can be:

authorised to take up posts which involve proximity to public figures at particular risk of attack by terrorist organisations, or which give access to information or material assessed to be of value to terrorists;

granted unescorted access to certain military, civil and industrial establishments assessed to be at particular risk of attack by a terrorist organisation.

The purpose of such checks is to prevent those who may have connections with terrorist organisations, or who may be vulnerable to pressure from such organisations, from gaining access to certain posts, and in some circumstances, premises, where there is a risk that they could exploit that position to further the aims of a terrorist organisation. A CTC will include a check against Security Service records. Criminal record information may also be taken into account.

Departments and agencies generally assure themselves, through the verification of identity, and written references from previous employers, that potential recruits are reliable and trustworthy. Such Basic Checks (BC) are already standard procedure for many departments and agencies. Where access needs to be granted to Government information or assets at CONFIDENTIAL level, departments, agencies and contractors engaged on government work are required to complete such checks. In some cases, at the CONFIDENTIAL level, where relevant, the Basic Check may be augmented with some of the checks normally carried out for security clearances.

Terms of Reference for the Security Vetting Appeals Panel (Updated October 2000)

1. The current policy on security vetting as announced in the Prime Minister's statement to the House of Commons on 15 December 1994, [see above]...

2. Where an amployee of a department, agency or other organisation specified in the Annex is aggrieved by the withdrawal or refusal of security clearance, and has exhausted appropriate internal appeal mechanisms, they may appeal to the Security Vetting Appeals Panel. The Panel will:

i.   Examine whether the appeal falls within the remit of the Panel; if so, it will:
ii. examine the procedure by which the vetting authority obtained and assessed the information underpinning the adverse vetting decision;
iii. examine the merits of the vetting decision, taking into account the interests of national security and the rights of the individual;
iv. produce a report of their recommendations for the Head of Department or equivalent; and
v.   produce a report for the complainant. As far as is possible, this should duplicate that sent to the Head of Department or equivalent.

Details of the Security Vetting Appeals Panel's operations are shown at Annex.

SECURITY VETTING APPEALS PANEL

Background
1. All departments and agencies should have in place an internal appeals process to consider challenges by individuals to security vetting decisions. The process should include an ultimate right of appeal to the Head of Department or equivalent. The appeals process should be available to all staff employed by the department or agency, or by its contractors, who are subject to vetting (but not to candidates for employment).
2. An independent Security Vetting Appeals Panel has been established to provide a final means of challenging a decision to refuse or withdraw security clearance. It is available to hear appeals from individuals in departments and other organisations, or those employed by contractors of those departments and organisations, who have exhausted the internal appeals process and who remain dissatisfied with the outcome.

Organisations covered by the Security Vetting Appeals Panel
3. All staff of the following organisations (excluding members of the Security and Intelligence Agencies, who are subject to different arrangements), who have been refused security clearance or have had it withdrawn, and who have exhausted the internal procedures for challenging the decision, have the right to appeal to the Security Vetting Appeals Panel:

> The Civil Service
> The Diplomatic Service
> The Armed Forces
> Other organisations and their subsidiaries which are listed in the Arrangements under section 2(3) of the Security Service Act 1989. These include:
>> the Police Forces;
>> the UKAEA;
>> the Civil Aviation Authority;
>> the Post Office;
>> British Telecommunications plc;
>> The Bank of England; and
>> Contractors of the above organisations.

Separate independent avenues of appeal against adverse vetting decisions are available to directly employed staff on the Security and Intelligence Agencies (and to those of their contractors) through the Security Service or Intelligence Services Tribunals as appropriate.

Access to the Security Vetting Appeals Panel
4. Security Division of the Cabinet Office provides the Secretariat for the Security Vetting Appeals Panel and handles the mechanics of the appeals process. The Panel will be convened to hear cases as they arise.
5. Departments and other organisations are responsible for drawing the attention of staff to the existence of the Panel when individuals are informed of the arrangements for the internal appeals process. It is the responsibility of Security Division to explain the Panel's procedures to these individuals. They should be told to write to The Secretary, Security Vetting Appeals Panel, Room 209, 4 Central Buildings, Matthew Parker Street, London SW1H 9NL.

How the Panel will operate

6. An appellant will be allowed to put their case to the Panel in person, accompanied, if they so wish, by a "friend". As the issues to be considered by the Panel are not matters of law, formal legal representation is not permitted. The role of the "friend" is confined to helping the appellant to present their case. A member of the Panel will not hear a case where there is a possible conflict of interest.

7. The defending department or organisation can also present their case in person to the Panel. Appellants should be provided, as far as possible and in advance of the hearing, with the reasons for the decision to refuse or withdraw security clearance, unless considerations of security or confidentiality prohibit this. When it is not possible to provide the appellant with the full reasons, the defending department or organisation should nevertheless submit them to the Panel in the normal way.

8. The Panel will follow an informal procedure. The hearing will be confidential to the parties concerned. A party to an appeal may submit information or make representations to the panel in the absence of the other party.

9. The department or organisation must disclose or give to the Panel such documents or information as they may require to carry out their functions.

10. The Panel is required to carry out their functions in such a way as to ensure that no document or information given to them by any person is disclosed, without the originator's consent, to any other person.

11. The Panel will produce a report of their findings. The report will include their recommendations, if any. Subject to the need to withhold any information in accordance with paragraph 10, the report will be published in full to both the appellant and the Head of the defending department or organisation.

Recommendations open to the Security Vetting Appeals Panel

12. The Panel will make recommendations to the Head of the department or organisation in the light of its findings. It can recommend:
— that the decision to refuse or withdraw security clearance should stand; or
— that security clearance should be granted or restored.
The Panel may also comment on the adequacy of the internal appeals process and make recommendations.

13. The department or organisation will inform the Panel's Secretary of the subsequent action taken.

14. The Panel will consider the merits of an appeal against a decision to refuse or withdraw security clearance. It will not become involved in examining any subsequent action which may be taken by the department or organisation over the continued employment of the appellant and will not therefore be concerned wit questions of compensation. No department or organisation can be required to retain an individual in whom they have lost confidence. However, it would be open to an individual who feels that they have been unfairly dismissed as a result of a decision to refuse or withdraw security clearance, to use existing procedures for challenging the decision.

15. More generally, any person who believes that the Security Service has disclosed information about them for use in determining whether they should be employed, or continue to be employed, by any person or in any office or capacity, may complain to the Security Service Tribunal asking them to investigate the complaint. Further information is available from The Security Service Tribunal, PO Box 18, London SE1 0TZ.

NOTES

1. PV procedures were considered in the report of the *Committee on Security Procedures in the Public Service* chaired by Lord Radcliffe[4] and the *Statement on the Recommendations of the Security Commission.*[5] Furthermore, the Security

4 Cmnd. 1681, 1961.
5 Cmnd. 8540, 1982.

Commission reported on the operation of procedures in the case of two persons convicted under the Official Secrets Acts who had received PV clearance:[6] Lord Bridge reported on the PV clearance of Commander Trestrail, who resigned as Queen's Police Officer following the revelation of his homosexuality. Information is also contained in memoranda to the Defence Committee[7] although the Committee did not have time to complete its work.[8] The 1994 guidelines replaced guidelines published in 1990.[9] While the procedures have been streamlined, the policy is generally similar, except that it applies to people whose work is vital to the 'interests' rather than the 'security' of the state; there is a general reference to susceptibility to pressure or improper influence (not just pressure from a subversive organisation, a foreign intelligence service or a hostile power); character defects that expose the person to blackmail or other influence by a subversive organisation or foreign intelligence service are no longer expressly mentioned as indications of unreliability (but presumably still are). There seems to be an intention to apply a higher degree of scrutiny (including financial checks) to a narrower range of personnel.[10]

2. In 1950 it was contemplated that PV would be applied to about 1,000 posts.[11] By 1982 the number of posts covered had risen to 68,000.[12] The Commission noted that the procedure was expensive and time-consuming, and recommended that the number of PV posts should be reviewed. In particular PV should no longer be an automatic requirement for officials of Under-Secretary rank and above and officials in the private offices of ministers. It remains a requirement for all members of the Diplomatic Service and the police special branches. It is also used in the UK Atomic Energy Authority and in firms which have contracts involving access to classified material. Following the review, some 2,000 posts were removed from the PV category.[13] Records of the number of posts subject to security vetting are, however, not kept centrally (information from the Cabinet Office). It is not government policy to reveal the numbers of persons subject to vetting checks, but in 1999–2000, 926 people were refused a CTC or had such a clearance withdrawn.[14] The Defence Vetting Agency (see below) carries out some 130,000 vetting checks and investigations each year.[15]

PV clearance does not apply to political ministers, although on appointment they are given specific instructions upon security problems and procedures. It does, however, apply to special advisers to ministers where they have regular access to highly classified information.

On 1 April 1997, various service units were combined to form the Defence Vetting Agency. It conducts vetting for the armed forces, MoD and defence industries and may undertake such work for other government departments.[16] Each of the security and intelligence agencies retains a small team of vetting officers.[17]

---

6 Geoffrey Arthur Prime (Report of May 1983, Cmnd. 8876), Philip Leslie Aldridge (Report of March 1984, Cmnd. 9212) and Steven John Hayden (Report of February 2000, Cm. 4578).
7 1982–83 HC 242.
8 See generally M. Hollingsworth and R. Norton-Taylor, *Blacklist: The Inside Story of Political Vetting* (1988); S. Fredman and G. S. Morris, *The State as Employer* (1989), pp. 232–236; I. Linn, *Application Refused: Employment Vetting by the State* (1990).
9 177 HC Deb, 24 July 1990, cols. 159–161, written answer.
10 See *Independent*, 16 December 1994.
11 P. Hennessy and I. Brownfeld, op. cit., p. 969.
12 Cmnd. 8540, p. 5.
13 I. Linn, op. cit., p. 21.
14 HC Deb, 25 January 2001, col. 693W.
15 HC Deb, 21 July 1999, col. 537, written answer.
16 HC Deb, 20 March 1997, col. 857, written answer; *Defence Vetting Agency Framework Document*, April 1997.
17 An arrangement endorsed in the Annual Report of the Intelligence and Security Committee 1999–2000 (Cm. 4897, 2000), para. 38.

3. *Criteria for clearance.* These are summarised in the 1994 statement. The policy on homosexuality was reviewed in 1991:[18]

> 'Because homosexual acts, even between consenting adults, remain criminal offences in a number of overseas countries, evidence of homosexuality, even if acknowledged, has been treated under this policy as a bar to clearance at PV(TS) – positive vetting (top secret) – or enhanced positive vetting (EPV) level in overseas posts and therefore as a bar to recruitment to certain areas of employment, including the diplomatic service. In the light of changing social attitudes towards homosexuality in this country and abroad, and the correspondingly greater willingness on the part of homosexuals to be open about their sexuality, their lifestyle and their relationships, the Government have reviewed this policy and concluded that in future there should be no posts involving access to highly classified information for which homosexuality represents an automatic bar to security clearance, except in the special case of the armed forces where homosexual acts remain offences under the service disciplinary Acts.
>
> The susceptibility of the subject to blackmail or pressure by a foreign intelligence service will continue to be a factor in the vetting of all candidates for posts involving access to highly classified information. An individual assessment is made in each case, taking account of the evidence which emerges in the course of the vetting process and the level of security clearance required.'

4. *Appeals.* An independent Security Vetting Appeals Panel was established on 1 July 1997 'to hear appeals against refusal or withdrawal of clearance at SC or DV levels and to advise the head of the organisation concerned. The Panel is available to all those, other candidates for recruitment, in the public and private sectors and in the armed forces who are subject to security vetting at these levels, have exhausted existing appeals mechanisms within their own organisations and remain dissatisfied with the results.' Staff of the security and intelligence agencies are to have recourse to the appropriate Service Tribunal (now the Tribunal under RIPA). The Panel replaced the Three Advisers. It is chaired by Sir Anthony May, and includes a High Court judge and other panel members with a background at a senior level in the Civil Service, the armed forces, the trades unions and industry, and related experience in security matters.[19] It heard two appeals in 1998 and two in 1999. It has 'stressed the need for as much openness as possible about the reasons for any doubts, giving the appellant opportunity to comment. Where decisions involve sensitive information, real efforts must be made to obtain the authority of the source to disclose or to agree a disclosable edited version.'[20] Formal legal representation is not permitted 'as the issues to be considered by the panel are not matters of law'.[1]

5. The limitations of judicial review as a mechanism for protecting the interests of those refused PV clearance were shown in *R v Director of Government Communications Headquarters, ex p Hodges.*[2] H, who had been employed at GCHQ since he was 16, informed his employers, when he was 21, that he had concluded that he was homosexual. Although he was entirely open about this, and had a current steady relationship, his PV clearance was removed as it was thought he might be subject to blackmail because of his lifestyle. The Divisional Court rejected his application for judicial review holding (1) that, in the light of the decision of the House of Lords in *Council of Civil Service Unions v Minister for the Civil Service,*[3] the court was not entitled even to consider whether the decision was *Wednesbury* unreasonable; and (2) that the procedure adopted was procedurally fair,

18 195 HC Deb, 23 July 1991, col. 474, written answer.
19 HC Deb, 19 June 1997, col. 243, written answer; 23 April 1998, col. 676, written answer.
20 Letter from the Secretary to the Panel, 13 October 2000.
 1 Ibid.
 2 (1988) Times, 26 July.
 3 [1985] AC 374.

notwithstanding that notes of an interview with his employers were not revealed. (H had been given a résumé of the facts, and had indeed been interviewed on a number of occasions.) In case he was wrong on point (1), Glidewell LJ also indicated that on the facts the Director's decision was not *Wednesbury* unreasonable.

6. In his report on the *Trestrail* case[4] Lord Bridge concluded that the PV procedures were not and could not be infallible: here, they were carried out efficiently and thoroughly. Where the subject was determined to conceal disqualifying factors this would present the PV investigator with an almost impossible task. They might be discovered by a 'system of random and covert surveillance of the subject's private activities'. However, this would '(a) add enormously to the cost of PV; (b) not necessarily be successful – this would depend on the length of the surveillance and the frequency of the subject's irregular behaviour; and (c) be strongly resented by most public servants as an unjustifiable invasion of their privacy'.[5] On the other hand, in the *Hayden* case the Security Commission was critical of a decision to overrule the recommendation of an investigator that Hayden's clearance be withdrawn. He was known to be in debt and a clear security risk. The Commission approved changes in vetting practice that the MoD had already implemented. It recommended that:

'(i) It should be standard practice for vetting authorities to consider whether to consult an individual's personnel or line managers, in order to ensure that the latter are aware of any particular vulnerabilities.

(ii) In cases where doubts emerge, it should be normal practice for regular consultations to take place between all those involved in assessing a clearance. Where the recommendations of Investigating Officers seem likely to be overridden for wider policy considerations of a non-security kind, there should invariably be a discussion between them and those responsible for making the assessment, so that options can be explored before final decisions are reached.

(iii) In risk cases where confidential medical reports exist on an individual, someone at an appropriately senior level should have the authority to see all the papers including a medical report on the individual's suitability to hold a DV clearance and thus be in a position to reach a proper assessment based on all relevant information.

(iv) More emphasis should be given to threats outside the traditional risk of an individual being vulnerable to approaches from a hostile foreign intelligence service. Threats from cheque-book journalism and industrial espionage should be given more emphasis in the current Field Investigation Officers Guide issued by the Cabinet Office, and in department guidance based upon it.

(v) The question of follow-up to Security Commission recommendations should be revisited to ensure that effective implementation of agreed recommendations takes place.'

Three recommendations were accepted in principle by the government.[6]

7. The 1990 reforms at least ensure that all candidates for vetting are aware that the procedures are to be carried out. They also expressly set out the procedure for individuals requiring access to less than Top Secret material (also in the past termed 'negative vetting').[7]

8. Following a major controversy in 1985, security vetting of staff in the BBC's domestic services has ended, except for those who may be invited to participate in the planning and operation of the wartime broadcasting service.[8]

---

4   1982–83 HC 59.
5   Ibid., pp. 21–22.
6   HC Deb, 17 February 2000, col. written answer 159.
7   See I. Linn, op. cit., pp. 17–21.
8   See M. Hollingworth and R. Norton-Taylor, *Blacklist* (1988), Chap. 5 and I. Linn, op. cit., pp. 49–50 and Appendix VII.

9. In *TD, DE and MF v UK*[9] the European Commission considered complaints that the applicants had been refused posts following adverse reports from security vetting. Complaints to the Security Service Tribunal were not upheld. The applicants alleged that information as to their private lives was kept on secret files by MI5 and/or police special branches and/or the PNC and/or GCHQ and that this infringed Art. 8(1) ECHR. The government submitted that TD and MF's job applications were not in fact referred to the Security Service or other agency as their long residence abroad rendered it impossible to carry out a satisfactory security clearance. The Commission concluded that they had failed to establish that there was a reasonable likelihood that the Security Service or other agency had compiled or retained information about their private life. The third case was adjourned for further examination of the facts, but was subsequently declared inadmissible on the ground that the legislative regime of the Security Service Act 1989 complied with Art. 8.[10]

6 The security and intelligence services

There is now a vast literature on the activities of the security and intelligence services, ranging from works of historical scholarship,[11] through books by knowledgeable observers apparently based on inside information[12] to journalistic pot-boilers. It has only been where the authors have themselves been members or former members of the relevant services that the government has taken serious steps to prevent publication, ultimately with comparatively little success.[13] With the growth in the amount of information about the services that has been made public has come increased concern at the constitutional position of the services, and at the illegality or impropriety of some of their activities. Examples of the latter include Peter Wright's claims that he and others 'bugged and burgled our way across London at the State's behest, while pompous, bowler-hatted civil servants in Whitehall pretended to look the other way';[14] his claims of an MI5 plot to destabilise the Wilson government;[15] and the revelations of Cathy Massiter.[16] The last of these led to an application for judicial review by three prominent CND members challenging *inter alia* the legality of the tapping of Cox's telephone: *R v Secretary of State for the Home Department, ex p Ruddock*.[17] The challenge ultimately failed, but was nevertheless embarrassing for the government. Moreover, in autumn 1988, the European Commission on Human Rights declared admissible a case brought by two former NCCL officers, Patricia Hewitt and Harriet Harman, complaining of their classification as 'subversive' by MI5, which had placed them under surveillance.[18] One of their grounds of challenge

9 Apps. Nos. 18600/91, 18601/92 and 18602/91, 12 October 1992.
10 *Eskester v UK* (App. No. 18601/91, 2 April 1993), below p. 890.
11 E.g. C. Andrew, *Secret Service* (1985); F. H. Hinsley and C. A. G. Simkins, *British Intelligence in the Second World War* (1990); I. Leigh and L. Lustgarten, *In from the Cold* (1994).
12 E.g. books by Nigel West (the pseudonym of Rupert Allason MP), including *MI5: British Security Service Operations 1909–45* (1981); *A Matter of Trust: MI5 1945–72* (1982); *MI6: British Secret Intelligence Service Operations 1909–45*; *Molehunt* (1986); *GCHQ: The Secret Wireless War 1909–86; The Friends: Britain's Post-War Secret Intelligence Operations* (1988); M. Smith, *New Cloak, Old Dagger* (1996).
13 See above, pp. 848–863.
14 *Spycatcher* (1987), p. 54.
15 Ibid., pp. 362–372; D. Leigh, *The Wilson Plot* (1988). According to *MI5 The Security Service* (3rd edn, 1998), p. 39, 'Wright himself finally admitted in an interview with BBC's *Panorama* programme in 1988 that his account had been unreliable'.
16 Above, p. 831.
17 [1987] 2 All ER 518 (see I. Leigh, [1987] PL 12).
18 *H and H v UK* App. No. 12175/86.

was the absence of any effective remedy for complainants. In May 1989, the Commission found that there had been breaches of Arts. 8 and 13 ECHR.[19] In response the government secured the passage of the Security Service Act 1989. This places the Security Service (MI5) on a statutory footing, but does little to answer the many concerns that have been expressed.

The Security Service operates at home and in the colonies, and has traditionally been concerned with counter-espionage. The Secret Intelligence Service (MI6), which mainly operates abroad, in co-operation with the Foreign Office, collects intelligence by covert means. Government Communications Headquarters (GCHQ) intercepts and analyses signals intelligence, including the communications of foreign countries, friendly and otherwise, companies and private individuals. SIS and GCHQ have now also been placed on a statutory basis by the Intelligence Services Act 1994. The work of the Security Service has been summarised in a glossy booklet issued by HMSO: *MI5, The Security Service.*[20] In 1997/98, direct expenditure on the Service's case areas was apportioned as follows: terrorism related to Northern Ireland, 25%; international terrorism, 15.5%; espionage, 12%; protective security, 7.5%; serious crime, 2.5% and proliferation (countering the threat posed by the spread of weapons of mass destruction), 2.0%.[1] The main changes in recent years are, first, that there are currently no investigations in the area of subversion. Since the late 1980s the threat from subversive (Communist, Trotskyists and Fascist) groups 'has declined and is now insignificant'. In 1997–98 only 0.3% of the Service's resources were devolved to 'the remnants of this work, predominantly to pay the pensions of retied agents'.[2] Secondly, the Security Service Act 1996 added supporting law enforcement agencies in work on serious crime to its statutory functions.[3] In October 1992, it took over from Special Branch lead responsibility for the intelligence effort against Irish Republican terrorism on the British mainland.[4]

Security Service Act 1989

1. The Security Service
(1) There shall continue to be a Security Service (in this Act referred to as 'the Service') under the authority of the Secretary of State.
(2) The function of the Service shall be the protection of national security and, in particular, its protection against threats from espionage, terrorism and sabotage, from the activities of agents of foreign powers and from actions intended to overthrow or undermine parliamentary democracy by political, industrial or violent means.
(3) It shall also be the function of the Service to safeguard the economic well-being of the United Kingdom against threats posed by the actions or intentions of persons outside the British Islands.
[(4) It shall also be the function of the Service to act in support of the activities of police forces, the National Criminal Intelligence Service, the National Crime Squad and other law enforcement agencies in the prevention and detection of serious crime.][5]
[(5) Section 81(5) of the Regulation of Investigatory Powers Act 2000 (meaning of "prevention" and "detection"), so far as it relates to serious crime, shall apply for the purposes

---

19 (1989) 14 EHRR 657, below, p. 890.
20 1993; 3rd edn, 1998.
1 *MI5, The Security Service* (3rd edn, 1998), pp. 6–7.
2 Ibid., pp. 18–19.
3 See below, p. 886.
4 Ibid., p. 14.
5 Inserted by the Security Service Act 1996, s. 1(1) and amended by the Police Act 1997, Sch. 9, para. 60.

of this Act as it applies for the purposes of the provisions of that Act not contained in Chapter 1 of Part 1.][6]

2. The Director-General
(1) The operations of the Service shall continue to be under the control of a Director-General appointed by the Secretary of State.

(2) The Director-General shall be responsible for the efficiency of the Service and it shall be his duty to ensure—

(a) that there are arrangements for securing that no information is obtained by the Service except so far as necessary for the proper discharge of its functions or disclosed by it except so far as necessary for that purpose or for the purpose of [the prevention or detection of][7] serious crime [or for the purpose of any criminal proceeding][8]; and

(b) that the Service does not take any action to further the interests of any political party; [and

(c) that there are arrangements, agreed with [the Director General of the National Criminal Intelligence Service][9] for co-ordinating the activities of the Service in pursuance of section 1(4) of this Act with the activities of police forces, [the National Criminal Intelligence Service, the National Crime Squad] and other law enforcement agencies.][10]

(3) The arrangements mentioned in subsection (2)(a) above shall be such as to ensure that information in the possession of the Service is not disclosed for use in determining whether a person should be employed, or continue to be employed, by any person, or in any office or capacity, except in accordance with provisions in that behalf approved by the Secretary of State.

[(3A) Without prejudice to the generality of subsection (2)(a) above, the disclosure of information shall be regarded as necessary for the proper discharge of the functions of the Security Service if it consists of—

(a) the disclosure of records subject to and in accordance with the Public Records Act 1958; or

(b) the disclosure, subject to and in accordance with arrangements approved by the Secretary of State, of information to the Comptroller and Auditor General for the purposes of his functions.][11]

(4) The Director-General shall make an annual report on the work of the Service to the Prime Minister and the Secretary of State and may at any time report to either of them on any matter relating to its work....

7. Short title, commencement and extent
. . . .

(3) This Act extends to Northern Ireland.

(4) Her Majesty may by Order in Council direct that any of the provisions of this Act specified in the Order shall extend, with such exceptions, adaptations and modifications as may be so specified, to the Isle of Man, any of the Channel Islands or any colony.

Intelligence Services Act 1994

The Secret Intelligence Service

1. The Secret Intelligence Service
(1) There shall continue to be a Secret Intelligence Service (in this Act referred to as 'the Intelligence Service') under the authority of the Secretary of State; and, subject to subsection (2) below, its functions shall be—

---

6 Inserted by the Regulation of Investigatory Powers Act 2000, Sch. 4, para. 4(1).
7 Inserted by ibid., Sch. 4, para. 4(2).
8 Inserted by the Intelligence Services Act 1994, Sch. 4, para. 1(1).
9 Substituted by the Police Act 1997, s. 12.
10 Inserted by the Security Service Act 1996, s. 1(2) and amended by the 1997 Act, Sch. 9, para. 61.
11 Inserted by ibid., para. 1(2).

(*a*)   to obtain and provide information relating to the actions or intentions of persons outside the British Islands; and

(*b*)   to perform other tasks relating to the actions or intentions of such persons.

(2) The functions of the Intelligence Service shall be exercisable only—

(*a*)   in the interests of national security, with particular reference to the defence and foreign policies of Her Majesty's Government in the United Kingdom; or

(*b*)   in the interests of the economic well-being of the United Kingdom; or

(*c*)   in support of the prevention or detection of serious crime.

2. The Chief of the Intelligence Service

(1) The operations of the Intelligence Service shall continue to be under the control of a Chief of that Service appointed by the Secretary of State.

(2) The Chief of the Intelligence Service shall be responsible for the efficiency of that Service and it shall be his duty to ensure—

(*a*)   that there are arrangements for securing that no information is obtained by the Intelligence Service except so far as necessary for the proper discharge of its functions and that no information is disclosed by it except so far as necessary—

  (i)   for that purpose;

  (ii)   in the interests of national security;

  (iii)   for the purpose of the prevention or detection of serious crime; or

  (iv)   for the purpose of any criminal proceedings; and

(*b*)   that the Intelligence Service does not take any action to further the interests of any United Kingdom political party.

[Subsections (3) and (4) follow the terms of s. 2(3A) and (4) of the Security Service Act 1989 (above, p. 879).]

GCHQ

3. The Government Communications Headquarters

(1) There shall continue to be a Government Communications Headquarters under the authority of the Secretary of State; and, subject to subsection (2) below, its functions shall be—

(*a*)   to monitor or interfere with electromagnetic, acoustic and other emissions and any equipment producing such emissions and to obtain and provide information derived from or related to such emissions or equipment and from encrypted material; and

(*b*)   to provide advice and assistance about—

  (i)   languages, including terminology used for technical matters, and

  (ii)   cryptography and other matters relating to the protection of information and other material,

    to the armed forces of the Crown, to Her Majesty's Government in the United Kingdom or to a Northern Ireland Department or to any other organisation which is determined for the purposes of this section in such manner as may be specified by the Prime Minister.

(2) The functions referred to in subsection (1)(*a*) above shall be exercisable only—

(*a*)   in the interests of national security, with particular reference to the defence and foreign policies of Her Majesty's Government in the United Kingdom; or

(*b*)   in the interests of the economic well-being of the United Kingdom in relation to the actions or intentions of persons outside the British Islands; or

(*c*)   in support of the prevention or detection of serious crime.

(3) In this Act the expression 'GCHQ' refers to the Government Communications Headquarters and to any unit or part of a unit of the armed forces of the Crown which is for the time being required by the Secretary of State to assist the Government Communications Headquarters in carrying out its functions.

4. The Director of GCHQ

(1) The operations of GCHQ shall continue to be under the control of a Director appointed by the Secretary of State.

(2) The Director shall be responsible for the efficiency of GCHQ and it shall be his duty to ensure—

(*a*) that there are arrangements for securing that no information is obtained by GCHQ except so far as necessary for the proper discharge of its functions and that no information is disclosed by it except so far as necessary for that purpose or for the purpose of any criminal proceedings; and

(*b*) that GCHQ does not take any action to further the interests of any United Kingdom political party.

[Subsections (3) and (4) follow the terms of s. 2(3A) and (4) of the Security Service Act 1989 (above, p. 879).]

Authorisation of certain actions

5. Warrants: general

(1) No entry on or interference with property or with wireless telegraphy shall be unlawful if it is authorised by a warrant issued by the Secretary of State under this section.

(2) The Secretary of State may, on an application made by the Security Service, the Intelligence Service or GCHQ, issue a warrant under this section authorising the taking, subject to subsection (3) below, of such action as is specified in the warrant in respect of any property so specified or in respect of wireless telegraphy so specified if the Secretary of State—

(*a*) thinks it necessary for the action to be taken [for the purpose of][12] in assisting, as the case may be,—

    (i) the Security Service in carrying out any of its functions under the 1989 Act; or

    (ii) the Intelligence Service in carrying out any of its functions under section 1 above; or

    (iii) GCHQ in carrying out any function which falls within section 3(1)(*a*) above; and

(*b*) is satisfied that [the taking of the action is proportionate to what the action seeks to achieve;][13] and

(*c*) is satisfied that satisfactory arrangements are in force under section 2(2)(*a*) of the 1989 Act (duties of the Director-General of the Security Service), section 2(2)(*a*) above or section 4(2)(*a*) above with respect to the disclosure of information obtained by virtue of this section and that any information obtained under the warrant will be subject to those arrangements.

[(2A) The matters to be taken into account in considering whether the requirements of subsection (2)(*a*) and (*b*) are satisfied in the case of any warrant shall include whether what it is thought necessary to achieve by the conduct authorised by the warrant could reasonably be achieved by other means.][14]

[(3) A warrant issued on the application of the Intelligence Service or GCHQ for the purposes of the exercise of their functions by virtue of section 1(2)(*c*) or 3(2)(*c*) above may not relate to property in the British Islands.

(3A) A warrant issued on the application of the Security Service for the purposes of the exercise of their function under section 1(4) of the Security Service Act 1989 may not relate to property in the British Islands unless it authorises the taking of action in relation to conduct within subsection (3B) below.

(3B) Conduct is within this subsection if it constitutes (or, if it took place in the United Kingdom, would constitute) one or more offences, and either—

(*a*) it involves the use of violence, results in substantial financial gain or is conduct by a large number of persons in pursuit of a common purpose; or

(*b*) the offence or one of the offences is an offence for which a person who has attained the age of twenty-one and has no previous convictions could reasonably be expected to be sentenced to imprisonment for a term of three years or more.][15]

(4) Subject to subsection (5) below, the Security Service may make an application under section (2) above for a warrant to be issued authorising that Service (or a person acting on its behalf) to take such action as is specified in the warrant on behalf of the Intelligence Service or GCHQ

---

12 Substituted by the 2000 Act, s. 74.
13 Substituted by the 2000 Act, s. 74.
14 Inserted by the 2000 Act, s. 74.
15 Inserted by the Securities Services Act 1996, s. 2.

and, where such a warrant is issued, the functions of the Security Service shall include the carrying out of the action so specified, whether or not it would otherwise be within its functions.
(5) The Security Service may not make an application for a warrant by virtue of subsection (4) above except where the action proposed to be authorised by the warrant—

- (a)   is action in respect of which the Intelligence Service or, as the case may be, GCHQ could make such an application; and
- (b)   is to be taken otherwise than in support of the prevention or detection of serious crime.

6. Warrants: procedure and duration, etc.
(1) A warrant shall not be issued except—

- (a)   under the hand of the Secretary of State [or, in the case of a warrant by the Scottish Ministers (by virtue of provision made under section 63 of the Scotland Act 1998), a member of the Scottish Executive;];[16] or
- (b)   in an urgent case where the Secretary of State has expressly authorised its issue and a statement of that fact is endorsed on it, under the hand of a senior official [...];[17] or
- (c)   in an urgent case where, the Scottish Ministers have (by virtue of provision made under section 63 of the Scotland Act 1998) expressly authorised its issue and a statement of that fact is endorsed thereon, under the hand of a member of the staff of the Scottish Administration who is in the Senior Civil Service and is designated by the Scottish Ministers as a person under whose hand a warrant may be issued in such a case.][18]

(2) A warrant shall, unless renewed under subsection (3) below, cease to have effect—

- (a)   if the warrant was under the hand of the Secretary of State [or, in the case of a warrant issued by the Scottish ministers (by virtue of provision made under section 63 of the Scotland Act 1998), a member of the Scottish Executive,][19] at the end of the period of six months beginning with the day on which it was issued; and
- (b)   in any other case, at the end of the period ending with the second working day following that day.

(3) If at any time before the day on which a warrant would cease to have effect the Secretary of State considers it necessary for the warrant to continue to have effect for the purpose for which it was issued, he may by an instrument under his hand renew it for a period of six months beginning with that day.
(4) The Secretary of State shall cancel a warrant if he is satisfied that the action authorised by it is no longer necessary.
(5) In the preceding provisions of this section 'warrant' means a warrant under section 5 above.
(6) As regards the Security Service, this section and section 5 above have effect in place of section 3 (property warrants) of the 1989 Act, and accordingly—

- (a)   a warrant issued under that section of the 1989 Act and current when this section and section 5 above come into force shall be treated as a warrant under section 5 above, but without any change in the date on which the warrant was in fact issued or last renewed; and
- (b)   section 3 of the 1989 Act shall cease to have effect.

7. Authorisation of acts outside the British Islands
(1) If, apart from this section, a person would be liable in the United Kingdom for any act done outside the British Islands, he shall not be so liable if the act is one which is authorised to be done by virtue of an authorisation given by the Secretary of State under this section.
(2) In subsection (1) above 'liable in the United Kingdom' means liable under the criminal or civil law of any part of the United Kingdom.
(3) The Secretary of State shall not give an authorisation under this section unless he is satisfied—

---

1 6 Inserted by S.I. 1999 No. 1750, Sch. 5, para. 14.
1 7 The words 'of his department' were repealed by the Regulation of Investigatory Powers Act 2000, Sch. 5.
1 8 Inserted by S.I. 1999 No. 1750, Sch. 5, para. 14.
1 9 Inserted by S.I. 1999 No. 1750, Sch. 5, para. 14.

    (*a*) that any acts which may be done in reliance on the authorisation or, as the case may be, the operation in the course of which the acts may be done will be necessary for the proper discharge of a function of the Intelligence Service; and

    (*b*) that there are satisfactory arrangements in force to secure—

        (i) that nothing will be done in reliance on the authorisation beyond what is necessary for the proper discharge of a function of the Intelligence Service; and

        (ii) that, in so far as any acts may be done in reliance on the authorisation, their nature and likely consequences will be reasonable, having regard to the purposes for which they are carried out; and

    (*c*) that there are satisfactory arrangements in force under section 2(2)(*a*) above with respect to the disclosure of information obtained by virtue of this section and that any information obtained by virtue of anything done in reliance on the authorisation will be subject to those arrangements.

(4) Without prejudice to the generality of the power of the Secretary of State to give an authorisation under this section, such an authorisation—

    (*a*) may relate to a particular act or acts, to acts of a description specified in the authorisation or to acts undertaken in the course of an operation so specified;

    (*b*) may be limited to a particular person or persons of a description so specified; and

    (*c*) may be subject to conditions so specified.

(5) An authorisation shall not be given under this section except—

    (*a*) under the hand of the Secretary of State; or

    (*b*) in an urgent case where the Secretary of State has expressly authorised it to be given and a statement of that fact is endorsed on it, under the hand of a senior official [...].[20]

(6) An authorisation shall, unless renewed under subsection (7) below, cease to have effect—

    (*a*) if the authorisation was given under the hand of the Secretary of State, at the end of the period of six months beginning with the day on which it was given;

    (*b*) in any other case, at the end of the period ending with the second working day following the day on which it was given.

(7) If at any time before the day on which an authorisation would cease to have effect the Secretary of State considers it necessary for the authorisation to continue to have effect for the purpose for which it was given, he may by an instrument under his hand renew it for a period of six months beginning with that day.

(8) The Secretary of State shall cancel an authorisation if he is satisfied that any act authorised by it is no longer necessary.

The Intelligence and Security Committee

10. The Intelligence and Security Committee

(1) There shall be a Committee, to be known as the Intelligence and Security Committee and in this section referred to as 'the Committee', to examine the expenditure, administration and policy of—

    (*a*) the Security Service;

    (*b*) the Intelligence Service; and

    (*c*) GCHQ.

(2) The Committee shall consist of nine members—

    (*a*) who shall be drawn both from the members of the House of Commons and from the members of the House of Lords; and

    (*b*) none of whom shall be a Minister of the Crown.

(3) The members of the Committee shall be appointed by the Prime Minister after consultation with the Leader of the Opposition, within the meaning of the Ministerial and other Salaries Act 1975; and one of those members shall be so appointed as Chairman of the Committee.

(4) Schedule 3 to this Act shall have effect with respect to the tenure of office of members of, the procedure of and other matters relating to, the Committee; and in that Schedule 'the Committee' has the same meaning as in this section.

---

20 Repealed by the Regulation of Investigatory Powers Act 2000, Sch. 5.

(5) The Committee shall make an annual report on the discharge of their functions to the Prime Minister and may at any time report to him on any matter relating to the discharge of those functions.

(6) The Prime Minister shall lay before each House of Parliament a copy of each annual report made by the Committee under subsection (5) above together with a statement as to whether any matter has been excluded from that copy in pursuance of subsection (7) below.

(7) If it appears to the Prime Minister, after consultation with the Committee, that the publication of any matter in a report would be prejudicial to the continued discharge of the functions of either of the Services or, as the case may be, GCHQ, the Prime Minister may exclude that matter from the copy of the report as laid before each House of Parliament....

12. Short title, commencement and extent

....

(3) This Act extends to Northern Ireland.

(4) Her Majesty may by Order in Council direct that any of the provisions of this Act specified in the Order shall extend, with such exceptions, adaptations and modifications as appear to Her to be necessary or expedient, to the Isle of Man, any of the Channel Islands or any colony.[21]

Regulation of Investigatory Powers Act 2000

59. Intelligence Services Commissioner

(1) The Prime Minister shall appoint a Commissioner to be known as the Intelligence Services Commissioner.

(2) Subject to subsection (4), the Intelligence Services Commissioner shall keep under review, so far as they are not required to be kept under review by the Interception of Communications Commissioner—

(a) the exercise by the Secretary of State of his powers under sections 5 to 7 of the Intelligence Services Act 1994 (warrants for interference with wireless telegraphy, entry and interference with property etc.);

(b) the exercise and performance by the Secretary of State, in connection with or in relation to—

(i) the activities of the intelligence services, and

(ii) the activities in places other than Northern Ireland of the officials of the Ministry of Defence and of members of Her Majesty's forces,

of the powers and duties conferred or imposed on him by Parts II and III of this Act;

(c) the exercise and performance by members of the intelligence services of the powers and duties conferred or imposed on them by or under Parts II and III of this Act;

(d) the exercise and performance in places other than Northern Ireland, by officials of the Ministry of Defence and by members of Her Majesty's forces, of the powers and duties conferred or imposed on such officials or members of Her Majesty's forces by or under Parts II and III; and

(e) the adequacy of the arrangements by virtue of which the duty imposed by section 55 is sought to be discharged—

(i) in relation to the members of the intelligence services; and

(ii) in connection with any of their activities in places other than Northern Ireland, in relation to officials of the Ministry of Defence and members of Her Majesty's forces.

(3) The Intelligence Services Commissioner shall give the Tribunal all such assistance (including his opinion as to any issue falling to be determined by the Tribunal) as the Tribunal may require—

(a) in connection with the investigation of any matter by the Tribunal; or

(b) otherwise for the purposes of the Tribunal's consideration or determination of any matter.

21 See the Intelligence Services Act 1994 (Channel Islands) Order 1994, S.I. 1994 No. 2955; the Intelligence Services Act 1994 (Dependent Territories) Order 1995, S.I. 1995 No. 752, as amended by S.I. 1996 No. 2896.

(4) It shall not be the function of the Intelligence Services Commissioner to keep under review the exercise of any power of the Secretary of State to make, amend or revoke any subordinate legislation.

(5) A person shall not be appointed under this section as the Intelligence Services Commissioner unless he holds or has held a high judicial office (within the meaning of the Appellate Jurisdiction Act 1876).

(6) The Intelligence Services Commissioner shall hold office in accordance with the terms of his appointment; and there shall be paid to him out of money provided by Parliament such allowances as the Treasury may determine.

(7) The Secretary of State shall, after consultation with the Intelligence Services Commissioner and subject to the approval of the Treasury as to numbers, provide him with such staff as the Secretary of State considers necessary for the carrying out of the Commissioner's functions
...

(9) On the coming into force of this section the Commissioner holding office as the Commissioner under section 8 of the Intelligence Services Act 1994 shall take and hold office as the Intelligence Services Commissioner as if appointed under this Act—

    (*a*) for the unexpired period of his term of office under that Act; and

    (*b*) otherwise, on the terms of his appointment under that Act.

(1) Subsection (7) of section 41 shall apply for the purposes of this section as it applies for the purposes of that section.

60. Co-operation with and reports by s. 59 Commissioner

(1) It shall be the duty of—

    (*a*) every member of an intelligence service,

    (*b*) every official of the department of the Secretary of State, and

    (*c*) every member of Her Majesty's forces,

to disclose or provide to the Intelligence Services Commissioner all such documents and information as he may require for the purpose of enabling him to carry out his functions under section 59.

(2) As soon as practicable after the end of each calendar year, the Intelligence Services Commissioner shall make a report to the Prime Minister with respect to the carrying out of that Commissioner's functions.

(3) The Intelligence Services Commissioner may also, at any time, make such other report to the Prime Minister on any matter relating to the carrying out of the Commissioner's functions as the Commissioner thinks fit.

(4) The Prime Minister shall lay before each House of Parliament a copy of every annual report made by the Intelligence Services Commissioner under subsection (2), together with a statement as to whether any matter has been excluded from that copy in pursuance of subsection (5).

(5) If it appears to the Prime Minister, after consultation with the Intelligence Services Commissioner, that the publication of any matter in an annual report would be contrary to the public interest or prejudicial to—

    (*a*) national security,

    (*b*) the prevention or detection of serious crime,

    (*c*) the economic well-being of the United Kingdom, or

    (*d*) the continued discharge of the functions of any public authority whose activities include activities that are subject to review by that Commissioner,

the Prime Minister may exclude that matter from the copy of the report as laid before each House of Parliament.

(6) Subsection (7) of section 41 shall apply for the purposes of this section as it applies for the purposes of that section.

NOTES

1. Schedules 1 and 2 to the 1989 Act and Schs. 1 and 2 to the 1994 Act made provision for the investigation of complaints. Any person aggrieved by anything which he believed the respective Services had done in relation to him or his property could complain to a Tribunal (one established in respect of each Service). The Tribunal was obliged to investigate it unless they considered it frivolous or vexatious. In the case of the Security Service, the Tribunal had to decide if there were reasonable grounds for any inquiries made about the complainant, and for believing any information disclosed to an employer to be true. Any complaint concerning property was to be referred to the Security Service Commissioner; any warrant issued under the Acts was to be reviewed by him, which he did applying judicial review principles. He also was required to investigate cases referred by the tribunal in which, although there was no determination in favour of a complainant, it appeared to the Tribunal that there were grounds for an investigation into whether the Service had acted unreasonably in any other respect in respect to the complainant and his property, and to make an annual report. The Tribunal had power to order inquiries to be ended, to direct the payment of compensation and to quash a warrant where the Commissioner found that it had not been properly issued. Similar arrangements applied in respect of the Intelligence Service and GCHQ under the 1994 Act. The Security Service Commissioner and Intelligence Services Commissioner had to be a person who held or had held high judicial office. Stuart-Smith LJ held both appointments from their inception and was succeeded by Simon Brown LJ. Each Tribunal comprised between three and five lawyers of ten years' standing. The President was Simon Brown J (subsequently LJ).

These arrangements have been superseded by the appointment of a single Intelligence services Commissioner for all three Services and a Tribunal with functions extending across the various regulatory regimes established by the Regulation of Investigatory Powers Act 2001.[1]

2. The Security Service Act 1996 extended the role of the Security Service to include that of acting in support of the activities of the police and other law enforcement agencies in the prevention and detection of serious crime. Co-ordination arrangements are agreed between the Director General of NCIS and the Director-General of the Security Service. The provisions of the Act have been criticised by P. O'Higgins[2] who argues that they contravene the ECHR; reverse the fundamental constitutional principle established by *Entick v Carrington*[3] (by providing for executive warrants outside the national security context); are open to abuse, given the absence of a definition of 'serious crime,' with, for example, words limiting its scope to 'organised crime' as apparently intended by the government; and will lead to difficulties given the very different legislative regimes governing the Security Service and the police. Primacy remains with the law enforcement agencies and the Security Service is tasked by or through NCIS.[4]

The Security Service is intended to 'bring a distinct package of skills to this arena (intelligence acquisition, processing, assessment and exploitation); its approach would be characterised by long-term investigation and analysis aimed at gaining a strategic advantage over organised crime targets'.[5] The Committee's view is that the Service can best be used in support of work against 'serious organised crime', which is their preferred term.[6] In its view the agencies have made a 'valuable contribution' here, particularly in the fight against drug trafficking, but it has been told that in the light of resources serious crime work may need to be scaled down.[7]

1 See above, pp. 884–885, below, p. 1013.
2 *Current Law Statutes Annotated 1996.* See also P. Duffy and M.Hunt, (1997) EHRLR 11.
3 Above, p. 84.
4 Intelligence and Security Committee, *Security Service Work Against Organised Crime* (Cm. 3065, 1995); Annual Report for 1996 (Cm. 3574, 1997), Appendix 2.
5 Ibid., para. 6.
6 Annual Report for 1995 (Cm. 3198), para. 26.
7 Annual Report for 1998-99 (Cm. 4532, 2000), paras. 67–71.

In his tenth and final report as Security Service Commissioner[8] Stuart-Smith LJ reported that as of 31 December 1999 the Tribunal had considered 338 complaints, with 3 outstanding. In 42 cases the complainants were the subject of a Security Service personal file and in 85 cases he or she had corresponded with the Service or had been the subject of a vetting disclosure. In no case had the tribunal made a determination in favour of the complainant. He had considered as Commissioner 141 property complaints over the ten years. A warrant had been issued in one case only. Aside from complaint cases, the Commissioner had discovered a small number of warrants authorised by a Secretary of State under the urgency procedure to be issued to an official of another department; s. 6(1)(b) of the 1994 Act, as originally drafted, contemplated such warrants being issued under the hand of a senior official 'of his department.' The Commissioner's view was that this meant that, although properly targeted, they were 'technically flawed' and he advised that they be reissued.[9] The Commissioner also discovered other errors.[10] He has concluded that it would not be in the public interest to publish statistics of warrants.[11] In interpreting s. 1(2) of the Act he noted that the term 'national security' was not defined in the Act, and was not limited to the matters listed 'in particular' in that subsection:[12]

'The concept of national security ... is wider than this and is not easily defined; indeed it is probably undesirable that I attempt an all embracing definition. In my opinion it includes the defence of the realm and the government's defence and foreign policies involving the protection of vital national interests in this country and abroad. In this regard I would draw a distinction between national interests and the interests, which are not necessarily the same, of the government of the day. What is a vital national interest is a question of fact and degree, more easily recognised when being considered than defined in advance.'

In his 1992 Report, Stuart-Smith LJ noted that, while being unable to be categorical, it was his opinion that unauthorised operations were not undertaken. His reasons were:[13]

'First, I believe that very tight control over such operations as are conducted is exercised by those in managerial positions in the Service. Secondly, technical operations of this kind are complex and expensive in money and human resources; it is unlikely that such resources would be squandered on unauthorised as opposed to authorised operations. Thirdly, such is the complexity of most technical operations that it would not be feasible to conceal from the management and colleagues the number of people, use of equipment and time which would need to be deployed on such unauthorised activity. Fourthly, if the target is a legitimate one within the functions of the Service, there should be no difficulty in obtaining a warrant; the Service can have no interest or reason to conduct unauthorised operations which, if discovered, would give rise to possible legal action and certain scandal.'

He was also of the view that the internal application procedure worked effectively, involving a number of checks at senior level, both within the Service and in the Warrantry Department, before submission to the Home Secretary or the Secretary of State for Northern Ireland.[14] His working methods over the years included the examination of security files relating to warrants, the examination of the product of

8 Report for 1999, Cm. 4779, para. 37. For earlier reports see Cm. 1480, 1946, 2174, 2523, 2827, 3253, 3679, 4002, 4365.
9 Ibid., paras. 25–28.
10 Ibid., para. 43: (1) an operational team deployed outside the target location specified in the property warrant; 'an unauthorised intrusion had clearly occurred'; (2) operation continued after warrant was cancelled where paperwork was delayed; 'all product received in this unwarranted period has been destroyed.' See also Cm. 4365, paras. 14–18.
11 1990 Report, paras. 12 and 14; 1999 Report, para. 18.
12 Ibid., para. 10.
13 Cm. 2174, para. 8; reaffirmed Cm. 4002, para. 27.
14 Report for 1999, Cm. 4779, paras. 7–13.

operations and interviews with officers of the Service. Reports as Commissioner under the 1994 Act similarly revealed no case where a complaint was upheld.[15]

4. The reception of the Security Service Act 1989 and the Intelligence Services Act 1994 has generally been critical.[16] Among the criticisms of the 1989 Act made by Leigh and Lustgarten,[17] were:

(1) The broad definition of 'subversion' reflected in s. 1(2): 'Actions intended to overthrow or undermine parliamentary democracy by political, industrial or violent means.' This was based on, but even broader than a definition given by Lord Harris when a Home Office Minister in a House of Lords debate:

> 'activities which threaten the safety or wellbeing of the state, and are intended to undermine or overthrow parliamentary democracy by political, industrial or violent means.'[18]

Leigh and Lustgarten argue that this is unacceptably broad given the inherent right-wing bias of security agencies.[19] While 'subversion' does not at present account for any of the Service's work[20] the involvement of the Service and Special Branch in the past in the surveillance of such bodies as the NCCL[21] and in covert operations against the NUM in the miners' strike[1] is not reassuring.[2]

(2) Lack of clarity in the arrangements for ministerial responsibility and control.[3] The Act failed to acknowledge the central place of the Prime Minister in the security and intelligence scheme, and left unclear the extent to which the Director-General may be given direct orders and the extent to which, conversely, ministers should be consulted by the Director-General. See now n. 8, below.

(3) Absence of any form of parliamentary oversight, or even a non-parliamentary oversight committee comprising privy councillors.[4] See now n. 11, below.

(4) The broad legal powers conferred by s. 3 (see now ss. 5, 6 of the 1994 Act).[5] Warrants are issued by the Secretary of State rather than a judicial officer; unlike under PACE there are no privileged or exempted categories of information;[6] and there are no requirements as to the degree of detail required in warrant applications.

> 'The section amounts to statutory authorisation of ministerial general warrants for reasons of state necessity of the kind which the common law disapproved in the celebrated case of *Entick v Carrington*.'[7]

---

15 Cm. 3288, 3677, 3975, 4361.
16 On the 1989 Act, see I. Leigh and L. Lustgarten, (1989) 52 MLR 801; P. Birkinshaw, *Reforming the Secret State* (1990), pp. 34–43. On the 1994 Act, see J. Wadham, (1994) 57 MLR 916; M. Supperstone, [1994] PL 329.
17 (1989) 52 MLR 801.
18 357 HL Deb, 26 February 1975, col. 947; endorsed by the Home Secretary, Merlin Rees, 947 HC Deb, 6 April 1978, col. 618: see R. J. Spjut, (1979) 6 BJLS 254.
19 See (1989) 52 MLR 801, 805–809.
20 Above, p. 878.
21 Above, p. 831.
 1 See S. Milne, *The Enemy Within: MI5, Maxwell and the Scargill Affair* (1994).
 2 See also the accounts, from an earlier era, of the surveillance of the Communist Party of Great Britain, the National Unemployed Workers Movement and the NCCL: R. Thurlow, *The Secret State* (1994), Chap. 5 ('Reds in the Bed'); 'British Fascism and State Surveillance 1934-45' (1988) 3 *Intelligence and National Security* 77; and ' "A Very Clever Capitalist Class". British Communism and State Surveillance 1939-45' (1997) 12 Intelligence and National Security 1; J. Morgan, *Conflict and Order* (1987), Chap. 8 ('The Police and the Unemployed Marchers, 1918–1939'); Liberty, *Agenda*, Summer 1993, pp. 10–11.
 3 (1989) 52 MLR 801 at 810–814.
 4 Ibid., pp. 814–822.
 5 Ibid., pp. 822–828.
 6 See above, pp. 225–227.
 7 Above, p. 84.

It is also uncertain whether the royal prerogative may continue as a source of legal power for the service (cf. *R v Secretary of State for the Home Department, ex p Northumbria Police Authority*[8]).

(5) The inadequacy of the complaints mechanism.[9] Particular difficulties include how a person will know whether he has been 'bugged, burgled or investigated' (service personnel who feel they have been asked to behave improperly in this way are *not* permitted to complain to the Tribunal or Commissioner); the complainant will not be given reasons for the Tribunal's decision; judicial review is excluded.

A further general cause for concern is these arrangements provide insufficient basis for satisfaction that appropriate systems are in place for the co-ordinated circulation and evaluation of intelligence in an effective and timely manner. Details of this work do not normally come into the public domain; an exception is provided by the Report of the Scott Inquiry[10] which revealed an 'appalling chronicle of intelligence failure.'[11]

4. One of the areas of concern has been the process by which the Service creates and maintains files on individuals. It currently holds about 440,000 files opened at some time since 1909; 290,000 relate to people who may have been investigated within the last 90 years. Of these, staff have access to 40,000 only for specific research purposes; 230,000 are closed so that staff may use them where necessary for current work but may not make enquires about the files' subjects; 20,000 relate to individuals who may be under current investigation of which 13,000 relate to UK citizens. Records must be kept of enquiries made about a complainant, or if any disclosure made for vetting purposes, since December 1989, so that they can be provided to the Tribunal. There are also arrangements for the transfer of records of historical interest to the Public Record Office. Between 1909 and the early 1970s, over 175,000 files were destroyed as they became obsolete following a major contraction in the Service; from the early 1990s, a further 110,000 files have been destroyed or earmarked for destruction.[12] It is possible that an individual may have a right under the Data Protection Act 1998 to discover whether personal data is held about him or her.[13]

5. In *R v Security Service Tribunal, ex p Hewitt*,[14] Kennedy J refused to hold that the retention of records by the Service necessarily meant that there was no 'discontinuance' of 'inquiries,' giving the tribunal jurisdiction under the 1989 Act, Sch. 1, para. 9, to deal with the question whether files on the applicants were still open and in the possession of the service. His Lordship refused leave to apply for judicial review, having accepted 'for today's purposes' that it is arguable that in certain circumstances the court could entertain such an application notwithstanding s. 5(4) of the 1989 Act (which provided that decisions of the Tribunal and Commissioner '(including decisions as to their jurisdictions) shall not be subject to appeal or liable to be questioned in any court').

In *R v Security Service Tribunal, ex p Clarke*,[15] the Court of Appeal rejected C's application for leave to move for judicial review of the Tribunal's decision to reject a complaint by her that the Service had infringed 'every single one of her human rights.' The court held that s. 5(4) was an 'insuperable bar' and there was no

---

8 [1988] 1 All ER 556.
9 (1989) 52 MLR 801, 828–835.
10 *Export of Defence Equipment and Dual-Use Goods to Iraq and Related Prosecutions* (1995–96 HC 115). See R. Austin (ed.), *Iraqgate: The Constitutional Implications of the Matrix-Churchill Affair* (1996); A. Tomkins, *The Constitution After Scott* (1998); [1996] PL Autumn issue.
11 Tomkins, op. cit., p. 130.
12 MI5, *The Security Service* (3rd edn, 1998), pp. 24–25.
13 *Baker v Secretary of State for the Home Department* (2001) Telegraph, 9 October, Information Tribunal (blanket exemption certificate for the Security Service held unlawful).
14 Unreported, 14 February 1992.
15 Unreported, 20 May 1998.

requirement for the Tribunal to give reasons, except in accordance with the Act. At first instance, Sullivan J had held that even if s. 5(4) did not apply in a case of fraud or bad faith, there was no evidence of that whatsoever. The equivalent of s. 5(4) is s. 67(8) of the Regulation of Investigatory Powers Act 2000.[16]

6. In three cases, the European Commission of Human Rights has rejected as inadmissible complaints of breaches of Arts. 8 and 13 ECHR holding that the structure of the 1989 Act was sufficiently certain for interference with private life arising from surveillance to be 'in accordance with the law' and necessary in a democratic society in the interests of national security under Art. 8 ECHR.[17] It took a similar view in respect of the regime established by the Interception of Communications Act 1985.[18]

7. Given the absence, prior to the 1989 Act, of any specific legal powers, the Security Service has in practice operated in conjunction with the Special Branches attached to each police force. According to the *Guidelines on Special Branch Work in Great Britain*:[19]

> 'Special Branches exist primarily to acquire intelligence, to assess its potential operational value, and to contribute more generally to its interpretation. They do so both to meet local policing needs and also to assist the Security Service.'

Its single most important function is counter-terrorism.[20] An investigation into Special Branch by the House of Commons Home Affairs Committee was hampered by limitations on the information made available to it.[1]

8. The Intelligence Services Act put the Secret Intelligence Service (sometimes known as MI6) and GCHQ on the same statutory footing as the Security Service. Points (4) and (5) made by Leigh and Lustgarten in relation to the 1989 Act (see n. **4**) remain relevant here. However, there has been some clarification of the arrangements for ministerial responsibility,[2] and some provision for external oversight (see n. **9**). The Prime Minister is responsible for intelligence and security matters overall, supported by the Secretary of the Cabinet. The Home Secretary is responsible for the Security Service, the Foreign Secretary for SIS and GCHQ and the Secretary of State for Defence for the Defence Intelligence Staff. There is a Ministerial Committee on the Intelligence Services, assisted by the Permanent Secretaries' Committee on the Intelligence Service (PSIS). The Joint Intelligence Committee, based in the Cabinet Office, sets the UK's national intelligence requirements and produces a weekly survey on intelligence. It includes senior officials, the heads of the three services and the Intelligence Co-Ordinator. Its chairman, also currently the Co-ordinator, has direct access to the Prime Minister.

The existence of GCHQ was formally acknowledged by the Prime Minister after the Prime affair.[3] The decision to ban trade unionism at GCHQ led to litigation that

---

16 Below, p. 1013.
17 See *Esbester v United Kingdom* (App. No. 18601/91, 2 April 1993), *Redgrave v United Kingdom* (App. No. 20271/92, 1 September 1993) and *Hewitt and Harman v United Kingdom* (App. No. 20317/92, 1 September 1993) (a further application), discussed by Stuart-Smith LJ in his 1993 Report (Cm. 2523).
18 *Christie v United Kingdom* App. No. 21482/93, 27 June 1994.
19 Home Office, Scottish Office, July 1994.
20 On the historical background see R. Allason, *The Branch: A History of the Metropolitan Police Special Branch 1883–1983* (1983); and B. Porter, *The Origins of the Vigilant State* (1987).
1 *Fourth Report from the Home Affairs Committee*, 1984–85 HC 71. See also H. M. Inspectorate of Constabulary in Scotland, *'For Police Eyes Only' Special Branch Thematic Inspection 2000* (www.scotland.gov.uk/hmic/docs/fpeo).
2 See the booklet on the *Central Intelligence Machinery* published by HMSO in 1993 replaced by a document on *National Intelligence Machinery* in 2000 with a 2nd edition in September 2001 (www.official-documents.co.uk/document/caboff/nim/natint.htm).
3 See above, p. 826.

was ultimately unsuccessful[4] and the dismissal of some employees.[5] The ban was lifted by the Labour government in 1997.

Section 7 of the 1994 Act is the 'statutory equivalent of James Bond's "licence to kill"'.[6]

9. It was formerly government policy to prevent access to industrial (now employment) tribunals by members of the intelligence services. This was changed in 1996 so that cases were reviewed on a case-by-case basis to see whether national security considerations could be met by measures short of a certificate under (ultimately) s. 193 of the Employment Rights Act 1996 (as originally enacted) excluding the individual from bringing tribunal proceedings. This power has now been repealed.[7] Members of the intelligence services are, however, expressly excluded from bringing proceedings under Part IVA and s. 47B of the 1996 Act (whistleblowing) and from rights under ss. 10–13 of the 1999 Act in respect of the right to be accompanied at disciplinary or grievance hearings.[8]

10. The nationality rules for employment by the intelligence services have been relaxed. An applicant or employee must (as before) be a British citizen and hold no other citizenship and at least one parent must be British or have substantial ties with the UK.[9]

11. The Intelligence Services Act 1994 also introduced an element of independent oversight (the Intelligence and Security Committee). The government did not accept a proposal by the Home Affairs Select Committee that it should provide oversight, and declined to respond in detail to the Committee's view that the Service in any event fell within its jurisdiction as an associated body of the Home Office.[10] Detailed provision for the Committee is made by Sch. 3. A member of the Committee holds office for the duration of the Parliament in which he is appointed, but must vacate office if he ceases to be an MP or member of the House of Lords or becomes a Minister, may be replaced by the Prime Minister or may resign. If the Committee seeks information from any of the heads of the intelligence services, he must either disclose it in accordance with arrangements approved by the Secretary of State, or inform the Committee that it cannot be disclosed (i) because it is sensitive information which in his opinion should not be made available, or (ii) because the Secretary of State has determined that it should not be disclosed. The Secretary of State may override the head of service's view under (i) if he 'considers it desirable in the public interest'.[11] He may not make a determination under (ii) 'on the grounds of national security alone', and, subject to that, 'he shall not make such a determination unless the information appears to him to be of such a nature that, if he were requested to produce it before a Departmental Select Committee of the House of Commons, he would think it proper not to do so' (para. 3(4)). Disclosures under para. 3 are to be regarded as disclosures necessary for the proper discharge of the functions of the

---

4 *Council of Civil Service Unions v Minister for the Civil Service* [1985] AC 374.
5 See S. Fredman and G.S. Morris, *The State as Employer* (1989), pp. 98–102; K. D. Ewing and C. Gearty, *Freedom under Thatcher* (1990), pp. 130–136; H. Canning and R. Norton-Taylor, *A Conflict of Loyalties: GCHQ 1984–1991* (1991).
6 J. Wadham, (1994) 57 MLR 916, 922, noting that 'the Minister has stated that: "It is inconceivable that, *in ordinary circumstances*, ... the Secretary of State ... would authorise the use of lethal force"' (emphasis supplied), HC Standing Committee E, col. 34, 3 March 1994.
7 See above, pp. 840–841.
8 1999 Act, s. 15.
9 HC Deb, 5 February 1998, col. 753, written answer.
10 See the 1st Report of the HAC, 1992–93 HC 265, *Accountability of the Security Service*, and Government Reply, Cm. 2197, 1993.
11 Para. 3(3).

respective services, for the purposes of the 1989 and 1994 Acts.[12] 'Sensitive information' is defined as:[13]

'(a) information which might lead to the identification of, or provide details of, sources of information, other assistance or operational methods available to the Security Service, the Intelligence Service or GCHQ;

(b) information about particular operations which have been, are being or are proposed to be undertaken in pursuance of any of the functions of those bodies; and

(c) information provided by, or by an agency of, the Government of a territory outside the United Kingdom where that Government does not consent to the disclosure of the information.'

It will be noted that while the Committee is comprised of Members of Parliament, it is appointed by and responsible to the Prime Minister, although its reports are to be laid before Parliament in the same way as those of the Tribunals and Commissioners under the 1989 and 1994 Acts. The members are to be notified under s. 1(1)(b) of the Official Secrets Act 1989.[14] Why should the Committee's access to information be more restricted than the Commissioners?[15] The chairman, from the establishment of the Committee to 2001, was Tom King MP, the former Defence Secretary. In 2001, he was succeeded by Ann Taylor MP.

These arrangements may be compared with those in other jurisdictions. In Canada, the domestic security service was put on a statutory basis by the Canadian Security Intelligence Service Act 1984, with oversight provided by an Inspector-General and a Security Intelligence Review Committee comprising Privy Councillors who are not members of the Senate or the House of Commons. The Australian Security Intelligence Organisation Act 1956 (Cth) put ASIO on a statutory basis. In 1986, two oversight mechanisms were established. The Inspector-General of Intelligence and Security's remit includes inquiry into ASIO's compliance with the law, ministerial directions and human rights, and the propriety of their activities. The Parliamentary Joint Committee on ASIO comprises seven members, with a majority of government members, and a majority from the House of Representatives, appointed after consultation with the leaders of each political party represented in Parliament. The latter development was controversial, but the Committee's powers are circumscribed.[16]

It is difficult to judge the effectiveness of this Committee given that it operates within the 'ring of secrecy' and its published reports are edited. It has been criticised for its limited comments on the Scott Inquiry's report on intelligence deficiencies.[17] However, it has been energetic, has addressed a wide range of topics and has included Parliamentarians of recognised independence of mind. It has appointed an Investigator to assist with its work. The Director General of the Security Service has indicated that on occasions, he felt able to go further than the law required in terms of providing information to the Committee.[18] Not all of its recommendations have been palatable to the government.

---

12 Para. 3(5).

13 Para. 4.

14 Above, p. 811: see J. Wadham, (1994) 57 MLR 926–927.

15 See J. Wadham, op. cit., at p. 926.

16 See H. P. Lee, (1989) 38 ICLQ 890; Lustgarten and Leigh, op. cit., pp. 455–458; H. Barnett, 'Legislation-based National Security Services: Australia' (1994) 9 *Intelligence and National Security* 287.). On Canada's arrangements, see Lustgarten and Leigh, op. cit., pp. 458–466; A. Goldsmith, [1985] PL 39; J. Ll. J. Edwards, (1985) 5 OJLS 143; M. Rankin, (1986) 36 UTLJ 249; S. Farson, [1992] PL 377 and (2000) 15(2) *Intelligence and National Security* 225.

17 A. Tomkins, *The Constitution After Scott* (1998), pp. 159-162.

18 Cited by Dale Campell-Savours MP (a Committee member), HC Deb, 29 March 2001, col. 1154.

The Home Affairs Committee[19] has described the ISC as a 'great step forward over previous arrangements in providing democratic accountability'. Its reports 'have shed light on areas of security service activity which hitherto had lain in darkness'. However, it should be replaced by a special Parliamentary select committee. While the differences between these two models were small, a change would address 'the absence of openness and of an overt independence in the present system'. The government 'is not convinced that there is a strong case for change in the fundamental structure of these arrangements now', notwithstanding that some of its members took the other view when in opposition.[20]

12. The new Intelligence and Security Committee must be distinguished from the Security Commission, a body that advises the Prime Minister, normally on breaches of security.[1]

7 Access to information

There has for many years been pressure for the creation of a general public right of access to official information.[2] There has been a steady increase in the number of specific rights of access created by legislation.[3] In 1994, the Conservative Government introduced a new *Code of Practice on Access to Government Information*.[4] Subject to an extensive list of exemptions, this commits departments and public bodies under the jurisdiction of the Parliamentary Commissioner for Administration to publish the facts and analysis behind the major policy proposals and decisions; to publish explanatory material on departments' dealings with the public; to give reasons for administrative decisions to those affected; to publish comparable information on the running of public services; and to release, in response to specific requests, information relating to policies, acts and decisions and other matters related to their areas of responsibility. There is no commitment that pre-existing documents, as distinct from information, will be released. Charges may be made. A complaint that information which should have been provided was not, or that unreasonable charges have been demanded, should be made first to the department or body concerned: if the applicant remains dissatisfied, a complaint can be made via an MP to the PCA.

Many overseas jurisdictions have enacted freedom of information laws, including the US, Sweden, Norway, Denmark, New Zealand, Australia and Canada. The UK has now followed suit, with the Freedom of Information Act 2000, which will be fully implemented by January 2005, starting with central government in November 2002. This is a large and complex piece of legislation and it is only possible to reproduce key sections here.

19 Third Report, 1998-99 HC 291, *Accountability of the Security Service.*
20 Government Reply (Cm. 4588, 2000).
 1 See I. Leigh and L. Lustgarten, 'The Security Commission: Constitutional Achievement or Curiosity?' [1991] PL 215 and Lustgarten and Leigh, op. cit., pp. 476–491.
 2 See generally J. Michael, *The Politics of Secrecy* (1982); K. G. Robertson, *Public Secrets* (1982); N. S. Marsh (ed.), *Public Access to Government Held Information: A Comparative Symposium* (1987); R. Chapman and M. Hunt (eds.), *Open Government* (1987); P. Birkinshaw, *Freedom of Information* (3rd edn, 2001) and *Government and Information* (2nd edn, 2001); D. Vincent, *The Culture of Secrecy: Britain, 1832-1998* (1998); A. McDonald and G. Terrill, *Open Government* (1998); P. Birkinshaw and A. Parkin, 'Freedom of Information', in R. Hazell and R. Plant (eds.), *Constitutional Reform* (1999); J. Beatson and Y. Cripps (eds.), *Freedom of Expression and Freedom of Information* (2000), Part II.
 3 E.g. the Local Government (Access to Information) Act 1985; Access to Personal Files Act 1987; Access to Medical Reports Act 1988; Environment and Safety Information Act 1990; Access to Health Records Act 1990. See now the Data Protection Act 1998.
 4 Following the White Paper, *Open Government* (Cm. 2990, 1993). See HC Research Paper 97/69.

Freedom of Information Act 2000

<small>PART I</small>

<small>ACCESS TO INFORMATION HELD BY PUBLIC AUTHORITIES</small>

Right to information

1. General right of access to information held by public authorities
(1) Any person making a request for information[5] to a public authority is entitled—
  (*a*) to be informed in writing by the public authority whether it holds information of the description specified in the request, and
  (*b*) if that is the case, to have that information communicated to him.
(2) Subsection (1) has effect subject to the following provisions of this section and to the provisions of sections 2, 9, 12 and 14.
(3) Where a public authority—
  (*a*) reasonably requires further information in order to identify and locate the information requested, and
  (*b*) has informed the applicant of that requirement,
the authority is not obliged to comply with subsection (1) unless it is supplied with that further information.
(4) The information—
  (*a*) in respect of which the applicant is to be informed under subsection (1)(*a*), or
  (*b*) which is to be communicated under subsection (1)(*b*),
is the information in question held at the time when the request is received, except that account may be taken of any amendment or deletion made between that time and the time when the information is to be communicated under subsection (1)(*b*), being an amendment or deletion that would have been made regardless of the receipt of the request.
(5) A public authority is to be taken to have complied with subsection (1)(*a*) in relation to any information if it has communicated the information to the applicant in accordance with subsection (1)(*b*).
(6) In this Act, the duty of a public authority to comply with subsection (1)(*a*) is referred to as "the duty to confirm or deny".

2. Effect of the exemptions in Part II
(1) Where any provision of Part II states that the duty to confirm or deny does not arise in relation to any information, the effect of the provision is that where either—
  (*a*) the provision confers absolute exemption, or
  (*b*) in all the circumstances of the case, the public interest in maintaining the exclusion of the duty to confirm or deny outweighs the public interest in disclosing whether the public authority holds the information,
section 1(1)(*a*) does not apply.
(2) In respect of any information which is exempt information by virtue of any provision of Part II, section 1(1)(*b*) does not apply if or to the extent that—
  (*a*) the information is exempt information by virtue of a provision conferring absolute exemption, or
  (*b*) in all the circumstances of the case, the public interest in maintaining the exemption outweighs the public interest in disclosing the information.
(3) For the purposes of this section, the following provisions of Part II (and no others) are to be regarded as conferring absolute exemption—
  (*a*) section 21,
  (*b*) section 23,
  (*c*) section 32,
  (*d*) section 34,
  (*e*) section 36 so far as relating to information held by the House of Commons or the House of Lords,

---

5   *Ed.* "'Information' (subject to ss. 51(8) and 75(2)) means information recorded in any form': s. 84.

(f) in section 40—
  (i) subsection (1), and
  (ii) subsection (2) so far as relating to cases where the first condition referred to in that subsection is satisfied by virtue of subsection (3)(*a*)(i) or (*b*) of that section,
(g) section 41, and
(h) section 44.

3. Public authorities
(1) In this Act "public authority" means—
  (a) subject to section 4(4), any body which, any other person who, or the holder of any office which—
    (i) is listed in Schedule 1,[6] or
    (ii) is designated by order under section 5, or
  (b) a publicly-owned company as defined by section 6.
(2) For the purposes of this Act, information is held by a public authority if—
  (a) it is held by the authority, otherwise than on behalf of another person, or
  (b) it is held by another person on behalf of the authority.

4. Amendment of Schedule 1
(1) The Secretary of State may by order amend Schedule 1 by adding to that Schedule a reference to any body or the holder of any office which (in either case) is not for the time being listed in that Schedule but as respects which both the first and the second conditions below are satisfied.
(2) The first condition is that the body or office—
  (a) is established by virtue of Her Majesty's prerogative or by an enactment or by subordinate legislation, or
  (b) is established in any other way by a Minister of the Crown in his capacity as Minister, by a government department or by the National Assembly for Wales.
(3) The second condition is—
  (a) in the case of a body, that the body is wholly or partly constituted by appointment made by the Crown, by a Minister of the Crown, by a government department or by the National Assembly for Wales, or
  (b) in the case of an office, that appointments to the office are made by the Crown, by a Minister of the Crown, by a government department or by the National Assembly for Wales.
(4) If either the first or the second condition above ceases to be satisfied as respects any body or office which is listed in Part VI or VII of Schedule 1, that body or the holder of that office shall cease to be a public authority by virtue of the entry in question.
(5) The Secretary of State may by order amend Schedule 1 by removing from Part VI or VII of that Schedule an entry relating to any body or office—
  (a) which has ceased to exist, or
  (b) as respects which either the first or the second condition above has ceased to be satisfied.
(6) An order under subsection (1) may relate to a specified person or office or to persons or offices falling within a specified description.
(7) Before making an order under subsection (1), the Secretary of State shall—
  (a) if the order adds to Part II, III, IV or VI of Schedule 1 a reference to—
    (i) a body whose functions are exercisable only or mainly in or as regards Wales, or
    (ii) the holder of an office whose functions are exercisable only or mainly in or as regards Wales, consult the National Assembly for Wales, and
  (b) if the order relates to a body which, or the holder of any office who, if the order were made, would be a Northern Ireland public authority, consult the First Minister and deputy First Minister in Northern Ireland.
(8) This section has effect subject to section 80.
(9) In this section "Minister of the Crown" includes a Northern Ireland Minister.

6 *Ed.* Sch. 1 lists 64 bodies within central and local government, the NHS, maintained schools and other educational institutions and the police, and a host of other agencies, boards, councils, committees and bodies.

5. Further power to designate public authorities

(1) The Secretary of State may by order designate as a public authority for the purposes of this Act any person who is neither listed in Schedule 1 nor capable of being added to that Schedule by an order under section 4(1), but who—

    (*a*) appears to the Secretary of State to exercise functions of a public nature, or

    (*b*) is providing under a contract made with a public authority any service whose provision is a function of that authority.

(2) An order under this section may designate a specified person or office or persons or offices falling within a specified description.

(3) Before making an order under this section, the Secretary of State shall consult every person to whom the order relates, or persons appearing to him to represent such persons.

(4) This section has effect subject to section 80.

6. Publicly-owned companies

(1) A company is a "publicly-owned company" for the purposes of section 3(1)(*b*) if—

    (*a*) it is wholly owned by the Crown, or

    (*b*) it is wholly owned by any public authority listed in Schedule 1 other than—

        (i)   a government department, or

        (ii) any authority which is listed only in relation to particular information.

(2) For the purposes of this section—

    (*a*) a company is wholly owned by the Crown if it has no members except—

        (i)   Ministers of the Crown, government departments or companies wholly owned by the Crown, or

        (ii) persons acting on behalf of Ministers of the Crown, government departments or companies wholly owned by the Crown, and

    (*b*) a company is wholly owned by a public authority other than a government department if it has no members except—

        (i)   that public authority or companies wholly owned by that public authority, or

        (ii) persons acting on behalf of that public authority or of companies wholly owned by that public authority.

(3) In this section—

"company" includes any body corporate;

"Minister of the Crown" includes a Northern Ireland Minister.

7. Public authorities to which Act has limited application

(1) Where a public authority is listed in Schedule 1 only in relation to information of a specified description, nothing in Parts I to V of this Act applies to any other information held by the authority.

(2) An order under section 4(1) may, in adding an entry to Schedule 1, list the public authority only in relation to information of a specified description.

(3) The Secretary of State may by order amend Schedule 1—

    (*a*) by limiting to information of a specified description the entry relating to any public authority, or

    (*b*) by removing or amending any limitation to information of a specified description which is for the time being contained in any entry.

(4) Before making an order under subsection (3), the Secretary of State shall—

    (*a*) if the order relates to the National Assembly for Wales or a Welsh public authority, consult the National Assembly for Wales,

    (*b*) if the order relates to the Northern Ireland Assembly, consult the Presiding Officer of that Assembly, and

    (*c*) if the order relates to a Northern Ireland department or a Northern Ireland public authority, consult the First Minister and deputy First Minister in Northern Ireland.

(5) An order under section 5(1)(*a*) must specify the functions of the public authority designated by the order with respect to which the designation is to have effect; and nothing in Parts I to V of this Act applies to information which is held by the authority but does not relate to the exercise of those functions.

(6) An order under section 5(1)(*b*) must specify the services provided under contract with respect to which the designation is to have effect; and nothing in Parts I to V of this Act applies to information which is held by the public authority designated by the order but does not relate to the provision of those services.

(7) Nothing in Parts I to V of this Act applies in relation to any information held by a publicly-owned company which is excluded information in relation to that company.

(8) In subsection (7) "excluded information", in relation to a publicly-owned company, means information which is of a description specified in relation to that company in an order made by the Secretary of State for the purposes of this subsection.

(9) In this section "publicly-owned company" has the meaning given by section 6.

8. Request for information

(1) In this Act any reference to a "request for information" is a reference to such a request which—

    (*a*) is in writing,

    (*b*) states the name of the applicant and an address for correspondence, and

    (*c*) describes the information requested.

(2) For the purposes of subsection (1)(a), a request is to be treated as made in writing where the text of the request—

    (*a*) is transmitted by electronic means,

    (*b*) is received in legible form, and

    (*c*) is capable of being used for subsequent reference.

9. Fees

(1) A public authority to whom a request for information is made may, within the period for complying with section 1(1), give the applicant a notice in writing (in this Act referred to as a "fees notice") stating that a fee of an amount specified in the notice is to be charged by the authority for complying with section 1(1).

(2) Where a fees notice has been given to the applicant, the public authority is not obliged to comply with section 1(1) unless the fee is paid within the period of three months beginning with the day on which the fees notice is given to the applicant.

(3) Subject to subsection (5), any fee under this section must be determined by the public authority in accordance with regulations made by the Secretary of State.

(4) Regulations under subsection (3) may, in particular, provide—

    (*a*) that no fee is to be payable in prescribed cases,

    (*b*) that any fee is not to exceed such maximum as may be specified in, or determined in accordance with, the regulations, and

    (*c*) that any fee is to be calculated in such manner as may be prescribed by the regulations.

(5) Subsection (3) does not apply where provision is made by or under any enactment as to the fee that may be charged by the public authority for the disclosure of the information.

10. Time for compliance with request

(1) Subject to subsections (2) and (3), a public authority must comply with section 1(1) promptly and in any event not later than the twentieth working day following the date of receipt.

(2) Where the authority has given a fees notice to the applicant and the fee is paid in accordance with section 9(2), the working days in the period beginning with the day on which the fees notice is given to the applicant and ending with the day on which the fee is received by the authority are to be disregarded in calculating for the purposes of subsection (1) the twentieth working day following the date of receipt.

(3) If, and to the extent that—

    (*a*) section 1(1)(*a*) would not apply if the condition in section 2(1)(*b*) were satisfied, or

    (*b*) section 1(1)(*b*) would not apply if the condition in section 2(2)(*b*) were satisfied,

the public authority need not comply with section 1(1)(*a*) or (*b*) until such time as is reasonable in the circumstances; but this subsection does not affect the time by which any notice under section 17(1) must be given.

(4) The Secretary of State may by regulations provide that subsections (1) and (2) are to have effect as if any reference to the twentieth working day following the date of receipt were a reference to such other day, not later than the sixtieth working day following the date of receipt, as may be specified in, or determined in accordance with, the regulations.

(5) Regulations under subsection (4) may—

    (*a*) prescribe different days in relation to different cases, and

    (*b*) confer a discretion on the Commissioner.

(6) In this section—
"the date of receipt" means—
    (*a*) the day on which the public authority receives the request for information, or
    (*b*) if later, the day on which it receives the information referred to in section 1(3);
"working day" means any day other than a Saturday, a Sunday, Christmas Day, Good Friday
    or a day which is a bank holiday under the Banking and Financial Dealings Act 1971 in
    any part of the United Kingdom.

11. Means by which communication is to be made

(1) Where, on making his request for information, the applicant expresses a preference for
communication by any one or more of the following means, namely—
    (*a*) the provision to the applicant of a copy of the information in permanent form or in
        another form acceptable to the applicant,
    (*b*) the provision to the applicant of a reasonable opportunity to inspect a record containing
        the information, and
    (*c*) the provision to the applicant of a digest or summary of the information in permanent
        form or in another form acceptable to the applicant,
the public authority shall so far as reasonably practicable give effect to that preference.
(2) In determining for the purposes of this section whether it is reasonably practicable to
communicate information by particular means, the public authority may have regard to all the
circumstances, including the cost of doing so.
(3) Where the public authority determines that it is not reasonably practicable to comply with
any preference expressed by the applicant in making his request, the authority shall notify the
applicant of the reasons for its determination.
(4) Subject to subsection (1), a public authority may comply with a request by communicating
information by any means which are reasonable in the circumstances.

12. Exemption where cost of compliance exceeds appropriate limit

(1) Section 1(1) does not oblige a public authority to comply with a request for information if the
authority estimates that the cost of complying with the request would exceed the appropriate limit.
(2) Subsection (1) does not exempt the public authority from its obligation to comply with
paragraph (*a*) of section 1(1) unless the estimated cost of complying with that paragraph alone
would exceed the appropriate limit.
(3) In subsections (1) and (2) "the appropriate limit" means such amount as may be prescribed,
and different amounts may be prescribed in relation to different cases.
(4) The Secretary of State may by regulations provide that, in such circumstances as may be
prescribed, where two or more requests for information are made to a public authority—
    (*a*) by one person, or
    (*b*) by different persons who appear to the public authority to be acting in concert or in
        pursuance of a campaign,
the estimated cost of complying with any of the requests is to be taken to be the estimated total
cost of complying with all of them.
(5) The Secretary of State may by regulations make provision for the purposes of this section
as to the costs to be estimated and as to the manner in which they are to be estimated.

13. Fees for disclosure where cost of compliance exceeds appropriate limit

(1) A public authority may charge for the communication of any information whose
communication—
    (*a*) is not required by section 1(1) because the cost of complying with the request for information
        exceeds the amount which is the appropriate limit for the purposes of section 12(1) and (2), and
    (*b*) is not otherwise required by law,
such fee as may be determined by the public authority in accordance with regulations made by
the Secretary of State.
(2) Regulations under this section may, in particular, provide—
    (*a*) that any fee is not to exceed such maximum as may be specified in, or determined in
        accordance with, the regulations, and
    (*b*) that any fee is to be calculated in such manner as may be prescribed by the regulations.
(3) Subsection (1) does not apply where provision is made by or under any enactment as to
the fee that may be charged by the public authority for the disclosure of the information.

14. Vexatious or repealed request

(1) Section 1(1) does not oblige a public authority to comply with a request for information if the request is vexatious.

(2) Where a public authority has previously complied with a request for information which was made by any person, it is not obliged to comply with a subsequent identical or substantially similar request from that person unless a reasonable interval has elapsed between compliance with the previous request and the making of the current request . . .

16. Duty to provide advice and assistance

(1) It shall be the duty of a public authority to provide advice and assistance, so far as it would be reasonable to expect the authority to do so, to persons who propose to make, or have made, requests for information to it.

(2) Any public authority which, in relation to the provision of advice or assistance in any case, conforms with the code of practice under section 45 is to be taken to comply with the duty imposed by subsection (1) in relation to that case.

Refusal of request

17. Refusal of request

(1) A public authority which, in relation to any request for information, is to any extent relying on a claim that any provision of Part II relating to the duty to confirm or deny is relevant to the request or on a claim that information is exempt information must, within the time for complying with section 1(1), give the applicant a notice which—

    (*a*) states that fact,

    (*b*) specifies the exemption in question, and

    (*c*) states (if that would not otherwise be apparent) why the exemption applies.

(2) Where—

    (*a*) in relation to any request for information, a public authority is, as respects any information, relying on a claim—

        (i) that any provision of Part II which relates to the duty to confirm or deny and is not specified in section 2(3) is relevant to the request, or

        (ii) that the information is exempt information only by virtue of a provision not specified in section 2(3), and

    (*b*) at the time when the notice under subsection (1) is given to the applicant, the public authority (or, in a case falling within section 66(3) or (4), the responsible authority) has not yet reached a decision as to the application of subsection (1)(*b*) or (2)(*b*) of section 2,

the notice under subsection (1) must indicate that no decision as to the application of that provision has yet been reached and must contain an estimate of the date by which the authority expects that such a decision will have been reached.

(3) A public authority which, in relation to any request for information, is to any extent relying on a claim that subsection (1)(*b*) or (2)(*b*) of section 2 applies must, either in the notice under subsection (1) or in a separate notice given within such time as is reasonable in the circumstances, state the reasons for claiming—

    (*a*) that, in all the circumstances of the case, the public interest in maintaining the exclusion of the duty to confirm or deny outweighs the public interest in disclosing whether the authority holds the information, or

    (*b*) that, in all the circumstances of the case, the public interest in maintaining the exemption outweighs the public interest in disclosing the information.

(4) A public authority is not obliged to make a statement under subsection (1)(*c*) or (3) if, or to the extent that, the statement would involve the disclosure of information which would itself be exempt information.

(5) A public authority which, in relation to any request for information, is relying on a claim that section 12 or 14 applies must, within the time for complying with section 1(1), give the applicant a notice stating that fact.

(6) Subsection (5) does not apply where—

    (*a*) the public authority is relying on a claim that section 14 applies,

    (*b*) the authority has given the applicant a notice, in relation to a previous request for information, stating that it is relying on such a claim, and

    (*c*) it would in all the circumstances be unreasonable to expect the authority to serve a further notice under subsection (5) in relation to the current request.

(7) A notice under subsection (1), (3) or (5) must—
- (*a*) contain particulars of any procedure provided by the public authority for dealing with complaints about the handling of requests for information or state that the authority does not provide such a procedure, and
- (*b*) contain particulars of the right conferred by section 50 . . .

PART II
EXEMPT INFORMATION
21. Information accessible to applicant by other means
(1) Information which is reasonably accessible to the applicant otherwise than under section 1 is exempt information.
(2) For the purposes of subsection (1)—
- (*a*) information may be reasonably accessible to the applicant even though it is accessible only on payment, and
- (*b*) information is to be taken to be reasonably accessible to the applicant if it is information which the public authority or any other person is obliged by or under any enactment to communicate (otherwise than by making the information available for inspection) to members of the public on request, whether free of charge or on payment.

(3) For the purposes of subsection (1), information which is held by a public authority and does not fall within subsection (2)(*b*) is not to be regarded as reasonably accessible to the applicant merely because the information is available from the public authority itself on request, unless the information is made available in accordance with the authority's publication scheme and any payment required is specified in, or determined in accordance with, the scheme.

22. Information intended for future publication
(1) Information is exempt information if—
- (*a*) the information is held by the public authority with a view to its publication, by the authority or any other person, at some future date (whether determined or not),
- (*b*) the information was already held with a view to such publication at the time when the request for information was made, and
- (*c*) it is reasonable in all the circumstances that the information should be withheld from disclosure until the date referred to in paragraph (*a*).

(2) The duty to confirm or deny does not arise if, or to the extent that, compliance with section 1(1)(a) would involve the disclosure of any information (whether or not already recorded) which falls within subsection (1).

23. Information supplied by, or relating to, bodies dealing with security matters
(1) Information held by a public authority is exempt information if it was directly or indirectly supplied to the public authority by, or relates to, any of the bodies specified in subsection (3).
(2) A certificate signed by a Minister of the Crown certifying that the information to which it applies was directly or indirectly supplied by, or relates to, any of the bodies specified in subsection (3) shall, subject to section 60, be conclusive evidence of that fact.
(3) The bodies referred to in subsections (1) and (2) are—
- (*a*) the Security Service,
- (*b*) the Secret Intelligence Service,
- (*c*) the Government Communications Headquarters,
- (*d*) the special forces,
- (*e*) the Tribunal established under section 65 of the Regulation of Investigatory Powers Act 2000,
- (*f*) the Tribunal established under section 7 of the Interception of Communications Act 1985,
- (*g*) the Tribunal established under section 5 of the Security Service Act 1989,
- (*h*) the Tribunal established under section 9 of the Intelligence Services Act 1994,
- (*i*) the Security Vetting Appeals Panel,
- (*j*) the Security Commission,
- (*k*) the National Criminal Intelligence Service, and
- (*l*) the Service Authority for the National Criminal Intelligence Service.

(4) In subsection (3)(*c*) "the Government Communications Headquarters" includes any unit or part of a unit of the armed forces of the Crown which is for the time being required by the Secretary of State to assist the Government Communications Headquarters in carrying out its functions

(5) The duty to confirm or deny does not arise if, or to the extent that, compliance with section 1(1)(*a*) would involve the disclosure of any information (whether or not already recorded) which was directly or indirectly supplied to the public authority by, or relates to, any of the bodies specified in subsection (3).

24. National security

(1) Information which does not fall within section 23(1) is exempt information if exemption from section 1(1)(*b*) is required for the purpose of safeguarding national security.

(2) The duty to confirm or deny does not arise if, or to the extent that, exemption from section 1(1)(*a*) is required for the purpose of safeguarding national security.

(3) A certificate signed by a Minister of the Crown certifying that exemption from section 1(1)(*b*), or from section 1(1)(*a*) and (*b*), is, or at any time was, required for the purpose of safeguarding national security shall, subject to section 60, be conclusive evidence of that fact.

(4) A certificate under subsection (3) may identify the information to which it applies by means of a general description and may be expressed to have prospective effect.

25. Certificates under ss. 23 and 24: supplementary provisions

(1) A document purporting to be a certificate under section 23(2) or 24(3) shall be received in evidence and deemed to be such a certificate unless the contrary is proved.

(2) A document which purports to be certified by or on behalf of a Minister of the Crown as a true copy of a certificate issued by that Minister under section 23(2) or 24(3) shall in any legal proceedings be evidence (or, in Scotland, sufficient evidence) of that certificate.

(3) The power conferred by section 23(2) or 24(3) on a Minister of the Crown shall not be exercisable except by a Minister who is a member of the Cabinet or by the Attorney General, the Advocate General for Scotland or the Attorney General for Northern Ireland . . .

30. Investigations and proceedings conducted by public authorities

(1) Information held by a public authority is exempt information if it has at any time been held by the authority for the purposes of—

    (*a*)   any investigation which the public authority has a duty to conduct with a view to it being ascertained—

        (i)   whether a person should be charged with an offence, or

        (ii) whether a person charged with an offence is guilty of it,

    (*b*)   any investigation which is conducted by the authority and in the circumstances may lead to a decision by the authority to institute criminal proceedings which the authority has power to conduct, or

    (*c*)   any criminal proceedings which the authority has power to conduct.

(2) Information held by a public authority is exempt information if—

    (*a*)   it was obtained or recorded by the authority for the purposes of its functions relating to—

        (i)   investigations falling within subsection (1)(*a*) or (*b*),

        (ii)   criminal proceedings which the authority has power to conduct,

        (iii) investigations (other than investigations falling within subsection (1)(*a*) or (*b*)) which are conducted by the authority for any of the purposes specified in section 31(2) and either by virtue of Her Majesty's prerogative or by virtue of powers conferred by or under any enactment, or

        (iv) civil proceedings which are brought by or on behalf of the authority and arise out of such investigations, and

    (*b*)   it relates to the obtaining of information from confidential sources.

(3) The duty to confirm or deny does not arise in relation to information which is (or if it were held by the public authority would be) exempt information by virtue of subsection (1) or (2).

(4) In relation to the institution or conduct of criminal proceedings or the power to conduct them, references in subsection (1)(*b*) or (*c*) and subsection (2)(*a*) to the public authority include references—

    (*a*)   to any officer of the authority,

    (*b*)   in the case of a government department other than a Northern Ireland department, to the Minister of the Crown in charge of the department, and

    (*c*)   in the case of a Northern Ireland department, to the Northern Ireland Minister in charge of the department . . .

31. Law enforcement

(1) Information which is not exempt information by virtue of section 30 is exempt information if its disclosure under this Act would, or would be likely to, prejudice—

  (*a*) the prevention or detection of crime,
  (*b*) the apprehension or prosecution of offenders,
  (*c*) the administration of justice,
  (*d*) the assessment or collection of any tax or duty or of any imposition of a similar nature,
  (*e*) the operation of the immigration controls,
  (*f*) the maintenance of security and good order in prisons or in other institutions where persons are lawfully detained,
  (*g*) the exercise by any public authority of its functions for any of the purposes specified in subsection (2),
  (*h*) any civil proceedings which are brought by or on behalf of a public authority and arise out of an investigation conducted, for any of the purposes specified in subsection (2), by or on behalf of the authority by virtue of Her Majesty's prerogative or by virtue of powers conferred by or under an enactment . . .

(2) The purposes referred to in subsection (1)(*g*) to (*i*) are—

  (*a*) the purpose of ascertaining whether any person has failed to comply with the law,
  (*b*) the purpose of ascertaining whether any person is responsible for any conduct which is improper,
  (*c*) the purpose of ascertaining whether circumstances which would justify regulatory action in pursuance of any enactment exist or may arise,
  (*d*) the purpose of ascertaining a person's fitness or competence in relation to the management of bodies corporate or in relation to any profession or other activity which he is, or seeks to become, authorised to carry on,
  (*e*) the purpose of ascertaining the cause of an accident,
  (*f*) the purpose of protecting charities against misconduct or mismanagement (whether by trustees or other persons) in their administration,
  (*g*) the purpose of protecting the property of charities from loss or misapplication,
  (*h*) the purpose of recovering the property of charities,
  (*i*) the purpose of securing the health, safety and welfare of persons at work, and
  (*j*) the purpose of protecting persons other than persons at work against risk to health or safety arising out of or in connection with the actions of persons at work.

(3) The duty to confirm or deny does not arise if, or to the extent that, compliance with section 1(1)(*a*) would, or would be likely to, prejudice any of the matters mentioned in subsection (1).

36. Prejudice to effective conduct of public affairs

(1) This section applies to—

  (*a*) information which is held by a government department or by the National Assembly for Wales and is not exempt information by virtue of section 35, and
  (*b*) information which is held by any other public authority.

(2) Information to which this section applies is exempt information if, in the reasonable opinion of a qualified person, disclosure of the information under this Act—

  (*a*) would, or would be likely to, prejudice—
    (i)   the maintenance of the convention of the collective responsibility of Ministers of the Crown, or
    (ii) the work of the Executive Committee of the Northern Ireland Assembly, or
    (iii) the work of the executive committee of the National Assembly for Wales,
  (*b*) would, or would be likely to, inhibit—
    (i)   the free and frank provision of advice, or
    (ii) the free and frank exchange of views for the purposes of deliberation, or
  (*c*) would otherwise prejudice, or would be likely otherwise to prejudice, the effective conduct of public affairs.

(3) The duty to confirm or deny does not arise in relation to information to which this section applies (or would apply if held by the public authority) if, or to the extent that, in the reasonable opinion of a qualified person, compliance with section 1(1)(*a*) would, or would be likely to, have any of the effects mentioned in subsection (2).

(4) In relation to statistical information, subsections (2) and (3) shall have effect with the omission of the words "in the reasonable opinion of a qualified person".

(5) In subsections (2) and (3) "qualified person"—

    (*a*) in relation to information held by a government department in the charge of a Minister of the Crown, means any Minister of the Crown,

    (*b*) in relation to information held by a Northern Ireland department, means the Northern Ireland Minister in charge of the department,

    (*c*) in relation to information held by any other government department, means the commissioners or other person in charge of that department,

    (*d*) in relation to information held by the House of Commons, means the Speaker of that House,

    (*e*) in relation to information held by the House of Lords, means the Clerk of the Parliaments,

    (*f*) in relation to information held by the Northern Ireland Assembly, means the Presiding Officer,

    (*g*) in relation to information held by the National Assembly for Wales, means the Assembly First Secretary,

    (*h*) in relation to information held by any Welsh public authority other than the Auditor General for Wales, means—

        (i) the public authority, or

        (ii) any officer or employee of the authority authorised by the Assembly First Secretary,

    (*i*) in relation to information held by the National Audit Office, means the Comptroller and Auditor General,

    (*j*) in relation to information held by the Northern Ireland Audit Office, means the Comptroller and Auditor General for Northern Ireland,

    (*k*) in relation to information held by the Auditor General for Wales, means the Auditor General for Wales,

    (*l*) in relation to information held by any Northern Ireland public authority other than the Northern Ireland Audit Office, means—

        (i) the public authority, or

        (ii) any officer or employee of the authority authorised by the First Minister and deputy First Minister in Northern Ireland acting jointly,

    (*m*) in relation to information held by the Greater London Authority, means the Mayor of London,

    (*n*) in relation to information held by a functional body within the meaning of the Greater London Authority Act 1999, means the chairman of that functional body, and

    (*o*) in relation to information held by any public authority not falling within any of paragraphs (a) to (n), means—

        (i) a Minister of the Crown,

        (ii) the public authority, if authorised for the purposes of this section by a Minister of the Crown, or

        (iii) any officer or employee of the public authority who is authorised for the purposes of this section by a Minister of the Crown.

(6) Any authorisation for the purposes of this section—

    (*a*) may relate to a specified person or to persons falling within a specified class,

    (*b*) may be general or limited to particular classes of case, and

    (*c*) may be granted subject to conditions.

(7) A certificate signed by the qualified person referred to in subsection (5)(*d*) or (*e*) above certifying that in his reasonable opinion—

    (*a*) disclosure of information held by either House of Parliament, or

    (*b*) compliance with section 1(1)(*a*) by either House,

would, or would be likely to, have any of the effects mentioned in subsection (2) shall be conclusive evidence of that fact . . .

40. Personal information

(1) Any information to which a request for information relates is exempt information if it constitutes personal data of which the applicant is the data subject.

(2) Any information to which a request for information relates is also exempt information if—

    (*a*) it constitutes personal data which do not fall within subsection (1), and

    (*b*) either the first or the second condition below is satisfied.

(3) The first condition is—

    (a) in a case where the information falls within any of paragraphs (a) to (d) of the definition of "data" in section 1(1) of the Data Protection Act 1998, that the disclosure of the information to a member of the public otherwise than under this Act would contravene—

        (i) any of the data protection principles, or

        (ii) section 10 of that Act (right to prevent processing likely to cause damage or distress), and

    (b) in any other case, that the disclosure of the information to a member of the public otherwise than under this Act would contravene any of the data protection principles if the exemptions in section 33A(1) of the Data Protection Act 1998 (which relate to manual data held by public authorities) were disregarded.

(4) The second condition is that by virtue of any provision of Part IV of the Data Protection Act 1998 the information is exempt from section 7(1)(c) of that Act (data subject's right of access to personal data).

(5) The duty to confirm or deny—

    (a) does not arise in relation to information which is (or if it were held by the public authority would be) exempt information by virtue of subsection (1), and

    (b) does not arise in relation to other information if or to the extent that either—

        (i) the giving to a member of the public of the confirmation or denial that would have to be given to comply with section 1(1)(a) would (apart from this Act) contravene any of the data protection principles or section 10 of the Data Protection Act 1998 or would do so if the exemptions in section 33A(1) of that Act were disregarded, or

        (ii) by virtue of any provision of Part IV of the Data Protection Act 1998 the information is exempt from section 7(1)(a) of that Act (data subject's right to be informed whether personal data being processed).

(6) In determining for the purposes of this section whether anything done before 24th October 2007 would contravene any of the data protection principles, the exemptions in Part III of Schedule 8 to the Data Protection Act 1998 shall be disregarded.

(7) In this section—

    "the data protection principles" means the principles set out in Part I of Schedule 1 to the Data Protection Act 1998, as read subject to Part II of that Schedule and section 27(1) of that Act;

    "data subject" has the same meaning as in section 1(1) of that Act;

    "personal data" has the same meaning as in section 1(1) of that Act.

41. Information provided in confidence

(1) Information is exempt information if—

    (a) it was obtained by the public authority from any other person (including another public authority), and

    (b) the disclosure of the information to the public (otherwise than under this Act) by the public authority holding it would constitute a breach of confidence actionable by that or any other person.

(2) The duty to confirm or deny does not arise if, or to the extent that, the confirmation or denial that would have to be given to comply with section 1(1)(a) would (apart from this Act) constitute an actionable breach of confidence.

NOTES[7]

1. Special arrangements apply where information is, or if it existed would be, contained in a 'transferred public record'.[8] Every public authority must adopt,

---

7   See the White Paper, *Your Right to Know* (Cm. 3818, 1997); Public Administration Committee Report on *Your Right to Know* (1997-98 HC 398) and *Government Response* (1997–98 HC 1020); *Freedom of Information* Consultation on Draft Legislation (Cm. 4355, 1999); Report of Select Committee on Draft FOI Bill, 27 July 1999; O. Gay, HC Research Paper 00/89.

8   ss. 15, 66.

maintain and review a publication scheme and publish information in accordance with it; it must have regard to the public interest in allowing public access to information held by it and in the publication of reasons for its decisions.[9] The scheme (or model scheme to which it conforms) must be approved by the Information Commissioner.[10] The Secretary of State must issue a code of practice with respect to the discharge to public authorities of their functions under Part I; the Lord Chancellor must issue a code of practice concerning the keeping, management and destruction of records.[11] The Information Commissioner[12] must promote good practice,[13] and has power to give a 'practice recommendation' to any public authority where it appears to him that it does not conform to the codes of practice.

Exemptions

2. Part II sets out a long list of cases where information is exempt from disclosure and (except in the case of s. 21) the duty to confirm or deny does not apply.

Apart from those extracted above, they include:

s. 26   (defence) where disclosure would, or would be likely to, prejudice (a) the defence of the British Islands or of any colony or (b) the capability, effectiveness or security of the armed forces;

s. 27   (international relations) where disclosure would, or would be likely to prejudice relations between the UK and any other State, or any international organisation or court, the interests of the UK abroad, or the promotion or protection by the UK of those interests, or if it is confidential information obtained from another State etc.;

s. 28   (relations within the UK) where disclosure would, or would be likely to prejudice relations between any UK administration (i.e. the UK government, the Scottish Administration, the Executive Committee of the Northern Ireland Assembly or the National Assembly for Wales);

s. 29   (the economy) where disclosure would, or would be likely to prejudice the economic interests of the UK or any part of it or the financial interest of any UK administration;

s. 32   (court records) various court records and documents and documents concerning an inquiry or arbitration;

s. 33   (audit functions) where disclosure would, or would be likely to prejudice the exercise by a public authority of audit functions in respect of other public authorities;

s. 34   (parliamentary privilege) where exemption is required to avoid an infringement of the privileges of either House;

s. 35   (formulation of government policy etc.) where information relates to the formation or development of government policy (including the policy of the Executive Committee of the NI Assembly and of the National Assembly for Wales); ministerial communications, including Cabinet and Cabinet Committee proceedings; Law Officers' advice; the operation of any ministerial private office;

s. 37   (communications with Her Majesty etc. and honours) where information relates to communications with the Queen, other members of the Royal Family or the Royal Household or the conferment of any honour or dignity;

---

9 s. 19.
10 ss. 19, 20.
11 ss. 46, 47. Drafts have been published: see HO and LCD websites.
12 Appointed under s. 18. Formerly the Data Protection Commissioner.
13 s. 47.

s. 38   (health and safety) where disclosures would, or would be likely to, endanger the physical or mental health or the safety of any individual;

s. 39   (environmental information) where the public authority holding the information is obliged by regulations under s. 74 to make it available to the public in accordance with the regulations, or would be so obliged but for any exemption contained in the regulations;

s. 42   information protected by legal professional privilege;

s. 43   (commercial interests) information which constitutes a trade secret or whose disclosure would, or would be likely to, prejudice the commercial interests of any person (including the public authority holding it);

s. 44   (prohibitions on disclosure) where disclosure (otherwise under the Act) by the public authority holding it is prohibited by or under any enactment,[14] is incompatible with any Community obligation, or would constitute or be punishable as a contempt of court.

3. *Enforcement.* The enforcement process established by the Act provides for applications by a complainant to the Information Commissioner for a decision whether, in any specified respect, a request for information made by the complainant to a public authority has been dealt with in accordance with the requirements of Part I. The Commissioner must make a decision unless it appears to him that the complainant has not exhausted any complaints procedure provided in conformity with the Code of Practice under s. 45, that there has been undue delay in making the application, or that the application is frivolous or vexatious or has been withdrawn or abandoned. The Commissioner must either: (a) notify the complainant that he has not made any decision as a result of the application, and why; or (b) serve a 'decision notice' on the complainant and the public authority. If he finds that the authority has failed to communicate information, or to provide confirmation or denial, where required by s. 1(1), or has failed to comply with any of the requirements of ss. 11–17, the decision notice must specify the steps to be taken and the period within which they must be taken. The Commissioner may obtain information about a public authority's practice by serving an 'information notice'. If he is satisfied that a public authority has failed to comply with any of the requirements of Part I he may serve an 'enforcement notice' requiring specified steps to be taken.[15] Accordingly, the Commissioner may take a different view from that of the authority on matters such as the balance of public interests. However, a decision or enforcement notice served on a government department, the National Assembly for Wales or a public authority designated by an order made by the Secretary of State, and which relates to a failure: (a) to comply with s. 1(1)(a) in respect of information which falls within any provision of Part II stating that the duty to confirm or deny does not arise; or (b) to comply with s. 1(1)(b) in respect of exempt information, ceases to have effect if a ministerial certificate is given to the Commissioner within 20 days. This certificate must be signed by a Cabinet Minister, the Attorney General, the Welsh Assembly First Secretary or the First Minister and deputy First Minister in Northern Ireland acting jointly, and must state that he has on reasonable grounds formed the opinion that there was no failure under s. 1(1)(b).[16] Non-compliance with a decision notice requiring steps to be taken, an information notice or an enforcement notice may be certified by the Commissioner to the High Court for the court to deal with as if there had been a contempt of court.[17]

---

14 The Secretary of State has a general power to repeal or amend such an enactment for the purpose of removing or relaxing the prohibition: s. 75.

15 ss. 50–52.

16 s. 53.

17 s. 54.

The Commissioner may obtain a warrant from a Circuit judge authorising entry and inspection.[18] The Act confers no right of action in civil proceedings.[19]

The complainant or the public authority may appeal to the Information Tribunal[20] against a decision notice; an authority may appeal against an information or enforcement notice. The permitted grounds of appeal are that the notice is not in accordance with the law or (to the extent that the notice involved an exercise of discretion by the Commissioner that he ought to have exercised his discretion differently. A further appeal on a point of law lies to the High Court.[21] The Commissioner or any applicant affected may appeal to the Tribunal against a national security certificate.[22]

4. *Historical records.* A record becomes a 'historical record' at the end of a period of 30 years beginning with the calendar year following that in which it was created; all the records in one file are treated as having been created when the latest record was created. Information in a historical record cannot be exempt information by virtue of ss. 28, 30(1), 32, 33, 35, 36, 37(1)(a), 42 or 43. Compliance with s. 1(1)(a) in relation to a historical record is not to be taken as capable of having any of the effects mentioned in ss. 28(3), 33(3), 36(3), 42(2) or 43(3). A 60-year period is specified in relation to s. 37(1)(b)(honours), and 100 years in relation to s. 31 (law enforcement). Information in a historical record cannot be exempt information by virtue of ss. 21 or 22.[1]

Where a PRO recieves a request for information which relates to information which is, or if it existed would be, contained in a public record which has been transferred to it, and either the duty to confirm or deny is excluded (but not absolutely) or the information is exempt information (but not absolutely), the PRO must copy the request to the 'responsible authority' that transferred the record.[2] Unless that authority has designated information in a record as 'open information for the purposes of this section' the PRO must consult the authority before determining whether: (a) it falls within any provision of Part II relating to the duty to confirm or deny; or (b) is exempt information. Any question as to the application of s. 2(1)(b) or (2)(b) (where there is no absolute exemption) is to be determined by the responsible authority after consulting the Lord Chancellor.[3]

The new statutory regime replaces the regime of access to and closure of records in the Public Record Office which largely depended on the discretion of the Lord Chancellor. Records were not normally available for public inspection for 30 years; longer periods were prescribed for certain categories.[4]

5. *Criticisms.* The FOI Bill was regarded as a disappointment by comparison with the White Paper and even the Code.[5] Concerns that remain with the provisions ultimately enacted include the fact that a Minister may have the last word on the public interest;[6] the number of exemptions that are class based, and the use of 'prejudice' rather than 'substantial harm' as a test where harm has to be established; and the existence of

---

18 s. 55, Sch. 3.
19 s. 56.
20 Formerly the Data Protection Tribunal. See Sch. 4.
21 ss. 56–59. Appeals are dealt with in accordance with procedures in the Data Protection Act 1998, Sch. 6, as amended by the 2000 Act, Sch 4, s. 61.
22 s. 60. See ss. 23(2), 24(3).
1 ss. 62, 63, 64.
2 s.15.
3 s.66.
4 See White Paper on *Open Government* (Cm. 2290, 1993), Chap. 9.
5 See O.Gay, HC Research Paper 99/61, pp. 38–40; CFI Press Release, 24 May 1999).
6 s. 53.

broadly drafted exemptions in such areas as the formulation of government policy and prejudice to the effective conduct of public affairs.[7]

6. There are many specific statutory provisions preventing the disclosure without lawful authority of information acquired from citizens.[8]

7. Government information may be protected from disclosure by a claim of public interest immunity.[9] In *Balfour v Foreign and Commonwealth Office*[10] the Court of Appeal held that while the court must always be vigilant to ensure that a claim of public interest immunity is raised only in appropriate circumstances and with appropriate particularity, once a Minister certifies that disclosure of documents poses a risk to national security, the court should not exercise its right to inspect those documents. The PII claims in the course of the prosecution of Matrix Churchill executives for deception in obtaining licences to export machine tool to Iraq, for use in armaments manufacture were particularly controversial.[11] The Labour government has affirmed the approach of its predecessor that PII will not be asserted by the government unless the relevant Minister believes that disclosure of a document or piece of 'information will cause real damage to the public interest. The test will be applied rigorously. Where public interest immunity applies, Ministers will nevertheless make voluntary disclosure if they consider that the interests of justice outweigh the public interest in withholding the document or information in question. In all cases, a Minister's claim for public interest immunity is subject to the court's power to order disclosure. The approach will be followed in both criminal and civil cases.'[12]

8. It is argued that the 'right to know' cannot be an integral part of freedom of expression, on the ground that the freedom would then be claimed 'where there is no willing speaker'.[13] There are other views on this point.[14] Article 10(1) ECHR does not confer a general right to freedom of information against state bodies.[15] However, a right of access to such information as is necessary for enjoyment of the rights conferred by Art. 8 ECHR is implicit in that article.[16]

---

7 ss. 35, 36.
8 See Y. Cripps, [1983] PL 600, 628–631, and the lists of statutes set out in Birkinshaw, *Government and Information* (1990), pp. 345–348. Annex B to the White Paper on *Open Government* lists over 200 provisions concerning disclosure of official information, most protecting third-party information.
9 See P.P. Craig, *Administrative Law* (4th edn, 1999), pp. 821–833; Simon Brown LJ, [1994] PL 579; and A. Tomkins, *The Constitution after Scott* (1998), Chap. 5.
10 [1994] 1 WLR 681.
11 See G. Ganz, (1993) 56 MLR 564, (1995) 58 MLR 417; T. R. S. Allan, [1993] Crim LR 660; I. Leigh, [1993] PL 630; and A. Tomkins, ibid., p. 650.
12 HC Deb, 11 July 1997, cols. 616-617, written answer by the Attorney-General, referring to a paper placed in the Libraries of the House on 18 December 1996.
13 E. Barendt, *Freedom of Speech* (1987), pp. 82–83, 107–113.
14 For a different view, see P. Bayne, 'Freedom of Information and Political Free Speech' in T. Campbell and W. Sadurski (eds.), *Freedom of Communication*, Chap. 10 and the discussion by Sir Anthony Mason in J. Beaton and Y. Cripps (eds.), *Freedom of Expression and Freedom of Information* (2000), Chap. 13.
15 *Leander v Sweden* (1987) 9 EHRR 433; *Guerra v Italy* (1998) 26 EHRR 357, para. 53.
16 *Guerra v Italy*; *McGinley and Egan v United Kingdom* (1998) 27 EHRR 1.

CHAPTER 9

The right to privacy

1 Introduction[1]

The right to privacy was described by Cooley as 'the right to be let alone'.[2] Both the Justice Report[3] and the Younger Committee Report[4] pointed out the difficulty of finding 'a precise or logical formula which could either circumscribe the meaning of the word "privacy" or define it exhaustively'.[5] Each, however, suggested a working definition. The Justice Report[6] understood privacy as meaning

'that area of a man's life which, in any given circumstances, a reasonable man with an understanding of the legitimate needs of the community would think it wrong to invade.'

Cf. the definition adopted by A. F. Westin:[7]

'Privacy is the claim of individuals, groups, or institutions to determine for themselves when, how, and to what extent information about them is communicated to others. Viewed in terms of the relation of the individual to social participation, privacy is the voluntary and temporary withdrawal of a person from the general society through physical or psychological means, either in a state of solitude or small-group intimacy or, when among larger groups, in a condition of anonymity or reserve.'

The Younger Committee[8] 'conceived of the right of privacy as having two main aspects':

'The first of these is freedom from intrusion upon oneself, one's home, family and relationships. The second is privacy of information, that is the right to determine for oneself how and to what extent information about oneself is communicated to others.'

More recently, the Calcutt Committee[9] adopted the following, similar, working definition of the right to privacy:

---

1   On the right to privacy, see Lord Bingham, [1996] EHRLR 450; P. Birks (ed.), *Privacy and Loyalty* (1997), particularly the chapters by E. Barendt, D. Feldman and R. Bagshaw; D. Feldman, (1994) 47(2) CLP 41; H. Fenwick and G. Phillipson, (1996) 55 CLJ 447; S. Goode, *The Right to Privacy* (1983); P. Jones, (2000) 6 EPL 275; B. Markesenis, (1990) 53 MLR 802; ibid. (ed.), *Protecting Privacy* (1999), particularly the chapters by B. Neill and R. Singh; ibid., (1999) 115 LQR 47; D. McLean, *Privacy and its Invasion* (1995); H. Nissembaum, (1998) 17 Law and Philosophy 559; E. Paton-Smith, (1998) 61 MLR 318; M. Richardson, 19 MULR 673; F. D. Schoman, *Privacy and Social Freedom* (1992); D. J. Siepp, (1983) 3 OJLS 325; R. Wacks, *The Protection of Privacy* (1980); ibid., *Personal Information: Privacy and the Law* (1989); ibid., *Privacy and Press Freedom* (1995).
2   *Torts* (2nd edn, 1888), p. 29.
3   *Privacy and the Law* (1970), p. 5.
4   *Report of the Committee on Privacy* (1972), Cmnd. 5012, p. 17.
5   Justice Report, p. 5.
6   Ibid.
7   *Privacy and Freedom* (1970), p. 7.
8   Report, p. 10.
9   *Report of the Committee on Privacy and Related Matters*, Cm. 1102 (1990), p. 7.

'The right of the individual to be protected against intrusion into his personal life or affairs, or those of his family, by direct physical means or by publication of information.'[10]

The concept underlying and justifying the right to privacy is a matter of debate. Writers have championed, *inter alia*, the notions of seclusion, individual autonomy and human dignity.[11] In *Douglas v Hello! Ltd*,[12] Sedley LJ suggested that privacy is a 'legal principle drawn from the fundamental value of personal autonomy'.

The 'principal areas of complaint with regard to intrusions into privacy' *in the private sector* were identified by the Younger Committee[13] as follows: (i) unwanted publicity (by the press and broadcasting); (ii) misuse of personal information (by credit rating agencies, banks, employers, educational institutions (student records) and the medical profession (particularly in industry)); (iii) intrusions on home life (by prying neighbours, landlords, the press, doorstep and postal and telephone sales and promotional methods and private detectives); and (iv) intrusion in business life (industrial espionage).[14] To these may be added *in the public sector* (i) intrusion in the course of the administration of the criminal law, for example, by personal and property searches (the law as to which is considered in Chap. 2), telephone tapping and bugging, fingerprinting, and the use of breathalysers and (ii) the misuse of personal information held by public authorities such as income tax, census, social security, council housing and family welfare authorities and the police.

In the absence of a general right to privacy,[15] the protection afforded to privacy by English law has been piecemeal, incomplete and indirect. Concern about the adequacy of the protection given has long been voiced[16] and has in recent years reached the point where it has been the subject of three reports and several private members' bills. The reasons for this activity were identified by the Younger Committee Report as follows:[16a]

'18 To some extent the new public concern on this subject is the direct result of new technological developments. Numerous sophisticated electronic devices have been invented and marketed, which greatly increase the possibilities of surreptitious supervision of people's private activities and of spying upon business rivals. Computers have been designed which facilitate the centralisation of information about people's private affairs and its dissemination for purposes other than those for which it was supplied. And, accompanying these technical developments, there has been a spectacular growth in the collection and distribution of information as a commercial activity, which has given rise to anxiety in connection with the granting of credit, mail-order business and other forms of promotion.

19 Furthermore, but by no means least important, there has been a fairly steady flow of complaints about intrusions into privacy by the mass information media. This is a subject as old as the popular press, but its importance has been enhanced in the context of radio and television and by the growing tendency of all media to engage increasingly in "investigative journalism". Press and broadcasting organisations see themselves as the watchdogs of the public in investigating and exposing conduct of many kinds which, though not necessarily

---

10 See also the definitions in the *US Restatement*, below, p. 914, and in the conclusions of the 1967 Nordic Conference on the Right of Privacy (Justice Committee Report, Appendix B, and S. Stromholm, *Right of Privacy and Rights of the Personality* (1967), p. 237). And see W. A. Parent, (1983) 2 Law and Philosophy 305.

11 For differing views, see E. Bloustein, (1964) 39 NYULR 962; D. Feldman, (1947) 2 CLP 41; P. Jones, (2000) 6 EPL 275; and J. Inness, *Privacy, Intimacy and Isolation* (1992), p. 46.

12 [2001] 2 All ER 289, below, p. 929.

13 Report, p. 7.

14 The problems posed by press conduct, which have been the most persistent and serious cause for concern, were identified in detail by the Calcutt Committee (Report, p. 10).

15 But see *Douglas v Hello!* below, p. 922.

16 See, e.g., Winfield, (1931) 47 LQR 23.

16a p. 6.

involving breaches of the law, may arguably be considered of concern to society and therefore fair game for revelation and public comment in the press or on the air. This may involve the reporting of intimate details of the lives of individuals which would not normally be thought of as being in the public domain.

20 From a wider point of view concern for the protection of privacy has been stimulated by the growing pressures exerted by modern industrial society upon the home and daily life, including such factors as the density of urban housing, the consequent difficulty of escaping from the observation of neighbours, the annoyance of commercial advertising and the increasing inquisitiveness of social surveys, polls and market research about the lives of private citizens.'

Although each of these reasons remains valid, it is probably correct to say that concern about the threat posed by computers has declined,[17] while exasperation with unethical or irresponsible press conduct has increased, as indicated by the appointment of the Calcutt Committee.

2 A general right of privacy?

Kaye v Robertson [1991] FSR 62, Court of Appeal

The plaintiff, the star of 'Allo! Allo!', a popular television comedy series, underwent extensive surgery to his head and brain after injuries resulting from storm debris falling on his car. In the interests of Mr Kaye's health, which remained a matter of serious concern, the hospital authorities placed a notice on the door of Mr Kaye's private room asking visitors to contact a member of the hospital staff before visiting. Acting on the instructions of their editor, a journalist and a photographer from *Sunday Sport*, a national newspaper, went to the hospital and, ignoring the notice on the door, entered Mr Kaye's room. They interviewed him and took photographs showing the injuries to his head. This, the editor claimed, was a 'great old-fashioned scoop'. The plaintiff obtained an injunction, based mainly upon *Tolley v J S Fry & Sons Ltd*,[18] requiring the first and second defendants, the newspaper editor and publisher respectively, to refrain from publishing the interview and photographs. The defendants appealed to the Court of Appeal.

Glidewell LJ: It is well-known that in English law there is no right to privacy, and accordingly there is no right of action for breach of a person's privacy. The facts of the present case are a graphic illustration of the desirability of Parliament considering whether and in what circumstances statutory provision can be made to protect the privacy of individuals.

In the absence of such a right, the plaintiff's advisers have sought to base their claim to injunctions upon other well-established rights of action. . . .

1. Libel
The basis of the plaintiff's case under this head is that the article as originally written clearly implied that Mr. Kaye consented to give the first 'exclusive' interview to *Sunday Sport*, and to be photographed by their photographer. This was untrue: [according to medical evidence] Mr. Kaye was in no fit condition to give any informed consent, and such consent as he may appear to have given was, and should have been known by *Sunday Sport*'s representative to be, of no effect. The implication in the article would have the effect of lowering Mr. Kaye in the esteem of right-thinking people, and was thus defamatory.

The plaintiff's case is based on the well-known decision in *Tolley v J S Fry & Sons Ltd* . . .

17 The problem is tackled by the Data Protection Act 1998. See the annual reports of the Data Protection Commissioner, which are published as House of Commons papers. See I. Walden, (1998) 3 Communications Law 207.
18 Below, p. 945.

Mr. Milmo for the defendants submits that, assuming that the article was capable of having the meaning alleged, this would not be a sufficient basis for interlocutory relief. In *William Coulson & Sons v James Coulson & Co* (1887) 3 TLR 846, this court held that, though the High Court has jurisdiction to grant an interim injunction before the trial of a libel action, it is a jurisdiction to be exercised only sparingly.[19] . . .

This is still the rule in actions for defamation, despite the decision of the House of Lords in *American Cyanamid Co v Ethicon Ltd* [1975] AC 396 in relation to interim injunctions generally. This court so decided in *Herbage v Times Newspapers Ltd*, unreported but decided on 1 May 1981.[20] . . .

It is in my view certainly arguable that the intended article would be libellous, on the authority of *Tolley v Fry*. I think that a jury would probably find that Mr. Kaye had been libelled, but I cannot say that such a conclusion is inevitable. It follows that I agree with Mr. Milmo's submission and in this respect I disagree with the learned judge; I therefore would not base an injunction on a right of action for libel.

2. Malicious falsehood

The essentials of this tort are that the defendant has published about the plaintiff words which are false, that they were published maliciously, and that special damage has followed as the direct and natural result of their publication. As to special damage, the effect of section 3(1) of the Defamation Act 1952 is that it is sufficient if the words published in writing are calculated to cause pecuniary damage to the plaintiff. Malice will be inferred if it be proved that the words were calculated to produce damage and that the defendant knew when he published the words that they were false or was reckless as to whether they were false or not.

The test in *Coulson v Coulson (supra)* applies to interlocutory injunctions in actions for malicious falsehood as it does in actions for defamation. However, in relation to this action, the test applies only to the requirement that the plaintiff must show that the words were false. In the present case I have no doubt that any jury which did not find that the clear implication from the words contained in the defendants' draft article were false would be making a totally unreasonable finding. Thus the test is satisfied in relation to this cause of action.

As to malice I equally have no doubt from the evidence, including the transcript of the tape-recording of the 'interview' with Mr. Kaye in his hospital room which we have read, that it was quite apparent to the reporter and photographer from *Sunday Sport* that Mr. Kaye was in no condition to give any informed consent to their interviewing or photographing him. Moreover, even if the journalists had been in any doubt about Mr. Kaye's fitness to give his consent, Mr. Robertson [the first defendant] could not have entertained any such doubt after he read the affidavit sworn on behalf of Mr. Kaye in these proceedings. Any subsequent publication of the falsehood would therefore inevitably be malicious.

As to damage, I have already recorded that Mr. Robertson appreciated that Mr. Kaye's story was one for which other newspapers would be willing to pay 'large sums of money'. It needs little imagination to appreciate that whichever journal secured the first interview with Mr. Kaye would be willing to pay the most. Mr. Kaye thus has a potentially valuable right to sell the story of his accident and his recovery when he is fit enough to tell it. If the defendants are able to publish the article they proposed, or one anything like it, the value of this right would in my view be seriously lessened, and Mr. Kaye's story thereafter be worth much less to him.

I have considered whether damages would be an adequate remedy in these circumstances. They would inevitably be difficult to calculate, would also follow some time after the event, and in my view would in no way be adequate. It thus follows that in my opinion all the preconditions to the grant of an interlocutory injunction in respect of this cause of action are made out. . . .

3. Trespass to the person

. . . The plaintiff's case in relation to this cause of action is that the taking of the flashlight photographs may well have caused distress to Mr. Kaye and set back his recovery, and thus caused him injury. In this sense it can be said to be a battery. . . . I am prepared to accept that

---

19 *Ed*. Cf. *Bonnard v Perryman*, below, p. 945.
20 *Ed*. See also *Herbage v Pressdram* [1984] 2 All ER 769, CA.

it may well be the case that if a bright light is deliberately shone into another person's eyes and injures his sight, or damages him in some other way, this may be in law a battery. But in my view the necessary effects are not established by the evidence in this case. Though there must have been an obvious risk that any disturbance to Mr. Kaye would set back his recovery, there is no evidence that the taking of the photographs did in fact cause him any damage.

Moreover, the injunction sought in relation to this head of action would not be intended to prevent another anticipated battery, since none was anticipated. The intention here is to prevent the defendants from profiting from the taking of the photographs, i.e. from their own trespass. Attractive though this argument may appear to be, I cannot find as a matter of law that an injunction should be granted in these circumstances....

4. Passing off
Mr. Caldecott submits . . . that the essentials of the tort of passing off, as laid down by the speeches in the House of Lords in *E Warnink BV v J Townend & Sons (Hull) Ltd* [1979] AC 731, are satisfied here. . . . I think that the plaintiff is not in the position of a trader in relation to his interest in his story about his accident and his recovery, and thus fails from the start to have a right of action under this head. . . .

Bingham LJ: The defendants' conduct towards the plaintiff here was 'a monstrous invasion of his privacy' (to adopt the language of Griffiths J in *Bernstein v Skyviews Ltd* [1978] QB 479 at 489G). If ever a person has a right to be let alone by strangers with no public interest to pursue, it must surely be when he lies in hospital recovering from brain surgery and in no more than partial command of his faculties. It is this invasion of his privacy which underlies the plaintiff's complaint. Yet it alone, however gross, does not entitle him to relief in English law.

Leggatt LJ: . . . In view of the importance of the topic I add a note about the way in which the common law has developed in the United States to meet the need which in the present case we are unable to fulfil satisfactorily....

It [the right to privacy] is manifested in several forms.... One example is such intrusion upon physical solitude as would be objectionable to a reasonable man. So when in *Barber v Time Inc* 159 SW 2d 291 (1942) the plaintiff was confined to a hospital bed, the publication of her photograph taken without consent was held to be an invasion of a private right of which she was entitled to complain. Similarly, a so-called 'right of publicity' has developed to protect the commercial interest of celebrities in their identities.... *Carson v Here's Johnny Portable Toilets Inc* 698 F 2d 831 (1983) at page 835.

We do not need a First Amendment to preserve the freedom of the press, but the abuse of that freedom can be ensured only by the enforcement of a right to privacy. This right has so long been disregarded here that it can be recognised now only by the legislature. Especially since there is available in the United States a wealth of experience of the enforcement of this right both at common law and also under statute, it is to be hoped that the making good of this signal shortcoming in our law will not be long delayed.

NOTES

1. Although the Court of Appeal was unanimously of the opinion that an interlocutory injunction should be granted on the basis of malicious falsehood, the appeal was allowed in part, the original injunction being discharged as having been wrongly granted on the basis of the claim of libel.[1] In accordance with the law of malicious falsehood, the new injunction was more limited than the original one. It allowed the publication of the story and certain less objectionable photographs (one of Mr Kaye lying in bed asleep was published) provided that it was not claimed that the plaintiff had given his consent.

---

1 On *Kaye v Robertson*, see D. Bedingfield, (1992) 55 MLR 111; B. S. Markensis, (1992) 55 MLR 118; and P. Prescott, (1991) 54 MLR 451.

2. Exemplary and aggravated damages are available in malicious falsehood: per Sir Michael Kerr in *Joyce v Sengupta*.[2] In that case, the *Today* newspaper had wrongly alleged that Princess Anne's maid had stolen her letters, an allegation that was both defamatory and a malicious falsehood. A case may be brought in malicious falsehood rather than defamation at the discretion of the plaintiff in order to obtain legal aid, which is not available in defamation proceedings: ibid. Unlike defamation, jury trial is not available in malicious falsehood.

3. The Court of Appeal's acknowledgement in *Kaye v Robertson* that there is no right to privacy in English Law follows similar pronouncements by judges in earlier cases.[3] Later, in 1996, in *R v Brown*[4] Lord Hoffmann stated that 'English common law does not know a general right of privacy and Parliament has been reluctant to enact one'. Soon afterwards, however, three members of the House of Lords preferred to leave the question open in *R v Khan*[5] and the UK government argument in the Strasbourg case of *Spencer v United Kingdom*[6] caused others to think again. In view of the *Spencer* case and following the enactment of the HRA, in *Douglas v Hello!*[7] the Court of Appeal indicated that the time might have come for the judicial development of a tort of invasion of privacy. The *Douglas* case is considered later in this section of this chapter.[8] The extracts that follow immediately mainly tell the story of the unsuccessful efforts to introduce a statutory tort prior to the *Douglas* case.

4. As noted by Leggatt LJ, the position in English law on the protection of privacy contrasts sharply with that in the US where the courts in most jurisdictions have long since developed a tort of invasion of privacy or one has been provided by legislation. The inspiration to do so came from an article by Warren and Brandeis[9] prompted by the press coverage of the wedding of the daughter of one of the authors. Somewhat ironically, the article argued for the existence of a right of privacy in tort largely on the basis of English precedents such as *Prince Albert v Strange*.[10] The tort – or more accurately the four interrelated torts – that has developed in the US is defined in the *Restatement, 2d, Torts* as follows:[11]

'(1) One who invades the right of privacy of another is subject to liability for the resulting harm to the interests of the other.
(2) The right of privacy is invaded by
    (*a*)   unreasonable intrusion upon the seclusion of another . . .; or
    (*b*)   appropriation of the other's name or likeness . . .; or
    (*c*)   unreasonable publicity given to the other's private life . . .; or
    (*d*)   publicity that unreasonably places the other in a false light before the public.'

---

2 [1993] 1 All ER 897, CA. And see *Khodaparast v Shad* [2000] 1 All ER 545, CA. See, however, the ruling on exemplary damages in the *AB* case, below, p. 937.
3 E.g. per Sir Robert Megarry V-C in *Malone v Metropolitan Police Comr* [1979] 1 Ch 344, Ch D, and Lord Denning MR in *Re X (A Minor)* [1975] Fam 47, CA.
4 [1996] 1 All ER 545 at 556, HL.
5 [1997] AC 558, HL. Lords Browne-Wilkinson, Slynn and Nicholls.
6 See below, p. 934.
7 Below, p. 922.
8 Ibid.
9 (1890) 4 Harv LR 193.
10 Below, p. 959.
11 1977, para. 652A. The Restatement represents the preponderance of opinion in American jurisdictions. See further on American privacy law, F. V. Harper, F. James, and O. Gray, *The Law of Torts* (2nd edn, 1986), vol 2, p. 626ff. For the view that American privacy law is ineffective, see D. Anderson, in B. S. Markesenis (ed.), *Protecting Privacy* (1999), Chap. 6. On the strong protection of privacy in French and German law, see respectively E. Picard, op. cit., Chap. 3 and H. Stoll, op. cit., Chap. 2.

5. When rejecting the claim in passing off in *Kaye v Robertson*, the Court of Appeal accepted that it applied only to unfair trading competition. The Court did not, however, refer to *Sim v Heinz*[11a] in which the question whether an action for passing off lies for the unauthorised use by impersonation of an actor's voice (in that case the impersonation of Alaister Sim's voice in an advertisement) was left open. B. S. Markesinis[12] asks 'if that could be done for the voice of an actor, why not for his image, especially when the appropriation of the likeness is used to enrich another person?'

Report of the Committee on Privacy and Related Matters, Chairman: David Calcutt QC[13]

12.5 We have concluded that an overwhelming case for introducing a statutory tort of infringement of privacy has not so far been made out and that the better solution lies with the measures set out elsewhere in this report. We therefore *recommend* that such a tort should not presently be introduced. . . . We make our recommendation on the assumption that the improved scheme for self-regulation recommended . . . will be made to work. Should this fail, the case for a statutory tort of infringement of privacy might have to be reconsidered.

12.6 . . . if unwarranted intrusion is taking place and sufficient remedy is lacking, there must be a case in principle for seeking to fill this gap. We are satisfied that the absence of sufficient protection for the individual against intrusion by the press satisfies the criterion of 'pressing social need'. . . . This need is especially pressing in the case of individuals who are vulnerable to exploitation because, for example, of age, immaturity, infirmity, grief or the need to undergo medical treatment. There is a clear precedent in the law of defamation for providing compensation for distress, hurt feelings and anxiety without it having to be established that a plaintiff has suffered actual damage. We see no difficulty in principle in the adoption of such an approach for intrusions into privacy.

12.7 We have considered, however, whether the pressing social need requires the creation of a new tort or whether it would be better met by the proposals elsewhere in this report. . . .

12.9 Any consideration of a possible tort of infringement of privacy must begin with the definition of the proposed tort and of the defences to it. This is the issue on which all other proposed legislation has foundered. . . .

12.10 The problem was clearly expressed by the Vice-Chancellor, Sir Nicolas Browne-Wilkinson, in his address to the International Press Institute assembly in Istanbul in 1988, as follows:

'I think it is extremely difficult for a legal system to apply a general concept of privacy, because it is hard to distinguish what is meant by it. On the other hand, it seems to me impossible to draw a comprehensive list of those things which, in any one society, are to be treated as private. As a legal technician, I would be unhappy dealing with the law of privacy. . . .'

12.12 We accept that it would be impracticable to create a general wrong of infringement of privacy, since this would give rise to an unacceptable degree of uncertainty. However, this would not necessarily rule out the formulation of a tort directed towards the publication of personal information to the world at large. The absence of a precise or exhaustive definition has not presented insuperable problems in the areas of negligence and defamation. . . . Concepts such as 'the reasonable man' and 'right-thinking members of society' are to be found there in daily use. . . . Our grounds for recommending against a new tort do not, therefore, include difficulties of definition. . . .

11a [1959] 1 WLR 313, CA.
12 (1990) 53 MLR 802, 803.
13 Cm. 1102, 1990.

12.17 We are satisfied that it would be possible to define a statutory tort of infringement of privacy. This could specifically relate to the publication of personal information (including photographs). It could follow Mr. Browne's approach rather than Mr. Cash's in excluding physical intrusion (for which we make specific recommendations . . .).[14] Personal information could be defined in terms of an individual's personal life, that is to say, those aspects of life which reasonable members of society would respect as being such that an individual is ordinarily entitled to keep them to himself, whether or not they relate to his mind or body, to his home, to his family, to other personal relationships, or to his correspondence or documents.

12.18 We would not see any advantage in laying down a more detailed definition of personal information on the face of any statute. The courts could develop their interpretation on a case by case basis. . . .

12.19 All proposals for a tort of infringement of privacy have included a number of defences. These have been of two kinds: the specific and the general. Specific defences have included consent, legal privilege, lawful authority and absence of intent. Defences of this kind would clearly be necessary if a tort were ever to be introduced. . . .

12.22 . . . we have serious reservations about a general defence merely labelled 'public interest'. We would not consider it appropriate for any tort of infringement of privacy. A defence to cover the justified disclosure of personal information would, however, clearly be necessary, but it would need to be tightly drawn and specific. The possible definition of personal information which we have set out (see *paragraphs 12.17–12.18*) would already provide for flexible interpretation by the courts. We would see difficulty in introducing a further variable which would be likely to mean different things to different people. . . .

12.24 . . . We do not accept that such a tort would be the thin end of a wedge leading towards censorship. A law designed solely for the protection of individual citizens and their personal lives should offer no scope for Government interference. Furthermore, there is no necessary inter-relationship between protection of individual privacy (in the terms in which we discuss it in this report) and censorship by Government. We cannot, therefore, accept the argument that no tort of infringement of privacy should be introduced unless balanced by some provision for the entrenchment of freedom of speech or a Freedom of Information Act.

12.25 Nor do we agree that a narrowly-drawn tort would inhibit serious investigative journalism or that responsible newspapers would suffer for the misdeeds of others. Serious investigative journalism would be outside the scope of such a law, especially when exposing serious wrong-doing. There is a clear distinction between infringements of privacy deriving from prurient curiosity and those associated with legitimate journalism. . . . Most people have little difficulty in recognising where the boundary lies.

12.26 Many of those opposed to the creation of a statutory tort argued that it would be disproportionate and an undue restriction upon freedom of speech in the light of our treaty obligations. We cannot accept the argument that Article 10 of the European Convention on Human Rights must be regarded as conclusive against a law of privacy. Due weight must be given to Article 8 in which privacy is described as a 'right'. Furthermore, Article 10(2) provides for legitimate exceptions to freedom of expression, including the protection of the rights of others. We note that a number of our European partners have had laws for the protection of privacy for many years and reconcile this with adherence to Article 10. . . .

12.27 Although Article 10 does not form part of our domestic law, it is clear that it is having an impact upon our jurisprudence (see . . . *A-G v Guardian Newspapers Ltd*)[15] . . .

---

14 The references are to the Right of Privacy and Protection of Privacy bills introduced in the sessions 1987/88 and 1988/89 by Messrs Cash and Browne MPs respectively. For the texts of these bills, see *Infringement of Privacy*, Lord Chancellor's Dept. Consultation Paper, 1992, Annex D.

15 Above, p. 850.

In any case, freedom of speech has long been recognised as of fundamental importance in the English common law. The clearest example is the so-called rule in *Bonnard v Perryman*[16] . . .

12.28 On the other hand, we are conscious that a tort of infringement of privacy would mark a new departure in the law. It might extend restrictions on the press even to situations where the information was not only true but also where it:

(a) would not necessarily cause any significant or lasting harm;
(b) had been obtained by reputable means; and
(c) was already known within the complainant's own circle of acquaintances.

12.29 In addition a tort might have the effect of stifling reports about the failings of people in the public eye who use the media to promote themselves. We have the impression that many people would agree with the sentiments expressed by Lord Denning, the Master of the Rolls, in *Woodward v Hutchins*[17] . . . .

12.30 One of the main arguments in favour of a new tort of infringement of privacy is that the courts would be able to grant an injunction to restrain publication. Such an injunction would be of far greater value to a plaintiff than an apology or compensation after an intrusion into his privacy. . . .

12.31 It has been argued that, when applied to true personal information, such a restraint upon the press would be excessive. Some mechanism would be necessary to guard against those with guilty secrets obtaining such an injunction. The availability of injunctions could, therefore, be restricted in England and Wales by imposing a limitation comparable to that which already exists in defamation cases. . . . Prior restraint of publication, in particular on the basis of an *ex parte* interlocutory injunction, is, however, undoubtedly still a major restraint upon press freedom. . . .

12.32 As well as the arguments of principle in *paragraphs 12.24–12.31*, we have considered whether a new statutory tort would be the most effective way to tackle the problems [of physical intrusion and the publication of intrusive material by the press that have led to complaints]. . . . We have concluded that the need could be met by a combination of the more sharply-focused remedies recommended elsewhere in this report. . . .

12.33 . . . we do not consider that physical intrusion as such is best tackled by means of a civil remedy. That is why we propose the creation of new criminal offences and why we would exclude such intrusion from the definition of infringement of privacy in any tort (see *paragraph 12.17*). A civil remedy would, however, be valuable against the imminent or actual publication of material obtained by means of physical intrusion. Accordingly, . . . we recommend that anyone having a sufficient interest should be able to seek an injunction and damages in respect of the publication of private material or photographs obtained by committing any of the proposed offences. . . . We consider that such a tightly-drawn civil remedy, closely linked to acts that most people would regard as clearly wrong, would tackle many of the worst forms of infringement of individual privacy. . . .

12.34 Any form of legal action in tort suffers from a number of limitations. The individual who has been wronged has the daunting task of mounting and pursuing an action in the courts. Many find the financial risks a deterrent. One of the main shortcomings of a tort of infringement of privacy would be that it would not provide a readily accessible remedy. Even if legal aid were made available, which we would consider essential, many would still fall outside its scope. . . . we set ourselves the test of asking whether any proposed remedy would satisfy the criteria of speed, cheapness and readiness of access. We are not persuaded that a tort of infringement of privacy would perform very well against such criteria. We consider this a major weakness.

16 See below, p. 945.
17 See below, p. 987.

12.35 On the other hand, the provision of a legal remedy in tort would provide a more certain redress, particularly for those seeking prior restraint (see *paragraphs 12.30–12.31*). It would also enable the courts to award compensation. Furthermore, it can be argued that the introduction of a new form of legal protection should not be rejected on what are essentially administrative grounds.

12.36 Nevertheless, an improved form of self-regulation, under which, once the initial complaint had been made, action was taken forward by the proposed non-statutory Press Complaints Commission . . ., would undoubtedly be less daunting to many people than having to use a new tort. The people whose privacy we consider most needs protecting should they, for example, become the victims of a crime or a disaster, or suffer from a disfiguring illness, are precisely those who hold no office, play no prominent role in society, have no publicity agent and also probably lack the means to sue. Thus, while we have not based our rejection of a general tort of infringement of privacy on accessibility alone, it is, nevertheless, an important factor in deciding whether the case for a tort has been made out. . . .

NOTES

1. The Calcutt Committee Report is the third report on privacy in the past 30 years. It follows the Justice Report (1970) and the Younger Committee Report (1972).[18] The Justice Report, which was privately sponsored, considered the threat to privacy posed by both state and private action and prepared a draft bill recommending a general statutory right of action for invasion of privacy. The Younger Committee, which was government appointed, was called upon to consider privacy in the private sector only (the press, private detectives, etc.). It came out against a general right of privacy, *inter alia*, because of the difficulty that the courts would face in handling 'so ill-defined and unstable a concept';[19] the effect upon freedom of speech; and the unrealised potential of the existing law (particularly breach of confidence) to respond to invasions of privacy.

The Younger Committee did, however, favour strengthening and adding to existing legal and extra-legal rules and remedies. Its main recommendations for changes in the law were for:

'(i) a criminal offence of surreptitious unlawful surveillance by means of a technical device;
(ii) a tort of unlawful surveillance by such means;
(iii) a tort of disclosure or other use of information unlawfully acquired;
(iv) a legally enforceable right of access to information held by a credit agency about oneself (implemented by the Consumer Credit Act 1974, s. 158).'

18 For references to these reports, see above, p. 909.
19 Report, p. 206. The Committee stated:
  'We have found privacy to be a concept which means widely different things to different people and changes significantly over relatively short periods. In considering how the courts could handle so ill-defined and unstable a concept, we conclude that privacy is ill-suited to be the subject of a long process of definition through the building up of precedents over the years, since the judgments of the past would be an unreliable guide to any current evaluation of privacy. . . .'
  On the 'unstable' nature of privacy, contrast the reaction now and 40 years ago to the information that an unmarried couple are living together. Note also that the revelation of a person's income was placed only below the revelation of facts about his sex life as an invasion of privacy in the public opinion survey done for the Younger Committee (Report, p. 239). In contrast, in Sweden one's income is a matter of public record in the sense that it is possible to buy a book which lists the income tax that everyone pays. The land ownership list kept by the Land Registry identifies the owner and mortgagee of land subject to registration in England and Wales. Access to the list became open to the public on written application in 1990 after having always been confidential.

The Committee also recommended changes in the working of the former Press Council (which were implemented); the taking of steps by the institutions and persons concerned to improve the confidentiality of personal information held by banks, universities and employers; the licensing of private detectives; and the adoption of a voluntary code by computer users.[20] Only where indicated above have the Committee's proposals been implemented.

The Younger Committee was not unanimous. Mr Lyon and Mr Ross appended dissenting opinions. Mr Lyon presented the advantages of a general tort as follows:

17. *First*, . . . Parliamentary time is restricted and every new advance demands a long and sometimes exhausting campaign. It is much better to set out the principles on which the courts can act and leave them to develop the law as need requires . . . .

19. *Second*, it gives a remedy to all those seriously prejudiced by intrusions into privacy . . . .

20. *Third*, it gives teeth to many of our other recommendations. If a computer operator knew that his activities might lead to a suit for damages, he would be more likely to respond to the code of principles we enunciate.

21. *Fourth*, it allows juries to set the standards in a constantly changing area of human values. If private enquiry agents are to lose their certificates of registration for unreasonable intrusion into privacy, who is to decide what is reasonable? The Home Office? The police? I would prefer a jury as more representative of public opinion.

22. *Fifth*, it would provide an effective remedy for any unreasonable behaviour. Not only would damages reimburse financial loss or mollify injured feelings, but an injunction would be a useful deterrent to prevent anticipated intrusions into privacy . . . .

23. *Sixth*, no general remedy is likely to gain Parliamentary approval if it did not include government activities. The result of my colleagues' recommendations is that the government has succeeded in keeping its activities to itself although many would agree that government intrusion is potentially more dangerous and annoying. A general tort would easily have been amended to cover all those government activities which were not authorised by law . . . .

24. *Seventh*, we would have fulfilled our obligations under the United Nations Declaration of Human Rights and the European Convention. One of the ironies of the majority report is that the European Court may choose in time to give a remedy for English litigants which my colleagues would deny to them[21] . . .

26. Early in my researches on this subject I came across the case of a Mrs X whose policeman husband took a mistress. The wife prevailed upon him to give up the mistress and they were reconciled. The jealous lover told a national newspaper. When their reporter was rebuffed by Mrs X, they printed the story under the headlines 'The love life of a detective'. The family had to move; the husband had to give up his job; the child was teased at school. What do I now tell Mrs X? 'Truth must prevail'. 'We cannot protect privacy except where there has been a breach of confidence or the intruder used offensive new methods like bugging devices.' 'A reformed Press Council will censure the newspaper!'

2. The Calcutt Committee, which was appointed by the government following mounting concern about the conduct of the press, was required:

'to consider what measures (whether legislative or otherwise) are needed to give further protection to individual privacy from the activities of the press and improve recourse against the press for the individual citizen.'[22]

Like the Younger Committee, the Calcutt Committee recommended against a general right of privacy, for reasons both of principle and practicality. Although, in accordance with its terms of reference, the Committee had particularly in mind ill-

20 See now the Data Protection Act 1998. On the Act, see below, p. 1020.
21 *Ed.* See the *Malone* case, below, p. 1013.
22 Report, p. 1.

conduct *by the press*, its discussion of the question of a general right has wider application. The Committee would appear to have found the arguments fairly evenly balanced and its recommendation was, in a sense, a provisional one – dependent upon the success of the new system of self-regulation that it proposed. Following the Calcutt Committee Report, a Press Complaints Commission was established by the industry in place of the Press Council, although the Commission is not composed or functioning in the way that the Calcutt Committee Report proposed.[1] Other changes proposed by the Committee have been postponed by the government pending the outcome of the new arrangements for self-regulation. The particular changes in the criminal law recommended by the Calcutt Committee to combat physical intrusion were that the following acts be criminal offences:[2]

'(a) entering private property, without the consent of the lawful occupant, with intent to obtain personal information with a view to its publication;

(b) placing a surveillance device on private property, without the consent of the lawful occupant, with intent to obtain personal information with a view to its publication; and

(c) taking a photograph, or recording the voice, of an individual who is on private property, without his consent, with a view to its publication and with intent that the individual shall be identifiable.'

Would these criminal offences have been of assistance in *Kaye v Robertson*?[3] The Committee also made certain recommendations for legal restrictions to protect the privacy of individuals from the press reporting of court proceedings:[4]

'5. Consideration should be given to amending the legislation on the non-identification of minors in England and Wales to eliminate any inconsistencies or uncertainties. . . .

6. The statutory prohibition on identifying rape victims in England and Wales should be extended to cover the victims of the sexual assaults listed at *appendix H*.[5] . . .

7. In any criminal proceedings in England and Wales, the court should have the power to make an order prohibiting the publication of the name and address of any person against whom the offence is alleged to have been committed, or of any other matters likely to lead to his or her identification. This should only be exercised if the court believes that it is necessary to protect the mental or physical health, personal security or security of the home of the victim.
. . .'

The Committee, however, recommended against the establishment of a statutory right to reply.[6]

3. How do you reconcile the fact that the Court of Appeal in *Kaye v Robertson* was clearly of the opinion that Parliament should act to introduce a statutory remedy for invasion of privacy when the Calcutt Committee, and the Younger Committee before it, recommended otherwise?

4. The Calcutt Committee regarded the Press Complaints Commission that it proposed as providing the 'final chance' for the press 'to prove that voluntary self-regulation can be made to work'.[7] Should the Commission fail, it proposed a statutory Press Complaints Tribunal applying a statutory code of practice with powers to award

---

1   See below, p. 992.
2   Report, p. ix.
3   Above, p. 911.
4   Report, p. ix.
5   *Ed*. These include intercourse with under age girls, incest and indecent assaults. See now the Sexual Offences (Amendment) Act 1992, s. 2, which provides for anonymity for victims of these offences. Anonymity for victims of rape is provided by the Sexual Offences (Amendment) Act 1976, s. 4, as amended. There is no anonymity for persons accused of rape.
6   Report, pp. x, 44.
7   Report, p. x.

compensation.[8] Elsewhere in its Report (p. 46), the Committee stated that if the Press Complaints Commission system of voluntary self-regulation fails, 'the case for a statutory tort of infringement of privacy might have to be reconsidered'.

5. As proposed when the Calcutt Committee Report was published, Sir David Calcutt was asked some 18 months after the new regime of voluntary self-regulation had become operational by the then Home Secretary, Mr David Mellor, to conduct a review of the effectiveness of the new regime and to consider whether the arrangements 'should be modified or placed on a statutory basis'. In his *Review of Press Self-Regulation*,[9] Sir David Calcutt was highly critical of the Press Complaints Commission. He found its composition, methods of work and bias in favour of the press unsatisfactory. He considered that it had been ineffective in protecting privacy in a number of cases concerning both private individuals and persons in public life and that in some high profile cases the individuals whose privacy had arguably been invaded had not sought to invoke its jurisdiction.[10] Sir David Calcutt's conclusion was the new regime had not proved an effective regulator and that the Government should introduce a statutory regime. In particular, he proposed a remedy for individuals against the press for infringements of privacy before a statutory Press Complaints Tribunal along the lines suggested in the Calcutt Committee Report. The Tribunal would be fully independent of the press, with a judge or senior lawyer appointed by the Lord Chancellor as chairman. It would draw up a statutory code of practice and have powers to restrain publication in breach of the code and receive complaints alleging breaches of it. The Commission would be able to award compensation and costs, impose fines and require the printing of apologies, corrections and replies. Sir David Calcutt also recommended that the Government give further consideration to the introduction of a statutory tort of infringement of privacy that would apply not only to the press. His view was that the proposed Tribunal, dealing only with the press, should be established at once; it would be open to the Government if it thought fit to allow this tailor-made remedy to continue in parallel with any general tort that it introduced.

6. Sir David Calcutt's proposals have not been implemented by the Government. In 1993, the Lord Chancellor's Department published a Consultation Paper, *Infringement of Privacy*, which invited comments on the 'proposal that the right to privacy should now be recognised, as a matter of principle, in English law and in Scots law'. Following the consultation period, the government published a white paper in which it rejected the idea of a statutory tort of invasion of privacy.[11]

---

8 Report, p. xi.

9 Cmnd. 2135, 1993.

10 One case in which no complaint had been brought concerned the (then) politician Mr David Mellor and the actress Ms Antonia de Sancha in which *The People* published a story of an affair that came to light after a telephone conversation had been recorded by electronic bugging. Another case concerned the publication in the *Daily Mirror* of compromising long-lens pictures of the Duchess of York and a Texan friend at a villa in France. The Duchess obtained damages in a French court for invasion of privacy; there would have been no legal liability in English law. A third case, to which the Chairman of the Press Complaints Commission responded by a statement reminding the press of the threat of government intervention, concerned press publicity about Mr. Paddy Ashdown's affair with his secretary. Mr Ashdown, then the leader of the Liberal Democratic Party, had obtained an injunction to prevent the publication of the story in England, which had been obtained following the theft of documents in a break-in. He admitted the affair when *The Scotsman*, which was not bound by the injunction, published details.

11 *Privacy and Media Intrusion: the Government's Response*, Cmnd. 2918, 1995. The Home Secretary (Mr Straw) maintained this position in 315 HC Deb, 2 July 1998, col. 541. The House of Commons National Heritage Select Committee has published a report (*Privacy and Media Intrusion*, Fourth Report, (1993), HC 291-1), which proposes the enactment of a Protection of Privacy Act, which would contain civil and criminal remedies for invasion of privacy and would apply not only to the press.

Douglas v Hello! Ltd (2000) 9 BHRC 543, [2001] 2 All ER 289, Court of Appeal

The first and second claimants were the film stars Michael Douglas and Catherine Zeta-Jones. They had sold to the third claimant, the proprietors of the magazine *OK!*, the exclusive rights to the photographs of their wedding in New York for publication in *OK!*. Under the contract, the first and second claimants had (i) agreed to use their best efforts to ensure that no other media would be present at the wedding and that no guests or anyone else at the wedding would be allowed to take photographs and (ii) retained rights of approval over any photographs published in *OK!*. The defendants were the proprietors of *Hello!*, a rival magazine, which had obtained unauthorised photographs of the wedding and were planning to publish them in the next issue of *Hello!*, before the publication of the authorised wedding photographs in *OK!*. It was not clear whether *Hello!*'s photographs had been taken by a guest or other person permitted to be at the wedding, or by an intruder. The claimants instituted proceedings in breach of confidence, malicious falsehood and interference with contractual relations, and obtained an interim injunction from Grant J to prevent publication of the unauthorised photographs before the case went to trial.

The Court of Appeal unanimously discharged the injunction. *Hello!* thereupon printed the photographs, thereby, as Brooke LJ pointed out, running the risk of substantial damages if *OK!* were to win its case at trial. In discharging the injunction, the Court of Appeal focused on the breach of confidence claim and on the possibility of a case being made out by the claimants for invasion of privacy.

Brooke LJ:

49 . . . It goes without saying that this is a case concerned with freedom of expression. Although the right to freedom of expression is not in every case the ace of trumps, it is a powerful card to which the courts of this country must always pay appropriate respect.[12]

50. What, then, are the principles which should govern the exercise of our discretion? The House of Lords has laid down a general rule which governs most cases in which a court is invited to grant an interim injunction restraining the defendant until the trial of the action from doing the things of which the claimant makes complaint. (See *American Cyanamid Co v Ethicon Ltd* [1975] 1 All ER 504, [1975] AC 396.) Once a judge has decided that there is a serious issue to be tried, he is required to weigh the respective risks that injustice may result from his deciding one way or the other on necessarily incomplete and untested evidence. On the one hand there is the risk that if the injunction is refused but the claimant succeeds in establishing at the trial his legal right, for the protection of which the injunction had been sought, he may in the meantime have suffered harm and inconvenience for which an award of money can provide no adequate recompense. On the other hand there is the risk that if the injunction is granted but the claimant fails at the trial, the defendant in the meantime may have suffered harm and inconvenience which is similarly irrecompensable. This is what is sometimes described as the balance of convenience . . .

52. Occasionally Parliament intervenes to make clear its wishes in particular contexts . . .

54. Parliament resorted to a different drafting technique in s 12(3) of the Human Rights Act 1998. This subsection reads:

'No [relief which, if granted, might affect the exercise of the convention right to freedom of expression] is to be granted so as to restrain publication before trial unless the court is satisfied that the applicant is likely to establish that publication should not be allowed.'

I agree with what Keene LJ says about the effect of this statutory provision in paras 150–154 of his judgment, to which I have nothing to add.

57. On the facts of the present case, using the *American Cyanamid* test, there is clearly a serious issue to be tried in relation to the claims made by all three claimants . . .

58. . . . it would certainly be arguable, if the appropriate facts were established at trial, that 'unauthorised' images were taken on this private occasion by someone in breach of his or her

---

12 *Ed.* Cf. The statement by Lord Hoffmann cited by Sedley LJ, para. 136, below, p. 931.

duty of confidence, and that they therefore constituted 'confidential information' as to what
was going on at the wedding and the wedding reception . . .

59. I cannot, however, exclude the possibility that the trial judge might find, as Sedley LJ
has suggested in para 112 of his judgment, that the photographer was an intruder with whom
no relationship of trust or confidence had been established. In that event the court would have
to explore the law relating to privacy when it is not bolstered by considerations of confidence.

60. In this context art 10(2) of the convention provides a potential justification for denying
the right to freedom of expression not only by restrictions that are necessary 'for preventing
the disclosure of information received in confidence', but also those that are necessary 'for
the protection of the reputation or rights of others'. On the hypothesis I have suggested in
para 59 above, the question would arise whether Mr Douglas and Ms Zeta-Jones had a right
to privacy which English law would recognise.

61. It is well known that this court in *Kaye v Robertson* [1991] FSR 62 said in
uncompromising terms that there was no tort of privacy known to English law. In contrast,
both academic commentary and extra-judicial commentary by judges over the last ten years
have suggested from time to time that a development of the present frontiers of a breach of
confidence action could fill the gap in English law which is filled by privacy law in other
developed countries. This commentary was given a boost recently by the decision of the
European Commission of Human Rights in *Earl Spencer v UK* (1998) 25 EHRR CD 105,
and by the coming into force of the Human Rights Act 1998.

71. It is well settled, then, that equity may intervene to prevent the publication of
photographic images taken in breach of an obligation of confidence. In other words, if on
some private occasion the prospective claimants make it clear, expressly or impliedly, that no
photographic images are to be taken of them, then all those who are present will be bound by
the obligations of confidence created by their knowledge (or imputed knowledge) of this
restriction. English law, however, has not yet been willing to recognise that an obligation of
confidence may be relied on to preclude such unwanted intrusion into people's privacy when
those conditions do not exist.

81. ... the convention ... seems to be primarily concerned with giving individuals rights
against the state (to be equated with public authorities in the language of art 8(2)). Thus
art 8(2) is concerned only with the circumstances in which a public authority may legitimately
interfere with the exercise by an individual of his right to private and family life, and s 8 of the
Human Rights Act is concerned only with the power of a court to award compensation against
acts of public authorities for unlawful acts which are incompatible with a convention right.
The Human Rights Act gives the court no such statutory power to order one private entity to
pay compensation to another in respect of a breach of convention rights.

82. An English judge interpreting the Human Rights Act and the convention is therefore
confronted with something of a dilemma. On the one hand, art 8(1) of the convention appears
to create a right, exercisable against all the world, to respect for private and family life. On the
other hand, art 8(2) of the convention, s 8 of the Human Rights Act, and the general philosophy
of both the convention and the Act (namely that these rights are enforceable only against
public authorities), all appear to water down the value of the right created by art 8(1).

83. In a series of decisions the European Court of Human Rights has addressed this dilemma
by relying on the positive duty imposed on the member states by art 1 of the convention ...
A vivid example of this technique at work can be seen in the judgment of the court in *A v UK*
(1998) 5 BHRC 137 when it was concerned with a complaint under art 3 by a boy who had
been hit by his stepfather with a garden cane. The court said:

'The court considers that treatment of this kind reaches the level of severity prohibited by art 3
... It remains to be determined whether the state should be held responsible, under art 3, for
the beating of the applicant by his stepfather ... The court considers that the obligation on the
high contracting parties under art 1 of the convention to secure to everyone within their
jurisdiction the rights and freedoms defined in the convention, taken together with art 3, requires
states to take measures designed to ensure that individuals within their jurisdiction are not
subjected to torture or inhuman or degrading treatment or punishment, including such ill-
treatment administered by private individuals ...' ((1998) 5 BHRC 137 at 141 (paras 21–22)).

84. In other words, the court was saying that the boy had the right under art 3 of the
convention not to be subjected to inhuman or degrading treatment or punishment, and although

it was his stepfather who had administered the treatment which breached that right, he was entitled to make a complaint against the state for its failure, in breach of art 1, to secure his art 3 right.

85. From time to time the court at Strasbourg has adopted a similar approach when applicants have complained to it that their art 8(1) right to respect for their private and family life has been violated . . . In *X v Netherlands* (1985) 8 EHRR 235 at 239–240 (para 23) the court said:

'The Court recalls that although the object of Article 8 is essentially that of protecting the individual against arbitrary interference by the public authorities, it does not merely compel the State to abstain from such interference: in addition to this primarily negative obligation, there may be positive obligations inherent in an effective respect for private or family life. These obligations may involve the adoption of measures designed to secure respect for private life even in the sphere of the relations of individuals between themselves.'

86. In *A v UK* it was the deficiencies of the common law, in relation to the physical chastisement of children, which led the court to conclude that the United Kingdom had violated the convention. This country narrowly escaped a similar finding by the European Commission of Human Rights in *Earl Spencer*'s case. A photograph of Lady Spencer had been taken with a telephoto lens while she was walking in the grounds of a private clinic at which she was receiving treatment. This photograph was published under the caption: 'SO THIN: Victoria walks in the clinic grounds this week.' Relying on the decision of this court in *Kaye v Robertson*, she did not pursue a claim in the English courts, but the commission held that she should have pursued her remedies in these courts first. It appears that the eloquence of the advocate for the United Kingdom government persuaded the commission that English law provided her with a potentially satisfactory remedy in an action for breach of confidence.

87. In this respect the commission relied heavily on the strong and detailed case of the applicants in the domestic proceedings which pointed to their former friends as the direct source of the essential confidential information that had been published. Its determination ended in these terms:

'Accordingly, the Commission considers that the parties' submissions indicate that the remedy of breach of confidence (against the newspapers and their sources) was available to the applicants and that the applicants have not demonstrated that it was insufficient or ineffective in the circumstances of their cases. It considers that, in so far as relevant doubts remain concerning the financial awards to be made following a finding of a breach of confidence, they are not such as to warrant a conclusion that the breach of confidence action is ineffective or insufficient but rather a conclusion that the matter should be put to the domestic courts for consideration in order to allow those courts, through the common law system in the United Kingdom, the opportunity to develop existing rights by way of interpretation.' (See (1998) 25 EHRR CD 105 at 117–118.)

88. The commission appears to be saying that since the authorities in this country have been content to leave it to the judges to develop the law in this sensitive field, it is the judges who must develop the law so that it gives appropriate recognition to art 8(1) rights. Whether they do so in future by an extension of the existing frontiers of the law of confidence, or by recognising the existence of new relationships which give rise to enforceable legal rights (as has happened in relation to the law of negligence ever since the 3–2 decision of the House of Lords in *Donoghue (or M' Alister) v Stevenson* [1932] AC 562, [1932] All ER Rep 1) is not for this court, on this occasion, to predict . . .

89. Recent annual reports of the Law Commission show how successive governments have been content to leave the development of the law in these fields to the judges. As long ago as 1981 the Law Commission recommended to Parliament that the law of confidence should be reformed and codified (see its *Report on Breach of Confidence* Law Com No 110 (1981)), but although this recommendation was accepted by a former government it was never implemented. The Commission's *Thirty-third Annual Report 1998* (Law Com No 258, p 5) describes how in 1998, following the *Earl Spencer* decision, a new government rejected that report 'because developing case law since its publication had clarified the scope and extent of the breach of confidence action, as confirmed by the European Commission on Human Rights'.

90. In its *Twenty-eighth Annual Report 1993* (Law Com No 223, p 25) the Law Commission described how one of the commissioners had recently assisted in the preparation of a

government consultation paper on the infringement of privacy (which did not lead to the enactment of legislation). The Commission's anxieties, if the law of privacy was put on a statutory basis but not the law of confidence, were clearly articulated in para 2.25 of that report. In the event, the executive and the legislature took the line of least resistance and left the development of both these fields of law to the judiciary, and that is how matters now stand. That members of the Appellate Committee of the House of Lords are uneasy about the present condition of our law is evident from the observations of Lord Browne-Wilkinson and Lord Nicholls in *R v Khan (Sultan)* [1996] 3 All ER 289 at 291, 302, [1997] AC 558 at 571, 582–583. On other occasions during the last 20 years some of our most senior judges have underlined the importance of the right to privacy: see Lord Scarman in *Morris v Beardmore* [1980] 2 All ER 753 at 763, [1981] AC 446 at 464 ('fundamental'), Lord Denning MR in *Schering Chemicals Ltd v Falkman Ltd* [1981] 2 All ER 321 at 333, [1982] QB 1 at 21 ('fundamental') and Lord Keith of Kinkel in *A-G v Guardian Newspapers Ltd (No 2)* [1988] 3 All ER 545 at 639, [1990] 1 AC 109 at 255 ('clearly one which the law should in this field seek to protect').

91. One difficulty which will confront the courts when they have to tackle this problematic issue head-on is that art 1 of the convention,[13] on which a state's positive duty is founded when it is brought before the international court which has the duty of enforcing member states' duties under the convention, does not find its way into the Schedule to the Human Rights Act which sets out the 'Convention rights' referred to in ss 2, 3, 4, 6 and 7 of the Act. On the other hand, when a court determines a question which has arisen in connection with a convention right, it must take into account any relevant judgment of the European Court of Human Rights (s 2(1)(a) of the Human Rights Act), and those judgments have made it clear that the law-making body of the member states has the positive duty identified in the judgments to which I have referred. Where Parliament in this country has been so obviously content to leave the development of the law to the judges, it might seem strange if the absence of art 1 from our national statute relieved the judges from taking into account the positive duties identified by the court at Strasbourg when they develop the common law. In this judgment, however, I have the luxury of identifying difficult issues: I am not obliged to solve them.

92. One matter, however, is clear, and this makes the task of the court that much easier on the present occasion. One of the Law Commission's anxieties in 1993 was that the law might develop in such a way that breaches of privacy, but not breaches of confidence, would be subject to statutory defences which the common law had not yet clearly recognised. In this respect, at least, Parliament has now intervened to provide that where proceedings relate to material which the respondent claims, or which appears to the court, to be journalistic, literary or artistic material, the court must have regard, among other things, to any relevant privacy code (s 12(4) of the Human Rights Act). In this context we were shown by Mr Tugendhat [for the claimants] the Code of Practice ratified by the Press Complaints Commission in November 1997, which states that all members of the press have a duty to maintain the highest professional and ethical standards, and that the code sets the benchmarks for those standards: 'It both protects the rights of the individual and upholds the public's right to know'.

93. The code covers 16 discrete topics, the third of which [clause 3[14]] is 'Privacy'...

94. It appears to me that the existence of these statutory provisions, coupled with the current wording of the relevant privacy code, mean that in any case where the court is concerned with issues of freedom of expression in a journalistic, literary or artistic context, it is bound to pay particular regard to any breach of the rules set out in cl 3 of the code, especially where none of the public interest claims set out in the preamble to the code is asserted. A newspaper which flouts cl 3 of the code is likely in those circumstances to have its claim to an entitlement to freedom of expression trumped by art 10(2) considerations of privacy. Unlike the court in *Kaye v Robertson* [1991] FSR 62, Parliament recognised that it had to acknowledge the importance of the art 8(1) respect for private life, and it was able to do so untrammelled by any concerns that the law of confidence might not stretch to protect every aspect of private life.

---

13 *Ed.* Art. 1 ECHR reads: 'The High Contracting Parties shall secure to everyone within their jurisdiction the rights and freedoms defined in Section 1 of the Convention.'
14 For text of Clause 3, see below, p. 993.

95. It follows that on the present occasion it is not necessary to go beyond s 12 of the Human Rights Act and cl 3 of the code to find the ground rules by which we should weigh the competing considerations of freedom of expression on the one hand and privacy on the other. So far as privacy is concerned, the case of the first and second claimants is not a particularly strong one. They did not choose to have a private wedding, attended by a few members of their family and a few friends, in the normal sense of the words 'private wedding'. There is nothing in the court's papers to belie the suggestion at p 88 of the disputed issue 639 of Hello! that they invited 250 guests, and the trappings of privacy in this context are identical with the trappings of confidentiality to which I have alluded earlier in this judgment. Although by cl 6 of their agreement with OK! they undertook to use their best efforts to ensure that their guests 'shall not publish and/or broadcast ... or write any article about, or give any extended comment, report or interview to any media concerning the Wedding', there is no evidence before the court which shows that they took any steps to enforce that undertaking, so far as their guests were concerned.

96. ... Either the claimants will establish at trial that this particular occasion successfully retained the necessary indicia of confidentiality, so far as the taking of photographic images is concerned, or they will not. I do not consider that their privacy-based case, as distinct from their confidentiality-based case, adds very much. I am satisfied, however, that on the present untested evidence the claimants are 'likely to establish that publication should not be allowed' on confidentiality grounds. This is not, however, the end of the matter, as I must turn to other factors affecting the balance of convenience and the manner in which the court should exercise its equitable jurisdiction...

99. It ... appears to me that the balance of convenience, as between OK! and Hello!, ... favours Hello! because it might be very difficult for Hello! to compute its losses in money terms if issue 639 was killed, whereas OK! did not appear to face the same difficulties if publication was allowed. There was no suggestion in the evidence that Hello! might be unable to pay the huge sums it might be held liable to pay (whether as damages or by way of an account of profits) if this action succeeded at trial.

100. As between these two parties, therefore, the balance of convenience appeared to favour leaving OK! to assert its legal rights at the trial of what is essentially a commercial dispute between two magazine enterprises which are not averse to exercising spoiling tactics against each other. I am not sorry to reach this conclusion because although it would have been wrong to withhold relief on equitable grounds alone, features of OK!'s past conduct, even making allowance for the fact that it did not have much time to defend itself against Hello!'s charges, appear to have made it an unattractive suitor for the bounty of a court of equity ...

101. The matter which gave me greater cause for hesitation was whether having decided that the balance of convenience favoured the withholding of injunctive relief so far as OK! was concerned, Mr Douglas and Ms Zeta-Jones were nevertheless entitled to the protection of an injunction. In the end I came to agree with the views expressed on this issue by Sedley LJ, to which I have nothing to add.

Sedley LJ:

Is there today a right of privacy in English law?

109. The common law, and equity with it, grows by slow and uneven degrees. It develops reactively, both in the immediate sense that it is only ever expounded in response to events and in the longer-term sense that it may be consciously shaped by the perceived needs of legal policy. The modern law of negligence exemplifies both senses.

110. The history of the law of confidence, however, while it displays many instances of the first kind of reactivity, has shown little of the second. The courts have done what they can, using such legal tools as were to hand, to stop the more outrageous invasions of individuals' privacy; but they have felt unable to articulate their measures as a discrete principle of law. Nevertheless, we have reached a point at which it can be said with confidence that the law recognises and will appropriately protect a right of personal privacy.

111. The reasons are twofold. First, equity and the common law are today in a position to respond to an increasingly invasive social environment by affirming that everybody has a right to some private space. Secondly, and in any event, the Human Rights Act 1998 requires the courts of this country to give appropriate effect to the right to respect for private and family life set out in art 8 of the European Convention for the Protection of Human Rights

and Fundamental Freedoms (Rome, 4 November 1950; TS 71 (1953); Cmd 8969) (the convention). The difficulty with the first proposition resides in the common law's perennial need (for the best of reasons, that of legal certainty) to appear not to be doing anything for the first time. The difficulty with the second lies in the word 'appropriate'. But the two sources of law now run in a single channel because, by virtue of ss 2 and 6 of the Human Rights Act, the courts of this country must not only take into account jurisprudence of both the European Commission of Human Rights and the European Court of Human Rights which points to a positive institutional obligation to respect privacy; they must themselves act compatibly with that and the other convention rights. This, for reasons I now turn to, arguably gives the final impetus to the recognition of a right of privacy in English law.

112. The reason why it is material to this case is that on the present evidence it is possible that the photographer was an intruder with whom no relationship of trust had been established. If it was a guest or an employee, the received law of confidence is probably all that the claimants need.

Common law and equity

113. Lawyers in this country have learned to accept that English law recognises no right of privacy. It was for this express reason that counsel for the actor Gordon Kaye instead put his case against the Sunday Sport, whose reporter and photographer had shamefully invaded the hospital room where Mr Kaye was recovering from serious head injuries, not as a breach of privacy, which it plainly was, but as a case of libel, malicious falsehood, trespass to the person and passing off. He managed only to hold an injunction to stop the paper claiming, by way of malicious falsehood, that Mr Kaye had voluntarily given an interview. But this court in *Kaye v Robertson* [1991] FSR 62 did not affirmatively consider and decide whether there is a right of privacy in English law. The court adopted—for it plainly shared—counsel's assumption that there was none.

[**Sedley LJ** quoted passages from the three judgments, for which see above, and continued:]

116. Nobody supposes that the members of the court which expressed this view were unfamiliar with the body of cases of which the best-known is *Prince Albert v Strange* (1849) 1 Mac & G 25, 41 ER 1171 or therefore that their assent to counsel's concession was per incuriam. But it is unhelpful now to speculate whether they would have maintained their view had the point been argued before them. The legal landscape has altered.

117. The argument would not have been that a right of privacy had been spelt out by the courts: plainly it had not. It would have been, as it has been in Mr Tugendhat's condensed but convincing submission, that the tort of breach of confidence contains all that is necessary for the fair protection of personal privacy, and that it is now a relatively small step to articulate it in that way—as was done four years after *Kaye v Robertson* by Laws J in *Hellewell v Chief Constable of Derbyshire* [1995] 4 All ER 473 at 476, [1995] 1 WLR 804 at 807:

> 'I entertain no doubt that disclosure of a photograph may, in some circumstances, be actionable as a breach of confidence ... If someone with a telephoto lens were to take from a distance and with no authority a picture of another engaged in some private act, his subsequent disclosure of the photograph would, in my judgment, as surely amount to a breach of confidence as if he had found or stolen a letter or diary in which the act was recounted and proceeded to publish it. In such a case, the law would protect what might reasonably be called a right of privacy, although the name accorded to the cause of action would be breach of confidence.'

118. This was of course obiter, but it has been understandably influential in the thinking of lawyers and commentators since it was said. The examples given by Laws J of invasions of privacy in the absence of some extant confidential relationship are taken from the speech of Lord Goff of Chieveley in *A-G v Guardian Newspapers Ltd (No 2)* [1988] 3 All ER 545 at 658–659, [1990] 1 AC 109 at 281:[15] ...

119. This passage, it seems to me, dulls the edge of the decision of Griffiths J in *Lord Bernstein of Leigh v Skyviews and General Ltd* [1977] 2 All ER 902, [1978] QB 479, a decision which in any event assumed that there was no legal right to privacy and focused

---

15 *Ed.* For the relevant part of Lord Goff's speech, see below, p. 967.

instead on whether the law of trespass could fill the gap (see in particular [1977] 2 All ER 902 at 907–908, [1978] QB 479 at 488).

120. I do not propose to go through the body of recent extra-judicial writings by judges on the subject, which Mr Tugendhat [for the claimants] has put before us. While these are valuable indicators to those who read them of changes in the legal climate, their authors would be the first to stress that they are not a source of law. It would be less than candid, however, not to acknowledge a debt to two particular essays. One is the survey of the field as it lies at present in Sir Brian Neill's essay 'Privacy: a challenge for the next century' in *Protecting Privacy*, ed Basil Markesinis (1999). The other is the celebrated essay by Samuel D Warren and Louis D Brandeis (at that time partners in a Boston legal practice; the latter to become an associate justice of the Supreme Court), 'The right to privacy' (1890) 4 Harv LR 193, deriving from chiefly English case-law what they memorably named 'the right of the individual to be let alone' as a free-standing right independent of property rights. As all these authors recognise, law emerges case by case from issues which have been argued out.

121. The cases in which the entitlement to the protection of confidences has been argued out are, in fact, numerous. In the leading case of *Margaret, Duchess of Argyll v Duke of Argyll* [1965] 1 All ER 611 at 616–619, [1967] Ch 302 at 318–322, Ungoed-Thomas J considered in detail *Prince Albert*'s case . . . And he described the case as one 'where the privacy is the right invaded' (the first 'the' may be a printer's interpolation).

122. Whether or not the fusion of law and equity would by itself have been sufficient to introduce an entitlement to damages for the violation of this right, in the *Guardian Newspapers* case, Lord Goff said:

'The remedy of an account is alternative to the remedy of damages, which in cases of breach of confidence is now available, despite the equitable nature of the wrong, through a beneficent interpretation of the Chancery Amendment Act 1858 (Lord Cairns' Act) ...' (See [1988] 3 All ER 545 at 662, [1990] 1 AC 109 at 286.)

123. This passage was cited, along with much other relevant English law, by the commission in *Earl Spencer v UK* (1998) 25 EHRR CD 105. By its decision the commission declared inadmissible the complaint of the Earl and Countess that English law failed to protect their privacy against what on any view had been hurtful and invasive publicity. The reason was that the United Kingdom government had submitted successfully that, although 'there is no law of privacy, as such, in England and Wales' (see *Kaye v Robertson*), the tort of breach of confidence was now well established; that its scope and extent, in particular as to damages (see *Malone v Comr of Police of the Metropolis (No 2)* [1979] 2 All ER 620, [1979] Ch 344 per Megarry V-C) were still in issue; but that the remedy 'was available to the applicants and the applicants have not demonstrated that it was insufficient or ineffective in the circumstances of their cases'.

124. Of course neither Her Majesty's government, which has the conduct of the United Kingdom's cases in Strasbourg, nor the commission (during its lifetime), had power to determine what the law of England and Wales is; but the fact that this unanimous conclusion could emerge from a detailed consideration, after written and oral argument, of the state of the extant English authorities by a body of distinguished European jurists is of real persuasive force. It would not be a happy thing if the national courts were to go back without cogent reason on the United Kingdom's successful exegesis of its own law. It was while *Earl Spencer*'s case was pending in the commission that the House of Lords heard and decided *R v Khan (Sultan)* [1996] 3 All ER 289, [1997] AC 558. There Lord Nicholls of Birkenhead said:

'I prefer to leave open for another occasion the important question whether the present, piecemeal protection of privacy has now developed to the extent that a more comprehensive principle can be seen to exist.' (See [1996] 3 All ER 289 at 302, [1997] AC 558 at 582–583.)

125. I would conclude, at lowest, that Mr Tugendhat has a powerfully arguable case to advance at trial that his two first-named clients have a right of privacy which English law will today recognise and, where appropriate, protect. To say this is in my belief to say little, save by way of a label, that our courts have not said already over the years. It is to say, among other things, that the right, grounded as it is in the equitable doctrine of breach of confidence, is not unqualified. As Laws J said in *Hellewell v Chief Constable of Derbyshire* [1995] 4 All

ER 473 at 476, [1995] 1 WLR 804 at 807: 'It is, of course, elementary that, in all such cases, a defence based on the public interest would be available.'

126. What a concept of privacy does, however, is accord recognition to the fact that the law has to protect not only those people whose trust has been abused but those who simply find themselves subjected to an unwanted intrusion into their personal lives. The law no longer needs to construct an artificial relationship of confidentiality between intruder and victim: it can recognise privacy itself as a legal principle drawn from the fundamental value of personal autonomy.

127. It is relevant, finally, to note that no Strasbourg jurisprudence contra-indicates, much less countermands, the establishment in national legal systems of a qualified right of privacy; and that the courts of France and Germany, to take two other signatories of the convention, have both in recent years developed long-gestated laws for the qualified protection of privacy against both state and non-state invasion (see Etienne Picard, 'The right to privacy in French law' in *Protecting Privacy*, ed Basil Markesinis (1999); Basil Markesinis *The German Law of Torts: A Comparative Introduction* (3rd edn, 1994) pp. 63–66).

The Human Rights Act 1998

128. The Human Rights Act was brought into force on 2 October 2000. It requires every public authority, including the courts, to act consistently with the convention. What this means is a subject of sharp division and debate among both practising and academic lawyers: does it simply require the courts' procedures to be convention-compliant, or does it require the law applied by the courts, save where primary legislation plainly says otherwise, to give effect to the convention principles? This is not the place, at least without much fuller argument, in which to resolve such a large question. But some attitude has to be taken to Mr Tugendhat's submission that, whatever the current state of common law and equity, we are obliged now to give some effect to art 8, among other provisions, of the convention.

129. It is helpful, first of all, to see how much change he is soliciting. If he is right in his primary submission then the law is today adequately configured to respect the convention. If it is not—for example if the step from confidentiality to privacy is not simply a modern restatement of the scope of a known protection but a legal innovation—then I would accept his submission (for which there is widespread support among commentators on the Human Rights Act: see in particular Murray Hunt 'The "Horizontal Effect" of the Human Rights Act' [1998] PL 423) that this is precisely the kind of incremental change for which the Human Rights Act is designed: one which without undermining the measure of certainty which is necessary to all law gives substance and effect to s 6 of that Act:[16]

130. Such a process would be consonant with the jurisprudence of the European Court of Human Rights, which s 2 of the Human Rights Act requires us to take into account and which has pinpointed art 8 of the convention as a locus of the doctrine of positive obligation. Thus in *X v Netherlands* (1985) 8 EHRR 235 at 239–240 (para 23), the court said:

> 'The Court recalls that although the object of Article 8 is essentially that of protecting the individual against arbitrary interference by the public authorities, it does not merely compel the State to abstain from such interference: in addition to this primarily negative obligation, there may be positive obligations inherent in an effective respect for private or family life. These obligations may involve the adoption of measures designed to secure respect for private life even in the sphere of the relations of individuals between themselves.'

131. More immediately to the present point is s 12 of the Human Rights Act. This provides:[17]

132. There is no need to look at the parliamentary genesis of this section in order to see that it, with s 13 of the Human Rights Act, is of a different kind from the rest of the Act. It descends from the general to the particular, singling out one convention right and making procedural and substantive provision for litigation in which the right is directly or indirectly implicated. The convention right in question is the right to freedom of expression [in Article 10 ECHR[18]]…

---

16 *Ed.* For the text of s. 6, see above, p. 14.
17 *Ed.* For the text, see above, p. 17.
18 *Ed.* For the text, see above, p. 22.

133. Two initial points need to be made about s 12 of the Human Rights Act. First, by sub-s (4) it puts beyond question the direct applicability of at least one article of the convention as between one private party to litigation and another—in the jargon, its horizontal effect. Whether this is an illustration of the intended mechanism of the entire Act, or whether it is a special case (and if so, why), need not detain us here. The other point, well made by Mr Tugendhat, is that it is 'the Convention right' to freedom of expression which both triggers the section (see s 12(1)) and to which particular regard is to be had. That convention right, when one turns to it, is qualified in favour of the reputation and rights of others and the protection of information received in confidence. In other words, you cannot have particular regard to art 10 without having equally particular regard at the very least to art 8:[19]

134. Mr Carr QC was disposed to accept this; so far as I can see he had no choice, although it is perhaps unexpected to find a claimant relying on s 12 of the 1998 Act against a publisher rather than vice versa. But he balked at what Mr Tugendhat QC submitted, and I agree, was the necessary extension of the subsection's logic. A newspaper, say, intends to publish an article about an individual who learns of it and fears, on tenable grounds, that it will put his life in danger. The newspaper, also on tenable grounds, considers his fear unrealistic. First of all, it seems to me inescapable that s 12(4) makes the right to life, which is protected by art 2 of the convention and implicitly recognised by art 10(2), as relevant as the right of free expression to the court's decision; and in doing so it also makes art 17 (which prohibits the abuse of rights) relevant. But this in turn has an impact on s 12(3) which, though it does not replace the received test (or tests) for prior restraint, qualifies them by requiring a probability of success at trial. The gauging of this probability, by virtue of s 12(4), will have to take into account the full range of relevant convention rights.

135. How is the court to do this when the evidence—viz that there is and that there is not an appreciable risk to life—is no more than evenly balanced? A bland application of s 12(3) could deny the claimant the court's temporary protection, even if the potential harm to him, should the risk eventuate, was of the gravest kind and that to the newspaper and the public, should publication be restrained, minimal; and a similarly bland application of s 12(4), simply prioritising the freedom to publish over other convention rights (save possibly freedom of religion: see s 13 of the Human Rights Act), might give the newspaper the edge even if the claimant's evidence were strong. I agree with Mr Tugendhat that this cannot have been Parliament's design. This is not only, as he submits, because of the inherent logic of the provision but because of the court's own obligation under s 3 of the Act to construe all legislation so far as possible compatibly with the convention rights, an obligation which must include the interpretation of the Human Rights Act itself. The European Court of Human Rights has always recognised the high importance of free media of communication in a democracy, but its jurisprudence does not—and could not consistently with the convention itself—give art 10(1) of the convention the presumptive priority which is given, for example, to the First Amendment in the jurisprudence of the United States' courts. Everything will ultimately depend on the proper balance between privacy and publicity in the situation facing the court.

136. For both reasons, and in agreement with paras 150 to 154 of the judgment of Keene LJ and para 94 of the judgment of Brooke LJ, I accept that s 12 of the Human Rights Act is not to be interpreted and applied in the simplistic manner for which Mr Carr contends. It will be necessary for the court, in applying the test set out in s 12(3), to bear in mind that by virtue of s 12(1) and (4) the qualifications set out in art 10(2) of the convention are as relevant as the right set out in art 10(1). This means that, for example, the reputations and rights of others—not only but not least their convention rights—are as material as the defendant's right of free expression. So is the prohibition in art 17 on the use of one party's convention rights to injure the convention rights of others. Any other approach to s 12 would in my judgment violate s 3 of the Act. Correspondingly, as Mr Tugendhat submits, 'likely' in s 12(3) cannot be read as requiring simply an evaluation of the relative strengths of the parties' evidence. If at trial, for the reasons I have given, a minor but real risk to life, or a wholly unjustifiable invasion of privacy, is entitled to no less regard, by virtue of art 10(2), than is accorded to the right to publish by art 10(1), the consequent likelihood becomes material under s 12(3). Neither

19 *Ed.* For the text, see above, p. 22.

element is a trump card. They will be articulated by the principles of legality and proportionality which, as always, constitute the mechanism by which the court reaches its conclusion on countervailing or qualified rights. It will be remembered that in the jurisprudence of the convention proportionality is tested by, among other things, the standard of what is necessary in a democratic society. It should also be borne in mind that that the much-quoted remark of Hoffmann LJ in *R v Central Independent Television plc* [1994] 3 All ER 641 at 652, [1994] Fam 192 at 203 that freedom of speech 'is a trump card which always wins' came in a passage which expressly qualified the proposition (as Lord Hoffmann has since confirmed, albeit extra-judicially, in his 1996 Goodman Lecture) as lying 'outside the established exceptions (or any new ones which Parliament may enact in accordance with its obligations under the Convention)'. If freedom of expression is to be impeded, in other words, it must be on cogent grounds recognised by law.

137. Let me summarise. For reasons I have given, Mr Douglas and Ms Zeta-Jones have a powerful prima facie claim to redress for invasion of their privacy as a qualified right recognised and protected by English law. The case being one which affects the convention right of freedom of expression, s 12 of the Human Rights Act requires the court to have regard to art 10 of the convention (as, in its absence, would s 6 of that Act). This, however, cannot, consistently with s 3 of the Human Rights Act and art 17 of the convention, give the art 10(1) right of free expression a presumptive priority over other rights. What it does is require the court to consider art 10(2) along with art 10(1), and by doing so to bring into the frame the conflicting right to respect for privacy. This right, contained in art 8 and reflected in English law, is in turn qualified in both contexts by the right of others to free expression. The outcome, which self-evidently has to be the same under both articles, is determined principally by considerations of proportionality.

The injunction

138. In his opening argument Mr Carr, having submitted (acceptably for present purposes) that this case is a case of breach of confidence or nothing, sought to stifle that cause of action at birth by arguing that pictures such as the defendant was proposing to publish were not information at all. This had the makings of an own goal, since it might well have excluded art 10 of the convention and with it s 12 of the Human Rights Act from the defendants' own armoury. But it is plainly wrong. The offending photographs convey the simple information: 'This is what the wedding and the happy couple looked like'.

139. It is also as information, however, that the photographs invade the privacy of Mr Douglas and Ms Zeta-Jones: they tell the world things about the wedding and the couple which the claimants have not consented to. On the present evidence, whoever took the photographs probably had no right to be there; if they were lawfully there, they had no right to photograph anyone; and in either case they had no right to publicise the product of their intrusion. If it stopped there, this would have been an unanswerable case for a temporary injunction and no doubt in due course for a permanent one; perhaps the more unanswerable, not the less, for the celebrity of the two principal victims. Article 8 of the convention, whether introduced indirectly through s 12 or directly by virtue of s 6 of the Human Rights Act, will of course require the court to consider 'the rights and freedoms of others', including the art 10(1) right of Hello!. And art 10, by virtue of ss 6 and 12, will require the court, if the common law did not already do so, to have full regard to Hello!'s right to freedom of expression. But the circumstances in which the photographs must have been obtained would have robbed those rights and freedoms of substance for reasons which should by now be plain.

140. The facts, however, do not stop here. The first two claimants had sold most of the privacy they now seek to protect to the third claimant for a handsome sum. If all that had happened were that Hello! had got hold of OK!'s photographs, OK! would have proprietary rights and remedies at law, but Mr Douglas and Ms Zeta-Jones would not, I think, have any claim for breach of the privacy with which they had already parted. The present case is not so stark, because they were careful by their contract to retain a right of veto over publication of OK!'s photographs in order to maintain the kind of image which is professionally and no doubt also personally important to them. This element of privacy remained theirs and Hello!'s photographs violated it.

141. Article 8 of the convention, however, gives no absolute rights, any more than does the law of breach of confidence or privacy. Not only are there the qualifications under art 8(2);

what para (1) requires is respect for, not inviolability of, private and family life. Taking it for the present that it is the state, represented by the court, which must accord that respect, what amounts to respect must depend on the full set of circumstances in which the intrusion has occurred. This intrusion was by uncontrolled photography for profit of a wedding which was to be the subject of controlled photography for profit.

142. Thus the major part of the claimants' privacy rights have become the subject of a commercial transaction: bluntly, they have been sold ... The retained element of privacy, in the form of editorial control of OK!'s pictures, while real, is itself as much a commercial as a personal reservation. While it may be harder to translate into lost money or an account of profits, it can readily be translated into general damages of a significant amount.

144. In the present case, and not without misgiving, I have concluded that although the first two claimants are likely to succeed at trial in establishing a breach of their privacy in which Hello! may be actionably implicated, the dominant feature of the case is that by far the greater part of that privacy has already been traded and falls to be protected, if at all, as a commodity in the hands of the third claimant. This can be done without the need of an injunction, particularly since there may not be adequate countervailing redress for the defendants if at trial they stave off the claim for interference with contractual relations. The retained element of the first two claimants' privacy is not in my judgment—though I confess it is a close thing—sufficient to tilt the balance of justice and convenience against such liberty as the defendants may establish, at law and under art 10 of the convention, to publish the illicitly taken photographs.

Keene LJ:

149. It is not in dispute that s 12(3) is applicable in this case. Mr Tugendhat QC's submission is that the phrase 'likely to establish' does not mean 'more probable than not', because that interpretation in certain circumstances could bring it into conflict with the European Convention for the Protection of Human Rights and Fundamental Freedoms (Rome, 4 November 1950; TS 71 (1953); Cmd 8969) (the convention) itself by giving priority to art 10, the right to freedom of expression, over art 8, the right to respect for private and family life. Such an automatic priority, it is said, would not be in conformity with the convention. Since s 3(1) of the Human Rights Act requires the court to construe legislation in a way which is compatible with the convention rights 'so far as it is possible to do so', s 12(3) itself must be read in a way which avoids giving precedence to art 10 rights. It is argued on behalf of the claimants that the words 'likely to establish' in that subsection should be taken to mean 'not fanciful' or 'on the cards'.

150. For my part, I do not accept that there is any need for conflict between the normal meaning to be attached to the words in s 12(3) and the convention. The subsection does not seek to give a priority to one convention right over another. It is simply dealing with the interlocutory stage of proceedings and with how the court is to approach matters at that stage in advance of any ultimate balance being struck between rights which may be in potential conflict. It requires the court to look at the merits of the case and not merely to apply the *American Cyanamid* test. Thus the court has to look ahead to the ultimate stage and to be satisfied that the scales are likely to come down in the applicant's favour. That does not conflict with the convention, since it is merely requiring the court to apply its mind to how one right is to be balanced, on the merits against another right, without building in additional weight on one side. In a situation such as the one postulated by Mr Tugendhat, where the non-art 10 right is of fundamental importance to the individual, such as the art 2 right to life, the merits will include not merely the evidence about how great is the risk of that right being breached, but also a consideration of the gravity of the consequences for an applicant if the risk materialises. The nature of the risk is part of the merits, just as it would be at trial when the balance had to be struck. That is as relevant at the interlocutory stage as it would be at trial. But that does not require any strained interpretation of s 12(3).

151. Certainly s 12(3) is making prior restraint (ie before trial) more difficult in cases where the right to freedom of expression is engaged than where it is not. That is not a novel concept in English law. As was said by Laws J in *R v Advertising Standards Authority Ltd, ex p Vernons Organisation Ltd* [1993] 2 All ER 202 at 205, [1992] 1 WLR 1289 at 1293:

'... there is a general principle in our law that the expression of opinion and the conveyance of information will not be restrained by the courts save on pressing grounds. Freedom of expression is as much a sinew of the common law as it is of the European Convention on Human Rights ...'

152. Perhaps more to the point, the jurisprudence of the European Court of Human Rights is generally hostile to prior restraint by the courts. Prior restraints on publication are not prohibited by the convention, as the European Court of Human Rights made clear in *Observer v UK* (1991) 14 EHRR 153, the 'Spycatcher' case, but in that same case it went on to say (at 191 (para 60)):

'On the other hand, the dangers inherent in prior restraints are such that they call for the most careful scrutiny on the part of the Court. This is especially so as far as the press is concerned, for news is a perishable commodity and to delay its publication, even for a short period, may well deprive it of all its value and interest.'

153. It is impossible to accept that a statutory provision requiring a court to consider the merits of the case and to be satisfied that the balance is likely to be struck in favour of the applicant before prior restraint is to be granted is incompatible with the convention. It follows that no strained reading of the language of s 12(3) is needed to render it compatible with convention rights. The wording can be given its normal meaning. Consequently the test to be applied at this stage is whether this court is satisfied that the applicant is likely to establish at trial that publication should not be allowed. Even then, there remains a discretion in the court.

[After ruling that the claims in malicious falsehood and interference with contracting relations did not justify an interim injunction, **Keene LJ** continued:]

Breach of confidence
164. It is [breach of confidence] which has formed the main plank of the claimants' case. The claim is put in terms of breach of confidence in the particulars of claim, but it was said in argument by Mr Tugendhat that the case has more to do with privacy that with confidentiality.

165. It is clear that there is no watertight division between the two concepts. *Margaret, Duchess of Argyll v Duke of Argyll* [1965] 1 All ER 611, [1967] Ch 302 was a classic case where the concept of confidentiality was applied so as, in effect, to protect the privacy of communications between a husband and wife. Moreover, breach of confidence is a developing area of the law, the boundaries of which are not immutable but may change to reflect changes in society, technology and business practice . . .

166. Since the coming into force of the Human Rights Act, the courts as a public authority cannot act in a way which is incompatible with a convention right: s 6(1). That arguably includes their activity in interpreting and developing the common law, even where no public authority is a party to the litigation. Whether this extends to creating a new cause of action between private persons and bodies is more controversial, since to do so would appear to circumvent the restrictions on proceedings contained in s 7(1) of the Act and on remedies in s 8(1). But it is unnecessary to determine that issue in these proceedings, where reliance is placed on breach of confidence, an established cause of action, the scope of which may now need to be approached in the light of the obligation on this court arising under s 6(1) of the Act. Already before the coming into force of the Act there have been persuasive dicta in *Hellewell v Chief Constable of Derbyshire* [1995] 4 All ER 473, [1995] 1 WLR 804 and *A-G v Guardian Newspapers Ltd (No 2)* [1988] 3 All ER 545, [1990] 1 AC 109, cited by Sedley LJ in his judgment in these proceedings, to the effect that a pre-existing confidential relationship between the parties is not required for a breach of confidence suit. The nature of the subject matter or the circumstances of the defendant's activities may suffice in some instances to give rise to liability for breach of confidence. That approach must now be informed by the jurisprudence of the convention in respect of art 8. Whether the resulting liability is described as being for breach of confidence or for breach of a right to privacy may be little more than deciding what label is to be attached to the cause of action, but there would seem to be merit in recognising that the original concept of breach of confidence has in this particular category of cases now developed into something different from the commercial and employment relationships with which confidentiality is mainly concerned.

167. Because of these developments in the common law relating to confidence and the apparent obligation on English courts now to take account of the right to respect for private and family life under art 8 when interpreting the common law, it seems unlikely that *Kaye v Robertson* [1991] FSR 62, which held that there was no actionable right of privacy in English law, would be decided the same way on that aspect today. It is noteworthy that no claim for breach of confidence was mounted in that case, and that the *Duchess of Argyll's* case and the

Guardian Newspapers case do not seem to have been cited to the court. In the latter decision the House of Lords had made it clear that a duty of confidence could arise from the circumstances in which the information was obtained, so that the recipient was to be precluded from disclosing it to others. Consequently if the present case concerned a truly private occasion, where the persons involved made it clear that they intended it to remain private and undisclosed to the world, then I might well have concluded that in the current state of English law the claimants were likely to succeed at any eventual trial.

168. But any consideration of art 8 rights must reflect the convention jurisprudence which acknowledges different degrees of privacy. The European Court of the Human Rights ruled in *Dudgeon v UK* (1981) 4 EHRR 149 at 165 (para 152) that the more intimate the aspect of private life which is being interfered with, the more serious must be the reasons for interference before the latter can be legitimate. Personal sexuality, as in that case, is an extremely intimate aspect of a person's private life. A purely private wedding will have a lesser but still significant degree of privacy warranting protection, though subject to the considerations set out in art 8(2) of the convention. But if persons choose to lessen the degree of privacy attaching to an otherwise private occasion, then the balance to be struck between their rights and other considerations is likely to be affected.

169. In the present case, it is of considerable relevance that very widespread publicity was to be given in any event to the wedding very soon afterwards by way of photographs in OK! magazine. The occasion thereby lost much of its private nature. The claimants were by their security measures and by their agreements with the service companies seeking not so much to protect the privacy of the first two claimants but rather to control the form of publicity which ensued . . .

170 . . . Indeed, it was made clear by Mr Tugendhat in his submissions that what was complained of here was the loss of control over the photographs to be published, leading to damage to the image of the first and second claimants because of unflattering photographs.

171. It may be that a limited degree of privacy remains in such a situation and it could be that at trial the claimants would succeed in obtaining a permanent injunction. There must still be some doubt about that. But even if the claimants had passed that threshold of showing that it is likely that they would obtain an injunction at trial, this court in exercising its discretion at this interlocutory stage must still take account of the widespread publicity arranged by the claimant for this occasion. When that organised publicity is balanced against the impact on the defendants of an injunction restraining publication, I have no doubt that the scales come down in this case against prior restraint. This is a matter where any damage to the claimants can adequately be dealt with in monetary terms. In those circumstances I would allow this appeal and discharge the injunction.

Appeal allowed.

NOTES

1. Although only a case concerning an interim injunction, *Douglas v Hello!* is likely to prove the breakthrough case that leads to the establishment of an independent tort of invasion of privacy, although this need to be confirmed by the House of Lords. Emboldened and inspired by the combination of the HRA's incorporation into English law of the Art. 8 ECHR guarantee of the right to respect for private life and the position taken by the British government at Strasbourg in the *Spencer* case (see paras. 86–88, 124, *Douglas* judgments) as to the capacity of English law to protect the applicants' Convention right to privacy through the law of breach of confidence, the three Lord Justices in the *Douglas* case, by different routes and with different degrees of certainty, support the idea that a new tort of invasion of privacy is emerging, with the law of breach of confidence as its midwife.
2. On the HRA aspects of the *Douglas* case, see above, p. 32.
3. What role and weight is given to the Press Complaints Commission's voluntary Code of Practice by Brooke LJ?

3 Indirect remedies in law for invasion of privacy

The established remedies relevant to the protection of privacy that exist in English law are found in various parts of the criminal and, particularly, the civil law. In terms of the two main kinds of invasion of privacy, protection from physical intrusion is offered mainly by the torts of trespass and nuisance. Informational privacy is to some extent safeguarded by the law of defamation, the court's jurisdiction to protect juveniles, breach of copyright and breach of confidence.

(A) TRESPASS

Hickman v Maisey [1900] 1 QB 752, 69 LJQB 511, 82 LT 321, Court of Appeal

The plaintiff owned and occupied land on which for a fee he allowed a racehorse trainer to train horses. The defendant, a racing tout, observed the horses from a highway that crossed the plaintiff's land. The plaintiff brought an action in trespass for damages and an injunction. The jury found for the plaintiff, awarding damages of one shilling, and the judge granted an injunction. The defendant appealed to the Court of Appeal.

A. L. Smith LJ: . . . Many authorities shew that prima facie the right of the public is merely to pass and repass along the highway; but I quite agree with what Lord Esher MR said in *Harrison v Duke of Rutland* [1893] 1 QB 142 . . . namely, that, though highways are dedicated prima facie for the purpose of passage, 'things are done upon them by everybody which are recognised as being rightly done and as constituting a reasonable and usual mode of using a highway as such'; and, 'if a person on a highway does not transgress such reasonable and usual mode of using it', he will not be a trespasser; but, if he does 'acts other than the reasonable and ordinary user of a highway as such' he will be a trespasser. For instance . . . if a man took a sketch from the highway, I should say that no reasonable person would treat that as an act of trespass. But I cannot agree with the contention of the defendant's counsel that the acts which this defendant did, not really for the purpose of using the highway as such, but for the purpose of carrying on his business as a racing tout to the detriment of the plaintiff by watching the trials of race-horses on the plaintiff's land, were within such an ordinary and reasonable user of the highway as I have mentioned. . . . In the case of *Harrison v Duke of Rutland* [1893] 1 QB 142 the point which arises in this case was not precisely similar to that in the present case. In that case the plaintiff went upon a highway, the soil of which was vested in the defendant, while a grouse drive was taking place on adjoining land of the defendant, for the purpose of interfering with the drive, which the defendant's keepers prevented him from doing by force. The plaintiff thereupon brought an action for assault against the defendant, and the defendant counter-claimed in trespass. . . . It was clear upon the facts that he was not using the highway for the purpose of passing or repassing along it, but solely for the purpose of interfering with the defendant's enjoyment of his right of shooting over his land, and it was held therefore that the plaintiff's user of the highway was a trespass. I cannot see any real distinction between that case and the present. . . . I do not agree with the argument of the defendant's counsel to the effect that the intention and object of the defendant in going upon the highway cannot be taken into account in determining whether he was using it in a lawful manner. I think that his intention and object were all-important in determining that question.

Collins and **Romer LJJ** delivered concurring judgments.

Appeal dismissed.

NOTES

1. It was crucial in this case that the defendant was using the highway for commercial purposes to the detriment of the plaintiff. The case concerned a highway the soil of which was the property of the plaintiff. In most cases (a private road would be an exception), the soil will be vested in a highway authority: a local authority or the Secretary of State. Although the same rule (ordinary and reasonable user) applies, it will be unlikely in such cases that a person who wishes to rely upon it will be as fortunate as the racehorse trainer in *Hickman v Maisey* was in persuading the owner of the soil to bring proceedings.

2. The trainer could not have brought an action in trespass to land because he was not in possession of the land. Similarly, in *Kaye v Robertson*,[21] the hospital authorities could have brought proceedings in trespass, but not the patient or his family. So also, 'the ordinary overnight visitor at an hotel may sleep in but does not "occupy" the bedroom allotted to him and hence has no remedy against an intruder who plants a microphone in the room; the hotel proprietor will have an action in trespass but he may be unwilling to bring it; indeed he may have put the microphone in the room himself or be in collusion with someone who did so'.[1] But 'where there is a contract between a hotel guest and the hotel proprietor it might be argued that it is an implied term of such a contract that the former's room should be free from devices intruding on his privacy'.[2] This, of course, would only give a claim against the hotel.

3. The plaintiff would not have had a remedy in trespass to land if the defendant had watched the horses from land that was not the plaintiff's. There has to be a physical presence on the plaintiff's land.[3] The Younger Committee[4] suggested that a 'method of spying which involved the projection into airspace above the plaintiff's land of beams (as for radar) could presumably be treated as trespass to land or perhaps nuisance'. The Committee added:

'An entry is unauthorised . . . if permission to enter is obtained by fraud, as when an enquiry agent posing as a post office engineer obtains entry to a building and puts a bugging device in a telephone receiver; and an entry lawfully made may become trespassing when the entrant takes advantage of the occasion to do things (e.g. to carry out a search of the premises) not covered by his permission to enter.'

See the Press Council cases[5] in which reporters have been invited into a house and then taken a photograph without consent.

4. In addition to the limitations upon trespass to land as a remedy for invasion of privacy noted above, trespass has two other limitations. Firstly, although an injunction may be granted to prevent a future trespass, one may not be available to prevent the publication of information or a photograph obtained as a result of a trespass: *Kaye v Robertson*.[6] Secondly, there is also the question of the measure of damages. As the Younger Report states:[7]

'In any case where invasion of privacy is the real issue, there is not likely to be any substantial claim for damage to the land, at least by comparison with what the plaintiff is likely to feel he ought to receive for the invasion of privacy. Damages for the latter can only be covered by a claim for aggravated or for punitive (or exemplary) damages i.e. for a sum which will offer the plaintiff some recompense for the attack made on his feelings and dignity or which will punish the defendant for the outrageous form which the trespass has taken. . . . It would seem

21 Above, p. 911.
 1 Younger Report (above, p. 909), p. 290.
 2 Ibid.
 3 *Sheen v Clegg* (1961) *Daily Telegraph*, 22 June, cited in the Younger Committee Report, p. 289 (microphone placed by trespass over plaintiff's marital bed) and *Greig v Greig* [1966] VR 376, S Ct Vict (microphone placed in plaintiff's flat by trespass). See also *Francome v Mirror Group Newspapers Ltd*, below, p. 988.
 4 p. 289.
 5 E.g. 18th Report 1971, p. 49. This may have been the situation in *Douglas v Hello!* above, p. 922.
 6 Above, p. 911.
 7 p. 290.

that . . . a journalist, for example, who forced his way into a house to get a story for his newspaper might find himself liable to pay substantial damages, even though he had done little or no damage to the house. However, the cases in which punitive damages may be awarded appear to have been severely limited by the House of Lords in *Rookes v Barnard* [1964] AC 1129 and *Cassell & Co v Broome* [1972] AC 1027.'

Aggravated and exemplary (or punitive) damages are distinct and different concepts. *Aggravated* damages were awarded in *Jolliffe v Willmett & Co*,[8] in which a private detective acting for the husband in a matrimonial dispute gained entry to the matrimonial home where the wife only was still living by deceit and force. The defendant pretended to be the postman and, when the door was opened, pushed past the wife to discover evidence of the sleeping arrangements. £250 damages were awarded for an 'insolent and high-handed trespass'. In *Rookes v Barnard*, Lord Devlin stated that *exemplary* damages were available only in: (i) cases of 'oppressive, arbitrary or unconstitutional action by the servants of the government' (the government includes local government and the police: *Cassell v Broome*); (ii) cases 'in which the defendant's conduct has been calculated by him to make a profit for himself which may well exceed the compensation payable to the plaintiff'; and (iii) where 'exemplary damages are expressly authorised by statute'. Exemplary damages are not available in respect of causes of action for which they had not been awarded before 1964.[9] Some privacy cases involving, for example, police or press action will come within the first or second of Lord Devlin's categories.[1]

5. In 1965 the *Sunday Express* and *The People* published pictures of the Queen and Princess Margaret showing them water-skiing at the Great Pond, Sunninghill Park. The Park is Crown land but has a public footpath running through it some distance from the lake and from which part of the lake can be seen. The pictures had been bought from a professional photographer who claimed to have taken them from the footpath with a telephoto lens. The case was investigated by the Press Council[2] which found 'that the photographs . . . were taken surreptitiously by Mr. R. Bellisario when the Queen and the Princess obviously were unaware that the pictures were being taken and that Mr. Bellisario was trespassing on the private ground of Her Majesty [i.e. off the footpath] at the time'. After concluding that the newspapers had acted in good faith, having been deceived by the photographer, the Council 'unreservedly' condemned the photographer. It also censured a *Daily Express* photographer who was one of two photographers discovered 'hidden in the undergrowth lying on the ground, with their cameras trained on the hut where Her Royal Highness was changing her clothes'. Clearly actions in trespass could have been brought to protect privacy on these facts. Could one have been brought against Mr Bellisario if his claim to have taken the pictures from the footpath had been correct?

6. Another Press Council case[3] in which there would have been a remedy in trespass was that in which the *Daily Sketch* published a reporter's story of how she had gatecrashed the Duke of Kent's 21st birthday party in the boot of a car. The editor

---

8   [1971] 1 All ER 478, QBD. Cf. *Thompson v Metropolitan Police Comr* [1997] 3 WLR 403, CA (aggravated and exemplary damages awarded for assault, false imprisonment and malicious prosecution by the police).

9   *AB v South West Water Services Ltd* [1993] QB 507, CA.

1   See, e.g., *John v MGN Ltd* [1997] QB 586, CA (exemplary damages for defamatory story about Elton John where reckless disregard for the truth calculated to make a profit). For a privacy case of breach of copyright in which punitive damages were awarded, see *Williams v Settle*, below, p. 957.

2   12th Report 1965, p. 3.

3   4th Report 1957, p. 22.

was found 'guilty of a flagrant violation of good manners'. In one case, the Council[4] condoned trespass by deception when a *News of the World* reporter claimed to be homeless to gain admission to the Centrepoint hostel in London to check a story that homeless youngsters were sleeping in a mixed-sex dormitory. The Press Council ruled that 'the use of subterfuge can be justified in cases involving public interest or the exposure of crime'. However, the Council found against the *Sunday People* in a case in which reporters had posed as hospital volunteers to investigate allegations of sexual promiscuity among mental patients. The public interest defence was defeated by the need to maintain confidence in the system of voluntary helpers.[5] Journalists should generally disclose that they are such when seeking information.[6]

7. In *Baron Bernstein of Leigh v Skyviews and General Ltd*,[7] the plaintiff's land was flown over and an aerial photograph of his house taken without his knowledge or consent. He refused the offer to sell him the photograph and sued the defendant in trespass and invasion of privacy instead. Rejecting the claim, Griffiths J stated:

'I can find no support in authority for the view that a landowner's rights in the air space above his property extend to an unlimited height. In *Wandsworth Board of Works v United Telephone Co Ltd* [1884] 13 QBD 904 Bowen LJ described the maxim, usque ad coelum, as a fanciful phrase, to which I would add that if applied literally it is a fanciful notion leading to the absurdity of a trespass at common law being committed by a satellite every time it passes over a suburban garden. . . . The problem is to balance the rights of an owner to enjoy the use of his land against the rights of the general public to take advantage of all that science now offers in the use of air space. This balance is in my judgment best struck in our present society by restricting the rights of an owner in the air space above his land to such height as is necessary for the ordinary use and enjoyment of his land and the structures upon it, and declaring that above that height he has no greater rights in the air space than any other member of the public.

Applying this test to the facts of this case, I find that the defendants' aircraft did not infringe any rights in the plaintiff's air space, and thus no trespass was committed. It was on any view of the evidence flying many hundreds of feet above the ground and it is not suggested that by its mere presence in the air space it caused any interference with any use to which the plaintiff put or might wish to put his land. The plaintiff's complaint is not that the aircraft interfered with the use of his land but that a photograph was taken from it. There is, however, no law against taking a photograph, and the mere taking of a photograph cannot turn an act which is not a trespass into the plaintiff's air space into one that is a trespass.

The present action is not founded in nuisance for no court would regard the taking of a single photograph as an actionable nuisance. But if the circumstances were such that a plaintiff was subjected to the harassment of constant surveillance of his house from the air, accompanied by the photographing of his every activity, I am far from saying that the court would not regard such a monstrous invasion of his privacy as an actionable nuisance for which they would give relief.'

8. The public opinion survey done for the Younger Committee[8] showed that 'callers at the door' were regarded as invading privacy, with Jehovah's Witnesses being mentioned in particular. In *Robson v Hallett*[8a] Diplock LJ stated that:

---

4   23rd Report 1976, p. 113. Cf. the case in which journalists took undercover video footage at a private party for employees of the TV series *Emmerdale*: Press Complaints Commission Report No 53, Jan.–March 2001, p. 10 (breach of Code, clause 4 (harassment)).

5   26th Report 1979, p. 68. See also the case in which a complaint by Ms Germaine Greer that a *Mail on Sunday* journalist had gained admission to her house by pretending to be homeless was upheld: Press Complaints Commission Report No 23, Jan.–Feb. 1994, p. 18.

6   *Daily Mail* condemned because journalists failed to do so when seeking an interview with hospital patient: 27th/28th Reports 1980/81, p. 177.

7   [1978] QB 479. See R. Wacks (1977) 93 LQR 491. For doubts about this case, see Sedley LJ in *Douglas v Hello!*, above, p. 922.

8   Report, Appendix E.

8a   [1967] 2 QB 939 at 953–954, DC.

'when a householder lives in a dwelling house to which there is a garden in front and does not lock the gate of the garden, it gives an implied licence to any member of the public who has lawful reason for doing so to proceed from the gate to the front door or back door, and to inquire whether he may be admitted and to conduct his lawful business.'

Diplock LJ stated that such an implied licence may be rebutted, as by a notice on the gate (e.g. 'No hawkers').

9. The above materials concern trespass to land. With statutory exceptions,[9] trespass to land is not a criminal offence. When Michael Fagan climbed into Buckingham Palace and surprised the Queen by sitting on her bed, he thereby committed no offence. He was charged and acquitted of burglary in respect of an entry into the Palace a month earlier when he had stolen wine.[10] Following the second incident, the enactment of an offence of trespassing on residential property in a 'manner likely to cause the occupier alarm or distress', was considered but no government bill has resulted.[11] Trespass to goods may also occasionally provide a remedy for invasion of privacy, as where a document is taken.

10. See also the additional criminal offences suggested by the Calcutt Committee,[12] which respond to certain of the above limitations on the law of trespass.

(B) NUISANCE

Hunter v Canary Wharf Ltd [1997] AC 655, [1997] 2 All ER 426, House of Lords

The plaintiffs sued in private nuisance, *inter alia*, for interference with television reception in their homes caused by the building of the Canary Wharf Tower on land developed by the defendants. In the Court of Appeal it was held that occupation of property as a home allowed the occupier to sue in private nuisance; it was not necessary to show a proprietary interest in the land. Thus, a member of the householder's family or a lodger with just a contractual interest as a licensee could sue as well as the householder. The House of Lords, by four votes to one, allowed an appeal against this ruling. In doing so, it overruled *Khorasandjian v Bush*,[12a] in which the question had been relevant in a privacy context.

> **Lord Goff of Chieveley**: ... Subject to this exception, however, it has for many years been regarded as settled law that a person who has no right in the land cannot sue in private nuisance. For this proposition, it is usual to cite the decision of the Court of Appeal in *Malone v Laskey* [1907] 2 KB 141, [1904–7] All ER 304. ...
>
> The decision in *Malone v Laskey* on nuisance has since been followed in many cases ... .
> Recently, however, the Court of Appeal departed from this line of authority in *Khorasandjian v Bush* [1993] 3 All ER 669, [1993] QB 727, a case which I must examine with some care.
> The plaintiff, a young girl who at the time of the appeal was 18, had formed a friendship with the defendant, then a man of 28. After a time the friendship broke down and the plaintiff decided that she would have no more to do with the defendant, but the defendant found this impossible to accept. There followed a catalogue of complaints against the defendant, including assaults, threats of violence, and pestering the plaintiff at her parents' home where she lived. As a result of the defendant's threats and abusive behaviour he spent some time in prison. An injunction was granted restraining the defendant from various forms of activity directed at the plaintiff, and this included an order restraining him from 'harassing, pestering or communicating with' the plaintiff. The question before the Court of Appeal was whether the judge had jurisdiction to grant such an injunction, in relation to telephone calls made to the plaintiff at

---

9 E.g. trespass using violence to secure entry (Criminal Law Act 1977, s. 6) and aggravated trespass (Criminal Justice and Public Order Act 1994, ss. 68–69).
10 *The Times*, 24 September 1982.
11 Calcutt Report, p. 10.
12 Above, p. 920.
12a [1993] QB 727, CA.

her parents' home. The home was the property of the plaintiff's mother, and it was recognised that her mother could complain of persistent and unwanted telephone calls made to her; but it was submitted that the plaintiff, as a mere licensee in her mother's house, could not invoke the tort of private nuisance to complain of unwanted and harassing telephone calls made to her in her mother's home. The majority of the Court of Appeal (Peter Gibson J dissenting) rejected this submission, relying on the decision of the Appellate Division of the Alberta Supreme Court in *Motherwell v Motherwell* (1976) 73 DLR (3d) 62. In that case, the Appellate Division not only recognised that the legal owner of property could obtain an injunction, on the ground of private nuisance, to restrain persistent harassment by unwanted telephone calls to his home, but also that the same remedy was open to his wife who had no interest in the property. In the Court of Appeal Peter Gibson J dissented on the ground that it was wrong in principle that a mere licensee or someone without any interest in, or right to occupy, the relevant land should be able to sue in private nuisance.

It is necessary therefore to consider the basis of the decision in *Motherwell v Motherwell* that a wife, who has no interest in the matrimonial home where she lives, is nevertheless able to sue in private nuisance in respect of interference with her enjoyment of that home. The case was concerned with a claim for an injunction against the defendant, who was the daughter of one of the plaintiffs, the other two plaintiffs being her brother and sister-in-law. The main ground of the complaint against the defendant was that, as a result of a paranoid condition from which she suffered which produced in her the conviction that her sister-in-law and her father's housekeeper were inflaming her brother and her father against her, she persistently made a very large number of telephone calls to her brother's and her father's homes, in which she abused her sister-in-law and the housekeeper. The Appellate Division of the Alberta Supreme Court, in a judgment delivered by Clement JA, held that not only could her father and brother, as householders, obtain an injunction against the defendant to restrain this activity as a private nuisance, but so also could her sister-in-law although she had no interest in her husband's property. Clement JA said (at 78):

'Here we have a wife harassed in the matrimonial home. She has a status, a right to live there with her husband and children. I find it absurd to say that her occupancy of the matrimonial home is insufficient to found an action in nuisance. In my opinion she is entitled to the same relief as is her husband, the brother.'

This conclusion was very largely based on the decision of the Court of Appeal in *Foster v Warblington UDC* [1906] 1 KB 648, [1904–7] All ER Rep 366, which Clement JA understood to establish a distinction between 'one who is "merely present"' and 'occupancy of a substantive nature', and that in the latter case the occupier was entitled to sue in private nuisance. However, *Foster v Warblington UDC* does not, in my opinion, provide authority for the proposition that a person in the position of a mere licensee, such as a wife or husband in her or his spouse's house, is entitled to sue in that action. This misunderstanding must, I fear, undermine the authority of *Motherwell v Motherwell* on this point; and in so far as the decision of the Court of Appeal in *Khorasandjian v Bush* is founded upon *Motherwell v Motherwell* it is likewise undermined.

But I must go further. If a plaintiff, such as the daughter of the householder in *Khorasandjian v Bush*, is harassed by abusive telephone calls, the gravamen of the complaint lies in the harassment which is just as much an abuse, or indeed an invasion of her privacy, whether she is pestered in this way in her mother's or her husband's house, or she is staying with a friend, or is at her place of work, or even in her car with a mobile phone. In truth, what the Court of Appeal appears to have been doing was to exploit the law of private nuisance in order to create by the back door a tort of harassment which was only partially effective in that it was artificially limited to harassment which takes place in her home. I myself do not consider that this is a satisfactory manner in which to develop the law, especially when, as in the case in question, the step so taken was inconsistent with another decision of the Court of Appeal, viz *Malone v Laskey* [1907] 2 KB 141, [1904–7] All ER Rep 304, by which the court was bound. In any event, a tort of harassment has now received statutory recognition (see the Protection From Harassment Act 1997). We are therefore no longer troubled with the question whether the common law should be developed to provide such a remedy. For these reasons, I do not consider that any assistance can be derived from *Khorasandjian v Bush* by the plaintiffs in the present appeals.

It follows that, on the authorities as they stand, an action in private nuisance will only lie at the suit of a person who has a right to the land affected. Ordinarily, such a person can only sue if he has the right to exclusive possession of the land, such as a freeholder or tenant in possession, or even a licensee with exclusive possession. Exceptionally however, as *Foster v Warblington UDC* shows, this category may include a person in actual possession who has no right to be there; and in any event a reversioner can sue in so far as his reversionary interest is affected. But a mere licensee on the land has no right to sue ...

For all these reasons, I can see no good reason to depart from the law on this topic as established in the authorities. I would therefore hold that *Khorasandjian v Bush* must be overruled in so far as it holds that a mere licensee can sue in private nuisance, and I would allow the appeal or cross-appeal of the defendants in both actions and restore the order of Judge Havery on this issue.

Lords Lloyd, Hoffmann and **Hope** delivered speeches concurring on this point. **Lord Cooke** delivered a speech dissenting on this point.

NOTES

1. The *Khorasandjian* case had allowed a person who had no proprietary interest in the land to bring a claim in private nuisance as a victim of persistent telephone calls to her in her home. The case was overruled in the *Hunter* case on this point on the basis that it was inappropriate to extend the tort of nuisance beyond its purpose of protecting the quiet enjoyment of a person's land; the remedy was to develop a tailor-made remedy focusing on harassment. None the less, nuisance remains available as a remedy for a householder for persistent[13] telephone calls.[14] As noted by Lord Goff, the Protection from Harassment Act 1997, s. 3, establishes a statutory tort of harassment. Under this, a course of conduct which the defendant knows or ought to know constitutes harassment is actionable for damages for, *inter alia*, 'any anxiety caused by the harassment and any financial loss resulting' therefrom. As well as persistent telephone calling, this covers conduct such as stalking. As Lord Goff notes, the result of the new statutory tort is that the development of a common law tort of harassment is unnecessary.[15]

2. Before the *Khorasandjian* case, the limited potential of the tort of nuisance as a remedy for invasion of privacy by way of physical intrusion was explained in the Younger Committee Report[16] as follows:

'Private nuisance, giving rise to a civil action at the suit of an aggrieved individual, has on occasions been very widely defined to cover virtually any unreasonable interference with that individual's enjoyment of land which he occupies. But an action for private nuisance is normally brought for *some physical invasion of the plaintiff's land by some deleterious subject-matter*—such as noise, smell, water or electricity—in circumstances which would not amount to trespass to land. It is much more doubtful if it would cover an activity which had no physical effects on the plaintiff's land, although it detracts from the plaintiff's enjoyment of that land. Thus spying on one's neighbour is probably not in itself a private nuisance although watching and besetting a man's house with a view to compelling him to pursue (or not to pursue) a particular course of conduct has been said to be a nuisance at common law. With regard to the latter type of conduct, however, it must be admitted that it is concerned with a situation very

---

13 A single telephone call, even in the middle of the night (see 11th Press Council Report 1964, pp. 32, 35), is not a nuisance.
14 Cf. *Stokes v Brydges* (1958) 5, S Ct Queensland, in which the defendant, annoyed by the noise made by milkmen, retaliated by making telephone calls to the homes of the directors of the milk company to disturb their sleep. The directors were granted an injunction.
15 For an earlier move in that direction, see *Burris v Azadani* [1995] 1 WLR 1372, CA.
16 Appendix I, para. 18.

different from the typical case in which complaint is made of an invasion of privacy. The eavesdropper or spy does not seek to change the behaviour of his victim; on the contrary he hopes that it will continue unchanged, so that he may have the opportunity of noting it unobserved....

As a remedy for invasions of privacy private nuisance has the same basic disadvantages as the action for trespass to land, namely that it can only be brought by the person who is from a legal point of view the 'occupier' of the land, enjoyment of which is affected by the nuisance.'

3. In *Robbins v Canadian Broadcasting Corpn*,[17] the plaintiff wrote to the producer of a television programme criticising it. The letter was read on the programme and viewers were invited to telephone (the number was given) or write to the plaintiff to cheer him up. For three days afterwards, the plaintiff's telephone rang nonstop until he was obliged to change his number. He also received 102 letters and had pranks played upon him. He was awarded damages by the Quebec Superior Court under the Quebec Civil Code for damage caused by the fault of another. Cf. a Press Council case[18] in which the *Daily Sketch* was censured for publishing the home telephone number of Christine Keeler at the height of the Profumo affair causing 'a constant stream of abusive calls'.

4. The criminal law also controls persistent telephone calls. A person commits a summary offence contrary to the Telecommunications Act 1984, s. 43, if he 'for the purpose of causing annoyance, inconvenience or needless anxiety to another ... persistently makes use for that purpose of a public telecommunications system'. It is also a summary offence to send to another person with intent to 'cause distress or anxiety' a letter or other article which conveys, *inter alia*, an indecent or grossly offensive message, a threat or information which is known or believed to be false: Malicious Communications Act 1988, s. 1. In addition, the Protection from Harassment Act 1997 has added offences of harassment. It is a summary offence to pursue a course of conduct 'which amounts to harassment of another' and 'which he knows or ought to know' amounts thereto (ss. 1, 2). The offence becomes an indictable one, with a possible penalty of five years imprisonment, if the course of conduct 'causes another to fear, on at least two occasions, that violence will be used against' that person (s. 4). In *R v Ireland*[19] the House of Lords held that silent telephone calls that cause psychiatric injury to a victim may amount to an assault contrary to the Offences Against the Person Act 1861, s. 47. In doing so, it recognises that a conviction for the s. 4 offence under the Protection from Harassment Act 1997 may not be easy to obtain in the case of a silent telephone caller because the woman will have to fear violence.

5. In *Victoria Park Racing and Recreation Grounds Co Ltd v Taylor*,[20] the first defendant owned land adjacent to the plaintiff's racecourse. The second defendant erected a platform on the land and broadcast descriptions of the races from it. The plaintiff was refused an injunction to prevent the broadcasts. Latham CJ stated at 494–496:

'Any person is entitled to look over the plaintiff's fences and to see what goes on in the plaintiff's land. . . . The court has not been referred to any principle of law which prevents any man from describing anything which he sees anywhere if he does not make defamatory statements, infringe the law as to offensive language, &c, break a contract, or wrongfully reveal confidential information. . . .

The claim under the head of nuisance has also been supported by an argument that the law recognizes a right of privacy which has been infringed by the defendant. However desirable

17 (1958) 12 DLR (2d) 35, Quebec Sup Ct.
18 12th Report 1965, p. 97.
19 [1997] 4 All ER 225, HL.
20 (1938) 58 CLR 479 (Aust HC).

some limitation upon invasions of privacy might be, no authority was cited which shows that any general right of privacy exists.'

Winfield[1] suggests that 'peeping Toms', however persistent, do not commit a nuisance. But they may be bound over to be of good behaviour.[2] 'Peeping Toms' would be liable for invasion of privacy in the form of 'intrusion upon seclusion' in the sense of the *Restatement, 2d, Torts*.[3]

6. Would the conduct of newspaper reporters who gather at the door of a person's house and will not go away unless they are given an interview or a picture be actionable in nuisance? On constant surveillance as nuisance, see the *Bernstein* case.[4] In the Yorkshire Ripper case, the Press Council concluded:[5]

'18.29 . . . in this case the relatives of those at the centre of the story—victim and accused—were subjected to wholly unacceptable and unjustifiable pressures by journalists and other media representatives anxious either to interview or photograph them or to bid for the right to publish their stories. The conduct of journalists who laid siege to their homes in the circumstances described above can best be characterised in the old phrase—watching and besetting. The targets of this attention were people in deep personal grief or grave anxiety and they were harassed by the media ferociously and callously.

18.30. The descriptions of the attempts by reporters and photographers to make contact with Mr and Mrs Hill and Mrs Szurma-Sutcliffe cannot be read without a feeling of revulsion.'

See also the *Christine Keeler* case.[6] Would the conduct of the press in the *Yorkshire Ripper* or *Christine Keeler* cases constitute a criminal offence contrary to s. 241, Trade Union and Labour Relations Act 1992? The Calcutt Committee considered that, although aimed at harassment during industrial disputes, the offence in s. 7[7] 'could be committed by journalists following someone or surrounding his house', although in practice 'it is unlikely to be invoked against the press', the police normally limiting themselves 'to moving the press aside so that someone can pass'.[8] A 'non-molestation order' may be granted by a court prohibiting one 'associated person' from molesting another or a 'relevant child'. 'Associated persons' include spouses and former spouses, cohabitants and former cohabitants, persons living in the same household and relatives.[9] 'Molesting' does not necessarily imply violence; it 'applies to any conduct which can properly be regarded as such a degree of harassment as to call for the intervention of the court'.[10] The Calcutt Committee suggested that the offences in the Public Order Act 1986, ss. 4 and 5 might apply in some press harassment

1 (1931) 47 LQR 23, 27.
2 See below, p. 992.
3 Above, p. 914.
4 Above, p. 938.
5 *Press Conduct in the Sutcliffe Case* (1983), Press Council Booklet No. 7, pp. 162–163.
6 Below, p. 949.
7 s. 241 reads:
  'Every person who, with a view to compel any other person to abstain from doing or to do any act which such other person has a legal right to do or abstain from doing, wrongfully and without legal authority . . .
  2. Persistently follows such other person about from place to place; or . . .
  4. Watches or besets the house or other place where such other person resides, or works, or carries on business, or happens to be, or the approach to such house or place; or,
  5. Follows such other person with two or more other persons in a disorderly manner in or through any street or road . . .
  [commits an offence].'
8 Report, p. 18.
9 Family Law Act 1996, s. 42.
10 *Horner v Horner* [1982] 4 FLR 50, per Ormrod LJ. It does require an intention to cause distress or harm: *Johnson v Walton* [1990] 1 FLR 350.

cases.[11] A trader who secretly videoed women in his changing room trying on swimwear he was selling was guilty of an offence under Public Order Act 1986, s. 5, as a sort of technological 'peeping Tom'.[12] In particular, the setting up and allowing to run of a camera in such a place was 'insulting behaviour … within the hearing or sight of a person likely to be caused harassment, alarm or distress thereby'.

7. The Broadcasting Complaints Commission upheld a complaint concerning Channel 4's 'The Big Breakfast' programme.[13] The presenter Mr Keith Chegwin and a camera crew arrived unannounced in the early morning on the doorstep of Mr Mike Smith and Ms Sarah Greene. They sought to attract attention by shouting through the letter box, etc. When the occupants failed to respond, the broadcasting team continued with their live broadcast and did not leave the property. The Commission held that the manner of obtaining material for the broadcast and its showing was an invasion of the complainant's privacy in breach of broadcasting standards.

(C) DEFAMATION

Corelli v Wall (1906) 22 TLR 532, Chancery Division, Swinfen Eady J

The plaintiff, a well known authoress and a resident of Stratford-on-Avon, sought an interlocutory injunction to restrain the defendants, publishers in the same town, from publishing a series of postcards depicting imaginary scenes in the private life of the plaintiff. The injunction was sought pending the hearing of a libel action based upon the cards. The scenes included the plaintiff feeding ponies, on the river Avon in a gondola, and in an imaginary garden. The plaintiff's annoyance reached its height when the defendants hired sandwich men to parade through Stratford, particularly near the plaintiff's home, to advertise the postcards.

Swinfen Eady J: The real ground of the plaintiff's motion is that the cards constitute a libel upon her and that their sale ought to be restrained on that ground. Although it is well settled that a person may be defamed as well by a picture or effigy as by written or spoken words, I am not satisfied that the cards are libellous; and in any event the case is not so clear as to justify the Court intervening before the fact of libel has been established. The case of *Bonnard v Perryman* [1891] 2 Ch 269 shows how careful the Court should be in granting interlocutory injunctions in cases of alleged libel. It is also urged that the plaintiff as a private person was entitled to restrain the publication of a portrait of herself which had been made without her authority and which, although professing to be her portrait, was totally unlike her. No authority in support of this proposition was cited. The plaintiff has not established, for the purpose of this motion, that she has any such right. Under these circumstances I do not see my way to grant any interlocutory injunction. When it is known that the sale of the postcards is in direct opposition to the plaintiff's wishes, and is the subject of grave annoyance to her, most respectable persons will probably do as Messrs. W. H. Smith and Son have done, and refuse to have anything to do with them.

Motion dismissed.

NOTES

1. The case illustrates that even if an action in defamation is available, the remedy may be limited to damages. Although an interlocutory injunction will often be much the more effective remedy from the privacy point of view, one will only be granted

---

11 Report, p. 18.
12 *Vigon v DPP* (1997) Times, 9 December, QBD.
13 See the Broadcasting Complaints Commission adjudication of 20 April 1994.

under the rule in *Bonnard v Perryman*[14] 'in the clearest cases, where any jury would say that the matter complained of was libellous . . .'. An interlocutory injunction will not be granted if the defendant's defence is justification.[15]

2. Did *Corelli v Wall* decide that there was no remedy in English law for invasion of privacy in the form of the 'appropriation' of a person's 'name or likeness'?[16] Or only that an injunction could not be granted on the facts of the case?

3. In *Monson v Tussauds* [1894] 1 QB 671, CA the plaintiff had been tried and acquitted of murder. He sued the defendants for libel for including in their exhibition a wax model of him with the gun that was thought to be the murder weapon close-by. Under the rule in *Bonnard v Perryman*, the Court of Appeal refused an injunction pending trial of the libel action. In the Divisional Court, Collins J expressly left open 'the question whether a private person can restrain the publication of a portrait or effigy of himself which has been obtained without his authority'.[17] In the Court of Appeal, Lord Halsbury touched upon the question of invasion of privacy in more general terms:[18]

'If I understand the argument correctly, it comes to this—that the exhibition in question is dedicated to the gratification of public curiosity in regard to every person or event which may for the moment be interesting. I confess I regard such a claim with something like dismay. Is it possible to say that everything which has once been known may be reproduced with impunity in print or picture; every incident of a criminal or other trial be produced, and its publication justified; not only trials, but every incident which has actually happened in private life, furnish material for the adventurous exhibitor, dramatized peradventure, and justified because, in truth, such an incident did really happen? That it is done for gain does not in itself make it unlawful if it be in other respects legitimate; but it is not altogether immaterial as excluding such a publication from the category of those which are made in the fulfilment of some moral or legal duty.'

4. In *Tolley v J S Fry & Sons Ltd*,[19] the defendants published an advertisement for their chocolate showing, without his knowledge or consent, a caricature of the plaintiff, a well known amateur golfer, playing golf with a packet of their chocolate in his pocket. The plaintiff recovered damages in defamation on the basis that the advertisement carried an innuendo that he had prostituted his amateur status by advertising the defendant's goods for reward. On the question whether a remedy would have existed if the advertisement had not been defamatory, Greer LJ stated in the Court of Appeal:[20]

'Some men and women voluntarily enter professions which by their nature invite publicity, and public approval or disapproval. It is not unreasonable in their case that they should submit without complaint to their names and occupations and reputations being treated as matters of public interest, and almost as public property. On the other hand a great many people outside the professions I have referred to resent any attempt to utilize their names or their doings as public property. And I can very well imagine that an amateur sportsman, though success necessarily brings about a certain amount of publicity, strongly objecting to the use of his name in connection with an advertising campaign aimed at increasing the sales of a commodity which he may either dislike, or at any rate in which he is not the least interested. I have no hesitation in saying that in my judgment the defendants in publishing the advertisement in question, without first obtaining Mr. Tolley's consent, acted in a manner inconsistent with the decencies of life,

---

14 [1891] 2 Ch 269 at 284, CA.
15 See, e.g. Fox LJ in *Francome v Mirror Newspapers* [1984] 2 All ER 408 at 414, CA.
16 *Restatement, 2d, Torts*, above, p. 914.
17 p. 679.
18 p. 687.
19 [1931] AC 333, HL.
20 [1930] 1 KB at 477–478.

946   *The right to privacy*

and in doing so they were guilty of an act for which there ought to be a legal remedy. But unless a man's photograph, caricature, or name be published in such a context that the publication can be said to be defamatory within the law of libel, it cannot be made the subject-matter of complaint by action at law: *Dockrell v Dougall* and *Corelli v Wall* [above].'

In *Dockrell v Dougall*[1] the defendant had used the plaintiff's name without his knowledge or consent in an advertisement for a quack medicine ('Dr Dockrell says "Nothing had done his gout so much good"'). After a jury had held that the advertisement was not libellous, the plaintiff unsuccessfully sought an injunction. Smith LJ stated:

'If it could be made out that a man has a property in his own name *per se* and there has been an unauthorised use of his name, then the plaintiff might be entitled to an injunction. In order, however, to be entitled to an injunction, it seems to me that the plaintiff must show injury to him in his property, business, or profession. Upon that ground I think that the appeal fails.'

5. A man who opened a copy of a medical textbook in a public library was surprised to find a full frontal nude photograph of himself giving his initials, hospital record number and details of his case, all without his consent. The Health Service Commissioner, or Ombudsman, found that there had been a breach of confidentiality by the Health Authority.[2]

The Goolagong Case[3]

Publication by the *Sun* of drawings purporting to show Miss Evonne Goolagong, the Australian tennis player, in the nude, was an infringement of privacy said the Council after the All England Lawn Tennis and Croquet Club had complained that the *Sun* published the drawings without Miss Goolagong's knowledge and consent and that the drawings caused her great distress. . . . The drawings . . . were published under the heading 'On Wimbledon's opening day Goolagong in the Altogether'.

Miss Goolagong wrote to the Secretary of the All England Club (Major A. D. Mills) saying (inter alia) that when she went on court on the first Tuesday she felt all eyes were turned on her and that she was being undressed publicly. . . . Major Mills protested to the Editor [Mr. Lamb] about the drawings and the Editor's Personal Assistant . . . replied that they were published because they believed they had artistic merit and were in no way offensive. They had had no complaint from Miss Goolagong. They would be distressed to think they had upset her. The newspaper was the first to note her charm, professional potential and appeal in 1971. . . .

Mr. Lamb replied that his information was that Miss Goolagong was distressed not so much by the drawings as the behaviour of a fellow competitor who publicly accused her of having posed for them. He was unable to accept that the drawings, which were wholly sympathetic, were below 'acceptable standards' or that they constituted an infringement of privacy. . . .

The adjudication was: In the view of the Press Council the publication of drawings purporting to portray Miss Goolagong in the nude without her knowledge and consent was an infringement of her privacy. The complaints against the *Sun* are upheld.

NOTE

1. Would there have been a remedy at law on these facts?

1   (1899) 80 LT 556 at 557, CA. See also *Blennerhassett v Novelty Sales Services Ltd* (1933) 175 LT Jo 393. On appropriation of personality, see T. Frazer, (1983) 99 LQR 281.
2   *Report of the Health Service Commissioner, Selected Investigations Oct. 1984–Mar. 1985*, p. 35. Liability for invasion of privacy was established in a somewhat similar US case: *Banks v King Features Syndicate* 30 F Supp 352 (1939) (surgical clamp left accidentally in a patient's abdomen; press photograph of the clamp in situ without the patient's knowledge or consent).
3   20th Press Council Report 1973, p. 44.

Melvin v Reid 112 Cal App 285 (1931) 297 Pac 91, District Court of Appeal, 4th District, California

The plaintiff, a prostitute, was acquitted of murder in 1918. Thereafter, she abandoned her former way of life and became a respectable married housewife. She made many friends who did not know of her past. In 1925, the defendants made a film without the plaintiff's knowledge or consent based upon her earlier life and trial and identifying the plaintiff by using her maiden name. The plaintiff sued in the California state courts inter alia for invasion of privacy. The plaintiff appealed against the judgment of the trial court rejecting her claim.

Marks J: ... the use of the incidents from the life of appellant in the moving picture is in itself not actionable. These incidents appeared in the records of her trial for murder, which is a public record, open to perusal of all. . . . Had respondents, in the story of 'The Red Kimono,' stopped with the use of those incidents from the life of appellant which were spread upon the record of her trial, no right of action would have accrued. They went further, and in the formation of the plot used the true maiden name of appellant. If any right of action exists, it arises from the use of this true name in connection with the true incidents from her life together with their advertisements in which they stated that the story of the picture was taken from true incidents in the life of Gabrielle Darley, who was Gabrielle Darley Melvin.

In the absence of any provision of law, we would be loath to conclude that the right of privacy as the foundation of an action in tort, in the form known and recognized in other jurisdictions, exists in California. We find, however, that the . . . right to pursue and obtain happiness is guaranteed to all by the fundamental law of our state [Article 1(1) Calif. Const.]. This right by its very nature includes the right to live free from the unwarranted attack of others upon one's liberty, property and reputation. . . .

. . . [E]ight years before the production of 'The Red Kimono' appellant had abandoned her life of shame, had rehabilitated herself, and had taken her place as a respected and honored member of society. This change having occurred in her life, she should have been permitted to continue its course without having her reputation and social standing destroyed by the publication of the story of her former depravity with no other excuse than the expectation of private gain by the publishers. . . .

We believe that the publication by respondents of the unsavoury incidents in the past life of appellant after she had reformed, coupled with her true name, was not justified by any standard of morals or ethics known to us, and was a direct invasion of her inalienable right guaranteed to her by our Constitution, to pursue and obtain happiness. Whether we call this a right of privacy or give it any other name is immaterial, because it is a right guaranteed by our Constitution that must not be ruthlessly and needlessly invaded by others. . . .

Barnard PJ and **Jennings J** concurred.

Judgment reversed.

NOTES

1. This would have been a case of invasion of privacy in the form of 'unreasonable publicity' for a person's 'private life' according to the classification of invasion of privacy in the *US Restatement, 2d, Torts*.[4] The *Restatement* states that publicity is not actionable if it is on a 'matter of legitimate public concern'. It also states that the private lives of both voluntary (e.g. politicians, actors, criminals) *and* involuntary (e.g. relatives of criminals, victims of crime, witnesses of catastrophes) public figures are such matters 'to some reasonable extent'. Some American courts are less protective

4   Above, p. 914.

of privacy than others. Contrast *Melvin v Reid* with *Sidis v F-R Pub Corpn*.[5] In the US it has been held that there can be no liability for invasion of privacy for publishing a matter of public record: *Cox Broadcasting Corpn v Cohn*.[6] This case may protect freedom of the press unduly. A distinction may be drawn between cases in which information is available for those who go and seek it out in public records and cases in which it is conveniently made available for the public at large in a newspaper or on television. Even though a matter is generally a matter of public knowledge, much distress may also be caused by repeated invasions of privacy.[7] An interesting case in this regard is recorded by Paton-Smith[8] as follows:

> 'The "practical obscurity" of much public record information is amply demonstrated by the success of Pauline Parker in establishing a new life in Britain, until her recent exposure by the media. In 1954, at the age of sixteen, Parker became a focus of media attention after she and her friend Juliet Hulme bashed Parker's mother to death with a half-brick. After serving a five-year prison sentence, Parker changed her name and completed a Bachelor of Arts degree at Auckland University, where fellow students were unaware of her past. She moved to Britain in 1965, settled in a quiet village, and put her past behind her. Despite the success in 1994 of the feature movie Heavenly Creatures, which revived public interest in the killing, her present identity and whereabouts remained a secret until a New Zealand journalist found her new name on the public record and tracked her down. Clearly the mere presence of her change of name on the public record did not prevent her from leading a quiet, private life, until the media publicised her new identity.'

2. There would have been no liability in defamation in English law in *Melvin v Reid* because justification, or truth, is always a defence.[9] 'Newspapers are free in this country to rake up a man's forgotten past, and ruin him deliberately in the process, without incurring tortious liability.'[10] In 1981, the Press Council severely censured the *Lancashire Evening Post* for a 'sordid piece of journalism' when it recalled details about a woman murdered several years earlier and published her parents' name and address, noting that the parents had refused to answer the newspaper's questions.[11] In most Australian jurisdictions truth is only a defence to defamation if the publication is for the 'public benefit' or in the 'public interest'.[12] Dworkin[13] suggests that if such a limitation were introduced into English law, cases of invasion of privacy of the 'unjustified publicity' kind which were not controlled by law would be 'reduced to negligible proportions'.

3. Under the Rehabilitation of Offenders Act 1974, a conviction leading to a sentence of no more than 30 months' imprisonment becomes 'spent' after a period of time ranging from 5 to 10 years. The effect of a conviction becoming 'spent' is, *inter alia*, that the convicted person (i) need not reveal it in judicial proceedings or for employment or insurance purposes and (ii) may recover in defamation against a person who reveals the conviction provided that he proves that the publication is made 'with malice'.[14] There are some exceptions. For a case in which malice was not shown, see

---

5 113 F 2d 806 (2d Circ, 1940) (a cruel 'where are they now' article on a failed childhood prodigy; no liability).
6 420 US 469 (1975) (name of a rape victim discovered in court records and broadcast on TV).
7 See *R v Broadcasting Complaints Commission, ex p Granada Television*, below, p. 997.
8 (1998) 61 MLR 318, 327. Footnotes omitted.
9 But see the Rehabilitation of Offenders Act 1974, n. 3 on this page.
10 Street, *Torts* (8th edn, 1988), p. 405.
11 27th/28th Reports, 1980/81, p. 184. For other 'raking up the past' cases, see ibid., pp. 108, 173.
12 See Fleming, *The Law of Torts* (8th edn, 1992), p. 557.
13 2 U Tas LR 418 at 425 (1967).
14 s. 8.

Herbage v Pressdram Ltd.[15] A case that does not fall within the 1974 Act may nonetheless infringe the Press Code of Practice. The *North-West Daily Mail* was condemned for the prominent way in which it reported that a man had lost his job when it became known he had been convicted of a murder some 14 years earlier.[16]

4. In *Re X (A Minor) (Wardship: Jurisdiction)*,[17] Lord Denning noted that a dead person could not be defamed:

> 'Suppose the mother of the child were to bring an action for defamation on the ground that the passages were untrue and a gross libel on her dead husband. Many might think she should be able to prevent the publication, especially as it would bring such grief and distress to his relatives, and, in addition, emotional damage to his child. But the law of defamation does not permit any such proceedings. It says simply that no action lies for a libel on a dead man: on the ground that on balance it is in the public interest that no such action should lie: see *R v Topham* (1791) 4 Term Rep 126; *R v Ensor* (1887) 3 TLR 366.

The Calcutt Committee rejected a suggestion that a right of action be allowed to close relatives for defamation of the dead:[18]

> 'However, distress and hurt feelings are central to defamation claims; a dead person can have no hurt feelings. In practice, the most immediate impact is upon the grieving relatives. The truth would be even more difficult than usual to establish in such cases. Problems would also arise over the discovery of documents. Furthermore, any change in the law would need to include clear guidance on the length of time after death during which a person could be libelled and whether any time limit should start from the events referred to or from the death of the individual. Some of the problems are illustrated by the play which falsely alleged, some years after his death, that Sir Winston Churchill had been responsible for the death of the Polish exiled leader, General Sikorski, during the Second World War. A time limit would have to be set, if only to permit research by historians. We do not consider that extending the law of defamation to cover the dead would provide a practical solution to intrusions into privacy.
>
> . . . We consider, however, that the immediate family of a person who is recently dead should be entitled to have recourse for intrusive press coverage, but only insofar as the intrusion infringes their own privacy. Stories about the private lives of the recently dead and their immediate families, and the reporting methods used to obtain those stories, should fall within the scope of the proposed expanded code of practice [for journalists].'

5. Christine Keeler had been a prominent figure in the Profumo Affair in the early 1960s. In spite of a request by her, several newspapers published her new name and address when she married several years later. The Press Council[19] considered that her request had been 'a reasonable one' and regretted 'that this was either overlooked or disregarded by a number of newspaper editors'. The complainant 'told the Council that from the Saturday afternoon on which her whereabouts were discovered by the Press, until the following Monday afternoon, reporters and photographers were almost continually outside her house. Repeated requests that she and her husband should pose for photographs were refused'. Eventually the photographers went away after Miss Keeler and her husband agreed to walk from the house to their car while photographs were taken. The Council did not comment specifically upon this harassment but noted that it 'was inevitable that Miss Keeler's marriage should be

---

15 [1984] 2 All ER 769, CA.
16 Press Council Press Release, 17 May 1988. The report caused the family distress and made re-employment unlikely. The case was decided under the Press Council's Declaration of Principle on Privacy.
17 [1975] Fam 47. For the facts, see Neill LJ in the *Central Independent Television plc* case, below, p. 951.
18 Report, p. 30.
19 13th Report 1966, p. 95.

950   *The right to privacy*

reported as a matter of public interest'. Would these facts give a remedy in English law? Should they?

6. The Press Council has ruled upon a lot of complaints about the revelation of current information about a person's life. In one case[20] the *Sunday Mercury* was censured for revealing, contrary to a coroner's request, the name of a married mother who had had an affair with a man who had committed suicide. The woman then committed suicide herself, apparently because of the revelation. In another case, the Council censured the *Daily Mail* for revealing 'the name, age and school of a six year old girl from whom her parents had kept the opinion of doctors that she would die from a rare blood disease before she reached teen-age'.[1]

In 1977, the Council[2] rejected a complaint that the *Daily Mail* had invaded the privacy of Ms Maureen Colquhoun (then an MP, later defeated in the 1979 election) by revealing in its Diary that Ms Colquhoun had left her matrimonial home to share a house with a close woman friend. Applying its Declaration of Principle on Privacy,[3] the Council considered that whereas her status as an MP would not by itself have justified the story, the fact that Ms Colquhoun was an MP 'who has taken a very strong stand on feminist issues and has not been loath to publicise her views upon them' did. It brought the story into 'the area of those matters which the public is entitled to know as being capable of affecting the performance of her public duties or affecting public confidence in her views as a Member of Parliament'. Recently, the Press Complaints Commission has upheld complaints by public figures of revelations of their private lives where there was no public interest justification. In two cases, it found that articles revealing publishing detailed accounts of the sexual activities two *Coronation Street* TV stars could not be justified on this ground or on the basis that the actresses had placed this aspect of their public lives in the public domain.[4] The Commission also upheld a complaint by the Prime Minister and Mrs Blair about an article in the *Daily Sport* entitled 'Horny Blair', with accompanying photograph, about their son, aged under 16, kissing a girl at a party.[5]

7. Under the Supreme Court Act 1981, ss. 124 and 125 entitle members of the public to inspect and obtain copies of wills admitted to probate, in the interests of persons who might have a claim under a will or the intestacy laws. For an unsuccessful attempt in Parliament to restrict by law the publication in the media of the details of wills, see the suggestion by Sir Anthony Meyer in 1975.[6] In the public opinion survey conducted for the Younger Committee[7] publication of the details of a large legacy left to a person was regarded by most people as an invasion of privacy that ought to

---

20 6th Report 1959, p. 30.
  1 9th Report 1962, p. 36. Cf. the case in which a newspaper revealed the name of a 16-year-old girl whose mother had hanged herself after her son had committed suicide: Press Complaints Commission, Report No. 46, April–June 1999, p. 16 (breach of Code, clause 6 (protection of children)).
  2 24th Report 1977, p. 72.
  3 The Declaration preceded the present Press Code of Practice. A public interest defence was rejected in another case concerning the MP Ms Clare Short: Press Complaints Commission Report No. 1, Jan.–June 1991, p. 9. In that case, the *News of the World* had interviewed Ms Short's former boy-friend and published a story headed "MP Clare's Ex-Boyfriend was Gun Murder Victim", in which his convictions for serious criminal offences were revealed. The Press Complaints Commission could find no public interest reason for this story.
  4 Complaints against the *News of the World* and the *Sunday Sport*: Press Complaints Commission Report No 49, Jan.–March 1999, p. 15, and ibid., No. 51, July–Sept. 2000, p. 5 (breaches of PCC Code, clause 3).
  5 Press Complaints Commission Report No 49, Jan.–March 2000, p. 5.
  6 895 HC Deb, 14 July 1975, col. 1059.
  7 Report, p. 238.

be prohibited by law. The Press Complaints Commission has issued guidance to the press on the treatment and identification of National Lottery winners.[8]

8. In a case of false attribution, the Press Council[9] upheld a complaint against the *Daily Express* in respect of the publication of 'an article on abortion purporting to have been written by Labour MP Mrs Helene Hayman, when in fact she was not the author and was not consulted about the presentation of her views in that way'. The *Express* had telephoned Mrs Hayman and asked for comments on the then current controversy in Parliament on abortion. Mrs Hayman's comments were used as the basis for an article under her name without her knowledge or consent that they would be used in this way. Had Mrs Hayman written the article, she would have presented her views in a very different way. 'The Council strongly criticised the practice of presenting interviews as if they were the personal contribution of the interviewee'. Would there have been a remedy for defamation in this case? Or for the tort of passing off?[10] In the US this would have been a case of invasion of privacy by placing a person in a 'false light' in the sense of the *Restatement, 2d, Torts*.[11]

(D) COURT JURISDICTION TO PROTECT MINORS

R v Central Independent Television plc [1994] Fam 192, Court of Appeal

The defendant company was responsible for a series of television programmes called 'Scotland Yard' that depicted the work of the police. One programme in the series concerned the investigation by the Obscene Publications Squad of a man who was eventually convicted of offences involving indecency with young boys and sentenced to six years' imprisonment. When the plaintiff saw a trailer of the programme, she recognised the man as her former husband and the father of her daughter, then five years old. In order to avoid potential harm to the daughter, who knew nothing of her father's offences, the plaintiff sought to have the programme altered so as to prevent it being possible to identify the man as her father. Following negotiations, the defendant agreed to remove from the broadcast any picture showing the exterior or interior of the plaintiff's house where the man had been arrested and to exclude pictures of the plaintiff and her daughter. When the defendant refused to agree to obscure pictures of the man so that he could not be recognised, the plaintiff obtained an injunction from Kirkwood J to the effect that the programme could only be broadcast if 'moving pictures of the father are obscured'. The Court of Appeal unanimously allowed an appeal by the defendant.

> **Neill LJ:**... The jurisdiction of the court to protect minors has been recognised for many centuries. The basis of the jurisdiction was explained ... by Lord Halsbury LC in *Barnado v McHugh* [1891] AC 388, 395:
>
> > '[A court of equity] interferes for the protection of infants, qua infants, by virtue of the prerogative which belongs to the Crown as parens patriae, and the exercise of which is delegated to the Great Seal....'
>
> The law which restricts the publication of information relating to proceedings in private is now statutory. Section 12(1) of the Administration of Justice Act 1960 ... provides ...:

---

8   PCC Press Release, 4 April 1995. For a Press Council case on unwanted publicity for football pool winners, see 13th Report 1966, p. 80.

9   23rd Report 1976, p. 111.

10 See above, p. 915.

11 Above, p. 914. For a 'false light' case in which defamation provided a remedy in English law, see *Fry v Daily Sketch* (1968) Times, 29 June. See also the Press Council ruling in the same case: 15th Report 1968, p. 100.

'The publication of information relating to proceedings before any court sitting in private shall not of itself be contempt of court except in the following cases, that is to say—(*a*) where the proceedings—(i) relate to the exercise of the inherent jurisdiction of the High Court with respect to minors; (ii) are brought under the Children Act 1989; or (iii) otherwise relate wholly or mainly to the maintenance or upbringing of a minor; ...'

Other statutory restrictions on newspaper reports of proceedings affecting children are contained in section 39(1) of the Children and Young Persons Act 1933 ... and in section 49(1) of the Act of 1933, amended by section 10(1) of the Children and Young Persons Act 1969 and Schedule 11 to the Criminal Justice Act 1991.

In *In re F (A Minor)* [1977] Fam 58 ... in the context of contempt proceedings to which section 12 of the Act of 1960 applied the Court of Appeal was careful to confine the protection of the ward to 'information relating to the wardship proceedings.'

In several cases decided in the last 10 years, however, the jurisdiction to protect the ward has been exercised on a somewhat wider basis. In *In re X (A Minor) (Wardship:Injunction)* [1984] 1 WLR 1422 the ward's mother had achieved notoriety in 1968 when, as a child [aged 11], she had been found guilty of the manslaughter of two small boys [aged 3 and 4]. On her release from prison she changed her name. In May 1984 the mother gave birth to a child and almost immediately the local authority for the area in which the mother was living applied for the child to be made a ward of court.... In July 1984 the birth came to the attention of a newspaper which wished to publish an article about the mother, though they offered undertakings that the new name of the mother and the names of the ward and other relatives would not be published. In the light of these undertakings the judge refused to make an order to prevent the publication of the fact that 'as Mary Bell' she had had a daughter....

A few days later, however, the newspaper made a further application to the court contending that there was no jurisdiction to prevent publication of material which might identify Mary Bell by her new name and thus the ward. In the course of his judgment Balcombe J. referred to the decision of the Court of Appeal in *In re F* [1977] Fam 58 and concluded that without an order of the court there could be no objection to the publication of the present identity of Mary Bell or the child, or of the child's father. He then turned to consider whether he was entitled to prevent publication in the exercise of the wardship injunction. He continued, at pp. 1425–1426:

'it seems to me that I have jurisdiction in this case to make an order which has the effect of prohibiting publication by anybody of details which would enable the present identity of Mary Bell and her child to become known....

I come next to the decision in *In re C (A Minor)(Wardship:Medical Treatment)(No 2)* [1990] Fam 39. In that case the child concerned was terminally ill. A national newspaper wished to publish an article relating to her care and treatment, though it was accepted on behalf of the newspaper that nothing should be published which might identify the child or her parents. The newspaper did wish, however, to refer in the article to the hospital and to the medical practitioners and staff who were looking after the child, and to be free to carry out interviews with the staff. It was said that in view of her condition the child herself would never be capable of understanding anything written about her, and that if an injunction in wide terms were granted it would have the effect of protecting from criticism or comment public authorities which should be accountable to the public for the decisions they take. Nevertheless, the Court of Appeal imposed an injunction which prevented the newspaper from identifying those who had looked after the child in the past, as well as those who were currently caring for her and from soliciting information from them. Nicholls L.J. said, at p. 55, that the terms imposed represented:

'a sensible balance, in a case of considerable public importance, between on the one hand the right of the public to be kept informed of what is going on in court and, on the other hand, the need for the welfare of baby C not to be put at risk by public identification of her, her parents and those who are or have been involved in her care....'

[After referring to *In re M and N (Minors)* (see below), **Neill LJ** continued:]

In re W [1992] 1 WLR 100 was a similar case. A boy of 15 with a disturbed background, and who had been involved in the past in homosexual activities with older men, had been made a ward of court and placed in the care of a local authority. The local authority decided to foster the boy with two men who had had a stable homosexual relationship with each other for many years. A national newspaper learnt of the placement and wished to publish an article about it. In this case also the Court of Appeal approved the grant of an injunction, though to a more limited extent than had the judge. It was held that the newspaper should be allowed to include in the article all the ingredients of the story which were of public concern, but that the article should not identify the boy or his foster parents nor give any other particulars which might directly lead to the identification either of him or of the foster parents. It was in this context that in *In re W* I set out the guidelines which should be taken into account when in a case involving a ward the court is asked to restrain the publication of material relating to him.

The crucial point about these cases, however, was that the publications restrained related to the care and upbringing of children over whose welfare the court was exercising a supervisory role. It is true that the restraints imposed went further than to prevent only publication of accounts of the wardship proceedings which had already taken place, but the activities restrained were not only likely to affect the welfare of the ward himself but also the ability of the carers to carry out their obligations to the court for the care of the ward. The court itself therefore had an interest in the integrity of its own wardship jurisdiction.

The present case, however, is quite different. The programme was in no way concerned with the care or upbringing of S. Indeed, the present case is much nearer to *In re X (A Minor)(Wardship:Jurisdiction)* [1975] Fam 47. In that case the stepfather of a girl aged 14 made her a ward of court for the purpose of applying for an injunction to restrain the publishers and author of a book which was on the point of publication from publishing it, so long as it contained an account describing the aberrant private activities and practices of the ward's deceased father.

Latey J. granted an injunction on the basis that the book might come to the attention of the ward and that grave injury would be caused to her emotional psychological health. The Court of Appeal discharged the injunction....

In the Court of Appeal Lord Denning M.R. rejected the idea that there was any balancing exercise to be carried out in such a case. He referred to the importance of the freedom of the press and continued, at pp. 58–59:

'... I do not think the wardship jurisdiction should be extended so as to enable the court to stop publication of this book. The relatives of the child must do their best to protect her by doing all they can to see the book does not come into her hands.... In my opinion it would be extending the wardship jurisdiction too far and infringing too much upon the freedom of the press for us to grant an injunction in this case.'

Counsel for Mrs R, however, drew our attention to passages in the judgments of Roskill LJ and Sir John Pennycuick in *In re X* [1975] Fam 47, which suggested that even in that case a balancing exercise had to be carried out and that the court had to weigh the interests of the child against the rights of free speech. Thus ... Sir John Pennycuick ... said ...

'The court must hold a proper balance between the protection of the ward and the rights of outside parties. Specifically, it seems to me, the court must hold a proper balance between the protection of the ward and the right of free publication enjoyed by outside parties and should hesitate long before interfering with that right of free publication. It would be impossible and not, I think, desirable to draw any rigid line beyond which the protection of a ward should not be extended....'

For my part, ... I am unable to accept the proposition that a balancing act has to be carried out in every case where a threatened publication may be likely to affect a ward. In my view the judgments of Roskill LJ and Sir John Pennycuick in *In re X (A Minor)(Wardship: Jurisdiction)* [1975] Fam 47, when read as a whole, do not support so wide a proposition.

A balancing exercise only becomes necessary where the threatened publication touches matters which are of direct concern to the court in its supervisory role over the care and upbringing of the ward. Whether in any particular case the relevant publication is in this category will depend on the facts and on the nature of the publication. In the earlier cases to which I have referred the court was closely concerned with the impact of the threatened publicity on the future care of baby X, of the dying baby C, of the two boys M and N in their new foster homes and of the boy W with his two male foster parents.

In the present case, as I have already observed, the programme had nothing whatever to do with the care or upbringing of S. There was nothing to put in the balance against the freedom to publish. I am reminded of the words of Lord Donaldson of Lymington MR in *In re M and N* [1990] Fam 211, where he said, at p. 231:

> '... I regard injunctive protection of children from publicity which, though inimical to their welfare, is not directed at them or at those who care for them, but is an incidental part of life, as being in a special category ...'

For these reasons I thought it right to uphold the television company's submission that they were entitled to publish the programme in full, and that there was no legal bar to prevent them from including pictures of the place of arrest.

On the other hand, I would wish to applaud, and to say nothing to discourage, the responsible attitude taken by the television company in this case. They did what they could to reduce the risk of identification and the risk of harm to the welfare of S. One would hope that in similar circumstances others would act in a similar way. The press and broadcasters are entitled to publish the results of criminal proceedings and questions as to what should be left out are in the main a matter for editorial decision. It is always to be remembered, however, that the families of those convicted have a heavy burden to bear and the effect of publicity on small children may be very serious....

The motives which impel judges to assume a power to balance freedom of speech against other interests are almost always understandable and humane on the facts of the particular case before them. Newspapers are sometimes irresponsible and their motives in a market economy cannot be expected to be unalloyed by considerations of commercial advantage. Publication may cause needless pain, distress and damage to individuals or harm to other aspects of the public interest. But a freedom which is restricted to what judges think to be responsible or in the public interest is no freedom. Freedom means the right to publish things which government and judges, however well motivated, think should not be published. It means the right to say things which 'right-thinking people' regard as dangerous or irresponsible. This freedom is subject only to clearly defined exceptions laid down by common law or statute.

Furthermore, in order to enable us to meet our international obligations under the Convention for the Protection of Human Rights and Fundamental Freedoms (1953) (Cmd 8969), it is necessary that any exceptions should satisfy the tests laid down in article 10(2).... It cannot be too strongly emphasised that outside the established exceptions, or any new ones which Parliament may enact in accordance with its obligations under the Convention, there is no question of balancing freedom of speech against other interests. It is a trump card which always wins.

This is why I respectfully think that Lord Denning MR was right in *In re X (A Minor)(Wardship:Jurisdiction)* [1975] Fam 47 when he said that the wardship jurisdiction did not permit the courts to balance the competing interests of the child and the freedom of the press. The exceptions to freedom of speech were, he said, at p. 58F 'already staked out by the rules of law.' Section 12(1)(*a*) of the Administration of Justice Act 1960 prohibits the publication of information relating to a private court hearing in proceedings which concern children. It does not however apply to information which relates to the child but not to the proceedings: see *In re F (orse A) (A Minor) (Publication of Information)* [1977] Fam 58. It would be wrong, said Lord Denning MR in *In re X (A Minor) (Wardship:Jurisdiction)* [1975] Fam 47, 58 to extend the law:

> 'so as to give the judges a power to stop publication of true matter whenever the judges— or any particular judge—thought that it was in the interests of a child to do so....'

It is true that in a series of decisions commencing with *In re C (A Minor) (Wardship:Medical Treatment) (No 2)* [1990] Fam 39 the courts have, without any statutory or, so far as I can see, other previous authority, assumed a power to create by injunction what is in effect a right of privacy for children. The power is said to be based on the powers of the Crown as parens patriae and the 'machinery for its exercise' is the wardship jurisdiction: see Butler-Sloss LJ in *In re M and N (Minors) (Wardship:Publication of Information)* [1990] Fam 211, 223. The novelty of this jurisdiction is shown by the fact that as recently as 1977, Scarman LJ in *In re F* [1977] Fam 58, 99 was able to say that apart from section 12(1)(*a*) of the Administration of Justice Act 1960, 'the ward enjoys no greater protection against unwelcome publicity than other children.' In *In re M and N* Butler-Sloss LJ said, at p. 224, that the power to restrain publication was needed because:

'There has, since *In re X* [1975] Fam 47, been an upsurge in investigative journalism with an interest in situations affecting children which has led the media to publish or attempt to publish more widely and more frequently than ever contemplated in the early 1970s.'

I would not for a moment dispute either this perception or the fact that a right of privacy may be a legitimate exception to freedom of speech. After all, other countries also party to the Convention have a right of privacy for grown-ups as well. But we do not and there may be room for constitutional argument as to whether in a matter so fundamentally trenching upon the freedom of the press as the creation of a right of privacy, it would not be more appropriate for the remedy to be provided by the legislature rather than the judiciary. In recent years Parliament has not been slow to act in the interests of children. However that may be, the existence of a jurisdiction to restrain publication of information concerning a child and its upbringing is no longer open to dispute in this court.

But this new jurisdiction is concerned only with the privacy of children and their upbringing. It does not extend, as Lord Donaldson of Lymington MR made clear in *In re M and N*, at p. 231B to 'injunctive protection of children from publicity which, though inimical to their welfare, is not directed at them or those who care for them.' It therefore cannot apply to publication of the fact that the child's father has been convicted of a serious offence, however distressing it may be for the child to be identified as the daughter of such a man. If such a jurisdiction existed, it could be exercised to restrain the identification of any convicted criminal who has young children. It may be that the decision of Balcombe J in *X County Council v A* [1985] 1 All ER 53 can be brought within Lord Donaldson of Lymington MR's language because the child's mother, at whose past the intended publication was directed, was actually caring for the child at the time of the application. But the events in question had happened long before the child was born. The publication was not directly concerned with the child or its upbringing, and for my part I think that the judge, for wholly commendable reasons, was asserting a jurisdiction which did not exist....

Waite LJ delivered a concurring judgment.

NOTES

1. The *Central Independent Television plc* case concerned the prerogative power of the Crown *parens patriae*, exercisable through the courts, to protect children. This power is normally used in respect of a child whom a court has decided to make a ward of court. As the present case illustrates, it may also be invoked to request a court order to protect other children. Although the power was invoked unsuccessfully in the present case, the courts have in several cases in recent years used their wardship jurisdiction to make orders protecting children in cases raising privacy or related issues, as several of the cases considered by Neill LJ indicate. In the *Central Independent Television plc* case, the Court of Appeal drew a distinction between cases where the publication that is challenged contains information (e.g. concerning the child's medical treatment) that has a direct bearing upon a child and his welfare, for which the courts are responsible, and cases where the publication has a less direct connection (e.g. where personal details are given about a close relative). In the former kind of case, the prerogative jurisdiction *parens patriae* is available to censor a publication provided that on balance this should be done. In other kinds of cases, such as the *Central Independent Television plc* case, no balancing act is called for: freedom of expression simply prevails. The guidelines applicable when considering the former kind of case were set out by Neill LJ in the earlier case of *Re W (a minor)*[12] as follows:

---

12 [1992] 1 All ER 794, CA. See also *Re H-S (Minors: Protection of Identity)* [1994] 3 All ER 390, CA (parent could write in press about his sex change operation, subject to restrictions to safeguard the identity of the children).

'(1) The court will attach great importance to safeguarding the freedom of the press....

(2) The court will also take account of art 10 of the Convention for the Protection of Human Rights and Fundamental Freedoms....

(3) These freedoms, however, are subject to exceptions, which include restrictions upon publication which are imposed for the protection of children.

(4) In considering whether to impose a restriction upon publication to protect a ward of court the court has to carry out a balancing exercise. It is to be noted, as Butler-Sloss LJ pointed out in *Re M and anor (minors)(wardship: freedom of publication)* [1990] 1 All ER 205 at 210, [1990] Fam 211 at 223, that: "In this situation the welfare of the child is not the paramount consideration."

(5) In carrying out the balancing exercise the court will weigh the need to protect the ward from harm against the right of the press (or other outside parties) to publish or to comment. An important factor will be the nature and extent of the public interest in the matter which it is sought to publish. A distinction can be drawn between cases of mere curiosity and cases where the press are giving information or commenting about a subject of genuine public interest.

(6) It is to be anticipated that in almost every case the public interest in favour of publication can be satisfied without any identification of the ward to persons other than those who already know the facts. It seems to me, however, that the risk of *some* wider identification may have to be accepted on occasions if the story is to be told in a manner which will engage the interest of the general public.

(7) Any restraint on publication which is imposed is intended to protect the ward and those who care for the ward from the risk of harassment. The restraint must therefore be in clear terms and be no wider than is necessary to achieve the purpose for which it is imposed. It also follows that, save perhaps in an exceptional case, the ward cannot be protected from any distress which he may be caused by reading the publication himself.'

2. A feature of the *Central Independent Television plc* case is that the Court of Appeal accepted the defendant's submission that it was 'entitled to publish the programme in full and that there was no legal bar to prevent them from including pictures of the place of arrest' (Neill LJ). In fact, the programme was broadcast without any of the deletions as to the place of arrest, etc, to which the defendant had agreed during negotiations. What is remarkable about this statement by the Court of Appeal is that, as the Court was aware, the pictures inside the house that were included in the film had been obtained without consent by means of a concealed camera and sound recording equipment. An action in trespass in respect of this entry by deceit was dropped when the defendant agreed in negotiations to exclude the material thus illegally obtained. Commenting on the case, J. Gardiner,[13] states:

'The pictures of the place of arrest were obtained by a trespass and included pictures and words of people not concerned in the arrest at all.

These pictures were then included in a documentary film about the work of the police. The fact of the suspect's conviction and sentence was the culmination of a thirty-minute film broadcast some eighteen months after the arrest. The local newspaper had not found the integrity of its contemporaneous report of the proceedings compromised in any way by omitting reference to the man's identity. As far as Mrs R is aware, no other media person had found her ex-husband's case of any interest to the general public.

Neill LJ's comment concerning the television company's entitlement to publish the programme in full suggests that the Court of Appeal will never be prepared to intervene to prevent publication of "fly-on-the-wall" film material. If the publication of such material really has anything to do with the freedom of the press, then one wonders whether it is now time for press freedoms to be defined and limited: not for the protection only of politicians and other public entertainers, but also of real people doing their best to bring up children and live their lives out of range of the apparently insatiable information industry.'

---

13 (1995) 145 NLJ 225, 226.

The Broadcasting Complaints Commission dismissed a complaint of invasion of privacy brought by the plaintiff in the *Central Independent Television plc* case, ruling that the broadcast of the full programme was justified in the public interest.

2. The Mary Bell case to which Neill LJ refers reached the courts again when the former Mary Bell sold her story to an author who published a book based upon it.[14] This generated renewed media interest and the possibility arose of Scottish newspapers, which were not subject to the court order made in the English High Court in *Re X (A Minor) (Wardship: Injunction)*, which applied only in England and Wales, publishing the identity of the former Mary Bell's child in Scotland. An interdict was granted by a Scottish court to prevent this happening.[15] The court rejected arguments that a considerable amount of information about the case had already been published in the press; that the press and her neighbours knew who and where Mary Bell was; and that the child had recently become aware of her mother's crime.[16] Instead it preferred on balance arguments that further public knowledge of the child's identity would be emotionally disturbing to the child and that there was a risk of physical injury to her and of demonstrations leading to public disorder if the location of the child's home became widely known. The same Scottish-English dimension to cases arose in 2000, when an injunction was granted by the English courts to prohibit the publication of a story about drug-taking by the son of Jack Straw, the Home Secretary. When, in the absence of an interdict, the story was published in the Scottish press, the English court injunction was lifted because the information was now in the public domain.[17]

4. See also *Re Z (a minor) (freedom of publication)*[18] in which, without disagreeing with *R v Central Independent Television plc*, Ward LJ approached the question of court restrictions on publicity concerning children on the different, Children Act 1989, basis of parental responsibility.

5. In *Venables v News Group Newspapers Ltd*[19] an injunction was granted under the law of breach of confidence to continue beyond the age of 18 a ban on media publicity about the two persons convicted of a notorious child murder.

(E) BREACH OF COPYRIGHT

Williams v Settle [1960] 1 WLR 1072, [1960] 2 All ER 806, Court of Appeal

The defendant, a professional photographer, took the photographs at the plaintiff's wedding. Two years later, when the plaintiff's wife was pregnant, her father was murdered. The case attracted publicity and, when the national press came looking for photographs, the defendant sold them copies of the wedding photographs. He did so without the knowledge or consent of the plaintiff, who held the copyright. One of the photographs—a family group with the father in it—was published five days after the wife gave birth with captions identifying the persons in it. One newspaper gave a particular description of the plaintiff's wife. The plaintiff successfully sued the defendant for breach of copyright in the county court. He was awarded £1,000 damages. The defendant's appeal to the Court of Appeal on the ground that the county

---

14 See G. Sereny, *Cries Unheard* (1998)

15 See note, (1998) 23 *Communications Law* 155.

16 Mary Bell was forced to reveal her identity to her daughter after journalists had camped outside the family home at the time of the publication of the book.

17 Loc. cit. at n. 15.

18 [1995] 1 All ER 961, CA (injunction to prevent media from revealing identity of handicapped child receiving special education care and treatment, despite mother's wishes that it be discharged).

19 Below, p. 973.

958   *The right to privacy*

court had lacked jurisdiction to award such a high amount of damages was rejected. The following extract concerns the appeal on the amount of damages.

Sellers LJ: In the present action the judge was clearly justified, in the circumstances in which the defendant, in breach of the plaintiff's copyright, handed these photographs to the press knowing the use to which they were going to be put, in awarding substantial and heavy damages of a punitive nature. The power so to do, quite apart from the ordinary law of the land, is expressly given by statute. By section 17(3) of the Copyright Act 1956, it is provided: 'Where in an action under this section an infringement of copyright is proved or admitted, and the court, having regard (in addition to all other material considerations) to—(a) the flagrancy of the infringement, and (b) any benefit shown to have accrued to the defendant by reason of the infringement, is satisfied that effective relief would not otherwise be available to the plaintiff, the court, in assessing damages for the infringement, shall have power to award such additional damages by virtue of this subsection as the court may consider appropriate in the circumstances.' It seems that this is not a case where there is any effective relief which could be given. The benefit which can be shown to have accrued to the defendant is meagre . . . It is the flagrancy of the infringement which calls for heavy damages, because this was a scandalous matter in the circumstances, which I do not propose to elaborate and about which I do not propose to express a view. It is sufficient to say that it was a flagrant infringement of the right of the plaintiff, and it was scandalous conduct and in total disregard not only of the legal rights of the plaintiff regarding copyright but of his feelings and his sense of family dignity and pride. It was an intrusion into his life, deeper and graver than an intrusion into a man's property.

Willmer and **Harman LJJ** delivered concurring judgments.

Appeal dismissed.

NOTES

1. The plaintiff also obtained £52 10s damages and costs from the *Daily Express*, an apology and undertakings from the *Daily Mail* and a ruling in his favour from the Press Council.[20] The power to award 'additional damages' in s. 17(3) of the 1956 Act has been re-enacted in similar terms in s. 97(2), Copyright, Designs and Patents Act 1988.
2. The first owner of the copyright in a 'work', including a photograph or letter, is its author (other than in the case of an employee acting in the course of his employment): Copyright, Designs and Patents Act 1988, s. 11. A person 'who for private and domestic purposes commissions the taking of a photograph or the making of a film has, where copyright subsists in the resulting work, the right not to have', *inter alia*, 'copies of the work issued to the public' or 'the work exhibited or shown in public'.[1] This right may, however, be waived, by contract or otherwise.[2]
3. The *Daily Mail* was sued for breach of copyright by Princess Margaret's lady in waiting for publishing photographs taken by her at a private house party which showed Princess Margaret dressed as Mae West and a Valkyrie and her friend Mr Llewellyn as a wizard.[3] The photographs had been taken from the plaintiff's home by her son and sold to the *Daily Mail* without her knowledge or consent. A court order was made against the defendant requiring the return of the photographs. Damages were agreed out of court.

20 See [1960] 1 WLR 1074–1075. On the case, see (1961) 77 LQR 12 and G. Dworkin, (1961) 24 MLR 185. On the public interest defence available in breach of copyright cases, see the *Woolgar* case, below, p. 982.
1 1988 Act, s. 85.
2 1988 Act, s. 87.
3 *Lady Anne Tennant v Associated Newspapers Group Ltd* [1979] FSR 298.

See also *Barrymore v News Group Newspapers Ltd*[4] in which the *Sun* printed extracts from letters written by a TV personality, 'in which he plainly owns the copyright', to a homosexual friend who had given them to the newspaper. Jacobs J stated:

'The Sun newspaper, manifestly knowing that what they were doing was likely to be a breach of copyright, nonetheless decided to publish portions of those letters. The financial consequences will no doubt be a matter for the court to decide in due course. I can say no more at this stage other than that newspapers which think that they can pay their way out of breach of copyright may find it more expensive than it is worth to print the material.'[5]

(F) BREACH OF CONFIDENCE

Prince Albert v Strange (1849) 1 Mac and G 25, 1 H & TW 1, Court of Chancery

Queen Victoria and the plaintiff had for their private amusement made etchings of their children and other subjects of personal interest. The defendant obtained copies and planned to exhibit them and to publish a catalogue listing and describing the etchings for profit. The etchings had been kept privately by the Royal Family, although a few copies had been given to friends. The plates for the etchings had been entrusted to a printer in Windsor for him to make further impressions. It appeared that, without the printer's knowledge or consent, one of his employees had made unauthorised copies of the etchings and the defendant had purchased these. The plaintiff obtained an injunction preventing the exhibition and the publication of the catalogue. In these proceedings, the defendant, who accepted that the exhibition should not proceed, applied to have the injunction amended to allow him to publish the catalogue. He appealed to the Lord Chancellor against the refusal of his application by Knight Bruce V-C[5a] who had referred in his judgment to 'sordid spying into the privacy of domestic life':

Lord Cottenham LC: . . . the Defendant insists that he is entitled to publish a catalogue of the etchings, that is to say, to publish a description or list of works or compositions of another, made and kept for the private use of that other, the publication of which was never authorised, and the possession of copies of which could only have been obtained by surreptitious and improper means. It was said by one of the learned counsel for the Defendant, that the injunction must rest upon the ground of property or breach of trust; both appear to me to exist. The property of an author or composer of any work, whether of literature, art, or science, in such work unpublished and kept for his private use or pleasure, cannot be disputed . . . the Plaintiff is entitled to the injunction of this Court to protect him against the invasion of such right and interest by the Defendant, which the publication of any catalogue would undoubtedly be; but this case by no means depends solely upon the question of property, for a breach of trust, confidence, or contract, would of itself entitle the Plaintiff to an injunction . . . and upon the evidence on behalf of the Plaintiff, and in the absence of any explanation on the part of the Defendant, I am bound to assume that the possession of the etchings by the Defendant . . . has its foundation in a breach of trust, confidence, or contract . . . upon this ground also I think the Plaintiff's title to the injunction sought to be discharged, fully established. The observations of Vice-Chancellor Wigram in *Tipping v Clarke* ((1843) 2 Hare 383) are applicable to this part of the case. He says: 'Every clerk employed in a merchant's counting-house is under an implied contract that he will not make public that which he learns in the execution of his duty as clerk. If the Defendant has obtained copies of books, it would very probably be by means of some clerk or agent of the Plaintiff; and if he availed himself surreptitiously of the information which he could not have had except from a person guilty of a breach of contract in communicating it, I think he could not be permitted to avail himself of that breach of contract.

4   [1997] FSR 600, Ch D. See further on this case, below, p. 972.
5   At 601.
5a (1848) 2 De G and Sm 652 at 698.

. . . This was the opinion of Lord Eldon, expressed in the case of *Wyatt v Wilson* in 1820, respecting an engraving of George the Third during his illness, in which, according to a note with which I have been favoured by Mr. Cooper, he said, 'If one of the late king's physicians had kept a diary of what he heard and saw, this court would not, in the king's lifetime, have permitted him to print and publish it.'

Motion refused.

NOTES[6]

1. The Younger Committee[7] considered that the 'law on breach of confidence offers the most effective protection of privacy in the whole of our existing law, civil or criminal'. In its opinion 'the extent of its potential effectiveness is not widely recognised'. Although this has been shown to be true by recent cases, the value of breach of confidence as a remedy is inevitably limited in that it only concerns informational privacy; it does not extend to physical intrusion. Breach of confidence was referred to the Law Commission, which produced its Report in 1981. It recommended that the present law of breach of confidence be replaced by a statutory tort of breach of a duty of confidence, binding on the Crown as well as others.[8] However, the 'Government do not propose, particularly in the light of recent judgments which restate that law, to give its implementation high priority at present'.[9] The Calcutt Committee recommended against the introduction of a statutory tort of breach of confidence, preferring to allow the judge-made law to develop.[10] Although the Law Commission accepted the close relationship between breach of confidence and privacy where confidential information is involved, it stressed that the two are not identical. For example, the obligation of confidence will not always be owed to the person whose privacy is at risk.[11]

2. *Prince Albert v Strange* is the seminal case in the development of the equitable doctrine of breach of confidence. Insofar as judgment was given for the plaintiff on a basis other than that of his property right in the etchings, was it given purely because of breach of confidence or because of an implied term in the rogue employee's contract of employment? As the cases Lord Cottenham refers to at the end of the above extract indicate, the common law has, in the absence of an express term, implied a term in a contract of employment by which an employee may not divulge confidential information obtained during employment to any third party without consent while he is still employed and thereafter. In practice this has mainly been relevant (as has the law of breach of confidence) in the context of trade secrets, but it can apply to more personal matters, as the unreported case of *Wyatt v Wilson*,[12] indicates. The conditions of service of members of the Royal Household contain a confidentiality clause.[13]

---

6 See on breach of confidence, H. Fenwick and G. Phillipson, [1996] 55 CLJ 447; F. Gurry, *Breach of Confidence* (1984, reissued in 1991); and M. Richardson, (1994) 19 MULR 673; Meagher, Gummow and Lehane, *Equity Doctrines and Remedies* (3rd edn, 1992), Chap. 41; And see Law Commission Report on Breach of Confidence (1981), Report No. 110, Cmnd. 8388. On the Law Commission Report, see M. W. Bryan, [1982] PL 188; G. Jones, [1982] CLJ 40; J. Michael, (1981) 131 NLJ 1201; A. M. Tettenborn, (1983) 34 NILQ 248.
7 Report, p. 26.
8 Report No. 110, p. 102.
9 148 HC Deb, 2 March 1989, WA col. 257. The government position has not changed.
10 Report, p. 32.
11 See the Law Commission obituary example, Law Commission Working Paper No. 58, para. 75.
12 Above, on this page.
13 See the Press Council's 2nd Report 1955, p. 35, in connection with a case in which the *Sunday Pictorial* had published the memoirs of the Duke of Edinburgh's valet.

Duchess of Argyll v Duke of Argyll [1967] Ch 302, [1965] 1 All ER 611, [1965] 2 WLR 790, Ungoed-Thomas J

The first defendant, the Duke of Argyll and former husband of the plaintiff, Margaret, Duchess of Argyll, had published in *The People* the first two of a series of articles in which he wrote of their married life. The plaintiff sought injunctions against the first defendant and against the editor and publisher of *The People* to prevent the publication in the remaining articles of 'secrets of the plaintiff relating to her private life, personal affairs or private conduct, communicated to the first defendant in confidence during the subsistence of his marriage to the plaintiff and not hitherto made public property'.

Ungoed-Thomas J: . . . it is clear that the court may restrain breach of confidence arising out of contract or any right to property. The question whether the court's protection is limited to such cases was considered in two authorities to which I shall refer.

[His Lordship discussed *Prince Albert v Strange*,[14] and *Pollard v Photographic Co.*[15] Referring to the latter, he said:]

. . . In that case a photographer, who had taken a negative likeness of a lady to supply her with copies for money, was restrained from selling or exhibiting copies, both on the ground that there was an implied contract not to use the negative for such purposes, and also on the ground that such sale or exhibition was a breach of confidence. . . .

These cases, in my view, indicate (1) that a contract or obligation of confidence need not be expressed but can be implied; (2) that a breach of confidence or trust or faith can arise independently of any right of property or contract other, of course, than any contract which the imparting of the confidence in the relevant circumstances may itself create; (3) that the court in the exercise of its equitable jurisdiction will restrain a breach of confidence independently of any right at law.

. . . Marriage is, of course, far more than a mere legal contract and legal relationship, and even legal status; but it includes legal contract and relationship. If, for the court's protection of confidence and, contrary to my view, the confidence must arise out of a contractual or property relationship, marriage does not lack its contract. It is basically a contract to be and, according to our Christian conception of marriage, to live as man and wife. It has been said that the legal consideration of marriage—that is the promise to become and to remain man and wife—is the highest legal consideration which there is. And there could hardly be anything more intimate or confidential than is involved in that relationship, or than in the mutual trust and confidences which are shared between husband and wife. The confidential nature of the relationship is of its very essence and so obviously and necessarily implicit in it that there is no need for it to be expressed. To express it is superfluous; it is clear to the least intelligent. So it seems to me that confidences between husband and wife during marriage are not excluded from the court's protection by the criteria appearing in the cases to which I have referred. . . .

[His Lordship then considered and distinguished *Rumping v DPP*,[16] in which the House of Lords ruled that an intercepted communication between a husband and wife was admissible in evidence in criminal proceedings against the husband.]

It thus seems to me that the policy of the law, so far from indicating that communication between husband and wife should be excluded from protection against breaches of confidence given by the court in accordance with *Prince Albert v Strange* strongly favours its inclusion, and in view of that policy it can hardly be an objection that such communications are not limited to business matters. . . . if there are communications which should be protected and which the policy of the law recognises should be protected, even to the extent of being a foundation of the old rule making husband and wife incompetent as witnesses against each other, then the court is not to be deterred merely because it is not already provided with fully developed principles, guides, tests, definitions and the full armament for judicial decision. It is sufficient that the court recognises that the communications are confidential, and their publication within the mischief

14 Above, p. 959.
15 (1888) 40 Ch D 345, Ch D.
16 [1964] AC 814, HL.

which the law as its policy seeks to avoid, without further defining the scope and limits of the jurisdiction; and I have no hesitation in this case in concluding that publication of some of the passages complained of is in breach of marital confidence. . . .

Should the plaintiff be denied the injunction which she would otherwise get because she has herself to an extent broken confidence and because she, after the confidences of whose breach she complains, adopted an immoral attitude towards her marriage? A person coming to Equity for relief—and this is equitable relief which the plaintiff seeks—must come with clean hands: but the cleanliness required is to be judged in relation to the relief that is sought.

First, I do not consider that the plaintiff's own articles [written in another Sunday newspaper before the defendant's articles and revealing information about him] justify the objectionable passages in the Duke's articles or, of themselves, should disentitle the plaintiff to the court's protection.

Secondly, with regard to the plaintiff's immorality. . . . [it] is not in my view just that adultery should have retrospective operation on a marriage and not only break the marriage for the future but nullify it for the past. The plaintiff's adultery, repugnant though it be, should not in my view license the husband to broadcast unchecked the most intimate confidences of earlier and happier days.

It is in my view established by *Lord Ashburton v Pape* [1913] 2 Ch 469, in accordance with the references already made to *Prince Albert v Strange*, that an injunction may be granted to restrain the publication of confidential information not only by the person who was a party to the confidence but by other persons into whose possession that information has improperly come.

Injunction granted.

NOTES

1. Breach of confidence was extended in *Argyll v Argyll* to provide a basis for a claim in equity in the absence of any express or implied term in a contract in order to protect confidential information which the policy of the law recognises should be protected, including marital secrets.

2. In *Saltman Engineering Co Ltd v Campbell Engineering Co Ltd*[17] (a trade secrets case), Lord Greene MR stated[18] that, for the law of breach of confidence to apply, the information must have 'the necessary quality of confidence about it, namely, it must not be something which is public property and public knowledge'. The 'public domain' doctrine was applied in *Woodward v Hutchins*.[19] See also *Lennon v News Group Newspapers Ltd*,[20] in which John Lennon was refused an injunction to prevent the publication in the *News of the World* of an article by his former wife about their married life. Distinguishing *Argyll v Argyll*, Lord Denning MR stated:

'The reasoning of that case, it was said, was put on the fact that marriage has been said to be the highest legal consideration and the court will protect the confidences arising out of it.

That may well be in normal marriages, but I cannot say, looking at this case, that either of these two parties have had much regard for the sanctity of marriage. . . . we have been shown a whole series of articles from various newspapers—some by the former wife, Cynthia Lennon, talking to newspapers about their relationships; some by Mr. Lennon himself talking about their relationships—going into the most intimate affairs, accusing one another, obviously just for the satisfaction of the public and, no doubt, for their own reward.

It seems to me as plain as can be that the relationship of these parties has ceased to be their own private affair. They themselves have put it into the public domain.'

---

17 [1963] 3 All ER 413, CA.
18 p. 415.
19 Below, p. 987.
20 [1978] FSR 573, CA. See also *Khashoggi v Smith* (1980) 130 NLJ 168, CA (application by Mrs K for an injunction to prevent publication in the *Daily Mirror* of an article by her former housekeeper refused partly because Mrs K had courted publicity).

Confidential information revealed in open court ceases to be subject to the law of breach of confidence.[1] Court proceedings are generally in public, despite the embarrasment that may result for parties or witnesses.[2] An order for a hearing in camera will only be granted where it is shown that 'the paramount object of securing justice is done would really be rendered doubtful of attainment if the order were not made'.[3]

Although information is in the public domain, questions none the less arise concerning republication or more extensive publication.[4] In *R v Broadcasting Complaints Commission, ex p Granada Television Ltd*,[5] a television company applied for judicial review of a Commission ruling that television programmes, in which images and information about two children in distressing cases had been broadcast without informing the parents, was a breach of relevant broadcasting standards. In both cases there had been previous publicity two to three years earlier. In one case, the programme rebroadcast footage shown earlier of the police investigation of a child's rape. In the other case, the story of the child's death from an allergy had been told earlier in a local newspaper and in a medical journal. When the application for judicial review was rejected, it was held *inter alia*, that 'the fact that a matter has once been in the public domain cannot prevent its resurrection, possibly many years later, from being an infringement of privacy'. As to more extensive publication, what if medical information about X that was published in a local newspaper following a breach of confidence by X's doctor were to be republished in a national newspaper? Would the national newspaper be liable in breach of confidence?[6] On more extensive publication, see also *Stephens v Avery*[7] and *Barrymore v News Group Newspapers Ltd*.[8]

Should a gay person be protected from the revelation in a newspaper that he frequents gay bars on the basis that the right to privacy protects him from further publication of this information to persons who do not frequent such bars, e.g. members of his family? How would a 'reasonable expectation of privacy' test apply in such a case? To what extent should the right to privacy apply to the filming for security or crime detection purposes of members of the public in shops or other public places?[9]

In *Malone v Metropolitan Police Comr*[10] (a police telephone tapping case), Sir Robert Megarry V-C questioned whether telephone conversations are confidential for the purposes of the law of breach of confidence:

'It seems to me a person who utters confidential information must accept the risk of any unknown overhearing that is inherent in the circumstances of communication. Those who exchange confidences on a bus or a train run the risk of a nearby passenger with acute hearing or a more distant passenger who is adept at lip-reading. . . .

---

1 *Chantry Martin v Martin* [1953] 3 QB 286, CA. The publication of information compulsorily discovered in court proceedings is not contempt of court.
2 *Scott v Scott* [1913] AC 417, HL. Cf. *A-G v Leveller Magazine Ltd* [1979] AC 440, 449–450, HL. For the permitted exceptions and restrictions on reporting in criminal cases (to protect juveniles, etc.), see *Blackstone's Criminal Practice 2000*, para. D2.47. For recent cases concerning HIV sufferers, see note, (1998) 3 *Communications Law* 192.
3 Per Lord Haldane in *Scott v Scott* [1913] AC 417, 439.
4 See E. Paton-Simpson, (1998) 61 MLR 318.
5 [1995] EMLR 163, 168 CA. Per Balcombe LJ.
6 See Law Commission Report No. 110, p. 90. On the liability of third parties, see below, p. 968.
7 Below, p. 969.
8 Below, p. 972.
9 For the view that the right to privacy should in some circumstances apply in public places, see H. Nissenbaum, (1998) 17 Law and Philosophy 559.
10 [1979] Ch 344, 376. This dictum is doubted in the *Francome* case, below, p. 988.

When this is applied to telephone conversations, it appears to me that the speaker is taking such risks of being overheard as are inherent in the system . . . . the Younger Report referred to users of the telephone being aware that there were several well-understood possibilities of being overheard, and stated that a realistic person would not rely on the telephone system to protect the confidence of what he says. That comment seems unanswerable. In addition, so much publicity in recent years has been given to instances (real or fictional) of the deliberate tapping of telephones that it is difficult to envisage telephone users who are genuinely unaware of this possibility. No doubt a person who uses a telephone to give confidential information to another may do so in such a way as to impose an obligation of confidence on that other: but I do not see how it could be said that any such obligation is imposed on those who overhear the conversation, whether by means of tapping or otherwise.'

3. In *Coco v A N Clark (Engineers) Ltd*,[11] Megarry J listed three elements that are required for a claim in breach of confidence to succeed: confidential information; an obligation of confidence; and unauthorised use. Of the second element, he suggested, in the *Coco* case, a 'reasonable man' test:

'It seems to me that if the circumstances are such that any reasonable man standing in the shoes of the recipient of the information would have realised that upon reasonable grounds the information was being given to him in confidence, then this should suffice to impose upon him the equitable obligation of confidence.'

The Law Commission[12] rejected the 'reasonable man' test in favour of one based on express or inferred acceptance of an obligation of confidence by the recipient. In *Malone v Metropolitan Police Comr*,[13] a claim challenging telephone tapping under a Home Office warrant for the police failed to meet the second and third requirements.

4. In *R v Department of Health, ex p Source Informatics Ltd*,[14] the applicant company collected data on the drugs prescribed by doctors which it then passed on commercially to drug companies. To do this, it paid pharmacists a fee for information from doctors' prescriptions. This contained details of the prescribed drugs, but with the patients' names omitted. In this case, it was held that the disclosure of the information did not infringe the pharmacists' duty of confidence to patient customers. After hearing elaborate argument concerning the question whether the release of anonymous information was a breach of the duty where there was detriment to the patients and other questions, Simon Brown LJ stated:

'To my mind the one clear and consistent theme emerging from all these authorities is this: the confidant is placed under a duty of good faith to the confider and the touchstone by which to judge the scope of his duty and whether or not it has been fulfilled or breached is his own conscience, no more and no less. One asks, therefore, on the facts of this case: would a reasonable pharmacist's conscience be troubled by the proposed use to be made of patients' prescriptions? Would he think that by entering Source's scheme he was breaking his customers' confidence, making unconscientious use of the information they provide?...
    This appeal concerns, as all agree, the application of a broad principle of equity. I propose its resolution on a similarly broad basis. ... I would stand back from the many detailed arguments addressed to us and hold simply that pharmacists' consciences ought not reasonably to be troubled by co-operation with Source's proposed scheme. The patient's privacy will have been safeguarded, not invaded. The pharmacist's duty of confidence will not have been breached.'

11 See the extract from that case quoted in *Stevens v Avery*, below, p 969. Cf. the same judge, Sir Robert Megarry V-C, in *Malone v Metropolitan Police Comr* [1979] Ch 344, 375.
12 Report No. 110, p. 106.
13 [1979] Ch 344 at 376, Ch D.
14 [2000] 1 All ER 786 at 796–797, CA.

5. As to whether a doctor who revealed to the parents of a 15-year-old patient that she was on the pill would be in breach of confidence in law, see below, p. 972.
6. Could a person who, without the knowledge or consent of the person or persons concerned, accidentally or intentionally, reads a document or witnesses conduct be liable in *breach of confidence* (as opposed to trespass, etc.) for revealing information that he has improperly obtained? Suppose a husband were to publish information obtained from his wife's private diary which she kept locked in a drawer, the key to which he had stolen? Would the law of breach of confidence provide a remedy?[15] See the *Francome* case,[16] in which an injunction was granted against the *Daily Mirror* preventing it from publishing information obtained from tapes resulting from illegal private telephone tapping. See also in this connection the Younger Committee's proposal[17] for a new tort of disclosing or using information unlawfully obtained:

'632. There is another type of situation which, although it may be partially covered by the law relating to breach of confidence, raises problems which cannot be entirely solved by an application of that branch of the law, at least as it is generally understood. We think that the damaging disclosure or other damaging use of information acquired by means of any unlawful act, with knowledge of how it was acquired, is an objectionable practice against which the law should afford protection. We recommend therefore that it should be a civil wrong, actionable at the suit of any person who has suffered damage thereby, to disclose or otherwise use information which the discloser knows, or in all the circumstances ought to have known, was obtained by illegal means. It would be necessary to provide defences to cover situations where the disclosure of the information was in the public interest or was made in privileged circumstances. We envisage that the kinds of remedy available for this civil wrong would be similar to those appropriate to an action for breach of confidence.'

The Law Commission proposed[18] that breach of confidence should be extended to impose an obligation of confidence in respect of improperly obtained information.
7. For the view that the publication of a photograph of a private act taken by telephoto lens may be a breach of confidence, see Laws J in *Hellewell v Chief Constable of Derbyshire*:[19]

'I entertain no doubt that disclosure of a photograph may, in some circumstances, be actionable as a breach of confidence. If a photographer is hired to take a photograph to be used only for certain purposes but uses it for an unauthorised purpose of his own, a claim may lie against him: *Pollard v Photographic Co.* (1888) 40 Ch. D. 345. That case concerned portrait photographs of a lady taken for her private use by a hired photographer who then used one of the pictures for a Christmas card which was put on sale in his shop. North J upheld the plaintiff's claim, both in contract and breach of confidence. If someone with a telephoto lens were to take from a distance and with no authority a picture of another engaged in some private act, his subsequent disclosure of the photograph would, in my judgment, as surely amount to a breach of confidence as if he had found or stolen a letter or diary in which the act was recounted and proceeded to publish it. In such a case, the law would protect what might reasonably be called a right of privacy, although the name accorded to the cause of action would be breach of confidence. It is, of course, elementary that, in all such cases, a defence based on the public interest would be available.'

---

15 On criminal liability, see *Oxford v Moss*, below, p. 992.
16 Below, p. 988. The duty of confidence arises only in respect of *illegal* telephone tapping, as in *Francome*; the police owe no duty of confidence in respect of information obtained by means of authorised telephone tapping: *Malone v MPC* [1979] Ch 344, Ch D. See G. Wei, (1992) 12 LS 302 and M. Richardson, (1994) MULR 673.
17 Report, p. 194.
18 Report No. 110, p. 122.
19 [1995] 1 WLR 804, 807, QBD. On photographic invasions of privacy generally, see C. R. Munro, (1977) Entertainment LR 197.

Would this cover the Press Council/Complaints Commission cases where newspapers have printed photographs of the royal family or other celebrities without trespassing upon land but in circumstances where there would be a reasonable expectation of privacy in the absence of a telephoto lens? In 1982, the Press Council condemned the publication by the *Daily Star* and the *Sun* of pictures taken by long-lens photography of the Princess of Wales sun-bathing in a bikini on a beach on holiday in the Bahamas when five months pregnant as 'a gross intrusion into her personal privacy'.[1] The Council stated: 'Whether the beach was public or private is immaterial to this offence. There was no legitimate public interest to excuse that intrusion. Personal consent would have been required for the publication of pictures in these circumstances of any woman who was pregnant.' The *Sun* apologised, reprinting the offending pictures to demonstrate its offence. In a 1994 royal family case, the Press Complaints Commission ruled that five national daily newspapers were in breach of the Press Code of Practice when they printed a picture of Prince Edward and his girl friend kissing outside a house on the private Balmoral estate.[2]

8. There have been two recent reported cases in which injunctions have been granted under the law of breach of confidence to prevent the publication of photographs on grounds of the *commercial* harm to the plaintiffs that might on different facts apply to invasions of privacy in a more personal sense.[3] In *Shelley Films v Rex Features Ltd*[4] the defendant photographic and news agency had supplied *The People* newspaper with a photograph of Robert de Niro on the film set of *Shelley's Frankenstein* in a special effects costume. The photograph had been taken on the set, where there were signs that indicated that photographs were prohibited. Granting an interim injunction to the plaintiffs to prevent further publication of such photographs, Martin Mann QC rejected the argument that there was no duty of confidence on the facts as follows:

'Counsel for Rex argues that the notorious case of *Kaye v Robertson*[5] is contrary authority. Relying on the judgment of Bingham LJ at page 70 he derives the proposition that absent some identifiable relationship between plaintiff and defendant English law does not impose any such obligation not to impart information in circumstances such as those now in issue. For my part, I have distinct difficulty seeing how that holding can stand in the light of Lord Goff's discourse in *Attorney-General v Guardian Newspapers*[6] if Bingham LJ was there referring to any of the categories of incident which Lord Goff had in mind, but I venture that he was adverting solely to invasions of 'privacy' as a possible branch of the law of tort and

---

1   *The Times*, 4 March 1982.
2   Press Complaints Commission Report No. 25, May–July 1994, p. 6. The Code as then drafted, which expressly provides that the 'use of long-lens photography to take pictures of people in private places without their consent is unacceptable'. For other royal family cases in which breaches of the Code involving long-lens photographs were found, see the *Bellassario* case, and the case in which *The People* published a picture of the Duke of York's baby daughter running naked in a high-walled garden: Press Complaints Commission Report No. 2, July–Sept. 1991, p. 18. In other, non-royal family cases, *The Sun* was condemned by the Press Council for publishing long-lens pictures of Brigitte Bardot sunbathing topless by her private swimming pool (*The Times*, 12 April 1984) and of David Niven showing him in a distressed state shortly before his death (*The Times*, 12 January 1984). More recently, *OK* magazine was in breach of PCC Code, clause 3, for publishing a paparazzi photograph of Prince William in the wilds of Chile on his year off because the trip was to a place where he had a reasonable expectation of privacy: Press Complaints Commission Report No. 52 Oct.–Dec. 2000, p. 8. However, the same magazine and the *Daily Mail* were not in breach of the same clause when the published a long lens photograph of the TV personality Anna Ford and her new male companion on a secluded but public beach in Majorca: ibid., p. 11.
3   See also *Douglas v Hello!* above, p. 922.
4   [1994] EMLR 134, Martin Mann, QC, sitting as a deputy High Court judge.
5   *Ed.*, above, p. 911.
6   *Ed.*, below, next note.

not to predations of confidential information which is primarily an equitable doctrine and a very different question. Of course, ... the photographer in the present case ... was not an invitee and assuming that he saw the signs at the entrance to Shepperton Studios as well as those within the set (I am not convinced that it would be fatal to Shelley's case if he did not – there is in any event an issue, which I cannot resolve, as to precisely which signs were visible on 18 November 1993), it is impossible for present purposes not to conclude that what he saw and understood from his location might not have fully and sufficiently fixed him with knowledge according to any of the relevant standards that the studio and Shelley considered these signs necessary for some good reason connected with filming and the filming of "Mrs Shelley's Frankenstein", in particular, which he was not unilaterally at liberty to impart to others.'

In *Creation Records Ltd v News Group Newspapers Ltd*[7] the Oasis pop group had arranged a photo session at a hotel for the cover of their new album. The *Sun* newspaper published a photograph commissioned by it from the defendants that was taken during the session and was very similar to that selected for the cover. The photographer had registered as a guest in the hotel and was therefore allowed in the area where the photo session occurred. Granting an interim injunction to prevent further publications, Lloyd J stated:

'Mr. Garnett argues that, despite all of that, no arguable case is made out for breach of confidence, or indeed for the existence of confidentiality, and says correctly that merely because a well-known person tries to stop people taking photographs of him or her it does not follow that any picture taken in evasion or defiance of those attempts is in breach of confidentiality. That seems to me to be a perfectly sound proposition but very far from this case. Here, while admittedly Mr. Seeburg was lawfully at the hotel and with others was able to gain access to the restricted area and his presence there was tolerated and even the taking of photographs was tolerated before the shoot as such began, the plaintiffs' evidence, if accepted, shows that thereafter a tighter regime of security was imposed as regards preventing photograph, the tight ring of security men and minders of which *The Sun's* first article spoke. It would of course have been clearer if each of the strangers to the shoot who were allowed to stay in the restricted area had been told that they may not take photographs thereafter. But what the plaintiffs' witnesses depose to amounts to much the same as that, although in a more general and less explicit form. I accept also that they were of course allowed to observe the scene and could therefore have gone away and told the world the ingredients of the picture, or even made a sketch of it from memory. But being lawfully there does not mean that they were free to take photographs and it seems to me that to be able to record it as a photographic image is different in kind, not merely in degree, from being able to relate it verbally or even by way of a sketch. That is above all because it was in photographic form that it was intended to be preserved for the group. It is the photographic record of the scene, the result of the shoot in fact, that was to be confidential.

I accept it as well arguable that the nature of the operation together with the imposition of security measures as described by the plaintiffs' witnesses made it an occasion of confidentiality at any rate as regards photography. In that context I also accept it as sufficiently arguable that in order to get his picture Mr. Seeburg must have conducted himself a good deal less openly than he suggests and indeed surreptitiously, as the plaintiffs suggest. If so, it is an easy inference that he did so because he knew that photography was not permitted and that he was being allowed to remain in the restricted area only on the basis that photographs would not be taken of the actual shoot. On that footing it seems to me that the plaintiffs do have a sufficiently arguable case for saying that the taking of the photograph and its publication is in breach of confidence and that future publication can be restrained by injunction at any rate until the image is fully released into the public domain, presumably on publication of the album, if it does come out with this cover.'

9. Distinct from the situation where a person improperly obtains confidential information is that in which a person lawfully happens upon such information. For the view that a duty of confidence exists in the latter situation provided the person has notice of the confidential nature of the information, see the following dictum by Lord Goff in *A-G v Guardian Newspapers Ltd (No 2)*:[8]

'I start with the broad general principle (which I do not intend in any way to be definitive) that a duty of confidence arises when confidential information comes to the knowledge of a person (the confidant) in circumstances where he has notice, or is held to have agreed, that the information is confidential, with the effect that it would be just in all the circumstances that he should be precluded from disclosing the information to others. I have used the word "notice" advisedly, in order to avoid the (here unnecessary) question of the extent to which actual knowledge is necessary; though I of course understand knowledge to include circumstances where the confidant has deliberately closed his eyes to the obvious. The existence of this broad general principle reflects the fact that there is such a public interest in the maintenance of confidences, that the law will provide remedies for their protection.

I realise that, in the vast majority of cases, in particular those concerned with trade secrets, the duty of confidence will arise from a transaction or relationship between the parties—often a contract, in which event the duty may arise by reason of either an express or an implied term of that contract. It is in such cases as these that the expressions "confider" and "confidant" are perhaps most aptly employed. But it is well settled that a duty of confidence may arise in equity independently of such cases; and I have expressed the circumstances in which the duty arises in broad terms, not merely to embrace those cases where a third party receives information from a person who is under a duty of confidence in respect of it, knowing that it has been disclosed by that person to him in breach of his duty of confidence, but also to include certain situations, beloved of law teachers—where an obviously confidential document is wafted by an electric fan out of a window into a crowded street, or where an obviously confidential document, such as a private diary, is dropped in a public place, and is then picked up by a passer-by. I also have in mind the situations where secrets of importance to national security come into the possession of members of the public ...'

10. Would a person who is subject to a duty of confidence who reveals information negligently, not intentionally, be liable in breach of confidence? In *Swinney v Chief Constable of the Northumbria Police*,[9] the plaintiff had informed on a criminal to the police, requesting measures to be taken to prevent him learning of her identity as he was known to be violent. The police recorded her name as the informant in a file that was left in an unattended police vehicle, from which the file was stolen. The plaintiff was threatened with personal violence and arson and suffered psychiatric injury. The Court of Appeal agreed that a claim in breach of confidence could go forward to trial. Hirst LJ quoted dicta by Lord Goff in *A-G v Guardian Newspapers Ltd (No 2)*[10] favouring liability for negligent breach of confidence, but quoted the Law Commission view that the question was undecided:[11]

'There does not appear to be any clear answer in the present state of the law to the question ... *whether a person who is under a duty of confidence*, but is not in any contractual relationship with the person to whom it is owed, can be liable for *breach of confidence* if the information to which the duty relates is disclosed or used owing to his negligence.'

11. Suppose that a newspaper buys a story reasonably, but incorrectly, believing that it has been obtained without a breach of confidence on the part of the writer? Can the newspaper be liable for breach of confidence?[12]

8 [1990] 1 AC 109 at 281, HL.
9 [1996] 3 All ER 449, CA.
10 [1990] 1 AC 109, 287, HL.
11 Law Commission Report No. 110, p. 26.
12 On the position of innocent third parties, see Jones, (1970) 86 LQR 463, 477–481; Meagher, Gummow and Lehane, *Equity Doctrines and Remedies* (3rd edn, 1992), pp. 880–881; Law Commission Report No. 110, p. 25. Was the defendant in *Prince Albert v Strange*, above, or the editor of *The People* in the *Argyll* case, above, an innocent third party?

Stephens v Avery [1988] Ch 449, [1988] 2 WLR 12 80, [1988] 2 All ER 477, Chancery Division

Mrs S, the plaintiff, confided in Mrs A, her close friend and the first defendant, about her lesbian relationship with Mrs T, for the killing of whom Mr T had been convicted of manslaughter. The plaintiff expressly stated when communicating the information that it was being given in confidence and should go no further, and the first defendant agreed. Mrs A allegedly informed *The Mail on Sunday* (the editor and publishers of which were the other defendants) of the relationship. The newspaper published details, revealing for the first time that the plaintiff was the woman whom Mr T had claimed at his trial to have found in a compromising position with his wife. When the plaintiff brought proceedings for breach of confidence, the defendants applied to have the action struck out as disclosing no reasonable cause of action. When the master refused, the defendants appealed.

Sir Nicolas Browne-Wilkinson V-C: Three requirements have to be satisfied before a court will protect information as being legally confidential. They were laid down by the Court of Appeal in *Saltman Engineering Co Ltd v Campbell Engineering Co Ltd* (1963) 65 RPC 203, and were summarised by Megarry J, in *Coco v A N Clark (Engineers) Ltd* [1969] RPC 41, 47, in this way:

> 'In my judgment, three elements are normally required if, apart from contract, a case of breach of confidence is to succeed. First, the information itself, in the words of Lord Greene MR in the *Saltman* case on p. 215, must "have the necessary quality of confidence about it." Secondly, that information must have been imparted in circumstances importing an obligation of confidence. Thirdly, there must be an unauthorised use of that information to the detriment of the party communicating it. . . .'

On this hearing I am not concerned with the third of those requirements, but with the first two only.

As to the first of those requirements, Mr. Wilson submits that the law does not protect information which relates to the sexual conduct or proclivities of an individual, save to the extent that such conduct takes place between married partners. He submits that such information is mere gossip or trivial tittle-tattle outside the protection of the law. He says that the law does not protect information relating to grossly immoral behaviour, and relies by analogy on the refusual of the courts to enforce copyright in literary works of a grossly immoral nature. Further, he submits that any sexual conduct whether heterosexual or homosexual—and he draws no distinction between the two—necessarily lacks the quality of confidentiality because, by taking part in the sexual activity itself, both sexual partners know what has happened, and accordingly neither of them can claim that the information is confidential to either of them. . . .

In my judgment those arguments are not well-founded. As to the submission that the law will not enforce a duty of confidentiality relating to grossly immoral conduct, the submission is founded on *Glyn v Weston Feature Film Co* [1916] 1 Ch 261. In that case Elinor Glyn complained that the defendants had made a film based on a book written by her. Younger J took a very unfavourable view of both the plaintiff's book and the defendants' film, regarding them both as indecently offensive. On that ground, amongst others, he refused the plaintiff any relief. . . .

I entirely accept the principle stated in that case, the principle being that a court of equity will not enforce copyright, and presumably also will not enforce a duty of confidence, relating to matters which have a grossly immoral tendency. But at the present day the difficulty is to identify what sexual conduct is to be treated as grossly immoral. In 1915 there was a code of sexual morals accepted by the overwhelming majority of society. A judge could therefore stigmatize certain sexual conduct as offending that moral code. But at the present day no such general code exists. There is no common view that sexual conduct of any kind between consenting adults is grossly immoral. I suspect the works of Elinor Glyn if published today would be widely regarded as, at the highest, very soft pornography.

The sexual conduct of the plaintiff was not so morally shocking in this case as to prevent the third defendant, a major national Sunday newspaper, from spreading the story all over its front and inside pages. The submission on behalf of these defendants that the actions of the plaintiff in this case are so grossly immoral as to produce a tendency towards immoral conduct and thereby to be without the law lies ill in their mouths, since they have themselves spread the news of such conduct nationwide for their own personal profit.

If it is right that there is now no generally accepted code of sexual morality applying to this case, it would be quite wrong in my judgment for any judge to apply his own personal moral views, however strongly held, in deciding the legal rights of the parties. The court's function is to apply the law, not personal prejudice. Only in a case where there is still a generally accepted moral code can the court refuse to enforce rights in such a way as to offend that generally accepted code.

As to the submission that there is no confidentiality in tittle-tattle and gossip, Mr. Wilson relied on a passage in the *Coco* case [1969] RPC 41, 48, where Megarry J said:

> '. . . I doubt whether equity would intervene unless the circumstances are of sufficient gravity; equity ought not to be invoked merely to protect trivial tittle-tattle, however confidential.'[13]

Since the *Coco* case was exclusively concerned with information which was of industrial value, those remarks were plainly obiter dicta. Moreover, I have the greatest doubt whether wholesale revelation of the sexual conduct of an individual can properly be described as 'trivial' tittle-tattle. Again, although it is true that the passage I have quoted occurs in that part of the judgment which deals with the nature of information which can be protected, it is to be noted that the judge appeared to be considering when equity would give a remedy, not dealing with the fundamental nature of the legal right. If, as I think he was, Megarry J was saying that the discretion to grant an injunction or to award damages would not be exercised in a case which was merely trivial, I agree. But the exercise of such a discretion can only be decided in the light of all the circumstances. Those cannot be known until there has been a trial.

Next, I consider the submission that because in all cases of sexual conduct both parties are aware of the facts, information relating to those facts cannot in law be confidential. In my judgment this submission is wholly misconceived. It is based on the premise that as between unmarried sexual partners there is no duty of confidentiality. Therefore, both parties are free to discuss the matter with the whole world. I will assume that submission to be correct, but without expressing any view on its correctness in law. Even on that assumption, the fact that the other partner to a sexual relationship *may* disclose what has happened does not mean that he or she had done so. To most people the details of their sexual lives are high on their list of those matters which they regard as confidential. The mere fact that two people know a secret does not mean that it is not confidential. If in fact information is secret, then in my judgment it is capable of being kept secret by the imposition of a duty of confidence on any person to whom it is communicated. Information only ceases to be capable of protection as confidential when it is in fact known to a substantial number of people.

That this is the law is shown by . . . the Court of Appeal in *A-G v Guardian Newspapers Ltd (No 2)* [1990] 1 AC 109, [1988] 2 WLR 805 . . . Sir John Donaldson M.R. said, at p. 868:

> 'As a general proposition, that which has no character of confidentiality because it has already been communicated to the world, i.e., made generally available to the relevant public, cannot thereafter be subjected to a right of confidentiality . . . However, this will not necessarily be the case if the information has previously only been disclosed to a limited part of that public. It is a question of degree.' . . .

In principle, therefore, I can see no reason why information relating to that most private sector of everybody's life, namely sexual conduct, cannot be the subject matter of a legally enforceable duty of confidentiality. Mr. Wilson submits that there is no case in which confidentiality of such information has been enforced. This is true. But it is equally true that no one has previously suggested that just because information related to the sexual conduct of an individual it was in someway different to any other information. In a number of cases where the point could

---

13   *Ed.* Cf. Lord Goff in *A-G v Guardian Newspapers Ltd (No 2)* [1990] 1 AC 109 at 282: '...the duty of confidence applies neither to useless information, nor to trivia.'

have been argued it was not: see, for example, *Woodward v Hutchins*.[14] In *Khashoggi v Smith*,[15] the point was apparently argued. Sir David Cairns said that:

'He was by no means satisfied that the duty of confidentiality was inappropriate to protect matters involving the plaintiff's sexual misconduct.'

Therefore, I can see nothing either in principle or authority to support the view that information relating to sexual conduct cannot be the subject matter of a duty of confidence.

I turn to the second attack made by Mr. Wilson, namely that the circumstances in which the plaintiff is alleged to have communicated the information to Mrs. Avery are not such as to raise a duty of confidence: . . .

Mr. Wilson submits that in the absence of either a legally enforceable contract or a pre-existing relationship—such as that of employer and employee, doctor and patient, or priest and penitent—it is not possible to impose a legal duty of confidence on the recipient of the information merely by saying that the information is given in confidence. In my judgment that is wrong in law. The basis of equitable intervention to protect confidentiality is that it is unconscionable for a person who has received information on the basis that it is confidential subsequently to reveal that information. Although the relationship between the parties is often important in cases where it is said there is an implied as opposed to express obligation of confidence, the relationship between the parties is not the determining factor. It is the acceptance of the information on the basis that it will be kept secret that affects the conscience of the recipient of the information. I quote again from the judgment of Bingham LJ in the *Spycatcher* case, where he said, at p. 904:

'The cases show that the duty of confidence does not depend on any contract, express or implied, between the parties. If it did, it would follow on ordinary principles that strangers to the contract would not be bound. But the duty "depends on the broad principle of equity that he who has received information in confidence shall not take unfair advantage of it:" *Seager v Copydex Ltd* [1967] 1 WLR 923, 931, *per* Lord Denning M.R. "The jurisdiction is based not so much on property or on contract as on the duty to be of good faith": *Fraser v Evans* [1969] 1 QB 349, 361, per Lord Denning M.R.'

If, as is here alleged, the information was communicated and accepted expressly in confidence, the conscience of Mrs. Avery is just as much affected as in any other case. In my judgment the express statement that the information is confidential is the clearest possible example of the imposition of a duty of confidence. . . .

Therefore, on the specific grounds argued, in my judgment it has not been demonstrated that there is no legal basis for the plaintiff's claim. I therefore decline to strike out the statement of claim.

However, in reply, Mr. Wilson tried to expand the ambit of his attack into more general fields of public policy. To my mind this case undoubtedly does raise fundamental difficulties as to the relationship between on the one hand the privacy which every individual is entitled to expect, and on the other hand freedom of information. To many, the aggressive intrusion of sectors of the press into the private lives of individuals is unpalatable. On the other hand, the ability of the press to obtain and publish for the public benefit information of genuine public interest, as opposed to general public titillation, may be impaired if information obtained in confidence is too widely protected by the law. Moreover, is the press to be liable in damages for printing what is true? I express no view as to where or how the borderline should be drawn in such a case. . . .

Appeal dismissed with costs.

NOTES

1. *Stephens v Avery* confirms the decision in *Argyll v Argyll*[16] that information concerning a person's sexual life may be protected by the law of breach of confidence.

14 Below, p. 987.
15 Above, p. 962, n. 20.
16 Above, p. 961: *Argyll v Argyll* was cited in argument but not referred to in Sir Nicolas Browne-Wilkinson's judgment.

In this connection, it is interesting that the court limits the scope and effect of Megarry J's exclusion of 'tittle-tattle' in the *Coco* case, so that it would not prevent a remedy in breach of confidence for the 'wholesale revelation of the sexual conduct of an individual', as on the facts of the case.

2. Whereas the decision in *Argyll v Argyll* was predicated upon the fact that the information was disclosed during marriage, an institution which the law seeks to protect, this was not the basis for the decision in *Stephens v Avery*. Nor does it involve any fiduciary relationship (doctor-patient, bank manager-client, etc.) recognised by the law. As in Lord Keith's speech in *A-G v Guardian Newspapers Ltd (No 2)*,[17] the court in *Stephens v Avery* supposes instead that it is the policy of the law to uphold the moral quality of an undertaking not to disclose information given in confidence, whatever the existing relationship between the persons concerned.[18] Would it have mattered in *Stephens v Avery* if the obligation of confidence had been an implied rather than an express one?

3. Would a doctor who revealed to the parents of a 15-year-old patient that she was on the pill or pregnant be in breach of confidence? What if he revealed to a patient's partner that the patient was HIV positive?[19] In *X v European Commission*[20] the European Court of Justice held that the right to respect for private life in Art. 8 ECHR includes the right to keep the state of one's health secret (so an AIDs screening test of applicants for employment requires consent).

4. *Stephens v Avery* was followed and applied in *Barrymore v News Group Newspapers Ltd*,[21] in which the *Sun* printed extracts from letters written by a TV personality to a homosexual friend who had given them to the newspaper. Granting an injunction on a breach of confidence basis, Jacobs J stated:

> '...I think that there is a strongly arguable case that the details of the relationship between Mr. Barrymore and the second defendant, Mr. Wincott, should be treated as confidential. I say that because, firstly, common sense dictates that, when people enter into a personal relationship of this nature, they do not do so for the purpose of it subsequently being published in *The Sun*, or any other newspaper. The information about the relationship is for the relationship and not for a wider purpose. It is well established that in many cases the law will spell out a duty of confidence when information is given for a limited purpose.
>
> Secondly, there is the authority of *Stephens v Avery* [1988] 1 Ch. 449. ...'

Quoting the statement by Sir Nicolas Browne-Wilkinson in *Stephens v Avery* that '(I)nformation only ceases to be capable of protection as confidential when it is in fact known to a substantial number of people', Jacobs J continued:

> 'The information presented in *The Sun* newspaper's article today was not known to a substantial number of people before *The Sun* newspaper published it. That was why *The Sun* claimed the whole story as "an exclusive"...
>
> Mr. Caldecott seeks to distinguish *Stephens v Avery* on several bases. First, that it was a strike out case in which it was pleaded that the recipient of the information, who was not the opposite partner in the sexual relationship the subject of the action, expressly received the information under a seal of confidence: the private conduct of the plaintiff was based on the understanding and agreement that the knowledge gained by the first defendant was entirely secret. I regard that as a distinction without a difference. Of course, if something is expressly said to be confidential, then it is much more likely to be so held by the courts, but it by no means follows that something that is not so expressly stated to be confidential is not confidential. The whole question turns on the relationship between the parties. The fact is that

---

17 Above, p. 850.
18 For criticism of this wider approach, which clearly strengthens the law of breach of confidence as a means of controlling the press, see W. Wilson, (1990) 53 MLR 43.
19 See *Gillick v West Norfolk and Wisbech Area Health Authority* [1986] AC 112, HL.
20 1995 IRLR 320, ECJ.
21 [1997] FSR 600, Ch D.

when people kiss and later one of them tells, that second person is almost certainly breaking a confidential arrangement. It all depends on precisely what they do. If they merely indicate there has been a relationship, that may not amount to a breach of confidence and that may well be the case here, because Mr. Barrymore had already disclosed that he was homosexual, and merely to disclose that he had had a particular partner would be to add nothing new.

However, when one goes into detail (as in *The Sun* article), about what Mr. Barrymore said about his relationship with his wife and so on, one has crossed the line into breach of confidence. I think that there is a very strong arguable case of breach of confidence and I grant an injunction for such period as may be discussed with counsel.'

The view that publication of information that is already to some extent known to others will not be in breach of confidence unless it is known by a 'substantial number' of others, is put somewhat differently by Lord Keith in *A-G v Guardian Newspapers Ltd*,[22] who suggests that the test is whether further publication would be 'more harmful'. An injunction was granted against newspapers on a basis of breach of confidence (and breach of contract) to prevent their publication of photographs of the Princess of Wales exercising in a gymnasium club where the photographs had been taken by the gymnasium owner without her knowledge or consent.[1] In this case, the information in the photographs was known to club members, but not the general public.

Venables v News Group Newspapers Ltd and others [2001] 1 All ER 908, Family Division

The plaintiffs had been convicted at the age of 11 of murdering a 2-year-old boy in a notorious murder case. During their trial, media reporting restrictions had been imposed by Morland J under s. 39, Children and Young Persons Act 1933. Following their convictions, the judge lifted the restrictions so as to allow the media to inform the public of the plaintiffs' names and background. However, acting under s. 39 and the High Court's inherent jurisdiction to deal with children, the judge granted comprehensive injunctions restricting the publication of any other information about the two boys for an unlimited period of time. He explained his reasons as follows:

'It is necessary for me to balance the public interest in lifting reporting restrictions and the interests of the defendants. I lifted the reporting restrictions as set out in my order of 24 November. I did this because the public interest overrode the interest of the defendants following the murder and I considered that the background in respect of the two boys' family, lifestyle, education and the possible effect of violent videos, on the defendants' behaviour ought to be brought out into the open because there was a need for an informed public debate on crimes committed by young children. However, public interest also demands that they have a good opportunity of rehabilitation. They must have an opportunity to be brought up in the units in a way so as to facilitate their rehabilitation.'

The present proceedings were instituted because the plaintiffs were now 18, so that Morland J's injunction had expired, and tariff recommendation made by Woolf CJ meant that in 2001 the Parole Board would make a decision about their release and reintegration into the community. The plaintiffs sought an injunction for a continuation of restraints upon publicity for an unlimited period.

---

22 Above, p. 850.
1 *HRH Princess of Wales v MGN Newspapers Ltd* (1993), Drake J, Ch D, unreported. The case did not go to trial on the breach of confidence and breach of contract claims, the *Daily Mirror* apparently paying £1m or so in settlement: (1995) 145 NLJ 1286. Cf. *Shelley Films Ltd v Rex Features Ltd*, above, p. 966.

Dame Elizabeth Butler-Sloss P:

24. Before turning to the question of whether there is jurisdiction to grant injunctions, the preliminary issue is whether the [European] convention [on Human Rights] applies to this case. It is clear that, although operating in the public domain and fulfilling a public service, the defendant newspapers cannot sensibly be said to come within the definition of public authority in s. 6(1) of the 1998 Act. Consequently, convention rights are not directly enforceable against the defendants; see ss. 7(1) and 8 of the 1998 Act. That is not, however, the end of the matter, since the court is a public authority, see s. 6(3), and must itself act in a way compatible with the convention, see s. 6(1),and have regard to European jurisprudence, see s. 2. In a private family law case, *Glaser v UK* [2000] 3 FCR 193, the European Court, sitting as a Chamber, declared admissible an application by a father seeking the enforcement of contact orders made in private law proceedings between him and the mother of his children. They considered the potential breach of the father's rights under Arts. 8 and 6. The court said (at 208–209 (para. 63)):

'The essential object of Art. 8 is to protect the individual against arbitrary interference by public authorities. There may however be positive obligations inherent in an effective "respect" for family life. These obligations may involve the adoption of measures designed to secure respect for family life even in the sphere of relations between individuals, including both the provision of a regulatory framework of adjudicatory and enforcement machinery protecting individuals' rights and the implementation, where appropriate, of specific steps, (see among other authorities, *X and Y v Netherlands* (1985) 8 EHRR 235 (para. 23)), and, mutatis mutandis, *Osman v UK* (5 BHRC 293 at 321 (para. 115)). In both the negative and ... positive contexts regard must be had to the fair balance which has to be struck between the competing interests of the individual and the community, including other concerned third parties, and the state's margin of appreciation (see, among other authorities, *Keegan v Ireland* (18 EHRR 342 at 362 (para. 49)).'

25. The court held that, in that case, the authorities, including the courts, struck a fair balance between the competing interests and did not fail in their responsibilities to protect the father's right to respect for family life. This decision underlines the positive obligations of the courts including, where necessary, the provision of a regulatory framework of adjudicatory and enforcement machinery in order to protect the rights of the individual. The decisions of the European Court in *Glaser's* case and *X v Netherlands* (1985) 8 EHRR 235, seem to dispose of any argument that a court is not to have regard to the convention in private law cases. In *Douglas v Hello! Ltd* [2001] IP & T 391 at 425 (para. 133) Sedley LJ held that s. 12(4) of the 1998 Act—

'puts beyond question the direct applicability of at least one article of the convention as between one private party to litigation and another—in the jargon, its horizontal effect.'

26. In the light of the judgments in *Douglas'* case, I am satisfied that I have to apply Art. 10 directly to the present case.

27. That obligation on the court does not seem to me to encompass the creation of a free-standing cause of action based directly upon the articles of the convention, although that proposition is advanced by Mr. Fitzgerald as a fall-back position, if all else fails. The duty on the court, in my view, is to act compatibly with convention rights in adjudicating upon existing common law causes of action, and that includes a positive as well as a negative obligation....

28. It is accepted by all the parties, and it is clearly right, that the basis upon which the injunctions were granted by Morland J on 26 November 1993 no longer exists. He based his decision on the inherent jurisdiction of the Family Division of the High Court to protect minors, and on the statutory provisions in s. 39 of the 1933 Act. If there is any jurisdiction to grant injunctions it has to be found elsewhere. The principal submission in favour of the existence of the court's power is based upon the law of confidence, taking into account the implementation of the 1998 Act. ...

30. As I have already said, in my view, the claimants in private law proceedings cannot rely upon a free-standing application under the convention. In their submissions, the claimants, supported by the Attorney General and the Official Solicitor, relied upon the common law right to confidence. The tort of breach of confidence is a recognised cause of action. ...

34. Article 10,[2] as applied to the media, is central to this case. ...

---

2   *Ed.* For the text of Art. 10, see above, p. 22.

35. In s. 12 of the 1998 Act, special provisions are made in relation to applications to restrict freedom of expression. Section 12(4) states: 'The court must have particular regard to the importance of the Convention right to freedom of expression ...'

36. There is no doubt, therefore, that Parliament has placed great emphasis upon the importance of Art. 10 and the protection of freedom of expression, inter alia for the press and for the media. The 1998 Act and the convention do not, however, establish new law. They reinforce and give greater weight to the principles already established in our case law. In *R v Secretary of State for the Home Dept, ex p Simms* [1999] 3 All ER 400 at 408, [2000] 2 AC 115 at 126, Lord Steyn said:

'Freedom of expression is, of course, intrinsically important: it is valued for its own sake. But it is well recognised that it is also instrumentally important. It serves a number of broad objectives. First, it promotes the self-fulfilment of individuals in society. Secondly, in the famous words of Holmes J (echoing John Stuart Mill), "the best test of truth is the power of the thought to get itself accepted in the competition of the market": *Abrams v US* (1919) 250 US 616 at 630 per Holmes J (dissent). Thirdly, freedom of speech is the lifeblood of democracy. The free flow of information and ideas informs political debate. It is a safety valve: people are more ready to accept decisions that go against them if they can in principle seek to influence them. It acts as a brake on the abuse of power by public officials. It facilitates the exposure of errors in the governance and administration of justice of the country: see Stone, Seidman, Sunstein and Tushnett *Constitutional Law* (3rd edn, 1996) pp. 1078–1086.'

37. Hoffmann LJ said, in *R v Central Independent Television plc* [1994] 3 All ER 641 at 651–653, [1994] Fam 192 at 202–204:

'The motives which impel judges to assume a power to balance freedom of speech against other interests are almost always understandable and humane on the facts of the particular case before them. Newspapers are sometimes irresponsible and their motives in a market economy cannot be expected to be unalloyed by considerations of commercial advantage. And publication may cause needless pain, distress and damage to individuals or harm to other aspects of the public interest. But a freedom which is restricted to what judges think to be responsible or in the public interest is no freedom. Freedom means the right to publish things which government and judges, however well motivated, think should not be published. It means the right to say things which "right-thinking people" regard as dangerous or irresponsible. This freedom is subject only to clearly defined exceptions laid down by common law or statute ... It cannot be too strongly emphasised that outside the established exceptions (or any new ones which Parliament may enact in accordance with its obligations under the convention) there is no question of balancing freedom of speech against other interests. It is a trump card which always wins ... no freedom is without cost and in my view the judiciary should not whittle away freedom of speech with ad hoc exceptions. The principle that the press is free from both government and judicial control is more important than the particular case.'

38. Munby J in *Kelly v BBC* [2001] 1 All ER 323 at 337, [2001] 2 WLR 253 at 264 said:

'... if those who seek to bring themselves within para. 2 of Art. 10 are to establish "convincingly" that they are—and that is what they have to establish—they cannot do so by mere assertion, however eminent the person making the assertion, nor by simply inviting the court to make assumptions; what is required ... is proper *evidence* ...' (Munby J's emphasis.)

39. In *Sunday Times v UK* (1979) 2 EHRR 245 at 281 (para. 65) the European Court said:

'The Court is faced not with a choice between two conflicting principles, but with a principle of freedom of expression that is subject to a number of exceptions which must be narrowly interpreted.'

40. However, more recently, in *Douglas v Hello! Ltd* [2001] IP & T 391 at 426–427 (paras. 136–137),[3] Sedley LJ said: ...

41. In his Goodman Lecture, (22 May 1996), Lord Hoffmann referred to his judgment in *R v Central Independent Television plc* and said:

3   *Ed.* Reprinted below, pp. 930–931.

'Some people have read that to mean that freedom of speech always trumps other rights and values. But that is not what I said. I said only that in order to put [in] the balance against freedom of speech, another interest must fall within some established exception which could be justified under Article 10 of the European Convention.'...

42. Mr. Desmond Browne submitted that that it was not a balancing operation between the right to freedom of expression against any legitimate aim falling within Art. 10(2). It would seem to me however that, whether it is called a balancing process or any other description, the conflict that may arise between Art. 10(1) and Art. 10(2) has to be resolved and the legitimate aim in restricting freedom of expression within the exceptions in Art. 10(2) given appropriate weight according to the facts of the individual case. Sedley LJ said in *Douglas v Hello! Ltd* [2001] IP & T 391 at 426 (par. 136): '...the qualifications set out in Art. 10(2) are as relevant as the right set out in Art. 10(1).'

43. There would not however be such a juggling act in a case which did not fall within the exceptions set out in Art. 10(2). It is clear however that, to obtain an injunction to restrain the media from publication of information, it requires a strong case. Brooke LJ said in *Douglas'* case [2001] IP & T 391 at 403 (para. 49):

'Although the right to freedom of expression is not in every case the ace of trumps, it is a powerful card to which the courts of this country must always pay appropriate respect.'

And Sedley LJ said at 427 (para. 137): 'If freedom of expression is to be impeded ... it must be on cogent grounds recognised by law.'

44. The onus of proving the case that freedom of expression must be restricted is firmly upon the applicant seeking the relief. The restrictions sought must, in the circumstances of the present case, be shown to be in accordance with the law, justifiable as necessary to satisfy a strong and pressing social need, convincingly demonstrated, to restrain the press in order to protect the rights of the claimants to confidentiality, and proportionate to the legitimate aim pursued. The right to confidence is, however, a recognised exception within Art. 10(2) and the tort of breach of confidence was the domestic remedy upon which the European Commission, in *Earl Spencer v UK* (1998) 25 EHRR CD 105, declared inadmissible an application by Lord and Lady Spencer on the basis that they had not exhausted their domestic remedies.

45. I turn to the three other articles of the convention [Articles 2, 3 8] which are said by the claimants to be engaged in this case, and which clearly I must consider alongside Art. 10. ...

46. If the claimants' case is made out, Art. 2[4] is clearly engaged. In *Osman v UK* (1998) 5 BHRC 293, the European Court held that the provisions of Art. 2 enjoined a positive obligation upon contracting states to take measures to secure the right to life. In that case it was the failure of the police to act to protect a family from criminal acts including murder. The European Court said (at 321 (paras 115–116)):

'The court notes that the first sentence of Art. 2(1) enjoins the state not only to refrain from the intentional and unlawful taking of life, but also to take appropriate steps to safeguard the lives of those within its jurisdiction ... it must be established ... that the authorities knew or ought to have known at the time of the existence of a real and immediate risk to the life of an identified individual or individuals from the criminal acts of a third party and that they failed to take measures within the scope of their powers which, judged reasonably, might have been expected to avoid that risk ...' ...

47. Article 3[5] is equally potentially applicable, if I am satisfied as to the strength of the claimants' case. Other than in the specified exceptions in Art. 2, there is to be no derogation from the rights set out in those two articles. ...

48. Article 8[6] is also potentially applicable. ...

49. In *X v Netherlands* (1985) 8 EHRR 235, the European Court held that, in a case where the prosecutor took no action on a complaint by a father of a sexual assault on his mentally incapacitated daughter of 16, that the state had failed to protect a vulnerable individual from

4   *Ed*. For the text, see above, p. 20.
5   *Ed*. For the text, see above, p. 20.
6   *Ed*. For the text, see above, p. 22.

a criminal violation of her physical and moral integrity by another private individual. A violation of Art. 8 was found. The court said (at 239 (para. 23[7])):

50. Sedley LJ said in *Douglas v Hello! Ltd* [2001] IP & T 391 at 425–426 (paras. 133–134):[8]
...

51. Although the Court of Appeal was concerned with an entirely different situation, the observations of Sedley LJ are highly relevant to and helpful in the task facing me in the present case where I have to resolve a potential conflict between Art. 10 on the one hand and Arts. 2 and 3 and 8 on the other hand. ...

76. I am, of course, well aware that, until now, the courts have not granted injunctions in the circumstances which arise in this case. It is equally true that the claimants are uniquely notorious. On the basis of the evidence presented to me, their case is exceptional. I recognise also that the threats to the life and physical safety of the claimants do not come from those against whom the injunctions are sought. But the media are uniquely placed to provide the information that would lead to the risk that others would take the law into their own hands and commit crimes against the claimants.

77. The starting point is, however, the well-recognised position of the press, and their right and duty to be free to publish, even in circumstances described by Hoffmann LJ in *R v Central Independent Television plc* [1994] 3 All ER 641, [1994] Fam 192. As Brooke LJ said in *Douglas'* case (see para 43 above) it is a powerful card to which I must pay appropriate respect. I am being asked to extend the domestic law of confidence to grant injunctions in this case. I am satisfied that I can only restrict the freedom of the media to publish if the need for those restrictions can be shown to fall within the exceptions set out in Art. 10(2). In considering the limits to the law of confidence, and whether a remedy is available to the claimants within those limits, I must interpret narrowly those exceptions. In so doing and having regard to Arts. 2, 3 and 8 it is important to have regard to the fact that the rights under Arts. 2 and 3 are not capable of derogation, and the consequences to the claimants if those rights were to be breached. It is clear that, on the basis that there is a real possibility that the claimants may be the objects of revenge attacks, the potential breaches of Arts. 2, 3 and 8 have to be evaluated with great care.

78. What is the information sought to be protected and how important is it to protect it? The single most important element of the information is the detection of the future identity of the claimants in the community. All the other matters sought to be protected for the present, and for the future, are bound up in the risk of identification, whether by photographs, or by descriptions of identifying features of their appearance as adults, and their new names, addresses and similar information. That risk is potentially extreme if it became known what they look like, and where they are. The risk might come from any quarter, strangers such as vigilante groups, as well as the parents, family and friends of the murdered child. In the present case, the public authority, the court, has knowledge of the risk to the claimants. Does the risk displace the right of the media to publish information about the claimants without any restriction imposed by the court?

79. As I have set out, Art. 10(2) recognises the express exception 'for preventing the disclosure of information received in confidence'. None the less, in order for it to be used to restrict freedom of expression, all the criteria in Art. 10(2), narrowly interpreted, must be met. Taking each limb in turn. ...

80. I am satisfied that, taking into account the effect of the convention on our law, the law of confidence can extend to cover the injunctions sought in this case and, therefore, the restrictions proposed are in accordance with the law. There is a well-established cause of action in the tort of breach of confidence in respect of which injunctions may be granted. The common law continues to evolve, as it has done for centuries, and it is being given considerable impetus to do so by the implementation of the convention into our domestic law. I am encouraged in that view by the observations of Brooke LJ in *Douglas v Hello! Ltd* [2001] IP & T 391 at 405–406 (para. 61):

---

7   *Ed*. For the text of para. 23, see above, p. 924.
8   *Ed*. Reprinted above, p. 930.

'It is well known that this court in *Kaye v Robertson* [1991] FSR 62 said in uncompromising terms that there was no tort of privacy known to English law. In contrast, both academic commentary and extra-judicial commentary by judges over the last ten years have suggested from time to time that a development of the present frontiers of a breach of confidence action could fill the gap in English law which is filled by privacy law in other developed countries. This commentary was given a boost recently by the decision of the European Commission on Human Rights in *Earl Spencer v UK* (1998) 25 EHRR CD 105, and by the coming into force of the Human Rights Act 1998.'

Keene LJ said:

'…breach of confidence is a developing area of the law, the boundaries of which are not immutable but may change to reflect changes in society, technology and business practice.' (See [2001] IP & T 391 at 433 (para. 165).)

81. The duty of confidence may arise in equity independently of a transaction or relationship between parties. In this case it would be a duty placed upon the media. A duty of confidence does already arise when confidential information comes to the knowledge of the media, in circumstances in which the media have notice of its confidentiality. An example is the medical reports of a private individual which are recognised as being confidential. Indeed it is so well-known that medical reports are confidential that Mr. Desmond Browne submitted that it was not necessary to protect that information by an injunction. It is also recognised that it is just in all the circumstances that information known to be confidential should not be disclosed to others, in this case by publication in the press (see Lord Goff in *A-G v Guardian Newspapers (No 2)*). The issue is whether the information leading to disclosure of the claimants' identity and location comes within the confidentiality brackets. In answering that crucial question, I can properly rely upon the European case law and the duty on the court, where necessary, to take appropriate steps to safeguard the physical safety of the claimants, including the adoption of measures even in the sphere of relations of individuals and/or private organisations between themselves. Under the umbrella of confidentiality there will be information which may require a special quality of protection. In the present case the reason for advancing that special quality is that, if the information was published, the publication would be likely to lead to grave and possibly fatal consequences. In my judgment, the court does have the jurisdiction, in exceptional cases, to extend the protection of confidentiality of information, even to impose restrictions on the press, where not to do so would be likely to lead to serious physical injury, or to the death, of the person seeking that confidentiality, and there is no other way to protect the applicants other than by seeking relief from the court….

82. It is a very strong possibility, if not, indeed, a probability, that on the release of these two young men, there will be great efforts to find where they will be living and, if that information becomes public, they will be pursued. Among the pursuers may well be those intent on revenge. The requirements in the convention that there can be no derogation from the rights under Arts. 2 and 3 provides exceptional support for the strong and pressing social need that their confidentiality be protected. …

83. Although injunctions have not been granted in such circumstances in the past, I am satisfied that, to protect information requiring a special quality of protection, injunctions can be granted. I gain support for that conclusion from the judgment of Lord Woolf MR in the *Broadmoor* case,[9] and the fact that over the past 30 years or so the jurisdiction of the court to grant injunctions, where it has been demonstrated to be necessary and in accordance with general equitable principles, has been exercised. The provision of injunctions to achieve the object sought must be proportionate to the legitimate aim. In this case, it is to protect the claimants from serious and possibly irreparable harm, which would, in my judgment, clearly meet the requirement of proportionality. As I have already said above, there is a positive duty upon the court to take such steps as may be necessary to achieve that aim. In *Osman's* case, the European Court held that a breach of Arts. 2 and 3 would be established if the authorities knew, or ought to have known, of the existence of a real and immediate risk to the life of an identified individual, from criminal acts of a third party, and they failed to take measures, within the scope of their powers, which might have been expected to avoid that risk. In that

9   Ed. *Broadmoor Hospital Authority v R* [2000] QB 775, CA.

case, the authority was the police. In the present case, the authority is this court. I know of the existence of a real risk, which may become immediate if confidentiality is breached.

84. Lord Woolf MR said in *R v Lord Saville of Newdigate, ex p A* [1999] 4 All ER 860 at 872, [2000] 1 WLR 1855 at 1857:

'...when a fundamental right such as the right to life is engaged, the options available to the reasonable decision-maker are curtailed. They are curtailed because it is unreasonable to reach a decision which contravenes or could contravene human rights unless there are sufficiently significant countervailing considerations. In other words, it is not open to the decision-maker to risk interfering with fundamental rights in the absence of compelling justification.'

With that warning from Lord Woolf in mind, in my judgment, the appropriate measures to be taken, within the scope of my powers, would be to grant injunctions. This would have the effect of substantially reducing the risk to each of the claimants.

85. I do not see that this extension of the law of confidence, by the grant of relief in the exceptional circumstances of this case, as opening a door to the granting of general restrictions on the media in cases where anonymity would be desirable. In my judgment, that is where the strict application of Art. 10(2) bites. It will only be appropriate to grant injunctions to restrain the media where it can be convincingly demonstrated, within those exceptions, that it is strictly necessary.

86. I am uncertain, for instance, whether it would be appropriate to grant injunctions to restrict the press in this case if only Art. 8 were likely to be breached. Serious though the breach of the claimants' right to respect for family life and privacy would be, once the journalists and photographers discovered either of them, and despite the likely serious adverse effect on the efforts to rehabilitate them into society, it might not be sufficient to meet the importance of the preservation of the freedom of expression in Art. 10(1). It is not necessary, however, for me to come to a conclusion as to the weight of a breach of Art. 8, since I am entirely satisfied that there is a real and serious risk to the rights of the claimants under Arts. 2 and 3. Subject, therefore, to my assessment of the strength of the evidence presented to the court, and the possibility that some protection less than injunctions might be proportionate to the need for confidentiality, I find that, in principle, I have the jurisdiction to grant injunctions to protect the claimants in the present case. ...

89. ...Since the relief sought is to restrict the freedom of expression of the press, I approach the assessment of future risk to each of the claimants on the basis that the evidence supporting the case has to demonstrate convincingly the seriousness of the risk, but in order to assess the future, I cannot by the very nature of the task, have concrete facts upon which to rely, nor can I predict upon the basis of future probability.

90. The evidence, which I have set out above, demonstrates to me the huge and intense media interest in this case, to an almost unparalleled extent, not only over the time of the murder, during the trial and subsequent litigation, but also that media attention remains intense seven years later. Not only is the media interest intense, it also demonstrates continued hostility towards the claimants. I am satisfied from the extracts from the newspapers: (a) that the press have accurately reported the horror, moral outrage and indignation still felt by many members of the public; (b) that there are members of the public, other than the family of the murdered boy, who continue to feel such hatred and revulsion at the shocking crime and a desire for revenge that some at least of them might well engage in vigilante or revenge attacks if they knew where either claimant was living and could identify him. There also remains a serious risk from the Bulger family, and the father was quoted as recently as October 2000 saying that upon their release he would 'hunt the boys down'; (c) that some sections of the press support this feeling of revulsion and hatred to the degree of encouraging the public to deny anonymity to the claimants. The inevitable conclusion to which I am driven, in particular, by the editorial from the *News of the World* (one of the newspapers in the first defendant group), is that sections of the press would support, and might even initiate, efforts to find the claimants and to expose their identity and their addresses in their newspapers. I have in mind, for example, the coupon campaign run by the *Sun*, demanding that the boys remain in detention for life and the recent *News of the World* campaign 'naming and shaming' paedophiles. The response of some members of the public to emotive newspaper reporting has created highly emotional and potentially dangerous situations. The misidentification of a female member of the public,

thought erroneously to be the mother of one of the claimants, was potentially very dangerous and demonstrates the probable reaction of members of the public to the knowledge that one of the claimants and his family were living nearby. I also bear in mind that the media coverage has been international as well as national. The information might be gathered from elsewhere and presented to an English national or local newspaper. Once in the public domain, it is a real possibility, almost a probability, that there would be widespread reporting by the press. If photographs are taken, and they would be likely to be taken, the claimants would find it difficult to settle anywhere safely, at least within the United Kingdom. It would, however, be fair to point out that there have also been, particularly recently, thoughtful and objective articles in the newspapers, and a reasoned debate over the correct period of detention for child offenders who commit appalling murders.

91. The evidence provided by the Secretary of State supported and affirmed much of the reporting in the press. It is most significant that this is only the second time ever that the Home Office has thought it necessary to provide a new identity for child murderers when they leave detention, the other being Mary Bell in 1980. This is a clear indication of the seriousness with which the authorities view the possibility that either claimant may be recognised with the consequences that they fear.

92. The Attorney General and the Official Solicitor both submitted that there is a high risk of serious physical harm and the real possibility that a claimant might be killed if identified. Morland J and Pill LJ felt it necessary to grant injunctions to protect the children during their detention in secure accommodation. In 1993 Morland J considered that there was a very real risk of revenge attacks upon them from others. Lord Woolf CJ in his statement on the tariff in October 2000 confirmed, from the information presented to him on the tariff, that that remained the situation (see [2001] 1 All ER 737 at 739). I heard evidence, in chambers, which supported the conclusion to which Lord Woolf CJ came, that there are solid grounds for concern that, if their identities were revealed on release, there might well be an attack or attacks on the claimants, and that such an attack or attacks might well be murderous.

93. At the moment, the claimants are not at risk. First, the injunctions are still in force. Second, there is no current photograph of either claimant, or any current description of the appearance of either in the public domain. The photographs that are available were taken when they were children and they are now adults. When they are released from detention with new names, so long as they are not identified, they will be living in the community, under life-long supervision, but with the opportunity for rehabilitation and reintegration.

94. I consider it is a real possibility that someone, journalist or other, will, almost certainly, seek them out, and if they are found, as they may well be found, the media would, in the absence of injunctions, be likely to reveal that information in the newspapers and on television, radio, etc. If the identities of the claimants were revealed, journalists and photographers would be likely to descend upon them in droves, foreign as well as national and local, and there would be widespread dissemination of the new names, addresses and appearance of the claimants. From all the evidence provided to me, I have come to the clear conclusion that if the new identity of these claimants became public knowledge it would have disastrous consequences for the claimants, not only from intrusion and harassment but, far more important, the real possibility of serious physical harm and possible death from vengeful members of the public or from the Bulger family. If their new identities were discovered, I am satisfied that neither of them would have any chance of a normal life and that there is a real and strong possibility that their lives would be at risk.

95. The claimants seek injunctions effectively for the rest of their lives. Is the grant of injunctions proportionate to the risk which I have identified? Mr. Desmond Browne argued that the editors of the newspapers that he represented could be trusted not to reveal information that would lead to the identity of the claimants. Editorial judgment should be respected and trusted. That brings in the question whether it is necessary, in order to achieve anonymity, to require injunctions. Although I recognise that editors do exercise judgment and restraint in some of the stories they run, I do not consider that editorial restraint can be the answer here. I am prepared to believe that editors of some newspapers might well hesitate to reveal this information. I do not see how editorial judgment would be able to restrain all the newspapers, particularly those now calling for that information to be made available. I also find it difficult to accept the case of the newspapers that they should be trusted not to publish when, at the same time, their counsel

submitted that it was wrong for the claimants to have the advantages of anonymity and to be allowed to live a lie. No offer has been made to the court not to publish. On the contrary, I am satisfied from the editorial in the *News of the World* (29 October 2000), that one newspaper at least would wish to publish information about identity or address if that information became available to them. Once one paper gives the information, all the papers will obviously be likely also to publish all the information they can obtain which remains live news. The judgment of editors cannot be an adequate protection to meet the risk I have identified.

96. The Press Code, as applied by the Press Complaints Commission, is not, in the exceptional situation of the claimants, sufficient protection. Criticism of, or indeed sanctions imposed upon, the offending newspaper after the information is published would, in the circumstances of this case, be too late. The information would be in the public domain and the damage would be done. The Press Code cannot adequately protect in advance. The risk is too great for the court to rely upon the voluntary Press Code. To do so would not be a sufficient response to the principles enunciated in *Osman's* case. I do not consider that the provisions of the 1997 Act would or could be adequate to protect the claimants if their identities became known. Recourse to the courts after the event would be too late—for example because they would have by then, almost certainly, been photographed, and would then be recognised everywhere.

97. These uniquely notorious young men are and will, on release, be in a most exceptional situation and the risks to them of identification are real and substantial. It is therefore necessary, in the exceptional circumstances of this case, to place the right to confidence above the right of the media to publish freely information about the claimants. Although the crime of these two young men was especially heinous, they did not thereby forfeit their rights under English law and under the convention. They have served their tariff period and when they are released, they have the right of all citizens to the protection of the law. In order to give them the protection they need and are entitled to receive, I am compelled to grant injunctions. ...

98. The submission of the defendants was, that even if there was jurisdiction to grant injunctions against them in this case, there was no jurisdiction to grant those injunctions against the world at large. The general principle was stated by Lord Eldon LC in *Iveson v Harris* (1802) 7 Ves 251 at 257, 32 ER 102 at 104: '...you cannot have an injunction except against a party to the suit'. ...

100. Although the dictum of Lord Eldon LC has been generally followed for nearly 200 years, in light of the implementation of the 1998 Act, we are entering a new era, and the requirement that the courts act in a way that is compatible with the convention, and have regard to European jurisprudence, adds a new dimension to those principles. I am satisfied that the injunctive relief that I grant should, in this case, be granted openly against the world. ...

104. In my judgment, there are compelling reasons to grant injunctions to protect, in the broadest terms, the following informtion. (i) Any information leading to the identity, or future whereabouts, of each claimant, which includes photographs, description of present appearance and so on. (ii) In order to protect the claimants on their release from detention, it is necessary to have injunctions to protect their present whereabouts, any information about their present appearance and similar information. That protection must include any efforts by the media to solicit information from past or present carers, staff or co-detainees at their secure units until the claimants' release from detention. (iii) In order further to protect their future identity and whereabouts, no information may be made public or solicited from their secure units that might lead to the identification of the units for a reasonable period after their release. It would seem to me that twelve months from the date of the release of each claimant would be a sufficient period to protect that information, subject to any further argument from counsel. (iv) It is not necessary, in my judgment, to protect other information relating to their period in the secure units when they were under 18 for two reasons. Firstly, the important information, from the medical/health professionals, including therapists and from social workers and other carers and from co-detainees who shared the confidential situations is already covered by confidentiality. Secondly, the other information is not covered by the necessity/imperative to keep it out of the public domain and their time in their secure units is not of itself confidential. There is much, after the twelve month embargo on information, that would be appropriately made public, such as the regime in the units. (v) I recognise the concerns, however, of the claimants as to what is and what is not confidential in the past information. I would be prepared

therefore to set out, if requested, a preamble to my order on the information setting out the categories of information which are confidential.

105. I am, of course, aware that injunctions may not be fully effective to protect the claimants from acts committed outside England and Wales resulting in information about them being placed on the internet. The injunctions can, however, prevent wider circulation of that information through the newspapers or television and radio. To that end, therefore, I would be disposed to add, in relation to information in the public domain, a further proviso, suitably limited, which would protect the special quality of the new identity, appearance and addresses of the claimants or information leading to that identification, even after that information had entered the public domain to the extent that it had been published on the internet or elsewhere such as outside the United Kingdom.

I am also aware that the Parole Board will soon be making inquiries and compiling a report for consideration at the Parole Board hearing. It is, in my view, essential that the nature of the inquiries, the content of the report and the hearing itself must be covered by the injunctions.

Injunction granted.

NOTES

1. This case is of interest because of its consideration of the impact of the HRA 1998 and its extension of the law of breach of confidence. As to the former, Dame Elizabeth Butler-Sloss P relied upon Sedley LJ in *Douglas v Hello!*[10] in balancing, on the one hand, the right to freedom of expression in Art. 10(1) and, on the other hand, the limitations on that freedom in Art. 10(2), together with the other relevant convention rights in Art. 2, 3 and 8 ECHR.

2. As to the extension of the law of breach of confidence, Dame Elizabeth Butler Sloss again found support in *Douglas v Hello!* for a duty of confidence on the part of the press not to disclose the identity or whereabouts of the two convicted murderers. As in the development of the law of confidence concerning photographs and situations where a person lawfully happens upon confidential information,[11] it is arguable that the better approach is to formulate a totally new tort of invasion of privacy, rather than artifically force the facts into the breach of confidence mould.

Woolgar v Chief Constable of the Sussex Police [1999] 3 All ER 604, Court of Appeal

The appellant, a registered nurse and the matron of a nursing home, was arrested and interviewed by the police on suspicion of having given an overdose of drugs to a patient who had died. The police decided not to prosecute for lack of evidence, but the UK Central Council for Nursing (UKCCN) initiated disciplinary proceedings against the appellant in respect of the alleged overdose and other allegations of maltreatment of patients and, following its normal practice, asked the police for any relevant information. The appellant sought to overturn a court decision refusing her an injunction to prevent the police disclosing the tape of her police interview to the UKCCN, she having refused to give consent thereto.

Kennedy LJ:
Undoubtedly when someone is arrested and interviewed by the police what he or she says is confidential. Plainly it may be used in the course of a criminal trial if charges are brought arising out of that investigation, but if it is not so used the person interviewed is entitled to believe that, generally speaking, his or her confidence will be respected. If authority be required

10 Above, p. 922.
11 See above, p. 967.

for that proposition, it can be found in *Taylor v Serious Fraud Office* [1998] 4 All ER 801, [1998] 3 WLR 1040 but, as all of the authorities cited to us indicate, there are exceptional circumstances which justify the disclosure by the police, otherwise than in the course of a criminal trial, of what has been said by a suspect during the course of an interview, in circumstances where the suspect, or former suspect, does not consent to such disclosure. The question which arises in this case is whether, if the regulatory body of the profession to which the suspect belongs is investigating serious allegations and makes a formal request to the police for disclosure of what was said in interview, the public interest in the proper working of the regulatory body is or may be such as to justify disclosure of the material sought. If the answer to that question is in the affirmative how, as a matter of procedure, should contentious issues in relation to disclosure be resolved?

... Under English law the position now is that records such as fingerprints and photographs obtained during the course of an investigation are destroyed unless the suspect is convicted or cautioned. A taped interview does not suffer a similar fate. One sealed copy is retained and para. 6.3 of the *Code of Practice on Tape Recording of Interviews with Suspects* (Code E) issued in accordance with s. 60 of the Police and Criminal Evidence Act 1984 provides:

'Where no criminal proceedings result it is the responsibility of the chief officer of police to establish arrangements for the breaking of the seal on the master tape, where this becomes necessary.'

Obviously the rule contemplates the possibility that breaking of the seal may become necessary, but that possibility can arise in circumstances other than those with which we are concerned. In 1986 the Home Office issued a circular (Police Reports of Convictions and Related Information, Home Office circular 45/1986) to police forces giving guidance on the disclosure of previous convictions and related information. This was recognised to be an area where the duty to maintain confidence could conflict with, for example, a public interest in safeguarding children, and para. 2 of the circular begins:

'The general principle governing disclosure remains that police information should not be disclosed unless there are important considerations of public interest to justify departure from the general rule of confidentiality. The 3 areas in which exceptions are made are the protection of vulnerable members of society; the need to ensure probity in the administration of law, and national security.'

The respondents invite us to note the reference to 'vulnerable members of society' ...

The first of the English authorities we were invited to consider is *Beloff v Pressdram Ltd* [1973] 1 All ER 241, and Mr. Wadsworth [for the appellant] submits that it should now be read in the light of later authorities. It concerned a breach of copyright, and Ungoed-Thomas J when dealing with the submission that public interest might justify disclosure, cited (at 260) from Lord Denning MR's judgment in *Initial Services Ltd v Putterill* [1967] 3 All ER 145 at 148, [1968] 1 QB 396 at 405, where Lord Denning MR said that the exception which justified disclosure—

'should extend to crimes, frauds and misdeeds, both those actually committed as well as those in contemplation, provided always—and this is essential—that the disclosure is justified in the public interest.'

Ungoed-Thomas J then looked at later cases and continued ([1973] 1 All ER 241 at 260):

'The defence of public interest clearly covers and, in the authorities does not extend beyond, disclosure, which as Lord Denning MR emphasised must be disclosure justified in the public interest, of matters carried out or contemplated, in breach of the country's security, or in breach of law, including statutory duty, fraud, or otherwise destructive of the country or its people, including matters medically dangerous to the public; and doubtless other misdeeds of similar gravity.'

Here again the respondents invite our attention to 'matters medically dangerous to the public'. ...

In *A-G v Guardian Newspapers (No 2)* [1988] 3 All ER 545, [1990] 1 AC 109 (the 'Spycatcher' case) the claim was for an injunction to restrain future publication of information derived from a former member of the security services. Lord Griffiths said ([1988] 3 All ER 545 at 649–650, [1990] 1 AC 109 at 268–269):

'The courts have … always refused to uphold the right to confidence when to do so would be to cover up wrongdoing. In *Gartside v Outram* (1856) 26 LJ Ch 113 it was said that there could be no confidence in iniquity. This approach has been developed in the modern authorities to include cases in which it is in the public interest that the confidential information should be disclosed: see *Initial Services Ltd v Putterill* [1967] 3 All ER 145, [1968] 1 QB 396, *Beloff v Pressdram Ltd* [1973] 1 All ER 241 and *Lion Laboratories Ltd v Evans* [1984] 2 All ER 417, [1985] QB 526. This involves the judge in balancing the public interest in upholding the right to confidence, which is based on the moral principles of loyalty and fair dealing, against some other public interest that will be served by the publication of the confidential material. Even if the balance comes down in favour of publication, it does not follow that publication should be to the world through the media. In certain circumstances the public interest may be better served by a limited form of publication perhaps to the police or some other authority who can follow up a suspicion that wrongdoing may lurk beneath the cloak of confidence. Those authorities will be under a duty not to abuse the confidential information and to use it only for the purpose of their inquiry. If it turns out that the suspicions are without foundation, the confidence can then still be protected …'

Lord Goff said ([1988] 3 All ER 545 at 659, [1990] 1 AC 109 at 282):

'…although the basis of the law's protection of confidence is that there is a public interest that confidences should be preserved and protected by the law, nevertheless that public interest may be outweighed by some other countervailing public interest which favours disclosure. This limitation may apply … to all types of confidential information. It is this limiting principle which may require a court to carry out a balancing operation, weighing the public interest in maintaining confidence against a countervailing, public interest favouring disclosure.'

In both speeches there is recognised the possibility of countervailing public interests, and of the need to balance one against the other …

In *R v Chief Constable of the North Wales Police, ex p AB* [1998] 3 All ER 310, [1999] QB 396 convicted paedophiles sought declarations that the decision of the police to inform a caravan site owner of their convictions was unlawful. They failed. In the Divisional Court Lord Bingham CJ said ([1997] 4 All ER 691 at 698, [1999] QB 396 at 409–410):

'When, in the course of performing its public duties, a public body (such as a police force) comes into possession of information relating to a member of the public, being information not generally available and potentially damaging to that member of the public if disclosed, the body ought not to disclose such information save for the purpose of and to the extent necessary for performance of its public duty or enabling some other public body to perform its public duty.'

After referring to two authorities, Lord Bingham CJ continued ([1997] 4 All ER 691 at 699, [1999] QB 396 at 410):

'It seems to me to follow that if the police, having obtained information about an individual which it would be damaging to that individual to disclose, and which should not be disclosed without some public justification, consider in the exercise of a careful and bona fide judgment that it is desirable or necessary in the public interest to make disclosure, whether for the purpose of preventing crime or alerting members of the public to an apprehended danger, it is proper for them to make such limited disclosures as is judged necessary to achieve that purpose.'

It is worth noting in passing that there is no suggestion that it is necessary for the police to seek court approval for making a disclosure. …

'…information acquired by the police in their capacity as such, and when performing the public law duties that Lord Bingham CJ has set out, cannot be protected against disclosure in the proper performance [of] those public duties by any private law obligation of confidence. That is not because the use and publication of confidential information will not be enjoined when such use is necessary in the public interest, though that is undoubtedly the case. Rather, because of their overriding obligation to enforce the law and prevent crime the police in my view do not have the power or vires to acquire information on terms that preclude their using that information in a case where their public duty demands such use.'

The Court of Appeal upheld the decision of the Divisional Court. Lord Woolf MR giving the judgment of the court, said ([1998] 3 All ER 310 at 321, [1999] QB 396 at 429):

'The issue here is not the same as it would be in private law. The fact that the convictions of the applicants had been in the public domain, did not mean that the police as a public authority were free to publish information about their previous offending absent any public interest in this being done. As Lord Bingham CJ stated, before this happens it must at least be a situation where in all the circumstances it is desirable to make disclosure. Both under [the European Convention on Human Rights] and as a matter of English administrative law, the police are entitled to use information when they reasonably conclude this is what is required (after taking into account the interests of the applicant), in order to protect the public and in particular children.'

Another recent example to which we were referred is *Bunn v BBC* [1998] 3 All ER 552. A plaintiff who had faced trial for conspiracy to defraud tried to stop the defendants from including in a broadcast and in a book admissions he had made when interviewed by the police which had been referred to in open court. He failed because the material was already in the public domain, but Lightman J (at 557) recognised that:

'There is a substantial public interest in an accused person being able to make full disclosure in a statement to the police without fear of that statement being used for extraneous purposes.'

...

Essentially Mr. Wadsworth's submission was and is that when the appellant answered questions when interviewed by the police she did so in the reasonable belief that what she said would go no further unless it was used by the police for the purposes of criminal proceedings. The caution administered to her so indicated, and in order to safeguard the free flow of information to the police it is essential that those who give information should be able to have confidence that what they say will not be used for some collateral purpose.

However, in my judgment, where a regulatory body such as the UKCC, operating in the field of public health and safety, seeks access to confidential material in the possession of the police, being material which the police are reasonably persuaded is of some relevance to the subject matter of an inquiry being conducted by the regulatory body, then a countervailing public interest is shown to exist which, as in this case, entitles the police to release the material to the regulatory body on the basis that save in so far as it may be used by the regulatory body for the purposes of its own inquiry, the confidentiality which already attaches to the material will be maintained. As Mr. Horan said in para. 14 of his skeleton argument:

'A properly and efficiently regulated nursing profession is necessary in the interest of the medical welfare of the country, to keep the public safe, and to protect the rights and freedoms of those vulnerable individuals in need of nursing care. A necessary part of such regulation is the ensuring of the free flow of the best available information to those charged by statute with the responsibility to regulate.'

Putting the matter in convention terms Lord Lester submitted, and I would accept, that disclosure is 'necessary in a democratic society in the interests of ... public safety or ... for the protection of health or morals, or for the protection of the rights and freedoms of others.'

Even if there is no request from the regulatory body, it seems to me that if the police come into possession of confidential information which, in their reasonable view, in the interests of public health or safety, should be considered by a professional or regulatory body, then the police are free to pass that information to the relevant regulatory body for its consideration.

Obviously in each case a balance has to be struck between competing public interests, and at least arguably in some cases the reasonableness of the police view may be open to challenge. If they refuse to disclose, the regulatory body can, if aware of the existence of the information, make an appropriate application to the court. In order to safeguard the interests of the individual, it is, in my judgment, desirable that where the police are minded to disclose, they should, as in this case, inform the person affected of what they propose to do in such time as to enable that person, if so advised, to seek assistance from the court. In some cases that may not be practicable or desirable, but in most cases that seems to me to be the course that should be followed. In any event, in my judgment, the primary decision as to disclosure should be made by the police who have the custody of the relevant material, and not by the court.

I would therefore dismiss this appeal.

Otton LJ and **Waller LJ** concurred.

Appeal dismissed.

NOTES

1. The *Woolgar* case concerns the third of Megarry J's three requirements in the *Coco* case, viz. the 'unauthorised use of that information to the detriment of the party communicating it', which is expressed in the *Woolgar* case in terms of a 'public interest' defence. As indicated, in the quotation from Lord Griffiths in the *Guardian Newspapers* case, the defence was formerly limited to cases where the disclosure would reveal 'iniquity', which was understood at one time to include only criminal conduct, but was gradually extended beyond that to other cases of misconduct. Now, as in the *Woolgar* case, the language of iniquity has been abandoned and the question is one of balancing the public interest in protecting confidences against other kinds of public interest.[12] Although, on its facts, the *Woolgar* case concerns the situation where the police respond to a request for information, the rule in the case is expressed more widely, so as to allow the police to volunteer information (e.g. about the presence of a paedophile).

2. In *Hellewell v Chief Constable of Derbyshire*,[13] as a part of a campaign to reduce shoplifting and harassment in shops, the police gave local traders copies of photographs of suspects, including a 'mug shot' of the plaintiff when he was arrested for theft. A claim by the plaintiff for declaratory relief and an injunction to prevent his photograph being disclosed to members of the public in this way was struck out. Laws J stated:

> '...In my judgment, having regard to the general principles of the law of confidence...where the police take a photograph of a suspect such as that in question here, and do so at the police station in circumstances where at least the suspect's consent is not required, they are not, by law, free to make whatever use they will of the picture so obtained. Such a photograph will, as I have said, convey to anyone looking at it the knowledge that its subject is or has been known to the police. That is not what I may call a public fact. It may be described, prima facie at least, as a piece of confidential information. The circumstances in which the photograph is taken, where the suspect has no choice, save to insist that physical force be not used upon him, impose obligations on the police, breach of which may sound in an action at private law. ...
>
> In my judgment, the use which the police may make of a photograph such as this is limited by their obligations to the photograph's subject as follows. They may make reasonable use of it for the purpose of the prevention and detection of crime, the investigation of alleged offences and the apprehension of suspects or persons unlawfully at large. They may do so whether or not the photograph is of any person they seek to arrest or of a suspected accomplice or of anyone else. The key is that they must have these and only these purposes in mind and must, as I have said, make no more than reasonable use of the picture in seeking to accomplish them.
>
> ...where the use in question is decided upon by the honest judgment of professional police officers, that will, of itself, go a long way to establish its reasonableness. Provided these bounds of principle are not transgressed, there will be an obvious and vital public interest in the use made of such photographs which the courts will uphold. It is perhaps confusing to put the matter on the basis that, in the celebrated dictum, "there is no confidence in iniquity"; some little difficulty has been caused in the past by the question whether the iniquity must be proved or it is enough that it is the result only of reasonable suspicion.
>
> The better analysis is in terms of the public interest defence, which is always available where the facts support it, against a confidence claim.

---

12 *Lion Laboratories Ltd v Evans* [1984] 2 All ER 417, [1985] QB 256, CA, was the first in which a public interest defence was upheld in a breach of confidence case when there was no evidence of 'iniquity' on the facts.
13 [1995] 1 WLR 804, QBD. See Ng-Loy Wee Loon, [1996] 5 EIPR 307.

The short point, at all events, is that common sense and law alike dictate that the police should be subject to no legal sanctions if they make honest and reasonable use of a suspect's photograph in the fight against crime. I take Sir Robert Megarry V.-C. to be of the same view in *Malone v Metropolitan Police Commissioner* [1979] Ch. 344, 377, which was concerned with telephone tapping. Where the use made of such photographs lies within these bounds, the police will have a public interest defence to any action brought against them for breach of confidence. ...

On the undisputed facts of the present case, it is, in my judgment, plain beyond the possibility of argument that the use made by the police of the plaintiff's photograph was lawful. There is no dispute as to their good faith. As I have said, the picture's dissemination was limited to parties having a reasonable concern to see it. There is, in my judgment, no issue here fit to be tried. The police have acted well within the scope of such obligation as the law imposes upon them in relation to the plaintiff's photograph. What they did was obviously and unarguably in the public interest: it was reasonably directed to the prevention of crime.'

3. In *Hubbard v Vosper*,[14] the first defendant had written a book in which he revealed damaging facts about scientology based upon his former membership. The disclosures were held to be justified in the public interest as arguably revealing 'medical quackery of a dangerous kind'. In *Woodward v Hutchins*,[15] the plaintiff 'pop' singers (Tom Jones, Englebert Humperdinck and Gilbert O'Sullivan) were refused an injunction to prevent the publication by their former public relations officer of embarrassing details of their personal lives in the *Daily Mirror* on grounds of public interest and public domain. Lord Denning MR stated:[16]

'There is no doubt whatever that this pop group sought publicity. They wanted to have themselves presented to the public in a favourable light so that audiences would come to hear them and support them. Mr. Hutchins was engaged so as to produce, or help to produce, this favourable image, not only of their public lives but of their private lives also. If a group of this kind seek publicity which is to their advantage, it seems to me that they cannot complain if a servant or employee of theirs afterwards discloses the truth about them. If the image which they fostered was not a true image, it is in the public interest that it should be corrected. In these cases of confidential information it is a question of balancing the public interest in maintaining the confidence against the public interest in knowing the truth. . . .

There is a further point. The injunction . . . speaks of 'confidential information'. But what is confidential? As Bridge LJ pointed out in the course of the argument, Mr. Hutchins, as a press agent, might attend a dance which many others attended. Any incident which took place at the dance would be known to all present. The information would be in the public domain. There could be no objection to the incidents being made known generally. It would not be confidential information. So in this case the incident on this jumbo jet was in the public domain. It was known to all the passengers on the flight. Likewise with several other incidents in the series.'

4. In *X v Y*,[17] the plaintiffs, a health authority, sought an injunction preventing the defendants, a reporter and newspaper publisher, from, *inter alia*, publishing the identity of two doctors who had AIDS who were continuing with their general practice or, as the defendants claimed in argument was now their sole intention, from revealing that two *unnamed* doctors with AIDS were continuing to practise. The information had been obtained from confidential hospital AIDS patients' records which had been leaked to the reporter by health authority employees. Granting the injunction, Rose J rejected a 'public interest' defence:

'I keep in the forefront of my mind the very important public interest in freedom of the press. And I accept that there is some public interest in knowing that which the defendants seek to

14 [1972] 2 QB 84, CA.
15 [1977] 1 WLR 760, CA.
16 pp. 763–764.
17 [1988] 2 All ER 648, QBD.

publish (in whichever version). But in my judgment those public interests are substantially outweighed when measured against the public interests in relation to loyalty and confidentiality both generally and with particular reference to AIDS patients' hospital records. There has been no misconduct by the plaintiffs. The records of hospital patients, particularly those suffering from this appalling condition should, in my judgment, be as confidential as the courts can properly keep them in order that the plaintiffs may 'be free from suspicion that they are harbouring disloyal employees'. The plaintiffs have 'suffered a grievous wrong in which the defendants became involved . . . with active participation'. The deprivation of the public of the information sought to be published will be of minimal significance if the injunction is granted; for, without it, all the evidence before me shows that a wide-ranging public debate about AIDS generally and about its effect on doctors is taking place among doctors of widely differing views, within and without the BMA, in medical journals and in many newspapers. . . . Paraphrasing Templeman LJ in the *Schering* case, the facts, in the most limited version now sought to be published, have already been made available and may again be made available if they are known otherwise than through the medium of the informer. The risk of identification is only one factor in assesing whether to permit the use of confidential information. In my judgment to allow publication in the recently suggested restricted form, would be to enable both defendants to procure breaches of confidence and then to make their own selection for publication. This would make a mockery of the law's protection of confidentiality when no justifying public interest has been shown. These are the considerations which guide me, whether my task is properly described as a balancing exercise, or an exercise in judicial judgment, or both.'

5. In *Francome v Mirror Group Newspapers Ltd*,[18] the *Daily Mirror* was offered by unnamed persons tapes of telephone conversations conducted on the home telephone of the champion National Hunt jockey. The tapes, which allegedly revealed breaches of the rules of racing, were obtained by means of a 'bug'.

Pending the hearing of their claim against the Mirror Group for exemplary damages for breach of confidence and for trespass, the plaintiffs, who were the champion jockey and his wife, sought an interlocutory injunction restraining the publication by the defendants of articles based upon the tapes. In granting the injunction, Sir John Donaldson MR stated:[19]

'The defendants . . . say that the plaintiffs have no right of action against them. So far as trespass is concerned, they were not parties to it. This may well be right. They go on to say that there is no cause of action against them or the eavesdroppers for breach of an obligation of confidentiality. The authority for this rather surprising proposition is said to be *Malone v Metropolitan Police Comr (No 2)*. Suffice it to say that Sir Robert Megarry V-C expressly stated that he was deciding nothing on the position when tapping was effected for purposes other than the prevention, detection and discovery of crime and criminals or by persons other than the police. . . . This is thus a live issue.

The defendants then go on to submit that, whatever their obligations towards the plaintiffs on grounds of confidentiality, they can rely on the classic, but ill-defined, exception of what is quaintly called 'iniquity'. The basis of this exception is that, whilst there is a public interest in maintaining confidentiality, there is a countervailing public interest in exposing conduct which involves a breach of the law or which is 'anti-social'. I use the term 'anti-social', without defining it, to describe activities which, whilst not in breach of the law, are seriously contrary to the public interest. In the defendants' submission the tapes revealed breaches by Mr. Francome of the rules of racing and, bearing in mind the large sums of money which are staked on the results of the races, this conduct they say is 'anti-social' within the meaning of the iniquity rule and may also involve criminal offences. Let me say at once it is not for me to say whether the tapes bear this interpretation and I express no view on that point. That will also be an issue. . . .'

---

18 [1984] 2 All ER 408, CA.
19 pp. 411–414.

6. In *W v Edgdell*,[20] the plaintiff who had killed five persons and suffered from paranoid schizophrenia, obtained a report from an independent psychiatrist in the course of preparing an application for release from a secure mental hospital. The psychiatrist was so concerned about the plaintiff's mental condition that he disclosed the report to the plaintiff's medical officer. The plaintiff was refused an injunction to prevent the defendant psychiatrist making further disclosures. Although the psychiatrist owed the plaintiff a duty of confidentiality, disclosure might be justifiable in the public interest. Bingham LJ stated:

'It has never been doubted that the circumstances here were such as to impose on Dr. Egdell a duty of confidence owed to W. He could not lawfully sell the contents of his report to a newspaper, as the judge held ante, p. 389B–C. Nor could he, without a breach of the law as well as professional etiquette, discuss the case in a learned article or in his memoirs or in gossiping with friends, unless he took appropriate steps to conceal the identity of W. It is not in issue here that a duty of confidence existed. ...

The decided cases very clearly establish: (1) that the law recognises an important public interest in maintaining professional duties of confidence; but (2) that the law treats such duties not as absolute but as liable to be overriden where there is held to be a stronger public interest in the disclosure. Thus the public interest in the administration of justice may require a clergyman, a banker, a medical man, a journalist or an accountant to breach his professional duty of confidence. ...

There is one consideration which in my judgment, as in that of the judge, weighs the balance of public interest decisively in favour of disclosure. It may be shortly put. Where a man has committed multiple killings under the disability of serious mental illness, decisions which may lead directly or indirectly to his release from hospital should not be made unless a responsible authority is properly able to make an informed judgment that the risk of repetition is so small as to be acceptable. A consultant psychiatrist who becomes aware, even in the course of a confidential relationship, of information which leads him, in the exercise of what the court considers a sound professional judgment, to fear that such decisions may be made on the basis of inadequate information and with a real risk of consequent danger to the public is entitled to take such steps as are reasonable in all the circumstances to communicate the grounds of his concern to the responsible authorities. I have no doubt that the judge's decision in favour of Dr. Egdell was right on the facts of this case.'

7. *The need for detriment.* The 'detriment' part of the third of Megarry J's three requirements in the *Coco* case has been doubted by some and given a very modest meaning by others.[1] In *A-G v Guardian Newspapers Ltd (No 2)*, Lord Keith took the view that 'it is in the public interst that confidences should be respected', so that there was no need for the plaintiff to show 'specific detriment to himself'.[2] The requirement was explained and applied by Rose J in *X v Y*,[3] as follows:

'In my judgment detriment *in the use of* the information is not a necessary precondition to injunctive relief. Although in *Seager v Copydex Ltd* the Court of Appeal held, by reference to the facts of that case, that the confidential information could not be used as a springboard for activities detrimental to the plaintiff, I do not understand any member of the court to have been saying that detrimental use is always necessary. I respectfully agree with Megarry V-C that an injunction may be appropriate for breach of confidence where the plaintiff may not suffer from the use of the information and that is borne out by more recent observations in the Court of Appeal and House of Lords ...(in particular in *Lion Laboratiries Ltd v Evans* [1984]

20 [1990] Ch 359 at 419, 424, CA.
1 As noted by Simon Brown LJ in *R v Department of Health, ex p Source Informatics Ltd* [2000] 1 All ER 786 at 790 CA, on 'the very next page of his judgment' in the *Coco* case, 'Megarry J expressly kept open the possibility that 'detriment' was not, after all, required'.
2 See the extract from his speech, above, p. 450. Lord Griffiths briefly, ([1990] 1 AC 109 at 269) stated that detriment was required. Lord Goff (at 281) preferred to leave the question open.
3 Above, p. 987.

2 All ER 417, [1985] QB 526, *Schering Chemicals Ltd v Falkman Ltd* [1981] 2 All ER 321, [1982] QB 1 and *British Steel Corp v Granada Television Ltd* [1981] 1 All ER 417, [1981] AC 1096), which contain no reference to the necessity for detriment in use and, indeed, point away from any such principle. In the present case, detriment occurred to the plaintiffs because patients' records were leaked to the press in breach of contract and breach of confidence, with the consequences, even without publication, to the plaintiffs and the patients listed by counsel for the plaintiffs. If use were made of that information in such a way as to demonstrate to the public (by identifying the hopsital) the source of the leak, the plaintiffs would suffer further detriment. But use of the information (as the defendants now seek) in a way which identifies neither the hospital nor the patients does not mean that the plaintiffs have suffered no detriment. Significant damage, about which the plaintiffs are entitled to complain, has already been done. This is also the answer to the additional submission of counsel for the first defendant that, though there was a breach of confidence in obtaining the information there is, on the evidence, none in publishing it, if the doctors are not identified. In my judgment it is, in the present case, the initial disclosure and its immediate consequences, not subsequent publication, which found the plaintiffs' claim in breach of contract and breach of confidence.'

8. On *damages for breach of confidence* (which will be the only satisfactory remedy where publication has already occurred), Sir Robert Megarry V-C stated in *Malone v Metropolitan Police Comr*:[4]

'This is an equitable right which is still in course of development, and is usually protected by the grant of an injunction to prevent disclosure of the confidence. Under Lord Cairns' Act 1858 damages may be granted in substitution for an injunction; yet if there is no case for the grant of an injunction, as when the disclosure has already been made, the unsatisfactory result seems to be that no damages can be awarded under this head: see *Proctor v Bayley* (1889) 42 Ch D 390. In such a case, where there is no breach of contract or other orthodox foundation for damages at common law, it seems doubtful whether there is any right to damages, as distinct from an account of profits.[5] It may be, however, that a new tort is emerging (see *Goff and Jones, The Law of Restitution* (2nd edn, 1978), pp. 518, 519, and Gareth Jones (1970) 86 LQR 463 at 491), though this has been doubted: see *Street, The Law of Torts* (6th edn, 1976), p. 377.'

Damages were awarded in *Seager v Copydex* (a trade secrets case).[6] They were to be 'assessed on the basis of reasonable compensation for the use of confidential information' (Lord Denning MR). In *Seager v Copydex (No 2)*,[7] Winn LJ stated that the damages were to be recovered 'on a tortious basis' and Lord Denning MR drew an analogy with conversion. Relying upon this case, North[8] argues that breach of confidence, which developed as an equitable principle, is now a tort at common law.[9] Presumably, if damages may be awarded for commercial loss (as in *Seager v Copydex*) they may be awarded for material loss in a privacy context (e.g. for dismissal when confidential information is passed on to an employer).[10] There is, however, despite the analogies that exist,[11] 'no authority to support an award of damages for mental stress'.[12] The Law Commission recommends that mental suffering be a head of damages for breach of confidence.[13]

---

4 p. 360.
5 A newspaper was ordered to make an account of profits in respect of an article published in breach of confidence in *A-G v Guardian Newspapers Ltd (No 2)* [1990] 1 AC 109, HL.
6 [1967] 2 All ER 415, CA.
7 [1969] 2 All ER 718, CA.
8 (1972) 12 JoSPTL 149.
9 On the Law Commission's proposal for a statutory tort, see above, p. 960.
10 See Law Commission Report No. 110, p. 67.
11 See *Williams v Settle*, above, p. 957, and s. 57(4), Race Relations Act 1976.
12 Ibid., p. 68.
13 Ibid., p. 152.

9. With regard to interlocutory injunctions (i.e. those granted pending the hearing of a case on the merits), the Calcutt Committee commented critically on their effect on third parties:[14]

> 'These injunctions are to all intents and purposes binding on a third party as soon as that party is notified of its terms. In *A-G v Newspaper Publishing plc* [1988] Ch 333 (the Spycatcher case) the Court of Appeal held that newspapers, which were not party to an injunction, could be guilty of contempt at common law if they published the information covered by the injunction, provided the relevant *mens rea* (criminal state of mind) was present. The purpose of the original injunction was to protect the position pending trial because the claim of confidentiality could only be tested at that stage. However, if someone else published the information in the meantime, the proceedings would become pointless and the Court's purpose in granting the temporary injunction would be defeated.
> ... We are persuaded that, in general terms, it is unjust for a newspaper to be restricted by the terms of an injunction without having an opportunity to argue against it. While the reasoning of the Court of Appeal in the Spycatcher case has been widely misunderstood, we nevertheless consider that the practical consequences for third parties, whose freedom of speech is undoubtedly restricted, should be urgently addressed, possibly by the Supreme Court Procedure Committee.'

(G) OTHER REMEDIES IN LAW

It has been suggested[15] that the tort of *intentional infliction of physical harm* (other than by trespass) established in *Wilkinson v Downton*,[16] could be developed to provide a remedy. In that case, as a practical joke the defendant told the plaintiff that the plaintiff's husband had broken his legs in an accident. The plaintiff suffered nervous shock causing 'serious and permanent physical consequences'. Wright J awarded her damages on the following basis:

> 'The defendant has wilfully done an act calculated to cause physical harm to the plaintiff— that is to say, to infringe her legal right to personal safety, and has in fact thereby caused physical harm to her. That proposition without more appears to me to state a good cause of action, there being no justification alleged for the act. This wilful *injuria* is in law malicious, although no malicious purpose to cause the harm which was caused nor any motive of spite is imputed to the defendant.'

The decision was approved and relied on by the Court of Appeal in *Janvier v Sweeney*.[17] In that case, the defendants, private detectives, sought to persuade the plaintiff to hand over letters to which she had access by telling her falsely that she was wanted by Scotland Yard for corresponding with a German spy. The plaintiff recovered damages for physical illness resulting from shock. Cf. the Press Council case[18] in which the press contacted a young girl and correctly informed her in the absence of her mother that her estranged father whom she had not seen since she was a baby had been granted a right of access to her by a court order. The girl 'suffered a serious emotional upset which required medical attention'.

Might there be liability in tort for *negligent misstatement* if a reporter failed to check his facts and published an inaccurate statement about someone's personal life (e.g. that he takes heroin or has a mistress) that causes him to lose his job? Is there a duty of care? In a Press Council case,[19] *The Sunday Times* mistakenly reported that

---

14 Report, p. 34.
15 See Dworkin, (1967) 2 U Tas LR 418, 444, and Neill, (1962) 25 MLR 393, 402.
16 [1897] 2 QB 57, QBD.
17 [1919] 2 KB 316, CA.
18 11th Report 1964, p. 36.
19 14th Report 1967, p. 53.

a person had committed suicide when the coroner's verdict was otherwise. What if his widow suffered physical injury resulting from shock?

Breach of contract may provide a remedy in some cases.[20]

In *criminal law*, eavesdroppers and 'peeping Toms' may be bound over to be of good behaviour.[21] A compulsive 'nosey parker' who had been seen peeping through many a window and who had been trapped with her hand in someone's letter box was bound over to keep the peace. She had earlier had buckets of water and snowballs thrown at her by neighbours.[1] Eavesdropping is not a criminal offence.[2] In *DPP v Withers*[3] the defendants were private detectives. They were convicted on two counts of conspiracy to effect a public mischief by (on the first count) obtaining confidential information from banks and building societies about private accounts by making telephone calls pretending to be officials from other banks, etc., and (on the second count) by obtaining confidential information from the Criminal Records Office, vehicle registration authorities and the Ministry of Defence. The information in relation to the second count was obtained either by deceit or by persuading a public official to act contrary to his duty. The convictions were quashed by the House of Lords on the ground that conspiracy to effect a public mischief was not a crime.[4] A majority of the House of Lords in *DPP v Withers* thought the defendants might have been guilty on the second count of a conspiracy to defraud. Two members—Lord Reid and Viscount Dilhorne—would appear to have taken the same view in respect of the first count. The Criminal Law Act 1977 retains conspiracy to defraud as an offence, but does not resolve the question whether private detectives (and others) may commit it only if they deceive public officials or defy public officials for this purpose. One situation which criminal law does not cover is that in which a person 'steals' information (by, for example, photographing a document). In *Oxford v Moss*,[5] a university student dishonestly obtained a copy of the proof of an examination paper and read and returned it. It was held that he could not be guilty of theft because information was not 'property' that could be stolen.[6]

4 Invasion of privacy by the media

In addition to such remedies at law as may exist, the following regulatory bodies have powers to receive and pronounce upon (in a legally non-binding way) invasions of privacy by the press and in broadcasting.

(A) PRESS COMPLAINTS COMMISSION

Code of Practice

The Press Complaints Commission is charged with enforcing the following Code of Practice which was framed by the newspaper and periodical industry and ratified by the Press Complaints Commission, 1 December 1999. All members of the press have a duty to maintain the highest professional and ethical standards. This Code sets the benchmarks

---

20 See, e.g., *Pollard v Photographic Co*, above, p. 965. On express or implied terms in contracts of employment, see above, p. 960.
21 See *R v Wyres* (1956) 2 *Russell on Crime* (12th edn, (1964)) 1397 (spying on woman undressing).
1 *Guardian* 6 November 1979.
2 Criminal Law Act 1967, s. 13(1)(a). The Official Secrets Acts 1911–89, above, p. 808ff, protect confidential information about private individuals in official hands. For other statutory provisions, see the Younger Committee Report, Appendix I.
3 [1975] AC 842, HL.
4 The decision is confirmed by the provisions on conspiracy (ss. 1, 5) in the Criminal Law Act 1977.
5 (1978) 68 Cr App Rep 183, DC.
6 See A. M. Tettenborn, (1979) 129 NLJ 967. On the Younger Committee's recommendation for a new tort of disclosure or other use of information unlawfully acquired, see above, p. 918.

for those standards. It both protects the rights of the individual and upholds the public's right to know. The Code is the cornerstone of the system of self-regulation to which the industry has made a binding commitment. Editors and publishers must ensure that the Code is observed rigorously not only by their staff but also by anyone who contributes to their publications. It is essential to the workings of an agreed code that it be honoured not only to the letter but in the full spirit. The Code should not be interpreted so narrowly as to compromise its commitment to respect the rights of the individual, nor so broadly that it prevents publication in the public interest. It is the responsibility of editors to co-operate with the PCC as swiftly as possible in the resolution of complaints. Any publication which is criticised by the PCC under one of the following clauses must print the adjudication which follows in full and with due prominence.

1. Accuracy
  (i) Newspapers and periodicals must take care not to publish inaccurate, misleading or distorted material including pictures.
  (ii) Whenever it is recognised that a significant inaccuracy, misleading statement or distorted report has been published, it must be corrected promptly and with due prominence.
  (iii) An apology must be published whenever appropriate.
  (iv) Newspapers, whilst free to be partisan, must distinguish clearly between comment, conjecture and fact.
  (v) A newspaper or periodical must report fairly and accurately the outcome of an action for defamation to which it has been a party.

2. Opportunity to reply
A fair opportunity to reply to inaccuracies must be given to individuals or organisations when reasonably called for.

*3. Privacy
  (i) Everyone is entitled to respect for his or her private and family life, home, health and correspondence. A publication will be expected to justify intrusions into any individual's private life without consent.
  (ii) The use of long-lens photography to take pictures of people in private places without their consent is unacceptable.
Note — Private places are public or private property where there is a reasonable expectation of privacy.

*4. Harassment
  (i) Journalists and photographers must neither obtain nor seek to obtain information or pictures through intimidation, harassment or persistent pursuit.
  (ii) They must not photograph individuals in private places (as defined in the note to Clause 3) without their consent; must not persist in telephoning, questioning, pursuing or photographing individuals after having been asked to desist; must not remain on their property after having been asked to leave and must not follow them.
  (iii) Editors must ensure that those working for them comply with these requirements and must not publish material from other sources which does not meet these requirements.

5. Intrusion into grief or shock
In cases involving grief or shock, enquiries must be carried out and approaches made with sympathy and discretion. Publication must be handled sensitively at such times, but this should not be interpreted as restricting the right to report judicial proceedings.

*6. Children
  (i) Young people should be free to complete their time at school without unnecessary intrusion.
  (ii) Journalists must not interview or photograph children under the age of 16 on subjects involving the welfare of the child or of any other child, in the absence of or without the consent of a parent or other adult who is responsible for the children.
  (iii) Pupils must not be approached or photographed while at school without the permission of the school authorities.

    (iv) There must be no payment to minors for material involving the welfare of children nor payment to parents or guardians for material about their children or wards unless it is demonstrably in the child's interest.

    (v) Where material about the private life of a child is published, there must be justification for publication other than the fame, notoriety or position of his or her parents or guardian.

*7. Children in sex cases

    (i) The press must not, even where the law does not prohibit it, identify children under the age of 16 who are involved in cases concerning sexual offences, whether as victims, or as witnesses.

    (ii) In any press report of a case involving a sexual offence against a child —
        (a) The child must not be identified.
        (b) The adult may be identified.
        (c) The word "incest" must not be used where a child victim might be identified.
        (d) Care must be taken that nothing in the report implies the relationship between the accused and the child.

*8. Listening devices
Journalists must not obtain or publish material obtained by using clandestine listening devices or by intercepting private telephone conversations.

*9. Hospitals
    (i) Journalists or photographers making enquiries at hospitals or similar institutions must identify themselves to a responsible executive and obtain permission before entering non-public areas.

    (ii) The restrictions on intruding into privacy are particularly relevant to enquiries about individuals in hospitals or similar institutions.

*10. Reporting of crime
    (i) The press must avoid identifying relatives or friends or persons convicted or accused of crime without their consent.

    (ii) Particular regard should be paid to the potentially vulnerable position of children who are witnesses to, or victims of, crime. This should not be interpreted as restricting the right to report judicial proceedings.

*11. Misrepresentation
    (i) Journalists must not generally obtain or seek to obtain information or pictures through misrepresentation or subterfuge.

    (ii) Documents or photographs should be removed only with the consent of the owner.

    (iii) Subterfuge can be justified only in the public interest and only when material cannot be obtained by any other means.

12. Victims of sexual assault
The press must not identify victims of sexual assault or publish material likely to contribute to such identification unless there is adequate justification and, by law, they are free to do so.

13. Discrimination
    (i) The press must avoid prejudicial or pejorative reference to a person's race, colour, religion, sex or sexual orientation, or to any physical or mental illness or disability.

    (ii) It must avoid publishing details of a person's race, colour, religion, sexual orientation, physical or mental illness or disability unless these are directly relevant to the story.

14. Financial journalism
. . .

15. Confidential sources
Journalists have a moral obligation to protect confidential sources of information.

*16. Payment for articles
    (i) Payment or offers of payment for stories or information must not be made directly or through agents to witnesses or potential witnesses in current criminal proceedings

except where the material concerned ought to be published in the public interest and there is an overriding need to make or promise to make a payment for this to be done. Journalists must take every possible step to ensure that no financial dealings have influence on the evidence that those witnesses may give. (An editor authorising such a payment must be prepared to demonstrate that there is a legitimate public interest at stake involving matters that the public has a right to know. The payment or, where accepted, the offer of payment to any witness who is actually cited to give evidence must be disclosed to the prosecution and the defence and the witness should be advised of this.)

(ii) Payment or offers of payment for stories, pictures or information, must not be made directly or through agents to convicted or confessed criminals or to their associates — who may include family, friends and colleagues — except where the material concerned ought to be published in the public interest and payment is necessary for this to be done.

THE PUBLIC INTEREST
There may be exceptions to the clauses marked * where they can be demonstrated to be in the public interest.

1. The public interest includes:
   (i) Detecting or exposing crime or a serious misdemeanour
   (ii) Protecting public health and safety
   (iii) Preventing the public from being misled by some statement or action of an individual or organisation.
2. In any case where the public interest is invoked, the Press Complaints Commission will require a full explanation by the editor demonstrating how the public interest was served.
3. There is a public interest in freedom of expression itself. The Commission will therefore have regard to the extent to which material has, or is about to, become available to the public.
4. In cases involving children editors must demonstrate an exceptional public interest to override the normally paramount interests of the child.

NOTES

1. Established in 1991 following the Calcutt Committee Report, the Press Complaints Commission replaced the Press Council, which had existed since 1953. The Council had an independent chairman and an otherwise equal number of press and lay members. It was the subject of much criticism because of its limited powers and impact in curbing press intrusion into individual privacy.

2. Like its predecessor, the Press Complaints Commission is a non-statutory body established by the newspapers and periodicals industry with the object, *inter alia*, of hearing complaints about the conduct of the press. It has an independent chairman (Lord Wakeham) and eight non-press members and seven editors. Any person may complain to the Commission of an invasion of privacy, whether personally affected or not. The Commission does not conduct oral hearings. It has no formal conciliation procedure, although it does informally advise the parties as to a solution where appropriate. The Commission has not adopted the 'hotline' procedure recommended by the Calcutt Committee, whereby complainants would have access to editors via the Commission prior to the publication of material in the press. The Commission decided that this would involve unacceptable censorship. Nor has the Commission formally adopted the 'fast track' procedure for the correction of significant factual errors recommended by the Calcutt Committee. It does not, however, require a complainant to waive any legal right of action, as the Press Council was criticised for doing. Instead, the Commission may call upon a complainant to wait until his case has been heard before resorting to law. The Commission has the same limited sanctions as the Press Council formerly had. It may censure a newspaper or journalist, but it has no power to fine or award compensation. Newspapers are expected to publish an adverse adjudication 'in full and with due prominence', although they are under no legal obligation to do so. In fact, newspapers normally co-operate.

3. The Code of Practice was prepared by a committee of editors acting for the newspapers and periodicals industry. As far as the protection of privacy is concerned, it replaces the more detailed Press Council Declaration of Principle on Privacy.[7] The Code is revised periodically. The present version of the Code was adopted in 1999.

4. The number of complaints of invasion of privacy dealt with by the Press Council was not high. The same is true of the Press Complaints Commission.[8] In its first year of operation, only 80 of the 1,000 or so complaints found to present a prima facie case concerned privacy. Even so, as the Younger Committee Report, p. 44, stated in respect of the Press Council, although the percentage of complaints which the Council received that were on privacy are 'a tiny proportion of the whole', they are sufficient in number and diversity to indicate the hazards that press coverage present for the protection of privacy – as the examples in this chapter taken from the Council's and the Commission's practice show.

5. In his Foreword to the Press Council's 22nd Report 1975, Lord Shawcross (Chairman) was critical of gossip columns and referred approvingly to Sir Harold Wilson's suggestion 'that the test of what is permissible might be that the Press would accord to public men and women the degree of privacy they would give to their own proprietors or to their own or other editors'. Cf. the following comment by Street:[9]

> 'What is more sinister is that the privacy of certain persons only is invaded: we are told nothing of the private lives of newspaper proprietors...But let Mrs Gilliatt expose the methods of the leading gossip columnists in an article in *Queen*, and she will be hounded by squads of reporters from the *Daily Telegraph* and other dailies who will report her minute-by-minute movements in the company of playwright John Osborne.'

In his Foreword in the following year, Lord Shawcross quoted the Royal Commission on the Press's opinion 'that the way in which a few national newspapers treat some private lives is one of the worst aspects of the performance of the press'.[10] Later, the Chairman (P. Neill QC) singled out harassment by the media as a problem:[11]

> 'cases which cause the most anxiety are those where the target of persistent inquiries is a person in a vulnerable position who has no organisation to protect him or her. Repeated badgering is particularly abhorrent where the victim is innocent of fault and has become an object of notoriety through some chance circumstance. But there may be cause for concern also in cases where the victim holds a public position.'

6. In his *Review of Press Self-Regulation*, 1993, p. 24, Sir David Calcutt emphasised that the Commission was significantly different from the new body that had been proposed in the Calcutt Committee Report: it was appointed by a body that represented the press industry; the Code it operated had been adopted by the

---

7   23rd Press Council Report 1976, p. 150.
8   In the Commission's practice in privacy cases, see L. Blom-Cooper and L. R. Pruitt, (1994) 23 Anglo-American LR 133.
9   *Freedom, the Individual and the Law* (5th edn, 1982), p. 262.
10   *Final Report of the Commission* (1977), p. 100.
11   27th/28th Press Council Reports, 1980/81, Foreword.

industry and had, *inter alia*, too wide a public interest defence; the Commission was not operating a hot-line; it was unwilling to initiate inquiries; generally, it was over-emphasising press freedom to the detriment of fairness to the individual. **7.** The question whether the Press Complaints Commission is subject to judicial review was left open in *R v Press Complaints Commission, ex p Stewart-Brady*.[12]

(B) BROADCASTING STANDARDS COMMISSION

The Broadcasting Standards Commission, which consists of up to 15 members, is a body independent of the broadcasting industry, provided for by the Broadcasting Act 1996.[13] It is competent to 'consider and adjudicate on complaints' *inter alia* of 'unwarranted infringement of privacy in, or in connection with the obtaining of materials included in', BBC or independent licensed television or sound broadcasts.[14] The Commission receives only a small number of invasion of privacy complaints annually. The Commission's decisions are not legally binding and there is no power to fine or award compensation. But, if it finds that there has been an unwarranted invasion of privacy, the Commission may give directions requiring the broadcasting body or licence holder to publish in, for example, the *Radio Times*, or broadcast a summary of the complaint and the Commission's findings.[15] Although the number of invasion of privacy cases is small, some are upheld annually.

In *R v Broadcasting Complaints Commission, ex p Granada Television Ltd*,[16] it was held that the Commission had not acted unreasonably under the *Wednesbury* principle in taking the view that there was an unwarranted infringement of privacy even though the material that was broadcast was in the public domain. In that case, parents of deceased children had complained to the Commission of a television programme called 'The Allergy Business' that had shown clips of their children without forewarning them, causing them great distress. Dismissing an application for judicial review of a decision made under s. 143, 1990 Act, Popplewell J held that it was not unreasonable for the Commission to decide that the recall in the film of what was in the public domain could intrude upon the parents' privacy.

The secret filming of transactions in a shop for the purposes of a consumer protection programme (*Watchdog*) may amount to an invasion of privacy even though the public have access to the shop and the events filmed are not private in character.[17] The Commission may only consider complaints when programmes have been broadcast; it has no anticipatory jurisdiction, whether to prevent a broadcast or otherwise. A company may make a complaint of invasion of privacy, as well as individuals.[18] The Commission's decisions are subject to judicial review.[19]

---

12 (1996) Times, 22 November, CA.
13 See further on the Commission, above, p. 676.
14 1996 Act, s. 110. The relevant standards are detailed in the Commission's Code of Practice on Fairness and Privacy.
15 1996 Act, s. 119(3).
16 (1993) Times, 31 May, QBD.
17 *R v Broadcasting Standards Commission, ex p BBC* [2000] EMLR 587, CA. It was also held that a company may complain of invasion of privacy.
18 *R v Broadcasting Complaints Commission, ex p Barclay* [1997] EMLR 62, QBD.
19 See the cases cited in the preceding footnotes.

5   Interception of communications

Regulation of Investigative Powers Act 2000

PART I: CHAPTER I

1. Unlawful interception

(1) It shall be an offence for a person intentionally and without lawful authority to intercept, at any place in the United Kingdom, any communication in the course of its transmission by means of—

(*a*)   a public postal service; or

(*b*)   a public telecommunication system.

(2) It shall be an offence for a person—

(*a*)   intentionally and without lawful authority and

(*b*)   otherwise than in circumstances in which his conduct is excluded by subsection (6) from criminal liability under this subsection,

to intercept, at any place in the United Kingdom, any communication in the course of its transmission by means of a private telecommunications system.

(3) Any interception of a communication which is carried out at any place in the United Kingdom by, or with the express or implied consent of, a person having the right to control the operation or the use of a private telecommunication system shall be actionable at the suit or instance of the sender or recipient, or intended recipient, of the communication if it is without lawful authority and is either—

(*a*)   an interception of that communication in the course of its transmission by means of that private system; or

(*b*)   an interception of that communication in the course of its transmission, by means of a public telecommunication system, to or from apparatus comprised in that private telecommunication system.

(4) Where the United Kingdom is a party to an international agreement which—

(*a*)   relates to the provision of mutual assistance in connection with, or in the form of, the interception of communications,

(*b*)   requires the issue of a warrant, order or equivalent instrument in cases in which assistance is given, and

(*c*)   is designated for the purposes of this subsection by an order made by the Secretary of State,

it shall be the duty of the Secretary of State to secure that no request for assistance in accordance with the agreement is made on behalf of a person in the United Kingdom to the competent authorities of a country or territory outside the United Kingdom except with lawful authority.

(5) Conduct has lawful authority for the purposes of this section if, and only if—

(*a*)   it is authorised by or under section 3 or 4;

(*b*)   it takes place in accordance with a warrant under section 5 ('an interception warrant'); or

(*c*)   it is in exercise, in relation to any stored communication, of any statutory power that is exercised (apart from this section) for the purpose of obtaining information or of taking possession of any document or other property;

and conduct (whether or not prohibited by this section) which has lawful authority for the purposes of this section by virtue of paragraph (*a*) or (*b*) shall also be taken to be lawful for all other purposes.

(6) The circumstances in which a person makes an interception of a communication in the course of its transmission by means of a private telecommunication system are such that his conduct is excluded from criminal liability under subsection (2) if—

(*a*)   he is a person with a right to control the operation or the use of the system; or

(*b*)   he has the express or implied consent of such a person to make the interception.

(7) A person who is guilty of an offence under subsection (1) or (2) shall be liable—

(*a*)   on conviction on indictment, to imprisonment for a term not exceeding two years or to a fine, or to both;

(*b*)   on summary conviction, to a fine not exceeding the statutory maximum.

(8) No proceedings for any offence which is an offence by virtue of this section shall be instituted—

(*a*) in England and Wales, except by or with the consent of the Director of Public Prosecutions;

(*b*) in Northern Ireland, except by or with the consent of the Director of Public Prosecutions for Northern Ireland.

2. Meaning and location of 'interception' etc

(1) In this Act—

'postal service' means any service which—

(*a*) consists in the following, or in any one or more of them, namely, the collection, sorting, conveyance, distribution and delivery (whether in the United Kingdom or elsewhere) of postal items; and

(*b*) is offered or provided as a service the main purpose of which, or one of the main purposes of which, is to make available, or to facilitate, a means of transmission from place to place of postal items containing communications;

'private telecommunication system' means any telecommunication system which, without itself being a public telecommunication system, is a system in relation to which the following conditions are satisfied—

(*a*) it is attached, directly or indirectly and whether or not for the purposes of the communication in question, to a public telecommunication system; and

(*b*) there is apparatus comprised in the system which is both located in the United Kingdom and used (with or without other apparatus) for making the attachment to the public telecommunication system;

'public postal service' means any postal service which is offered or provided to, or to a substantial section of, the public in any one or more parts of the United Kingdom;

'public telecommunications service' means any telecommunications service which is offered or provided to, or to a substantial section of, the public in any one or more parts of the United Kingdom;

'public telecommunication system' means any such parts of a telecommunication system by means of which any public telecommunications service is provided as are located in the United Kingdom;

'telecommunications service' means any service that consists in the provision of access to, and of facilities for making use of, any telecommunication system (whether or not one provided by the person providing the service); and

'telecommunication system' means any system (including the apparatus comprised in it) which exists (whether wholly or partly in the United Kingdom or elsewhere) for the purpose of facilitating the transmission of communications by any means involving the use of electrical or electro-magnetic energy.

(2) For the purposes of this Act, but subject to the following provisions of this section, a person intercepts a communication in the course of its transmission by means of a telecommunication system, if and only if, he—

(*a*) so modifies or interferes with the system, or its operation,

(*b*) so monitors transmissions made by means of the system, or

(*c*) so monitors transmissions made by wireless telegraphy to or from apparatus comprised in the system,

as to make some or all of the contents of the communication available, while being transmitted, to a person other than the sender or intended recipient of the communication.

(3) References in this Act to the interception of a communication do not include references to the interception of any communication broadcast for general reception.

(4) For the purposes of this Act the interception of a communication takes place in the United Kingdom if, and only if, the modification, interference or monitoring or, in the case of a postal item, the interception is effected by conduct within the United Kingdom and the communication is either—

(*a*) intercepted in the course of its transmission by means of a public postal service or public telecommunication system; or

(*b*) intercepted in the course of its transmission by means of a private telecommunication system in a case in which the sender or intended recipient of the communication is in the United Kingdom.

(5) References in this ct to the interception of a communication in the course of its transmission by means of a postal service or telecommunication system do not include references to—

(*a*) any conduct that takes place in relation only to so much of the communication as consists in any traffic data comprised in or attached to a communication (whether by the sender or otherwise) for the purposes of any postal service or telecommunication system by means of which it is being or may be transmitted; or

(*b*) any such conduct, in connection with conduct falling within paragraph (*a*), as gives a person who is neither the sender nor the intended recipient only so much access to a communication as is necessary for the purpose of identifying traffic data so comprised or attached.

(6) For the purposes of this section references to the modification of a telecommunication system include references to the attachment of any apparatus to, or other modification of or interference with—

(*a*) any part of the system; or

(*b*) any wireless telegraphy apparatus used for making transmissions to or from apparatus comprised in the system.

(7) For the purposes of this section the times while a communication is being transmitted by means of a telecommunication system shall be taken to include any time when the system by means of which the communication is being, or has been, transmitted is used for storing it in a manner that enables the intended recipient to collect it or otherwise to have access to it.

(8) For the purposes of this section the cases in which any contents of a communication are to be taken to be made available to a person while being transmitted shall include any case in which any of the contents of the communication, while being transmitted, are diverted or recorded so as to be available to a person subsequently.

(9) In this section 'traffic data', in relation to any communication, means—

(*a*) any data identifying, or purporting to identify, any person, apparatus or location to or from which the communication is or may be transmitted,

(*b*) any data identifying or selecting, or purporting to identify or select, apparatus through which, or by means of which, the communication is or may be transmitted,

(*c*) any data comprising signals for the actuation of apparatus used for the purposes of a telecommunication system for effecting (in whole or in part) the transmission of any communication, and

(*d*) any data identifying the data or other data as data comprised in or attached to a particular communication,

but that expression includes data identifying a computer file or computer programme access to which is obtained, or which is run, by means of the communication to the extent only that the file or program is identified by reference to the apparatus in which it is stored.

(10) In this section—

(*a*) references, in relation to traffic data comprising signals for the actuation of apparatus, to a telecommunication system by means of which a communication is being or may be transmitted include references to any telecommunication system in which that apparatus is comprised; and

(*b*) references to traffic data being attached to a communication include references to the data and the communication being logically associated with each other;

and in this section 'data', in relation to a postal item, means anything written on the outside of the item.

(11) In this section 'postal item' means any letter, postcard or other such thing in writing as may be used by the sender for imparting information to the recipient, or any packet or parcel.

3. Lawful interception without an interception warrant

(1) Conduct by any person consisting in the interception of a communication is authorised by this section if the communication is one which, or which that person has reasonable grounds for believing, is both—

(*a*) a communication sent by a person who has consented to the interception; and

(*b*) a communication the intended recipient of which has so consented.

(2) Conduct by any person consisting in the interception of a communication is authorised by this section if—

(*a*) the communication is one sent by, or intended for, a person who has consented to the interception; and

(*b*)   surveillance by means of that interception has been authorised under Part II.
(3) Conduct consisting in the interception of a communication is authorised by this section if—
 (*a*)   it is conduct by or on behalf of a person who provides a postal service or a telecommunications service; and
 (*b*)   it takes place for purposes connected with the provision or operation of that service or with the enforcement, in relation to that service, of any enactment relating to the use of postal services or telecommunications services.
(4) Conduct by any person consisting in the interception of a communication in the course of its transmission by means of wireless telegraphy is authorised by this section if it takes place—
 (*a*)   with the authority of a designated person under section 5 of the Wireless Telegraphy Act 1949 (misleading messages and interception and disclosure of wireless telegraphy messages); and
 (*b*)   for purposes connected with anything falling within subsection (5).
(5) Each of the following falls within this subsection—
 (*a*)   the issue of licences under the Wireless Telegraphy Act 1949;
 (*b*)   the prevention or detection of anything which constitutes interference with wireless telegraphy; and
 (*c*)   the enforcement of any enactment contained in that Act or of any enactment not so contained that relates to such interference.

4. Power to provide for lawful interception
(1) Conduct by any person ('the interceptor') consisting in the interception of a communication in the course of its transmission by means of a telecommunication system is authorised by this section if—
 (*a*)   the interception is carried out for the purpose of obtaining information about the communications of a person who, or who the interceptor has reasonable grounds for believing, is in a country or territory outside the United Kingdom;
 (*b*)   the interception relates to the use of a telecommunications service provided to persons in that country or territory which is either—
  (i)   a public telecommunications service; or
  (ii)   a telecommunictions service that would be a public telecommunications service if the persons to whom it is offered or provided were members of the public in a part of the United Kingdom;
 (*c*)   the person who provides that service (whether the interceptor or another person) is required by the law of that country or territory to carry out, secure or facilitate the interception in question;
 (*d*)   the situation is one in relation to which such further conditions as may be prescribed by regulations made by the Secretary of State are required to be satisfied before conduct may be treated as authorised by virtue of this subsection; and
 (*e*)   the conditions so prescribed are satisfied in relation to that situation.
(2) Subject to subsection (3), the Secretary of State may by regulations authorise any such conduct described in the regulations as appears to him to constitute a legitimate practice reasonably required for the purpose in connection with the carrying on of any business, of monitoring or keeping a record of—
 (*a*)   communications by means of which transactions are entered into in the course of that business; or
 (*b*)   other communications relating to that business or taking place in the course of its being carried on.
(3) Nothing in any regulations under subsection (2) shall authorise the interception of any communication except in the course of its transmission using apparatus or services provided by or to the person carrying on the business for use wholly or partly in connection with that business.
(4) Conduct taking place in a prison is authorised by this section if it is conduct in exercise of any power conferred by or under any rules made under section 47 of the Prison Act 1952, section 39 of the Prisons (Scotland) Act 1989 or section 13 of the Prison Act (Northern Ireland) 1953 (prison rules).
(5) Conduct taking place in any hospital premises where high security psychiatric services are provided is authorised by this section if it is conduct in pursuance of, and in accordance

with, any direction given under section 17 of the National Health Service Act 1977 (directions as to the carrying out of their functions by health bodies) to the body providing those services at those premises.

(6) Conduct taking place in a state hospital is authorised by this section if it is conduct in pursuance of, and in accordance with, any direction given to the State Hospitals Board for Scotland under section 2(5) of the National Health Service (Scotland) Act 1978 (regulations and directions as to the exercise of their functions by health boards) as applied by Article 5(1) of and the Schedule to The State Hospitals Board for Scotland Order 1995 (which applies certain provisions of that Act of 1978 to the State Hospitals Board).

(7) In this section references to a business include references to any activities of a government department, of any public authority or of any person or office holder on whom functions are conferred by or under any enactment.

(8) In this section—

"government department" includes any part of the Scottish Administration, a Northern Ireland department and the National Assembly for Wales;

"high security psychiatric services" has the same meaning as in the National Health Service Act 1977;

"hospital premises" has the same meaning as in section 4(3) of that Act; and

"state hospital" has the same meaning as in the National Health Service (Scotland) Act 1978.

(9) In this section "prison" means—

(a)   any prison, young offender institution, young offenders centre or remand centre which is under the general superintendence of, or is provided by, the Secretary of State under the Prison Act 1952 or the Prison Act (Northern Ireland) 1953, or

(b)   any prison, young offenders institution or remand centre which is under the general superintendence of the Scottish Ministers under the Prisons (Scotland) Act 1989,

and includes any contracted out prison, within the meaning of Part IV of the Criminal Justice Act 1991 or section 106(4) of the Criminal Justice and Public Order Act 1994, and any legalised police cells within the meaning of section 14 of the Prisons (Scotland) Act 1989.

5. Interception with a warrant

(1) Subject to the following provisions of this Chapter, the Secretary of State may issue a warrant authorising or requiring the person to whom it is addressed, by any such conduct as may be described in the warrant, to secure any one or more of the following—

(a)   the interception in the course of their transmission by means of a postal service or telecommunication system of the communications described in the warrant;

(b)   the making, in accordance with the international mutual assistance agreement, of a request for the provision of such assistance in connection with, or in the form of, an interception of communications as may be so described;

(c)   the provision, in accordance with an international mutual assistance agreement, to the competent authorities of a country or territory outside the United Kingdom of any such assistance in connection with, or in the form of, an interception of communications as may be so described;

(d)   the disclosure, in such manner as may be so described, of intercepted material obtained by any interception authorised or required by the warrant, and of related communications data.

(2) The Secretary of State shall not issue an interception warrant unless he believes—

(a)   that the warrant is necessary on grounds falling within subsection (3); and

(b)   that the conduct authorised by the warrant is proportionate to what is sought to be achieved by that conduct.

(3) Subject to the following provisions of this section, a warrant is necessary on grounds falling within this subsection if it is necessary—

(a)   in the interests of national security;

(b)   for the purpose of preventing or detecting serious crime;

(c)   for the purpose of safeguarding the economic well-being of the United Kingdom; or

(d)   for the purpose, in circumstances appearing to the Secretary of State to be equivalent to those in which he would issue a warrant by virtue of paragraph (b), of giving effect to the provisions of any international mutual assistance agreement.

(4) The matters to be taken into account in considering whether the requirements of subsection (2) are satisfied in the case of any warrant shall include whether the information which it is thought necessary to obtain under the warrant could reasonably be obtained by other means.

(5) A warrant shall not be considered necessary on the ground falling within subsection (3)(*c*) unless the information which it is thought necessary to obtain is information relating to the acts or intentions of persons outside the British Islands.

(6) The conduct authorised by an interception warrant shall be taken to include—

(*a*) all such conduct (including the interception of communications not identified by the warrant) as it is necessary to undertake in order to do what is expressly authorised or required by the warrant;

(*b*) conduct for obtaining related communications data; and

(*c*) conduct by any person which is conduct in pursuance of a requirement imposed by or on behalf of the person to whom the warrant is addressed to be provided with assistance with giving effect to the warrant.

6. Application for issue of an interception warrant

(1) An interception warrant shall not be issued except on an application made by or on behalf of a person specified in subsection (2).

(2) Those persons are—

(*a*) the Director-General of the Security Service;

(*b*) the Chief of the Secret Intelligence Service;

(*c*) the Director of GCHQ;

(*d*) the Director General of the National Criminal Intelligence Service;

(*e*) the Commissioner of Police of the Metropolis;

(*f*) the Chief Constable of the Royal Ulster Constabulary;

(*g*) the chief constable of any police force maintained under or by virtue of section 1 of the Police (Scotland) Act 1967;

(*h*) the Commissioners of Customs and Excise;

(*i*) the Chief of Defence Intelligence;

(*j*) a person who, for the purposes of any international mutual assistance agreement, is the competent authority of a country or territory outside the United Kingdom.

(3) An application for the issue of an interception warrant shall not be made on behalf of a person specified in subsection (2) except by a person holding office under the Crown.

7. Issue of warrants

(1) An interception warrant shall not be issued except—

(*a*) under the hand of the Secretary of State; or

(*b*) in a case falling within subsection (2), under the hand of a senior official.

(2) Those cases are—

(*a*) an urgent case in which the Secretary of State has himself expressly authorised the issue of the warrant in that case; and

(*b*) a case in which the warrant is for the purposes of a request for assistance made under an international mutual assistance agreement by the competent authorities of a country or territory outside the United Kingdom and either—

(i) it appears that the interception subject is outside the United Kingdom; or

(ii) the interception to which the warrant relates is to take place in relation only to premises outside the United Kingdom.

(3) An interception warrant—

(*a*) must be addressed to the person falling within section 6(2) by whom, or on whose behalf, the application for the warrant was made; and

(*b*) in the case of a warrant issued under the hand of a senior official, must contain, according to whatever is applicable—

(i) one of the statements set out in subsection (4); and

(ii) if it contains the statement set out in subsection (4)(*b*), one of the statements set out in subsection (5).

(4) The statements referred to in subsection (3)(*b*)(i) are—

(*a*) a statement that the case is an urgent case in which the Secretary of State has himself expressly authorised the issue of the warrant;

(*b*) a statement that the warrant is issued for the purposes of a request for assistance made under an international mutual assistance agreement by the competent authorities of a country or territory outside the United Kingdom.

(5) The statements referred to in subsection (3)(*b*)(ii) are—

(*a*) a statement that the interception subject appears to be outside the United Kingdom;

(*b*) a statement that the interception to which the warrant relates is to take place in relation only to premises outside the United Kingdom.

8. Contents of warrants

(1) An interception warrant must name or describe either—

(*a*) one person as the interception subject; or

(*b*) a single set of premises as the premises in relation to which the interception to which the warrant relates is to take place.

(2) The provisions of an interception warrant describing communications the interception of which is authorised or required by the warrant must comprise one or more schedules setting out the addresses, numbers, apparatus or other factors, or combination of factors, that are to be used for identifying the communications that may be or are to be intercepted.

(3) Any factor or combination of factors set out in accordance with subsection (2) must be one that identifies communications which are likely to be or to include—

(*a*) communications from, or intended for, the person named or described in the warrant in accordance with subsection (1); or

(*b*) communications originating on, or intended for transmission to, the premises so named or described.

(4) Subsections (1) and (2) shall not apply to an interception warrant if—

(*a*) the description of communications to which the warrant relates confines the conduct authorised or required by the warrant to conduct falling within subsection (5); and

(*b*) at the time of the issue of the warrant, a certificate applicable to the warrant has been issued by the Secretary of State certifying—

(i) the descriptions of intercepted material the examination of which he considers necessary; and

(ii) that he considers the examination of material of those descriptions necessary as mentioned in section 5(3)(*a*), (*b*) or (*c*).

(5) Conduct falls within this subsection if it consists in—

(*a*) the interception of external communications in the course of their transmission by means of a telecommunication system; and

(*b*) any conduct authorised in relation to any such interception by section 5(6).

(6) A certificate for the purposes of subsection (4) shall not be issued except under the hand of the Secretary of State.

9. Duration, cancellation and renewal of warrants

(1) An interception warrant—

(*a*) shall cease to have effect at the end of the relevant period; but

(*b*) may be renewed, at any time before the end of that period, by an instrument under the hand of the Secretary of State or, in a case falling within section 7(2)(*b*), under the hand of a senior official.

(2) An interception warrant shall not be renewed under subsection (1) unless the Secretary of State believes that the warrant continues to be necessary on grounds falling within section 5(3).

(3) The Secretary of State shall cancel an interception warrant if he is satisfied that the warrant is no longer necessary on grounds falling within section 5(3).

(4) The Secretary of State shall cancel an interception warrant if, at any time before the end of the relevant period, he is satisfied in a case in which—

(*a*) the warrant is one which was issued containing the statement set out in section 7(5)(*a*) or has been renewed by an instrument containing the statement set out in subsection (5)(*b*)(i) of this section, and

(*b*) the latest renewal (if any) of the warrant is not a renewal by an instrument under the hand of the Secretary of State,

that the person named or described in the warrant as the interception subject is in the United Kingdom.

(5) An instrument under the hand of a senior official that renews an interception warrant must contain—

    (*a*) a statement that the renewal is for the purposes of a request for assistance made under an international mutual assistance agreement by the competent authorities of a country or territory outside the United Kingdom; and

    (*b*) whichever of the following statements is applicable—

        (i) a statement that the interception subject appears to be outside the United Kingdom;

        (ii) a statement that the interception to which the warrant relates is to take place in relation only to premises outside the United Kingdom.

(6) In this section 'the relevant period'—

    (*a*) in relation to an unrenewed warrant issued in a case falling within section 7(2)(**a**) under the hand of a senior official, means the period ending with the fifth working day following the day of the warrant's issue;

    (*b*) in relation to a renewed warrant the latest renewal of which was by an instrument endorsed under the hand of the Secretary of State with a statement that the renewal is believed to be necessary on grounds falling within section 5(3)(*a*) or (*c*) means the period of six months beginning with the day of the warrant's renewal; and

    (*c*) in all other cases, means the period of three months beginning with the day of the warrant's issue or, in the case of a warrant that has been renewed, of its latest renewal.

...

CHAPTER II
21. Lawful acquisition and disclosure of communications data

(1) This Chapter applies to—

    (*a*) any conduct in relation to a postal service or telecommunication system for obtaining communications data, other than conduct consisting in the interception of communications in the course of their transmission by means of such a service or system; and

    (*b*) the disclosure to any person of communications data.

(2) Conduct to which this Chapter applies shall be lawful for all purposes if—

    (*a*) it is conduct in which any person is authorised or required to engage by an authorisation or notice granted or given under this Chapter; and

    (*b*) the conduct is in accordance with, or in pursuance of, the authorisation or requirement.

(3) A person shall not be subject to any civil liability in respect of any conduct of his which—

    (*a*) is incidental to any conduct that is lawful by virtue of subsection (2); and

    (*b*) is not itself conduct an authorisation or warrant for which is capable of being granted under a relevnt enactment and might reasonably have been expected to have been sought in the case in question.

(4) In this Chapter 'communications data' means any of the following—

    (*a*) any traffic data comprised in or attached to a communication (whether by the sender or otherwise) for the purposes of any postal service or telecommunication system by means of which it is being or may be transmitted;

    (*b*) any information which includes none of the contents of a communication (apart from any information falling within paragraph (*a*)) and is about the use made by any person—

        (i) of any postal service or telecommunications service; or

        (ii) in connection with the provision to or use by any person of any telecommunications service, of any part of a telecommunication system;

    (*c*) any information not falling within paragraph (*a*) or (*b*) that is held or obtained, in relation to persons to whom he provides the service, by a person providing a postal service or telecommunications service.

(5) In this section 'relevant enactment' means—

    (*a*) an enactment contained in this Act;

    (*b*) section 5 of the Intelligence Services Act 1994 (warrants for the intelligence services); or

    (*c*) an enactment contained in Part III of the Police Act 1997 (powers of the police and of customs officers).

(6) In this section 'traffic data', in relation to any communication, means—

    (*a*) any data identifying, or purporting to identify, any person, apparatus or location to or from which the communication is or may be transmitted, (*b*) any data identifying or selecting, or purporting to identify or select, apparatus through which, or by means of which, the communication is or may be transmitted,

    (*c*) any data comprising signals for the actuation of apparatus used for the purposes of a telecommunication system for effecting (in whole or in part) the transmission of any communication, and

    (*d*) any data identifying the data or other data as data comprised in or attached to a particular communication,

but that expression includes data identifying a computer file or computer program access to which is obtained, or which is run, by means of the communcation to the extent only that the file or program is identified by reference to the apparatus in which it is stored.

(7) In this section—

    (*a*) references, in relation to traffic data comprising signals for the actuation of apparatus, to a telecommunication system by means of which a communication is being or may be transmitted include references to any telecommunication system in which that apparatus is comprised; and

    (*b*) references to traffic data being attached to a communication include references to the data and the communication being logically associated with each other;

and in this section 'data', in relation to a postal item, means anything written on the outside of the item.

22. Obtaining and disclosing communications data

(1) This section applies where a person designated for the purposes of this Chapter believes that it is necessary on grounds falling within subsection (2) to obtain any communications data.

(2) It is necessary on grounds falling within this subsection to obtain communications data if it is necessary—

    (*a*) in the interests of national security;

    (*b*) for the purpose of preventing or detecting crime or of preventing discorder;

    (*c*) in the interests of the economic well-being of the United Kingdom;

    (*d*) in the interests of public safety;

    (*e*) for the purpose of protecting public health;

    (*f*) for the purpose of assessing or collecting any tax, duty, levy or other imposition, contribution or charge payable to a government department;

    (*g*) for the purpose, in an emergency, of preventing death or injury or any damage to a person's physical or mental health, or of mitigating any injury or damage to a person's physical or mental health; or

    (*h*) for any purpose (not falling within paragraphs (*a*) to (*g*)) which is specified for the purposes of this subsection by an order made by the Secretary of State.

(3) Subject to subsection (5), the designated person may grant an authorisation for persons holding offices, ranks or positions with the same relevant public authority as the designated person to engage in any conduct to which this Chapter applies.

(4) Subject to subsection (5), where it appears to the designated person that a postal or telecommunications operator is or may be in possession of or be capable of obtaining, any communications data, the designated person may, by notice to the postal or telecommunications operator, require the operator—

    (*a*) if the operator is not already in possession of the data, to obtain the data; and

    (*b*) in any case, to disclose all of the data in his possession or subsequently obtained by him.

(5) The designated person shall not grant an authorisation under subsection (3), or give a notice under subsection (4), unless he believes that obtaining the data in question by the conduct authorised or required by the authorisation or notice is proportionate to what is sought to be achieved by so obtaining the data.

(6) It shall be the duty of the postal or telecommunications operator to comply with the requirements of any notice given to him under subsection (4).

(7) A person who is under a duty by virtue of subsection (6) shall not be required to do anything in pursuance of that duty which it is not reasonably practicable for him to do.

(8) The duty imposed by subsection (6) shall be enforceable by civil proceedings by the Secretary of State for an injunction, or for specific performance of a statutory duty under section 45 of the Court of Session Act 1988, or for any other appropriate relief.

(9) The Secretary of State shall not make an order under subsection (2)(*h*) unless a draft of the order has been laid before Parliament and approved by a resolution of each House.

    …

PART III

49. Notices requiring disclosure

(1) This section applies where any protected information—

    (*a*) has come into possession of any person by means of the exercise of a statutory power to seize, detain, inspect, search or otherwise to interfere with documents or other property, or is likely to do so;

    (*b*) has come into the possession of any person by means of the exercise of any statutory power to intercept communications, or is likely to do so;

    (*c*) has come into the possession of any person by means of the exercise of any power conferred by an authorisation under section 22(3) or under Part II, or as a result of the giving of a notice under section 22(4), or is likely to do so;

    (*d*) has come into the possession of any person as a result of having been provided or disclosed in pursuance of any statutory duty (whether or not one arising as a result of a request for information) or is likely to do so; or

    (*e*) has, by any other lawful means not involving the exercise of statutory powers, come into the possession of any of the intelligence services, the police or the customs and excise, or is likely so to come into the possession of any of those services, the police or the customs and excise.

(2) If any person with the appropriate permission under Schedule 2 believes, on reasonable grounds—

    (*a*) that a key to the protected information is in the possession of any person,

    (*b*) that the imposition of a disclosure requirement in respect of the protected information is—

        (i) necessary on grounds falling within subsection (3), or

        (ii) necessary for the purpose of securing the effective exercise or proper performance by any public authority of any statutory power or statutory duty,

    (*c*) that the imposition of such a requirement is proportionate to what is sought to be achieved by its imposition, and

    (*d*) that it is not reasonably practicable for the person with the appropriate permission to obtain possession of the protected information in an intelligible form without the giving of a notice under this section,

the person with that permission may, by notice to the person whom he believes to have possession of the key, impose a disclosure requirement in respect of the protected information.

(3) A disclosure requirement in respect of any protected information is necessary on grounds falling within this subsection if it is necessary—

    (*a*) in the interests of national security;

    (*b*) for the purpose of preventing or detecting crime; or

    (*c*) in the interests of the economic well-being of the United Kingdom.

(4) A notice under this section imposing a disclosure requirement in respect of any protected information—

    (*a*) must be given in writing or (if not in writing) must be given in a manner that produces a record of its having been given;

    (*b*) must describe the protected information to which the notice relates;

    (*c*) must specify the matters falling within subsection (2)(*b*)(i) or (ii) by reference to which the notice is given;

    (*d*) must specify the office, rank or position held by the person giving it;

    (*e*) must specify the office, rank or position of the person who for the purposes of Schedule 2 granted permission for the giving of the notice or (if the person giving the notice was entitled to give it without another person's permission) must set out the circumstances in which that entitlement arose;

    (*f*) must specify the time by which the notice is to be complied with; and

    (*g*) must set out the disclosure that is required by the notice and the form and manner in which it is to be made;

and the time specified for the purposes of paragraph (*f*) must allow a period for compliance which is reasonable in all the circumstances.

(5) Where it appears to a person with the appropriate permission—

    (*a*) that more than one person is in possession of the key to any protected information,

    (*b*) that any of those persons is in possession of that key in his capacity as an officer or employee of any body corporate, and

(c)   that another of those persons is the body corporate itself or another officer or employee of the body corporate,

a notice under this section shall not be given, by reference to his possession of the key, to any officer or employee of the body corporate unless he is a senior officer of the body corporate or it appears to the person giving the notice that there is no senior officer of the body corporate and (in the case of an employee) no more senior employee of the body corporate to whom it is reasonably practicable to give the notice.

(6) Where it appears to a person with the appropriate permission—

(a)   that more than one person is in possession of the key to any protected information,

(b)   that any of those persons is in possession of that key in his capacity as an employee of a firm, and

(c)   that another of those persons is the firm itself or a partner of the firm,

a notice under this section shall not be given, by reference to his possession of the key, to any employee of the firm unless it appears to the person giving the notice that there is neither a partner of the firm nor a more senior employee of the firm to whom it is reasonably practicable to give the notice.

(7) Subsections (5) and (6) shall not apply to the extent that there are special circumstances of the case that mean that the purposes for which the notice is given would be defeated, in whole or in part, if the notice were given to the person to whom it would otherwise be required to be given by those subsections.

(8) A notice under this section shall not require the making of any disclosure to any person other than—

(a)   the person giving the notice; or

(b)   such other person as may be specified in or otherwise identified by, or in accordance with, the provisions of the notice.

(9) A notice under this section shall not require the disclosure of any key which—

(a)   is intended to be used for the purpose only of generating electronic signatures; and

(b)   has not in fact been used for any other purpose.

(10) In this section 'senior officer', in relation to a body corporate, means a director, manager, secretary or other similar officer of the body corporate; and for this purpose 'director', in relation to a body corporate whose affairs are managed by its members, means a member of the body corporate.

(11) Schedule 2 (definition of the appropriate permission) shall have effect.

50. Effect of notice imposing disclosure requirement

(1) Subject to the following provisions of this section, the effect of a section 49 notice imposing a disclosure requirement in respect of any protected information on a person who is in possession at a relevant time of both the protected information and a means of obtaining access to the information and of disclosing it in an intelligible form is that he—

(a)   shall be entitled to use any key in his possession to obtain access to the information or to put it into an intelligible form; and

(b)   shall be required, in accordance with the notice imposing the requirement, to make a disclosure of the information in an intelligible form.

(2) A person subject to a requirement under subsection (1)(b) to make a disclosure of any information in an intelligible form shall be taken to have complied with that requirement if—

(a)   he makes, instead, a disclosure of any key to the protected information that is in his possession; and

(b)   that disclosure is made, in accordance with the notice imposing the requirement, to the person to whom, and by the time by which, he was required to provide the information in that form.

(3) Where, in a case in which a disclosure requirement in respect of any protected information is imposed on any person by a section 49 notice—

(a)   that person is not in possession of the information,

(b)   that person is incapable, without the use of a key that is not in his possession, of obtaining access to the information and of disclosing it in an intelligible form, or

(c)   the notice states, in pursuance of a direction under section 51, that it can be complied with only by the disclosure of a key to the information,

the effect of imposing that disclosure requirement on that person is that he shall be required, in accordance with the notice imposing the requirement, to make a disclosure of any key to the protected information that is in his possession at a relevant time.

(4) Subsections (5) to (7) apply where a person ('the person given notice')—

   (*a*) is entitled or obliged to disclose a key to protected information for the purpose of complying with any disclosure requirement imposed by a section 49 notice; and

   (*b*) is in possession of more than one key to that information.

(5) It shall not be necessary, for the purpose of complying with the requirement, for the person given notice to make a disclosure of any keys in addition to those the disclosure of which is, alone, sufficient to enable the person to whom they are disclosed to obtain access to the information and to put it into an intelligible form.

(6) Where—

   (*a*) subsection (5) allows the person given notice to comply with a requirement without disclosing all of the keys in his possession, and

   (*b*) there are different keys, or combinations of keys, in the possession of that person the disclosure of which would, under that subsection, constitute compliance,

the person given notice may select which of the keys, or combination of keys, to disclose for the purpose of complying with that requirement in accordance with that subsection.

(7) Subject to subsections (5) and (6), the person given notice shall not be taken to have complied with the disclosure requirement by the disclosure of a key unless he has disclosed every key to the protected information that is in his possession at a relevant time.

(8) Where, in a case in which a disclosure requirement in respect of any protected information is imposed on any person by a section 49 notice—

   (*a*) that person has been in possession of the key to that information but is no longer in possession of it,

   (*b*) if he had continued to have the key in his possession, he would have been required by virtue of the giving of the notice to disclose it, and

   (*c*) he is in possession, at a relevant time, of information to which subsection (9) applies,

the effect of imposing that disclosure requirement on that person is that he shall be required, in accordance with the notice imposing the requirement, to disclose all such information to which subsection (9) applies as is in his possession and as he may be required, in accordance with that notice, to disclose by the person to whom he would have been required to disclose the key.

(9) This subsection applies to any information that would facilitate the obtaining or discovery of the key or the putting of the protected information into an intelligible form.

(10) In this section 'relevant time', in relation to a disclosure requirement imposed by a section 49 notice, means the time of the giving of the notice or any subsequent time before the time by which the requirement falls to be complied with.

NOTES

1. The Regulation of Investigatory Powers Act 2000 (RIPA 2000), Part I, Chapter I, ss. 1–20, on *interception*, regulates the interception of communications that are made by telephone or by a public postal service.[1] It controls communications by mobile

---

1 On the RIPA 2000, see Y. Akdeniz, N. Taylor and C. Walker, [2001] Crim LR 73. See also the Home Office consultation paper, *Interception of Communications in the United Kingdom*, Cm. 4368, 1999, that preceded the RIPA 2000. On the consultation paper, see M. Colvin, (1999) 149 NLJ 1067. The RIPA 2000 replaced the Interception of Communications Act 1985, which it repealed. Prior to the 1985 Act, the interception of communications was not regulated by statute, but by Home Office administrative practice that was given oblique recognition by Post Office Act 1969, s. 80. The 1985 Act was introduced partly to comply with the Strasbourg judgment in *Malone v United Kingdom*: see below, p. 1013. The 1985 Act complied with Art. 8 ECHR in respect of *public* telecommunication systems: *Christie v United Kingdom*, 78A DR ECommHR 119 (1994). The RIPA 2000 was introduced partly to comply with *Halford v United Kingdom* (1997) 24 EHRR 523 concerning *private* telecommunication systems: see below, footnote 10. As well as the ECHR, the EU Telecommunications Data Protection Directive 1997 (97/66/EC), (1998) OJL 24, p. 1, requires member states to secure the confidentiality of communications on public telecommunications systems. The Directive is implemented by the Telecommunications (Data Protection and Privacy) Regulations 1999, S.I. 1999 No. 2093.

and cordless or portable telephones and communications by email, the Internet and pagers.[2] RIPA 2000, in Part I, Chapter II, ss. 21–25, regulates *access to metered communications data*.[3] The use of electronic bugging devices is controlled not by RIPA 2000, but by the Police Act 1997, ss. 91 ff[4] in so far as it involves 'entry on or interference with property or with wireless telegraphy'.[5] However, the use of electronic devices (e.g. long-distance activated microphones) that does *not* involve such conduct is regulated by RIPA 2000, Part II (ss. 26–48), on *surveillance*.[6] Access to *encrypted electronic data* is regulated by RIPA 2000, Part III (ss. 49–56).[7] The Data Protection Act 1998 regulates the storing of and access to *personal data*.[8]

2. *Warrants for interception.* RIPA 2000, s. 1, makes it an offence 'intentionally and without lawful authority' to intercept in the UK any communication in the course of its transmission by means of a 'public' or 'private telecommunications system', or by means of a 'public postal service'.[9] Private telephone communications systems include 'an office or hotel network, or the telephones in a domestic household.[10]

3. An interception is 'without lawful authority' unless: (i) it is authorised by warrant;[11] or (ii) there are reasonable grounds to believe that it is with the consent of the sender and the intended recipient;[12] or (iii) it is with the consent of either the sender or the recipient and it is authorised under the surveillance provisions of Part II the RIPA 2000;[13] or (iv) in certain other cases.[14]

4. Applications for a warrant may be made by a police Chief Constable or other similar office-holder listed in RIPA 2000, s. 6. The Act leaves the authority to issue a warrant with the competent Secretary of State (s. 5); proposals[15] that warrants should be issued by a judge were not accepted.[16]

5. The grounds for issuing a warrant are indicated in RIPA 2000, s. 5(3). A 'serious crime' is defined in s. 81(3) as one that satisfies either of the following tests:[17]

---

2   See the definition of 'telecommunication system' in s. 2(1) and s. 2(7).

3   For access to communications data, see below, p. 1011.

4   See above, note 1, pp. 261–262.

5   Police Act 1997, s. 92(1).

6   See above, pp. 265ff.

7   See below, p, 1012.

8   See below, pp. 1020ff.

9   These terms are defined in RIPA 2000, s. 2. Prosecution for the s. 1 offence is only with the consent of the DPP. The penalty is up to two years' imprisonment or an unlimited fine. For the exception permitting employers to monitor phone calls and emails by employees, see below, p. 1013, note 1.

10 613 HL Deb, 12 June 2000, col. 1421 (Lord Bassam, for the Government). In *Halford v United Kingdom* (1997) 24 EHRR 523, the applicant was an Assistant Chief Constable of the Merseyside Police Force who was in dispute with her police force. It was held that the interception by the Merseyside Police Force of her communications on her internal office phone was a breach of Art. 8, ECHR. This was because they were not 'in accordance with law', as Art. 8(2) required, since the Interception of Communications Act 1985 did not apply to private telephone systems and there was no other UK law that regulated them.

11 RIPA 2000, s. 5.

12 RIPA 2000, s. 3(1).

13 RIPA 2000, s. 3(2).

14 RIPA 2000, s. 3(3).

15 See the Justice Report, *Under Surveillance* (1998), p. 21.

16 Although it is 'in principle desirable to entrust supervisory control to a judge', the ECHR does not require judicial authorisation: other independent authorisation or post-authorisation review procedures may suffice: see *Klass v Federal Republic of Germany* below, p. 1016. Judicial authorisation may not by itself be sufficient in the absence of precisely worded powers and other safeguards: *Kruslin v France*; (1990) 12 EHRR 547. Note that 'sensitive' surveillance authorisations have to be approved by an independent Commissioner under s. 97 of the Police Act 1997: see above, note 1, pp. 261–262.

17 Cf. the identical definition of 'serious crime' in s. 93(4) of the Police Act 1997: see above, note 1, pp. 261–262.

(a) that the offence is one of the offences that is or would be constituted by the conduct is an offence for which a person who has attained the age of twenty-one and has no previous convictions could reasonably be expected to be sentences to imprisonment for a term of three years or more;

(b) that the conduct involves the use of violence, results in substantial financial gain or is conduct by a large number of persons in pursuit of a common purpose.

As to 'economic well-being', a government spokesman[18] stated during the passage of the same wording in the earlier Interception of Communications Act 1985:

'It is concerned with the interception that is necessary for the effective protection of the country's economic interests at the international level. It is an important part of our foreign policy to protect the country from adverse developments overseas which may not necessarily affect our national security so directly as to justify interception on that ground but which may have damaging consequences for our economic well-being ... If I refer in a general way to a threat to the supply from abroad of a commodity [eg oil] on which our economy is particularly dependent, I hope that your Lordships will accept that I have gone ... as far as I can by way of offering an example.'

The term 'national security' is not defined.

Warrants may be issued only when the Secretary of State considers that the warrant is 'necessary' on one of the above grounds and the authorised conduct is 'proportionate to what is sought to be achieved'.[19]

6. Warrants may be issued under the RIPA 2000 for the interception of communications to or from the persons or to or from the premises described in the warrant.[20] In 1966, the Prime Minister (Mr Wilson) announced that he had given instructions after taking office that MPs' telephones were to be immune from tapping.[1] The Secretary of State may certify that the required description in the warrant of the person or premises to be targeted may be dispensed in the case of 'external communications',[2] i.e. communications to or from outside the British Isles.[3] Warrants are issued for three months, renewable for a further six months.[4]

7. In 1999, under the 1985 Act, 1,734 warrants (1,645 for telecommunications intercepts, 89 for the interception of letters) were issued by the Home Secretary; 522 warrants were in force at the end of 1999.[5] Most warrants concerned 'serious crimes'.

8. Under RIPA 2000, s. 17, evidence obtained from interceptions of communications made under a warrant issued under the RIPA 2000 is inadmissible in legal proceedings.[6] Section 17 follows the same rule in s. 9 of the 1985 Act, although the wording is not identical.[7]

9. *Metering.* RIPA 2000, ss. 21–25 regulate the disclosure of telephone or postal communications data resulting from metering[8] to a 'relevant public authority', such

18 Lord President of the Council (Lord Hailsham) HL Deb 6, 6 June 1985, col. 879.

19 RIPA 2000, s. 5(2). The terms 'necessary' and 'proportionate' echo the limitations on interferences with privacy in Art. 8(2) ECHR.

20 RIPA 2000, s. 8(1).

1 736 HC Deb, 17 November 1966, col. 639. Cf. Mr. Heath 803 HC Deb, 16 July 1970, col. 1723.

2 RIPA 2000, s. 8(4). For safeguards in respect of such certified warrants, see s. 16, RIPA 2000.

3 RIPA 2000, s. 20.

4 RIPA 2000, s. 9(6).

5 Annual Report of the Interception of Communications Commissioner for 1999, Cmnd. 4778, Annex.

6 Certain exceptions are allowed by RIPA, s. 18. The contents of lawful interceptions made under RIPA 2000, ss. 1(5)(c), (3), (4) fall within these exceptions: RIPA 2000, s. 18(4).

7 On s. 17, see P. Mirfield, [200] Crim LR 91. On s. 9 of the 1985 Act, see *R v Preston* [1994] 2 AC 130, HL and *Morgans v DPP* [2000] 2 All ER 522, HL.

8 I.e. data resulting from the collection of information about, for example, the traffic on a telephone, including the numbers dialled and the time and duration of calls, or the address on a postal communication.

as the police, the inland revenue and customs and excise.[9] Access to communications data may be authorised on grounds of the detection of crime, etc.[10] by a 'designated person' within the 'relevant public authority'.[11] There is no provision for authorisation or approval by a judge or other independent person.

10. *Encrypted electronic data.* RIPA 2000, Part III, ss. 49–56 regulates access by investigating authorities to encrypted electronic data ('protected information'). It covers the situation, for example where the police gain access to computer files by a lawful search but are unable to read them because they are encrypted. Where a 'person with appropriate permission' within an investigating authority (the police, customs and excise, the intelligence services) has reasonable grounds to believe that 'a key to the protected information is in the possession of any person, a disclosure notice may be issued under RIPA 2000, s. 49(2), requiring that the person in possession disclose the encrypted information or the key to gain access to it. The notice may be issued only where disclosure is 'necessary' in the interests of 'national security', the prevention or detection of crime, or the 'economic well-being' of the UK.[12] A notice under s. 49 must be issued by a circuit court judge, except where access to the encrypted data has been obtained through the use of a lawful search, interception, surveillance or other warrant which grants the required permission to have access to encrypted electronic data.[13]

11. *Interception of Communications Commission.* RIPA 2000 provides for independent supervision of the operation of the system of warrants for the interception of communications and authorisations for the disclosure of communications data in Part I of the Act and of the system for access to encrypted data in Part III of the Act. The supervision is the responsibility of an Interception of Communications Commissioner appointed by the Prime Minister.[14] The Commissioner must report annually to the Prime Minister, the report being presented to Parliament and published as a command paper.[15] A part of the report need not be presented to Parliament if its presentations would be 'contrary to the public interest' or 'prejudicial to – (a) national security, (b) the prevention or detection of serious crime, (c) the economic well-being of the United Kingdom, or (d) the continued discharge of the functions of any public authority whose activities include activities that are subject to review'.[16] The Commissioner has no

---

9 The system under RIPA 2000, ss. 21–25 replaces the less rigorous, permissive system under the Telecommunications Act 1984, s. 45 and the Data Protection Act 1998, s. 29. In *Malone v United Kingdom*, below, p. 1013, the disclosure to the police by the Post Office of its records of metering was a breach of Art. 8 ECHR because there was no legal regulation of this interference with privacy.

10 The list of grounds is longer than that for the interception of communications. It includes 'national security', 'preventing or detecting crime', 'preventing disorder', 'economic well-being', 'public safety', 'public health', collecting tax and preventing death or injury in an emergency: RIPA 2000, s. 22(2). Requirements of 'necessity' and 'proportionality' apply: RIPA 2000, ss. 22(5), 23(8).

11 For definitions, see RIPA 2000, s. 25. The data may be ordered to be disclosed by a postal or telecommunications operator to, for example, the police by the designated police officer, or it may already be in the hands of the police as a result of a lawful police operation, with the self-authorisation providing a legal safeguard. A list of designated persons, indicating the level of office-holder so authorised, will be provided by statutory instrument.

12 RIPA 2000, s. 49(3). There is also a 'proportionality' requirement: RIPA 2000, s. 49(2).

13 RIPA 2000, Sch. 2.

14 RIPA 2000, s. 57(1). The Commissioner must hold or have held 'high judicial office': RIPA 2000, s. 57(5). A similar office existed previously under the 1985 Act. The current Commissioner is Swinton Thomas LJ. Other commissioners with comparable roles are the Intelligence Services Commissioner, the Security Service Commissioners, and the Chief Surveillance Commissioner. There is also an Investigatory Powers Commissioner for Northern Ireland. It would make sense for these offices to be merged.

15 RIPA 2000, s. 58.

16 RIPA 2000, s. 58(7).

power to authorise, approve or cancel warrants, etc. Instead his function is to monitor and report upon practice. The reports of his predecessor under the 1985 Act have revealed a number of unlawful interceptions of communications, resulting, for example, from errors in the transcription of telephone numbers or from the tapping of a telephone after it has been transferred to a different subscriber. They do not reveal any case of a warrant being issued when this was not justified on the grounds listed in the 1985 Act.

12. RIPA 2000, s. 65 establishes a Tribunal that has jurisdiction to hear complaints from individuals arising out of the operation of the arrangements for: (i) the interception of communications and the disclosure of communications data under Part I, RIPA; and (ii) the release of encrypted data under Part III of the RIPA 2000.[17] Tribunal members must hold or have held 'high judicial office' and are appointed for five-year terms.[18] If the Tribunal finds, applying judicial review principles, that the required procedures have not been complied with, it may make an order awarding compensation, or quashing the warrant or authorisation, or requiring the destruction of the intercepted material.[19] The remedy before the Tribunal is final; it is not subject to appeal or judicial review in the courts.[20]

13. RIPA 2000, s. 1(3) creates a statutory tort of unlawful interception of a communication by means of a private telecommunications system by or with the consent of a person with the right to control the system. The tort might, for example, be committed by an employer who unlawfully intercepts communications made by employees on an internal office system, as where employees are not made aware that monitoring may take place.[1] The statutory tort established by s. 1(3) applies in situations where the tortfeasor is exempt from the offence in RIPA 2000, s. 1(3).[2]

Malone v United Kingdom, ECtHRR A 82 (1984), 7 EHRR 14, European Court of Human Rights

Having lost in the High Court in *Malone v Metropolitan Police Comr*,[2a] the applicant took his case to Strasbourg. He alleged violations of Art. 8 resulting from the tapping of his telephone and interference with his correspondence. He also claimed that details of calls he had made which the Post Office had obtained by 'metering' for its own record purposes had been passed on to the police contrary to Art. 8. The Commission expressed the opinion, by 11 to 0, with one abstention, that the applicant's rights

---

17 The Tribunal also has jurisdiction in complaints arising out of the operation of the surveillance system in RIPA 2000, Part II as to which, see above, p. 265. The Tribunal is exclusively competent to determine any action brought under s. 7(1)(a) of the Human Rights Act 1998 claiming that conduct under the RIPA 2000 is incompatible with Convention rights (e.g. the right to privacy) RIPA 2000, s. 65(2). The Tribunal established by s. 65 is the successor to the one that operated under the Interception of Communications Act 1985. It also has jurisdiction to consider complaints under the Security Services Act 1989, the Intelligence Services Act 1994, and the Police Act 1997. The tribunals that formerly considered complaints under these other statutes are replaced by the present Tribunal established by the RIPA.

18 RIPA 2000, Sch. 3, para. 1.

19 RIPA 2000, s. 67(7).

20 RIPA 2000, s. 67(8). The remedy before the Tribunal is also the exclusive first instance judicial remedy to challenge compliance with the relevant statutory procedures.

1 See the Telecommunications (Lawful Business Practices) (Interception of Communications) Regulations 2000, S.I. 2000 No. 2699, which permit an employer to intercept employees' phone calls, internet use and emails at work for stated purposes, including determining whether they are relevant to the employer's business, by a business (including a government department). Interceptions are only permitted provided that 'all reasonable efforts' have been made to inform employees that communications may be intercepted.

2 See RIPA 2000, s. 1(6).

2a [1979] Ch 344, Ch D.

under Art. 8 had been infringed 'by reason of the admitted interception of his telephone conversations and the law and practice governing the interception of postal and telephone communications on behalf of the police'.

JUDGMENT OF THE COURT
63 ... the present case 'is directly concerned only with the question of interceptions effected by or on behalf of the police' — and not other government services such as H.M. Customs and Excise and the Security Service — 'within the general context of a criminal investigation, together with the legal and administrative framework relevant to such interceptions' ...
66. The Court held in [the] *Silver* [case, E Ct HRR A61 (1983)] ... that, at least as far as interferences with prisoners' correspondence were concerned, the expression 'in accordance with the law/*prévue par la loi*' in paragraph 2 of Article 8 should be interpreted in the light of the same general principles as were stated in the *Sunday Times* [case, (1979–80) 2 EHRR 245] ... to apply to the comparable expression 'prescribed by law/*prévues par la loi*' in paragraph 2 of Article 10 ...
[The Court restated the *Sunday Times* principles and continued:]
67. ... The Court would reiterate its opinion that the phrase 'in accordance with the law' does not merely refer back to domestic law but also relates to the quality of the law, requiring it to be compatible with the rule of law, which is expressly mentioned in the preamble to the Convention (see, *mutatis mutandis*, the ... *Silver* [case] ..., and the *Golder* [case] ... The phrase thus implies — and this follows from the object and purpose of Article 8 — that there must be a measure of legal protection in domestic law against arbitrary interferences by public authorities with the rights safeguarded by paragraph 1. ... Especially where a power of the executive is exercised in secret, the risks of arbitrariness are evident (see the ... *Klass* [case]) ... Undoubtedly, as the Government rightly suggested, the requirements of the Convention, notably in regard to foreseeability, cannot be exactly the same in the special context of interception of communications for the purposes of police investigations as they are where the object of the relevant law is to place restrictions on the conduct of individuals. In particular, the requirement of foreseeability cannot mean that an individual should be enabled to foresee when the authorities are likely to intercept his communication so that he can adapt his conduct accordingly. Nevertheless, the law must be sufficiently clear in its terms to give citizens an adequate indication as to the circumstances in which and the conditions on which public authorities are empowered to resort to this secret and potentially dangerous interference with the right to respect for private life and correspondence.
68. There was also some debate in the pleadings as to the extent to which, in order for the Convention to be complied with, the 'law' itself, as opposed to accompanying administrative practice, should define the circumstances in which and the conditions on which a public authority may interfere with the exercise of the protected rights ... in the case of *Silver* ... the Court held that 'a law which confers a discretion must indicate the scope of that discretion', although the detailed procedures and conditions to be observed do not necessarily have to be incorporated in rules of substantive law. ... The degree of precision required of the 'law' in this connection will depend upon the particular subject-matter (see the ... *Sunday Times* ... [case]). Since the implementation in practice of measures of secret surveillance of communications is not open to scrutiny by the individuals concerned or the public at large, it would be contrary to the rule of law for the legal discretion granted to the executive to be expressed in terms of an unfettered power. Consequently, the law must indicate the scope of any such discretion conferred on the competent authorities and the manner of its exercise with sufficient clarity, having regard to the legitimate aim of the measure in question, to give the individual adequate protection against arbitrary interference. ...
69. Whilst the exact legal basis of the executive's power in this respect was the subject of some dispute, it was common ground that the settled practice of intercepting communications on behalf of the police in pursuance of a warrant issued by the Secretary of State for the purposes of detecting and preventing crime, and hence the admitted interception of one of the applicant's telephone conversations, was lawful under the law of England and Wales. The legality of this power to intercept was established in relation to telephone communications in the judgment of Sir Robert Megarry dismissing the applicant's civil action. ... and, as shown by the independent findings of the Birkett report ..., is generally recognised for postal communications.

70. The issue to be determined is therefore, whether, under domestic law, the essential elements of the power to intercept communications were laid down with reasonable precision in accessible legal rules that sufficiently indicated the scope and manner of exercise of the discretion conferred on the relevant authorities ...

[The Court then reviewed English law on the interception of communications and continued:]

79. The foregoing considerations disclose that, at the very least, in its present state the law in England and Wales governing interception of communications for police purposes is somewhat obscure and open to differing interpretations. The Court would be usurping the function of the national courts if it were to attempt to make an authoritative statement on such issues of domestic law. ... The Court is, however, required under the Convention to determine whether, for the purposes of paragraph 2 of Article 8, the relevant law lays down with reasonable clarity the essential elements of the authorities' powers in this domain.

Detailed procedures concerning interception of communications on behalf of the police in England and Wales do exist. ... What is more, published statistics show the efficacy of those procedures in keeping the number of warrants granted relatively low, especially when compared with the rising number of indictable crimes committed and telephones installed. ... The public have been made aware of the applicable arrangements and principles through publication of the Birkett report and the White Paper and through statements by responsible Ministers in Parliament.

Nonetheless, on the evidence before the Court, it cannot be said with any reasonable certainty what elements of the powers to intercept are incorporated in legal rules and what elements within the discretion of the executive. In view of the attendant obscurity and uncertainty as to the state of the law in this essential respect, the Court cannot but reach a similar conclusion to that of the Commission. In the opinion of the Court, the law of England and Wales does not indicate with reasonable clarity the scope and manner of exercise of the relevant discretion conferred on the public authorities. To that extent, the minimum degree of legal protection to which citizens are entitled under the rule of law in a democratic society is lacking ...

82. ... In view of its foregoing conclusion that the interferences found were not 'in accordance with the law', the Court considers that it does not have to examine further the content of the other guarantees required by paragraph 2 of Article 8 and whether the system complained of furnished those guarantees in the particular circumstances.

83. The process known as 'metering' involves the use of a device ... which registers the numbers dialled on a particular telephone and the time and duration of each call ...

84. As the Government rightly suggested, a meter check printer registers information that a supplier of a telephone service may in principle legitimately obtain, notably in order to ensure that the subscriber is correctly charged or to investigate complaints or possible abuses of the service. By its very nature, metering is therefore to be distinguished from interception of communications, which is undesirable and illegitimate in a democratic society unless justified. The Court does not accept, however, that the use of data obtained from metering, whatever the circumstances and purposes, cannot give rise to an issue under Article 8. the records of metering contain information, in particular the numbers dialled, which is an integral element in the communications made by telephone. Consequently, release of the information to the police without the consent of the subscriber also amounts, in the opinion of the Court, to an interference with a right guaranteed by Article 8. ...

87. Section 80 of the Post Office Act 1969 has never been applied so as to 'require' the Post Office, pursuant to a warrant of the Secretary of State, to make available to the police in connection with the investigation of crime information obtained from metering. On the other hand, no rule of domestic law makes it unlawful for the Post Office voluntarily to comply with a request from the police to make and supply records of metering. ... The practice described above, including the limitative conditions as to when the information may be provided, has been made public in answer to parliamentary questions. ... However, on the evidence aduced before the Court, apart from the simple absence of prohibition, there would appear to be no legal rules concerning the scope and manner of exercise of the discretion enjoyed by the public authorities. Consequently, although lawful in terms of domestic law, the interference resulting from the existence of the practice in question was not 'in accordance with the law', within the meaning of paragraph 2 of Article 8. ...

88. This conclusion removes the need for the Court to determine whether the interference found was 'necessary in a democratic society' for one of the aims enumerated in paragraph 2 of Article 8 ...

FOR THESE REASONS, THE COURT

1. *Holds* unanimously[3] that there has been a breach of Article 8 of the Convention; ...

NOTES[4]

1. The Court had no difficulty in treating telephone tapping as an interference with 'correspondence' (see para. 63).

2. When the *Malone* case was decided, telephone tapping in the UK was regulated by administrative practice, the up-to-date details of which were not readily accessible to the public. There was no express statutory authorisation or regime. Nor was there a common law basis. The position was essentially that telephone tapping was lawful because there was no law (it involved no trespass, no breach of confidence, etc.) prohibiting it: *Malone v Metropolitan Police Comr.*[4a] As a matter of practice, the Home Secretary authorised telephone tapping in accordance with internal, government guidelines, the details of which only became known to the public from time to time through reports such as the Birkett Report,[5] in 1957 in response to telephone tapping incidents giving cause for concern.

3. The legality of the interception of postal communications and telephone tapping under the Convention had earlier been considered by the Court in *Klass v Federal Republic of Germany.*[5a] There the Court held that the West German law permitting the interception of postal and telephonic communications in national security cases was consistent with Art. 8; although an 'interference by a public authority' with the 'right to respect for' a person's 'private and family life ... and his correspondence', it was justified as being necessary 'in the interests of national security' and/or for 'the prevention of disorder or crime'. The Court accepted that some power of interception was permissible to prevent espionage and terrorism and, bearing in mind the 'margin of appreciation' doctrine, concluded that the controls built into the West German system to prevent abuse were sufficient. Under that system, permission to intercept communications is given by a government minister applying certain criteria as to 'reasonable suspicion', etc. An independent Commission, chaired by a person qualified for judicial office, reviews and may reverse the Minister's decisions. A Board composed of government and opposition members of parliament keeps a more general watch on the system. A person whose communications are intercepted must be told that this has happened afterwards if national security allows. He may challenge the legality of current or past interceptions in the courts (so far as he is aware of their occurrence). Although the Court stated that it was 'in principle desirable to entrust supervisory control to a judge', the above safeguards were sufficient, at least in a national security context. An interesting aspect of the *Klass* case was that the Court regarded the applicants as 'victims' able to bring a claim under Art. 25 even though their telephones had not been tapped. Whereas an applicant under Art. 25 normally cannot challenge the validity in law *in abstracto* (as a state can under Art. 24) but has to show that the law 'has been applied to his detriment', the position is different in a case in which 'owing to the secrecy of the measures objected to, he cannot point to any concrete measure specifically affecting him'. In such a case the need to make

3   *Ed.* The case was heard by the full Court.
4   On the *Malone* case, see J. Michael, (1984) 134 NLJ 646, 669, 698. For other cases in which arrangements for telephone tapping were in breach of the 'in accordance with the law' requirement, see *Huvig v France* (1990) 12 EHRR 528 and *Kruslin v France* (1990) 12 EHRR 528.
4a [1979] Ch 344, Ch D.
5   Cmnd. 283.
5a (1978) 2 EHRR 214. See P. J. Duffy and P. T. Muchlinski, (1980) 130 NLJ 949.

the application procedure effective dictates that the 'individual may, *under certain conditions*, claim to be the victim of a violation occasioned by the mere existence of secret measures or of legislation permitting secret measures. ...' Moreover, the Court stated, the mere prospect that a telephone may be tapped is such as to inhibit conversation and thereby directly interfere with respect for privacy. In the *Malone* case, the Court similarly did not find it necessary to establish that interception or metering of the applicant's postal or telephonic communications had actually occurred. (Only one instance of telephone tapping and no metering had been admitted by the defendant government.) The Court observed that, as a suspected receiver of stolen goods, the applicant was a member of a class of persons whose privacy was likely to be invaded in these ways. It is not clear from the Court's judgment whether it was necessary for the applicant to have been a member of such a class (as opposed to any person making a telephone call, etc.) where a system of secret surveillance was in operation to have been a 'victim' and for Art. 8 to apply.

4. In the *Malone* case, the Court was prepared to accept that the interception of communications could be justified under the Convention as being necessary to prevent crime (para. 81) as well as (see the *Klass* case) for reasons of national security. Because of its ruling on the 'in accordance with the law' point, the Court did not find it necessary to specify what procedural safeguards were required in criminal cases. They must be at least as stringent as those spent out in the *Klass* case for national security cases.

5. In order to comply with the *Malone* case, the UK enacted the Interception of Communications Act 1985. In *Christie v United Kingdom*[6] the Commission held that the Act met the 'in accordance with the law' requirement in Art. 8(2). It also held that, 'having regard to the wide margin of appreciation ... in this area', the procedural safeguards provided by the Act (Commissioner, Tribunal, etc.) were sufficient for a case such as that before it where the applicant was a trade unionist with links with communist Eastern Europe whose telephone was being tapped on 'national security' and 'economic well-being' grounds. The complaint under Art. 8 was declared inadmissible.

6 Personal data: its electronic and manual storage and privacy

NOTES

1. The question of safeguarding privacy in the use of computerised data banks containing personal information about individuals in the private sector was considered in 1970 by the Younger Committee.[7] The Committee stated that 'of all the forms of invasion of privacy which have been cited in evidence to us that involving the use or misuse of computers has been the least supported in concrete terms'.[7a] The Committee could not on the evidence before it 'conclude that the computer as used in the private sector is at present a threat to privacy, but we recognise that there is a possibility of such a threat becoming a reality in the future'.[8] In recognition of the potential threat, the Committee formulated ten principles – the Younger Principles – which it proposed computer users should adopt in the handling of personal information. In 1975, the Government published a White Paper in which it stated that 'the time had come when those who use computers to handle personal

---

6 (1994) 78–A DR E Com HR 119.
7 Report, Chap. 20.
7a Ibid., p. 179.
8 Ibid., p. 191.

information, however responsible they are, can no longer remain the sole judges of whether their own systems adequately safeguard privacy.[9] The government therefore established the Data Protection Committee (the Lindop Committee), which reported in 1978 on the form that legislation should take.[10] Not all of its recommendations are followed in the 1984 Act.

2. The areas in which computers are used in the *public* sector to store personal information are described by the Lindop Committee. Summarising the *central government* position, the Lindop Committee stated:[11]

> '6.05. ... Certainly the government now collects and holds 'a good deal of information' about individuals; indeed, paragraph 10 of the Supplement rightly describes the total list as 'formidable'. There are some huge operations covering large sections of the total population. For example, the Department of Health and Social Security (DHSS) does not have files on every individual, but the systems dealing with National Insurance, Pensions and Child Allowances hold some 48 million records. The Department of National Savings (DNS) handles about 10 million National Savings Bank accounts; the Department of Education and Science (DES) has collected the records of some 3.5 million students for the Further Education Statistical REcord (FESR); and the Office of Population Censuses and Surveys (OPCS) aims to collect, for statistical purposes, information about every individual in the country. Many routine tasks in relation to such a volume of information can, for all practical purposes, only be carried out by computer. However, the amount of personal information held about each individual is usually small, and the operations themselves are straightforward. Often the names and addresses of individuals are not stored on computer files because they are not needed there and some identifier, such as an account number, can be used to link the information held on computer with that held in manual files.'

On the use of computers by the *police*, the Lindop Committee stated:[12]

> '8.07. The PNC [Police National Computer] holds five major files: the index to national records in the Criminal Records Office (CRO), a file of vehicle owners, a file of stolen and suspect vehicles, an index to the national fingerprint collection and a file of wanted or missing persons.
> ...
> 8.13. The PNC is connected, by a network of private lines provided by the Post Office, to some 300 wholly dedicated terminals situated in police premises and operated by police forces in Great Britain; thus police information on the PNC is available only within the police service. Local forces can input, alter and delete data on the stolen and suspect vehicles and wanted and missing persons files. The chief officer of a force which receives information from the PNC is responsible for ensuring that it is dealt with in accordance with the practices which apply to police information generally. The Home Office has recently issued notes for the guidance of chief officers of police on privacy precautions in police systems handling personal information; these deal mainly with the security of records.
> 8.14. The Home Office said in evidence that the PNC has no computer links with any other central government department and that no such links are planned. ...'

An indication of the kind of information stored on the Police National Computer appeared in a report in the *Guardian*, 20 September 1979 on 'jury-vetting'. Information on 19 of the 93 potential jurors in a conspiracy case with political overtones at the Old Bailey was given to the prosecution by the police for 'jury-vetting purposes'. The information identified people who had friends or relations with criminal records, had complained against the police, were squatters, had 'spent' convictions under the Rehabilitation of Offenders Act 1974 or had been the victims of crime. The jurors concerned were not aware that the information was being passed

---

9 *Computers and Privacy*, Cmnd. 6353, p. 8.
10 Cmnd. 7341.
11 Ibid., p. 53.
12 Report, pp. 80–84.

on to the prosecution. Was this a case of information collected for one purpose being used for another purpose? Would you object to information about you being collected and used in this way?

The Lindop Committee also described the use of computers by *local government,* the *nationalised industries* and in *schools* and *higher education.* As far as local government is concerned, the Committee stated:[13]

'The conflict between efficiency in the performance of those tasks and respect for the privacy of the individual is, in principle, the same as it is in central government. But it is much more acute because a smaller community is administered, and there is no legal separation of departments which established their independence from each other. Departments of State infrequently pass information about identifiable persons between one another; departments of a local authority rely upon such transfers for the proper exercise of their functions. And there is no doubt that local government comes closer to the lives of ordinary people than any other body in the public or private sectors.'

In the *private* sector, the Committee described the use of computers in employment, consumer credit, banking, insurance and direct marketing and by building societies.

3. As the government White Paper states, 'none of the functions carried out by computers within an information system is different in kind from those which are, or could in principle be, carried out by traditional means'.[14] The reasons why they nonetheless present a problem for the protection of privacy requiring special treatment are stated in the White Paper as follows:[15]

'6. The speed of computers, their capacity to store, combine, retrieve and transfer data, their flexibility, and the low unit cost of the work which they can do have the following practical implications for privacy:

(1) they facilitate the maintenance of extensive record systems and the retention of data in those systems;

(2) they can make data easily and quickly accessible from many distant points;

(3) they make it possible for data to be transferred quickly from one information system to another;

(4) they make it possible for data to be combined in ways which might not otherwise be practicable;

(5) because the data are stored, processed and often transmitted in a form which is not directly intelligible, few people may know what is in the records, or what is happening to them. ...

8. The principal potential dangers to privacy come from three main sources:

(1) inaccurate, incomplete or irrelevant information;

(2) the possibility of access to information by people who should not or need not have it;

(3) the use of information in a context or for a purpose other than that for which it was collected.

Any of these dangers can come about either intentionally, or by accident, and properly designed safeguards must therefore provide against both eventualities.'

The storing of inaccurate information results from human error and can be countered by a right of subject access. Cases in which the person about whom inaccurate information is compiled is not made aware of this fact[16] present the greatest problems. As far as the other two 'principal potential dangers' to which it refers are concerned, the White Paper states:[17]

---

13 Ibid., p. 94.
14 Cmnd. 6353, pp. 5–6.
15 Ibid.
16 See, e.g., those in Hewitt, *The Information Gatherers* (1977), pp. 1–2.
17 Cmnd. 6353, pp. 5–6.

'14. The very complexity of computers and their operations creates problems for anyone who tries to gain authorised access to them ...

15. Where data are printed out in human readable form, computer based systems share the security weaknesses of manual systems.

16. Whre someone with authorised access to information uses that information for an improper purpose, it is a breach of confidence ... and our law already provides a number a remedies for it ... The additional fear that arises from the development of computers is that someone will make improper use of the computer's capacity for storing, processing and transferring data so as to combine information from a number of sources about individuals without their knowledge and consent. ...

18. The confidentiality of personal information held in a computer system can of course also be put at risk through accident, carelessness or sheer lack of foresight. In practice, that is the way in which confidentiality – and also accuracy – are most likely to be compromised in the foreseeable future. Any computer system which is properly designed and operated must therefore ensure that risks of this kind have been foreseen, and that adequate safeguards are maintained to obviate them.'

Commenting on the combining and transferring of information, the Lindop Committee noted:[18]

'6.07. The prospect which seems to cause most public alarm is the possibility that the government might, with the aid of computers, collate and centralise all the government-held inforamtion about an individual to form a personal dossier. Such a collation and centralisation, for however beneficial purpose, would, in our view, be thoroughly undesirable. It would give any government too great a potential power over its citizens and it would be dangerous if it fell into the wrong hands. It is therefore important that some independent body should be able to ensure that reasonable limits are placed on the possible collation of information.'

The Committee could see that in some cases the transfer of information from one computer-based information system to another could be justifiable in the public interest. It quoted the following case:[19]

'6.11. On 17 January 1977, the *Daily Mail* had a story under the heading 'Taxmen Use Driving Licence Computer to Spy' and a version of the same story was also reported in other papers. There was at that time a public outcry over the fact that the Driver and Vehicle Licensing Centre (DVLC) at Swansea, whose records are held on computer, supplied the Inland Revenue with individuals' addresses. This was taken by some to be a new and clandestine scheme, to which the involvement of computers lent Orwellian overtones. In fact, since 1931 the driving and vehicle licence authorities have supplied the IR on request with individuals' current addresses in order to trace tax-evaders. This use of computerised information was noted in the White Paper Supplement, and it involves the transfer of information which the IR needs to carry out its statutory duties and which it has reason to believe is being deliberately withheld.

6.12. There is nothing underhand about this procedure and many regard it as highly desirable. It is a pity, therefore, that it should have given rise to public suspicion.'

Data Protection Act 1998

1 Basic interpretative provisions

(1)   In this Act, unless the context otherwise requires—

'data' means information which—

(*a*)   is being processed by means of equipment operating automatically in response to instructions given for that purpose,

(*b*)   is recorded with the intention that it should be processed by means of such equipment,

---

18   Report, p. 54.
19   Ibid., p. 57.

    (*c*) is recorded as part of a relevant filing system or with the intention that it should form part of a relevant filing system, *or*

    (*d*) does not fall within paragraph (*a*), (*b*) or (*c*) but forms part of an accessible record as defined by section 68; [*or*

'data controller' means, subject to subsection (4), a person who (either alone or jointly or in common with other persons) determines the purposes for which and the manner in which any personal data are, or are to be, processed;

'data processor', in relation to personal data, means any person (other than an employee of the data controller) who processes the data on behalf of the data controller;

'data subject' means an individual who is the subject of personal data;

'personal data' means data which relate to a living individual who can be identified—

    (*a*) from those data, or

    (*b*) from those data and other information which is in the possession of, or is likely to come into the possession of, the data controller,

and includes any expression of opinion about the individual and any indication of the intentions of the data controller or any other person in respect of the individual;

'processing', in relation to information or data, means obtaining, recording or holding the information or data or carrying out any operation or set of operations on the information or data, including—

    (*a*) organisation, adaptation or alteration of the information or data,

    (*b*) retrieval, consultation or use of the information or data,

    (*c*) disclosure of the information or data by transmission, dissemination or otherwise making available, or

    (*d*) alignment, combination, blocking, erasure or destruction of the information or data;

'relevant filing system' means any set of information relating to individuals to the extent that, although the information is not processed by means of equipment operating automatically in response to instructions given for that purpose, the set is structured, either by reference to individuals or by reference to criteria relating to individuals, in such a way that specific information relating to a particular individual is readily accessible.

(2) In this Act, unless the context otherwise requires—

    (*a*) 'obtaining' or 'recording', in relation to personal data, includes obtaining or recording the information to be contained in the data, and

    (*b*) 'using' or 'disclosing', in relation to personal data, includes using or disclosing the information contained in the data.

(3) In determining for the purposes of this Act whether any information is recorded with the intention—

    (*a*) that it should be processed by means of equipment operating automatically in response to instructions given for that purpose, or

    (*b*) that it should form part of a relevant filing system,

it is immaterial that it is intended to be so processed or to form part of such a system only after being transferred to a country or territory outside the European Economic Area.

(4) Where personal data are processed only for purposes for which they are required by or under any enactment to be processed, the person on whom the obligation to process the data is imposed by or under that enactment is for the purposes of this Act the data controller.

2. Sensitive personal data

In this Act 'sensitive personal data' means personal data consisting of information as to—

    (*a*) the racial or ethnic origin of the data subject,

    (*b*) his political opinions,

    (*c*) his religious beliefs or other beliefs of a similar nature,

    (*d*) whether he is a member of a trade union (within the meaning of the Trade Union and Labour Relations (Consolidation) Act 1992,

    (*e*) his physical or mental health or condition,

    (*f*) his sexual life,

(*g*)   the commission or alleged commission by him of any offence, or

(*h*)   any proceedings for any offence committed or alleged to have been committed by him, the disposal of such proceedings or the sentence of any court in such proceedings.

3. The special purposes

In this Act 'the special purposes" means any one or more of the following—

(*a*)   the purposes of journalism,

(*b*)   artistic purposes, and

(*c*)   literary purposes.

4. The data protection principles

(1) References in this Act to the data protection principles are to the principles set out in Part I of Schedule 1.

(2) Those principles are to be interpreted in accordance with Part II of Schedule 1.

(3) Schedule 2 (which applies to all personal data) and Schedule 3 (which applies only to sensitive personal data) set out conditions applying for the purposes of the first principle; and Schedule 4 sets out cases in which the eighth principle does not apply.

(4) Subject to section 27(1), it shall be the duty of a data controller to comply with the data protection principles in relation to all personal data with respect to which he is the data controller.

7. Right of access to personal data

(1) Subject to the following provisions of this section and to *sections 8 and 9* [*sections 8, 9 and 9A*], an individual is entitled—

(*a*)   to be informed by any data controller whether personal data of which that individual is the data subject are being processed by or on behalf of that data controller,

(*b*)   if that is the case, to be given by the data controller a description of—

(i)   the personal data of which that individual is the data subject,

(ii)   the purposes for which they are being or are to be processed, and

(iii)   the recipients or classes of recipients to whom they are or may be disclosed,

(*c*)   to have communicated to him in an intelligible form—

(i)   the information constituting any personal data of which that individual is the data subject, and

(ii)   any information available to the data controller as to the source of those data, and

(*d*)   where the processing by automatic means of personal data of which that individual is the data subject for the purpose of evaluating matters relating to him such as, for example, his performance at work, his creditworthiness, his reliability or his conduct, has constituted or is likely to constitute the sole basis for any decision significantly affecting him, to be informed by the data controller of the logic involved in that decision-taking.

(2) A data controller is not obliged to supply any information under subsection (1) unless he has received—

(*a*)   a request in writing, and

(*b*)   except in prescribed cases, such fee (not exceeding the prescribed maximum) as he may require.

[(3)   Where a data controller—

(*a*)   reasonably requires further information in order to satisfy himself as to the identity of the person making a request under this section and to locate the information which that person seeks, and

(*b*)   has informed him of that requirement,

the data controller is not obliged to comply with the request unless he is supplied with that further information.]

(4) Where a data controller cannot comply with the request without disclosing information relating to another individual who can be identified from that information, he is not obliged to comply with the request unless—

(*a*)   the other individual has consented to the disclosure of the information to the person making the request, or

(*b*)   it is reasonable in all the circumstances to comply with the request without the consent of the other individual.

(5) In subsection (4) the reference to information relating to another individual includes a reference to information identifying that individual as the source of the information sought by the request; and that subsection is not to be construed as excusing a data controller from communicating so much of the information sought by the request as can be communicated without disclosing the identity of the other individual concerned, whether by the omission of names or other identifying particulars or otherwise.

(6) In determining for the purposes of subsection (4)(*b*) whether it is reasonable in all the circumstances to comply with the request without the consent of the other individual concerned, regard shall be had, in particular, to—

    (*a*)   any duty of confidentiality owed to the other individual,

    (*b*)   any steps taken by the data controller with a view to seeking the consent of the other individual,

    (*c*)   whether the other individual is capable of giving consent, and

    (*d*)   any express refusal of consent by the other individual.

(7) An individual making a request under this section may, in such cases as may be prescribed, specify that his request is limited to personal data of any prescribed description.

(8) Subject to subsection (4), a data controller shall comply with a request under this section promptly and in any event before the end of the prescribed period beginning with the relevant day.

(9) If a court is satisfied on the application of any person who has made a request under the foregoing provisions of this section that the data controller in question has failed to comply with the request in contravention of those provisions, the court may order him to comply with the request.

(10) In this section—

    'prescribed' means prescribed by the Secretary of State by regulations;

    'the prescribed maximum' means such amount as may be prescribed;

    'the prescribed period' means forty days or such other period as may be prescribed;

    'the relevant day', in relation to a request under this section, means the day on which the data controller receives the request or, if later, the first day on which the data controller has both the required fee and the information referred to in subsection (3).

(11) Different amounts or periods may be prescribed under this section in relation to different cases.

10. Right to prevent processing likely to cause damage or distress

(1) Subject to subsection (2), an individual is entitled at any time by notice in writing to a data controller to require the data controller at the end of such period as is reasonable in the circumstances to cease, or not to begin, processing, or processing for a specified purpose or in a specified manner, any personal data in respect of which he is the data subject, on the ground that, for specified reasons—

    (*a*)   the processing of those data or their processing for that purpose or in that manner is causing or is likely to cause substantial damage or substantial distress to him or to another, and

    (*b*)   that damage or distress is or would be unwarranted.

(2) Subsection (1) does not apply—

    (*a*)   in a case where any of the conditions in paragraphs 1 to 4 of Schedule 2 is met, or

    (*b*)   in such other cases as may be prescribed by the Secretary of State by order.

(3) The data controller must within twenty-one days of receiving a notice under subsection (1) ('the data subject notice') give the individual who gave it a written notice—

    (*a*)   stating that he has complied or intends to comply with the data subject notice, or

    (*b*)   stating his reasons for regarding the data subject notice as to any extent unjustified and the extent (if any) to which he has complied or intends to comply with it.

(4) If a court is satisfied, on the application of any person who has given a notice under subsection (1) which appears to the court to be justified (or to be justified to any extent), that the data controller in question has failed to comply with the notice, the court may order him to take such steps for complying with the notice (or for complying with it to that extent) as the court thinks fit.

    (5)   The failure by a data subject to exercise the right conferred by subsection (1) or section 11(1) does not affect any other right conferred on him by this Part.

13. Compensation for failure to comply with certain requirements
(1) An individual who suffers damage by reason of any contravention by a data controller of any of the requirements of this Act is entitled to compensation from the data controller for that damage.
(2) An individual who suffers distress by reason of any contravention by a data controller of any of the requirements of this Act is entitled to compensation from the data controller for that distress if—

  (a)   the individual also suffers damage by reason of the contravention, or
  (b)   the contravention relates to the processing of personal data for the special purposes.
(3) In proceedings brought against a person by virtue of this section it is a defence to prove that he had taken such care as in all the circumstances was reasonably required to comply with the requirement concerned.

14. Rectification, blocking, erasure and destruction
(1) If a court is satisfied on the application of a data subject that personal data of which the applicant is the subject are inaccurate, the court may order the data controller to rectify, block, erase or destroy those data and any other personal data in respect of which he is the data controller and which contain an expression of opinion which appears to the court to be based on the inaccurate data.
(2) Subsection (1) applies whether or not the data accurately record information received or obtained by the data controller from the data subject or a third party but where the data accurately record such information, then—

  (a)   if the requirements mentioned in paragraph 7 of Part II of Schedule 1 have been complied with, the court may, instead of making an order under subsection (1), make an order requiring the data to be supplemented by such statement of the true facts relating to the matters dealt with by the data as the court may approve, and
  (b)   if all or any of those requirements have not been complied with, the court may, instead of making an order under that subsection, make such order as it thinks fit for securing compliance with those requirements with or without a further order requiring the data to be supplemented by such a statement as is mentioned in paragraph (a).
(3) Where the court

  (a)   makes an order under subsection (1), or
  (b)   is satisfied on the application of a data subject that personal data of which he was the data subject and which have been rectified, blocked, erased or destroyed were inaccurate,
it may, where it considers it reasonably practicable, order the data controller to notify third parties to whom the data have been disclosed of the rectification, blocking, erasure or destruction.
(4) If a court is satisfied on the application of a data subject—

  (a)   that he has suffered damage by reason of any contravention by a data controller of any of the requirements of this Act in respect of any personal data, in circumstances entitling him to compensation under section 13, and
  (b)   that there is a substantial risk of further contravention in respect of those data in such circumstances,
the court may order the rectification, blocking, erasure or destruction of any of those data.
(5) Where the court makes an order under subsection (4) it may, where it considers it reasonably practicable, order the data controller to notify third parties to whom the data have been disclosed of the rectification, blocking, erasure or destruction.
(6) In determining whether it is reasonably practicable to require such notification as is mentioned in subsection (3) or (5) the court shall have regard, in particular, to the number of persons who would have to be notified.

32 Journalism, literature and art
(1) Personal data which are processed only for the special purposes are exempt from any provision to which this subsection relates if—

  (a)   the processing is undertaken with a view to the publication by any person of any journalistic, literary or artistic material,
  (b)   the data controller reasonably believes that, having regard in particular to the special importance of the public interest in freedom of expression, publication would be in the public interest, and

    (*c*) the data controller reasonably believes that, in all the circumstances, compliance with that provision is incompatible with the special purposes.

(2) Subsection (1) relates to the provisions of—

    (*a*) the data protection principles except the seventh data protection principle,

    (*b*) section 7,

    (*c*) section 10,

    (*d*) section 12,

    [(*dd*)section 12A,] and

    (*e*) section 14(1) to (3).

(3) In considering for the purposes of subsection (1)(b) whether the belief of a data controller that publication would be in the public interest was or is a reasonable one, regard may be had to his compliance with any code of practice which—

    (*a*) is relevant to the publication in question, and

    (*b*) is designated by the Secretary of State by order for the purposes of this subsection.

(4) Where at any time ('the relevant time") in any proceedings against a data controller under section 7(9), 10(4), 12(8)[, 12A(3)] or 14 or by virtue of section 13 the data controller claims, or it appears to the court, that any personal data to which the proceedings relate are being processed—

    (*a*) only for the special purposes, and

    (*b*) with a view to the publication by any person of any journalistic, literary or artistic material which, at the time twenty-four hours immediately before the relevant time, had not previously been published by the data controller,

the court shall stay the proceedings until either of the conditions in subsection (5) is met.

(5) Those conditions are—

    (*a*) that a determination of the Commissioner under section 45 with respect to the data in question takes effect, or

    (*b*) in a case where the proceedings were stayed on the making of a claim, that the claim is withdrawn.

(6) For the purposes of this Act 'publish", in relation to journalistic, literary or artistic material, means make available to the public or any section of the public.

  Section 4(1) and (2)

SCHEDULE 1

THE DATA PROTECTION PRINCIPLES

PART I

THE PRINCIPLES

1. Personal data shall be processed fairly and lawfully and, in particular, shall not be processed unless—

    (a) at least one of the conditions in Schedule 2 is met, and

    (b) in the case of sensitive personal data, at least one of the conditions in Schedule 3 is also met.

2. Personal data shall be obtained only for one or more specified and lawful purposes, and shall not be further processed in any manner incompatible with that purpose or those purposes.

3. Personal data shall be adequate, relevant and not excessive in relation to the purpose or purposes for which they are processed.

4. Personal data shall be accurate and, where necessary, kept up to date.

5. Personal data processed for any purpose or purposes shall not be kept for longer than is necessary for that purpose or those purposes.

6. Personal data shall be processed in accordance with the rights of data subjects under this Act.

7. Appropriate technical and organisational measures shall be taken against unauthorised or unlawful processing of personal data and against accidental loss or destruction of, or damage to, personal data.

8. Personal data shall not be transferred to a country or territory outside the European Economic Area unless that country or territory ensures an adequate level of protection for the rights and freedoms of data subjects in relation to the processing of personal data.

NOTES

1. Following the *Lindop Report*, Parliament enacted the Data Protection Act 1984. This incorporated the Younger Principles, on the Data Protection Principles, and adopted most of the Lindop recommendations. The Data Protection Act 1998 replaced the Data Protection Act 1984, which it repealed.[20] The 1998 Act follows the pattern of the 1984 Act, but contains some important differences, partly in response to the EU Data Protection Directive 1995,[1] which it implements. Most significantly from a privacy standpoint, the law now extends to some manually processed data, as well as data that are processed by computer, and the 'data subject' (i) has a more extensive right of access to personal information held by the 'data controller' and (ii) may prevent the processing of personal data information where this would be likely to cause damage or distress or the information is of a sensitive personal kind.

2. The Act applies only to 'personal data'.[2] As well as computer-based data, the 1998 Act applies to information that 'is recorded as part of a relevant filing system or with the intention that it should form part of' such a system (s. 1(1)(c)). This includes manually prepared files, such as employee record files.[3]

3. A 'data subject' has a right of access to 'personal data' of which he or she is the subject.[4] Under the 1998 Act, this includes information about the source of the data. The information must be provided, for a fee, by the 'data controller', who is the person who controls the data storage operation concerned.[5] The data subject may prevent the processing of personal data that is likely to cause substantial distress or damage.[6] The processing of 'sensitive personal data'[7] is also prohibited, unless it satisfies one or more of a large number of specified conditions.[8] Journalists, who have extensive personal data files, whether computer or manually based, are exempt from key parts of the Act, including those providing for the rights of the data subject to access to stored information and to prevent the publication of data that is likely to cause substantial distress or damage.[9] The data subject is entitled to compensation from a data controller for the damage or distress caused by a breach of the Act, including the storage of inaccurate information.[10] The processing of personal data must be conducted in accordance with the Data Protection Principles.[11]

4. The Act is administered by the Data Protection Commissioner. The Commissioner maintains a register of data processing operations, which, subject to certain exemptions, cannot be conducted unless they are notified to the Commissioner.[12] The Commissioner monitors compliance with the Act by data processors. The Data Protection Tribunal may hear appeals against action taken by the Commissioner.

---

20 On the 1998 Act, see P. Carey, *Data Protection in the UK* (2000).
1 (1995) OJ L 43, p. 1.
2 For the definition of 'personal data', see s. 1(1) of the 1998 Act.
3 For the definition of a 'relevant filing system', see s. 1(1), of the 1998 Act. Manually prepared files that pre-date the 1998 Act benefit from a transitional period ending in 2007.
4 1998 Act, s. 7.
5 For the definition of a 'data controller', see s. 1(1) of the 1998 Act.
6 1998 Act, s. 10.
7 For the definition of 'sensitive personal data', see s. 2 of the 1998 Act. 'Sensitive' data include data about a person's racial or ethnic origin, sexual life, health and criminal record.
8 For the conditions, see Sch. 2 of the 1998 Act and the relevant statutory instruments. They include consent, public knowledge and statutory authority.
9 1998 Act, s. 32.
10 1998 Act, s. 13.
11 1998 Act, s. 3 and Sch. I.
12 1998 Act, s. 17. For the exemptions, see ss. 28–38, of the 1998 Act.

CHAPTER 10

Freedom of religion

1 Introduction[1]

One element of freedom of religion is freedom from discrimination between religions. The Church of England's status as the established church means some preference in law for it over other denominations, although establishment carries disadvantages too. Religious toleration has reached the point where almost all the disabilities formerly suffered by dissenters have been removed and atheism is within the policy of the law. In addition to the aid to religion that the establishment of a particular church represents, the state provides support to religion generally or to particular denominations in other ways as well. The provision made for religion in schools, for exemption from taxation and by the law of blasphemy are good examples. *Private* discrimination on religious grounds is mostly uncontrolled. There is no statute like the Race Relations Act 1976 prohibiting it in Great Britain,[2] although the concept of indirect racial discrimination in that Act may provide a remedy in some cases. This has been the case for Muslims and Sikhs especially.[3]

Freedom of religion also includes freedom of worship and expression and freedom to conduct one's life in accordance with one's religious beliefs. Freedom of worship is now virtually complete. Freedom of expression on religious matters is limited only by the remnants of the law of blasphemy. The Christian morality underlying English law means that most Christians have no difficulty in practising their religion in their daily lives. Members of some minority Christian and non-Christian denominations lack the same facility, as the sections in this chapter on criminal law, employment, religious holy days and immigration show.[4] Immigration from the new Commonwealth since the 1950s has provided further evidence of the link between Christianity and the law. The same development of a more multi-racial (and hence multi-religious[5]) society has increased the importance of freedom of religion.

---

1   On the legal aspects of freedom of religion see, A. Bradney, *Religions, Rights and Laws*, (1993); P. Cumper, in J. Van Der Vyver and J. Witte (eds.), *Religious Human Rights in Global Perspectives*: *Legal Perspectives* (1996), p. 205; J. Montgomery, in B. Hepple and E. M. Szyszczak (eds.), *Discrimination: The Limits of the Law* (1992) Chap. 11; S. Poulter, ibid., Chap. 10; and St. J. Robilliard, *Religion and the Law* (1984). On freedom of religion in Northern Ireland, which is too large and complex a subject to be considered here, see S. Livingstone, in B. Dickson, ed., *Civil Liberties in Northern Ireland* (3rd edn, 1997), Chap. 12.

2   For proposals for reform in this area, see B. Hepple and T. Choudhury, *Tackling Religious Discrimination*: *Practical Implications for Policy-Makers and Legislators*, Home Office personal study 221, (2001). Private discrimination in employment is illegal in Northern Ireland: Fair Employment (NI)Acts 1976 and 1989.

3   See, e.g., *Walker v Hussain*, below, p. 1064, and the *Mandla* case, below, p. 1116. As to Rastafarians, see the *Dawkins* case, below, p. 1123.

4   On the problems that face ethnic minorities, see S. Poulter, *Asian Traditions and English Law: a Handbook* (1990) and ibid., *Ethnicity, Law and Human Rights* (1998).

5   In terms of community (as opposed to active) members, there are approximately 38.1 million Christians; 1.3 million Muslims; 0.5 million Hindus; 0.4 million Sikhs; and 0.3 million Jews: P. Weller (ed.), *Religions in the UK 2001–03* (2001), p. 34.

The Human Rights Act 1998, s. 13, requires that 'particular regard' be paid to the importance of the right to freedom of thought, conscience and religion when court decisions are taken affecting the exercise of that right by religious organisations. The significance of this provision is considered in Chapter 1.[6] A key question that arises is the policy that the law should follow in respect of the treatment of religious minorities. In a report to the United Nations, the United Kingdom government explained its approach to the treatment of ethnic minorities generally as follows:

> 'It is a fundamental objective of the U.K. Government to enable members of ethnic minorities to participate freely and fully in the economic, social and public life of the nation, with all the benefits and responsibilities which that entails, while still being able to maintain their own culture, traditions, language and values.'[7]

2   What is a religion?

Re South Place Ethical Society; Barralet v A-G [1980] 3 All ER 918, [1980] 1 WLR 1565, QBD

The South Place Ethical Society sought a declaration that its objects were charitable, as being for the advancement of religion or otherwise. The objects of the society were 'the study and dissemination of ethical principles and the cultivation of a rational religious sentiment'. Counsel for the society described it as 'a wholly learned society with a deep and thoughtful philosophy'; it was 'agnostic about the existence of any god'. The society had abandoned prayer in 1869. In the society's objects, the word 'religious' was 'used in a sense which eschews all supernatural belief'. The society's beliefs were an aspect of humanism and in the Platonic tradition. The society held Sunday meetings open to the public at which lectures were given. There were also ancillary social activities. The following extract concerns the question whether the society could be regarded as charitable on religious grounds.

> **Dillon J**: . . . The Society says that religion does not have to be theist or dependent on a god; any sincere belief in ethical qualities is religious, because such qualities as truth, love and beauty are sacred, and the advancement of any such belief is the advancement of religion.
>
> One decision [cited to the court] is the decision of the Supreme Court of the United States in *United States v Seeger* (1965) 380 US 163.[8] That was concerned with the exemption of a conscientious objector from conscription on the grounds of religion. . . . The judgment of the court (delivered by Clark J) gives as the ratio (at 176) that in the opinion of the court—
>
> > 'A sincere and meaningful belief, which occupies in the life of its possessor a place parallel to that filled by the God of those admittedly qualifying for exemption on the grounds of religion comes within the statutory definition.' . . .
>
> In a free country . . . it is natural that the court should desire not to discriminate between beliefs deeply and sincerely held, whether they are beliefs in a god or in the excellence of man or in ethical principles or in Platonism or some other scheme of philosophy. But I do not see that that warrants extending the meaning of the word 'religion' so as to embrace all other beliefs and philosophies. Religion, as I see it, is concerned with man's relations with God, and ethics are concerned with man's relations with man. The two are not the same, and are not made the same by sincere inquiry into the question, what is God. If reason leads

---

6   Above, p. 36.
7   13th UK Report to CERD, UN DOCS. CERD/C/263/Add.7 and Add.7, Part II, p. 2.
8   *Ed.* In *Wisconsin v Yoder* (1972) 406 US 205, the Supreme Court later adopted a narrower conception of religion than in *United States v Seeger* distinguishing between 'secular considerations' and 'religious belief.' See *Penalver* (1997) 107 Yale LJ 791, 798.

people not to accept Christianity or any known religion, but they do believe in the excellence of qualities such as truth, beauty and love, or believe in the Platonic concept of the ideal, their beliefs may be to them the equivalent of a religion, but viewed objectively they are not religion. The ground of the opinion of the Supreme Court in *Seeger's* case, that any belief occupying in the life of its possessor a place parallel to that occupied by belief in God in the minds of theists is religion, prompts the comment that parallels, by definition, never meet.

In *Bowman v Secular Society Ltd* [below, p. 1036], Lord Parker, in commenting on one of the objects of the society in that case, namely to promote the principle that human conduct should be based upon natural knowledge and not on supernatural belief, and that human welfare in this world is the proper end of all thought and action, said of that object:

'It is not a religious trust, for it relegates religion to a region in which it is to have no influence on human conduct.'

That comment seems to me to be equally applicable to the objects of the society in the present case, and it is not to be answered in my judgment by attempting to extend the meaning of religion. Lord Parker has used the word 'in its natural and accustomed sense'.

Again, in *United Grand Lodge of Ancient, Free and Accepted Masons of England v Holborn Borough Council* [1957] 3 All ER 281 at 285, [1957] 1 WLR 1080 at 1090 Donovan J, delivering the judgment of the Divisional Court, after commenting that freemasonry held out certain standards of truth and justice by which masons were urged to regulate their conduct, and commenting that, in particular, masons were urged to be reverent, honest, compassionate, loyal, temperate, benevolent and chaste, said:

'Admirable though these objects are, it seems to us impossible to say that they add up to the advancement of religion.'

Therefore I take the view that the objects of this society are not for the advancement of religion.

There is a further point. It seems to me that two of the essential attributes of religion are faith and worship; faith in god and worship of that god. This is supported by the definitions of religion given in the Oxford English Dictionary, although I appreciate that there are other definitions in other dictionaries and books. The Oxford Dictionary gives as one of the definitions of religion:

'a particular system of faith and worship . . . recognition on the part of man of some higher, unseen power as having control of his destiny and as being entitled to obedience, reverence and worship.'

In *R v Registrar General, ex p Segerdal* [1970] 3 All ER 886 at 892, [1970] 2 QB 697 at 709, which was concerned with the so-called Church of Scientology, Buckley LJ in his judgment said this:

'Worship I take to be something which must have some, at least, of the following characteristics: submission to the object worshipped, veneration of that object, praise, thanksgiving, prayer or intercession.'

He went on to say that, looking at the wedding ceremony of the scientologists, he could find nothing in the form of ceremony which would not be appropriate in a purely civil, non-religious ceremony such as is conducted in a registry office, and that it contained none of the elements which he had suggested were necessary elements of worship. . . .

The society really accepts that worship by that definition, which in my view is the correct definition in considering whether a body is charitable for the advancement of religion, is not practised by the society because, indeed, it is not possible to worship in that way a mere ethical or philosophical ideal. . . .

One of the matters that has been pressed in argument and which weighed with Douglas J in *Seeger's* case is the position of Buddhism, which is accepted by everyone as being a religion. It is said that religion cannot be necessarily theist or dependent on belief in a god, a supernatural or supreme being, because Buddhism does not have any such belief. I do not think it is necessary to explore that further in this judgment because I do not know enough about Buddhism. It may be that the answer in respect of Buddhism is to treat it as an exception, as Lord Denning MR did in his judgment in *R v Registrar General* . . . Alternatively, it may be that Buddhism is not an exception, because I have been supplied with an affidavit by his

Honour Judge Christmas Humphreys QC, an eminent English Buddhist, where he says that he does not accept the suggestion that 'Buddhism denies a supreme being'. I would not wish to suggest in any way that Buddhism is not a religion.

The society therefore fails in my judgment to make out its case to be charitable on the ground that its objects are for the advancement of religion. . . .

[Dillon J then held that the society was charitable as being for purposes beneficial to the community and as being for the advancement of education.]

Declarations accordingly.

NOTES

1. This case defines 'religion' in the context of the law of charities. In *R v Registrar General, ex p Segerdal*[9] [1970] 2 QB 697, the Court of Appeal had adopted a similar approach when deciding whether the chapel of the Church of Scientology at East Grinstead was a 'place of meeting for religious worship' so as to qualify for registration within the Places of Worship Registration Act 1855. That Act applies to places of worship of all denominations except the Church of England. Registration is not compulsory, but carries with it important advantages. By registration, Lord Denning stated,[10] the church 'will have taken one step towards getting a licence to celebrate marriages there; they will be outside the jurisdiction of the Charity Commissioners; and the building itself may become exempt from paying rates'. Refusing the applicants mandamus to require the Registrar General to register the chapel, Lord Denning continued:[11]

> '. . . the combined phrase, "place of meeting for religious worship" . . . connotes to my mind a place of which the principal use is as a place where people come together as a congregation or assembly to do reverence to God. It need not be the God which the Christians worship. It may be another God, or any unknown God, but it must be a reverence to deity. There may be exceptions. For instance, Buddhist temples are properly described as places of meeting for religious worship. . . .
> Turning to the creed of the Church of Scientology, I must say that it seems to me to be more a *philosophy* of the existence of man or of life, rather than a *religion*. Religious worship means reverence or veneration of God or a Supreme Being. I do not find any such reverence or veneration in the creed of this church, or, indeed, in the affidavit of Mr. Segerdal. There is considerable stress on the spirit of man. The adherents of this philosophy believe that man's spirit is everlasting and moves from one human frame to another; but still, so far as I can see, it is the spirit of man and not of God. When I look through the ceremonies and the affidavits, I am left with the feeling that there is nothing in it of reverence for God or deity, but simply instruction in a philosophy.'

Winn and Buckley LJJ delivered concurring judgments. In *Church of the New Faith v Comr for Pay-Roll Tax*[12] it was held that scientology *was* a religion so as to attract tax exemption. The definition of religion adopted by Mason ACJ and Brennan J (two members of a five man court) was:

> '. . . for the purposes of the law, the criteria of religion are twofold: first, belief in a supernatural Being, Thing or Principle; and second, the acceptance of canons of conduct in order to give effect to that belief, though canons of conduct which offend against the ordinary laws are outside the area of any immunity, privilege or right conferred on the grounds of religion.'[13]

9 [1970] 2 QB 697.
10 Ibid. at 704.
11 Ibid.
12 (1983) 57 ALR 785, Aust H Ct.
13 Ibid., 789.

In so far as belief in a 'principle' could suffice, this definition was wider than that in *Re South Place Ethical Society*.[14]

2. The charitable status of the South Place Ethical Society was important for tax purposes. A charity, whether for the advancement of religion or for other charitable purposes, is largely exempt from tax.[15]

3. The charitable status of the Exclusive Brethren has been the subject of scrutiny. An investigation conducted on behalf of the Charity Commissioners by Mr. H. Francis QC into the Brethren concluded that a faction of the Brethren which followed the teachings of James Taylor Jnr could not be regarded as charitable because it applied the 'separation from evil' doctrine in such a way that 'the advancement of such a religion, far from being beneficial to the community, is inimical to the true interests of the community'[16] In *A-G v BBC*,[17] Lord Salmon gave this picture of the sect:

'On September 26, 1976, the BBC broadcast on television what purported to be the habits, teaching and attitudes of a religious sect called the Exclusive Brethren which adhered to the principles laid down by an American called James Taylor Jnr. The broadcast was extremely hostile to the sect; it made it plain that the sect taught that anyone who is not one of its members is necessarily evil, and accordingly decreed that the sect's members must dissociate themselves from any such persons whosoever they may be—husband, wife, father, mother, brother or sister. They must not even talk to them nor eat with them. According to the broadcast, this doctrine was applied so strictly that it caused the deepest distress amongst many and led in Andover to two deaths which the coroner described as murder and suicide.'

In that case, the House of Lords rejected an application for an injunction to prevent the re-broadcast of the BBC programme pending the hearing of a case before a local valuation court concerning a claim to exemption from rates because such a court was not protected by the law of contempt.[18] Following the Francis Report (but before the *BBC* case), in *Holmes v A-G*[19], Walton J granted a declaration requested by the Brethren to the effect that they were entitled to be registered as a charity. The Brethren were clearly a religion and the presumption that their purposes were therefore charitable was not rebutted by the evidence presented to the court on the question whether the furtherance of their activities was contrary to public policy.

4. The charitable status of the Unification Church, or 'Moonies' (after their founder, Sun Myung Moon), has also been questioned.[20] In a libel action brought by the spiritual leader of the Moonies in the UK against the *Daily Mail*, which had printed an article claiming that the sect broke up families and brainwashed converts, the jury found for the defendant and added a rider to their verdict calling for the charitable status of the Moonies to be investigated on the ground that they were a political

14 See on the New Faith case, Sadurski, (1989) 63 LJ 834. Scientology is probably not eligible to be registered as a charity under English law: see G. Moffat, *Trusts Law: Text and Materials* (3rd edn, 1999), p. 727. See also on scientology, *Hubbard v Vosper*, above, p. 987; *Church of Scientology of California v Kaufman* [1973] RPC 635 at 658 ('pernicious nonsense'); and the immigration section below, p. 1066.
15 See G. Moffat, ibid., p. 704.
16 1976 Charity Commissioners Report, 1976–77 HC 389, p. 35.
17 [1981] AC 303 at 340, HL.
18 See above, pp. 742–743.
19 (1981) Times, 12 February, QBD.
20 See on the Moonies, A. Swetland, *Escape from the Moonies* (1982) and E. Barker, *The Making of a Moonie* (1984). On the Children of God Sect, which is registered as a charity, see the immigration section, below, p. 1067. See also H. Picarda, (1981) 131 NLJ 436, 1064. On new religions generally, see E. Barker, *New Religious Movements* (1989).

organisation[1]. The Charity Commissioners considered the matter but decided that the sect should continue to be registered. In a debate in Parliament on the Moonies, a Home Office Minister (Dr S. Summerskill), responding to allegations that the Moonies tended to separate vulnerable teenagers from their families and to obtain funds by fraud, stated:[2]

> 'If the Government as a Government took action against organisations which they regarded as wrong-headed or even worse, we should be living in a rather different kind of society. The cost of such freedom is that some people will spend their money foolishly, be led astray by charlatans and even misunderstand the motives and feelings of their families and true friends. But when we decide that people should be treated as adults from the age of 18, this meant that they had the right to make their own choice on the way they wished to lead their lives and to make their own mistakes.'

5. Whereas the courts do consider what qualifies as a religion for various purposes, they tend not to consider whether a particular person is a follower, etc, of a recognised religion or what the tenets of the religion are, preferring to leave this to the person or the religion concerned.[3]

6. No abstract definition of the term 'religion' in Art. 9 ECHR has been spelt out in the Strasbourg jurisprudence. No doubt this is partly because of the difficulty of the task. It may also be for the reason there is in many cases no need to draw a line between religion and other kinds of belief since Art. 9 extends indiscriminately in its text to 'freedom of thought, conscience and religion' and the freedom to 'manifest one's religion or beliefs'. Similarly, the European Commission on Human Rights has not ruled upon the status of a number of particular claimant religions.[4]

3   Church and the state

(A) THE ESTABLISHED CHURCH

The Canons of the Church of England (Canons Ecclesiastical promulgated by the Convocations of Canterbury and York in 1964 and 1969)

CANON A1
The Church of England, established according to the laws of this realm under the Queen's Majesty, BELONGS to the true and Apostolic Church of Christ; . . .

CANON A7
We acknowledge that the Queen's most excellent Majesty, acting according to the laws of the realm, is the highest power under God in this kingdom, and has supreme authority over all persons in all causes, as well ecclesiastical as civil.

---

1   The *Times*, 1 April 1981.
2   926 HC Deb 23, February 1977, cols. 1597–8.
3   See J. Montgomery, in B. Hepple and E. M. Szyszczak, *Discrimination: The Limits of the Law* (1992), Chap. 11. See, e.g., the *Mandla* case, below, p. 1114, where the House of Lords accepted 'what the Sikhs themselves say' as to the requirements of the Sikh religion.
4   See *X v UK* (1978) 11 DRECommHR 55 (Wicca, 1990); *X and Church of Scientology v Sweden* (1979) 16 DRECommHR 68; *Chappell v UK* 53 DRECommHR 241 (Druidism).

NOTES[5]

1. Although the Church of England had become the established church in England long before the 16th century, it is with the Reformation statutes of that time, which severed the link with Rome and stated the doctrine of royal supremacy, that one associates the idea of establishment in its present form.[6] None of these statutes, which are now mostly repealed, expressly 'establishes' the Church of England. The above extract from the Canons of the Church of England recognises the fact of establishment as clearly as any other legislative source. Canon law is a part of the ecclesiastical law of the Church of England; it is binding upon the clergy of the Church, not the laity.[7]

2. The Sovereign is the head of the Church of England: Canon A7, Canons of the Church of England, above. The Act of Supremacy 1558, s. 9, now repealed, referred to the Sovereign as 'the Supreme Governor of the Realm in all spiritual and ecclesiastical causes as well as temporal'. Under the Coronation Oath Act 1688 the Sovereign undertakes to maintain 'the Protestant Reformed Religion established by law'. The Act of Settlement 1700, s. 3, provides that

> 'whosoever shall hereafter come to the possession of this crown shall join in communion with the Church of England as by law established.'

The same Act (s. 2) also provides that

> 'all and every person and persons who shall or may take or inherit the said crown by virtue of the limitation of this present Act and is are or shall be reconciled to or shall hold communion with the see or church of Rome or shall profess the popish religion or shall marry a papist'

are disqualified from being the Sovereign. In 1978, Prince Michael of Kent renounced his claim to the throne upon marrying a Roman Catholic. In 1980, the amendment of s. 2 was discussed when Prince Charles was considering marriage. It was then understood that any such amendment would by convention require the approval of all Commonwealth countries accepting the monarch as such. The government indicated that it had no plans for amendment.[8]

3. The Church of England's position as the established church gives it certain privileges in law. The Archbishops of Canterbury and York, the Bishops of London, Durham and Winchester and 21 other diocesan bishops by seniority in office are members of the House of Lords[9]. These arrangements survived the 1999 alterations in the composition of the House of Lords, the government White Paper[10] having

---

5 On establishment, see R. Davies, (1976) 7 Cambrian LR 11; C. Garbett, *Church and State in England* (1950); E. G. Moore, *An Introduction to English Canon Law* (1967), Chap. II; and D. Grant, in R. Blackburn, (ed.), *Constitutional Studies* (1992) Chap. 11. See also *Church and State* (1970), a Report of the Archbishops' Commission (Chadwick Commission) and the resulting House of Lords debate on establishment: 314 HL Deb, 20 January 1971, cols. 485–501, 506–562. For the case for disestablishment, see T. Benn, in D. Reeves (ed.), *The Church and the State* (1984). Mr. Benn unsuccessfully introduced a Bill for disestablishment in 1988. The current Archbishop of Canterbury (Dr. Carey) strongly favours establishment: *Observer*, 4 April 1993, p. 7.

6 See, in particular, the Ecclesiastical Appeals Act 1531; the Submission of the Clergy Act 1533; the Appointment of Bishops Act 1533; the Ecclesiastical Licences Act 1533; and 26 Hen 8 c 2 (Supremacy of the Crown) (1534).

7 The Church in Wales was disestablished by the Welsh Church Act 1914. On the special status of the Church of Scotland, see F. Lyall (1976) JR 58, 65.

8 989 HC Deb, 29 July 1980, written answers, col. 607.

9 *Erskine May* (22nd edn, 1997), p. 12. Leaders of other denominations and faiths have sometimes been made life peers.

10 *Reforming the House of Lords* (1999), Cm. 4183, p. 39.

proposed no changes during the transitional period of the reform of the House. In 2000, the Wakeham Royal Commission took the view that there should be continued religious representation in the House of Lords but that this 'should be broadened to embrace other Christian denominations, in all parts of the United Kingdom, and other faith communities'.[11] The justification given by the Royal Commission for religious representation of any kind in the House of Lords, which is 'unique in the democratic world' among national legislatures,[12] was that religious belief is 'an important part of many people's lives and it is desirable that there should be a voice, or voices, in the second chamber to reflect that aspect of people's personalities and with which they can identify'.[13] However, in order to reflect the multi-religious nature of the United Kingdom, the Royal Commission recommended both that *ex officio* Christian representation should extend beyond the Church of England and that there should be representation of other religions. Accordingly, it recommended that the present 26 *ex officio* religious representatives should be retained but redistributed: there should be: (1) 21 representatives from England, of which 16 should be from the Church of England and five from other Christian denominations; and (2) five representatives from Scotland, Wales and Northern Ireland altogether, chosen to represent in proportion the different denominations in these parts of the United Kingdom. In addition, there should be five other House of Lords members 'selected to represent the various non-Christian faith communities'.[14] The reasons given by the Commission for the continued large Church of England representation were its status as the established church and 'its unique place in English society and wider constitutional framework of the country'.[15] The 'lords spiritual' are free to debate and vote on any matter before the House, not only on matters of direct concern to the Church.[16] The ecclesiastical law of the Church of England is a part of the law of the land[17] and is enforced by the state. The Sovereign is crowned by the Archbishop of Canterbury.[18]

4. The price that the Church pays for these and other privileges is a certain degree of state involvement in its affairs. The state has control over law-making by the 'parliament' of the Church of England, the General Synod (formerly the National Assembly). *Canons* (which cannot be contrary to the prerogative or statutory or other law of the realm[19]) passed by the General Synod require the royal assent to be law[20]. *Measures* (which have the force of statute and hence may change any law) passed by

---

11   A House for the Future (2000), Cm. 4534, p. 152

12   Ibid., p. 150.

13   Ibid., p. 151.

14   Ibid., p. 154.

15   The Report states (p. 152): 'Some 50 per cent of the population of England are baptised members of the Church of England and it is the Christian denomination to which they claim to belong and with which they identify, regardless of the regularity of their church attendance. The church serves the whole of England through 13,000 parishes. It runs 5000 primary schools … and 200 secondary schools … While there is no direct or logical connection between the establishment of the Church of England and the presence of Church of England bishops in the second chamber. their removal would be likely to raise the whole question of the relationship between Church, State and Monarchy, with unpredictable consequences.'

16   See D. Shell and D. Beamish, *The House of Lords at Work* (1993), p. 58.

17   *Mackonochie v Lord Penzance* (1881) 6 App Cas 424, 446 HL.

18   In 1994, the Archbishops of Canterbury and York stated that they would welcome the participation of minority religious leaders in the coronation: *Daily Mail*, 11 July 1994, p. 7, cited by P. Cumper, op. cit., p. 216.

19   Submission of the Clergy Act 1533, s. 3.

20   Synodical Government Measure 1969, s. 1.

it have to be approved by the two Houses of Parliament as well as obtain the royal assent.[1] It is rare for Parliament not to approve a proposed measure.[2]

Archbishops and bishops are appointed by the Crown[3] on the advice (by convention) of the Prime Minister. As of 1977, the newly established Church of England Crown Appointments Commission puts forward two candidates (in order of preference if it thinks fit) for the Prime Minister's consideration. The understanding is that he will recommend one of these candidates, normally the 'first choice' candidate if there is one. In 1981, the second choice candidate for the office of Bishop of London was, somewhat controversially, put forward by the then Prime Minister. Otherwise, Mrs. Thatcher and Mr. Major accepted almost every preferred candidate of the Commission. Mr. Blair, however, rejected three preferred candidates in three years.[4] The arrangement applies only to Archbishops and diocesan bishops; in the case of suffragan bishops, the appointment is made on the basis of a recommendation from the diocesan bishop. The Crown is also the patron of a larger number of benefices, or livings. Appointments to these are made after consultation with the Church.

'No person having been ordained to the office of priest or deacon' in the Church of England or minister of the Church of Scotland may be an MP: House of Commons (Clergy Disqualification) Act 1801. The prohibition extends beyond the Church of England to all episcopally ordained clergymen:[5] Roman Catholic priests are also excluded.[6] Ministers of non-conformist churches (e.g. Dr Ian Paisley) may be MPs. The Chadwick Commission[7] recommended that the prohibition be lifted. The 1801 Act was explained in *Re MacManaway*[7a] in terms of the spiritual, and hence non-political, nature of the priest's office. The historical evidence indicates that the intention was to prevent priests representing their patrons and to exclude one particular demagogic priest at the time.

(B) TOLERATION OF OTHER DENOMINATIONS

Lord Chancellor (Tenure of Office and Discharge of Ecclesiastical Functions) Act 1974

1. For the avoidance of doubt it is hereby declared that the office of Lord Chancellor is and shall be tenable by an adherent of the Roman Catholic faith.
2. In the event of the office of Lord Chancellor being held by an adherent of the Roman Catholic faith it shall be lawful for Her Majesty in Council to make provision for the exercise of any or all the visitational or the ecclesiastical functions normally performed by the Lord Chancellor, and any patronage to livings normally in the gift of the Lord Chancellor, to be performed by the Prime Minister or any other Minister of the Crown.

1 Church of England (Assembly) Powers Act 1919.
2 In 1927 and 1928, Parliament rejected proposed measures for the revision of the Prayer Book passed by the National Assembly. In 1975, the Incumbents (Vacation of Benefices) Measure was rejected, although later passed as revised. In 1990, the House of Commons approved the Clergy (Ordination) Measure, which allows a remarried man whose former spouse is still alive to be ordained as a Church of England priest, 167 HC Deb, 20 February 1990, col. 882, after having earlier rejected it: 157 HC Deb, 17 July 1989, col. 174.
3 See 1 Co Inst 134 and the Appointment of Bishops Act 1533, s. 3.
4 *Sunday Times*, 2 July 2000, p. 2.
5 *Re MacManaway* [1951] AC 161, HL (Church of Ireland priest).
6 Roman Catholic Relief Act 1829, s. 9.
7 Chadwick Commission Report, p. 58.
7a [1951] AC 161, HL.

NOTES

1. At the time of the Reformation settlement, a consequence of the establishment of one denomination was inevitably the proscription of others. Since then the church has lost most of its temporal power and attitudes have mellowed to the point where it is not illegal to profess or practise any religion and nearly all of the other disabilities to which non-conformists were subject (e.g. exclusion from Parliament) have been removed.[8] The Prime Minister may be of any religion or none. So may the Lord Chancellor, as the Lord Chancellor, etc., Act 1974 makes clear. The Act was expressed in terms only of Roman Catholics because there was felt to be no doubt that adherents of other religions were eligible. And at least one Lord Chancellor had been 'a devoutly practising atheist'.[9] But the Sovereign must, as noted above, be a member of the Church of England and his or her consort may not be a Roman Catholic.[10]

2. Another result of religious toleration is the Oaths Act 1978 which provides (s. 5):

> '5.—(1) Any person who objects to being sworn shall be permitted to make his solemn affirmation instead of taking an oath.
>
> (2) Subsection (1) above shall apply in relation to a person to whom it is not reasonably practicable without inconvenience or delay to administer an oath in the manner appropriate to his religious belief as it applies in relation to a person objecting to be sworn.'

Bowman v Secular Society [1917] AC 406, House of Lords

The appellants challenged the validity of a testamentary gift to the respondent company on the ground that the latter's objects were illegal so that the gift was for an illegal purpose. Its objects were 'to promote . . . the principle that human conduct should be based upon natural knowledge, and not upon super-natural belief, and that human welfare in this world is the proper end of all thought and action'.

Lord Sumner: My Lords, the question is whether an anti-Christian society is incapable of claiming a legacy, duly bequeathed to it, merely because it is anti-Christian. . . . is the maxim that Christianity is part of the law of England true, and, if so, in what sense? If Christianity is of the substance of our law, and if a Court of law must, nevertheless, adjudge possession of its property to a company whose every action seeks to subvert Christianity and bring that law to naught, then by such judgment it stultifies the law. . . .

My Lords, with all respect for the great names of the lawyers who have used it, the phrase 'Christianity is part of the law of England' is really not law; it is rhetoric . . . One asks what part of our law may Christianity be, and what part of Christianity may it be that is part of our law? Best CJ once said in *Bird v Holbrook* (1828) 4 Bing 628 at 641 (a case of injury by setting a spring-gun): 'There is no act which Christianity forbids, that the law will not reach: if it were otherwise, Christianity would not be, as it has always been held to be, part of the law of England'; but this was rhetoric too. Spring-guns, indeed, were got rid of, not by Christianity, but by Act of Parliament. 'Thou shalt not steal' is part of our law. 'Thou shalt not commit adultery' is part of our law, but another part. 'Thou shalt love thy neighbour as thyself' is not part of our law at all. Christianity has tolerated chattel slavery; not so the present law of England. Ours is, and always has been, a Christian State. The English family is built on Christian ideas, and if the national religion is not Christian there is none. English law may well be called a Christian law, but we apply many of its rules and most of its principles, with equal justice and equally good government, in heathen communities, and its sanctions, even in Courts of

---

8 See, mainly, the Toleration Act 1688 (protestant non-conformists); the Roman Catholic Relief Acts 1791 and 1829; and Religious Disabilities Act 1846 (Jews).

9 352 HL Deb, 11 June 1974, written answers, col. 417.

10 Other minor disabilities (mostly affecting Roman Catholics) are listed in Moore, *An Introduction to English Canon Law* (1967) pp. 161–162.

conscience, are material and not spiritual. . . . . In the present day reasonable men do not apprehend the dissolution or the downfall of society because religion is publicly assailed by methods not scandalous. . . . Accordingly I am of opinion that acts merely done in furtherance of paragraph 3(A) and other paragraphs of the respondents' memorandum are not now contrary to the law, and that the appeal should be dismissed.

Lords Dunedin, Parker of Waddington, and **Buckmaster** delivered concurring speeches. **Lord Finlay LC** delivered a dissenting speech.

Appeal dismissed.

NOTES

1. *Bowman v Secular Society* was one of two cases decided in the space of three years in which the House of Lords adjusted the policy of the common law to reflect the change in the relationship between church and state that has occurred since the Reformation. The other was *Bourne v Keane*,[11] in which it was held (overruling *West v Shuttleworth*[12] that a trust for the saying of Roman Catholic masses for the dead was valid. In these cases, the old idea that the 'Church must help the State to maintain its authority, and the State must help the Church to punish nonconformists and infidels'[13] gave way to one emphasising freedom of conscience instead. Nonetheless, although, in Lord Sumner's famous dictum, it may only be 'rhetoric' to say that 'Christianity is part of the law of the land', most of English law remains firmly based on Christian moral values. Consequently, members of the main Christian denominations are unlikely to find themselves out of step with the law as they practise their religion in their daily lives. As the cases later in this chapter show, the same may not be true of members of some of the minority Christian sects[14] or of non-Christian denominations, whether the latter are denominations that have long been well represented in the community[15] or denominations that are now more common because of recent patterns of immigration.[16]

2. In *Cowan v Milbourn*[17] an owner of a room refused to honour a letting when he discovered that it was to be used by the Liverpool Secular Society (not to be confused with the Liverpool Football Club, which is a religious society) for a lecture questioning Christian doctrine. The Court of Exchequer Chamber held the refusal to be justified as the intended use was for an unlawful purpose, Christianity being a part of the law of the land. The case was overruled in *Bowman v Secular Society.*

(C) ASSISTANCE TO RELIGION

(i) Education

School Standards and Framework Act 1998

. . .

69. Duty to secure due provision of religious education
(1) Subject to section 71, in relation to any community, foundation or voluntary school—

---

11 [1919] AC 815, HL.
12 (1835) 2 My & K 684.
13 W. Holdsworth, (1920) 35 LQR 339.
14 See, e.g., *R v Senior*, below, p. 1055.
15 See, e.g., *Ostreicher v Secretary of State for the Environment*, below, p. 1063.
16 See, e.g., *Ahmad v Inner London Education Authority*, below, p. 1058.
17 (1867) LR 2 Exch 230.

(*a*)   the local education authority and the governing body shall exercise their functions with a view to securing and

(*b*)   the head teacher shall secure,

that religious education is given in accordance with the provision for such education included in the school's basic curriculum by virtue of section 352(1)(a) of the Education Act 1996.

(2) Schedule 19 has effect for determining the provision for religious education which is required by section 352(1)(a) of that Act to be included in the basic curriculum of schools within each of the following categories, namely—

(*a*)   community schools and foundation and voluntary schools which do not have a religious character.

(*b*)   foundation and voluntary controlled schools which have a religious character, and

(*c*)   voluntary aided schools which have a religious character.

(3) For the purposes of this Part a foundation or voluntary school has a religious character if it is designated as a school having such a character by an order made by the Secretary of State.

(4) An order under subsection (3) shall state, in relation to each school designated by the order, the religion or religious denomination in accordance with whose tenets religious education is, or may be, required to be provided at the school in accordance with Schedule 19 (or, as the case may be, each such religion or religious denomination). ...

70. Requirements relating to collective worship

(1) Subject to section 71, each pupil in attendance at a community, foundation or voluntary school shall on each school day take part in an act of collective worship.

(2) Subject to section 71, in relation to any community, foundation or voluntary school—

(*a*)   the local education authority and the governing body shall exercise their functions with a view to securing, and

(*b*)   the head teacher shall secure,

that subsection (1) is complied with.

(3) Schedule 20 makes further provision with respect to the collective worship required by this section, including provision relating to—

(*a*)   the arrangements which are to be made in connection with such worship, and

(*b*)   the nature of such worship.

71. Exceptions and special arrangements; provision for special schools

(1) If the parent of a pupil at a community, foundation or voluntary school requests that he may be wholly or partly excused—

(*a*)   from receiving religious education given in the school in accordance with the school's basic curriculum,

(*b*)   from attendance at religious worship in the school, or

(*c*)   both from receiving such education and from such attendance,

the pupil shall b e excused until the request is withdrawn.

(2) In subsection (1)—

(*a*)   the reference to religious education given in accordance with the school's basic curriculum is to such education given in accordance with the provision included in the school's basic curriculum by virtue of section 352(1)(a) of the Education Act 1996, and

(*b*)   the reference to religious worship in the school includes religious worship which by virtue of paragraph 2(6) of Schedule 20 takes place otherwise than on the school premises.

(3) Where in accordance with subsection (1) a pupil has been wholly or partly excused from receiving religious education or from attendance at religious worship and the local education authority are satisfied—

(*a*)   that the parent of the pupil desires him to receive religious education of a kind which is not provided in the school during the periods of time during which he is so excused,

(*b*)   that the pupil cannot with reasonable convenience be sent to another community, foundation or voluntary school where religious education of the kind desired by the parent is provided, and

(*c*)   that arrangements have been made for him to receive religious education of that kind during school hours elsewhere, the pupil may be withdrawn from the school during such periods of time as are reasonably necessary for the purpose of enabling him to receive religious education in accordance with the arrangements.

(4) A pupil may not be withdrawn from school under subsection (3) unless the local education authority are satisfied that the arrangements there mentioned are such as will not interfere with the attendance of the pupil at school on any day except at the beginning or end of a school session (or, if there is only one, the school session) on that day. ...

(7) Regulations shall make provision for securing that, so far as practicable, every pupil attending a community or foundation special school

    (*a*)   receives religious education and attends religious worship, or

    (*b*)   is withdrawn from receiving such education or from attendance at such worship in accordance with the wishes of his parent.

. . .

SCHEDULE 19

REQUIRED PROVISION FOR RELIGIOUS EDUCATION

Introductory

1.—(1) In this Schedule "the required provision for religious education", in relation to a school, means the provision for pupils at the school which is required by section 352(1)(a) of the Education Act 1996 to be included in the school's basic curriculum.

(2) In this schedule "agreed syllabus" has the meaning given by section 375(2) of that Act.

Community schools and foundation and voluntary schools without a religious character

2.—(1) This paragraph applies to—

    (a)   any community school; and

    (b)   any foundation or voluntary school which does not have a religious character.

(2) Subject to sub-paragraph (4), the required provision for religious education in the case of pupils at the school is provision for religious education in accordance with an agreed syllabus adopted for the school or for those pupils.

(3) If the school is a secondary school so situated that arrangements cannot conveniently be made for the withdrawal of pupils from it in accordance with section 71 to receive religious education elsewhere and the local education authority are satisfied—

    (a)   that the parents of any pupils at the school desire them to receive religious education in the school in accordance with the tenets of a particular religion or religious denomination, and

    (b)   that satisfactory arrangements have been made for the provision of such education to those pupils in the school, and for securing that the cost of providing such education to those pupils in the school will not fall to be met from the school's budget share or otherwise by the authority.

the authority shall (unless they are satisfied that because of any special circumstances it would be unreasonable to do so) provide facilities for the carrying out of those arrangements.

(4) If immediately before the appointed day the school was a grant-maintained school (within the meaning of the Education Act 1996), and in relation to the school or any pupils at the school the appropriate agreed syllabus as defined by section 382 of that Act was a syllabus falling within subsection (1)(c) of that section, then until—

    (a)   the end of such period as the Secretary of State may by order prescribe, or

    (b)   such earlier date as the governing body may determine,

the required provision for religious education in the case of the school or (as the case may be) those pupils is provision for religious education in accordance with that syllabus.

(5) No agreed syllabus shall provide for religious education to be given to pupils at a school to which this paragraph applies by means of any catechism or formulary which is distinctive of a particular religious denomination (but this is not to be taken as prohibiting provision in such a syllabus for the study of such catechisms or formularies).

Foundation and voluntary controlled schools with a religious character

3.—(1) This paragraph applies to any foundation or voluntary controlled school which has a religious character.

(2) Subject to sub-paragraph (4), the required provision for religious education in the case of pupils at the school is provision for religious education—

    (a) in accordance with any arrangements made under sub-paragraph (3), or

    (b) subject to any such arrangements, in accordance with an agreed syllabus adopted for the school or for those pupils.

(3) Where the parents of any pupils at the school request that they may receive religious education—

    (a) in accordance with any provisions of the trust deed relating to the school, or

    (b) where provision for that purpose is not made by such a deed, in accordance with the tenets of the religion or religious denomination specified in relation to the school under section 69(4).

the foundation governors shall (unless they are satisfied that because of any special circumstances it would be unreasonable to do so) make arrangements for securing that such religious education is given to those pupils in the school during not more than two periods in each week.

(4) If immediately before the appointed day the school was a grant-maintained school (within the meaning of the Education Act 1996), and in relation to the school or any pupils at the school the appropriate agreed syllabus as defined by section 382 of that Act was a syllabus falling within subsection (1)(c) of that section, then until—

    (a) the end of such period as the Secretary of State may by order prescribe, or

    (b) such earlier date as the governing body may determine,

that syllabus shall be treated for the purposes of sub-paragraph (2)(b) as an agreed syllabus adopted for the school or (as the case may be) those pupils.

Voluntary aided schools with a religious character

4.—(1) This paragraph applies to any voluntary aided school which has a religious character.

(2) The required provision for religious education in the case of pupils at the school is provision for religious education—

    (a) in accordance with any provisions of the trust deed relating to the school, or

    (b) where provision for that purpose is not made by such a deed, in accordance with the tenets of the religion or religious denomination specified in relation to the school under section 69(4), or

    (c) in accordance with any arrangements made under sub-paragraph (3).

(3) Where the parents of any pupils at the school—

    (a) desire them to receive religious education in accordance with any agreed syllabus adopted by the local education authority, and

    (b) cannot with reasonable convenience cause those pupils to attend a school at which that syllabus is in use,

the governing body shall (unless they are satisfied that because of any special circumstances it would be unreasonable to do so) make arrangements for religious education in accordance with that syllabus to be given to those pupils in the school.

(4) Religious education under any such arrangements shall be given during the times set apart for the giving of religious education in the school in accordance with the provision for that purpose included in the school's basic curriculum by virtue of section 352(1)(a) of the Education Act 1996.

(5) Any arrangements under sub-paragraph (3) shall be made by the governing body, unless the local education authority are satisfied that the governing body are unwilling to make them, in which case they shall be made by the authority.

(6) Subject to sub-paragraph (3), the religious education given to pupils at the school shall be under the control of the governing body.

SCHEDULE 20

1. In this Schedule "the required collective worship", in relation to a school, means the collective worship in that school which is required by section 70.

2.—(1) This paragraph applies to any community, foundation or voluntary school.

(2) The arrangements for the required collective worship may, in respect of each school day, provide for a single act of worship for all pupils or for separate acts of worship for pupils in different age groups or in different school groups. ...

3.—(1) This paragraph applies to—
    (a) any community school; and
    (b) any foundation school which does not have a religious character.
(2) Subject to paragraph 4, the required collective worship shall be wholly or mainly of a broadly Christian character.
(3) For the purposes of sub-paragraph (2), collective worship is of a broadly Christian character if it reflects the broad traditions of Christian belief without being distinctive of any particular Christian denomination.
(4) Not every act of collective worship in the school required by section 70 need comply with sub-paragraph (2) provided that, taking any school term as a whole, most such acts which take place in the school do comply with that sub-paragraph.
(5) Subject to sub-paragraphs (2) and (4)—
    (a) the extent to which (if at all) any acts of collective worship required by section 70 which do not comply with sub-paragraph (2) take place in the school,
    (b) the extent to which any act of collective worship in the school which complies with sub-paragraph (2) reflects the broad traditions of Christian belief, and
    (c) the ways in which those traditions are reflected in any such act of collective worship,
shall be such as may be appropriate having regard to any relevant considerations relating to the pupils concerned which fall to be taken into account in accordance with sub-paragraph (6).
(6) Those considerations are—
    (a) any circumstances relating to the family backgrounds of the pupils which are relevant for determining the character of the collective worship which is appropriate in their case, and
    (b) their ages and aptitudes.
(7) In this paragraph references to acts of collective worship in the school include such acts which by virtue of paragraph 2(6) take place otherwise than on the school premises.
4.—(1) This paragraph applies where a standing advisory council on religious education have determined (under section 394 of the Education Act 1996) that it is not appropriate for the requirement imposed by paragraph 3(2) to apply in the case of any school to which paragraph 3 applies or in the case of any class or description of pupils at any such school.
(2) While the determination has effect—
    (a) paragraph 3 shall not apply in relation to the school or (as the case may be) the pupils in question, and
    (b) the collective worship required by section 70 in the case of the school or pupils shall not be distinctive of any particular Christian or other religious denomination;
but paragraph (b) shall not be taken as preventing that worship from being distinctive of any particular faith.
5. In the case of a foundation school which has a religious character or a voluntary school, the required collective worship shall be—
    (a) in accordance with any provision of the trust deed relating to the school, or
    (b) where—
        (i) provision for that purpose is not made by such deed, and
        (ii) the school has a religious character,
in accordance with the tenets and practices of the religion or religious denomination specified in relation to the school under section 69(4).

NOTES[18]

1. The statutory provisions on religion in schools apply to all of the three kinds of primary and secondary schools maintained by the state: community schools, foundation schools and voluntary schools.[19] Community schools are schools

---

18 See generally *Religious Education and Collective Worship*, Department of Education Circular 1/94, most of which continues to apply despite the later legislative changes.
19 School Standards and Framework Act 1998 (hereafter the 1998 Act), s. 20.

established by the state. Foundation and voluntary schools are schools that have been established privately but that have voluntarily been brought within the state system and as a result are, to varying degrees, financially maintained by local authorities and subject to their control. Foundation and voluntary schools are divided into two categories: those that have a religious character, and those that do not. Voluntary schools are further divided into controlled and aided schools. The rules governing religious education varies between these categories, with schools within different categories being subject to greater or lesser state control. Most of the 7,000 foundation or voluntary schools are of a religious character and, with the exception of a small number of Jewish, Methodist and other schools, nearly all of these are Roman Catholic or Church of England. Although several Muslim schools had applied to the Secretary of State for Education for voluntary aided status over a number of years, none of these applications were successful[20] until 1998, when two primary schools in Birmingham and Brent were accepted as voluntary schools. There are 40 or so private Muslim schools in Great Britain.[1] Some Sikh schools in the London area were approved as voluntary schools in 1999.[2]

2. *Religious education.* Religious education is a compulsory part of the basic curriculum in all state maintained schools.[3] It is not, however, a part of the national curriculum so that there are no national attainment requirements or tests. Religious education must follow a non-denominational locally 'agreed syllabus',[4] except that provision is made for religious education to be of a particular denomination or faith in foundation and voluntary schools of a religious character.[5] The 1998 Act refers to religious 'education', not 'instruction', in order to emphasise that the intention is to inform children about religion as a part of their social education rather than to indoctrinate them in the tenets of a particular religion.

In recent years, the main problem in practice has not been the nature of the religious education provided but ensuring that schools comply with their legal obligation to provide religious education at all. An HMI report indicates that in at least 20% of primary schools inspected 'the teaching of RE was negligible' and that the 'vast majority of secondary schools did not provide enough time to teach the agreed syllabus'.[6] The HMI report states that religious education often does not comply with the agreed syllabus or the new criterion in the 1988 Act. Inspection revealed that there was very limited teaching of the world's non-Christian religions and that much 'RE teaching is confined to a rather dull exposition of basic Christian beliefs, with little attempt to examine Christianity as a major world faith'.[7]

3. *Religious worship.* In all maintained schools, there must be a daily act of worship.[8] In foundation schools with a religious character and all voluntary schools, provision

---

20 In 1993, an application from a primary Muslim school in Brent was rejected because there were surplus places in state funded schools in Brent. Judicial review proceedings in the case failed in *R v Secretary of State for Education, ex p Yusar Islam* (1992) Times, 22 May.

1 M. Parker-Jenkins, *Children of Islam* (1995) p. 12.

2 Information from the Department for Education and Employment.

3 1998 Act, s. 69(1). See also the Education Act 1996, s. 352(1)(a).

4 The agreed syllabus is drawn up by the local Standing Advisory Council on Religious Education (SACRE), which includes representatives of the Christian and other religions in the locality and of teachers' organisations. See *The Impact of New Agreed Syllabuses on the Teaching and Learning of Religious Education* (OFSTED Publication, 1997).

5 1998 Act, Sch. 19, paras. 2(2), (5) and 3(2).

6 *Religious Education and Collective Worship 1992–3*: Report of Her Majesty's Inspector of Schools, pp. 4–5.

7 Ibid., p. 40.

8 1998 Act, s. 70(1).

is made for the act of worship to be denominational.[9] In community schools and foundation schools that do not have a religious character it must be 'wholly or mainly of a broadly Christian character'.[10] It will be such if it 'reflects the broad traditions of Christian belief without being distinctive of any particular Christian denomination'.[11] Not every act of worship need comply with this requirement; it will be sufficient if, 'taking any school term as a whole, most such acts' do so.[12] Allowance is made for the non-Christian student body of a particular community school or foundation school without a religious character by the 'family background' provision in the 1998 Act,[13] Sch. 20, para. 3(6). Moreover, such a school that does not have a religious character may apply for exemption from the 'broadly Christian' requirement to the local SACRE (see above). Such exemption will allow a school with a largely non-Christian student body to hold its own acts of worship for all or some students. These acts of worship may be 'distinctive of any particular faith' (e.g. the Muslim faith) but not 'distinctive of any particular Christian or other religious denomination' (e.g. Roman Catholic or Sunni Muslim).[14]

Compliance with the religious worship requirement is far from perfect. HMI has reported that 40% of the secondary schools inspected 'were identified as not complying with the legal requirements regarding collective worship and in the remainder there were difficulties and tensions'.[15] Commenting on the provisions for collective worship, Poulter states:[16]

'... there would seem to be extremely persuasive arguments in favour of removing worship from school life altogether.... Collective *worship* is not primarily or essentially educational and is almost certainly an activity which is best organized by the faith concerned within the child's local community and subject to the continuing direction and supervision of parents ...'

4. *The right of withdrawal.* The parent of a child at a maintained school has the right to withdraw a child from its acts of collective worship or its religious education classes.[17] The HMI report states that 'very few parents exercised their right to withdraw children from RE'.[18] Parents may also withdraw their children from school 'on any day exclusively set apart for religious observance by the religious body to which his parents belong'.[19] The Department for Education and Employment will not allow parents to withdraw their children in maintained schools from classes in secular subjects on grounds of religion or conscience.[20] This position was taken in connection with a request by Plymouth Brethren parents that they be allowed to withdraw their children from classes involving the use of computers or television.

5. In *Watson v Hertfordshire County Council*[1] a teacher who was the head of religious studies in a comprehensive school in Hertfordshire was dismissed when he refused

---

9 1998 Act, Sch. 20, para. 5.
10 1998 Act, Sch. 20, para. 3(2).
11 1998 Act, Sch. 20, para. 3(3).
12 1998 Act, Sch. 20, para. 3(4).
13 Sch. 20, para. 3(6).
14 1998 Act, Sch. 20, para. 4(2).
15 *Religious Education and Collective Worship 1992–3*: Report of Her Majesty's Inspector of Schools, p. 30. The position in primary schools was more satisfactory.
16 (1990) 2 Education and the Law 1, 9.
17 1998 Act, s. 71.
18 Op. cit. at n. 1, above, p. 20. A 1975 survey found that most children withdrawn are Jehovah's Witnesses: Religious Education, Assistant Masters Association Survey, (1975).
19 s. 39(2), 1944 Act. E.g. Ascension Day (for members of the Church of England or Roman Catholics) or the Day of Atonement (for Jews). And see *Marshall v Graham* [1907] 2 KB 112, DC.
20 In its view, the European Convention on Human Rights, Art. 2, First Protocol, does not require this: 158 HC Deb, 23 October 1989, written answers, col. 321.
1 Summarised in (1977) 150 Education 170.

to give an undertaking to teach the story of the creation in Genesis as 'myths and legends' which did not conflict with evolutionary theories, as the 'agreed syllabus' required. He lost his claim for unfair dismissal before an industrial tribunal.

6. Mixed sex schools have presented problems for Muslim parents. In 1972, a Muslim parent in Blackburn was convicted of failing to cause his daughter to receive efficient full-time education when he kept her away from a co-educational secondary school because he 'believed that, having regard to the tone of present-day society, she would lose her virtue and become unmarriageable'.[2] The parent was fined £5. Similarly, when Peterborough amalgamated two single sex schools in 1973 in the course of local government reorganisation, the parents of Muslim children who were allocated to a co-educational secondary school appealed unsuccessfully to the Minister on the ground their religion forbade mixed schooling.[3] In the same year, a Muslim family in Bradford returned to Pakistan to avoid mixed schooling.[4]

7. A child's religion and his or her religious education are generally matters for the parents within a marriage to decide until he or she reaches the age of discretion.[5] The mother has an equal voice and responsibility with the father in the matter.[6] In the case of a child whose parents are not married at the birth, the parental responsibility for the matter is one just for the mother, unless there is agreement to the contrary or the father makes a successful court application.[7] If a dispute concerning the religious upbringing of a child should reach the courts, it must be decided in accordance with the welfare of the child.[8]

8. *Parental choice of schools.* The duty in the Education Act 1980, s. 6(2), as amended to comply with parental choice in the allocation of school places does not prevent an oversubscribed voluntary aided school from operating an admissions policy that gives preference to children of a particular religion. In *Choudhury v Governors of Bishop Challoner Roman Catholic Comprehensive School*,[9] two girls, a Hindu and a Muslim, were not admitted to a single sex Catholic school because they did not meet the admissions criteria, which gave preference to Catholics and other Christians in that order. It was held that the admissions policy was lawful under s. 6(3)(a) by which parental preference need not be respected if it would 'prejudice the provision of efficient education'. This permitted a limit to be set on pupil numbers and it was reasonable when applying such a limit to take account of the religious character of the school. Section 76 of the 1944 Act (children 'to be educated in accordance with the wishes of their parents') has proved to be of limited value as a means of ensuring compliance with the religious wishes of the parents.[10]

---

2 G. R. Barrell, *Teachers and the Law* (5th edn, 1978) p. 27, referring to a report in the *Daily Mail*, 3 November 1972.

3 The 'Islamic doctrine of purdah (seclusion) prescribes the separation of the sexes from puberty onwards': Cumper, loc. cit. at p. 1027, n. 1, above, p. 389. See also G. Sarwar, *British Muslims and Schools* (rev. edn, 1994) p. 24.

4 *Times*, 15 December 1973.

5 Exceptionally, a court may make a 'prohibited steps' order preferring the child's wishes concerning religious education: see *Re T* [1995] ELR 1.

6 Children Act 1989, s. 2.

7 Children Act 1989, ss. 2, 4.

8 Children Act 1989, s. 1. On the granting of custody of children to parents belonging to minority sects such as the Jehovah's Witnesses, see F. Bates, (1981) 131 NLJ 1139. The religion of the natural family is a relevant background factor when a child's adoptive parents are selected: *Re P* [1999] 3 All ER 755.

9 [1992] 3 All ER 277, HL. See also *R v Lancashire County Council, ex p Foster* [1995] 1 FCR 210, QBD.

10 *Watt v Kesteven County Council* [1955] 1 QB 408, CA, and *Cumings v Birkenhead Corpn* [1972] Ch 12, CA.

(ii) Blasphemy and Blasphemous Libel

R v Chief Metropolitan Stipendiary Magistrate, ex parte Choudhury [1991] 1 All ER 306, [1990] 3 WLR 986, Queen's Bench Divisional Court

This case concerned the novel *The Satanic Verses* written by Salman Rushdie and published by Viking Penguin, the first and second respondents.[11] The Chief Magistrate refused the applicant a summons against the respondents alleging the common law offences of blasphemous libel and seditious libel. The applicant sought, by way of judicial review, an order of certiorari to quash the Chief Magistrate's decision and an order of mandamus directing him to issue the summons.

Watkins LJ (for the Divisional Court): 'The Satanic Verses' is a book, said to be a novel, published by Viking Penguin in 1988. In that year the book won the Whitbread Prize for Literature. It has been translated into 15 different languages.

The book has achieved considerable notoriety. It has been banned, so we were told by Mr. Azhar, counsel for the applicant, in all Muslim countries, in South Africa, China and India. He said that there had been demonstrations abroad against the book in which people had died, notably in Bombay which is Mr. Rushdie's place of birth, in Lahore and in Kashmir; that Muslims have demonstrated against the book in the United Kingdom—there are two million of that faith here—and that Muslims, otherwise of good character, have been arrested and convicted of offences against public order arising out of those demonstrations, in particular where the demonstrations by Muslims against the book have encountered groups demonstrating in favour of the book.

There can be little doubt that the contents of the book have deeply offended many law abiding Muslims who are United Kingdom citizens. . . .

The particulars [of the complaint against the book] can be summarised under six headings. First, God is described as 'The Destroyer of Man'. Secondly, the book vilifies the prophet Abraham, who is, as 'Ibrahim', a prophet revered by Muslims, by recounting the story of Abraham, Hagar and Ishmael, their son, and commenting adversely on Abraham's behaviour towards Hagar and Ishmael. Thirdly, the book refers to Muhammad as Mahound, which is a word having the meaning of a devil; that elsewhere in the book Muhammad is called 'a conjurer', a 'magician', and 'a false prophet'. Fourthly, the book grossly vilifies and profoundly insults the wives of Muhammad by calling some whores after their names. Muslims hold the prophet's wives in the highest esteem as mothers of the faithful. Fifthly, the book vilifies the close companions of Muhammad (calling them 'some sort of bums from Persia' and 'clowns') whereas the Koran recounts that they were men of high moral character and righteousness. Sixthly, the book vilifies and ridicules the teachings of Islam as containing too many rules and as seeking to control every aspect of day to day life. Moreover, insult is added to injury by the liberal use of an offensive four letter word.

Mr. Robertson [for the first respondent] pointed out that those passages form part of Gibreel's dreams and are, for the most part, words spoken by characters in the book who appear in Gibreel's dreams, some of whom have not been converted to Islam at the moment they make the utterances to which objection is taken.

That appears to be so but, in our opinion, a statement will not necessarily be prevented from being a blasphemous libel simply because the statement is put into the mouth of a character, even a disreputable character, in a novel.

. . . it appears . . . that this is the first case in which a would-be prosecutor has claimed that the offence of blasphemy is applicable to religions other than Christianity. . . .

Before the Restoration in 1660 the offence of blasphemy was dealt with in the ecclesiastical courts; it was akin to heresy, though punished less severely. The common law offence traces its origins from *Taylor's* Case[12] (1676) 1 Vent 293. . . .

---

11 On the background to the case, see R. Atel, *Speaking Respect: Respecting Speech* (1998), pp. 21–43.

12 *Ed.* The accused, who was mentally disturbed, was convicted of blasphemy for 'uttering diverse blasphemous expressions, horrible to hear, viz. that Jesus Christ was a bastard, a whoremaster, religion was a cheat'.

For the next hundred years or so following *Taylor's Case*, the basis of prosecutions was that the defendant had aspersed the Christian religion. . . .

The most explicit statement of the law is to be found in Alderson B's direction to the jury in *Gathercole's Case*[13] (1838) 2 Lewin 237, 254, where he said:

'A person may, without being liable to prosecution for it, attack Judaism, or Mahomedanism, or even any sect of the Christian Religion (save the established religion of the country); and the only reason why the latter is in a different situation from the others is, because it is the form established by law, and is therefore a part of the constitution of the country. In like manner, and for the same reason, any general attack on Christianity is the subject of criminal prosecution, because Christianity is the established religion of the country.' . . .

By the middle of the 19th century the essential elements of the offence were beginning to change. This was no doubt as a result of the revolution in thought brought about by Darwin and others. It was no longer blasphemous to make a sober reasoned attack on the Christian religion; it had to be a scurrilous vilification of that religion. . . .

This change in the law was firmly established by 1883 . . . in *R v Ramsey and Foote*[14] (1883) 15 Cox CC 231. . . .

It is . . . clear from the speeches in *Bowman v Secular Society Ltd* [above, p. 1036] that the House of Lords were dealing with the offence only in relation to the Christian religion. Lord Sumner after referring to Alderson B's dictum in *Gathercole's Case*, said, at pp. 459–460:

'it only shows that the gist of the offence of blasphemy is a supposed tendency in fact to shake the fabric of society generally. Its tendency to provoke an immediate breach of the peace is not the essential, but only an occasional, feature. After all, to insult a Jew's religion is not less likely to provoke a fight than to insult an Episcopalian's . . .'

Bowman v Secular Society Ltd was a civil action. Since that time there have been only two prosecutions for blasphemy. The first was *R v Gott*[15] (1922) 16 Cr App Rep 87. Avory J's direction to the jury included the following passage, at p. 89:

'What you have to ask yourselves in this case is whether these words which are published, these matters which are published in these two pamphlets are, in your opinion, indecent and offensive attacks on Christianity or the Scriptures or sacred persons or objects, calculated to outrage the feelings of the general body of the community and so lead possibly . . . to a breach of the peace.' . . .

The second was *R v Lemon* [1979] AC 617, the 'Gay News' case, the blasphemy in which related to a poem about Christ on the Cross. Mr. Azhar has referred us to a ruling by the trial judge, Judge King-Hamilton, in that case on a motion to quash the indictment on the ground that blasphemy was no longer an offence. In the course of that he said:

'In my judgment, therefore, the offence of blasphemous libel today occurs when there is published anything concerning God, Christ or the Christian religion in terms so scurrilous, abusive or offensive as to outrage the feelings of any member of or sympathiser with the

---

13 *Ed.* The accused was convicted of blasphemous libel for referring to certain Roman Catholic nunneries as 'houses of prostitution' and 'popish stews', inquiring 'how many popish priests enter the nunneries . . . each week . . . and how many infants are born in them . . . and whether the innocents are murdered'.

14 *Ed.* The accused published the *Freethinker*, a paper that promoted the views of some members of the secularist movement at the end of the nineteenth century. Walter states that 'the most objectionable material it published was a series of "Comic Bible Sketches" . . . which were crudely anti-religious and anti-semitic cartoons of appropriate biblical events – very effective, but also very offensive': Walter, *Blasphemy Ancient and Modern* (1990) p. 51. One such cartoon is printed on the back cover of Walter's book. In the reported case, the jury disagreed and the charge was dropped.

15 *Ed.* The accused had been found in a public place selling papers entitled 'The Rib Tickler' and 'The Liberator' containing pamphlets that described Jesus as entering Jerusalem 'like a circus clown on the back of two donkeys'. Upholding the accused's conviction for blasphemous libel and sentence to nine months' hard labour, Trevethin LCJ noted that the pamphlets contained other passages that were 'equally offensive to anyone in sympathy with the Christian religion'.

Christian religion and would tend to lead to a breach of the peace. I would be prepared to extend the definition to cover similar attacks on some other religion, as we have now become a multi-religion state, but it is not necessary for me to go so far for the purpose of the present case.'

[This] . . . sentence, as the judge recognised, was obiter and was unnecessary for the decision in the case. Nevertheless, we must say that if it was intended to be a statement of the existing law it was, in our view, plainly wrong. . . . But this dictum, which was not repeated in the judge's summing up, received no support from the Court of Appeal [1979] 1 QB 10, nor the House of Lords [1979] AC 617. The only issue that arose on appeal related to the mens rea of the offence. As to that Lord Diplock said in his speech in the House of Lords, at p. 632:

'The only question in this appeal is whether in 1976 the mental element or mens rea in the common law offence of blasphemy is satisfied by proof only of an intention to publish material which in the opinion of the jury is likely to shock and arouse resentment among believing Christians or whether the prosecution must go further and prove that the accused in publishing the material in fact intended to produce that effect upon believers, or (what comes to the same thing in criminal law), although aware of the likelihood that such effect might be produced, did not care whether it was or not, so long as the publication achieved some other purpose that constituted his motive for publishing it.'

It was held, affirming the Court of Appeal, that an intention to publish the material was sufficient. Although counsel suggested to the House, at p. 620н, that the offence might no longer be restricted to Christianity, there is nothing in any of the speeches to support this. On the contrary the definitions of the offence in their Lordships' speeches refer only to the Christian religion . . . Lord Scarman[16] made it plain that, in his view, it extends only to the Christian religion and that any change in the law was a matter for Parliament. . . .

'My Lords, I do not subscribe to the view that the common law offence of blasphemous libel serves no useful purpose in the modern law. On the contrary, I think that there is a case for legislation extending it to protect the religious beliefs and feelings of non-Christians. The offence belongs to a group of criminal offences designed to safeguard the internal tranquillity of the kingdom. In an increasingly plural society such as that of modern Britain it is necessary not only to respect the differing religious beliefs, feelings and practices of all but also to protect them from scurrility, vilification, ridicule and contempt.

. . . My criticism of the common law offence of blasphemy is not that it exists but that it is not sufficiently comprehensive. It is shackled by the chains of history.

'While in my judgment it is not open to your Lordships' House, even under [the 1966 House of Lords Practice Statement] . . . to extend the law beyond the limits recognised by the House in *Bowman v Secular Society Ltd*, or to make by judicial decision the comprehensive reform of the law which I believe to be beneficial, this appeal does offer your Lordships the opportunity of stating the existing law in a form conducive to the social conditions of the late 20th century rather than to those of the 17th, the 18th, or even the 19th century. This is, my Lords, no mere opportunity: it is a duty.' . . .

In 1914 Sir John Simon, the Attorney-General, was asked to advise the Home Office on the current state of the law. In the course of his opinion he said:

'It seems certainly to be the fact that no offence is committed if the religious beliefs which are attacked are not those of the Church of England; this seems a gross anomaly.'

With that comment we entirely agree; but the anomaly arises from what Lord Scarman called 'the chains of history', the origins of the law in the ecclesiastical courts, and the fact that the Anglican religion is the established law of the country. Perhaps more important, and certainly more recent, are the views of the Law Commission set out in their Working Paper No. 79, Offences against Religion and Public Worship. They report, at p. 82, para. 6.9:

16 *Ed.* Lord Scarman later changed his mind, now favouring abolition of the offence because of uncertainty about the meaning of religion and a preference for freedom of speech; the matter should be dealt via public order law: see S. J. D. Green, *Encounter*, June 1990, pp. 12, 15.

'Another shortcoming—or at any rate an anomaly—in the present law of blasphemy is the narrow scope of its protection. As we have seen, it is clear that that protection does not extend beyond the Christian religion, but it is less clear whether in the law of England and Wales it also protects the tenets of Christian denominations other than the established Church. Having regard to the authorities, it seems probable that at most other denominations are protected only to the extent that their fundamental beliefs are those which are held in common with the established Church.' . . .

We have no doubt that as the law now stands it does not extend to religions other than Christianity.

Can it in the light of the present conditions of society be extended by the courts to cover other religions? In our judgment where the law is clear it is not the proper function of this court to extend it; particularly is this so in criminal cases where offences cannot be retrospectively created. It is in that circumstance the function of Parliament alone to change the law. This was the view of Lord Scarman in the passage already quoted. . . .

. . . If the law is uncertain in interpreting and declaring the law the judges will do so in accordance with justice and to avoid anomaly or discrimination against certain classes of citizens; but taking that course is not open to us, even though we may think justice demands it, for the law is not, we think, uncertain. . . .

We think it right to say that, were it open to us to extend the law to cover religions other than Christianity, we should refrain from doing so. Considerations of public policy are extremely difficult and complex. It would be virtually impossible by judicial decision to set sufficiently clear limits to the offence, and other problems involved are formidable. These are considered at length in the Report of the Law Commission No. 145. We need only mention a few briefly.

Among other matters consideration would have to be given to the kinds of religions to be protected and to how religion is to be defined, see for an illustration of this problem *Church of the New Faith v Comr for Pay-Roll Tax* (1983) 57 ALJ 785 in which it was held that Scientology was a religion. Although an English jury may be expected, or certainly were in the last century, to understand the tenets of Christianity, this would not be so with other religions. There would be a need for expert evidence, no doubt for both prosecution and defence. If different sects of the same religion had differing views and the published material scandalised one sect and not another, how would the matter be decided? Since the only mental element in the offence is the intention to publish the words complained of, there would be a serious risk that the words might, unknown to the author, scandalise and outrage some sect or religion.

In any event, in the light of the majority opinion of the Law Commission in favour of abolition of the offence, it would, in our judgment, be wholly wrong to extend the law, even if, which we do not, we had the power to do so.

The resourceful Mr. Azhar [referred the Court to Articles 9, 10 and 14 ECHR]. . . . He maintained that the magistrate failed to consider and, therefore, take account of, the fact that we are a signatory to that Convention which, among many other things, guarantees freedom of religion to all citizens in equal terms. That being so, it is to be assumed, he said, that there must be a provision in our law to enforce such a freedom. If the law of blasphemy is designed to protect Christianity alone, it means, he went on, that other religions have been left unprotected ever since the Convention was signed in 1950. . . .

Mr. Lester [for the second respondent] responded impressively to Mr. Azhar's attempt to show that the absence of a domestic law of blasphemy relating to Islam would or might be in breach of the Convention.

He accepted that the obligations imposed on the United Kingdom by the Convention are relevant sources of public policy where the common law is uncertain. But, he maintained, the common law of blasphemy is, without doubt, certain. Accordingly, it is not necessary to pay any regard to the Convention. Nevertheless, he thought it necessary, and we agree, in the context of this case, to attempt to satisfy us that the United Kingdom is not in any event in breach of the Convention. Indeed, he went further and asserted that if this application were to succeed and result in successful prosecutions, the rights of Mr. Rushdie and of Viking Penguin, as protected by articles 7 and 10 of the Convention, would be violated. . . .

What the applicant seeks to do, Mr. Lester said, is to interfere with a well founded right to freedom of expression, a kind of interference never at any time foreshadowed by the common law of this country. Moreover, it would be an interference such as would contravene article 7 by creating ex post facto a criminal offence: see *Gay News Ltd v United Kingdom* (1982) 5 EHRR 123. Nothing in Mr. Azhar's argument could possibly bring either Mr. Rushdie or 'Gay News' within one of the exceptions in article 10(2). The test of necessity, if that could be said to be relevant, requires, he contended, the existence of a pressing social need for an interference with free speech for one of those purposes: see *Sunday Times v United Kingdom* (1979) 2 EHRR 245. Nothing in the book calls for additional protection of public order, or the freedom of everyone, Muslims included, to worship just as they please.

. . . freedom of religion [in Article 9, ECHR] is not absolute. It must tolerate certain restrictions including that, Mr. Lester submitted, of it not including the right to bring criminal proceedings for blasphemy where it cannot be shown that a domestic law has been offended against. There might be, Mr. Lester said, a breach of article 9 if criticism or agitation against a church or religious group reached such a level that the church or its members were prevented from manifesting their beliefs in the way set out in article 9. Nothing remotely like that had been demonstrated by the applicant.

If no law of blasphemy protects Muslims, Mr. Azhar maintained that they would be plainly discriminated against in that they would be denied the enjoyment of the rights and freedoms under the Convention. Mr. Lester dealt at length with that contention. Article 14, he said, read alongside article 9 clearly indicated that there was no such discrimination: see *Church of X v United Kingdom* (1968) 29 Collection of Decisions of the European Commission of Human Rights 70, and *Gay News Ltd v United Kingdom* 5 EHRR 123, 131, where the Commission decided that it is inadmissible to complain of discrimination in breach of article 14, read with article 9, on the ground that the law of blasphemy protects only the Christian but no other religion.

Mr. Lester [also submitted] that even if there is discrimination in the exercise of freedom of religion, it has an objective and reasonable justification and therefore involves no breach of article 14. The offence of blasphemous libel is an offence of strict liability. It is no defence that the defendant did not intend to blaspheme. As it stands, the offence is capable of resulting in unreasonable interferences with freedom of expression in breach of article 10. If the offence is extended to cover attacks upon religious doctrines, tenets, commandments, or practices of religions other than Christianity, the existence of such an extended law of blasphemy would encourage intolerance, divisiveness and unreasonable interference and interferences with freedom of expression. Fundamentalist Christians, Jews or Muslims could then seek to invoke the offence of blasphemy against each other's religion, doctrines, tenets, commandments, or practices; for example, for denying the divinity of Jesus Christ; or for denying that the Messiah has yet to come; or for denying the divine inspiration of the Prophet Mohammed, and so on. An extended law of blasphemy which applied to all religions could be used as a weapon between Protestants and Roman Catholics in Northern Ireland, or by fringe religions, such as the Church of Scientology. The fact that the offence was committed only in cases of scurrilous attacks would mitigate, but not eliminate, the resulting intolerance, divisiveness, and unreasonable interference with freedom of expression. To the extent that it has been submitted by the applicant that there is no relevant difference in Christianity, Judaism and Islam, it is clear that there are fundamental differences which would be capable of setting one religion against another under an extended law of blasphemy.

We agree that extending the law of blasphemy would pose insuperable problems and would be likely to do more harm than good. We cannot think that the makers of the Convention could have had in mind such an extension of the law in this country in giving expression to the right of freedom of religion as it has in the various articles we have referred to.

Mr. Lester has persuaded us convincingly that the Convention does not demand within any of those articles the creation of a law of blasphemy for the protection of Islam so that as signatory to the Convention the United Kingdom be in conformity with it. Thus, Mr. Azhar's attempt to invoke the assistance of the Convention is, in our judgment, unavailing.

[The court then rejected the applicant's claim based upon seditious libel on the ground that the book did not disclose any intent to incite persons to violence against the state.]

Application dismissed

NOTES[17]

1. After lying dormant for half a century,[18] the offence of blasphemous libel has been the object of a reported case twice in more recent years. The first case was in *Whitehouse v Lemon*,[19] from the speeches in which extracts are quoted in *Ex p Choudhury*. *R v Lemon* concerned the poem 'The Love that Dares to Speak its Name', by James Kirkup, an established poet and a Fellow of the Royal Society of Literature. The poem 'purports to describe in explicit detail acts of sodomy and fellatio with the body of Christ immediately after his death and to ascribe to Him during his lifetime promiscuous homosexual practices with the Apostles and with other men' (per Lord Diplock). Mrs. Mary Whitehouse brought a private prosecution for blasphemous libel against the editor and publisher (Gay News plc) of *Gay News*, which had published the poem together with an illustration of the fantasy it contained.[20] Both defendants were convicted. The editor was given a suspended sentence of nine months' imprisonment that was quashed by the Court of Appeal. Fines of £1,000 and £500 on the editor and Gay News plc respectively and an order for prosecution costs were upheld. The House of Lords' ruling, when dismissing the appeal, that there was no need to prove a specific intent to shock believing Christians was by three to two, Lords Diplock and Edmund-Davies dissenting. It had been strongly argued by the defence that neither the author of the poem nor the defendants had intended to offend Christians; their intention was instead to put a homosexual point of view.

Although, as demonstrated by the conviction in *R v Lemon*, the offence of blasphemy inevitably limits freedom of expression, as at present defined under English law it is in breach of the guarantee of freedom of expression in Art. 10 ECHR.[1]

2. An application in the *Choudhury* case under Arts. 9 and 14 ECHR, claiming discrimination in the protection of freedom of religion, was declared inadmissible by the European Commission of Human Rights as manifestly ill-founded because Art 9 could not be read as including a positive obligation upon states to protect religious sensibilities.[2] *Ex p Choudhury* raises a question that has become increasingly relevant as the United Kingdom has become a more multi-religious

17 On blasphemy and blasphemous libel, see L. Blom-Cooper and G. Drewry, *Law and Morality* (1976), pp. 294–60; R. Buxton, [1978] Crim LR 673; P. Jones, (1980) 10 BJ Pol S 129; C. Kenny, (1922) CLJ 127; S. Poulter, [1991] PL 371; C. L. Ten, (1978) 5 BJ Law and Soc 89; Walter, *Blasphemy Ancient and Modern* (1990); R. Webster, *A Brief History of Blasphemy* (1990); *Law, Blasphemy and the Multi-Faith Society* (1990), Report of a CRE-Inter Faith Network Seminar, CRE Discussion Paper 1. See also *Criminal Law: Offences against Religion and Public Worship*, Law Commission Report No. 145 (1985). This was preceded by Law Commission Working Paper No. 79 (1981) (same title). On the Working Paper, see J. R. Spencer, [1981] Crim LR 810; G. Robertson, [1981] PL 295; and St. J. Robilliard, (1981) 44 MLR 556. On the *Choudhury* case, see M. Tregilas-Davey, (1991) 54 MLR 294.
18 Blasphemy was described as 'a dead letter' by Lord Denning in *Freedom under the Law* (1949) p. 46. Criminal proceedings were contemplated or attempted in certain cases in the early 1970s before the *Lemon* case; see the Law Commission Working Paper, n. 1, above, p. 18.
19 [1979] AC 617, HL.
20 For a full account of the prosecution, see M. Tracy and D. Morrison, *Whitehouse* (1979) pp. 3–17.
 1 See *Wingrove v UK* (1996) 24 EHRR 1. See also *Otto-Preminger Institute v Austria* (1995) 19 EHRR 34 (Austrian blasphemy law use as a basis for film seizure consistent with Art. 10 ECHR).
 2 *Choudhury v UK* No 17349/1990, 12 HRLJ 172 (1991). There may be a breach of the equality before the law guarantee in Art. 26, ICCPR: see P. Cumper, in D. Harris and S. Joseph, (eds.), *The International Covenant on Civil and Political Rights and United Kingdom Law* (1995), p. 368.

society. Is it defensible that in *R v Lemon* the publisher of a poem that offended Christians could be guilty of blasphemy when in *Ex p Choudhury* the publishers of a novel that contained passages that were at least equally offensive to Muslims could not? The Law Commission addressed this question in their 1985 Report[3] when recommending the abolition of the offences of blasphemy and blasphemous libel (the written form of blasphemy). The Report reads (footnote omitted):

'2.4 [Law Commission] Working Paper 79 examined the rationales for retaining in the criminal law an offence penalising insults directed against religion. It distinguished four arguments— (i) the protection of religion and religious beliefs, (ii) the protection of society, (iii) the protection of individual feelings, and (iv) the protection of public order. Of these, the working paper concluded that (iii) was the most persuasive. Even so, it found that the arguments were quite evenly balanced and, in particular, that, while the presence of a pressing social need might justify the imposition of penalties for incitement to racial hatred, there was no corresponding need in the context of religion which might justify an offence of blasphemy.

2.5 Accordingly, the working paper examined the form which a new offence might take in order to assess whether there were insuperable difficulties in specifying with precision its possible constituent elements, for 'where the case for a law is finely balanced, the inability to state clearly what the law requires can be allowed to weigh against it.' The paper came to the conclusion that, while an offence of wounding or outraging the feelings of adherents of any religious group could be envisaged, it seemed impossible to construct a sufficiently precise definition of what was meant by 'religion' in this context, and that other elements would also have an unacceptable degree of imprecision; this shortcoming, in the view expressed by the working paper, fatally flawed this possible offence. . . .'

Two of the five members of the Commission (Gibson J, Chairman, and Mr. B. Davenport) dissented. In their Note of Dissent, they stated:

'We agree with the substance of the main criticisms of the existing common law offence of blasphemy and with the recommendation that it should be abolished. We attach particular importance to the defect in the existing offence that it affords protection to one religion only. Our view, however, is that in abolishing the common law offence of blasphemy the preferable course would be to enact a new offence which would be free of the defects of the present law. . . .

We agree that if there is no argument which may properly be regarded as sufficiently powerful to justify the derogation from freedom of expression which any offence of blasphemy must occasion, then no such offence should have a place in the criminal law. In our view, however, that argument is to be found in what we think should be seen as the duty on all citizens, in our society of different races and of people of different faiths and of no faith, not purposely to insult or outrage the religious feelings of others.'

In the view of the two dissenting Law Commissioners, the drafting of a new, satisfactory offence, although difficult, could be achieved.

In 1994, a House of Lords amendment proposed by Lord Lester to a bill that would have abolished the offence of blasphemy was withdrawn in the face of Government opposition.[4] Do the difficulties of drafting a new offence extending to all religions support the Law Commission's conclusions that none should be enacted? Does the high value placed upon freedom of speech in western societies do likewise? Or should it be recognised that a person may value his or her religion so highly that verbal attacks may cause such offence to reasonable believers that the law should make blasphemous words a criminal offence and do so without regard to their tendency to

---

3 Loc. cit. at n. 17 above.
4 See the debate on Lord Lester's amendment and the Government response by Earl Ferrers, who noted a lack of consensus and foresaw practical difficulties: 555 HL Deb, 16 June 1994, cols. 1891–1909.

1052   *Freedom of religion*

cause a breach of the peace?[5] Would you agree with J. C. Smith's comments,[6] on Lord Scarman's speech in *R v Lemon*?

'Should the law protect all religions, however weird and potentially harmful to the community, from vilification, ridicule and contempt? It is submitted that vilification, ridicule and contempt may be decidedly in the public interest. Should it not be possible to attack in the strongest terms religious beliefs that adulterers should be stoned to death and that thieves should have the offending hand lopped off, however offensive that may be to the holders of the beliefs?'

Do these comments apply to the offence caused by *The Satanic Verses*?

An Archbishop of Canterbury's Working Group, chaired by the Bishop of London, agreed with the dissenting members of the Law Commission that the offence should be extended to other religions, although it is understood that, since the Salman Rushdie Affair, at least some members of the Working Group have changed their mind. The Government position is that, in the absence of any consensus, no change in the law is appropriate.

3. In its 1985 Report, the Law Commission identified other weaknesses in the present law of blasphemy, in addition to its application only to Christianity:[7]

'2.18 The defects in the common law analysed in the working paper may be summarised as follows—
  (i)   The law is to an unacceptable degree uncertain. As we put it—
       'Once the judge has directed the jury as to the ingredients of the offence, it is for the jury to say whether the matter is "scurrilous" or "abusive" or "insulting" in relation to the Christian religion and thereby has a tendency to induce a breach of the peace . . . It is hardly an exaggeration to say that whether or not a publication is a blasphemous libel can only be judged *ex post facto* . . . Delimitation of a criminal offence by reference to jury application of one or more of several adjectives (all of which necessitate subjective interpretation and none of which is absolute) is hardly satisfactory . . . While matter which is merely abusive is ignored in the law of defamatory libel, it becomes of the essence in blasphemous libel, provided that the jury finds it sufficiently scurrilous to amount to the offence.'
  (ii) In so far as the law requires only an intention to publish the offending words and not an intention to blaspheme, the offence is to an undesirable extent one of strict liability. Furthermore, the absence of a mental element of an intent to blaspheme runs contrary to the general principle developed during the past century that a mental element is normally required as to all the elements of the prohibited conduct both in common law and statutory crimes, save in special cases of regulatory offences. The practical consequence of the exclusion of any requirement as to the intent of the defendant to blaspheme is that he cannot give admissible evidence as to what he claims to be his beliefs and purpose. It is thus quite possible for the offence to be committed by someone with profound religious beliefs and with entirely sincere motives, provided that the language in which he expresses himself is sufficiently shocking and insulting to be held blasphemous by a jury. . . .
We see no reason now to differ from the views expressed in the working paper.'

Other aspects of the present law that the Commission criticised or noted were that there is no defence of 'public good' comparable to that under the Obscene Publications

---

5   See A. Weale, in *Free Speech* (1990), Report of a CRE-Policy Studies Institute, CRE Discussion Paper 2, p. 49. Cf. the problem with incitement to racial hatred: below, p. 1152 Arguing for an extension of the law of blasphemy to eliminate discrimination against Muslims, see A. Bradney, (1993) 143 NLJ 434. See also *Otto-Preminger Institute v Austria* (1995) 19 EHRR 34.
6   [1979] Crim LR 311 at 313.
7   Loc. cit. at p. 1050, n. 17, above. As to whether the law protects only the established church or Christianity generally, the Law Commission stated in its Working Paper, para. 3.2, that it 'seems that the Christian religion in general is protected, together with the doctrines and rituals of the Church of England but not those of other religions or other Christian bodies'.

Act 1959, s. 4; that publication to just one other person may constitute an offence; that there 'is no authority on the question whether statements made on television or in other broadcasts' are prohibited, although 'in principle' there 'seems to be no reason why statements or visual images' on television or radio should not be subject to the law; and that a prosecution may be brought by any member of the public without the consent of, for example, the DPP (as in *R v Lemon*)[8]. As to whether a tendency to a breach of the peace is a necessary element in the offence, the Law Commission stated (para. 6.2)

> '. . . if this element survives, it means in this context no more than that the publication must be such as 'to provoke or arouse angry feelings, something which is a possibility, not a probability'.[9] If blasphemy is to be regarded as an offence 'designed to safeguard the internal tranquility of the kingdom', which according to the most recent authority is still its primary function,[10] the exiguous or non-existent burden laid upon the prosecution to prove some possibility of disturbance to public order compares unfavourably with the position in other areas of the law. [For example, there are] the limits imposed by section 5 of the Public Order Act 1936, where a subjective intent to cause a breach of the peace or an objective likelihood of a breach of the peace is required.[11] If the requirements of section 5 were held to be satisfied by a requirement that the behaviour complained of might possibly, not probably, arouse angry feelings, we believe that its unacceptable character would be readily apparent and that it would be regarded as a gross infringement of freedom of expression.'

4. Muslims objected when the Mecca chain of bingo halls opened a new hall in their town in the chain's name; the use of the name of their holy city in connection with alcohol and gambling was profane.[12] Should it be illegal?

(iii)   Other forms of assistance

Apart from the assistance given in schools, the law aids religion in many other ways. The Sunday Observance Act 1780, as amended, prohibits public entertainments and amusements on Sundays for which an admission charge (as opposed to a charge for a programme or car parking) is made. Its rigours have been reduced somewhat by the Sunday Entertainments Act 1932 (museums, picture galleries, zoological gardens, etc, may open) and, more recently, the Sunday Theatre Act 1972 and the Cinemas Act 1985, s. 9, as amended, which permit the opening of theatres and cinemas subject to certain limitations. In 1976, seven people were convicted under the Sunday Observance Act 1780. The Home Office consolidated circular to the police on crime states that it is assumed that the police will take the view that prosecutions under the Act can best be brought by private persons rather than the police.[13]

The Sunday Trading Act 1994 withdrew the assistance to religion that had been provided by the general prohibition on Sunday trading in the Shops Act 1950. Under the 1994 Act, large shops (defined in terms of floor area) are permitted to open for six hours on Sundays; small shops may open all day. Large shops occupied by persons of the Jewish religion are not subject to the six hours limit if they close on the Jewish Sabbath. Shopworkers may, for reasons of conscience or otherwise, decide not to work on Sundays and must not be disadvantaged for doing so.

The law allows religions to have single sex ministries: Sex Discrimination Act 1975, s. 19 excludes employment or the granting of authorisations or qualifications 'limited to one sex so as to comply with the doctrines of the religion or avoid offending

---

8 Loc. cit. at p. 1050, n. 17, above, paras. 3.5–3.9.
9 *R v Lemon*, per Judge King-Hamilton QC, transcript of summing-up, para. 11a.
10 See *Whitehouse v Lemon* [1979] AC 617 at 658 and 662 per Lord Scarman.
11 *Ed.* see now, Public Order Act 1986, s. 4, above, p. 471.
12 *The Times*, 6 January 1998.
13 952 HC Debs, written answers 21 June 1978, col. 204.

the religious susceptibilities of a significant number of its followers' from the prohibition of sexual discrimination in the Act.

Account is taken of the increased diversity of religions in the United Kingdom by the Matrimonial Causes Act 1973, s. 47, by which Parliament changed the policy of the law so that matrimonial relief is now available to a party to a polygamous marriage celebrated abroad. This is, however, discrimination between religions in law in respect of the recognition of marriages celebrated in accordance with religious traditions in the United Kingdom.[14]

A Roman Catholic priest is probably not privileged in the law of evidence in respect of what is said to him in the confessional.[15] In the Irish case of *Schlegel v Corcoran and Gross*,[16] it was held that consent to the assignment of a lease was not 'unreasonably withheld' by a Roman Catholic widow who refused her consent to the assignment to a Jewish dentist of a tenancy of rooms used for a dental practice in the house which she owned and in which she lived. There is no comparable English case interpreting the same 'consent not to be reasonably withheld' provision in Landlord and Tenant Act 1927, s. 19(2). Cf. the Race Relations Act 1976, s. 24.[17] A person who is unable to vote at a parliamentary or local election 'by reason of religious observance' may vote by post.[18]

Some allowance for religious beliefs is made in the case of jury service. Although a 'serious conscientious objection arising out of a religious belief, on its own, would be unlikely to amount to a "good reason" for being excused jury service', it may do so 'if the applicant's religious beliefs, for example, would be likely to prevent her from performing her duty in a proper way'.[19]

Arrangements exist to hear appeals by members of the regular Armed Forces whose claim for discharge on grounds of conscientious objection has been rejected by the Service authorities. Such appeals go to the Advisory Committee on Conscientious Objectors, an independent, non-statutory body established in 1970[20] whose members are appointed by the Lord Chancellor. The Committee, which hears argument in public, has advised acceptance of 8 out of 33 appeals. Its advice is normally followed.[1]

Although neither the BBC nor commercial broadcasting are legally obliged to broadcast religious programmes, there is a strong tradition that they should.

Places of worship are protected by the criminal law from 'riotous, violent or indecent behaviour'.[2] It is also an offence to use force to prevent a Minister from celebrating divine service.[3]

On freedom of religion in prisons, see St. J. Robilliard.[4]

---

14 See S. Poulter, loc. cit. at p. 1027, n. 1, above, pp. 176–178. E.g. polygamous marriages celebrated in the UK are not recognised and no concession is made to the Muslim religion as to the place or formalities of the marriage. Likewise a Muslim divorce by talaq that occurs in the UK is not valid. On the claim to a separate Islamic system of personal law in the UK, see ibid., in Mallat C and Connor J (eds.), *Islamic Family Law* (1990) p. 140.

15 *Cross and Tapper on Evidence* (9th edn, 1999), p. 463.

16 [1942] IR 19, H Ct Ireland.

17 Below, p. 659.

18 Representation of the People Act 1983, s. 19(1)(c).

19 *R v Crown Court at Guildford, ex p Siderfin* [1989] 3 All ER 7 at 12, CA, per Watkins LJ (Plymouth Brethren member would not have been able to have talked the case over with her fellow jurors).

20 See 807 HC Deb, 2 December 1970, col. 423.

 1 For a successful appeal by an army captain who objected to the British military presence in Northern Ireland, see *The Guardian*, 16 May 1979.

 2 Ecclesiastical Courts Jurisdiction Act 1860, s. 2, interpreted in *Abrahams v Cavey*, [1968] 1 QB 479 and *R v Farrant* [1973] Crim LR 240.

 3 Offences against the Person Act 1861, s. 36.

 4 *Religion and the Law* (1984), pp. 132–137.

4 Religion and the criminal law

R v Senior [1899] 1 QB 283, Court for Crown Cases Reserved

The defendant was a member of a Christian religious sect called the 'Peculiar People'. Following its beliefs, he refused to allow his child, aged nine months, to be treated by a doctor. The child died and the defendant was convicted of manslaughter for having caused the death by an unlawful act—'wilful neglect' of a child in his custody contrary to the Prevention of Cruelty to Children Act 1894, s. 1. The defendant was the father of 12 children, of whom seven had died. More than one would appear to have died because of the defendant's religious beliefs. The following extract concerns solely the question whether these beliefs could provide a defence to the charge.

Lord Russell of Killowen CJ: . . . Mr Sutton contended that because the prisoner was proved to be an affectionate parent, and was willing to do all things for the benefit of his child, except the one thing which was necessary in the present case, he ought not to be found guilty of the offence of manslaughter, on the ground that he abstained from providing medical aid for his child in consequence of his peculiar views in the matter; but we cannot shut our eyes to the danger which might arise if we were to accede to that argument, for where is the line to be drawn? In the present case the prisoner is shown to have had an objection to the use of medicine; but other cases might arise, such, for instance, as the case of a child with a broken thigh, where a surgical operation was necessary, which had to be performed with the aid of an anæsthetic; could the father refuse to allow the anæsthetic to be administered? Or take the case of a child that was in danger of suffocation, so that the operation of tracheotomy was necessary in order to save its life, and anæsthetic was required to be administered.

Conviction affirmed.

NOTES

1. The 1894 Act offence is now found in s. 1, Children and Young Persons Act 1933. The father would not now be guilty of manslaughter by unlawful act, because his unlawful act was an omission.[5] A genuine lack of understanding that the child requires medical care (which was not present on the facts in *R v Senior*) is a good defence to the 1933 Act offence.[6] A Rastafarian couple, Beverley and Dwight Harris, whose religious belief caused them to refuse their diabetic daughter insulin were convicted of manslaughter by gross negligence. They believed insulin was produced from pigs and hence unclean.[7]
2. Before the Suicide Act 1961 (which abolished the offence), a person who refused medical treatment for himself for religious or other reasons with the result that he died was guilty of suicide. A person who aids, abets, counsels or procures another to commit suicide is still guilty of the offence of complicity in suicide (Suicide Act 1961, s. 2). As a matter of criminal or civil law, a person may refuse medical treatment for religious or other reasons, provided that the refusal is not the result of undue influence by another.[8] The courts may, however, authorise medical treatment to A despite A's religious beliefs to save the life of another,[9] or to save A's own life where she is a child.[10]

5 *R v Lowe* [1973] QB 702, CA.
6 *R v Sheppard* [1981] AC 394, HL.
7 *Runnymede Bulletin* 271, p. 7 (1994).
8 *Re T* [1992] 4 All ER 649, CA.
9 *Re S* [1992] 4 All ER 671, Fam D ('Born-again' Christian's refusal to have caesarian birth overriden).
10 *Re L (Medical Treatment: Gillick Competency)* [1998] 2 FLR 810, CA (14-year-old Jehovah's Witness girl in life-threatening situation: her refusal of blood transfusion overridden because of her sheltered life within Jehovah's Witness community).

3. In *R v John*[11] the Court of Appeal held that a motorist's religious beliefs cannot constitute a 'reasonable excuse' for his failure to provide a specimen of blood contrary to the Road Traffic Act 1972, s. 9(3). The appellant was a Mesmerist and believed that he was possessed of certain faith healing powers derived from the presence in his blood of certain divinely given gifts. The court followed *R v Lennard*[12] in which it was held that 'no excuse can be adjudged a reasonable one unless the person from whom the specimen is required is physically or mentally unable to provide it or the provision of the specimen would entail a substantial risk to his health'. Similarly, in *Blake v DPP*,[13] it was held that a genuinely held belief was not a 'lawful excuse' under the Criminal Damage Act 1971. So, a vicar who wrote words from the bible on a concrete pillar in protest at the use of force in the Iraq war was guilty of the offence of criminal damage.

4. A Muslim Ugandan Asian was fined £20 by Burnham Magistrates for stopping illegally on the hard shoulder of the M4. He had been found there beside his car at sunset praying as his religion required.[14]

5. Religious belief is a statutory defence for Sikh motor-cyclists and Sikhs on construction sites. It is a principle of his religion that a Sikh wear a turban in public. The wearing of a crash helmet with or without a turban is a breach of this principle. After a series of cases[15] in which Sikhs were convicted (one more than 30 times) of riding motor-cycles with turbans and without crash-helmets, the Motor-Cycle Crash-Helmets (Religious Exemption) Act 1976 s.1, provided an exemption for 'any follower of the Sikh religion while he is wearing a turban'. The Employment Act 1989, s. 11, exempts a Sikh from any legal requirement to wear a safety helmet while on a construction site when he is wearing a turban. However, no such exemption has been provided for Sikhs working in industry who are required to wear a safety helmet under health and safety legislation.[16]

Under the Criminal Justice Act 1988, s. 139(5), a person charged with the offence of having a knife in a public place has the defence that he has it for 'religious reasons', which might be the case of a Sikh carrying a kirpan.

6. The Abortion Act 1967, s. 4, provides:

> '**4.**—(1) Subject to subsection (2) of this section, no person shall be under any duty, whether by contract or by statutory or other legal requirement, to participate in any treatment authorised by this Act to which he has a conscientious objection:
>
> Provided that in any legal proceedings the burden of proof of conscientious objection shall rest on the person claiming to rely on it.
>
> (2) Nothing in subsection (1) of this section shall affect any duty to participate in treatment which is necessary to save the life or to prevent grave permanent injury to the physical or mental health of a pregnant woman. . . .'

Section 4(1) offers a defence against criminal liability for a doctor, nurse, etc, who is unable to carry out an abortion for reasons of conscience.[17] A doctor's secretary who types a letter referring a patient to a consultant with a view to an abortion does not

---

11 [1974] 1 WLR 624, CA.
12 [1973] 1 WLR 483, 487, CA.
13 (1993) Times, 19 January, DC.
14 *Daily Telegraph*, 7 September 1976.
15 See, e.g., *R v Aylesbury Crown Court, ex p Chahal* [1976] RTR 489, DC.
16 *Singh v British Rail Engineering Ltd* [1986] ICR 22, EAT and *Dhanjal v British Steel*, ET, in IDS, *Racial Discrimination: Employment Law Handbook* (1999), p. 149.
17 Cf. the Human Fertilisation and Embryology Act 1990, s. 38, which has a similarly worded conscience clause.

'participate' in treatment for abortion for the purposes of s. 4.[18] In that case a receptionist and secretary was dismissed by the Authority for refusing to type such a letter on the ground that as a Roman Catholic she believed abortion to be morally wrong. She applied for judicial review of the Authority's decision on the ground that by virtue of the Abortion Act 1967, s. 4, her contract of employment did not require her to type correspondence concerning abortions, but was unsuccessful. The House of Commons Social Services Committee recommended that the s. 4 conscience clause be extended to some ancillary staff.[19] It also recommended that the burden of proving a conscientious objection should not be on the person claiming it. These recommendations have not been made law.

Cf. the limitation in s. 4(2) with the summing up by Macnaghten J in *R v Bourne*:[20]

'. . . there are people who, from what are said to be religious reasons, object to the operation being performed under any circumstances. That is not the law either. On the contrary, a person who holds such an opinion ought not to be an obstetrical surgeon, for if a case arose where the life of the woman could be saved by performing the operation and the doctor refused to perform it because of his religious opinions and the woman died, he would be in grave peril of being brought before this Court on a charge of manslaughter by negligence. He would have no better defence than a person who, again for some religious reason, refused to call in a doctor to attend his sick child, where a doctor could have been called in and the life of the child could have been saved.'

7. *R v Blaue*[1] concerned the religious beliefs of the victim. The question was whether a Jehovah's Witness who had been stabbed by the defendant and who refused a blood transfusion that would have saved her life had broken the chain of causation by her action so that the defendant was not guilty of manslaughter. The Court of Appeal held that she had not:

'It has long been the policy of the law that those who use violence on other people must take their victims as they find them. This in our judgment means the whole man, not just the physical man. It does not lie in the mouth of the assailant to say that his victim's religious beliefs which inhibited him from accepting certain kinds of treatment were unreasonable. The question for decision is what caused her death. The answer is the stab wound.'

8. See also the Slaughterhouses Act 1974, s. 36(3), and the Slaughter of Poultry Act 1967, s. 1(2), as amended, which exempt from the provisions of those Acts 'that impose criminal liability' the slaughtering of animals and birds by the methods used by Jews and Muslims in the preparation of their food provided that unnecessary suffering is not inflicted.
9. The use of marijuana by Rastafarians[2] as a part of their faith is not permitted by law. 'The true Rastafarian is deeply religious . . . He believes it is as legitimate to smoke cannabis as to drink alcohol and less likely to lead to unruly behaviour; but . . . the true Rastafarian accepts the law of the land.'[3] Should the law make an exception for him in respect of drugs offences?
10. Following the custom of the Yoruba tribe, Mrs. Adesanya had small incisions cut into the cheeks of her two sons at puberty. This occurred at a family ceremony in England at which hymns were sung and there was 'just rejoicing in the name of the Lord'. Mrs Adesanya was convicted of assault, but given an absolute discharge.[4]

18 *Janaway v Salford Health Authority* [1989] AC 537, HL.
19 10th Report HC 123 (1989–90).
20 [1939] 1 KB 687.
1 [1975] 1 WLR 1411, CA.
2 See E. Cashmore, *The Rastafarians* (Minority Rights Group Report 64, 1992), p. 4.
3 *Scarman Report on the Brixton Disorders 10–12 April 1981*, Cmnd. 8427, p. 44.
4 (1974) 124 NLJ 708.

Female genital mutilation is a criminal offence under the Prohibition of Female Circumcision Act 1985.[5]

11. In 1986, the Severn Trent River Authority informed Indian families who had approached the Authority for permission to scatter funeral ashes in a river that they could be prosecuted under Part II of the Control of Pollution Act 1974 for polluting controlled waters. Ashes could be scattered at selected tidal points on the Trent and the Severn with Ministry of Agriculture dispensation.[6]

5 Religion and employment

Ahmad v Inner London Education Authority [1978] QB 36, [1977] 3 WLR 396, [1978] 1 All ER 574, Court of Appeal

The appellant, a devout Muslim, was employed as a full-time schoolteacher by the ILEA. From 1968 to 1974, he taught at a school that was too far away from a mosque for it to be necessary for him in accordance with his religion to attend one on Fridays for prayer. Upon being transferred by the ILEA to a school only 20 minutes away from a mosque, he went there for prayers on Fridays as his religion required. This meant that he missed 45 minutes of teaching time, during which his teaching had to be done by someone else. The school's work was to that extent disrupted and his colleagues objected. The ILEA informed the appellant that if he continued to go to the mosque, he would have to give up his full-time post for a part-time one at a lower salary. The appellant thereupon resigned and applied to an industrial tribunal for compensation and for reinstatement on the ground that the ILEA's conduct had forced him to resign and amounted to unfair dismissal contrary to the Trade Union and Labour Relations Act 1974. The tribunal held against him on the ground that the employer had not acted unreasonably so that the dismissal was not unfair. The Employment Appeal Tribunal rejected his appeal. The appellant appealed further to the Court of Appeal. He relied upon section 30 of the Education Act 1944, which reads:

'Subject as hereinafter provided, no person shall be disqualified by reason of his religious opinions, or of his attending or omitting to attend religious worship, from being a teacher in a county school or in any voluntary school, or from being otherwise employed for the purposes of such a school; and no teacher in any such school shall be required to give religious instruction or receive any less emolument or be deprived of, or disqualified for, any promotion or other advantage by reason of the fact that he does or does not give religious instruction or by reason of his religious opinions or of his attending or omitting to attend religious worship: Provided that, save in so far as they require that a teacher shall not receive any less emolument or be deprived of, or disqualified for, any promotion or other advantage by reason of the fact that he gives religious instruction or by reason of his religious opinions or of his attending religious worship, the provisions of this section shall not apply with respect to a teacher in an aided school or with respect to a reserved teacher in any controlled school or special agreement school.'

Lord Denning MR: . . . On the appeal, Mr. Ahmad relied much on section 30 of the Education Act 1944. . . . If the words were read literally without qualification, they would entitle Mr Ahmad to take time off every Friday afternoon for his prayers without loss of pay. I cannot think this was ever intended. The school time-table was well known to Mr Ahmad when he applied for the teaching post. It was for the usual teaching hours from Monday to

5   FGM is a cultural tradition rather than a religious one.
6   *The Times*, 23 September 1986, p. 9.

Friday, inclusive. If he wished to have every Friday afternoon off for his prayers, *either* he ought not to have applied for this post: *or* he ought to have made it clear at the outset and entered into a 4¹/₂-day engagement only. . . .

I think that section 30 can be applied to the situation perfectly well by reading it as subject to the qualification 'if the school time-table so permits.' . . . It has been so interpreted by the great majority of Muslim teachers in our schools. They do not take time off for their prayers. . . . The industrial tribunal said: '. . . none of the other education authorities has ever received such a request from Muslim staff and the problem would seem to be unique to the applicant, Mr Ahmad.' . . .

During the argument Scarman LJ drew attention to article 9 of the European Convention on Human Rights. . . .

The convention is not part of our English law, but . . . we will always have regard to it. We will do our best to see that our decisions are in conformity with it. But it is drawn in such vague terms that it can be used for all sorts of unreasonable claims and provoke all sorts of litigation. As so often happens with high-sounding principles, they have to be brought down to earth. They have to be applied in a work-a-day world. I venture to suggest that it would do the Muslim community no good—or any other minority group no good—if they were to be given preferential treatment over the great majority of people. If it should happen that, in the name of religious freedom, they were given special privileges or advantages, it would provoke discontent, and even resentment among those with whom they work. As, indeed, it has done in this very case. And so the cause of racial integration would suffer. So, whilst upholding religious freedom to the full, I would suggest that it should be applied with caution, especially having regard to the setting in which it is sought. Applied to our educational system, I think that Mr. Ahmad's right to 'manifest his religion in practice and observance' must be subject to the rights of the education authorities under the contract and to the interests of the children whom he is paid to teach. I see nothing in the European Convention to give Mr Ahmad any right to manifest his religion on Friday afternoons in derogation of his contract of employment: and certainly not on full pay. . . .

I would dismiss the appeal.

Scarman LJ: The true construction of s. 30 is at the heart of this case . . . The reasons for its 30 years of immunity from judicial interpretation are not hard to see. First, and foremost, local education authorities, like the ILEA in this case, have treated it as no more than of negative intent—forbidding discrimination on the ground of religion in the selection and employment of teachers, but not obliging them to ensure that religious minorities are represented amongst their teachers. The ILEA, we have been told, have sought to comply with the section by not asking questions, the theory being that, if you do not know a man's religion, you cannot discriminate against him on that ground. Secondly, there were until recently no substantial religious groupings in our country which fell outside the broad categories of Christian and Jew. So long as there was no discrimination between them, no problem was likely to arise. The five-day school week, of course, takes care of the Sabbath and of Sunday as days of special religious observance. But with the advent of new religious groups in our society section 30 assumes a new importance. . . .

When the section was enacted, the negative approach to its interpretation was, no doubt, sufficient. But society has changed since 1944; so also has the legal background. Religions, such as Islam and Buddhism, have substantial followings among our people. Room has to be found for teachers and pupils of the new religions in the educational system, if discrimination is to be avoided. This calls not for a policy of the blind eye but for one of understanding. The system must be made sufficiently flexible to accommodate their beliefs and their observances: otherwise, they will suffer discrimination—a consequence contrary to the spirit of section 30, whatever the letter of that law. The change in legal background is no less momentous. Since 1944 the United Kingdom has accepted international obligations designed to protect human rights and freedoms, and has enacted a series of statutes designed for the same purpose in certain critical areas of our society. These major statutes include the Trade Union and Labour Relations Act 1974, the Employment Protection Act 1975, the Sex Discrimination Act 1975, and the race relations legislation.

They were enacted after the United Kingdom had ratified the European Convention on Human Rights . . . and in the light of our obligations under the Charter of the United Nations.

Today, therefore, we have to construe and apply section 30 not against the background of the law and society of 1944 but in a multi-racial society which has accepted international obligations and enacted statutes designed to eliminate discrimination on grounds of race, religion, colour or sex. Further, it is no longer possible to argue that because the international treaty obligations of the United Kingdom do not become law unless enacted by Parliament our courts pay no regard to our international obligations. They pay very serious regard to them: in particular, they will interpret statutory language and apply common law principles wherever possible, so as to reach a conclusion consistent with our international obligations.
. . .

With these general considerations in mind, I conclude that the present case, properly considered, begins but does not end with the law of contract. It ends with a very difficult problem—the application to the particular circumstances of this appellant of the new law associated with the protection of the individual's human rights and fundamental freedoms.
. . .

The ILEA submits that because of its context, coming as it does as a final saving for the position of teachers at the end of a set of sections dealing with religious education in schools, the section is to be read as limited to attending or omitting to attend worship in school. . . .

Although I see the force of the submission, I reject it; because fundamentally a narrow construction of the section is in conflict with the developments in our society to which I have already referred—developments which are protected by statutes to which I have also referred. A narrow construction of the section would mean that a Muslim, who took his religious duty seriously, could never accept employment as a full-time teacher, but must be content with the lesser emoluments of part-time service. In modern British society, with its elaborate statutory protection of the individual from discrimination arising from race, colour, religion or sex, and against the background of the European Convention, this is unacceptable, inconsistent with the policy of modern statute law, and almost certainly a breach of our international obligations. Unless, therefore, the language of section 30 forces one to adopt the narrow construction, I would think it wrong to do so. But it does not: the section, linguistically speaking, can be construed broadly or narrowly. No doubt, Parliament in 1944 never addressed its mind to the problem of this case. But, if the section lends itself, as successful human rights or constitutional legislation must lend itself, to judicial interpretation in accordance with the spirit of the age, there is nothing in this point, save for the comment that Parliament by refusing to be too specific was wiser than some of us have subsequently realised. The choice of construction, while it must be exercised judicially, is ours: for the reasons which I have attempted to formulate, the decision must be in favour of the broad construction.

Construed broadly and as part of the teacher's contract for full-time service, the section means that the teacher is not to receive less emoluments by reason only that during school hours he attends religious worship. It is immaterial whether he does so in the school or elsewhere; but the right to go to church, chapel, temple or mosque whether it be inside or outside the school, which the section confers on the teacher, has to be read into his full-time contract. In the context of such a contract the right is to be exercised in such a way as not to conflict with the duty of full-time service. . . .

Nor do I think there is any substance in the point that a broad construction of section 30 imposes an unfair burden upon the teacher's colleagues. . . . If, however, my view of section 30 is correct, all that is necessary is that the authority should make its administrative arrangements on the basis of that view. It may mean employing a few more teachers either part-time or full-time, but, when the cost is compared with the heavy expenditure already committed to the cause of non-discrimination in our society, expense would not in this context appear to be a sound reason for requiring a narrow meaning to be given to the words of the statute. The question, therefore, as to whether Mr Ahmad broke his contract ultimately depends upon an examination of the particular circumstances of his case. . . . I therefore would allow the appeal . . .

Orr LJ delivered a judgment concurring with **Lord Denning MR.**

Appeal dismissed.

NOTES

1. The appellant also lost his claim under the ECHR.[7] The European Commission dismissed the case at the admissibility stage: in relying upon the applicant's contract of employment, the ILEA had not arbitrarily disregarded the applicant's freedom of religion as protected by Article 9, ECHR.

2. In *Esson v United Transport Executive*,[8] a bus conductor refused to work on Saturdays after he had become a Seventh Day Adventist. His dismissal was held not to be unfair because he was in breach of contract and because his failure to take his share of Saturday work placed an unreasonable burden upon his fellow employees. Similarly, in *Storey v Allied Breweries*,[9] in which it was held that it was not unfair to dismiss a chambermaid who refused to do new Sunday rota work in order to take the elderly to church on Sunday mornings, since her refusal imposed a burden on other chambermaids and she could attend Sunday evening services.

3. British government contracts (unlike Federal government contracts in the United States) do not require that the firm awarded the contract not follow an employment policy that discriminates on religious grounds.[10]

4. In *Yassin v Northwest Homecare Ltd*[11] the applicant, a Muslim, was dropped from a sales representative training course after requesting an hour off to attend Friday prayers at the Mosque. The Tribunal awarded him £3,000 compensation for injury to feelings and loss of potential earnings for discrimination contrary to the Race Relations Act 1976. The Tribunal stated:

'The requirement not to attend the Mosque ... seems to us to be wholly unreasonable. In a working day of 12 or 13 hours there had to be breaks of refreshment and rest. The working day was not strictly defined. One hour a week to visit the Mosque (and the hour included travelling time) could easily be accommodated, even when a high commitment to the job was required.'

Can this case be distinguished from the Ahmad case? Other employment cases concerning Muslims and Sikhs that have been considered as indirect racial discrimination under the Race Relations Act.[12]

6 Religious holy days

Prais v EC Council Case 130/75 [1976] ECR 1589, [1976] 2 CMLR 708, European Court of Justice

The plaintiff, a British national, applied for a job in the European Communities as a translator. By a letter of 23 April 1975 she was told that the written examination would be on 16 May 1975. By a letter of 25 April 1975, the plaintiff informed the Council that she was unable to attend on 16 May because she was Jewish and that day was a Jewish holy day. The application form had no place for an applicant's religion and the plaintiff had not otherwise informed the Council of her religion. By a letter of 5 May, the Council replied that the plaintiff could not be given an alternative date for the examination for security and administrative reasons. In her

7 *Ahmad v United Kingdom* (1982) 4 EHRR 126.
8 [1975] IRLR 48, Int. Trib.
9 (1976) 84 IRLIB 9, Int. Trib.
10 See C. Turpin, *Government Contracts* (1972) pp. 257–258.
11 CRERep 1993, p. 21, Ind Trib.
12 See below, pp. 1100–1101.

application to the European Court of Justice, the plaintiff sought the annulment of the decisions taken against her and damages.

JUDGMENT OF THE COURT

The plaintiff claims that Article 27 of the Staff Regulations ['Officials shall be selected without reference to race, creed or sex'] is to be interpreted in such a manner that the defendant should so arrange the dates of tests for competitions to enter its service as to enable every candidate to take part in these tests, whatever his religious circumstances. Alternatively the right of freedom of religion guaranteed by the European Convention [Article 9] so requires. . . .

The defendant does not . . . seek to suggest that the right of freedom of religion as embodied in the European Convention does not form part of the fundamental rights recognized in Community law, but says that neither the Staff Regulations nor the European Convention are to be understood as according to the plaintiff the rights she claims.

The defendant submits that such an obligation would force it to set up an elaborate administrative machinery. Article 27 does not limit its application to any particular creeds by enumerating them, and it would be necessary to ascertain the details of all religions practised in any Member State in order to avoid fixing for a test a date or time which might offend against the tenets of any such religion and make it impossible for a candidate of that religious persuasion to take part in the test. . . .

When the competition [for posts] is on the basis of tests, the principle of equality necessitates that the tests shall be on the same conditions for all candidates, and in the case of written tests the practical difficulties of comparison require that the written tests for all candidates should be the same.

It is therefore of great importance that the date of the written tests should be the same for all candidates.

The interests of participants not to have a date fixed for the test which is unsuitable must be balanced against this necessity.

If a candidate informs the appointing authority that religious reasons make certain dates impossible for him the appointing authority should take this into account in fixing the date for written tests, and endeavour to avoid such dates.

On the other hand if the candidate does not inform the appointing authority in good time of his difficulties, the appointing authority would be justified in refusing to afford an alternative date, particularly if there are other candidates who have been convoked for the test.

If it is desirable that an appointing authority informs itself in a general way of dates which might be unsuitable for religious reasons, and seeks to avoid fixing such dates for tests, nevertheless, for the reasons indicated above, neither the Staff Regulations nor the fundamental rights already referred to can be considered as imposing on the appointing authority a duty to avoid a conflict with a religious requirement of which the authority has not been informed.

In so far as the defendant, if informed of the difficulty in good time, would have been obliged to take reasonable steps to avoid fixing for a test a date which would make it impossible for a person of a particular religious persuasion to undergo the test, it can be said that the defendant in the present case was not informed of the unsuitability of certain days until the date for the test had been fixed, and the defendant was in its discretion entitled to refuse to fix a different date when the other candidates had already been convoked.

Application dismissed.

NOTE

In his opinion in the case, the Advocate General (Mr J-P Warner) summarised British practice in regard to examinations:

'It seems to be the invariable practice of professional and academic bodies in the United Kingdom to make, when requested, alternative arrangements for observant Jewish candidates whose examinations fall on Jewish holy days. . . . The letter from the Civil Service Commission shows that its practice is quite different. Under the heading of "Criteria observed when setting examination dates" it states:

"Known factors which could affect particular groups of candidates would be taken into account as far as is possible when constructing the programme. For example, the Board of Directors of British Jews have for many years provided the Commission with a list of dates on which Jewish Holy days are given . . . [However]

   (i)   The Commission expects all candidates to make arrangements to attend the examination on the date(s) set.

   (ii) An examination is not deferred, or the date altered, to suit the needs of individual candidates.

  (iii) Special separate sittings are not arranged for individuals who cannot attend on the examination dates.'"

Ostreicher v Secretary of State for the Environment [1978] 3 All ER 82, [1978] 1 WLR 810, Court of Appeal

The applicant, a devout Jewess, lodged an objection through her surveyor, Mr L, to a compulsory purchase order made by the second respondent, a local authority, which applied to houses which she owned. By a letter of 5 February 1976, Mr L was informed that the inquiry would be held on 21 April 1976. This was one of 11 annual Jewish festival days on which the applicant was forbidden to work or to employ anyone to work for her. On 1 April 1976, Mr L wrote to the first respondent stating that the applicant was unable to attend the hearing for religious reasons. He did not mention the question of representation. In the letter, Mr L indicated the reasons for the applicant's objection to the order and asked for a special hearing at which they could be put orally in respect of one of the houses.

On 7 April, the first respondent rejected this request and suggested that the applicant could be represented at the inquiry. The inquiry was held on the scheduled day and the order confirmed. By notice of motion, the applicant applied under the Housing Act 1957, Sch. 4, para. 2, for the order to be quashed for non-compliance with the rules of natural justice in not giving her an opportunity of being heard by the inspector who held the inquiry. The applicant appealed to the Court of Appeal against an order dismissing her application.

Lord Denning MR: It is one of the elementary principles of natural justice, no matter whether it is in a judicial proceeding or an administrative inquiry, that everything should be done fairly: and that any party or objector should be given a fair opportunity of being heard. . . . Sometimes a refusal of an adjournment is unfair, but quite often it is fair. It depends on the circumstances of each particular case. . . . There is a distinction between an administrative inquiry and judicial proceedings before a court. An administrative inquiry has to be arranged long beforehand. There are many objectors to consider as well as the proponents of the plan. It is a serious matter to put all the arrangements aside on the application of one objector out of many. The proper way to deal with it, if called on to do so, is to continue with the inquiry and hear all the representatives present; and then, if one objector is unavoidably absent, to hear his objections on a later day when he can be there. There is ample power in the rules for the inspector to allow adjournments as and when reasonably required.

   . . . it seems to me that the men at the department acted perfectly reasonably in what they did. First, they acted reasonably in arranging the date of 21st April, the Wednesday after Easter Monday. . . . I cannot think that even in Hackney [with its high Jewish population] it would be wrong for the Secretary of State to give that date as a suitable date for the inquiry. Indeed, no objection was ever taken to it by anyone until two or three months later when this letter of 1st April 1976 was written on behalf of Mr and Mrs Ostreicher. In that letter the surveyors do not say that they could not attend themselves or that anyone else could not attend on behalf of Mr and Mrs Ostreicher to look after their interests. Moreover that letter only refers to one house, no 16. . . . The Secretary of State's representative wrote back quite reasonably. He said: 'Should your clients deem it necessary they are open of course to arrange to be represented at the inquiry in their absence.' . . . There was no reply to that letter. If

Mr and Mrs Ostreicher or their representative thought that there ought to be a postponement or an adjournment, so far as their houses were concerned, they could have written back and said so. . . .

Second, the inspector acted reasonably in going on with the inquiry as he did. No representative turned up on behalf of Mr and Mrs Ostreicher. It seems to me that the inspector could well have understood from what had happened that they were content to leave the position as it was on the papers. . . . I see no want of natural justice whatever in what the inspector did either at the inquiry and later on in making his report.

. . . I would dismiss the appeal accordingly.

Shaw LJ concurred. **Waller LJ** delivered a concurring judgment.

Appeal dismissed.

NOTES

1. At first instance, Sir Douglas Frank QC, sitting as a deputy High Court judge, had rejected an argument based upon the freedom of religion guarantee in Art. 9 ECHR on the ground that it was 'of little assistance because it does not apply and moreover it is in vague terms'.[13] He also referred to the dictum in *Prais v EC Council*, above, that the administration must be given notice in good time of an objection to a proposed date.

2. In *J H Walker Ltd v Hussain*.[14] Muslim employees from the Indian subcontinent of ten years' standing who had always been allowed to take off Eid, a religious holiday, as a part of their annual holiday or as unpaid leave were no longer allowed to do so following a change in the firm's holiday arrangements that affected all workers. This was held to be indirect discrimination contrary to the Race Relations Act 1976. It was otherwise not illegal, as direct religious discrimination is not prohibited.

7　Religion and the law of trusts and succession

Re Lysaght[15] [1966] Ch 191, [1965] 3 WLR 391, [1965] 2 All ER 888, Buckley J

By her will, the testatrix established a trust for scholarships tenable at the Royal College of Surgeons. To qualify, a student had to be 'of the male sex and a British born subject and not of the Jewish or Roman Catholic faith'. Buckley J rejected the College's submission that the religious discrimination clause was void for uncertainty. He then considered in the following extract a submission by another beneficiary under the will that the trust as a whole was contrary to public policy.

Buckley J: . . . I accept that racial and religious discrimination is nowadays widely regarded as deplorable in many respects and I am aware that there is a Bill dealing with racial relations at present under consideration by Parliament, but I think that it is going much too far to say that the endowment of a charity, the beneficiaries of which are to be drawn from a particular faith or are to exclude adherents to a particular faith, is contrary to public policy. The testatrix's desire to exclude persons of the Jewish faith or of the Roman Catholic faith from those eligible for the studentship in the present case appears to me to be unamiable, and I would accept Mr Clauson's suggestion that it is undesirable, but it is not, I think, contrary to public policy. . . .

13　[1978] 1 All ER 591.
14　[1996] IRLR 11, EAT.
15　On *Re Lysaght*, see (1965) 29 Conv 407, (1966) 82 LQR 10.

[Buckley J then, after holding that it was an essential part of the testatrix's intention that the College should be a trustee and noting that the College felt itself unable to be such if it discriminated on religious grounds, ordered by way of scheme that the trust should be administered by the College with the offending words omitted.]

Declaration accordingly.

Blathwayt v Baron Cawley [1976] AC 397, [1975] 3 WLR 684, [1975] 3 All ER 625, House of Lords

One question in this case was whether a forfeiture clause in a trust established by the will by which a beneficiary forfeited his interest if he 'be or become a Roman Catholic' was invalid for reasons of public policy. The following extract concerns this question only.

Lord Wilberforce: . . . Finally, as to public policy . . . it was said that the law of England was now set against discrimination on a number of grounds including religious grounds, and appeal was made to the Race Relations Act 1968 which does not refer to religion and to the European Convention on Human Rights of 1950 which refers to freedom of religion and to enjoyment of that freedom and other freedoms without discrimination on the ground of religion. My Lords, I do not doubt that conceptions of public policy should move with the times and that widely accepted treaties and statutes may point the direction in which such conceptions, as applied by the courts, ought to move. It may well be that conditions such as this are, or at least are becoming inconsistent with standards now widely accepted. But acceptance of this does not persuade me that we are justified, particularly in relation to a will which came into effect as long ago as 1936 and which has twice been the subject of judicial consideration, in introducing for the first time a rule of law which would go far beyond the mere avoidance of discrimination on religious grounds. To do so would bring about a substantial reduction of another freedom, firmly rooted in our law, namely that of testamentary disposition. Discrimination is not the same thing as choice; it operates over a larger and less personal area, and neither by express provision nor by implication has private selection yet become a matter of public policy.

Lord Cross of Chelsea: . . . Turning to the question of public policy, it is true that it is widely thought nowadays that it is wrong for government to treat some of its citizens less favourably than others because of differences in their religious beliefs; but it does not follow from that that it is against public policy for an adherent of one religion to distinguish in disposing of his property between adherents of his faith and those of another. So to hold would amount to saying that though it is in order for a man to have a mild preference for one religion as opposed to another it is disreputable for him to be convinced of the importance of holding true religious beliefs and the fact that his religious beliefs are the true ones.

Lord Simon, Lord Edmund-Davies and **Lord Fraser** delivered speeches to the same effect.

NOTES

1. Contrast the refusal of the courts in these cases to find private religious discrimination contrary to public policy with the Race Relations Act 1976 which prohibits private racial discrimination on grounds of colour in charitable trusts.[16]
2. Trusts for the advancement of religion are valid whatever the religion benefited.[17] They are also charitable.[18] This is probably true of all religions, although the cases

16 See below, p. 1152.
17 See *Bowman v Secular Society*, above, p. 1028, and *Bourne v Keane*, above, p. 1037.
18 See *Re South Place Ethical Society*, above p. 1036. On the charitable status of the Exclusive Brethern and the Unification Church, see above, p. 1031.

are as yet limited to Christianity and the Jewish religion. To be charitable a trust must be for the public benefit.[19] A trust for a Roman Catholic order of strictly cloistered and contemplative nuns is therefore not charitable.[20]

3. In *Re Remnant's Settlement Trusts, Hooper v Wenhaston*,[1] clauses in a will by which grandchildren would forfeit their interests under it if they became Roman Catholics were deleted under the Variation of Trusts Act 1958. The clauses were regarded as undesirable in the particular circumstances of the family and their deletion was to the advantage of all possible beneficiaries. In *Re Tepper's Will Trusts*[2] grandchildren received gifts under a will 'provided that they shall remain within the Jewish faith and shall not marry outside the Jewish faith'. Responding to an argument that the proviso contained a condition subsequent that was void for uncertainty, Scott J adjourned the summons to allow evidence to be adduced as to the religion practised by the testator which might make it possible to conclude with sufficient certainty what the expression 'the Jewish faith' meant. This approach was used to avoid *Clayton v Ramsden*[3] where a majority of the House of Lords considered that the phrase 'of the Jewish faith' was uncertain so that a similar condition subsequent was void for uncertainty. In neither case would it appear to have been argued that the limitation was contrary to public policy as being restrictive of freedom of religion.

8   Religion and immigration

Home Office Policy on Religion and Immigration 424 HC Deb 5 July 1946 cols 2580–2

Mr Ede (Home Secretary)

I am not prepared to apply religious or political tests to people who desire to come into this country unless it can be established that they desire to come here to carry on subversive propaganda as defined by the Acts concerned with seditious practices. . . .

I desire that the ancient record of this country as a place of free speech, where the flow of ideas from all parts of the world is welcome, may be maintained; and while I will not guarantee that some of the people I admit may not be charlatans, may not . . . even be false prophets on occasion, I desire to impose no censorship other than that which the law entitles me to impose against subversive propaganda on any person who desires to come to this country to meet people of his own persuasion. I am confident of this, that as far as this particular movement is concerned, there are some people in this country who gain spiritual sustenance from it. . . . Therefore I desire to live and let live in this particular matter.

NOTES

1. The 'particular movement' to which the Home Secretary referred was Moral Re-Armament, or the Oxford Group Movement, founded by Dr Buchman, an American evangelist. The statement was made following criticism in Parliament of Mr Ede's decision to admit into the UK a number of aliens who were members of the Movement and who intended to further its cause here. The persons admitted had committed no

---

19 *Re Hetherington* [1990] Ch 1, Ch D (a trust for the saying of masses which would in practice be said in public a valid charitable trust).
20 *Gilmour v Coats* [1949] AC 426, HL. See *Tudor on Charities* (7th edn, 1984) pp. 43–82.
1   [1970] Ch 560, Ch D.
2   [1987] Ch 358, Ch D.
3   Below, p. 1152.

crime under UK law. The criticism was based mainly on the fact that certain leading members of the Group had been Nazi sympathisers.

2. It would seem that the 1946 statement still represents Home Office policy. In 1976, the Home Office was not prepared to exclude American members of the Children of God when police inquiries had produced no evidence of criminal activities in the UK (apart from minor street collection, etc, offences). Allegations that young people over 18 had been estranged from their families did not raise any issue of criminal law: Home Office Minister (Dr S. Summerskill).[4] The Home Secretary's discretionary power to exclude aliens and other non-'patrials' from the UK is based upon the Immigration Act 1971, s. 3 and is exercised in accordance with Immigration Rules made by him under that section. The Rules provide for the admission of ministers of religion, missionaries and members of religious orders coming to work as such, including those engaged in teaching.[5] On scientology, see below. On the special position under the Treaty of Rome of EU citizens who wish to enter the UK for employment, see *Van Duyn v Home Office*.[6] In 1976, when rumour had it that a Danish film maker, Jens Thorsen, was planning to enter the UK to make a film portraying the sexual life of Christ, the Under Secretary of State for the Home Department pointed out that were Thorsen, a Common Market national, actually to seek entry into the UK the question would arise whether he could be excluded under the Treaty of Rome on grounds of 'public policy'.[7]

3. In 1968, the Minister of Health (Mr Robinson) announced[8] that the government had decided that scientology was 'socially harmful' (although not illegal) and that foreign nationals seeking entry to work or study at scientology establishments in the UK would be refused admission. The Minister described scientology as 'a pseudo-philosophical cult'; he did not refer to it as a religion. It was described by Sir John Foster in his government-sponsored *Enquiry into the Practice and Effects of Scientology*,[9] as a form of psychological medicine or therapy. Sir John Foster criticised the 1968 ban on the ground that 'the mere fact that someone is a Scientologist is . . . no reason for excluding him . . . when there is nothing in law to prevent his fellows who are citizens in this country from practising Scientology here.'

In *Schmidt v Secretary of State for Home Affairs*[10] the Court of Appeal held that the plaintiffs, who had been refused an extension of their permits to enter the United Kingdom to study at the Hubbard College of Scientology at East Grinstead in accordance with the new policy, had no cause of action in English law; the Home Secretary had acted properly within his power to exclude aliens under the Aliens Order 1953. In *Van Duyn v Home Office*[11] a Dutch secretary was refused entry into the United Kingdom to work at the same College. The European Court of Justice ruled that the refusal was not contrary to Art. 48 of the Treaty of Rome (by which nationals of European Communities countries have, subject to certain limitations, freedom of movement for employment purposes within the Communities); it could be justified as being 'on the grounds of public policy' (Art. 48(3)). An application to Strasbourg by the Church of Scientology under Art. 9 ECHR also failed because it does not protect companies (such as the Church).[12]

In 1980, the Home Secretary (Mr Whitelaw) lifted the general ban on Scientologists[13] so that scientology students are admitted.

4   905 HC Deb, 11 February 1976, cols. 584–8.
5   See below, note 3.
6   Below, n. 3.
7   918 HC Deb, 26 October 1976, cols. 239–248.
8   769 HC Deb, 25 July 1968, written answers, col. 189.
9   1971–72 HC 52, Chap. 9.
10   [1969] 2 Ch 149, CA.
11   Case 41/74 [1975] Ch 358, ECJ.
12   *Church of X v UK* 12 YBECHR 306 (1969).
13   988 HC Deb, 16 July 1980, written answers, col. 578.

CHAPTER 11

Freedom from racial discrimination

1 Introduction[1]

(A) THE BACKGROUND TO THE RACE RELATIONS ACT 1976

The Race Relations Act 1976 (the 1976 Act) is the third Act of Parliament on racial discrimination. It repealed the Race Relations Act 1968 and what remained of the Race Relations Act 1965. In much of its form and its content, the 1976 Act follows the pattern of the Sex Discrimination Act 1975. It was understood that the two might later be merged, but there are no current plans for this.[2]

The common law had only incidentally and exceptionally offered protection against racial discrimination before Parliament acted.[3] In the words of Lord Simon in *Applin v Race Relations Board*:[4]

'The common law before the making of the first Race Relations Act (1965) was that people could discriminate against others on the ground of colour, etc., to their hearts' content. This unbridled capacity to discriminate was the mischief and defect for which common law did not provide. The remedy Parliament resolved and appointed was to make certain acts of discrimination unlawful. The reason for the remedy must have been that discrimination was thought to be socially divisive (indeed, section 6 of the Act of 1965 [incitement to racial hatred] suggests, potentially subversive of public order) and derogatory to human dignity.'

The arrival of immigrants from the West Indies and later India and Pakistan to take jobs in the 1950s and 1960s resulted in friction and discrimination. Racial incidents such as the Notting Hill riots in 1958 and the example of the Civil Rights Act 1964 in the US led Parliament, after much hesitation, to enact the Race Relations Act 1965. This made it illegal to discriminate in certain places of public resort (e.g. pubs and

---

1 On the law of racial discrimination generally, see G. Bindman, in R. Blackburn (ed.), *Constitutional Studies* (1992), Chap. 7; C. Bourne and J. Whitmore, *Anti-Discrimination Law in Britain* (1996); A. Lester and G. Bindman, *Race and Law* (1972); J. Gregory, *Sex, Race and the Law* (1987); B. Hepple and E. M. Szyszczak (eds.), *Discrimination: the Limits of the Law* (1992); C. McCrudden, in C. McCrudden and G. Chambers (eds.), *Individual Rights and the Law in Britain* (1994), Chap. 13. On the limitations of law as a means of tackling racial inequality, see L. Lustgarten, (1986) 49 MLR 68. For a critical review of the working of the 1976 Act, see C. McCrudden, D. J. Smith and C. Brown, *Racial Justice at Work* (1991). The CRE has published a *Second Review of the Race Relations Act 1976* (1992) *and Reform of the Race Relations Act 1976* (1998), which both make recommendations for changes to the Act. For recommendations for the reform of UK anti-discrimination law, see B. Hepple et al., *Improving Equality Law: the Options* (1997), a report by Justice and the Runnymede Trust and *Equality: A New Framework* (2000), a report by the Cambridge Centre for Public Law and the Judge Institute of Management Studies.
2 A single anti-discrimination law is recommended in *Equality: A New Framework*, op. cit., at n. 1.
3 See, e.g. *Constantine v Imperial Hotels Ltd*, below, p. 1135, and *Scala Ballroom Ltd v Ratcliffe*. [1958] 3 All ER 220, CA (officials of Musicians' Union did not commit the tort of conspiracy by refusing to allow members to play in a ballroom with a colour bar to protect livelihood of its coloured members).
4 [1975] AC 259 at 286, HL.

dance halls) and in the disposal of tenancies, and created an offence of incitement to racial hatred. Conciliation procedures operated by the Race Relations Board (RRB) and local conciliation committees were the key to enforcement of the Act, with recourse to the courts by the Attorney-General available as a last resort. These modest provisions soon proved insufficient and were replaced or supplemented by those of the Race Relations Act 1968. This was enacted in the light of evidence[5] that much discrimination existed in areas not covered by the law and that the 1965 Act enforcement procedures needed strengthening. The violent riots in Watts in Los Angeles and elsewhere in the US in the mid-1960s also cast their shadow. The 1968 Act, which was influenced by the favourable assessment in the Street Report[6] of the effectiveness of US race legislation, extended the prohibition of discrimination to include goods, facilities and services generally, employment, housing and advertisements and modified the system of enforcement mainly by allowing the RRB to take cases to court instead of the Attorney General if conciliation failed. The Act also established a Community Relations Commission (CRC) to promote good race relations. The 1968 Act, in its turn, soon came to be seen as inadequate. The government White Paper[7] introducing the present 1976 Act contains the following passages justifying legislation on racial discrimination generally and suggesting the new direction it should take:

'4. . . . The Government's proposals are based on a clear recognition of the proposition that the overwhelming majority of the coloured population[8] is here to stay, that a substantial and increasing proportion of that population belongs to this country, and that the time has come for a determined effort by Government, by industry and unions, and by ordinary men and women, to ensure fair and equal treatment for all our people, regardless of their race, colour, or national origins. Racial discrimination, and the remediable disadvantages experienced by sections of the community because of their colour or ethnic origins are not only morally unacceptable, not only individual injustices for which there must be remedies, but also a form of economic and social waste which we as a society cannot afford. . . .
23. Legislation is the essential pre-condition for an effective policy to combat the problems experienced by the coloured minority groups and to promote equality of opportunity and treatment. It is a necessary pre-condition for dealing with explicit discriminatory actions or accumulated disadvantages. Where unfair discrimination is involved, the necessity of a legal remedy is now generally accepted. To fail to provide a remedy against an injustice strikes at the rule of law. To abandon a whole group of people in society without legal redress against unfair discrimination is to leave them with no option but to find their own redress. It is no longer necessary to recite the immense damage, material as well as moral, which ensues when a minority loses faith in the capacity of social institutions to be impartial and fair. . . .
25. Legislation is capable of dealing not only with discriminatory acts but with patterns of discrimination, particularly with patterns which, because of the effects of past discrimination, may not any longer involve explicit acts of discrimination. Legislation, however, is not, and can never be, a sufficient condition for effective progress towards equality of opportunity. A wide range of administrative and voluntary measures are needed to give practical effect to the objectives of the law. But the legislative framework must be right. It must be comprehensive in its scope, and its enforcement provisions must not only be capable of providing redress for the victim of individual injustice but also of detecting and eliminating unfair discriminatory practices. . . .

5   See the PEP Report, *Racial Discrimination in Britain* (1967).
6   H. Street, G. Howe and G. Bindman, *Report on Anti-Discrimination Legislation* (1967).
7   *Racial Discrimination*, Cmnd. 6234.
8   *Ed.* The 1991 census indicated that the 'ethnic' population of Great Britain was 3,015,000 ('white' population 51,874,000). This was divided as follows: 27.9% Indian; 15.8% Pakistani; 5.4% Bangladeshi; 5.2% Chinese; 6.6% 'other Asian'; 16.6% Caribbean; 7% African; 5.9% 'other black'; 9.6% 'other': *Whitaker's Almanack* (1994), p. 119.

31. It is not possible to provide a quantifiable measure of the practical impact of the 1968 Act. Generally, the law has had an important declaratory effect and has given support to those who do not wish to discriminate but who would otherwise feel compelled to do so by social pressure. It has also made crude, overt forms of racial discrimination much less common. Discriminatory advertisements and notices have virtually disappeared both from the press and from public advertisement boards. Discriminatory conditions have largely disappeared from the rules governing insurance and other financial matters, and they are being removed from tenancy agreements. It is less common for an employer to refuse to accept any coloured workers and there has been some movement of coloured workers into more desirable jobs. . . .

33. And yet, at the end of the decade, both statutory bodies have forcefully drawn attention to the inability of the legislation to deal with widespread patterns of discrimination, especially in employment and housing, a lack of confidence among minority groups in the effectiveness of the law, and a lack of credibility in the efficacy of the work of the Race Relations Board and the Community Relations Commission themselves. The continuing unequal status of Britain's racial minorities and the extent of the disadvantage from which they suffer provide ample evidence of the inadequacy of existing policies.'

Evidence of the 'continuing unequal status' and 'disadvantage' in employment and other areas had been produced in a series of PEP Reports.[9] A strike by Asian workers in the Mansfield Hosiery Mills in 1972, which revealed that skilled jobs were being reserved exclusively for whites,[10] was also important.

(B) THE AREAS OF CONDUCT CONTROLLED BY THE 1976 ACT

The areas covered by the 1976 Act are essentially those covered in 1968 although there are a number of particular changes, including the extension of the law to cover contract workers (s. 7), partnerships (s. 10) and clubs (s. 25).[11] The principle that the law should not apply to 'personal and intimate relationships' is retained.[12] The definition of discrimination is widened to include discrimination on the ground of nationality (s. 3) and, in accordance with the new strategy of attacking 'patterns of discrimination' (such as that in the Mansfield Hosiery Mills case) as well as particular 'discriminatory acts', 'indirect discrimination' (s. 1(1)(b)) and 'discriminatory practices' (s. 28) are prohibited too.

The remainder of this chapter deals with most aspects of the 1976 Act, but does not consider in detail the provisions of Part II of the Act on employment and related matters. Although discrimination in employment is of prime importance, it is best seen as an area of employment law and is fully treated in books on that subject.[13]

---

9 D. Smith, *Racial Disadvantage in Employment* (1974); N. McIntosh and D. Smith, *The Extent of Racial Discrimination* (1974); D. Smith and A. Whalley, *Racial Minorities and Public Housing* (1975), and D. Smith, *The Facts of Racial Disadvantage* (1976). See since the 1976 Act, *Racial Disadvantage*, 5th Report of the Home Affairs Committee, 1980–81 HC 424–I; the *Scarman Report on the Brixton Disorders* 10–12 April 1981, Cmnd. 8427; and *Racial Discrimination: 17 Years After the Act*, a study by the Policy Studies Institute for the CRE (1985).
10 RRB Report 1972, p. 10.
11 The 1976 Act originally did not make illegal discrimination by or in respect to barristers. A 1990 amendment makes unlawful discrimination on racial grounds in relation to the offering of a pupillage or tenancy or the giving of instructions to a barrister: Race Relations Act 1976, s. 26A. In 1993, racial discrimination was made a specific professional disciplinary offence for solicitors: CRE 1993 Annual Report, p. 9. In 1998, the Lord Chancellor wrote to heads of chambers asking them to encourage more ethnic minority lawyers to put themselves forward for silk or for judicial appointment: (1998) 148 NLJ 394.
12 Cmnd. 6234, p. 15. E.g. the Act does not apply to employment in a private household (s. 4(3)) or to accommodation in small premises (s. 22).
13 See, e.g., I. T. Smith and J. Wood, *Industrial Law* (7th edn, 2000), Chap. 5.

It may be noted, in connection with employment that, although not required by the 1976 Act,[14] central government contracts contain a term by which contractors must comply with the non-discrimination provisions of the 1976 Act in respect of their workforce.[15] Local authorities have commonly followed a similar practice, although their freedom to do so has been considerably restricted by the Local Government Act 1988, ss. 17–18, which, subject to certain exceptions reflecting s. 71 of the 1976 Act, require them not to take 'non-commercial matters', which include the terms and conditions of employment of a contractor's workforce, into account in their contracts.

(C) THE COMMISSION FOR RACIAL EQUALITY AND REMEDIES UNDER THE 1976 ACT

As in the 1968 Act, discrimination is treated as a statutory tort. Apart from the offences of incitement to racial hatred[16] and certain minor offences,[17] the remedies provided by the law remain civil, not criminal. In other respects the enforcement machinery in the 1976 Act differs markedly from that which predated it. The emphasis in the earlier legislation had been on enforcement by conciliation by the RRB following complaints by individuals of particular 'discriminatory acts'. Three major changes were made. Firstly, conciliation was largely abandoned; nearly all complaints may be taken straight to court instead. Secondly, the decision to take a case to court is in most cases in the hands of the individual complainant; the CRE is there simply to offer assistance if the complainant wants it. The CRE may take legal proceedings in a few 'reserved' cases. Thirdly, in keeping again with the realisation that underlying 'patterns of discrimination' need to be tackled as well as (and perhaps more than) individual cases of 'discriminatory acts', the CRE is given wide-ranging authority to conduct formal investigations on its own initiative. Armed with a new power to subpoena evidence in 'named person investigations', the CRE may investigate 'discriminatory acts' or 'patterns of discrimination' and may issue non-discrimination notices that are binding in law. Unfortunately, the power to conduct formal investigations has been seriously undermined by judicial interpretation.[18] For this and other reasons the formal investigation procedure has not proved a great success.

(D) STEPHEN LAWRENCE INQUIRY

This has had a considerable impact upon government and public attitudes to race relations and the law. It arose out of the murder in 1993 of Stephen Lawrence, an 18 year old black youth, who was stabbed to death by a gang of white youths while waiting for a bus in Eltham, London. A police investigation did not lead to any public prosecution. In 1996, a private prosecution was brought by the deceased's parents, leading to the trial of three youths, who were acquitted in the absence of firm or sustainable evidence.[19] The deceased's parents then led a campaign alleging racial discrimination on the part of Metropolitan Police in the investigation of the case. In 1997, the unanimous verdict of the jury in the inquest into Stephen Lawrence's death

---

14 The CRE has recommended that persons tendering for contracts should be subject to the 1976 Act: *Reform of the Race Relations Act 1976* (1998).
15 *Second Review of the Race Relations Act 1976* (1992) p. 41. However, Whitehall does not monitor compliance: ibid.
16 Now in the Public Order Act 1986, below, p. 1152.
17 E.g. that in the 1976 Act, s. 29(5) below, p. 1150.
18 See the *Prestige* and *Amari* cases, below, pp. 1163 and 1165.
19 The case against two other youths was dismissed at the committal stage.

was that he had been 'unlawfully killed in a completely unprovoked racist attack by five white youths'. A Government Inquiry was then established by the Home Secretary to inquire into matters arising from the death of Stephen Lawrence 'particularly to identify the lessons to be learned for the investigation and prosecution of racially motivated offences'. The Macpherson Report[20] found that there was 'institutional racism' in the Metropolitan Police and recommended a number of reforms. One recommendation was that police forces generally should be made subject to the Race Relations Act 1976, a recommendation that has been implemented by the Race Relations (Amendment) Act 2000. The following extract from the Macpherson Report defines and considers 'institutional racism'.

'6.1 A central and vital issue which has permeated our Inquiry has been the issue of racism. The chilling condemnation, made by and on behalf of Mr & Mrs Lawrence at and after the Inquest in February 1997 ... of the police and of the system of English justice, has sounded through all the months of our consideration of the evidence Mr & Mrs Lawrence allege and fervently believe that their colour, culture and ethnic origin, and that of their murdered son, have throughout affected the way in which the case has been dealt with and pursued. ... These allegations are plainly supported by many people, both black and white, in our Public Gallery and in the community at large. ...

6.3 In this Inquiry we have not heard evidence of overt racism or discrimination, unless it can be said that the use of inappropriate expressions such as 'coloured' or 'negro' fall into that category. The use of such words, which are now well known to be offensive, displays at least insensitivity and lack of training. A number of officers used such terms, and some did not even during their evidence seem to understand that the terms were offensive and should not be used.

6.4 Racism in general terms consists of conduct or words or practices which disadvantage or advantage people because of their colour, culture, or ethnic origin. In its more subtle form it is as damaging as in its overt form. ...

6.7 In 1981 Lord Scarman's Report into The Brixton Disorders was presented to Parliament. In that seminal report Lord Scarman responded to the suggestion that '*Britain is an institutionally racist society,*' in this way:—

'*If, by* [institutionally racist] *it is meant that it* [Britain]*is a society which knowingly, as a matter of policy, discriminates against black people, I reject the allegation. If, however, the suggestion being made is that practices may be adopted by public bodies as well as private individuals which are unwittingly discriminatory against black people, then this is an allegation which deserves serious consideration, and, where proved, swift remedy*'. (Para 2.22, p. 11 — Scarman Report). ...

6.12 Lord Scarman further said:—

'*All the evidence I have received, both on the subject of racial disadvantage and more generally, suggests that racialism and discrimination against black people — often hidden, sometimes unconscious — remain a major source of social tension and conflict.*' (Para 6.35, p. 110).

6.13 Thus Lord Scarman accepted the existence of what he termed '*unwitting*' or '*unconscious*' racism. To those adjectives can be added a third, namely '*unintentional*'. ...

6.27 The MPS Black Police Association's spokesmen, in their written submission to the Inquiry, para 3.2, said this:—

'*...institutional racism...permeates the Metropolitan Police Service. This issue above all others is central to the attitudes, values and beliefs, which lead officers to act, albeit unconsciously and for the most part unintentionally, and treat others differently solely because of their ethnicity or culture*' ...

6.28 ...We believe that it is essential that the views of these officers should be closely heeded and respected. ...

---

20 Cmnd. 4262. The inquiry was conducted by Macpherson J, retired High Court judge. See A. Rutherford, 149 NLJ 345, and S. Hall, *Connections*, Spring 2000, 14.

6.34 For the purposes of our Inquiry the concept of institutional racism which we apply consists of:

> The collective failure of an organisation to provide an appropriate and professional service to people because of their colour, culture, or ethnic origin. It can be seen or detected in processes, attitudes and behaviour which amount to discrimination through unwitting prejudice, ignorance, thoughtlessness and racist stereotyping which disadvantage minority ethnic people. ...

> It persists because of the failure of the organisation openly and adequately to recognise and address its existence and causes by policy, example and leadership. Without recognition and action to eliminate such racism it can prevail as part of the ethos or culture of the organisation. It is a corrosive disease. ...

6.45 Institutional racism is in our view primarily apparent in what we have seen and heard in the following areas:—

    (a) in the actual investigation including the family's treatment at the hospital, the initial reaction to the victim and witness Duwayne Brooks, the family liaison, the failure of many officers to recognise Stephen's murder as a purely *'racially motivated'* crime, the lack of urgency and commitment in some areas of the investigation.

    (b) countrywide in the disparity to 'stop and search figures'. Whilst we acknowledge and recognise the complexity of this issue and in particular the other factors which can be prayed in aid to explain the disparities, such as demographic mix, school exclusions, unemployment, and recording procedures, there remains, in our judgment, a clear core conclusion of racist stereotyping;

    (c) countrywide in the significant under-reporting of 'racial incidents' occasioned largely by a lack of confidence in the police and their perceived unwillingness to take such incidents seriously. Again we are conscious of other factors at play, but we find irresistible the conclusion that a core cause of under-reporting is the inadequate response of the Police Service which generates a lack of confidence in victims to report incidents; and

    (d) in the identified failure of police training; as evidenced by the HMIC Report, *'Winning the Race'* and the Police Training Council Report, and the clear evidence in Part I of this Inquiry which demonstrated that not a single officer questioned before us in 1998 had received any training of significance in racism awareness and race relations throughout the course of his or her career. ...

6.54 Racism, institutional or otherwise, is not the prerogative of the Police Service. It is clear that other agencies including for example those dealing with housing and education also suffer from the disease. If racism is to be eradicated there must be specific and co-ordinated action both within the agencies themselves and by society at large, particularly through the educational system, from pre-primary school upwards and onwards.'

Finally, the Macpherson Report defines a 'racial incident' as 'an incident which is perceived to be racist by the victim or any other person'.[21]

(E) EUROPEAN CONVENTION ON HUMAN RIGHTS

With the incorporation of the ECHR into United Kingdom law by the Human Rights Act 1998, the protection provided by the ECHR now supplements that in the Race Relations Act 1976. Unfortunately, the ECHR does not have a free standing guarantee of freedom from racial discrimination, ie one that applies to discriminatory acts in all areas of conduct. Instead, Art. 14 ECHR provides only that the 'enjoyment of the rights and freedoms set forth in this Convention shall be secured without discrimination on any ground such as ... race, colour, ... national ... origin ... association with a national minority, ... or other status'. Thus the ECHR just prohibits discrimination within the ambit of a Convention right. For example, it prohibits

---

21 Report, p. 238.

racially discriminatory juries,[22] because Art. 6 ECHR guarantees the right to a fair trial, but it does not prohibit discrimination in employment, because the ECHR does not include the right to work. However, in addition to Art. 14, there is a guarantee of freedom from 'degrading treatment', which clearly has the potential to control racial discrimination.[23] The 12th Protocol to the ECHR, was adopted in 2000, will improve the protection against racial discrimination afforded the ECHR considerably for the parties to it when it enters into force.[24] It provides the missing free standing 'equal protection' guarantee, by which discrimination by the state in any area of conduct is prohibited. If the United Kingdom were ever to ratify the 12th Protocol, the Human Rights Act would need to be amended to incorporate it into United Kingdom law.[25]

(F) EUROPEAN UNION LAW

Article 13 of the Treaty of Rome[26] empowers the Council, after consultation with the Parliament, to act to combat discrimination 'based on sex, *racial or ethnic origin,* religion or belief, disability, age or sexual orientation'.[27] Directive 2000/43/EC[28] implementing the principle of equal treatment between persons irrespective of racial or ethnic origin (the race directive) has been adopted under Art. 13.

2 Liability and duties of public authorities

(A) LIABILITY FOR DISCRIMINATION

Race Relations Act 1976

19A. Discrimination by planning authorities
(1) It is unlawful for a planning authority to discriminate against a person carrying out their planning functions. ...

19B. Discrimination by public authorities
(1) It is unlawful for a public authority in carrying out any functions of the authority to do any act which constitutes discrimination.
(2) In this section 'public authority'—
    (*a*) includes any person certain of whose functions are functions of a public nature; but
    (*b*) does not include any person mentioned in subsection (3).
(3) The persons mentioned in this subsection are—
    (*a*) either House of Parliament;
    (*b*) a person exercising functions in connection with proceedings in Parliament;
    (*c*) the Security Service;
    (*d*) the Secret Intelligence Service;
    (*e*) the Government Communications Headquarters; and

---

22 See *Sander v United Kingdom*, below, p. 1176.
23 In *East African Asians v United Kingdom* (1977) 3 EHRR 76, the refusal to admit into the UK British citizens from East Africa was found to be 'degrading' in the special circumstances of the cases. See also *Hilton v United Kingdom* (1978) 3 EHRR 104. These are rare cases, Art. 3 could be used more in racial discrimination cases. On Art. 8 ECHR, see *Chapman v United Kingdom* below, p. 1123.
24 For the text of the 12th Protocol, see (2001) 8 IHRR 300. The 12th Protocol will enter into force when ratified by ten ECHR parties. There have been no ratifications yet. The UK is not expected to become a party in the foreseeable future.
25 On the application of the ECHR and the 12th Protocol to private as opposed to state acts of discrimination, see above, p. 32.
26 As added by the 1999 Treaty of Amsterdam.
27 Italics added.
28 29 June 2000, (2000) OJL 180/22.

    (*f*)   any unit or part of a unit of any of the naval, military or air forces of the Crown which is for the time being required by the Secretary of State to assist the Government Communications Headquarters in carrying out its functions.

(4) In relation to a particular act, a person is not a public authority by virtue only of subsection (2)(a) if the nature of the act is private.

(5) This section is subject to sections 19C to 19F.

(6) Nothing in this section makes unlawful any act of discrimination which—

    (*a*)   is made unlawful by virtue of any other provision of this Act; or

    (*b*)   would be so made but for any provision made by or under this Act.

19C. Exceptions or further exceptions from section 19B for judicial and legislative acts etc

(1) Section 19B does not apply to—

    (*a*)   any judicial act (whether done by a court, tribunal or other person); or

    (*b*)   any act done on the instructions, or on behalf, of a person acting in a judicial capacity.

(2) Section 19B does not apply to any act of, or relating to, making, confirming or approving any enactment or Order in Council or any instrument made by a Minister of the Crown under an enactment.

(3) Section 19B does not apply to any act of, or relating to, making or approving arrangements, or imposing requirements or conditions, of a kind falling within section 41.

(4) Section 19B does not apply to any act of, or relating to, imposing a requirement, or giving an express authorisation, of a kind mentioned in section 19D(3) in relation to the carrying out of immigration and nationality functions.

(5) In this section—

    "immigration and nationality functions" has the meaning given in section 19D; and

    "Minister of the Crown" includes the National Assembly for Wales and a member of the Scottish Executive.

19D. Exception from section 19B for certain acts in immigration and nationality cases

(1) Section 19B does not make it unlawful for a relevant person to discriminate against another person on grounds of nationality or ethnic or national origins in carrying out immigration and nationality functions.

(2) For the purposes of subsection (1), "relevant person" means—

    (*a*)   a Minister of the Crown acting personally; or

    (*b*)   any other person acting in accordance with a relevant authorisation.

(3) In subsection (2), "relevant authorisation" means a requirement imposed or express authorisation given—

    (*a*)   with respect to a particular case or class of case, by a Minister of the Crown acting personally;

    (*b*)   with respect to a particular class of case—

        (i)   by any of the enactments mentioned in subsection (5); or

        (ii)   by any instrument made under or by virtue of any of those enactments.

(4) For the purposes of subsection (1), "immigration and nationality functions" means functions exercisable by virtue of any of the enactments mentioned in subsection (5).

(5) Those enactments are—

    (*a*)   the Immigration Acts (within the meaning of the Immigration and Asylum Act 1999 but excluding sections 28A to 28K of the Immigration Act 1971 so far as they relate to offences under Part III of that Act);

    (*b*)   the British Nationality Act 1981;

    (*c*)   the British Nationality (Falkland Islands) Act 1983;

    (*d*)   the British Nationality (Hong Kong) Act 1990;

    (*e*)   the Hong Kong (War Wives and Widows) Act 1996;

    (*f*)   the British Nationality (Hong Kong) Act 1997; and

    (*g*)   the Special Immigration Appeals Commission Act 1997;

and include any provision made under section 2(2) of the European Communities Act 1972, or any provision of Community law, which relates to the subject-matter of any of the enactments mentioned above.

[Section 19E provides for the appointment by the Secretary of State of a "monitor" who will check on the operation of the immigration and nationality exception in s. 19C and make an annual report.)]

19F. Exceptions from section 19B for decisions not to prosecute etc

[Section 19B does not apply to—

  (*a*) a decision not to institute criminal proceedings and, where such a decision has been made, any act done for the purpose of enabling the decision whether to institute criminal proceedings to be made;

  (*b*) where criminal proceedings are not continued as a result of a decision not to continue them, the decision and, where such a decision has been made—

   (i) any act done for the purpose of enabling the decision whether to continue the proceedings to be made; and

   (ii) any act done for the purpose of securing that the proceedings are not continued.

NOTES

1. As originally enacted and interpreted by the courts, the 1976 Act only applied to discrimination by public authorities to a limited extent.[1] They have always been subject to sections of the 1976 Act covering particular areas of activity such as their employment of staff (s. 4) and the provision by them of education (ss. 17, 18) and public housing (s. 21). More generally, 'the services of … any local or other public authority' are controlled (s. 20(1)(g)),[1a] but this wording has been narrowly interpreted to mean only 'acts which are similar to acts that could be done by private persons'.[1b] It therefore excludes acts of the police, the prison service, the immigration authorities, and tax inspectors, etc, in the exercise of their functions, with certain exceptions where the acts are seen as the performance of a service rather than acts of control or regulation. Although this limited interpretation reflected the intention of Parliament in 1976, the result is an important gap in the scope of coverage of the Act.[2] As a result of the failings of the police in the Stephen Lawrence case, the Race Relations Act 1976 was amended by the Race Relations (Amendment) Act 2000 to extend to discriminatory acts by the police, and other public authorities, in the exercise of their functions generally.[3]

2. Section 19B makes any discriminatory act (or omission) by a public authority when carrying out any of its functions a breach of the 1976 Act. This unqualified obligation adds substantially to s. 20(2)(g), which remains good law. For the purposes of s. 19B, a discriminatory act has the normal 1976 Act meaning, covering direct and indirect discrimination and victimisation.[4] A 'public authority' is defined as 'any person certain of whose functions are functions of a public nature' (s. 19B(2)(a)).[5] This includes private persons who perform public functions, such as companies operating prisons. The 'public authorities' that are exempt from the 1976 Act are listed in s. 19B(3). They include the Houses of Parliament, the Intelligence and Security Services and GCHQ.[6] The result of s. 19B is that the 1976 Act now extends,

---

1   In contrast, discrimination by private persons has always been fully covered.

1a   Below, p. 1134.

1b   Per Lord Fraser, in the *Amin* case, below, p. 1138.

2   See below, p. 1140.

3   The MacPherson Report on the Lawrence case, see above, p. 1072, recommendation 11, recommended that the 1976 Act be fully extended to the police. The 2001 Act entered into force on 26 March 2001: S.I. 2001 No. 566. The general extension of the RRA 1976 to the functioning of public authorities generally by the 2001 Act was preceded by the addition of s. 19A 1976 Act by the Housing and Planning Act 1986, which concerns planning authorities in particular and which remains in force.

4   The government had originally intended to exclude indirect discrimination, but agreed to include it during the passage of the 2001 Act in Parliament.

5   Cf. the definition in s. 6(3) HRA, above, p. 14. An act of a public authority does not give rise to liability if 'the nature of the act is private': s. 19B(4).

6   The Act does not apply to discriminatory acts, including speech protected by parliamentary privilege, in 'proceedings in parliament': s. 19B(3)(b). Parliament and others exempted by s. 19B(3) continue to be subject to the employment provisions of the 1976 Act.

inter alia, to the functioning of the police (investigation, search and seizure, arrest, etc), the prison service (discipline, searching visitors, treatment of prisoners generally), the probation service, immigration and nationality officials (subject to s. 19D, below), licensing authorities (liquor, street trading, etc) and income tax and customs authorities.[7] In addition, chief officers of police are made vicariously liable for the acts of police constables.[8] Exceptionally, by s. 19D, an immigration or nationality official may discriminate 'on grounds of nationality or ethnic or national origins' when 'carrying out nationality or immigration functions'.[9] An exception is also made by s. 19C for 'judicial acts'. This refers to judicial decisions, including jury verdicts.[10]

By s. 19F, decisions not to initiate or to discontinue a prosecution are exempt from the 1976 Act.

3. Claims of discrimination contrary to s. 19B may be brought before a county court in accordance with the arrangements for other non-employment claims under the 1976 Act.[11]

4. In addition to the provisions concerning public authorities in s. 19B that establish police liability under the 1976 Act, there is provision for the monitoring of discrimination in the criminal justice system in the Criminal Justice Act 1991, s. 95(1). This was introduced before the police were brought within the 1976 Act by the 2000 Act, but still applies. Section 95(1) reads:

> 'The Secretary of State shall in each year publish such information as he considers expedient for the purpose of—
>
> ...
>
> (b) facilitating the performance by ... persons [engaged in the administration of criminal justice] of their duty to avoid discriminating against any persons on the ground of race or sex or any other improper ground.'

The 'duty' referred to does not arise from other legislation. Whether it was intended to establish such a legal duty incidentally in the course of imposing a different and more general information-giving duty upon the Secretary of State is debatable. The CRE has recommended that 'the vague non-discrimination duty applicable to the whole of the criminal justice system should be made more explicit', and should be 'backed by code-making powers together with proper ways of airing grievances'.[12]

Race Relations Act 1976

41. Acts done under statutory authority etc.
(1) Nothing in Parts II to IV shall render unlawful any act of discrimination done—
    (*a*) in pursuance of any enactment or Order in Council; or
    (*b*) in pursuance of any instrument made under any enactment by a Minister of the Crown; or

---

7 Crown appointments (i.e. those not within the employment provisions of s. 4) and honours awards are also covered more extensively than previously by the original s. 7 of the 1976 Act by a new s. 76 of the 1976 Act, substituted by the 2000 Act, s. 3.
8 Section 76A of the 1976 Act, as inserted by s. 4 of the 2000 Act.
9 Discrimination on these grounds may occur, for example, when distinguishing between EU and other nationals for immigration purposes, when applying the 1951 Refugee Convention or when granting nationality to persons of a particular origin. Section 19C was considered necessary because of the narrow interpretation of the court of s. 41 below, p. 1078, by which acts done under statutory authority are excluded only if they are necessary, and not if they involve an exercise of discretion, as many acts by immigration and nationality officials will do.
10 Racially biased verdicts by juries are thus not illegal under the RRA. See, however, the ECHR jury bias cases, below, p. 1176.
11 s. 57 of the 1976 Act, as amended by the 2000 Act.
12 *Second Review of the Race Relations Act 1976* (1992), p. 31.

    (*c*)   in order to comply with any condition or requirement imposed by a Minister of the
        Crown (whether before or after the passing of this Act) by virtue of any enactment.
References in this subsection to an enactment, Order in Council or instrument include an
enactment, Order in Council or instrument passed or made after the passing of this Act.
(2) Nothing in Parts II to IV shall render unlawful any act whereby a person discriminates
against another on the basis of that other's nationality or place of ordinary residence or the
length of time for which he has been present or resident in or outside the United Kingdom or
an area within the United Kingdom, if that act is done—

    (*a*)   in pursuance of any arrangements made (whether before or after the passing of this
        Act) by or with the approval of, or for the time being approved by, a Minister of the
        Crown; or
    (*b*)   in order to comply with any condition imposed (whether before or after the passing
        of this Act) by a Minister of the Crown.

42. Acts safeguarding national security
Nothing in Parts II to IV shall render unlawful an act done for the purpose of safeguarding
national security. [If the doing of the act was justified by that purpose].[13]

NOTES

1. Section 41 was restrictively interpreted by the House of Lords in *Hampson v
Department of Education and Science*,[14] so that the wording 'in pursuance of' refers
only to acts that are 'acts done in necessary performance of an express obligation in
the instrument' and does not include discretionary acts done under the instrument.
In that case, the Education (Teachers) Regulations 1982, a statutory instrument made
by the Secretary of State in the exercise of a power under the Education Act 1980,
provided that a person could not be employed as a teacher unless he was qualified.
The Regulations provided further that a person would be so qualified if he had
successfully completed an 'approved' course, viz. one approved by the Secretary of
State, in his discretion, as being 'comparable to a course within sub-paragraph (a)' of
the Regulations. Lord Lowry, for the House, decided that s. 41 did not provide a
defence, explaining his approach to the interpretation of s. 41 as follows:

    'Balcombe LJ framed the question clearly when, having summarised the respondent's point
    on s. 41, he said ...

        'This argument, which succeeded below, is controvertible if the words 'in pursuance of
        any instrument' are apt in their context to include, not only acts done in necessary
        performance of an express obligation contained in the instrument (the narrow construction)
        but also acts done in exercise of a power of discretion conferred by the instrument (the
        wide construction). Both constructions are possible.'

    ...s. 41 ... introduces over a wide field, namely the subject matter covered by Pts II to IV of
    the 1976 Act, as exceptions to the Act's general purpose of outlawing discrimination, five
    cases in which an act of discrimination shall not be unlawful and in each such case the relevant
    enactment, Order in Council, instrument, condition, requirement or arrangement may be either
    pre- or post-Act. In view of the wide sweep of these provisions, the exceptions ought therefore,
    I suggest, to be narrowly rather than widely construed where the language is susceptible of
    more than one meaning. The next point which strikes me is that the words 'in pursuance of'
    occur in sub-ss. (1)(a) and (b) and in sub-s. (2)(a). I take note, too, of the words 'in order to
    comply with' in sub-ss. (1)(c) and (2)(b) and the words 'by virtue of' also in sub-s. (1)(c).
    Even allowing for the variation of expression which may be attributed to the dictates of grammar
    or style, it seems to me that the phrase 'in pursuance of', while not limited to describing an act

13 As amended by the Race Relations (Amendment) Act 2000, s. 7.
14 [1991] 1 AC 171. The House of Lords reversed the Court of Appeal. For the facts of the case
    further, see below, p. 1098.

which is done *in order* to comply with an enactment etc, is more limited in its meaning than 'by virtue of', a phrase with which it could in a different context be synonymous ... The inference to be drawn is that, if the discriminatory act is specified in an enactment, order or instrument, but not otherwise, it is done 'in pursuance of' that enactment, order or instrument and protected by s. 41.

It is, however, the consideration of the wider context that demonstrates the need to adopt the narrow construction of the words 'in pursuance of', since the wide construction is seen to be irreconcilable with the purpose and meaning of the 1976 Act. ... The most important weapons contained in Pts II and III of the Act would be irretrievably blunted and, indeed, would not make sense. ...

My Lords, the alleged act of discrimination ... was to decide the appellant's application by reference to a test of acceptability of her teacher training course (in statutory language, 'a requirement') which indirectly discriminated against her within the meaning of s. 1(1)(b)(i) and (iii) of the 1976 Act. That requirement was no doubt applied 'in pursuance of' the 1982 regulations according to the wide construction, as defined by Balcombe LJ, but it was not so applied according to the narrow construction, under which the requirement must be found in the regulations as, for example, is true of the courses described in para. 2(a)(i) of Sch. 5. On the other hand, the approval of a course as 'comparable to a course within sub-paragraph (a)' involved the application of a requirement (whether established or ad hoc) which was based on administrative practice and discretion and was not a requirement laid down by the regulations. Therefore the requirement of a course consisting of three consecutive years' training, assuming that it was discriminatory and also not justifiable under s. 1(1)(b)(ii), was not protected by s. 41(1)(b).

There is a sound argument, based on public policy, for drawing the line in this way. I refer to the need and the opportunity for parliamentary scrutiny. Balcombe LJ put the matter aptly ([1990] 2 All ER 25 at 32, [1989] ICR 179 at 188):...

'If an enactment, Order in Council or statutory instrument imposes requirements compliance with which may lead to racial discrimination, those requirements can be debated in Parliament and their justification considered there. Similarly, if a minister of the Crown imposes a condition or requirement compliance with which could lead to racial discrimination (see s. 41(1)(c) of the 1976 Act) he can be made answerable in Parliament for his action. If what is done is not *necessary* to comply with a statutory requirement, then there can be no valid reason why it should not have to be justified before an industrial tribunal...'

What I would venture to describe as the fallacy of [the Court of Appeal's] approach can be recognised when one reflects that almost every discretionary decision, such as that which is involved in the appointment, promotion and dismissal of individuals in, say, local government, the police, the national health service and the public sector or the teaching profession, is taken against a statutory background which imposes a duty on someone, just as the 1982 regulations imposed a duty on the Secretary of State. It seems to me that to apply the reasoning of the majority here to the decisions I have mentioned would give them the protection of s. 41 and thereby achieve results which no member of the Court of Appeal would be likely to have thought acceptable.

2. Section 42 exempts acts done 'for the purpose of safeguarding national security', provided that 'the doing of the act was justified by that purpose'. The 2000 Act repealed the provision in the 1976 Act, s. 69(2)(b) by which a certificate from a government Minister certifying that an act was for 'national security' purposes was conclusive evidence for the purposes of s. 42.[15] Instead, alternative arrangements are made in a new s. 67A for a procedure to be followed by the court where it considers this expedient in the interest of national security.

15 s. 69(2)(b) was repealed because a similar national security certificate provision had been found to be in breach of the right of access to a court in Art. 6(1) ECHR in *Tinnelly & Sons v United Kingdom* (1999) 27 EHRR 249.

Race Relations Act 1976

75. Application to Crown etc

(1) This Act applies—

    (*a*)   to an act done by or for purposes of a Minister of the Crown or government department; or

    (*b*)   to an act done on behalf of the Crown by a statutory body, or a person holding a statutory office,

as it applies to an act done by a private person.

(2) Parts II and IV apply to—

    (*a*)   service for purposes of a Minister of the Crown or government department, other than service of a person holding a statutory office; or

    (*b*)   service on behalf of the Crown for purposes of a person holding a statutory office or purposes of a statutory body; or

    (*c*)   service in the armed forces,

as they apply to employment by a private person, and shall so apply as if references to a contract of employment included references to the terms of service.

[[(2A) Subsections (1) and (2) do not apply in relation to the provisions mentioned in subsection (2B).

(2B)   Sections 19B to 19F, sections 71 to 71E (including Schedule 1A) and section 76 bind the Crown; and the other provisions of this Act so far as they relate to those provisions shall be construed accordingly (including, in particular, references to employment in Part IV).][16]

NOTE

Section 75 is the standard statutory provision that indicates whether the Crown is subject to an Act. Section 75(1) answers this question generally in the affirmative, although the extent of that liability depends on other particular provisions such as s. 19B and s. 20(2)(g).[17] Section 75(2) concerns the extent of liability in respect of Crown employment.

(B) DUTIES OF PUBLIC AUTHORITIES

Race Relations Act 1976

71. Specified authorities: general statutory duty

[(1) Every body or other person specified in Schedule 1A or of a description falling within that Schedule shall, in carrying out its functions, have due regard to the need—

    (*a*)   to eliminate unlawful racial discrimination; and

    (*b*)   to promote equality of opportunity and good relations between persons of different racial groups.

(2) The Secretary of State may by order impose, on such persons falling within Schedule 1A as he considers appropriate, such duties as he considers appropriate for the purpose of ensuring the better performance by those persons of their duties under subsection (1).

(3) An order under subsection (2)—

    (*a*)   may be made in relation to a particular person falling within Schedule 1A, any description of persons falling within that Schedule or every person falling within that Schedule;

    (*b*)   may make different provision for different purposes.

(4) Before making an order under subsection (2), the Secretary of State shall consult the Commission.

(5) The Secretary of State may by order amend Schedule 1A; but no such order may extend the application of this section unless the Secretary of State considers that the extension relates to a person who exercises functions of a public nature.

16 s. 75(2A)(2B) were added by the Race Relations (Amendment) Act 2000, Sch. 2.
17 See above, p. 1074.

(6) An order under subsection (2) or (5) may contain such incidental, supplementary or consequential provision as the Secretary of State considers appropriate (including provision amending or repealing provision made by or under this Act or any other enactment).
(7) This section is subject to section 71A and 71B and is without prejudice to the obligation of any person to comply with any other provision of this Act.]

71A. General statutory duty: special cases

[(1) In relation to the carrying out of immigration and nationality functions (within the meaning of section 19D(1)), section 71(1)(b) has effect with the omission of the words 'equality of opportunity and'.
(2) Where an entry in Schedule 1A is limited to a person in a particular capacity, section 71(1) does not apply to that person in any other capacity.
(3) Where an entry in Schedule 1A is limited to particular functions of a person, section 71(1) does not apply to that person in relation to any other functions.]

71C. General statutory duty: codes of practice

[(1) The Commission may issue codes of practice containing such practical guidance as the Commission think fit in relation to the performance by persons of duties imposed on them by virtue of subsections (1) and (2) of section 71. ...

NOTES

1. As substituted by the 2000 Act, s. 71(1) imposes a general statutory duty upon specified authorities to have 'due regard' to the need to eliminate unlawful racial discrimination and to promote equality of opportunity and good relations among members of different racial groups. Originally, s. 71 imposed such a duty only upon local authorities, but it was amended beyond this by the 2000 Act. The specified authorities, or kinds of authorities, are listed or characterised in Sch. 1A in a long list of 60 authorities. They include Ministers of the Crown and government departments, the armed forces, health authorities, local authorities, planning committees, probation committees, police authorities and magistrates' committees. The new s. 71 is different also in that some specific duties, in addition to the general duty, may be spelt out by statutory instrument (s. 71(2)). Provision is also made, again for the first time, for codes of practice (s. 71C). Finally, a system of enforcement is provided, also for the first time, by way of compliance notices issued by the CRE (s. 71D), backed by the possibility of a court order (s. 71E).
2. The 'due regard' duty in the original s. 71(1), the wording of which is essentially repeated in that of the present s. 71(1), was interpreted by the courts in two cases in which local authority action in opposition to apartheid in South Africa was found not to be justified by s. 71(1).
The scope of s. 71 was first considered in *Wheeler v Leicester City Council.*[18] Leicester Rugby Football Club had had its licence to use a council administered recreation ground terminated after it had failed to comply with requirements imposed by the council. These requirements followed the decision of three of the club's players to take part in a rugby tour of South Africa. The club was willing to comply with the council's demand that it should condemn apartheid. It did not, however, comply with the council's requirement that it put pressure on the players not to take part in the tour. It regarded itself as having no such jurisdiction over its players. The club sought *certiorari* to quash the council's decision revoking its licence. The council argued that it had, in exercising its discretionary powers as regards the licensing of the ground, properly taken into account and been guided by its duty under s. 71 of the 1976 Act to

18 [1985] AC 1054, HL. See on the *Wheeler* case, T. R. S. Allan, (1986) 49 MLR 121 and A. Hutchinson and M. Jones (1988) 15 J Law Soc 263.

discharge its functions in such manner as would tend to promote good relations between persons of different racial groups. The Court of Appeal, by a majority, accepted this reasoning, holding that on the facts and in view of the ethnic mix in the city of Leicester it was not possible to categorise the decision of the council as improper or unreasonable in the *Wednesbury* sense.[18a] Browne-Wilkinson LJ dissented in strong terms. He stressed the fact that the actions of the players were in no way unlawful, and also noted the importance to be placed upon the liberty of freedom of speech and of conscience. The council's requirements of the club, in his opinion, went beyond its powers of administration of the ground for the general public benefit, and improperly sought to discriminate against a licensee on the grounds of that person's (lawful) views and beliefs. These matters were, he held, irrelevant considerations to the proper exercise of the licensing power. Browne-Wilkinson LJ did not regard s. 71 as sufficient to authorise what the council had done. To so hold, as the majority had done, was to permit the council to impose a 'penalty' on the club for behaviour which was not unlawful within the terms of the principal provisions of the 1976 Act. Section 71 should not, given its rather general terms, be interpreted as giving to local authorities such a power of punishment. The club appealed successfully to the House of Lords. Lord Roskill acknowledged that s. 71 required the council in exercising its powers to have regard to the interests of race relations. But this did not make any course of action decided upon immune from judicial review. His Lordship regarded the action of the council as unreasonable and procedurally unfair, given its inflexible attitude as regards strict compliance with all of the requirements it had imposed. Lord Templeman's opinion was founded on the improper purpose of the council in seeking to punish the club which had, it was stressed, committed no wrong. Lords Bridge, Brightman and Griffiths concurred with both speeches. Then, in *R v Lewisham London Borough Council, ex p Shell UK Ltd*[19] it was held that, given the multi-racial character of the borough, the council was entitled, in view of s. 71, to adopt a policy of not trading with a company that had links with South Africa. However, to adopt such a policy, as the council had done, in order to bring pressure to bear on the company to sever links with South Africa was to abuse power in the same way as in the *Wheeler* case.

It may be that the specific duties to be introduced by delegated legislation or, more likely, that any Codes of Practice that are adopted will address the issues raised in the *Wheeler* and *Shell* cases.

3   The meaning of discrimination

(A)   GENERALLY

Race Relations Act 1976

1. Racial discrimination
(1) A person discriminates against another in any circumstances relevant for the purposes of any provision of this Act if—
>   (*a*)   on racial grounds he treats that other less favourably than he treats or would treat other persons; or
>   (*b*)   he applies to that other a requirement or condition which he applies or would apply equally to persons not of the same racial group as that other but—
>>   (i)   which is such that the proportion of persons of the same racial group as that other who can comply with it is considerably smaller than the proportion of persons not of that racial group who can comply with it; and

---

18a*Associated Provincial Picture Houses Ltd v Wednesbury Corpn* [1948] 1 KB 223.
19 [1988] 1 All ER 938, QBD.

(ii)   which he cannot show to be justifiable irrespective of the colour, race, nationality or ethnic or national origins of the person to whom it is applied; and

(iii)   which is to the detriment of that other because he cannot comply with it.

(2) It is hereby declared that, for the purposes of this Act, segregating a person from other persons on racial grounds is treating him less favourably than they are treated.

2. Discrimination by way of victimisation

(1) A person ('the discriminator') discriminates against another person ('the person victimised') in any circumstances relevant for the purposes of any provision of this Act if he treats the person victimised less favourably than in those circumstances he treats or would treat other persons, and does so by reason that the person victimised has—

(*a*)   brought proceedings against the discriminator or any other person under this Act; or

(*b*)   given evidence or information in connection with proceedings brought by any person against the discriminator or any other person under this Act; or

(*c*)   otherwise done anything under or by reference to this Act in relation to the discriminator or any other person; or

(*d*)   alleged that the discriminator or any other person has committed an act which (whether or not the allegation so states) would amount to a contravention of this Act,

or by reason that the discriminator knows that the person victimised intends to do any of those things, or suspects that the person victimised has done, or intends to do, any of them.

(2) Subsection (1) does not apply to treatment of a person by reason of any allegation made by him if the allegation was false and not made in good faith.

NOTES

1. Discrimination in any of the three forms prohibited by ss. 1–2 (direct and indirect discrimination and victimisation) is only illegal if it occurs in one of the areas of conduct or activity covered by Part II (employment and related matters), Part III (education; goods, facilities or services; housing; clubs), or Part IV (advertisements) of the 1976 Act. Racial questions that raise issues of discrimination may arise in other areas of the law. For example, a jury may be racially prejudiced in court,[20] and in adoption proceedings, the welfare of a mixed race or black child may justify preferring a black couple as the adoptive parents instead of the child's white foster parents on the basis that adoptive parents should be of the same racial group as the child.[1]

2. *Positive action.* Sometimes called 'affirmative action', 'positive discrimination' or 'reverse discrimination', positive action means discrimination in favour of a racial group whose members suffer from extensive racial discrimination. An employment training programme or a quota of reserved places in higher education are examples. Although writers have made constructive attempts to distinguish between the above terms, unfortunately usage varies.[2] There is no one or more recognised term or terms in English law. The government White Paper[3] was against positive action and the definition of 'discrimination' in s. 1 makes it generally illegal. Thus in *Riyat v London Borough of Brent*,[4] a tribunal held that an employer had infringed the 1976 Act by discriminating in favour of black applicants for employment. Likewise, in *Lambeth*

20   See *Sander v United Kingdom* below, p. 1176.

1   *Re P (A Minor) (Adoption)* [1990] 1 FLR 260, CA. The 1976 Act does not apply to the fostering of children, s. 23(2) below or adoption. The Children Act 1989, s. 22(5)(c), requires local authorities to give due consideration to a child's 'religious persuasion, racial origin and cultural and linguistic background' when taking decisions concerning children being looked after by them.

2   Contrast, e.g., B. Parekh and G. Pitt, in Hepple and Szyszczak, op. cit., at p. 1068, n. 1, above, Chaps. 15 and 16 respectively.

3   Cmnd. 6234, p. 14.

4   (1983), cited in *IDS Racial Discrimination Employment Law Handbook* (1984), p. 24.

London Borough Council v Commission for Racial Equality,[5] Balcombe LJ indicated that the policy of the Act was not such as generally to authorise positive action:

> 'It is undoubtedly the case that certain sections of the Act encourage positive action to meet the special needs of particular racial groups in certain defined fields, by providing that acts of discrimination that would otherwise be unlawful shall not be so if done for those purposes. [ss. 35–38, below] . . . It is also correct that s. 71 imposes on local authorities the duty to promote equality of opportunity between persons of different racial groups, although this is expressly stated to be 'without prejudice to their obligation to comply with any other provision of this Act'.
>
> Nevertheless . . . I am wholly unpersuaded that one of the two main purposes of the Act is to promote positive action to benefit racial groups. . . .
>
> However, I should make it clear that . . . I express no view of the case for or against positive action in favour of ethnic minorities in order to counter the effects of past discrimination; I confine my attention to the present meaning of the 1976 Act.'

As Balcombe LJ states, the 1976 Act, ss. 35–38, allows for some exceptions. Thus it is not unlawful to afford 'persons of a particular racial group access to facilities or services to meet the special needs of persons of that group in regard to their education, training or welfare, or any ancillary benefit' (s. 35) and special training schemes (public or private) to boost the number of members of a racial group in an occupation in which their number is disproportionately low are lawful (ss. 37–38). Employers are also permitted to encourage applications from members of particular racial groups where these are under-represented in their workforce (ibid). Special provision 'for the benefit of persons not ordinarily resident in Great Britain in affording them access to facilities for education or training' is also permitted (s. 36). As to s. 35, English language instruction is an obvious case. Bindman states[6] that a 'number of "special access courses" have been introduced with the encouragement of the Department of Education and Science in colleges of further education and polytechnics' and that while 'a number of these courses are foundation courses which are not related to specific kinds of work, others are designed to direct members of ethnic minorities into specific occupations such as teaching'. As to ss. 37 and 38, training may be provided by public bodies such as the Manpower Services Commission or by private employers. Preference by way of *training* only may be given; the clear intention is that there should be no positive action in the *selection* or *promotion* of employees.[7]

Parekh[8] suggests, however, that practice is ahead of the law in that places on some public bodies are reserved for members of ethnic minority groups (and women) and that similar employment quotas are common:

5   [1990] IRLR 231, 234, CA.
6   (1980) *New Community* 248.
7   See, however, the facts of the *Cardiff Women's Aid* case, below, p. 1151, where a job was advertised as just for a 'black or Asian woman'. This would seem to cross the line between legal encouragement under s. 38 and an act of discrimination contrary to s. 1. It could only be lawful if the job came within s. 5(2), which permits selection for employment on racial grounds where this is 'a genuine occupational qualification for a job'. See, e.g., *Tottenham Green Under Fives Centre v Marshall (No 2)* [1991] ICR 320, EAT. An example of a scheme within the Act was one involving the reservation of nearly half of the places on a BBC regional radio news training scheme: *Runnymede Bulletin* No. 179 (1994) p. 3. Following a formal investigation that revealed considerable under-representation of ethnic minorities in management, supervisory and clerical grades in the hotel industry, the CRE recommended that ss. 37 and 38 be used by hotel groups to improve the situation: *Working in Hotels*, F Invest Rep 1991.
8   Hepple and Szyszczak, op. cit., at p. 1068, n. 1, above, p. 279. London Underground has set equality targets (15%) for the employment of ethnic minority senior managers following a CRE formal investigation (*Lines of Progress*, 1990) that concluded that the selection procedures involved indirect discrimination: *Race and Immigration, Runnymede Bulletin*, No. 241, (1991) p. 5.

'For years the Home Office has ensured that one of the ten governors of the BBC is black. There is no reason to believe that the black appointee is among the top ten "most distinguished" men and women in the country or is "uniquely equipped" to look after black interests.... The same is true of the appointments of blacks and women to the Independent Broadcasting Authority, the Equal Opportunities Commission, the Commission for Racial Equality, and to countless other government bodies. Local authorities are guided by similar considerations when they appoint school governors. And all political parties, albeit in different ways and with different degrees of enthusiasm, appoint blacks and women to important committees or select them as their local and parliamentary candidates.

Several private and public organizations too ... set informal quotas (or what are euphemistically called targets) and go out of their way to recruit black and female staff, sometimes to important positions and in preference to equally or more qualified whites and males. Although their motives are mixed, they include a sense of social responsibility, the need to integrate blacks and other disadvantaged groups into mainstream society, the desire to encourage and tap talent, and the concern to counter the still pervasive preferential treatment of the traditional racist and sexist kind.'

Positive action was considered by Lord Scarman in his *Report on the Brixton Disorders 10–12 April 1981*[9] in the following paragraph, which attracted a good deal of public attention:

'6.32. This leads me to the question how far it is right to go in order to meet ethnic minority needs. It is clear from the evidence of ethnic minority deprivation I have received that, if the balance of racial disadvantage is to be redressed, as it must be, positive action is required. ... Given the special problems of the ethnic minorities, exposed in evidence, justice requires that special programmes should be adopted in areas of acute deprivation. In this respect, the ethnic minorities can be compared with any other group with special needs, such as the elderly, or one-parent families. I recognise the existence of a legitimate and understandable fear on the part of both public and private institutions that programmes which recognise and cater for the special needs of minority groups will stimulate a backlash from the majority. ... Nevertheless, it must not be allowed to prevent necessary action. Certainly special programmes for ethnic minority groups should only be instituted where the need for them is clearly made out. But need must be the criterion, and no other. The principle has already been recognised by Parliament (ss. 35, 37, 38 of the Race Relations Act 1976), and must be made effective.'

Noting that ss. 35–38 have not been used as much as was anticipated, the CRE has recommended that they be amended so as to make clearer the kind of training that is permitted. This should include training for the exclusive benefit of members of a particular racial group, reserving places on courses that are open to persons generally, training bursaries and on-the-job and apprenticeship training for up to two years.[10]

Affirmative action is permitted to some extent in other legal systems. It is not per se unconstitutional, under United States law, but a 'strict scrutiny test' now applies so that it is very difficult to justify.[11] Similarly, EU sex discrimination law treats affirmative action as *prima facie* illegal, but does permit it in exceptional cases.[12]

---

9 Cmnd. 8427.
10 *Reform of the Race Relations Act 1976* (1998).
11 *Adarand Constructors v Pena* 115 S Ct 2097 (1995) and *City of Richmond v Croson* 488 US 469 (1989). These are race discrimination cases in which the Supreme Court, after earlier jurisprudence in which it was more sympathetic to affirmative action, moved to a stricter approach, seemingly on the basis that affirmative action had not had the desired results and was unfair to individuals who had themselves not been guilty of discrimination.
12 See *Kalanke v Freie Hansestadt Bremen* (Case C-450/93) [1995] ECR I-3051, ECJ; *Marschall v Land Nordrhein-Westfalen* (Case C-409/95) [1997] ECR I-6363, ECJ; *Hill v Revenue Comrs* (Case C-243/95) [1998] ECR I-3739, ECJ.

(B) DIRECT DISCRIMINATION

Nagarajan v London Regional Transport [1994] 4 All ER 65, House of Lords

The appellant, of Indian origin, applied unsuccessfully for a job with the LRT, by which he had been employed previously. The interviewers were aware that he had earlier brought unsuccessful racial discrimination proceedings against LRT. In this case, he claimed victimisation in breach of s. 2(1)(a) of the Race Relations Act 1976, arguing that he had been treated less favourably because of the earlier proceedings. The question for the House of Lords was whether s. 2(1) requires conscious motivation on the part of the alleged discriminator. Allowing an appeal from the Court of Appeal on this point, the House held that it does not. The following speech by Lord Nicholls examines the relevance of motive in both s. 1(1)(a) and s. 2 of the Race Relations Act.

Lord Nicholls of Birkenhead:
Section 2 should be read in the context of s. 1. Section 1(1)(a) is concerned with direct discrimination, to use the accepted terminology. To be within s. 1(1)(a) the less favourable treatment must be on racial grounds. Thus, in every case it is necessary to enquire why the complainant received less favourable treatment. This is the crucial question. Was it on grounds of race? Or was it for some other reason, for instance, because the complainant was not so well qualified for the job? Save in obvious cases, answering the crucial question will call for some consideration of the mental processes of the alleged discriminator. Treatment, favourable or unfavourable, is a consequence, which follows from a decision. Direct evidence of a decision to discriminate on racial grounds will seldom be forthcoming. Usually the grounds of the decision will have to be deduced, or inferred, from the surrounding circumstances.

The crucial question just mentioned is to be distinguished sharply from a second and different question: if the discriminator treated the complainant less favourably on racial grounds, why did he do so? The latter question is strictly beside the point when deciding whether an act of racial discrimination occurred. For the purposes of direct discrimination under s. 1(1)(a), as distinct from indirect discrimination under s. 1(1)(b), the reason why the alleged discriminator acted on racial grounds is irrelevant. Racial discrimination is not negatived by the discriminator's motive or intention or reason or purpose (the words are interchangeable in this context) in treating another person less favourably on racial grounds. In particular, if the reason why the alleged discriminator rejected the complainant's job application was racial, it matters not that his intention may have been benign. For instance, he may have believed that the applicant would not fit in, or that other employees might make the applicant's life a misery. If racial grounds were the reason for the less favourable treatment, direct discrimination under s. 1(1)(a) is established.

This law, which is well established, was confirmed by your Lordships in *Equal Opportunities Commission v Birmingham City Council* [1989] 1 All ER 769, [1989] AC 1155, a case concerning similar provisions in the Sex Discrimination Act 1975. In that case the answer to the question I have described as the crucial question was plain. The council did not treat all children equally. Girls received less favourable treatment than boys.[13] Your Lordships decided that, this being so, the reason why the girls were discriminated against on grounds of sex was irrelevant. Whatever may have been the motive or intention of the council, nevertheless it was because of their sex that the girls received less favourable treatment, and so were the subject of discrimination: see Lord Goff of Chieveley ([1989] 1 All ER 769 at 774, [1989] AC 1155 at 1194).

The same point was made in *James v Eastleigh BC* [1990] 2 All ER 607, [1990] 2 AC 751.[14] . . .

I turn to the question of subconscious motivation. All human beings have preconceptions, beliefs, attitudes and prejudices on many subjects. It is part of our make-up. Moreover, we do not always recognise our own prejudices. Many people are unable, or unwilling, to admit even to themselves that actions of others may be racially motivated. An employer may genuinely believe that the reason why he rejected an applicant had nothing to do with the applicant's race. After

---

13 *Ed.* Higher pass mark requirement for girls for grammar school entry because fewer girls' places was direct discrimination.
14 *Ed.* See below, p. 1088.

careful and thorough investigation of a claim members of an employment tribunal may decide that the proper inference to be drawn from the evidence is that, whether the employer realised it at the time or not, race was the reason why he acted as he did. It goes without saying that in order to justify such an inference the tribunal must first make findings of primary fact from which the inference may properly be drawn. Conduct of this nature by an employer, when the inference is legitimately drawn, falls squarely within the language of s. 1(1)(a). The employer treated the complainant less favourably on racial grounds. Such conduct also falls within the purpose of the legislation. Members of racial groups need protection from conduct driven by unrecognised prejudice as much as from conscious and deliberate discrimination. Balcombe LJ adverted to an instance of this in *West Midlands Passenger Executive v Singh* [1988] 2 All ER 873 at 877, [1988] 1 WLR 730 at 736. He said that a high rate of failure to achieve promotion by members of a particular racial group may indicate that 'the real reason for refusal is a conscious or unconscious racial attitude which involves stereotyped assumptions' about members of the group.

Thus far I have been considering the position under s. 1(1)(a). I can see no reason to apply a different approach to s. 2. 'On [racial] grounds' in s. 1(1)(a) and 'by reason that' in s. 2(1) are interchangeable expressions in this context. The key question under s. 2 is the same as under s. 1(1)(a): why did the complainant receive less favourable treatment? The considerations mentioned above regarding direct discrimination under s. 1(1)(a) are correspondingly appropriate under s. 2. If the answer to this question is that the discriminator treated the person victimised less favourably by reason of his having done one of the acts ('protected acts') listed in s. 2(1), the case falls within the section. It does so, even if the discriminator did not consciously realise that, for example, he was prejudiced because the job applicant had previously brought claims against him under the Act. In so far as the dictum in *Aziz v Trinity Street Taxis Ltd* [1988] 2 All ER 860 at 870, [1989] QB 463 at 485 ('a motive which is consciously connected with the race relations legislation') suggests otherwise, it cannot be taken as a correct statement of the law. *Aziz's* case, it should be noted, antedates the decisions in the *Equal Opportunities* and *James'* cases. Although victimisation has a ring of conscious targeting, this is an insufficient basis for excluding cases of unrecognised prejudice from the scope of s. 2. Such an exclusion would partially undermine the protection s. 2 seeks to give those who have sought to rely on the Act or been involved in the operation of the Act in other ways.

Decisions are frequently reached for more than one reason. Discrimination may be on racial grounds even though it is not the sole ground for the decision. A variety of phrases, with different shades of meaning, have been used to explain how the legislation applies in such cases: discrimination requires that racial grounds were a cause, the activating cause, a substantial and effective cause, a substantial reason, an important factor. No one phrase is obviously preferable to all others, although in the application of this legislation legalistic phrases, as well as subtle distinctions, are better avoided so far as possible. If racial grounds or protected acts had a significant influence on the outcome, discrimination is made out. Read in context, that was the industrial tribunal's finding in the present case. The tribunal found that the interviewers were 'consciously or subconsciously influenced by the fact that the applicant had previously brought tribunal proceedings against the respondent'.

Lord Steyn delivered a concurring speech. **Lords Hutton** and **Hobhouse** concurred. **Lord Browne-Wilkinson** delivered a dissenting speech.

Appeal allowed.

NOTES

1. The terms 'direct' and 'indirect' discrimination are used to distinguish between the two forms of discrimination in s. 1(1)(a) and s. 1(1)(a) and s. 1(1)(b) respectively. Although, on its facts, the *Nagarajan* case concerns victimisation contrary to s. 2, Lord Nicholls' speech discusses questions of motive and intention relevant to direct discrimination contrary to s. 1(1)(a) also. As Lord Nicholls indicates, neither motive nor intention are crucial when deciding whether a person has been treated less favourably 'on racial grounds' contrary to s. 1(1)(a). Instead, the test used is the 'but for' test that was adopted in the *Equal Opportunities Commission* and *James* sex discrimination cases.[15] In the *James* case, a husband and wife, both aged 61, went to a public swimming bath where persons of retirement age were admitted free of charge. Because of the different retirement ages for men and women (65 and 60) in UK law, the wife qualified for free entry; the husband did not. In the Court of Appeal it was held that this situation was not direct discrimination contrary to the Sex Discrimination Act 1975 because the intention was not to discriminate 'on the ground of sex'. The crucial question was not the result of applying a retirement age rule but the reason for doing so. In this case, the reason for the retirement age rule was not to discriminate against men but, Sir Nicolas Browne-Wilkinson stated, to benefit those whose resources would be likely to have been reduced by retirement. The House of Lords, by the narrow majority of three to two (Lords Griffiths and Lowry dissenting), took a different approach and held that there had been direct discrimination. The majority applied a 'but for' test. Lord Goff stated:

> '...as I see it, cases of direct discrimination under s. 1(1)(a) can be considered by asking the simple question: would the complainant have received the same treatment from the defendant but for his or her sex? This simple test possesses the double virtue that, on the one hand, it embraces both the case where the treatment derives from the application of a gender-based criterion, and the case where it derives from the selection of the complainant because of his or her sex; and on the other hand it avoids, in most cases at least, complicated questions relating to concepts such as intention, motive, reason or purpose, and the danger of confusion arising from the misuse of those elusive terms. I have to stress, however, that the "but for" test is not appropriate for cases of indirect discrimination under s. 1(1)(b), because there may be indirect discrimination against persons of one sex under that subsection, although a (proportionately smaller) group of persons of the opposite sex is adversely affected in the same way.'

The two dissenting judges rejected the majority's adoption of an objective test, arguing that the wording 'on racial grounds' suggested a subjective test. In terms of causation, there is authority for the view that when applying the 'but for' test, it does not have to be established that the victim's race was the sole reason for his less favourable treatment: it is sufficient that racial grounds are 'an important factor' or 'a substantial reason for what has happened'.[16]

2. Racial harassment may be less favourable treatment contrary to s. 1(1)(a). Several claims of racial harassment at work have succeeded. One such case is *Jones v Tower Boot Co Ltd*,[17] in which an employer was held liable under s. 1(1)(a) and s. 32 for acts of physical and verbal harassment by his employees against a fellow employee on the basis that this was action 'in the course of' their employment. In *Burton and Rhule v De Vere Hotels*,[18] the defendants were held liable under s. 1(1)(a) and s. 4 for harassment in a workplace by third parties. The facts were that two black waitresses served at table at a Round Table dinner at which the main speaker was Bernard Manning, a comedian with a reputation for making racist jokes. On seeing the waitresses, he made sexually racist remarks about them, following which some guests made other such remarks directly to the waitresses and one of the waitresses was physically harassed. An assistant manager intervened and the waitresses were offered work behind the bar, but no guest was

---

15 Cf. Rose LJ in *R v Tower Hamlets London Borough Council, ex p Mohib Ali* (1993) 25 HLR 218 at 225, CA: 'it is common ground that this does not depend on intention or motive, but simply on whether "but for" their race, persons would have been more favourably treated.'

16 *Owen and Briggs v James* [1982] ICR 618 at 622, 626, CA. Although this case pre-dates the adoption of the 'but for' test, it is likely to apply in cases where there is more than one reason for the defendant's action.

17 See the extract below, p. 1105.

18 [1996] IRLR 596, EAT. See R. Mullender, (1998) 61 MLR 236, who points out that Mr Manning's remarks might also have been an offence under s. 5, Public Order Act 1986, above, p. 472 (abusive or insulting behaviour likely to cause harassment, alarm or distress). See also on the *Burton and Rhule* case, K. Monaghan and M. Javaid, (1997) 147 NLJ 350.

required to leave. The employer later wrote apologising to the complainants, but they brought tribunal claims alleging that they had been discriminated against contrary to s. 4(2)(c), 1976 Act by being 'subjected' to 'detriment' by the employer. The Employment Appeal Tribunal allowed an appeal against a tribunal decision dismissing their claim. The EAT held that an employer 'subjects' an employee to the detriment of racial harassment in breach of s. 4(2)(c) if he, by the application of good employment practice, could have prevented the harassment occurring in the workplace. In this case, the employer could have warned his assistant managers to monitor Mr Manning's speech and to withdraw the waitresses before matters had proceeded so far.

Words of discouragement also may amount to racial discrimination.[19] Although aimed at stalking, not discrimination, the Protection From Harassment Act 1997[20] can extend to the latter. A local authority is not liable in common law nuisance or negligence for continuous racial harassment by tenants of a council housing estate.[1]

3. For there to be illegal direct racial discrimination, it is necessary to show that discrimination in the sense of s. 1(1)(a) of the 1976 Act has occurred in the context of some other provision of the Act. In *De Souza v Automobile Association*,[2] a coloured employee overheard the manager tell a clerk to give some typing to the 'wog', viz. herself. The Court of Appeal was prepared to hold that the applicant had been treated less favourably for the purposes of s. 1(1)(a) provided that 'he intended her to overhear the conversation in which it was used, or knew or ought reasonably to have anticipated that the person he was talking to would pass the insult on or that the employee would become aware of it in some other way'. The question was then whether the discrimination was to the applicant's 'detriment' as an employee contrary to s. 4 of the Act, which concerns discrimination in employment. Holding that it was not, May LJ stated for a unanimous court:

> '...the detriment or disadvantage to the employee ... [must be] in connection with ... his employment context ... I think that this necessarily follows upon a proper construction of section 4, and in particular section 4(2)(c) of the Act. Racially to insult a coloured employee is not enough by itself, even if that insult caused him or her distress; before the employee can be said to have been subjected to some "other detriment" the court or tribunal must find that by reason of the act or acts complained of a reasonable worker would or might take the view that he had thereby been disadvantaged in the circumstances in which he had thereafter to work.'

4. Failure to follow the standards of a reasonable employer in dismissal procedures does not lead to a presumption that an employer is treating the dismissed employee less favourably than other employees for the purposes of the Race Relations Act 1976; such a conclusion must be based on a comparison with the procedures followed in the case of other employees.[3] Moreover, if less favourable treatment is proven, it cannot be concluded that this is on 'racial grounds' without hearing the employer's explanation.[4]

5. Section 1(2) makes it clear that segregation (e.g. in public houses) is illegal. In *Furniture, Timber and Allied Trades Union v Modgill; Pel Ltd v Modgill*,[5] only Asians were employed in a factory paintshop. White employees had worked there, but as vacancies had arisen they had been filled by Asians who had been alerted to their

---

19 *Simon v Brimham Associates* [1987] ICR 596, 600, CA, per Balcombe LJ. See also *Tower Hamlets London Borough Council v Rabib* [1989] ICR 693, EAT. The cases concerned remarks that Jews or persons who could not work on Saturdays might have difficulty in being employed.
20 Above, p. 941.
 1 *Hussain v Lancaster City Council* [1999] 4 All ER 125, CA (Asian shopkeeper's premises on council estate subject for years to physical and verbal racial abuse by tenants, leading to some criminal convictions).
 2 [1986] ICR 514, CA. See H. Carty, (1986) 49 MLR 653.
 3 *Strathclyde City Council v Zafar* [1998] 2 All ER 953, HL. See A. Korn, (1997) 141 SJ 1213.
 4 Ibid.
 5 [1980] IRLR 142 at 166 EAT. For a comment on the case, see (1981) 97 LQR 10.

existence by Asians already employed in the paintshop. For two years, all vacancies had been filled 'by word of mouth' in this way, without the employer having to advertise for candidates or otherwise take the initiative. An allegation of segregation contrary to the Act made by some of the Asian paintshop workers was rejected:

> '...had there been evidence of a policy to segregate, and of the fact of segregation arising as a result of the company's acts, that might well have constituted a breach of the legislation; but it does not seem to us that there was evidence to support that position. We do not consider that the failure of the company to intervene and to insist on white or non-Asian workers going into the shop, contrary to the wishes of the men to introduce their friends, itself constituted the act of segregating persons on racial grounds within the meaning of s. 1(2) of the Act.'

In *Qadus v Henry Robinson (Ironfounders) Ltd*,[6] it was held by an industrial tribunal that the defendant had infringed s. 1(1)(a) by having separate toilets for Asian and white employees.

Showboat Entertainment Centre v Owens [1984] 1 WLR 384, Employment Appeal Tribunal

The appellant, who was white, was dismissed from his post as the manager of an amusement centre for failure to obey an order to exclude black youths. He was awarded £1,350 compensation for discrimination against him contrary to ss. 1(1)(a) and 4(2)(c) (employment provision) of the 1976 Act. The employer appealed.

Browne-Wilkinson J (for the Tribunal): In essence, the question raised by this appeal is whether, for the purposes of the Act of 1976, A can unlawfully discriminate against B on the ground of C's race. . . .

The racially discriminatory instructions given by the employers to the applicant were unlawful by virtue of s. 30.[7] But under s. 63 only the Commission for Racial Equality has the right to bring proceedings based on such illegality. The applicant can only bring a complaint if he brings himself within s. 54(1)(*a*) by showing that there has been unlawful discrimination 'against' him. Therefore the question is whether the racially discriminatory instruction not to admit blacks (which constituted discrimination 'against' the blacks excluded) can also be regarded as discrimination 'against' the applicant.

In *Zarczynska v Levy* [1979] 1 WLR 125, the circumstances were broadly the same as in the present case: an employee [a barmaid in a pub] who had not got the necessary qualifying period to complain of unfair dismissal was dismissed because of her refusal to obey an instruction not to serve black customers. This appeal tribunal held that she had been unlawfully discriminated against contrary to s. 4(2)(*c*) of the Act of 1976. . . .

In our judgment, the words of section 1(1)(*a*) are capable of two possible meanings, the one reflecting the broad approach of Mr Hytner and the other the narrower approach of Mr Harvey. It is plain that the person 'against' whom there has been discrimination is the person who is being treated less favourably by the discriminator, i.e. the words 'that other' in paragraph (*a*) refer back to 'another' in the phrase 'a person discriminates against another' at the beginning of the subsection. Therefore the only question is whether the applicant was treated less favourably 'on racial grounds.' Certainly the main thrust of the legislation is to give protection to those discriminated against on the grounds of their own racial characteristics. But the words 'on racial grounds' are perfectly capable in their ordinary sense of covering any reason for an action based on race, whether it be the race of the person affected by the action or of others.

. . . The fact that the giving of racialist instructions is dealt with separately in section 30 in a part of the Act headed 'Other unlawful acts' is in our judgment explicable without requiring the words 'on racial grounds' to be given a narrow meaning. . . . [A]part from s. 30, the mere giving of the instruction unaccompanied by an action pursuant to such an instruction which falls within Parts II or III would not be rendered unlawful by Parts II or III of the Act. Therefore

6   (1980) CRE Report 1980, p. 84.
7   *Ed.* For s. 30, see below, p. 1104.

s. 30 by making unlawful the giving of the instruction itself is creating another unlawful act, namely, the mere giving of the instruction. Moreover there is nothing manifestly absurd in giving the Commission for Racial Equality the right to take proceedings to stop the giving of such instructions . . . at the same time as giving a right to individual redress to someone who has actually suffered as a result of such instruction.

At this stage we should note a point . . . which has caused us some hesitation. . . . It seems to us clear that in relation to indirect discrimination under sub-s. (1)(*b*) the discrimination must relate to the race of the person against whom it is exercised. Thus, the requirement or condition is applied to 'that other'; it is the racial group of 'that other' whose ability to comply with the requirement has to be considered; it is detriment to 'that other' which has to be shown. . . . it might be argued that the same must also be true in relation to direct discrimination under s. 1(1)(*a*). However . . . Mr Hytner provided the answer. He said that if, for example, an employee refused to carry out an indirectly discriminatory recruitment policy on the ground that it was racially discriminatory and was dismissed for such refusal, his dismissal would be 'on racial grounds' within s. 1(1)(*a*) not withstanding that his refusal was a refusal to be a party to indirect discrimination within s. 1(1)(*b*).

. . . We find it impossible to believe that Parliament intended that a person dismissed for refusing to obey an unlawful discriminatory instruction should be without a remedy. It places an employee in an impossible position if he has to choose between being party to an illegality and losing his job. It seems to us that Parliament must have intended such an employee to be protected so far as possible from the consequences of doing his lawful duty by refusing to obey such an instruction. . . .

We, like the appeal tribunal in the *Levy* case, gain considerable support from certain remarks made in the Court of Appeal in *Race Relations Board v Applin* [1973] QB 815.[8] That case was concerned with incitement by Mr Applin to stop foster parents taking in coloured children placed with them by the local authority. . . .

The Court of Appeal held that such conduct [by the foster parents] would have amounted to discrimination against the children themselves. But Lord Denning MR said that they would also have discriminated against the local authority. Counsel had put to the Court of Appeal the example of two white women who were refused entrance to a public house if accompanied by coloured men. After quoting section 1 of the Act of 1968, Lord Denning MR said, at p. 828:

'That definition of discrimination is wide enough to cover the case of the two women. They are treated less favourably than other women on the ground of colour. Similarly in this case [the foster parents] would discriminate against the local authorities on the ground of colour if they said: "We will take white children only."'

Stephenson LJ [agreed] . . .

We therefore agree with the decision in *Zarczynska v Levy* . . . (although for rather different reasons) and hold that on the facts as found by the industrial tribunal . . . the applicant had been unlawfully discriminated against.

Appeal dismissed.

NOTES

1. In *Zarczynska v Levy*, to which the Tribunal refers, the CRE took proceedings in the county court against a publican for a declaration that his instruction not to serve coloured men had been contrary to s. 30. Kilner Brown J stated:

'Can it not be said in the instant case that in dismissing the one barmaid because she wanted to serve some coloured men, and not dismissing a barmaid who was prepared to apply the embargo, the employer treated the one less favourably than the other on racial grounds? We recognise that s. 1(1) of the Act of 1976 has to be read in conjunction with the other provisions to which reference has been made and that a broad approach to s. 1(1) may be prevented or delimited by the effect of other provisions. If we could say, however, that such other provisions are explanatory of or provide remedies for instances of breach of the general principle, then the general principle would not be restricted. This might involve reading into section 1 the

8   See on this case, below, p. 1143.

purposive intent of Parliament to make it a section which overrides subsequent sections which might otherwise be deemed to limit the provisions of that section. If this is not done the strict interpretation of the relevant sections taken as a whole may well create an absurd—or unjust situation which Parliament would not have intended if they had contemplated its possibility.

. . . We are of opinion here that if Parliament had had pre-knowledge of this unfortunate complain-ant's predicament they would have made clear that the great civilised principle upon which the Act was based was one which overrode all apparent limitations expressed in other sections which had the effect of denying justice to someone who was victimised.'

Earlier, Kilner Brown J had referred to s. 2(1)(d). Would it have been possible to have decided either the *Levy* or the *Owens* case (as to which see above, p. 1088) in favour of the claimant under s. 2?

2. In *Wilson v TB Steelwork Co Ltd*,[9] a white woman was held by an industrial tribunal to have been discriminated against contrary to the 1976 Act when she was refused employment because she was married to a West Indian.

(C) INDIRECT DISCRIMINATION

Section 1(1)(b) made indirect racial discrimination illegal in English law for the first time. The government White Paper[10] explained the reason for this and gave examples:

'One important weakness in the existing legislation is the narrowness of the definition of unlawful discrimination upon which it is based. . . . [I]t is insufficient for the law to deal only with overt discrimination. It should also prohibit practices which are fair in a formal sense but discriminatory in their operation and effect. . . .

The new Bill . . . will, for example, cover the situation where an employer requires applicants to pass an educational test before obtaining employment if (a) the test operates to disqualify coloured applicants at a substantially higher rate than white applicants and (b) it cannot be shown to be significantly related to job performance. The employer will be required to stop using such a test. . . . The provision will similarly apply to requirements concerning the clothing worn by employees (e.g. preventing the wearing of turbans or saris) or their minimum height, where such requirements cannot be shown to be justifiable.'

The concept was consciously imported from US law. In *Griggs v Duke Power Co*,[11] the US Supreme Court used it in the employment context to rule against a requirement for certain jobs in a power station that the occupant have graduated from high school or have passed an intelligence test. The Court stated:

'Congress has now provided that tests or criteria for employment or promotion may not provide equality of opportunity merely in the sense of the fabled offer of milk to the stork and the fox. . . . The Act proscribes not only overt discrimination but also practices that are fair in form, but discriminatory in operation. The touchstone is business necessity. If an employment practice which operates to exclude Negroes cannot be shown to be related to job performance, the practice is prohibited.'

Indirect discrimination was introduced into English law in the Sex Discrimination Act 1975 which contains in s. 1(1)(b) the same provision *mutatis mutandis* as the Race Relations Act 1976, s. 1(1)(b). The case law that has developed under the Sex Discrimination Act is helpful in interpreting the Race Relations Act.

(i) Discriminatory practices

The prohibition of indirect discrimination in s. 1(1)(b) is supplemented by that in s. 28. This provides:

9 (1978), cited in IDS *Racial Discrimination Employment Law Handbook 28* (1984), p. 7.
10 Cmnd. 6234, pp. 8, 13.
11 (1971) 401 US 424, 431.

'(1) In this section "discriminatory practice" means the application of a requirement or condition which results in an act of discrimination which is unlawful by virtue of any provision of Part II or III taken with section 1(1)(*b*), or which would be likely to result in such an act of discrimination if the persons to whom it is applied included persons of any particular racial group as regards which there has been no occasion for applying it.

(2) A person acts in contravention of this section if and so long as—

    (*a*) he applies a discriminatory practice; or

    (*b*) he operates practices or other arrangements which in any circumstances would call for the application by him of a discriminatory practice.'

The purpose of s. 28 is indicated in the government White Paper:[12]

'It will also be unlawful to apply a requirement or condition which results or would be likely to result in an act of discrimination as defined above, irrespective of whether the requirement or condition is actually applied to a particular victim. . . . This will, for example, cover the situation where an employer operates recruiting arrangements which result in there being no coloured applicants for job vacancies and thus no act of discrimination against any individual victim.'

Section 28 is enforceable only by a non-discrimination notice issued by the CRE after a formal investigation;[13] it is not enforceable by court proceedings. Thus in the *Barlavington Manor Children's Home* case,[14] a private children's home which had made it known that it was not prepared to accept black children from local authorities so that no such children had been sent to it was found to have operated a discriminatory practice contrary to s. 28 and a non-discrimination notice was issued.

Perera v Civil Service Commission (No 2) [1983] ICR 428, Court of Appeal

The appellant was a Sri Lankan national who had been educated in Sri Lanka. On coming to the United Kingdom, he had qualified as a barrister and been employed as a civil servant in the executive grade. He had applied unsuccessfully for the post of legal assistant in the Civil Service. A person appointed to this post *had* to be a barrister or solicitor. In addition other considerations were taken into account, including command of English and experience in the United Kingdom. In his claim of indirect racial discrimination, the question arose whether these additional considerations were 'requirements or conditions' in the sense of s. 1(1)(b). The following extract concerns just this point.

Stephenson LJ: According to the appeal tribunal, it was clear from the evidence before the industrial tribunal that in making their selection the board took four factors into account among others: whether the complainant had experience in the United Kingdom, whether he had a good command of the English language, whether he had British nationality or intended to apply for it, and his age. His interview with the board lasted for about half an hour. He was asked a number of questions and he was graded under four letters, A to D. C meant only fair and D meant poor. The four qualities, or heads, in respect of which he was marked were: personal qualities, ability to communicate, intellectual capacity and potential. The marking that he received from all three members of the interview board was C in respect of the first three and D in respect of the last. The board therefore assessed him as an unsuitable candidate and marked his papers "never to be seen again.". That marking was held by the industrial tribunal to be objectionable and has happily since been discarded altogether.

    The chairman's report on him was in these terms:

12 Cmnd. 6234, p. 13.
13 See below, p. 1162.
14 F Invest Rep 1979.

'Experience is essentially centred in Sri Lanka. Bar exams but no practical legal experience in four years in U.K., and had apparently made little attempt to keep up to date on his legal knowledge. His answers generally lacked point. Ponderous in style, deliberate in communication, but regrettably clearly short of minimum recruitment standard.'...

The matters which have to be established by an applicant who claims that he has been discriminated against indirectly are, first of all, that there has been a requirement or condition, as the complainant put it, a "must": something which has to be complied with. Here there was a requirement or condition for candidates for the post of legal assistant in the Civil Service: it was that the candidate should be either a qualified member of the English Bar or a qualified solicitor of the Supreme Court of this country—an admitted man or a barrister; and those conditions or requirements—those "musts"—were fulfilled by the complainant. But, as he admitted in his argument before the appeal tribunal and before this court, there is no other express requirement or condition, and he has to find a requirement or condition in the general combination of factors which he says the interview board took into account. He cannot formulate, as in my judgment he has to, what the particular requirement or condition is which he says has been applied to him and to his attempt to obtain a post of legal assistant. That is the hurdle which, as it seems to me, he is unable to get over.

I do not find that the industrial tribunal singled out the four factors which are singled out by the appeal tribunal and on which the complainant so strongly relies. But in my opinion none of those factors could possibly be regarded as a requirement of a condition in the sense that the lack of it, whether of British nationality or even of the ability to communicate well in English, would be an absolute bar. The whole of the evidence indicates that a brilliant man whose personal qualities made him suitable as a legal assistant might well have been sent forward on a short list by the interview board in spite of being, perhaps, below standard on his knowledge of English and his ability to communicate in that language.

That is only an illustration, but once it appears clear from the evidence that the industrial tribunal were entitled to conclude that it was personal qualities for which the interviewing board were mainly looking, and it was personal qualities, as stated in the chairman's report and as was made clear by the markings of all the members of the board, which, in the opinion of the board, the complainant lacked, and that that was the reason for not sending him forward on the short list, the case of indirect discrimination which the complaintant seeks to make, in my opinion, falls to the ground.

O'Connor LJ delivered a concurring judgment. **Sir George Baker** concurred.

Appeal dismissed.

NOTES

1. The approach to the meaning of 'requirement or condition' in the *Perera* case has been followed subsequently. It has been criticised as being too strict, placing minorities at a serious disadvantage.[15] In *Meer v London Borough of Tower Hamlets*,[16] although following it as a binding precedent, Balcombe LJ stated that there were 'strong arguments' for saying that the *Perera* case 'may not be consistent with the object of the Act'. The *Perera* case was avoided in the sex discrimination case of *Jones v University of Manchester*,[17] when the tribunal found that a preference ('preferably aged 25–35') was really a 'requirement' because the evidence revealed that it was such in fact.

2. In many cases, a person may not appreciate that a 'requirement or condition' that he has imposed is indirectly discriminatory. Although he is nonetheless liable under

15 See M. Connolly, (1995) Cambrian LR 83.
16 [1988] IRLR 399 at 403, CA. See Sylvester, (1989) 23 Law Teacher 202.
17 [1993] ICR 474, CA. With some hesitation, the Court of Appeal accepted the tribunal's finding of fact. See M. Connolly, (1997) 18 Stat LR 160.

the Act, allowance is made by the rule that damages may not be awarded if there is 'no intention of treating the claimant unfavourably on racial grounds' (s. 57(3)). A declaration or other civil remedy is available in such cases.[18]

Orphanos v Queen Mary College [1985] AC 761, [1985] 2 All ER 233, [1985] 2 WLR 703, House of Lords

The plaintiff, a Cypriot national, was required to pay an 'overseas student' university tuition fee of £3,600. Had he been 'ordinarily resident' in the EEC for the preceding three years (which then meant residence for purposes other than purely educational purposes), he would have had to have paid only the home/EEC student fee of £480. He claimed, inter alia, that this 'requirement' amounted to indirect discrimination contrary to ss. 1(1)(b) and 17, Race Relations Act 1976.

In the following extract from his speech, Lord Fraser considered whether the ordinary residence requirement fell within the three conditions set by s. 1(1)(b).

Lord Fraser: That requirement will only be discriminatory within the meaning of paragraph (*b*) [of s. 1(1), 1976 Act] if it falls within all three sub-paragraphs (i), (ii), (iii). Clearly it does fall within sub-paragraph (iii) because Mr. Orphanos, not having been 'ordinarily resident' in the area of the EEC for three years before 1 September 1982, cannot now comply with that requirement. Sub-paragraph (i) is more doubtful, but the college has conceded that it also applies.

. . . Strictly speaking the House could proceed simply on the basis of the admission [i.e. concession] without considering whether it had made correctly, but as this is a test case, and as the point does not seem to be covered by any authority, I think it is right to attempt to clarify a somewhat obscure provision. The draftsman of the notice of admission evidently had in mind section 3(2) of the Act of 1976 . . . which provides in effect that a racial group may comprise two or more distinct racial groups.

The admission seems to be made on the footing that Mr. Orphanos belongs to three racial groups (Cypriot, non-British, and non-EEC) and that it makes no difference which of these groups is chosen for the comparison required by section 1(1)(*b*)(i). I agree that Mr. Orphanos belongs to each of these groups, and that each is a 'racial group' as defined by section 3(1) as extended by section 3(2). But I do not agree that it makes no difference which of these groups is used for the comparison under section 1(1)(*b*)(i). The comparison must be between the case of a person of the same racial group as Mr. Orphanos and the case of a person not of that racial group, but it must be such that 'the relevant circumstances in the one case are the same, or not materially different, in the other': see section 3(4). The 'relevant circumstances' in the present case are, in my view, that Mr. Orphanos wished to be admitted as a pupil at the college, so the comparison must be between persons of the same racial group as him who wish to be admitted to the college, and persons not of that racial group who so wish. Consider first the two largest groups—namely persons of non-British and non-EEC nationality (omitting the reference to national origins *brevitatis causa*.) I have no doubt that the proportion of persons of non-British and non-EEC nationality who wish to attend the college and who can comply with the requirement of having ordinarily resided in the EEC area for three years immediately before 1 September 1982 is substantially smaller than the proportion of persons not of that group (i.e., persons who *were* British or EEC nationals) who wish to attend the college and who can comply with it. That seems obvious and causes no difficulty. But consider now the group consisting of persons of Cypriot (or Greek Cypriot) nationality and compare it with the group consisting of persons not of Cypriot (or Greek Cypriot) nationality, i.e., consisting of all persons (except Cypriots) of every nationality from Chinese to Peruvian inclusive. If the comparison is between persons of those groups who wish to be admitted to the college as pupils I do not see how any sensible comparison can be made because it would be impracticable to ascertain the numbers of persons so wishing. On the other hand if it is limited to persons

---

18 See, e.g. the *Orphanos* case, below.

who actually apply to the college for admission it would omit all those who may have been deterred from applying because they knew that they would not comply with the residence qualification. A comparison limited to applicants would, in my view, be entirely unsatisfactory.

I am accordingly of opinion that the concession should not have been made with regard to persons of Cypriot nationality. But the omission of that part of the concession would make no difference to the result because in terms of section 3(1), references to a person's racial group refer to *any* racial group into which he falls. As Mr. Orphanos falls into two racial groups, both of which are caught by section 1(1)(*b*)(i), that is enough to make that paragraph apply to his case.

On the assumption that the residence qualification is therefore caught by section 1(1)(*b*)(i), it is necessary to consider under 1(1)(*b*)(ii) whether the requirement is 'justifiable irrespective of the colour, race, nationality or ethnic or national origins of the [student] to whom it is applied.' Nationality is the only one of these grounds which is in question in this appeal. 'Justifiable' means, in my opinion, 'capable of being justified.' 'Irrespective of' in that subsection means 'without regard to,' as I said in *Mandla (Sewa Singh) v Dowell Lee* [below, p. 1114], and I see no reason to alter that opinion. No doubt the main reason for introducing the residence requirement was, as Mr. Scrivener said, to curtail public expenditure on education in the interest of economy. That reason itself did not involve discrimination on racial grounds.

. . . But the economy was to be effected at the expense of foreign students. That may have been a perfectly reasonable and justifiable policy for the British Government to adopt but in my opinion the college, on whom the onus lies under section 1(1)(*b*)(ii), has not been able to justify the requirement without having regard to the nationality of the applicants at whose expense the policy was carried into effect. The typical example of a requirement which was caught by section 1(1)(*b*)(i) but which was nevertheless justifiable irrespective of racial grounds was *Panesar v Nestlé Co Ltd* [1980] ICR 144 where it was held that a rule forbidding the wearing of beards in the respondent's chocolate factory was justifiable on hygienic grounds notwithstanding that the proportion of Sikhs who could conscientiously comply with it was considerably smaller than the proportion of non-Sikhs who could comply with it. The justification there was purely a matter of public health and nothing whatever to do with racial grounds. But in the present case the discrimination is in accordance with a policy directed against persons who are not ordinarily resident in the EEC area, and ordinary residence is in my view so closely related to their nationality that the discrimination cannot be justified irrespective of nationality.

For these reasons I agree . . . that the college did discriminate on racial grounds against Mr. Orphanos.

NOTES

1. Although deciding that indirect racial discrimination had occurred,[19] Lord Fraser dismissed the plaintiff's appeal against the decisions of the county court and the Court of Appeal rejecting his claim to restitution of the difference between the overseas and home student fee because the discrimination was not intentional: see s. 57(3) of the 1976 Act, below, p. 1168. Lord Fraser's speech was concurred in by the other four members of the House of Lords.[20] The following notes concern the 'considerably smaller' requirement in s. 1(1)(b)(i). The justification defence is considered below in the notes following the *Hampson* case, below, p. 1098.

2. When considering the proportion of members of V's 'racial group' who can comply with a 'requirement or condition', the comparison must, in terms appropriate to an employment context, be with the 'pool of qualified persons', not the population at

19 Note that higher overseas student fees are now authorised by the Education (Fees and Awards) Act 1983 and delegated legislation thereunder so that s. 41, 1976 Act, see above, p. 1077, excludes liability under the Act.
20 See on this aspect of the case, I. Leigh, (1986) 49 MLR 235.

large: *Price v Civil Service Commission.*[1] In *Perera v Civil Service Commission (No 2),*[2] Stephenson LJ stated that this was made clear by s. 3(4) of the 1976 Act,[3] and continued:

'... you do not compare all the population of, in this case, Sri Lanka with all the population of England or any other racial group; you compare the persons in those two groups similarly qualified, and if you do that it is quite plain that in this case there was no evidence to prove that a substantially smaller proportion of persons from Sri Lanka who had got over the hurdle of Bar examinations or solicitor's final examinations than the proportion of barristers or solicitors from other racial groups could comply with anything that might be called a requirement or condition which would satisfy these examiners, as it were, of their suitability for the post of legal assistant.'

If an Englishman complained of the refusal of a publican in Wales to serve anyone who did not speak Welsh, what comparison would be made? Between Welsh and non-Welsh persons who could comply? Or between Welsh and English persons? In addition to the *Orphanos* case, see the *Bohon-Mitchell* case.[4]

3. In the *Mandla* case,[5] it was established that 'can comply' means 'can in practice' or 'can consistently with the customs and cultural conditions of the racial group'; it does not mean 'can physically'.

4. *Considerably smaller.* The comparison here is between the number of qualified persons of the victim's racial group and the number of qualified persons not of that group: the number of the former who can comply with the requirement or condition must be "considerably smaller" than the number of the later. The phrase 'considerably smaller' has been given a 'common sense' meaning.[6] There is no required method of proof. Judicial notice has been taken of well known facts about the population.[7] Because of the cost, elaborate statistical evidence is not required, at least not in all cases.[8] In cases in which statistics have been relied upon, no particular threshold percentage has been identified. In *Meeks v National Union of Agricultural and Allied Workers*[9] a female part-time typist complained that a lower hourly rate of pay for part-time, as opposed to full-time, typing was indirect discrimination under the Sex Discrimination Act. Although rejecting her claim on another ground, the industrial tribunal accepted her contention that the 'considerably smaller' criterion had been fulfilled. It did so on the basis of statistical evidence showing that 97% of employed men were in full-time employment (and hence satisfied the requirement for the higher rate of pay) but that only 68% of female employees were in such employment. Statistical evidence was also used in *Hussein v Saints Complete House Furnishers.*[10] It was held in *Wong v GLC*[11] that a 'requirement or condition' that *no* member of a racial group can comply with cannot be indirect discrimination because the Act imagines 'a smaller proportion who can comply, not zero':[12] Slynn J stated, obiter,

---

1 [1978] ICR 27 at 32, EAT (sex discrimination).
2 Above, p. 1093.
3 Below, p. 1109.
4 Below, p. 1101.
5 Below, p. 1114.
6 *Clarke v Eley (IMI) Kynoch Ltd* [1982] IRLR 131, 137, Ind Trib (sex discrimination).
7 *Perera v Civil Service Commission (No 2),* above.
8 Ibid.
9 [1976] IRLR 198, Ind Trib.
10 Below, p. 1100.
11 (1980) EAT, cited in IDS *Racial Discrimination: Employment Law Handbook* (1984), p. 11
12 Contrast *Wetstein v Misprestige Management Services Ltd* EAT 523/91, EAT (5 to 10% fewer Jews able to comply than non-Jews: not considerably smaller) and *Greater Manchester Police Authority v Lea* (1990) IRLR 372, EAT (4.1% difference between men and women was considerably smaller). These cases are cited in IDS, *Race Discrimination: Employment Law Handbook* (1999), p. 25.

that it was 'obvious that someone who is brown cannot comply at all with the condition [imposed in the case] that the candidate has to be white' so that it was 'quite impossible to look for a smaller proportion of people who are able to satisfy the condition'. This dictum has, however, been doubted. In *Greencroft Social Club and Institute v Mullen*,[13] a sex discrimination case, Waite J stated:

> 'It will be sufficient to say of this citation that we are satisfied that the appeal tribunal did not intend in that case to lay down any general principle to the effect that nil can never for discrimination purposes be a proportion of the whole. If there was any such intention, we would feel justified in declining to follow it, because now that the matter has been raised before us for direct consideration powerful arguments come to our mind to the contrary. It would, in our view, run counter to the whole spirit and purpose of the sex discrimination legislation if a requirement or condition which otherwise fell within the definition in section 1(1)(*b*) because a negligible proportion of women as against men could comply with it was held to lie outside the legislation if the proportion was so negligible as to amount to no women at all.'

In most such cases, however, a claim of direct discrimination will be available. The dictum in the *Wong* case might be crucial, however, in claims of 'discriminatory practices' in the sense of s. 28 of the 1976 Act.[14] As noted above, s. 28 forbids discriminatory practices that amount to indirect discrimination. It is designed to meet the situation where, because of a known requirement, no applicants have applied for a job, house, etc. In the absence of individual victims, the – CRE instigated – procedure is applicable. The procedure does not apply where the discrimination which would have been practised is direct, not indirect, discrimination. In such cases there may be no victims so that a direct discrimination claim cannot be brought. For example, in the *Percy Ingle Bakeries Ltd* case,[15] a non-discrimination notice requiring a company not to contravene s. 28 by refusing to employ Pakistanis or black persons to serve in their bakery shops was quashed by an industrial tribunal. On the authority of *Wong v GLC*,[16] it was considered that such discrimination would have been direct, not indirect. Only one shop employee out of 140 was black, although there was a high ethnic minority population in the area. A manageress reported no job applications from black persons in three years.

Hampson v Department of Education [1989] ICR 179, [1990] 2 All ER 25, Court of Appeal

The appellant, of Hong Kong Chinese origin, had qualified as a teacher in Hong Kong, having taken a two year teacher training course there. In 1978, after teaching for eight years, she took a further one year teacher training course in Hong Kong and then became a teaching inspector. In 1984, the appellant came to the United Kingdom, where her application for qualified teacher status was rejected, *inter alia*, on the ground that her initial training did not meet a Department of Education requirement of a three year teacher training course. In this connection, the 1978 course that the appellant had taken was not regarded as an integral part of her initial training. The appellant claimed that the Department of Education requirement amounted to indirect discrimination contrary to ss. 1(1)(*b*) and 12, 1976 Act.[1] In argument before the Court of Appeal, it was accepted that the three year rule was a 'requirement' for the purposes of s. 1(1)(*b*) and that it had, in terms of s. 1(1)(*b*)(i), a disproportionate effect upon persons of the appellant's racial origin. The following extract concerns the justification defence under s. 1(1)(*b*)(ii).

---

13 [1985] ICR 796, 802, EAT.
14 Above, p. 1092.
15 CRE F Invest Rep 1983; IDS, *Race Discrimination: Employment Law Handbook* (1999), p. 78.
16 Above, p. 1097.
  1 For s. 12, see below, p. 1101.

Balcombe LJ: In *Ojutiku v Manpower Services Commission* [1982] ICR 661 this court was concerned with the meaning of 'justifiable' where it appears in section 1(1)(*b*)(ii) of the Act of 1976 and of course that decision is binding on us in so far as it decides that meaning. . . . However, I regret that I do not find, in two of the judgments in *Ojutiku*, any clear decision as to that meaning. . . . With all due respect to Eveleigh and Kerr LJJ, I derive little help from these judgments. 'Justifiable' and 'justify' are words which connote a value judgment, as is evident from the dictionary definition cited by Eveleigh LJ—'to produce adequate grounds for,' but neither Lord Justice indicates what test should be applied. Kerr LJ says it applies a lower standard than 'necessary,' but does not indicate how much lower. It was, however, accepted by Mr. Carlisle, and rightly so, that whatever test is to be applied it is an objective one: it is not sufficient for the employer to establish that he considered his reasons adequate. However I do derive considerable assistance from the judgment of Stephenson LJ. At p. 674, he referred to:

> 'the . . . judgment of the appeal tribunal given by Phillips J. in *Steel v Union of Post Office Workers* [1978] ICR 181, 187–188 . . . What Phillips J. there said is valuable as rejecting justification by convenience and requiring the party applying the discriminatory condition to prove it to be justifiable in all the circumstances on balancing its discriminatory effect against the discriminator's need for it. But that need is what is reasonably needed by the party who applies the condition; . . .'

In my judgment 'justifiable' requires an objective balance between the discriminatory effect of the condition and the reasonable needs of the party who applies the condition. This construction is supported by the recent decision of the House of Lords in *Rainey v Greater Glasgow Health Board* [1987] ICR 129, a case under the Equal Pay Act 1970, and turning on the provisions of section 1(3) of that Act . . .

The House of Lords held, applying the decision of the European Court in *Bilka-Kaufhaus GmbH v Weber von Hartz* (Case 170/84) [1987] ICR 110, that to justify a material difference under section 1(3) of the Equal Pay Act 1970, the employer had to show a real need on the part of the undertaking, objectively justified, although that need was not confined to economic grounds; it might, for instance, include administrative efficiency in a concern not engaged in commerce or business. Clearly it may, as in the present case, be possible to justify by reference to grounds other than economic or administrative efficiency. . . .

Mr. Sedley constructed an elaborate argument designed to show that *Ojutiku* had been overruled by *Rainey*. . . . However I do not find it necessary to consider this argument further here. For my part I can find no significant difference between the test adopted by Stephenson LJ in *Ojutiku* and that adopted by the House of Lords in *Rainey*. Since neither Eveleigh LJ nor Kerr LJ in *Ojutiku* indicated what they considered the test to be—although Kerr LJ said what it was not—I am content to adopt Stephenson LJ's test as I have expressed it above, which I consider to be consistent with *Rainey*. It is obviously desirable that the tests of justifiability applied in all these closely related fields should be consistent with each other.

NOTES

1. Nourse and Parker LJJ concurred in the judgment of Balcombe LJ on the interpretation of the justification defence. The case went on appeal to the House of Lords on a separate question whether the Department of Education had a defence under s. 41, 1976 Act on the basis that its refusal to recognise the appellant's course was an act done under lawful authority. The House of Lords reversed the Court of Appeal's decision, Balcombe LJ dissenting, that the Department of Education was immune by virtue of s. 41[2] and remitted the case to an industrial tribunal for a rehearing. The House of Lords did not consider the Court of Appeal's interpretation of the justification defence.

2. The 'justification' defence in s. 1(1)(b) has been the subject of disagreement. In *Steel v Union of Post Office Workers*[3] Phillips J stated:

2   See further on this point, above, p. 1077.
3   [1978] ICR 181, EAT (a sex discrimination case).

'. . . it is right to distinguish between a requirement or condition which is necessary and one which is merely convenient and for this purpose it is relevant to consider whether the employer can find some other and non-discriminatory method of achieving his object'.

This is consistent with the 'business necessity' test adopted in the American employment case[4] from which the concept of indirect discrimination derives, but is probably not what Parliament intended.[5]

Since *Steel*, a less demanding test has evolved. The approach that first prevailed was that indicated by Eveleigh LJ in *Ojutiku v Manpower Services Commission*:[6]

'For myself, it would be enough simply to ask myself: is it justifiable? But if I have to give some explanation of my understanding of that word, I would turn to a dictionary definition which says "adduce adequate grounds for"; and it seems to me that if a person produces reasons for doing something, which would be acceptable to right-thinking people as sound and tolerable reasons for so doing, then he has justified his conduct.'

In the course of applying the *Ojutiku* approach in *Clarke v Eley (IMI) Kynoch Ltd*,[7] Browne-Wilkinson J was critical of the discretion that a 'right-thinking people' test left to industrial tribunals on such emotive matters as racial or sex discrimination. In the *Hampson* case the Court of Appeal has itself responded to this criticism. Eveleigh LJ's 'acceptable to right-thinking people' formula in *Ojutiku* has now been replaced by the *Hampson* 'balancing' test.[8] The new test places a greater onus of proof upon the defendant than its predecessor. Even so, the test is not as strict as the unavoidable necessity test suggested earlier in *Steel*.

3. The following are examples of 'requirements or conditions' that have been held, by courts or tribunals not always applying the same test, to be justified: a rule prohibiting beards in a chocolate factory, for reasons of public hygiene;[9] a requirement that a person have managerial experience to be sponsored for a management course, because persons without such experience were unlikely to gain employment subsequently;[10] and a requirement that a Sikh factory employee wear a hard-hat in place of his turban.[11] It was also justifiable under the *Hampson* balancing test for a Church of England school to advertise for a committed communicant Christian as headmaster.[12]

Cases in which a justification defence has been rejected include the *Mandla* case;[13] *Hussein v Saints Complete House Furnishers*,[14] and *Bohon-Mitchell v Common Professional Examination Board*.[15] In the *Hussein* case, an employer decided not to employ youths from the 'City Centre' of Liverpool because 'lads who live within

---

4   *Griggs v Duke Power Co*, above, p. 1092.
5   In the drafting of the provision parallel to s. 1(1)(b) in the Sex Discrimination Act 1975, amendments to replace 'justifiable' by 'necessary' were rejected as being too strict: HC, Standing Committee B, 24 April 1975, cols. 64–79 and 362 HL Deb, 14 July 1975, cols. 1013–1020. On the justification defence, see L. Lustgarten, (1983) 133 NLJ 1057 and (1984) 134 NLJ 9.
6   [1982] ICR 661, 667–668, CA. Cf. Kerr LJ in the same case.
7   [1983] ICR 165, 174–175, EAT.
8   In *Webb v EMO Air Cargo* [1993] 1 WLR 49, the House of Lords approved the *Hampson* test as replacing that of Eveleigh LJ in *Ojutiku*. On the *Hampson* case, see E. Ellis, [1990] PL 461 and B. W. Napier, [1989] CLJ 187.
9   The *Panesar* case, above.
10   The *Ojutiku* case, above.
11   *Dhanjal v British Steel General Steels* (1993) Ind Trib, cited in G. Welhengama, 144 NLJ 671 (1994). The statutory exception for construction workers on religious grounds, see above, p. 1056, did not apply.
12   *Board of Governors of St Matthias Church of England School v Crizzle* [1993] ICR 401, EAT.
13   Below, p. 1114.
14   [1979] IRLR 337, Ind Trib.
15   [1978] IRLR 525, Ind Trib.

walking distance of our shop have a lot of friends out of work who stand in front of the shop, distracting their mates and putting customers off'. When the requirement was imposed, approximately 50% of the people in the City Centre were black whilst outside that zone the percentage of black residents was no more than 2%. It was held that the requirement could not be justified under the 1976 Act. In the *Bohon-Mitchell* case, the claimant was an American national and a graduate of an American university. She was married to a UK citizen and had been resident in the UK for five years overall. It was held that a requirement that she should, as a non-law graduate of a university other than a British or an Irish one, have to take a 21 month course to qualify for the Bar when non-law graduates of British or Irish universities need only take a course lasting 12 months, was indirect discrimination contrary to ss. 1(1)(b) and 12 of the Act.[1] The tribunal considered that the proportion of graduates not of British or Irish nationality who could qualify for the shorter course was 'considerably smaller' than those who were of such nationality and, applying *Steel*, that the Council's aim of ensuring that barristers be familiar with the English way of life could be attained in a way that was less detrimental to overseas graduates (by assessing their familiarity on a case by case basis) and was therefore not 'justifiable'. The defence was also unsuccessful in the *Orphanos* case.[2] The House of Lords there rejected the College's attempt to justify charging overseas students a higher tuition fee on economic grounds. Economic considerations could not justify the choice of a policy that was racially discriminatory. See also *Malik v British Home Stores*[3] in which a shop uniform that did not permit trousers was held to be unjustified. The tribunal 'accepted the evidence of an expert witness that the wearing of skirts without trousers by mature Muslim girls was forbidden and that some 14% of Blackburn's population was of Indian or Pakistani origin, mainly of the Muslim faith'.
4. 'Detriment' in s. 1(1)(b)(iii) does not require financial or other material loss. It simply means being put 'under a disadvantage', provided it is not *de minimis*.[4]
5. *Racial Justice at Work*[5] concluded that the extension of the law to control indirect discrimination has not proved as effective as had been expected:

> 'A central finding [of the present study] is that the attempt to extend the law to cover something wider than direct discrimination has not worked; and this has been one factor limiting the success of the strategic approach to combating institutional discrimination. The vast majority of cases heard by industrial tribunals were concerned only with direct discrimination, hence the tribunals were articulating concepts only in that area. ... In its role of assisting individual complainants, the CRE also concentrated on direct discrimination. ... In its strategic role ... it has since 1983 concentrated on direct discrimination in formal investigations of specified organisations; though the recommendations to employers following such investigations typically went wider, the investigations themselves were almost exclusively concerned with direct discrimination, so it was over direct discrimination that the main battles were fought. ...'

The CRE has recommended that the definition of indirect discrimination be changed to the following:[6]

1   s. 12 prohibits discrimination by authorities or bodies 'which can confer an authorisation or qualification which is needed for, or facilitates, engagement in a particular profession or trade'.
2   Above, p. 1095.
3   (1980) CRE Report 1980, p. 78. In *Kingston and Richmond Area Health Authority v Kaur* [1981] ICR 631, EAT, it was held that a requirement, based upon statutory authority, that if nurses wore a uniform it must not include trousers, was justified. The requirement has since been abolished: S.I. 1981 No. 1533.
4   *BL Cars Ltd v Brown* [1983] ICR 143 at 147, EAT, following *Ministry of Defence v Jeremiah* [1980] ICR 13 at 26, CA (a sex discrimination case: detriment was employment in dirty conditions). See also *De Souza v Automobile Association*, above, p. 1089.
5   Op. cit. at p. 1068, n. **1**, above, p. 271.
6   *Reform of the Race Relations Act 1976* (1998).

'Indirect discrimination occurs where an apparently neutral provision, criterion, practice or policy which is applied to persons of all racial groups cannot be as easily satisfied or complied with by persons of a particular racial group, or where there is a risk that the provision, criterion, practice or policy may operate to the disadvantage of persons of a particular racial group, unless the provision, criterion, practice or policy can be justified by objective factors unrelated to race.'

This definition would allow a claimant to prove indirect discrimination without having to rely on statistics or establish a suitable pool for comparison, as is the position at present.

(D) VICTIMISATION

Aziz v Trinity Street Taxis [1989] QB 463, Court of Appeal

The appellant taxi driver, who was of Asian origin, was a member of an organisation of taxi operators. During industrial tribunal proceedings in which he complained that the fee he was being charged to operate a taxi was racially discriminatory, he disclosed that he had tape recordings of private conversations with members of the organisation who were sympathetic to his case but were not prepared to speak out in public. It was after they had learnt of the tapes that the organisation expelled the appellant, who, in the present case, claimed victimisation contrary to s. 2(1)(c).

Slade LJ for the court:
The wording of paragraph (c) is 'otherwise done anything under or by reference to this Act in relation to the discriminator or any other person'. Slynn J in *Kirby v Manpower Services Commission* [1980] 1 WLR 725, 730, said, in relation to the word 'under': 'For it to be done under the Act one must find a specific statutory provision under which the report was made, and there is none'. On this appeal the correctness of this statement has not been challenged and no reliance has been placed by the complainant on the word 'under'. The question is whether he made his tape recordings 'by reference to the Act'.

...as we read their decision, [the tribunal] at least found, expressly or by necessary inference, that at the time when he made the recordings (i) the complainant considered that he was being unfairly treated by T.S.T. by reason of the imposition of the £1,000 fee; (ii) the possibility was beginning to form in his mind that this might amount to a form of racial discrimination and that correspondingly some form of legal redress might be available to him; (iii) he considered it possible that the secretly taken tape recordings might assist him if and when he chose to pursue that redress.

In our judgment, this was enough to entitle the industrial tribunal as a matter of law to find that the complainant, in making the tapes, had done an act 'by reference to' the Act in relation to T.S.T. The phrase 'by reference to' is, in our judgment, a much wider one that 'under' and should be read accordingly. An act can, in our judgment, properly be said to be done 'by reference to the Act' if it is done by reference to the race relations legislation in the broad sense, even though the doer does not focus his mind specifically on any provision of the Act. The inapposite reference by the industrial tribunal to discovery in March 1984 does not, in our judgment, vitiate their conclusion on this point, which should stand. ...

The complainant has, in our judgment, shown that he has done a protected act falling within category (c). However, in order to show that there has been discrimination by victimisation within section 2(1) of the Act, he still has to satisfy us that, in expelling him from membership, T.S.T. (1) 'in any circumstances relevant for the purposes of any provision of this Act[treated the complainant] less favourably than in those circumstances [it] treats or would treat other persons', and (2) did so *by reason that* the complainant had 'otherwise done anything ... by reference to this Act in relation to the discriminator ...' within the meaning of section 2(1)(c). We shall now turn to the first of these two issues and conclude by dealing with the issue of causation...

It is common ground that the opening words of section 2(1), containing the phrase 'less favourably than', necessitate a comparison of some kind or another. ...

The key to the correct relevant comparison, in our judgment, lies in correctly identifying the relevant 'circumstances' for the purpose of section 2(1) (in the present case in the context of a complaint under section 11(3)(*b*))[7] ...

The wording of section 2, in our judgment, plainly contemplates that the relevant circumstances will already subsist at the time when the treatment complained of occurs. Thus in our judgment in the present case, while the complainant's former membership of T.S.T. clearly is a relevant circumstance, the expulsion itself, being itself the treatment complained of, clearly is not.

The next question is whether the relevant circumstances include the circumstances giving rise to the termination of the complainant's membership or employment, as the Employment Appeal Tribunal considered in *Kirby v Manpower Services Commission* [1980] 1 WLR 725. A complaint made in reliance on section 2 necessarily presupposes that the complainant has done a protected act. If the doing of such an act itself constituted part of the relevant circumstances, a complainant would necessarily fail to establish discrimination if the alleged discriminator could show that he treated or would treat all other persons who did the like protected act with equal intolerance. This would be an absurd result and, in view of the separate, second limb of section 2(1), directed to the questions of causation to which we are about to come, such a construction is not, in our judgment, required for the protection of persons who might otherwise be found to have discriminated unlawfully by virtue of the subsection. In our judgment, for the purpose of the comparison which section 2(1) makes requisite, the relevant circumstances do not include the fact that the complainant has done a protected act.

In our judgment therefore, Mr Sedley is right in submitting that the respective tests applied by the Employment Appeal Tribunal in *Kirby v Manpower Services Commission* and in the present case, for the purpose of effecting the comparison made requisite by the opening words of section 2(1), were not the correct tests. The treatment applied by the alleged discriminator to the complainant has to be compared with the treatment which he has applied or would apply to persons who have *not* done the relevant protected act.

Applying this test, it is clear that on the facts of the present case and in the circumstances relevant for the purposes of sections 2 and 11(3)(*b*), i.e. the complainant's membership of T.S.T., T.S.T. *has* treated the complainant 'less favourably than in those circumstances [it] treats ... other persons,' i.e. by expelling him from membership. On this point the complainant's argument is, in our judgment, well founded. ...

[The Court of Appeal then considered the question of causation and held against the appellant on the ground that the evidence did not show that the fact he had made the recordings was the reason why he had been expelled from the organisation. For this reason the appeal was dismissed. Comments made by the Court in this case on the relevance of racial motivation were disapproved in the *Nagarajan* case.[8]]

Appeal dismissed.

NOTES

1. The fear of victimisation and the absence of any protection from it was identified by the RRB as one of the reasons why minority groups had been reluctant to complain under the 1968 Act.[9] Section 2 covers victimisation by a third person as well as the person against whom proceedings have been brought, etc. It also protects persons who are not themselves victims of direct or indirect discrimination.

2. Racial motivation for the discriminatory act of victimisation is not required; instead a 'but for' test applies.[10] The 'but for' test was applied in *Chief Constable of West*

7 *Ed.* Section 11 concerns discrimination by organisations, such as the taxi organisation in this case.
8 Above, p. 1086.
9 RRB Report 1973, p. 14.
10 *Nagarajan* case, above, p. 1086.

Yorkshire v Khan.[11] In that case, a police sergeant was applying for a job with a different police force. The police force in which he was serving allegedly victimised him contrary to s. 2 by refusing to give him a reference because he was also bringing a racial discrimination claim against them in respect of promotion procedures. The force stated that its motivation was not racial; its policy was to refuse a reference to any person bringing legal proceedings against it, whether racial discrimination proceedings or proceedings of another kind. The Court of Appeal held that s. 2(1)(a) applied; the reference would not have been refused 'but for' the bringing of the proceedings. In the same case, the Court of Appeal held that the correct comparison was not with other persons who had brought proceedings against the force, but with other officers requesting references.
3. The CRE has recommended that the offence of victimisation be extended so as to make it unlawful to victimise a former employee by providing a negative reference or by varying his or her pension where the initial complaint had been made during the course of employment.[12]

(C) INSTRUCTIONS AND PRESSURE TO DISCRIMINATE, VICARIOUS LIABILITY AND AIDING

Race Relations Act 1976

30. Instructions to discriminate
It is unlawful for the person—
    (*a*)   who has authority over another person; or
    (*b*)   in accordance with whose wishes that other person is accustomed to act,
to instruct him to do any act which is unlawful by virtue of Part II or III, or procure or attempt to procure the doing by him of any such act.

31. Pressure to discriminate
(1) It is unlawful to induce, or attempt to induce, a person to do any act which contravenes Part II or III.
(2) An attempted inducement is not prevented from falling within subsection (1) because it is not made directly to the person in question, if it is made in such a way that he is likely to hear of it.

32. Liability of employers and principals
(1) Anything done by a person in the course of his employment shall be treated for the purposes of this Act (except as regards offences thereunder) as done by his employer as well as by him, whether or not it was done with the employer's knowledge or approval.
(2) Anything done by a person as agent for another person with the authority (whether express or implied, and whether precedent or subsequent) of that other person shall be treated for the purposes of this Act (except as regards offences thereunder) as done by that other person as well as by him.
(3) In proceedings brought under this Act against any person in respect of an act alleged to have been done by an employee of his it shall be a defence for that person to prove that he took such steps as were reasonably practicable to prevent the employee from doing that act, or from doing in the course of his employment acts of that description.

33. Aiding unlawful acts
(1) A person who knowingly aids another person to do an act made unlawful by this Act shall be treated for the purposes of this Act as himself doing an unlawful act of the like description.
(2) For the purposes of subsection (1) an employee or agent for whose act the employer or principal is liable under section 32 (or would be so liable but for section 32(3)) shall be deemed to aid the doing of the act by the employer or principal.
(3) A person does not under this section knowingly aid another to do an unlawful act if—

---

11 [2000] IRLR 324, CA.
12 *Reform of the Race Relations Act 1976* (1998).

(*a*)   he acts in reliance on a statement made to him by that other person that, by reason of any provision of this Act, the act which he aids would not be unlawful; and

(*b*)   it is reasonable for him to rely on the statement.

(4) A person who knowingly or recklessly makes a statement such as is mentioned in subsection (3)(*a*) which in a material respect is false or misleading commits an offence, and shall be liable on summary conviction to a fine not exceeding [level 5 on the standard scale].

NOTE

Sections 30–33 of the 1976 Act provide for liability for racial discrimination under the Act for secondary involvement in acts of discrimination by others. The most important in practice is the provision of vicarious liability for employers in s. 32.

Jones v Tower Boot Co Ltd [1997] 2 All ER 407, CA

The appellant, a 16-year-old boy of mixed ethnic parentage, went to work at a shoe factory. After being subjected to persistent verbal and physical racial abuse by fellow workers, he resigned after four weeks of employment. An industrial tribunal awarded him £5,000 compensation from his employer under the Race Relations Act 1976 on the basis that the employer was responsible for each employee's conduct because it occurred 'in the course of his employment' (1976 Act, s. 32(1)). The appellant appealed to the Court of Appeal against the decision of the Employment Appeal Tribunal to overturn the tribunal's decision in his favour. In the Employment Appeal Tribunal's view, the offending acts had not been committed 'in the course of his employment'. The Court of Appeal unanimously allowed the appeal.

Waite LJ: In April 1992, a 16-year-old boy started work at the employers' shoe factory, as a last operative. He was of mixed ethnic parentage and was joining a workforce which had not previously employed anyone of ethnic minority origin. From the outset, he was subjected by fellow employees to harassment of the gravest kind. He was called by such racially offensive names as 'chimp' and 'monkey'. A notice had been stuck on his back reading 'Chipmonks are go'. Two employees whipped him on the legs with a piece of welt and threw metal bolts at his head. One of them burnt his arm with a hot screwdriver, and later the same two seized his arm again and tried to put it in a lasting machine, where the burn was caught and started to bleed again. Unable to endure this treatment the boy left the job after four weeks. He made a complaint against the employers of racial discrimination, contending that his fellow employees had subjected him to a discriminatory detriment on racial grounds under s. 4(2)(c) of the Race Relations Act 1976 (racial harassment), for which the employers were responsible by virtue of s. 32(1) of the Act as representing acts done by the employees in the course of their employment. The employers sought to resist the claim on the ground that the relevant acts had been outside the scope of the employees' employment; or, on the alternative ground that all reasonably practicable steps to avoid them for the purposes of s. 32(3) (the reasonable steps defence) had been taken.

On appeal to the Employment Appeal Tribunal, the employers did not challenge the industrial tribunal's primary findings of fact as to the treatment given to the complainant or the finding that such treatment amounted to racial harassment (see [1995] IRLR 529). Nor was any challenge directed to the industrial tribunal's finding that the reasonable steps defence had not been made out. The sole ground of appeal was that the industrial tribunal had been wrong to regard the racial harassment as having been 'done by a person in the course of his employment' for the purposes of s. 32(1) …

In this appeal, the complainant, with the backing of the Commissioner for Racial Equality, …bases it … upon a challenge to the entire notion that the words 'in the course of his employment' in s. 32(1) are to be given a restricted meaning which would limit them to instances where the impugned conduct on the part of the employee would attract tortious liability to the employer under the common law doctrine of vicarious liability. …

Two principles [of statutory interpretation] are, in my view, involved. The first is that a statute is to be construed according to its legislative purpose, with due regard to the result which it is the stated or presumed intention of Parliament to achieve and the means provided for achieving it (the purposive construction); and the second is that words in a statute are to be given their normal meaning according to general use in the English language unless the context indicates that such words have to be given a special or technical meaning as a term of art (the linguistic construction). It will be convenient to deal with those separately.

The legislation now represented by the Race and Sex Discrimination Acts currently in force broke new ground in seeking to work upon the minds of men and women and thus affect their attitude to the social consequences of difference between the sexes or distinction of skin colour. Its general thrust was educative, persuasive, and (where necessary) coercive. The relief accorded to the victims (or potential victims) of discrimination went beyond the ordinary remedies of damages and an injunction—introducing, through declaratory powers in the court or tribunal and recommendatory powers in the relevant commission, provisions with a proactive function, designed as much to eliminate the occasions for discrimination as to compensate its victims or punish its perpetrators. These were linked to a code of practice of which courts and tribunals were to take cognisance. Consistently with the broad front on which it operates, the legislation has traditionally been given a wide interpretation: see e.g. *Savjani v IRC* [1981] 1 All ER 1121 at 1125, [1981] QB 458 at 466–467, where Templeman LJ said of the 1976 Act—

'...the Act was brought in to remedy very great evil. It is expressed in very wide terms, and I should be very slow to find that the effect of something which is humiliatingly discriminatory in racial matters falls outside the ambit of the Act.'

Since the getting and losing of work and the daily functioning of the workplace are prime areas for potential discrimination on grounds of race or sex, it is not surprising that both Acts contain specific provisions to govern the field of employment. Those provisions are themselves wide-ranging—as is evidenced, for example, by the inclusion of contract workers without employee status within the scheme of the legislation. There is no indication in the 1976 Act that by dealing specifically with the employment field, Parliament intended in any way to limit the general thrust of the legislation.

A purposive construction, accordingly, requires s. 32 of the 1976 Act (and the corresponding s. 41 of the 1975 [Sex Discrimination] Act) to be given a broad interpretation. It would be inconsistent with that requirement to allow the notion of the 'course of employment' to be construed in any sense more limited than the natural meaning of those everyday words would allow.

Mr Buckhaven's argument is attractively simple. Vicarious liability is a doctrine of tortious liability which has been applied by the common law to the employment context. Part III of the 1976 Act applies expressly to discrimination in the employment field. The two fields are the same. Words and phrases that have acquired a familiar and particular meaning through case law applied to employers' liability in the former context must, therefore, have been intended by Parliament to have the same meaning when applied to employers' liability in the latter context.

Mr Robin Allen QC, while acknowledging that there is a broad conceptual similarity between the employers' responsibility that applies in both contexts, submits that substantial differences emerge when vicarious liability in tort is analysed and contrasted with the statutory scheme of which s. 32 forms part. The employer's authority, for example, is a crucial element in vicarious liability in tort, as evidenced by the statement in *Salmond and Heuston on the Law of Torts* (20th edn, 1992) pp. 456–457:

'A master is not responsible for a wrongful act done by his servant unless it is done in the course of his employment. It is deemed to be so done if it is either (1) a wrongful act authorised by the master, or (2) a wrongful and unauthorised way of doing some act authorised by the master.'

That is to be contrasted with the position under s. 32(1) of the 1976 Act, where all actions by a person in the course of employment are attributed to the employer 'Whether or not ... done with the employer's knowledge or approval'. Mr Allen points to other distinctions, such as the greater range of remedies available under the statute (including damages for injury to feelings), than those available in tort against an employer at common law, and the total absence from the concept of vicarious liability in tort of any provision corresponding to the reasonable steps defence under s. 32(3).

I am persuaded that Mr Allen's submission is to be preferred, and that there is here no sufficient similarity between the two contexts to justify, on a linguistic construction, the reading of the phrase 'course of employment' as subject to the gloss imposed on it in the common law context of vicarious liability.

Both approaches to statutory construction, therefore, lead to the same interpretation. But even more compelling, in my view, is the anomaly which would result ... from adopting any other interpretation. Mr Buckhaven accepts ... the fact that an inevitable result of construing 'course of employment' in the sense for which he contends will be that the more heinous the act of discrimination, the less likely it will be that the employer would be liable. That, he argues, is all to the good. Parliament must have intended the liability of employers to be kept within reasonable bounds.

I would reject that submission entirely. It cuts across the whole legislative scheme and underlying policy of s. 32 of the 1976 Act (and its counterpart in sex discrimination), which is to deter racial and sexual harassment in the workplace through a widening of the net of responsibility beyond the guilty employees themselves, by making all employers additionally liable for such harassment, and then supplying them with the reasonable steps defence under s. 32(3), which will exonerate the conscientious employer who has used his best endeavours to prevent such harassment, and will encourage all employers who have not yet undertaken such endeavours to take the steps necessary to make the same defence available in their own workplace. The decision of the Employment Appeal Tribunal in *Burton v De Vere Hotels* [1996] IRLR 596 provides a useful illustration of the matters to which employers need to be alert if they are to be able to take advantage of the reasonable steps defence in a harassment context.

Mr Buckhaven submits that the whole question is in any event concluded by authority at the level of this court which is binding on us, *Irving v Post Office* [1987] IRLR 289. That was a case in which a Post Office employee had neighbours who were black. He fell into dispute with them. While sorting mail at his place of work, he came across a letter addressed to them, and made use of that opportunity to write a racially offensive remark on the envelope before it was placed for delivery. The neighbours, having received the letter in the ordinary course of post, complained to the Post Office, who conducted an investigation, identified the culprit and disciplined him. The neighbours brought a complaint of racial discrimination against the Post Office, which was heard in the county court by an assistant recorder sitting with two assessors. The complaint was dismissed, and the Court of Appeal (Fox LJ and Sheldon J) dismissed the neighbours' appeal from that decision.

No record of the arguments heard on that appeal has survived. It is undoubtedly the case, however, that both judgments proceeded on the basis that any issue as to the liability of the Post Office for the action of their employee depending upon establishing vicarious liability in the sense in which that concept is used in the law of tort. It is also the case, however, that in neither judgment is a single reference made to s. 32 of the 1976 Act. Indeed, the Act itself is not mentioned at all in Sheldon J's judgment, and only in general terms by Fox LJ at the beginning and end of his judgment. There is a reference to s. 32(1) at the head of the law report, but it is evident from glancing at other reports in the series that such references are introduced by the editors for the assistance of their readers and for indexing purposes, and form no part of any judicial statement.

The only realistic inference that can be drawn, in my judgment, is that the Court of Appeal in that case dealt with the issue on the basis of vicarious liability as applied in the law of tort because both counsel invited them to do so. The issue that is now before the court, therefore, never arose for consideration. *Irving's* case is, accordingly, not an authority for the purpose for which reliance is sought to be placed upon it. It does not preclude us from holding that the majority of the Employment Appeal Tribunal was in error, and that there is no authority which requires the reference to 'course of employment' in s. 32(1) to be construed restrictively by reference to the case law governing an employer's vicarious liability in tort.

It would be particularly wrong to allow racial harassment on the scale that was suffered by the complainant in this case at the hands of his workmates—treatment that was wounding both emotionally and physically—to slip through the net of employer liability by applying to it a common law principle evolved in another area of the law to deal with vicarious responsibility for wrongdoing of a wholly different kind. To do so would seriously undermine the statutory scheme of the Discrimination Acts and flout the purposes which they were passed to achieve.

The tribunals are free, and are indeed bound, to interpret the ordinary and readily understandable words 'in the course of employment' in the sense in which every layman would understand them. This is not to say that when it comes to applying them to the infinite variety of circumstance which is liable to occur in particular instances—within or without the workplace, in or out of uniform, in or out of rest-breaks—all laymen would necessarily agree as to the result. That is what makes their application so well suited to decision by an industrial jury. The application of the phrase will be a question of fact for each industrial tribunal to resolve, in the light of the circumstances presented to it, with a mind unclouded by any parallels sought to be drawn from the law of vicarious liability in tort.

I ... would allow the appeal and restore the order of the industrial tribunal.

McGowan LJ wrote a judgment to the same effect. **Potter LJ** agreed with both judgments.

Appeal allowed.

NOTES

1. *Section 32: vicarious liability. Jones v Tower Boot Co Ltd* adopts a broad and common sense interpretation of the key phrase "in the course of his employment" in s. 32 that fits the race relations context in which it applies and generally signals a continuation of the purposive approach to interpretation of the 1976 Act adopted in the *Savjani* case.[13] The *Jones* case was applied in *Sidhu v Aerospace Composite Technology Ltd*,[14] where it was held that a company social function was not 'in the course of employment'.

2. *Sections 30, 31: instructions and pressure to discriminate.* In *Commission for Racial Equality v Imperial Society of Teachers of Dancing*,[15] the words 'induce' in s. 30 and 'procure or attempt to procure' in s. 31 were read widely:

'The industrial tribunal stated their conclusion ...:

"We think the word 'induce' must imply an element of 'stick or carrot', a mere request, which is the highest that Mrs McBride's words could be put at, comes far short of an attempt to induce as covered by the section."

With great respect to the industrial tribunal we for our part do not consider that the word "induce" in section 31 can be so limited. There may be cases where inducement involves the offer of some benefit or the threat of some detriment, but in their ordinary meaning the words 'to induce' mean 'to persuade or to prevail upon or to bring about'. In our judgment the intimation by Mrs McBride that 'she would rather the school did not send anyone coloured' as 'that person would feel out of place as there were no other coloured employees' did constitute an attempt to induce Mrs Patterson not to send coloured applicants for interview. We consider that the word 'induce' is apt to cover the facts found by the industrial tribunal in the present case; we see no reason to construe the word narrowly or in a restricted sense.

We turn to the alleged contravention of section 30. ...

The industrial tribunal came to the conclusion ... that an expression of a preference was not an attempt to procure. On this matter we regret to say that we disagree with the industrial tribunal. It seems to us that in the context the words 'procure' and 'attempt to procure' have a wide meaning and are apt to include the use of words which bring about or attempt to bring about a certain course of action.'

13 Below, p. 1138.
14 (2000) Times, 21 June.
15 (1983) ICR 473, 476 EAT.

See also on s. 30, the *Showboat Entertainment Centre* case,[16] and *Zarczynska v Levy*.[16a]

3. *Section 33: knowingly aids unlawful acts.* The meaning of 'knowingly aids' was considered in *Anyanwu v South Bank Student Union*.[17] In that case, the applicants, who were of black African origin, were students who were employed by the student union of their university. When they were expelled from the university following a disciplinary hearing on matters unconnected with their employment, they were dismissed by the student union because they were now barred from university premises. The applicants brought proceedings before an industrial tribunal against the union and the university alleging racial discrimination. The Court of Appeal struck out the claim against the university, which was based on s. 33 of the 1976 Act. On the meaning of 'knowingly aids', Butler-Sloss LJ stated:

'In ordinary language a person who aids another person is one who helps, supports or assists the prime mover to do the act. On the present facts the university took steps to expel the applicants for its own reasons, justified or unjustified. Those expulsions, carrying with them the prohibition against entering any part of the university buildings including the students' union, cannot in ordinary language be said to be knowingly aiding the students' union to dismiss the applicants within s. 33(1). In this case the prime mover of the dismissal of the applicants was students' union but its acts were effectively dictated to it by the prior decision of the university to expel the applicants. It seems clear to me that the students' union had no alternative but to dismiss the applicants after the university expelled them. In ordinary language can that conceivably be said to be knowingly aiding? I would answer No.'

In the *Cottrell and Rothon* case,[17a] an estate agent was found by the CRE to have 'aided' vendors and landlords in breach of s. 33 by accepting discriminatory instructions from them.

Race Relations Act 1976

3. Meaning of 'racial grounds', 'racial group' etc.

(1) In this Act, unless the context otherwise requires—

'racial grounds' means any of the following grounds, namely colour, race, nationality or ethnic or national origins;

'racial group' means a group of persons defined by reference to colour, race, nationality or ethnic or national origins, and references to a person's racial group refer to any racial group into which he falls.

(2) The fact that a racial group comprises two or more distinct racial groups does not prevent it from constituting a particular racial group for the purposes of this Act.

(3) In this Act—

    (*a*) references to discrimination refer to any discrimination falling within section 1 or 2; and

    (*b*) references to racial discrimination refer to any discrimination falling within section 1, and related expressions shall be construed accordingly.

(4) A comparison of the case of a person of a particular racial group with that of a person not of that group under section 1(1) must be such that the relevant circumstances in the one case are the same, or not materially different, in the other.

---

16 Above, p. 1090.
16a Above, p. 1091.
17 [2000] 1 All ER 1 at 13, CA.
17a (1980) CRE F Invest Rep.

NOTES[18]

1. The term 'national origins' as it appeared in the 1968 Act was examined by the House of Lords in *Ealing London Borough Council v Race Relations Board.*[19] In that case the appellants had refused to put a person of Polish nationality – a Mr Zesko – on their council housing waiting list because he was not, as their rules required, a British subject. The House of Lords held that discrimination based upon nationality was not discrimination on the ground of 'national origins' and, since discrimination on the ground of 'nationality' was not prohibited, the 1968 Act had not been infringed. Lord Simon said:[20]

'The Acts of 1965 and 1968 do not provide a complete code against discrimination or socially divisive propaganda. The Acts do not deal at all with discrimination on the grounds of religion or political tenet. It is no offence under the Acts to stir up class hatred. It is, therefore, unquestionably with a limited sort of socially disruptive conduct that the Acts are concerned, and it is, on any reading, within a limited sphere that Parliament put its ameliorative measures into action.

... Moreover, "racial" is not a term of art, either legal or, I surmise, scientific. I apprehend that anthropologists would dispute how far the word "race" is biologically at all relevant to the species amusingly called homo sapiens. ...

The ["colour, race or ethnic or national origins"] is rubbery and elusive language— understandably when the draftsman is dealing with so unprecise a concept as "race" in its popular sense and endeavouring to leave no loophole for evasion.

... "Origin", in its ordinary sense, signifies a source, someone or something from which someone or something else has descended. "Nation" and "national", in their popular in contrast to their legal sense, are also vague terms. They do not necessarily imply statehood. For example, there were many submerged nations in the former Hapsburg Empire. Scotland is not a nation in the eye of international law, but Scotsmen constitute a nation by reason of those most powerful elements in the creation of national spirit—tradition, folk memory, a sentiment of community. ...

... To discriminate against Englishmen, Scots or Welsh as such, would, in my opinion, be to discriminate against them on the ground of their national origins. To have discriminated against Mr Zesko on the ground of his Polish descent would have been to have discriminated against him on the ground of his national origins.

There is another situation which the phrase is apt to cover, namely, where a person of foreign nationality by birth has acquired British nationality or where a person of British nationality by birth is descended from someone of foreign nationality. There are those who are apt to say "The leopard cannot change his spots; once an Erehwonian always an Erehwonian." To discriminate against a British subject on the grounds of his foreign nationality by birth or alien lineage would be to discriminate against him on the ground of his national origins. To have discriminated against Mr Zesko on the ground of Russian nationality by birth (if such was his case, which is not clear) would have been to have discriminated against him on the ground of his national origins. ...'

Lord Cross said:[1]

'There is no definition of "national origins" in the Act and one must interpret the phrase as best one can. To me it suggests a connection subsisting at the time of birth between an individual and one or more groups of people who can be described as a "nation"—whether or not they also constitute a sovereign state. The connection will normally arise because the parents or

one of the parents of the individual in question are or is identified by descent with the nation in question, but it may also sometimes arise because the parents have made their home among the people in question. Suppose, for example, that a man of purely French descent marries a woman of purely German descent and that the couple have made their home in England for many years before the birth of the child in question. It could, I think, fairly be said that the child had three "national origins": French through his father, German through his mother and English not because he happened to have been born here but because his parents had made their home here. Of course, in most cases a man has only a single "national origin" which coincides with his nationality at birth in the legal sense and again in most cases his nationality remains unchanged throughout his life. But "national origins" and "nationality" in the legal sense are two quite different conceptions and they may well not coincide or continue to coincide.
... It is not difficult to see why the legislature in enacting the Race Relations Act 1965 used this new phrase "national origins" and not the word "nationality" which had a well-established meaning in law. It was because "nationality" in the strict sense was quite irrelevant to the problem with which they were faced. Most of the people against whom discrimination was being practised or hatred stirred up were in fact British subjects. The reason why the words "ethnic or national origins" were added to the words "racial grounds" which alone appear in the long title was, I imagine, to prevent argument over the exact meaning of the word "race". For example, a publican who had no objection to West Indians might refuse to serve Pakistanis. He would hardly be said to be discriminating against them on grounds of colour and it might well be argued that Pakistanis do not constitute a single "race". On the other hand, it could hardly be argued that they did not all have the same "national origin".'

What emerges from these speeches is that the terms used in s. 3 are to be understood in their popular rather than their scientific meaning (insofar as there is an agreed scientific meaning for them):[2] and to be read as covering, under one head or another, members of all of those minority groups that might popularly be regarded as having a racial character. This approach is in tune with the statement made by the Home Secretary (Sir Frank Soskice) when the 1965 Bill was before Parliament:[3]

'It is an objective which is of prime importance in the Bill that no grouping of citizens of whom one could, in ordinary English parlance, predicate that they have, or are thought to have, or are merely represented to have, some common feature or characteristics or origins that, broadly speaking, one relates to the stem from which they proceed ... should be excluded.
The word "colour" is one which ordinarily would be understood. ...
The word "race" is perhaps a little more ambiguous. The words "ethnic or national origin" are deliberately introduced into the Clause to make certain that no one is left out of the description "colour or race". We want to be certain that, because of some accident of language, some ambiguity of outline attaching to the words "colour or race", we do not fail to cover anybody who could possibly have fallen outside the ambit of these two words.'

2. Discrimination on the ground of 'nationality' was added by the 1976 Act in the light of the *Ealing* case. The 1976 Act s. 78(1) provides that 'unless the context otherwise requires, "nationality" includes "citizenship"'.[4] Discrimination against aliens by legislation or with legislative authority in areas covered by the Act (e.g. higher tuition fees for overseas students) is protected by the 1976 Act, s. 41;[5] other laws (e.g. those preventing an alien from owning a British ship or voting) are not within the Act because their subject-matter does not fall within its scope.
3. Discrimination on religious or political grounds is not covered by the Act: see Lord Simon in the *Ealing* case, above and Lords Fraser and Templeman in the *Mandla* case, below. Lord Templeman supposed that Parliament 'considered that the amount

2　See A. Dickey, (1974) JR 282.
3　716 HC Deb, 16 July 1965, cols. 970–1.
4　See further on both concepts in the context of United Kingdom law, British Nationality Act 1981, s. 11.
5　See above, pp. 1077, 1098.

of discrimination on religious grounds does not constitute a severe burden on members of religious groups'. An attempt to include discrimination on religious grounds in the 1976 Act was unsuccessful, the government arguing that a separate tailor-made bill would be necessary to deal with all of the issues peculiar to religion that would arise and that the Act's prohibition of indirect racial discrimination would (like that of direct discrimination) deal with a lot of cases of religious discrimination.[6] Although some cases may be caught in this way (e.g. a 'No Hindus' rule would be indirect racial discrimination against Indians and the requirement in the *Malik* case[6a] was similarly discriminatory for Muslims), there are many cases that would escape. A 'No Catholics' rule would not be illegal if applied to an English Catholic. Whether a case is to be seen as religious or racial discrimination will in some cases turn upon the view of the court as to whether a person is being discriminated against by reference to his religion or his ethnic status.[7]

Northern Joint Police Board v Power [1997] IRLR 610, Employment Appeal Tribunal

The respondent applied for the post of Chief Constable of the Northern Constabulary, a police force in Scotland. He brought a claim under the Race Relations Act alleging a breach of its employment discrimination provisions before an industrial tribunal on the ground that he had not been shortlisted because he was English, not Scots. On a preliminary point, the tribunal held that the Act applied to the case for the reason that discrimination against a person because he was English, not Scots, was discrimination against him because of his 'national origins'. At the same time, the tribunal held that the English were not an 'ethnic group', so that the Act did not also apply on an 'ethnic origins' basis. The EAT rejected the Police Board's appeal on the 'national origins' point; it upheld the Tribunal's ruling on the 'ethnic origins' point.

Lord Johnston:
In seeking to address this matter, we confess that we do not find the discussion by Lord Simon,[8] ... to be particularly helpful, other than to point to the nature of the elements which may enter the equation determining whether or not, in a particular context of England and Scotland, there are national attributes. On the other hand, it is perfectly clear that the phrase 'national origins' has to be given a different context and meaning within the legislation from the word 'nationality', but we have no difficulty with this concept. Nationality, we consider, has a juridical basis pointing to citizenship, which, in turn, points to the existence of a recognised state at the material time. Within the context of England, Scotland, Northern Ireland and Wales the proper approach to nationality is to categorise all of them as falling under the umbrella of British, and to regard the population as citizens of the United Kingdom. Against that background, what context, therefore, should be given to the phrase 'national origins'? It seems to us, so far as there needs to be an exhaustive definition, what has to be ascertained are identifiable elements, both historically and geographically, which at lease at some point in time reveals the existence of a nation. Whatever may be difficult fringe questions to this issue, what cannot be in doubt is that both England and Scotland were once separate nations. That, in our opinion, is effectively sufficient to dispose of the matter, since thereafter we agree with the proposition that it is for each individual to show that his origins are embedded in such a nation, and how he chooses to do so requires scrutiny by the tribunal hearing the application.

---

6   See HC, Standing Committee A, 29 April 1976 and 4 May 1976, cols 84–118. On developments concerning religious discrimination, see above, pp. 1027–1028.
6a   Above, p. 1101.
7   *Tower Hamlets London Borough Council v Rabin* [1989] ICR 693, EAT (Jewish faith or being a Jew).
8   *Ed.* In the *Ealing* case, see above, p. 1110.

In our opinion, whatever factors are put forward to satisfy the relevant criteria will be self-evidently relevant or irrelevant as the case may be. There is, therefore, no need for the tests such as enunciated by Lord Fraser in *Mandla*[9] ... with regard to the question of groups based on ethnic origins in relation to the issue of national origins, since the former by definition need not have, although it might have, a defined historical and geographical base. It is perfectly possible that the two defined groups may overlap, but that does not affect the issue which is required to be approached in each context from a different direction. The existence of a nation, whether in the present or past, is determined by factors quite separate from an individual's origins, and those factors are easily established in any given case by reference to history and geography. That the same cannot be said in relation to groups based on ethnic origins creates the need for Lord Fraser's test.

We are also entirely satisfied that it is legitimate, assuming there is any doubt in the matter as to whether Parliament intended to include the constituents within the United Kingdom, as part of the 'races' to be considered within the legislation, to examine the surrounding materials in order to determine the intention, and indeed the mischief being addressed. On doing so, it is manifest that Parliament's intention was to include the constituent races, so-called, within the United Kingdom under the umbrella of the legislation. The matter is, therefore, put beyond doubt.

As a matter, therefore, of general jurisdiction as to whether or not the industrial tribunal has the power to entertain an allegation of discrimination against an Englishman per se, or for that matter a Scotsman, based on national origins, we consider the industrial tribunal came to the correct decision.

With regard to the secondary question raised in this matter in the context of 'ethnic origins', we heard comprehensive argument in this matter in the recent case of *Mark Boyce and three others v British Airways plc* (EAT/385/97),[10] and concluded that it was not appropriate to regard, in that case, the Scots (but equally the English) as comprising a group falling within the definition of 'racial group' on that basis alone. We would therefore simply adopt the reasoning that we put forward in that case which applies mutatis mutandis to the present case since, in our opinion, there is no distinction on the question of general principle. In that case we said:

'...the issue that we have to address is one of statutory construction. Each of the definitions of racial group must be regarded as separate and alternative, and although it is possible for a person to fall under more than one of the heads the characteristics of one head should not be included in that of another by definition. However, having said that, it is plain that within the context of 'racial group' ethnic origins must, as the House of Lords have indicated, have a racial flavour to it. Whether it is correct to categorise that factor as an essential precondition to determining whether the definition is satisfied seems to us to beg the essential question, which relates to whether or not the group being identified *has* common characteristics within all its members of a racial nature and not, by contrast, members drawn from various ethnic backgrounds. Thus, not having to decide whether the Scots should be regarded as a race, we are equally driven to the position that, given the wide variations in origin, background and, indeed, race, within Scotland, all of whom can be categorised as 'Scots', we cannot find the common racial element within the group being addressed as Scots which meets the test plainly laid down by the House of Lords *before* the individual tests enunciated by Lord Fraser are considered. It is our opinion, therefore, that to go straight to those tests, as contended for by the appellants, to see whether the Scots meet them is to ignore the essential purpose, and indeed intention, of the Act, which is to prevent racial discrimination. Putting the matter simply as a matter of construction, once race is not being relied upon as the appropriate definition within the categories of such as a matter of construction, racial group defined by ethnic origin must be something else easily identifiable as, for example, amongst the Sikh or Gypsy communities which share common characteristics and origins. Non constat that the Welsh should be regarded as such and, in so far as it is so stated in *Gwynedd*,[11] we would not agree that the Welsh should be regarded

9 *Ed. Mandla v Dowell Lee*, below, p. 1114.
10 *Ed.* Unreported.
11 *Ed.* See below, p. 1114.

as a racial group based on ethnic origins within the meaning of the Act. Looking at the question as a matter of construction, whatever may be the general intention of Parliament, in our opinion the Scots, the English and the Welsh do not fall into the definition of a racial group based on ethnic origins; and, repeating that what we are concerned to do is not to discuss the way in which the Scots may be identified on a national basis, but rather merely as to whether Parliament has included them as a matter of construction in a piece of legislation in relation to a particular category, viz ethnic origins, we determine that it has not.

Furthermore, we recognise the argument that, as far as an employer is concerned, if he is required to address the question of Scottishness on grounds of discrimination with regard to ethnic groups, it may be an impossible task for him to determine in an individual case whether or not the person in question is Scots or regards himself or herself as such. We consider it would be an impossible task to seek to define what tests should be applied by an employer to an individual case in this context. While this in itself is not a bar to an exercise of statutory construction achieving a certain result, it may be an indication that that result ought not to be achieved if the consequences are unworkable.'

Accordingly, if this case depended upon resolution in favour of the respondent on the basis of 'ethnic origins', we would have found against the respondent and sustained the provisional views of the tribunal.

For these reasons, this appeal will be refused, and the matter remitted back to the industrial tribunal for further consideration of the two issues that are, in our opinion, live, namely whether or not the respondent can establish that he has national origins based upon his assertion that he is English and, equally importantly, that in fact he was discriminated against in that context.

NOTES[12]

1. While not finding the approach of Lord Simon in the *Ealing* case 'particularly helpful', the EAT reached the same conclusion as Lord Simon, viz. that the English and the Scots are nations so that discrimination against an Englishman or a Scot because he is such is discrimination against him because of his 'national origins'. The EAT does not provide any guidance as to how a claimant should show that his 'origins are embedded in such a nation'. As Lord Cross suggested in the *Ealing* case, the nationality of either of a person's parents and the place where they have settled are key considerations. What if the respondent in the *Power* case had been discriminated against not because he was English but because he was not a Scot, when the Board was not prepared to appoint anyone who was not Scottish?
2. On the question of 'ethnic origins', the EAT did not follow an earlier EAT ruling in *Gwynedd County Council v Jones*[13] in which it was held that the Welsh were 'a nation and an ethnic group'. Was the EAT approach in the *Gwynedd* or the *Power* case preferable?

Mandla v Dowell Lee [1983] 2 AC 548, [1983] 1 All ER 1062, [1983] 2 WLR 620, House of Lords

A Sikh solicitor resident in Birmingham applied for his son's admission to a private school. The application was refused because, as an orthodox Sikh, the son would have had to have worn a turban, contrary to school rules. The father complained to the CRE which supported county court proceedings, *inter alia*, for a declaration that the refusal was indirect discrimination contrary to ss. 1(1)(b) and 17(a) of the 1976 Act. The county court rejected the claim. The Court of Appeal, [1983] QB 1, dismissed

---

12 On the *Power* and *Boyce* cases, see A. O'Neill, 1997 SLT 101 and K. Miller, (1997) JR 67.
13 [1986] ICR 833.

an appeal on the ground that Sikhs were not a 'racial group' in the sense of s. 3(1), 1976 Act. The House of Lords unanimously allowed the appeal. The interval between the Court of Appeal and House of Lords hearings was marked by demonstrations indicating the strength of feeling in the Sikh community.

Lord Fraser. . . . the first question is whether the Sikhs are a racial group . . .

It is not suggested that Sikhs are a group defined by reference to colour, race, nationality or *national* origins. In none of these respects are they distinguishable from many other groups, especially those living, like most Sikhs, in the Punjab. The argument turns entirely upon whether they are a group defined by *'ethnic* origins.'. . .

The *Oxford English Dictionary* (1897 ed) gives two meanings of 'ethnic'. The first is 'Pertaining to nations not Christian or Jewish; gentile, heathen, pagan.' That clearly cannot be its meaning in the Act of 1976, because it is inconceivable that Parliament would have legislated against racial discrimination intending that the protection should not apply either to Christians or (above all) to Jews. . . . The second meaning . . . was 'Pertaining to race; peculiar to a race or nation; ethnological.' A slightly shorter form of that meaning (omitting 'peculiar to a race or nation') was given by the *Concise Oxford Dictionary* in 1934 and was expressly accepted by Lord Denning MR as the correct meaning for the present purpose. Oliver and Kerr LJJ also accepted that meaning as being substantially correct, and Oliver LJ . . . said that the word 'ethnic' in its popular meaning involved 'essentially a racial concept—the concept of something with which the members of the group are born; some fixed or inherited characteristic.' . . .

My Lords, I recognise that 'ethnic' conveys a flavour of race but it cannot, in my opinion, have been used in the Act of 1976 in a strictly racial or biological sense. For one thing, it would be absurd to suppose that Parliament can have intended that membership of a particular racial group should depend upon scientific proof that a person possessed the relevant distinctive biological characteristics (assuming that such characteristics exist). The practical difficulties of such proof would be prohibitive, and it is clear that Parliament must have used the word in some more popular sense. For another thing, the briefest glance at the evidence in this case is enough to show that, within the human race, there are very few, if any, distinctions which are scientifically recognised as racial. . . .

I turn therefore, to the third and wider meaning which is given in the *Supplement to the Oxford English Dictionary* (1972). It is as follows: 'pertaining to or having common racial, cultural, religious, or linguistic characteristics, esp. designating a racial or other group within a larger system; . . .' . . . The 1972 meaning is, in my opinion, too loose and vague to be accepted as it stands. It is capable of being read as implying that any one of the adjectives, 'racial, cultural, religious, *or* linguistic' would be enough to constitute an ethnic group. That cannot be the sense in which 'ethnic' is used in the Act of 1976, as that Act is not concerned at all with discrimination on religious grounds. . . . But in seeking for the true meaning of 'ethnic' in the statute, we are not tied to the precise definition in any dictionary. The value of the 1972 definition is, in my view, that it shows that ethnic has come to be commonly used in a sense appreciably wider than the strictly racial or biological. That appears to me to be consistent with the ordinary experience of those who read newspapers at the present day. In my opinion, the word 'ethnic' still retains a racial flavour but it is used nowadays in an extended sense to include other characteristics which may be commonly thought of as being associated with common racial origin.

For a group to constitute an ethnic group in the sense of the Act of 1976, it must, in my opinion, regard itself, and be regarded by others, as a distinct community by virtue of certain characteristics. Some of these characteristics are essential; others are not essential but one or more of them will commonly be found and will help to distinguish the group from the surrounding community. The conditions which appear to me to be essential are these: (1) a long shared history, of which the group is conscious as distinguishing it from other groups, and the memory of which it keeps alive; (2) a cultural tradition of its own, including family and social customs and manners, often but not necessarily associated with religious observance. In addition to those two essential characteristics the following characteristics are, in my opinion, relevant; (3) either a common geographical origin, or descent from a small number of common ancestors; (4) a common language, not necessarily peculiar to the group; (5) a common literature peculiar to the group; (6) a common religion different from that of neighbouring groups or from the general community surrounding it; (7) being a minority or being an oppressed or a dominant group within a larger community, for example a conquered people (say, the inhabitants of England shortly after the Norman conquest) and their conquerors might both be ethnic groups.

A group defined by reference to enough of these characteristics would be capable of including converts, for example, persons who marry into the group, and of excluding apostates. Provided a person who joins the group feels himself or herself to be a member of it, and is accepted by other members, then he is, for the purposes of the Act, a member. That appears to be consistent with the words at the end of s. 3(1): 'references to a person's racial group refer to any racial group into which he falls.' In my opinion, it is possible for a person to fall into a particular racial group either by birth or by adherence, and it makes no difference, so far as the Act of 1976 is concerned, by which route he finds his way into the group. This view does not involve creating any inconsistency between direct discrimination under paragraph (*a*) and indirect discrimination under paragraph (*b*). A person may treat another relatively unfavourably 'on racial grounds' because he regards that other as being of a particular race, or belonging to a particular racial group, even if his belief is, from a scientific point of view, completely erroneous.

Finally . . . I think it is proper to mention that the word 'ethnic' is . . . derived from the Greek word 'ethnos', the basic meaning of which appears to have been simply 'a group' not limited by reference to racial or any other distinguishing characteristics . . . I do not suggest that the meaning of the English word in a modern statute ought to be governed by the meaning of the Greek word from which it is derived, but the fact that the meaning of the latter was wide avoids one possible limitation on the meaning of the English word.

. . . The conclusion at which I have arrived by construction of the Act itself is greatly strengthened by consideration of the decision of the Court of Appeal in New Zealand . . . in *King-Ansell v Police* [1979] 2 NZLR 531. . . . If it had been before the Court of Appeal it might well have affected their decision. In that case the appellant had been convicted by a magistrate of an offence under the New Zealand Race Relations Act 1971, the offence consisting of publishing a pamphlet with intent to incite ill-will against Jews, 'on the ground of their ethnic origins.' . . . The decision of the Court of Appeal was that Jews in New Zealand did form a group with common ethnic origins within the meaning of the Act.

. . . Richardson J. said . . . :

'a group is identifiable in terms of its ethnic origins if it is a segment of the population distinguished from others by a sufficient combination of shared customs, beliefs, traditions and characteristics derived from a common or presumed common past, even if not drawn from what in biological terms is a common racial stock. It is that combination which gives them an historically determined social identity in their own eyes and in the eyes of those outside the group. They have a distinct social identity based not simply on group cohesion and solidarity but also on their belief as to their historical antecedents.'

My Lords, that last passage sums up in a way upon which I could not hope to improve the views which I have been endeavouring to express . . .

. . . [Sikhs] were originally a religious community founded about the end of the 15th century in the Punjab by Guru Nanak . . . but the community is no longer purely religious in character. Their present position is summarised sufficiently for present purposes in the opinion of the learned judge in the county court in the following passage:

'The evidence in my judgment shows that Sikhs are a distinctive and self-conscious community. They have a history going back to the 15th century. They have a written language which a small proportion of Sikhs can read but which can be read by a much higher proportion of Sikhs than of Hindus. They were at one time politically supreme in the Punjab.'

The result is, in my opinion, that Sikhs are a group defined by a reference to ethnic origins for the purpose of the Act of 1976, although they are not biologically distinguishable from the other people living in the Punjab. . . . It is, therefore, necessary to consider whether the respondent has indirectly discriminated against the appellants in the sense of section 1(1)(*b*) of the Act. . . .

It is obvious that Sikhs, like anyone else, 'can' refrain from wearing a turban, if 'can' is construed literally. But if the broad cultural/historic meaning of ethnic is the appropriate meaning of the word in the Act of 1976, then a literal reading of the word 'can' would deprive Sikhs and members of other groups defined by reference to their ethnic origins of much of the protection which Parliament evidently intended the Act to afford to them. They 'can' comply with almost any requirement or condition if they are willing to give up their distinctive customs and cultural rules. On the other hand, if ethnic means inherited or unalterable, as the Court of Appeal thought it did, then 'can' ought logically to be read literally. The word 'can' is used with many shades of meaning. In the context of section 1(1)(*b*)(i) of the Act of 1976 it must, in my opinion, have been intended by Parliament to be read not as meaning 'can physically,' so as to indicate a theoretical possibility, but as meaning 'can in practice' or 'can consistently with the customs and cultural conditions of the racial group.' The latter meaning was attributed to the word by the Employment Appeal Tribunal in *Price v Civil Service Commission* [1978] ICR 27, on a construction of the parallel provision in the Sex Discrimination Act 1975. I agree with their construction of the word in that context. Accordingly I am of opinion that the 'No turban' rule was not one with which the second appellant could, in the relevant sense, comply.

The word 'justifiable' occurs in section 1(1)(*b*)(ii). It raises a problem which is, in my opinion, more difficult than the problem of the word 'can'. . . . Regarded purely from the point of view of the respondent, it was no doubt perfectly justifiable. He explained that he had no intention of discriminating against Sikhs. In 1978 the school had about 300 pupils (about 75 per cent boys and 25 per cent girls) of whom over 200 were English, five were Sikhs, 34 Hindus, 16 Persians, six negroes, seven Chinese and 15 from European countries. The reasons for having a school uniform were largely reasons of practical convenience—to minimise external differences between races and social classes, to discourage the 'competitive fashions' which he said tend to exist in a teenage community, and to present a Christian image of the school to outsiders, including prospective parents. The respondent explained the difficulty for a head-master of explaining to a non-Sikh pupil why the rules about wearing correct school uniform were enforced against him if they were relaxed in favour of a Sikh. In my view these reasons could not, either individually or collectively, provide a sufficient justification for the respondent to apply a condition that is prima facie discriminatory under the Act.

An attempted justification of the 'No turban' rule, which requires more serious consideration, was that the respondent sought to run a Christian school, accepting pupils of all religions and races, and that he objected to the turban on the ground that it was an outward manifestation of a non-Christian faith. Indeed he regarded it as amounting to a challenge to that faith. I have much sympathy with the respondent on this part of the case and I would have been glad to find that the rule was justifiable within the meaning of the statute, if I could have done so. But in my opinion that is impossible. The onus under paragraph (ii) is on the respondent to show that the condition which he seeks to apply is not indeed a necessary condition, but that it is in all circumstances justifiable 'irrespective of the colour, race, nationality or ethnic or national origins of the person to whom it is applied'; that is to say that it is justifiable without regard to the ethnic origins of that person. But in this case the principal justification on which the respondent relies is that the turban is objectionable just because it is a manifestation of the second appellant's ethnic origins. That is not, in my view, a justification which is admissible under paragraph (ii). The kind of justification that might fall within that provision would be one based on public health, as in *Panesar v Nestlé Co Ltd (Note)* [1980] ICR 144, where the Court of Appeal held that a rule forbidding the wearing of beards in the respondent's chocolate factory was justifiable within the meaning of section 1(1)(*b*)(ii) on hygienic grounds, notwithstanding that the proportion of Sikhs who could [sc. conscientiously] comply with it was considerably smaller than the proportion of non-Sikhs who could comply with it. Again, it might be possible for the school to show that a rule insisting upon a fixed diet, which included some dish (for example, pork) which some racial groups could not conscientiously eat was justifiable if the school proved that the cost of providing special meals for the particular group would be prohibitive. Questions of that sort would be questions of fact for the tribunal of fact, and if there was evidence on which it could find the condition to be justifiable its finding would not be liable to be disturbed on appeal.

But in the present case I am of opinion that the respondents have not been able to show that the 'No turban' rule was justifiable.

Before parting with the case I must refer to some observations by the Court of Appeal . . . which suggest that the conduct of the Commission for Racial Equality in this case has been in some way unreasonable or oppressive. Lord Denning MR . . . merely expressed regret that the Commission had taken up the case. But Oliver LJ . . . used stronger language and suggested that the machinery of the Act had been operated against the respondent as 'an engine of oppression,' Kerr LJ . . . referred to notes of an interview between the respondent and an official of the Commission which he said read in part 'more like an inquisition than an interview' and which he regarded as harassment of the respondent.

My Lords, I must say I regard these strictures on the Commission and its officials as entirely unjustified. The Commission has a difficult task, and no doubt its inquiries will be resented by some and are liable to be regarded as objectionable and inquisitive. But the respondent in this case, who conducted his appeal with restraint and skill, made no complaint of his treatment at the hands of the Commission. . . . Opinions may legitimately differ as to the usefulness of the Commission's activities, but its functions have been laid down by Parliament and, in my view, the actions of the Commission . . . were perfectly proper and in accordance with its statutory duty.

I would allow this appeal. . . .

Lord Templeman: I agree with the Court of Appeal that in this context ethnic origins have a good deal in common with the concept of race just as national origins have a good deal in common with the concept of nationality. But the statutory definition of a racial group envisages that a group defined by reference to ethnic origins may be different from a group defined by reference to race, just as a group defined by reference to national origins may be different from a group defined by reference to nationality. In my opinion, for the purposes of the Race Relations Act a group of persons defined by reference to ethnic origins must possess some of the characteristics of a race, namely group descent, a group of geographical origin and a group history. The evidence shows that the Sikhs satisfy these tests. They are more than a religious sect, they are almost a race and almost a nation. As a race, the Sikhs share a common colour, and a common physique based on common ancestors from that part of the Punjab which is centred on Amritsar. they fail to qualify as a separate race because in racial origin prior to the inception of Sikhism they cannot be distinguished from other inhabitants of the Punjab. As a nation the Sikhs defeated the Moghuls, and established a kingdom in the Punjab which they lost as a result of the first and second Sikh wars; they fail to qualify as a separate nation or as a separate nationality because their kingdom never achieved a sufficient degree of recognition or permanence. The Sikhs qualify as a group defined by ethnic origins because they constitute a separate and distinct community derived from the racial characteristics I have mentioned. They also justify the conditions enumerated by my noble and learned friend, Lord Fraser of Tullybelton. The Sikh community has accepted converts who do not comply with those conditions. Some persons who have the same ethnic origins as the Sikhs have ceased to be members of the Sikh community. But the Sikhs remain a group of persons forming a community recognisable by ethnic origins within the meaning of the Act.

I agree that the appeal should be allowed.

Lords Edmund Davies, Roskill and **Brandon** concurred in both of the above speeches.

Appeal allowed.

NOTES[14]

1. This case makes it clear that Sikhs are protected by the 1976 Act, as a 'group of persons defined by reference to . . . ethnic origins'. This would appear to have been the intention of Parliament.[15] Sikhs must comply with 'five Ks': they must leave

---

14 For comments on the case, see H. Beynon and N. Love, (1984) 100 LQR 120; M. Jefferson, (1983) 5 Liverpool LR 75; I. B. McKenna, (1983) 46 MLR 759; St. J. A. Robilliard, [1983] PL 348; Saunders, (1983) 7 Trent LJ 23.

15 See the reference to Sikhs by the government spokesman (Lord Harris), 373 HL Deb, 27 September 1976, col. 73. For further discussion of the cultural distinctiveness of the Sikh people, see the Court of Appeal judgment in the case, [1983] QB 1.

their hair uncut (hence the turban to keep it in order); secure it with a comb; wear a long undergarment and a steel bracelet; and carry a symbolic dagger.
2. Is the meaning of 'ethnic origins' adopted by Lords Fraser and Templeman the same? Does Lord Templeman mention the second of Lord Fraser's two 'essential' characteristics (a 'cultural tradition')? Are all of the three necessary characteristics listed by Lord Templeman ('group descent', 'group of geographical origin', 'group history') regarded as essential by Lord Fraser? Does Lord Templeman refer to the other relevant characteristics referred to by Lord Fraser? Note that (1) Lord Templeman does say that Sikhs do 'justify the conditions enumerated by' Lord Fraser and (2) that the other three judges concurred in both speeches.[16] In 1965, the Home Secretary (Sir Frank Soskice), when asked what the word 'ethnic' added in the phrase 'colour, race or ethnic or national origins', replied:[17]

> 'We have chosen that connotation [quaere "combination"] of words to try to ensure that we include every possible minority group in the country . . . We hope, by the use of the word "ethnic", to cover everybody who is neither of a particular national origin nor of a particular racial origin but [quaere "or"] who would be distinguishable by colour'.

In 1976, the government spokesman (Lord Harris) explained that the wording 'ethnic or national origins' was intended to 'cover the examples which do not fit comfortably into "colour" or "race"' and that this formula 'gets away from the idea of physical characteristics which inform the words "colour" and "race" and introduces the idea of groups defined by reference to cultural characteristics, geographic location, social organisation and so on'.[18]
3. *Mandla* also confirms that Jews are a 'racial group' within the 1976 Act. The definitions of 'ethnic origins' in both speeches include Jews. See too the specific references to Jews by Lord Fraser and in the Court of Appeal. In *Seide v Gillette Industries Ltd*,[19] alleged employment discrimination against a Jew was said to be within the Act if 'what happened . . . was not because Mr Seide was of the Jewish faith but [as was held] because he was a member of the Jewish race or of Jewish ethnic origin'. The absence of discrimination on religious grounds from the Act had raised the question whether Jews are protected by it.[20] In the debate on the 1965 Act, the Home Secretary had no doubt:[1]

> 'It is certainly the intention of the Government that people of Jewish faith should be covered. The words have to be construed in law according to the ordinary canons of construction, as an ordinary person would read ordinary English language. I would have thought a person of Jewish faith, if not regarded as caught by the word "racial" would undoubtedly be caught by the word "ethnic", but if not caught by the word "ethnic" would certainly be caught by the scope of the word "national", as certainly having a national origin.'

Hepple[2] suggests the following approach in cases where it is unclear whether a person is being less favourably treated because of his race or his religion:

---

16 In the *Dawkins* case, below, p. 1123, the Court of Appeal stated that the two speeches in the Mandla case (1) were not to be read as the closely drafted text of a statute and (2) had the same meaning. In fact, Lord Fraser's speech was the one cited in Dawkins.

17 711 HC Deb, 3 May 1965, col. 932.

18 373 HL Deb, 27 September 1976, col. 74. There is a hotel in Glencoe which has a notice saying 'Positively no Campbells' (373 HL Deb, 27 September 1976, col 75. (Lord Hailsham)). Is this contrary to the 1976 Act?

19 [1980] IRLR 427, 430, EAT.

20 See Jewish Employment Group, [1983] PL 4.

 1 711 HC Deb 3 May 1965 cols 932–3. Some members were sceptical, believing that 'the Jewish identity is essentially a religious one' (Mr N. St. John-Stevas, Standing Committee B, col. 70, 27 May 1965.

 2 *Race, Jobs and the Law* (2nd edn, 1970), p. 37.

'... [T]he problem is not really one of definition but of proof ... it is erroneous to lay down, in the abstract, whether discrimination against Jews or Sikhs is on racial grounds rather than for religious reasons. In each case, ... the actual relationship of the parties must be examined to determine whether the discriminator believed his victim to be a member of some distinct race and for that reason discriminated against him.'

Cf. the approach of the RRB in the following case:[3]

'Two complaints dealt with in the field of private education concerned allegations that children had been refused admission to certain schools because of their Jewish ethnic origin. The Act does not deal with discrimination on religious grounds; and it was maintained by the schools complained against that to admit more than a certain proportion of children of the Jewish faith would affect the Christian character of their schools, and that the schools therefore operated Jewish quotas which varied from 25 to 50 per cent. Enquiries showed that one of the schools was established by its charter as an Anglican foundation. The Christian character of the other school was not so apparent, but enquiries showed that the parents of the children concerned had answered "Jewish" to questions on the school's application form which asked for their religious denomination. In both of these cases the Board concluded that the discrimination was religious and not ethnic.'

What if D were to discriminate against V in the belief that V was a French national and for that reason when V was in fact a British citizen? Would that be direct discrimination? Can one rely on the understanding and motive of the discriminator in respect of *indirect* discrimination? Or is it necessary to decide to what 'racial group' V actually belongs?

4. In the *Ealing* case,[4] the House of Lords understood the phrase 'national origins' to refer to a connection *at birth*.[5] Neither speech in the House of Lords imposes such a limitation when interpreting 'ethnic origins'. Sikhs were held to be a 'racial group' even though, as was acknowledged, the Sikh (like the Jewish) community accepts converts and excludes apostates.

5. On the meaning of 'can comply' and the 'justification' defence, see above, pp. 1097, 1198.

6. There were echoes of the *Mandla* case on its facts in a 1990 incident concerning two Muslim sisters who were refused permission to wear a hijab, or headscarf, to Altrincham Grammar School in accordance with their religious beliefs because this was contrary to school uniform rules. Following an approach from the CRE and much publicity, the school allowed the sisters to wear hijabs in the school colours.[6]

Commission for Racial Equality v Dutton [1989] QB 783, [1989] 2 WLR 17, [1989] 1 All ER 306, Court of Appeal

The defendant was the licensee of the 'Cat and Mutton', Hackney. Having previously had trouble with persons who lived in illegally parked caravans, he put up a 'No Travellers' notice in his pub window. A local resident informed the CRE,

---

3 RRB Report 1970–71, p. 7.
4 Above, p. 1110.
5 Cf. Oliver and Kerr LJJ in the Court of Appeal in *Mandla v Dowell Lee*.
6 CRE Report 1990, p. 44. On this case and similar French cases, see S. Poulter, (1997) 17 OJLS 43. Muslims do not constitute a racial group: see *J. H. Walker v Hussain* [1996] IRLR 11, EAT. But see K. S. Dobe and S. S. Chokar, (2000) 4 Int J Discrimination and Law 369, who argue that *British* Muslims have sufficient distinctive cultural traditions to make them a racial group. A claim of racial discrimination against a Muslim may be successful in some cases as indirect discrimination by reference to 'national origins' (e.g. persons with national origins in Pakistan or Bangladesh).

who, acting under s. 63, 1976 Act, brought proceedings seeking a declaration that the notice was an unlawful advertisement contrary to s. 29. The claim having been rejected in the county court (gipsies not a racial group), the CRE appealed to the Court of Appeal.

Nicholls LJ: One of the difficulties in the present case, in my view, is that the word 'gipsy' has itself more than one meaning. The classic dictionary meaning can be found as the primary meaning given in the *Oxford English Dictionary* (1933):

'A member of a wandering race (by themselves called *Romany*), of Hindu origin, which first appeared in England about the beginning of the 16th c. and was then believed to have come from Egypt.'...

Alongside this meaning, the word 'gipsy' also has a more colloquial, looser meaning. This is expressed in the *Longman Dictionary of Contemporary English* (1984), where two meanings are attributed to 'gipsy'. The first meaning is along the lines I have already quoted. The second is: 'a person who habitually wanders or who has the habits of someone who does not stay for long in one place': in short, a nomad.

I can anticipate here by noting that if the word 'gipsy' is used in this second, colloquial sense it is not definitive of a racial group within the 1976 Act. To discriminate against such a group would not be on racial grounds, namely on the ground of ethnic origins. As the judge observed, there are many people who travel around the country in caravans, vans, converted buses, trailers, lorries and motor vehicles, leading a peripatetic or nomadic way of life. They include didicois, mumpers, peace people, new age travellers, hippies, tinkers, hawkers, self-styled 'anarchists', and others, as well as Romany gipsies. They may all be loosely referred to as 'gipsies', but as a group they do not have the characteristics requisite of a racial group within the Act....

Like most English words, the meaning of the word 'traveller' depends on the context in which it is being used. It has one meaning when seen on a railway station ... In my view, in the windows of the Cat and Mutton 'No travellers' will be understood by those to whom it is directed, namely potential customers, as meaning persons who are currently leading a nomadic way of life, living in tents or caravans or other vehicles. Thus the notices embrace gipsies who are living in that way. But the class of persons excluded from the Cat and Mutton is not confined to gipsies. The prohibited class includes all those of a nomadic way of life mentioned above....

For this reason I cannot accept that Mr Dutton's notices indicate, or might reasonably be understood as indicating, an intention by him to do an act of discrimination within s. 1(1)(*a*). Excluded from the Cat and Mutton are all 'travellers', whether or not they are gipsies. All 'travellers', all nomads, are treated equally, whatever their race. They are not being discriminated against on racial grounds....

That suffices to dispose of the claim based on s. 1(1)(*a*) of the 1976 Act, but ... I must now turn to consider s. 1(1)(*b*), ...

On this the first question which arises is whether gipsies are a racial group....

The definition of 'racial group' in s. 3(1) includes a group of persons defined by reference to 'ethnic ... origins'. This definition was considered by the House of Lords in *Mandla v Dowell Lee* [above, p. 1114].

... with all respect to the judge, I am unable to agree with his conclusion on what have been called the *Mandla* conditions when applied, not to the larger amorphous group of 'travellers' or 'gipsies' (colloquially so-called), but to 'gipsies' in the primary, narrower sense of that word. On the evidence it is clear that such gipsies are a minority, with a long shared history and a common geographical origin. They are a people who originated in northern India. They migrated thence to Europe through Persia in medieval times. They have certain, albeit limited, customs of their own regarding cooking and the manner of washing. They have a distinctive traditional style of dressing, with heavy jewellery worn by the women, although this dress is not worn all the time. They also furnish their caravans in a distinctive manner. They have a language or dialect, known as 'pogadi chib', spoken by English gipsies (Romany chals) and Welsh gipsies (Kale) which consists of up to one-fifth of Romany words in place of English words. They do not have a common religion, nor a peculiar, common literature of their own, but they have a repertoire of folk-tales and music passed on from one generation to the next. No doubt, after all the centuries which have passed since the first gipsies left the Punjab, gipsies are no longer derived from what, in biological terms, is a common racial stock, but that of itself does not prevent them from being a racial group as widely defined in the 1976 Act.

I come now to the part of the case which has caused me most difficulty. Gipsies prefer to be called 'travellers' as they think that term is less derogatory. This might suggest a wish to lose their separate distinctive identity so far as the general public is concerned. Half or more of them now live in houses, like most other people. Have gipsies now lost their separate, group identity so that they are no longer a community recognisable by ethnic groups within the meaning of the Act? The judge held that they had. This is a finding of fact.

Nevertheless, with respect to the judge, I do not think that there was before him any evidence justifying his conclusion that gipsies has been absorbed into a larger group, if by that he meant that substantially all gipsies have been so absorbed. . . . In my view the evidence was sufficient to establish that, despite their long presence in England, gipsies have not merged wholly in the population, as have the Saxons and the Danes, and altogether lost their separate identity. They or many of them, have retained a separateness, a self-awareness, of still being gipsies. . . .

Having concluded that gipsies are a racial group, each of sub-paras (i) to (iii) in s. 1(1)(*b*) of the 1976 Act must be satisfied before the conduct complained of amounts to discrimination within the meaning of the Act. . . .

Clearly the proportion of gipsies who will satisfy the 'no travellers' condition is considerably smaller than the proportion of non-gipsies. Of the estimated gipsy population in the United Kingdom of some 80,000, between one-half and two-thirds now live in houses. But this still means that a far higher proportion of gipsies are leading a nomadic way of life than the rest of the population in general or, more narrowly, than the rest of the population who might wish to resort to the Cat and Mutton.

Counsel for Mr Dutton submitted that the word 'can' in the expression 'can comply' in sub-para (i) means 'can comply without giving up the distinctive customs and cultural rules of gipsies'. He submitted that gipsies can cease to be nomadic, and become house-dwellers, and comply with the 'no travellers' condition, without giving up their customs and cultures and that, therefore, sub-para (i) is not satisfied in this case. I do not accept this. Lord Fraser's words in *Mandla*'s case . . . were used in the context of a 'no turban' condition being applied in relation to a Sikh. Lord Fraser was rejecting the submission that 'can' meant 'can physically'. But that does not assist the solution of the present case. Indeed, gipsies can and do cease to be nomadic, but that will be of little use to a particular nomadic gipsy when he chances on the Cat and Mutton and wishes to go in for a drink. At that stage he is, in practice, unable to comply. In the present case the problem is a different one: at what moment of time does ability to comply fall to be judged? Is it when the condition is invoked (in this case, when the gipsy is outside the public house wishing to enter) or is it at some earlier date (which would give the gipsy sufficient opportunity to acquire housing accommodation for himself before turning up at the Cat and Mutton)?

A similar question was considered by the Employment Appeal Tribunal in *Clarke v Eley (IMI) Kynoch Ltd* [1983] ICR 165 with regard to s. 1(1) of the Sex Discrimination Act 1975, the wording of which does not differ materially from s. 1(1)(*b*) of the 1976 Act. Browne-Wilkinson J delivered the judgment of the tribunal to the effect that the relevant point of time at which the ability or inability to comply has to be shown is the date at which the requirement or condition has to be fulfilled. I find his reasoning compelling, and I agree with his conclusion (see [1983] ICR 165 at 171–172).

In my view, therefore, sub-para (i) is satisfied in the present case.

Sub-paragraph (iii) requires the applied condition to be to the relevant person's detriment because he cannot comply with it. Rightly, it was not disputed that sub-para (iii) is satisfied in the present case, by the hypothetical nomad gipsy being excluded from the Cat and Mutton (I say hypothetical, because there was no evidence that there were any gipsies among the travellers on the nearby sites). . . .

In these circumstances for my part I would remit the action to the county court for the judge to determine whether s. 1(1)(*b*)(ii) is satisfied in the present case and, if it is, for him to make such order as he considers appropriate. I would allow this appeal accordingly.

NOTES

1. The decision in the *Dutton* case that gipsies are a racial group follows clearly from the reasoning in the *Mandla* case. It has also been the view of the CRE. Acting on this basis, in the *Brymbo* Case,[7] the CRE had issued non-discrimination notices after local residents had urged that a gipsy family not be re-housed in council housing.
2. In *Crown Suppliers (PSA) v Dawkins*,[8] it was held that Rastafarians are not an ethnic group in the sense of the *Mandla* case, so that failure to employ the applicant as a van driver because, as a Rastafarian, he refused to cut his dreadlocks was not discrimination contrary to the 1976 Act. Neill LJ stated:

'It is clear that Rastafarians have certain identifiable characteristics. They have a strong cultural tradition which includes a distinctive form of music known as reggae music. They adopt a distinctive form of hairstyle by wearing dreadlocks. They have other shared characteristics of which both the industrial tribunal and the appeal tribunal were satisfied. But the crucial question is whether they have established some separate identity by reference to their ethnic origins. In speaking about Rastafarians in this context I am referring to the core group, because I am satisfied that a core group can exist even though not all the adherents of the group could, if considered separately, satisfy any of the relevant tests.

It is at this stage that one has to take account of both the racial flavour of the word "ethnic" and Lord Fraser's requirement of a long shared history. Lord Meston submitted that if one compared Rastafarians with the rest of the Jamaican community in England, or indeed with the rest of the Afro-Caribbean community in this country, there was nothing to set them aside as a separate *ethnic* group. They are a separate group but not a separate group defined by reference to their ethnic origins. I see no answer to this submission.

Mr. Whitmore quite rightly stressed that this case is concerned with identity. The question is: have the Rastafarians a separate *ethnic* identity? Do they stand apart by reason of *their* history from other Jamaicans?

In my judgment it is not enough for Rastafarians now to look back to a past when their ancestors, in common with other peoples in the Caribbean, were taken there from Africa. They were not a separate group then. The *shared* history of Rastafarians goes back only 60 years or so. One can understand and admire the deep affection which Rastafarians feel for Africa and their longing for it as their real home. But, as Mr. Riza recognises, the court is concerned with the language of the statute.'

Chapman v United Kingdom, Judgment of 18 January 2001, European Court of Human Rights

The applicant, a gypsy, lived in a caravan on her own land in Hertfordshire. She had always lived in a caravan in the area, moving from place to place with her family. After several years unsuccessfully on a waiting list for a place on a permanent gypsy site in the area, in 1985 she bought a piece of land. She applied for planning permission to live there with her family in a caravan, and began living there illegally before the application was decided. She made this change in her way of life because the constant problem of being moved on by the police and local authorities was detrimental to her family's health and her children's education. In 1986, the planning application was rejected and enforcement notices for the removal of the caravan were issued. The applicant's appeal against the refusal of planning permission was rejected by a Ministry inspector after an inquiry, on the ground that the land was in the green

7 F Invest Rep 1981.
8 [1993] ICR 517 at 528. Neill LJ's judgment was concurred in by a unanimous court. On the *Dawkins* case, see N. Parpworth, (1993) 143 NLJ 610. On Rastafarians, see M. Banton, (1989) 16 *New Community* 153, and E. Cashmore, *The Rastafarians* (1992). See generally on state education and the 1976 Act, L. Lustgarten and V. Giles, (1981) 4 Urban Law and Policy 55.

belt and national and local planning considerations should override the personal needs of the applicant. Although there was no local authority or private official gypsy site in the local authority area, there were such sites for which the applicant could apply elsewhere in the county. When the applicant remained in her caravan because she had nowhere else to go she was fined in 1990 for failure to comply with the enforcement notices. She then resumed a nomadic way of life with her family, but returned to the caravan on her land in 1992, whereupon enforcement notices were issued against her again and a further planning appeal by her was rejected by a government inspector.

Judgment of the Court:

73. The Court considers that the applicant's occupation of her caravan is an integral part of her ethnic identity as a gypsy, reflecting the long tradition of that minority of following a travelling lifestyle. This is the case even though, under the pressure of development and diverse policies or from their own volition, many gypsies no longer live a wholly nomadic existence and increasingly settle for long periods in one place in order to facilitate, for example, the education of their children. Measures which affect the applicant's stationing of her caravans have therefore a wider impact than on the right to respect for home. They also affect her ability to maintain her identity as a gypsy and to lead her private and family life in accordance with that tradition.

74. The Court finds therefore that the applicant's right to respect for her private life, family life and home are in issue in the present case ...

78. Having regard to the facts of this case, it finds that the decisions of the planning authorities refusing to allow the applicant to remain on her land in her caravans and the measures of enforcement taken in respect of her continued occupation constituted an interference with her right to respect for her private life, family life and home within the meaning of Article 8 § 1 of the Convention. It therefore examines below whether this interference was justified under paragraph 2 of Article 8 as ... pursuing a legitimate aim or aims and as being 'necessary in a democratic society' in pursuit of that aim or aims ...

82. ... the Court finds that the measures pursue the legitimate aim of protecting the 'rights of others' through preservation of the environment. It does not find it necessary to determine whether any other aims were involved. ...

92. [As to whether the interference is 'necessary in a democratic society, the] judgment in any particular case by the national authorities that there are legitimate planning objections to a particular use of a site is one which the Court is not well equipped to challenge. It cannot visit each site to assess the impact of a particular proposal on a particular area in terms of impact on beauty, traffic conditions, sewerage and water facilities, educational facilities, medical facilities, employment opportunities and so on. Because Planning Inspectors visit the site, hear the arguments on all sides and allow examination of witnesses, they are better situated than the Court to weigh the arguments. Hence, as the Court observed in *Buckley* (ECtHRR 1996 – IV p. 1271, 1292 § 75 *in fine*), 'in so far as the exercise of discretion involving a multitude of local factors is inherent in the choice and implementation of planning policies, the national authorities in principle enjoy a wide margin of appreciation', although it remains open to the Court to conclude that there has been a manifest error of appreciation by the national authorities. In these circumstances, the procedural safeguards available to the individual applicant will be especially material in determining whether the respondent State has, when fixing the regulatory framework, remained within its margin of appreciation. In particular, it must examine whether the decision-making process leading to measures of interference was fair and such as to afford due respect to the interests safeguarded to the individual by Article 8 (see the *Buckley* judgment, cited above, p. 1292–3, §§ 76–77).

93. The applicant urged the Court to take into account recent international developments, in particular the [European] Framework Convention for the Protection of Minorities,[9] in reducing the margin of appreciation accorded to States in light of the recognition of the problems of vulnerable groups, such as gypsies. The Court observes that there may be said to be an emerging international consensus amongst the Contracting States of the Council of Europe

---

9   *Ed.* (1995) 34 ILM 351; (1995) 2 IHRR 217.

recognising the special needs of minorities and an obligation to protect their security, identity and lifestyle ... not only for the purpose of safeguarding the interests of the minorities themselves but to preserve a cultural diversity of value to the whole community.

94. However, the Court is not persuaded that the consensus is sufficiently concrete for it to derive any guidance as to the conduct or standards which Contracting States consider desirable in any particular situation. The Framework Convention, for example, sets out general principles and goals but signatory states were unable to agree on means or implementation. This reinforces the Court's view that the complexity and sensitivity of the issues involved in policies balancing the interests of the general population, in particular with regard to environmental protection and the interests of a minority with possibly conflicting requirements, renders the Court's role a strictly supervisory one.

95. Moreover, to accord to a gypsy who has unlawfully established a caravan site at a particular place different treatment from that accorded to non-gypsies who have established a caravan site at that place or from that accorded to any individual who has established a house in that particular place would raise substantial problems under Article 14 of the Convention.

96. Nonetheless, although the fact of being a member of a minority with a traditional lifestyle different from that of the majority of a society does not confer an immunity from general laws intended to safeguard assets common to the whole society such as the environment, it may have an incidence on the manner in which such laws are to be implemented. As intimated in the *Buckley* judgment, the vulnerable position of gypsies as a minority means that some special consideration should be given to their needs and their different lifestyle both in the relevant regulatory planning framework and in arriving at the decisions in particular cases (*loc. cit.,* pp. 1292–95, §§ 76, 80, 84). To this extent there is thus a positive obligation imposed on the Contracting States by virtue of Article 8 to facilitate the gypsy way of life (see *mutatis mutandis* the *Marckx v Belgium* judgment of 13 June 1979, Series A no. 31, p. 15, § 31; ...).

97. It is important to appreciate that in principle gypsies are at liberty to camp on any caravan site which has planning permission; there has been no suggestion that permissions exclude gypsies as a group. They are not treated worse than any non-gypsy who wants to live in a caravan and finds it agreeable to live in a house. However, it appears from the material placed before the Court, including judgments of the English courts, that the provision of an adequate number of sites which the gypsies find acceptable and on which they can lawfully place their caravans at a price which they can afford is something which has not been achieved.

98. The Court does not, however, accept the argument that, because statistically the number of gypsies is greater than the number of places available in authorised gypsy sites, the decision not to allow the applicant gypsy family to occupy land where they wished in order to install their caravan in itself, and without more, constituted a violation of Article 8. This would be tantamount to imposing on the United Kingdom, as on all the other Contracting States, an obligation by virtue of Article 8 to make available to the gypsy community an adequate number of suitably equipped sites. The Court is not convinced, despite the undoubted evolution that has taken place in both international law, as evidenced by the Framework Convention, and domestic legislations in regard to protection of minorities, that Article 8 can be interpreted to involve such a far-reaching positive obligation of general social policy being imposed on States (see paragraphs 93–94 above).

99. It is important to recall that Article 8 does not in terms give a right to be provided with a home. Nor does any of the jurisprudence of the Court acknowledge such a right. While it is clearly desirable that every human being has a place where he or she can live in dignity and which he or she can call home, there are unfortunately in the Contracting States many persons who have no home. Whether the State provides funds to enable everyone to have a home is a matter for political not judicial decision.

100. In sum, the issue for determination before the Court in the present case is not the acceptability or not of a general situation, however deplorable, in the United Kingdom in the light of the United Kingdom's undertakings in international law, but the narrower one whether the particular circumstances of the case disclose a violation of the applicant's, Mrs Chapman's, right to respect for her home under Article 8 of the Convention.

101. In this connection, the legal and social context in which the impugned measure of expulsion was taken against the applicant is, however, a material factor.

102. Where a dwelling has been established without the planning permission which is needed under the national law, there is a conflict of interest between the right of the individual under Article 8 of the Convention to respect for his or her home and the right of others in the community to environmental protection ... When considering whether a requirement that the individual leave his or her home is proportionate to the legitimate aim pursued, it is highly relevant whether or not the home was established unlawfully. If the home was lawfully established, this factor would self-evidently be something which would weigh against the legitimacy of requiring the individual to move. Conversely, if the establishment of a home in a particular place was unlawful, the position of the individual objecting to an order to move is less strong. The Court will be slow to grant protection to those who, in conscious defiance of the prohibitions of the law, establish a home on an environmentally protected site. For the Court to do otherwise would be to encourage illegal action to the detriment of the protection of the environmental rights of other people in the community.

103. A further relevant consideration, to be taken into account in the first place by the national authorities, is that if no alternative accommodation is available, the interference is more serious than where such accommodation is available. The more suitable the alternative accommodation is, the less serious is the interference constituted by moving the applicant from his or her existing accommodation.

104. The evaluation of the suitability of alternative accommodation will involve a consideration of, on the one hand, the particular needs of the person concerned — his or her family requirements and financial resources — and, on the other hand, the rights of the local community to environmental protection. This is a task in respect of which it is appropriate to give a wide margin of appreciation to national authorities, who are evidently better placed to make the requisite assessment.

(b) Application of the above principles

105. The seriousness of what is at stake for this applicant is demonstrated by the facts of this case. The applicant followed an itinerant lifestyle for many years, stopping on temporary or unofficial sites. She took up residence on her own land by way of finding a long-term and secure place to station her caravans. Planning permission was however refused for this and she was required to leave. The applicant was fined twice. She left her land but returned as she had been moved on constantly from place to place. It would appear that the applicant does not in fact wish to pursue an itinerant lifestyle. She was resident on the site from 1986 to 1990 and between 1992 and these proceedings. Thus the present case is not concerned as such with traditional itinerant gypsy life styles.

106. It is evident that individuals affected by an enforcement notice have in principle, and this applicant had in practice, a full and fair opportunity to put before the Planning Inspectors any material which she regarded as relevant to her argument and in particular her personal financial and other circumstances, her views as to the suitability of alternative sites and the length of time needed to find a suitable alternative site.

107. The Court recalls that the applicant moved onto her land in her caravans without obtaining the prior planning permission which she knew was necessary to render that occupation lawful. In accordance with the applicable procedures, the applicant's appeals against refusal of planning permission and enforcement notices were conducted in two public enquiries by Inspectors, who were qualified independent experts. The Inspectors in both appeals saw the site themselves and considered the applicant's representations. As is evidenced by the extension of the time period for compliance, some notice was taken of the points which the applicant advanced.

108. The first Inspector had regard to the location of the site in the Metropolitan Green Belt and found that the planning considerations, both national and local, outweighed the needs of the applicant .... The second Inspector considered that the use of the site for the stationing of caravans was seriously detrimental to the environment, and would 'detract significantly from the quiet rural character' of the site, which was both in a Green Belt and an Area of Great Landscape Value. He concluded that development of the site would frustrate the purpose of the Green Belt in protecting the countryside from encroachment. ...

109. Consideration was given to the applicant's arguments, both concerning the work that she had done on the site by tidying and planting and concerning the difficulties of finding other sites in the area. However, both Inspectors weighed those factors against the

general interest of preserving the rural character of the countryside and found that the latter prevailed.

110. It is clear from the Inspectors' reports that there were strong, environmental reasons for the refusal of planning permission and that the applicant's personal circumstances had been taken into account in the decision-making process. The Court also notes that appeal to the High Court was available in so far as the applicant felt that the Inspectors, or Secretary of State, had not taken into account a relevant consideration or had based the contested decision on relevant considerations.

111. The Court observes that during the planning procedures it was acknowledged that there were no vacant sites immediately available for the applicant to go to, either in the district or in the county as a whole. The Government have pointed out that other sites elsewhere in the county do exist and that the applicant was free to seek sites outside the county. Notwithstanding that the statistics show that there is a shortfall of local authority sites available for gypsies in the country as a whole, it may be noted that many gypsy families still live an itinerant life without recourse to official sites and it cannot be doubted that vacancies on official sites arise periodically.

112. Moreover, given that there are many caravan sites with planning permission, whether suitable sites were available t the applicant during the long period of grace given to her was dependent upon what was required of a site to make it suitable. In this context, the cost of a site compared with the applicant's assets, and its location compared with the applicant's desires are clearly relevant. Since how much the applicant has by way of assets, what outgoings need to be met by her, what locational requirements are essential for her and why they are essential are factors exclusively within the knowledge of the applicant, it is for the applicant to adduce evidence on these matters. She has not placed before the Court any information as to her financial situation, or as to the qualities a site must have before it will be locationally suitable for her, nor does the Court have any information as to the efforts she has made to find alternative sites.

113. The Court is therefore not persuaded that there were no alternatives available to the applicant besides remaining in occupation on land without planning permission in a Green Belt area. As stated in the *Buckley* case, Article 8 does not necessarily go so far as to allow individuals' preferences as to their place of residence to override the general interest (judgment cited above, p. 1294, § 81). If the applicant's problem arises through lack of money, then she is in the same unfortunate position as many others who are not able to afford to continue to reside on sites or in houses attractive to them.

114. In the circumstances, the Court considers that proper regard was had to the applicant's predicament both under the terms of the regulatory framework, which contained adequate procedural safeguards protecting her interest under Article 8 and by the responsible planning authorities when exercising their discretion in relation to the particular circumstances of her case. The decisions were reached by those authorities after weighing in the balance the various competing interests. It is not for this Court to sit in appeal on the merits of those decisions, which were based on reasons which were relevant and sufficient, for the purposes of Article 8, to justify the interferences with the exercise of the applicant's rights.

115. The humanitarian considerations which might have supported another outcome at national level cannot be used as the basis of a finding by the Court which would be tantamount to exempting the applicant from the implementation of the national planning laws and obliging governments to ensure that every gypsy family has available for its use accommodation appropriate to its needs. Furthermore, the effect of these decisions cannot on the facts of this case be regarded as disproportionate to the legitimate aim being pursued.

(c) Conclusion

116. In conclusion, there has been no violation of Article 8 of the Convention …

FOR THESE REASONS, THE COURT

1. *Holds* by ten votes to seven that there has been no violation of Article 8 of the Convention;
2. *Holds* unanimously that there has been no violation of Article 1 of Protocol No. 1 to the Convention;
3. *Holds* unanimously that there has been no violation of Article 6 of the Convention;
4. *Holds* unanimously that there has been no violation of Article 14 of the Convention.

Joint dissenting Opinion of **Judges Pastor Ridruejo, Bonello, Tulkens, Stráznická, Lorenzen, Fischbach and Casadevall**

1. We regret that we are unable to share the opinion of the majority that there has been no violation of Article 8 in this case. This is one of five cases brought before our Court concerning the problems experienced by gypsies in the United Kingdom. There are more pending our examination. All disclose elements of hardship and pressure on a vulnerable group within the community. While complaints about the planning and enforcement measures imposed on a gypsy family who occupied their own land without planning permission have a precedent in the case of *Buckley v the United Kingdom* (judgment of 25 September 1996, *Reports* 1996–IV, p. 1271) which concluded in a finding of no violation, we consider that this cannot bind the Court, whose first task is to implement effectively the Convention system for the protection of human rights. We must pay attention to the changing conditions in Contracting States and give recognition to any emerging consensus in Europe as to the standards to be achieved. We would note that the *Buckley* case was decided four years ago by a chamber of the Court prior to the reforms instituted by Protocol No. 11. Its finding of no violation was reached by six votes to three. This Court, constituted as a Grand Chamber of seventeen judges, has the duty to review the approach adopted in the *Buckley* case in light of current conditions and the arguments put forward by the parties and, if it is necessary, adapt that approach to give practical effect to the rights guaranteed under the Convention.

2. We agree with the majority as to the scope of the rights under Article 8, which are affected in this case (see paragraphs 73–74). The traditional form in which the applicant exercises her home, private and family life attract the protection of this provision. We also agree with the majority that there has been an interference with the enjoyment by the applicant of these rights under Article 8 of the Convention. We would recall however that, although the essential object of Article 8 is to protect the individual against arbitrary action by public authorities, there may in addition be positive obligations inherent in an effective 'respect for private and family life and home'. The boundaries between the State's positive and negative obligations do not lend themselves to precise definition and, indeed, in particular cases such as the present, may overlap. The applicable principles are nonetheless similar. In both contexts, regard must be had to the fair balance which has to be struck between the competing interests of the individual and of the community as a whole; and in both contexts the State enjoys a certain margin of appreciation. While it is therefore not inappropriate to examine the impact of the measures affecting the applicant in terms of the second paragraph of Article 8 of the Convention, we consider that this examination must take into account that positive obligations may arise and that the authorities may, through inaction, fail to respect the balance between the interests of the individual gypsy and the community.

3. Our principal disagreement with the majority lies in their assessment that the interferences were 'necessary in a democratic society'. We accept that the examination of planning objections to a particular use of a site is not a role for which this Court is well-suited (paragraph 92). Where town and country planning is concerned, the Court has previously noted that this involves the exercise of discretionary judgment in the implementation of policies adopted in the interest of the community (see the *Buckley v the United Kingdom* judgment, cited above § 75; *Bryan v the United Kingdom* judgment of 22 November 1995, Series A no. 335–A, p. 18, § 47). It is indeed not for us to substitute our own view of what would be the best policy in the planning sphere or the most appropriate individual measure in planning cases, which involve a multitude of local factors.

In the *Buckley* case (*loc. cit.,* § 75) it was stated that in principle national authorities, for the above reasons, enjoyed a wide margin of appreciation in the choice and implementation of planning policies. In our view, this statement cannot however apply automatically to any case which involves the planning sphere. The Convention has always to be interpreted and applied in the light of current circumstances (see the *Cossey v the United Kingdom* judgment of 27 September 1990, Series A no. 184, p. 17, § 42). There is an emerging consensus amongst the member States of the Council of Europe recognising the special needs of minorities and an obligation to protect their security, identity and lifestyle (see paragraphs 55–67 above, in particular the Framework Convention for the Protection of Minorities), not only for the purpose of safeguarding the interests of the minorities themselves but also in order to preserve a cultural diversity of value to the whole community. This consensus includes a recognition that the protection of the rights of minorities, such as gypsies, requires not only that Contracting States refrain from policies or practices which discriminate against them but that also, where necessary, they should take positive steps to improve their situation through, for example, legislation or specific programmes. We cannot therefore agree with the majority's assertion that the consensus is not sufficiently concrete or with their conclusion that the complexity of the competing interests renders the Court's role a strictly supervisory one (see paragraphs 93–94). This does not reflect in our view the clearly recognised need of gypsies to protection of their effective enjoyment of their rights and perpetuates their vulnerability as a minority with differing needs and values from the general community. The impact of planning and enforcement measures on the enjoyment by a gypsy of the right to respect for home, private and family life therefore has a dimension beyond environmental concerns. Having regard to the potential seriousness of an interference which prohibits a gypsy from pursuing his or her lifestyle at a particular location, we consider that, where the planning authorities have not made any finding that there is available to the gypsy any alternative, lawful site to which he or she can reasonably be expected to move, there must exist compelling reasons for the measures concerned.

4. In the present case, the seriousness of what is at stake for this applicant is readily apparent. The applicant and her family followed an itinerant lifestyle for many years, stopping on temporary or unofficial sites and being increasingly moved on by police and local authority officials. Due to considerations of family health and the education of the children, the applicant took the step of buying land on which to station her caravans with security. Planning permission was however refused for this and they were required to leave. The applicant was fined twice and left her land. She returned though, as they had again been moved on constantly from place to place. She and her family remain on their land subject to the threat of further enforcement measures. Her situation is insecure and vulnerable.

We would observe that during the planning procedures it was acknowledged that there were no alternative sites available for the applicant to go to either in the district or in the county as a whole. The Government referred to other sites in the county and said that the applicant was free to seek sites outside the county. It is apparent however that, notwithstanding the statistics relied on by the Government (see paragraph 53), there was still a significant shortfall of official, lawful sites available for gypsies in the country as a whole and that it could not be taken for granted that vacancies existed or were available elsewhere. It is also apparent that the legislation and planning policies which have been introduced over the last half century have drastically reduced the land on which gypsies may station their caravans lawfully while travelling. Following the latest legislation, the Criminal Justice and Public Order Act 1994, unauthorised campers—persons who station a caravan on the highway, on occupied land without the owner's consent or on any other unoccupied land—commit a criminal offence if they fail to comply with directions to move on.

The Government have argued that the applicant's applications for planning permission for a bungalow should be taken into account as showing that her accommodation needs attract no very special considerations. We are not persuaded of the relevance of this argument. The applicant applied for permission for a bungalow after her application for her caravans had been refused and when she was facing imminent removal from her land. Nor does the fact that she has shown an intention to settle on land on a long-term basis detract from the seriousness of the interference. The pressure on the historic nomadic lifestyle of gypsies from the legislation passed from 1960 onwards has had the effect of inducing many gypsies to adopt the solution of finding a secure, long-term base for their caravans on their own land, while maintaining the ability to travel seasonally or from time to time. Indeed, it may be noted that the official policy for some decades has been to encourage gypsies to find their own private sites (see paragraphs 38–40, 46).

The applicant, in adopting this course for her own family, did not however obtain planning permission for stationing her caravans on her land. Furthermore, the land in question was in a Green Belt area. The Inspectors who conducted the planning inquiries found that, notwithstanding the tidying, improving and screening of the site, her occupation of the land detracted significantly from the quiet, rural character of the countryside which the Green Belt was intended to preserve from encroachment. It is not for us to dispute this assessment.

The Government have further placed significant weight on the safeguards afforded by the planning procedures, submitting that the applicant's interests were properly and fairly taken into account by the Inspectors in reaching their decisions that the environmental interests outweighed hers. We note however that the Planning Inspectors reach their decisions having regard to the applicable planning laws and policies. These indicated that there was a general presumption against inappropriate development in the Green Belt, that gypsy sites were not regarded as appropriate developments in the Green Belt and that very special circumstances would be required to justify such an inappropriate development. Having regard to the fact that in this case it was accepted that no other official sites were available to the applicant to station her caravan and that she had worked to improve and screen the site, we consider that the burden placed on the applicant to prove very special circumstances is extremely high, if not insuperable. We are accordingly not persuaded that the planning framework was able to give anything more than marginal or token weight to the applicant's interests or to the associated public interest in preserving cultural diversity through protection of traditional ethnic lifestyles.

We have therefore weighed the seriousness of the interference with the applicant's rights with the environmental arguments which militate against her occupation. While the latter are not of negligible importance, they are not, in our view, of either a nature or degree as to disclose a 'pressing social need' when compared with what was at stake for the applicant. There was no indication in the planning procedures that the applicant had anywhere else to which she could reasonably be expected to move her caravan. The local authority had been found in breach of their duty to make adequate provision for gypsies in the area in 1985 and had been under a direction from the Secretary of State to comply with their statutory duty, without any concrete improvement of the situation resulting since. In these circumstances, we find that the planning and enforcement measures exceeded the margin of appreciation accorded to the domestic authorities and were disproportionate to the legitimate aim of environmental protection. They cannot therefore be regarded as 'necessary in a democratic society'.

5. In reaching this conclusion, we have given consideration to whether, as the Government warned, this would be tantamount to excluding gypsies from planning enforcement mechanisms and giving them carte blanche to settle wherever they choose. The long-term failures of local authorities to make effective provision for gypsies in their planning policies is evident from the history of implementation of measures concerning gypsy sites, both public and private (see paragraphs 36–37, 46, 49). Recognition has been given domestically to the difficulties of the gypsies' situation through the 'toleration' of some unlawful sites and the sensitivity urged on local authorities as regards the exercise of their 'draconic' enforcement powers (see paragraphs 47–48). This indicates that the Government is already well aware that the legislative and policy framework does not provide in practice for the needs of the gypsy minority and that their policy of leaving it to local authorities to make provision for gypsies has been of limited effectiveness (see paragraphs 49–52). The complexities of the problem have been adverted to above and it is not for us to impose any particular solution on the United Kingdom. However, it is in our opinion disproportionate to take steps to evict a gypsy family from their home on their own land in circumstances where there has not been shown to be any other lawful, alternative site reasonably open to them (see, *mutatis mutandis*, the *Buckley v the United Kingdom* judgment, cited above, §§ 26 and 81, where the problems of vandalism alleged to exist on the official site 700 metres from the applicant's land did not appear to pose any specific threat to her or her family's health or security). It would accordingly be for the authorities to adopt such measures as they consider appropriate to ensure that the planning system affords effective respect for the home, private life and family life of gypsies such as the applicant.

6. The reference by the majority to the alleged liberty of gypsies to camp on any caravan site with planning permission (paragraph 97) ignores the reality that gypsies are not welcome on private residential sites which are, in any event, often prohibitively expensive. Nor are they able to use such private residential sites for seasonal or temporary transit. The planning authorities themselves recognise that the only practicable options open to gypsies are local authority owned sites or privately owned gypsy sites. It is not a question of gypsies imposing particular preferences as to location and facilities without realistic reference to their own resources (see paragraph 112). The options open to them are, as in this case, severely limited, if existing at all.

7. We would also take issue with the relevance or validity of the statement in paragraph 99 of the judgment to the effect that Article 8 does not give a right to be provided with a home. In this case, the applicant had a home, in her caravan on her land but was being prevented from settling there. Furthermore, it is not the Court's case-law that a right to be provided with

a home is totally outside the ambit of Article 8. The Court has accepted that there may be circumstances where the authorities' refusal to take steps to assist in housing problems could disclose a problem under Article 8 — see for example the case of *Marzari v Italy*, where the Court held a refusal of the authorities to provide housing assistance to an individual suffering from a severe disease might in certain circumstances raise an issue because of the impact of such refusal on the private life of the individual (no. 3644/97, decision of 4 May 1999). Obligations on the State arise therefore where there is a direct and immediate link between the measures sought by an applicant and the latter's private life (*Botta v Italy* judgment of 24 February 1998, *Reports* 1998–I, p. 422, §§ 33–34). ...

9. In conclusion, we would reiterate that it is not a necessary consequence of finding a violation in this case that gypsies could, freely take up residence on any land in the country. Where there were shown to be other sites available to them, the balance between the interests of protecting the environmental value of the site and the interests of the gypsy family in residing on it would tip more strongly towards the former. United Kingdom legislation and policies in this area have long recognised the objective of providing for gypsies' special needs. The homeless have a right under domestic legislation to be provided with accommodation (see paragraph 54). Our view that Article 8 of the Convention imposes a positive obligation on the authorities to ensure that gypsies have a practical and effective opportunity to enjoy their rights to home, private and family life, in accordance with their traditional lifestyle, is not a startling innovation.

10. We conclude that there has been a violation of Article 8 of the Convention.

NOTE

The *Chapman* case confirmed and developed the decision of a Chamber of the old Court in the gypsy case of *Buckley v United Kingdom*, which was similar on its facts. Would it have made any difference if the applicant had not moved on to her land and lived there illegally before the planning decision was taken? Or if the land had not been green belt land? Should the burden of proof have been upon the applicant to show that she had nowhere else to live, as the Court held, or upon the state to show that an official site location was available? Was the Court fair to the applicant in noting that she was willing to abandon the gypsy nomadic life? Might living in a gypsy caravan on a permanent site be all that is reasonably possible in the manner of the gypsy way of life in a society such as that in England and Wales?

4 Education

Race Relations Act 1976

17. Discrimination by bodies in charge of educational establishments
It is unlawful, in relation to an educational establishment falling within column 1 of the following table [omitted], for a person indicated in relation to the establishment in column 2 (the 'responsible body') to discriminate against a person—
  (a) in the terms on which it offers to admit him to the establishment as a pupil; or
  (b) by refusing or deliberately omitting to accept an application for his admission to the establishment as a pupil; or
  (c) where he is a pupil of the establishment—
      (i) in the way it affords him access to any benefits, facilities or services, or by refusing or deliberately omitting to afford him access to them; or
      (ii) by excluding him from the establishment or subjecting him to any other detriment.

18. Other discrimination by local education authorities
(1) It is unlawful for a local education authority, in carrying out such of its functions under the [Education Acts] as do not fall under section 17, to do any act which constitutes racial discrimination. ...

NOTES

1. Section 17 applies, by virtue of the Table attached to it, to all state and independent primary and secondary schools in England and Wales, including private schools for children with special needs and private community homes (education). It also applies to most institutions of higher education. Universities, polytechnics, colleges of education, colleges of further education and designated institutions (such as the College of Nursing and the Co-operative College) are within the section. Other non-designated institutions are controlled by s. 20,[10] not s. 17.

2. Although the 1968 Act did not contain any provision comparable to s. 17 dealing just with discrimination in education, a number of cases arose under the equivalent provision to the 1976 Act, s. 20, below, in respect of educational facilities. A case in which a private preparatory school was found by the RRB to have unlawfully refused to admit a child of Iranian origin[11] would now come within s. 17(1)(b).[12] The RRB also examined under the 1968 Act the London Borough of Ealing's dispersal policy for immigrant children. By this policy, Asian children were not admitted to local schools in Southall but 'bussed' to 'white' schools elsewhere within the Borough's jurisdiction. White children were not 'bussed'. After obtaining the opinion of an expert assessor, the RRB reported on the policy as follows:[13]

> '30. In his report Professor Kogan explained that dispersal was introduced in Ealing in the mid-1960s. In 1976 nearly 3,000 Asian children of primary school age were sent by coach every day to other parts of the Borough. In the great majority of cases the dispersal was on educational grounds, but there was evidence which suggested that a number of these children were dispersed away from their neighbourhood schools even though their knowledge of the English language was perfectly adequate. The local authority argued that any such Asian children were dispersed because of cultural needs. The Board formed the opinion that such children were being treated less favourably than other children for no other reason than their ethnic origins. Attempts at conciliation failed and the Board determined to bring proceedings.'

After legal proceedings had been instituted against the Borough,[14] an out of court settlement was reached:[15]

> 'The central feature of the settlement was that in future no child would be "bussed" except on the basis of educational need, and a special assessment procedure was introduced to enable the language needs of children entering the education system for the first time to be individually defined. Moreover, no additional children would be "bussed" after September 1979 and it was expected that new school building in the Southall area would enable "bussing" to be completely phased out by 1981.'[16]

What would have to be proved to establish that 'bussing' in these dispersal cases was direct or indirect discrimination? Note the dictum in *Cumings v Birkenhead Corpn*[16a] that the allocation of children to particular schools on the basis of the colour of their skin would be unlawful as an 'abuse of power' (quite apart from race relations legislation).

Another issue has been the testing and classification of school children as educationally subnormal and their placement in special schools. Following a complaint concerning Haringey, 'the Board noted that West Indian children in the

---

10 Below, p. 1134.
11 Case 6, RRB Report 1974, p. 36.
12 For the 'Jewish quota' case, see above, p. 1120.
13 RRB Report 1975–76, p. 6.
14 See *Race Relations Board v Ealing London Borough (No 2)* [1978] 1 WLR 112, CA.
15 CRE Report 1978, p. 101.
16 See also the dispersal case reported in RRB Report 1974, p. 6.
16a [1972] Ch 12, CA.

borough concerned, and in a number of other local education authority areas, were over-represented in the group considered to be educationally sub-normal. The evidence suggested that this situation had come about because the intelligence tests in general use do not effectively distinguish the educationally sub-normal from those whose performance is at a similar level as a result of educational or cultural deprivation'.[17] The RRB did not consider that there had been any unlawful discrimination contrary to the 1968 Act. Might there be *indirect* discrimination under the 1976 Act?

In the *Teaching of English as a Second Language* case,[18] Calderdale, in West Yorkshire, had required all children whose language at home was not English to undergo language scrutiny, with the likely consequence of being placed in separate language units instead of the usual school classes. Such units might be located at places requiring pupils to be bussed to school; their curriculum was also more restricted than the normal curriculum. The CRE concluded that these arrangements could not be justified on educational grounds and amounted to indirect discrimination.

In another complaint to the RRB it was alleged (but not proven) that a head-master had discriminated in the protection of school children from assault by other children.[19] Would this be unlawful discrimination under any part of s. 17?

3. Unlike s. 17, ss. 18 and 19 apply only to 'racial discrimination', which excludes victimisation contrary to s. 2.[20] The allocation of local authority grants for higher education is subject to s. 18. A three year residence condition for eligibility for such grants was considered by the RRB to work harshly against some immigrant pupils seeking further education but was not thought to be contrary to the 1968 Act.[1] It is lawful under s. 41.[2]

4. In the *Secondary School Allocations in Reading* case,[3] the CRE investigated allegations of discrimination in new school zoning arrangements adopted by Berkshire LEA. Although it did not find the arrangements to be discriminatory, the CRE did conclude that 'the Authority had carried out no analysis of what the consequence of their scheme would be for ethnic minority pupils. . . . To that extent the Authority had taken insufficient account of their duties under [ss. 19 and 71 of the] Race Relations Act'.[4] In 1982, the CRE considered a complaint that a group of parents of children at the Greenfield Primary School, Hyde, had attempted to induce the local authority to limit the number of children of Asian origin attending the school. It concluded that s. 31 of the 1976 Act had been infringed. The parents accepted this finding and undertook not to contravene the Act again.[5]

The 1976 Act imposes no duty of positive action upon a local education authority to ensure that there are Asian children in a school's catchment area.[6]

An admissions procedure by which parents were required to give at least four reasons for the admission of their children to particular schools was indirect

---

17 RRB Report 1970–71, p. 7.
18 CRE F Invest Rep 1986.
19 Case 5, RRB Report 1972, p. 35.
20 See s. 3(3) above, p. 1110.
1 RRB Report 1969–70, p. 9.
2 1976 Act, above, p. 1077.
3 F Invest Rep 1983, p. vi.
4 Report, p. vi. S. 19 has since been repealed by the Race Relations (Amendment) Act 2000, Sch. 3.
5 CRE Report 1982, p. 12.
6 *R v Bradford Metropolitan Borough Council, ex p Sikander Ali* (1993) Times, 21 October.

discrimination against Asian parents because of their difficulties with English and their relative lack of knowledge and experience of the British education system.[7]
5. For a case arising under s. 17 concerning tuition fees for overseas students, see the *Orphanos* case.[8]
6. The Race Relations Act provides a special regime for the enforcement of ss. 17–19.[9]
7. The duty of a local education authority under the Education Act 1996, s. 411, to comply with a parent's request to transfer a child to another school is not limited by s. 18 of the Race Relations Act. In *R v Cleveland County Council, ex p Commission for Racial Equality*,[10] an education authority complied with a mother's request to transfer her five year old daughter, who was of mixed English and African descent, from a primary school that had nearly all Asian pupils to one that was predominantly white. The request was made for fear that the daughter would learn a Pakistani language at the expense of her English. It was held that the education authority had not committed an act of discrimination contrary to s. 18; its duty to transfer the child was not limited by s. 18 (since the duty fell under s. 17) and, in any event, the transfer was not, as argued, an act of segregation contrary to s. 2 of the Race Relations Act so that the authority had not committed any act of racial discrimination. The CRE had reached the contrary conclusion in a formal investigation report.[11]

5 Goods, facilities and services

Race Relations Act 1976

20. Discrimination in provision of goods, facilities or services
(1) It is unlawful for any person concerned with the provision (for payment or not) of goods, facilities or services to the public or a section of the public to discriminate against a person who seeks to obtain or use those goods, facilities or services—
    (*a*) by refusing or deliberately omitting to provide him with any of them; or
    (*b*) by refusing or deliberately omitting to provide him with goods, facilities or services of the like quality, in the like manner and on the like terms as are normal in the first-mentioned person's case in relation to other members of the public or (where the person so seeking belongs to a section of the public) to other members of that section.
(2) The following are examples of the facilities and services mentioned in subsection (1)—
    (*a*) access to and use of any place which members of the public are permitted to enter;
    (*b*) accommodation in a hotel, boarding house or other similar establishment;
    (*c*) facilities by way of banking or insurance or for grants, loans, credit or finance;
    (*d*) facilities for education;
    (*e*) facilities for entertainment, recreation or refreshment;
    (*f*) facilities for transport or travel;
    (*g*) the services of any profession or trade, or any local or other public authority.

NOTES

1. *Goods, facilities or services.* These terms are not defined in the Act. A. Lester and G. Bindman[12] suggest:

7 *Secondary Schools Admissions*, F Invest Rep 1992.
8 Above, p. 1095.
9 See below, p. 1171.
10 (1993) 91 LGR 139, CA. The case concerned the duty under the Education Act 1980, s. 6, now Education Act 1996, s. 411.
11 *Racial Segregation in Education* (1989).
12 *Race and Law* (1972), p. 260.

'They must be given their ordinary and natural meaning. "Goods" are any movable property, including merchandise or wares. "Facilities" include any opportunity for obtaining some benefit or for doing something. "Services" refer to any conduct tending to the welfare or advantage of other people, especially conduct which supplies their needs. Each of these expressions is deliberately vague and general; taken together, they cover a very wide range of human activity.'

Manufacturers, wholesalers and retailers are all subject to s. 20. Thus a wholesaler who refused to supply a retailer (retailers being a 'section of the public') with goods on racial grounds would be in breach of the Act. In *Dockers' Labour Club and Institute Ltd v Race Relations Board*,[13] Lord Diplock stated that 'normally' (now 'normal' in the 1976 Act) indicated that the Act was not intended to deal with persons who supplied goods, etc., 'on an isolated occasion'; it concerned only persons who did so 'regularly'.

2. Section 20(2) gives certain examples of 'facilities and services'. Places 'which members of the public are permitted to enter' include shops, banks, public houses, restaurants, public parks, dance halls, and theatres. This first example overlaps with the subsequent ones in that many of the places that come within it (e.g. public houses) provide a 'facility' (e.g. refreshment) listed in another. The place may be publicly or privately owned. There need be no legal right of entry; a licence to enter is sufficient. The test is whether the public or a section of it (e.g. persons over 18) are customarily or on a particular occasion (e.g. garden open to the public one day in the year) 'permitted to enter'.[14] Would the organisers of the meeting in *Thomas v Sawkins*,[15] have been entitled to exclude a black member of the public from the meeting because of his colour? A District Registrar provides 'facilities or services' when carrying out 'his duties' in the course of applications for marriage licences.[16] Prison work is a 'facility' for prisoners, who constitute a 'section of the public', for the purposes of s. 20.[17]

3. 'Hotel' in the phrase 'hotel, boarding house or other similar establishment' can be taken to have the meaning that it has in the Hotel Proprietors Act 1956, s. 1(3):

'An establishment held out by the proprietor as offering food, drink and if so required sleeping accommodation, without special contract, to any traveller presenting himself who appears able and willing to pay a reasonable sum for the services and facilities provided and who is in a fit state to be received.'

This definition is also that of an inn at common law. An innkeeper is obliged at common law to receive allcomers without discrimination. Thus in the famous case of *Constantine v Imperial Hotels Ltd*,[18] judgment was awarded against an innkeeper for refusing to accommodate a well known black West Indian cricketer (and later a member of the Race Relations Board) during the Second World War for fear of upsetting members of the US armed forces. The case would now fall within the 1976 Act, s. 20 and the plaintiff would have to bring proceedings under the Act and not at common law.[19] The wording 'boarding house or other similar establishment' includes bed and breakfast establishments and other establishments insofar as they offer *short-*

---

13 [1976] AC 285 at 297, HL.
14 See further A. Lester and G. Bindman, *Race and Law* (1972), pp. 261–262, and M. Supperstone, *Brownlie's Law of Public Order and National Security* (2nd edn, 1981), pp. 33–34.
15 Above, p. 548.
16 *Tejani v Superintendent Registrar for the District of Peterborough* [1986] IRLR 502, CA. See J. Gardner, (1987) 50 MLR 345.
17 *Alexander v Home Office*, below, p. 1172.
18 [1944] 1 KB 693, KBD.
19 See the 1976 Act, s. 53, below, p. 1168.

term (see 'similar') residential accommodation for travellers. A holiday camp might qualify; it might also be said to offer facilities for 'recreation'. The longer term 'facilities' offered by private or residential hotels, 'bed-sits', and university halls probably fall within s. 21, below, and not s. 20.[20] But the examples listed in s. 20(2) are not exhaustive[1] and it could be that as far as accommodation is concerned there is some overlap between ss. 20 and 21, below. In that case, the generality of the wording of s. 20 ('facilities for . . .') might in a few cases make it more useful than the more precise wording of s. 21. In the *Hackney* case,[2] an enforcement notice was issued in respect of both ss. 20 and 21. In the *Racial Discrimination in Liverpool City Council Housing Department* case,[3] in which the CRE found that the Housing Department had consistently allocated poorer quality council housing to ethnic minority applicants, the enforcement notice was in respect of s. 20 only. The 'small premises' exception in s. 22, below, applies to both s. 20 and s. 21.

4. The prohibition of discrimination in respect of the making of 'loans' includes the granting of mortgages. In the *Race and Mortgage Lending* case,[4] the CRE found that certain rules applied in the allocation of mortgages by building societies in Rochdale (e.g. no mortgages for houses without front gardens, which were mostly city centre houses where ethnic minorities tended to live) was indirect discrimination contrary to s. 20.

5. Although s. 20 refers to 'facilities for education' without qualification, the 1976 Act, s. 23(1), provides that s. 20 does not apply to discrimination in education rendered unlawful by ss. 17–18, above. As a result, s. 20 has only a modest role. It applies to establishments not covered by s. 17, such as driving schools, foreign language schools, crammers, and to piano lessons (whether in the pupil's home or that of the teacher).

6. For a case of discrimination by a restaurant ('facilities for refreshment'), see the *Genture Restaurants Ltd* case,[5] (restrictions on black persons and Chinese: illegal discrimination).

7. 'Facilities for transport and travel' include sleeping cabins for passengers on board ship. The 1968 Act, s. 7(6), permitted the segregation of persons of different 'racial groups' in such cabins as a result of pressure from British shipping companies to protect them from international competition. As with innkeepers, the obligation of the common carrier at common law to accept allcomers is placed upon a statutory basis and any proceedings against him for racial discrimination must be brought under the 1976 Act, s. 53.[6]

8. 'Trade' in the phrase 'the services of any profession or trade or any local or other public authority' includes 'any business'.[7] Estate agents and accommodation bureaux come within this wording (they *may* be subject to s. 21 too, see below). A PEP Report in 1974[8] showed that discrimination by estate agents against Asian and West Indian house buyers had dropped a lot in the five years since the law was extended to cover housing in 1968. There had been discrimination in 64% of cases in tests conducted in 1967. In tests in 1973 there was discrimination in one form or another in 17% of

20 But note that a *long-term* private children's home was treated by the CRE as being within s. 20 in the *Barlavington Manor Children's Home* case, F Invest Rep 1979.
1   See Lord Simon in *Applin v Race Relations Board* [1975] AC 259, 291, HL.
2   Below, p. 1146.
3   CRE F Invest Rep 1989.
4   CRE F Invest Rep 1985.
5   CRE F Invest Rep 1978.
6   Below, p. 1168.
7   1976 Act, s. 78(1).
8   McIntosh and Smith, *The Extent of Racial Discrimination* (1974).

cases. According to one manager of an accommodation agency, '95 per cent of landlords using the agency gave racially discriminating instructions'.[9] The CRE has issued non-discrimination notices in several cases against estate agents.[10] Estate agents are also controlled in respect of racial discrimination by the Estate Agents Act 1979.[11] An estate agent is defined as 'a person who, by way of profession or trade, provides services for the purpose of finding premises for persons seeking to acquire them or assisting in the disposal of premises'.[12] An estate agent (or accommodation bureau) may rely upon the 'small premises' exception[13] even if the property does not fall within it if he has taken 'all reasonable steps in the circumstances to ensure that the accommodation with which he is concerned and in respect of which racial stipulations are sought to be imposed falls within' it.[14] Normally, 'the agent could be expected in relation to each property to ascertain and record the specific facts relevant to section 7[15] and would, where any doubt existed, carry out further investigation to satisfy himself that the criteria in the section were met'.[16]

The 1976 Act is supplemented by the Consumer Credit Act 1974, s. 25(2)(c), which provides that in determining whether an applicant for a licence to carry on a consumer credit or consumer hire business is a 'fit person', account must be taken of evidence that he has practised discrimination on grounds of sex, colour, race or ethnic or national origins in or in connection with the carrying on of any business.

9. The wording 'local or other public authority' covers discrimination in the provision of public housing (as does s. 21) and other 'services'.[17] In *Hillingdon London Borough Council v Commission for Racial Equality*,[18] the Council was obliged by statute to house homeless persons within its area, which included Heathrow airport, at ratepayers' expense. In protest, a Councillor drove a Kenyan Asian family, then recently arrived, to Whitehall and left them on the steps of the Foreign Office. A white Rhodesian family that arrived in the same period was housed without difficulty. It was accepted in argument that s. 20 had been infringed. In *Commission for Racial Equality v Riley*[19] it was held that the granting of planning permission was a 'service' or 'facility' (injunction restraining National Front officer from bringing pressure to bear (contrary to s.31) on the planning authority to refuse planning applications from black persons). Following the *Amin* case,[20] doubts were expressed as to the correctness of this decision. These doubts have been resolved by s. 19A, 1976 Act, added by the Housing and Planning Act 1986, by which 'it is unlawful for a planning authority to discriminate against a person in carrying out their planning functions'. The police were intended by Parliament to be covered only in the few areas where they offer 'services' (e.g. crime prevention advice); discrimination in the course of their operational duties was understood to be subject not to s. 20 of the 1976 Act, but to

---

9 RRB Report 1974, p. 12.
10 See, e.g. *Racial Discrimination in an Oldham Estate Agency*, F Invest Rep 1990, and *Allen's Accommodation Bureau* case, F Invest Rep 1980.
11 The Director General of Fair Trading may stop a person from doing estate agency work if he is satisfied that the person has been discriminating: 1979 Act, s. 1(3)(b). The Director may also revoke a licence to grant mortgages of an estate agent who has practised discrimination: Consumer Credit Act 1974, s. 25(2).
12 1976 Act, s. 78(1).
13 1976 Act, s. 22, below.
14 *Race Relations Board v Furnished Rooms Bureau*, Westminster C Ct (1972) RRB Report p. 38.
15 1968 Act, see now the 1976 Act s. 22.
16 Ibid.
17 See, e.g., the *Hackney Council Housing* case, below, p. 1146.
18 [1982] AC 779, HL.
19 (1982) CRE Report 1982, p. 18, Manchester C Ct.
20 Below, p. 1138.

the police complaints procedure under other legislation.[1] The work of other public servants such as immigration officers, public health inspectors and Inland Revenue officials likewise was understood not to constitute a 'service'.[2]

In *Savjani v IRC*,[3] however, the IRC had a policy by which a taxpayer born in the Indian subcontinent who was claiming tax relief for the first time for a child born in the UK had to provide a full birth certificate, which gave details of the parents and cost £2.50. In the case of other taxpayers, a short birth certificate, which gave no such details and cost nothing, was sufficient. The policy had been introduced because fraudulent claims to relief had been made by persons originating from the Indian subcontinent based upon false documents. The Court of Appeal held unanimously that, in its operation of the tax relief system, the Inland Revenue was providing a 'service' in the sense of s. 20(2)(g), which was infringed on the facts of the case. Templeman LJ stated:

> '. . . the board and the inspector are performing duties. . . . The duty is to collect the right amount of revenue; but, in my judgment, there is a service to the taxpayer provided by the board and the inspector by the provision, dissemination and implementation of regulations which will enable the taxpayer to know that he is entitled to a deduction or a repayment which will entitle him to know how he is to satisfy the inspector or the board if he is so entitled, and which will enable him to obtain the actual deduction or repayment which Parliament said he is to have. For present purposes, in my judgment, the inspector and the board provide the inestimable services of enabling a taxpayer to obtain that relief which Parliament intended he should be able to obtain as a matter of right subject only to proof.
>
> Now if the inspector or the board make it more difficult for a taxpayer—who is entitled to relief if he does satisfy all the conditions—to obtain that relief than they do for other taxpayers, they are discriminating in the provision of the service to the public and the service to him of enabling tax relief to be obtained.'

It was pointed out by the Court of Appeal that it would have been possible for the Minister concerned to have sanctioned the illegal policy in accordance with s. 41(2)(a).[4]

The Court of Appeal in the *Savjani* case distinguished *R v Immigration Appeal Tribunal, ex p Kassam*,[5] in which it was held that the Home Secretary was not providing a 'facility' in the sense of s. 29 of the Sex Discrimination Act 1975 (the equivalent provision to s. 20) when exercising powers under the Immigration Act 1971 in respect of entry to the UK. In that case, Stephenson LJ stated:

> 'The kind of facilities with which the sections of the Acts of 1975 and 1976 are concerned is of the same order as goods and services, and though it may not always be easy to say whether a particular person (or body of persons) is a person concerned with the provision of any of those three things to the public or a section of the public and although a Minister of the Crown or a government department might be such a person (for instance, in former days the Postmaster General . . .), I am clearly of the opinion that the Secretary of State in acting under the Immigration Act and Rules is not such a person, and he cannot be held to have discriminated against the appellant by refusing to give him leave to remain here while his wife was a student, or by refusing to interpret or alter the immigration rule . . . which is relevant to this appeal. He is operating in a field outside the fields in which Parliament has forbidden sex discrimination.'

Both the *Kassam* and *Savjani* cases were approved by the House of Lords in *Re Amin*.[5a] In that case, an Asian woman who was a UK citizen was refused a special entry voucher for admission to the UK because she was not a head of household. Her

---

1   See above, p. 47: cf. 374 HL Deb, 29 September 1976, col. 525.
2   Cf. ibid.
3   [1981] QB 458, CA.
4   See above, p. 1078.
5   [1980] 2 All ER 330, [1980] 1 WLR 1037, CA.
5a   [1983] 2 AC 818.

claim that this was sex discrimination contrary to the 1975 Act was rejected by the House of Lords by the narrow majority of 3 to 2. Lord Fraser, giving the only speech for the majority, stated:[6]

> My Lords, I accept that the examples in s. 29(2) are not exhaustive, but they are, in my opinion, useful pointers to aid in the construction of subsection (1). S. 29 as a whole seems to me to apply to the direct provision of facilities or services, and not to the mere grant of permission to use facilities. That is in accordance with the words of subsection (1), and it is reinforced by some of the examples in subsection (2). Example (*a*) is 'access to *and use of* any place' and the words that I have emphasised indicate that the paragraph contemplates actual provision of facilities which the person will use. Example (*d*) refers, in my view, to the actual provision of schools and other facilities for education, but not to the mere grant of an entry certificate or a special voucher to enable a student to enter the United Kingdom in order to study here. Example (*g*) seems to me to be contemplating things such as medical services, or library facilities, which can be directly provided by local or other public authorities. So in *Savjani*, Templeman LJ took the view that the Inland Revenue performed two separate functions—first a duty of collecting revenue and secondly a service of providing taxpayers with information. . . . In the present case the entry clearance officer in Bombay was in my opinion not providing a service for would-be immigrants; rather he was performing his duty of controlling them.
>
> Counsel for the appellant sought to draw support for his contention from section 85(1) of the Act of 1975 [cf. s. 75(1), 1976 Act, above, p. 615: identical wording] . . . . That section puts an act done on behalf of the Crown on a par with an act done by a private person, and it does not in terms restrict the comparison to an act *of the same kind* done by a private person. But in my opinion it applies only to acts done on behalf of the Crown which are of a kind similar to acts that might be done by a private person. It does not mean that the Act is to apply to any act of any kind done on behalf of the Crown by a person holding statutory office. There must be acts . . . done in the course of formulating or carrying out government policy, which are quite different in kind from any act that would ever be done by a private person, and to which the Act does not apply. I would respectfully agree with the observations on the corresponding provision of the Race Relations Act 1976 made by Woolf J in *Home Office v Commission for Racial Equality* [1982] QB 385 at 395B–C. Part V of the Act of 1975 makes exceptions for certain acts including acts done for the purpose of national security (s. 52 [cf. s. 42, 1976 Act]) and for acts which are 'necessary' in order to comply with certain statutory requirements: s. 51 [cf. s. 41, 1976 Act]. These exceptions will no doubt be effective to protect acts which are of a kind that would otherwise be unlawful under the Act. But they do not in my view obviate the necessity for construing s. 29 as applying only to acts which are at least similar to acts that could be done by private persons.'

In *Home Office v Commission for Racial Equality*, Woolf J had stated:

> 'In relation to [s. 75] sub-s. (1) it was contended on behalf of the Home Office that that only applies to acts which could be done by a private person. . . . Thus, in the course of argument, Mr Scott contended that if an immigration officer treated coloured immigrants in a wholly different manner from the way in which he treated white immigrants, this would not be an act to which section 75 referred, because it was not an act capable of being done by an individual.
>
> I cannot accept this restricted interpretation of section 75. It is true that only an immigration officer and not a private person can purport to exercise immigration control. However, the type of act to which I have just made reference is one which a private person in a different capacity is quite able to perform, for example a doorkeeper at a nightclub, and so it seems to me that that would be an act falling within section 75. After all it is only a government department who can engage immigration officers. A private individual cannot do that. But the Home Office concedes that such an engagement would be an act within section 75.
>
> . . . It appears to me that an act, for the purposes of section 75, which is defined in section 78 as including a deliberate omission, means some act which, while not necessarily the same, is one similar to the kind of act which can amount to unlawful discrimination under the Act of 1976.'

---

6 p. 835.

What emerges from Lord Fraser's speech in the *Amin* case is that an act by a public official or body may involve a service within s. 20 if it is one that a private person may perform. This approach was followed in *Farah v Commissioner of Police of the Metropolis*.[7] In that case the plaintiff was a Somali refugee living in London who called for police assistance when she was attacked by white teenagers near her home. Instead of detaining the attackers, the police arrested the plaintiff and charged her with affray. No evidence was offered and she was acquitted. Thereupon she brought proceedings in tort at common law and also alleged a breach of the Race Relations Act. On a preliminary point, it was held that the claim fell within s. 20 of the 1976 Act because that part of the police officers' duties that involved assisting and protecting the public amounted to a 'service'. The Court of Appeal accepted that the assistance and protection sought by the plaintiff was similar to acts that might have been performed by a private person, such as a security firm.

Now, however, the problem has been tackled by Parliament by a new provision – s.19B, RRA 1976[8] – making public authorities liable generally under the RRA 1976 in respect of discriminatory acts committed in the exercise of their functions; this supplements s. 20, RRA 1976, which has been left unamended.

What if an income tax official were to discriminate when investigating a person's income? Would this be contrary to s. 20? Is the *Riley* case, above, consistent with the interpretation of ss. 20 and 75 of the 1976 Act in the *Amin* case?

Prior to the amendments to the RRA 1976 by the Race Relations (Amendment) Act 2000, the CRE had recommended that the *Amin* decision be reversed by Parliament, so that s. 20 should apply to 'all areas of governmental and regulatory activity, whether central or local, such as acts in the course of immigration control, the prison and police services, and planning control'.[9] The particular areas of the public sector listed above were ones in which there had been allegations and some proven instances of racial discrimination. As the CRE stated, the lack of a remedy in most of the public sector was serious given the importance of many of the decisions taken for individuals and the fact that, in contrast with the case of discrimination by a private person, there was usually no opportunity to go elsewhere.

10. An early problem in cases referred to the RRB was discrimination in motor and life insurance. A number of complaints revealed that it was common for insurance companies to refuse car hire insurance if the applicant was born abroad. The Board took the view that this was illegal discrimination ('national origins')[10] and negotiated an agreement with Lloyd's Motor Underwriters' Association by which members of the Association would replace their 'born abroad' test by one of three years' residence together with appropriate driving experience.[11] A 'born abroad' restriction was imposed in *Kelsall v National Motor and Accident Insurance Union*[12] (named driver restriction in car insurance for German born car owner resident in UK 16 years; liability under s. 20 admitted). On the question of residence, the CRE takes the view that, with the introduction of indirect discrimination in 1976, a general three years' residence requirement, which remains common practice, may be illegal.[13] In respect

---

7 [1997] 1 All ER 289, CA.
8 See above, p. 1074.
9 *Second Review of the Race Relations Act 1976* (1992) p. 30. Planning control is subject to the 1976 Act to a small extent: see s. 19A. As to the control of discrimination in the criminal justice system, see above, p. 1077.
10 RRB Report 1968–69, p. 14.
11 RRB Report 1969–70, p. 50.
12 (1980) CRE Report 1980, p. 84, Westminster C Ct.
13 *Zone Insurance Co Ltd* case, F Invest Rep 1982, p. 13.

of life insurance, the RRB took up a case in which a form used by a life assurance society asked the proposer to state whether he was 'Caucasian, Negroid or Asian'. The company agreed to abandon this question and to ask instead about the proposer's length of residence in the United Kingdom. The Board took the view that 'dubious anthropological concepts such as caucasian, or negroid, can have no actuarial relevance to life or sickness assurance'[14] and that discrimination based upon them was illegal.[15]

Discrimination in pubs may take various forms.[16] In 1973, the RRB reported 'an increase in the number of complaints in which it was alleged that licensees told Asian customers they would only be served if they and their friends talked to each other in English'. The Board stated that 'to refuse any group merely for speaking a language other than English is unreasonable; where the real ground for the refusal is racial, it is also unlawful'.[17] Summarising the effect of the 1968 Act, the RRB stated:[18]

> 'We are of the view that the Act has worked well in relation to public houses and that whereas before 1968 members of minorities were never sure whether they would be served, they can now enter the vast majority of public houses reasonably confident that they will be treated in the same way as others. Since 1968 brewers and the National Union of Licensed Victuallers have done a great deal to ensure that licensees are made familiar with the Act and we believe that their work has played an important part in reducing discrimination.'

Complaints about discrimination in dance halls (like some complaints about pubs) have raised the question whether it is lawful for the owner to exclude all persons belonging to a particular 'racial group' because one or more members of that group have caused 'trouble' in the past. In *Race Relations Board v Mecca Ltd (Hammersmith Palais)*,[19] at the time that the complainant, a West Indian, was refused admission to the Palais 'a temporary ban had been imposed on West Indians and the Company claimed that the ban was imposed following a disturbance involving some coloured youths'. Judge Ruttle gave judgment for the Board. Repeating what he had said in *Race Relations Board v Morris*,[20] he stated:

> '... I think he [the licensee] has to consider them as individuals and not jump to the conclusion because a man happens to come from a particular country that he will be in the gang. He has to bring his judgment to bear upon the individuals as such as distinct from being of a particular colour, race or ethnic origin'.

There have not been many complaints of discrimination in shops. In *Race Relations Board v Beckton*,[1] a declaration was made against a shopkeeper who 'lost his temper and went beyond the bounds of proper behaviour when he shouted at Mrs Robinson and ordered her out of his shop' because 'colour was a matter which played a very large part in the defendant's conduct'. In another case,[2] a complaint was made against

---

14 RRB Report 1971–72, p. 9.
15 RRB Report 1970–71, p. 9.
16 E.g. overcharging (*Antwerp Arms Public House* case, F Invest Rep 1979), discrimination in the time allowed for drinking (*Race Relations Board v Royal Oak Public House, London E15*, Westminster C Ct, 1977 CRE Report, p. 118, or refusal to serve (*Race Relations Board v White Hart Public House, Kent* Westminster C Ct (1973) RRB Report p. 42).
17 RRB Report 1973, p. 4.
18 RRB Report 1975–76, pp. 5–6.
19 Westminster C Ct, 1974 RRB Report, p. 39.
20 Reported in 1973 RRB Report, p. 42, as *Race Relations Board v White Hart Public House, Kent*. See also the *Rank Leisure Ltd* case, F Invest Rep 1983, and *Hussain v Canklow Community Centre* (1980) CRE Report, p. 85, Leeds C Ct (refusal to let hall for Pakistani wedding illegal).
1 Leeds C Ct, 1975–1976, RRB Report, p. 52.
2 RRB Report 1970–71, p. 44.

a hairdresser who charged more for cutting 'Asiatic' and 'Negroid' hair. The local conciliation committee appointed an assessor who 'gave it as his opinion that there was no technical difference between the cutting of European and the cutting of Asian hair. Negroid hair required a different technique, but this could be learnt and, once learnt, could be carried out as quickly as cutting European hair'. The committee took the view that unlawful discrimination had occurred. 'The respondent gave an assurance against future unlawful discrimination and removed the words "Asiatic" and "Negroid" from his price list.'

In *Commission for Racial Equality v Marr, Cleanersweep Ltd*,[3] the Newcastle County Court issued a declaration against a chimney sweep who refused to sweep a Pakistani chimney ('we don't deal with you people').[4]

Are Irish jokes prohibited by s. 20, or any other part of the 1976 Act?

11. The meaning of a 'section of the public' in s. 2, 1968 Act (now s. 20, 1976 Act) was considered by the House of Lords in several cases. In *Charter v Race Relations Board*,[5] the complainant was an Indian living in East Ham. He applied for membership of the East Ham South Conservative Club. As a Conservative male of 18 or more, he was eligible for admission. The Club committee rejected his application on the casting vote of the Chairman. The vote was taken after the Chairman had said, in reply to a question from a committee member, that he regarded the applicant's colour as relevant to the decision. It was held that the members of a club were not a 'section of the public' so that s. 2 did not apply. The ruling was extended to associate club members in the *Dockers' Labour Club* case.[6] Although clubs therefore can be taken not now to be within s. 20, 1976 Act, they have been brought within the law by s. 25, 1976 Act,[7] which in effect reverses *Charter*. The above is true only of what might be called genuine clubs. A club that does not have a 'genuine system of personal selection of members' (Lord Reid's phrase) falls on the public side of the division that the House of Lords sought to draw between public and private groups. It is thus 'a section of the public' and subject to s. 20, not s. 25. The RAC (*associate* membership: contrast *full* membership) and the London (and other) Co-operative Societies are examples. They do not under their constitutions apply a 'genuine system of personal selection': they take all motorists or all comers. A club which provides for 'personal selection' in its rules but in which 'in practice the rules are disregarded' (Lord Reid) is similarly not a genuine club. An example of the latter kind is to be found in the facts of *Panama (Piccadilly) Ltd v Newberry*.[8] The proprietor of the Panama Club appealed against convictions for keeping premises for public dancing, etc., without a licence on the ground that only members and guests were allowed to enter the club. The appeal was rejected because any member of the public was in fact admitted at the door upon payment of a 25s. annual membership fee. Although there was provision for the nomination and seconding of applicants, the procedure was not followed. To Lord Parker CJ's mind, it was 'open to any member of the public to go in, pay 25s. and see the show'. The case was referred to by two members of the House of Lords in *Charter* as that of a club that would be 'a section of the public' for the purposes of s. 2. Although the distinction between genuine and other clubs drawn in *Charter* would appear to survive the 1976 Act in law, it is no longer important in view of s. 25 (unless the more general wording of s. 20 offers a fuller remedy).

3   CRE Report 1977, p. 120.
4   See also *Race Relations Board v Botley, Motor Vehicle Repairs*, Westminster C Ct, ibid., p. 118 (declaration against garage for refusal to re-spray car: 'You're coloured and that's enough for me').
5   [1973] AC 868.
6   Above, p. 1135.
7   Below, p. 1147.
8   [1962] 1 WLR 610, DC.

12. In *Applin v Race Relations Board*,[9] Mr and Mrs W had for many years fostered children in care of local authorities. They normally had four or five children in their home, each staying for about three weeks. About 60 per cent of the children were coloured. The appellant, a member of the National Front, learnt of this and brought pressure to bear upon Mr and Mrs W to stop fostering coloured children. The RRB sought a declaration that the appellant's conduct was incitement to commit an act of unlawful discrimination, contrary to the 1968 Act, s. 12 (now the 1976 Act, s. 31). The House of Lords ruled in favour of the Board on the ground that the fostering of children in care was the provision of facilities or services to a 'section of the public' (children in care) so that the refusal to take in children because of their colour would be unlawful discrimination. After studying the examples given in s. 2(2) of the 1968 Act (now s. 20(2) of the 1976 Act), Lord Wilberforce drew the following conclusion as to its scope:

> 'What it suggests, in combination with section 2(1), is that the area in which discrimination is forbidden is that in which a person is concerned to provide something which in its nature is generally offered to and needed by the public at large, or a section of it, which is offered impersonally to all who choose to go through the doors or approach the counter: things which, in their nature, would be provided to anyone, and the refusal of which to persons of different colour etc., could only be ascribed to discrimination on grounds of colour etc. Conversely, they do not extend to matters, the provision of which is a private matter, as to which the motives of the refusing provider may reasonably have nothing to do with colour etc., at all.'

The decision in the *Applin* case was reversed by the 1976 Act, s. 23(2) which creates an exception to s. 20:

> 'Section 20(1) does not apply to anything done by a person as a participant in arrangements under which he (for reward or not) takes into his home, and treats as if they were members of his family, children, elderly persons, or persons requiring a special degree of care and attention.'

In *Conwell v Newham Borough Council*,[10] it was held that s. 20 does apply to the acts of a local authority that is looking after children in its care: looking after children was a 'service' and the exception in s. 23(2) did not apply to a child who was being looked after by a local authority, which did not have a 'home' or a 'family'.

13. A national health trust hospital in Sheffield accepted the donation of a human organ from the body of a white person for transplant purposes that was made on condition that it would only be transplanted into a white human being.[11] Was the acceptance a breach of s. 20? Or any other provision of the 1978 Act? What about compliance with the condition by the hospital in the selection of recipients and the conduct of the transplant? Or the making of the condition by the deceased person's relatives? Should any or all of these be illegal acts?[12]

6 Housing, etc

Race Relations Act 1976

21. Discrimination in disposal or management of premises
(1) It is unlawful for a person, in relation to premises in Great Britain of which he has power to dispose, to discriminate against another—
    (*a*) in the terms on which he offers him those premises; or

9 [1975] AC 259.
10 [2000] 1 All ER 696, EAT.
11 See (1999) 149 NLJ 1125. For comment, see A. R. Maclean, ibid., at 1250.
12 The Human Tissue Act 1961, which governs transplants, does not expressly prohibit such a racially discriminatory condition, although considerations of public policy might be invoked.

(*b*) by refusing his application for those premises; or

(*c*) in his treatment of him in relation to any list of persons in need of premises of that description.

(2) It is unlawful for a person, in relation to premises managed by him, to discriminate against a person occupying the premises—

(*a*) in the way he affords him access to any benefits or facilities, or by refusing or deliberately omitting to afford him access to them; or

(*b*) by evicting him, or subjecting him to any other detriment.

(3) Subsection (1) does not apply to a person who owns an estate or interest in the premises and wholly occupies them unless he uses the services of an estate agent for the purposes of the disposal of the premises, or publishes or causes to be published an advertisement in connection with the disposal.

NOTES

1. *'Premises'*. These 'include land of any description'.[13] The use (residential, business, recreational, etc.) to which the land is put does not matter, although racial discrimination is mostly a problem of housing. In *Race Relations Board v Geo Haigh & Co Ltd*,[14] it was held that a builder who refused to sell a house under construction on a housing estate to the complainant because of his colour had acted contrary to the 1968 Act, s. 5(a), which prohibited discrimination in the disposal of 'housing accommodation, business premises or other land'. The partly built house was 'housing accommodation' although not ready for occupation. The case would have the same outcome on this point under the different wording of s. 21. After the case, the builder stated that he would 'reluctantly' change his policy and sell to coloured applicants.[15]

2. *Power of disposal.* A 'power of disposal' includes the power to grant a right to occupy the premises.[16] Generally, the 'disposal' of premises would appear to include the sale of a fee simple, the assignment or granting of a lease or tenancy, and the granting of a licence to occupy premises. Public housing authorities have the 'power to dispose' of housing within their control. An estate agent or accommodation bureau will be subject to s. 21 (as well as s. 20) if, as is sometimes the case, he or it is given a 'power to dispose'.

3. Would a covenant by which land may not be sold to persons 'not of the caucasian race' be unlawful under s. 21? Or at common law on grounds of public policy?[17]

4. Section 21(1) does not apply to disposals of property that come within s. 21(3). This was an exception that would have been available to the defendant in *Race Relations Board v Relf*,[18] had he, when selling his house, refrained from advertising it as well as from using an estate agent. Since a 'for sale' or 'vacancies' notice on the premises is an advertisement, the exception is a very narrow one. The 'small premises' exception in s. 22, below, also applies to s. 21(1).

---

13 1976 Act, s. 78(1).

14 (1969) Times, 11 September, Leeds C Ct.

15 *Guardian*, 11 September 1969, quoted in A. Lester and G. Bindman, *Race and Law* (1972), p. 235.

16 1976 Act, s. 78(1).

17 See S. Cretney (1968) 118 NLJ 1094; J. F. Garner, (1972) 35 MLR 478; and J. D. A. Brooke-Taylor, (1978) 42 Conv(ns) 24. And see the public policy cases in Chap. 10, section 7, above, p. 1065. See also *Shelley v Kraemer* 334 US 1 (1948).

18 Below, p. 1151.

5. *Management of premises.* A case of discrimination in the management of premises under the 1968 Act that would now come within the 1976 Act, s. 1(2) was reported by the RRB as follows:[19]

> 'During the year the Board formed the opinion that a local authority had acted unlawfully by treating a Cypriot tenant less favourably than other tenants. The complainant received a letter from the local housing manager concerning his children's behaviour which stated that because of his limited residence in the country he was fortunate to have local authority accommodation, and indicated that his tenancy might be terminated if a further complaint were received. No such warning was sent to an English tenant whose children had also been the subject of adverse reports by the same caretaker. The Council apologised to the tenant and gave an assurance against further acts of unlawful discrimination.'

Other examples suggested by I. A. Macdonald,[20] are 'separate toilet or bathroom facilities for coloured tenants in a boarding house or the situation where the landlord sends a rent collector to white families but makes the coloured families call in at the rent office'.

6. Examples of discrimination in the terms on which premises are offered[1] that occurred under the 1968 Act are the refusal on racial grounds to allow a house purchaser mortgage facilities available to other purchasers[2] and insistence upon a coloured house purchaser buying both houses in a two house development (for fear that the other house would otherwise be difficult to sell) when such a requirement would not have been placed upon a white purchaser.[3] Charging a higher purchase price would be another obvious example. Refusal to renew a lease,[4] to rent a flat,[5] or to sell a house[6] come within s. 21(1)(b).[7] Section 21(1)(c) applies to waiting lists kept, for example, by a caravan site owner or a local authority.

7. *Discrimination in the allocation of public housing.* Local authority waiting list rules were the subject of several investigations by the RRB. Wolverhampton Corporation's 'housing waiting list rule which, broadly speaking, treated people on the waiting list who were born outside the country less favourably than others by applying to them a longer qualifying waiting period' was declared by the RRB to be unlawful and later abandoned by the Corporation.[8] The rule was replaced by one which applied a residence (as opposed to a place of birth) test, a longer qualifying waiting period being applied to persons who had lived in the United Kingdom for less than 10 years. This rule was dropped after the RRB began an investigation of it.[9] It was reported in 1975[10] that a number of local authorities in the London area required an applicant for council housing to have lived within its area for five years. Might such a rule be indirect discrimination (the 1976 Act, s. 1(1)(b))? What of a rule by which residence in a borough is effective for waiting list purposes only from

---

19 RRB Report 1970–71, p. 11.
20 *Race Relations – The New Law* (1977), p. 90.
1 s. 21(1)(a).
2 RRB Report 1969–70, p. 13.
3 Case 7, RRB Report 1974, p. 36.
4 *Race Relations Board v Wharton*, 1977 CRE Report, p. 119.
5 RRB Report 1974, p. 11.
6 Case 8, RRB Report 1975–76, p. 46.
7 RRB Report 1969–70, p. 12 and RRB Report 1970–71, p. 11. On nationality restrictions, see the *Ealing* case, above, p. 1110. A rule whereby priority for public housing on a new estate was given to the largely white residents of an existing estate was indirect discrimination: *Out of Order*, F Invest Rep 1990. For an investigation into the practices of a housing association, see *Racial Discrimination in Hostel Accommodation*, F Invest Rep 1992.
8 RRB Report 1970–71, p. 11.
9 RRB Report 1970–71, p. 10.
10 Smith and Whalley, *Racial Minorities and Public Housing* (1975) p. 36.

the date that the applicant is joined by his family? In the *Hackney Council Housing* case,[11] a non-discrimination notice was issued against the Council for breaches of ss. 20(1)(b) and 21(1)(c). The CRE concluded that Council officials had discriminated between black and white persons when allocating accommodation (newer housing, houses and maisonettes as opposed to flats, ground floor flats as opposed to high rise flats predominantly for whites). Hackney was selected not because of any complaints against it. It was chosen 'as an inner-city area with a large ethnic minority population' that could be considered as a 'suitable and representative borough on which to concentrate a comprehensive investigation of the causes of' the discrimination and disadvantage in public sector housing 'that research had shown ethnic minorities had suffered'.[12] The findings of the CRE, which were accepted by the Council, were for the first time in any formal investigation based solely upon statistical evidence:

> 'Until now, findings of discrimination have generally been centred on individual acts of discrimination. The practical difficulty of relying on this approach is that the scope for comparison, to determine whether there has been less favourable treatment on racial grounds, is necessarily narrow. When one finds less favourable treatment there will often be factors present which might appear to explain away the differences on non-racial grounds. However, when large numbers of cases are examined statistically, and less favourable treatment of a racial group is established, and one then examines all possible non-racial explanations statistically, it becomes possible to say with statistical certainty whether they can in fact explain the difference. In practice, non-racial explanations start falling away when subject to this kind of scrutiny. This is the reason why the Commission is insistent that ethnic record keeping and monitoring are essential to securing equality of opportunity, not only in the housing field, but elsewhere. And it is for this reason also that this investigation represents a significant milestone on the long road toward eliminating racial discrimination.'

8. *Discrimination in the private sector.* A formal investigation of racial discrimination in the private sector revealed that discrimination was practised by about 20% of the accommodation agencies investigated.[13] There was less discrimination by private landlords and very little by guesthouses and private hotels.

9. Section 24 makes it illegal (subject to a 'small premises' exception) for a landlord to discriminate in refusing to agree to the assignment of a tenancy.[14]

Race Relations Act 1976

22. Exceptions from ss. 20(1) and 21: small dwellings

(1) Sections 20(1) and 21 do not apply to the provision by a person of accommodation in any premises, or the disposal of premises by him, if—

    (*a*) that person or a near relative of his ('the relevant occupier') resides, and intends to continue to reside, on the premises; and

    (*b*) there is on the premises, in addition to the accommodation occupied by the relevant occupier, accommodation (not being storage accommodation or means of access) shared by the relevant occupier with other persons residing on the premises who are not members of his household; and

---

11 F Invest Rep 1984. See Bryan, [1984] PL 194. For a finding of illegal segregation in public housing, see *Housing Allocation in Oldham* (1993). See also the *Homelessness and Discrimination in the London Borough of Tower Hamlets* case, F Invest Rep 1988, in which an enforcement notice was issued in respect of ss. 20(1)(b) and 21(1)(c) on the ground of discrimination against Bangladeshi families in need of emergency rehousing.

12 *Report*, p. 5.

13 *Sorry Its Gone*, F Invest Rep 1990.

14 See also the Landlord and Tenant Act 1927, s. 19, and *Schlegel v Corcoran*, above, p. 1054.

(c) the premises are small premises.

(2) Premises shall be treated for the purposes of this section as small premises if—

(a) in the case of premises comprising residential accommodation for one or more households (under separate letting or similar agreements) in addition to the accommodation occupied by the relevant occupier, there is not normally residential accommodation for more than two such households and only the relevant occupier and any member of his household reside in the accommodation occupied by him;

(b) in the case of premises not falling within paragraph (a), there is not normally residential accommodation on the premises for more than six persons in addition to the relevant occupier and any members of his household.

NOTE

The exception in s. 22 applies to s. 21(2) as well as s. 21(1), the management of premises being covered by the wording 'the provision by a person of accommodation in any premises'. A person is a near relative of another 'if that person is the wife or husband, a parent or child, a grandparent or grandchild, or a brother or sister of the other (whether of full blood or half blood or by affinity), and "child" includes an illegitimate child and the wife or husband of an illegitimate child'.[15] 'Accommodation . . . shared'[16] includes a bathroom, kitchen, or toilet; it does not include a stairway. 'Hotels, boarding houses and other similar establishments' that would otherwise be subject to the 1976 Act, s. 20 are exempt from it if they can be brought within the 'small premises' exception in s. 22.

7 Clubs

Race Relations Act 1976

25. Discrimination: associations not within s.11

(1) This section applies to any association of persons (however described, whether corporate or unincorporate, and whether or not its activities are carried on for profit) if—

(a) it has twenty-five or more members; and

(b) admission to membership is regulated by its constitution and is so conducted that the members do not constitute a section of the public within the meaning of section 20(1); and

(c) it is not an organisation to which section 11 applies [trade unions, etc].

(2) It is unlawful for an association to which this section applies, in the case of a person who is not a member of the association, to discriminate against him—

(a) in the terms on which it is prepared to admit him to membership; or

(b) by refusing or deliberately omitting to accept his application for membership.

(3) It is unlawful for an association to which this section applies, in the case of a person who is a member or associate of the association, to discriminate against him—

(a) in the way it affords him access to any benefits, facilities or services, or by refusing or deliberately omitting to afford him access to them; or

(b) in the case of a member, by depriving him of membership, or varying the terms on which he is a member; or

(c) in the case of an associate, by depriving him of his rights as an associate, or varying those rights; or

(d) in either case, by subjecting him to any other detriment.

---

15 1976 Act, s. 78(1)(5).
16 s. 22(1)(b).

(4) For the purposes of this section—

    (*a*) a person is a member of an association if he belongs to it by virtue of his admission to any sort of membership provided for by its constitution (and is not merely a person with certain rights under its constitution by virtue of his membership of some other association), and references to membership of an association shall be construed accordingly;

    (*b*) a person is an associate of an association to which this section applies if, not being a member of it, he has under its constitution some or all of the rights enjoyed by members (or would have apart from any provision in its constitution authorising the refusal of those rights in particular cases).

26. Exception from s. 25 for certain associations

(1) An association to which section 25 applies is within this subsection if the main object of the association is to enable the benefits of membership (whatever they may be) to be enjoyed by persons of a particular racial group defined otherwise than by reference to colour; and in determining whether that is the main object of an association regard shall be had to the essential character of the association and to all relevant circumstances including, in particular, the extent to which the affairs of the association are so conducted that the persons primarily enjoying the benefits of membership are of the racial group in question.

(2) In the case of an association within subsection (1), nothing in section 25 shall render unlawful any act not involving discrimination on the ground of colour.

NOTES

1. As noted earlier,[17] in the *Charter* case, it was held that genuine clubs were not subject to the 1968 Act's prohibition of discrimination in the provision of goods, facilities and services. In enacting the 1976 Act, Parliament decided that such clubs should be controlled in this respect. It decided to achieve this result not by amending the section on goods, facilities and services (now the 1976 Act, s. 20), but by adding a new section—s. 25—specifically dealing with clubs. The government White Paper explained its reason for wanting to bring clubs within the Act as follows:[18]

'72 . . . Some 4,000 working men's clubs, with a total membership of about $3\frac{1}{2}$ million people, are affiliated to the Club and Institute Union and are not covered by the 1968 Act. In some towns they have replaced public houses as the main providers of facilities for entertainment, recreation and refreshment. In addition, thousands of golf, squash, tennis and other sporting clubs registered as members' clubs are, almost certainly, also outside the 1968 Act, except in so far as they may offer only limited playing facilities to the public generally. Many clubs do not discriminate on racial grounds but at present they may lawfully do so. The Government considers that it is right that all clubs should be allowed to apply a test of personal acceptability to candidates for membership, but it considers that it is against the public interest that they should be entitled to do this on racial grounds. The Government believes that the relationship between members of clubs is no more personal and intimate than is the relationship between people in many situations which are rightly covered by the 1968 Act; for example, the members of a small firm or trade union branch, children at school, or tenants in multi-occupied housing accommodation. In principle it is justifiable to apply the legislation in all these situations because of the inherently unjust and degrading nature of racial discrimination and its potentially grave social consequences. In practice the objectives of the legislation will be seriously undermined if its protection does not extend beyond the workplace and the market-place to enable workers and other members of the public to obtain entertainment, recreation and refreshment together on the basis of equality, irrespective of colour or race.

    The Bill will therefore make it unlawful for a club or other voluntary body to discriminate as regards the admission of members or the treatment accorded to members. Subject to this

17 Above, p. 1142.
18 Cmnd. 6234, p. 18.

the Bill will not, of course, affect the right of such a body to withhold membership or facilities from someone who does not qualify for them in accordance with its rules. Small voluntary bodies will be exempted from this provision so as to avoid interference with the kind of regular social gathering which is genuinely private and domestic in character. In addition, there will be an expectation to enable bona fide social, welfare, political or sporting organisations whose main object is to confer benefits on a particular ethnic or national group to continue to do so.'

A club that is not a genuine club in the sense of the *Charter* case, so that its members are a 'section of the public', is subject to s. 20 and not s. 25.

2. Section 25(3) reverses the *Dockers' Labour Club* case,[19] so that discrimination by a club against an associate member is prohibited by the 1976 Act. The RRB reported in 1974 that there were about one million members of working mens' clubs who held associate member cards valid in other clubs that are members of the Working Men's Club and Institute Union.[20] The CRE takes the view that discrimination against a member's guest is discrimination against the member contrary to s. 25.

3. The exemption for small clubs[1] was set at 25 members because that is the minimum number of members that a club must have to qualify for registration under the Licensing Acts. It was suggested in debate in Parliament that there will be few clubs with a list, as opposed to an active, membership of less than 25.[2]

4. Section 26 safeguards such clubs as the Caledonian Club, the London Welsh Rugby Club and the Indian Workers' Association.[3] It would not allow a person who was otherwise qualified for membership of such a club to be excluded because of his colour. It would, however, allow him to be excluded on 'racial grounds' other than colour.

5. The CRE has issued non-discrimination notices in several cases of discrimination in respect of club membership. In *Handsworth Horticultural Institute Ltd v CRE* (1992),[4] a social club had a rule (rule 7) whereby an applicant for membership had to be sponsored by two members and approved by a selection committee. Although 60% of the local population was non-white, no non-white person had ever applied for membership. Following a formal investigation, the CRE found that rule 7 constituted a discriminatory practice involving indirect discrimination in breach of ss. 28 and 1(1)(b). The club's appeal against the resulting non-discrimination notice was rejected by the Birmingham County Court:

'It seems to us that given the circumstances in which the Club finds itself ..., surrounded by a population of half black and half white, the evidence is clear, that, whether intended or not, experience has shown that not a single black person has ever been proposed for membership of the Club of 1500 members, and that leads us to the view that while the rule remains in being it has an adverse impact, and it is not likely that one will be proposed. It is true that black people can comply, ie become members, but in practice one will not be asked. Further we are of the view that the failure of the Club committee ever formally to discuss the matter between themselves, and their failure ever to raise the situation with the members once the Commission had drawn attention to it, exhibited clear disingenuousness.

... We accept that no other system is quite as satisfactory as that set out in Rule 7. However, looking at the matter objectively, we have asked ourselves whether what we accept are marginal

---

19 Above, p. 1142.
20 RRB Report 1974, p. 4.
 1 s. 25(1).
 2 374 HL Deb, 29 September 1976, col. 538.
 3 See Standing Committee A, Race Relations Bill, 9th Sitting HC Deb, col. 400, 25 May 1976.
 4 Birmingham County Court judgment reported in Ruled Out, F Invest Rep 1992, Appendix C. See also the *Woodhouse Recreation Club, Leeds*, F Invest Rep 1980. A Sikh was awarded £150 damages by the Birmingham County Court for exclusion from a golf club on racial grounds: *The Guardian* 25 February 1984.

disadvantages of a reference system, as an alternative method of applying for membership, sufficiently outweigh the desirability of maintaining good order as effected by the present sponsorship system. We have come to the conclusion that they do not, and accordingly we hold that the Club cannot show that the rule which provides for the sole means of entry by proposer and seconder can in all the circumstances of the case be justified.'

8 Advertisements

Race Relations Act 1976

29. Discriminatory advertisements

(1) It is unlawful to publish or to cause to be published an advertisement which indicates, or might reasonably be understood as indicating, an intention by a person to do an act of discrimination, whether the doing of that act by him would be lawful or, by virtue of Part II or III, unlawful.

(2) Subsection (1) does not apply to an advertisement—

    (*a*) if the intended act would be lawful by virtue of any of sections 5, 6, 7(3) and (4), 10(3), 26, 34(2)(*b*), 35 to 39 and 41; or

    (*b*) if the advertisement relates to the services of an employment agency (within the meaning of section 14(1)) and the intended act only concerns employment which the employer could by virtue of section 5, 6 or 7(3) or (4) lawfully refuse to offer to persons against whom the advertisement indicates an intention to discriminate.

(3) Subsection (1) does not apply to an advertisement which indicates that persons of any class defined otherwise than by reference to colour, race or ethnic or national origins are required for employment outside Great Britain.

(4) The publisher of an advertisement made unlawful by subsection (1) shall not be subject to any liability under that subsection in respect of the publication of the advertisement if he proves—

    (*a*) that the advertisement was published in reliance on a statement made to him by the person who caused it to be published to the effect that, by reason of the operation of subsection (2) or (3), the publication would not be unlawful; and

    (*b*) that it was reasonable for him to rely on the statement.

(5) A person who knowingly or recklessly makes a statement such as is mentioned in subsection (4)(*a*) which in a material respect is false or misleading commits an offence, and shall be liable on summary conviction to a fine not exceeding [level 5 on the standard scale].

NOTES

1. The number of discriminatory advertisements would appear to have dropped considerably since 1968 when they were first prohibited.[5] Nonetheless, in 1998 the CRE disposed of complaints about 83 advertisements; 43 complaints were considered to be well founded and the complaint was settled informally in all cases.[6] In 1982, there were several complaints about notices refusing service to Argentinians during the Falklands War. The CRE considered these illegal, but took no action.[7]

5   RRB Report 1973, p. 13. Comparing advertisements in one London newspaper in July 1968 and July 1969, the Board noted that it had 18 discriminatory advertisements ('no coloured', 'Europeans wanted', 'coloured only', 'Jew preferred') in 1968 and none a year later (RRB Report 1969–70, p. 53). A similar survey of newsagents' noticeboards in 1970 revealed one discriminatory accommodation advertisement out of 36: ibid.

6   CRE 1998 Annual Report, p. 28.

7   CRE Report 1982, p. 25.

2. 'Advertisement' is defined very widely. Section 78(1) of the 1976 Act reads:

'"advertisement" includes every form of advertisement or notice, whether to the public or not, and whether in a newspaper or other publication, by television or radio, by display of notices, signs, labels, showcards or goods, by distribution of samples, circulars, catalogues, price lists or other material, by exhibition of pictures, models or films, or in any other way, and references to the publishing of advertisements shall be construed accordingly;'

The inclusion of the display of a 'notice' was the reason for the well-publicised case of *Race Relations Board v Relf*,[8] in which a notice in a house window: 'For sale to an English Family' was held contrary to the 1968 Act by the county court. An advertisement indicates an 'intention to do an act of discrimination' if that is the natural and ordinary meaning of the words as they would be understood by a reasonable person.[9]

3. The 'Scottish porridge' case also illustrates the wide field of application of s. 29. It was reported by the RRB as follows:[10]

'Here a Scottish doctor living in Eastbourne sought a "daily" able to cook plain Scottish food. But he advertised for a "Scottish daily". There can be few who would regard such a restriction as anything but innocuous, but a member of the public insisted that the Board should investigate a complaint. The regional conciliation committee understandably formed the opinion that the advertisement contravened section 6 of the Act [now the 1976 Act s. 29]. Having called the doctor's attention to section 6 of the Act, the committee proposed to do no more.'

Would the doctor have infringed the Act if he had advertised for a 'daily' who could cook plain Scottish food?

4. Partly because of cases like the 'Scottish porridge' case, enforcement of s. 29 is placed solely in the hands of the CRE, which may issue a non-discrimination notice after a formal investigation[11] or bring legal proceedings for a declaration or an injunction.[12] Damages may not be awarded. Placing an advertisement for a post 'designated for a black or Asian woman under the terms of s. 38' of the 1976 Act was not an act of discrimination within s. 4 of the 1976 Act (employment discrimination); instead it fell within s. 29, so that only the CRE could enforce it.[13] The Tribunal did not consider the question whether the case fell within s. 38. If an advertisement is published by someone (e.g. a newspaper) other than the advertiser, the publisher is liable under s. 29 as well as the advertiser. The publisher has a defence of 'reliance' in such cases.[14]

5. Section 29 has been criticised for making it illegal, subject to s. 29(2), to advertise something that may in itself be perfectly lawful, as in the case of a letting of accommodation exempted from the Act by the 'small premises' exception.[15] The justification for this in the government White Paper[16] was that 'the public display of racial prejudices and preferences is inherently offensive and likely to encourage the spread of discriminatory attitudes and practices'.

8 RRB Report 1975, p. 56. The 'no travellers' notice in the *Dutton* case, above, was an advertisement.
9 *Race Relations Board v Associated Newspapers Group Ltd* [1978] 3 All ER 419, CA.
10 RRB Report 1969–70, p. 6.
11 s. 58.
12 ss. 63, 64.
13 *Cardiff Women's Aid v Hartup* [1994] IRLR 390, EAT. On s. 38, see above, p. 1084.
14 s. 29(4).
15 s. 22.
16 Cmnd. 6234, p. 19.

9 Charities

Race Relations Act 1976

34. Charities
(1) A provision which is contained in a charitable instrument (whenever that instrument took or takes effect) and which provides for conferring benefits on persons of a class defined by reference to colour shall have effect for all purposes as if it provided for conferring the like benefits—

   (a) on persons of the class which results if the restriction by reference to colour is disregarded; or

   (b) where the original class is defined by reference to colour only, on persons generally;

but nothing in this subsection shall be taken to alter the effect of any provision as regards any time before the coming into operation of this subsection.

(2) Nothing in Parts II to IV shall—

   (a) be construed as affecting a provision to which this subsection applies or;

   (b) render unlawful an act which is done in order to give effect to such a provision.

(3) Subsection (2) applies to any provision which is contained in a charitable instrument (whenever that instrument took or takes effect) and which provides for conferring benefits on persons of a class defined otherwise than by reference to colour (including a class resulting from the operation of subsection (2)). . . .

NOTE

Quite a number of charitable trusts apply in areas covered by the Act, particularly education and housing. Section 34 only concerns those that discriminate on grounds of colour. Others that do so on grounds of race, etc.[17] are not affected, although they may be void at common law for reasons of uncertainty or public policy. As to uncertainty, see, for example, *Clayton v Ramsden*,[18] in which a condition subsequent in a will by which a beneficiary was to forfeit a legacy upon marrying a person 'not of Jewish parents and not of Jewish faith' was held void for uncertainty. As to public policy, see *Re Lysaght*.[19]

10 Incitement to racial hatred

Public Order Act 1986[20]

17. Meaning of 'racial hatred'
In this Part 'racial hatred' means hatred against a group of persons in Great Britain defined by reference to colour, race, nationality (including citizenship) or ethnic or national origins.

18. Use of words or behaviour or display of written material
(1) A person who uses threatening, abusive or insulting words or behaviour, or displays any written material which is threatening, abusive or insulting, is guilty of an offence if—

   (a) he intends thereby to stir up racial hatred, or

   (b) having regard to all the circumstances racial hatred is likely to be stirred up thereby.

(2) An offence under this section may be committed in a public or a private place, except that no offence is committed where the words or behaviour are used, or the written material is displayed, by a person inside a dwelling and are not heard or seen except by other persons in that or another dwelling.

---

17 See s. 3.
18 [1943] AC 320, HL.
19 Above, p. 1064.
20 These sections are printed as amended by the Broadcasting Act 1990.

(3) A constable may arrest without warrant anyone he reasonably suspects is committing an offence under this section.

(4) In proceedings for an offence under this section it is a defence for the accused to prove that he was inside a dwelling and had no reason to believe that the words or behaviour used, or the written material displayed, would be heard or seen by a person outside that or any other dwelling.

(5) A person who is not shown to have intended to stir up racial hatred is not guilty of an offence under this section if he did not intend his words or behaviour, or the written material, to be, and was not aware that it might be, threatening, abusive or insulting.

(6) This section does not apply to words or behaviour used, or written material displayed, solely for the purpose of being [included in a programme service].

19. Publishing or distributing written material

(1) A person who publishes or distributes written material which is threatening, abusive or insulting is guilty of an offence if—

    (*a*) he intends thereby to stir up racial hatred, or

    (*b*) having regard to all the circumstances racial hatred is likely to be stirred up thereby.

(2) In proceedings for an offence under this section it is a defence for an accused who is not shown to have intended to stir up racial hatred to prove that he was not aware of the content of the material and did not suspect, and had no reason to suspect, that it was threatening, abusive or insulting.

(3) References in this Part to the publication or distribution of written material are to its publication or distribution to the public or a section of the public.

[Ss. 20–22 contain offences similar to that in s. 19 concerning the public performance of a play (s. 20), the distribution, showing or playing of a recording (s. 21) and the broadcasting of programmes (not BBC and IBA programmes) (s. 21).]

23. Possession of racially inflammatory material

(1) A person who has in his possession written material which is threatening, abusive or insulting, or a recording of visual images or sounds which are threatening, abusive or insulting, with a view to—

    (*a*) in the case of written material, its being displayed, published, distributed, [or included in a cable programme service], whether by himself or another, or

    (*b*) in the case of a recording, its being distributed, shown, played, [or included in a programme service], whether by himself or another,

is guilty of an offence if he intends racial hatred to be stirred up thereby or, having regard to all the circumstances, racial hatred is likely to be stirred up thereby.

(2) For this purpose regard shall be had to such display, publication, distribution, showing, playing, [or inclusion in a programme service] as he has, or it may reasonably be inferred that he has, in view.

(3) In proceedings for an offence under this section it is a defence for an accused who is not shown to have intended to stir up racial hatred to prove that he was not aware of the content of the written material or recording and did not suspect, and had no reason to suspect, that it was threatening, abusive or insulting.

NOTES[21]

1. These sections of the Public Order Act 1986, on incitement to racial hatred replace s. 5A, Public Order Act 1936. As the government White Paper leading to the 1986

---

21 On the earlier law and incitement to racial hatred generally, see G. Bindman, (1982) 132 NLJ 299; id., in S. Coliver (ed.), *Striking a Balance: Hate Speech, Freedom of Expression and Non-discrimination* (1992), Chap. 28; R. Cotterrell, [1982] PL 278; A. Dickey, [1968] Crim LR 489; Gordon, *Incitement to Racial Hatred* (1982), Runnymede Trust publication; Khan, (1978) 122 Sol Jo 256; P. Leopold, [1977] PL 389; D. G. T. Williams, [1966] Crim LR 320; *Review of the Public Order Act 1936 and Related Legislation* (Cmnd. 7891), pp. 29–31. On the 1986 Act, see W. J. Wolffe, [1987] PL 85.

Act[1] makes clear, the general purpose remains the protection of public order, not the prevention of the expression of offensive views:

> 'A variety of amendments to the section were suggested, many of which would alter the basis of the offence, so that the criminal law would be used against the production of material or the expression of views which are offensive in a multi-racial society. The Government believes that the reasonable exercise of freedom of expression should be protected, however unpleasant the views expressed, and has concluded that section 5A should continue to be based on considerations of public order.'

This approach has been criticised:[2]

> 'The assumption underlying the incitement offence is that hate speech should be regulated by the law insofar as it has implications for public order, and not with respect to any direct impact it might have on the feelings of the victims.
>
> A distinction is thereby made between indirect hate speech, which may be deemed unlawful, and direct hate speech, which is not prohibited. This kind of distinction was outlined by the majority of the Canadian Supreme Court in the case of *R v Keegstra* (which concerned the prosecution of a high school teacher for the use of antisemitic material, including Holocaust denial, in his history classes),[3] and can be elaborated as follows:
> - Direct hate speech: A's hate speech is directly communicated to victim group C. This does not require C actually to hear the speech, but can include C becoming aware of the existence of the speech.
> - Indirect hate speech: A's hate speech is communicated to B, encouraging B to hate victim group C and to carry out acts based on that hatred.
>
> The prohibition, in English law, of incitement to racial hatred rather than of hate speech *per se* arises from concerns about the legitimacy of restricting free speech in a democratic society. The rationale for the distinciton between indirect and direct speech which follows can, however, be questioned. It seems to be an anomaly that a neo-Nazi can be prosecuted if he harangues an audience of fellow neo-Nazis, but not an audience of Jews, on the subject of the Holocaust. Gerry Gable recounted to the Panel his experience of being 'told by the police, the Crown Prosecution Service (CPS) and successive attorney-generals … that no action can be taken when hate material [involving Holocaust denial] is sent to Jews, as Jews cannot be turned into antisemites'. And yet, the direct impact of hate speech upon its victims can be extremely harmful, as the *Keegstra* judgment made clear:
>
> > [W]ords and writings that wilfully promote hatred can constitute a serious attack on persons belonging to a racial or religious group. A response of humiliation and degradation from an individual targeted by hate propaganda is to be expected. A person's sense of human dignity and belonging to the community at large is closely linked to the concern and respect accorded the groups to which he or she belongs. The derision, hostility and abuse encouraged by hate propaganda therefore have a severely negative impact on the individual's sense of self-worth and acceptance.'[4]

2. The offence of incitement to racial hatred in Public Order Act 1936, s. 5A had replaced the same offence in the Race Relations Act 1965, s. 6. Referring to incitement to racial hatred and to the similar offence in section 5 of the Theatres Act 1968,[5] the government White Paper explained its reason for moving the former offence from the Race Relations Act to the Public Order Act as follows:[6]

---

1   Cmnd. 9510, p. 39.
2   Institute for Jewish Policy Research, *Combating Holocaust Denial Through Law in the United Kingdom* (2000), p. 8.
3   [1990] 3 SCR 697.
4   Ibid., at 748–749.
5   Now replaced by s. 20, Public Order Act 1986.
6   Cmnd. 6234, p. 30.

'125. These offences are entirely separate from the anti-discrimination provisions of the race relations legislation. They deal with the stirring up of racial hatred rather than with acts of racial discrimination; they are criminal rather than civil; and they are enforced in the criminal courts rather than by the Race Relations Board in the civil courts. In several respects they are similar to the offence under section 5 of the Public Order Act 1936 of using threatening, abusive or insulting words, in any public place or at any public meeting, with intent to provoke a breach of the peace or whereby a breach of the peace is likely to be occasioned. They are concerned to prevent the stirring up of racial hatred which may beget violence and public disorder.'

3. As defined in the 1965 Act, s. 6, the offence of incitement to racial hatred had required an 'intent to stir up hatred' against a racial group. As redefined in s. 5A of the Public Order Act 1936, it no longer required this subjective intent. It was necessary only to prove that hatred was likely to be stirred up by the defendant's act; no mention was made of intent. The government White Paper justified this widening of the offence as follows:[7]

'126. Relatively few prosecutions have been brought under section 6 of the 1965 Act . . . However, during the past decade, probably largely as a result of section 6, there has been a decided change in the style of racialist propaganda. It tends to be less blatantly bigoted, to disclaim any intention of stirring up racial hatred, and to purport to make a contribution to public education and debate. Whilst this shift away from crudely racialist propaganda and abuse is welcome, it is not an unmixed benefit. The more apparently rational and moderate is the message, the greater is its probable impact on public opinion. But it is not justifiable in a democratic society to interfere with freedom of expression except where it is necessary to do so for the prevention of disorder or for the protection of other basic freedoms. The present law penalises crude verbal attacks if and only if it is established that they have been made with the deliberate intention of causing groups to be hated because of their racial origins. In the Government's view this is too narrow an approach. . . . It therefore proposes to ensure that it will no longer be necessary to prove a subjective intention to stir up racial hatred.

127. The present law does not, however, penalise the dissemination of ideas based on an assumption of racial superiority or inferiority or facts (whether true or false) which may encourage racial prejudice or discrimination. It is arguable that false and evil publications of this kind may well be more effectively defeated by public education and debate than by prosecution and that in practice the criminal law would be ineffective to deal with such material. Due regard must also of course be paid to allowing the free expression of opinion. The Government is not therefore at this stage putting forward proposals to extend the criminal law to deal with the dissemination of racialist propaganda in the absence of a likelihood that group hatred will be stirred up by it. It recognises, however, that strong views are held on this important question and will carefully consider any further representations that may be made to it.'

4. Under s. 18(1)(b) and s. 19(1)(b), 1986 Act it remains the case that an intention to stir up racial hatred is not required where racial hatred is in fact likely to be stirred up. However, the 1986 Act amends the law as it existed previously so that, by virtue of s. 18(1)(a) and s. 19(1)(a), a person may be guilty of an offence where he intends to stir up racial hatred even though the stirring up of such hatred is not a likely effect of his conduct.[7a] The White Paper leading to the 1986 Act[8] explained the reason for this further extension of the offence:

'6.6 One area in which difficulties have been experienced with section 5A is where circulation of the material is to selected groups of people, such as clergymen or Members of Parliament who might be thought unlikely to be incited to racial hatred. At present, the more level-headed the recipients of racially inflammatory material, the more difficult it is to show that racial

---

7   Cmnd. 6234, p. 30.
7a The position under ss. 18(1)(a), (b) and 19(1)(a), (b) is also found in the new possession offence in s. 23.
8   Cmnd. 9510, p. 39.

hatred is likely to be stirred up, even when the material itself is so threatening, insulting or abusive that this was clearly the intention of the distributor. The public order consideration is relevant here since the material may well find its way to other, less equable, audiences, although not directly distributed to them, and its effect may be to stir up racial hatred. The Government proposes that section 5A should be re-cast to penalise conduct which is either *likely* to stir up racial hatred or which is intended to do so. The offence will then be in similar terms to the main section 5 offence of conduct which is *likely* or *intended* to cause a breach of the peace.'

5. Amendments to the offence introduced by the 1986 Act are that there are now two separate offences of *using* threatening, etc., words or behaviour and of *publishing* threatening, etc., written material (ss. 18 and 19) and a new offence of possessing racially inflammatory material has been introduced (s. 23).[9] Other changes are (i) that the s. 18 offence may be committed in a 'public or a private place' (other than a dwelling); previously it could only be committed 'in any public place or at any public meeting' and (ii) that the exception in respect of publication or distribution of written material to members of an organisation to which the publisher or distributor belongs is not retained in s. 19. This omission is justified in the White Paper (p. 39) as follows:

> This provision was intended to protect freedom of expression within a group holding particular views, but it is possible that even those who already hold racialist views may be incited or incited further to racial hatred, and the mischief at which section 5A is aimed could occur. The Government sees no justification for allowing material to be circulated privately when it would be open to prosecution if circulated more generally and may have the same effect in both cases; accordingly it proposes to remove the exemption for material circulated to members of an association.'

Offences under ss. 18–23 of the Public Order Act 1986 carry a prison sentence of up to two years.

6. Offences under ss. 18–23 of the Public Order Act 1986 apply only to incitement to racial hatred; they do not extend to incitement to religious hatred, for example against Muslims. Prosecutions may only be brought 'by or with the consent of' the Attorney-General. In practice, all complaints are referred for investigation to the local police, who may, if they find a complaint to have substance, refer it back to the Attorney-General, through the Crown Prosecution Service. Although there are quite a number of complaints, there are usually only a few prosecutions a year. Under the 1986 Act, the Attorney-General had by mid-2000 given his consent for prosecution in 51 cases and there had been 41[10] convictions. One reason for the small number of prosecutions is that racist literature has not been so intemperate since the 1986 Act as previously. Cases under the Act have concerned incitement to hatred against black persons or, increasingly, Jews. In 1990, following the choice of John Taylor as a Conservative parliamentary candidate for Cheltenham, a Major Galbraith, a party member, was charged with incitement for calling Mr Taylor a 'bloody nigger', although the defendant died before the trial. In 1994, Lady Birdwood, aged 80, was convicted of the offence for distributing anti-semitic literature (the holocaust was a 'holohoax'; Jack the Ripper was Jewish, etc.). She was given a three months suspended sentence.

7. The common law offence of sedition and ss. 4–5 of the Public Order Act 1986,[11] also control conduct tending to cause racial hatred. Sections 18 and 19 have effectively replaced sedition, although the latter may still be of use if it extends to conduct causing hatred against religious groups within society. In *R v Caunt*[12] the jury was directed that an article aimed at Jews could be seditious.

---

9   There is a power to search premises in connection with this offence of possession: 1986 Act, s. 24.
10 Letter from the Attorney-General's Chambers, 27 July 2000.
11 Above, pp. 471–472.
12 (1947). See (1948) 64 LQR 203.

8. *Holocaust denial.* In 1997, a private Member's Bill was introduced to make holocaust denial a criminal offence, but was unsuccessful.[13] This would have made it an offence 'to claim, whether in writing or orally, that the policy of genocide against the Jewish people committed by Nazi Germany did not occur'. Six European states have such offences.[14] Should English law make holocaust denial a criminal offence, or is the offence of incitement to racial hatred sufficient? This question was considered in a Report of the Law Panel of the Institute for Jewish Penal Policy.[15] The Report concluded that a holocaust denial offence should not be introduced on the grounds that: (i) it could be seen as an illegitimate limitation on freedom of expression; (ii) the evidence of other states with such an offence was inconclusive as to its value; (iii) there were problems in defining holocaust denial and in giving the holocaust priority over other cases of genocide; and (iv) the resulting publicity might work to the advantage of holocaust denial. The Report proposed instead that the incitement to racial hatred offence should be amended, primarily so as to include direct hate speech.

9. The problem of racial abuse at football matches is dealt with by the Football (Offences) Act 1991, s. 3, as follows:

'**3.**—(1) It is an offence to take part at a designated football match in chanting of an indecent or racialist nature.

(2) For this purpose—

> (*a*) "chanting" means the repeated uttering of any words or sounds in concert with one or more others; and
>
> (*b*) "of a racialist nature" means consisting of or including matter which is threatening, abusive or insulting to a person by reason of his colour, race, nationality (including citizenship) or ethnic or national origins.'

There are regularly convictions for the offence, which is punishable by fine.

11 Racially aggravated offences[16]

Crime and Disorder Act 1998

28. Meaning of "racially aggravated"

(1) An offence is racially aggravated for the purposes of sections 29 to 32 below if—

> (*a*) at the time of committing the offence, or immediately before or after doing so, the offender demonstrates towards the victim of the offence hostility based on the victim's membership (or presumed membership) of a racial group; or
>
> (*b*) the offence is motivated (wholly or partly) by hostility towards members of a racial group based on their membership of that group.

(2) In subsection (1)(a) above—

> "membership", in relation to a racial group, includes association with members of that group;
>
> "presumed" means presumed by the offender.

(3) It is immaterial for the purposes of paragraph (a) or (b) of subsection (1) above whether or not the offender's hostility is also based, to any extent, on—

> (*a*) the fact or presumption that any person or group of persons belongs to any religious group; or
>
> (*b*) any other factor not mentioned in that paragraph.

13 The Holocaust Denial Bill was introduced by Mike Gapes MP, but failed for lack of parliamentary time. See G. Bindman, (1997) 147 NLJ 466.

14 A conviction under the French holocaust denial law was held not to infringe the freedom of expression guarantee in Art. 19 ICCPR by the UN Human Rights Committee: *Faurisson v France* (1997) 4 IHRR 350. See also *Lehideux v France*, E Ct HRR 1996–VII 2864.

15 Loc. cit., above at n. 2, p. 23. Cf. G. Bindman, (1997) 147 NLJ 466.

16 See also above, p. 501.

(4) In this section "racial group" means a group of persons defined by reference to race, colour, nationality (including citizenship) or ethnic or national origins.

29. Racially-aggravated assaults

(1) A person is guilty of an offence under this section if he commits—

(*a*)   an offence under section 20 of the Offences Against the Person Act 1861 (malicious wounding or grievous bodily harm);

(*b*)   an offence under section 47 of that Act (actual bodily harm); or

(*c*)   common assault,

which is racially aggravated for the purposes of this section.

(2) A person guilty of an offence falling within subsection (1)(a) or (b) above shall be liable—

(*a*)   on summary conviction, to imprisonment for a term not exceeding six months or to a fine not exceeding the statutory maximum, or to both;

(*b*)   on conviction on indictment, to imprisonment for a term not exceeding seven years or to a fine, or to both.

(3) A person guilty of an offence falling within subsection (1)(c) above shall be liable—

(*a*)   on summary conviction, to imprisonment for a term not exceeding six months or to a fine not exceeding the statutory maximum, or to both;

(*b*)   on conviction on indictment, to imprisonment for a term not exceeding two years or to a fine, or to both.

30. Racially-aggravated criminal damage

(1) A person is guilty of an offence under this section if he commits an offence under section 1(1) of the Criminal Damage Act 1971 (destroying or damaging property belonging to another) which is racially aggravated for the purposes of this section.

(2) A person guilty of an offence under this section shall be liable—

(*a*)   on summary conviction, to imprisonment for a term not exceeding six months or to a fine not exceeding the statutory maximum, or to both;

(*b*)   on conviction on indictment, to imprisonment for a term not exceeding fourteen years or to a fine, or to both.

(3) For the purposes of this section, section 28(1)(a) above shall have effect as if the person to whom the property belongs or is treated as belonging for the purposes of that Act were the victim of the offence.

(4) A person guilty of an offence falling within subsection (1)(a) or (b) above shall be liable—

(*a*)   on summary conviction, to imprisonment for a term not exceeding six months or to a fine not exceeding the statutory maximum, or to both;

(*b*)   on conviction on indictment, to imprisonment for a term not exceeding two years or to a fine, or to both.

(5) A person guilty of an offence falling within subsection (1)(c) above shall be liable on summary conviction to a fine not exceeding level 4 on the standard scale.

(6) If, on the trial on indictment of a person charged with an offence falling within subsection (1)(a) or (b) above, the jury find him not guilty of the offence charged, they may find him guilty of the basic offence mentioned in that provision.

(7) For the purposes of subsection (1)(c) above, section 28(1)(a) above shall have effect as if the person likely to be caused harassment, alarm or distress were the victim of the offence.

31. Racially-aggravated public order offences

(1) A person is guilty of an offence under this section if he commits—

(*a*)   an offence under section 4 of the Public Order Act 1986 (fear or provocation of violence);

(*b*)   an offence under section 4A of that Act (intentional harassment, alarm or distress); or

(*c*)   an offence under section 5 of that Act (harassment, alarm or distress), which is racially aggravated for the purposes of this section.

(2) A constable may arrest without warrant anyone whom he reasonably suspects to be committing an offence falling within subsection (1)(a) or (b) above.

(3) A constable may arrest a person without warrant if—

(*a*)   he engages in conduct which a constable reasonably suspects to constitute an offence falling within subsection (1)(c) above;

(*b*)   he is warned by that constable to stop; and

(*c*)   he engages in further such conduct immediately or shortly after the warning.

The conduct mentioned in paragraph (a) above and the further conduct need not be of the same nature.

32. Racially-aggravated harassment etc.

(1) A person is guilty of an offence under this section if he commits—

(*a*)   An offence under section 2 of the Protection from Harassment Act 1997 (offence of harassment); or

(*b*)   an offence under section 4 of that Act (putting people in fear of violence),

which is racially aggravated for the purposes of this section.

(2) In section 24(2) of the 1984 Act (arrestable offences), after paragraph (o) there shall be inserted—

"(p) an offence falling within section 32(1)(a) of the Crime and Disorder Act 1998 (racially-aggravated harassment);"

(3) A person guilty of an offence falling within subsection (1)(a) above shall be liable—

(*a*)   on summary conviction, to imprisonment for a term not exceeding six months or to a fine not exceeding the statutory maximum, or to both;

(*b*)   on conviction on indictment, to imprisonment for a term not exceeding two years or to a fine, or to both;

(4) a person guilty of an offence falling within subsection (1)(b) above shall be liable—

(*a*)   on summary conviction, to imprisonment for a term not exceeding six months or to a fine not exceeding the statutory maximum, or to both;

(*b*)   on conviction on indictment, to imprisonment for a term not exceeding seven years or to a fine, or to both.

(5) If, on the trial on indictment of a person charged with an offence falling within subsection (1)(a) above, the jury find him not guilty of the offence charged, they may find him guilty of the basic offence mentioned in that provision.

(6) If, on the trial on indictment of a person charged with an offence falling within subsection (1)(b) above, the jury find him not guilty of the offence charged, they may find him guilty of an offence falling within subsection (1)(a) above.

(7) Section 5 of the Protection from Harassment Act 1997 (restraining orders) shall have effect in relation to a person convicted of an offence under this section as if the reference in subsection (1) of that section to an offence under section 2 or 4 included a reference to an offence under this section.

82. Increase in sentences for racial aggravation

(1) This section applies where a court is considering the seriousness of an offence other than one under sections 29 to 32 above.

(2) If the offence was racially aggravated, the court—

(*a*)   shall treat that fact as an aggravating factor (that is to say, a factor that increases the seriousness of the offence); and

(*b*)   shall state in open court that the offence was so aggravated.

(3) Section 28 above applies for the purposes of this section as it applies for the purposes of sections 29 to 32 above.

NOTES[17]

1. The Crime and Disorder Act 1998 introduces the concept of racially aggravated offences into English law. Attempts to introduce such offences had previously been

17 On the racially aggravated offences in the Crime and Disorder Act 1998 and such offences generally, see F. Brennan, 1999 Crim LR 17; I. Hare, (1997) 17 OJLS 415; and J. Holroyd, (1999) 149 NLJ 722.

made unsuccessfully. In 1994, proposals[18] for a specific offence of racially motivated violence were rejected by the government on the basis that violence was already the subject of a number of offences; that special treatment for minorities might be resented by others and that racial motivation might be difficult to prove. A 1994 private Members' Bill[19] that would have strengthened the existing offence of incitement to racial hatred and introduced an offence of group defamation – by which it would have been an offence to publish offensive written material intended to vilify a racial group – failed for lack of government support. The government decided instead to provide a measure of protection for the population at large, by adding the offence of intentionally causing harassment, alarm or distress to the Public Order Act 1986.[20]

2. But the problem did not go away. Following the MacPherson Report on the Lawrence case[1] and continued reliable evidence of: (i) large and increasing numbers of racially motivated attacks upon members of racial groups, particularly black people and Asians, and upon persons supporting them; and (ii) many incidents of racial abuse and sustained harassment,[2] a different government decided to introduce the concept of racially aggravated offences in the Crime and Disorder Act 1998.

3. There are two approaches in the 1998 Act. New offences of racially aggravated assault, criminal damage, public disorder and harassment are created in ss. 29–32. Each of these attracts a higher possible sentence on conviction than the equivalent non-racially aggravated offence carries. In addition, under s. 82 a person convicted of any other offence may be given a higher sentence than otherwise because the offence was racially aggravated. Section 82 places on a statutory footing the approach that the courts had already developed in *Attorney-General's Reference (Nos 29, 30 and 31 of 1994)*.[3] In that case, a black man had been assaulted by three white men when he stopped at a petrol station because his girl friend, who was with him, was white. Taylor LCJ increased the trial court sentence for the ordinary offence of causing grievous bodily harm from five to seven years imprisonment. Section 82 is of value in giving this approach the backing of Parliament and in requiring that a court 'state in open court that the offence was so aggravated' (s. 82(2)(b)). Prosecutions in racial incident cases using either of these two approaches are increasing.[4]

The term 'racially aggravated' for the purposes of both ss. 29–31 and s. 82 is defined in s. 28. The definition of 'racial group' in s. 28 is that in the Race Relations Act, s. 3, except for the addition of the word 'citizenship', which presumably derives from the EU concept of citizenship. This link with the Race Relations Act means that the 1998 Act does not apply to cases where the motivation is religious rather than racial. Thus violence, harassment, etc., against persons because they are 'Muslims' would on the face of it would not be included; it would need to be established that the motivation, which is generally hard to prove, was in fact racial.[5] Could the offence be used in cases of offences against members of such organisations as the British National Party? Should that be possible?

18 See the House of Commons Home Affairs Committee, *Racial Attacks and Harassment*, 27 HC 71–I (1993–4), recommendation 27; CRE, *Second Review of the Race Relations Act 1976*, p. 74; and the Association of Chief Police Officers' proposal, *Runnymede Bulletin* 23, p. 3.

19 The Racial Hatred and Violence Bill, introduced by Mr Hartley Booth.

20 On s. 4A of the Public Order Act 1986, see above, p. 472. On racial harassment at work as discrimination under the Race Relations Act 1976, see above, p. 1088.

1   See above, p. 1071.

2   E.g. in 1995–96, over 12,000 racial attacks and other incidents (e.g. racial insults or threats) were reported to the police: *Racial Violence and Harassment: A Consultation Document* (Home Office, 1997), p. 2.

3   *R v Ribbans, Duggan and Ridley* (1995) 16 Cr App Cas (S) 698, CA.

4   2,417 cases were sent for prosecution in 1999–2000, as opposed to 1,603 in 1998–99. Over 40% of the offences prosecuted were the new racially aggravated crimes brought in under the Crime and Disorder Act 1998: CPS Press Release, 1 March 2001.

5   On the overlap or connection between racial and religious discrimination in some cases, see above, p. 1027.

12 The Commission for Racial Equality

Race Relations Act 1976

43. Establishment and duties of Commission

(1) There shall be a body of Commissioners named the Commission for Racial Equality consisting of at least eight but not more than fifteen individuals each appointed by the Secretary of State on a full-time or part-time basis, which shall have the following duties—

    (*a*) to work towards the elimination of discrimination;

    (*b*) to promote equality of opportunity, and good relations, between persons of different racial groups generally; and

    (*c*) to keep under review the working of this Act and, when they are so required by the Secretary of State or otherwise think it necessary, draw up and submit to the Secretary of State proposals for amending it.

NOTES[6]

1. The CRE has its full complement of 15 members. The Chair is Gurbux Singh. Extra commissioners may be appointed *ad hoc* for the purposes of a particular investigation.[7] The CRE is a body corporate.[8] It is wholly independent of the government. It is 'not an emanation of the Crown, and shall not act or be treated as the servant or agent of the Crown'.[9]

2. The CRE replaces and merges the enforcement and promotional functions of the RRB and the CRC.[10] In carrying out the very wide duties listed in s. 43, it is authorised (i) to 'give financial and other assistance to any organisation appearing to the Commission to be concerned with the promotion of equality of opportunity, and good relations, between persons of different racial groups';[11] (ii) to 'undertake or assist (financially or otherwise) the undertaking by other persons of any research and any educational activities, which appear to the Commission necessary or expedient for the purposes of s. 43(1)';[12] (iii) to issue codes of practice aimed at the elimination of discrimination in employment and/or 'the promotion of equality of opportunity in that field between persons of different racial groups' and in respect of housing;[13] (iv) to give assistance to an individual bringing a claim under the Act,[14] and (v) to conduct formal investigations, as to which see below. The CRE's work is summarised in its annual reports.

6 On the CRE, see G. Bindman, (1976) 3 Br Jo of Law and Soc 110; I. Leigh, (1982) 132 NLJ 24; L. Lustgarten, [1982] PL 229; *A Review of the Race Relations Act 1976*, Runnymede Trust (1979).

7 s. 49(2).

8 1976 Act, Sch. 1.

9 Ibid.

10 On these bodies, see above, p. 1069.

11 s. 44(1).

12 s. 45(1).

13 s. 47(1). Section 47 was amended to extend to housing by the Housing Act 1988, s. 137 (rented housing), and the Local Government and Housing Act 1989, s. 180 (other housing). There are Statutory Codes on Employment, S.I. 1983 No. 1083; Rented Housing (1991), S.I. 1991 No. 227; and Non-Rented (Owner Occupied) Housing 1992, S.I. 1992 No. 619. As the legal significance of s. 47 codes, s. 47(10) reads: '(10) A failure on the part of any person to observe any provision of a code of practice shall not of itself render him liable to any proceedings; but in any proceedings under this Act before an industrial tribunal any code of practice issued under this section shall be admissible in evidence, and if any provision of such a code appears to the tribunal to be relevant to any question arising in the proceedings it shall be taken into account in determining that question.' There are also non-statutory CRE Codes on Education and Primary Health Care. On s. 47 codes, see C. McCrudden (1988), 51 MLR 409.

14 s. 66, and see below, p. 675.

3. The *First Report of the Home Affairs Committee*, 1981–82 HC 46–I contained many criticisms of the CRE's work. One general criticism was of the CRE's tending to see itself as a spokesman for ethnic minorities and to prefer this role to its 'true one of a quasi-judicial Statutory Commission'.[15]

13 Formal investigations

Race Relations Act 1976

48. Power to conduct formal investigations
(1) Without prejudice to their general power to do anything requisite for the performance of their duties under section 43(1), the Commission may if they think fit, and shall if required by the Secretary of State, conduct a formal investigation for any purpose connected with the carrying out of those duties. . . .

49. Terms of reference
(1) The Commission shall not embark on a formal investigation unless the requirements of this section have been complied with.
(2) Terms of reference for the investigation shall be drawn up by the Commission or, if the Commission were required by the Secretary of State to conduct the investigation, by the Secretary of State after consulting the Commission.
(3) It shall be the duty of the Commission to give general notice of the holding of the investigation unless the terms of reference confine it to activities of persons named in them, but in such a case the Commission shall in the prescribed manner give those persons notice of the holding of the investigation.
(4) Where the terms of reference of the investigation confine it to activities of persons named in them and the Commission in the course of it propose to investigate any act made unlawful by this Act which they believe that a person so named may have done, the Commission shall—
  (*a*) inform that person of their belief and of their proposal to investigate the act in question; and
  (*b*) offer him an opportunity of making oral or written representations with regard to it (or both oral and written representations if he thinks fit);
and a person so named who avails himself of an opportunity under this subsection of making oral representations may be represented—
  (i)   by counsel or a solicitor; or
  (ii) by some other person of his choice, not being a person to whom the Commission object on the ground that he is unsuitable.
(5) The Commission or, if the Commission were required by the Secretary of State to conduct the investigation, the Secretary of State after consulting the Commission may from time to time revise the terms of reference; and subsections (1), (3) and (4) shall apply to the revised investigation and terms of reference as they applied to the original.

50. Power to obtain information
(1) For the purposes of a formal investigation the Commission, by a notice in the prescribed form served on him in the prescribed manner—
  (*a*) may require any person to furnish such written information as may be described in the notice, and may specify the time at which, and the manner and form in which, the information is to be furnished;
  (*b*) may require any person to attend at such time and place as is specified in the notice and give oral information about, and produce all documents in his possession or control relating to, any matter specified in the notice.
(2) Except as provided by section 60 [investigations as to compliance with non-discrimination notices], a notice shall be served under subsection (1) only where—
  (*a*) service of the notice was authorised by an order made by the Secretary of State; or

---

15 Ibid., p. xiv. On the strongly critical comments on the CRE's conduct by the Court of Appeal in *Mandla v Dowell Lee* – comments rejected by the House of Lords in that case – see above, p. 1114.

(*b*) the terms of reference of the investigation state that the Commission believes that a
person named in them may have done or may be doing acts of all or any of the following
descriptions—
  (i) unlawful discriminatory acts;
  (ii) contraventions of section 28; and
  (iii) contraventions of sections 29, 30 or 31,
and confine the investigation to those acts.

NOTES

1. The CRE's power to conduct formal investigations was a key part of the conception
of the 1976 Act.[16] In practice, however, this has not proved to be the case. Formal
investigations may be initiated by the Secretary of State (none so far) or by the CRE.[17]
They may be conducted for any purpose connected with the execution of the CRE's
duties under s. 41(1). In *Home Office v Commission for Racial Equality*,[18] Woolf J
held that the CRE was entitled to conduct a formal investigation into racial
discrimination in the immigration service. Such an investigation could not be seen
as coming within s. 43(1)(a) because 'discrimination' there referred to discrimination
within the 1976 Act and the court was bound by the ruling in the *Kassam* case[19] that
discrimination in immigration practice was outside the Act. It did, however, come
within s. 43(1)(b) as being aimed at 'promoting "good relations . . . between persons
of different racial groups"'. Woolf J pointed out that the CRE's powers to conduct
the investigation would be limited in that it would only be able to require the Home
Office to produce evidence if the Secretary of State authorised it to do so.[20] In fact,
the Home Office co-operated fully.[21] One incident which led the CRE to undertake
the investigation was the disclosure that Asian women had been required by
immigration officials to undergo virginity tests before entry into the UK.[1]
2. The procedure to be followed in the conduct of formal investigations is indicated
in ss. 49–50 of the Act. The meaning of these sections, which have proved difficult
to interpret, has been considered in two House of Lords cases: the *Hillingdon* and
Prestige cases,[2] with the one speech in each case being delivered by Lord Diplock.
The cases established, *inter alia*, that the CRE is subject to judicial review in the
exercise of its statutory powers in respect of formal investigations.
3. The Act provides for named person and general investigations. A *named person
investigation* may only occur if the CRE has a 'belief' that the person named has
acted illegally.[3] In the *Hillingdon* case, it was said:[4]

16 On formal investigations, see Appleby and Ellis, [1984] PL 236; ibid., (1984) 100 LQR 349;
    M. Coussey, in Hepple and Szyszczak, op. cit. at p. 1068, n. 1, Chap. 3; C. McCrudden, in
    R. Baldwin and C. McCrudden (eds.), *Regulation and Public Law* (1987) p. 227; *Racial
    Justice at Work*, op. cit. at p. 1068, n. 1, above, Chaps. 3 and 4; Pardoe, (1982) 132 NLJ 670.
17 s. 48(1).
18 [1982] QB 385, QBD.
19 Above, p. 1138.
20 s. 50(2)(a).
21 See *Immigration Control and Procedures: Report of a Formal Investigation*, F Invest Rep
    1985.
 1 *The Guardian* 20 July 1979.
 2 *Hillingdon London Borough Council v Commission for Racial Equality* [1982] AC 779 (see
    above, p. 1137 for the facts) and *Re Prestige Group plc, Commission for Racial Equality
    v Prestige Group plc* [1984] 1 WLR 335. On the *Prestige* case, see M. Munroe, (1985) 14
    Anglo-American LR 187.
 3 s. 49(4).
 4 p. 791.

'... to embark upon the full investigation it is enough that there should be material before the Commission sufficient to raise in the minds of reasonable men, possessed of the experience of covert racial discrimination that has been acquired by the Commission, a suspicion that there may have been acts by the person named of racial discrimination of the kind which it is proposed to investigate.'

In the *Prestige* case, Lord Diplock added:[5]

'... it should be a condition precedent to the exercise by the CRE of its power to conduct named persons investigations that the CRE should in fact have already formed a suspicion that the persons named may have committed some unlawful act of discrimination and had at any rate *some* grounds for so suspecting, albeit that the grounds upon which any such suspicion was based might, at that stage, be no more than tenuous because they had not yet been tested.'

In the *Prestige* case, a non-discrimination notice was quashed because the CRE had had no 'belief' at all that the company had acted illegally when it decided to conduct an investigation into 'the employment of persons of different racial groups by the Prestige Group Ltd.' The House of Lords rejected the CRE's view that there could be a second, non-accusatorial kind of named person investigation within the Act, to which s. 49(4) did not apply, of the sort represented by the facts of that case.

The decision in the *Prestige* case was a considerable blow to the CRE which had a number of similar investigations pending. They were all investigations into a particular sector of activity which seemed to merit inquiry (e.g. because of the small number of black persons employed in an industry or allocated public housing) and in which the CRE had chosen to investigate a particular company or body as a test case. In each case, the named company or body was chosen not because it was believed to have been discriminating but because it would, for one reason or another, make a good subject for study. One such case was the *Hackney Council Housing* case.[6] This case was completed and a non-discrimination notice issued. Although the decision to conduct it could almost certainly have been quashed under the *Prestige* case, the Council decided not to challenge the notice and agreed to comply with it. As a result of the *Prestige* case, in which the House of Lords showed its concern for a named person who would appear to many to have been accused, such test cases can only be conducted as general investigations, in respect of which the CRE has no automatic right to subpoena evidence and from which a non-discrimination notice cannot result. If, in the course of a general investigation, a belief emerges that discrimination has occurred, a separate named person investigation may be initiated, after the framing of new named person terms of reference. The CRE has called for the repeal of s. 49(4), with the result that the *Prestige* case would be reversed and the CRE would be free to conduct formal investigations for any purpose connected with the carrying out of its duties.[7]

In a named person investigation proceedings begin with a preliminary inquiry,[8] the purpose of which was described in the *Hillingdon* case as being to 'give the persons named in the terms of reference an opportunity of making written or oral representations or both . . . that the proposed full investigation should not be proceeded with at all, or that its terms of reference should be made narrower . . . or as to the manner in which the full investigation should be conducted'. In other words, Lord Diplock stated, '*audi alteram partem*, the first rule of natural justice, is expressly required to be observed . . .'. The named person is entitled to be legally represented

---

5   p. 342.
6   Above, p. 1146.
7   *Second Review of the Race Relations Act* (1992), p. 43.
8   s. 49(4).

at an oral hearing, although he has no right to cross-examine witnesses against him.[9] The oral hearing in the *Hillingdon* case took over three days. In the *Prestige* case, the CRE had infringed s. 49(4) because it had not conducted a preliminary inquiry. If the CRE decides to proceed with a named person investigation after the s. 49(4) inquiry, a full investigation occurs. CRE staff question individuals and collect documentary evidence, backed by the power to subpoena persons to give evidence or to produce documents.[10] Lord Denning MR described these powers as 'immense' and, in somewhat exaggerated fashion, has stated: 'You might think that we were back in the days of the Inquisition'.[11] The Act contains no provision giving the named person a right to a hearing at the full investigation stage. The reason for this can be traced to the drafting history of s. 49(4). This was intended by its author (Lord Hailsham) to apply at the full investigation stage; it was included in s. 49 and phrased in terms of a preliminary inquiry by mistake, as Lord Denning MR acknowledged in the *Hillingdon* case.[12] It is by virtue of this drafting error that the preliminary inquiry stage and many of the difficulties in the working of the formal investigation procedure exist. In the *Hillingdon* case, in the Court of Appeal, Griffiths LJ stated[13] 'if the Act is to be construed as giving a right of audience and legal representation before the formal investigation even commences, it must be implicit that there is a similar right during the course of the formal investigation itself'. In practice, although the named person will be allowed to make written and oral representations, there is no formal oral hearing in the sense that this can occur at the preliminary inquiry stage until the 'minded' stage is reached.[14]

The CRE may issue a non-discrimination notice (other than in education cases within s. 58(6)) following a named person investigation.[15] Before a notice is issued, the CRE must, if 'minded' to make one, offer the person who will be subject to it the chance to make representations.[16] In *R v Commission for Racial Equality, ex p Cottrell and Rothon*,[17] it was held that there was no right at this stage to cross-examine witnesses relied upon by the CRE. The rules of natural justice applied to formal investigations but in the view of Lord Lane LCJ in that case they meant only 'that the proceedings must be conducted in a way which is fair . . . in all the circumstances' and that in an investigatory process of a largely administrative kind which did not lead to the imposition of criminal sanctions, the right to cross-examine was not required.[18] A non-discrimination notice is subject to judicial review which may occur before an appeal is made in the case.[19] There is a right of appeal against a notice to an industrial tribunal or a county court (s. 59). This allows the person concerned to challenge the CRE's findings of fact as well as raise points of law.[20] Commenting on the court's 'finding of fact' jurisdiction, Griffiths LJ stated:[1]

---

9 See *R v Commission for Racial Equality, ex p Cottrell and Rothon*, below, which presumably applies at the preliminary inquiry stage as well as later.
10 s. 50(2)(b).
11 *Science Research Council v Nassé; Leyland Cars Ltd v Vyas* [1979] QB 144 at 172, CA.
12 [1982] QB 276, 285, CA.
13 Ibid., at 297.
14 Below.
15 s. 58.
16 s. 58(5).
17 [1980] 1 WLR 1580, QBD.
18 *Quaere* whether this approach is consistent with Lord Diplock's emphasis on natural justice later in the *Hillingdon* case.
19 *R v Commission for Racial Equality, ex p Westminster City Council* [1985] ICR 827, CA.
20 *Commission for Racial Equality v Amari Plastics Ltd* [1982] QB 1194, CA.
1 pp. 1204–5.

'There is no doubt that before a non-discrimination notice is served, the Commission have carried out a searching inquisitorial inquiry to satisfy themselves of the truth of the facts upon which the notice is based and have given at least two and probably three opportunities to the person to put his case, either orally or in writing, either by himself or through solicitors, counsel or any person of his choice. This is necessarily an expensive and a time-consuming process. In the present case it has already been going on over four years, and I can understand the frustration that the commissioners must feel if the Act requires that their findings of fact are liable to be reopened and reversed on appeal.

. . . If it were not for the plain wording of section 59(2), I should be most sympathetic to the commission's argument. If Parliament empowers a body to carry out a formal investigation and hedges the procedure with safeguards to ensure that the person investigated shall have every opportunity to state his case and then requires that body to publish its findings, one might be forgiven for thinking that Parliament intended that that would be the end of the matter. But it is to my mind clear from the language of this statute that such is not the case.'

Lord Denning also appreciated the CRE's difficulty:[2]

'The machinery [of formal investigations] is so elaborate and cumbersome that it is in danger of grinding to a halt. I am very sorry for the Commission, but they have been caught up in a spider's web spun by Parliament, from which there is little hope of their escaping.'

He noted, however, that under the *Cottrell and Rothon* case,[3] the company would have had no opportunity to cross-examine witnesses before the CRE and that the hearing before the court or tribunal would be the one occasion on which it would be able to put its case to a body other than the CRE.

The CRE must keep a register of non-discrimination notices and make it available for public inspection.[4] It is kept in the CRE's library in London. A non-discrimination notice will require the person named not to commit further discriminatory acts. If, during the following five years, it appears likely to the CRE that discrimination persists, it may apply for an injunction to enforce the notice.[5] At the end of 1999, there was just one non-discrimination notice in force.

A named person investigation is completed by the adoption of a report, to which any non-discrimination notice may be appended. A formal investigation report must be published by the Secretary of State if the investigation was one required by him.[6] Otherwise the CRE has the choice of publishing the report or simply making it available for inspection.[7] The reports made so far have been published. The CRE may make recommendations in its report, including recommendations for a change in the law.[8]

4. In the case of a *general investigation*, once the terms of reference have been adopted, the CRE begins its full investigation, interviewing individuals and collecting evidence. In general investigations, the power of subpoena is only available if the Secretary of State agrees.[9] The question of a right to a hearing for any interested party is not dealt with by statute and has not as yet been considered judicially. In the case of some general investigations, although no person is named in the terms of reference (they must not be: the *Hillingdon* and *Prestige* cases), the nature of the investigation (e.g. specific to the immigration service) or the way in which the investigation develops (so as to focus upon a particular person) suggests

2   p. 1203.
3   Above, p. 1165.
4   s. 61.
5   s. 62(1).
6   s. 51(3).
7   s. 51(4).
8   s. 51(1).
9   s. 50(2)(a).

that a right to representation should exist, even though the reasoning in the *Hillingdon* and *Prestige* cases indicates that the CRE may not issue a non-discrimination notice following a general investigation. The outcome of a general investigation is a report which is otherwise subject to the same rules as a report resulting from a named person investigation. A draft of the report is submitted to any interested party for comment.
5. By mid-2000, the CRE had completed 63 formal investigations resulting in 24 non-discrimination notices. Several investigations were pending, including investigations of the Crown Prosecution Service and the Immigration Service. Most formal investigations have been in employment or housing, particularly the former. Whereas in the early years the great majority of investigations were 'named person' investigations, following the *Prestige* case the number of general investigations has increased. The response to the *Prestige* case has been for most general investigations to be narrower in scope, following the success of the *Beaumont Leys* case.[10] Coussey[11] has described the post-*Prestige* strategy for general investigations as follows:

> 'The investigation must be narrowly-defined, either by industry or organised structure or by function or geographical location. It must include in its scope employers regarded as a model or leader by others, and it must focus on an issue or practice about which the industry itself has a concern, to maximise self interest and the potential for negotiating change.'

In the mid-1990s, a further shift in strategy occurred, so that the Council's present approach is, 'wherever possible, to resolve complaints of institutional discrimination through preliminary enquiries, followed by negotiation and voluntary agreement and to use its powers of formal investigation only as a last resort.[12] As a result, the Council spends most of its time in this area of activity on informal approaches to institutions and the achievement of voluntary changes without resorting to the more confrontational mechanism of a formal investigation. Even if a formal investigation is begun, the strong preference is for the adoption of a voluntary agreement or informal change in practice rather than a non-discrimination notice. At the end of 1998, only one formal investigation was in progress and no new investigation had been opened during the year.

Overall, formal investigations have not played the key enforcement role that was envisaged for them under the 1976 Act and their importance has declined significantly in recent years. This has been partly because of the *Prestige* case and delays and upsets that have resulted from legal challenges through judicial review or appeals against non-discrimination notices. It is also partly to do with a lack of resources and different views within the CRE as to the relative importance of its enforcement and promotional roles. As is concluded in *Racial Justice at Work*[13] the result is that, contrary to Parliament's intentions, the individual complaint is a more effective means of enforcement than the formal investigation:

> 'Formal investigations are not playing the central role now that might have been expected. On the other hand, the use of the CRE's power to assist individual complainants has expanded over the period since it was established in 1977, in spite of the legislators' intention to reduce the dominance of the law enforcement agency and give individuals direct access to the tribunals and courts. This may be to do with the failure of alternative legal strategies. As one senior officer said: "Complaints were regarded as the scout cars of the CRE powers, whereas formal investigations were supposed to be the tanks. What has happened is that the scout cars have become the more ... effective".'

10 CRE F Invest Rep 1985. The general investigation there was into the numbers of black employees in shops, including leading stores, at a new Leicester shopping precinct.
11 Loc. cit. at p. 1163, n. 16, above, p. 45.
12 CRE 1998 Annual Report, p. 27.
13 Op. cit. at p. 1068, n. 1, above, p. 275.

14 Enforcement in the courts

Race Relations Act 1976

53. Restriction of proceedings for breach of Act[14]

(1) Except as provided by this Act [or the Special Immigration Appeals Commission Act 1997 or Part IV of the Immigration and Asylum Act 1999] no proceedings, whether civil or criminal, shall lie against any person in respect of an act by reason that the act is unlawful by virtue of a provision of this Act [or the Special Immigration Appeals Commission Act 1997 or Part IV of the Immigration and Asylum Act 1999].

(2) Subsection (1) does not preclude the making of an order of certiorari, mandamus or prohibition. ...

[Sections 54–6 provide for remedies in employment and similar (partnerships, trade unions, etc) cases arising under Part II (ss. 4–16) of the Act. A person alleging discrimination against him may take his case directly to an employment (formerly industrial) tribunal (s. 54(1)). If conciliation through ACAS (s. 55) proves unsuccessful, the tribunal will hear the case and may make an order declaring that discrimination has occurred, award compensation, or recommend action to rectify the wrong done (s. 56).]

57. Claims under Part III

(1) A claim by any person ('the claimant') that another person ('the respondent')—
- (*a*) has committed an act of discrimination against the claimant which is unlawful by virtue of Part III [ss. 17–27]; or
- (*b*) is by virtue of section 32 [vicarious liability of employers and principals] or 33 [aiding unlawful acts] to be treated as having committed such an act of discrimination against the claimant,

may be made the subject of civil proceedings in like manner as any other claim in tort or (in Scotland) in reparation for breach of statutory duty.

(2) Proceedings under subsection (1)—
- (*a*) shall, in England and Wales, be brought only in a designated county court; and
- (*b*) shall, in Scotland, be brought only in sheriff court;

but all such remedies shall be obtainable in such proceedings as, apart from this subsection and section 53(1), would be obtainable in the High Court or the Court of Session, as the case may be.

(3) As respects an unlawful act of discrimination falling within section 1(1)(*b*), no award of damages shall be made if the respondent proves that the requirement or condition in question was not applied with the intention of treating the claimant unfavourably on racial grounds.

(4) For the avoidance of doubt it is hereby declared that damages in respect of an unlawful act of discrimination may include compensation for injury to feelings whether or not they include compensation under any other head. . . .

NOTES

1. Section 53 excludes the few common law remedies that might be available, e.g. a claim in tort against an innkeeper.[15] The prerogative orders remain available where they apply and may be cheaper and quicker to use in some cases.

2. The Act provided for the first time[16] for direct and immediate access to court for an aggrieved individual to challenge acts of discrimination contrary to the Race

---

14 *Ed.* S. 53 is printed as amended by the Race Relations (Amendment) Act 2000, Sch. 2.
15 See above, p. 1135.
16 Except for unfair dismissal cases under (now) the Employment Protection (Consolidation) Act 1978, as amended. The CRE has recommended that the time limit be extended to six months: *Reform of the Race Relations Act 1976* (1998).

Relations Act. Under the 1968 Act, the only remedy was to complain to the RRB which attempted conciliation and took the case to court if conciliation failed. This approach was criticised as 'paternalistic' and an individual may now take a case claiming a breach (either directly or by virtue of ss. 32 or 33) of Part II (employment and related matters) to an employment tribunal and of Part III (education, acts of public authorities, goods, facilities, services, housing, and clubs) to a county court. The CRE has recommended a radical change in these arrangements.[17] It has proposed that a single 'discrimination division within the industrial tribunal system should be established to hear both employment and non-employment race and sex discrimination cases'. It has also recommended that class actions should be permitted where the discrimination complained of affects a number of persons.[18]

3. The limitation period is very short. Cases must be brought within three months of the alleged act of discrimination before any employment tribunal[19] and within six months before a county court, except for public sector education cases under ss. 17–18 (eight months) and cases where assistance is sought from the CRE (eight or nine months).[20] The claimant does not have to inform the CRE that he is bringing proceedings, although he will obviously do so if (as in practice he normally does) he seeks the assistance which the CRE can give him.[1] In 1998, the CRE received 1,657 applications for assistance, over two thirds of which concerned employment and provided full or limited representation in 264 court or tribunal cases. In such cases, the claimant retains control over his case in the sense that he is always free to terminate proceedings.

Legal aid is available in county court cases. Guidance to local legal aid committees has suggested that legal aid should be given in accordance with the importance of the case to the individual and not the likely amount of damages (which may not be great). Legal aid is not available in the much more numerous employment tribunal cases—which makes CRE assistance particularly important.[2] The 'green form' legal advice scheme applies, however, and trade union representation may be available. In *Freeman v Salford Health Authority*,[3] an industrial tribunal argued in favour of extending legal aid to employment cases as follows:

'So much of an applicant's case depends upon in-depth cross-examination of the respondent's witnesses. Such a cross-examination can in most cases only be conducted by a skilled advocate. Fortunately in this case the applicant's representation was financed by the Commission for Racial Equality. Unfortunately their resources only permit them to represent in selected cases. There must clearly be a case for the availability of legal aid, with proper safeguards, in discrimination cases.'

17 *Second Review of the Race Relations Act 1976* (1992), p. 48. Cf. the similar proposal made by the Home Office sponsored Policy Studies Institute study: *Racial Justice at Work* (1991), pp. 227–8. The CRE has been concerned at the very small number of non-employment cases going to county courts, with their inappropriately formal procedures, and the problems in race cases before industrial tribunals (see below).
18 *Reform of the Race Relations Act 1976* (1998).
19 s. 68(1).
20 s. 68(2)–(4). The time limit may be waived if this would be 'just and equitable' (s. 68(6)). It does not prevent a claim being brought in the case of a continuing act of discrimination: see *Barclays Bank plc v Kapur* [1991] 1 All ER 646, HL. See also *Sougrin v Haringey Health Authority* [1991] IRLR 447.
1 s. 66.
2 Legal aid is available on appeal to the Employment Appeal Tribunal.
3 Quoted in *Second Review of the Race Relations Act 1976*, p. 52. The CRE has recommended that legal aid be available in industrial tribunal cases. The Home Office sponsored Policy Studies Institute study reached the same conclusion: *Racial Justice at Work* (1991), p. 277.

The absence of legal aid in employment cases is one reason for the low success level of racial discrimination claims. Other reasons that apply to employment and other cases include the fact that '[r]acial discrimination is not normally practised openly.... It may take a whole variety of subtle forms that are not easy to uncover'.[4] There are also problems as to the burden of proof. Under the Act, this is the normal civil law burden of proof upon the balance of probabilities.[5] It falls upon the claimant, although in a case of indirect discrimination the burden of proving that a requirement or condition is 'justifiable' is upon the defendant.[6]

Although recognising the particular problem of proving racial discrimination, the courts have declined to adopt an approach whereby the burden of proof would shift to the defendant once less favourable treatment consistent with discrimination is proved; instead, it is for the court to draw its own conclusion as to whether there has been unlawful racial discrimination on the basis of the findings of fact, taking into account any failure of the defendant to prove a convincing explanation. The position was explained in *King v GB China Centre*:[7]

'(1) It is for the applicant who complains of racial discrimination to make out his or her case. Thus if the applicant does not prove the case on the balance of probabilities he or she will fail. (2) It is important to bear in mind that it is unusual to find direct evidence of racial discrimination. Few employers will be prepared to admit such discrimination even to themselves. In some cases the discrimination will not be ill-intentioned but merely based on an assumption that "he or she would not have fitted in." (3) The outcome of the case will therefore usually depend on what inferences it is proper to draw from the primary facts found by the tribunal. These inferences can include, in appropriate cases, any inferences that it is just and equitable to draw in accordance with section 65(2)(b) of the Act of 1976 from an evasive or equivocal reply to a questionnaire. (4) Though there will be some cases where, for example, the non-selection of the applicant for a post or for promotion is clearly not on racial grounds, a finding of discrimination and a finding of a difference in race will often point to the possibility of racial discrimination. In such circumstances the tribunal will look to the employer for an explanation. If no explanation is then put forward or if the tribunal considers the explanation to be inadequate or unsatisfactory it will be legitimate for the tribunal to infer that the discrimination was on racial grounds. This is not a matter of law but, as May LJ put it in *North West Thames Regional Health Authority v Noone* [1988] ICR 813, 822, "almost common sense." (5) It is unnecessary and unhelpful to introduce the concept of a shifting evidential burden of proof. At the conclusion of all the evidence the tribunal should make findings as to the primary facts and draw such inferences as they consider proper from those facts. They should then reach a conclusion on the balance of probabilities, bearing in mind both the difficulties which face a person who complains of unlawful discrimination and the fact that it is for the complainant to prove his or her case.'

Commenting on the low success level in racial discrimination claims, the CRE has stated:[8]

'The Commission has long expressed concern at the low number of ethnic minority chairs and members in industrial tribunals. During the year the President of Tribunals and the Department of Employment agreed that more ethnic minority chairs and members were needed.... The approach some tribunals took towards applicants alleging racial discrimination,

---

4   Per Lord Diplock in *Hillingdon London Borough Council v Commission for Racial Equality* [1982] AC 779, HL.
5   *Strathclyde City Council v Zafar* [1998] 2 All ER 953, HL.
6   See above, p. 1100.
7   [1992] ICR 526 at 528, CA, per Neill LJ for a unanimous court. Applied in the *Zafar* case, above, n. 5. See M. Chapman, (1999) 149 NLJ 572.
8   CRE 1993 Annual Report, p. 9. Only 15% of racial discrimination claims heard by industrial tribunals succeeded in 1990–91: *Second Review of the Race Relations Act 1976*, p. 22.

and the quality of some tribunal decisions, also gave us cause for concern.... In recent years, cases taken to the Employment Appeals Tribunal have met with little success. Whether this was because the cases were weak, or the issues of law misunderstood, was a matter much debated.... There was a worrying number of cases where the industrial tribunal found discrimination but this was then overturned at the EAT—in some cases because the tribunal had issued a defective written decision. This reinforces the need to improve training for tribunal members.'

4. There are special arrangements for the enforcement of the education provisions in ss. 17–19. Sections 17 and 18 cases arising in the public sector (i.e. mainly cases concerning LEAs, but excluding universities and independent schools) must be taken first to the Minister for Education.[9] They may be referred to a county court if no satisfactory solution has been reached within two months. The general duty in s. 19 is not enforceable under the Act through the courts or by a non-discrimination notice (although a formal investigation is possible).[10] It is enforceable instead by the Secretary of State for Education acting under his Education Act 1944 powers.[11]

5. By s.75(8), 1976 Act, a member of the armed forces has no remedy before an employment tribunal or in the courts. Instead any complaint of racial discrimination contrary to the Act must be considered through internal armed forces procedures. When considering a racial discrimination complaint from a serving soldier, the Army Board of the Defence Council must allow the complainant to see all of the evidence seen by the Board and allow him a proper opportunity to respond, which will require the Board to consider in its discretion giving the complainant an oral hearing.[12] In 1993, the Army Board awarded a soldier £8,500 compensation from the Ministry of Defence for racial bullying and constant racial abuse and physical violence.[13] The Ministry has issued a Code of Practice for the Armed Forces that deals with racial discrimination.[14]

6. *Evidence.* The question of discovery of documents has been dealt with encouragingly by the courts. In *Science Research Council v Nassé*; *BL Cars Ltd v Vyas*[15] it was held that discovery must be ordered, notwithstanding confidentiality, where this was 'necessary for disposing fairly of the proceedings'.[16] In an important ruling it has also been held that the discovery of statistical material as to the ethnic composition of an employer's workforce may be ordered in a case of direct (as well as indirect) discrimination as probative evidence of a policy of racial discrimination that may have been applied to the plaintiff.[17] In that case, a coloured bus inspector who had failed in his application for promotion, successfully sought an order requiring his employer to disclose a schedule indicating the number of white and non-white persons who had applied for and been appointed to the post of traffic supervisor for which he had applied.[18] A separate question concerns the s. 65 questionnaire procedure. A standard questionnaire[19] has been provided by the Secretary of State

---

9 s. 57(5).
10 See the *Reading* case, above, p. 1133.
11 1944 Act, s. 19(4).
12 *R v Army Board of Defence Council, ex p Anderson* [1991] 3 All ER 375, DC (Army Board decision quashed on judicial review for failure to consider oral hearing and to allow discovery).
13 CRE Report 1993, p. 9.
14 Ibid., p. 22.
15 [1980] AC 1028, HL. See also *Metropolitan Police Comr v Locker* [1993] ICR 440, EAT.
16 Lord Wilberforce, at p. 1065.
17 *West Midlands Passenger Transport Executive v Singh* [1988] ICR 614, CA.
18 See Gardner, (1989) 105 LQR 183.
19 The questionnaire is in the Race Relations (Questions and Replies) Order 1977, S.I. 1977 No. 842.

under s. 65 which a complainant or intending claimant may use as a basis for questioning the alleged discriminator. The questions and the replies may be used in evidence in court or tribunal proceedings. A defendant is not obliged to complete the questionnaire properly, although if he does not the court or tribunal may draw any inference 'that it considers just and equitable'. The CRE has recommended that the court or tribunal should be under a duty to draw the appropriate inference.[20]

7. The remedies available to an individual in a county court are those available in any tort claim.[1] Damages, which are unlimited, may include damages for injured feelings.[2] As noted above,[3] no damages may be awarded for indirect discrimination if there is no wrongful intention.[4] In employment cases, a declaration or compensation corresponding to damages that could have been ordered in the case by a county court may be awarded by an industrial tribunal.[5] There is now no statutory limit to the amount of damages that may be awarded by an industrial tribunal in a claim under the 1976 Act.[6] A tribunal may recommend that the victim be offered employment or reinstated. The recommendation is not legally binding, but the tribunal may award further compensation if it is not carried out. Unlike a county court, a tribunal has no power to issue an injunction against a defendant to prevent acts of discrimination.

The measure of damages in racial discrimination cases was discussed in *Alexander v Home Office*.[7] In that case, the plaintiff, who was black, was a convicted prisoner who successfully complained of direct racial discrimination contrary to s. 20, 1976 Act, by being refused employment in the prison kitchens because of his colour. Relevant to his treatment were initial assessments of him by the prison authorities, of which the appellant only became aware during the legal proceedings, which contained racial stereotyping remarks, in particular that he displayed 'the usual traits associated with people of his ethnic background being arrogant, suspicious of staff, anti-authority, devious and possessing a very large chip on his shoulder.' The Court of Appeal allowed an appeal against the quantum of damages, increasing the damages from £50 to £500. On the measure of damages, May LJ stated:[8]

'As with any other awards of damages, the objective of an award for unlawful racial discrimination is restitution. Where the discrimination has caused actual pecuniary loss, such as the refusal of a job, then the damages referable to this can be readily calculated. For the injury to feelings, however, for the humiliation, for the insult, it is impossible to say what is restitution and the answer must depend on the experience and good sense of the judge and his assessors. Awards should not be minimal, because this would tend to trivialise or diminish respect for the public policy to which the Act gives effect. On the other hand, just because it is impossible to assess the monetary value of injured feelings, awards should be restrained. To award sums which are generally felt to be excessive does almost as much harm to the

---

20 *Second Review of the Race Relations Act 1976* (1992), p. 55. For criticism of the s. 65 procedure, see L. Lustgarten, *Legal Controls of Racial Discrimination* (1980), p. 205.

1 s. 57(1).

2 s. 57(4).

3 See above, p. 1095.

4 The CRE has recommended that compensation should now be available for indirect discrimination even in cases of unintentional discrimination on the basis that the victim suffers injury in all cases and that people generally should by now be aware of the likely effect for racial groups of any requirement or condition that they impose: *Third Review of the Race Relations Act 1976* (1998).

5 s. 56(1).

6 Race Relations (Remedies) Act 1994. Interest may be included in a compensation award: S.I. 1996 No. 2803.

7 [1988] 1 WLR 968, CA.

8 pp. 975–976.

policy and the results which it seeks to achieve as do nominal awards. Further, injury to feelings, which is likely to be of a relatively short duration, is less serious than physical injury to the body or the mind which may persist for months, in many cases for life.

Nevertheless damages for this relatively new tort of unlawful racial discrimination are at large, that is to say that they are not limited to the pecuniary loss that can be specifically proved. Further, even where exemplary or punitive damages are not sought, nevertheless compensatory damages may and in some instances should include an element of aggravated damages where, for example, the defendant may have behaved in a high-handed, malicious, insulting or oppressive manner in committing the act of discrimination: see per Lord Devlin in *Rookes v Barnard*. . . .

Although damages for racial discrimination will in many cases be analogous to those for defamation, they are not necessarily the same. In the latter the principal injury to be compensated is that to the plaintiff's reputation: I doubt whether this will play a large part in the former. On the other hand, if the plaintiff knows of the racial discrimination and that he has thereby been held up to 'hatred, ridicule or contempt,' then the injury to his feelings will be an important element in the damages. That the injury to feelings for which compensation is sought must have resulted from knowledge of the discrimination is clear from the decision of this court in *Skyrail Oceanic Ltd v Coleman* [1981] ICR 864: see per Lawton LJ, at p. 871. (This was a case concerned with sex discrimination and not racial discrimination, but in my opinion the principle must be the same.)'

Whereas May LJ countenanced the possibility of exemplary damages in racial discrimination cases, it has since been established that such damages are not available for torts, such as the statutory tort of racial discrimination, that have been established since 1964.[9] Aggravated damages remain available so that when assessing compensatory damages the court 'can take into account the motives and conduct of the defendant where they aggravate the injury done to the plaintiff'.[10] Since the *Alexander* case, the level of damages in racial discrimination cases has increased. Although a very high award of £5,000 was reduced to £3,000 in *Noone v North West Thames Regional Health Authority*,[11] the Court of Appeal in that case, which included May LJ, reaffirmed the general statement of principle in the *Alexander* case. £500 is the minimum that should be awarded for injury to feelings.[12]

8. Enforcement through the CRE by formal investigation and non-discrimination notices has been dealt with in the previous section. Although it lacks the power the RRB had to refer cases in any area covered by the Act arising out of individual complaints to the courts, the CRE retains an important enforcement role in the courts, particularly in giving assistance to claimants bringing their own cases. The CRE also has the exclusive right to bring legal proceedings before a county court or industrial tribunal to enforce ss. 29 (advertisements), 30 (instructions to discriminate), and 31 (inducement to do so). In each of these cases the tribunal or court may only make a declaration or issue an injunction; no damages or compensation may be awarded.[13]

9. Assessing the value of the individual complaint system under the 1976 Act, *Racial Justice at Work*, pp. 156–7, concludes:

'The number of complaints of racial discrimination made to the tribunals has increased substantially over the period since the 1976 Act came into force, and the number of complaints

9 *Deane v Ealing Borough Council* [1993] ICR 329, applying *AB v South West Water Services Ltd* [1993] 2 WLR 507, CA.
10 Per Lord Devlin in *Rookes v Barnard* [1964] AC 1027, 1221, HL.
11 [1988] IRLR 195.
12 *Sharifi v Strathclyde Regional Council* [1992] IRLR 259, EAT.
13 s. 63. On the power to seek injunctions when persistent discrimination continues following non-discrimination notices, see above, p. 1166.

upheld (though not the proportion) has also increased. The system seems to have attracted complaints from a broad cross-section of the population belonging to non-white ethnic minorities. The system has proved far more popular with ethnic minorities than the comparable system has with women.

... Complaints of ... race discrimination have tended to be against organisations in the public sector, which are trying to introduce equal opportunity policies, and in this sector the success rate of complainants has been low; too few complaints have been made against private sector organisations, although the success rate in this sector has been higher. It may be that organisations that pursue equal opportunity policies tend to raise the level of consciousness of racial discrimination, thereby stimulating complaints, while those which allow discriminatory policies to continue are relatively untouched.

... The CRE is much better equipped than any other organisation to provide advice and representation to complainants, and it is the major source of free representation. At the same time, it has a limited budget to spend on this aspect of its work. The result is that a twin-track system has developed. Applicants who are granted assistance by the CRE have a substantially better chance of success than others, for at least three reasons: first, the CRE tries to select the stronger cases; second, it is likely to provide more effective advice and representation than any other body; third, and perhaps most important, it provides moral support to the applicant throughout the earlier stages, thus greatly reducing the chance that he or she will withdraw. Because the minority of applicants who are granted CRE assistance have a substantial advantage, the determining factor becomes the CRE's decision about whether or not to assist. This means that the CRE retains a dominant and quasi-judicial function. Another consequence is that there has been no development of campaigning organisations which sponsor individual complaints, although the CRE is currently making efforts to develop a complainant aid organisation.

The industrial tribunal process is simpler and quicker than most processes of civil action through the courts. Three-quarters of cases took up to six months from start to finish. Yet the objective of creating an informal system which would be worth entering for the prospect of modest rewards has not really been achieved....

The prospects of success for racial discrimination cases in the industrial tribunal system are much lower than for other types of cases, such as unfair dismissal.... For the cases included in the PSI database, which mostly fall within the 12 months ending 31 March 1988, 18 per cent ended in a judgment or settlement in which the applicant was paid £500 or more. (It is possible that the level of financial awards has tended since to increase, following the *Alexander* and *Noone* cases.) It seems clear from these results that a rational person would not embark on the process of making a complaint of racial discrimination to a tribunal simply for the prospect of securing monetary compensation.... To achieve a further substantial increase in the number of complaints it will probably be necessary to increase the prospects of success and the size of the remedies.[14]

Evidence presented in later chapters suggests that honour and self-respect are at stake more than monetary compensation.'

15 The impact of the 1976 Act on racial discrimination

B. Hepple, 'Have Twenty-Five Years of the Race Relations Acts in Britain been a Failure?' in Hepple and Szyszczak, op. cit. at p. 1068, n. 1, pp. 19–20 (footnotes omitted)

Judged in terms of the aims expressed in the White Paper on *Racial Discrimination*[15] – to reduce discrimination and by so doing to help break the 'familiar cycle of cumulative disadvantage' – the ineffectiveness of the Race Relations Act 1976 is irrefutable. The Policy Studies Institute's (PSI) third survey (1982–85) showed a continued gap in the unemployment rates, job levels, earnings, household income and quality of housing between black and white

---

14 *Ed.* The limit on employment tribunal compensation has since been lifted: see above, p. 1075.
15 *Ed.* Above, p. 1069.

people.[16] This has been confirmed by successive Labour Force Surveys.[17] Seventeen years after the Act of 1968, the PSI found that 'even at a conservative estimate' there were still 'tens of thousands of acts of racial discrimination in job recruitment every year'.[18] The most recent report by Colin Brown[19] shows that differential unemployment rates between whites and ethnic minorities cannot be explained by differences in levels of qualifications. They reflect instead employer discrimination against ethnic minorities and the concentration of workers from minority groups in jobs that are most vulnerable to redundancy. While there has been some narrowing of the gap between white and ethnic minority unemployment rates in recent years, this mainly reflects the tendency for unemployment among minorities to rise faster than white unemployment during economic downturns and to fall faster during periods of growth. Brown points out that ethnic minorities might benefit from changes in labour supply conditions in the next few years but one cannot expect lasting improvement without a serious assault on racial discrimination.

Even the severest critics of the Acts would concede that they have broken down some barriers for individuals in their quest for jobs, housing and services and that they have driven underground those overt expressions of discrimination which were current twenty years ago. Yet most of the reformers expected more than this from the legislation. They usually acknowledge the obvious difficulties in ascribing to an Act of Parliament specific responsibility for any degree of social change, especially where the long-term aim of the Act is to alter entrenched attitudes and behaviour. But they tend to focus their critique, and strategies for future changes, on the perceived weaknesses of the legislation and its enforcement. If only the Act had 'more teeth', imposing cost-deterrent sanctions on discriminators, there would be more significant impacts upon discrimination and disadvantage, according to this line of argument.

This approach shows little familiarity with the insights provided by sociologists into law as an instrument of social change. If these scholars teach us anything, it is that law is more likely to be effective in facilitating action which people want to take than in creating new rights to protect weaker parties.[20] The lack of social change following the Race Relations Acts is not unique. It is characteristic of most legislation which seeks to protect those who lack economic and social power, through the mechanism of individual rights enforced by private litigation.

NOTE

The 'serious assault' to which Hepple refers would require Government action. For the view that the Government's policy on racial discrimination in recent years has been one of 'benign neglect', McCrudden[1] also quotes and agrees with the following critical assessment by J. Solomos:[2] 'The translation of policies into practice has been hampered by a weak legal framework, organisational marginality and a lack of political legitimacy'. Government action could be required by European Union legislation comparable to that which has led to remarkable advances in the UK law on sex discrimination.[3]

16 C. Brown, *Black and White Britain: The Third PSI Survey* (London, Policy Studies Institute, 1984).
17 'Ethnic Origin and the Labour Market' (1991) Employment Gazette 59–72; compare 'Ethnic Origin and Economic Status' (1987) *Employment Gazette* 18–29.
18 Policy Studies Institute *Racial Discrimination: Seventeen Years after the Act* (London, Policy Studies Institute, 1985), p. 31.
19 C. Brown, *Racial Discrimination in the British Labour Market* (London, Employment Institute Economic Report, Vol. 5, No. 4, June 1990).
20 This distinction is made and developed in the context of the Race Relations Acts by L. Lustgarten, 'Racial Discrimination and the Limits of Law' (1986) 49 MLR 68 at p. 71.
1 See McCrudden, loc. cit. at p. 1068, n. 1, above, p. 439.
2 67 Pub. Admin. 79, 90 (1989).
3 See Lord Lester and S. L. Joseph, in D. Harris and S. Joseph, (eds.) *The International Covenant on Civil and Political Rights and UK Law* (1995), Chap. 17. For the view that the legal basis for such a development of European Union law exists, see C. Docksey, [1991] ILJ 258. See also *Second Review of the Race Relations Act 1976* (1992), p. 68.

16 Racial bias by juries

Sander v United Kingdom (2000) 8 BHRC 279l, European Court of Human Rights

The applicant and another accused, who were both of Asian origin, were tried before Birmingham Crown Court for conspiracy to defraud. During the judge's summing up, a jury member sent a note to the court stating that at least two jury members had been making racist remarks and jokes. The judge rejected a defence submission that the jury should be discharged. Instead, he read out the complaint to the jury, reminded them of their oath to decide the case according to the evidence and asked each of them, after a night's reflection, to inform the court if they could not in conscience decide the case without prejudice. The morning produced two letters: one from all twelve jurors, including the complainant juror, refuting the allegations and confirming that they would decide the case according to the evidence; and one from one juror seemingly accepting that he had made racist jokes. Thereupon, the judge decided not to discharge the jury but reminded them again of their duties.

The applicant was found guilty and sentenced to five years imprisonment; his co-accused was acquitted. The Court of Appeal rejected the applicant's appeal, *inter alia*, approving the trial judge's actions.

The applicant alleged a breach of the 'impartial tribunal' guarantee in Art. 6(1), ECHR:

Judgment of the Court:

22. The Court recalls that it is of fundamental importance in a democratic society that the courts inspire confidence in the public and above all, as far as criminal proceedings are concerned, in the accused. To that end it has constantly stressed that a tribunal, including a jury, must be impartial from a subjective as well as an objective point of view (see the above-mentioned *Gregory* judgment, p. 308, § 43).

23. The Court also recalls that the present case concerns clear and precise allegations that racist comments had been made by jurors called upon to try an Asian accused. The Court considers this to be a very serious matter given that, in today's multicultural European societies, the eradication of racism has become a common priority goal for all Contracting States (see, *inter alia*, Declarations of the Vienna and Strasbourg Summits of the Council of Europe).

24. The Court notes that the allegations in question led the applicant to the conclusion that he was tried by a racially prejudiced jury. The applicant's complaint is, therefore, that there was subjective bias on the part of some jurors.

25. The Court recalls that the personal impartiality of a judge must be presumed until there is proof to the contrary (see the *Piersack v Belgium* judgment of 1 October 1982, Series A no. 53, pp. 14–15, § 30). The same holds true in respect of jurors.

26. In the circumstances of the applicant's case, a member of the jury submitted a note alleging that two fellow jurors "[had] been making openly racist remarks and jokes" and stating that he feared that "they [were] going to convict the defendants not on the evidence but because they were Asian". Another juror, being confronted with these allegations, accepted that "he might have done so" and stated that "he was sorry if he had given any offence". The Court, therefore, considers that it was established that at least one juror had made comments that could be understood as jokes about Asians. In the Court's view, this does not on its own amount to evidence that the juror in question was actually biased against the applicant. Moreover, the Court notes that it was not possible for the trial judge to question the jurors about the true nature of these comments and the exact context in which they had been made. It follows that it has not been established that the court that tried the applicant was lacking in impartiality from a subjective point of view.

27. This is not, however, the end of the Court's examination of the applicant's complaint. The Court must also examine whether the court was impartial from an objective point of view, i.e. whether in the circumstances there were sufficient guarantees to exclude any objectively justified or legitimate doubts as to the impartiality of the court. Although the standpoint of the accused is important in this connection, it cannot be decisive (see the above-mentioned *Gregory* judgment, p. 309, § 45).

28. The Government submitted that there existed such guarantees. They referred in principle to the redirection of the jury by the judge and to the unequivocally positive assurance of impartiality that the judge sought and received from the jurors.

29. As regards the latter, the Court recalls that, the morning after the submission of the note about the racist jokes, all the jurors signed a letter to the effect that the allegations in question were unfounded. However, the Court considers that this letter cannot on its own discredit the allegations contained in the original note, for the following reasons.

First, one of the jurors wrote a separate letter indirectly admitting that he had been making racist jokes. The Court considers that this is a matter that cannot be taken lightly since jokes of this nature, when made by jurors in the context of judicial proceedings, take on a different hue and assume a different significance from jokes made in the context of a more intimate and informal atmosphere.

Secondly, the collective letter was also signed by the juror who had submitted the note. In the Court's view, this in itself casts some doubt on the credibility of the letter. The note, which was the product of a genuine, spontaneous reaction, the honesty of which has not been questioned, expressed fear that the defendants could be convicted because they were Asian. The letter, which reflected the common position of a number of persons with not necessarily the same interests in mind, denied any possible racial bias. The two cannot be reconciled and the Court considers the note more reliable. In addition, the Court notes that the juror who had submitted the note had been treated in such a way that it had become obvious to the other jurors that he was the one who had made the allegations. It is obvious that this must have compromised his position *vis-à-vis* his fellow jurors.

Thirdly, the Court considers that the collective letter does not discredit the allegations contained in the original note because openly admitting to racism is something which the average person would have a natural tendency to avoid. *A fortiori*, an open admission of racism cannot be easily expected from a person in jury service, the latter being generally regarded as important civic duty.

Given all the above, the Court finds that the collective denial of the allegations contained in the note could not in itself provide a satisfactory solution to the problem.

30. Moreover, in the present case the Court is not prepared to attach very much weight to the judge's redirection to the jury. The Court considers that, generally speaking, an admonition or direction by a judge, however clear, detailed and forceful, would not change racist views overnight. Although in the present case it cannot be assumed that such views were indeed held by one or more jurors, it has been established that at least one juror had been making racist comments. In these circumstances, the Court considers that the direction given by the judge to the jury could not dispel the reasonable impression and fear of a lack of impartiality, which were based on the original note.

31. As for the rest, the Court is not prepared to attach much weight to the fact that the judge had direct contact with the jurors either. The Court has already noted that, under domestic law, the judge could not question the jurors on the allegations contained in the note. Nor can G.C.'s acquittal be of decisive importance, since there is nothing to indicate that the two cases were comparable. Finally, the fact that the Court of Appeal rejected the applicant's appeal applying principles that corresponded to the Convention case-law can offer only limited assistance to the Court in the present case.

32. The Court therefore, considers that the allegations contained in the note were capable of causing the applicant and any objective observer legitimate doubts as to the impartiality of the court, which neither the collective letter nor the redirection of the jury by the judge could have dispelled.

33. In this connection, the Court observes that the facts of the applicant's case can be distinguished from the above-mentioned *Gregory* judgment, in which the Court found no violation of the Convention. In the latter case there was no admission by a juror that he had made racist comments, in the form of a joke or otherwise; there was no indication as to who had made the complaint and the complaint was vague and imprecise. Moreover, as opposed to *Gregory v the United Kingdom*, in the present case the applicant's counsel insisted throughout the proceedings that dismissing the jury was the only viable course of action.

34. The Court has accepted that, although discharging the jury may not always be the only means to achieve a fair trial, there are certain circumstances where this is required by Article 6 § 1 of the Convention (see the above-mentioned *Gregory* judgment, p. 310, § 48). In the present case the judge was faced with a serious allegation that the applicant risked being condemned because of his ethnic origin. Moreover, one of the jurors indirectly admitted to

making racist comments. Given the importance attached by all Contracting States to the need to combat racism (see paragraph 23 above), the Court considers that the judge should have reacted in a more robust manner than merely seeking vague assurances that the jurors could set aside their prejudices and try the case solely on the evidence. By failing to do so, the judge did not provide sufficient guarantees to exclude any objectively justified or legitimate doubts as to the impartiality of the court. It follows that the court that condemned the applicant was not impartial from an objective point of view.

35. There was, therefore, a violation of Article 6 § 1 of the Convention. ...

For these reasons, the Court:

1. *Holds* by four votes to three that there has been a violation of Article 6 § 1 of the Convention;
2. *Dismisses* unanimously the applicant's claims for just satisfaction.

Partly concurring, partly dissenting Opinion of **Judge Loucaides**:
While I am in agreement with the majority that there has been a violation of Article 6 § 1 of the Convention in that the court which condemned the applicant was not impartial from an objective point of view, I disagree that it has not also been established that the same court was lacking in impartiality from a subjective point of view.

I believe that there is sufficient proof in this case to rebut the presumption that the court was impartial. This proof consists of the evidence that at least one of the jurors admitted that he was making openly racist jokes and comments in respect of the accused, who was an Asian. It is true that the judge tried to neutralise the danger emerging from such an incident but, as rightly observed in the decision of the majority "an admonition or direction by a judge, however clear, detailed and forceful, would not change racist views overnight" (paragraph 30 of the judgment).

I am convinced that a juror who, in the context of carrying out his duties, makes racist jokes or comments in respect of the accused cannot reasonably be impartial as regards the trial of the latter. Evidently such attitude implies that the juror considers the accused an inferior person because of his race. As a result of such prejudice the accused could not have received an impartial treatment by one of the persons who, together with the other jurors, condemned him. Consequently the applicant was not tried by an impartial tribunal as required by Article 6 § 1 of the Convention.

Dissenting Opinion of **Judge Sir Nicolas Bratza** joined by **Judges Costa** and **Fuhrmann**:
I regret that I am unable to agree with the majority of the Court that there has been a violation of Article 6 § 1 of the Convention in the present case.

...in contrast to the decision of the Court in the *Gregory* case, the majority have concluded that the fact that a juror made racist jokes in the present case gave rise to justified and legitimate doubts as to the impartiality of the trial court and that sufficient guarantees did not exist to exclude or dispel these doubts.

I cannot agree. While I readily accept that the making of racial jokes is unacceptable in any circumstances, and particularly in the context of a jury trial, such comments as may have been made cannot in my view be seen in isolation and without regard to the steps subsequently taken by the trial judge to dispel any risk of bias.

The majority of the Court attach little weight to the letter signed by each member of the jury, or to the judge's redirection of the jury on two occasions or to the fact that the judge had direct contact with the members of the jury and thus was arguably in a better position to assess what measures were called for.

I do not share this view. The collective letter was written in response to an express reminder to the jury of their oath or affirmation as jurors and to the instructions by the trial judge that they were to indicate if, after reflection, they felt they were unable to try the case solely on the evidence or to put aside any prejudices they might have. The letter contained an explicit assurance that the jury intended to reach a verdict solely according to the evidence and without racial bias, thus responding both to the fears and concerns expressed in the note and to the judge's admonition.

Unlike the majority, I find no inconsistency between the note and the letter. Nor can I accept that the reliability or credibility of the letter is undermined by the fact that it was signed by the juror who had written the note. There is no evidence to suggest that the fact that his identity must have been known to the other jurymen might have compromised his position or subjected him to pressure to drop his allegations. His signing of the letter seems to me to be at least equally consistent with is acknowledgment that his fears and concerns that certain jurymen would reach a verdict on a racial basis were dispelled. That this was the true position seems to me to be borne out by the fact that the jury acquitted one of the applicant's co-defendants, a matter to which I, like the Court of Appeal, attach some, if not decisive, importance.

Again, unlike the majority of the Court, I place considerable weight on the fact that a highly experienced trial judge, having presided over the trial for several days and having been able to observe the jurors as the trial progressed, considered that it was inappropriate to discharge the jury immediately on receiving the note but chose rather to resolve the matter by giving a firm direction and admonition to the jury. I attach weight, also, to the fact that having reviewed the position, as he indicated he would, in the light of the collective letter and separate letter from one juryman, he took the view that the case could be safely left to the jury without any danger of bias causing injustice to the defendants — a view which was fully endorsed by the Court of Appeal.

The majority of the Court, while acknowledging that their conclusion is at variance with that of the Court in the *Gregory* case, seek to distinguish the two cases on their facts. Two such grounds of distinction are suggested. In the first place, it is pointed out that the complaint of bias in the *Gregory* case was vague and imprecise while, in the present case, there was an admission by a juror that he might have made racist jokes. While this is true, it is not to my mind a material point of distinction, the important question in each case being whether sufficient steps were taken to dispel any objectively justified fears that a verdict would be reached on grounds of racial prejudice. Secondly, it is said that in the present case, unlike in *Gregory*, the applicant's counsel insisted throughout the proceedings that the discharge of the jury was the only proper course. I do not find this point compelling either. It was certainly the recollection of defence counsel in the *Gregory* case that he had asked the judge to discharge the jury.[4] More importantly, the fact that the trial judge, having consulted counsel for all parties, did not accept the view of the defence but chose a different course does not mean that a fair trial was not guaranteed. As the Court noted in its *Gregory* judgment, safeguards other than the discharge of a jury, including a carefully worded redirection to the jury, may be sufficient. In my view, it was sufficient in the present case.

In conclusion, I fully endorse the importance to be attached to the need to combat racism. What I cannot accept is that this consideration should have caused the trial judge in the present case to have reacted "in a more robust manner" or that only the discharge of the jury could have satisfied the requirements of Article 6 § 1.

NOTES[5]

1. The case was the second English jury case to be decided by the European Court of Human Rights on the question of racial discrimination. In the earlier case of *Gregory v United Kingdom*,[6] no breach of the 'impartial tribunal' guarantee in Art. 6 had been found. In that case, the applicant, who was black, was convicted by a jury, by 10 to 2, of robbery and sentenced to six years imprisonment. While the jury was deliberating, a jury member had passed a note to the trial judge that read: 'Jury showing racial overtones. One member to be excused'. After seeking the views of prosecution and defence counsel, the judge called the jury back and redirected them, emphasising their duty to decide on the evidence alone. In ruling that there had been no breach of Art. 6, the European Court stated:

---

4   *Ed.* On this point, see further the passage from the *Gregory* case, below.
5   On the *Sander* case, see Zander, (2000) 149 NLJ.
6   (1998) 25 EHRR 577. None of the seven judges in the *Gregory* case were in the *Sander* case.

'46. As regards the situation which arose at the trial, the Court in applying the objective test to the facts at issue must have particular regard to the steps taken by the trial judge on receipt of the note from the jury. His immediate reaction was to seek the views of both prosecution and defence Counsel and not to dismiss the allegation outright. As an experienced judge who had observed the jury throughout the trial, he was no doubt aware of the possibility of either discharging the jury at that stage or asking the jury in open court whether they were capable of continuing and returning a verdict on the evidence alone. He chose neither of these courses of action, and it is significant that defence Counsel did not in fact press for them. It may be reasonably inferred that defence Counsel himself did not consider that either was warranted in the circumstances. At the most defence Counsel would appear to have asked the judge to investigate the circumstances which motivated the writing of the note.[7] However, such an investigation would not have been possible under English law.

47. The trial judge chose to deal with the allegation by means of a firmly worded redirection to the jury having had the benefit of submissions from both Counsel. His statement was clear, detailed and forceful. He was anxious to ensure that his words were understood, and he deliberately broke off on occasions to satisfy himself that such was the case. He sought to impress on the jury that their sworn duty was to try the case on the evidence alone and that they must not allow any other factor to influence their decision.

Admittedly, the judge did not make any reference in his direction to the words "racial prejudice". However, it is to be noted that he instructed the jury to put out of their minds "any thoughts or prejudice of one form or another". The meaning of such words must have been clear, in particular to any juror whose conduct may have given rise to the allegation of racial overtones. It is significant that on no subsequent occasion was there any further suggestion of racial comment. The judge could reasonably consider therefore that the jury had complied with the terms of his redirection and that any risk of prejudice had been effectively neutralised.

48. The Court's assessment of the facts leads it to conclude therefore that, in the instant case, no more was required under Article 6 to dispel any objectively held fears or misgivings about the impartiality of the jury than was done by the judge. While the guarantee of a fair trial may in certain circumstances require a judge to discharge a jury it must also be acknowledged that this may not always be the only means to achieve this aim. In circumstances such as those at issue, other safeguards, including a carefully worded redirection to the jury, may be sufficient. The Court considers that it is confirmed in this conclusion by the view taken of the judge's handling of the note by the judges on appeal in application of legal principles which corresponded closely to its own case law on the objective requirements of impartiality.

49. The Court further observes that the facts at issue are to be distinguished from those which led it to find a violation in the abovementioned *Remli* case.[8] In that case, the trial judges failed to react to an allegation that an identifiable juror had been overheard to say that he was a racist. In the present case, the judge was faced with an allegation of jury racism which, although vague and imprecise, could not be said to be devoid of substance. In the circumstances, he took sufficient steps to check that the court was established as an impartial tribunal within the meaning of Article 6(1) of the Convention and he offered sufficient guarantees to dispel any doubts in this regard.

50. The Court concludes therefore that there has been no violation of Article 6(1) in the circumstances of the case.'

---

7   *Ed.* Earlier in its judgment the Court had stated: '11. There is some uncertainty as to the stance taken by defence Counsel with regard to the follow-up to be given to the note. Prosecution Counsel recalls that defence Counsel did not raise strong objections to the approach which the judge indicated he intended to pursue, namely to recall the jury and give clear directions on their duty to return a verdict on the basis of the evidence alone. However defence Counsel seems to recall that he did in fact ask the trial judge to discharge the jury in the circumstances, but his application was refused. Defence Counsel based his recollection on the grounds of appeal and advice on appeal which he drafted shortly after the trial on 10 December 1991. However, neither of these documents suggests that defence Counsel made an express request to the judge to discharge the jury.'

8   *Ed. Remli v France* (1996) 22 EHRR 391. The French court held that it had no power in law to intervene, when the matter was drawn to its attention because the remark suspecting bias had been made in a corridor, not in court proceedings.

2. In *R v Ford* [9] it was held that a jury must be chosen at random in order best to ensure a fair trial; a court has no residual power to interfere with the random selection of jury members to achieve a multiracial jury. In that case, it was decided that a trial judge was correct to reject a request by a black accused for black jury members. Herbert [10] is critical of the approach in the *Ford* case:

'In January 1989 the defence right to the use of up to three peremptory challenges was abolished on the pretext that the pooled exercise was making the jury "too defence orientated". The decision of the Court of Appeal in *R v Ford* completed the process, for black defendants, of limiting the right of trial by a jury of one's peers. The Court went on to hold that a judge has no power to influence the composition of the jury panel, as that power was the sole preserve of the Lord Chancellor under s. 5 of the Juries Act 1974:

The decision in *Ford* forces one to rely instead on the principles of "random selection" and the "common man" to guarantee impartiality. There is a clear reluctance on the part of the Lord Chief Justice to see any advantage in providing for a multi-racial jury. In a speech to the Leeds Race Issues Advisory Council, [11] the Lord Chief Justice said that multi-racial juries represented the "thin edge of a particularly insidious wedge ... we must on no account introduce measures which allow the State to start nibbling away at the principle of random selection."

However, Professor J Gobert [12] found that:

"Studies consistently show an under-representation of ethnic minorities, young persons and women on jury panels."

Similarly, a survey (initiated by the Society of Black Lawyers and conducted by the Lord Chancellor's Department in 1990) of 15 court centres in Coventry and Birmingham, found that 7.5 per cent and 9.3 per cent respectively of all excusals were of Asians on the basis that English was not their first language.

The "randomness" principle is already distorted by cases involving black defendants being moved from inner city courts out to Maidstone, Aylesbury and Kingston, areas with a low ethnic minority population.

For example, the *"Cardiff Three"* [13] were tried by an all white Swansea jury trying three black men from a community in Cardiff of which they had no concept. This resulted in a conviction later overturned by the Court of Appeal. ...

Professor J Gobert commented:

"A randomly selected jury is not an end in itself, it is only a means to an end. The end is the empanelling of an impartial jury." [14]

The United States Supreme Court, not known for its liberal views in recent years, acknowledged the problem when it commented. [15]

"Securing representation of the defendant's race on the jury may help to overcome racial bias and provide the defendant with a better chance of having a fair trial."

The abolition of the right of preemptory challenge enabled judges prior to *Ford* to exercise their discretion to obtain a multi-racial jury. ...'

9 [1989] QB 868, CA (Cr D).
10 P. Herbert, (1995) 144 NLJ 1138.
11 *The Times*, 1 July 1995.
12 *"The Peremptory Challenge – An Obituary"* (1989) Crim LR 528.
13 *R v Parris* (1989) 89 CR App R 173.
14 See n 12.
15 *Georgia v McCullom*, 112S. CT 2348, 2364 (1992).

Index

Abortion
  refusal to carry out, religious reasons for, 1056, 1057
Abuse of rights
  prohibition, provisions of European Convention on Human Rights, 23
Administration of justice
  contempt of court. *See* CONTEMPT OF COURT
  improper interference and obstruction, protection from, 717
  offences relating to, 717
Advertisements
  broadcast–
    control of, 670
    general provisions, 670
  discriminatory–
    definition, 1151
    enforcement, 1151
    lawful discrimination, in relation to, 1151
    notice as, 1151
    number of, 1150
    statutory provisions, 1150
Alcohol
  minors, sale to, 392
  public places, prohibited consumption in, 392
  sporting events, control at, 408, 409
  under-18-year-old, confiscation from, 517
Aliens
  political activity, prohibition on imposing, 22
Armed forces
  conscientious objectors, 1054
  racial discrimination, complaint of, 1171
Arrest
  acquittal of offence, effect on lawfulness of, 289, 290
  aggravated trespass, for, 522, 523
  anticipated breach of the peace, for, 177
  arrestable offences–
    list of, 276, 277
    public law, in context of, 391
    serious offences, including, 290
    statutory provisions, 275–277
  breach of the peace, for–
    anticipatory, 465–469
    powers of, 460–465
  complete offence, in relation to, 289

Arrest—*contd*
  compulsion, words indicating, 282
  conditions, 277
  detention for questioning as, 287
  discretion, exercise of, 287
  dispersal of assembly, in course of, 525
  disposition after, 294
  entry on premises for purposes of, 229
  fact of, arrestee informed of, 282
  failure to answer to police bail, for, 307
  fingerprinting of offenders, 278
  further offence, for, 280
  general condition, satisfaction of, 293
  grounds for–
    explaining, 283–287
    informing arrestee of, 283
    particular offence, details of, 284, 285
    time for informing suspect of, 286
  information to be given on, 278
  minor offences, for, 291
  necessary, power being, 291
  obstruction, for, 176, 284, 293
  Official Secrets Acts, under, 809, 816
  other than at police station, 279
  person helping with enquiries, and, 296
  police dogs, use of, 198
  private person, by, 294
  public assemblies, in relation to, 441, 442
  purpose of, 211
  reasonable force, use of–
    batons, use of, 197
    common law, at, 201
    excessive, effect of, 200
    extent of, 197
    justification, 197
    objective concept of, 197
    statutory provisions, 196, 201
  reasonable suspicion, on–
    application of test, 184–186
    arrestable offence, of, 187
    basis of, 190
    circumstances of case, depending on, 192
    concept of, 178
    definition, 178
    fleeting glimpse eyewitness evidence, based on, 191
    grounds for, 284
    high and low exercises of discretion, 189

1183

Racial discrimination—*contd*
  Commission for Racial Equality—*contd*
    assistance from, 1071
    criticisms of, 1162
    duties of, 1161
    establishment of, 1161
    formal investigations by, 1071, 1162–1167
    members, 1161
    non-discrimination notice, issue of, 1093, 1098, 1149, 1165, 1166
    register of non-discrimination notices, 1166
  common law protection against, 1068
  contract compliance, 1071
  course of employment, offending acts in, 1105–1108
  courts, enforcement of provisions in–
    armed forces, relating to, 1171
    burden of proof, 1170
    claims, 1168
    common law remedies, exclusion of, 1168
    damages, 1172, 1173
    education provisions, of, 1173
    evidence, 1171
    individual complaint system, evaluation of, 1173, 1174
    legal aid, 1169, 1170
    limitation period, 1169
    low level of success, 1170
    proceedings, restriction of, 1168
    remedies, 1172
    statutory provisions, 1168
  criminal justice system, in, 1077
  Crown, application of provisions to, 1080
  damages for, 1172, 1173
  dance halls, in, 1141
  degrading treatment, freedom from, 1074
  detriment, to, 1101
  direct–
    conscious motivation for, 1086–1088
    detriment, to, 1089
    dismissal procedures, in application of, 1089
    exclusion of black youths, dismissal for failure to obey order for, 1090–1092
    segregation as, 1089, 1090
  discouragement, words of, 1089
  education, in–
    admissions procedure, 1133
    application of provisions, 1132
    courts, enforcement of provisions in, 1171
    facilities, provision of, 1132, 1136
    language scrutiny, 1133
    special schools, placement of children in, 1132, 1133
    statutory provisions, 1131
    transfer, parent's request for, 1134
    victimisation, exclusion of, 1133
    zoning arrangements, 1133

Racial discrimination—*contd*
  employment, in, 1070
  English origin, on grounds of, 1112–1114
  equal treatment Directive, 1074
  ethnic group, against, 1113–1118
  ethnic origins, meaning of, 1119
  European Convention on Human Rights, provisions of, 1073, 1074
  European law, under, 1074
  formal investigations–
    Commission for Racial Equality, by, 1071, 1163
    enforcement by, 1173
    general, 1166, 1167
    named person, 1163–1166
    non-discrimination notice, issue of, 1165, 1166
    number of, 1167
    preliminary inquiry, 1164
    procedure, 1163
    role of, 1167
    Secretary of State, by, 1163
    statutory provisions, 1162
  forms of, 1083
  gipsies–
    against, 1120–1123
    general laws, compliance with, 1125
    private and family life, right to respect for, 1123–1131
    racial group, as, 1120–1131
    sites for, 1123–1131
  goods, facilities and services, in provision of–
    accommodation, 1135, 1136
    dance halls, in, 1141
    education, for, 1132, 1136
    estate agents, by, 1136, 1137, 1144
    examples of, 1135
    fostering, 1143
    hotel, meaning, 1135
    human organs, donation of, 1143
    innkeeper, obligations of, 1135
    loans, granting of, 1136
    meaning, 1134, 1135
    motor or life insurance, 1140
    public housing, 1137
    public official or body, by, 1149, 1140
    pubs, in, 1141
    refreshment, 1136
    section of the public, meaning, 1142
    shops, in, 1141, 1142
    statutory provisions, 1134
    tax official, by, 1140
    tax relief, claim for, 1138
    trade, meaning, 1136
    transport and travel, 1136
  illegal, scope of, 1083
  impact of provisions on, 1174, 1175
  indirect–
    change of definition, recommendation for, 1101, 1102